LITERARY CULTURES OF
LATIN AMERICA

A COMPARATIVE HISTORY

LITERARY HISTORY PROJECT

UNDER THE AUSPICES OF THE SOCIAL SCIENCES
AND HUMANITIES RESEARCH COUNCIL OF CANADA
AND THE UNIVERSITY OF TORONTO

RESEARCH DIRECTOR
Mario J. Valdés, University of Toronto

CODIRECTOR
Linda Hutcheon, University of Toronto

Hutcheon, Linda, and Mario J. Valdés, eds.
Rethinking Literary History: A Dialogue on Theory.
New York: Oxford University Press, 2002.

Valdés, Mario J., and Djelal Kadir, eds.
Literary Cultures of Latin America: A Comparative History.
3 vols. New York: Oxford University Press, 2004.

Cornis-Pope, Marcel, and John Neubauer, eds.
History of Literary Cultures in East-Central Europe.
Forthcoming.

LITERARY CULTURES OF LATIN AMERICA

A COMPARATIVE HISTORY

Mario J. Valdés
and
Djelal Kadir
Editors

Volume III
LATIN AMERICAN LITERARY CULTURE:
SUBJECT TO HISTORY

OXFORD

UNIVERSITY PRESS

2004

Page Design & Production
Publication Services

Project Manager
Susan Yates

Designer
Lori Martinsek

Editorial Manager
Rob Siedenburg

Editorial Staff
Jerome Colburn, Al Davis, Philip D. Hamer, David Mason, Jennifer Putman,
Scott Stocking, Rebecca Taylor

Production Manager
Foti Kutil

Production Staff
Kelly Applegate, Pamela J. Broderick-Rhoades, Elisa Laird, Carol McGilliuray,
Paul Mitchell, Steven Sansone, James Torbit, Eric R. Tucker

Indexing Staff
Alysia Cooley, Benjamin Moreland, Louise Toft, Joyce Wiehagen,
Debora Mori Benencase Ayers, Neil Ching

Art
Ben Coblentz, Jason Pankoke, Guoliang Wu

OXFORD
University Press

Oxford   New York
Auckland Bangkok Buenos Aires Cape Town Chennai
Dar es Salaam Delhi Hong Kong Istanbul Karachi Kolkata
Kuala Lumpur Madrid Melbourne Mexico City Mumbai
Nairobi São Paulo Shanghai Taipei Tokyo Toronto

Library of Congress Cataloging-in-Publication Data

Literary cultures of Latin America : a comparative history / edited by
Mario J. Valdés and Djelal Kadir.
    v. ; cm.
  Includes bibliographical references and index.
  Contents: v. 1 Configurations of literary culture -- v. 2
Institutional modes and cultural modalities -- v. 3 Latin American
literary culture.
  ISBN 0-19-512621-1 (set : alk. paper) -- ISBN 0-19-517540-9 (v. 1 :
alk. paper) -- ISBN 0-19-517541-7 (v. 2 : alk. paper) -- ISBN
0-19-517542-5 (v. 3 : alk. paper)
  1. Latin American literature--History and criticism. 2. Literature
and society--Latin America. I. Valdés, Mario J. II. Kadir, Djelal.
  PQ7081.A1L525 2004
  860.9'98--dc22
                              2003027353

Printing Number: 9 8 7 6 5 4 3 2 1

Printed in the United States of America
on acid-free paper

Contents of Volume III

Latin American Literary Culture:

Subsect to History

PART THREE

LIMINALITY AND CENTRALITY OF LITERARY CULTURES IN THE TWENTIETH CENTURY

CONTENTS OF OTHER VOLUMES

Volume I
Configurations of Literary Culture

INTRODUCTION: BEYOND LITERARY HISTORY
Mario J. Valdés

SERIES OVERVIEW: RETHINKING LITERARY
HISTORY–COMPARATIVELY
Mario J. Valdés and Linda Hutcheon

COEDITOR'S INTRODUCTION:
HISTORY AFTER HISTORY
Djelal Kadir

INTRODUCTION TO VOLUME I: FOR A MORE INCLUSIVE
LITERARY HISTORY OF LATIN AMERICA
Luisa Campuzano

PART ONE

PARAMETERS OF LITERARY CULTURE

PART TWO

FROM THE MARGINS OF LITERARY HISTORY

PART THREE

PLURALITY OF DISCOURSE IN LATIN AMERICAN CULTURE

Volume II
Institutional Modes and Cultural Modalities

INTRODUCTION
Walter D. Mignolo

PART ONE

CULTURAL INSTITUTIONS

PART TWO

TEXTUAL MODELS AND THEIR TRANSFORMATIONS

PART THREE

THE CULTURAL CENTERS OF LATIN AMERICA

INTRODUCTION TO VOLUME III

Wander Melo Miranda

Within literary historiography the construction of Latin American literatures has always been beholden to the idea of a cultural dependency on the legacy of European colonization; and it has therefore been inscribed within a theoretical framework marked by the concepts of source and influence. Even after the various movements toward political independence in the nineteenth century and the advent of the twentieth century, critics and historians have not ceased to stress the former colonies' debt to the metropolis, establishing a hierarchical relation that deems the diverse national literatures of the New World inferior in comparison with a foreign model. This configuration, which results from the convergence of an evolutionary concept of history and the notion of universal standards for aesthetic evaluation, has favored a binary type of comparativism that has been circumscribed in a realm of unilateral symbolic exchanges and in which the asymmetry of the terms of comparison reaffirms exclusionary rules.

The *Literary Cultures of Latin America: A Comparative History,* edited by Mario J. Valdés and Djelal Kadir, presents a new form of literary history. It works out possibilities of historiographical inquiry that are not restricted to the binary oppositions that have always substantiated these fables of identity in traditional literary histories of Latin America: categories such as the universal and the particular, the center and the periphery, nativism and cosmopolitanism. This work considers Latin America as a space inscribed within the folds of a cultural fabric that spans the region's ever-present social contradictions and political struggles. The *Comparative History* presupposes the elaboration of a theory of cultural difference understood as an intermittent process of translation, whereby the migration of modernity's values and meanings betrays the mobility that defines them and that transforms difference into a frontier under constant dislocation and erasure. Only in this manner may literary history recuperate a narrative knowledge that is conditioned by the point of view of the agent who produces it, and that is revealed as relative rather than universal knowledge. This *Comparative History* affirms a discourse on Latin America that is relational, critical, and deconstructive, working not to lapse into essentialism or essentialist particularities. It marks a conceptual advance over previous forays into the historiography of Latin American literatures, for it submits neither to an organic vision of unitary national cultures nor to the notion of a transnational Latin American system. This work seeks rather to reflect upon the unequal determinants of the conditions that regulate knowledge (or lack thereof) of a Latin American*ism*, by stressing the critical task necessary to recuperate what was silenced by the dominant nexus of power and knowledge and its sustaining ideology.

The fifty-four chapters that constitute this third volume demonstrate from various perspectives how the multiplicity of sites of enunciation (hitherto subsumed under the common rubric of a Latin American discourse of unity) challenges the old monological discourse and the epistemic strategies responsible for its stability (see Mignolo). In this way these essays call into question the limits of a prior disciplinary knowledge that sought to sustain a politics of identity, effectively deconstructing that prior discourse's defining history and conditions of production. The contributions included here constitute a complex and sustained discussion of the processes that go to make up literary cultures in Latin America, and this introduction will be able to highlight only some of these decisive interventions.

From the struggles for political independence in the nineteenth century, the Latin American nations' need for cultural differentiation beyond the common embrace of Western values pointed to the overcoming of submission to a European imaginary (see Candido 1969). Hence the insertion of works and authors into a linear and continuous temporality that evolved through successive stages, within a system that integrated facts and events until it formed a discursive tradition that pointed solidly to a referent. Hence the constitution of a literary history that, forged under the specter of the nation and predicated on the metaphor of organic growth, attempts to reconcile the literary and the social. This kind of literary history entails a concept of representation that presupposes a certain focus on the physical reality of Brazil in order to define the constitutive values of its historical identity–like the "mapa del Imperio, que tenía el tamaño del Imperio y coincidía puntualmente con él" (Borges 1972, 143) ("Map of the Empire whose size was that of the Empire, and which coincided point for point with it"; 1998, 325).

From this vantage point, the literary history of Brazil, for example, can be described as the evolutionary process of the emancipation of forms and content from the metropolis. The metropolis dictated the parameters that, in contradiction to the national context, define history as the realization of civilization in the shape of the modern European model. It is thus that the composition of a Brazilian national identity articulates itself–above all from the advent of Romanticism on–in accordance to an exercise in (un)real rhetoric that marginalizes and de-legitimizes "desafetos nacionais" (Rouanet 293) ("national preoccupations"). What is denied legitimacy is out of focus and outside history, situated in the non-place between something called Brazil and the idealized image of a recently politically emancipated country. The de-legitimized insist on making opaque the transparency that would allow Brazilians to observe and be observed. Still, in Romanticism, the task of describing the nation and making it visible for its inhabitants fell to foreign travelers (see Gomes et al., Chapter 51 in this volume), who, armed with palette, pencils, brushes, and ink, delineated a cartographic landscape of the country through which they passed.

In this context emerges the nationalist narrator of Brazilian fiction, the spokesman of–"o 'amadurecimento' como processo contínuo, a nacionalidade como essência meta-histórica" (Süssekind 19) ("the notion of 'maturation' as a continuous process, the idea of nationality as a meta-historical essence"). In the twentieth century this task of description fell to the Modernists of the first wave, armed with the belief or illusion of being more advanced and, as such, closer to a rational project of development, education, and emancipation. Thus Oswald de Andrade (1890–1954) proclaimed, half seriously, that "A massa, meu caro, há de chegar ao biscoito fino que fabrico" (quoted in Boaventura 39) ("the masses, my dear, will yet eat from this fine biscuit that I create").

The making of a nation and the making of a literature are simultaneous processes in the trajectory of the "espírito do Ocidente, buscando uma nova morada nesta parte do mundo" (Candido 1969, 10) ("spirit of the West, seeking a new home in this part of the world"). Nonetheless this "spirit of the West" ultimately turns into a specter, at once seductive and the greatest cause of the dilemma that, in general, accompanies the formation of cultures on this side of the Atlantic. The tragedy of the Brazilian and American musical traditions, notes Mario de Andrade (1893–1945), is that they were not allowed to develop "mais livre de preocupações quanto à sua afirmação nacional e social" (11) ("freer from preoccupations pertaining to their affirmation of a social and national identity") Thus in a certain way Brazilians remain beholden, as Roberto Schwarz noted in 1977, to a conception of their cultural life as inauthentic and artificial. Octavio Paz (1914–1998) affirmed that, despite attempts throughout the centuries to remain within the Western compass, Latin Americans represent "um extremo do Ocidente–um extremo excêntrico, pobre e dissonante" (1980, 3) ("an extremity of the West–an extremity at once eccentric, poor and dissonant"). The question for this poet and critic is whether Spanish American literature–however rich and original–constitutes a modern literature, since it lacks a conceptually grounded reflection that is at once critical, moral, and philosophical. Latin Americans, Paz laments, lack "movimentos intelectuais originais" ("original intellectual movements") and "intelectualmente no passado" ("intellectually live in the past") (1980, 3).

Paz's dilemma resolves itself in the temporal and spatial displacement of literature as an art of conjunction, a displacement worked by the synchronic dynamic of "la Poética del ahora" (1984, 204) ("the poetics of now"). This proposition's strategic universalism allows the critic to solve, or at least suspend, the question of whether Latin American literatures are original or backward, a question undone by the "voz de la *otredad*" (Paz 1984, 207) ("voice of *otherness*") articulated in the poetic language that defines the possibility of a Latin American identity. The paradigmatic norms established by hegemonic thought would conclude that they are always other, that they constitute pure difference. In contrast, the notion of "vivência de uma opção cultural" (Morse 14) ("experiencing a cultural option") contains the concept of a civilizing process that does not relapse into universalist extremes or reductive nationalisms, but rather articulates simultaneous yet distinct experiences of historical temporality. Further, the idea of "experiencing a cultural option" forgoes macro-structural explanations that situate power in a fixed and unique site. This idea rather unveils the particular Anglo-American ideal of humanity as one among many, and its pretension to unify all others as an aspiration that could only be achieved through violence.

By the mid-nineteenth century, if not before, a model for the independent nation-state was available to be copied: a mixture of elements borrowed from the ideals of the French Revolution and those articulated in the Constitution of the United States of America. From this point onward the "nation" proved itself an invention impossible to copyright, for its constituent elements did not admit significant deviations, however varied and even foreseen its appropriations. It is the style of these appropriations, rather than the opposition between the false and the authentic, which will come to distinguish "nationness" (Anderson 77). In the Americas the creation of nations in the image of European utopian visions of the New World forms part of this process of copying, a process interwoven with the Latin American novel at the start of its formation and which constructed the novel as the complement or corrective to a history of non-productive events. The literature of this period takes on the political and ideological function of legitimating the emergent nation after Independence, extrapolating the emergent nation's future from an ideal history conceived in accordance with a European model of progress and of prosperity. In the "irresistible romance" of the founding fiction of Latin America, sentimental and erotic rhetoric performs a key role: The domestic novel is taken as a model for national homogenization, as conciliation is achieved by means of a Liberal leadership that acts as a bridge between antagonistic races, regions, and political groups (see Sommer). In this fashion the novel's stylistic appropriation of a model seemingly dominant among nations follows the constitutive logic of national integration that seeks to conceal differences under the alibi of a civilizing modernization.

In the case of Brazilian literature, writers such as Gonçalves Dias (1823–1864) and José de Alencar (1829–1877) note the vanishing point for the ethnocentric vision imposed by the hegemonic culture (for the example of Alencar, see Figueiredo, Chapter 6 in this volume). Dias and Alencar accomplish this through the recuperation of the misrepresented Other, that is, through the salvaging of the authentic and the national. In this context the figure of the native comes to represent this emerging alterability and is considered a symbol of national affirmation. In their capacity as the weakest in the clash between cultures, natives suffer immediately the consequences of what Freyre terms a "contacto dissolvente" (2000, 327) ("that contact [which] was dissolvent in effect"; 1966, 106). In any event, the dramatization of the native question allows Alencar, in his novel *Iracema*, to "estabelecer, desenvolver e codificar por escrito e reflexivamente os novos valores que vão surgindo anarquicamente, ou seja, os que seriam em última instância determinantes da estrutura social do país e da hierarquia entre seus habitantes" (Santiago 1982, 90) ("establish, develop, and codify, reflexively and in writing, the new values that emerge anarchistically, that is, those values that would ultimately prove determinant of the country's social structure and of the hierarchy among its inhabitants").

In the 1920s the Modernist project of Oswald de Andrade took up this question from the vantage point of the practice of "anthropophagy," the Tupi Indians' ritualistic act of devouring brave enemies captured in battle. "Só me interessa o que não é meu" (13) ("Only what is not mine interests me"), proclaims Andrade in the 1928 *Anthropophagic Manifesto*. Thus he expresses, by means of the anthropophagic desire for appropriation and expropriation, the mitigation of Brazil's cultural dependence on the hegemonic culture of Europe. Andrade's powerful transformation of taboo into totem constitutes at once a diagnosis and a therapy:

> *diagnóstico* da sociedade brasileira como sociedade traumatizada pela repressão colonizadora que condicionou seu crescimento . . . ~~wrapdoudux~~ por ~~melo dessa reação violenta e sistemática, contra os~~ mecanismos sociais e políticos, os hábitos intelectuais, as manifestações literárias e artísticas, que, até à primeira década do século XX, fizeram do trauma repressor, de que a Catequese constituiria a causa exemplar, uma instância censora, um Superego coletivo. (Nunes xxvi)

> a *diagnosis* of Brazilian society as a society traumatized by the colonial repression which conditioned its growth . . . and a *therapy*, for it prescribes a systematic and violent reaction against the social and political mechanisms, the intellectual habits, and the literary and artistic manifestations that until the first decade of the twentieth century made of the repressive trauma (whose exemplary case would be the Catechism) an instance of censorship, a collective Superego.

For Oswald de Andrade only a local primitivism could restore to "cansada cultura européia o sentido moderno, quer dizer, livre da maceração cristã e do utilitarismo capitalista" (Schwarz 1987, 37) ("the exhausted European culture the meaning of the modern, that is, a meaning free of Christian mortification and Capitalist utilitarianism"). If Andrade's proposal seems naïve and jingoistic, the notion of anthropophagy nonetheless transcends his historical predicament and comes to act as an operative concept in more recent theoretical formulations. Anthropophagy, translation, and intertextuality have come to be associated with a synchronic perspective on Brazilian (and by extension Latin American) culture, a perspective no longer anchored in the category of nation. In the domain of historiography, the concept of anthropophagy points to the cosmopolitanism present in Brazilian literature since its origins. Brazilian literature was born already sharing and articulating the most celebrated artistic code of the time, the Baroque. As Maria Consuelo Cunha de Campos (Chapter 4 in this volume) notes, the work of Gregório de Matos (1633?–1696) and Antonio Vieir (1608–1697) a is thus related to that of Tejeda and Caviedes in the Spanish American world. From this perspective, the Baroque comes to delineate a tradition of rupture and difference in Brazil, as in other Latin American countries. In the twentieth century the Baroque came to be understood as an operative concept of vast critical and ideological range and was affirmed by critics and historians as a standard for artistic reference and evaluation in processes of literary canonization.

If the Baroque proved, strictly speaking, to be the key to the foundation of literatures throughout Latin America, its transnational character produced in its sites of enunciation a displacement that called into question the homogeneity of the space of the production of literary models. The copy supplements rather than merely replicates the original, through an operation in which the European culture of reference loses its hierarchical status. The decolonized text of Latin American culture comes to possess an unforeseen energy, "*por conter em si uma representação do texto dominante e uma resposta a esta representação no próprio nível da fabulação, resposta esta que passa a ter um padrão de aferição da universalidade tão eficaz quanto os já conhecidos e catalogados*" (Santiago 1982, 23) ("*since it contains both a representation of the dominant text and an answer to this representation at the same level of the production of tales,* an answer that comes to possess a standard for the assessment of

universality just as efficient as those already known and catalogued"). The reversal of values such as backwardness and originality makes possible the emergence of a discursive "in-between" that belies the endogenous character of cultural exchange among texts. This discourse of the "in-between" proves more interested in the hiatus inherent in a vision both close to and removed from its cultural object than it is in the certainties that lead to theories of identity (Santiago 1978, 11–28 and 1982, 13–24).

If globalization frees local identities from the weight of national culture, the residual power of the latter can prevent the former from becoming a fetish. Thus a space is made available for the evaluation of the culture of the Other that does not seek to delegitimize the heterogeneity that makes the Other irreducible. For Antonio Candido the "reality" of underdevelopment is demystified once it is understood as an alibi for a literary nativism that postulates the identity of the Latin American subject as beholden to local values. In his 1972 essay on "Literatura e subdesenvolvimento" ["Literature and Underdevelopment"], Candido proposes instead the notions of cultural interdependence and reciprocal assimilation, which–since they do not posit any universalist content– would allow Latin American discursive production to be approached as a space of tension and exchange between heterogeneous values. It follows that for a literary history of Latin America not to reduce this literature to the dead archive of an unfractured totality, it is necessary for literature to be conceived of as the loss of memory of the continuum of history. The concept of history as a unitary stream must be exposed as a construction by the dominant social groups and classes of what was relevant in the past *to them.* One must recognize the cultural construction of the diverse "nations" grouped under the name of Latin America as a broad form of social and textual affiliation crisscrossed by truths and (perhaps unintended) falsehoods capable of exceeding the margins of literary conventions and the common places of ideology.

In Latin American thought this sense of cultural mobility is articulated through the concept of transculturation (see Ortiz; Rama). On the horizon made available by this operative category, one can perceive the extent to which transcultural processes contribute, by virtue of their own dynamic, to the creation of new theoretical objects. In turn, the creation of these new objects calls into question their production in Latin America, whether this production is considered under the sign of heterogeneity (see Cornejo Polar) or of hybridity (see García Canclini). As Moreiras notes (in his introduction to Part Two of this volume), the return to transculturation makes sense, then, only if it is conceived as a meta-critical operation–if transculturation signals at once the closure and liminality of cultural difference, as is markedly evident in the case of José María Arguedas (1911–1969) (see *El zorro de arriba y el zorro de abajo* [1996; *The Fox from Up Above and the Fox from Down Below*, 2000]). This concept of transculturation deserves a hearing that aims not at repetition but rather at being one capable of infiltrating its fabric of signifiers, so that its repressed contents may emerge and give rise to the work of re-elaborating the cultural formations of Latin America. This task entails placing in check the very concept that feeds interpretation and questioning the historical (if not historiographical) validity of the modernizing ideology of the nation-state that witnessed the concept's birth. Only thus may one reach a result freer of the restrictions of hegemonic knowledge and less compromised by the discoursive forces that aim to encompass proceedings of this nature in a totality or in a hierarchy of predetermined values.

The a posteriori theoretical construction of transculturation allows for a consideration of the other traces of meaning that have been attributed to this concept, thus inserting it into a historical perspective. This process highlights the double mandate of transculturation–its meta-theoretical force and its meta-historiographical demands–that is pragmatically oriented toward the battle of values in the contemporary scene. Operating among cultures and discourses in an "in-between" place, its conceptual activity can be effected only through an enunciation in which the experience of alterity is conceived as the interlocutor's (nontransferable) alterity. In this attempt at a transcultural and interdisciplinary comprehension of Latin America, cultural difference intervenes to transform the site of the past and present enunciation of conflicting terms and values, reorienting knowledge through the vantage point of the Other who resists undifferentiated totalization. Through a process of displacement, substitution, and projection, the disjunctive forms of representation of a possible "Latin Americanness" (strictly speaking, a form of Latin American counter-discourse) interfere with justifications of progress and homogeneity in the world of globalization, revealing authoritarian and normative tendencies pursued in the realm of culture in the interests of ethnic and state prerogatives.

In turn, the transformations worked by the dissemination of information on a planetary scale contribute to the rupture of cultural isolation and reproportion the identity of rural or urban communities to the extreme point of the erasure of each tradition's distinctive traits. In this context, the current embrace of local traditions in Latin America represents a mnemonic act of recovery that challenges the notion of a uniform and centralizing cultural unit, making possible the distinction or individualization of hitherto marginalized practices. It is a labor of memory interested in the apprehension of mechanisms through which diverse traditions–of erudite, popular, or mass culture–are transformed (or are deconstructed) as they conform to society. The cultural agency and exchange that ensue from this labor allow for a measure of how the reception of intra- or international models supplements local models, and of the extent to which this process propels the emergence of new values that question cultural boundaries and run counter to a mere cult of the past.

The emergence of differentiated cultural products translates into the formation of a space of de-centered meaning, open to residual or alternative modalities of knowledge. In this sense the national or macro-regional element is understood as a cultural component that acquires value as a framework of reference only in light of the heterogeneity that constitutes it and makes it unique within the cluster of representations in which it is situated. To conceive of Latin America as a theoretical site for a proposal of alternative knowledge is to vindicate a performative practice capable of opening critical reason to a political reason and a critique of knowledge, at the precise moment in which the hegemonic culture perpetuates its epistemic authority as the extension of its social and political dominance (see Moreiras 2001). The need to locate an outside to the global system points to a residual conception of exteriority, capable of explaining the lingering desire for singularity as the virtual expression of a certain distance or inadequacy with the process of assimilation to a culture of globalization.

In this third volume of the *Literary Cultures of Latin America*, divided into four parts, the reader will find multiple avenues for the further investigation of these and other questions that pertain to the exploration of a cultural imaginary more than five centuries old: questions that pertain to its transnational dynamic and to the material conditions of the production, distribution, circulation, and consumption of literary, artistic or cultural objects. Read in conjunction with one another, these texts offer effective possibilities for an enunciation not founded on the horizon of critical consensus, but rather on a process of signification understood as a conjectural wager that "takes advantage of highly contextualized and relative practices of interpretation with their liminality and hybrid configuration" (Ortega, Chapter 54 in this volume).

Part One, "Fissured Foundations: Nostalgia and New Beginnings," analyzes the precarious and unstable nature of the foundation of nations in Latin America, subject as they were from colonial times to the pressures of modernization. Literature here was the vehicle for the institutionalization of tastes and values, as well as a pedagogical tool to form ideal citizens for the newly independent republics of the nineteenth century. As the eight texts that make up this part demonstrate in different ways, the process of national foundation sought to open a crack in the European tradition as a strategy for the invention of a local variant, a paradoxical form of deletion of the European tradition by means of a transgressive inscription within it.

The volume's second and most extensive part, "Internal Borders: Cultural Conflicts and State Discourse," is composed of twenty-three chapters, all directly or indirectly engaged in the debates on transculturation. Understood as a reaction to the violent process of Westernization set in motion in Spanish and Portuguese America, transculturation is pressed into service as a concept key for the reading of the contradictions, conflicts, and paradoxes of a modernity that consumes itself before its full formation. These essays approach distinct aspects of this question: the "lettered mediation" that characterized the colonial period, the construction of national communities in the nineteenth century, the "inversion of social Darwinism," and the clash between modernity and modernization in the process of the formation of cultural identity in the twentieth century. The conceptual apparatus afforded by the national and popular phenomenon of transculturation makes evident the loss of the heterogeneous components specific to the struggle between hegemony and alterities in favor of a synthesis between the archaic and the modern.

In turn, the third part, "Liminality and Centrality of Literary Cultures in the Twentieth Century," considers indigenous literatures and cultures as subjects of knowledge that possess memories of colonization and muster them to produce alternative forms of knowledge. Rather than taking their cue from a merely anthropological approach, these texts present indigenous production in dialogue with the academic community, attesting to an enunciation that runs counter to the inequality and asymmetry then prevalent. In a comparable fashion, the analysis of Latino literary cultures in the United States reveals fractures and discontinuities in the contemporary transformation of these same cultures. One sees here the workings of a complementary logic that intervenes against the force of calculations that aim at negating distinct cultural manifestations through recourse to the notion of a unifying resemblance.

Finally, the fourth part, "Literary Culture in the Twentieth Century," privileges migrant theoretical trajectories, discursive and ideological displacements that highlight the transformations of literary culture in the course of the twentieth century. By effecting a methodological distortion along spatial and temporal axes that is analogous to the dynamic of travel narratives, these displacements set in motion a new reading of the various Latin American projects of modernization, the role played by the avant-garde, and the postmodern relation between the new and the traditional.

Whether the result of a preference for a comparativist methodology or simply a reflexive consideration of the premises for such inquiry, all four parts of this volume demonstrate how literary objects are liminal forms of social representation and of the reconceptualization of political practices, whose value can be ascertained only when a disciplinary or cultural frontier is crossed. This point of intersection reveals that identities are always virtual in the sense that they are located "entre o não ser e o ser outro" (Gomes 77) ("between non-being and being another"), to recover a familiar formulation but not as stigma, rather as the very prerequisite for the possibility of Latin American literary cultures. This formulation points to the provocative alternative of a practical and theoretical journey to a "non-place" that is productive in its critical negativity. Perhaps there lies the originality of the literary cultures in question, as well as the force of the writing of a new history.

Translation by Paulo Lemos Horta

Works Cited

Anderson, Benedict. 1991. *Imagined Communities*. London: Verso.

Andrade, Mário de. 1991 [1939]. "Evolução social da música social no Brasil." *Aspectos da música brasileira*. Belo Horizonte: Villa Rica. 11–31.

Andrade, Oswald de. 1972 [1928]. "Manifesto antropófago." *Obras completas*. Vol 6: *Do Pau-Brasil à antropofagia e às utopias: manifestos, teses de concursos e ensaios*. Rio de Janeiro: Civilização Brasileira. 11–19.

Arguedas, José María. 1996 [1969]. *El zorro de arriba y el zorro de abajo*. Ed. Eve-Marie Fell. Mexico City: ALLCA XX/Fondo de Cultura Económica.

——. 2000. *The Fox From Up Above and the Fox From Down Below*. Trans. Frances Horning Barraclough. Ed. Julio Ortega. Pittsburgh: University of Pittsburgh Press.

Boaventura, Maria Eugenia. 1995. *O salão e a selva: uma biografia ilustrada de Oswald de Andrade*. Campinas: Ed. Unicamp.

Borges, Jorge Luis. 1972. "Museo." *El hacedor*. Madrid, Buenos Aires: Alianza, Emecé. 143–44.

——. 1998. "Museum." *Collected Fictions: Jorge Luis Borges*. Trans. Andrew Hurley. New York: Penguin Books. 325.

Campos, Haroldo de. 1983. "Da razão antropofágica: diálogo e diferença na cultura brasileira." *Boletim Bibliográfico da Biblioteca Mário de Andrade* (São Paulo) Vol. 44: 107–27.

Candido, Antonio. 1969 [1957]. *Formação da literatura brasileira (momentos decisivos)*. Vol. 1 and 2. São Paulo: Martins.

——. 1972. "Literatura e subdesenvolvimento." *América Latina em sua literatura*. Ed. César Fernández Moreno. São Paulo: Perspectiva. 343–62.

Cornejo Polar, Antonio. 2000. *O condor voa: literatura e cultura latino-americanas*. Ed. Mario J. Valdes. Belo Horizonte: Ed. UFMG.

Freyre, Gilberto. 1966. *The Masters and the Slaves. A Study in the Development of Brazilian Civilization*. 2nd ed. rev. Trans. Samuel Putman. New York: Alfred A. Knopf.

——. 2000 [1933]. *Casa-grande & senzala*. Ed. Silviano Santiago. Vol 2 of *Intérpretes do Brasil*. Rio de Janeiro: Nova Aguilar.

García Canclini, Néstor. 1995 [1992]. *Culturas híbridas; estrategias para entrar y salir de la modernidad*. Buenos Aires: Sudamericana.

Gomes, Paulo Emílio Salles. 1973. "Cinema: trajetória no subdesenvolvimento." *Argumento* (São Paulo) 1: 55–67.

Martín-Barbero, Jesús. *De los medios a las mediaciones*. Santafé de Bogotá: Convenio Andrés Bello.

Mignolo, Walter D. 2000. *Local Histories/Global Designs: Coloniality, Subaltern Knowledges, and Border Thinking*. Princeton: Princeton University Press.

Moreiras, Alberto. 2001. *A exaustão da diferença; a política dos estudos culturais latino-americanos*. Trans. Eliana L. Reis and Gláucia R. Gonçalves. Belo Horizonte: Ed. UFMG.

Morse, Richard M. 1988. *O espelho de Próspero; cultura e idéias nas Américas*. Trans. Paulo Neves. São Paulo: Companhia das Letras.

Nunes, Benedito. 1972. "Antropofagia ao alcance de todos." *Do Pau-Brasil à antropofagia e às utopias* by Oswald de Andrade. Rio de Janeiro: Civilização Brasileira. xi–liii.

Ortiz, Fernando. 1978 [1940]. *Contrapunteo cubano del tabaco y el azúcar*. Caracas: Ayacucho.

Paz, Octavio. 1980. "Hispano-América: literatura e história." *O Estado de São Paulo: suplemento literário* 14 (Sept.): 3.

——. 1984. *Os filhos do barro: do romantismo à vanguarda*. Trans. Olga Savary. Rio de Janeiro: Nova Fronteira.

Rama, Ángel. 1984. *La ciudad letrada*. Hanover: Ediciones del Norte.

Rouanet, Maria Helena. 1991. *Eternamente em berço esplêndido: a fundação de uma literatura nacional*. São Paulo: Siciliano.

Santiago, Silviano. 1978. *Uma literatura nos trópicos; ensaios sobre dependência cultural*. São Paulo: Perspectiva.

——. 1982. *Vale quanto pesa; ensaios sobre questões político-culturais*. Rio de Janeiro: Paz e Terra.

Schwarz, Roberto. 1977. *Ao vencedor as batatas; forma literária e processo social nos inícios do romance brasileiro*. São Paulo: Duas Cidades.

——. 1987. *Que horas são?* São Paulo: Companhia das Letras.

Sommer, Doris. 1990. "Irresistible Romance: The Foundational Fictions of Latin America." *Nation and Narration*. Ed. Homi K. Bhabha. London, New York: Routledge. 71–98.

Süssekind, Flora. 1990. *O Brasil não é longe daqui: o narrador, a viagem*. São Paulo: Companhia das Letras.

Literary Cultures of
Latin America

A Comparative History

PART ONE

FISSURED FOUNDATIONS: NOSTALGIA AND NEW BEGINNINGS

INTRODUCTION

Doris Sommer and Maria Consuelo Cunha Campos

Throughout Latin America, where whole indigenous civilizations were apparently erased and replaced and where modern cultures have developed by leaving traditions to an Old World, foundations can seem precarious and unstable. Seen from the losing side or from the abandoned homelands, the foundations of both autochthonous and Europeanizing empires crumble under the pressures of modernization in its successive stages, from the early colony to Baroque, Enlightened, Romantic, and contemporary forms. The successors sometimes develop a tragic sense of history too, when they reflect on the rhythm of replaceability that can augur the victor's own future loss of ground. Their very success in overthrowing foundations makes grounding insecure. This dangerous supplement of adding new beginnings to old ones can seem to open onto an uncontrollable chain of foundations that are convenient though short-lived fictions. Nevertheless, fictions have some staying power, and they inform social relations along with creative sensibility, even when their political institutions feel the overload of supplements. This precariousness—for example, Aztec, Incan, Spanish, Portuguese, imperial, and republican institutions, despite the cultural continuities from stage to stage—points to a typical irony of writing (in) Latin America: Successive generations presume to establish lasting cultural and political structures even when they may sense expiration dates. If the new founders imagine themselves to be setting bases that can endure, other American founders had imagined the same.

Jorge Luis Borges (1899–1986) jokes about the circularity and the impossible pride of starting anew in "The Wall and the Books" (1950), his story about the emperor of China who built the Great Wall and burned all books written before his reign only to sense that a future emperor would erase his epoch-founding work with another new beginning. Borges is evidently amused, but also fascinated, by a tradition written into the efforts to erase the past. In Silviano Santiago's recent Brazilian version of this Americanist paradox, Latin America has been, since colonial times, a copy or simulacrum, becoming more and more similar to the original model by the paradoxical erasure of its own originality. The gradual elimination of original traces and the stimulus to forget violent erasures—a stimulus that comes with a desire to survive violence—produce the phenomenon of duplication. European conquerors seem to multiply their foundations in the New World, through cities, for example, that have European names whose ironic originality consists in the marker of repetition "New": Nueva

España, Nova Friburgo, New England, and so on. It is the same irony on which Borges made his "New Refutation of Time," because newness is already a symptom of time and of unshakable precedents.

Already at the end of the nineteenth century, Brazilian Machado de Assis (1839–1908) had gotten the joke about starting anew. In his novel *Dom Casmurro* (1899), an old man named Bentinho aims at rebuilding his childhood by building—elsewhere—a replica of his old family house, originally located in downtown Rio de Janeiro, on Mata-Cavalos Street. Its walls decorated with medallions of Roman emperors, the corners of the ceiling with tropical paintings of little flowers and big birds, the house as a whole suggests an allegory of the foundation of the nation itself, by the juxtaposition of Western imperial foundations as an inheritance from Portuguese colonization with the local South American flora and fauna. At its first location on Mata-Cavalos Street (named for the many dangerous potholes that threatened horse-and-buggy travelers), the old house was Bentinho's home at the beginning of Brazil's Second Empire, when the national economy was based on natural products, coffee and sugar. That was before engines and railways modernized production and commercialization. In the 1870s, when modernization was in full process, Bentinho moved to the suburb of Engenho Novo, named for the large "new sugar plantation" in the neighborhood. But the "agricultural" name literally means "new engine." So Bentinho's dream of re-establishing local agricultural traditions founders in a changing language in which even agriculture has been modernized and mechanized.

Many moments make up this confounding rhythm of razing one foundation to raise another. In the repeating efforts toward occidentalization, there are countervailing efforts that syncopate with the dynamic models bent on continuous change. The three fundamental moments featured here—both in Hispanic America and in Brazil—are certainly not exhaustive; but they are the foci of investigation for our contributors, and they represent obviously important conjunctures of our Latin Americas for readers to consider and add to.

At the time of the conquest, José Antonio Mazzotti tells us, Spanish adventurers were thinking backward rather than forward. They were reviving medieval hopes of glory while, in response, indigenous practices made sure to keep the local past alive. The conquerors' nostalgia is not so much geographical, as we may have imagined; it is more temporal, Mazzotti argues. The past, before a consolidated crown

1

reduced autonomous gentlemen into mere subjects, becomes the object of impossible desire for adventurers who tried to reconquer autonomy in America. That doubling back of the past as a future would characterize the ambition of indigenous historians too, as they revive the glories of conquered empires through the modern codes that promise to preserve the past. These histories thereby create a new form of writing, through rhythms and semantic fields that Spanish historians had not imagined.

On the Brazilian side, Guillermo Guicci and Marcelo Rocha Wanderley focus on the problem of the national foundation as an a posteriori construction, showing how a chance discovery in 1500 of what seemed to be simply an unknown island on the way to India became the foundational event for Portugal's future progeny. They also show how the documents of discovery were re-read in 1900, during the fourth centenary, as a refounding of Brazil's national identity in light of the new republican modernization.

For the Baroque period, Stephanie Merrim shows how Spanish American cityscapes inherit the nolstalgia that had driven the conquerors to reconquests of autonomy. But by now, their sons confront past losses by flaunting their new-world achievements. She reads the public spectacle of festivals and ceremonies as a symptom of cultural volatility, a mechanism for overwhelming *criollo* anxieties with the energy of extravagance and complexity. Her productive observation yields a new taxonomy of the urban Baroque imaginary: sublime, marginal, scandalous, panic-stricken, sinful, and nocturnal cityscapes, where protagonists locate themselves more through spectacular transculturated events than through the constants of city planning. Both distant Spain and the local empires fuel the feelings of a general style that Merrim describes as American dependent plenitude. The style embraced both colonists and the metropolis through a shared desire to bridge a riven community. Each Baroque spectacle had two ideal publics—one here, another there—and two ideal receptions—as an extension of Spanish tradition, and as a New World departure from it.

Taking the Baroque cultural center of Salvador as her starting point, Maria Consuelo Cunha Campos shows how the space fostered a uniquely brilliant dichotomy between international and local writers. To focus the tensions she considers the polemics surrounding the sermons by the Jesuit preacher Antônio Vieira (1608–1697); they extended like concentric circles around Salvador, through much of Latin America (think of Sor Juana in Mexico) and through much of Europe (especially Portugal and Italy).

Given the paradox of new foundations, Spanish American Independence is, logically, something of an oxymoron, with the "American" adjective still depending on the "Spanish" one. Beatriz González Stephan goes so far as to describe the foundation of official Spanish American cultural traditions as doubled, or self-reflexive, produced for two mutually vigilant publics: for local fellow citizens who might be critical of European

models and for Europeans skeptical about the worth of American creativity. Her specific texts are literary histories, which can stand in as synecdoches for an ambitious general cultural construction of legitimate rebelliousness. Literature was the vehicle for institutionalized tastes and values; its pedagogical ambition was to model ideal citizens for the new republics. These states founded their legitimacy both on approval from Europe and on independence from seeking that approval; they located a gap in (European) tradition as an opportunity to invent a local variation. And the destabilizing variations carry a thrill of anxiety whether the founding language is Spanish or Portuguese.

In Vera Follain de Figueiredo's convincing comparison, Brazil's nationalist elite, like Mexico's, needed a literary tradition to anchor its claim of cultural and political autonomy. Inventing a tradition and building a national identity were two faces of the same coin, not only for Brazilian Romantic writers but also for their contemporary patrons. Follain de Figueiredo develops the dynamic of mutual support, with particular attention to Brazilian and Mexican penchants for representing indigenous peoples as Romantic builders of a postcolonial nation.

Doris Sommer adds her observations about mid- to late-nineteenth-century national romances that helped to consolidate republics by celebrating a particular country, paradoxically in the universally modern terms of heterosexual erotics and laissez-faire. The contradiction between being particular and being universally modern produced a *double consciousness* that parallels the tensions described by Merrim's anxious Baroque affirmations and by González Stephan's double-dealing histories of legitimate literature, which excluded the risky contemporary novels. Those histories wanted to claim modernity by documenting it, while the novels agitated to produce bourgeois modernity in the forms of political stability, commerce, and legitimate children. The novels were training manuals, intentionally paced over newspaper installments to gradually wean the public away from fruitless passions and then to quicken the pulse of productive desire. A typical plot begins with an easy erotic hook for conventional readers. But then the narrative veers away from aristocratic tangles and carries the enchanted audience over the murderous differences of class, region, and race toward new and liberal passions.

To bring these changes into focus today, Victor Hugo Adler Pereira points out that the characteristics of the Brazilian modernization when the Republican period began at the end of the nineteenth century are again models of neo-liberal policies. In his essay, the republican practices of discrimination, including the marginalization and exclusion of the ex-slaves, the homeless, and the landless, were very similar to the streamlining efforts of Brazil's economy—*vis-à-vis* the working classes—at the end of twentieth century. Both moments are, for Adler Pereira, two acts of the same play, in which Repression and Resistance are the main protagonists.

CHAPTER 1

EPIC VOICES
NON-ENCOUNTERS AND FOUNDATION MYTHS

José Antonio Mazzotti

The Necessary Expansion of the Corpus

The definition of epic poetry as a literary genre has been problematic since its beginnings; this situation has not been resolved in the discussion inspired by the Aristotelian definition of the lengthy heroic poem or the introduction of the *romanzo* by Boiardo and Ariosto in the sixteenth century, though that broke the thematic unity of the classic poem and left the door open for the inclusion of fantastic passages, apparently unconnected with the central argument. In addition, the categories of "poem" and "the heroic" can themselves become relative given the interdisciplinary expansion within the field of colonial literary studies and the contributions of folklore studies during recent years, which have both influenced the definition of the term "epic poetry" and the concept of "epical" itself. This section will therefore consider an extensive corpus that will include, as well as the commonly accepted genre of epic poetry, examples of other discoursive typologies, especially those that relate to the area of Americanist historiography based on indigenous versions of conquered peoples' past.

It is important here to examine a series of formulations of social or community space from the perspective of the subject of the writing, who focalizes the heroic deeds narrated in each text. Hence these formulations must include those written expressions of ancestral and primordial definition (endemic to heroic discourse in general), derived from Amerindian oral sources. These, as far as one knows, imply modalities of production, diffusion, and consumption that are connected to other modes of expression such as ritual representations, choruses, and music; frequently these links are clear from their plots or their formulaic structures based on ways of inscribing and registering collective memory, such as the *amatl*, or Mesoamerican codex, and the Andean *quipu*. Rarely does the totality of these non-literary expressions remain transcribed in the historiographic texts derived from them, but even so, the texts still conserve something of their origin in the written configurations handed down to us from the sixteenth century.

Following this line of argument a simple division of the material under study would include at least these two categories:

1. Epic poetry based on European discourse. This body of work includes two subcategories defined according to the degree of their relationship with the tradition of medieval Spanish romance and Italian models of the Renaissance period. In both cases can be found components of the epic of the conquerors (according to the Virgilian paradigm) and the epic of the conquered (following that of Lucan). These are the definitions proposed by David Quint (in his introduction to *Epic and Empire*) and sketched out in the Hispanic context by Frank Pierce (21–22) and Antonio Prieto (see 1975; 1980, 119). A study of both the strong popular Spanish oral tradition and the European theoretical frameworks of the sixteenth century (and their cultural manifestations by poets who heroicized events of the conquest) could throw light on the peculiarities of many of the works to be investigated. But as a result of the peripheral context of their New World production, these works contribute new elements as well as reorganizations of Medieval and Renaissance topics made in the interests of the new social subject whose perspective is being presented. While the increase of European epic poetry during the sixteenth century revealed a nostalgic vision of the martial aristocracy in the face of the increasing power of the royal houses (Quint 3–18), it is worth investigating to what point poems of Americanist origin not only coincide in the exaltation of the martial and cultural aspects of the Spanish invasion, but also act as a symbolic space to reformulate those knightly ideals already on the wane in the Iberian Peninsula. In certain cases, we will also see here the creation of a *criollo* feeling of connection to the land, a desire for permanence and dominion, that arose even prior to the appearance of the *criollos* as a social group (Lafaye 7–8; Lavallé 1978, 39–41; Durand 1953).

2. Epic narratives with indigenous roots. This corpus includes texts written within the conventions of historiography but which contain an obvious exemplificatory or hero-making intent, especially in relation to their indigenous and *mestizo* sources and interests. This category includes the *Suma y narración de los Incas* [c.1548–1556; *Narrative of the Incas*] by Juan Díez de Betanzos (1510–1576), the *Instrucción* by Titu Cussi Yupanqui (sixteenth century) [1570?; *Instruction*]; Books III, VIII, and XII of the *Historia general de las cosas de la Nueva España* [1560; General History of the Things of New Spain] by Bernardino de Sagahún (1500?–1590); the analogous chapters of the *Historia de las Indias de Nueva España e islas de Tierra Firme* [1581; The History of the Indies of New Spain] by Diego Durán (1537–1587); the *Historia de Texcoco* [1608; History of Texcoco] by Fernando de Alva

Ixtlilxóchitl (1578–1650); the *Crónica mexicana* [1598; Mexican Chronicle] by Fernando Alvarado Tezozómoc (1530?–1600?); and the martial chapters of the *Comentarios reales* [1609 and 1617; The Royal Commentaries of Peru] of El Inca Garcilaso de la Vega (1539–1616), which refer to the expansionist work of the Incas, among others. If, on the one hand, these works, along with other similar examples, attempt to be taken primarily as histories and so assume the criterion of truth (transcendental, if not factual) as the basis of their narrative, it is clear, on the other hand, that the limits of the genre in which they are usually classified are transcended—here as a result of the oral components that contained heroic indigenous elements. Such an expansion clearly exceeds the standard paradigm of the canonical heroic, but it proves highly fruitful for research on indigenous self-definition, the sense of identity of an ancestral community based on a foundation myth and on a form of ethnic nationality (or nation, as the term was interpreted by the Spanish culture of the sixteenth century).

Such works *sui generis* constitute part of the corpus of Colonial historiography, but here will be examined in light of the "residues of oral tradition" (Zumthor 1987, 37) with which they reconstruct the heroic conduct of their conquered subjects in terms of both the pre-Hispanic past and the Conquest. Nevertheless, this examination will not try to show just the reflection of a lost oral or primordial tradition in the texts. Of even more consequence, it will reveal both the discursive foundations of a pluricultural polyphony, one that made room for other discursive intertexts in the original Amerindian narrative systems, and also the ways in which peninsular historiography attempted to understand this phenomenon. Thus, this second category presupposes a re-evaluation of the traditional concept of epic poetry and of epic voice (see Bynum 70; also Zumthor 1990, 81), in order to allow the inclusion of written and *transformed* events from these other sources in the final form of their historiographic narrative.

This section will explore the limits and characteristics of the historiographic genre of the period and its connections to the epic form, according to the peninsular conception of heroic discourse in general. In this context the ideas of Joseph Pellicer on the epic prose poems (167) are important, as are the theories of Pinciano, Sebastián Minturno, and other contemporary authorities on the possibility of developing heroic narrative in prose form, an idea that seemed to be already contemplated in Aristotle's *Poetics* within the category of "impossible verisimilitude" and in Tasso's *Discorsi del'arte poetica e del poema eroico* [1964; *Discourse of the Heroic Poem*], where he points out that this form could be written "senza obligo alcuno di rime" (106) ("without any obligation to rhyme"). Although the concept of heroic prose narrative was formulated in the sixteenth century with reference to texts written with entertainment in mind (as does Pinciano, with respect to *Amadis*), it suggests a rhetorical connection to the expressive possibilities of the genre of historiography at the time.

In studying both categories, however, the focalization, which points to specific definition of the social whole, will be given precedence. In so doing, it is easy to foresee that in many of the texts in the first category, the *criollo* ideal will prevail as a strategy for the formulation of their own identity through the heroizing elevation of their ancestors. For this reason, it is no exaggeration to speak of a "*criollo* nation" (Pagden 91) (in the previously mentioned ethnic sense of the word), even though the study of epic poetry has to date been barely used as a focus to investigate the theme in any depth. This is perhaps because of its similarity to, rather

than difference from, European models that have been sought, and also because the importance of the Indian context has not been considered in its true dimensions—since the modes of European discourse are repeated and re-semanticized in accordance with the historical variables of the colonizing experience. Moreover, if we make a direct and anachronistic application of so-called post-Colonial theory (based on the British and French experience in Africa and India during and after the Enlightenment), the specificity of the *criollo* and *mestizo* production risks being lost, assimilated to similar categories that actually deserve a serious reformulation within the very specialized field of pre-Enlightenment Spanish America. The re-semanticization of the European canon can be seen in some poems, and at different moments in the same poem, says Quint; a work can faithfully follow the canonical tradition and at the same time react to the immediate historical situation: "I distinguish between where the text responds to historical occasion and where it repeats a generic convention or commonplace, although it may do both simultaneously" (15). As far as the second category is concerned, one can see that despite the fact that the authors, translators, or writers from the dominant colonial group act as intermediaries in certain cases, some features of the indigenous discourse—though transformed—are still visible as part of the subtext of the works. (For a definition of the category of subtext, see Mazzotti 1996 *Coros mestizos*, Introduction.)

To facilitate matters, I propose to dislocate the American reference as a fundamental point of departure for the works of both the first and the second category—at least in relation to the constituent elements of the academic institution that pretends to take responsibility for it. In the majority of cases because of tradition and authorial provenance, this discourse is one of the clearest instances of the "lettered city" (Rama, chaps. 1–3); it is thus logical to suppose that the general orientation of its narrative would be written in terms of the topics and rhetorical strategies that made the same genres part of a symbolic practice of European cultural self-affirmation. Even so, on being moved into the American frame of reference, these same genres undergo substantial modifications (especially those of the second category) on account of the nature and rhetorical format of the Amerindian sources. Thus the term "non-encounter" in the title of this section alludes not only to the conquest with its well-known anecdotes of lack of communication and genocide, but also to the notable differences in systems of historicization that produced works that are basic to the subsequent traditions of Latin American discourse.

The Epic of European Extraction

Some time ago, José Toribio Medina (1918, vii–xii), Ramón Menéndez Pidal (7–13), Winston Reynolds (1978, 15) and Cedomil Goic (431–32), among others, pointed out that the popular tradition of the chivalric romance arrived in the New World with the conquistadors, who in addition to repeating tales of the Carolingian cycle and of El Cid, spontaneously composed verse narratives recounting their own misfortunes and exploits and broadcast them by word of mouth. It should therefore come as no surprise that the initial compositions of epic character composed by Europeans in America have an evident medieval flavor in terms of rhythm, meter, and subject matter: So too could one characterize the protagonists of these tales as being the medieval knights struggling between the Goddess Fortune and Christian Providence. Miguel Nieto Nuño (xviii–xix) rightly points out that the heroes, such as

Francisco Pizarro in *La conquista de la Nueva Castilla* [The Conquest of New Castile] (an anonymous 1537 poem also known as *La conquista del Perú* [Conquest of Peru]), are presented in terms of an opposition of values that finds its greatest antecedent in the *Laberinto de fortuna* [1444; Labyrinth of Fortune] of Juan de Mena (1411–1456). An examination of the *Romancero de Hernan Cortés* [Ballads of Hernán Cortés], compiled by Winston Reynolds (1967), makes clear that the image of the *dux populi* elaborated there fits in very well with a pre-established pattern. Nevertheless, such an example of martial prowess and Christian virtue acquires the dimensions of a foundational myth for the hereditary lineage of the New World. (See also Reynolds 1978, 113–44 for a detailed list of the works of the Golden Age that put Cortés center-stage, including the Cortés epic cycle, which will be examined later.)

For this reason, although it is relatively simple to investigate the crosscurrents that make possible the genesis and shaping of this first Spanish epic in the New World, the problem does not by any means end with textual genealogy. Historians such as Anthony Pagden have underlined that these soldiers and their captains, when offering Masses for the soul of the champion El Cid, were indicating their determination for a ruling autonomy subject to the Crown but administered by them; they "considered themselves to be the founders of a new kingdom that would be a fief of the Spanish crown but in all important respects a self-governing polity" (53). Moreover these same individuals came to New Spain "to act out the role of the great magnates of the Old Spain" (53). Cortés has been described as the instigator of a popular rebellion (see Giménez Fernández) and his heir Martín Cortés, the second Marquis del Valle de Oaxaca, the inspiration behind a *criollo* conspiracy whose defeat would be meticulously and gloomily recounted by Juan Suárez de Peralta (1536–1589?), nephew of the first Marquis, in his *Tratado del descubrimiento de las Indias* [1589; Treatise on the Discovery of the Indies]. Thus, beyond the transmission of some common ideals and the identification with a familiar kind of discourse, for the peninsular army, the poetic heroization of military leaders also played its part as political affirmation and was thus very much in tune with new aspirations. Years later these would lead to irreconcilable and at times bloody confrontations with the Crown, when the latter began to limit the power of the new *encomienda* aristocracy and to strengthen a bureaucratic apparatus of direct control over the indigenous population through the local jurisdictions and the settlement of converted Indians (see Millones 1995).

In the case of Peru, the previously mentioned poem, *La conquista de la Nueva Castilla* (written in double hendecasyllabic quatrains), presents a Pizarro superior even to classic heroes. Francisco de Jerez (1497–1564?), the author of one of the first chronicles to record Pizarro's victory over Ataw Wallpa in 1532, included at the end of *La conquista del Perú* (published in Seville two years later) a poem "Al Emperador que es el Rey Nuestro Señor" ("To the Emperor Who Is Our Lord the King"), in which he praises the entire business of conquest and explains to Charles V that the wealth of his crown and Seville's magnificence is due to the triumphs of the Spanish soldiers in their role as participants in private enterprise overseas. (See Varón Gabai for a recent hypothesis about the Pizarro brothers' concept of enterprise in Peru.) Seville is thus counted "por maravilla," since "della salen, a ella vienen/ciudadanos labradores/de pobres hechos señores/pero ganan lo que tienen/por buenos conquistadores" (Jerez 38) ("marvelous, [since] they leave her, they come to her/working

citizens/from poor men made lords/but they earn what they have/by being good conquistadors"). This is a symptomatic expression of that mentality of contractual subjection that is set up between the king and his vassals, whose fidelity was measured through owed recompense, and whose effort and overwhelming investment granted them implicit virtue and nobility. For this reason, even though the chronicle in its entirety is a narrative of events from the legal and historical perspective of an eyewitness, it includes deeds so extraordinary that the poem is allowed to say that the action of Francisco Pizarro is "cosa/digna de escribir en prosa/y en metro como la embio" (38) ("a matter/worthy of writing down in prose/and in meter as I am indeed transmitting it"). This suggests the flexible limits of the genre and places the work within the old peninsular tradition of rhyming chronicles for popular consumption.

The concept of Pizarro as a founding father (despite the ignominy suffered by his family after the revolt of his half-brother Gonzalo in 1544 to 1548 against the Leyes Nuevas [New Laws]) would endure until the seventeenth and eighteenth centuries. In 1630, for example, Fray Buenaventura de Salinas (d. 1653), a Franciscan *criollo* and author of *Memorial de las historias del Nuevo Mundo Pirú* [1630; Memoir of Histories of the New World, Peru], one of the most representative reformist and pro-localist chronicles in the debate between *criollos* and peninsular Spanish, demanded a "Spanish Virgil" who would take up the theme of the exploits of Pizarro to imbue the dispirited descendants of the conquistadors with the authority and prestige necessary for their aspirations toward atavistic heroism. As Salinas says:

> De Piçarro, que nauegò por entre perlas del Sur, y corriò por sedientos arenales dãdo fuerça a sus trabajos, y possession a su esperança, y animosamente se arrojò a quitar de la frente, y manos de Atagualpa el supremo señorio de la America, arroxandola a los pies del cetro, y sobre los ombros Catolicos de España. Apenas se oye su nombre en el Pirú, apenas se cuentan sus hazañas, ni se pondera su coraje, y valentia. Quien a sabido referir las singulares, y no creydas hazañas destos Conquistadores, a quienes la desecha fortuna del mar, y tierra hizo exploradores de los frutos, y riquezas del Pirú? Que Virgilio Español a tomado a su cargo esta nauegacion, como el otro, que cantò la de Eneas, por el Mar Tirreno? Que Valerio Flaco de aquesta insigne Vniuersidad de los Reyes a querido celebrar el bellozino de oro, que hallaron tantos Iasones, y mares nauegados por tantos Argonautas valerosos? (Salinas f. n. n.)

> Of Pizarro, who navigated between the pearls of the south, and ran past quicksands, lent strength to his work, and full of hope he spiritedly ventured to take the supreme lordship of America from the brow and hands of Atahuallpa, casting it at the feet of the scepter and on the Catholic shoulders of Spain. His name is barely mentioned in Peru, and his adventures are hardly retold; nor are his courage and valor considered. Who has known to mention the singular and unbelievable adventures of these conquistadors, who a turn of fortune made explorers of the fruits and wealth of Peru? What Spanish Virgil has taken up this voyage, like that other poet who sang of Aeneas in the Tyrrhenian Sea? What Valerius Flaccus from that splendid University de los Reyes has wanted to celebrate the beauty of gold discovered by so many Jasons and seas navigated by so many valiant Argonauts?

This highly declamatory encomium was to receive a response adequate to its demands only a century later, when Pedro de Peralta y Barnuevo (1663–1743), another prominent *criollo*, published his *Lima Fundada, o Conquista de Perú* [Lima Founded, or the Conquest of Peru] in 1732, using the *Aeneid* as a model. He was proclaimed, in the "Aprobación" ["Approval"] of his fellow artist Pedro Bermúdez de la Torre y Solier (b. 1665), the "Spanish Virgil" whom the *criollo* nation had long awaited.

This prolongation of the heroic paradigm of Pizarro would, however, be discredited from the moment of its appearance by texts exalting, instead, other figures of the Conquest who were opposed to his leadership; in time, he became the proto-*criollo* Aeneas. For example, a highly critical vision of the Pizarros appeared in the *Muerte del adelantado Don Diego de Almagro* [1541; The Death of Governor Don Diego de Almagro] written by the polemical "ruined knight" Alonso Henríquez de Guzmán (1499–1547) and described by Clemente Palma as the "primer poema sobre la conquista de América" (12–13) ("first poem on the conquest of America"). This critique can be explained by Henríquez's service under the banner of Almagro el Viejo, who was decapitated in 1538 after the defeat of Salinas on the orders of Hernando Pizarro: Almagro is praised as the true vassal, faithful to the king, and the Pizarro brothers become the traitors. Furthermore, Henríquez laments that the Pizarros were to blame for the fact that the Indians dared to call "tyranos/a muchos d'España por esta ocasión" (Palma 42) ("tyrants/many of Spain on this occasion"). This same loyalty to the king and the magnificence of his exploits made Almagro "otro Gran Capitán" (67) ("another great captain") with "hechos de notar,/tales que por cualquier dellos/se debe coronizar" (68) ("deeds of note,/ such that any single one/was worthy of a crown"). There is, as Bermúdez Gallegos (13) points out, a clear tone of political dissidence (or at least of ambiguity), which could be the combination of nostalgia for political autonomy and the desire for a local king "crowned" in accordance with the majesty endowed by his own warlike exploits and moral virtues. Not for nothing does the medievalization of Henríquez allude to the "arte [que] se ha de cantar al tono de 'El Buen Conde Hernán González'" ("art that must be sung to the tune of 'The Good Count Hernán González'").

Yet another aspect can be seen in the anonymous poem, baptized as "La batalla de Chupas" ["The Battle of Chupas"] (only published in 1906 by Carlos A. Romero), a direct homage to the Governor Vaca de Castro, who was sent to Peru to defeat Diego de Almagro, "El Mozo," *mestizo* son of the associate of Francisco Pizarro (who, as we have seen, was indirectly responsible for the latter's assassination in 1541). Almagro el Mozo was thus able to exact vengeance for the death of his father, but he was finally defeated at the battle of Chupas in 1542. Like his progenitor, he was decapitated shortly afterwards. The author of the poem, an anonymous soldier, exclaims, "Perú, de tu libertad/este [Vaca de Castro] fue inventor primero" ("Peru, your liberty/was first created by this man [Vaca de Castro]"). In a vein very clearly in support of the Pizarro cause, he deploys a long eulogy of the loyal *encomenderos* who participated in the overthrow of Almagro "El Mozo": "Allí vieras los galanes/ mostrarse valientes hombres/y esforzados capitanes,/que pueden llamar Roldanes" (Vargas Ugarte 26) ("There you could see the gallant ones/ showing themselves to be valiant men/and captains of endeavor,/who could be called Rolands"). Even when applied to those *encomenderos* loyal to the king, the medieval knightly concept maintained its relevance, providing an excellent framework within which to define the self-assumed identity of these plebeians and followers, elevated after a few years to a military (and almost legendary) stardom.

In the case of Mexico, an examination of some passages of the *romances* (ballads) based on the story of Cortés is sufficient to uncover similar formulations concerning the military and spiritual paradigm of glorification. In the "Romance a Cortés" ["Ballads to Cortés"] (see Reynolds 1967, 30), for example, Jerónimo Ramírez states that the conquistador could with his lance alone humiliate proud kings and that he gave to Spain ships laden with silver to relieve the world of all human poverty. This restorer of the lost order of the golden age (an inveterate topic of chivalric romance [Lulio 160]) is nevertheless the most loyal servant of the king, despite the fact that in practice "quita y pone leyes" ("he annuls and imposes laws") with the same wisdom and moderation as a monarch and without keeping anything back "para sí solo, [salvo] el pregón de la fama" ("for himself, [except] the proclamation of his fame"). In another ballad, anonymous this time, Cortés "dejó de ser rey,/por ser a sus reyes firme" ("rejected kingship,/to be loyal to his own monarchs") (Reynolds 1967, 61). And in the work of the erudite Gabriel Lobo Lasso de la Vega, he even appears as a crusader ordering the devil to abandon Mexico to save the souls of the indigenous population (Reynolds 1967, 40). The *dux populi* is here once again transformed by legend into the rank of a monarch, to the point of even striking fear into the real king, as one sees in the celebrated ballad "En la corte está Cortés" ["Cortes Is in the Royal Court"] (attributed by some to Mateo Rosas de Oquendo; see Reynolds 1967, 57–60).

Thus it can be seen that there is no thematic homogeneity, even if there is a similarity of perspective in the great variety of poems that were recited and written, based on popular peninsular models. In fact many of these remained unedited up until the nineteenth century, and the large majority have been lost or buried in archives. The tradition that places the Christian hero within an imaginary space similar to that of the *Reconquista* (reconquest of southern Spain from the Moors) still allows one to espy the edge of a decentralized subjectivity that would characterize later generations, especially sections of the *criollo* population. With all its ambiguities, the so-called cultivated epic poem would shortly after this address some of the same concerns, though in a more concealed way. In some cases however, like that registered by José Toribio Medina (1918), the popular vein would give way to the cultured. One need only think, for example, of *Los romances basados en La Araucana* [Ballads Based on the *Araucana*], which began to be collected and published scarcely two years after the appearance of the third part of Ercilla's work in 1589.

The study of this poem, considered by some to be the only true epic poem in Spanish American literature, must take into account the fact that the concept of heroism had very clear definitions for authors of the time, who recognized the autonomous and superior status of epic and heroic fiction, subject only to the laws of its own world. In addition to the masters already mentioned, such as Tasso, Pinciano, and Minturno, Fray Jerónimo Román (1536–1597) wrote at the end of the sixteenth century that:

> La diosa Iuno se llama en Griego Hera, y Iuno tuvo un cierto hijo (segun las fabulas) que se llamó Heros, el qual denota ayre, y porque el ayre de la fama sube a los hombres al alto lugar quando son Ilustres en sus hechos, por esso son llamados Heroycos, o Heroas, porque el ayre es dedicado a Iuno, y todas las cosas que participan de los dioses, tienen como dizen los Poetas cierta parte de diuinidad. . . . (Román f. 293v).

The Goddess Juno was called Hera by the Greeks, and Juno had a son (according to the fables) who was called Heros which meant [of] air, and because the air of fame raised men to the highest place when made illustrious through their deeds, for this reason they are called Heroic or Heroes, since the air is dedicated to Juno, and all the things that participate in the gods have, as the Poets say, a certain element of divinity. . . .

Heroism in the end implies the raising and separation of the protagonist of a narrative, which results in his entering a dimension that in the twentieth century would be described by Lukàcs and Bakhtin respectively as a closed world and absolute past. In effect the autonomy and independence of the hero and his circumstances were accentuated from the time of the introduction of the *romanzo* as part of the Renaissance epic; it was then transformed into a fertile field for thematic variety, fantastic passages and journeys, and structural dislocation (as in the case of the cave of the magician Fitón and the appearance of the Battle of Lepanto in the second part of *La Araucana*). Without trying to reproduce the long history of the precepts, polemics, and poetic theory of the Renaissance (see Pierce, Introduction, for Spanish epic in general; see Cevallos for *La Araucana* specifically), I will only point out that in the first poem published (not, however, the first to be written) on the discovery and conquest of the New World–Cantos XI–XV of *Carlo famoso* [1566; Famous Carlo] by Luis Zapata (1526–1595)–Cortés is not really human but almost a supernatural personality. He is capable of overcoming monsters such as gigantic eagles and sharks (Zapata 66–74) in order to protect and win the respect and veneration of the indigenous population (a theme from the *Orlando furioso* transferred to the Indian context, as pointed out by Reynolds 1984, 4).

It is not relevant here to repeat in detail all the poems that make up the corpus of the Americanist cultivated epic. On the contrary, I just want to emphasize how the uses of European topics and verse modalities often obey concerns that lie beyond mere aesthetics and respond in the historical process to two constant threats to the "Republic of Spaniards" during the viceregal period: on the one hand, the overwhelmingly larger numbers of the indigenous population and, on the other, the attacks of pirates and corsairs that attempted to cut off the flow of minerals to the peninsula.

I will present some of these features as expressed in certain poems of which a minimal list would include *La Araucana* [1569, 1578, 1589; La Araucana: The Epic of Chile], by Alonso de Ercilla (1533–1594); *Arauco Domado* [1596; Arauco Tamed] by Pedro de Oña (1570?–1643?); *Argentina y conquista del Río de la Plata* [1602; Argentina and the Conquest of the River Plate] by Martín del Barco Centenera (1535–1601); *Armas Antárticas* [1604–1608; Antarctic Weapons] by Juan de Miramontes y Zuázola (1560–1614); *Elegías de varones ilustres de Indias* [1589; Elegies of Illustrious Men of the Indies] by Juan de Castellanos (1522–1607); *Poema heroyco hispano-latino panegyrico de la fundación, y grandezas de la muy noble, y leal ciudad de Lima* [1687; Panegyrical Hispanic-Latin Heroic Poem of the Foundation and Grandeur of the Very Noble and Loyal City of Lima] by Rodrigo de Valdés (1609–1682); *Lima Fundada* by Pedro de Peralta y Barnuevo, previously mentioned; *Cortés Valeroso* [1588; Courageous Cortés] and *Mexicana* (1594) by Gabriel Lobo Lasso de la Vega (1559–1615); *Nuevo Mundo y Conquista* [ca. 1580; New World and Conquest] by Francisco de Terrazas (ca. 1524–1600) (whose only known fragments appear in the *Sumaria relación de las cosas de la Nueva España*

[1604; Summary Report of the Things of New Spain] by Baltasar Dorantes de Carranza (fl. 1550–1604); *El peregrino indiano* [1599; The Pilgrim from the Indies] by Antonio Saavedra y Guzmán (fl. 1599); the *Historia de la Nueva México* [1610; History of the New Mexico] by Gaspar Pérez de Villagrá (1555–1620) and *México Conquistada* [1798; Conquered Mexico] by Juan de Escoiquiz (1762–1820). The greater part of these particular poems, in one form or another, gives an account of the glorious ideals of the enterprise of Conquest, while reinforcing the ideology of the peninsular aristocracy in some cases and in others that of the *encomenderos* raised to the aristocracy and their descendants in America. (A more comprehensive list, though still incomplete, that includes peninsular and Hispano-American production up until 1700 can be seen in Pierce 327–62.) This latter social group found in the aforementioned poems the best expression of their motives (the spread of Christianity, the task of civilization, the pursuit of fame and honor), placed as a discursive barricade in the face of accusations by Bartolomé de Las Casas and the "Black Legend" regarding the cupidity and cruelty of the conquistadors. As they formulated this argument and affirmed the profile of a type of overseas Hispanic identity in the sixteenth century, they cleansed their family honor and conferred an authoritative discourse on their demands for the continuation of the *encomienda* system.

In some of these same texts it is also possible to discover elements that acknowledge the nobility of the conquered people, their moral high ground (in terms of war and social organization), and the possibility of seeing in them the viability of a new and alternative society to that of the peninsula. At the same time, in various of these poems there exists in embryonic form the perspective of a social subject grounded in its control over the American land and in the previously mentioned (*criollo*) sentiment that differentiates between the heirs of the conquistadors and the administrators and bureaucrats of the viceregal organization immediately after the expansion of the *encomienda* system. (Aspects of this dispute are discussed in Liss, chap. 6, for Mexico and Lavallé 1993 for Peru.)

Some religious poems (which are no less heroizing) could also be considered within this category that uses divine or godlike figures to formulate and order space. These include *La Christiada* [1611; Christ Crucified] by Diego de Hojeda (1570?–1615); the *Vida de Santa Rosa de Santa María* [1711; The Life of Saint Rosa of Santa María] by Luis Antonio de Oviedo y Herrera or the Conde de la Granja (1636–1717); the *Santuario de Nuestra Señora de Copacabana* [1641; Sanctuary of Our Lady of Copacabana] by Fernando Valverde (1599?–1658); the *Oriental planeta evangélico* [1668; Eastern Evangelical Planet] and the *Triunfo parténico* [1683; Virginal Triumph], both by Carlos Sigüenza y Góngora (1645–1700); and the *Nueva Jerusalén María* [1662; New Jerusalem Mary] by Antonio de Escobar y Mendoza (1589–1669). In some of these, the concept of epic poetry within the peninsular tradition leads to the creation of local icons (such as in the poems of Fernando de Valverde and Luis Antonio de Oviedo) that define their own symbolic space within the context of an emerging *criollo* tradition. These authors make use of the concept of the "Christian epic" to exalt personalities of cultural and geographic proximity whose spiritual deeds overshadowed the soldiers of the Conquest and thus elevated them both literally and figuratively to divine status, a requirement for the attainment of the status of genuine epic hero. The scriptural subject that focused on the triumphs of the faith would, little by little, put the finishing touches on its own spiritual interests versus those of the dominant peninsular paradigm, in the same way as had subtly happened to the epic poem with a mainly martial or military theme. I will refer briefly to some aspects of these works, beginning with the glorification of Spanish military heroism in the face of foreign threats and the negation of the important role played in the military defense by the indigenous, mulatto, *mestizo,* and black troops whose participation is mentioned in numerous chronicles and documents of the period. In almost all these cases, the *criollo* class took the opportunity to create a martial ideal that might compete in terms of authorship and reference to homologous works describing Spanish triumphs within Europe.

Using the long and varied epic poem of Pedro de Oña as an example, we can examine certain *cantos* to reveal a *criollo* perspective, whether through the theme of the *encomienda* or through that of the struggles with the English corsairs, that motivated a partisan concealment of the role of the indigenous, *mestizo,* and mulatto Peruvian soldiers who participated in the conflicts. This insistence on the purity of blood derives from an actual source: A considerable percentage of *mestizos* assimilated into the *criollo* class during the first generations after the Conquest. It was for this reason that the peninsular Spaniards felt a growing lack of confidence in these "sons of the land," however much the latter were included within the "republic of Spaniards" (see Schwartz; Kuznesof). *Criollo* discourse naturally reacted by negating such biological and cultural links with the subjected "others." To do so they inflated themselves, not only as a focus for the heroization of Spanish arms in general, but also as the materialization of a subject self-constituted as the authorized and sanctified voice of a model of conduct located in the here and now of the New World. In the process they suggested economic reforms within the *encomienda* system, thereby setting themselves in opposition to the viceregal state's unsympathetic reorganization of the system, from its initial introduction into the Andean jurisdiction in 1564.

As far as one knows, the *Arauco Domado* by Pedro de Oña was partially conceived as a reaction to the minimal recognition that Alonso de Ercilla accorded to Don García Hurtado de Mendoza (1535–1609), firstborn son of the viceroy of Peru, in *La Araucana* (published in three parts in 1569, 1578, and 1589) during the latter's campaign in Chile (1557–1559), in which Ercilla was a participant. De Oña apparently corrected his poem during the printing process (see Victoria Pehl Smith 1984), revealing to the world a vision of martial heroism principally centered on the individuality of the protagonist. (For relevant comments on the *Arauco Domado,* see Alegría [Chap. 2], Dinamarca; Durán-Cerda; Morton [Chap. 2]; Raviola Molina; Rodríguez; Seguel; and Vega, among others.)

From the moment of its publication, Ercilla's text was a paradigm for the epic poem in the New World, and its importance has been underscored by numerous studies, with an emphasis on the heroic image of some Spanish captains and Araucanian chiefs. Relevant studies of *La Araucana* in this context include those of Corominas and Pastor, who take opposing viewpoints. This duality is due in part, according to Quint (especially 157–85), to the Virgilian and Lucanian nature of the basic models used by Ercilla; through transposition they identify the diminished military peninsular aristocracy with the emergent Araucana society of heroes, free of the monarchic yoke. Even so, Ercilla's ambiguity should also be framed within the context of Las Casas's thought, with its

strong criticism of the avarice of the conquistadors. Such a viewpoint finally favored the enterprise of imperial expansion directly regulated by the Crown, with common principles and values with regard to particular aspects of the official discourse against the *encomenderos* (see Mejías-López). Together with de Oña's poem and the *Argentina* by Barco Centenera, *La Araucana* belongs to what Luis Alberto Sánchez calls "el ciclo araucano" ("the Araucanian cycle") of the Colonial epic. To this short list must be added *Araucana II* by Fernando Álvarez de Toledo (1550?–1633) of which only eleven eight-line stanzas are known to survive within the *Histórica relación del reino de Chile* [1646; Historical Report of the Kingdom of Chile] by Alonso de Ovalle (1601–1651) and the extensive *Purén Indómito* [first years of the seventeenth century; Indomitable Purén], now properly attributed to Diego Arias de Saavedra (b. 1558?) (see Ferreccio Podestá).

A young soldier, aged twenty-six when the poem was published, de Oña based his work on the events of the expedition of Don García Hurtado de Mendoza (see particularly Cantos I to XIII) and eulogized his reforms and rational control of the *encomienda* system (especially in Canto III). De Oña's praise is dedicated to making the control of tribute, the age limit, improvements in mining work, and other measures in favor of the the Indians attributed to Don García into an implicit enumeration of remedies for the *criollo* situation. Quint (173) also notes this, a point that without doubt sets de Oña's position apart from the latent assumption of Las Casas that can be found in some passages of Ercilla's poem (Held 41–44; Rodríguez 80–81). De Oña's position is coherent with what he understands as the immanent capacity of the Araucanian Indians to convert themselves into subject workers under the control of the *encomenderos* "without excesses" (Quint 174). The condition of rustic or dependent subjects (as the laws governing the Indies catalogued the natives), along with the obligation to provide them with both material and spiritual protection, naturally favored in the long term the situation of the *criollo* descendants of these first *encomenderos.* This, on the other hand, generated the development of a tradition of *criollo* literature of paternalistic defense of the indigenous population (Mazzotti 1996c and 1998b).

The attitude of the authorities evident in their withdrawal of the first edition–apparently because of the poem's treatment of *encomenderos* and the inhabitants of Quito in the sales tax revolt of 1594 (Canto XVI, recounted through the dream of the indigenous Quidora)–would support this reading. (See also Seguel 49–50 and Victoria Pehl Smith, 16–17; for the historical event see Lavallé 1992.) Moreover the mourning for those unjustly executed is described in an extremely hyperbolic manner (the weeping of the women "reaches the stars"), while an ambiguous stance is revealed in terms of emotional solidarity (not political solidarity, which is unequivocally on the side of the crown). As far as it is possible for us to understand, the disorder of the generalized lament that ensued reached the heavens and destabilized the foundation of the naturally accepted order. The tremendous scope of this image could be challenged, if one was so inclined, but it is difficult not to see the discomfort and deep melancholy felt over the deterioration of the "common good" in the repression of the rebels. In addition the dispute between the viceroy and the Archbishop of Lima, Toribio de Mogrovejo, predisposed the Church to take a contrary attitude to the poem, which heroized the marquis' loyalty and implicated some members of the clergy in the rebellion. José Toribio Medina (1963, 1:

47–69) reproduces the documents of the process to which both poem and author were subjected. The second edition of the *Arauco domado* was published in Madrid without the expurgated fragments in 1605; de Oña went on writing poetry, completing three further volumes (*El temblor de Lima de 1609* [1609; Lima's 1609 Earthquake], *Ignacio de Cantabria* [1639] and *El Vasauro* [1635; The Vasauro] before his death in 1640.

De Oña's discussion of the foreign enemy is to be found in the two last cantos of his work (XVIII and XIX) in which he narrates the arrival of the English pirate Richard Hawkins on the Peruvian coast in 1594. Any mention of the help and participation of the indigenous and black soldiers in the Spanish military actions is eliminated from his text. It is not surprising that, as part of the dialogue of the time, as much in the struggle against the Araucanos as in that against Hawkins, de Oña would emphasize a particular form of heroism that was propitious to the legitimization of the merits that the already diminished *encomenderos* and their offspring, the *criollos*, would propose as the premise for any kind of establishment of social order in the Colonial period. It is worth mentioning that Seguel (44–45) remarks on de Oña's awareness of an American nation in the sense of a kingdom like Galicia or Catalonia in terms of the Spanish throne. In fact, in the "Prólogo al Lector" ["Prologue to the Reader"], de Oña confesses that his writing was motivated by "el solo desseo de hazer algun servicio a la tierra donde nasci (tanto como esto puede el amor de la patria)" ("the sole desire to render some service to the land where I was born [such as love of the fatherland can inspire]"). This pro-Chile aspect of de Oña, so much a foreshadowing of the later republican state, is a matter whose anachronism certainly constitutes a theme worthy of discussion. (For an opposing viewpoint of the Colonial mentality of *Arauco Domado,* see Rodríguez 80 and Alegría 57–59.)

Nevertheless the structure of the work itself, with its extraordinary length, reveals an indication of this difference, notably "the new fashion for eight-line stanzas" announced by de Oña himself in his "Prologue." The conventional order of the rhymes is altered, apparently only for the purpose of appearing to be different. Thus the poem is presented as a harsh variant of the canonic model, a discourse that is impeded by its own sonority, that would include juridical digressions (such as the reforms of the *encomienda* in Canto III) and those of a Romantic turn (as in the celebrated passage describing the bath of Caupolicán and Fresia in Canto V). In addition, the work includes numerous indigenous terms and a final glossary in which he explains their meanings. All these elements combine to suggest the development of an alternate voice, non-centralized and "Hesperic" (de Oña 4), that finds epic discourse an ideal vehicle for its own diction and the reconfiguration of *criollo* identity somewhere between ambiguity and celebration.

In another epic ensemble, dubbed "the Antarctic cycle" by Porras Barrenechea (1971), there appears a long poem by Juan de Miramontes y Zuázola entitled *Armas Antárticas.* Published for the first time in 1921, it has since been the subject of various studies that all coincide in acknowledging its remarkable literary quality. The first edition was issued in Quito by Gijón and Caamaño; three years later, in Chile, José Toribio Medina reproduced Cantos XVIII and XIX, which cover the expedition of Pedro Sarmiento de Gamboa to the Straits of Magellan. (Among more recent studies are those of Miró and Firbas, which provide numerous bibliographic references;

moreover, Firbas convincingly argues the need for a new critical edition of the poem.) Like the majority of the epics written during the viceregal period, *Armas Antárticas* glorifies the military prowess and evangelizing mission of the Spaniards. Here the poem makes special reference to the role of the Spanish forces in defense of the northernmost border of the viceroyalty of Peru, notably the region that encompasses modern Panama, against the invading forces of John Oxenham, one of Drake's lieutenants. Oxenham attempted to open a passage through the isthmus and blockade the port of Panama in order to expedite Drake's sacking of Lima and other Spanish cities along Peru's coast. He was successively defeated by expeditions under the command of Pedro de Ortega and Diego de Frías Trejo (Miró xiv–xv). The poem also addresses other themes, such as the love story between the young Incas Chuquiaquilla and Corioyllur, narrated by the Spanish general Arana on the triumphant army's return journey to Lima (Cantos X to XVII), and the expedition of Pedro de Sarmiento de Gamboa in 1580, sent by the Viceroy Francisco de Toledo across the Straits of Magellan to request the backing of the Spanish Crown with an eye to installing a permanent population in the remote Antarctic regions bearing the picturesque name of Filipópolis (Canto XVIII). Drake, as is known, arrived at the Peruvian coast by crossing these dangerous straits. It was the viceroy's intention to prevent a similar occurrence. Unfortunately for the Spaniards, the Filipópolis project was not successful because of the severity of the climate and the hostility of the inhabitants of the region. Miramontes y Zuázola concluded with two final Cantos narrating the arrival in 1587 of the pirate Cavendish, but the poem ends without completing the description of the historical developments connected with this event. (This leads one to believe that the poet did not actually complete the work.)

In the first section of the poem it is obvious that the runaway slaves helping Oxenham fulfill a role that contrasts with that symbolized by the impeccable whiteness of the Hispanic heroes. Only for a moment in the pursuit of Cavendish (Canto X, lines 1681–1704) do the Indians collaborate with the Spaniards on the Island of Puná offshore from Guayaquil, leaving their belongings and treasure at home. The English, confident of a speedy victory, celebrate that night and are surprised–and defeated–at dawn by the Spanish troops (among whom there is no mention, of course, of any soldier "of color").

As can be seen, the lengthy poem fulfills its objective of stressing what Miramontes would consider as "Antarctic arms." The brief allusions to non-white soldiers provide minimal evidence of the black and indigenous elements in the Spanish forces. The outstanding heroes are both peninsular and *criollo,* and not any subordinate personnel of color, who in fact are barely mentioned. This exclusion is made more evident in the two poems that follow, which provide a clearer idea of the mechanisms of discourse that complement the social and racial domination of the Spanish over the indigenous groups and the so-called "castes," with their varying degrees of African blood. In contrast to the epic poetry of other regions of Spanish America (for example the contemporary Cuban work, *Espejo de paciencia* [1608; Mirror of Patience] by Silvestre de Balboa [1563–1648], in which the hero is a black slave), this epic of Lima fulfills a highly defined political function in the context of the reorganization of the *mestizo* elite of Incan origin who, as the years passed, would constitute the driving force behind numerous revolts within the so called national Inca movement of the eighteenth century (see Rowe).

Almost a century later, a religious poem, the *Vida de Santa Rosa de Santa María* (1711), appeared in Madrid, not only with a historical theme but with references to events dating from the sixteenth through to the beginning of the seventeenth century. The author was Luis Antonio de Oviedo y Herrera, Conde de la Granja, a title this Spanish general acquired in Lima after many years of residence in Peru. At the age of thirty-two, he arrived as *corregidor* (chief magistrate) of Potosí in 1668. He stayed in Peru until he died in 1717, honored as a poet and soldier by *criollos* and peninsulars alike. His *Vida de Santa Rosa,* consisting of twelve cantos, covers the early historical periods in the history of Peru such as Incan genealogy and the arrival of Pizarro. These events occurred prior to the birth of the Lima saint (1586–1617), who immediately after her death became the object of a cult for the local population. Numerous miracles were attributed to her both during her lifetime and afterwards, leading to her rapid beatification (1668) and canonization (1671), as well as her receiving the titles of Patroness of the Americas and of the Philippines. A group of *criollos* played a major and direct role in this process, seeking thereby to secure their own ecclesiastical and symbolic support, which paralleled in the mid-seventeenth century the beginning of their involvement with manufacturing and haciendas (see Hampe Martínez 1995 and 1998 for a documented inventory of this hardly innocent procedure). Certainly Rosa is the best-known Peruvian (if not American) saint in the Catholic calendar of saints. Oviedo's poem endeavors to place itself within the rank of epic or heroic poetry because of the elevated theme with which it deals. This attitude is not uncommon in Christian epic poetry, which uses the original meaning of the word *heroic* to present saints, martyrs, and Christ himself as the main theme of their texts, as has already been pointed out. Even so, the interesting point here is how, in the events of the poem that refer to martial conflict with various English corsairs, Oviedo calls on the general expedient of completely ignoring the participation of the colored forces used to defend the viceroyalty of Nueva Castilla.

The first case in the narrative is that of Richard Hawkins, who appears off the Peruvian coast in 1594. According to the poem, on Hawkins's arrival in Peru, "faltan Buques, y sobran Peruanos" (Canto X, f. 378) ("there were not enough [Spanish] ships, and there were too many Peruvians [on land]"). Hence the saint intercedes with her "husband" Christ, for his support of the Spanish expedition under the command of Don Beltrán de la Cueva y Castro, who succeeds in defeating Hawkins and imprisons him after various days of fighting. The salvation of Lima, achieved by Rosa's prayers in this instance, seems to be an element of clearly fictional nature, given the youth of the future saint; Rosa was only eight years old when Hawkins's raid took place, and she lived in the Andean village of Quives, where her father managed an *obraje* (mill). According to calculations she would return to Lima, her place of birth, only in 1605, when she was nineteen years old (Millones 1993, 60). But in the case of a poem of praise, fidelity to real events matters less than glorifying the merits of the protagonists.

For this reason, Drake's visit to the Caribbean coast of Panama on his second expedition (1596–1597) is mentioned later in the text, while the raid of the Dutch pirate Spielbergen (1615), which blockaded the port of Callao in Peruvian waters but without managing to come ashore, is described in greater detail. The Lima Saint "era . . . la única esperanza/de Lima" (Canto XII, line ix) ("was . . . the only hope/for Lima"), says Oviedo, since the Spanish fleet that set sail to attack Spielbergen was defeated by the latter in Cañete to the south of Lima, leaving both the port of Callao and the capital without naval defense. (This was the combat in which Catalina de Erauso, the celebrated "Monja Alférez" ["Lieutenant Nun"] supposedly took part and was one of the few survivors of the shipwrecked flagship of the Spanish captain.) In the face of this threat Rosa succeeded in keeping the enemy at a distance so that it did not invade the city, thanks to the power of her prayer to invoke divine will to protect the city from the Dutch heretics. Any mention of the participation of indigenous, *mestizo,* black, and mulatto soldiers in all these events is glaringly absent. What can certainly be assumed is that many were involved in the general conscription, as had occurred in the defense of Concepción, Chile, where 300 Indians were included in a defense contingent of 1,200 soldiers to prevent the disembarkation of Spielbergen's forces (Bradley 37). It seems that the Dutch observed a superior defense consisting of eight companies of cavalry and some 4,000 infantry defending Callao and decided against attempting a landing (Bradley 41; Spielbergen 78–79). But the majority of the defenders were untrained troops, including some 300 priests and many young students who must have substituted in quantity but not experience for the soldiers who left with the defeated fleet and the fleet that had set sail for Panama with the royal treasure days before Spielbergen's arrival. One witness from the period pointed out that the soldiers thus mustered on an improvisatory basis might not have totaled more than two or three thousand (Álvarez de Paz, qtd. Bradley 42). Even though extant documentation does not mention the number of non-white soldiers who participated in the last-minute defense prepared by the viceroy (the Marquis de Montesclaros), we can suspect that many may have been *mestizos,* mulattos, and blacks, given that this was the general practice for conscription. (The first battalion of mulattos was created precisely in 1615.) The poem, as discussed above, gives most of the credit for the victory to the power of Rosa's prayers and the superiority of the Catholic faith over the "Luciferan" deviations of Protestantism and the rebel Indians (as in the frustrated rebellion of Yupanqui and Bilcaoma [*sic*], Inca prince and priest respectively, in Cantos VI to IX). Attacked on both fronts, internally and externally, the security of peninsulars and *criollos* alike would require the creation of their own cultural icons to sustain their control in terms of discourse. In this sense, Granja's poem, like those examined previously, fulfills a highly useful social role in its presentation of the war as a proof of legitimacy. The colored soldiers, given their links to sectors that were religiously suspect and racially despised by the dominant group, would not easily be given credit, however frequent or brave their participation in defense of these same Spaniards.

To conclude this section, it is worth mentioning certain aspects of the *Lima Fundada, o, Conquista del Perú* [1732; Lima Founded, or the Conquest of Peru]. The author, Don Pedro de Peralta y Barnuevo, was responsible for a number of works, including over forty treatises, histories, scientific studies, meteorological reports, books of poetry, and political essays. However, the most outstanding of his works is the lengthy epic poem of ten cantos that presents the history of Peru from the arrival of Pizarro to the period of the Marquis de Castelfuerte, the viceroy to whom Peralta dedicated his work and for whom Peralta fulfilled the important role of councillor as he had done with previous holders of the office. In this *criollo* version of Peruvian history, those passages recounting the arrival of various pirates to the coasts of Peru are of interest. While the thematic unity of the work is based on the events of the Conquest, in other words from the arrival of Pizarro (1532) to the foundation of Lima, Peralta rearranges these to present a lengthy prognostication of events that would take place in the kingdom during the 200 years from the episode of Cajamarca (the capture of Ataw Wallpa) and the moment of the publication of the poem (1732). This prediction, a common rhetorical stratagem in the poems that follow the Virgilian model, is announced by an angel or "genius of Lima." From Canto III onward, the angel recounts to Pizarro the grandeur and the glory of the kingdom that he will found on the laying of the first stones of the capital, notably the City of Kings, or Lima.

Among the events presented as predictions, I will linger briefly on those that refer to the appearance of the pirates Drake, Cavendish, Hawkins, Van Noort, Spielbergen, and L'Hermite in different passages of Cantos V and VI. As we shall see, the hesitation of previous poets (such as Miramontes) in recognizing the merits and the participation of colored soldiers in defense is converted, in Peralta's case, into an absolute denial of their presence. This, of course, should not surprise anyone, given the discriminatory views of the Peruvian *criollo* elite. This prejudice permits a necessary pause for a final reflection on the legitimacy of the glorificatory discourse of war (as is the case with epic poetry), so much part of the general strategy of political control by a supposedly white privileged social stratum, that of the *criollo*. For example, in the cases of Drake and Oxenham (Canto V, lines xl–xlvii), the only mention of the Peruvian defense is that of the "Martes de Lima" who fought against Oxenham and the runaway slaves in Panama. It remains implicit that this defense included only peninsulars and *criollos*. When referring to Cavendish's raid (Canto V, line lv) in one of his multiple explicatory notes to the poem, Peralta mentions that the viceroy, Count del Villardompardo, armed "la nobleza y demás gente en el Callao" ("the nobles and other inhabitants of Callao") without entering into details of the composition of the defending forces. The defeat of Hawkins is apparently due to the courage of Don Beltrán de la Cueva y Castro, brother-in-law of the viceroy, the Marquis de Cañete, who was sent by the latter to pursue the pirate (Canto V, line xlix). When in 1600 the then viceroy, the Marquis de Salinas, sent three ships to pursue the Dutch pirate Oliver Van Noort, no mention was made of the social make-up of the navy (Canto V, lines lxv–lxvi). When it comes to Spielbergen, he mentions only that "contra él pronto armamento peruano/el gran Marqués destinará celoso" (Canto V, line lxxx) ("against him soon/The Great Marquis would station Peruvian armaments that would bravely resist"). The term "Peruvian," applied in this period exclusively to the *criollos*, reduced the social component of the defending troops to only those sectors corresponding to the "Republic of Spaniards." Finally, so as not to lengthen this inventory further, I will only point out that in the narrative describing the blockade of Lima by the Dutch pirate L'Hermite in 1624, the only allusion to the defense forces was a mention of the absence of sufficient defensive walls in the port of Callao. Peralta says that "del fuerte Heremita a los furores/sin muros se opondrá muro inminente" (Canto VI, line iii) ("the fury of the powerful L'Hermite/was opposed by

an imminent bulwark without walls")–in other words a human force sufficiently large to prevent the disembarkation of the Dutch. Even though the poem does not mention the fact, it is well known that more than 4,000 men were brought together, including free blacks and mulattos, as part of the conscription ordered by the viceroy, the Marquis of Guadalcázar (Bradley 62).

Lima Fundada presents diverse images of the indigenous world in relation to the activities of Pizarro and his troops, but it mainly has recourse to a metonymic feminization of the Incas to emphasize the romance between Pizarro and an Inca princess, the sister of Ataw Wallpa, in Canto III (Mazzotti 1996, 66–68). He would marry her, according to the poem (in Canto VIII), and it would be this princess who would warn him of the preparations for the great revolt of Manco Inca. Thus, the only way indigenous society appears in the poem is as the enemy of the Spaniards (as Incan warriors) or as the spouse to satisfy the conquistador's appetite for women. From there, the ideal unity between Spaniards and Indians is achieved by means of a subaltern structure that also implies gender domination. Thus the presence of the indigenous soldiers and other groups within the poem only can belong to the domains of barbarity and idolatry. Their participation as part of the Spanish defense forces would be contradictory, since the image of heroism was reserved only for the members of the "Republic of Spaniards."

The individual responsible for consecrating these local heroes was a prominent *criollo* intellectual who elevated his native city to the heights of an almost mythical domain. Bermúdez's poem, "Aprobación," is revelatory in this sense: Each canto of the poem corresponds mathematically to a celestial sphere, so that this demonstration of *criollo* discourse becomes a simulacrum of the cosmic order, taking as the center of the empire a point actually existing on the periphery, notably the capital of the Peruvian viceroyalty, presented as the new *axis mundi* of the Spanish peoples. Thus the continuity of *criollo* discourse in Lima was strengthened when the pronouncements describing the capital as the sum of the civilizing virtues of the empire were well articulated. This had been done previously (in 1687) by the Jesuit *criollo* Rodrigo de Valdés in his *Fundación y Grandezas de Lima*. And even prior to that, in 1680, Clarinda, the unknown author of "Discurso en loor de la poesía" ["Discourse in Praise of Poetry"], had pointed out that the *axis mundi* of Spanish civilization had been transferred to Lima, whose *criollo* intellectuals were none other than the greatest exponents of the *republica humanitas* of the Renaissance ideal (see Colombí-Monguió).

Malaise and Praise: The Dual Face of the Epic in New Spain

The extensive bibliography that deals with the formation of *criollo* identity in New Spain (for example the notable works of Lafaye; Brading [especially Chapters 16 and 17]; Liss [particularly Chapter 7], and Alberro), concentrates above all on texts and documents that rarely include poems in the genre traditionally known as epic. Similar to their Peruvian homologue, this area of Spanish letters is framed in general terms within peninsular and Italian premises and models (*ottava rima* is only the visible manifestation of this mimicry). In contrast to the epic of New Castile, that of New Spain had a far more illustrious and less questionable hero in Cortés than the former had in Francisco Pizarro. The biographies of Cortés unfailingly include his sojourn at Salamanca University and his basic command of Latin; so too does the direct testimony of the legal and historical record in the *Cartas de relación* [1519–1526; *Five Letters from Mexico*] that cast the convenient illiteracy of Pizarro into the shadows. In addition, the praises heaped up by Francisco López de Gómara (1511–1564) along the line of the classic histories of the individual hero–as well as his attributing to Pizarro the dishonor of illegitimacy and a shameful job as a swineherd–should not be forgotten. In brief, Cortés was a far more ideal candidate for heroization, on account of his military virtues as much as his spiritual and intellectual ones. For this reason the degree of loyalty the Marquis del Valle showed for the crown matters little in comparison with the manipulation of his persona by some descendants of the conquistadors. These seized on the prestigious genre of epic poetry to exalt their own ancestors who accompanied Cortés, while subtly promoting their own demands on the back of old family merits.

The most important two cases for this kind of political and socio-historical reading of the use of cultured epic on American soil are Francisco de Terrazas's (ca. 1524–1600) *Nuevo Mundo y conquista* and Antonio Saavedra y Guzmán's *El peregrino indiano*. Both authors were numbered among the resentful *criollos* described by Peña (220), who possibly participated, along with Baltasar Dorantes de Carranza (fl. 1550–1604), González de Eslava (1534–1601), and other poets, in the informal group around the conspiring Martín Cortés in the 1560s. This is not to say that the complimentary poems by Gabriel Lobo Lasso de la Vega, *Cortés valeroso* and *Mexicana* (which also form a central part of the ten poems that make up the so-called "Cortés cycle" and were published prior to those of Francisco de Terrazas and Antonio de Saavedra) have no importance for this investigation. However, what is certain is that what approximates being a *criollo* protest and the expression of a collective malaise in the works of Lobo Lasso is the actual list of the conquistadors who accompanied Cortés. He names 113 in *Cortés valeroso* and 170 in *Mexicana*. But given that both works have the indisputable aim of transforming Cortés into a paradigm of Spanish heroism (in addition to the concrete interests of Martín Cortés and his son Fernando, which intervened during the composition of the works, as noted by Amor in xx–xxvii), it is logical that neither text enlarges on the protests over the dispossession of *encomiendas* and the loss of privileges suffered by the other conquistadors. Even so, in both works several actions of Jéronimo de Aguilar and Pedro Alvarado are highlighted, while the majority of the soldiers remain in the background; this treatment is very similar to that in López de Gómara's *Conquista de México* [1552; Conquest of Mexico]. This last, highly individual vision of the Conquest must have given rise to some of the recriminations of Bernal Díaz del Castillo that considerably preceded the complaints voiced by both Terrazas and Saavedra (even though the work of the former was published in 1632, long after his death).

The 175 eight-line stanzas of the *Nuevo Mundo y conquista* that have survived were included by Baltasar Dorantes de Carranza in the *Sumaria relación de las cosas de la Nueva España* [Summary Report of the Matters of New Spain], written between 1601 and 1604 but published only in 1902. For this reason, the exact date of the poem's composition is unknown, even though it is assumed that Terrazas, who died around 1600 according to Dorantes, would have been working on his text from the 1580s on. Recent research nevertheless pinpoints the date of his death as 1600 (see Lasarte 1997), hence

the doubt regarding Terrazas's authorship of the verses collected by Dorantes. However, notwithstanding his prestige and the appreciation of his work articulated in that of others (he even merited a eulogy by Miguel de Cervantes in his *Canto de Calíope*), Terrazas unfortunately did not leave a notable impression in Golden Age literature. Francisco de Terrazas was the son of the conquistador of the same name, an important figure among Cortés's military avatars and one of his closest collaborators. (He ended up becoming *alcalde ordinario* [mayor] for Mexico.) His birth in New Spain and his role as prime witness to both the glory and the decline of the *encomienda* system, which he calls in his poem "the golden age" of this initial period of Colonial organization, make it understandable that his praise of Cortés is constantly interrupted by criticism of his non-fulfillment of promises made to his collaborators and reproaches aimed at the crown for the paltry compensation that the remaining conquistadors and their descendants finally received. Dorantes included twenty-one fragments of Terrazas's poem in his work, of which undoubtedly the most explicit concerning the theme of *criollo* identity is number 20, entitled by Castro Leal "Allegation in Favor of the Sons of the Conquistadors."

In this section Terrazas proposes a comparison of the bad luck that has dogged the conquistadors and their descendants with the glorious destiny reserved for the Roman generals after their conquests and the Spanish nobles who helped their king in the War of Reconquest. Thus the Crown's dispossession of the *encomiendas* of New Spain was presented as an aberration of natural law and tradition, since "lleno está el siglo de guardar las leyes/de generosas pagas de los reyes" (Terrazas 84) ("the age is full of examples of keeping laws/concerning the generous payments of kings"). Mexico, from this point of view, was born dislocated from world history, and from its beginnings, has been a place of exception with an anomalous future: "sólo a ti, triste México, ha faltado/lo que a nadie en el mundo le es negado" (85) ("only you, unhappy Mexico, have lacked/what has been denied to no one the world over"). The destiny of all people in New Spain is that of having their own sons treated as foreigners, and treating foreigners as their own sons: "Madrastra nos has sido rigurosa,/y dulce madre pía a los extraños" (87) ("You have been strict stepmother to us,/and a sweet mother to all foreigners"). Thus the scarcely 300 descendants of the conquistadors who remained in Mexico, according to Terrazas (even though Pagden [56] notes the number 733 for 1604) are condemned to disappear along with the possibility of hegemony for this group of old vassal lords condemned to historical failure and, with it all the ideals of a world of chivalric ancestry overtaken by a distant and arbitrary state–a monstrosity that regenerates itself again and again, and its image is not only different each time but more devastating.

Terrazas ends his poem begging that if the kingdoms promised by Cortés (here no longer functioning in the paradigm developed by Gómara, Cervantes de Salazar [1514?–1575]), and Lobo Lasso, but transformed into a problematic foundational figure) are not going to be bestowed, then at least the crown should allow the *encomiendas* to be hereditary. This would permit, for reasons of dignity and proper pride, the survival of those whom the poem considers the legitimate heirs of power and wealth in Mexico, the *criollos*, who like Terrazas were born imbued with virtue because of the heroic blood coursing through their veins. From this moment up until the end of the seventeenth century, in works such as

1: EPIC VOICES 13

Parayso occidental [1684; *Western Paradise*] by Carlos Sigüenza y Góngora, the religious fervor of New Spain would be exalted over that of Europe, a fitting amplification by those who knew in their time how to confront face to face the Devil, supposedly present amidst the indigenous population in their pagan religious beliefs.

Terrazas undoubtedly presents a relatively early expression of the malaise that reveals a new point of view in which melancholy would become one of the notable characteristics; simultaneously this is one in which eulogizing the exploits of the Conquest would have a double edge that reaffirmed royalist loyalty, while denouncing historical injustice. With this double gesture the bases were laid for a discourse using a genre of high prestige—such as the cultivated epic–to create a genuinely decentralized vision of power, identity, and the foundations themselves.

Antonio de Saavedra y Guzmán was another notable *criollo* linked to this same perspective, who published *El peregrino indiano* in 1599. This poem has, however, survived intact, and for this very reason provides us with an opportunity to understand the complexity and development of a complete drama–in this case the expedition of Cortés, concluding with his triumph over Cuauhtémoc–in twenty cantos. Saavedra, like Terrazas, also could borrow from his ancestors. He was great grandson of the first Count of Castelar and the son of one of the first Spanish settlers in Mexico. Moreover he married a grandaughter of Jorge de Alvarado, brother of the terrifying Pedro de Alvarado, leading protagonist in the enterprise of the Conquest.

From Saavedra's long poem (frequently maltreated by literary criticism, which finds in it less aesthetic merit than in the work of Lobo Lasso and Terrazas), there are several sections of enormous interest in the context of the current discussion. In particular, the first seventeen eight-line stanzas of Canto XV present a direct defense of the *criollo* descendants of the conquistadors and an implacable series of arguments against the forfeiture of their privileges. Criticism is now converted into begging Philip III to protect these descendants and correct the evils of the kingdom since:

> ay como yo otros muchos olvidados
> hijos, y nietos, todos descendientes
> de los conquistadores desdichados,
> capitanes y alferez valientes:
> los mas destos están arrinconados,
> en lugares humildes diferentes,
> sin tener en la tierra más que al cielo,
> de quien sólo esperando están consuelo.

> Like myself there are many forgotten
> sons, and grandsons, all descendants
> of the unfortunate conquistadors
> valiant captains and lieutenants:
> most of them are down on their luck,
> in different humble places,
> having no more on the earth but the sky,
> who only wait for comfort.

(Saavedra 402)

The problem of the decay and misery of the *criollos* is not just limited to a particular and minority issue but also transforms Mexico into a "mala Madrastra" (403) ("wicked Stepmother"), the same as in Terrazas's poem. Even though recognizing the efforts of the king to maintain good government through wise decrees, these latter, says Saavedra, are rarely complied with in the New World. Moreover the legitimate Spanish heirs have not only been despoiled of Mexico's wealth but each viceroy also distributes it arbitrarily "a quien . . . quisiere darlo" (404) ("on whomever . . . he wishes to bestow it").

"El peregrino indiano," initially referring to Cortés, is a formula that emphasizes the journey westwards and with it the *translatio imperii* to the New World. However, little by little it comes to denote the figure of Saavedra himself, who puts himself forward in Spain, east of Mexico, to reclaim his rights and carve out a compensatory literary fame. The poem first appeared in Madrid, published at the press of the well-known printer Pedro Madrigal. In the re-semanticization of the title of the poem it is possible to observe the internal echoes of an identity that is dislocated in both geographical and social terms. The virtue of the military and religious pilgrimage of the poem's hero, Cortés, can thus be understood as the other face of a mendicant pilgrimage, that of the author, in the opposite direction. The reaction comes two generations later, but in a warped way. And this distortion will once again assume, as in Terrazas, a questioning of the purported glorious foundation and homogeneity of the dominant discourses of social agents with their own interests, even though they have been obliged to adapt to them.

As a compensatory reaction, Bernardo de Balbuena (1563?–1627), a *criollo* peninsular (who arrived from Spain at the age of three), published his *Grandeza mexicana* [1604; Mexican Greatness], a prophetic poem that does not belong, in the strict sense of the word, to the epic genre but shows some of its features in its enthusiastic glorification of Mexico City in terms of its many buildings that are finer than their Spanish or European counterparts. Thus "esta ciudad famosa/[es] centro de perfección, del mundo el quicio" (Balbuena 5) ("this famous city/[is] the center of perfection, the pivot of the world"). The re-centering (acting as a momentary cure for melancholy) is exercised through an alternate code that re-signifies the paradigm. "Todo en este discurso está cifrado" ("All this discourse is encoded"), says Bernardo de Balbuena. In fact through this variant (the city as "hero"), the malaise of Terrazas and Saavedra can assume a facet of self-glorification that reveals its own inferiority.

Historiographic Polyphony

Included in this literary canon are some authors of indigenous and *mestizo* origin who appeared contemporaneously with the mature *criollo* voices proclaiming through the printed word their pride in the New World and their restless malaise. For the majority of the Andean authors who took up the pen to set down their own version of the indigenous past or to protest against the abuse of the Spaniards, their very heterogenous status made them quite unique within the world of letters. Even though many were unknown until the end of the nineteenth or beginning of the twentieth century, it is salutary to recognize that they were already adapting the alphabetic script to their own tonalities, semantic fields, and narrative structures–without which they naturally would have been distanced from the forms of European discourse hallowed at the time.

Among these is the *Instrucción* (also known as the *Relación de la conquista de Perú* [1570; Report on the Conquest of Peru]) by Tito Cusi Yapanqui. Its format, as a report of services rendered and judicial allegations, its oral diction (it was dictated in Quechua), and the dialogue-style structure all bring the text much closer to indigenous forms of discourse. It is also of some significance that many of the semantic categories of time, space, and enumerative procedures correspond to Cuzco tradition and bear an even closer relationship to the epic mode of historical repertory current at the Inca court. (For a study of these aspects see Lienhard 235–41 and Mazzotti 1996a, 85–100.) In the *Manuscrito de Huarochirí* [c. 1608; Huarochirí Manuscript], the Quechua text compiled by Francisco de Ávila (ca. 1573–1647) and his scribes, serves as a means of entry for many dire warnings, while undoubtedly maintaining many native narrative and symbolic structures. These latter recount the exploits of the gods and *apus* or forces that inhabit the mountains; together these constitute the primordial population responsible for the deeds of the foundation myth recorded there. Though it lacks a specific epic resonance, the title of *Nueva corónica y buen gobierno* [c. 1615; *New Chronicle and Good Government*] by Guamán Poma de Ayala (1524?–1613), conveys the idea of adjustment and search for universal order in the hands of Philip III, to whom the work is addressed. There is also a reformist vein to this text, which was conceived "para enmienda de vida para los cristianos y los infieles" ("to rectify the life of Christians and unbelievers"), followed by an extensive list of the abuses of the *corregidores, encomenderos,* scribes, priests responsible for Indian parishes, and all those representatives of colonial organization who in practice distanced themselves to a large extent from contributing to the material or spiritual salvation of the native population. But Guamán Poma's text, despite its insertion into a context referring to the elimination of idolatries and demands for reform so frequent in the period, and in spite of the not always obvious influence of Spanish culture (see Adorno 1978), does include many linguistic, iconographic, and structural elements that make it an undeniable example of the modification of the discursive models of its time, as well as being a privileged source of information about Quechua poetic forms collected by the author (see Husson 1985). In addition, his voice is completely indigenous and regionalist in the diatribes against the *mestizos,* and the mention of the Incan religion and the demands for legitimacy for his family group, descendants of the Yaru Willka. Finally there is the paradigmatic case of El Inca Garcilaso de la Vega, in whose *Comentarios reales* some forms of symbolic organization can be discerned that suggest resonances of pre-Hispanic Cuzco; in addition, certain elements of the narratives about Incan conquests simulate a form of native authority in their prosodic distribution in syntactic/semantic pairs or doublets proper to some Andean styles of poetic composition (see Mazzotti 1996a, Chap. 2). This undoubtedly does not eliminate the Cuzco-centric or elitist features of this discourse (what could be described as a discriminating indigenism); nor does it mean that the overwhelming evidence for the Renaissance reading of El Inca should be ignored. But it does present a means of escape from the trap into which the majority of contemporary criticism of his work has fallen on the topic of the definition of the *mestizo* subject matter of the work, almost always reducing it to a flourishing acculturation, but no more than that.

At this point, before passing on to some Mexican examples, it seems valid to refer to two examples of this interweaving of discourse, notably the *Suma y narración de los Incas* by the Spaniard Juan Díez de Betanzos and the previously mentioned "martial" chapters of the *Comentarios reales.* In the former case it is worth pointing out that Betanzos was one of the first Spaniards to compile information from indigenous sources, in particular the *panaka* or royal family of Pachakutiq

Inka Yupanqi (the ninth Incan governor, according to most of the genealogies). The result was a historical version of Cuzco's ethnic past and a narrative of the civil wars between Waskar and Ataw Wallpa, shortly before the arrival of Pizarro in 1532.

Betanzos undertook his investigations and wrote at the end of the 1540s and the beginning of the next decade at the behest of Viceroy Antonio de Mendoza. He states in the dedication of the *Suma* that the book will preserve "la manera y orden del hablar destos naturales" ("the manner and speaking order of those who are native-born"). First published in 1880 with only one part of the sixteen chapters, it was described by many researchers, such as Luis Valcárcel, José de la Riva Agüero (qtd. in Bendezú 10), Raúl Porras Barrenechea (1970), and others as the literal translation of an Incan epic poem. A more complete version, based on another manuscript, appeared only in 1987, including the second part covering the war between Waskar and Ataw Wallpa. In an earlier study (see Mazzotti 1994), I referred to the inexactitude of the claim of direct transposition and the supposed literalness in relation to an indigenous epic, since there are numerous interventions by the "translator" Betanzos, who makes value judgments about and comparisons to the Incan way of life and religious beliefs. Generally such comments reveal an obvious Eurocentrism, given that the text is interrupted by commentaries expressing various viewpoints that differ from one another; the superimposition of numerous voices allows one to call this variant of historiography with an Americanist theme a "choral text." On the other hand, with the new edition, in which the text is not punctuated (thereby respecting the original manuscript), it is clearer that the voices are truly superimposed, and it can be very difficult to determine the narrative subject of some passages. An Andean subtext filters through into the prose of the *Suma* through the use of verbs in the present tense and in the first person—when an Incan person is speaking—with no warning, let alone quotation marks (which actually only began to be used from the eighteenth century); this produces the effect of direct quotation that in turn alludes back to what is known about collective, ritual and sung presentations of historic "poems." (See Lisi for a characterization of this kind of representation of historical memory in *El señorío de los incas* [1548–1550; Kingdom of the Incas] by Pedro Cieza de León [1518–1554]). The descendants of Pachakutiq Inka Yupanqi possibly reclaimed a version that was favorable to the founder of the dynasty, as was the custom within the system of official preservation of historical memory among the Cuzco royal families. Betanzos, who was married to a princess of the *panaka* of this Inca and was one of the few Europeans who succeeded in mastering Quechua in the first decades of the Spanish conquest, took advantage of his access to information—which was in the process of disappearing, given that, after the dismantling of the Incan state, the material support of many of the descendants diminished considerably and consequently the state subsidy granted by the Cuzco governors to the composers, recorders (*khipukamayuq*) and interpreters of the historical and glorifying stories of their royal families no longer existed. Betanzos's *Suma* thus appears as an example of a kind of heterogeneous historiography, a discourse of unresolved polarities and superimpositions that illustrates very well the non-encounters and discursive foundations of the first decades of the European intervention in the Andean region (see Lienhard 230–35; Mazzotti 1994).

A different but at the same time similar issue involving related principles can be seen in El Inca Garcilaso's main work. It would be wrong to ignore the extensive mediation of topics and styles that have their source in European humanism, for the latter influence many specific passages as well as narrative and descriptive structures in the *Comentarios reales*—including the tradition of the *vires illustres* and Garcilaso's own admiration for Ariosto and Boiardo. From the celebrated commentaries of Marcelino Menéndez y Pelayo (1856–1912) on the "utopian novel" character of the work to more recent studies, the erudition of El Inca and his complex use of the cultural baggage of the Renaissance have been recognized. (See Arocena; Durand 1976; Pupo-Walker; Zamora, among many others.) Even so, little attention has been paid to the criteria used in the selection of particular narrative and symbolic strategies of European origin that could have some kind of consonance with the modes of discourse and cultural particularities of the Cuzco ethnic group. This topic is immense and complex, but it is worth mentioning in relation to Betanzos's work and the relatively analogous circumstances (in the Cuzco version of Quechua during the 1550s) in which Betanzos and Garcilaso collected their information. Even though, in the case of the Inca, there is an enormous geographical and temporal distance from the moment of his youth until the composition of the work (end of the sixteenth and beginning of the seventeenth centuries), the simulation of particular rhythms of the foundational narratives is visible in some passages in the *Comentarios* after the first edition of 1609 (see Mazzotti 1996a). Once again, a bipolar subject appears, along with a conflict-ridden identity that indirectly reveals the flaws in communication, politics, and culture during the first decades of the westernization of the Andean world.

In the Mexican context there existed even more sources identifiable as epic tales that were collected by different chroniclers throughout the sixteenth century. One of the pioneering and organizational works in creating this panorama is that of Ángel María Garibay K., who recovered previous contributions such as those of Salvador Flores Toscano, Alfred Chavero, and Joaquín García Icazbalceta and systematized what he called a "Nahuatl epic." Composed of three cycles, the Tenochca, the Tezcoco, and the Tlaxcala, this corpus is really taken from sources written after 1521; as Garibay himself points out, of the twenty actual pre-Hispanic codices that have survived, the two that deal with mythic-historical themes belong to the Mixtec culture (Garibay [1945] 1993, v). The organization of the story and the perspective taken in the handling of foundation themes in these codices are comparable to the sources that (after the Conquest) compiled heroic versions of the human and divine past of the people of the central valley of Mexico in the Latin alphabet (in both Nahuatl and Spanish). (A rich compilation on the theme of writing "without words" can be seen in Mignolo and Hill Boone. For the transposition of oral material in general to writing in the Andean instance, see Adorno 1982.)

The history of this transmission goes back to the celebrated meeting in 1524 between the twelve Franciscan friars sent by the Spanish Crown and the Aztec wise men who held a prolonged discussion on their religious beliefs and worldviews. Around 1564 Fray Bernardino de Sahagún compiled these dialogues, added his own interpretations in his *Coloquios y doctrina cristiana* [Colloquies and Christian Doctrine], which were only published in 1924 (see Mignolo, Chap. 2). Fray Diego Durán, Fernando de Alva Ixtlixóchitl, Fernando Alva-rado Tezozómoc, and Diego Muñoz Camargo (1529–1599) extracted information from this material and many other sources, some now lost, along with other Spanish, indigenous, and *mestizo* chroniclers (who introduced or paraphrased various narratives in the historiographical genre), and recorded the foundational narratives or debates about primordial heroes. Although the interest of these authors was to explain the past of the indigenous people within dominant frames of discourse, the verse composition of the native text and the formulaic organization (attributable to a narrative system that was not necessarily Spanish) is traceable in some features of their prose.

To quote two out of many possible examples, in Chapter 1 of Book VIII of his *Historia general de las cosas de la Nueva España*, Sahagún introduces a tale concerning "Los señores y gobernadores que reinaron en México desde el principio del reino hasta el año de 1560" ("The Lords and Governors who ruled in Mexico from the beginning of the kingdom until 1560"). The theme is not surprising in itself, given the character of the process to which Sahagún subjected his indigenous informants. Indeed, beyond being what has been often called a true ethnographic study, this work also reveals old medieval themes as in the supposed "portents" and supernatural warnings received by the Aztecs regarding the arrival of the Spaniards. (See Rozat Dupeyron, especially 77–193, for a refutation of the authenticity of the "portents.") Without making an attempt to exhaust a debate that deserves a separate chapter, Sahagún transposes fragments of discourse in various parts of his extensive work that, because of their repetitive nature, evoke a formulaic narrative system. The narrative entitled "The Beginning of the Gods" in Book III not only compiles information from indigenous sources but also appears to a certain extent to be stylistically modified by what could be seen as an Amerindian model of discourse and not just raw material from the task of compiling information. It is undeniable that within the biographies of the Kings of Castile (like those of Fernando del Pulgar and Fernán Pérez de Guzmán), the echo of a popular oral tradition is also discernible. But in some aspects Sahagún's prose, precisely that in the most "imperfect" books, as Garibay calls them (see the prologues to Books III and VIII in the 1956 edition), it is clear that their "translation" of original versions in Nahuatl or oral versions based on codices is heavily mediated by a narrative register in which the heroism of the personalities is the central theme, and the presentation of successive Aztec kings is structured in function of an oral, repetitive transmission, similar to a litany, that is only interrupted when Sahagún introduces his two versions of the portents, especially in the paragraph dedicated to Moctezuma II. (For a selection of the epic sources of many Mexican chronicles, see Garibay 1993 [1945].)

As a second example, it seems fitting to mention the case of Fernando Alvarado Tezozómoc and his *Crónica mexicayotl o mexicana* [Mexicayotl or Mexican Chronicle] in which he claims to have derived much information directly from indigenous chroniclers. This access was thanks to his privileged position as the grandson of Moctezuma through matrilineal descent and as the son of Diego Alvarado Huanitzin, governor of Ehecatepec for nineteen years and *tlatoani* or "chief of men" of Mexico-Tenochtitlan between 1539 and 1541 (as the author declares in another source written in Nahuatl studied by Mariscal [xiv–xxxiv]). According to Mariscal (xli), the *Crónica mexicana* was originally written in Nahuatl and then translated by its author or someone else into Spanish; it is also possible that it was dictated by Alvarado Tezozómoc. What is certain is the presence of multiple syntactical forms foreign to Spanish and the repetition of names corresponding to homonyms in Nahuatl, suggesting that the translation reveals a smaller vocabulary in the written Spanish. The version that has survived to the present day includes lexical errors in the transcribed Nahuatl terms, which suggests the activity of an intermediate author or scribe, making this similar to the composition process of Titu Cusi's *Instrucción*.

It is interesting to note some features of the original sources in Nahuatl as they appear in the Spanish version of Alvarado Tezozómoc. Epic resonances of the text are found, for example, in Chapter XXI of the work, which covers the actions of Moctezuma "El Viejo," the fourth Aztec *tlatoani*, concerning the foundation of the temple of Huitzilopóchtli, or in the detailed description of the jewels and adornments of the same ruler found in Chapter XXXVI. In both cases there is a long list of items that suggests the existence of a version in Nahuatl previously codified according to the usual parameters of the sound links within formal epic stories containing fixed lists of objects to help the memory of the oral narrator. Allusion to the *arietos*, the songs and dances of the Tenochca population to celebrate various festivities, are also frequent. Possibly, as Garibay suggests, some of these songs might have contained foundational narratives and myths of the origin of the gods, such as the "Poem of Huitzilopóchtli" in Tezozómoc's version that is "la más bella y cercana a los originales por su sabor" (Garibay xviii) ("on account of its flavor, the most beautiful and the closest to the originals").

Conclusions

It is not an easy task to categorize the complex and varied range of texts that can be called epic in accordance with the wide (and orally focused) definition proposed at the beginning of this section. If a large part of the traditional so-called "cultivated" epic maintained its links with its Spanish and Italian models, at the same time it also served as a vehicle for a problematic articulation of martial glory. Here was a poetic subject located on the periphery and seen from a binary *criollo* perspective, one that does not succeed in fully ridding itself of its peninsular heritage, while still proclaiming the superiority of its new surroundings. On the other hand, many historical texts show signs of the material presence of indigenous systems of narration that go considerably beyond the purely oral. In some cases, intervention in terms of dialogue or the presence of the indigenous source itself modifies the character of the chronicles to create a truly heterogeneous form of writing.

There are many other texts that would contradict this interior dispersion of perspectives among *criollo* or adopted *criollo* epic poets and chroniclers who based themselves on a formally structured indigenous oral tradition. But despite the old prejudices (certainly sometimes with foundation) about the acute differences between the so-called Colonial texts and the metropolitan models, in both cases the epic voices succeeded in offering a glimpse of an even greater problem than that of the simple classification of types of discourse. I refer here to what happens when perspectives do not coincide but act to create local images and symbologies that, with the passage of centuries are better defined within the concept of pre-Enlightenment ethnic nationality–that is, without the egalitarian and all-embracing sense implied by the modern concept of the nation. (For a criticism of this last view, represented to a large extent by Benedict Anderson, see Anthony Smith's Introduction.) Defining the nation as an ethnic group and its discourse (at the margin of the historical identity of the authors) can be used as a point of departure for the invention of cultural traditions and genealogies that, by the Enlightenment and the Romantic periods, explain the Hispano-American difference. A well-known case is that of the manipulation, during the nineteenth century, of the *Espejo de paciencia* [Mirror of Patience] of Silvestre de Balboa by those Cuban and *criollo* intellectuals based in Cuba into an antecedent to a "national" literature (see González Echevarría). The way in which the *Comentarios reales* served as a source of inspiration for a neo-Inca nationalism in Cuzco during the eighteenth century is also well known (Rowe; and Durand 1979). This latter text was also manipulated by Lima intellectuals to their own ends in the imaginary construction of a social totality by accepting from Garcilaso only the material grandeur of the Inca empire and his eulogy of particular individuals among the conquistadors-*encomenderos*. (See Mazzotti 1998a and Guíbovich for a retelling of the Andean reception of the *Comentarios reales*.)

But at the margin of these manipulations, not knowing the specificity of the epic texts can lead one to the opposite extreme of assigning a present origin to traditions that have responded in different historical moments to the necessities of their group of origin. Another problem is that the proto-hegemonic groups (the *criollo* and the *mestizo*) triumphed with the nineteenth-century foundation of the Spanish American republics, but this theme, on account of its breadth, must remain just mentioned here. What is certain is that the *criollo* production of epic poetry and the part of the chronicles based on indigenous foundation narratives realize the early subjectivities that do not openly question either the Spanish presence or identity. In the first case, they instead try to overcome it, thereby converting the social subject into a new spiritual paradigm within the Empire. In this sense the epic voices of the period prior to the Bourbon reforms of the second half of the eighteenth century do not directly express a typical colonial situation, not at least in the current sense given the term (Klor de Alva; Adorno 1992). The criteria of reproduction for the kingdoms of the Spanish Crown in the New World (equality with respect to its other European kingdoms) have been generally ignored in nationalist bibliographies, which underline the pillaging aspects of the Spanish presence in their viceroyalties (thereby prolonging the discourse of the Black Legend). Without trying to evaluate the moral meaning of such a complex historical experience, it is useful to examine the internal dialogue of *criollo, mestizo,* and indigenous cultural productions and explain how what Cornejo Polar (89) calls a relational identity exists in each one of them. Each of these groups would elaborate through epic and historical discourse its own proto-hegemonic projects and its own symbolic foundations (for example, the Virgin of Guadalupe or Santa Rosa in Lima), which with the passing of the centuries would come to form a substantial part of the nationalist discourses of the Enlightenment, trapped between a future of doubtful oligarchic continuity and a dispersed and protean past.

Translation by Jessica Johnson

Works Cited

Adorno, Rolena. 1978. "Las otras fuentes de Guamán Poma: sus lecturas castellanas." *Histórica* 2.2: 137–58.

——, ed. 1982. *From Oral to Written Expression.* Syracuse: Maxwell School of Citizenship and Public Affairs.

——. 1992. "Reconsidering Colonial Discourse for Sixteenth- and Seventeenth-Century Spanish America." *Latin American Research Review* 27: 135–45.

Alberro, Solange. 1992. *Del gachupín al criollo. O de cómo los españoles de México dejaron de serlo*. Mexico City: El Colegio de México.

Alegría, Fernando. 1954. *La poesía chilena. Orígenes y desarrollo del XVI al XIX*. Mexico City: Fondo de Cultura Económica.

Alvarado Tezozómoc, Hernando. 1943. *Crónica mexicana. Prólogo y selección de Mario Mariscal*. Mexico City: Imprenta Universitaria.

Amor y Vásquez, José. 1970. "Introducción." *Mexicana de Gabriel Lobo Lasso de la Vega*. Madrid: Biblioteca de Autores Españoles. xiii–lviii.

Anderson, Benedict. 1983. *Imagined Communities: Reflections on the Origin and Spread of Nationalism*. London: Verso.

Arocena, Luis. 1949. *El Inca Garcilaso y el humanismo renacentista*. Buenos Aires: Centro de Profesores Diplomados de Enseñanza Secundaria.

Bakhtin, Mikhail M. 1981. "Epic and Novel." *The Dialogic Imagination: Four Essays*. Ed. Michael Holquist. Trans. Caryl Emerson and Michael Holquist. Austin: University of Texas Press. 3–40.

Balbuena, Bernardo de. 1992 [1604]. *Grandeza mexicana*. Mexico City: Universidad Nacional Autónoma de México.

Bendezú, Edmundo. 1986. *La otra literatura peruana*. Mexico City: Fondo de Cultura Económica.

Bermúdez de la Torre y Solier, Pedro José. 1732. "Aprobación." *Lima Fundada, o, Conquista del Perú*. By Pedro de Peralta y Barnuevo. 2 vols. Lima: Imprenta de Francisco Sobrino y Bados. N. pag.

Bermúdez Gallegos, Marta. 1992. *Poesía, sociedad y cultura: diálogos y retratos del Perú colonial*. Potomac: Scripta Humanistica.

Betanzos, Juan Díez de. 1987 [1548–1556]. *Suma y narración de los Incas*. Ed. María del Carmen Martín Rubio. Madrid: Ediciones Atlas.

Brading, David A. 1991. *Orbe indiano. De la monarquía católica a la república criolla, 1492–1867*. Mexico City: Fondo de Cultura Económica.

Bradley, Peter T. 1989. *The Lure of Peru. Maritime Intrusion into the South Sea, 1598–1701*. London: Macmillan.

Bynum, David E. 1976. "The Generic Nature of Oral Epic Poetry." *Folklore Genres*. Ed. Dan Ben-Amos. Austin: University of Texas Press. 35–58.

Castellanos, Juan de. 1944 [1589]. *Elegías de varones illustres de Indias*. Madrid: Ediciones Atlas.

Castro Leal, Antonio. 1941. "Prólogo." *Poesías*. By Francisco de Terrazas. Mexico City: Porrúa. ix–xxvii.

Centenera, Martín del Barco. 1998 [1602]. *Argentina y conquista del Río de La Plata*. Buenos Aires: Instituto de Literatura Hispanoamericana, Facultad de Filosofía y Letras, Universidad de Buenos Aires.

Cevallos, Francisco Javier. 1992. "Don Alonso de Ercilla y la teoría poética del Renacimiento." *Crítica y descolonización: el sujeto colonial en la cultura latinoamericana*. Eds. Beatriz González Stephan and Lúcia Helena Costigan. Caracas: Academia Nacional de la Historia. 199–217.

Cieza de León, Pedro de. 1880. *Segunda Parte de la Crónica del Perú que trata del Señorío de los Yncas, Yupanquis y de sus grandes hechos y gobernación*. Ed. Marcos Jiménez de la Espada. Madrid: Biblioteca Hispano-Ultramarina.

Colombí-Monguió, Alicia. 1996. "El Discurso en loor de la poesía, carta de ciudadanía del humanismo sudamericano." *Mujer y cultura en la colonia hispanoamericana*. Ed. Mabel Moraña. Pittsburgh: Instituto Internacional de Literatura Iberoamericana. 91–110.

La conquista del Perú: poema heróico de 1537. 1992. Ed. Miguel Nieto Nuño. Cáceres: Institución Cultural "El Brocense" de la Excma. Diputación Provincial de Cáceres.

Cornejo Polar, Antonio. 1994. *Escribir en el aire. Ensayo sobre la heterogeneidad socio-cultural de las literaturas andinas*. Lima: Editorial Horizonte.

Corominas, Juan María. 1980. *Castiglione y La Araucana. Estudio de una influencia*. Madrid: Porrúa Turranzas.

Dinamarca, Salvador. 1952. *Estudio del Arauco Domado de Pedro de Oña*. Nueva York: Hispanic Institute.

Dorantes de Carranza, Baltasar. 1902. *Sumaria relación de las cosas de la Nueva España*. Mexico City: Editorial Porrúa.

Durán-Cerda, Julio. 1978. "*Arauco Domado,* poema manierista." *Revista Iberoamericana* 44.104–05: 515–25.

Durand, José. 1953. *La transformación social del conquistador*. 2 vols. Mexico City: Porrúa y Obregón.

——. 1976. *El Inca Garcilaso, clásico de América*. Mexico City: Sepsetentas.

——. 1979. "Presencia de Garcilaso Inca en Túpac Amaru." *Cuadernos Americanos* 6.18 : 172–77.

Ercilla, Alonso de. [1569, 1578, 1589] 1803. *La Araucana*. 2 vols. Madrid: Imp. De Matero Repullés.

Ferreccio Podestá, Mario, ed. 1984. *Purén Indómito*. By Diego Arias de Saavedra. Concepción: Biblioteca Nacional, Universidad de Concepción, Seminario de Filología Hispánica.

Firbas, Paul. 1995. "Piratas, cimarrones e indígenas en el discurso épico colonial americano: Estudio de Armas Antárticas, poema de Juan de Miramontes y Zuázola." Diss. University of Notre Dame, Indiana.

Garcilaso de la Vega, El Inca. 1999. *Comentarios reales*. Ed. Enrique Pupo-Walker. Madrid: Cátedra.

Garibay K., Ángel María. 1993 [1945]. *Épica náhuatl*. Mexico City: Universidad Nacional Autónoma de México.

Giménez Fernández, Manuel. 1948. *Hernán Cortés y su revolución comunera en la Nueva España*. Sevilla: Escuela de Estudios Hispanoamericanos.

Goic, Cedomil. 1988. "El romancero en Hispanoamérica." *Historia y crítica de la literatura hispanoamericana*. Vol. 1: *Época colonial*. 3 vols. Barcelona: Editorial Crítica. 431–44.

González Echevarría. 1987. "Reflexiones sobre el *Espejo de paciencia* de Silvestre de Balboa." *Nueva Revista de Filología Hispánica* 35: 571–90.

Guamán Poma de Ayala, Felipe. 1943. *Nueva corónica y buen gobierno*. Ed. Luis Baudizzone. Buenos Aires: Editorial Nova.

Guíbovich, Pedro. 1991. "Lectura y difusión de la obra del Inca Garcilaso en el virreinato peruano (siglos XVII–XVIII). El caso de los Comentarios reales." *Revista Histórica* (Órgano de la Academia Nacional de la Historia, La Academia de Perú) 37: 103–20.

Hampe Martínez, Teodoro. 1995. "El proceso de canonización de Santa Rosa (nuevas luces sobre la identidad criolla en el Perú colonial." *Boletín de Lima* 99: 25–38.

——. 1998. *Santidad e identidad criolla. Estudio del proceso de canonización de Santa Rosa*. Cuzco: Centro de Estudios Regionales Andinos Bartolomé de las Casas.

Held, Barbara. 1983. *Studien zur Araucana von Don Alonso de Ercilla*. Frankfurt: Haag und Herchen.

Husson, Jean-Philippe. 1985. *La poésie quechua dans la chronique de Felipe Waman Puma de Ayala: de l'art lyrique de cour aux chants et danses populaires*. Paris: L'Harmattan.

Jerez, Francisco de. 1983. *La conquista del Perú*. Madrid: El Crotalón. facsim. ed. de la edición princeps de 1534.

Klor de Alva, Jorge. 1992. "Colonialism and Postcolonialism as (Latin) American Mirages." *Colonial Latin American Review* 1.1–2: 3–23.

Kuznesof, Elizabeth Anne. 1995. "Ethnic and Gender Influences on 'Spanish' Creole Society in Colonial Spanish America." *Colonial Latin American Review* 4.1: 153–76.

Lafaye, Jacques. 1976 [1974]. *Quetzalcoatl and Guadalupe: The Formation of Mexican National Consciousness, 1531–1813*. Trans. Benjamin Keen. Chicago: University of Chicago Press.

Lasarte, Pedro. 1997. "Francisco de Terrazas, Pedro de Ledesma y José de Arrázola: algunos poemas novohispanos inéditos." *Nueva Revista de Filología Hispánica* 45.1: 45–66.

Lavallé, Bernard. 1978. "Del 'espíritu colonial' a la reivindicación criolla o los albores del criollismo peruano." *Histórica* 2.1: 39–61.

———. 1992. *Quito et la crise de l'alcabala* (1580–1600). París: Éditions du Centre National de la Recherche Scientifique.

———. 1993. *Las promesas ambiguas. Ensayos sobre el criollismo colonial en los Andes.* Lima: Fondo Editorial de la Pontificia Universidad Católica del Perú.

Lienhard, Martin. 1990. *La voz y su huella. Escritura y conflicto étnico-social en América Latina (1492–1988).* Havana: Casa de las Américas.

Lisi, Francisco L. 1990. "Oralidad y escritura en la crónica de Pedro [de] Cieza de León." *Hispamérica* 56–57: 47–55.

Liss, Peggy K. 1986 [1975]. *Orígenes de la nacionalidad mexicana, 1521–1556. La formación de una nueva sociedad.* Trans. Agustín Bárcena. Mexico City: Fondo de Cultura Económica.

Lobo Lasso de la Vega, Gabriel. 1588. *Primera parte de Cortés valeroso, y Mexicana.* Madrid: Pedro Madrigal.

———. 1594. *Mexicana.* Madrid: Luis Sánchez.

Lukács, Gyorgy. 1963. *La théorie du roman.* Trans. Jean Clairvoye. Geneve: Editions Gonthier.

Lulio, Raimundo. 1975. "Libro de la Orden de Caballería." *Floresta española de varia caballería.* Ed. Luis Alberto de Cuenca. Madrid: Editora Nacional. 149–206.

Mariscal, Mario. 1943 [1598]. "Prólogo." *Crónica mexicana.* By Fernando Alvarado Tezozómoc. Mexico City: Universidad Nacional Autónoma de México. ix–xlvi.

Mazzotti, José Antonio. 1994. "Betanzos: de la 'épica' incaica a la escritura coral. Aportes para una formulación del sujeto colonial en la historiografía andina." *Revista de Crítica Literaria Latinoamericana* 40: 239–58.

———. 1996a. *Coros mestizos del Inca Garcilaso. Resonancias andinas.* Lima: Fondo de Cultura Económica.

———. 1996b. "Sólo la proporción es la que canta: poética de la nación y épica criolla en la Lima del XVIII." *Revista de Crítica Literaria Latinoamericana* 43: 59–76.

———. 1996c. "La heterogeneidad colonial peruana y la construcción del discurso criollo en el siglo XVII." *Asedios a la heterogeneidad cultural. Libro de homenaje a Antonio Cornejo Polar.* Eds. José Antonio Mazzotti and U. Juan Zevallos Aguilar. Philadelphia: Asociación Internacional de Peruanistas. 173–96.

———. 1998a. "Garcilaso and the Origins of Garcilasism: The Role of the Royal Commentaries in the Development of a Peruvian National Imaginaire." *Garcilaso Inca de la Vega: An American Humanist. A Tribute to José Durand.* Ed. José Anadon. Notre Dame, Indiana: University of Notre Dame Press. 90–109.

———. 1998b. "Indigenismos de ayer: prototipos perdurables del discurso criollo." *Indigenismo hacia el fin de milenio. Homenaje a Antonio Cornejo Polar.* Ed. Mabel Moraña. Pittsburgh: Instituto Internacional de Literatura Iberoamericana. 77–102.

Medina, José Toribio. 1918. *Los romances basados en* La Araucana. Santiago de Chile: Imp. Elzeviriana.

———. 1963 [1897]. *Biblioteca hispano-chilena, 1523-1817.* 3 vols. Santiago de Chile: Fondo Histórico y Bibliográfico José Toribio Medina. facsim. ed.

Mejías-López, William. 1995. "La relación ideológica de Alonso de Ercilla con Francisco de Vitoria y Bartolomé de las Casas." *Revista Iberoamericana* 170–71: 197–217.

Mena, Juan de. 1979 [1444]. *Laberinto de fortuna.* Madrid: Cátedra.

Menéndez Pidal, Ramón. 1939. *Los romances de América.* Buenos Aires: Austral.

Menéndez y Pelayo, Marcelino. 1948. *Historia de la poesía hispano-americana.* Ed. Enrique Sánchez Reyes. 2 vols. Santander: Consejo Superíor de Investigaciones Científicas.

Mignolo, Walter D. 1996. *The Darker Side of the Renaissance: Literacy, Territoriality and Colonization.* Ann Arbor: University of Michigan Press.

——— and Elizabeth Hill Boone, eds. 1994. *Writing without Words: Alternative Literacies in Mesoamerica and the Andes.* Durham: Duke University Press.

Millones, Luis. 1993. *Una partecita del cielo. La vida de Santa Rosa de Lima narrada por Don Gonzalo de la Maza, a quien ella llamaba padre.* Lima: Editorial Horizonte.

———. 1995. *Perú colonial: de Pizarro a Túpac Amaru II.* Lima : Fondo Editorial de COFIDE.

Miramontes y Zuázola, Juan de. 1978 [ca. 1608]. *Armas Antárticas.* Caracas: Biblioteca Ayacucho.

Miró, Rodrigo. 1978. "Prólogo." *Armas Antárticas.* By Juan de Miramontes y Zuázola. Caracas: Biblioteca Ayacucho. ix–xxvii.

Morton, Frederick Rand. 1958. "The Spanish Renaissance Epic in America on American Themes." 2 vols. Diss. Harvard University.

Nieto Nuño, Miguel. 1992. "Introducción." *La conquista del Perú (poema heroico de 1537).* Anonymous. Cáceres: Instituto Cultural El Brocense. ix–xxviii.

Oña, Pedro de. 1944. *Primera Parte del Arauco Domado.* (Ed. fac. 1596). Madrid: Ediciones Cultura Hispánica.

Pagden, Anthony. 1987. "Identity formation in Spanish America." *Colonial Identity in the Atlantic World, 1500–1800.* Eds. Nicholas Canny and Anthony Pagden. Princeton: Princeton University Press. 51–93.

Palma, Clemente. 1935. *Don Alonso Henríquez de Guzmán y el primer poema sobre la conquista de América.* Lima: Comisión Municipal del Centenario de Lima.

Pastor, Beatriz. 1984. *Discursos narrativos de la conquista. Mitificación y emergencia.* Havana: Casa de las Américas.

Pellicer de Tovar, Joseph de. 1989. "Epílogo de los preceptos del poema heroico." *La teoría poética en el manierismo y el barroco españoles.* Ed. Alberto Porqueras Mayo. Barcelona: Puvill Libros. 166–69.

Peña, Margarita. 1992. *Literatura entre dos mundos. Interpretación crítica de textos coloniales y peninsulares.* Mexico City: Universidad Nacional Autónoma de México.

Peralta y Barnuevo, Pedro de. 1732. *Lima Fundada, o, Conquista del Perú.* 2 vols. Lima: Imprenta de Francisco Sobrino y Bados.

Pierce, Frank. 1968. *La poesía épica del siglo de oro.* Trans. J. C. Cayol de Bethencourt. 2d ed. Madrid: Gredos.

Porras Barrenechea, Raúl. 1970 [1962]. *Los cronistas del Perú.* Lima: Banco de Crédito.

———. 1971 [1951]. *Mito, tradición e historia en el Perú.* Lima: Peisa.

Prieto, Antonio. 1975. "Del ritual introductorio en la épica culta." *Estudios de literatura europea.* Madrid: Narcea. 15–72.

———. 1980. *Coherencia y relevancia textual. De Berceo a Baroja.* Madrid: Editorial Alhambra.

Pupo-Walker, Enrique. 1982. *Historia, creación y profecía en los textos del Inca Garcilaso de la Vega.* Madrid: Porrúa Turranzas.

Quint, David. 1993. *Epic and Empire: Politics and Generic Form from Virgil to Milton.* Princeton: Princeton University Press.

Raviola Molina, Víctor. 1967. "Observaciones sobre el *Arauco Domado* de Pedro de Oña." *Stylo* 5: 71–113.

Rama, Ángel. 1984. *La ciudad letrada.* Hanover: Ediciones del Norte.

Reynolds, Winston A. 1967. *Romancero de Hernán Cortés. Estudio y textos de los siglos XVI y XVII.* Madrid, Alcalá.

———. 1978. *Hernán Cortés en la literatura del siglo de oro.* Madrid: Centro Iberoamericano de Cooperación.

———. 1984 [1566]. "Palabras preliminares." *Carlo famoso. El primer poema que trata del descubrimiento y conquista del Nuevo Mundo (Cantos XI a XV).* By Luis Zapata. Madrid: José Porrúa Turranzas. 1–7.

Rodríguez, Mario. 1981. "Un caso de imaginación colonizada: *Arauco Domado* de Pedro de Oña." *Acta Literaria* 6: 79–91.

Román, Jerónimo. 1595 [1575]. "República de las Indias Occidentales." *Repúblicas del mundo.* Salamanca: en Casa de Juan Fernández.

Rowe, John Howland. 1976 [1954]. "El movimiento nacional inca del siglo XVIII." *Túpac Amaru II–1780.* Ed. Alberto Flores Galindo. Lima: Retablo de Papel. 13–66.

Rozat Dupeyron, Guy. 1993. *Indios imaginarios e indios reales en los relatos de la conquista de México.* Mexico City: Tava Editorial.

Saavedra y Guzmán, Antonio de. 1880 [1599]. *El peregrino indiano.* Mexico City: Sandoval.

Sahagún, Fray Bernardino de. 1956. *Historia general de las cosas de la Nueva España.* 2 vols. Ed. Ángel María Garibay K. Mexico City: Porrúa.

Salinas [y Córdoba], Buenaventura de. 1630. *Memorial de las Historias del Nuevo Mundo Pirú: Méritos y Excelencias de la Ciudad de Lima, Cabeça de sus Ricos, y Estendidos Reynos, y el estado presente en que se hallan. Para inclinar a la Magestad de su Catholico Monarca Don Felipe IV Rey Poderoso de España, y de las Indias, a que pida a Su Santidad la canonizacion de su Patron Solano.* Lima: Por Geronimo de Contreras, Microfilm en la Colección José Toribio Medina de la Biblioteca Rockefeller, Brown University, Providence.

Sánchez, Luis Alberto. 1974 [1921]. *Los poetas de la Colonia.* Lima: Editorial Universo.

Schwartz, Stuart. 1995. "Colonial Identities and Sociedad de Castas." *Colonial Latin American Review* 4.1: 185–201.

Seguel, Gerardo. 1940. *Pedro de Oña. Su vida y la conducta de su poesía.* Santiago de Chile: Editorial Ercilla.

Sigüenza Góngora, Carlos de . 1995 [1684]. *Parayso Occidental.* Facsimile ed. Mexico City: UNAM, Centro de Estudios de Historia de Mexico.

Smith, Anthony D. 1986. *The Ethnic Origins of Nations.* London: Basil Blackwell.

Smith, Victoria Pehl. 1984. "Pedro de Oña's *Arauco domado*: A Study and Annotated Edition Based on the Princeps Edition (Spanish Text)." Diss. University of California, Berkeley.

Spielbergen, Joris van. 1906 [1619]. *The East and West Indian Mirror.* Trans. J. A. J. de Villiers. London: The Hakluyt Society.

Suárez de Peralta, Juan. 1949. *La conjuración de Martín Cortés y otros temas.* Ed. Agustín Yáñez. Mexico City: Universidad Nacional Autónoma de México.

Tasso, Torquato. 1964 [1594]. *Discorsi dell'arte poetica e del poema eroico.* Bari: Laterza e Figli.

Terrazas, Francisco de. 1941. *Poesías.* Ed. Antonio Castro Leal. Mexico City: Porrúa.

Valcárcel, Luis. 1939. *Garcilaso el Inca. Visto desde el ángulo indio.* Lima: Museo Nacional.

Vargas Ugarte, Rubén, ed. 1951. *Nuestro romancero.* Vol 4. Lima: Colección Clásicos Peruanos.

Varón Gabai, Rafael. 1997. *La ilusión del poder. Apogeo y decadencia de los Pizarro en la conquista del Perú.* Lima: Instituto de Estudios Peruanos e Instituto Francés de Estudios Andinos.

Vega, Miguel Ángel. 1970. *La obra poética de Pedro de Oña.* Santiago de Chile: Editorial Orbe.

Yapanqui, Titu Cussi. *Instrucción al licenciado Don Lope García de Castro: (1570).* Ed. Liliana Regalado de Hurtado. Lima: Pontificia Universidad Católica del Perú, Fondo Editorial.

Zamora, Margarita. 1988. *Language, Authority and Indigenous History in the* Comentarios reales. Cambridge: Cambridge University Press.

Zapata, Luis. 1984 [1566]. *Carlo famoso. El primer poema que trata del descubrimiento y conquista del Nuevo Mundo (Cantos XI a XV).* Ed. Winston A. Reynolds. Madrid: José Porrúa Turranzas.

Zumthor, Paul. 1987. La lettre et la voix: *De la "littérature mediévale."* Paris: Éditions du Seuil.

———. 1990 [1983]. *Oral poetry: An Introduction.* Trans. Kathryn Murphy-Judy. Foreword by Walter J. Ong. Minneapolis: University of Minnesota Press.

CHAPTER 2

FRAGMENT AND TOTALITY
NARRATING COLONIAL ENCOUNTERS

Guillermo Giucci and Marcelo Rocha Wanderley

How can we narrate colonial encounters? How can we interpret them? These questions are especially pertinent when we consider a historic episode with profound repercussions, such as the arrival of the Portuguese in what is today Brazil, itself a subject undergoing radical revision. A first approach might be through political chronology. Brazilian history in the sixteenth century could be viewed as an integral part of Portuguese seaward expansion, which is usually divided into four clearly distinct phases: 1500–1532, 1532–1549, 1549–1580, and 1580–1640. Each period exhibits clear defining elements. The first period marks the arrival of the Portuguese and, comprising the first three decades of the sixteenth century, is commonly referred to as the pre-Colonial period. Its basic markers are the symbolic possession of land, the inaugural contact of cultures previously unknown to each other, and the incipient exchange of raw materials for manufactured goods.

The "Capitanias Hereditárias" ("Hereditary Captaincies")–the earliest administrative regions–were established in 1532 and signal the beginning of Portuguese colonial rule in the New World. Historians concur that Brazil begins in 1530 or 1532, according to whether one uses the date of the Martim Afonso de Sousa expedition or that of the foundation of the Hereditary Captaincy of Sao Vicente (Barreto 170; Calógeras 8; Silva 27). The Hereditary Captaincies mark a significant change in the relationship between cultures, because they mark the start of settlement. Occupation, or the effective realization of the colonizing project, would be the motivating factor for the change in the relationship between the protagonists of the encounter.

The Hereditary Captaincies' failure, thanks to unremitting attack by indigenous peoples and thus the Captaincies' continuous demands to Lisbon for resources, obliged the Portuguese government to send a new type of emissary to defend the interests of the crown. The Governor General arrived in Salvador in 1549, endowed with far greater power than the *Capitão Donatário,* the administrator of the Hereditary Captaincies, and established a more centralized administration. The Portuguese empire was already under duress because of the disastrous 1578 expedition of King Dom Sebastião to North Africa–from which the term *Sebastianismo* originates, denoting delirious messianism–and the death of most of the imperial court; it was to suffer through problems of succession that would eventually lead to its incorporation into the Spanish Empire. Portugal would recover its independence only in 1640.

There is a second, literary approach to narrating and understanding colonial encounters that would discard the politically chronological divisions as irrelevant. The literary model would generally admit to the existence of the national state without questioning it. This approach might include the cultural production of the sixteenth century as a whole under the label "Brazilian colonial literature" but would exclude non-Portuguese texts that were influential in Brazil. Such a literary approach offers a broad survey, but deeper analysis is

deemed unnecessary, and there are few surprises. The first examples include Pero Vaz de Caminha's fifteenth-century *Carta* (Letter), along with the historical and ethnographic travel writings of Fernão de Magalhães (Magellan) (d. 1521), Gândavo, Soares de Sousa, Teixeira Pinto, Fernandes Brandão, and finally the writings of the Jesuit and Franciscan Orders (Nóbrega, Anchieta, Cardim, Vicente do Salvador). If the political model can be accused of granting excessive importance to legal form to the detriment of the quotidian and studies of the imaginary, the literary model in its turn suffers from the limitations of formalism and problematic anachronisms, in part, because of the proliferation of readings based on codes of Brazilian nationalism and underlying premises with regard to the natural and the social, which are then applied anachronistically to the past. The primary sources on Brazilian history in the sixteenth century present us much less with a "Brazilian" intellectual scene than with the encounter of European expeditions with indigenous groups of different socio-cultural development (Giucci 1993, 12).

Critics have not been sparing in their efforts to try to date the beginning of Brazil's intellectual history. Wilson Martins opens his voluminous *História da inteligência brasileira* (Brazilian Intellectual History) with the following phrase: "A história da inteligência brasileira começa em 1550, quando Pe. Leonardo Nunes inicia os estudos rudimentares de Latim no Colégio dos Meninos de Jesus, em São Vicente" (1:13) ("Brazilian intellectual history begins in 1550, when Father Leonardo Nunes starts rudimentary Latin classes at the Colégio dos Meninos de Jesus, in São Vicente"). Formulations such as these are currently being revised under the influence of multiple critical approaches that challenge the Eurocentrism of these remarks. Once the indigenous cultures have been incorporated into the literary field, Latin American colonial history must be redefined. Symptomatic in this respect are critical approaches such as those found in Rolena Adorno's article, "Cultures in Contact: Mesoamerica, the Andes, and the European Tradition," where she interrogates the modes of cultural production, or even the modes of contemporary colonial history. Adorno states that "without the inclusion of native American voices and related subject positions (such as those taken by *mestizo* writers), there can be no full history of colonial Spanish American culture as manifest in the spoken and written word" (Adorno 33). Situated within the same interpretive framework is Martin Lienhard's book, *La voz y su huella: escritura y conflicto étnico-cultural en América Latina, 1492–1988,* which focuses on the marginalization of oral literatures, and Gordon Brotherston's study on the Amerindian vision of conquest. Finally, yet another approach to interpreting colonial literature warrants mentioning, for it is also indicative of profound changes in subject matter, in this case with regards to the form of colonial discourse; we refer here to the work of Walter Mignolo and Stephanie Merrim (Chap. 3, this volume). This chapter will offer a different approach again to the cross-pollination between history and literature. Initially it will examine the written accounts of the historical encounter: the narratives of the first encounter between the Portuguese and the Tupiniquin natives in April 1500. The second part of this essay is an analysis of the historiography, civic accounts, and speeches taken from the formal celebration of the discovery of Brazil in 1900. The aim is to demonstrate the relationship between the icons of identity that were disseminated in the nineteenth century and the historic event of the Semana de Vera Cruz ("Week of the True Cross") by analyzing selected topics, such as definitions of Brazilian nature and character.

Semana de Vera Cruz ("Week of the True Cross")

Three letters bear witness to the discovery of Terra de Vera Cruz ("Land of the True Cross"); these are Pero Vaz de Caminha's *Carta*, Mestre João's letter, and the Anonymous Pilot's *relação* ("report"). Caminha's (1450?–1500) and Mestre João Faras's (15th/16th century) letters are dated 1 May 1500, written during the armada's sojourn in Brazil, and refer exclusively to events that take place in Vera Cruz. In contrast, the Anonymous Pilot describes both legs of the voyage of Cabral's expedition to and from India in his report, which includes a few pages concerning the stop the squadron makes in the land of Vera Cruz (Giucci 1993, 28). The first problem to note when interpreting the encounter between the Portuguese and Tupiniquins along the Brazilian coastline in 1500 is geographic: The members of the Portuguese fleet were ignorant of the local geography. Edmundo O'Gorman, in his classic study *La invención de America* (*The Invention of America*), examined the process by which America was created as a historical entity and demonstrated the epistemological error that was contained in the statement "Christopher Columbus discovered America on 12 October 1492." The event named the "Discovery of Brazil" shares this example's imposition of a retrospective frame that confers meaning on the encounter of the Portuguese overseas expansion with the native peoples of the coast. Certainly vision and appropriation become intertwined in the discovery episode. As in the Columbus example, the process of legitimization operates by naming (e.g., Monte Pascoal ["Easter Mount"] and Terra de Vera Cruz), by the placement of the royal banner, and by the celebration of the first Mass. However, according to the Anonymous Pilot's report, the crew could not even tell whether they were on an island or on the mainland. Explorers, on the other hand, considered the Land of Vera Cruz a simple stop on route to the wealth of the Orient. In this way, a modest encounter (even if portending profound repercussions) would be transformed a posteriori into the founding event of the nation. Such processes of attributing meaning became especially evident in chronicles and in the projects for the construction of national memory.

The second problem is the absence of a common language between the Portuguese and the native peoples of the coast. The need for information often leads one to consider objects and gestures as substitutes for words. Christopher Columbus, who faced a similar problem in the Caribbean, resorted to capturing and transporting ten natives to the Old World with the intention of accelerating their learning of the Spanish language. Portuguese expeditionaries tried diverse means to collect information. One of these consisted in offering manufactured goods such as hats, shirts, mirrors, and knives—objects intended to allow for the exchange of information. The reverse tactic of displaying samples of gold and silver to the natives turned out to be useless. If the encounter is understood as a seeking of information, it can be seen as less of a process of miscegenation and more of an effort to overcome mutual distrust. There are multiple indications of this distrust throughout Pero Vaz de Caminha's letter. A clear example is to be found in the figure of the seaman who is obliged to learn the ways of the natives and obtain information regarding the riches of the land.

The third problem concerns the armada's destination: It sped toward the fabulous Orient, that is, Calcutta, India. In contrast, the Land of Vera Cruz seemed uninteresting and lackluster, even with the promise of agricultural bounty. The Land of Vera Cruz was relegated to being a simple stop on the route to Oriental riches. It would be an attractive resting place according to Caminha's definition, or a place of "refreshment" for Lusitanian ships on their way to India according to the King, Dom Manuel. A few years later, in 1505, in a letter to Fernando o Católico ("Ferdinand the Catholic"), the Spanish King, Dom Manuel would reiterate the new land's condition as a stopping place. Referring to the armada that had left Lisbon on 10 April 1501 under Gonfalon Maletra's command, the King of Portugal writes: "porque já havia noticia d'aquella nova terra chamada de Santa Cruz, ahi foram ter para tomar algum refresco, pois certo a dita terra é muito necessária para essa viagem. E d'ahi foram montar o Cabo da Boa Esperança; e não encontrando nenhuma das nossas náos, foram sem demora até a India" (Academia Real 21) ("because there were already news of that new land called Santa Cruz, they had stopped there to take refreshments; certainly the mentioned land is very necessary to this trip. And from there they went on to navigate the Cape of Good Hope; and not finding any of our ships, left in haste for India").

The fourth interpretive problem to be faced involves the differentiation between symbolic possession and actual conquest. The discovery (by accident) of the Land of Vera Cruz did not imply a project of conquest or colonization. It differs from the Hispanic example, in which Columbus took possession of the new lands in the name of the Castilian Crown with the prospect of establishing himself there. The "discovery" of Brazil, in contrast, implies solely a ritualized act of symbolic possession, and this changes the relationship between the parties involved profoundly. In fact, this ritualized act of symbolic possession is the key to understanding the peaceful character of the encounter, the perception of mere symbolic possession that would rule out native resistance. A careful reading of Caminha's letter shows that he did not concern himself with the discovery of the noble savage, or an edenic paradise. Bereft of both Christianity and clothing, the indigenous peoples had to be incorporated into the Luso-Christian world. Prior to any open hostilities, the foundation of future conflicts would be established. The Week of the True Cross, however, did not offer adequate time for any conversion. The motivation behind the cordiality expressed in that week was more of an indication of the absence of a colonizing project than it was a sign of a bucolic vision of the discovery. Caminha announces the great potential the new land has for a colonial project. The well-watered land was so rich, he reported, that it could grow everything. These observations were repeated endlessly to announce the discovery of a bucolic paradise, but, in fact, what they do is point out the vast gulf between a European viewpoint and Brazilian reality; this was a contradiction that prevailed throughout the sixteenth century. (See Arroyo.) Impervious to the implications of symbolic possession, both historians and literary critics have contributed to an idyllic vision of the first encounter between the Portuguese and Tupiniquin natives. One consequence of this was the creation of the insidious thesis of a subsequent rupture, a transition from paradise to the infernal, by the institution in 1532 of the Hereditary Captaincies. These bucolicizing readings, which ignore the ambiguities present in Caminha's letter, became second nature to Brazilian historiographers toward the end of the twentieth century.

Celebrations of the Week of the True Cross: The Fourth Centennial of the Portuguese Landing in Brazil and the Invention of the Promised Land

The national anthem is one of the civic symbols that popular tradition has imposed with particular intensity on the Republic. Composed by Franscisco Manuel da Silva in 1831 on the occasion of the Emperor Dom Pedro I's abdication, the anthem would only attain popular acclaim at a later date, during Dom Pedro II's coronation festivities (Ferreira Neto 110–14). The proclamation of the Brazilian Republic in 1889 began the process of institutionalizing the symbols of the new regime, including the official anthem. Charged with this purpose, the provisional government opened a competition in 1890. Even though the first prize was awarded to the composition of the conductor Leopoldo Miguez–with lyrics by Medeiros de Albuquerque–this victory did not make the song into the national anthem. In fact, it was left with a lesser function, that of saluting the new Republic. The audience present during the competition at the Teatro Lírico voted in favor of the older composition by Francisco Silva, demanding its performance. This was reason enough for President Deodoro da Fonseca to sign a decree that would make it the Brazilian national anthem (José Carvalho 126–27). The last symbolic touch would be the inclusion of new words extolling Brazilian nationalism. Its main stanzas are significant because they would become the representation of national identity disseminated during the Centennial of the Discovery in the year 1900.

The images disseminated throughout the different genres produced during the nineteenth century in Brazil–from historiography to literature–point to a common trend among intellectuals involved with the topic of national identity: to promote idyllic and epic themes in their formulations of the nation. The idyllic and the epic, adopted as a strategy of representation, endeavored to create and accentuate an aura of grandeur around the subject being evoked. Another topic that purportedly explained the foundations of Brazilian civilization was an appreciation of the ethnic and psychological make-up of the Brazilian people. The idyllic can easily be seen in Francisco Adolfo Varnhagen's (1816–1878) work. A member of the Instituto Histórico e Geográfico Brasileiro (Brazilian Historical and Geographic Institute) and considered one of the founders of Brazilian national historiography, Varnhagen dedicated the first chapter of his *História geral do Brasil* [General History of Brazil], written between 1854 and 1857, to the geographic and geological studies of the environment, highlighting the characteristic make-up of this tropical area. This focusing on idyllic natural phenomena charged the geographic descriptions with considerable expressive power, so much so that exuberant nature became the basic icon of national identity. The depiction of nature as benevolent, abundant, and fertile, as illustrated in this text, is exemplary of this view:

O firmamento ostenta-se no Brasil em toda a sua esplêndida magnificência. O hemisfério austral é, segundo sabemos, mais brilhante que o do norte, ao menos nas altas latitudes, donde se não pode ver a bela constelação do cruzeiro, de todas as do firmamento a que mais atrai a atenção, ainda dos menos propensos a admirar a criação, nessas miríadas de mundos, que confundem o miserável habitante deste nosso pequeno planeta.

A vegetação é sucessiva: poucas árvores perdem as folhas; algumas delas carregam de flores, ... Nos terrenos de formação de gnaisse, em vigorosa decomposição pela ação fortíssima da atmosfera e das chuvas torrenciais, há mais umidade, e a vegetação é mais luxuriosa, sendo aí mais admiráveis as mata-virgens. (Varnhagen 15)

The firmament flaunts itself in Brazil in all its splendid magnificence. The southern hemisphere is, to our knowledge, more brilliant than the northern one, at least in those northern latitudes, where one cannot observe the beautiful constellation of the Southern Cross, which of all the constellations in the heavens is the one to attract the most attention, even from those of us who are less inclined to admire creation and those myriad worlds, that confuse the miserable inhabitants of this, our small planet.

The vegetation is coniferous: Few trees lose their leaves; some have flowers . . . . In terrain where compost forms, with vigorous decomposition due to the powerful forces of the atmosphere and torrential rains, there is more humidity, and the vegetation is more luxurious, engendering the most admirable virgin forests.

Poetry inspired by the national anthem intertwines with the wild exuberance accentuated in Varnhagen's text, be it in the celestial spectacle, in the regenerating climate, or the rich earth–all purportedly essential qualities of the land claimed by the Portuguese in 1500. The exaggeration of natural attributes in the selection above, condensed in the magnanimous vision of its lines, did not limit itself to instilling the emblematic quality of the territory, but also initiated a second level of discourse which was that of the natural environment as a potential source of wealth. Territorialization at this stage, connected to a sort of aesthetics of the fauna and flora, canceled out the possible attraction of foreign landscapes, making the natural environment emblematic of the nation. Nature thus stimulated symbolic recognition, nullifying the very real disarticulation of the nation in the sphere of daily life, as well as serving to identify the Brazilian monarchy with a civilizing enterprise in this savage world.

Varnhagen's text at first presents nature as permanently benevolent; however, once the initial presentation is made, a second point of view takes over, the historical one, in which elements of nature are interposed with the Portuguese colonizing presence:

Apesar de tanta vida e variedade das matas-virgens, apresentam elas um aspecto sombrio, ante qual o homem se contrista, sentindo que o coração se lhe aperta, como no meio dos mares, ante a imensidão do oceano. Tais matas, onde apenas penetra o sol, parecem oderecer mais natural guarida aos tigres e aos animais trepadores do que ao homem; o qual só chega a habitá-las satisfatoriamente depois de abrir nelas extensas clareiras, onde possa cultivar os frutos alimentícios ou preparar prados e pastos, que dêem sustento aos animais companheiros inseparáveis da atual civilização. (Varnhagen 16)

In spite of the abundance of life and variety of virgin forests, they present us with a somber aspect, in face of which man suffers hardship and distress, feeling his heart tighten with fear, as when in the midst of raging seas, he faces the immensity of the ocean. These forests, barely pierced by sunlight, seem to offer a more natural lair for tigers and climbing beasts than for man, who will only be able to inhabit them satisfactorily after having opened extensive clearings where he may plow the land and cultivate foodstuffs and pastures that will nourish his animals, all of which are required for present-day life.

This interpretation of Brazilian nature as a hostile environment is coupled with a celebration of the Portuguese crowning achievement: its civilizing enterprise (and the incessant struggle to subjugate nature), which tempered the strength of the paradisiacal image spread by the inaugural literature on Brazil.

This hypothesis finds support in another source through which the thematics of identity were disseminated–civic didactic writings. Intended for classes on moral and civic ethics in schools throughout the federal district at the end of the nineteenth century, these texts divulged a positive, generous vision of the country, formulated around simple plots, almost standardized, where the line of reasoning, steeped in nationalist sentiment, would lead the reader intuitively to imbibe unprecedented patriotism. This specific form of literature, created by the literary critic José Veríssimo, who was concerned with creating Brazilian books on national topics, was used at the time in the education of primary school students. These school texts all expressed the same background themes: nature at the same time hostile and bounteous, territorial greatness, epic national constitution and the heroic performance of Brazilians, whether born to the nation or adopted as immigrants. Waves of immigration are thus given a role in the development of the country, for they were all included in this message of *abrazileiramento*, or Brazilianization.

In the spirit of disseminating didactic texts that would be beneficial to civic conduct, Olavo Bilac (1865–1918) and Henrique Coelho Netto (1864–1934) wrote *Contos Pátrios* (Stories of the Nation), published at the beginning of the century and intended for children and young adults. Civic qualities of honesty, diligence, and respect for authority emerge in narratives linked to themes such as natural riches, military exploits, the sagas of popular heroes, the existence of unique Brazilians and, finally, the powerful victory of civilization. Stories such as "A fronteira" ("The Border"), "O Bandeirante" ("The Frontiersman") and "A Civilização" ("Civilization") are good examples of texts that follow scenarios developed around such themes. Concerned with highlighting the most salient aspects of nationality, Netto begins the short story "A fronteira" with a galloping horse carrying a messenger towards a hut deep in the farthest reaches of the interior. The dominant image is of savage nature with strong visual content, yet the natural world is depicted as a passive spectator to the unfolding travails of the modern heroes. The story's message was, in fact, the need to defend the territorial borders as they had been established historically–a reminder of the border disputes with Bolivia and Peru in the last decade of the nineteenth century, which had been won by the Brazilian Foreign Office under the tutelage of the Baron of Rio Branco. In the following excerpt, the focus turns to the power of nature:

Noite alta e morna: o rio rolava vagarosamente as suas grandes aguas, e a veneranda seiva, de troncos virgens, enchia a solidão com o seu murmurio solemne, quando chegou ao povoado um cavalleiro . . . algum acontecimento grave o levava a emprehender tão arriscada viagem, atravez da floresta percorrida pelos animaes bravios. (Bilac and Netto 7–8)

Night is deep and warm: The river's great waters rolled slowly, and sacred sap, from virgin trunks, filled the solitude with its solemn murmur, when a horseman arrived at the little village. . . . a serious event must have spurred him to face such a perilous journey, through a forest alive with wild beasts.

A foreign expedition had landed, threatening to take possession of that piece of national soil. The horseman arrived asking the townsfolk for help. The *sertanejo* (a popular cowboy-like figure considered natural to the arid lands of the *sertão*) who greets him at the door is promptly convinced of the urgency to take up arms and fight the usurpers. Although they will be outnumbered, they find encouragement in the messenger's call for sacrifice for the fatherland.

Elles ahi vêm: não ha tempo a perder! Se morrermos, todos os nossos corpos ficarão marcando a fronteira da Patria. Pelas nossas ossadas e pelas cinzas de nossas cabanas, os que vierem mais tarde conhecerão o limite do Brasil. Vamos! Falta-nos uma bandeira; temos, porém, o céo, o grande céo; e o choro assustado de nossos filhos excita-nos mais do que os clarins de guerra. Vamos! (Bilac and Netto 9–10)

They (the intruders) are on their way, there is no time to lose! If we die, our bodies will mark the border of our fatherland. Those who come after us will be able to tell, on seeing our bones and the ashes of our huts, what the limits of Brazil are. Let us go! If we lack a banner, we have the sky, the great sky; and we have the cries of our children, which will move us more than war horns. Onward!

Cries of "Viva o Brasil" ("Long live Brazil!") rang out as the heroic defenders of the land, which the foreigners thought abandoned, fell on their enemies, making them retreat to their ships–all under the watchful eyes of Brazilian women and children. The final triumphant scene is accentuated by the animistic image of a forest's maternal approval of those who defended the land: "E a selva grande e veneranda parecia aplaudir os seus filhos valentes com sua grande voz murmurosa e constante" (Bilac and Netto 12) ("And the great, venerable forest seemed to applaud its valiant sons with its immense and constant murmuring voice"). The theme persists in the sequence of stories written by the poet Olavo Bilac, with their recurring oscillation between the idyllic and the epic, as is seen especially in "O Bandeirante" ("The Frontiersman"). The plot centers on the life of the intrepid seventeenth-century frontiersman Fernão Dias Paes Leme, who penetrated the unknown *sertões* region of Minas Gerais in search of emeralds. To brave the wild, in the context of this story, means coming into contact with the vastness of nature, which works to undermine Paes Leme's enterprise.

Following the trail of the illusion of riches, and facing all sorts of adverse conditions–fierce animals, savage Indians, fevers, and abrupt changes in weather–the frontiersmen opened up the interior of Brazil, making possible the expansion of settlements. Civilization, as represented by the *bandeirantes*, was confronted with the destructive side of nature's power, the forest, as it threatened to overpower man's intervention. Bilac notes how Europeans pick up semi-savage habits during their expeditions:

. . . convivendo com os animaes ferozes e com os indios anthropophagos, entendendo e falando os idiomas de varias tribus, acostumados a não temer a odiosidade dos povos indomaveis e as inclemencias da natureza primitiva da America, tinham ficado corajosos como esses povos, rijos e primitivos como essa natureza. Quando a secca abrasava os mattos, os bandeirantes, para mitigar a sêde que os agoniava, bebiam o sangue dos animaes que matavam. Comiam fructas, cascas de arvores, sapos, lagartos, cobras. (Bilac and Netto 152)

... cohabiting with fierce animals and cannibalistic Indians, understanding and speaking the languages of various tribes, growing accustomed to not fearing the odiousness of the indomitable native peoples and the cruelties of the primitive nature of Brazil, they had become courageous like these people, inflexible and primitive like nature. When drought hit, the frontiersmen, to quench the thirst that tortured them, would drink the blood of animals they killed. They would eat fruits, the bark of trees, frogs, lizards, snakes.

Desire for wealth, courage and the spirit of adventure came together in the person of Paes Leme, and all would be pitted against the perverse demands of the environment. In particular, personal ambition as a motivating factor was played down in favor of the *bandeirante*'s heroics. It was the *bandeirantes* who brought the civilization of the nation to the backlands and who brought the savage forces of nature into submission. It is in Bilac's vision that the ability of man to conquer nature justified the perpetuation of his symbolic status, so much so that the story culminates in an apotheosis of the civilizing process:

O filho enterrou-o, piedosamente, em plena selva, no meio d'aquella admiravel natureza cujos segredos o seu olhar atrevido fôra o primeiro a devassar . . . . E se Fernão Dias paes Leme não teve a gloria de descobrir esmeraldas no Brasil, teve em compensação a gloria mais alta de ter lançado a semente da civilização nos sertões de Minas Geraes, fazendo oito cidades rebentarem de seu solo inculto. (Bilac and Netto 155–56)

His son buried him, piously, in the thick forest, in the midst of that wonderous nature whose secrets he was the first to encroach . . . . And if Fernão Dias Paes Leme was not awarded the glory of discovering the first emeralds in Brazil, he had a higher glory still, of having sown the first seeds of civilization in the *sertões* of Minas Gerais, bringing forth eight cities that sprouted from its uncultured soil.

This short story suggests a predilection for this theme in the work of Olavo Bilac. "A Civilisação" ("Civilization") is another one that articulates, with even greater polish, an intense fusion between the natural world, the march of civilization, and national greatness. A conversation between a father and son, set in a dining room where the family is gathered at a large table, is sparked when Octávio, the young student, after reading extensively the accounts of European explorers in Africa and Asia, asks his father to define the word "civilization." Octávio's second question is if the men of Africa and Asia are men just like his own countrymen. The response is elucidating: "São homens como nós, meu filho, mas não são civilizados como somos" (Bilac and Netto 272) ("They are men like us, son, only not as civilized as we are"). On the one hand, we find a recognition of the parity of individuals as a genus, through a naturalized conception of their physical constitution; on the other hand, there is a much more problematic view of the place these other peoples hold in the basic order of the developed world.

The same logic would take the lack of civilized traits among the peoples of Africa and Asia as irrefutable proof of another deficiency–the absence of a collective history marked by the transforming force of progress. In the father's explanation, we find an argument that presents progress as a continuous process and elucidates Olavo Bilac's understanding of civilization:

A civilisação, que é a diffusão das riquezas materiaes, intellectuais e moraes, não pode nunca, sem um longo trabalho de reforma paciente, tomar conta de um paiz. Para que um povo tenha civilisação, é necessario que o moroso passar dos seculos vá aperfeiçoando o caracter d'esse povo. Assim, se a terra brasileira é hoje prospera e forte, foi necessario para isso o esforço collectivo e anonymo das gerações que se tem succedido. Tu, que nasceste em plena civilisação, gosando os beneficios que o trabalho dos teus antepassados preparou, concentra teu espirito, e, contemplando o presente e lembrando o passado, compara-os, admirando o que foi esse lento progresso. (Bilac and Netto 272)

Civilization, which is the diffusion of material, intellectual and moral wealth, could never, unless by the protracted labor of patient reform, take over a nation. For a people to be in possession of civilization, it is necessary that the slow passing of centuries perfect its character. If Brazilian lands are today strong and prosperous, it is due to the collective and anonymous efforts of successive generations. You, who were born into full civilization, enjoying the benefits of the work of your forefathers, must concentrate your spirit, and looking at the present and remembering the past, compare them, in admiration of what this slow movement toward progress has been.

To Bilac, Brazil's four centuries of existence proved the success of the civilizing process. To civilize meant to domesticate the land and to cancel out the intimidation of the unknown. Civilization further represented the submission of those human beings identified with the hostile environment, the barbarians of the time prior to the knowledge of civility. Following the suggestion articulated to Octávio, Bilac's narration compares past to present, and praises the social and material evolution of the Brazilian people in contrast to the land's original inhabitants and to the slave population:

E o que era a vida social d'esses tempos, diziam-no claramente as caveiras dos inimigos mortos em combate, espetadas nas Acaiçáras. Compara esses tempos ao tempo de agora! Vê como a terra brasileira está coberta de uma população de mais de dezoito milhões de homens; o esforço humano venceu a hostilidade da natureza. As florestas abriram-se; desvendou-se o mysterio das serras; as pontes arrojadas de margem a margem dominaram os rios; as féras recuaram; e o arado, rasgando victoriosamente a terra, deixou-a submissa e amiga . . . . De extremo a extremo do paiz, a civilisação estendeu essa rêde prodigiosa, que é como a ramificação de uma arvore immensa . . . . E repara agora como, acompanhando as locomotivas que voam pelos trilhos, se estendem os fios telegraphicos, constantemente vibrando, conduzindo a electricidade invisivel e poderosa, que transmitte o pensamento, e que congrega num mesmo ideal de ordem, de disciplina, de submissão ao governo da lei todos os cerebros . . . . A sua habitação não é a rude *taba* do selvagem, nem a feia *senzala* dos escravos, onde em promiscuidade immunda os desherdados da fortuna penavam e morriam. (Bilac and Netto 273–76)

And what an illustration of life in those days is to be found in the skulls of enemies killed in combat, stuck atop the *caiçaras* (Indian palisade). Compare those days to our days! See how the Brazilian lands are covered with a population more than eighteen million strong; human effort overcame nature's hostility. Forests were opened; the mysteries of the mountain ranges unveiled; bridges thrust from shore to shore dominating rivers, beasts retreating into the forests and the plow, tearing victoriously at the earth, leaving her submissive and friendly . . . . From one end of the nation to the other, civilization extended its prodigious net like the branches of an immense tree . . . . And notice that following closely on the tracks of our locomotives, telegraph lines unravel, constantly vibrating, conducting electricity, invisible and powerful, which transmits thoughts and which brings together all our brains in a single ideal of order, discipline, and submission to the government of laws . . . . And take note of the comfort of working people. Their houses are no longer the rude *taba* [Indian village or settlement] of the savage, not the ugly *senzala* [dwelling] of the slaves, where in filthy promiscuity those who were disinherited by fortune suffered and died.

The reign of Dom Pedro II drew sustenance from the fact that monarchy, both as a symbol and agent of European civilization, had been transplanted to the tropics (R. de Carvalho 308). The relationship of civilization-state to physical-natural space (Salles 100–101) was determined by the self-designated modernizing image of the state, and it elevated the abundance of nature to the status of a national symbol, especially of the backwardness of the nation. Nevertheless, once the monarchy came to an end in 1889, the state faced a Republican cataclysm; its omnipotence as an entity was compromised and, there appeared an opportunity for reorganizing existing forms.

The subjection of the Brazilian natural world was a topic that found wide dissemination in the channels of culture from 1900 onward, thus consolidating the notion of nature as passive and scenic, appropriate for contemplation. Nature, however, would no longer be subordinated merely to the civilizing dynamo of the state, but more simply, to that of modernity. Progress with a material, technical, and moral basis was based in the shaping labor of the population. The controlling effect material progress had over the environment finally made it compatible with the ideal of the modern social order. In the previous excerpt (Bilac and Netto 273–76), the civilized discipline imposed on individuals was extended to the natural world, modifying its original essence. As a hostile natural world was brought to civilized order, the stark contrast between the social collectivity and the natural world was lessened, and the benign notion of nature as a source of riches was strengthened, thus endorsing the notion of progress. Society had to follow the inexorable laws of change in the historical process, and this rapidity inspired a sense of permanent dependence to public order and to the authority vested in the nation.

Replacing the paradigm formerly used to promote social modernization by a more progressive critical stance had significant consequences for the interpretation of the nation. This change stimulated a critique of the historic value of the state, a revision of its contributions toward the course of the moral and material advances of the nation. The immediate result of this revision was a greater interest in social studies, especially when confronting social, political, and technological backwardness as obstacles that compromised the future. Two distinct schools of thought emerged on the viability of Brazil, based on a revised view of the nation's cultural and ethnic heritage. The first focused on the obstacles in the divisions of race and propagated a negative image of the people based on fatalistic considerations. In clear opposition was a second school of thought, intent on an exalted and optimistic view of Brazil, that promoted a certain self-congratulatory spirit (Maio and Santos 27–29). Both contributed to popularizing the concept of national change and supported urban reform and sanitary campaigns in Rio de Janeiro at the beginning of the century. However, for the purposes of creating images of national representation, the dominant trend was the imagery of patriotism, images of nationalism that would be endowed with much greater power and effect during the twentieth century. The reification of the bucolic was a direct result of and, in part, a compensation for the rapid destruction

of the land. Adorned with the allegory of abundant natural riches and consolidated into the main metaphor used by Brazilian authors throughout the nineteenth century, the theme of the Promised Land was derived, in a manner not without its polemics, from the writings of the first chroniclers and then projected toward the future as a type of "utopia do tempo" (Le Goff 351) ("temporal utopia"). In this sense, the return to the distant past is not marked by nostalgia. Instead, the search for original roots was justified as a summoning of historical references to the aid of contemporary national purposes. They celebrated the success of nation building, the epic grandeur of the opening of the backlands, in order to confirm Brazil's youth and its great appetite for growth in the twentieth century.

The Quotidian Made Mythical

The celebrations of the Centennial held in 1900 brought this nationalist iconography to the masses with imagery exalting the role of nature, those European cultural origins, the unique history of Brazil's nineteenth century, and the noble character of the Brazilian people. The insistence on these topics demonstrates a determination to create a Brazilian nationalism, to have it incorporated into the collective tradition, and to allow for its diffusion a posteriori. The idea of nation was a rational construct that responded to social demands for group identity, but it had to appear to the people as an inherent attribute of the land. Manuel Antonio Moreira de Azevedo (1832–1903), author of one of the entries in the *Livro do Centenário* (Book of the Centennial), notes:

> Mostra ter perdido a consciência de sua nacionalidade o povo que não lembra as suas datas históricas, não preza o seu passado e não rende homenagem a seus feitos e, a seus heróes. A nação que olvida os acontecimentos celebres de sua existencia perdeu o sentimento de dignidade histórica. (I: iii)

> A people that ignores its history and does not esteem its past, and fails to pay homage to its victories and its heroes, has lost consciousness of its nationality. A nation that forgets the famous events of its existence has lost its sense of historic dignity.

The "Patria" ("fatherland") as a fact of consciousness (Bethencourt 31–47) is the result of long labor and much intellectual elaboration of national characteristics. Nation builders stimulated an expansion of social consciousness by personifying the nation as the community. They invited its members to identify the specific elements that would promote their sense of belonging to a unique collectivity. In the case of the "Discovery" jubilee, the selected elements reinforced the predilection for an identity that is visual, emotive, strongly consensual, and structured on a series of images and basic notions such as abundance, wealth, hospitality, generosity, and the Promised Land. These are presented as being the ideal pillars of civilization and progress in Brazil. They permeate the diffuse fabric of the reformist culture prevalent at the time, which was obsessed with establishing modernity. Modernity was to be the enticement to reach those sectors of society disillusioned with political projects, most especially with literature as political propaganda. The celebrations of the Discovery concentrated on an energetic pretension of renewing the foundations of national identity, associated with the consecration of modernization. The strong influence of positivism and scientificism contributed to this effect, for these doctrines were entrusted with disseminating the idea of history as the collective memory.

Analyzing the speeches given at the celebrations, one must keep in mind that identity was a central issue for intellectuals in 1900. They understood identity as an object of fixed and natural characteristics. And this identity-object is imagined as a singular entity, shaped by a people or a group's common inheritance, as qualified by space, time, and culture (Gillis 28–30). However, when analyzing the specific intellectual sense of identity, one is theoretically obliged to come up with a key concept that will enable us to understand its operations. Take, for instance, the concept of the naturalization of identity. Its validity arises from the recognition of a thick mythical substratum that centers on the normalization of the quotidian. This mythical medium is clear in the many elaborations of the purported national character of Brazilian civilization that one finds dispersed in newspaper articles, poems, and ceremonial speeches of the time. Such is the importance of this that it suggests an anthropological hypothesis at work in the elaboration of the national edifice, supplanting the utilitarian version of the de facto population of the nation-state.

The committed intellectual would see in the commemorations a powerful instrument for transforming the humbling realities of the nation. Political crises, civil wars, strikes, yellow fever, and urban needs such as the paving of streets and sewers, drainage of swamps, and clean water supplies illustrate the entropy of everyday life. This was the subject matter of newspaper headlines during the fourth Centennial, contrasting strongly with the festive spirit. Journalists did not limit themselves to the issues at hand but extended their attacks to cultural deficiencies. An epidemic breakout in Santos became, by extension, a denunciation of the contradiction of everyday life in Brazil. The disparity between a country of illiterates and those doctors of science would not pass unnoticed by newspaper reporters of the day.

It was thought necessary to establish a hegemonic structure in an attempt at overcoming impotence. The strategy was to displace instant identification with the events around the Discovery celebration, to allow forces that constitute the collective memory to be redirected to topics and facts of far greater social significance. By denying any mere apology for the past, by focusing on immediate experience, it became possible to stimulate a projection of social reforms that would cancel out the entropy. National sentiment became accessible through icons charged with ideological values and reproduced as part of everyday experience. National memory acted in accordance with consoling myths, allusions to national origins, which recovered an ideological agenda essential to the Week of the True Cross: the myth of Brazil as the Promised Land. A guarantee of perpetuation in memory, of confidence in national stability, of the vindication of pressing ahead into the future, this myth borrowed its logic from the testimony of the first chroniclers, especially in the statements of promise selected directly from their texts.

Myths such as the Promised Land, the cordial Brazilian, and even the myth of Brazil being the nation of the future, emerged at this point as being the solution to all the problems deriving from the nation's origins, and its historical obstacles. These myths undermined the dichotomies of nature versus civilization, race versus progress, and spirituality versus progress.

The Myth of the Promised Land, Modern Submission

"Porque me ufano do meu país" ("Why I am proud of my nation"): These are the words of the monarchist Afonso Celso (1860–1938), from the title of one of the contributions to the commemoration of the Centennial of the Discovery of Brazil. These very words, especially the use of the term *ufanar* as a synonym of high patriotic sentiment, were eventually to have great repercussions in later years, becoming an enduring landmark of Brazilian nationalism in the version of patriotism known as *Ufanista* thought. Published in the Centennial year, with several subsequent re-editions, this work was used to instruct future generations in the appropriate teachings intended to strengthen patriotic sentiment, similar to the way in which Olavo Bilac and Coelho Netto had employed fiction in *Contos Pátrios*. Celso, however, was concerned with social psychology; he wanted to remove the stigma of the inferiority complex attributed to Brazilians, demonstrating to that end the basic aspects of Brazilian nationality.

His therapeutic crusade resorted to a series of meditations on the realities of foreign lands, the fruit of countless trips and studies he undertook throughout his aristocratic life. Paradoxically, it was his experience as a modern world traveler with a refined sense of cosmopolitan observation that conferred authority on his ideas within the national scenario. From the confrontation with the Other emerged the territory made sacred by the virtual effect of the myth of the Promised Land: "Vários existem mais prósperos, mais poderosos, mais brilhantes que o nosso. Nenhum mais digno, mais rico de fundadas promessas, mais invejável" (Celso 10) ("There are many nations more prosperous, more powerful, more brilliant than ours. But none has more dignity, or is richer in the fundamental promise of the future and therefore more enviable"). Physical grandeur, paradisiacal beauty, rich flora, and fertile soil would be the foundation of national excellence, thus becoming signs of identity. Brazil's geography, converted into the promise of the future, found sustenance throughout Afonso Celso's work, based ostensibly on two different sources of inspiration: Divine Providence and the extent of the nation's natural resources.

Divine Providence existed in the first instance as a guarantee of the sense of the Brazilian extraordinary, which was attributed to natural opulence. This was the case even though the notion of divine intervention hinted at the residue of a theological past. The first signal of the divinity's privileged affection for Brazil was expressed in one of the primary aspects of its superiority–territorial vastness. Brazil was deemed to be outstanding among countries around the globe and in the Americas, having primacy among all the nations of the "Latin race." Brazilian territory benefited from the blessings of a harmonious geography hospitable to human development, capable of promoting social relations and the physical needs of a population in safety. Providentialism deepened the contrasts to an even greater extent, endowing the nation with an evolution devoid of any wars of considerable impact, and thus intense divisiveness and dispersive violence, and allowing for the attainment of a unified nation.

Since the image of a land without conflict helped to break the commonplace reputation of aggressiveness inherent in the histories of territorial conquest and the consolidation of territories, it was decided that the suppression of news about natural and man-made catastrophes would further promote a history devoid of problems. There would be no records of occurrences such as cyclones, floods, earthquakes, volcanoes, or even the long cycles of plagues and hunger. The portrait of nature as a benign domain was to prevail, since the hostile essence of nature was banished a priori by the Creator's hand, and not by man's prodigious transformation. The confrontation between individual and nature thus nullified by Providence's generous hand, we find prefigured the initial setting of the theme of earthly paradise, determining the representation of nature as *mátria* ("motherland"), to distinguish it from *patria* ("fatherland"), and as land (Da Matta 98–99):

> Já assinalamos que nas florestas são relativamente em número insignificante os animais ferozes. Os que existem raro agridem o caminhante. Limitam-se a defender-se, tirando escassas vidas, fazendo estragos de pouca monta. Em suma: oferecendo ao homem condições de vida sem igual, a natureza brasileira em nada lhe é hostil ou áspera. Póde o habitante confiar nela, com segurança. Não o trae, não o surpreende, não o amedronta, não o maltrata, não o aflige. Dá-lhe tudo quantopóde dar, mostrando-se-lhe sempre magnanima, meiga, amiga, maternal. (Celso 55)

> We have already noted that in the forests there is a relatively insignificant number of fierce animals. The ones that do exist rarely attack travelers. They are limited to defending themselves, taking few lives, and causing damage of negligible worth. To sum up: Offering men incomparable living conditions, Brazilian nature will in no form be hostile or rough. The inhabitant may freely count on nature, with certainty. Nature will not betray him, surprise him, threaten him, make him afraid, or be a source of affliction. Nature will afford him everything in its power to provide, showing itself always magnanimous, tender, friendly, maternal.

As previously noted, the allusion to God as the causal entity persists in the selection of noteworthy interpretations in colonial writings. Even chronologies dedicated to structuring national history were in keeping with some form of the providential vision disseminated especially through letter writers and the Jesuit missionary chronicles (Dias Malheiro 1–2). Historical events such as the Discovery, the formal possession of the land, and colonization became the symbolic events of a sacred foundational narrative that portrayed yet another proof of supernatural election—paradisiacal beauty. Numerous edenic motifs were picked up by Affonso Celso, who created another order of Brazilian excellence. This acclaim for unprecedented aesthetic beauty was derived not only from colonial descriptions but also from the impressions of nineteenth-century foreign travelers (collected by historians through their research) and also from the exuberance of Romantic poetry. The numerous sources of this tradition—Americo Vespucio's (1451–1512) and Pero Vaz de Caminha's letters, the Jesuit Simão Vasconcelos's (1597–1671) chronicle, Sebastião da Rocha Pitta's (1660–1738) *História da América portuguesa* [History of Portuguese America], the German naturalist Alexander von Humboldt's observations, and the verses of Antônio Gonçalves Dias' (1823–1864) "Canção do Exílio" ["Song from Exile"]–as presented by Celso, all allow him to bring a modern adjustment to the topos of terrestrial paradise allied to a mythic belief in El Dorado (Celso 18). His statement, however, which refers to two models of the historical formulation of the marvelous, has the limited purpose of serving as a projection for the testimonies capable of substantiating the superiority of Brazilian phenomena, as popularized by the author:

> Infindos campos, tapisados de macia e fresca relva, suavemente ondulados, constelados de flôres selvagens, povoados de codornas e perdizes e aprazíveis em qualquer estação; as pampas do sul, . . . , incomensuráveis savanas núas, de face impassível, sem rugas nem sorrisos, atravessadas por armentos de poldros

indômitos e pelo gaucho, de originalidade, bravura e independência legendárias; amplas cavernas cheias de mistério; elevados picos, fácilmente acessíveis, donde se descortinam perpectivas soberbas; centenas de angras recortadas com esmero artístico; jardins incomparáveis; flora opulenta; fáuna inestimavel, sobretudo em matéria de aves, notaveis pela delicadeza das fôrmas, suntuosidade das plumagens, doçura do canto e primor da nidificação–aves que não emigram de bem que se acham onde nasceram: eis outras belezas do Brasil, digna cada qual de lhe assinalar posto de primazia no mundo. (Celso 39–40)

Endless fields, carpeted with soft and fresh grass, softly undulating, covered with wild flowers, populated with quails and partridges and pleasant in any season; the *pampas* [plains region] to the south . . . the incommensurable bare savannas, its face impassive, without wrinkles or smiles, crossed by droves of indomitable horses and *gauchos* [regional cowboys], of legendary originality, courage and independence; large caves full of mystery; high peaks, easily accessible, from which superb perspectives unfold; hundreds of bays chiseled to artistic perfection; incomparable gardens; opulent flora; inestimable fauna, especially with regard to birds, notable for delicacy of form, sumptuousness of plumage, sweetness of song and nesting excellence–birds that do not migrate, so happy do they find themselves where they were born: here among many others are the beauties of Brazil, each one with the capacity of conferring on the nation a place of primacy in the world.

Ufanista (Celsian high patriotic) thought finds perpetual room for growth in the confluence of paradise and a natural abundance that will be the guarantee of his great expectations. Suggesting that territorial extension and the portent of abundance goes along with material wealth, the *ufanista* discourse sets itself up to articulate an irreversible road to prosperity, displaying the material foundations that would reward patriotic devotion.

Considerations of Brazilian riches–the third motive for national preeminence–allow us to appreciate the transition from a narrative of threatening nature, to another one that presents us with the raw materials for economic transformation. In this case, the transition was far from being an appeal to ecological conservation, a transition that would champion the rational use of available resources. What in fact prevailed was a predatory disposition to exploit resources, put at the service of national prosperity, because of the certainty of an infinite regeneration of the terrestrial sources:

> O milho e a mandioca já eram cultivados pelos índios. O arrôs silvestre em várias regiões. Prestam-se a qualquer cultura as terras do Brasil, de fertilidade proverbial. Verdadeira maravilha a uberdade da terra roxa que o calor e a umidade bastam a fecundar. As laranjeiras produzem, sem trato. Alguns pés, em Mato Grosso, as laranjas, já muito doces, que murcham no galho, reamadurecem dulcíssimas,–verdadeira ressurreição. (Celso 44–45)

> Corn and manioc had already been cultivated by the Indians, wild rice too in various regions. Brazilian lands are appropriate for any cultivation, for they are of proverbial fertility. This rich, purple earth is truly a marvel, and the heat and humidity are enough to make it fecund. Orange trees produce without any need for care. Some trees in Mato Grosso, whose oranges, already very sweet, wither on their branches, ripen once again in renewed sweetness–truly a resurrection.

In a sudden change, the language that had described green fields, an extraordinary variety of fauna and flora, has been transformed into images of the earth as propitious for farming and pastoral activities, of forests as reserves of plants and fine wood useful for medicine, industry, and commerce. Natural treasures and mineral and vegetable resources were also seen as a guarantee of Brazil's economic vitality and independence vis à vis the rest of the world. In Celso's terms, with a destiny so marked by success, Brazilian opulence would find itself threatened only by the corrupting intervention of the mismanagement of government or by an inability to perceive the benefits that would arise in the long term in such a way as to hinder the intelligent and prudent exploitation of the special qualities of the nation's land (Celso 48).

Behind the futuristic images of Brazil as the world's granary and supplier of inexhaustible raw materials for industrial production, we find the proposition that work was an ideal of civic virtue, able to ensure a well-balanced industrious initiative, most especially dissipating the danger of class disputes that had disgraced the Old World. The naked distortions of a more mature capitalism, which was to be the climax of this fictive Brazil, were saluted as constituting the most perfect acclimatization of natural laws and rights. It was hoped that Brazilian society would be exempted from the negative effects of aggressive, segregating competition, as well as from the specter of internal strife in the name of the redistribution of wealth. These arguments originated from an eloquent belief in the country's predestined harmony and vocation for prosperity, and above all provided the ballast for realizing social justice and public welfare, which would be sustained by unprecedented ethical deportment, refined by the education of the native character:

As nossas condições econômicas hão de ser breve forçosamente aproveitadas, em virtude da ação de fôrças inflexiveis. Acresce que circunstâncias especiais operam no Brasil a distribuição da riqueza conforme as leis naturais do trabalho, o que, numa sociedade laboriosa, suficientemente esclarecida, onde a liberdade de cada um seja protegida contra a fraude e a violência, é o ideal, no dizer dos economistas.

Não conhecemos proletariado, nem fortunas colossais que jámais se hão de acumular entre nós, graças aos nossos habitos e sistema de sucessão. Nem argentarismo, pior que a tirania, nem pauperismo, pior que a escravidão. No Brasil, com trabalho e honestidade, conquistam-se quaisquer posições. Encontra-se a mais larga acessibilidade a tudo, no meio de condições sociais únicas, sem distinção e divergência de classes, em perfeita comunicação e homogeneidade da população. A esperança constante de uma situação melhor anima a todos, e é esse o eficaz incentivo da indústria humana.

Temos, pois o estado mais propício ao progresso da riqueza pública. No Brasil, o trabalho anda à procura do homem e não o homem à procura do trabalho. Ninguem, querendo trabalhar, morrerá de fome. Parece país de milionários, tão largamente se gasta. (Celso 48)

Our economic resources are soon to be greatly exploited, by virtue of the inexorable forces of progress. Add to that the special conditions that operate the distribution of wealth in Brazil according to the natural laws of labor, in a sufficiently enlightened working society, where every person's freedom is protected against fraud and violence, which is the economist's ideal. We have no proletariat to speak of; nor do we have colossal fortunes, which can never be accumulated among us, thanks to our customs and system of government. *Monetarism* is worse than tyranny, and pauperism is worse than slavery. Any job can be won in Brazil through work and honesty. There you will find the most open accessibility to everything, in unique social conditions, without distinction of classes, in perfect communication and a homogenous population. There is constant expectation of

improvement, which motivates everyone and is the most efficient incentive for human industriousness. We have therefore, the most auspicious prospect for progress in the general public's prosperity. Work is in search of men in Brazil, instead of men being in search of work. No one who is willing to work will die of hunger. Brazil has the appearance of being a nation of millionaires because the people are spending so much.

Edenic appeal (originally represented in Genesis in metaphors of the Garden of Delights)–a land destined to protect purity, one which has perfect accord among all its creatures (Holanda 149–84)–insinuates itself into this utopic creation. This is an environment that is resistant to the adversity inherent in the struggle for survival. This image of terrestrial paradise, however, was immediately followed by its extension, the "El Dorado Brasílico"–the copious nation of treasures.

The virtues of hard work with improved technology are part of a new version of the paradisiacal, now as a futuristic projection. Engineers argued that it was urgent that the nation improve workers' skills, thereby giving them the means to increase the exploitation of the inexhaustible resources. On another level, the mystique of free enterprise, inherent in the discourse of the empowered elites, promised prosperity to all by functioning as a means of offsetting the lack of initiative, which was considered a manifestation of Brazilian workers' indolence. Brazilian indolence was actually a well-rooted notion in the mentality of the elites ever since colonial times, seen as the corrupting effect of racial miscegenation, slavery, and the climate.

As we can see, the image of Brazil as God's generous creation–later incorporated into the national imaginary as the notion that "God is Brazilian"–mitigated the civilizing urgency. Myriad resources awaited, almost untouched, the exploitation of labor and technique. A new phase was begun, opposed to centuries of colonizers and adventurers, who had experienced the frustration of their expectations of immense wealth, finding instead racial violence, hunger, and sickness. The imagery of the heroism of basic exploration of a fascinating paradise gave way to a new order, that of workers, modern methods and techniques, and large factories, which led to visionary investors measuring Brazil's cornucopia with the sophisticated development prospects of modern capitalism. We find combined in the representation of a prodigious nature (the main element in the myth of the Promised Land), aestheticism, and utilitarianism (now greatly inflated with the perspective of future material exploitation). The use of images of a new El Dorado therefore served to reinforce this utilitarian vision. The director and eminent member of the "Associação do Quarto Centenário do Descobrimento do Brasil" ("The Fourth Centennial of the Discovery of Brazil Association"), Benjamin Franklin Ramiz Galvão (1846–1938), stated in his speech at the opening of the Engineering Conference in 1900:

Nem há extranhar este asserto; o sólo que a Providencia entregou á nossa actividade mede 8 1/2 millhões de kilometros quadrados, e só o pedaço de territorio, que o patriotismo e saber do Emerito Rio Branco acabam de conquistar com tanta glória, ao dirimir-se o pleito secular da nossa fronteira do Norte, (*applausos prolongados*) equivale em superficie a mais de dez vezes a Belgica. As nossa riquezas mineraes são estupendas; coleiam enormes serpentes de ouro pelo amago da terra ou á flôr dos valles, desde a Bahia até Matto-Grosso; Minas dir-se-hia um gigante de ferro com o dorso salpicado de turmalinas, topazios e diamantes; nas entranhas do Rio Grande do Sul e Sancta Catharina dormem

jazidas de carvão de pedra que valem thesouros e só aguardam o alvião industrial para transformar-se em luz, calor, movimento e vida. Nas cachoeiras espumantes dos nossos rios palpita a força motriz de geradores electricos colossaes; nas mattas profundas e a perder de vista campeiam sucupiras, ipés e acapús que, transformados em dormentes, dariam o leito de muitas estradas transcontinentaes do Atlantico ao Pacifico. Por toda a parte a materia prima preciosa das industrias mais variadas e remuneradoras, a pedir capitaes, braços e coragem para converter-se em instrumentos de riqueza e civilização.
(Associação do Quarto Centenário IV, 361)

Here is a truth that is not to be underestimated; the earth that Providence provided to us for our nation measures 8 1/2 million square kilometers, and that portion alone of our territory, which the intelligence and patriotism of the honourable Rio Branco treaty has only recently and so gloriously won for Brazil, on resolving the dispute at our northern borders (*prolonged clapping*), has a surface that is the equivalent of more than ten Belgiums. Our mineral riches are stupendous; enormous sinuous serpents of gold in the heart of the earth break out to the surface of the fields, extending from Bahia to Mato Grosso; of Minas one could say it is an iron giant whose back is incrusted with tourmalines, topazes, and diamonds; in the entrails of Rio Grande do Sul and Santa Catarina sleep beds of coal worth treasures lying in wait for industrial mining to be transformed into energy for light, heat and transportation. In the great waterfalls of our rivers there is the palpitating, driving force to move colossal electric generators; in our deep forests we find endless reserves of *sucupiras, ipês,* and *acapus* [Brazilian trees], which, made into sleeper cars, will serve many transcontinental railroads from the Atlantic to the Pacific. Everywhere there is precious raw material awaiting the most varied and profitable industries, waiting for captains of industry with means and courage to convert them into instruments of wealth and civilization.

The Brazilian El Dorado thus formed the horizon of expectation represented by progress and civilization. It reduced the temporal lag between Brazil and the industrialized nations, since the acquisition of technical and scientific knowledge served to stabilize the march of industrial progress, creating opportunities for those who wished to join in. Brazil, taking its own historical trajectory into account, and given its peculiar natural make-up, had the advantage of being a politically young nation. Increasing Brazil's positive outlook were a purported racial integration, cultural and linguistic identity, and common interests, and especially the ennobling character of Brazilians. The trope of cultural solidarity, present especially in Affonso Celso's essay, demonstrates a fixation on the fictive notion of stability taken from the readings on the foundations of Brazil (such as Pero Vaz de Caminha's narrative).

In de Caminha's letter the Indian nations' submission to the principles of the Luso-Christian world and their announced acculturation are all implicit, whereas in Affonso Celso the specter of national unity and supposition of non-violence serve to dilute diversity, bringing Brazilians into a unity of patriotism, civilization, and prosperity. The commemoration of the Centennial aimed, above all, to celebrate the images of the Brazilian people: cordial, fond of order, patient, resigned, sweet, natural, selfless, charitable, and tolerant. All of this marked the potential for progress and a reversal of the national sense of inferiority (Celso 77).

As for the question of defining character, the speeches of the other Centennial publicists differ from the example above only insofar as they instilled a more explicit link to that inaugural vision of Brazil. We therefore find in the modern image of cordiality indications of an insistence on the topics of hospitality and the redemptive mission, which were taken from Caminha's narrative. The attorney Francisco João Evangelista Saião de Bulhões de Carvalho's opening speech to the solemn inaugural session of the Judicial Assembly on 3 May 1900 proposed that the Portuguese navigator Pedro Alvarez Cabral was a model of the peaceful contact with the native population.

From this text there emerges a reading of the encounter between Christian civilization and edenic paradise, clothed in indigenous hospitality, crystallizing the memory of the founding colonizers. Indian hospitality suggests the land's and peoples' virtual adaptation to civilization, a concept that elevated the Portuguese founders' mission to the category of redemption and was fulfilled in the success of the emergence of the Brazilian nation, thus justifyng the consecration of the discoverers. If the interpretation of the Promised Land was to have far-reaching effects starting from the events of 1500, it would be only in 1900 that the birth of Brazil would be symbolically sanctioned, opening then the doors to a future of promise.

Translation by Lis L. P. Horta Moriconi

Works Cited

Academia das Ciências de Lisboa. Commissão Portuguesa da Exposição Colombina de Madrid. 1892. *Centenário do Descobrimento da América.* Memórias da Comissão Portuguesa. Lisbon: Typ. da Academia Real das Sciencias.

Adorno, Rolena. 1996. "Cultures in Contact: Mesoamerica, the Andes, and the European Tradition." *The Cambridge History of Latin American Literature.* Vol 1: *Discovery to Modernism.* Eds. Roberto González Echevarría and Enrique Pupo-Walker. Cambridge: Cambridge University Press. 33–57.

Arroyo, Leonardo. 1971. *A Carta de Pero Vaz de Caminha: ensaio de informação a procura de constantes válidas de método.* São Paulo: Melhoramentos.

Associação do Quarto Centenario do Descobrimento do Brasil. 1900–1902. *Livro do centenario (1500–1900).* 4 vols. Rio de Janeiro: Imprensa Nacional.

Barreto, Luís Felipe. 1983. *Descobrimentos e renascimento: Formas de ser e pensar nos séculos XV e XVI.* Lisboa: Imprensa Nacional-Casa da Moeda.

Bethencourt, Francisco, and Diogo Ramada Curto, eds. 1991. *A memória da nação: Colóquio do gabinete de estudos de simbologia realizado na Fundação Calouste Gulbenkian, 7–9 outubro, 1987.* Lisbon: Livraria Sá da Costa Editora.

Bilac, Olavo, and Henrique Coelho Netto. 1932. *Contos pátrios.* 28th ed. São Paulo: Francisco Alves.

Brotherston, Gordon. 1992. *Book of the Fourth World: Reading the Native Americas through Their Literature.* New York: Cambridge University Press.

Calógeras, João Pandiá. 1972. *Formação histórica do Brasil.* São Paulo: Companhia Editora Nacional.

Carvalho, José Murilo de. 1993. *A formação das almas: O Imaginário da República no Brasil.* São Paulo: Companhia das Letras.

Carvalho, Maria Alice Rezende de. 1989. "República Brasileira: Viagem ao mesmo lugar." *Dados–Revista de Ciências Sociais* (Rio de Janeiro) 32.3: 303–20.

Celso de Assis Figueiredo, Affonso. 1937. *Porque me ufano do meu país.* 11th ed. Rio de Janeiro: F. Briguiet & Cia.

Da Matta, Roberto. 1993. *Conta de mentiroso: Sete ensaios de antropologia brasileira.* Rio de Janeiro: Rocco.

Dias Malheiro, Carlos, ed. 1921–24. *História da colonização portuguesa do Brasil.* 3 vols. Porto Litografia Nacional.

Ferreira Neto, and Edgar Leite. 1989. "O improviso da civilização. A nação republicana e a construção da ordem social no final do século XIX." Diss. Universidade Federal Fluminense.

Galvão, Benjamin Franklin Ramiz. 1900–1902. "Memoria historica dos trabalhos da Associação do Quarto Centenario do Descobrimento do Brasil." *Livro do centenário, 1500–1900.* Vol 4. Rio de Janeiro: Associação do Quarto Centenário do Descobrimento do Brasil; Imprensa Nacional. 1–391.

Gillis, John R, ed. 1994. *Commemorations: The Politics of National Identity.* Princeton: Princeton University Press.

Giucci, Guillermo. 1992. *Viajantes do maravilhoso: O novo mundo.* São Paulo: Companhia das Letras.

———. 1993. *Sem fé, lei ou rei: Brasil 1500–1532.* Rio de Janeiro: Rocco.

Holanda, Sérgio Buarque de. 1992. *Visão do paraíso: Os motivos edênicos no descobrimento e colonização do Brasil.* 5th ed. São Paulo: Brasiliense Editora.

Le Goff, Jacques, ed. *Memória-História.* Lisboa: Imprensa Nacional-Casa da Moeda, 1984. Vol. 1 of *Enciclopédia Einaudi,* 1984.

Lienhard, Martin. 1992. *La voz y su huella: Escritura y conflicto étnico-cultural en América Latina,* 1492–1988. Lima: Editorial Horizonte.

Maio, Marcos Chor, and Ricardo Ventura Santos. 1996. *Raça, ciência e sociedade.* Rio de Janeiro: Ed. Fiocruz/Centro Cultural Banco do Brasil.

Malheiro, Agostinho Marques Perdigão. 1850. *Índice chronologico dos factos mais notáveis da historia do Brasil desde seu descobrimento em 1500 ate 1849* . . . Rio de Janeiro: Typographia de Francisco de Paula Brito.

Martins, Wilson. 1976. *História da inteligência brasileira.* Vol. 1: 1550–1794. São Paulo: Cultrix.

Mignolo, Walter D. 2000. *Local Histories/Global Designs.* Princeton: Princeton University Press.

———. 1994. "Signs and Their Transmission: The Question of the Book in the New World." *Writing Without Words.* Eds. Elizabeth Hill Boone and Walter D. Mignolo. Durham: Duke University Press.

Moreira de Azevedo, Manuel Antonio. 1900–1902 "O descobrimento do Brasil. Intuitos da viagem de Pedro Alvares Cabral." *Livro do centenário,* 1500–1900. Vol 1. Rio de Janeiro: Associação do Quarto Centenario do Descobrimento do Brasil; Imprensa Nacional. iii–xvi.

O'Gorman, Edmundo. 1972. *The Invention of America: An Inquiry into the Historical Nature of the New World and the Meaning of Its History.* Westport: Greenwood Press.

Salles, Ricardo. 1996. *Nostalgia imperial: A formação da identidade nacional no Brasil do Segundo Reinado.* Rio de Janeiro: Topbooks.

Silva, Francisco Carlos Teixeira da. 1992. "Portugal. Das origens agrárias às grandes navegações." *Ciência Hoje* 15.86: 27.

Varnhagen, Adolfo. 1991. *História geral do Brasil: Antes de sua separação e indepêndencia de Portugal.* 5 vols. Belo Horizonte: Itatiaia.

CHAPTER 3

SPECTACULAR CITYSCAPES OF BAROQUE SPANISH AMERICA

Stephanie Merrim

Fin de Siècle

"Is the idea of a Spanish-American baroque an oxymoron?" asks Kathleen Ross (1993, 1). Ross's question neatly brings into focus the diffracted responses of recent literary and cultural scholars to the Latin American seventeenth century. Also at the end of the century, John Beverley (1992) parses the debate to which Ross refers into the poles of a continuum, inflected as either American or Spanish. He asks (1992, 290) whether the Latin American Baroque is "heterodoxia frente a la tradición castiza española" ("heterodoxy confronting the most entrenched Spanish tradition"), as Octavio Paz (1914–1998) stated in *Las peras del olmo* [1957; The Pears of the Elm], or "estilo importado por la monarquía española como parte de una cultura estrechamente ligada a su ideología imperialista" ("a style imported by the Spanish monarchy as part of a culture closely tied to its imperial ideology"), as Leonardo Acosta stated in *El barroco de Indias* [1984; The Baroque of Indies]. Unpacking Beverley's question, we can surmise that the first construction of the Baroque he mentions would include the works of Chang-Rodríguez, González Echevarría (1993), Moraña, Paz, Picón-Salas, Roggiano, and Ross. (See the bibliography to this chapter for references to all texts mentioned and cited.) These scholars highlight in a panoply of ways the difference of the Latin American Baroque from the Spanish and Portuguese Baroque. Subversion and resistance and contestation, alterity and marginalization, identity, cultural syncretism and hybridity—in sum, the redimensionalizing of the Spanish Baroque—entail their guiding paradigms and José Lezama Lima's (1910–1976) battle cry in *La expresión americana* (1957; American Expression), arguably their guiding light: "Ahora, gracias al heroísmo y conveniencia de sus símbolos, precisamos que podemos acercarnos a las manifestaciones de cualquier estilo sin acomplejarnos ni resbalar, siempre que insertemos allí los símbolos de nuestro destino" (54) ("Today, thanks to the heroism and the usefulness of its symbols, we can state that we can approach the expressions of any style without error or inferiority, as long as we include the symbols of our destiny"). The second construction of the Baroque, by materialist scholars such as Acosta, Beverley (who nevertheless has embraced both positions; see Beverley 1992), Concha, Maravall, Rama (1983), and Vidal, emphasizes not heterodoxy but hegemony, articulating the imperial power structures that configure New World colonial regimes and their ineluctable impact on cultural production.

Each group's approach to the Baroque as a *colonial* phenomenon ensues organically from the matrix established over the course of the twentieth century by Irving A. Leonard's (1896–1996) landmark studies of the Spanish American Baroque. In the study that most concerns us here, *Baroque Times in Old Mexico: Seventeenth-Century Persons, Places, and Practices* (1959), and in other works, Leonard challenged what he called the myth of Spanish obscurantism. "I found out," he states, "that what historians had been saying about Spain's cutting the Indies off from European ideas, books, or literature was entirely false" (see TePaske 246). Leonard's meticulous documentation of the book trade proves that Spain's stranglehold on New World culture and thought, while indeed formidable, was far from absolute. Secular literary works and even isolated shreds of Cartesian thought made their way through the semi-permeable curtain of cultural embargo, creating small rifts in the monolithic enterprise of the Baroque, whose main thrust, according to Leonard, "was immobility, spiritual, intellectual, cultural, social, political and economic" (1959, 223). From this dim but hardly inconsequential dialectic between absolutism and challenge emerges the larger design of *Baroque Times*, which is framed between the spectacular entry into Mexico City in 1623 of Archbishop Fray García Guerrero, as emblem of the absolutist machine, and the proto-Enlightenment thinking and *criollo* patriotism of Carlos de Sigüenza y Góngora (1645–1700) at the end of the century, as a harbinger of things to come. From here also, as my preceding remarks suggest, emerges the source of much recent theorizing about the "Barroco de Indias."

No less captivating have been the glittering, multidimensional portraits of the Spanish American Baroque drawn by Leonard in *Baroque Times*. To imbue historiography with a vivid "phosphorescence of learning" (TePaske 248), Leonard imported the engaging dramatic style of Romantic historians Francis Parkman and W. H. Prescott into the twentieth century. As a result, Leonard capitalizes to great effect on the gilded *fin de siècle* opulence of the viceregal world, highlighting its spectacle-ridden and spectacular nature, and at the same time succeeds in enlivening even such ponderous subjects as Baroque neo-Scholasticism. If this Romantic stylistic energy accounts for the continuing appeal of *Baroque Times*, it is no doubt the monograph's special mix of literary history and history itself into cultural history that guarantees the work's ongoing intellectual currency. In effect, the interdisciplinarity of *Baroque Times* builds bridges between early- and late-twentieth-century methodological practices.

The present essay bears in mind the gamut of recent approaches to the "Barroco de Indias" and will work them explicitly into and through the lines opened up by *Baroque Times*, principally, the lines dealing with what could be called the Baroque's will to spectacle. I map out an approach to vice-regal culture that perpetuates not only Leonard's interdisciplinarity but also the driving force evident in the subtitle of his work, *Seventeenth-Century Persons, Places and Practices*—a sense of the Baroque "as an historical epoch *and a way of life*" (ix; emphasis added). As distinct from the familiar, formalistic investigations of *la diferencia americana*, I particularly wish to recuperate this emphasis on the praxis of the Baroque in the Indies. The essay begins by building on Leonard's discussions of the Baroque as a way of life in order to lay the groundwork for the spectacular cityscapes rendered in prose and poetry by transplanted Spaniards and New World *criollos* to which the remainder of its pages are devoted.

Baroque Times in Spanish America

As does this essay, *Baroque Times* focuses the seventeenth century through *criollo* life and culture rather than through the lives and cultures of the indigenous peoples of Latin America. (José Antonio Mazzotti's essay complements mine in this regard.) If lacking an indigenous perspective, *Baroque Times* does succeed in providing the blueprint for a southern-hemispheric one in terms of what Paz has called "el siglo criollo" (1982, 63) ("the century of the *criollo*" [1988, 40]). Leonard begins by setting up the by now indelible framework (see Picón-Salas; Simpson; Lafaye; Lavrin) in which that century must be viewed, belying the disregard into which it had fallen: "in comparison to the Age of Discovery and Conquest and the later period of intellectual ferment foreshadowing the political separation from Spain," it is often said that "the intervening seventeenth century is a 'forgotten' or 'neglected' era" (1959, vii). He then immediately regroups the era, edged out of prominence by the more visibly heroic ages that precede and follow it, with one of his most powerful formulations: While in Europe it was a time of ferment,

> for the peoples who lived out their days in these remote regions of the New World it was a formative period of ethnic and cultural consolidation. It was a quiet era, comparatively speaking, when the process of hybridization, cultural absorption, and psychological growth shaped the matrix whose imprint on the human elements of present-day Hispanic America is recognizable. (vii)

Several interrelated dimensions of colonial life underlie both Leonard's statement and the specifically cultural development of the period and thus warrant brief discussion here: Stabilization, economic development, urbanization, and *criollo* consciousness.

If within fifty years of Columbus's landfall the sedentary areas of Latin America had been conquered by Spain (see Merrim 1996), the next fifty years would witness the consolidation, and the next one hundred the exploitation, of the colonial situation. During the seventeenth century, the "período de la Estabilización Colonial" (Vidal 25) ("period of colonial stabilization"), with administrative and labor structures in place and the native peoples largely pacified,

Church and state would turn their sights to maintaining the wealth of the New World and to enjoying its fruits. The indigenous populations began a slow but sustained demographic recovery (Lavrin 296). Sustained by the labor force they provided, it was indeed a time of relative complacency, considerable leisure, and security for those possessed of capital, although, as will become evident, it was also a time intermittently punctuated by uprisings and natural disasters.

The exorbitant, disproportionate wealth of the New World upon which Jesuit historian Bernabé Cobo (1580–1657) comments in his 1639 *Fundación de Lima* (Foundation of Lima)— "Porque hombres tiene Lima de a trescientos y cuatrocientos mil ducados de hacienda, y de ahí para arriba, y no se llama rico a boca llena el que no pasa de cien mil; ... están en opinión de pobres las personas de calidad y obligaciones que no llega su hacienda a veinte mil pesos" (321) ("Lima has men with an income of three to four hundred thousand gold ducats and from this level upwards, and in all honesty, no one who has less than one hundred thousand ducats can call himself a rich man; ... persons of quality and responsibility who do not have twenty thousand pesos are considered to be poor")— stood at the absolute epicenter of colonial life, ruling all of its practices. Yet economic historians have found that there was a decline in trade between Spain and its colonies beginning in the first half of the seventeenth century and have questioned whether the New World suffered an economic depression corresponding to that of Spain. Recent investigations (Lynch; TePaske), however, have attributed the downswing in trade to the increasing diversification and independence of the thriving New World economies. As the inequities of the Spanish monopoly became more flagrant (Lynch 212), the colonies became more self-sustaining. Their economies diversified beyond mining to agriculture and cattle-raising as early *encomiendas* grew into the *haciendas* that would determine Spanish America's profile for centuries to come. Spanish America increasingly traded with partners other than Spain and intracontinentally, and Spanish Americans invested capital abroad. The viceroyalty of Mexico diversified more notably and earlier than that of Peru, yet all told it can be said that "[t]he crisis in the *carrera de Indias* occurred not because the American economies were collapsing but because they were developing and disengaging themselves from their primitive dependence on the mother country. This was the first emancipation of America" (Lynch 211). Not the American economies but the colonial regime, we see, was ultimately in jeopardy.

Spanish American wealth for the time being joined with the colonial regime to support the solidification of the major New World urban centers, especially the capitals of the viceroyalties. Cobo noted that "luego que cesó el ruido de las armas, abonanzó el tiempo, y comenzaron los españoles a gozar de paz y quietud. ... Respiró esta ciudad y comenzó a ir en tan grande aumento ... " (305) ("when the turmoil of war ended and the times became calm, Spaniards began to enjoy peace and quiet. ... The city breathed and it began to grow"). That great enlargement of the city could be found in Lima or in Mexico City, whose population had climbed from about 15,000 in the 1620s to 50,000 by the end of the century. The central urban administrative centers grew at a faster rate than smaller ones (Morse 78) and were the preferred dwellings of whites, even of those with rural estates (Morse 90). Ethnic and racial groups converged in the daily commerce of the city. Trade, power, and culture were all brokered there. Cities replicated European-style civilization and constituted the locus of production and consumption of cultural goods. It was in the city, center of learning and court patronage, that all of the major writers of the period (Spanish, *criollo*, and *mestizo* alike) produced their works.

The highly engineered Baroque cities of the New World were designed for ideological consolidation, social stratification, and ostentation. In the blueprint of the city could be read that of the planned society originally set out by the orderly sixteenth-century *trazas* (city plans), with their grid design–Ángel Rama's *ciudad ordenada* (1984) (well-ordered city). The center of the city notoriously contained the icons of power: The church, the *cabildo* (municipal council), the viceregal palace, the marketplace, and the plaza. Cities radiated out in concentric circles that moved from the wealthy and sources of wealth, such as commercial establishments, to the furthermost tier, which housed the disenfranchised Spanish and those Indians not lodged in the homes of the rich that they served. Commerce between the inner and outer tiers was strictly regulated, with the schedule suspended only for festivals (see Vidal 103–104). Broad avenues joined the tiers, and large parks (the "Alamedas" of Mexico City and Lima) ringed the outskirts of the city. Together with the plazas, they furnished the backdrop for parades of an official and an unofficial nature, the latter comprising the splendid carriages and their retinues on which so many writers of the period remarked with awe (for example, Gage 67, 73; Cobo 321). Plazas, avenues, and parks in the New World Baroque city took on vaster and showier dimensions than their Spanish counterparts, laid out for the public performance of status and power. As Roberto González Echevarría well observes, "Viceregal cities . . . were designed for representation, not for life" (1996, 207).

For these were aristocratic cities, or more aptly, cities with aristocratic pretensions. In them dwelt and prevailed the newly rich Spaniards who styled themselves as nobles, as *hidalgos*. "He who was a peasant in Spain takes on airs of gentility, and the commoner tries to look like a noble," noted Bartolomé Arzáns de Orsúa y Vela (1676–1736) of the boomtown, Potosí (1975, xxiv–v). Though their riches often derived from mercantile activities, these would-be *hidalgos* effaced the bourgeois sources of their wealth and invested themselves with the trappings of nobility (see Romero, Ch. 3). They flaunted their aspired-to status through the conspicuous consumption of jewelry, clothing, liveries, and home furnishings. Cities, in imitation of the Spanish noble ideal, were the chosen habitat of the parvenus, who utilized urban structures as the stage on which to perpetuate their fiction.

From a more prescient perspective, it can nevertheless be said that in the city and in general, this was the century of the *criollo*. José Lezama Lima's storied *criollo*, "el Señor Barroco" ("Mr. Baroque"), represents "un triunfo de la ciudad y un americano allí instalado" ("a triumph of the city and the installation of a Spanish American"); this "americano señor barroco, auténtico primer instalado en lo nuestro, . . . aparece cuando ya se han alejado del tumulto de la conquista" (31–32) ("this Spanish American Baroque man, authentically inserted in our culture, comes when the turmoil of the conquest has passed"). Lezama's "Señor Barroco" conjoins the triumph of the city with the age of the *criollo* and of stabilization in a foundational myth for a syncretic America, situating its first plenitude in the seventeenth century. Yet even when divested of mythic proportions, that century still appears to have been foundational for the *criollo* spirit. Fundamental to any story of

the age is an understanding of the tensions that arose between *criollos* and Spaniards, especially the bureaucracy and the heirs of the conquerors, as the *criollo* economy took on a life of its own. *Criollos* gained in wealth, wealth-based power, and education only to be curtailed by the colonial glass ceiling that generally prevented them from attaining high office in the church, the state, or the military. Such tensions found a positive outlet in the sentiments or nascent ideology of what is best called *criollo* patriotism or consciousness. Leonard writes that "the *criollos* thought of themselves more and more as Mexican Americans and sought compensatory pride in their homeland" (1959, 225). Paz draws a line between this *criollo* pride or awareness and factual *criollo* separatism or nationalism, noting that seventeenth-century *criollos* remained loyal to the Crown (1976, xvi–xvii). I will examine at length issues related to Mexican *criollo* consciousness in the works of Balbuena and Sigüenza y Góngora; for now, I offer these words written in 1662 by the Peruvian *criollo* Juan de Espinosa Medrano ("Lunarejo") (1620?–1688), apologist for Góngora and for his own *patria*: "habiendo heredado la cumbre más alta del mundo, podríamos enorgullecernos de nuestra tierra y nuestro cielo" ("having inherited the summit of world culture, we Peruvians could be proud of our land and our skies"), for in Peru we have been born "grandes hombres en letras, en ingenio, en doctrina, en amenidad de costumbres y en santidad" (xlii) ("great in letters, in wit, in doctrine, in the amenity of our customs, and in holiness").

Espinosa Medrano's words confirm from a *criollo* perspective that during the period of stabilization there were manifold reasons for self-exaltation and for celebration. Indeed, the various New World circumstances summarized in the previous paragraphs further inflamed the propensity to spectacle of the already "celebratory universe of the Spanish Baroque" (Díez Borque 11), a universe constantly involved in exorbitant displays of grandeur and power in festivals, church ceremonies, court rituals, and so on. Leonard writes, "'To make of life a drama, and of drama, life' was, in a sense, a fundamental principle of the Baroque age. [. . .] If the mother country was fatally engaged in making of life a tragic drama, its remote and sheltered possessions, dwelling in relative peace and settled order, felt impelled to make of diverting drama a more pulsating way of life" (1959, 117). These diverting dramas or celebratory spectacles stand at the very heart of Leonard's conception of the Baroque. For him, they emblematize an age full of drama and pomp but signifying nothing more than its own forced immobility (1959, 28). We now turn our attention to the New World spectacles that, despite Leonard's caveats, prove to be essential to the texture of New World life, to its ideological underpinnings, and to its cultural imaginary.

The celebratory universe of the Spanish Baroque took on new meaning in the New World, where, like the actual city of Mexico/Tenochtitlán, it was erected upon the foundations of indigenous civilizations. Leonard notes the love of show common to the conqueror and the conquered (1959, 118), and Frederick Luciani tells us that Colonial society "inherited from both of the principal lines of its cultural patrimony–the indigenous and the Hispanic–a delight in elaborate public ceremony, tantamount to communal, civic theatre" (266) and states that evidence of forms of theatrical activity has been found in some thirty-four indigenous American languages (261). The conquering Spaniards were at pains to match the magnitude of indigenous displays so that Christianity would not appear inferior and as a proselytizing tool for the natives whom famed Franciscan historian Juan de Torquemada deemed "ceremoniáticos" (Brading 287). A report from the Council of Lima in 1583 quoted by Robert Ricard observes that "es cosa cierta y notoria que esta nación de yndios se atraen y provocan sobremanera al conocimiento y veneración de nuestro sumo Dios con las ceremonias exteriores y aparatos del culto divino; procura mucho los obispos y también en su tanto los curas, que todo lo que toca al culto divino se haga con la mayor perfection [sic] y lustre que puedan . . ." (317) ("it has been established that this nation of indigenous people are attracted to and have an extraordinary interest in the knowledge and veneration of our supreme God through the ceremonies and ritual of divine worship; the bishops as well as the priests take great care to ensure that all matters pertaining to divine worship be done with the utmost perfection and brilliance possible. . ."). Ricard even goes so far as to attribute the over-ornateness of later Spanish spectacles to the desire to satisfy indigenous proclivities.

In festive Baroque times, occasions of the most varied sorts prompted public celebration. First and perhaps foremost were the religious festivals that commemorated Corpus Christi and the many other holy events, the dedication of new churches or additions to existing structures, the investiture or departure of religious officials, the transfer of relics or sacred images, beatifications and canonizations, articles of doctrine, patron saints of the cities or their organizations, and so forth. The state ritualized its activities large and small, personal and private, colonial and imperial, praiseworthy and punitive. Hence, everything from the private events of the royal family in Spain or in the colonies to the arrival of new fleets, and especially the entries and farewells of viceroys, gave rise to spectacle. Hangings, floggings, and penitential parades constituted their own kind of exhibitionist theater, attracting a large public. Nor were popular festivals of a traditional nature, such as those marking the seasons, neglected. Moreover, festivals overflowed organized bounds and spilled into a daily life punctuated by paseos, masquerades, and other public recreations involving display. Colonial society needed no formal pretext to indulge in its insatiable taste for show.

The most extraordinary wealth and splendor–jewels, luxurious costumes, fabulously elaborate floats and special effects, even streets paved with silver (Mugaburu, 215)–characterized official festivals. Private individuals, trade guilds, confraternities, and merchants were increasingly called upon to bear the ever more onerous costs that Colombian Juan Rodríguez Freyle (1566–1642?) lamented in *El Carnero* [1936; The Sheep]: "Hízose al presidente un solemne recibimiento [in 1569], con grandes fiestas, que duraron por quince días y con excesivos gastos, que los sufría mejor la tierra por ser nueva. En la era de agora [1638] no sé cómo los lleva; lo que veo es que todos se huelgan, y que los mercaderes no han dejado de cobrar" (214) ("The president was given a formal reception [in 1569] with splendid celebrations that lasted fifteen days at an excessive cost that the country suffered better because it was so new. Today [in 1638] I do not know how the country can afford such expenses; what I see is that everyone has leisure time and merchants have not stopped charging for goods"). The prominence accorded to material riches vitiated the spirituality of religious processions, profaning them and rendering them profane. Lima poet Juan del Valle y Caviedes (1652–1692) critiqued the dual profanation of the festival of Corpus Christi in his "Coloquio entre una vieja y Periquillo a una procesión celebrada en esta ciudad" ["Conversation

between an old woman and Periquillo about a procession that was celebrated in this city"]: "También vi en la Compañía [the Jesuits]/por adorno de la iglesia,/colgados muchos rebozos/de brocato y de bayeta,/porque femeniles galas,/a desplegadas banderas,/hagan de profanidades/aun en los templos ostenta" (206) ("I also saw that the church of the Jesuits/was decorated with the presence of many shawls/of brocade but also of cotton,/because women's apparel,/like unfurled flags,/profane though they may be, even in church are ostentation").

Other categories were conflated in the all-melding festivals. State dignitaries participated in religious festivals, and religious dignitaries participated in civic celebrations. Sumptuary laws were suspended, erasing some of the visible boundaries between classes. Torquemada, recalling our discussion of the would-be *hidalgos*, remarked with umbrage that "en la diferencia de los Hombres, el Domingo, y día de Fiesta, no se halla entre ellos distinción; porque tan Ilustre parece el Oficial, como el que no lo es por Nobleza, y Sangre . . ." (Book 3, Ch. XXVI, n.p.) ("in contrast among men, on Sunday and on feast days, there is no distinction to be seen among them, for the government official appears as distinguished as those who do not share aristocratic blood . . ."). Elite culture jostled with popular culture in the festival, whose processions included elegant masquerades and displays of equestrian skills together with raucous *mojigangas* (masquerades) and cross-dressing of a carnivalesque ilk. Hieroglyphs piqued the educated mind, and visual pageantry stimulated the unlettered. Sor Juana Inés de la Cruz (1648–1695) wrote of her arch for the entry of the Bishop in 1680 that its inscriptions captivated "la atención de los entendidos, como sus colores los ojos de los vulgares" (4: 374) ("the minds of those who can distinguish them, while the common man discerns only the colourful").

Perhaps most interesting, officially sponsored festivals provided a forum for both praise and critique of the colonial regime. The laudatory poetry produced for the occasions could be declaimed alongside biting satires, purely frivolous masquerades performed next to burlesques. Leonard states that the "*máscara a lo faceto* was frequently a useful medium of criticism, and it provided opportunities to pillory prominent officials and unpopular dignitaries" (1959, 121). Mexican proto-journalist Antonio de Robles details an "indecentísima" masquerade in Puebla in 1666, unchecked by its bishop: "en que sacaron en estatuas al conde virrey y a la condesa su mujer, en forma en que se hacía justicia de ambos, con pregón de muchas y grandísimas injurias, haciendo paseo por las calles" (1: 29) ("and they carried statues of the viceroy and the condesa, his wife, in a manner that did justice to both, to the shouts of many and most insulting words as they were paraded through the streets").

In festival times, banners, rich cloth hangings, temporary façades, altars, fireworks, and ephemeral architecture such as artificial arches, mountains, pyramids, and columns displaced everyday reality, temporarily transforming the entire city into a large-scale theater. If all the world became a stage, all constituencies of the festival's universe participated in the vast dramatic production. The poor were fed in large banquets that assumed the cast of a mass secular communion in worship of the Empire. Entertainments were provided for all according to their wont. Nuns were at times allowed to break their encloisterment to ride in floats (see Mugaburu 77); parades marched through the convents. The various classes and races also participated in the parades, with indigenous contingents (as my later discussions will establish) sometimes assuming an imposing role. Spanish spectacles not only replicated the magnificence of indigenous ceremonies but also incorporated tribal dances and music.

Racially syncretic and artistically synesthetic, spectacles held profound significance for literary culture. The festivals embodied and apotheosized New World culture, providing a singular venue for creative endeavors. A great array of texts, the very bedrock of the festival, were commissioned for its events: liturgical poetry and lyrics, sermons, a variety of theatrical and paratheatrical productions, *saraos* (private entertainments with music and dance), hieroglyphic epigrams and emblems, announcements, satires, *relaciones* (reports), and, of course, poetry. Poetry represented the pinnacle of elite culture, or even of culture per se. Poets and poetasters therefore strove to advertise their erudition with abstruse, Gongoresque contrivances to be declaimed in poetic competitions. These competitions were spectacles unto themselves, often involving parades and magnificent prizes that concretized the metaphors contained in the spectacular poems. However, the most valuable prize for the writer conceivably lay in the publications and upward mobility that ensued from the spectacle. Festivals gave rise to the published *relaciones* that lauded and immemorialized its events; the entries in poetry contests often made their way into published volumes such as the *Triunfo parténico* (Parthenon Triumph) of 1682 edited by Sigüenza. The importance of festivals for writers cannot be underestimated. In a world where publication was extraordinarily costly and difficult, especially for secular works, and where the entry of *criollos* into the highest circles was severely limited, spectacle-allied literary works furnished opportunities to break both barriers.

Although it is a private text, and one that remained unpublished until 1917, the diary of Josephe de Mugaburu (d. 1686) suggests the seduction that spectacles exercised on writers, interested or disinterested. Mugaburu held the position of sergeant of the guard for the viceroy's palace in Lima's Plaza de Armas, and between 1640 and 1686 registered the goings-on of the plaza in his diary. His physical vantage point translates into a literary one as Mugaburu faithfully records, to the exclusion of nearly all else, the ceremonial life of the State. In the represented world of Mugaburu's chronicle, spectacle and city become one, as the Baroque City amply fulfills the designs that underlie its very construction. The sentry's diary is an utter delirium of spectacles recorded in ample objective detail, with one spectacle following upon another in rapid succession, each more extravagant and elaborate than the previous one. Herein we find minute descriptions of floats and of the participation of the several racial groups in festivals, as well as step-by-step transcriptions of *octavarios* (week-long festivals); moreover, herein we find unequivocal, even numbing, proof of the seamless tissue of spectacles that in many ways dominated the urban life of Baroque Spanish America.

This said and established, it behooves us to ask *why*, beyond the blazoning of wealth or outdoing of indigenous rituals, spectacle had attained such pre-eminence in the New World. A ready answer will present itself to anyone familiar with Antonio Maravall's study of absolutism and cultural shaping, *La cultura del barroco* [*Culture of the Baroque*]. Maravall understands the Hispanic Baroque as a culture of crisis. To staunch the overwhelming religious and political turmoil of the seventeenth century, to foreclose on political and social change, Spain imposed an absolutist monarchy, together with its correlate, the guided culture of the Baroque. The seventeenth century ushered in the epoch of the masses, the first in modern history, and absolutism utilized the "expedients" (*resortes*), or organs, of culture to guide, control, and integrate the masses. Thus did Baroque culture emerge "as a complex of resources to overcome the forces of deviance or of opposition present in the society of the epoch" (125).

Coterminous with its guided culture, the statecraft of the Baroque swelled into a hypertrophic, omnivorous art form. Baroque statecraft theatricalized power in full recognition that power lives in representation and that representation generates more power. Spectacles of all sorts, almost needless to say, made up the principal dramatic artillery of what had become a thespian state. Although the Baroque's metaphysics claimed the ephemerality of all worldly phenomena, its statecraft insisted on the incessant, extravagant, controlled spectacles that I have described. Their frequency and calculated excess dazzled and suspended the will of spectators and participants alike, sublimating their passions and interpellating them as subjects for the State. Spectacles left those caught up in them, as Sigüenza well put it in *Glorias de Querétaro* [1660; The Glories of Querétaro], "extáticos," that is, ex-static, standing outside themselves and thus free to be filled up. The controlled, meticulously orchestrated nature of the spectacles, furthermore, meant that whatever transpired within the privileged confines of the festival, however transgressive, took place under the sanction of the State. This, of course, is an essential feature of Bakhtin's and Paz's notion of the carnival/fiesta, and it explains the conflation of categories and the presence of carnivalesque elements in the festivals as discussed above. It is important, nonetheless, to underscore one essential difference between carnival and the spectacles under study (as attested to by George Foster's statement that "carnival observances were recognized as a threat to morality and order, and they were discouraged . . . in America and Spain" [15]): Carnival stands alone, on its own entirely transgressive if externally sanctioned bounds. The multiform spectacles of the Baroque thespian state, on the other hand, absorb elements of carnival into their own network, making those elements but one piece of a Machiavellian contrivance that in its entirety traduces the originally transgressive nature of the carnival.

Rather than being fully betrayed, at least one carnivalesque element acquired a certain potency in the spectacles enacted in a Hispanic colonial setting: the egalitarianism of carnival. By incorporating the many constituents of the most racially complex society the world had yet known into its festivals, the guided culture of the American Baroque sought to resolve concrete tensions in symbolic but palpable form. Spectacles both represented and created a mixed, blended collectivity. Paz sees New World festivals as confirming both the horizontal and the vertical bonds of society, as "la fusión de los distintos elementos que componen la sociedad y la reafirmación de los vínculos entre el señor y sus vasallos" (1982, 199) ("the fusion of the different elements composing society and the affirmation of the bonds between the lord and his vassals") (1988, 144). In view of the spectacle's function as a cog in the machinery of a guided culture, it can be said that, in spectacles, the New World was simultaneously worshiping itself in effigy (especially in the case of the multi-ethnic parades mentioned above) and in a utopian projection desired by and for the State. The spectacular was both specular and a simulacrum. Spectacles propagandizing the providentialism of the Conquest, such as the one described by Mugaburu in which an impressive file of splendidly clad Incas offer to the Viceroy's newborn son a globe veined in New World silver and gold (51), exemplify my, and Paz's, point. The tensions created by the spectacle itself between specularity and hegemonic speculation (or, within its very specularity, between a spectacular performance and its performativity), will reach interesting expression in spectacle-allied literary works.

The efficacy, or inefficacy, of state theater and of Baroque guided culture at large depended to a far greater degree on their *aesthetic of amazement* (my term embraces the phenomena of *asombro* [astonishment] and *lo raro* [the strange] absorbed into this extreme, multifaceted Baroque construct) than on their equivocal egalitarianism. Both dazzling and bedazzling, spectacles incarnate and generate the amazement that, as Maravall tells us, played such a fundamental role in the absolutist machine. His exegesis of the function of that aesthetic helps us understand its volatility. In Maravall's explanation (see Chapter 9 of *Culture of the Baroque*), the conservative Baroque sought to rechannel the dangerous appeal of the new that had attained such prominence in the Renaissance by consigning the new and surprising to the sphere of art, as its subject matter and/or as the effect it intended to produce in its public: "The irruption of outlandish elements in poetry, literature, and art compensated for the deprivation of novelty elsewhere" (138). Thus displaced and cordoned off, novelty could safely satisfy public tastes as art shocked and excited the public with its wonder-provoking outlandishness. Thus defined, the novelty that motivated the aesthetic of the outlandish or amazement was one of the guided culture's prime weapons for what I call the *managing of modernity*. As John Beverley notes of Maravall's theory, "[e]n su visión, el barroco incorpora y reintegra las energías de estas nuevas formas, evitando su articulación como contracultura" (1992, 296) ("in his view, the Baroque incorporates and reintegrates the energy of new forms, thus avoiding the articulation of a counterculture").

Perhaps any aesthetic predicated on awe and wonder–according to Descartes, categories prior to moral judgment–is bound to escape the confines of a particular ideology (Stephen Greenblatt writes that the "experience of wonder seems to resist recuperation, containment, ideological incorporation . . . ," 17). In any case, the extreme Baroque aesthetic of amazement, designed, as I have argued, to manage modernity, contained the seeds of its own implosion. On the threshold of a new age, Baroque awe attempted to harness into art the vibrancy of change, movement, and dynamism proscribed to society. This literal and figurative container of modernity was thus an even more acutely volatile aesthetic than it could be on solely philosophical grounds, one wrought of tensions and fraught with the potential for self-destruction. It follows, too, that if that art in which resides the aesthetic of amazement were the only free space for modernity, it would be the historically productive one as well. Maravall himself acknowledges the inevitability that this aesthetic would implode: "It was unavoidable that the passion for the unknown, for the new and extraordinary, and, finally for its corruption in the outlandish would go to such extremes, already beyond its permitted limits . . ." (230). The Spanish historian cites as exemplary of the instability of the aesthetic of amazement (and, I add, of its historical productivity) the case of Francisco de Quevedo (1580–1645), who, "not being satisfied with his 'rarities,' with his novelties or freedom on the literary plane . . . tried to use his freedom to criticize the government" (230).

The fact that Quevedo's works proved so influential for New World satirists leads us to another near inevitability–the final and a most crucial plank in the scaffolding for the spectacular cityscapes that follow. That plank is the even greater likelihood that the aesthetic of amazement would short-circuit in the New World. I base my statement precisely on the transfer of the Baroque from a literary style to a lifestyle, that is, on the fact that the New World's very being incarnated what the Spanish Baroque had attempted to sublimate into art. Dynamism and change, along with novelty and exoticism and outlandishness, irrepressibly characterized the colonial world. Similarly, the New World amply concretized what, given the ongoing decline of the Spanish Empire (impelled, as we have seen, by the evolution of colonial economies), was in the Metropolis only, the stuff of poetic metaphors or spectacular masquerades: unlimited wealth and grandeur. It stands to reason, then, that the irrepressible should find expression in New World writings, that the repressed would return under the aegis of the aesthetic of amazement that purported to subsume it. And so it was, as our texts will firmly substantiate, that New World writers seized on the novel and the astonishing as an authorizing conduit for the representation of New World reality, re-territorializing them and launching what can be called the supplementary (and historical) productivity of the aesthetic of amazement.

In so doing, and in very Baroque ways, New World writers essentially decolonized the aesthetic of amazement willed to them by the Spanish Renaissance chroniclers. Sixteenth-century writers such as Columbus (ca. 1451–1506) and Gonzalo Fernández de Oviedo (1478–1557) had funneled their perceptions of the otherness of the New World through the Renaissance *admiratio* exemplified in novels of chivalry (on Renaissance novelty in the New World see Greenblatt; Merrim 1996), thus colonizing the marvelous. Several seventeenth-century New World writers, the most crucial of whom we will examine here, would redirect *admiratio* into the tropes of strangeness and monstrosity so proper to the extreme Baroque sensibility. Self-exoticizing and self-othering would be one important literary platform on which *criollos* would erect their flailing, nascent self-identity. Paz asserts that in "este amor por la extrañeza están tanto el secreto de la afinidad del arte barroco con la sensibilidad criolla como la razón de su fecundidad . . ." (1982, 86) ("such love for the strange we find both the secret of the Baroque art's affinity with the *criollo* sensibility and the source of its fruitfulness . . .") (1988, 58; see also González Echevarría 1993, Ch. 6, and 1996; Sabat de Rivers 1992, 40). An impressive example of Baroque historiography by Antonio de León Pinelo (1590?–1660), a Spaniard who preferred to claim that he was from Lima, sets up a fascinating syllogism that both embraces the New World's exoticism and revisits a Renaissance "classic" of wonder. In *El Paraíso en el Nuevo Mundo* (1650; Paradise in the New World), León Pinelo expands on Columbus's *Relación del tercer viaje* (1498; Report of the Third Voyage) to conclude that since Paradise lies in the East, and the East is the New World, then the New World/Paradise is the seat of "infinitas cosas peregrinas y singulares" ("an infinite number of strange and singular things") for which reason it occupies "la primacia del Orbe . . ." ("the primary place of the world. . .") (Book 4, Ch. I, 3). As he decolonizes the marvellous, and with it Columbus, León Pinelo situates his own work in the intertextual tradition of reframing Renaissance works that Kathleen Ross insightfully identifies as the salient feature of Baroque *criollo* historiography (see 1993, Ch. 2; 1996).

I purport to approach Baroque colonial historiography and literature in my essay not principally through the lens of intertextuality but rather through the matrix of three of the elements on which the preceding pages have expounded: the aesthetic of amazement, cities, and spectacles. Each one of these elements galvanized colonial writers. As just seen, the protean *aesthetic of amazement* held tremendous potential for the destabilizing of received cultural forms and constructs of identity. It invited "mimicry," mobility within ostensible imitation. The site of the patronage, consumption, and production of literature, *cities* themselves naturally emerged as the subjects of literature, the inspiration for some of the first secular literature produced in an orthodox religious world. Through the city per se and the literature that represented it, Latin America achieved a cultural presence and a signature. The profound investment of the colonial Baroque City and Baroque *spectacle* alike in self-dramatization and performance lent itself to literature. Like the city, spectacles furnished a venue for publication as well as for a gamut of literary forms and for a range of postures in the colonial subject, from exaltation to critique. In gathering the many elements of colonial society into a collectivity—real, desired, or both—spectacles moreover activated a crucial dimension of the cultural imaginary, that is, what Benedict Anderson has called an "imagined community." Leonardo García Pabón writes that in spectacles, "[d]e alguna manera asistimos al despliegue de una comunidad que se reconoce y se descubre sólo en/por ese acontecimiento" (1995, 436) ("in some way, we participated in the display of a community that recognizes itself and discovers itself only in/through this event"). The splendor and dazzlement incited as much by spectacles as by the spectacular Baroque City also indelibly engrave the two phenomena in the cultural imaginary and wed them to the aesthetic of amazement, confirming the intimate relationship between all three of the pivotal elements.

The interplay between the three elements of the matrix I have assembled from the theory, the physical setting, and the praxis of the colonial Baroque, together with the multiplex nature of spectacles, sustains the argument that informs my literary discussions, that not just the aesthetic of amazement but also the spectacles so deeply ingrained in the Baroque colonial way of life as well as in its imaginary were instrumentalized as a platform for *criollo* consciousness and/or *critique by colonial authors writing in and about cities*. While Hernán Vidal, not unlike Leonard, views spectacles as signs of the superficiality of colonial society (108), I will continue to carve out a deeper role for them here. The elements of the matrix outlined above also reflect and articulate what I consider to be a vital, though certainly not all-embracing, corpus of seventeenth-century texts, one that encompasses a spectrum of genres, works canonized and uncanonized, some previously seen as interrelated and some not. Each of the texts that I will examine relies on the spectacular (the positive or negative aspects of amazement), involves actual spectacles (by representing them, by being materially associated with them, or both), and imagines a different kind of city (the taxonomy of which the rest of my essay aims to provide). This tripartite configuration will carry us from Mexico southwards, from the beginning to the end of the seventeenth century, from the Sublime City to its antithesis, from Gongoresque poetry to

prose influenced by the popular genres of the theater and exemplary novel, and from there to satirical poetry.

The Sublime City

"La grandeza mexicana" [1604; "Mexican Greatness"], the extravagant paean to Mexico City, to the viceregal regime, and to poetry by the man who would later be the bishop of Puerto Rico, has long been viewed as a watershed in colonial literature. And rightly so, as only the second work to see print in Mexico in the seventeenth century (the first has been lost), "La grandeza mexicana" inaugurated both the century and, as Leonard (1959, 65) and many others have observed, the infusion of Baroque characteristics into New World literary production. Despite its nature as a literary watershed, "Grandeza" has only recently begun to receive the analytical scrutiny that it requires (for example, Beverley 1987; González Echevarría 1996; Sabat de Rivers 1992; Vidal). This essay will appropriate "Grandeza" as a paradigmatic text, as a motherlode for Mexican literature of the viceregal period, and as a touchstone for its readings of literary cityscapes from throughout Spanish America.

Any scrutiny of Bernardo de Balbuena's (1563?–1627) work, I believe, gains from situating the poem in the context of the larger phenomenon that was the city itself. For the poem, originally written as a guide to Mexico City for Balbuena's perhaps erstwhile love interest, Isabel de Tovar, in anticipation of her profession as a nun in Mexico City, was significantly repackaged for publication. Having encountered difficulties in publishing the poem, Balbuena changed its overt addressee from Tovar to the recently arrived archbishop of Mexico, Fray García de Mendoza y Zúñiga, and bundled it into a volume that also included various prefatory materials, a poem of praise to the archbishop and its extensive gloss in prose, and the first treatise on poetry to originate in the New World, the "Compendio apologético en alabanza de la poesía" ["Apologetic Compendium in Praise of Poetry"]. The personal circumstances and interests of Balbuena resonate throughout the three major texts that constitute the volume. Having been remanded from Mexico City, where he had spent many pleasant months, to Guadalajara as chaplain of its Audiencia, the Spanish-born Balbuena appears to have wished to return to Mexico's capital. To further his interests, Balbuena exalts, as we will eventually see, the city, its power-brokers, poetry, and the poet.

The first two texts of "Grandeza," if not all three, ostentatiously and organically emerge from the spectacle of the entry of García de Mendoza into Mexico City that had taken place just eight days before Balbuena composed his elegy to the prelate. Balbuena, clearly availing himself of the *entrada* as an expedient for publication, describes this "bellísimo teatro de hermosura" (33) ("most beautiful theater of beauty"), with the magnificent cloth hangings, arches, commotion, music, trumpets, and finery that incited the "admiración y espectáculo del pueblo" (13–14) ("admiration and spectacle of the people"). In a fawning, tedious, pedantic manner, Balbuena plays into the power dynamics that underwrite the spectacle. His short poem to the archbishop and the inordinately long gloss that unpacks its hidden meanings engage in the most fulsome praise of its addressee (e.g., "si no eres Dios, en su lugar veniste" (15) ["if you are not God, in his place you have come"]). Balbuena at the same time offers up "La grandeza mexicana" as the poetic equivalent of the recent spectacle: "Que yo con la Grandeza Mexicana/coronaré tus sienes/de heroicos bienes y de gloria ufana" (16) ("For I with Mexican

Greatness/will crown your temples/with heroic gifts and with proud glory").

While "Grandeza" extols the Empire in no uncertain terms, it principally magnifies Mexico City in truly spectacular fashion. Its more than 2,000 verses, composed of elaborately wrought tercets, write Mexico City into the classical lines of the panegyric. Like the traditional panegyric, "Grandeza" begins with a panoramic view of the site (*asiento*) of the city; it then broadens out to include in its encyclopedic purview chapters on the origins and greatness of the city, its elegant streets and customs, its elevated culture and occupations, its many recreations, its pastoral beauty, its illustrious government, and its impressive religious and state institutions. Fabulous exhibition and excess characterize the poem's structure. Upon reaching the end of its all-embracing survey, the poem actually restarts in an Epilogue that may have been the original poem but that in any case revisits *all* of the topics celebrated in the body of the poem. "Todo en este discurso está cifrado" (59) ("All in this text is coded"): we encounter a rhythm of contraction and expansion throughout the poem as, in a reflection of its totalizing panegyric ambitions, it repeatedly and self-statedly ciphers the whole (of Mexico, of the poem) into metonymic abbreviations and the city's central features into *recopilaciones* (recapitulations).

The festival parades a city's wealth and eminence. Analogously, Balbuena composes poetry of overt civic pride. His is an especially spectacular manifestation of a New World genre that derived not only from the classics, but also, more directly, from Spanish praise of Seville, portal to the colonies. David Brading writes that "the inflated hyperbole of this rhetoric found immediate echo in the Indies, where it was employed to celebrate both Lima and Mexico City in a vein of civic patriotism . . ." (300). Alfonso Reyes notes the superabundance of civic poetry devised by participants in officially sponsored festivals (97). Already present in the sixteenth century (see with respect to Mexico City, Eugenio de Salazar y Alarcón and Juan de la Cueva, excerpted in Becco), the poetry of civic pride grew in prominence and rhetorical effulgence in the seventeenth century (Rodríguez Fernández 205), motivated by increased urbanization and *criollo* patriotism, and electrified by the Baroque sensibility. Indeed, much as the question of Balbuena as Mannerist or Baroque poet has been debated, there is no mistaking the hallmarks of the extreme Baroque sensibility in Balbuena's turn-of-the-century praise of what he calls *nuestro México* (our Mexico). Balbuena's first direct characterization of the city in the poem, "centro de perfección, del mundo el quicio" (62) ("center of perfection, threshold to the world"), marks the shift from Renaissance encomium to Baroque hyperbole (Rama 1983, 16), which pervades the poem. "La grandeza mexicana" manufactures for the city an elaborate, urbane rhetorical system that features the *sobrepujamiento* (excellence) of Mexico City surpassing that of all other places past and present and includes the use of the superlative, the ennobling simile, synecdoche, anaphora, chaotic enumeration, aporia, and the *brevitatis formula* (the last five techniques suggesting the inexhaustibility and ineffability of Mexico City's merits).

I say specifically that the poem "manufactures" this rhetorical system in order to signal the *avant la lettre* quality of Balbuena's seemingly Baroque stylistics. Though he mentions Góngora in the *Compendio* (141), Balbuena is unlikely to have known anything other than the Spanish poet's early *romances*, if that (Schons 23). How then to explain Balbuena's deviations

from Renaissance equanimity? As other scholars have asserted in somewhat different terms (see Rama 1983; Sabat de Rivers 1992; González Echevarría 1996), I would argue that Balbuena arrived at his *barroquismo* through channels largely independent of cultural importation from the Metropolis. His *barroquismo* appears to me as a natural outgrowth if not necessarily of the spectacle with which the poem explicitly joins forces, then most likely of the spectacular urban environment and the redoubtable power dynamics of the city to which the panegyric pays tribute. Balbuena's Baroque literary city, in this interpretation, would antedate by almost a century the architectural presence of the Baroque in the real city and usher in the Baroque literary style before it was heavily imported precisely because of the force of the Baroque way of life.

Balbuena endows that way of life with nobility and transcendence as he frames a Sublime City characterized by "hermosura" ("beauty"), "nobleza" ("nobility"), "virtud" ("virtue"), "deseo" ("desire"), and "discreción" ("discretion"), all enhanced by art (93). Its towers, sharing the dream of Gothic churches, emblematically fuse with the heavens (72). For Balbuena, it is a post-heroic society no longer shaken by war (80, 118) that spawns such a heavenly climate. The heroic world gives way in "Grandeza" to a demilitarized, otherly, "feminized" city given over to pleasure, art, and culture. Such delights acquire their own nobility through the humanist poetic tradition in which Balbuena locates his poetic city, a tradition that sees the imperial city as a center of virtue, pleasure, civilization, and culture (Sabat de Rivers 1992, 52, 75). And only a suitably sublime and noble poetry, Balbuena tells us in the "Compendio," befits a city of this ilk: "De manera que mi poesía, en estilo heróico y grave trata de la más noble, de la más rica y populosa ciudad desta nueva América . . ." (146) ("And thus it is that my poetry, in grave and heroic style, treats the most noble, richest, and most populated city of this new America . . ."). Like Góngora and Lunarejo, Balbuena advocates for the imperial city an elevated poetic discourse, one of "gravedad, honestidad, altivez y espíritu" (145) ("seriousness, honesty, arrogance, and spirit"). Also like Góngora, his poetry sounds an intensely elitist note: "acierte a salir éste del gusto de los discretos, para quien se guisó" (6) ("this one succeeded in pleasing the taste of the discreet for whom it was prepared"). Elitism goes hand in hand with the erudition that Balbuena prescribes for the poet–"el poeta tiene obligación a ser general y consumado en todo" (131) ("the poet has the obligation of being aware of and master in everything") –and that he is himself at great pains to display in his gloss, with its approximately 159 references to authors or texts (Van Horne 124). The shibboleth of erudition, in turn, takes on another form as Balbuena praises the "gran legalidad" of the "suma de escribientes y escribanos," "plumas y manos/llenas de fe . . ." (103) ("great legality of the sum of writers and notaries, pens and hands/full of faith . . ."). We see that the Sublime City countenances and happily contains the *ciudad letrada* (lettered city), ennobling its bureaucratic elitism and erudition.

Elitism, erudition, nobility, and the *ciudad letrada* all conspire in Balbuena's larger project for the Sublime City and for Mexico City per se: to depict and to promote the coming into Culture of the New World through poetry. Numerous passages in the three components of "Grandeza" establish that Mexico City has achieved the heights of "Parnassus" (35) as a center of education, the arts, and intellectual activity. A poetic contest held there attracted 300 participants. (Balbuena, expectably, took the prize.) The poet urges the prelate to support the cultivation of learning (22), and in the "Compendio" (Abridgement), goes on to make a stunning, if hardly disinterested, case for poetry as the prime mover of civilization: "la ciudad noble ha de acoger y sustentar los poetas como una cosa de grande utilidad y provecho suyo" (127) ("the noble city must welcome and support poets as a resource that is of great usefulness and benefit for it"). Given Balbuena's aspirations for the Sublime City, a Platonic notion of poetry as vehicle of the ideal and divine prevails in the "Compendio." Its sublime properties, significantly, render poetry a key civilizing force, "porque la tierra . . . no quedase inculta y bárbara" (129) ("so that the land . . . not remain uncultured and barbaric"). The Platonic and civilizing attributes of a poetry that signifies for Balbuena a coming into Culture, I should note, find their exact equivalents in the tercets of the "Discurso en loor de la poesía" ("Discourse in praise of poetry") written only four years after "Grandeza" by the anonymous female poet of Peru (reproduced in Becco). While according to both authors poetry will conquer the barbarism of their respective cities, only Balbuena audaciously suggests that poetry has replaced proselytizing or religion in this effort (139).

Through poetry, then, the Sublime City sublimates "primitive" impulses into a culturally higher activity. Similarly and lamentably, the ideal poetic universe of Balbuena's Sublime City sublimates or reinflects those aspects of the New World it considers to be beneath itself. Chapter II of "Grandeza" treats the fraught issues of the indigenous peoples and the overweening presence of greed in Mexico City. Because the elitist Balbuena has already established that he understands poverty to reflect a lack of virtue (28), he explicitly declines to recount the history of the Indians (69). His Sublime City thus appears basically to have been born ex nihilo with the arrival of the Spaniards. Born from nothing, this utopian world would also appear to derive its prosperity from nothing but nature's bounty, in that Balbuena at the same time obliterates almost all traces of the labor forces that produce its wealth. (See Beverley 1987, 74ff.) The greed and self-interest that dominate the New World, on the other hand, do not escape Balbuena's attention. He names and bemoans them; for example: "Por todas partes la cudicia a rodo,/que ya cuanto se trata y se pratica/es interés de un modo o de otro modo" (65) ("Everywhere greed lurks/so that whatever is dealt with or done is done so/out of self-interest one way or the other"). Yet he also tweaks them, twisting them into the motor of the New World, source of its positive contributions. Avid materialism is ultimately and improbably held responsible for the splendor, generosity, heroism, culture, and religious conversions of the New World. In rehabilitating greed and in effacing the native populations, this paean to wealth accords with the pretensions of the nouveaux *hidalgos* discussed earlier. Romero terms the poem a "[s]util breviario de la hidalguía barroca" (90) ("subtle breviary of baroque nobility"). If their city is a fiction, then "Grandeza" enshrines a fiction within a fiction.

Balbuena's early literary city-building leaves yet another important element in its wake, the countryside. Oft-noted is the disparagement of the countryside and the praise of the city found in Chapter IV of "Grandeza." Here we find an early poetic satire of the provincial town, later to be matched, for similarly personal reasons, by Colombian Hernando Domínguez Camargo's (1606–1659) piquant sonnet, "A Guatavita" ("To Guatavita"). Critics generally see in Balbuena's rejection of the countryside an inversion of the

Renaissance topic, introduced by Antonio de Guevara, of "menosprecio de la corte/alabanza de la aldea" ("disdain of the court/praise of the village"). While undoubtedly true, the binary framework of the topic, however construed, obscures what I consider to be one of the most interesting aspects of Balbuena's watershed attempts to build a sublime poetic city: how, in the effort to construct a truly sublime space and its equivalent discourse, Balbuena imports pastoral topics into the city. In other words, now that the consecrated heroic discourse, the epic, no longer applies for post-Conquest Mexico, Balbuena must forge a new noble language for the city. Despite its obvious inconvenience, that language will be another extant sublime, the pastoral. Hence, nature becomes the principal source of metaphor or simile for the city of "Grandeza." Women are the city's flowers, the convent its garden or "paradise" (probably the source of Sigüenza's *Paraíso Occidental*), and, importantly, the city is recrafted into a *locus amoenus*.

The last transformation mentioned involves some particularly ingenious maneouvres. Transporting Fray Luis de León's "vida retirada" ("the quiet life") into the inimical realm of "mundanal ruido" ("the world's noise"), Balbuena converts the city into a "golfo de bienes y de males calma" (85) ("repository of good and relief of ill") by dint of the variety of the city; anyone can enjoy anything there in an "honesta vida, recogido trato" (89) ("honest life and retired relations"). The implausible rebalancing act from Chapter V that we have just seen reaches a silent crisis point in the explicitly pastoral Chapter VI, "Primavera inmortal y sus indicios" ("Immortal spring and its signs"), ironically enough, the most anthologized chapter of "Grandeza." There, as pastoral topics assert themselves in full force to depict an idealized harmonious world of natural abundance and pleasures, a basic question arises in the reader's mind: *where* does all of this take place? The poet's previous disparagement of the countryside would rule it out as the seat of such pleasures. Balbuena gives us ample temporal markers (e.g., it is springtime), but in terms of space, he only makes a vague passing reference to a "real jardín" (99) ("royal garden"). Hence, it would appear that the all too literary pastoral idyll takes place in a *city* park. Balbuena, himself in a liminal discursive space, has, as it were, written himself into a corner and created from pastoral topics a near utopia. Waves "como espejos quebrados alteradas" (Ch. VI, 98) ("like altered broken mirrors")–this line neatly encapsulates Balbuena's break with the Renaissance aesthetic together with his fracturing of Renaissance topics as they are forcibly lodged in the Sublime City.

An easier fit between sweet nature and the divine city, and a more characteristically Baroque transformation, is Balbuena's repeated metamorphosis of the natural into the artificial. Balbuena invokes the master of metamorphoses and later model for the Baroque, Ovid, in his gloss (26), situating the classical poet's Age of Gold, which of course preceded the formation of cities, in viceregal Mexico City. He then proceeds throughout "Grandeza" to transmute natural phenomena into the artifice (see González Echevarría 1996, 210) that epitomizes the high level of civilization attained by the Sublime City. For example, horses, the vestiges of the heroic age and the crowning glory of the animal world, become the equivalent of mannequins who march down the runways of the city's broad avenues parading their owners' wealth in their fine trappings (75). Capitalism also leaves its imprint on the Renaissance New World topic of abundance: "aquel pródigamente darlo todo,/sin reparar en gastos excesivos,/las perlas, oro, plata y seda a rodo" (77) ("that generous giving away of everything/without taking notice of the excessive cost,/pearls, gold, silver, and silk in abundance"). Artisans turn gold into jewelry; *obrajes* weave cotton into fine clothes, "artificio que el humano curso . . . sustenta" (82) ("artifice that the course of human events . . . sustains"). The fertile country-side is domesticated into a garden (92) or park. Nature's bounty, such as the exotic fruits that so captivated the chroniclers of the previous century, now becomes prepared food, the analogue of Lévi-Strauss's cooked meat, standard-bearer of civilization. And, in a wonderfully telling dual metamorphosis worthy of Góngora, fruits become a "*mina* de conservas rica" (92; emphasis added) ("mine rich in preserved foods").

The final transfer from nature to culture that we will examine in "Grandeza" involves Balbuena's quintessentially Baroque *and* New World activation of the aesthetic of amazement. He formulates his *avant la lettre* concept of that aesthetic as part of the of the *ars poetica* of the "Compendio": "lo ordinario y común dicho por modo particular y extraordinario, y lo que más es, las cosas extraordinarias, nuevas y difíciles por modo ordinario y fácil" (131) ("the ordinary and the common-place said in a particular and extraordinary way, and what is more, things that are extraordinary, new and difficult said in an ordinary and easy way"). The poet's rhetorical system, as we have seen, fulfills this precept. His larger presentation of Mexico City also marries the ordinary with the extraordinary by alienating the topic of wonder from its prior location in nature and resituating it in mercantile culture. Balbuena associates "lo raro" (that which is "rare") with wealth ("sus cosas raras, su riqueza y trato" [63] ["his rare things, his wealth and manner"]) and, as the reader will have gathered, transforms his text into a wonder cabinet both miscellaneous and encyclopedic for the sublime American marvels wrought by mercantile endeavors.

In so doing, the Balbuena who refrained from utilizing "exotic" indigenous names for the now civilized fruits (Sabat de Rivers calls this "nihil admirari" [34]) exoticizes Mexico to notable effect. His Mexico is the emporium city described by Leonard (1959, 76), the insatiable consumer of the luxury goods that regularly arrive from the Orient. From its real connection with the Orient, Balbuena's feminized Mexico City gains an exotic splendor and opulence that radiate "orientalism": "Es la ciudad más rica y opulenta,/de más contratación y más tesoro,/que el norte enfría . . ." (see the whole second movement of Ch. II) ("It is the richest and most opulent city/with more trade and more treasure,/that the north knows . . ."). The Sublime City has rejected its Aztec past, surpassed the classical world, and aligned itself with the exotic Orient. Curiously enough, Mexico City's alignment with exotic orientalism and with the Orient itself assigns the New World city a pivotal place in the globe. By virtue of its extraordinary commercial dealings, the Mexico that Balbuena described in the poem's "Introducción" as ex-centric– "estos acabos de mundo, remates de lo descubierto y últimas extremidades deste gran cuerpo de la tierra" (55) ("these ends of the earth, this finishing off of the discovery and most remote areas of this great land")–obtains from "lo raro" ("the rare") an apocalyptic centrality: "En ti se junta España con la China,/Italia con Japón, y finalmente/un mundo entero en trato y disciplina" (see 91) ("It is in you that Spain is joined with China, and Italy with Japan, and finally an entire world

in relations with all and in discipline"). So central in fact is the Mexico situated conveniently near the Equator that Balbuena even implies that it displaces Spain: "Oh pueblo (Mexico) ilustre y rico, en quien se pierde/el deseo de más mundo . . ." (77) ("Oh people (Mexico) illustrious and rich in whom one loses/the desire for more of the world . . .").

In sum, this text, forged under the aegis of the spectacular by a staunch imperialist inserting himself in the power dynamics of the spectacle, has succeeded in creating an apocalyptic, sublime, hyperbolic portrait of his New World city. Balbuena, we have seen, can hardly be taken to be a purveyor of *criollo* consciousness in a political sense. Thus it need not be said that he mimics the discourse of the colonizers but rather that, to do justice to the vibrant urban life of which he wishes again to be part, Balbuena evolves a proto-Baroque poetic discourse that fully complies with the Imperial project, so much so that it obliterates the Indians. Taken unwaveringly to its logical consequences, however, that discourse spins off its axis geographically and rhetorically. It results in an inflated artifact over-swollen with civic pride, and in an indeterminate performativity. Because it subverts without subverting, Balbuena's poem, wittingly or not, acquires a double edge or functionality. It, together with the reams of other poetry that bespoke civic pride and wielded the aesthetic of amazement in service of encomium, could hardly fail to magnify not only the Empire, but its colonial subjects' sense of place and self as well. One cannot help but question the effect of civic spectacles and poems, and especially Balbuena's spectacular poem, upon their consumers; one cannot help but envision the supplementary productivity of the wonder-full representations of the New World's grandeur.

The City of the Margins

In the fall of 1680, Mexico City readied itself for another grand celebration: the entry of the new viceroy, the Count de Paredes. Two up-and-coming *criollo* and *criolla* intellectuals, Carlos de Sigüenza y Góngora (1645–1700) and Sor Juana, had been commissioned to design triumphal arches for the occasion. Sigüenza's stood at the traditional entry point of dignitaries in the Plaza de Santo Domingo, Sor Juana's in the center of the city over a portal of the still-unfinished Cathedral. Sigüenza's wooden arch rose 90 feet. Corinthian pillars supported its three levels and sixteen niched pedestals bearing painted effigies of Aztec kings (Brading 362). Sor Juana's arch, made of wood, cloth, and plaster, had a single façade some 30 yards high composed of eight murals depicting legends associated with Neptune, including one featuring Minerva, goddess of wisdom. Pillars of various architectural styles, adorned with simulated jasper and bronze, supported it. (See Sabat de Rivers 1983, 73 for a diagram of the arch.) The two authors also composed verbal explanations of their allegorical arches, later to be published. Sigüenza's prose work, featuring three lengthy preludes and an explanation of each Aztec king's significance, bore the title of *Teatro de virtudes políticas que constituyen a un príncipe* (1680; Theatre of Political Virtues That Represent a Prince). Sor Juana's *Neptuno alegórico* (1680; Allegorical Neptune) contained two twin texts, one in prose and one in verse (circulated on the occasion and recited, though not by Sor Juana). Both authors' redundant texts evinced an almost insufferable Baroque excess and erudition. Perhaps for this reason, neither text has traditionally been elevated into the canon of its author's works. It is these two spectacle-allied official texts (and works related to them), nonetheless, that will afford us a vision of the reconfigured city that I call the City of the Margins.

Sigüenza and Sor Juana had their own marginalization to overcome as they devised their contributions to the state spectacle. Sigüenza had been expelled from the Jesuits, and his petition to re-enter the Company of Jesus had been rejected. Sor Juana, of illegitimate birth and limited financial means, sought a patron to sponsor and sanction her intellectual pursuits (Paz 1988, 150); the *Neptuno* was one of her earliest published works. Both availed themselves of the occasion as an opportunity to present not just their works but also themselves, as intellectuals, to the Viceroy. The excessive erudition that, from Balbuena's era to their own, had come to signify the height of culture would be their passport to recognition. It would identify them as icons of Culture worthy of the Viceroy's support. Sigüenza writes in the prohemio to *Teatro*, "Glorioso premio de mis estudios, reconozco la ocasión en que me puso mi dicha" ("The glorious reward of my studies, I acknowledge the occasion that gave me happiness"), an occasion that allows him to prostrate himself at the feet of the Viceroy "para ensalzar mi fortuna" (167) ("in order to extol my fortunes"). Sor Juana more subtly allies herself with knowledge and power, saying, "Este, Señor, triunfal arco,/ que artificioso compuso más el estudio de amor/que no el amor del estudio" (IV, 403; all references to Sor Juana follow the numbering and pagination of Méndez Plancarte's four-volume edition of her works) ("This triumphal arch, Sir,/that was the ingenuous creation more of the study of love/than the love of study"). I will return to the equivocations bound up in her self-presentation.

The two colonial intellectuals had far more in common than their aspirations for the 1680 occasion. As María Luisa Bemberg's film on Sor Juana, "Yo, la peor de todas" (1990; I, the Worst of All) dramatizes, they appear to have maintained frequent contact for many years, exchanging ideas and writings. Sor Juana may have obtained from Sigüenza's incipient Cartesianism (so underscored by Leonard) the tendency toward empiricism that surfaces in the *Respuesta a sor Filotea de la Cruz* (1691; *A Woman of Genius: The Intellectual Autobiography of Sor Juana Inés de la Cruz*) and the *Primero sueño* (1686; First Dream). Sigüenza delivered the funeral oration (now lost) for Sor Juana. In any case, the 1680 celebration furnishes tangible proof of their collaboration. The two writers read and critiqued each others' texts. Sor Juana praises Sigüenza's *Teatro* in her Sonnet 204. Sigüenza lauds Sor Juana at length in his *Teatro*. He explains that his patriotic emphasis on Mexican *history* should not be taken as a criticism of the *mythological* nature of her arch and that in fact, Neptune was no "quimérico rey o fabulosa deidad sino sujeto que con realidad subsistió con circunstancias tan primorosas como son el haber sido el progenitor de los indios americanos" (177) ("fantastic king or fabulous god but rather a human subject who in reality existed with circumstances as beautiful as having been the father of American Indians").

Octavio Paz states, "Nada más alejado de las interpretaciones patrióticas e históricas de Sigüenza que el arco ideado por Sor Juana" (1982, 212) ("Nothing could be further from the patriotic and historical interpretations of Sigüenza than the arch devised by Sor Juana" [1988, 155]). On the face of things, Paz's statement holds true. Yet when we overlay the two works, several unexpected commonalities emerge. Both authors share Balbuena's vision of their city as imperial; both use their works to advocate (as did Balbuena [24]) for the

incoming ruler the same characteristics of liberality, pacificism, prudence, and benevolence toward the weak. Far more interesting, I believe, is the following matter. As Sigüenza and Sor Juana presented themselves to the Viceroy, they drew not only on their erudition but also on their own particular bailiwicks as their calling cards. Taking the festival as their personal stage, both dared to flaunt as the centerpieces of their texts and as defining or secondary elements of their arches a different marginalized element: the Aztecs for Sigüenza, the learned woman for Sor Juana. The official entry thus became a forum for a special pleading for each author's defining concern *and* a spectacle of marginality. The Indian whom the colonial regime had relegated to the outer circles of the city and its society and the woman encloistered in either the home or the convent were temporarily brought out of exile and installed, respectively, in the ceremonial and power centers of the city. For a few days, through the ephemeral architecture of the spectacles, they stood at the centers of the theater-city. Yet even after the city had returned to normal and its triumphal arches were torn down, the texts that reproduced them remained. *Teatro* and *Neptuno* thus immemorialize the ephemeral City of the Margins, giving enduring life to the upside-down, carnivalesque world.

David Brading's magnificent 1991 study, *The First America: The Spanish Monarchy, Creole Patriots, and the Liberal State 1492–1867*, exhaustively demonstrates that by the era of independence, New World writers had created an intellectual tradition that rescued pre-contact history from oblivion and served the needs of *criollo* patriotism. The *Comentarios reales* [1609; *The Royal Commentaries of Peru*] of El Inca Garcilaso de la Vega (1540–1616), the *Monarquía indiana* [1615; Indian Monarchy] of Juan de Torquemada, and the works of several Jesuits figure prominently in that tradition. So do, as they should, certain works of the Jesuit-trained Sigüenza y Góngora, whom the "Aprobación" to *Glorias de Querétaro* aptly deems the "dueño de lo pretérito" ("master of the past"). From his earliest years with the Jesuits on, Sigüenza evidenced a fascination with Aztec history and with his own nation. (He wrote a tribute to the Virgin of Guadalupe, *Primavera indiana* [Indian Spring], in his late teens.) The characteristic Jesuit syncretism at work in Sigüenza's seemingly sui generis claim for Neptune as progenitor of the Mexican Indians (see Preludio III of *Teatro* for its exposition; also Paz 1988, Ch. 3 on Jesuit syncretism) allowed Sigüenza to place Mexican Indian history on the global, universal stage where the Jesuits viewed Christianity as having unfolded and to establish such odd linkages. Sigüenza and several other vindicators of pre-contact history, many of whom the erudite Mexican often quotes, would syncretically set biblical, mythological, classical, and historical sources, and the East and the West, on the same continuum, in effect finding in Jesuit universalism authorization for Balbuena's orientalism. The *criollo* patriotism that Sigüenza frequently championed—often, as the prefatory material of *Teatro* suggests, in terms of the need to rescue Aztec history or the need for Mexicans to write a comprehensive history of their own country—thus dovetailed with Jesuit syncretism, and the two together qualify Sigüenza as a key player in the trajectory detailed by Brading.

Neither Brading nor another important scholar of early Mexican nationalism, Jacques Lafaye, gives its due to a seminal text written by Sigüenza in 1680, *Glorias de Querétaro*. This spectacle-allied cityscape fortifies their lines of inquiry, my lines of inquiry, and, quite directly, *Teatro*. It thus merits our attention. *Glorias* chronicles the efforts of the provincial city of Querétaro to establish a temple for the Virgin of Guadalupe, efforts that culminated in a festival celebrating the accomplishment that provides much fodder for the text and the springboard for its publication. In reporting these glories, the text covertly purports to win patronage and charity for the temple. Accordingly, as my earlier mention of the "ecstasy" *Glorias* invokes suggested, the chronicle abounds in locutions of awe. The awe that originally interpellated spectators now summons patrons and monumentalizes whatever allegedly inspired it. Monumental in themselves, the miracles wrought by the Virgin, which *Glorias* minutely describes, carry amazement onto its neighboring plane of the supernatural. These miracles and the heightened presence of awe also indicate the overt agenda of the text: to render homage to the Virgin of Guadalupe as a unique icon of America, "único imán suave de los americanos afectos" (10) ("unique gentle magnet of American affection"). As Lafaye and others have established, Spain sanctioned the Virgin of Guadalupe and then, in the "frenesí guadalupano" (Paz 1982, 63) ("Guadalupe frenzy") of the seventeenth century (1988, 40), she emerged as the first *criolla* emblem. Sigüenza condenses the full dynamics of that movement into his short, fervent text, but he particularly underscores the devotion of the Indians to Guadalupe (generally understood to have been viewed as the reincarnation of indigenous fertility goddess Tonantzín). "[N]uestra indiana Guádalupe" (13) ("Our American Guadalupe") becomes a cult figure for the native peoples and thus a rallying point for the unity of Indians, *criollos,* and Spaniards.

Sigüenza's rendition in Chapter 7 of the dedication of the church to Guadalupe awards special prominence to the contribution of the Indians. The masquerade composed solely of Indians that Sigüenza meticulously recounts proffers a living primer of their history, from which the *criollo* author draws various morals. In the masquerade participate the "wild" Chichimecs of the mountains, an infantry company of 108 Indian boys dressed in Spanish finery (and marching with an admirable discipline that proves that they are not "incapaces de disciplina" [50] ["incapable of discipline"]), followed by a magnificently attired parade of Chichimec and Aztec kings in chronological order, at the end of which, providentially, marches what must have been an Indian representing Carlos V. Sigüenza's commentary on the masquerade validates Indian history and the native aesthetic as appropriate vehicles for the exaltation of Christianity. One need not, he says, look to foreign customs on this noble occasion given that the "rica y galante" "contextura" ("rich and gallant context") of the Indians' "extraordinarios adornos" (51) ("extraordinary adornments") suits its needs. The "gentile" "grandeur" (51) that Sigüenza detects in the Indians recontextualizes Balbuena's "grandeza mexicana," ascribes an equally Baroque aesthetic to the Indians, and recognizes the continuity between the Spanish and Indian penchants for spectacles. Sigüenza goes on to interpret the allegorical floats accompanied by native music and dances that capped the parade. Principal among them was a float bearing the image of Guadalupe. Worshiping Guadalupe, surrounded by angels, knelt an Indian girl in native dress "en que se ideaba no tanto lo común en la América, cuanto con especialidad estas Provincias Septentrionales, que llamó la gentilidad Anáhuac" (52) ("in which not only the commonplace in America was thought of much as the special characteristics of these northern provinces, which he called the grace of Anáhuac [the central

plateau of Mexico]"). The apotheosis of American syncretism in the float, together with the protagonism assigned to the Indians, constitutes a potent reappropriation of the spectacle by the New World and its *criollo* chronicler.

At the same time as Sigüenza installs the Indians in the center of the festive city, he fashions the town of Querétaro into a new center for Mexico. Its historical function as guardian of the outskirts of the Aztec empire recommends the growing town, as do the fertility of the land, delightful climate, great prosperity, many churches, varied population, and other contemporary attributes he describes in Chapter 1. In the course of the text, the floating motif of paradise attaches itself to Querétaro, its convents, and its churches. We can see that Sigüenza, in yet another New World recasting of Guevara's topic, is praising the marginal "aldea" ("village") as containing the best of the city and the countryside. Moreover, Sigüenza mentions various aspects of Querétaro, the third city of the country, that equal those of the first, Mexico City. Sigüenza thus positions Querétaro as a foil to the viceregal Spanish capital. The Querétaro that he has presented throughout *Glorias* as a showcase of Indian culture and devotion, as the frontier zone that it was under the Aztec empire, will, he leads us to imagine, soon take its place as the urban center representing the new Mexico's syncretism.

Sigüenza delivers the glories of Querétaro directly unto Mexico City in his arch and its accompanying text, *Teatro*. To my knowledge, the direct connections between the two spectacles and the two texts, though patent and meaningful, have gone unnoticed. Querétaro's church to Guadalupe opened in May 1680; the Count de Paredes entered Mexico in December 1680. The chronological proximity of the two events translates into the thematic kinship between the two texts. Sigüenza's *Teatro* and his arch adopt as their themes the central portion of the Indian masquerade in Querétaro, that is, the historical parade of Aztec kings whose magnificent dress so impressed Sigüenza. The arch, with its niches of effigies, recreates that parade for the eye. The text also recreates it point by point and adds, for the mind, an allegorical reading of the meaning of each Aztec king.

Several important implications issue from the intimate relationship between *Glorias* and *Teatro*. First, *Teatro* is a doubly spectacle-allied text that layers one festival on top of another, instrumentalizing both of them. Hence, the correctness of its title, heralding the *mise en abîme* of theatricality that the text houses, and the fact that its allegorical effigies all but reproduce festival actors. Hence, too, and paradoxically, the reality of Sigüenza's daring text, based as it is on an actual performance by the Indians themselves. The Indians play different but always principal and thus subversive roles in both texts, performing and dominating the parade of Aztec history in *Glorias*, as the sole subject of *Teatro*. The tension between specularity and speculation to which I referred above gains concrete form here as the all-embracing nature of spectacles gives rise to New World enactments or literary re-enactments of them dominated by Indians, to an extraordinary imagined community. Second, *Teatro*, despite the absence of Guadalupe from its panorama, bears the *criollo* and Guadalupan message of *Gloria* in its aura. Its aura joins with the exhortations in *Teatro* to Mexicans about their own history, mentioned above, to reinforce the *criollo* patriotism of the second text. Especially in *Teatro,* Sigüenza uses *indigenous* symbols as an expression of *criollo* patriotism. (See García Pabón on the spectacles of Potosí [1995, 426].)

The indigenous symbols of Sigüenza's *Teatro*, in fact, serve multiple purposes, most of them dangerous and counterintuitive. By far the boldest aspect of the text is its holding up of the Aztec leaders as exemplars of the virtues the new Viceroy should himself incarnate. One by one, from Huitzilopochtli to Cuauhtémoc, *Teatro* rehabilitates the eleven Aztecs who precede the crowning figure (twelve being the magical number of Pythagoras [187]), the Viceroy whom the text weaves into the royal Aztec lineage and whom it intends as the culmination of Aztec and Spanish-American history. Each verbal portrait of an Aztec leader follows the same pattern, including historical information on his deeds, an explanation of the virtues of the king arising from them, and a gloss of the symbols in the arch's painting. From within the set pattern, Sigüenza reforms Aztec leaders into models of non-violent, clement, generous leadership. The portrait of the first Mexican king, Acamapich, allows Sigüenza provocatively to sing the praises of freedom and to baptize the Mexicans as a "Gentum expectantem" (201), as do those of other virtuous Aztecs. Sigüenza's task becomes even more formidable and treacherous when he turns his sights to the figures that have been most problematic for the Spaniards. Nevertheless, fully in keeping with Jesuit syncretism and supported by quotes from the Old Testament, Sigüenza manoeuvres Huitzilopochtli, Aztec god of war, into an avatar of the Christian messiah for having led his people to their motherland, Mexico. Moctezuma (the Second) comes to symbolize absolute monarchy, magnificence, generosity, and affability—the quintessence of the greatness of Mexico that derives from its Aztec past. And even Cuauhtémoc, who resisted the Spanish to the last, is regenerated into an "alma constante" (228) ("steadfast soul"), tenacious in the face of adversity, and into a martyr.

The stark contrasts between *Teatro* and "Grandeza" throw Sigüenza's program into relief. Clearly, where Balbuena obliterated the Indian past, Sigüenza brings it to the fore. Balbuena buttressed his Sublime City with a Platonic notion of poetry; Sigüenza bolsters his theatre of Aztec history by invoking Plato's phrase that true praise is praise of *origins* (231). Sigüenza's particular slant on history detraumatizes the origins of Mexico City; that of Balbuena arose ex nihilo with the arrival of the glorious Spanish empire. With Sigüenza, we have moved from Balbuena's civic pride to *criollo* patriotism and pride in history, as well as to the past as a source of Mexico's "grandeza." Sigüenza adheres to Balbuena's grand characterization of Mexico City as equivalent to Imperial Rome, but elevates pre-contact Tenochtitlán into an Imperial city. Eliding the Conquest, Sigüenza instates continuity between Imperial Tenochtitlán and Imperial Mexico City (Paz 1988, 152–53).

At this point, one might be asking how it was that Sigüenza's audacious City of the Margins, deviating so notably from Balbuena's Sublime City, avoided being razed by official Mexico. My discussion has already suggested some answers to the question. The tide of *criollo* patriotism, the trend of resuscitating indigenous history, Jesuit syncretism, the providentialism invariably built into the Indian-dominated spectacles (actual and verbal), and the exaltation of Empire all to a degree authorized Sigüenza's two texts. Yet two further matters salvage his City of the Margins. The first is perhaps expectable: the exotic parade of magnificent Indians in the arch and in *Teatro*, Sigüenza says, appeals to the spectacular aesthetic of festival. He intends that spectators "quedan atónitos con tal espectáculo" (187) ("are amazed with such spectacle"). The second is rather surprising but necessary to round out our picture of Sigüenza and his times: as Lafaye notes, "Sigüenza's Indian is a dead Indian" (65), not the Indian of the present. The redemption of the Indian past undertaken by Sigüenza and his fellow *criollos*, Lafaye also notes, may paradoxically indicate the death of the Indian empire, the fact that it has lost its subversive force (65–66). Moreover, in various of his texts, Sigüenza excoriates the present degraded state of the Indians, for example, "no hay instante del día ni de la noche en que no sólo se cometa lo que tengo dicho [embriaguez], sino infinitos robos, muertes, sacrilegios, sodomías, incestos y otras abominaciones mucho mayores" (1995, 48) ("there is no moment of day or night in which what I have said [drunkenness] takes place, but also an infinity of robberies, killings, sacrilege, sodomy, incest, and other worse abominations"). Despite Sigüenza's mixed view, we should note in conclusion, it was the "dead Indian" who lived on. Like Sigüenza's selective vindication of the Indians, history itself can be felicitously discriminating. A century later, a different group of criollo patriots would claim Sigüenza's historical works in support of Mexican Independence.

Unlike Sigüenza, when Sor Juana Inés de la Cruz set out to present herself to the Viceroy in 1680, she found little sustenance for her cause in either the present or the past of Mexico. No Mexican mores, indigenous or viceregal, explicitly countenanced the learned woman. She knew herself to be, at least in terms of Mexico, sui generis. At this early stage in her career and throughout her later life, she undertook to forge an authorizing tradition for herself and for women in general. Two qualities intrinsic to Baroque culture and epitomized by Sor Juana—vast learning and boundless ingenuity—afforded a rich playing field for such efforts. In the *Respuesta* (1691), for example, Sor Juana would not only appeal to the techniques and topics of the *querelle des femmes* initiated by Christine de Pisan in the fourteenth century but also cleverly piece together—often from decontextualized strands of Spanish, Mexican, classical, biblical, and patristic sources—a legitimating framework for female intellectual endeavors.

In the *Neptuno alegórico*, Sor Juana grounds her case, as she frequently does, in that wellspring of strong male *and* female heroes, mythological tradition. The shared qualities of Neptune and the Viceroy constitute the overall ostensible motivation of her three contributions to the festival. Yet in the prose text, Sor Juana shifts the focus quickly and with unmistakable alacrity onto Isis, who occupies almost half of the "Razón de la fábrica alegórica y aplicación de la fábula" ("Reason of allegoric configuration and the use of fable"). Strategically, the nun-writer first presents Isis in her pertinent, inoffensive role as mother of Neptune, as *Magna Mater* of all the gods. The maternal Isis, however, quickly gives way to Isis as queen of learning. Sor Juana, in an argument akin to Pisan's on Minerva and Isis in *The City of Women* (Pt. 1, Chs. 37–38), then spirals out into Isis as inventor of "letras" (letters), discoverer of food staples, and embodiment of all wisdom. Through a logic too elaborate to recount here, Sor Juana also recasts all the goddesses of classical mythology as incarnations of Isis. And through an etymological analysis of Isis's name, which allegedly means "dos veces hombre" (366) ("two times man"), she recasts Isis as embracing both sexes. With this last touch, Sor Juana has dealt Isis an anomalous centrality not only in mythic history and in the *Neptuno* but also in a patriarchal world.

If the foregrounding of Isis in the "Razón de la fábrica alegórica" threatens to eclipse Neptune, and thus the Viceroy, in the "Argumento del séptimo lienzo" Minerva actually defeats Neptune. Sor Juana describes the contest to name Athens, in which Minerva's contribution triumphs over Neptune's. Minerva's victory over the Viceroy/Neptune suits Sor Juana's feminism but leaves the author in a situation as slippery as Sigüenza's vindication of Cuauhtémoc. The nun-writer cuts this Gordian knot by treating Neptune's defeat as another kind of victory. To accept defeat as he did, Sor Juana tells us, is a triumph of reason, "que es la verdadera libertad" ("which is true liberty") over inferior "ímpetus desordenados" (391) ("disordered impetus"). Sor Juana adds that since Minerva/Isis and Neptune are just two sides of the same coin, victory can hardly be ascribed to either separately (391).

The privileging of reason and the doubling of Neptune with Minerva prove central to the example that the nun holds up for the Viceroy to emulate. Concretely, she would have him embody the characteristics I mentioned earlier (and complete the Cathedral and the drainage of Mexico City). At the same time, the cultural agenda that Sor Juana consistently promotes bestows on the new ruler the qualities of Isis and urges him to support learning, the arts, and intellectuals. Sor Juana's repeated pleas that the Viceroy sponsor intellectual undertakings, Paz points out, oddly transform the stormy god of the seas into a "deidad civilizadora" (1982, 219) ("civilizing deity" [1988, 161]). Her ideal ruler, we see, must continue to carry forth the coming into culture of Mexico that Balbuena proposed for García de Mendoza. Yet, from the margins and more than a half century after "Grandeza," Sor Juana interjects a jarring comment on the not-so-sublime structures of patronage that sustain colonial intellectuals, saying that "nunca el beneficiado puede tener el mérito de obrar libre" (386) ("never can the recipient have the condition of acting independently").

What affects the colonial intellectual, of course, directly affects the text's author. Sor Juana sets up the connection by writing herself into the *Neptuno*. As can be ascertained from the lines "mas el estudio de amor/que no el amor del estudio" ("more the study of love/than the love of study"), her self-presentation heeds the verbal protocols allotted to women, that is, an attitude and topics of humility characterize Sor Juana's few first-person interventions in the text. The *conceptismo* of those lines, however, goes far in exposing her stance as a mere posture. Throughout the text, Sor Juana will domesticate her "I" but flaunt her worldly erudition and wit. The very first paragraph of the "Razón de la fábrica alegórica" unveils the strategy that in fact underlies many of Sor Juana's works. As would seem fitting, Sor Juana attempts to explain why she, a woman, was contributing to the important festival. Tapping into the topic of *vos me coegistis*, Sor Juana claims that she could not disobey the town council, which, she reasons, appears to have preferred the "blandura inculta de una mujer" ("uncultivated meekness of a woman") over "la elocuencia de tantas y tan doctas plumas" ("the eloquence of so many learned pens") (358). She concludes the paragraph with the example, orchestrated by quotes in Latin, of a woman "no conocida, ignorante y pobre" ("not known, ignorant, and poor") chosen to plead the case of Absalom to King David (358). Sor Juana's brilliant opening act has placed her person immediately in view, as the uncultured woman she manifestly was not and as the modest woman she of necessity purported to be.

The unabashed erudition of the *Neptuno* inevitably links its author to its central female figure, Isis, thereby appointing Sor Juana a prominent place in the text/festival. Scattered details of the text, transplanted from Sor Juana's own life into the text's goddesses, cement the association. It is in this regard that Isis's alleged nature as "dos veces hombre" ("two times man") takes on considerable importance. Isis, while a laudable "manly woman," is also something of a hybrid monster, a freak—as was Sor Juana in her context. By the early 1680s, Sor Juana had already acquired great renown as the "Phoenix" or "Tenth Muse of Mexico." In her first play, *Los empeños de una casa* (The Undertakings of a House), performed in 1683 during the celebrations of the arrival of another dignitary (the archbishop of Mexico, Francisco Aguiar y Seijas), Sor Juana's textual mask, Leonor, bemoans *and* announces that "fui celebrada por milagro" (4: 37) ("miraculously I was given recognition"). Sor Juana was a spectacle unto herself, a "monstrous" combination of nun, writer, and the first New World intellectual to obtain international fame. Mexico for a time condoned her anomaly and allowed Sor Juana (while physically absent) to be omnipresent in the city's spectacles as its unofficial poet laureate, its passport to Metropolitan culture. Spain would take her up as the appropriately freakish icon of the sideshow that was New World culture.

Sor Juana was a spectacle and therefore allowed to *be*. The nun, ever aware of the dangers from which fame insulated her, did not fail to cultivate it. She did so in part precisely by trading on her anomaly through the creation of self-inscriptions such as Isis that broadcast rather than concealed her eccentricity. Sor Juana, in the *Neptuno* and beyond, juggled the two scripts open to writing women of her time, humility and exceptionality or oddity. As I have discussed in detail elsewhere (Merrim 1991; 1999, Ch. 1), the nun-writer recognized in the extreme Baroque sensibility, in its taste for "monsters," one culturally available resource for self-promotion. She, like the Peruvian defender of Góngora, the mestizo "Lunarejo," would parlay her own eccentricity into a trademark. "Lunarejo" made of his physical deformity, his birthmark, the mark of his personal and national identity. (See González Echevarría 1993, Ch. 7.) Sor Juana transformed her personal circumstances as an asexual nun, a famed woman writer, a prodigy, a *rara avis*, into an iconography of anomaly. Isis takes her place in this line alongside many more explicit and daring feats of self-exoticizing. Sor Juana playfully deploys her iconography of anomaly in such poems as Romances 19, 48, and 49, and frames it in a manner designed to elicit pathos in *Empeños* and the *Respuesta*, among other texts. The truly stirring lines of Sor Juana's last poem, "Romance 51," trenchantly articulate the potency that Sor Juana, and other subalterns, discerned in the aesthetic of amazement to which the City of the Margins owes a special debt: "Si no es que el sexo ha podido/o ha querido hacer, por raro,/que el lugar de lo perfecto/obtenga lo extraordinario" ("For it is not that gender has been able/or has strived to make perfection as rare/to be taken as the extraordinary").

The City of the Mind

At the end of Sigüenza's most familiar text, the early testimonial narrative entitled *Los infortunios de Alonso Ramírez* (1690; The Misfortunes of Alonso Ramírez), the protagonist, Alonso Ramírez, finally receives recompense for his travails in an enlightened Mexico City. Its Viceroy (now the Count de Galve), versed in geography and hydrography, readily grants

Ramírez the rights to his beached frigate. In our last glimpse of Ramírez, he is departing for Veracruz to rescue the ship, having told his tale to Sigüenza (cosmographer, professor of mathematics, chaplain of the charity hospital of Mexico City) and accompanied by Juan Enríquez Barroto, "mancebo excelentemente consumado en la hidrografía, docto en las ciencias matemáticas" (71) ("a young man extraordinarily knowledgeable in hydrography, and learned in mathematical science").

This final snapshot from Mexico City caps off a text that harbors a subtle polemic between knowledge and faith, Mexico and Puerto Rico. The uneducated Puerto Rican, Ramírez, has had his oral tale recorded in writing by the erudite Mexican, Sigüenza. In the text that results from their collaboration, *Infortunios,* Sigüenza demonstrates his encyclopedic knowledge of literary forms by successively filtering Ramírez's story through the picaresque novel, the Byzantine novel, the shipwreck tale, and the chronicles of the sixteenth century. (See Santiago-Díaz.) He imposes his scientific expertise in geography and navigation on his interlocutor's tale by technically charting the course (73–74) that Ramírez blindly followed as a captive of British pirates and later as the dazed pilot of his own frigate. (See Gimbernat de González and Sacido Romero, on the two voices in *Infortunios.*) On the other hand, according to *Infortunios* what saves Ramírez is his faith. God and the Virgin of Guadalupe repeatedly rescue him from the most dire situations: "Creo hubiera sido imposible mi libertad, si continuamente no hubiera ocupado la memoria y afectos en María Santísima de Guadalupe de México, de quien siempre protesto viviré esclavo por lo que le debo" (48) ("I believe that my freedom would have been impossible if I had not continuously filled my thoughts with the memory and love of most Holy María of Guadalupe of Mexico, to whom I confess I shall always live beholden for what I owe her"). The sentimental, superstitious, medieval Ramírez ends up as the spiritual leader of his company, as a martyr to faith.

Ramírez has suffered tremendously, maybe inordinately– "A las lágrimas de regocijo por la libertad conseguida se siguieron las que bien pudieran ser de sangre, por los trabajos pasados" (48) ("The tears of joy for the liberty gained where followed by tears that could have been of blood because of the suffering I had endured"). Why? The text insinuates, with Sigüenza perhaps putting his own words into Ramírez's mouth, that a good deal of Ramírez's suffering arises from his ignorance: "No se espante quien esto leyere de la ignorancia en que estábamos de aquellas islas, porque, habiendo salido de mi patria de tan poca edad nunca supe–ni cuidé de ello después–qué islas son circunvecinas y cuáles sus nombres" (54; also see 53) ("Let no one who reads this be shocked by the ignorance in which we lived on those islands, because I left my country at such a young age that I never knew–nor did I ever take care later to learn–what islands are near and what their names are"). Ramírez has only a primitive understanding of navigation and no useful map; he doesn't understand the pirates' route; he constantly loses his way. His faith suffices to rescue him but not to avert his suffering.

Sigüenza's *Infortunios* has "framed" Ramírez by setting forth his story and by setting him up as the protagonist of a moral tale of the limitations of a faith not allied with knowledge. The collaboration of Sigüenza and Ramírez remedies the Puerto Rican's shortcomings after the fact. *Infortunio's* Mexico City, initially praised by Ramírez–"Lástima es grande el que no corran por el mundo grabadas a punto de diamente en láminas de oro las grandezas magníficas de tan soberbia ciudad" (33) ("It is a great shame that diamond-point metal engravings do not circulate in the world depicting the magnificent greatness of such a proud city")–confirms for the future the benefits of knowledge as well as its own superiority over a Puerto Rico that has been bled dry by the conquerors (31) and left only with the faith that sustains Ramírez. The symbolic configuration with which *Infortunios* closes, of the man of faith marching off with the man of science, intimates that a dialectic between the two ensures "las grandezas magníficas" ("the magnificent greatness") of the viceregal capital.

Infortunio's enlightened Mexico City and Sigüenza's ostentatious, polymorphous erudition both stand at the end of a century that witnessed the full installation of the Baroque in Mexico City's architecture and culture, heralded by Balbuena in 1604. Both aspects of *Infortunios* stand as heirs, and as the apogee, of Balbuena's project for a sublime, intellectual Mexico City. Into this constellation I would now like to insert Sor Juana's *summa,* the "Primero sueño" (1692), as an abstract world, a pure City of the Mind. I hasten to state that rather than treating the mental landscape of the "Sueño" as an actual cityscape (Sor Juana, cloistered in her convent, wrote *for* Mexico City but rarely *of* the city per se), I will be positioning the "Sueño" within the *coordinates* of the spectacular cityscapes examined thus far, as a logical consequence of them. To place the infinitely rich "Sueño," the best-studied of all our texts, within those coordinates is barely to touch on many major aspects of the text (in particular, on most of the feminist aspects on which I and others have already commented extensively; see, for example, my 1991 edited collection and Merrim 1999, Ch. 5) but to unlock a few others. From this vantage point, it will be seen that the "Sueño" represents a climax, like *Infortunios, and* a terminus of the Sublime City set in motion by Balbuena.

Sor Juana divulges in the *Sueño* (according to the nun, the only work she wrote for her own pleasure) the deepest, most prized treasures of her complex mind. She exercises her own polymorphic erudition on the poem's various scenarios, which move from the coming of nightfall to the dream, from the body to the mind, and then range over the epistemological landscape of the early modern Hispanic world, back to the body, and into the coming of day. With a syncretism akin to Sigüenza's but more closely related to the Neoplatonic hermeticism that also fed the Jesuits' universalism, Sor Juana weaves together in each of these varied scenarios the diverse languages and bodies of early modern knowledge: science (astronomy, astrology, optics, empiricism, mechanism), religion, mythology, history, politics, jurisprudence, philosophy, poetics, and metaphysics. As the famous summary of the *Sueño* by Diego Calleja (1638–1725?), in his "Aprobación" to Sor Juana's *Fama y obras póstumas* (1700; Fame and Posthumous Works), presents it, "soñé que de una vez quería comprender todas las cosas de que el universo se compone" (Paz 1982, 471) ("I dreamed that I wanted to understand totally and instantly all the things of which the universe is composed" [1988, 359]). Sor Juana's encyclopedic *silva* recalls the origins of the metrical form as a miscellanea, a *selva.* The nun shapes her miscellanea into a curio cabinet, stocked with wonders: the Egyptian pyramids, the lighthouse of Alexandria (one of the seven wonders of the ancient world), the magic lantern, and so on. Balbuena's poem had erected a mercantile wonder cabinet. Sor Juana's wonder cabinet, for once having nothing to do with wealth, is a repository of the awe-inspiring human achievements that she has encountered over the course of her intellectual journeys.

In the central portion of the poem, the Soul (intermittently and ultimately identified with the "yo"; I will therefore view the Soul as feminine) takes an awed journey through a purely ideational dreamscape. By turns astonished, exhilarated, or aghast at what she sees, the Soul witnesses what is manifestly a *spectacle* of metaphysical entities. First the Platonic method and then the Aristotelian (neo-scholastic) parade before her, their abstract principles attaining a breathtaking corpo*reality* in concrete symbols such as the pyramid, the ladder, and the rose. The Soul, questing for knowledge, attempts to encompass the Platonic pyramid in her mental glance, to climb the Aristotelian ladder, and thus to enter the spectacle. Sor Juana stages the spectacle in a poetic cosmos that features not only an idiosyncratic iconography but also the alternative textual practices that befit a dreamworld. Perhaps modeling her dream realm on Neptune's watery "ciudad" (4: 377) in the *Neptuno alegórico*, she crafts another otherly realm in which predominate female figures (even figurations of the Divinity as feminine) and fluidity. The rigid phallogocentric lines of the twilight and morning that lie outside the nightworld of the dream give way in its confines to a textual universe in which metaphor prevails over metonymy, ambiguity and contradictions over clarity, digressions over linearity, chiaroscuro over color. (See Merrim 1999, Ch. 5 for textual examples, too imbricated to present here.) The reader is left astonished, sometimes lost, in this decentered space, as is the Soul in her confrontation with the cosmos's floating bodies of knowledge.

The foregoing discussion allows us to set the "Sueño" over/against the texts that have preceded it. Balbuena and Sor Juana's encyclopedic poems cipher whole worlds, be they the world of Mexico City or the world of knowledge, into their reaches, evolving new textual practices as a function of their designs. The aesthetic of amazement, the spectacle, and overweening pedantry clearly inform Balbuena's, Sigüenza's, and Sor Juana's texts. Yet it is the distance of the eminently Baroque "Sueño" from its predecessors rather than its similarities to them that most concerns us in terms of the City of the Mind. Where "Grandeza" and *Infortunios* depict real cities infused with much-desired ideas, the supremely erudite "Sueño" depicts a world wrought of nothing but ideas. It is thus at once a reification, a projection, an abstraction, and, as I have said, a climax of the cultured Sublime City. Lacking the concrete referentiality of its predecessors' efforts, the colorful vivacity of "Grandeza," or even that poem's pastoral sublimity, the universe of the "Sueño" towers over the referential world in the same way that St. Augustine's invisible kingdom of God hovers over the visible kingdom of earth. The Sublime City presented by Balbuena has engendered the ideational mindscape of Sor Juana's "Sueño."

In the final analysis, however, from her lofty place at the end of the century, the daughter devours the father. The chiaroscuro abstractions of the "Sueño" gesture away from the Baroque and toward the pure Cartesian thought that Sigüenza sporadically embraced. Whether or not Sor Juana shared her companion's inclinations, it can be argued that the "Sueño" effects a critique of the two main, and by metonymic inference *all*, the epistemologies that prevailed in her times. In the central portion of the poem, as suggested above, the Soul fails to achieve total knowledge through either Platonic or Aristotelian means. Do the Soul's failures arise from her own inadequacies or from those of the methods themselves? Sor Juana, for obvious reasons, waffles on the matter. Among many ways, she equates the Soul with Phaeton to accentuate her hubris. Conversely, Sor Juana intimates that the world itself is too complex to be subsumed into Plato's ideal forms and that the "mentales fantasías" (1: 595) ("mental fantasies") of Aristotelianism belie the diversity of the world when empirically apprehended. The Soul witnessing the spectacle of knowledge from outside the world and Sor Juana, with a *fin de siècle* perspective that ventriloquizes the Baroque's own characteristic attitude of *desengaño* ("disabusal"), both realize that the present state of philosophical knowledge is just not sufficient. All told, Sor Juana's first dream is a last dream, the final burst of radiance of the Sublime City before its philosophical bases actually give way to new modes of thought.

Panic City

Not just at the end, but throughout the seventeenth century, the tensions and anxieties of a world in turmoil channeled themselves into forms inimical to the pure City of the Mind or to the exalted Sublime City yet still intrinsic to the Baroque aesthetic of amazement. I refer to the voracious taste for bizarre, salacious, outlandish phenomena that permeated the historiography, proto-journalism, and satires of the century. Maravall tells us that the "interplay of harsh constriction and permitted expansions" of the Baroque Age led to a "free enthusiasm for outlandishness" that "developed monstrously among peoples who found their ways blocked to a rational criticism of social life" (228–29). "The outlandishness, the frenzy that went from inconceivable crime to the most nonsensical tales of miracles, was common to all of Europe in the seventeenth century" (229), causing the bizarre to override truth or verisimilitude as a didactic tool. Two private seventeenth-century diaries later published, Jerónimo de Barrionuevo's (1587–1671?) *Avisos* (1654–1658; Notices) from Spain and its more temperate New World counterpart, Antonio de Robles's *Diario de sucesos notables* (1665–1700; Diary of Significant Events) from Mexico, convey a picture of what aspects of current life sensibility construed as worthy of note. Reports of miracles, witchcraft, supernatural apparitions, bizarre matters of "human interest," human "monstrosities" (birth defects), crimes large and small, scandals public and private, sexual wrongdoings, and public punishments unproblematically coexist with copious accounts of public ceremonies and state affairs in both texts.

The *Avisos* and the *Diario*, as just summarized, bring into play both poles of amazement—negative or sensationalistic and positive awe. The texts examined in the previous three sections of the present essay basically manoeuvre within the positive pole; the texts that occupy the rest of our discussion (none of which was published in its author's lifetime) acerbically exploit the negative pole. Be they the local histories to which we now turn or the satires that end our excursion, like the "máscaras a lo faceto" ("witty masks") built into spectacles, they engage with the disillusioned outer edges of amazement to advance their ever more biting critiques of cities in crisis, of colonial misrule. These sensation-driven colonial texts deploy Baroque *desengaño* (disabusal) in extreme games predicated on the scandal-sheet criterion that is operative—albeit far more moderately and lacking the ideological spleen of works like *El Carnero* or Rosas de Oquendo's (b. 1559?) satire—in Robles and Barrionuevo. In sum, aided by the darker side of "lo raro," seventeenth-century historiographies and satires "spectacularize" the ills of New World societies, exoticizing their societies through scandal.

As the foregoing suggests, Baroque colonial historiography took as keen an interest in the present of its societies as it did in their past. Colonial cities had burgeoned into effervescent, complex metropolises. Historiography met them with texts that, unlike the multi-regional compendiums of the sixteenth century, would center on the evolution and daily life of the local urban environment. One such text, that of Fray Bernabé Cobo (cited earlier), depicts the bustling Baroque city of Lima as overflowing the "orden y concierto" (306) ("order and concert") of its original *traza* ("design"). Similarly, the urban historiographies of the century would annex onto the scaffolding of official storytelling the "menudencias" ("trifles") that Cobo so prizes (280), resulting in texturized, unidealized accounts of New World cities. Certainly the most famous of these is *El Carnero* (1638, first published in 1859), written by Colombian *criollo* Juan Rodríguez Freyle at the venerable age of seventy. Freyle inaugurates the *criollo* literary history of Colombia with an ambitious, Baroque chronicle of the first one hundred years of the capital city of Nueva Granada, Santafé de Bogotá. The disillusioned son of a conqueror, Freyle lays bare the inner workings of a Panic City constantly rocked by crises in a text that, like the city, sharply deviates from order and harmony as it bodies forth the "thick" history of colonial society.

Instead of registering the physical dimensions of Bogotá, Freyle x-rays the city. His infra-history takes us behind the walls of colonial life, into what happens *inside* the great *cabildos* (municipal council), cathedrals, or homes of the city's Spanish residents whose exteriors Balbuena celebrated in Mexico. Freyle penetrates those façades and reveals a human landscape seething with passion, greed, and vices. People, the *petites histoires* of Bogotá's inhabitants, dominate his literary city. Their base motivations have materialized El Dorado into a decadent metropolis, lacking higher culture and ruled by gold and sex and power-mongering. The prose in which Freyle renders his city is relatively limpid for a seventeenth-century text; what makes the Bogotá of *El Carnero* a Baroque city is the excess, dynamism, and unchained ferment of its inhabitants' lives.

Only two physical "monuments" gain dimensionality in *El Carnero*, more as icons of the text's overriding concerns than as occupants of extra-textual space. The first operates by enigmatic implication—it is the *carnero* mentioned only in the title and left hanging there without further explanation. Although what the title actually means has given rise to much speculation (Darío Achury Valenzuela lists some seventeen possible meanings for *carnero* in his prologue to the Ayacucho edition), most critics concur that it refers to the common graves of a city's hospitals and churches and/or to the trashbin into which old, useless papers are thrown instead of being incinerated. These meanings accord with the text's mission of rescuing from the grave or trashbin the general history of Colombia, "porque nadie lo ha hecho" (3) ("because nobody has done it"), and in particular with the history of all the transgressions that have been buried, all the laws moral and civic that have fallen by the wayside. The crimes of all those involved in the Juana García case, except of the woman herself, for example, remained unpunished, for "la tierra era nueva, y que era mancharla con lo proveído" (214) ("the land was new and it would be stained with the ruling"), while official texts related to her case ended up in the "archivo del fuego" (221) ("the fire's archive"). González Echevarría calls Freyle "the theoretician of the Archive" (1990, 99), a denomination well borne out by a central passage in which Freyle defines his task as an historian: "La razón me dice que no me meta en vidas ajenas; la verdad me dice que diga la verdad. Ambas dicen muy bien,

pero valga la verdad; y pues los casos pasaron en audiencia y en cadalsos públicos, la misma razón me da licencia que lo diga, que peor es que lo hayan hecho ellos que lo escriba yo" (236) ("Reason tells me not to meddle in the lives of others; truth tells me to say the truth. Both are correct, but truth is more important, and since the cases occurred in court and in public prisons, reason itself gives me the licence to speak about it, for it is for worse that they have done it than that I write it down"). This "true" history counterweighs the heroic histories of Colombia (of Juan de Castellanos and Pedro Simón) that Freyle often cites. As the calculated chronological inversion of the text's subtitle, *El Carnero: Conquista y descubrimiento del Nuevo Reino de Granada . . .* (The Ram: Conquest and Discovery of the Kingdom of New Granada . . .), indicates, it purports to uncover what previous narratives have suppressed (Chang-Rodríguez, 49; emphasis added).

As *El Carnero* invades "others' lives" and exhibits their crimes, it assumes the function of the text's second physical icon, the "cadalso" ("gallows") that Freyle mentioned in the passage cited above. The text becomes a panopticon that performs the surveillance and, like the gallows or pillory, the verbal punishment through exposé and moralizing of one hundred years of crimes and scandals in Bogotá. Wielded by Freyle in the shadow of the gallows, the Baroque asthetic of amazement undergoes notable transformations. The "maravilla" ("marvel") that, as the author tells us, he equates with virtue, practically disappears, while the "novedades" ("news") that he identifies with sin prevail (393). And as the text unrelentingly parades and punishes these "novedades," it occupies the space of the public square that houses the gallows. Freyle indirectly equates *El Carnero* with the plaza as he rails against criminal Juan de Mayorga: "sacaste a pública plaza las faltas y flaquezas de los tuyos, que tiempo y olvido tenían acabadas" (390) ("you took the faults and weaknesses of your people that time and oblivion had done with and exposed them in the public square"). In *El Carnero*, crimes repeatedly take place, are broadcast or rumored by common folk, and are punished by the State in the plaza. Freyle recounts only one celebratory official spectacle and, as the reader will recall, he does so censoriously. In the place of the celebratory festival, Freyle offers the macabre spectacle of punishment. He changes the sign of both the spectacle and the plaza and offers his text as the theatre or "tablado" (371) ("stage") in which the spectacle will be enacted for the edification of his reader and the enhancement of history.

Into *El Carnero*'s punitive spectacle enter every possible sort of crime and all the players of the colony, be they Indians, common folk, men or women, or even church or state officials. Like Bartolomé de Las Casas (1474–1566), Freyle openly vents his ire against the Spaniards for raping Colombia's resources and against "[e]sta golosina del mandar" (371) ("this sweet morsel of rule"). He castigates them for not providing a model of Christianity for the Indians whom he, as distinct from Las Casas, sees as the handiwork of the Devil. On the other hand, Freyle details at length and extols the efforts of the colonial regime to impose order, justice, and reason on the wayward colonies: "La justicia es raíz de la vida, porque de la manera que es un cuerpo sin entendimiento y razón, es una ciudad sin ley ni gobierno" (Freyle quoting San Inocencio, 315) ("Justice is the basis of life itself, for in the same way that a body without understanding and reason lives, so does a city without law or government"). Yet try as they might to implant these values, the efforts of the few honest

Spanish leaders and the few admirable Spanish laws (such as reforms of the *encomienda*) miscarry. They fail, like rejected skin grafts, invariably overcome by the chaos endemic in colonial Bogotá. "Alboroto" ("Turmoil") is the word that echoes most insistently and resoundingly throughout the text. The city constantly erupts into a pandemonium whose tide the fragile official scaffolding of order is utterly unable to staunch and to which it invariably gives way. In Panic City, the unceasing uprisings from all quarters in New Granada and other viceroyalties, the private scandals that explode onto the public scene, the disruptive and unproductive official audits, the ineffectual system of justice, the internecine power struggles, and the incorrigible criminality of gold-rich Bogotá all wreak havoc on law and order: "Con esto se ardía esta ciudad y toda la tierra, y no se veía el fuego sino sólo el gigante del miedo y temor que causaba el nombre del alzamiento. Estaba esta ciudad muy disgustosa, porque los buenos bien conocían el engaño y falsedad; los malos, que eran el mayor bando, gustaban del bullicio y alzábanlo de punto" (260) ("And with this the city was burning and one did not see the fire but only the giant of fear and dread that the very name of the uprising caused. The city was repugnant, because the good people were well-acquainted with deceit and falsehood; and the evil, who were in the majority, took great pleasure in the turmoil and increased it"). Only God, and not the fundamentally flawed colonial regime, can bring order to this Baroque city of deceptions and panic and disorder, "porque cuando falta la justicia en la tierra, la envía Dios del cielo por el camino que él es servido" (225) ("for when justice is absent on earth, God sends it through the means that he chooses").

The panic that convulses the extra-textual Bogotá also destabilizes the narrative of *El Carnero*. We witness in the text yet another internecine struggle, between official historiography and the earthy, scandalous *casos* (occurrences) conveying the stuff of individual lives. (See González Echevarría 1990, Ch. 2 on this quarrel.) The parting of the ways between the two could hardly be more self-evident or more dramatic. First, we have the rigid chronological framework of the text meted out into the regimes of Colombia's rulers, the lengthy formal chapter headings that announce those demarcations, the formulaic or schematic narration of official comings and goings, and the desiccated catalogues of names of noteworthy figures. In contrast, we have the protracted *petites histoires* or *casos* based on files from Bogotá's archives, recounted with a punctilious relish that follows every twist and turn of these tangled, non-linear situations. Barely hinted at in the chapter titles, downplayed in the text's title as "algunos casos sucedidos en este Reino, que van en la historia para ejemplo, y no para imitarlos por el daño de la conciencia" ("some of the cases that occurred in this kingdom, which are in history as an example not to be imitated lest there be harm to one's conscience"), the "thick" history imparted by the *casos* threatens to overwhelm official history.

As Freyle elaborates the *casos*, literature makes inroads into history, further shaking it. Most critical treatments of *El Carnero* have discussed the literary devices derived from the Baroque novella, the comedia, and the picaresque of which Freyle skillfully avails himself in plotting these shocking tales of passion and vice. (See, for example, Pupo-Walker.) In brief, these devices include suspenseful foreshadowing, simultaneous plots, invented dialogue, moralizing commentary, themes of honor, and much reliance on disguise and deception. *El Carnero*'s literary contrivances, clearly transcending

the factual mode of narration of the archives, tangibly bear out Leonard's contention (1949) that secular literary works were read in the colonies. Freyle finds in the *casos* an outlet for his literary impulses, a means of effectively combating another prohibition, of 1531, against the writing of fiction in the colonies. We, in turn, find in the *casos* of *El Carnero* a shift away from the erudite Baroque and into its popular manifestations. Staunch adversary of the bureaucratic *ciudad letrada* (Freyle remarked that the paperwork sent to Spain outweighed the gold [314]), he gravitates toward the relative transparency, melodramatic theatricality, and vulgar naturalism of Baroque comedias and novellas. With his use of oral sources, colloquial language, and the gossip that circulates incessantly in the plaza, Freyle liberates the New World Baroque from both its elite language and its themes, bringing it to bear on the populace. Moreover, as I have already stated, the tabloid criterion of sensationalism propels much of *El Carnero*, and particularly its *casos*. It is thus the negative pole of amazement that produces the New World's earliest forays into prose fiction, fiction that issues, significantly enough, from the public square rather than from the *ciudad letrada*. Freyle terms these forays, the *casos* with which he allegedly "adorns" his history, "flowers" (36). *El Carnero* once again takes a pastoral topic to the city, but to places, heights, and depths antithetical to "La grandeza mexicana."

The feminine connotations of Freyle's pastoral image signal that the moralistic *casos* of *El Carnero* will impute ultimate blame for the depths to which Bogotá has fallen to women rather than to the colonizers. Freyle disingenuously introduces his flower-like *casos* and the story of Eve's diabolical deceptions in the same chapter (Ch. 5). And indeed, women lie at the heart of many of the convoluted *casos* and constitute the prime target of the verbal punishments that Freyle effects through his heated moralizing comments. Nevertheless, the text itself makes it difficult for us to accept women as the root evil of Panic City, to take Freyle's misogyny at face value. Women don't incite *all* of the scandals presented in the *casos;* the men are often as guilty as the women and are guilty of not keeping women in check; the women can be innocent and wrongly victimized; the moralizing comments are often contradictory or take on a comical air; the aged Freyle even notes the absurdity of his apparent obsession with women (329) and identifies the world, the devil, *and* the flesh as man's principal enemies (392). All of these equivocations make Freyle's misogyny suspect (though they fail to cancel it out) and bid the reader to understand his "other" otherwise. Freyle, I maintain, is scapegoating women, using them as a hook for his readers' conceivable prurience and as a smokescreen for the lack of reason and fragility of order characteristic of the colonial world as he sees it. What better, more available, more sanctioned vehicle could there be for the tenuousness of the colonial Panic City than a woman's honor, "sujeta a mil calamidades" (390) ("subject to a thousand calamities")? Freyle all but discloses his emblematizing of Panic City through women when, after criticizing them as a "casta de víboras" ("caste of snakes"), he states ambiguously, "La casa a donde sólo la voluntad es señora, no está segura la razón ni se puede tomar punto fijo. Esto fue el origen y principio de los disgustos de este Reino, y pérdida de haciendas, y el ir y venir de los visitadores y jueces . . ." (259) ("Reason is not safe in a house where will is the sole mistress nor can one be confident of anything. This was the origin and beginning of the difficulties of this kingdom, and the loss of haciendas and the constant coming and going of royal visitors and judges . . ."). Like so many seventeenth-century male writers, Freyle targets women as the height of disorder, holding them accountable in metaphorical or real terms for the turmoil of the times (Merrim 1999, xxx). As do other colonial writers we will examine, he draws on the prevailing misogyny as a conduit through which to channel his critique of colonial misrule.

For a cameo of this and other aspects of *El Carnero* discussed here, I return to the case of Juana García, lone culprit charged with a crime of which other guilty parties were exculpated and whose criminal history was burned, to Juana García converted into a spectacle, mounted on a stage in the plaza of Santo Domingo and declaring: "'Todas [las personas], todas lo hicimos, y yo sola lo pago'" (214) ("'Everyone, we all did it, and only I pay for it'").

Sin City

The nature of the spectacles represented in a text, as we have seen, indexes its cityscape and its ideological bent. In the case of Bartolomé Arzáns de Orsúa y Vela's *Historia de la villa imperial de Potosí* [*Tales of Potosí*] (written between 1705 and 1736, but not published in full until 1965), the many festivals chronicled in the text, like everything else it contains, are larger than life. The *criollo* Arzáns, who spent his entire life in Potosí and is not lacking in civic pride, recounts festivals so lavish, so extravagant, as almost to defy imagining. When, for example, Potosí celebrated the marriage of Philip II to Margarita of Austria in 1556, it mounted a festival that lasted twenty-four days and cost eight million pesos (Hanke 1956, 2). In 1600, the city quite literally worshipped its own grandeur:

> The fiestas began on the eighteenth of June with a showy and sumptuous masque by the famous miners of the Mountain, in which there were admirable figures, very costly floats, splendid costumes, marvelous embroideries, precious stones and pearls of inestimable value, spirited horses, and splendid trappings. The last float (which was extremely large and rich, and was drawn by twelve white horses) represented the rich Mountain of Potosí, all made of fine silver, and at its feet was the imperial city in the form of a grave and beautiful maiden wearing a dress of silver cloth covered with diamonds, emeralds, zircons, amethysts, and rubies, and kneeling before a portrait of His Majesty Felipe II, which was placed on a sumptuous throne under a canopy. . . (171–72; to promote study of this remarkable, little-analyzed text, I quote from the easily available excerpted translation of the text, *Tales of Potosí*, rather from the scarce full edition).

Potosí devotes more space and gives more weight to spectacles than any other general work of the times. Lewis Hanke writes, "If one had to select the one symbolic institution through which the ethos of this silver city could best be seen, that institution would probably be the fiesta and the *History* documents its history admirably" (1965a, 40). Arzáns zealously documents the festivals in his history of Potosí from 1545 to 1736, an annalistic text that for the most part bears an uncanny resemblance to *El Carnero*. I take the position that *Potosí* overlaps with but ultimately swerves from *El Carnero* precisely because of the ethos of Potosí that its festivals reflect; I locate the muse of the quintessentially Baroque *Potosí* in the spectacle.

Potosí, in fact, abounded in everything but muses. Antonio de Calancha described it in 1638 as "único en la opulencia, primero de la magestad, último fin de la codicia" (Hanke 1956, 36) ("unique in opulence, first in majesty, culmination of greed"). Beginning in 1545, the rich silver mines of the mountain of Potosí attracted Spaniards from all regions and

walks of life together with Indians from all parts of the viceroyalty of Peru of which Potosí formed part. By 1610, Potosí, with a population of 160,000, was the largest and richest city in the New World, the center of wealth and trade in South America. The phrase "vale un Potosí" had entered common parlance as an expression of unlimited wealth. Situated in a region so remote and high as to be almost uninhabitable, Potosí developed from its extraordinary prosperity the tenor of a Wild West boomtown. Its newly rich inhabitants, the would-be *hidalgos* described with words from Arzáns above, consumed luxury goods with a vengeance and indulged their passions and vices with equal fervor. Gambling, prostitution, violence, and ethnic rivalries defined the social climate of this melting pot. The boomtown produced silver and social institutions such as brothels and dance halls, but notably little literary culture. As it has come down to us through Arzáns's text and other sources, Potosí was probably the least "cultured" New World city of its time. Bogotá's cultural developments go unmentioned in the selective *El Carnero*; Potosí simply had little to boast of. It lacked a university or institutions of higher learning, an *audiencia* or a printing press. While there is evidence of a couple of lone poets in residence in Potosí, of theatrical productions, and (via Leonard) of books having been shipped there from Spain, no new plays seem to have been written in Potosí, no treatises or histories published in the city. The principal cultural manifestations of this materialistic boomtown were the spectacles that vaunted its wealth and grandeur.

In the cultural wasteland of Potosí, the schoolteacher and autodidact Arzáns wrote his history of Sin City, a fallen city that had abandoned all morality. By the time Arzáns wrote, the city had quite concretely fallen into economic decline. Nostalgic for its greatness, remorseful of its decline, the *criollo* author imputes the city's fall to the sins occasioned by its wealth. He inscribes Potosí's history in a biblical framework according to which God, as Arzáns tells us, had visited divine vengeance on Sin City in the form of three scourges: the War of the Vicuñas in 1622, a flood caused by the collapse of the Caricari dam in 1626, and the devaluation of currency around 1650. Although Arzáns had originally planned to call his work "Las tres destrucciones de la Villa Imperial de Potosí" (Hanke 1965b, 59) ("The Three Devastations of the Imperial City of Potosí"), the sins of Potosí's citizens rather than the three plagues primarily occupy the text. It is here that the similarities between *Potosí* and *El Carnero* assert themselves. As did that of his Colombian forebear, Arzáns's infra-history takes up the gauntlet of exposing, in an unbroken chronological framework based on the official regimes of Potosí, the lawlessness, scandals private and public, sin, greed, criminality, and chaos that ran rampant in his city. In Arzáns's view, R. C. Padden tells us, "sex and sin are coterminous, if not synonymous" (xxxi). As in *El Carnero*, private scandals, minutely divulged, burst onto the public scene. Here too, the colonial regime proves ineffectual in stemming the chaos or imposing order. Yet Arzáns is rather less concerned than Freyle with indicting the government and more so with exposing the social and ethnic tensions proper to his milieu. Tensions between Basques, Estremadurans, Andalusians, *criollos*, and Indians constantly erupt in private disputes, seditious acts, civil tumults, and outright civil wars. If Potosí possesses any virtue, it lies in the Christian charity that the city's wealth promotes, but uncontainable rancor often undoes even that saving grace.

Arzáns presents the Indians as particular victims of the greedy Sin City. He pleads for reform of the *mita*, or conscription, that forces them to work in the mines under inhumane conditions; he defends their intelligence and achievements and repeatedly registers the miracles wrought upon the Indians by the Mother of God of Candelaria and others. While here Arzáns starts to sound like Sigüenza y Góngora, with the important caveat that the Potosino's Indians are alive and real, the role of the Indians in the festivals that he describes probably exceeds Sigüenza's wildest dreams. Similar to the Indian masquerade of Querétaro, but with the presence of Indians magnified a hundredfold and a common occurrence, in Potosí's spectacles the native peoples parade their splendor and history on an equal footing with the Spanish, albeit with the expectable providential reverence for the Spanish regime. (See García Pabón's excellent 1995 article on Potosí's fiestas.) In these festivals, and only in them, are the tensions of Sin City temporarily alleviated.

Both the miracles and the hypertrophied festivals just mentioned are symptomatic of Arzáns's wild, extreme text. Although Arzáns wrote in the early eighteenth century, his portrait of a decadent society epitomizes the Baroque sensibility, bearing no signs of the Enlightenment. *Potosí* contains not only the pandemonium and ferment of *El Carnero* but also frequent supernatural occurrences, hyperbolic "monstrous" protagonists demonstrating the society's lawlessness, utterly implausible events, violent crimes of the most grotesque nature recounted in naturalistic detail verging on the obscene, and Baroque locutions of wonder, shock, and surprise. The scandal-sheet criterion apposite to Sin City rivals the positive awe occasioned by the festivals; the predominant cast of the text is marvellous, prodigious, beyond belief, in a word, spectacular. Under the aegis of the Baroque spectacles that the text privileges, *Potosí* leads one to believe that in the prodigiously wealthy boomtown, anything is possible. The fabulous and fabulation authorize each other, suspending the criterion of verisimilitude and naturalizing history into fiction.

Much as the very nature of the Potosí might appear to warrant his fabulations, Arzáns, like Freyle, invokes the protection of history. Claiming to have read everything written on Potosí, the apparently erudite Arzáns cites a wide array of sources throughout the text. He takes special pains to attribute the accounts of miracles to the archives. Nevertheless, and significantly, it is now believed that Arzáns fabricated some of his main sources, for no trace of them has been found. (See Hanke 1965b, 62–64.) *Potosí* thus reproduces in a New World historiographic context *Don Quijote*'s appeal to fictionalized historical sources. García Pabón (1992), moreover, has established that Arzáns took considerable liberties even with those sources that were not apocryphal.

When Arzáns turns his creative impulses to the, at least in part, apocryphal wrongdoings of Sin City, full-blown *novelas ejemplares* ("exemplary novels") result. The *Tales of Potosí*, probably the most outright entertaining works to have been produced in the colonial New World besides its relatively few comedias, transcend the literary plotting of the *casos* of *El Carnero*. They adopt a Cervantine thematics that centers on the dangers of constraining freedom or the ways in which God's will supersedes human planning ("el hombre propone pero Dios dispone"). Their multipart plotting, their unspeakably cruel mothers, tortures, obscene dismemberments, rapes, and so on, however, reveal an even greater kinship with the decadent peninsular novellas of María de Zayas (1590–1661)

or Alonso de Castillo Solórzano (1584–1648?) that sensationalized Cervantes's (1547–1616) *Novelas ejemplares* (1613). Castillo Solórzano in particular imposed perfunctory morals on his works of sheer entertainment to placate the censors. Arzáns, for his part, works in a moralizing mode that permits tremendous literary mobility. Similar to *El Carnero*, in Arzáns's tales, God always intervenes to punish a culprit or to bring a sinner to grace. As distinct from *El Carnero*, Arzáns's God generally intervenes in private, can do so at any moment in a person's life (even in a final moment of repentance, at the end of a wholly despicable life), and can rescue even the most unlikely subjects. *Potosí*'s free-floating moralizing in essence allows for any kind of story to be told and somehow to be transfigured into a moral tale. With the aid of the divine "escape clause," Arzáns can narrate his spectacular sinful stories at will and with gusto, for they need not illustrate any moral other than God's seemingly capricious benevolence nor need they have an overtly moralistic shape. The same zest for spectacular storytelling renders Arzáns's position on women unseizable. While he often inveighs against women and imputes blame to them for men's sins, as does Freyle, Arzáns also celebrates the outrageous exploits of "manly women" and includes praise of them that echoes the pro-female *querelle des femmes*. Simply put, these stories are too wonderful not to be told, and not to be told with admiration.

Potosí's tales are equally irreducible to a single paradigm. Aside from the constant of divine intervention and a few stock characters (e.g., the "monster" man, the cruel mother), they refuse to adhere to a single mould. Each story shifts gears from the previous one, successively giving us black protagonists, Indian protagonists, would-be noble protagonists, cross-dressing women, murderers and murderesses, New World Don Juans, ghosts and angelic apparitions, witches, and so on, seemingly ad infinitum. Only the variety and infinite ingenuity designed to shock and surprise at every turn define *Potosí*. This unremittingly variegated text thus takes on the dimensions of a literary sampler, a sin-full encyclopedia of literary figures and plots transplanted from the Metropolis into a New World setting. Arzáns has produced from his cultural wasteland a coming into culture similar to that desired for Mexico by Balbuena and realized in the encyclopedic urges of Sigüenza's *Infortunios*, to which *Potosí* bears a telling resemblance. Potosí, the represented world, lacks its own literary culture and boasts only spectacles; like *El Carnero*, but in the more concerted and spectacular vein that befits the boomtown's ethos, Potosí absorbs culture into its textual representations. Arzáns, a New World storyteller against all odds, has naturalized history into fiction, invented his historical sources, freed up the Baroque exemplary novella, and imbued his Sin City with a fabulous literary culture.

The Nocturnal City

The final stage of our excursion takes us to the poetic satires of Lima by Mateo Rosas de Oquendo and Juan del Valle y Caviedes. Leonardo Acosta observes, "Quizás sea en el Perú donde la enajenación colonial llegó a su máximo grado" (1972, 46) ("Perhaps it was in Peru that the colonial alienation reached its maximum degree"). Perhaps this is due to the more strictly "colonial" nature of Peru's economy, less diversified in the seventeenth century than Mexico's (Lynch 201, 205). Hanke, in fact, has suggested that it was the silver production of Potosí that chained Peru's economy to mining and kept agriculture from developing (1956, 38). In any case, the two disillusioned poets satirize the colonial Lima and undertake to *purge* the colonial world of its manifold ills. Each does so by means of a time-worn ritualistic structure, Rosas through carnival and Caviedes through the plague. Both symbolize the ills of colonial Lima through the body. Their purges literally and figuratively desublimate colonial tensions by venting them, alleviating them through bodily functions, and voicing them in an unbound satirical register devoid of any conceivable sublimity. In these degraded counterparts of the Sublime City and the City of the Mind, the collective spectacles that allow for a taxonomic review of society and thus lend themselves to satire continue to play a major role, but as through a glass, darkly.

One of the earliest and most significant colonial satires, the *Sátira hecha por Mateo Rosas de Oquendo a las cosas que pasan en el Pirú, año de 1598* (Satire Written by Mateo Rosas de Oquendo or What Occurred in Peru in 1598) has only recently begun to come into its own, largely thanks to the superb critical edition by Pedro Lasarte published in 1990. Lasarte imparts what biographical information there is on Rosas, who was born in Spain (ca. 1563), participated in the founding of Tucumán, and resided in Lima and later in Mexico, probably dying there. More important, Lasarte's detailed notes and commentary make the long (2,120 verses), difficult, and palimpsestic *romance* intelligible, revealing its multidimensionality. Perhaps the *Sátira*'s time has finally come. The scatological subtext that Lasarte brings to light, the text's carnivalesque dimensions, its scathing critique of yet another colonial Sin City, are all as inviting to our critical climate as they were inimical to its own.

At the beginning of the *Sátira*, "Mateo Rosas de Oquendo" convenes all of Lima to hear his denunciation of arrogant Peru, "tan rrico como ynorante" (2) ("as rich as ignorant"), on the day of his departure. A self-styled town crier, a self-statedly reformed rogue who had previously studied the arts of magic, the narrator immediately plunges his audience into the necromantic world of the Nocturnal City that he purports to indict. If *El Carnero* and *Potosí* show us the hidden entrails of the colonial world where sex fed scandal, the *Sátira* guides us through a sexualized world turned inside out and upside down. This is the devil-ruled domain of "libianos de noche" (4) ("lustful of the night"), of nighttime sallies, seductions, recreation rather than work, bedrooms, and streets. The nocturnal world given over to libidinous activity inverts the diurnal world, purges its ills ("qué de soles ai dañosos,/serenos medizinales") (5) ("there are harmful sun/and serene ones that cure"; the orthography of the text is highly irregular), discharges its hidden desires, and unmasks its disguises ("qué de corderos de día/y de noche gauilanes,/de noche sin capirotes/y de día con disfrases") (4) ("sheep by day/and hawks by night,/at night without hoods/and by day in disguise"). The narrator's exposé of the Nocturnal City takes place, fittingly enough, during Carnival time: "Mas pues biene la Quaresma/y tengo de confesarme" (43) ("For it is Lent/and I have to take confession"). As Lasarte indicates in his discussion of the contradictory elements brought together by the text (see also Julie Greer Johnson's discussion of Rosas, Ch. 2), and as we will explore here among other things, the *Sátira* folds Bakhtin's carnivalesque mode into the colonial New World.

The *Sátira*, itself a carnivalesque spectacle of "fiestas de noche" (33) ("nighttime festivities") convoked by a streetwise narrator, mocks and replays official spectacles. The narrator tells us how official festivals collapse into carnival disorder,

"qué de holguras se ordenan/por sólo desordenarse" (7) ("that by merriment they become ordered/only by being disordered"). Similarly, the two bizarre spectacles that Rosas actually portrays in his text unthrone what is held on high, giving full rein to the subversive charge latent in the festivals dominated by Indians and described by Sigüenza and Arzáns. Rosas's first spectacle takes place on the grandest of religious holidays, the festival of Corpus Christi. In a parody of the transubstantiation of the Eucharist celebrated that day, Rosas stages an aberrant allegorical procession of nocturnal women warriors, prostitutes, each wearing some cryptic insignia of her profession. To decipher their insignia is, perversely, to partake of the metaphorical mechanisms of the Eucharist. The second spectacle shifts from celebration to penitence, and from an allegorical to a plausibly real festival organized by the trade guilds (*cofradías*) during Lent. Rosas transposes this lofty exhibition by freighting it with the sexual innuendo that turns its ostensible mortification of the flesh into an orgy.

Rosas's deviant renditions of holy festivals cue us into the *Sátira*'s sexual obsessions and the "erotics" of its language. Women and the flesh dominate this *avant la lettre* Quevedesque text and, as one by now expects, serve as a venue for satires of religion (e.g., worship and pilgrimages as pretexts for sexual activity), society (e.g., men's alleged effeminacy after the Conquest), and politics (e.g., men purporting to be distinguished conquerors to make a sexual conquest). We recall Balbuena's *avant la lettre* Gongorism: Once again it can be said, in the words of the neo-Baroque *Tres tristes tigres* (1967; Three Trapped Tigers), that "el barroquismo viene con la cultura" (Cabrera Infante 399) ("the Baroque comes with culture") rather than from across the seas. As is the case with Quevedo's and many other phobic, misogynist texts, Rosas's text paradoxically invests women, such as the nocturnal warriors, with hyperbolic powers. His is a carnivalesque matriarchy in which women command men's servitude and men live off women's sexually gotten gains. And as in Quevedo's erotic satires, love is wholly reduced to the body, to the all-devouring grotesque body and its lowest functions. It is from this polymorphous perversity, with its desublimation of colonial tensions, that the *Sátira* derives its most unique aspect, its polysemia. The language of the poem, as Lasarte painstakingly documents, is shot through with sexual double entendres. It pulsates with the crudest obscenity. Wordplay, slang, and extended metaphors insistently remand the knowing reader to the corporeal subtext. Often the sexual innuendo directly counters the moralistic literal meaning. For example, the narrator cautions his friends against sexual conquest inside a woman's own home, saying, "le diremos que se harme [arme],/porque si le coxen dentro/pueda libralla y librarse" (3) ("we shall tell him to arm himself, / because if they get him inside/he might free her and free himself"). Given that in street slang *armar* means to have an erection and *librarse* to reach orgasm, the narrator is at the same time egging his friends on. The ambiguous subtext dynamites the literal text, dragging it into the debased geography of the Nocturnal City. Rosas, we should note, also explodes the seeming monologism of official texts. On several occasions he lambastes the inflated claims of the *relaciones de servicios y méritos* (reports of services and merits) presented to the Viceroy by the undistinguished Spaniards who settled this bad, rather than brave, New World.

As it decenters language and releases repressed passions, the *Sátira* breaks down boundaries. Not unlike the nightworld of Sor Juana's *Sueño*, the nocturnal *Sátira* embodies fluidity; if *El Carnero* posits a fragile scaffolding of order, constantly being challenged and giving way, in the *Sátira* boundaries are dismantled, infinitely permeable, of no account. The *Sátira* announces its fluidity with persistent sexual wordplay around nautical themes based on the concept of navigation. In popular parlance, to navigate means both to sail and to engage in sexual intercourse. Broken locks (e.g., on doors and on chastity belts), and doors, windows, and walls that fail to contain, also make their appearance at several moments in the text. All of this feeds into the essential thrust of the *Sátira*: to attack the unconscionable upward mobility, knowing no limits or reason, of the would-be nobles of Lima. About two thirds into the poem, the *Sátira* leaves off its sexual foreplay to engage in an overt tongue-lashing of those who come from an impoverished Spain bringing nothing but claims of a non-existent noble ancestry (all, supposedly, "son hidalgos finos/de conosidos solares," [38] ["are fine noblemen/from well-known estates"]), who cheat their way into rewards and wealth, who but replicate the insidious class structure of Spain that had condemned them to poverty, who parade their sham nobility in exorbitant finery, whose desire for power matches or is symbolized by their desire for sex. "Malditos seáis de Dios/enbusteros charlatanes!" (40) ("May you be dammed by God/cheats, charlatans"), rails Rosas at these New World *pícaros*. This is the real upside-down world, a fluid, unstable city in which morality and class lines hold no sway. And Rosas's narrator would restore the suspended, ineffectual boundaries. He advocates a work ethic that will instate a worthy nobility and return the Spaniards to their peasant origins (40), and urges rewards only for those who (like Rosas) actually reaped them through blood (41).

The narrator who here and elsewhere assumes so rigid a moralistic stance is nevertheless "himself" a fluid, carnivalesque construct. Much as he purports at the beginning and end of the poem to have renounced the vices of the Nocturnal City, to have abandoned his degraded identity as Juan Sánches and now to be reclaiming his upstanding persona as Mateo Rosas de Oquendo, the narrator continues incongruously to be contaminated by the nightworld's not inconsiderable charms. He rejects the nightworld's sinful ways but does not cease to be complicitous with it, giving advice to women on how to enhance their seductions (12), offering to be their go-between (for friends from Potosí [12]), letting himself be fooled by women and enjoying fancy clothing (20), exhorting men to have sex (27), and so on. The narrator presents himself as a chameleon who adjusts to and is seduced by his surroundings: "Lo que de mí sé dezir/es que soy tan miserable/que en comensándose el son/comienso a desatacarme" (31) ("What I can say about myself/is that I am so miserable/that as soon as the *son* begins,/I begin to unburden myself"). His position as both a spectator of and participant in the "fiestas de noche" ("night celebrations") represents a breakdown of the boundaries that separate the moralist or satirist from his or her material. This is not hypocrisy, as Lasarte astutely notes, but rather yet another manifestation of the contradictory logic that runs through the text (xxi), the gleeful moralizing of a rogue who, despite himself, disseminates the carnival spirit.

What, if anything, levels the discrepancies of the narrator's position is knowing, laughing, and marveling. The narrator has intimate knowledge of the Nocturnal City he would leave behind and he revels in his knowledge. He transmits it with pleasure and humor. (Johnson calls the *Sátira* a "sermon joyeux" [35].) The narrator of the *Sátira*, incapable of wholly condemning what he sees ("muerto yo por estas cosas,/gusto de oír sus dislates [disparates]" [18] ["I die for these things/pleasure of hearing nonsense"]), instead dissolves into laughter: "el más amigo se rríe/de su proseder infame!" (2) ("the best friend laughs/at his terrible actions"). Laughter in general and in the carnivalesque mode eases tensions, blurs boundaries, and harmonizes contradictory impulses. In the *Sátira*, laughter goes hand in hand with "maravilla": "Quando le vi desta suerte/comensé a marabillarme:/. . ./rreíme, Dios me perdone,/de ber aquel personaxe,/y por no soltar la rriza,/me fui la calle adelante" (38) ("When I saw him in this state/I was amazed,/. . ./I laughed, may God forgive me,/on seeing that person,/so not to burst out laughing,/I went to the street ahead"). Here, for the first time in our trajectory, we encounter a text that not only aims to inspire laughter but also thematizes it, carrying the marvel in its wake. Baroque novelty, on the other hand, acquires a dark demeanor in the *Sátira*. It turns into a symbol of the medieval wheel of fortune (48, ll.1939–42) and of bodily illness: "que el pecho de más asiento/se muere por nobedades,/porque son sus mouimientos/humores asidentales" (48, ll. 1943–46) ("for the most sensible person/is dying for something new,/because his movements are/accidental moods"). When toward the end of the poem, Rosas paints a pathos-ridden picture of the ill fortune of the displaced soldiers (like himself) forced to live in the homes of the would-be nobles and to *laugh* hypocritically at their hosts' jokes, the marvel and laughter shade into "nobedades" and knowledge, shutting down the carnivalesque nightworld with a strong dose of a very present reality.

The City of the Plague and Conclusions

The canon of Spanish-American colonial literature that has in most cases ignored Rosas de Oquendo does admit another wild satirist, Juan del Valle y Caviedes, but tends to project a skewed, incomplete picture of his work. Caviedes, born in Spain but reared from an early age in Peru, has become known as the "Quevedo of America" because of the outrageous Baroque satires of doctors that occupy much of his *Diente del Parnaso* and that have passed into literary anthologies. In *Diente*, which circulated in manuscript during his lifetime and was only published in full in 1984, Caviedes lashes out against doctors in comically mordant poems, arguing, as any beginning student of his poetry will know, that doctors bring death rather than life, are the allies of the Empress Death, kill more victims than war or soldiers, issue death warrants with their prescriptions, know nothing but flaunt an empty erudition, defraud the poor, milk the rich for profit, and so on. Caviedes uses any ammunition he can muster to decimate his target. The poems *à clef* of *Diente* (90 percent of the doctors he mentions have been identified [Reedy, Prologue to Caviedes, xxi]) conflate medical malpractice, mortifying anecdotes of the doctors' personal lives and manners, and their physical deformities. Caviedes embeds this shocking roster of malignities in his no less astonishing, unrelenting skeins of wicked Baroque *conceptista* wordplays, which, like Rosas's *Sátira* but more overtly, can indulge in crude obscenity. His invective, his ingenuity, nor his ire against doctors, it would appear, respect any bounds.

From Rosas's palimpsestic figurations of sexuality, we have moved into Caviedes's uncontrollable, almost diseased, *conceptismo*. From the *Sátira's* subterranean nocturnal transgressions and epidemic sexuality, we walk into the sickness, the real sickness, that erupts day and night in *Diente* and shapes its Lima into the City of the Plague. The heading, or perhaps original title, of the text announces the plague ambiguously, as either a metaphorical phenomenon (i.e., the doctors as a pestilence) or as a real one: "Guerra Física, Proezas Medicales, Hazañas de la Ignorancia, sacadas a luz del conocimiento por un enfermo que milagrosamente escapó de los errores médicos por la protección de señor San Roque, abogado contra médicos *o* contra la peste que tanto monta" (5; emphasis added) ("Physical war, medical exploits, feats of ignorance, exposure by a patient who miraculously escaped from medical errors though the protection of St. Roch [healer of the plague], advocate against doctors or against the plague that is intensifying"). Another of the text's various references to the plague makes it clearer that the city has more afflictions to contend with than its doctors: "Bástenos, señor Doctor,/la peste de que morimos,/sin usted . . ." (Poem 26, 65; I follow the numeration assigned by Reedy) ("Let it suffice, Sir Doctor,/that the plague is killing us,/without also suffering you . . ."). Of course it stands to reason that if doctors wield such power, so too must disease. At the same time, so compulsive is Caviedes's focus on doctors, so punishing are his attacks on them, so generally unspecified are the diseases that doctors fail to cure, that we begin to suspect that *Diente* is, as "plague" texts do, actually *scapegoating* not, for once, women, but doctors. In his *romance* 43, Caviedes assembles an extensive catalogue of the complaints levied against doctors by classical and Spanish authors, a veritable history of the targeting of doctors. When at the end of the poem Caviedes suggests that doctors be made to wear distinctive clothing on the Day of the Dead for their sins, or at the end of Poem 27 when he banishes them to the cemetery outside of the city, we hear echoes of the oracle's words from *Oedipus the King* cited by René Girard as defining the mechanisms and motivations of scapegoating: "'A murderer is in your midst; get rid of him and you will be rid of the plague'" (145).

The preceding association with Oedipus and the medical satires of *Diente* themselves raise the questions of exactly what plague the doctors are unable to cure, of why Caviedes targets or scapegoats them. One needs to look beyond the familiar corpus of medical poems for an answer, that is, for the key to the City of the Plague. When we range outside the medical poems, we find in Caviedes's *oeuvre* a portrait of a wholly sick city, a sick colonial society, suffering from a variety of illnesses that, in truth, no medical doctor could cure. Caviedes's Lima revolves around the characteristically Baroque "illnesses" generated by its matrix of appearances versus reality: lies, hypocrisy, posturing, adulation, deceit, materialism, pretension to nobility, and lack of honor. Wealth stands at its heart as the root of its evils. In a series of philosophical-moral sonnets (Poems 199, 200, 201, 206, 207, 212), the poet makes his neo-Stoical case against the materialism endemic in Peru and in general; for example: "De la vida enemiga es la riqueza,/porque es centro del vicio la abundancia;/y así es la muerte del hombre, si en sustancia/facilita la gula y la torpeza" (Poem 201, 386) ("Wealth is the enemy of life,/because abundance is the center of vice;/and thus it is with man, (if) of substance/greed and awkwardness follow"). His special sympathy, accordingly, lies with the poor. He leaves no doubt that *society* scapegoats the poor, attributing to them all the defects of the falsely noble or erudite: "El pobre es tonto, si calla,/y si habla es majadero;/si sabe, es sólo hablador,/y si afable, es embustero"

(Poem 102, 286) ("The poor man is a fool if he is silent,/ and if he speaks he is stupid;/if he knows something, he is just a gossip,/and if he is good-natured, he is a cheat"). Caviedes undoes that scapegoating with his own scapegoating of doctors. Yet in a handful of poems, and notably in his longthiest one (Poem 56, "Remedio para ser lo que quisieres, que son observaciones del autor" ["The remedy for being what you would like to be, which are the author's observations"]), Caviedes's poetic persona doles out ironic prescriptions to all those who wish to succeed in colonial society, becoming none too benign a doctor in his own right. Poem 56 lays out a map of Lima's most representative characters–hypocrites, false nobles, scholars, prostitutes, doctors–and caustically provides each character with the code of his or her mendacious occupation. Elsewhere, lawyers, painters, clerics, mulattoes, Indians, drunks, devout women, duennas, individuals with physical deformities, and false virgins all fall under Caviedes's satirical scalpel. Far from being an isolated malignancy, clearly scapegoated for their pretensions to healing, doctors thus take their place in the large company that Caviedes dissects. Like that great equalizer, the Dance of Death, the satirist appropriates in his blanket condemnation of society what Girard calls the "undifferentiation" (148) intrinsic to a collapsed, plague-ridden society.

While "La grandeza mexicana" posits Mexico City as a Parnassus, and the famed literary academy of Lima (the Academia Antártica) issued a work entitled *Primera parte del Parnaso Antártico* (1608), Caviedes's *Diente del Parnaso* evokes a diseased, abscessed tooth that must be removed. That tooth, no doubt, is the ills of society. Caviedes, retaining the exalted role that his cohorts in Parnassus assigned the poet, asserts that *he* can cure society's ills–by purging them through laughter. In the Prologue to *Diente* we read, "Más médico es mi tratado/que ellos, pues si bien lo miras,/divierte que es un remedio/que cura de hipocondría" (Poem 9, 20) ("My essay is more of a doctor/than they are, for if one considers it well,/laughter is a medicine/that cures the hypochondriac"). The poem ends with the following good counsel to its reader: "Ríete de todo, puesto/que, aunque de todo te rías,/tienes razón. Dios te guarde,/sin médicos ni botica" (21) ("Laugh at everything for,/even though everything makes you laugh,/you are right. May God keep you,/from doctors and pharmacy"). Caviedes exempts only the poor and the poet from complicity with the pestilence that rages in colonial Lima. For Caviedes, the poet redresses the vacuousness of others' mere, or false, erudition by creatively deploying knowledge: "No alcanzan sus relevantes/primores los que profesan/estudiar letras, sino/aquéllos que hacen las letras" (Poem 43, 112) ("Those who study letters/will not reach the relevant pleasures [of nature's secrets],/for that is reserved for those who write literature"). Poem 214, "Que no hay más felicidad en esta vida que el entendimiento" ("There is no greater happiness in this life than understanding"), informs the reader that since poetry, not wealth, brings true contentment, ". . . el que tuviere entendimiento/el más feliz será que hay en el suelo" (394) ("he who has understanding / will be the happiest person on earth"). Replacing the ineffectual doctor with the effectual poet, and wealth with poetry, Caviedes valorizes Parnassian intellectual endeavors.

An exact contemporary of Sigüenza y Góngora and Sor Juana, Caviedes counters the City of the Plague with the City of the Mind. Moreover, in addition to laughter and poetry, Caviedes proposes the reason and empiricism espoused by his Mexican counterparts as remedies for his own Baroque City of the Plague, so rife with deceptions. That is to say, we find in Caviedes a reprise, even a self-conscious one, of the two Mexican luminaries' philosophical arguments, now invoked as an antidote to the City of the Plague. In his Sonnets 197 and 206, Caviedes lauds reason over passion and over lies, respectively. Sonnet 213, "Que los temblores no son castigo de Dios" ("Earth tremors are not punishment from God"), and *romance* 263, "Juicio de un cometa que apareció hecho por el autor" ("Opinion written by the author on a comet that appeared"), evince an Enlightenment scientific perspective that, in striking contra-distinction to Caviedos's other contemporary, Arzáns, pro-nounces these phenomena to be natural occurrences rather than divine punishments. The second poem treats the same comet of 1681 that sparked the famous debate in Mexico between Austrian Jesuit Eusebio Kino and Sigüenza (incited by Sigüenza's *Manifiesto filosófico contra los cometas despojados del imperio que tienen sobre los tímidos* ["Philosophical mani-festo against the exposed comets that rule over the timid"]), and in precisely the same terms as those of the Mexican savant. It is not entirely unlikely that Caviedes had read Sigüenza's pamphlet, given that he knew Sor Juana's works, corresponded with her, and established an intertextual dia-logue with her as well. Sor Juana's boundless flow of Baroque conceits attracted Caviedes, making their way ver-batim into his poetry (see Poems 12, 43, 64), as did her philosophical bent. Caviedes's Sonnet 203, "No hay cosa cierta en esta vida" ("There is nothing certain in this life"), replays the wordplay of Sor Juana's signature philosophical sonnet, "Verde embeleso de la vida humana" (Poem 152) ("Green Enchantment of Human Life"), and recapitulates its critique of illusion and deception. This unlikely cross-fertiliza-tion between two, or perhaps three, largely dissimilar Baroque New World writers attests that resistance to the Baroque realm of deceptions and to the stranglehold of neo-Scholasticism was spreading through the colonies on the wings of the muse.

The earthquake that prompted Caviedes's scientific reflec-tions also gave rise to one of his two "spectacle" poems. "Al terremoto de Lima el día 20 de octubre de 1687" (Poem 261) ("To Lima's earthquake on 20 October 1687") depicts a natu-ral event in spectacular terms, as a spectacle. Its spectator-nar-rator bears horrified witness to the two awesome tremors that decimated Lima, punctuating his testimony with an anguished *ubi sunt*:

¿Qué se hicieron, Lima ilustre,
tan fuertes arquitecturas
de templos, casas y torres,
como la fama divulga?
¿Dónde están los artezones
cincelados de moduras,
portadas, bovedas, arcos,
pilastros, jaspes, columnas?

Illustrious Lima, what happened to
the powerful architecture
of temples, houses and towers,
such as fame divulges?
Where are the caissons,
chiseled moulds,
façades, domes, arches,
pilasters, jasper columns?

(465)

The earthquakes, a real "Dance of Death," treat everyone equally ("Detenga un temblor el grave/que mayor que otro se juzga,/y si no, piense que todos/tenemos igual fortuna" [465] ["Let the serious person contain an earth tremor/for he judges himself to be superior to others,/and if not, he thinks that we all have the same fortune"]), convening all of the city's inhab-itants in a macabre parody of the quasi-equalizing festival: "El plebeyo, el pobre, el noble,/sin excepción de ninguna/per-sona, se atropellaban/por adelantar la fuga" (465) ("The com-mon man, the poor, the noble,/without any exception,/trample each other/in order to get away"). The medieval-sounding scourge that levels the city and its inhabitants impels Caviedes to retreat somewhat from his previously held (Poem 213) scientific position on the meaning of natural disas-ters. Natural disasters may not, he says, be sent by God, but they should cause us to meditate on our sins: "Asústenos los pecados/no la tierra que fluctúa" (466) ("Our sins frighten us/not the earth that moves"). It is *as if* the earthquakes were Judgment Day or the Biblical flood ("*como* cuando en el diluvio/vengó de Dios las injurias," [464; emphasis added] ["*as with* the deluge,/God's vengeance for the offences"]) and thus as if the tremors had purged the sinful city, leaving it, as does the plague, in ruins and purified of all but the poet-witness.

In his "Coloquio entre una vieja y Periquillo a una pro-cesión celebrada en esta ciudad" (Poem 64) ["Colloquy between an old woman and Periquillo on a procession cele-brated in this city"], Caviedes revisits an official rather than a natural spectacle. Like Rosas, he satirizes the grand festival of Corpus Christi, which now becomes a "mojiganga burlesca" (210) ("burlesque masquerade"). An old woman, representing Curiosity, plies a young boy, a truth-telling innocent, with questions about the festival he has witnessed in Lima. From their exchanges emerges the scathing commentary on the profanation of the festival by the overly splendid Jesuits that I cited above, together with equally scathing condemnations of the *tapadas*, false piety, bombastic sermons (206), the upwardly mobile male population, and prostitutes of the Lima the poem terms "Babel" (212). As it turns the procession into one of Folly and Vanity, the "Coloquio" lays bare the effi-cacy of conjoining spectacle and satire. And in what I con-sider to be its most interesting movement, the poem cynically conjugates the Fiesta of Corpus with the Baroque lexicon of *desengaño* (disabusal) to decorporealize the bodily City of the Plague. The old woman asks Periquillo if he perchance saw those who ". . . primero niegan/doce artículos de fe/que uno de caballeresco" (". . . they will first deny/twelve articles of faith/rather than one of the nobility"), and he maliciously replies that he only espied airy devils who feed off the wind, chameleons, goblins lacking in form, frivolous apparitions, gallant phantoms from a play (209). Shortly thereafter, the old woman follows the boy's lead and sums up his report of the festival by asking Periquillo if all the seeming pomp of the fes-tival enacted in this fabulous Crete, imaginary Memphis, fan-tastic Athens are indeed nothing more than "perspectivas aparentes/de humo que el viento subleva/en ficticios obelis-cos/a desvanecida esfera" (212) ("apparent perspectives/of smoke that the wind subverts/into fictitious obelisks/in dissi-pated spheres"). When the boy replies that truly he has wit-nessed nothing but "cascos vanos, tripas huecas,/mucho ruido, pocas nueces" (212) ("vain heads, empty stomachs,/much noise, little substance"), the old woman responds that henceforth she will give no credence whatsoever to any offi-cial reports of any official events.

The conclusion of Caviedes's second "spectacle" poem provides a fitting ending to the plague-beset Baroque city of Lima as well as to our excursion through Baroque cityscapes. The pomp and splendor of the festival and its city have dissolved into the smoke, dust, shadows, and ultimate nothingness of Góngora's and Sor Juana's famed sonnets. Lima's final hallucinated nothingness reimagines the mystery of the Eucharist from transubstantiation into the desubstantiation of a city so fraught with Baroque disease that it evanesces into a dis-illusioned phantasmagorical realm. Both of Caviedes's "spectacular" poems, we see, end by wiping out the City of the Plague. This is the ultimate effect of the plague and also the fate augured for Panic City, Sin City, and the Nocturnal City by the potent forces that threaten to undo them. In each case, the city appears as a vulnerable construct plagued by New World ills. These ills, as we have seen, find natural and organic expression in the philosophical disposition, lexicon, and aesthetic of the Baroque. Freyle, Arzáns, Rosas, and Caviedes each "spectacularize" the tensions of their societies in a wholly Baroque idiom, subverting the city without recourse to subversion on literary grounds. That the Baroque purveyed by absolutist Spain as a means of maintaining its hegemony has proven equally enabling for texts designed not to disparage but to celebrate the New World places an ironic spin on the final caveat emptor of the "Coloquio"–which in this light could read, "*Seller* beware"–and prompts a final assessment of Leonard's *Baroque Times in Old Mexico.*

Incongruous as it may sound, Leonard's conception of the Baroque Age communes with Caviedes's City of the Plague. Caviedes discerns a resistance to novelty in his stagnant milieu: "Cosa nueva en esta edad/difícilmente lo apruebo:/lo ya dicho hacerlo nuevo/es sólo la novedad" (Poem 151, 329) ("Something new in our time/that with difficulty do I approve:/to make new what has already been said/is the only development"). Leonard all too similarly sees the Baroque as an intellectual disease in view of its

> tendency to shift from content to form, from ideas to details, to give new sanction to dogmas, to avoid issues, and to substitute subtlety of language for subtlety of thought; it served to repress rather than liberate the human spirit, and to divert by spectacles, by overstatement, and by excessive ornamentation. Such, in essence, was the spirit of the so-called "Baroque Age" as manifested in the Hispanic world. (1959, 28)

Caviedes satirizes a Baroque spectacle and leaves no doubt as to the diseased nature of his Baroque city. Leonard again devalues the spectacles of the Baroque state, saying (with some truth) that the *criollo* "often frittered away his talents on pageant-like ceremonies, ceremonious functions, and versified panegyrics designed to flatter its vanity" (1959, 33). In sum, as Kathleen Ross has noted with her customary perspicacity (1993; 1994), Leonard displays a not inconsiderable discomfort, or, as our discussion would have it, dis-ease, with the Baroque. Much as he revives and verbally reinvigorates the "forgotten century," Leonard tends to see it as a stepping stone to the Enlightenment that purged it, as an age redeemed in intellectual terms by whatever shards of Enlightenment thinking can be teased out of Sigüenza's works or Sor Juana's, or–were Leonard to have extended his framework to Lima–Caviedes's. Leonard's tutelary figure of Sigüenza straddles Renaissance humanism and the Enlightenment (1959, 213), curiously discounting, as does *Baroque Times* in the ways just mentioned, the very era that both spawned the Mexican writer and, as my discussion hopes to have established, provided him and others with efficacious tools.

The author of the present essay, together surely with many other colonial era scholars, in any case owes to Leonard her first awakening to the seventeenth century. My essay owes to *Baroque Times*, among many things, its primary focus on Baroque spectacles and *criollo* consciousness, two phenomena that Leonard largely views as inimical but that, as I have shown, can be intimately enmeshed. Especially when instrumentalized by literary works and aligned with the aesthetic of amazement that it is engineered to inspire, the redimensionalized spectacle acquires a contestatory potency, a destabilizing energy that assumes a different guise in each cityscape. Even the most official spectacle thus imparts a carnivalesque charge. The neo-Romantic Leonard, who has led us into the exorbitant world of the colonial Baroque, may well have been arrested by its very spectacularity. When we now focus our sights on the spectacular literary and social practices of the several centers of the viceregal New World, we are newly compelled by the productivity that *Baroque Times*, the colonial Baroque, and spectacle each in its own way promotes, by the manner in which each surreptitiously voices the vital mobility that managed to underwrite the period of colonial stabilization or forgotten century on its own Baroque terms.

Works Cited

Achury Valenzuela, Darío. 1979. "Prólogo." *El Carnero.* By Juan Rodríguez Freyle. Caracas: Ayacucho. ix–lxxxv.

Acosta, Leonardo. 1972. "El barroco americano y la ideología colonialista." *Unión* (Havana) 11.2–3: 30–63.

——. 1984. *El barroco de Indias y otros ensayos.* Havana: Casa de las Américas.

Anderson, Benedict. 1983. *Imagined Communities: Reflections on the Origin and Spread of Nationalism.* London: Verso.

Arzáns de Orsúa y Vela, Bartolomé. 1965. *Historia de la villa imperial de Potosí.* Eds. Lewis Hanke and Gunnar Mendoza. 3 vols. Providence: Brown University Press.

——. 1975. *Tales of Potosí.* Ed. and Introduction by R.C. Padden. Trans. Frances M. López-Morillas. Providence: Brown University Press.

Bakhtin, Mikhail. 1984. *Rabelais and His World.* Trans. Hélène Iswolsky. Bloomington: Indiana University Press.

Balbuena, Bernardo de. 1985. *La grandeza mexicana y compendio apologético en alabanza de la poesía.* Mexico City: Porrúa.

Barrionuevo, Jerónimo de. 1968. *Avisos (1654–1658).* Biblioteca de Autores Españoles. Vol. 221. Madrid: Atlas.

Becco, Horacio Jorge, ed. 1990. *Poesía colonial hispanoamericana.* Caracas: Ayacucho.

Beverley, John. 1987. *Del Lazarillo al Sandinismo: Estudios sobre la función ideológica de la literatura española e hispanoamericana.* Minneapolis: The Prisma Institute.

——. 1992. "Nuevas vacilaciones sobre el barroco." *Crítica y descolonización: El sujeto colonial en la cultura latinoamericana.* Eds. Beatriz González Stephan and Lúcia Helena Costigan. Caracas: Academia Nacional de la Historia. 289–301.

Brading, D[avid] A. 1991. *The First America: The Spanish Monarchy, Creole Patriots, and the Liberal State 1492–1867.* Cambridge: Cambridge University Press.

Cabrera Infante, Guillermo. 1967. *Tres tristes tigres.* Barcelona: Seix Barral.

Chang-Rodríguez, Raquel. 1982. *Violencia y subversión en la prosa colonial hispanoamericana, siglos XVI y XVII.* Madrid: Porrúa Turanzas.

Cobo, Bernabé. 1956. *Fundación de Lima.* Obras. Madrid: Atlas. 2: 279–460.

Concha, Jaime. 1976. "La literatura colonial Hispano-Americana: Problemas e hipótesis." *Neohelicon* 4.12: 31–50.

Díez Borque, José María. 1985. "Relaciones de teatro y fiesta en el Barroco español." *Teatro y fiesta en el barroco: España e Iberoamérica.* Ed. José María Díez-Borque. Sevilla: Ediciones del Serbal. 11–40.

Domínguez Camargo, Hernando. 1960. *Obras.* Ed. Rafael Torres Quintero. Bogota: Instituto Caro y Cuervo.

Espinosa Medrano, Juan de. 1982. *Apologético.* Trans. Rafael Blanco Varela. Ed. Augusto Tamayo Vargas. Caracas: Ayacucho.

Foster, George M. 1960. *Culture and Conquest: America's Spanish Heritage.* New York: Wenner-Gren Foundation for Anthropological Research.

Gage, Thomas. 1958. *Thomas Gage's Travels in the New World.* Ed. J. Eric S. Thompson. Norman: University of Oklahoma Press.

García Pabón, Leonardo. 1992. "Pensamiento andino y tradición historiográfica americana en la f(ec)undación de la ciudad colonial: *La historia de Potosí* de Bartolomé Arzáns (1676–1736)." *Crítica y descolonización: El sujeto colonial en la cultura latinoamericana.* Eds. Beatriz González Stephan and Lúcia Helena Costigan. Caracas: Academia Nacional de la Historia. 493–513.

———. 1995. "Indios, criollos y fiesta barroca en la *Historia de Potosí* de Bartolomé Arzáns." *Revista Iberoamericana* 61.172–73: 423–39.

Gimbernat de González, Ester. 1980. "Mapas y texto: Para una estrategia del poder." MLN 95: 388–99.

Girard, René. 1978. *'To Double Business Bound': Essays on Literature, Mimesis and Anthropology.* Baltimore: Johns Hopkins University Press.

González Echevarría, Roberto. 1990. *Myth and Archive: A Theory of Latin American Narrative.* Cambridge: Cambridge University Press.

———. 1993. *Celestina's Brood: Continuities of the Baroque in Spanish and Latin American Literature.* Durham: Duke University Press.

———. 1996. "Colonial Lyric." *The Cambridge History of Latin American Literature.* Eds. Roberto González Echevarría and Enrique Pupo-Walker. Cambridge: Cambridge University Press. 1: 191–230.

Greenblatt, Stephen. 1991. *Marvelous Possessions: The Wonder of the New World.* Chicago: University of Chicago Press.

Hanke, Lewis. 1956. *The Imperial City of Potosí: An Unwritten Chapter in the History of Spanish America.* The Hague: Martinus Nijhoff.

———. 1965a. *Bartolomé Arzáns de Orsúa y Vela's History of Potosí.* Providence: Brown University Press.

———. 1965b. "El otro tesoro de las Indias: Bartolomé Arzáns de Orsúa y Vela y su *Historia de la villa imperial de Potosí.*" *Actas del Segundo Congreso Internacional de Hispanistas.* Eds. Jaime Sánchez Romeralo and Norbert Poulussen. Nijmegen, Netherlands: The Spanish Institute of the University of Nijmegan. 51–72.

Johnson, Julie Greer. 1993. *Satire in Colonial Spanish America: Turning the New World Upside-Down.* Austin: University of Texas Press.

Juana Inés de la Cruz, Sor. 1951–1957. *Obras completas.* Eds. Alfonso Méndez Plancarte and Alberto G. Salceda. Vol. 1: *Lírica personal;* Vol. 4: *Comedias, Sainetes y Prosa.* 4 vols. Mexico City: Fondo de Cultura Económica.

Lafaye, Jacques. 1976. *Quetzalcóatl and Guadalupe: The Formation of Mexican National Consciousness,* 1531–1813. Trans. Benjamin Keen. Chicago: University of Chicago Press.

Lavrin, Asunción. 1996. "Viceregal Culture." *The Cambridge History of Latin American Literature.* Eds. Roberto González Echevarría and Enrique Pupo-Walker. Cambridge: Cambridge University Press. 1: 286–335.

León Pinelo, Antonio de. 1943. *El Paraíso en el Nuevo Mundo.* 2 vols. Ed. Raúl Porras Barrenechea. Lima: Comité del IV Centenario del Descubrimiento de Amazonas.

Leonard, Irving A. 1929. *Don Carlos de Sigüenza y Góngora, A Mexican Savant of the Seventeenth Century.* Berkeley: University of California Press.

———. 1949. *Books of the Brave.* Cambridge: Harvard University Press.

———. 1959. *Baroque Times in Old Mexico: Seventeenth-Century Persons, Places, and Practices.* Ann Arbor: University of Michigan Press.

Lezama Lima, José. 1969. *La expresión americana.* Santiago de Chile: Editorial Universitaria.

Luciani, Frederick. 1996. "Spanish American Theatre of the Colonial Period." *The Cambridge History of Latin American Literature.* Eds. Roberto González Echevarría and Enrique Pupo-Walker. Cambridge: Cambridge University Press. 1: 260–85.

Lynch, John. 1981. *Spain under the Habsburgs.* Vol. 2. 2nd ed. New York: New York University Press.

Maravall, José Antonio. 1986. *Culture of the Baroque: Analysis of a Historical Structure.* Trans. Terry Cochran. Minneapolis: University of Minnesota Press.

Merrim, Stephanie. 1996. "The First Fifty Years of Hispanic New World Historiography: The Caribbean, Mexico, and Central America." *The Cambridge History of Latin American Literature.* Eds. Roberto González Echevarría and Enrique Pupo-Walker. Cambridge: Cambridge University Press. 1: 58–100.

———. 1999. *Early Modern Women's Writing and Sor Juana Inés de la Cruz.* Nashville: Vanderbilt University Press.

———, ed. 1991. *Feminist Perspectives on Sor Juana Inés de la Cruz.* Detroit: Wayne State University Press.

Moraña, Mabel. 1994. "Introducción." *Relecturas del Barroco de Indias.* Ed. Mabel Moraña. Hanover: Ediciones del Norte. i–xii.

Morse, Richard. 1984. "The Urban Development of Colonial Spanish America." *The Cambridge History of Latin America.* Ed. Leslie Bethell. Cambridge: Cambridge University Press. 2: 67–104.

Mugaburu, Josephe, and Francisco Mugaburu. 1975. *Chronicle of Colonial Lima: The Diary of Josephe and Francisco Mugaburu,* 1640–1697. Trans. and ed. Robert Ryal Miller. Norman: University of Oklahoma Press.

Padden, R. C. 1975. "Editor's Introduction." *Tales of Potosí.* Ed. R. C. Padden. Trans. Frances M. López-Morillas. Providence: Brown University Press. x–xxxvi.

Paz, Octavio. 1957. *Las peras del olmo.* Mexico City: Impr. Universitaria.

———. 1976. "Foreword: The Flight of Quetzalcóatl and the Quest for Legitimacy." *Quetzalcóatl and Guadalupe: The Formation of Mexican National Consciousness,* 1531–1813. By Jacques Lafaye. Trans. Benjamin Keen. Chicago: University of Chicago Press. ix–xxii.

———. 1982. *Sor Juana Inés de la Cruz, o, Las trampas de la fe.* Barcelona: Seix Barral.

———. 1988. *Sor Juana, or, The Traps of Faith.* Trans. Margaret Sayers Peden. Cambridge: Harvard University Press.

Picón-Salas, Mariano. 1975 [1944]. *De la Conquista a la Independencia: Tres siglos de historia cultural hispanoamericana.* Mexico City: Fondo de Cultura Económica.

Pizan, Christine de. 1982. *The Book of the City of Ladies.* Trans. Earl Jeffrey Richards. New York: Persea.

Pupo-Walker, Enrique. 1982. *La vocación literaria del pensamiento histórico en América.* Madrid: Gredos.

Rama, Ángel. 1983. "Fundación del manierismo hispanoamericano por Bernardo de Balbuena." *University of Dayton Review* 16.2: 13–22.

———. 1984. *La ciudad letrada.* Hanover: Ediciones del Norte.

Reyes, Alfonso. 1948. *Letras de la Nueva España.* Mexico City: Fondo de Cultura Económica.

Ricard, Robert. 1947. *La conquista espiritual de México.* Trans. Angel María Garibay K. Mexico City: Jus.

Robles, Antonio de. 1946. *Diario de sucesos notables*. 3 vols. Ed. Antonio Castro Leal. Mexico City: Porrúa.

Rodríguez Fernández, Mario. 1961. "El tópico de la alabanza en la poesía barroca americana." *Atenea* 143.393: 202–25.

Rodríguez Freyle, Juan. 1979. *El Carnero*. Ed. Darío Achury Valenzuela. Caracas: Ayacucho.

Roggiano, Alfredo. "Para una teoría de un Barroco hispanoamericano." *Relecturas del Barroco de Indias*. Ed. Mabel Moraña. Hanover: Ediciones del Norte. 1–16.

Romero, José Luis. 1976. *Latinoamérica: Las ciudades y las ideas*. Mexico City: Siglo Veintiuno.

Rosas de Oquendo, Mateo. 1990. *Sátira hecha por Mateo Rosas de Oquendo a las cosas que pasan en el Pirú, año de 1598*. Ed. Pedro Lasarrte. Madison: The Hispanic Seminary of Medieval Studies.

Ross, Kathleen. 1993. *The Baroque Narrative of Carlos de Sigüenza y Góngora: A New World Paradise*. New York: Cambridge University Press.

——. 1994. "Carlos de Sigüenza y Góngora y la cultura del Barroco hispanoamericano." *Relecturas del Barroco de Indias*. Ed. Mabel Moraña. Hanover: Ediciones del Norte. 223–43.

——. 1996. "Historians of the Conquest and Colonization of the New World: 1550–1620." *The Cambridge History of Latin American Literature*. Eds. Roberto González Echevarría and Enrique Pupo-Walker. Cambridge: Cambridge University Press. 1:101–42.

——. 1992. *Estudios de literatura hispanoamericana: Sor Juana Inés de la Cruz y otros poetas barrocos de la colonia*. Barcelona: PPU.

Sabat de Rivers, Georgina. 1983. "El *Neptuno* de Sor Juana: Fiesta barroca y programa político." *University of Dayton Review* 16.2: 63–73.

Sacido Romero, Alberto. 1992. "La ambigüedad genérica de los *Infortunios de Alonso Ramírez* como producto de la dialéctia entre discurso oral y discurso escrito." *Bulletin Hispanique* 94.1: 119–39.

Santiago-Díaz, Eleuterio. 1992. "*Infortunios de Alonso Ramírez* Texto enciclopédico de la Ciudad letrada." Diss. Brown University.

Schons, Dorothy. 1939. "The Influence of Góngora on Mexican Literature During the Seventeenth Century." *Hispanic Review* 6 (Jan.): 22–34.

Sigüenza y Góngora, Carlos de. 1945. *Glorias de Querétaro*. Querétaro: Ediciones Cimatario.

——. 1945. *Triunfo parténico*. Mexico City: Ediciones Xochitl.

——. 1984a. *Los infortunios de Alonso Ramírez*. Eds. J. S. Cummins and Alan Soons. London: Tamesis.

——. 1984b. *Teatro de virtudes políticas que constituyen a un Príncipe. Seis obras*. Ed. William G. Bryant. Prologue by Irving A. Leonard. Caracas: Ayacucho.

——. 1995. *Paraíso Occidental*. Ed. Margarita Peña. Mexico City: Cien de México.

Simpson, Lesley B. 1963. "Foreword." *Land and Society in Colonial Mexico: The Great Hacienda*. By François Chevalier. Trans. Alvin Eustis. Berkeley: University of California Press. v–ix.

TePaske, John J. 1983. "An Interview with Irving A. Leonard." *Hispanic American Historical Review* 63.2: 233–53.

—— and Herbert S. Klein. 1981. "The Seventeenth-Century Crisis in New Spain: Myth or Reality." *Past and Present* 90: 116–35.

Torquemada, Juan de. 1969. *Monarquía indiana*. Mexico City: Porrúa.

Valle y Caviedes, Juan del. 1984. *Obra completa*. Ed. and Prologue by Daniel Reedy. Caracas: Ayacucho.

Van Horne, John. 1940. *Bernardo de Balbuena: Biografía y crítica*. Guadalajara: Font.

Vidal, Hernán. 1985. *Socio-historia de la literatura colonial hispanoamericana: Tres lecturas orgánicas*. Minneapolis: Institute for the Study of Ideologies and Literature.

Yo, la peor de todas. 1990. Dir. María Luisa Bemberg. Argentina.

CHAPTER 4

THE DISCOURSE OF MELANCHOLY IN A CULTURE OF LOSS

Maria Consuelo Cunha Campos

The city of Salvador, in Bahia–situated on a hill, in an area of many springs, protected by forts and embedded between the port and plantations, many of which were the size of some of the European kingdoms of the time–became the seat of the colonial government in the seventeenth century and is the oldest cultural center in Brazil. This was the period of the single-crop sugar plantations, which were responsible for the economic development of the region. As capital of Portuguese America, colonial Salvador spread in an unruly fashion between the sea, the hill, and the swamp, without any previous planning–in that sense, quite unlike other capitals-to-be of the Brazilian Republic in the twentieth century such as Belo Horizonte and Brasília. Many Portuguese who were driven out of the metropolis flocked to Salvador, lured by the possibility of quickly acquiring either wealth and a life of luxury in the tropics or a life free from the moral restrictions of the Counter-Reformation in the metropolis. In the Portuguese imagination, Colonial Brazil was a means for transforming unsuccessful men into plantation owners and even nobles. A century earlier, cattle and the first sugar cane plants had been brought from São Vicente, in Cape Verde, to Brazil, where both flourished. The Bahian climate was appropriate for sugar cane, which became, for this very reason, its main source of wealth and made possible the opulent lifestyle of the lords of the sugar mills. As rich men, they spent money like petty kings in their dominions and gradually formed a kind of rural pseudo-aristocracy, one rather jealous of its blood relations; for this reason they avoided marrying outside their peer group (despite furtive male relations with women from other ethnic groups). The life of these sugar mill owners therefore was most notable for its greed, ambition, and sensuality.

Salvador was founded by Tomé de Sousa in 1549, and was strategically located in a place from which one could see the Atlantic Ocean; from the beginning, it displayed the features of an untamed city, where houses, churches, and chapels were built randomly with no urban plan along its narrow, winding, dirty streets, which lacked water, sewage systems, and lighting. It was the dwelling place of a multi-racial and culturally heterogeneous population: Blacks, *mestizos*, Indians, Portuguese, Jews, gypsies, and Moors. As administrative seat, Colonial Salvador was the home of the Governor General, the highest position in the local hierarchy, who, to reinforce his authority, also had a military guard and a corps of musketeers and riflemen. The complex Portuguese colonial administrative bureaucracy required scriveners, notaries, investigators, accountants, treasurers, warehouse keepers, officers, justices of the peace, and bailiffs. All of these (generally underpaid) co-inhabited the city along with members of the Roman Catholic clergy–canons, chaplains, curates, friars, monks, priests–and members of the municipal government–alderman, judges, solicitors, and inspectors.

Local trade, in which Jews predominated, was carried out not only in shops and warehouses, but also by travelling salesmen and peddlers. There were also workers from the necessary trades: Saddlers, colliers, bricklayers, lumbermen, carpenters, blacksmiths, tailors, bleeders, apothecaries, masons, and clockmakers, among others. Vendors traveled on burros in pack trains into the heart of the backlands, reaching the sugar mills in the Recôncavo region, where there was a considerable market for manufactured goods. Labor was gender divided: Women were lace-makers, embroiderers, seamstresses, confectioners, bakers, midwives, and healers.

Despite the colonizers' attempts to control religious practices, African religions, as well as witchcraft and superstition, abounded in multi-racial and multicultural Salvador. Slavery, the sugar crop, and the master's house–a kind of transposed late-European medieval castle–were emblematic of the local power relations. Small wares and luxury goods were brought from Portugal. This kind of commerce was maintained with every kind of vessel known at the time: Galleons and galliots, hookers, caravels, brigantines, among others. Canoes were used to cross short distances, along the shore or up and down rivers, between sugar mills. In short, water travel was the most common means of transportation, and the Atlantic coast was the usual route between plantations.

Private space was not characterized by luxury; in contrast to the magnificence of religious festivals, houses had only a few pieces of furniture. Ostentatious celebrations by the colonial authorities were the result of budget surpluses in the growing colonial society. Salvador, with its violent streets, alleys, and squares, where thieves ruled, suffered an epidemic of late-night robberies and assaults. A person with any possessions moved at his own risk when alone in the streets. The colonial elite, who lived on isolated rural properties like veritable autocrats, were occasionally visited by traveling salesmen to supply them with imported goods and, of course, additional supplies of staple goods when it was necessary. Besides native fruits–the mango, *mangaba, cajá, jabuticaba,* passion fruit, cashew fruit–they could also get wine from Madeira and the Canary Islands, as well as various kinds of meat, seafood from the Bay of All Saints, and manioc flour, a staple item from the local cuisine.

The younger generation from the colonial elite went to Salvador for education, usually attending Jesuit schools, and went on to higher education in Portugal since there were no colleges in Brazil at the time. Thus it is that a man from the local ruling class could go from the sugar-growing Recôncavo area to the capital, and from there to Coimbra and Lisbon. Women from the same social levels were educated at home. Under their mother's guidance, and guarded from the eyes of strangers by closed windows and locked doors, the daughters of the sugar aristocracy formed a world of mantillas and were generally married very young or went into colonial religious seclusion.

This seventeenth-century society, strongly hierarchical and repressed, found relief from such pressures mainly through festivals, during which the upper class consorted socially with inferiors. The black population in Salvador and in the plantations was so large that Bahia was referred to as a New Guinea. The white minority of slave owners, originally from distant and largely exhausted European agricultural lands, spread over the nearly boundless colonial territory and benefited from the continuous work of black slaves from the Nau, Hausa, Gege, and Sudanese areas of West Africa. This was the Bahia de São Salvador that, in 1616, the future Jesuit Antônio Vieira (1608–1697), author of the most important Baroque prose in Brazil, encountered with his family (for he was still a boy). His religious training took place in the colony, where he was ordained a Roman Catholic priest and eventually became the first overseas intellectual and writer from Portugal to gain an international reputation.

In 1641, when the Portuguese monarchy was restored after a period of Spanish domination (1580–1641), Antônio Vieira returned to Portugal. He was part of a cortege that accompanied the king, Dom João IV, and became preacher of the Royal Chapel in Lisbon, capital of the Portuguese empire. Vieira was later appointed ambassador, and was sent twice to France as well as to Holland and Rome. Upon his return to Brazil as a missionary, Father Vieira went to Maranhão but was later banished because of disagreements with the estate rulers regarding the enslavement of Native Americans. After being sent back to Lisbon, he was exiled to Oporto and was then imprisoned for a time by the Inquisition in Coimbra. In his travels, Vieira went to Rome, where he preached his sermons both in Portuguese and in Italian, preaching even to Queen Kristina, who had converted to Roman Catholicism and abdicated the throne of Sweden, and for whom Vieira acted as confessor. Vieira spent the last years of his life in Salvador, as Jesuit Inspector General. No other intellectual in seventeenth-century Colonial Brazil achieved the influence of Vieira; as a royal counselor, he reached the top positions of power in Portugal; Vieira was also unique in the Portuguese colonial empire for his defense of the natives and the Jews, who had been marginalized by Lisbon. In *Vieira e a visão trágica do barroco* [1986; Vieira and the Tragic Vision of the Baroque], Luís Palacin defends the provocative thesis that the Jesuit represented the highest moral consciousness possible at the time with regard to marginalized groups. This social consciousness represented the application of attainable knowledge by the erudite Jesuit to the question of basic justice in the colonial system and its view of the Other, keeping in mind the various cultural constraints that would have shaped his view. In fact, like no one else at his time, Vieira analyzed the ethical and political predicaments of the colonialist system, which he nevertheless did not condemn but rather tried to reform. He turned into a kind of millennary prophet of a Portuguese empire to come, along the lines of the Sebastian myth that had such an impact on the Portuguese.

Besides being a preacher, Vieira was one of the most astute politicians of his time, and the vast experience he acquired in Europe made him stand out among the colonials. In his work, Vieira strongly and passionately denounced illegal transactions and the injustices committed by colonial authorities. His sermons established a comparison between Roman imperialism in antiquity and Portuguese imperialism in his own time. Based on this comparison, Vieira could understand the fundamental role played by geographical distance in an entirely new context. The ocean that separated the two continents effectively made a difference; the Portuguese overseas empire gradually reached, first, islands and archipelagos on the route to Africa, and, later, India, Timor, and China. Meanwhile, as the Portuguese advanced on three eastern continents, they also moved toward the west and reached a fourth continent, the American, and from the coast they penetrated inland into the area that would later form Brazil. The Roman Empire, in its turn, originated in the Italian peninsula with the conquest of Latium and spread along the Mediterranean, romanizing as it went; it gradually incorporated the north of Africa and the Middle East, as well as southern Europe, but all its territory could be reached by the Mediterranean or by land. The ocean separating Brazil from Portugal, however, only aggravated the problems caused by distance, because the further away metropolitan government was from the colony, the greater the need for local, subordinate authorities to make decisions without consulting the metropolis. This fact contributed to a feeling of superiority and to corruption in Brazil, which, in Vieira's view, was an intrinsic part of colonialism.

In his large and varied production, which included exegeses, sermons, prophecies, epistles, and political reports, Vieira not only revealed significant political contradictions but also expressed his personal preference for mercantilism, still in its infancy. Commerce should be the true independent variable in developing a nation's wealth, he felt. Vieira witnessed the multiplication of colonialist powers in Europe, and later would also live to see the decline of the Portuguese Empire. Holland turned into a rival power, first of Spain, under whose rule Portugal found itself, and then in the seventeenth century of Portugal itself, especially in Brazil's Northeast during the sugar cane conflicts. While the seventeenth-century discoveries glorified the Portuguese nation, the somber misery that permeates the last cantos of Camões' epic poem then came over the metropolis. When the Spanish domination ceased and the monarchy was restored in Portugal, a dispute over continental hegemony between the colonialist powers in Europe was well under way, played against a weakened Christianity in the throes of the Catholic Counter-Reformation, in which the Vatican opposed both Reformists and Protestants. In this new European political order, Portugal became a peripheral, second-order colonial metropolis that depended on its Empire and on European alliances for its survival. The Portuguese decline, and the dream of a return to ancient grandeur, was precisely the key question for Vieira. Messianic and prophetic, he clashed with the Inquisition because of his belief in the return of the already deceased monarch Dom João IV. Although, on the one hand, his prediction of a fifth Portuguese Empire did not occur, on the other hand, he tacitly and with a sense of vision advocated the end of colonialism, although he never lived to see it himself. He proposed that everything produced by the area of the colonial empire called Bahia should be left there for its own benefit and not be sent back to Portugal, and also that anything taken from Brazil should be of concomitant benefit to Brazil.

The discovery of the gold mines in the eighteenth century can be traced in Vieira's discourse. Long before the discovery of gold in Tripuí that set off the gold rush to the *minas gerais* (general mines), Vieira had already pointed out the chance of finding precious metals in Brazil. In 1665, the news was brought to Belém that an expedition in search of such metals had failed. Vieira, who was in Belém at the time, preached to the disappointed population, claiming that what they thought to be a misfortune was in reality a blessing for the colony. According to Vieira, had gold been discovered, Portugal would have undoubtedly charged more taxes, besides putting into practice other metropolitan measures to ensure the extraction, transportation, and shipment of the goods overseas. Consequently, this would have turned plantation owners into mere administrators. Moreover, the Portuguese kingdom itself, on the periphery of European geopolitics, would turn into a mere conveyer of wealth to the true hegemonic centers of Europe. Alfredo Bosi acutely notes that Father Antônio Vieira not only understood the irreversible nature of the *máquina mercante* (mercantile machine)–a term borrowed from Gregório de Matos (1633?–1696), a Baroque poet of Vieira's time–but also, as a consequence, put his best efforts into turning mercantilism into an asset for Portugal in the dispute for dominance among the new colonial empires of Europe. Bosi places the Jesuit "no centro nervoso da política colonial do tempo" (120) ("at the heart of colonial politics of the time"); he was responsible for the creation of a Portuguese *Companhia das Indias Ocidentais* (Company of the West Indies), mainly with Portuguese Jewish funds. Despite the strong opposition on the part of the Portuguese Inquisition, the *Companhia* began its operations in 1649. The first fleet departed from the Tagus River, thus launching a regular maritime connection between Lisbon and the colonial ports of Bahia and Rio de Janeiro.

One can readily see that the strategic models of Portugal's rivals in the colonial enterprise, Holland and England, were being carefully studied by the royal counselor. However, in a society like the Portuguese in the seventeenth century, where bourgeois thought was not yet pervasive–contrary to what was going on in the Protestant kingdoms–Vieira found an environment of suspicion and even of open hostility toward his ideas. Consequently, it was up to him to persuade not only the monarch, but also the noblemen, men of letters, and theologians, and, of course, to overcome the opposition of the Portuguese Inquisition. In order to achieve this goal, Vieira wrote the Sermon of São Roque. Bosi refers to this as a "singular simbiose de alegoria bíblico-cristã e pensamento mercantil" (120) ("unique symbiosis of biblical-Christian allegory and mercantile thought"). The sermon begins with the story of St. Roch, a French nobleman, and his return from Italy to France at the time that a war was being fought between the two countries. St. Roch was not recognized by his fellow countrymen and was taken to be a spy; he was imprisoned and indicted on the basis of a series of alleged charges against him. The facts, however, came to the surface later and redeemed him. St. Roch thus went from prison to a position of providential helper to his people.

Basing this sermon on this hagiography, Vieira then builds a network of verbal analogies. He reproaches Portugal for its mistrust of the Jews and of Jewish capital, motivating the country to accept this badly needed support, and thus check its anti-mercantile and anti-Semitic prejudices. Yet, colonialist interests were not always uppermost in the concerns of Vieira's sermons. In the famous Epiphany Sermon, for instance, he sided with the Maranhão Indians against colonists who wanted to enslave them for the benefit of the mercantile enterprise. Vieira preached this sermon in Portugal, in the royal chapel itself, in the presence of the widowed queen Dona Luísa, after his expulsion from Maranhão and subsequent return to Portugal. With this sermon, Vieira tried to win the support of the widowed queen and of the crown prince for the return of the Jesuits to Maranhão, where he felt autonomous missions ought to be established, independent of pro-slavery colonists. Bosi considers this sermon "exemplar como xadrez de conflitos sociais, dados os interesses em jogo, obrigando o discurso ora a avançar até posições extremas, ora a compor

uma linguagem de compromisso" (134) ("an illustration of social conflicts, given the interests at stake, forcing discourse to advance at times to radical positions, at other times to compose a language of commitment").

In effect, the condemnation of Indian slavery could also be found in other pontifical documents, including the 1537 *Sublimis Deus* edict, of Pope Paul III; at this time, there was a debate going on in Spain about the nature of Native Americans. On the other hand, in Vieira's time there was already a political engagement between colonists and Jesuits, with the missionaries accompanying the settlers on their journeys inland. As a result, the year was divided between catechism with the Jesuits and field work in the service of colonizers. The Indians had to work in the fields for six months, and for the rest of the year could stay in their villages and receive religious instruction. Yet, as agricultural work prospered, the Indians inevitably had to dedicate more and more time to it, and consequently break the original pact and neglect Jesuit interests. As the Jesuits began to rebel against this, they were driven from Maranhão. Bosi also argues that "o pacto entre o colono e o jesuíta mostra a sua precariedade" (137) ("the pact between colonists and Jesuits emphasizes its very precariousness"), thus leading to a conflict between the two in the context of unequal powers, the temporal and spiritual, invested in them.

Father Antônio Vieira himself no longer had such advantages as he had enjoyed during Dom João IV's life. While Portugal was becoming more and more secularized–a 1663 law imposed a strict separation between the powers–Vieira suffered under the Inquisition and was forbidden to preach in Portuguese territory because of his prophecies. His concern was not only Indian slavery; African slavery was also the topic of several of his sermons. He was also especially devoted to the praying of the rosary. This was probably because many religious brotherhoods were devoted to the rosary at the time; brotherhoods in Bahia and Pernambuco were primarily made up of Africans and their descendants. His most formidable enemy, however, was the racism that dominated Bahia. Racial segregation was conspicuous. Some other brotherhoods welcomed only white people; still others were made up exclusively of *mestizos*.

Father Vieira's sermons on the topic of race were also preached to slaves themselves, as was the case of Sermon XIV of the Rosary, delivered in 1633 on a Bahian sugar plantation. He blamed the greed of slave owners for the physical suffering of the slaves and for the plundering of the fruits of their labor, and he also reflected upon the origin of the inequality among people that was the basis of any society of masters and slaves. From his religious point of view, Vieira referred to the original Fall, to a deviation from the Creator's will, but his thoughts on slavery must be taken in the context of his times. In another sermon, he spoke of a theory of compensation for the sacrifice of slaves, making possible a providential approach to the institution within the colonialist context of slavery, and thus legitimizing it, even if indirectly, in favor of the masters' interests. How could human beings, originally created by God as equals, come to such inequality? In Sermon XXVII he spoke of African enslavement as God's own will, so that the Africans could become Christians. From the African coast as point of departure to America as point of arrival, Africans were in fact journeying toward the redemption of their souls: Had they stayed in their continent of origin, they would have remained non-Christians, whether animist or Muslim.

Luís Palacin points out the revival of Counter-Reformation authoritarianism during the Portuguese crisis, a point that helps to explain some of the contradictions in Vieira. According to Palacin, "estes reflexos da crise, um tanto atenuados nos países em ascensão onde fermentava a afirmação burguesa e capitalista, como Holanda e Inglaterra, foram particularmente rigorosos nos países em processo de irremediável decadência como Portugal" (59) ("these consequences of the economic crisis, which were somewhat weakened in countries where capitalist bourgeoisie was gaining ground, like Holland and England, were especially severe in countries that were undergoing a process of political decadence, like Portugal"). Not only was Portugal declining, but a sharp divide had also been developing since the Restoration between an aristocratic state structure and its markedly mercantile orientation; values historically associated with the nobility were incontestable obstacles in the ongoing dispute for colonialist hegemony and the struggle against political and economic decline. The contempt for work and for mercantile agreements, and the preference for ostentation and idleness, are good examples of this clash in values between the aristocracy and the new bourgeoisie.

Vieira's discourse conveys the deep, unresolved opposition between a desire for modernization and the basic acceptance of conservative thought. This can be verified again in his sermons, specifically the Sermon for the Success of Portuguese Arms against Holland, written under the threat of a Dutch invasion in Bahia: "A estratégia do texto consistirá em usar do discurso profético em defesa e justificativa de um tipo de colonialismo (português, país católico) ameaçado por outro (holandês, país protestante) sem colocar em jogo a origem (a colonização européia)" (M. Campos, 58) ("The text's strategy was to use a prophetic discourse to defend and account for one kind of colonialism [Portuguese, a Catholic nation] threatened by another [Dutch, a Protestant nation] without putting the origin at stake [European colonization]"). Many of Vieira's sermons that were translated into other European languages had a far-reaching impact during the seventeenth century. Of the numerous ones that were published in Spanish, one had consequences far removed from its original utterance in the Royal Chapel; here, Vieira's specific concern was the "Mandato" sermon on the topic of Christ's perfection. In New Spain this sermon became a target for ecclesiastic politics. The archbishop of Mexico, Aguiar y Seijas (d. 1698), was so taken with the sermon that he ordered that it be reproduced and distributed to the clergy. It was on this sermon that the brilliant Sor Juana Inés de la Cruz (1648–1695) was induced to debate. She wrote the renowned *Carta atenagórica* ("Athenagoric Letter") for private circulation, but it was promptly published without her permission.

Vieira's renown reflected the prestige of the Society of Jesus and the Brazilian Jesuits specifically. As Octavio Paz (1914–1998) wrote: "En México los jesuítas no sólo dominaban la educación superior sino que, a través del arzobispo Francisco Aguiar y Seijas, ejercían una influencia muy profunda en la Iglesia y en el Estado" (1982, 524) ("In Mexico the Jesuits not only dominated higher education but, through Archbishop Francisco Aguiar y Seijas, exercised a very profound influence over Church and state" [1988, 401]). Father Antônio Vieira was indeed much admired by Aguiar y Seijas, to whom he dedicated two volumes of his sermons, published in Madrid in 1675 and 1678; the Archbishop's *Conclusiones a toda la teología* (Conclusions to All Theology), published by the Real y Pontificia Universidade de Mexico in 1683, was dedicated to Vieira as a return favor to the Brazilian Jesuit, then fallen into disfavor in Lisbon. These publications, followed in 1685 by "Heracles Defended," another sermon by Vieira, were praised by Aguiar y Seijas; these facts are seen by Paz as clear indications that, in Sor Juana's letter, the target was not the Jesuit, but the Archbishop of Mexico. Sor Juana's text, therefore, served as a form of attack in the rivalry between two prelates, whose probable cause was the dispute over Mexico's See. The controversy created by the nun's text encompassed, in reality, a fight for power, in which Sor Juana served the purpose of angering Aguiar, who hated and despised women. The Bishop of Puebla betrayed Sor Juana and used her debate with Vieira for his own purposes–to oppose the Archbishop of Mexico.

Father Antônio Vieira himself, however, was never aware of the controversy caused by his "Mandato" sermon; delivered in 1650 in Lisbon, as part of the Royal Chapel series, it was not until forty years later that it became the object of intellectual debate thanks to the Mexican nun. Sor Juana's response was published at the end of 1690 and entitled *Carta atenagórica de la madre Juana Inés de la Cruz, religiosa profesa de velo, y coro en el mui religioso convento de San Jerónimo... Que imprime y dedica a la misma Sor Philotea de la Cruz, su estudiosa aficionada en el convento de la Santisima Trinidad [Letter after the manner of Athenagoras by Mother Juana Inés de la Cruz, member of a religious order in the very religious convent of San Jeronimo... Printed and dedicated to Sor Philotea de la Cruz, her devout scholar in the convent of the Holy Trinity]*. In this text Sor Juana worked out a criticism of the Jesuits' theological argument, which was to cost her dearly. In the beginning of the text, Juana emphasizes her condition as a woman, a fact that puts her at a disadvantage in relation to the Jesuit preacher. The commentary on Sor Juana's text by Sor Philotea–a transparent disguise of Manuel Fernández de Santa Cruz (1637–1699), Bishop of Puebla, confessor to Sor Juana and enemy of the Archbishop of Mexico–turned the debate away from Vieira's argument on the divine attributes of Christ and redirected the focus to the proper comportment of a religious woman in the service of God. The duplicity of Fernández de Santa Cruz (even 300 years later) ranks as extreme perfidy in the history of colonial New Spain, for Sor Juana had written the Vieira critique only after insistent demands by Fernández de Santa Cruz. She was the victim of entrapment designed to help Fernández de Santa Cruz embarrass his ecclesiastic rival and superior; it was treachery Vieira most likely never knew about. Sor Philotea (i.e., Fernández de Santa Cruz) praised Vieira's sermon on the topic of Christ's perfection, offering duplicitous praise to Juana's criticism only to raise the issue of the appropriateness of intellectual pursuits for a nun. He turned to Saint Paul's teachings on the submission of women, arguing that Juana should give priority to religious duties and prayer over all intellectual concerns. Sor Juana wrote the *Carta atenagórica* as a form of obedience to her confessor (Fernández de Santa Cruz) and under the condition that her text remain unpublished. Nevertheless Fernández de Santa Cruz published it, for his own purposes.

Towards the end of the seventeenth century, Sor Juana's New Spain was going through a social and historical crisis. Sor Juana went through her own personal, intellectual, and psychological crisis as a result of her entrapment; she was forced to choose between her religious state and her intellectual aptitude, within the context of her condition as a woman in an overwhelmingly misogynist society. In the end, she was forced to abandon her writing and give up her library and scientific and musical instruments as penance for her alleged sin of intellectual pride. She died a few years later at the age of forty-seven, a victim of the virulent but unidentified (Matlazahuatl) epidemic that swept through New Spain, which she contracted working in the infirmary.

The *Carta atenagórica* triggered a sharp, impassioned controversy that even crossed the Atlantic. In the wake of this controversy, in 1727, an "Apology for R. P. Antonio Vieira" was published; an Augustinian nun, Sor Margarida Inácia, was the alleged author of this new pamphlet. It was her brother, Luís Gonçalves Pinheiro (d. 1727), who actually wrote the work and hid behind the name of a woman, as Puebla's bishop had done earlier in a different way. The most significant result of the initial Sor Juana–Antonio Vieira debate (at a distance of forty years) was that Sor Juana felt compelled to defend herself and defend women's right to intellectual pursuits. In 1691 she wrote the "Respuesta," a response to Sor Filotea; this text was not only unique to New Spain, but it is one of the most important texts written anywhere in the long history of the struggle for women's rights. In part it was an autobiographical self-defense, but it is much more, for in it she denounced all those who continued to keep women ignorant and offered a powerful rational argument for the human mind as a gift from God that must be used to its fullest for His greater glory. Therefore, to deny women access to writing and intellectual pursuits was a sin against God.

In her article "Freiras no Brasil" ("Nuns in Brazil"), from *História das mulheres no Brasil* (History of Women in Brazil), Maria José Rosado Nunes establishes an interesting parallel between the religious situation of women in the Spanish colonies and women in the Portuguese colony in America. According to Nunes, the founding of convents for women took place in Brazil not only much later, but also much slower than in Spanish America. In 1677, when the first convent was established in Portuguese America, there were already over seventy such institutions in the Spanish colonies, due to economic and political factors and, above all, population density. The founding and maintenance of these convents required a great capital investment. (See also Ch. 33, Volume I, this *History*) Whereas Spanish colonial America produced wealth very early on from agriculture and cattle raising, as well as from gold and silver mines (which created a social class of wealthy aristocrats able to support this kind of enterprise), in Portuguese America, this wealth came much later. The political and social power of the Catholic Church at the time turned the support of this kind of enterprise into an effective means of gaining or maintaining prestige: "Na América portuguesa, a política da Metrópole em relação à economia da Colônia, nos seus primeiros anos, dificultou a criação das condições econômicas necessárias à construção e manutenção dos conventos" (Nunes 483) ("In Portuguese America, metropolitan politics regarding the colonial economy, in its first years, hindered the development of the necessary economic conditions for the construction and maintenance of convents"). This was because

> enquanto a Metrópole espanhola desenvolvia, desde o início, uma política de povoamento com *vistas à formação* de uma colônia permanente, a Coroa portuguesa tinha como objetivo a exploração das riquezas naturais. Quando *essa* política foi mudada e o despovoamento da Colônia passou a ser um problema, a escassez de mulheres brancas foi apresentada como um obstáculo para construção de conventos femininos. (Nunes 484; emphasis mine)

while the Spanish metropolis established, from the beginning, a politics of settlement with *the aim of establishing* a permanent colony, the Portuguese Crown aimed at the exploitation of natural resources. *These* politics were changed and the depopulation of the colony turned into a problem, the scarcity of white women considered an obstacle to the construction of women's convents.

There was, in short, a demographic purpose in prohibiting women's convents. Mixing races and concubinage with Indian and Negro women, without the counterweight of a white, European-descended population, were seen as threats to the Crown's project for settling the colony. Female orphans of the kingdom, especially the poor and those without any dowry, were reproductive, biologically and socially speaking, and were considered more valuable to that end. In this sense, convents would hinder such an aim, since they would remove the fertile female population from their reproductive activity.

In Brazil, however, there were plenty of religious retreats, and "pure blood" was not a requirement for a woman to be accepted into them; new Christians and women of mixed race were allowed to join this deeply diverse and unequal society. Because they were not ecclesiastically established, these houses of retreat did not claim to be such, but they were among the few places where women could learn to read and write. Many aspects (especially the erotic) of these female religious retreats in the colonial period were the themes of the satiric poems of Gregório de Matos. Matos was a contemporary of Father Antônio Vieira; he had a chance to meet the Jesuit and much admired his work. When both were older and living in Salvador, Matos became a kind of counterpoint to Vieira. Bosi sees Matos immersed in a kind of "piccolo mondo," that is, nearly always limited to chronicling Bahian infamies; this clearly put Matos at the opposite end of the spectrum from Vieira, who was an intellectual concerned with the great issues of his time on an international scale.

While the Jesuit preacher realized early on the inevitability of mercantilism, and thus the uselessness of a discourse of melancholy in a culture of loss (given mercantile intrusion into the ports of the Portuguese colony), Gregório de Matos's attitude regarding this issue was precisely the opposite, and his poems reveal his feeling of loss and his longing for the old state of affairs. His sonnet "À Bahia" ["To Bahia"], written in the last quarter of the seventeenth century, shows this:

> Triste Bahia! ó quão dessemelhante
> Estás, e estou do nosso antigo estado!
> Pobre te vejo a ti, tu a mi empenhado,
> Rica te vejo eu já, tu a mi abundante.
>
> A ti tocou-te a máquina mercante,
> Que em tua larga barra tem entrado,
> A mim foi-me trocando, e tem trocado
> Tanto negócio, e tanto negociante.
>
> Deste em dar tanto açúcar excelente
> Pelas drogas inúteis, que abelhuda
> Simples aceitas do sagaz Brichote.
>
> Oh se quisera Deus, que de repente
> Um dia amanheceras tão sisuda
> Que fora de algodão o teu capote!
>
> *(1990a, 333)*

Sad Bahia! how different
You and I are from our old state!
You are now poor, while I am in debt,
But you were once rich, while I enjoyed abundance.

The mercantile machine has changed you,
it has touched your own shores.
Both business and businessmen have
changed me and keep changing me.

You have given so much superb sugar
In exchange for useless drugs, which you
hastily accept from the clever Brichote.

I wish to God that you would suddenly wake up
one day so prudent that your overcoat
were made of cotton!

This poem on the decadence of Bahia also shows his own place in the local social hierarchy. Sad, melancholic, unhappy, miserable, and disgraced, the lyric voice and his Bahia were both victims of the decline of the old state.

At that time, merchant ships from England, France, and Holland brought their luxury merchandise from the Indies and Europe, sailing into the Bay of All Saints. Open in the sense of both territory and morals, Bahia became a victim of the metonymy of mercantilism. In a frenzy of commercial exchange, the Colony was itself "exchanged," changed, altered by a fateful commerce that brought to it only "os européis de um luxo funesto" (Bosi 97) ("the tinsel of a fateful luxury"), which a smart "Brichote" (probably a corruption of "British") imposed on simple-minded Bahia. Gregório de Matos witnessed the mid-century economic crisis, when the price of Brazilian sugar dropped drastically because of Antillean competition. During Matos's childhood and formative years, the sugar plantations had increased and a local aristocracy had been consolidated in the Recôncavo region to the benefit of the plantation owners; during his adulthood, protectionist politics declined "à medida que a economia portuguesa entrava na órbita da Inglaterra" (Bosi 99) ("as the Portuguese economy began to be controlled by England"). During the time of Dom Sebastião of Portugal and Philip II of Spain, when Portugal was under Spanish domination, only ships from the metropolis could cast anchor in Salvador, but when the Bahian port was later opened to ships from other countries, the mercantilist politics practiced by Dom João IV (the same king who protected Vieira) changed the capital of the colony. With this, the poet's family lost the means of official, unrestricted support that they had enjoyed in the first decades of the century.

In this culture of loss–loss of the prosperity of the old state in Bahia, coveted by Holland during the sugar war–Matos and Vieira signify two possible solutions to the uprooted intellectual in Portuguese America: the melancholic and satirical discourse, which turns to the lost past, and the prophetic discourse, which seeks to probe the future to realize its dreams of glory. As intellectuals in the colony, Father Antônio Vieira and the poet Gregório de Matos were two sides of the same Portuguese colonial elite class. In the Jesuit, who came to Brazil as child, one finds the side of those who were either born in Portugal or descended directly from those who were. Vieira returned to Portugal after the Restoration as an adult and cleric. Contrary to most people who returned to Portugal after becoming wealthy, Vieira went back to Portugal as a cleric whose character and professional views were still being formed, and then returned to Brazil where he spent most of his long life as a missionary and preacher, often opposing colonialist interests. The poet, however, exemplified another, more common side of this class: that of the Brazilian born of European parents. Matos left Bahia at the age of sixteen in order to study law in Coimbra, and only returned to Brazil at a very mature age.

Vieira quickly adopted the Eurocentric perspective that continued to prevail in the seventeenth century and went on to fulfill his mission once the power structures were altered from those that existed prior to Iberian unification. The players at that time were the kingdoms disputing colonialist hegemony over the New World. Gregório de Matos, on the contrary, upon his return to his native Bahia, turned into an uprooted man, an intellectual exiled in his own homeland, in a colony lacking universities, and having only isolated courses in higher education; there were no publications in Brazil until the beginning of the nineteenth century. The non-existence of local literary production, of which his poetic *oeuvre* would have been a part, plus Matos's feeling of social displacement as an intellectual in a peripheral, colonial society in which orality predominated (as Salvador was at that time), contributed to turning him into an eccentric, that is, not only an intellectual situated on the margin of the great cultural centers of his time, but also a displaced individual caught in the middle of a struggle between bureaucrats and clerics.

Unlike the merely flattering, eulogist poetry of other seventeenth-century writers in the colony, and not sharing Vieira's prophetic view of the land, Matos's poetic work departed markedly from this celebratory mode and therefore shows us a very different Bahia. This was not the Bahia that had been the boomtown during the great years of (sugar) prosperity; it was still as backward and poor as it had ever been, little more than a backwater town run by a bureaucratic and religious ruling class. It was also a place of intense sexual commerce and of tense interethnic relations among diverse social strata. This exchange between two worlds, the upper and the lower, is visible in his texts, where at times they merge into one. One finds in Matos's poetry a mixture of Baroque conventions and the more informal register of sixteenth-century Portuguese spoken language, developed by multicultural and multiethnic, subaltern classes for everyday use. This mix contributed, in this colonial environment, to the circulation of his poems in manuscript form (given the lack of printing presses in the colony and the impossibility of printing this kind of poetry in the metropolis) and consequently also explains the semi-clandestine dissemination of his poetry.

Contrary to the hegemonic discourse that praised the flora and fauna of the New World and mystified this continent into an El Dorado or tropical paradise, Matos's poetry presents the dystopia of a topsy-turvy world, a kind of hell instead of heaven, much closer to the misfortunes of contemporary post-utopian and dystopian life in the Third World today (despite the hundreds of years that separate the poet from us). This is a poetry that transcends the myths on which Latin American nationalisms were founded and brings the reader face to face with the despair of exploitation as a way of life. According to Antônio Dimas,

> ao contrário dessa prostração perante a natureza, desse embasbacamento que louvaminha aipins e ananases, pitangas e peixes, melões e mariscos, batatas e bananas, Gregório preferiu vasculhar os interstícios da sociedade, surpreendendo–a naquilo que ela tivesse de mais contraditório, de mais irônico, de mais incongruente. Ativo, perseguiu a arriscada construção social, rejeitando a contemplação anestesiada do natural. (345)

instead of this prostration before nature, this amazement that praises manioc and pineapples, *pitangas* and fish, melons and shellfish, potatoes and bananas, Gregório de Matos preferred to investigate the interstices of society, revealing its most contradictory, ironic, and incongruous aspects. He delineated a daring picture of the social fabric and rejected the anesthetized contemplation of nature.

Born on the periphery–Portuguese America in the seven-teenth century–and thus considered to be inferior in Europe as well (since Portugal was under Spanish domination throughout the seventeenth century), the poet wandered from periphery to periphery, from his exile in Angola after a time in Bahia, to his definitive return to Brazil, though this time to Recife instead of Salvador. Although forgotten throughout all of the eighteenth century and part of the nineteenth, Matos's satirical writings would become the cultural source for parody in the twentieth century. Matos's poetry comes back with the 1922 Modernists, and appears in works such as *Memórias senti-mentais de João Miramar* [1924; *Sentimental Memoirs of John Seaborne*] by Oswald de Andrade (1890–1954), and *Macunaíma* (1928), by Mário de Andrade (1893–1945).

The poet was nicknamed "Boca do Inferno" ("Mouth from Hell") because of his biting wit, and although he was unique in the Brazilian setting, he was somewhat similar to the Peru-vian poet Juan del Valle Caviedes (1652–1692), whose work "Diente del Parnaso" [1873; The Tooth of Parnassus] lam-basted Lima society, as Haroldo de Campos (1929–2003) has noted (55). Matos and Caviedes, both Baroque poets from the same colonial century prior to the geo-political concept of Latin America, were well known during their lifetime, but their works were published only about two centuries later. There have been some problems legitimizing the authorship of their works, as is to be expected given the fact that no signed manuscripts exist, yet the works of both poets have become a fundamental part of literary culture.

Situated in a kind of interval between the anonymous popu-lar oral tradition and the literariness of canonical forms of high literature, Gregório de Matos's works form a strong counter-point to Vieira's, even though Matos's works were incorpo-rated into the Brazilian literary canon much later than Vieira's works, which were already classics by the time of his death. Having grasped the inevitability of mercantilism *vis-à-vis* the old state, Vieira put the whole verbal apparatus of his splendid Baroque prose into his sermons in the service of Portugal, at a time when all the European empires were engaged in the com-petition for hegemony over an Old World divided between Catholics and Protestants. As a result, Vieira inspired the Portu-guese to adopt strategies similar to those of their adversaries, the Spanish and the Dutch. Matos, on the other hand, was more interested in the misfortunes brought on by transconti-nental imperialism. He wrote of the dramatic story of Angola, which he referred to as "armazém de pena, e dor" ("warehouse of pity and pain") and which made him wish that "Leve o diabo o dinheiro,/por cujo sangue queimado/tanta queimação de sangue/padecem negros, e brancos" (1990a, 1183) ("the devil take the money/for whose burned blood/so much burn-ing of blood/has been experienced by blacks and whites"). He also wrote on the theme of the "terra de gente oprimida" ("land of oppressed people") to which he adds the story of Recife, "que o Belga edificou ímpio tirano" (1990a, 1191) ("built by the impious Belgian tyrant").

When writing about the trans-Atlantic journey taken by "Christ's poor fellows" (that is, those deprived of possessions) from Portugal to Brazil in search for wealth, the "Mouth from Hell" chose to emphasize the fact of social metamorphosis that affected these men, instead of focusing on the epic aspect of discovery and praising and glorifying the victory of men and their nautical technology. In a book fundamental to the understanding of the development of Brazilian political patronage, *Os Donos do Poder* [1975; *The Owners of Power*],

Raymundo Faoro, referring to the Portuguese overseas voy-ages, reminds us that

> Portugal–e a Europa do século XVI–não era apenas a próspera mercancia, a riqueza fácil. A aventura da Índia, as navegações de intermediação para o norte e o sul da Europa, ao tempo que consumiam as ambições e as cobiças, deixavam, à borda da sociedade opulenta, uma larga faixa de espuma de pobres, desditados, ressentidos com a fácil riqueza alheia que mais lhe afrontava a miséria. Para esta gente, desprezada, faminta, esfarrapada, expulsa dos campos, não aquinhoada pelos nobres altivos ou pelos comerciantes retirados das navegações, desajustada nas cidades, para ela era necessário, em favor da tranquilidade de todos, um escoadouro. A visão paradisíaca, criada pelo grupo dominante, filtrada da imaginação dos letrados, servia para calar os ódios guardados. Longe, em outros hemisférios, fora do caldeirão das cobiças, havia terras virgens, habitadas de bons selvagens, onde a vida se oferece sem suor, para glória de Adão antes do pecado. (1:100–101)

> Portugal was not the only prosperous trading center of sixteenth century Europe; a place of easy wealth. Maritime adventures such as those to India or those that went to the north and the south of Europe at the same time fulfilled men's ambitions and desires. But alongside an opulent society there was also a wide fringe of poor, wretched, resentful people, who felt more miserable at the sight of the wealth of others. It was necessary, for the good of all, to find an outlet for this group of despised, hungry, ragged people, driven from the countryside and displaced in the cities, not compensated by the nobles or rewarded by merchants. The paradisiacal image created by the elite dominant group and lettered men, was used to appease the underlying hatred on the part of the wretched masses in Portuguese society. The tale was repeated constantly, far away in another hemisphere, away from the
> caldron of desires and jealousies, there were virgin lands inhabited by noble savages, where life could be lived without sweat, like that of Adam before the Fall.

Upon arriving in Brazil, the Portuguese destitute found in "Senhora Dona Bahia,/nobre e opulenta cidade, madrasta dos naturais/e dos estrangeiros madre" (Matos 1990b, 334) ("Our Lady Bahia, a noble and opulent city, step-mother of the natives,/and mother of the foreigners"). Yet, even before disembarking, while they were still on the ocean, a kind of metamorphosis had already begun and the poor men began to give themselves airs and conceal their subaltern past. Once on land, they used the most diverse tricks to become what they were not and this deception colored everything: politics, economics, social life, and even the private sphere. It allowed them to take advantage of the natives and to turn themselves quickly into the new colonial "great ones," as well as become key elements in the mercantile system, all without showing any intrinsic merit or accomplishment of their own. The fig-ure of the magnate, the sixteenth-century forefather of the emblematic *marajá* (maharajah) in the contemporary Brazil-ian scene, is the object of Matos's satire, and was seen by the poet as an authentic product of the "terra/sempre propícia aos infames" (1990b, 334) ("land/always propitious to the infamous") as well as to the appropriation of public goods, turning them into their own possessions. The "desgoverno da república" (1990b, 334) ("misgovernment of the republic"), with the manipulation of foreign currency exchange so as to create stability at the cost of general impoverishment and even hunger in the colony, is all part of the powerful social denunciation in Matos's work. The main theme of his poems was always colonialism's predatory effect upon the colony and the colonized.

Like Vieira and also within the frame of mind of his time, Gregório de Matos added his own contradictions to Baroque paradoxes. The deconstruction of the discourse of colonial conquest, achieved through the disclosure of its predatory aspect and the melancholic lament of the colonized in a culture of loss, as a kind of denunciation of the perverse face of European prosperity, is as present in Matos's works as his clear sexist racism (Queiroz 31), especially with regard to creating a literary stereotype of the mulatto woman as a sexual object. This stereotype has persisted into the twentieth century and can be found, for instance, in the fiction of another Bahian, Jorge Amado (1912–2001), whose *Grabriela, Cravo e Canela* [1958; Gabriela, Clove, and Cinnamon] so aptly associates the female with two oriental spices, the demand which motivated the great overseas voyages.

**Translation by Thomas LaBorie Burns and
Gláucia Renate Gonçalves**

Works Cited

Bosi, Alfredo. 1992. *Dialética da colonização*. São Paulo: Companhia das Letras.

Campos, Haroldo de. 1989. *O sequestro do barroco na formação da literatura brasileira: O caso Gregório de Mattos*. Salvador, Bahia: Fundação Casa de Jorge Amado.

Campos, Maria Consuelo Cunha. 1978. "Sermão pelo bom sucesso das armas de Portugal contra as de Holanda (Vieira): Uma leitura." *Convergência* 2.4: 51–60.

Dimas, Antônio. 1993. "Gregório de Matos. Poesia e controvérsia." *América Latina, Palavra, Literatura e Cultura* Vol. 1. *A situação colonial* Ed. Ana Pizarro. Campinas: Editora da Unicamp. 335–57.

Faoro, Raymundo. 1975. *Os donos do poder. Formação do patronato político brasileiro*. 2 vols. Porto Alegre: Editora Globo.

Matos, Gregorio de. 1990a. "À Bahia." *Gregório de Matos: Obra poética*. Vol. 1. Eds. James Amado and Emanuel Araújo. 2nd ed. Rio de Janeiro: Record. 333.

———. 1990b. "Descreve com mais individuação a fiducia, com que os estranhos sobem a arruinar sua república." *Gregório de Matos: Obra poética*. Vol. 1. Eds. James Amado and Emanuel Araújo. 2d ed. Rio de Janeiro: Record. 334–39.

Nunes, Maria José Rosado. 1997. "Freiras no Brasil." *História das mulheres no Brasil*. Ed. Mary del Priore. São Paulo: Editora Contexto, Editora da UNESP. 482–509.

Palacin, Luís. 1986. *Vieira e a visão trágica do barroco: Quatro estudos sobre a consciência possível*. São Paulo: Editora Hucitec.

Paz, Octavio. 1982. *Sor Juana Inés de la Cruz, o, las trampas de la fe*. Barcelona: Seix Barral.

———. 1988. *Sor Juana: Or, The Traps of Faith*. Trans. Margaret Sayers Peden. Cambridge, MA: Harvard University Press.

Queiroz Júnior, Teófilo de. 1982. *Preconceito de cor e a mulata na literatura brasileira*. São Paulo: Ática.

SECTION III
NARRATIVES OF LEGITIMATION:
THE DISCOURSE OF HEGEMONY AND THE
HERMENEUTICS OF GLOBALIZATION

CHAPTER 5

NARRATIVES OF LEGITIMATION
THE INVENTION OF HISTORY–MONUMENT
AND THE NATION-STATE

Beatriz González Stephan

By taking for granted its distancing from tradition and the social body, in the last resort historiography is based upon a power that in effect distinguishes it from the past and from the whole of society. "The making of history" is buttressed by a political power which creates a space proper (a walled city, a nation, etc.) where a will can and must write (construct) a system (a reason articulating practices) . . . . [T]his discourse "legitimizes" the force that power exerts; it provides this force with a familial, political, or moral genealogy; it accredits the prince's current "utility" while transforming it into "values" that organize the representation of the past. . . . It is through a sort of fiction, however, that the historian is accorded this place. . . . Thus historians can write only by combining within their practice the "other" that moves and misleads them and the real that they can represent only through fiction.

–Michel de Certeau 1988, 6, 7, 8, 14

Historiographic Writing: *Criollo* Awareness and the Elimination of the Imperial Catalogue

The invention of a form of writing that could represent a changing political economy–in other words, the invention of a technology of time or the writing of national history–was entrusted to a group of *criollos*, distant descendants of Iberian conquistadors, who, by the mid-eighteenth century, regarded themselves, given their economic power, as the masters of their political destinies. The invention of cultural historiography in the Spanish American continent had a political dimension that, on the one hand, linked it to the Spanish-speaking lettered city yet, on the other hand, emerged as a dissident gesture of a social class that wished to be identified as distinct from the European continent, that is, similar but not identical. The learned *criollos*, as the new subjects of an early modernity, sought the end of a social and political order that, until the eighteenth century, had seemed immutable.

Linked to this wish to become decolonized, that is, to be both different and separate from the fixed colonial categories, the *criollos* turned to a specific form of writing for this undertaking: The genre of literary historiography. The overthrow of the hierarchy of the colonial order was a crucial political project that left its mark on a certain type of discourse, which would encompass an imponderable array of varied interests including *belles lettres*, a love of European high culture, and its current cultural imaginary. Independence and political change, together with recognition within the Western European orbit of influence, encouraged historiographic invention, which was used as powerful propaganda to authenticate

the delicate balance of similarity and difference in the emancipatory operations of the *criollo* aristocracy. Historical writing in Spanish America thus became a timely display of symbolic capital.

Colonial institutions, far from being mimetic reproductions of those of the metropolis, triggered a *criollo* opposition that created cultural sensitivities and social formations that anticipated the new centers of national power. The *Carta persuasiva al Señor Don Ignacio de Escandón . . . sobre asunto de escribir la historia-literaria de la América meridional* [The Persuasive Letter to Mr. Ignacio de Escandón . . . on the Writing of Literary History in South America] (dated Cádiz 1768 and reprinted in Lima in 1769) by José Eusebio de Llano Zapata (1721–1780), mentions the urgent need "de componer una Obra, que en la América hace falta, y en la Europa se desea. Es ella la *Historia de Nuestros Escritores*, que con menoscabo de las Ciencias, y deshonor de la Literatura, yacen olvidados" (González 1993, 50) ("to compose a Work, which America requires and Europe desires. This was the *Historia de Nuestros Escritores* [History of Our Writers] who, to the detriment of Science and the dishonor of Literature, have been forgotten"). This is the first known document, which not only expresses the functionality of the literary historical genre, but is also an early expression of the creation of a new social class and its mentality.

The idea of a literary history emerges as a responsive statement in the midst of powerful debates, dating from the time of the first colonial foundations, on the relative intelligence and culture of the Old and New Worlds; various arguments aimed at defending or denying the spread and propagation of *civitas* in the New World or affirming the human and rational quality of Amerindian cultures. The historical project was originally conceived of as a regional appendix to the *Historia literaria de España* [(1779–1791) Literary History of Spain], directed at first by Father Raphael Rodríguez Mohedano, who noted:

> No obstante la distancia, no podemos mirar, como Extraños, ni dexar de apreciar, como grandes los progresos de la Literatura, conque se ha enriquecido una Región, no menos fecunda en Ingenios, que en Minas . . . Para desempeñar este assunto con exactitud posible. . . . [I]mploramos eficazmente el socorro de Nuestros Sabios Americanos . . . que tengan especial instrucción, o interés en la Historia-Literaria de Indias. (in González 1993, 54)

> Despite the distance, we cannot look on, as strangers, nor fail to appreciate the greatness of the progress of the Literature with which they (Spanish Americans) have enriched a Region, no less fertile in Wit than in Mines. . . . In order to perform this task with every accuracy . . . we beg for the assistance of Our American Scholars . . . who may have special knowledge or interests in the Literary History of the Indies.

The dynamic tension between center and periphery produced a complex pattern of crossed perspectives and of policy shifts that eliminated the one-sidedness of the colonizing impulse. "Europa desea" ("Europe desires") that this literary history be written because in its drive to control the Other, Europe (and its historians) sought to inscribe the "strange"(extraña) new culture within its own history because for Europeans, to write meant to appropriate and therefore to shorten "la distancia" (the distance) from the outer limits of empire, which were dangerous because of possible desertions from the European center. Metropolitan historiographic writing globalizes because, like "los thesoros de Oro, y Plata, que continuamente nos vienen de las Indias, y esperamos de su generosidad . . . nos proveeran abundantes Noticias y Memorias-Manuscritas, como de Libros-Impressos que en España son bien raros de Authores Americános" (González 1993, 54) ("the golden and silver treasures, which are continually sent to us from the Indies and which we expect owing to their generosity . . . will also supply us with abundant details and records and manuscripts, and printed books by American authors, which are extremely rare in Spain"). At the same time, "América le hace falta" ("America requires") this literary history because it will serve as a written platform for *Sabios Americanos* (American scholars) in which they will be able to recognize themselves "porque la Patria se ilustra con sus Literatos. . . nada más conviene al aliento de la juventud en la Carrera de las Letras, que el recuerdo de los Sabios Patricios, cuyo exemplo obra con más eficacia" ("because the fatherland is illuminated by her Literati . . . nothing benefits the breath of youth pursuing a degree in literature better than the memory of the patrician scholars, whose example works more effectively")–because it interiorizes the writing of the Other (i.e., of the colonizer), in order to separate and exclude itself from it. Thus, for the learned *Criollos,* writing meant recovering "las Memorias de los Varones Literatos de este Reyno . . . y que qualquier tinta es mejor que el polvo, y más vale una mala memoria, que el olvido" ("the memories of the literate men of this kingdom . . . since any ink is better than dust, and even a poor memory is better than oblivion") (González 1993, 47).

A double game is involved here: Being oneself for others and engaging in the act of writing to be able to recognize oneself as subject and thus to make oneself known to Europeans.

Llano Zapata emphasizes the fact that "la distancia es causa, que nos tengan por dormidos, quando quizá estámos bien despiertos" ("the distance is the reason why they think we are asleep, whereas we may in fact be wide awake"). History keeps the dead literary bodies alive in "Memorias y Archivos" ("Records and Archives") (González 1993, 52). Through writing, the fiction of the past is revived and "awakens" the dead bodies from its pages. Literary history is an operation that has more to do with the present; writing from the past is dramatized to create an interest in the present. A national literary history also means symbolically "shaking off" imperial ties and using historiographical writing to pave the way for independence. The point is not only to write one's own literary culture, but to write it down as a historical representation; thus by representing one's place in the past, it becomes possible to imagine the future. Moreover, the European tradition appears to focus only on written texts and forms of cultural logic; other discursive genres that are not recorded in writing do not exist–they think we are asleep whereas we are in fact wide awake (González 1993, 52).

However, Spanish American literary history, which functioned as a letter of introduction to Western Europe for the *criollo* lettered elite, was based entirely on written texts in the European languages. For this reason, Llano Zapata recommended, for the compilation of a true literary history, that if the "mejores Monumentos, Libros, y Memorias, que han acumulado allí el estudio, la curiosidad, y el tiempo" ("best of our monuments, books, and memories, accumulated there by study, curiosity, and time") did not suffice to fill a history, "la falta de algunas noticias se suplirá con las Pinturas, ó Retratos de nuestros Sabios. . . . De estas se formará una *Historia Iconographica*, que servirá de grande luz, si se le acompañan las Inscripciones del merito de cada uno, de su edad, patria, profession, y dignidad" ("the lack of texts could be compensated by the inclusion of portraits of our scholars. . . . These will be used to create an *Iconographic History*, which will serve as a great light, if it is accompanied by inscriptions of the merits of each, his age, country, profession, and dignity") (González 1993, 52). Thus literary history served as the birth certificate of an incipient bourgeois modernity, an identity card and foundational book for both the agents–the men of letters and a post-colonial culture. This history thus constructed the appearance of an official culture through portraits of writers and works of literature; it was to serve as symbolic capital for the imminent foundation of nation-states. Graphemic writing and historical iconographics constituted the pre-national *criollo* subjects, just as the writing of national constitutions would do decades later. Portraits of great men combined with biographical sketches to establish the profile of virtues and heroism of the nobility of talented wit who would be the future founders of the "fatherland." Historiography and painting were the identifiable signs of the sphere of power of a class that was preparing the validation for its claim to legitimacy. It meant that the awakening nationalism was accompanied by a written/iconographic record and that everything outside this discourse would simply be a faceless non-identity without representation, without a language, without history, and without literature: In other words, all Amerindian and popular literary culture did not exist in the new *criollo* canon.

Inclusion in the national hierarchy was granted through historiography, though the portraits of men of letters–"patrician scholars," "enlightened men"–the face and above all the proper use of language created the enlightened ruling class's self-legitimation. A century later in the expanding space of national historiographies, another excluded subject, women, would negotiate their entry into the field of the interpretative power of the word. The lettered *criolla* would do so as a part of the Enlightenment. Women had had no face or identity; they were protected subjects in a subordinate position. Domitila García de Coronado published her *Album poético fotográfico de escritoras y poetisas cubanas* [Havana 1872; Poetic and Photographic Album of Cuban Women Writers and Poets], emphasizing the absence of women in the historiography of the time and thereby forcing recognition of the displaced subjects through her reconfiguration of women's faces in the photographic album and through the appropriate language in the "album of female writers and poets." A century earlier, in Llano Zapata's *Carta persuasiva*, the *criollo* subject had been at a political disadvantage. And from this situation of subordination, the *criollo* was forced into an alliance with lettered *criollas* and finally acknowledged the existence of learned women. Indeed, there must have been many lettered women who undoubtedly played an important role in colonial life. Otherwise, it would be difficult to account for Llano Zapata's interest in including women within the plan of literary history:

> Por el deseo en que está el Suplicante, previene, á toda la Nación, porque el interés comprehende sin excepción a nadie, ni aun del otro Sexo, pues este no le pone fuera de la instruccion. . . . Y más quando en este Pais de las dichas, al presente, y en todos tiempos se han visto esclarecidas Heroynas en Lenguas, Artes, y Ciencias, y casi por cada viviente se conoce el fondo clarísimo de su viveza mental. (González 1993, 48)

> This writer wants to give notice to the entire nation, that literature includes everyone, with no exception, not even those of the other Sex, since their sex does not exclude them from instruction. . . . And particularly so, because both now and in the past, this felitious country has witnessed distinguished heroines in arts, languages, and sciences, and because the fullness of their mental alertness is recognized and acknowledged by all.

With the establishment of the Republic, there was a return to more conservative measures regarding intellectual women, who were again assiduously restricted to the home and excluded from participation in national literary culture. In this respect, mid-nineteenth-century literary historiography broke its alliance with the "distinguished heroines of language" and limited the space, functions, and genres of literary culture in keeping with the nation's division of civic life into distinct polarities: Public versus private, male versus female and, most significantly, speaking versus silence. The new modern bourgeois sensitivity, a century after Llano Zapata's letter, had taken a step backward.

This proves that, as much as writing displays and explains, it also forgets and silences; history distends, suppresses, and has an ulterior, political motive, in keeping with the interests of those in authority. History is a dramatic genre (see White 1985, 1992; de Certeau 1988), and historians write a script ensuring that certain actors (who represent only a fraction of reality) appear to be the only active agents. Eighteenth-century *criollos* understood the artificial yet real political power of literary history:

> Las pruebas, que más califican en el Tribunal de la Literatura, son la demostración de los talentos, del ingenio, del juicio. . . . Lo demás de calidad, que llaman buena o mala no es de la inspección de aquel Juzgado. . . Es grande impertinencia, en estos casos, gastar el tiempo en remover alcuñas. . . De las fuentes donde se há de beber una verdad . . . se sacaran la

> Profession, y Progressos de cada uno, sus Escritos, Impressos, o Manuscritos, sus Peregrinaciones, o Viages, sus Descubrimientos . . . y la Edad. (González 1993, 50–51)

> The evidence with the greatest weight in the court of literature is the demonstration of talent, ingenuity, and keen judgment, . . . The question of aesthetic quality, whether good or bad, is not the responsibility of that court. . . . In these cases, it is a great impertinence to waste time looking for the lineages of noble families. . . . From the historical sources . . . we shall obtain the information on the profession and progress of men of letters, their writings, printed matter or manuscripts, their pilgrimages or voyages, their discoveries . . . and their age.

The demonstration of talents and keen judgment that could be capable of breaking with the colonial legacy was important, since it could bring to light a symbolic *thesoro* (treasure) of sufficient importance to ensure that people would value their independence. This treasure, however, had to be skillfully given a cosmetic makeover to gain credibility. It was strategically important—Llano Zapata suggests—that literary history should "se deberá dár en un estilo, que no declíne á las baxezas de humilde, ni se eleve á las sobervias de hinchado. . . . La magestad de la Eloquencia no se viste de adornos afectados, que la desfiguren . . . ni gastar el tiempo en remover alcuñas . . . que como los gusanos se alimentan de roer huesos" (González 1993, 50–51) ("be written in a particular style, neither descending to the language of the street nor soaring to the arrogance of the vain elite. . . . [T]he majesty of eloquence is not draped in affected adornments that disfigure it . . . nor does it waste time in turning lineages that, like worms, feed on the dead").

The depiction of America as being rich in gold and silver mines fostered its exploitation by the empire; the depiction of America as being rich in wit and talents made the colonial situation untenable and facilitated the introduction of a new politico-cultural entity: Scholars and literature, which made colonial subordination more difficult, in addition to giving the future nation a face (portraits of our scholars*)* and a national discourse. *Criollos* of letters were aware of the advantages of historico-literary writing because they saw in it the political strength of its very fictionality as the national "majesty of eloquence." The correlation between nation-state and literary historiography (the fatherland is enlightened by its literati) had already been outlined by the *criollo* humanists of the Enlightenment just as the cultural imaginary of a nation was already beginning to take a leading role in the political function that literature was to have.

Yet even before the Spanish American nations had been established as such, this project was already evident in private circles. Llano Zapata wrote a letter to persuade Ignacio de Escandón of the advisability of devising a public "circular-letter" in order to share information with a larger circle of *criollos* and *criollas*. One might surmise that the process of acquiring a learned historical awareness for oneself was gradually developing, at first through private communication, where the subject (a merchant of the elite class), aware of the foundational historical project, might write an autobiography to portray himself before turning to other publications. The Llano Zapata letter was the manifesto of a pre-modern/pre-national Western European *criollo* and *criolla* vanguard. In this respect, it could be regarded as slightly subversive, since the fact that it existed in a private sphere meant that it escaped official control. It galvanized the learned male and female lettered population born in American territory; it aimed to use a mass of information that lay buried in the "archives of certain families" as the basis for citizenship in the new Republic. The plan called for the use of a body of literature in a time sequence containing a before and an after, which upset the atemporal fixed categories of the seventeenth century.

Historico-cultural reflections acquire various forms of textual formalization through a combination of factors: The epistemological horizon of the intellectual subject and the sociopolitical motivation behind the selection of available historical discursive genres. In this respect, historiographic modalities change with the times; they alter the way culture is represented in time. The nineteenth century witnessed the use of a (modern) historico-discursive modality, which we recognize under the general heading of "history," that does not contradict other possible forms of exercising this form of creative imagination. The era of nationalism (the nineteenth century) created a type of historiography (as well as of literary historiography) to which we are still indebted. Nevertheless, the desire to collect in order subsequently to display the cultural wealth of the American territories that had been claimed by Spain and Portugal was first evident among the Spaniards themselves (both conquistadors and missionaries). Subsequently among the Jesuits and Spanish Americans such display became a demonstration of the expansive and self-generating nature of the civilizing Western European project, as well as the triumphal power of *humanitas* over a form of nature regarded as a corrosively destructive force. It was the dominant, enlightened peninsular or Hispanic sectors of the lettered city that began to collect cultural or literary materials in order to validate their own habitat as an enunciative *locus* and to accredit their being within the European geo-political radius. On the one hand, economic wealth was extracted, thereby impoverishing the Latin American continent; on the other, attempts were made to offset this alienating process through this kind of symbolic enrichment.

Catalogue compilation was the great wall that enclosed peninsular and *criollo* subjects of the Americas in the "library" of the colonial lettered city. It did not suffice merely to possess ostentatious libraries (the public libraries in Seville were much smaller than the private treasures kept in Lima); it was also necessary for this lettered culture to be reproduced in the order of discourse. The citizens of the lettered city, ignoring their surroundings, collected and enclosed their literary wealth, producing "catalogues" and "compendiums" to be read in Europe–as a means of legitimizing the fruits of the colonial undertaking. The collection of literary material in the colonized areas of Spanish America was undertaken by groups socially linked to religious orders, the crown, or the economic power of the *criollo* elite.

The stability of the imperial order found its most subjugating and deceptive instrument of domination in these catalogues: like botanists, they drew the map of printed species in Latin and Spanish. In 1608, Andreas Schottus (1552–1629) wrote *Hispaniae illustratas seu Rerum urbiumque. Hispaniaie, Lusitanias, Aethiopie et Indiae, scriptores varii*; in 1629, Antonio de León Pinelo (1590?–1660) published his *Epítome de una Biblioteca Oriental y Occidental náutica y geográfica, en que se contiene los escritores de las Indias Occidentales* [Epitome of an Oriental and Occidental Nautical and Geographic Library, Which Contains the Writers from the West Indies]; 1672 saw the publication of *Bibliotheca hispana sive hispanorum* by Nicolás Antonio (1617–1684), while in 1755, Juan José Éguiara y Eguren's (1696–1763) *Bibliotheca Mexicana* [*Mexican Library*]

was published in Latin. These are just a few examples of works that consistently supported not only European culture in contact zones, but also the cultural wealth and complexity of Indian societies.

These seventeenth- and eighteenth-century catalogues and libraries would seem like silent monoliths to us, almost inert in their monumentality, if we did not realize that they were, in fact, the traces of aggressive polemics against the George Louis Leclere, Comte de Buffon (1707–1788) and Cornelius de Pauw (1739–1799), who were the principal spokesmen of the argument that rejected the possibility either that Spanish America might constitute a locale for the flowering of a society with European roots or that forms of cultural expression might exist among the aboriginal peoples. The tendency to discredit the Indian legacy–on the assumption that it had been an inferior culture which had lacked alphabetical writing–was strongly contested by the *criollos*. The pretext that was used by Europeans like Buffon was the ominous influence exerted by the climate, the fauna, and the flora, in producing an unredeemably backward culture, and this now served as a key device in the appraisal of Spanish American colonial culture. De Pauw's assumptions threatened the disseminating, redemptive impulse of the imperial mission and its multiplying capacity and therefore had to be contested vigorously.

The political agenda which controlled the *criollo* bibliographic catalogue form was, however, limited to the defense of colonial Spanish America's reproduction of metropolitan culture. Ideologically speaking, this meant the total legitimization of the latter's values, in addition to refuting the argument that restricted European culture to the European continent. It fought against the colonies' possible–and indeed inevitable–ideological deviation from the metropolitan centers. However, this displacement was not merely speculative. The rupture caused by the cultural transfer to the Americas produced a transculturation of the spheres of intellectual production and consequently the transformation of Western discursive forms into new forms provoked by unexpected situations in the colonial periphery.

These bibliographic catalogues, like the botanists in natural history, unfolded the map of Imperial taxonomic knowledge; they preferred historical imagination to geographical space, for it could describe and include a kind of temporal "space." Hence it would seem that the work of bibliographical collection was closely linked to a strategy that, by enumerating the cultural and literary wealth of the New World, aimed to translate the so-called American "cornucopia" into discourse. In other words, catalogues and compendiums, particularly in the seventeenth century, were genres that produced an effect homologous to a system of rhetoric that sustained the greatness and magnificence of the Spanish empire at the time; it served as a rhetorical counterweight to the imminent decadence of Spanish power–and the empire, which was beginning to show signs of collapse in terms both of overseas trade and of the internal economic and social control within the colonies.

Small wonder, then, that these bibliographical catalogues, which compiled only works printed in Latin and Spanish, were the great archives that eliminated the American temporality from their narrative. Accumulation of intellectual capital and the extension of the Imperial limits were the distinctive traits of the genre. León Pinelo must have recognized this relationship in the *Discurso Apologético*, which opens his *Epítome*:

... no sólo juntó nombres de Escritores para esta
Biblioteca ... que en quarenta Lenguas, i más de mil Autores
forman este Epítome ... comprendidos desde la Provincia de
Santa Cruz del Brasil, hasta los Reinos de Malaca, i Archipiélagos
del Moluco: i Occidental, desde donde demarca el verdadero
Meridiano , hasta salir por el Occidente a nuestro Océano
Atlantico; abraçando ... los dos famosos continentes de la
duplicada América, ó Ibérica ... (unpaginated)

... not only were the names of Writers collected for this
Library ... which, in forty Languages and over a thousand
Authors, comprise this Compendium ... ranging from the
Province of Santa Cruz in Brazil to the Kingdoms of Malacca
(Malaya) and the Archipelagos of Molucca: and the West, where
the true Meridian is located ..., emerging in the West in our
Atlantic Ocean; embracing ... the two famous continents of the
duplicated America or Iberian America ...

Catalogues have the same function as atlases: the display
of learning is subject to the Imperial gaze. They offer a worldwide, panoramic view that, in a single gesture, links the
appraisal of knowledge ("a thousand authors," "forty languages") to vast territorial extensions ("from Brazil to the
Kingdoms of Molucca"). Discourse that advances by naming
geographical places not only extends the imaginary spheres
of the Conquest but also implies expansion through the accumulation of an indiscriminate collection of data. The intellectual landscape of the Imperial library, despite the fact that the
organization reveals a varied panorama, offers the same information and perspective, and not that of each different region.
Thus the universalizing, abstract logic of metropolitan hegemonic culture becomes globalized by erasing particular distinguishing details.

Nevertheless, the implantation of Spanish Imperial culture
in Spanish America does not follow the same dynamics or
enunciatory interests and horizons as in Europe. Indeed,
although the bibliographical work that founded a historiographical tradition in the Latin American continent was
undertaken by the Spanish elite with close links to the
metropolis, it demonstrated a new awareness among these
intellectuals, which led them to acknowledge that the accumulation of knowledge, such as influential books, leading
authors, and libraries of ancient and modern works (like the
accumulation of merchandise) represented a form of power
that was as legitimate and necessary as the capital represented
by gold and silver. "La gloria del reinar" ("the glory of reigning"), said León Pinelo,

es el deseo de saber, acariciar letras, es asegurar aciertos. . . Como
si fueran indices del poder, tanto los muchos Soldados, en los
Campos, como los numerosos Libros, en la Biblioteca.
Alabança es de esta edad, ver la Nobleça bien ocupada . . . no
solo de Pinturas, sino adornados de Libros . . . como de las Indias
solo se apetece Plata, i Oro, están sus Escritores tan Olvidados,
como sus Historias poco vistas. . . . (unpaginated)

is the desire to know, to caress letters, and to ensure success. . . .
Both the many Soldiers, in the Fields, and the many books in the
Library, are regarded as indices of power. It is most praiseworthy,
at this time, to see the Nobility fully occupied . . . not only with
Paintings, but also with Books. . . . Since all that appeals from the
Indies is their Silver and Gold, their Writers are as Neglected as
their Histories are unknown. . . .

By the seventeenth century, a distinction had already been
established between the *criollos,* who had economic power, and
the peninsular group, whose political power was undergoing a
crisis or, at least, was threatened. This new configuration of
power led to the emergence of a *criollo* sensibility, which was
not necessarily anti-Spanish or even anti-colonial, and which
regarded success in life as being able to acquire knowledge
and erudition of the same quality and quantity as they could
possess in material wealth. One could say that, to a certain
extent, this accumulation of books and authors, stored
according to the same criterion with which material possessions were gathered, was the result of the emergence of bourgeois social relations. This *criollo* sensibility was riddled with
subtle contradictions, making it difficult to classify it in dualistic terms as being either for or against the Iberian Imperial
undertaking. Exaltation of the "capitalizing" of symbolic
goods in Spanish America was a compensatory strategy
responding to the draining of the continent's wealth by Spain,
and it reveals a sense of guilt over the Conquest ("de las
Indias sólo se apetece Plata, i Oro" ["all that appeals from the
Indies is their Silver and Gold"]), a sentiment that would soon
deprive the peninsular Spaniards of their power. For this reason, the Conquest constitutes a form of unjustified violence
that is questioned in the catalogues. Yet the wish to appropriate, possess, and display wealth continued, the object merely
being transferring from material to cultural riches. The discourse of libraries as the accumulation of knowledge replaces
the discourse of violence and conquest (both the military
destruction and the administrative indices of power) with the
discourse of the anti-Conquest and anti-extraction of wealth.
The catalogue replaces material wealth with words; yet it also
exercises a non-violent form of domination, since by taking
possession of books and authors, it establishes its power over
knowledge ("la gloria del reinar, es el deseo de saber" ["the
glory of reigning is the desire for knowledge"]). It is the
expression of the desire for knowledge and a *criollo* authority
created through the conspicuous consumption of objects,
which the discourse of power transforms into the status symbols of privilege. In other words, for the moment, the possession of libraries establishes a learned nobility; subsequently,
the latter will share its knowledge in exchange for political
autonomy. At the same time, this colonial subject reproduces
the same egocentric desire for possession as the Empire had.
The difference lies in the type of wealth accumulated: gold
and silver alienate; libraries enrich. The limits between an
imperial subject's loyalty and independent allegiances are not
easy to distinguish; they are full of nuances and gray areas.

The double aspect of the catalogues suggests the ambivalent behavior of transculturation. On the one hand, as the
repositories of knowledge, they would seem to reproduce the
immutable stability of the colonial order in an absolute
present; they do not suggest the passage of time; there is no
past or future. On the other hand, they also serve as a
counter-discourse to the natural histories that stripped the colonized lands of their history, humanity, and culture. Conversely, catalogues saturate this imaginary empty space with
books and libraries; they humanize the landscape of the New
World to attract travelers and men of science. This discourse
does not stop being a dialogue between Empire and periphery, but it begins to look differently at these relations.
Although Spanish and Portuguese colonial authorities
decided to construct a cultural vacuum in their respective colonies, the *criollo* men of letters responded in abundance.

Yet there was more: León Pinelo was not merely content
with recounting the "many books"; in the colonies he also
considered the need to rescue forgotten writers and histories.
Beyond mere taxonomy, he developed a narrative genre that

would historicize historical works and authors. He began to perceive the culture of the colonial world as a possible dynamic space, rather than merely as an objectified appendix to the metropolis. Subtly conceiving of the American world as a historical space also meant wishing it had a different history–not one marked by the domination of Western hegemonies. Yet it was only 1629, and the crack in colonial Hispanic mentality was just beginning to widen. Nor is it coincidental that most of the catalogues were written in Latin, unlike León Pinelo's *Epítome*. Latin was the first language of the European scientific community, which indirectly implied the exclusion of Amerindian cultures and therefore made them invisible in both the present and the past. Thus, these catalogues were the first founding gestures that eliminated Amerindian cultures because of their orality and because they had other forms of written codification that were not understood. The form of these catalogues both in regard to the choice of language (whether Latin or Spanish) and the arrangement of the material involved (whether alphabetical, regional, or historical) is semantically and politically significant. The absolute present of the catalogues served as a strategic restriction for eliminating the idea of the past.

Yet the homogenous grid of the inventory of this period of colonial stability (in the seventeenth century) could not remain unaffected by the escalation of Indian uprisings (such as the Andean uprising led by Tupac Amaru) and anarchistic movements (such as Toussaint Louverture's rebellion in Haiti) that shook the continent between 1740 and 1790; the expulsion in 1767 of the Jesuits, whose dissatisfaction with imperial policies led them to promote ideologies oriented toward social reform, with a deep concern for living conditions of Amerindian societies and cultures; the circulation of new trends of humanistic rationalism, which prompted the understanding and acceptance of the diversity of languages and cultures; not to mention the already-established power of the *criollo* patricians. These different concerns not only critically disturbed the colonial order but also catalyzed the configuration of a historical awareness that permeated all social sectors, although only the white learned *criollos* formalized in their enlightened culture the idea of a type of discourse that would interpret this desire for change.

For the first time, cultural reality was regarded as a process, while the representation of space was envisaged in historical terms; people thought in terms of stages, each of which was qualitatively preparatory for the great final leap entailed by Independence. José Eusebio de Llano Zapata's 1768 *Carta persuasiva* was a forceful indication–and by no means the only one–of the presence of a white *criollo* subject who clearly visualized his attachment to these lands and wished that they were countries and nations with their own identities. Moreover, the *criollos'* wish to feel that they were the legitimate masters of this world that did not as yet rule itself politically fostered a whole ideological operation, which led to the authentication of class interests. Conjuncturally speaking, despite being profoundly indebted to the Western European Hispanic tradition, this group neither was able nor wished to identify with the immediate hegemonic present and past. It had to produce its own distinctness, or at least the effect of being distinctive. The invention of a past that was genealogically different from the Spanish past was the imaginary key to a differentiated identity that was distinct from that of the white Spaniards but would nevertheless enable the *criollos* to justify a national social project different from the colonial one.

Their prospective historical perspective led them to propose a different representation of the past and to place their roots in pre-Hispanic antiquity. Moreover, they depicted Amerindian cultures as having an antiquity, a past (rather than a present), and as offering a useful antechamber to the Hispanic tradition, a move that enabled them at their discretion to situate the natives always in the past. Thus, the *criollos'* cultural originality would be temporally indebted to a past that had been excluded from the catalogues of the previous century, allowing them rhetorically and with no further commitments to authenticate their ethnic-cultural differences from peninsular Spaniards. They could thus appear as the symbolic inheritors of the Amerindian cultures.

The diligent study and enthusiastic defense of Amerindian cultures found its expression in Juan José Eguiara y Eguren's *Bibliotheca Mexicana* (1755), which, in addition to its two thousand references to American authors, constituted a major effort to develop an alternative canon. By attempting to set out the historical stages of the region's cultural processes, it necessarily authenticated Amerindian cultures:

> Cierto es que "los indígenas" desconocieron el uso de los caracteres alfabéticos, de que las naciones europeas y cultas se sirven para comunicar a la posteridad la memoria de sus hechos . . . mas no por eso ha de tachárselos de brutos e incultos, ignorantes de todas las ciencias y desconocedores de libros y bibliotecas. (Eguiara y Eguren 61–2)

> It is true that the "natives" were unfamiliar with the use of alphabetical letters, which cultured European nations use to communicate the memory of their deeds to posterity . . . yet this is no reason to classify them as stupid and uncultured, ignorant of all the sciences and unaware of books and libraries.

Undoubtedly, chronicles since the time of the Conquest had compiled numerous references to Amerindian cultures, from Pedro Cieza de León's (1518-1554) *Crónica del Perú* [1552; *Chronicle of Peru*] and *Relación de las fábulas y ritos de los incas* [1575; *Report on the Fables and Rituals of the Incas*] by Cristóbal de Molina, *el cuzqueño* (1494?–1578), to Father Andrés de Olmos's (1491–1571?) *Cantares mexicanos* [*Songs of the Aztecs*], published in Spanish much earlier, in 1532. It was not until the eighteenth century, however, with the pre-eminence of the new scientific spirit (in addition to the *criollo* aspirations to power) that the historiographical task of reconstituting pre-Hispanic culture achieved a degree of formalization. This drive successfully combined the exhaustiveness of previous methods of cataloguing with a Spanish American sensibility capable of revisiting and exploiting the subaltern side of the Amerindian presence. In other words, what had been hidden by Spanish domination, but also repressed by the hegemonic *criollo* culture itself–which (in order to appear Westernized) had sought to erase any traces that might reveal any cultural hybridity–now came to the fore. Despite the dynamics of unidirectional metropolitan transfer to the colonies, cultural life necessarily produced transculturated processes, whose multiple folds gave rise to cultural resistance and, at certain moments, contested the metropolitan elite for interpretative power.

The interest in the study of pre-Hispanic codices and paintings reflected not only the nostalgia for an ancient Imperial greatness and the wish to base a Spanish American style on it, but also the desire to show that the emerging social project was supported by a reality that not only had greater historical density than had been heretofore acknowledged, but was by no means barbarous. In other words, Spanish America was a world that was hardly new and that, far from owing its existence to the Europeans, comprised societies with an ancient history and a complex culture, despite the ahistorical and irrational nature attributed to them by the ignorant. Let us return to Eguiara y Eguren's enthusiasm for Amerindian cultures:

Los mexicanos cultivaron además la poesía, la retórica, la oratoria, la aritmética, la astronomía y otras disciplinas, de las que nos quedan los monumentos insignes y testimonios dignos de entero crédito. . . . Entre los cinco libros más importantes de la nación se contaban las "Ruedas" pintadas con arte primoroso. Cada una de ellas abarcaba el espacio de un siglo, con perfecta distinción de años, meses, semanas y días. . . . En lo que a librerías se refiere, no es extraño que los indios tuvieran cantidad de ellas. . . . Una circunstancia que acrecía el mérito de estos libros mexicanos, era haber perpetuado mediante representaciones figuradas, la cronología y exacta sucesión de los siglos de su historia. (74, 78)

The ancient Mexicans also cultivated poetry, rhetoric, oratory, mathematics, astronomy, and other disciplines, of which distinguished monuments and reliable testimonies remain. . . . The five most important books of the nation included the exquisitely illustrated *Ruedas*. Each of these spanned a century, in which years, months, weeks and days were perfectly distinguished. . . . As far as libraries are concerned, it is by no means strange that the Amerindians should have had many of these. . . . One circumstance that increased the merit of these Mexican books was the fact that, by means of figured representations, they had perpetuated the chronology and exact succession of the centuries of their history.

This historiographic work fostered a type of rhetoric whose aim was precisely to produce a historical and cultural past. The reconstruction of the codices, maps, icons, rituals, and texts of the Amerindian cultures from within the learned city implied not only a mechanism of persuasion but also a strategic means of configuring new subjectivities (see Rabasa). What led the Spanish American elite to situate their origins in Amerindian cultures was certainly not any humanitarian recognition of the cultural legacy of the conquered, but rather a political recognition—not uninfluenced by fear—of the strength of these groups and the advisability of taking them into account. This fictitious operation of creating a past depicted these as heirs and included them in the proto-national project, while at the same time successfully concealing their real distance from the elite. This rhetoric also served as a means of establishing timely distinctions between the white peninsular Spaniards and the *criollo* power base.

However, this *criollo* sensibility, which appears to have affiliated itself with secondary cultures as a means of establishing its Americanness, deployed a series of artifices which converted the logic of Amerindian cultures into Western rationality: They have books and libraries, therefore they are civilized. The Amerindian culture was registered within the parameters of the lettered city ("as far as libraries are concerned, it is by no means strange that the [Amerindians] should have had many of these"). In other words, they saw Indian culture through the prism of the European learned institution ("they cultivated poetry, rhetoric, oratory, mathematics"). Their cultural forms and practices were made literary as a result of a process of transfer by the learned *criollos* themselves, who needed to project the same onto the other: books, libraries, and writing. But they were still unable to incorporate orality into lettered culture. In this respect, it was the scriptural gesture itself that converted/perverted the

world of Amerindian and popular cultures into a realm of ethnographic and historical artifacts. Registering Amerindian society within the framework of writing meant turning it into a simultaneously historical and ethnographic affair: This move canceled its historicity in the present, turning it into a remote, closed past. The reification experienced by these cultures as a result of the Eurocentric rhetoric of the learned sector was reflected in their being immobilized like monuments. It is no coincidence that *Bibliotheca Mexicana* was written in Latin.

And it was precisely at this intersection that literary or cultural historiography emerged in Latin America. This "other" material—different and distant—permitted the imagination of the past to unfold ("the five most important books of the nation included the *Ruedas*. Each of these spanned a century") and take the form of serialized periodization: the past, the present, and the future. It generated a narrative that was unable to place the other and the same at the identical time in contemporary temporal spaces. The linear arrangement of historiographic writing elegantly solved the problem by placing an earlier, Amerindian non-Hispanic temporality within a Hispanic temporal space and thus creating a chronological illusion. The proximity of opposites suggested a relationship between them, rather than contamination. The technique of historiographic writing solved a crucial problem of identity for the *criollos* by placing them midway between the purely Amerindian cultures and the white Iberian cultures. Eighteenth-century historiography still kept these borders quite separate. Nineteenth-century literary historiography would attempt to establish cultural hybridization through the ideology of miscegenation. The desire for power and a new correlation of forces between the various social sectors served as the background to the transformation of bibliographic historiography; here was the potential of a narrative genre whose artifice enabled heterogeneity to be handled within the chronological time of linear writing. The invention of this past was part of the game of this rhetoric.

Both writing that opted for the formal arrangement of the catalogue inventory and the narrative that produced a representation of social reality were strategies based on the representational power of writing itself. Both were fictional in form: the fiction of a sense of order and space that was static and the fiction of a space in time that could be represented only through change. This is why the invention of literary historiography as a discipline attached to the institution of literature itself finds one of its decisive founding moments in the emergence of a hegemonic learned social class, which appropriated the genre in order to shape its politico-cultural identity (emancipated from colonizing management) and to project an agenda conducive to the formation of cultural nationality. At this point, historiography had implications for cultural autonomy that were not necessarily pro-Independence. However, what interests us here is the praxis of the enlightened *criollo* subject, who debated his identity and remained in power within a new world economy, where countries gained separate recognition though their regionally differentiated literatures, yet were subject to the same homogenizing logic of the same economy of writing.

The century that elapsed between Llano Zapata's *Carta persuasiva* (1768) and the various national literary histories (the first of which were published in the 1850s), once the Spanish American national states had been constituted and stabilized, presents a no less lengthy process of examination and appraisal of this scriptural process, which required specific socio-cultural conditions for its implementation. The period between the project implied by the *Carta persuasiva* (which could well be interpreted as the manifesto of an intellectual avant-garde that had already prophesied its Independence) and the reification of this desire in the historiographic gesture itself, saw decades of emancipatory wars, the confusing early stages of State founding, economic and institutional precariousness, internal instability, together with the burden and survival of colonial habits and sensitivities. These tended to promote another type of foundational writing that complied more with the urgency of the moment than with any proto-Independence movement. Thus, for the moment, anthologies and collections of poems, together with incisive articles and fierce polemics, not only occupied the space of historico-literary reflection, but also configured a first horizon that permitted the historiographic undertaking–once civic life had been re-arranged.

Undoubtedly, what was important was both the pressing needs and prospects of eighteenth-century pre-Independence considerations of the rights of man and the construction of new national states. Once the process of modernization in the new states was well underway, *criollo* men of letters used their historiographic writing to structure a national culture that legitimized the State apparatus they had created to maintain power. These new Republics extolled their national sovereignties through a form of modernization that would in time immerse them in new types of colonization. By the mid-nineteenth century each historian had visualized the political power that this historiographic narrative could achieve from his own point of view. Historiography and cultural autonomy, historiography and the national project, historiography and the nation-state: These pairs effectively summarize three key periods of the Spanish American historiographical process as the expression of the emergence of a specific subject configured as a means of obtaining power in and through the genre of literary historiography; this enabled it to work on and construct a new apparatus of power (the nation-state) on the basis of the effects attributable to the literary and cultural apparatus. Consequently, the historiographical genre, as we know it and have inherited it, was (and to a certain extent continues to be) a hegemonic practice closely linked to the undertaking of the modern-day State. It has proved to be a mechanism that could manufacture and represent time in keeping with the changing nature of new Western epistemological systems, which moved inexorably toward the horizon of the future utopia of modernity. Latin American intellectuals saw themselves as prisoners of peripheral zones distant from the metropolitan centers. They were thus moved to dismiss their cultural identity and embark on an endless race to camouflage themselves with purportedly trans-Atlantic cultural patterns.

In the middle of the eighteenth century, Llano Zapata's *Carta* had been merely a letter of intention of a historical subject caught up in the process of social change; this change would only be realized, in fact, with the triumph and consolidation of the bourgeois project of the nation-state. Between the still private expression of the hopes of a class (which implies the letter as a genre), and its historical triumph (which signifies a historiographic book as an object and also as both an official and a public genre), there was a temporal gap that would mark the destruction of the Imperial project; the rise of the *criollo* subject with his vocation for an autonomous, nationalistic modernity; and, finally, the establishment of the national project.

The merging of historiographic writing and the national state took place within the framework of a power dynamics: National historiography was a powerful manifestation of the patriarchal subject who pushed the expressions of popular, female, non-white, and non-learned subjects towards the edges of "non-history." And it was precisely in this respect that the *Carta* was a pretext that was doubly subordinate to historiographic writing: It intended to include, as pointed out earlier, both female and male learned subjects and, to a certain extent, it constituted a counter-hegemonic narrative by seeking to define a different cultural identity with its back to, yet open to, Spanish Imperial power (see Guha 1997a and b; Rodríguez). During its celebratory period, a century later, during the last third of the nineteenth century, literary historiography contained no expressions of protest. On the contrary, it was one of the most highly-treasured trophies of hegemonic power. It wallowed in its official monumentalism; the glorious rigidity of the walls of the lettered city intensified the use and abuse of the fictions of the past.

The Traces of Memory and the Production of Patriotic Glory

The configuration of national literatures–in other words, their canonization in historiography–was one of the innumerable gestures of the complex fabric of symbolic practices that proliferated in the new urban spaces as manifestations of modern life in the no less recent nation-states that began their civic life during the first decades of the nineteenth century. It was the period of greatest intensity for the historical imagination, simultaneously regulated by the languages of patriotic monumentalism and by the compulsion to manufacture founding origins out of the vertiginous situation of the moment that threatened to dissolve the solid traditions on which long-term identities were based.

Spanish American literary historiography originated within a landscape marked by the Independence Day celebrations, which began to replace the calendar of religious festivities of earlier times with the now sacred but nevertheless banal and prosaic celebrations of the nation. The history of everyday life that was experienced in a low-key fashion until the middle of the century began to be celebrated on a large scale with the centenaries of the birthdays, saints's days, and deaths of the Liberators, the Declarations and Wars of Independence; the anniversaries of the illustrious, national heroes; the first and the last day of the year, the 12th of October, and carnivals. . . . The construction of the State apparatus was marked by an uncontrolled celebratory spirit, which encouraged an expansion of public works and increased communication, for public adornment as well as cultural activities. The celebration of the Mexican *Grito de Dolores* [Call for Independence] was able to synchronize on the same date the opening of the National Theater and its staging of Verdi's *La Traviata*, the inauguration of the aqueduct and the central drainage system of Mexico City, a banquet for 3,000 people to fête Prince Henry of Prussia, and the presentation of a laurel wreath to the writer of the best ode to Porfirio Díaz, Cuauhtémoc, or Christopher Columbus, accompanied by a dramatic performance of *La Libertad*, a tableau comprising the elegant ladies of the choicest Aztec society. The same audience was as delighted to watch the inauguration of the drainage system as it was to drain a glass of the finest Moët et Chandon, or–without making too many distinctions, since it was all a question of good taste and love of art–to toast the recently-elected poet laureate or the ample bosom of the new soprano.

Despite the entirely apocryphal nature of my example here, it actually resembled less fictitious events of the time. Modern times brought with them new technologies and comforts to everyday life, which co-existed with a mixture of styles that were often imitative caricatures of what was deemed to be modern. Cities grew, and with them, their population. For the first time ever, there was a perception of the existence of crowds, which had to be contained or repressed or, at best, disciplined using pedagogical means and channeled through the modeling influence that art could exert. Grandiloquence and theatricality characterized many of the cultural manifestations of social life, particularly those controlled and subsidized by the State. Because of new architectural scenarios–courts of justice, public squares, statues, avenues, parks, theaters, shops, markets, spas, and hippodromes–urban space now permitted unusual human agglomerations, which had to be brought together around showy public celebrations that bore the disingenuous stamp of self promotion of the person who had organized them: the nation was embodied in the incumbent governor, who consecrated his personality through national rituals–and vice versa. State and nation, as abstract artifacts, were now personalized in the figure of the illustrious citizen; the parade of such figures occasionally bordered on that tasteless exhibitionism so in vogue at the time. During his administration (1870–1888), the Venezuelan Guzmán Blanco, the "Regenerator of the Republic," used to enjoy comparing himself to Simón Bolívar, in a vertiginous game of assimilations that ended up fusing both personages (see Rama 1984, 1985; Silva 1993).

The secularization of religious life paralleled the consecration of the fatherland, and the worship of the fatherland was the result of the identification of a State that was trying to consolidate itself with various inter-class alliances: the old oligarchy, the new sectors of the commercial bourgeoisie and the popular masses. As Rafael Gutiérrez Girardot has pointed out:

la "sacralización" de lo que la burguesía llamaba la "patria". . .no era otra cosa que la abusiva identificación de su estado con el "pueblo," con la Nación, con el Estado. Y esta Nación, esta patria tuvo sus "símbolos," celebró ritos y cultos y creó normas tácitas, pero eficaces: el "amor a la patria," "todo por la patria," el "sacrificio en el altar de la patria" etc. etc. Es decir, se secularizó el vocabulario de la misa y de la praxis religiosa, y se sacralizó a la Nación y a la patria. (84)

the "consecration" of what the bourgeoisie called the "fatherland". . .was nothing more than the abusive identification of their State with the "people," the Nation and the State. And this Nation, this fatherland, had its "symbols," celebrating rites and cults, and created unspoken, but effective rules: "love of the fatherland," "everything for the fatherland," "sacrifice on the altar of the fatherland," and so on. In other words, the vocabulary of mass and religious practice was secularized, while the Nation and the fatherland were consecrated.

A particular taste for histrionic performance, not devoid of fanfare and fireworks, was linked to the desire for legitimization of a rising class, which, lacking its own lifestyle (in keeping with the new economic and political power it was beginning to enjoy), saw fit to loot and indiscriminately appropriate forms from other historical times and geographical spaces. It was clear that a society of posturing was emerging (see Rama 1985), together with an acute awareness of the symbolic power of words and their subsequent use as a mechanism for shaping

sensibilities, appealing to loyalty, making groups cohere, and above all, manipulating audiences. Let us imagine the impact that the performance of the allegory *Apoteosis de Bolívar* [Apotheosis of Bolívar], to commemorate the centenary of the hero's birth, must have had on the Caracas public, which, in 1883, had still not shaken off its parochialism: Inside the Teatro Guzmán Blanco (see **Figure 1**), Bolívar was to appear "coronado de laureles, por dos ángeles suspendidos en la parte principal del templete; lluvias de flores caen desde lo alto; Marte desciende de la altura en nube de oro y púrpura" (Castellanos 2: 97–8) ("crowned with laurels, suspended by two angels over the main part of the stage; streams of flowers cascaded onto the stage, Mars descended from above in a cloud of gold and purple"). The evening before, the outside of the theater "aparecería la víspera engalanado de flámulas, banderolas y escudos triunfales con los nombres de Miranda, Ribas, Arismendi, Guzmán Blanco . . ." ("would be swathed in pennants, streamers, and triumphal coats of arms with the names of Miranda, Ribas, Arismendi, Guzmán Blanco . . ."). And in the center of the square, lit up for the very first time by electric light, "una guirnalda colosal de flores con las iniciales S.B. y G.B. hecha toda de rosas y claveles" (Castellanos 2: 98) ("a colossal garland of flowers with the initials S.B. and G.B made up of roses and carnations"). At the same time, Felipe Tejera had composed the long epic poem, *La Boliviada*, which was to be recited in honor of the occasion; its author, together with other luminaries of national literature, on the same day were to celebrate the founding of the Venezuelan National Academy of the Language. It is hardly surprising that in this "chorus of perpetual adoration" of the illustrious Spanish American–Simón Bolívar–the historians of national literature were among them. On this occasion, reality beggared fiction.

The consolidation of the state apparatus and its consensual validation, with the aim of creating what is now called an imagined community, was the result of numerous factors: economic, military, bureaucratic, and the reintegration of the nation into the international community. The role played by public verbal-symbolic forms (the press, advertising, architecture, plastic and musical arts, theater, parades, and literature–from the private reading of newspaper serials to public contests and street lampoons) proved decisive in the process of national configuration (consult Anderson; Romero; Silva 1993; Baczko). The learned, political subject of the modern State perceived the high yields that could be obtained from gestures alluding to the representational quality of things, in terms of both the democratic process (to exist for the other) and the theatrical process (to be another than oneself). In this last respect, one of the key moments of simulation in the politics of affectation was achieved through the strength of appearances, disguises, and manners (one should recall the success of Manuel Antonio Carreño's [d. 1874] *Manual de urbanidad y buenas maneras* [1854; Manual of Urbanity and Good Manners]) and a national fiction in which signs replaced action: Statues replaced heroes; portraits replaced men; money replaced patricians; railways replaced progress; historiography replaced culture; and hymns replaced nations.

The limited influence and legitimacy of the new social protagonists had to be hidden under a veneer of cultural forms; among these, the exhumation of history was the most effective disguise for concealing the impact of the changes caused by modernity by means of the elaboration of imaginary traditions and pasts. The "revival" of various historical styles effortlessly permitted the construction of this academic,

Figure 1.

The Teatro Guzmán Blanco in Caracas, named for the president of Venezuela, Antonio Guzmán Blanco, c. 1890. (Archive of the author)

monumentalist, courtly, and laudatory art so dear to elites unfamiliar with actual historical detail. The patricians of the earlier years of the newly constituted Republics were unlikely to have been as compulsively concerned with creating a prestigious "past" for themselves. Indeed, they were a class that did not have to justify its authority by flaunting its ancestry and origins; they had the power to ignore the past. The discourse of the past was an invention of bourgeois modernity: Its various historiographical genres constituted the technologies of the lettered city used to authenticate the project of the nation-state for this new sector. In the words of Angel Rama, "la democratización que va creciendo a lo largo del siglo, se pone a revisar la Historia como una guardarropía de teatro" (1985, 83) ("the democratization that developed throughout the century used History as though it were a wardrobe of theatrical costumes").

Performing history as though it were a script or offered characters from a particular work could give rise to myths, or at least grandiloquence; above all, it could produce a claim to truth on the basis of this past in the service of the present. Inventing the past was a demagogic instrument that included not only the cultured formats of historiographic writing (such as biography, political, intellectual, and literary history, as well as other historical narratives) but also the more popular genres (such as the librettos of operas and certain carnival processions). Patricians probably did not need to see themselves depicted among Egyptian pyramids and Celtic ruins, as Roman emperors or medieval knights, or in invented geographical or temporal settings whose anachronistic lack of

precision ended up revealing the popular origins of the new taste for expropriating the "text" of the past, without rhyme or reason, as a means of adapting its secrets to their ends (see Hobsbawm and Ranger). Past and present could be haphazardly exchanged in everyday experiences, shifting easily into a chain of successive events as fiction-history-fiction. What difference could there be, for these sensibilities, between having imaginary walks with Radamès among the Egyptian temples of *Aida*, and having strolled through the Caracas residence of the Benítez, who had brought in a few camels to facilitate the transfer of building materials for their magnificent mansion with its spacious garden (Calcaño 310), or spending the weekend at the Schiaffinos' house in Mexico, decorated in the style of Pompeii, with an Aztec room to give it an exotic touch, where a daguerreotype might capture the owners in Japanese kimonos (Rama 1985, 84–5).

Obviously, this asymmetry in the use and abuse of the past did not affect all cultural expressions in the same way. The wall around the lettered city shielded it from the multi-colored and carnivalesque excess of historicist fiction; it strove to maintain a sobriety and coherence in its own discourse, to produce at least the necessary effects of "scientific truth" that would permit the credibility of the institutional apparatus (academies of history, geography, medicine and language; university chairs, schools, ministries, secretariats) that it was establishing as the mainstay of the national State itself. Indeed, the use of the "fiction of the past" that occurred at this level developed methodological categories and operations (such as the fetishization of data, the overuse of documentation and the archive, excessive quotations of irrelevant authorities, the creative invention of sources, and in general the philological strategy of overwhelming the user with detail, map making, the exhibition of case histories, statistics, and photographs) that established the bases of the modern acquisition of knowledge. These gave rise to the series of academic disciplines whose limitations and boundaries we are now questioning. In this respect, the scholars who assumed responsibility for the "invention of the past" had the power to invest genealogical arguments with a cohesive function for the new national entities.

Then, amid great tension, modernity made an aggressive technological novelty converge with ancient traditions that had resisted modernization. It was the consumption of luxury goods by an increasingly cosmopolitan society that had plunged the culture into the rapid internationalization of a series of social rites and practices intended to establish traditions that were artificially old. The old and the new crisscrossed and overlapped. And herein lay one of the greatest charms of the historiographic genre: Writing about the past shifted people's gaze toward past events, while concealing the social apparatus that produced them. It was a highly effective disguise (see de Certeau 1995), able to conceal the fears and desires of the new oligarchy that historical circumstances themselves called into question. Torn between vanishing traditions and lifestyles, with which they no longer wanted to be identified, and the increasingly irresistible attraction of Westernization, in order to keep pace with industrialized countries, paradoxically, they also felt that they were obliged, in this world economy, to have an identity of their own. In this, the production of a national literature by the lettered class would play a significant role. Representations that concealed violent contradictions, such as the discourses that expressed asymmetries and hybridizations, were one of the matrices that characterized the cultural forms of this period in Spanish America, the result of a double vision, torn between *mestizo* habits and traditions acculturated over time and the demands of the present to redefine his cultural logic. The Janus-like face of this modernity sometimes seemed dramatically paradoxical or even schizophrenic.

As one of the legitimizing narratives of the institutional apparatus, national literary historiography began to emerge during the second half of the century, closely linked to the slow stabilization of the national State, when the latter managed to impose relative social peace, under the positivist slogan of order and progress. In 1844, José Manuel Valdez y Palacios (1812–1854) published *Bosquejo sobre el estado político, moral y literario del Perú en sus tres grandes épocas* [Outline of the Political, Moral, and Literary State of Peru in Its Three Great Epochs]. José Ignacio Víctor y Eyzaguirre's (d. 1875) elegant, three-volume *Historia eclesiástica, política y literaria de Chile* [Ecclesiastical, Political, and Literary History of Chile] was published in 1850 at the Imprenta del Comercio in Valparaíso. In 1867, José María Vergara y Vergara (1831–1872) humored the Colombian oligarchy with his *Historia de la literatura en Nueva Granada, desde la Conquista hasta la Independencia, 1538–1820* [History of the Literature of New Granada from the Conquest to Independence]; in 1868, Ecuador and Mexico could boast of having their *Ojeada histórico-crítica sobre la poesía ecuatoriana desde su época más remota hasta nuestros días* [Historical-Critical Review of Ecuadorian Poetry from the Most Remote Period to Our Time], written by Juan León Mera (1832–1894), and *Del movimiento literario en México* [On the Literary Movement in

Mexico] by Pedro Santacilia (1826–1910), both published by the printing presses of their respective governments. In the isolated Paraguay of José Gaspar Rodríguez de Francia (1766–1840), Ildefonso Antonio Bermejo (1820–1892) was able to write *Enciclopedia mensual y popular de ciencias, artes y letras* [Monthly and Popular Encyclopedia of Science, Arts, and Letters] in 1860. Even in Cuba, which would still have to wait a few more decades for its Independence, the pre-Independence winds of the time fostered considerable cultural reflection, leading Antonio Bachiller y Morales (1812–1889) to publish his *Apuntes para la historia de las letras y de la instrucción pública en la isla de Cuba* [Notes for a History of Letters and Public Education in Cuba] between 1859 and 1861; these were hardly "notes," since the three volumes are virtually an extended defense of Cuban intellectual autonomy.

Rather than being foundational narratives that could have accompanied the creation of Republics in the years immediately after Independence, these works were in fact constituted genres that, by their very nature, required more highly structured circumstances for their production, as regards both the necessary infrastructure and the conditions of politico-cultural concentration. One should recall that these books were published in deluxe editions, with embossed, fine leather covers; their very appearance had to fulfill certain protocols in representing official culture. By the end of the century, there was a heightened awareness of the representativeness that a nation's cultural capital could have, in the eyes, for example, of foreign travelers. These editions were also regarded as valuable objects that could be acquired and displayed on the shelves of private libraries or else exhibited in Universal Exhibitions. They lacked the ephemeral nature of newspaper articles, almanacs, chapters of serials, poems, or broadsheets. They were veritable monuments to the State's investment in printing presses as the heritage of a "nation," both because of their ambitious content and the very size of the books. Together with constitutions, grammars, and anthologies, they could serve as the new sacred books aimed at founding equally new modern identities, that is, of the nation (see Achugar).

However, the vagaries of the emergence and zenith of national literary histories (between 1850 and 1914, approximately) reveal that their most prolific stage was reduced to the last two decades of the nineteenth century and the first decade of the twentieth. In other words, they were produced at a time of intense display of civic imagination by States, as a result of both an internal process of affirmation and centralization of patriotic fervor and a greater insertion in the international market (and therefore a substantial increase in currency and the expansion of a taste for consumption in the capital cities). All this permitted the timely exploitation of the series of centenaries of heroes' birthdays and Independence, together with the creation of new centennials such as the "Day of Discovery" and "Columbus Day" to promote innumerable activities that, in the end, were intended to demonstrate the degree of civilization and progress achieved. Efforts were to be intelligently divided between bridges, abattoirs, statues, poorhouses, and telegraph lines *and* dictionaries, grammars, literary journals, operas, waltzes, and histories.

In 1892, October 12 was legislated as a national holiday in all Spanish-speaking countries in the Americas, and, of course, there was no shortage of new literary histories published to celebrate links with the former mother country, such as Isidoro Laverde Amaya's (1852–1903) *Literatura colombiana* [1892;], published in Madrid. Several histories were published in Chile, including *La alborada poética en Chile, después del 18 de septiembre de 1810* [1892; Poetic Dawn in Chile, after 18 September 1810] by Miguel Luis Amunátegui (1828–1888); *La literatura chilena: bosquejo histórico desde la colonia hasta nuestros días, escrito para América Latina* [1891; Chilean Literature: A Historical Outline from the Colonial Period to Our Days, Written for Latin America] by Pedro Pablo Figueroa (1857–1909); *Bosquejo del desarrollo intelectual de Chile* [1889; Outline of the Intellectual Development of Chile] by Augusto Orrego Luco (1848-1933); and the monumental *Historia de la literatura colonial de Chile* [1878; History of Colonial Chilean Literature] by José Toribio Medina (1852–1930); César Nicolás Penson's (1855–1901) *Reseña histórico-crítica de la poesía en Santo Domingo* [1878; Historic-Critical Review of Poetry in Santo Domingo]. Guatemala concentrated its historiographic production during this anniversary, with Agustín Gómez Carrillo's (1842–1915) *Reseña historico-crítica de la literatura guatemalteca* [1893; Historic-Critical Review of Guatemalan Literature], Antonio Batrés Jáuregui's (1847–1929) *Literatos guatemaltecos* [Guatemalan Writers of Literature]; *Landívar e Irisari; con un discurso preliminar sobre el desenvolvimiento de las ciencias y las letras en Guatemala* [1896; Landívar and Irisari; with a Preliminary Speech on the Development of Sciences and Letters in Guatemala] and Ramón Salazar's (1852–1914) three-volume *Historia del desenvolvimiento intelectual de Guatemala desde la fundación de la primera escuela de letras europeas hasta la inauguración del Instituto Nacional de Indígenas* [1897; History of Intellectual Development of Guatemala from the Foundation of the First School of European Letters to the Inauguration of the National Institute of Indian Affairs]. This increasingly hispanophilic climate at the end of the nineteenth-century was accompanied by other signs of reconciliation, such as the foundation of a series of *Academias de la lengua* ("Academies of the [Spanish] Language"), corresponding to the one in Spain, beginning with the Colombian *Academia* in 1871; this climate had its peninsular counterpart in the no less immense *Antología de poetas hispanoamericanos realizada por la Real Academia Española* [1893–95; Anthology of Hispano-American Poets Published by the Royal Spanish Academy] by Marcelino Menéndez y Pelayo (1856–1912), who continued to reinforce the neo-Hispanic perspective that framed virtually all the historiographic writing on the other side of the Atlantic. Spain recovered her intellectual dominance over its former colonies by peaceful means, and the latter accepted–through sophisticated scriptural operations–the historiographic fiction that offered a link and a rapprochement with Europe.

Other centenaries also proved useful in providing the State and the founders of the nation, both past and present, with enormous works that evaluated and compiled the country's cultural life. Virtually all Venezuelan literary historiography was organized around the centenary of the birth of Simón Bolívar: José Güell y Mercader (1839–1905) dedicated the two volumes of his *Literatura venezolana* [1883; Venezuelan Literature] to the "regenerator" of the nation, a gesture repeated by Ramón Hernández, with his *Literatura Venezolana* (1883). Shortly afterwards, Julio Calcaño (1840–1918) completed his *Reseña histórica de la literatura venezolana escrita expresamente para la América Latina* in 1888 [Historic Review of Venezuelan Literature Written Expressly for Latin America]. In 1895, combining various centenaries, the El Cojo printing press issued *El primer libro venezolano de literatura, ciencias y bellas artes* [The First Venezuelan Book of Literature, Science, and Fine

Arts], whose thousands of references made it more of an encyclopedia than a history book (see **Figures 2** and **3**). The autocratic government of Guzmán Blanco turned certain dates into significant national events, thereby promoting a social dynamic framed by a series of anniversaries. He constructed the country's memoirs on the basis of staged events as permanent dates to be remembered in the future, thus magnifying each aspect of the material transformation of the nation.

As far as literary historiography specifically is concerned, the modern State created the necessary social conditions for the development of this genre; yet at the same time, this historiography underpinned the legitimacy of the State apparatus with its verbal-symbolic capital. In this way, the work of the Argentinean Ricardo Rojas (1882–1957), *La literatura argentina: ensayo filosófico sobre la evolución de la cultura en el Plata* [1917–1922; Argentinean Literature. Philosophical Essay on the Evolution of Culture in the Plate Region] in four volumes, and of the Uruguayan Carlos Roxlo (1860–1926), *Historia crítica de la literatura uruguaya* [1911–1920; Critical History of Uruguayan Literature] in seven volumes, have constituted the

Figure 2.

Cover of El primer libro venezolano de literatura, ciencias y bellas artes, offered in memory of General Antonio José de Sucre on the centenary of his birth, Caracas, 1895. (Archive of the author)

Figure 3.

The inside cover of El primer libro venezolano de literatura, ciencias y bellas artes depicts the coat of arms of the National Association of Science, Literature and the Fine Arts. The publisher was the literary magazine El cojo ilustrado (1892–1915). (Archive of the author)

clearest expression to date of celebrating the centenary of the founding of Latin American nations.

In short, the materialization of historiographic writing in books and this mutual influence of historiography-book-national consecration, which one can clearly see in about 1900, was the result of a lengthy earlier process characterized by burning polemics and lucid reflections by learned men, as yet uncommitted to the State apparatus, who, basically through the medium that the press provided, planned what would eventually become the corpus of national literature, its possible origins, stages of development, and social function. Indeed, the early emergence of anthologies (one should recall that the first continental anthology was Juan María Gutiérrez's [1809–1878] *América Poética* [1846; Poetic America]), collections of poems–liras, garlands, and albums–made a significant contribution to the construction of literary traditions and took the risk of establishing a link between the creative imagination and the idea of the nation that was being founded.

The construction of the literary system should therefore be regarded as a process that clearly acquired its institutional form during the last third of the nineteenth century, but it cannot be fully appreciated unless it is linked to a series of related practices, such as the establishment of free, compulsory public education; the dissemination of literacy through special education programs (see Ramos 1989); the creation of normal schools for training teachers; the increased numbers of printing presses and newspapers; the expansion of a reading public that was particularly fond of literature and poetry (see Rama 1985; Silva 1993); the emergence of institutions that guaranteed the expression of an official culture (academies of language, art, music, and science) that supported intellectuals and artists through generous patronage; the fashion of literary cafés, which stimulated the discussion and reading of both political and literary texts; the organization of public libraries and reading rooms; the emergence of athenaeums, in some cases directed by learned women; an increased taste for competitions and contests. All this suggests a markedly strategic function of culture, which in many cases permitted individual social climbing, as well as more complex operations of political legitimation.

Art and literature represented abundant symbolic capital, thanks to the new popularity that high culture had acquired. An aesthetic of appearances, manners, and elegant form was one of the golden rules of the new era of world capitalism. The politics of affectation would be added to the politics of high culture. Thus, the historiographic book was a type of cultural merchandise par excellence, a museum-shop displaying what had been chosen as the sum of national values. At a glance, one could see and possess (the illusion of) the "entire" evolution of the literary achievement of a country and appreciate the degree of civilization achieved through the imaginary forms expressed by words. It was the era of the textual museum, which could gather the scattered fragments of time into the homogenous order of a national discourse. To a certain extent, literary historiography shared a number of features with museums and universal exhibitions, in the sense of having served as the new expression (both for this period and later on) of the accumulative appetite of the bourgeois spirit of conspicuous consumption, which transformed any object, torn from its original context, first into merchandise and then, since these objects had no functional value, into relics, fetishes, and *objects d'art* (see Guidieri). In their locales, whether art galleries or newspaper pages, the scraps of culture, in a sort of disparate cramming together of objects, entered into the new capitalist order of acquisition; this demorphologized things, turning them into an analogous chronological series of status symbols, governed by the same logic that homogenized them as merchandise, fetishes, and trophies. But with time, the social market made them heterogeneous again, and they acquired greater value as primitive or exotic specimens on display for the crowd. Museums, albums, anthologies, and histories, turned the past into fragments. This diversity of forms was an essential part of the modern perception of the transculturated and transgeographical diorama of the past as an arbitrary collection of fragments.

Let us compare certain events. As mentioned earlier, the case of Venezuela is once again paradigmatic in this respect: the compilation and construction of the canon was combined with the year of the centenary of Simón Bolívar's birth (1883). It was not only the inaugural moment of literary historiography but also the year of the first Universal Exhibition, which several European countries attended as observers (see **Figure 4**). The fair was the showcase for the world to get to know and appreciate the nation, and as such, had to fill the building designed for this purpose with objects of the most varied origins, ranging from pianos produced by Triemer, Hiller, and Rodríguez, coffee grinding machines, revolvers, carriages, typewriters, sugar mills, and paintings by Venezuelan artists commissioned to paint the memory and face of national history to soap, candles, tobacco, silk-worm cocoons, animals from Zulia, both live and embalmed, and trivialized versions of national heroes represented in affordable paperweights. It served as a showcase for putting on display for foreigners not only the results of the country's material progress but also its moral progress, understood in terms of literary and artistic knowledge. The exhibition was an architectural gesture and as a socio-cultural event, reduced to the unidimensional perspective of national achievement. It was just as fitting to display the sewing machines produced by Winkelman Bros (an expression of technological progress) as it was to show an extensive collection of oil paintings that retrospectively created the

cultural imaginary of the national past. "La firma del acta de independencia" ["The Signing of the Act of Independence"] and "La batalla de Carabobo" ["The Battle of Carabobo"], by Martín Tovar y Tovar (1828–1902), hung next to "La muerte de Guaicaipuro" ["The Death of Guaicaipuro"], painted in the same bombastic, heroic style. In honor of the occasion, artists created a visible body of national history. This showcase or museum of national glory demonstrated the artificial nature of the historical past, placed there with the same surreal effect as placing a sewing machine and an umbrella on a dissecting table. Likewise and with the same logic, historiography, like the Exhibition palace, compiled vast lists of university graduates, doctors, public speakers, writers, physicians, historians, and Venezuelan jurists who filled out the nation's skeleton.

To convert the patriarchal structures of the rural population of the plains, deserts, mountain ranges, and forests into an urban modernity by means of fairly complex operations of symbolization, supported primarily by a culture of images, was

Figure 4.

Certificate of first place award in the Venezuelan Exposition of 1883, which celebrated the centenary of the birth of Simón Bolívar and was presided over by the president of Venezuela, Antonio Guzmán Blanco. (Archive of the author)

one of the most conspicuous tasks of the body of learned men working in the service of the state. The capacity of poetic language to create an illusion meant that Bolívar could easily appear in the same exhibition hall as the Teque and Caraca Indians. Thus dolled up, the nation could offer itself on the world market; the country had to make itself attractive to foreign investments and immigration and, for the moment, it was giving notice, at least in general terms, of being able to provide habitable conditions for a non-Spanish-speaking population.

The popularity among the ruling class for imported social forms of elegance and good taste was in evidence in the obligatory "masked ball," but it can also be seen as the expression of something more serious–the rapidly advancing globalization of Latin America. Modern times were revolutionizing all the means of travel and communication (by land and sea; visual and auditory). The development of the world economy began to reduce the asymmetry of the producing structures of Western countries, momentarily linking the peripheral elites to the comings and goings and the modalities of the metropolitan centers. This internationalization, part of the new phase of capitalism, was (and is) simultaneously centrifugal (because it was globalizing, and its operative conditions were the same everywhere) and centripetal (because it tended to make the magnetizing axis and the one that controlled goods a single center). The need to bring together (and thus to persuade, convince, mobilize) and galvanize the media was one of the rallying cries and needs of the new political parties, as well as a response to the characteristics of the global market of symbolic goods. Both teaching people to read and write, through compulsory schooling, and the installation of railway networks, bridges, telegraph and telephone lines, and steamboats were results of this same, though apparently different, logic of modernization and globalization (see **Figure 5**).

Modern mass media thus came together as a technology that disciplined subjectivities and territories, with a view to homogenizing both as spaces to be governed and exploited. As early as 1847 Andrés Bello (1781–1865) had recognized the importance of standardizing a single language throughout the continent to facilitate "la difusión de las luces, la administración del Estado, y la unidad nacional" (1951, 4:12) ("the dissemination of enlightenment, the administration of the state, and national unity"). Within this new political economy, a unified language established a correlation between linguistic and territorial identities in favor of inter-American commerce. An inadequate system of regulation of mass media facilitated globalization and promoted the development of a common market. It is therefore by no means surprising that throughout Spanish America governments should have constructed significant buildings for post and telegraph offices, railway stations and customs offices, not to mention the virtual palaces dedicated to the national academies of the Spanish language.

The subject of language and all the debates concerning its stabilization, cleansed of "irregularidades dialectales, licenciosas y bárbaras" (Bello 1951, 4:12) ("dialectal, licentious and barbarous irregularities") were the most visible aspects of the new communication technologies. The obsession with linguistic

Figure 5.

Grade school classroom shortly after the establishment of compulsory education, c. 1860. (Archive of the author)

correctness that absorbed grammarians, teachers and politicians established an implicit correlation between language and social status (and work): speaking, entering the social space governed by the law of correct usage, was concomitant with the person's incorporation into the labor force. Consequently, the wish to subject and purify language occurred primarily on the pedagogical level, within the framework of a policy aimed at national unification (see Ramos 1993; Balibar and Laporte).

It was here that literature would play a distinctly historical role not only in providing symbolic, well-written contents, conducive to informing the new collective imagination (see Anderson; Sommer) but also in coordinating and reducing the profound contradictions of a heterogeneous and multicultural society at the representational level. Literary works would set the standard for a disciplined national language; in these texts, the representation of the hierarchy of correct usage in the linguistic market would be defined in dominant and subordinate registers. Thus the construction of the paradigmatic axis of these models of language, literature, and nation was the task of literary historiography, whose function, among other things, was to establish the canon of authors and works to be converted into the society's symbolic capital. It would be rather like the new sacred book that would be the moral bastion (a secular version of religious heritage) of the nation.

As a result, education, as a space for the disciplinary procurement of persons, languages, and souls for the nation, would teach as part of its curriculum methods for becoming familiar with the new languages of artistic communication. The construction of the national literary canon, a task controlled by the historiographic establishment, was closely linked to the need to construct a cultural imaginary comprising collective subjectivities created by pedagogical means. It is not surprising that at the same time as literary histories emerged, institutes and academies of Fine Arts, with their respective schools of music and painting, were also established in every country. Within this context, the first chairs of literature were also created. In Venezuela, for example, a mere ten years elapsed between the foundation of the Institute of Fine Arts (1877) and the establishment of a Center of Literary Studies (1887) in Valencia, where young writers could read systematically and be exposed to the Latin classics, Spanish texts and, obviously, the work of Venezuelan writers (see Silva 1993). At the same time, by the last decade of the century, the female population, which, according to surveys, surpassed the male in reading, already directed athenaeums, literary journals, reading circles, and orchestras and had already established schools for girls and young women. However, despite the astonishing breadth of women's cultural production, the task of writing the history of national literature was an exclusively male concern. It was the same with the national pantheon, which was reserved exclusively for the remains of the fathers of the nation. Women built their own private cemeteries, just as they created their own cultural space. The fashion for poetic albums allowed them to collect fragments of poetry for domestic consumption.

Teaching literature–as the privileged use of language that would provide citizens with new coordinates of social life– also required a specific plan for implementation. What was the point of consecrating symbolic capital if it was not circulated, consumed, interiorized, and recapitalized? In his article "La enseñanza de la literatura" [1908; "The Teaching of Literature"], José Enrique Rodó (1871–1917) designed a strategy for disseminating the various meta-discursive operations already under way in the literary system. The field of literary production was undoubtedly being disciplined both by the pigeonhole classifications of discursive typologies and through the academic training in their use. Rodó felt that the teaching of literature should be supported by an "aesthetic science," which, unlike ancient rhetoric, should focus on the study of "American" literary forms of modern times:

> Ningún retórico se ha detenido a pensar, por ejemplo, que, variando la importancia relativa de los géneros literarios según las condiciones de las diferentes épocas, caducando y decayendo unos, suscitándose o realzándose otros, las clasificaciones de las retóricas clásicas deben ser revisadas y adaptadas al orden de la realidad literaria actual. . . . Abatir esa armazón vetusta de clasificaciones y jerarquías; probar a distribuir el variadísimo contenido de la actividad literaria propia de la civilización y cultura modernas, según un orden fundado en las formas que realmente viven. . . . (582; 533)

> No rhetorician has paused to think, for example, that, since the relative importance of literary genres varies according to the conditions of the various eras, some falling into disuse and decay, others emerging and becoming more prominent, the classifications of classical rhetoric should be revised and adapted to the standards of current literary reality. . . . This old framework of classifications and hierarchies should be dismantled and attempts made to distribute the highly varied contents of literary activity characteristic of modern civilization and culture, on the basis of their actual living forms. . . .

Yet the teaching of literature could be successful only if it were complemented by two other, no less important instruments:

> una *Antología* compuesta con objeto y plan esencialmente didácticos y ajustada al ordenado desenvolvimiento del libro de *teoría*, para corroborarlo con la eficacia irremplazable de los ejemplos; y un texto de *historia literaria*, parco en nombres y en juicios bibliográficos, y en el que se atendiese debidamente a la relación de la actividad literaria con los caracteres de raza, de país, de sociabilidad, de instrucción, que concurren a imprimir el sello en la literatura de cada nación y cada época. (533, my emphasis)

> an *anthology* compiled on the basis of an essentially didactic purpose and plan and adjusted to the orderly development of *literary theory*, in order to corroborate it with the irreplaceable examples; and a *literary history*, sparing in names and bibliographical opinions, and giving due attention to the relationship between literary activity and the characteristics of race, country, social class, and educational level of instruction, which combine to stamp the hallmark of each nation and era on literature.

Rodó's proposals were the result of the intellectual and ideological context of his time, on the one hand, but they also founded and arranged the literary field within the institutional apparatus, on the other, while emphasizing the obvious link between the political aspect of the teaching of literature and the making of the nation-state. Literature prepared subjects for the public arena, situating them in a hierarchical order; at the same time, it was an ideal channel for the re-structuring of social sensibilities and forms, whose standardization would inevitably lead to a collective identity. This pedagogical operation, as an activity that was closely linked to the localized needs of a national project, also demanded the regionalized establishment of its agenda. This is the only explanation for the fact that, among the subjects taught, history and geography were so profoundly marked by territoriality. On the other hand, literary history would constitute the ideal point of convergence of nation, society, racial characteristics, and literary activity that would seal the particularity of each nation and each era. In other words, the pedagogical machines would seal the *literature-nation-history* concept and put it into operation: hence the importance of the chronological arrangement of the subject; the linear series of works would construct the qualitative evolution of the nation.

Thus the distinctive feature of modern times was the result of a genesis; it involved coming into existence in history. The dynamics imposed by the new communication technologies required the changing nature of things and their capacity for transformation for progress as Rodó claimed, the relative importance of literary genres varies according to the conditions of the various eras, some falling into disuse and decay, others emerging or becoming more prominent (582). The displacement of rhetoric (dismantling that old framework of classification and hierarchies) was a gesture that sought to get rid of atemporal universals to make way for the prolific construction of effects of the past which merely praised the modern present. Thus, the genre of literary historiography operated within these coordinates as a multivalent mechanism—at the pedagogical level, as an "orthopedic" device in the construction of the national imaginary by offering a series of molds to channel deflected sensibilities, and at the market level, by providing symbolic goods with an exchange value (by placing them at the same level as the discourse of the national exhibition and commercial showcase). At the political or State level, it operated by turning literature into a book-mausoleum, a sarcophagous or crypt of the immortal remains of the nation's men of letters, the virile body of the law—and the correct use of language; but it also functioned as a fictionalizing creation of national origins, an artifice of the past, a receptacle of memories, a control center for what was said and unsaid, an arena of patrimonies, and of identity of the visible body of the nation. It proved to be a writerly ritual par excellence in the consolidation of the modern Spanish American State apparatus, since it provided it with axioms, coherence, and density, making up, at least verbally, for the noticeable fissures and shortages in its actual configuration. The symbolic power that its accumulative effect could produce, as well as offering the required temporal diorama of national culture, turned literary historiography into the consecrational discourse of the fatherland, whose genealogical methods (not all that different from religious and hagiographic exegesis) filled the vacuum left by the demythologizing tendencies of the modern world.

Spanish America's nations built their State apparatuses as a response to the logic of Western European modernity, responding only partly and with enormous difficulties and limitations to the new internal and external realities; there was a confrontation between an inward-facing country, basically designed around regional loyalties and distinctly oralized cultures that were highly suspicious of the lettered city, and another, outward-facing country, concentrated in the cities, which was transformed according to international fashions and markets and which, as modernization progressed, compulsively sought to wash away any vestiges of rural roots or racial hybridization. Spanish America was straddling two powerful, virtually opposite, historico-cultural formations (on the one hand the attraction toward and the demands of a North Atlantic interlocutor, and on the other the vast and complex set of peasant, popular, Indian, and *mestizo* societies) whose only hope of solution was to

develop forms of representation in their symbolic and discursive practices that would use imaginary compensation to mesh the intractable contradictions of a project and a historical subject that wished it were a single, white, homogeneous, and Western nation (but knew it was not). The structure that separated the hinterland from the pressures of the new urban international situation (i.e., the rural from the urban, the great wealth from the bazaars and small trades) placed the learned subject in a dilemma of living in a double vision, which was required to satisfy the conditions of reception of a cosmopolitan audience (an audience that wished to see its history notarized), for whom literature served as the landmark of material progress, but at the same time, it had to continue to accommodate regionally marked cultural particularities, using sophisticated mechanisms involving cuts, adjustment, disguise, and obliteration.

How could one produce effects that would soften or muffle the recent surge of nationalism? How could one come to grips with the continuation of colonial literary traditions in a postcolonial society and with the challenge of the creation of identities based on heterogeneous, multilingual cultures, with multiple disruptions and violent interruptions in their historical processes? How could one reach a sense of where the origins of this national literature lie? Which historical past was the basis for national identity, and how could the legacy of non-Western cultures be incorporated into the scenario of learned bourgeois culture? These and many more questions would remain unresolved throughout the twentieth century.

Inclusions and exclusions, erasures and celebrations—all these occupied literary historiography during the time of its emergence, turning it into a highly complex laboratory for the construction and establishment of the bases of national canonical cultures and an invaluable prop for the credibility of the State apparatus. Fractures had to be healed, contradictions glossed over, paradoxes resolved, and vacuums filled. It seemed that the Gordian knot of the national issue was lying in wait for the historiographic exercise. For the *criollo* elites, both aristocratic and bourgeois, Conservative and Liberal, who were interested in this historical configuration, the project of the modern nation-state involved a moderate political and bureaucratic organization that would grant them, without substantially altering the deep structures of the productive system, land ownership, the distribution of social privileges, and their incorporation into the new market economy, with its vast profits. Throughout the nineteenth century, the elites developed a form of behavior that was Liberal and cosmopolitan in foreign policy matters; from their position as world market consumers, they tended to camouflage themselves with all forms of technological modernity. At the same time, however, as regards domestic policy, these same elites proved extremely cautious and reticent about transforming the old structures and lifestyles inherited from colonial times (consult Kaplan; Halperin Donghi; González 1987).

Insertion into the world economy involved the distribution of unequal roles: Latin America would be responsible for providing raw materials; which, contrary to the rules of Liberal ideology, would not only make every nation a single producer but would also expand and extend the large estates (the most profitable socio-economic system within the new interdependency) and guarantee cheap labor. The creation of the Republics was obviously based more on an apparatus of discursive fictions—the formality of verbal practices and symbolic rituals—than on the creation of national markets or development of a powerful middle class, comprising both industrialists and craftsmen or free citizenry, and including the equitable redistribution of land, the secularization of education, the diversification of the economy, greater participation in political affairs, the capacity to incorporate the nonwhite, non-Spanish-speaking majorities, or the more effective spread of schools and literacy. On the contrary, large estates increased and slavery or forms of indentured servitude were maintained, while entailed estates, sales taxes, the Church's tithes, local *caudillismo* (strong man rule), authoritarian regimes, and social structures that combined feudal, precapitalist and bourgeois forms and sensibilities continued.

It was the elites, historically more closely linked to trade with Europe, who were the most interested in modernizing their countries; they at least sought to leave a visible mark on the spheres with the highest concentration of political power (cities) and certain areas of communication and trade (ports, trains, ships, the telegraph). They spoke constantly of progress and understood progress to mean creating their nations in the image and likeness of Europe (Paris and London) and North America (New York, Chicago) (see **Figure 6**). This sector obviously needed to create its own vital scenario of economic liberalism as an extension of the centers of this cosmopolitan culture. Poised between the advance of globalization and ever more marginalized zones, they had no qualms about whitewashing the façades of their countries to attract increasing amounts of foreign capital, since by the sec-

ond half of the century, they not only controlled banking, communications, customs, and business but also were the owners of vast stretches of land (see Bradford Burns).

As the demands for economic Liberalism grew, the impact of a far from benevolent modernization also extended over less visible areas of Spanish American countries; it spread its railroads throughout the national territory, configuring its arbitrary expropriatory and exploitative drive and depriving the peasant and Indian communities of their lands. For the popular masses, modernization meant misery and poverty, coupled with the loss of roots, identity, and assets. Deprived of their lands, separated from their communities, decimated by hunger, prostitution, and crime, by the end of the century the masses realized that all effective means of intervention had evaporated. It is hardly surprising, then, that the process of State consolidation should have been systematically undermined and resisted by the immense majority, who expressed their disagreement with the national project (in other words, the modernizing project), since it constituted an attack on their values and lifestyle.

The Mexican case was the most extreme example of this reaction: Between 1876 and 1910, over 96 percent of peasants in villages lost their lands. The nation-state of the Díaz regime and the capitalist forces of modernization often engaged in brutal negotiations to achieve social calm; the policies of social order (to ensure capitalist progress) used genocidal solutions to eliminate native resistance or simply to "whiten"

Figure 6.

Architectural pastiche, end of the 19th century. (Archive of the author)

the population. The spread of railroads (the symbol of progress) was accompanied by massacres of the Amerindian peoples of Mexico's Northwest and more perverse forms of neo-colonial dependence. Meanwhile, governments celebrated the anniversaries of national Independence and blessed Christopher Columbus for having given them a Christian language, while artists used their pens and paintbrushes to (re)-compose the faces of Indians and gauchos, brought under control by the language of art. At the same time, the elites and the middle classes enjoyed a cosmetic modernization that increased their immediate comfort and improved the image they had of themselves, enabling them to blame the "barbarous" masses for delaying and frustrating the advance of progress. Only a few intellectuals, such as Juan Bautista Alberdi (1810–1884), José Martí (1853–1895), Manuel González Prada (1844–1918) and, in the decade of the 1920s, José Carlos Mariátegui (1894–1930) noted the disconcerting paradox of modernization and the Liberal project, in which literature was barely able to conceal the lacerations caused by this political and economic period, pointing out the ironic, and extremely fictitious, nature of the learned project itself; on numerous occasions, this had served only to accommodate and imaginatively fill in cracks and vacuums in the fictional panorama of a modern Latin America. Language muffled dissent with a whole range of intellectual theories drawn from Western logocentrism to minimize the unequal conditions of this exchange of goods and services. It concealed the dark side of progress by branding expressions of protest as "barbaric." The counter-culture of modernization was reduced to "barbarity," while European and Anglo-American modalities signified "civilization."

In short, modernization throughout the continent was achieved by means of a conservative progressivism, at great cost to the general population (see González 1987; Bradford Burns); in other words, Liberalism was introduced in a conservative fashion, since, like a two-faced Janus, national oligarchies and bourgeoisies engaged in a dual form of behavior: modern and progressive, cosmopolitan and bourgeois in their economies, tastes, and lifestyles–when it was a question of interacting on the international scene–yet rural and retrograde when it came to keeping as many structures of the colonial past as possible virtually intact during the process of national formation. These were Republics based on constitutions that were merely a written document, while the social order continued to be one allowing slavery. They talked of free trade when a national currency had as yet to be established (in many places, people were still paid in sacks of salt). A furious anti-colonialism was preached with regard to Spain, without regard to the new situations of English and French domination. In the name of secularization, the power of the Church was reduced, yet the lands expropriated from the latter were used to swell those of the landed oligarchy estate-owners. The political elite was Liberal toward the international market, whereas on the national market they favored exploitation by despotic governments that essentially maintained the traditional status quo. Modern, yet resistant to change and still undecided, these new oligarchies, once the colonial monarchical authority had disappeared, did not know how to make the transition. Centrifugal forces split the territories into numerous sovereignties regulated by various types of rationality, more in keeping with the colonial traditions that had centered aboriginal, Hispanic, and African elements around strong patriarchal and tribal structures. The

lack of a national market and genuine socio-economic interdependence encouraged isolation during the foundational period of the newly constituted Republics.

The idea of nation was a notion devised by the European bourgeoisie and the capitalist market, a notion that the Spanish American oligarchy incorporated as part of its historical plans for power. In Spanish America, it was imposed from above, by decree, as in the case of Bolivia (see Kaplan; Lukács), which created noticeable gaps between the manifestos of the elite's imagined community and what the territory with its inhabitants was really like. The nation functioned in the imagination of this minority group, which preached a barely credibly unity, in the midst, moreover, of noticeably pro-foreign tendencies, on the one hand, and non-Spanish-speaking majorities on the other.

Here literature, and particularly historiography, which constructed a national literary culture, played a far from insignificant role in designing various elements of cultural unity through a standard written language, the making of a common past, the totalizing forms of geography, a pantheon of national heroes, the differential representation of social and ethnic groups, and the ethical determinations of the forces of good (the nation) and evil (anything that might disrupt the national project). In other words, the moral distribution of Amerindian and Western cultures was in keeping with a hierarchical scale from bottom to top, from pagan deviation to salvation, from materiality to spirituality, from emptiness to abundance, from madness to reason. These narratives created the discursive links between "barbarous America" and "civilized Europe"; they wove the arguments of Spanish American progress in terms of a pilgrimage or symbolic displacement, and of a mutation in time and space. They designed reasons that enabled the elites to imagine an ascending evolutionary line that led the continent from the level of backwardness and obscurantism to the level of the Industrial Revolution, the world of trade and electricity and modern technology.

The cultural distance separating Latin American from European rationalism had to be disguised using extremely effective self-deception. Historiographic writing was the means created by Western rationalism that provided the illusion of an evolutionary process arranged in terms of stages shared by all humanity. The teleological conception of the time-line was part of the globalizing script that regarded material well-being as progress and saw the accumulation of capital as the ultimate goal of society. The ideology of progress was associated with the capitalistic notion of evolution, which represented both the expansion of production for the hegemonic centers and the strangulation of any production in the peripheries that was not connected with the extraction of raw materials. The imitation of the center by the periphery only translated into an approximation of the external forms of modernization, meaning that the enormous difference and monstrous disparity created by economic Liberalism had to be replaced by a powerful narrative that reconciled the interests and fantasies of European hegemonies. To this end, the historicism of Georg Wilhelm Friedrich Hegel's (1770–1831) *The Philosophy of History* (1857), the apex of European rationalism, controlled the writing of Spanish American history writing. These historians were able to select and organize, with a satisfactory degree of coherence, the necessary body of traditions, past events, and purported origins of the fragile nation-states, and thus display their historically arranged cultural heritage in the international concert of nations.

Knowledge of the cultural imaginary of this crossroads is necessary, if we are to gain an understanding not only of the emergence of the literary historical genre in Spanish America, but also of its epistemological orientation. The argumentative framework of Hegelian thought was appropriated for the State narrative, which historians compiled to give shape to and explain their respective national literatures; thus they constructed these narratives historically and organically within a script that would serve to justify the State policies of the present as well as, and above all, to provide the coherent discursive counterpart to economic Liberalism. In other words, Hegel's philosophy of history became the cultural side of the imaginary of the elites, which explained the policies of the New World economy. It was Reason that arranged the asymmetries, in discourse as in any narrative history (see White 1985; Colmenares), by its very sequential and linearly ordering nature; this is what made it easy to offer the fiction of rising (chronological) growth curves (from "childhood" to "maturity") and centripetal movements (from "barbarity" to "civilization," from the edges to the center, from outside to inside), with the understanding that these took shape because of their reality *and* their longed-for Utopia. Historians consequently constructed the literary histories of their nations on the basis of European models. Just as the rules of the market globalized economies, the German philosopher's theory embraced the entire world through the indivisibility of the "universal spirit." At this level, just as the new modality of capitalism was Liberalism and its political expression was the formation of the nation-state, the historiographical genre was one of the discursive forms of this modernity. If Liberalism aspired to world markets, historiography could elaborate the national literature's place within world literature, using the same conceptual framework as was displayed in Europe: This was one of the macro indicators in the drive toward modernity.

In *Lectures on the History of Philosophy* (1828), Hegel argued that the evolution of history implied a teleological development of the Universal Spirit (single and indivisible), which had shifted (in other words, progressed) from the Oriental civilizations, passing through Greece and Rome, and eventually reaching its final stage of plenitude and maturity with the European bourgeoisie and the modern nation-state. In the wanderings of this Spirit, Latin America and Africa had been excluded from its route–in other words, excluded from history and civilization. The Spirit had neglected to wander through them, and thus they remained as a kind of no man's land or natural zone that had to be conquered, subjugated, and (re)populated by the rational world. Consequently, universal geography was divided into historical and non-historical zones; the latter were incapable of producing rational forms despite all attempts to do so. On the contrary, the most highly rational (spiritual) area was located in countries that had produced the Industrial Revolution, whose forms were seen as a higher expression of this Spirit. History was condensed in these areas–the Old World– whereas, because of its permanent immaturity, America would always be the New World. The consequences were predictable: Latin America, Africa, and Australia would never be part of History. Latin America was thus situated within Hegelian thought as a space of non-historicity, and could ironically be the land of where everything had yet to be done. Therefore Latin America had to draw up a replacement version of its own possible history. And Hegel had himself anticipated one substitute for a national history: Everything that happens in the Americas has its origins in Europe.

This Hegelian universal Spirit had been perfectible in time; it had passed through reified forms and periods that had led to progress, until it achieved the supreme form of freedom of self-awareness: in the Prussian State and economic Liberalism. The underlying determinism in Hegel's philosophy authorized the Imperial mobility of the West in relation to the other natural spaces, conceived of as passive, sterile zones waiting to be civilized/colonized. The ideological defects in Hegel's language would soon trap the Latin American intelligentsia, and it was none other than Domingo Faustino Sarmiento (1811–1888) who repeated the German philosopher almost in unison:

> [H]emos de abandonar un suelo de los más privilegiados de la América a las *devastaciones* de la *barbarie*, mantener cien ríos navegables *abandonados* a las aves acuáticas. . . Hemos de cerrar voluntariamente la puerta a la inmigración europea . . .para *poblar* nuestros *desiertos*? . . . Después de la Europa, hay otro mundo cristiano civilizable y *desierto* que la América? (16, my emphasis)
>
> Should we abandon one of the most privileged soils in America to the *devastation* of *barbarity*, and *abandon* a hundred navigable rivers to aquatic birds? . . . Should we voluntarily shut the door to European immigration . . . to *populate* our *deserts?* . . .After Europe, is there another Christian world more capable of being civilized and *more unpopulated* than America?

Reflecting like concave mirrors, much of the learned sector modeled Spanish American geography, history, and culture in accordance with European Imperial perspectives.

Hegel's *Lectures* was not the only text responsible for shaping this view, although it was certainly one of the most articulate expressions and therefore able to serve as a model for these colonized sensibilities. To take an obvious example, beginning in the eighteenth century, several European travelers, men of science, ranging from Buffon and de Pauw to Charles-Marie de La Condamine (1701–1774) and Baron von Humboldt (1767–1835), created an important horizon of references through their writings, drawings, and engravings; in these America was consistently depicted as a sort of Eden, a space of exuberant nature and exotic plants, where the human element was barely visible amidst the eruption of volcanoes and earthquakes (see **Figure 7**). The natural histories or outlooks implied by the itineraries of these travelers intentionally stripped the continent of its social and historical life in order to repopulate it with plant and animal species (see Pratt 1992). The scientific knowledge that converted these lands into a well-supplied botanical garden prepared European desires–and to a certain extent those of the *criollo* elite of the Republics–for another conquest of the New World, this time supported by the technologies of science.

Thus, Hegel is only one link–albeit an essential one–in the long chain of virtually identical collective imaginations. The Hegelian link is important in that it served as the hinge that was able to formalize and reconcile the views and interests of both hegemonic groups (at once the local lettered elite and those in the metropolitan center with economic and political ambitions) within the order of social and discursive practices and thus served to rationalize the State enterprise within the project of Liberalism. Hegel's philosophy resolved the disparities caused by modernity by providing a narrative framework that would enable both the historiographic and the novel genres–the latter also regarded as historical in the nineteenth century–to justify backwardness and raise expectations for the creation of European imitations.

Figure 7.

Engraving by Karl Appun, c. 1858, depicting a "new world" without history, where nature ruled supreme. (Archive of the author)

The total freedom of the Hegelian Spirit, which equated the greatest development of the material forces of capitalism with the European model of civilization, constituted a sophisticated rhetorical framework that the modern bourgeoisie encouraged as one of the most serious and profitable systems for authenticating its New World hegemony. It legitimized geopolitical disparities in its inversely proportional and oblique relationships. While one of the parties was said to provide meaning and reason, it alienated the other; and while the latter surrendered its riches, it believed it was receiving civilization and progress in return. The mirage that made the elite see a process of mimetic progress toward the developed forms of other times lowered real living conditions in Spanish America. The gap between the elite and the common people, between writing and orality, between cities and the countryside, widened dramatically, confirming an agenda that would not only encourage the co-existence of heterogeneous cultural systems that contradicted each other but would also reveal the inorganic and artificial way in which the concept of nature was invoked during this period.

One of the fundamental premises offered by this philosophy of history was based on the way Hegel conceived the concept of period–not merely as a lapse of time, but in the sense of a step in a staircase; thus forcing a re-thinking of the arrangement and appreciation of events in terms of a teleological line, in which each stage is regarded as another step up a long staircase. The arrangement from bottom to top often led to an assessment that denigrated the past by arranging social processes according to a dramatic (or tragic) script. Thus the life of societies could shift (evolve) from obscurity or the gloomy times of slavery, colonialism, or feudalism, toward the light, associated with modern times, with free trade and the accumulation of capital, which guaranteed the realization of the Republic as a political form. Writing history according to these guidelines made it much easier for Latin American men of letters, regardless of whether they were Liberal or Conservative, to be able to recover the colonial past and understand it as a necessary stage in their historical process. For many, it was a completely expendable stage, oppressed by its unenlightened conditions as regards culture (see, for example, *Historia crítica de la literatura uruguaya* [1912–1916; Critical History of Uruguayan Literature] by Carlos Roxlo; *La literatura argentina: ensayo filosófico sobre la evolución de la cultura en el Plata* [1924; Argentinean Literature: A Philosophic Essay on Cultural Evolution of the River Plate] by Ricardo Rojas, and *La literatura venezolana en el siglo diez y nueve* [1906; Venezuelan Literature in the Nineteenth Century] by Gonzalo Picón Febres [1860–1918]); yet for many others, it was a long period characterized by a dichotomy of light and dark, which, rightly or wrongly, formed part of the background of what would be the movement toward Independence: a period of incubation and important legacies, such as the language and Judeo-Christian rationality of the colonizers (see *Historia de la literatura en Nueva Granada, desde la Conquista hasta la Independencia, 1538–1820* [1867; Literary History of New Granada from the Conquest to Independence] by José María Vergara y Vergara; *La literatura chilena: bosquejo histórico desde la colonia hasta nuestros días* [1891; Chilean Literature: Historical Summary from Colonial Time to Our Day] by Pedro Pablo Figueroa; *Historia de la literatura colonial de Chile* [1878; History of Colonial Chilean Literature] by José Toribio Medina; *Carácter de la literatura del Perú independiente* [1905; Character of the Literature of Independent Peru] by José de la Riva Agüero (1885–1944); *Bosquejo sobre el estado político, moral y literario del Perú en sus tres grandes épocas* [1844; Summary of the Political, Moral, and Literary State of Peru During Its Three Great Epochs] by José Manuel Valdez y Palacios).

History was understood to be a perfectible process, which, in its dialectical spiral (a highly productive Hegelian concept) gradually removed obstacles, including both the Inquisition and deserts populated with Indians, until it achieved the rationality of the culture of the industrial age. If the fetal stage corresponded to a remote Indian past (pre-Hispanic) of doubtful historicity, maturity was identified with the appropriation of trans-Atlantic historical forms. In this respect, periodization became an extremely useful tool, since it restored, re-arranged, and ensured the possibility of historiographical writing in post-colonial societies; this writing above all, was strategically important to the State for its symbolic validation. Thus, national histories could display a range of periods from the present to the past (pointing toward the low points of distant origins) and thereby provide recent States with a fictional genealogy. Time could be divided into logical fragments (and a period would constitute the beginning or the end of a process), rather than merely neutral chronological cuts. The interpretation of history became a valuable political weapon indicating the triumph or failure of an ideological project. Thus, Liberalism and historiography constituted two sides of the same coin of modern culture.

It is symptomatic that Andrés Bello (1965 [1848]) should have placed such a strong emphasis on the way of writing history, a new technology responsible for fictionalizing facts and reconstructing the narration of facts. Exhibiting a modernity related to that of the current historiographic theories of Hayden White and Michel de Certeau, the Venezuelan writer, trusting in the effectiveness of the narrative model as a rhetoric for re-establishing chains of events, credited this scriptural art with a representational power capable of accommodating and reducing the profound fissures and paradoxes entailed by the hegemonic project of modernization. Faced with the sometimes almost schizophrenic disparities between the social and discursive practices involving the narration of events, history was able to use the narrative form of historical representation to achieve a tranquil linearity where the very order of discourse composed the non-existent *Gestalt*. One should not forget that Bello was also the father of the grammar of American Spanish. The law that governed correct speech (see Ramos 1989) also regulated the language of events; the machine of language fabricated a realistic illusion

by expelling the heterogeneity of reality itself from its texture. And it is precisely this modality that established the form of writing history that would remain throughout the nineteenth century.

Although Bello eschewed the implementation of a philosophy of history ("la filosofía de la historia de Francia . . . carece de sentido aplicada . . . al pueblo chileno" [1965, 177] ("the philosophy of the history of France . . . lacks meaning when applied . . . to the Chilean people"), in those neutral declarations which he tried to construct for the genre, the Hegelian episteme still left its mark: "la filosofía general de la historia, la ciencia de la humanidad, es una misma en todas partes" (1965, 173) ("the general philosophy of history, the science of humanity, is the same everywhere"). The teleological design–the matrix of Liberal thought which the Venezuelan writer shared, with his contemporaries–supported this historical narrative strategy. Moreover, it guaranteed the methodological rigor of the operation and the genre, by ensuring greater reliability in historical writing than in novels. Historiographic practices always revolved around power, either to establish or to legitimize it. All in all, Bello not only wrote in 1847 his *Gramática de la lengua castellana destinada al uso de los americanos* [Grammar of the Castilian Language Destined for Use by the American People]; he had also drafted the first outline of a *Resumen de la historia de Venezuela* [1809; Summary of the History of Venezuela]. In short, the key to historiographic writing, according to Bello, lay in the way it is written–with a rhetorical strategy capable, on the one hand, of structuring the possibilities of each local process (a lesson learned from Herder) through the description of events and, on the other, of arranging the periods of these national processes according to the laws that Western reason had universalized. History thereby managed to wedge the representation of the local American diversities into the vertical structure required to make the New World history one-dimensional. Literature could arrange, or at least provide a soothing explanation for the cultural asymmetries of heterogeneous societies.

The nation-state in Spanish America was gradually consolidated throughout the century, despite countless obstacles and acute ideological indecision and ambiguity. It was a relatively new project, indebted to Western European modernity, that the *criollo* elite (most inclined towards European customs) had imported and implanted as one of many moves to Europeanize their respective countries. In the midst of these intractable contradictions, nations became fragile structures, constantly threatened by the same disintegration by internal forces, their lack of real cohesion, and the complex pressures of foreign monopolies. How could one possibly conceive the idea of a nation based on homogenous, standardizing categories (one language, one ethnic population, one territory, one culture, one religious creed), when American realities belied every aspect of that European project? The power of writing eventually produced a body of fiction that was able to sew up the tears, stitch up gaps, mitigate contradictions, fill vacancies, silence annoyances, and solve conflicts. Historical narrative was the mechanism on which national culture was based, and became the fabricator of its most cherished myths; history endowed that recent apparatus–the Spanish American nation–with age-old traditions, prestigious antiquities, a remote past, and origins to which its multiple identities could be attached.

The aggressive modernity of the national structure, its markedly cosmopolitan and pro-foreign nature, required compensatory discursive operations that would provide the State with long, dense narratives to support a tradition that was barely able to emerge and organize itself during earlier decades of the century. What was new or recent had to be disguised as ancient so that it could help constitute a tradition; the impulse to absorb the most recent import had to appear as the natural continuation of a long established process. In other words, the modern nation had to be the result of a refined past that was in some way congruent with a present that was fascinated by the vertigo of its own cosmopolitanism (see **Figure** 8). Reconciling a distinguished past with this modernity, finding a point of origin that would determine the beginning of a historical process, fabricating a history or a narrative that would describe the richness of its heritage and the happy ending to this project in the present—this was the difficult task of literary historiography. On the one hand, nations wished to see themselves as relieved of the weight of colonial, Indian, *mestizo,* and rural traditions; on the other, they sought to recompose these carefully in a form of writing that saw fit to choose only the least conflictive threads and those that were least out of harmony with the new, Euro-centric and Anglo-centric tradition being established.

What aspects of the past should they choose? How should they design the past? What memories were to be selected as the symbolic capital of the nation? The oxymoronic moment through which the institutionalization of the State and its historiographic practices were obliged to pass oscillated between

Figure 8.

Drawing of the proposed palace of the 1883 Universal Exposition of Caracas. It was to be a neo-gothic cathedral to the new consumer economy. (Archive of the author)

the condition of a modernity (that could be assimilated by the industrialized nations) and the weight of an unwanted past (from which the country had recently separated itself, and which historians were still at a loss as to how best incorporate into the modern experience); this oscillation created distinct traditions that were totally unlike the European societies they wished to emulate. In short, how could one have a nation-state without a literature that endorsed its physiognomy and a past that guaranteed its place among civilized nations and its existence in the future? There was a risk of being a political State without being a nation, of being without a corpus of writings that, in its verbal-symbolic capital, would provide the weight of the representation of the avowed national features. The aim was to be modern yet with tradition, up to date but with a past (see González 1987; Cornejo Polar; Hobsbawm; Valdés; Franco Carvalhal).

However, in the years following the Wars of Independence, the immediate agenda for consolidating the nation-state encountered serious pitfalls that jeopardized both the accreditation of the State and the possibility of historiographic writing itself. It was impossible to construct a past when the past was foreign and involved the colonial state against which they had fought. For the moment, the national imaginary was incapable of nationalizing the colonial experience. Although in everyday life, societies continued to be attached to both the Hispanic and the Amerindian way of life, behavior, and values, the image that the lettered class wished to create of itself as a modern nation was less easy to find. The starting point for a national literary history did not merely follow the logic of European Liberal historicism, for if the identity of a nation was based on its linguistic unity, which had been supported by a corpus of written literary works in that language for some time, the new Spanish American nations necessarily had to claim their origins in the Spanish language and its literature. Philological works strove to establish the authenticity of these foundational national texts (the myth of national origins in epic poems, for example). The history of this literature summarized the character of a nation because it managed to create the necessary effect of identity through the accumulation of books and authors arranged in thematic analogical sequences. The texts became documents (thanks to philology), which in turn permitted the production of a past, and gave temporal depth to the national tradition, whose roots were seen to have distant origins in the peninsula's Middle Ages.

This logic was established early on by European nationalism, and became a more organic project with the development of the forces of the Liberal market; it could fabricate a lost unity (of language and native soil) in the middle ages, in a past that was depicted as heroic, patriarchal, and virile. It served as the starting point for not only that illusory linguistic unity but also the nostalgic space of magnified values of a supposed historic nationality, lost in modern times, yet recoverable since the Spirit was one and indivisible. The nation as such seemed to come from the past: great, heroic, united. This ideological construction of national European pasts enabled the modern Liberal bourgeoisies to conceal the tremendous class conflicts generated by a rapacious industrial society. The cohesion of the people had to be elaborated through a complex framework of mechanisms, one of them being the unity of this people in the past. For this reason, the middle ages were depicted as the foundational space, sweetened by a mythical version of Christianity, which could serve as a counterweight to aggressive modern times in which an increasingly profiteering and materialistic mentality was beginning to take hold. Historiography, which constructed national literatures and the past for the State, based its coherence on the idea of a single language, a single people, and one history: literary works objectified this identity. Despite their own inner contradictions, the processes of cultural homogenization in the European context did not seem to differ blatantly from the Spanish American versions.

Yet, in their craving to "whiten" themselves through more Westernized forms, the learned men of Spanish American countries, who were responsible for choosing the origin and past of their nations, were horrified to see that their present identities lay in the past of Indian cultures. Moreover, with the exception of José Martí and Manuel González Prada, they thought that the Indians of the present were a disruptive element and an obstacle to the realization of the national project: They constituted an element of backwardness that would have to be either eliminated or incorporated through education. Prestigious historians, such as the Peruvian José de la Riva Agüero, tirelessly repeated that "la raza quichua es haragana, desconfiada y astuta" ("the Quechua race is lazy, distrustful, and astute") and that the black race ("no puede reconocérsele nada que se asemeje siquiera a un ideal literario") ("has nothing that even resembles a literary ideal") (50 and 53).

The nature of the literature of the new nations that were being developed had to have a coherence that could be adjusted to the other processes of Western modernization. The problem of Indian cultures was therefore a thorny one, since its nature effectively contravened the logic of Liberalism. It was consequently thought preferable to silence these cultures:

> aquellas civilizaciones o *semicivilizaciones* ante-hispanas *murieron*, se *extinguieron*, y no hay modo de reanudar su tradición, puesto que *no dejaron literatura*. Para los criollos de raza española, son *extranjeras* y peregrinas, y nada nos liga a ellas; y extranjeras y peregrinas son también para los mestizos o indios cultos, porque la educación que han recibido los ha europeizado por completo. (Riva Agüero 71; my emphasis)

> those pre-Hispanic civilizations or *semi-civilizations died*, and became *extinct* and there is no way of renewing their traditions, since *they left no literature*. For the *criollos* of Spanish descent, they are *foreign* and alien, and nothing links us to them; and they also seem foreign and alien to cultured Indians and *mestizos* of our time, since the education they have received has fully Europeanized them.

The same writing that was deemed foundational was also responsible for eradicating the pre-Hispanic (*they left no literature*). At the same time as Riva Agüero described the Indian cultures as semi-civilizations, he buried them—"murieron" ("they died")—casting them into a non-historical periphery—"ante-hispana" ("pre-Hispanic"); in a doubly alienating twist, Spanish literature had turned its own people into outsiders—"son extranjeras y peregrinas" ("they are foreign and alien")—separating the subjects from their identities—"porque la educación que han recibido [los indios] los ha europeizado" ("since the education that [the Indians] have received has fully Europeanized them")—and producing self-destructive schizophrenic shifts at various levels.

It seemed that in the areas where the substratum of Indian civilizations had achieved a notable development in the past, and where their cultures were still alive because their population was numerically larger than the white *criollo* population, the latter, feeling its class identity threatened, developed racist arguments that supported native disqualification in terms of a clinical pathology (they were "sick," "degenerate," or "polluting" cultures) or an exotic re-appraisal of the past—through archaeological arguments which, although they seemed to acknowledge the splendor and grandeur of these cultures, continued to relegate them to a remote, extinct past, in addition to exiling them by subsuming them within Oriental civilizations:

> opacas, incoherentes y misteriosas tradiciones de gentes bárbaras o degeneradas que para los mismos americanos de hoy resultan más extrañas, menos familiares y menos interesantes que las de los asirios, los persas o los egipcios. (Riva Agüero 83)

> opaque, incoherent, and mysterious traditions of barbarous or degenerate peoples who are stranger, less familiar, and less interesting even to the Americans of today than those of the Assyrians, the Persians and the Egyptians.

Conceiving a national literature with two linguistic registers or in the language of certain subordinate majorities (Quechua, Náhuatl, Aymara) would have been virtually tantamount to placing the nation in a position in which civilization and history were denied: Unity would be destroyed by diversity; "barbarie" ("barbarity") would rule. It was important to emphasize the "carencia de obras literarias" ("lack of literary works") in these cultures:

> No habiendo escritos en quichua no puede haber literatura quichua... el quichua ha sufrido también cambios y adulteraciones notables con la introducción del castellano, y á la vuelta de un siglo será lengua muerta que nadie tratará de aprender, porque no cuenta con obra ninguna que la inmortalice como el griego y el latín. (León Mera 19)

> The absence of writings in Quechua means that there can be no Quechua literature... Quechua has also undergone noticeable changes and alterations as a result of the introduction of Spanish, and within a century, it will be a dead language which no one will attempt to learn, because there are no books that immortalize it, in contrast to Greek or Latin.

León Mera went on to reassert that the Quechua language was in the process of becoming extinct:

> Lo que en estas tierras vivirá más que las razas puras europea y americana, son la lengua y las costumbres extranjeras. El elemento español tiene que preponderar en su mezcla con el indígena, y acabará por absorberlo todo.... El quichua no solamente va adulterándose, sino desapareciendo.... Eso me alegra mucho.... [N]o cabe duda que el indio para civilizarse necesita adoptar un idioma culto. (23)

> Foreign languages and customs will outlive those that are pure European or Amerindian in these territories. The Spanish element will predominate in its mixture with the Indian and will eventually absorb everything... Quechua is not merely being adulterated, it is actually disappearing.... That gives me a great deal of pleasure.... There can be no doubt that, in order to become civilized, Indians need to adopt a refined language.

The cultural horizon of print culture was focused on books, thereby fostering a disingenuous historical blindness that condemned the oral nature of the cultures of the Amerindians of both the past and the present. This in turn led a number of historians to eliminate these cultures with one delighted stroke of the pen. Witness the *Cuadro Histórico de la Producción Intelectual de Chile* [1890–1910; Historical Summary of Chilean Intellectual Production] by the Chilean Jorge Huneeus y Gana (1866–1926) (who held a number of high positions, such as Deputy of the National Congress, Minister of Justice and Public Education, Chairman of the Board of Literature and Fine Arts, and Member of the Library of Chilean Writers). In order to depict the origin of the country's cultural life, Huneeus y Gana designed a portico whose inscription read: "Estado de la raza indígena de Chile: su nulidad intelectual histórica" ("The status of the Indian race in Chile: an historical intellectual nothingness"). In other cases, the pressure of living Indian cultures was so noticeable on the collective imagination of these elites that, in order to avoid it, they shifted their idea of their cultural roots toward the national Colonial era or directly toward the Republic. The *Historia del desenvolvimiento intelectual de Guatemala desde la fundación de la primera escuela de letras europeas hasta la inauguración del Instituto Nacional de Indígenas* [published in three volumes in 1897; History of the Intellectual Development of Guatemala from the Foundation of the First School of European Letters to the Inauguration of the National Institute of Indian Affairs] by Ramón A. Salazar, reveals the paradoxes faced by this same learned man in having to struggle with his own phobias and commitments to the present:

> El día lunes 25 de julio del año de 1524, el capitan don Pedro de Alvarado, después de haber recorrido el país con sus armas victoriosas y cometido los excesos y crueldades de que la historia lo acusa y la humanidad se duele, dispuso . . . hacer pie firme en Iximché y fundar allí, a nombre del rey de España, la capital de los dominios que acababa de conquistar. . . . Con este objeto convocó a todos sus valientes, en aquel día memorable de nuestra historia. (7)

> On 25 July 1524, Captain Pedro de Alvarado, having traveled the length of the country with his victorious army and having committed the excesses and acts of cruelty of which history accuses him and over which humanity grieves, decided . . . to set foot in Iximché and establish, in the name of the king of Spain, the capital of the dominions which he had just conquered. . . . To this end, he summoned all his brave men, on that memorable day of our history.

Civilizing foundational literature arguably exerted the same degree of violence as the Spanish Imperial Conquest, since, by constructing the past, it immolated memories with the sowing of oblivion. Like a small sickle, it harvested a social alienation that was only negotiable within the formality of colonial institutional space. The irony of the historiographic gesture lay in the fact that it was precisely the Instituto Nacional de Indígenas (National Institute of Indian Affairs) that eliminated the past and present of the cultures that the institution itself symbolically represented.

The force of writing, like the armed conquest, also imposed its empire on memory, making referents and scriptural operations coincide. The Conquest of Guatemala by Pedro Alvarado is reproduced in the words of the historian; the use of the words "victorious armies" and "our history" assimilate the double foundational gesture—of European literature and violence—within the same operation: The Captain set *foot* in Iximché and *founded*, in the name of the *king of Spain*, the capital of the *dominions* (my emphasis). This historiographic writing is therefore equivalent to the gesture of colonization that it evokes, it is just as colonizing of the modern imaginary. It was the monopolizing action of the new nation-state that, unlike the *criollos* in previous centuries, decided to erase (or distance the nation as far as possible from) the disruptive, despised non-European elements. The national project had to recall Europe and, to this end, writing created

the sphere of a whitened, historical imagination (the Spanish element will predominate).

However, there were also less categorical voices among the historians. Although a national literature could not be based on the language of the conquered, a language that distanced it from Europe, a language that stifled the imagination of a national culture for which a minority longed, there were other, more benign operations that did not contradict the essence of hard-line Eurocentric positions and that acknowledged the "poetic talent" of these Indian cultures; while purging them of the barbarian overtones of what would eventually become the original substrate of the Spanish American historical process. In his *América poética* (1846), Juan María Gutiérrez included an enthusiastic defense of the high faculty of the human spirit seen in those remains of ancient civilization. He acknowledged the fact that the bards of those "primitive" languages had produced poems that, like history, would serve to perpetuate the memory of events (vi). However, not only does he include this high praise in the prologue to his magnum opus, but, in the limits of his understanding, he establishes them as the distant forerunners of the true national literary formation, which began during the colonial era:

> la elocuencia y la poesía fueron cultivadas por los súbditos de Montezuma, y Atahualpa, siglos *antes que la civilización europea* echara en molde cristiano la inteligencia de mejicanos y peruanos. (Sarlo 104; my emphasis)

> eloquence and poetry were cultivated by the subjects of Motecuhzoma and Atahuallpa, centuries *before European civilization* cast the intelligence of Mexicans and Peruvians in a Christian mold.

The exponents of Liberal thought most anxious not to lose sight of Americanist elements were keen to recover them by means of ideological miscegenation: casting "the intelligence of Mexicans and Peruvians in a Christian mold" or asserting that "the Spanish element will predominate in its blend with the Indian." Less dogmatic about pure categories, they understood that the total elimination of the heterogeneous might entail a dangerous loss of identity for Spanish America, even in its drive to be European and modern. In this respect, rhetoric reconciles the clashes and tensions of societies in conflict by reconciling these opposites by, on the one hand, blending in the human element of the Indians (their intelligence), yet sacrificing their culture and language and, on the other, casting them in a "Christian mold" and forcing them to adopt a cultured language.

Certain, less aggressive Liberals understood that the most effective processes of whitening should revolve around discipline rather than fascist extermination policies. Obviously both means involved a fair measure of violence. Thus the most flexible historiography in this respect situated these cultures in an extinct past, at least on paper:

> si hemos citado unas pocas estrofas en este idioma quechua, ha sido porque convenía al buen desenvolvimiento del plan que nos hemos propuesto seguir: era preciso introducirse algo en las *profundidades de lo pasado*, para examinar el *grado de progreso* de la poesía ecuatoriana en los siglos de la dominación española. (León Mera 26; my emphasis)

> If we have quoted a few lines in the Quechua language, it is because it was necessary to the development of the plan we have proposed to follow: It was essential to delve into the *depths of the past*, to examine the *degree of progress* of Ecuadorian poetry during the centuries of Spanish domination.

This differential otherness is brought onto the scene of writing, yet at the same time, controlled by it. Another historian, Adolfo Valderrama (1843–1902), would say that "propiamente la literatura de los aboríjenes pertenece a los dominios de la etnología. . . . [N]uestra literatura nacional no es sino rama desprendida del fecundo árbol de la literatura española" (91–92) ("Properly considered, the literature of the aborigines belongs to the realm of ethnology. . . . [O]ur national literature is merely a branch that has broken loose from the fertile tree of Spanish literature"). It was not enough to push the other toward a primitive pre-history–a sort of preverbal unconscious. There was a sense that anything that created discomfort within the homogeneous limits of literature had to be driven into other spheres of modern knowledge; Amerindian, popular, and African cultures became exotic animals to be exhibited in the new zoos, the new museums. The scientific disciplines of ethnology and anthropology would engage them in the grids of their knowledge. But this did not refer to Amerindians, Africans, or popular literary cultures in the actual Americas but only the Incas, the Aztecs, and the Maya of the past.

Thus, in order to maintain the teleological coherence of the evolution of Western reason, Juan María Gutiérrez himself would conclude many years after in his reflections in the 1846 *Prólogo* that

estas biografías concurrieron a la formación de una historia de la literatura antigua de la América poblada por los españoles, en la persuasión de que un trabajo semejante sería de honra para los nacidos en el Nuevo Mundo e indispensable para colocar a la luz adecuada ciertos grupos oscurecidos en el cuadro de la vida colonial que tanto nos interesa conocer bien y por entero. (1957, 9)

these biographies came together in the formation of a history of the ancient literature of an America populated by Spaniards, in the conviction that a work of this nature would be an honor to those born in the New World and indispensable for providing an accurate portrait of certain groups of writers who have been overshadowed in the accounts of colonial life that we are so concerned with exploring in depth.

When it came to suggesting systems of periodization, most were content to visualize the stages of American culture as including a first stage of foundation (a period of imitation), which was anchored in the Spanish Conquest; a second heroic period (chaotic, with armed struggles), marked by the years of the Wars of Independence; and a third, "la edad de la razón severa" ("the age of strict reason"), as Esteban Echeverría (1805–1851), Florencio Varela (1807–1848), and José María Torres Caicedo (1830–1889) would call it, which was peaceful, industrious, the result of freedom, and which possessed a literature that could be regarded as national, because of its local themes and local color. The most ancient history recognized was eventually the Hispanic, and thus it could honor those born in those new lands.

However, the assimilation of the colonial past and Hispanic culture into the republican process then underway led to lengthy disputes and misunderstandings and not very many agreements among the makers of national historiography, whose Liberal and Conservative factions held opposing views: Conservatives regarded it as a splendid and fruitful period in the foundation of the nation, since it lent the future nation the hallmark of Christian values, the glitter and politeness of the Golden Age of the peninsula, together with a civilized language that managed to emend and catechize–in the opinion of the Mexican politician

Francisco G. Cosmos–the miserable and abject Indian race. Liberals would have preferred to eliminate the colonial period altogether, since it represented an ominous past of slavery, darkness, and inexplicable obstacles to free trade and the circulation of enlightened knowledge, a period whose surviving elements still prevented the progress of nations. Both the impassioned defense of the Colonial period and its absolute disparagement made it difficult to create the narrative coherence that would make it possible to represent this as the essential past for the present of these nation-states.

Modernity in the nineteenth century was a time of relentless pursuit by the urban public of the novelty of French fashions that were totally unrelated to Hispanic and Amerindian traditions. Riva Agüero writes,

Continuando con esta tarea de afrancesamiento literario, que la juventud americana ha emprendido con ardor tan irracional, concluiremos por ser ramas desgajadas del árbol español, arrastradas por todos los vientos de la veleidosa moda; vendremos a ser como hijos pródigos que, apartados de la casa paterna, vestiremos extrañas libreas y adoraremos extraños fetiches. (286–87)

Continuing this task of literary gallicization, which American youth had undertaken with such irrational fervor, we shall end up becoming branches torn from the Spanish tree, swept along by the fickle winds of fashion; we shall appear as prodigal sons who, separated from the paternal home, wear strange dress and worship strange fetishes.

The sense of loss created a feeling of nostalgia about those same traditions among many, causing them to express their unconditional defense of the Conquest and the Colonial period:

La evangelización de los pueblos conquistados, su ingreso en el regazo de la civilización europea, constituyeron el primer *desideratum* que se presentó a los poseedores de la nueva España. . . . A este progreso intelectual que bien puede llamarse extraordinario . . . a la vez se alzaba majestuosa la Metrópoli de Nueva España sobre las ruinas de la antigua Tenochtitlán. (Vigil 31 and 29).

The evangelization of the conquered peoples, together with their entry into the lap of European civilization, constituted the first *desideratum* presented to the masters of New Spain. . . . At the same time as this intellectual progress was unfolding, which could well be called extraordinary, the Metropolis of New Spain rose up majestically over the ruins of ancient Tenochtitlán.

At the same time, however, other voices less caught up in this melancholic nostalgia for past times disparaged any such fictitious view of the past. They were committed to the present and modernity:

Enigma fué que pude resolver del siguiente modo: la literatura en México había nacido con su independencia y libertad política [1820], y en 1865 una y otra habían muerto á los golpes de la intervención francesa y el imperio. La corta edad de la fenecida literatura habíamela revelado la historia del país posterior á la conquista. . . . Pero, reducidos á la impotencia los virreyes– estorbada la creación de colegios, vacía de ciencia la Universidad, prohibida la adquisición de libros, qué literatura podía existir en Nueva España? . . . Pero una vez iniciada la lucha de Independencia, en cada hijo de México se reveló un poeta . . . que en algunos años consiguieron ensalzar el talento nacional sobre el silencio de tres siglos de dominación. (Olavarría y Ferrari 14, 23, 26)

It was an enigma that I was able to solve as follows: Literature in Mexico had emerged together with its political independence and freedom [in 1820], and in 1865, both died as a result of the onslaught of French intervention and the Empire. The nature of this now-extinct literature of such short duration was revealed to me by the history of the colonial period after the Conquest. . . . But with the Viceroys reduced to impotence, the creation of schools obstructed, the University lacking in science, and the purchase of books prohibited, what literature could possibly exist in New Spain? . . . Yet once the struggle for Independence had begun, a poet was revealed in every son of Mexico . . . who, in a few years, were able to establish and enhance national talent after the silence of three centuries of domination.

The field was once again plagued with polarizations, which, nonetheless, had a subtle point of convergence: Both positions sought desperately not to sever their Western European ties, either by making links with the ancient metropolis or with the new industrial empires. Historians maintained firm connections with the old continent, and their Liberal or Conservative modernity was expressed precisely through nostalgia for the past or through futuristic ideals (see Olalquiaga 1998).

This atmosphere created a further problem for the writing of a literary history: If one categorically rejected the Colonial period, adopting an anti-Spanish position–since all that was Spanish was, according to José Victorino Lastarria (1818–1888), full of lackluster temperaments, immoral interests, a corrupting element, and vices due to the backwardness of the era–then what language could be used to construct this national literature? Both Liberals and Conservatives undoubtedly felt that an Indian language would be unsuitable, since its "irrationality" would mar their insertion into Western rationality as well as hinder their ability to follow Hegelian logic: It would have meant having no literature, history, or State. And adopting a new foreign language (whether French or English) constituted a brusque move that was unworthy of the social function of these symbolic practices.

The way was gradually opened for a sensible negotiation that would establish the limits of anti-Spanish and anti-colonialist positions, the latter seeming more viable and productive to the mentality of the lettered class. Both Liberals and Conservatives had to moderate their radical positions; for the latter the recovery and preservation of the Spanish language (paradoxically in its traditional purity) constituted the umbilical cord that ensured a sense of belonging to the Latin community, the ancient Roman world, the civilized world, and, by this means, language served as a legitimate passport to the European community. For Liberals the colonial political situation had constituted an error of the historical Spirit and a deviation from progress; yet, fortunately, its culture had a written and rational language and could therefore aspire to writing or arranging their respective histories as part of the universal concert of developed nations. Panic at not being European at a key point in the modernizing ideology forced both sides to agree and defend Spanish as the language of their national literatures, searching for arguments that could accommodate a series of problematic issues: to acknowledge the language of the colonizers in order to construct their own cultural identities; to operate within the integrity of this language to the detriment of its political implications; and to link the "pure" categories (such as the defense of the correctness of the Spanish language) with the *criollo* and *mestizo* element that would represent the compulsory mark of distance from Spanish

literature. In short, they were compelled to enter the game of modernity and sovereignty with traditional, dependable weapons–by pretending to be in the West, using borrowed pure categories, yet with hybrid and heterogeneous realities. The case of the Venezuelan historian Gonzalo Picón Febres (1860–1918) may be paradigmatic. On the one hand, he is categorically anti-Hispanic in the political sphere:

> Las monstruosidades y los horrores cometidos por los conquistadores castellanos en las tribus indígenas de América; la destrucción de los hogares de los indios y de sus propiedades; la matanza de los hombres que morían combatiendo con la flecha por defender el suelo sagrado de la Patria. . . . Tal conducta, verdaderamente criminal, produjo aquel estado semibárbaro en que se encontraban las colonias en las postrimerías del pasado siglo. (226, 84)

> The monstrosities and horrors committed by the Spanish conquistadors on the Indian tribes of America; the destruction of the Indians' homes and their property; the killing of men who died fighting with bows and arrows to defend the sacred land of the fatherland. . . . This truly criminal behavior was responsible for the semi-barbarous state of colonial Spanish America at the end of the last century.

At the same time, however, he expressed his enthusiasm for the new patterns of European culture:

> Fué admirable el fomento que este *contacto con los extranjeros* dio en breve a la civilización en Venezuela. Junto con sus artefactos, los *franceses* y *norteamericanos* llevaron una gran cantidad de libros, que despertaron la afición a la lectura. . . . Los *libros importados*, la visita de viajeros ilustrados, el desarrollo del *comercio con las naciones extranjeras* . . . fueron otras tantas causas que contribuyeron a levantar el espíritu de una juventud destinada a representar los destinos de la Patria. (87 and 88; my emphasis)

> There was an admirable energy that this *contact with foreigners* gave to civilization in Venezuela in a very short time. Together with their artifacts, the *French* and *North Americans* brought with them vast quantities of books, which sparked an interest in reading. . . . *Imported books*, visits by enlightened travelers, and the development of *trade with foreign nations* . . . were some of the other causes that helped raise the spirit of a youth that was destined to represent the destinies of the fatherland.

And finally, he advocated the conservation of the purity of the Spanish language as an authentic value of literary nationality:

> Si de algún poeta venezolano puede decirse muy en alto que *no tiene manchas ni defectos*, es de Manuel Fombona Palacio. . . . *Versadísimo en la lengua castellana*, y extensamente sabio en su literatura desde los más lueñes orígenes, trabajó sobre aquélla, con *verdadera corrección, noble cultura* y *elegancia*. (306; my emphasis)

> If there is one Venezuelan poet who can claim that he *has no stains or defects*, it is Manuel Fombona Palacio (1857–1903). . . . *Extremely well-versed in the Spanish language* and extremely knowledgeable about its literature, from its earliest origins, he worked on it, with *veritable accuracy, noble culture*, and *elegance*.

Here was a man dislocated by the very requirements of modernity, split between a bookish solidarity with aboriginal cultures (the Indians who died defending the sacred land of the fatherland), which acted as an imaginary counterweight to the new cosmopolitanism (contact with French and North American foreigners), and also with a language that was both alien and their own (the Spanish language, veritable accuracy, noble culture, and elegance). He seems like an ego with a schizophrenic identity fused in the crucible of nineteenth-century Venezuela, in a chain of substitute, compensatory othernesses. Within this vertiginous situation, a curious political metaphor represents the drama of Spanish American postcolonial cultures: At the base of all linguistic Hispanicism lay the obscure desire to become modern Europeans, in other words, like the French or English. Synecdoche both conceals and substitutes one for the other: The Hispanic mode served as the means of situating oneself in the First World. Consequently, Hispanicism was the version in the literary historical sphere of economic Liberalism. Language, among other forms, was one of the best-preserved masks of the cultural whitening of the hegemonic class:

> conservemos la lengua, esta magnífica lengua, fuerte como una encina, sólida como el mármol, brillante como el fuego, sonora como la mar; conservémosla en la integridad de su genio. . . . El idioma es un vigoroso fundamento de la tradición; y mientras no se altere, un gran vínculo subsiste. (Riva Agüero 44)

> let us preserve language, that magnificent language, as strong as an oak, solid as marble, brilliant as fire, as sonorous as the sea; let us preserve it in the integrity of its genius. . . . Language is a vigorous basis of tradition; and as long as it is not altered, a great link subsists.

In short, in the political sphere, an anti-Hispanicism was professed, a fairly widespread anti-colonialism, which envisaged Imperial situations only in the past, yet failed to perceive the new colonialism of the present with sufficient clarity, regarding it as progress and modernity.

So far, Hispanic affiliation might appear to be a Conservative solution within the range of Liberal possibilities. However, during this period, the profile of Hispanicism was more complex, virtually constituting a bastion of resistance of a fairly ambiguous ideological hue. After 1870, diplomatic relations between Spain and Spanish American countries were increasingly reactivated, a rapprochement that intensified during the war of 1898. Given the loss of Cuba and Puerto Rico to the United States, Spanish American intellectuals were more concerned than ever before with the threatening presence of the United States, a new imperial force, both admired and feared. They fostered the forging of closer links with Spain, which not only suggested a political alliance but also an acknowledgment of belonging to an extensive Hispanic cultural community, with extremely old links that could create a cultural oppositional bloc against the U.S. And it is precisely at this point that language and the assimilation of the colonial past as part of national history—essentially cultural aspects—became real political strategies.

This Pan-Hispanicism, mainly encouraged by Spain, symbolically attempted to recover its territories through both the linguistic and the ethnic link (the exaltation of the Iberian race). The Yankeephobia which the peninsula continued to encourage sought to draw these countries nearer and to create a common front through the "Ibero American Union" (1884). This would culminate in the festivities of the Fourth Centenary of the Discovery, which, in addition to introducing the defense of the figure of Columbus and the consecration of the fatherland, served as an important counterweight to the growing presence of Anglo-American culture and power. Thus, in this turn-of-the-century context, to a greater or lesser degree, the Hispanophilia, of historiography should perhaps be interpreted as a political defense of the integrity of certain continental traditions against the risks of new imperial subordinations. The defense of Spanish and the Spanish Colonial undertaking effectively proved to be a Conservative move if one takes only local factors into account. Yet if we broaden our range of vision, the status of Spain was an intense point of discussion within the

scenario of international politics. At stake was the defense of the old colonialism–Spain was in a position of having lost the Philippines, Cuba, and Puerto Rico–vis-à-vis the emergence of the new imperial ambitions represented by England, France, and the United States. This is why the whole problem concerning the continuity or break with Spain was merely the expression of how to conceive a national culture at a time when the world was beginning to experience the modern impact of new forms of distributing territory–thanks to the insatiable expansionism of the United States.

The context of 1898 undoubtedly fostered historiographical reflections that might appear Conservative in another light, since they involved a hypertrophied appraisal of the Spanish Discovery, Conquest, and colonization of the continent. Moreover, literary histories and the foundation of Academies of the Language jointly undertook the task of configuring the canon of literary works in the national tradition on the basis of being monuments of the purest expression of the Spanish language. Not surprisingly, several historians were numbered among the original members of the Academy of the Language. Moreover, literary history has probably been the least inclined to support most modern literary modalities, such as the novel (in its versions as Romantic or Naturalistic melodrama), theater, serial stories (chapbooks), written and oral popular forms, and above all, the literary activity of women. In this respect, although not exclusively so, historiographic writing preserved the most traditional literary forms of the lettered city; it was a field that was noticeably more inclined toward the defense of practices and genres inherited from the Hispanic tradition. It is not uncommon to find in these works that sacred and profane oratory, treatises on rhetoric and grammar, travel reports, books on history and geography, reports by religious orders and scientific societies, histories of printing, universities and athaeneums, jostle for space with poets, playwrights, and novelists. Depending on how one looks at them, the various aspects of literary historical work constituted either a form of contestation or a Conservative ideology.

The learned men in charge of preserving the heritage of emerging nations were not exactly in the vanguard of national culture. Tending instead to belong to old, patrician families of the land-owning oligarchy, they found the framework of the sensibility of Hispanicism to be in keeping with their aristocratic values. Modern times questioned and shattered these traditional fashions, introducing what was for them a dangerous mannerism or "feminization" of culture (see Douglas; Montaldo; Silva 1998). Many attributed this inauspicious deformation to the influence of the fashion for and readings of French authors, which were particularly pernicious for the female sector of society. The basically patriarchal sensibility of this learned group viewed this aspect of modernization with concern, particularly the democratizing process, which popularized culture among the middle classes, particularly among women. This specific conditions of the present led these intellectuals, who were more resistant to change, to choose and wield arguments that would counteract what for them was a weakening or degeneration of culture.

Thus, by defending Spanish as the language of the national literary project, they poured their (phallocratic) patriarchal fantasies into it, turning it into a practice shot through with gendered markings, where Spanish, the language of tradition and the Conquest, came to mean, within the tense framework of new sensibilities, the strong, solid, integrated, vigorous element (as Riva Agüero would put it) in national culture; it was a virile language which, stamped by the mark of the epic gesture (of the father's house), was able to counteract a language adulterated by foreign words that might engender a weak, sickly, and affected national literature. The latent homoerotic panic in these lines, together with an evident unwillingness to create national literature as a heterosexual locale—in other words, the fear of allowing learned women into the canon (which only occurred in very few cases)— closed the walls of national memory around a jealously guarded male canon:

> Lo que sí parece que puede sentarse como un hecho es que no carecemos de literatura puesto que nadie puede poner en problemas que tanto en la época colonial como en la subsiguiente *nacieron y vivieron en el seno de nuestra sociedad varios hombres de talento que dejaron notorios vestigios en la tradición de sus escritos.*
> (Sarlo 85; my emphasis)

> What does seem to be an undeniable fact is that we do not lack a literature, since no one can possibly doubt that during the colonial era and the period following it, *various men of talent were born into and lived in the bosom of our society who left noticeable traces in the tradition of their writings.*

Although Juan María Gutiérrez was one of the very few to have acknowledged Sor Juana Inés de la Cruz (1648–1695), in *Estudios biográficos y críticos* [1865; Biographical and Critical Studies], the majority of the learned community thought that the health of national literature depended on a corpus of male works, both as regards their authorship and the literary genre:

> Nosotros concebimos que la literatura en una nación joven, es uno de los más eficaces elementos de que puede valerse la educación pública. . . . Para nosotros su definición debe ser más social, más útil, más del caso, será el retrato de la individualidad nacional. . . . Pensamos, que las Repúblicas Americanas, hijas del *sable* y del movimiento progresivo de la inteligencia democrática del mundo, necesitan una literatura fuerte y varonil, como la política que las gobierna, y los brazos que las sostienen. (Cané 135; my emphasis)

> We believe that literature in a young nation is one of the most effective elements available for public education. . . . For us, the definition must be more social, more useful, and more precisely, it will be the portrait of national individuality. . . . We think that the American Republics, the daughters of the sword and the progressive movement of the democratic intelligence of the world, need a vigorous, male literature, like the politics that governs them and the arms that sustain them.

The learned elite regarded literature as a strong and manly production of nationality; the portrait of the individuality of the nation would be provided by the world of male intelligence. Literary production was a matter for men and a public affair, like the politics that govern them; it was a matter of State. Learned men were public men, whose swords were the words they used to record both the chaos of the common people and the danger of the dissolution of modern times within the order of discourse. For this reason, it ought to have manly arms to support this young nation. Many historians regarded the soft genres, such as novels and newspaper serials, as suspect in terms of public morals, stirring female readers' unrestrained passions. The aim was to channel the melodramatic imagination towards historical narration, which was more pedagogical and ethical.

Although the more Conservative tendency in historiography regarded the Colonial period as the origin of the nation, and while the Liberal trend preferred to regard the Independence movements as the foundational period, both had their reservations as regards the iconoclastic frenzy of modernity, since in either case, exaltation of the past, whether Colonial or pro-Independence, was achieved by transferring the imaginary need to belong to an aristocratic, patrician family genealogy to another locale. In both cases, there was a need for the learned class to establish itself as a hegemonic entity that distanced itself both from the professional and tradesman cadres of the bourgeoisie and from the new francophile intellectuals and artists of *modernismo*. They obtained the stamp of prestige not only from their insertion into institutional apparatuses, but also by the way in which they fashioned their own discoursive practices: Colony and Independence, in the genealogical matrix of historiographers, both emerged as epic, grandiloquent pasts. From Cortés to Bolívar, from Pizarro to San Martín, from the *Diario de Colón* to Bello's *silvas*, the historiographic imagination restored the same nostalgic need for acts of heroism and class prestige that modernity would displace. The displacement that was already beginning to make itself felt simultaneously triggered this historiographic fiction, which consolidated the present by remaking the past. And Hispanicism was the mark of distinction of the group that was most committed to keeping effective political power.

Among the polemics concerned with solving the question of the originality of national literatures, pan-Hispanic fervor did little to promote the creation of a Spanish American cultural map distinct from that of the peninsula. If "la vida de la América es la vida del pueblo español, modificada por circunstancias locales" (359) ("the life of [Spanish] America is the life of the Spanish people, modified by local circumstances"), as the Chilean Francisco Vargas Fontecilla (1824–1883) thought, what would determine the different forms of identity of countries that shared the same language, or what would encourage decolonization at the level of symbolic forms and determine the specifically national and independent nature of these cultures?

The site of the construction of national literature was once again caught in the crossfire, whose dangerous horizon was the monumental *Antología de poetas hispanoamericanos* [Anthology of Spanish American Poets] compiled by Marcelino Menéndez y Pelayo between 1893 and 1895, which included the former colonies in the same literary territory as the fatherland. This colonial museum capitalized on its mechanism of accumulation in two different directions: It added value to those who were excluded, since they would now form part of the canon-treasure, and at the same time, it would add patrimony to the Spanish canon by expanding its scope. This collection was obviously aimed at strengthening Spanish identity in the Americas, which expanded at the expense of the appropriation of French and English literary objects, and obviously to the detriment of a blurring of the literary territorialities of Spanish American countries.

Rather like a pendulum, the Hispanic link had to be nuanced with what one could call the ideology of criollization or miscegenation of literatures, which would eventually give nations a particular local color that would distinguish them one from the other. In this new turn of events, given the overwhelming Westernization of historiographic imaginaries, the point was now to create an effect of local (re)insertion:

> Se puede decir que la América Latina posee hoy una literatura nacional por el tema y el color local, literatura rica y variada . . . fecunda como nuestro suelo.
> (José María Torres Caicedo, qtd. in Ardao 225)

One can say that Latin America today has a national literature because of its theme and local color, its rich and varied literature . . .as fertile as our soil.

The demands of modernity of the nation-state had led to the development of written genres that narrowed the gap between the new centers and the peripheries. Historiography was one of those strategically modern and cosmopolitan exercises, more inclined to meet the expectations of a metropolitan clientele curious to find out about the peculiar features of these newly independent areas.

From Bello to Rodó, their reflexive recommendation was to use European models to a certain extent, while beginning to scrutinize their own models. From Alberdi to Martí, there was the same insistent demand for a decolonized, autonomous perspective:

Depuremos nuestro espíritu de todo color postizo, de todo traje prestado, de toda parodia, de todo servilismo. Gobernémonos, pensemos, escribamos, y procedamos en todo, no a imitación de pueblo ninguno de la tierra, sea cual fuere su rango, sino como lo exige la combinación de las leyes generales del espíritu humano, con las individualidades de nuestra condición nacional. (Alberdi 21)

Let us cleanse our spirit of all false color, all borrowed clothes, all parody, and all servility. Let us rule, think, write, and proceed in all matters, not by imitating any people on earth, regardless of its rank, but as required by the combination of the general laws of the human spirit with the individualities of our national condition.

However the need for Latin America to have an original and authentic identity that would distinguish it from the homogenizing languages of mass consumption was an illusion. What passed for authentic and original in culture was an artificial style of writing, and exaggerated emphasis on local flora and fauna, the display of indigenous communities that had remained alienated for centuries and were still excluded from the process of Westernization. The historiography constructed by a national literary heritage was not that far removed from certain taxidermal procedures, because of its ability to catch and fossilize specimens of organic life, as well as being tangentially contaminated by a fondness for souvenirs, because of their ability to extrapolate and miniaturize aspects of human and social life (see Olalquiaga). The mass of discourse that the lettered men circulated on the matter not only suffered from numerous, profound contradictions, whose possible basis could be found within a cross-eyed or Janus-like image of modernization–with elites unconditionally attached to European tastes (whether Hispanic or North Atlantic), on the one hand, and a nationalistic sensibility based on the exotic exaltation of provincial localities, on the other. This last point opens up a dramatic new paradox, based on the responsibility of the Spanish American intelligentsia for endorsing, albeit silently, the State policies that liquidated the Indian and peasant populations in a variety of ways, in order to pave the way for large landed estates, railroads, and foreign companies.

Ironically, Domingo Faustino Sarmiento believed that literary nationality would be based on an "arte socialista que hiciese concurrir la ciencia, el arte y la política al único fin de mejorar la suerte de los pueblos . . . de rehabilitar al pueblo, al mulato y a todos los que sufren" (in Donoso 1980, 128, 136) ("on a socialist art that would bring together science, art, and politics with the sole aim of improving the fate of peoples . . . rehabilitating the people, the mulatto, and all those who suffer"). No doubt Indians had no time to suffer, since for Sarmiento they were not even a people, they were

nothing. . . . The national project of the national States was not only contradictory but extremely fragile, since it had to use nationalistic rhetoric to cover up and disguise not only the progressive decapitalization being suffered by Latin American countries but also to produce an efficient metonymic effect whereby the part that was able to use words (the elite) did so on behalf of everyone (the people). The latter constituted an overwhelming majority of rural peasants, with no say in the matter, and who only had an ambiguous presence that literature would project as a concocted figuration that in fact summarized the inadequacies and anxieties of the elite towards its otherness. The authority the written word enjoyed easily enabled the elite to identify what was "authentically" national through the production of subaltern types or "exotic" geographical locales (Indians in the jungles, gauchos in the plains, and *mestizos* in the sierras):

las poesías, las novelas, los cuentos i las narraciones de toda especie en que figuran, cantan, lloran o combaten los *descendientes de los héroes de Arauco*, i de los Conquistadores españoles, constituyeron las obras más *orijinales* i *jenuinas* que se han producido entre nosotros. (Amunátegui Solar 8; my emphasis)

poems, novels, stories, and all kinds of narrations in which the *descendants of the heroes of Arauco* represent, sing, cry, or fight, and of the Spanish conquistadors, constituted the most *original* and *genuine* works that have been produced among us.

The ideology of miscegenation, which produced a sweetened blend of opposing ethnic groups and cultures at the discourse level, concealing the Hispanic bases of mediation, was the key to literary criollism, which was, after all, an aesthetic effect of a populist nature of Liberal thought designed to include the social sectors marginalized in this national project as merely a form of representation (both in the sense of *Darstellung* and *Vertretung*). In view of all the racist, misogynistic ideology of the lettered city, the *criollo* experiment undoubtedly constituted a significant step forward, since it provide a space within literature for the exploration of heterogeneous cultures (see Ramos 1993), obviously controlled by a corresponding hierarchy achieved on the basis of all kinds of circumventions that used commas, dashes, italics, bold type, footnotes, and lengthy glossaries of native words to distance and control the disciplined inclusion of the other.

Thus, what was typically national came to mean this popular ingredient, incorporating into non-Hispanic ethnic features, which was accommodated at the discourse level in order to make it appear sufficiently strange–exotic, extravagant, and distant to Western eyes–and yet at the same time, close and consubstantial for the national collectivity. In other words, historians glossed over the tense conflictive components of popular and rural reality. The non-Hispanic ethnic features of the population were so stylized that they became objectified. A descriptive code developed that would create a world compatible to what was considered Western. Juan Cruz Varela (1794–1839) went so far as to draw up a prescriptive glossary on how national literature should describe the American landscape: "una vegetación rápida y prodigiosa. Un suelo siempre verde y florido . . . todos estos objetos son propios para inflamar la imaginación de los poetas y producir grandes y bellas descripciones" (Sarlo 123) ("a rapid and prodigious vegetation. A soil that is always green and florid . . . all these objects are suitable for inflaming the imagination of poets and producing beautiful, impressive descriptions"). The key to local color was to use the panorama of "green and florid," fertile soils to inflame the expansionist imagination of the West. The idea of this torrid, fertile zone was maintained throughout the century. It was easier to turn everything into vegetation, into vast still-life paintings (that is, into objects) for universal exhibitions and for museums: to a certain extent, literature, and the discipline that canonized it, historiography, was the sarcophagus in which pieces of these popular cultures were embalmed; they were fragmented, divided between an aesthetic aura of art and a very different disenchanted response to serialized production of kitsch. The historical imperative of a social and civilizing literature for the propagation of new ideas (that were democratic and popular as Alberdi and Echeverría had ordained) would collapse in the face of the Euro-Imperial desire to turn these territories into lands that would always be Edenic and ahistorical, with plains that were forever green. This Utopian hinterland was the imaginary and ideological counterweight to cosmopolitan modernization.

The *criollo* interpretation of the conflictive heterogeneity of Spanish American countries was an imaginary negotiation of the learned sector. This cultural imaginary simplified differences and adulterated issues in its representation of the other, which it could no longer ignore given the enormous pressure that workers' demands began to exert at the end of the nineteenth century in the urban centers of Spanish America. These workers were no longer those distant hordes of bandits (Canudos, Yaquis, Huaichu, Tzotziles, Cruzob, Cabanos, and Maribondos) who rioted along the border, but craftsmen who inhabited the same spaces as the creators of patriotic symbols. On the basis of the affirmation of State power, cities attracted both those who designed the rhetorical apparatus for their consecration and a growing mass of workers who, through their anonymous efforts, provided the changes in the new urban scenario. Yet this was the popular group closest to the learned ones, and obviously to historians too, who were no less frightened by the magnitude of this social force, which they probably understood yet repressed in their historical imagination:

> Algunos también sueñan con emprenderla contra el capital y en propagar el socialismo. Sería para el Perú la última desgracia, el último absurdo, la última plaga. Desde que aquí *no hay* todavía cuestión obrera, desde que aquí *no existe ninguna* de las causas económicas que en los demás países producen el socialismo, introducirlo por manía simiana, sería, a la vez que ridículo e insensato, criminal en alto grado. (Riva Agüero 248; my emphasis)

> Some also dream of taking on capitalism and propagating socialism. For Peru, this would be the ultimate misfortune, the ultimate absurdity, the ultimate plague. Since *there are no* workers' issues here, since *there are none* of the economic causes that produce socialism in other countries, introducing it here in simian fashion would be both ridiculous and foolish, and absolutely criminal.

Like the ghost of Hamlet's father (see de Certeau 1995), everything that is repressed returns, yet to a different scene than the scene of the crime; literary historiography removed the popular from the present scene and hid it at the bottom of the trunk. The subjects of Moctezuma and Atahuallpa cultivated poetry centuries before European civilization cast the intelligence of Mexicans and Peruvians in a "Christian mold," as Juan María Gutiérrez would claim; yet he disguised that art as Incan and Aztec, thereby placing an artificial construction in the space left by the eradication of the actual. It was a fetish that, from the unconscious of this particular class, staved off the tensions that it was unable to resolve on its own.

Without abandoning the scene of the crime, the representation of the people was sweetened by banishing it to the countryside: This is the poetry of the people; these are tunes of peasants, the *corridos* of the countryside (see Adolfo Valderrama). The popular is turned into a literary subject, a "costumbrista" sketch, fetishized by the mechanism of the typical Juan Cruz Varela would himself make a brief adjustment to his literary manifesto, which is somewhat ironic:

> yo no creo que para que la literatura sea nacional es necesario que tome en la patria todos los asuntos que trata, que copie *solamente nuestra naturaleza,* que refleje siempre *nuestros caracteres,* nuestras costumbres. (qtd. in Sarlo 62; my emphasis)

> in order for literature to be national literature, I do not believe that it needs to include the fatherland in all the issues it explores; nor *should it only copy our nature,* and always reflect *our characters,* our customs.

The social conflict of the nineteenth-century popular struggles was officially depicted in national literature by characters who previously had been constrained, sweetened, and gagged. The literary institution psychologized social dissidence, reconverting the subaltern subject into a tropical rarity, just as biology would do with animal species (see **Figure 9**).

Figure 9.

Music-sheet of a popular ballad recycled in a zarzuela and thus reconciling the music of the social barrier between the elite and the popular. (Archive of the author)

That this concept of national literature canonized by its historiography eventually prevailed is hardly surprising: It agreed with the Conservative turn that Liberalism had taken in the middle of the nineteenth century. The historiographic model based national literary historicity on the motifs and works that provided a naturalized image of reality, in other words, on the bearers of an oligarchical-bourgeois perspective that turned popular culture into folklore. This revealed a problem of identity that would muffle the foreign-leaning sensibility of the elites, fonder of the technological modernity of cities and the luxury of their private lives than of images that showed up the falsity of their preferences. The restoration of pristine nature and an ingenuous, spontaneous peasant was, in the last analysis, merely another object for international consumption, or proved useful for a community with a split identity in which literature could serve as the site for compensatory representations. The process of cosmopolitanization that took place in the late nineteenth century compelled the learned sectors to re-think, not entirely without contradictions, the question of representation. Hence the opposing options of criollism and cosmopolitanism were polarized expressions of a deeper problem, characterizing the postcolonial condition of cultures that have been colonized for many years, which enter a world economy in a subaltern position, with unequal development of their social structures; this in turn accelerates the co-existence of polarities (traditional as opposed to international modes; different forms of cultural logic). And within this web of lines of flight fostered by modernization, historiography appears to create a bridge between a complex present that erased long-established traditional patterns and writing which wove an imaginary past. Perhaps, as in ancient times, historiographic writing has been a monument of modern times marked by nostalgia and melancholy.

Translation by Suzanne Stephens

Works Cited

Achugar, Hugo, ed. 1998. *La fundación por la palabra: letra y nación en América Latina en el siglo XIX*. Uruguay: Universidad de la República, Facultad de Humanidades y Ciencias de la Educación, Departamento de Publicaciones.

Alberdi, Juan Bautista. 1964. *Escritos sobre estética y problemas de la literatura*. Buenos Aires: Ediciones La Rosa Blindada.

Amunátegui Solar, Domingo. 1915. *Bosquejo histórico de la literatura chilena*. Santiago de Chile: Imprenta Universitaria.

Anderson, Benedict. 1993. *Comunidades imaginadas: reflexiones sobre el origen y la difusión del nacionalismo*. Trans. Eduardo L. Suárez. Mexico City: Fondo de Cultura Económica.

Antonio, Nicolás. 1672. *Bibliotheca hispana, sive. Hispanorvm qvi vsqvam vnqvamve sive Latinâ sive populari sive aliâ qvávis lingvâ scripto aliqvid consignaverunt: notitia, his qvae praecesservnt locvpletior et certior brevia elogia, editorum atque ineditorum operum catalogum dvabvs partbvs partibvs continents, qvarvm haec ordine qvidem rei posterior, conceptu verò prior duobus tomis de his agit, qvi post annvm secvlarem MD usque ad praesentem diem floruere . . .* Rome: Ex officina Nicolai Angeli Tinassii.

Ardao, Arturo. 1980. *Génesis de la idea y el nombre de América Latina*. Caracas: Centro de Estudios Latinoamericanos Rómulo Gallegos.

Baczko, Bronislaw. 1991. *Los imaginarios sociales: memorias y esperanzas colectivas*. Trans. Pablo Betesh. Buenos Aires: Ediciones Nueva Visión.

Balibar, Renée and Dominique Laporte. 1974. *Le français national*. Paris: Hachette.

Bello, Andrés. 1951. *Gramática de la lengua castellana destinada al uso de los americanos. Obras completas*. Vol 4. Caracas: Ministerio de Educación.

——. 1965 [1848]. "Modo de escribir la historia." *Antología de Andrés Bello*. Ed. Raúl Silva Castro. Santiago de Chile: Ed. Zig-Zag. 166–178.

Bradford Burns, E. 1990. *La pobreza del progreso, América Latina en el siglo XIX*. Mexico City: Siglo XXI.

Calcaño, José Antonio. 1985. *La ciudad y su música*. Caracas: Monte Avila Editores.

Cané, Miguel. 1838. "Literatura." *El Iniciador* 3 (15 May): 133–36.

Castellanos, Rafael Ramón. 1983. *Caracas 1883. (Centenario del Natalicio del Libertador)*. 2 vols. Caracas: Academia Nacional de la Historia (Estudios, Monografías y Ensayos).

Certeau, Michel de. 1988. *The Writing of History*. Trans. Tom Conley. New York: Columbia University Press.

——. 1995. *Historia y psicoanálisis: entre ciencia y ficción*. Trans. Alfonso Menidola. Mexico City: Universidad Iberoamericana.

Colmenares. Germán. 1989. *Las convenciones contra la cultura*. 2nd ed. Colombia: Tercer Mundo Edit.

Cornejo Polar, Antonio. 1989. *La formación de la tradición literaria en el Perú*. Lima: Centro de Estudios y Publicaciones.

Donoso, Armando. 1980. *Sarmiento en el destierro*. Buenos Aires: M. Gleitzer Edit.

Douglas, Ann. 1988. *Feminization of American Culture*. New York: Anchor Books.

Eguiara y Eguren, Juan José. 1944. Prólogos a la *Biblioteca Mexicana*. Ed. Agustín Millares Carlo. Mexico City: Fondo de Cultura Económica. 55–213.

Figueroa, Pedro Pablo. 1891. *La literatura chilena: bosquejo histórico desde la colonia hasta nuestros días*. Santiago de Chile: Imp. de el Correo.

Franco Carvalhal, Tania. 1997. "Literatura e Historia: a ficção latino-americana." *La Torre* 2.4-5: 321–29.

García de Coronado, Domitila. 1926 [1868]. *Album poético fotográfico de escritoras y poetisas cubanas*. Havana: Imprenta de "El Figaro."

González, Beatriz. 1987. *La historiografía literaria del liberalismo hispanoamericano del siglo XIX*. Havana: Premio Casa de las Américas.

——. 1993. "Sujeto criollo/conciencia histórica: La historiografía literaria en el período colonial." *Ruptura de la conciencia hispanoamericana*. Ed. José Anadón. Mexico City: Fondo de Cultura Económica. 15–57.

Guha, Ranajit. 1997a. "Sobre algunos aspectos de la historiografía colonial de la India." *Debates postcoloniales: una introducción a los estudios de la subalternidad*. Ed. Silvia Rivera Cusicanqui and Rossana Barragán. La Paz, Bolivia: Edit. Historias. 25–32.

——. 1997b. "La prosa de contra-insurgencia." *Debates Postcoloniales: una introducción a los estudios de la subalternidad*. Ed. Silvia Rivera Cusicanqui y Rossana Barragán. La Paz-Bolivia: Edit. historias. 33–72.

Guidieri, Remo. 1997. *El museo y sus fetiches: crónica de lo neutro y de la aureola*. Trans. Isabelle Touet de Matallana. Madrid: Edit.Tecnos.

Gutiérrez, Juan María. 1957 [1865]. "Advertencia preliminar." *Escritores coloniales americanos*. Ed. Gregorio Weinberg. Buenos Aires: Raigal. 219–21.

——. 1846. "Prólogo." *América Poética*. Valparaiso: Imprenta del Mercurio. i–xii.

Gutiérrez Girardot, Rafael. 1983. *Modernismo*. Barcelona: Montesinos.

Halperin Donghi, Tulio. 1977. *Historia contemporánea de América Latina*. Madrid: Alianza.

Hegel, Georg Wilhelm Friedrich. 1857. *Philosophy of History*. Trans. John Sibree. New York: P.F. Collier and Son.

———. 1990 [1828]. *Lectures on the History of Philosophy: The Lectures of 1825–1826.* Ed. Robert F. Brown. Trans. R. F. Brown, J. M. Stewart, and H. S. Harris. Berkeley: University of California Press.

Hobsbawm, Eric J. 1992. *Naciones y Nacionalismo desde 1780.* Trans. Jordi Deltran. Barcelona: Grijalbo.

——— and Terence Ranger. 1983. *The Invention of Tradition.* Cambridge: Cambridge University Press.

Kaplan, Marcos. 1969. *Formación del estado nacional en América Latina.* Buenos Aires: Amorrortu Edit.

León Mera, Juan. 1893 [1868]. *Ojeada histórico-crítica sobre la poesía ecuatoriana.* Barcelona: Imp. de José Cunill Sala.

León Pinelo, Antonio de. 1973. *Epítome de una Bibliotheca Oriental, y Occidental, naútica, y geográfica, etc. Tomo 2. En que se contienen los escritores de las Indias Occidentales especialmente del Perú, Nueva España, La Florida, El Dorado, Tierra Firme Paraguay y el Brasil y Viajes a ellos, y los autores de Navegación y sus materiales apéndices.* 3 vols. Ed. Fascimile Carlos Sanz López. Madrid: Oficina de Francisco Martínez Abad.

Llano Zapata, José Eusebio de. 1769. *Carta persuasiva al Señor Don Ignacio de Escandón . . . Sobre asunto de escribir la historia-literaria de la América meridional.* Lima: Oficina de los niños huérfanos.

Lukács, Georg. 1969. *Historia y consciencia de clase: estudios de dialéctica marxista.* Trans. Manuel Sacristán. Mexico City: Grijalbo.

Medina, José Toribio. 1878. *Historia de la literatura colonial de Chile.* 3 vols. Santiago de Chile: Imprenta de la Librería del Mercurio.

Menéndez y Pelayo, Marcelino. 1927–1928 [1893–1895]. *Antología de poetas hispanoamericanos.* Madrid: Tip. de la "Revista de archivos."

Montaldo, Graciela. 1994. *La sensibilidad amenazada. Fin de siglo y modernismo.* Rosario: Beatriz Viterbo Edit.

Olalquiaga, Celeste. 1998. *The Artificial Kingdom: a Treasury of the Kitsch Experience.* New York: Pantheon Books.

Olavarría y Ferrari, Enrique de. 1878. *El arte literario en México: noticias biográficas y críticas de sus más notables escritores.* 2nd ed. Madrid: Espinoza y Bautista Edit.

Picón Febres, Gonzalo. 1947 [1906]. *La literatura venezolana en el siglo diez y nueve (ensayo de historia crítica).* Buenos Aires: Edit. Ayacucho.

Pratt, Mary Louise. 1992. *Imperial Eyes: Travel Writing and Transculturation.* London: Routledge.

Rabasa, José. 1993. *Inventing America: Spanish Historiography and the Formation of Eurocentrism.* Norman: Oklahoma University Press.

Rama, Angel. 1984. *La ciudad letrada.* Montevideo: Fundación Angel Rama.

———. 1985. *Las máscaras democráticas del modernismo.* Montevideo: Arca.

Ramos, Julio. 1989. *Desencuentros de la modernidad en América Latina. Literatura y política en el siglo XIX.* Mexico City: Fondo de Cultura Económica.

———. 1993. "El don de la lengua." *Casa de las Américas* 193: 13–25.

Riva Agüero, José de la. 1962. *Estudios de literatura peruana: carácter de la literatura del Perú independiente. Obras completas.* Vol 1. Lima: Universidad Católica del Perú.

Rodó, José Enrique. 1967. "Enseñanza de la literatura." *Obras completas.* Madrid: Edit. Aguilar. 525–84.

Rodríguez, Ileana. 1998. "Hegemonía y dominio: subalternidad, un significado florante." *Teorías sin disciplina: Latinoamericanismo, poscolonialidad y globalización en debate.* Ed. Santiago Castro-Gómez y Eduardo Mendieta. Mexico City: Miguel Angel Porrúa. 101–20.

Rodríguez Mohedano, Rafael. 1770–1801. *Historia literaria de España.* 10 vols. Madrid: Ibarra.

Rojas, Ricardo. 1922. *La literatura argentina: ensayo filosófico sobre la evolución de la cultura en el Plata.* 4 vols. Buenos Aires: Imprenta de Coni Hnos.

Romero, José Luis. 1984. *Latinoamérica: las ciudades y las ideas.* Mexico City: Siglo XXI.

Roxlo, Carlos. 1936. *Historia crítica de la literatura uruguaya.* 7 vols. Montevideo: A. Barreiro y Ramos.

Salazar, Ramón A. 1951 [1897]. *Historia del desenvolvimiento intelectual de Guatemala desde la fundación de la primera escuela de letras europeas hasta la inauguración del Instituto Nacional de Indígenas.* Guatemala: Biblioteca de Cultura Popular.

Sarlo, Beatriz. 1968. *Juan María Gutiérrez: historiador y crítico de nuestra literatura.* Buenos Aires: Edit. Escuela.

Sarmiento, Domingo Faustino. 1969. *Facundo. Civilización y barbarie.* Buenos Aires: Editorial Universitaria de Buenos Aires.

Schottus, Andreas. [1608]. *Hispaniae illustras seu Rerum urbiumque. Hispaniae, Lusitanias, Aethiopie et Indiae, scriptores varii.* Francofvrti: C. Marnium & haeredes Iohannis Aubrij.

Silva, Paulette. 1993. *Una vasta morada de enmascarados. Poesía, cultura y modernización en Venezuela a finales del siglo XIX.* Caracas: Ediciones La Casa de Bello.

———. 1998. "¿De qué hablaban cuando hablaban de amor? Narrativas sentimentales médicas en Venezuela." Diss. Universidad Simón Bolívar de Caracas.

Sommer, Doris. 1991. *Foundational Fictions: The National Romances of Latin America.* Berkeley: University of California Press.

Valderrama, Adolfo. 1866. *Bosquejo histórico de la poesía chilena.* Santiago de Chile: Imp. Chilena.

Valdés, Mario. J. 1997. "The Hermeneutics of Historical and Literary Remembering." *La Torre* 2.4-5: 209–22.

Valdés y Palacios, José Manuel. 1971. *Bosquejo sobre el estado político, moral y literario del Perú en sus tres grandes épocas.* Trans. Carmen Sologuren. Lima: Biblioteca Nacional del Perú.

Vargas Fontecilla, Francisco. 1853. "Discurso de recepción pronunciado ante la facultad de humanidades por Don Francisco Vargas Fontecilla el 12 de julio de 1852." *Anales de la Universidad de Chile* (January): 359.

Vergara y Vergara, José María. 1905 [1867]. *Historia de la literatura en Nueva Granada, desde la Conquista hasta la Independencia, 1538–1820.* Bogota: Librería Americana.

Vigil, José María. 1892. *Reseña histórica de la literatura mexicana.* Mexico City: np.

White, Hayden. 1985. *Tropics of Discourse. Essays in Cultural Criticism.* Baltimore: The Johns Hopkins University Press.

———. 1992. *Metahistoria. La imaginación histórica en la Europa del siglo XIX.* Trans. Stella Mastrangelo. Mexico City: Fondo de Cultura Económica.

CHAPTER 6

CREATING THE NATIONAL IMAGINARY

Vera Follain de Figueiredo

The literary period conventionally called Romanticism can be considered the first to witness the emergence of a full-fledged proposal to imbue the Brazilian nation's history with meaning. It is the first time that such a proposal takes on the characteristics of a program, as writers enlist in its ranks to forge a national imaginary. This is the spirit in which Domingos José Gonçalves de Magalhães's (1811–1882) article for the *Revista Niteroi* (published in Paris in 1836 and with the motto "Tudo pelo Brasil e para o Brasil" ["Everything in the name of Brazil, and for Brazil"]) articulates the national cry for literary independence. Magalhães points out the need to create a Brazilian poetry that "cortando as amarras com um passado de cópia e imitação" (Miguel Pereira 147) ("cuts through the shackles of a past of imitation and copies"). From that point on, in the pages of Antônio Gonçalves Dias's (1823–1864) *indianista* (nativist) poetry, José de Alencar's (1829–1877) novels, and Antônio de Castro Alves's (1847–1871) socially conscious poetry, to mention but a few of the works of the most notable authors, we find the intellectual elite's efforts to vindicate the newly independent nation's promise of future greatness by endowing it with an equally grandiose past.

Modernity, a state of mind fixated on a linear concept of time, as Octavio Paz (1914–1998) observed (1974, 39–40), and lulled by a belief in progress, presupposes a causal relation between past, present, and future. The Brazilian nation must therefore adjust itself to this historical perspective. It becomes necessary to signal the nation's rupture with the colonial powers in order to consolidate its political emancipation in the cultural sphere, and it is imperative to establish continuity in the nation's historical trajectory. This continuity, true to modern temporality, should vindicate the notion of a meaningfully directed process that moves towards an optimum end. Castro Alves formulates an interrogation in the poem "O livro e a America" ("America and the Book") that becomes paradigmatic. In the poem's opening pair of stanzas, the poet de-historicizes the Conquest of America, accentuating the continent's pristine quality. Still wet from the Flood, America emerges from the waters by power of Columbus's hands, the man who "unveils the new land" with Jehovah's council. The recourse to the mythic sphere acts as a ruse, covering the gaps deliberately left in history. Pre-Columbian peoples go unmentioned in an elision of the violence of the Conquest, a strategy that makes *tabula rasa* of a past that the poet is not interested in recovering:

Molhado inda do diluvio,
Qual Tritão descommunal,
O continente desperta
No concerto universal.
Dos oceanos em tropa
Um–traz-lhes as artes da Europa, . . .
E os Andes petrificados,
Como braços levantados,
Lhe apontam para a amplidão.
Olhando em torno então brada:
Tudo marcha!. . . O' grande Deus!
As cataractas–para terra,

As estrellas–para os céos.
Lá, do polo sobre as plagas,
O seu rebanho de vagas
Vai o mar apascentar . . .
Eu quero marchar com os ventos,
Com os mundos . . . co'os firmamentos!!!
E Deus responde–Marchar!

(Castro Alves 19–20)

Still wet from the Flood,
Like immense Triton,
The continent awakens
To the universal concert.
From the oceans in masse
One brings the arts of Europe to it, . . .
And the Andes carved in stone,
Like arms raised high,
Show the place where vastness lies.
Looking about, then, it thunders:
All is marching! . . . O great Creator!
Cataracts plummet waters to earth,
Like stars in the heavens.
There, from atop the pole of countries,
Herds of waves
Run to pasture in the seas . . .
I want to march with the wind,
With worlds . . . with the firmaments!!!
And the Lord's answer–March!

The poem unveils a nation ready to march toward progress. The use of the verb *march* is noteworthy because it conveys the period's universal certainty that the world would indeed forge ahead, that is, it would be moving ever closer to an ideal state. However, in the case of Brazil, the question remained: From which point in Western history would it begin its march? Would the nation have to return to the primordial moments of that history? As a new continent–all references to pre-Columbian peoples erased–should Brazil adopt Western civilization's own designated starting point–classical antiquity–and thus begin climbing upward? Castro Alves, embedded in a linear vision of time, finds himself at a problematic juncture. The poet's solution uses an argument that is, in principle, at odds with modern rationality, since it is based on chance, on the fortuitous:

Por uma fatalidade,
Dessas que descem de além,
O sec'lo que viu Colombo,
Vio Gutenberg tambem.
Quando no tosco estaleiro
Da Alemanha o velho obreiro
A ave da imprensa gerou . . .
O Genovez salta os mares
Busca um ninho entre os palmares
E a *patria da imprensa achou.*

(Castro Alves 21–22)

100

It was per chance,
Like one descending from up above,
The century that saw Columbus,
Also witnessed Gutenberg.
When in the shipyards
The old worker from Germany
Created the bird of the press . . .
The Genovese rides the seas
Searching to nest among the palm trees
And discovered the *homeland of the printing press.*

Since Columbus's discovery of the Atlantic route to the Americas and Gutenberg's invention of the printing press are contemporaneous, Brazil was to leap directly into the Enlightenment. The imagined connections among Columbus, Gutenberg, and America, based on a temporal coincidence, point to two important issues pertaining to temporality. On the one hand, they are attuned to a modern mentality, with that dimension of simultaneity—measured on the face of a clock—that belongs to the homogeneous and empty temporal dimension inaugurated with modernity, and that allows for the juxtaposition of articles in a newspaper, for example. On the other hand, this imagined alliance of discoverer, inventor, and continent constitutes an attempt to escape a causal scheme based on the successiveness of time, by electing to allow simultaneity to attenuate the contrasts that characterize the nation's entrance into the modern world, synthesized in the image of the iron train that chases away the naked *caboclos* (indigenous Brazilian).

It does not take much to see how the world view that directed the project of modernity, including the homogenization of time according to European experience, clashed with the heterogeneous and contradictory Brazilian reality: Iron trains and machines share the landscape with naked *caboclos.* Nevertheless, it is equally understandable that the very concept of progress, one of the pillars of modern thought, was well suited to fulfilling the expectations of a young, newly independent country, ready to take on the task of transforming itself into a modern nation fashioned in the European mold. The issue at hand was that, if there was grandeur and great promise in the future, there was conversely a nagging deficiency, the absence of a glorious past from which to take root. This past had to be created. As Lúcia Miguel Pereira observed, "não foi para criar uma espécie de Idade Média americana—servil imitação européia—que nossos escritores se voltaram para os índios, mas para se certificarem de que podiam ter confiança no futuro" (146) ("our writers did not turn to the natives in an attempt to create a sort of Brazilian Middle Ages—in servile imitation of Europe—but to convince themselves that they could believe in the future").

The Brazilian intellectual elite in the nineteenth century found itself, continuously and in different ways, in search of an answer to the question formulated by the poet Castro Alves. In other words, to march, but from where? Writers of the Romantic period took it upon themselves to choose a starting point for this march toward progress, a taste that was to define a historical beginning and invent a tradition that would mold the country into a cohesive nation. To better understand this movement, it is necessary to situate it in the larger context of the Western world in the nineteenth century, taking into account that in inaugurating the project of inventing the Brazilian nation, the country's intellectual elite was in perfect consonance with events occurring in developed regions. The construction of national identities was, at the time, a requirement of modernity—for various reasons, including those motivated by the economic order, such as the demands of liberal capitalism. One should keep in mind, however, that the American colonies, in their struggle against the colonial powers, developed such a nationalist sentiment well ahead of the Old World. The effort to define a historical origin and extend a supposedly continuous timeline to justify the nation had, in Europe, the function of replacing the deteriorating ties that held pre-modern societies together. Empowered elites worked to create a network of imaginary relations capable of guaranteeing social cohesion. In Europe as well as in Brazil, there was a concerted investment in creating narratives that would legitimize the nation-state. This meant providing the people inhabiting lands newly determined as nations with elaborate accounts of a distinct historic past; it meant interpreting facts in particular ways, augmenting meaning in some, diminishing or suppressing meaning in others. Understood as "imagined communities," to use Benedict Anderson's expression (13), nations draw sustenance from beliefs that look to cultural artifacts for their foundations. Therefore there was an incentive both to produce and to consume a form of literature that would define a common identity. Walter Scott presented the British nation as a historical society that arose from adventures in foreign lands and intense domestic conflicts to develop into an established state, capable of resisting both internal and external upheaval. In Portugal, Almeida Garret and Alexandre Herculano gave shape to the myth of origin of the Lusitanian nation. Romanticism, centering on the remote and mysterious past as a theme, created fertile ground for budding national mythologies.

In Europe, as in the American nations, it was up to the elites to create the constitution of the modern state; they enacted social and ideological concepts to constitute the nation according to specific principles. A decisive point was the creation of a territorial imaginary, since the land was perceived as an integral physical dimension that manifested the spirit of the state, and was thus associated with national sovereignty. As an imaginary based on geography began to take form, along with related interests in legitimizing borders, fresh ground opened up in literature for the topic of travel, stimulating the description of landscapes and the creation of records of natural resources.

The invention of tradition in Brazil meant managing both unfavorable conditions that arose from the manner in which the country was brought into the modern context and its own particular status conferred by its recent colonial past. It was simultaneously necessary to create a proto-history that would justify the nation's existence, and work with the idea of a rupture from Portugal to consolidate the political emancipation that had recently occurred. The harmonious, organic image being tailored for the nation-state clashed with the country's abrupt irruption into the Western world and with the break imposed by the colonizer's undermining of indigenous cultures so that the unity of Christian civilization would prevail. That image contrasted, by the same token, with a society based on slavery, a society that excluded blacks, excusing them (because of their servile condition) from the cast of builders who were to raise up the young nation under the gaze of the West.

In a utilitarian reconstruction of the past, two paths appeared that were, to a certain extent, in opposition to each other. The first path would be to create a proto-history starting from the native, as was done, for example, in Mexico. As

Octavio Paz noted, official Mexican history presents a categorical refutation of the Colonial period, which is considered an interregnum, a period usurped, a phase of historical illegitimacy. Independence was consequently seen as restoration: With Independence the continuity of historical discourse was reestablished after three centuries of colonial interruption, and the Aztec past and the pre-Hispanic world were rescued (1979, 60–61). Meanwhile, the conservative character of Brazil's process of political independence and the marginal reality of native indigenous cultures in the nation made it impossible for the radical Mexican reading to take root. Thus, while Brazil opted for such an interpretation, it adopted it as an attenuated solution, one that recovered the indigenous past without excluding the Portuguese inheritance, searching for success in the symbiotic and favoring the sense of continuity. The second path, aimed more toward the future than the past, would situate the beginning of Brazil's proto-history at the threshold of its entrance into the Western world. Expatriate Europeans, as well as Brazilians, would take it upon themselves, given the impossibility of founding a modern nation with the elements provided by their own autochthonous tradition, to create it according to standards imported from Europe or the United States. This move placed the emphasis on suppressing both the indigenous past and the Portuguese colonial inheritance, so that a new model for civilization could be championed, a model that could guarantee the nation's place in modernity.

The first path can be identified with José de Alencar's proposal and the second path with that of Joaquim Nabuco (1849–1910). These authors constructed the paradigms that would provide an enduring framework for the differing representations of the Brazilian nation. Each writer would define a specific type of identity discourse in defense of a particular ideological stance. The opposition between these paradigms in Hispanic America has many times found expression in the Shakespearean characters of Caliban and Ariel from *The Tempest*. A rereading of the play suggests that to choose Caliban as the inaugural character for Latin American culture meant to affirm a pre-colonial essence, or, in a less radical interpretation, to accept a *mestizo* past. The choice favoring Ariel, alternatively, implies inclusion in Prospero's culture, in other words, an opting for white culture. In the case of Brazil, the two opposing propositions, which in the sphere of culture were, at times, quite distinctly evident, were related in one fundamental aspect: Neither of them suggested profound changes that would challenge the social order. This created the paradox enunciated by Florestan Fernandes:

> Dessa perspectiva a independência pressupunha, lado a lado, um elemento puramente revolucionário e outro elemento especificamente conservador. O elemento revolucionário aparecia nos propósitos de despojar a ordem social, herdada da sociedade colonial, dos caracteres de heteronômicos aos quais fora moldada, requisito para que ela adquirisse a elasticidade e a autonomia exigidas por uma sociedade nacional. O elemento conservador evidenciava-se nos propósitos de preservar e fortalecer, a todo custo, uma ordem social que não possuía condições materiais e morais suficientes para engendrar o padrão de autonomia necessário à construção e ao florescimento de uma Nação. (32)

> From this perspective, independence presupposed there existing, side by side, a purely revolutionary element and another specifically conservative one. The revolutionary element was present in propositions to divest the social order, inherited from colonial society, of the heteronymic characteristics with which it was

shaped, a requisite for the necessary autonomy and elasticity of a national society. The conservative element became evident in proposals to preserve and strengthen, at any cost, a social order that did not possess the sufficient material or moral conditions to engender the autonomy necessary for the constructing and flourishing of a nation.

The polemics between José de Alencar and Joaquim Nabuco serve in an exemplary manner to illustrate the differences between the positions they held, and, at the same time, allow us a glimpse of the common ground from which they spring, since both points of view inscribe themselves in the American paradox mentioned previously. If one ignores the more regrettable aspects–personal attacks, personal vanity at play– of the discussions between the writers, we can say that the debate centered on a basic question: What is worthy of being represented in Brazilian literature? The core of Joaquim Nabuco's criticism of Alencar was more relative to *what* the fiction writer chose as his topics, rather than *how* he did so. It's not without reason that Nabuco began his criticism of Alencar's fictional works with an *indianista* (nativist) book; he asserted that *O Guarani* was Alencar's first novel, and deliberately declined to mention *Cinco Minutos* and *Viuvinha*, both written prior to *O Guarani*, although sharing the same year of publication (1857). Nabuco wrote,

> Que futuro, que relação com o país, que razão de ser, que direito de chamar-se brasileira, tinha essa falsa literatura tupi, é o que eu discutirei, não hoje, mas a propósito de *Iracema* e *Ubirajara*. (in Coutinho 84)

> What future, what relation to the nation, what reason for being, what right to call itself Brazilian, this false Tupi literature has, that is what I shall discuss, not today, but with respect to *Iracema* and *Ubirajara*.

The concern here is to determine what has the right to be called Brazilian, to draw and establish the boundaries for representing certain topics, and, in this particular case, the critic sees *indianismo* (nativism) as being Tupi, but not Brazilian. This polemic brings two visions of nationality into confrontation; two different cultural projects fight for supremacy. In the same way that he tried to exert control over the representation of the native in Brazilian literature, Nabuco, in an article for the *O Globo* newspaper dated 24 October 1875, condemned the choice of a black heroine to articulate the drama of maternity:

> Não era nessa raça infeliz que o Sr. J. de Alencar devia ter procurado o ideal da mãe; entre os animais ser-lhe-ia fácil descobrir casos de heroísmo materno mais tocantes, do que o dessa escrava que se fez sem sacrifício, vender pelo filho. (in Coutinho 112)

> It is not in this unhappy race that Mr. Alencar should have looked for the ideal of motherhood; it would be easier for him to find cases of more touching maternal heroism among animals than in this slave woman who gives herself without sacrifice to be sold in place of her son.

One can perceive here, as elsewhere, the contradictions with Nabuco's abolitionism, inspired by English sources, arising from a universalism that is abstract, linked to a rhetoric of a civilizing mission, but does not prevent a feeling of superiority towards blacks, even when his discourse is marked by affection, such as in the chapter "Missangana" in *Minha Formação* [My Upbringing], in which he confesses to a singular nostalgia for the slave (153). Nabuco wrote elsewhere,

Quando leio o teatro do Sr. J. de Alencar, ponho-me a pensar que foi por estar dominado pela idéia de fundar a literatura tupi que ele quis desacreditar a sociedade brasileira, a vida civilizada do nosso país, os elementos de poesia que pode ter em si a raça européia que o povo ou e que, pela ação lenta do meio exterior, já tornou-se verdadeiramente americana. (in Coutinho 114)

When I read Mr. José de Alencar's plays, the thought occurs to me that it was because he was dominated by the idea of founding a Tupi literature that he wanted to discredit Brazilian society, our country's civilized life, the elements of poetry that may be intrinsic to the European race that peopled it, and that, under the slow action of the environment, has already become truly American.

The accusation in this passage consists in situating Alencar as a person against civilization, an opponent of the European race. Elsewhere he accuses the author of *Iracema* of having a certain inclination for parties at which human flesh is served. Nabuco then proposes to take it on himself to re-educate Alencar, bringing him back to the true doctrine. The project for building the Brazilian nation, in Nabuco's eyes, meant idealizing white urban society. Alencar idealized the native, and because of his urban writing, as in *Lucíola* (1862), for example, he would be accused of a realism devoid of moral elevation and thus opposed to the principles of a healthy society.

Apart from the exhaustive debates with the young Nabuco, the other polemics in which Alencar took part allow us to conclude that the path he chose, even if conciliatory in character, was not a very comfortable one at the time:

Ora sou acusado de barbarizar a nossa literatura, tornando-a tupi e selvagem, separando-a do mundo civilizado pela linha negra da escravidão; criando um teatro como nunca existiu; ora, não tenho a menor originalidade, e sou apenas o tradutor dos livros europeus. (in Coutinho 151)

One moment I am accused of barbarizing our literature, making it Tupi and savage, isolating it from the civilized world with the black border of slavery; creating theater as it has never been known; the next, I am not in the slightest original, and am just the slavish translator of European books.

The contradictions of the critics were fed by Alencar's own attitude, however. His response to accusations would be to change from one extreme to the other, which was clearly the only possible course of action at a time when originality was greatly prized, with the caveat that, in a nation such as Brazil, it had to be backed by the literary conventions in use in Europe. Thus, if he was accused of barbarizing Brazilian literature, he responded with European examples that could legitimize his conduct: If white Cecília loved the native Peri, Desdemona loved Othello. His reliance on foreign models, which he was unable to break, became clear, especially because of his own education. If the ideal was to create a "native Eve" to follow Milton's example, or a Helen emulating Homer (as he demanded of Gonçalves de Magalhães on occasion of the publication of *A Confederação dos Tamoios* [1855; The Confederation of the Tamoios]), Alencar, in a letter appended to the 1875 novel *Senhora*, stated that it was necessary to tailor characters to the dimensions of *fluminense* society (belonging to Rio de Janeiro), which did not admit of giants, in order to guarantee national color.

Looking at the criticism José de Alencar received and his replies, one finds evidence of an inferiority complex in relation to the European literary tradition, and of the unease he experienced feeling that he at once belonged and was extraneous to this tradition. The issue of imitation took on great importance in this context. In a passage of *Como e porque sou romancista* [How and Why I Am a Novelist], Alencar held up French literature as a great model and praised imitation as a tool that allowed for flexibility of spirit in the same way that gymnastics developed flexibility in the body. At another point in the same text, he refuted accusations of plagiarism by opposing Brazilian nature, which was his true master, to Chateaubriand's works, which were his models. The opposing elements belong to different orders, one to the order of external referents to the literary work, that is, to that which becomes a topic (nature), and the other to what is more rightly the literary order (the French author's texts). Alencar's resolution of this impasse comes in the form of a metaphor: Nature is also a book, from which *O Guarani* issued forth. For want of a national literary tradition that he could guiltlessly call on, Alencar uses nature as a substitute:

Quanto à poesia americana, o modêlo para mim ainda hoje é Chateaubriand; mas o mestre que eu tive, foi esta esplêndida natureza que me envolve, e particularmente a magnificência dos desertos que eu perlustrei ao entrar na adolescência, e foram o pórtico majestoso por onde minha alma penetrou no passado de sua pátria . . .

Daí, dêsse livro secular e imenso é que eu tirei as páginas de *O Guarani*, as de *Iracema*, e outras muitas que uma vida não bastaria a escrever. (1959a, 148, 149)

With respect to American poetry, I still hold Chateaubriand as a model; but the master I truly had is the splendid nature that envelops me, particularly the magnificence of the deserts that I traversed on the threshold of my adolescent years, and which were the majestic portals through which my soul penetrated the past of its fatherland.

From there, from this vast, timeless book, I took the pages of *O Guarani*, as those of *Iracema*, and many others of which a single lifetime is too short to write.

The ambiguities that permeate the positions held by both Alencar and Nabuco characterize, in truth, the elite's own condition as an instrument for the maintenance and transformation of the social structures of the Imperial State, and are also present in the most diverse ranks of Brazilian society during the reign of Pedro I (1822–1889):

Tanto as idéias e valores que predominam entre a elite, como as instituições implantadas por esta mesma elite mantinham relação de ajuste e desajuste com a realidade social do país: uma sociedade escravocrata governada por instituições liberais e representativas; uma sociedade agrária e analfabeta dirigida por uma elite cosmopolita voltada para o modelo europeu de civilização. (Carvalho 383)

The ideas and values prevalent in the elite, as well as the institutions they established, were often in an incongruous relation to the social reality of the nation: a slave society governed by Liberal and representative institutions; an illiterate agrarian society directed by an elite that was cosmopolitan and turned toward a European model of civilization.

Those elites, preoccupied with the development of the nation, neglected the development of its people, from which they were socially and culturally distant:

Pelo que eram e de onde se achavam, era um Brasil especial o que viam e o que julgavam dever representar. Esse Brasil era um sistema heliocêntrico, dominado pelo sol do Estado, em torno do qual giravam os grandes planetas do que chamavam as "classes conservadoras" e, muito longe, a miríade de estrelas da grande massa do povo. (Carvalho 345)

For what they were, and for where they were, it was a special Brazil that they saw, and that they judged they ought to represent. This Brazil was a heliocentric system, dominated by the sun of the State, around which the great planets of the so-called "conservative classes" gravitated, and, at a great distance, the myriad stars that composed the great mass of the people.

The Imperial system can be defined accordingly as a game of appearances, of false realities. As José Murilo de Carvalho states, it generated a complex game between reality and fiction in which both dimensions were frequently merged:

> As crises podiam advir seja do excesso de ênfase no realismo, em geral marca dos conservadores, seja do excesso de ênfase na ficção, tendência comum entre liberais. O difícil, no entanto, era distinguir a ficção da realidade. (388)

> The crises could arise from either the excess of emphasis on the realist, in general a mark of the Conservatives, or from the excess of emphasis on the fictive, a common trend among Liberals. The difficulty would then lie in distinguishing fiction from reality.

It becomes impossible not to equate the play between fiction and reality that marks the Brazilian context at the time with the game between realism and idealization that characterized Alencar's literature, although one must be aware that both these extremes were present in Romantic literature in general. This tension, however, becomes an idiosyncratic reality in the person of the Brazilian intellectual who is brought up with a European education and standards, is isolated from the masses or the collectivity, and becomes a naive admirer of the formidable legacy of Western culture. In turning toward his own land, he felt as if he were creating from almost nothing, as if all depended on his own willpower and imagination.

If it is a nationalist myth to imagine the nation as a natural way in which to classify people, to delimit a community, in the Brazilian case, in light of the enormous gap that separated the elites from the people, to this character of invention one must add the dimension of fiction. These are the contextual characteristics that help us to evaluate the importance that José de Alencar conferred on the foundation, through literature, of "his" fictional nation, which evidently differed from other Brazilian nations, built in other narratives, that were fighting for supremacy in the local imaginary. Adopting Miroslav Hroch's division of historical nationalist movements into three phases, Eric J. Hobsbawm considers that nationalism in Europe evolves from a purely cultural, literary, and folkloric point, through a second stage of political nationalism, in which militancy for a national cause begins to develop, to a third and final stage, during the last third of the nineteenth century, when nationalistic programs become rooted in mass participation (11–12). The notion of sovereignty based on collectivity gains strength in European countries throughout the entire nineteenth century, however, and it will determine issues such as the eradication of slavery, the promotion of universal education, the expansion of voting rights, and so forth. In Brazil, the first and second phase of nationalism as described by Hobsbawm were combined and the third would be found only in the twentieth century, specifically in the thirties, when the masses become a focal point for developing and encouraging nationalist sentiment. Unlike in Europe, there was no gradual inclusion of the people during Brazil's nineteenth century. One finds, consequently, a more extreme sense of a nation staged by the elites, and thus a dissonance with the local economy, administration, technology, and politics.

What we would like to highlight, however, is José de Alencar's increasing awareness of the invented character of the nation, as well as the ideological nature of historic discourse, all of which came as a consequence of the disputes over the power to narrate and create images. His works demonstrate a preoccupation with constructing an image of Brazil that would meet all the criteria set by the period for the existence of a nation. It must not be overlooked that at a time when the map of Europe was being drawn along new lines, according to the principle of nationality, an intense debate arose about the criteria to be employed in deciding which peoples would have the right to become integrated nations, which nations were, in fact, viable. The first criterion, as Hobsbawm explains, is the budding nation's historic association with an existing state, or a state with a recent and reasonably enduring past. The second criterion was defined by the existence of a firmly established cultural elite, with roots extending into the past, in possession of an administrative and literary vernacular idiom. The third criterion expressed the future nation's capacity for conquest, or its vocation for imperialism. These were the basic requirements postulated by ideologues for the recognition of a nation in the era of triumphant bourgeois Liberalism, that is, between 1830 and 1880, the period that covers all of Alencar's literary production. One must add that to belong to a well-established nation was a condition for progress and a prerequisite for entering modernity.

From José de Alencar's point of view, the status of truth in official historical discourse becomes relative when the purpose is that of creating a national imaginary. This premise shows up clearly in a series of four articles published in *O Globo* in 1875. Stimulated by Joaquim Nabuco's comments on the reception of the play "O Jesuíta" ["The Jesuit"], being staged at the time, Alencar wrote about his creative process in writing the text. The play was originally written in 1861, and intended for staging at the S. Pedro de Alcântara Theater during national festivities celebrating the anniversary of Brazil's Independence on the 7th of September. The author described the difficulties he faced in the creative process, the first being the choice of subject matter, which he wanted to be that of a people enthusiastic for the glory of the homeland. He studied historic texts about Brazil's colonial period in search of an episode that would adequately suit his objectives. Alencar considered the historical figure of Bartolomeu Bueno da Ribeira, only to conclude that he lacked the greatness that is traditionally conferred such a personage. He was further disappointed on perusing records of the Dutch war; the officially elected and promoted hero, to use Alencar's words, was João Fernandes Vieira, a Portuguese man who became wealthy at the beginning of Dutch dominion by associating with the invaders, and later changed sides for his own benefit. Instead, Alencar would find true war heroes in Brazilians, uncelebrated by history, such as André Vidal de Negreiros:

> A platéia do Teatro de S. Pedro, então como hoje, não suportaria semelhante reivindicação histórica. Dou-lhe toda razão; é portuguesa na máxima parte; e tanto deve comprazer-se na comemoração de suas glórias nacionais como aborrercer-se dos confrontos desfavoráveis. (in Coutinho 30)

> The audience at the S. Pedro Theater, then as now, would find such a historical claim unacceptable. I would have to agree; since the audience is mostly Portuguese; and it must be entertained by commemorating its own national glories as well as be annoyed with disagreeable confrontations.

He then added,

> Seria longo dar conta da excursão que fiz pela história pátria a busca de um assunto; basta dizer que não achei então um fato que me inspirasse o drama nacional, como eu o cogitava. Resolvi portanto criá-lo de imaginação, filiando-o à história e à tradição, mas de modo que não as deturpasse. (in Coutinho 30)

> It would take too long to recount the journey I made through the nation's history in search of a theme; suffice it to say that I did not find an event that would inspire in me the national dramaturgy as I conceived of it. I decided then to create it from the imagination, incorporating it into history and tradition, but in a manner so as not to create distortions.

These excerpts betray the author's awareness of the manipulation of historical discourse by those who are in power, as well as the role that he grants literary imagination in creating a nationalist alternative to history as narrated by the colonizer. It is also evident that the author nevertheless prefers to evade any "disagreeable confrontations," and does not venture so far as to challenge the theater audience with a play whose protagonist was André Vidal de Negreiros, electing instead to create a completely fictional hero.

One finds in the articles comprised in the polemic with Joaquim Nabuco, written toward the end of Alencar's life, emerging traits of anti-Lusitanianism (anti-Portuguese sentiment) and anti-cosmopolitanism, which in the realm of fiction engendered the novel *Ubirajara* (1874):

> Mas os brasileiros da corte não se comovem com essas futilidades patrióticas; são positivos e sobretudo cosmopolitas, gostam do estrangeiro; do francês, do italiano, do espanhol, do árabe, de tudo, menos do que é nacional. Isto apenas serve para a eleição.

> No meio da chusma que se diverte e enche os espetáculos, há um creme; valerá ela mais do que o coalho? A sociedade fina é uma seleção de Darwin, e muito próxima do primitivo, ainda está muito símia. Na alta roda vive-se à moda de Paris; e como em Paris não se representam dramas nem comédias brasileiras, eles, *ces messieurs*, não sabem que significa teatro nacional.
> (in Coutinho 24)

> However, the Brazilian members of the court were not moved by these patriotic futilities; they are positivists and above all cosmopolitan; xenofiles, they like the French, the Italian, the Spanish, the Arab, everything but what is national. The last is only useful during elections.

> Amid the crowd that amuses itself and throngs the performances is the cream; has it more value than the curd? Sophisticated society is a Darwinian selection; it is very close to the primitive, it is still very simian. In the high circles one lives in the manner of the Parisians; and since in Paris no Brazilian comedies or dramas are staged, they, *ces messieurs*, are ignorant of the meaning of national theater.

José de Alencar opposes the provinces, where the presence of national sentiment is still felt, to the city, turned as it is toward foreign influences; he contrasts the people with an elite that is simian and Frenchified. However, throughout his career as a writer, Alencar tried to avoid radical oppositions, and his work shows a prevailing conciliatory stance. This kind of stance characterized the attitude of Brazilian intellectuals on the whole in the Romantic period, since their overriding concern was the nation's unity.

Although choosing not to privilege the segregating forces, Alencar did employ *indianista* (nativist) themes, as well as use words extracted form Tupi-Guarani, and both engendered varied criticism of his *oeuvre*. His election of native cultures as one of the components of Brazilian nationality meant affirming the irreducible difference between "us" and the Europeans, a move that irritated intellectuals with Westernizing inclinations—even though his natives were depicted with the traits of medieval knights, thus paying tribute to Eurocentrism by undermining difference. In order to contest the chroniclers who saw the first inhabitants of American lands as barbarian and ferocious, the writer endeavored to prove the existence of affinities between natives and Europeans. It was in the cultural sphere that tellurian nationalism and liberal cosmopolitanism entered into combat in Brazil; more specifically, this occurred within literature, since in all remaining spheres the country had already opted for the European model. Contrary to what happened in Argentina, no exclusive formulations–civilization or barbarism, as Domingo Faustino Sarmiento (1811–1888) termed it–developed. In Brazil, the fact that the native as a protagonist was associated with the remote past, and therefore not threatening to the present, allowed for the use of his image, even if in controversial manner, as a symbol for Brazilian nature; it would be offered as an alternative to compensate for the country's inferiority complex *vis-à-vis* European culture.

Despite some critics' contention that Alencar's *indianista* novels were an attempt at barbarizing Brazilian literature, nativism was also accused of being artificial, since the indigenous character, suffering impending extinction, was really no more than an exotic figure. This is what transpires in the irony and disdain with which Joaquim Nabuco refers to the existence of "um ou outro índio do Amazonas" ("one or the other Amazonian Indian"), in the following passage.

> Sempre me pareceu um esforço mal compensado esse que emprega o Sr. J. de Alencar para formar uma língua, que só pode ser falada por ele e por um ou outro índio do Amazonas que venha ver o último dos seus pajés e recolher o idioma sagrado. (in Coutinho 70)

> It has always seemed to me a poorly rewarded effort, the one that Mr. José de Alencar employs to create a language that can be spoken only by him and one or another Amazonian Indian who comes to see the last of their shamans in order to collect the sacred idiom.

However, the native was treated, in nineteenth-century Brazil, as a type of mythical ancestor, and the traits that were attributed to him, such as courage and nobility of character, did not clash with the patriotic ideals of progress; on the contrary, they served to reinforce them. In the case of Brazil in that century, despite the depiction of the countryside and forests as venues where the American land best expressed its power, one cannot speak of a confrontation between a rural and an urban ideology, as in Argentina. This opposition would only become more evident at the beginning of the twentieth century. The opposition between civilization (urban life) and barbarism (rural life) in Argentina betrayed the presence of two competing ideologies in the conflicts that took place after Argentinean Independence. It underlined the clash of two distinct national projects that were extrapolated to the terrain of culture and implied different political and economic paths: one entrenched in patriarchal values, of binding telluric character, and the other, with a Liberal and cosmopolitan stamp. It was only after the urban ideology had gained ground and begun to translate itself into a civilizing politics that excluded the *gaucho* that this figure was allowed to become a symbol of

Argentinity. Being expelled from history enabled the *gaucho* to become a literary myth, a sort of atemporal essence, the image of an ideal, embodying an archetypical national identity. At this point, he went through the same process that had already been undergone by Brazilian Romanticism's native Indian, a process that is explicit in José de Alencar's own words:

> No *O Guarani* o selvagem é um ideal, que o escritor intenta poetizar, despindo-o da crosta grosseira de que o envolveram os cronistas, e arrancando-o ao ridículo que sôbre êle projetam os restos embrutecidos da quase extinta raça. (1959a, 149)

> In *O Guarani* the savage is an ideal that the writer tries to poeticize, divesting him of the crude image with which the chroniclers enveloped him, and removing him from the ridicule that is projected on to him as the brutish remainder of an almost extinct race.

The writer rejects the chroniclers' past depiction of the native, denouncing it as deforming, while he also refuses the image of the present Indian because it would reflect the race's decadence. The image that he defends is, therefore, emptied of its historical concreteness so that it may serve as an incentive for the future nation.

José de Alencar, writing at a time when the European model of civilization was utterly victorious in Brazil, was able to rescue nature and the indigenous past, and opted for a historical reconstruction that Alfredo Bosi calls "simbiose luso-tupi" (181) ("Luso-Tupi symbiosis"). The project of an idealized nation acted as a guide for the interpretation of the past. To provide better foundations for a future of grandeur, Alencar chose the product of a communion between the best of the native and the best of the Portuguese. The specific conditions of the Brazilian Declaration of Independence, in 1822, in which there was no violent confrontation with Portugal (I refer here to the process of transferring the crown to the Prince Regent, and not to the events following D. Pedro I's abdication, when urban and rural revolts broke out, some of which marked anti-Lusitanian sentiment), opened up a space for a literary depiction of the colonizer who favored the notion of harmony among the diverse elements that constituted the national population. It is evident that a solution based on the suppression of conflict, so as to solidify the image of a peaceful and cohesive nation, was to create a lack of definition of the boundaries between history and legend. The historical framework served, in truth, as the foundation for forging the desired myth.

Considering that a novel such as *O Guarani* is characterized more by an immediate commitment to the national imaginary and by the intention to highlight national difference rather than registering the conflict between historical facts and the grandiose plots borrowed from the great European novels of the time, there is an apparent discord between the historical and mythic dimension within the work itself—an apparent discord, because whereas history betrays conflicts and points to the tensions that marked the colonial past, myth instead interprets the events narrated and sublimates them so that an idealized vision of history prevails. It is important to stress the fact that what is predominant in literature with a nativist theme is not a recourse to that European exoticism of the native, but the disposition to create the myths of Brazilian nationality with an awareness of the need to stamp them with true historical grounding. In other words, when Alencar wrote *O Guarani* he did not slip from the realm of history into

that of myth, but rather history is present so as to provide consistency to myth; it is an integral part of, and provides the background for, mythic discourse.

When Augusto Meyer stated that he did not see Alencar's work as what one could identify as historical fiction (in the style of Sir Walter Scott's novels, for example) because of the preponderance of fantasy over documented fact, he was alluding indirectly to the fact that for the Brazilian writer the question was not one of faithfully establishing an origin, but conferring on it a fictional foundation:

> A intenção de criar o romance histórico brasileiro, ao modo de Walter Scott, agiu no seu caso como simples incitamento; a intuição criadora arrastando-o a francas liberdades, em virtude dos arroubos incontidos da sua fantasia, . . . No *Guarani*, por exemplo, só com muita complacência . . . poderíamos ver uma ficção histórica em que se refletem as relações do conquistador com o indígena, no período inicial de povoamento. (301)

> The aim of creating the Brazilian historical novel, after the manner of a Walter Scott, functioned in his case as a simple incentive; creative intuition led him to take liberties with historical facts due to his unrepressed deliriums of imagination. . . . In Alencar's *O Guarani*, for example, it is only with a great deal of poetic license . . . that we can find historical elements that depict the relations between conqueror and native in the initial colonial period.

In Augusto Meyer's reading, however, the "arroubos incontidos de fantasia" ("unrepressed deliriums of imagination"), in Alencar's fiction, ended up undoing the initial proposal of writing a historical novel:

> Eu por mim confesso humildemente que não vejo indígenas na obra de Alencar, nem personagens históricas, nem romances históricos; vejo uma poderosa imaginação que transfigura tudo, a tudo atribui um sentido fabuloso e não sabe criar senão dentro de um clima de intemperança fantasista. (298)

> For myself, I humbly confess that I do not see natives in Alencar's *oeuvre*, neither historical characters, nor historical novels; I see a powerful imagination that transfigures all, that instills in all things a sense of the fabulous, and does not know how to create if not from within a climate of intemperate fantasy.

History transfigured by imagination leads the critic, who isolates and compartmentalizes history and imagination, to see neither natives nor historical characters in the author's novels. The essays as well as the notes, prefaces, afterwords, and admonitions that Alencar adds to his novels show that the writer worked on the relativization of the boundaries between history and fiction (e.g., his commentaries on writing *O Jesuíta* [The Jesuit]). He is aware that the historiography on which he bases his work is in keeping with the European chroniclers' point of view, that historical discourse is not neutral, although he does not dissolve the markers that separate it from fiction completely: "É indispensável sobretudo escoimar os fatos comprovados, das fábulas a que serviam de mote" (1959e, 327) ("It is indispensable, above all, to winnow verified facts from the fables that grew around them"), he says, in "Advertência" ["Admonition"] to *Ubirajara*. Similarly, in *O Guarani*, Alencar selects what he finds most convenient in the texts of the ancient chroniclers and corrects what seems to be wrong, as can be read from his notes:

> O que dizem alguns cronistas a respeito da ignorância absoluta dos indígenas, sôbre a astronomia, me parece inexato. Os guaranis tinham conhecimentos rudes, filhos da observação. (1959c, 278)

What some chroniclers say regarding the natives' complete ignorance of astronomy seems to me inexact. The Guarani have some rough knowledge, the fruit of observation.

The data Alencar collects from historiography were important but not sufficient; it was necessary to arrange them in such a way as to instill greatness in the nation's past. Imagination served the purpose of creating myth so as to iron out and refresh the official history, creating another history just as transformed as the first, but emerging from a point of view that would belong neither to the defeated (native) nor to the conquerors (Lusitanian), but to the Brazilian who needs to consolidate the nation with the cement of nationalist sentiment. Thus, in Alencar's work, legend enters into dialogue with history: They are two sides of the same coin. The historical dimension based on documented fact is only superficially prevalent, because the author's main concern was not with restoring the past, but with constructing the future, and to that end, he needed to create myths that would sustain the nation's pride:

> Em direção oposta à dos *Primeiros Cantos* e dos *Timbiras*, o romance histórico de Alencar voltou-se não para a destruição das tribos tupis, mas para a construção ideal de um nova nacionalidade: o Brasil que emerge do contexto colonial. (Bosi 186)

> Taking the opposite direction from *Primeiros Contos* [First Stories] and *Timbiras*, the historical romance of Alencar centered not on the destruction of the Tupi tribes, but on the ideal construction of a new nationality: a Brazil that emerges from the colonial context.

Historical discourse is revisited for this purpose, so that it may provide elements that give consistency to myth. *O Guarani* illustrates this process more fully than any other of Alencar's works; in both *Iracema* and *Ubirajara*, which are presented as legends, the relationship between myth and history is less evident.

O Guarani, José de Alencar's first *indianista* novel, has as protagonists Peri and Cecília, two idealized characters who rise above contingencies and break through cultural barriers. They are atemporal essences who serve as a basis for creating the myth of a society destined for greatness; they are gestures. As Roland Barthes put it, myth in so-called historical societies is a language that appropriates a sign and empties it of its meaning, transforming it into form and distancing it from contingency (109). It is a two-way system that needs historical meaning for sustenance, even if it is a history in parentheses. It constitutes a meta-language, a way to enunciate a history that is defined by its intention: Peri and Cecília, articulated in the language of myth, remain concepts, and through them a whole new history is implanted in myth, containing values that do not rely on truth for their sanctioning.

The novel's secondary characters are drawn with a more realist palette. D. Antônio Mariz's nobility is not unblemished; the fact that he has a daughter out of wedlock (Isabel, officially his niece) and his cordial relations with smugglers both speak against him. Nothing is comparable to Peri and Cecília's purity. Abstract figures instead of concrete individuals, they represent the ideal that must guide the future and supplant historical foundations: Peri is not merely the Indian and Cecília is not simply the white woman, offspring of the colonizers. Peri is nature itself, in communion with Cecília, the Christian spirit incarnate. The de-eroticized quality of their relationship suggests an atmosphere of moral elevation that nature can attain as God's creation. This notion is repeated in various passages that center on forest scenery, for instance in the associating of dusk in the wild to the Hail Mary:

> Um concêrto de notas graves saudava o pôr do sol e confundia-se com o rumor da cascata, que parecia quebrar a aspereza de sua queda e ceder à doce influência da tarde.
> Era a ave-maria.
> Como é solene e grave no meio das nossas matas a hora misteriosa do crepusculo, em que a natureza se ajoelha aos pes do Criador para murmurar a prece da noite! (1959c, 51)

> A concert of bass notes saluted the sunset and became interwoven with the rumors of the waterfall, which seemed to soften its harsh fall and give way to the evening's sweet influence.
> It was the *Hail Mary*.
> How solemn and grave in midst of our forests the mysterious hour of dusk is, when nature kneels at the feet of the Creator to murmur its night prayers!

Cecília provokes another instance: While Loredano wants to take her body violently, and Álvaro desires amorous possession of it, Peri contemplates and adores her. In the text's words,

> Assim, o amor se transformava tão completamente nessas organizações, que apresentava três sentimentos bem distintos: um era uma loucura, o outro uma paixão, o último uma religião.
> Loredano desejava; Álvaro amava; Peri adorava. O aventureiro daria a vida para gozar; o cavalheiro arrostaria a morte para merecer um olhar; o selvagem se mataria, se preciso fôsse, só para fazer Cecília sorrir. (1959c, 60)

> Thus love transformed itself so completely in these forms, that it presented three very distinct sentiments: one madness, the other a passion, and the last a religion.
> Loredano desired; Álvaro loved; Peri adored. The adventurer would give his life for pleasure; the gentleman would face death in exchange for the honor of a single gaze; the savage would kill himself, if so required, in order to make Cecília smile.

The novel thus structures itself around two different axes: a foundational axis that is close to historical discourse and enacted through the action of peripheral characters, and a mythical axis that detaches itself from the first to circumscribe the sphere in which the hero and his chosen one inhabit, where there is no contradiction between Brazilian nature and Christian civilization. The second axis, where the two realities, nature and Christianity, come into harmony, is also responsible for generating similar narratives, such as that of the Flood, which can be found in biblical narrative as well as in indigenous myth. The book ends ambiguously and the final question is whether God will grant complete victory to the forces of nature that have rebelled against the evils of civilization (and as a consequence Peri and Cecília would be destined for salvation only in heaven) or (as in the case of Noah and Tamandaré) will instead grant humanity on earth a second chance. In leaving this second hypothesis open, the novel suggests a second foundation that would correct the first.

In *O Guarani* the waters of the Flood purify the country of its spurious past, leaving Cecília's and Peri's future open to speculation; they are the potential founders of a new nation built on unique foundations, where one would find a communion of the best of Western culture and the best of the realm of nature. Peri and Cecília embody these ideals, and for that reason neither one is bound by their original culture. Both are characterized as being open to the Other. Peri is above the contingencies of his tribe and his culture, placing himself at the service of a white woman. Cecília is beyond the prejudices of Western civilization, both when she has an affectionate relationship with the *mestiza* Isabel and when she becomes attached to the native, distancing herself from Álvaro. Álvaro is the perfect example of the dignity of the white man, but is also the perfect example of a man inextricably connected to his own cultural codes. The difference between Álvaro and Peri becomes explicit in the following passage.

> –Se tu a amasses, matarias teu irmão para livrá-la de um perigo.
>
> –Peri, talvez não compreendas o que vou dizer-te. Daria a minha vida sem hesitar por Cecília; mas minha honra pertence a Deus e à memória de meu pai. (1959c, 154)
>
> "If you loved her, you would kill your own brother to save her from danger."
>
> "Peri, you might not understand what I am about to tell you. I would give my life without hesitation for Cecília; but my honor belongs to God and the memory of my father."

And the narrator then comments, anticipating the novel's ending,

> Em Álvaro, a honra e um espírito de lealdade cavalheiresca dominavam todas as suas ações; não havia afeição ou interêsse que pudesse quebrar a linha invariável, que êle havia traçado, e era a linha do dever.
>
> Em Peri a dedicação sobrepujava tudo; viver para a sua senhora, criar em tôrno dela uma espécie de providência humana, era a sua vida; sacrificaria o mundo se possível fôsse, contanto que pudesse, como o Noé dos índios, salvar uma palmeira onde abrigar Cecília. (1959c, 154)
>
> In Álvaro, honor and the spirit of a gentleman's loyalty dominated all his actions; there was no affection or interest that could mar that unchanging line, drawn by his own hand, which was the line of duty.
>
> In Peri, dedication surpassed everything; to live for his lady, to create around her a sort of human providence, was his life; he would sacrifice the world if it were possible, so long as he could, like an Indian Noah, save a palm tree where he could shelter Cecília.

Two parallel universes unfold in the novel: Western Christian civilization and the one belonging to the native. Both have characters who are good and evil, but the encounter between whites, as represented by the Mariz family, and the natives, represented by the Aimoré tribe, results in mutual destruction. To create an ideal nation it would be necessary to take this story as a starting point and imagine a world that surmounts its problems. If cultural difference generates conflict and violence, it becomes necessary to create two archetypical figures who will overcome cultural barriers. In the last pages of the novel, Cecília abandons the canoe that would take her to her brother, a symbolic gesture through which she undoes the ties that bind her to the civilized world. She chooses to reward Peri's selfless devotion:

> Disse então que entre seus dois irmãos era justo que acompanhasse antes aquêle que só vivia para ela, que não tinha um pensamento, um cuidado, um desejo que não fôsse inspirado por ela.
>
> D. Diogo era um fidalgo, herdeiro do nome de seu pai; tinha um futuro diante de si, tinha uma missão a cumprir no mundo; êle escolheria uma companheira para suavizar-lhe a existência.
>
> Peri tinha abandonado tudo por ela; seu passado, seu presente, seu futuro, sua ambição, sua vida, sua religião mesmo; tudo era ela, e ùnicamente ela; não havia pois que hesitar. (1959c, 269)

She said then that in choosing between her two brothers it was fair that she should accompany the one who lived only for her, who had no other thought, no other care, no desire that was not inspired by her.

D. Diogo was a nobleman, and would inherit his father's name; he had a future ahead of him, had a mission to carry out in the world; he would chose a companion to make his existence more agreeable.

Peri had abandoned everything for her; his past, his present, his future, his ambitions, his life, his religion even; all for her, and solely for her; there was no motive for hesitation.

From her education, the heroine keeps the Christian faith, which she intends to transmit to the native:

> Depois, Cecília tinha ainda um pensamento que lhe sorria: queria abrir ao seu amigo o céu que ela entrevia na sua fé cristã; queria dar-lhe um lugar perto dela na mansão dos justos, aos pés do trono celeste do Criador. (1959c, 269)
>
> Afterwards, Cecília still entertained a thought that made her smile: she wanted to open to her friend the heavens she glimpsed through her Christian faith; she wanted to offer him a place near her in the mansion of the just, at the feet of the celestial throne of the Creator.

The book ends, thus, with a scene in motion–if, according to Peri's expectations, it were possible to find the place, the "*entre-lugar*" ("mid-place"), to use Silviano Santiago's expression (1978, 11), where the communion between Brazilian nature and Christianity would reach its full realization, the *entre-lugar* would be neither city nor forest (as a manifestation of a menacing and indomitable force). The solution in the form of indigenous myth is in dialogue with utopian narratives inspired by the discovery of America, since it points to an ideal society that results from the fertile encounter of two different worlds. Peri and Cecília, unattached as they are to the material world, to gold and sex, which motivate the villain Loredano's behavior, embody the possibilities of this encounter that would create a rupture in the historical continuum. At this juncture, the central characters evoke a path that could have been followed at the crossroads of the sixteenth century with the discovery of America, a path which fiction recovers in the form of utopia. The utopian project makes obligatory the implosion of D. Antônio Mariz's castle, together with its hierarchical immobility, and with it, the obliteration of the Aimorés and their spirit of revenge.

The story's dramatic focus is on the romance, so that it may be transcended; otherwise D. Antônio Mariz's death would be unnecessary. His heroism, his good intentions, and noble sentiments were not sufficient to prevent the tensions underlying the colonizing enterprise from exploding in conflict. If the medieval castle that he built in the tropics were to be fully harmonious with the environment, it would not need to be defended with battlements, even if, paradoxically, these walls were created by nature itself. The protection from external threat, however, did not prevent its collapse from the inside. The causes of its destruction were not restricted to Loredano's ambition or D. Diogo's "imprudence," but also rested on Isabel's own resentment; born a *mestizo*, of a love that offered no redemption for the agony of living with racial difference, she was seen by the Mariz clan as having a much lower status than themselves. This led her to disown the two races that created her:

–Sabeis o que eu sou; uma pobre órfã que perdeu sua mãe muito cedo, e não conheceu seu pai. Tenho vivido da compaixão alheia; não me queixo, mas sofro. Filha de duas raças inimigas devia amar a ambas; entretanto minha mãe desgraçada fêz-me odiar a uma, o desdém com que me tratam fêz-me odiar a outra. (Alencar 1959c, 145)

"Knowest thou what I am; a poor orphan who lost her mother very early and did not know her father. I have lived on the compassion of others; I do not complain but I do suffer. Daughter of two enemy races, I should love both of them; and yet my unhappy mother made me hate one, and the disdain with which I am treated made me hate the other."

This *mestiza*, denied identity, lacking a defined place in the feudal castle of the Mariz, is neither native nor white. Therefore, she must invent herself. Because of this, she would better represent the matrix of the Brazilian character, and Alencar does not go as far as to exclude Isabel from his fictional universe. However, he does suppress her importance: She is relegated to the plane of secondary characters so as to place at the center the myth of Cecília, whose purity pushes aside Isabel's marred existence.

The order created by D. Mariz was thus precarious, destined for destruction; at the same time, the possibility of another order, based on a communion between nature and culture, was being built in a mythic dimension. It does not wait to make its appearance at the end of the book; it starts being woven during the development of Peri and Cecília's relationship. Thus without evasion the novel registers the racial tensions generated by the Conquest, but the narrative point of view is similar to Cecília's perspective some time after the catastrophe that befell her family:

Ela mesma não saberia explicar as emoções que sentia; sua alma inocente e ignorante tinha-se iluminado com uma súbita revelação; novos horizontes se abriam aos sonhos castos do seu pensamento.

Volvendo ao passado admirava-se de sua existência, como os olhos se deslumbram com a claridade depois de um sono profundo; não se reconhecia na imagem do que fôra outrora, na menina isenta e travêssa. (Alencar 1959c, 260)

She herself would not know how to explain the emotions she felt; her innocent and ignorant soul had been lit up by a sudden revelation; new horizons opened themselves to the chaste dreams of her thoughts.

Turning to the past she marveled at her own existence, as if with eyes dazzled with daylight after deep sleep; she could not recognize herself in the image of what she had been before, that free and mischievous girl.

The past is drained of its strength in face of the future. The future, however, will come into being or will not, depending on the faith bestowed on the myths that may deliver it: Is Brazil to be the civilization founded by Peri and Cecília?

We agree with Silviano Santiago's observation that Alencar does not obliterate conflict, but at the same time, does not privilege it in his work (1982, 109). The attempt to obtain a delicate balance between continuity with and rupture from the colonizer's tradition reflects in another dimension the drama of the Brazilian elites of the time, who were also divided between the desire to maintain the colonial order practically unchanged, so as not to see their privileges threatened, and the need to update themselves, to shorten the distance that kept them from the European elites. Alencar tried, analogously, to transmit through fiction the notion

of a transformation that also implies continuity; to do so, he resorted to myth. The difficulty in adjusting a modern historical perspective to the trajectory of turmoil experienced by the newly independent nation determined that the dimension of space would prevail over the dimension of time. The utopian vision of harmonious synthesis was translated as the search for a place where the reconciliation of the various contenders could somehow come about.

Iracema (1865), like *O Guarani*, is also a novel in which the spatial dimension is dominant. The protagonist migrates from the heart of the country towards the coast, and as she moves away from the interior, she begins to die, suggesting the impossibility of determining a pure origin for the nation. The survivors will be those born on the beach, at the geographical point where the encounter between native and Portuguese took place; they will be creatures of the border, the only possible point of departure for a hybrid nationality. The emergence of this border creature demands, however, the sacrifice of indigenous culture in favor of the culture of the colonizer. The indigenous identity that takes part in the symbiosis is represented as a force of nature.

The novel sets out the problem of the conflict between cultures, but Alencar's conciliatory stance interprets the relationship between native and conqueror, the process of domination of the indigenous by the Portuguese, as being a game of seduction. It is not by accident that in *Iracema* the native protagonist of the romantic pair is a woman, a different choice from that made in *O Guarani*. In this instance, we find a foundational narrative that is set at the time of the first contact of the Portuguese with Brazilian lands, depicted in terms of a relationship of erotic possession: The conqueror, the white warrior ego, will be at the same time a phallic ego, the complete opposite of Peri. And, in a counter-gesture to Cecília's, the white man will not abandon his culture, push his canoe away downriver: Martim's eyes are ever turned toward the sea. He possesses, knows (in the biblical sense) the body that belongs to the land/female, and that possession legitimizes his epistemological superiority. To know Iracema's body is to know the land, its rivers, forests, and everything else entailed in it, so as to mark it anew, distancing it/her from predestined ends. To mark it is to create a body of knowledge that will mold a new being, Moacir, impregnating it with values and objectives different from those that guided the natives. Iracema is a metaphor for nature, but she also represents her tribe's culture, and in doing away with it she is left with no heritage but her blood to offer her son. The text of the legend strives to define a Brazilian identity that is hybrid but undivided, relegating traumatic tensions to the subplot.

Almost ten years would go by, after *Iracema*, before José de Alencar's publication of *Ubirajara* (1875), a legend that reverts to the period before the arrival of the Portuguese, receding even further into the past than the settings of his previously published *indianista* novels. From the "Advertência" ("Foreword") to the numerous and extensive notes that close the book, Alencar sheds light on his aim: A severe criticism of the historians, chroniclers, and European travelers, here accused of denigrating the image of the indigenous peoples, out of intolerance or because they needed to justify the violence used against the native peoples.

Already in *O Guarani* the author established an interaction with the textual sources he investigated in search of information about the Brazilian colonial past, and with which he sometimes disagreed. In *Ubirajara* a notable change occurs:

Here the author stresses the need for a critical reading of the European accounts and chooses to emphasize discord. The entire book constitutes a passionate defense of indigenous culture, from the plot's efforts to illustrate the greatness of this people to explanatory notes describing native customs most exploited by Europeans in their accusations of native barbarism. One example is Alencar's attempt to explain anthropophagy, as he tries to combat what he considers an incorrect Eurocentric vision. As Silviano Santiago puts it, Alencar pits himself against *quinhentista* (the mentality of the 1500s) blindness:

> Por outro lado, é com segurança e destemor que Alencar, muito antes do ensaio pioneiro de Métraux sobre a antropofagia e do mais complexo e abrangente estudo de Florestan Fernandes sobre os tupinambás, tenta enquadrar a antropofagia como ritual entre os indígenas brasileiros, e não como uma forma sangüínea e bárbara de comportamento. (1981, 7)

> On the other hand, it is with firmness and without shrinking that Alencar, long before Métraux's pioneering essay on anthropophagy and the more complex and inclusive study authored by Florestan Fernandes on the Tupinambá, attempts to place anthropophagy as a ritual among Brazilian natives, and not as a barbarous and bloodthirsty form of behavior.

Alencar, in his critical rereading of both the chronicles and missionary writings, is bold enough to refer to Europeans in his notes as the invading race that tried to justify its own brutality by relegating the aborigines to the condition of beasts that must be subjugated. The author calls attention to the importance of the narrator's viewpoint, which amounts to relativizing Old World values; this can be seen in the *Advertência* with which the book opens:

> Narrados com êste pessimismo, as cenas da cavalaria, os torneios e justas não passariam de manejos inspirados pela sensualidade. Nada resistiria à censura ou ao ridículo. (1959e, 328)

> Narrated with such pessimism, the scenes of knighthood, tournaments and jousting would not pass for more than horse play inspired by sensuality. Nothing would resist censorship and ridicule.

There is an evident change in tone in this late novel, a greater concern with affirming the native through cultural traits (that is, no longer limited to natural benevolence) and offering more overt protest. This protest extended itself to those who, sharing the Brazil of his time, would have acquired an aversion to the indigenous element in the literature; the extreme response would have eliminated it completely. He further defended natives by comparing their customs to those of European civilization, and did not limit himself to comparing them to the medieval model, thus legitimizing them through similarity. His comparison also served to criticize Western culture and, in an inversion of colonial discourse, demonstrated the superiority of the native. Alencar used the Bible to illustrate this: He invokes the native practice in which a young woman's suitors serve her father for a certain period of time in the expectation of marriage and compares it to the biblical tale of Jacob:

> Aí está a lenda bíblica de Jacó, servindo [sete] anos para obter por espôsa a Raquel. Não consta porém que os selvagens usassem da esperteza do pai de Lia para descartar-se de uma filha defeituosa; se tal acontecesse entre os tupis, de que ridículas indignações não se encheriam os cronistas? (1959e, 372 note 54)

> There is the biblical tale of Jacob, who served for seven years in order to marry Rachel. It does not come about, however, that among the savages Lia's father would use his wiles in order to rid

himself of an unattractive daughter; if such a thing were to happen among the Tupi, what amount of ridiculous indignation would not fill the pages of the chroniclers?

If one can sense in *Ubirajara* a certain regression on Alencar's part in search for ethnic purity, it must be taken into consideration that toward the end of his life (while writing the novel), his disappointment with the civilized nation, which his own fiction helped legitimize, led him to increase his criticism. This critical stance also meant shedding a more naive understanding of the European conceptual framework that was used by Brazilians to evaluate their reality and constituted the first step toward a critical revision of the nation's history, which would be undertaken by the Brazilian modernists at the beginning of the twentieth century:

> Alencar, no radicalismo final de *Ubirajara*, prenuncia já a técnica de composição dos textos da poesia Pau-Brasil, pelo mesmo tipo de apropriação crítica dos textos escritos por europeus sobre os primórdios do Brasil. (Santiago 1981, 6)

> Alencar, in *Ubirajara*'s late radicalism, anticipates the techniques of textual composition that are present in Pau-Brasil poetry, in the same kind of critical appropriation of European writings on the origins of Brazil.

In questioning the place of the enunciation, in relativizing concepts and forms of knowledge that were articulated during the Colonial period, and in intuiting the power of the narratives, Alencar's anti-colonialist attitude found its strongest articulation. For Alencar the construction of the Brazilian nation was associated with achieving the freedom to create an ethnic self-image, even if this self-image was created in an ambiguous manner and demanded qualifications. On the one hand, by relativizing the truth-value of the colonizer's discourse, *indianismo* (nativism) remained the mark of difference that must not be surrendered in defense of a place that is hybrid, but nevertheless belongs to the Brazilian nation, and which is irreducible to pure Western tradition (as defended by, for example, Joaquim Nabuco). On the other hand, there is an emphasis not on the violence that occurred in the process of the Conquest of America, but on conciliation between invaded and invader, in the name of the higher goal of forging an undivided cultural identity. This goal led Alencar to represent the nation as the product of a unifying process undertaken with the co-participation of the parties involved. It was necessary to relativize the indigenous tribes' defeat so as to elevate the native to the category of active participant in the construction of nationality; Alfredo Bosi (179) identifies in the novel the sacrificial myth that has this function. In the construction of a new world, the sacrifice of the native was interpreted as a voluntary gesture of greatness, although one in which the natives were co-authors of their own demise.

José de Alencar's work inspired evaluations in the established literary criticism of his time. Since then, every literary period has responded to Alencar's fiction, and the reception of his work has always been polemical in nature. At the start of the twenty-first century, when Brazilian nationalist sentiment is diminishing and the concept of nation is being relativized historically, when it is fashionable to question the inherited literary canon, Alencar's work once again provokes challenges and elicits new interpretations, and this, most certainly, confirms the importance of the place he has held in this culture.

Translation by Lis Horta Moriconi

Works Cited

Alencar, José Martiniano de. 1959a. "Como e porque sou romancista." *Obra completa.* Vol. 1: *Romance urbano.* Rio de Janeiro: Editora José Aguilar. 125–55.

———. 1959b. "Senhora." *Obra Completa.* Vol. 1: *Romance urbano.* Rio de Janeiro: Editora José Aguilar. 941–1214.

———. 1959c. "O Guarani." *Obra Completa.* Vol. 2: *Romance histórico–Alfarrábios.* Rio de Janeiro: Editora José Aguilar. 25–280.

———. 1959d. "Iracema." *Obra Completa.* Vol. 3: *Romance histórico, lendas indianistas, romance regionalista e fragmentos.* Rio de Janeiro: Editora José Aguilar. 223–320.

———. 1959e. "Ubirajara." *Obra Completa.* Vol. 3: *Romance histórico, lendas indianistas, romance regionalista e fragmentos.* Rio de Janeiro: Editora José Aguilar. 321–404.

Anderson, Benedict. 1983. *Imagined Communities: Reflections on the Origin and Spread of Nationalism.* London: Verso.

Barthes, Roland. 1972. *Mythologies.* Trans. Annette Lavers. New York: Hill and Wang.

Bosi, Alfredo. 1992. *Dialética da colonização.* São Paulo: Companhia das Letras.

Carvalho, José Murilo de. 1996. *A construção da ordem: A elite política imperial; Teatro de sombras: A política imperial.* Rio de Janeiro: Editora da Universidade Federal do Rio de Janeiro e Relume-Dumará.

Castro Alves, Antônio de. 1913. "O livro e a America." *Espumas fluctuantes.* Rio de Janeiro: Livraria Garnier. 19–23.

Coutinho, Afrânio, ed. 1978. *A polêmica Alencar-Nabuco.* Rio de Janeiro: Tempo Brasileiro.

Fernandes, Florestan. 1976. *A revolução burguesa no Brasil: Ensaio de interpretação sociológica.* Rio de Janeiro: Zahar Editores.

Hobsbawm, Eric J. 1992. *Nations and Nationalism Since 1780: Programme, Myth, Reality.* Cambridge: Cambridge University Press.

Meyer, Augusto. 1986. *Textos críticos.* Ed. João Alexandre Barbosa. São Paulo: Editora Perspectiva; Instituto Nacional do Livro, Fundação Nacional Pró-Memória.

Miguel Pereira, Lúcia. 1992. *A leitora e seus personagens: Seleta de textos publicados em periódicos (1931–1943) e em livros.* Ed. Luciana Viégas. Rio de Janeiro: Graphia Editorial.

Nabuco, Joaquim. 1995. *Minha formação.* Porto Alegre: Paraula.

Paz, Octavio. 1974. *Los hijos del limo: Del romanticismo a la vanguardia.* Barcelona: Seix Barral.

———. 1979. *El ogro filantrópico: Historia y política, 1971–1978.* Barcelona: Editorial Seix Barral.

Santiago, Silviano. 1978. "O Entre-lugar do discurso Latino-americano." *Uma literatura nos trópicos: Ensaios sobre dependência cultural.* São Paulo: Perspectiva e Secretaria de Cultura, Ciência e Tecnologia do Estado de São Paulo. 11–28.

———. 1981. "Introdução." *Ubirajara.* 7th ed. By José Martiniano de Alencar. São Paulo: Ática. 3–8.

———. 1982. "Liderança e hierarquia em Alencar." *Vale quanto pesa: Ensaios sobre questões político-culturais.* Rio de Janeiro: Paz e Terra. 89–115

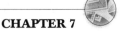

CHAPTER 7

NATIONAL INSTALLMENTS

THE EROTICS OF MODERNITY IN SPANISH AMERICA

Doris Sommer

Vainly, Spain had tried to instill corporatist habits of feeling in its heterogeneous American subjects. But, colonial subjects recognized the contradictions between their dynamic society and a political culture that would anchor unequal rights and obligations in unyielding differences of caste. (*Casta* is a Spanish word adapted as *caste* for Anglo-India.) The struggles for Independence that followed, lasting variously from the first to the third decade of the nineteenth century, brought their own contradictions and often civil wars, because the emancipatory impulses of liberalism became mired in regional rivalries and in the lingering caste-consciousness of leaders for whom liberalism was an idea out of place. Argentina's Sarmiento, and then nation-builders throughout Latin America, contrasted "civilization" to "barbarism" (also called "Americanism") to describe the conflict between elite and popular tendencies. The conflict expresses a general contradiction in the project of modernity (Lenin later called it modernity's Janus face) that requires both normalization of universal practices and a national specificity that grounds patriotism and dedication. A modern nation should be the same as others to promote liberal relations, yet it should be different to justify citizens' loyalty.

Desire and Flexibility

Nation-builders evidently sensed the conflicting demands as a paradox, an apparent inconsistency that has the almost mystical charm of a secular religion. Legal codes and constitutions can copy those of other countries without forfeiting their local authenticity, and the cultural vehicles of modernity similarly overlap from one country to another even while they develop particular, apparently autochthonous, characteristics. The most successful of these vehicles was surely the national novel. Often, before they were published in book form, and long before they became required reading in public schools, national novels circulated in newspaper columns and supplements. The short installments that engaged the reading (politically active) population over a long period of time functioned as sentimental training for new dynamic structures of feeling based on desire. Heroes and heroines fell in love across class, color, and regional barriers; they yearned to and struggled to overcome the archaic distances imposed by parental (colonial) restrictions and to celebrate the sentimental laissez-faire that would fuel other expressions of modern freedom.

Why else, it is worth asking, would all of the national novels of Latin America be love stories? What has love got to do with the state and with civic education? Why were so many nation-builders also novelists? Bartolomé Mitre (1821–1906), José Mármol (1817–1871), Juan Bautista Alberdi (1810–1884), Alberto Blest Gana (1830–1920), Ignacio Manuel Altamirano (1834–1893), Manuel de Jesús Galván (1834–1911), José de Alencar (1829–1877), Juan Mera (1832–1894), José Milla (1822–1882), and Eugenio María de Hostos (1839–1903) are among them. Even now, at the beginning of the twenty-first century, after the patriotic feelings associated with independence and consolidation have been challenged by the disappointments of history, the plots and structures of feeling established in the national novel recur to shore up optimism or pride through historical *telenovelas*, delivered in installments like serialized novels. Today people are more likely to watch *novelas* than to read them. And writers who had written off the sentimental tradition of earlier narrative are returning to that tradition, not only through historical novels, but also sometimes through television. With the characteristic impatience of his boom generation, Gabriel García Márquez (b. 1927) used to dismiss national love stories, but in 1991 he wrote the script for a miniseries based on Isaacs's *María* (1867) for Colombian television. What accounts for the erotic investment of nation in narration?

In fact, by the nineteenth century, sexual desire had become the shorthand for human association and therefore "the explanation for everything" in modernity, to use Foucault's words (78). Desire fuelled modernity, which was more a dynamic adventure than an enactment of enlightened principles. But, adventure and reason were coming together, making nations, babies, and alliances. Desire legitimated conquest, regicide, independence, and acquisition—the very longing for change and for growth that traditional societies had inhibited.

In national romance, the political and personal levels represent and fuel one another. If passion is unrequited, it produces a surplus of energy that can hope to overcome the political interference between the lovers. At the same time, the enormity of the social abuse, the unethical power of the obstacle, invests the love story with an almost sublime sense of transcendent purpose. As the story progresses, the pitch of sentiment rises along with the cry of commitment, so that the din makes it ever more difficult to distinguish between our erotic and our political fantasies for an ideal ending.

Ingenious, indeed brilliant, is the fact that one libidinal investment ups the ante for the other. And every obstacle that the lovers encounter heightens more than their mutual desire to (be a) couple, more than our voyeuristic but keenly felt passion; it also heightens their/our love for the possible nation in which the affair could be consummated. The two levels of desire are different, which allows us to remark on an allegorical structure, but they are not discrete. Desire weaves between the public (family) and the individual in a way that shows the terms to be contiguous–coextensive as opposed to merely analogous. And the desire keeps weaving, or simply doubling itself at personal and political levels, because the obstacles it encounters threaten both levels of happiness. These obstacles are almost always a social convention or a political impasse; that is, they are public and interpersonal rather than intimate and particular differences between the lovers. The lovers almost never quarrel, probably because of the vestigial aristocratic character of these romances; the heroes and heroines appear on the scene full-blown, immutable, and easily distinguished from the masses of servants and supporters. Romantic heroes don't develop in the way we expect from the heroes of modern open-ended novels. Instead, they move the narrative as a magnet moves unanchored metals, selectively and at the center. When the novel form was imported by Latin Americans, the genre suffered some sea changes, along with its companion ideology of liberal democracy. The Latin American elite wanted to modernize and to prosper, yes, but it wanted at the same time to retain the practically feudal privilege it had inherited from colonial times. For some evidently cautious and controlling reason, the Latin American Romantic novel's heroes are not the self-reflexive, naive, and developing protagonists that European theorists expect in the novel. Instead, they are unerringly noble, by birth and by talent. Non-white lovers are more often than not indigenous or imported princes, like Sab's mother (Gómez de Avellaneda's *Sab*), José de Alencar's Guaraní, Enriquillo, Tabaré, and the African lovers in Isaacs's *María*.

Perhaps more daring as a narrative feature even than the racial crossings, in countries whose official pronouncements on race can celebrate *mestizaje* as the solution to racial strife, are the gender crossings. Not that male and female protagonists choose anyone but heterosexual partners (except for an occasionally tortured variant such as José Martí's [1853–1895] *Amistad funesta* [Deadly Friendship] or Adolfo Caminha's [1867–1897] *Bom crioulo* [*The Black Man and the Cabin Boy*]). When homosocial relationships prosper, as in Alencar's *Iracema*, domestic desire flags dangerously. After all, the patriotic projection of new alliances was literally to become fathers of new generations, after centuries of colonial, inter-regional, racial, and partisan strife. "Gobernar es poblar" (To govern is to populate), in Alberdi's famous formulation. But the attractive young men and women of these novels share, surprisingly, many physical and spiritual charms. The overlaps ensure a bond between the lovers. The men are typically delicate, now that military heroism is anachronistic. Why reduce the population to dead soldiers, Alberdi taunted, when the nation needs live citizens? Daniel Bello (in Mármol's *Amalia*) has a hand so white that any coquette would envy it; and Efraín is easily moved to tears, as are his ideal readers. The women, on the other hand, are surprisingly strong to readers who expect faltering femininity in traditional heroines. Amalia defies the police chief; María mounts an unmanageable horse; Cumandá saves her bumbling lover from dangers in the air, on water, and on land; Iracema greets hers with an arrow shot. At mid-century, when rigid corporatist hierarchies of race and class were softening into the hegemonic relationships that liberalism needed, gender assignments in the national romances were suitably flexible. This eased the tensions in tales of transition and secured the bonds by which men and women, the rulers and the ruled, could overlap and prosper.

A wonderfully graphic, almost pornographic, example may suggest this general lesson in flexibility. It occurs in *Amalia*, long after the initial battle between the dictator Rosas's death squad and the two surviving liberals who are preparing for the next battle from the safe distance of Amalia's country house: Daniel Bello will reveal his winning weapon, calling it a *casse-tête*, which translates in Spanish as *rompecabezas*, literally, a head breaker but also a puzzle for permanent disaggregation. The detail is important, because the neologism evidently associates Bello with the Francophile opposition to Rosas. This admiration for France was not only typical for young intellectuals, modeling themselves after French Romantics; it was also a response to France's punitive blockade of Buenos Aires (while Rosas continued to traffic with England to the point of stifling home industry; see Mayer 109, 194) and to its promises of support for the resistance. But the weapon itself, with its wicker handle connecting two ropes tipped by iron balls and covered by a fine net of soft leather, turns out to be uncannily familiar. I am referring to the visual joke it produces when Amalia's curiosity about Daniel's hidden weapon finally makes him expose what looks like artificial genitalia:

—Qué arma es ésa, Daniel, que usas tú y con la que has hecho a veces tanto daño?

—Y tanto bien, podrías agregar, prima mía.

—Cierto, cierto perdona; pero respóndeme; mira que he tenido esta curiosidad muchas veces.

—Espera, déjame terminar este dulce.

—No te dejo ir esta noche sin que me digas lo que quiero.

—Casi estoy por ocultártelo entonces.

—Cargoso!

—Daniel, what is that weapon that you use and that sometimes causes such harm?

—And as much good, you could add, my dear cousin.

—True, true, excuse me; but answer me; I have long been curious.

—Wait a minute, let me finish these sweets.

—I will not let you leave tonight until you tell me what I want to know.

—I am almost of a mind not to tell you.

—You are insufferable!

The joke, so characteristic of Mármol's flair for dialogue but perhaps lost on generations of forced readers, is of course prepared earlier in the same conversation, when Daniel hopes out loud that Eduardo has given up his unwieldy sword for something less troublesome, to which Eduardo condescends, "Yo no uso armas misteriosas, caballero" ("Sir, I do not use mysterious weapons"), as if these were a woman's weapons. "Así será" ("That may well be"), Daniel retorts, "pero son más eficaces; sobre todo más cómodas" ("but they are more efficient; and above all easier to use") (391).

The familiarity I am referring to is also the structural and strategic similarity between this new and improved phallus and the gaucho's traditional "lasso," or *bolas*. The device is a triple rope tipped by three hard balls that wrap around the victim's legs. Structurally, Daniel's weapon displaces power from the rigid center (which Eduardo still prefers) to a multiple periphery, just as the *bolas* do, the difference between two balls and three being one measure of the plurivalence achieved once phallocentrism gives in to dissemination. And strategically, Daniel's discreet masculinity, borne close to the heart in his breast pocket (and turning upside down Freud's quip about the heart being at the genitals) is more potent than Eduardo's sword, much as the ensnaring *bolas* are. (They had, in fact, made the Unitarian cause hopeless after General Paz's horse was caught in the whirling ropes of Rosas's Gaucho troops; see Crow 582.) The analogy is ambiguous to be sure. It may even leave the reader incredulous at the transgression of a French signifier, *casse-tête*, pointing to a "barbarous" signified. Nor do we easily imagine that elite ends (saving Eduardo) are served by popular means (gaucho equipment). But this lack of imagination, Alberdi was arguing, had more to do with a doctrinal narrowness he associated with Sarmiento than with the country's political economy. Gauchos, after all, should hardly be eliminated in a clean sweep of barbarism by civilization, since they were the rural workers who produced the nation's wealth and who kept its cities in business (Alberdi 33).

Dialectical Allegory

By assuming a kind of translatability between romantic and republican desires, writers and readers of Latin America's canon of national novels have in fact been assuming what amounts to an allegorical relationship between personal and political narratives. *Allegory* is a vexed term, but unavoidable to describe how one discourse consistently represents the other and invites a double reading of narrative events. The difficulty with the term *allegory* here is that the shuttling from one level to another is not a simple matter of round trips between the same two points or lines, but is more loom-like, in that the thread of the story doubles back and builds on a previous loop. Love plots and political plotting keep overlapping with each other. Instead of the metaphoric parallelism, say between passion and patriotism, that readers may expect from allegory, we will see here a metonymic association between romantic love that needs the state's blessing and political legitimacy that needs to be founded on love. Walter Benjamin provides a lead out of this terminological impasse through his unorthodox matchmaking between allegory and dialectic. It resonates with the equally unorthodox practices of national novelists, statesmen who trained their fellow citizens in the productivity of private desire. Allegory here, as for Benjamin's Baroque variety as the vehicle for time and dialectics, is a narrative structure in which one line is a trace of the other, in which each helps to write the other. A more standard interpretation describes allegory as a narrative with two parallel levels of signification. These are temporally differentiated, with one revealing or repeating the anterior level of meaning (either trying desperately to become the other or looking on from a meta-narrative distance at the futility of any desire for stable meaning). But Latin America's national novels describe an interlocking, not a parallel, relationship between erotics and politics.

Although Benjamin never made his dialectic count for anything constructive ("history does not assume the form of the process of an eternal life so much as that of irresistible decay. . . . Allegories are in the realm of thoughts, what ruins are in the realm of things"; quoted in Jennings 177–78), we

can willfully misread him in order to sustain the possibility of mutually constructing terms. Without looking back at the crumbling structure of political ill-fitting narratives, we may sense how these foundational fictions work. It is far more important for us to suggest *how* these books achieved their persuasive power than to determine *if* they had any right to do so. The foundational fictions are philosophically modest, even sloppy, or, one could say, post-philosophical (Rorty 28). Lacking the rigor that would either keep levels of meaning discrete or show how that was impossible, these novels hypostatize desire as truth and then slide easily between them. These novels are not trapped in unproductive impasses. Even the tragic *María* includes an afterlife of productive tenant farmers. The novels do not actively worry about any incommensurability between truth and justice, because they know themselves to be performing and seducing. Their object is to win at love and at politics, not to anchor the narrative or to reckon the cost of winning. Content to construct personal and public discourses "upon each other in a circle without end," as Pascal had described his own mundane allegorizing (de Man 1981, 17), with no stable philosophical ground to either violate or desire, foundational novels are precisely those fictions that try to pass for truth and to become the ground for political association.

If the novelists had closely followed a popular model such as Rousseau they might have worried about what they were doing. Rousseau fretted over the referential error of the word *love*. He sensed that love was not the cause of desire but desire's effect: "Love is a mere illusion: it fashions, so to speak, another Universe for itself; it surrounds itself with objects that do not exist or that have received their being from love alone; and since it states all its feelings by means of images, its language is always figural" (quoted in de Man 1979, 198). But, the nation-building novelists didn't fret. The possibility that hypostatized passion would be taken for empirical reality was hardly a danger at all, but was precisely their opportunity to construct a legitimating national culture. Whereas Rousseau's *Julie* contrasts passion with piety in a way that must have seemed too classical to Latin-American writers from the middle of the nineteenth century on, the nation-building novelists were making a virtue of love. For Rousseau erotic passion may well have been pathological; for them it was the cure to the pathology of social sterility.

Despite their admiration for fashionable French and English styles, Latin Americans dared to adjust imported patterns. Balzac's Chilean disciple, Blest Gana, explicitly adapts the master to local material in *Martín Rivas*: "The French . . . say: *l'amour fait rage et l'argent fait mariage* (love makes rage and wealth makes marriage), but here love makes both: *rage et mariage*" (Blest Gana 249). This improvement does not mean that the national novels represent any literary advance over great European novels; on the contrary, they are far more conventional. More predictable, and understandably less challenging to read, these novels set up a dialectic between love and the state, as does *Julie* in the first part, but never stop, as *Julie* does, to turn around (in the Augustinian sense of converting; see Burke 51) and look back.

They look relentlessly forward, like the mortals Benedict Anderson leaves with their backs to his nostalgic Angel of History (Anderson 147), and so do not draw desire into the regress of loss that seems inevitable in allegory. (See Fineman 26–60.) Instead, they set desire into a spiral or zigzagging motion inside a double structure that keeps projecting the narrative into the future while eroticism and patriotism pull each other along. Rather than rue their artificiality, these novels celebrate their own handiwork as revolutionary departures. There is no crisis associated with the loss/castration that triggers the telling. Instead this loss opens a space, because it is the father who has been castrated, not the hero. I am suggesting that some allegories, such as the ones the founding fathers wrote, may have no pre-existing and eternal level of referentiality, but, like Nietzsche's point about the fiction of empirical moorings, make themselves up, all the while attempting to produce an illusion of stability.

If I read a double and corresponding structure between personal romance and political desiderata, it is not with any priority for either register. I am suggesting that Eros and Polis are the effects of each other's performance, something like the Marquis de Sade's explanation of sexual desire as the effect of another's commotion (although the analogy would certainly have scandalized the Latin-American founders; see Bersani 145). Erotic interest in these novels owes its intensity to the very prohibitions against the lovers' union across racial or regional lines. And political conciliations, or deals, are transparently urgent, because the lovers "naturally" desire the kind of state that would unite them. For example, histories still debate the political portrayal of Juan Manuel de Rosas. Was he a bloodthirsty and vindictive barbarian who singled out Argentina's intelligentsia for terror and torture? Or was he a sophisticated defender of Argentine cultural and economic autonomy, no more bloody than his equally extravagant opponents who wanted to Europeanize the country as soon as possible? If we "know" from reading *Amalia* that Rosas was an unscrupulous dictator, our knowledge is to a considerable degree a political articulation of the erotic frustration we share with Amalia and Eduardo. And we feel the intensity of their frustration because we know that their obstacle is the horrible dictator. Our erotic and political fantasies fuel one another.

Feeling Survives

Of course, the allegories will appeal rhetorically to some legitimating, a priori principle. Being a justification for modern and anti-authoritarian projects, that principle is often Nature, which has been conveniently redefined since the days of enlightened Independence as interactive rather than hierarchical. If erotic desire seemed to be the natural, and therefore eternal, grounding for happy and productive marriages (including national families by extension), it was thanks to these redefinitions. Nature was no longer the classical realm of predictable law but the realm of flux, where energy could meet obstacles and turn frustration into excess. It was a world that produced angels and monsters, not clockwork. The allegories will strain at points against these redefinitions. For one thing, the writing elite was loath to give up its hierarchical privilege to conciliatory projects; and for another, compelling characters may exceed or somehow miss an ideally assigned meaning.

But the observation I am making is far more fundamental than any demonstration of the allegory's partial failures. I am simply registering the incredible measure of its success. In many cases, the double-dealing romance actually helped to give a cognitive expression and an emotive mooring to the social and political formations it articulates. The historical romances became national novels in their respective countries, a term that refers not so much to their market popularity (although to be sure many of these novels were immediately popular) as to the fact that they became required reading by

the first decades of the twentieth century. Perhaps their promise of a nationalizing embrace was particularly appealing after massive immigration in some countries seemed to threaten a cultural core and after Latin-American regimes decided on patriotic programs for economic and civic development as responses to the Depression and to competing "foreign" ideologies. These states, in other words, tacitly accepted the nineteenth-century pot-boilers as founding fictions that cooked up the desire for authoritative government from the apparently raw material of erotic love.

Works Cited

Alberdi, Juan Bautista. 1967. *Proceso a Sarmiento*. Buenos Aires: Ediciones Caldén.

Alencar, José de. 1979. *Iracema*. São Paulo: EDUSP.

———. 1994. *O guaraní*. Coimbra: Livraria Almedina.

Anderson, Benedict. 1983. *Imagined Communities: Reflections on the Origin and Spread of Nationalism*. London: Verso.

Bersani, Leo. 1981. "Representation and Its Discontents." *Allegory and Representation*. Ed. Stephen Greenblatt. Baltimore: Johns Hopkins University Press. 145–62.

Blest Gana, Alberto. 1977. *Martín Rivas (Novela de costumbres político-sociales)*. Ed. Jaime Concha. Caracas: Biblioteca Ayacucho.

Burke, Kenneth. 1961. *The Rhetoric of Religion: Studies in Logology*. Boston: Beacon Press.

Caminha, Adolfo. 1895. *Bom crioulo*. Rio de Janeiro: Olive Editor.

Crow, John A. 1980. *The Epic of Latin America*. 3rd ed. Berkeley: University of California Press.

de Man, Paul. 1979. *Allegories of Reading: Figural Language in Rousseau, Rilke, Nietzsche and Proust*. New Haven: Yale University Press.

———. 1981. "Pascal's Allegory." *Allegory and Representation*. Ed. Stephen Greenblatt. Baltimore: Johns Hopkins University Press. 1–25.

Fineman, Joel. 1981. "The Structure of Allegorical Desire." *Allegory and Representation*. Ed. Stephen Greenblatt. Baltimore: Johns Hopkins University Press. 26–60.

Foucault, Michel. 1980. *The History of Sexuality*. Vol. 1: *An Introduction*. Trans. Robert Hurley. New York: Vintage Books.

Galván, Manuel de Jesús. 1964. *Enriquillo: Leyenda histórica dominicana*. New York: Las Américas Publishing Company.

Gómez de Avellaneda, Gertrudis. 1997. *Sab*. Ed. José Servera. Madrid: Cátedra.

Isaacs, Jorge. 1946. *María*. Buenos Aires: Editorial Castelar.

Jennings, Michael W. 1987. *Dialectical Images: Walter Benjamin's Theory of Literary Criticism*. Ithaca, NY: Cornell University Press.

Mármol, José. 1984. *Amalia*. Ed. Teodosio Fernández Rodríguez. Madrid: Editora Nacional.

Martí, José. 1994. *Amistad funesta*. Ed. Carlos Javier Morales. Madrid: Cátedra.

Mayer, Jorge M. 1973. *Alberdi y su tiempo*. 2nd ed. Buenos Aires: Biblioteca de la Academia Nacional de Derecho y Ciencias Sociales de Buenos Aires. 2 vols.

Rorty, Richard. 1989. "Comments on Castoriadis's 'The End of Philosophy.'" *Salmagundi* 82–83: 24–30.

Rousseau, Jean-Jacques. 1997 [1763]. *Julie, or, The New Heloise: Letters of Two Lovers Who Live in a Small Town at the Foot of the Alps*. Trans. Philip Stewart and Jean Vaché. Series eds. Roger D. Masters and Christopher Kelly. Hanover: Dartmouth College, University Press of New England.

CHAPTER 8

IN THE PUBLIC EYE
NATURALISM AND BRAZILIAN LETTERS

Victor Hugo Adler Pereira

The rise of cities under new government policy in Brazil at the close of the nineteenth century brought about profound changes and upset the traditional domination of the country by the rural, patriarchal way of life. Regional urban centers developed into alternative poles to the rural power base of the landed aristocracy, especially from the point of view of cultural life. The growth of regional cultural centers subsequently countered the hegemony Rio de Janeiro had enjoyed since 1808; Rio itself was shaken by changes in social interaction among the ruling elites, and by the radical physical transformation the urban landscape was undergoing. The turn of the century is therefore marked by the influence exercised by government projects that proposed to bring the nation up to par with the centers of the Western world. If we take the city of Rio de Janeiro, for example, governmental policies such as the urban reform headed by Pereira Passos, authoritarian and exclusionist in character, show up in different guises in the following decades, such as the policy of killing beggars in the name of urban hygiene or the extreme approach adopted by the civil and military police in dealing with the needy population or with minorities.

The modernizing project begun at the end of the nineteenth century still prevailed at the end of the twentieth century; the authorities of both periods enlisted policies of discrimination and exclusion, and evinced a version of social Darwinism applied to social relations in which the individuals and sectors of society most vulnerable to the economic sphere's savage global competition have been relentlessly pressed into more extreme levels of marginality. The racism implicit in modernizing thought a century ago developed as pseudo-scientific cant undervaluing the Brazilian worker, considered indolent by nature and purportedly ethnically unprepared to carry out any activities more sophisticated than physical labor. The mental make up of the Brazilian seemed foreign to work, believed Araripe Júnior (1848–1911) who went so far as to state, "O tropical não pode ser correto. A correção é fruto da paciência e dos países frios; nos países quentes, a atenção é intermitente" (in Sodré 206) ("What is tropical cannot be fully developed. Complete development is the fruit of patience and of nations with cold climates; in countries of warm climates the attention-span is intermittent").

This perspective is not altogether absent even in today's Brazil; it is present in the passive role imposed on workers as a whole, in face of the technological innovations that are enlisted in order to bring the nation up-to-date. This negative attitude is present when local culture is underrated and implicitly considered lacking in the capacity to incorporate the changes of the new millennium; there is today a new version of the strategy of obsolescence that drives the market of consumer goods that now also includes cultural production. This racist view is also inherent in the still pervasive notion of the Brazilian population's racial inferiority, which translates into cultural inferiority in the general viewpoint of the public. This purported cultural inferiority,

of course, can be put forward with much less political risk, as the justification for the policy of total eradication of regional differences as part of the government's modernizing mission.

Yet another point in which we find echoes of continuity between these two historically distinct modernizing projects (overcoming racial inferiority and regional differences) is the importance given to sexuality. One of the manifestations of this is the championing of sexual freedom as a symptom of progress as in, for example, nineteenth-century Naturalism in literature and the latest pornographic films. They both illustrate a series of mechanisms that come into play, inciting and exploring the effects of sexual liberalization. These mechanisms are in turn closely related to the recrudescence of the repression of sexually deviant behavior, such as the nineteenth-century practice of considering homosexuality to be a clinical problem, or the current violence against same-sex sexuality. The ambiguities around the subject of repression have already been aptly analyzed and amply demonstrated by Michel Foucault in his "repression hypothesis" (1988) but, in the case of Brazil, one must not ignore the further complication of social class. The social disparities that have followed on the heels of the liberalization of sexual behaviour have increased the opportunities for and diversified the forms of enslavement of the poorest sector of the population, especially through child prostitution.

This evidence of the continuity between ideas implanted in Brazil in the positivist nineteenth century and their current versions, as well as the metamorphosis they have undergone, can reveal their acclimatization to the current climate. They were not, "fora do lugar" ("out of place"), in reference to Roberto Schwarz's (b. 1938) famous essay "As idéias fora do lugar" ["Ideas Out of Place"]. These ideas have taken root from the time of their original introduction because they met with varying conditions, not uniformity; they adapted to contradictions and developed a unique history in the Brazilian environment.

The arguments about the transformation that nineteenth-century Brazilian society underwent throughout the various stages of the development of international capitalism can best be explained by a close examination of the dominant idea of progress. To study the cultural changes brought about by the boom of modernization at the close of the nineteenth century inevitably entails a discussion of progress as a legacy of Romanticism. The task at hand is to situate some of the contradictions that are part of Brazilian cultural life as a whole, and that result from the modernization project based predominantly on European ideas and their Brazilian acclimatization. We will begin with a presentation of some of the innovative aspects of the way in which modernization was begun in Brazil, just as the nation breaks with the Empire's hegemonic control (1822–1889), and how this control diffuses into regional identity. We will examine the ways in which the adoption of Naturalism as a literary current, supplanting the transformative drive of Romanticism, was deemed necessary by the social and intellectual conditions intrinsic to Brazil. We will examine Naturalism and the process of social normalization that aimed at establishing a more homogeneous nation, in part through literary nationalism's function as entertainment and/or erotic stimulus. We will finally try to explain why the vigor that Naturalism evinced in prose fiction never translated into the theater. This last topic is of particular interest for the discussion of the specific role the theater has had, and for questioning the notion that the arts should have an evolutionary dynamic in Brazil comparable to the one witnessed in European cultural centers.

The Space of Modernization

The inauguration of the Republic near the turn of the century in Brazil (the new constitution was promulgated in 1891), created in the capital, Rio de Janeiro, an urgent need for urban surgery. The *carioca* capital underwent a modernization project that illustrates some of the fundamental elements of the tension between repression and cultural resistance. As the city was modernized architecturally, it simultaneously underwent a series of measures designed for public hygiene and intended to discipline the population. This project of such ambitious proportions has been traditionally associated with the personal legacy of Pereira Passos, but his relationship to the vested interests of different sectors of society and the political forces behind them has been largely left unexamined. The novel *Memórias de um sargento de milícias* [Memoirs of a Militia Sergeant: A Novel] written by Manuel Antônio de Almeida (1831–1861) in 1855, for example, presents us with a panorama of disorder in Rio de Janeiro's urban space that moves Vidigal, the policeman, to take action in an attempt to have some control over the reigning disruptions. The comedy depicts grotesque disparities generated when an administrative hierarchy is lacking and cultures are jumbled; but underlying its comic design it is possible to detect a pervasive dissatisfaction with a daily life riddled with disorganization.

Oswaldo Porto Rocha's study of the governmental policies implemented at the beginning of the century, in his aptly entitled *A era das demolições (1870–1920)* [1995; The Demolition Era], highlights the contributions intellectuals made to that project of urban reform through their own organizations. None of these entities surpassed the importance of the Clube de Engenharia (Engineering Club), an offshoot of the Escola Politécnica (Polytechnic School) (42). The engineer Francisco Pereira Passos was one of the leading figures who witnessed its foundation in 1880, and the sessions the institution held were routinely preoccupied with the topic of urban reform. The 1887 report created by the Inspetoria Geral de Higiene (The General Hygiene Inspectorship) for the Imperial Minister induced the Engineering Club to set up a special commission to review the report's proposal for urban sanitation. The Engineering Club was characterized by its active participation in the decisions of the city administration, gaining a prominent power base in the city's political and social scene, as Oswaldo Porto observes, because of two factors: "devido à inoperância e ineficácia da municipalidade com relação aos projetos e obras" ("because the municipality was inoperative and inefficient regarding the projects and works") and "não é somente uma entidade profissional, mas de classe" (51) ("because (the club) was not just a professional entity, but above all one of social class"). Oswaldo Porto Rocha adds a further explanation:

Não são apenas engenheiros e arquitetos os seus filiados, mas também comerciantes, industriais e proprietários de firmas de construção civil. Não temos dúvida alguma em reconhecer o clube como um agente social, órgão de uma classe dirigente. (51)

The (club's) affiliates are not restricted to engineers and architects, but they extend to retailers, captains of industry, and owners of construction companies. We have not the slightest doubt that the club acted as a social agent, an organ of the ruling class.

Paulo de Frontin became the president of the Engineering Club in 1901, and according to Oswaldo Rocha, represented the interests of the large construction companies in opposition to the small builders and contractors. Small building contractors were the preferred targets of some of the administrative measures implemented in the capital of the Republic. Pereira Passos became the Mayor of Rio de Janeiro in 1903 at the invitation of president Rodrigo Alves; he accepted with the condition that he suffer no interference from the city administration. Pereira Passos presented himself as a man above politics who wanted his administration to run on scientific principles of technological expertise.

Some of the practices that Pereira Passos instituted as mayor, as described by Edgar Carone, were so penetrating and widespread, having an effect on such minute aspects of community life, that it forces the question of the type of power being established:

Proprietário da "ditadura financeira," isto é, podendo dispor do dinheiro da prefeitura, o prefeito age livremente durante o período de plenos poderes. Daí tomar apressadamente medidas complementares e fundamentais: proíbe o comércio de bilhetes de loteria; baixa regulamento para a Diretoria de Higiene e Assistência Pública e fixa sua verba; assina novo regulamento sobre infrações e posturas e leis municipais; regula a construção e consertos de prédios; proíbe que os mendigos perambulem pela cidade; cria serviço de "turmas (que) percorrerão as ruas da cidade, acompanhadas de um ou mais caminhões de limpeza pública. As visitas domiciliares serão feitas sistematicamente em todas as habitações e, daí, tudo quanto for encontrado no seu interior, que seja julgado prejudicial à higiene, será incontinenti removido para aqueles carros." Posteriormente, lança a campanha pela extinção dos cães vadios. (in Rocha 213)

Empowered with a "financial dictatorship," availing himself of City Hall funds, the mayor acted freely during his mandate because of his complete power. That motivated his hurried adoption of fundamental and auxiliary measures: lottery tickets were banned; a budget was created for the Directory of Hygiene and Public Assistance and its regulations were laid down; the mayor signed new regulations for infractions of municipal law; enacted building, maintenance, and construction codes; outlawed loitering beggars; created a service "of a crew that will sweep city streets followed by one or more public sanitation trucks. This includes a systematic sanitary inspection of homes and the prompt removal of anything deemed prejudicial to hygiene." These measures were followed by a public campaign to exterminate stray dogs.

These measures functioned as what Michel Foucault (1926–1984) identified as disciplinary forms of power (1979, 219). In this sense the proposal to sanitize the city was implemented through the organization of public space, which implied, with other forms of organizing behavior, taking control of the traffic of individuals, exercising control over their circulation.

Michel Foucault drew attention to the role of the general preoccupation with the growth of cities in his research on the emergence of the discourse that will become Social Medicine in Europe. For Cabanis, as for the eighteenth century and for a whole tradition that was already familiar in the Renaissance, the knowledge of life was based on the essence of the living (Foucault 1975, 145).

As the new concerns and practices got a foothold in the administration of public life and grew more complex, they engendered urban medicine, which as Foucault points out, is not a medicine of the body, but of things, of air, water, waste, fermentation: A medicine of living conditions and of the medium of life. The emergence of the notion of cleanliness appears at the end of the eighteenth century, and becomes the foundation of public hygiene as a technique for the control and modification of the environment, which, in its turn, is considered an agent of intervention in the health of individuals and the collectivity. It is no longer a question of determining the factors by which the disease can be recognized, but of restoring, at least by words, a history that covers the total being of public life (Foucault 1975, 95).

The measures implemented by Pereira Passos have characteristics in common with Foucault's argument that cannot be ignored; the mayor was an attaché to the Brazilian delegation to France at exactly the period in which Haussmann was directing the modernization of Paris. He thus had opportunity to come into close contact with members of Haussmann's team (Rocha 57). Richard Sennett, in *Flesh and Stone*, links the urbanist ideas and policies implemented throughout the eighteenth-century to the new capitalist ideas regarding the flux of individuals into a society, and to William Harvey's theories on the circulation of blood (introduced in a 1628 study). Sennett explains the authorities' growing fears and provides a few examples of their representative measures in London and Paris:

> The desire to put into practice the healthy viruses of respiration and circulation transformed the look of cities as well as the bodily practices in them. From the 1740s on, European cities began cleaning dirt off the streets, draining holes and swampy depressions filled with urine and faeces, pushing dirt into sewers below the street. . . .
>
> These changes can be charted in a series of municipal health laws in Paris. In 1750, the city of Paris obliged people to sweep away the dung and debris in front of their houses; in this same year it began to sluice down major public walkways and bridges; in 1764, it took steps to clear overflowing or blocked gutters throughout the city; in 1780 it forbade Parisians to throw the contents of their chamber pots into the streets. Within houses, Parisian artchitects used smooth plaster on walls for the same purpose; the plaster sealed the wall surface, making it easy to clean. (263)

In *Discipline and Punish* Michel Foucault states that the system of procedures being perfected and generalized in Europe, especially from the eighteenth century onwards—procesures that intervened in the organization of space, in architecture, in the traffic of people, and even in domestic hygienic practices—accompanied the need to create productive individuals, and make better use of the social forces available at the time. He clarifies: "In this task of adjustment, discipline had to solve a number of problems for which the old economy of power was not sufficiently equipped" (1979, 219). He adds that, with the intent of making individual and collective elements more manageable and availability more profitable, there was a move to introduce a "discipline that fixes; it arrests or regulates movements; it clears up confusion; it dissipates compact groupings of individuals wandering about the country in unpredictable ways; it establishes calculated distributions" (1979, 219).

It is not surprising therefore, that the capital of the Brazilian Republic should undergo the systematic implementation of disciplinary practices associated with a modernizing discourse, which was promoted by the Engineering Club, a club whose political actions and social make-up–captains of industry, merchants, and engineers–led it to be identified by Rocha as "um agente social, órgão de uma classe dirigente" (51) ("a social agent, an organ of a ruling class"). The measures implemented by Pereira Passos and by the sanitary engineer Oswaldo Cruz had varied repercussions and consequences for the future design of the city of Rio de Janeiro and for the plight of its population. Even so, the city's unruly population growth, escalated because of the rural exodus that took place at the beginning of the century, escaped the control of the measures and modernizing propositions that it inspired. There was, therefore, an especially telling *carioca* phenomenon that arose from the capital's population growth, and the exemplary character of resistance to power and the projects of urban regimenting. The Praça Onze, or Onze Square, situated close to downtown Rio de Janeiro nowadays, was initially urbanized in 1846 and was an aristocratic stronghold up until the 1870s. During that decade the tram allowed the wealthy to build their mansions in the more removed neighborhood of Tijuca, and the proliferation of tenements started to give the Onze neighbourhood a more proletarian character. The tenement houses occupied what were previously aristocratic mansions and mushroomed with the accelerating exodus of the wealthy between the end of the nineteenth century and the beginning of the twentieth century. They housed ex-slaves, freed in 1888 with abolition, arriving from the interior of the *fluminense* (Rio de Janeiro) state, and, with the end of the *Canudos* war, ex-soldiers-turned-migrants in search of better living conditions in the Southern regions of the country.

Settling in the vicinity of the Praça Onze, in the Saúde neighbourhood, was a population that originated in the State of Bahia (in Brazil's Northeast), employed mostly as stevedores on the nearby docks. Its culture, transplanted from Bahia, was described by Edigar de Alencar, a historian of Brazilian popular music:

> Nos fins do século passado, o bairro da Saúde era reduto de costumes e usanças africanas transportadas da Bahia. Pequenas mas inúmeras famílias baianas ali se acumulavam, trazendo para o Rio hábitos da velha metrópole, com marca das reminiscências do continente negro, entre as quais, cantigas e danças próprias, festas, comidas, ritos e crendices. Havia nas cercanias, babalaôs <autoridades religiosas> de fama, que realizavam sambas (festas de dança) e candomblés. Eram todos conhecidos como "tios" e "tias". . . . Essas reuniões, embora freqüentes, não contavam com a simpatia das autoridades, dada a confusão que, de quando em quando, geravam. Por vezes se realizavam na moita, clandestinamente, o que lhes dava maior sabor e sedução. . . .
> Na segunda década do século atual, até 1926, a praça Onze era, no dizer de Heitor dos Prazeres, uma África em miniatura. Nas suas proximidades, na rua Visconde de Itaúna, No. 1117, morava a Tia Ciata (Hilária de Almeida), babalaô-mirim acatada, vinda da rua da Alfândega para ali assentar sua tenda festiva e movimentada.
> Naquela rua e na Senador Eusébio, que lhe ficava paralela e noutras adjacentes, funcionavam sociedades dançantes que mais tornavam rumoroso e festivo o local. Os sambas (danças) transbordavam dos casinhotos para os quintais e ruas. Daí provavelmente surgir a praça Onze como autêntico berço de samba (música e canto). E a casa da Tia Ciata viria a ser precisamente o local do nascimento do samba feito música. Composição melódica e não dança de grupo. Nascimento ruidosos, discutido, como sua importância exigia, pois marcaria o advento de nova e expressiva fase damúsica popular brasileira. (Rocha 80)

At the end of the last century, the *Saúde* neighborhood was a haven of African customs and usages transported from Bahia. Small but numerous Bahian families accumulated there, bringing to Rio habits of the old capital of Bahia, marked by the reminiscences of the African continent, among which were their own songs and dances, festivities, foods, rites, and beliefs. The neighborhood had renowned *Babalaôs* (religious authorities), who conducted *sambas* (festivities which had dancing) and *candomblés* (religious rites). They were all known as *tios* and *tias* (uncles and aunts). . . . These meetings, although frequent, did not please the authorities because of the confusion they created from time to time. They were sometimes held underground, in hiding, a fact that gave them even more appeal and a seductive attraction. . . . In the second decade of the current century, up until 1926, *praça Onze* was, as Heitor dos Prazeres phrased it, a miniature Africa. The tiny and revered *Babalaô tia* Ciata, Hilaria de Almeida, took up residence in the nearby street *Visconde de Itaúna*, number 117. She had arrived from *Alfândega* Street, her festive and busy tent in tow. Dancing Societies sprang up in *Visconde de Itaúna*, and the parallel street *Senador Eusébio*, as well as in other adjacent ones, making the region more festive and noisy. The *sambas* (dances) would spill out from the little houses onto the backyards and the streets. That is how *praça Onze* became the probable birthplace of the samba (music and song). And *tia* Ciata's house would become precisely the place where samba is born as a musical form, as a composer's melody instead of existing as a group dance. A noisy, polemic birth, as its importance merited, because it would mark the advent of a new and expressive stage in Brazilian popular music.

The samba of Praça Onze can be taken as a form of cultural resistance that runs parallel to the modernizing project overseen by a sector of the empowered elite. Oswaldo Rocha (81) observes that, once the "Demolition Era" was over, Praça Onze kept its socio-economic characteristics, even accommodating a much larger population. There was a spirit of solidarity that directed the influx of Bahian migrants to find housing and work in the social network of their countrymen, and it kept them arriving in Rio de Janeiro.

The relationship this community had with the police and the empowered authorities was ambiguous, and this was illustrated in the lyrics of the first sambas. Some of the *terreiros de Candomblé* (the places where Candomblé rituals are held) were frequented by intellectuals and political figures, some of whom were also connected to the nation's modernizing projects: Pinheiro Machado, Paulo de Frontin, Irineu Machado, and Lopes Trovão are some of the notables that Oswaldo Rocha names (82). The musician João da Baiana is the protagonist of a story that reveals the contradictions inherent in the relations between the neighborhood and the authorities. The composer had his *pandeiro* (tambourine) routinely destroyed by the police at parties in the neighborhood of Penha, because the samba was then considered an infraction of the law. On the occasion of his invitation to senator Pinheiro Machado's house in the upper-class neighborhood of Laranjeiras, he was asked by his host why he had not brought along his *pandeiro*. His explanation prompted the politician to have him call in on the senate the following day, where he was given a *pandeiro* inscribed with the senator's own dedication; this marked the end of João's problems with the police.

Another factor of importance in the Praça Onze community was men's attire. A badly dressed man could be easily mistaken for someone who was unemployed, and this could turn into an arraignment for vagrancy and eventually imprisonment. This problem led some members of the community to adopt a characteristic mode of dress, in which refinement and display of wealth were used to counteract the image of the outlaw.

The factors that allowed that part of the city to develop its own culture and its complex relations with the society of the time also accentuated the neighborhood's isolation and social exclusion, which rested on the population's economic origins (linked to activities considered marginal or subaltern), on its ethnicity (predominantly Afro-Brazilian from the state of Bahia), and finally on its construction of an identity cohesive enough to be recognizable from both the inside and the larger society. In a process similar to the one Richard Sennett used to describe Jews in Venice during the Renaissance (244), the construction of this identity meant concentrating certain group characteristics that were reinforced by their seclusion in a differentiated space. There are similarities in how this process unfolds in history, as Sennett exemplifies, between the multitudes that went to Leon de Mondena's synagogue, attracted by his enormously successful sermons at the beginning of the seventeenth century, and an analogous contemporary phenomenon: ". . . like modern European tourists going to Harlem in New York, the visit was a matter of voyeurism, a voyage to a forbidden culture" (246). The analogy suggests the same phenomenon at work when members of Rio de Janeiro's intellectual and political elite turned up at the Saúde neighborhood.

Another more direct victim of Pereira Passos's urban reform was the neighborhood of Lapa, pushed into social exclusion by the demolition of residences in order to open the Mem de Sá Avenue and the elimination of Lapa beach, again, to build the Beira Mar Avenue—all this following the exodus of the wealthy to the city's periphery, facilitated by the burgeoning network of trams. In *Antologia da Lapa* (Lapa Anthology) Gasparino Damata (b. 1918) defines the transformation: "A partir de 1910, a Lapa tinha dupla personalidade: as residências familiares misturavam-se às pensões das decaídas, embora estas de portas fechadas" (10) ("Starting in 1910, Lapa acquired a double personality: family residences were interspersed with run down boarding houses, which kept their doors closed"). Lapa suffered the same process of becoming a haven for a peculiar lifestyle and developing a special relationship with the rest of the city:

> A partir de 1915, as ruas adjacentes—Conde de Laje, Taylor, Joaquim Silva, bem como o decantado Beco dos Carmelitas—começaram a infestar-se de casas suspeitas. Nascia, então uma nova Lapa: de crimes passionais, de boemia desenfreada, de malandragem, de desordeiros perigosos e prostituição em alta escala. Mas era também a Lapa dos cabarés e cassinos famosos . . . , centro da vida noturna da capital, freqüentados pelo mundo elegante, por famílias mais progressistas. (Damata 10–11)

> From 1915 on, the adjacent streets—*Conde de Laje, Taylor, Joaquim Silva*, as well as the renowned *Beco das Carmelitas*—started being overrun with houses of ill repute. That year witnessed the birth of a new *Lapa*: known for its crimes of passion, bohemian lack of restraint, vagrancy, unruly behaviour, and finally high class prostitution. It was also, however, the *Lapa* of the famous cabarets and casinos, . . . the center of the capital's nightlife, frequented by elegant people, by progressive families.

Rodolfo Paschoal's study of two novels by Luís Martins (1907–1981), *Lapa* (1937) and *Noturno da Lapa* [1944; Nocturnal Lapa], focuses on the censures and interdictions imposed on this neighborhood and on a part of the intellectual elite that breached them. It is interesting to note the distinction that is established between Lapa, the bohemian neighborhood, known in its golden years as the tropical Montmartre, and Mangue, an area of low-class prostitution, close to Praça Onze and devoid of the charm of being geographically associated with downtown Rio de Janeiro. Paschoal points out the ambiguities of the author's attempt at understanding his relation to a neighborhood as strange to his own upbringing as it was strange to the handful of intellectuals who frequented it. The need to establish markers of distance becomes transparent in the author's assertion that they were bohemian because of their youth, but "nossas almas e os nossos caracteres não se contaminaram, não se macularam, não se deformaram" (Martins 171) ("our souls and our characters were not contaminated, they escaped unblemished, not defiled"). Sennett too articulates the fear of contamination that goes hand in hand with venturing into the ghetto (236–37); fascination and infection become inseparable when an insecure society fears not being able to offer any resistance, when coming into contact with the strangeness of the Other. This preoccupation is often turned into the metaphor of illness–leading to Sennett's own conclusion regarding the social mechanisms often triggered by the AIDS virus. The writer Luís Martins, as read by Paschoal, creates a system of self-reference to explain the elite's contacts with prostitutes. Bohemian intellectuals enriched their lives through transgressive contact with the prohibited domain of the city. The author, however, allows the reader a glimpse of the small indiscretions that entail closer contact between the two groups:

> Em geral, nada mais inocente que estas excursões; a presença de cad um, por uma questão de respçetio humano, inibia os demais. Sentávamos a uma das mesas, bebíamos cervejas, brincávamos com as raparigas e ficávamos nisso, como se fossemos (em verdade, não éramos) austeros observadores do vício, apenas interessados na sua contemplação. (Martins 141)

> In general, there is nothing more innocent than these excursions; each person's presence was enough to inhibit their fellows out of mutual respect. We would sit at the same table, drink beer, and play with the girls and keep it at that, just as if we were (which in truth we weren't) austere observers of vice, interested solely in its contemplation.

As Sennett theorizes, the greatest peril in coming into contact with the marginalized group is expressed through the sense of touch. To contemplate it, however, is as dangerous as the temptation to breach the limits that stop impurities from circulating in the urban blood.

Luís Martins's works offer us a privileged opportunity to observe the mechanisms that *carioca* (born in Rio de Janeiro) youth used to establish safe limits in their contact with a population that was marginalized, but which could not be exiled from the city and therefore had to be kept under control. Martins's novels also show the implausibility of the notion that *carioca* society had an easy, festive, and unproblematic relationship with prostitution. They detail the exclusionary maps drawn in the memoirs of an intellectual's formative years, and the author's consequently painful attempts at unraveling them. *Lapa*, published in 1936, intersected with national politics when a copy was annotated and sent to president Getúlio Vargas by a self-professed fascist sympathizer. Luís Martins, taking precautionary refuge in São Paulo the following year, found himself being sought by the police, and his books being apprehended and destroyed. The author himself could not understand why his books were considered subversive and dangerous instead of merely pornographic. It is Paschoal's

contention that the danger seen in the book was precisely in the contact it established between two traditionally separate worlds on the verge of the outbreak of intolerance–many times disguised by the cordiality that habitually cloaked repression and violence in Brazil.

The Map of Naturalism

Flora Süssekind states, "sucesso de público das obras naturalistas demonstrava que atendiam a condições internas, que estavam organicamente ligadas à sociedade brasileira de fins do século passado" (59) ("as public successes, Naturalist works demonstrated that they were fulfilling internal needs that were organically linked to Brazilian society at the end of the last century"). The very choice of Zola as an artistic model over a disdained Flaubert, and the privileging of Comte and Spencer to the detriment of Marx, suggest the presence of criteria intrinsic to the Brazilian intellectual sphere in action. Nelson Werneck Sodré explains the Naturalist school's prestige at the turn of the nineteenth century as being based on its elaboration of a language that expressed social transformations linked to the decadence of old rural structures, the growth of middle-class urban sectors, and the bourgeoisie's search for its own role in the emergent political and economic scene (59). Naturalism, in short, served to convey new ideas and to voice social unrest in Brazil. It is important, however, to underscore the fact that the destabilization that was felt at the end of the nineteenth century fostered the ripe conditions for the emerging regional centers. They broke away from the imperial capital's leash and began to articulate their own cultural activities with their own interpretations of foreign ideas and intellectual fashions. These regional centers found that the need to acknowledge the foreign origin of new ideas was no longer incompatible with a nationalist thrust to engender new proposals to reorganize the nation.

The States of Ceará and Recife in the Northeast became two important centers for the spread of Naturalist ideas. In Ceará, these ideas found expression in the Academia Francesa (French Academy) founded in 1872, and ten years later in the Padaria Espiritual (Spiritual Bakery), which expressed, not without some naiveté, a preoccupation with Brazilian cultural traditions (policing, for example), the use of foreign words in its meetings, and repudiating any work that mentioned animals or plants extraneous to Brazilian flaura and fauna (Sodré 197). This latter group's literary influence reached much further and was responsible for at least two writers becoming well-known throughout the nation: Adolfo Caminha (1867–1897) and Antônio Sales (1868–1940). The Escola de Recife (Recife School), founded in 1868 and grouped around the Law School, was led by Tobias Barreto (1839–1889) and Sílvio Romero (1851–1914). Sílvio Romero's career covered many activities, including literature during the 1860s, criticism and philosophy from 1870 to 1877, and law from 1878 onwards (Sodré 198). His intent to steer the group toward militancy led him to state, "Não escrevo pelo gosto de escrever, senão com o sentimento de ser útil à minha pátria" (quoted in Sodré 199) ("I do not write for the pleasure of writing, but I am motivated by the sentiment of serving my nation"). Romero believed it was his responsibility to attenuate the discrepancies and ignorance that tore apart the different regions and social classes of Brazil. He extended Tobias Barreto's pioneering ideas past the immediate jurisdiction of Pernambuco to the whole nation, stating, "No Rio de Janeiro, só de 1874 em diante é que, pela primeira vez, os nomes de Darwin e

Comte foram pronunciados em público, em conferências e escritos" (in Sodré 201) ("only after 1874 do we hear in Rio de Janeiro the names of Darwin and Comte being mentioned in public, in conferences and in writing"). Lúcia Miguel Pereira states that the nature of Tobias Barreto's and Sílvio Romero's criticism, in conjunction with that of José Veríssimo, "feita com bases científicas, e já não apenas impressionista como fora no período romântico" (57) ("was built on scientific bases, and no longer merely impressionistic, as during the Romantic period"). In her view, their criticism helped to confer on the literature of the final two decades of the last century "prestígio talvez sem precedentes entre nós" (57) ("a prestige perhaps unprecedented among us [Brazilians]").

Normative Criticism

Lúcia Pereira also believes that the new school's overriding merit with respect to literature was introducing Brazilian intellectuals to more rational methods of evaluation and analysis, which were anchored in other scientific disciplines; this is what gave Naturalism its unprecedented prestige. She does, however, concede that the subsequent literary output exhibits certain deficiencies because of what she considers the writers' scientific pretensions. Pereira observes that their subservience to literary fashion turned out to be detrimental to their work. In analyzing Lenita, a character from Júlio Ribeiro's (1845–1889) *A carne* (1888, The Flesh), she interprets her as being "tão inexistente, com o seu corpo demasiadamente exigente, como as incorpóreas heroínas românticas" (131) ("just as improbable, with her insatiable body, as the incorporeal Romantic heroines"). Sodré also criticizes Naturalism for what he calls a fixation on hysteria, almost to the point of literary cliché: "Magdá, Lenita, Ester são, no fim das contas, um estereótipo que o Naturalismo coloca em primeiro plano, um motivo com poucas variações, um mote, uma constante" (219) ("Magda, Lenita, Ester are, in sum, a stereotype that Naturalism places center stage, a motif with little variation, a motto, a constant"). He adds, "Criando as rebeladas, ainda que pela histeria, os naturalistas levantavam um protesto, cuja forma era inócua, pela falsidade da deformação, mas que não deve ser esquecido. Era errônea, sem dúvida, a formulação, porque se fazia em torno de um mito, apesar de bases pretensamente científicas" (221) ("In depicting rebellious women as hysterical, the Naturalist writers' descriptions were so false that their creation turned out to be an innocuous form of protest, which should not be forgotten. It was fundamentally flawed, because it rested on a myth, regardless of its supposed scientific pretensions"). Sodré does not spare the writers' anticlericalism either, considering it yet another artificial instance of subservience to Émile Zola's literary model.

The arguments offered by both critics show a good understanding of the novels and the relationship between Naturalism as a literary school and the intellectual ideas at the time. This perspective is theoretically lacking, however, when it is limited to the analysis of literature in terms of its homologous portrayal of social and cultural reality. As Flora Süssekind has observed, concerning the different Naturalisms that influenced Brazilian letters, critics focused on the inadequacy of literary form seen as a copy of reality. They stopped short of analyzing the literary function that female hysteria had for its readership–something that guaranteed the novels' success, whether or not approved by the critics.

Katia Muricy, taking a different approach, studies the changes that affected daily life, "ainda que com fundamentais

diferenças, o século XIX brasileiro viu surgir novas formas de organização social que nos aproximavam do processo de racionalização, que, nas reformas sanitárias e pedagógicas desse século, na Europa, ganhou características que permitiram chamá-lo de *normalização*" (14) ("despite some fundamental differences from the European experience, nineteenth-century Brazil saw the emergence of new forms of social organization that came close to [European] rationalization which, by means of educational and sanitary reforms, became known as *normalization*"). The social and economic transformations mentioned by Sodré, brought about by the gradual urbanization of the nation during the nineteenth century, are re-examined in light of the new demands of the urban elites. The same anticlericalism professed by Naturalist writers, and disparaged by Sodré as being an inauthentic copy of French social issues resulting from stylistic obedience, acquires unexpected depth in the new social order, commanded by medicine's hygienic policies. In Muricy's view, the prominence once granted the priest, enabling him to wield control over all the patriarchal family, "foi sendo eclipsada pela presença do médico na vida da família urbana" (14) ("was gradually being eclipsed by the doctor's presence in the urban family's life"). As Sodré points out, the Naturalist novel is narrated from the implicit point of view of the doctor: The new gaze evaluates what is conducive to fostering healthy family relationships and to circumscribing what is deviant and therefore detrimental to society. This results in the establishing of increasingly rigorous borders between public and private life. The emerging perspective is thus based on a set of rules that do not necessarily coincide with any religious viewpoint. The priest must be fought because he becomes an obstacle to the new social order, or more simply, is a contender for public guidance who represents a set of guidelines for life that are deemed outdated.

The most startling aspect of Naturalist literature, what has attracted the attention of critics then and now (apart from the description of clinical cases and the medical language that its pages are steeped in), was the insistence on the topic of feminine hysteria. Women were being consigned to new social functions on the heels of capitalist transformations, urbanization, and the changed nature of the family (as the nuclear family). In Muricy's words, "A série de restrições das funções econômicas e políticas da família, com os primórdios da industrialização, e a sua concentração em funções da procriação e do disciplinamento do impulso sexual caracterizam o advento da família moderna. A família conjugal moderna é típico produto da urbanização" (60) ("The beginnings of industrialization brought about a series of restrictions on the economic and political functions of the family, now concentrated on procreation and the disciplining of sexuality, which characterized the advent of the modern conjugal family unit, a typical product of urbanization"). Muricy goes even further:

> "Se a família passa a ser sinônimo de intimidade, os sujeitos serão vistos como indivíduos, diferentes uns dos outros e requerendo um tratamento distinto. Nessa demanda abre-se o espaço para a intervenção médica na privacidade da família. Foram as mulheres, as 'enclausuradas das más alcovas' (cf. Luís Azevedo Correa em 1872), a porta de entrada para os médicos na casa familiar" (61)

> "The family becomes synonymous with intimacy, its subjects are then understood as differentiated individuals in need of distinct (medical) treatment. This opens the door for the medical intervention

in the privacy of the family. Women, 'encloistered in bedrooms' (see Luiz Azevedo Correia in 1872), are the conduit for doctors into the home."

Jurandir Freire Costa shows us in *A face e o verso* [The Face and the Verse] how the Enlightenment provided the first and decisive contribution to the historical construction of sexual differentiation in the West. Based on Thomas Laqueur's work, he states that because of Neoplatonism women were understood as inverted men for two millennia: "Havia um modelo metafísico ideal do corpo humano, cujo grau de perfeição era alcançado pelo homem. A mulher era um homem invertido e inferior. A forma feminina do sexo era um índice de inferioridade na escala da perfeição metafísica" (Costa 100) ("There was a metaphysical ideal model of the human body, which attained its highest degree of perfection in man. Woman was an inferior and inverted man. The female sexual form was indicative of inferiority in the scale of metaphysical perfection"), an inferiority explained by its less intense *"calor vital"* (Costa 100) ("vital heat, or energy"). This conception was predominant in France during the entire *ancien régime*. The Enlightenment and the Revolution raised the issue of the equality of the sexes, only to witness anatomical differences being interpreted as a new basis for inequalities. Once women were determined to be fragile by nature, their sphere of action was separated from that of men and limited to private life. Sexual difference was imbued in this way with political interests during the nineteenth century. Sexual behavior was charged with varying political meaning, but mostly it was used for distinctions of class–establishing the difference between *bourgeois* management of procreation and property and proletarian promiscuity. Women's physiology, their bone structure and the psychological reactions considered unique to their gender, such as *vapores* (vapours)– understood as a mild fit of hysteria (mostly an affliction of noble women and interpreted as a sign of their superior nervous sensibility)–were investigated with the aim of providing a scientific basis for the notion of female fragility and a justification for that restriction of agency to private life (Costa 113). These were attempts at substituting hysteria for the *calor corporal* (bodily heat) theory, a legacy of the now dying and outdated Neo-Platonism.

In a development parallel to the establishing of sexuality as an arena for the regulation of individual behavior and a principle for family organization, female behavioral studies were conducted in order to establish the limits of its normalcy. The strategic aim of this line of research was to organize the *bourgeois* family around the right to property–its inherent claim to the recognition of paternity, as well as its implied right of inheritance, which can only be guaranteed by a woman's complete fidelity to her spouse, the patriarch. Costa highlights the contrast between the social and economic importance of controlling female sexuality and the toleration of other deviant behavior during the nineteenth century. Contrary to prevalent contemporary belief, Charcot contended that hysteria was not an exclusively female phenomenon, affirming that it was possible to observe the same symptoms in men subjected to harsh living conditions, and concluding that "entre os agentes provocadores da histeria, ao lado das grandes perturbações morais, dos traumatismos, das intoxicações etc, há lugar para colocar a miséria, a miséria com todas suas durezas, suas cureldades" (Costa 124) ("among the agents that cause hysteria, great moral

disturbances, traumas, intoxications, etc., one must place penury, destitution in all its cruel harshness"). However, as Costa notes, the almost exclusive scientific investment in female hysteria, to the point of considering it a phenomenon observable only among women, was evidently political:

O cuidado teórico com a histeria da mulher e o descuido com a histeria dos mendigos, trabalhadores, ferroviários etc., tinha como motor a preocupação com a família e a descendência. A histérica era a anti-mãe burguesa; mas o histérico não era o anti-pai burguês. Era um desclassificado, um sem-família, cuja sorte patológica interessava pouco à constituição da "raça" e da moral das *ruling classes*. (Costa 124)

the theoretical concern with female hysteria to the detriment of hysteria in beggars, workers, railway workers etc., was motivated by a preoccupation with the family and inheritance. A hysterical woman was the anti-bourgeois mother, whereas a hysterical man was not the equivalent, anti-bourgeois father. He had no social standing, a man without family, whose pathological destiny provided little interest for the constitution of the race and the morals of the ruling classes.

This comment originates in the field of sexuality, from a theoretical perspective that had a great influence on Naturalist literature. It did not, however, exhaust the influences at work in the creation of Naturalist literary techniques or in the choice of topics in its stylistic canon; nor would it be the sole explanation for the interest aroused in these literary works.

Ana Christina Chiara has re-examined the Naturalist movement based on an analysis of how Júlio Ribeiro's novel *A carne* was received by its readers. She reminds us of the erotic undercurrent always threatening to surface in material originally intended to satisfy an intellectual appetite. Chiara cites John Bende who used Foucault's comparisons of illustrations in anatomical atlases with pornographic material, to conclude, "apesar do aparato do olhar científico tentar neutralizar os aspectos libidinais em representações do corpo humano anatomizado, a violência erótica irrompe como um suplemento estranho à imparcialidade científica" (in Chiara 135) ("although the scientific gaze tries to neutralize the libidinous content of anatomic representations of the human body, erotic violence erupts in the form of the foreign supplement to scientific impartiality").

Hysteria, the ubiquitous literary topic, tended to satisfy various social needs. The frequency of its appearance can be explained by a rising interest in investigating female functions (or dysfunctions) in a changing society, a society concerned with establishing hierarchy and certain regulatory norms for the nuclear family. There was also a proliferation of sexual themes, ranging through a variety of sexually deviant behaviors; ultimately sexuality achieved a new status in the definition of human nature (Foucault 1988, 3:115). We must not, however, ignore a different set of motivations that made the Naturalist novel attractive to the public, especially to its male readership. Brito Broca points out the emergence of a specific market for literature in the 1880s for which the main attractions were precisely the traits characteristic of the movement:

Parece-nos significativo o fato de encontrarmos em vários números da *Gazeta de Notícias*, em 1888, um dos anos mais fecundos para o Naturalismo entre nós, quando causava grande escândalo *A carne*, de Júlio Ribeiro, um anúncio sob este título: "Leitura para homens". Em que consistiam tais leituras? Em novelas fesceninas de autores anônimos, algumas decerto adaptadas de outros idiomas, pura obscenidade sem qualquer valor literário.

Eis aqui os títulos de algumas delas: *Clarita, Beatriz, As Sete Noites de Lucréia, Os Prazeres de Rosália, Morgadinha das Delícias. . . . Camarões Elétricos* e *Mexilhões Incendiários . . .* (111–12)

It is significant that the year of 1888, one of the most productive in Brazilian Naturalism, when Júlio Ribeiro's *A carne* was scandalizing society, was the same year in which many issues of the newspaper *Gazeta de Notícias* carried an advertisement entitled: "Men's Literature." What did it consist of? Licentious literature, anonymously authored, some surely translated from other languages, pure obscenity, devoid of any literary value. Some of the titles included: *Clarita, Beatriz, Lucretia's Seven Nights, Rosália's Pleasures, Morgadinha's Delicacies. . . . Electric Shrimps and Incendiary Mussels . . .*

Brito Broca's commentary calls attention to the transformations that took place in Brazilian cultural life towards the end of the nineteenth century. There was an incipient marketing logic similar to that of best sellers today, the exploitation of a literary fashion through stylized imitation. There is also an indirect association with the exploitation of the human body for commercial ends to sell products, a practice that culminates in real and symbolic prostitution of the female body.

Machado de Assis's (1839–1908) novel *Quincas Borba* (1891) provides us with an example of this new role of sexuality in social relationships through the character of Sofia. The narrator compares her behavior to a lamp suspended above the entrance of an inn, and in doing so refers to the power of seduction that she uses for furthering her husband's business. The image Machado chooses also illuminates her subaltern condition: She is subject to her husband's decisions and control. She never fails to obey him, even if from a position of liminality and risk, as noted in the novel.

Fashion, as Katia Muricy suggests, became a symptom of changes not only in women's roles but also in the treatment of the body, at a time when members of the family were undergoing the process of individualization and when women started to compete in the game for individual prestige and money that was played out in the public sphere (61). Muricy contrasts the turn-of-the-century reality with the situation in colonial times, noting that in colonial times while in public, one mimicked power by an extravagant affectation, in the private sphere, one would mimic equality to disguise relations of dominance: "Homens e mulheres eram absolutamente negligentes quanto ao seu vestuário doméstico e aos seus cuidados higiênicos: as mulheres passavam quase todo o tempo descalças e de camisolas, e os homens, de ceroula, camisas e chinelas" (58) ("Men and women were completely negligent with regards to their domestic attire and their personal hygiene: Women passed almost their entire time barefoot and in their sleeping gowns, and men in their underpants, shirt, and slippers").

As urban habits took hold and Brazil embraced city life, questions arose about the status of literature in relation to the journalistic press and about the modes of thought that were being disseminated along with the new media. In this sense, there was a gradual transition from a phase in Western culture defined by the search for truth (carried out through scrupulous investigation of physical phenomena in order to transcend reality through the act of observation itself) to another phase, that of the *compulsive* search for truth.

The question seen from Ana Chiara's perspective is that of the contamination of *voyeurism* by a pretentious pseudo-medical gaze. In instances where one would expect to find a pure, unmediated search for knowledge, one discovered instead the pleasure of viewing, which is what characterizes pornography. Medical narrators, the profane prophets of the new order, thus established a pact with the reader that discouraged the critical analysis encouraged in the representation of reality, and dared him to give himself over to the pleasure of the text, of the evoked reality that this type of writing promised to deliver.

Some of the criticism of Naturalism was related to this promise of satisfaction and the loss of the limits of subjectivity. The Naturalist novel presupposed a position on the part of its readers, as its receivers, that can be associated with the attitude the consumer has towards a commodity. As Flora Süssekind remarks, "Oculta-se dessa escrita transparente o seu caráter de produção, como numa mercadoria manufaturada se escondem também os traços do trabalho operário que a produziu" (101) ("Its transparent writing hides the character of its production in the same way that manufactured commodities conceal the traces of the proletarian labor that produced it"). Süssekind bases her assertion on Karl Marx's concept of commodity fetishism, which cloaks the relations of production that make it possible (1:43–58). The fallacy of the Naturalist trend in literary production is exposed and denounced most clearly when its privileging of the visible is condemned: "Ao literário e àquele que o escreve cumpre negar o trabalho com a e na linguagem para que o leitor, dominado por 'desejo irresistível de ver', pareça estar em contato direto com 'o' real" (101) ("The literary object and the person who writes it is obliged to deny the labor performed with and to language so that the reader, dominated by the 'irresistible desire to see,' will feel in direct contact with the real").

In an attempt to characterize the status of the visible in modernity, Martin Jay states in "The Rise of Hermeneutics and the Crisis of Ocularcentrism" that Western philosophy is the outcome of a continuous struggle between visual codes and the word as the originators of truth. This tension can be detected in two of the most influential sources of the West's dominant culture: in Jewish civilization, Moses's rejection of idolatry, his defense of the truth of the word revealed to him by God against the Hebrew worship of images; and in Greek culture, the Platonic criticism of the illusionary character of appearances, which engendered a series of political and pedagogical proposals to promote truth and censure the corrupting influence of the seduction and trickery of images (Jay 1993a).

Jay's essay discusses the French theologian Jacques Ellul's hypothesis that the current relationship between images and words in Western culture was first defined in the fourteenth century. The adhesion of the Church to this view contributed to the gradual establishment of a state that the theologian defines as that of the "debauchery of images." Ellul proposes that the dominance of the image is replaced by the passive reception of the word as source of supreme truth, the return of the authority of the Divine Word. Jay uses Ellul to illustrate what he presents as the dominant trend among French thinkers and artists: a denunciation of so-called ocularcentrism (1993a, 99–100). According to Jay, vision has been profoundly discredited ever since Bergson, and this trend can be found in the works of philosophers such as Sartre and Lyotard, film critics like Metz and Baudry, thinkers such as Sarah Kofman and Luce Irigaray, literary critics like Bataille and Blanchot, and finally literary writers such as Robbe-Grillet and Bonnefoy. After a long period in which culture was greatly interested in the gaze, the trend was reversed in twentieth-century France, according to Jay, to the extent that even the visual arts began to treat the gaze with suspicion–as proved, for example, by Marcel Duchamp's work. In another essay on the same topic, "From the Empire of the Gaze to the Society of the Spectacle: Foucault and Debord," Jay states that while the reasons are unclear, it is possible to speak of a change in the discursive paradigm of French twentieth century thought, in which "the denigration of the gaze" supplants its previous exaltation (1993b, 434).

In light of this theory of ocularcentrism, we can see how Machado de Assis argued for the demise of Naturalism in two critical essays he published in 1878 on José Maria Eça de Queirós's (1845–1900) novel *O primo Basílio* [1878; Cousin Basílio]; he bases his argument on the appeal to the senses for the expression of the intellect. The essays became a kind of manifesto refuting Naturalism as the model to supplant Romanticism. They expressed his own choice for a new path, away from literary fashion, on which he would embark a few years later in 1881 with the publication of *Memórias póstumas de Brás Cubas* [*Epitaph of a Small Winner* or *The Posthumous Memoirs of Brás Cubas*]. In his analysis, Naturalism privileged what were only accessory elements and was dominated by description (1959, 3:908), creating scenes that did not deepen conflicts for characters; this led him to the conclusion that the Naturalist novel relegated characters and their conflicts to a secondary plane. This spurred him on to counter with an aesthetic model in which human passions were privileged: "O drama existe, porque está nos caracteres, nas paixões, na situação moral dos personagens: o acessório não domina o absoluto . . ." (1959, 3:910) ("Drama exists, because it is inherent to the characters, their passions, their moral situations: What is accessory should not take precedence over what is absolute . . ."). From Machado's perspective the fortuitous hand of chance should not be the dominant force in a narrative plot's development, because it prevents a deeper comprehension of the character's subjective universe and interferes in the unfolding of events. His analysis of the aesthetic problems caused by the defects in composition that were encouraged by Naturalism as a literary fashion led Machado de Assis, especially in the second article he devotes to the topic, to moralistic conclusions. In the great works of literature, Machado concludes, the moral beauty of certain characters is superimposed on the depiction of human degradations; this conjunction of "high and low" (which had already been sanctioned by Victor Hugo in his theory on Romanticism in the preface to *Cromwell*) differs greatly from the emphasis on only the "low" found in the new style championed by Eça de Queirós:

> Diferente coisa é a indecência relativa de uma locução, e a constância de um sistema que, usando aliás de relativa decência nas palavras, acumula e mescla tôda a sorte de idéias e sensações lascivas; que, no desenho e colorido de uma mulher, por exemplo, vai direito às indicações sensuais. (1959, 3:912)

> Quite another thing is the relative indecency of a locution, and the constantly recurring system that with fairly decent wording accumulates and mixes all sorts of lascivious ideas and sensations; which, in the depiction of a woman, for example, goes directly into sensuality.

Machado's criticism rejects the construction of scenes in Naturalist literature designed to draw the reader in, which provoke lascivious thoughts and sensations by the recurrent use of words that refer to vision or the other senses.

György Lukács also condemned the Naturalist privileging of visuality, as well as what he sees as Naturalism's defective concept of the novel, with its emphasis on the accidental (which corresponds to Machado de Assis's "accessory"). He associates both traits with a superficial approach to human conflicts–with the additional criticism, in his case, of the novel's distance from historical reality. Like Machado, Lukács links the knowledge of human passions and destiny to a study of the circumstances that generate individual *praxis*, consigning the incidence of chance to a secondary role. His major preoccupation, like Flora Süssekind's, is with the generalized reifying mechanism that takes control of artistic production. Note his criticism of the importance given to things over individuals and their conflicts: "As coisas só têm vida poética enquanto relacionadas com acontecimentos de destinos humanos. Por isso, o verdadeiro narrador épico não as descreve e sim conta a função que elas assumem na vida humana" (78) ("Things will only have poetic life while they are related to the events in human destinies. That is why the true epic narrator does not describe them, but narrates the function that they fulfill in human life"). Lukács does not, however, see any relevance in the moral dimension that is so important to Machado de Assis; he is concerned instead with the exploitation of the senses that he finds predominant, for example, in the culture industry.

The discussions precipitated by Naturalism are still pertinent today, especially since they bring back some of the most penetrating criticism still applicable to today's culture industry. One wonders, therefore, whether some of the criticism set in motion with the reception of Naturalism somehow foreshadows the present-day response to current themes and topics, or whether we are in the midst of a literature with new modes of perception in which oppositions such as surface/depth have lost their meaning. However, there is also the long view: The pleasure of contemplating the world, which threatens to weaken the ego, is a danger that has been feared in Western culture since the time of St. Augustine, and is not limited to its manifestation in the erotic object. The observation of life as a succession of sense impressions is the topic explored by Naturalist literature.

The same contradiction between the compulsion to know all and the pleasure of unmediated contemplation, which is present in the literature of the body and of eroticism, is revealed when the literary object shifts to the lower classes. The depiction of the lower classes in Realist literature can express this two-way impulse: On the one hand, the promise of access to a sector of the population that has been hitherto absent from literary representation of the nation; on the other, the pleasure awarded by the spectacle of a world in which social relations are not yet dictated by the rigid codes enforced in *bourgeois* circles, which the *petit bourgeoisie* feels compelled to imitate. Trying to define the attitude of the reader toward Émile Zola's (1840–1902) work, Nelson Werneck Sodré foresees a form of voyeuristic pleasure, similar to what we have been endeavoring to characterize here; he states,

> De uma forma geral, o que caracterizou o papel de Zola foi a curiosidade universal, curiosidade que se explicava pela necessidade de dar guarida a tudo aquilo que vinha afetando, de forma tão profunda, a vida da sociedade. Curiosidade que chegou aos limites da bisbilhotice, que se perdeu, por isso mesmo, em inúmeros detalhes, desmandando-se em minúcias desprovidas de significação, perdendo-se em pesquisas estéreis, despojadas de importância, para a vida como para a literatura. Ver bem não era ver tudo, já naquele tempo. (238–39)

In a general manner, what characterized Zola's image was a universal curiosity, a curiosity that was explained by the need to encompass everything that bore an influence on life in society in such a profound way. A curiosity that goes to the limit of prying, and for that same reason finds itself trammeled in infinite, insignificant detail, losing its way in sterile searches, divested of importance for life, as well as for literature. To see well, even then, did not mean to see everything.

The curiosity that is close prying, as defined by Sodré, is evidence of the compulsive trend mentioned previously, which seems to have set the tone for contemporary visuality as Jean Baudrillard emphasized, the need to show everything, even if this act had already lost all hope of uncovering any hidden meaning (as was proposed in the initial phase of this process two centuries ago). Such an attitude differs from the one Walter Benjamin identified with the *flâneur* and his *oisive* availability to penetrate meaning inherent in things through a fortuitous observation of the environment. The current concept of the gaze as an instrument for truth (which made Zola sing the praises of the advent of experimental science (122) and was mirrored in his passion for collecting photographs) solidifies differentiations in the ways in which it is exercised. João do Rio's definition of the *flâneur*, as noted by Renato Cordeiro Gomes, also presupposed observation as its goal, an insight into the reverse of a scene, that leads us to a reflection on the contrast between this configuration of the gaze and the one we associate with obscene compulsion:

> Flanar é ser vagabundo e refletir, é ser basbaque e comentar, ter o vírus da observação ligado ao do vadiagem. . . . Flanar é a distinção de perambular com inteligência. . . . O flâneur . . . acaba com a idéia de que todo o espetáculo da cidade foi feito especialmente para seu gozo próprio. . . . E de tanto ver o que os outros quase não podem entrever, o flâneur reflete. . . . Quando o flâneur deduz, ei-lo a concluir uma lei magnífica por ser para seu uso exclusivo, ei-lo a psicologar, ei-lo a pintar os pensamentos, a fisionomia, a alma das ruas. (Gomes 68–69)

> *Flâner* is to be a vagabond and to reflect, it is to be stupefied and to make comments, to harbor the virus of observation linked to the bacteria of idleness. . . . *Flâner* is the distinction of strolling with intelligence. . . . The *flâneur* . . . ends up believing that the whole spectacle of the city was created for his own pleasure. . . . And with eyes brimming with what others can barely glimpse, the *flâneur* reflects. . . . In the *flâneur*'s conclusion is a magnificent law, for it was deduced for his own–exclusive–purpose, a psychologist, an artist of thought, of the physiognomy, the soul of the streets.

The *flâneur* lacks, therefore, two defining elements of the Naturalist gaze: An a priori commitment to a system of interpretation of reality, and the pretension of reaching an ultimate, definitive truth–this last trait inherent in the first stages of the process that engendered the contemporary compulsion with the obscene.

The Stage: Mirroring the Audience?

In commenting upon the difficulty of creating a theater out of the Naturalist movement's foundations, Émile Zola suggested that "The naturalistic formula, however complete and defined in the novel, is very far from being so on the stage, and I conclude from that that it will be completed, that it will assume sooner or later there its scientific rigor, or else the stage will become flat . . ." (141–42). Zola observed that one of the problems faced by most of the representative contemporary playwrights was the difficulty they had in freeing themselves from the self-imposed task of transforming action into a duel. He

was ". . . waiting for them to rid us of fictitious characters, of conventional symbols of virtue and vice, which possess no value as human data" (143). Contrary to what happened to the novel as it disseminated a new form of conceiving human life, the difficulty in establishing a relationship with the theater audience became one of the focal points in the struggle to transmit new artistic ideas. "The public remains cold and unresponsive when their passion for an ideal character, for some combination of loyalty and honor, is not satisfied" (155). He added, however, the hopeful belief in a sort of inevitable evolution that would lead the public not only to accept, but to demand, the new forms of de-idealized characters.

The Brazilian public had, in the 1856 opening of Alexander Dumas's (1824–1895) *A Dama das Camelias* [*Camille*], four years after the play's opening in France, its first introduction to theatrical renewal. With it came the hope of superseding the by now well-worn Romanticism, a chance to follow a path already established in the novel. This play became a model for innovative theatrical productions, as Décio de Almeida Prado described:

> O problema da alta prostituição, retomado e discutido exaustiva e ardorosamente por dezenas de outras peças, iria ainda firmar ante as platéias um novo gênero: a peça de tese, munida do seu "raisonneur," porta-voz do autor, e encarregada de encarar uma questão social e defender um ponto de vista. Nunca uma palavra de ordem partida da França repercutiu aqui com tanta intensidade. (14)

> The problem of high class prostitution, taken up once again and discussed exhaustively and arduously in scores of other plays, was to establish for successive audiences a new genre: a play with a thesis, armed with its own *raisonneur*, the author's spokesman, entrusted with facing a social problem and defending a point of view. Never had the order of the day in France had such great repercussions (in Brazil).

Dumas's play inspired copious productions of what the public nicknamed black-tie dramas, centered on modern characters, although melodramatic in tone. The Ginásio dramático (Dramatic Gymnasium), the renamed Teatro de São Francisco (Saint Francis Theater), certainly renamed in homage to the Paris Gymnase Dramatique, staged some of the productions, and its contribution on diverse fronts acted as a reviving theatrical force. The company that took over the management of the theater house announced in 1855 its intention "estabelecer o verdadeiro e apurado gosto pela representação do vaudeville e da comédia" (Faria 78) ("to establish the true and refined taste for staging the vaudeville and comedy"). The history of the company was marked by various innovating ventures–for example, its preoccupation with opening up a discussion of Realism on the stage. The company's repertoire, however, was of a didactic and moralizing quality, which differed from Romantic theater in Brazil by focusing on current topics of its time. They staged plays written by fashionable French Realists (in translation), as well as Brazilian and Portuguese authors. Among the company's contributions to theatrical renewal was its inaugural staging in 1857 of José de Alencar's (1829–1877) *O demônio familiar* [The Familiar Demon], which, in João Roberto Faria's view, was "um autêntico divisor de águas, pois marca, a um só tempo, a ruptura com o romantismo teatral e o início de uma dramaturgia voltada para a discussão de problemas sociais" (Faria 167) ("an authentic watershed, for it marked simultaneously the rupture with Romantic theater and the beginning of a dramaturgy directed toward the discussion of social problems").

José de Alencar's theatrical work had limited impact and fell short in its ambition to treat polemic topics; this is in sharp contrast to the skill and even audacity with which he wrote his novels. It was a problem he shared with other writers of Realist theater in Brazil. Alencar's *As asas de um Anjo* [1860; Wings of an Angel], an attempt at recreating Dumas's successful *La dame aux camélias*, despite the audacity of the topic and dialogues that exposed some of the harsh realities of prostitution, nevertheless illustrated the strict limitations in Brazilian theater at the time. The moralizing tone and conclusion of the plot, completely circumscribed by a patriarchal perspective, were praised in a review issued by the Conservatório dramático (Dramatic Conservatory) in 1858. This is proof of the existence in Brazilian theater of the same kind of limitations that Émile Zola denounced in French theater, which, even in its anti-Romantic manifestations, could not get rid of its manichean characters, its didactic function, or its set of moral values shared tacitly with the audience. José de Alencar, for his part, contrasted the psychological conditions that were propitious for treating the topic of prostitution in his successful novel *Lucíola*, in 1862, with the timidity that inhibited him while writing the play *As Asas de um Anjo*: "Já tinham passado as veleidades teatrais . . ." ("my theatrical flight of ambition had already elapsed . . ."), Alencar concluded, adding ". . . já me havia de sobra convencido que a platéia fluminense estava em anacronismo de um século com as idéias do escritor" (in Prado 16) (". . . I had already more than convinced myself that the *fluminense* [pertaining to Rio de Janeiro] audience was a century out of synchrony with the author's ideas").

Machado de Assis, however, expressed admiration for the moral content of Alencar's plays, as befits his own attempts as a playwright. According to theater critic Quintino Bocaiúva, Machado de Assis's first plays follow the model of French proverbs (one-act plays illustrating a maxim). Décio de Almeida Prado believes that it was the novelist's very concept of the human psyche that made a venture into the theater impossible: "É pouco provável que jamais a voz interior, a conversa das diferentes personalidades que coexistem entre nós, o 'cochicho do nada,' o apêlo da loucura, pudessem ser transmitidos, sem distorção, . . . por êsse instrumento poderoso e, no fundo, pouco sensível, que é o palco" (24) ("It is not likely that the inner voice, the conversation of different personalities that coexist inside us, the 'nothing that whispers,' the appeal of madness, could ever be transmitted without distortions, . . . by this powerful and, ultimately, hardly sensitive instrument that is the stage"). For years critics had believed unanimously that Oswald de Andrade's (1890–1954) plays were impossible to stage. Prado's conclusion, apart from showing his limited grasp of theater's potential, ignores the other ways Machado de Assis had of engaging in theatrical exercises. Sonia Brayner noticed on examining Machado's short stories that the small moralizing fables in which a certain theory is presented take on the appearance of the "teatro do mundo" ("theater of the world") (434). The relationship between Machado's short stories and the theater is also noted by Sábato Magaldi: "O exercício de síntese que fez na dramaturgia aplicou magistralmente no conto, que por muitos aspectos se aproxima da peça de um ato, sem a obrigação de utilizar o homem inteiriço" (119) ("The exercise in synthesis that Machado carried out in his plays, he applied masterfully to the short story, which in many respects is similar to a one-act play without the obligation of using people in their physical entirety"). There was a latent development in the author's work of an aesthetic concept that was similar to that of contemporary theater, closer to the traditions of the narrative-epic genre.

Machado de Assis's short stories, contrary to most Naturalist fiction, however, embodied a skeptic's view of human beings and included the theme of mutability that was a constant throughout his life. Machado did not take up the analysis of pathological cases from the medical point of view; turning away from Naturalism, he instead chose to denounce the unreason that directs human lives, and the dimension of the absurd in the rationalist ideals of his time. Machado de Assis's passion for the stage (which, to the dismay of some critics, never flourished in a theater of note) was generalized into a view of existence as the *theatrum mundi*. Doubtless, elements of this concept are present in his appreciation of didacticism and even in the timid moralism found in the first years of his youthful participation as a chronicler and playwright of Rio de Janeiro's theater life; later this view would unfold in great, detailed sketches in which the ideas and passions of his time are polyphonically staged.

Whether because of the difficulty in breaking through the barriers of tradition or because of the short time that Naturalism actually dominated Brazilian letters, the movement never found theatrical expression in the nation. Décio de Almeida Prado expresses dismay that a process he had thought inevitable never came to be:

> O teatro brasileiro parecia estar pronto para receber o Naturalismo: contava com um núcleo relativamente forte de autores dramáticos e passara pela indispensável iniciação realista. *Mas êsse passo, lógico e natural, nunca chegou a ser dado.* O nôvo movimento de idéias, apesar da imediata influência que exerceu sôbre o romance brasileiro, e mesmo sôbre a poesia, jamais alcançou os nossos palcos. (18, emphasis added)

> Brazilian theater seemed ready to receive Naturalism: it boasted a relatively strong nucleus of dramatic authors and had gone through the indispensable Realist initiation. *But this logical and natural step was never taken.* The new movement of ideas, in spite of the immediate influence it exercised over the Brazilian novel, and even its poetry, never reached the stage.

This critic seems disappointed with the failure of Brazilian theater to take the next "logical and natural step," which would have meant a repetition of the history of European theater, most especially, French theater. Our current perspective might lead us to analyze the specific reasons why Brazilian theater audiences, leaving behind the taste for black-tie dramas, embraced musical theater. A study of this transition would possibly elucidate the functions fulfilled by this new form of theater in experimenting with new forms of visuality or in the constitution of a Brazilian tradition in the construction of plots and interpretive styles (as has already been noted by some critics and actors). Considering the importance of minor genres may provide us with elements that will enrich our understanding of the ways in which the Brazilian theater articulated elements borrowed from other cultural centers and adapted itself to the transformations of the quotidian experiences of history.

Translation by Lis Horta-Moriconi

Works Cited

Assis, Machado de. 1959. "Crítica–Eça de Queirós: *O Primo Basílio*." *Obra completa*. Ed. Afrânio Coutinho. Rio de Janeiro: Editôra José Aguilar. 3:903–13.

——. 1975. *Quincas Borba*. Rio de Janeiro: Civilização Brasileira.

——. 1998. *Quincas Borba*. Trans. Gregory Rabassa. New York: Oxford University Press.

Baudrillard, Jean. 1987. *Forget Foucault*. New York: Semiotext(e).

Brayner, Sonia. 1982. "Metamorfoses machadianas; o laboratório ficcional." *Machado de Assis*. Eds. Alfredo Bosi, José Carlos Garbuglio, Mario Curvelho, and Valentim Facioli. São Paulo: Editora Ática. 426–37.

Broca, Brito. 1991. *Naturalistas, parnasianos e decadistas: Vida literária do realismo ao pré-modernismo*. Ed. Luiz Dantas. Campinas: Editora da Universidade Estadual de Campinas.

Chiara, Ana Cristina de Resende. 1996. "Leituras malvadas." Diss. Pontifícia Universidade Católica do Rio de Janeiro.

Costa, Jurandir Freire. 1995. *A face e o verso; estudos sobre o homoerotismo II*. São Paulo: Editora Escuta.

Damata, Gaspiano. 1978. *Antologia da Lapa: Vida boêmia no rio de ontem*. Rio de Janeiro: Editôra Codecri.

Faria, João Roberto. 1993. *O teatro realista no Brasil: 1855–1865*. São Paulo: Editora Perspectiva.

Foucault, Michel. 1975. *The Birth of the Clinic: An Archaeology of Medical Perception*. Trans. A. M. Sheridan Smith. New York: Vintage Books-Random House.

——. 1979. *Discipline and Punish: The Birth of the Prison*. Trans. Alan Sheridan. New York: Vintage Books-Random House.

——. 1988. *The History of Sexuality*. Vol 3: *The Care of the Self*. Trans. Robert Hurley. New York: Vintage Books-Random House.

Gomes, Renato Cordeiro. 1996. *João do Rio: Vielas do vício, ruas da graça*. Rio de Janeiro: Relume-Dumará.

Jay, Martin. 1993a. "The Rise of Hermeneutics and the Crisis of Ocularcentrism." *Force Fields: Between History and Cultural Critique*. New York: Routledge. 99–113.

——. 1993b. "From the Empire of the Gaze to the Society of the Spectacle: Foucault and Debord." *Downcast Eyes: The Denigration of Vision in Twentieth-Century French Thought*. Berkeley: University of California Press. 381–434.

Lukács, György. 1971. "Narrate or Describe?" *Writer & Critic, and Other Essays*. Ed. and trans. Arthur D. Kahn. New York: Grosset & Dunlap. 110–48.

Magaldi, Sábato. 1972. *Panorama do teatro brasileiro*. Brasilia: Ministério de Educação e Cultura. Departamento de Assuntos Culturais. Fundação Nacional de Arte. Serviço Nacional de Teatro.

Martins, Luís. 1964. *Noturno da Lapa*. Rio de Janeiro: Editôra Civilização Brasileira.

Marx, Karl. 1962. *Capital*. Trans. Eden and Cedar Paul. 2 vols. London: Dent.

Muricy, Katia. 1988. *A razão cética: Machado de Assis e as questões de seu tempo*. São Paulo: Companhia das Letras.

Paschoal, Rodolfo Treitel. 1997. "A cidade proibida; Madame Satã e outros personagens da Velha Lapa." Diss. Pontifícia Universidade Católica do Rio de Janeiro.

Pereira, Lúcia Miguel. 1988. *História da literatura brasileira: Prosa de ficção, de 1870 a 1920*. Belo Horizonte: Editora Itatiaia; São Paulo: Editora da Universidade de São Paulo.

Prado, Décio de Almeida. 1968. "A evolução da literatura dramática." *A literatura no Brasil*. Vol 6: *Teatro, Conto, Crônica, A nova literatura*. Ed. Afrânio Coutinho. Rio de Janeiro: Editorial Sul Americana. 7–37.

Rocha, Oswaldo Porto. 1995. *A era das demolições; cidade do Rio de Janeiro 1870–1920*. Rio de Janeiro: Departamento Geral de Documentação e Informação Cultural, Secretaria Municipal de Cultura, Divisão de Editoração.

Schwartz, Roberto. 1987. *Qué horas são? ensaios*. São Paulo: Companhia das Letras.

——. 1992. "Brazilian Culture: Nationalism by Elimination." *Misplaced Ideas*. Ed. John Gleason. New York: Verso. 1–18.

Sennett, Richard. 1994. *The Body and the City in Western Civilization*. New York: W.W. Norton.

Sodré, Nelson Werneck. 1992. *O naturalismo no Brasil*. Belo Horizonte: Oficina de Livros.

Süssekind, Flora. 1984. *Tal Brasil, qual romance?: Uma ideologia estética e sua história, o naturalismo*. Rio de Janeiro: Achiamé.

Zola, Émile. 1964. *The Experimental Novel*. Trans. Belle M. Sherman. New York: Haskell House.

INTERNAL BORDERS: CULTURAL CONFLICTS AND STATE DISCOURSE

INTRODUCTION: THE CONFLICT IN TRANSCULTURATION

Alberto Moreiras

Transculturation is the original sin of cultural production in the same sense in which Karl Marx said that primitive accumulation is the original sin of political economy: no capitalism without primitive accumulation; no Latin-American culture without transculturation. Hence, of transculturation we can also say that it is written in the annals of Latin-American history in letters of blood and fire. Transculturation is the very violence of culture, a primitive or originary device of ceaseless separation and expropriation for which no account can properly be given, as it is itself what accounts for any kind of historical account. Transculturation is the reason for cultural reason—at the same time culture's principle of sufficient reason and its abyss; a power within culture superior to culture itself, a force always in excess of itself that interpreters can only ignore at their own risk but with which no adequate coming-to-terms is ever possible. As a map for the understanding of Latin-American symbolic production, whether in literature, thought, or the visual arts—and even in political action—a detailed-enough history of transculturation would be as vast as the territory it would purport to cover. The history of Latin-American transculturation is the history of Latin-American culture—but precisely, not seamlessly, so. The gap between map and territory, between transculturation and culture, cannot be written away. And as with all such gaps, if you stare at it long enough, it will end up staring right back at you.

As the reader will find out in the essays that follow, Fernando Ortiz (1881–1969) invented the term *transculturation* about 1940 in the context of a continent-wide inversion of social Darwinism that had everything to do with the need to develop a new hegemonic ideology to go with the massive sociohistorical shift from neocolonial economies and state formations to dependency development and national-populist articulations. Through Ortiz' materialist approach, the link was made between transculturation and primitive accumulation: transculturation emerges in the Caribbean as a result of the vast machinery of expropriation which is simultaneously cause and effect of the fetishization of tobacco and sugar in Cuban history. And transculturation expropriates, too, as it becomes a commodity in itself, a form of valuation and exchange and a payment against the theft of time. Transculturation happens, says Ortiz, or it has happened and will con-

tinue to happen, and it is in any case, by now, a destiny. Why, then, oppose it? Or, by the same token, why not oppose it? In the name of what, in either case?

The historical task was, around 1940, elsewhere. No notion of cultural purity had ever become state discourse in Latin America, and it was unlikely that any new resistance to transculturation could find cultural or historical productivity. Accordingly, not less but more transculturation was needed, beyond rejecting or endorsing its originary violence, for the sake of communal integration and of the conversion of a mongrel multitude into a people who might then be in a better position to reverse expropriation and arrest their loss of historical time. As transculturation becomes ideology, an ideology of the intellectual class if not a state ideology *tout court*, not opposed to but rather in the wake of the historically previous ideology of national and continental whitening, transculturation also becomes a dream for the productive containment of the social—beyond the state but not beyond history, beyond class but not beyond culture, beyond the nation but not beyond community. The stage was set for the next half-century of literary and critical production—including the necessary reinterpretation of previous history.

Once the concept of transculturation came into its own, it could only stage its productivity not just within but also beyond the particular social and historical conditions that made it a necessity; it became the plane of immanence within which to think the fear and trembling of cultural contact among any and all human groups and historical forces that turned Latin America into what Antonio Cornejo Polar (1936–1997) would later call a contradictory totality. But, with that, the concept itself glimpsed its own disaster. Its absolutization gave it a peculiar transcendence: if transculturation could explain it all, what would explain transculturation itself? This, far from being merely a philosophical question, found its political urgency in the historical terrain. Granted that transculturation was procedure and not foundation, the work of transculturation had to be carefully explicated at every point of its emergence and at all levels of the Latin-American social and political constitution—including intranational levels. But in the name of what? Was it an enterprise of knowledge, or did knowledge carry over into a historical program and a desire for social stasis? Could transculturation survive its own conditions of conceptual production in the national-popular state form? What of transculturation, say, today?

Those are some of the questions that led Wander Melo Miranda, Iris Zavala, and myself to accept our commission from the editors. This was to be an alternative sort of literary history and, in particular, this was to be a history that would attempt to interrogate its own ideological presuppositions. The notion of transculturation was not going to be simply the master concept around which or in subservience to which our contributors would be asked to shape their contributions. Transculturation would itself be the object of theoretical and interpretive speculation, and not in view of some predecided take but precisely without it. At three meetings in Toronto, under the hospitable auspices of Mario and María Elena Valdés and the University of Toronto, we set out a number of guidelines meant to establish a historiographic framework. In retrospect, our editorial guidelines, which would eventually become simply the heading of this Part Two, along with a number of subheadings that follow the history of the Latin American state, from the colonial state ("Lettered Mediations"); to the post-independence state ("People's Communities and Nation Building"), the national-popular state ("The Inversion of Social Darwinism"), and the Latin-American version of the Keynesian or welfare state ("Modernization and the Formation of Cultural Identities"); to the contemporary state form. Our overall purpose would not be an exhaustive drawing of either the strategies or the events of transculturation from 1492 to the present but rather a symptomatic study. This is what we have attempted to do. We had a meeting at Duke University in 1998 in which many of our contributors participated. Some contributions only reached us later, as a result of editorial process. The reader will judge the general effect of this cluster of essays. My own mission in this introduction is not to summarize them all but rather to set the stage for particular readings—or, I should say, to set a stage, one of many possible ones, from a perspective that insists rather tenuously not so much on transculturation as on the infinite problematicity of its force, which is also its richness. I will not give a historical account here, since I leave that for the essays that follow. This introduction will be speculative and theoretical, and it aims at nothing but to provide the beginning of a framework for discussion.

There are two main uses of the word *transculturation*: In a loosely anthropological sense it is a descriptive word for any kind of cultural mixing (some gain, some loss, and some creation are always ingredients in it, as well as some expropriation, some violence, and its compensatory counterparts). And then transculturation also refers to a different use as a critical concept—that is, to an active, self-conscious use of cultural combination as a tool for aesthetic or critical production. In the sense developed by Ángel Rama (1926–1983) from Ortiz's first use, literary transculturation is a "revitalized examination of local traditions, which had become sclerotic, in order to find formulations that would allow for the absorption of external influences. External influences would thus be diluted into larger artistic structures that can still translate the problematics and the peculiar flavors they had continued to preserve" (1982, 207). Transculturation is thus a form of "cultural plasticity," an active receptivity, as it were, that regulates "the incorporation of new elements . . . through the total rearticulation of the regional cultural structure" (208). In

Rama's use, literary transculturation is a form for the promotion of cultural survival undertaken as a reactive response to modernization. As he puts it, it comes to strengthen and co-constitute the contemporary "Latin American literary system, understood as a field of integration and mediation, and with enough leeway for self-regulation" (217).

In Rama's definition, transculturation has come to fulfill a foundational role for contemporary Latin American cultural critique. As a foundational notion, transculturation is and is not a return to Latin-American cultural origins. It is *not* a return because, as Silvia Spitta argues, post-Ortiz transculturators—the kind of people about whom Rama wrote his own book on transculturation—"open the door to a radical rewriting of the tradition" (10). But it *is* a return because once that rewriting is done, it would finally be established that transculturation is indeed at the traumatic source of everything that is literary and not-so-literary in Latin America. In other words, at the teleological end of the transculturating process, its technical, critical, or literary use would revert to its anthropological use, now understood as infinitely accomplished. If the critical insistence on transculturation is meant to counter the colonialist whitening of Latin American culture, against which Ortiz warned, but which he in fact could only continue by other means, the task at hand for transculturation analysts is to radicalize Ortiz's enterprise by reinterpreting and reconstructing the tradition so that the transculturated Latin-American subject can survive within a full, and fully known, representational genealogy. In Rama's work, the political epistemics of transculturation go beyond the description or the incorporation of a given state of affairs into a willed critical interference with its very conditions of possibility. In other words, literary transculturation (and, for that matter, for Rama, transculturation in the extended anthropological sense) is not simply a response to modernization, understood as an "external influence," but it is necessarily also a critical relationship to it. Literary transculturation is oriented transculturation.

Such a critical relationship, however, has some limitations that Rama could not fully see. Transculturation analysts must realize, following the very logic of their practice, that transculturation, as oriented transculturation, is in itself always already transculturated; that transculturation, in their sense, does not name a "natural" or primary fact, but is itself an *engaged* representation; that it does not simply refer to a social relation, but rather is "itself a social relation, linked to the group understandings, status, hierarchies, resistances and conflicts that exist in other spheres of the culture in which it circulates" (Greenblatt 6). As a hermeneutic concept, transculturation is as historically produced as the phenomena it would seek to interpret. To that extent, there is no such thing as a stable or accomplished reinterpretation or reconstruction, or a proper genealogy, of the transculturated subject. The possibility that a full Latin American subject in its complex historicity can emerge or be constituted, even at the level of literary representation, through more or less exhaustive analysis or critique is simply not given—and it would not be given even if we were to replace, as indeed we must, the notion of *a* Latin-American historical subject with a sufficient plurality of them: subject*s*. There is no transparency in transculturation, which means that literary transculturation, as oriented, is simultaneously always beyond control and always outside its function as a technical device for the integration of external influences into an enterprise of cultural preservation and renewal.

Transculturation, as a genealogical critical apparatus for a certain cultural and historical expression, will have extreme difficulty protecting itself from the history it attempts to critique or vanquish (the history of hierarchically differentiated cultural domination) for the sake of the history it attempts to preserve in mediated form (the history of subaltern attempts to temper cultural domination), because both histories, and not just the latter, are simultaneously part of its own constitution: Transculturation cannot step outside of itself so as to establish clear-cut "objective" or disengaged distinctions. As a radical concept, insofar as it is oriented toward a possible restitution, preservation, or renewal of cultural origins and not toward a mere phenomenology of culture, transculturation runs into the theoretical wall that marks its conditions of possibility as heterogeneous with respect to itself; the critical concept of transculturation, paradoxically enough, does not seem to originate in the anthropological concept, but rather in a different, nontransculturated realm of truth: The realm of ideology. There is no critical transculturation without an end or a limit of transculturation, through which the critical concept of transculturation appears as something other than or beyond what it is purported to be. Without its explicit critique, transculturation loses its edge and is good, at best, as a concept for factual analysis.

Although Rama is quite aware of the difference between literary and anthropological transculturation, for him transculturation is still something "to be accomplished" rather than something that simply and ceaselessly happens. In that sense, he thought of José María Arguedas's (1911–1969) work as "a reduced model for transculturation, where one could show and prove the eventuality of its actualization, so that if it was possible in literature it was also possible in the rest of the culture" (1976, 15). All of this, of course, depends upon Rama's notion of transculturation as necessarily successful transculturation, that is, a transculturation where the dominated culture is able to register itself on or inscribe itself into the dominant. That an inscription into the dominant culture as such may be considered to constitute a success (and the noninscription therefore a failure) implies a strong ideological positioning concerning transculturation as an everyday anthropological phenomenon; in fact, it ultimately implies the acceptance of modernization as ideological truth and world destiny. For Rama, therefore, and not only for Rama, transculturation is always excessive with respect to itself, and it always already incorporates a certain goal. Such a goal may or may not be shared by other subjects of transculturation, who may have different goals or may be blind to their goals or may not have a goal. But if they do not have a goal, they are not transculturators in the critical sense, only in the anthropological sense.

On the one hand, in Rama's determination, which is generally shared by his critical generation, the end of critical transculturation must be understood as a historical self-subjecting to Eurocentric modernity. This does not happen counterintentionally, but is rather part and parcel of the relatively unexamined ideology of modernization that most Latin American intellectuals endorsed from pre-Independence days to very recent times. On the other hand, that same end of transculturation can also be understood as an opening toward an aporetics of meaning. Once the second sense is realized, however, transculturation comes to the end of itself and must mutate into alternative forms of confronting the materiality of history and its cultural precipitate. As oriented, in other words, transculturation necessarily reaches a final de-orientation. But only the de-oriented use of transculturation has the potential of being put to use for a critique of the present—whereas its oriented use falls right into its ideological articulations. This split within the concept—namely, its ability to function simultaneously as a tool of ideology and of ideology critique, as a constituted as well as constituent force, as construction and deconstruction—is rehearsed in multiple ways in the essays that follow. There can be no such thing as a blanket negation of the critical potentiality of the concept—and with this, we follow tradition. By the same token, however, there can be no enthusiastic endorsement of its tremendous plasticity without paying attention to its limits, where, in a sense, everything is decided—and with this, we follow tradition too. The conflict in transculturation is critically more important than transculturation itself—but then, transculturation is nothing but conflict.

In his foreword to the English translation of Néstor García Canclini's *Culturas híbridas*, Renato Rosaldo remarks about the critical concept of cultural hybridity that there is always a conceptual polarity involved in it: "Hybridity can imply a space betwixt and between two zones of purity in a manner that follows biological usage that distinguishes two discrete species and the hybrid pseudospecies that results from their combination. . . . [H]ybridity can [also] be understood as the ongoing condition of all human cultures, which contain no zones of purity because they undergo continuous processes of transculturation" (xv). The concept of transculturation is naturally entangled in the same unresolved and ultimately unresolvable polarity. The militant or critical version of literary transculturation must posit both a (utopian) zero-degree and a full-degree of transculturation, a point of origin and a goal, which are always and equally unreachable, but without which transculturation would find itself deprived of a teleological reason for its own practice. The phenomenological usage of transculturation, on the other hand, can survive safely within the second term of the polarity, which ultimately makes it redundant or merely tautological, in the sense that if everything were transculturation, then the concept itself would seem to have no particular critical validity. The conditions of possibility of critical transculturation, to the very extent that they refer back to or ground themselves in the anthropological notion as their natural ground, are therefore aporetic; the critical concept is only made possible by the invocation of a reason for transculturation that is itself beyond the reach of transculturation: Transculturation is always already transculturated. The way out of the aporetic conflict is of course always pragmatic: The end of every transculturating practice or analysis determines in every case its specific relevance as a hermeneutic tool. But that is no excuse to stop reflecting on the theoretical difficulty.

In Spitta's definition, "[t]he transculturated subject is someone who, like [José María] Arguedas, is consciously or unconsciously situated between at least two worlds, two cultures, two languages, and two definitions of subjectivity, and who constantly mediates between them all" (24). Transculturation would then organize that "ambivalent and indeterminate space" (24) where the transculturating artist or critic would be free to give herself over to the task of, in Rama's words, "recomposing from [previous cultural] material a superior discourse that could match or confront the most hierarchic products of a universal literature" (1982, 228). Perhaps our historical times, different from Rama's, no longer advise or enable us to be so relentlessly upbeat in the evaluation of the cultural power of the world's semiperiphery—at least not in the sense invoked by Rama. The celebratory or heroic telos of oriented transculturation would not be able to respond to a rather simple question: What if that indeterminate space of betweenness should prove to be, not the purveyor of a new historical coherence, but rather a mestizo space of incoherence? In the definition of Claudio Lomnitz-Adler, "Mestizaje is the process wherein communities are extracted from their cultures of origin without being assimilated into the dominant culture. This is a process that entails fracturing the coherence of a subordinate . . . culture. It also entails undermining the conditions for the creation of a new, independent, coherent culture" (39). Hasn't transculturation theory assumed for too long that meaning is always already available, always already to be either found or produced? Such an insistence comes at the price of a certain foreclosure. What if transculturation were shown to be not a path to meaning, but rather a path into the implosion of meaning? In other words, what if a given transculturating practice turned toward the site of its impossibility and not toward its possibility? Rama preferred to dwell on an optimistic or celebratory possibility, understanding the end of transculturation as the "ample overcoming of modernization" from a Latin-American or regional perspective (1982, 215), and perhaps that is what he had to do. It may now be time to examine an alternative side.

Dreams have a tendency to turn into nightmares—the night need be only long enough. Let us imagine a situation in which militant transculturation succeeds totally. What would accomplished transculturation in fact accomplish? The political parameters of transculturation in modernity have been defined by the space obtaining between nature and the state. The originary or primitive violence of transculturating expropriation is the violence of absolute sovereignty and relentless domination for which the state, as Leviathan, is already merely a cipher and a substitute formation: The domination of the sovereign over nature as standing reserve, as total availability. In his *Brevísima relación de la destrucción de las Indias,* Bartolomé de Las Casas (1474–1566) asks Prince Philip to bring to an end the savage extraction of capital from the Indies on the basis of the need to preserve the integrity of the imperial *dominium*. It is a question, says Las Casas, of avoiding destruction, since destruction will damage the empire. Las Casas denounced the ongoing historical process as precisely the wrong kind of primitive accumulation—much better to christianize the Indians, to show a Christian attitude toward them, and that way they will be persuaded to cooperate; the work of transculturation would have started. Las Casas's politics met with relative success, and the massacres stopped or diminished. Primitive accumulation, from the initial to the second phase of the Conquest, went from being understood as the brutal and indiscriminate extraction of gold, silver, pearls, and precious stones to the perception that the very Indians being wasted in the mining endeavors could become profitable labor. The separation of the producer from the means of production went from outright murderous abuse to the kind of tributary slavery disguised as *mitas, repartimientos,* and other kinds of labor exploitation. This second phase of the Conquest initiates transculturation proper, in the sense that with it, the conditions are created for the inhabitants of the New World to participate in their own domination. From the absolute separation implied in the radical expropriation of land and life, a relative separation ensued, based upon the constant threat of reversion. Transculturation starts in the operationalization of empire: In order for empire to function, subjects must be created rather than erased. If that is the case, is a throughly accomplished transculturation anything but the most proper success of imperial reason itself?

The moment when the New World natives were led to admit that Lascasian politics—or what comes to the same, the politics given force of law in the 1542–1543 *Leyes nuevas* and other royal measures, were no doubt absolutely better than the practices of the cruel tyrants Alvarado or Pedrarias Dávila, that is the moment when imperial reason starts to become hegemonic reason; reasonable reason, post-terror reason. Reason after terror, but reason based upon terror: Without the original terror, primitive accumulation would never have gone into its second stage and transculturation proper would not have commenced. Las Casas would never have converted a single native. The *imperium* as the realm of the *verum* could never have come into its own. From the necessary but impossible thought of primitive accumulation as the ground of ground, the history of colonial conflict cannot be understood as the history of a hegemony formation. Rather, the history of every process of hegemony is always already the history of a forgetting: Hegemony is always the forgetting of primitive accumulation, the original sin of political economy. And then what about the state, every state, insofar as every state is necessarily founded upon colonial territorialization, territorial reason, imperial reason—insofar as every state reproduces itself through internal colonialism? The history of the state in Latin America, whatever else it may also be, is the history of an ongoing colonialism of transculturation that we can perhaps identify as the politico-cultural translation of primitive accumulation in its myriad varieties. Undoing the translation is tropology in reverse, and it is always necessarily allegorical in that it refers to the unthinkable of terror as originary expropriation. Transculturation always incorporates the memory of this unrecordable terror.

But even before Las Casas wrote his memorial to the Prince, the process of transculturation as a cultural politics of empire had started. "I have been bitten," says Gonzalo Fernández de Oviedo (1478–1557) in the chapter he devotes to Central American vampires in *Sumario de la natural historia de las Indias* (113). If *Sumario* is, as it could be argued, an address to the Emperor Charles aiming, among other things, to warn him tenuously of the dangers in the modality of primitive accumulation the Spaniards had been practicing in the New World during the first phase of the Conquest, then the chapter on vampires has a sinister ironic function. The Captain's narrative can be understood as a synecdoche of the totality of the work if we allow that *Sumario* is entirely invested in the promotion of a new relationship to the conquered land and in the consolidation of a colonial process based upon exploitive devices alternative to the ones that were initially carried out.

Fernández de Oviedo's great antagonist or specular figure and nemesis was Pedrarias Dávila, Governor of Darién, with whom Oviedo traveled to the Indies on 4 April 1514, and under whom he served as Lieutenant Governor. Oviedo would later repeatedly denounce him before the imperial court. With regard to "Pedrarias Dávila, instigator of an assassination attempt against our Captain, which he miraculously survived, Las Casas says that he was an 'infelicitous governor, most cruel tyrant, . . . instrument of divine wrath,' who depopulated and killed great lands and realms, throwing an immense amount of their people to hell" (Fernández de Oviedo 95). Pedrarias Dávila's strategy of primitive accumulation can no doubt be defined as vampiric, as it is told *in nuce* by Las Casas in the following anecdote:

> Upon a cacique or lord giving them [Pedrarias's people], both of his own will and through fear (as it is more truthful), nine thousand Castillian pesos, not content with this, they arrested the said lord and they tied him to a pole sat upon the ground, and his feet stretched out, they gave them fire so that he would give more gold, and the lord sent to his home and they fetched another three thousand *castellanos*. They went back to give him torments, and the lord, not giving more gold as he did not have it, or because he did not want to give it, was held in that guise until the bone marrow came out of his soles, and thus he died.
> (Fernández de Oviedo 98)

But Oviedo himself was not above such exploits. Thus he tells the Emperor how, since 1514, he served in Tierra-Firme as a "supervisor of the gold works and a supervisor of mines . . ., and for this reason I have seen very well how gold comes to be extracted . . . and I have had gold extracted for me with my Indians and slaves" (161). In any case, in 1525, Oviedo writes his *Sumario* in order to "bring to the royal memory" (47) the need for an alternative relation to the conquered land that can be ciphered under the word *perseverar* [to persevere]. Oviedo criticizes those "young men," "friends of novelty," who would refuse, for instance, to settle the already depopulated Hispaniola "because since other new lands have been discovered and are discovered every day, it seems to them that in those lands they can fill up their bags all the sooner" (54). But some, says Oviedo, are now starting to think about "persevering in the land" (54), that is, about "sowing wheat and planting vineyards" (55)–hence, literally, about transcultivating and transculturating. It is to these that Oviedo dedicates the most important work of his life, that is, his great *Historia general y natural de las Indias,* in which the description of the American flora and fauna is set at the service of a presentation of the New World as a standing reserve, that is, the New World as naturally available to long-term Christian exploitation. Thus Oviedo criticizes those who:

> their consciences and the fear of human and divine justice deferred, have done things, not of men, but of dragons and of infidels, for without observing or having any kind of human respect, they have been the cause that many Indians who could have been converted and saved died in diverse forms and manners, and in case those who so died had not converted, they could still have been useful, living, for the service of your majesty, and for the profit and utility of the Christians, and some parts of this land would not have been totally depopulated, that for this reason are almost void of people, and those who have been the cause of this damage call pacified what is depopulated, and I, rather than pacific, call it destroyed. (81–82)

The natives are here understood as pure labor, that is, as human capital at the service of the enrichment of Caesar Charles's *monarchia universalis*. Oviedo will praise the new laws and regulations, such as the establishment of the Council of Indies in 1525, meant to amend errors leading into genocide and depopulation and to set things in such a way that the kingdoms of Spain could be "very enriched and increased by means of that land, since God made it so very rich, and God kept it hidden for you since He formed it, in order to make your majesty the universal and only monarch in the world" (82). In his "Conclusion," Oviedo will lament that the gold that goes from the Indies to Spain is only good to make other

European nations richer: "The witnesses are those doubly minted *ducados* that your majesty throws around the world, and that come out of these realms but never return to them" (177). Oviedo's recommended form of primitive accumulation, based upon a systematic exploitation of natural resources, to describe which he writes his major opus, can be understood as an alternative and apotropaic form of vampirism– a vampirism meant to stem the excessive flow of gold and blood, and one for which *Sumario*'s Chapter 35, entitled "Bats," gives us a splendid tropology. In "Bats," primitive accumulation is subjected to an apotropaic conversion by means of which terror is naturalized as hegemony and destruction becomes transculturation. The background is given in Chapter 10, "On the Tierra-Firme Indians," in which Oviedo remarks that the Indians, who are "in continuous conversation and dealings with the devil" (80–81), have come to give the Spaniards a nickname, "*tuyra,* for they call the devil thus" (81). The Spaniards are placed in the position of that to which the Indians "make sacrifices in many places of blood and human life" (81).

Pedrarias Dávila's 1514 Darién expedition was meant to relieve the Adelantado of the Southern Seas, Vasco Núñez de Balboa. Fernández de Oviedo tells us that the Darién vampires had been wreaking havoc among Núñez de Balboa's men: for they were very dangerous to the Christians . . . when Darién was won, because, since the easy and safe remedy against the bat's bite was not known then, some Christians died then, and others were in danger of dying, until it was found out from the Indians how to cure someone who had been bitten by them" (112). The danger of the vampire's bite consisted not only of the anticlotting quality in its saliva, which induced a considerable loss of blood, but also of the more alarming fact that "if they bite one man among one hundred one night, the following night, and the next, the bat does not bite but the one it had already bitten, even if he is among many other men" (112). The sucking quality of the bat is brutally persistent and persevering–perhaps only comparable to that of the men under the command of Pedrarias Dávila in relation to the Tierra-Firme gold, or even to capital itself: "Capital is dead labour which, vampire-like, lives only by sucking living labour, and lives the more, the more labour it sucks" (Marx 1:342).

The application of fire to the feet, popular in Spain in the early sixteenth century through the practices of the Holy Office of the Inquisition, was a choice tool of the Spaniards for their operations of accumulation. Just as the poor cacique would lose his bone marrow to fire before being killed in the Spanish sacrifice, so the Spaniards would lose the blood that was accumulated by the extracting bat–until a remedy is found in cauterization, through fire itself, or through boiling water. Fire plays here a role directly opposite to the one it played in Spanish accumulation. Whereas fire was used as a gold-extracting device by the Spaniards against the Indians, the Indians thought the Spaniards to use it as an instrument that prevents blood accumulation by the vampires: not an extracting but a preserving function, then, learned from the Indians, taken from them.

"I have been bitten." The modern reader cannot avoid thinking that the one speaking to the Emperor has therefore become a blood-extracting vampire and *tuyra* devil who has come to live off the "sacrifices . . . of blood and human life" involving the Indians. Oviedo, however, tells us that he was cured of the vampiric process through the boiling-water remedy. Having learned from the Indians how to rid himself of his bloodletting and loss of substance, he then proceeds to set the remedy at the service of a mimetic project of appropriation and of incorporation of his new domain's natural resources. Just after the sentence "I have been bitten, and I have been cured through water," he rather uncannily says, "There are other bats in the island of San Juan, and they are eaten, and they are very fat, and in very hot water they are easily skinned, and they come to resemble the little birds that are skewered and roasted in Spain, and they are very white and very fat and of a very good taste, according to the Indians, and even according to some Christians who also eat them, especially those who are fond of trying whatever they see others do" (113). As Christian transculturation is thus accomplished, the model is set for a general economy of transculturating practices.

The politico-rhetorical figure of apotrope refers to a defense mechanism that consists of the appropriation and incorporation of a small part of that against which one wants to defend oneself precisely in order to defend oneself against the totality from which that small part is taken. Fernández de Oviedo's apotropaic appropriation is complex. In the first place, the Indians use fire as a cauterizing device to defend themselves from the terminal bloodletting caused by the "round little morcels of flesh" that vampires eat (112). Thus, a smaller pain prevents a greater evil. The same remedy that is used by the Captain not to die bloodless–boiling water, water subjected to the principle of fire–will also be used by him and his people to imitate "what they see others do": that is, to eat the vampires, in order to establish a relationship to the New World that places the latter in the position of a standing reserve, apt for a mimetic conquest and appropriation of natural resources. Against Pedrarias Dávila's or Núñez de Balboa's depopulating vampirism, Oviedo will suggest a type of colonization based upon progressive digestion: Eat something, we could say, in order not to eat everything. This is of course consistent with his recommendation to "persevere in the land" and with the general outlook of his memorial to the Emperor. It gives us a model of imperial reason that will become dominant in the New World in the second phase of the Conquest: from the dominance of terror to the terror of hegemony. Oviedo shares it with Las Casas; both write their work in order to request the mediating intervention of the imperial state so that early primitive accumulation can be controlled and the destruction of the Indies avoided. This destruction was foreseeable not only in 1542, when Las Casas handed over his *Brevísima relación* to Prince Philip, but already in 1525, when Oviedo wrote his *Sumario*. The latter, through his uncanny story of Tierra-Firme bats, succeeds in symbolically turning the page of primitive accumulation, which is, according to Marx, "written in the annals of humankind in letters of blood and fire" (875). It is still blood and fire for Fernández de Oviedo, but now apotropaically controlled, mimetically attuned, and put at the service of a more perfect exploitation of the imperial *dominium*. Imperial reason has started to produce itself as its own critique. It has now become transculturation as imperial enterprise.

For centuries the process developed, and it continues to develop as well as to be resisted. The essays in this section will tell you about some important segments of that story as it affects the history of Latin-American letters. These essays are written from today's perspective. Can transculturation today do anything but at most contest hegemonic thinking or react

to it? Isn't transculturation originally and structurally bound by the impossibility of offering itself as an alternative to hegemonic thinking, in the radical sense of a thinking whose political directive is not an integration into any kind of hegemonic articulation–a thinking otherwise from hegemony, a nonhegemonic thinking? Transculturation, as oriented transculturation–that is, as a critical praxis–is a praxis of thought of which both the conditions and the horizon of possibility are determined by both historical and situational consciousness. It is, moreover, a thinking of situational consciousness that remains radically open to transnational influences and articulations. It maintains that it can establish fundamental distinctions between kinds of cultural hybridity, that is, that it can elaborate something like a typology of the cultural hybrid–as well as, of course, of the nonhybrid wherever it exists–by mapping historico-situational consciousness onto it. It is a sort of cognitive mapping that conceives of itself as the force behind the necessary drawing of a gigantic grid, tendentially coincidental both in time and space with the history of the planet Earth, upon which ideologies can be traced as exhaustively definable in terms of their relational position. In other words, it is a thinking of translation and of the difficulties of translation, a thinking for which translation is all there is, in the sense that, within its parameters, nothing is recognized beyond translation–whether from the subject to community, from community to the subject, from subject to subject, or from one community to another following the pertinent vectors of force. It is a communicational thinking of culture, in the strong sense in which it could be said that no thinking exists outside culture and that culture, as communication, exhaustively defines thinking without remainder. As thinking of/in the ruins of the local, it is translational or translative because it vindicates the trace of either subjugated culture and subjugated identity or of dominant culture and dominant identity in any given thought formation. Correspondingly, it succeeds in mobilizing the ideological analysis of thought and of all cultural production as geopolitical analysis in terms of the dominant-versus-subjugated binary. And it sides with the subjugated every time it must choose because the dominant always already enjoys a regime of visibility. To ensure the visibility of the nonvisible, or the thinkability of the nonthinkable, is always already to rehearse the binary dominant/subjugated in favor of the latter. The thinking of transculturation, even there where it is practically indistinguishable from imperial reason, is subalternist thinking, because nothing but attention to the nondominant can begin to account exhaustively for historico-situational consciousness in a world perspective. It is, after all, in the interest of empire that its subjects cooperate in the task of their own domination. Empire is always a subalternist.

But through this provisional definition, which the following essays will amply supplement, we can perhaps initiate a critique. For a thinking of transculturation, it is always a matter of vindicating the sheer (utopian) possibility of a retrieval of what Walter Benjamin would have called "pure language" by means of the labor of translation–understanding translation as the infinite opening to history. If history is, among other things, the story of power and resistance, then transculturational thinking undertakes to retrieve the historicity of resistance as itself a form of power. We could alternatively describe this by repeating that transculturational thinking is already a thinking of expropriation, of history's expropriation, and of the expropriation of the thinker as well. The labor of translation undertakes to liberate what the late Julio

Cortázar (1914–1984) would have referred to as a sort of intersemiotic ghost: If the ghost is precisely that which can never leave the place of erstwhile dwelling, the rooted trace of history, then the thinker of transculturation is the thinker for whom what remains at stake is precisely what remains. And what remains can only be found, through translative digging, at the very crossing of intersemiotic systems–for instance, at the crossing of colonial discourse and subaltern negation. But translation is never simply a procedure. The minute translation comes to its own end–that is, the minute the labor of translation transmutes into a result, fulfilling its structural goal–is also the minute when translational thinking abandons its vocation as a ruinous thinking, a thinking of the ruins of thinking, and becomes ruined thinking. When expropriation turns into property, there is no place left for the intersemiotic ghost, who chokes and must return to the underground. A fulfilled translation cancels the crossing at the cost of the structural conversion of subaltern negation into colonial discourse. A fulfilled translation, a work of appropriation, is always necessarily colonial discourse. It can alter hegemony only at the price of reconstituting it, because recognition is all it seeks.

The maximum accomplishment of the translational thinking of transculturation is also its total defeat: an adequate integration into the circuits of conformity, when all further translation becomes unnecessary, when language no longer exists as such. If it is necessary to translate so that what is alien does not expropriate us, and if it is necessary to translate so that what is ours does not kill us, it is also crucial to understand that translation is not the final horizon of thinking and that transculturation cannot be the ultimate goal of cultural affirmation. An untranslative excess, then, must mark cultural reflection as its last condition of critical existence. Jorge Luis Borges (1899–1986) already understood all of this when, around the same years in which Fernando Ortiz conceived his own theory of transculturation as material constraint, he wrote "The Lottery in Babylon" (1941).

In that short story, Borges interprets the Keynesian state, which in Latin America, as elsewhere, is a direct result of the 1929 Black Thursday. As Tulio Halperín Donghi puts it, "[after 1929] national states were . . . the only economic entities rugged enough to navigate in such high seas . . . and Latin-American states began to exercise functions and adopt techniques unimaginable only a few years before. . . . The multiplication of state functions signaled a total abandonment of the laissez-faire principles that had guided neocolonial economic policy. Awareness of the emergency was so widespread that . . . none disputed the expansion of state power per se" (209–10). The state that started its new life after 1929 is the planning state, whose most acute phase was in Argentina the Peronist national-populist state, and which would only find its final collapse during the debt crisis of 1982. Borges, in his short story, radicalizes historical phenomena into a proleptic understanding of what was, for him, the postcontemporary: the passage from the interventionist state into the state of control as the teleological truth of the modern state. Its Latin-American contemporary manifestation, euphemistically called "neoliberal," has meant, among other things, a drastically accelerated pull toward globalization, whereby the Latin-American dependency upon transnational corporations increases exponentially. In late-capitalist times, the Latin-American states become subsidiaries of a perhaps nonexistent, but nevertheless effective transnational state apparatus whose function is merely to ensure the ceaseless reproduction of labor power through and for "functional integration between internationally dispersed activities" (Gereffi and Hempel 19). The spectral transnational state of flexible accumulation replaces the national-popular state and its old legitimacies. What obtains is a new social regime "of perpetual metastability" based upon the market as final mechanism of control (Deleuze 4). The Borgesian notion of the lottery in its last stage, there where it comes up against the limit of its own nonexistence (when the lottery no longer really matters, for its effects are all-pervasive already), is an allegory of perpetual social metastasis (what neoliberal theoreticians call simply "the market") as a regime of total social control.

"The Lottery in Babylon" is the account given to us by an obscure narrator (who happens to find himself temporarily outside Babylon) of a very peculiar state institution and its history: the lottery, in its Babylonian form. The narrator tells us early on that in Babylon "the Lottery is a major element of reality" (Borges 1999, 101). How it has come to be such a principal part of reality is his topic–a topic, by the way, that the logic of the story leads us to believe has been given to him by the lottery system itself, a result of its hazardous but rigorous prize distribution. The lottery develops historically from a game sponsored by a private corporation–the narrator calls it "the Company" (102)–to the total administration of experience by the "shadowy corporation" (106). If at its historical beginning the lottery is an institution of civil society dependent upon market mechanisms, by the end the very notion of civil society has become impossible and unsustainable because the lottery has merged with life to the point where they are experientially undistinguishable: The results of the lottery affect or determine every facet of human and even cosmic events. The lottery, at the end of its evolution, has become such a "major element of reality" that it is in fact the primary mechanism of the real. At the end of the story, the narrator hints that it is undecidable whether the lottery should be considered the primary mechanism of the real or, on the contrary, the real as primary mechanism: "It makes no difference whether one affirms or denies the reality of the shadowy corporation, because Babylon is nothing but an infinite game of chance" (106).

Since the very writing of the story could (or could not) be a result of the lottery itself, the truth of this statement is infinitely suspended. The very statement already suspends historical truth, but that suspension is itself suspended, in double undecidability. The reader is called forth to make a preliminary ideological judgment, faced with at least three options: (1) The lottery exists, and the narrator is its unwitting servant; (2) the lottery no longer exists, but the narrator is unable to decide upon its nonexistence; or (3) the lottery exists, and the narrator is willingly mystifying us. The real choice for the reader is not to decide in favor of one of them or in favor of their negations. The reader must instead enter an alternative order of decision that the first (and false) choice at the same time announces and introduces: if the truth of the narrator's statement is infinitely postponed and can never be ascertained, then it is up to the reader to let himself remain caught in perpetual entanglement or else to break free and refuse the very terms of the question. The latter requires, as it is usually the case in Borges, a complicated act of metacritical analysis in which the text's general theoretical perspective finds itself at stake.

Right at the point in Babylonian history at which the pressure of the people clamoring for equality succeeds in imposing "a *novus ordo seclorum*, a necessary stage of history," "the Company" is asked to assume "all public power" and becomes the state or its substitute (103): "The fair and reasonable desire that all men and women, rich and poor, be able to take part equally in the Lottery inspired indignant demonstrations–the memory of which, time has failed to dim. Some stubborn souls could not (or pretended they could not) understand that this was a *novus ordo seclorum*, a necessary stage of history. . . . There were disturbances, there were regrettable instances of bloodshed, but the masses of Babylon at last, over the opposition of the well-to-do, imposed 'their will; they saw their generous objectives fully achieved. . . . [T]he Company was forced to assume all public power" (103). "A new order," that populist triumph, an accomplished national-popular integration operated by the Company at the apparent prompting of the multitude, is then the remote beginning of the society of control. The state, which is in principle nothing but the corporation running the lottery, keeps its extraordinary expansion (constantly necessary to keep the lottery running ever more smoothly and consistently) until a moment is reached where every human act happens as a function of state power. Transculturation, that is–now understood by Borges, following state logic, as the absolute conversion of life into administration–has now reached full immanence. It is then that the narrator affirms that the total and real subsumption of life into the state form has been accomplished, perhaps in order to claim further that such an accomplishment also marks the point at which the state form becomes subsumed into the total reality of life. A dialectical inversion has taken place: The planning state has metamorphosed into its own spectrum in order to better saturate the field of the real, which is now equivalent to the spectral. Proleptic anticipation is thus accomplished in Borges's text: The society of control, our present, is announced in the 1941 text as a teleological consequence of the development of the state apparatus from its national-popular configuration. Transculturation is here subjected to an extreme critique.

But Borges also offers a solution, beyond transculturation, to the conflict in transculturation. His ironic disengagement, or the narrator's stated "indifference," does not hide but in fact reveals the all-determinant difference; the passage from an interventionist lottery to a total lottery is also a passage into the total domination of the human, and it is, epistemologically, a passage from history into its reification as ontology. "To affirm or deny the reality of the shadowy corporation" is precisely not indifferent, because it makes all the difference. "To affirm" means to opt for history and to keep open the difference between knowledge and experiential consciousness; "to deny" means to opt for the reification of history and to collapse knowledge into experience. Granted that "Babylon is nothing but an infinite game of chance," everything depends upon deciding that the game of chance is fated to occur through ultimately human determination because it is orchestrated by the state form as a site of power, or that such human determination is or becomes nature itself and as such it cannot be alternatively imagined. The very notion of historical freedom is at stake in the metacritical decision that the narrator paradoxically offers to us by claiming that there is no decision to be made or that the decision is indifferent. What is at stake, in other words, is the theoretical possibility of an outside to ideology or, as Louis Althusser would put it in his autobiography, "how to escape the circle while remaining within it" (319)–in the story's terms, "how to escape the lottery while remaining

within it," or if you want, how to escape the state of control while remaining within it. The text's historical-critical consciousness thus depends upon the possible form or forms of responding to the question it embodies.

It is naturally only the theoretical possibility of an escape that will leave open the possibility of historical change, and the final destruction of what we understand, through this reading, to be the late-capitalist mode of production under the allegory of total state lottery (only a future possibility for Borges in 1941). If the lottery exists, then to understand it as a contingent and not as a necessary historical fact is fundamental. But even if the lottery no longer exists, realizing that such is the case is what matters. Is "The Lottery in Babylon," as a total textual act, meant to contribute to the reproduction of state power, by now thoroughly linked to capitalist exploitation, by ideologically sustaining it through either submission to it or through its naturalization as equivalent to life itself? Or is it, on the contrary, a way of opening into the subjectless process of history, into the outside of interpellation by the lottery apparatus, into a rupture of the order of the signifier, and into a beyond of transculturation? The narrator of "The Lottery in Babylon" tells us a monstrous story, monstrous because it encompasses all stories to the same extent that it kills them all, by voiding them of autonomy. If the lottery orders and determines every human event, every story is simply *that* story and no alternative perspective can ever be developed. The total administration of life through an infinite and unceasing lottery means that life is thoroughly denarrativized, because it responds in every one of its moments to an order issuing from above, from state power in its guise as the absolute administrator of thoroughly universalized capital. Leviathan has absolutely coopted culture as life. From the perspective of the total lottery, life is always already heteronomous, nothing but an infinite game of chance–and, therefore, a realm of absolute compulsion. But there is an alternative perspective. Paradoxically but inevitably, the thorough denarrativization of life as the ideological apotheosis of the global lottery returns us to an alternative possibility of understanding. The final closure of the story–that is, the successful allegorization of social totality as always already alienated, always already disappropriated–"redirects," in words that Fredric Jameson applies to a different context, "our attention toward history itself and the variety of alternative situations it offers" (Jameson 288). There is certainly, in Borges's text, no affirmation of human autonomy; there is only, through the metacritical dimension of the text, a loosening up of radical heteronomy, which is, to an extent, also a (nonhumanist) affirmation of the human potential for freedom. "The ignorant assume that infinite drawings require infinite time; actually, all that is required is that time be infinitely subdivisible, as in the famous parable of the Race with the Tortoise" (Borges 1999, 105). In another text on the Greek paradox, Borges says: "We (the undivided divinity that operates in us) have dreamed the world. We have dreamed it resistant, mysterious, visible, ubiquitous in space and firm in time; but in its architecture we have allowed tenuous and eternal interstices of unreason in order to know that it is false" (Borges 1980, 204). Such falsities destroy ontology. Through the destruction of ontology, history returns, and with it historical consciousness.

A militant concept of transculturation, first developed by Ortiz, adopted and developed by Rama, and embraced by successive generations of Latin-American(ist) critics and cultural producers (it is a dominant ideologeme in the Latin

American boom novel, for instance), showed its main historical productivity, as several of the contributions that follow will establish, in the context of the national-populist integration that was a state project for a good part of the Latin-American twentieth century. It was an attempt at reaching social closure in the cultural realm. But present times are different, and the contemporary distribution of power in the world economy no longer calls for strong state arbitration in the semiperiphery of the world system. Hybridity has now come to substitute for transculturation as the master concept of cultural analysis. It is genealogically linked to the historically antecedent notions of transculturation and heterogeneity. Heterogeneity, a concept developed by Antonio Cornejo Polar in the 1970s in a double relationship of antagonism and supplementarity with transculturation, had as its main strategic function to insist upon a critique of the national-popular ideology as it was already coming undone through its very failure to accomplish the intended national integration. It signaled the fact that, from the point of view of what was heterogeneous to the dominant social articulation (for instance, indigenous identities), transculturation was a powerfully threatening instrument of social subordination, not of redemption. The Latin-American-dominant state formation starts to change in a major way after the public debt crisis of 1982, which is not just concomitant with real changes in the structure of world capitalism but is also partially caused by them. Hybridity as a master concept for Latin-American social thought develops in the late 1980s in the work of Néstor García Canclini as the epistemological anchor for a cultural politics that could control or adjust to a number of epiphenomena derived from the then emergent neoliberal state formations, and it is co-constituted through a multiplicity of trans-state processes that the new configuration of capital–finance capitalism–made unavoidable.

Hybridity, in the influential work of García Canclini and many others, refers first of all to the impossibility of identitarian closure in the social or national sphere. Its political force is presented as the basis for a new counterhegemonic articulation–the very possibility of a new chain of equivalences where democratic struggles undertaken from various loci of enunciation articulate with one another until they constitute the basis of a new "popular front," as well as for cultural practices associated with it. Hybridity would open up the very possibility of new alliances that would then be constitutive of an antiracist, antisexist, antinationalist, antielitist change in late-capitalist hegemonic articulations. We should not dismiss such political promises. But is it possible that hybridity, far from being the unsuturing of the neoliberal closure, can be precisely understood as a militant concept, as the particular historical form of neoliberal suture? What if neoliberalism wanted to have nothing to do with ideologies of social purity and had always already embraced a radical form of transnational transculturation as its own cultural politics? The question is significant enough for us to keep in mind just as we embark on a passage through practices of cultural translation in Latin American letters.

Works Cited

Althusser, Louis. 1993. *The Future Lasts Forever: A Memoir.* Trans. Richard Veasey. New York: New Press.

Benjamin, Walter. 1968. "The Task of the Translator." *Illuminations. Essays and Reflections.* Ed. Hanna Arendt. Trans. Harry Zohn. New York: Schocken. 69–82.

Borges, Jorge Luis. 1980. "Avatares de la tortuga." *Prosa completa.* Barcelona: Bruguera. 1:199–204.

——. 1999. "The Lottery in Babylon." *Collected Fictions.* Trans. Andrew Hurley. New York: Penguin. 101–06.

Cornejo Polar, Antonio. 1994. *Escribir en el aire: ensayo sobre la heterogeneidad socio-cultural en las literaturas andinas.* Lima: Editorial Horizonte.

Cortázar, Julio. 1984. "Apocalipsis de Solentiname." *Nicaragua tan violentamente dulce.* Buenos Aires: Muchnik. 18–24.

Deleuze, Gilles. 1992. "Postscript on the Societies of Control." *October* 59: 3–7.

Fernández de Oviedo, Gonzalo. 1986. *Sumario de la natural historia de las Indias.* Ed. Manuel Ballesteros. Madrid: Historia 16.

Gereffi, Gary and Lynn Hempel. 1996. "Latin America in the Global Economy: Running Faster to Stay in Place." *NACLA Report on the Americas* 29.4:18–27.

Greenblatt, Stephen. 1991. *Marvelous Possessions: The Wonder of the New World.* Chicago: University of Chicago Press.

Jameson, Fredric. 1997. *Postmodernism, or, The Cultural Logic of Late Capitalism.* Durham: Duke University Press.

Halperín Dongui, Tulio. 1993. *The Contemporary History of Latin America.* Trans. John Chasteen. Durham: Duke University Press.

Las Casas, Bartolomé de. 1987. *Brevísima relación de la destrucción de las Indias.* Ed. André Saint-Lu. Madrid: Cátedra.

Lomnitz-Adler, Claudio. 1992. *Exits from the Labyrinth: Culture and Ideology in the Mexican National Space.* Berkeley: University of California Press.

Marx, Karl. 1977. *Capital: A Critique of Political Economy.* Vol 1. Trans. Ben Fowkes. New York: Vintage.

Ortiz, Fernando. 1987. *Contrapunteo cubano del tabaco y el azúcar.* Caracas: Biblioteca Ayacucho.

Rama, Ángel. 1976. "José María Arguedas transculturador." *Señores e indios: acerca de la cultura quechua.* By José María Arguedas. Montevideo: Arca. 7–40.

——. 1982. "Los procesos de transculturación en la narrativa latinoamericana." *La novela en América Latina. Panoramas 1920–1980.* Veracruz: Universidad Veracruzana/Fundación Angel Rama. 203–33.

Rosaldo, Renato. 1995. "Foreword." *Hybrid Cultures: Strategies for Entering and Leaving Modernity.* By Néstor García Canclini. Trans. Christopher Chiappari and Silvia L. López. Minneapolis: University of Minnesota Press. xi–xxi.

Spitta, Silvia. 1995. *Between Two Waters: Narratives of Transculturation in Latin America.* Houston: Rice University Press.

CHAPTER 9

DOCUMENTS OF THE FIRST ENCOUNTER OF EUROPEANS WITH THE NEW WORLD

LEXICONS, MISSIONS, VOYAGES, AND RESISTANCES

Ettore Finazzi-Agrò

Where were you when I laid the earth's foundations?
Tell me, since you are so well informed.
Who decided the dimensions of it, do you know?
Or who stretched the measuring line across it?
 —*Job 38.4–5*

The time is out of joint.
 —*Shakespeare, Hamlet, 1.5.189*

In analyzing the first documents of the New World's colonization, scholars have at times neglected to take into account the impact of that immense, apparently immeasurable territory upon European culture's conception of space. In particular, what seems to be lacking is an evaluation of the radical change of habits and especially of that conceptual framework that affects the private sphere of possession, of habitat–of *habere* as *habitare* (for in Latin, as we know, the second verb is but a frequentative of the first)–of the modification of the established concepts of "having" and "living," upon which personal identity largely depends (Klein 507–22). All of this was provoked precisely by the perception that there was a land without boundaries, without visible confines, which disperses into an inaccessible distance.

It would appear that the Americas did, in fact, present themselves to their astonished "discoverers," to their lost explorers, as a totally unforeseen and ineffable earthly dimension–unpredictable, in spite of its centuries-old anticipation. It is true that the continent's existence became a fantasy-turned-reality from a geographical mythology elaborated and assimilated throughout the Middle Ages, as the European imaginary absorbed slowly the wonder and amazement of the sailors; it was no less true, however, that the concrete experience of the Americas exceeded and eluded all expectations, surpassing all the repertories of *mirabilia* and *monstrua* produced during the Middle Ages, shuffling those propositions upon which were based all the constellations of images, all the figurative

conceptions of the world and the universe elaborated by the cartography and the astronomy of more than fifteen centuries. And it is within this imperfect, ultimately poetic dialectic–between the waiting for "something" and the surprise provoked by the appearance and the experience of "everything other than the anticipated thing"–that the idea of the New World *fills a place* (in the fullest sense of the word): an idea that slowly penetrates and undermines the cultural certainties upon which it was based, entangling, so to speak, the mental maps thanks to which it was located and to which it led, maps which had "situated" it, in both a spatial and a temporal sense.

The new land presented itself as a dimension of time and space open to the *beyond*, moving to the *outside*, a place in which established categories did not apply, in which traditional distinctions of space did not work, in which distances and locations were confused by a profusion of bewildering and contradictory indications, in which both distance and proximity lost all meaning. For all these reasons, the Americas appear on the European horizon as the domain of pure possibility or of fantasy, an empty space by European norms but already filled with a plethora of contradictory, interwoven signs yet to be interpreted. And the visible consequence is a hesitation before this new territory, between the imposition of known meanings and the patient deciphering of a confused and unexpected sense of space. These are operations that not only create the basic conditions for the realization of an ambiguous process of transculturation, in which the sheer force of overlapping conceptual orders (mental, linguistic, or religious) paradoxically associates a welcoming gesture–an incomprehensible cultural modality–with the empirical weakness of the other. But, above all, these are operations that, in their combinations and contradictions, nonetheless delineate a hermeneutical trajectory in which an American "lived space" justly seeks–and finally finds–its own spatial enunciation, subverting, at this trajectory's end, all the suppositions or traditional European values with which it began.

The discovery of a *terra incognita* produced devastating effects upon the "ethical" chronology and the "moralized" topology elaborated by the Middle Ages: a harmonious whole, illuminated by divine certainty, from which came a European world vision of humanity's existence and place within it. The discovery disarticulated logical or ideological sets, forcing a rethinking of spiritual hierarchies and material taxonomies and inevitably leading to the formulation of an infinitely problematic open universe without limits that laid waste to the old certainties, unsettled the boundaries of the closed, rigorously organized world within which medieval society and culture were entrenched (Koyré 65–90). The theocratic geography that medieval science (not without controversies and contradictions) had succeeded in defining contemplated an Earth with three continents, three seas, five climates, and twelve winds (Zumthor 229–30). This imaginary geography, which had been able to establish the emblematic economy of its measurements and the symbolic perfection of its numbers, suddenly loses its axiological and interpretive validity with regard to the real. All things on earth consequently become "oblique," that is, everything becomes hazardous, the shadow of doubt and uncertainty spreads over all reality, and the darkness of possible error and chaos extends over all things (Santillana 11–49).

It is certain that the loss of centrality, the irremediable tilting of the axis around which medieval knowledge and practices were organized, did not immediately register, given that European culture and its agents in the new land (explorers and colonizers of every stripe) attempted an obstinate defense of their citadel of received knowledge: That is, they continued for a long time (and, in part, continue still) to think of themselves as "central". But it is also certain that in the compactness of this defense apparatus–which, in turn, assaults and rationalizes the *other* in relation to the European–there is also an *elsewhere* in relation to its here, the colonial lettered city. The certainty of truth in the citadel of knowledge cannot hide its uneasiness with rigorous interrogation and a new hypothesis; nor can it mask its hesitation in the face of the unknown. Furthermore there is the nebulous and disturbing perception of an alterity that is unassimilable and immeasurable in terms of the old measurements. All of these penetrate the citadel almost immediately: European thinking has been shaken to its foundation. There is no lack of answers, just as there is an abundance of attempts to suppress inquiry by representing it (and by concretizing it) in the figure of a disturbing heretical perception of a world without measure. This ambiguous work of the challenge to received truth by an extracanonical alterity is seen throughout the sixteenth century in art and literature. One need only seek out these subversives and study them according to the historical method that, paradoxically, represents one of the most important and precious legacies of European civilization in the New World.

I have attempted to read and interpret at least one of these cartographic signs by making use of the readings and interpretations that produced it: the image of the Island. So present in the first and, obviously, imaginary cartography of the Americas, the Island so obsessively sought after and so often fallaciously identified by its discoverers can serve us well in this inquiry into the breakup of European space (Finazzi-Agrò 1–20). The representation of the New World as a gigantic archipelago (of which Brazil would be not more than a small portion [Lestringant 218–34]) may be justly considered as a macroscopic, ostentatious, geographical symptom of the unease that takes European culture by surprise on the threshold of a threatening, unfathomable dimension, of a space apparently without history, unforeseen by anyone anywhere, of which there had been no trace in medieval treatises or maps, in texts by Latin or Greek authors, or in the authorities who had both directed knowledge and established space during the Middle Ages.

According to medieval tradition, the Sea of Darkness could contain only islands. Islands were consequently what the navigators saw, endlessly witnessing and redesigning a geography of desire, forever placing within known, controllable, tranquilizing dimensions this enormous newness they confronted. There is a will to understand this nameless continental space, the extension of space without boundaries that is pushed to the very limits in so many partial, undefined places upon which the imprimatur of a proper name has been imposed. But confronting these everyday figures of curiosity, there is the incomprehensibility of an unusual and extreme experience for which nothing could have prepared the first European arrivals (Baudry 279–82). This need to bestow names signifies, beyond this, the possibility of bestowing meaning (once again, a *proper* meaning) upon the senselessness of an apparently infinite space, of finding, then, the words to control it–thus making it a place, a localizable, topical dimension within the geographical discourse and the ideological system elaborated by medieval culture.

It is not, therefore, by chance, that Pero Vaz de Caminha (1450?–1500), after having witnessed the visibly immeasurable nature of the land discovered by Cabral–"Pelo sertão, nos pareceu do mar muito grande, por que, a estender olhos, não podíamos ver se não terra e arvoredos, que nos parecia mui longa terra" (in Unali 76–77) ("The backlands appeared to us larger than the sea, because, in extending our gaze, we could not see but land and groves of trees, which appeared to us to be a very long expanse of land")–after having twice repeated the word "land" which, as we know, was synonymous with *terra firma*, and after having qualified it as "very large" and "very long," closes his text "da vossa ilha de Vera Cruz" (Unali 77) ("from thine Island of Vera Cruz"). None of this is accidental, precisely because the island, as a specific and localizable dimension, may be denominated and the king may appropriate it ("thine island"); on the contrary, land, as unlimited space, could not be comprehended, and would elude any appropriation and thus contradict the appellation of any proper name, remaining undefined and ineffable.

Similarly, in reading the successive Portuguese chronicles in which Brazil had already acquired the geographical profile and contours of a *terra firma*, it is easy to discover that, in the description of this huge country, attention appears always to be focused almost obsessively upon the islands. One need only consult Pero Magalhães de Gândavo's (d. 1576) *Tratado da Terra do Brasil* [1570; Treatise on the Land of Brazil] or his *História da Província de Santa Cruz* [1576; History of Santa Cruz Province], works in which–as regards at least four of the eight captaincies (Bahia, Tamaracá, Espírito Santo, and São Vicente)–the author forcefully underlines not so much the wealth of its interior but, above all else, the existence of many, indeed countless, islands upon which rise the *feitorias* ("trading posts") or the principal establishments. For example, there is the description of Bahia from the History: "Tem dentro em si muitas ilhas de terras mui singulares. Divide-se em muitas partes, e tem muitos braços e enseadas por onde os moradores se servem em barcos para suas fazendas" (Gândavo 89) ("[The harbor of Bahia Salvador] contains many unique islands. It is divided into many parts, and has many arms and bays, which the inhabitants use to reach their homesteads by boats.") What is presented to the Portuguese reader's eyes is a fairly fragmented topography, a broken territory, a sort of archipelago of "terras singulares" ("singular lands"), infinitely more tranquilizing, at bottom, than a space without measure, without name.

It is, in fact, precisely because of this that, after having used the designation *Brazil* in the title of his first text, Gândavo returns to the matter of naming in his *History*, eventually deciding in favor of *Santa Cruz* as a denomination. It is precisely because he realizes that only a *proper* name (that is, one taken from the European cultural and religious code) can eliminate all and any ambiguity, all and any doubt with regard to a territory marked by an uncertain, multiple (and therefore diabolical) designation. To confirm or re-establish the sacred name means, as he writes, to remove the colony from the domain of the Devil "que tanto trabalhou e trabalha para extinguir a memória da Santa Cruz" (Gândavo 80) ("who has long worked and works still to extinguish the memory of the Santa Cruz [the Holy Cross]"). Evidently, the denomination functions here to exorcize division and alterity as the certain, "symbolic" delimitation of a territory threatened by a demoniacal indeterminacy and an infernal incomprehensibility (Souza 1993, 21–57).

A determinate, comprehensible designation must be invoked if the new land is to have European cultural meaning and have a place in cultural memory; this can be achieved only by exorcizing that nonfinitude in which diabolical confusion hovers (in the fullest sense); this designated space must become contiguous to the customary places and must be capable of being assimilated by them, thereby repressing or denying that there is an unbridgeable distance–for this is not only unthinkable but is destructive to the perspective itself. The geography of the Americas was, in fact, for a long time subordinated to this attempted approximation or even homologation, which achieves its clearest expression in the Rabelaisianism *tout comme chez nous*, a phrase which sums up, as everyone knows, the experience of Alcofribas in the *nouveau monde* he discovers inside Pantagruel's mouth. This episode clearly records the Old World opening up to the vastness and distance of the New (Auerbach 3–27), just as it returns us, not by chance, in a parodic, carnivalized register to the epochal climate marked by the stupefied perception of a space unmeasurable and unthinkable by Europeans as a consequence of the geographic discoveries. Except that, in this case, the *elsewhere* is presented as an extension of the *here*, as a sort of imaginative reproduction and continuation of the well-known places, imitating both their qualities and their defects. Alcofribas needs to walk no more than two leagues upon the giant's tongue before entering a universe that, though other, claims its paradoxical freedom and priority with regard to the "outside"–so much so that, when his

discoverer inquires of a peasant inhabitant of this "oral" dimension if it is a new world, the latter replies:

> Certes . . . il n'est mie nouveau; mais l'on dist bien que hors d'icy y a une terre neufve où ils ont et soleil et lune, et tout plein de belles besongnes; mais cestuy-cy est plus ancien.
> (Rabelais [1532] 1973, 345)

> Sure . . . it is never a jot new, but it is commonly reported, that without this there is an earth, whereof the inhabitants enjoy the light of a sun and moon; and that it is full of, and replenished with, very good commodities; but yet, this is more ancient than that. (Rabelais 1871?, 213–14)

To inhabit a place beyond a threshold, while nevertheless retaining the essential characteristics of that which lies this side of it, seems finally to distort and alter every spatial and temporal perspective, corrupting and confounding categories of *within* and *without*, of *here* and *there*, of *before* and *after*, until these concepts are indistinguishable–despite distinctions of spaces and of times (because, after all, Alcofribas does both enter and leave Pantagruel's mouth). Something similar, moreover, happens in many chronicles of discovery and exploration, in which a sensation of unrest may be experienced over a humanity that places itself in line with the foundations of time, at the lower end of history, appearing, because of this, to live a sort of past that never was for Americans–therefore a past without redemption–updating itself, however, and stirring under European eyes to claim an alien heritage as their own. The inhabitant of the New (World) thus simultaneously presents himself as an emblem of the Old: the agent of a primitive, natural time (the Golden Age) from which Europeans have distanced themselves through their guilt, pursuing and attaining an ideal of "innovation," which appears to make them, paradoxically, older than that young and innocent humanity that surrounds them. And in this apparent turnaround of the times, in this progressive destruction of chronology and history, the European spatial canons are also, obviously, reverted and subverted until they threaten the established frontiers, until they confound the distinct, circumscribed places created, throughout the centuries, by logical, ethical, juridical, and above all, theological discriminations.

What is in crisis, in other words, is European manicheanism, which had rigorously categorized and ordered the world both horizontally and vertically; which had fixed, within unquestionable hierarchies and paradigms, the places of good and evil, of the just and the unjust, of the holy and the damned, of master and slave. The confusion of these categories, the erasure of accepted limits, in the interior of an apparently unlimited territory, provokes in Europeans a sort of endless vertigo that constantly forces them to reaffirm the purported correct and univocal meaning of established truth, to re-establish an orthodoxy that, in that heterodoxical context of the Americas, would run the risk of vanishing, of losing its certainty, casting the colonizer into the infinite abyss of self doubt, the "immeasurability" of a boundary-less space. For a concrete example of this we need only remember José de Anchieta's (1534–1597) poem, "Do Santíssimo Sacramento" (Of the Holiest Sacrament), which in its subject matter and treatment seems to show exactly–as Alfredo Bosi has pointed out–the "pavor de recair em algum escuro e vertiginoso poço pré-histórico submerso mas não abolido aquém do limiar da consciência individual" (84) ("the horror of falling into some dark, vertiginous prehistoric underground well that exists just this side of the threshold of individual consciousness"). Or rather, to write a poem about the Eucharist in a land of cannibals may also be considered a way of exorcizing fear and the confusion of practices that, in the profusion of the unexplained experiences of an excessive world, would run the risk of becoming completely disoriented.

The poem was more an apophatic gesture, more an act of exorcism, then, than a work of poetry, more a way of reaffirming the legitimacy of the sacramental mystery against the diabolical illegitimacy of cannibalism, than a text inspired solely by Catholic orthodoxy and spirituality. Nonetheless, it is precisely within the mesh of this asseverative discourse, this frightened "reaffirmation," that the discourse of the other insinuates itself; Anchieta's text is, in fact, born of a categorical logic, from an obligation to exemplarity, inspired by rigid European cultural and lettered canons, which is suddenly forced to feed on another experience, on other examples, on other *logoi* that escape the one, the only and always identical logic of orthodoxy. This is a discourse, after all, moving and evolving in a dimension that reopens and questions the established models, becoming fatally ambiguous, somehow stained by the indeterminacy of the other to whom it directs itself and to the elsewhere from which it begins. Moreover, all of the poem "Do Santíssimo Sacramento," despite its markedly spiritual accents, is nonetheless impregnated by a disturbing materialism in which the physical attributes of the body are manifested in an opaque and triumphant plenitude: "fome, comida, sabor, entranhas" ("hunger, food, taste, entrails")–words that define a semantic scope linked to *apetite* (appetite), as an alimentary isotopy running through the work (Anchieta 366–72). We ought to consider the strongly sensorial or even sensual nature of the mystical Iberian tradition of which Anchieta's poetry is the fruit, but we cannot forget the fact that, in it, the poet confronts an experience (lived or merely imagined, it matters very little) in which the corporeality and the entire sphere of physical urgency, of carnal instinct–of appetite, once again, in all its possible senses–appear as central facts of culture. Indeed, the interpretation of indigenous culture under the prism of corporeality, of absence–more generally, of all metaphysical unease–is an integral part of the first European vision of the Americas. In it, sexual hunger and the voracity of human flesh play a key role, until, for instance, all of Brazil is reduced–in Nóbrega's cutting image–to a *boca infernal* ("hellish mouth") (see Souza 1989, 64–66): The familiar and soothing representation *of* the new world, as used by Rabelais, now becomes impossible, and Pantagruel's welcoming mouth thus becomes a diabolical, all-swallowing, all-destroying abyss. In short, to live *elsewhere* (and, besides this, to adopt, as did Anchieta, the language of the *other*), is not, nor could it be, an innocent act, a choice without consequences for Europeans or for the literature they produced, for what awaited them might also have been a tremendous absorption of the Self and its Voice, a terrible annihilation of its cultural identity in this immeasurable space without rules.

This is, in fact, a crisis of the European world vision or, better yet, of this old *episteme*: It is ideology that had made medieval Europe a continent traversed and tormented by frontiers, in which the population's predominant spatial limitation (very few persons left their place of birth) had been slowly transformed (and, by it, in turn, confirmed) into a rigorous code of admitted or prohibited behaviors (Zumthor 31–47), largely determined by territorial, social, physical, and juridical place of birth. (We need only think of medieval

Portugal's set of rights and obligations, which went under the name of *natural law*, forever linking the individual to his origin in all senses.) It is because they were coming from a "closed" system and moving toward the interior of an apparently unlimited dimension that Europeans were able neither to orient themselves nor to orient their gaze: They found it impossible to define fully, to comprehend, that unmeasured alterity dominated by a very different *natural law* whose rules they did not know. Suffice it to say, it was from this perspective that one can explain the incessant accusations of evangelizing clerics and colonizers against the Brazilian Indians: Their transiency, their nomadism, the fact that they had no roots or attachment to places condemned them to the realm of the incomprehensible, as did their purported absence of ideals, their unencumbered movement through limitless space. All of this presumably meant that they lacked moral will and the material means to become established (Castro 22–34).

As a matter of fact the connection between this nomadism and marginality (whether social, ethical, or mental) also comes from the medieval imaginary, within which spiritual distance was verified in spatial terms, in the sense of a vagrancy, a distancing from places established by the norm; indeed, such a way of life meant the abandonment of any normality and any moral habit (Zumthor 150–66). And it is precisely within this perspective that we frequently find the condemnation of indigenous nomadism in the Jesuit letters–as in that of Father Luís de Grã written to Ignatius of Loyola dated 27 December, 1554:

> Andan pellas Aldeas muchos que erão christanos y moravão en una Aldea que estava aquí junto de la cibdade (Baía) entre los quales los Padres, que aqui estuvieron al principio teníam casa y heremita y allí los enseñavan a grandes y pequeños, honbres y mugeres. Y como su costumbre sea mudárense mui amenudo, que no tienen más que por qualquer antojo quemar su lanço en que moran 'y ninguno le va a la mano aunque aian de quemar toda l'aldea' mudáronse muchos y finalmente toda la Aldea se mudó. Por éstos trabajava yo más, pero de todo están sin señal de christianos en los costumbres, qu en la fee ni teinen ellos en que la mudar; dexan escaecer todo. (quoted in Leite 135–36)

> There are many [natives] who were Christians who lived in a village that was adjacent to the city [Baía] in which priests, who were here at the beginning, had a house and hermitage and there they would teach the old and the young, men and women. But because they have a custom of frequently moving about, when they leave for no apparent reason they burn the houses where they have lived–and no one seems to care even though they might burn down the entire village; in time many move away and finally the entire village moves. I worked with these people but they are completely without signs of Christianity in their customs. In faith, they do not believe that they have to change. They allow themselves to forget everything they have left behind.

A clear accusation against Indian nomadism–regarded here from an explicitly economic perspective–can still be found in Gândavo's previously evoked *Treatise*:

> Uma das cousas porque o Brasil não floresce muito mais, he pelos escravos que se alevantarão e fugirão pera suas terras e fogem cada dia: e se estes indios não foram tão fugitivos e mudaveis, não tivera comparação a riqueza do Brasil. (Gândavo 42)

> One of the reasons why Brazil no longer flourishes is because of the slaves that have fled and flee everyday to their own communities, and if the Indians were not such fugitives and so unreliable, there would be no comparison in the world to the richness of Brasil.

To Europeans, the Indians remain atypical and unclassifiable, just as they are ahistorical, outside time and beyond social norms. The frequent denunciation of their laziness, as we know, will become proverbial (until its ironic reutilization in *Macunaíma*), constituting, in fact, one of the most persistent traces of the colonizer's racial prejudice against the colonized. The incessant accusation regarding the Indians' propensity toward wasting their time derives precisely, in my opinion, from this inability to recognize, in the temporality of the other, an analogous but different sense of time that contains equivalent cadences to European temporality. While European time was divided into distinct phases, between a time for celebration and a time for work, the temporality of the "savages" presented itself, on the contrary, as a temporality out of step and diffused, apparently without distinction, and thus impossible to dedicate to a specific task. In a paleo-bourgeois sense, the Indians did not use time, did not "capitalize" their time, but instead lost it or, once more, wasted it. This attitude is already clearly denounced by the priests of the Society of Jesus in their letters: "Isto lhes acontece por serem naturalmente muy priguisossos (*sic*), e taes que o que lhes é necessário pera seu mantimento por esta cause o deixão de buscar" (Leite 354) ("This happens to them for being naturally very lazy, to the extent that they will not do what is necessary for their basic maintenance and will abandon striving for it").

Within the scope of missionary literature, moreover, examples of European attempts to delimit the apparently uninterrupted time of autochthonous culture, to measure the chronological flux of this humanity strikingly "outside time," may be easily found. José de Anchieta's writings in Tupi may once again be taken as an example in which, from the standpoint of catechesis, the effort of adopting the Indian's language is counter-balanced through the use of rhyme. Meter is, in fact, a resource which tends, perhaps unconsciously, to regiment the disordered speech of the other; to finally set, in a traditional rhythm–once again in an "old meter"–an expression and a voice that seem, also from phonic and auditive standpoints, to elude any temporal division, to ignore known cadences, to founder in indistinctness and babble. As a matter of fact, the first contact between the Portuguese and the Indians (described by Caminha in his *Letter*) already shows nicely how the absence of a known linguistic "order" not only impedes comprehension between the two groups but also embarasses the European ear: "ali não houve mais fala nem entendimento com eles, por a berberia deles ser tamanha que se não entendia *nem ouvia* ninguém" (Unali 95) ("there was no way to speak or understand them, for their barbarism was such that you could not understand or even bear to *listen* to anyone"). To measure, as did Anchieta, the possible meaning of speech through the tempo of diction is part of the problem. Diction, in this sense, is an attempt at perceiving the other, receiving them, that is, lending them an ear and giving them a voice, but only within the scope of proper European (auditive and expressive) norms. *Língua geral* (the general language; a Latin grammatical structure encompassing the Tupi-Guarani language) was an attempt by the Jesuits to introduce European norms, to delimit the incomprehensibility and plurality of the American languages; this represents the ineluctable foundation of all and every process of transculturation.

In fact, as long as the Indians (and their language) continued to elude both the Church and the authorities who imposed forced labor in the plantations, as long as they continued to disperse into the interior and ignore the distinctions established by the religion and culture of Portugal, they would be accused of living in complete disorder. This accusation, unceasingly repeated, also ends up taking on a proverbial tone; this is based on a paradoxical linguistic or, better yet, phonetic-referential determinism, invented and illustrated by the previously quoted Pero Magalhães de Gândavo: "[*A língua dos índios*] carece de tres letras, convem a saber, nam se acham nella F, nem L, nem R, cousa digna despanto porque assi nam têm Fé, nem Lei, nem Rei, e desta maneira vivem desordenatamente sem terem alem disto conta, nem peso, nem medido" (Gândavo 124) ("It should be known that [the Indian language] lacks three letters; in it neither F nor L nor R are to be found, an amazing thing for thus it is that the Indians cannot have either Faith or Law or King, and this is the way they live"). This clearly underlines the association between the absence of social order and a lack of personal constraints, in which life without European phonetic or alphabetic norms leads ipso facto to a plunge into disorder, to a regression into chaos, and to the impossibility of participating in civilized society. The conclusion drawn from this paradoxical phonological premise is that these inhabitants ignore all the principles of order and any axiology; therefore, they do not fit into any human paradigm and must remain outside all possible social norms. As we may see, anthropological misunderstanding passes through linguistic misunderstanding, leaving the Indians suspended in an undefinable space and time, in a condition that immediately appears to be beyond measure and without rules.

The European sense of abnormality, with regard to the nature of the *other* and a space that is outside the rational world, resulted from the very real threat to European notions of space and time provoked by the discovery of America; this was a profound rupture to the established sense of proportion. The incalculable distances of the new world, its lack of limits and dimensions, ended up being compensated for, at the imaginary level, through recourse to fantasies of the immeasurable and the deformed. It is not by chance that objects, trees, animals, and people, either too small or too large by European standards, inhabit the chronicles of the explorers; nor is it by chance that the European literature of that period is filled with giants and dwarfs; traditional characters, certainly, but characters who enjoy a sort of ideal re-semantization in the sixteenth century, lending themselves, in the deformity of their bodies, to incarnating the enormous and abnormal nature of this new space (Zumthor 260–66). The model may once again be Rabelais's masterpiece or, perhaps, Camões's *Adamastor*, but, above all the multitude of these configurations of enormity or extreme smallness in the chivalric romances that were still popular with the lettered class and had been absorbed by the popular imagination.

With regard to the Rabelaisian text, Erich Auerbach's masterful reading has underlined the symbolic value of Pantagruelian "immeasurability" and its relationship to the discovery of the New World, but as far as I know we are still lacking a study on the frequency of such gigantic or minuscule figures in sixteenth century chivalric narratives, which were parallel to the European loss of proportion that was provoked, precisely, by geographical discoveries. As the most popular literary genre of the time (to the point of influencing, as we know, American topological nomenclature ranging from the Amazon to California), it is not difficult to believe that, on the one hand, chivalric romances compensated on a level of fantasy (within collective imagination) for the disagreements on physical dimension and the epistemological crises that resulted and ran through

European culture, and, on the other hand, these works of fiction rendered plausible or even inevitable the generalized recourse to abnormal images in the wide range of chronicles and travel literature that fed an insatiable European appetite for the fantastic-made-real. From this perspective, giants and dwarfs are no more than emblematic figures of an alterity that, through them, may eventually be domesticated, may eventually become habitual and comprehensible to Europeans. The idea of an unknown Other, colored with the notion of the infra-human, the immense difficulty of imagining a world outside of the familiar known world and the disruption of the sense of proportion, come together to produce an extreme situation that finally finds a traditional and amazingly tranquilizing meaning in the fantastic.

Standing upon the slippery ground of the European literary imagination and familiar with the marvellous and the fantastic, the reader of chronicles and treatises on the New World should be able to realize the distance and recognize the European's perception of his own cultural superiority regarding a world and its inhabitants, which opens up beyond the threshold of European habitual space. What Europeans are not able to restore, however, is precisely the traditional measure of things, their identity guided by that which surrounds them, their ingenuous trust in a space that respects the laws of faith and desire. And what awaits Europeans is a radically changed culture that has lost its axiological and transcendental nature; what awaits them, in the end, is a geography thrown out of order, one which no longer has a center; it is a world that has fallen off its axis and will condemn Europeans to a long pilgrimage through the unmeasured and marginal territories of search and doubt.

For a long time, Europeans will be forced to inhabit this non-locatable and non-habitual dimension, painfully re-adapting their cultural order to the laws and measures of a "strange" culture, ceaselessly redesigning the confines of *having* a place and *being there*, that is, of being in relation to those inhospitable and improper places that Europeans will slowly, with brutality and awe, appropriate and falsify and, with equal brutality and awe, will irreversibly alienate from their original identity.

Translation by Stephen A. Berg

Works Cited

Anchieta, José de. 1954. *Poesias (Manuscrito do séc. XVI, em Português, Castelhano, Latim e Tupi).* Ed. and trans. Maria de Lourdes de Paula Martins. São Paulo: Comissão do IV Centenário da Cidade de São Paulo, Serviço de Comemorações Culturais.

Auerbach, Erich. 1956. *Mimesis. Il realismo nella letteratura occidentale.* Vol. 2. Trans. Alberto Romagholi and Hans Hinterhäuser. Torino: Einaudi.

Baudry, Robert. 1997. 'L'île carrefour du merveilleux.' *Île des merveilles: Mirage, miroir, mythe.* Ed. Daniel Reig. Paris: L'Harmattan. 279–95.

Bosi, Alfredo. 1992. *Dialética da Colonização.* São Paulo: Companhia das Letras.

Castro, Eduardo Viveiros de. 1992. 'O Mármore e a Murta: Sobre a inconstância da alma selvagem.' *Revista de Antropologia.* 35: 21–74.

Finazzi-Agrò, Ettore. 1993. *Invenção da Ilha: Tópica literária e topologia imaginária na descoberta do Brasil.* Rio de Janeiro: PUC-Rio.

Gândavo, Pero de Magalhães. 1980. *Tratado da Terra do Brasil–História da Província de Santa Cruz.* Belo Horizonte-São Paulo: Itatiaia-Edusp.

Klein, Robert. 1975. *La forma e l'intelligibile.* Torino: Einaudi.

Koyré, Alexandre. n.d. *Do mundo fechado ao universo infinito.* Lisboa: Gradiva.

Leite, Serafim. 1954. *Cartas dos primeiros Jesuítas do Brasil.* Vol. 2. São Paulo: Comissão do IV Centenário da Cidade de São Paulo.

Lestringant, Frank. 1981. 'Fictions de l'espace brésilien à la Renaissance: L'exemple de Guanabara.' *Arts et légendes d'espaces: Figures du voyage et rhétoriques du monde.* Eds. Christian Jacob and Frank Lestringant. Paris: Presses de l'École Normale Supérieure. 205–56.

The New Jerusalem Bible. 1985. Ed. Henry Wansbrough. New York: Doubleday.

Rabelais, François. 1871?. *The Works of Rabelais.* Gustave Doré 1876? *The Work of Rabelais:* faithfully trans. from the French, with variorum notes: and numerous illustrations by Gustoave Doré. Nottingham: Printed for private circulation.

——. [1532] 1973. *Oeuvres complètes.* Paris: Seuil.

Santillana, Giorgio de. 1983. *Fato antico e fato moderno.* Milano: Adelphi.

Shakespeare, William. 1997. *Hamlet.* Ed. Harold Jenkins. New York: Arden Shakespeare.

Souza, Laura de Mello e. 1989. *O Diabo e a terra de Santa Cruz.* São Paulo: Companhia das Letras.

——. 1993. *Inferno Atlântico. Demonologia e colonização séculos XVI–XVIII.* São Paulo: Companhia das Letras.

Unali, Anna. 1984. *La Carta do achamento di Pero Vaz de Caminha.* Milano: Cisalpino-Goliardica.

Zumthor, Paul. 1993. *La Mesure du monde.* Paris: Seuil.

CHAPTER 10

INDIGENOUS, *MESTIZO,* AND IMPERIAL REASON

Marco Luis Dorfsman and Lori Hopkins

Toward the end of the fifteenth century, the encounter between two cultures, the European and the Amerindian, took place. This text will attempt to retrace some aspects of the trajectory of the sixteenth century along which these two cultures interpenetrated each other to form a conglomeration of elements now known as colonial culture. First of all, it is worth recalling that neither of these cultures was monolithic. The American continent was inhabited by a very large number of ethnic groups, some closely related and others extremely different. There was a great variety of communities that had distinct political, economic, and social organizations, as well as diverse languages and customs. However, they all inhabited what was, in principle, a relatively comprehensible universe. That is to say, the conceptions of time, space, and reality held by Mayas, Mixes, and Mexicas (including the Incas, for example), were not radically different. The encounter with the Europeans was devastating for the Amerindian cultures not only because it destroyed the communities themselves through conquest and epidemics, but also and especially because it foreclosed the possibilities for an indigenous perception of the universe. In a way, it abolished the universe itself in which these cultures were constituted. The irruption of the European world into the pre-Hispanic world was the irruption of an absolute and incomprehensible otherness in the very texture of the universe. The so-called New World also became new for its old inhabitants, who suddenly found that their world no longer existed. This does not mean, of course, that nothing survived or was adapted to the new situation—it would be absurd to make such an assertion. It does mean, however, that indigenous thought confronted the limits of its possibilities in a new universe where the old norms no longer functioned. The colonial world that began to take shape over the next few centuries was one in which the Mexica, Maya, or Inca as such could no longer survive.

We shall not retrace here a new history of the devastation of the Indies, but rather, we will simply review a few moments of what could be called the deculturation of the Nahuas. It is worth asking, first, what the operative concept of culture is throughout this discourse. *Culture* is more than the grouping of beliefs, rites, customs, artifacts, languages, ways of everyday life, etc., but less than communal identity. As Inga Clendinnen has said, culture is not ideology, but neither is it something as passive as worldview (2). Yet this leaves us with a term that is too vague and flexible to be very useful critically. In Western thought, *culture,* at least since Romanticism, has been the unquestioned ground of all artistic and intellectual production of peoples. It is assumed that each community *has* a culture, whatever this might be, but at the same time, it is assumed that it *is* a culture. We should note that, by this logic, the term is intimately related to a concept of communal identity that is not far from that of the (national) subject. More recently, critical discourse has distinguished between popular and hegemonic cultures. Whereas the first emerges spontaneously from everyday practices of the people,

the latter is imposed from above by the dominant classes. At any rate, within a single culture there seem to operate various processes of division, dialogue, exchange, negotiation, and mobility—in other words, processes of acculturation and transculturation. We bring this up not to enter into a debate with or about culture and cultural studies, but to underline the complexity and ambivalence of the very notions operative within Western discourse when it attempts to speak about indigenous cultures and their transculturation.

Within the context of Latin American Cultural Studies, the term *transculturation,* which was put in circulation by Fernando Ortiz (1881–1969) and retaken by Ángel Rama (1926–1983), attempts to respond to some of the problems outlined above. Rama quotes Ortiz:

> Entendemos que el vocablo *transculturación* expresa mejor las diferentes fases del proceso transitivo de una cultura a otra, porque este no consiste solamente en adquirir una cultura, que es lo que en rigor indica la voz anglo-americana *aculturación,* sino que el proceso implica también necesariamente la pérdida o desarraigo de una cultura precedente, lo que pudiera decirse una parcial desculturación, y, además, significa la consiguiente creación de nuevos fenómenos culturales que pudieran denominarse *neoculturación.* (1982, 33)

> We understand that the term *transculturation* better expresses the different stages of the transitive process from one culture to another, for it consists not only in acquiring a culture, which is what in all rigor the Anglo-American term "acculturation" indicates, but that the process also and necessarily implies the loss or deracination of a preceding culture, which could be called a partial deculturation, and, also, it means the consequent creation of new cultural phenomena, which could be named *neoculturation.*

The critical value of the term transculturation consists in that it does not merely celebrate the new cultural phenomenon (today called hybrid), but that it also emphasizes, while recognizing the power relations operative between hegemonic and popular cultures, the loss of culture that every transculturation by necessity implies. But again, we must ask, what or who is the subject of this partial deculturation? And further, that which has already been partially deculturated—is it culture per se, or could it be something else? Rama has a fairly optimistic view of the process, which he elsewhere calls "un esfuerzo transculturador de tal magnitud, como es la forja de un pueblo nuevo a partir de diversas culturas puestas en contacto" (1985, 19) ("a transculturating effort of such magnitude, as is the forging of a new people out of diverse cultures placed in contact").

The concept of transculturation is an essentially dialectical (and hence Romantic) one. It responds, as does Latin America throughout the nineteenth century, to a need for independence. Already in Rama, one can sense an almost epic tone, in which the battle between master and slave is played and replayed until, in the same way as in Hegel, the slave manages to inscribe himself in a process that is larger than him and thus turns his defeat into an ironic victory for the process

145

or the product themselves. The sixteenth-century encounter between European and Amerindian cultures can no doubt be productively described in such terms. However, doing so immediately locks the indigenous peoples into a historical process that is essentially alien to their own conception of the universe. It turns them into auxiliary and ancillary beings to Western culture, recovering their otherness for the simple renovation and strengthening of hegemonic culture. Rama says, "Es justamente esa capacidad para elaborar con originalidad, aún en difíciles circunstancias históricas, la que demuestra que pertenece a una sociedad viva y creadora" (1982, 34) ("It is precisely that capacity to develop originally, even under difficult historical circumstances, that demonstrates that it belongs to a creative and lively society"). Who belongs? Latin America, which "que es un producto largamente transculturado y en permanente evolución" (1982, 34) ("is a product of a long and slow transculturation and continues to be in permanent evolution"). We aren't suggesting that Rama ignores the destruction of indigenous cultures; quite on the contrary, his reading is brilliant, nuanced, and effective. However, in privileging the process of transculturation and locating it in "difficult historical circumstances," Rama merely puts indigenous cultures at the symbolic service of a historicity that is definitely not theirs. In lesser thinkers than Ortiz or Rama, or in ideologists of *criollismo*, mestizaje, or national populism, the very term *transculturation* has become, as Martin Lienhard has pointed out, "sinónimo del gastado concepto de 'mestizaje cultural'" (1991, 97) ("synonymous with the worn-out concept of 'mestizaje cultural'").

Let us take one of the elements from Ortiz's formulation, that of a "partial deculturation." This concept might be useful to us, as Western subjects already more or less transculturated, but it is irrelevant to pre-Hispanic cultures, and it is alien even to contemporary indigenous cultures, even though it accurately describes their historical situation. First of all, the term *deculturation* already assumes that the peoples of America were "cultures." Culture, however, is a regional, Western concept. Of course, Amerindian groups cultivated the earth, had different religious cults, and their languages were full of metaphors that distinguished between urban and rural inhabitants. Nevertheless, this does not imply that they saw themselves as "cultures." That is our definition, not theirs. It is important to underline the differences, in part to correct the notion that Indians are mere contributors to Western knowledge about them and in part to alienate all knowledge that can be produced here by us. What view of themselves did the pre-Hispanic peoples have? Obviously, the question is paradoxical and oxymoronic. First of all, it is impossible to speak of a single view since there were many different populations and ethnic groups with obviously diverse views, who had internal divisions and hierarchies. Trying to reduce this to one vision, whether of the vanquished or of something else, would be a mistake. We can nevertheless try to reconstruct some aspects of self-definition in some of the traditions, as long as we keep in mind that adopting the position of absolute otherness is phenomenologically impossible.

Let us follow Miguel León Portilla's reconstitution of the notion of *toltecáyotl*, which shall here serve as an exemplary model. With this word, León Portilla tries to utter a pre-Hispanic concept somewhat parallel to Western concepts of culture or civilization. Literally, *toltecáyotl* means "the essence," or, more precisely, "the heart of a Toltec," and it alludes to the great civilization that built the city of Tula, from which the Mexicas

claimed ancestry. León Portilla translates the term as "Toltec-hood" (*toltequidad*), that is to say, the series of qualities that identify a group as belonging to the Toltec tradition. Being a Toltec did not simply mean belonging to that civilization in particular, but rather, in more general terms, it meant being an inhabitant of a city (*tollán*, hence *tolteca*). In even more abstract and general terms, being a Toltec meant being a cultivated or civilized being. It was also synonymous with being an artisan or a sage. León Portilla says, "nos inclinamos a pensar que su connotación mucho se acerca a la que tiene, desde el punto de vista histórico y antropológico, el término civilización. Este último se deriva de *civitas*, en latín. *Toltecáyotl* viene en última instancia de *Tollan* que así mismo quiere decir metrópoli" (1980, 19) ("we are inclined to believe that its main connotation is very close to the one possessed by the term civilization, from a historical and anthropological point of view. This latter derived from *civitas*, meaning citizenship in Latin. *Toltecáyotl* comes finally from *tollán*, which also means metropolis").

While León Portilla offers here an important parallel, it is necessary to also underline the differences. Toltec-hood might be analogous to civilization and culture; it is composed of elements that are also present in Western traditions: Art, writing, wisdom, and morality. But Toltec-hood is also something else: "el legado de Quetzalcóatl y los toltecas abarcaba la tinta negra y roja–la sabiduría–escritura" (1980, 7) ("the legacy of Quetzalcoatl and the Toltecs included the red and black ink–wisdom, writing"). León Portilla translates the Nahuatl term *in tlilli in tlapalli*, the color red and the color black, as "saber que sobrepasa la comprensión ordinaria" (1966, 392) ("a knowledge that is above ordinary comprehension"). Nahuatl wisdom (or science) was said to belong to the *tlacuilos* (writers, notaries, painters), who were in charge of the red and black ink, the materials and instruments for painting/writing. They were the ones who painted the codices (*amoxtli*) and kept charge over the memories of the community. There is a metonymic displacement between the instruments of inscription and the production of knowledge itself. Knowledge is the process of the production of knowing; and it also is the instrument that gives form to that knowing. Like *toltecáyotl*, "civilization," *tlilli tlapalli*, "knowledge," is in essence material. Within the model postulated by León Portilla, one can translate (or reconstruct) a formulation that groups together these concepts as follows: "(Nahuatl) culture consists in knowledge (writing)." However, it would also be correct to emphasize a hyperliteral translation as follows: "the heart of those who inhabit the city is the red and the black." And there are further variants, like "it is citizens that know," "city people write," "the essence of knowledge is painting," "culture is writing." No doubt this is beginning to sound like a game of puns and bad philology, but what we are trying to point out is that the concept of Toltec-hood is alien to us, even if loosely translatable and familiarizable around a cluster of Western concepts.

Toltec-hood, then, was the essence of civilized being for the Nahuas. But, unlike culture in the West, it was never something that simply belonged to them. It was more like a responsibility, something they had to bear, to carry on their backs. And it was, more than anything else, a constant ongoing and unfinished process. If it belonged to anyone, it belonged to others. "Los toltecas eran experimentados,/acostumbraban dialogar con su propio corazón" (León Portilla 1980, 29) ("The Toltecs were experienced/they carried a dialogue with their own heart").

This ongoing dialogue is not a concept or abstract thought; it is a way of being. It is a material process that takes place in things themselves, in the books or codices *(amoxtli)*, for example. The process by which the scribes *(tlacuilos)* paint or inscribe these books is not independent from nor derivative of this dialogue with the heart (their own heart as well as the essence of things). Therefore, when it is said that the *tlacuilos* bear the black ink and the red ink, it is also implied that they carry with them knowledge itself. In a way, carrying the red and the black is already being involved in a dialogue with the heart. This dialogical process comes full circle with those who read *(pohua)*, those who, in talking with their hearts, actualize and account for knowledge and wisdom. It is the reader that guides, who can see and transform what is seen into sound. In Sahagún's (1500?–1590) *Colloquios y doctrina christiana* (1564; Christian Doctrine and Colloquies), the readers are described as follows:

Los que están mirando (leyendo)
los que cuentan (lo que leen)
los que vuelven ruidosamente
las hojas de los libros de pinturas
los que tienen en su poder
Ellos nos llevan, nos guían,
la tinta negra y roja, las pinturas
nos dicen el camino.

Those who are looking (reading)
those who relate
those who noisily turn
the leaves of the books
those who constantly carry
the black ink and the red ink, the color
They are carrying us, guiding us,
they cause the earth to speak to us.

(León Portilla 1966, 76)

The reader here is the *tlamatini*, "he who has the wisdom of the word" (Mignolo 103), he who knows things. It is important to note that the *tlamatini* is not the *tlacuilo*; the skills and responsibilities of those who participate in the dialogue with the heart are quite different. The *tlamatinime* are the Nahuatl sages, those who "leen y comentan la doctrina contenida en los codices" (León Portilla 1966, 78) ("read and comment upon the doctrines contained in the codices"), as León Portilla says. However, the manner in which the knowledge is actualized here is not one that is adequately described by concepts such as reading or commentary, much less doctrine. These are terms that our tradition, in following Sahagún and other Renaissance compilers, has imported into and superimposed onto processes that may be quite different. The *tlamatinime* are simply looking, not necessarily reading in the sense of deciphering a code. This looking is a modality of the dialogue with the heart of things. And the looking operationalizes an oral component. For in looking, they are also relating; that is, they are telling a story and giving an account, counting the days and events and organizing them into a narrative.

More important, they are giving the colors poetic sense. Their dialogue organizes knowledge in time and space. It is here that orality and writing are synthesized, although the concept of synthesis is perhaps also inadequate. At any rate, they are joined together. For the *tlamatine* and the *tlacuilo*, the oral and the written are not different concepts, attitudes, or acts, although they may imply different skills. But the dialogue with the heart is both. What for us might be merely a

metaphor, "vuelven ruidosamente las hojas de los libros" ("they noisily turn the leaves of the books"), is a true identity for the Toltec (a name taken by all Nahuatl-speaking people as master scholar or artist). No doubt we can hear "el ruido característico" ("the characteristic sound") of dry *amate* paper, which "evocaba a la figura del sabio" ("evokes the figure of the sage") (León Portilla 1966, 78) as it unfolds, as León Portilla points out. But it is necessary to note as well that noisily turning the leaves can also mean making the *amate* speak. The *tlamatine* (scholar) gives sound to the *tlacuilo* (*amate* painted books). Their looking is the way in which they "cause the earth to speak to us." This is not a mere vocalization; rather, there is an inextricable juncture and combination between the image and the word (Gruzinski 13). This kind of reading (*amoxpohua*) effects a transformative process that has the power to turn painting into song and knowledge. The song is imbricated in the painting. It is neither its translation nor its supplement but its performance; and the painting is constituted of song, without being its mere illustration. *Tlacuilo* and *tlamatini*, inscription and performer, embody the "dialogue with the heart" (*tlatolyotl*). As a poem from *Cantares mexicanos* puts it, the god *Ometéotl*, the giver of life, is also referred to as a Toltec artist who created us by:

ontlantoc amoxtliya moyollo
ya onaya moch
onahciticac oo toltecayootl
A ycaya ninemiz ye nicã ayyo.

pronunciándonos como una flor
pintándonos como una canción
el libro se ha terminado
vuestro corazón está completo

pronouncing us like a flower
painting us like a song
the book is finished
your heart is complete

(Bierhorst 221)

It is not a matter of finding a new, more or less interesting or sophisticated synesthesia, but rather of recognizing a way of thinking and conceptualizing that is radically different. Being is pronounced and painted, in a book, by a Toltec. This is the heart and the essence of being completed. To read is to dialogue with the heart, and to dialogue with the heart is to sing and paint. The tlamatini "él mismo es escritura y sabiduría" (León Portilla 1966, 65) ("is himself writing and wisdom").

Let us stop for a moment on this formulation. The sage himself is wisdom and writing, in Nahuatl, *in tlilli in tlapalli*. León Portilla comments that "a la letra significa que el sabio es tinta negra y roja" ("literally this means that the sage is red and black ink"); however, he hastens to add that it is better to look at ("obvio sentido metafórico: escritura y sabiduría") ("its obvious metaphorical meaning: writing and wisdom") (1966, 65). We do not believe there is anything obvious here. On the contrary, it seems essential, though perhaps impossible, to maintain the literalness of the metaphors. If the sage is painting, and the painting is book, and the book is being, and being is culture, we have here a series of notions that demand to be articulated in some way, not necessarily by means of the Latin copula or Spanish and imperial grammar, but rather as a bundle, like the *Xiumolpilli*, or bundle of years, by which the Nahuas organized their calendric systems. The chain is not metonymic but rather temporal. The indigenous text does not confront the literal-versus-figural binary. There is no literality, or else it is all literal. This is another way of attempting to recuperate the materiality of Amerindian thought. Such thought is not symbolic, although most studies of pre-Hispanic cultures are used to reading it as such. For it is worth noting that all these things, from ink to codices to wisdom, in other words the *toltecáyotl* itself, were quite literally the bundles that the Toltec sages carried on their backs as they left Tula. They were said to bear the people themselves as well: ("Hay quienes nos guían, nos gobiernan, nos llevan a cuestas . . .") (León Portilla 1966, 76) ("There are those who guide us, govern us, carry us. . ."). These are the people who can see. And they were in charge of culture, tradition, or what we call civilization, but which they merely referred to as the bundle or the load of what should be preserved.

Surprisingly, perhaps, this skill (which was the essence of Toltec identity) was something that, for the Mexicas at least, had already been lost long before the arrival of the Spaniards. Sahagún's informants tell of an event during the long trek toward Tenochtitlan–when the Mexica people arrived at a place they called Tamounchan ("we search for home"), they found that the sages who possessed the codices had left, leaving them dispossessed. As they departed,

se llevaron la tinta negra y roja,
los códices y las pinturas
se llevaron todas las artes, la toltecáyotl
la música de las flautas

they took with them the black and red ink
the codices and paintings
they took all the arts, the *toltecáyotl*
the music of the flutes

(León Portilla 1980, 22)

Toltecáyotl had to be invented all over again. In a way, to be a Toltec meant to be capable of doing so. Such is the paradoxical logic of all traditions and legacies: Culture is always already the loss of culture. For the Mexica in particular, we could say that they had already suffered a de-toltequization at least once, before the arrival of the Spaniards. Their history is full of destructions, comings, and goings of empires and civilizations. Even book burnings were not for them a new phenomenon. However, the main difference lies in that before the Spanish Conquest, none of the changes had affected the very texture of the universe. Peoples and cultures fell, but the world, which could accommodate a great deal of destruction, continued. The de-toltequization that began to take place after the Conquest was different. After this new trauma, there seems to be little possibility of reinvention;

Todo esto pasó con nosotros,
nosotros lo vimos,
nosotros tuvimos que admirarlo.
Con esta lamentosa y triste suerte nos vimos angustiados
Golpeábamos en tanto los muros de adobe
y fue nuestra herencia una red de agujeros.
Pero nuestra soledad
ni con escudos pudo ya sostenerse.
Dejadnos morir,
dejadnos ya perecer
puesto que ya nuestros dioses han muerto . . .

All this happened with us
we saw it,
we had to look upon it.
With this sorrowful and sad fate we felt anguished

We struck back as the adobe walls fell,
and our legacy was a net of holes.
But our solitude,
even with shields could not be sustained.
Let us die,
let us perish already
since our gods are dead . . .

(León Portilla 1980, 32)

We could perhaps describe the phenomenon of the sixteenth century no longer as an encounter between two cultures, but rather as a radical misunderstanding between a culture and a *toltecáyotl.* What happens when a culture encounters a *toltecáyotl?* The two belonged to heterogeneous universes that intersected violently, forming a net full of holes. The power relations between the two were completely unequal, and, by destroying established hierarchies, also provided for tremendous changes. The encounter, then, is a trauma that marks a radical heterogeneity. In considering this trauma, we should underline two important problems: That of representation, and that of communication. The net full of holes can be a metaphor for the destroyed world, for it gives the impression of tattered remains, of shredded material. But at the same time, it is worth recalling that a net is, in essence, a conglomeration of holes. Are we then talking of the perennial question of whether a glass is half full or half empty? We could compare the notion of the net with the idea of transculturation, because both attempt to maintain the viability of both the empty and the full, being and non-being. The net marks the field of interpenetration between the two cultures but in a radically ambivalent and indecisive context. Perhaps only in cultural discourse can one valorize the torn remains of a net as an aesthetic object without taking into account the flow of conquest that left it shredded in the first place.

Seamus Deane has noted that Western thought in the post-Holocaust era has passed through a series of crises in which it has had to question such matters as the possibility of the representation of the horrible, the morality of such an attempt, the complicity of the attempt to represent catastrophe discursively, etc. However, he notes, there has not been a similar anxiety in reference to the representation of the crimes of imperialism. On the other hand, he writes:

the West has discovered in postcoloniality a form of discourse that is irrepressibly given to misrepresentation of the Other. Such misrepresentation has been accorded an ontological status. The claim that representation is always misrepresentation can lead to a depoliticized celebration of heterogeneity that ignores or subdues the cultural power and political purposes of racial stereotypes, caricatures, and other, subtler, rhetorical strategies. (356)

It seems to us that the danger is at least two-fold, and we should not forget the traps entrenched in this supposed "depoliticized celebration of heterogeneity" and in the name of the "other": First, as has already been said, the dismembering of the devastation in the name of cultural survival, and second, the essentializing of indigenous expression as a possible interference against the negativity of conquest. It is therefore crucial to reexamine the project of transculturation, taking into account these warnings against such attractive but potentially facile praxes.

If we agree with Sylvia Spitta's definition of tranculturation as "the complex processes of adjustment and re-creation–cultural, literary, linguistic, and personal–that allow for new, vital, and viable configurations to arise out of the clash of cultures and the violence of colonial and neo-colonial appropriations" (2), how can these observations about transculturation help us to understand the catastrophe that was the Conquest and its disastrous consequences? What can these supposedly transcultural practices, which testify to cultural survival, which call attention to the instances of cultural resistance, which recuperate a previously unknown text, or which discover the articulations of indigenous dynamism, tell us about the hegemonic relationships in the cultural clash? Perhaps they tell us nothing, because cultural discourse has no mechanism to articulate the power structures, except, as Deane points out, in ontological terms, as either existent or not. Thus, if there is an expression of non-Occidental culture, if there is survival of a cultural artifact, if there exists a residue of cultural material, it exists and it is good in itself. That is to say, the catastrophe of cultural imperialism has mostly been disarticulated in the cultural field. It has been possible, and relatively easy, to discuss the destruction of conquest in terms of the economic devastation of preexisting systems, of the loss of life and the dispossession of land, of the political obliteration of previous governing systems, of the destruction of communal relations and the production of foodstuffs: This documentation provides us with tangible information and evidence of conquest as an extremely destructive force. Perhaps the only thing that can be said of the critical practice of transculturation is that it is a discourse of guilt–it attempts to lighten in the cultural field what can hardly be interpreted positively (in terms of the preservation of indigenous civilization) in any other discursive field. It would be difficult to celebrate the survival of a malnourished people that nevertheless continues practicing the agricultural techniques of its forebears, and yet it has been easy to depoliticize the literary/aesthetic product of indigenous texts as material reminders of the Other. Therefore, as Deane points out, the territories of these writers

> are still disputed and colonized territories, are still economically and politically marginalized while being granted a canonical or semicanonical place in culture. This bespeaks no emancipation from an oppressive situation; it merely indicates how competently the imperial world, now rechristened the First World, can incorporate cultural material from the Third World and process it for world wide consumption–just as it does with raw material for industrial and commercial purposes. (368)

In the cultural field, the questions of power and destruction remain unanswered, and in fact, unasked. For example, how can the interpenetrations of the cultural domain be read in a writer like Guamán Poma (1524?–1613) without making judgments about levels of indigenousness versus hispanicness, and would we even want to take such measurements? Instead of reading the texts from the sixteenth century as instances of transcultural resistance and survival, which allows them an affirmative and celebratory reading, what would be the benefit of reading them as instances of cultural genocide and literary destruction? If the cultural is simply a field, in opposition to the powers that be, how is it that such power is so undeniable? And is it possible to read the points of interpenetration without the gesture of valorizing positively the instances of supposedly indigenous enunciations and, as a corollary, devaluing any perception of Spanish imposition?

Spitta reminds us that the colonizer and colonized "nevertheless change at a different rate and with a different sense of urgency" (2) and warns that the transcultural approach must keep in mind the imbalance of power intrinsic to the study of the vanquished culture. This is obviously an important point; however, we should also ask, how are these differences measured from within the cultural field? What can we do with the information that registers qualitative or quantitative differences? We must question the simple ontological naming of otherness in colonial texts as that which automatically confers value, for in such a way we limit thought's capacity. The simple celebration of any representation of cultural difference risks erasing the real destruction of imperialist practices. We are not denying the affirmative and constestatory use of the transcultural process: Culture has been used as a space of resistance against the political destruction so undeniable in other fields. By appropriating and recuperating these spaces as contestatory forces against the power of imperialism, it has been possible to mark these spaces as points of resistance, as loci of refuge. However, neutralizing the cultural clash as a mere encounter, while reserving the martial and violent codes of other discursive fields risks the complete depoliticization (and possible abuse at the hands of the status quo) of the cultural, transforming it into mere creative and joyful energy, ready to be consumed. How can sixteenth-century texts be read transculturally without falling into the trap of conferring or not conferring a certain authentic voice of the Other to the text in question? How can we avoid this essentialist movement, which confers more value to what is judged to be more authentically indigenous? This last movement seems to us the most obvious example of transcultural studies as a discourse of guilt that nevertheless does very little to change the relations of power, since that which is more highly valued culturally is what is most oppressed socially, politically, economically, and historically. It is evident that the cultural is opposed to other discourses by means of an inverted value: That which is least valued in economic terms is most valued in cultural terms. But if this value is limited only to the cultural field, this means that it can serve as an excuse for inaction, even for the mistaken belief that the cultural value offsets political oppression.

And if the transcultural process is founded on the idea that at least two intrinsically separate beings enter into a process of unequal relationship, it is worth considering that between the two cultures under consideration here there was also a series of superficial similarities that facilitated the process of acculturation. One must note that for the Nahuas, for example, writing was of prime importance. There is no doubt that it also had a considerable influence in establishing and maintaining the relations of power. The accounts of the days were kept, but so too were those of tributes and histories, as well as those of genealogies that legitimated the rule of one or another faction. Similarly, for the Spaniards in the sixteenth century, writing is crucial. One could almost say that the Spanish *toltecáyotl* is letters, and in particular, legal letters. As González Echevarría writes, "In the sixteenth century writing was subservient to the law... [T]he legal system [of the Empire] ... redefined the relationship between the individual and the body politic and held a tight rein on writing.... Legal writing was the predominant form of discourse in the Spanish Golden Age" (45).

A key example of the confrontation between orality and writing, and of their inevitable mutual misunderstanding, is that of the infamous "Requerimientos" (Injunctions of expropriation), which were duly recited to the natives before and during every taking of possession of their lands. The text is full of legalisms that mark, from the start, the problematic morality of the situation. They also emphasize the incommensurability and incomprehension that existed between the two worlds. The function of the text was to legalize the claim of possession of the New World. The text speaks, first of all, in the name of those who are not there but who nevertheless claim to be masters and sovereigns of that domain (notions that, in any case, are alien). Before a soldier could appropriate lands and peoples, he was required (hence the name) to read the following: "De partes del rey D. Fernando y de la reina doña Joana, su hija, reina de Castilla y León etc., domadores de gentes bárbaras . . . os notificamos . . ." (Las Casas 1967, 3: 26–27) ("On behalf of King Ferdinand and of the queen Juana, his daughter, Queen of Castilla and Leon, tamers of barbarian peoples, we their servants, put you on notice" (Las Casas 1971, 192–93; the following quotations are all from this text). The attitude and tone of the text already imply that its content is communicable, that the language and concepts included therein give legal notice as to some particulars, as if it were possible for the Amerindians to know what a king is and where Castille might be located. Leaving aside the fact that the communicative situation is more than problematic, we can at least note that the rhetoric of the text itself seems to highlight a certain disquiet, a certain communicative anxiety: "y hacemos saber como mejor podemos" ("and we let you know, as best we can"). After this self-referential moment, which points toward the limits of communication, and hence which attempts to exculpate and justify itself by its rhetoric, the text goes on to inform the natives: "que Dios, Nuestro Señor, vivo y eterno, crió el cielo y la tierra y un hombre y una mujer" ("that God, our Lord, living and eternal, created Heaven and Earth, and a man and a woman"), from whom all are descendants. The text informs of the existence of God, which is taken for granted. Note how the rules of evidence operate. It is assumed that there is a creator; what needs to be communicated is how, from this creator, "de quien vosotros y nosotros y todos los hombres del mundo fueron y son descendientes" ("you and us and all men of the world are and were descended"). The genealogy alluded to establishes a certain kinship between Europeans and Indians; in principle, one could even say that the rhetoric of universal brotherhood may begin to point toward a potential equality. The first (long) sentence ends by alluding to a future of peace and coexistence between the two peoples, as long as the new situation admits and recognizes the preceding genealogy.

The text continues by pointing out how the pope, a direct inheritor of Saint Peter, has declared the Catholic kings sovereigns of these newly "discovered" lands. The expropriation is immediate and de facto: ". . . a quien esto ha sido notificado, han recibido a sus Altezas y les han recibido y servido de buena voluntad y sin ninguna resistencia, luego sin dilación, como fueron informados de lo susodicho, obedecieron" ("Whosoever has already been notified of all this has received their majesties and served them in good will, without any resistance, promptly and without delay as soon as they were informed of the aforementioned, they obeyed. . . ."). All of this happening here, seems to imply, is also happening all around you; this destruction of your world is being accepted and understood by all others; you too should be so pliant. It then puts forth an ultimatum, according to which the Indians should take "tiempo que fuere justo" ("a time deemed to be just") to think about it, and then they should accept the new order so as to receive "privilegios y exenciones" ("privileges and exemptions"). But it also proffers a threat: "i no lo hicierdes, y en ello dilación maliciosamente pusierdes" ("but if you should not do what we demand, and if you maliciously attempt to delay matters"). The tone begins to become almost

hysterical; the function of the discourse seems to be less and less one of communication and more and more one of self-justification. It tries desperately to legitimize what it seems also to declare, at some level, unjustifiable. There is only one proper response to this call, and no delay is acceptable.

To any possible interlocutor, the rules of this language game must be incomprehensible: "certificoos que con la ayuda de Dios entraremos poderosamente contra vosotros y os haremos guerra por todas las partes y maneras que pudiéremos . . . y tomaremos vuestras personas y de vuestras mujeres e hijos haremos esclavos . . . y vos haremos todos los males que pudiéremos" ("be it certified that with God's help, we shall make powerful war upon you and we shall attack you everywhere that we may be able to find you, and we shall take your own persons, and your wives and children we shall enslave, and we shall inflict upon you every evil we may imagine"). In other words, we shall kill and maim and rape and pillage, which is in fact what they did do. But, and this is an important disavowal, ". . . protestamos que las muertes y daños que dello se recrecieren sea a vuestra culpa y no de sus Altezas, ni nuestra, ni destos caballeros" ("we protest that all the deaths and damages that may ensue from this shall henceforth be your own fault and not fall upon the shoulders of us or these knights or their Highnesses in Castille"). The rhetoric is instructive because it marks the limits of the relationship between language and power. The "requirement" is infamous not because it is effective (or ineffective: las Casas had already remarked on the absurdity of the situation), but because it marks what we could perhaps call the "rules of engagement." The forced legalisms reveal to what extent the Spanish Crown was preoccupied with the justice of its own actions. There is a certain unsettledness about the whole colonial project. The text of the "Requerimiento" shows an awareness of the very destruction it puts in motion. This awareness is already somewhat nostalgic, like that of Bernal Díaz, for example, when he contemplates the now lost world he himself helped to destroy. At any rate, the reading of the "Requerimiento" must be duly notarized: "pedimos al presente escribano que nos lo dé por testimonio signado . . ." ("we ask that the secretary and scribe give signed testimony etc., etc., etc. . . ."). And with such signatures, the legality of conquest, if not its morality, is formalized. Writing and power become inseparable.

Even though the "Requerimiento" might seem an easy text to demystify because of its obvious absurdity, and even though its practical power with each reading (i.e., each actualization) might be minimal in the end, it is important to remember that each time the drama of the text is represented (i.e., performed), the world itself is marked by the order of writing. It is through writing itself that the project of conquest is effected and later also destabilized. By *writing*, we do not mean simply the representation of ideas in alphabetical order, but rather, the material constitution of a modality of thought. The fact that in each reading of the "Requerimiento" there is an absolute failure of communication is important, because upon this failure all possibilities of understanding, as well as all possible misunderstandings, are constructed. Moreover, upon this very failure the structures of power that will determine future relations are also formed. Figures as diverse as Las Casas, Motolinía (1490?–1565?) (*Relaciones de la Nueva España* [1541; Reports on New Spain]), José de Acosta (1540–1600) *Historia natural y moral de las indias* (1591; Natural and moral history of the Indies), , and Diego de Landa (1524–1579) (*Relaciones de las cosas de Yucatán* [1566; *Yucatan Before and After the Conquest*, 1979]) very quickly recognized this situation.

Conquest and evangelization both depended on writing. Even though there were, from the very beginning, different opinions about whether or not the Indians had writing, there was no doubt that they had obvious and recognizable means of notation and archival record keeping. It is precisely there, in the textual field of writing, a field in essence mystified by both sides, that the battle between the two worlds took place. Note, for example, that the burning–the wholesale burning– of indigenous codices was based on the same type of fetishization that gives the object itself, the text as artifact, a certain magical, or satanic, power that threatens the order of things. The reading of the "Requerimiento," whether pro forma or not, and the burning of Pre-Hispanic documents are two sides not so much of the conflict between orality and writing, but of the disavowal of the textual constitution of the battlefield.

The "Requerimiento" is situated at the origin of transculturation, and it marks the guidelines by which the two cultures would henceforth interact. The famous dialogue at Cajamarca between the Inca Atahualpa and the priest Valverde and the subsequent and disastrous defeat of the Incas under the forces of Pizarro are paradigmatic of the encounter between heterogeneities. Antonio Cornejo Polar refers to these events as the "punto en el cual la oralidad y la escritura no solamente marcan sus diferencias extremas sino que hacen evidente su mutua ajenidad y su recíproca y agresiva repulsión" (28) ("point at which orality and writing not only mark their extreme differences but also make evident their mutual heterogeneity and their reciprocal and aggressive repulsion"). There are various extant versions of the facts of this encounter, but, generally, it is known that Pizarro and his men were guests of Atahualpa, that the Incan troops were immensely superior in number, and that at the beginning of their dialogue, Father Valverde presented Atahualpa with a version of the "Requerimiento." Valverde indicated that the doctrine is clearly set forth in a breviary; Atahualpa requested the object itself for inspection and, depending on the version, was unable to open it, opened it and claimed it said nothing or clarified nothing since it spoke not, and ended up throwing it on the ground. This act was then taken as the ultimate insult by Pizarro's troops and became the signal to begin the surprise attack in which the Spanish massacred six or seven thousand Indians and took Atahualpa prisoner (Hemming 40). It is worth noting that in the most schematic version of events, what is most evident is that the dominant mode of relationships is that of misunderstanding (whether one allows for good or bad faith).

The scene presents us with an impossible communicative situation. Leaving aside the fact that the verbal exchange is at any rate mediated by translators, it is obvious that there are numerous errors of interpretation at all levels. As Cornejo Polar has pointed out, the majority of the Spanish chroniclers interpret the event as a failure of orality and hence the proof of Inca barbarism. Atahualpa fails to marvel before the power of the Word, which justifies his destruction. However, the event can also be read inversely, as "como la historia del fracaso del propio libro" (39) ("the history of the failure of the book itself") that indeed did not speak. It would be strange to catalogue the reaction of marveling before a magical, sacred, though inert object as the only adequately civilized reaction. On the contrary, it is Pizarro's men, most of whom could not read, who should be properly called superstitious or primitive, for it is they who expected the book to exert some sort of power or spell. As Lienhard has noted, it is the West that fetishized writing, in order to then project a false ingenuity on

non-literate cultures (1991, 12). In any case, the encounter between Atahualpa and Valverde is important not so much for what happens at the semantic level, where bad interpretations are in the end irrelevant, but for what happens at the level of a ritual act, a performance. The characters are playing a role in which they think they know the script (or the rhythm). Valverde and Pizarro needed to comply with the "Requerimiento" in order to legalize their taking possession of the lands. They needed, also, to plant calculated insults to establish an adequate *causus belli*. From his own perspective, Atahualpa played a similar role. He was not particularly worried about the threat posed by two or three hundred Spaniards. On the contrary, the intrigues against his brother Huascar presented a much more immediate political affront. His main error was not his misunderstanding of the book, but rather his underestimation of Pizarro himself. Within the performative game of diplomacy, his insult too was quite calculated. According to his own nephew, Titu Cusi Yupanqui, the gesture of throwing the breviary was a direct response to a previous affront, when the Spaniards had spilled the "chicha" that had been offered to them earlier. (See Seed.) This interpretation puts the events in a very different context, where the speech acts operative within Inca diplomacy end up being heterogeneous to the rules from the Christian-Imperial language game. Titu Cusi, for his part, has already learned the lesson when he describes his own father, Manco Inca, Atahualpa's brother, as someone capable of functioning in both registers (Lienhard 1992, 165). That is to say, unlike Atahualpa, who expects to communicate with his guests, and unlike Pizarro, for whom communication is irrelevant as long as the formality (and formalism) of the "Requerimiento" is adhered to, Manco Inca manipulates his own discourse so that the Spaniard understands one thing and the Indian another. This marks the reemergence of Colonial indigenous discourses, which more than representing transculturation, actually mark an inevitable disglossia.

Both Felipe Guamán Poma de Ayala and Inca Garcilaso de la Vega (1539–1616) confront, recount, and reinterpret this same set of events. For Guamán Poma, the encounter marks not so much an incompatibility of discourses as an inversion of the relations of power and a turning upside down of the world. Guamán Poma describes the encounter as follows:

> Y preguntó el dicho Ynga a fray Uicente quién se lo auía dicho. Responde fray Uicente que le auía dicho euangelio, el libro. Y dixo Atagualpa: 'Dámelo a mí el libro para que me lo diga.' Y ancí se la dio y lo tomó en las manos y comensó a oxear las ojas del dicho libro. Y dize el dicho Ynga: 'Qué, cómo no me lo dize? (Ni me habla a mí el dicho libro!' Hablando con grande magestad, asentado en su trono, y lo echó el dicho libro de las manos el dicho Ynga Atagualpa. (392)

> And the Inca asked Fray Vicente (Valverde) who had told him so. Fray Vicente responds that the Gospel had told him so, the book. And Atahualpa said: "Give it to me, the book, so that it can tell me." And so he took it in his hands and began to peruse the pages of the aforementioned book. And the Inca says: "How come it does not tell me? It doesn't talk or say anything, this book." Speaking with great majesty, sitting high on his throne, the said Atahualpa Inca flung the said book from his hands.

Guamán Poma also illustrates the encounter, and he draws Atahualpa sitting in his throne while Pizarro and Valverde appear before him as supplicants. While the drawings seems to emphasize the majesty of the Inca, as Rolena Adorno has shown, the hierarchical order of the characters has been inverted. Adorno states: "By disordering the signs of Andean spatial representation, Guamán Poma symbolizes the threat to Andean political order occasioned by this event" (93).

There are various levels of incoherence that stage an interpretative aporia. On the one hand, we witness the tension between the narrative and the illustrations: The inversion of hierarchies is codified but not made explicit; the overthrow of Atahualpa's throne is narrated but not drawn, etc. On the other hand, the most obvious tension is that between orality and writing. Guamán Poma does not resolve these tensions. He presents his text as a translation from the oral to the written, making passing references to the *khipus*, mnemonic devices that force him to organize his thoughts differently. However, he visualizes his text not as a revocation of a culture now happily merged with the European one, but as an intervention, in the form of a letter to the sovereign, in search of his own survival: "'Desde aquí de ueynte años no abrá yndio en este rreyno de que se cirua su corona rreal y defensa de nuestra sante fe católica. Porque cyn los yndios, vuestra Magestad no uale cosa porque se acuerde Castilla es Castilla por los yndios'" (982) ("'From here until twenty years from now, there will be no Indian in this kingdom by which your royal crown and the defense of our holy Catholic faith might be served. Because without the Indians, your Majesty is not worth anything. Because one must remember that Castille is Castille because of the Indians'" [Adorno 29]). To a certain extent, his own attempted dialogue repeats the failure of the one begun in Cajamarca. As Beatriz Pastor has pointed out, "La *Nueva crónica* es, en ese sentido, una exploración minuciosa–lingüística, cultural y política–de la imposibilidad del diálogo en la sociedad colonial" (343) ("The *Nueva crónica* is a minute, detailed, linguistic, cultural and political exploration of the impossibility of dialogue in colonial society").

Unlike Guamán Poma, Inca Garcilaso de la Vega is compelled to construct some kind of subject that is intelligible to a community of European readers. However, this subject is marked by an unreadable otherness. His own interpretation of the events at Cajamarca offers us a third, now conciliatory version. Garcilaso alleges that the misunderstanding could have been avoided if only there had been better translators. His version even denies that Atahualpa ever tossed down the book (he moreover claims that this event is pure invention by Spanish historians), although he does admit that there are various conflicting versions of the story. Garcilaso thus presents himself as the best interpreter, capable not of inventing but simply of translating the sequence of events. His own *Comentarios reales* (1609; *The Royal Commentaries of Peru*), in fact, does not pretend to offer another point of view but rather a concordant one, which merely clarifies some discrepancies from the Indian side: "Para atajar esta corrupción me sea lícito, pues soy indio, que en esta historia yo escriba como indio" (1976, 7) ("I, being an Indian, may properly avoid this corruption, and write this history as an Indian" [1963, viii]). Garcilaso, writing from Spain, attempts to insert Indian culture into Spanish culture, whereas Guamán Poma presents a world in which the Indian worldview ceases to be an organizing principle.

We should pause for a moment to consider Garcilaso Inca's problematic use of personal pronouns in the *Comentarios reales*, a text that seems to want to assert an Indian/Mestizo subjectivity. Already, in his preface, the mestizo writer claims a privileged role conferred upon him as a descendant from both Spanish and Inca cultures, which, he states, authorizes his text.

This text, moreover, does not try to correct the Spanish histories, but merely to clarify certain inconsistencies of translation:

> En el discurso de la historia protestamos la verdad de ella, y que no diremos cosa grande que no sea autorizándola con los mismos historiadores españoles que la tocaron en parte o en todo, que mi intención no es contradecirles, sino servirles de comento y glosa, y de intérprete en muchos vocablos indios, que como extranjeros en aquella lengua interpretaron fuera de la propiedad de ella. (1976, 5–6)

> In the text of the history I protest (sic) concerning its truth, and that I affirm no important circumstance that is not authorized by the Spanish historians, either in part or altogether. My intention is not to contradict them, but to supply a commentary and gloss, and to interpret many Indian words which they, as strangers in that land (sic) gave a mistaken meaning. (1963, v–vi)

Garcilaso will insist over and over again throughout his gloss that his text, and hence Inca civilization itself, is a supplement to and not a replacement of Spanish history. His commentaries are a synecdoche of Indian civilization in relation to the Spanish conquest: They do not contradict, they merely add. But when we see how the author portrays his own research in the question he poses to his old uncle, a sage who is keeper of the Inca histories, we can easily see that his chosen role of translator and glosser will not easily remain within the confines of a supplement:

> Inca, tío, pues no hay escritura entre vosotros, que es lo que guarda la memoria de las cosas pasadas, ¿qué noticias tenéis del origen y principio de nuestros reyes? Porque allá los españoles y las otras naciones sus comarcanas, como tienen historias divinas y humanas, saben por ellas cuándo empezaron a reinar . . . Empero vosotros, que carecéis de ellos, ¿qué memoria tenéis de vuestras antiguallas? ¿Quién fue el primero de nuestros Incas?, ¿cómo se llamó?, ¿qué origen tuvo su linaje?, de qué manera empezó a reinar?, ¿con qué gente y armas conquistó este grande imperio?, qué origen tuvieron nuestras hazañas? (1976, 37)

> Ynca, my uncle, *you* have no writings which preserve the memory of past events; but what accounts have you of the origin of *our* kings? For the *Spaniards*, and other people who live on their borders, have divine and human histories, and they know through them when their kings began to reign. . . . But *you*, who have no books, what memory have you preserved respecting *your* ancestors? Who was the first of *our* Yncas? What was his name? What was his origin? In what manner did he begin to reign? With what people and arms did he conquer this great empire? What beginning had *our* history? (1963, 62–63, emphasis added)

In these almost violent changes between nationalities, between dominant and dominated communities, we see underlined the position/counterposition of the translator, conscious or unconscious. This is illustrated by the binary oppositions into which the glosser has trouble fitting, making it difficult for him to remain a mere and impartial linguistic supplement. Garcilaso's main problem, in the final analysis, is a problem of translation. Besides redeeming the Inca world, he also wants to present it as a model. Garcilaso offers the Europeans a lesson on how to conquer and civilize other peoples correctly, vying first for their love rather than for their resentment. By necessity, the translator finds himself in alternating positions. As much as Inca Garcilaso de la Vega wants to insert Inca civilization into the pages of official histories of the Spanish Conquest, his project cannot remain innocent and harmless; the task of the translator brings with it an obligation. Translation, transference, and transculturation always replace, reposition, cancel, and lack something; they cannot escape loss. In the end

Garcilaso will refer to Inca civilization as "esta república, antes destruida que conocida" (1976, 46) ("this empire, which was destroyed as soon as it was known" [1963, 78])–a statement that severely questions his own claim to be offering merely a friendly amendment to the text.

The sixteenth century is filled with discourse of disaster. Bartolomé de las Casas (1474–1566) is not the only writer who speaks of devastation. Writing enters the continent and becomes omnipresent. Colonial America produces (and destroys) an unimaginable quantity of documents of all types, particularly legal and litiginous documents. Sahagún produces his *Historia general de las cosas de la Nueva España* [General History] (started in 1547), codices and annals are updated, and the indigenous communities, now forming new and distinct social organizations, enter into the field of writing and written legitimation. By the middle of the seventeenth century, the so-called *Primordial Titles* are produced. In these, the histories of different towns, families, and genealogies are reconstructed. These primordial titles are official documents, anonymously written for the purpose of legitimizing the recognition of particular borders and domains of certain towns (Lockhart 1992, 20–21; Gruzinski 98). By this time, the Spanish, *criollo,* and *mestizo* populations were growing and gaining a firm foothold. The indigenous population was also recovering to a certain extent from the previous century's devastation and beginning to demand new rights under the new infrastructure (See Lienhard 1992). They entered into territorial disputes by appealing to colonial justice. Often in these documents, a history is related concerning how a town was granted the domain of this or that territory, by mercy of such and such authority. These titles pretend to have been written in the sixteenth century in order to establish precedence among the different disputes. In some cases, the text itself proclaims its own authenticity: "This writing is not new nor made yesterday. . . . because it was done an immemorial time ago" (Gruzinski 101). The authors reconstructed titles by using archaic rhetoric and century-old paper to enter into disputes not so much with the crown but more often with neighboring towns. Lockhart mentions a title factory and Gruzinski discusses their falsehood. Presenting stylistic anachronisms, Lockhart compares the text of an existing title with what it would say if it had in fact been written in the sixteenth century: "'ninotlimachiotia notoca notonal. Ton Locax te xantiaco tlacuilo:' 'I sign my name and rubric. Don Lucas de Santiago, notary,' a real one would read 'ninofirmayotia don Lucas de Stiago escribano'" (1992, 414). What matters is not that the titles were false documents but rather that they give us an idea of the degree to which the indigenous peoples had been assimilated and/or had comprehended the new order after only 150 years of the Conquest. The discourse is the same as that of the "Requerimiento," but from the point of view of those who arrived after the devastation had taken place. What we have here is a kind of appropriation of writing and its forms of power for new, creative, and different purposes.

The Jesuit Joseph de Acosta (1540–1600) had already recognized that the problem of translation was central to the project of evangelization. Translation and transculturation were intimately joined, and without resolving the former, the latter would fail. Acosta observed that the indigenous languages seemed to lack concepts to express certain universal abstractions: Truth, Justice, God. He wrote,

Porque si queremos en lengua de indios hallar vocablo que corresponde a este Dios, como en latín responde Deus y en griego Theos, y en hebreo El y en arábigo Alåa, no se halla en lengua del Cuzco, ni en lengua de México, por donde los que predican o escriben para los indios usan el mismo nuestro español, Dios. (13)

Because if we want to find, in the language of the Indians, a term that corresponds to this God, as in Latin we have Deus, and in Greek Theos, and in Hebrew El, and in Arabic Allah, you won't find it either in the tongue of Cuzco or in the tongue of Mexico, where those who preach or write for the Indians use our own Spanish term, Dios.

In his classification of the different genres of idolatry, Acosta tells us that the Indians always venerate specific things, whether they be natural phenomena, particular objects, or deceased people. The *huacas* of the Incas, for example, are objects or places considered sacred because they fall outside the norm. Generally, they are either very big or very ugly or simply very unusual things: "Cualquier cosa que tenga extrañeza les parecía que tenía divinidad" (Acosta 18) ("Anything that seems strange seemed to the Indians that it had divinity"). In their evangelizing and pedagogical project, the Spaniards transformed the specific (and satanic) divinity of certain *huacas* into the model of abstract, universal Christianity. Acosta offers us the following example: "Para fundir una campana grande tuvimos en la Ciudad de los Reyes, necesidad de leña recia y mucha, y cortóse un arbolazo disforme, que por su antigüedad y grandeza había sido largos años adoratorio y guaca de los indios" (18) ("to forge a large bell, we had in Ciudad de los Reyes the need for much strong firewood, and we cut a huge and deformed tree that, because of its age and size, had been for many years shrine and *huaca* to the Indians"). This is a true act of translation. We could almost say that it is a kind of transubstantiation, whether alchemical or theological. In any case, the interpellation of the bell will find that it is mediated by the pagan divinity. As Edmundo O'Gorman has pointed out in his introduction, Acosta's book creates a rigorous and congruent system of the universe, the world, nature, and man (Acosta xv). Within this system, idolatry itself, as a satanic parody of the Christian order, serves, in the final analysis, as a function of Providence that will redeem itself–although not before undergoing a process of violent transculturation. Together with evangelization, there operates a project of rather less spiritual conquest. The extirpation of idolatry and plunder are complementary. As Pierre Duviols has pointed out, it is not surprising that "extirpation was a convenient and providential pretext for pillage, since objects of gold were abundant, especially in the 'temples of Satan'" (90). By 1550 almost all important temples had been destroyed (Duviols 90), and the majority of the documents had been lost.

The pre-Hispanic world was a world full of documents. In Mesoamerica, Aztecs and Mayas, among others, had developed highly sophisticated writing systems that were central to their culture, gathering together memoirs, histories, the records of tributes, and so forth. Today, however, most pre-Hispanic documents have been lost, or very few have survived, and even many of these are of doubtful authority. A system of hieroglyphic writing of great complexity was developed, and it found itself grafted and recontextualized in the new world of alphabetic writing. What has survived is a plethora of copies and already hybrid texts produced after the Conquest and responding to later needs. The work of Sahagún is invaluable, but it responds to a specific gathering and its specific context. It is therefore necessary to read it in relation to that new context, for there is no doubt that it includes it.

The text is and remains always contextual. The text (as with any legal document) is always a response to a particular situation, even when the latter cannot be (or can no longer be) fully articulated. The text always contains its context in some form; it enframes it. As Stephen Greenblatt puts it, literary texts "contain directly or by implication much of the situation [in which they were produced] within themselves, and it is this sustained absorption that enables many literary works to survive the collapse of the conditions that led to their production" (227). That is not to say that their significance lies only in their context, but that the context too can and must be read through. The context is part of the text, not vice versa. But in the case of the sixteenth-century Americas, we often have to read artifacts that are not exactly texts. Nahuatl hieroglyphic writing, for example, was constituted in various modalities. On the one hand, there were pictograms, paintings that more or less represented directly what they were attempting to portray: a god, for example, or a particular event. There were also specific ideograms: stylizations of things like water, stone, mountain, and so forth. The complexity of relationships between the different elements produced changes in meaning. There were, finally, elements that played a phonetic as well as a mimetic role. They functioned, as Gruzinski points out, like a rebus (30). A famous example, cited by Lockhart, is the use of the ideogram for buttocks (*tzintli*), which is a small drawing of the lower part of the body; when used in conjunction with another ideogram, it signals the diminutive, since the phonetic suffix -*tzin* performs that function (1992, 328). Thus, visual punning and wordplay, in general, played a very important role in the production of meaning.

It is not yet known to what extent the Nahuatl phonetic system was elaborated, although it is known that the Mayas used it even more, compiling very complex syllabaries. What is clear is that after the Conquest, the role of the phonetic elements within hieroglyphic writing grew considerably. In order to cite Christian names, for example, there soon appeared very current codifications. *Francisco*, to offer just one example, was represented by the glyphs for *pantli*, banner, *cilin*, seashell, and *comitl*, pot. Thus it could be read *Pan-ci-co*, Francisco, which becomes *Pancho* (Lockhart 1992, 332). These artifacts are structured like texts, that is to say, they possess a fluidity and adaptability that allows something like transculturation to take place in them.

It is worth noting, as Jacques Lafaye points out, that a transcultural process is set in motion from the very beginning of colonial times. In his investigations about the story of Topiltzin, fray Diego Durán finds that "[an old Indian] began to tell me the content of chapter 14 of Exodus. If an old Indian recited Exodus in telling the story of Quetzalcóatl's flight, one can imagine what the accounts of young acculturated Indians must have been like. In any case, even before Durán, the image of Quetzalcoatl must have been markedly syncretic?" (160).

Just as many indigenous histories and songs were translated and glossed by Sahagún and other Franciscan missionaries, many Christian texts were rendered into Nahuatl. There exists, for example, a sixteenth-century "translation" or transliteration of the *Pater Noster* into hieroglyphic writing. The text begins with the glyph for the word *pantli* (in Nahuatl, a banner or flag of sorts) followed by the glyph for *nochtli* (in Nahuatl, the cactus fruit or tuna); and so it continues, phoneticizing syllables in a like manner until it ends with the symbols for *atl* (water) and *metl* (agave), amen (Gruzinski 30; Picón Salas 82). The idea is that the Indian is supposed to read *pantli nochtli* phonetically, and not to see the images of the hieroglyph. A proper reading of the pictographic writing would of course produce pure, absurd gibberish, while the phonetic reading produces a distorted Latin. It is worth recalling that the majority of the Indians, even those who would have been able to "read" and recite the *Pantli Nochtli*, would not have been able to understand Latin in any case, although in the *calmecac* of Tlatelolco, for example, the sons of the Mexica nobility, at least, were beginning to be educated in Latin, Hebrew, Spanish, and Nahuatl. In any case, it is precisely the fact that this new hybrid is incomprehensible that gives it both its sacred and its poetic power. At this stage, the scribes, the *tlacuilos*, could still adapt certain aspects of their old art to the new context and produce novel meanings.

A text that clearly reveals the play of text and context between the problem of representation in general and the problem of deculturation in particular is the sixteenth-century Quiché Mayan cosmogony and epic entitled the *Popol Vuh* (first published in 1857). The *Popol Vuh* has gained great importance given that it is one of the few texts from the period under question that has survived. But in the context of Mayan culture in general, it is not a particularly important text. The Quiché people were merely one of many ethnic groups of Maya-related peoples that inhabited the region of modern Chiapas, Yucatan, Guatemala, Belize, and Honduras at the time of the Spanish arrival. They may have been descendants of the Classical Mayas who built cities like Palenque and Tikal but who had already disappeared by the ninth century. The Quiché were not a civilization of great pyramids, but they were a people of writing. The *Popol Vuh* was one of their central texts. The original book, now lost, must have been quite an artifact, a hieroglyphic codex in which there was inscribed the origin of the universe, various etiological myths, and the lineage and history of a particular people, along with their relations with their various neighbors. We can only imagine what the artifact looked like, but it was probably very elaborate, colorful, and full of illustrations. The book was an instrument and called such: a seeing instrument. Its purpose was to give sight or understanding. The text was read on specific occasions and according to rigorous protocols in order to shed light on particular situations.

This is not the text we have now. In the sixteenth century a number of anonymous Quichés who were literate in Spanish produced a transcribed version of the hieroglyphic text, still in Quiché but now rendered in the Roman alphabet. What they transcribed, however, was not the hieroglyphs directly, but a singular oral performance that took its cues from the hieroglyphs, that is to say, a particular reading among a variety of possible ones. This reading was already dematerialized, since it divided the songs from the images, which, as we have seen, should have been inseparable. This first "Westernized" text probably had a number of illustrations accompanying the Quiché transcript, for there are various references that seem to indicate and explicate one particular image or another. We do not have this version either. It, or a copy of it, was found in the small parish of Chichicastenango by a friar, Francisco Ximénez (1666–ca. 1722), who copied the Quiché text along with his own Spanish translation of it into two columns in the early eighteenth century. This is the earliest documented version we have, and it is held today at the Newberry Library in Chicago. During the nineteenth and early twentieth centuries, the standard edition of the *Popol Vuh* was in French. Ironically, the most widely available Spanish edition for a good part of the twentieth century was Miguel Ángel Asturias's (1899–1974) 1927 translation of the French version by Georges Reynaud. Today, the definitive edition, perhaps in any language, is the English translation by Denis Tedlock, published by Simon and Schuster in 1985. The reason we trace this textual history is to point out the multiplicity of "scenes of writing," all of which allude to an original locus of enunciation that is now irremediably and irretrievably lost. This is not to say that the text can no longer be contextualized, but that the text has always already been a play of contexts, recontextualizations, translations, and interpretations.

In an almost uncanny prefiguration of its own (con)textual history, the *Popol Vuh* stages a scene in which the difficulties with the transmission of messages are played out. Two of the book's heroes, boys named Hunahpu and Xbalanque, are summoned to the underworld, Xibalba, because their ball playing makes too much noise and annoys the lords of the underworld. The lords send forth the owl messengers, who meet up with the boys' grandmother and inform her of the summons. She then turns and charges a louse with going to get the boys. Along the way, the louse is eaten by a toad, who is then eaten by a snake, who in turn is eaten by a falcon, who finally, and coincidentally, perches himself near the ball game where the boys are playing. The boys, unaware of the cybernetic chain, shoot the falcon with their blowguns. The wounded falcon tells them, "Traigo un mensaje en mi vientre. Curadme primero el ojo y después os diré" (1971, 77) ("My word is contained in my belly. But heal my eye first, then I'll name it" [1985, 132]). After they tend to him, however, articulate speech does not come forth. He does eventually regurgitate the snake, who repeats the gesture, ("Aquí está el mandado en mi vientre . . ." (1971, 78) ("My word is contained in my belly . . ." [1985, 133]) and so on. But when we get to the toad we are told that "Y en seguida hizo esfuerzos, pero no pudo vomitar; solamente se le llenaba la boca como de baba, y no le venía el vómito" (1971, 78) ("then he tried to throw up, but there was no vomit, he just sort of drooled. He was trying, but there was no vomit" [1985, 133]). So "dándole de puntapiés en el trasero, y el hueso del anca le bajó a las piernas. Probó de nuevo, pero sólo la baba le llenaba la boca" (1971, 78) ("they kicked him in the rear, and they crushed the bones of his rear end with their feet. When he tried again, he just sort of spit" [1985, 133]). They do finally get the louse out, who does in fact deliver the message—correctly—but the story is nevertheless symptomatic of the problem of transporting, translating, and metaphorizing across contexts. It acts as a striking example of a fable of transculturation. It is also a testimony, albeit a comic one, to the very real problems associated with a variety of loci of enunciation. The text is self-referential and proleptic in ways that none of the various authors and reiterators could have intended.

If we briefly look at the preamble of the *Popol Vuh*, we can begin to see how this process is already at work. It opens with a prologue that could not have been a part of the hieroglyphic version: "Este es el principio de las antiguas historias de este lugar llamado Quiché" (1971, 21) ("This is the beginning of the Ancient word, here in this place called Quiché" [1985, 71]). The text immediately alludes to its context, invoking a "this" and a "here." But what is the status of the "this" and the "here"? What is the "this" in "this is the beginning"? The beginning of the book? The beginning of the performance

that is being transcribed into the book? The beginning of the elocution that will articulate the beginning of the world? The summons to begin? Where does the text begin? The Quiché text reads "*Are uxé oher tzih*" ("This Root Old Saying"). The word for beginning is already a metaphor, root, but it is a root of something even older, the ancient word, which is language, saying. The deictic, "this," then is pointing to a before-the-beginning, to the foundation, root, origin, source, and so on, not necessarily of the universe but of the language that says the universe—although by a curious logic, this ancient word becomes the source itself as well. But on a more pragmatic level, the "this" and the "here" are indices, markers that point to the place where the contexts merge, where the enunciation, or the writing, is reoperationalizing earlier beginnings. This is the text itself; "here" is the place where it is being written. The indices mark the frame, but they also mark the place where the text goes beyond its frame to connect to its outside, its earlier iteration, and thus to prepare the way for the possible reframings of its later iteration. For the Mayas, these divisions were not problematic in the way that they might be for "us."

The text continues as follows: "Aquí escribiremos y comenzaremos las antiguas historias, el principio y el origen de todo lo que se hizo en la ciudad de Quiché, por las tribus de la nación quiché" (1971, 21) ("Here we shall inscribe, we shall implant the Ancient Word, the potential source for everything done in the citadel of Quiché, in the nation of Quiché people" [1985, 71]). The word may be ancient, but it needs to be reinscribed, replanted, so it can be a root, a further beginning for other iterations. The text already sees itself essentially as writing and as agriculture. It is a written artifact through and through, and yet it is permeated with orality, the saying of the here and now. There is an appropriation of a different medium, a different kind of writing, which is antithetical to the time and space of its composition, as Walter Mignolo has pointed out. If any true transculturation were to have been possible, the sixteenth century marks the end of its possibilities. The indigenous elites adapted themselves, to a large extent, to the European Renaissance, instituted under the guidance of the Franciscan schools in which grammar, rhetoric, and theology were taught in indigenous as well as classical languages (Gruzinski 62). Many Indians collaborated diligently in the Christianizing process. However, since they could not themselves become priests, they remained forever neophytes. At times, the Church was more afraid of the production of new texts than of the discovery of old texts.

The prologue of the *Popul Vuh*, which replants the agricultural metaphor of writing, is a magnificent catachresis. But it is not merely a figure of speech; it is quite literally the beginning. It goes on: "Esto lo escribiremos ya dentro de la ley de Dios, en el Cristianismo; lo sacaremos a luz porque ya no se ve" (1971, 21) ("We shall write about this now amid the preaching of God, in Christendom now. We shall bring it out because there is no longer a place to see it" [1985, 71]). Again, the text constantly points to a context that is now, if not lost, at least in need of reconstruction and reinterpretation. And yet, by definition, that is precisely the meaning of a text. The text speaks, as trace of otherness and heterogeneity. The *Popol Vuh* was a seeing book, a theoretical book, so we can see the irony of the fact that the preface of the text now being transcribed points to the absence or invisibility of the original text. What we have is a seeing instrument that is nowhere to be seen. The fact that the hieroglyphic or oral text needs to be transcribed is testimony to a lack, a loss in the context of the original artifact. It does not speak. It just sort of drools.

To speak of transculturation in the sixteenth century is to fall into an anachronism. As we have pointed out, the peoples submitted to conquest and colony were not, strictly speaking, cultures, in the sense of the Western definition of the term, however widely it is defined. Nonetheless, pre-Hispanic peoples did form networks of production, transmission, and manipulations of meanings. From this point of view, one of the most important phenomena of this period was the production, by means of violent impositions as well as failed seductions, of a new series of signifying conglomerations that today we could call transcultural. However, it must be recalled that transculturation is intimately linked to a movement that is, in the final analysis, homogenizing–to a state project, that is, to a recuperation of a certain political meaning–which is then attributed a posteriori to elements that represented, instead, the absolute and radical failure of meaning. The networks of meaning from the Tahuantinsuyu to the Mixteca slowly disintegrated. Populations saw themselves decimated, not only by wars, epidemics, hunger, or slavery, but also and especially because their systems of production of cultural meaning stopped functioning and reproducing themselves. In the new colonial world, the values that were hitherto highest were completely devalued. It would perhaps make more sense to speak of nihilism than of transculturation. From the indigenous point of view, the end of the world is the end of the world. To speak of the vision of the vanquished is already to fall into a project of the recuperation of meaning, which actually serves other interests. Any interpretation of the terrible events of the encounter, from Sahagún's informants to León Portilla, becomes, in the final analysis, a rescue operation. However, the culture here rescued, as a network of signifiers, is by definition salvageable. That is to say, it is open to making signifying connections, to translation, transformation, interpretation, and misinterpretation and to submerging itself in new signifying processes (which nevertheless remain historical, and result in a transcultural situation). We can recognize that transculturation, as an operation to rescue lost and expired meanings and values, is an essentially Western and nihilist project, incapable of thinking the destroyed alterity even while remaining haunted by it.

Works Cited

Acosta, Joseph de. 1962. *Historia natural y moral de las indias en que se tratan de las cosas notables del cielo/elementos/metales/plantas y animales dellas/y los ritos/y ceremonias/leyes y gobierno de los indios.* Ed. Edmundo O'Gorman. Mexico City: Universidad Nacional Autónoma de México.

Adorno, Rolena. 1986. *Guamán Poma: Writing and Resistance in Colonial Peru.* Austin: University of Texas Press.

Benavente, Fray Toribio de (Motolinía). [1541] 1964. *Relaciones de la Nueva España.* Mexico City: Universidad Nacional Autónoma de México.

Bierhorst, John. 1985. *Cantares mexicanos: Songs of the Aztecs.* Stanford, CA: Stanford University Press.

Casas, Bartolomé de las. 1967. *Historia de las Indias.* 3 vols. Ed. Agustín Millares Carlo. Mexico City: Fondo de Cultura Económica.

——. 1971. *History of the Indies.* Trans. Andrée Collard. New York: Harper and Row.

Clendinnen, Inga. 1991. *Aztecs: An Interpretation.* Cambridge: Cambridge University Press.

Cornejo Polar, Antonio. 1994. *Escribir en el aire: Ensayo sobre la heterogeneidad cultural en las literaturas andinas.* Lima: Editorial Horizonte.

Deane, Seamus. 1995. "Imperialism/Nationalism." *Critical Terms for Literary Study.* Eds. Frank Lentricchia and Thomas McLaughlin. 2nd ed. Chicago: Univeristy of Chicago Press. 354–68.

Duviols, Pierre. 1977. *La destrucción de las religiones andinas: Conquista y colonia.* Trans. Albor Maruenda. Mexico City: Universidad Nacional Autónoma de México.

Garcilaso de la Vega, Inca. 1963. *First Part of the Royal Commentaries of the Yncas.* Trans. Clements R. Markham. New York: B. Franklin.

González Echevarría, Roberto. 1990. *Myth and Archive: A Theory of Latin American Narrative.* New York: Cambridge University Press.

——. 1976. *Comentarios reales de los Incas.* Vol. 1. Ed. Aurelio Miró Quesada. Caracas: Biblioteca Ayacucho.

Greenblatt, Stephen. 1995. "Culture." *Critical Terms for Literary Study.* Eds. Frank Lentricchia and Thomas McLaughlin. 2nd ed. Chicago: University of Chicago Press. 225–32.

Gruzinski, Serge. 1993. *The Conquest of Mexico: The Incorporation of Indian Societies into the Western World, 16th–18th Centuries.* Cambridge: Polity Press.

Guamán Poma de Ayala, Felipe. 1987. *Nueva crónica y buen gobierno.* Eds. John V. Murra, Rolena Adorno, Jorge L. Urioste. Madrid: Historia 16.

Hemming, John. 1970. *The Conquest of the Incas.* New York: Harcourt Brace Jovanovich.

Lafaye, Jacques. 1976. *Quetzalcóatl and Guadalupe: The Formation of Mexican National Consciousness.* Chicago: The University of Chicago Press.

Landa, Diego de. [1566] 1938. *Relación de las cosas de Yucatán.* Mexico City: Editorial Pedro Robredo.

León Portilla, Miguel. 1966. *Filosofía náhuatl estudiada en sus fuentes.* Mexico City: Universidad Nacional Autónoma de México.

——. 1980. *Toltecáyotl: aspectos de la cultura náhuatl.* Mexico City: Fondo de Cultura Económica.

Lienhard, Martin. 1991. *La voz y su huella: escritura y conflicto étnico-social en América Latina, 1492–1988.* Hanover: Ediciones del Norte.

——. 1992. *Testimonios, cartas y manifiestos indígenas: desde la conquista hasta comienzos del siglo XX.* Caracas: Biblioteca Ayacucho.

Lockhart, James. 1992. *The Nahuas after the Conquest: A Social and Cultural History of the Indians of Central Mexico, Sixteenth through Eighteenth Centuries.* Stanford: Stanford Universtiy Press.

Mignolo, Walter D. 1995. *The Darker Side of the Renaissance: Literacy, Territoriality, and Colonization.* Ann Arbor: University of Michigan Press.

Pastor Bodmer, Beatriz. 1996. *El jardín y el peregrino: Ensayos sobre el pensamiento utópico latinoamericano, 1492–1695.* Amsterdam: Rodopi.

Picón Salas, Mariano. 1958. *De la conquista a la independencia: Tres siglos de historia cultural latinoamericana.* Mexico City: Fondo de Cultura Económica.

Popul Vuh: Las antiguas historias del Quiché. 1971. 7th ed. Ed. and trans. Adrián Recinos. Mexico City: Fondo de Cultura Económica.

Popul Vuh: The Definitive Edition of the Mayan Book of the Dawn of Life and the Glories of Gods and Kings. 1985. Trans. Denis Tedlock. New York: Simon and Schuster.

Rama, Ángel. 1982. *Transculturación narrativa en América Latina.* Mexico City: Siglo Veintiuno.

——. 1985. "La señal de Jonás sobre el pueblo mexicano." *La crítica de la cultura en América Latina.* Eds. Saúl Sosnowski and Tomás Eloy Martínez. Caracas: Biblioteca Ayacucho. 19–65.

Sahagún, Bernardino de. [1569] 1985. *Historia general de las cosas de Nueva España.* Barcelona: Tusquets: Círculo de Lectores.

Seed, Patricia. 1991. "'Failing to Marvel': Atahualpa's Encounter with the Word." *Latin American Research Review* 26.1: 7–32.

Spitta, Silvia. 1995. *Between Two Waters: Narratives of Transculturation in Latin America.* Houston: Rice University Press.

CHAPTER 11

"A VERY SUBTLE IDOLATRY"
ESTANISLAO DE VEGA BAZÁN'S AUTHENTIC TESTIMONY OF COLONIAL ANDEAN RELIGION

Kenneth Mills

hasta aora se avia entendido, que los Indios adoravan a los cerros, se ha descubierto, q. no los adoran, porq. Tales ofrendas las hazian al dicho Huari, y no a los cerros, y tienen a los idolos por representaciones del Huari. . . .

Until now, it has been understood that the Indians worshiped hills. (Now,) it has been discovered that they do not worship them, because offerings are made to the said Huari, and not to the hills. And they (the Indians) have idols as representations of Huari. . . .

—Estanislao de Vega Bazán

aora vendran los santos, y nos diran lo que emos de hazer.

Now the saints will come, and tell us what we have to do.
—Felipe Ramos, according to Estanislao de Vega Bazán

Like other evangelized populations before and after them, many indigenous people in colonial Spanish America set about recomposing kinds and parts of Christianity for themselves without completely giving up existing systems of belief and practice. For their ingenuity and resilience, such Indians were often repaid with expressions of disappointment, blanket condemnations of their supposed perversions, and punishments meted out by one or another guardian of the Christian faith's purity. Particularly in the century or so following the Council of Trent (the last session of which was in 1563), visions of salvageable native religious notions and of pre-Hispanic practices merging with Catholic Christianity seemed to fall beneath the advance of a narrower and more demanding vision of what was licit and what forbidden. Much documentation has survived from this period that is ostensibly about colonial Indians, their misguided ways of seeing, and the urgent need for instruction and reform. It is tempting to distrust the capacity of such documents to teach us about anything apart from their repressive and bipolar selves.

In the essay that follows, I want to avoid this temptation and to consider such a text and its author (and their broader context and meanings) with what I hope is an open mind. My essay takes us to the middle of the seventeenth century and to a mountainous region in the northeast of the vast Archdiocese of Lima, in the southernmost viceroyalty of Peru in the Spanish Indies. Although the author and document in my sights are, undeniably, local representatives of the post-Tridentine Church's concern with the reformation of error among (largely Quechua-speaking) native Andean parishioners, I contend that this is only the beginning of what they can be for their students. In this case, a very subtle idolatry of colonial Indians is perceived and recorded by a *criollo* priest as a delicate and multifaceted thing. His principal sources are the oral testimonies of native Andeans–these testimonies as filtered through his and others' judgmental gazes and notarial ink. The fact of this inquisitorial scenario and process of filtering, and our knowledge that this man's record was produced at the veritable height of his and other churchmen's investigation of these same native Andeans' beliefs and practices in order to bring about their end, do not go away. But this colonial documentary reality, more than disqualifying this churchman's perception and record, makes it urgent and invaluable.

The author is anchored before a complex religious reality that he is at pains to capture. The result is that, with uncertainty and for ends very different from our own, the author carries his reader within an emerging regional religiosity and culture in the colonial Andes.

Estanislao de Vega Bazán's *Testimonio auténtico de una idolatría muy sutil que el demonio avia introducido entre los Indios de las provincias de Conchucos y Guamalíes* [Authentic Testimony of a Very Subtle Idolatry That the Devil Had Introduced Among the Indians of the Provinces of Conchucos and Guamalíes] of 1656 is a short report, crammed with information rather than an elegant text, written to illuminate mid-seventeenth-century native Andean religious error for contemporary churchmen. The *Testimonio auténtico* alone cannot represent the variety of information surrounding and generated by priests who–like Vega Bazán himself–sought or accepted commissions as inspector-judges and extirpators of native Andean religious error ("visitadores generales de idolatría") during the sporadic anti-idolatry initiatives sponsored by certain prelates in the seventeenth- and early eighteenth-century Archdiocese of Lima. That surviving documentation is more diverse than is usually imagined. It ranges from theological treatises and religious chronicles, through catechisms, confessionals, and sermons, to occasional letters and reports, and, of course, the bundles of idolatry trial evidence themselves. It includes a bilingual (Quechua and Spanish) edition of St. Robert Bellarmine's catechetical manual for teachers prepared by the experienced priest-extirpator Bartolomé Jurado Palomino, as well as the more famous Francisco de Avila's bilingual cycle of sermons, and even the native-language collection of regional sacred histories, the Huarochirí Manuscript, the production of which was at least partly influenced by the same Avila (see Bellarmino; Avila 1646–1648; Salomon and Urioste). Within this varied corpus, Vega Bazán's *Testimonio auténtico* offers a fathomable set of details and issues, and an inviting line from which readers–some of whom may be somewhat or wholly unfamiliar with the extirpation of idolatry, the evangelization of Indians, and the immediate, central Andean historical context–can descend into the thickets of colonial religion and culture.

Thickets are difficult going. But the worst tangles of frustration are reserved for those with less interest in the colo-

157

nial thickets themselves than in the recovery from them of "reliable" information about the continuity of a pre-Hispanic native Andean religious tradition, as if the latter could remain a pure and separated thing, as little touched by time as by Christianity and the other exigencies of colonial Indian life—existing either to resist alteration or be destroyed. If such aims are foremost in mind, a participant-teller such as Vega Bazán—an active extirpator of idolatry claiming to have and publishing revelations about native Andean religion—will beg to be distrusted. He will seem only a self-serving cleric who would invent almost any depiction of native Andeans and their beliefs so long as it would gain him notice. Vega Bazán and his published text can seem to confirm that the "Andean religion of the extirpators of idolatry [was] an abstract construction," an illusory "anti-idolatry discourse" arising from the bureaucratic and institutional climate in seventeenth-century Lima (Urton 1996, 144; see also Urbano).

A questioning attitude is necessary for any student of colonial documentation. But there is virtue in adding to the mix of our requisite caution and suspicion a certain alertness to prospects—an openness to how apparent inconsistencies and contradictions got pulled together by colonial writers who (not surprisingly) often tripped on their way across the categories we and our historian-predecessors have erected for them. Given the interwoven relationship between the genres of literature and history, and thus of fictionality and truth in medieval and early modern Western European tradition (see Mignolo 1995, esp. Part 2, Chs. 3, 4; Kristeller; Spiegel), what, in contemporary terms, would an abstract construction be? What separated a supposed formation of the mind (a text) from what was ostensibly more grounded and factual (the referent)? Might not many documents from the colonial Andes be both, and might not both aspects be meaningful? Potential examples are many, deriving from a wide variety of authors.

Although the characters who speak in the secular priest Pedro de Quiroga's *Coloquios de la verdad* [Colloquies of Truth] from the early 1560s are imagined, neither the force of their dialogues nor the evidence of their author's deep familiarity with key contemporaries and the state of sixteenth-century evangelization and Andean life is diminished (see Quiroga, on evangelization, esp. 117–18, 122–29, 52, 63–64; Cerrón Palomino, esp. 395–96; Santo Tomás 1951a, 188–207; and the relationship neatly discussed by Dedenbach-Salazar Saenz 1997b, 195–96, 205n.1; compare José de Acosta 199–209, 231–43; Guamán Poma de Ayala; see also Pagden 1993, 38–41). In his artful way, Quiroga enters into a discourse that would be revisited by a great many commentators. Some, like the late sixteenth-century priest from Charcas, Bartolomé Álvarez, would write with devastating clarity directly to their sovereign (see Álvarez). More to the point, is a text composed by a seventeenth-century priest and extirpator of idolatry—or, more commonly, brought to light because of his investigations—more constructed, suspect, or limited in its potential as a historical source than, say, an audiencia judge's letter (e.g., Padilla), a missionary's treatise, or many other sources one could name?

My intention is not to deny the biases of Vega Bazán, the intellectual high-handedness of many Spanish commentators, their frequent misunderstandings of native Andean social and religious logic, or what Frank Salomon has succinctly called the anti-Andean axiomatic foundations of much of the written record (see Salomon 1995, 315). Nor do I wish to pretend for a moment that native Andeans could not dissemble and dis-

tort matters as expertly as any extirpator (see García Cabrera 1996; Mills 1997, 1994b; and see the disarming contemporary realizations of Arriaga [[1621] 1920, 116–17]). I want to demonstrate that the *Testimonio auténtico* (like a host of related documents) defies the notion that priest-extirpators, and others from the dominant and educated elite in colonial society, bequeathed only their convenient fabrications and fixed illusions about Indians to posterity. Rather, sources produced by many participant-tellers of Spanish descent—and not only active extirpators of idolatry—are invaluable keys to meanings and possibilities in a colonial history that includes native peoples and their rituals, not just what these were imagined to be. A significant rise up the ecclesiastical career ladder, even when it (infrequently) did occur for a priest-extirpator, was not the sole concern. While there is no such thing as direct or unproblematic access through texts to historical persons or events, one need not be restricted, as Peter Gose has put it, to "the critical evaluation of Spanish sources as an end in itself" (1995b, 36). The partiality of minds, categories, and cultural paraphernalia is fruitfully seen as the very stuff of colonial sources, the points of view and context of colonial history. These are characteristics, ingredients, before they are barriers or literary devices. In the era of the extirpation of idolatry, undeniably destructive purposes coexisted with—indeed, were served by—curiosity and diligence. Texts by active extirpators, like the findings of many idolatry investigations, are related to evangelization and are far more varied in their details, apparently disordered, and uncontrolled by official interests than is often assumed. There are tensions, slips, and silences that challenge us to think harder and more widely.

With their prescribed and tighter-than-normal definitions of what constituted religious error, many idolatry inspectors cut a vicious swath through the parishes they targeted in the seventeenth- and eighteenth-century parishes of the Archdiocese of Lima. Yet, if the documentation from their investigations serves up constant reminders of intimidation, punishment, and violence, it also features much evidence—sometimes half-buried—of a religion and culture that was not exclusively in the hands of Spanish Christian parish priests and extirpators. Confrontation seemed ensured as it grew clear that native Andean interest in Christian elements and ideas came most often without a will to abandon older religious conceptions. The apparently fragmented rituals and unfinished religious creations—the informal accretions and refinements of what Tristan Platt, working on rural Potosí, has called colonial Indians' "original Andean configuration of Christianity" (1987; 1988)—raised mostly the eyebrows of and alarm in many seventeenth-century churchmen. But these same men kept looking and writing. To such officials, a reliable and steadfast conversion of indigenous parishioners seemed delayed. And what was worse, baptized and at least rudimentarily instructed native people appeared to be falling away from an orthodox Christianity. The colonial religious creations in parishes of Indians rose into view as worrisome anti-achievements—perversions rather than conversions—Frankenstein's monsters that called for redoubled effort to stamp them out. Idolatry inspectors were frequently conceived of as physicians charged with the task of severing diseased parts from the body of colonial native Andean society (see Arriaga [1621] 1920; Villagómez). The inspectors commonly called the range of what they found idolatry, heresy, apostasy, superstition, and a host of other elastic terms—all approximations for what many of these observers understood as both native Andean survivals and misunderstandings of the Christian faith.

Yet even as extirpating churchmen such as Vega Bazán identified error and demonic intervention in colonial Indians' beliefs and practices, they described what they found in ways that were not fixed or formulaic. The descriptions that were undertaken in the service of more effective eradication should not be overlooked simply because of that service or because of our dissatisfaction with the few available words–the blanket terms–that extirpators used to defend themselves in the face of an increasingly multiform enemy. I focus on how Vega Bazán's recurring insertions of skepticism and disbelief actually enabled, rather than diminished, his descriptions of the "very subtle idolatry" he discerned. By this method, he effectively freed himself from caution and constant argument and was able to give a deeper and fuller account. Vega Bazán's doses of skepticism often come through his use of the adjective *aparente* ("apparent") and the verb *aparecer* ("to seem like")–in ways that play ingeniously between meanings of actual appearance or visibility, on the one hand, and something that seems to be real or true but clearly is not, on the other. Vega Bazán's *aparente*, in particular, works like a legal alleged, in these instances assuring his clerical readers that as a judge of idolatry, he is not persuaded by the things he is considering in detail.

There is another way in which extirpators' descriptions and interpretations do not exist only on some hermetically sealed plane of discourse as prejudicial barriers or distorting shadows cast over what might otherwise be seen. The descriptions also suggest ideas that were transmitted over time and that became influential and increasingly untethered understandings of indigenous people themselves. The new understandings were shared or–more often–half-shared values, terms, and associations, concepts, and practices that were preached and taught and talked about–ideas that traveled the uneven and unequal spaces between Spaniards and native Andeans, between writers and readers, between speakers and hearers, and that themselves became cultural and religious catalysts in ways we are only beginning to comprehend. (Good examples of widening and dynamic approaches to the study of colonial religion and culture are demonstrated by W. B. Taylor 1996, 2000, 1998, 1994a, 1994b; Gruzinski 1992, 1999; Sallnow; Moreno Yánez; Millones esp. 1979a, 1979b; Cahill; Mujica Pinilla; Harris 1995b; Adorno 1986, 1991, 1994; Cummins 1988, 1995, 1998, among others).

Estanislao de Vega Bazán was a *criollo* from Lima with papers to prove his descent from the Spanish conquerors of Peru. In the middle of the seventeenth century, he became the parish priest of the some 1,300 native Andean parishioners spread between Santa Ana de Cinga (or Singa, in the *corregimiento* [colonial tribute jurisdiction] of Guamalíes [Huamalíes]) and its two annexes of Punchau and Cuquibamba, in the Andes mountains a little less than 300 miles northeast of Lima (*Archivo General de Indias* [AGI] Audiencia de Lima 304, Pedro de Villagómez to the king, Lima, 20 November 1664). With his early education by Jesuits, a bachelor's degree from the University of San Marcos, and competence in the Quechua language, Vega Bazán's preparation was not outstanding among the secular clergy (many of whom were *licenciados*) competing for vacant parishes in his day. If he intended his relatively remote parish at Cinga to be an early step up the ecclesiastical ladder, his ultimate rise ended up being of a middling kind (see Mills 1997, Ch. 5, and further discussion below). Soon a comissary of the Holy Office of the Inquisition in Huamalíes, by the 1650s he had gained a further commission as

inspector and judge of native Andean religious error (*visitador general de la idolatría*) over a wider area, the jurisdictions of los Conchucos and Huamalíes. The latter commission made Vega Bazán one of about fifteen key extirpators of idolatry during the decades of the 1650s and 1660s, the very height of the era of idolatry investigations revived and enthusiastically sponsored by the current archbishop of Lima (1641–1671), Pedro de Villagómez (Mills 1997). He was not among the most active extirpators in his time, but by 1662, Vega Bazán turns up in the documentary record as an overseer of the extirpating work of another (Juan Sarmiento de Vivero) and a willing provider of specific advice on procedure for his prelate (Vega Bazán [1662] 1971, 390–93).

In most of the resettled Indian towns that Vega Bazán visited in the mid-seventeenth century, life within a parish under the gaze of a priest was an established norm. In Conchucos, the sustained spread of diocesan structures and monastic foundations had largely followed the pioneering efforts of the Augustinians, especially Fray Ernando García Vicario and Fray Juan de Pineda, in the 1560s and 1570s. Even so, the region, which the Augustinian Antonio de la Calancha likened to a redoubt of the Devil and a rebel Flanders because of the persistent religious errors of its native inhabitants, maintained a negative reputation among many Catholic churchmen well into the seventeenth century (Calancha, vol. 3, 1059–60 and Ch. 32). For native Andeans in Conchucos, the scrutiny of their beliefs and practices by visitors from outside would soon have been something known and–according to evidence from neighboring regions–well remembered (Mills 1994b).

As was the case with a number of his fellow extirpators at mid-century, Vega Bazán's extirpating efforts and experiences came not in fresh territories but in revisitations to parishes of Indians, such as those in Conchucos, that had been suspected of error and had drawn investigations by predecessors at least once and sometimes twice before. The earlier waves of idolatry *visitas* had come over three decades before, during the tenures of two other archbishops who supported centralized campaigns of extirpation: 1609–1620, Bartolomé Lobo Guerrero and, more briefly, 1625–1626, Gonzalo de Campo. According to the Jesuit Pablo Joseph de Arriaga, the region that fell under Vega Bazán's jurisdiction in the mid-1650s had first been visited by an idolatry inspector in 1617. Dr. Diego Ramírez, a priest from the urban parish of Santa Ana in Lima, had proceeded with an eventful commission that had been unfulfilled when its original appointee, Francisco de Avila, had fallen ill (Arriaga [1621] 1920, Ch. 1, 12–13). Arriaga also tells of another *visitador*, Juan Delgado, parish priest of Huaráz, who had been active in the region. Delgado heard confessions in the settlements of Cahuana and Tauca, Conchucos, about great Andean ancestor-beings, one named *Chanca* and another *Catequilla*, among many other things (Ariaga [1621] 1920, 15, 23–25, 36–37; also on Chanca and the celebrated Catequilla, Calancha vol. 3, 1065, 1062–64; *Relación*, San Pedro).

The *Testimonio auténtico* is composed in the third person in the form of a notarial telling of the insights and accomplishments of "the said Bachiller Don Estanislao Vega Bazán." That said, there is no doubting who the compiler and author was, and it is entirely appropriate to treat the text as Vega Bazán's work. The third-person point of view is a contemporary convention that, along with expressions of modesty and self-sacrifice, heightened for his community of readers the sense of a credible, authorized objectivity. In his prefatory *aprobación* of the *Testimonio auténtico*, the Augustinian Juan de

Ribera deepened this sense of authority, comparing Vega Bazán with the apostle Paul among the Romans and churches of Galatia (Ribera in Vega Bazán, *Testimonio*, fol. 2r). For his own part, Vega Bazán claimed to have discovered a number of essential things about the religious beliefs and practices of the indigenous peoples he served. *Descubrió* ("discovered") was the powerful word he chose to describe and introduce his achievements. He employed the word in a calculated manner that recalls the better-known narratives of earlier would-be discoverers of crypto-idolatry in Spanish America such as Francisco de Avila in Huarochirí and Diego de Landa in Yucatan, or, for that matter, a discoverer of heresy in Spain such as the Inquisitor-General Fernando de Valdés, whose political fortunes rested on his mid-sixteenth-century reports to King Philip II telling of all the Lutherans active in Valladolid, Seville, and Salamanca (see Avila, "Prefacion" to *Tratado* [1646–1648]; [1611] 1904, 385–89; Clendinnen; Memorials and letters of Valdés to king, Archivo General de Simancas, Valladolid: section Estado, leg. 129, fols. 110–12, 128, cited in Kamen 1997, 73, with wider discussion in Kamen 1998, 83–102). Vega Bazán insisted just as conventionally on his service to God and man, his "continua predicacion" ("continuous preaching") and "mucho cuidado en el oficio de Cura" ("great care in the office of priest"). He stressed the authority that came from the fact that his investigations (into obscure things in remote and difficult regions) had been conducted in person, sometimes on foot, in difficult conditions, and without self-interest. The only sustenance for himself and his entourage of assistants, he reminded his readers, came from his own pockets (see Álvarez on the problem of priestly incomes).

Along with Vega Bazán's published *Testimonio auténtico*, two surviving letters from May 1656 and December 1662 form a timely little corpus to court archiepiscopal favor in hope of a canonry in the cathedral of Lima. Vega Bazán appears to have read with special care the Archbishop of Lima Pedro de Villagómez's published pastoral letter, the first part of which was an exhortation to vigilant eyes and ears in the mountain parishes and a call for individual initiatives in the extirpation of native religious error—the evil lost to view (Villagómez). Augustinian Juan de Ribera, who, as mentioned above, contributed a prefatory stamp of approval for Vega Bazán and his *Testimonio auténtico* in 1656, laid it on even more thickly when he noted that the extirpator's extraordinary labors had unmasked an idolatry "no conocida hasta aora en estos Reynos" (Ribera in Vega Bazán, *Testimonio* fol. 2r) ("not hitherto known in these kingdoms"). Villagómez's own words were not only being attended to, they were also being projected back at him by a priest in the provinces and his friar-supporter.

There may have been further need to court favor. Vega Bazán's reputation as an idolatry inspector was not unblemished. After gaining his commission as *visitador general de idolatría*, his extirpating career was soon distinguished mostly by its interruptions. Already by the mid-1650s, despite the fact that Villagómez's extirpating teams were operating in a number of regions of the archdiocese, all was not well in his war against Andean idolatry. The *visitas* were variable affairs, extremely uneven in the diligence of their efforts and coverage of regions. *Visitador* Vega Bazán was part of the problem. The archbishop wrote bitterly of Vega Bazán's desertion from duty, and this when a number of other idolatry inspectors were being forced to cease their activities for reasons ranging from failing health to serious charges of excesses and corruption in the course of duty (AGI Lima 59, Letters from Villagómez to the king, Lima, 24 June, 1656 and 26 June, 1657; see Acosta Rodríguez 1987b; Mills 1996). The *Testimonio auténtico*, dated and signed in Lima on 19 October 1655 and published in 1656, appeared at virtually the same time as these problems and Villagómez's penned frustration.

Seeking to move through available institutional channels to a higher position in Lima, Vega Bazán is one of the cadre of *letrados* evoked so memorably by Ángel Rama—an urban-oriented intellectual producer who, through his skills and manipulations, might gain a measure of power, but who was just as much a dependent servant to it (Rama 30–31; and on priestly careers in New Spain and beyond, see W. B. Taylor 1996, esp. 88–96 and Chs. 5, 6). As I have hinted above, Vega Bazán recalls other, better-known extirpators of native Andean idolatry and their career quests: Fernando de Avendaño, who became the prime assistant-of-choice to a succession of Lima prelates in the first half of the seventeenth century; Francisco de Avila, who sought and belatedly received a place in the cathedral chapter of Lima; and, long before them, Cristóbal de Albornoz, a canon in the cathedral at Cuzco, who sought and never received a see of his own (see Acosta Rodríguez 1987a; essays within Millones 1990; also Ramos 1993). Certain other extirpators—mostly the seventeenth-century big four of Francisco de Avila, Fernando de Avendaño, Bernardo de Novoa, and (to a slightly lesser extent) Juan de Sarmiento Vivero—and their intellectual formations and orbits have become of steadily more interest to investigators (see esp. Guibovich Pérez; Hampe Martínez 1996; García Cabrera 1993; Mills 1994b, 1997, Ch. 5; Rivera de Tuesta; Duviols 1966). Yet there has been significantly less attention to the ways in which Jesuit education, intellectual associations, and books in libraries may have both mattered and been transformed by experience. Did the ideas of Alcalá and Lima remain rigid, or did they bend and move, and perhaps explode, in a parish of Indians? A sustained answer to that question demands evidence we often do not have. As a result, with the possible exception of Francisco de Avila—with his hand in an expansive collection of native Andean traditions, an artful cycle of sermons, his letters (G. Taylor; Salomon and Urioste; Avila 1646–1648; also Estenssoro Fuchs 1994, 1996), and his happy intersection with the best overall study of an Incaic and colonial Andean region (see Spalding)—idolatry inspectors still often appear in monochrome, as if these parish priests' commissions somehow molded them into a uniformly stiff concentrate of post-Tridentine policy and prejudice. As I have hinted, it can be particularly tempting to pass off a relatively minor extirpator with a small paper trail such as Estanislao de Vega Bazán. Only his text beckons us forward.

Vega Bazán does not offer up what might be called a generalized Andean religion. He does not pretend that a pre-Hispanic native cosmology is accessible to his enquiries and containable in a quick few sentences. This may not seem a remarkable restraint until one recalls how easy it was for a contemporary Spanish Christian commentator to go not much further than a prejudicial label for the suspect religiosity of subject peoples, whether idolatry or superstition or deception of the Devil. Of course, Vega Bazán is not completely immune to such labeling, but he is also more curious and thorough in his attempts to describe. Native Andeans' beliefs and practices make up "a very subtle idolatry," Vega Bazán asserts with an unsettling combination of admiration and loathing. He is also stalling, playing up the suspense in preparation for his revelations. For him, idolatry is a number of things at once: Hateful and deserving of denigration, of course, but also delicate in its difficulty, with a great and fluid range of stubbornly emergent meanings. It has been miscast by others. It requires attention.

Vega Bazán's *Testimonio auténtico* is a concentrated assemblage of information. It resembles a report or account most often dubbed a *relación* or *descripción* and most often generated by a person of entirely or largely Spanish ancestry. Such an account might also be contained within a letter to a superior, prelate, or monarch. A number of vaguely similar reports were produced by seventeenth-century priest-extirpators, though unlike Vega Bazán's *Testimonio auténtico,* they were not formally printed. Thanks to the modern transcriptions of Pierre Duviols and José Toribio Medina in particular, several of these other documents are easily accessible for comparative purposes (beyond the letter from Vega Bazán himself ([1662] 1971), see Avendaño ([1614] 1971 and [1617] 1986; Hernández Principe; F. de Medina; Bauer de Castro, among others). Among the most outstanding of these reports—and to be entirely truthful, the close rival to Vega Bazán's *Testimonio auténtico* as I considered what was to be my focus for this essay—is Felipe de Medina's "Relación" from the coastal region north of Lima and written in March 1650. It is a gripping and detailed narrative of Medina's discovery of various *mallquis* (the mummified and revered bodies of native Andean dead) and idols, as well as a sizeable declaration and denunciation of the accused persons. Even more typical (because more workmanlike and less expansive) is a document such as Fernando de Avendaño's "Testimonio" of 1614, a fascinating, brief inventory of the names of Andean dead that had been revealed by living relatives and exhibited during the course of one of his multi-parish investigations, or Diego Bauer de Castro's 1655 sketch of his principal movements and sentences as an idolatry judge in the Jauja valley a year before. Yet while the *Testimonio auténtico* shares a number of properties with these and other roughly contemporary reports and letters, it also differs from them. It offers a more complicated and ranging narrative, and it is interesting to consider why this is so.

A letter that Vega Bazán sent to Archbishop Villagómez in 1662 (to be discussed later) demonstrates that the extirpator was as capable of a methodical sketch or a terse inventory as Avendaño, Medina, or Bauer de Castro had been. In comparison to these other texts, the *Testimonio auténtico* is disorienting, almost a gathering of wayward narrative leaps. It has distinct and coherent segments, to be sure, but it appears to proceed in its different directions almost at random and sometimes to double back on itself, like a whole of many parts just put together.

Many of the historical chronicles produced in the early and mid-colonial Indies were composed by writers with some degree of Renaissance humanistic training who would have seen as obvious the need to record, organize, and otherwise compile "miscellaneous knowledge." And many went much further than that, effectively rethinking established written and pictorial forms in the face of such challenges as complex indigenous oral traditions and performative culture, bringing about a mixing of genres (Mignolo 1995, 204–15). The meeting of established European and native Andean genres has been studied mostly in the context of chronicles written in the sixteenth century. Vega Bazán's *Testimonio auténtico,* although

a minor work and much less sustained than a chronicle, can fruitfully be seen as a similar kind of creation from the significantly later, extirpating moment in the mid-seventeenth-century archdiocese of Lima.

The European encyclopedic enthusiasm is evident in the text, but it is only the beginning. In its general choppiness, and its mixed narrative and informational character, the *Testimonio auténtico* appears to have been cobbled together, especially from the testimonies of native witnesses that Vega Bazán and others (with their notaries and interpreters to help) had heard and recorded as judges and inspectors of idolatry (among the expanding number of published examples of such testimonies to consider, see esp. Duviols 1986 and 1971, Appendix 7, 367–86; Sánchez; García Cabrera 1994; Gose 1995a; Mills and Taylor 236–49; Mills 1992). Perhaps most significant are the points at which the text closely resembles the *tradiciones* (the sacred histories and explanatory myths) related by Indian informants and witnesses, sometimes collected by Jesuit missionaries (some of whom traveled as pedagogical complements to the idolatry judges) and included in expansive letters to superiors in Lima and Rome. There are relations of incidents from case evidence involving people with names mixed with precise information on ritual practices and reference to Andean divine personages, sacred regional histories, and beliefs as remembered and transforming into mid-colonial times. There is a gradual accumulation of insights and memories, with the repetitions occurring, like refrains, to provide further details on matters already raised. A reader of Vega Bazán's text has the distinct sense of a person—or, more probably, people—talking, providing answers to questions, a number of which have to be repeated or clarified in different ways to elicit a more detailed response. Some of the answers grow expansive; others are curt and seem to carry the text almost nowhere. More than a testimony, as advertised in its title, the *Testimonio auténtico* is a testimonial document, though decidedly not the expression of a tightly controlled or unitary point of view (Dedenbach-Salazar Sáenz 1997a, 149–50, working from Lanser 13–14).

Of course, the indigenous people of los Conchucos and Huamalíes who may have informed Vega Bazán's Conchucos and Huamalíes text could not have possessed anything like the creative and editorial agency that the redactor(s) of the famous early seventeenth-century Quechua manuscript from Huarochirí appears to have had (Salomon and Urioste; Dedenbach-Salazar Sáenz 1997a, 1994), nor can they be treated as source-equivalents of named and acknowledged native scholars, artists, and informant-participants, such as those now so increasingly well studied in sixteenth-century central Mexico (amid a burgeoning interdisciplinary literature, see esp. Burkhart; Peterson). Vega Bazán's Indian confessants and informants—of whom only two are mentioned by name in the *Testimonio auténtico* (see later in this article)—were probably non-literate persons either themselves accused of idolatrous practices or suspected of possessing information about others who engaged in them. On top of this, the effects of the translation of their Quechua oral testimonies—and who knows how many local meanings and allusions—into written Castilian, and the extent of redactorial influence and filtering by the extirpator and his functionaries, can never be fully appreciated.

Following this line, it could be argued that the resemblance between parts of Vega Bazán's text and the recorded testimonies of witnesses before idolatry inspectors and missionaries suggests nothing so much as a creeping standardization of accounts during the era of systematic extirpation, and thus the great extent of clerical and notarial influence in the act of recording and translating (hence, even the manufacture, the construction of) Indians' testimonies about their beliefs and practices. As important as it is to keep such cautions in mind, it is arguably even more essential not to pretend a formulaic and controlled nature in the different accounts and in Vega Bazán's *Testimonio auténtico* does not exist. Resemblance is quite another thing. It is more plausible that a number of Indian witnesses, or at least their translated and recorded testimonies, heard or known by Vega Bazán, became his principal founts of information and that, as fed into the account, they contribute to the meandering nature of significant portions of the *Testimonio auténtico*.

An example of mediated native Andean information in the *Testimonio auténtico* is Vega Bazán's narration of an oral tradition or sacred history of origin about the important regional ancestor-divinity named Huari. The instance also serves as an important preface to further discussion of the slippery textual roles and meanings of Christian terminology, especially God and the Devil, within the interactive environment of a parish of Indians. According to Vega Bazán, native Andean ministers in the regions of Huamalíes and Conchucos in the middle of the seventeenth century taught people of the wrath of an ancient God. *Dios* is capitalized and described as the "criador de la tierra" ("creator of the earth"). God, in this portion of the text, is a term interchangeable with Huari, the name of the native Andean ancestor-divinity of whom Vega Bazán would have learned from Indian elders (fols. 4r, 3v; further, Duviols 1973; also Mills 1994a). The description of Huari (and, indeed, of other trans-regional making and ordering divinities such as his better-known Conchucos neighbors Catequilla and Chanca, or the even more famous Viracocha, Pacha Camac, and Paria Caca, about whom Spanish observers had learned) has a monotheistic, a Christian, ring (Calancha, vol. 3, 1062–66; and, amid a huge secondary literature, esp. Pease G. Y.). Early chroniclers and missionaries found purchase, not to mention interpretative and spiritual comfort, in these apparent Andean equivalents to God.

Our understanding of the divine hierarchies of colonial Andean numina within regional cosmologies is not confident. Yet the supremacy of founding figures such as Huari is not so badly served by the epithet of creator, especially if the creation in mind is permitted a strongly local (or regional) as well as a metaphysical resonance. It is possible that Vega Bazán recorded the story of origin as it was related to him. The God Huari had seen fit to punish the land with a great flood, effectively remaking the land and its peoples. The Indians who lived in the lowlands were drowned by the rising waters, while those in the high mountains survived, taking refuge in caves. They remained there for one year, at which point the waters had receded enough for the Indian families to descend from the fastnesses and live safely. These survivors were believed to be the forefathers of those living in the seventeenth century. The caves from which the forefathers emerged, the *paccarinas*, which is to say *nacimientos* (places of origin) could still be seen and were venerated "porque los Indios entendian que avian nacidos de las cuevas" (fol. 4r) ("because the Indians believe they were born from the caves") (further on *pacarinas*: see Arriaga [1621] 1920, 21; Gose 1995b). There was much to do. In that time "toda la tierra

[fue] lodosa" ("the earth was all muddy"). The God Huari appeared as a giant, three *varas* [over eight feet] in height, to help his people "en todo, allanado la tierra, produciendo los frutos de ella, governandola, y dando buelta a toda ella cada dia" *Testimonio* (fol. 4r)("in everything, smoothing out the land, cultivating its fruits, giving it order, and walking all around it each day"). Traveling about thus, as a benevolent force and supervisor, the giant Huari gained many admirers. His initiating and organizing tasks complete, he found a high place above the *pueblos* to sit on a stone seat close to some altars, where he could see the offerings the people made. And today, the tradition concludes, racing neatly (if ominously) into mid-Colonial times,

> El dicho Huari se convierte oy en dia en muchas formas de hombre, y de culebras, y en especial se convierte en ayre rapido, y que en esta forma de ayre anda todos los dias governando el mundo, y dando buelta por el, y entrando enfermedades, culebras, y otras cosas a los que no le adoran, ni le sirven, y dando vida, y salud a los que le sirven, dogmatizando que era Dios, y criador de la tierra. (fol. 4r)

> The said Huari transforms himself into many human forms, into serpents, and especially into strong winds. And as the wind, every day, he goes all about governing the land, causing illnesses, snakes, and other things to befall those who do not worship him, and giving life and health to those who do, teaching that he is God and creator of the world.

Various aspects of this narrative have more companions within the contemporary documentation than I have space in this essay. Suffice it to say that similar giant-forefather divinities roamed and contributed to the landscape and order of other regions (for another Jesuit relation concerning Huari, see "Misión a las provincias" 452–53; and Mills 1997, 51), floods were said to have cleansed and initiated human eras in the Huarochirí myths (Salomon and Urioste Ch. 3, 51–52), and other ancestor-beings were said to move as wind (Archivo Arzobispal de Lima [AAL], Leg. 4, Exp. 14, Caujo, in the parish of Pomacocha, Canta; and see Mills 1997, 231–32, 236–37). One by one, *huacas* (in this context, ancestors turned to stone and present as extraordinary—and occasionally sculpted and painted—features in the regional landscape) such as Huari had taken their places in regional sacred landscapes. Their living histories were retold and integrated into oral traditions and festive seasonal calendars that often remained vital, transforming components of regional Andean life into colonial times and well beyond (see Salomon and Urioste; Mills 1997, esp. Chs. 2, 7–9; Gose 1996; Howard-Malverde 1990; Bastien). The nature of this regional God seems Christlike. He feels the crises of his people, he exacts his punishments from on high, and he then appears on earth as a guide—a giant among normal men and women, and one who attracts followers—before ascending to a spot from which to see, administer, and receive offerings. Is this Christlike nature adequately explained as only Vega Bazán's or his notary's imposition of a Christian character and frame upon an Andean sacred history?

Why is the Huari story recorded and included? The history of the people's origins, of Huari's creative contributions, and the explanation of how this divinity came to inhabit his mountain place provide essential information about a central feature within these peoples' kind of idolatry, namely the ancestral or *huaca* dimension. The sacred history lays out in a memorable way just what this divine ancestor-being and founder, "el Dios fingido, que llaman Huari" (*Testimonio* fol. 3r) ("the false God whom they call Huari"), means to the Indians, who connect themselves and their whole environment to him and his supposed actions. Vega Bazán presents these beliefs as the product of the people's credulity. Moreover, when the extirpator engages in such commentary, pushing the purpose of his narrative further, God, the creator of the earth, becomes not only a false God, but also quite firmly the Devil or the Devil Huari. This particular move by Vega Bazán (and by other priest-extirpators of idolatry and many other clerical commentators) has long caught the imagination of scholars, arguably distracting them from other elements that also repay attention.

Pierre Duviols has emphasized the diabolic aspect within Vega Bazán's *Testimonio auténtico*, tacking on an important 1986 discussion to what he had more briefly proposed in 1971 (see Duviols 1986, lxxi–lxxii). The full title of the work invites this emphasis, with its reference to the "idolatría muy sutil" ("very subtle idolatry") as something "que el demonio avia introducido entre los Indios de las provincias de Conchucos, y Guamalies" ("which the Devil has introduced among the Indians of the provinces of Conchucos and Huamalíes"). Duviols takes Vega Bazán at his word and puts him and the *Testimonio auténtico* within a larger diabolizing frame. He demonstrates that the mental categories of a number of influential Spanish and *criollo* writers in early seventeenth-century Peru (especially the Jesuits Pablo Joseph de Arriaga and Luis de Teruel [see Romero 1918] and the Augustinian Antonio de la Calancha) were affected by their peninsular readings (see the widely known manual for inquisitors, the *Directorium Inquisitorum* of Nicolaus Eymerich [Eymericus, reprinted with Francisco Peña's commentaries in 1503, and some seven more times between 1578 and 1608] and Jacob Sprenger and Heinrich Kramer's *Malleus maleficarum* [Sprenger and Institoris 1928], edited some thirty-one times between 1587 and 1689) and by knowledge of famous contemporary events involving the Devil and witches in Spain, especially the extraordinary (for Spain) revelations from the famous witch trials in the Basque Country, notably in Zugarramurdi, which culminated in the *auto de fe* at Logroño in 1610. Ironically, the subsequently successful effort of the inquisitorial inspector Salazar y Frias, the advocate of witches, to discredit the procedure and findings of the Basque witch trials appears not to have registered with at least these particular readers who had traveled to Peru (see Henningsen).

Statements within Arriaga's resource for priests of Indians and guide for idolatry inspectors and judges in the central Andes, along with his general vision of *visitas de idolatría* as a solution for suspect Indian religiosity (*La extirpación* of 1621), do suggest the influence of Western European strains of diabolism and witch-hunting. And these combine with a precise comparison between the findings of the inquisitors in Zugarramurdi and those of early seventeenth-century extirpators in the town of Huarmey ("Guarmey") in the coastal parish of La Barranca, Peru, in a lost manuscript attributed to Arriaga's Jesuit contemporary Luis de Teruel (at least summarized, and perhaps copied, by the Augustinian *criollo* Antonio de la Calancha; see Calancha vol. 4, 1422–27). There is basis for Duviols's diabolic emphasis thus far.

But how far can it extend as a generalization about later priest-extirpators? Did Teruel's notions of malicious covens of witches, of orgiastic nocturnal gatherings "como las del Aquelarre de tierra de Burgos, en el pueblo Cegarramurde" ("like those of the Aquelarre in the town of Zugarramurdi in the

region of Burgos"), and of a vile Devil-participant who appeared as a "leon, perro, [y] cabron" (Teruel [attributed] in Calancha vol. 4, 1425) ("lion, dog, (and) he-goat") among other forms, which had sparked the minds of the two Jesuits on the coast of Peru in the second decade of the seventeenth century, hold the same kind of potency for people such as Estanislao de Vega Bazán in the highlands at mid-century, as Duviols also contends? Calancha's interest in and inclusion of the Jesuit's text in his chronicle do suggest an extended currency for these ideas. And this currency appealingly disregards the walls of a historiographical ghetto that is too often reserved for seventeenth-century Jesuits and priest-extirpators in the Andes, as if they, and the era and process of the extirpation, were somehow separate from other churchmen and the wider process of the evangelization of Indians. But, as Sabine MacCormack has argued through a juxtaposition of the views of Calancha and his fellow Augustinian Alonso Ramos Gavilán, contemporaries' beliefs in the Devil and in demonic possession were not uniform—even when the individuals were rough contemporaries in the same religious order, serving in the same part of the world (see MacCormack 377–82).

Duviols may be too little concerned with multiplicity of opinion and with changing conceptions of the Devil, not to mention the possible effects of extended experience in parishes of Indians on churchmen over the course of the first half of the seventeenth century. Duviols makes Estanislao de Vega Bazán's *Testimonio auténtico* of 1656, as well as the contents of the letter the extirpator wrote to Villagómez six years later, a principal case in point. For Duviols, Vega Bazán's treatment of the regional cult of the divinity Huari, assertions of pacts between the Devil and native Andean religious specialists, and descriptions of women's roles in rites purported to involve the Devil all combine to suggest the continued sway that the *Directorium*, the *Malleus Maleficarum*, and other European texts held over this extirpator and, by inference, over others into the 1660s (see Duviols 1986, lxxi–lxxii).

On the surface, Duviol's argument about the diffusion of intellectual formations and milieux—and even his stretch between the preoccupations of Arriaga and Teruel and those of Vega Bazán—seems incontestable. Indeed, as intellectual historians of different stripes and concerns have been suggesting for some time, it would be far more surprising if a formally educated *criollo* from Lima such as Vega Bazán, a priest working as a *visitador de idolatría* and attempting to make sense of intricate native Andean beliefs and rituals en route to their eradication, had completely cast off inherited modes of thought or somehow failed to think, to a certain extent, analogically (see Mignolo 1989, 1995; Pagden [1982] 1986, 1993, Chs. 1, 2; Elliott; Greenblatt; MacCormack; W. B. Taylor 1989; Grafton; Hodgen). Yet, as was once the case with roughly contemporary witch-finders in Western Europe and not so unlike assumptions about native and Afro-American peoples' sense-making in colonial and post-colonial times, there is risk of assuming a homogeneity of opinion among extirpators of idolatry—a changelessness in conception and reaction over time—that did not exist (Harris 1995a, 1995b; Rappaport 1990; Urton 1996; Price; on witch-finders esp. Briggs; Clark; Larner). Vega Bazán's attitude toward native Andean numina and religious specialists is not cut from some common cloth of early modern extirpating opinion— whether from the *Información* on the Taki Onqoy movement collected by Cristóbal de Albornoz in south-central Andes in the 1560s, the extirpating treatise of Pablo Joseph de Arriaga, or the evidence from the idolatry trials conducted by Bernardo de Novoa in Cajatambo at mid-century, to mention only three of the principal looms from which the assumed fabric has most often been imagined to come (see Albornoz in Millones 1990; Arriaga [1621] 1920; Novoa).

The ways in which Vega Bazán employs ideas about the corrupting role of the Devil and the existence of explicit pacts between native Andean "sorcerers" and Satan in the *Testimonio auténtico* are instructive and demand closer attention. Vega Bazán made his belief in these notions just as clear in the succinct letter, already noted above, that he sent to archbishop Villagómez some six years after the publication of the *Testimonio* (Vega Bazán [1662] 1971, 390–93). Vega Bazán's letter of December, 1662 is, at base, a report on the recent activity of his particularly indefatigable extirpating colleague, Juan Sarmiento de Vivero, in the region of the parish of San Jerónimo de Sayan, Chancay. In the role of overseer, Vega Bazán commended Sarmiento's careful service to God before going on to explain and approve the different sentences meted out to five native Andeans, among them the famous regional love specialist "María Arriera" (or María de Arriero, alias María Sussa Ayala) (AAL Leg. 5, Exp. 7; and see Sánchez; Mills 1997, 111–13, 116–24, 272–73 n. 13, 1994b). Yet in another, perhaps largely self-appointed (though, as noted above, certainly encouraged), role of adviser to his Lima-bound prelate, the correspondent Vega Bazán grew more expansive. He told of various deficiencies he had observed in general extirpating procedure (without stating that Arriaga's guidelines were being abandoned or implying that Sarmiento was any less effective than other judges). And he made specific recommendations for reform. The details of each part of the letter need not concern us here, but suffice it to say that Vega Bazán's points on extirpating procedure help us to gain an impression of the man. He writes with an insider's knowledge and a shrewd understanding of human nature, appreciating the potential for corruption and feelings of futility among idolatry inspectors. And he kept a ruthless eye out for loopholes native Andeans might be able to discern in the contemporary investigations of their religiosity.

Within these points in the letter is Vega Bazán's most sustained discussion of the pacts people might seal with the Devil, as well as his recommendation of the most suitable punishments for native Andeans who succumbed to such temptation. By Vega Bazán's time, lettered persons in Western Europe and its various colonial domains who were persuaded by the ideas of demonic influence and activity in the world (for not all were persuaded in anything like equal measure) understood the diabolic pact as a promise made by a person to the Devil, usually in exchange for certain powers commanded or gifted by him (see Clark 466–71, 478–85; Cervantes Chs. 1, 2). Vega Bazán wrote that although the existence of a pact was difficult to determine, there were signs and, moreover, ways of perceiving it clearly that he would explain (Vega Bazán [1662] 1971, 391). The Indian specialist who was guilty of accepting a pact, the extirpator maintained, would betray her or his link with the Devil. The guilty were diviners who would act,

Por la mayor parte para divinar cosas futuras suelen llamar por sus nombres a los Ydolos que adoran, Piedras, cerros, Sol, Luna, Lucero dandoles renombre del criador, y soberano sobre todas las cosas, en que consiste el pacto. (Vega Bazán [1662] 1971, 391)

for the most part, to foretell things in the future, summoning by name their idols, which they worship, [as well as] stones, hills, the sun, moon, and morning star, praising them as creator and sovereign over all things—the pact consists of this [act of summoning and praising something not deemed to be the Christian God as creator].

Thus beckoned, "por parte del Demonio se aparece una araña, o otra qualquiera sabandixa" ([1662] 1971, 391) ("the Devil would appear as a spider, or some other crawling insect"), Vega Bazán continued. The divining specialist would examine the condition of its legs, keeping to a ritual process described more fully in the *Testimonio auténtico* (and to be discussed below), in order to learn of things that lay in the future for a person or persons (the most common examples concern health) or the answer to some question.

Like many Christian missionaries among originally non-Christian populations before and after him, Vega Bazán believed that local religious elites—an obstinate few, and usually elders—held up conversion in the seventeenth-century central Andes. Earlier in the seventeenth century, Calancha told of "un gran echizero maestro de los encantamientos, i artes mágicas, llamado Charimanga" ("a great sorcerer, maestro of spells and the magical arts, named Charimango"), who had lived in Tauca, Conchucos, and who had defied Christ and gathered followers, and whose memory lived on in the region (Calancha, vol. 3, 1066; 1066–67). These corrupting elders had to be identified and defeated in native society in order for Christianity to win and maintain its own. Ordinary Indian parishioners were cut some slack. In the 1662 letter, Vega Bazán argued that only the teacher and spreader of error, the "dogmatizador de dha. supersticion" ("dogmatizer of the said superstition"), was guilty of sealing a "pacto . . . explicito con el Demonio" ("explicit pact with the Devil"). The dogamatizer's pact was "expreso" ("clear"). Only this kind of person was deserving of the maximum sentences decreed by the Lima Church: A public shaming and varying dose of corporal punishment, followed by banishment from the region of their influence, either to the sorcerers' prison in the Cercado district of Lima or to serve a term of work in an urban hospital. People who consulted the specialists, though "tacitamente" ("tacitly") worshiping the Devil, were judged to have committed a lesser offence. They had submitted to an "implicito" ("implicit") pact through their intentional recourse to such a person's powers. As an example to all, Vega Bazán recommended that these offenders ought to be punished only a little less harshly than those guilty of explicit pacts, meaning that public flogging and lengthy exiles would still be enforced ([1662] 1971, 391). Thus, while, for Vega Bazán, serious corruption came in two varieties, he maintained that both could be severed from the Andes by diligent and properly informed extirpators who applied the appropriate penalties.

Very much a man of his time and place (the era presided over by Archbishop Pedro de Villagómez in the Archdiocese of Lima), Vega Bazán held that intensive programs of Christian teaching and public refutation of errors would probably be wasted on Indians guilty of pacts with the Devil. Some of these native Andean ministers, specialists, and dogmatizers were remarkably well informed about Christian ideas (the Devil being only a well-documented and exceptionally potent one of these), and they twisted these ideas and elaborated upon them. Because their understandings of aspects of Christianity and the practices they generated were unsanctioned, often mixed with older Andean rituals, and sometimes directly countered the efforts that Catholic priests made to regularize ritual observance in their parishes, the ministers and dogmatizers were, unsurprisingly, offered no part to play in Vega Bazán's vision of a Christian Andean future. Yet, as we shall see later, the priest-extirpator could not help but notice and reflect these individuals' importance to regional society. Details of a few of their teachings and doings form a kind of culmination in the *Testimonio auténtico.*

According to Vega Bazán, the teaching of doctrine was most fruitfully reserved for the many other Indians who, while guilty of practicing idolatry, were viewed as the pitiable followers–people like Sebastián Quito el viejo, who was tried by *Visitador* Sarmiento in Chancay and found to have backslid into error. In his report to Villagómez, Vega Bazán carefully plucked the example of this man from the testimonial corpus of his colleague's investigations. The old Indian man might mumble errors about the mysteries of the Christian faith, Vega Bazán admitted, but his sin "no fue mas que una ignorancia" ("was nothing more than ignorance"). In his capacity as adviser and overseer, Vega Bazán concluded that Sebastián Quito el viejo did not deserve as long an exile from his town as the zealous Sarmiento had judged appropriate. The priest-extirpator showed the depth of his experience in the mountain parishes in viewing a native Andean love specialist such as Quito, as well as the many participants in his regional ritual system, as a lesser evil–part of a misguided but vibrant customary dimension. Vega Bazán advanced no diabolic generalization, recommending rather that in such cases idolatry inspectors would need to judge for themselves whether pacts with the Devil were in evidence ([1662] 1971, 392; for the 1662 idolatry trial from Sayan, Chancay, involving both the elder Quito and his son, and much more, AAL Leg. 5, Exp. 7; Mills 1997, 118, Ch. 4).

Vega Bazán's belief in the existence of demonic pacts and apparitions was not exclusively an imported matter in the way that Duviols's treatment suggests. Vega Bazán includes no discussion of witches' sabbats, nor evidence to suggest a close following of Arriaga's earlier descriptions of such things as divination rituals, let alone precise information from the *Directorium* or the Zugarramurdi testimonies from the Basque country. Vega Bazán's general ideas about the deceptions of the Devil derived originally from European books and theories, but these grew more distant as he marshaled before himself remarkable evidence of the Devil's doings on the ground in the Andes, evidence that, however filtered, came from Quechua-speaking witnesses whom he or his colleagues had heard. Moreover, the undeniable diabolic element in Vega Bazán's documents is not an isolated or predominant feature; in fact, it often pales beside his attempts to describe what the native Andean parishioners' errors entailed. Vega Bazán partook of contemporary ideology and its labels, but he also admitted details that leave much more than demonology and flat labels to ponder.

When the Devil does take center stage in the narrative of the *Testimonio auténtico,* summoned by native ministers' and healers' invocations to Andean gods and sealing his pacts with this specialist elite, he does so as both an ingrained and an ambiguous force. True to his native Andean sources, and because of them, Vega Bazán does not suppress that ambiguity. The Devil is also called Huari, who is also called God. The Devil, as he appears in the *Testimonio auténtico,* brings to mind nothing so much as the many other *huaca-demonios*–the omnipresent protagonists of some colonial Indians' visions and dreams–about which so many native Andean specialists and wisepersons (often identified as diviners and healers) left evidence in these mid-colonial years and thereafter (see Salomon and Urioste, Chs. 20, 21, and Salomon 1990; Mills 1997, Ch. 7, 1999; Pérez Bocanegra; and strongly suggesting modern connections in the region of Andahuaylillas, department of Cuzco: Mannheim; Lira).

According to Vega Bazán, the kind of idolatry practiced by seventeenth-century devotees of Huari in the regions of los Conchucos and Huamalíes often centered on elaborate healing sessions and ritual performances of healing and divination in people's homes (*Testimonio* fol. 3r). On the basis of the *Testimonio auténtico,* it must remain unclear whether ritual was quite so domestic in pre-Hispanic times, though one can presume, as others have done in other parts of colonial Spanish America, that a need for secrecy and various adaptations toward a more private ritual complex increased in colonial times, as native observances became both known to and forbidden by churchmen (see Farriss Chs. 10, 11). In Huamalíes and los Conchucos, a "ministro de esta idolatría" ("minister of idolatry") would enter the home of the person or persons he came to heal, Vega Bazán writes. And soon after, a "muy horrible" ("very hideous") spider would make an appearance, "trepando por encima de la cama" ("climbing over the sickbed"). Or else some worms would appear on the wall, striking fear into the *enfermo* (sick person). At this point, the minister is said to have spoken to the one who was ill. He spoke formally, threatening a divine wrath, according to Vega Bazán's Castilian account of what would be said:

> No os espantis, porque nuestro Dios Huari, y criador te ha embiado esta araña, para que te coma, porq. no le has adorado, ni servido, y te ha criado muchas culebras dentro de tu cuerpo, que son causa de tu dolencia; pero como tengas proposito de adorarle, y servirle de aqui adelante, observando lo que yo te enseñare, te sacarè e virtud del Huari todas las culebras, arañas, y gusanos, que ha criado en tu cuerpo. (*Testimonio* fol. 3r)
>
> Do not be afraid that our God and creator Huari has sent this spider to eat you because you have not worshiped and served him, and also nurtured in your body many snakes that are the cause of your illness. For as you intend to worship and serve him from now on, abiding by what I have taught you, by virtue of Huari, I will remove all the snakes, spiders, and worms that he has grown in your body.

Having secured the *enfermo*'s intention to be more mindful of Huari, the specialist minister would proceed. Taking the spider in his hand, he would walk through the home with it before finally tossing it into the air. When it was thrown, according to Vega Bazán, the spider "ni caìa en el suelo, ni se iba por el ayre" ("neither fell to the ground, nor passed through the air"). It simply vanished ("se desuanecia, y se perdia al arrojarla") (*Testimonio* fol. 3r; compare with ritual descriptions and apparent aims from other central Andean regions in Mills 1997). The illness, apparently brought on at least in part by ritual negligence, was cast away and disappeared through the performance. Thirty-five years earlier, in his careful inventory of "ministers of idolatry," the Jesuit Pablo José de Arriaga had noted a similar central Andean specialist, the Pacharícuc (with the alternative Quechua spellings Pacchacátic or Pachacuc for the spider-diviner), even if he described the ritual examination differently and in less detail (Arriaga [1621] 1920, Ch. 3, 34–35), further suggesting that Vega Bazán's account was put together mostly from regional evidence he or his contemporaries had gathered.

A second descriptive passage of colonial Andean healing practices and the extractions of ills in the *Testimonio auténtico* both confirms and builds upon the one just related. Here is an excellent example of Vega Bazán's enabling of his description through the recurring insertion of a dose of skepticism, particularly the use of *aparente* and *aparecer,* which I mentioned above. He asserts that he has discovered the pact that the said dogmatizers and ministers of this idolatry make with the Devil. He has found it in the formal appeal and incantation the specialist ministers were said to make to Huari:

> A Señor Huari, à criador, y soberano sobre todas las cosas: yo te adoro, dame tu favor para sacar estos gusanos. (*Testimonio,* fol. 3v.)

> To Lord Huari, the creator and sovereign over all things: I worship you; give me your favor [that I might] remove these worms.

Grains of maize and coca leaves were then cast into a fire, "para que aquel humo fuesse ofrecido al dicho Huari" ("in order that their smoke would be offered to the said Huari"). The specialist ministers would then make "unas cuchilladas aparentes" ("some apparent stabs"), or else they would make a scratch "con un pedernal, o otra cosa" ("with flint or some other thing"), in the region of the person's afflicted part, from which it then seemed that the ministers removed "culebras, arañas, y otras sabandijas, piedras, y pedaços de huessos, todas ellas aparentes" ("snakes, spiders, and other such bugs and insects, stones, and pieces of bone, all of them (seemingly) there to see"). They would do this while informing the *enfermos* that their illnesses were being removed and thrown into a consuming fire. At other times, Vega Bazán asserted, the specialists would carry their extractions away and cast them to the hills, "pidiendo al dicho Huari, que no les bolviesse essa enfermedad" (*Testimonio* fol. 3v) ("asking of Huari that the illness not return to them").

To Vega Bazán's mind, such things amounted to a fearsome and disgusting performance, one that arose and survived because of the unhappy meeting of the Devil's deceptive capacity with the native people's credulity. The extirpator's language–particularly in these renderings of what the ministers are to have spoken to *enfermos* and to Huari–features some particularly wicked parody not only of Christian catechetical and liturgical language, but also of prayers that contemporary Catholics were encouraged to make only before authorized images of saints and their relics. And the Devil's aping was apparent in more than words. Later in Vega Bazán's account, when he tells of an *auto de fe* (in this case, a ceremonial burning, smashing, and burying of movable local divinities) in the town of Santo Domingo, he describes one of Huari's temples as a near-perfect inversion of a Christian church, darkness as opposed to light. Three stone idols were discovered in a "comun adoratorio de los Indios ("a common place of native Andean worship"), a large, dark cavern, "todo debaxo de tierra con unos callejones, y laberintos muy dilatados, hechos de piedras muy grandes, y muy labradas" (*Testimonio* fols. 5r–5v) ("all underground with some extensive passages and labyrinths cut expertly through very large rocks"). Vega Bazán saw confirmation that the Devil was tireless in his efforts to imitate, and thus thwart, God and his Church. But that is not all.

The priest also recorded religious information and a terminology that were increasingly shared with native Andeans. By the mid-seventeenth century, and a good deal earlier in certain cities and towns and well-evangelized regions, originally Spanish Christian ideas, terms, and practices had seen permutations and found local purchase. They became both Christian and native Andean concepts, part of an emerging colonial orientation. As degrees of cultural religious mixture became the norms into which native people were born and through which many lived, the provenance of such ideas, symbols, and language mattered less and less (see Harris 1995b, 112–13). The Quechua dictionaries of Domingo Santo Tomás ([1560] 1951a and [1560] 1951b) and Diego González Holguín, combined with the trilingual (Quechua, Aymara, and Castilian) "Christian doctrine" (1584), two catechisms and a sermon collection (1585) published and disseminated after the Third Provincial Council of Lima of 1582–1583 (*Doctrina Christiana*), as well as sources such as the "Huarochirí Manuscript" and many idolatry trials themselves (see Salomon and Urioste; Mills 1997) provide an expanding base of evidence suggesting that originally Christian concepts and terminology (sometimes untranslated for fear of misunderstanding and heresy, and many other times expressed through what missionaries hoped were near-equivalents in the principal native Andean tongues) would have been familiar to mid-seventeenth-century native Andeans, people who had grown up in established parishes receiving at least basic indoctrination and observing the principal sacraments (see Dedenbach-Salazar Sáenz 1997b). Catholic Christianity was not a new religion with an unfamiliar ritual language of expression to most of these people, nor for many of their immediate forbears.

An attitude that reflected (even if it did not acknowledge) religious mixture was not monopolized by Indians. The information about colonial Andean religion that Vega Bazán was compiling clearly set him to thinking, and not here about diabolic intervention, but about something he himself presented as a breakthrough. It concerned his emerging understanding of Andean divinities as symbolic or representational. "Hasta aora," ("Until now,") the account affirms, in the third person, and slipping into the triumphant tone of revelation,

> se avia entendido, que los Indios adoravan a los cerros, se ha descubierto, q. no los adoran, porq. Tales ofrendas las hazian al dicho Huari, y no a los cerros, y tienen a los idolos por representaciones del Huari, lo qual assi missmo à descubierto el dicho Bachiller Don Estanislao de Vega Bazan.
> (*Testimonio* fols. 3v–4r)

> it has been understood that the Indians worshiped hills. [Now,] it has been discovered that they do not worship them, because offerings are made to the said Huari, and not to the hills. And they [the Indians] have idols as representations of Huari, which the said Bachiller Don Estanislao de Vega Bazán has also discovered.

As Pierre Duviols recognizes briefly in a footnote (in terms of fetishism-versus-animism, which may raise more problems than it solves), Vega Bazán's discovery is no small thing and was highly controversial in his day. In marked contrast to Fernando de Avendaño's, and indeed other extirpators', insistence on the fetishism of Andean religion (people being deluded into worshiping stones, springs, mountains, and other objects), Duviols contends, "E. de la Vega Bazán [sic] was perhaps the first to 'discover' the fundamental animism of Peruvian religion" (Duviols 1971, 289 n. 24). Duviols's "perhaps" is warranted, in that a number of earlier and roughly contemporary thinkers–Las Casas, Blas Valera, Luis Jerónimo de Oré, El Inca Garcilaso de la Vega, and Bernabé Cobo foremost among them–had entertained significant thoughts on both the more abstract possibilities of Andean religious forms and the prospect of a creative convergence of Andean religious forms and Christianity (see MacCormack). Yet unlike Vega Bazán, these other commentators were not making their suggestions while engaged as active idolatry inspectors. While Vega Bazán obviously did not intend his statement about the representations of Huari within native Andean religious activity to be part of a case for the legitimacy of native Andean beliefs concerning *huacas* and *mallquis* or the cure of illnesses, his statement was as potentially explosive as it was perceptive–explosive because he attempts to understand colonial Andean religion in a way that tests closely a distinction between Catholic veneration of sacred images and native Andean idolatry. Granting the capacity for symbolism to native Andean religious practitioners by describing Huari and idols as representations opens the way for a challenge to one of the arguments most commonly enlisted in refutation of native Andean religion, namely the charge that the divinities and forces in the supposed Andean religious imagination were exclusively secondary things, that is, nothing more than they were–worldly, material, and therefore powerless. In the context in which it was written, the description of Huari and other idols as representations, and the connection–albeit implicit–between representative images of Christian saints (whose veneration as intermediaries between God and his human creations was approved of) and native idols (whose veneration was forbidden as a usurpation of God's right), was dangerous.

Experienced Christian authorities in early and mid-colonial Peru, who saw such convergences of the sacred happening, also saw the prospect of close control over Indian religious activity seeming to recede. Following the pertinent decrees from the Council of Trent (1545–1563), the pastoral complements published in the wake of the Third Provincial Council of Lima (1582–1583) made explicit most contemporary Church leaders' concerns about encouraging only a proper and uncontaminated veneration of sacred images among all Catholics, especially those who were believed to fall easily into error, such as Indian neophytes (*Doctrina Cristiana*, i.e., sermon 19; from the twenty-fifth session of the Council of Trent: Tanner 774–76). And among active extirpators of idolatry and a host of other Spanish and Andean Christian observers in the seventeenth century, preoccupation about the appearance and roles of images (sculpted or painted) of saints, crosses, and sacred objects in Indian devotions had grown even more acute ("Constituciones sinodales, Lima, 1614" 513; also in Duviols 1986, Appendix 1, 517; Estenssoro Fuchs 1994; Mills 1994a, Chs. 4–6; Cummins 1998; W. B. Taylor 1994b; Rappaport and Cummins). In the *Testimonio auténtico*, Vega Bazán was partaking of what Tom Cummins has called a common language, a largely unsanctioned relationship that was developing between Indian idolatry and Christian sacred art (principally images and symbols) (1998; also Marzal 1992, 73–79; [1983] 1988), and using it to elaborate his description. Whether he completely realized his act or its implications (see further discussion below) is perhaps unanswerable and beside the point. The priest-extirpator was exploring one of the most potent dimensions of an emerging colonial Indian religiosity, one that would have been recognized–perhaps intimately–by many native Andean parishioners in their own ways and according to their own understandings. This colonial religiosity had numerous dimensions, but among these, one of its most meaningful was becoming the local sacred image: the physical object that was a colonial intercessor with God, resembling a sacred or divine

being, named one thing or many things, and connecting to larger forces and older histories–something housed in a shrine that might be visited, seen, and called upon in times of need.

Near the end of the *Testimonio auténtico*, Vega Bazán refers to two native Andean religious offenders by name. His specificity signals not only the explicit use of case evidence from idolatry investigations, as noted earlier, but also the author's arrival before the most perplexing information in the document. As is also suggested by contemporary idolatry trial evidence from other regions of the central Andes, in Huamalíes and los Conchucos, religious specialists–ministers of Huari, healers, and diviners–were at the center of processes of transformation that had long been animated both by stimuli from priests and missionaries and by what might be called the Indians' gradual self-Christianization (Mills 1997, 254–66, Chs. 4, 7).

An Indian named Felipe Ramos was said by Vega Bazán to have been kept by the Devil for a number of days in a cave, sustained only by black maize and blue-colored water. The Devil's purpose was presented as clearly didactic, for when Felipe Ramos was eventually released from his initiation and sent into the world, he began preaching of this infernal sect. Rather than a simple confirmation of Vega Bazán's imported diabolism, the story seems to reveal a churchman wrestling with what he perceived to be native Andean delusion and error. In the story, the Devil sits ambiguously once again in place of Huari or, rather, in place of what in another region might have been not only a powerful and knowledge-laden *huaca*, but, increasingly, also the Virgin Mary or a familiar patron saint. The story of Felipe Ramos's short pedagogical abduction strongly resembles other colonial Andean descriptions of the choosing, appointment, and training of dogmatizers and specialist ministers often carried out through visions or dreams involving a growing complement of Andean and Christian spiritual beings, among whom the Devil was only one force (see Mills 1997, esp. 221–24, 240, 226, 234, 61–62; Salomon 1990; Mannheim). Fittingly, this is not the end of Vega Bazán's discussion of Felipe Ramos's consultations and seeking of divine favors.

Related to Ramos's incessant dogmatizing before groups of Indians were this man's special skills as a healer. Ramos was regularly consulted by the people of his town and region, much like the specialists described earlier who divined from the legs of spiders. Yet his procedures were cause for a new level of alarm. At night, Vega Bazán related, Felipe Ramos constructed altars for images of the saints and of Our Lady the Virgin. Before his makeshift images, he would make consultations, learning what was needed for his curing of the sick. According to Vega Bazán, Ramos would say: "aora vendran los santos, y nos diràn lo que emos de hazer" (*Testimonio* fol. 4v) ("now the saints will come, and tell us what we have to do"). His act of supplication and petition before the representantive sacred images recalls the invocation to the idol Huari (who also had altars near his stone seat) that Vega Bazán had identified as the typical summons that sealed a pact with the Devil. Viewed from another angle, Ramos's raising of makeshift altars in honor of images of Mary and of other saints was a genuine form of contemporary Catholic piety, an expression not only of his trust in these Christian forces but also of his need to show gratitude and beg favors before them.

The extirpator's account continued. A candle that Felipe Ramos had lit on the altars would go out, and the Devil would appear, not in one of his usual guises, but in the figure of Adam, God's first creation. The Devil-as-Adam would command that everyone should believe and do just as Felipe Ramos instructed, because it was the wisdom of God. After a number of these *representaciones* (the account, here, may refer to the Devil's statements, or perhaps to his appearance in other forms), the candle would again be lit and Felipe Ramos would preach to a gathering of native Andean men and women. The wisdom of God, as spoken by Ramos the dogmatizer, amounted to a well-informed, local counter-evangelization, a native refutation of a steadily pervading Christianity that prompts comparison with the messages of steadfast teacher-minister Hernando Hacas Poma and his less well-known contemporaries in San Pedro de Acas, Cajatambo (Huertas Vallejos 1981, 107; Duviols 1986, 135–262; Mills 1994a, esp. 55–63; and arguing further: Cummins 1998). Ramos is said to have taught people that

> se devia adorar al dicho Hauri [sic], y que no se devia adorar a Iesu Christo nuestro Redentor, ni oyessen Missa, ni Dotrina; porque el dicho Huari era criador de los hombres, y dava salud, y vida, y sanava las enfermedades. (*Testimonio* fols. 4v–5r)

> one should worship Huari, and not Jesus Christ Our Redeemer, [and that one should] neither hear Mass nor attend *doctrina*, because the said Huari was the creator of men and the one who gave health and life and healed illnesses.

Felipe Ramos also gave people special baths—superstitious baths, Vega Bazán insists—as part of his healing sessions. During the baths, he set about removing stones and other things from the sick person, in the manner described above. The extractions were duly taken to hills where Huari was invoked by Ramos with the said pact (using the appeal and incantation also noted above). Ramos would be asking Huari what he needed to do in the case at hand, just as he had done with the images of Our Lady and the saints. The Devil would then appear again to Felipe Ramos, but this time in the form of a mulatto (in contemporary terms, a man of African and either Spanish or Indian descent). The Devil-as-mulatto told the specialist not to look at him—to turn his back—while he spelled out what Ramos had to do (fol. 5r).

The range of Ramos's consultations is staggering both in place and in form, and one seems to catch Vega Bazán in the act of trying to record as many as possible. The hills (and perhaps the place of the all-seeing seat noted above) were where one usually contacted Huari, but Felipe Ramos would also conduct divinations at certain springs in the area (similarly suggesting the importance of "sorcerers" connected to marvelous springs in Conchucos, and on "Puquio" near Lamellín in particular, see Calancha vol. 3: 1061–62). According to Vega Bazán's account, from one of these springs a great snake would routinely emerge and give him a lick. The method of learning from these particular encounters was reported as follows: If the great snake left the water and then slid back into the spring, it was an indication that whatever the consultation concerned would happen, but if the snake left for some other place, the thing would not occur.

Vega Bazán's sketch of the evidence against Felipe Ramos leads directly into that concerning another Indian, Juan Pérez, whom Vega Bazán had discovered during the course of his preaching (*Testimonio*, fol. 5r). Pérez is described as a priest (*sacerdote*) of the said Huari, who, among his other offences, had initiated his own aunt as a minister and ritual specialist. He was said to have taken his aunt to another local spring in order to give her a superstitious bath, while calling out to Huari. His invocations had summoned from the water (not a

great snake or a mulatto, but) Huari, this time "en figura de un Padre [probablemente un Jesuita], con ropones largos, de tres varas de alto" ("in the figure of a *padre* [probably a Jesuit father], three *varas* [over eight feet] tall, with a long outergarment,") followed by a slither of "culebras, y lagartijas, y lamieron a la dicha su tia, y al dicho Iuan Perez" ("snakes and lizards, [all of] which licked his said aunt and the said Juan Pérez). Notably, the giant *padre* was precisely the same height as the giant Huari in the origin myth was said to have been. And as the account of the former continues, the two divine beings merge completely. That is to say, the named identity of the now multiform Andean God Huari returns. In the presence of the *padre* and his slimy retinue, the minister instructed his aunt for a time, teaching her how to remove snakes from the sick and advising her to do just as he taught. All this, the account reads, before "el dicho Huari se bolvió a entrar en el manantial" (*Testimonio* fol. 5r) ("the said Huari went back into the spring").

Pablo Joseph de Arriaga had written almost four decades before Vega Bazán's *Testimonio auténtico* was published that the native Andeans in the highlands of this region had no understanding of the first parents of humankind, Adam and Eve (Arriaga [1621] 1920, Ch. 2, 24; and Teruel [attributed], as reported by Calancha vol. 3, 930–31). If the implications of his claim were true even in 1621, then it does not appear to have been strictly so by the 1650s. Not that Vega Bazán's evidence of Felipe Ramos's understanding or kind of knowledge of the first parents would have been seen by churchmen as an advance! But, native Andeans' very subtle idolatry, as Vega Bazán chose to dub the colonial religiosity in los Conchucos and Huamalíes, was altering, along with local oral traditions and ritual practices. Perhaps there was a painting of the temptation in Eden in a local church, or, one might reasonably presume, a priest who had spoken of Adam in indoctrination (Hartmann; and parallels in New Spain: Williams). What is clear is that Huari—or God, or the Devil (Vega Bazán alternates between and among the terms, as I believe his sources did)—now appeared to his ministers and specialists in the figure of Adam as readily as that of a serpent, or a hairy spider. He might also emerge from his spring as a giant Jesuit, or he could appear as a mulatto, and after invocations were made before the images of Christian saints—merged forces and figures from colonial times, with healing knowledge, who knew how to proceed. Huari was the older regional creator, who could be everywhere, like a strong wind. He was also acquiring new meanings and manners of address and response, combining gradually with Spanish Christian symbols and practices that—because of evangelization and its unpredictable aftermaths—were also meaning more to Indians as religious boundaries grew less clearly marked.

From the perspective of an upholder of official Christianity, perhaps this was an instance of what George M. Foster referred to as the stripping down, the simplification of Spanish Catholicism as bits of it took root in the Americas (Foster 12–17). One sees Foster's point, yet it is difficult to see here only reduction and loss, even if our gaze widens to include those whom Foster, in 1960, was content to call the principal recipient culture, the native Andean people who clearly lost so much. Huari, represented by an idol, by the hills, by the winds, was not unseated in the middle of the seventeenth century. But neither was he a lone or heroically changeless source of healing power and knowledge in his mountain realm. For the minister and specialist Felipe Ramos, images of the Virgin

Mary and unspecified saints, who were arrayed on altars erected by the Indian himself, might also become authentic and responsive channels. From Ramos's perspective, such ritual actions may have felt like a sensible, perhaps even a very necessary, move in difficult times; the makeshift altar, and the consultation of images of the Virgin and saints emerged from his own understandings of just where sacred power now resided. The idol Huari, the Devil, and images of Mary and some unspecified saints all appear to have been meaningful players in a colonial religion that, in William Taylor's words, "podían abarcar la separación entre la religión institucional y la devoción popular, participando en ambas" (2000, 185) ("could span the separations between institutional religion and popular devotion by partaking of both").

Even Vega Bazán, albeit for his own reasons, would have wanted to take Foster's point about the stripping down of Christianity a good deal further. The apparent religious creativity and convergence in a case such as that involving Felipe Ramos might be presented as the height of disorder by the extirpator: A native minister and specialist was invoking representations of the Virgin Mary and saints in similar ways and for similar reasons as he had called upon native divinities (the Devil). But only the names appeared to have changed—and this, in itself, is perhaps a more profound suggestion than it may at first sound.

Native Andeans in colonial times probably did not need much encouragement or guidance in this matter. But, often unwittingly and even in contradiction with themselves, Spanish Christians had effectively invited native Andeans toward profound religious mixture (other examples in Mills 1997, esp. Chs. 4, 8). The issue of naming, and instructions about the names of forbidden divinities and Christian saints, had even featured among the guidelines meant to assist *visitadores generales de idolatría* set down by Padre Arriaga in 1621. What indigenous people were called—their names—mattered. These names were believed to connect people to the divinities whom they understood, sought, and consulted in times of need. "De aquí adelante," ("From this moment forward"), the Jesuit had commanded,

> Ningún Indio, ny India se llamaré con nombre de las Huacas, ny el Rayo: y assí no se podrá llamar Curi, Manco, Missa, Chacpa, ny Líbiac ny Santiago, sino Diego; y al que a su hijo pusiere alguno de estos nombres le serán dados cien açotes por las calles, y el Cura, y Vicario de esta Dotrina procederá contra él, como contra relapso en la Idolatría, y a los que hasta aquí se han llamado con algunos de los dichos nombres mando se los quiten, y se acomoden a llamarse con otros sobre nombres, de los Españoles, o de Santos. ("Constituciones que dexa el visitador," in Arriaga, 203; also reprinted in Duviols 1986, Appendix 1, 517)

> no Indian man or woman shall be named after the *huacas* or the lightning, nor ought they to be named Curi, Manco, Missa, Chacpa, or Líbiac or Santiago, but Diego; and the priest or vicar of the [given] parish can administer one hundred lashes in the street to anyone who names their child one of those [forbidden] names, proceeding as if against a backslider [*relapso*] into idolatry; and it is ordered that those persons who have had those names up to now cease to be known by them and adjust themselves to being called by other names, those of Spaniards or the saints.

There is plenty of evidence to suggest that personal, or Christian, names were widely taken by colonial Indians at baptism; evidence from later in the seventeenth century, and into the eighteenth century and beyond, suggests that many Andean last names were changed much less readily. Not that it appears to have mattered in the way that Arriaga and other

churchmen may have hoped. If the adopted saints' and Spaniards' names were meant as neat substitutes for native Andean identities (which were to be extirpated along with memory of the old gods), they became nothing of the kind in practice. Of this, Vega Bazán, before his evidence of the beliefs and ritual practices of persons named Felipe Ramos and Juan Pérez, would hardly have needed reminding. The names, however, can still be seen as markers of a more complicated kind of change, signs that not much was as it seemed. Divine beings and their reputations and competences, like names and religious identities, were combining in these times. They were still being called upon by this society's specialists—in a pattern of change and persistent vitality that modern evidence suggests has continued in parts of the wider Andean cultural zone to this day (Harris 1982; Gose 1995b; and on ritual sessions convened by shamans or *yatiri* and modern cults of Santiago de Bombori [or Pumpuri] and a number of his saintly associates in the highlands on the northwestern boundaries of the territory of the Macha people, in North Potosí, Bolivia, see esp. Platt 1988, 1997; Grosso).

Evidence of colonial Andean religious change (here, not the penetration of one belief system by another so much as a fluid set of understandings and a gradual adjustment of concepts and practices that might involve, and be capitalized upon by, the impulses of native Andeans and Spaniards) comes from imperfect sources and almost always ends too soon. Although seventeenth-century churchmen with long experience in Andean parishes knew about the mixing, it remained something with which it was difficult for them to engage in a sustained manner. For them, it represented confusion and error far worse than persistent pre-Hispanic ways, for the latter were thought to flow predictably from an ignorance that, while offensive to God, might still be partly excused. Engaging with religious mixture meant entertaining, among other things, their predecessors' failures, the complex ramifications of evangelization (including native self-Christianization), and perhaps even the futility of their own continuing task.

One learns most about Indian religious change from sources that, even in the midst of refutation and condemnation, gave a degree of play to information gained from native Andeans, and in which (however imperfectly and fleetingly) native Andeans are active as individuals instead of as a faceless group of uniformly resistant or accommodating *indios*. Vega Bazán's *Testimonio auténtico* manages to be one of these documents, in spite of itself. For it is not as if the condemnatory tinge, the living acceptance of demonic mimicry of God in the world and of the caves of damnation reserved for those in error, ever goes away. But, because of Vega Bazán's curiosity and his effort to portray a number of different dimensions within a very subtle idolatry by putting together what he has learned from interrogations of native Andeans, his text unleashes more than barriers for his readers' consideration. Complementing the earlier reporting on Conchucos by religious commentators such as the Jesuit Pablo Joseph de Arriaga and the Augustinian Antonio de la Calancha, Vega Bazán has produced an authentic testimony of transforming mid-colonial understandings that, whether stumbled upon or hard won, were summonable by native Andeans as well as by a parish priest and extirpator of idolatry. The text allows the changes occurring within colonial religion to be glimpsed and for the document to be more than simply a churchman's convenient invention. This kind of seeing and suggestion, at least as we might understand it, was certainly not the point of the *Testimonio auténtico*. It was not what Estanislao de Vega Bazán intended. Perhaps precisely because of this—because, as with the Devil who appeared as a mulatto to Felipe Ramos, the witness is supposed to look away and not see such things—one cannot help but remember them and think over what they may have meant.

Works Cited

Acosta, José de. [1588] 1984. *De Procuranda Indorum Salute.* Ed. and trans. Luciano Pereña et al. Madrid: Consejo Superior de Investigaciones Científicas.

Acosta Rodríguez, Antonio. 1987a. "Francisco de Avila, Cusco 1573(?)–Lima 1647." *Ritos y tradiciones.* Ed. Gerald Taylor. Lima: Instituto de Estudios Peruanos and Institut Français d'Etudes Andines. 551–616.

———. 1987b. "La extirpación de las idolatrías en el Perú. Origen y desarrollo de las campañas. A propósito de *Cultura andina y represión* de Pierre Duviols." *Revista andina* 9: 171–95.

Adorno, Rolena. 1986. *Guaman Poma: Writing and Resistance in Colonial Peru.* Austin: University of Texas Press.

———. 1991. "The Image of the *Indio ladino* in Early Colonial Peru." *Transatlantic Encounters: Europeans and Andeans in the Sixteenth Century.* Eds. Kenneth J. Andrien and Rolena Adorno. Berkeley: University of California Press. 232–70.

———. 1994. "The Art of Survival in Early Colonial Peru." *Violence, Resistance, and Survival in the Americas: Native Americans and the Legacy of Conquest.* Eds. William B. Taylor and Franklin Pease. N. Y., Washington and London: Smithsonian Institute Press. 67–97.

Álvarez, Bartolomé. [1588] 1998. *De las costumbres y conversión de los indios del Perú. Memorial a Felipe II.* Eds. María del Carmen Martín Rubio, Juan J. R. Villarías Robles, and Fermín del Pino Díaz. Madrid: Ediciones Polifemo.

Archivo Arzobispal de Lima (AAL), Lima, Peru. Sección de Hechicerías e Idolatrías (manuscript sources).

Archivo General de Indias (AGI), Seville, Spain. Audiencia de Lima (manuscript sources).

Arriaga, Pablo José de. [1621] 1920. *La extirpación de la idolatría en el Perú.* Ed. Horacio H. Urteaga. Colección de libros y documentos referentes a la historia del Perú. Series 2, vol. 1. Lima: Imprenta y Librería San Martín.

———. [1621] 1968. *The Extirpation of Idolatry in Peru.* Trans. L. Clark Keating. Lexington: University of Kentucky Press.

Avendaño, Fernando de. [1614] 1971. "Testimonio de los cuerpos muertos que el Maestro Avendaño hizo exhibir en el pueblo de San Francisco de Musca." *La Lutte Contre les Réligions Autochtones dans le Pérou Colonial. 'L'Extirpation de L'Idolâtrie' entre 1532 et 1660* by Pierre Duviols. Lima: Institut Français d'Etudes Andines. Appendix doc. 1, 355–56.

———. [1617] 1986. "Relación de las idolatrías de los indios de Hernando de Avendaño." *Cultura andina y represión. Procesos y visitas de idolatrías y hechicerías Cajatambo, siglo XVII.* Ed. Pierre Duviols. Cusco: Centro de Estudios Rurales Andinos "Bartolomé de Las Casas." 441–47.

———. [1653] 1971. "El Dr. Fernando de Avendaño a S. M." *La Lutte Contre les Réligions Autochtones dans le Pérou Colonial. 'L'Extirpation de L'Idolâtrie' entre 1532 et 1660* by Pierre Duviols. Lima: Institut Français d'Etudes Andines. Appendix doc. 5, 363–65.

Avila, Francisco de. [1611] 1904. "Relación que yo, el Doctor Francisco de Avila, presbítero, cura y beneficiado de la ciudad de Huánuco, hice por mandado del Señor Arzobispo de los Reyes acerca de los pueblos de indios de este arzobispo donde se ha descubierto la idolatría y hallado gran cantidad de ídolos, que los dichos indios adoraban y tenían por sus dioses." *La imprenta en Lima* (1584–1824). Ed. José Toribio Medina. Santiago, Chile: Impreso y grabado en casa del autor. Vol. 1: 386–89.

———. 1646–1648. *Tratado de los evangelios que nuestra Madre la Yglesia nos propone en todo el año. Desde la primera dominica de Adviento hasta la última Missa de Difuntos, Santos de España, y añadidos en el nuevo rezado. Explicase el Evangelio, y en cada uno se pone un sermon en lengua castellana y la General de los Indios deste Reyno del Perú, y donde conviene da lugar la materia se refutan los errores de idolatría.* Lima: n.p.

Bastien, Joseph W. [1978] 1985. *Mountain of the Condor: Metaphor and Ritual in an Andean Ayllu.* Reprint, Prospect Heights, IL: Waveland Press.

Bauer de Castro, Don Diego de. [1653] 1971. "Ynforme del visitador Don Diego de Bauer de Castro sobre actuaciones sobre hechicerías." *La Lutte Contre les Réligions Autochtones dans le Pérou Colonial. 'L'Extirpation de L'Idolâtrie' entre 1532 et 1660* by Pierre Duviols. Lima: Institut Français d'Etudes Andines. Appendix doc. 6, 365–67.

Bellarmino, Roberto Francesco Romolo. [1598] 1649. *Declaracion copiosa de las quatro partes mas essenciales, y necessarias de la doctrina christiana, compuesto por orden del Beatissimo P. Clemente Octavo de felice memoria por el eminentissimo Cardenal Roberto Belarminio de la compania de Jesus, con las adiciones del maestro Sebastian de Lirio, catedratico de Prima de Griego en la Universidad de Alcala . . .* Trans. from Spanish into Quechua by Bartolomé Jurado Palomino. Lima: Jorge López de Herrera.

Briggs, Robin. 1996. *Witches and Neighbours: The Social and Cultural Context of European Witchcraft.* London: Harper Collins.

Burkhart, Louise M. 1996. *Holy Wednesday: A Nahua Drama from Early Colonial Mexico.* Philadelphia: University of Pennsylvania Press.

Cahill, David. 1996. "Popular Religion and Appropriation: The Example of Corpus Christi in Eighteenth-Century Cuzco." *Latin American Research Review* 31: 67–110.

Calancha, Antonio de la. [1638] 1974–1981. *Crónica moralizada. [Corónica moralizada del orden de San Augustín en el Perú, con sucesos egenplares en esta monarquía. Dedicada a Nuestra Señora de Gracia, singular Patrona i Abogada de la dicha Orden. Compuesta por el muy reverendo Padre Maestro Fray Antonio de la Calancha de la misma Orden, i Definidor actual].* Ed. Ignacio Prado Pastor. Lima: Imprenta de la Universidad Nacional Mayor de San Marcos. 6 vols.

Cerrón Palomino, Rodolfo. 1991. "Un texto desconocido del quechua costeño (s. XVI)." *Revista Andina* 9: 393–413.

Cervantes, Fernando. 1994. *The Devil in the New World: The Impact of Diabolism in New Spain.* New Haven and London: Yale University Press.

Clark, Stuart. 1997. *Thinking with Demons: The Idea of Witchcraft in Early Modern Europe.* Oxford: Clarendon Press.

Clendinnen, Inga. 1987. *Ambivalent Conquests: Maya and Spaniard in Yucatan, 1517–1570.* Cambridge: Cambridge University Press.

"Constituciones sinodales, Lima, 1614." 1986. *Cultura andina y represión. Procesos y visitas de idolatrías y hechicerías Cajatambo, siglo XVII.* Ed. Pierre Duviols. Cusco: Centro de Estudios Rurales Andinos "Bartolomé de Las Casas." Appendix 1, pp. 511–14.

Cummins, Tom (Thomas B. F.). 1988. "Abstraction to Narration: Kero Imagery of Peru and the Colonial Alteration of Native Identity." Dissertation. University of California, Los Angeles.

———. 1995. "From Lies to Truth: Colonial Ekphrasis and the Act of Cross-Cultural Translation." *Reframing the Renaissance: Visual Culture in Europe and Latin America, 1450–1650.* Ed. Claire Farago. New Haven and London: Yale University Press. 152–74.

———. 1998. "El lenguaje del arte colonial: Imagen, ekfrasis e idolatría." *I Encuentro Internacional de peruanistas: Estado de Estudios Histórico-Sociales sobre el Perú a fines del Siglo XX.* Lima: Unversidad de Lima y Fondo de Cultura Económica, 23–45.

———. 1997a. "Point of View and Evidentiality in the Huarochirí Texts (Peru, 17th Century)." *Creating Context in Andean Cultures.* Ed. Rosaleen Howard-Malverde. Oxford and New York: Oxford University Press. 149–67.

Dedenbach-Salazar Sáenz, Sabine. 1994. "El arte verbal de los textos quechuas de Huarochirí (Perú, siglo XVII) reflejado en la organización del discurso y en los medios estilísticos." *Andean Oral Traditions: Discourse and Literature/Tradiciones orales andinas: Discurso y literatura*. Eds. Margot Beyersdorff and Sabine Dedenbach-Salazar Saenz. Bonn: Holos. 21–49.

———. 1997b. "La terminología cristiana en textos quechua de instrucción religosa en el siglo XVI." *Latin American Indian Literatures: Messages and Meanings*. Ed. Mary H. Preuss. Lancaster, CA.: Labyrinthos. 195–209.

Doctrina Christiana y catecismo para instruccion de indios . . . [y] Tercero Cathecismo . . . [1584–1585] 1985. Facsimilie of the trilingual text. Ed. Luciano Pereña et al. Corpus Hispanorum de Pace. Vol. 26-2. Madrid: Consejo Superior de Investigaciones Científicas.

Duviols, Pierre. 1966. "Estudio bio-bibliográfico." *Dioses y hombres de Huarochirí: Narración quechua recogida por Francisco de Avila*. Ed. and trans. José María Arguedas. Lima: Museo Nacional de Historia and Instituto de Estudios Peruanos. 218–40.

———. 1971. *La Lutte Contre les Réligions Autochtones dans le Pérou Colonial. L'Extirpation de L'Idolâtrie' entre 1532 et 1660*. Lima: Institut Français d'Etudes Andines.

———. 1973. "Huari and Llacuaz: Agricultores y pastores, un dualismo prehispánico de oposición y complementaridad." *Revista del Museo Nacional* 39: 153–91.

———. 1977. *La destrucción de las religiones andinas (conquista y la colonia)*. Trans. Albor Maruenda. Mexico: Universidad Nacional Autónoma de México.

———, ed. 1986. *Cultura andina y represión. Procesos y visitas de idolatrías y hechicerías Cajatambo, siglo XVII*. Cusco: Centro de Estudios Rurales Andinos "Bartolomé de Las Casas."

Elliott, Sir John H. 1970. *The Old World and the New, 1492–1650*. Cambridge: Cambridge University Press.

Estenssoro Fuchs, Juan Carlos. 1994. "Descubriendo los poderes de la palabra: Funciones de la prédica en la evangelización del Perú (siglos XVI–XVII)." *La venida del reino: Religión, evangelización y cultura en América, siglos XVI–XX*. Ed. Gabriela Ramos. Cusco: Centro de Estudios Regionales "Bartolomé de Las Casas." 75–101.

———. 1996. "Les pouvoirs de la parole: La prédication au Pérou de l'évangelisation à l'utopie." *Annales HSS* 6: 1225–57.

Eymerich, Nicolaus [Eymericus]. 1503. *Directorium inquisitorum. Seguuntur decretales tituli de summa trinitate et fide catholica*. Barcelona [Barchinone]: Iohanem Iuschner.

Farriss, Nancy M. 1984. *Maya Society under Colonial Rule: The Collective Enterprise of Survival*. Princeton: Princeton University Press.

Foster, George M. 1960. *Culture and Conquest: America's Spanish Heritage*. New York: Wenner-Gren Foundation for Anthropological Research.

García Cabrera, Juan Carlos. 1993. "Apuntes para una biografía del bachiller Rodrigo Hernández Príncipe, extirpador de idolatrías." *Catolicismo y extirpación de idolatrías, siglos XVI–XVIII: Charcas, Chile, México, Perú*. Eds. Gabriela Ramos and Henrique Urbano. Cusco: Centro de Estudios Regionales Andinos "Bartolomé de Las Casas." 241–61.

———, ed. 1994. *Ofensas a Dios, pleitos e injurias: Causas de idolatrías y hechicerías, Cajatambo siglos XVII–XIX*. Cusco: Centro de Estudios Regionales Andinos "Bartolomé de Las Casas."

———. 1996. "Por qué mintieron los indios de Cajatambo? La extripación de idolatrías en Hacas entre 1656–1665." *Revista Andina* 27: 7–39. (With comments by Antonio Acosta, Josep M. Barnadas, José Antonio Benito, Iris Gareis, Peter Gose, and Teodoro Hampe Martínez, 40–52).

Gareis, Iris. 1987. *Religiöse Spezialisten des zentralen Andengebietes zur Zeit der Inka und während der spanishen Kolonialherrschaft*. Hohenschäftlarn: Klaus Renner Verlag.

González Holguín, Diego. [1608] 1989. *Vocabulario de la lengua general de todo el Peru llamada lengua Qquichua o del Inca*. Facsimilie ed. of the 1952 version. Lima: Universidad Nacional Mayor de San Marcos.

Gose, Peter. 1995a. "Contra Paqual Haro: Un proceso de idolatrías, Cusco, 1697." *Ciencias Sociales (Revista del Instituto de Investigaciones Históricas Sociales, Lima)* 1.1: 203–18.

———. 1995b. "Les Momies, les Saints et les Politiques D'inhumation au Pérou, au XVIIe Siècle." *Recherches Amérindiennes au Québec* 25.2: 35–51.

———. 1996. *Deathly Waters and Hungry Mountains: Agrarian Ritual and Class Formation in an Andean Town*. Toronto: University of Toronto Press.

Grafton, Anthony, with April Shelford and Nancy Siraisi. 1992. *New Worlds, Ancient Texts: The Power of Tradition and the Shock of Discovery*. Cambridge, MA. and London: Belknap Press of Harvard University Press.

Greenblatt, Stephen J. 1991. *Marvelous Possessions: The Wonder of the New World*. Oxford: Clarendon Press.

Grosso, José Luis. 1995. "La suerte de lo andino, sus saberes y poderes. Adivinación y mestizaje en el Norte de Potosí," Master's thesis. Universidad del Valle, Cali, Colombia.

Gruzinski, Serge. 1992. "Vision et christianisation: L'expérience mexicaine." *Visions indiennes, visions baroques. Les métissage de l'inconscient*. Ed. Jean Michel Sallman. Paris: Presses Universitaires de France. 117–49.

———. 1999. *La pensée métisse*. Paris: Fayard.

Guamán Poma de Ayala, Felipe. [ca. 1615] 1980. *El primer nuevo corónica y buen gobierno*. Eds. John V. Murra and Rolena Adorno. 3 vols. Mexico City: Siglo XXI editores.

Guibovich Pérez, Pedro. 1993. "La carrera de un visitador de idolatrías en el siglo XVII: Fernando de Avendaño (1580?–1655)." *Catolicismo y extirpación de idolatrías, siglos XVI–XVIII: Charcas, Chile, México, Perú*. Eds. Gabriela Ramos and Henrique Urbano. Cusco: Centro de Estudios Regionales Andinos "Bartolomé de Las Casas." 169–240.

Gutiérrez Arbulú, Laura. 1993. "Indice de la sección hechicerías e idolatrías del Archivo Arzobispal de Lima." *Catolicismo y extirpación de idolatrías, siglos XVI–XVIII: Charcas, Chile, México, Perú*. Eds. Gabriela Ramos and Henrique Urbano. Cusco: Centro de Estudios Regionales Andinos "Bartolomé de Las Casas." 105–36.

Hampe Martínez, Teodoro. 1996. *Cultura barroca y extirpación de idolatrías. La biblioteca de Francisco de Avila (1648)*. Cusco: Centro de Estudios Regionales Andinos "Bartolomé de Las Casas."

Harris, Olivia. 1982. "The Dead and the Devils among the Bolivian Laymi." *Death and the Regeneration of Life*. Eds. Maurice Bloch and Jonathan Parry. Cambridge: Cambridge University Press. 45–73.

———. 1995a. "'The Coming of the White People.' Reflections on the Mythologisation of History in Latin America." *Bulletin of Latin American Research* 14: 9–24.

———. 1995b. "Knowing the Past: Plural Identities and the Antimonies of Loss in Highland Bolivia." *Counterworks: Managing the Diversity of Knowledge*. Ed. Richard Fardon. London and New York: Routledge. 105–23.

Hartmann, Roswith. 1991. "Christian Religious Pictographs from the Andes: Two Examples." *Latin American Indian Literatures Journal* 7: 172–91.

Henningsen, Gustav. 1980. *The Witches' Advocate: Basque Witchcraft and the Spanish Inquisition* (1609–1614). Reno, NV: University of Nevada Press.

Hernández Príncipe, Rodrigo. [1621–1622] 1986. "Visitas de Rodrigo Hernández Príncipe." *Cultura andina y represión. Procesos y visitas de idolatrías y hechicerías Cajatambo, siglo XVII*. Ed. Pierre Duviols. Cusco: Centro de Estudios Rurales Andinos "Bartolomé de Las Casas." 461–507.

Hodgen, Margaret T. 1964. *Early Anthropology in the Sixteenth and Seventeenth Centuries*. Philadelphia: University of Pennsylvania Press.

172 KENNETH MILLS

Howard-Malverde, Rosaleen. 1990. The Speaking of History: *'willa paakush ayki'* or Quedma Ways of Telling the Past. London: University of London.

Huertas Vallejos, Lorenzo. 1981. *La religión en una sociedad rural andina (siglo XVII).* Ayacucho: Universidad Nacional de San Cristóbal de Huamanga.

Kamen, Henry. 1997. *Philip of Spain.* New Haven and London: Yale University Press.

———. 1998. *The Spanish Inquisition: A Historical Revision.* New Haven and London: Yale University Press.

Kristeller, Paul Oskar. 1980. *Renaissance Thought and the Arts.* Princeton: Princeton University Press.

Lanser, Susan Sniader. 1981. *The Narrative Act: Point of View in Prose and Fiction.* Princeton: Princeton University Press.

Larner, Christina. 1981. *Enemies of God: The Witch-hunt in Scotland.* London: Chatto and Windus.

Lira, Jorge A. 1950. "El demonio en los Andes." *Tradición* 1.2: 35–40.

MacCormack, Sabine. 1991. *Religion in the Andes: Vision and Imagination in Early Colonial Peru.* Princeton: Princeton University Press.

Mannheim, Bruce. 1987. "A Semiotic of Andean Dreams." *Dreaming: Anthropological and Psychological Interpretations.* Ed. Barbara Tedlock. Cambridge: Cambridge University Press. 132–53.

Marzal, Manuel María. [1983] 1988. *La transformación religiosa peruana.* Lima: Pontificia Universidad Católica del Perú.

———. 1992. "Daily Life in the Indies." *The Church in Latin America, 1492–1992.* Ed. Enrique Dussel. Tunbridge Wells, Kent: Burns and Oates; Maryknoll, NY: Orbis Books. 69–80.

Medina, Felipe de. 1904. "Relación del Licenciado Felipe de Medina, visitador general de las idolatrías del arzobispado de Lima, inviada al ilustrísimo y reverendísimo Señor Arzobispo della, en que le da cuenta de las que se han descubierto en el pueblo de Huacho, donde ha comenzado á visitar desde 19 de febrero hasta 23 de marzo de 1650 (Se acompaña la anterior relación con carta del Arzobispo de Lima, su fecha en 9 de Marzo de 1650)." *La imprenta en Lima* (1584–1824). Ed. José Toribio Medina. Santiago, Chile: en casa del autor. Vol. 1: 215–21.

Medina, José Toribio, ed. 1904–1907. *La imprenta en Lima* (1584–1824). Santiago, Chile: en casa del autor. 4 vols.

Mignolo, Walter D. 1989. "Colonial Situations, Geographical Discourses and Territorial Representations: Toward a Diatopical Understanding of Colonial Semiosis." *Dispositio* 36–38: 93–140.

———. 1995. *The Darker Side of the Renaissance: Literacy, Territoriality, and Colonization.* Ann Arbor: University of Michigan Press.

Millones, Luis. 1969. "Introducción al estudio de las idolatrías." *Letras* 78–79.27: 5–40.

———. 1979a. "Los ganados del señor: mecanismos de poder en las comunidades andinas, siglos xviii y xix." *América Indígena* 39.1: 107–45.

———. 1979b. "Religion and Power in the Andes: Idolatrous Curacas of the Central Sierra." *Ethnohistory* 26: 143–263.

———. 1984. "Shamanismo y política en el Perú colonial: los curacas de Ayacucho." *Histórica* 8: 131–49.

———, ed. 1990. *El retorno de las huacas: Estudios y documentos sobre el Taki Onqoy, siglo XVI.* Lima: Instituto de Estudios Peruanos.

Mills, Kenneth. 1992. "Persistencia religiosa en Santiago de Carhuamayo (Junín), 1631." *Testimonios, cartas y manifiestos indígenas (época colonial y primer período republicano).* Ed. Martín Leinhard. Caracas: Biblioteca Ayacucho. 222–31.

———. 1994a. *An Evil Lost to View? An Investigation of Post-Evangelisation Andean Religion in Mid-Colonial Peru.* Liverpool: Institute of Latin American Studies.

———. 1994b. "The Limits of Religious Coercion in Mid-Colonial Peru." *Past and Present* 145: 84–121.

———. 1996. "Bad Christians in Colonial Peru." *Colonial Latin American Review* 5: 183–218.

———. 1997. *Idolatry and Its Enemies: Colonial Andean Religion and Extirpation, 1640–1750.* Princeton: Princeton University Press.

———. 1999. "Diego de Ocaña e la organizzazione del miracoloso a Potosí." *Il Santo e la Città.* Ed. Giovanna Fiume. Venice: Marsilio Editrice. 384–402.

———, and William B. Taylor, eds. 1998. *Colonial Spanish America: A Documentary History.* Wilmington, Delaware: Scholarly Resources.

"Misión a las provincias de Ocros y Lampas del corregimiento de Cajatambo." [1619] 1986. *Cultura andina y represión. Procesos y visitas de idolatrías y hechicerías Cajatambo, siglo XVII.* Ed. Pierre Duviols. Cusco: Centro de Estudios Rurales Andinos "Bartolomé de Las Casas." 449–57.

Moreno Yánez, Segundo E. 1991. "Los doctrineros 'wiracochas' recreadores de nuevas formas culturales: Estudios de caso en el Quito colonial." *Reproducción y transformación de las sociedades andinas, siglos XVI–XX.* Eds. Segundo E. Moreno Yánez and Frank Salomon. Quito: Ediciones ABYA-YALA and Movimiento Laicos para América Latina. 529–53.

Mujica Pinilla, Ramón. 1992. *Ángeles apócrifos en la América Virreinal.* Mexico City: Fondo de Cultura Económica.

Novoa, Bernardo de. [1664] 1971. "Bernardo de Noboa a S. M." *La Lutte Contre les Réligions Autochtones dans le Pérou Colonial. 'L'Extirpation de L'Idolâtrie' entre 1532 et 1660* by Pierre Duviols. Lima: Institut Français d'Etudes Andines. Appendix 11, 393–94.

Padilla, Juan de. [1657] 1971. "Trabajos, agravios e injusticias que padecen los indios en lo espiritual y temporal." *Historia general del Perú* by Rubén Vargas Ugarte. 2nd rev. ed. Lima: Editor Carlos Milla Batres. Vol. 3, Appendix.

Pagden, Anthony. [1982] 1986. *The Fall of Natural Man: The American Indian and the Origins of Comparative Ethnology.* 2nd rev. ed.. Cambridge: Cambridge University Press.

———. 1993. *European Encounters with the New World: From Renaissance to Romanticism.* New Haven and London: Yale University Press.

Pease G. Y., Franklin. 1973. *El dios creador andino.* Lima: Mosca Azul.

Pérez Bocanegra, Juan. 1631. *Ritual formulario e institución de curas para administrar a los naturales de este reyno, los santos sacramentos del baptismo, confirmación, eucaristía y viatico, penitencia, extrema unción y matrimonio, con advertencias muy necesarias.* Lima: Jerónimo de Contreras, junto al convento de Santo Domingo.

Peterson, Jeanette F. 1993. *The Paradise Garden Murals of Malinalco: Utopia and Empire in Sixteenth-Century Mexico.* Austin: University of Texas Press.

Platt, Tristan. 1987. "The Andean Soldiers of Christ. Confraternity Organization, the Mass of the Sun and Regenerative Warfare in Rural Potosí (18th–20th Centuries)." *Journal de la Société des Américanistes* 73: 139–92.

———. 1988. "Cultos milagrosos y chamanismo en el cristianismo sur-andio. Iglesia, religión y sociedad en la historia latinoamericana." *Actas del VIII Congreso de la Asociación de Historiadores Latinamericanistas en Europa.* Szeged: n. p. 119–37.

———. 1997. "The Sound of Light: Emergent Communication through Quechua Shamanic Dialogue." *Creating Context in Andean Cultures.* Ed. Rosaleen Howard-Malverde. Oxford: Oxford University Press. 196–226.

Price, Richard. 1983. *First-Time: The Historical Vision of an Afro-American People.* Baltimore: Johns Hopkins University Press.

Quiroga, Pedro de. [1562] 1922. *Libro intitulado Coloquios de la verdad. Ttrata de las causas e inconvenientes que impiden la doctrina xpiana e conversion de los indios de los reinos del Piru. Otrosi ttrata de la entrada y conquista de aquel Reino y de los daños e males e agravios que los indios padeçen y el estado en que al presente esta la justiçia e doctrina que se les administra. Compuesto por un saçerdote que en aquellos reinos a residido. Dirigido al muy illustre Señor Doctor Gaspar de Quiroga, Presidente del Consejo Real de los Estados de Italia, del Consejo Real de Su Magestad, y de la Sancta y General Inquisiçion.* Ed. Julián Zarco Cuevas. Seville: Tipografía Zarzuela.

Rama, Ángel. 1986. *La ciudad letrada.* Hanover, N.H: Ediciones del Norte.

Ramos, Gabriela. 1993. "Política eclesiástica y extirpación de idolatrías: discursos y silencios en torno al Taqui Onqoy." *Catolicismo y extirpación de idolatrías, siglos XVI–XVIII: Charcas, Chile, México, Perú.* Eds. Gabriela Ramos and Henrique Urbano. Cuoco: Centro de Estudios Regionales Andinos "Bartolomé de Las Casas." 137–68.

———, and Henrique Urbano, eds. 1993. *Catolicismo y extirpación de idolatrías, siglos XVI–XVIII: Charcas, Chile, México, Perú.* Cusco: Centro de Estudios Regionales Andinos "Bartolomé de Las Casas."

Rappaport, Joanne. 1990. *The Politics of Memory: Native Historical Interpretation in the Colombian Andes.* Cambridge: Cambridge University Press.

———, and Tom Cummins. 1998. "Between Images and Writing: The Ritual of the King's *Quillca*." *Colonial Latin American Review* 7: 7–32.

Relación de la religión y ritos del Perú hecha por los primeros religiosos Agustinos que allí pasaron. [ca. 1560]. Colección de documentos inéditos relativos al descubrimiento, conquista y colonización de las posesiones españolas en América y Oceanía. Vol. 3: 5–58.

Rivera de Tuesta, María Luisa. 1996. "Francisco de Avila y la extirpación de la idolatría en el Perú." *Logos Latinoamericano* (Lima) 2: 33–56.

Romero, Carlos A.., ed. 1918. "Idolatrías de los indios Huachos y Yauyos" (attributed to Padre Luis de Teruel). *Revista Histórica* 6: 180–97.

———. [1919] 1920. "El padre Pablo Joseph de Arriaga." *La extirpación de la idolatría en el Perú* by Pablo Joseph de Arriaga. Ed. Horacio H. Urteaga. Lima: Imprenta y Librería San Martín.

Saignes, Thierry. 1999. The Colonial Condition in the Quechua-Aymara Heartland (1570–1780). *The Cambridge History of the Native Peoples of the Americas.* Vol. 3. *South America.* Part 2. Eds. Frank Salomon and Stuart B. Schwartz. Cambridge: Cambridge Unviersity Press. 59–137.

Sallnow, Michael J. 1987. *Pilgrims of the Andes: Regional Cults in Cusco.* Washington, D.C. and London: Smithsonian Institute Press.

Salomon, Frank. 1990. "Nightmare Victory: The Meanings of Conversion among Peruvian Indians (Huarochirí, 1608?)." Department of Spanish and Portuguese, University of Maryland, College Park, Working Papers, no. 7.

———. 1995. "'The Beautiful Grandparents': Andean Ancestor Shrines and Mortuary Ritual as Seen Through Colonial Records." *Tombs for the Living: Andean Mortuary Practices.* Ed. Tom D. Dillehay. Washington, D.C.: Dumbarton Oaks Research Library and Collection. 315–53.

———, and George L. Urioste, eds. and trans. 1991. *The Huarochirí Manuscript: A Testament of Ancient and Colonial Andean Religion.* Austin: University of Texas Press.

Sánchez, Ana, ed. 1991. *Amancebados, hechiceros y rebeldes (Chancay, siglo XVII).* Cusco: Centro de Estudios Regionales Andinos "Bartolomé de Las Casas."

San Pedro, Juan de. [ca. 1560] 1992. *La persecución del demonio. Crónica de los primeros agustinos del norte del Perú.* Preliminary studies by Luis Millones, John Topic, and José L. Gonzalez. Málaga: Algazara y CAMEI editores.

———. [1560] 1951b. *Lexicon, o vocabulario de la lengua general del Perú llamada Quichua.* Facsimile ed. Lima: Universidad Nacional Mayor de San Marcos.

Santo Tomás, Domingo de. [1560] 1951a. *Grammatica o arte de la lengua general de los indios de los reynos del Peru.* Facsimile ed. Lima: Universidad Nacional Mayor de San Marcos.

Spalding, Karen. 1984. *Huarochirí: An Andean Society Under Inca and Spanish Rule.* Stanford: Stanford University Press.

Spiegel, Gabrielle M. 1997. *The Past as Text: The Theory and Practice of Medieval Historiography.* Baltimore and London: Johns Hopkins University Press.

Sprenger, Jacob, and Institoris (Henricus) (Heinrich Kramer). 1928. *Malleus Maleficarum.* Trans. Montague Summers. London: John Rodker.

Tanner, Norman P. S. J., ed. 1990. *Decrees of the Ecumenical Councils.* Vol. 2. *Trent to Vatican II.* London and Washington, D.C.: Sheed and Ward and Georgetown University Press.

Taylor, Gerald, ed. and trans. 1987. *Ritos y tradiciones de Huarochirí (manuscrito quechua de comienzos del siglo XVII).* Lima: Instituto de Estudios Peruanos and Institut Français d'Etudes Andines.

Taylor, William B. 1989. "... de corazón pequeño y ánimo apocado': Conceptos de los curas párrocos sobre los indios en la Nueva España del siglo XVIII." *Relaciones* 39: 5–67.

———. 1994a. "Santiago's Horse: Christianity and Colonial Indian Resistance in the Heartland of New Spain." *Violence, Resistance, and Survival in the Americas: Native Americans and the Legacy of Conquest.* Eds. William B. Taylor and Franklin Pease G. Y. Washington and London: Smithsonian Institute Press. 153–89.

———. 1994b. "Colonial Religion and Quincentennial Metaphors: Mexican Santiagos and *Cristos de Caña*." *Mesoamerican and Chicano Art, Culture and Identity.* Ed. Robert C. Dash. Salem, Oregon: Willamette Journal of the Liberal Arts Supplemental Series 6 (Bilingual ed.). 26–49.

———. 1996. *Magistrates of the Sacred: Priests and Parishioners in Eighteenth-Century Mexico.* Stanford: Stanford University Press.

———. 1998. "Nuestra Señora del Patrocinio y Fray Francisco de la Rosa: Una intersección de religión, política y arte en el México del siglo XVIII." *Relaciones* 73: 281–312.

———. 2000. "La iglesia entre la jerarquía y la religión popular: Messages from the Contact Zone." *Historia de América Latina.* Vol 1: *La época colonial.* Ed. Brian F. Connaughton. Mexico City: Universidad Nacional Autónoma de México. 177–226.

Urbano, Henrique. 1993. "Idolos, figuras, imágenes: La representación como discurso ideológico." *Catolicismo y extirpación de idolatrías, siglos XVI–XVIII: Charcas, Chile, México, Perú.* Eds. Gabriela Ramos and Henrique Urbano. Cuzco: Centro de Estudios Regionales Andinos "Bartolomé de Las Casas." 7–30.

Urton, Gary. 1996. "Rituales andinos y discurso antiidolátrico (s. XVI–XVII)." *Estudios sobre el sincretismo en América Central y en los Andes.* Eds. Bernd Schmelz and N. Ross Crumrine. Bonn: Bonner Amerikanistische Studien/Holos. 137–52.

Vargas Ugarte, Rubén. 1959–1962. *Historia de la Iglesia en el Perú.* 5 vols (1953–1962). Vol. 1, Lima: Imprenta Santa María, 1953; Vols. 2–5, Burgos: Imprenta de Aldecoa.

Vega Bazán, Estanislao de. 1656. *Testimonio autentico de una idolatria muy sutil que el demonio avia introducido entre los Indios de las pronincias [sic] de Conchucos, y Guamalies, sus sacerdotes, idolos, templo de baxo de tierra de admirable arquitectura, otros adoratorios, altaresgmas falsos, y supersticiones, que nuevamente descubrio el Bachiller Don Estanislao de Vega Bazan, Cura beneficiado de la Dotrina de Santa Ana de Cinga, Comissario de la Santa Cruzada en el partido de Guamalies, y Visitador general de la idolatria en este Arzobispado, en la visita, y escrutinios que hizo. Por Comision, y Particulares Instrucciones, que le dio el Illustris. y Reverend. Señor Doctor D. Pedro de Villagomez Arzobispo de Lima del Consejo del Rey N. Señor.* Lima: Imprenta de Iulian Santos.

———. [1662] 1971. "El Bachiller Estanislao de la Vega Bazán al Arzobispo." *La Lutte Contre les Réligions Autochtones dans le Pérou Colonial. 'L'Extirpation de L'Idolâtrie' entre 1532 et 1660* by Pierre Duviols. Lima: Institut Français d'Etudes Andines. Appendix doc. 10, 390–93.

Villagómez, Pedro de. [1649] 1919. *Carta pastoral de exortación e instrucción acerca de [sic: contra] las idolatrías de los indios del arzobispado de Lima.* Ed. Horacio H. Urteaga. Colección de libros y documentos referentes a la historia del Perú, vol. 12. Lima: Imprenta y Librería San Martín.

Williams, Jerry M. 1991. "Iconography and Religious Education in New Spain." *Revista Canadiense de Estudios Hispánicos* 5: 305–22.

CHAPTER 12

THE THREE FACES
OF THE BAROQUE IN MEXICO
AND THE CARIBBEAN

Iris M. Zavala

The center of gravity in this world is located in the future . . .
—*Bakhtin 1990, 99*

What I propose to address in this chapter is the articulation of influential, even dominant, traditions of literary and popular expression as they pass from Europe to the colonies in America. The paradoxical form of this transfer and its appropriation, by what we now call the people of Latin America in their construction of a civil society, is but one of the issues involved in the critical debate that surrounds the term transculturation. Focusing on the Baroque will help us see the relationships among values, poetics, and history in cultural history that is as rich on one side of the Atlantic as the other; I will explore the inner anatomy of the Baroque and try to present a synchronic section of its world so that we can then confront its historical genesis in the form of the accumulation of signifiers of power, and thereby explore the complex relationships of the cultural imaginary and cultural identity.

I will proceed by looking at three faces of the Baroque in the Caribbean and Mexico in the seventeenth century, at the end of the nineteenth century, and in the second half of the twentieth century. If we conceive of the making of the nation as the traumatic element around which fantasies are woven, Sor Juana's (1648–1695) texts indeed represent the struggle for a new rhetoric of the *self.* (See Zavala 1997.) The idea of *race* becomes established in each of the areas according to how a particular discourse preserves the colonial symbolic order; this is the basis for the radical heterogeneity that could account for the articulation of a neo-Baroque postcolonial discourse in both Mexico and the Antilles, which in turn has created a new space of action through the concept of a synchrony of heterogeneities as simultaneous collective action. (See Cornejo Polar.)

The First Face of the Baroque

The Baroque brings together often incompatible positions; not without some skepticism, it has been referred to as an aesthetic sensibility of high culture, a style of representation, and a periodizing concept that, in Spain itself, is used to describe often conflicting and apparently exclusionary ideologies of writers ranging from Quevedo (1580–1645) to Calderón (1600–1681) and Góngora (1561–1627). It is almost superfluous to point out the scandalous character of the extreme form the Latin-American Baroque reached as a culminating point in a long anti-colonial process and also as a kind of ethical response to metropolitan exploitation, for it was used to undermine the foundations of power and the authority of Church and State, at the same time as it appeared to support them. By relying heavily on metaphor, conceit, hyperbole, rich colorful images, mythological allusions, and Latinistic vocabulary and syntax–even forms of grotesque pedantry–the Baroque makes mimetic narration an impossibility. Its

ambivalence and ambiguity are used as a form of resistance to the Spanish State's concept of the order of the world, thus posing a danger to colonial legislators and administrators. Reinforced by what Mikhail Bakhtin (1986) would call "heteroglossia," in colonial Latin America it made evident a constitutive flaw in the colonial structure, revealing a kind of impasse. The Baroque in the Caribbean involves the subject's radical splitting into separate and at times opposing cultural identities. The exploration of this tension during the seventeenth century leads to the very center of the problematic of the subject as split self, but the question was posed at that time in terms of artistic creativity, not articulated in moral or philosophical discourse. By relying on metaphor, colonial Baroque discourse speaks with the voice of another, multiplies voices, and clearly establishes a dialectic relationship of presence and absence.

Now, if the term *Baroque* were used only to define an artistic style–a *modern* style, to be more precise–we would miss the point of the staged social action involved. Given the term's long and complex history and the reality of its use over more than three centuries, it is fitting to locate its tensional power in the context of an inherently conflictual action-oriented belief system. Baroque art emerges out of a bricolage, a plurality of voices, a dialogy of difference, irreducible to the concepts of identity and representation. On this level, the Baroque defines a specific form of subjectivity. Traditionally (that is, in Europe), it refers to a style that prevailed between 1580 and 1750 and was employed as a synonym for the grotesque. It was the work of J. Burckhardt and H. Wölfflin that gave the Baroque historical limits, freeing it of pejorative associations.

It is difficult to imagine a style of representation better suited to capturing the paradoxes of seventeenth-century colonial life than the Baroque, which created an evanescent, yet objectively real, entity that organized perception and framed the empirically visible. The Baroque constitutes something like a surplus of signifiers, a space of exegetical excess, enabling, through interpretive multiplicity, the formalizing of the ideological dilemma of writing national identities through a polyphonic structure of language, wherein several voices are heard in one "melodic" line. Its effect hinges on the metaphorical condensation of a multitude of voices into that one line. The excesses of this Baroque "fugue" underscore the articulation of a subject whose voice condenses much bricolage. The most elementary understanding of local ideological identification–of *mestizo, criollo,* mulatto–rests in the whole series of articulated but provisional combinational possibilities of identifying with a virtual place in discourse. Within the framework of this conceptual background it is now possible to

174

reformulate the logic of the Baroque as that which was always already there and also as the new *Zeitgeist* formed through the influence of antiquity (both European and Latin American). Like the rhizome, that vegetal arborescence, and like the grotesque, the Baroque brings with it a dimension of extreme exaggeration.

Its first flowering in New Spain made the symbolic order visible in the heteroglossia and heterogeneity used in the articulation of the subject. The community of differences within differences became symbolically structured, looking to the future (and, in a radical sense, an imagined future). The most evident contradictory extremes can be found in Sor Juana's (1648–1695) texts and the famous poem *Grandeza mexicana* (1604; Mexican Grandeur) by the Spanish poet Bernardo de Balbuena (1563?–1627), who employs Baroque literary strategies to unite ideological and material territories, to keep them tightly unified for the crown. This philosophical poem aims at territorialization, while Sor Juana's texts (e.g., *Divino Narciso* [*The Divine Narcissus,* 1998] and *Los empeños de una casa* [*The House of Trials,* 1997], both published in 1692) tell another story of heterogeneity through oblique and elliptical links and multiple rhythms and resonances. (See Zavala 1992, 815.) Each individual expression is a link in the chain of communication and has clear-cut boundaries that are determined by the change of subjects. But within these boundaries these expressions–"Baroque *Zeitgeist*" or "Baroque strategies" (like Leibniz's monads)–reflect the creative process linking the expression of many other poets. Sometimes close and sometimes very distant, these expressions are united by their very incorporation into the artistic creation, addressed to the future.

Although the limited scope of this text cannot fully engage the multiple manifestations of the Baroque in the architecture, music, and art of New Spain and the Caribbean, perhaps a few examples of the kind of artistic appropriation to be found in this part of Spanish America will suffice. Among the musical achievements of the Spanish American Baroque we can single out "Maitines para Nuestra Señora de Guadalupe" ["Matins for Our Lady of Guadalupe"], composed sometime in the 1740s by Ignacio de Jerusalem (1707–1769) and performed with great success in Mexico City's Basilica de Guadalupe in 1749. But perhaps the most outstanding Baroque composer was Esteban Salas y Montes de Oca (1725–1803), who was born in Havana of a Spanish father and a *criolla* mother and died in Santiago de Cuba. Like so much of the artistic achievement of Colonial Spanish America, his work was unknown in Spain and has emerged only in the twentieth century with the reconsideration of the Colonial period in the Caribbean. It was Alejo Carpentier (1904–1980) who, in *La música en Cuba* (1946; Music in Cuba), rediscovered the extraordinary genius of Esteban Salas buried in the archives of the cathedral in Havana. Cuban musicologists have since completed the work begun by Carpentier in a number of significant publications. (See Hernández Balaguer.)

Esteban Salas lived during one of the most tumultuous periods in the history of the Caribbean: This was the time of the rationalism of the Enlightenment, the Bourbon reforms in the Spanish empire and the imposition of a centralized bureaucracy, the occupation of Havana by the British (1762–1763), the expulsion of the Jesuits by Charles III in 1767, and the French Revolution in 1789, with its aftermath. Salas lived under four Spanish kings–Philip V (1700–1746), Ferdinand VI (1746–1759), Charles III (1759–1788), and Charles IV (1788–1808). (This period forms the historical background to Alejo Carpentier's *El*

siglo de las luces [1962; *Explosion in a Cathedral,* 1989].) When Salas died in 1803, he had been ill for some time and had been abandoned by the authorities, who had deprived him of his small pension. Although his music is steeped in the tradition of the church music of the great cathedrals of Seville, Toledo, Granada, and Naples (then a Spanish possession–from 1442 with a hiatus between 1713–1759), it is also influenced by Cuban street music. His highly original art of the classical fugue for voices and popular instruments far exceeds that of any other composer in Spanish America in defining an American Baroque. For example, his *Villancico* (Christmas Song) of 1791 reveals a marked departure from Spanish *villancicos.* Amidst the most difficult days of food shortages in Havana, he wrote a *villancico* for performance on 1 December 1791, called "Una nave mercantil" ["A Merchant Ship"]. It was scored for polyphonic performance of three voices and violins. The first part consists of three stanzas of three lines, each designated "Moderato couplets en duo"; the second part is "Allegro-Fugue à trois." The words of this fugue give a clear indication that this is a different kind of Christmas carol:

> Llegue pronto una tal nave
> en que nos viene el remedio,
> pues la hambre nos acaba
> y nos consume el aliento.
>
> Mas ya esa sola noticia
> nos deja muy satisfechos.
>
> May the ship arrive soon,
> for it brings relief
> hunger is killing us
> and our very breath is consumed.
>
> Even the good word of its coming
> gives us great happiness.
>
> *(Salas)*

Sociopolitical factors related to colonial control tended to curtail literary expression or, at best, limit it to occasional poetry; they restricted theater to religious plays aimed at evangelization and, of course, held painting to religious themes. But there was one art form that was given every means of private and public support: architecture. It is for this reason that the most extraordinary expression of the Latin-American Baroque is to be found in the churches and related buildings of the eighteenth century. Mexican Baroque architecture was at first modeled on Spanish architecture of the previous century, but the mutations began almost at once, so that, by the height of the building activity in the eighteenth century, a most distinctive mode of architectural expression had developed, using new building materials, both exaggerating and expanding tendencies already present in Spain, and mixing in pre-Hispanic designs in a syncretic explosion of form. Let us begin with the building materials. The basic stone used in colonial construction was *tezontle,* a volcanic stone of an intense red color, which was set in vivid contrast with *chiluca,* a white limestone; polychrome plasterwork was adopted from Hispanic mural ornamentation; glazed tiles originating in Andalusia were developed for the arabesque tile-works used on domes and on entire façades in startling blends of red, blue, and yellow. The forms were audacious, the expression unrestricted, and the blaze of color was the hallmark of Mexican Baroque architecture.

One of the outstanding examples of Mexican Baroque architecture is Santa Prisca, built between 1751 and 1758 in

Taxco by Don José de la Borda. The architect was Durán Bernecos. The ornamentation of the façade is overwhelming; there is no rest for the eye. The dome is faced with glazed tile from Puebla. Perhaps the most elaborate architectural extravagance of Baroque Mexico is the Cathedral of Zacatecas, begun in 1752 and completed in 1761. Leopoldo Castedo describes an encounter with the syncretic masterpiece:

> la sopresa del espectador, estimulada por la forma de enmarcar el conjunto, la novedad de prescindir de los paños laterales como encuadramiento y, sobre todo, un hieratismo permanente que culmina en las figuras del remate del frontis, en las que se enlazan las raíces románicas y la composición planiforme indígena, en las representaciones del Padre Eterno rodeado por ocho ángeles músicos. (1970, 127–28)

> Shock and surprise are generated by the frame that surrounds the entire façade, by the novelty of omitting the flanking panels, and above all, by a continuous hierarchical ascension that culminates in the representation of the Eternal Father surrounded by eight angelic musicians, in a style that mingles Romanesque origins with the indigenous composition. (1969, 121)

My third example is considered by scholars to be the greatest achievement of Mexican architecture in the eighteenth century: The Sagrario Chapel, next to the Cathedral of Mexico City, built by Lorenzo Rodríguez between 1749 and 1760 (see **Figure 1**). The façade is carved in white *chiluca* limestone, while the walls are of bright red *tezontle*.

Figure 1.

Façade of the Sagrario Chapel adjacent to the Cathedral of Mexico City facing the Zócalo, architect Lorenzo Rodríguez, built between 1749 and 1760. (Courtesy of Mario J. Valdés)

There are twenty-two major architectural masterpieces in the area around Mexico City, including Santa María Jolapan, San Luis Tzicatlán, and Santa María Tlancualpicán. On the façade of Santa María Jolapan the columns sport intertwined serpents (the most important earth symbol in pre-Hispanic Mexican culture); the stone curtains represent exotic birds; the *estipites* (a pilaster in the shape of a truncated pyramid inverted to rest on the smaller base) are in human form; and the symbols of the sun and the moon (also pre-Hispanic symbols—e.g., Teotihuacan) are visible amidst the incredible profusion of forms in this Mexican *mestizo* work. My last example is the façade of San Francisco Acatepec, to the southwest of Mexico City; it is entirely covered in glazed tile, predominantly blue and yellow. The originality of the design lies not in the fact that the tile was applied to a basic structure consisting of twists and turns, but rather that the façade itself was conceived and built up through the tiles. To cite Castedo once again,

> las piezas de cerámica que constituyen, en sí mismas, capiteles, molduras, roleos, estípites, estrellas y lóbulos. La discreta concavidad de la fachada, en su conjunto, destaca la versión popular de un evidente dinamismo barroco. (1970, 138)

> The pieces of ceramic that made up the façade were actually fashioned into capitals, moldings, volutes, *estípites*, stars, and lobules. The slight concavity of the façade as a whole enhances the evident Baroque dynamism expressed here in popular adaptation. (1969, 132)

The passion for color that is part of both Mexican art and its popular culture achieves monumental dimensions in the nation's Baroque architecture.

The Second Face of the Baroque

A second stage of this Baroque fugue or polyphonous structure of speech came with the *modernistas* Manuel Gutiérrez Nájera (1859–1895), Salvador Díaz Mirón (1853–1928), José Asunción Silva (1865–1896), and José Antonio Pérez Bonalde (1846–1892); these new voices related to each other in their mode of questioning authority and in ironic overtones. It is a first step in the articulation of a postcolonial subject, a first manifestation of neo-Baroque postcolonial discourse, now directly addressed to a different form of governance, a republican democracy. If during the colonial epoch the Baroque was pure republican ambivalence, for the *modernistas* its meaning was twofold, as it was addressed to both French colonization in Mexico (1864–1867), Spanish in the Antilles (until 1898), and the United States's neo-colonialism. The *modernistas'* neo-Baroque texts in fact delineated the inherent limitations of the Liberal political ethic and its paradoxes.

What both the seventeenth-century Baroque and the turn-of-the-nineteenth-century neo-Baroque exhibit is the fantasy-space within which a community organizes its mode of enjoyment. Once again, we must consider the role played by conflictive tensions at work in defining identity. In contrast to a universe of pure positivism and instrumentalization, the nineteenth-century neo-Baroque postcolonial writers hope to organize their way of life through the self-sufficient forms of ethnic communities, even as they caricature and parody old forms of identification. We must be particularly attentive to the background of inherent racism that has structured the social space as the exclusive antagonism between "us" and "them." The dialogic of the Baroque specifically involves this antagonism, always re-enacted and rewritten, thus providing new answers. This fantasy-space is present in neo-Baroque novels from the turn of the century to the 1920s and 1930s—a period of obvious capitalism. Elzbieta Sklodowska has delineated the great modernizing leap some traditional novels–by Federico Gamboa (1864–1939), Mariano Azuela (1873–1952), and José Eustasio Rivera (1888–1928)–propose and their dreams of nationalism, a desperate search for new roots in an organic community, with all the predictable inherent paradoxes.

It is not surprising that Latin American writers would return to Baroque sensibilities less than a hundred years after the Wars of Independence (which originated in Haiti in 1804). We now move to a more direct, more exaggerated Baroque, a new Baroque with an imaginary that goes beyond the long history of allegorical indirection written under the pressure of totalitarian colonial censorship. I am referring directly here to the pioneering work of Ramón Emeterio Betances (1827–1898), Eugenio María de Hostos (1839–1903), José Martí (1853–1895), Lola Rodríguez de Tió (1843–1924), and that entire generation of the anti-colonial struggle. The "logical terrorists" (to politicize a term used by George Steiner) reanimated and reaccentuated semantic and grammatical resources in order to project political utopias against the Manichaean allegories of the colonizers. Epistemic metaphors are literally made into different shapes, yet without losing their literary aura in the process.

National identities were indissolubly linked to narrating undecidabilities against the inhabited, fixed world of colonial fictions. Since the dawn of modernity, Caribbean Baroque culture has fought against the imperial ideology's negation of the possibility that the colonized world had its own cultures and could create its own destiny. The reductive, subaltern, passive subject–imaginary and composite–is a product of a monological discourse, aiming at a monolithic uniform dependency, essentially unmodifiable. In fact, monology is the political fantasy of the colonialist imaginary. In a reverse emancipatory venture, Baroque art has been an important agent in the transmission of culture, patterning the ways by which human beings transgress the roles assigned to them.

In the general symbolic economy of Caribbean "knowable communities" (to redirect Raymond Williams's coinage), different from each other in this sea of many lands and languages, the circulation of cultural material has often been unpredictable and highly disturbing. *Modernismo*, for example (and I now limit myself to the Spanish Caribbean), as a mode of cultural production, reaccentuated and reimagined a joint history even within the powerful constraints created by colonial fragmentation and geographic diversity. In the Spanish Caribbean, the Spanish language has become (since the Spanish-American War of 1898) a marker to define cultural identity, a wellspring of emotional identification as both the official language and common language of the streets. Nowhere is this more in evidence than in neo-Baroque texts. This is in contrast to the non-Hispanic Caribbean, descended from the northern European tradition, in which there is invariably a difference between the official and the common languages: French and Creole in Haiti, English and Anglo-Creole or French-Creole in the Commonwealth Caribbean, Dutch and Papiamento or Anglo-Creole in the Dutch colonies. Heteroglossia and polyglossia are part of the non-Hispanic Antillean tradition.

The Hispanic Caribbean asks how it is that subjects of Anglo-America cannot think of themselves as plural. In the polyphonic Caribbean world, many island histories resemble that of the Dominican Republic (the first American territory to establish a university, in 1538, predating by centuries the United States). Before 1492, Santo Domingo was Taino and Caribe; after 1492 and until 1795 it was Spanish; then it became French, then Haitian; next it was French again; and soon thereafter it was Spanish once more. By 1821, affected by the winds of Independence, it proclaimed itself part of Bolívar's Federation of Colombia under the name of The Independent State of Spanish Haiti–a situation that lasted only two months, expiring when the Haitians swarmed across the border and began an occupation that continued for twenty-two years, until 1844. When it was independent again, a *caudillo* returned the territory to Spain in 1861, which misgoverned the island until 1865. In 1869–70 efforts were made to annex the country to the United States (thwarted mainly by the racial prejudice of the U.S. Senate); from 1882 to 1889 it was under the total control of a tyrant; and between 1905 and 1940, the United States administered Dominican financial and political affairs. The will to be Caribbean and part of the Hispanic world never lessened, in spite of the multiplicity of encounters with its Anglo-American neighbor.

The truth of the matter is that, in succession, Spain, England, France, Holland, and the United States have fragmented, muted, divided, subdivided, possessed, and repossessed the Caribbean with their many names and geographies and peoples and dreams. Islands have been, historically, the site of struggle, the battling arena of hegemonies, a cacophony of many different discourses uttered by many voices whose descriptions change so frequently that it is impossible to assign an origin to the utterances. What is positive is that islanders know from way back that those cacophonous invaders are fortunately not substantial, enduring, consistent, or part of the original landscape of their world. Everything changes into its opposite and back again. Reversal rules; everything is possible in the encounter of evaluative utterances that constitute subjects and identities. No construct is fixed forever. Subjectivity and identities are created and creative; colonialism unleashes heterogeneity. Such is the nature of this essentially Baroque culture.

The Third Face of the Baroque

A third stage is to be found in what we know as neo-Baroque literatures after the 1940s, and here Severo Sarduy (1937–1993) has been the pivotal influence. What this latest phase of the postcolonial neo-Baroque suggests is a defense of the celebratory, of enjoyment–*jouissance*, even–quite specifically through the heterology of popular music. A whole set of alternative histories is interwoven in the texts of Sarduy (and of Guillermo Cabrera Infante [b. 1929] and Miguel Barnet [b. 1940], among others) through *cha cha chas, boleros*, and *sones*. Music is presented as the conventional stereotype in its relation to Antillean identity.

Wave after wave of rational forces have failed: Descartes, Euclidean geometry, and Ptolemaic panoptics have been unable to silence the voices of difference. Islanders have the knowledge that all these sciences falsify the world. Many an *Odyssey* and many a Ulysses have brought their arrogant, enlightened, technocratic, bourgeois ideology to the islands. According to Derek Walcott (b. 1930), they are

the traitors
who, in elected office, saw the land as views
for hotels and elevated into waiters
the sons of others, while their own learnt something else.

(289)

The many ideas and questions pertaining to identity (and how to think through the subject of the colonial experience) rely upon different strategies, but two imaginaries intersect in simultaneity: One is the poetical/political utopia; the other, the creation of the entropy of the Colonial through a Baroque poetics. What is important is that each neo-Baroque text provides the reader with imaginative materials that provoke reactions and force objections into flux, always circling back to make words now true now false, echoing with the ambivalence and undecidability of a permanent uncertainty: We have always been "sea-moralists" to use Walcott's term.

What is at issue is the question of how the multiple Caribbean discourses should be positioned with respect to the competing ethics and imaginary identities thrust upon the region by colonial and neocolonial power. Identity is not a topic or a trope, but is constituted by a discourse. Both national identities and nationalism have emerged through texts, as some subjects identify themselves as members of the community of readers implied in the symbolic values of the printed form. But speech has its own space; no human event is developed or resolved within the bounds of a single medium. Caribbean cultural utterances aimed at opening an understanding of subjective and social identities are also to be found in the heteroglossic, multivoiced popular songs.

Popular culture, and especially music, are forms of mass culture about which some literary critics are still skeptical. Heteroglossic and polyphonic Caribbean music introduces irony as a way of life and offers a sustained rehearsal of dialogism between interrelated cultural universes. Dialogism articulates the mixtures of literary and nonliterary, elitist and popular, written and oral, literate and non-literate. Caribbean popular music—from *merengue* and *salsa* to *calypso*, *plena*, *reggae*, and the *bolero*—are an essential part of the social imaginary that is the symbolic center of social life, and therefore at the forefront of the overthrow of oppressive colonial structures and the replacement of degraded imposed identities. An almost obsessive Baroque cultural imaginary strives to undo the caricatures catering to metropolitan audiences, very often making a series of political, social, and ideological textual interruptions to remind the reader that representations are not a given but are, instead, produced. Because those stories are not convincing, the Caribbean writer's social imaginary must often deal with the gift of wonder and mystery in order to offer her or his vision of the world and project a truly postcolonial identity. Prototypes are newly examined; many do not do away with identification but examine it critically, using a multiplicity of techniques to show that no representation is fixed and final. Michelle Cliff (b. 1951), for example, includes the spectator/reader to show that the producer is really the one at the receiving end of literary representation (as in her *Claiming an Identity They Taught Me to Despise* [1980] and *No Telephone to Heaven* [1987]).

The point is that, in the multiple space of many languages with many inflections, writing is meant to offer a radically new set of ideological proposals in social imaginaries that are projects to alter the basic conditions of life. As a part of the productive transformation of other forms of cognition, writing in Latin America (certainly in the Caribbean) has been a Baroque emancipatory expression of an independent cultural imaginary, a will toward action, and an embattled fight against colonial domination. Luisa Capetillo (1879–1922) in turn-of-the-twentieth-century colonial Puerto Rico knew plainly that sexual relations and gendered roles reproduce the conflicts and alliances found in colonial social and economic realities. All of her work as a socialist and feminist intellectual centered on these problems. Her writing stands even today, in the twenty-first century, as a reminder of the island's independent cultural imaginary.

The Baroque as a cultural condition rather than a style or a historical period of art is deeply rooted in the social reality of the Caribbean. Understood as a means of knowing and transforming the social structure, culture is an arena to be occupied. Questions are raised through texts, often against the myths (racial, patriarchal, colonial) that separate peoples, along with their histories. The social imaginary is not only a conviction but also a changing notion, not simply a cognitive difference, but one based on differences in rhetorical organization, intonation, accentuation, semantics, grammar, and syntax. The uses of language acquire social meaning and political significance only in particular situations.

The Caribbean neo-Baroque of both Lezama Lima (1910–1976) and García Márquez (b. 1927) poses yet other challenges. Lezama Lima's poetical system of the universe has been described by Cruz-Malavé as sliding into metaphor and metonymy. The metonymical displacement is propelled by elements of *négritude*, homosexuality, and nation; his neo-Baroque demonstrates the importance of contingency. García Márquez's neo-Baroque *Cien años de soledad* [1967; *One Hundred Years of Solitude*, 1970] makes the reader oscillate between two extremes: On the one hand, there is the question of how the manuscripts we are presumably reading get to us, especially because the man who finally reads them perishes; and on the other, there is the question of the presence of speech as truth in its personification in Melquiades. Truth appears as action, as a presence beyond language, yet paradoxically exists only through language. Historical research of Latin-American colonization reveals an obscure and somber story of violent expropriation and plunder, of merchant adventurers, a story we do not have to know in detail to grasp its meaning. Within this framework, the accumulation of incidents that seem to be the life-history of the Buendías is nothing but a vicious circle of a myth produced by capitalism retroactively explaining its own genesis. In a voyage into the past, the novel's fictive reader fills in the missing links of his genesis by enabling him and us to jump into the past and appear to be in touch with the source, because the manuscripts were always there. García Márquez's form of the neo-Baroque creates and recreates history as myth and myth as history.

What each of the three stages of the Baroque have, to paraphrase Hegel, is that the concept of time is the time of the human experience of things. Now, if we accept that Caribbean literatures can be described as Baroque, that the Baroque is linked to the grotesque, and that both form rhizomes of signifiers, then we can use Lacan's reflections on the signifier in order to follow the rhizome. The proliferations of signifiers are forms of identity—different from those of both European discourse and its American offshoot. The signifier is unfolding into a Master signifier, which, as a virtual reality, creates false identities. The signifier is turned upside-down; it is a distorted image. Anamorphosis then can help us understand these cultures, which simultaneously identify with the *criollo*, *mestizo*, and mulatto signifiers. This is the obscene signifier of the Baroque. What this obscenity reveals is that some communities can best rely on decentering knowledge and figuring doubt. These decentering ideas and doubts present both the hyperbolic gesture of suspending every content heterogenous to them and the proof that there is some traumatic, insistent kernel of objective certainty.

If speech is the transmission of need and desire, then the Baroque, within its metamorphoses, is a mode of discourse through interlineation. During the seventeenth-century colonial experience, the Baroque was used to organize a discourse of grotesque identity in order to reveal the non-sayable by means of a certain disorder, certain ruptures, and certain intentional discordances, slips, lacunae, and repetitions. This discourse thereby expressed the manner in which the cultural identity of a new community was organized. The Baroque, in its three distinct but linked stages, developed this conception to the point of heroism in Mexico and especially in the Caribbean.

Works Cited

Bakhtin, Mikhail. 1986. *The Dialogic Imagination: Four Essays.* Ed. Michael Holquist. Trans. Caryl Emerson and Michael Holquist. Austin: University of Texas Press.

———. 1990. *Art and Answerability. Early Philosophical Essays by M. Bakhtin.* Eds. Michael Holquist and Vadim Liapunov. Trans. Vadim Liapunov. Supplement trans. Kenneth Brostrom. Austin: Texas University Press.

Balbuena, Bernardo de. 1988. *Grandeza mexicana.* Ed. José Carlos González Boixo. Roma: Bulzoni.

Benjamin, Walter. 1999. *Illuminations.* Ed. Hannah Arendt. Trans. Harry Zorn. London: Pimlico.

Burckhardt, Jacob. 1958. *The Civilization of the Renaissance in Italy.* 2 vols. Trans. S. G. C. Middlemore. New York: Harper.

Capetillo, Luisa. 1911. *Mi opinión sobre las libertades, derechos y deberes de la mujer como compañera, madre y ser independiente: La mujer en hogar, en la familia, en el gobierno.* San Juan, Puerto Rico: Times Publishing Company.

Carpentier, Alejo. 1946. *La música de Cuba.* Mexico City: Fondo de Cultura Económica.

———. 1968. *El siglo de las luces.* Mexico City: Compañía General de Ediciones.

Castedo, Leopoldo. 1969. *A History of Latin American Art and Architecture from Pre-Columbian Times to the Present.* Trans. Phyllis Freeman. New York: Praeger.

———. 1970. *Historia del arte y de la architectura latinoamericana desde la epoca precolombina hasta hoy.* Rev. ed. Santiago de Chile: Editorial Pomaire.

Cliff, Michelle. 1980. *Claiming an Identity They Taught Me to Despise.* Watertown, MA: Persephone Press.

———. 1987. *No Telephone to Heaven.* New York: Vintage Books.

Cornejo Polar, Antonio. 1994. *Escribir en el aire: Ensayo sobre la heterogeneidad socio-cultural en las literaturas andinas.* Lima: Editorial Horizonte.

Cruz-Malavé, Arnaldo. 1994. *El primitivo implorante. El 'sistema poético del mundo' de José Lezama Lima.* Amsterdam: Rodopi.

Hernández Balaguer, Pablo. 1986. *Los villancicos, cantadas y pastorelas, de Esteban Salas.* Havana: Editorial Letras Cubanas.

Jerusalem, Ignacio de. 1997. *Matins for the Virgin of Guadalupe.* Chanticleer Teldec Digital Audio 3984-2189-2. Los Osos, CA: Russell Editions.

Juana Inés de la Cruz, Sor. 1951, 1952, 1955, 1957. *Obras completas de Sor Juana Inés de la Cruz.* 4 vols. Ed. Alfonso Méndez Plancarte. Mexico City: Fondo de Cultura Económica.

Lacan, Jacques. 1977. *Ecrits: A Selection.* Trans. Alan Sheridan. New York: Norton.

Salas y Montes de Oca, Esteban. 1995. "Una nave mercantil." *Les Grandes heures du Baroque Cubain. Choral Music.* Madrid: AMS NEVE Audiofile et Logic 1 and Kash Productions 74321-34549-2. Colombes, France: Editions Jade.

Walcott, Derek. 1990. *Omeros.* New York: Farrar Straus Giroux.

Wölfflin, Heinrich. 1932. *Principles of Art History: The Problem of the Development of Style in Later Art.* Trans. M. D. Hottinger. London: G. Bell and Sons.

Zavala, Iris M. 1992. "Metáforas epistemológicas coloniales: 'En breve cárcel'." *Estudios de folklore y literatura dedicados a Mercedes Díaz Roig.* Eds. Beatriz Garza Cuarón and Yvette Jiménez de Báez. Mexico City: El Colegio de México. 803–16.

———. 1997. "'Vano artificio del cuidado': Polifonía de polifonías en la escritura de Juana Inés de la Cruz." *Paraula de dona. Actes del colloqui dones, literatura i mitjans de comunicació: Tarragona del 26 al 29 d'abril de 1995.* Ed. Margarida Aritzeta i Abad and Montserrat Palau Martí. Tarragona: Diputació de Tarragona. 15–28.

CHAPTER 13

THE BAROQUE AND TRANSCULTURATION

Mabel Moraña

Instances of Transcultural Theorizing

Just four years after the publication of *Contrapunteo cubano del tabaco y el azúcar* [1940; *Cuban Counterpoint, Tobacco and Sugar* 1995], in which Fernando Ortiz (1881–1969) posited the idea of transculturation as an operative concept for explaining the various factors that contributed to the emergence of dependent capitalism in the Cuba of the time, the Venezuelan Mariano Picón Salas (1901–1965), in his classic work *De la conquista a la independencia* (1944; *A Cultural History of Spanish America, from Conquest to Independence*, 1962), took up the category that the Cuban had thrown into the arena of cultural studies, converting it into the starting point of a historiographical project of enormous scope that would have a profound effect on Latin American thought. Three decades later, Uruguayan Ángel Rama (1926–1983) took up the concept of transculturation, applying it to neo-regionalistic narrative production. He was primarily concerned with exploring the phenomenon of cultural transfer or transitiveness on the basis of which vernacular elements (both differential and relatively stable, and linked to popular cultures) combined with the "pulsión de homogeneización" ("tendency towards homogenization") introduced by "la aceleración modernizadora" ("modernizing acceleration") (Rama 1986, 206).

Whereas in Ortiz's text the national allegory, elaborated on the basis of the main products of the Cuban economy, had already introduced a model that could be applied to the interpretation of neo-Colonial structure at the Latin American continental level, in Picón Salas and Rama, the scheme was expanded and redefined in a disciplinary fashion, focusing on an analysis of the forms of hybridization on the basis of which cultural miscegenation emerges and is developed as an expression of the vernacular and exogenous aspects that lead to the emergence and development of national formations in Latin America. Anthropological in Ortiz, historicist in Picón Salas, cultural in Rama, and functionalist in all its applications, the concept of transculturation, particularly in the last two types of theorizing, focuses on lettered agency as the space in which the legitimizing strategies and representational practices of hegemonic discourse, in its various stages of institutional consolidation have emerged.

The theory of transculturation seeks to describe the processes on the basis of which the various subjects who figure in the drama of Western insertion at the continental level are located and positioned, highlighting both the mediations and the operations that take place within the modernizing process. This cognitive platform is used to explore the various levels crucial to an understanding of the emergence and consolidation of nationalities in Latin America: The definition of collective subjectivities (autochthonous, foreign, itinerant, migrant, and interstitial), processes of identity (sectorial, national, and regional awareness; otherness), ideological locations regarding the structure of power (hegemony, subalternity, marginalization, peripheral insertion), and practices of cultural integration (imitation, resistance, syncretism, hybridization,

mimicry). The bases for a perception of Latin America that is both global and particular are thereby established (see Spitta; Moraña 1997).

The ideology of miscegenation is presented, from its early colonial origins, as the means by which the *criollo* elite structures, implement, and legitimize their hegemonic project. As cogently explained in Picón Salas's proposal and subsequently developed by Angel Rama in *Los procesos de transculturación en la narrativa latinoamericana* [1982; The Process of Transculturation in the Latin American Narrative] and more extensively in *La ciudad letrada* [1984; *The Lettered City*, 1996], the destabilization of the modernizing projects would increasingly reveal the need to undertake a critique of transculturating discourse. As an ideological construct, it was capable of subsuming the antinomies inherent in Latin American "totalidades contradictorias" (contradictory totalities) (see Cornejo Polar) in a discourse that, by emphasizing the strategies and results of cultural integration, reduced the questioning and catalyzing nature of social and ideological antagonisms, envisaging them as a "difference" and thereby paving the way for the liberal notion of multiculturalism as a theoretical space of pluralistic conciliation.

For this critique of transculturation, it is therefore essential to focus on the notion of the subject and that of learned mediation, on which the interpretation of cultural interrelationships and transfers are based, and which, since the establishment of *criollo* society, have demarcated the integration of "the popular" into the legitimizing discourse of the elites and into the process of Latin American cultural institutionalization. To this end, it is useful to explore the theoretical findings of Picón Salas's work regarding colonial transculturation, particularly the epistemic parameters that were formalized, as Rama reaffirmed following the guidelines of the Venezuelan critic, during the period when "Baroque culture" was consolidated as a foundational stage of *criollo* identity.

This period not only saw the centralization and reinforcement of the bureaucratic and educational bases for the dissemination of the idea of the sociocultural unification of the colonial world, but also witnessed the development, on the overseas periphery, of the massive strategies–of popular appeal–to consolidate the viceregal elite as the depository of a power that was still dependent on metropolitan structures but on the way to achieving autonomy. Although it is true that by delegating power to the *criollo* elite, the empire succeeded in internalizing its domination by creating a subsidiary apparatus of colonial control, it is an undeniable fact that by doing so, it strengthened this sector both politically and ideologically, providing the bases for the emergence of counter-hegemonic projects that would eventually subvert the order from which they emanated. This delegation of power, therefore, politically reinforced the duality that was already implicit in the *criollo* elite by virtue of its Spanish American genealogy. In the seventeenth and eighteenth centuries, the process of *criollization*, which, as Picón Salas accurately noted, began with the first forms of colonialist transculturation, was replaced by the emergence and consolidation of a new hegemony, which, in accordance with the imperial model, colonized the American social space, progressively imposing its own agendas both inside and outside the social formations of the Colonial period.

Historicism and Transculturation

Picón Salas opens the fourth chapter of his aforementioned work, entitled "De lo europeo a lo mestizo: Las primeras formas de transculturación" ["From European to a Mixed Culture: The First Forms of Transculturation"], with the following consideration: "Las formas de la cultura europea penetran desde el comienzo en los centros urbanos que se fundan en América en el siglo XVI aunque la originalidad del ambiente impone, como ya lo veremos, el precoz aparecimiento de formas mestizas" (1982, 69) ("European culture first permeated Spanish America in the urban centers established in the sixteenth century, although the peculiarities of the surroundings, as will presently be noted, quickly imposed modifications" [1962, 42]). This paragraph contains a summary of the principal considerations that, ever since the emergence of *criollo* society, have governed the complex process of cultural transplantation and assimilation in America and the tense relationship linking vernacular cultures to the metropolitan centers. What in Fernando Ortiz's theorizing is presented as a model of interpretation of the transformations that accompanied the American insertion into the Utopian horizon of modernity, within a political, economic, and cultural conjuncture determined by the changes wrought at an international level primarily from the First World War onwards, is proposed, in the Venezuelan's view, as the identification of a paradigm that stretches back to the very origins of American Westernization. This lent the continent a historically established feature of identity: Its transculturated condition (syncretic, hybrid, and *mestizo*) resulting from the dialog linking the structures of Imperial power to the cultures subalternized by the imposition of colonialism.

Picón Salas establishes the core of the process: The European matrix as a mechanism of ideological penetration and imposition within the context of the colonial relationship; the urban centers as primary spheres of cultural reception and reproduction; the American environment as the site of an otherness that asserts its particularity in the face of imperial penetration; and miscegenation as the synthesis that resolves the historical dialectic. In effect, the Venezuelan points to the terms of this process, just as Ángel Rama would three decades later, in his application of the category of transculturation to the neo-regionalistic narrative corpus–as a bilateral negotiation in which the conquered cultures managed, in turn, within the parameters of colonial domination, to impose a transforming impulse on the colonizing trend. In Picón Salas's view, the earliest stages of the Conquest coincided with the beginning of the history of resistance, hybridization, and cultural responses that opposed the project of Imperial unification, giving rise to the emergence of collective subjectivities that are more than the sum of their parts and which contain, in the same blend that defines them, a specific value, capable of subverting and redimensioning the primary elements that produced them. Emphasis, however, is placed less on the resistance of the vernacular cultures and the cultural systems that coexisted with the dominant culture than on the synthesis of American *criollization*–in other words, on the cultural combination that emerges as the seed of future nationalities.

In binary terms, the transculturating process can be regarded as the link established between spaces, subjects, practices, and cultural identities located at either end of a spectrum defined on the basis of power relations (hegemony/ marginalization, universalism / particularity, civilization barbarity, Occidentalism / Americanism, metropolis / colony, Christianity / paganism, modernity / primitivism). But the historical perspective tends to focus more on the instances, metamorphoses, and exchanges produced at the epistemic intersection of cultures in conflict and the negotiations that take place within them. From this perspective, transculturation is therefore an interstitial experience that both problematizes and relativizes, in a single movement, the historical "agencies" that interrelate within the colonial combination. Without overlooking the violence inherent in the process of cultural encounter, appropriation, and reformulation that accompanied imperial management in America, the transculturating view proposed by Picón Salas values the receptive instance in which, as in the theorization of Ortiz and Rama, the popular base is promoted as a space where, paradoxically, the processes of differentiation are integrated into a new synthesis. Here the components are all affected and modified by the cultural combination, so effectively illustrated by the image of the potato and chili stew in Ortiz's proposal. However, one should not overlook the fact that, far from constituting a harmonious and ideologically conciliatory mixture, the transculturating process sometimes exacerbates particularities; this is a result of the oppositions and displacements that it causes, exposing the qualities inherent in each of the historically linked components.

The concept of transculturation therefore enables one to visualize difference as both the result of a globalizing segregation and a possibility for the gestation of a counter-imaginary strengthened by the vindication of American nature, one projected as the foundation of an anti-universal episteme on the basis of which the limits that separate and connect the colonized periphery and colonizing Occidentalism are negotiated. American otherness and miscegenation (as the absorption and re-dimensioning of hegemonic identities) constitute a representational paradigm as an alternative to the dominant one that, through the process of its constitution, influences and modifies the disciplining, homogenizing, and universalizing imagination imposed from the position of power. However, by prioritizing the function of *criollo* agency and the strategies of learned discourse in the establishment of nationalities, the narrative of transculturation remains powerfully attached to the discourse of power, even though the plurality of the regional cultures that form part of this process maintains an opposing dynamic capable of eroding the supposed unity of modernized culture in its various historical contexts.

Both approaches to Latin American transculturation, however, start from distinct notions of cultural subject and agency. In Picón Salas's interpretation, which is of the greatest interest for the historical approach to the period analyzed here, the category of transculturation highlights the operations through which hegemonic culture is superimposed over the American matrix. This is part of a process in which the project of ideological reproduction of the learned elite and that of spiritual colonization converge (pensamiento pedagógico [pedagogical thought], missionary practices). This, in turn, results in the emergence of "... las primeras expresiones de criollización..." (Picón Salas 1982, 78) ("the earliest expressions of *criollization*"), guided by the desire "[de] conciliar dos sociedades y dos mundos opuestos–el del conquistador ensoberbecido y el del indio medroso…" (Picón Salas 1982, 77) ("to harmonize contrasting societies and worlds of the haughty conqueror and the timorous Indian…" [1962, 48]), a desire experienced at either end of the political and social spectrum of colonial life. Borrowing Fernando Ortiz's "útil neologismo" ("useful neologism") of transculturation, the Venezuelan critic notes

> Desde tan tempranos días se plantea allí el que todavía parece permanente y no resuelto enigma de la cultura hispanoamericana, o sea el de la imitación y transplante de las formas más elaboradas de Europa en que siempre se esmerará una clase culta pero un poco ausente de la realidad patética de la tierra, y la intuición que despunta en algunos frailes y misioneros extraordinarios–un Vasco de Quiroga, un Pedro de Gante, un Sahagún–de que hay que llegar al alma de la masa indígena por otros medios que el del exclusivo pensamiento europeo, mejorando las propias industrias y oficios de los naturales, ahondando en sus idiomas, ayudándolos a su expresión personal. (Picón Salas 1982, 75)

> Hubo una pedagogía, una estética y hasta un sistema económico de la evangelización cuyo estudio parece aún hoy, mucho más que curiosidad erudita, ejemplo o experiencia aprovechable en el camino de incorporar a la cultura y la técnica las masas indígenas todavía irredentas. (Picón Salas 1982, 85–86)

> Dating from early times is the still-unresolved conflict of Spanish American culture. On the one hand, the cultivated classes, always a little out of touch with reality about them, tried diligently to transplant and imitate the most elaborate ways of European living. On the other hand, a few exceptional friars and missionaries–such as Vasco de Quiroga, Pedro de Gante, and Sahagún–intuitively realized that ideas other than the purely European were necessary to reach the soul of the aboriginal elements. More suitable methods, for example, were needed for teaching the natives to improve their own trades and crafts, for studying their languages, and for helping them to express their own unique personalities. (Picón Salas 1962, 47)

> They developed a methodology, a code of ethics, and even an economic system of evangelizing that, far more than as an intriguing bit of antiquarianism, would seem to merit study even now as a useful experiment or model for the still-unfinished task of incorporating the Indian into modern technological civilization. (Picón Salas 1962, 55)

Transculturating practices are, in Picón Salas's view, a "method" for the implementation of the project of colonial assimilation, through which "…las formas europeas no pretendían suplantar a lo indígena, sino que se trataba de incluirlas dentro de las necesidades e imperativos de una nueva cultura" (1982, 88) ("…[European cultural modes] did not undertake to substitute… for native ones, but tried to absorb these within the needs and imperatives of a new culture" [1962, 57–58]). By focusing on the process of Westernization from the perspective of Hispanic values, Picón Salas favors the pole of domination and the agency through which cultural transplantation was effected, thereby sidestepping the practices of vernacular resistance and colonial acculturation. Thus, the cultures subdued by the Conquest constitute an "unredeemed" redoubt of otherness, which, while maintaining its capacity to influence the episteme of the conqueror–through the syncretic and conciliatory process of miscegenation–is compelled to submit to the dictates, strategies, and ends of the dominant, subsuming differential and particular elements within the ahistorical space of universal elements.

What in Ortiz's anthropological and highly allegorical theorizing appears as a paradigm of the negotiation inherent in the processes of capitalistic modernization, in the historicist conceptualization of Picón Salas, is linked to the notion of origin (the European culture that penetrated urban centers from the outset, the precocious emergence of miscegenation). This lent the colonial transculturating experience a foundational value: That which promotes the entry of conquered America into the Euro/ethnocentric epistemic space that is, in turn, transformed in the process of its colonial reproduction.

In both authors, the core of cultural interpretation lies in the constant dynamic that alternately destabilizes and reestablishes a power that looks at itself in the distorting mirror of otherness in order to recognize its own image. This other is always placed across the abyss of a history that continuously erases cultural borders, making them, as in Fernando Coronil's image, not separate islands but fluid, provisional artifices written on the sands of history and subject to continuous transformations (Coronil xv). Likewise, for both critics, American nature is the basis of an authenticity that is both precarious and permanent; this last refuge of what is particularly American has been held onto with intensity following demographic explosion of the cities, the superimposition of capitalism, and the lettered rejection of the other. Thus, because of historical circumstances, this redoubt constitutes a zone of negotiation in which disadvantage, exploitation, and marginalization are differential elements harboring the destabilizing ferment that any periphery contains vis-à-vis the centers by which it is determined.

Baroque, *Criollo* Identity, and Transculturation

Although this process can be traced from the earliest episodes and representations of the practices of territorial appropriation, spiritual colonization, and discursive domination of the American colonies, it was not until the period of viceregal stabilization that the full force of a unified, centralized cultural power, institutionally established in the learned centers of the colony, began to be felt. It was precisely in the establishment of the Baroque city that Angel Rama located the transculturating effort exercised by an elite that, from a complex bureaucratic, ecclesiastic, and educational apparatus, reproduced its ideology and cultural forms on a vast scale. Although its existence was directly dependent on the metropolitan centers and models, it was guided by its own dynamics, which were becoming increasingly transgressive and counter-cultural. It was no longer, as it had been during the early stages of imperial settlement, a colonial periphery organized from a locus outside the continent, whose power was phantasmagorically projected over the colonial empire; rather, it was the consolidation of a social formation of hybrid genealogy and interests, different from both those of the Iberian Peninsula and those of the Indians or African-Americans who existed within the internal margins of colonial totality. The political, social, and cultural agenda of this new sector began to develop internally, giving rise to the emergence of a *criollo* self-awareness, on the basis of which new forms of hegemony and subalternity would develop.

Historically, this process corresponds to the changes that took place throughout the seventeenth century, after the death of Philip II (1598) and up to the reign of Charles II, the last member of the Hapsburg dynasty. During this period, the policy of the Spanish state toward America was substantially modified and channeled into fiscal objectives. Without altering the bases of monopolistic mercantilism, the Crown adopted a philo-aristocratic policy with profound social consequences in

America. On the one hand, the region saw the growth and development of a Spanish American nobility, based on entailed estates, marriage alliances, and the monopolization of lands by illegal means (exorbitant concessions by the Town Councils; nepotism; the usurpation of lands belonging to Indian communities). This group strove for social recognition through whatever means were available to it, whether legitimate or not, gradually accumulating titles of the Spanish nobility, whether bought or granted; membership in the military orders; frequently false coats of arms; titles of association with the Inquisition; positions in religious brotherhoods; posts in the viceregal court; honorary military ranks; and the patronage of monasteries and charity institutions. At the middle-class, social level, *criollos* also made aggressive progress, in the various professions, the clergy, and bureaucracy, and became a satellite power of the elite, both peninsular and *criollo*, that dominated the colonial centers. In the midst of these centers (whose very urban design reflected the social hierarchies, the spaces of interaction, and marginalizing practices), the core of the lettered city emerged—constantly besieged, as Rama pointed out, by the requirements and dangers of the royal city.

Following—albeit with few express references—the design of transculturating practices pointed out by Picón Salas for the colonial period and—more openly in José Antonio Maravall's classic study on *La cultura del barroco* [1975; *Culture of the Baroque*, 1986]—Rama attributed the supremacy of the lettered city to the existence and cohesion of the intellectual elite established in those urban enclaves and to the development of mass, propagandistic forms of ideological indoctrination and cultural reproduction, which, through various means, reached the vast public that gathered around the religious, administrative, and court center. The lettered elite, trained in the ancient tradition of Roman law (already codified since the *Siete Partidas* [*The Siete Partidas*, 2001] of Alfonso el Sabio (Alfonso X, 1221–1284) as the administrator of "la ciencia de las leyes" ["the science of laws"]), had the power to convert utopia into reality, defining the nature of the conquest and the order that would guarantee its continued existence (Malagón-Barceló 8). In these early functions as scribes or lawyers or merely providing administrative support for political power, the learned were present throughout American civil society, especially because of their mastery of the skills of judiciary maneuvers that would exert such a great influence over rhetorical-literary discourse during the stages of consolidation of the *criollo* imaginary. *Criollo* culture, however, would always be challenged by the coexistence of various systems of cultural production that came into conflict within the broader context of American culture.

The circuits of production and consumption of high culture were restricted to the closed enclaves of religious, court, bureaucratic, and educational institutions where "los dueños de la letra" (Rama 1984, 30) ("owners of the written text") engaged in writing as a closed self-serving and self-celebratory practice. But culture spread and transcended these parameters through multiple strategies of symbolic representation that were integrated into the Baroque fiesta. Within this context of carnivalization and performance, the face of power was disguised by various masks, and assumed the seductive forms of ephemeral art, ostentation, and parody, precisely for the benefit of the heterogeneous captive audiences who formed part of colonial society, and have to be addressed by diversified representational strategies.

Dramatizations, symbols, triumphal arches, processions, allegorical parades, and civil and religious commemorations attracted a people trained in the communicative resources that disseminated the prestigious models of the metropolis through the filters imposed by the lettered *criollos*—who thus maintained their representational monopoly in a world both subjected to and seduced by the monumentality of power. This is how the Baroque operated; in addition to being a product of and for the elites, it was public art (propagandistic, demagogic, dogmatic, and repressive). As a result of its communicational scope, it also constituted a form of art that is open to the kingdom of man (sensual, parodic, and challenging), particularly in its updated American form, which was heavily dependent on the irreducible materiality of the social as subjected to imperial power. Practiced "en una suerte de religión secundaria" (Rama 1984, 33) ("[in a kind of] secondary religion" [1996, 24]) , writing was only one of its instruments—although undoubtedly the most select and privileged, comprising as it does the principal transculturating apparatus. The Baroque city was the center of a series of concentric circles from which emanated the legitimizing rituals and discourses of power (which were transferred to the viceregal authorities as depositories of the universals that sustained the episteme of the conqueror).

In seventeenth-century American culture, superimposed on the drama of castes, exploitation, and marginality, peninsular paradigms were presented as a spectacle of all the chiaroscuros and polarities that had been regarded as canonical features of European Baroque. In the face of colonial fragmentation, and an unredeemed and potentially dangerous subalternity, the Baroque served as a narrative of centralization, of fusion, based on a utopian idea of the trans-historical and trans-cultural created by the lettered city. The Baroque program was therefore originally a state ideology—affirmed in the great discourses of Scholasticism, Counter-Reformation policy, and the aesthetics of Góngora—as privileged languages of imperial power. Through the appropriation and exhibition of these codes (through which Western rationality was manifested), prestige was transferred from metropolitan culture to its colonial representatives, who thereby avoided civil and religious censure, affirming the bases of a new "Americanist" imaginary that was still a tributary of metropolitan sources. Yet within the circle of *criollo* power, the indigenous, black, or *mestizo* peoples' identities, marginalized and repressed in lettered culture, survived, developing their own parallel communication systems, absorbing the influences of the dominant trends, yet also imbuing them with their own culture.

Within this dynamic of cultural and political transfer and representation, the *criollo* elite would play a vicarious role; it was defined by the ambiguities of a problematic genealogy—peninsular and American, elitist and subordinate, central and marginalized, depending on the point of view (whether imperial or American) adopted in each case to understand their position within the context of colonial totalization. On the basis of these determining factors, it would fall to this group to implement transculturating processes to a lesser degree, since the ideological message of Empire, reproduced by the Baroque machinery, would be mediated by the *criollo* perspective. The latter incorporated into the ideological and cultural models received as part of the colonizing baggage the marginalized knowledge and representational styles of colonial subalternity. In this respect, rather than being a contact zone, the *criollo* nation was a battlefield in which a growing awareness of the *criollo* difference began to redefine and negotiate the terms of miscegenation as a starting point for the forging of a new identity, in which race, class, gender, and language acquired a new importance and significance. The *criollo* project challenged the epistemological bases of transculturation, understood as a conciliatory, homogenizing strategy, as yet unable to detach itself from the utopian ideal of a unification that would, over and above any subaltern counter-rationality, permit the politicoinstitutional centralization in America from which a new concept of the state and its power relations would gradually begin to emerge.

Criollo Production: Transcultural Strategies and Subalternity

In the terms of the time, Baroque culture constituted a project of globalization inside which the many fragments composing the colonial totality coexisted uneasily. American otherness, constructed since the early stages of the Conquest as a resource for defining the position of the dominator, objectivized—indeed fetishized—the colonial subject, while at the same time defining another cognitive *locus* presented as an alternative to the discourses of reason, civilization, and revealed truth, which linked marginalized knowledge to hegemonic models. The mysterious space opened up by vernacular languages, the threatening materiality of the *encomienda* and slave quarters that besieged urban centers, the counter-models of paganism and the indigenous rebellions that plagued the processes of viceregal stabilization, constituted a sociocultural system that resisted a definitive, civilizing reduction by exposing the antagonisms that had separated dominators and the dominated since the origins of the Conquest and which continued to interact within viceregal society. Interposed between these two epistemes, Baroque culture in America corresponded to the foundation of a transculturated, transculturating discursive enclave in which the *criollo* was both the object and the active subject of the processes of redefining the collective identities that were produced as a response to rationalistic modernity. Consequently, the representational strategies adopted by *criollo* culture at the height of the Baroque model were crucial to understanding the forms of integration and resistance of the American periphery of this period and its historical projections.

Picón Salas noticed the historiographical and more particularly the ideological problem entailed by the transcultural, transhistorical, and transdisciplinary use of the term *Baroque*. According to the Venezuelan critic, in Spain, the Baroque was transformed into "... estilo nacional; es anti-Renacimiento y anti-Europa en cuanto España estaba negando, o planteando de otra manera, aquellos valores de la conciencia moderna" (Picón Salas 1982, 122) ("... a national style. So far as Spain was denying more modern concepts or was construing them differently, its artistic expression was anti-Renaissance and anti-European" [1962, 86]). Yet in American transculturation, adapting the term, without any further clarification, could prove even more dangerous:

En Hispanoamérica el problema presenta nuevas metamorfosis, debido al aditamento de un medio más primitivo, a la influencia híbrida que en la obra cultural produce el choque de las razas y la acción violenta del trasplante. (Picón-Salas 1982, 122)

The baroque underwent further changes in Spanish America because of a more primitive environment and the hybrid influences that were inevitable in the collision of races and the violence of transplantation. (Picón-Salas 1962, 86)

Metamorphoses, contradictions between rationality and modern aesthetics—on the one hand, American "primitivism," multi-ethnic and multi-linguistic hybridization, and the violence of transculturation, on the other—mark the process of transposing topics, types of compositions, rhetorical forms, images, and metropolitan worldviews to the colonial environment; hence the Venezuelan's coining of the hybrid formula "Baroque of the Indies" to describe the elements composing the *criollo quiasmo*. This also explains why he regarded it as the product of a rationality that was both visionary and alienated: like the monologue delivered by Segismundo (Calderón de la Barca's [1600–1681] *La vida es sueño* [1636; *Life is a Dream*, 1985]), who, in his prison of images, shifts between dream and reality and between the utopias and the disillusionment of power (Picón Salas 1982, 126). For this reason, he sees Bernardo de Balbuena, (1563?–1627) the author of *Grandeza mexicana* (1604; Mexican Greatness) and *El Bernardo* [1624], as the figure who establishes the border between two epistemes determined by the different stages of colonial settlement: the epic, which would correspond to the territorial Conquest during the early stage of the Conquest, and the more contemplative, sedentary, and urban stage, coeval with the consolidation of *criollo* society. The "ciudad ilustre, rica y populosa" (64) ("arrogant and populous city") described by Balbuena as a "fénix de galas, ... museo de ciencias ..., jardín de Venus" (53) ("phoenix in full dress, ... a museum of science ..., a garden of Venus") was the arrogant machine that achieves the ideal synthesis of culture and nature, always imagined by the Old World. The seat of civilization and power, the city thereby acquired the symbolic value that Rama would develop as a metaphor for the spaces and processes of cultural institutionalization and a means through which the phenomenon of transculturation was implemented at the various stages of American history.

It was from this civic inscription that the colonial subject, from the parameters and models of Baroque culture, tested the forms of historical projection that would be assumed by *criollo* identity—still a tributary of the ideological constructs formalized since the time of the discovery as the legitimization of colonial domination. Iris Zavala has highlighted the importance of the representational forms that, from the earliest stages of the Conquest, were used to create the negative image of the American *other*; this occurred through the notions of savagery, primitivism, monstrosity, and degeneration that served as the basis for the characterization and taxonomy of subaltern ethnic groups, creating a common denominator that homogenized difference from a position of supposed epistemological privilege. According to Zavala:

The identity of the colonized subject was thus represented through the power of a borrowed language, introduced by technologies of knowledge: the authorities of myths (as in Fracastoro's poem), the authority of theology, of science, and of rhetoric. (332)

Within this context, it is interesting to see how the learned *criollos*, from a position of relative power, applied these representational strategies to their own construction of identity (rather than merely to the subjected ethnic groups under their control), since they take personally the insulting epithets that place them at the outer edge of civilizing spaces. Juan de Espinosa Medrano, "El Lunajero," (1620?–1688), a priest from Cuzco who wrote and preached in Quechua and Spanish, and who is best known as the author of the erudite *Apologético en favor de don Luis de Góngora* (1662; Apologetics in Favor of Don Luis de Góngora), refers, for example, to the condition of the American subject from the point of view of the dominator, expressing the terms of the *criollo* agenda as follows:

> Ocios son éstos que me permiten estudios más severos. pero (qué puede haber bueno en las Indias?)Que puede haber que contente a los europeos, que desta suerte dudan? Sátiros nos juzgan, tritones nos presumen, que brutos de alma, en vano se alientan a desmentirnos máscaras de humanidad. (Espinosa Medrano 17)

> This is leisure indeed that allows me to pursue more rigorous studies: But what good can there be in the Indies? What can there be that would please the Europeans, who doubt us so? They brand us as satyrs, assume we are newts and, with their brutish souls, vainly encourage themselves to deny our masks of humanity.

González Echevarría (1993), among other critics, has also noted this link between themes of racial monstrosity and cultural barbarity as a contributing factor in the legitimizing nature of *criollo* intellectul discourse; the *criollo* appropriated the cultural models of the dominator as a means of affirming the group's intellectual competence and forming a contra-hegemonic construction of the *criollo* subject to counteract the distorted identity attributed to them and symbolized by the wart found on Espinosa, nicknamed El Lunarejo, or by Juan Ruiz de Alarcón's hump, visible manifestations of the *criollo* "anomaly" and their hybrid socio-cultural status.

According to González Echevarría (1993), the rhetorical figure that best illustrates this atypical and unclassifiable quality of the *criollo* subject is the chiasmus, which involves exchanging the terms of one proposition with those of the next, meaning that the latter is therefore linked to the first through a relationship of antithesis. This reverse order, in which one term alters a parallel order (producing both opposition and synthesis between the components, without either of them dominating the other), serves as a metaphor for the relationship established between the two cultural and ideological factors that gave rise to *criollo* identity. There are certain discursive features–the cliché of American backwardness, the rhetoric of self-defense, the transition from mimesis to representational mimicry, the uses of irony, parody, and satire, together with operations to secure the discursive recovery of American territory (the wealth and variety of nature, urban monumentality), vernacular ethnicity (studies of pre-Hispanic languages and culture) and *criollo* cultural production incorporated into Western historical and scientific reason through the libraries, compendia, naturalists' catalogue, and historiographical records drawn up by the viceregal elite–that serve as expressions of the distance that existed between the paradigms of Eurocentric rationality and the revindication of the peripheral discursive space summarized in "we, the *criollo*s," an expression that appears, either explicitly or implicitly, in many of texts of the time.

Criollo "Difference": Power and Marginalization in the Construction of Colonial Knowledge

Criollo "difference" determined the development of an agenda that was inevitably ambiguous and oscillated between the loyalty due to the metropolitan system (the protector and organizer of the colonial periphery) and the American social reality, which was located on the liminal space between knowledge of America and peninsular power; hence the image of Janus, which has been used to symbolize the dual, conflictive nature of the *criollo* scholar, an organic intellectual of a system that grants him a disintegrated identity alienated

from his own American roots. In America, the construction of colonial knowledge is a process that must begin by examining its own roots: the tradition handed down by the dominator; the authority in the language in which this tradition is transmitted; the function of this knowledge as an instrument of subjection or liberation vis-à-vis the metropolitan powers; and the place of vernacular cultures in the synthesis presided over by *criollo* power. It was during this process that social actors began to define their identity as subjects of a differentiated history that was also a tributary, at various levels, of the imperial matrix.

As the creator and ideologist of this mixed system of loans, impositions, and cultural decanting, the *criollo* man of letters was forced to consolidate a discourse of identity, which, from our historical perspective, we can interpret as Americanist and proto-national. This discourse comprised a volatile mixture of elements from the Western source with others linked to American reality, both pre-Hispanic and *criollo*. Baroque production in America reveals the tension that is characteristic of the colonial situation and the emergence and progressive consolidation of a new American hegemony in the context of imperial domination. From the late sixteenth and early seventeenth centuries, the figures of the Incan Garcilaso de la Vega (1539–1616) and Guamán Poma de Ayala (1524?–1613) had already been projected as an obvious challenge to peninsular dominance and to the project for the "civilization" of America by Western rationalization and power. The Inca Garcilaso was canonized by traditional historiography as a paradigm, in both his life and work, of the transculturating processes and the hybrid and bidirectional condition of the colonial subject. His own genealogy linked him to aspects of both the dominated and the dominator. Born under the name of Gómez Suárez de Figueroa, the Incan Garcilaso was descended, on his mother's side, from the Incan princess Isabel Chimpu Ocllo (granddaughter of the Emperor Tupac Inca Yupanqui and niece of Huayna Capac, under whose government the Incan Empire would reach its peak) and, on his father's side, from the illustrious Spanish poet Garcilaso de la Vega, whose name he would adopt as a sign of his assimilation into metropolitan culture. However, his work, primarily the *Comentarios reales* [*The Royal Commentaries of Peru*, 1688] (the first and second part of which were published in 1609 and 1617 respectively) focused on the history and culture of the Inca period represented as the otherness that questioned the Western world's claim to be the greatest civilizing force in the Old World. Combining his mastery of Renaissance discourse with his aim of creating an American historiography by recording the memoirs of the survivors of the Conquest, the Incan Garcilaso constructed the *Comentarios* as the first real alternative to European models. Consequently, the *Historia general del Perú* [General History of Peru], to which the *Comentarios Reales* belong, emerged as the finest colonial example of inter-culturalism, in which European and American sources contributed equally to the historical reconstruction of the space destroyed by the empire. From this view of pre-Hispanic history, which was both nostalgic and revindicatory, the *criollo* imaginary would draw much of the emancipatory ideology that would move the Andean elite toward independence, projecting it as part of proto-national thought and praxis in subsequent centuries.

During the same period that saw the production of *Historia general del Perú*, Guamán Poma de Ayala would work on his *Primer nueva corónica y buen gobierno* [1612–1615; *Letter to a*

King: A Peruvian Chief's Account of Life under the Incas and under Spanish Rule, 1978], which provided a more belligerent view than the Incan Garcilaso's of the effects of the Spanish Conquest. Recently rediscovered in the 1920s, several centuries after it was written, Guamán Poma's work describes to Philip III Incan genealogy as the legitimization of a lineage destroyed by colonialist domination. Hybrid in its very composition and linguistic framework, the *Primer nueva corónica* includes both pictographic writing and words in Quechua and Aymara, together with a Castillian Spanish that bears traces of orality—thereby diversifying the communicative effectiveness of the work. As Rolena Adorno points out, when the colonial subject was set up as the producer of historical discourse, a de-feminization of native culture (which was perceived as weak, spontaneous, and instinctive) began to take place; this occurred when it was evaluated from the perspective of the supposed rationality and military force of the conquistador. Recovering the history of conquered civilizations and their resistance to Spanish dominion placed this emerging American historiography within the process of a construction of identity that depicted the other as the border of the collective ego and its practices as transgressions within the space of pre-Hispanic rationality. In this respect, Guamán Poma's text, like the *Comentarios reales,* achieves a veritable colonization of the peninsular imaginary, now "contaminated" by the literary and ideological force of this colonial counterdiscourse—in other words, by the language, history, and worldview of the dominated, who, in a complex process of cultural appropriation and reformulation, begins to formulate the ideological construct of their own American otherness as a formula for identity with which to challenge Western thought.

Although these criticohistoriographical testimonies described, with unusual eloquence, the history and complaints of the cultures subdued by Imperial domination (on the basis of the written praxis of transculturated subjects who were still representative of a time and a space prior to the Conquest), the Baroque writers, who began to produce later in the century in the major colonial centers, would provide a different view of the enclave that the *criollo* nation constituted within the American Western world. The political, ideological, and discursive negotiations from which American Baroque literature emerged would result in different characteristics that were heavily influenced by the social dynamics of the time and by the project for the consolidation of a *criollo* hegemony within the colonial world. While this project was being defined and gaining political and social ground through emancipatory action, the *criollo* elite would provide various forms and degrees of colonial awareness, depending on its representatives and the way they were linked to the existing powers.

Juan Ruiz de Alarcón (1581–1639), a dramatist from New Spain whose American identity is called into question by many critics of American literary history because of his residence in Spain for much of his life, is in many respects paradigmatic of the ambiguous condition of the lettered *criollo,* whose intellectual trajectory is always marked by a dual sociocultural affiliation and in many cases by a lack of territorialization and diglossia. His work, published in Madrid in two volumes in 1628 and 1634, constitutes an indictment against provincialism and a vote in favor of the anti-nobility social values and lay morals that would take root so firmly in America. In *La verdad sospechosa* [1634; The Truth Suspected] and other of his plays (*El semejante a sí mismo* [1628; Similar to Himself], *La*

crueldad por el honor [1634; Cruelty for the Sake of Honour], *La prueba de las promesas* [1634; The Proof of Promises]), he focuses on the theme of a class-ridden society and the principles of honor and community ethics that govern metropolitan and, to a lesser extent, Colonial society.

Although, as has already been pointed out, Ruiz de Alarcón's work "no expresa explícitamente una conciencia criolla subalterna y subversiva sino un discurso asimilativo imperial" (Sandoval 284) ("does not explicitly express a subaltern and subversive *criollo* awareness but rather an assimilatory, imperial discourse"), it does, however, exemplify the anomaly of being off-center, developed as a paradigm of colonial marginalization. As Jaime Concha notes, "la deformidad corporal [de Juan Ruiz de Alarcón] se transforma, mediante la alquimia dolorosa de su obra, en esa monstruosidad cultural y social que supone haber nacido en Ultramar" (39) ("the physical deformity [of Juan Ruiz de Alarcón] is transformed, through the painful alchemy of his work, into that cultural and social monstrosity that is entailed in being born abroad"). The dramatist's cultural difference would be projected onto both the form adopted by the criticism of his plays at one stage and his subsequent literary canonization—in which his perspective as a foreigner removed from both the colony and the metropolis is always cited as a significant fact. However, it was precisely his status as a Spanish American in Spain and virtually as a Spaniard in viceregal society that would fuel his scathing criticism of the social system.

Alarcón effectively distanced himself (as is clear in the dedications of his works) from both the nobility to which he could have belonged, yet which rejected him because of his lack of wealth and influence, and from the common people who constituted his public at various levels, and whom he reprimanded for their decadent customs and lack of values. In many cases, his plays dramatized the conflicts that affected the society of his time, particularly metropolitan society, which constituted his immediate public; in some cases (*Los favores del mundo* [1628; The Favors of the World]) he himself represented the qualities of virtue and personal bravery by portraying himself, Garci Ruiz de Alarcón, as a protagonist in his own fictitious world. With a foot in both spheres of the Spanish empire, the representations of the works of this man of letters—alienated from both his native land and the Old World, which accepted him without, however, fully acknowledging him—serve as a constant reminder of *criollo* hybridity and the Baroque mask; this symbolic transaction between various forms of social affiliation and identification was always incomplete, strange, and unsatisfactory.

In the Peruvian viceroyalty, the *mestizo* man of letters, Juan de Espinosa Medrano, had already revealed his exceptional erudition and creative capacity, together with his gifts as a preacher, which earned him the nickname of "Doctor Sublime." In addition to the aforementioned *Apologético en favor de don Luis de Góngora,* which studies the various forms of hyperbaton and other rhetorical figures characteristic of peninsular *culteranismo,* he also wrote *autos sacramentales* (mystery plays) in Quechua (*El hijo pródigo* [The Prodigal Son], *El rapto de Proserpina y el sueño de Endimión* [The Abduction of Proserpina and the Dream of Endimión]). The latter are clear examples of the *criollo* project to link classical, peninsular, and American features in a syncretic means of expressing the cultural and ideological negotiation on which the new society was based.

In New Spain, a land, in the words of Méndez Plancarte, "de especial fertilidad barroca" (xxvi) ("of particular Baroque fertility"), other lettered men also exemplified other aspects of *criollo* consciousness by expressing forms of group awareness that were absolutely representative of the American condition and the process of progressive differentiation from the peninsular matrix that occurred throughout the seventeenth century. Carlos de Sigüenza y Góngora (1645–1700) is one of the best-known viceregal literati, both because of the breadth of his intellectual interests and because of his close friendship with Sor Juana Inés de la Cruz, whose work complements his so well with its narrative, scientific, and anthropological contributions. With his solid, copious work, Sigüenza y Góngora, dubbed "a Mexican savant" by Irving Leonard (1984) in one of his laudatory studies, refutes, in his prolific and solid work, the skeptical, contradictory considerations of his critic, for whom *mestizo* society had not yet, at that stage of its development, produced its own cultural history (as distinct from peninsular history). His *Primavera Indiana* (1668; Spring of the Indies) is an epic poem of a historico-religious nature, focusing on the figure of the Virgin of Guadalupe, the emblem of American religiosity; in this epic the early seeds of nationalism and *criollo* pride were sown. In it, as in other compositions, he expresses the particularities of the historical and cultural development of New Spain, the seat of both the viceroyalty and the vestiges of ancient Aztec society, aspects that *criollo* historiography was eager to include as part of the utopia of a possible synthesis between the civilizations that were interlinked in the transculturating process.

As part of this project, in his *Teatro de virtudes políticas que constituyen a un príncipe* [1680; Theater of Political Virtues which Make a Prince], Sigüenza y Góngora linked numerous references to Aztec monarchs and gods to European references, acknowledging the role of both in the construction of Mexico. The *Teatro* is an excellent example of cultural syncretism, since it blends the sources of Renaissance historiography with contributions from American history, turning its author into the mediator and privileged spokesman of combined traditions and providing a historicoideological basis for a transculturated *criollo* society.

A similar syncretism, albeit with a different purpose, informs his *Parayso occidental* [1684; Occidental Paradise], in which the author himself delves into the history of the founding of Mexican convent space (the Convent of Jesús María), by describing throughout the text the defining characteristics of colonial society in its various aspects–linked to religiosity, gender, race, and social class (as Kathleen Ross notes in her detailed analysis). This text not only gives women prominence as protagonists in Mexican history, but also combines various cultural and ethnic realities that harmonize within both the Christian religion and its ecclesiastic practices. The combination of all these factors occurs in the convent, which is converted into an allegorical (paradisiacal) space of an American Christianity created through the link with the paradigms of faith and Imperial reason. Aimed at both the female audience of *criollo* nuns (from its male perspective) and at the King of Spain (from its position of colonial subalternity), Sigüenza's text exposes the historiographical artifices typical of Spanish-American chronicles: the representation of the voices and histories of "others" who cannot or will not speak for themselves (*Parayso* is, in the author's words, a history "of and for women"); the appeal to various audiences; the fixing of a memory that gradually constructs a past that it is different from (yet still a tributary of) the metropolitan past; and the subjugation, even at that stage, to peninsular models and expectations.

Sigüenza y Góngora is also known as the author of the pseudo-autobiographical novel entitled *Infortunios de Alonso Ramírez* [1690; Misfortunes of Alonso Ramírez], in which he narrates the vicissitudes of a Puerto Rican rogue (and therefore, from the viceregal margins), the son of an Andalusian and a native woman of the island. Disguised as the tale of a journey, the story is an implicit denunciation of the ineffectiveness of the Imperial project, which has turned the legendary wealth of Borinquen into poverty. Subjected to the degradation of misery, voluntary exile, and fear, Alonso testifies to the social disintegration of a milieu that remains unredeemed by the Imperial powers. In this respect, the roguish "I" represents an ideological "we": that of the Americans clamoring for a more effective and beneficial insertion into the sociopolitical system that surrounds them. The same strategy of the pseudo-autobiography is what moves Alonso to hand over the oral account of his life to a lettered man, so that he can retell it as if it were his own, in the first person, thus enlisting him in his defense before the viceroy. This strategy dramatizes the mediating position of the American intellectual and the varying degrees of subalternity that co-exist within the imperial project. It also reveals the dominance of vice, heresy, injustice, and a lack of productivity, and describes the place of lettered men in the institutions and the social dynamics of the viceroyalty. Sigüenza y Góngora constructs a powerful version of American "otherness" and its relegation to the margins of the empire, as perceived by a belligerent *criollo* consciousness.

Within this same interrogation of the restlessness of Colonial society and having recourse to the genre of the chronicle, Sigüenza y Góngora, in *Alboroto y motín de México* (Uprising and Riot in Mexico; a letter on the uprisings of 8 June 1692), describes the chaos caused by "plebe tan en extremo plebe" (148) ("the truly common people") clamoring for a return to the urban layout established by Cortés at an early stage of the Conquest, in which the Spanish and *criollo* quarters were separated from those of the Indians as a means of keeping the disciplined population safe from popular barbarity. In the form of a letter addressed to Andrés de Pez, at the court of Madrid, Sigüenza y Góngora describes the politicoeconomic, social, and climatic conditions that led to the popular uprisings that threatened the stability of the viceregal order represented by the viceroy, the Count of Galve. Kathleen Ross has suggested that Cortés's second "carta de relación" ("Letter of Report") is a subtext of the *Alboroto*; in a complementary fashion, Cogdell has highlighted the importance of the social context to an interpretation of the written expression of the learned Mexican in this particular text. The account offers a vivid testimony of the dynamic unrest affecting stratified viceregal society and the interaction of the various sectors with each other and the metropolitan powers. Warning of the dangers of miscegenation, this representation of the Lettered City–threatened by the tumultuous advances of the royal city–introduces into the utopian vision of the city, extolled in texts such as the aforementioned *Grandeza mexicana,* the alarmed *criollo* perspective, which, faced with both the benefits of the viceregal order and the subversive materiality of the subaltern classes, studies the likelihood of survival of the project of centralized unification in a society that is still largely made up of radical social heterogeneity and dominated by a centrifugal military power, contrary to the homogenization of Western rationality. In this respect, the text exemplifies the ideological ambiguity of the *criollos* and their desire to negotiate, under the best possible terms, the contents and influence of their cultural intervention on the colony.

Sigüenza y Góngora's work is, therefore, one of the finest examples of the flourishing of Western rationality in America, expressed as easily in scientific codes as in religious rhetoric, historical chronicles, or anthropological research. He presents himself to the European world primarily through his polemic with the Jesuit Kino on the scientific explanation of the trajectory of comets. Beyond any perfunctory respect for the prestige of the cultural authority of the European Jesuit, in his *Libra astrónomica y filosófica* [1690; Astronomical and Philosophical Calculations], Sigüenza y Góngora argues for the value of demonstration and proof as the basis of scientific thought, and the rigour of an elaboration of the great critico-intellectual scope that emerged in far-off overseas Spain. Through this type of debate, as well as through his command of Gongorist rhetoric, Jesuitic hermeneutics, or the discussion of values through the theater, poetry, or the varied forms of art, the learned *criollo* gradually succeeds in linking his colonial location to the discourse of universals that governed both religious and profane rationality in the Old World, drawing up, in the terms of his European interlocutors, oppositional agendas of non-conformism and demands expressed through satire, mime, or the appropriation and adaptation of peninsular culture according to specifically American needs.

In seventeenth-century Lima, the caustic verses of *Diente de Parnaso* [1689; Tooth of Parnassus] by Juan del Valle Caviedes (1652–1692), a Spaniard who had settled in the Peruvian viceroyalty in his youth, constituted a virtual clandestine questioning of the values, medical profession, and habits of the time, revealing the cracks in a social system built on the false premise of exploitation, appearance, and personal ambition. The "Peruvian Quevedo," whose work was rediscovered and published in 1873 by Manuel de Odriozola and Ricardo Palma, also incorporated genuinely American complaints into these caustic texts, refocusing the peninsular satirical tradition in compositions that reflect the progress of *criollo* consciousness as a belligerent identity in relation to metropolitan models, earning him the title of first *criollo* of the New World.

At the same time, the critical narrative that forms the basis of *El cautiverio feliz* [1673; The Happy Captive] by Francisco Núñez de Pineda y Bascuñán (1607?–1676) and the ironic, picaresque frieze of the society of New Granada that Juan Rodríguez Freyle (1566–1642) describes in *El carnero* [1636; The Ram] also contain representations of the subject and colonial spaces, but in a literary (and ideological) tone that contrasts sharply with the monumentality of the canonical Baroque, by introducing demystifications of the colonial order at different levels; these reveal the vitality of a society left to the ups and downs of its own popular and peripheral dynamic. Núñez de Pineda y Bascuñán provides an autobiographical account that reconstructs, forty years after the events, his captivity among the Araucanian Indians in 1629, offering a history composed of ethnographic observations, personal reflections on the social system of his captors, and an account of his activities during his forced stay in the land of Indians, a people whose excesses he criticizes as sharply as those of the Spanish oppressors.

Rodríguez Freyle's stories, together with those of Núñez de Pineda y Bascuñán, Sigüenza y Góngora, and others, have been rightly studied as examples of colonial historiography, since they incorporate community behaviors and values (see Zamora; Bost) at a time when historical writing was not yet fully distinguishable from the telling of anecdotes and the description of customs. *El carnero* includes numerous genres–chronicle, autobiography, and fiction–blending them in a vivid, intriguing frieze of the society of the time, very much in the tradition established in Spain by *El libro de buen amor* [*The Book of Good Love*], *La Celestina* [*The Celestina*] and *El Conde Lucanor* [*Count Lucanor*]. Yet, as an American text, Rodríguez Freyle reveals, above all, the social vicissitudes of his time, which combines orality, popular and high culture, domestic and public spheres, morality and humor, imagination and history, and erudition and the observation of customs; together these elements make up one of the most interesting and illustrative narrations of the Colonial period.

As Julie Greer Johnson has noted, the function of satire is defined in the New World by the adoption and social restructuring (sometimes through inversion) of peninsular models, placed at the service of an emerging critical and revindicatory awareness of the rights of *criollos*. In a broad spectrum ranging from the most innocent comicality to the grotesque, American satirists not only recovered the everyday colonial life that went beyond the themes and style of Baroque discourse, but also chose to counter the latter through the use of a "minor" theme and an ironic, colloquial language, sometimes loaded with vulgarities and obscene allusions; this was intended as a representation of *criollo* non-conformism and of their perception of the colony as a repressive, decadent (dis)order. Both in the aforementioned text from New Granada and in the case of *Infortunios de Alonso Ramírez*, critics have highlighted the role of the picaresque: The direct, displaced adoption of the peninsular genre revealed how to imitate the metropolis. They often ignored the importance acquired, within these stories, by the construction of a *criollo* subjectivity, at both the individual and collective level, and the significance of an anti-heroic protagonist whose social mutations challenged the repressive, homogenizing, organizing project that accompanied Imperial domination in the colonies (see Moraña 1998).

Yet no work from the Baroque period better expresses the transculturating influence and dual identity of the learned *criollo* than that of Sor Juana Inés de la Cruz, born Juana Ramírez de Asbaje (1648–1695), with its multiple cultural attachments to the discursive, social spaces of religiosity, court life, and the politico-ecclesiastic institutions that regulated the functioning of the world of New Spain. Her work exposed the complex interconnections existing between scholasticism reaffirmed by the Counter-Reformation, Gongorist rhetoric, popular culture, and the celebration of everyday life in the viceroyalty; yet it is also presented as striving to promote what today we would call interdisciplinarity and multiculturalism as transgressive elements capable of challenging the dominant, compartmentalized models of knowledge and cultural praxis. Through her texts, Baroque codes are confirmed as the language of an elite, initiated in the mysteries and privileges of the written word, exercised as an instrument of social and ideological control; through them, however, one can also glimpse the *criollo* agenda as a revindicatory program through which a new concept of the colonial subject and its relations with power and subaltern groups is defined. Sor Juana's work is projected through an immense variety of genres and literary forms: courtly compositions, Christmas carols, *autos sacramentales* (mystery plays), theater, hieroglyphics, epistles, ballads, celebratory poetry, and highly metaphorical poems. This variety of poems covers a broad spectrum ranging from jesuitic hermeneutics to medleys parodying the language of Indians and slaves, with their phonetic alterations of Spanish, together with the insertion of verses in Náhuatl and Latin. These are blended in a verbal carnivalization that contrasts with the solemnity of the rites of politicoecclesiastic power, as exemplified by her *Villancicos* [1676–1601; Christmas Carols] dedicated to San Pedro Nolasco or to St. Catherine. Yet together with mocking dialogism, the courtly game, and Baroque monumentality, her works also express that *criollo* consciousness that seeks ways of integrating the fragments of colonial society from a position of rising power; this includes the demand for a place where women could also make their contributions to the construction of American knowledge. Her own intellectual praxis constituted a definite intervention in the spaces controlled by viceregal high culture, while serving as a paradigm of the program that the *criollos* would develop, increasingly effectively, to consolidate their power.

Among the challenges contained in the work of the tenth Muse, the praises that precede the mystery plays *El divino Narciso* [*The Divine Narcissus*], published in Mexico in 1688, and *El Cetro de José* [The Sceptre of José], first published in 1692, specifically express the nun's opinions regarding the Conquest of Mexico, by allegorically representing the position of the Indians' and the *criollos*' revindication with regard to the issues of colonial appropriation and the ethics of war. By linking the figures of Christ and Huitzilopochtli ("the great God of the Seeds"), as well as the Eucharist and cannibalism, Christianity and American "idolatries," Sor Juana dramatically raises the issue of cultural conflict and *criollo* positioning, with an aggressive relativism that increasingly distances the *criollos* from the dominant peninsular position. As Sabat de Rivers's studies have so effectively demonstrated, Sor Juana's is a discourse of transgression and *criollo* affirmation, cleverly filtered through the prestigious metropolitan models.

Sor Juana's lengthy poem, *Primero Sueño* [First Dream], a 975-line work first published in 1692 in the second volume of the Hieronymite nun's *Obras* (but probably written in or about 1685), exemplifies the desire for appropriation and influence in Western thought through its concern with themes linked to intellectual and empirical knowledge and to the world of faith, mythology, and Classical-Scholastic philosophy. The poem is offered as a lyrical exploration of the limits and domains of knowledge and as a story of the pilgrimage of the spirit in its impossible quest for a knowledge that cannot be encompassed. In this composition, Sor Juana also exemplifies the *criollo* adoption and reformulation of Classical sources and motifs, sending the material received back to Europe as part of colonial transculturation.

According to Octavio Paz (1914–1998), *La Respuesta* [*The Answer*, 1994] written to Sor Filotea de la Cruz in 1691, although published posthumously is the complement of *Primero sueño*, since it extends to the duration of an entire life what the long poem offered as the story of a pilgrimage embarked on by the soul in a single night (Paz 481). The letter is clear evidence of the system imposed on colonial society and of the persecution suffered by the Hieronymite nun as a result of her transgressive intellectual practices. Other epistolary documents–*Carta Atenagórica* [1690; Letter Worthy of Athena], the letter to Father Núñez (discovered in Monterrey in 1980 by Aureliano Tapia Méndez and dated 1682 [see Alatorre] as well as the enigmatic epistle discovered by Elias Trabulse in 1995, signed with the pseudonym

of Serafina de Cristo and dated 1 February 1691 [see Trabulse])–have revealed unusual aspects of the nun's intellectual project and her complex relations with the society of the time. Yet *La respuesta*, addressed to the Bishop of Puebla, Manuel Fernández de Santa Cruz (who used the pseudonym of Sor Filotea), is to this day the most direct testimony to the limitations and challenges facing the nun as a result of her subaltern condition vis-à-vis the peninsular powers and the patriarchal authoritarianism that governed the court and the convent. An unusual display of erudition and social awareness, *La respuesta* makes individual circumstances (a reconstruction of convent dynamics, the integration of personal memoirs, the reference to public spaces) the reflexive axis around which it weaves an intricate network of relationships imposed by the spirit of the Counter-Reformation, patriarchal authoritarianism, scholastic tradition, and the advent of modern rationality in the culture of the era.

In Sor Juana's work, epistolary discourse and lyrical, dramatic, or religious discourses revolve around the construction of individual and collective subjectivity, which, within the context of viceregal politics, refers to the process of consolidation of *criollo* consciousness. Although this personal-public link is evident in her letters, it is no less obvious when expressed in a poetic code, in her ballads or rondels, in which female subjectivity is expressed at numerous levels (emotional, intellectual, and social), revealing the achievements and conflicts of *criollas* in the spaces of the court or ecclesiastic life and in the everyday popular life of the colony. This explains why the autobiographical element (as with the "I" construction in *Infortunios de Alonso Ramírez*) has a central value in Sor Juana's texts, serving as a point of intersection between the public and private sphere, hegemony and marginalization, the utopia of Imperial "order" and "unredeemed" American barbarity, the adhesion to metropolitan models and the construction of a *criollo* consciousness that was increasingly oppositional and distinct from the peninsular matrix. This urgency in the (self-)construction of *criollo* subjectivity is the common denominator that the learned *criollos* elaborated and hoisted as a banner in their process of historical ascension as the only means of countering the negative identity foisted on Americans by the conquerors ever since the discovery; they thereby constructed a new utopian horizon that has been carried to the present and expressed so precisely by El Lunarejo from his position of besieged marginality:

> Pues los europeos sospechan seriamente que los estudios de los hombres del Nuevo Mundo son bárbaros . . . . Más qué si habré demostrado que nuestro mundo no está circundado por aires torpes, y que nada cede al Viejo Mundo?
> (Espinosa Medrano 325)

> The Europeans seriously suspect that studies by men from the New World are barbarous . . . . Yet what if I have proved that our world is not surrounded by sluggish airs and that it is in no way inferior to the Old World?

This statement not only illustrates the fundamental problem of colonial America, relegated to the periphery, displaced by Western rationality, but is also projected forward onto following centuries as a possible agenda for the Latin American periphery to counter the new projects of transculturating globalization. In any case, one should recall that the construction of *criollo* identity was conjuncturally determined, at that particular point in American social development, by the challenge imposed by colonialism, and the heavily protected, collective subjectivity it provoked. The "we, the *criollos*" that guided the learned project in the colony would, in turn, become the formula for the new means of homogenization and social control of the other subaltern groups, in various ways and to varying degrees, because of the political, economic, and cultural power of this new ruling class. The ideal of a fixed, totalizing identity based on the various stages of a continental history was always to the detriment of the ethnic heterogeneity and cultural pluralism inherent in American social formations; despite these efforts at cultural leveling and conciliation, numerous opposing agents, discourses, and sectorial agendas always coexisted. Baroque transculturation was therefore only one example–although perhaps the most monumental and artistically productive–in the historical process of anti-hegemonic transgression and the construction of an alternative to the dominant imaginary, yet it sought, in turn, to transform into power what had begun as marginalization, subjugation, and resistance.

Translation by Suzanne Stephens

Works Cited

Adorno, Rolena. 1988. "El sujeto colonial y la construcción cultural de la alteridad." *Revista de crítica literaria latinoamericana* (Lima) 14.28: 13–28.

Alatorre, Antonio. 1987. "La *Carta* de Sor Juana al P. Núñez (1682)." *Nueva revista de filología hispánica* 35: 591–673.

Balbuena, Bernardo de. [1624] 1852. *El Bernardo: Poema heróico.* Madrid: Gaspar.

——. [1604] 1988. *Grandeza mexicana.* Ed. José Carlos González Boixo. Roma: Bulzoni.

Bost, David H. 1996. "Historians of the Colonial Period: 1620–1700." *Cambridge History of Latin American Literature.* Vol 1: *Discovery to Modernism.* Eds. Roberto González Echevarría and Enrique Pupo-Walker. Cambridge: Cambridge University Press. 143–90.

Cogdell, Sam. 1994. "Criollos, gachupines, y 'plebe tan en extremo plebe': Retórica e ideología criollas en *Alboroto y motín de México,* de Sigüenza y Góngora." *Relecturas del barroco de Indias.* Ed. Mabel Moraña. Hanover: Ediciones del Norte. 245–80.

Concha, Jaime. 1976. "La literatura colonial hispanoamericana: Problemas e hipótesis." *Neohelicón* (Budapest) 4.1–2: 31–50.

Cornejo Polar, Antonio. 1994. *Escribir en el aire: Ensayo sobre la heterogeneidad socio-cultural en las literaturas andinas.* Lima: Editorial Horizonte.

Coronil, Fernando. 1995. "Introduction: Transculturation and the Politics of Theory: Countering the Center, Cuban Counterpoint." *Cuban Counterpoint: Tobacco and Sugar.* By Fernando Ortiz. Durham and London: Duke University Press. ix–xi.

Espinosa Medrano, Juan de. 1982. *Apologético.* Ed. Augusto Tamayo Vargas. Caracas: Biblioteca Ayacucho.

Garcilaso de la Vega, Inca. 1985. *Comentarios reales de los incas.* Caracas: Biblioteca Ayacucho.

González Echevarría, Roberto. 1990. *Myth and Archive: A Theory of Latin American Narrative.* Cambridge: Cambridge University Press.

——. 1993. *Celestina's Brood: Continuities of the Baroque in Spanish and Latin American Literature.* Durham: Duke University Press.

Guamán Poma de Ayala, Felipe. 1980. *Nueva corónica y buen gobierno.* 2 vols. Ed. Franklin Pease. Caracas: Biblioteca Ayacucho.

Johnson, Julie Greer. 1993. *Turning the New World Upside Down. Satire in Colonial Spanish America.* Austin: University of Texas Press.

Leonard, Irving. 1984. *Don Carlos de Sigüenza y Góngora. Un sabio mexicano del siglo XVII.* Mexico City: Fondo de Cultura Económica.

Malagón-Barceló, Javier. 1961. "The Role of the *Letrado* in the Colonization of America." *The Americas* 18: 1–17.

Maravall, José Antonio. 1975. *La cultura del barroco: análisis de una estructura histórica.* Barcelona: Ed. Ariel.

Méndez Plancarte, Alfonso. 1951–1957. "Introducción." *Obras completas.* By Juana Inés de la Cruz. Ed. Alfonso Méndez Plancarte. Vol 1: *Lírica personal.* Mexico City: Fondo de Cultura Económica. i–lxviii.

Moraña, Mabel, ed. 1997. *Angel Rama y los estudios latinoamericanos.* Pittsburgh, PA: Instituto Internacional de Literatura Iberoamericana, Universidad de Pittsburgh.

——. 1998. *Viaje al silencio: Exploraciones del discurso barroco.* Mexico City: Universidad Nacional Autónoma de México.

Núñez de Pineda y Bascuñán, Francisco. 1974. *El cautiverio feliz y razón individual de las guerras dilatadas del Reino de Chile.* Ed. Alejandro Lipshutz and Alvaro Jara. Santiago de Chile: Editorial Universitaria.

Ortiz, Fernando. 1963. *Contrapunteo cubano del tabaco y el azúcar.* Havana: Consejo Nacional de Cultura.

Paz, Octavio. 1995. *Sor Juana Inés de la Cruz, o, las trampas de la fe.* Barcelona: Seix Barral.

Picón Salas, Mariano. 1962. *A Cultural History of Spanish America, from Conquest to Independence.* Trans. Irving A. Leonard. Berkeley: University of California Press.

——. [1944] 1982. *De la conquista a la independencia.* Mexico City: Fondo de Cultura Económica.

Rama, Ángel. 1984. *La ciudad letrada.* Hanover, NH: Ediciones del Norte.

——. 1986. "Los procesos de transculturación en la narrativa latinoamericana." *La novela en América Latina: panoramas 1920–1980.* Mexico City: Universidad Veracruzana/Fundación Angel Rama. 203–34.

——. 1996. *The Lettered City.* Ed. and trans. John Charles Chasteen. Durham, NC: Duke University Press.

Rodríguez Freyle, Juan. 1979. *El carnero.* Ed. Darío Achury Valenzuela. Caracas: Biblioteca Ayacucho.

Ross, Kathleen. 1993. *The Baroque Narrative of Carlos Sigüenza y Góngora: A New World Paradise.* Cambridge: Cambridge University Press.

Ruiz de Alarcón, Juan. 1957–1968. *Obras Completas.* Edición, prólogos notas de Agustin Millares Carlo. 3 vols. Mexico City: Fondo de Cultura Económica.

Sabàt de Rivers, Georgina, ed. 1982. *Inundación castálida.* By Sor Juana Inés de la Cruz. Madrid: Editorial Castalia.

——. 1988. *El "Sueño" de sor Juana Inés de la Cruz. Tradiciones literarias y originalidad.* London: Tamesis.

Sandoval, Alberto. 1988. "Aportes para una canonización de Juan Ruiz de Alarcón en la literatura latinoamericana." *Revista de crítica literaria Latinoamericana* 14.28: 281–90.

Sigüenza y Góngora, Carlos. 1940. "Alboroto y motín de México del 8 de Junio de 1692." *Relaciones históricas.* Ed. Manuel Romero de Terreros. Mexico City: Ediciones de la Universidad Nacional Autónoma de México. 91–172.

Spitta, Silvia. 1995. *Between Two Waters. Narratives of Transculturation in Latin America.* Houston, TX: Rice University Press.

Trabulse, Elías. 1995. *El enigma de Serafina de Cristo. Acerca de un manuscrito inédito de Sor Juana Inés de la Cruz (1691).* Toluca: Instituto Mexiquense de Cultura.

Zamora, Margarita. 1987. "Historicity and Literariness: Problems in the Literary Criticism of Spanish American Colonial Texts." *Modern Language Notes* 102: 334–46.

Zavala, Iris M. 1989. "Representing the Colonial Subject." *1492–1992: Re/Discovering Colonial Writing.* Ed. René Jara and Nicholas Spadaccini. Minneapolis: University of Minnesota Press. 323–48.

CHAPTER 14
THE BAROQUE GAZE

Raúl Antelo

One of the keenest political thinkers of the nineteenth century, Juan Bautista Alberdi (1810–1884), born in Tucumán—a contact zone between Spanish colonization and Inca culture—repeatedly attempted to appease his contemporaries by reminding them not to fear "la confusión de razas y de lenguas. De la Babel, del caos, saldrá algún día brillante y nítida la nacionalidad sudamericana" (3: 436) ("the confusion of races and languages. Some bright and clear day the South-American nationality will emerge out of Babel, out of chaos"). This metaphor introduces not only the letter of politics but also a politics of the letter, one that begins to be disseminated in the eighteenth century, at times threateningly, at other times auspiciously.

As a politics of the letter, America-as-Babel displays not only the always incipient but also the unfinished. It reveals the very pretension or impossibility of the desire to conclude and totalize. It unmasks the illusion of saturation or completion of any initiative in the order of construction, insofar as Babel demands a paradigmatic reading. On the other hand, in regard to writing, the metaphor of Babel not only allows for satire, but it also triggers it, for the coexistence of multiple discourses—in other words, intertextuality in its literal sense—proves to be bound to fail because of its abusive ambition of totality. Or, in other words, this failure persuades us that intertextuality as a merely linguistic totality is nothing but minuscule and, strictly speaking, satiric, for it always rests on a wish for a divine *correspondence* that is drastically confronted with stammering and silence. From the Benjaminian theory of translation we know, precisely, that all possibility of comparison between two terms, let us say, metropolis and colony, can be effected only through a third term, the *tertium comparationis*, a metalinguistic term that gathers and unifies them. However, once the unity of the paradisiacal language is lost, along with the necessary and natural relation between sign and referent, the *etymo* becomes the only alternative for the (re)cognition of the true. Nevertheless, in America the *etymo* is itself a *post-factum* construct and, as such, is threatened by dissent. Far from grounding the stability of the comparison, the third term founds a *mestizo* philosophy. Romantic historians were precisely the first ones to make an effort to provide full representations of the "American," the third term. The basis for that attempt was the (imaginary) harmony between sound and meaning, nature and culture. One of the literary historians of the period, the pioneering Juan María Gutiérrez (1809–1878), pointed out that the ideal concept of the time was the harmonious and gallant relations between women and men, much like the pine tree and the palm.

One could thus think that American men of letters abhor and condemn the Babelic aspect of the colony, since it expresses itself in non-metropolitan languages, as attested to by the work of Pedro de Cieza de León (1518–1554), José de Acosta (1540–1600), and Cristóbal de Molina (1494?–1578) in Peru, the Hispanic-Latin mixes to be found in the Lima panegyric signed by the Jesuit Rodrigo de Valdés (1609–1682), or, in the case of Brazil, José de Anchieta's (1534–1597) catechetical literature. Even the Peruvian Juan del

Valle y Caviedes's (1652–1692) transgressive poetry already betrayed this multilingual impact. Such is the case with the "bey-oca rendiya" (508–509) or "Portrait of a Lima belle" by using the common hoax proper to the patricians of that city, the "y" instead of the "ll" (the title of the poem is a pun on "belloca" [pretty woman] and "redondilla" [a popular Spanish verse form], which uses the phonetic equivalence in Spanish between the "ll" and the pre-vocalic "y"), or a poem dedicated to the wedding of a tinker and composed in "Indian language" ("jonto al novia,/ tan ridondo y ella larga,/como en los trocos di juego,/taco, bola in mis[m]a cama" [539] ["next to the groom/so round, she is so long,/like the game's stick,/and ball in the same bed"]). The poem satirically compares the bride to a stick and the groom to a ball, and is written with non-standard spelling.

Be that as it may, it is nevertheless necessary to point out that the reference to Babel has not always denoted corrosive mixes. The Babelic indeed designates, in the beginnings of the Western tradition, human *construction* (Genesis I: 1–9), and it is only in the Middle Ages that the idea of *confusio linguarum* is popularized, first through fifth- and sixth-century codices. (This meaning is well illustrated by Welislaw's Bible from the 1300s.) The Renaissance celebrated the human initiative and intelligence presupposed by the Babelic endeavor to such an extent that several Dutch engravings from the 1500s and the 1600s—such as those by Harenbout in the Guimani Breviary or the vision of Saint John of Cornelius Antonisz (1547)—highlight those traits of ambition. Contemporary with the colonization of America, Cesare Ripa's *Iconologia* [1593; Iconology] describes Babel with the by-then canonical emblem of *confusio labii et universae terrae*, that is, with the traits of an indigenous young woman, "confusamente vestita de diversi colori, che havendo i capelli mal composti, posì la destra sopra quattro elementi confusamente uniti e la sinistra sopra la torre di Babel co'l motto, che dicca, *Babilonia undique*" (82) ("confusedly clad in multiple colors, with poorly combed hair, her right hand poised on four elements confusedly united and her left on the tower of Babel, with the motto that read *Babilonia undique*"). Operative in this description, undoubtedly, is the sensitive representation of uncouth tongues to be found in the beginning of the *Inferno* (III, 25–30), when Dante alludes to

Diverse lingue, orribili favelle,
parole di dolore, accenti d'ira,
voci alte e fiocche, e suon di man con elle
Facevano un tumulto, il qual s'aggira
sempre in quell'aura senza tempo tinta,
como la rena quando turbo spira.

Uncouth tongues, horrible shriekings of despair,
Shrill and faint voices, cries of pain and rage,
And, with it all, smiting of hands, were there,
Making a tumult, nothing could assuage,
To swirl in the air that knows not day or night,
Like sand within the whirlwind's eddying cage.

(28–31)

The whole question of the entrance into another culture, of the hybridism of codes, and the estrangement of representation

191

itself conspires in this construct to fuse the foreigner (*barbarus*) with the stutterer (*babbus*). After all, Babel is built against them. It should come as no surprise, then, that in the colonization of America this fable of the social as a construct not only demonizes the barbarian stammering, but also, at the same time, consecrates the colonizers' salvational enterprise.

Thus, the Jesuit José de Acosta (1540–1600)–upon whom Euclides da Cunha (1866–1909) would later base his own interpretation, put forth in *Os sertões* [1902; *The Rebellion in the Backlands,* 1944]–sustains in *Historia natural y moral de las Indias* [1590; *The Natural and Moral History of the Indies,* 1970] that the Indians of New Spain were descendants from the exodus of Jerusalem. In his turn, the Franciscan Jerônimo de Mendieta (1525–1604) goes so far as to affirm in his *Historia eclesiastica indiana* [1596; *Historia Eclesíastica Indiana: A Franciscan's View of the Spanish Conquest of Mexico,* 1997] that the tower of Babel was to be found in the Anahuac valley (present day Mexico City). He says,

> Los indios de Cholula, dando en la locura de los de la Torre de Babel, quisieron hacer uno de estos teucales o templos de los dioses que excedise en altura a las más altas sierras de esta tierra . . . y para este efecto comenzaron a plantar la cepa que hoy día tiene al parecer de planta un tiro de ballesta, con haberse desboronado y deshecho mucha parte de ella, porque era de más anchura y longitud y mucho más alta. Y andando en esta obra . . . los confundió Dios, aunque no multiplicando las lenguas como a los otros, sino con una terrible tempestad y tormenta cayendo entre otras cosas una gran piedra en figura de sapo que los atemorizó. (1973, 1: 54)

> The Indians of Cholula [Cholula has the highest pre-Hispanic pyramid] fell victims to the madness of the builders of the Tower of Babel by attempting to raise one of their temples to the height of the highest mountain range in the land . . . In order to achieve this objective, they began to erect a pyramid; but today it has only modest measurements, for the greater part of it has crumbled or been demolished; originally it was much wider, longer and higher. The ancients relate that as they proceeded with their work, God confounded them, not by confusing their tongues but with a terrible storm, thunder and lightening, with large blocks of stone coming down like hailstones, some in the shape of toads, events which naturally frightened them. (1997, 39)

References to the tower of Babel are to be found in Mariano Veytia's (1718–1780?) *Historia antigua de México* [1886; History of Ancient Mexico], Juan de Torquemada's (ca. 1557–1664) *Monarquía indiana* [1615; Indian Monarchy], Diego Durán's (1537–1588?) *Historia de las Indias de Nueva-España* [1579–1581; History of the Indies of New Spain, 1994], Francisco Javier Clavijero's (1731–1787) *Historia antigua de México* [1780–1781; *The History of Mexico,* 1979], William Hickling Prescott's (1796–1859) *History of the Conquest of Mexico* (1843), Alexander von Humboldt's (1769–1859) *Researches, Concerning the Institutions and Monuments of the Ancient Inhabitants of America* (1814), and even Fernando de Alva Ixtlilxochitl's (1578–1650) manuscript *Sumaria relación de todas las cosas que han sucedido en la Nueva España* [1608; Summary Report of All Things That Have Occurred in New Spain]. Manuel Orozco y Berra (1816–1881) points out in his *Historia antigua y de la conquista de México* [1880; Ancient History and History of the Conquest of Mexico]:

> El objeto era alzar una torre como la de Babel para librarse de un nuevo diluvio, intento que los dioses burlaron impidiendo la conclusión de la obra y confundiendo las lenguas de los trabajadores: rayos ó una gran piedra en figura de sapo, mutilaron lo ya terminado. (3: 16–17)

The purpose was to erect a tower such as the one in Babel, in order to escape another flood, an attempt mocked by the gods, who prevented its conclusion and confounded the workers' languages; thundering and an immense toad-shaped rock mutilated that which had been finished.

It should not be forgotten that a particular version of this fantasy of barbarism–an element still active in Europe's historical imaginary at the time–appeared in one of the sonnets by Luis de Camões (1524?–1580), the greatest Portuguese poet of the sixteenth century who crafted the equation Babel = Babylon = labyrinth:

> Cá nesta Babilónia, donde mana
> Matéria a quanto mal o mundo cria;
> Cá onde o puro amor não tem valia
> Que a Mãe, que manda mais, tudo profana;
> Cá onde o mal se afina e o bem se dana,
> E pode mais que a honra a tirania;
> Cá onde a errada e cega Monarquia
> Cuida que um nome vão a desengana;
> Cá neste labirinto, onde a nobreza,
> Com esforço e saber pidindo vão
> Às portas da cubiça e da vileza;
> Cá neste escuro caos de confusão,
> Comprindo o curso estou da natureza.
> Vê se m'esquecerei de ti Sião!

> *(1984, 270)*

> Here in this Babylon where enough raw ill
> Springs to supply the needs of the whole earth;
> Here where pure Love has forfeited his worth
> To his more powerful mother who soils all;
> Here where ill is refined and good is blamed,
> And tyranny has seized the upper hand;
> From honor, here where kingship wandering blind
> Takes care that reputations are defamed;
> Here in this labyrinth where nobility,
> Panting and knowledge cap in hand must come
> Before the gates of greed and villainy;
> Here in this murky pandemonium
> The law of the jungle rules: ah, woe is me
> If I forget you, O Jerusalem!

> *(1990, 69)*

At first Babylon represents exile (that is, India) whereas Zion (that is, Jerusalem) stands for the Portuguese metropolis. As we know, Jerusalem represents the decisive moment in Judaic urbanization. It refers us back to the Jahveh pact, the alliance with David, and to Solomon's construction of two buildings, which were to house the two powers: a temple to lodge religion and a palace where royal sovereignty would reign. In a word, the tiara and the throne. The whole medieval imaginary rests, therefore, upon the tension between a city condemned to destruction (Babylon) and a sacred one with origins in Zion (Jerusalem), which would become the new Jerusalem and later, as an abyssal point in the eschatological encounter between nations, the celestial Jerusalem. In some poems from this period, the two cities, Jerusalem and Babylon, appear intertwined in rather problematic ways. In "Sôbolos rios, chora por ti, Sião divina"–another Camões poem dedicated to Babylon, which begins "Sôbolos rios que vão/ Por Babilónia, me achei,/Onde sentado chorei" (Camões 1963, 1) ("Beside the rivers that stream/Through Babylon, there I stepped/And there I sat down and wept"), in dialogue with Saint John's "Super fluminem Babilonis," Zion is the bygone time and Babylon is the present evil; the past is a time of glory and the present is the abode of grief. In the above-quoted sonnet, however, Zion itself *is* Babylon, which allows us to present reality proper to the past itself, or as a sort of sublimation of effective privations and sacrifices. But to these arguments we must add the discoursive one. Babylon is Babel because the sonnet's anagrammatic character articulates the following notion: The metropolis, from which the matter of Evil springs, the Mother who dominates and corrupts–for love in her no longer possesses any value–this absolute Evil that destroys hierarchies and undoes dynasties, in other words imperial power, mixes profanation and putrefaction. Babel-Babylon is an allegory of Baroque temporal identity, which still echoes in "Son los ríos," in which Borges (1899–1986), centuries later, tells us "Y sin embargo hay algo que se queda/y sin embargo hay algo que se queja" (3: 463) ("and yet there's something that remains/and yet there's something that laments").

However, being a cipher of time Babel is also a figure of speech–a labyrinth–a chaotic, confusing, arduous, and even unintelligible figure, such as the "Sator arepo tenet opera rotas." It is worth highlighting the presence of the same anagram of the word "sapo" ("toad") already noted in Cholula's Babel, readable also in the interstices of "Sator arepo," an anagram that reappears in the figure of the founding god of the post-flood era, *Macunaíma*, in the versions of Mário de Andrade (1893–1945) and Alejo Carpentier (1904–1980). Although it is a figure of speech, Babel is also a figure of absolute reversibility, much like evil, or modernity itself. The two political fictions we are treating here become fused in it. On the one hand, Babel provides us with a psychological-linguistic model of relative incapacity for effective comprehension in which, however, meaning goes beyond the text itself. Signs convey more than information. In his *Reflexões sobre a vaidade dos homens* [1752; Reflections on Men's Vanity], Matias Aires (1705–1763) wrote

Os que amam não têm livre o espírito para dizerem o que sentem, e sempre acham que o que sentem é muito mais do que o que dizem; o mesmo amor entorpece a idéia e lhes serve de embaraço: os que não amam, mal podem discorrer sobre uma impressão que ignoram; os que amaram, são como a cinza fria, donde só se reconhece o efeito da chama, e não a sua natureza; ou também como o cometa, que depois de girar a esfera, sem deixar vestígio algum desaparece. (167–68)

Those who love are not free in their spirit to say what they feel, and they always think that what they feel is much more than what they say; love itself inebriates the idea, and ends up functioning as an obstacle: Those who do not love can barely say anything about a feeling they ignore; those who have loved are like cold ashes, where one can recognize the flame's effect, but not its nature; or like the comet, which after the turn of the wheel disappears without any traces.

But, whereas Babel is the emblem of *hiponóia* or fiction, for it sustains the suspicions held by reason against the will, Babel's supplement–the labyrinth–offers a plural cultural model, not only as missed routes but also as a search for an end to a voyage, which, after all, turns out to be a point of no return and an irreversible relaxation of norms.

That period's proliferating cartographies and grammars attempt, therefore, to contain Babels and labyrinths that are threatening to European reason. It is along these lines–the maintenance of *opera rotas*–that one can read José da Costa Miranda's Atlantic letters, or *Cartas del cantino* (1502), Lopo Homem's (fl. 1517–1565) *Atlas Miller* (1515–1519), the *Quarta*

orbis pars, mundus novus (1558), Martin Waldseemüller's (1470–1521?) *Tabula terrae novae* (1513), Jacques de Vall de Claye's maps (Dieppe, 1759), Diogo Soares's (1513–ca.1565) excursions, or those by the scientist priests through the Amazon around 1730. It is within this framework that we should evaluate Antonio de Nebrija's (1441? 1522) effort in regard to the Spanish language, or those of João de Barros (1496–1570) in relation to Portuguese. Both are anti-Babelic crusaders, although it is necessary to point out, as a differential mark, the belated and tolerant stance of the Portuguese vis-à-vis Babel. In fact, only in 1757 do we see the appearance of the first official legislation curbing the advance of Tupi-Guaraní, the general language. Furthermore, that legislation–made normative by grammarians such as Jerônimo Contador de Argote (1676–1749) for vocabulary, and Luis de Monte Carmelo (d. 1785) for phonology–was restricted to Pará and Maranhão, lands more Spanish than Portuguese.

In these cases, grammarians and cartographers attempted, with great effort, as Peruvian Pedro de Peralta Barnuevo (1663–1743) said in French, "renfermer dans un point un abîme" (quoted in Gutiérez 119) ("to enclose an abyss in a dot"), that is, to control heteroglossia. It is interesting to highlight that this cultural and discoursive mix was not aleatory; it emerged from more tolerant practices, which had turned America not only into a land of refuge but also–and precisely because of that–into a land of the future, that is, a space of what was yet-to-come and a no less virtual democracy. Juan del Valle y Caviedes's (1652–1692) allegory compellingly captures the tone of this entreaty. Old Curiosity interrogates her grandson, Disillusionment, "Experience's child," about the structure and life of the city of Lima, this supreme Cairo, this "new Babylon":

con quien Roma es un cortijo;
Nápoles, una aldehuela;
Londres, un zaquizamí;
París, una choza yerma.

(492)

along with which Rome is a parade,
Naples, a little village;
London, a tiny closet;
Paris, a deserted hut.

The recounting of experience reveals, in modern fashion, the disillusionment with the breach established between identity and difference. This disillusionment is translated in certain stammering (by the *babiecas*, the simpletons from Babel); from word to deed there was always

muy notable diferencia,
y en cualquier tierra de Babia
suelen mentir sus babiecas.
Y más, éstos, que por dar
a sus errores más fuerza,
dirán que el cielo es pintado
sobre cristalino néctar;
que es de tela de cebolla,
bordada de lentejuela;
que hay en cada nube un astro
y es un sol cada planeta.
Siendo así, que las más veces,
cubierto de opaca niebla,
puede competir al limbo
o apostar con la Noruega.

(494)

a very notable difference
and in any land of Babel.
Its fools tend to lie
and even more, to give their
errors more strength
they will say that the sky is painted
upon crystal-clear nectar;
that it's made of onion thin fabric,
embroidered with sequins;
that in each cloud there's a star
that each planet is a sun.
Being thus, most of the time
covered with opaque fog
it can compete with limbo
or challenge Norway.

The coeval Brazilian version of this disillusionment by poet Gregório de Matos (1633?–1696)–in whose work, as Araripe Jr. has pointed out, all seventeenth-century poetry coalesces–describes, in poems such as "Soneto à cidade da Bahia" ["Sonnet to the City of Bahia"], the state of decadence reached by the Brazilian capital, a formerly powerful colonizing center: "'Pobre te vejo a ti, tu a mim empenhado/. . ./A ti trocou-te a máquina mercante/Que em tua larga barra tem entrado" (1986, 83–84) ("I see you in debt/for you've been traded away by mercantile machine/that has onto your soil made an entrance"). Just as much can be inferred from pieces such as "Senhora dona Bahia" ["Lady Bahia"] or "A cada canto um grande conselheiro" ["On Each Corner a Great Advisor"]. However, consistent with the Enlightenment's emancipatory project, later poets rapidly abandon the satire of manners in favor of direct description. For example, in Caramuru (1781)–the theme of which is precisely the colonization and population of the Bahia coast–José de Santa Rita Durão (1720–1784) informs us that "Engenhos, povoações que descobria,/Eram como ornamentos da cidade,/de que se ergue no plano a majestade" (186) ("sugar-cane mills, villages one discovered/ were like ornaments to the city/against whose outline it rises in majesty"). This celebratory note remains true even if one of the Arcadian poets from Minas Gerais, Tomás Antônio Gonzaga (1744–1807), expresses such laments or raptures tinged with disillusionment. In the case of Rio de Janeiro, it is not, in fact, a matter of an urban or social sore spot; it is the rationalist reconstruction of the city that is mitigated by nature. Santa Rita Durão himself extols it in Canto VIII of Caramuru, whereas other Arcadian poets, such as Alvarenga Peixoto (1748–1798) in poems like "Tu onde o vento e o mar a fúria esbarra" ["You, Where Wind and Sea Clash with Fury"] or Silva Alvarenga (1749–1814) in "O desertor" ["The Deserter"], seem to concentrate their gaze on the Pão de Açúcar (Rio de Janeiro's Sugar Loaf mountain).

Since these examples place us at the heart of the pragmatic spirit of the Enlightenment, it should come as no surprise to us that the city is seen as a land to be civilized by the resolute urbanistic intervention of the governor, who disciplines the roughness of rustic nature. The target becomes, therefore, the enlightened figure of the viceroy Luis de Vasconcelos, during whose administration the dock, the customhouse, the fountain, and the public promenade are built. In order to contain the excesses of all kinds that threaten the city, the combined power of technology and capital appears magnified through the artifices of reason. Not surprisingly, the built space becomes more and more powerful the closer it is to areas of cultural contact with the Other. It is necessary, by any means, to curb Babel. This curbing is, however, equally useless.

Architecture offers several examples of these anti-Babelian endeavors, which are always, by the way, saturated with multicultural content. This tendency was already noticeable in Europe, where the austerity of Jesuit churches deprived of cupolas, such as those of Saint Roc in Lisbon or Saint Paul in Braga, correspond to the basic structures found in East Europe, Georgia, or Armenia, and later in Córdoba del Tucumán. These stripped-down forms contrast the ornamental excess of the Bahia churches, such as the Saint Francis convent, which displays an explosion of plateresque, full of columns with exaggerated twists and turns where nothing is left unembellished. The same articulation between several architectural styles is to be found in the School of the Jesuits in Salvador–adorned by Gregório de Matos's brother, Friar Eusébio da Soledade Matos (1629–1692)–or in the work of the Hungarian architect, Carlos Mandel, who transplanted various solutions that coexisted with the style of Mediterranean architects from Spain, such as Juan de Herrera, or from Italy, such as Filippo Terzi, in a kind of stylistic discourse of diverse forms also observable in the Sabará church in Minas Gerais. Therefore, Babel points to a field of transformations in the colonial relationship. The metropolis is not unified. There is also a dispute between metropolises, and not only between languages. Whereas Brueghel's Babel, announcing Rimbaud's postutopian "Cities," turned out to be the result of an intertextual juxtaposition of the Roman coliseum, in Herodotus's tale, and the contemporary machines that built the Dutch harbors–to which Latin American gold would flow–the Baroque Babel was an unequivocal sign of the emerging city as a cosmopolitan stage of modernity in which it is often incumbent upon theological discourse (innocuously and inconsequentially) to attempt to sublimate the falsity of the message.

Without explicitly referring to the city of Salvador, in Bahia, Gregório de Matos laments, in allegorical fashion, the losses implied in these ongoing transformations in colonial society:

Ó cháos confuso, labyrinto horrendo,
Onde não tópo luz, nem fio amando;
Lugar de glória, aonde estou penando;
Casa da morte, aonde estou vivendo!
Ó voz sem distinção, Babel tremendo,
Pesada fantasia, somno brando,
Onde o mesmo que tóco, estou sonhando,
Onde o própio que escuto, não entendo!
Sempre és certeza, nunca desengano,
E a ambas pretensões com igualdade
No bem te não penetro, nem no dano.
És ciúme martírio da vontade,
Verdadeiro tormento para engano,
E cega presumpção para verdade.

Oh! Confusing chaos, horrendous labyrinth,
Where no light or thread is to be found;
Place of glory, where I am grieving;
House of death, where I am living!
Oh! indistinct voice, trembling Babel,
Heavy fantasy, light sleep,
Where what I touch has me dreaming,
Where what I hear has me confounding!
You are always certainty, never undeceived,
And in both pretensions, be it in Good,
or in Evil, I fathom you not.
You are ambition, a martyrdom of the will;
True torment to deceive;
And the blind presumption of truth.

(1981, 60–61)

In the colonial city–this drama of contradictory drives–the crisis of rationalist voluntarism ("és ciúme martírio da vontade" ["you are ambition, a martyrdom of the will"]) exposes, on the other hand, the crisis of rationality as a basis for social organization. The decline of *cogito ergo sum*, or simply its strange and foreign condition in the periphery of the empire, turns it into an irreverent and transgressive *ubi non cogito, sum*, which generates a double oxymoron: that of deceit as a true torment and that of truth as blind presumption. Both are lies that trigger the two basic lines of action, that of the pursuit of knowledge and that of power. As an illustration, we remind the reader that in the River Plate region, between 1663 and 1680, Luis de Tejeda (1604–1680) composed a ballad (romance) about his life, *El peregrino en Babilonia* [The Pilgrim in Babilonia], where his birth place, Córdoba–which was, by the way, as important as, or even more than, the capital of viceroyalty–is represented as

La ciudad de Babilonia,
aquella confusa Patria,
encanto de mis sentidos,
laberinto de mi alma;

The city of Babylon,
that confusing Fatherland,
wonder of my senses,
labyrinth of my soul;

(83)

There is certainly something topical about this urban representation, extracted from Saint John's Apocalypse (chapters XIV: 8; XVII: 5 and XVIII), from Saint Augustine, and even from Cervantes's *Galatea*. One can see here the echoes of the allegory found in Luis Góngora's (1561–1627) erotic adventures in the *Fábula de Píramo y Tisbe* [1618; Fable of Pyramus and Thisbe], which evokes "la ciudad de Babilonia/famosa no por sus muros" (287) ("the city of Babylon/not famous for its walls"). Those walls had, by the way, also been praised in a sonnet to the fatherland's military glory–"Oh siempre gloriosa patria mía/tanto por plumas, cuanto por espadas!" (105) ("Oh, my always glorious fatherland/in pens, as in swords")–reminiscent of that valiant Cordoba in the avant-garde of the Moorish wars, elliptically reduced to its military boundaries:

Oh excelso muro, oh torres coronadas
De honor, de majestad, de gallardía!

Oh, supreme walls, oh crowned towers
of honor, majesty, grandiosity!

(105)

In this fusion of erotic adventures and misadventures, of distant lands and wars, the Tajo and the Suquia babelically confound in Tejeda. Both of these strands lead to the *soledades* composed by another contemporary pilgrim, Manuel de Falla, in the Argentinean Cordoba, where he laments the loss of the first one by taking the same Góngora sonnet as support. We could say that the loss of exile–with nothing fortuitous about it–implies, for all émigrés, a loss of power and a dissociation of will, which anamnesically and catastrophically comes to reinstate the experience of origins as an experience of the ever-lasting enigma.

As we know, the enigmatic character of these statements consists in the fact that they affirm an immanent meaning and conceal another, which transgresses this limitation. Theodore Adorno (1903–1969) argues that this character is coextensive with the mimicries of a clown, a figure to which he, by the way, attributed a resemblance to monkeys. This resemblance between clown and animal–he writes in his *Aesthetic Theory*–reminds him of human resemblance to monkeys to the point of turning the animal/madman/clown into a crucial component of modern art. The enigma, therefore, harks back to mimesis as a double strategy of confirmation/transformation of the colonial status. It is certainly not only individual and it presupposes an always effective sociability, insofar as it rests upon an institutional game. In the same Cordoba/Babylon found in Tejeda, no less hybrid and enigmatic voices were heard, such as that of Domenico Zipoli. Unlike other European musicians relocated to America in the service of the Crown–such as Juan de Araujo or Tomás de Torrejón y Velasco, whose aesthetic, consecrates the power of the peninsular elite–Zipoli, from Tuscany, composed music that only seemingly simplifies the Baroque (learned from Scarlatti), and in fact privileges a no less enigmatic style that attempts to make Catholic dogma intelligible to indigenous ears through music. This is what can be heard in "Missa de Santo Inácio" ["Mass of Saint Ignatius"], in praise of the founder of the Company of Jesus, and transmitted in that region at length through the oral tradition. In it, the alternation between homophony and counterpoint movements, next to the mosaic of brief quasi-autonomous moments within the sequence, structurally shows the enigmatic hybridity of the language chosen by Zipoli. In what language–the Italian musician must have asked himself–can we utter Christ and make him accessible to the monkey-men? Probably in a *bambocciata* diction, similar to the one he himself learned in Naples. (Let us not forget that Neapolitans invented the *opera buffa*, just as they defended, in their Baroque painting, the *stain*, a figure deprived of fixed structure superimposed on a harmonious background so as to further highlight the contrast.) In sum, Zipoli inaugurates, in his own way, American Orphism. He descends to the netherworld in search of the ideal, but this fiction not only offers a kernel of truth for his language, but it also models the beauty he produces, which symptomatically becomes hybrid. It should be remembered that this hybridity, besides pointing to the spheres of power and knowledge, also interrogates desire. One of the major manifestations of this hybridity is its gender ambivalence. In effect, in Europe itself, Baroque art inherits and takes up the Renaissance ephebus, which is often embodied in images of the martyrdom of Saint Sebastian, such as that of Sodom and Gomorrah, or the fair, young Saint John, as in the painting by Leonardo da Vinci. In America, there is a certain air of *l'après midi d'un faune* in these figures that proliferates in Jesuit art, seducing hearts through rapture and ecstasy. Uncontested testimony to this is provided by the images of Saint Sulpicius or by the widespread dissemination of the representations of the Sacred Heart.

Therefore, if we consider the origin no longer as an instance of absolute beginning but as an ambivalent start, if we place in perspective and in movement that which was believed to be stable or well-known, and if we articulate body and history with this genealogy, it is in this hybrid event that the emergence (never the culmination, always the return) of a difference can be verified. Our contention is, therefore, that in all manifestations of colonial symbolic life in America we confront this structural duplicity, which, after all, demands a specific politics of truth in order to be read: It is a question of reading in these figures the elliptical syntax of the complex discoursive filigree. The understanding of the filigree demands considering a serial structure, but one in which individual works in the series necessarily operate in the simultaneity of at least two other simultaneous series coming from that ambivalent distant starting point. In other words, all serial form is rigorously multi-serial, being itself composed of numerous other series, not identical among themselves, but functioning differentially: One always operates as signifier to the other, the signified.

Taking that as our assumption, a work of art, let us say a sonnet, unequivocally aligned on the plane of expression, migrates away from this specific space of reception–in a guided fashion and due to a signifying excess–toward the plane of designation, thereby composing the paradox of value, which becomes irreducible to both series. Indeed, if we take for example "Desenganos da vida humana metaforicamente" ["Disillusion of Human Life Metaphorically"], a poem in which Gregório de Matos defines vanity as a rose, as a plant, and as a ship–thereby offering us images of a victorious colonial power that is, however, confronted by obstacles and destined for decline–we can see that this referent fable is rearticulated, in a serial arabesque, in *Reflexões sobre a vaidade dos homens*, by Matias Aires, where the moralist establishes that

> cada um de nós tem duas vontades sempre opostas entre si; ao mesmo tempo queremos e não queremos; ao mesmo tempo condenamos e aprovamos; ao mesmo tempo buscamos e fugimos; amamos e aborrecemos . . . . A vaidade é uma espécie de concupiscência; não se lhe resiste com as forças do corpo, com as do espírito sim; a carne não é frágil só por um princípio mas por muitos, e a vaidade não é o menor deles. (82–83)

> each one of us has two wills always opposed to each other; at the same time we want and do not want; we love and we abhor . . . . Vanity is a sort of concupiscence; one cannot resist it with the strength of the body, but with that of the spirit; the flesh is fragile not only for one reason, but for many, and vanity is not the smallest of them.

In the same way, if we invert our perspective, a treatise unabashedly devoted to direct designation can offer us an unexpected grammar of cultural expression. Nobody hesitates to classify Fr. Antonio Vieira's (1608–1697) *História do futuro* [1697; History of the Future] as a political text. This is a work that presents us with a prophetic reflection of unmistakable Hebrew roots, in tune with John's apocalyptic thought and foreseeing a catastrophe that, in the end, would bring about an era of happiness, the millennium of angelical life. It is undoubtedly a treatise about life in the polis. However, the highly complex system of this Jesuit priest assumes the translation between languages insofar as the difference rests, in its turn, upon the idea of an ur-language. The desire for translation of the several spheres (the transitory concupiscence of which moralist Matias Aires speaks) is unthinkable without the correspondence with the thought of God. Just as Jesuit linguists allude to the question of an ur-historical center–which they identify with the language of the heathen (as in Ludovico Bertonio, *Arte de la língua aymará* [1603; *The Art of the Aymara Language*])– Vieira writes *História do futuro* with the purpose of prophesying the fifth empire and therefore translating the signs to come into a degraded social experience, that of colonization.

We thus infer that each enunciative colonial series is, in sum, multi-serial. It operates coextensively with other series by articulating truth in the form of a paradigm that begs to be reconstructed from its differing and deferred effects. Let us look at a specific case. In a romance dedicated to an Inquisition doctor, the Peruvian Valle y Caviedes recovers this dual and breached discoursive structure of truth through nominalism and poetic equivocality:

> Ya los autos de la fe
> se han acabado sin duda,
> porque de la Inquisición
> médico han hecho a Machuca.
>
> The trials have ended
> they are surely over,
> for the Inquisition
> has made Machuca a doctor.
>
> *(104)*

Let us offer yet another example of a cultural paradigm. In 1638, in the sermon of Saint Anthony, preached by Father Vieira in Bahia, we confront another tropological reading in a quotation from the Second Book of the Kings, commonly called the Fourth Book of Kings chapter 19, verse 34: "For I will defend this city, to save it, for mine own sake, and for my servant David's sake." Following Sérgio Buarque de Holanda, we would say that in this passage God persuades us that he will take the city of Jerusalem under his protection, thereby alluding to the siege of the sacred city by Senaqueribe. But the Jesuit preacher adds that the protection of Bahia from the Dutch undoubtedly possesses more significance and force for Brazilians. What matters here is that the truth, ciphered in all aspects, is revealed to us only through a poetic procedure. In Father Vieira's interpretation, God promises to save the city, *salvabo eam*, and this contains the truth because this *urbem* is the city of Salvador. The effect and the work are thereby confirmed: The Savior's action is to save. Furthermore, much as the city is saved *propter me, propter David*, the hill of Jerusalem, the *Civitas David*, is also saved. In a *mise en abime*, we see that the Bahian Zion was a hill where the chapel of Saint Anthony was located, the very chapel where Father Vieira was preaching that sermon. Therefore, if David can stand for Saint Anthony, he can stand for any and all saints. From this reading (which is simultaneously writing) we conclude that much as Babel is a field of transformations not unlike war, this event located between emptiness and sameness, i.e., the city itself– now Babylon, now Salvador–takes on its specific incompleteness due to its nature as representation of a representation.

Once the unity of the ur-language, as well as the natural and necessary relation between sign and referent, are lost, the imposition of a limit–be it an archaic *etymo* or a future *telos*– becomes indispensable in order to fix the true. This is so despite the recognition of the provisional nature of this task, since all totalization decidedly appears, on the plane of the construction of a language, as an elusive operation. If, on the one hand, this provides us with a principle of unlimited interpretation and semiosis–exemplified, by the way, by Sor Juana (1648–1695) in her *Respuesta a Sor Filotea de la Cruz* [1691; *The Answer to Sor Filotea de la Cruz*]–on the other hand, the ceaseless displacement of elements from one series to the other shows that neither of them possesses an absolute location, or better put, that this absolute location (its value) bestowed on them is defined in relation to an ethical and verbal distance and does not cease to be displaced from itself, in such a way that the paradox is never where one looks for it, and it is never found where it actually is. In other words, value lacks its own place, or, in other words, the subject lacks (an) identity. This idea–that identity exists only insofar as it is the identity of the non-identical–allows, in its turn, for an evaluation of the Baroque transdiscoursivity as a peculiar Latin American response to the challenges of modernity. It also allows us to understand it as a subtle elaboration of colonial identity, defined as a place between truth and desire.

Several series, therefore, coalesce there: subjects, spaces, temporalities. In the allegories of the colonial world, we come across indications that these include more than individuals. Public space becomes the center of the administrative capital, the headquarters of the central power or (by default), in a subaltern province, a mere gratuitous complement to the capital. These cities, Cordoba or Vila Rica, Salvador or Recife, need to protect and defend themselves due to the growing hostilities in the territorial wars against other colonial powers or against insurrection by the native population. On the one hand, therefore, the Baroque city becomes an organism opened by the crossing of roads; but on the other, this cosmopolitan initiative is not derived from the spontaneity of the migration of citizens to the city nor from the local, municipal authority, but rather from the response to the restrictive authority of specific colonial policies. Knowledge, always tied to the power of the capital, is located in the unequivocal authority of the monarch and in the imperial apparatus connected with him. What defines the value of the city is not, therefore, its physical extension, or even its borders, but its power of control over its dwellers. Why isn't Duarte Coelho's well-policed Pernambuco, for example, the capital of the kingdom? According to Gregório de Matos

> Por entre o Beberibe e o Oceano
> Em uma areia sáfia e legadiça
> Jaz o Recife, povoação mestiça,
> Que o belga edificou ímpio tirano.
> O Povo é pouco, e muito pouco urbano

> Between Beberibe and the Ocean
> On a rough and steamy sand
> Lies Recife, *mestizo* borough,
> put up by the Belgian impious tyrant.
> People are scarce, and barely urban

(1986, 171)

It is for this reason, by the way, that the capital of Brazil would cease to be Salvador and would be, within a few years, displaced to Vila Rica, in Minas, a remarkably more contained and cautious city. It is for the same reason that the later colonial cathedrals take on the openly neo-Classical, stripped-down form of Rio's Candelária or the Buenos Aires Cathedral, both of them designed by Brigadier José Custódio de Sá e Faria, whose fusion of military and religious idioms would be adopted by the Estrela Basilica in Lisbon, revealing the union between temporal and ecclesiastic powers in a challenge to colonial power. In this Babel of flux and reflux, it is the court that copies the colony, even though the ties of coercion and discipline that subordinate the latter are not any looser.

Once the parameters of the city had been rationalized and ethical values had been personalized, the economic power of circulation and distribution of goods and services concentrated political power in the city (already the effective locus of accumulation); however Vila Rica's power derived from the honesty of its citizens. In this moment of the conflict between secession and union, administrative and economic power converge in one place as Pedro de Peralta Barnuevo points out:

> Es la moneda el espíritu universal que anima el cuerpo del comercio, y la inteligencia material que mueve la esfera del Imperio. Sin ella la plata y el oro que producen las minas serían más adorno que riqueza y ofrecerían más esplendor que utilidad. Y aunque por si no lo requería éste ni aquel metal, sin embargo, ha sido bien que en ella la excelencia que le presta la materia acompañe el valor que le da el cuño. Por esto es la imagen más adornada que tienen los príncipes y consistiendo en ella la mayor regalía del dominio y la mayor fe de la república, viene a ser el sacramento político de la majestad, cuyas ofensas son de aquella criminalidad que trae esta circunstancia agravante del real sacrilegio. (quoted in Gutiérrez 80)

> Money is the universal spirit animating the body of trade, and the material intelligence that moves the sphere of Empire. Without it the silver and gold produced by the mines would be more an ornament than riches, and would offer more spectacle than usefulness. Even though it is not of itself required by either gold or silver, nonetheless it has been felicitous that the excellence that accompanies the metal endows value to the coin. This is why it is the most adorned image possessed by princes, and why it constitutes the greatest luxury of the power and faith of the republic. It thus comes to be majesty's political sacrament, any offenses to which qualify as criminal circumstances aggravating sacrilege.

If, however, money draws up these circuits of interchange that lie at the foundation of power over the world–leading us to judge, as Matias Aires said, that even nature is a perpetual and singular metamorphosis–it is impossible to infer that being in constant change, this metamorphosis is deprived of discipline and tumultuously presents itself, all of a sudden, before our eyes. It is this *chaotic image*, certainly, that gets demonized. It is a tumult of perceptions. Precisely in October of 1687, when the earthquake that destroys Lima takes place, Valle y Caviedes sees a sign, a signal: This quake is a punishment for the excesses of the city, one that demanded reflection and regret from its contemporaries: "Asústennos los pecados/no la tierra que fluctúa" (608) ("may sins threaten us/not the moving ground"). There is more than a simple correspondence between individual comportment and universal harmony. The circuit of exchange is under the watchful eyes of the state, which places the greatest importance on the loss suffered by the adulteration of precious metals and the consequent increase in smuggling. But the *criollo* elite by then perceives–and articulates it as a political fable–out of the earthquake a new power in which language was born, a power by which language, in a broad sense, becomes a mechanism regulated by excess, homologous to the city and to the colonial state itself.

Peralta Barnuevo, in his urban genealogy *Lima fundada* [1732; Foundation of Lima], presents us with this relatively stable model in which "la máquina del universo no consta de muchos todos, sino de uno solo compuesto de variedade de muchas partes; máquina de infinitas piezas gobernadas por un solo resorte que simboliza la divinidad de quien la formó" (quoted in Gutiérrez 137) ("the machine of the universe does not consist of many wholes, but of one made up of many parts, a machine of infinite parts governed by a single resource that symbolizes the divinity of its creator"). However, this seemingly lasting and stable celestial engineering is unsettled by the drifting of fiction. In the love of Aeneas and Dido, for example, (both of them regulated by the stars) Peralta Barnuevo sees a case of betrayal and negligence by Virgil himself. This is the surrogate creative divinity that, even after sending Mercury to wrest Aeneas from Dido's arms, still describes the stain that remains on the queen. However, Peralta Barnuevo admits that it is true that Virgil condemns the love of Aeneas and Dido, but condemns it as he sings its praises; this, as an accepted break in the rules, is seen as a fictional copy that resembles colonial transculturation. In sum, it is transgression that founds the interdiction; it also begets, however, a language that offers (however partially) an autonomous space. Being doubled in this dichotomy of knowledge/power, its logic exceeds and differs from monological discourse, which operates through identification, description, variation, and exclusion of contradictions, and is unequivocal and conclusive in its affirmation of truth. But it is always worth noting that this dialogic heterogeneity–although implicit and unfolding in every dialogue–is itself constantly transgressed by the discursive order. By absorbing interdiction, transgression demonstrates the ambivalence of representation. In it we have, on the one hand, science's monological discourse–let us not forget, for example, that Peralta Barnuevo, author of *El cielo en el Parnaso* [1736; Heaven in Parnassus], is a scientist and cosmographer dedicated to the study of mathematics, chemistry, and botany, as well as modern and ancient languages–coexisting with, on the other hand, poetry's dialogical discourse–that of Valle y Caviedes, for example, dedicated in great part to the erosion of medical knowledge. The same could be said of the Antonio Vieira/Gregório de Matos pair. Vieira writes the future without the present; Matos, in his turn, writes the present without the future. The same could also be said of the "Eucharistic Triumphs," the ostentatious processions that staged the celestial and earthly machines in Vila Rica. The famous one from 1733 consecrated communion as a symbolic elaboration of difference and a sublimation of subalternity. In the pompous gathering that accompanies the ark and the banner with the saying "Eucharistia Translatione Victrix"–in which they were announcing, as it were, future carnivals with their allegorical carriages–the sun was foregrounded.

In cases such as these, we can see that the interdiction founds the law, with the proviso that when a deviation is normalized, it is simultaneously transgressed, revealing the structural historicity of discourses. In the functioning of these discourses, oppositions such as nature/culture, culture/society, and society/individual are more than determinate historical folds, since by acting as oppositional dyads, they nevertheless bring out new distinctions (the unconscious/repression, autonomy/censorship), which do not cease to unfold new tensions themselves, according to the logic of signification. Transculturation is, therefore, a deferred effect of the coexistence of the order of discourse and the subject of the unconscious.

In *Highlands of the Brazil*, Captain Burton (1821–1890) belittles the Aleijadinho sculptures of the Calvary procession in Congonhas as "caricatures", yet these are works that are a true tableau of bodily passions. Modernists would, on the contrary, turn this subaltern defect into a value, an expressionistic eulogy, since these grotesque figures served–as Mário de Andrade (1893–1945) would say–as an anamnesic force that fixed a tradition in the popular unconscious. This duplicitous register (normalizing vision, deviating diction) is recurrently noted in the poetic representation of the colonial city. It obeys this scopic regime of distance, which, however, is translated into satire's moral centrality. In the case of

Gregório de Matos, for example, satire can come to occupy three positions: (a) prosopopeia, with a full personification of the city and consequent representation of its discourse in indirect speech; (b) a vocative interpretation, either as "Senhora" ("Mrs.") or "Sodoma" ("Sodom"), in which even the positive marking implies a lowering in register involving undesirable confrontations (such as the chiasmus "madrasta dos Naturais,/ e dos Estrangeiros madre" (1981, 18) "a stepmother to the Natives/a mother to Foreigners"); and (c) narration or description in which the "torpe cidade" ("vile city") is materialized, "de dous ff se compõe/. . . /um furtar, outro foder/ . . . / esta cidade a meu ver" (1981, 16) ("composed of two f's/ . . . / one stealing [*furtar*], the other fucking [*foder*]/. . . /what my sights see in this city"). This latter case is particularly emblematic. If the signal is double (ff), but the value is single, it is because that in spite of tropological instability and imperial coercion, the city organizes itself as a paradigm, in far more stable fashion than one would expect judging from the first chroniclers. Gândavo (d. 1576), in his *Tratado da terra do Brasil* [1576; Treatise on the Land of Brazil], pointed out the nominalist substratum of a conception of an indigenous culture whose language "carece de tres letras–*scilicet*, não se acha nela F, nem L, nem R, cousa digna de espanto, porque assi não tem Fé, nem Lei, nem Rei" (24) ("lacked three letters–*scilicet*, one does not find an F or an L or an R, a truly astonishing thing, since they therefore have no Faith or Law or Royalty"). Gabriel Soares de Sousa (ca. 1540–1591) would later repeat the same observation:

> faltam-lhes três letras das do ABC, que são F, L, R grande ou dobrado, coisa muito para se notar; porque se não tem F, é porque não têm fé em nenhuma coisa que adorem; nem os nascidos entre os cristãos e doutrinados pelos padres da companhia têm fé em Deus Nosso Senhor, nem têm verdade, nem lealdade a nenhuma pessoa que lhes faça bem. E se não têm L na sua pronunciação é porque não têm lei alguma que guardar, nem preceitos para se governarem; e cada um faz lei a seu modo, e ao som de sua vontade; sem haver entre eles leis com que se governem, nem têm leis uns contra os outros. E se não têm essa letra R na sua pronunciação, é porque não têm rei que os reja, e a quem obedeçam, nem obedecem a ninguém . . . nem o filho ao pai e cada um vive ao som de sua vontade. (364–65)

> In their ABC three letters are missing, and they are F, L, R, neither double nor capitalized, a rather noteworthy thing; for if they do not have an F, they have no Faith in anything they love; not even those born among Christians and indoctrinated by the priests of the Company have any faith in God our Lord; they have no truth, nor loyalty to any person who has done them good. And if they have no L in their pronunciation it is because they have no Law to keep, nor precepts to govern them; and each one makes law his own way and follows the direction of his own will; having no laws to govern them they have no laws against each other. If they have no letter R in their language, it is because they have no Royal authority [*Rei*] to reign over them, to whom they would obey; each one lives according to his own will, for nobody obeys anybody, children do not obey their parents . . .

In this regard, it should be pointed out that the troubadour poet Guilherme de Aquitânia, toward the end of the eleventh century, narrated a situation similar to this one: Two ladies looking for adventure come across a stammering wanderer who–incapable of speaking and responding to demands–can only babble, in disconnected fashion: "babariol, babariol, babarian." Similarly, the encounter between Indians and colonizers–not deprived of sexual violence, by the way–also alludes to the solitude and incommunicability of amorous bliss. It is still to be evaluated how the scopic regime and the semiotic regime are connected in this paradoxical process of *eulalia* and *aleluia*.

One could hypothesize that in the very idea of language as infinite productivity, in the notion of the paradigm, and in that of the literary text as an anathema, that is, as a network of connections unfolded in identical and complementary moments–that of writing and that of reading–we can find, in a word, the articulation between function and value in colonial society. On the one hand, the chronicles inform us that the letter F is missing in the natives' language; on the other, the lettered administrator concludes that the evils of the colony derive, on the contrary, from the excess of F's, noted in the acts of *furtar* (stealing) and *foder* (fucking), that is, in advances upon others' property. In this subtle paradigmatic numerology, there is no residue or singularity but only the two and the whole. The unit is empty and does not add up, while the 1 is a zero, but it signifies, for it centralizes and consequently hierarchizes. However, the paradigm does not attribute stable meaning to this representation, for the unit–if it possesses any unity–is far from being a fusion of one with the other (say, of excess and lack), but rather separates the terms opposed to each other, which are, at the same time, linked with each other in a proliferating tension. The oppositional dyad does not signal, therefore, the passage from the limited to the unlimited, or even from the undefined to the determinate. It marks, on the contrary, the passage from the disordered to the centered and from the chaotic to the hierarchized. The transculturating discourse ceaselessly produces these new units by replacing irreducible differences with nonexcluding oppositional dyads, where the tension between the interdiction and transgression shows that the singular does not function as a unit, but as a totality, with the proviso that we understand that this whole is double.

By refusing to become stable as a system, without F, L, and R, in other words, being doubled (endowed with two Fs), transculturation negates itself. But insofar as it negates itself as a transgressive moment, it affirms itself as a disseminated negativity, one that floats, suspended, in the fog. Fernando Pessoa (1888–1935) takes up this image in "Nevoeiro" ["Mist"], the poem that closes *Mensagem* [1934; Message]. In it he admits that

Nem Rei, nem lei, nem paz nem guerra,
Define com perfil e ser
Este fulgor baço da terra
Que é Portugal a entristecer

No king, no law, no peace or war
Defines the profile and being
Of this dark splendor of the soil,
Which is a saddened Portugal

(98)

The mist is the suspended materialization of the new, the accumulation of an energy forever ready to explode and expand by contesting the conventional representation of the norm.

Pascal, a contemporary of Father Vieira, wrote that "L'univers est un cercle dont le centre est partout et la circonférence nulle part" (quoted in Blanqui 37) ("the universe is a circle whose center is everywhere and the circumference is nowhere"). Important at that moment was to make sure that the truth of a salvation that would unify the nation for the next millennium could circulate unimpeded. At the end of the nineteenth century Louis Auguste Blanqui (1805–1881) was

concerned, much like Marx, with the proliferation of the truth of a proletarian politics; he amends Pascal and, in the search for a celestial Jerusalem, writes in *L'éternité par les astres*: "L'univers est une sphere dont le centre est partout et la surface nulle part" (37) ("the universe is a sphere whose center is everywhere and surface is nowhere"). However, we now know (thanks to the Touneur edition) that Pascal characterized that sphere as *effroyable*, a word that, through the *ex fragor* violence, exposes the fragility of the system, its fractures and fragments, its persistent resistances, and the folds in which its opposite is juxtaposed. We thus contend that through these Babelic fictions the Baroque gaze, mixed with the gaze of the undifferentiated and indiscriminate city, poses the question of the compatibility between divine infinity and the finite, substantialist, and medieval ontology of traditional thought. Even though the positions of many of these intellectuals–Tejeda, Valle y Caviedes, and Gregório de Matos, to mention the most representative ones–can be interpreted as conservative due to their adherence to the colonial regime, it would still be necessary to intervene in the debate between identity and citizenship by considering, along with Lacan, that although no religions are true, Christianity is the one closest to the truth insofar as, for most people, it does not advocate a life of contemplation or quietest knowledge, but the direct–and in these cases satirical–intervention that verifies that truth is breached, folded, and fragmented. The politics of the letter shows that, in truth, there are always two. Furthermore, by resorting to multiple referents and anachronism, the letter of politics is equally duplicitous.

At the gates of the Inferno Dante heard *orribili favelle*. Euclides da Cunha (1866–1909), as a correspondent accompanying the Army and witnessying the State's repression of Antonio Conselheiro and his celestial Jerusalem, described the complete and wanton destruction of this community, as well as the destruction of favela housing in Rio de Janeiro's slums. Carlos Drummond de Andrade (1902–1987) described this "Morro da Babilônia" [1941; "Babylon Hill"]:

À noite, do morro
descem vozes que criam o terror
(terror urbano, cinqüenta por cento de cinema
e o mais que veio de Luanda ou se perdeu
na língua geral)

At night, on the hill
voices descend that create terror
(urban terror, 50% cinema
plus whatever came from Luanda or got
lost in the general language)

(70)

Elisabeth Bishop (1911–1979), in her turn, verified in "The Burglar of Babylon" (1965) that

On the fair green hills of Rio
There grows a fearful stain:
The poor who come to Rio
and can't go home again.

. . .

There's the hill of Kerosene,
and the hill of Skeleton,
the hill of Astonishment,
and the hill of Babylon.

(132)

Even in the basement of a house belonging to the emerging Buenos Aires bourgeoisie, in Armando Discépolo's (1887–1971) *Babilonia* [1925; *Babylon*], pilgrims from various continents dream of making it in the big city. However, in this peripheral modernity, the image of the city as a utopian space of mixture turned out to be decisively and irreversibly shocked and silenced. To compensate for it, contemporary post-utopian eclecticism seems to realize perfectly the phantasmagoria of the Baroque gaze: a public sphere emptied out in the name of an increasingly privatized world, home to a catastrophic superposition of Babel and Babylon, labyrinth and barbarism.

Translation by Idelber Avelar

Works Cited

Acosta, José de. 1998. *Historia natural y moral de las Indias*. Ed. Antonio Quilis. Madrid: Ediciones de Cultura Hispánica.

Adorno, Theodore W. 1997. *Aesthetic Theory*. Ed. Gretel Adorno and Rolf Tiedemann. Trans. Robert Hullot-Kentor. Minneapolis: University of Minnesota Press.

Aires, Matias. 1761. *Reflexões sobre a vaidade dos homens*. Lisboa: Officina de Antonio Vicente da Silva.

Alberdi, Juan Bautista. 1886. *Organización de la Confederación Argentina*. *Obras completas*. Vol. 3. Buenos Aires: Imp. de "La Tribuna Nacional." 371–580.

Alvarenga Peixoto, Inacio José de. 1960. *Vida e obra de Alvarenga Peixoto*. Ed. Manuel Rodrigues Lapa. Rio de Janeiro: Instituto Nacional do Livro, Ministério da Educação e Cultura.

Andrade, Carlos Drummond de. 1983. *Nova reunião: 19 livros de poesia*. Rio de Janeiro: Livraria J. Olympio Editora em convênio com o Instituto Nacional do Livro, Fundação Nacional Pró-Memória.

Bertonio, Ludovico. 1879. *Arte de la língua aymará*. Facsimile ed. Leipzig: B. G. Teubner.

Bishop, Elizabeth. 1969. *The Complete Poems*. New York: Farrar Straus Giroux.

Blanqui, Louis Auguste. 1996. *L'éternité par les astres*. Paris: Editions Slatkine.

Borges, Jorge Luis. 1989. "Son los ríos." *Obras completas*. Vol. 3. Mexico City: Emece. 463.

Burton, Richard Francis. 1869. *Highlands of the Brazil*. London: Tinsley.

Camões, Luis de. 1963. *Babel e Sião*. Ed. Hernâni Cidade. Lisbon: Livraria Sá da Costa Editora.

———. 1984. *Sonetos*. Ed. Maria de Lourdes and José Hermano Saraviava. Mem Martins: Europa Lisboa América.

———. 1990. *Epic and Lyric*. Ed. L.C. Taylor. Trans. Keith Bosley. Manchester: Carcanet.

Clavijero, Francisco Javier. 1917. *Historia antigua de México*. Trans. J. Joaquin de Mora. Mexico City: Departamento Editorial de la Dirección General de las Bellas Artes.

Cunha, Euclides da. 1985. *Os sertões*. Ed. Walnice Nogueira Galvão. São Paulo: Editora Brasiliense.

Dante Alighieri. 1933. *Inferno*. Bilingual ed. Trans. Laurence Binyon. London: Macmillan.

Discépolo, Armando. 1970. *Giácomo. Babilonia. Cremona*. Buenos Aires: Talía.

Durán, Diego. 1867–1880. *Historia de las Indias de Nueva-España y islas de Tierra Firme*. Mexico City: Imprenta de J. M. Andrade y F. Escalante.

Gândavo, Pero de Magalhães. 1995. *Tratado da terra do Brasil*. Ed. Leonardo Dantas Silva. 2 vols. Recife: Fundação Joaquim Nabuco, Editora Massangana.

Góngora y Argote, Luis de. 1986. *Antología poética (Polifemo, Soledad primera, Fábula de Píramo y Tisbe, y otros poemas)*. Ed. Antonio Carreira. Madrid: Editorial Castalia.

Gutiérrez, Juan María. 1957. "Pedro de Peralta Barnuevo." *Escritores coloniales americanos*. Ed. Gregorio Weinberg. Buenos Aires: Editorial Raigal. 7–212.

Humboldt, Alexander von. 1814. *Researches, Concerning the Institutions and Monuments of the Ancient Inhabitants of America: With Descriptions and Views of Some of the Most Striking Scenes in the Cordilleras!* Trans. Helen Maria Williams. London: Longman, Hurst, Rees, Orme & Brown, J. Murray & H. Colburn.

Matos, Gregorio de. 1981. *Gregório de Matos*. Ed. Antônio Dimas. São Paulo: Abril Educação.

———. 1986. *Gregório de Matos*. Ed. Higino Barros. São Paulo: L & PM Editores Ltda.

Mendieta, Gerónimo de. 1973. *Historia eclesiástica indiana*. 2 vols. Ed. Francisco Solano y Pérez-Lila. Madrid: Biblioteca de Autores Españoles.

———. 1997. *Historia eclesiástica indiana: A Franciscan's View of the Spanish Conquest of Mexico*. Ed. and trans. Felix Jay. Lewiston: Edwin Mellen Press.

New Jerusalem Bible. 1985. London: Darton, Longman & Todd.

Orozco y Berra, Manuel. 1880. *Historia antigua y de la conquista de México*. 4 vols. Mexico City: Tipografía de Gonzalo A. Esteva.

Peralta Barnuevo, Pedro de. 1732. *Lima fundada o conquista del Perú: Poema heroico en que se decanta toda la historia*. Lima: Imprenta de Francisco Sobrino y Bados.

Pessoa, Fernando. 1941. *Mensagem*. Lisbon: Editorial Ática.

Prescott, William Hicking. 1856 [1843]. *History of the Conquest of Mexico: With a Preliminary View of the Ancient Mexican Civilization, and the Life of the Conqueror, Hernando Cortés*. Boston: Phillips, Sampson and Co.

Ripa, Cesare. 1970. *Iconologia: Overo descrittione di diverse imagini cavate dall' antichità, e di propria inventione*. Hildesheim: George Olms Verlag.

Santa Rita Durão, José de. 1945. *Caramuru: Poema épico do descobrimento da Bahia*. São Paulo: Edições Cultura.

Silva Alvarenga, Manuel Ignacio da. 1774. *O desertor: Poema heroi-comico*. Coimbra: Na Real Officina da Universidade.

Sousa, Gabriel Soares de. 1938. *Tratado descriptivo do Brasil em 1587*. Ed. Francisco Adolpho de Varnhagem. São Paulo: Companhia Editora Nacional.

Tejeda, Luis de. 1916. *El peregrino en Babilonia y otros poemas*. Buenos Aires: Librería La Facultad, J. Roldán.

Torquemada, Juan de. 1943. *Monarquía indiana*. Mexico City: Editorial Salvador Chavez Hayhoe.

Valle y Caviedes, Juan del. 1990. *Obra completa*. Ed. Daniel R. Reedy. Caracas: Biblioteca Ayacucho.

Veytia, Mariano. 1984. *Historia antigua de México*. Ed. Francisco Ortega. Mexico City: Editorial Leyenda.

Vieira, António. 1718. *História do futuro*. Lisbon: Antonio Pedrozo Galram.

CHAPTER 15

FRANCISCO XAVIER CLAVIJERO AND THE ENLIGHTENMENT IN MEXICO

José Emilio Pacheco

Pre-Hispanic civilizations flourished without any apparent connection with the rest of the world; Spain prohibited her colonies from having any dealings with other European countries; a nostalgia for the original primitive state and an uneasiness about the use of books (instruments that belong to all of humanity, yet which were regarded as articles of contraband) burdened those who tried to speak of a national culture in Latin America. In addition to these problematic issues there is the ubiquitous presence of what no one can escape: Anglo-American culture. Any attempt at analysis must begin with the colonial situation. In this regard, a comparison with the African experience is enlightening if we do not mechanically transfer its lessons to a different historical sphere. In his 1961 classic work on anticolonialism, *The Wretched of the Earth*, Frantz Fanon (1925–1961) defines national culture as "the sum of the efforts made by a people on an intellectual level, to describe, justify and glorify the actions by which the nation was formed and maintained" (214). Six years earlier, in *Guatemala, las líneas de su mano* [1955; Guatemala, the Lines of Its Hand], Luis Cardoza y Aragón (1904–1992) wrote a few lines that are as applicable to Mexico as to Guatemala:

> Tenemos una comunidad formada históricamente dentro de un territorio compartido sin sólida vinculación económica y cultural: hay inmensas mayorías que viven una economía casi neolítica que, por su número y arraigo, nos dan rasgos que expresan particularidades de lo que deberíamos llamar cultura nacional, como resultado de las condiciones de su existencia en el transcurso de los siglos. Esta situación no permite hablar, en propiedad, de una verdadera cultura nacional compartida, porque la cultura dominante es la de una muy escasa minoría semifeudal dueña de la tierra, con raíces antagónicas y metas diferentes de aquella de las inmensas mayorías explotadas colonialmente. Los rasgos nacionales los constituyen esta pugna, la prolongación de tal infamia. (184)

> We have a community historically formed within a shared territory without solid economic or cultural ties: There are a great many who live in an almost neolithic economy, and who, by virtue of their numbers and their roots, give us traits that express characteristics of what we should call a national culture, as a result of their existence through the centuries. This situation does not allow us rightfully to speak of a true, shared national culture, because the dominant culture is that of a small semi-feudal minority of landowners, with contrasting origins and different goals from those of the large, colonially exploited majority. This conflict, the continuation of such infamy, constitutes a national characteristic.

And in 1969, Leopoldo Zea (b. 1912) saw in the national culture

> así en en abstracto, sería un "mirlo blanco" de que hablaba González Casanova; pero un "mirlo blanco" que deja de serlo en cuanto esa cultura se concretiza, se expresa en obras, las que realiza un determinado hombre o, más ampliamente, un determinado pueblo. (8)

> an abstract term that would be that "impossible dream" about which Pablo González Casanova spoke: But an "impossible dream" (something indefinable and at the same time non-existent),

which ceases to be so once that culture is made concrete, is expressed in works, those of one specific man, or, in broader terms, of a specific people.

The three quotations from Fanon, Cardoza y Aragón, and Zea are sufficient evidence to demonstrate that the term "national culture" has undergone a process of semantic erosion: It means so many things that it no longer means anything. If we ask anthropologists or sociologists about the term, they will say that nothing like that exists in Mexico, that there are different specific cultures and subcultures, different modes of learned behavior. People without a great awareness of the hundreds of definitions of culture will take the part as meaning the whole; they will think of the arts, of science, of ideas; they will answer that, in effect, Mexico has a national culture that is able to include the works exhibited in the Museum of Anthropology, the murals, the architecture of the Viceroyalty, Teotihuacán, Palenque, Chichén Itzá, the poetry of Sor Juana Inés de la Cruz and Octavio Paz, the paintings and novels of the Revolution, the sugar skulls, the University City, the books of José Vasconcelos and Alfonso Reyes–all manifestations different from those of other Latin-American countries, each of which can present its own separate set of traits.

There are images of the past that we unconsciously accept as part of national culture, a *mestizo* culture (as defined from the *criollo* point of view), which may be the only means of unifying a plurality of ethnic groups and social classes. The bases of the national culture, in this limited sense of a *criollo* creation made prestigious by indigenous elements, were established by Francisco Xavier Clavijero (1731–1787). (See **Figure 1**.) His great work, the *Historia antigua de México* [1780–1781; *Ancient History of Mexico*] constituted the cornerstone of the vindication of the indigenous world–or, more precisely, the Aztec world–from the triple perspective of Catholicism, classical culture, and the modern culture of the eighteenth century. If, in accordance with David A. Brading's assessment, Clavijero expropriated the Indian past to serve *criollo* ideology (23), and thus contributed to the establishment of a national plan that, in the liberation of the oppressed, came to mean only a change of exploiters, its history served, in spite of everything, a liberating function that has not lost its usefulness, and which must be redeemed.

Clavijero is not responsible for the revolutionary uses to which his *Historia* was put. We can read it only from a contemporary viewpoint and try to understand it by putting ourselves in his place and time. Given the shadow that is presently cast over the Age of Enlightenment, it is easy to forget Clavijero: He was not radical enough; he did not give the same answers as Fanon or Guevara; he invented a rhetoric that has served to synthesize the races in the colony under the abstraction of *mestizo* and has thus perpetuated the oppression of the Indians. To challenge him in this way, however, would reveal a lack of critical acumen no less acute than that presented by a

Figure 1.

Francisco Javier Clavijero (1731–1787), c. 1755. (Archive of the author)

historical approbation of his views. In 1959, Fanon himself wrote against the custom of "minimizing the actions of our fathers, pretending a lack of comprehension in the face of their silence or passivity. They fought as they could, with the weapons they had at the time" (188).

Henry Miller (1891–1980) has said that the greatest misfortune ever to befall the white race took place on this continent. It was their refusal to fill the role that the aborigines expected when they welcomed them (xiii). Instead of a peaceful fusion that would have created a new world and a true *mestizo* culture, military violence brought about the disappearance of native religion, science, arts, writing, and above all, political institutions. The vastness of the territory and the resistance put up by many indigenous groups made it difficult for European culture to be transmitted in the way, for instance, that Roman culture had spread throughout Europe. Simply by virtue of transplantation, it was necessary to adapt the European ways to the new lands, and so the local traditions managed to survive in daily domestic life (Henríquez Ureña 25–26). This process of acculturation was described in 1957 by Gonzalo Aguirre Beltrán: The conquerors imposed those elements of their culture they considered capable of maintaining the permanent exploitation of human and natural resources. By means of political-religious control, an interdependence was created whereby the worst part always fell to the conquered peoples. With their cultures destroyed, the latter were tied to

their old world masters, prisoners of a feudal economy that levied charges (and taxes) against them and made it impossible for them to undertake commercial activities, for they were monopolized by the Spaniards. In addition, they were denied access to higher education, the priesthood, Spanish medicine, trade in Spanish goods, the use of Spanish clothing, houses of masonry and tile, Western food, horses, arms, and heraldry, and even the right to the Spanish designation of *don*. Thus, the Indians had available to them only those cultural elements that institutionalized their dependence and forced them into a collective system. But the contact unleashed reciprocal forces, and so there were native influences on the *mestizo* and Spanish cultures. The gendered nature of the dominant group—first only men and later a few peninsular women—brought about a racial mixture, and a cultural *mestizaje* was soon instituted that could not be stopped, even by all the measures taken to keep the domination uncontaminated: The Inquisition persecuted magic in much the same way as it did illicit union with Indian women.

The culture shock induced by the destruction of their traditional values led to an acute disorganization among the native ethnic groups. They suffered from demoralization, rejection, procrastination, and an apocalyptic fatalism—all of which helped prevent them from resisting the European diseases; a half-century after their meeting with the Europeans, they had been reduced to one-quarter of their original number and by the end of the century had reached the low point of one-tenth. A system was imposed that gave support (and continuity) to the small ruling group. Rigid in matters of religion and social control, the system was less strict about questions of economy, domestic and community organizations, education, language, and art. But in all respects, the Spanish were more satisfied with the native religious conversion on the level of form than of content. For this reason, the native cultures conserved many of their original elements. They had changed in appearance, but at heart, in their meaning and customs, they continued to be the same. They arrived at the twentieth century different from the pre-Columbian cultures from whence they had come, but different too from the European cultures and, to a lesser degree, from the *mestizo* (Aguirre Beltrán 1957, 27ff). (New points of view on this topic can also be found in the work of Pedro Carrasco, Alesandra Moreno Toscano, Andrés Lira and Luis Muro.) A few years after the work of Aguirre Beltrán, a significant study appeared that documents and confirms the steps of the acculturation process that must be taken into account along with the tragic truthfulness of the "black legend"—Charles Gibson's *The Aztecs Under Spanish Rule (1619–1810)* (1964). A chronicle dealing with the more contemporary situation has been written by Fernando Benítez in *Los indios de México* [(1967–1972) The Indians of Mexico]. Ricardo Pozas and Isabel Horcasitas de Pozas, in *Los indios en las clases sociales de México* [1971; Indians in Mexico's Social Classes], have written about native participation in national development.

During the first century of the colony's existence, the missionaries succeeded in transmitting European literary culture to some descendants of the conquered nobility, but without completely eclipsing their tradition. Such historians as Hernando Alvarado Tezózomoc, Diego Muñoz Camargo, and Juan Bautista Pomar helped to prevent the complete loss of this heritage. Nevertheless, a considerable number of texts were lost. Colonial interests triumphed before a *mestizo* figure comparable to the Inca Garcilaso de la Vega (1539–1616) could arise in New Spain. The great contribution of the Indians to the culture of New Spain was made manifest primarily through the imaginative skill as stone cutters and masons who enriched and modified the European architectural projects. Deprived of the voice that writing could give them, they had to entrust their defense to the peninsular priests and to the *criollos* and express their sensibility in the colonial buildings with which they filled the region.

For their part, the *criollos* used the Imperial tongue from the very beginning in order to protest against their position within the colonial political order. Heirs of the conquerors, dispossessed by the merchants coming from Europe to make themselves rich through the looting of a country they despised, the *criollos* wrote what appear to be the first Spanish verses written by someone born in the land that is today called Mexico. Francisco de Terrazas (circa 1524–1600) contemplated the "Llorosa Nueva España que deshecha,/te vas en llanto y duelo consumiendo" ("Tearful New Spain, destroyed,/consuming yourself in tears and sorrow"). He saw around him "miserias, hambre y pobreza" ("miseries, hunger, and poverty"), fruits of exploitation: "Si los más que te habitan son tratantes/que te agotan la sangre de las venas" ("Most of those who inhabit you are merchants/who suck the blood from your veins"). This is so because:

Madrastra nos has sido rigurosa
y dulce madre pía a los extraños;
con ellos de tus bienes generosa,
con nosotros repartes de tus daños.

You have been a stern stepmother to us
and a sweet kind mother to the foreigners;
you are generous to them with your goods,
with us you share your injuries.

Terrazas formed for himself a typical colonial relationship where the *criollo*, oppressor of the Indian and oppressed by the peninsular, was left out in the cold in no-man's land, but in some way remained linked with the fate of those who "con estrago y muerte/un número infinito que acabado" ("[were] with destruction and death/an infinite number wiped out"), or, if they survived, found themselves "en miseria y en afrenta" ("in misery and insulted") (Terrazas 85–87).

In 1954, Francisco López Cámara observed that, as part of their domination strategy, the Spaniards considered the *criollos* (theoretically Spanish Americans) to be inferior because of their original sin of having been born in America, and of having something of the Indian in them, if not in the blood then at least in customs and mentality. Divorcing the *criollos* from everything European, the Spaniards associated them with the conquered and vanquished Indian peoples. When the *criollos* finally became an autonomous social class, they entered into conflict with Spaniards from the peninsula, who had a political and social monopoly (24–26).

In 1971, Severo Martínez Pelaez analyzed certain elements in the case of Guatemala that are also applicable to New Spain:

Unos y otros tenían el propósito común de extraer el máximo de riqueza de la tierra a base del trabajo de los indígenas, y por eso se estorbaban. . . . Quiere decir, pues, que la ideología de clase de los criollos—el criollismo—no entrañaba únicamente fórmulas justificadoras de una situación de privilegio—prejuicios de superioridad–, sino también, y ésto reviste la mayor importancia para nuestro estudio, fórmulas veladas de ataque y defensa frente a lo español. . . . frente a indios, mestizos y mulatos, ellos eran

dominadores y explotadores en diversas formas; frente a las autoridades españolas eran parcialmente dominados aunque no explotados. . . . La idea de patria . . . es la patria del criollo. Es un producto ideológico de la lucha que sostenían los criollos con la madre patria, con España. Como cualquiera otra idea política, esta idea era la expresión de un complejo de intereses de clase que tenía su origen en una situación económica. Los criollos estaban defendiendo su patrimonio de herederos de la conquista, y ese patrimonio fue la base material de la que surgió entre ellos la idea de patria. (37–38, 43)

The common aim is to extract maximum riches from the earth using indigenous labor. As unsatisfied participants in the system of colonial exploitation, the *criollo* slowly develops a class ideology– *criollismo*–with feelings of superiority to justify his privileges and plans of attack and defense in the face of the Spanish. . . . in relation to Indians, *mestizos*, and mulattoes, the *criollos* are dominators and exploiters in various ways. In relation to the royal authorities, they, in turn, are dominated but not exploited. . . . The idea of homeland . . . was the homeland of the *criollos*, ideological product of the battle going on with Spain and which, as all political ideas, expresses a complex of class interests based on an economic situation. The *criollo* defends his patrimony as heir of the conquest. This patrimony is the base material from which arises in him the idea of country.

The *criollos* found their natural ideological apologists in the most learned sector: that of the Jesuits, who monopolized education and many productive branches in New Spain, and were the greatest developers of the haciendas and masters over the best administered and most flourishing properties of the viceroyalty (Florescano 85, 88, 90).

The eighteenth century opened for Spain with the ascent to the throne of the Bourbons and with the Treaty of Utrecht, which marked the end of Spanish authority in Europe. The riches from its American empire arrived in Europe by two routes: the monopolies of Cádiz and the English, Dutch, and French pirates. The mines of Mexico and Peru produced the riches that gave rise to capitalism, which in turn brought about the international division of labor–between the sites of raw material production and the industrial nations. As an intermediary, at first prospering from what it did not produce, Spain was suffocated by European economic expansion. Due to Spain's lack of industrial development, it was incapable of supplying its colonies; because of the actions of the monopolies, prices in America were double or triple those in the peninsula, and created favorable conditions not only for poverty and discontent, but also for smuggling and dishonesty–which corrupted all economic and administrative relations.

With the Bourbons, the Age of Enlightenment also arrived in Spain. A more reflective intelligencia came to realize that the vast and sudden arrival of bullion in Spain brought about the disastrous economic decline of the seventeenth century in a nation that was already stretched to its limits with the establishment and maintenance of its American empire. The negative impact of the exploitation of the Spanish-American gold and silver mines was also felt in political and moral terms. The wealth of the New World merely passed through Spain ending up with Spain's enemies in payment of the goods needed for the colonial enterprise that Spain, with its depleted manpower, could not produce. And in moral terms the "black legend" did not spare Spain the world's condemnation for the violent oppression of the Indian workers in the mines of Potosi and New Spain. The Hispanic version of the Age of Enlightenment rejected all anti-Christian ideas, as well as all political and social change. It was limited to the spreading of artistic and scientific news, to developing industry and commerce, and to promoting economic expansion. Improvements in education and training became anti-scholastic and anti-Aristotelian. The Age of Enlightenment was thus reduced in the Spanish Empire to a program of empirical reform. The political reforms in Spain increasingly aimed at linking America to Spain and making it a more productive source of riches and power (Humphreys and Lynch 10–11).

All the European powers exploiting the lands of the new continent took measures to get the best economic return from their domains. In the final analysis, such measures had the effect of speeding up independence in the north as well as in the south. Michèle Duchet's *Antropología e historia en el Siglo de las Luces* [1971; Anthropology and History in the Enlightenment] shows that the reforms effected in the colonies were an attempt to solve the problems of the system of slavery–the excessive mortality, the abortions, the passivity of the slaves–and to protect the slaveholders from a slave insurrection. By giving back to the slaves a small portion of their rights, it was hoped the tax on the duties owing to the crown would be obtained with greater assurance. The self-serving humanism of the Bourbons was based on the reports by colonial administrators. The object was to implement new means of exploitation that would reconcile humanitarian sentiment and self-interest. Thus was conceived a practice and a colonial ideology that offered to bourgeois humanitarian sentiments an alternative solution.

In 1762, the English took possession of Manila and Havana, the fortress guarding the transfer of silver from Mexico. In 1763, the Seven Year War ended in the Treaty of Paris, which relegated Spain to a new lower status as a third-rate power. The reign of Carlos III (or the political policy enacted in his name and used to describe the actions of the Spanish enlightened, such as Aranda, Campomanes, Florídablanca and Jovellanos) began with the royal decree of 16 October, 1765, initiating the period known as the Bourbon reforms. New Spain attained her Golden Age and became the principal colony of the empire. The reforms gave rise to three processes:

> un rapidísimo crecimiento económico que descoyunta las estructuras sociales forjadas a través de un siglo de lento reacomodo y hace más evidentes las desigualdades existentes; una inflexibilidad casi total de la fábrica política y social para dar cabida a los nuevos grupos y absorber las contradicciones y expectativas creadas por el proceso anterior; y una difusión también acelerada de las ideas de la modernidad que le darán fundamento a los grupos marginados para proyectar y racionalizar sus reivindicaciones. No es un azar que el área de El Bajío y Michoacán, que experimentó el mayor crecimiento económico, concentró el número más alto de criollos y albergó a los focos más avanzados de renovación intelectual, haya sido la matriz de la insurrección que encabezó Hidalgo.
> (Florescano and Gil Sánchez 301)

> a very rapid economic growth that throws out of kilter the social structures, forged over a century of slow rearrangement, and makes the existing inequalities more evident; an almost total inflexibility on the part of the social and political fabric to make room for the new groups and absorb the contradictions and expectations created by the previous process; and an accelerated diffusion of the ideas of modernity that supplied marginal groups with a base for projecting and rationalizing their claims. It was no accident that the area of Bajío and Michoacán, which experienced the greatest economic growth, had the greatest concentration of *criollos*, and housed the most advanced centers of intellectual restoration, was to be the seat of the insurrection led by Hidalgo.

The *Compañía de Jesús* (i.e., Jesuits) was an international organization that extended to three continents and was composed of members from all of the European countries and the American colonies. Their obedience to the Vatican put them in conflict with the Bourbon "enlightened despotism." Philosophers saw the Jesuits as representatives of the obscurantist spirit, which had to be combated before the Enlightenment of that century could descend upon humanity. The Jesuits were also accused of being conspirators and economically self-sufficient. The brilliance and dedication of the company aroused jealousy and resentment even among the clergy, who, with few exceptions, longed for the removal of their most important rivals. This campaign triumphed and the Jesuit order was suppressed in Portugal (1759), France (1764), and Spain and her possessions (1767); it was dissolved in 1773 and restored in 1814. In Latin America, the Jesuits constituted the primary cultural body and one of the greatest economic and political powers, whose interests began to overlap with those of the *criollo* class. Even before obtaining the approval of Pope Clement XIV, Charles III ordered the confiscation and liquidation of Jesuit possessions; their riches passed into the hands of the landed establishment and were incorporated into the regular economy. For this reason, it was in the interest of the property holders to maintain a gulf between themselves and the Jesuits.

But the Jesuits were the teachers of the *criollo* society: Their missions and colleges constituted the highest-ranking intellectual and educational centers in New Spain. Their expulsion was a political measure that had a variety of consequences. It disturbed Latin American intellectuals so much that historians consider it to be one of the decisive preludes to the movement toward emancipation. Hundreds of *criollo* families with sons and brothers in the *Compañía* were affected, and almost all *criollos* considered the expulsion an atrocious injustice that diminished their loyalty and respect for the crown. One concrete example of the despotism against which it was essential for them to rebel was the famous edict from the viceroy Marquis de Croix (26 July 1767) in which the exile of the Jesuits was justified as a means of maintaining a subordinate nation whose inhabitants "nacieron para callar y obedecer y no para discurrir, ni opinar en los altos asuntos del gobierno" (León Portilla et al 358) ("were born to keep quiet and obey, and not to think about or offer opinions on high matters of government").

The Marquis Charles François de Croix (1699–1786) was born in Belgium and during his adolescence became a lieutenant in the Guardias Valonas under Felipe V, the first Bourbon king of Spain, and the one who had to accept the independence of the Low Countries from Spain. Croix participated in the Spanish wars with Italy and Africa and gained the confidence of the future Carlos III when the latter was simply the king of the Two Sicilies. In 1741 Croix joined a military freemasons lodge, but we cannot attribute to freemasonry the future expulsion of the Jesuits, for that was done for reasons of state. While he was Captain General of Galicia, Croix was summoned by Carlos III to become the viceroy of New Spain, with the specific mission of expelling the Compañía de Jesús. Because of his military experience and his enlightened ideas, the king considered his friend Croix to be invulnerable to corruption and thus the most suitable administrator for carrying out martial and administrative reforms in the colony. A letter from the ambassador in Madrid to Louis XV suggests the possibility that Croix, without impairing his services to the Spanish Crown, may also have been an agent of French politics (introduced into New Spain to counter the ambitions of England). As viceroy (1766–1771), Croix reorganized finances, combated bureaucratic immorality, crushed the pro-Jesuit rebellion at Guanajuato, created the Legion of San Carlos for the purpose of repressing the insurrections of the miners, and, with the visitor José de Gálvez, recruited the *criollo* militia, which, as time passed, became the core of the insurgent army's officers.

The ideas and books of the Enlightenment reached New Spain with the Central European Jesuits. Teaching science and modern philosophy, the Jesuits changed the worldview held by the *criollo* elite. Interest in knowledge itself was replaced by the study of its practical applications and the search for rationality and efficiency in economic production. The Jesuits introduced the idea of progress, but, to make progress possible, it was necessary to be familiar with its nature before exploiting it. Intellectual work, which had previously been almost exclusively literary, in the New Spanish eighteenth century became oriented towards other fields. At the same time, the Jesuits expressed the philanthropic sentiment of the Enlightenment, which was related to the missionary traditions that were comparatively more favorable to the indigenous peoples than to the autocratic thinking of the Spanish authorities. Their theories of popular sovereignty turned out to be contrary to the absolutism of Carlos III. Consequently, not only were their huge properties confiscated, but the circulation of their doctrines was also prohibited. Of the close to 2,000 Jesuits expelled from Spanish America, about 600 came from New Spain, among them 450 *criollos*. Many were old men, but among the exiles was also found the most brilliant intellectual generation produced by the viceroyalty: Francisco Xavier Clavijero (1731–1787), Francisco Xavier Alegre (1729–1788), Andrés Cavo (1739–1803), Andrés de Guevara y Basoazábal (1748–1801), Pedro José Márquez (1741–1820), Manuel Fabri (1737–1805), Juan Luis Maneiro (1744–1802), to name only the "Humanistas del siglo XVIII" (Humanists of the Eighteenth Century) assembled by Gabriel Méndez Plancarte in his 1941 anthology of that name.

Clavijero was born in Veracruz on 6 September, 1731, the son of Blas Clavijero, a Spaniard from León who had studied in Paris, and Isabel Echegaray, a *criolla* of Basque descent. His father served as mayor in predominantly indigenous regions such as Teziutlán and Jicayán in Mixteca. From childhood, Clavijero had contact with the natives of the country and learned their language. At the age of sixteen he entered the Jesuit novitiate at Tepozotlán, perhaps because only the Church in New Spain could offer an appropriate environment for his intellectual calling. He was a professor in Puebla, Valladolid (Morelia), Guadalajara, and San Ildefonso in the city of Mexico. Another Jesuit, Rafael Campoy, showed him the codices and documents of Mexican antiquities deposited by Carlos de Sigüenza y Góngora (1645–1700) in the convent of San Pedro y San Pablo. In addition to his work in the field of library research, Clavijero studied Descartes, Leibnitz, and Newton, renewed the teaching of philosophy and science, wrote a course in Physics (now lost but believed to be his fundamental work), taught the Indians, in Nahuatl, at the college of San Gregorio, and with his Spanish reading and his knowledge of classical and modern languages, forged for himself a style that was (according to his biographer, Juan Luis Maneiro) "enteramente seguro, simple, grave, que fluía fácilmente, más cercano a lo conciso, no mezclado de afectación, sino lleno de dignidad y hermoso con sencillez" (131)

("completely sure, uncomplicated, serious, which flowed easily, predominantly concise, unencumbered by affectation, but filled with dignity and beautiful in its simplicity"). When Clavijero established himself in Bologna, after some time in Ferrara, all factors were favorable for the writing of his *Historia antigua de México* [1780–1781; History of Ancient Mexico].

According to the Aristotelian tradition defended by Juan Ginés de Sepúlveda (1490–1573) against Fray Bartolomé de las Casas (1474–1566), barbarism–that is, the lack of culture– made the Indians slaves by nature, and it was therefore just and necessary for the Spaniards to subjugate them. Since their religion came to be seen as demonic by the Spaniards, the Conquest acquired the characteristics of a new Crusade: Spreading the Christian faith morally justified all of the violence (Hanke 46–61). The Franciscan Juan de Torquemada (1557?–1664), in his *Monarquía indiana* [1615; Indigenous Monarchy], defended the humanity of the American Indian. He denied their savagery, although not the demonic character of their religion; he drew an analogy between aboriginal and Roman antiquity; he interpreted the Conquest in terms of providentiality and millenarianism–in order to neutralize Las Casas' criticism. Above all he proclaimed the missionaries, not the conquistadores, to be the true founders of New Spain.

Miguel León Portilla has published a critical edition of the *Monarquía indiana* and prior to this, in 1969, wrote an introduction to the second of the three volumes of the facsimile edition, and even earlier, published an anthology of selections from the *Monarquía indiana*. The vindication of Torquemada was begun by Alejandra Moreno Toscano's *Fray Juan de Torquemada y su "Monarquía indiana"* [1963; Juan de Torquemada's "Indian Monarchy"]. Like all historians, Torquemada had freely at his disposal the material accumulated by his predecessors. Clavijero, in turn, relied on him more perhaps than on any other author. However, the claim that Clavijero plagiarized *La monarquía indiana* seems exaggerated. Charles E. Ronan formulates this charge against him in his 1973 article "Francisco Javier Clavijero, 1731–1787." Of course, in the eighteenth century, there was none of the acute consciousness of copyright that exists today, especially in North America. Clavijero declared on the frontispiece of the first edition that his *Historia* had been unearthed from "los mejores historiadores españoles y de los manuscritos y de las pinturas antiguas de los indios" ("the best Spanish historians, the manuscripts and ancient paintings of the Indians").

In spite of a vast social and economic gulf that separated the indigenous population and the *criollo* clergy, they were united in their veneration of the Virgin of Guadalupe. Before acquiring a *mestizo* identity, she had been Tonantzin, the goddess of life on earth. Our Lady of Guadalupe conferred an autonomous spiritual base on the church of New Spain and made the country a privileged one in the Catholic sphere; if she justified the Conquest as an undertaking destined to make possible her appearance in Tepeyac, she also affirmed the rights of the *criollos* in the face of Spanish privilege (Brading 12–14). Sigüenza y Góngora, an intellectual who, like Sor Juana Inés de la Cruz (1648–1695), is a forerunner of the *criollo* mentality of the eighteenth century, began to retrieve the indigenous religion from its consignment to the infernal powers: Developing a hypothesis of the Peruvian Antonio de la Calancha (1584–1654), he identified Quetzalcoatl with the apostle Saint Thomas. Masters of a classical past governed by a natural religion and of a Christian present inspired by the Virgin of Guadalupe, *criollos* were freed of their Hispanic origins

(Brading 14). An Indian uprising was an ever-present threat in the colony; few had ever witnessed an uprising and still fewer in the capital of the viceroyalty. Sigüenza y Góngora understood that if the *criollos* did not take the lead in the future revolt, the storm would destroy them (145–54).

The *Historia antigua de México* builds upon this underground tradition to give to *criollo* thought its master work and to Fray Servando Teresa de Mier (1763–1827) and Carlos María de Bustamante (1774–1848) the point of departure for their elaboration of the theory of Mexican nationalism. There are various treatises within this one text: a historical, polemical, geographical, geological, climatological, mineralogical, botanical, zoological, characteriological, anthropological, ethnographic, theological, juridical, sociological, educational, economic, artistic, literary, linguistic, architectural, medical, and calendrical, as well as a political treatise. As with all Hispanic literature of the late fifteenth century to the early nineteenth, Clavijero's book was written in the face of the censorship of the Inquisition. *The Storia antica del Messico, cavata da' migliori storici spagnuoli e de' manuscritti e dalle pitture antiche degl'indiani; divisa in dieci libri e corredata de carte geografiche e di varie figure e dissertazioni sulla terra, sugli animali e sugli abitatori del Messico, opera dell' abate D. Francesco Saverio Clavigero* [1780–1781; The History of Mexico, Collected from Spanish and Mexican Historians, from Manuscripts, and Ancient Paintings of the Indians; Together with the Conquest of Mexico by the Spaniards, with Critical Dissertations on the Land, Animals, and Inhabitants of Mexico] appeared originally in its author's Italian version; the four volumes were printed by Gregorio Biasini (Cesena). It was translated into English, German, and other European languages. It first became known in the Spanish-speaking world through the translation by José Joaquín de Mora (London and Mexico, 1826). This translation was subsequently published in Jalapa Mexico in 1868 by A. Ruiz and in Mexico City by Dirección General de Bellas Artes (1917) but it was not widely disseminated in Mexico until 1945 in the Colección de Escritores Mexicanos by Porrúa. It is the text invariably quoted in this article, except where the "Disertaciones" is used; the original Spanish manuscript has been lost, as has almost all of Clavijero's work. Pablo González Casanova has said that:

> La Inquisición es un supuesto de la cultura española y no se le puede entender si no se advierte que es una burocracia más que una filosofía. La represión administrativa y física que ejerce es quizás de menor significado que la represión ideológica, ética y metafísica. (131)

> The Inquisition is the exercise of power in Spanish culture and it cannot be understood if one is not aware that it is a repressive bureaucracy more than a philosophy. The administrative and physical repression it exercises is perhaps less important than the ideological, ethical, and metaphysical repression.

The violence perpetrated by the crown–in the form of banishment, the visible manifestation of despotism,–converted the king into an enemy of the *Compañía de Jesús*, as well as of the papacy and the rest of the Catholic Church. Clavijero's loyalties no longer lay with the Spanish throne, but with his ethnic group, his class. But he continued to belong to the *Compañía*, which, although formally dissolved, maintained a spiritual existence. Clavijero tried to reconcile the concrete interests of *criollismo* with the orthodoxy of his

religion. He aspired to be read throughout that country to which he restored the status it had the day preceding the conquest: He recognized the legitimacy of the Aztecs; he omitted the other peoples (probably, at least in part, because his scientific scruples prevented him from speaking about matters of which he had no direct knowledge), and called his land *México*, not New Spain. He drew up a list of the country's riches for his compatriots, whom he referred to as *mis nacionales* (p. xxii). That is, he suggested that *criollos* take command of what can be exploited and expropriated in nature (Villoro 1963, 549). This appears to be the common preoccupation of the exiled Jesuits; even Rafael Landívar's *Rusticacio Mexicana*, a poem in Latin verse, can be considered an economic description. The expulsion converted the colonial hell into a "paradise lost"–to which the Jesuits could not return, yet which was completely recoverable for their *criollo* brothers. The attributes of the Golden Age were appropriated by the remote colony and by her indigenous antiquity. Everything that the adversary–the European–tried to impose as a stigma of inferiority was transformed by a dialectical operation into a reason for pride.

The *Historia* was the Mexican "Encyclopedia" of the eighteenth century. Through it, New Spain finally joined the Golden Age, and its author took the lead in the New World Enlightenment. It is true that his original intention was to compile his material in dictionary form. Later, on the advice of a friend–apparently his future biographer Maneiro–Clavijero decided to put it into the form of an essay and historical narration. The paradox of the encyclopedist was to be part of the enlightened vanguard in the New World and to be at the same time a Jesuit priest; the Enlightenment implied a secular vision of the universe and of society based on a new natural science and a new natural law. He wrote his *Historia* from Europe, after the shock of meeting the dominant, ethnocentric culture, and was in a polemic with precisely the thinking of the European enlightened; he defended the Spaniards against their protestant enemies and the Spanish Americans–the term that brings together *criollos*, Indians, and blacks–against the colonial power of the Spanish; he offered the Indian a complicit view of their subjugation, which they could not read, and a plan, also complicit, which, if carried out, would divest the colonial society of its very foundations.

Luis Villoro's 1950 study has served as a basis for those who have subsequently dealt with Clavijero. Villoro considers the *Historia* to be the first American attack against the arrogance of the Europeans–a rebellion against the archetype of Europe's purported ethnic superiority. The dominated become the accusers against the dominant power and utilize the same code that sought to enslave them. Security replaces inferiority, and, in the *Historia* (where all supernatural dimensions seem to have disappeared), Clavijero provides an epic, heroic vision; he judges the Conquest from the perspective of the indigenous peoples and presents them with a classic model capable of being followed by any rational person:

> La misma Europa es, pues, la causa de lo que le echa en cara a América. La organización política creada por España en el nuevo continente es responsable de la accidental inferioridad del indio. El ideal pedagógico de Clavijero entraña así necesariamente un inconsciente ideal político. No adivinamos acaso aquí las ideas fundamentales de la emancipación americana? (Villoro 1963, 115)

> Europe herself is responsible for that with which she reproaches America. The political organization created by Spain on the new continent is responsible for the accidental inferiority of the Indian. Clavijero's pedagogical ideal (education as the sole

salvation of the indigenous people) of necessity carries within it an unconscious political ideal. Can we not perhaps perceive here the fundamental ideas of the American emancipation?

In effect, as has been illustrated, Clavijero sees in ignorance the source of all evil. He has an absolute faith in education and insists on the necessity of spreading teaching everywhere. In a paragraph referring to the Indians and not to the *criollos*, he affirms

> las almas de los americanos no son en nada inferiores a las de los europeos; que son capaces de todas las ciencias, aun de las más abstractas, y que si seriamente se cuidase de su educación; si desde niños se instruyesen en seminarios, bajo la dirección de buenos maestros, y si fuesen protegidos y estimulados con premios, se verían entre ellos filósofos, matemáticos y teólogos que podrían revalizar con los más famosos de Europa. Pero es harto difícil, por no decir imposible, hacer grandes progresos en las ciencias en medio de una vida miserable y servil, y bajo el peso de continuos males. (2: 365)

> that the souls of Mexicans are in no way inferior to those of Europeans; that they are capable of all the sciences, even the most abstract ones, and if their education were attended to, if from childhood they were raised in seminaries under good teachers, and if they were protected and encouraged with prizes, they would be found among the American philosophers, mathematicians, and theologians who could compete with the most famous ones in Europe. But it is very difficult, if not impossible, to make progress in the sciences while surrounded by a miserable, servile life and constant ills.

In Clavijero's view Europeans have had no greater advantage over the Mexicans than that of being better educated. That is to say that, as indicated by Antonello Gerbi, the obstacle that impedes development is not natural but social: "Not stupidity, but poverty: 'It is very difficult, not to say impossible, to make great progress in learning in the midst of a wretched and servile life and continued discomforts'" (204). The negative features of their character, he claims, can be corrected through education. Clavijero does not hide the fact that his objective is the defense of

> los propriamente americanos, que son los más injuriados y los más indefensos. Si a esta tarea me indujese alguna pasión o interés, me hubiera encargado más bien de la causa de los criollos, que, además de ser la más fácil, es la que más de cerca me toca. He nacido de padres españoles y no he tenido la menor afinidad ni consanguinidad con indios, ni espero el menor galardón de su miseria. Así que, sólo el amor a la verdad y el celo en favor de la especie humana, me hace abandonar la causa propia y abrazar la ajena, con menos peligro de errar. (2: 339–40)

> the rightful Americans (the Indians) as they are the ones most slandered and with the fewest defenses. If, on writing this history, I was moved by some passion or self-interest, it would have been the defense of the *criollo*, since, in addition to being much easier, it would be of more personal interest. I was born of Spanish parents and have no affinity with or blood relationship to the Indians; nor can I expect any reward from them, given their poverty. Thus, there is no motive behind my history other than love of truth and ardor for humanity, which has moved me to abandon my own cause to defend that of others.

In his defense of the Indians, Clavijero judges them superior to the blacks and the orientals, using arguments that suffer from the same racism of which he accuses the Europeans (2: 344) and that contrast with the sympathy showed by Francisco Xavier Alegre (55–57) towards the Africans in America. In spite of it all, Clavijero admits to the "gran talento y de la capacidad de los mulatos para toda clase de ciencias" (2: 364)

("great talent and capabilities of the mulattoes for the learning of all the sciences"), and far from closing his eyes to the actual situation of the Indians, he clearly says of them

> son los verdaderos labradores; ellos son los que aran, siembran, escardan y siegan el trigo, el maíz, el arroz, las habas, las habichuelas y todos los otros granos y legumbres; ellos los que cultivan el cacao, la vainilla, el algodón, el añil y todas las plantas útiles al sustento, al vestido y al comercio de aquellas provincias. Sin su ministerio no se hace nada. . . . Aun puedo decir algo más: ellos son los que cortan y transportan de los bosques toda la leña y madera que se consume; ellos los que cortan, transportan y elaboran la piedra; ellos los que hacen la cal, el yeso y los la drillos. Ellos son los que construyen todos los edificios de aquellos pueblos . . . ellos son los que abren y componen los caminos; los que limpian las ciudades; los que trabajan en las innumerables minas de plata, oro, cobre y otros metales . . . . en una palabra, ellos son los que llevan todo el peso de los trabajos públicos, como es notorio a cuantos han estado en aquellas regiones. Esto hacen los débiles, flojos e inútiles americanos, mientras el vigoroso Mr. de Pauw y otros infatigables europeos se ocupan en escribir contra ellos amargas invectivas. (2: 351)

> they are the ones who work the land, the ploughmen, the sowers, weeders, and harvesters of the wheat, corn, rice, coffee beans, beans, and other grains and vegetables; they cultivate the cacao, vanilla, cotton, indigo, and all the other plants useful for nourishment, clothing, and commerce of those provinces, and without them, nothing can be done . . . . But that is still little: They are the ones who cut down and clear all the necessary wood from the forest; the ones who cut, transport, and dress the stones, and the ones who make the lime, plaster, and bricks. They are the ones who construct all the buildings in that kingdom . . . . They are the ones who open and build roads, the ones who make the canals and dams, and the ones who clean the cities. They work in many gold, silver, copper, and other mines. In a word, they are the ones who carry the entire weight of the public works, as is well known in all those provinces. This is done by the weak, lazy, useless Americans, while the vigorous [Cornelius de] Pauw and other indefatigable Europeans are busy writing invectives against them.

What alarms Clavijero is that, through ignorance or lack of thinking, many Spaniards and *criollos* share a contempt for the indigenous peoples; he is indignant over the charge of cowardice levied against the Aztecs, and he affirms that Tenochtitlán was not conquered through lack of heroism on the part of its defenders but rather because of internal divisions and the superiority of European arms (2: 366–67).

The anti-colonial treatise implicit in the *Historia* exalts the shining aboriginal past in order to contrast it with the degradation of the present. Colonial destruction acquires its true significance in comparison with classical antiquity when Texcoco was the Athens of the Anahuac and Nezahualcoyotl the Solon of those peoples (1: 202). The order and harmony of the cities was far superior to that of ancient Europe, but the Spaniards left almost nothing standing. The conquest of Tenochtitlan ended on 13 August 1521, 196 years after the city was founded by the Aztecs. The destruction of the city has been compared to the destruction of Jerusalem in the demolition of the most magnificent buildings of Mexican antiquity. The siege had lasted seventy-five days. The utter destruction of the city is partially explained by the religious fanaticism of the Spaniards and in part by their urgent need to use the stone to erect their own buildings. It is only in the testimony of the soldiers who destroyed the magnificent residences and gardens that we have notice of what was, for the beauty of these architectural accomplishments have disappeared without a trace (2: 203). Clavijero takes great pains to demonstrate, through documentation, that the ancient Mexicans had a culture, that they did not live in a natural state (and it was therefore neither just nor necessary to conquer them), but rather were outstanding in their religion, economy, and policing (policing in the sense of good order, which is observed and guarded in the most advanced cities and republics, in accordance with laws and ordinances established for their better government).

To know which one of all the definitions of culture Clavijero had in mind, it is useful to consult the twenty-first edition (1992–1994) of the Real Academia Española's *Diccionario de la lengua Española* (1726), which still reflects the mentality of Bourbon Spain where it began to take shape. Culture is "el resultado o efecto de cultivar los conocimientos humanos y de afinarse por medio del ejercicio de las facultades intelectuales del hombre" (624) ("the result or effect of cultivating human knowledge and of refining, through exercise, the human intellectual faculties"). The (pre-) anthropologist in Clavijero leads him to work out a still fuller concept in which culture covers all that humanity generates in its domination of nature, all that separates it from the ethnocentric notion of barbarism and draws it closer to the paradigm of Greco-Roman antiquity. Consulting the entry on nation, we note that the first and fourth definitions in the *Diccionario* present significant shades of meaning that illuminate Clavijero's usage. Nation can mean the whole group of inhabitants of a country ruled by the same government, including *criollos*, Indians, and other races. But as a term meaning a group of persons with the same ethnic origin, who generally speak the same language and who have a common tradition, it can be applied only to the *criollos*–Mexicans not by blood but by nation in the sense that they were born in the land that Clavijero refuses to continue calling New Spain.

As a Catholic, he cannot justify the Aztec religion; however, it does not seem as cruel, superstitious, and childish to him as the religion of the ancient Greeks and Romans, the founders of the Western world (2: 451, 453). Nor does he neglect to condemn the human sacrifices (2: 457). He alleges, on the other hand, that, like all the cultured peoples of the world, the Mexicans had temples and believed in a Supreme Being and in the immortality of souls (2: 377). In the Sixth Treatise, where he takes on the diatribes of Cornelius de Pauw (1739–1799) against the culture of the Aztecs, Clavijero reminds his antagonist that the European nations were also at some time in their history uncivilized, barbarian, and savage, while, when the Europeans discovered them, the peoples of Anahuac and Peru

> reconocían un Ser Supremo y Omnipotente, aunque su creencia era, como la de otros muchos pueblos idólatras, un tejido de errores y supersticiones. Tenían, sin embargo, un sistema fijo de religión; sacerdotes, templos y sacrificios; ritos encaminados al culto uniforme de la Divinidad. Tenían reyes, gobernadores y magistrados; ciudades y poblaciones tan grandes y tan bien ordenadas como haré ver en otra Disertación. Tenían leyes y costumbres de cuya observancia cuidaban las autoridades públicas. Ejercían el comercio y se esmeraban en hacer respetar la equidad y la justicia en sus tratos. Sus tierras estaban distibuidas y aseguradas a cada uno la propiedad y la posesión de su terreno. Practicaban la agricultura y las otras artes, no sólo las necesarias a la vida, sino también las de deleite y lujo. (2: 377–78)

recognized a supreme and omnipotent being, even if their belief was, like that of other idolatrous nations, corrupted by a thousand errors and superstitions. They had a system of religion, priests, temples, sacrifices, and rites organized to ensure worship of the divinity. They had a king, governors, and magistrates; they had many large and well-ordered cities and towns, as I will show in another Treatise. They had laws and customs watched over by magistrates and governors; they had trade and were very careful about equity and justice in their contracts; they had their lands distributed and each owner was assured of his rights to and possession of his territory; they practiced agriculture and other arts, not only those necessary to life, but even those that serve only the senses and promote luxury.

Clavijero describes in detail the Aztec social organization and praises it, but he directs his greatest tribute to the Mexican language, capable of allowing the flourishing of orators and poets so excellent that he claimed that even amidst the humiliation they suffered and the almost complete lack of instruction in their own language, which they had previously received, they were still able to exhibit such good reasoning and such moving poetry that they astonished everyone who heard them. Their culture manifested itself as well in the theater, in dance, and in the plastic arts. It was imperfect but admirable, and it was destroyed before it had a chance to develop. For Clavijero's neoclassical taste, the Aztecs created monstrous and deformed sculptures; however, that in no way justified the inference that Mexicans lacked artistic talent:

> Pero aun concediendo a Mr. de Paw que la industria de los americanos en sus artes sea inferior a la de los otros pueblos del mundo, nada debe inferirse de aquí contra las calidades mentales de aquellos pueblos. (2: 406)

> But even conceding to Mr. Paw (sic Pauw) that the artistic creation of Americans (native Mexicans) might be inferior to that of other peoples in the world, it should not be inferred from this that there was any deficiency in the mental capacity of these people.

Books VIII, IX, and X, the best in the work, offer a history of the Conquest based on Spanish sources, but favorable, nevertheless, to the Aztecs. As much as Clavijero justifies the undertaking of the Conquest in the name of Divine Providence, which gave Spaniards the mission of being an instrument of justice and mercy to those nations, punishing the few for their superstition and cruelty and illuminating the many others with the light of the Gospel, it seemed to him a disastrous example of divine justice because the indigenous peoples, in spite of the prudent laws of the Catholic monarchs, were cast into the most abject poverty, oppression, and contempt:

> Los mexicanos, con todas las naciones que contribuyeron a su ruina quedaron, a pesar de las cristianas y humanísimas disposiciones de los Reyes Católicos, abandonados a la miseria, a la opresión y al desprecio, no solo de los españoles, sino también de los más viles esclavos africanos . . . castigando Dios, en la miserable posteridad de aquellos pueblos la injusticia, la crueldad y la superstición de sus antepasados: ¡horrible ejemplo de la justicia divina y de la instabilidad de los reinos de la tierra! (2: 204)

> The Mexicans with all the (Indian) nations that contributed to their downfall ended up, despite the most Christian and humane dictates of the Catholic Monarchs (Fernando and Isabella), abandoned to misery, oppression, and scorn not only of the Spaniards but even of the lowest of African slaves . . . God's punishment on the miserable posterity of these peoples for the injustice, cruelty, and superstition of their ancestors: a horrible example of Divine justice and of the instability of the kingdoms of this world!

The nine treatises that end the *Historia antigua de México* constitute an argument by *criollo* Enlightenment against European Enlightenment, personified by Jean Louis Leclerc, Count of Buffon (1707–1788), Guillaume-Thomas Raynal (1713–1796), William Robertson (1721–1793) and above all, the abbot Cornelius de Pauw (1739–1799), author of the *Recherches philosophiques sur les Américains, ou mémoires intéressants pour servir à l'histoire de l'espèce humain* (1768; Philosophic Research on the American Peoples or Interesting Memoirs to Inform the History of the Human Race). The great capabilities for polemic in the *Compañía de Jesús* are put to use in an ironic and devastating denunciation of Eurocentrism. In classical Jesuitical form he argued that

> Si algún filósofo de Guinea emprendiese una obra por el estilo de la de Mr. de Paw, con el título de "Recherches Philosophiques sur les européens" (Indagaciones filosóficas sobre los europeos) podría valerse del mismo argumento para censurar el clima de Europa y las ventajas del de Africa. . . .) Qué son el caballo y el buey, los mayores de sus animales, comparados con nuestros elefantes, con nuestros rinocerontes. (2: 273–74)

> If any philosopher in Africa were to undertake a study of Europeans based on de Pauw's thinking, he would be able to demonstrate the unhealthy nature of the Northern European climate and the advantages of that of Africa. . . . He could also point out that while the horse and ox are the largest European animals, when compared with elephants, rhinoceroses, they are insignificant.

To refute the view that all in the New World is inferior, Clavijero gives a portrayal of the natural "prodigiosa fertilidad de su suelo" (2: 284) ("prodigious fertility of those lands"), which have an advantage even over European lands in relation to their animals, plants, and fruits (2: 287). If America had no wheat, "El maíz se cultiva en Europa; pero es mucho más pequeño, y de inferior calidad que el de América" (2: 287) ("the corn cultivated in Europe is much smaller and of inferior quality").

Clavijero demonstrates the superiority of his own scientific knowledge in drawing up a list of the species confused by or unknown to the naturalist Buffon (2: 334–37). Clavijero's best argument (and his greatest advantage over his adversaries) is his first-hand experience. Thus he answers de Pauw that while he himself learned the Mexican tongue among the Indians, and heard it spoken for many years, de Pauw never left his study in Berlin and has no right to believe that he knows more about America than the Americans themselves; nor does his knowledge of the aboriginal tongues exceed that of those like Clavijero, who speak them fluently (2: 408): "Reconozca, pues, su error Mr. de Paw, y aprenda a no decidir en las materias que ignora" (2: 414) ("Paw should therefore recognize his error, and learn not to make decisions in matters of which he has no knowledge"). If there is no opposition he can offer to de Pauw's condemnation of human sacrifice, Clavijero states that the same denunciation can be made of institutional torture practised in Europe by the authorities during the eighteenth century. And, even so, the Mexican laws were less cruel than those of the Greeks and Romans (2: 421).

The purpose of the treatises–to prove scientifically the culture and rationality of the Indians–is summarized at the end of the sixth one:

> Este es un breve, pero verdadero ensayo de la cultura de los habitantes de Anáhuac, sacada de su historia antigua, de sus pinturas, de las relaciones de los más fidedignos y exactos historiadores

> españoles. Así se gobernaban aquellos pueblos que Mr. de Paw cree los más salvajes del mundo; aquellos pueblos inferiores en industria y sagacidad a los más groseros del antiguo continente; aquellos pueblos de cuya racionalidad dudaron algunos europeos. (2: 428)

> This is a brief but true example of the culture of the Mexicans, taken from their ancient history, from the paintings and stories of the most exact Spanish historians. Thus it is that these people governed themselves in a way not inferior in industry and sagacity to the most primitive peoples of the Old Continent. Thus those peoples whose rationality was questioned by some Europeans, governed themselves.

Aguirre Beltrán notes that Clavijero takes a direct stand with regard to the rationality of the Mexican Indian and the highly developed capacity for abstract thought of the Nahautl language but to no avail:

> Las autoridades administrativas de la colonia desalentaron, primero; contradijeron, después, la política misionera. Ordenes, que en el transcurso de las centurias se hicieron cada vez más imperiosas, obligaron a la enseñanza del castellano y, al pulsar los escasos avances obtenidos, llegaron a prohibir el uso de las lenguas indígenas. La política de concentración lingüística tuvo así origen y desarrollo, alcanzado la más extrema rigidez durante el gobierno ilustrado de Carlos III. Para entonces, la Ilustración había postulado la inferioridad genética del hombre y del mundo americanos y, en la formulación, quedaron incluidos los idiomas nativos. En vano el mexicano Clavigero se apresuró a demostrar la admirable perfección del nahua que, sin recurrir a préstamos extraños, era capaz de expresar con aptitud los abstrusos conceptos de la metafísica occidental y de la propia. (1970, 81–82)

> The colonial administrative authorities first discouraged and then contradicted the policies of the missionary orders. Administrative orders that with the passing of centuries became more and more imperious in making the teaching of Spanish mandatory, and on recognizing the scant success obtained came to a complete prohibition of the indigenous languages. This policy of linguistic dominance had this long process of development but it attained its most rigid and arbitrary expression during the enlightened reign of Carlos III. By this time the Enlightenment had decreed the genetic inferiority of the American world and population, and, of course, this formulation included the Amerindian languages. In vain did the Mexican Clavijero hasten to demonstrate the admirable perfection of the Nahuatl language, which without recourse to foreign loan words was perfectly capable of fully expressing the most abstract concepts of Western metaphysics as well as its own.

The affirmations of David Brading cannot be denied: *Criollo* patriotism is indeed the manifestation of a class and not of a nation, and expresses the sentiments of a sector that was denied its birthright–the governing of its country. Clavijero expropriates indigenous history for the patriotic ends of his class and recognizes the social distance separating the *criollo* élite from the indigenous masses (Brading 20–23). However, unlike other testimonies of *criollismo*, the *Historia* insists that the economy of New Spain–the principal support of the Spanish economy and to a large extent, of the European–rests on the work of the Indians. He asks for education for them, and that obviously cannot be supplied without prior liberation. If the ancient Mexicans had a culture, then by creating better socioeconomic conditions for their descendants–that is, liberating them from colonial servitude and from racism (which, as is well known, turns out to be the inevitable ideology of the practice of selling cheaply to the mother country the products of the soil and subsoil, and of buying manufactured articles at high prices)–they can assimilate, in a short time, the culture of the Age of Enlightenment and its faith in progress and under the guidance of the *criollo* clergy can begin to make of Mexico a nation that reaps the benefits of its own riches.

This is the project of a national culture to be inferred from the *Historia*. In such a project, *mestizaje* appears more as a very long-term utopia: the creation of a new human who will one day inherit the homeland emancipated and built by the *criollos*, the only ones who are historically in a position to carry out this change. At no time does Clavijero present *mestizaje* as something that has already occurred or is in process, but rather as something in the realm of the possible but which, in times prior to his, was not carried out or even proposed. To Clavijero's mind a much greater degree of intermarriage between European male subjects and Mexican women would have made a more unified nation in demographic terms. It must be remembered that at the time Clavijero was writing in Bologna the demographic recovery of the Mexican *mestizo* was just beginning to make a difference (see Sánchez Albornoz, Vol. I, Ch. 7, this *History*).

Thus, in the condition to which colonial oppression has reduced them, neither the Indians nor any other group can place themselves at the head of a popular struggle for independence. In the name of a hypothetical common good, the sharing of which shall be indefinitely postponed, the *criollos* confer on themselves this historical mission and believe themselves able to fulfill it without recourse to armed rebellion. Hence their surprise in the face of the Rebellion of 1810–1816, which, once transformed into a class war, sweeps over them and forces them to ally themselves with the most reactionary Spanish factions. Mexican Independence shall not be, as in South America, the fruit of victory over the royalist army, but rather, once the Revolution of José María Morelos is put down, the product of a military rebellion by *criollo* officers, headed by Agustín de Iturbide.

Clavijero died two years prior to the French Revolution, and his limitations are the limitations of his time. His fundamental importance to Mexican culture consists in his being the first in the Age of Enlightenment to suggest an image that no longer has the European at its center, an initial attempt to show that there are other cultures and other human groups than the Greco-Latin paradigms. His silent ambition is Promethean: to seize from Europe the instruments of her culture to serve other projects. In this field, the *Historia antigua de México* is the equivalent of a declaration of intellectual independence. Clavijero dares to engage in controversy with the sages of the Old World. Not only does he dare to speak as an equal to the attackers of America, but when he does so, he affirms his intellectual superiority. He had an indispensable function, without which liberation could not even have been considered: to defeat the negative vision that the Mexicans had of themselves, which Spanish colonial culture had imposed upon them from birth in the colonies. The most conclusive proof of his argument is the *Historia* itself—by virtue of the precision of its scientific information and the craft of its prose. If a *criollo* from New Spain, educated completely in the seminaries of his country, is capable of producing such a work, a book which demonstrates a prodigious assimilation of European culture and personal research that notably advances the state of knowledge in his time, then no one with the power of reason can continue to scorn Americans for the original sin of having been born in the New World. No one can repeat, with the viceroy's arrogance, that they were only

born to be silent and obey, that they are simians or at least savages, unfit to govern themselves.

A master of dialectical argument, Clavijero gives his countrymen the intellectual foundation for the *criollo* homeland, which seeks its legitimization by ideologically developing a *mestizo* culture. In the contrast between their past splendor and their present dejection, he gives to the natives (who, I repeat, cannot read it) the consciousness of their oppression. The colonized individuals reading these pages, instead of feeling inferior, feel proud, worthy of being the subject and no longer simply the object of history: Their social and cultural orphanhood finds an ancestry. The Conquest ceases to be a crusade come to save them, and becomes an undertaking, this one truly demonic, that ended with the Golden Age and instituted the reign of tyranny, exploitation, and contempt. With Clavijero's work, the storm, the beginnings of which date from 1521, begins to break. The road is opened to national independence, indeed, to *rational* independence. Whether consciously or not, such is the political significance of the *Historia*.

The work of Frantz Fanon was necessary for us to understand Clavijero's role as the beginning of a process that achieved its radicalization only with Morelos, and would later be diverted by the reactionary *criollo* forces of Iturbide and Santa Anna. If the fact of the existence of an Aztec civilization did not change the meager diet of the peasant in 1782 (or today), the search for and recovery of a culture prior to the Conquest establishes a claim to the reinstatement of contact with the most ancient and anti-colonial energy. The recovery of a history previous to colonization—a history annihilated, distorted, and disfigured by the colonist—is not a discovery of shame but of dignity, glory, and solemnity; it justifies a future national culture, provokes in colonized individuals a significant change, breaks down the idea that colonialism pulled them out of the darkness of night, and that to leave them to their own devices would mean a return to barbarism, to degeneracy, to an animal-like state of being. Faced with the condemnation of the dominators, Clavijero nevertheless assumes a Mexican culture. He cannot speak of a "national culture" when the nation does not yet exist and there is only a politically unified territory, without any ethnic, social, economic, or geographical homogeneity. He can, on the other hand, present a past that can be shared by all who live in that land. To the continental condemnation, the Jesuits, exiled by absolutism, offer, in turn, a continental reply: *Ensayo sobre la historia natural de Chile* [1781–1795; *The Geographical, Natural and Civil History of Chili*, 1808] by Juan Ignacio Molina (1740–1829); *Historia del reino de Quito en la América Meridional* [1789; History of the Kingdom of Quito] by Juan de Velasco (1727–1792); *Historia de la provincia del Gran Chaco* [1789, History of the Gran Chaco] by José Jolís (1728–1790).

We still do not have in-depth research on how the *Historia* was read by the *criollos* and the Spaniards. There are great contradictions and ambiguities surrounding the production as well as the reception of the book. In "Un airado mentís a Clavijero" ["An Angry Refutation of Clavijero"], Elías Trabulse studies in exemplary fashion the criticism of another ex-Jesuit who considered the *Historia* injurious to the Spaniards and contributed to its not being published in its original language until half a century later. In 1784, Ramón Diosdado Caballero wrote a few "Observaciones americanas y suplemento crítico..." ["American Observations and Critical Supplement"], which were never printed, although they were adapted for a book published by him in 1806, *L'eroismo di Ferdinando Cortese* [The Heroism of Hernán Cortés], in Italian, to combat Clavijero on his own ground. On the other hand, Maneiro tells the story (171–72) that on receiving the copies sent by Clavijero, the professors of the University of Mexico, the archbishop, the president of the Real Audiencia, and the viceroy himself, Bernardo de Gálvez, heaped praise on the *Historia* and were proud that its author was a native of New Spain. With regard to his work's influence on the insurgents of 1810, Gastón García Cantú has written

> Todo movimiento popular ha sido precedido por la crítica del regimen establecido, sus instituciones, sus mentiras y exhortaciones públicas. La crítica de la colonia es lanzada por Hidalgo. Utiliza la obra de Clavijero. La *Historia antigua de México* sirve de fundamento a sus páginas más intensas: la respuesta de Guadalajara o el discurso a los Comanches en Saltillo. (10)

> Every popular movement has been preceded by criticism of the established regime, its institutions, its lies and public exhortations. The criticism of the colony is levied by Hidalgo. He makes use of Clavijero. The *Historia antigua de México* gives rise to one of his most intense pages: the reply of Guadalajara or the address to the Comanches in Saltillo.

Clavijero did not reach the stage of describing a national literature, a task completed perhaps by no one other than Juan Pablo Viscardo y Guzmán (1748–1798) in Peru, who tried to convince the Church to send an expedition of support for the rebellion of Tupac Amaru, and who summarized in four words the history of three centuries: "ingratitude, injustice, slavery and destruction" (Batllori 70). However, in the *Historia antigua de México*, in the prose of Francisco Javier Clavijero, the language of domination began to be transformed into the language of liberation.

Works Cited

Aguirre Beltrán, Gonzalo. 1957. *El proceso de aculturación.* Mexico City: Universidad Nacional Autónoma de México.

——. 1970. *El proceso de aculturación y el cambio sociocultural en México.* Mexico City: Editorial Comunidad, Instituto de Ciencias Sociales.

Alegre, Francisco Xavier. 1994. "El comercio de esclavos negros." "Rebelión victoriosa de los negros." *Humanistas del siglo XVIII.* Intr. and ed. Gabriel Méndez Plancarte. 2nd ed. Mexico City: Universidad Nacional Autónoma de México. 55–57, 69–74.

Batllori, S. J., Miguel. 1965. "The Role of the Jesuit Exiles." *The Origins of the Latin American Revolutions, 1808–1826.* Ed. R.A. Humphreys and John Lynch. New York: Knopf. 60–72.

Benítez, Fernando. 1967–1972. *Los indios de México.* 4 vols. Mexico City: Era.

Brading, David. 1985. *The Origins of Mexican Nationalism.* Cambridge: Cambridge University Press.

Caballero, Ramón Diosdado. 1806. *L'eroismo di Ferdinando Cortese confermato contre le censure nemice.* Rome [private printing].

Cardoza y Aragón, Luis. 1955. *Guatemala, las líneas de su mano.* Mexico City: Fondo de Cultura Económica.

Carrasco, Pedro. 1975. "La transformación de la cultura indígena durante la colonia." *Historia mexicana.* 25.2: 175–203.

Clavijero, Francisco Xavier. 1917. *Historia antigua de México.* 2 vols. Ed. Luis González Obregón. Trans. J. Joaquín de Mora. Mexico City: Departamento Editorial de la Dirección General de las Bellas Artes.

Duchet, Michèle. 1975. *Antropología e historia en el siglo de las luces.* Trans. Francisco González Aramburo. Mexico City: Siglo XXI.

Fanon, Frantz. 1963. *The Wretched of the Earth.* Trans. Constance Farrington. New York: Grove Press.

Florescano, Enrique. 1971. *Estructuras y problemas agrarios de México (1500–1821).* Mexico City: SepSetentas.

Florescano, Enrique, and Isabel Gil Sánchez. 1976. "La época de las reformas borbónicas y del crecimiento económico: 1750–1808." *Historia general de México.* Ed. Daniel Cosío Villegas. Vol. 2. Mexico City: El Colegio de México. 185–301.

García Cantú, Gastón. 1970. "La crítica, tradición nacional." *Siempre* 424 *"La cultura en México"* (March 25): 10.

Gerbi, Antonello. 1973. *The Dispute of the New World: The History of a Polemic, 1750–1900.* Ed. and trans. Jeremy Moyle. Pittsburgh: University of Pittsburgh Press.

Gibson, Charles. 1964. *The Aztecs Under Spanish Rule: A History of the Indians of the Valley of Mexico, 1519–1810.* Stanford: Stanford University Press.

González Casanova, Pablo. 1958. *La literatura perseguida en la crisis de la Colonia.* Mexico City: El Colegio de México.

Hanke, Lewis. 1959. *Aristotle and the American Indians.* Chicago: Henry Regnery.

Henríquez Ureña, Pedro. 1966. *A Concise History of Latin American Culture.* Trans. Gilbert Chase. New York: Frederick A. Praeger.

Humphreys, R.A., and John Lynch, eds. 1966. *The Origins of the Latin American Revolutions, 1808–1826.* New York: Knopf.

Landívar, Rafael. 1924 [1782]. *Rusticación mejicana.* 2nd ed. Trans. Ignacio Loureda. Mexico City: Sociedad de Edición y Librería Franco Americana.

León Portilla, Miguel et al. 1964. *Historia documental de México.* Vol. 1. Mexico City: Universidad Nacional Autónoma de México.

Lira, Andrés, and Luis Muro. 1988. "El siglo de la integración." *Historia general de México.* Ed. Daniel Cosío Villegas. Vol. 1. Mexico City: El Colegio de México. 371–469.

López Cámara, Francisco. 1969. *La génesis de la conciencia liberal en México.* 2nd ed. Mexico City: Universidad Nacional Autónoma de México.

Maneiro, Juan Luís, and Manuel Fabri. 1956. "Javier Clavijero." *Vidas de mexicanos ilustres del siglo XVIII.* Ed. and trans. Bernabé Navarro. Mexico City: Universidad Nacional Autónoma de México. 119–79.

Martínez Peláez, Severo. 1973. *La patria del criollo: Ensayo de interpretación de la realidad colonial guatemalteca.* 2nd ed. San José de Costa Rica: Editorial Universitaria Centroamericana.

Méndez Plancarte, Gabriel, ed. 1941. *Humanistas del siglo XVIII.* Mexico City: Universidad Nacional Autónoma de México.

Miller, Henry. 1963. "Preface." Haniel Long. *The Marvelous Adventure of Cabeza de Vaca. Malinche.* New York: Ballantine Books. xii–xx.

Moreno Toscano, Alesandra. 1988. "El siglo de la conquista." *Historia general de México.* Ed. Daniel Cosío Villegas. Vol. 2. Mexico City: El Colegio de México. 289–369.

——. 1963. *Fray Juan de Torquemada y su Monarquía indiana.* Xalapa: Universidad Veracruzana

Pozas, Ricardo, and Isabel Horcasitas de Pozas. 1971. *Los indios en las clases sociales de México.* Mexico City: Siglo XXI.

Real Academia Española. 1992–1994. *Diccionario de la lengua española.* 21st ed. Madrid: Real Academia Española, Editorial Espasa Calpe.

Ronan, Charles E. 1973. "Francisco Javier Clavijero, 1731–1787." *Handbook of Middle American Studies.* 13: 276–97.

Sigüenza y Góngora, Carlos. 1940. *Relaciones históricas.* Ed. Manuel Romero de Terreros. Mexico City: Universidad Nacional Autónoma de México.145–54.

Terrazas, Francisco de. 1941. *Poesía*. Ed. Antonio Castro Leal. Mexico City: Porrúa.

Torquemada, Juan de. 1975–82. *Monarquía indiana*. Ed. Miguel León Portilla. Mexico City: Universidad Nacional Autónoma de México.

Trabulse, Elías. 1975. "Un airado mentis a Clavijero." *Historia Mexicana*. 25.1: 1–40.

Villoro, Luis. 1963. "La naturaleza americana en Clavijero." *La palabra y el hombre*. (28 Oct.–Dec.) 543–50.

——. 1950. *Los grandes momentos del indigenismo en México*. Mexico City: El Colegio de Mexico.

Zea, Leopoldo. 1969. "Definición de la cultura nacional." *Características de la cultura nacional*. Ed. Leopoldo Zea et al. Mexico City: Fondo de Cultura Económica. 7–13.

CHAPTER 16

NEW THINKING
FROM THE ENLIGHTENMENT
TO INDEPENDENCE

The generation responsible for the Independence movement in the Caribbean reformulated an imaginary in which the local was better than the European, or in any case had the possibility of being so. Thus the Colonial pact founded on a "Utopian happenstance," in which the dreams of the Old World could become a reality, ended up becoming a fundamental inducement to put an end to the Colonial regime. To be new, to be young, and to be Other from Imperial power was almost an invitation for rupture and change, but in this case a change in which the one-time subalterns could think of themselves as superior or equivalent to the center of power. Those colonies that would in a few short years become independent nations of the New World would achieve this by undertaking a transcultural process of the first order, understood in this case as a practice involving symbolic negotiations and adaptations of ideas that, once passed through this transcultural sieve, would be both similar to and different from their originals. The similarity to the ideas of the French Revolution, European Enlightenment, and Independence of the United States has meant that criticism may have maintained neo-Colonial analytical models and, as a result, in the context of Latin-American Independence, encountered the (somewhat corrupted) heirs of the West, reproducing Occidental logic and ignoring the fact that in the process of adaptation, there are local factors that have at least as much weight as the foreign ideas with which they had commerce.

I propose in this section to use this concept as a filter through which to present the tensions expressed by center/periphery and educated creoles/the popular sector. Young, new, rich, and resentful at the lack of opportunities allowed them by the Spanish Crown in their own countries (given that administrative, commercial, and ecclesiastical preferments were reserved for peninsulars), the *criollos,* by taking advantage of such discourse, were able to legitimize their demands for social ascent. This they achieved by combining the language of the Enlightenment with a mix of *criollo* Catholicism, a practical reformism that was potentially capable of unleashing Liberalism, Scientism as a doctrine that challenged Thomism, the vocabulary of the French Revolution, and a practical autonomy that could deal with the racial peculiarity and its attendant demands in each region. *Criollo* enthusiasms were universal (for 'universal' read Occidental), considering themselves dominant within their intellectual sphere. This approach went against the imperialist habit of rearticulating Latin-American reality by possessing and explaining it within the parameters of the centers of power where all thought derives from its own image (any similarities and differences being related to its own model of development), as if the local people had no personal dimension of similarities and differences (their own minorities, their own national borders) or their own coordinates of power.

To study the history of ideas in the Caribbean and Mesoamerica in that moment is thus to question the assumption that these countries, upon liberating themselves from the Spanish Empire, were constituted as nations and surrendered to rules and influences substituted from other international economic interests (such as those of England); that they put together their national identities according to the image of the European model and therefore as inferior to that model (interpreting a filial relationship as imitation, the son would always be considered inferior or subaltern). But this logic in the relationship of center and periphery is only structured thus or thought out from the center position. In an illuminating and polemical analysis, Partha Chattarjee comments on the "Creole nationalisms" of the Americas as being the product of the ambition of those classes whose economic interests were oriented toward the metropolis and for whom the model they sought to emulate remained incomplete "because it lacked linguistic communality and its state was both retrograde and congruent with the arbitrary administrative boundaries of the imperial order" (Chatterjee 20). The definition of *incomplete,* in spite of coming from a theory of Third World culture, is tendentious. Incomplete in relation to what? To an original or "pure" model that it transforms, derives from, and transmutes into other versions and other models of reality? Why does "transmuted" (transculturated/the crossing of cultures) have to be seen as something incomplete and without value in itself? Chatterjee also states that self-evaluation after Independence in accordance with the values of progress and organization borrowed from France and England (and not changing the basic structure of the countries on a profound level) implies a moral and epistemic foundation that perpetuates "in a real and not merely a metaphorical sense, a colonial domination" (11). It is difficult not to agree with this postcolonial reading with its more complex mechanism. In fact, not everything occurs in relation to the hegemonic center; the so-called periphery (conceived as such only from the center) has its own center, periphery, logic, and rules. While they will participate in the international economic chessboard in a subaltern position, these national cultures have never viewed themselves as existing on the periphery of other nations.

This essay will attempt to revise "new thinking" of the Enlightenment in the light of these ideas of dependence, traffic, and transit, taking into consideration the sieving action of transculturation. I understand the latter in terms of those strategies designed to integrate the contradictions of a local present (totally distinct from that of Napoleonic Europe) with indigenous masses, slaves, mulattos, and *criollos* of different social classes, with religious traditions and their own social logic that varies within the diverse countries that make up the Caribbean region. It is true that Latin American nations did not manage to apply their pronouncements in favor of justice and equality, which were introduced by liberationist thought: Thus the social framework less than a century after Independence was one of misery for the majority. But this does not mean that one should look at Latin America through the lens of either progress or underdevelopment. This is a Western viewpoint and one that is interested solely in operating within its own parameters. Transculturation might explain how each region takes, appropriates, and becomes influenced by another, adapting, negotiating, and modifying in an interrelationship in which each part is affected and changes permanently. Thus the generation of Latin American emancipation is related to that of Europe, its heir only in terms of its own social and cultural appropriations, among which can be included the mythification of Europe. This point of departure is important, given that only through it can one attempt to come close to the processes in operation from the end of the eighteenth to the beginning of the twentieth century. Otherwise, they would be viewed solely as an imitation or clumsy copy of the European. It is worth retracing the journey, the transit, and the transmission of ideas during the period, understanding it more as an interested dialogue between men of letters (traffic) than as a product of center/periphery interdependency. Transit and traffic occur in different directions, each one marking its own peculiarities and demands. This movement outwards brought in regional pressure groups and brought together different classes and races who were possible allies in the war against Spain and in the establishment of a new government: Other *criollo literati* (who cannot be assumed to be a group with a homogenous ideology) and other Europeans (especially the French and English) and their social projects, with which the Spanish Americans felt they were on familiar terms (when not superseding them).

An Example

There are many examples of transcultural and unifying mechanisms during this period among those who considered themselves on an equal footing with the Empire, while fighting for their rights and trying to forge a better future. Such is the case of the "Oath Sworn on Monte Sacro," which featured Simón Bolívar (1783–1830) confronting his teacher Simón Rodríguez (1771–1854) on a hill in Rome in 1805 where Bolívar, at the age of twenty-two, mythically sealed his commitment to American freedom. The power of that scene had (and still has) a profoundly respectful effect, reinforced invariably by one of the two oil paintings by the Venezuelan Tito Salas depicting the scene of the oath. While the image *par excellence* of the Conquest of America is that of Christopher Columbus (ca. 1451–1506) and his men planting an enormous cross in the earth with the three ships as the back drop, the "Oath Sworn on Monte Sacro" is, without a doubt, a kind of foundational scene that organizes and condenses the identity of nations (see **Figure 1**). The Father of His Country (or of various countries, as is the case here) promised to resolve the problem of humanity in a state of freedom in the New World, on the basis that throughout the history of the great Roman Empire and the civilization that blew from the East, nothing had been done for the emancipation of the human spirit or for the abolition of man's inhumanity to man. Here he alludes to the central issues of nineteenth-century thought: The desirable model of government, in comparison with the European model; history as a leap from Classical Europe to grade zero in the America of the Emancipation period; and the New World as a vacuum, an unknown, a novelty without a past, a non-existent entity. Latin America is as it will be so frequently interpreted later: A project, an action without past or present, just a future. It is the place of potential and redemption, the

Figure 1.

Painting of Simón Bolívar taking an oath on the Aventine Hill, Rome, to dedicate his life to American independence from Spain. (Archive of the author)

land of freedom, understanding by this term something as broad as the definitive perfection of reason. Rome thus becomes both backdrop and witness, while Bolívar is the image and symbol of rebirth that is the Old World's notion of utopia expressed as desire in America and transformed in the space of the New, given its own value and purpose, and now conceived as the transcendence of Europe and not as subordination, even though it takes its form from the latter.

The position assumed by the burgeoning republics in the context of history, heirs supposedly *avant la lettre* of the Hegelian concept of what we now call the West (when emancipation was a movement produced prior to Hegelian definitions on the sharing out of the world), becomes evident in the "Oath Sworn on Monte Sacro." Hence, their image as the continuing of a tradition rather than as a total rupture from it. One must recall that the original plan of the majority of the rebel *criollos* was not that of total independence from Spain but autonomous government. The locals wanted power-sharing, but they did not conceive of themselves as entities totally different from Europe but rather as their equals and, in every case, as new countries (with regard to the realization of Western fantasies of society and utopia). History would seem to begin with the declaration of independence rooted in the Latinity (more than Hispanism) of America, as observed in the scene at Monte Sacro. The awareness of an indigenous pre-Columbian history would be incorporated later with variations according to the region and the ethnic composition of the countries, becoming a well-structured discourse only after the Mexican Revolution.

The nuances would also depend on the specific region, since the struggles for national liberation were not the same. Ricaurte Soler (1980) distinguished three types of tendencies: That which arose from an agrarian demand combined with a call for democracy; that emerging from the *criollos* and middle levels of society with Liberal characteristics when it came to public welfare and national affirmation; and that which organized the nation through *caudillos* and the strengthening of the State apparatus. These three tendencies, it must be added, were occasionally superimposed.

The Logic of Dependent Thought

It should be recalled that the Independence generation was brought up in the period when it was customary to denigrate the American continent. Understanding this adds a further dimension to the task facing these nations, as well as revealing how even today the interpretation of history still continues to be tainted by this logic of inferiority. If George Louis Leclerc, Comte de Buffon (1707–1788); Cornelius de Pauw (1739–1799); Guillaume-Thomas Raynal (1713–1796); and William Robertson (1721–1793) had impressed on the European culture and imaginary that the American subject was not even an immature animal or a child but rather a degenerate, then how can one accept the prestige of an individual such as Francisco de Miranda (1750–1816) and his role in European and North American history? Miranda's father was a native of the Canaries and his mother was from Caracas. He did military service in Africa, Melilla, and Havana and participated in the War of Independence of the United States in the context of the Franco-Spanish War against England. While in the process of carving out the great country of Colombia, he traveled to Holland, Prussia, Italy, Greece, Asia Minor, the Ottoman Empire, Switzerland, and the Nordic countries. He became an intimate friend of Catherine the Great of Russia and met Washington, Jefferson, and Lafayette. Later remembered as *Generalísimo* and *El Precursor*, he was in France when the Revolution broke out. This did not exactly mean that he would then export such ideas to New Granada, but rather that it produced an interesting exchange of ideas. Miranda chose to fight on the side of the Revolutionary Army since this allowed him to promote the cause of Spanish American Independence. In London he published the weekly *El colombiano*. Later he would be the leader of an invasion of Venezuela that ended in disaster. Even though he would die in prison many years before Independence became a reality, he became a member of the Sociedad Patriótica (Patriotic Society) and his name appears among the signatories of Venezuela's Declaration of Independence.

Within the logic of the conventional relationships between center and periphery, in his heroic actions one can discern in Miranda a member of the Spanish army fighting against France and perhaps glimpse his contact with European literature, which is also a certainty. Moreover, his revolutionary leadership changed the role of subalterns in the period. Miranda, of course, has been held responsible for the concept of unity implied by the phrase "our America," which appeared as early as 1806: ". . . that the day will come, when our America, recovering her sovereign independence, her sons will be able freely to show to the universe their exalted spirit" (quoted in Biggs 125). While Jean-Jacques Rousseau (1712–1778) dreamed of the lost innocence of the aborigines, Georges-Louis Léclerc [Count] of Buffon, declared in his

Histoire naturelle, générale et particulière [1748–1804; *Natural History, General and Particular,* 1780–1785] that American degeneracy was so extreme that men in the New World suffered from sexual frigidity, while their passivity when confronted with nature placed them on the same level as the animals. This kind of thesis was not uncommon. David Hume (1711–1776) in his essay *Of National Characters* (1748 and 1754), for example, commented that "There was never a civilized nation of any other complexion than white, nor even any individual eminent either in action or speculation" (quoted in Chukwudi Eze 33). Johann Gottfried Herder (1744–1803) is one of the few pluralists among the great European thinkers of the age who did not view one culture as inferior to another but rather thought that each one should be considered in accordance with its own value and truth. His suggestions for a revision of historical theory appeared in his *Reflections on the Philosophy of the History of Mankind* (1784–1791).

The intense and influential debate on the New World followed the ancient Aristotelian notions on the inferior conditions of life in the tropics. The Enlightenment exaggerated the arguments, claiming that rational law was universal (and that being universal, it should be interpreted according to its own image). This struggle to define who is more rational, or rather who is the true civilized being, summarized the struggle for geopolitical power between the European metropolises. In his *Histoire philosophique et politique des établissements et du commerce des européens dans les deux Indes* [1770; *A Philosophical and Political History of the Settlements and Trade of the Europeans in the East and West Indies,* 1776], Abbé Raynal directly attacked Spain. His book contains allegations against the cruelty of the colonizers and a denunciation of the immense suffering of the indigenous peoples. Denis Diderot (1713–1784) took up this line, accusing the Spanish Conquest of America of producing ignorance, evangelizing fanaticism, and abuses. Thus the colonized world and the fiercely determined colonizers (Spain) were made inferior; the struggle was for the possession of the world. François Marie Arouet de Voltaire (1694–1778), Jean-François Marmontel (1723–1799), and the Scot William Robertson, in his *History of America* (1777), all participated in such attacks.

The cultural framework here is complex. The moment of the crystallization of innovatory thought thus includes not only the inferiorization of the New World from the European point of view but also the attacks against Spain (also despised, and moreover accused of excesses of cruelty). In the colonial center the monarchy and the Church were declining, while general discontent reigned in the colonies on account of the tribute paid to the Crown, the misery of the *campesinos* and indigenous peoples, the rise of new popular classes as a product of *mestizaje* without a defined position in society, and the disgraces and tensions of the slave regimes. Throughout the continent the peninsular minority controlled the bureaucratic apparatus, while the freeing up of trade decreed by Carlos III did not benefit the *criollo* merchants. Even worse, the opening up of the new ports fragmented the intercontinental relationship to such an extent that the regions were communicating more with the metropolis than between themselves.

In reality the designation "Spanish Americans," used both before and during the Independence period, embraced a block of emerging social classes for whom no role was anticipated within the colonial system. These included discontented landowners and merchants, the middle classes who had no possibility of ascending the political or social ladder.

Spanish-American identity had an increasing part in creating a national, or at least regional, consciousness, as evidenced by the writing of the first provincial histories, whether that of Fray Pedro Simón (1574–1627) or José de Oviedo y Baños (1671–1738). If one adds the Napoleonic invasion of Spain to the mix, the conditions for change can be observed parallel to what was being produced in other Western latitudes.

The Traffic of Ideas

One cannot interpret the period without taking all these debates into account or realizing that the Independentist generation read Benito Jerónimo Feijóo (1676–1764) as well as Georges-Louis Leclerc Comte de Buffon, Charles-Louis de Secondat Baron Montesquieu (1689–1755), Jean-François Marmontel, and Robertson. Moreover, it is worth pointing out that, in the region, reading these texts had the glamour of the forbidden. Ideas were censored. The Index of 1780 banned the reading of Montesquieu, Jean-Jacques Rousseau, and Voltaire, as well as limiting works by Étienne Bonnot de Condillac (1714–1780) and Cornelius Jansenius (1585–1638), while the importation of novels to America was prohibited. This does not mean that no texts circulated, but it is inevitable that they did so with the ideological charge of the forbidden, independent of content. The relative isolation of the colonies from outside, combined with a higher education based almost entirely on Catholic theology, provided a very particular context for the reading of such concepts. Moreover, the movement of ideas should also be seen as taking place between the new Republics, despite their limitations. One should not underestimate the symbolic power of the Virgin of Guadalupe on the doctrine of Simón Bolívar or the figures of Padre Hidalgo and Bolívar himself in the union of Central American Republics and their conflictive relationship with Guatemala and Mexico.

To complicate this framework of symbolic capital, it is also useful to record that many liberationist ideas were received with a certain ambiguity by *criollo* society: These ideas gave them the possibility of engendering autonomous thought that took pride in itself and of abandoning their presumed inferiority; but at the same time, it is undeniable that many individuals effectively had economic interests in the neo-Imperial centers and that fundamentally they were not too interested in modifying the status quo, especially in terms of caste privileges. Many aristocrats had been honestly idealist, while others used Liberal discourse more as part of the intellectual traffic of ideas of the times rather than because of any belief in their validity. As an explanation of the contradictory juxtaposition of slavery with Liberal premises, Roberto Schwarz observes that in Brazil during the nineteenth century, "Once the European ideas and motives took hold, they could serve and very often did, as a justification, nominally 'objective,' for what was unavoidably arbitrary in the practice of a favor" (23). Long before Brazilian Liberalism, Simón Rodríguez (1771–1854) had already in his work fiercely denounced the traffic of ideas in Great Colombia (present day Colombia and parts of Venezuela, Ecuador, and Panama) after Independence. According to him, the words were dead; they were epitaphs and ought to be resuscitated (see Rotker). In *Sociedades americanas* [1828; American Societies], Rodríguez gives an explanation that frees up (or by chance perhaps reaffirms) the coherence between the word and power. Here one is dealing with commerce in words, realized by "una clase intermedia de sujetos, únicamente empleada–ya en *cortar toda*

comunicación entre el pueblo y sus representantes,–y en *tergiversar el sentido* de las providencias que no pueden ocultarse, . . . –ya en *exaltar la idea* de la soberanía para exaltar al pueblo . . . y *servirse de él* en este estado" (1: 273, emphasis added) ("an intermediate class of subjects, uniquely employed–to cut all communication between the people and their representatives,–and to shift the meaning of measures that now cannot hide themselves, . . . –exalting the idea of sovereignty to excite the people . . . and to take advantage of them in this state").

This is the other face of the mechanics of crossing cultures, seen now not from the imperial center but from within the new nations when the movement of contamination, borrowing, and fusion was handled by the elite through a practice said to be representative but which, in reality, canceled differences and imposed a hegemonic project. Subsequently, such commerce was accentuated further when Positivism was assimilated to Liberal discourse. Nothing seems more difficult in the analysis of Latin American political thinking of the nineteenth century than to distinguish a Liberal Conservative from a Conservative Liberal (Romero and Rombero 115–62). The Cuban Enrique José Varona (1849–1933) saw this from his own perspective when, in 1888, he mockingly remarked

> No te has fijado, amigo, en que siempre le pegan a la libertad un adjetivo, como una ventosa? Libertad verdadera, libertad posible, libertad adecuada, libertad necesaria, libertad moral, libertad civil, ya hasta libertad provisional, de quita y pon. La única que no encuentras por parte alguna es la libertad, monda y lironda. (in Sánchez Reulet 45)

> Have you not noticed, friend, that freedom is always stuck to an adjective, like a cupping glass? True freedom, possible freedom, adequate freedom, necessary freedom, moral freedom, civil freedom, even provisional freedom that can be shrugged on and off. The only word that one does not find anywhere is freedom, pure and unadulterated.

In this sense it is certain that transculturation was also a political phenomenon that allowed the strengthening of power of some classes/races over others in America, adapting a convenient vocabulary for such ends (such as "new" and "change"–a vocabulary used to preserve class privileges). This is the Lacanian catacresis, a traffic in metaphors in the cognitive-political sphere functioning as empty signifiers and mobilizers (see Laclau; Žižek).

The freedom movements constructed their language in the molds of Enlightenment ideology and Liberal democracy. The discourse borrowed from Rousseau, Voltaire, Montesquieu, Diderot, John Locke (1632–1704), Jeremy Bentham (1748–1832), (Jean Joseph) Benjamin Constant (1767–1830), Antoine Louis Claude [Comte] Destutt de Tracy (1754–1836), Joseph Blanco White (1775–1841), Feijóo, and the United States's Declaration of Independence (1776). Opposition to the colonial system was a promise of progress; it meant going against the clergy, the king, and Spain. The opposite was seen as retrograde and reactionary. But this discourse had two sides: *Liberty* meant the struggle against colonial power and at the same time implied the replacement of one hegemonic group with another. The new power base had to legitimize itself in terms of discourse. Thus the import of prestigious vocabulary was not sufficient; local conditions also had to be taken into account, even on a minimal basis, and so a very strange amalgam was created that in many cases was contradictory. Bolívar himself accurately summed this up when he stated that "somos un pequeño género humano" (1968, 1: 64) ("we [Latin Americans] are a young people" [1951, 1: 110]). The great advocate of the abolition of slavery in 1825 warned of the risk that "la pardocracia, que es la inclinación natural y única, para exterminio después de la clase privilegiada" (1968, 2: 114) ("the darker-skinned elements should rule. This is a natural obsession that will ultimately lead to the extermination of the privileged class" [1951, 2: 490]) He also anxiously commented that "Guinea y más Guinea tendremos . . . el que escape con su cara blanca será bien afortunado" (1968, 2: 429) ("we shall have more and more of Africa . . . for anyone with a white skin who escapes will be fortunate" [1951, 2: 625]).

The contradictions are revealing. Discussions regarding the abolition of slavery began in 1810, but emancipation was not initiated until after the 1820s and at first only in countries such as Chile, Central America, and Mexico, where slavery was an issue of marginal importance. In Venezuela and Colombia, abolition became a reality between 1840 and 1850; in Puerto Rico slavery was abolished by decree in 1878, while in Cuba this was achieved only in 1886. (In Cuba and Brazil trafficking in slaves continued until well into the 1870s.) But while the example of slavery shows how practices and ideas were molded to local conveniences, Bolívar himself is a perfect example of the contradictions implied by the transcultural pact, in the sense that symbolic traffic in plurality is one thing, concrete practice in the same is quite another. Thus in Bolivia's constitution a perpetual president is created who "como el Sol que, firme en su centro, da vida al Universo" (Bolívar 1968, 3: 765) ("becomes the sun which, fixed in its

orbit, imparts life to the universe" [Bolívar 1951, 2: 598]). This supreme authority was to be exercised in a Republic that should have an unchecked love of liberty, yet political rights were limited to those citizens who could read and possessed property, requirements that left the indigenous majority out of the picture. It seems surprising to think that Bolívar's declaration of independence had elicited accusations of Jacobinism. In Bolívar's words one can find many examples that reflect how his generation used European ideas, adapting only the part that served their convenience. His project of 1826 for the creation of the federation of Spanish American republics in Panama invoked Montesquieu to support the Confederate Republic as the state form most fitted to survive the inevitable conflicts in isolated provinces. This argument was proved wrong only four years later with the dissolution of Great Colombia (Venezuela, Colombia, and Ecuador; see **Map 1**).

The best way to illustrate the history of the foundation period as a game of traffic, transits, and appropriations is to quote from Bolívar himself. Another method that would open up into a literary connection essential to later Latin American culture is the semi-quotation that would later become the displaced and apocryphal quotations penned by Domingo F. Sarmiento (1811–1888) or, much later, by Jorge Luis Borges (1899–1986) and José Lezama Lima (1910–1976). Bolívar quotes what suits him, modifying it as he does so. He takes a comment from Montesquieu, who in turn repeats something previously stated by Rousseau: ". . . nunca se ha convertido un pueblo corrompido por la esclavitud, tampoco las naciones han

Map 1.

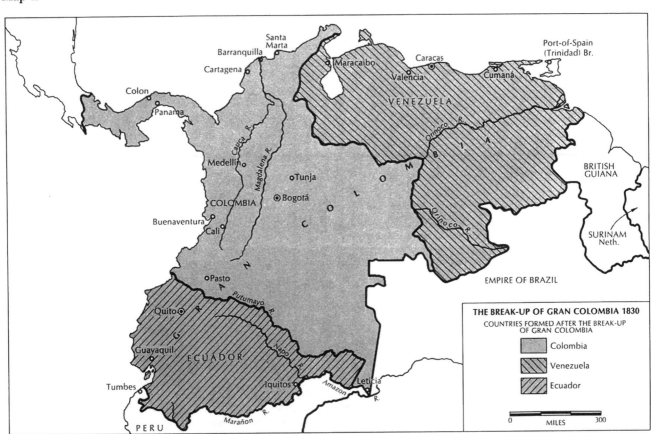

Map of the breakup of Gran Colombia, 1830. (Archive of the author)

podido tener sino conquistadores y de ninguna manera libertadores" (1968, 2: 821) ("... it has never been possible to reform a people corrupted by slavery, and such nations, have only had conquerors never liberators" [1951, 2: 689]). To be emperor was, for Bolívar, to be unworthy of his destiny; he thought that to be liberator was much better. He borrowed from Montesquieu what was convenient and omitted the rest (Bolívar 1968, 2: 323).

To conclude this section on the supposed dependence on ideas derived from the French Revolution and the Enlightenment, let us consider another element in the transcultural mechanism of new thought: the revaluation of the crafts and craftsmen in America during the Independence period. Strictly the idea was not original, regional, or French, given that it was the main contribution of the Spanish Catholic Enlightenment (a contradiction in itself) and the reforms of Carlos III (apart from the scientism already brought by Padre Feijóo during the eighteenth century). The importance of this observation is not so much in thinking how Latin America appropriated and adapted colonial Spanish ideas that brought with them the germ that led to the fall of the colonial power, but in questioning why this emphasis and continuing influence of French and English thought survived; in other words, in interpreting history as a reaction to or a manifestation of neo-colonial logic itself.

The Journey (Crossing) and Appropriations

In 1797 the first attempt at independence was made in La Guaria and Caracas, led by Manuel Gual, José María España, and his wife Joaquina Sánchez, a group of *criollos,* peninsulars, whites, mulattos, and blacks from different social strata, who had allied with Spaniards involved in the failed San Blas Conspiracy against the Spanish monarchy (and were sent into exile in the Venezuelan colony). This is fascinating as a transcultural experience, even though it collapsed very quickly. The revolutionary leaders transmitted their impressions and way of understanding reality through the writings of Juan Bautista Picornell. This Madrid Freemason and republican combined their ideas with his own revolutionary knowledge and was to a large extent responsible for writing the manifestos. The conspiracy led by Gual and España used the *Carmañola* (revolutionary song) and the *Marseillaise* (in their *criollo* versions) to whip up the enthusiasm of the masses. The American song invoked the new brotherhood, which now embraced the new citizens, Indians, blacks, and mulattos (see Grases 126–27). Despite this kind of revolutionary rhetoric, it is a simplification to state that everything was influenced by France, but the French example was strong and not only in the Caribbean region. In Buenos Aires, for example, the uprising provoked by the *mestizo* José Díaz in 1795 was called "The French Conspiracy." Others took place in Chile, even though they had a very indigenous basis, such as the Tupac Amaru rebellion of 1780. In Venezuela the movement of José Leonardo Chirininos and José Caridad González (1795) was carried out under the proclamation of the law of the French Revolution of 1789.

All this demonstrates the mechanisms of legitimacy and prestige coeval with those of transculturalism. The conspiracy of Gual and España modified the emblem of "Liberty, Equality, Fraternity," broadening this triangular dynamic to encompass four points: "Equality, Liberty, Property, and Security," replacing Fraternity with a recovery of the defense of private property and order, and at least pretending to abolish slavery.

The Venezuelan flag was also to have four colors (white, blue, yellow, and red) representing the four races (whites, mulattos, Indians, and blacks). The removal of the term "Fraternity" without doubt had its origin in the terror of Jacobinism, a terror that gained ground throughout the nineteenth century because of the uprising of the Haitian blacks. The tension between the desire for a more extreme change and the wish to conciliate was resolved more in terms of conciliation (Mexico is a clear example), but this does not deny the existence of attempts of another kind. In the state of Cartagena, for example, Gabriel Gutiérrez de Piñeres, a rich *criollo* and vice-president of the state in 1811, was said "predicaba por todas partes la igualdad absoluta, ese dogma destructor de todo orden social. Siempre se le veía cercado de negros y mulatos sin educación" (Liévano Aguirre 864) ("to preach everywhere absolute equality, that dogma so destructive of all social order. He was always to be seen surrounded by uneducated blacks and mulattos"). A careful reading of texts on the Revolution fomented by Gual and España (probably written by Picornell, a prisoner in La Guaira during the period of the revolt) makes clear the way in which the republican rhetoric that the prisoner brought from Spain was altered by ideological needs connected to a local actuality–notably the additions to the text concerning the equality of races. These addenda give the declarations a very different flavor from the pure European Republican discourse.

But this kind of conciliatory tendency toward multiple races–as founders of a national project on the basis of *mestizaje*–was unsuccessful at these very early stages. José María España was quartered and his remains displayed in various urban areas. Subsequently, the head of the revolutionary, José Félix Ribas, a man feared by the Caracan Mantuans during his lifetime, was publicly fried in oil by the Spaniards and exhibited as an example to all. Demographic make-up is not a minor detail in these accounts. In the ambit of Great Colombia, Venezuela ran the greater risk of surrendering herself to mulattocracy, as Bolívar warned, given that more than 60 percent of the inhabitants were mulattos, free blacks, slaves, and runaways. Such were the class interests that, contrary to what occurred in Mexico, the initiative for agrarian expropriation was not taken by the independentist leaders but rather by the populist royalists headed by José Tomás Boves. The attempts at the abolition of slavery, as has already been mentioned, also deserve some careful consideration, for abolitionists and anti-abolitionists were among the ranks of both independentists and royalists.

The Clergy and the Enlightenment

No doubt as a result of the commercial sugar interests, the wealth derived from the slave trade, and the social fear engendered by the Haitian Revolution, the cultural development of the Spanish-speaking islands had a different rhythm from that of the rest of the region. The forging of a national culture from the end of the eighteenth century took on a certain aspect of resistance to the Scholastic or Thomist philosophy that was predominant in school and university teaching, the result of the pressure from the Catholic Church. The inclusion of scientific language, the introduction of the explicative method in pedagogy, and the cultivation of the natural sciences served to open up the issue of the despotic and feudal dominion of Spain. Among the *criollo* landholding and bourgeois classes in Cuba arose a so-called avant-garde philosophical thinking (the new) seen as patriotic self-consciousness in gestation that went against the military bureaucracy of the peninsulars. A closer look at the Cuban social class structure will help explain the peculiarities of the period. Plantation society was a form of feudalism mixed with modern forms of sugar production and, of course, contemporary economic theory. In order to avoid the error of attributing Liberal or Illuminist ideas to what was a happenstance of economic reformism one should keep in mind that the plantations were totally dependent on slavery. The slave revolts, contraband, pirates, the struggle against Napoleon, and the Spanish reforms of Riego (1820–1823) were all part of the background to the philosophy of José Agustín Caballero (1762–1835), Félix Varela (1788–1853), and the Sociedad Patriótica (Patriotic Society), as much as the anti-Scholasticism of Francis Bacon (1561–1626) and René Descartes (1596–1650), John Locke, and Bonnot de Condillac (1715–1780). In fact the anti-Scholastic philosophers were later also responsible for designing the project for the autonomous government of Cuba. But the consolidation of independence would have to wait until the end of the nineteenth century. (The peculiarity of the three Spanish-speaking islands of the Caribbean will be discussed in another section.)

The role of the Sociedades Económicas (Economic Societies) in Central America was decisive in the formation of innovative thought at the end of the eighteenth century and the first half of the nineteenth century. This innovative thinking was also furthured by the enlightened bishops and by the radicalization (in the face of the cautious proposal of the landowning *criollos*) of the *mestizo* middle class, whose only hope (unless there were significant revolutionary change) was to carry on, depending on their salaries as minor employees. Confronted by Mexico's powerful annexationism, the region sustained the dream of Central-American unity for some years (Honduras, Nicaragua, El Salvador, Costa Rica) but still kept the Indians totally marginalized; they were not included under the description "American." In this region, in short, transculturation, understood as the traffic and transit of ideas, took the form of a rationalizing Enlightenment discourse that legislated the first constitutional measures applied to the Catholic Church as well as instituting property rights and the control of education. This process differed from that of Mexico and the Caribbean, given that Central America did not obtain independence as a result of unified struggles against the Captain Generalcy, but was rather the consequence of the general reaction against the 1820 Liberal Revolution in Spain. When Central America declared independence, Mexico's Emperor Iturbide sent an army to recover the isthmus for Mexico. After the latter's defeat, the five Central American provinces again declared independence in 1823. The Constitution of 1824 was written under Liberal influence and, despite the antecedents, with limited input from the clergy. This federation would survive strong divisions and confrontations between Liberals and Conservatives, such as Manuel José Arce, Francisco Morazán, and Rafael Carrera, until it dissolved in 1837.

Without doubt the most interesting personality of the period was José Cecilio del Valle (1777–1834), a kind of Enlightened Liberal, the owner of the most important private library in Central America and one of those who drew up the Act of Independence. Author of imaginary satirical dialogues (such as those between Columbus and Rousseau, Hernán Cortés [1485–1547] and Montesquieu) and proposals for continental unity in the style of Bolívar, he renewed the idea of the appropriation of American history. An outstanding member of the new government and founding father of the region, he supported the prosperity of the Indians as a condition for the prosperity of the country as a whole—an approach that was not, of course, characteristic of Liberalism in other Latin American countries. José Cecilio del Valle was a kind of Central American Andrés Bello (1781–1865). Both were learned men; both had an important relationship with Jeremy Bentham (1748–1832), a fact that Valle chose to ignore other than to mention Bentham's influence on Bolívar's thinking. Among Valle's proposals was the need to Americanize the language: "La lengua castellana, hablada por naciones independientes de Castilla, se irá mudando insensiblemente. Cada estado americano tendrá su dialecto: se multiplicarán los idiomas; y cada idioma será un método nuevo de análisis" (2: 186) ("The Spanish language spoken by nationals independent of Spain would imperceptibly undergo alteration. Each American state would have its dialect: The languages would multiply; and each language would become a new method of analysis"). Just as Gual and España, in their own way, had tried to do in vain, Valle recovered the rights of man and the citizen learned from France and the United States, and went on to adapt them:

> Una población heterogénea, dividida en tantas castas y diseminada en territorios tan vastos, llegará a unir sus votos sobre el gobierno que debe constituirse? Las clases que han gozado serán bastante justas para dividir sus goces con las demás? Las que han sufrido serán bastante racionales para no excederse en sus peticiones? (1: 165, 174–75)

> Would a heterogeneous population, divided up in so many castes and disseminated over such vast tracts of land, succeed in uniting their votes on the type of government needed? Would those social classes that had enjoyed possessions be sufficiently fair to divide these up with the rest? Would those who have suffered be sufficiently rational not to exceed themselves in their petitions?

Internal transculturation still had a long way to go, and I am not assuming here an interchange or a balanced contact between so many castes; on the contrary, in the will to Americanize the language also lies the will to homogenize under the control of a group placed above the others, something one could not but expect from this period. Nevertheless, José Cecilio del Valle, in his desire to nationalize/Americanize, does not marginalize the so-called silent minorities: Indians, workers, and women. His transcultural thesis of history as a traffic and transit of ideas does not subordinate the new states to imperial models in a new disguise. The beginning of Latin American nationalism can be seen in the 1820s when the countries began to develop their own mode of organization after the wars of independence and sought to establish distinctive national traits. In Europe meanwhile, as Eric Hobsbawm has noted, this was not the case until the middle of the nineteenth century.

The *Criolla* Virgin

The independence of New Spain was largely connected with an awareness of its own superiority. Mexico knew that it was enormously rich in natural resources; its educational institutions were outstanding among those in the Spanish empire, and its past was an ever-increasing source of pride. History began to be rewritten. At the end of the sixteenth century the *criollos* began nostalgically to record the Conquest period of the early sixteenth century, whose heroism and legacy they claimed as descendants of the conquistadors. The clergy now argued that the Aztec Empire was the principal glory of the Mexican fatherland. Bernardo de Sahagún (1500?–1590), for example, was a Franciscan priest whose monumental work *Historia general de las cosas de Nueva España* [1579; *General History of the Things of New Spain*, 1950–1982] established beyond a doubt the depth and richness of the pre-Hispanic civilization. The foundation of Mexico as a nation was initiated by a theological issue. If the discovery of the Indies was, as Gomara states, the best event since the creation of the world, leaving out the incarnation and death of the One who created it, this fact was so important that it should already have been written into the sacred texts. At the beginning of the seventeenth century, the Dominican monk Gregorio García (d. 1627) and the Augustine Order, through Fray Antonio de la Calancha (1584–1654), stood firmly behind the idea that there had been pre-Conquest evangelization, deducing that it would be an insult to the mercy of God's justice to think that between the coming of Jesus and the arrival of the Spaniards, God would have left the Indians so many centuries without light. The Franciscans took the opposite view, which was imposed as the official one: The Indians had been kept in darkness for fifteen centuries to be enlightened on a particular day, chosen by the Lord, by a King and by a chosen people, the Spaniards. The providential right of the Spaniards appears like a divine grace promising the arrival of universal salvation mediated by the Catholic monarchs.

Despite Franciscan opposition, the devotion paid to a specifically native Virgin began. Bishop Montúfar ordered an investigation and in 1555 founded the first Basilica of Our Lady of Guadalupe (Nuestra Señora de Guadalupe). Almost a century would pass before the Guadalupe cult would be formalized in writing. In 1648 Miguel Sánchez Requejo (d. 1615) published *Imagen de la Virgen María Madre de Dios de Guadalupe, milagrosamente aparecida en la Ciudad de México . . . [Image of the Virgin Mary, Mother of God of Guadalupe, Miraculous Appeared in Mexico City . . .*, 1998], in which he explained the miracle: The Virgin Mary appeared in person at Tepeyac, near the City of Mexico, to the illiterate Indian Juan Diego (canonized saint, 2002). As proof she left her image on the Indian's *tilma* or cloak. If the Virgin had chosen to come personally to Mexico and bless it as God's land, the providentialist role of the Spaniards in Mexico was reduced. To the *criollos* the apparition of the Virgin conferred a noble title on Mexico, in this case a nobility of grace that came not from the King but directly from God. The mother of God was now championed as the founder and patron of the Mexican Church—a cult inspiring both enormous religious devotion and unlimited patriotic sentiment was born (Brading 356–61). The diffusion of the Guadalupe cult was also identified with Quetzalcoatl (the eighth-century Toltec king), who from the seventeenth century was regarded as the incarnation of St. Thomas the Apostle. These ecclesiastics who were at the forefront of this *criollo* Mexican nationalism included the already mentioned figures of Bernardino de Sahagún, Diego Durán (1537–1587), Juan de Tovar (ca. 1546–ca. 1626), and the celebrated scholar and poet Carlos Sigüenza y Góngora (1645–1700).

In 1747 the diocese of New Spain had already declared Our Lady of Guadalupe as its patron; all the provincial capitals constructed special altars, frequently located in the open air in imitation of Tepeyac (see **Figure** 2). None of these authors or the followers of the Mexican Virgin dared to formulate any theory of the prior evangelization of America, however. Until Fray Servando Teresa de Mier's (1763–1827) famous sermon of 1794, the basis of the Spanish Conquest for

more than two centuries had been evangelization. (This sermon was to earn him thirty years of persecution.) In it, he links two traditions, claiming that the Virgin appeared to St. Thomas instead of the Indian Juan Diego. In one blow Fray Servando Teresa wiped out the justification for the Conquest of America. Moreover, he continued, if the conquistadores had recognized the Mexican religion as a variant or transfiguration of the Christian faith, the Conquest would not have required the shedding of a single drop of blood. In fact the Spaniards destroyed the same religion that they professed. His ideas were judged heterodox, and Fray Servando Teresa was harshly punished by the Tribunal of the Holy Office of the Inquisition, although his transgression was more political than religious. A fervent defender of Mexican freedom, he illustrated in his ideas how countries were revising their discourse to support political revolution:

> Digo esto porque algunos me acusaban de que había intentado quitar a los españoles la gloria de haber traído el Evangelio. Cómo pude haber pensado en quitarles una gloria que es muy nuestra, pues fué de nuestros padres los conquistadores, o los primeros misioneros, cuya sucesión apostólica está entre nosotros? (Fray Servando Teresa de Mier 21)

> I state this because some accuse me of having tried to take away from the Spaniards the glory of having brought the Gospels. How could I have thought of removing a glory that is very much our own, since it came from our fathers, the conquistadors or the first missionaries, whose apostolic succession remains with us.

It is certain that Fray Servando Teresa de Mier contributed, for example, to *El Español*, published in London by José María Blanco y Crespo (1775–1841) (known as Blanco White) and that this publication also greatly influenced Bolívar. But the echo of his attacks against Bonaparte and Catholic religious culture does not explain why Mexican Independence is rooted in religious grounds. It is also certain that the ideas of the Enlightenment arrived in the region and that the debating and defining of what was found in the Guadalupan creed show that Mexicans were open to outside influences. But the Virgin of Guadalupe, as one of the major examples of syncretism and *mestizaje*, involved much more. Something similar occurred with the Virgen del Cobre in Cuba, at least according to the description of Onofre de Fonceca, reconstructed at the end of the eighteenth century.

The reforms of the government of Carlos III meant, in the long term, the end of the Spanish monarchy. There was a necessity for economic reform. Bishop Manuel Abad y Quiepo wanted to apply the ideas of Jovellanos in Mexico, which stated that if the government provided equal rights under the law and equality in land distribution, all individuals, independent of class or race, would respond to economic incentives. This implied investigation into injustices in the allocation of land. The bishop supported the monarchy and not independence, but he too was accused of being responsible for the number of rebel priests in Michoacan and was imprisoned by the Inquisition. On the other hand, the Crown in 1804 ordered that Church properties in New Spain be sold and the funds deposited in the royal coffers. The loss of Church privileges was fatal. Many *criollos* considered that America's role was to conserve a religion that was being exterminated in Europe and to defend the religious orders that were outlawed in Spain. When the priest Miguel Hidalgo y Costilla (1753–1811) called for mass revolt in 1810, Indians, ranchers, artisans, and miners rallied to the standard of Our Lady of Guadalupe.

Figure 2.

Painting of the Virgin of Guadalupe by María Luisa de Villa. (Courtesy of María Luisa de Villa)

The elite landowners were frightened by the sacking and the popular character of the uprising led by Father Hidalgo and had him executed. In the south another cleric emerged, the parish priest José María Morelos (1765–1815), who demanded the abolition of ethnic castes, proclaimed the equality and common identity of the Mexicans, and demanded the expulsion of the Europeans and obedience to the Virgin of Guadalupe. Morelos wanted to return property to the Mexicans and lost power to the priests, who, he considered, ought to govern in both temporal and spiritual spheres. His measured policies urged leaders to achieve their ends through means that were straightforward and secure, avoiding the spilling of blood on both sides; these ideas had no match in the continent. The enemies of the State were no longer only the *gachupines* (Spaniards) but also the rich, noble, and employed *criollos* who were addicted to the European system. Morelos, moreover, decreed the abolition of the *latifundia* system and the destruction of over-large haciendas, so that many more might benefit from agriculture.

Mexico is a country where concepts of transculturation and cultural hybridism and/or *mestizaje* have been more apparent because of the necessity to negotiate with the *mestizo* and Indian majorities. The "new" here did not correspond to

Enlightened discourse, except for the capacity of syncretism to achieve political mobilization on the path to national autonomy. The creed of the Virgin of Guadalupe, Fray Servando Teresa de Mier's failure as a negotiator on a symbolic level, and the pressure of popular demands incarnated in Fathers Hidalgo and Morelos led to the proclamation of the Emperor Augustin Iturbide (1783–1824) and his coronation with the crown of Anahuac, a figure quickly defeated by his enemies but also himself an expression of transculturation.

Translation by Jessica Johnson

Works Cited

Biggs, James. 1810. *The History of Don Francisco de Miranda's Attempt to Effect a Revolution in South America.* Boston: E. Oliver.

Bolívar, Simón. 1951. *Selected Writings of Bolívar.* Compiled by Vicente Lecuna. Ed. Harold A. Bierck, Jr. Trans. Lewis Bertrand. 2 vols. New York: Colonial Press.

———. [1968] *Obras completas.* Ed. Pedro Grases. 3 vols. Caracas: E. Requena Mira.

Brading, David. 1991. *The First America: The Spanish Monarchy, Creole Patriots and the Liberal State, 1492–1867.* Cambridge: Cambridge University Press.

Chatterjee, Partha. 1986. *Nationalist Thought and the Colonial World: A Derivative Discourse.* Minneapolis: University of Minnesota Press.

Chukwudi Eze, Emmanuel, ed. 1997. *Race and the Enlightenment: A Reader.* Cambridge: Blackwell's.

Fonceca, Onofre. 1853. *Historia de la aparición milagrosa de Nuestra Señora de la Caridad del Cobre, sacada de un manuscrito que el primer capellán que fue de ella, presbítero D. Onofre de Fonceca, componía por el año de 1703 y sacaba de los autos que en el de 1688 se formaron ante juez competente, los cuales se hallan en el archivo de la santa casa.* [Santiago de] Cuba: Imprenta de la Viuda e hijos de Espinal.

Grases, Pedro. 1959. "Estudio sobre los 'derechos del hombre y del ciudadano.'" *Derechos del hombre y del ciudadano.* Caracas: Academia Nacional de la Historia. 103–246.

Hobsbawm, Eric. 1992. *Nations and Nationalism Since 1780: Programme, Myth, Reality.* Cambridge: Cambridge University Press.

Laclau, Ernesto. 1996. *Emancipación y diferencia.* Buenos Aires: Ariel.

Liévano Aguirre, Indalecio. 1966. *Los grandes conflictos sociales y económicos de nuestra historia.* Bogota: Tercer Mundo.

Miranda, Francisco de. 1992. *América espera.* Ed. J. L. Salcedo Bastardo. Caracas: Biblioteca Ayacucho.

Rodríguez, Simón. 1975. *Obras completas.* 2 vols. Caracas: Universidad Simón Rodríguez.

Romero, José Luis, and Luis Alberto Rombero, eds. 1978. *Pensamiento conservador (1815–1898).* Caracas: Biblioteca Ayacucho.

Rotker, Susana. 1996. "Nation and Mockery: The Oppositional Writings of Simón Rodríguez." *The Places of History: Regionalism Revisited in Latin America.* Ed. Doris Sommer. Trans. Sophia McClennen. *Modern Language Quarterly* (Special Issue) 57.2: 253–68.

Sánchez Reulet, Aníbal. n.d. *La filosofía latinoamericana contemporánea.* Mexico City: Unión Panamericana.

Schwarz, Roberto. 1992. *Misplaced Ideas: Essays on Brazilian Culture.* Ed. and trans. J. Gledson. London and New York: Verso.

Soler, Ricaurte. 1980. *Idea y cuestión nacional latinoamericanas de la independencia a la emergencia del imperialismo.* Mexico City: Siglo XXI.

Teresa de Mier Noriega y Guerra, Fray José Servando. 1917. *Memorias de Fray Servando Teresa de Mier.* Madrid: Editorial América.

Valle, José Cecilio del. 1929–1930. *Obras de José Cecilio del Valle.* 2 vols. Ed. José del Valle and Jorge del Valle Matheu. Guatemala: Tipografía Sánchez y De Guise.

Žižek, Slavoj. 1989. *The Sublime Object of Ideology.* London and New York: Verso.

CHAPTER 17

LITERARY *CRIOLLISMO* AND INDIGENISM

Horacio Legrás

The *criollista* canon (basically composed of works dating between 1900 and 1940) sought to assert Latin-American culture and advertise its difference from both European and a purported universal culture. *Criollista* strategy has therefore had recourse to representing aesthetically an abundance of characters, signs, and social symbols considered characteristic of a country or region (e.g., the Venezuelan *llanero*, the Argentine gaucho, the Chilean *huaso,* and the Brazilian *sertanejo*). Faced with the cosmopolitan nature of urban expansion at the beginning of the century, *criollismo* presented such characters as national icons, preferring to locate fictional drama in regions of the country still untouched by modernization. This reaction to cosmopolitanism should not lead to the erroneous conclusion that *criollismo* was an anti-modern movement. On the contrary, it asserted national idiosyncrasy as a means of assimilating the nation, and indeed Latin America, into the modernizing process.

In a continent composed of dissimilar and heterogeneous national cultures, this intent to reduce diversity to a common denominator was a complex operation with unpredictable results. The very genesis and evolution of the word *criollo* is indicative of the problem of how to discern the differential aspect of what is American. While, in the Caribbean, *criollo* was the name given to the descendants of black slaves born in America, later on the term evolved to designate the offspring of Spaniards born in America. But by the twentieth century some authors were already describing everyone on the continent as *criollo* in simple opposition to the foreigner. In the countries where *criollismo* was politically dominant, the term underlines locality over origin and sociopolitical position over lineage. There is nothing accidental about the fact that *criollismo* appeared after the rejection of the nineteenth-century explanatory models of Latin American culture based on concepts such as race or heritage. *Mestizaje,* reviled throughout the nineteenth century as the producer of inferior groups, was elevated as the basis for a utopian future for America in works such as *La raza cósmica* [1925; *The Cosmic Race,* 1997] by the Mexican José Vasconcelos (1881–1959).

The *criollista* enterprise marked its difference from "America" (as a term now appropriated by the United States) by using an element that was both transcendent and invariable: The land. For this reason *costumbrismo* (customs and manners), tellurism, or regionalism became categories that were superimposed on the traditional understanding of *criollismo.* But *criollismo* was not only a literary movement; it was fundamentally a complex ideological device. As such it incarnated what Roland Barthes called the essential function of ideology: To live as *natural* what is in fact *historical.* The historical institution that *criollismo* sought to naturalize was the modern nation-state and its representational apparatus–of which literature, especially the *criollista* version, was an essential component.

While *criollista* writers formed or aspired to form part of the elite of their respective countries, the *criollista* novel selected popular groups who had been excluded up until that time

from consideration as representative types: The gaucho in Argentina, the *llanero* or plainsman of Venezuela, the *huaso* in Chile, and the *sertanejo* of Brazil. *Criollista* writing subsequently moved from employing typical social symbols to a more denunciatory social mode (Martin 35–64; Arias 757); primarily it became a constituent element of cultural nationalism (Altamirano and Sarlo 72). The *criollista* decision to select from among the most marginalized sectors the representatives of national idiosyncrasy alerts us to a fundamental change in the concept of the nation as the nineteenth century moved into the twentieth. Unlike the exclusionary logic prevalent during the earlier Independence period (1820–1900), now there was an attempt to integrate all the inhabitants of the territory into a national body. José Rodó (1871–1917) popularized a *criollista* conviction when he wrote in the introduction to *El Terruño* [1916; Native Soil], a novel by his fellow countryman Carlos Reyles (1868–1938): "La misteriosa 'voluntad' que nos señala tierra donde nacer y tiempo en que vivir, nos impone con ello una solidaridad" (xiii) ("The mysterious 'will' that indicates the land where we are to be born, and where we spend our lifetime, imposes a solidarity on us").

Jorge Luis Borges (1899–1986) can be considered an avant-garde *criollista.* In 1932 he examined the consequences of fifty years of *criollista* experience in Argentina; he was critical of the reductive representational character of the movement and he considered it an unjustifiable imposition. In "El escritor argentino y la tradición" ["The Argentinean Writer and Tradition"], Borges begins by implying that the ideal reader of *criollista* works is European or a Europeanized American and therefore unfamiliar with Latin American peculiarities and idiosyncrasies. For Borges, *criollista* writers were creators of exoticism whose Eurocentric America was an extension of their fantasies. In the same work Borges uses his well-known example of the Koran (in which, despite the indubitable Arabic character of the text, there is no mention of camels) in order to refute the representational pretensions of the *criollistas*: "Mahoma, como árabe, no tenía por qué saber que los camellos eran especialmente árabes . . . un falsario, un turista, un nacionalista árabe, lo primero que hubiera hecho es prodigar camellos . . ." (1: 270) ("Muhammad, being Arab, did not have any reason to state that camels were particularly Arabic . . . the first thing an imposter, a tourist, an Arab nationalist, would have done would have been to feature camels on a lavish scale").

Borges's dismantling of *criollismo* is, paradoxically, a profoundly *criollista* act. *Criollismo,* as mentioned previously, seeks to naturalize the social relationships that it proposes. For this reason it constructs language, land, or some idiosyncrasy as destiny–that "mysterious will" referred to by Rodó. Significantly, Benedict Anderson underlines the point that the historically contingent form of the nation-state is considered by its inhabitants as fate and destiny (Anderson 12; see also Balibar and Wallerstein 86). Such a destiny takes on the form of an ideology, to the extent that it is not thought out by the social actors who incarnate and endure it. As Carlos Alonso has pointed out in his commentary on Borges's text, the evidence that Muhammad, being an Arab, did not represent camels as part of Arabic culture relies on the presupposition that camels *are* an essential element in the definition of Arabness (!). In the same way, Borges's dismantling of a dominant cultural representation of national character does not deny but rather affirms the existence of the same.

Moreover, Borges presupposes that the implied reader of *criollista* literary works is a foreigner, when in fact the public is overwhelmingly a national one. *Criollismo* is aimed at the very heart of the community, offering images for cultural identification and inviting its readers to see themselves reflected in the cultural imaginary. This dimension of *criollista* praxis allows us to differentiate it from nineteenth-century Romanticism, which was also suffused with an enthusiasm for representation. Esteban Echeverría (1805–1851) had announced that the destiny of Americans was to have one eye fixed on their societies and the other on Europe. The *criollista* of the next century might say that their literature emerged in the moment that both eyes were turned to the peculiarities of the landscape of their respective countries. This sustained attention to the local was accompanied by a new definition of the people that was inseparable from and complementary to the already mentioned redefinition of nation. In political terms the nineteenth-century conception of the people actively excluded the illiterate, women, ethnic minorities, and the dispossessed. To represent them to the implied European reader meant to expose the internal deficiencies that Latin American modernization should, in the best of cases, overcome and, in the worst (e.g., the indigenous peoples), exterminate. The eugenic rhetoric dominant in the continent at the end of the nineteenth century constituted the form in which the elite took charge of a people, defined in advance as atavistic and ineducable (see Stepan). This ideology could not constitute a discourse for *speaking to the people*, or a discourse capable of describing the social conditions of production. The twentieth century, on the other hand, transformed this policy of exclusion into an attempt at maximum inclusion. What had changed to bring about such a result?

The key to change was found in the incorporation of Latin America into the world capitalist market as a producer of raw materials. This change began to dominate Latin America around 1880, inaugurating what Tulio Halperín Donghi called the period of neo-Colonial maturity (288–368). The trilogy of foundational *criollista* novels—*Doña Bárbara* (1929) by Rómulo Gallegos (1884–1969), *La Vorágine* [1924; The Vortex] by José Eustasio Rivera (1888–1928), and *Don Segundo Sombra* (1926) by Ricardo Güiraldes (1886–1927)—clearly fit into the movement and created this ideological horizon. In their respective texts a new Latin America appears at odds with the past, given the appearance of new forms of production, an incipient accumulation of capital, and the effective legislative power of the nation-state. By proposing a limited but representative group as characteristic of a national totality, *criollismo* fulfilled a homogenizing function that was vital to the success of the enterprise of modernization. The relationships between the intellectual and the people would not continue in the form of the nineteenth-century polarity of civilization and barbarism but, rather, as Rodó once again exemplified, there was a civic duty to modernize, which meant a close correlation between educators and pupils, wherein the entire nation was transformed into a gigantic classroom.

While William Rowe defines *criollismo* as a "nacionalismo estético" ("aesthetic nationalism") (1994, 707) following Ricardo Latcham (1903–1965), one should understand such a statement in the sense that the nation-state and one's belonging to it are imagined, fundamentally, on an aesthetic basis. But who grants writers this point of privileged enunciation in the imaginary construction of the nation? As Carlos Altamirano and Beatriz Sarlo have noted, the privileging of literature in this process was already written into *criollista* ideology, which made the land into the transcendent principle of nationality. The land was set up as a secret meaning in search of a hermeneutic; the writer was granted the privilege of unraveling that meaning. Borges ironically described both *criollismo* and its demise in his celebrated definition of the aesthetic event as that moment at which the pampas are on the point of telling us something, but the revelation of meaning is not forthcoming.

The transformation of the writer at the turn of the century has been seen as a move from amateur avocation to professionalization (Altamirano and Sarlo; Ramos). Professionalization, though, does not distance the writer from the sphere of influence of the State, but rather achieves the opposite, since the nation-state, by recodifying its relationship with the writer—as the maker of the imagined community—absorbs them more than ever. While, in the nineteenth century, the authority of the intellectual derived from superior sensibility (Romanticism) or scientific knowledge (Naturalism) or, later, from being a purveyor of high culture (*modernismo*), the authority of the *criollista* writer issued from the very notion of the nation-state itself. The Mexican Martín Luis Guzmán (1887–1977), in his administrative position in the post-Revolutionary government, made Pancho Villa in one of his novels say "vamos a la lucha como revolucionarios concientes, como hombres que saben que se batirán por el bien del pueblo y de los pobres, contra los ricos y poderosos, y que por ser ignorantes, pues nadie los ha enseñado, necesitan que los que más saben los manden y los guíen" (27) ("let us enter the struggle as conscious revolutionaries, as men knowing that they are fighting for the good of the people and the poor, against the rich and powerful, and who, being ignorant, since no one has instructed them, need those with greater knowledge to give them orders and guide them"). The notion that Guzmán puts in Pancho Villa's mouth reveals the transition that *criollismo* as an institutional literary project wished to incarnate: From revolutionary struggle to education, from confrontation to persuasion, or (to sum up) from domination to hegemony. A similar view was held by Euclides da Cunha (1866–1909) in *Os sertões* [1902; *Rebellion in the Backlands*, 1944]: When reflecting on the destruction of the city of Canudos by the federal army, he reflected on the idea that the schoolteacher is a more effective weapon than the army to achieve national unification.

This adaptation of intellectuals to the demands of the popular nation-state did not entail only their function as educators of the masses but also the re-education of the writers themselves. Rodó's *Ariel*, to be discussed at length below, was aimed at the educated elite rather than at the general population. Euclides da Cunha (in *Os sertões*), Santos Luzardo (in *Doña Barbara*), or Arturo Cova (in *La Vorágine*) are all intellectuals who began a voyage of discovery of a profound reality, intimate but unknown, that ended up by also transforming them. But this does not mean that the writers were fully successful in removing the eugenic prejudice or intellectual dependence on Europe that had characterized their education up to the beginning of the century. It seems indicative that Fernando Ortiz (1881–1969), responsible for the concept of transculturation, began his intellectual career with a text that argued the impossibility of incorporating a good part of the black population into the Cuban society (*Los Negros brujos* [1906; The Black Sorcerers]), and that the Peruvian Francisco García Calderón (1883–1953) decided to write *Les democraties latines de l'Amerique* [1912; The Latin Democracies of America] in French and publish it in Paris, assuming that his intended readers, if not actually in France, would be educated in French. If there were no biological determinants for this nascent *criollismo*, if the determining program was cultural and education-oriented, and if in many cases different eugenic doubts remained (a lack of confidence in the possible constitution of the people), then *criollismo* must be understood as re-interpreted nineteenth-century ideology (i.e., Positivism or Social Darwinism). In the places where racial determinist discourse disappeared in favor of a cultural approach, what was actually taking place was the replacement of one intellectual elite by another. While Justo Sierra (1848–1912) himself completed the trajectory from ideologue and political partisan of eugenic Positivism in Mexico to defender of the *mestizo* within Mexican society (312), the triumph of the *criollista* paradigm occurred through the replacement of its leadership by members of the Ateneo de la Juventud, such as José Vasconcelos. In the River Plate region, where, as Martin Stabb has pointed out (14), racial determinism and atavism were never dominant in the ideology of the emergent middle class, the replacement of paradigms reflects in this case a replacement of the very make-up of the intellectual camp.

One significant element in the evolution of *criollismo* was continentalization, the concept of a Latin American culture. In this sense it is not an exaggeration to state that *Ariel* (1900), by the Uruguayan writer José Rodó, established *criollismo* as a possible Latin American ideology. *Ariel* was published two years after the Spanish-American War (1898), an event that made manifest the now sustained penetration of United States capital into the Americas and the military domination over what was now Latin America. This historical context determined the interpretation of the book more than any other element. *Ariel* was thus read as an indictment of U.S. capitalism, which Rodó opposed by reasserting a Latin American identity, with spirituality as its distinctive feature. In his exhaustive introduction to Rodó's text, Gordon Brotherston has shown that the context in which the work was produced was rather different from that in which it was received (5).

Even though *Ariel* proposed to characterize Latin American culture as one confronted by U.S. expansionism, it was obvious that Rodó's proposal posed enormous problems for intellectuals. *Ariel* stressed a reclaiming of the Hispanic tradition on a continent where the indigenous, *mestizo*, or black presence refuted the possibility of such an all-embracing representation. On the other hand, as Roberto Fernández Retamar (b. 1930) would note in his *Calibán* (1971) (a text that complements and inverts Rodó's teleology), *Ariel* did not recognize the need for incorporating the people as a whole into the democratic process. The large population of the suburbs of the time was as distant from (and contrary to) Rodó's viewpoint as the materialist idiosyncrasies of U.S. investors. Even though it was esteemed by Latin American intellectuals, Rodó's text ought to have engaged in dialogue with different local realities; it was at the local level that it suffered either drastic adaptations or was practically ignored, and this was

especially true in those regions of greatest economic dynamism. Even its most enthusiastic admirer, Pedro Henríquez Ureña (1884–1946), felt the need to note *Ariel*'s deficiencies in terms of the modernizing process and did so in the introduction that he wrote for the Mexican edition of *Ariel* published in 1907. Despite all of this, the Latin American novel did not lose its sense of cultural kinship and, in turn, fostered the continental phenomenon of what literary criticism for a long time called, ironically, the regionalist novel.

Criollista Maturity

In 1929 two basic texts representative of Latin American *criollismo* and the modern Venezuelan novel were published, *Memorias de Mamá Blanca* [*Mama Blanca's Souvenirs*, 1959] by Teresa de la Parra (1889–1936) and Rómulo Gallegos's *Doña Barbara*. Both novels were written in the context of the modernizing process experienced by contemporary Venezuelan society, despite the fact that they were set in more remote historical periods. *Memorias de Mamá Blanca* represents the tension between an aristocratic rural world that was disappearing and the new commercial world and its relationships, made painfully clear with the relocation of the protagonist's family to Caracas. Teresa de la Parra is explicitly sympathetic toward the old methods of production (the sugar mill with its ominous echo of slavery) in contrast with modern industrial forms of production. Details of this kind have been offered to support the somewhat prevalent conviction regarding the reactionary character of *Memorias*. Doris Sommer (314), like other contemporary literary critics, has rightly disputed such a reductive characterization. Economic and social modernization, as *Doña Bárbara* would make all too clear, did not consider the inclusion of women within the national economic community. Sylvia Molloy also points out that the politically reactionary narrative focus of *Memorias* can be read as a reaction to the limitations of a cynical modernization.

On the other hand, *Memorias* also indicated a terrible condemnation of Venezuelan landed aristocracy through the character of Cousin Juancho who is the prototype of the vain individual, as implied by his useless peripheral knowledge: "Tal era primo Juancho: un Larousse desencuadernado y des-encadenado con todas las hojas sueltas . . . incapaz de orga-nizar ni crear nada que no fuese el caos" (1983, 75) ("That was Cousin Juancho–an unbound Larousse, with all the pages loose, and upside down . . . incapable of organizing or creating anything but chaos" [1959, 50]). Cousin Juancho incarnates the Latin American figure of the wealthy modern aristocrat. He travels to Europe and brings back customs that are absurd and out of place (e.g., a London parasol for four o'clock tea in the midst of the powerful summer sun of the Venezuelan prairies). This negative characterization rapidly gives way to an elegy to futility. In the best style of *Ariel*, Teresa de la Parra counterpoints the useless trappings of modernity with the true value of Cousin Juancho as the symbol of "el alma idealista de la raza" (1983, 86) ("the idealistic soul of my race" [1959, 58]). The Conservative nucleus of *Memorias*, echoing *Ariel*, is precisely the identification of *criollismo* with the landed aristocracy of Hispanic heritage, the traditional values of Hispanism and the Spanish language, which it opposes to a dangerous rush toward modernization.

The counterpart to Cousin Juancho is Vicente Cochocho, a mix of Indian and black, described by the narrator with almost religious fervor. Cochocho is the last peon of the hacienda; he is loyal to the old ways of life on the prairies and speaks the rural Spanish of Venezuela, both traits that are highly praised by the narrator: "Vicente decía, como en el magnífico siglo XVI, *ansina*, en lugar de así; *truje*, en lugar de traje . . . , su español, en una palabra, era del Siglo de Oro" (1983, 107–08) ("Vicente's Spanish (*ansina* instead of *así*; *truje* instead of *truje*) was that of the Golden Age" [1050, 73]). The obvious problem with such a strategy is that it identifies as its utopia a past that the same text will end up declaring irrecoverable. Contrary to what has so frequently been pointed out, Hispanism did not constitute an integral part of the *criollista* project, but rather almost always figured as an ideological weapon used by the old oligarchies to slow down the advance of the middle classes and the threat of the burgeoning proletariat. Its inspiration also derives, paradoxically, from José Rodó's seminal text.

In contrast to Parra, who delighted in the use of the word *bárbaro* ("barbarous"), Rómulo Gallegos aimed to construct a dialectic between civilization as the principal guide, and barbarism as the truth and primordial force of the prairies. The prairie land, now fallen into barbarism and lawlessness, was once a happy place. Its ruin was the result of a fratricidal struggle between José Luzardo and his son Félix, provoked by the Spanish-American War of 1898. José, "fiel a su sangre" ("true to his race"), sympathized with Spain, while his son Félix, "síntoma de los tiempos que ya empezaban a correr, se entusiasmaba por los yanquis" (1990, 74) ("a symbol of the new times, took the part of the 'Yankees'" [1948, 20]). This tension between "race" and "modernity" (where, in terms of race, the point of view expressed by *Ariel* competed with tellurism) is postulated as the textual past of *Doña Bárbara*. Santos Luzardo arrives on the prairies to find himself reduced to the will of the dominant Doña Bárbara. In contrast to *La vorágine*, in which the ferocity of capitalist exploitation is at the forefront, Santos Luzardo finds the work of primitive capital accumulation already monopolized by the landowner. Santos Luzardo ends up becoming a recodifier of the laws of the territory. His modernization is limited to demarcating property limits, putting justice into action, and existing capital into circulation; Doña Bárbara does not invest her money; she buries it—perhaps an unconscious elliptical reference by Gallegos to the future scenario of Venezuelan economic modernization: the exploitation of petroleum.

The conflict in *Doña Bárbara* surfaces when, as in almost all *criollista* works, the novel describes the work of the people. Here a woman, Marisela, represents the people: She is the daughter, abandoned almost at birth by Doña Bárbara, whom Luzardo will take into his charge as a means of demonstrating the efficacy of his modern educational theories. This equivalence between Marisela and the people will prove to be problematic in a novel that is packed with nearly all of the clichés of patriarchalism. Gallegos fails to rid himself of the millstone of the eugenic tradition or to overcome a reductive paternalistic attitude that is reflected in the stereotyped character of Santos Luzardo. The narrator draws our attention to the fact that Doña Bárbara is *mestiza* and has Indian blood. The sorcerer, the most dangerous male character, in the novel represents "alguna semilla tártara caída en América" (1990, 60) ("a strain of Tartar blood mysteriously introduced into South America" [1948, 4]). This obliges the narrative voice to present both Doña Bárbara and the sorcerer as foreign to the prairie. Once again it is the action of outsiders that brings ruin to the rural scene, which would have maintained itself in a state of idyllic harmony had there not been external forces (the war between the United States and Spain, the migrations

in Venezuela). The ambiguity about and the lack of confidence that the narrator has in the people also affects Marisela, who is the unwitting recipient of the civilizing attention of Santos Luzardo. From the transformation of the young woman and her subsequent union with her civilizing father-husband, Luzardo will bring about the reunification of the prairies. In a first instance Marisela is a representative "del alma de la raza, abierta como el paisaje a toda acción mejoradora" (1990, 213) ("of the soul of the Plainsman, open as the prairie and improved by every experience" [1948, 185]). But when Luzardo must seriously consider the possibility of marrying her, eugenic arguments dominate the scene: "Marisela, fruto de una unión inmoral y acaso heredera de las funestas condiciones paternas y maternas, no podía ser la mujer en quien pusiera su amor un hombre sensato" (1990, 293) ("Marisela, offspring of an illegitimate union and possibly inheritor of the regrettable qualities of both father and mother, could not be the woman in whom a judicious man would center his love" [1948, 282]). Thus, even though *Doña Bárbara* appears to be a more decided gamble on the side of modernization than *Memorias*, the novel still maintains a latent hostility to the possibility of new social groups invading the political field. In 1940 Rómulo Gallegos was elected president of Venezuela; it is undoubtedly anecdotal but indicative that the same doubts regarding the populism that plagued his novel also came to the surface during his short term as president.

Argentinean *Criollismo*

Criollismo emerged in Argentina prior to other *criollista* manifestations on the continent. The reason for this is partly the early entrance of the River Plate region into the world markets and the modernizing vigor of the zone. By 1880 the model, but not canonic, text of the genre made its appearance with *Juan Moreira* by Eduardo Gutiérrez (1851–1889). Curiously, literary criticism has generally preferred to ignore this first example of popular *criollismo* and has postulated *Don Segundo Sombra* by Ricardo Güiraldes as the seminal text of Argentinean *criollismo*. But the latter is fundamentally an expression of an attempt to make *criollismo* aristocratic, born out of a closed circle of urban letters and preceded by a long history of popular *criollista* production. William Rowe and Vivian Schelling relativize the canonic story of *criollismo* by counterpointing it with others' works: "Aunque las historias de la literatura enfatizan el rol de Don Segundo Sombra, mucho más leído en ese momento fueron las novelas populares producidas por escritores como Eduardo Gutiérrez para un creciente público urbano y masivo" (46) ("Although histories of literature emphasize *Don Segundo Sombra*, popular novels produced by writers such as Eduardo Gutiérrez, for what was becoming a mass urban public, were far more widely read at the time"). The reference to "ese momento" ("at the time") contrasts *Juan Moreira* of 1880 with *Don Segundo Sombra* of 1926, a period of forty-six years. What happened during these years? This is the time it took for that cultural nationalism, motivated by the oligarchy, to appropriate the productive symbolic apparatus of popular *criollismo*.

The serial story by Eduardo Gutiérrez was the fictionalization of the adventures of a bad gaucho, Juan Moreira, whose life had been followed in some detail by the newspapers of the period. Gutiérrez's character is not a bandit; nor is he someone incapable of adapting himself to the new conditions imposed by modernization. On the contrary, Moreira is a prosperous merchant who is forced into banditry because of the lack of institutional guarantees. For Gutiérrez, Moreira is not the rural or semi-urban subject presented as anti-modern, but the Argentinean state itself that is anti-modern (the Latin American exemplar of a successful modernization around 1880). The serial novel, emerging as a critique against an oligarchy resistant to broadening the democratic base, was also transformed into a cultural expression of *campesino* migrant and European immigrant groups who maintained a hostile relationship with the group in power. Given this political articulation, it would be erroneous to interpret Moreira's rebellion as a negation of modernization; rather, it deals with the incorporation of that modernization through confrontation. The novel, moreover, thematizes precisely this transition to new forms of daily life regulated by abstract entities such as the State and the marketplace. Thus toward the end, Moreira, who is dressed in a manner "que no es de ciudad ni de campo" (126) ("that is neither from the city nor the country"), will install himself at a crossroads to keep vigil over the railroad that connects the countryside and the city. This liminal position gives a special dimension to his death. Killed by a police sergeant, Moreira becomes a sacrificial hero, transforming his liminality into transitional movement. Readers understood this; adding to the immense popularity of the serial story, Moreira's image was constantly reproduced in Carnival disguises.

In his notable study of Argentinean *criollismo*, Adolfo Prieto observed that, around 1910, Rubén Darío (1867–1916) had the opportunity to record the proliferation of Moreira's story in his chronicles of the Carnival held in Buenos Aires. From the end of the nineteenth century, the street and the Carnival had been transformed into the constituent environments of Argentina's *criollista* citizenry. Social resentment and political protest became embodied in the Moreira disguise. That kind of spectacle soon reached the stage. The year that the Podestá brothers first presented *Juan Moreira* (1886) marked the birth of Argentinean theater–before the horrified gaze of an elite that had tried for decades to create a national theater. A commentator of the period warned the cultural producers of the elite that "este pueblo . . . al par de otros, tiene derecho a elegir sus espectáculos, irá a Juan Moreira hasta que ustedes, señores, no lo reemplacen con otro" (Schiaffino 36) ("these people . . . like others, have the right to choose their spectacles, they will attend *Juan Moreira* until you, sirs, replace it with another work").

Later Argentinean culture echoed the call of this commentator. Intellectuals of the oligarchy and the burgeoning middle class immediately set themselves the task of replacing the pernicious spectacle of *Juan Moreira* with more edifying work. The urgency was not just aesthetic. The political opposition entitled their newspaper *Juan Moreira*; the anarchists were writing texts, pretending to be *criollista* and calling on the popularity of the *campesino* hero. Meanwhile, those attending the performances were leaving the auditorium eager to shout verbal challenges to the first police authorities who came to hand. In Argentina the *criollo* enterprise thereby fulfilled its mediating and shaping role in the broadest manner possible, but did so using a means that the elite had not been able to predict.

On the other hand, the dramatic success of *Juan Moreira* signified the elevation of the theater to the space of social experimentation, where it offset the long-standing sense of the popular with its modalities, limits, and antagonisms. Ten years after Gutiérrez's work, Martiniano Leguizamón (1858–1935) began the project of replacing *Juan Moreira*. His drama *Calandria, costumbres campestres* [1896; *Calandria, A Drama of Gaucho Life,* 1932] was greeted with fervor by the entire Liberal press and all Conservative critics. No one was ignorant of the fact that the piece responded to *criollista* notions that were basically rooted in the anti-Moreira camp. Calandria was presented as a man pursued by injustice "un infelís gaucho que no tenía quien diera la cara por [él]" (25) ("an unhappy gaucho shunned by all"). While Moreira did not ask for anyone's mediation, particularly that of an intellectual, Calandria from the very first scene appears as if in need of State tutelage and oligarchic paternalism. It is a secondary issue to debate whether the work fulfilled its ideological objectives. More to the point is the fact that, from *Calandria* onward, it was evident that *criollismo* had to be refuted in its own camp–that of *criollo* and popular expression.

With the start of the twentieth century Argentinean *criollismo* would follow fundamentally two routes. On the one hand, it would act to guarantee the emergent middle-class or libertarian ideas of European derivation. Alberto Ghiraldo (1874–1946), for example, published *Alma Gaucha* [1907; Gaucho Soul] as a means of diffusing anarchist ideology, while the Uruguayan Florencio Sánchez (1875–1910) tackled the need for an alliance between the immigrant colonizer and the worker *criollo* against the oligarchic elite in a work such as *La gringa*. This is evident from the setting of the play in the Pampas on small parcels of land worked by immigrants and not in *latifundista* (estate) Buenos Aires. Immigrant groups simultaneously found a vehicle of expression in *criollismo* as well as an entry into a new society. Such was the case of Alberto Gerchunoff (1883–1950), who published *Los gauchos judios* [The Jewish Gauchos of the Pampas] around 1910. The second *criollo* wave was identified with a cultural nationalism that alternated progressive postures–Ricardo Rojas (1882–1957)–with more conservative and pro-oligarchic themes–Leopoldo Lugones. The *criollismo* promoted by Lugones (1874–1938) through, among other things, his reinterpretation of *Martín Fierro* (1872) as a national hero, aimed at the depoliticization of *criollismo*. Even so, such a work was placed at the service of a growing xenophobic nationalist discourse that was shot through with what Nestor García Canclini calls a "reactionary ontology" (18). The identification of *criollismo* and nationalism (non-existent in the primitive popular version) served the landowning oligarchy as an ideological weapon against growing labor agitation and organizations whose most outstanding leaders were, without exception, European-born.

Early popular *criollismo* had achieved an extraordinary representational power that transformed it into an indispensable cultural device for the state's nationalist discourse in spite of the fact that it had initially despised state power. *Criollismo* seemed to offer the nationalists, and not only Argentineans (even though the illusion was more intense in Argentina), the possibility of imagining total representation. Nationalism, anchored almost always in traditionalism, had to construct a system of exclusions. Internally, one could add, the emphasis of these same *criollista* novels on patriarchy gave the lie to the pretension to universal representation. Proof is plentiful: the desubjectivization of Marisela at the hands of Santos Luzardo, the forgetting of Juan Manuel (by no means accidentally assimilated into a statue of Bolívar) by his little girls in *Memorias de Mamá Blanca*, the suicide of "the negress" in *El inglés de los güesos* [1924; The English Bone Collector] by Benito Lynch (1880–1951), or Moreira's wife, begging on her knees "mátame, mi Juan, mátame" ("kill me, my Juan, kill me") in Gutiérrez's novel (72). In the end, *criollismo* was never anything other than politics among brothers.

Indigenism: The Unrepresented Remainder

Indigenism arose, like *criollismo*, as a cultural response to capitalist integration and the development of the modern nation-state. This process occurred in the Andean region (Peru, Ecuador, and Bolivia) from the second decade of the twentieth century (see Cueva; Cornejo Polar 1989; Caravedo Molinari). Unlike Uruguay or Argentina, whose population presented a high degree of European unification, the *criollo* sectors in the Andean countries were confronted with a vigorous indigenous population: To recall the words of José Carlos Mariátegui (1894–1930), they could "ni eliminarla, ni absorberla" (1976, 169) ("[not] eliminate it, or absorb it" [1971, 164]). Antonio Cornejo Polar (1936–1997), the most lucid analyst of Indigenism, insists that this is not the reference that primarily or exclusively defines the Indigenist novel. The colonial texts that deal with indigenous episodes are not Indigenist, nor is the idealizing of the indigenous, which, orientating itself to the past, forgets the contemporary exploitation of these groups. This basically nineteenth-century literature is categorized under the label of "Indianism" and includes novels such as *Enriquillo* (1882) by Manuel Galván (1834–1911) and *Cumandá* (1879) by Juan León Mera (1832–1894). In other words, the Indigenist problem arises only in relation to the modern State and its representational vocation.

Literature as an institution sought to understand itself as the incarnation of a universal reason, the cross-cultural apparatus of the nation-state, which represented national space as being beyond all strong cultural determination. The word that Cornejo Polar uses to combat this pretension is heterogeneity. Literature, the expression of European values in terms of universalized particulars, cannot represent indigenous otherness without violating it. The fact that many indigenous novels begin with a white intrusion into the balance of an indigenous community is not a thematic coincidence for Cornejo Polar. The indigenous world is revealed through an act of aggression: "En su coherencia o en sus conflictos interiores, ese universo resulta ajeno al indigenismo" (Cornejo Polar 1982, 98) ("In its coherence or its interior conflicts, that universe is distant from Indigenism").

The need to take into account indigenous cultures in an elaboration of a national Peruvian modernity harks back to the work of José Carlos Mariátegui. Mariátegui systematized more general or inconsistent pro-indigenous currents, like that of Manuel González Prada (1848–1918), who had published "Nuestros indios" ["Our Indians"] some months prior to the former's return from Europe, or Luis Valcárcel (1891–1987), whom Mariátegui supported but debated in his prologue to *Tempestad en los Andes* [1927; Tempest in the Andes]. In his *Siete ensayos de interpretación de la realidad peruana* [1928; *Seven Interpretative Essays on Peruvian Reality*, 1971] Mariátegui for the first time introduced a series of precise areas in which Indigenism would no longer be overlooked. First, he denied that Peruvian literature was an organic whole, since Peru as a nation was not a whole. Secondly, Mariátegui differentiated between Indigenist literature produced by *mestizos* and Indigenous literature produced and consumed by indigenous people themselves–a project that, in his view, still lay in the future. Cornejo Polar has criticized the restricted use of the word "literature" in Mariátegui's work; nevertheless, such a restriction helps to illuminate the cultural (Western) historical specificity of the literary institution. As a Marxist, Mariátegui did not hesitate to encourage the incorporation of indigenous groups (identified in Peru as the workers) into the terrain of hegemony. He had written that only the individual who spoke the Indian language could gain the confidence of the indigenous people. It is with tragic irony, perhaps, that in *Yawar Fiesta* (1940) José María Arguedas (1911–1969) includes a scene in which the *serranos* (mountain people), having arrived at the coast, swear together before a portrait of Mariátegui to defend their Indian brothers, only to end up, once returned to the mountains, involuntarily allied to the source of power and the landowners against the customs of their own people.

The basic tensions of the Indigenist project had emerged by the end of the nineteenth century with the publication of *Aves sin nido* [1889; *Torn from the Nest*, 1998] by Clorinda Matto de Turner (1852–1909), which is considered to be the first text written in the genre. Cornejo Polar has objected that what little of the indigenous universe is saved in the novel is achieved through its total transference to the white world that threatens to destroy it (1994b, xxiv–xxv). This criticism does not put in question the progressive character of Matto de Turner's work, especially if one takes into account that *Aves sin nido* was published in an intellectual environment dominated by Positivist and racist ideas that propagated allegations of the natural inferiority of the indigenous people: *Continente enfermo* [1899; Sick Continent] by César Zumeta (1860–1955) in Venezuela; *Nuestra América* [1903; Our America] by the Argentinean Carlos Bunge (1875–1918); and the ferocious *Pueblo enfermo* [1909; Sick Nation] by the Bolivian Alcides Arguedas (1879–1946). These racist positions, whose predominant format was the essay, were answered from the perspective of an equally Positivist fervor–for education–by other contemporary essayists. Franz Tamayo (1879–1956), one of the intellectuals influenced by Nietzschean vitalism, proclaimed the superiority of the indigenous in *La creación de la pedagogía nacional* [1910; The Creation of National Pedagogy], an effort similar to that of Guillermo Francovich (1901–1990) in *Pachamama* (1942) and Fernando Díez de Medina (1908–1990) in *Thunupa* (1947) and "Sariri" (1954). Remarkably, many of these texts are both Indigenist and anti-Arielist, rejecting the function that the intellectual elites granted themselves in the Latin American modernizing process.

The Modern Indigenist Novel

Huasipungo (1934), by the Ecuadorian Jorge Icaza (1906–1978), articulated the Indigenist tension in a tragic resolution that would be a constant in later Indigenist work. *Huasipungo* describes the land where an indigenous community lives, while they work in almost slave conditions for the landowner. In the first chapters the interior monologues of the whites are opposed to the laconic expression of the indigenous people, who are brutalized by their poor living conditions. The solitude of the indigenous community, who, driven by hunger and worn out by unremunerative toil, decide to attack the hacienda of the landowner, is here complete. The Church, the Quito press, the army, the landowners, and U.S. capital (in the figure of Mr. Chapy), all come together against the *huasipungueros*. The novel culminates, as do the majority of Indigenist texts, in a massacre that is apocalyptic in tone.

The responsibility for the defeat of the Indians in this novel lies to a great extent in their incapacity, during their struggle, to transcend the limits of the hacienda and their ancestral practices. Even in the midst of the revolt, Icaza does not allow his heroes any expression other than the duplication of the voice of the master. The indigenous personalities in the novel are represented as existing in the most absolute degradation. Jean Franco would find fault with Icaza on this point. How could the narrative elicit a sense of solidarity for these wretched beings if it presents them almost on the edge of atavism? Jean Franco points out a key problem here in Indigenist portrayal: the dominance of wretchedness in the intellectual code (see Yúdice). Agustín Cueva would insist, even so, that the knowledge of indigenous otherness is attained only through the rejection of the familiar categories of the intellectual. The literary conscience, wrote Cueva, comes from the "polo social hegemónico" ("social hegemonic pole") and for this reason fails in the "plasmación de aquella materia prima, que, naturalmente, posee su propio espesor, vale decir, su propia forma" (16) ("depiction of that raw material that naturally possesses its own density, in other words, its own form").

The problem of *Huasipungo* finds an echo in what is considered to be the first modern novel of the Peruvian Indigenist cycle: *El mundo es ancho y ajeno* [1940; *Broad and Alien Is the World*, 1941] by Ciro Alegría (1909–1967). As in *Huasipungo*, the conflict begins with the inexorable expropriation of communal lands by prosperous landowners. The community interprets these events, clearly linked to the incorporation of Peru into the dynamic of international capitalism, through ancestral schema, such as the offering and augury. The novel concludes with Benito Castro, who has lived among the whites, directing the revolt against the landowners. Nevertheless, isolation returns to play the determining role in the defeat of the community. From Clorinda Matto to Icaza to Ciro Alegría, the tension is perpetuated between defending the communal life that ought to be defended and the cost of entering into struggles that imply rules and alliances totally alien to the indigenous world. This world extracts from its difference the negativity that allows it to confront the burgeoning capitalist organization. The paradox is that it can confront this organization only by renouncing that difference and liquidating its negativity.

From Testimony to *Testimonio*: José María Arguedas and Rigoberta Menchú

José María Arguedas's work marks the culmination of the tensions of Indigenism. Bilingual in Quechua and Spanish, Arguedas seemed, from his early short stories, to be the writer destined to reveal this immeasurable border of otherness represented by the Indian. His first novel *Yawar Fiesta* declares, through the disjunction of its title, the dual dynamic that structures the text. The conflict that the novel orchestrates is the state prohibition of the bullfight in Puquio. For the indigenous people the bullfight is an opportunity to transcend the social stereotypes to which they are condemned (above all, passivity). Arguedas does not oppose this wretchedness that has dominated the representation of the Indian with a positive image, but rather creates the scenario for a struggle for recognition. The prohibition is backed by the lords, the Mistis, and the Cholos, ex-Indians who now live in Lima and return to their Puquio for the community fiestas. Arguedas takes the indigenous side against the development-oriented discourse of the government and of the Indians transformed by their experience on the coast. In opposition to the *criollista* project, the distance between the Indians and the circuit of communication that unites, though poorly, the state and the *criollos* is remarkable. The notice prohibiting the bullfight concerns only the Mistis, who aspire to be within the hegemonic framework and, for this reason, feel attracted to the power structure. Nevertheless, even among the Mistis the notice functions as a fetish, an

emanation from a distant state that acts more by domination and violence than on the basis of representation and consensus. For the indigenous people, the notice (and the state that thereby makes its presence felt) is simply incommensurate with their life.

In Arguedas's later novels such as *Los ríos profundos* [1958; *Deep Rivers*] and *Todas las sangres* [1964; *All the Bloods*], the problem persists of the non-incorporation of the indigenous person into the community that constitutes the nation as its horizon of meaning. After the publication of *Todas las sangres*, Arguedas was criticized regarding the veracity of his representation of the mountain communities. In his bitter response to these accusations, Arguedas stated that "Si no es (Todas las sangres) un testimonio, entonces yo he vivido por gusto, he vivido en vano o no he vivido" (quoted in Cornejo Polar 1973, 299) ("If it (*Todas las sangres*) is not a testimony, then I have lived as a whim, I have lived in vain, or I have not lived at all"). It is necessary to look into this polemic further, since it makes evident the confrontation between a testimonial truth and the literary device of speaking the truth. It is revelatory that Cornejo Polar fails, in his exegesis of Arguedas, to prove the realistic basis of this narrative. In *Los universos narrativos de José María Arguedas*, the Peruvian critic has to conclude that Realism does not here refer to the "representación de la realidad; significa, en lo esencial, revelación del sentido de la realidad" (1973, 82) ("representation of reality; it signifies, essentially, revelation of the sense of reality"). Thus Cornejo Polar seems to accept the claim that Arguedas could not offer an accurate representation of the indigenous world precisely because, invoking a radical realism, he imposed a horizon of meaning and interpretation of the indigenous world completely alien to that of narrative codes of the written text.

Arguedas's final novel, *El zorro de arriba y el zorro de abajo* [1968; *The Fox from Up Above and the Fox from Down Below*, 2000], marked a substantial change of direction for literary Indigenism. For the first time, claimed Martin Lienhard, indigenous rationalism provides a rationale for Western modernism (322). Such interpretations are supported by the intertextual relationships that this last novel shares with *Huarochiri*, the indigenous text of the seventeenth century that Arguedas translated from Quechua into Spanish. Even so, it remains for critics to elucidate the nature of that intertextuality. Does a message perhaps exist at the foxes' heart that awaits the critic and has yet to be deciphered? There are strong reasons to see in this an allusion to the Latin American literary institution. *Yawar Fiesta* revolves around a governmental notice that was structurally incapable of speaking to the indigenous population of Puquio. Literary texts are created in linguistic affinity with that notice. But the same is true of the literary conventions and resources such as genres, characters, or diverse narrative styles. The literary system of expression, on which our interpretations depend, implodes in Arguedas's universe. It has been said that in texts written prior to *El zorro*, Arguedas's hero is the community and that this explains the expressive inarticulateness of particular indigenous characters, such as Rendón Wilka in *Todas las sangres*. Arguedas's final novel, unlike the previous ones, is a perpetual conversation among different characters, but that discursiveness dissipates before it confirms the ideology of an individual speaking subject. The answer to Michel Foucault's provocative question (what does it matter who is speaking?) is of some consequence. It matters, because speech outside of discourse, with a voice that cannot be reduced to a specific speaker, is the voice of a non-subject of absence. There are characters in *El zorro* whose only function is to speak and who, indeed, do so publicly. Such is the case of the madman Moncada, a character who speaks in plazas and markets, articulating utopia *and* the frustration of a non-existent public discursive sphere. Moncada proclaims his sermons, trying to make himself heard without any other form of legitimation other than that reminiscent of nineteenth-century popular religion in the style of Conselheiro in *Os sertões,* whose discourse, incidentally, was also classified as that of a madman. Literary criticism has tried to find a coherent thread in this discourse and, of course, has partially found it (Cornejo Polar 1973, 180). But the extraordinary coherence of the madman Moncada points out the impossibility of an alternative discourse presented in any way other than that of the alienated voice. In the same way the excellent chapter in which Don Diego, a fox from below, and the businessman Don Angel speak confirms (rather than refutes) that devastating rejection by Arguedas of the literary subject. In a chapter where the word "understand" appears dozens of times, the characters come to an agreement that ends up being totally alien to the rules of rationality and communication as we understand them in modern society. They enunciate discourses that remain fixed in a state of non-understanding and reveal, in the same act, the fiction of the understanding of peripheral modernity, frequently based on the blackmail of "concealed violence" (a simulacrum of understanding).

Julio Rodríguez-Luis has said that Indigenism triumphed by making the national citizenry conscious of the sharp alienation and exploitation of the indigenous person, but it failed to give an internal and true image of the Indian (44). In this more radical vision of heterogeneity, the alternative to non-communication appears a false dilemma. In Arguedas's work, literature cannot express the other because the very notion of voice is revealed as an ideological element of the dominant culture. The concept of heterogeneity elaborated by Cornejo Polar must be extended to the subject itself, to show that the idea of an internal make-over was a greater and more profound co-opting of indigenous otherness. This is the lesson that the reader is offered in the sustained meditation that makes up Arguedas's last novel. Is Indigenism then only a remainder without effective representation? If Indigenism is to be considered as existing within the limits of the rationale of the nation-state, the reply is affirmative: Indigenism has always insisted, knowingly or not, on the need to transcend those limits. *El zorro de arriba y el zorro de abajo* is a text that Arguedas had not completed when he committed suicide. In a lucid commentary on the closed internal causes of Arguedas's suicide in the context of this last novel, Alberto Moreiras interprets his death as the closing down of the possibility of expression, as the implosion of meaning in the face of the definitive limits of transcultural possibility (227). The tragic sign under which it was formulated for the first time would come to life again in the final triumph of Indigenism.

After Arguedas's suicide, Peruvian Indigenism basically took two routes. On the one hand, there appeared a so-called neo-Indigenism, fundamentally defined in terms similar to the standardization of Latin American literature that resulted from the boom: artifice, complex drama, the decentering of the narrator—all elements, as Cornejo Polar observed, already present in Arguedas's work (1994a, 736). Its principal exponent was Manuel Scorza (1928–1983) with his cycle of novels entitled *La guerra silenciosa* [1970–1978; Silent War]. On the

other hand, there appeared a proliferation of testimonies that often implied the work of ethnographers or intellectuals as mediators between the non-authorized voice of the indigenous person and the social representation to which it acceded through writing in the idiom and language of hegemony.

The appearance of *Me llamo Rigoberta Menchú y así me nació la conciencia* [1983; *I, Rigoberta Menchú: An Indian Woman in Guatemala,* 1984] (the testimony of Rigoberta Menchú [b. 1959] edited by Elizabeth Burgos) marked the closure of the Indigenist problem as it was imagined by restitution-oriented intellectuals. George Yúdice has noted the affinity between the testimonial genre and postmodernity: Both depend on the weakening of grand narratives, in this case the narrative of the nation as the horizon of meaning (whether positive or negative) of *criollismo* and Indigenism (44). We have seen in this narrative how a desire for national community granted the writer a place of enunciatory authority. In this sense it is symptomatic that the discussion of *testimonio* in the academic environment was contemporary with the discussion of the nation as an imagined community. Rigoberta Menchú and Benedict Anderson present two poles of one and the same constellation of problems. Like Andean Indigenism, the text of Rigoberta Menchú had vast effects at the social level and accompanied a growing discussion about the autonomy of indigenous minorities within national communities.

The first critical reactions to Menchú's text revolved around traditional questions in literary criticism, notably problems of referentiality, authenticity, and mediation. These debates were strangely similar to those that had accompanied the discussion of autobiography a little earlier and had been solved through the concept of autobiographical contract. I say "strangely" here because, while autobiography is the consummation of the ideology of a subject and of Liberal expression, *testimonio* rears its head precisely as a problem resulting from that concept. Very soon it was recognized that the traditional categories of literary criticism could not be applied in this field, because, as John Beverly noted in 1993, among other reasons the appearance of the *testimonio* prejudiced the trajectory of the literary institution in the continent. The new understanding of Menchú's testimony was then centered on the crisis of the representative model and the possible conditions for the emergence of a subaltern voice (see the texts on *testimonio* edited by Gugelberger in *The Real Thing*).

Just when the debates on the testimonial genre seemed to have reached a certain theoretical fatigue, a critique by anthropologist David Stoll in 1999, accusing Menchú's text of false references and imprecise facts, revived interest in the work, perhaps taking its interpretation to its completion. In Beverley's 1999 response to Stoll's critique, the emphasis was placed on the disciplinary issues relevant to an interrogation of the disciplinary subject as privileged in the use of an authorized voice. Why, asked Stoll, of all the Maya lives in existence, do we have to give Rigoberta Menchú the status of representative of the voice and the problems of a people? It is the same possibility that had been demanded of Arguedas as a virtue (to speak for the Indians), which was now considered to be a defect. Also, remarkably, what Arguedas considered as a testimony from life and not a novel, was, remarkably like Menchú's testimony, understood in turn as literature and stripped of its authority from the viewpoint of the practice of the social sciences.

Beverley's appreciation of the fact that the entire discussion revolved around who has the right to make a public declaration seems correct. To deny Menchú's text the possibility of confronting other discourses because it represents her people, argues Beverley, "is to deny the possibility of political struggle as such, since a hegemonic project by definition points to a possibility of collective will and action that depends precisely on transforming the conditions of cultural and political disenfranchisement that underlie these contradictions" (1999, 76). These comments could well express the imaginative thinking behind contemporary academic discussion–its uncomfortable movement between the mere statement of what exists and the affirmation of an inscrutable subalternity. It only remains to point out that *criollismo* and Indigenism have undoubtedly played a vital role in the formation of this imaginary.

Translation by Jessica Johnson

Works Cited

Alegría, Ciro. 1941. *El mundo es ancho y ajeno*. Santiago de Chile: Edicones Ercilla.

Alonso, Carlos. 1990. *The Spanish American Regional Novel: Modernity and Autochthony*. Cambridge: Cambridge University Press.

Altamirano, Carlos, and Beatriz Sarlo. 1983. "La Argentina del centenario: Campo intelectual, vida literaria y temas ideológicos." *Ensayos argentinos: De Sarmiento a la vanguardia*. Buenos Aires: Centro Editor de América Latina. 69–105.

Anderson, Benedict. 1991. *Imagined Communities*. London: Verso.

Arguedas, José María. 1992. *El zorro de arriba y el zorro de abajo*. Ed. Eva Marie Fell. Mexico City: Archivos.

Arias, Arturo. 1994. "La novela social: Entre la autenticidad del subdesarrollo y la falacia de la racionalidad conceptual." *América Latina, palavra, literatura e cultura. Vol 2: Emancipacão do discurso*. Ed. Ana Pizarro. Sao Paulo: Universidade Estadual de Campinas. 757–86.

Balibar, Etienne, and Immanuel Wallerstein. 1998. *Race, Nation, Class: Ambiguous Identities*. London: Verso.

Beverley, John. 1993. *Against Literature*. Minneapolis: Minnesota University Press.

——. 1999. *Subalternity and Representation: Arguments in Cultural Theory*. Durham: Duke University Press.

Borges, Jorge Luis. 1975. "El escritor argentino y la tradición." *Obras Completas*. Buenos Aires: Emecé Editores. 1: 267–74.

Brotherston, Gordon. 1967. "Introduction." *Ariel*. By José Rodó. Cambridge: Cambridge University Press. xii–xxviii.

Caravedo Molinari, Baltazar. 1980. "Economía, producción, trabajo." *Historia del Perú*. Lima: Juan Mejía Baca. 8: 189–361.

Cornejo Polar, Antonio. 1973. *Los universos narrativos de José María Arguedas*. Buenos Aires: Losada.

——. 1982. "La novela indigenista: Una desgarrada conciencia de la historia." *Sobre literatura y crítica latinoamericanas*. Caracas: Universidad Central de Venezuela. 93–107.

——. 1989. *La formación de la tradición literaria en el Peru*. Lima: Centro de Estudios y Publicaciones.

——. 1994a. "Indigenismo andino." *América Latina, palavra, literatura e cultura*. Ed. Ana Pizarro. São Paulo: Universidade Estadual de Campinas. 2: 719–38.

——. 1994b. "Prólogo: Aves sin nido como alegoría nacional." *Aves sin nido*. Clorinda Matto de Turner. Caracas: Biblioteca Ayacucho. ix–xxv.

Cueva, Agustín. 1974. "Para una interpretación sociológica de *Cien años de soledad*." *Revista Mexicana de Sociología* 26.1: 3–22.

Cunha, Euclides da. 1987. *Os sertões*. Rio de Janeiro: Ediouro.

Fernández Retamar, Roberto. 1974. *Calibán: Apuntes sobre la cultura de nuestra América*. Mexico City: Diógenes.

Foucault, Michel. 1998. "What Is an Author?" *Contemporary Literary Criticism: Literary and Cultural Studies*. Eds. Robert Davis and Ronald Schleifer. New York: Longman. 365–76.

Franco, Jean. 1985. *La cultura moderna en América Latina*. Mexico City: Grijalbo.

Gallegos, Rómulo. 1948. *Doña Barbara*. Trans. Robert Malloy. New York: Peter Smith.

——. 1990. *Doña Bárbara*. Madrid: Espasa Calpe.

García Canclini, Néstor. 1995. "Narrar la multiculturalidad." *Revista de Crítica Literaria Latinoamericana*. 21.42: 9–20.

Gugelberger, George M., ed. 1996. *The Real Thing: Testimonial Discourse and Latin America*. Durham: Duke University Press.

Gutiérrez, Eduardo. 1967. *Juan Moreira*. Buenos Aires: Centro Editor de América Latina.

Guzmán, Luis Martín. 1978. *Memorias de Pancho Villa*. Mexico City: Porrúa.

Halperín Donghi, Tulio. 1996. *Historia contemporánea de América Latina*. Barcelona: Alianza Editorial.

Henríquez Ureña, Pedro. 1907. "Nota de edición al *Ariel* de Rodó." *Ariel*. By José Rodó. Monterrey, Mexico: Talleres Lozano.

Icaza, Jorge. 1976. *Huasipungo*. Madrid: Espasa Calpe.

Leguizamón, Martiniano. 1977. "Calandria." *Teatro Rioplatense: (1886–1930)*. Ed Jorge Lafforgue. Caracas: Biblioteca Ayacucho. 23–59.

Lienhard, Martin. 1990. "La 'andinización' del vanguardismo urbano." *El zorro de arriba y el zorro de abajo*. By José María Arguedas. Ed. Eve Marie Fell. Paris: ALLCA XX; Colección Archivos. 321–32.

Mariátegui, José Carlos. 1971. *Seven Interpretive Essays on Peruvian Reality*. Trans. Marjory Urquidi. Austin: University of Texas Press.

——. 1976. *Siete ensayos de interpretación de la realidad peruana*. Barcelona: Editorial Crítica.

Martin, Gerald. 1989. *Journeys Through the Labyrinth: Latin American Fiction in the Twentieth Century*. London: Verso.

Menchú, Rigoberta. 1983. *Me llamo Rigoberta Menchú*. Ed. Elizabeth Burgos Debray. Havana, Cuba: Ediciones Casa de Las Américas.

Molloy, Sylvia. 2000. "La cuestión del género: Propuestas olvidadas y desafíos críticos." *Latinoamérica, debates teóricos para el nuevo siglo*. Round Table. Latin American Studies Association Congress. Hyatt Regency. Miami. March 16.

Moreiras, Alberto. 1997. "José María Arguedas y el fin de la transculturación." *Angel Rama y los estudios latinoamericanos*. Ed. Mabel Moraña. Pittsburgh: Instituto Internacional de Literatura Iberoamericana. 213–31.

Parra, Teresa de la. 1959. *Mama Blanca's Souvenirs*. Trans. Harriet de Onis. Washington, D.C.: Pan American Union, General Secretariat, Organization of American States.

——. 1983 [1929]. *Las memorias de Mamá Blanca*. Caracas: Monte Avila.

Prieto, Adolfo. 1988. *El discurso criollista en la formación de la Argentina moderna*. Buenos Aires: Sudamericana.

Ramos, Julio. 1987. *Desencuentros de la modernidad en América Latina*. Caracas: Monte Avila.

Rodó, José. 1916. "Prólogo." *El terruño*. By Carlos Reyles. Montevideo: Renacimiento. xiii–xxix.

Rodríguez-Luis, Julio. 1990. "El indigenismo como proyecto literario: Revaloración y nuevas perspectivas." *Hispamérica* 19.55: 41–50.

Rowe, William. 1994. "El criollismo." *América Latina: Palavra, literatura e cultura. Vol 2: Emancipacão do discurso*. Ed. Ana Pizarro. São Paulo: Universidade Estadual de Campinas. 703–17.

Rowe, William, and Vivian Schelling. 1991. *Memory and Modernity: Popular Culture in Latin America*. London: Verso.

Schiaffino, Eduardo. 1933. *La pintura y la escultura en la Argentina*. Buenos Aires: Kraft.

Sierra, Justo. 1977. "México social y político (apuntes para un libro)." *Evolución política del pueblo mexicano*. Prologue and chronology by Abelardo Villegas. Caracas: Biblioteca Ayacucho. 295–328.

Sommer, Doris. 1991. *Foundational Fictions: The National Romances of Latin America*. Berkeley: University of California Press.

Stabb, Martin. 1967. *In Quest of Identity. Patterns in the Spanish American Essay of Ideas, 1890–1960*. Chapel Hill: University of North Carolina Press.

Stepan, Nancy Leys. 1991. *The Hour of Eugenics: Race, Gender and Nation in Latin America*. Ithaca: Cornell University Press.

Stoll, David. 1999. *Rigoberta Menchú and the Story of All Poor Guatemalans*. Boulder, Colo.: Westview Press.

Yúdice, George. 1996. "Testimonio and Postmodernism." *The Real Thing. Testimonial Discourse and Latin America*. Ed. George M. Gugelberger. Durham: Duke University Press. 42–57.

PEOPLES, COMMUNITIES, AND NATION BUILDING

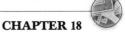

CHAPTER 18

PROJECTS OF LATIN AMERICAN EMANCIPATION
THE CARIBBEAN, 1800–1850

Latin American emancipation began with an independence struggle that was, at its root and for the most part, a struggle against slavery. In 1804, after more than a decade of protracted battles between insurgent slaves, their free allies, and colonial armies, Jean Jacques Dessalines (1758–1806) declared Saint Domingue independent from France. Under the name of Haiti, the first black state in the Americas realized a complete reversal of imperial hierarchies and social goals: The territory's European name had been obliterated; slaves had become masters; and the process of capitalist development through the industrialization of agriculture had been severely disrupted (Blackburn 161–264; Knight 193–220).

There was a general consensus among settlers of European descent in the region that Haiti was not a commendable model of emancipation. In response to the revolution, a *cordon sanitaire* was drawn around the island to interrupt the flow of information and people. The colonial authorities in Cuba prohibited the introduction of "French" slaves and even of the mere mention of the events in Haiti (on the epistemological difficulties of acknowledging the political agency of slaves, see Trouillot). As the only newly independent state in the Americas to have unequivocally abolished slavery, Haiti was also the only one that was not invited to the Pan-American Conference in 1826.

Yet Haiti's regional isolation was undercut even as it was being imposed. The Revolution set off waves of migrations that carried the story of the successful slave uprising from island to island. French settlers from Saint Domingue moved to Cuba's Oriente province first, then on to other islands or to Louisiana. In permanent fear of Haitian incursions, *criollos* from Spanish Santo Domingo continued to leave the island throughout the first few decades of the nineteenth century; they settled anywhere from Venezuela to Cuba. Indeed, Dominican literary histories typically contain a chapter on "Emigrants" or "Emigrations" and point out that some of the most prominent families and figures in Caribbean cultural history were Dominican, among them, most importantly, the Heredias and the Del Montes. The Spanish prohibitions on the introduction of "French" slaves apparently did not work either. A rebellious slave was once brought in front of the

governor of Puerto Príncipe (Cuba). Showing clear signs of being a "French" slave, he declared "haughtily, with various expressions typical of an ignorant person puffed up with very foolish though seditious principles and ideas, that the blacks of Cap Français all were free, because they had won [*adquirido*] their liberty." The next day, all other "French" slaves were gathered in the town square to watch as he was given one hundred lashes. A sign around his neck said: "This is the fruit of the imaginary liberty of the French slaves: True freedom is found in virtue" (Geggus 137).

If one reaction to the Haitian Revolution was the attempt to cut Haiti off from the other islands and the mainland, the opposite design existed as well. The new Haitian state subscribed to what we might call an internationalist ethos: Haiti's first constitutions invited immigration by guaranteeing immediate freedom for anybody of African or Amerindian descent who set foot on Haitian soil, and after Simon Bolívar's visit to Haiti, Alexandre Pétion (1770–1818) provided him with supplies and soldiers in exchange for a promise that slavery would be abolished in all liberated territories (a promise that was promptly broken). As fears of Haitian agents and Haitian ships swept through the region, and as the new Haitian heads of state were celebrated in black popular cultures from Louisiana to Northern Brazil, several post-revolutionary constitutions contained a provision–unique in the Americas–to the effect that Haiti would abstain from any interference in other countries' affairs.

The reactions to the Haitian events exemplify a contradiction that later nationalist narratives of emancipation in the Caribbean often took pains to deny. Slavery and colonialism produced two distinct emancipatory projects: The struggle against slavery or the slave trade, and the struggle for independence or some form of autonomy. Although the two projects occasionally generated close alliances, the relation between them remained highly problematic and exposed to the contingencies of social and political circumstances. The relation was further complicated by the fact that the emancipatory visions of the local elite's abolitionist movement and those of slave resistance were by no means identical–witness, for instance, Bolívar's fear of unwittingly promoting a *pardocracia* (black majority rule) (Blackburn 347–8). Even where the elite's anti-slavery sentiment and desire for autonomy appear to join forces, the negotiations between them took place within a space defined by the nightmare of black self-liberation.

The fact that Spain was able to hold on to its Caribbean possessions long after the colonies on the mainland had gained independence can be explained, at least in part, by the importance of slavery to the local economies and by the threats posed by local and international antislavery movements to white domination. In the first decades of the nineteenth century, any movement against the Spanish authorities had to be weighed against the possible loss of security and profit that might result (see, for instance, Arango y Parreño's "Reflexiones de un habanero sobre la independencia de esta Isla" [1824; "Reflections by a Citizen of Havana on the Independence of This Island"]). Although the slave trade appears to have stopped by 1870–many years after international treaties had officially outlawed the "odious commerce"–slavery itself was not abolished until 1873 in Puerto Rico and 1886 in Cuba. Cuba did not gain independence until 1902, after two wars of independence (1868–78 and 1895–98) and two years of U.S. occupation. The Dominican Republic finally established itself in 1864, after years of Haitian occupation (1822–44) and a brief return to Spanish rule (1861–64). Puerto Rico never gained independence, having been ceded to the United States in 1899.

Temperamentally, abolitionism and the *criollo* struggle for self-representation were not particularly well suited to each other. Abolitionism tended to have an internationalist orientation and appealed to universalist moral standards. It allowed fancy to roam the oceans, envisioned slaves as long-suffering lovers, and extracted empathy in the form of blood and tears. The movements for autonomy or independence, on the other hand, encouraged an introspective gaze that would roam the rugged hinterlands and register picturesque populations, and that would not dream of crossing the borders. It demanded an aesthetic of national realities, promoted the individual's subjection to the new nation's discipline, and tended to rely on particularistic political reason. Yet the fault lines of these conflicts are not always easily recognizable. Those who opposed slavery were often also the same people who promoted local identity and favored increased autonomy, if not independence, from the metropolis. The elite discourse that was emerging in the nineteenth-century Caribbean thus ran the two projects together at times, and the retrospective desire to cast national history as a history of emancipation *tout court* has further complicated the issue. The cultures of former slaves become the guarantor of national difference vis-à-vis former (and future) colonizers: The liberation of slaves liberated the national spirit; national literature is born in the struggle against slavery.

Fernando Ortiz's (1881–1969) account of Cuban history as a history of "intermeshed transculturations" (98) in *Cuban Counterpoint: Tobacco and Sugar* (1940) is a particularly interesting and complex example. The great merits of Ortiz's formulation over other attempts to account for cultural processes in the Caribbean are well known (see Coronil for an excellent discussion). The present context, however, requires that we also consider the blind spots that this account tends to generate. Ortiz's description of the interactions between the various transplanted cultures in colonial Cuba exemplifies the tendency to assimilate different forms of oppression:

> Todos convivientes, arriba o abajo, en un mismo ambiente de terror y de fuerza; terror del oprimido por el castigo, terror del opresor por la revancha; todos fuera de justicia, fuera de ajuste, fuera de sí. Y todos en trance doloroso de transculturación a un nuevo ambiente cultural. (Ortiz 1978, 96)

> Everybody, those above and those below, lives together in the same atmosphere of terror and oppression, the oppressed in terror of punishment, the oppressor in terror of reprisals; everybody outside justice, unadjusted, beside themselves. And everybody [caught] in the painful process of transculturation in a new cultural environment. (Ortiz 1995, 102)

The antagonisms that separate various kinds of Cubans are sublated in the pain and struggle they share. By overriding and transcending the divisions of class and ethnicity, transculturation is the medium by which slaveholders and slaves, and Cubans of all colors, are linked and integrated–a transhistorical force quite beyond the reach of particularistic interest. There is no outside to transculturation: Even the genocide of the indigenous populations in the Caribbean is designated, disconcertingly, as a "transculturación fracasada" (1978, 94) ("failed transculturation" [1995, 100]). Where a more politically nuanced narrative would have pointed to antagonisms, victories, and losses, the culturalist narrative suggests an imagery of absorption and incorporation: Within the national territory, culture has taken on the role of politics as the vehicle for resolving divisions. The political, and specifically the idea of emancipation, can only be thought of in the context of colonial and neocolonial oppression.

We may even wonder whether the integrationist tendencies of this account are not stronger than Ortiz himself would have desired. The process of transculturation is driven, after all, by the forces of capitalist modernization, that is, by economic expansion and technological development. Like transculturation, modernization is a process beyond the reach of any particularistic interests. And like transculturation, it is irresistible. Sugar and tobacco are at the same time the backbone of the Cuban economy and the symbols of the mixed heritage that comes to form Cuban culture: The former, the symbol of the foreign capital, colonial plantation economy, mass production, and slave labor; the latter, the symbol of European and indigenous individualism, artisanal forms of production, and ultimately Cuban independence. Yet while transculturation leads to national integration and reconciliation, modernization leads to the erasure of national difference. Integrationism does not stop at national borders; what consolidated and unified the nation internally can also erase the difference that in a sense produced independence. It may have been this probably unintended and undesirable implication that prompted Ortiz to offer two rather different endings in the famous opening essay of *Counterpoint*. The first is a rather pessimistic ending for the history of modernization:

> Ya se ha visto cómo el tabaco y el azúcar han contrastado siempre hasta que las máquinas y el capitalismo financiero han ido aplanando sus diferencias, deshumanizando sus economías y equiparando más y más sus problemas. (1978, 87)

> We have seen the fundamental differences that existed between [sugar and tobacco] from the beginning until machines and capitalism gradually ironed out these differences, dehumanized their economy, and made their problems more and more similar. (1995, 93)

The second ending takes up the literary allegory that had driven part of the narration and imagines that out of the marriage of Doña Sugar and Don Tobacco, alcohol is born as a synthesis:

"Acaso canten un día los vates del pueblo de Cuba cómo el alcohol . . . hijo de tales padres, es fuego, fuerza, espíritu, embriaguez, pensamiento y acción" (1978, 88) ("It may be that one day the bards of Cuba will sing of how alcohol . . . the offspring of such parents, is fire, force, spirit, intoxication, thought, and action" [1995, 93]). Here, transculturation's powers of integration and synthesis once again save the difference upon which Cuban independence is built. In the face of the equalizing force of modernization in the first ending, however, the salvation of the second ending appears rather too rhetorical to be altogether persuasive.

Ortiz's account of Cuban history as the history of "intermeshed transculturations" bears witness to the problems that stem from ignoring the politics that mediates between modernization and culture. Accordingly, while relying on Ortiz's insight into the crucial role played by transculturation in Caribbean history, the following account tries to understand the emerging forms of cultural production in the nineteenth-century Caribbean in the context of contradictory cultural and political projects and practices. This of course can only be done on a case-by-case basis because demographic, political, and economic circumstances varied considerably from island to island. I will therefore focus on Cuba, the Spanish Caribbean island with the largest slave population and the most diverse literary and cultural life in the first decades of the nineteenth century, while also trying to maintain a pan-Caribbean perspective that takes into account, as much as possible, the structures of political, cultural, and economic exchange between the Caribbean islands and the three continents—Europe, Africa, and the Americas.

Until the end of the eighteenth century, the Spanish Caribbean islands had been little more than colonial outposts where ships on their way to the mainland would stop and replenish their provisions. After the collapse of the plantation economy in Saint-Domingue, however, Cuba seized the opportunity and, in the course of the first decades of the century, established itself as the main sugar producer in the region. Between 1792 and 1841 the slave population grew from 86,000 to 352,500, and sugar production increased from 18,500 to 162,500 tons (Knight 365). Cuba had become the richest Caribbean colony.

In 1790 the first Cuban newspaper, the *Papel Periódico*, appeared. A forum for the exchange of moderately reformist ideas, the newspaper was more concerned with hygiene, health, and agriculture than with cultural and literary matters. It is not that surprising, then, that one of the most interesting documents concerning the cultural and ideological production in those years and the forms of transculturation that had established themselves can be found not in the newspaper or the limited materials that were published, but among the unpublished manuscripts in the National Archive (for a history of Cuban publishing, see Fornet).

On 9 April 1812, José Antonio Aponte (a free black cabinet maker) and eight co-conspirators were found guilty of having planned a slave uprising with the aim of taking power in Cuba. In keeping with local custom, they were publicly executed and their severed heads were put on display in iron cages.

Part of the extensive record compiled through three weeks of interrogation relates to a variety of artifacts that were found in Aponte's possession (see Franco). In the transcripts of the interrogations a political and cultural geography emerges, one that is strikingly different from that of later *criollo* writers. Haitian connections became the center of the investigators' concern.

Portraits of Toussaint Louverture, Henri Christophe, and Dessalines were found in Aponte's house; one of the conspirators adopted the pseudonym Juan Francisco, after the Haitian general Jean François; and a suspected adviser to Aponte was Gil Narciso, who had fought in Haiti. One of the most notable objects discovered was an oversized book with seventy-two pictures, maps, drawings, and so forth. Resembling what we could perhaps call a revolutionary scrapbook, it contained a hugely eclectic array of drawings and sketches on topics ranging from classical mythology to world history and Christian religious themes, pictures with inscriptions in Spanish and Latin, maps, and figures and landscapes cut out from prints and fans. Many pictures seem to have had a narrative character, and they involved on one page figures as different as the Greek philosopher Diogenes, the Spanish King Rodrigo, and the Egyptian goddess Isis. As if in anticipation of *négritude* and other forms of pan-Africanism, Aponte celebrates Egyptian and Abyssinian achievements, the contributions of Africans to Western culture, African cardinals and librarians in the Vatican, and black armies:

> . . . se notan soldados blancos, y negros uno destos a cavallo con la cavesa de uno de aquellos en la punta de una hasta, y otro negro igualmente que tiene una cavesa cortada arrojando sangre hayandose aquí en situación, de vencido los blancos. (Franco 113)

> there were white soldiers and blacks, one of the the latter on a horse, with the head of one of the former on the point of a pike, and another black likewise who holds a severed head dripping blood, being here in the situation of having defeated the whites.

In response to the colonial slaveholders' structuring of the hemisphere through slave routes and slave markets, Aponte's radical syncretism suggests a Black Atlantic whose cultural imaginary mirrors the global scope of the slave trade and whose projects of emancipation converged, at least for a few years, around Haiti.

Now, of course, emancipation in the Caribbean did not follow the path sketched by Aponte: The self-liberation of slaves remained anathema to local abolitionists and reformists alike, and instead of looking outwardly toward social and cultural exchange following the old slave routes, Caribbean islands turned inward, searching for grounds of local difference. Aponte himself did not survive the revelation of his political and educational work. His picture book disappeared. The transcripts of the proceedings survived as part of Cuba's criminal archives rather than as its artistic patrimony. If we look for traces of Aponte in later years, we find very little. There may be a shadow of his erudite syncretism in the figure of the "negro catedrático" [Black Professor], always played in blackface, in the Teatro Bufo in the second half of the nineteenth century. The play that appears to have inaugurated this genre in 1868 ends as follows: "No soy más que un catedrático,/que busca con su gramática,/Elíptica y sistemática,/La rígida clave técnica,/Política, pirotécnica,/Quirúrgica, y problemática" (Francisco Fernández qtd. in Montes Huidobro 79) ("I am just a professor/who searches with his grammar,/ [which is] elliptical and systematic,/The rigid technical,/Political, pyrotechnical,/Surgical, and problematic key"). In the sequel, also from 1868, we witness the induction of a "Congo," whose garbled Spanish is barely intelligible, into the culture of "catedratismo." His Cuban-born teacher excuses the slowness of his progress: "Todavía no ha estudiado más que a Nebrija y Calepino y hojeado superficialmente a Cicerón. Sólo lleva dos cursos de universidad lírica, por cuya razón no luce en la plenitud de su entusiasmo" (85–86) ("Thus far he has only studied Nebrija and Calepino and has superficially leafed through Cicero. He has only taken two courses at the lyrical university, which is why he is not shining in the plenitude of his enthusiasm" [my translation]), to which the "Congo" replies, "Yo tá creyendo eso cosa matemáticamente sempiterna" (85–6) ("I believe this (to be) a mathematically sempiternal matter"). The racist nature of this kind of humor does not need to be expounded. What is worth pointing out, however, is that the jokes turn on the absurdity of people of African descent claiming erudite European culture as their own. It is not surprising, then, that in the third part of the play, the "Congo" becomes a positive figure in that he rejects the pretensions of the Creole Blacks and returns to work on the docks of Havana.

The events of the 1812 conspiracy themselves are called up again in 1901, on the eve of the declaration of the Cuban Republic, by Francisco Calcagno, the author of the first study of poets of color in Cuba and certainly no apologist for slavery. His historical novel *Aponte* opens with a gory depiction of the conspirator's severed head, surrounded by flies and an unbearable stench–a barbaric monster with "de alma tan negra como su rostro" (8) ("a soul as black as his face") and with savagely sharpened crocodile teeth who had modeled himself on Dessalines and Christophe. The novel's story, however, stays clear of Aponte and focuses on a fictional mulatto slave who joins Aponte after having been used as bait in a complicated plot of revenge that turns on class prejudice among whites. Calcagno articulates one more time the antagonisms and deep-seated apprehensions that underlie nineteenth-century negotiations of emancipation. Even after abolition, Independence is thinkable, it seems, only after the black insurgent is eliminated from the body politic.

Returning to the early decades of the nineteenth century, we can observe how a paradox took shape that in one way or another underlay all the negotiations between antislavery sentiment and the desire for autonomy. Slavery was seen as both the source of rapid development and the source of barbarism: The more slaves, the more development, the more barbarism. The following quote from a letter by the writer Tanco y Bosmiel articulates these concerns:

Qué esperanzas . . . de que nuestra tierra se mejore con estatutos, ni con Ayuntamientos nuevos . . . mientras nos están atarugando de negros por todas as partes? Qué civilización de mis pecados, ni que progreso had de haber entre nosotros, si esto es una cafrería, la más abominable región de la tierra? Permitiera Dios que estos brutos de negros se convirtieran todos en tigres, osos, serpientes . . . y no dejaran con vida a ninguno de la maldita raza caucásica . . . (Fernández de Castro 41)

What hopes [are there] . . . that our land will be better with statutes, or new town halls . . . while they are packing us with blacks? What manner of civilization is this–what progress will there be among us, if this is a savage place, the most abominable region on earth? If God would allow for these black brutes to be all transformed into tigers, bears, serpents . . . and not leave alive anyone of the cursed Caucasian race . . . (my translation)

Views varied a great deal, of course, about where barbarism was located and how it could be uprooted. The colonial authority's propensity for tight social and demographic control and occasional brutal crackdowns on antislavery insurgency and independence movements alike seemed to be predicated on the view that it was precisely the colonial regime that made slavery and development compatible. The politics of the liberal elite aimed at different solutions, reflecting

their more ambivalent attitudes toward both slavery and colonialism, to be sure, but also their fear that Cuba might become another Haiti (see, for instance, Del Monte, "Estado de la poblacion blanca y de color de la isla de Cuba, en 1839" ["The Situation of the White Population and the Population of Color on the Island of Cuba in 1839"] 1: 144–45). It is in the sphere of cultural politics and cultural production that the liberal *criollo* elites negotiated the two projects of emancipation. The standard discourse about the slaves' barbarism suggests that cultural production was and always had been the domain of white *criollos* and that the fears of the elite were directed at the possibility of culture being destroyed outright by the savages brought to Cuba as slaves. If we consider this claim in the light of the cultural practices that existed at the time, however, it appears that it entails a good measure of denial.

In the 1820s, Félix Varela (1788–1853) had complained about the fact that the arts and crafts were firmly in the hands of the colored population, and José Antonio Saco (1797–1879) in his famous *Memoria sobre la vagancia en Cuba* [1832; Memoir about Vagrancy in Cuba] reiterated this charge: The poor white population was idly sitting by, he claimed, while the free colored population took over all forms of cultural production. Music had become the domain of colored orchestras (Carpentier 107, 137 ff.; Lapique 27), painters and portraitists tended to be artisans of color, and even primary instruction had fallen into the hands of colored women who, according to contemporary testimony, often could barely read and write themselves. In response, the white *criollo* elite developed hegemonic strategies that aimed at promoting a *criollo* culture that was, above all, "in good taste." In 1818, the San Alejandro Academy for Drawing and Painting opened its doors. Under the tutelage of Vermay, a student of David who had run into political problems in post-Napoleonic France, the children of white *criollos* were introduced to European-style academic painting (Fischer, 1998). New aesthetic hierarchies slowly took root as a more European standard of taste–favoring perspectival painting, neoclassical styles, and sublime renditions of Cuban landscapes–replaced older popular styles of cultural production of which Aponte's syncretic pictures were but one example. In the 1920s, art historian Bernardo Barros described the San Alejandro Academy in its early years as a:

refugio de una pequeñísima legión de cultivadores del arte, cuna de esa débil renovación–pero renovación al fin–del buen gusto que va destruyendo prejuicios y creando el inicio de una nueva tendencia estética. Cuando muere Vermay, ya las artes no son patrimonio exclusivo de la raza de color. (25)

refuge of a very small group of cultivators of the arts, cradle of a weak rejuvenation–but rejuvenation it was–of good taste that goes on to destroy prejudices and to create the beginnings of a new aesthetic tendency. When Vermay dies, the arts are no longer the exclusive patrimony of the race of color.

It is difficult to estimate the efficacy of these hegemonic strategies, particularly because they were de facto supported by measures of brute repression; much of the violence in the aftermath of the supposed Conspiracy of La Escalera (the Ladder) (1844) was directed against the free colored population and further reduced the number of free people of color working in the various crafts (see Paquette and Deschamps Chapeaux). What seems clear, however, is that the new "aesthetic tendency" provided criteria for identifying and eliminating a barbarism located in the cultural practices of the free colored population and for recreating a local culture equal to and contemporaneous with European culture. For a variety of reasons, though especially perhaps because of its supposed associations with the forces of radical abolitionism, the unabashed syncretism of the practices of the free black populations did not become the backbone of transculturated Cuban culture. Cuban national culture was shaped not so much by transculturation per se as by struggles over what kind of transculturation was admissible.

The early literary efforts of the *criollo* elite seem to relate in a very different way to the societal antagonisms produced by slavery and colonialism. It is a common view that Cuban national literature in effect grows out of the writing against slavery (see Luis; Williams; and Fiol for an attempt to trace the origins of the Cuban novel back to poetry and drama), and in some sense this is undoubtedly true. Yet, at the same time, questions have been raised about the extent to which the early writings reflect a truly abolitionist stance. But more pressing for the history of literary culture than the question of the presence or absence of abolitionist intentionality is how the cultural ideals and activities became operative within the societal antagonism sketched above, and what impact they may have had on future cultural developments.

Between 1835 and 1842, literary life in Havana crystallized around the figure of Domingo del Monte (1804–1853) (see Martínez Carmenate and Schulman). Among the group of *criollo* intellectuals who exchanged their reformist views under his tutelage were Anselmo Suárez y Romero (1818–1878), the author of the antislavery novel *Francisco o Las delicias del campo* [Francisco, or The Delights of the Countryside] (written in 1839, published in England in 1840); Félix Tanco y Bosmiel (1797–1871), whose anti-slavery story "Petrona y Rosalía" was written in 1835 but not published until 1925; Cirilo Villaverde (1812–1894), whose *Cecilia Valdés* (written in exile in New York in the 1880s and set in Havana in the 1830s) came to be the most popular account of Colonial Cuba; the *costumbrista* (writer of sketches of customs and manners) José Victoriano Betancourt (1813–1875); and the poet and playwright José Jacinto Milanés. The circle was also frequented by the slave Juan Francisco Manzano (1797–1854), who had made a name for himself as a poet and who was commissioned by Del Monte to write his autobiography for the British abolitionist Richard Madden's antislavery dossier (see Williams on the international aspects of antislavery writing in Cuba).

The texts that grew out of Del Monte's circle locate barbarism in the institution of slavery itself and in the practices used to maintain it. In striking contrast with Victor Hugo's (1802–1885) *Bug-Jargal*–a novel that combined a portrait of a "noble savage" with a depiction of the events in Saint-Domingue as a rebellion of barbarians and that was acknowledged as a source of inspiration by Cuban writers–the fear of uprisings and of a repeat of the Haitian events left hardly any traces in the fictional texts. Instead, we find docile, peaceful slaves who are the object of the lascivious desires and self-indulgent sadism of their owners. Gertrudis Gómez de Avellaneda's (1814–1873) novel *Sab* (1841), a romantic novel written in Spain and prohibited in Cuba, preserves a small mark of this obliteration. The title hero, who is irredeemably in love with the daughter of his owners, explicitly renounces rebellion and eventually gives away the substantial sum of money he had won in the lottery–which could have helped him to establish himself as a free man, one would think–so that his beloved may realize her own romantic dreams.

Eliminating agency along with all traces of the free black population, which had been associated with most of the larger slave uprisings in the Caribbean, the antislavery narratives transform slavery from a political into a moral problem. In questions of morality, it is the conscience of the moral agent that matters, the victims' responses to the injury suffered are irrelevant to the assessment of guilt. Not so in political questions, where projects and goals need to be negotiated, or, as the case may be, solved by force. But whereas political discourse and measures of social control were largely driven by fear, the antislavery novel drew on more refined sentiments: love and compassion. The liberal *criollos* produced a literary fantasy that eliminated precisely that conflict which provided a justification for the continuation of colonialism at a time when the Spanish American mainland had long been independent. The fantasy of docile slaves who desire nothing more than to be with their beloveds can be read as an attempt to imagine a society where the forces of brute repression are not needed (on Manzano's self-portrait, see Molloy). One may of course wonder whether this fantasy was ever completely believed: The political writings and interventions of Del Monte offer plenty of grounds for doubt. Having had to abandon the island in 1842 because of his reformist views, Del Monte was accused, in absentia, of having participated in the supposed conspiracy of 1844. He was absolved, but he did not return to the island, because, according to a letter to the U.S. diplomat Alexander Hill Everett, he feared that some black might assassinate him as a traitor to a cause to which he never belonged (Paquette 263). Also, because he had left the island for fear of the colonial regime, he could not return for fear of the rage of the black population–an ironic reflection of the contradictions between the various projects of emancipation.

No doubt, the antislavery narratives were in part a societal fantasy. But perhaps they became operative in other ways as well. As literary texts they could do something that is beyond the reach of other forms of writing (for an analysis of the hierarchization of speech in antislavery novels, see Ramos). They provided reasons and occasions for a more refined emotional response. Tears and compassion certainly would have qualified as civilizing emotions. The descriptions of physical and psychological torture may very well indicate something more than a desire for realism: They transform terror and crude fear–the ubiquitous feeling that justified the continuation of the colonial regime–into awe in the face of the enormity of the slaves' physical suffering and of their endurance. Actual fear is contained aesthetically in the experience of the sublime. Fear is not a subtle emotion and is unlikely to become culturally productive; it certainly does not further reformist tendencies. By making the brutality of the slaveholding regime aesthetically available, these texts operated, in a less obvious way than the campaign for "good taste," on the sensibility of the reader or listener.

It is in this context that Del Monte's acerbic attack against the free mulatto poet Plácido (Gabriel de la Concepción Valdés [1809–1844]) gains its full meaning:

Pero yo prefería los cantos tristes del esclavo, a . . . [los] versos simples, aunque armoniosos del mulato libre, . . . porque . . . los principios de mi estética y de mi filosofía, se avienen más con el lamento arrancado del corazón del oprimido, que con el concierto estrepitoso del oficial laureado, del poeta envilecido, de Placido, en fin . . . (2: 150)

I preferred the sad songs of the slave [i.e., Manzano] to the . . . simple, though harmonious, verses of the free mulatto . . . ; the principles of my aesthetics and my philosophy concur more with the lament torn from the heart of the oppressed than with the ostentatious concert of the official laureate, the vile poet, in short, Plácido . . .]

The slave is sublime, the free mulatto is ridiculous (on the polemics surrounding Plácido, see Fischer "Plácido," and 2000). In a gesture reminiscent of the reforms that were directed against the cultural production of colored artisans, del Monte invokes aesthetic criteria that allow him to draw the line between the black slave poet and the free mulatto poet. (And it is worth remembering here that Manzano stopped writing soon after he was freed, whereas Plácido was executed as one of the supposed leaders of the Conspiracy of La Escalera.) In the same gesture of aesthetic ranking and containment, the assimilation of the experience of the slave and that of the colonized white *criollo* becomes emotionally persuasive. Slavery can become a metaphor for colonialism.

The reform of aesthetic criteria and the promotion of literature in the early nineteenth century in Cuba track the highly ambivalent and complicated relationship between two projects of emancipation: On the one hand there is the fantasy of the docile slave, a fable that facilitates the assimilation of ex-slaves into colonialism; it is the means of eliminating slavery's barbarism and of promoting Cuban culture as one of "good taste" and aesthetic sensibility. On the other hand there is the rejection of the more ostentatious cultural practices of the free black population (e.g., Santiago's Carnival). Emancipation thus becomes imaginable as one unified project rather than two conflictual projects; yet the very aesthetic standard that rejects slavery as barbarism concurs with the hegemonic strategies pitted against the colored population that only thinly hid the fear of the black other that both fantasies deny.

In his ambling epistolary novel *La Peregrinación de Bayoán* [1863; *The Pilgrimage of Bayoán*], the Puerto Rican writer and intellectual Eugenio María de Hostos (1839–1903) reflects, at a time when none of the Spanish Caribbean islands had achieved independence, on the aporias of Caribbean unity. Enacting the model of "foundational fictions" (see Sommer) in the mode of failure, the novel's main characters–barely veiled indigenist allegories of the three Spanish Caribbean islands–remain unsuccessful in their attempts to join forces through marriage. Contrary to the common tendency to ground arguments for Caribbean unity in similarities in socioeconomic structures and to ground arguments for its fragmentation in cultural and linguistic diversity (e.g., Mintz 19–20), Hostos seems to think of unity and fragmentation as a political issue. The cultural politics that surrounded the emergence of literary production in early nineteenth-century Cuba lend support to Hostos's view while putting his attempt to think unity on indigenist grounds in perspective. In the aftermath of the Haitian Revolution, both unity and fragmentation correspond to the conflicting political and social desires of the colonial authorities, the *criollo* elite, the free blacks, and the vast slave populations in the area and are thus intrinsically linked to the conflicts between the two projects of emancipation. Hostos's narrator articulates his frustrated desire for the unity of the Spanish Antilles while he sails back and forth between the islands and crosses the Atlantic. It is this perspective that neither *criollo* antislavery forces nor autonomists can entertain: They begin to write as they are turning inward.

Works Cited

Arango y Parreño, Francisco de. 1983. *Reflexiones de un habanero sobre la independencia de esta isla*. 2nd ed. Havana: Arazoza y Soler.

Barros, Bernardo G. 1924. "Discurso de ingreso como miembro de número de la sección de literatura presentado a la academia pocos días antes de morir por el Sr. Bernardo G. Barros." *Academia Nacional de Artes y Letras. Discursos pronunciados en la sesión celebrada por esta corporación a la memoria del académico fallecido Sr. Bernardo G. Barros y Gómez, el día 12 de mayo de 1924*. Havana: El Siglo XX.

Blackburn, Robin. 1988. *The Overthrow of Colonial Slavery* (1776–1848). London: Verso.

Calcagno, Francisco. 1901. *Aponte*. 2 vols. Barcelona: Tipografía de Francisco Costa.

Carpentier, Alejo. 1989. *La música en Cuba*. La Habana: Pueblo y Educación.

Coronil, Fernando. 1995. "Transculturation and the Politics of Theory: Countering the Center, Cuban Counterpoint." Introduction to *Cuban Counterpoint: Tobacco and Sugar*. By Fernando Ortiz. Trans. Harriet de Onis. Durham: Duke Uuniversity Press. ix–lvi.

Del Monte, Domingo. 1929. *Escritos*. 2 vols. Habana: Cultural.

Deschamps Chapeaux, Pedro.1971. *El negro en la economía habanera del siglo XIX*. Havana: Instituto Cubano del Libro.

Fernández de Castro, José Antonio. 1943. *El tema negro en las letras de Cuba* (1608–1935). Havana: Mirador.

Fiol, Roberto. 1968. "La novela cubana en el s. XIX." *Revista de la Unión de escritores y artistas de Cuba* 4, 7: 179–207.

Fischer, Sibylle. "Plácido: abyección y modernidad oblicua." Forthcoming in *Temas* (La Habana).

———. 2000. "Poetas en Haipacu: algunas reflexiones sobre estética y política en el Atlántico esclavista." *Roberto Fernández Retamar y los estudios latinoamericanos*. Eds. Elzbieta Sklodowska and Ben A. Heller. Pittsburgh: Instituto Internacional de Literatura Iberoamericana, Serie Críticas. 299–325.

———. 1998. "Sketches of a Colony: Cuba in the 1800s." *Journal of Latin American Cultural Studies* 7.1: 131–49.

Fornet, Ambrosio. 1994. *El libro en Cuba: siglos XVIII y XIX*. Havana: Letras Cubanas.

Franco, José Luciano. 1977. *Las conspiraciones de 1810 y 1812*. Havana: Ciencias Sociales.

Geggus, David P. 1997. "Slave Resistance in the Spanish Caribbean." *A Turbulent Time: The French Revolution and the Greater Caribbean*. Eds. David Barry Gaspar and David Patrick Geggus. Bloomington: Indiana University Press. 131–55.

Gómez de Avellaneda, Gertrudis. 1997 [1841]. *Sab*. Ed. José Servera. Madrid: Cátedra.

Hostos, Eugenio María de. 1988. *La peregrinación de Bayoán*. Vol. I: *Literatura*. San Juan; Rio Píedras: Instituto de Cultura Puertorriqueña, Universidad de Puerto Rico.

Knight, Franklin W. 1990. *The Caribbean: The Genesis of a Fragmented Nationalism*. 2nd ed. New York: Oxford University Press.

Lapique, Zoila. 1979. *Música colonial cubana en las publicaciones periódicas* (1812–1902). Havana: Letras Cubanas.

Luis, William. 1990. *Literary Bondage: Slavery in Cuban Narrative*. Austin: University of Texas Press.

Martínez Carmenate, Urbano. 1997. *Domingo Del Monte y su tiempo*. Havana: Unión.

Mintz, Sidney W. 1971. "The Caribbean as a Socio-cultural Area." *Peoples and Cultures of the Caribbean: An Anthropological Reader*. Ed. Michael M. Horowitz. Garden City, NY: The Natural History Press. 17–46.

Molloy, Sylvia. 1991. *At Face Value: Autobiographical Writing in Spanish America*. Cambridge: Cambridge University Press.

Montes Huidobro, Matías. 1987. *Teoría y práctica del catedratismo en "Los negros catedráticos" de Francisco Fernández*. Miami: Editorial Persona.

Ortiz, Fernando. 1978. *Contrapunteo cubano del tabaco y el azúcar*. Caracas. Ayacucho.

———. 1995. *Cuban Counterpoint: Tobacco and Sugar*. Trans. Harriet de Onis. Durham: Duke University Press.

Paquette, Robert L. 1988. *Sugar Is Made with Blood: The Conspiracy of the Escalera and the Conflict between Empires over Slavery in Cuba*. Middletown CT: Wesleyan University Press.

Ramos, Julio. 1993. "Cuerpo, lengua, subjetividad." *Revista de Crítica Latinoamericana* 19: 225–37.

Saco, José Antonio. 1974. *Memoria sobre la vagancia en Cuba*. Santiago de Cuba: Instituto Cubano del Libro.

Schulman, Iván. 1976. "Reflections on Cuba and Its Antislavery Literature." *Annals of the Southeastern Conference on Latin American Studies* 7: 59–67.

Sommer, Doris. 1991. *Foundational Fictions. The National Romance of Latin America*. Berkeley: University of California Press.

Trouillot, Michel-Rolph. 1995. *Silencing the Past: Power and the Production of History*. Boston: Beacon Press.

Varela, Félix. 1977. "Memoria sobre la esclavitud." *Escritos políticos*. Havana: Ciencias Sociales. 260–76.

Williams, Lorna Valerie. 1994. *The Representation of Slavery in Cuban Fiction*. Columbia: University of Missouri Press.

CHAPTER 19

TRANSCULTURATION AND THE DISCOURSE OF LIBERATION

Graciela Montaldo

New World, New Identities

The transition from Colonial to post-Colonial society in Latin America involved more than a change from one political order to another; it marked the redefinition of collective identities organized in accordance with new scales of power, dominance, and subordination. Without question, the reshaping of the political order at the end of the eighteenth century radically affected the Spanish colonies on the American continent. But this was due not only to the new political possibilities initiated by Independence but primarily to the necessity of working out, under the pressure of European powers, new methods of constructing political constitutions. Spain had segregated the American continent into great ethnocultural blocks that had no opportunity to express their identities politically; under the Colonial system the Spanish authorities had completely excluded all of the non-Spanish population from the public sphere, though with a number of internal gradations. Furthermore, a group of ethnic Spaniards and their subordinates was also excluded from political power but not all its privileges; the *criollos* were a cultural and economic elite, descended from Spaniards, who had been born on the continent with political aspirations but not political rights.

These were the intellectual elites who were partially aware of the new political and philosophical thinking of Europe after the French Revolution and restive in the face of the tremendous opportunities for exercising a political role in their own territories. These *criollos,* banned from exercising power in the colonies as a social class, gradually became the principal protagonists in the emancipation process, and in pursuit of these aims they expanded their influence through military action and the written word. Wars of Independence represented an irrevocable confrontation with Spain, while literature furnished the means of creating an awareness of cultural difference. The Enlightenment, and especially its diffusion of political rationalism, provided the *criollos* with an ideological weapon over the Colonial oppressor but also over the indigenous "barbarian." This was a world, inspired by reason, that had expanded ideologically from the ideals of liberty, equality, and fraternity to republicanism and revolution—and also to racism.

The struggle thus waged would be on the authority of reason; the patriots had adopted the claim that the entire world was beginning to establish itself as unified and hierarchical (see Smith). The writings of Alexander von Humboldt played a central role in this new geopolitical design. His redefinition of America as the New World, which was the result of his naturalist studies processed through a Romantic sensibility, had a pervasive effect on the discourse of the *criollo* elites during the first half of the nineteenth century (see Pratt). Perhaps it was Simón Bolívar (1783–1830) who explained these new interdependencies best in his celebrated "Carta de Jamaica" ["Letter from Jamaica"] of 1815, two years after having declared a war to the end against Spain. He begins by quoting from Humboldt and states:

La Europa misma, por miras de sana política, debería haber preparado y ejecutado el proyecto de la independencia americana; no solo porque el equilibrio del mundo así lo exige, sino porque éste es el medio legítimo y seguro de adquirirse establecimientos ultramarinos de comercio. La Europa que no se halla agitada por las violentas pasiones de la venganza, ambición y codicia, como la España, parece que estaba autorizada por todas las leyes de la equidad e ilustrada sobre sus bien entendidos intereses. (87)

Europe itself, with an eye to sane policy, should have planned and carried out the project of American independence: not only because the balance of power in the world so demands, but also because this is the legitimate and secure means of acquiring overseas business interests. Not disturbed by violent passions of vengeance, ambition, and avarice as Spain was, [the rest of] Europe appears to be authorized by all the laws of equality and enlightened reason concerning its well-understood interests.

Already Venezuela's Act of Independence (1811) had appealed for a broader international relationship (*Pensamiento* 1: 105). Thus, the revolutionary conflict was rapidly internationalized (see Rios), and the independent *criollos,* although militarily weak in their own country, sought external political and material support. Internationalization also implied establishing a complex of *criollo*-European alliances that had, as Bolívar clearly pointed out, an economic basis. The ideological program of Independence thus also implied the inclusion of Spanish America in the world of European rationalism (that had been extolled as universal).

There was a *criollo* conviction that there was nothing in Colonial Spanish America that might be considered politico-cultural rationality; this belief, combined with their political fragmentation, induced them to look toward Europe for political models as well as for material assistance. In fact, numerous pro-Independence patriots would travel to Europe and the United States asking for political help in exchange for future investment in America. The leading role played by Great Britain in Latin American Independence is well known; Francisco de Miranda (1750–1816) was one of the first to make an exploratory journey in search of possible alliances. Miranda—a friend of Thomas Jefferson, lover of Catherine the Great, General of the Girondists, agent of William Pitt, and political revolutionary chief in Venezuela—publicized internationally the impasse that existed between Spain and her American colonies.

These *criollo* elites were created by transcultural processes to no less a degree than were the indigenous and black populations of the continent, though their values were very different. The concept of transculturation, in the sense that Fernando Ortiz uses the word, is connected ethnographically to the recording of a series of differences within societies subjected to external processes of economic change, thus creating internal conflicts. In the critical discourse of Angel Rama (1982b), this process is linked to politico-cultural modernization, placing in the foreground the idea of intellectual mediation between the metropolitan cultural models and a purported local or regional authenticity. The consideration of the intellectual Spanish American elites of the Liberation period and their politico-cultural discourse in this section has the aim of establishing that historical field, so permeated by difference. In terms of the *criollo* elites' relationships, both abroad and at home, their ethnic and political nuclei were created out of rationalized self-interest, from which they renegotiated their identities and legitimated themselves as subjects of power, thereby initiating national processes of exclusion addressed to other peoples or nations of the continent.

The focus here is on the transculturation that operated at the educated cultural level at the beginning of the nineteenth century in Latin America as the (political) adhesion to a model of European reason. In this way the *criollo* elite acted to legitimate their own positions of power within their communities. It was from such a position of authority that they negotiated with Spain, England, and France and, inside their countries, suppressed the non-European ethnic populations. From this point of view, the liberation process did not develop in one direction, and the *criollos'* position was unstable. The elites shifted in one decade from being a marginal and excluded sector to becoming a dominant group that had to construct its authority. The *criollo* elite, seen in this context, had the overriding need to create their identity as the national identity even where they were by far in the minority, and to do so in terms of power that would provide them with links to the Europe of the Enlightenment.

The *Criollo* Elites

When the historian Halperín Donghi contemplated the Spanish American Independence period, he pointed out the bewilderment of the *criollo* elites, during the time of Revolution and Independence, on the discovery of legitimacy that allowed them to exercise power. This bewilderment was the product of their political limitations, in other words, their lack of an intellectual context within which to consolidate a modern political practice that would replace the old Colonial order. The boundaries between the social castes were firm because Colonial society limited Amerindians and blacks to being economic commodities. These tensions were connected, in Halperín Donghi's view, to the violence of antipeninsular feelings that swept the continent. The shattering of the Colonial order promised the transference of wealth and power from the Spanish elite into the hands of the *criollo* elite.

For this reason redistribution of political power posed few questions regarding legitimacy, as long as it could be kept under control and simple. It is from this point that the debates concerning which system to adopt in each region of the former Viceroyalties–monarchy, parliamentary monarchy, or republic–were disruptive, and without question the arguments were put together as the occasion demanded. This did not imply a lack of purpose but rather a negotiation between the elites. Halperín emphasizes that:

> Este edificio colonial que . . . había durado demasiado, entró en rápida disolución a principios del siglo XIX. . . . La lucha por la independencia sería en este aspecto la lucha por un nuevo pacto colonial, que–asegurando el contacto directo entre los productos hispanoamericanos y la que es cada vez más la nueva metrópoli económica [Gran Bretaña]–conceda a esos productores accesos menos limitados al mercado ultramarino y una parte menos reducida del precio allí pagado por sus frutos.

> Al lado de la reforma económica estaba la reforma político-administrativa. (1975, 74–75)

> The New World Empires of Portugal and Spain crumbled rapidly in the early nineteenth century. . . . The wars of independence may be viewed, in that respect, as a struggle by Spanish American producers to acquire better access to overseas markets and secure a larger share of the profits.

> The administrative reforms of the same period had created other sources of friction because of their centralizing tendencies and their preference for employing peninsular personnel. (1993, 42)

For Halperín Donghi the issue was not that of an ideological revolution:

> [E]sa renovación–colocada bajo el signo ilustrado–no tenía necesariamente contenido políticamente revolucionario. Por el contrario, se dio durante una muy larga primera etapa en el marco de una escrupulosa fidelidad a la corona. . . . La crítica de la economía o la sociedad colonial, la de ciertos aspectos de su marco institucional o jurídico no implicaban entonces una discusión del orden monárquico o de la unidad imperial. (1975, 76)

> For the most part, the ideological ferment of the Enlightenment had a less-than-revolutionary impact on political thinking in the Iberian world. New ideas advanced, during much of the century, in the context of scrupulous fidelity to the absolutist crowns. . . . Most criticisms of the colonial order implied no rejection of the monarchy or the ideal of imperial unity. (1993, 43)

Along with other historians, Halperín Donghi has pointed out that the revolt against the King rapidly took on the character of a social struggle. But in terms of revolutionary mechanics there was no "people"; the lower class of *mestizo* taxpayers simply did not count. The "people" was one of those modern subjects that was consolidated as a political reference to the French Revolution. In Latin America during the Liberation period, it was a kind of significant vacuum to be continually filled with the content of the multiple and ephemeral wartime alliances used by elites to generate their power positions. The initial idea behind Independence was the construction of autonomous political power in regions (the Viceroyalties) that were lacking completely in modern practical politics, where it was first necessary to define an identity. It is strange that Simón Bolívar himself had to clarify that: "no somos europeos, no somos indios sino una especie media entre los aborígenes y los españoles" ("we are not Europeans, we are not Indians but a species midway between the aborigines and the Spaniards"), adding that "nuestro pueblo es un compuesto de Africa y América más que una emanación de Europa. *Todos nuestros padres son extranjeros*" (89) ("our people are a composite derived from Africa and America rather than an emanation from Europe. *All our parents are foreigners*") (italics mine). Camilo Torres (1766–1816) from Great Columbia affirmed in *Memorial de Agravios* (1809) that "somos todos españoles" (27) ("we are all Spaniards") and added that "los naturales conquistados y sujetos hoy al dominio español, *son muy pocos o son nada en comparación con los hijos de europeos* que hoy pueblan estas ricas posesiones" (29) ("the natives who were conquered and who are today subject to Spanish domination are *very few or nothing in comparison to the sons of Europeans* who today populate these rich possessions") (italics mine). These disputes placed *criollo* subjects in an unstable position but, at the same time, gave them the advantage of opportunely choosing their identity. Obviously elites enjoy this kind of mobility. The native or Afro-Latin American population did possess an identity, but it was either secure or suspect. (There eventually existed in the immediate post-Revolutionary period over 30 intermediate degrees of blood intermixing that were scrupulously measured.) The antipeninsular alliances were never solid, because the elites had as little confidence as the Spaniards in the indigenous peoples and freed slaves. The liquidation of the white planters in the Caribbean island of Haiti served as an instructive example of the kind of alliances that could be constructed. In Mexico, the Indian and later the *mestizo* protest dominated the first stage of the Independence movement and led it to disaster when the protesters were faced with the combined opposition of Peninsulars and white *criollos*. For this reason the partisans did not feel they were rebels but rather heirs to the collapsed Spanish authority; that, in turn, meant that the native populations often sided with the Colonial authorities in the belief that they would have less to lose.

We could say that there are two general perspectives on Spanish American Independence: One interprets it as part of the process of European political struggle, and the other views it as resulting from the ancient and constant process of indigenous, black, and *criollo* revolt against the power of the Spanish crown. These views bring not only a historiographic polemic but also the ambiguous position of the *criollo* elites into the scenario. Even so, these elites do not seem to have had a strictly mediatory function in the transcultural process but rather a new role in expressing both worlds. The *mestizo* myth that began to develop–"somos otra cosa" ("we are something else"), "algo Nuevo" ("something new"), said Bolívar–and the original character of the Latin American conflict would result in a growing authoritarianism and militarism. On this, *criollo* leaders would end up constructing the post-Colonial state that would, appropriately, establish the military as its heroes. Likewise the literature of Independence would celebrate military triumph and initiate a hero cult.

The State, Lettered Culture

Contemporary post-Colonial criticism has largely outlined (see Said; Richards) the process of exclusion of the periphery by employing the values of European literary culture, especially in the nineteenth century. I am specifically interested here in the means by which this process of exclusion took place; by "exclusion" I am referring to that practiced by the elites on the same subjects that they were attempting to modernize and integrate into a culture that they would progressively call national and induce the nation to enter "civilization." Two cultural practices constructed as universal were science and art; these were the privileged expressions of modernity for the educated *criollos* and, therefore, became decisive areas for the expression of cultural projects in those countries that had recently become independent. The writings of Andrés Bello (1781–1865) and Domingo F. Sarmiento (1811–1888) that lay the foundations for the new forms of governance were fundamental in terms of their contribution to a Latin American lettered practice.

While the expansion of capitalism was clearly responsible for outlining the idea of the "world" at that moment, the recently independent Spanish colonies had to rethink their place in the new territorial arrangement and establish their continuity with the civilized regions of the earth. The *criollos* initiated a double-edged strategy. On the one hand, they promoted their inclusion in Western culture. Sarmiento did this clearly in *Facundo* (1845), which begins with the geopolitical location of the Argentinean Republic, and he reveals what Said has called orientalism in his comparison of Latin American barbarity with that of the nomads of the East in his attempt to state, in the language of civilization, that "no somos barbarie" ("we are not barbarian") because we recognize others as barbarians. As Julio Ramos points out, Sarmiento's orientalism "es así un gesto muy significativo: proyecta, por parte de quien no es europeo, un deseo de inscribirse en el interior de la cultura occidental. Implica un lugar de enunciación–ficticio–fuera de la 'barbarie' (lo no europeo), enfáticamente civilizado" (22) ("is thus a very significant act: It projects on the part of the non-European a wish to install himself within Western culture. It implies a–fictitious–place of expression beyond 'barbarism' (but non-European) that is emphatically civilized").

On the other hand, Sarmiento also tried to outline a space for culture and the "civilized region" within the nation-state itself. This process was highly complex, because, if he wished to construct the Argentinean citizen, he also knew that citizenship was not for all, and not all would approach it in the same way. The post-Colonial state was conceived as an extremely selective entity that was incapable of sharing all its power. Ángel Rama (1984) states that the educated *criollos* fulfilled a definitive function in the constitution of power in Latin America by mediating through the authority conferred by foundational texts, between the state and its subordinates, even though clearly aligning themselves with the former. The texts of the educated *criollos* were responsible for a process that we might call internal colonization in their respective territories. This process operated in different ways and with varying scopes. There was a colonization of the past, through the writing of history, and a colonization of difference. The latter was most obvious with the Indians, who for the *criollos* formed a kind of undifferentiated otherness that had to be sent to the periphery, to a frontier that the *criollos* themselves created through the exercise of geographic imagination and military strategy, particularly where black slaves were concerned.

The appropriation of European knowledge was on the agenda of the educated *criollos* as part of the process of territorial and population control. This was the direction taken by the alternately exact and generalized encyclopaedism of Andrés Bello, author of the *Gramática de la lengua Castellana* [1847; Grammar of the Spanish Language], who pointed out in his introduction: "La gramática de una lengua es el arte de hablarla correctamente, esto es, conforme al buen uso, que es el de la gente educada" (1981a 15) ("The grammar of a language is the art of speaking it correctly, that is, in accordance with good usage, which is that of educated people"). Bello was also the author of the civil code, a cosmography, notes for the writing of a history (all this in addition to his administrative work in Chile for various cultural undertakings). It is also notable that Sarmiento too gave such importance to the control of knowledge. His insistence on creating cultural and artistic institutions for the new Republic was based on a belief that these were parallel to public highways and railways, to developing navigable rivers and other mechanisms for imposing order on the chaos of the new Republic.

Such strategies were practiced from the position of the intellectual who played a central role in the construction of the national state in Latin American societies. For Ángel Rama (1984) and Julio Ramos, such an individual had both a didactic and a "modernizing" function to perform during the Independence period, if the new Republics were to enter a world of Eurocentric values. For this reason Ramos brings up the theme of the political function of literature: "El trabajo intelectual no es independiente de la vida pública, pero tampoco es idéntico a ella: cumple una función superior en la administración de la vida pública cristalizándose en esa especie de metainstitución, la nueva universidad, cuya tarea era reflexionar sobre los roles y operaciones de otras instituciones" (40) ("Intellectual work is not independent of public life, nor is it identical to it: It fulfills a higher function in the administration of public life, crystallizing in a kind of meta-institution, the new university whose task is to reflect on the roles and operations of other public institutions"). Perhaps this function should be understood in the double sense that all civilizing strategies suggest. If, as Ramos states, "escribir, en ese mundo, era dar forma al sueño modernizador; era 'civilizar': ordenar el sinsentido de la barbarie americana" (19) ("to write, in that world, was to give form to the dream of modernization; it was to 'civilize': To impose order on the illogicality of American barbarism"), one might add that to write also was to constitute barbarism as such because writing orders and codifies the new identity, one that was not problematic under the imperial regime of the Spanish Crown. To write was to produce a concrete form of barbarism (i.e., confrontation) and to do so to an even greater extent than before, given the kind of texts written—notably genres that were classical and/or authorized by the European tradition. From this point of view, mediation was not a mere relationship; *criollo* intellectuals used direct confrontation to claim intellectual authority. Literature could also be seen as an area in which the problem of intellectual identity was developed (José Martí [1853–1895] would do this in the 1890s); meanwhile, the specific practice of literature was legitimized by aesthetic criteria that were also hermetic and inaccessible to the nonlettered of society. However, in all instances, literature operated on the basis of symbolic modes of construction of social authority and political legitimacy from which degrees of civilization or barbarism would be defined, whether this implied entry into the world of culture or banishment to the savage region of irreversible otherness. The success of this formula of civilization versus barbarism (promoted by Sarmiento in 1845) shows how European literary culture was one of the most important forces in the definition of identity in Latin America.

The intelligentsia placed this question of identity (civilization/barbarism) within their field of knowledge. Outside literature, there was no possible room for negotiation on the theme of identity. Beyond this identity-as-civilization, there was only war, the nonlettered response to the authority of civilizing power. For *criollo* writers the authority of science (knowledge) was not the only attempt at homogenization through the written word. Another force, almost as powerful as scientific truth, was the universal authority of beauty; thus literature was promoted in which landscape occupied a fundamental place. Mitchell considers landscape as a medium for exchange between the human and the "other," as well as between humans. Landscape is a medium not only for expressing value but also for expressing meaning, for communication among persons—most radically, for communication between the human and the non-human. He thus suggests that it is an abstraction that, like money, enables the state to function. A large part of the literature of the Independence period placed the Latin American landscape and its natural history well into the foreground. (See Vol. 2, Ch. 20.)

Humankind: Bello

During times of open political struggle within a culture, the relationship with the land and its space (whether natural or constructed) defines many of the genres and topics of literature. In Latin America the natural space, linked to property, was the focus for the construction of writing and political reflection, because it became the basis on which projects for the organization of elites in the recently independent Republics were established. It is sufficient to consider here the cultural periodicals of the elites, always linked to land issues where economics, politics, art, and territory are categories that belong to the same configuration of vested interests. At an early stage of his career, Andrés Bello wrote a group of texts in which he restructured the relationship of the imagination to the land. It is worth remembering that the geographical fragmentation of the former Spanish Empire in America immediately after Independence was enormous. Communication among the different regions was virtually nonexistent; this was the legacy of a Colonial structure that had developed much better means of communication between each province and the metropolis than among the individual American provinces.

Bello, who had initially left Caracas as a member of Bolívar's delegation, was surprised (after arriving in Europe) by the fall of the Revolutionary government that had dispatched him on his diplomatic mission. Left without work or contacts in London, he rapidly became a State official in political exile. Despite his poverty and exclusion, he made every effort to gain access to a vast quantity of contemporary knowledge. At the same time, he recognized that it was necessary to construct the cultural tradition of Latin America within the European tradition, but from an American perspective, and thus update the archive. His writings on natural science were published in the *Biblioteca Americana* or *Miscelánea de literatura, artes y ciencias* and the *Repertorio americano*, the two periodicals he edited in London. In almost all cases, these writings on natural science follow the line of von Humboldt. Bello had met the German scientist in 1799 in Caracas, where he had briefly taken part in some expeditions from which he derived the idea of the natural history of Latin America as a basis for a distinctive identity–as well as legitimating the denomination of "New World," understood in the sense of a unified as well as paradisiacal land.

Julio Ramos examined Bello's highly disciplined use of learning to create a Spanish American paradigm of culture. This system appeared to be developing from the time of his earliest writings. He basically became the transmitter and translator of new scientific ideas, providing his own version of the new European theories of scientific and political culture. It was also Bello who selected the authors and the ideas of European knowledge that he considered most suitable for the political project of Latin American emancipation (see **Figure 1**). These theories provided the framework of a powerful adherence to the Western culture, especially what he considered the basis of the intellectual life in Western Europe; this was a Spanish American cultural project that we must examine in the light of its political context.

The poems entitled *Silvas americanas* [*American Silvas*], especially the "Alocución a la poesía" ["Allocution to Poetry"] of 1823 and the "Silva a la agricultura de la zóna tórrida" ["Silva to Agriculture in the Torrid Zone"], written by Bello in London in 1826, constitute fragments of a great epic poem to be titled *America* (a text he never completed), with which he intended to illustrate and reveal Latin American greatness. This fact seems relevant in the context of such foundational texts, for these two passages in particular make a gesture of negation. It becomes evident that one cannot rewrite America in the cultural codes of classical Western culture, even if the idea is stated as a foundational program, or precisely because it is proposed as such a program. The reason is that America already exists in this context; there is therefore no longer a need to write it. In "Alocución a la Poesía," Bello explicitly calls on a poet other than the enunciating lyric voice to write about the new lands of the Americas: "Tiempo vendrá cuando de ti inspirado/Algún Marón americano, !oh diosa!/ también las mieses, los rebaños cante" (1981b, 48). ("The time will come when inspired by you/Some American Virgil, O goddess!/Will sing of the cornfields, the flocks"). Later on he writes: "Despierte (oh Musa, tiempo es ya) despierte/algún sublime ingenio, que levante/el vuelo a tan espléndido sujeto" (51) ("Awaken–O Muse, the time is now–awaken/ Some sublime genius to soar/In flight worthy of such a splendid theme") and concludes by asking: "Mas no a mi débil voz la larga suma/de tus victorias numerar compete;/a ingenio más feliz, más docta pluma,/su grata patria encargo tal compete" (64) ("No more to my fragile voice do the large sum/Of your victories compete in number,/To a happier genius, a more learned pen,/His grateful country grants such a duty"). Some twenty years later Sarmiento would make a similar gesture when he asks in *Facundo* for the arrival of a certain A. de Tocqueville to penetrate Spanish American reality with his insight, because its complexity exceeds the capacity of Sarmiento himself (who called his book "obrita" [4] ["a minor work"]). All that would remain now for the *criollos* was to put into practice the idea of producing future intellectuals who would be effectively "Europeans in America." These writers in turn de-legitimate any other perspective; the impasse was that there were no intellectuals sufficiently capable, according to their own self-evaluation, of articulating the American reality. The poet and scientist in Latin America's lettered city were of European provenance and saw America through European ideas. One could write in America, it seems, only with the awareness of an absence.

In a form of writing as rhetorical as Bello's, one could take this expression of negation as indicative of the poet's humility. Even so, the rewriting of America also responds to the problem of the intellectual himself, who, in the same moment in which he voiced his own program, was questioning the very place he desired within Western culture. Bello knew that it was impossible to write the history of America through the perspective of European Western culture, but he was also convinced of the necessity of establishing a lettered nucleus in the independent Republics that would not diminish the commitment to a Eurocentric model of civilization. An interesting question arises: What was the point of the footnotes Bello added to his "Silva a la agricultura de la zona tórrida"? Touched by the urban/rural opposition (correlating with the moral corruption/virtuous life duality), the poem is written in pastoral style, including a description of exuberant nature, but Bello wrote a second text on top of the first. He added footnotes in a scientific ("universal") code to elucidate what already had been said in the "universal" language of art. Thus, for example, when describing the yucca in line 40, he notes: "No se debe confundir (como se ha hecho en un diccionario de grande y merecida autoridad) la planta de cuya raíz se hace el pan de casabe (que es la *Jatropha manihot* de Linneo,

Figure 1.

Photograph of painting of Andrés Bello teaching Simón Bolívar. (Courtesy Bank of Venezuela)

conocida ya generalmente en castellano bajo el nombre de yuca) con la *yucca* de los botánicos" (1981b, 66) ("One should not confuse, as has been done in a dictionary of great and recognized authority, the plant from whose roots cassava bread is made, which is the *Jatropha manihot* of Linnaeus, now generally known in Spanish under the name *yuca*, with the *yucca* of the botanists"). When he mentions the palm (line 37) he adds: "Ninguna familia de vegetales puede competir con las palmas en la variedad de productos útiles al hombre: pan, leche, vino, aceite, fruta, hortaliza, cera, leña, cuerdas, vestido, etc." (1981b, 66) ("No plant family can compete with the palm for its variety of products useful to man: Bread, milk, wine, oil, fruit, vegetable, wax, wood, rope, clothing, etc.").

The organizational and disciplinary will evident in Bello's writing consolidated various strategies at one and the same time: Those of bringing culture to America through poetry, publicizing her natural history, circumscribing its practices, and above all establishing a cultural continuum with the European model, and thereby naturalizing its adherence to Western culture. Here Bello exercised what one could call the double epistemological condition of practically all nineteenth-century Latin American intellectuals in their position as privileged spokesmen of a dual approach to knowledge, the local and the Eurocentric. They slid from one to the other with ease, establishing themselves in this dual role in order for information to circulate; yet they had no desire to claim intellectual equality with Europe, but rather subordinated Spanish American culture to that of Europe. This dual condition defined their identity.

The Bello who wrote the Silvas also translated work by Jacques Delille (1738–1813), the author of *Les jardins* and *Les trois règnes de la nature* (edited with notes "by Cuvier and other savants") for the journal he published in London. In his work Bello advocated a poetic program, of imitating nature (the topic of the useful and sweet), of seeing literature in a mimetic relationship with reality. Bello also retained the strong moral framework established by Delille, but in a world that had completely changed its values and tastes. Not from ignorance but for the purposes of his program, Bello chose Jacques Delille—a minor poet—as his master in his foundational texts. Even though his bibliographic archive contained the works of Virgil, Ovid, and other classic poets, Bello's references leaned toward the Enlightenment, and he opted for an image of the intellectual that oscillated between authoritarian modernity and premodernity. The significant paradox here is that there is no system more entrenched in colonialism than the celebratory poetry in praise of the heroes of Independence, since the purported values are almost entirely Eurocentric. One must keep in mind that the intellectual context for men like Bello was one in which classical poetry was dominant and served as a model for all literature during the entire colonial period. It cannot be repeated too often that all prose fiction, both European and American, was prohibited. There were contraband books of prose fiction, but nothing of this nature could be published.

On the one hand, in the Silva poems, particularly the second, Bello was responsible for defining a fundamental strategy of Colonial celebration. The "Alocución," on the other hand, is a poem that invokes poetry to abandon "the cultural excess" that exists in Europe and aim at "that place" (marking en route a place that is nonlocalized, non-American) where simplicity exists. Even though this is a commonplace of this kind of composition, in a programmatic work one cannot read "that place" without it being the imagined place selected by the writer. This is a place outside the territory that he postulates as a future reserve of culture, and poetry is exhorted to set it up, to create an aesthetic primarily derived from the innocence of nature (in combination with people who are imagined as existing on the first day of creation) but also from the glories of the patriotic heroes. With this mythologization of history and poeticization of nature, Bello defines a nonpolitical place, but he also takes a strong moralizing tack. The depoliticization of history becomes clear in the use that the poet makes of the indigenous past; in criticizing Spanish tyranny on the continent at the time of the Conquest, he asks (in lines 555–57): "Pudo a un Cortés, pudo a un Pizarro el mundo/la sangre perdonar que derramaron;/imperios con la espada conquistaron" (1981b, 57) ("Could the world forgive Cortés, forgive Pizarro/The blood that they shed;/The empires conquered by the sword"). This tack is reinforced in a footnote such as the one in which he mentions Caupolicán (line 661): "*Caupolicán*. Véase el poema de Ercilla, y particularmente su canto XXXIV" (1981b, 60) (*Caupolicán*. "See the poem by Ercilla and Canto XXXIV in particular"). History thus passes into literature and there is now nothing more to say about the indigenous past. It is now—as poetry—part of Western culture and should remain a closed subject. This laying to rest is necessary: If there was blame, the world has now pardoned it. One could mention, incidentally, that it is possible

to make the same reading of the literary criticism on Bello's work. The majority of studies take aspects of his cultural development literally. For example, it is customary to point out, as proof for his foundation of an independent discourse within and for America, his loyalty to the principle of imitating nature—without taking into consideration that for Bello literature was *discourse* and the natural world of America was what Linnaeus, Ercilla, or Humboldt had classified or poeticized. It is also rarely pointed out that he knew very little of Latin American geography when he wrote his Silvas, just as Sarmiento only knew his own province and a small part of Chile when he wrote *Facundo*. The reading of the classics into the local, using this code of references, is part of the codification of Western critical knowledge.

This strategy was made even more explicit in "Silva a la agricultura de la zona tórrida." Once again, when he mentions the ferocity of the war that killed so many Amerindians, Bello notes (in line 310): "Saciadas duermen ya de sangre ibera/las sombras de Atahualpa y Moctezuma" (1981b, 73) ("Satiated with Spanish blood they now sleep/The shades of Atahualpa and Moctezuma"): Thus he lays to rest the period prior to Independence. But it was in fact the *criollos* themselves who had created the need for vengeance through the genocide (though it was never mentioned as such) of the indigenous peoples. History prior to the wars of Independence thus becomes a closed chapter only to be read in books. Consequently, the present becomes history at the point of transference to the written word. The *criollos* are seen as the new, and only, American subjects who will propel history forward into the future.

Innocence, threshold, new world, point zero: Such were the different ways of conceiving of the developmental stage of liberation, and this is what was recorded in the writings of Latin American intellectuals. This *criollo* and lettered identity (that of the educated people) was adopted by the elite, who appointed themselves to govern these Adamic territories. The subjects appear belatedly in the Silvas; first the land, then the history, and finally the humans. The latter are presented in two basic categories: The anonymity of the crowd of plebeians on one side, and the virtuous citizens on the other. City and country are their respective environments, and these are interpreted on a moral basis. The crowd that lives in the cities is corrupt and base, succumbing to noxious idleness and servility. The countryside harbors a primordial innocence that will reward its cultivators by teaching them how to exercise power; the proposal of the poem as a whole is the return to the countryside, not as a referential space but as a zone of civic/moral virtue where "the citizens" are educated to exercise authority. With a perspective strongly marked by gender, Bello refers to the feminine corruption that dwells in the cities from which one has to extract future members of the political elite: "Y será que se formen de ese modo/los ánimos heroicos denodados/que fundan y sustentan los estados?" (lines 105–107) ("And will they develop thus/the intrepid heroic spirits/That found and sustain states?"). Here he refers to the sons of the elite, who seem to be more occupied with their personal grooming than the future of the country.

The Silva poems pointed toward a cultured form of nature to which industry and law should strive and to a poetic discourse by which poetry is superimposed onto reality, thus establishing an organized world for the new countries. As an heir to the Enlightenment, in "Alocución a la Poesía," Bello describes the path that literature must take in America: A retracing of the entire history of culture, beginning with the classical genres inspired by the epic form and fusing with this the point of view of reason. The nature that Bello proposed to imitate was that derived from books canonized by the European tradition. His fundamental strategy consisted of employing these models in the broad and open American political arena, as if they were universals.

Nature in America was not a referential but a moral space. It was the promise of order at this new stage in the evolution of these independent countries. Bello, an intellectual without a country, wrote from his exile in London, where he witnessed at close hand the evils and "corruption" of industrialization. London was at that time a "monster." According to Raymond Williams, between 1821 and 1841 (Bello lived in London between 1810 and 1829) the city expanded by 20 percent and was the center for both commerce and the distribution of goods within the United Kingdom, as well as the place in which the reality of the nation was forged. In London new political protest movements were evident, and Bello must have rapidly perceived that the poor who aimlessly wandered the city were regarded as potentially seditious. The project for America was thus that of a premodernized Europe, capable of avoiding the rabble and the threats that the criminal classes posed to capitalism. Agrarian life signified an ordered existence, and poetry's invitation to the new continent was in fact intended to draw attention to the dangers and threats that modernity brought in its wake. In the urban reality that Bello witnessed in London, the rabble symbolized the possibility of a disruption of harmony; from early on, he regarded the danger they represented as a threat to America, and the city as the environment where this threat was both created and disseminated. The return to the countryside was a call, not to the construction of a homogenous national identity based on the idea of ordered nature, but rather to the cohesion of the elites in the face of the threat of the plebeians. Traditionally agriculture was governed by the imperative to reform and subordinate Nature; for Bello, it is *human* nature that must be reformed and subordinated, that should take a look at itself in the moral mirror of ordered fields and not the bad example of the modernized city. If, as Williams points out, in England the problem of rural history was the problem of the class struggle, Bello, who witnessed and participated in this modernizing process, attempted to delay the threat of this and other conflicts through his writings. From this perspective his relationship with the Eurocentric tradition is highly selective; he did not just accept classic models, but rather revised them for an American context.

Bello was not alone. In "La victoria de Junín. Canto a Bolívar" ("Victory at Junín: Hymn to Bolívar") (first version published in Guayaquil 1825), José Joaquín Olmedo (1780–1847) produced a work inspired by the classic genres. The poem deals with the ongoing struggles for Independence as past history and calls on the future to judge the greatness of the new heroes. The canonization of masculine, warlike, and military values is complete: Bolívar himself, "hijo de Colombia y Marte" (125) ("son of Colombia and Mars"), wrote commentaries on the poem that Olmedo subsequently incorporated in the second version of his poem (1826), thereby clearly indicating the links between military power and the written word. This dialogue between arms and letters would become increasingly fluid. José María Heredia (Cuba, 1803–1839), in exile in the United States and Mexico, would incorporate the Romantic subject in his classic poems "En el Teocalli de Cholula" ("In the Teocalli of Cholula") (the definitive version

of 1832) and "Niágara" (1825). His reordering of Latin American geography from a subjective perspective meant that nature became the mute context for the contemplation of the past, a past that in its barbarian state must remain silent in the written word. Through the classic poetic trope of the meditation amid ruins, the image of Aztec human sacrifice is conjured up. Legitimate and illegitimate historical violence was also inflicted on the *criollo* elites and enumerated in the written texts. But above all there was an identity that created a bond in the face of difference.

The constitution of the post-Independent elite, its design for a map of worthy and unworthy subjects to participate in the new republican model, and the statute by which the selected would enter had already been denounced by an unusual individual, Fray Servando Teresa de Mier (Mexico, 1763–1827). Sensitive to the idea of power as a place that is first occupied, before becoming a part of the subjects who exercise it, he commented in a sonnet:

Cesó la Inquisición? Cesó el local,
varióse el nombre con el edificio
es hoy Capitanía General
lo que antes se llamaba Santo Oficio.
Con la Constitución todo es lo mismo:
mudóse el nombre, sigue el despotismo.

Did the Inquisition shut up shop? The premises closed,
the name of the building changed,
what today is called the General Captaincy
was previously called the Holy Office.
All is the same with the Constitution:
change the name, the despotism carries on as before.

(152)

Irony of this kind (radical in terms of the doubt cast on the Revolution) was unthinkable in the context of the insurgents in the River Plate region.

Transculturation and the Nation

While these first intellectuals of Independence committed themselves to a universal model of culture and made their declarations from what could hardly be considered local contexts (as seen above, many wrote from distant and lengthy exile), from early on another model arose in the River Plate region with the fundamental aim of national construction through written texts. These intellectuals did not propose to locate America or their Republic on the world map, but rather to establish the national content that defined their own community and use it as a tool in their own internal political struggles. This meant that changes in the universalist rhetoric began to appear in some regions of the continent only when the intellectuals established as their basis for reflection not just an independent political stand but also (and primarily) a national project that conflicted with that of other groups. In the River Plate region these changes became evident during the 1830s and 1840s, when Juan Manuel de Rosas (1793–1877) implemented at State level a *caudillista* tradition in the Argentine Republic. His populism and his refusal to "Europeanize" the country were responsible for setting against him a homogenous block of intellectuals (with only a few internal divisions). Rosas forced them into exile in neighboring countries (mainly in Uruguay and Chile). During the first years of Rosas's government, they were subsequently known as "the outlaws." Nation and exile came together for this first generation of literary

Argentineans who, absent from the *patria*, had to recreate it as a highly desirable and basically unpopulated entity. In contrast to those exiled during the wars of Independence, the Argentineans in exile during the reorganization period had to deal with a succession of different projects for their nation and varying perspectives on the types of alliances required by the elites to govern the Republic when the enemy lay within and was, in fact, a fellow citizen. Rosas represented the greatest threat because he questioned the lettered model and the traditional alliances of intellectuals with the elite, military, and commercial groups. The alliance that Rosas set up between the uneducated gauchos and the members of the "dangerous classes" of post-Colonial society openly confronted the Enlightenment-oriented elite with the authoritarian system of the *caudillo*.

In this context of extreme violence, Juan Cruz Varela (1794–1839) stands out among the first Argentine exiles. Along with his odes to Gutenberg and the freedom of the press, to progress and patriotic heroes, Varela, considered by his peers as Argentina's leading poet, was also able to incorporate difference into the homogenizing model of political modernization, in the knowledge that his enemy was the premodernism of Rosas. For Varela the literary project of the new nation was stamped by the canonic genres of tradition, echoing his own neo-Classical education. He wrote tragedies (*Dido, Argia*, fragments of *Idomeneo*) and translated Virgil, Horace, Ovid, Corneille, Boileau, La Fontaine, and Alfieri. His work as a journalist in exile placed him at the center of the first Argentinean intellectual generation to use the adjective *Argentinean* in the restrictive sense of citizenry. When it came to open struggle with the authoritarian government of Juan Manuel de Rosas, Varela's writings called for the elite to be united in their shared commitment to Enlightenment values and even incorporated the *criolla* woman into his texts, an element of difference that almost all poetry of the Independence period had expelled from the cultural sphere and Revolutionary history. Varela used the *criolla* woman (not in her subjectivity but as a symbol of private life, seen as the refuge from the struggles of history and fundamental to the constitution of the new citizenry. It was not difficult then, as it would not be difficult in the future, for the rhetoric and iconography of the French Revolution to identify the passive role of the female with that of the *patria* (both proof of the agency of men). The woman becomes a refuge in her contrast with the barbarism of the coarse and violent local political boss. In the ode "Al bello sexo argentino" [1831; "To the Argentinean Fair Sex"] Varela writes:

El campeón patrio, que en feroz milicia
pasó sus verdes años;
el ministro imparcial de la justicia;
el sabio que destruye los engaños,
consagrados tal vez por la malicia;
el mercadante activo y afanoso,
todos, todos, oh bellas,
a vuestro lado olvidan deleitoso
penas a un tiempo y la memoria de ellas.

The patriotic champion, who in the fierce militia
spends his years of youth;
the impartial minister of justice;
the wise man who roots out deceit,
perhaps consecrated by malice;
the active and enthusiastic man of commerce,

all, all, O fair ones,
In your enchanting company forget
their worries for a time and the memory of them.

(in Carilla 135)

Here Varela creates a masculine elite subject, subdivided in accordance with his life in the public sphere; the woman is the place where conflict, politics, and commercial competition cease. This alliance with the *criolla* also forms part of the strategy to integrate tolerable difference that was newly deployed by literary culture. If the Argentinean Republic was the place of barbarism for Varela, something of the nation survived within it to take on the qualification of "Argentinean" that the exiled intellectual located in the female figure, companion of the patriotic (nonpolitical) struggle. Women are to be found at the start of Argentinean literature. *La Cautiva* [1837; The Captive] by Esteban Echeverría and *Amalia* (published as a serial novel in 1851 and in 1855 as a book) by José Mármol (1817–1871) are two foundational texts that treat women as a passive emblem of the struggle for power and a nationalizing and civilizing element that opposes the barbarism of political violence displayed by their enemies. In the case of the historical aboriginals (only including the male sex) as well as the gauchos, the woman in elite discourse represents difference, the recipient of the characteristics granted by the hegemonic subject: passivity, domesticity, absence of agency and voice. Basically, literary discourse carried the weight of authority derived from the prestige of Classical learning and set the demarcation between those who could and could not enter the lettered scene. In this way women did play an active part in capturing and negotiating their own space through the expression of their difference.

While this first stage of exile was occurring, another group of young intellectuals held meetings in "The Literary Salon of 1837" (founded in Buenos Aires by the librarian Marcos Sastre), and their proposals were as much aesthetic as they were political. Their activities consisted of discussion groups, reading sessions, and the discussion of both texts and political projects. Juan Bautista Alberdi (1810–1884), Esteban Echeverría (1805–1851), and Juan María Gutiérrez (1809–1878) were among the more outstanding participants. During the inaugural discussions of the Salón, the need to create a national literature was seen as a necessity of nationhood. In the minds of these men Argentina required a mode of discourse and a mythic imagination in order to hold its own with European letters and thus bring to a close the isolated *criollismo* of the Rosas faction. During the 1960s (another important moment in the nationalization of culture), David Viñas (b. 1929) stated that: "La literatura argentina es la historia de la voluntad nacional. . . . [L]a literatura argentina comenta a través de sus voceros la historia de los sucesivos intentos de una comunidad por convertirse en nación. . . ." (14) ("Argentinean literature is the history of national will. . . . Argentinean literature comments through its spokesmen on the history of a community's successive attempts to convert itself into a nation. . ."). Perhaps this is a particular feature of River Plate cultures, preserved since the nineteenth century, cultures that exterminated the indigenous population and considered Europe their ethnocultural horizon; expressing the processes of transculturation in terms of processes of cultural nationalization, they argued that the legitimate agent of exchange with centralized cultures was the nation and not an ethnic, linguistic, or sexual identity. A century after the texts of the generation of 1837, Jorge Luis Borges (1899–1986) would also seek strategies to nationalize (through colloquial language, *criollo* mythology, and the myth of the land) forms of avant-garde modernization produced in the 1920s and 1930s and genres (such as the detective novel and the comic) of a flourishing cultural industry.

But this process had already begun in the post-Independence period when the importance of literature to national development was so great that it was not surprising that literary critic Juan María Gutiérrez would emerge early on to explain clearly the program of cultural nationalization when European Romanticism swept through Latin America at the beginning of the nineteenth century. The celebrated phrase of Esteban Echeverría's *Dogma Socialista* [*Socialist Dogma*]: "tendremos siempre un ojo clavado en el progreso de las naciones y el otro en las entrañas de nuestra sociedad" (1991, 254) ("we should always have one eye glued to the progress of nations and the other on the heartbeat of our society") defines this program. Nationalization would be effected from the perspective of dislocation, looking toward two different traditions that neither exchanged nor bartered with each other. For this game to work one needed basically an intellectual elite capable of expressing its perspective. Prior to exile, the elite had taken its shape from its struggle against the power implicit in the "Rosas phenomenon" (a mix between Romantic hero, *criollo caudillo,* and nomadic gaucho), while it sought for a means of sharing authority among the different power groups, while excluding the dangerous classes. The nation would be the instance from which one focused a normalizing perspective.

Cultural nationalism filled the vacuum left by the loss of colonial identity when the form that a particular country would assume was still very undetermined. This was not only the consequence of warring provinces headed by *criollo* factions promoting the autonomy of their own states, but also because they had not as yet stabilized their internal frontiers; the Indian still had not lost the great quantity of territory that at the time was increasingly coming under the control of the Argentinean state. For the lettered Argentinean elite the purported barbarism of the Indian and Rosas's gauchos became the prime target against which the production of a national literature would be constituted, effectively excluding both groups from consideration. *La cautiva* and *El matadero* [1871; *The Slaughter House*] by Echeverría and Mármol's *Amalia* are emblematic of the violence that laid the foundations of the nation as well as of the irreducible differences that composed it. It would be Rosas, interpreted as the generator of barbarism, who (according to Viñas) would frustrate the project of European-national synthesis and polarize it definitively, thereby eliminating the possibility of a pact between members of the elite to Europeanize the Republic. Then it would be impossible to forget their non-European origin, because the populist state emphasized national difference. The first attempt at modernization found Rosas (a member of the land-owning class) to be an obstacle; a pact was agreed upon for the purposes of interchange with the most problematic cultures of the center. More or less negotiated Europeanization would not be possible; the intellectuals had to recognize the existence of difference. Paradoxically, the barbarism of Rosas produced the actual elements of a nation in the process of being Europeanized by a lettered elite that had always to live with the problem of its premodernity (but not in the harmonious terms suggested by Rama [1982b] in the case of twentieth-century transculturation). Esteban Echeverría articulated the

program of national culture and identified it with Romanticism (in 1837): "La poesía romántica no es el fruto sencillo y espontáneo del corazón, o la expresión armoniosa de los caprichos de la fantasía, sino la voz última de la conciencia" (1944, 50) ("Romantic poetry is not the simple and spontaneous fruit of the heart or the harmonious expression of the caprices of fantasy but rather the last voice of conscience"). As voluntary cultural strategies of self-awareness, the demarcation of tradition and the processes of transculturation all have the nation as their privileged context for expression.

Gutiérrez, placing his discourse very close to the Romantic, described *La Cautiva* as "escenas de nuestra naturaleza y de nuestras costumbres, traídas a la admiración urbana y culta por la pluma mágica del bardo argentino" (93) ("scenes of our natural world and customs brought together for the admiration of the urban and cultured reader by the magic pen of the Argentine bard"); once again the polarity of country-city, nature-culture, oral-written, and civilization-barbarism finds its expression in the work of the intellectual and the nation. (The "Argentine bard" makes a notable contrast to Andrés Bello, who addressed "Poetry" and called for the appearance of an "American Virgil," in addition to despising the city in favor of the morality of the countryside.) The relationship of literature with the *patria* (fatherland) is the central aspect of Gutiérrez's cultural project that saw in elite fiction the means for expressing sentiments and values attributed to the nation:

> Al aceptar los hombres nuevos la doctrina literaria del autor de estos libros (se refiere a los de Echeverría), que era esencialmente emancipadora, se efectuó en ellos una especie de revelación de destinos desconocidos, pero seductores, a cuya conquista estuvieron dispuestos a lanzarse; y las dificultades se allanaron por sí mismas para la realización de tan patrióticos propósitos. (95)

> On accepting the essentially liberationist literary doctrine of the author of these books (referring to those of Echeverría), a kind of revelation of unknown but seductive destiny was effected in the new men who were disposed to launch themselves to conquer it; and the difficulties were smoothed out by themselves for the achievement of such patriotic proposals.

In fact the relationship between the elites and the *patria* would be constructed from this time forward as a natural alliance. As Echeverría always emphasized, this was the hegemonic place of the intellectuals in national cultural development: "La poesía sigue la marcha de los elementos de la civilización, y nutriéndose, como principalmente se nutre, de principios filosóficos, de ideas morales y religiosas, debe ceder al impulso que le dan las doctrinas dominantes en la época sobre aquellos tres puntos centrales del mundo de la humana inteligencia" (1944, 67) ("Poetry follows the march of the elements of civilization, and nurtures itself, as it did in the beginning, on philosophical principles, and moral and religious ideas, and should give in to the impulse granted by the dominant doctrines of the period regarding those three central points in the world of human intelligence"). For this reason there was little hesitation at the moment of selecting the content of the program; in 1837 at the inaugural discussion of the Salón Literario, Gutiérrez confirms:

> Nula, pues, la ciencia y la literatura española, debemos nosotros divorciarnos completamente con ellas y emanciparnos a este respecto de las tradiciones peninsulares, como supimos hacerlo en política, cuando nos proclamamos libres. Quedamos aún ligados por el vínculo fuerte y estrecho del idioma; pero éste debe aflojarse de día en día, a medida que vayamos entrando en el movimiento intelectual de los pueblos adelantados de la Europa.

Para esto es necesario que nos familiaricemos con los idiomas extranjeros y hagamos constante estudio de aclimatación al nuestro cuanto en aquellos se produzca de bueno, inteligente y bello. (in Altamirano and Sarlo 42)

Spanish science and literature are null and void; we should divorce ourselves totally from them and free ourselves from the peninsular traditions, as we knew how to on the political front when we declared ourselves to be free. We are still strongly connected by the powerful and tight link of language, but this should ease as time progresses in accordance with our gradual entrance into the intellectual movement of the advanced peoples of Europe. For this reason it is essential to familiarize ourselves with foreign languages and make a constant study of acclimatizing them to ours when something good, intelligent, and beautiful is produced in those languages.

The translation of 'the good' from Europe would be integrated into the education of the intellectual to finally create the culture of the nation.

Gauchesco Literature

Perhaps there is no celebratory, patriotic literature that more precisely illustrates the strategies of transculturation than the *gauchesca* (gaucho literature) employed by the literary *criollos* of the River Plate region. Part of this intellectual group used this genre for political effect and sought support, not from their peers but from the lower class, the uneducated *criollos*. What is known as *gauchesco* poetry is a nonhomogenous complex of compositions that, using the fiction of a Colonial and rural language, had wide circulation among the lower and less educated sectors of the coastal region of Argentina and the interior of Uruguay. The gauchos, subjects and objects of this literature, were a key element of this rural population. Generally *mestizos* of Spanish and Indian parentage, they were not recognized as fully belonging to either of these two ethnic groups; nor were they recognized by them. They were to be found in the lines of the regular *criollo* army and the *montoneros*, the armed groups that spontaneously rose up against one or another group in power, under the banner of some local *caudillo*. The gaucho was thus a subject subordinate to imperial power as much as to the Republican military, and completely tied into the power struggle during the Independence period and in the internal conflicts waged over the organization of the Republic.

The participation of the gauchos in the Independence armies was far from spontaneous—in fact quite the contrary. Nomadic and indifferent to the future constitution of the State (from which they could not benefit), the gaucho had no place in the Republican scheme. The elites of the Rio Plate region repeatedly used contingents from this group under coercion to make up the regular armies that initially fought against the Spaniards and later against centralized power in Buenos Aires, in favor of the different provincial hegemonies and finally against the Indians on the southern border of Argentina. As a result of the levies, a brutal process of recruitment, the *gauchos* formed part of the army. (All those who had no accreditation as a worker in some rural establishment were subjected to the levy.) During periods of civil war, this law, applied to illiterates, was in practice a means of arranging a permanent resource for the army (the most powerful elite group) at the lowest possible price; their maintenance cost next to nothing.

Josefina Ludmer, in her work on the *gauchesco* texts from the perspective of discourse, hypothesizes that this genre is a kind of writing that attempts to form an alliance between two social sectors, that of the intellectuals who provided a political program and the *gauchos* who supplied their point of view. The terms of that alliance were handled by the intellectuals, who tried to position the gaucho to take advantage of the different political opportunities that emerged during the Independence process. In this sense gauchesco literature offers a privileged context for investigating how many processes of transculturation were instigated in Latin America as nationalizing projects by the elites (with integration that excluded different groups). As Valentín Alsina pointed out in 1848: "como este género tiene tanta aceptación en cierta clase inculta de nuestras sociedades, puede ser un vehículo que una administración sagaz sabría utilizar para instruir a esas masas y transmitir los sucesos e ideas que, de otro modo nada saben ni nada les importa" (qtd. in Rama 1982a, 170) ("since this genre had such acceptance in a certain uneducated class of our societies, it could be a vehicle that a resourceful administration would know how to use in order to instruct these masses and transmit events and ideas that otherwise they would know nothing about or consider unimportant"). José Hernández (1834–1886) (author of the classic poetic denunciation on the abuses of Republican power used against the gauchos) comments in the letter-prologue of *Martín Fierro* (1872) to José Zoilo Miguens: "Es un pobre gaucho con todas las imperfecciones de forma que el arte tiene todavía entre ellos; y con toda la falta de enlace en sus ideas, en las que no existe siempre una sucesión lógica, descubriéndose frecuentemente entre ellas, apenas una relación oculta y remota" (191) ("He is a poor gaucho with all the formal imperfections that art still has among them; and all the lack of connection between ideas, in which there does not always exist a logical succession, frequently showing not even a hidden and remote relationship among them"). He then emphasizes his work as an intellectual in the process of transforming and dignifying the *gaucho*:

Me he esforzado, sin presumir haberlo conseguido, en presentar un tipo que personificara el carácter de nuestros gauchos, concentrando el modo de ser, de sentir, de pensar y de expresarse, que les es peculiar; dotándolo con todos los juegos de su imaginación llena de imágenes y de colorido, con todos los arranques de su altivez, inmoderados hasta el crimen, y con todos los impulsos y arrebatos, hijos de una naturaleza que la educación no ha pulido y suavizado. (191)

I have made an effort, without presuming to have achieved my aim, to present a type that personifies the character of our gauchos, concentrating on the way of being, feeling, thinking, and expressing that is peculiar to them; endowing them with all the play of their imagination replete with images and color, all the outbursts of their arrogance, immoderate to the point of crime, and with all their impulses and rages as sons of a natural environment that education has neither polished nor softened.

For this reason he also speaks of the gaucho as a type who "al paso que avanzan las conquistas de la civilización, va perdiéndose casi por completo" (192) ("will be lost almost completely as the conquests of civilization advance").

Thus the very element that neo-Classical rhetoric and the establishment of a pantheon of national heroes had banished was culturally integrated by a literary group whose achievements in transculturation would be rapidly taken advantage of by those in power. While in the first *gauchesco* texts there is represented an active participation in the struggle against the Spaniards, in the second half of the nineteenth century the scene would shift to the factional struggles in which the *gaucho* is even more fully represented. The writers of the elites, who progressively began to use the *gaucho* as a character in political, nationalist, and melodramatic fiction, felt that his incorporation into the literature of the intelligentsia required that such an entry be neutralized. Later, during different stages of modernization within River Plate culture, the *gaucho*, after having vanished from national life, began to represent the essence of the nation and was adopted to confront the changes generated by European immigration in the urban cultures of the region (fundamentally in Ricardo Rojas's (1882–1957) four volumes of *Historia de la literatura argentina*– 1917, 1918, 1919, 1922 [*History of Argentine Literature*] and in *El Payador* [1916; "The Ballad Singer"] by Leopoldo Lugones [1874–1938]).

The nineteenth century in Latin America reveals a broad complex of strategies that involve the progressive movements of modernization, nationalization, and democratization in political and cultural practices. Intellectuals played a central role in the creation and diffusion of these strategies, especially in terms of fixing the limits of the groups that shared in modernization and what was to be considered national and most significantly the discretionary control exercised in political and cultural practices under the banner of democracy. Forms of expression that we could call transcultural were actualized through the powerful alliance between political and military power and with the support of intellectuals. From this alliance new factors entered into the cultural imaginary that were blind to cultural difference, and ultimately legitimized an exclusionary culture in the name of the nation.

Translation by Jessica Johnson

Works Cited

Altamirano, Carlos, and Beatriz Sarlo. 1983. *Ensayos argentinos.* Buenos Aires: Centro Editor de América Latina.

Bello, Andrés. 1981a. *Gramática*. Vol. 4 of *Obras completas*. Caracas: Fundación La Casa de Bello.

——. 1981b. *Poesías*. Vol. 1 of *Obras Completas*. Caracas: Fundación La Casa de Bello.

Bolívar, Simón. 1977. "Carta de Jamaica (1815)." *Pensamiento político de la emancipación (1790–1825)*. Caracas: Biblioteca Ayacucho. 2: 83–99.

Carilla, Emilio, ed. 1979. *Poesía de la Independencia*. Caracas: Ayacucho.

Echeverría, Esteban. 1944. *Clasicismo y romanticismo. Los consuelos.* Buenos Aires: Sophos.

——. 1991. "Dogma Socialista." *Obras escogidas/Esteban Echeverría*. Ed. Beatriz Sarlo and Carlos Altamirano. Caracas: Biblioteca Ayacucho. 159–267.

Gutiérrez, Juan María. 1979. "Noticias biográficas sobre don Esteban Echeverría." *La literatura de mayo y otras páginas críticas* by Juan María Gutiérrez. Buenos Aires: Centro Editor de América Latina. 62–125.

Halperín Donghi, Tulio. 1975. *Historia contemporánea de América Latina*. Madrid: Alianza.

——.1993. *The Contemporary History of Latin America*. Ed. and trans. John Charles Chasteen. Durham: Duke University Press.

Hernández, José. 1977. "Martín Fierro." *Poesía gauchesca*. Caracas: Biblioteca Ayacucho.

Ludmer, Josefina. 1988. *El género gauchesco: un tratado sobre la patria.* Buenos Aires: Sudamericana.

Mitchell, W. J. T., ed. 1994. *Landscape and Power*. Chicago: University of Chicago Press.

Olmedo, José Joaquín. 1947. "La victoria de Junín. Canto a Bolívar." *Poesías completas*. Mexico City: Fondo de Cultura Económica. 122–52.

Ortiz, Fernando. 1987. *Contrapunteo cubano del tabaco y el azúcar.* Caracas: Biblioteca Ayacucho.

Pratt, Mary Louise. 1992. *Imperial Eyes: Travel Writing and Transculturation.* London: Routledge.

Rama, Ángel. 1982a. *Los gauchipolíticos rioplatenses*. Buenos Aires: Centro Editor de América Latina.

——. 1982b. *Transculturación narrativa en América Latina*. Mexico City: Siglo XXI.

——. 1984. *La ciudad letrada*. Montevideo: Fundación Internacional Ángel Rama.

Ramos, Julio. 1989. *Desencuentros de la modernidad en América Latina: literatura y política en el siglo XIX*. Mexico City: Fondo de Cultura Económica.

Richards, Thomas. 1993. *The Imperial Archive: Knowledge and the Fantasy of Empire.* London and New York: Verso.

Ríos, Alicia: 1997. "Prensa y Nación en la Venezuela independentista." *Estudios* 9 (Jan–Jun): 127–38.

Said, Edward W. 1993. *Culture and Imperialism*. New York: Knopf.

Sarmiento, Domingo Faustino. 1977. *Facundo o civilización y barbarie.* Caracas: Ayacucho.

Smith, Neil. 1990. *Uneven Development: Nature, Capital and the Production of Space*. Oxford: Basil Blackwell.

Torres, Camilo. 1977. "Memorial de agravios (1809)." *Pensamiento político de la emancipación (1790–1825)*. Caracas: Biblioteca Ayacucho. 1: 25–42.

Viñas, David. 1982. *Literatura argentina y realidad política*. Buenos Aires: Centro Editor de América Latina.

Williams, Raymond. 1973. *The Country and the City*. New York: Oxford University Press.

CHAPTER 20

TRANSCULTURATION AND NATIONHOOD

Idelber Avelar

Ricardo Piglia (b. 1941) once pointed out that the apocryphal quote at the beginning of Domingo Sarmiento's (1811–1888) *Facundo* (1845)–the French sentence "on ne tue point les idées" (Sarmiento 1977, 5) ("Ideas cannot be killed"; 1998, xi), written by Sarmiento on a wall after being attacked by a federalist gang–can be taken as an emblem of Argentine literature in its foundational moment, and that this is so not simply in its banal content, but primarily in its form and in the discursive economy that presides over its historical inscription. By relating how Juan Manuel de Rosas (1793–1877), "mandó una comisión encargada de descifrar el jeroglífico" (Sarmiento 1977, 5) ("sent a committee in charge of deciphering the hieroglyph"; Sarmiento 1998, ix), Sarmiento draws the line between civilization and barbarism with a mere epigraph: Barbarians are, of course, those unable to read the French. More than in the utopian vision it voices, "el contenido político de la frase reside en el uso de la lengua francesa" (Piglia 15) ("the sentence's political content resides in the use of the French language"). A voracious student of foreign languages, Sarmiento located in the transculturation of European sources a sine qua non condition for the construction of a modern, civilized, Argentine nation. Transculturation is, however, always already torn apart by aporias, not the least of which plagues the authorship of Sarmiento's epigraph. Sarmiento attributes it to Hippolyte Fortoul, but Paul Groussac (1848–1929) later argued that it was in fact taken from C. P. Volney, only to be contradicted by Paul Verdevoye, who noted that it does not appear either in Fortoul or Volney, but in Denis Diderot (1713–1784). The exercise in tracking down sources naturally does not matter in itself, but it is an emblem of the predicament of an entire national literature. Designed to found a nation by alienating, domesticating, and eventually transculturating that nation's originary barbarism, the *letrado's* (the lettered writer's) civilizing gesture is from the beginning contaminated by a savage, barbaric relationship with its sources, emblematized in recurrent erroneous and secondhand attributions.

Sarmiento's relationship with barbarism is thus not one of pure exteriority, because the task of transculturation is double: One must translate both the European source and the untamed vigor of the nation's barbaric essence. This double task had already been formulated by the members of the Salón Literario of 1837 and popularized by Esteban Echeverría's (1805–1851) famous dictum: "hay que tener un ojo puesto en la inteligencia europea y el otro en las entrañas de la patria" (qtd. in Weinberg 223) ("one must have one eye on European intelligence and the other on the entrails of the fatherland"). From the standpoint of Argentine liberalism, *Facundo* is the book that accomplishes this task. Sarmiento's insistence on the need to discipline barbarism through enlightened modern knowledge is no more central to his argument than the insistence on refusing the mere imitation of Europe, which he saw in so many of his liberal contemporaries. Echeverría, for example, is praised in *Facundo* for not

having repeated the error of Juan Cruz Varela (1794–1839) and Florencio Varela (1807–1848), who failed despite their "maestría clásica y estro poético . . . porque nada agregaban al caudal de nociones europeas" (Sarmiento 1977, 39) ("classic art and poetic fire . . . because they added nothing to the stock of European ideas"; 1998, 29). In contrast, Echeverría's *La cautiva* ["The Captive"] approached that "inmensidad sin límites . . . de una naturaleza solemne, grandiosa, incomensurable" (Sarmiento 1977, 39–40) ("immeasurable and boundless space, . . . of such natural scenery as is solemn, imposing, unusual"; 1998, 29) and thus envisioned a truly national literature, which for Sarmiento had to emerge from the "descripción de las grandiosas escenas naturales" (1977, 39) ("description of the mighty scenes of nature"; 1998, 28). It would be simple, of course, to show that Sarmiento's account of Argentine nature in Echeverría's poem and in the literature to come drew considerably more on the Kantian analytic of the sublime–by then already disseminated by European Romanticism, notably by Alexander von Humboldt's (1769–1859) highly influential writings on his equinoctial travels (Pratt; González Echevarría)–than on the pampa itself, with which, by the way, Sarmiento had not had firsthand contact. For the understanding of the economy of transculturation in its foundational moment, however, a more complex challenge presents itself: To demonstrate how the roots of Sarmiento's aporias lie, as I will argue below, in his perception that despite his best efforts this dialectic–to transculturate Europe while also transculturating barbarism, to translate the European source while remaining faithful to the truth of barbarism–could not be realized without leaving a remainder.

Justifying why he did not make any changes in this hastily produced work, Sarmiento confessed he was reluctant to polish such a shapeless work lest it might lose its formless and primitive physiognomy, willful audacity, and undisciplined conception, yet these are also the terms used by Sarmiento *to describe barbarism.* The civilizing, foundational text borrows from barbarism its very principle of construction. It is not gratuitous that in Sarmiento's metacommentary his work replicates the very (un)structure of the barbarism that is to be transculturated. Sarmiento legitimates himself not so much as the bearer of modern European knowledge–in this he was not unique among his Unitarian liberal compatriots–but as the *faithful translator of barbarism.* As he attempts to cancel barbarism while maintaining its truth, this being Sarmiento's view of translation, one particular operation becomes crucial: Taxonomy. Not by chance, the study of Juan Facundo Quiroga's (1790–1835) origins is prefaced by an inquiry into the Argentine characters among which Sarmiento discerns the tracker, guide, the bad gaucho, and the troubador. The gaucho appears as a vegetal or mineral species to be classified, organized, described to an alien observer; Sarmiento presupposes a traveler's gaze. Before explaining the origins of the barbarian *caudillo,* the grounds that made him possible, the reader must accept the *letrado's* taxonomic effort. That which can be classified can be tamed. The Nietzschean postulate of an organic relationship between grammar and power was never clearer than in Sarmiento. If the untamed dispersion of singularities can be subsumed under a handful of pseudo-Linnean categories, barbarism might yield to the *letrado's* civilizing mission and agree to cancel or maintain itself in the modern nation-state. Sarmiento's taxonomy announces the seed of the *gaucho bueno/gaucho malo* dichotomy that Lucio Victorio Mansilla (1831–1913) would popularize a few decades later, when the pseudo-Linnean table had already been reduced to a polarity between those inside and those outside the ideological universe encompassed by the nation state.

The most crucial taxonomy in *Facundo* emerges, however, in the introduction, when Sarmiento establishes one of the many connections and contrasts between Facundo and Rosas: The provincial Juan Facundo Quiroga (1790–1835), barbarian but "brave" and "audacious," has degenerated to the urban Rosas who devastates without feeling, with a cold heart, and is nothing more than calculated evil. In this American proto-version of the first-time-as-tragedy-second-time-as-farce axiom that Marx would formulate seven years later, the transculturator identifies a process of transculturation at the very heart of barbarism. Barbarism, misunderstood by many of Sarmiento's allies and later readership as the unchanging realm of untamed nature–a contention that is a crucial part of Sarmiento's own argument in the book–appears, in fact, as the agent of the originary transculturation, the mythical fall that provides Sarmiento with his point of departure and mechanism of legitimation. The seduction of Sarmiento's work derives from his ability to envision a utopia while narrating a fall. This fable of origin depicts a division of labor between the barbarian but truthful *caudillo* and his farcical, despicable reincarnation in the capital, and therein Sarmiento locates the very need for his endeavor: *Facundo* is necessary because Facundo has become Rosas. In other words, the civilizing transculturation carried out by the *letrado* is imperative because barbarism has proven to be able to disguise itself in the garb of civilization–to beat civilization, as it were, on its own terrain. Remarkably more complex than one would think at first, the fable of origin paints a barbarism originally "patriarcal y primitiva . . . pureza bárbara y hostil" (1977, 92) ("patriarchal and primitive . . . in all its purity and hostility"; 1998, 89), traits that are embodied in the gaucho's moral character, "fuerte, altivo, enérgico" (1977, 34) ("strong, haughty, and energetic"; 1998, 26). Facundo, faithful translator of a prelapsarian barbarism, is dictatorial but "un hombre de genio" (1977, 86) ("a man of genius"; 1998, 82), sheer "instintos de destrucción y carnicería" (1977, 83) ("destructive and sanguinary instincts"; 1998, 78) but "un hombre superior" (1977, 88) ("a man of superior ability"; 1998, 85), capable of nurturing legends about his omnipotence, whereas Rosas can now only impose himself through a mercenary gang of bullies.

How has the primitive truth of barbarism, savage and odious yet faithful to its essence, been transculturated into the sly, deceitful, cowardly barbarism of the urban *caudillo*? In a sense, the whole purpose of Sarmiento's enterprise is to solve this puzzle. If "Quiroga, en su larga carrera, en los diversos pueblos que ha conquistado, jamás se ha encargado del gobierno organizado, que abandonaba siempre a otros" (1977, 96) ("Quiroga, in his long run through the various towns which he conquered, never took upon himself the task of organizing governments; he always left that task to others"; 1998, 94), this is so because Facundo Quiroga remains truthful to the

essence of barbarism: As untamed destruction, barbarism cannot, by definition, organize a State. It cannot exist as a positive set of rules and laws. Barbarism is the realm of sheer negativity. When it *does* take charge of the State, it loses its truth, the haughtiness, energy, and purity that remained uncorrupted in Facundo, the prelapsarian translator. The protagonist of this fall is, of course, Rosas. In Sarmiento's narrative Rosas becomes the portrait of what happens to the barbarian *caudillo*, hitherto a faithful incarnation of the land's essence, when he takes charge of a civilized, modern State. This civilized State loses its truth, becomes barbarian–although the verb "to become" is misleading here, because there is obviously no previously constituted civilized State to be later corrupted by Rosas–but a correlative loss takes place *within barbarism itself.* The *caudillo* loses his untamed prelapsarian force and falls to the level of a despicable dictator. Sarmiento extracts his foundational fiction from this remarkably complex dialectic: If the barbarian ruling the State has corrupted the laws of civilization, his presence at the helm has also corrupted his own barbarism, which has thus lost its original truth. If the lawless *caudillo* turned chief of state has made of civilization a barbarian aberration, the need to administer civilization has produced an aberrant barbarism, a barbarism deprived of the vigor, force, and haughtiness most proper to it. Sarmiento's project, the project of Latin American modernizing liberalism is, then, to extract from this dialectic its moment of truth and turn it upside down, as it were.

The transculturator's self-imposed task is to stand the dialectic of barbarism on its head (to continue with the Marxist analogy). As we have seen, this operation for Sarmiento designates not a simple movement of "civilizing barbarism," but a considerably more complex one of forging the truth of civilization from the starting point of an already transculturated barbarism, a barbarism that has fallen away from its truth precisely by taking charge of civilization. There is no symmetry between these two terms, not only because civilization is the dominant, privileged pole in the binary, but more importantly because they entertain different relationships with truth. Barbarism has fallen out of truth–*renounced* its truth, so to speak–at the moment it ceased to be sheer destruction and negativity (a moment represented by Quiroga, the faithful translator) and accepted the positive role of taking charge of the State apparatus (a farcical moment represented by Rosas). In contrast, the truth of civilization, for Sarmiento, still has to be built; it has a utopian nature. The truth of civilization is the truth of what still is not. In other words, for Sarmiento the present is deprived of truth, both the truth of barbarism, located in a prelapsarian past, and the truth of civilization, projected to a future yet to be built by the enlightened elite. The transculturator sets to himself the mission of extracting a utopian truth from the residue of a barbarism that has fallen out of truth. The transculturator writes, then, in a present without truth.

This utopian, programmatic dimension separates *Facundo* from the entirety of the anti-Rosas writing that sets the grounds of national literature in Argentina. For much of that writing–José Mármol's (1817–1871) *Amalia* (1851), Esteban Echeverría's *El matadero* [1840; *The Slaughter House*]–presents its allegories of nationhood negatively, through a resolute negation of what is (Rosas), the monstrosity of which, however, precludes the imagining of what may be, or at best leaves that imagining to be done upon the ruins, the failure, of the enlightening projects they narrate. Only *Facundo* turns the void of the present (emblematized in the "intellectual barren land" into which Rosas has transformed Argentina, but also in the pampa's very emptiness, a transhistorical, atemporal origin for Sarmiento, who in this sense inaugurates a tradition that would culminate in Ezequiel Martínez Estrada [1895–1964]) into the basis for a positive program. *Facundo*'s uniqueness lies, then, not in its inscription "en la literatura al lograr el nivel de especificidad de lo literario" (Viñas 5) ("in literature by achieving the level of specificity of the literary")–for that specificity in Latin America is, of course, a transcultural retrospective construction several decades posterior to Sarmiento's work, as Julio Ramos has shown in his genealogical exploration of "literature" as a discursive formation in Latin America (Ramos 1989)–but rather in its vision of the transculturation of barbarism as a prerequisite for the liberal project of forging a modern nation-state.

In this sense, Sarmiento shares much with Daniel Bello, the hero of José Mármol's *Amalia* (1851). An emblem of integrity with flexibility, perseverance with equilibrium, commitment to ideals without sectarianism, Daniel Bello stands opposed not only to the dictator Rosas, but also to hasty Unitarians who have not learned the value of political reconciliation. Born to a family with Federalist credentials, Daniel must use them on several occasions to weave the political strategy that could bring an end to Rosist barbarism. Contrary to the lovers Belgrano and Amalia, models of virtue but also of naïveté, Daniel represents the maturing of that adolescent yearning for justice into an adult, virile sense of balance and prudence. In 1851 the Argentine elite, represented by Mármol, had already formulated the image of the *patricios* who would unify the state in 1880. After seeing his love for Florencia and Belgrano's for his cousin Amalia survive countless peripeteia related to the struggle against Rosas's persecution, Daniel is murdered, along with Belgrano, by Rosas's police during their final attempt to flee to Montevideo. As Doris Sommer points out, "Belgrano and Bello hold them off with unbelievable heroism and success, but not long enough for Bello's Federalist father to arrive and turn the police away. The two friends *could* have been saved by his conciliatory presence. The tragedy was not inevitable; it was rather a miscalculation" (101). If it is true that the "final scene plays on the reader's mind like some kind of possibility or promise" (Sommer 101), it is also true that this is all that is left of Daniel Bello: An example. Unlike *Facundo*, *Amalia* only imagines a nation negatively, as a by-product of what *might have happened* had Daniel's conciliatory strategy been followed to the full. Although Amalia ends the novel as a young widow, bearing in her womb the recently conceived heir to Belgrano and thus projecting to the future a nation-building process still incomplete, nothing in the novel guarantees the future success of Daniel's tactics of subsuming barbarism under civilization rather than opposing the two to each other.

The impossibility of rounding off the image of the nation as a coherent totality takes, for Mármol, the dimensions of a formal problem. The elusiveness of totalization in the civic sphere accounts for *Amalia*'s fragmented structure, its resistance to being a novel in the modern sense. For if not even Daniel's sensible negotiation of opposites has managed to trigger the *Aufhebung* that could consolidate a nation, if barbarism resists being subsumed under civilization as much as it resists being defeated by it, fiction will necessarily fail to conjure the impure residues of a pre-novelistic, pre-modern melange of discourses. Bello himself is not a novelistic hero,

insofar as he always *knows* what happens to him, as opposed to the incomplete, decentered, unauthorized character proper to the novel as a genre. Daniel Bello is little more than a replica of Mármol, an omniscient figure whose presence in the text eliminates all possibility of ironic distance. Furthermore, throughout *Amalia* the evolution of the plot is plagued by interruptions of all kinds: Political declarations, manifestos, chronicles, historical letters, autobiographical remarks, etc. This highly hybrid text replicates the very disassembled polis that it denounces. The failure of Daniel's project, emblematized in his murder at the end of the novel–despite the feeling that it was not inevitable, despite the strong authorial suggestion that his policy was the one that could lead Argentina to an enlightened modernity–represents, in itself, the failure of transculturation. Nothing guarantees that the fetus borne by Amalia will be the carrier of a fulfilled nation in the future. The *letrado*'s legacy remains uncertain, an uncertainty that resonates outside the text, in its publication history: On 25 October 1852, after Justo José de Urquiza's (1801–1870) victory over Rosas's army in Caseros, Mármol announced the interruption of the publication of *Amalia* as part of the *ni vencedores ni vencidos* (neither triumphant nor defeated) post-Caseros pact. Whereas Daniel's reasonable strategies of compromise earned him a place as a fictional model of moderation, historical moderation demanded the silencing of his voice lest the bourgeois-oligarchic pact that would eventually unify the nation be spoiled.

Remarkably different in its structure but expressing a similar historical predicament to *Amalia*, Colombia's national novel, *María* (1867), also imagines the nation negatively, in the void left by an unfulfilled allegory. In the only South American nation not to achieve national unification in the nineteenth century, Jorge Isaacs (1837–1895) embedded a national allegory in a frustrated love story in which the impossibility of romantic love is represented by the most unusual figure of an interdict without prohibition. Efraín, another image of the reasonable, enlightened, and modern male, loves and is loved by María, his bastard cousin. This is a love that cannot be fulfilled, not due to any of the social impediments one usually finds in romantic taboos (family prohibition, class difference, etc.), but simply because good sense, and discreet family encouragement, has sent Efraín to London, to acquire that modern enlightened knowledge that would make of him the emblem of the new ruling class. Suffering from epilepsy, María cannot bear the sight of her beloved during her seizures, and their second opportunity is lost on that account–Efraín is too sensible a young man to allow his passion to stand in the way of his concern for her health. Upon his definitive return, María's health has worsened, and he barely makes it in time to see her corpse. The timing of their frustrated re-encounter emblematizes the impossibility of the utopian junction: Either Efraín has wandered for too long in the cradle of civilization, or María has lingered for too long, too close to the native land, and finds herself eventually killed by a disease inherited from her mother. Efraín is either too far from her (in England, away from the Colombian oligarchic idyll) or too close (too immediately present and thus threatening her health). Travel, return, inheritance, proximity, and temporality are some of the axes that organize this sentimental allegory of an impossibility. Around these axes, the utopian junction is always traversed either by a lack or an excess.

Whereas *Facundo* understands transculturation through the model of subsumption–civilization has the task of capturing the barbaric truth while maintaining or canceling it under itself–and *Amalia* understands it as a reasonable negotiation of opposites epitomized in Daniel's moderate strategy, which attempts to defeat Rosas and attract the honorable side of Federalism, in *María* the alterity to be transculturated is a masked alterity, one permanently on the verge of proving to be just another facet of sameness. If subsumption and conciliation are the privileged figures for Sarmiento and Mármol, for Isaacs transculturation takes the form of conversion. Efraín's father, Jorge, is a converted Jew; his cousin and María's father, Salomón, give Jorge the task of converting the daughter, and changing her name from Esther to María. María is thus the image of that alterity that can only conform to the allegorical picture once it is converted back to sameness. As a figure for the otherness that sustains all fables of identity, she belongs to the family without really belonging, is a Christian without really being one. Her seemingly arbitrary death indicates that conversion is either not enough or too much: "Either María dies because her Jewishness is a sin, or she dies because conversion was a sin" (Sommer 190). The object to be transculturated is either untranslatable or redundant; María is either too much of the same–like Efraín, a white, slavocrat, oligarchic, converted Christian, or she is too much of an alterity–a convert from Judaism, after all, and as such unabsorbable in the national allegory. Isaacs's crucial move was to displace the locus of failure away from the terrain more immediately recognizable as political toward the female body. Unlike the Argentine allegories, we are confronted with an intra-class, not a multi-class, transculturation: The popular classes in Isaacs's novel are little more than part of the landscape, unable or unwilling to resist anything, too unimportant even to be the object of co-optive advances by the oligarchy. With a social hierarchy well established, but in a country still in need of national unification, family romance in *María* is self-contained, perfectly symbolized, of course, in the semi-incestuous relationship between these two cousins.

As in *Facundo* and *Amalia*, transculturation is not an external content that *María* depicts in a ready-made form. While it replicates the model of the sentimental novel, the absence of interdict, the unique racial composition, and the particular vision of nationhood it advances encourage us to view skeptically claims that the novel is a "mere imitation" of European Romanticism (González Echevarría 40, 103). If *María* does not replicate the natural scientific discourse that plays such a central role in *Facundo*, it is not because *María* is a servile imitation of Europe and *Facundo* some sort of original Latin American contribution, but rather because the model of travel available to Sarmiento can become in Argentina the instrument of transculturation in a way unthinkable in Colombia. Having achieved a degree of political and ideological unification unparalleled in other Latin American countries, the Argentine lettered elite could formulate its political task in a binary opposition that fit rather nicely with prevailing natural scientific discourse; in fact, the otherness to be transculturated takes, in *Facundo*, the locus of nature itself.

It should be emphatically stated, then, that interpreting *María* or *Amalia* as imitations of European Romanticism amounts to reading their plots while ignoring the discursive economy in which they are inscribed. Despite seeming to be a conventional sentimental novel, *María* is a rich source by which to grasp the Latin American *letrado*'s transculturation of Western literary forms for nation-imagining purposes. Critics have noted the novel's tremendous success (see McGrady), which is certainly not explainable solely by the catchy love story. More puzzling is the complete absence of a projected redemption of María's death: bearer of no children, carrier of no legacy, leaving behind a lover who simply gallops away through the solitary Pampas after hearing of her death. María is simply wrested away from the circuit of exchange by her death. Hers is a value that does not survive its own facticity, the particularity of its own existence; that is, it is a *use value*. As sheer use value, her name perishes with her passing; it only exists as an unexchangeable singularity. If transculturation depends, obviously, on the establishment of an economy whereby proper names can acquire exchange value–and thus transcend their immediate facticity–María's name is handed down as a pure gift, one that will not accrue dividends, and thus will remain alien to the realm of production. Such alienness to productivity finds its perfect emblem, of course, in Efraín and María's sterility as a couple. By making of family reproduction the privileged metaphor of the nation's foundational moment, the novel installs a dilemma: Sexual reproduction by definition requires an alterity, the very alterity erased, in a sense, by María's conversion. Alterity is necessary but impossible, an undecidable structure that allegorizes a deferred foundation. Transculturation is displaced from its terrain, that of economic interchange, for economy is here referred back to its roots: *oikos-nomia*, the managing of the house, which is, in *María*, the very image of a sameness that recoils from exchange, that will not tolerate any otherness, and that thus lingers on in the perpetual self-deferral of sterility.

If Sarmiento could say that "El mal que aqueja a la República Argentina es la extensión . . . el despoblado sin una habitación humana" (1977, 23) ("The evil from which the Argentine Republic suffers . . . wastes containing no human dwelling"; 1998, 9), the problem facing the Peruvian elites was evidently quite different. Whereas the project of transculturation can take a futuristic character for Argentine Liberalism, in Peru it had to be first and foremost played out on the terrain of memory. No hegemonic project of Peruvian nationhood could come into being without taking charge of the colonial and precolonial past. No fable of identity could be formulated without coherently transculturating the past. This is why *costumbrismo* (narratives of local customs and manners)–hegemonic in the first years following Independence, immersed in the immediacy of the present, at any rate more local than national–could not fulfill the nation-imagining task facing the Peruvian elites. Robert Bazin's hypothesis is enlightening in this context. Although Americanism in its most prestigious version, that of Andrés Bello (1781–1865), did not seem to channel the "most concrete realities", *costumbrismo* took it upon itself to voice that immediate empiricity: "si el costumbrismo no define más que la epidermis, es porque únicamente la epidermis era definable" (Bazin 31) ("if costumbrismo does not define more than the epidermis it is because only the epidermis was definable"). The limits of *costumbrismo* with regard to the nation-building task become apparent in the anecdote related by Jorge Basadre of how Sarmiento and Felipe Pardo y Aliaga (1806–1868) met by chance in Chile in the 1840s. While the former was writing *Facundo*–the utopian book par excellence–the second can only appeal to satire, colonialist nostalgia, and Hispanic racism in his struggle against the Peruvian-Bolivian Confederation (Cornejo Polar 30). A similar fate awaited *Incaísmo*, the ephemeral poetic and theatrical school that postulated the newly born republic as heir and avenger of the Inca empire (the latter interpreted fundamentally through el Inca Garcilaso's [1539–1616] *Comentarios reales* [1609; Royal Commentaries]). The nostalgic fiction was unmasked by Simón Bolívar (1783–1830) himself, for whom the liberating armies were, "aunque vengadores de su sangre (del Inca), descendientes de los que aniquilaron su imperio" (qtd. in Germán Wettstein 143) ("in spite of having avenged the Inca's blood, descendants of those who annihilated his empire"). It is the masterful erasing of everything uncanny, paradoxical, disturbing in this contradiction–the freeing of the oppressed by the descendants of the oppressors–that would later become the keystone of the constitution of a Peruvian national canon with Ricardo Palma (1833–1919).

It is with Palma and the inscription of tradition that Peruvian literature faces up to the nation-building task, because only Palma fulfills the need, crucial for the Peruvian elite, to nationalize the past. As Cornejo Polar notes, the recuperation of the colony was easier for liberals than for conservatives, for while the former could propose the republican *criollo* Peru as a rupture with Spanish despotism, but not with the entire colonial universe–especially not with its enlightened strand–the latter were forced to lay a claim to the legacy of the very colonizing process, including Spain's actions (65). Of the two, only liberalism could nationalize the past without renouncing its own Hispanism, that is, without opening the national project to those social sectors not represented by either of the two political forces. Palma's moderate liberalism, then, is not extraneous to the *Tradiciones*'s nation-imagining accomplishment. Conferring upon the *costumbrista* sketch the historical consciousness it had always lacked, but maintaining *costumbrismo*'s elusive, conflict-free approach to social relations, Palma manages to trace back from the republican present a continuous line with the colony. The colony appears almost as a *locus amoenus*, from which all guilt has been expelled. If the past comes across as a *locus amoenus*, however, it does not follow that the present is a fall: The immediacy inherited from *costumbrismo* allows Palma to narrate scenes from the colony almost from within, in an illusory but compelling presentness, thereby making of them household items to whose gregarious symbolic power the republican elite could now resort. The background for "Amor de Madre" ["Mother's Love"] offers one of the most recurrent images in the *Tradiciones*: "En los quince años y cuatro meses que duró el gobierno de Brazo de Plata, período a que ni hasta entonces ni después llegó ningún virrey, disfrutó el país de completa paz; la administración fue ordenada, y se edificaron en Lima magníficas casas"(117) ("In the fifteen years and four months that Brazo de Plata's government lasted–a term reached by nobody then or now–the country enjoyed complete peace; the administration was ordered, and magnificent houses were built in Lima"). With social contradictions dissolved in their purely anecdotal or humorous content, the past comes alive again in Palma, and this time the possibility of citing accrues dividends, namely for the liberal project of building the nation by claiming a rupture with Spanish despotism but claiming also a continuity with the *criollo* subject formed in and through the colony.

Palma's primary transculturating operation takes place, therefore, not so much upon Peru's indigenous masses or the European forms appropriated, but upon the past itself. The constitution of a national canon in Peru–consolidated with the publication of José Toribio Polo's (1841–1918) *El Parnaso Peruano* [1862; The Peruvian Parnassus], Peru's first specifically literary national anthology, and Juan de Arona's (1839–1895) *Diccionario de peruanismos* [1883; Dictionary of Peruvianisms]–owes much to Palma's invention of a past that has become narratable. Palma recuperates for a modern, secular world the pre-modern figure of the storyteller who tells from experience. It is within the horizon of this project–the recuperation of the past as symbolic capital for *criollo* nation-building–that Palma's conversational style, rambling commentaries, frequent digressions, and all sorts of pre-literary, pre-modern interruptions become legible. Palma is not a more personal narrator than, say, Blest Gana, because the former is subjective while the latter is objective, with that tautological explanation so proper to traditional historiography. For Palma, the constitution of a "nosotros" (we) around the axis of memory is possible only through a miming of the premodern storyteller who tells his tale by the fire and has communal bonds with his audience. The paradox of this genre is the paradox proper to all experience-informed storytelling: It presupposes the community that it constitutes. Hence the powerful myth of Palma as the good old grandfather, telling wisdom-filled stories to the new generations, an image constructed, needless to say, in and by Palma's stories themselves. As an essentially transcultural genre, the *tradición* thus takes up tasks usually ascribed to the novel. In fact, in its structure, temporality, characterization, underlying world view, and in much else, the *tradición* has very little to do with the novel. Rather, in its episodic, antiteleological immediatism it seems tributary of a pre-novelistic episteme. If it can fulfill novelistic tasks in Peru it is because it has transculturated the past by voiding it of all alterity.

Because of the *tradición*'s organic link with the translation of the oral to the written, one of its most powerful ideological effects stemmed from the impression that the reader was being told a story rather than reading it. The imagined community constructed by the *tradición* depended heavily on this effect of immediacy and unmediated presence. In the Andes, where the opposition between orality and writing remained more polarized than anywhere else in South America, Palma managed to produce a literary genre that incorporated an imaginary orality while keeping at bay the explosively political content implicit in the clash between oral and written forms. The reason behind the status of Palma's *tradiciones* as the first literary system to express a truly national project has much to do with the way he synthesizes the polarity between orality and writing within their own form without challenging–in fact, while reinforcing–the hegemony of the lettered *criollo* sectors over the oral Andean cultures.

Ricardo Palma's originality in the context of the nation-building discourses of the nineteenth-century Latin American elites resides, then, in this particular incorporation of the colonial past for an implicitly oral reinscription of the hegemony of writing, a gesture highlighted by the flair of Palma's prose. The *criollo* colonial subject is undoubtedly the great source of Palma's *tradiciones*. Both, elements that would perturb the affable stability of their world and elements of the past that fell outside the genealogy of that particular subject are excluded. In other words, the absence of the indigenous in Palma–of all the 500 *tradiciones*, only six deal with the Inca empire, and very few depict any indigenous subjects under colonialism–is not simply a matter of choice, but an organic component of his project. The system of the *tradiciones* allows Palma to develop a national project based on the colony that is not, however, Hispanist in the sense that would emerge later with José de la Riva-Agüero. As Cornejo Polar has argued, Palma's dissociation of colonialism and Hispanism–his privileging of the former as his major source without a necessary embrace of the latter–allows him, for example, room for the violent polemic against Spain's Real Academia regarding the validity of Americanisms. It is through the particular relationship he establishes with the colony, mediated by the ideological processes described above, that Palma manages to modernize the Peruvian literary system. Fundamentally defining his project neither in relation to Hispanism, as Riva-Agüero (1885–1944) would do later (despite the deliberate subjugation and silencing of the indigenous in Palma's work) nor in relation to modern European and Anglo-American literatures, as did Manuel González Prada (1844–1918) and Sarmiento, Palma's *tradiciones* accomplish the nation-imagining task usually fulfilled in other national traditions by the novel.

Since I assume a certain privileged relationship between nation-building and the novelistic–the latter expressed in novels in the traditional sense or in more hybrid transcultural forms such as *Facundo* or the *Tradiciones peruanas* (1872)–it might be useful to say a thing or two about how I conceive that relationship, which should bring us back to the concept of transculturation. Beginning in the 1840s and 1850s, the novel became the nation-imagining genre *par excellence* in Spanish South America. Analyzing it along with the newspaper, Benedict Anderson noted that these were "the two forms that provided the technical means for 're-presenting' the kind of imagined community that is the nation" (Anderson 25). First, the progressive, cumulative conception of time entailed by the novel–as opposed, say, to the episodic and discontinuous time of the epic or, in the case of Latin America, the historical chronicles–allows for the organicist, identity-unfolding development that creates the metaleptic illusion that the community being constituted precisely through that narrative is, in fact, always already given. Second, the particular relationship presupposed by the individual with the national collective is such that it invariably allows for a reading in an allegorical key whereby, again, one establishes a link by presupposing it. In this fashion the novel sets out to posit nationhood as an object of desire, as a futuristic construction, as the space of what still is not. Thus a second transcultural operation must be carried out by the nineteenth-century Latin American author (this word itself being a transcultural anachronism, since the professionalization of the field did not take place until late in the century): attempting to claim autochthony through mimesis–transculturating the very genre of European modernity–the writer must also draw the possible from the real, what will be from what is. There seems to be, then, a certain organic link between the novel and utopia in nineteenth-century Latin America, manifested clearly, as argued above, in Sarmiento's hybrid novel.

This perspective allows for a new look at the fate of the European literary movements in Latin America. For where traditional literary historiography has seen a contrast between a neoclassical Andrés Bello and a Romantic Sarmiento, the theoretical analysis informed by transculturation sees two projects of instrumentalization of literature for social control. Octavio Paz (1914–1998), for example, has claimed that Spain had no Romanticism for lack of a true Enlightenment to react against and that Spanish America was therefore doubly lacking, for it was a reflection of a reflection (Paz 122). Note how the attachment to sources and influences still operates here,

precluding an understanding of discursive production in the Americas in terms of which that production responded and not in terms of a quasi-transcendental succession of movements (neoclassicism, Romanticism, realism), which all literatures, Paz's text seems to assume, would necessarily have to follow. For the will to form in Bello has less to do with an attachment to neoclassical norms than with a model of citizenship in which language–*el bien decir*–became increasingly crucial for establishing social hegemony. The rift that separates Sarmiento from Bello is then one between a project (Sarmiento's) in which language, as such, plays no role autonomously–this is the reason that there is no conception of what it is to write well in Sarmiento–and another (Bello's) in which an incipient autonomization of the intellectual field (emblematized in the very institutions, such as the University of Chile, in whose foundation Bello played such a key role) demanded the formulation of a specific task for language in constructing the nation:

> Si en Sarmiento prevalece un concepto de la escritura como máquina de acción, transformadora de la "naturaleza" caótica de la barbarie y generadora de vida pública, en Bello constatamos el otro modelo dominante de "literatura" . . . : el concepto de las Bellas Letras que postulaba la escritura "literaria" como paradigma del *saber decir*, producción de efectos . . . ligados a la racionalización proyectada de la vida y . . . la lengua nacional. (Ramos 1989, 40–41)

> If in Sarmiento's thinking, writing is conceptualized as an instrument of action which can transform barbarism's chaotic nature and can generate a life of public service, in Andrés Bello we find the other dominant model . . . : the concept of "belles lettres" which held to the paradigm of literary writing as "knowing how to say it well" and thereby effectively generate a projected rationalization of life and of the national language.

Despite the fact that one cannot speak of Bello's work as partaking of a fully autonomous intellectual or literary field, it is true that Bello inaugurated a discursive configuration in which language as such played a role in the formation of the good citizen (Ramos 1996). From then on, the *letrado*'s transculturating effort has been inseparable from the disciplining of the body politic.

This brings us back full circle to the very concept of transculturation. Angel Rama's appropriation of Ortiz's concept claims that transculturation rests on the originality and independence of Latin American literature–"su flagrante autonomía respecto a las peninsulares" (Rama 12) ("its flagrant autonomy vis-à-vis the Peninsular literatures"). These concepts, in their turn, go hand in hand with the representability of a given singularity–a subject position, a region–with regard to the continental totality: "esa originalidad sólo podría alcanzarse . . . mediante la *representatividad* de la región en la cual surgía, pues esta se percibía como notoriamente distinta de las sociedades progenitoras" (Rama 13) ("this originality could only be achieved . . . through the *representativeness* of the region in which it came into being, because that region was perceived as clearly distinct from the progenitor societies"). Transculturation is thus, for Rama, inseparable from what one might call foundational Latin-American fiction, the very concept of Latin America as a positive totality endowed with common attributes. The analysis carried out here of the very moment in which these categories–originality, independence, representability–become productive for the articulation of social hegemony seems to suggest, then, a possible reversal of Rama's postulate: From the perspective we advance here, originality, independence, and representability are always already in themselves transcultural fictions. In Rama's still residually populist scheme, the discursive forms through which originality, independence, and representability were to be achieved (the novel, popular song, oral traditions, the visual arts, etc.) had of necessity to undergo a transcultural operation, but the achievement itself, the concepts describing the productivity of those discursive forms, remains immune, stable in its post-Kantian, Romantic meanings (hence the tension between our emphasis on transculturation's relationship with technologies of discipline and control and Rama's at times glowing description of transculturation's liberating powers, notably in his discussion of Arguedas). For originality, representability, and independence can only, of course, be taken as that which is Latin America's own–the properly Latin American, its proper property and propriety–once they have already been submitted to transcultural violence, that is, once the very contents they name–again, in all their Romantic glow–have been negated, canceled in the whirlwind of transculturation. The purity and univocity of these concepts is guaranteed by the masking of the violence that makes them possible. This volume, as I understand it, is the unveiling of this masking. This operation should bring us close to the abyss that Rama himself approached and that his belief in those three categories prevented him from embracing: the deconstruction of the very notion of Latin America.

Works Cited

Anderson, Benedict. 1983. *Imagined Communities: Reflections on the Origins and Spread of Nationalism.* London and New York: Verso.

Basadre, Jorge. 1929. *La iniciación de la República: contribución al estudio de la evolución política y social del Perú.* Vol. 2. Lima: F. y E. Rosay.

Bazin, Robert. 1963. *Historia de la literatura americana en lengua española.* Buenos Aires: Nova.

Cornejo Polar, Antonio. 1989. *La formación de la tradición literaria en el Perú.* Lima: Centro de Estudios y Publicaciones.

Echeverría, Esteban. 1926. *El matadero.* Buenos Aires: Imprenta de la Universidad.

———. 1941. *La cautiva, poema.* Buenos Aires: Editorial Araujo.

González Echevarría, Roberto. 1990. *Myth and Archive: A Theory of Latin American Narrative.* Cambridge: Cambridge University Press.

Isaacs, Jorge. 1986 [1867]. *María.* Ed. Donald McGrady. Madrid: Cátedra.

Mármol, José. 1944. *Amalia.* Ed. Adolfo Mitre. 2 vols. Buenos Aires: Ediciones Estrada.

McGrady, Donald. 1971. *Bibliografía sobre Jorge Isaacs.* Bogota: Instituto Caro y Cuervo.

Palma, Ricardo. 1977. *Cien tradiciones peruanas.* Caracas: Biblioteca Ayacucho.

Paz, Octavio. 1974. *Los hijos del limo: del romanticismo a la vanguardia.* Barcelona: Seix Barral.

Piglia, Ricardo. 1980. "Notas sobre *Facundo.*" *Punto de Vista* 8: 15–18.

Pratt, Mary Louise. 1992. *Imperial Eyes: Travel Writing and Transculturation.* New York and London: Routledge.

Rama, Ángel. 1982. *Transculturación narrativa en América Latina.* Mexico City: Siglo XXI.

Ramos, Julio. 1989. *Desencuentros de la modernidad en América Latina.* Mexico City: Fondo de Cultura Económica.

———. 1996. "El don de la lengua." *Paradojas de la letra.* Caracas: eXcultura. 3–21.

Sarmiento, Domingo. 1977 [1845]. *Facundo, o civilización y barbarie.* Caracas: Biblioteca Ayacucho.

———. 1998. *Facundo: or, Civilization and Barbarism.* Trans. Mary Mann. New York: Penguin Books.

Sommer, Doris. 1991. *Foundational Fictions: The National Romances of Latin America.* Berkeley: University of California Press.

Viñas, David. 1964. *Literatura argentina y realidad política.* Buenos Aires: Jorge Alvarez.

Weinberg, Félix. 1980. "La época de Rosas. El romanticismo." *Historia de la literatura argentina.* Vol.1: *Desde la colonia al romanticismo.* Ed. Susana Zanetti. Buenos Aires: Centro Editor de América Latina. 217–40.

Wettstein, Germán. 1984. "Lenguaje alegórico e ironía pedagógica en el quehacer político de Bolívar." *Casa de las Américas* 24.143: 18–32.

CHAPTER 21

THE BRAZILIAN CONSTRUCTION
OF NATIONALISM

Adriana Romeiro

Estará bem empregado todo o cuidado que V. S. mandar ter neste novo reino, pois está capaz para se edificar nele um grande imperio o qual, com pouca despesa destes reinos, se fará tão soberbo, que seja um dos Estados do mundo.

(Gabriel Soares de Sousa, Tratado Descritivo do Brasil
[Descriptive Treaty of Brazil], 40)

All the attention that Your Highness cares to provide to this new realm will be well employed, because it can be the foundation for building a large empire which, with a little expense of this kingdom, will be so superb that it will become one of the significant States of the world.

In 1440, Nicolau de Cusa (1401–1464) announced in his *De docta ignorantia* the relativity of the perception of space, demonstrating that an observer's image of the world is determined by the place he or she occupies in the universe, and that, therefore, none of these places can claim an absolutely privileged position–such as, for instance, that of being the center of the universe (Koyré 26). Such a formulation anticipated the Copernican revolution and clashed with the medieval notion of placing the earth in the center of the universe and Jerusalem at the center of the earth, beyond which there were only the unknown and the extraordinary, in the guise of the fantastic and the supernatural. In opposition to the center–the axis of reference and the criterion for what was natural–and to the geographical space of the known Old World–territory of light and faith–the dark areas opened themselves up to the marvelous and were filled with the dreams and nightmares of the imaginary of the West. The antipodes and the margins, the unknown, became a kind of dark and disturbing antiworld which, moving within the realm of the irrational, rejected reason and filled medieval maps with pictures of fantastic monsters and ill-shaped creatures. This move translated into images in the cultural imaginary of what lay beyond Europe and formed the unknown (to Europeans) in the huge collection of the *mirabilia* (Le Goff 1980, 275).

Toward the end of the fifteenth century, the discovery of new lands forced the Old World to see itself, the center of order, besieged by chaos and disorder, embedded in a dark and untamed wilderness with strange inhabitants living at the margins of culture, hiding in a wild world. Civilization, built up with great difficulty, was threatened throughout Europe by the *silva* (wilderness)–with both its geographical and symbolic connotations–and was now faced with the disturbing challenge of propagating faith and reason across a vast portion of the planet filled with the unknown (see Turner). Those unknown lands were now subjected to pagan and biblical concepts of hidden meaning and consequently placed in the unexplored territory of the image of the Garden of Eden. Travellers and chroniclers, profoundly influenced by what they expected, transformed the new lands into the Earthly Paradise (Holanda 1992). What was heretofore unknown now became known; the new and different were translated by means of the old patterns of the European imaginary and were thus incorporated into the repertoire of what had been foreseeable. What was imagined was projected onto what was new, thus creating a link between the recently discovered lands and the European cultural imagination (see Souza). Realization of the marvelous, place of hallucinations and last

bastion of the devil, the New World was situated in the liminal space between culture and wild nature. To go across the Atlantic was to travel a route with highly symbolic meaning, endlessly explored in medieval literature; it was to renounce civilization and plunge into the wilderness. To undergo this adventure in the wild imaginary of European fantasy could result either in purification–like that experienced by the heroes of chivalric romances–or in a physical and moral degradation caused by being far away from civilization and too close to wild populations (Le Goff 1985, 187).

For the Jesuits who traveled to Brazil, the adventure did not become a religious experience of mystical ecstasies and divine communions, such as that lived, amidst physical and spiritual suffering in the wilderness, by hermits who had believed in the biblical tradition of the desert as a place of religious revelation. At most, the new arrivals interpreted their suffering as an extension of the mortifications announced in the *Spiritual Exercises* by means of which they disciplined and purified the spirit, strengthening it against worldly temptations. The temptations of the devil, whose presence invested the earth with the negative connotations of the biblical desert, transformed it into the place of confrontation between man and the multiple disguises worn by a throng of demons. Faithful to that image, Anchieta warned his fellow priests of Coimbra to pack their bags full of religious fervor, because "em meio da maldade, onde convém e é necessário ser santo para ser irmão da Companhia" (Leite 1954, 161) ("amidst evil, it is necessary and convenient to be a saint in order to be a brother of the Society of Jesus"). It was believed that as a result of the devil's secular expulsion from Christian Europe, where crosses and religious temples prevailed and where men could always find shelter, he had taken refuge in the New World and governed the pagan peoples (Delumeau 260).

Even the cultivated reason of the lettered elite seemed to fall prey to animal instincts and subverting the notions of right and wrong. Few explored this idea with such subtlety and in such a synthetic way as Father Azpilcueta who, in an extraordinary passage, wrote: "A letra, que por essas partes me parecia clara, cá se me torna obscura, não sei si sera de andar entre gentes que continuamente se comen uns aos outros e andaren envoltos em sangue humano" (Leite 1940, 155) ("The alphabet, which in Portugal seemed so clear to me, here is darkened, I do not know whether it is as a result of traveling among these peoples who continuously eat each other and walk around covered in human blood"). Beyond the boundaries of civilization, divine light barely shone and reason could not make sense of what the senses ill perceived; this experience differed radically from that of the English puritans in North America who believed that they were recreating the cosmic drama of the Israelites, crossing the desert and facing heathen enemies.

For the Jesuits, missionary work was aimed at enlarging the frontiers of the Old World to such a degree that, at least in the early stages, the evangelization process presupposed the Europeanization of indigenous populations. Unlike Franciscan friars like Mendieta, the Jesuits never considered America as a shelter and a way to experience a more elevated religious life (see Phelan). Instead, they sadly referred to "las privaciones de este destierro y desamparo" ("the deprivations of this exile and abandonment"), and their reports do not cease to ponder the vicissitudes of the self-imposed exile. Their ideal was that of creating "um novo Portugal" ("a new Portugal") in the New World; the expansion of the Portuguese world–European and civilized–became intertwined with the work of catechism (Cardim 56). And even a Capuchin monk like Ivo d'Evreux, a member of the expedition led by Daniel de la Touche in 1612, was predisposed to see in the simplicity and rusticity of the American landscape the traces of what the primitive Church had been and did not shirk from the idea of founding an Equinoctial France in the New World. He was very impressed by the contrast between the simple wooden chapel covered with palm leaves, "mais semelhante ao presépio de Belém" ("but similar to Bethlehem's manger"), and the rich and luxurious European churches. His sympathetic attitude toward the Indians–who were advantageously compared to French peasants–did not prevent him from stating what kind of world he expected would be founded in Brazil: "ninguém pois poderá contestar-me, que não sejam estes fatos bastante para convencer-nos de que devemos esperar e acreditar ser esta nação, com o andar dos tempos, civilizada, honesta e muito aproveitada" (74) ("nobody will be able to tell me that these facts do not suffice to convince us that we must expect to be, in due time, a civilized, honest, and well-employed nation"). European-style cities, offices, trade, religious, and government institutions–that is, the transplantation of the European world to American lands–shaped the horizon of the French Capuchin. Even if the Capuchins kept some traces of the link between Amerindian dispossession and apostolic poverty (advocated by their order) well into the seventeenth century, in the end they bowed to the need to turn Amerindians into Europeans by trying to turn the New World into a pale copy of the Old.

The dream of recreating the values of European culture in the tropics quickly gave way to the realization that, in a world ruled by passion and barbarism, men tended to deny their original culture. The renowned figure of João Ramalho is emblematic of the white man who, leaving behind his cultural baggage, goes into the bush in order to live like an Indian, breaking with all the moorings of civilization. Toward the end of the sixteenth century, the notion was widely disseminated that the white man who had been transplanted in America had become different and was morally inferior to European man. Far from becoming a kind of moral counterpoint to the degenerate lack of values of an increasingly decrepit Old World–the aim of Jean de Léry–the society implanted in America was now defined as a perverse and disturbing antithesis of precisely that which should be its model. The New World became the negative image of Europe; Brazil, denied the millenarian utopias, revealed itself full of anti-utopias with a morally degraded and transformed population: This was the widespread conclusion of the critics of colonial society. This was to be an endless repetition of Shakespeare's *The Tempest*, a foreboding drama dealing with the fragility of moral codes and values lost on the brutish Caliban who turns against the European Prospero; but here it was the Europeans who became savages once the barriers and constraints of life in the metropolis were abandoned (Turner 190).

History seemed never to have taken place in this anti-world. As part of an atemporal world, everything remained in the same state for centuries; the most significant events of the history of humanity–Christ's incarnation, passion, and resurrection–did not seem to exist here. Father Simão de Vasconcelos (1597–1671), chronicler of the Society of Jesus, believed that divine Providence had first turned toward Asia, Africa, and Europe, where it had placed humanity, the earthly paradise and the patriarchs, whereas the rest of the world had remained without a paradise, without patriarchs, and without "sua divina presença humanada" ("His divine humanized presence"). The Creator's oblivion had lasted 6,691 years, at the end of which he "deu ordem como aparecesse este novo e encoberto mundo" ("ordered this new and hidden world to appear") so that Portugal could take to it the knowledge of the faith (Turner 50). Therefore, Brazil was inscribed in the course of history as an unfolding of Portugal's own history, because the geographical discovery was in fact the realization of the prophecies and predictions that foresaw the birth of a great empire, with Lisbon as its center. As a geographical space, devoid of autonomy, only understood as a part of a wider empire, Brazil was denied its own historicity. The underlying historical view of Portuguese myths was similarly Lusocentric, as the fulfillment of a promise made at the very foundation of the kingdom, just before the battle of the Ourique. In Brazil's origins, the future of the Portuguese was announced–a people chosen to experience great happiness. By giving the New World's time and space meaning, this imaginary imposed a collective pattern on the interpretation of reality, one in which Portugal would become a world empire and the Amerindian other would be defined as being outside of history and spatially peripheral to the center, Lisbon.

Within this Lusocentric cartography, the Brazilian colony remained circumscribed to the margins, condemned to the outskirts of the known world, its spatial existence defined only through its relationship with the metropolis. The vast continent was conceptually reduced to the dimensions of an island, represented in the geographical maps of the sixteenth and seventeenth centuries as a huge land extension comprised within river basins, most of the time those of the Plate and the Amazon, following the example of Father Simão de Vasconcelos, who referred to these rivers as "duas chaves que fecham o Brasil" (Cortesão 1958, 41) ("the two keys that lock Brazil up").

Earthly paradise, margin of the known world, container of enormous wealth, Brazil was inscribed on European maps as a Portuguese possession, as divine Providence's gift which confirmed the imperialist vocation of Portugal. As the center of the empire, Lisbon brought together–according to Father Antônio Vieira (1608–1697)–the necessary qualities to hold the scepter of a world empire because, within it "o céu, a terra, o mar, todos concorrem naquele admirável sitio tanto para a grandeza universal do Império, como para a conveniência também universal dos súditos" (1679–1748, 211) ("the sky, the earth, the sea, all of them concur in that wonderful place both for the universal greatness of the Empire and for the universal convenience of her subjects"). The geopolitical superiority of Lisbon over the rest of the capitals was evident, in his opinion, in the design of that "supremo Arquiteto" ("supreme Architect") who destined it to be "a fábrica de tão alto edificio" ("the constructer of such a high building") (Cantel 146).

The projection of edenic myths on the new land must also be considered from this perspective; from this viewpoint Brazil was an earthly paradise, but this cannot be separated from the wish to celebrate the power and opulence of Portugal, the place where all wealth should go. This is the meaning of the words conveyed by Gabriel Soares de Sousa (ca. 1540–ca. 1591) when he announced the rise of a great empire because "a terra é quase toda muito fertile, mui sadia, fresca e lavada de bons ares e regada de frescas e frias aguas" (Cantel 40) ("most of the land is fertile, wholesome, fresh and cleansed with fine airs and irrigated by fresh and cool waters"). The great empire proposed by Soares de Sousa was a geographical extension of the great Portuguese empire, to which it was inextricably bound. During the eighteenth century, Sebastião da Rocha Pita (1660–1738) from Bahia published his *História da América Portuguesa* [History of Portuguese America], an ambitious work which was to convey the history of Brazil from the time of the "discovery" to the more recent events witnessed by its author. The description of facts is presented in a panegyric register inspired by edenic myths, such as the episode in which he openly states that Bahia is situated in the Earthly Paradise. In fact, Rocha Pita's tone does not differ much from the general tone of the narrations and treatises of the previous centuries, in which the exaltation of local beauty was placed at the service of Portugal as the legitimate owner of the colony and the receiver of all the resources found in Brazil. It is not coincidental that he makes reference to the products which "saem da nossa América portuguesa para todos os portos do reino" (Cantel 71) ("leave our Portuguese America for all the ports of our kingdom"), implicitly suggesting that the wealth of Brazil belongs to the metropolis.

Rocha Pita was, however, an exception among the eighteenth-century authors, for in general these writers were less inclined to state the political implications of the edenic view of Portuguese America; they were much more concerned with correcting the metropolitan perspective, which reflected little or nothing of the colonial reality. A huge gap opened up between the collection of folklore (*mirabilia*) and everyday reality. Limited to the coastal regions, Portuguese colonization did not find the wealth of El Dorado that had been anticipated by early chroniclers. The Portuguese could only occupy the margins of this territory. They settled like crabs on the coasts, in order to "arranhar as freldas do mar" (Cantel 18) ("scratch the seaside"), to use the apt expression of Brother Vicente do Salvador (1564–1639?). Beyond this small coastal area, known and contained, was the *sertão*, the unknown land where the devil reigned. There the Jesuits risked their lives; brother Pero Correia wrote: "neste lugar tivemos muitos combates do demônio e ainda agora temos" (Leite 1954, 171) ("we fought and continue to fight many battles against the devil in this place"). As the border of the explored territory, the faint dividing line between the settlements of civilized life and the huge wilderness inhabited by purportedly wild Indians and monstrous beasts, the *sertão* was also thought to harbor sparkling El Dorados and the utopia of Christian purity. Around 1550, Father Nóbrega (1517–1570) told King João III about a wellspring of pure souls, a town inlaid with gold in the *sertão*, waiting for evangelizing action (Leite 1954, 15).

During the Colonial period, traversing the fringes of this coarse backland became an adventure that excited the imagination. Awed either by the promise of the treasure of pure souls or by the wealth of a distant El Dorado (both of which were located in the midst of the unknown continent), Jesuits and explorers went in search of a new epic story, traveling through a sea of rocks and bushes in an attempt to conquer it and deprive it of its wealth through a variety of cultural strategies that converged in the realization of Lusocentric ambitions. Rather than being objective and precise descriptions, these tales reveal the filters that were interposed between this wild world and those who opened it up, bringing attention to the interplay of meanings that conveyed a new definition of geographical space, one in which the land acquired an historical and symbolic significance. Marveling at the wonders of an unknown world opening itself up, powerfully and disturbingly extending itself beyond what could be perceived, these men deciphered the new through the grid of their own culture, softening its edges, adapting some things here and there, investing it with new meanings, transforming it, finally, into a tamed reality.

Even the *sertão* was destined to open itself up to human experience. If, from the geographical point of view, the colony remained an enigma for the Portuguese crown–which was still concerned with issues related to its limits, as a result of the Treaty of Tordesillas–the fact is that the work of the *bandeirantes* or explorers revealed the Brazil hidden in the *sertões*. By walking across the land, they became the depositories of a highly specialized knowledge, inheritors of a long indigenous tradition (Cortesão 1969, 316). They got to know unique geographical features; they learned how to distinguish rivers and basins; they worked with the secrets of the fauna and flora; they managed to identify the tribes and their respective regions, and were even able to reach the Spanish empire. It was not surprising, therefore, that the Jesuit Diogo Soares–designated to conduct a land survey of the Brazilian colony in preparation for negotiating the Treaty of Madrid–resorted to the valuable information collected by the explorers of the *sertão* (see Taunay). Once the geographical survey was carried out, that sense of the marvelous lost its efficacy as the proper instrument to perceive this reality (Giucci 12) and consequently moved into the realm of literature, where it forged and shaped the elements of the prodigious. Witness the poem "Vila Rica" ["Splendid Villa"], where Cláudio Manuel da Costa (1729–1789) presents a *sertão* sculpted in rock, immersed in a dense environment, made of darkness. From this profound gloom, the existence of disturbing animal life loomed up, one which could not be perceived by the eyes but only through the sinister sounds that broke the silence of the night (Costa 1903, 188).

It is in the diversity of the *sertão* that the explorers discovered the mines of El Dorado, transforming into reality the gold-filled dreams that had prevailed since the sixteenth century. However, at a very early stage, that sense of wonder was gradually dismantled in the face of a reality that refused to sustain the notion of an accessible wealth, ready to offer itself to the discoverer. It is at that moment that contemporary data (and later literature) began to convey the image of the *sertão* as an inhospitable and barren land, full of obstacles to human exploration. In fact, according to *Notícias dos primeiros descobridores das primeiras minas de ouro* [1899; News from the Earliest Discoverers of the First Gold Mines], crossing the *sertão* revealed the hard struggle of humanity against a hostile and sterile land where dreams of wealth gave way to hunger and major physical suffering: "o sertão da Casa da Casca era mui agro, e falto de víveres silvestres por serem tudo matos e aspérrimas brenhas e falto do mais favorável gênero de caças" (Taunay 25) ("the sertão of the Casa da Casca was very harsh, devoid of wild foodstuffs because it was full of bushes and rough brambles and lacked the most favorable kind of hunting game"). The landscape underlined human fragility; the explorers were faced with the vertigo of jagged mountains, steep rocks, and inaccessible peaks. This was "geografia ameaçadora que se expande para os céus, como uma terrível catedral gótica de formas pontiagudas e espinhosas" (Costa 1903, 188) ("a threatening geography which expands to the sky as a terrible gothic cathedral with sharp and thorny shapes"). Seventeenth-century Brazilian accounts took pleasure in their meticulous descriptions of the hardships endured by people who dared to woo "o coração da terra para haver seus haveres" (Taunay 25) ("the core of the earth in order to obtain its possessions"). It is thus possible to get a glimpse of the fascination of the strangely penitential nature of such adventures: There was a long succession of ordeals to be faced by the explorer, who accepted this as necessary for redemption.

This sertão, then, became a kind of revelation, because it had gone beyond the frontier of the unknown: The marvelous had given way to the known. The recently discovered mines did not evoke immeasurable treasures, with golden palaces, emerald rivers, and precious stones floating in their surfaces. There emerged, between the El Dorado and humanity, a huge abyss through which the frontiers between the imaginary and the real were translated. At the end of the gold-seeking adventure, people found hunger and misery, suffering and death, because in spite of its gold, this land was miserly in providing basic sustenance; thus, it was possible to find on the side of the roads "não poucos mortos com uma espiga de milho na mão, sem terem outro sustento" (Antonil 374) ("not a few dead people with a wheat tassel in their hands, but no other form of sustenance"). Or even "deixando a Divina Providência ao desvelo daqueles animosos vassalos da Coroa Portuguesa que pretendiam enriquecer com os haveres ocultos por aquelas largas e aspérrimas montanhas que a poder de perigo, fome, sede e trabalhos, romperam aqueles fragosos montes, e incultas brenhas" (Taunay 27) ("leaving to Divine Providence the welfare of those enthusiastic subjects of the Portuguese Crown who, seeking to become rich with the hidden wealth of those high and rugged mountains, faced peril, hunger, thirst, and exhaustion, opening the way through those mountains and rough brambles").

How was it possible to reconcile the tales of the prodigious and marvelous in a universe forbidden to man with the treasures now gained at the cost of constant sacrifice and painful work? If the marvelous was inscribed in the sphere of the unknown, how could it survive the opening of the sertão? A new perspective on Brazilian reality came to the fore. The imaginary of colonialism–understood as a set of ideas and values that constituted Brazil as a pole in its bipolar relationship with Portugal–came to a crisis point in the eighteenth century and was replaced by representations not linked to the colonial model: In response to the old images of Eden and the marvelous, Brazilians now reshaped Brazil in relation to their own experiences and concerns. To have a perspective implies that the observer has a determinate place and a cultural lens from which to observe and therefore is inexorably tied to everyday reality. The experience of living in a colony,

so different from living in the metropolis, gave rise to the production of images that could not fit European images and representations. In other words, this marked the emergence of a truly Brazilian perspective and culture, based on specific experiences and not on the superimposed cultural grids of Europe.

This is why the simple rhetorical register of the paradisiacal descriptions of the first two centuries was replaced by a more objective perception of reality; the new representations were of a clearly realistic character, concerned with taking inventory of the resources from an economic point of view. A good example is the 1705 publication of the Tuscan Jesuit Antonil's (1650–1716) work Cultura e opulência do Brasil por suas drogas e minas [Culture and Opulence of Brazil, Considering Its Drugs and Mines], in which a decisive innovation appears: Antonil introduces for the first time an essentially pragmatic and utilitarian view of the products of the land, a view placed within a wider reflection about the possibilities of economic exploitation. This small book shows the final failure of the discourse of the marvelous as a way to apprehend concrete reality, demonstrating that the transition from the unknown to the known was now concluded. Opulence does not appear here gratuitously, as a marvelous gift bestowed on man; on the contrary, it is the result of accomplishing a difficult task, and this new notion becomes the core of a certain praxis based on experience and technique. Thus, his book was intended to be "de alguma utilidade aos que nos engenhos de açúcar, nos partidos e nas lavouras de tabaco, e nas minas de ouro experimentam o favor do Céu com notable aumento dos bens temporais" (Antonil v) ("of some use to those who, working in the sugar plantations, cutting and preparing tobacco, and in the gold mines, enjoyed Heaven's favor in the form of a remarkable increase of temporal goods").

If, for João Capistrano de Abreu (1853–1927), Antonil's book "ensinava o segredo do Brasil aos brasileiros, mostrando toda a sua possança, justificando todas as suas pretensões, esclarecendo toda a sua grandeza" (Abreu 162) ("taught the secrets of Brazil to Brazilians, showing them its might, justifying its pretensions, and revealing its greatness"), the truth is that this new point of view–contrary to the marvelous and, in contrast, clearly pragmatic–emerged on both sides of the Atlantic. During the eighteenth century, the vague and disproportionate dimensions of the Brazilian territory were at the core of the attentions of King Dom João V, who directed his policy toward definitely establishing geographical borders. Thus, expeditions and mapping commissions were organized in order to study and reveal the true boundaries of the colony and, simultaneously, to take inventory of the land, describing its people, its fauna and its flora, and bringing the mapping techniques in line with the empirical knowledge of colonists and Indians. This was precisely the attitude behind Pombal's policies: In 1751, the Marquês de Pombal (1699–1782) made a recommendation to Gomes Freire regarding the need to keep the sertão free from foreign greediness, because it was its "segredo, e não a força, [que] teve o Brasil em segurança há mais de dois séculos" (qtd. in Maxwell 31) ("inaccessibility, and not force, that has kept Brazil in Portuguese control for more than two centuries"). In order to protect the Brazilian sertão, and to ensure its systematic exploitation, Pombal needed to impose the sovereignty of Portugal throughout the whole geographical space, something he began to do by building fortifications that were to contribute to the administrative success of gaining control of the country. Regarding such a huge space that escaped the control of metropolitan power, Pombal wrote that "e como este grande número de gente que é necessário para povoar, guarnecer e sustentar uma tão desmedida fronteira não pode humanamente sair deste reino e ilhas adjacentes; porque ainda que as ilhas e o reino ficassem inteiramente desertos, isso não bastaria para que esta vastíssima raia fosse povoada" (qtd. in Maxwell 31) ("the huge number of people necessary to inhabit, keep, and sustain such an immeasurable frontier cannot humanly come from this kingdom and its surrounding islands because even if the islands and the kingdom were to become entirely deserted, this would not be enough to inhabit this vast frontier").

Pombal's sober and realist tone greatly differs from the generalized enthusiasm that had characterized the period during the early eighteenth century when Portugal foretold the emergence of a new age. Amidst an economic crisis, the discovery of gold mines tended to be interpreted as the start of a period of endless wealth (see Boxer 1969). Shortly before his death, the chronicler and eulogist of King João V, Father Caetano de Sousa, described the realm to him as "um reinado feliz, que podia com propriedade chamar-se a idade de ouro, visto que as minas do Brasil continuavan a produzir uma abundância de ouro" (Boxer 1992, 166) ("a happy kingdom, which could appropriately be said to be in a golden age, as a result of the fact that Brazil's mines continued to produce a wealth of gold"). It was in this context of jubilation and even dizziness that we find both the old imaginary of the Fifth Empire and the announced greatness of Portugal, to be elevated to the highest position among nations. The myth of the chosen nation, receiver of rich veins of gold and destined to a material and spiritual pre-eminence over the world, is reborn. And it was thanks to the Brazilian mines that the prophecies were finally being fulfilled.

For many, the year 1700 was "verdadeiramente nesta terra a era dourada; e para Portugal a de maior felicidade" (Taunay 27) ("truly in this land a golden age, and for Portugal the period of greatest happiness"); it was as if the treasures kept in the Brazilian *sertão* had been put there by Divine Providence for the "dilatação de sua Monarquia e grandeza de seu Império" (Taunay 27) ("enhancement of the Monarchy and the greatness of its Empire"). This universe overflowing with precious metals was not bestowed gratuitously on its discoverers; on the contrary, this wealth was pursued and obtained with great difficulty. It was the product of the labor of people who struggled in the wilderness, who were less concerned with elevating the greatness of a distant Portugal than with guaranteeing Portugal's rights over it. The El Dorado of Minas Gerais had an impact upon the view that had prevailed that Portugal was the center of the world and Brazil was merely one more colony; Portuguese bureaucracy now saw itself forced to rethink its imperial model. Lisbon could no longer be the head of the empire emerging in the New World, because Lisbon and even Portugal itself were insignificant in comparison. Thus, if the country mapped by the *bandeirantes* had shown the Portuguese the vast extent of the territory in contrast to the smallness of the metropolis, the wealth of Minas Gerais would show them their relative poverty and misery.

In the end, as a result of the extent of the gold and diamond mines, which place would be the true head of the Portuguese empire? In 1738, the ambassador Dom Luiz da Cunha (1662–1740) wrote a secret memorandum in which he suggested that the Court be moved to Rio de Janeiro and that King João V take the title of Emperor of the West. His justification was that

o ditto príncipe para conservar Portugal necessita totalmente das riquezas do Brasil e de nenhuma maneira das de Portugal, que não tem para sustentar o Brasil, de que se segue que é mais comodo e mais seguro estar onde se tem o que sobeja, que onde se espera o de que se carece. (Boxer 1969, 333)

in order to keep Portugal, the prince needs the wealth of Brazil and not that of Portugal, which is not enough to sustain Brazil; therefore, it is more comfortable and more safe to be where one readily has access to the wealth, than to be where one has to wait for the leftovers.

In 1752, echoing such ideas, Duke Silva-Tarouca stated that Brazil would be "o Brasil onde os reis de Portugal podem vir sucessivamente a ter um Império, como o da China, e ainda maior que a França, Alemanha e Hungria, unidas se fossem em um só corpo" (Maxwell 32) ("the place where the kings of Portugal can successively come in order to have an Empire such as that of China, and even larger than that of France, Germany, and Hungary, united in a single country").

In 1732 one of the most experienced members of the Overseas Council, Antônio Rodrigues da Costa, wrote a long report on Brazil's goldmines and, among the inconveniences which they represented for the crown, he mentioned the huge number of people who had left the kingdom and the attendant threat of depopulation. This migration would make

ter o Brasil tantos vassalos brancos, como tem o mesmo Reino, e bem se deixa ver, que posto em uma balança o Brasil, e na outra o Reino, há de pesar com grande excesso mais aquela que esta, e assim a maior parte, e mais rica não sofrera ser dominada pela menor mais pobre, nem a este inconveniente se lhe poderá achar fácil remedio. ("Papel" 144)

Brazil has as many white subjects as the Kingdom, and it is obvious that, if Brazil is placed on one side of a balance scale and the Kingdom on the other, the former must be much heavier than the latter; thus, the largest and richest side will not long suffer to be dominated by the smallest and poorest, and it will not be easy to find a remedy to such an imbalance.

The basic premise of the counselor's analysis rested on the thesis that the material prosperity of the colony was enough of a factor to drastically subvert the interplay of forces with the metropolis. He sensed that Brazil's mineral wealth could give rise to interpretations that would differ from those that exalted Portugal as the great repository of the wealth (obtained from the other side of the Atlantic). Should the imaginary of colonialism be brought down, this rupture could easily promote the feeling that the colony was the real heir to its treasures, the only one chosen to profit from them, whatever the claims of the rest of the world. If this happened, Brazilian subjects would no longer recognize themselves as constitutive parts of a single empire, conceived as an indivisible body.

In this context, the history of the former miner Pedro de Rates Henequim is significant. Henequim was prosecuted by Lisbon's Inquisition and sentenced to death in 1744 for defending, among other things, the concept that a new empire should rise in Brazil. In his cosmology, a legacy of the millenarianism of Father Antônio Vieira, everything was inverted: The true receiver of the graces of Providence would be the colony, and not the metropolis; Brazil would reign sovereign not only over Portugal, but over all the nations (*Inquisição No. 4864*). With Henequim, the American space was transformed into a spiritual space, a kind of alpha and omega of the history of humanity, because the Earthly Paradise would also be the stage where the drama of salvation would come to an end, thus establishing the millennium announced by the Bible.

A contemporary of Henequim and, like him, a symbol of the process which Marcel Bataillon calls the spiritual emancipation of the New World, Father Manuel Lopes de Carvalho from Bahia presented himself in Lisbon as an enlightened prophet, destined to reveal to the Portuguese king the imminent end of the world. Like a new prophet Jonah, born on Brazilian soil, he claimed to be the instrument of good news, chosen by God in order to denounce the mistakes of the Catholic Church; he reserved for King João V the task of extinguishing such errors, so that Vieira's prophecies could be fulfilled and renewed by him, his zealous disciple.

Recapturing the millenarian imaginary that had placed Lisbon at the center of the political and religious map for centuries, these two men re-elaborated and subverted its meaning, reinterpreting, in an opposing political way, the place of the colony and the metropolis in time and space. In their own way, they filtered the reading of Father Antônio Vieira's *História do Futuro* [1697; History of the Future] and radically altered its perspective—be it in order to found the Fifth Empire in the tropics, or else to bestow the title of prophet on a *mazombo*, which was the pejorative name given by the Portuguese to those born in America of Portuguese parents (*Inquisição No. 9.255*). By questioning the transcendental foundations of colonial domination—the evangelizing mission and the Christian superiority of the metropolis—both prophets announced the crisis of colonialism on a symbolic plane and revealed the inventive and subversive function of the cross-cultural process in their forging together of the Portuguese cultural universe and their own millenarian system. In Henequim's case, it was the experience of working in the mines that suggested this move; in that of Lopes de Carvalho, it was his astronomical observations. Both men inverted the power relationships between Portugal and Brazil, reducing the importance of the former in order to celebrate the latter. With them, a belligerent opposition took over and the religious density of Portugal was put to the side. They thus sought to establish a privileged stage for a transcendental revelation that revealed the future of Brazil.

The millenarian expressions of the eighteenth century flourished best in the region of Minas Gerais, with its vertiginous Baroque processions and festivals, by means of which the new captaincy exhibited its splendor and glory, thus defying a poor and gloomy Portugal. The author of *Triunfo eucarístico* [1734; Eucharistic Triumph], Simão Ferreira Machado (18th century), could hardly disguise the ambiguity of his text, which, while purporting to feature the deeds of the Portuguese, presented Brazil on a level of equality or even superiority in relation to the Kingdom. Following the edenic tradition, he reported the temperance of the air, the fertility of the land, the eternal spring, but introduced a new and disturbing note: that the increasing Portuguese migration, together with the expansion of frontiers, would turn Brazil into "terreno capacíssimo para uma dilatada Monarquia" [an auspicious territory for a vast Monarchy]. The meaning of this image, concrete and tangible, is quite different from that foretold by Gabriel Soares de Sousa. Vila Rica is described as "cabeça de toda a América" ("head of America") and "pérola preciosa de Brasil" ("Brazil's precious pearl"), whose inhabitants enjoy a level of trade and importance which "excede sem comparação o maior dos maiores homes de Portugal" ("by far exceeds beyond comparison, the best of the best men of Portugal") (Ávila 169).

The treasures of Minas Gerais led the author of *Triunfo* to enthusiastic descriptive expressions such as "opulento Hemisfério das Minas" ("opulent hemisphere of the mines"), where there can be seen "mais que as riquezas, o fausto dos Templos, e a preciosidade dos Altares" ("more than wealth, the lavishness of the Temples and the preciousness of the Altars"). However, recognizing that the Portuguese were the great heroes of the conquest of Minas, the author did not hesitate to state that in turn Portugal owed Brazil "grandiosos auxílios, e quantiosos [sic] reditos . . . e afluencia das riquezas" ("substantial support and considerable revenues . . . and affluence of wealth"). And, if this was not enough, he observed that "em breve tempo [foi] transplantado meio Portugal" ("in a very short time, half of Portugal would be transplanted") to Minas, which would become a famous commercial center of the world (Ávila 169).

The American landscape did not fit the aesthetic models of Europe; Cláudio Manuel da Costa (1729–1789) underlined the lack of symmetry between the colony and the metropolis. Even if the banks of the Carmo were not as delightful as those of the Tejo, the Lima, and the Mondego, the river had "turva e feia a corrente" ("a muddy and strong current") and was the best of this captaincy ("o mais rico desta capitania") (Costa 1903, 45). And this land, in spite of being uncultivated, deserved to be praised as "o vasto empório das douradas Minas" ("the vast emporium of the gold mines"), whose wealth "têm derramado por toda a Europa, e pelo muito que socorrem com a fadiga dos seus habitantes ao comércio de todas as nações polidas" (Costa 1959, 105) ("has spilled throughout Europe, and has given succor to the commerce of civilized nations owing to the toil and fatigue of the inhabitants [of Minas]"). The wealth of the mines—from a pragmatic and utilitarian perspective—was in no way related to the marvelous. When considered together with the miserable condition of the local population, it gave rise to one of the first expressions of Brazilian nationalism, the *Inconfidência Mineira*, which was evident in the poetry of Cláudio Manuel da Costa and in that of another member of that movement, Alvarenga Peixoto (1748–1798):

Que fez a Natureza
em pôr neste país o seu tesouro,
das pedras na riqueza,
nas grossas minas abundantes de ouro,
se o povo miserável? . . . Mas que digo:
povo feliz, pois tem o vosso abrigo!

(42)

What of nature's
placing its treasure in this country,
stones of wealth,
in the great mines filled with gold,
if the population is poor? . . . I say:
happy people, you who have your shelter!

According to Joaquim José da Silva Xavier (d. 1789), also called Tiradentes, the natural resources of Minas Gerais were the greatest in the world; Brazil had everything it needed, so it did not depend on any other country. But poverty resulted from the fact that

a Europa, como uma esponja, lhe estivesse chupando toda a substância, e os Exmos. Generais de três em três anos traziam uma quadrilla, a que chamavan criados, que depois de comerme a honra, a fazenda, e os oficios que deviam ser dos habitantes, se iam rindo deles para Portugal. (Maxwell 153) like a sponge, Europe sucked the substance from Brazil, and The Honourable men-Generals every three years brought over a crew, which they called servants, and who after devouring the honor, the estate, and the trades of the land which should belong to its inhabitants, went back to Portugal, laughing.

Inseparable from this idea of exploitation by the Portuguese, there emerged, here and there, the notion of the motherland, understood in a very local sense of belonging to a place, a parish, a hamlet. And it was a love for his place of birth that shaped, for instance, the work of Manuel Botelho de Oliveira (1636–1711), "o primeiro filho do Brasil" ("Brazil's first son"), and led him to publish his first book. In 1705 the small book *Música do Parnasso* [Parnassus Music] was published by Manuel Menescal's press and was dedicated to the Duke of Cadaval. In the poem "Ilha da Maré" ["Island of Maré"], Botelho de Oliveira praised the Bahia island where he was born, describing its beauties. He compares Brazil to Portugal and concludes:

> Tenho explicado as fruitas e legumes,
> Que dão a Portugal muitos ciúmes;
> Tenho recopilado
> O que o Brasil contém para invejado
>
> *(134)*
>
> I have described the fruits and vegetables,
> Which make Portugal jealous;
> I have listed
> What Brazil offers to be envied

Tropical nature, with its fish, fruits, and vegetables, was the subject matter of this poetic praise. Even if we consider the small island of Maré as a "breve apodo" ("brief epithet") of all Brazil, the poet's particular and parochial feeling cannot be denied: The motherland, as Sérgio Buarque de Holanda has rightly pointed out, has "o significado restritivo, de simples lugar de nascimento ou residência" (Holanda 1991, 80) ("the specific meaning of the place of birth or residence").

The emergence of patriotic sentiment was linked to the incorporation of the Brazilian landscape into the poetical imagery: The contradiction between the European literary models and the coarseness of the Brazilian landscape is clearly present in Cláudio Manuel da Costa's work. José Basílio da Gama's (1740–1795) *O Uruguai* (1769) also offered a revealing eulogy of Brazil:

> um novo mundo onde não se teriam ainda desnaturado as imagens da vida bucólica e da liberdade campestre, caras à fantasia setecentesca, habitada de populações indígenas que o século de Laffitau, de Rousseau e do abade Raynal começava a prezar com interesse muitas vezes simpático. (Holanda 1991,125)
>
> a new world where the images of bucolic life and rural freedom had not yet been denaturalized, ideas–so dear to eighteenth-century fantasies–inhabited by indigenous populations which the century of Laffitau, Rousseau, and abbot Raynal valued with an interest that was often congenial–and that could often be congenial.

Even the members of the *Inconfidência Mineira* revealed a very particular notion of motherland, understood as the region of Minas Gerais, the place of birth; indeed, the whole *Inconfidência* movement was marked by its regionalist tone, which started by choosing São João d'El Rey as the proposed republic's capital (Maxwell 151).

A similar pride in the place of birth can be found in the first endeavors to write a local history, in which an American tradition was forged in order to offset the weight of the

European past. Once the space was conquered as free, the task remained simply to inscribe the colony into history, endowing it with its own temporality, one which, still lacking the notion of Brazil as physical, political, or even administrative entity, was divided into a series of particular local temporalities. This is the kind of nativism that shaped *Nobiliarquia paulistana, histórica e genealógica* [1902; São Paulo Nobility, History and Genealogy] written by Pedro Taques de Almeida Paes Leme (1714–1777), who, interested in tracing the genealogical line of São Paulo's families, wrote the history of Southern Brazil by means of the districts of São Paulo. Silvio Romero has rightly pointed out that it is the neighborhood or district spirit that gives the work its particular register: Recognizing and assuming himself as *paulista*, the author turned to the products of his land, attempting to bestow on them a tradition and an heroic origin, as if São Paulo's captaincy was also the cradle of great heroes, worthy of being paralleled with the seats of the highest of European nobility.

In a single work, Loreto Couto conveys a historiographic narration, a restitution of the historical validity to the rehabilitation of the *mazombo* (by means of a subtle nativism conceived as the praise of the motherland), the invention of a tradition, and an appraisal of the Pernambucan character. When explaining the reasons for the book, he writes categorically:

> pouco me vali dos livros que tratam do nosso Brasil, porque neles há muitas disminuições, muitos defeitos, muitas fábulas e bastantes calúnias, e estas me obrigam a dar ao meu livro o título de Desagravos do Brasil, assim como o de Glórias de Pernambuco às ilustríssimas ações de seus naturais. (Azevedo 241)
>
> I did not depend much on the books that deal with our Brazil, because they are full of defects, degradations, fables, and slanders, all of which force me to give my books the titles of *Apologies of Brazil,* and *Glories of Pernambuco* which is about the illustrious actions of its natural inhabitants.

What was at stake–as a constitutive part of the symbolic construction of the motherland–was the need to prove that Brazilians descended from people as talented or virtuous as those born in the metropolis, as well as the will to secure a history of Brazil cleansed of preconceptions and written from a local point of view. Thus, the particular and the local emerged as legitimate and appropriate perspectives with which to capture the knowledge of reality: The alphabet was no longer obscure for the young men of the eighteenth century, as Father Azpilcueta used to complain 150 years before. For the new historians it was sufficient to demand the validity of their worldview and to vindicate their insertion in the sphere of Western culture, in order to authorize them to produce relevant knowledge about the human universe.

In his *Cartas Chilenas* [1863; Chilean Letters], Tomás Antônio Gonzaga (1744–1807) displayed his knowledge of the colonial experience (and inappropriateness) of Portuguese laws and regulations about which he compiled the vast documentation he sent to Lisbon. He offered complaints, suggested changes, and firmly condemned the ineptitude of the governors and the local authorities and their inability to understand the singular nature of the colony. As a whole, these are ideologically reformist texts: They do not question colonialism, but only propose to correct and perfect the machinery of metropolitan control. In spite of this, they illustrate a stand that tended to intensify throughout the eighteenth century, which saw the emergence of the conviction that the colonists are better prepared to diagnose and identify local problems.

Confirming the appropriation/inversion/subversion mode inherent in the transcultural process, the marvelous that flourished at the time of the great discoveries offered raw material for the formulation of a new view of America, reintroducing myths related to the Earthly Paradise but now into a political perspective that was radically different, indeed oriented according to an exaggerated nativism. An instance of this process of returning to the fifteenth-century marvelous for the constitution of a discourse of exaltation of the motherland was present in the issues raised by the *Academia dos Renascidos* [The Academy of the Reborn], which appeared again in 1759 in Bahia, a center of nativist expression. There, scholars of the Academies debated the question: "se o dilúvio universal compreendeu esta parte do Novo Mundo chamada América, e se nele escaparam os seus habitantes"; "se a América é ilha ou terra firme"; "se tem alguma probabilidade a opinião de alguns autores que discorreram estava o paraíso terreal neste Novo Mundo" (Azevedo 232) ("whether the biblical flood included this part of the New World called America, and whether its inhabitants escaped it"; "if America can be considered to be an island or *terra firma*"; "whether the opinion of some European authors, that the Earthly Paradise was located in this New World, can possibly be true").

Significantly, this nativist notion of local experience, as it was formulated here, had nothing to do with rational proof or the advances of science; it looked back to the long-standing conviction that the firsthand contact with the realities of the New World offered a specific knowledge, unknown or undervalued by Europeans. This is how certain experiences were accepted, for instance, in order to validate the utilitarian kind of knowledge collected by surgeon Luís Gomes Ferreira in his book *Erário mineral* [Treasury of Mineral Wealth] published in Lisbon in 1730, in which he declared that all his work was founded upon experience, "a base fundamental da Medicina," ("the basic foundation of Medicine"), and also that he had learned more by experience than from the books brought from Portugal. It was experience itself that made him inquire into the American marvelous–those inexplicable cures and cases such as that of an eighty-year-old woman who breast-fed her own granddaughter.

It is possible to trace in the literature of the sixteenth century the timid emergence of a tension between an external perspective (what ought to be) and an internal one (what experience showed), a tension reflecting the dislocation between the projection of the European marvelous and the assertion of a Brazilian specificity, respectively. Experience, observation, and direct knowledge were the elements that justified, for example, the adoption in the Jesuit missions of techniques and procedures that greatly differed from (or were contrary to) those recommended by the Society of Jesus in Portugal. The detailed reports of the Jesuits are among the most interesting testimonies of the ways in which the specificity of the land and its inhabitants was captured and elaborated, gradually constituting a kind of interiorization. In this regard, it is worth remembering the pragmatic skepticism that gradually undermined the utopia of an America transformed by Christianity and integrated into Christendom. This is clear, for example, in the famous *Diálogo sobre a conversão do gentio* [1880; Dialogue on the Conversion of the People], when Father Manuel da Nóbrega (1517–1570), with the kind of authority given by experience, derided the unbridled optimism of the Jesuits who, imbued with strong missionary fervor, dreamed about catechizing the whole continent. For

Nóbrega–and later for the other Jesuits of that first generation–the process of acculturation revealed itself as impossible, because the Indians were not a *tabula rasa* on which the Word would be written in an inexorable and definitive way. Far from actually explaining the effective dynamics of cultural clashes, the concept of acculturation reveals the direction of the European colonizing project, oriented according to a reductionist logic in which cultural differences tended to be interpreted as absence. As an inadequate instrument, this concept disintegrated in the face of the difficulties of a complex and polysemic reality. Toward the end of the sixteenth century, the Jesuits outlined the first steps in a multifaceted strategy, endless and unfinished, that could well be seen to contain within it the concept of transculturation later developed by Angel Rama (1926–1983) from the work of Fernando Ortiz (1881–1969). Dancing naked to the rhythm of rustic instruments, singing Catholic prayers translated into the Tupi language, the Indians did not seem at all the model of the good Christians into which the Society of Jesus wanted to transform them. But neither were they the same after the Jesuits filled them with notions of the afterlife with the horrors of Hell, the trials of Purgatory, and the happiness of Heaven.

At the origin of transculturation lies, thus, alterity, the perceiving of difference at all levels. That internal perspective of Father Nóbrega is present, for instance, in the *Diálogo das grandezas do Brasil* [1618; Dialogue of the Glories of Brazil], when Ambrósio Fernandes Brandão (fl. 1585–1613) traces the opposition between two interlocutors: on the one hand, Brandônio, settled in a land full of local expertise that he could access; on the other, Alviano, the recently arrived immigrant, without local experience. The candor of the Portuguese immigrant, who sees the region through Old World eyes, not believing what is new and just being able to see absence and gaps, in comparison with Portugal, is counterpointed to the flexible spirit of Brandônio, who is willing to find a sense of novelty in a singular experience by exploring it and transforming it into the foundations of a new way of life. Facing a tree that produced a kind of fleece, the colonist thinks about using it for filling cushions, pillows, and mattresses; he is in fact the apologist of experience and novelty as means of reinventing different patterns of existence in different geographical conditions. The following passage of the *Diálogo* summarizes the basic opposition between the immigrant and the colonist. At one point, Alviano states that it is "porque o mundo é tão velho e os homens tão desejosos de novidades, que tenho para mim que não há nele coisa por descobrir, nem experiéncia que se haja de fazer de novo que já não fosse feita" ("because the world is so old and men so willing to entertain novelties, that I have decided that there is nothing left to discover, and that past experience which has to be repeated should not be lived again"). To which Brandônio replies, "ainda há muitas cosas por descobrir e segredos não achados que para diante se hão de manifestar" ("many a thing is yet to be discovered, as well as hidden secrets which are to be understood in the future") (28). What Brandão denounces in his work is not just the immigrant's ignorance and prejudice; he also suggests that the colonist's empirical knowledge does not agree with that of the preconceived notions of the metropolis, and thus the latter's external perspective is an obstacle to solving local problems.

After two centuries of cultural exchange, the old imaginary of the colonial empire seemed to collapse under the weight of the common perception in Brazil that the experience of life in the colony was completely different from that of the metropolis.

This everyday experience was responsible for the constitution of a specifically Brazilian culture, either as a site of the commingling of uneven cultural traditions, or as a space for new forms in which men could interrelate with the peculiarities of living in the tropics. Thus, the emergence of different imaginaries or concurrent representation systems pointed to the process by means of which local knowledge, accumulated and created throughout the colonial experience, confronted the repertory of representations which the Old World continued to project on America and its inhabitants. Employing Chartier's terms (17), the New World became, simultaneously, the place and object of the conflicts posed by concurrent representations. Unlike the notion of counter-culture, such systems of representation were not defined as autonomous and independent entities, as channels of resistance against and oppression by a dominant culture with which they did not have any links. On the contrary, it is impossible to approach independently the imaginaries in dispute in a society, because their force depends on the ability to formulate new readings and interpretations, to invent new meanings, in order to bring about fundamental displacements in the play of forces among them. In the end, the imaginaries are not born out of nothing; what actually takes place is the re-elaboration of meanings in a different cultural key or through the political re-appropriation of a previously given imaginary.

It is in the movement of these imaginaries in action that the multiple motherlands are conceived, defining different temporal and spatial dimensions: the rocky and prodigal motherland of Cláudio Manuel da Costa, the *bandeirantes*, and of Pedro Taques, the insular and paradisiacal motherland of Botelho de Oliveira, the warlike and heroic motherland of Loreto Couto, the motherland of the Fifth Empire of Henequim, the motherland of the prophet of the end of the time of Father Manuel Lopes de Carvalho, the independent and emancipated motherland of the *inconfidentes*. Out of this transcultural process, Brazil developed and discovered itself as a conflictive reality, reinvented every day and deconstructed in these fragmented motherland concepts; it became a conveyer of a new perspective about itself, one which arose from real and concrete experience. What the eighteenth century witnessed was the profusion of these new discourses that translated into a new imaginary.

Translation by Nair María Anaya-Ferreira

Works Cited

Abreu, Capistrano de. 1976. *Capítulos de história colonial.* Ed. José Honório Rodrigues. 6th ed. Brasília/Rio de Janeiro: INL/Civilização Brasileira.

Antonil, André João. [1705] 1968. *Cultura e opulência do Brasil por suas drogas e minas.* Text from the 1711 edition. French trans. and ed. Andrée Mansuy. Paris: Institut des Hautes Études de L'Amérique Latine.

Ávila, Affonso. 1967. *Resíduos seiscentistas em Minas: textos do século do ouro e as projeções do mundo barroco.* Vol. 1. Belo Horizonte: Centro de Estudos Mineiros.

Azevedo, J. Lúcio de. 1932. *Novas Epanáforas: estudos de história e literatura.* Lisbon: Livraria Clássica.

Bataillon, Marcel. 1976. *Estudios sobre Bartolomé de las Casas.* Barcelona: Ediciones Peninsula.

Boxer, Charles. 1969. *A idade de ouro do Brasil.* 2nd ed. São Paulo: Nacional.

———. 1992. *O Império marítimo português* (1415–1825). Lisbon: Edições 70.

Brandão, Ambrósio Fernandes. [1608] 1956. *Diálogo das giandezas do Brasil.* Intro. Capistrano de Abreu. Notes by Rodolfo Garcia. Salvador: Livraria Progresso.

Cantel, Raymond. 1960. *Prophétisme et messianisme dans l'oeuvre d'Antonio Vieira.* Paris: Ediciones Hispano-Americanas.

Cardim, Femão. 1980. *Tratados da terra e gente do Brasil.* Belo Horizonte/São Paulo: Itatiaia/Edusp.

Chartier, Roger. 1990. *A história cultural—entre práticas e representações.* Trans. Maria Manuela Galhardo. Lisbon: Difel.

Cortesão, Jaime. 1969. *A colonização do Brasil.* Lisbon: Portugália.

———. 1958. *Raposo Tavares e a formação territorial do Brasil.* Rio de Janeiro: Ministério da Educação e Cultura.

Costa, Cláudio Manuel da. 1903. *Vila Rica. Obras poéticas.* Vol. 11. Ed. João Ribeiro. Rio de Janeiro.

Delumeau, Jean. 1999. *O medo no Ocidente (1300–1800): uma cidade sitiada.* Trans. Heloisa Jahn. São Paulo: Companhia das Letras.

———. 1959. *Epicédios (à morte do Ilustríssimo e Excelentíssimo Senhor Gomes Freire de Andrade, Conde da Bobadela, Governador e capitão general do Rio de Janeiro e Minas). Obras.* Text based on the 1768 edition. Ed. Antonio Soares Amora; text's restitution by Ulpiano Bezerra de Meneses. Lisbon: Betrand. 100–131.

Evreux, Ivo d'. 1929. *Viagem do norte do Brasil feita nos anos de 1613 a 1614.* Ed. and trans. Ferdinand Diniz Marques. Rio de Janeiro: Livraria Leite Ribeiro.

Ferreira, Luis Gomes. 1735 [1730]. *Erário mineral.* Lisbon: Officina de M. Rodrigues.

Giucci, Guillermo. 1992. *Viajantes do maravilhoso: o Novo Mundo.* São Paulo: Companhia das Letras.

Holanda, Sérgio Buarque de. 1991. *Capítulos de literatura colonial.* Ed. Antonio Cândido. São Paulo: Brasiliense.

———. 1992. *Visão do paraíso: os motivos edênicos no descobrimento e colonização do Brasil.* 5th ed. São Paulo: Brasiliense.

Inquisição de Lisboa, Arquivo Nacional da Torre do Tombo [National Archive of the Tower of Tombo], Father Manoel Lopes de Carvalho's trial, no. 9.255.

Inquisição de Lisboa, Arquivo Nacional da Torre do Tombo [National Archive of the Torre do Tombo], Pedro de Rates Henequim's trial, no. 4864.

Koyré, Alexandre. 1979. *Do mundo fechado ao universo infinito.* São Paulo: Edusp.

Le Goff, Jacques. 1985. "Lévi-Strauss en Brocéliande." *L'imaginaire médiéval: essais.* Paris: Gallimard. 151–87.

———. 1980. "O Ocidente medieval e o Oceano índico: um horizonte onírico." *Para um novo conceito de Idade Média: tempo, trabalho e cultura no Ocidente.* Trans. Maria Helena da Costa Dias. Lisbon: Estampa. 263–81.

Leite, Serafim. 1940. *Novas cartas jesuíticas (de Nóbrega a Vieira).* São Paulo: Companhia Editora Nacional.

———. 1954. *Cartas dos primeiros-jesuítas do Brasil.* São Paulo: Comission for the IV Centenary of São Paulo.

Leme, Pedro Taques de Almeida Paes. 1980. *Nobiliarqui paulistana: histórica e genealógica.* 5th ed. Ed. Afonso de E. Taunay. Belo Horizonte/São Paulo: Itatiaia/Edusp.

Maxwell, Kenneth. 1978. *A devassa da devassa: a Inconfidência Mineira: Brasil e Portugal (1750–1808).* Trans. João Maia. Rio de Janeiro: Paz e Terra.

Oliveira, Manuel Botelho de. [1705] 1967. *Música do Parnasso.* Ed. Antenor Nascentes. Rio de Janeiro: Instituto Nacional do Livro.

"Papel que fez Antonio Rodrigues da Costa a Sua Majestade por consulta do Conselho Ultramarino. Ano de 1732." Biblioteca Pública e Arquivo Distrital de Évora, Codex CV/1-1, ff. 135–44v.

Peixoto, Alvarenga. 1960. *Vida y obra de Alvarenga Peixoto*. Ed. Manuel Rodrigues Lapa. Rio de Janeiro: Instituto Nacional do Livro, Ministério da Educação e Cultura.

Phelan, J. Leddy. 1970. *The Millennial Kingdom of the Franciscans in the New World*. Berkeley: University of California Press.

Pita, Sebastião da Rocha. 1976. *História da América Portuguesa*. Ed. Pedro Calmon. Belo Horizonte/São Paulo: Itatiaia/Edusp.

Rama, Ángel. 1985. *A cidade das letras*. Trans. Emir Sader. São Paulo: Brasiliense.

Salvador, Frei Vicente do. n.d. *História do Brasil* (1500–1627). São Paulo: Melhoramentos.

Sousa, Gabriel Soares de. 1971. *Tratado descritivo do Brasil*. 4th ed. Ed. Francisco Adolfo Varnhagen. São Paulo: Nacional-Edusp.

Souza, Laura de Mello e. 1986. *O diabo e a terra de Santa Cruz*. São Paulo: Companhia das Letras.

Taunay, Affonso de E., ed. 1981. *Relatos sertanistas*. Belo Horizonte/São Paulo: Itatiaia/Edusp.

Turner, Frederick. 1990. *O espírito ocidental contra a natureza: mito, história e as terras selvagens*. Trans. José Augusto Drummond. Rio de Janeiro: Campus.

Vasconcelos, Simão de. 1977. *Crônica da Companhia de Jesus*. 3rd ed. Ed. Serafim Leite. Petrópolis/Brasília: Vozes/Instituto Nacional do Livro.

Vieira, Antônio. 1679–1748. *Sermoens do Padre Antônio Vieira da Companhia de Iesu, Pregador de Sua Alteza*. 15 vols. Lisbon: Officina de Ioam da Costa.

———. 1992 [1697]. *História do Futuro*. 2nd ed. Ed. M.L. Carvalhão. Buescu. Lisbon: Imprensa Nacional-Casa da Moeda.

CHAPTER 22

NEGRISMO
THE AMERICAN "REAL"

Elzbieta Sklodowska

Negrismo: Definitions, Trajectory, Poetics

Negrismo, often seen as the Hispanic counterpart of the French-Antillean *Négritude*, is widely defined as a movement that flourished particularly in poetry but that also manifested itself in other areas of the arts and letters of the Hispanic Caribbean (Cuba, Puerto Rico, the Dominican Republic) in the 1920s and 1930s. What marked the ideological and aesthetic distinctiveness of this movement was the affirmation of African-based traditions (Matibag 91). Even though *negrista* poetry at times took the form of cultural and ethnic polarization–stressing rather than bridging the gap between cultures–many critics end up using designations such as *negrista* or *negroide* interchangeably with the "transculturated" terms *mulata*, *afrocubana*, *afrocriolla*, or *afroantillana*.

Discussions of *negrista* poetry often revolve around lengthy listings of formal characteristics, which include onomatopoeic phrasings, mythological references, Africanized vocabulary, imitation of drumbeat rhythms, and incorporation of the oral tradition (Matibag 93). The impact of music, dance, and aurality on *negrista* poetry deserves special attention because, as Iris Zavala has shown, Caribbean music especially has been richly syncretic and often signified a form of resistance, while Cuban *son* "has traditionally been used in Cuba to critique and parody dictators [and] . . . the Puerto Rican *plena* and the Dominican *merengue* have similar political intention" (Zavala 213n6; other references on syncretism in Caribbean music include Daniel, Garabís, and Glasser).

Even though the opinion that *negrista* writings are of marginal literary value and should be read chiefly for their social content or anthropological interest has long been refuted (see Kubayanda), the tenacity with which such ostensibly antiquated approaches keep resurfacing in contemporary publications should alert us to the difficulties that we face when attempting to rewrite literary history. I will limit myself to just one telling example: In a *Handbook of Latin American Literature*, Matías Montes-Huidobro argues that "Afro-Cuban poetry takes on its greatest authenticity when it coincides with the social poetry . . . although dogmatism, diatribe, and political propaganda may prevail" (244). So although there are many threads to follow here, going beyond the social parameters into the textual repertory of *negrismo* in order to explain the enduring appeal of some *negrista* works should become a touchstone throughout this study.

There seems to be a widespread belief (Jackson; Kutzinsky) that in Cuba the movement's forerunners were poets Felipe Pichardo Moya (1892–1957) and Agustín Acosta (1886–1979), known for their depiction of the world of sugar plantations, and that attempts to emphasize the African heritage were spearheaded almost simultaneously in 1928 by two poems: José Zacarías Tallet's (1893–1985) "La rumba" and Ramón Guirao's (1908–1949) "Bailadora de rumba" ["Rumba Dancer"]. However, a somewhat more attentive tracing of chronology allows critics such as Aníbal González (1989), Julio Marzán, and Mónica Mansour to credit one of the most prominent figures associated with *negrismo*, the Puerto Rican poet Luis Palés Matos (1898–1959), with the inauguration of the movement. Palés Matos had been known as the author of "Danzarina africana" [1918; "African Female Dancer"] and "Pueblo de negros" [1921; "Black People"] well before *Motivos de son* [1930; *Folk Song Motifs*], the landmark book by Cuban Nicolás Guillén (1902–1989), which was heralded as the most influential and accomplished example of *negrista* poetry.

The birth of *negrismo* was obviously not announced *urbi et orbi*; therefore, pinpointing the exact date of its emergence is bound to produce considerable anguish among critics interested in such details. What is quite evident, however, is that the apogee of *negrismo* took place in the 1930s. The clearest proof of this is the lengthy list of works inspired by African traditions and published during those years: Alejo Carpentier's (1904–1980) *Ecué-Yamba-O!: Novela afrocubana* [1933; Ekwé-Yamba-O! An Afrocuban Novel]; José Antonio Ramos's (1885–1941) *Caniquí* [1936; *Caniquí*]; Emilio Ballagas's (1908–1954) *Cuaderno de poesía negra* [1934; Book of Black Poetry]; Regino Pedroso's (1896–1983) *Nosotros* [1933; *Us*]. That this is a diverse list–in terms of aesthetics, ideology, literary genres, and ethnic origins (if not gender) of the authors–should serve as a reminder that the label *negrismo* covers a wide variety of approaches and brackets or conceals significant differences.

When establishing the pedigree of *negrismo*, the dominant approach is to view it in a broader scope, "impelled by a sense of black self-renewal and self-affirmation" (Kubayanda 12) that manifested itself in Marcus Garvey's movement back to Africa and in the Harlem Renaissance (see Cobb). Critics agree on the fact that the ground for *negrismo* had been prepared outside of the Hispanic Caribbean by publications ranging from Hannibal Price's *De la réhabilitation de la race noire par le peuple d'Haiti* [1900; On the Rehabilitation of the

Black Race by the People of Haiti] and W. E. B. du Bois's *The Souls of Black Folk* (1903) to Vachel Lindsay's *The Congo and Other Poems* (1914) and Blaise Cendrars' *Anthologie nègre* [1927; *The African Saga*]. The traditionally held opinion that *negrismo* drew on the European avant-garde that glorified "primitivism" as an alternative to the decline of the West no longer holds sway, although in a recent book Roy Armes attempts to make a claim that it was "the impact of surrealism" that "liberated the Caribbean and African poets of *Négritude* from the constraints of a borrowed language" (27). In contrast to such general statements, well-grounded studies of specific cases—such as Aníbal González's (1988) analysis of Spenglerian influences in *Tuntún de pasa y grifería* [1937; *Tuntún*] by Palés Matos—are by far more persuasive.

Basic aspects of the Eurocentric position favored by some critics are forcefully debated by Amy Fass Emery, who argues that "the ethnographic surrealism of the European avant-garde" had little impact on Latin American writers, because it "was out of sync with the social realities of post-Independence Latin America" (5). In her insightful analysis of Carpentier's (*Ecué-Yamba-O!: Novela afrocubana*–commonly used as a prime example of *negrista* narrative–Emery demonstrates how "the form and spirit of ethnographic surrealism" is forged by Carpentier in a virtuoso process of bricolage, which, I would add, appears to mirror the contradictions of transculturation itself:

> Carpentier draws on writings by ethnomusicologists, accounts of Afro-Cuban performances, photographs of Afro-Cuban instruments and artifacts, the writings of Fernando Ortiz on Afro-Cuban culture (as well as his documentary, ethnographic style), his knowledge of Afro-Cuban speech patterns, the primitivism of Parisian *négritude*, the naturalism of the nineteenth-century novel, and assorted literary devices derived from the avant-garde. (Emery 8–9)

Through the apt use of the metaphor of bricolage, Emery escapes the danger of measuring the degree of *negrismo*'s indebtedness to Parisian influences against Caribbean originality. With a refined sense of textual detail she shows Carpentier's inventiveness and invites reflection upon the dislocation of European aesthetic registers on the Latin American scale.

In order to surpass binary oppositions and also to keep the trajectory of *negrismo* in a historical perspective, it is important to consider its regional roots. To be sure, anchoring the movement locally has become the primary focus of research in recent years. For Puerto Rico, Juan Flores traces an extended genealogy of *negrismo* back to the nineteenth century (to Salvador Brau and Alejandro Tapia y Rivera) and gives special credit for placing the marginalized Afro-Puerto Rican culture within the scope of intellectual inquiry to the article "A los negros puertorriqueños" ["To Black Puerto Ricans"], published in 1903 by a "lesser-known working-class writer Ramón Romero Rosa" (192). With reference to Cuba, the tendency is to go at least as far back as Francisco Calcagno's (1827–1903) anthology *Poetas de color* [in four editions: 1868, 1878, 1879, 1887; *Poets of Color*] and José Martí's (1853–1895) manifesto of racial integration "Mi Raza" [1893; "My Race"]. It is widely acknowledged that the anthropological research of Fernando Ortiz (1881–1969) (*Hampa afrocubana: los negros brujos* [1906; Afrocuban Underworld: The Black Sorcerers]; *Los negros esclavos* [1906; Black Slaves]; *Glosario de afrocubanismos* [1924; A Glossary of Afrocuban Usage]), the formation of Sociedad de Estudios Afrocubanos (1936), and the high quality of articles published by the Sociedad's official journal

Estudios Afrocubanos were instrumental in heightening the awareness of Afro-diasporic cultures in Cuba and beyond (González Echevarría 46–50; Kutzinsky). As Kubayanda's informed study has shown, "in the intellectual context of the 1930s, no other Caribbean group seems to have devoted as much time as the Afro-Cuban Society to the studies of the African contributions to the so-called New World" (14). In decades afterward, Ortiz's pioneering endeavor was to inspire numerous works of cultural anthropology, folkloric literature, and testimony, from Lydia Cabrera's (1899–1991) *Cuentos negros de Cuba* [1936; Cuban Black Short Stories] to Miguel Barnet's (b. 1940) *Biografía de un cimarrón* [1966; *The Autobiography of a Runaway Slave*, 1973] and *Akeké y La Jutía* (1978).

The other major influence on Cuban *negrismo*, recognized, for example, by González Echevarría (44–46), was the historiographic work of Ramiro Guerra y Sánchez (*Azúcar y la población en las Antillas* [1927; *Sugar and Society in the Caribbean: An Economic History of Cuban Agriculture,* 1964]). The political origins of the Afro-Cuban movement, which gained momentum thanks to the black rights organization called the *Partido Independiente de Color*, are also worth exploring (Matibag 93) and can help further differentiate between *afrocubanismo* and other manifestations of *negrismo*. To complete the picture, Francine Masiello's exemplary research demonstrates that despite its somewhat erratic editorial position on the issue of race, the leading Cuban avant-garde periodical *Revista de Avance* (1927–1930) further fostered the interest in Afro-Cuban themes by publishing "sketches of and by Cubans of African descent, poems praising blackness, and celebrations of African heritage" (24). At the same time, the influential conservative daily *El Diario de la Marina* offered a more consistent treatment of black culture in a section titled "Ideales de una raza" ["Ideals of a Race"], which was later converted into a literary supplement (1928–1931).

While it is certainly illuminating to posit the development of Afro-Antillean writings through a prism of influences exerted locally and externally, it may be equally beneficial to look at it through a lens of differences. Because of the widespread homogenizing tendency to stress cultural affinities within the Caribbean, diverse chronologies are often collapsed for the sake of neat periodization, and local manifestations of *negrismo* become easily conflated under the umbrella term of *poesía afroantillana*. And yet even a cursory comparative look at the trajectories of *negrismo* in Cuba, Puerto Rico, and the Dominican Republic throws the differentiation into sharp focus.

According to Marzán, because critics have customarily treated *negrista* poetry from a political or ethnological point of view rather than an aesthetic one, the formally complex works of Puerto Rican Palés Matos have been overshadowed by the socio-political and "popular" dimension of Guillén's poetry (9–34). Indeed, for Josaphat Kubayanda, Guillén was the most successful of his generation in reclaiming Afro-Caribbean experience for aesthetic expression. In addition to intrinsic criteria of literary evaluation, Palés Matos's reception was influenced by the fact that in Puerto Rico the issue of African-based traditions versus the formation of national identity took a more openly controversial form than in Cuba, where it did not evolve into a full-fledged polemic. As Ben Heller has argued, Antonio Pedreira's *Insularismo* (1934) depicted the influence of the "black race" as an obstacle to Puerto Rican modernization, turning instead toward the "autochthonous" heritage of the Puerto Rican peasantry, the *jíbaros*. Overcoming the legacy of *insularismo* has been, as José Luis González and Juan Flores have shown, a long and complex process. According to Flores, "Discovering and valorizing African 'roots' has comprised a second stage, after the first one marked off by *Insularismo*, in the theoretical definition of Puerto Rican culture, and that stage has only come to full articulation in the past decade" (193).

In Cuba, by contrast, as Heller indicates in some detail, even José Lezama Lima's (1910–1976) well-known skepticism about the African heritage followed a much more nuanced, if still ambivalent, path:

> [H]e does assert that Cuban culture was too hasty in its incorporation of the "sensibilidad negra"–this was a brusque adoption of a foreign element, rather than the careful assimilation of the received, and the result was a superficiality, a musicality (reliance on the onomatopoeic) with no profound connection with Cuban sensibility. (Heller 398–399)

A look at the case of the Dominican Republic reveals analogous attitudes of ambivalence toward the African heritage. Racial stereotypes are imprinted in a vast repertory of texts, but once again with a local twist (Davis; Lizardo). According to James J. Davis, despite the fact that a considerable body of literature infused with African-based traditions was produced by recognized Dominican writers such as Manuel de Cabral (1907–1999), Rubén Suro (1916–1999), Francisco Domínguez Charro (1910–1943), and Tomás Hernández Franco (1904–1952), the national identity was defined in terms that either excluded the presence of African cultures from consciousness and discourse or relegated them to the undesirable "influence" of marginalized immigrants from neighboring Haiti or the English-speaking Antilles (Coulthard 38). For example, when the issue of "transculturative" processes comes up in Tomás Fernández Franco's celebrated epic poem *Yelidá* (1944), it is illustrated by the marriage between a black Haitian woman, Madam Suqui, and a Norwegian fisherman, Erick: "The title character of this poetic celebration of hybridism is quintessentially Caribbean. She is the daughter of an African mother and a European father, both of whom become free from nostalgia for their origins as their lives meld into Yelidá" (Sommer and Torres 276).

As these examples suggest, it may well be that suturing together different strands of *negrismo* will show how the term itself is increasingly wearing thin. The pervasive lines of difference and the startling juxtapositions at the very heart of the concept signal both the promises and the problems that await a postcolonial reader of *negrismo*.

Critical (Re)readings of *Negrismo*

As Kubayanda has demonstrated with remarkable insight, *negrismo* has to be understood in terms of what preceded it: "[T]he picture of blackness as primitivism was so pronounced that it influenced Caribbean poetic discourse of the 1920s and 1930s" (21). In other words, *negrismo* was not immune to vestigial colonialist attitudes; nor did it put an end to the perpetuation of racist tropes, from plays upon Eurocentric hierarchies of light/darkness or civilization/barbarism to the unwitting reduction of the cultural to the strictly biological (the main sources of reference here are Emery, Kubayanda, Mama, Marzán, and Matibag). Even when collective traditions of African community were not demonized but sanctified as a natural "antidote" for the decline of European values, for the most part (Guillén being an exception), little relevance was given to the real predicament of black people. Among the

ethnic stereotypes reinforced in some *negrista* texts are the romanticized notion of symbiotic links between nature and people of African ancestry, with particular emphasis on a libidinous, wild, primordial, earthbound image of a black woman. This insensitivity to gender issues and to the "double colonization" of women of color in particular makes *negrismo* an easy target for feminist critics. While specific arguments are too numerous and intricate to elaborate here, in recent years *negrista* poets–including the "canonical" authors such as Guillén–have been cited for their tendency to argue the primacy of race or class as the only determinants of oppression and for excluding the categories of gender and sexuality.

Even though the characteristics attributed to black people by the colonial discourse were for the most part recast by *negrista* writers "as positive gifts, or even superior attributes, rather than as signs of inferiority" (Mama 107), lingering prejudice was often visible in the patronizing vocabulary focused not only on unbridled sexuality, but also on magic, animism, superstitious rites, sacrifice, and trance. Curiously enough, despite its overall positive connotations, myth may be construed to emphasize the stereotype of the ontological ahistoricity of non-European people, for, as Peter Mason explains, myths "narrate those collective representations which are not ours and whose underlying causes seem strange to us" (1). Johannes Fabian echoes this view in asserting that Western anthropological discourse tends to place the images of the other outside the time of historical representation, thus transforming the other into a timeless archetype of primitivism.

To be sure, the importance of mythical and religious notions in *negrismo* certainly goes beyond a mere sign of exoticization. Working from different methodological angles, numerous critics (Cuervo-Hewitt, Fernández Olmos, Luis, Matibag, and Piedra) have shown how the suppression of African diasporic religions under slavery has resulted in complex operations of camouflage, masking, and selective appropriation of the dominant culture. Matibag, for example, frames his study by arguing that in the works by Carpentier, Ramos, and Lachatañaré, "Afro-Cuban religion–as social structure, doctrine, slave ideology, mythic archive, transcendence–fulfills its diverse vocations as a signifier of otherness in the bosom of Cuban culture, as its nationalist alter/native" (94).

Two recent studies–a collective work titled *Sacred Possessions: Vodou, Santería, Obeah, and the Caribbean* and Eugenio Matibag's already-mentioned *Afro-Cuban Religious Experience: Cultural Reflections in Narrative*–are particularly keen on demonstrating how texts employing Afro-Caribbean beliefs confront some readers with the need to "decode" the otherwise "defamiliarizing frame of reference" (Matibag 102). In broaching the subject of the transculturative recoding of African-derived beliefs, both *Sacred Possessions* and *Afro-Cuban Religious Experience* are designed to assist those readers in "an ethnologically informed understanding" (Matibag xiii).

The assumption that critics should provide cultural keys for (re)orienting an apparently disoriented reader shows how hybridity becomes a shaping force with respect to both producers and consumers of literature. The question of whether negrista texts were written for the culturally misinformed or for the initiated might seem irrelevant if it were not for the fact that ethnic experience and ancestry, of writers and readers alike, was crucial in configuring the movement and its reception. As a matter of fact, influential critics such as Kubayanda attribute the resurfacing of the most pernicious racial stereotypes in *negrista* poetry to the fact that many practitioners of the movement (Palés Matos, for example) "were essentially outsiders in Caribbean-African ethnic life" and therefore "no adequate emotional bond is forged between the poetic voice and the poetic object" (24). That experience and ethnicity are not simply relevant but crucial to Afro-Caribbean literature has been accentuated in the highly influential writings of Edward Kamau Brathwaite (b. 1930). His categories of "Rhetorical Africa," "Literature of African Survival," and "Literature of African Expression" (1974b) have become the order of the day for critics like Kubayanda, who are interested in drawing a distinction between exoticized versions of Africa and works nourished by a more genuine, African-based consciousness (Kubayanda 17–32).

The issue of the "intended" reader of Latin American texts–particularly those texts whose extensive use of folklore, ritual, and myth places them in the highly controversial category of "magic realism"–points to the links between *negrismo* and other contemporary discourses seeking to encompass the bewildering syncretism of Latin America's "real." For most critics, Carpentier's theory and practice of *lo real maravilloso americano* and his related construct of *lo barroco* epitomize these efforts (Zamora 136). Here I would like to posit the question of the "intended" readership not in terms of the European versus the Latin American, but in a manner that may help us broach the problem of transculturation with regard to reception.

The proximity of anthropology and literature in this case is evident enough to encourage me to borrow Kamala Visweswaran's differentiation between various types of ethnographic writing. More specifically, Visweswaran makes a distinction between normative/reflexive ethnography and deconstructive ethnography, by arguing that while the former rests on a "declarative mode" of imparting knowledge to a reader "whose position is stabilized by invisible claims to a shared discourse," the latter "disrupts the identity of the reader with a unified subject of enunciation by discouraging identification" (78).

When we look at other significant texts that emerged from the Hispanic Caribbean roughly at the same time as *negrismo*, it becomes obvious that the authenticating seal of the syncretic Caribbean was not imprinted on them in a "declarative mode." The earlier narrative of Carpentier, the *negrista* poems by Palés Matos, the lyrical meanderings of Dulce María Loynaz's (1902–1997) novel *Jardín* [1935; Garden], and the intricate poetic imagery of Julia de Burgos (1914–1953), offer some of the most notable examples of the ways in which the Latin American "real" is traced, fractured, and constantly reinscribed in the liminal space of hybridity.

Negrismo, Palés Matos, and the Hybridity of the "American Real"

Since Afro-Antillean poems by Guillén have been given their due in numerous studies, the most obvious choice for a rereading of *negrismo* is Palés Matos, not only because of the centrality of his poetry to Latin American literary history but also because of the complexity of his hybrid articulations of the Caribbean. It also seems to me that his writings stand to gain the most from recent theoretical insights, because, as I have just indicated, they do not conform to the simple dichotomies of a "declarative mode."

Unlike Guillén, who is considered the embodiment of the most genuine strands of *negrismo*, Palés was appreciated for his verbal virtuosity but also criticized for being a "cultured" poet given to "intellectual exercises" (Marzán 34). Aníbal González has also shown how Palés Matos was "furiously attacked" by some of his contemporaries for his Afro-Anti-lleanism (1992, 567). Marzán refers to two extreme contemporary critiques of Palés Matos' work ("El Llamado Arte Negro No Tiene Vinculación en Puerto Rico" ["The So-Called Black Art Has No Relevance to Puerto Rico"], by Luis Antonio Miranda, and "La Broma de Una Poesía Prieta en Puerto Rico" ["The Joke of a Black Poetry in Puerto Rico"], by Graciany Miranda Archilla), stressing the racialist bias of both pieces (29): "Because Palés Matos dared to claim that Puerto Rico is half-Spanish and half-African, he irritated tender sensibilities, and therefore his poetry provoked the counterattack of island conventions that played down African culture in Puerto Rico's official myths" (33). Several decades later, in an ironic inversion of opinions, Palés's poems "Esta Noche He Pasado" ["I Have Passed By Tonight"], "Lagarto Verde" ["Green Lizard"], and "Elegía del Duque de la Mermelada" ["Elegy of the Duke of Marmalade"] were chastised for being racist (see Isabelo Zenón Cruz).

It was Arcadio Díaz Quiñones who at that time significantly redefined Palés's poetry. In arguing that the poet's perspective initiated the process of affirmation of the African presence in Puerto Rican national culture, Díaz Quiñones opened up a fuller dialogue that reflected the interpretive concerns of the postcolonial era. From different angles, equally thoughtful rereadings of Palés Matos were offered by Aníbal González and Juan Antonio Corretjer. More recently, Marzán's insightful study has presented Palés Matos's variant of *negrismo* as a multilayered constellation of images that both reproduce and reconfigure hegemonic notions of ethnicity. In *Tuntún de pasa y grifería*, according to Marzán, transculturative process is all pervasive, because these poems "are not about black people or white people, real or fictive, but about the obsessive and continual encounter of a white persona with a black heritage and the images of it in the soul of his language, images that range from the ridiculously racist to those that are sublime" (43).

There are several points of contact between Marzán's argument, my previous discussion of hyphe-nation as a space of liminality, and the following comment by Díaz Quiñones, which brilliantly traces the dynamics of transculturative encounters as the structuring principle of Palés's most important *negrista* collection, *Tuntún de pasa y grifería*:

> Afterwards follow three parts that the poet titles "Trunk," "Branch," "Flower." Interpreted generally and unrigorously, "Trunk" refers to the ancestral African things in their purest state: dance, rhythm, temperament. In "Branch," he gathers the poems that deal with the results of resettling black people in the Caribbean. "Flower" groups the ironic poems, in which Palés eulogizes Puerto Rico, the racially mixed Antilles, and describes the tropical landscape. (15)

It should be evident by now that Díaz Quiñones and Marzán map out a different discursive space for *negrismo* than Kubayanda does. Whereas the latter offers an in all respects admirable examination of cross-cultural codes that have shaped Guillén's poetry, what he fails to recognize is the ambivalence that often characterizes the portrayal of African-based cultures of the Caribbean. Only in passing does the critic wonder whether Palés Matos's depiction of African primitivism should be taken at face value, or, perhaps, "[c]ould all this be said tongue-in-cheek, at the expense of a

Christianizing impulse rather than so-called primitive super-stition?" (23). However, Kubayanda quickly abandons this line of inquiry, "because the subtlety of the ironic mode seems altogether missing. What comes through more force-fully are the anti-Voodoo mocking overtones" (23–24). More important, Kubayanda attributes this lack of subtlety to the fact that "Palés Matos was handicapped for not knowing Africa first hand" (23), whereas, by contrast, Guillén was able "to bring to light the religious and creative importance of these symbols" due to his "vantage point of the more knowl-edgeable insider" (24).

While the significance of experience cannot be over-looked, I am reminded here of Foucault's statement that "it is necessary to include within one and the same form of knowl-edge all that has been *seen* and *heard*, all that has been *narrated* by nature or by men, by the language of the world, of tradi-tions or of poets" (qtd. in Mason 26). Even though Kubayanda displays a salutary self-doubt as to anybody's abil-ity to speak for the other, he downplays multiplicities that tend to occur at the intersection of the seen, the heard, and the narrated, and he eschews altogether the mediatory aspects of discourse production and reception.

Peter Mason points to a historically changing hierarchy in the triple alliance of "seeing, hearing, reading," with the emphasis on the visual well through the end of the nineteenth century (26). When placing *negrismo* historically and anchor-ing it in Latin American reality, we may want to consider George Yúdice's remark that a predilection for aural and musical metaphors reflects a shift in attention from the pre-dominantly visual poetics of modernity–based on perspectiv-ism and empirical evidence–to a "postmodern" space of the vocal as a means of "restoring voice to the voiceless" (Shohat and Stam 214). While it is not my intention to claim that *negrismo* was an early incarnation of postmodernism, the reli-ance on aural images and metaphors certainly helped prepare the ground for the enormous popularity of Latin American *testimonio* some thirty years later.

Since the publication of Kubayanda's important study, our postmodern wisdom has undermined the notions of "experi-ence" and "subjectivity" altogether while stressing the layer-ing of discursive meaning. It is here that transculturation–conceived as the transient space of exchange, presence, and absence–may render some critically productive results. I would like to suggest, however, that in order to achieve a more nuanced rereading of *negrismo*, the critic's arsenal of transculturated terminology has to be further enriched, in addition to the already-mentioned *bricolage* and hybridity, with such related theoretical or metaphorical concepts as hyphenation, signifying, Bakhtinian heteroglossia, cannibal-ism, and *cimarronaje*.

Hyphenated doubles, such as Afro-Antillean, in the view of some postcolonial critics, "bear witness to a dis-avowal of any crossing between white and black" (Young 174), while for others claiming the hyphen not only evokes "a movement between cultural identity and nation states" (Hus-sein 10), but also becomes a form of empowerment (Visverswa-ran 116). I find Nasser Hussein's comment on hyphenation as a space of liminality particularly illuminating and worth quoting *in extenso*:

Hyphens are radically ambivalent signifiers, for they simultaneously connect and set apart; they simultaneously represent both belonging and not belonging. What is even more

curious about a hyphenated pair of words is that meaning cannot reside in one word or the other, but can only be understood in movement. (10)

The metaphor of hyphenation could be further expanded by a more Caribbean notion of *cimarronaje cultural* ("cultural maroonization"), adopted by Zavala (156) from René Depes-tre and Brathwaite. Unlike the term "transculturation," which lends itself to highlighting assimilation and integration, the notion of *cimarronaje* conveys both resistance and a heteroge-nous layering of influences, with numerous codes and mes-sages, some partly camouflaged, some completely erased. In *Contradictory Omens*, Brathwaite has defined "psychic maroon-age" as the forging of "a syncretic vision of African patterns, symbols and communicative canons . . . which the subordi-nate maintains in everyday life even in the course of submit-ting to large-scale socioeconomic pressures of dominance" (qtd. in Fernández Olmos et al. 2). In art and literature, this subversive appropriation of master codes may appear in dif-ferent rhetorical guises, but it tends to retain an aesthetic that rejects formal harmony in favor of asymmetry, "strategic inflections," and "reaccentuations" (Lavie and Swedenburg 9).

Combined with Bakhtinian and Lacanian terminology, the metaphor of *cimarronaje* is exemplified in Zavala's argument concerning Palés Matos, whom she situates, along with Guillén and Julia de Burgos, within the frame of the discourse of anti-colonial resistance:

In *Tun tún de pasa y grifería* (1937), Palés Matos models heteroglossia, but also the seepages between boundaries of festive carnivalization and the castration of the uncanny. The mirror is emptied of optical content (I return to Lacan) and produces mirages rather than sensory images. . . . The remapping of the Antilles for Lloréns and Palés Matos is revealed in the form of bodies split into pieces, with language divided within itself by all the oppositions and differences it must convey. (183)

Zavala's argument brings to mind Bakhtin's overarching model of hybridity, which the critic himself defined as

a mixture of two social languages within the limits of a single utterance, an encounter, within the arena of an utterance, between two different linguistic consciousnesses, separated from one another by an epoch, by social differentiation or by some other factor. (358)

Bakhtin's approach underscores the subversive, carnivalizing force of hybridization, thus intersecting once again with "cre-olizing practices" associated with transculturation, whereby master codes of the hegemonic culture are appropriated, dis-articulated, and transformed (Young 25).

Zavala's focus on Bakhtin adds yet another twist to the notion of transculturation. Because Bakhtin's concepts of car-nival, heteroglossia, dialogic, and polyphony were created in response to a historical context completely different from the Hispanic Caribbean, we have to view the transplantation of his theories as yet another transculturative process. "Apply-ing" theories imported from Europe or North America to other contexts has become increasingly problematic in recent years, and Audre Lorde's famous dictum that "the master's tools will never dismantle the master's house" has also reso-nated among literary critics dealing with Latin America (see Vidal). Nonetheless, Bakhtin's ideas seem to have had an uncanny ability to travel and retain their illuminating power, as evidenced by Zavala's adaptations of Bakhtin to different areas of Hispanic letters. Similarly, Henry Louis Gates, Jr., has explored the contestatory potential of "double-voiced" strategies within African-American discourses. In *The Signifying Monkey* in particular, Gates "has developed a theory of the ironizing double-voiced 'trickster' discourse of the Black literary tradition in which one point of view is self-consciously layered palimpsestically on–and against–another" (Young 24). For Gates, it is the Yoruba trickster Eshu-Elegbara who embodies the deconstructive strategy of "signifying" in African-derived art forms (see Piedra for a Caribbean perspective on "signifying").

Certainly, critical possibilities inspired by Bakhtin may bifurcate into one more potentially productive metaphor: that of cannibalization. Even though the intersection of cannibalism and the avant-garde was first highlighted by European writers–from Alfred Jarry's (1873–1907) "Anthropophagie" [1902; "Anthropophagy"] to Francis Picabia's (1879–1953) less known "Manifeste Cannibale Dada" [1920; "Dada Cannibal Manifesto"]–the trope of cannibalism became a focus for Brazilian modernists of the 1920s. Oswald de Andrade's (1890–1954) memorable "Manifesto Antropofágico" [1928; "Anthropophagous Manifesto"] stressed the "digestive" aspect of Brazilian culture in relation to the European, echoing the authochtonous tradition of the Tupinamba Indians, who devoured their enemies in order to gain strength and vitality (see Emery; Heller).

Even though "cannibalistic" concepts never coalesced into a defined artistic movement in the Spanish-speaking countries of Latin America or the Caribbean, and none of the *negrista* writers appears to have subscribed to Andrade's anthropophagic ideas, it is not difficult to implicate Palés Matos in the practice of literary cannibalism. Images of food that eloquently speak of assimilation and resurrection, incorporation and violence, aggression and identification with the other (Kilgour 6–7) sustain, for example, "El menú" ["The Menu"], one of the most explicitly self-reflexive poems in the second edition of *Tuntún de pasa y grifería* (1950). As Marzán has shown in his splendid analysis of the poem, Palés Matos, appearing as the host of a restaurant, offers dishes whose multilayered flavoring attests to "the poetic possibilities of the Caribbean treasure of images from which the host is able to whip up unheard of creations" (Marzán 20):

Si a lo francés, prefieres lo criollo,
y tu apetito, con loable intento,
pírrase por ajiaco y ajopollo
y sopón de embrujado condimento,
toma este calalú maravilloso
con que la noche tropical aduna
su maíz estrellado y luminoso,
y el diente de ajo de su ajo de su media luna
en divino potaje sustancioso.

If to French, you prefer creole
and your appetite, with commendable designs,
craves hot sauce, seasoned chicken,
and a soup of bewitched condiments,
taste this enchanting calalú
in which the tropic night combines
its shining, star-like grains of corn
and its garlic-clove half moon
in a hearty celestial pottage.

(qtd. and trans. in Marzán 19–20)

The cannibalistic (meta)poetics of destruction, re-creation, and incorporation permeates Palés Matos's poetry, as all of the most insightful critics (Díaz Quiñones; Aníbal González 1989;

Marzán) have demonstrated. Behind the unstable boundary of words, Palés's poetry can be read as the result of a long–and painful–transculturative process of confrontation between unequal forces, from literary models (such as the "cultured" Baroque and *modernismo,* rather than the "popular") to sociopolitical systems. His poetry is a testimony, perhaps an unwitting one, to the possibilities and limits of cross-cultural encounters. In recent theoretical proposals, such as that of Shohat and Stam, the articulation of the intersecting issues of hybridization, hegemony, and resistance has become nuanced enough to help illuminate the contradictions inherent in Palés's world:

> A celebration of syncretism and hybridity per se, if not articulated with questions of historical hegemonies, risks sanctifying the fait accompli of colonial violence. For oppressed people, even artistic syncretism is not a game but a sublimated form of historical pain. . . . As a descriptive catch-all term, "hybridity" fails to discriminate between the diverse modalities of hybridity: colonial imposition, obligatory assimilation, political cooptation, cultural mimicry, and so forth. Elites have always made cooptive top-down raids on subaltern cultures, while the dominated have always "signified" and parodied as well as emulated elite practice. Hybridity, in other words, is power-laden and asymmetrical. . . . Hybridity is also cooptable. In Latin America, national identity has often been officially articulated as hybrid and syncretic, through hypocritically integrationist ideologies that have glossed over subtle racial hegemonies. (43)

If we approach Palés Matos's poetry not only as a manifestation of *negrismo*, but as part of a broader movement forging a postcolonial cultural autonomy for Latin America and the Caribbean, his writings acquire yet another dimension: that of anticolonial counterdiscourse, seeking to end the fabrication of non-European worlds for the European consumers (Hulme 2). Instead, in Yúdice's words, along with *indigenismo*, Brazilian Modernism, and the Nicaraguan *Vanguardia, negrismo* was a movement whereby "(elite) aesthetics in Latin America finally went beyond a mere *costumbrismo*, tapping local indigenous cultural forms in search of its own unalienated cultural capital" (13).

I began this essay with a brief discussion of recent advances in postcolonial theory, and I have used some of these newer insights in my rereading of *negrismo*, mindful of the fact that of the three options available to Pierre Menard in his task of (re)writing *Don Quijote*, the third, which consists in recreating the text from a contemporary perspective, is perhaps the only feasible one. What I hope to have suggested in these pages, in addition to what is ostensibly an "application" of contemporary theories to not-so-recent texts, is that the complex articulations of hybridity in the works of Carpentier, Guillén, Palés Matos, Loynaz, or Burgos should make us pause, put down our postmodern toolbox, and consider to what extent recent postcolonial theories may be regarded as deferred formulations of some of the artistic experiments that writers from the Hispanic Caribbean had already put into practice in the 1920s and 1930s.

Works Cited

Andrade, Oswald de. 1978 [1972]. *Do Pau-Brasil à Antropofagia e às Utopias: Manifestos, teses de concursos e ensaios.* 2nd ed. Rio de Janeiro: Civilização Brasileira.

Armes, Roy. 1987. *Third World Filmmaking and the West.* Berkeley: University of California Press.

Bakhtin, Mikhail. 1981. *Dialogic Imagination: Four Essays by M. M. Bakhtin.* Ed. Michael Hoquist. Trans. Caryl Emerson and Michael Holquist. Austin: Texas University Press.

Ballagas, Emilio. 1934. *Cuaderno de poesía negra*. Havana: Imprenta "La Nueva."

Barnet, Miguel. 1978. *Akeké y la jutía. Fábulas cubanas*. Havana: Ed. Unión de Escritores y artistas de Cuba..

Brathwaite. Edward Kamau. 1974a. *Contradictory Omens: Cultural Diversity and Integration in the Caribbean*. Mona, Jamaica: Savacou Publications.

——. 1974b. "The African Presence in Caribbean Literature." *Deadalus* 103. 2 (Spring): 73–109. Reprinted in *Africa in Latin America. Essays on History, Culture and Socialization*. Ed. Manuel Moreno Fraginals. Trans. Leonor Blum. 103–44. New York: Holmes and Meier, 1984.

Cabrera, Lydia. 1972. *Porqué. . . (Cuentos negros de Cuba)*. 2nd ed. Madrid: Ediciones CR.

Carpentier, Alejo. 1968. *Ecué-Yamba-O. Novela afrocubana*. Buenos Aires: Ed. Xanandú.

Cobb, Martha K. 1979. *Harlem, Haiti and Havana: A Comparative Critical Study of Langston Hughes, Jacques Roumain, and Nicolás Guillén*. Washington DC: Three Continents Press.

Coulthard, G. R. 1962. *Race and Colour in Caribbean Literature*. London: Oxford University Press.

Cuervo-Hewitt, Julia. 1988. *Aché, presencia africana. Tradiciones yoruba-lucumí en la narrativa cubana*. New York: Peter Lang.

Daniel, Yvonne. 1995. *Rubma: Dance and Social Change in Contemporary Cuba*. Bloomington: Indiana University Press.

Davis, James J. 1988. "Ritmo poético, negritud y dominicanidad." *Revista Iberoamericana* 142: 171–186.

Díaz Quiñones, Arcadio. 1970. *La poesía negra de Luis Palés Matos: realidad y conciencia de su dimensión colectiva*. San Juan, P. R.: Talleres Gráficos Interamericanos.

Emery, Amy Fass. 1996. *The Anthropological Imagination in Latin American Literature*. Columbia and London: University of Missouri Press.

Fabian, Johannes. 1983. *Time and the Other: How Anthropology Makes Its Object*. New York: Columbia Univesity Press.

Fernández Olmos, Margarite, and Lizabeth Paravisini-Gebert, eds. 1997. *Sacred Possessions: Voudou, Santería, Obeah, and the Caribbean*. New Brunswick, NJ.: Rutgers University Press.

Flores, Juan. 1992. "Cortijo's Revenge: New Mappings of Puerto Rican Culture." *On Edge: The Crisis of Contemporary Latin American Culture*. Eds.George Yúdice, Jean Franco, and Juan Flores. Minneapolis: University of Minnesota Press. 187–205.

Garabís, Juan Otero. 1996. "'Puerto Rico Is Salsa': Propositions, Appropriations and Interpretations of a Popular Genre." *Journal of Latin American Cultural Studies* 5.1: 25–31.

Gates, Henry Louis, Jr. 1988. *The Signifying Monkey: A Theory of African-American Literary Criticism*. New York: Oxford University Press.

Glasser, Ruth. 1995. *My Music Is My Flag: Puerto Rico Musicians and Their New York Communities, 1917–1940*. Berkeley: University of California Press.

González, Aníbal. 1988. "La (sín)tesis de una poesía antillana: Palés y Spengler." *Cuadernos Hispanoamericanos* 451–452: 59–72.

——. 1989. "Luis Palés Matos." *Latin American Writers*. Eds. Carlos Solé and Maria Isabel Abreu. Vol. 2. New York: Charles Scribners. 821–830.

——. 1992. "Puerto Rico." *Handbook of Latin American Literature*. Ed. David William Foster. 2nd ed. New York: Garland Publishing. 555–581.

González, José Luis. 1995. "The Four-Storeyed House: Africans in the Forging of Puerto Rico's National Identity." *Slavery and Beyond: The African Impact on Latin America and the Caribbean*. Ed. Darién J. Davis. Wilmington, DE.: Scholarly Resources. 173–194.

González Echevarría, Roberto. 1977. *Alejo Carpentier: The Pilgrim at Home*. Ithaca: Cornell University Press.

Guerra y Sánchez, Ramiro. 1927. *Azúcar y población en las Antillas*. Havana: Cultural, S. A.

Guillén, Nicolás. 1930. *Motivos de son*. Havana: Rambla & Bouza.

Heller, Ben. 1996. *Assimilation/Generation/Resurrection: Contrapuntal Readings in the Poetry of José Lezama Lima*. Lewisburg PA: Bucknell University Press.

Hulme, Peter. 1986. *Colonial Encounters: Europe and the Native Caribbean 1492–1797*. London: Methuen.

Hussin, Nasser. 1989. "Hyphenated Identity: Nationality, Discourse, History, and the Anxiety of Criticism in Salman Rushdie's *Shame*." *Qui Parle?* 3.2: 1–18.

Jackson, Richard L. 1976. *The Black Image in Latin American Literature*. Albuquerque: University of New Mexico Press.

Kilgour, Maggie. 1990. *From Communion to Cannibalism: An Anatomy of Metaphors of Incorporation*. Princeton NJ: Princeton University Press.

Kubayanda, Josaphat B. 1990. *The Poet's Africa: Africanness in the Poetry of Nicolás Guillén and Aimé Césaire*. New York-Westport CT: Greenwood Press.

Kutzinski, Vera M., ed. 1987. *Callaloo*. Special issue on Nicolás Guillén. 10.

Lavie, Smadar, and Ted Swedenburg, eds. 1996. Introduction. *Displacement, Diaspora, and Geographies of Identity*. Durham-London: Duke University Press. 1–26.

Lizardo, Fradique. 1978. *Cultura negra en Santo Domingo*. Santo Domingo: Sociedad Industrial Dominicana.

Luis, William, ed. 1984. *Voices from Under. Black Narrative in Latin America and the Caribbean*. Westport, CT: Greenwood Press.

Mama, Amina. 1995. *Beyond the Masks: Race, Gender and Subjectivity*. London and New York: Routledge.

Mansour, Monica. 1973. *La poesía negrista*. Mexico City: Ediciones Era, 1973.

Marzán, Julio. 1995. *The Numinous Site: The Poetry of Luis Palés Matos*. Madison-Teaneck: Fairleigh Dickinson University Press.

Masiello, Francine. 1993. "Rethinking Neocolonial Esthetics: Literature, Politics, and Intellectual Community in Cuba's *Revista de Avance*." *Latin American Research Review* 28.2: 3–31.

Mason, Peter.1990. *Deconstructing America: Representations of the Other*. London-New York: Routledge.

Matibag, Eugenio. 1996. *Afro-Cuban Religious Experience: Cultural Reflections in Narrative*. Gainesville: University Press of Florida.

Montes-Huidobro, Matías. 1992. "Cuba." *Handbook of Latin American Literature*. Ed. David William Foster. 2nd ed. New York: Garland Publishing. 227–269.

Ortiz, Fernando. 1973 [1906]. *Hampa afro-cubana: los negros brujos (Apuntes para un estudio de etnología criminal)*. Miami: Ediciones Universal.

——. 1995. *Cuban Counterpoint: Tobacco and Sugar*. Introduction Fernando Coronil. Trans. Harriet de Onís. Durham and London: Duke University Press.

Palés Matos, Luis. 1937. *Tuntún de pasa y grifería: poemas afroantillanos*. San Juan PR: Biblioteca de Autores Puertorriqueños.

Pedreira, Antonio S. 1973. *Insularismo*. Río Piedras, P.R.: Editorial Edil.

Piedra, José. 1997. "From Monkey Tales to Cuban Songs: On Signification." *Sacred Possessions: Voudou, Santería, Obeah, and the Caribbean*. Eds. Margarite Fernández Olmos and Lizabeth Paravisini-Gebert. New Brunswick, NJ: Rutgers University Press. 122–150.

Shohat, Ella, and Robert Stam. 1994. *Unthinking Eurocentrism: Multiculturalism and the Media*. New York and London: Routledge.

Sommer, Doris, and Esteban Torres. 1992. "Dominican Republic." *Handbook of Latin American Literature*. Ed. David William Foster. 2nd ed. New York: Garland Publishing. 271–286.

Vidal, Hernán. 1993. "The Concept of Colonial and Postcolonial Discourse: A Perspective from Literary Criticism." *Latin American Research Review* 28.3: 113–119.

Visweswaran, Kamala. 1994. *Fictions of Feminist Ethnography.* Minneapolis: University of Minnesota Press.

Young, Robert J. C. 1995. *Colonial Desire: Hybridity in Theory, Culture and Race.* London and New York: Routledge.

Yúdice, George. 1992. "Postmodernity and Transnational Capitalism." *On Edge: The Crisis of Contemporary Latin American Culture.* Eds. George Yúdice, Jean Franco, and Juan Flores. Minneapolis: University of Minnesota Press. 1–28.

Zamora, Lois Parkinson. 1997. *The Usable Past: The Imagination of History in Recent Fiction of the Americas.* Cambridge: Cambridge University Press.

Zavala, Iris M. 1992. *Colonialism and Culture: Hispanic Modernisms and the Social Imaginary.* Bloomington and Indianapolis: Indiana University Press.

Zenón Cruz, Isabelo. 1975. *Narciso descubre su trasero: el negro en la cultura puertorriqueña.* 2 vols. Humacao, PR: Editorial Furidi.

CHAPTER 23

THE LITERARY CULTURE OF THE "NEW ORDER"

MEXICO 1867–1910

Leopoldo Zea

On 16 September 1867, in the city of Guanajuato, an address was delivered that was to prove the beginning of a new and astonishing stage of Mexican thought and culture. The author of this civic oration was Dr. Gabino Barreda (1820–1881), and the theme was a Comtean interpretation of the history of Mexico. Dr. Barreda had become acquainted with Auguste Comte while taking a course that the French philosopher had given in Paris in 1845 on the general history of mankind. Other Latin Americans took the same course, and these, too, would become notable supporters of the positivist doctrine. The year 1867 was special in the history of Mexico, for it was the year in which the invading army of France withdrew, and the abandoned and disillusioned Austrian emperor fell prisoner and was shot on the hill named Campanas de Querétaro. That year, the Liberal Reform movement triumphed and a new phase of Mexican history began. A new order was finally going to take the place of the old colonial order, which had been defended to the very last moment by Mexican Conservatism, only to fall symbolically on Campanas.

Gabino Barreda spoke of Mexican history and of the liberal forces that were going to give rise to the new, Positivist order, with the metaphysics of liberty triumphing over the theological spirit implanted by the colonial authorities. The Positivist spirit was advancing Mexico along the road of progress. This struggle in Mexico was but a phase in the worldwide struggle between the negative and Positivist spirits, and the triumph of Mexican Liberalism was declared to be the triumph of the spirit of mankind.

The defeated Mexican Conservative forces had found it necessary to seek the support of one of the greatest representatives of regression in the history of humanity, Napoleon III. Barreda proclaimed that French intervention in Mexico was nothing less than the intervention of the forces of obscurantism in order to crush the positive spirit of progress. Mexico became, in Barreda's interpretation, the final outpost of progress. It would be here that the destiny not only of Mexico, but of the whole of humanity, would be decided. For this reason, in Barreda's opinion, the battle of 5 May 1867 and the Mexican triumph were but the expression of the titanic struggle between the powerful forces which disputed the destiny of mankind. The soldiers of the Republic in the Battle of Puebla, said Barreda, like the Greeks at Salamis, saved the future of civilization by saving the Republican principle which is the modern ensign of humanity. Europe, and with Europe the entire world, had fallen before the powers opposed to progress, and only Mexico had stood firm and confronted Napoleon III. The conflict between European retrogression and American civilization manifested the struggle of the monarchical principle against the Republican; this marked the last efforts of fanaticism against emancipation. The Republicans of Mexico stood alone.

Gabino Barreda had explained that the clergy and the military were the two great bodies of vested interests from the past; they were representatives of the negative forces, which corresponded to what Comte called the "theological stage." On the other side were the new social groups which, embracing the Liberal ideology, confronted the Conservatives in order to establish a new economic, political, social, and cultural order. This stage of combat, corresponding to what Comte called the metaphysical stage, was necessary to destroy and to displace or dislodge the forces that opposed progress and to establish the positive order. With the combative phase complete and victory won, the ideological bond that would make the new order work had to be created. The philosophical forces of Liberalism, as Barreda called them, were acutely conscious of this and were preparing themselves to meet the challenge. It was a question of a new order that, while respecting the ideals for which the Mexican Liberals had fought, would make possible the envisioned progress. This new order would be put in the service of the most authentic freedom, which had nothing in common with the anarchy the Mexican people had suffered for half a century.

In the future, total freedom of conscience, absolute freedom of expression, and exchange of ideas would permit the light of reason to spread in every quarter and make unnecessary, and indeed impossible, all upheaval that was not purely spiritual, every revolution that was not purely intellectual. Material progress was to be conserved at any price by the government and respected by the governed as the guarantor of progress and civilization. The age of revolutions had ended, Barreda claimed. The goal of the Liberal revolution had been achieved. Now would come the order that would facilitate the envisioned progress. The utopian spirit of the times is captured admirably in the novel *La Navidad en las montañas* [1870; Christmas in the Montains], by Ignacio Manuel Altamirano (1834–1893), and for the first time since Fernánez de Lizardi (1776–1827), literature was once again an important part of the foundational discourse. The transition, however, was not to be simple, for material progress, the supreme objective of every government as the instrument of civilizing society, did not take into account the idea of individual liberty, that which belonged to the tribunal of one's personal conscience. It was clear that this personal liberty would have to be subordinated to the good of society. However, before reaching this stage, Positivism would, for the moment, openly support Mexican Liberalism with its adherence to what Barreda called the "emancipation of conscience." It was necessary to free Mexicans from their servitude to colonialism, to theologism, as Comte would say. This would be achieved by means of an adequate education. The new order would emerge from this change in society.

On 2 December 1867, three months after this Positivist manifesto, the triumphant Republic, under the presidency of

Benito Juárez (1806–1872), promulgated the law that oriented and regulated public education in Mexico, from the elementary to the professional level, including the most important instrument for the formation of future citizens, the National Preparatory School. The man who was called upon to collaborate in this reform, which would proceed along Comtean lines, was Gabino Barreda. President Juárez had seen in Barreda's ideas an ideology capable of forming the Mexicans of the future and putting an end to the long period of anarchy that followed emancipation. But very soon sharp differences would become apparent that would divide triumphant Mexican Liberalism from Positivist ideology. Barreda himself had been careful to make these differences apparent in his Civic Oration. Liberalism represented the necessary metaphysical stage, capable of destroying the old theological order and of making possible the new, Positivist order that was to be constructed. For the time, Positivism had to be subordinated to triumphant Liberalism until its combative mission had been accomplished.

In the Civic Oration, Barreda had already changed the Comtean motto of love, order, and progress to liberty, order, and progress. Liberalism was triumphant, and now it had to carry out the task of establishing a social order that would lead to progress. Such was the dream of every Liberal, and Positivist philosophy was seen as a useful instrument to its realization by forming, through education, the men who would make it possible and who would create the society for which their ancestors had fought. However, liberty had a different meaning for Liberals than it had for Positivists. Liberty, taken in the sense of laissez-faire, the initial phase of Liberalism, was becoming impossible and proved contrary to the idea of a positive order. Order and liberty had to be reconciled.

Barreda argued that liberty is commonly represented as a faculty of doing or seeking anything whatsoever without subjection to law or to any force that might direct it; if such a freedom could be achieved, it would be both immoral and absurd because it would make discipline and, consequently, order impossible. Liberty is compatible with authentic Liberal order, if given a positive meaning, by which something is free when it follows its natural course. And this course is to be found in the law or laws which determine that thing, which are proper to its nature. Its liberty expresses itself in freely following what its laws dictate. Barreda cites an example from physics: When one speaks of a free-falling body, one is speaking of a body that follows the laws of gravity. The same holds true in the moral field, where man will act freely if he follows his moral impulses, which demarcate for him the distinction between what is and what ought to be, between good and evil. Man's task is to take freely the path that does not impede the realization of moral goals.

Society enters its highest expression: It is the state which, by means of education, fortifies the impulses that follow the moral law and limits those that oppose it. In this way, altruistic impulses can develop freely. Freedom thus is not laissez-faire or laissez-passer, but the expression of the unimpeded progress of the higher moral sentiments that society, of which the individual is a part, needs for its evolution. Liberty, understood in the limited sense given by Liberalism, would entail disorder and with it the destruction of the highest social goals that make a true Liberal order possible. It would mean the stimulation of the egotistic sentiments and the hampering of altruistic sentiments. For that reason, freedom that does not attend to ends that fortify society, and with it the individual who

makes society possible, is an egotistic liberty which must be made subject to the laws of societal development. The egotistic liberty of individuals must subordinate itself to social order.

These idealistic sentiments had common currency at the time. Six years earlier, in 1861, Nicolas Pizarro Suárez (1830–1895) published two novels: *El Monedero* [The Moneybag] and *La Coqueta* [The Coquette]. Pizarro was an ardent defender of the Reform movement, and his novels are full of Ignacio Manuel Altamirano's Romantic idealism: There is in *El Monedero* the presentation of a model community. The community as the instrument of governance exists for the good of all and cannot be reduced to individual interests. There is a kind of communal democracy where everyone has a voice in how the community should be run, and owing to the superior education everyone receives, there is no possibility of discord because of individual preference or possible personal gain. The utopian ideal of a communal democracy made possible by the high educational level of all citizens so vividly portrayed here was an important part of the Reform movement of Mexican Liberalism. José María Luis Mora (1794–1850) had expressed his belief in this goal for Mexico in his "Pensamiento sobre educación" (1844): "The objective of governments is to provide the governed with the highest number of benefits and this cannot be done without public education" (83). The isolation of this model community defends it from an outside world of greed and individual abuse of power.

Hence, the state must guarantee the moral education of Mexicans. It must prepare Mexicans to be good servants of society by stimulating their altruism. Mexicans, as individuals, may be Liberals or Conservatives, Catholics or Jacobins–this means nothing; what is important is that, independently of these individual attitudes, they must be good citizens, submitting their personal desires to the goal of the society. In doing so, they will, in due course, realize their own individual goals. In other words, the individual may think what he wishes, but he must work in accordance with the interests of society: He cannot hinder, by his freely held ideas, the free development of society and of the individuals who constitute it. This is of course the delicate issue of freedom of expression. It should be noted that Positivists consistently made freedom of expression conditional. If the ideas expressed in any way hindered or held back the free movement of society, they had to be censored. This is without a doubt a formula for absolutism, which later became part of the intellectual climate in the early years of the Díaz dictatorship. The most direct opposition to positivism in literature was in Arcadio Zentella's (1844–1920) *Perico* (1885). The rampant racism that would emerge some twenty years later during the dictatorship would be adamantly opposed by Liberals like Eligio Ancona (1836–1893), who never abandoned Liberal ideals. His Romantic novel *La mestiza* (1891) denounced Conservative views on the innate superiority of white people over the Mexican *mestizo*, who is envisioned as the future unification of the racial heterogeneity of Mexico.

The debate in the 1860s and 1870s centered on reconciling Liberalism and positivism. How far does or may the state intervene in the service of society? No further than the social order requires for the development of society, a development that stood in direct relationship to the material progress of each individual member. Of importance for the ideologists of Positivism would be this social order, which would put an end to the anarchy in which the country had wallowed since its political emancipation from Spain, would permit the material development of the most capable Mexicans. In other words, the state socialism advocated here went no further than the establishment of a social order enabling the material development of the social class that had been emerging since the beginning of Liberalism itself–the Mexican bourgeoisie, as Justo Sierra (1848–1912) called it.

Barreda maintained that the state should not intervene in private property. Only through education could altruistic sentiments be brought about and would proprietors direct private property toward the greater good of society. Only education and the fostering of enlightened self-interest should be undertaken by the state. It would, of course, be able to regulate the political order, which would put an end to anarchy, but not the economic order, which would remain at the free disposition of individuals. What the state had to do was to make the owners of wealth understand that, although morally authorized to hold capital that the social order had made possible for them to acquire, accumulate, and preserve, they should only keep what was necessary for their real needs and for the maintenance of their rank and dignity; they had the moral duty to use the excess for the public good.

Moral responsibility was understood as the conviction that wealth ought to benefit society as well as its owners. It does not imply state intervention except as a counsel for the disposition of such wealth. Barreda said that it would not be necessary to regulate wealth but to humanize the rich. Rich people should be able to do what they want with their wealth except divide it up, for to do so would obstruct the common good. Wealth is an instrument of the material development of society; for the sake of society, then, the state should create more opportunities for the wealthy. Although the rich were considered to be the depository of the wealth of society, there was no justification for the state to intervene, save morally, in the regulation of that wealth.

State regulation of capital would impede the free development of that wealth, which would naturally redound to the benefit of society. A society seeking to lay the foundation of a political order that would end anarchy would be obliged to abstain from impeding the material development of private wealth. Personal wealth was proclaimed an instrument of social progress when it was in the hands of those who understood the laws of development, and there it should remain. The only thing that should be of interest to society is that this wealth should also serve social progress. Wealth, because it is the instrument of progress, must, for the same reason, be protected by the state.

So far as the abuses that the owners of wealth may commit are concerned, the most that can be done is to appeal to the moral responsibility that comes with the possession of wealth. To attack wealth and those who know how to increase it would be to diminish and to extinguish their stimulus and, with it, the progress that the development of wealth implies. The most important principle for Positivism is the creation and development of political order. All of the state's powers should be directed to the establishment of that order. The State has no transcendent mission such as it claimed in the theological and metaphysical periods; even less has it the economic mission that socialism claimed for it, such as the distribution or organization of wealth. Its mission concerns only the conservation of the social order; it intervenes in education in order to create the kind of people who will make this order possible. The state as the instrument in the service of society, then, should not concern itself with people who are more or less rich, more or less poor, but only with people of order who make wealth possible, and without impeding their freedom of thought.

Let Mexicans think whatever they want to think; let them exploit others or permit themselves to be exploited. The primary goal was to guarantee the social order that makes economic progress possible. The free play of material interests would, according to Social Darwinian doctrine, demonstrate that the fit will prevail and that society will improve. Behind the neutrality of the State in the areas of personal ideologies and private property, defended by Barreda, emerge the interests of the Mexican bourgeoisie. This social class was nurtured by a doctrine that justified its economic and social privilege and, at the same time, created the political instrument that would prevent any alteration of this situation.

Amidst the turmoil brought out in Mexican education by the Positivists, the old ideals of personal freedom had returned with a vengeance as utopian Positivism was conveniently left behind. In 1871 José Tomás de Cuéllar (1830–1894) initiated an entirely different kind of narrative prose in a series called *La linterna mágica* [The Magic Lantern]. The novels of this series are replete with detailed descriptions of middle-class complicity with the demise of personal freedoms in exchange for personal enrichment. Cuéllar's weapon is satire. The central character in the novelistic series is the *pollo*, that irresponsible affluent youth who disclaims all public morality while seeking the immediate consummation of pleasure. Wealth is sought as a means of continuing his self-indulgence. The ideals of civic duty propounded by the Positivist education are completely foreign to him. If his wife had to prostitute herself for material gain, the *pollo* would usually choose to look the other way. Cuéllar's characters were a direct response to the cynical betrayal of the ideals of the Reform movement as constituted by Barreda's Positivists. Some of the more memorable novels in this series are *Las jamonas* [1871; The Fat Women], *Ensalada de pollos* [1871; Chicken Salad], *Historia de Chucho el ninfo* [1871; Story of Chucho the Nymph], *Gabriel el cerrajero o las hijas de mi papá* [1872; Gabriel the Locksmith or My Father's Daughters], *Las gentes que son así* [1872; People Who Are Like This], and *Baile y cochino* [1886; Dance and Feast].

The effects of Positivist education on the political order made themselves felt almost immediately. Porfirio Díaz had risen to power after a revolution that unseated President Sebastián Lerdo de Tejada (1823–1889), the heir of the revered Benito Juárez. By 1878 a new political group sprang up in the capital of Mexico that made its voice and its ideas heard in a newspaper entitled *La Libertad* and that carried the Comtean motto, "Order and Progress." A number of its editors had been students under Gabino Barreda or had been formed in the system of education he had established under the reforms introduced by President Benito Juárez in 1867. This new group concentrated on one idea: Social order. However, theirs was a new type of order that did not resemble in any way the colonial order broken by the Liberal triumph, and that was not the one upheld by the conservativism that had been annihilated on the hill of the Campanas. The new group called itself Conservative; however, they subscribed to a composite liberal conservativism. Their purpose was to attain liberty; however, their methods were deemed by them to be Conservative: They claimed to be conservators of order as an instrument for the achievement of authentic liberty, which was not and could not be the anarchy that had weighed upon the country for half a century. Liberty, they held, was to be achieved by way of free and natural development. Their motto was "not revolution, but evolution." Order was the precondition for the achievement of authentic liberty. According to these Liberal Conservatives, this was what Mexican Liberals had not been able to, and still did not, understand. They had tried to give the people liberties for which they were not ready; the result had been anarchy. The priority was to educate, to build a knowledge of liberty and of the obligations it implied. So long as Mexicans did not have this knowledge, they argued, all utopian laws and constitutions would be useless, alien to the reality of Mexico. Liberal constitutions and laws were incapable of creating responsible liberty.

But times had changed. Thanks to the educational reforms of Positivism, a generation–practical, positive, realistic–had grown up capable of directing the nation along the road to progress. This generation would establish the social order that would give birth to the liberties the Liberals had unsuccessfully tried to establish. This was a generation capable of creating the base of a democratic government resting upon authentic social freedom. The first step was to create the political and social order that would make possible, in the near future, the dreamed-of Liberal Conservative government. It was necessary to put an end to widespread anarchy, which continued despite the triumph of Liberalism over colonial Conservatism. The main obstacle was the Liberal Constitution of 1857. The ideal liberty advocated by the Constitution could not be attained until the habits and customs that would animate it were created within each Mexican.

Francisco G. Cosmes, one of the editors of *La Libertad*, took the offensive, attacking the older generation of Liberal thinkers as men of such retarded mentality that they still believed in the ideas of the 1857 Constitution. Justo Sierra, director of the same newspaper, wrote less heavy-handed criticism of the Constitution makers of 1857. He argued that Mexicans, as men of the Latin race, believe that a thing is certain and realizable if it is logical; they try to implement any ideal, by force, if necessary; they jump in one day from the absolute to the relative; and they force people to practice what is true only in the domain of pure reason. These men confused heaven and earth and created a noble and elevated code of governance in the constitution of 1857, but it is a code in which everything leads to the autonomy of the individual raised to the highest degree over the interests of society–that is, to the point at which the force of social duties ceases and everything is converted into the rights of individuals.

Sierra captured the spirit of Social Darwinism when he claimed that utopia must come to an end. A new period of history was approaching, a realistic period directed toward an order whose final term would be the realization of that which had been merely a utopia. The forces of the new generation, conscious of its historical mission, would march toward this end. No longer following Comte, but rather Spencer and, above all, Social Darwinism, this generation would hold firm to a belief in the necessity of strengthening Mexicans for the struggle for life and for the transition from the military era of the past, the era of order of the present, to the industrial era, the era of work and of the eventual triumph of the individual in the future.

A realistic Liberalism, a Liberalism of order, a Conservative Liberalism, was firmly opposed to utopian and anarchistic Liberalism. We desire, said Justo Sierra, the formation of a great Conservative party, composed of all the elements of order that in the country possess the capacity of rising to public life. We do not carry as our banner a person, but an idea. We plan to gather together in this political party all those who think that the time for realizing its aspirations by revolutionary violence is over, all those who think that the definitive moment has now arrived for organizing a party more devoted to practical than to declamatory liberty, and all those who are profoundly convinced that progress resides in the orderly development of society. With these words, he expressed the idea of the new, impersonal political order, whose force did not depend upon the will of a *caudillo* (strong man), but which was derived from the minds of enlightened Mexicans. However, this order remained, for the moment at least, a future goal. Above all, it was necessary to educate the people. To implement this education, any kind of order would be good. The problem seemed insoluble: Abandon an order that depended on the will of a *caudillo* while requiring someone of sufficient personal prestige to lay the bases of a new one. This someone, of course, would be only a simple instrument, something transitory, until Mexicans could acquire the mental habits necessary for an autonomous order–that is, an order free from any force external to it.

For the moment, Justo Sierra asserted the necessity of limiting liberties that were manifestly utopian in the current state of affairs. First, it was necessary to create confidence in the country and build the economic base, which was the only way to initiate a process of regeneration. Individual rights had already been rejected by Mexicans as a utopian luxury, Francisco G. Cosmes bluntly affirmed. Mexicans needed bread, not utopian dreams. In place of constitutions filled with sublime ideas, not one of which had been realized in practice, Mexico needed peace in which it would be possible to work tranquilly, with some security for the interests of those who would create work, and to know that, instead of launching the nation into the flight of the ideal, the authorities would hang the exploiters, the thieves, and the revolutionaries. Fewer rights and liberties in exchange for greater order and peace. No more utopias. Mexico needed order and peace, even at the price of all the rights that had cost it so dearly. Cosmes even went so far as to claim that the day was not distant when the country would say, I want order and peace at the price of my independence.

How to achieve this order and peace for which they called out in such urgent need? Not by means of one-man rule, they said. There is nothing more odious or more contrary to progress than the domain of one man, or several men, without *regla fija* (fixed norm). Nevertheless, the Mexican reality had given rise to dictatorships, to tyranny. To have done with that, it was necessary to transform that reality. In one editorial after another, *La Libertad* proclaimed that Mexico must establish a practicable constitution; however, since that was impractical in the prevailing circumstances, responsible persons were content to seek extraordinary authorizations for these extraordinary circumstances. Francisco G. Cosmes wrote in another of his articles that Mexico had already legislated an infinity of rights that produced only misery and distress in society. Now Mexicans were being asked to try a bit of honorable tyranny to see what effect it might produce. This honorable tyranny would prove to be that of General Porfirio Díaz (1830–1915).

The so-called honorable tyranny, with its implicit support of social injustice, did not take long to produce a very different kind of novelist, one no longer content with social satire. These were the writers of indignation and outrage of the

Porfiriato, writers such as Arcadio Zentella. In his novel *Perico*, he denounces the common brutality of the *hacendado* (landowner) toward his *peones* (laborers). Scenes of unmitigated brutality and inhumanity are presented as acceptable to the defenders of social progress. Other novelists who joined Zentella in this spirit of denunciation were José López Portillo y Rojas (1850–1923), the author of *La parcela* [1898; The Lot] and *Los precursores* [1909; The Forerunners], among others, and Rafael Delgado (1853–1914), author of *La calandria* [1890; The Lark] and *Angelina* (1893). But López Portillo and Delgado denounced individual abuse rather than, as Zentella did, the system that made possible its institutionalization.

The generation educated by Gabino Barreda, the men who were going to lead the nation toward progress, found itself confined by the limits of Comtean Positivism and moved on to new political thought. Comtean Positivism, no matter how hard Barreda had tried, could not justify the kind of political organization that had the greatest interest for the future Mexican bourgeoisie, the liberty to enrich itself, with no limits save those of the capability of each individual. Comteanism, in the strict sense, subordinated the individual to society in all the fields of material good. This was the meaning of Comte's sociocracy; this is what his Positivist politics would establish. Comte's politics, like the religion of humanity, had not been accepted by the Mexican Positivists because they considered them contrary to the interests for which Positivism itself had been imported. The objective was to form the directing class of the Mexican bourgeoisie, which was increasingly powerful as time passed. The model to which this class should conform was offered by the Anglo-Saxon countries.

The theoreticians of the Mexican bourgeoisie very soon found different political theories to justify their interests: those of the English political philosophers John Stuart Mill (1806–1873) and, especially, Herbert Spencer (1820–1903), and the evolutionism of Charles Darwin (1809–1882). These doctrines seemed to coincide most fully with the interests that needed to be justified. Moreover, these men represented the highest expression of that practical spirit the Mexicans so admired. English political philosophy, far from opposing the idea of individual freedom, justified it, as exemplified by the Liberal regimes in England and in the United States: Spencer opposed the coercive state, and Mill defended individual liberty. In both their theories, the State proved to be nothing else than what José María Luis Mora had advocated for some time: an instrument of protection for the individuals who composed society. The Spencerian idea of progress would make it possible to offer, at least for the future, an ideal of liberty, for which the nation had struggled on different occasions. To establish this promise, it was necessary only to make a determined degree of progress.

And here is the connection with the group of young Mexican political leaders who, through the pages of *La Libertad*, had demanded a new order and aspired to establish an honorable dictatorship. This group no longer followed Comte, but rather Mill and Spencer. How, then, could they justify ideas that seemed so contradictory? They would reconcile the contradictions between English Liberalism and honorable tyranny through Spencer's idea of evolution. Sierra would say that it was beyond doubt that society is an organism that, though different from others (the reason Spencer called it a super organism), had undeniable analogies with living organisms. Like animal organisms, society is subject to laws of evolution. In accordance with these laws, all organisms realize a movement toward integration and differentiation in a process that goes from the homogeneous to the heterogeneous, from the indefinite to the definite. In social organisms, the movement is from social homogeneity to individual differentiation, from complete order to complete liberty. Thus, the idea that the older Liberals had held about liberty was not completely rejected; what was opposed, on the basis of Herbert Spencer's *Principles of Sociology* (1876–1896) was the notion that Mexican society had reached the same high level of progress as England. Social Darwinists did not think, as had the Comteans, that this freedom was possible in the stage of metaphysical transition; rather, they were convinced that it was a goal yet to be achieved. It was not something of the past, but something of the future. In order that such a condition might come about, however, it was necessary that society should evolve in that direction. For this reason, the new conservatives, inspired by Darwin and Spencer, opposed the Constitution of 1857 as utopian—that is, outside its proper place in time. Such constitutions could be good only for countries like the United States with the high degree of progress they had achieved, not countries like Mexico, which found themselves at an inferior stage of development. Is it not contrary to common sense, they asked, to raise a great building on unstable ground without first constructing a solid foundation? The first thing to be done was to look to the material development of the country, for liberties are useless in a materially depressed country. When that future development is reached, liberty in its many forms will come about by natural evolution. These men stood for progress by way of evolution, not revolution.

The urgent demand was to strengthen and integrate society. To the degree that society became integrated, homogeneous, it would become more differentiated and defined. To the degree that social order became more permanent, individual liberty would take form. These new conservatists thought that Mexico had been a land without order and, therefore, a land that had not complied with the laws of progress as revealed by Spencer. For this reason it was necessary, before all else, to establish order. It was not possible to go from anarchy to true freedom. The demand for a strong state, which would assume the task of setting up the order so necessary for the progress of Mexico, became natural and justified. Justo Sierra said that it was a natural goal for a people who lived in the most miserable conditions to seek the invigorating force of a center that would serve to augment the power of cohesion. Otherwise, instability would become more pronounced every day, the social organism would not integrate, and the nation would be aborted. It was disorder, Sierra went on, that made the Mexican nation one of the most feeble and most defenseless social organisms in civilization. While Mexico went on destroying itself, there lived alongside it a marvelous collective animal, for whose enormous appetite there seemed not to be enough sustenance, and which was mightily armed and ready to devour Mexico. The Mexican nation was exposed to this colossus as living proof of Darwin's theory, and in the struggle for existence Mexico would find the future dubious at best.

Political evolution, the evolution of liberty, would be sacrificed on the altar of what Sierra called social evolution. In order to arrive at that supposed political liberty, all liberty was to be limited. To uproot the habits of disorder from the minds of Mexicans would be a very difficult task. Only a strong State would be able to bring about such a change. The day a group or political party succeeded as an organized body, political evolution would continue. All political power, and with it the freedom of Mexicans, would be turned over to a strong man, General Porfirio Díaz. Justo Sierra argued that in order for President Porfirio Díaz to complete the great task he had taken on, he needed the greatest concentration of power in his hands–not only the legal authority of the presidency, but political authority over the legislature (which would permit him to effectively direct political groups, the legislature, and state governments) and social authority over the nation. He would establish himself as the supreme judge of peace in Mexican society and, by general assent, the custodian of moral authority. This delegation of power to one man had to be compensated by the State in the field of education: The honorable tyranny was to be a means of educating Mexicans on the meaning of freedom.

On 26 November 1876, General Porfirio Díaz, who had risen up in arms against the government of Sebastián Lerdo de Tejada under the banner of "no reelection," made himself interim president. On December 5 of the same year, he ceded power to General Méndez, but reassumed it, provisionally, on 16 February 1877. On 25 September 1880, with his consent, General Manuel González was elected; however, in 1884 Díaz returned definitively to the presidency, where he was to remain until 25 May 1911, when he was forced out by the Mexican Revolution. All the country's political forces were grouped around General Díaz. He came to symbolize the peace and order for which men brought up on Positivism had clamored so loudly. Materialism was converted into a model for life by the generation that was formed during his regime: industry, money, railroads–and always more money. Progress seemed to triumph definitively. Social evolution seemed to march forward with giant steps. However, in this euphoria, it was forgotten that order had been established at the expense of freedom. Freedom of enrichment was a freedom in which not all classes could participate.

Absence of authentic liberty, Sierra was to protest, had necessarily brought about the denial of everything that had been gained in evolution. A new generation of Mexicans arose with "Porfirism," whose members, in contrast to the preceding Liberal generation, described themselves as scientists: men who studied logic through Mill and Bain, philosophy through Comte and Spencer, and science through Huxley and Tyndall, Virchow and Helmholtz. The new generation considered itself destined, by reason of its education, to guide and direct the nation. Its methods were sure, perfect, and precise: These were the methods of science, which they had learned in the schools reformed by Gabino Barreda. These methods, they said, would be applied to solve all of Mexico's problems, including the political ones. In 1881, they were already speaking in Mexico of the scientific school of politics. In 1886, a number of its members entered the Chamber of Deputies. Some were to become outstanding figures in the regime of Porfirio Díaz: Justo Sierra, Pablo Macedo, Rosendo Pineda, Francisco Bulnes, and others. All of them would put their mark on the period known as *porfirismo*. The era of the "scientists" had begun.

Justo Sierra's plea for a strong State and his readiness to turn over the freedom of the nation to the strong man had been heard many times before in many places. But it is important to note that even during the early Díaz period there was intense dissatisfaction with the dictatorship, and these sentiments were expressed in the novels of these years. Emilio O. Rabasa's (1856–1930) *Novelas Mexicanas* [1887–1888; Mexican Novels]: *La bola* [Disorder], *La gran ciencia* [The Great Science], *Moneda falsa* [Counterfeit Money], and *Cuarto poder* [The Fourth Power], in particular, stress the impassable divide that had separated the rhetoric of the politicians from the needs of the people. In 1892, the political party called Union Liberal issued a manifesto in support of the fourth reelection of Porfirio Díaz. A program intended to further the interests of the ever more powerful Mexican bourgeoisie was formulated. It spoke of analyzing the Mexican social situation, its problems, and their solutions from a scientific point of view. For this reason the opposition and the mass of the people in general, whose political rights had been trodden upon, began to refer to that party as the Party of the Scientists. The manifesto also spoke, among other things, of the necessity of conceding greater liberties to Mexican society, because Mexico seemed to have reached a higher level of progress. It seemed that the promised freedoms were to be granted at last. Recalling the slogans of the old Liberal party, this new union believed that liberty was not possible until a certain level of order had been attained. However, this order seemed to be achieved thanks to the government of Porfirio Díaz. With order established, it would be possible to take a further step in the attainment of liberty.

With this proposed increase of liberties it would become possible to decide whether Mexican society had attained that level of order necessary to gain still greater liberties. The new political party proposed a series of liberties; however, electoral liberty was not to be found among them, because it was considered neither important nor opportune. The people could have other, more important liberties. What was immediately sought was freedom of trade and an economic liberty which would permit the accumulation of capital. What was desired was the reduction of the intervention of the State in economic affairs. Political liberty was betrayed or sacrificed in exchange for the freedom of increasing wealth, a freedom, obviously, that could benefit only those who possessed resources capable of being increased. There was no question of granting the kind of liberty that had been of interest to the older Mexican Liberals.

Political order and economic freedom–such was the ideal of the Mexican bourgeoisie. Political order, maintained by General Díaz, was to be placed in the service of the economic freedom of the bourgeoisie. As far as political rights were concerned, the bourgeoisie would reserve its power to demand them only when an attempt might be made against the freedom of enrichment. Political freedom, the right to elect governors, could be limited for the good of an order that satisfied the interests of the Mexican bourgeoisie, and since the government of General Díaz ensured peace, its reelection was necessary. In this way, the bourgeois order identified itself with national order, and the bourgeois party with the people. With national order achieved, it would be necessary to ensure the liberty that served its interests. Díaz was the man called upon to grant this liberty and to see that it was not obstructed. The authors of the manifesto affirmed that if he were to be reelected for the fourth time, it was not because he was considered indispensable, but rather because in his previous three terms he had proven his ability to govern in accordance with the interests of the nation. In this manner, the bourgeoisie had succeeded in making Porfirio Díaz the honored tyrant who would satisfy its interests. For this reason, it had supported him and would continue to support him so long as he defended their interests.

From the beginning the political strategists of the bourgeoisie had distinguished between what they called personal dictatorship and social dictatorship. The first type of dictatorship was one that served the interests of a determined group or social body, such as the clergy or the military. The second was, simply, the dictatorship established to protect what the bourgeoisie called the interests of society–that is, its own interests. For his part, Porfirio Díaz, a power-oriented man with convictions of the kind that the educators of the bourgeoisie had sought to extirpate, was not satisfied to be a mere instrument of the bourgeoisie. He rejected the limits the bourgeoisie sought to impose on his political power. He was not disposed, consequently, to maintain the order that suited the Mexican bourgeoisie, but rather demanded the total transfer of that power to himself.

Without a doubt Federico Gamboa's (1864–1939) *Santa* (1903) remains the most influential literary work of the entire Porfiriato. As a novel, it creates a narrative world that clearly reflects the social reality of the Mexico of the day. As a sociohistorical document, it is without equal: The social problems of the lower classes, the marginal sectors of Mexico City, as well as the destitute, are all represented in the novel. The shallow rhetoric of the political establishment is created by and ineluctably entwined with the rationalization of absolutism. By the last years of the dictatorship it was evident that things were not going as planned. The proud boasting of a period of peace and order was proved wrong. To maintain appearances, the government had to resort to an increasing suppression of civil liberties and insist that the wealthy elite remain distant from the mass population if they wanted to retain their privileges. When Heriberto Frías (1870–1925) published his novel *Tomóchic* (1895), which dealt with the wanton destruction of an Indian village in northern Mexico, the newspaper *El Demócrata*, which published the novel in installments in 1895, was closed and Frías had to flee for his life.

Justo Sierra, with the brilliant intuition that made him stand out among the members of his generation, understood that this delegation of political liberties to the person of the dictator was dangerous for the future because it imposed habits contrary to those of self-government, without which one may have great men, but not great peoples. And he vowed that at this crossroads of its historical life the Mexican people would not err.

Works Cited

Altamirano, Ignacio Manuel. 1943 [1870]. *La Navidad en las montañas.* Mexico City: Porrúa.

Ancona, Eligio. 1956 [1891]. *La mestiza.* Mérida: Editorial Yucatanense, Club del Libro.

Barreda, Gabino. 1967. "Oración cívica, 1867." *Introducción a la ley orgánica de instrucción pública en el Distrito Federal.* Mexico City: Universidad Nacional Autónoma de México. 83–110.

Cuéllar, José Tomás. 1946 [1871]. *Las jamonas.* Mexico City: Porrúa.

——. 1946 [1871]. *Ensalada de pollos.* Mexico City: Porrúa.

——. 1946 [1872]. *Gabriel el cerrajero o las hijas de mi papá.* Mexico City: Porrúa.

——. 1946 [1886]. *Baile y cochino.* Mexico City: Porrúa.

Delgado, Rafael. 1947 [1893]. *Angelina.* Mexico City: Porrúa.

——. 1931 [1890]. *La calandria.* Mexico City: Ediciones de "La Razón."

Frías, Heriberto. 1960 [1895]. *Tomóchic.* Mexico City: Edinal.

Gamboa, Federico. 1987 [1903]. *Santa.* Mexico City: Grijalbo.

López Portillo y Rojas, José. 1978 [1898]. *La parcela.* Mexico City: Porrúa.

——. 1978 [1909]. *Los precursores.* Guadalajara: Ayuntamiento de Guadalajara.

Mora, José María Luis. 1941. "Pensamientos sueltos sobre educación pública." *Ensayos, ideas, retratos.* Mexico City: Universidad Nacional Autónoma de México. 91–99.

Pizarro Suárez, Nicolás. 1947 [1861]. *El monedero.* Mexico City: Porrúa.

——. 1947 [1861]. *La coqueta.* Mexico City: Porrúa.

Rabasa, Emilio. 1948 [1887]. *La bola.* Mexico City: Porrúa.

——. 1948 [1887]. *La gran ciencia.* Mexico City: Porrúa.

——. 1970 [1888]. *Cuarto poder.* Mexico City: Porrúa.

——. 1970 [1888]. *Moneda falsa.* Mexico City: Porrúa.

Sierra, Justo. 1940 [1910]. *Evolución política del pueblo mexicano.* Mexico City: Fondo de Cultura Económica.

Spencer, Herbert. 1882–1897. *The Principles of Sociology.* 3 vols. New York: D. Appleton.

Zentella, Arcadio. 1946 [1885]. *Perico.* Mexico City: Porrúa.

CHAPTER 24

THE TRANSCULTURAL MIRROR OF SCIENCE

RACE AND SELF-REPRESENTATION IN LATIN AMERICA

Gabriela Nouzeilles

Introduction

Between approximately 1870 and 1940 science was the language authorized to talk about the body. Its authority lay in the presumption that it provided a series of transparent lenses through which one could interpret human variety with certitude. The widespread contemporary conviction that races were cultural artifacts or "floating signifiers" (Hall 52–53) whose definition was in a state of continual flux to a certain extent prevents today's reader from understanding the almost unquestionable status and international prestige that scientific racism enjoyed until the Second World War. One of the few areas in which a critical response managed to take shape was through the intrusion of those who, like African Americans and Jews, were the favored targets of the racial stereotypes created by scientific discourse (Stepan and Gilman 171–72). For similar reasons, Latin American intellectuals also had a problematic relationship to the dominant discourse; as was the case with African Americans and Jews, the underlying geopolitics of racial science also placed them, by definition, outside the field of the production of knowledge. Their exclusion was part of the developmental process of this science, a result of racist assumptions: It was supposed that groups considered inferior were always objects of study and never producers of knowledge. In Latin America the legacy of Positivism is most notable on the issue of social identity where it was dominant until the publication of *Contrapunteo cubano del tabaco y el azúcar* [*Cuban Counterpoint: Tobacco and Sugar*] in 1940 by Fernando Ortiz (1881–1969). If, as Homi Bhabha suggests, in every postcolonial text the problem of identity returns unfailingly as the persistent questioning of the framework of representation (46), the objective of this section is in part to decipher how such a mechanism works, specifically in the discursive terrain of science, as an instrument of self representation within the Latin American periphery.

The success of resistance was always ambiguous. As we shall see, the nature of the scientific discourse itself would make it extremely difficult to formulate an efficacious and coherent questioning of the postulates about racial difference. The institutionalization of modern science and its epistemological principles required that scientific arguments could be refuted only by science itself, which meant that minority groups always found themselves outside and at a disadvantage. This subordinate position was especially disadvantageous if we take into account the fact that science, now converted into the dominant cognitive model of industrial society, was considered neutral, objective, empirical, and above all universal. One of the most disconcerting features was the acceptance–even in resistance–of almost all the negative norms by which scientific racism had defined Latin America. The internalization of this dominant ethnocentric representation generated forms of fragmentation of identity at a community level similar to what Sander Gilman calls classical forms of self-rejection (1986, 1–21).

Ortiz's theory of transculturation represents the apogee of this local critical genealogy and is at the same time an analytical instrument with which its functional logic can be understood. The concept of transculturation–understood as a fluid conceptual flow between center and periphery–articulates the persistence of scientific assumptions of Positivist origin and all those lesser forms of intellectual resistance, specifically with regard to issues of creativity and originality. If we take into account the premises of Latin American Positivism as cultural artifacts (for they are not very different from other symbolic artifacts such as literature), it is possible to conjecture that processes of transculturation took place there similar to those that controlled (according to Ángel Rama) the production of literary fiction in Latin America (33–34). As in literature, there also would have been "pérdidas, selecciones, redescubrimientos e incorporaciones" [losses, selections, rediscoveries, and incorporations] that all would have been resolved within a general restructuring of the dominant system of discourse (39). But in contrast to literature, the Positivist essay would have been subjected to far more severe and rigorous restrictions regarding what it was possible to say and not to say, according to the rules of scientific discourse at the time. For this reason, in the game of alternative representations that Latin American Positivism played in front of the mirror of science, only a reduced number of fractured images ever achieved definition.

Scientific Racism and Self-representation

> Self-hatred results from outsiders' acceptance of the mirage of themselves generated by their reference group–that group in society which they see as defining them–as a reality. (Gilman 2)

> Sealed into that crushing objecthood, I turned beseechingly to others. . . . But just as I reached the other side, I stumbled, and the movements, the attitudes, the glances of the other fixed me there, in the sense in which a chemical solution is fixed by a dye. (Fanon 109)

The formation of national societies in Latin America did not result from the political baptism of the popular classes, as the different national myths of origin insist. Rather it was the *criollo* elites, excluded from the juridical apparatus during the colonial period, who proposed to create cohesive communities through the transformation of the local populations (Anderson 50–51). From the *criollo* perspective, the invention of the nation was seen as an almost impossible challenge. This sense of impossibility was born out of the contradictory demands of modern nationalism. While on one hand, the constitution of the State was based on the acceptance of certain axiomatic values (progress, reason, liberty, industry) as being universally valid, on the other, its political legitimacy would require a common and unique identity that, without contradicting the values of modernity, would distinguish its population from that of other nation-states. This tension between universality and locality would characterize all the Latin American debates on national identity and the role of race within history.

From the margins of nineteenth-century imperial order, modernity seemed to be the natural effect of historical destiny in countries like France and England that lacked an indigenous or black population or that, as was the case of the United States, practiced a brutally segregationist policy. Homogeneity, Arianism, and progress made up the basic triad of the ideal national community. Faced with the apparent incontrovertibility of the racial "fact," in the eyes of local elites the heterogeneity of Latin American populations seemed to be an insurmountable obstacle on the road to progress. From the beginning, the question of the viability of the nation-state and its insertion in the international order would raise the issue of the relationship among the racially and culturally heterogeneous groups that inhabited the new Republics (Wade 10–11). In his famous message delivered at the Angostura Congress of 1819, "the Liberator," Simón Bolívar (1783–1830), would see racial diversity as both the source of Latin American identity and the origin of difficulties for future continental progress:

> Tengamos presente que nuestro Pueblo no es el europeo, ni el Americano del Norte, que más bien es un compuesto de África y de América, que una emanación de Europa; pues que hasta la España misma deja de ser Europea por su sangre africana, por sus Instituciones y su carácter. *Es imposible asignar con propiedad a qué familia humana pertenecemos.* La mayor parte del indígena se ha aniquilado: el Europeo se ha mezclado con el Americano y con el Africano, y éste se ha mezclado con el Indio y con el Europeo. *Nacidos todos de la misma madre, nuestros padres, diferentes en origen y en sangre, son extranjeros, y todos difieren visiblemente en epidermis: esta desemejanza, trae un relato de la mayor trascendencia.*
> (Bolívar 1968, 3:682, énfasis mío)

> We must keep in mind that our people are neither European, nor North American; rather, they are a mixture of African and the American who originated in Europe. Even Spain herself has ceased to be European because of her African blood, her institutions and her character. *It is impossible to determine with any degree of accuracy where we belong in the human family.* The greater portion of the native Indians has been annihilated: Spaniards have mixed with Americans and the Africans and Africans with Indians and Spaniards. *While we have all been born of the same mother, our fathers, different in origin and in blood, are foreigners, and all differ visibly as to the color of their skin: a dissimilarity which places upon us an obligation of the greatest importance.*
> (1951, 1:181, my italics)

Bolívar's observations are symptomatic of later debates on identity and race for two reasons. In the first place, the passage reveals the difficulty faced by intellectuals when they wished to make "America" enter the dominant parameters of classification: America was and was not Europe, was and was not Africa, was and was not Amerindian. In other words, the object "America" ended up being incomprehensible within the registers of Western intelligibility. In the second place, this same classificatory impossibility would lead Bolívar to connect the ambiguity of local identity with the chaotic effects of a series of erotic exchanges between an indigenous woman and an endless number of foreign lovers. The bodily dissimilarity rooted in promiscuity and racial mix (as well as in a perverse arrangement of family relationships) would, from that moment onward, be a crucial issue that would be responsible

for the dilemma of Latin American postcolonial modernity in terms of its relationships with Europe and the United States.

In the second half of the nineteenth century, Positivism, as the philosophy that supposedly made sense of Western progress determining the objective laws of history, would become the toolbox with which Latin American intellectuals would study the apparent ontological disorder of what it meant to be American—with the intention, once the task was completed, of designing and implementing those programs of transformation required to convert the perverse multiracial family described by Bolívar into a stable and productive one. It is not accidental that the process of State centralization would coincide with the progressive hegemony of Positivism in the official culture of the continent. The success and degree of notable influence achieved by Positivist philosophy in Latin America was due not to the intrinsic coherence of the doctrine as much as to its forceful entry on an institutional basis into the State apparatus in the form of classificatory and disciplinary practices (Terán 13–15). This official anchoring would manifest itself above all in the presence of scientists holding positions of responsibility in different State departments and in the creation of teaching and research organizations such as scientific societies, hospitals, museums, and university programs created, for instance, in Argentina under a formal oligarchic republican liberalism (Babini 63–127). Science was one of the agents employed to implement the machinery of State and its rationality. In his "Oración cívica" [Civic Oration] for example, Gabino Barreda (1818–1881) would explicitly adopt the ideals of Comtean Positivism as the political slogan of modern Mexico: "Conciudadanos: que en lo adelante sea nuestra divisa *libertad, orden y progreso*; la libertad como medio; el orden como base y el progreso como fin; triple lema simbolizado en el triple colorido de nuestro hermoso pabellón" (in Zea 1980, 296) ("Fellow citizens: Let our maxim from this time forward be *freedom, order, and progress*; liberty as the medium, order as the base, and progress as the end result; the triple motto symbolized by the triple coloring of our beautiful flag").

The main field of action of this alliance between science and politics on population issues was national society understood as a racial macro-organism within which the body of the citizen was an integral element and on whose physical health depended the stability of the biological system of which it formed a part. The mechanisms of demographic supervision activated by the State, with the aid of science, were oriented toward vigilance and the manipulation of the physical bodies of the citizenry—their health, illness, and sexuality—for the benefit of the common race. It was thus, contradicting the opinion broadly held in political philosophy, that the secularization of politics in modern times was always accompanied by the disembodiment of power (Lefort 17–19), that the legal fiction of the Latin American Positivist State tended to be confused with the biological fiction of the nation as a race.

The proliferation of essays on identity that characterized Latin American Positivism formed part of the struggle for hegemony through which the *criollo* sectors traced the exclusive borders of their national societies in racial terms. Given that the definition of corporal difference came from European science, its meaning varied according to how the *criollos* positioned themselves in terms of the problem of identity. As the strategy for the self-legitimation of the elite, positivist essays were almost always re-expressions of colonial forms of discrimination, though now translated into the language of science, within which the subordinate classes were re-categorized as biologically inferior beings, or intellectual minors whose supervision ought to remain the responsibility of those who were considered to be closer to the European racial ideal: The *criollos*. But when attempting to define the national community as a whole, in opposition to the metropolitan societies, the Positivist essays were above all conflict-ridden manifestations of self-rejection, accepting inferiority in forms of self-representation that incorporated the stereotypes fabricated by a dominant European scientific perspective.

From the Renaissance, the development of the idea of Europe had meant the creation of other negatives, in opposition to which Europeans defined themselves, using the features of a superior collective identity that justified the expansion and violence of the Imperial enterprise over the globe (see Said; Young 1–12). In the eighteenth century, science became the principal instrument with which Europe began to construct its others. The result of that intervention was the biological reification of difference and the articulation of racial hierarchies. Only by viewing the racialized body of the other could Europe think of itself as racially superior and consequently as the universal standard of a bodiless rationality. This radical opposition would remain set within a historiographical model, systematized in the nineteenth century by social Darwinism, according to which universal history consisted in the indefinite evolution of humanity toward more perfect forms within a process ruled by interracial war and the predominance of the rational superior: Europe. The *de facto* domination of European empires over extensive zones of the planet would in this way remain naturalized as a historical necessity.

From this geopolitical imaginary emerged two negative stereotypes of Latin America. According to the first, the predominance of inferior races had debilitated the potential of the new postcolonial states. Countries like Peru, Mexico, and Bolivia, in theory, suffered the disastrous consequences of an indigenous majority incapable of being educated as well as being resistant to the demands of progress; meanwhile, the incorporation of large numbers of Africans on Caribbean and Brazilian plantations had further worsened the already deteriorating racial economy of the ex colonies. According to some, the Spanish legacy of the process of colonization had also been pernicious. The English Darwinist, Francis Galton (1822–1911), stated that the Spaniards represented the most degraded stage of the European races, owing to their prolonged contact with the Orient and Africa and the irrationalism provoked by their religious fanaticism (343–45). He added to this somber diagnosis accusations of the degenerative effects caused by the extended *mestizaje* among Amerindians, blacks, and Spaniards. The most durable image of Latin American mestizos and mulattos was captured in 1879 by the famous Swiss naturalist Louis Agassiz (1807–1873), who described them as hybrids and unstable individuals who, when they were not sterile, took on the majority of the negative features of the most primitive races. The combination was even more negative when involving the indigenous races: "The hybrid between White and Indian, called Mammeluco in Brazil, is pallid, effeminate, feeble, lazy, and rather obstinate. . . . It is very remarkable how . . . the Indian impresses his mark more deeply upon his progeny than the other races, and how readily, also, in further crossings, pure Indian characteristics are reclaimed and those of the other races are thrown off," stated the Swiss polygenist (1868, 532).

The idea of the return to a more primitive stage would reappear later under different guises, always returning in one way or another to the same paranoid fantasy: The primitive body of the primordial other, imprisoned in the body of the racial hybrid.

The second Latin American stereotype is related to the reactivation of the classical theory of geographical determinism. Since the publication in 1761 of Volume IX of Buffon's (1707–1788) *Histoire naturelle, générale et particulière* [Natural History, General and Particular], the theory had gained acceptance that nature in America was inferior to that of Europe; the excessive heat and humidity of the former produced biological species reduced in size and lacking in vitality. Contact with this geographical zone, generator of monsters, negatively affected Europeans who, once exposed to its influence, degenerated irreversibly (Gerbi 3–34). A geographical hierarchy thus corresponded to the hierarchy of bodies; the two stereotypes were complementary. According to science, it was because of the racial inferiority of the native population and the negative influence of the local natural environment that the Latin American nations were at a distinct disadvantage in their efforts to participate in social, economic, and political progress.

The inclusion of these classic stereotypes of Latin America into Positivist reflections on Latin American identity was associated from the very beginning with the rhetoric of failure. Toward the end of the century, after varying decades of political independence, the stability of Latin American States was still threatened by the frail character of their public institutions and the continuous difficulties that slowed down modernization. In contrast, the United States had a booming economy and a strong democracy, at the same time as it increasingly presented itself as a new Imperialist threat to the rest of the continent. What were the causes of this difference in the two postcolonial models? Latin American Positivists would seek the answer to this question in the racial analysis of the population (Graham 1–2), and such an emphasis would provoke a radicalization of previous tendencies. The essays of Domingo F. Sarmiento (1811–1888) represent one of the clearest cases of this. In *Facundo* (1845), he had explained the internecine Argentine and Latin American wars as a struggle between civilization and barbarism or between the modernizing city and backward rural areas. If this opposition was founded on the ethnocentric axiology that identified civilization with Europe to the disadvantage of the local American situation, Sarmiento's causal system actually placed emphasis more on the effect of institutions on local customs than on biological determinism. In 1883, Sarmiento rewrote *Facundo* as *Conflicto y armonías de las razas en América* [Conflict and Harmony of Races in America], re-employing the formula of civilization and barbarism in a Darwinist version of history that explained the persistence of institutional chaos and the fragility of the hegemonic pact in South America caused by racial conflict (1946, 10–19). The epistemological anxiety with which Sarmiento opens the first chapter of his second essay underlines his discomfort as much as his desire to reformulate the question of identity strictly in corporeal terms:

Es acaso ésta la primera vez que vamos a preguntarnos quiénes éramos cuando nos llamaron americanos, y quiénes somos cuando argentinos nos llamamos.
Somos europeos?–¡Tantas caras cobrizas nos desmienten!
Somos indígenas?–Sonrisas de desdén de nuestras blondas damas nos dan acaso la única respuesta.
Mixtos?–Nadie quiere serlo, y hay millares que ni americanos ni argentinos querrían ser llamados.

Somos Nación?–Nación sin amalgama de materiales acumulados, sin ajuste ni cimiento.
Argentinos?–Hasta dónde y desde cuándo, bueno es darse cuenta de ello. (1946, 27)

Is this the first time that we ask ourselves who we were when we called ourselves Americans, and who we are when we call ourselves Argentines.
Are we Europeans?–So many copper-colored faces prove this to be untrue!
Are we indigenous?–Smiles of disdain from our blonde ladies perhaps provide us with the only response.
Mixed blood?–No one wishes to be so, and there are millions that do not wish to be called either Americans or Argentines!
Are we a nation?–A nation without an amalgam of accumulated goods, without organization or foundation.
Argentines?–It is worthwhile knowing to what extent and from when this is so.

Sarmiento's confusion to some extent reflects Bolívar's when, in 1819, he tried to imagine the demographic bases of the new Republics. Sarmiento's confusion stems from the incapacity to differentiate because he cannot see beyond the surfaces of the body.

The Positivist question of identity was basically an interrogation of the racial body placed in front of the mirror of science, whose reflective superficiality would eventually create precise images of the marginal subject. To be able to "see," the Latin American intellectual accepted the lens that Europe offered as efficacious and objective. This seeing oneself through different eyes was expressed in certain scientific fictions as a scene of apprenticeship in which a European savant–generally Darwin–presented the principles of scientific analysis to Latin American intellectuals and/or scientists. The story "Viaje a través de la estirpe" [1903; "Voyage through Race"] by the Argentine sociologist Carlos Octavio Bunge (1875–1918) is paradigmatic in this sense. Just as Virgil in *The Divine Comedy* explains to Dante the sense and order that organizes the world, Darwin in Bunge's fiction accompanies the protagonist on a voyage back in time during which the micro-stages of natural evolution come to life before his inexpert eyes and finally explain the racial composition of Argentina. This all-encompassing vision of science possessed the virtues of divine omniscience. Thus Sarmiento compares the Darwinist perspective with the point of view achieved by Moses when, according to the Bible, God allowed him to see six different stages of creation as if through a kaleidoscope (1946, 14). In the social sphere, the mediating function of the sage was manifested in the act of contracting of foreign scientists, the majority of European provenance (Babini 83–91).

The Positivist discourse of identity consisted above all of an uninterrupted succession of attempts at classifying society in accordance with the principles of the intelligibility of scientific racism; there were obsessive exercises whereby the fervent disciples of reason would try to make sense of the biological chaos they believed they were confronting. The racial catalogues included in the majority of the Latin American Positivist essays are textual effects of that meticulous translation of the real according to the purported order of scientific reason. Apart from Sarmiento's *Conflicto y armonías*, there was *Nuestra América* [1903; Our America] by the Argentine Carlos O. Bunge, *Sociología argentina* [1910; Argentine Sociology] by José Ingenieros (1877–1925), *El hombre y la historia (Ensayo de sociología venezolana)* [1891; Man and History: An Essay in

Venezuelan Sociology] by José Gil Fortoul (1861–1943), *Pueblo enfermo* [1909; Sick Nation] by the Bolivian Alcides Arguedas (1879–1946), *Hampa Afro-Cubana: los negros brujos* [1906: Afro-Cuban Underworld: The Black Witches] by Fernando Ortiz, *Cuba y su evolución colonial* [1907; Cuba and Its Colonial Evolution] by Francisco Figueras (1853–1909), *Los grandes problemas nacionales* [1909; Great National Problems] by the Mexican Andrés Molina Enríquez (1866–1940) and *El porvenir de las naciones latino-americanas* [1899; The Future of Latin American Nations] by another Mexican, Francisco Bulnes (1847–1924). Along with other examples, these all responded to a greater or lesser degree to this imperative.

Within the accepted epistemological framework, each race occupied a place in the chain of being. This *scala naturae*, an Aristotelian notion taken up again by Positivism, organized humanity according to a hierarchical pyramid which began with the white Europeans at the top and descended to the negroes and Amerindians, who were inevitably found on the bottom rung of the ladder of the species, scarcely differentiated from certain animal species such as the monkey (Stepan 1982, 6–7). Of the numerous systems of racial classification that circulated during this period which claimed a total number of races oscillating between three and thirty-four varieties, the categorization proposed by Linnaeus (1707–1778) of four groups (whites, Asiatics, negroes, and Amerindians) would predominate. The identification of each race would always be accompanied by a detailed description of their physical and psychological features, inspired by binaries derived from the basic opposition between nature and culture, the all-encompassing framework that gave meaning to racial hierarchy.

Even though the classificatory fiction was always the same, the emphasis varied according to the region involved. Each historico-cultural zone would produce its own phantasm of otherness in relation to the idea of nationhood. Thus, while the silent shadow of the indigenous individual preoccupied Andean and Mexican intellectuals, in the Caribbean the terrifying figure of the black would return again and again as a problem for Cuban and Puerto Rican thinkers. The obsession with this blind spot would produce a meticulous and contradictory iconography of difference, repeated in images of a body (simultaneously obvious and devious) on which were superimposed the masks of sickness and criminality. *Pueblo enfermo* (1909) by the Bolivian Alcides Arguedas and *Hampa Afro-Cubana* by the Cuban Fernando Ortiz were good examples of these variants. Of the four races that made up the Bolivian population (the white or the *criollo*, the *mestizo*, the Indian, and the black), according to Alcides Arguedas, the Indian was the origin of the sickness that attacked the national community as a whole, because of their numbers and ancestral influence. It was the predominance of indigenous blood that had prevented Bolivia from consciously directing her destiny and at least achieving the level of development of those Latin American countries without an indigenous majority, like Argentina and Chile. There seemed to be no way out. According to Arguedas, race and geography blocked every possibility of redemption. The situation was particularly alarming in the inter-Andean region where "vegeta[ba] desde tiempo inmemorial, el indio aymara, salvaje y huraño como bestia de bosque, entregado a sus ritos gentiles y al cultivo de ese suelo estéril en que ... concluir[ía] pronto su raza" (45) ("the Aymara Indian vegetated from time immemorial, savage and taciturn like a jungle beast, given to his heathen rituals and the cultivation of this sterile earth in which ... his race will soon end"). The iconography of racial inferiority displayed in this text focuses above all on the physique and impassivity of the face in which ancestral barbarism is said to be revealed. The pronounced coppery tone of the flesh, the rough and long locks of hair, and the aloof expression created a general effect diagnosed by Arguedas as pure absence. Trapped in the prison of a degraded and indolent body, the indigenous individual lacked the means, intelligence, and sensibility to facilitate any change.

In *Hampa Afro-Cubana,* Ortiz also would appeal to racial classifications to establish the particular status of the black race with respect to State law. Once again, it was an attempt to impose limits on a perceived danger. Of the four races populating Cuba (white [Spanish and *criollo*], Asiatic, blacks, and the indigenous), the blacks had most affected the national sociability, especially through their criminal influence, he argued, while white felons were biological exceptions, people who adopted a villainous life as a result of regressive anthropological factors that clouded their judgment or social deprivation that made them into casual lawbreakers; Afro-Cuban criminality was absolute. According to Ortiz, in Cuba the entire black race participated directly or indirectly in a criminal lifestyle, an aberration caused by the fact that they were so primitive, they had not yet acquired a sense of moral law. The black, as a type, had a primitive psyche that was evident in cultural and religious practices that were not only antisocial but also criminal (37). Not even the extreme discipline of slavery had been able to rescue them from every aspect of their savage condition (27). Even though, in contrast to Arguedas, Ortiz denied the existence of physical features that acted as indicators of racial inferiority, *Hampa Afro-Cubana* also presents an iconography of difference. But instead of the paradigmatic passivity of the indigenous population emphasized by Arguedas, Ortiz saw the primitive irrationalism of Afro-Cubans as being revealed in the convulsive gestures and movements of dance (360).

Together with this classical categorization of races that indicated internal diversity, the distinction most commonly used on an international basis was that established between Anglo-Saxons and Latins: This was popularized by, among others, the English historian Henry Thomas Buckle (1821–1862) in his voluminous *History of Civilization in England* [1857–1861]. Originally these terms, Anglo-Saxon and Latin, were just labels to refer to two linguistic branches, but by the second half of the nineteenth century they came to represent a racial code for the political and economic antagonism between northern and southern Europe. In Latin America, the north-south opposition was focused largely on the antagonism between the United States and Latin America. This alternative method of visualizing the geopolitical order complicated, without replacing, the America-European axis. The north-south difference grew out of the thesis of geographical determination applied to the American continent at the end of the eighteenth century, according to which temperature influenced physical and moral aspects of race. According to this argument the superiority of the Anglo-Saxons on both continents was due to the fact that they inhabited cold or temperate zones while the Latins suffered the pernicious effects of climate in the torrid zones. In the hierarchy of progress, the Anglo-Saxons stood out on account of their higher grade of intelligence, morality, and efficiency in contrast with the Latins who, subject to the primacy of the body and the passions, were closer to those races traditionally considered inferior on the racial scale. Faced with the supposed evidence of this vision of the world, all other hypotheses about humanity were rejected for one reason or another. In fact, as the Venezuelan-born José Gil Fortoul wrote:

> aun suponiendo con Locke que el hombre ha sido el mismo, en cuanto a dotes naturales, en todos los tiempos, o con Turgot, que las capacidades primitivas obran de un modo idéntico en los pueblos salvajes y en los civilizados . . . , la historia universal demuestra que los diversos grupos de pueblos se civilizan de modos muy diferentes, y que la evolución social no sigue en todos ellos la misma trayectoria ni se verifica con igual rapidez. (28–29)

> even supposing, with Locke, that man has always been the same in terms of natural gifts or, with Turgot, that primitive capacities work in an identical way in savage and civilized people . . . , universal history demonstrates that diverse groups of people become civilized in very different ways and that social evolution does not follow the same trajectory in all of them, nor can it be verified with equal rapidity.

Following the social theories of Herbert Spencer (1820–1903), the complete history of Latin America–from colony to the creation of the national State–was considered to be the result of racial war in all its forms. In each case, the Darwinist explanation of historical change justified the status quo. For Gil Fortoul the racial struggle explained both the inevitability of Spanish dominance over the Amerindians during the Conquest and the progressive disappearance of the tribes that still inhabited Venezuela (37–38). Bunge would argue that after Independence the civil confrontations that had devastated the new Republics, dividing their populations into enemy factions, had been the result of the successive metamorphoses of racial war during the process of developing the nation-state (156–60). Racial conflict was also used to explain the dependent position of Latin American postcolonial countries within the global order of modernity. According to Sarmiento, the territorial losses suffered by countries such as Mexico and Argentina were caused by the same problems:

> El conflicto de las razas en México le hizo perder a California, Tejas, Nuevo México, Los Pueblos, Arizona, Nevada, Colorado, Idaho, que son ahora Estados florecientes de los Estados Unidos. . . . Nosotros hemos perdido ya como Mexico, por conflicto de raza, la Banda Oriental y el Paraguay por alzamientos guaraníes, el Alto Perú por la servidumbre de los quichuas, y perderemos nuestra Alsacia y nuestra Lorena codiciadas de extraños por las demasías de poder como la Francia. (1946, 19)

> The racial conflict in Mexico caused the latter to lose California, Texas, New Mexico, the Pueblos, Arizona, Nevada, Colorado and Idaho, all now flourishing States within the United States . . . . We have now lost, like Mexico, on account of racial conflict, the Banda Oriental (present-day Uruguay) and Paraguay as a result of Guaraní uprisings, Upper Peru because of the submissiveness of the Quechuas, and we will lose our Alsace and our Lorraine, so coveted by foreigners made audacious by power in the same way France lost her eastern region.

While international politics was another of the infinite complications in the struggle for survival, racial conflicts that internally weakened the new societies had left them at the mercy of stronger nations such as the United States or England, whose territorial ambitions were a direct expression of their racial aggression.

But the most noxious form of biological warfare that worried Latin American Positivists was not so much the one occurring between clearly different groups, but the one that had been incarnated in those physical bodies where, through the processes of *mestizaje,* had come together every race on the continent. Faced with the impure heterogeneity of the mestizo, the list of examples of race types and their characteristics functioned more as an entelechy than as an effective description. The infinite mixes within bodies escaped representation as much as they did the control of the gaze. In this zone of the unknown and unclassifiable, this "gray area" to which Fernando Ortiz refers in *Hampa Afro-Cubana* (35), lived the contradictory beings, created by *mestizaje,* whose unstable nature held the key to the resistance to progress. The concern about *mestizaje* did not cancel the racism directed against the blacks and indigenous peoples, but rather prolonged and intensified it. The terror provoked by racial mixing was born out of the terrifying fantasy of the white stigmatized by the phantasm of the other race. Sameness and difference were confounded in the hybrid, producing a "scandal that was both ontological and biological at the same time" (Poliakov 179). As with the definition of uncleanness (Douglas 35–36), the notion of *mestizaje* supposed two conceptual conditions: the acceptance of a previous world order (the hierarchical scale of being) and the interruption of that order.

Given that there were no single categories that included the phenomenon of racial hybridization, Positivism called on two analogies that allowed the imprecision of the *mestizo* body to be fixed through its visualization. In the first analogy, *mestizaje* remained associated with the idea of the plague. To cross the acceptable limits of race was similar to contamination; that is, it was the same as the body being invaded by a foreign organism, against which the body has to fight for its survival. The persistence of racial conflict in the secret ambit of physiology created additional pathology through inheritance. In the analogical series that connected the idea of *mestizaje* with disease, the hybrid also evoked the instability of madness. Reason, incarnated in the white race, was lost in the *mestizo* body, as it was lost in the extreme destabilization of the madman. Inspired perhaps by *Las neurosis de los hombres célebres en la historia argentina* [1878; Neurosis of Famous Men] in which Doctor Ramos Mejía (1849–1914) had characterized madmen as contradictory beings who participated in two diametrically opposed races (92–93), Bunge declared psychological disharmony as being one of the defining features of the racial *mestizo* (131–32*).* Arguedas, following Bunge, would describe the emotional imbalance of Latin American *mestizos* as an explosive amalgam: "Del abrazo fecundante de la raza blanca, dominadora de los indios, y de los indios, la raza dominada, nace la mestiza, trayendo por herencia los rasgos característicos de ambas, pero mezclados en una amalgama estupenda a veces, porque determina contradicciones en ese carácter que de pronto se hace difícil de explicar" (81) ("From the fecund embrace of the white race, who had dominion over the Indians, and these Indians, the dominated race, the *mestizo* race was born, having as its legacy the characteristic features of both, but mixed in an occasionally marvelous amalgam, since certain contradictions exist in this character that suddenly make it difficult to explain"). From such contradictions supposedly emerged passions that were an obstacle to the exercise of the public freedoms of bourgeoisie democracy and impeded the consolidation of a lasting hegemonic pact in countries such as Bolivia.

The second analogy related *mestizaje* to women. The mulatto, as Bunge would also say, was "irritable y veleidoso como una mujer, y como mujer, como degenerado, como el demonio mismo, fuerte de grado y débil por fuerza" (140) ("irritable and capricious like a woman, and like a woman, as degenerate as the devil himself, strong willed and weak in physical strength"). In the racist scientific discourse of the nineteenth century and, because of it, in general discourse, the female shared with the *mestizo* or mulatto the fact of being perceived as a divided being who was sickly and in conflict with herself, and thus could not adjust to the universal definition of man, the model of the normality of the body (Stepan 1993, 361). This gendering of *mestizaje* also responded to the taboo of miscegenation. The superimposition of the two concepts alluded to the fact that occasionally the racial hybrid could be simultaneously a pathological monster and an erotic object that incited desire. In the Caribbean the figure of the attractive mulatto female synthesized this double orientation of representation. The Cuban writer Francisco Figueras would note with alarm that her physical charms, her voluptuousness, and her sexual talents were deceptive attractions that disguised the true nature of her morally corrupting body (242)–a trap in which the racial vigor of the *criollos* could be lost forever.

The basic features shared by mestizos, the infirm, and women involved biological phenomena in which the autonomy of the subject was negated, because they could cross the insulating borders of the body. Seen as a border where the inside always threatens to change into an outside, the surface of the skin was a seam that scarcely hid the precariousness of the subjectivity that lay beneath. The violation of corporeal borders unleashed a war whose armies were composed of every kind of bloodline. In narrative terms *mestizaje* implied the slow development of an abnormal macro-organism whose existence threatened the very structures of Western knowledge (nature-culture, feminine-masculine, human-animal, etc.). To the extent that the issue was grounded in racial antagonisms, its historical destiny depended on the result of the conflicts and harmonies of the races to which Sarmiento referred in the title of his last essay. Based on the pessimist prognosis of theorists like Gobineau and Agassiz, the narrative mode of this corporeal narrative was ruled by a dynamic that could be called "gothic," in the sense that it was impelled by a fear of the monstrous. In the context of scientific racism, the implication of the gothic was that all sexual contact that ignored the racial hierarchy of the chain of being produced infinite pathological deformations that led to progressive weakening and indeed to the disappearance of the peripheral nation.

The transformations produced by *mestizaje* corresponded to an inverted version of the Spencerian idea of history as progress. If the proper history of humanity distanced people from nature and moved them toward more perfect and rational manifestations, the regressive history of *mestizaje* moved them toward the most grotesque manifestations of the body. The deformed monster, in whom sooner or later all interracial exchange was to culminate, held in its image of physical corruption the internal social contradiction that could not be resolved. The gothic culmination predicted the annihilation of the hybrid in the hereditary impossibility of the monster. The repetition of interracial contact, in Bunge's opinion, created the possibility of the eventual disappearance of the entire national population:

> La hibridez en sí no se mantiene, no queda nunca como el pícaro de Quevedo . . . porque si queda, con continuos cruces entre mestizos semejantes, degenera, y degenera hasta producir lo que los psiquiatras llaman *la disolución de la especie por degeneración,* ó sea hasta engendrar tipos tan degenerados que resultan mediocres y aún nulamente aptos para la generación. (134, énfasis mío)

Hybridism does not maintain itself, it does not remain like Quevedo's rogue . . . since if it does stay, with continuous breeding with similar *mestizos*, it degenerates and degenerates until it produces what the psychiatrists call *the dissolution of the species through degeneration*, until it creates types so degenerate that it results in mediocrity and even an inability to procreate. (my italics)

The narrative logic of the Naturalist Latin American novel best displays the implications of the gothic narrativization of *mestizaje*. Appropriating the concepts and arguments of scientific racial discourse, Naturalism developed the paranoid phantasms of racial mixture as an experimental field for the literary imagination, taking them to the limit of representation (see Nouzeilles 1997). Novels such as *Sin rumbo* [1885; Without Direction] by the Argentinean Eugenio Cambaceres (1843–1890), *Libro extraño* [1894–1904; Strange Book] by Francisco Sicardi (1856–1927), another Argentine, and *La charca* [1893; Charca] by the Puerto Rican Manuel Zeno Gandía (1855–1930), are examples in which the sexual contact between incompatible races unleashes a pathological chain that potentially threatens the future of society as a whole. In each case, the example culminates with the apparition of the monstrous being whose detailed representation at the end of the novel forms a terrifying warning aimed at those *criollos* unconcerned with the consequences of a wrongly invested libido. But the success of the detective operation is always subject to doubt, for how is one to separate the other from what now forms a single entity? In the play of images activated by Positivist novels and essays, the monster destabilizes the objectivity of the narrative gaze, creating the suspicion that the detector of differences, the Realist narrator—or racist scientist on the periphery—would also prove to be contaminated by such a mixture. The image of the decaying cesspool without clearly defined limits that reproduces indefinite and indiscriminate degeneration was coined by Zeno Gandía to describe the population of Puerto Rico, constituting thereby perhaps the most complete image of the omnivorous and multiracial monster so feared by the Positivists (see Nouzeilles 1998).

The fictions of identity created by Latin American Positivism and its derivations were largely contradictory manifestations of self-rejection. Inside the game of perspectives created by self-rejection, subalterns perceive themselves from two simultaneous perspectives, their own and that of the cultural oppressor. This double perspective characterized the functioning of self perception in different types of subaltern groups. According to John Berger, this is the way women are viewed in a patriarchal system, in which the masculine gaze determines not only the hierarchical relationship between men and women but also that of women among themselves. The structure is simple: "men look at women. Women watch themselves being looked at" (47). The quotation from Fanon that introduces this section also refers to the effect of the rebounding of the gaze within a relationship of oppression, a reference to the racializing effect of the colonial gaze and how this affects the self-representation of the colonized. The perception of the self from the viewpoint of the European gaze internally divided subalterns and converted them into objects of themselves. A similar structure characterized the mechanisms of self-representation that the subaltern Latin American intellectuals activated when they defined themselves and the cultural community to which they belonged with the tools of racist scientific representation. As in the examples of Berger

and Fanon, the Positivist reflection on identity was also subject to specular relationships in which subjects as observers saw themselves reflected in the pupil of a foreign eye. The Europeans looked at the Latin Americans and the Latin Americans observed themselves as the object of looking. This schema began to duplicate itself inside Latin America, as well, when the rejected members of the local elite observed themselves from the dominant perspective of the *criollos*.

There were no apparent fissures on the surface of this mirror. The power of racist science in the language of representation remained unquestionable. The hierarchy of races, the condemnation (or ambivalence) provoked by *mestizaje*, the sexist analogue that linked women to primitive peoples, and the social Darwinist version of history as universal progress incarnated in the West—all of these premises of scientific racism would remain expressed in the Positivist formulations of local identity and their relationship with the social body. In certain cases, imitation of the hegemonic discourse attained such high levels that the authoritative reference would succeed in wiping out the particular perspective of the Latin American intellectual originally responsible for writing it. In his condemnation of *mestizaje* in *Conflicto y armonías*, for example, Sarmiento incorporated entire pages of the racist writings on Latin America by Prescott, Wilson, and Agassiz without any mediating commentary between his voice and that of the authorizing racist scientific material:

> Ahora oigamos al sabio Agassiz sobre el carácter moral de esas razas. Si alguna duda del mal de esta mezcla de razas, que venga al Brasil, donde el deterioro consecuente a la amalgamación, más esparcida aquí que en ninguna otra parte del mundo, va borrando las mejores cualidades del hombre blanco, dejando un tipo bastardo sin fisonomía, deficiente de energía física y elemental. (1946, 72)
>
> Now let us hear the erudite Agassiz on the moral character of these races. If anyone doubts the evil of this racial mix, let him come to Brazil, where the deterioration consequent on the amalgamation, more disseminated here than in any other part of the world, continually erases the best qualities of the white man, leaving a kind of bastard without physiognomy, lacking in physical and elemental energy.

The authority of the scientific perspective on the body functioned here as a sacred text with which one rediscovered the world of experience. The way in which Sarmiento introduces the quotation from Agassiz reveals the total subservience of the Latin American Positivist discourse to the epistemological models of the metropolis. It is thus very difficult to trace and prove the existence of transcultural processes in the local Latin American scientific versions. Originality and dissent were only valid within the rules of scientific discourse and its assumptions. Even so, despite general submission to the conceptual schema of scientific racism, Latin American Positivism did produce specific minor modalities of intellectual resistance that, without questioning the actual principals of racist science, reoriented and cannibalized some of its central hypotheses. The transcultural processes that interwove with the local versions of Positivism were to be found in these areas of significant negotiation.

Utopia, *Mestizaje*, and Intellectual Resistance

> Each [Latin American] historian, each period's social thinkers . . . have revealed their relation to the central question of national identity by how they have dealt not just with the "Indians" but especially with the hybrids. (Klor de Alva 244)

"Ser como otros, para poder dejar de ser lo que se había sido y se era" ("To be like others, to be able to leave off being what one has been and one was"), according to Leopoldo Zea, was the fundamental political and cultural problem of Latin Americans in the nineteenth century (xii). But even if, when reflected in the mirror of European science, Latin Americans perceived themselves as pallid, sick, degenerate, and destined to serve Prospero to the end of their days, they did not abandon the search for remedies that might vitalize their physiology. Thus texts such as Alcides Arguedas's *Pueblo enfermo* (1909), *El continente enfermo* [1899; Sick Continent] by the Venezuelan César Zumeta (1860–1955) and *Enfermedades sociales* [1905; Social Illnesses] by the Argentinean Manuel Ugarte (1878–1951) did not stop at including a diagnostic of Latin American pathologies in the style of a medical text, but also provided didactic instructions for the changing of the inhabitants into something else (Stabb 1967, 24–50). The projects for change were reduced to two possible forms of intervention in physical terms: one biopolitical, in terms of population, implemented through regulatory mechanisms over life in general and sexuality in particular, and the other, an anatomical policy based on the disciplining of the individual.

The first solution for achieving not only a cohesive but also a racially capable community consisted in promoting further miscegenation. According to some, the European programs of massive immigration offered an infallible recipe for radically transforming the local population, strengthening their capacity for participating in the struggle for survival and accelerating their assimilation into the white race. Even though this philosophy was prevalent throughout Argentina, such a project would also attract Positivist intellectuals from other countries, as is clear in the works of Alcides Arguedas (342), Gil Fortoul (186–87) and Prado (205). Another way of inducing beneficent forms of intermixing was the promotion of further *mestizaje* between the racial elements already present in the population. This would be the model that would predominate in Mexico during the (1876–1910) dictatorship of Porfirio Díaz. The fundamental difference between these two solutions was in the image they offered of the utopian body of the nation. While the first case was an attempt to lighten this body in an approximation of an increasingly white body, the biological ideal in the second case was based on the idea of the new social body as the racial hybrid.

Whatever the type of miscegenation, it was commonly agreed that its beneficent effects should be reinforced by state programs of compulsive education which, like orthopedic instruments, would remove deformities from the body politic by reducing the passions of the body to the dictates of modern reason. The school, the gymnasium, rows of children, in single file and marching to a rhythmic pattern would all diminish the convulsions of primitive impulses, while work would discipline the body for the good of progress (Sarmiento 1913, 378). To sum up, the school would be a factory of modern citizens that collaborated with the leveling of society and the creation of a national community in which all could recognize themselves. For these proposals to be viable within the schema of Positivist racism, it was necessary to question and readjust some of its basic assumptions. Within the narrow margin of epistemological negotiation that science left them, Latin American Positivists had to maneuver feverishly to mount a convincing alternative argument.

Two basic strategies were used to resist the negative ideas of Latin American societies constructed by scientific racism.

The first would call for the recontextualization of scientific facts and the elaboration of a scientific counter-discourse that argued from an "objective" questioning of the interpretation of facts. To relativize the accepted truth, the Positivists had to demonstrate the universal character of negative features attributed to a racial group, proving that they were also manifested in others. The second operation, complementary to the first, consisted in inverting the binary oppositions in which the stereotype of the racial *mestizo* was based. Even though more radical, this second strategy had the disadvantage that the shift of meanings still maintained the reifying marks of the original stereotype without making way for variation.

The querying of the interpretation of the facts was a recurrent strategy in Positivist essays. The deconstruction of a racial stereotype through the universalization of one or various of its negative features was a method used by Gil Fortoul, for example, when he observed that the immorality that French social scientists such as Le Bon (1841–1931) attributed to the South American mestizo societies also corroded the moral bases of metropolitan institutions:

> Aún admitiendo como sería la hipótesis gratuita (y anticientífica, puesto que el autor [Le Bon] no la basa en ningún estudio de etnografía comparada) de que la moralidad de las repúblicas sudamericanas sea infinitamente inferior a la de la república norteamericana y a la de los Estados europeos, la historia contemporánea demuestra que ciertos hechos de inmoralidad y política no son estigma especial de una sola raza. (52–53)
>
> Even taking seriously the gratuitous hypothesis (and anti-scientific, given that the author [Le Bon] did not base it on any comparative ethnographic work) that the morality of the South American Republics was infinitely inferior to that of North America and the European States, contemporary history shows that certain acts of social and political immorality are not the stigma of one race alone.

In this argument the subaltern scientist (Gil Fortoul) accuses his superior (Le Bon) of being anti-scientific, first for not rigorously following the methodology indicated for ethnographic research, and then for not correctly interpreting the facts. The neutrality attributed to science could be used to the benefit of the Latin American Positivists who sought to triumph using the same conceptual weapons that condemned them.

The theory of the innate inferiority of the Amerindians, widely accepted in Europe, was another of the preferred targets of Latin American Positivists. Given that many of the premises of racism continued to be accepted, this kind of refutation was always partial. So, while the pre-Columbian civilizations prior to the Conquest were vindicated, implying that in that period the indigenous races were as strong and healthy as the white population, this argument was always made to the detriment of the surviving Amerindian populations. This rejection did not contradict the celebratory recovery of the past. While the apparent degeneration of the contemporary indigenous people justified the prejudices of *criollo* racism, the superiority of the original tribes permitted a claim for the previous existence of racially stronger groups that could be assimilated into the rhetoric of the glorious national past. Alcides Arguedas, for example, also conceded that the backwardness of the indigenous tribes of Bolivia was more the effect of exploitation than an innate condition of its racial origin, even though he would still agree with the general opinion that they were now in all respects biologically inferior. As a means of justifying the contrast between past and present, Gil Fortoul attributed the decadence of the Amerindian communities that still inhabited Venezuela to the fact that only the more passive tribes, with less strength for fighting the *criollos*, would have survived the colonial wars (38). Apart from the symbolism of the gesture, an additional advantage of the distinction (by degree) between the two types of Amerindians was the possibility of suggesting the persistence of positive racial elements that, dormant in the genetic pool, could be reactivated through education, hygiene, or miscegenation with more capable branches of the racial tree. Mexican Indigenism in the 1930s would call on this argument frequently (see Knight 92–94).

These two strategies of resistance adopted to rebut the dominant racist scientific discourse were principally applied to the relativization of the thesis that affirmed that racial mixture, once a primitive race was involved, inevitably meant that the resultant progeny were subject to irreversible regression and the predominance of inferior features. On the contrary, it was pointed out, the mix could function as a means to improve and strengthen the population. It is worth repeating that the debate was concentrated only on certain aspects of the argument of scientific racism, leaving others intact. The supposedly degenerate condition of the popular classes and the existence of superior and inferior races were very rarely matters open to discussion. On the contrary, a parallel hierarchy of types of *mestizaje* was postulated and somehow inserted into the accepted racial scale. This argument, not new within scientific racism, was transformed by Latin Americans into the core of their defense. Such a maneuver allowed the design of narrativizations of *mestizaje* wherein interracial contact could be productive. This narrative model of *mestizaje* could be called "comic" in counterpoint to the "gothic" that characterizes the negative version of racial combinations. Thus, as the gothic finale paired Latin American Positivism with literary Naturalism, comic narratives of racial interchange connected up with what Doris Sommer has called the foundational fictions of Latin America. These include national romances like *Sab* [1841; *Sab and Autobiography*] by the Cuban Gertrudis Gómez de Avellaneda (1814–1873) or *Enriquillo* [1882; *The Cross and the Sword*] by the Dominican-born Manuel de Jesús Galván (1834–1911), which presented sentimental histories in which the erotic union of lovers belonging to racially antagonistic groups finally achieved consolidation in a single body–that of the national family.

Contrary to what one might think, the two ways of narrating *mestizaje* are not necessarily contradictory but rather form complementary aspects of the same dynamic of argumentation. The hegemonic demand for a holistic vision (representative of society as a whole) can only be satisfied by a doubled discourse that created a consensus, by working obsessively on the demarcation of limits and identifying those groups that ought to remain excluded from the body of the nation. In accordance with this dual approach, one can speak of two kinds of *mestizaje*, one that harkens back to a fusion without homogenous results, which can never reach the degree of cohesion characteristic of unions between compatible races (Sarmiento 1946, 70), and a second type in which the races manage to fuse themselves into an absolute and perfect form. Despite the democratizing impulse, the second notion of *mestizaje* also rests on a system of racist values by assessing the final results of the amalgam as corresponding to those of a superior racial type. The ideology of *mestizaje* as a resolution of contradictions was without a doubt the principal strategy used by the *criollo* elites to achieve (or impose) consensus on racial and culturally heterogeneous populations, without admitting more marginalized groups (Klor de Alba 250). The

notion of racial combination created the image of a collective organism in which all the sectors of society could in some way recognize themselves and through which the governing classes could maintain their hegemony. Externally, the celebration of the beneficial effects of the racial amalgam would serve in time to question the scientific stereotype that condemned Latin America to a subordinate position in the international order. In this context of the reassessment of the idea of *mestizaje*, one can distinguish three paradigms of resistance to scientific racism which correspond in general terms to the responses of Positivism in Argentina, Mexico, and Cuba, as we shall now see.

Survival of the Fittest in the Pampas

Perhaps the most polemical of the tactics of readaptation utilized in the Latin American response to scientific racism and its negative definition of *mestizaje* was that adopted by the Argentinean Positivists. One of the effects of self-rejection is the creation of internal fissures within a group of subjects who experience racial discrimination. This mechanism naturalized the differences between the upper and lower classes within each society individually, throughout the continent, and subsequently acted to reinforce those that existed among Latin American countries. Just as the governing elites were distinguished from the *mestizo* masses by representing themselves as more white, the discursive traditions of national self-definition created racialized oppositions in Latin America, at the regional level, between the north and south. Not all societies were equal; some were whiter than others. Social scientists such as Ingenieros, Ramos Mejía, and Bunge would attribute the Argentinean racial superiority and that of the Cono Sur (Southern Cone) countries over the rest of Latin American countries to three factors: the smaller number of Indians and blacks, the radical whitening of its mestizo population through European immigration, and the supposed advantages of its geographical location.

After Independence, Argentinean intellectuals perceived their national territory as almost an empty space, a *tabula rasa* on which it was possible to outline a perfect modern society. The rationalist gaze overseeing the natural space emptied it of content, ignoring the ostensible presence of the Amerindians who had populated the pampas from ancient times and proposing programs of transformation of the mestizo classes that had resulted from the colonial occupation. In *Bases y puntos de partida para la organización política de la República Argentina* [1852; Bases and Points of Departure for the Political Organization of the Argentinean Republic], Juan Bautista Alberdi (1810–1884) would compare the action of populating that void with the foundation of the new Republic. The theme would be "Gobernar es poblar" ("to govern is to populate")– that is, to populate with European immigrants, Anglo-Saxons where possible, who would help to exploit the natural wealth of the country and marry its women. This formula would result in the incorporation of European immigrants into Argentine society on a massive scale from 1875 on, and at the same time in the extermination campaign against the indigenous people that would conclude with the definitive conquest of Patagonia in 1879.

The racial pessimism of Sarmiento in *Conflicto y armonías* was in line with a period in which the therapeutic effect of European immigration was still not clear. The immigrants seemed to isolate themselves from the rest of national society, without their beneficial influence being evident and, what was more worrying, the majority of them came from Spain and

Italy, that is, from the Latin regions of Europe. Doubts existed as to whether this new biological force would help to form the new national race. This was not the attitude that would prevail, however. The majority of Argentine Positivists agreed that while disorder and irregularities were evident on a superficial level, the macro-process of *mestizaje* was not only promising but assured that, out of all the Spanish ex-colonies, Argentina was destined to be in the racial vanguard of the postcolonial history of the continent (see Zimmermann 28–32). In each case an organizing model of national history would be imposed that unfailingly culminated in the predominance of the whitest biological element within a general movement that pointed toward the future birth of "Argentine people."

In *Las multitudes argentinas* [1899; Argentine Multitudes], the doctor and sociologist José María Ramos Mejía presented Argentine history as a polemical succession of collective racial agents, the multitudes, each one incarnating different but complementary phases in the formation of the national race within a process that assured the final dominance of the strongest and fittest in the struggle for survival. The multitude of the colony and the Viceroyalty had organized itself in the cities and had been "genuinamente española" ("genuinely Spaniard"). The second were the petty *caudillos* who had emerged from the country's interior and had been "india, heterogénea como ninguna y completamente inculta" ("indian, heterogeneous like no other and completely uncultured") and "casi autóctona mestiza-española" ("almost indigenous mestizo-Spaniard") (1934, 239–40). In the process of transformation undergone by the racial body of the nation, this second multitude had the appearance of a monstrous hybrid, an intermediate stage that, in iconographic terms, was like a symbolic mermaid, "mitad gente, mitad animal" (1934, 240) ("half person, half animal"). The third multitude, still barely defined at the end of the century, was incarnated in the body of the immigrant in a state of metamorphosis—like a kind of embryo—and gradually growing and developing, aided by the fortifying effects of the local environment. It was true, conceded Ramos Mejía, that superior and inferior beings existed among the mass of mutant bodies ("Al lado de los leones y los elefantes, existen animales más pequeños que viven de sus restos" [1934, 257] ["Beside lions and elephants, much smaller animals exist that live off of them"]), but he was convinced that such manifestations, once lost from the race, would succumb to the determinism of biological law. Thus, even though the modern Argentine multitude still had neither consolidated itself nor rid itself of its most pernicious elements, it was only a matter of time. Education would help to accelerate the most cohesive tendencies of the national race in such a way that the stage would finally be reached in which a homogenous and strong collective body would come together to help to boost the country's progress.

Around 1910 the psychiatrist José Ingenieros, a disciple of Ramos Mejía, reinterpreted the evolution of the Argentine race as a long succession of racial battles in which different biological inheritances were gradually amalgamating. Given the predominance of the immigrant element from 1875 on, the leveling out of the social body largely manifested itself in the gradual whitening of native bodies until the indigenous and African elements were extinguished, thus erasing "el estigma de inferioridad étnica con que siempre se ha[bía] marcado en Europa a los sudamericanos, ignorando los diferentes resultados que el clima y la segunda inmigración blanca ha[bía]n determinado entre la zona templada y la zona

tropical" (1934, 262–63) ("the stigma of ethnic inferiority with which South Americans had always been branded in Europe, ignoring the different results that the climate and the second white immigration had provoked in the temperate and tropical zones"). The beneficial influence of pampas geography accelerated the natural tendency to whiteness, he argued, and in scarcely four generations, the descendants of white men and Indian women could consider themselves practically white and believe themselves of European origin (253). Echoing Ingenieros in *El juicio del siglo* [1810; Judgment of the Century], Joaquín Víctor González (1863–1923) would see one of the notable achievements of the first century of Argentine independence as the racial purification of the social organism, a transformation that guaranteed a population in which the mixing with Europeans had left the values of bourgeois modernity literally incarnated in the flesh:

> Eliminados los factores inadmisibles: negros e indios, quedaron los mestizos, pero a su vez, la evolución produjo la sangre criolla que es también europea, de donde saldrá el tipo étnico nacional similar al de la raza europea, pura por su origen y pura por la selección operada en nuestro suelo sobre la sangre criolla que es también la sangre europea. La enorme ventaja económica de esta evolución, no necesita acaso inventario o prueba: suprimidos los elementos de degeneración y corrupción, que significan debilidad, agotamiento, extinción, y en otro orden, ineptitud y falta de resistencia para el trabajo creador y productivo quedaba pues un producto selecto de sangre pura y blanca, pura o depurada, cuyo coeficiente o "ratio" de potencia mental, de labor, de energía y voluntad, y cuya asimilación a las altas formas de la cultura se hallan demostradas por los resultados históricos de las más grandes nacionalidades contemporáneas. (187)

> The inadmissible factors eliminated; blacks and Indians, mestizos remained, but in turn evolution produced *criollo* blood which is also European, from which will emerge the national ethnic type similar to the European race, pure because of its origin and pure as a result of the selection taking place on our soil on *criollo* blood which is also European blood. The enormous economic advantage of this evolution does not need to be inventoried or proved: once the elements of degeneration and corruption are suppressed that indicate weakness, exhaustion, extinction and, in another order, ineptitude and the lack of stamina for creative and productive work, there remained a select product of pure white blood, pure or cleansed, whose coefficient or "ratio" of mental potential, work, energy, and will and whose assimilation into the high forms of culture are demonstrated by the historical achievements of the greatest contemporary nations.

In this reformulation, the monster that threatened the future of mestizo families in the gothic tale of the race is reduced to a momentary phase of the collective body, a stage rapidly replaced and superseded by the dominance, in the struggle for existence, of the superior and virile elements of the white race. While the principles of the debate of scientific racism were maintained, whoever affirmed the white characters of a mestizo population always ran the risk of falling into paradox or contradiction. In their enthusiasm to avoid all suspicion, both Ingenieros and González made the logic of their arguments more flexible (European blood preceded and succeeded the immigrant intervention), having recourse to the almost obsessive repetition of a chain of associations that interested them most: white, European, *criollo*, Argentinean, and pure blood. This optimistic version of *mestizaje* defended by the Argentinean Positivists was principally based on the distinction between kinds of racial combinations. This differentiation maintained the racist axiology of science but modified certain aspects of the hegemonic argument, opening a space of relativization in the service of a defensive response. Contrary to the belief that underpinned European racist science, the sexual union between two compatible racial offshoots, the white and the *mestizo*–so common in the Cono Sur–could be fruitful and even a corrective to the atavistic deviations introduced by the inferior element. Even so, it was accepted that *mestizaje* could also generate counter-productive results. In contrast to the actual behavior of racial combinations in the Cono Sur, the multiple hybridism among three or more groups, so characteristic of the tropics, brought about the irreversible degeneration of the lineage and its eventual sterility, it was claimed (Bunge 137). Resistance to the principles of scientific racism clearly occurred within the limits of a discriminatory negotiation. For this reason, the querying of the uniform definition of *mestizaje* was always accompanied by distinctions derived from the theory of the correspondence between geography and race. Taking up again an idea that went back to Aristotle, both Ingenieros and Bunge defended the geographical thesis according to which the zones appropriated for the development of Western civilization and the white race were those of temperate climate; in the American continent these corresponded mainly to the Argentinean pampas and the North American prairies. The climate and vegetation of tropical regions that were inappropriate for European reason to flourish and debilitated Aryan vigor, favored the predominance of a population of Indian and African heritage. According to Ingenieros, it was for this reason that the mestizos of the pampas consistently tended to be whiter, while those of the tropics had a more Indian or mulatto appearance. The geographical thesis, of all the alternative arguments wielded by Latin American Positivists, introduced a crack in the image of the subaltern as reflected in the mirror of Western racist science. The others (according to the scientific rationale) who could eventually form part of Europe began to be distinguished, within the corporeal chaos characteristic of Latin America, from those others who, being "more" other, guaranteed the legitimacy of Positivist reason through their difference alone.

The Cosmic Race

In contrast to the Argentinean strategy aimed at readapting the theory of *mestizaje,* the racialist reformulations that placed the future of mankind in the tropical zone and in the eugenic effects of the multiracial mix of Latin America operated above all through the actual inversion of the racist argument that condemned *mestizaje*. In certain geographical contexts, the mestizo was not just equal but superior to the white. This was the principle argument of Mexican intellectuals, faced as they were by a sociocultural reality radically different from that of Argentina. The fantasy of the absolute foundation of a modern nation would obviously be inadequate in a country with a large population, the majority *mestizo* and indigenous, and with a territory occupied and marked by the prolonged activity of a multiplicity of peoples and traditions.

The most famous and influential rewriting of *mestizaje* is undoubtedly the essay *La raza cósmica* [1924; *The Cosmic Race*] by José Vasconcelos (1881–1959), in which the author provided post-Revolutionary Mexico with a physical image of national reconciliation centered in the figure of the *mestizo*. The appeal to *mestizaje* as the unificatory instance of a profoundly heterogeneous population was not new in Mexico. At the end of the nineteenth century, the *científicos* (Positivists

trained at the National Preparatory School) of the Porfiriato had already made use of the cohesive power of the mestizo image to create a sense of unity during the process of accelerated modernization introduced by the regime (Stabb 1959, 405–7). Justo Sierra, Minister of Education in Díaz's government, had also taken advantage of a reinterpretation of social Darwinism to demonstrate the inevitability of mestizo predominance in the constitution of the future Mexican race:

> La familia mestiza, llamada a absorber en su seno a los elementos que la engendraron, a pesar de errores y vicios que su juventud y su falta de educación explican de sobra, ha constituido el factor dinámico en nuestra historia; ella revolucionando unas veces y organizando otras, ha movido o comenzado a mover las riquezas estancadas en nuestro suelo. (299)

> The mestizo family, called to absorb in its core elements responsible for its generation, despite the errors and vices fully explained because of immaturity and lack of education, has been the dynamic factor in our history; having caused revolution at times, organization at other, (the *mestizo*) has shifted or begun to shift the unexploited wealth of our soil.

Taking an explicit stand against Gustave Le Bon's (1841–1931) statements in "La influencia de la raza en la historia" [1888; "The Influence of Race in History"], Sierra denied (298) that *mestizaje* necessarily implied a weakening of Spanish American societies. On the contrary, as Andrés Molina Enríquez (1866–1940) would add in *Los grandes problemas nacionales*:

> Es indudable que el elemento mestizo es el más fuerte, puesto que en una larga carrera que ha durado más de tres siglos, a través de inmensas dificultades, y en lucha con los demás elementos, ha llegado a preponderar. Su fuerza le viene de su sangre indígena, y como está en contacto íntimo y en constante cruzamiento con el elemento indígena que es todavía numeroso, puede renovar y renueva de un modo incesante sus energías. (358)

> Undoubtedly the mestizo element is stronger, given that over a long period, lasting more than three centuries, in the face of enormous difficulties and struggling against the remaining elements, it has eventually dominated. Its strength comes from its indigenous blood, and as this is in intimate contact and constantly interbreeding with the still numerous indigenous segment, it can renew and does renew its energies incessantly.

The *mestizo* had inherited from the indigenous peoples the capacity for geographical adaptation, an ability that could be bettered by no other racial group, even when strengthened by the beneficial influence of European blood. Once more the defense of *mestizaje* was based on an adjustment of the Darwinist interpretation of the survival of the fittest. Instead of restricting himself to one method of measuring the racial aptitude of a group–a mode insufficient to analyze the Mexican demographic phenomenon–Andrés Molina Enríquez proposed using two parameters. There existed races of more advanced evolution, such as the Europeans, characterized by their greater capacity for action, and races of better selection, featuring, like the *mestizos,* better adaptability to a specific environment. This important resistance meant that, though momentarily inferior, the *mestizo* was the best suited for surviving and developing in Mexican territory and thus the only viable foundation for the future national race (346–51). Relying on this biological advantage, the state should accelerate the evolution of this hybrid body through education, providing it with the most appropriate form to compete in the context of modernity. It was precisely this possibility of redemption through education that differentiated, according to Francisco Pimentel (1889–1942), the Indian from the *mestizo*:

> los defectos de los mestizos son de naturaleza diferente a los de los indios, y cuyo remedio pudiéramos comprender con un ejemplo tomado de la medicina. Es más fácil curar al hombre dotado de un exceso de robustez que volver a la vida un cuerpo exámine, debilitado, despues de larguísimas privaciones y trabajos. El mestizo puede corregirse con sólo que se le modere por medio de una saludable disciplina. (Stabb 1959, 407)
>
> The defects of the *mestizos* are of a different nature than those of the Indians, and the remedy can be understood with an example taken from medicine. It is easier to cure the man granted an excess of vigor than to treat an extremely lifeless body, weakened after long privations and toil. The *mestizo* can correct himself through moderation alone by means of healthy discipline.

Education should correct the primitive instincts of racial hybrids by submitting them to the principles of reason, at the same time as it offered an incentive to homogenization by the imposition of a common culture and encouraged *mestizaje* among those sharing a common existence governed by the classroom. Barreda, one of the most fervent critics of racial determinism derived from the Darwinist model of history, would recognize that school was the fitting place for the creation of new family links and perhaps the only method whereby eventually the unfortunate divisions of races might be extinguished (65).

The greatest celebration of *mestizaje* took place after the Revolution (Knight 86–92). Like the *científicos* who designed the rationalist mold of the Porfirian authoritarian State, the revolutionary intellectuals also proposed for themselves the task of "forging the fatherland," as the nationalist anthropologist Manuel Gamio expressed it. As in the Positivist regime, the figure of the mestizo acted as a cohesive element to establish hegemony over a population divided by violence, misery, and racism. Vasconcelos, in *La raza cósmica*, would manage definitively to establish the figure of the mestizo in the Mexican national imaginary through a radical inversion of that biological hierarchy anchored in racist science. To strengthen his argument, Vasconcelos went beyond the Mexican border by stating that his proposal was applicable to the entire geocultural system of which Mexico formed a part. Not only Mexico, then, but all of Latin America would be the scene of a new golden age, dominated by the cosmic race. The new racial combination would not be an addition to the organic order of humanity but rather its final consummation, the last stage of progress in which all the races of the planet would fuse together. The cosmic race would have to be Latin American, because only these continental regions contained all racial expressions and only there had the process of *mestizaje* occurred on a global scale of greater significance. Assuming an openly polemical attitude toward the Argentine Positivist tradition, Vasconcelos stated that the new evolutionary stage would require not the temperate plains but the tropics as its favored environment, the geographical zone in which Western culture had truly begun with the Greeks and the Egyptians ("Las grandes civilizaciones se iniciaron entre trópicos y la civilización final volverá al trópico" [63] ["The great civilizations began in the tropics and the final civilization will return to the tropics"; 23]). The new race would fulfill its destiny to the extent that it invented new technical means of combating the hostile aspects of the heat, while using all its beneficial powers for the production of life. In this primordial space, the racial blend would be carried out in accordance with the laws of social

convenience, sympathy, and beauty, all of which would lead to a racial type infinitely superior to those that had existed previously: "Por encima de la eugénica científica prevalecerá la eugénica misteriosa del gusto estético. . . . Los muy feos no procrearán, no desearán procrear" (70) ("Above scientific eugenics, the mysterious eugenics of aesthetic taste will prevail. . . . The very ugly will not procreate; they will have no desire to procreate"; 30). The consciousness of the species itself would gradually develop an astute form of natural selection in such a way that, as quickly as it was free of physical constraint, ignorance and misery, the monstrosities would disappear and what had been considered normal would eventually seem abominable. The "pupila del hombre rojo" (61) ("pupil of the red man") (21) of Atlantis, the drop of Negro blood, the mystery of the slanting eyes of the Mongol, the clear mind of the white man, the cunning of the Jews, and the melancholy of the Arab would come together in the aesthetic purity of the cosmic body and, emerging from all these elements, including them and elevating them, would come the fantastic intelligence of the superman.

The restating of the scientific theories of *mestizaje* runs through all the strategies of conceptual resistance from Sierra to Vasconcelos. Among them is an inversion that dominates the argument: Not only through rejecting the supposed negative effects of combination and geographical determination but also by positing *mestizaje* as the possible source of a superior race, to the new mestizo is attributed the racial excellence formerly attributed to whites by Positivist ethnocentrism. The democratic appearance of the argument according to which all races would eventually come together in a fraternal embrace should not make us lose sight of the fact that the celebration of the combination retained the discriminating principles of scientific racism. As Lomnitz-Adler has established, in the Mexican intellectual tradition the official consecration of the mestizo component as the foundation of the national race always implied the rejection and marginalization of certain ethnic groups. In the imaginary body of the cosmic race proposed by Vasconcelos, the mind continued to be white, Hispanic, and Christian (Vasconcelos 73–75), while in order to achieve the utopian stage of *mestizaje,* "Los tipos bajos de la especie ser[ía]n absorbidos por el tipo superior" (72) ("The lower types of the species will be absorbed by the superior type"; 32). The black could thus be redeemed and little by little, through voluntary extinction, the ugliest stock would give way to the most attractive. The inferior races would become less prolific after educating themselves, and the best specimens would ascend gradually up the scale of ethnic perfection. In the post-Revolutionary context, the cosmic race allowed one to imagine a cohesive community in which all the groups divided by war could learn to live together.

But the other face of this apparent all-embracing utopia was the continuation of the Darwinist selection postulated by Positivism that eliminated the ugly, the weak, and those whose difference could not be absorbed by the melting pot of the national citizenry. The conflict of Mexican races would remain contained in a fantastic and beautiful body that Vasconcelos could only visualize within the limits of his imagination as a mere aesthetic possibility. This insistence on the aesthetic values of racial *mestizaje* in the constitution of a future egalitarian society would also mark the corporeal representation in the nationalistic series of works by Mexican muralists such as Rivera and Orozco. Apparently completely different, the defense of whitening and that of cosmic *mestizaje* appealed to similar values. In both cases, the racial mix was governed by the law of natural selection that resulted in the cosmic resolution of its elements through the hierarchization of difference. Thus, while Vasconcelos referred to purification through continued racial miscegenation, and Ramos Mejía proposed the corporeal refutation of the gothic image of the self-destructive monster, both reinterpretations of *mestizaje* maintained the historical determinism of social Darwinism as valid, along with the geographical thesis of racial distribution and its hierarchies.

Caribbean Hybrids

In Cuba the attempts to reformulate and refute scientific theories of *mestizaje* were also related to the debates on the creation of the nation and, in particular, on the place that the black ex-slaves would occupy within the national community after Independence. As in other post-slavery societies, a marked difference existed between the egalitarian rhetoric of bourgeois Liberalism on which the modern State wished to be founded and the racism that, in fact, divided the population into blacks and whites. The concept of *mestizaje* as a unifying dynamic once again proposed itself as a solution to social conflicts within the country. Among the interpretations and projects offered, two main proposals can be distinguished. The prevalent one timidly resisted the premises of scientific racism; the other, expressed in Martí's essays, saw the discussion of the Positivist paradigm achieve a far more radical formulation that undermined the epistemological structure of racial science in its entirety.

In the case of the first proposal, despite the notable differences between Argentina and Cuba, the Cuban *criollo* elite adopted a reinterpretation of the hegemonic definition of *mestizaje* similar to that defended by the Argentine Positivists. The central element of this position was once again the negotiation of a negative view of all miscegenation. In the debate over the position that *mestizaje* inevitably occasioned the predominance of primitive elements it was stated that, in fact, the superior elements of the mix necessarily prevailed. As in Argentina, biological utopia was related to the slow whitening of the social body, rather than to the celebration of hybridism as an end in itself. Given that the process was slow and unequal, the State could aid the acceleration of the whitening of the colored classes through the introduction of more European immigrants and a rigorous education. This population plan gained even more support during the two U.S. military interventions (1898–1902, 1906–1909) that brought with them both the system of dual racial discrimination prevalent in the United States and an immigration system that prohibited the entry of blacks and Asians (Helg 94–97).

Cuba y su evolución colonial [1899–1906; Cuba and Its Colonial Evolution] by Francisco Figueras exemplifies this tendency well. According to Figueras, the lack of synthesis that could still be observed in the Cuban physiognomy, the battleground for the ferocious struggle between the Caucasian and African races, was temporary. It was a question of time; natural selection would complete the work that it had initiated through interbreeding, "eliminando de una vez y para siempre los últimos vestigios del tipo inferior" (242) ("eliminating once and for all the last vestiges of the inferior type"). In the inverse of the economic law that regulated the circulation of coins of different metals (so that the ones of less value eliminated the most valuable from the marketplace), the corporeal economy that presided over the palingenesis of the

races "condena[ba] a la inferior a una lenta, pero segura absorción por la superior" (242) ("condemned the inferior to the slower but sure absorption by the superior"). The fact that the strength of this general tendency could be verified did not imply that no artificial mechanisms existed to favor the general process. The abolition of slavery and the consequent interruption of African arrivals had obviously initiated "un proceso de blanqueo" ("a whitening process") that led to the reduction by a quarter of the number of colored inhabitants of Cuba in less than a third of a century (242–43). The superiority of the white element, on the other hand, justified the fact that certain mulattos had been able to leave their mark on the political sphere. The anthropological study of the skeleton and cranium of General Antonio Maceo (1845–1896), hero of the war against Spain, undertaken by an official commission in 1900, conveniently proved that the white heritage of the mulatto official predominated over the African side. Even though the exaggerated length of his extremities was characteristic of the black race, as the anthropometric study stated, the shape of his head indicated that his general type was closer to that of the white race and, moreover, this gave him the advantage (Helg 104–05).

With "Nuestra América" [1891; Our America], José Martí (1853–1895) inaugurated a line of debate, still very current within Caribbean identity politics, that sought to annul the terms of the racist scientific argument and replace them with those of humanist discourse (Pruna and García González 152), appealing to values such as justice, the soul, and universality:

No hay odio de razas, porque no hay razas. Los pensadores canijos, los pensadores de lámpara, enhebran y recalientan las razas de librería, que el viajero justo y observador cordial buscan en vano en la justicia de la naturaleza, donde resalta, en el amor victorioso y el apetito turbulento, la identidad universal del hombre. El alma emana igual y eterna de los cuerpos diversos en forma y en color. Peca contra la humanidad el que fomente y propague la oposición y el odio de las razas. (Martí 1979, 124; énfasis mío)

There is no such thing as race hatred, because there is no such thing as race. Feeble thinkers, armchair thinkers, categorize and speculate too much on the races they encounter on the bookshelf that the reasonable traveler and cordial observer seek for in vain in natural justice, where the universal identity of humanity is conspicuous in the triumph of love and the turbulence of appetites. The soul emanates equally and eternal from bodies that differ in shape and color. He who foments and propagates opposition to and hatred of races sins against humanity. (my italics)

In his denial of the validity of the concept of race, Martí puts two types of knowledge in confrontation with each other. He counterpoints that of the bookshelf, principally represented by the Western lettered tradition, with the clarity of the nonprejudiced eye, free of the spectacles of Imperial authority–suggesting the political and partial nature of the production of all knowledge. Following this same line of argument, Martí contrasts two modalities of travel, the nineteenth-century activity from which originated all appreciation of cultural difference and the scientific tourist who confirms what he already knows. Martí privileges the itinerant traveler who is involved and dialogues with the different people met. The efficacy of the rhetoric of this conceptual modification is based, in turn, on a parallel stylistic displacement in which scientific vocabulary and argumentation are replaced by the suggestive flexibility of the literary trope.

Martí's redefinition of *mestizaje* produced the phantasmagoric image of a *mestizo* America represented by an indefinite body by which biology and culture overlapped to such an extent that it was no longer possible to distinguish between them. Penetrating the multiple and successive cultural masks with which history had developed the nature of Spanish Americans did not hark back to a truer corporeality behind the masks; on the contrary, the human bodies were none other than the incarnation of those masks. Through a strategy of destabilization of representation, Martí redefined American *mestizaje* as a cultural interchange in which multiple traditions were fused together. The preservation of the idea of *mestizaje* nevertheless limited his critique. Questioned as to what was the desirable relationship between those cultures in contact in Latin America, Martí seemed to tend towards a notion of *mestizaje* that served to reconcile and unify the different ethnic groups through a national identity that embraced all. The politics of difference, even when they were defensive, threatened the integrity and stability of the State. This fear of division was possibly what led Martí to condemn, in "Mi raza" [1893; "My Race"], the efforts by certain Afro-Cuban groups to define an autonomous space for themselves:

> El hombre negro que proclama su raza, cuando lo que acaso proclama únicamente en esta forma érronea es la identidad espiritual de todas las razas, autoriza y provoca al racista blanco. La paz pide los derechos comunes de la naturaleza: los derechos diferenciales, contrarios a la naturaleza, son enemigos de la paz. El blanco que se aísla, aísla al negro. El negro que se aísla, provoca a aislarse al blanco. . . . *Cubano es más que blanco, más que mulato, más que negro.* (299, énfasis mío)

> When the black man proclaims his race, perhaps all that he is declaring in this erroneous form is that there is a spiritual identity of all races, authorized and provoked by the white racist. Peace demands the common rights of nature: differential rights, contrary to nature, are the enemies of peace. The white man who isolates himself isolates the black. The black who isolates himself provokes the white man to isolate himself. . . . *The Cuban is more than white, more than mulatto, more than black.* (my emphasis)

The superior status of the national State constituted the conclusive source for the legitimation of cultural *mestizaje* as defended by Martí. All conflicting cultural difference should remain subordinate to the demands of the nation. The redefinition of hybridity in Martí's texts produced a double orientation whose ambiguities would continue to be repeated in the debates on identity in the Caribbean throughout the twentieth century. Owing to this central indecision, the hybrid of joyful multiplicity would always run the risk of converting itself into the annihilation of all difference.

Conclusion

In *Contrapunteo del tabaco y el azúcar*, Fernando Ortíz took up Martí's critical program once more and took it even further. After all, the theory of transculturation was an attempt to resolve the two problems that had concerned Martí, that of the production of knowledge in peripheral societies and that of the role of science in the subalternization of those same societies. The concept of transculturation offered a similar response to both problems. On one hand, in order to emphasize the creativity of the dominated cultures and the selective resistance opposing modernizing homogenization, the idea of transculturation contradicted the metropolitan theories of contact that interpreted colonial situations as unidirectional processes of acculturation. On the other hand, in order to interpret the social as cultural interchange, the theory of transculturation returned to confront the socio-biological interpretations

developed by Positivism in favor of a socio-cultural model according to which Latin American mestizo identity was the result, not of racial determination, but of heterogeneous cultural practices generated by a transnational network of unequal economic and social exchanges. As in Martí's case, Ortiz would never go so far as to renounce the promises of the ideology of universal progress, or reject the principles of cultural nationalism as a source of State legitimacy (Coronil xix, xxii–xxiv). It is not strange, therefore, that the sexualization and racialization of cultural differences characteristic of social Darwinism would continue to be the fundamental tropes of textual rhetoric. Ortiz would end up describing the process of transculturation itself in terms of the effects of interracial coupling: "en todo abrazo de culturas sucede lo que en la cópula genética de los individuos: la criatura siempre tiene algo de ambos progenitores, pero también siempre es distinta de cada uno de los dos. En conjunto, el proceso es una *transculturación,* y este vocablo comprende todas las fases de su parábola" (1987, 96–97) ("the result of every union of cultures is similar to that of the reproductive process between individuals: The offspring always has something of both parents but is always different from each of them. In combination, the process is a *transculturation,* and this word embraces all the phases of its parabola"; 1995, 103). In the slippery territory of equivalencies, the metaphorical relation between bodily contact and transcultural exchange becomes literalized. Surreptitiously, the history of Cuban cultural productivity becomes indistinguishable from a racial history characterized by *mestizaje* and the predominance of the strongest corporeal blends:

> La verdadera historia de Cuba es la historia de sus intrincadísimas transculturaciones. *Primero la transculturación del indio paleolítico al neolítico y la desaparición de éste por no acomodarse al impacto de la nueva cultura castellana.* Después, la transculturación de una corriente incesante de inmigrantes blancos. . . . Al mismo tiempo, la transculturación de una continua chorrera humana de negros africanos, de razas y culturas diversas. . . . Y todavía más culturas inmigratorias, en oleadas esporádicas o en manaderos continuos, siempre fluyentes e influyentes y de las más varias oriundeces. (Ortiz 1987, 93, énfasis mío)

> The real history of Cuba is the history of its intermeshed transculturations. *First came the transculturation of the paleolithic Indian to the neolithic, and the disappearance of the latter because of an inability to adjust to the new culture brought in by the Spaniards.* Then the transculturation of an unbroken stream of white immigrants . . . . At the same time there was going on the transculturation of a steady human stream of African Negroes coming from all the coastal regions of Africa [literally of diverse ethnic groups and cultures]. . . . And still other immigrant cultures of the most varying origins arrived, either in sporadic waves or a continuous flow, always exerting an influence and being influenced in turn. (1995, 98, my italics)

The violent encounter of races at different stages of social evolution on the scale of progress–the disappearance of the weakest, the triumph of the strongest–these are all classical elements of the Latin American Positivist essay on identity. It is in this sense that one can confirm that the concept of transculturation was nothing more than a derivation already implicit in the discursive matrix of Darwinism in its indigenous per-version.

But despite its limitations, the theory of transculturation, as an analytical instrument, would continue to be illuminating. If we stick to the idea of transculturation not as a neutralizing form of self-improvement but as a contradictory tension that will never be resolved, the strategies of readaptation within the Latin American Positivist tradition become visible and acquire a dimension that transcends both the idea of the servile copy and that of absolute originality. In this sense, the concept of transculturation allows one to realize the transformatory incorporation of hegemonic cultural forms within Latin American symbolic production in its different regional expressions.

Among the multiple processes of discursive exchange that have taken place during the formation of post-colonial Latin American States, the case of Positivism represents an extreme instance in which the very modality of exchange (scientific authority) was always controlled by a fixed number of restrictive rules that limited the possibilities of transforming the dominant discourse. It is this same exceptional authority of scientific discourse that permits us to gain some insight into what occurred in all postcolonial cultural production, when the liberating impulse of strategic emphasis on cultural difference is nonetheless supported by the partial acceptance of the terminology of the cultural oppressor. In Latin American Positivism, the subaltern is the victim of a contradictory positioning that fragments its image in the transcultural mirror of science. The partial identification with the image of otherness is always contaminated by the variables in the continuous exchange that exists within the group that the excluded regard as homogenous. This illusion contains an inherent opposition: On the one hand the Liberal fantasy that all can form part of the dominant group if they accept its rules; on the other, the Conservative genocidal tendency that returns to marginalize the excluded (Gilman 2). The reification of identity by the inversion of the racist argument does not annul the persuasive force of the conceptual system that produces it. If, as Fanon anxiously declared, all ontology is unsustainable in a society that has arisen from a colonial system of discrimination (109), the only way out is to completely dismantle the imprisoning mirror.

Translation by Jessica Johnson

Works Cited

Agassiz, Louis. 1868. *A Journey in Brazil.* Boston: Ticknor and Fields.

Alberdi, Juan Bautista. 1966. *Bases y puntos de partida para la organización política de la República Argentina.* Buenos Aires: Editorial Universitaria de Buenos Aires.

Anderson, Benedict. 1989. *Imagined Communities: Reflections on the Origin and Spread of Nationalism.* London/New York: Verso.

Arguedas, Alcides. 1979 [1909]. *Pueblo enfermo.* La Paz (Bolivia): Gisbeit & Cía. S.A.

Babini, José. 1949. *Historia de la ciencia argentina.* Mexico City: Fondo de Cultura Económica.

Barreda, Gabino. 1967. "Oración cívica, 1867." *Introducción a la ley orgánica de instrucción pública en el Distrito Federal.* Mexico City: Universidad Nacional Autónoma de México. 83–110.

Berger, John, et al. 1977. *Ways of Seeing.* New York: Penguin Books.

Bhabha, Homi. 1993. *The Location of Culture.* London: Routledge.

Bolívar, Simón. 1951. *Selected Writings of Bolívar.* Compiled by Vicente Lecuna. Ed. Harold A. Bierck, Jr. Trans. Lewis Bertrand. 2 vols. New York: Colonial Press.

——. [1968] *Obras completas.* Ed. Pedro Grases. 3 vols. Caracas: E. Requena Mira.

Buckle, Henry Thomas. 1906. *History of Civilization in England.* 3 vols. London: G Richard.

Bunge, Carlos Octavio. 1905 [1903]. *Nuestra América: ensayo de psicología social.* Buenos Aires: Valerio Abeledo.

——. 1908. *Viaje a través de la estirpe y otras narraciones.* Buenos Aires: n.p.

Coronil, Fernando. 1995. "Introduction: Transculturation and the Politics of Theory: Countering the Center, Cuban Counterpoint." *Cuban Counterpoint: Tobacco and Sugar.* By Fernando Ortiz. Durham, NC: Duke University Press. ix–lvi.

Douglas, Mary. 1992. *Purity and Danger: An Analysis of the Concepts of Pollution and Taboo.* London: Routledge.

Fanon, Frantz. 1967. "The Fact of Blackness." *Black Skin, White Masks.* Trans. Charles Lam Markmann. New York: Grove Press. 109–40.

Figueras, Francisco. 1907. *Cuba y su evolución colonial.* Havana: Isla, S.A. Editores.

Galton, Francis. 1914 [1869]. *Hereditary Genius: An Inquiry into Its Laws and Consequences.* London: Macmillan and Co., Ltd.

Gerbi, Antonello. 1973. *The Dispute of the New World: The History of a Polemic, 1750–1900.* Ed. and Trans. Jeremy Moyle. Pittsburgh: University of Pittsburgh Press.

Gil Fortoul, José. 1916. *El hombre y la historia.* Madrid: Editorial América.

Gilman, Sander. 1986. *Jewish Self-Hatred: Anti-Semitism and the Hidden Language of the Jews.* Baltimore: Johns Hopkins University Press.

González, Joaquín Víctor. 1945. *El juicio del siglo.* Buenos Aires: Editorial Rosario.

Graham, Richard, ed. 1990. *The Idea of Race in Latin America, 1870–1940.* Austin: University of Texas Press.

Hall, Stuart. 1997. "Old and New Identities." *Culture, Globalization, and the World-System: Contemporary Conditions for the Representation of Identity.* Ed. Anthony D. King. Minneapolis: University of Minnesota Press. 41–68.

Helg, Aline. 1995. *Our Rightful Share: The Afro-Cuban Struggle for Equality, 1886–1912.* Chapel Hill: University of North Carolina Press.

Ingenieros, José. 1918 [1910]. *Sociología argentina.* Buenos Aires: Ediciones L. J. Rosso.

Klor de Alva, J. Jorge. 1995. "The Postcolonization of the (Latin) American Experience: A Reconsideration of 'Colonialism,' 'Postcolonialism,' and 'Mestizaje.'" *After Colonialism: Imperial Histories and Postcolonial Displacements.* Ed. Gyan Prakash. Princeton, NJ: Princeton University Press. 241–75.

Knight, Alan. 1990. "Racism, Revolution, and *Indigenismo*: Mexico, 1910–1940." *The Idea of Race in Latin America, 1870–1940.* Ed. Richard Graham. Austin: University of Texas Press. 71–113.

Lefort, Claude. 1988. *Democracy and Political Theory.* Trans. David Macey. Minneapolis: University of Minnesota Press.

Lomnitz-Adler, Claudio. 1992. *Exits from the Labyrinth: Culture and Ideology in the Mexican National Space.* Berkeley: University of California Press.

Martí, José. 1963. "Mi raza." *Obras Completas.* Havana: Editorial Nacional de Cuba. 2: 298–300.

——. 1979. "Nuestra América." *Páginas escogidas.* Ed. Alfonso M. Escudero. Madrid: Espasa Calpe. 118–24.

Molina Enríquez, Andrés. 1978 [1909]. *Los grandes problemas nacionales (1909) y otros textos (1911–1919).* Mexico City: Ediciones Era.

Nouzeilles, Gabriela. 1997. "Ficciones paranoicas de fin de siglo: naturalismo argentino y policía médica." *Modern Language Notes* 112: 232–52.

——. 1998. "El enigma del monstruo: modernidad e higiene racial en *La charca* de Zeno Gandía." *Latin American Literary Review* 25.50 (July–December): 89–107.

Ortiz, Fernando. 1917 [1905]. *Hampa Afro-cubana: los negros brujos (apuntes para un estudio de etnología criminal).* Madrid: Editorial América.

——. 1987. *Contrapunteo cubano del tabaco y el azúcar.* Caracas: Ayacucho.

——. 1995. *Cuban Counterpoint: Tobacco and Sugar.* Trans. Harriet de Onís. Durham, NC: Duke University Press.

Poliakov, Léon. 1975. *Hommes et bêtes: entretiens sur le racisme.* Paris: Mouton.

Prado y Ugarteche, Javier. 1941. *Estado social del Perú durante la dominación española (estudio histórico sociológico).* Lima: Librería e Imprenta Gil.

Pruna, Pedro M., and Armando García González. 1989. *Darwinismo y sociedad en Cuba: siglo XIX.* Madrid: Consejo Superior de Investigaciones Científicas.

Rama, Ángel. 1985. *Transculturación narrativa en América Latina.* Mexico City: Siglo Veintiuno Editores.

Ramos Mejía, José María. 1934 [1899]. *Las multitudes argentinas.* Buenos Aires: Talleres Gráficos Argentinos L. J. Rosso.

——. 1936 [1878–1882]. *Las neurosis de los hombres célebres en la historia argentina.* Buenos Aires: Ediciones Anaconda.

Said, Edward W. 1979. *Orientalism.* New York: Vintage Books.

Sarmiento, Domingo Faustino. 1900 [1886]. "Sobre instrucción popular." *Obras Completas.* Vol. 47: *Educar al soberano.* Buenos Aires: Imprenta y Litografia Mariano Moreno. 371–79.

——. 1946 [1883]. *Conflicto y armonías de las razas en América.* Buenos Aires: Editorial Intermundo.

Sierra, Justo. 1977. *Evolución política del pueblo mexicano.* Caracas: Biblioteca Ayacucho.

Sommer, Doris. 1993. *Foundational Fictions: The National Romances of Latin America.* Berkeley: University of California Press.

Stabb, Martin S. 1959. "Indigenism and Racism in Mexican Thought, 1857–1911." *Journal of Inter-American Studies* 1: 405–23.

——. 1967. *In Quest of Identity: Patterns in the Spanish American Essay of Ideas, 1890–1960.* Chapel Hill: University of North Carolina Press.

Stepan, Nancy. 1982. *The Idea of Race in Science: Great Britain 1860–1960.* Hamden, CT: Archon Books.

——. 1993. "Race and Gender: The Role of Analogy in Science." *The Racial Economy of Science: Toward a Democratic Future.* Ed. Sandra Harding. Bloomington: Indiana University Press. 359–76.

Stepan, Nancy Leys, and Sander L. Gilman. 1993. "Appropriating the Idioms of Science. The Rejection of Scientific Racism." *The "Racial" Economy of Science: Toward a Democratic Future.* Ed. Sandra Harding. Bloomington: Indiana University Press. 170–200.

Terán, Oscar. 1986. *En busca de la ideología argentina.* Buenos Aires: Catálogos Editora.

Vasconcelos, José. 1997. *The Cosmic Race/La raza cósmica: A Bilingual Edition.* Trans. Didier T. Jaén. Baltimore: Johns Hopkins University Press.

Wade, Peter. 1993. *Blackness and Race Mixture: The Dynamics of Racial Identity in Colombia.* Baltimore/London: Johns Hopkins University Press.

Young, Robert. 1990. *White Mythologies: Writing History and the West.* London: Routledge.

Zea, Leopoldo. 1980. *Pensamiento positivista latinoamericano.* 2 vols. Caracas: Biblioteca Ayacucho.

Zimmermann, Eduardo A. 1992. "Racial Idea and Social Reform: Argentina, 1890–1916." *Hispanic American Historical Review* 72.1: 23–47.

Zumeta, César. 1961 [1899]. *El continente enfermo.* Ed. Rafael Angel Insausti. Caracas: Editorial Arte.

CHAPTER 25

LITERARY EDUCATION AND THE MAKING OF STATE KNOWLEDGE

Juan Poblete

In what follows, I will discuss in three different cases (Chile, Colombia, and Argentina) the relationship between Positivism, state policies, and pedagogical practices in the production of subjects and knowledge within what I call the discipline and disciplining of literary education in the long nineteenth-century fin de siècle in Latin America. Because of the regional division and format of this volume, I have left out any consideration of two of the best-known Latin American examples of the confluence of Positivism and state policies: Mexico and Brazil. Limitations of space have also precluded the inclusion of, for example, the Uruguayan reform of education undertaken in 1877 under the inspiration of José Pedro Varela's (1845–1879) work (see Zea 1965 and 1980).

Positivism had been born in Europe as a result of the explosion of classical political philosophy that the French Revolution entailed. As a doctrine then, Positivism was a response to revolution, an attempt at dealing with the consequences of and preventing at least some of the effects attributed to the French Revolution. Because the Old Regime had gone down, Saint Simon and Comte reasoned, it was necessary to find new forms of social integration that would somehow functionally replace the work of religion and thus prevent revolution. And because until the French Revolution religion had been the social cement holding together the different structures of European societies, it was deemed essential to find an adequate replacement. It is thus not surprising that both Saint Simon and Comte ended up founding new secularized religions (see Therborn).

In Latin America Positivism was, it will be contended here, the state's response to the need to administer huge and racially, culturally, and economically diversified and increasingly urban populations. It was not as much an answer to revolution as it was a continuation of revolution's fundamental accomplishment, the preservation of the socioeconomic situation of the (now expanded) ruling elites in a new era of growing massification. The ever-expanding semiotic possibilities of the concepts of citizen, *pueblo*, political representation, and rights (see Jocelyn Holt) at the hands of increasingly difficult to control social sectors determined a certain minimal compromise on the part of the two contending political factions that divided the continent's power map. Liberals and conservatives, and at times coalitions and hybrids of both parties, began a process of state consolidation that required practical solutions to what were perceived on both sides as the inherent logistical problems of ruling and controlling the increasing demands of subaltern sectors of society. In this regard then, both liberals and conservatives were in fundamental agreement.

The motto of the Mexican Positivists, "poca política y mucha administración" (see Romero) ("less politics and more administration"), reflects a Latin American transaction between the liberal ideals of education–property, freedom, and work for (potentially) all–and a vested interest in keeping a fundamentally class-based society intact. As such, the Porfiristas motto is a call for science–social science, that is–to

transform political problems into technical or social ones (see Laclau) and to solve them by administrative decree rather than by political means.

What I would like to do now is not so much to explore in all its complexity and variety the liaison between politics and Positivism in Latin America as to posit, with some historical examples, a (theoretical) reconstruction of the place of literature (as a school subject) in the midst of different Positivisms, nascent social sciences, and emerging nationalisms. In its most essential formulation, my argument will be the following: Promoting a dependent national development that follows the dictates of the Euro-American model, Positivist policies, in particular those in the educational sphere, nevertheless end up developing increasingly nationalized forms of perception of what is from then on called "la realidad nacional" ("national reality"). Later on, these same perceptions generate in turn different questionings of Positivism's own universalizing and modernizing postulates. With its critique of what Liberalism had already termed the colonial scholastic, Positivism would promote social studies, a new type of disciplinary knowledge that borrowed its methodology from the natural sciences, would attempt to observe and formulate the scientific laws governing the social world. In this context, instruction in language and literature, modeled after the Positivist's faith in the method of observation and induction characteristic of the natural sciences, provided the grounds for a local and national sensibility to arise and be produced. This in turn created the cultural space for the emergence of a nationalistic (*criollo*) literature in the first decades of the twentieth century. This hypothesis, of course, should not be taken as a denial of the cultural agency of the subaltern sectors of society at the turn of the century and of its impact on and importance for the emergence of national literatures in Latin America (see Prieto). I am simply trying to study one important aspect of such an emergence, but by no means the only one.

Jorge Gracia has offered the following description of Positivism in Latin America:

> a rather peculiar hodgepodge of ideas borrowed from a wide spectrum of sources that included such figures as Comte, Spencer, Haeckel, and others, which seems to have developed into a kind of religion or cult in some countries and in others it became simply an ideological veneer used to justify political regimes. (115)

At least two defining traits of what was afterwards grouped under the rubric of Positivism should be underscored here: On the one hand, the heterogeneous nature of its doctrinal sources; on the other, the multiplicity of its political articulations and results depending on the different national context of its insertions.

Beyond the important differences between Mexican, Argentine, and Chilean Positivisms (Zea 1965; Subercaseaux), it will be contended here that in Latin America Positivism can be studied more generally as a somehow coherent system for the production of social meaning. As a result of religion's and, more to the point, of Catholicism's relative loss of validity in the production of social guidelines to confront the many problems that an incipient process of dependent development was bringing to the fore, the need arose, at least as perceived by some sectors of society at the long fin de siècle, for a secularized philosophy of (modern) life. This philosophy was Positivism, and many times its preferred variety was Herbert Spencer's substitution of evolution for revolution, which envisioned an industrial society (modeled after contemporary England) where science and religion would come together to provide the multiple answers demanded by material and moral progress.

One of the most important fields in which this crisis manifested itself was the humanities. The humanities had been based generally on the classical languages and literatures for the production of socially sanctioned knowledge that had symbolic effects. Latin had worked in two ways. Etymological reasoning in its classical version presupposed that behind many of the discursive (lexical, syntactic, and semantic) forms of the present there had to be an expression in a classic language, and in particular in Latin. This etymology worked as deduction much more than as induction; it was not so much the result of a linguistic observation as it was the authorized derivation from a model. Thus it always reinforced the model from which that authority emanated, therefore closing a circle of successive authorizations all stemming from the same classical–that is, traditional–space. On the other hand, Latin as a mental gymnastics was the instrument in and through which the student could exercise his brain using a universal reason free from temporal or geographical determinations.

When the place of Latin in the school curriculum came under attack, something that occurred to different degrees in many countries in the last quarter of the nineteenth century (see Solar Correa; Rivas), what was at stake was of course not simply the content of the educational plans but the question of what were the means of cultural production in relatively new countries as well as why, what for, and for whom those means were relevant.

The centrality of Latin in the curriculum reflected the role the Church played at the heart of traditional culture and in the texture of the political and everyday life of the elites and, by extension, of that of the rest of the population. The preservation of Latin, and above all of its formal hegemony in the school system, meant the persistence of the mediating role the priests had had until that moment as important arbiters of the meanings socially produced and circulating in the polity. During the many battles about the proper relations between the Church and the state (see Pike 1964), it was said frequently that it was precisely this ability of (organized) religion to cement and secure a social structuration that made it irreplaceable both at the school and more generally at the national level. In 1884, for example, Eduardo Wilde, Minister of Justice, Public Instruction, and Culture (a triad that had already been questioned in some countries and that would be challenged by many more in the coming years) declared:

> Es una cosa sabida y proclamada por todos los filósofos que no bastan las creencias morales para educar a las masas. Por qué? Porque las creencias morales tienen una forma abstracta. Es necesario que para las masas los elementos de moralización tengan, diré usando de metáforas, algo de tangible, de voluminoso y de concreto. La religión es conveniente con sus formas externas, para obtener el dominio de ciertos espíritus mediocres, que no alcanzan a las sublimidades de la abstracción. (Tedesco 126–27)

It was a well-known fact expressed by all philosophers that moral belief is not sufficient to educate the masses. Why? Because moral belief has an abstract nature. The masses require moral instruction, which, to say it metaphorically, has something tangible, of ubstance, and concrete. Religion, because of its external forms, is a convenient way to reach certain mediocre spirits who are incapable of grasping the sublime nature of abstraction.

What is most notable in this quotation is not simply the expression of the traditional defense of the role of religion for the preservation and constitution of an ordered society, but precisely the alteration such an argument suffers when it meets a secularized rationalism, for which religion is only a needed concession to the vulgarity of the masses incapable of understanding philosophy.

In the search for solutions to the moral and practical dilemmas posited by the elite's perception of the need for this social cement in an age of increasingly unruly and bigger populations, the state would find a new space for the exercise of its governmentality (see Burchell). Instruction on language and literature and eventually the promotion of a national literature and language would meet those needs in a long and convoluted process that takes many shapes in different countries. Before we proceed to the description of some of the organizing positions in such a process, it may be worth reiterating that my focus on educational reform and the role of language instruction is only one way to show part of the legacy of the confluence of Positivism and state governmentality at the turn of the century in Latin America. That conjunction also produced other legacies, such as, for example, the criminalization and racialization of subaltern populations by what was promoted as scientific discourse (see Nouzeilles in this volume; Terán).

In what follows, then, I will discuss three basic Latin American scenarios in which the relationships between traditional and modern nationalized humanisms are played out in the context of the influence of Positivism on educational thought and planning. I will refer to the Chilean and Colombian cases as delineating the two poles of a continuum resolved locally and differently in the other countries of the region. The case of Argentina will provide an example of the new nationalized humanisms that both Positivism and the pendular reactions to it made possible. What was at stake in all of these cases was the state's interest in (re)directing the creation of a national culture and, in particular, of a national sensibility grounded in nationalized forms of perception, reading, and writing. This in turn demanded attention to the school curriculum and more specifically to the language and literature instruction in it.

Chile

On 29 April 1889, the Instituto Pedagógico of Santiago was created to provide a rigorous disciplinary formation to secondary (high school) teachers. Its creation was part of what is known as the "German reform" of Chilean education. As if to consolidate its place in the regional context, the Chilean State, which had triumphed over its Peruvian and Bolivian counterparts in the Pacific War (1879–1883), attempted to modernize its educational base. Part of this effort was the implementation of the concentric method of organizing the curriculum (see Amunátegui) and along with it the creation of a new curricular subject: el castellano [Spanish language]. The latter's key professor was Rudolf Lenz (1863–1938), a German originally hired to teach French, who would end up becoming one of the essential figures in the resurgence of a cultural nationalism in Chile through his proposals and texts for the reform of Spanish-language instruction (as part of the curriculum) and for the creation and institutionalization of folk studies in Chile.

Spanish language as a school subject was destined to consolidate in one class the remnants of older and classics-oriented disciplines such as rhetoric, literary history, grammar, and poetics, along with the insights provided by the new human or social sciences (psychology, scientific pedagogy, school administration, etc.). Its fundamental innovation was a switch from deduction and normative instruction to induction and empiricism. Here practice was to replace rote memorization and repetition to give way to the natural expression of a subject firmly placed in a local and national reality. This was in stark contrast to the supposed universality of the classics.

Lenz's work on the Chilean context can be divided in two parts: The scientific-philological and the pedagogical and methodological. Both were inspired by a strong nationalistic undercurrent, which meant in practical terms a recuperation of Chilean popular and indigenous language and culture.

Attempting to explain his "Chilenische Studien" [1891–1892; "Chilean Studies"] on the popular speech in Chile, he commented:

Como noté luego que la gente culta, sobre todo los profesores de castellano, no tenían ningún interés por el estudio de "la jerigonza corrompida de la plebe," que simplemente despreciaban porque no comprendían. . . . Me resolví a publicar mis estudios fonéticos del dialecto chileno en revistas científicas alemanas. (Lenz 1940, 17)

I have noticed that educated people, especially professors of Spanish language, have no interest in studying "the corrupt slang of the lower classes," which they despise because they do not understand it. . . . I resolved to publish my phonetic studies of Chilean dialect in German scientific journals.

In 1894, in his "Ensayos filológicos americanos," he added: "en Chile parece faltar por completo entre la jente ilustrada ese amor e cariño al pueblo bajo, el cual, sin embargo, como hemos dicho en otra parte, es la base eterna de la fuerza nacional" (Lenz 1894, 358) ("Chile seems to be completely lacking in educated people who have love and affection for the lower classes, who, as I have said before, constitute the eternal foundation of national strength").

The first strand is manifested in publications such as "Chilenische Studien," "Nacionalidad y lenguaje" ["Nationality and Language"]–not coincidentally published in Buenos Aires in 1893–"Volkpoesie von Santiago" [1895; "Folk Poetry in Santiago"], and "Estudios Araucanos" [from 1895 on; "Araucanean Studies"], culminating in his "Programa de la Sociedad de Folklore" [1905 and 1909; "Program of the Folklore Society"]. In these endeavors, Lenz expanded the use of notions such as culture, literature, poetry, and grammar that up to that point had been limited to the study of the classics and the normative Spanish of Spain but that he now developed into new fields of study in the Chilean context, that is, urban popular literature and poetry, Mapuche oral literature, and language.

Lenz's work gives us an insight into the role played by instruction on (national) language and literature in the creation of a nationalized subjectivity capable of framing, describing, and valorizing its "realidad nacional" ("national reality") and, in so doing, preparing the cultural space for the production and reception of a national *criollo* literature.

In 1924, culminating a long list of pedagogical publications, Lenz faced their central issue with *La Composición escolar en lengua patria* [Student Writing in the National Language]. Commenting on the failure of primary and secondary writing education, he remarked: "Sin necesidad interior no habla sino el tonto, el charlatán y . . . el niño que recita su lección. . . . Pero aún el 'tema libre' sólo excepcionalmente da buen resultado, [ello ocurre] cuando en vez de ser libre está 'amarrado' a la vida del niño" (1924, 7) ("Only the fool, the charlatan, and . . . the child who recites his lesson speak without a reason. . . . Even 'open themes' only rarely give good results, and this happens only when they are 'linked' to the child's life").

The pedagogical and psychological challenge of this emerging nationalism is superbly expressed by Lenz's wording: The problem was, on the one hand, how to tie the topic to the child and, on the other, how to tie the child to the topic–a disciplinary conjunction for both educational and state interests. The challenge was to generate in the child, within the child, in her own subjectivity, the need to write and learn a national language. Lenz proposed:

Eduquemos a los niños a escribir sobre la vida real que los connmueve, a que ellos mismos vean lo que les interesa, que observen los detalles y nos presenten los resultados de su investigación como ellos mismos los sienten en su alma. Este es el camino que nos muestran los grandes escritores. (1924, 13)

Let us teach the children to write about real life as it affects them, so that they can recognize what interests them, so that they can observe the details and express the results of their inquiry as they themselves feel it. This is the road that great writers show us.

As can be glimpsed, Lenz was also transforming the traditional cultural hierarchy in which the Classical writer provided the model that was then supposed to be respected and followed as closely as possible by the student. This hierarchical imitation was viable while the elite did not possess aspirations to a national singularity and did not pretend to fully govern through cultural hegemony but instead used simple domination or a mix of both. In the wake of an ever-expanding educational system and the increasing massification of society, the need arose for a nationalized program shared across the complete social spectrum. At the same time, from the point of view of the state's capacity to govern, the expansion of a common bond and thus the potential expansion of common entitlements or rights demanded specific and effective forms of social control.

At the level of Spanish-language composition this meant a particular implementation of controlled expression, to facilitate the shift from mindless imitation and deduction to a new paradigm of inductive thinking and expression. In his *Proyecto de programa de Castellano* [1919; Project for a Program in Spanish-Language Instruction], Lenz advanced the use of standard notebooks and texts evenly distributed among the students. Emphasizing the importance of uniform and mandatory notebooks, he remarked:

El cuaderno en limpio tiene un propósito pedagógico general, a saber, de acostumbrar a los educandos a manejar papeles con limpieza i orden, i de conservarles hasta el sesto año la escritura caligráfica. Este último propósito se malogra por completo si se les permite usar como cuadernos unos papeluchos desaseados, apenas cosidos, sin tapa resistente. (Lenz 1899, 20)

The blank notebook has a pedagogical purpose, specifically, it will accustom the students to handle their papers cleanly and in an orderly manner, and thereby to continue their instruction in penmanship until the sixth grade. This aim is completely lost if the students are permitted to use scrap paper, barely sewn together, without a hard cover.

The notebook works here as a disciplined teaching device where personal subjectivity can manifest itself in many forms. It is, on the one hand, the space where the subjectivity of the student is expressed. On the other hand, it becomes a manifest representation of that interiority. As such, the *cuaderno de composición* (composition notebook) presents, from the point of view of state educational authorities, an invaluable asset by being simultaneously free expression of the student's subjectivity and a pedagogical space for control, study, and discipline.

The two most important processes marking Chilean modernity were increased schooling for a greater part of society in conjunction with rapid urbanization, and the transition from courses on language and literature based on the classics to logical induction that promoted the mastery over the national language and in the end was instrumental in creating the conditions at both the individual and the collective levels that made possible the production and appreciation of a national literature. Thus, this shift facilitated the development of a new, fully hegemonic form of relation between state, ruling elites, and popular culture that was to characterize the Latin American political scenario during the rest of the first half of the twentieth century (see Martin Barbero).

Nevertheless, the educational transformations brought about by the scientific spirit of Positivism—that is, in the case of Chile's German reform, the inductive method—were soon surpassed by the rapid succession of historical developments. It was not long after the complete overhauling of the Chilean educational curriculum that the scientific Positivism that had animated it was itself deemed too encyclopedic, too general, and not local enough for the real and national needs of the country. Suffice it to say that this critique came mostly from the new appreciations of *la realidad nacional*, which came into the national scene through implementation of the very social science tools that had been introduced by Positivism, such as statistical methods, used to evaluate, quantify, and measure that reality. Some thirty years later, this first wave of social sciences would in turn be criticized for their generality and abstraction when a new "sociología concreta, aplicada y práctica, que se preocupa de los problemas de cada nación y del continente Americano" (Poviña 20) ("concrete, applied, and practical sociology, which is concerned with the problems of each nation and of the American continent") emerged to displace what was then labeled as "academic sociology" (see Brunner).

Educational reform, psychology-based pedagogical methods, and social statistics were some of the most important technologies introduced for the effective education of complex populations. Therefore this entire process should be viewed as the gradual expansion of state-developed forms of formalized (i.e., school discipline) culture with the aim of engaging a popular culture and creating a national culture. Thus it is that the first national school programs of reading and writing opened up the opportunity for the emergence of a new *criollo* national literature that was more attuned to the times and challenges the Latin American states faced in the first half of the twentieth century. This development was to be an important element in the production of hegemonic

forms of government. While the Enlightenment in Latin America had produced a flourishing of new constitutions animated by a strong belief in the power of rational discourse to transform social mores, and while liberal Romanticism in turn had been a search for what Hegel termed "ethical substances" at the level of family and civil society (see Roig), Positivism can be thought of as the process of identification of that ethical substance with the state itself. This was perhaps the most important of the Latin American processes of state consolidation at the end of the nineteenth century

We have now seen how in Chile Positivist reforms meant a radical critique of traditional humanism. This critique derived, of course, not only from the new experiential and empirical foundation of the emerging scientific determinism but also from the political affiliations of those defending the changes. In fact the reform itself was part of a political attempt to confirm a secular turn in Chilean society and politics. Much to the dismay of Rudolf Lenz, who personally saw Latin as an integral component of the teaching of the romance languages, Latin had already become part of this struggle between the advocates of secular education and catholic forces, and the result was its suppression from the mandatory curriculum. More generally, at the popular level, Latin was identified with everything that needed to be eliminated from modern Chilean education: memorization, passivity, blind obedience to sterile models, and the burden of tradition and scholastic philosophy. The Colombian case is the proof, if it is needed, that the encounter between Positivism, Latin, religion, national culture, hispanism, and foreign influences could be articulated and presented differently.

Colombia

Most of the issues that concerned public education toward the end of the nineteenth century in other Latin American countries had already been introduced in the Colombian liberal republic of 1849 (mandatory, nonreligious, and State-run education). In 1870, for example, a German pedagogical mission of Pestalozzian orientation was brought by the government to create the first Escuela Normal (Teacher's College) (González G. 54; Loy; Zuluaga 1979, 97). These liberal efforts to secularize Colombian education were, however, followed after 1885 by conservative government attempts to reverse them. Education was thus at the heart of the liberal and conservative debates over the proper relationship of Church and state and at the center of their efforts to build a lasting political hegemony (Deas 28). Therefore, when the conservative movement known as La Regeneración [The Regeneration] took power in the last two decades of the nineteenth century, they presented the return to Catholic-dominated public and private education as part of the changes necessary to bring about real modernization. Rafael Nuñez (1825–1964), three-time president of Colombia (between 1880 and 1894) and leader of La Regeneración, would therefore claim that "la República espiritual con su aureola de esperanzas infinitas, debe venir en socorro de la república laica" (*Nueva Historia de Colombia* 4: 69) ("the spiritual Republic with its help of infinite hope should come forward to help the lay republic").

For Nuñez progress was an eclectic combination of science and religion, of innovation and tradition, of Catholicism and sociology. He found his spiritual inspiration in the work of Herbert Spencer:

Creemos . . . que los sociologistas (los de la escuela de Spencer a lo menos) profesan como uno de sus dogmas fundamentales el principio de la unidad moral del mundo. . . . Es por tanto, del amor a los semejantes, o sea, del desarrollo y ejercicio de la caridad cristiana, de lo que Spencer nos promete confiadamente la perfección del hombre. La aspiración a la unidad moral del mundo no podría determinarse en más preciso y claro lenguaje. (Nuñez 236–39)

We believe . . . that sociologists (at least those of Herbert Spencer's school) profess as one of their fundamental dogmas the principle of the moral unity of the world. . . . And thus it is, through the love of one's fellow man, or, that is, through the development and practice of Christian charity, that Spencer confidently promises the perfection of mankind. This aspiration to the moral unity of the world could not be expressed in clearer or more precise language.

Nuñez's government was oriented toward reconciling his sociological (i.e., quasi-Positivist) views with those of his more traditional Catholic allies. In what marked an important change in Nuñez's own views concerning science, religion, and progress, he conceded in 1890:

En otros tiempos nosotros pensábamos que la escuela laica . . . era uno de los agentes principales de moralidad en la vida pública; pero hoy, después de larga y desastrosa experiencia, hemos perdido toda fe en las combinaciones en que no prevalece la educación netamente religiosa. (Molina 146)

In another time we formerly believed that lay education . . . was one of the principal agents of public morality; but after a long and disastrous experience, we have lost all faith in educational policies in which fully religious education does not prevail.

Thus "centralism, strengthened institutional authority, and close Church-state cooperation composed the doctrinal core of the Regeneration" (Park 269). One of its ideologues, especially of this latter aspect, was Miguel Antonio Caro (1843–1909). He conceived of La Regeneración as a God-sent blessing that, undoing liberal policies, was able to correct the course of Colombian history and in particular that of Colombian education:

En punto a educación, por ley fundamental se declaró [1886] que la enseñanza pública sería conforme a la doctrina católica. [Además] la enseñanza quedó bajo la inspección de la Iglesia misma en lo concerniente a la fe y a la moral. (Caro 1962b, 1457)

With regard to education, the law of 1886 declared that all public education would be according to Catholic dogma. Further, all teaching would be subject to review by the Church regarding issues of faith and morals.

Although he was a Catholic doctrinaire militantly opposed to Positivism, Caro, who was first minister and then successor to Nuñez, was fully committed to the work of La Regeneración, as summarized by Nuñez's political motto: "centralización política y descentralización administrativa" ("political centralization and administrative decentralization"). At the educational level, this meant an undoing of the radical reforms of 1870 and a return to a Catholic-directed and -oriented school system. Robert V. Farrell provides a useful summary of this state of affairs:

During the "Regeneración" the Church and Catholicism permeated official and most private school curriculums. . . . Classical curriculums and educational elitism became guiding standards. Catholic pedagogy, with its emphasis on religious and academic activities, tight routines and schedules, competition and discipline, was again Colombia's educational model. (2–3)

The hegemony of this Catholic pedagogy charted a peculiar course for Colombia's fin de siècle. Rafael Gutierrez Girardot has talked of the "ficción del humanismo colombiano" ("fiction of Colombian humanism"), a "humanismo de sacristía y escuela" ("humanism of sacristy and school"), in an attempt to emphasize what he calls "la voluntad antihistórica de la república conservadora" ("the antihistorical will of the conservative republic") (Jaramillo Uribe 3: 448–50), which held tight to its faith in Catholicism and traditional social norms as the basis for the connections between state, society, and nation in modern Colombia. Classic humanism was an important stone in this edifice, and like Andrés Bello before him, Miguel Antonio Caro developed a personal agenda that expressed and directly influenced these political views:

La conquista estableció la unidad del culto y de la lengua. La emancipación acarreó un nuevo elemento de grandeza, la libertad. . . . Sin libertad el progreso se estanca por falta de motor. Pero sin unidad las fuerzas se fraccionan y descarrían, y el progreso social no sólo se entorpece sino que se hace imposible. . . . La corrupción creciente de una lengua arguye desorganización social. (Caro 1928a, 129)

The conquest instituted unity of religion and language. Independence added a new element: liberty. . . . Without liberty, progress stops because there is no motor. But without unity, national forces fragment and dissipate and social progress is not only impeded, it becomes impossible. . . . The growing corruption of the language bespeaks social chaos.

It is this continuity of language and politics—of language, race, and religion—that is here most relevant in Caro's views and that deserves further commentary. His complex thinking on the subject can be examined in three parts: (1) the relationship between Spanish-language use and learning policies and Colombian politics; (2) the connection between Colombian, and more generally the Spanish of the Americas, with peninsular Spanish; and (3) the relation between peninsular Spanish and Latin. As can be easily anticipated, this whole hierarchical structure was determined by its inclusion in a Catholic Church–dominated world view. In such a view there was no space for the modern (European) process of discursive autonomy that separates science, the state, and religion as specialized concerns and practices. On the contrary, it was their inextricable union and strength that Caro underlined: "Se ha temido que los rumores advenedizos y callejeros sean soplo potente a derribar el trono en que se asienta, con triple aureola de gloria, literaria, política y religiosa, la Lengua Castellana" (Caro 1928a: 5, 136) ("It has been feared by some that the speculative street rumors are strong enough to dislodge the Spanish language from its place of dominance achieved through its triple glory of its literature and its political and religious expression"). For Caro a grammar based on the classical models becomes a microparadigm for national politics in which: first, the one who knows is accepted and obeyed *because* he is the authority; second, Castilian Spanish turns into an indelible link with the Spanish (and eventually Latin or European meridional "race" and spirit); and third, Latin as a language and culture is the space where language, religion, and politics (insofar as Latin was the language of the Roman Catholic Church) intersect. This thought is developed in a series of tightly argued neoscholastic essays in which Caro defines language use, literature, and poetry and their study in classical humanities. His advocacy of a literary education was standard for his time in most centers of learning in Europe. This apology for learned studies of letters claimed that the study of literature, especially the classics, sharpens the wit, develops the mind, and in general enhances the natural intelligence of the individual. Therefore, he argued, any diminishment in the imparting of a classical education would have dire consequences for civilization, especially in democracies which are so prone to vulgarity and disorder (Caro 1962c, 1. 1382).

Whereas in Rudolf Lenz we saw the composition notebook becoming a space for both the expression and the control of modern subjectivities, here in Caro, classically oriented literature (and its study) constitute a space where traditional social, cultural, political, and racial hierarchies can be reproduced. The Republic of Letters becomes the paradigm for the Republic of politics.

Defining language use as "la forma que toma una lengua y el curso que lleva en boca de las gentes, entregada al instinto natural y a la imaginación irreflexiva y libre de la influencia directa de los libros" (Caro 1928b, 248) ("the form language takes and the course it develops in the speech of people given over to natural instincts and unreflective imagination when it is free from the direct influence of books"), Caro positioned literature as "la sal del lenguaje, el único poder que neutraliza e impide la acción disolvente del uso" ("the salt of language, the only power that neutralizes and impedes the dissolutory action of usage"). Literature as a space of social containment could then be redefined as "esta especie de nacionalidad que llamamos literaria" ("this kind of nationality that we call literary"). Therefore literature and language made possible participation in a higher level of citizenship: "Si la lengua es una segunda patria, todos los pueblos que hablan un mismo idioma, forman en cierto modo una cierta nacionalidad" (Caro 1952, 86) ("If language constitutes a second nationality, then all the people who speak the same language in a certain way make up a nationality"). This connection of Spanish, Latin (both language and "race"), and Catholicism, then, meant that Caro's cultural project was by definition supranational in scope. Celebrating the reemergence of Catholic youth associations, he declared:

> Nace de ahí el carácter de internacionales que distingue a estas asociaciones, y aquel espíritu de racional cosmopolitismo que debe animarnos, y que sin alterar el amor doméstico, el amor patrio, ningún afecto legítimo, ahoga sí el pagano orgullo nacional y personal. (Caro 1962a, 731)

> Thus is born the international character that distinguishes these associations and that spirit of cosmopolitan rationalism that should inspire us without in any way diminishing our love of our homeland, and thereby drowns out that pagan form of national and personal pride.

As is clear in this quotation, the national for Caro was simply the first and not necessarily the most important level of personal identification for a good citizen, but it could lend itself easily to a form of paganism when it became nationalism.

On the so-called *raza latina* (Latin race) unified by religion and language, he added: "¿Qué es pues eso que así llamamos? Un conjunto de pueblos y familias que se estrechan, confunden e identifican a virtud de una idea, y esta es la idea católica . . . dogma, tradiciones y afectos" (Caro 1962d, 735) ("What is it that we call [the Latin race]? It is an assembly of peoples and families that embrace, mix, and identify by virtue of an idea, and this idea is the Catholic idea . . . dogma, traditions, and affections"). Short of religious faith and commitment, this literary Catholic ideal was paradoxically most fully realized in the study of Classical poetry because it was there

that the worship of true authority coincided with models of Beauty, Good, and Truth. For this, Caro reread Virgil and Homer, and more generally epic poetry, as quintessentially religious texts: "La Eneida de Virgilio, por ejemplo, es como toda verdadera epopeya, un poema religioso" (Caro 1888, 316 and 321) ("the Aeneid of Virgil, for example, like all true epics, is a religious poem").

What in Rafael Nuñez had originally been a sociological aspiration, based on Spencer, to the moral unity of the polis became in Miguel Antonio Caro, his political successor and partner, an explicit reformulation of the Catholic medieval ideal of communitas, now connected to a racialized and militant "hispanism." Faithful to his deeply felt convictions, Caro was successively professor of Latin, a founding member of the Academia Colombiana de la Lengua, president of the Catholic University, and finally, president of Colombia. His was an extremely consequential effort to revive traditional Catholic and Hispanic social and cultural structures and to put them to the service of a particular project for modernizing Colombia. The role of language practice and learning was central in such an enterprise. There were two fundamental aspects of this influence of the literary on Colombian education under the conservative hegemony: a pedagogical system and a pedagogical concept of the student, which were closely connected.

The first and most general manifestation of this literary determination on the pedagogical system is what Ángel Rama has termed the "ciudad letrada" ("lettered city"). Here there was a radical distance between the lettered, who elaborated the laws and governed the country, and the rest of the population. But this characterization can be applied both to the liberal project of reform and secularizing modernization and to the conservative Catholic Regeneración that followed it (see von der Walde). In both cases the ideas are misplaced or out of touch with the everyday life of the vast majority of the people. Although it is true that the Colombian conservative republic of the Regeneración may have been the most perfect manifestation of Rama's model in the nineteenth century, I have tried to suggest that a closer look at this lettered city can take us beyond generalizations toward a deeper understanding of the concept of transnational Latin Americanism.

The classically oriented model of literary pedagogy proposed and implemented by Caro both reflected and made possible a certain authoritarian political model at the level of the lived experience of the student-citizen. At the religious level, there was only one existing truth from which all possible meanings derived, and there were only two specialized interpreters of this truth: priests and the lettered. At the literary level, this instruction promoted Catholicized classics; the paradigmatic genre was poetry in the two languages in which these classics were written: Latin and Spanish. The whole system was based on the paradigmatic nature of the model and on the hierarchically structured distance that separated the socially stratified citizens from the lettered elite. In this context, rote memorization and imitation of the models were not remnants from the past, as the liberals had contended, but were once again the *only* proper ways of preserving, transmitting, and recreating the humanistic values that organized the cultural aspects of La Regeneración. The student-citizen lived and knew his place in society by speaking properly and writing correctly in conjunction with these models.

Although both the German pedagogical mission (1870) and the previous Pestalozzian pedagogical turn in Colombian education, with their privileging of observation and direct experience as the basis of school knowledge, had rejected the humanistic paradigm based on rote memorization and the imitation of classical models, what turned out to be the most subversive aspect of this liberal view of education from the perspective of Caro's neotraditionalism was not that it privileged the daily contact with the national and with concrete everyday life and objects, but its liberal concept of the student. For in pedagogical liberalism the student was, regardless of his or her status, the psychopedagogical site of a universal process of development. Insofar as children were naturally determined to follow the same equalizing psychological evolution, they could become the democratically and scientifically uniform objects of a disciplinary knowledge and not the hierarchically ranked souls that Caro's neoscholastic and Hispanic project envisioned. The lasting rejection of those pedagogical liberal postulates in favor of a medieval concept of the Catholic ethnically, socially, and culturally stratified student was one of Caro's lasting legacies in Colombia. Thus conquering the desacralizing impulse of the liberal attempt to turn Catholic morality into one among many private forms of morality, Miguel Antonio Caro succeeded in confirming and identifying hispanic Catholicism as the heart of Colombian public life (Zuluaga 1987, 219). It is a measure of his success that the first article of Law 39 of 1903 (On Public Instruction) declared: "La Instrucción pública en Colombia será organizada y dirigida en concordancia con la religión católica" ("Public instruction in Colombia will be organized and directed in concordance with the Catholic religion"). Decree 491 of 1904 (by which the law of 1903 was regulated) stated in its Article 55: "[Los maestros] Procurarán, en consecuencia, explicar las lecciones por medio de ejemplos relativos a la geografía, a la historia y a las riquezas naturales de Colombia, así como a los hechos de la vida cotidiana" (Uribe 537 and 559) ("[Teachers] will, consequently, endeavor to teach their classes through examples taken from the geography, history, and natural wealth of Colombia, as well as from the reality of everyday life"). The conservative Catholic hegemony over Colombian education would not be seriously challenged until the arrival in Colombia of yet another German educational mission in 1924 (González 71–77).

At the turn of the nineteenth century, the influence of the state in the production of social knowledge seemed to have arrived at a defining moment in Latin American history. Positivism, which had reacted against what it perceived as the unscientific and metaphysical generalizations of Catholic-oriented classical education (despite its insistence on the appreciation of local realities) was itself always inherently running the risk of being perceived as another claim to universal reason, this time in the guise of science. In 1912, for example, the Peruvian Manuel Vicente Villarán stated:

No olvidemos que las universidades latinoamericanas tienen una misión nacional dentro del orden científico. En nuestras aulas debe estudiarse nuestra geografía, nuestro cielo, nuestra raza, nuestra historia, nuestra política, nuestras instituciones. Tópicos nacionales de esta índole ponen en consorcio la ciencia y el patriotismo; concilian el amor a la verdad con el interés por el bien público. (qtd. in Zea 1980, 1: 108)

Let us not forget that Latin American universities have a national mission to realize within the scope of scientific inquiry. It is our geography, our skies, our race, our history, our politics, and our institutions that must be studied in our classrooms. National topics of this kind make patriotism and science compatible; they therefore reconcile the love of truth with the interest in furthering the public good.

The challenge of the state's intervention in public education was to make the production of scientific (universal) knowledge compatible with national (locally oriented) values. The public national interest thus demanded a tangible negotiation between translocal science and specific local culture. National reality required not only scientific description but also practical forms of intervention. Thus even science had to be nationalized if this connection was to be made. If in this context we now focus on Argentina, we will see yet another turn in the articulation of national languages and literatures, Positivism, social sciences, humanities, and politics.

Argentina

In 1909 Ricardo Rojas (1882–1957), summarizing the conclusions to what he called a pedagogical plan, declared:

(a) Pedagogía de restauración nacionalista por medio de la historia y del neohumanismo.
(b) Nuestra enseñanza general de humanidades es un estéril ejercicio mecánico, cuya deficiencia finca, más que en los profesores, en la carencia de material pedagógico y de programas sistemáticos.
(c) Nuestra situación de pueblo nuevo y cosmopolita requiere del Estado argentino, hoy más que nunca, el culto de la tradición y la formación de un ambiente histórico nacional.
(d) Nuestro curso de humanidades, en la enseñanza general, exige una renovación nacionalista, inspirada en propósitos equivalentes a los que han organizado esta disciplina en otros países.
(Rojas 1971, 239–41)

(a) Our pedagogy must be a nationalist restoration through the study of history and neo-humanism.
(b) Our present general education in the humanities is a sterile, mechanical exercise, whose primary deficiency resides in the lack of pedagogical materials and of a systematic program of instruction rather than in the teachers.
(c) Our situation as a new and cosmopolitan nation requires that the Argentinean State, today more than ever, support and implement the cultivation of tradition and the development of a national historical awareness.
(d) Our national instruction in the humanities, in general education requires a nationalistic renovation inspired by similar programs that have organized this discipline in other countries.

What is particularly striking here about Rojas's plan is not so much the nationalistic impulse, at the time present across the continent, but his confidence in modernizing the country by fully nationalizing the humanities. By this time some Positivists were already missing the strong moral discipline the classical humanities had been supposed to provide. The Bolivian Ignacio Prudencio Bustillo, who had praised the Positivists' concentric method, for example, complained about the abandonment of the Classics:

Hemos imitado a Francia en la supresión de las letras clásicas, y en esto se ha cometido en ambos países un grave error. . . . En Bolivia debíamos cultivar estas lenguas, no para adquirir un conocimiento del idioma nacional, lo que es ya muy importante, tampoco para educar y refinar el gusto estético; únicamente para consolidar la enseñanza de la moral, designio importantísimo que es perseguido en Inglaterra. (qtd. in Zea 1980, 1: 135–36)

We have imitated France in the suppression of classical literature, and this is a grave error in both countries. . . . In Bolivia we should study the classical languages, not to gain knowledge of the national language, which is of primary importance, nor to educate and refine our aesthetic appreciation, but rather in order to consolidate our teaching of morality, a most important aim pursued in England.

Rojas's effort, which he termed "neohumanismo," was also in itself both a product of and a reaction against Positivism. It was a product of Positivism insofar as it borrowed a number of Positivist arguments against the classical humanities and their teaching methods (memorization, lack of local specificity, outdated and unscientific methods, etc.). But it was also a reaction to Positivism's general scientific rationality and to its faith in a singular model of international development. Thus Rojas warned against mistaking progress for civilization. Whereas progress was the external and constantly changing face of society, civilization was society's organic process of cultural and spiritual accumulation. Civilization was based on a vital and locally specific form of patriotism grounded in a "concepción de trascendencia ética y cívica" (Rojas 1971, 64) ("a transcendent concept of ethics and civics").

The originality of Rojas's neohumanism can be perceived when this neohumanism is contrasted with the ideas of orthodox Argentinean Positivists such as J. Alfredo Ferreira, who in his "Bases científicas de la educación moral" [1918; "Scientific Bases for Moral Education"], stated:

Cuando se perfeccione la ciencia social al igual que la astronomía, por ejemplo, será tan fácil predecir la aparición de un hombre representativo, como el paso del cometa Halley. . . . El punto de vista social da un nuevo aspecto a la moral humana, explica su origen, desenvolvimiento y caracter actual y hasta puede inducir sus caracteres futuros. (qtd. in Zea 1980, 2: 149)

When social science is perfected to the same level as astronomy, for example, it will be as easy to predict the development of a representative man as the appearance of Halley's comet. . . . The perspective of social science gives a new dimension to human morality; it explains its origins, development, and present character and will even predict its future characteristics.

This was the language and the scientific model of the first Positivist wave in the social sciences. It claimed, based mostly on psychology and biology, an ability to predict universal forms of behavior manifested locally at the social and individual level. Victor Mercante, another important Positivist educator, produced in 1891 one of the first Argentinean experimental attempts at studying the psychobiology of school children by analyzing 5,000 written compositions (Manganiello 149). It was partly against this type of Positivism in search of a scientific, universal basis for moral education that Rojas reacted with his nationalistic neohumanist proposal.

Rojas's *renovación nacionalista* (nationalist renovation) was also, in Argentina, part of a widespread elite response to what was perceived as the new coming of the barbarians in the form of hundreds of thousands of immigrants who did not speak Spanish. It is the presence of this second or alternative subaltern sector (the immigrants) that makes Rojas's call for renewal clearer as a form of governmental intervention in the field of national education in order to invent the cultural imaginary of the Argentinean nation. "Inventing" here does not refer to a fabrication of the national past (see Gagliano 291) but to a conscious attempt at articulating a coherent set of narratives of national development that could in turn be taught to and inculcated in all its citizens.

Rojas quotes a former minister of education of Argentina, Carballido, under Pellegrini:

Tan violenta ha sido la avenida inmigratoria que podría llegar a absorber nuestros elementos étnicos. . . . Ante el eclipse de todo ideal, sería para alarmarnos por el olvido de nuestras tradiciones: correría peligro la misma nacionalidad. . . . Y es, sin embargo, esta hora suprema la que algunos eligen para ensalzar la educación

utilitaria que nos ha traido donde estamos, y atacar la cultura clásica, que por si sola constituye una escuela de patriotismo y de nobleza moral.

Los razonamientos del señor Carballido eran todos exactos según se ve; pero me sorprende que al atacar el cosmopolitismo y defender las tradiciones argentinas, plantee la cuestión sobre las humanidades clásicas y el latín, en lugar de hacerlo sobre las humanidades modernas y la historia. Es que él era también una víctima del enciclopedismo internacional, (¡sin raíz de instinto aborigen!) (Rojas 1971, 111)

The massive arrival of foreign immigration has been so violent that it can soon get to the point when it will engulf our ethnic element. . . . Facing the eclipse of all ideals, the forgetting of our traditions, would be cause for alarm: our nationality itself would be at risk. . . . And nevertheless, some among us have chosen this hour of supreme danger to praise vocational education, which has brought us to the present crisis, and to attack the teaching of classical culture, which in of itself constitutes a school of patriotism and of moral nobility.

The reasoning of Mr. Carballido was evidently correct; but what surprises me is that in attacking cosmopolitanism and defending Argentine traditions he should have put the question [of survival] in terms of the [teaching of] classic humanities and Latin instead of doing so with regard to modern humanities and history. He was also the victim of international encyclopedism–with a trace of native instinct!

Thus Rojas shared the diagnosis but not the cure. For him it was modern humanities, centered on the teaching of history and of the Spanish language and literature as a nationalized pedagogy, that were needed to put a halt and provide a corrective to what he considered the corrupting influence of immigrants and European cosmopolitan culture on Argentina. Therefore traditional classicism and immigrants shared at least one trait in Rojas's view: They were both foreign.

Naturally, in Rojas's neohumanism, history took the most important place. In analyzing what he conceived to be the main properties of history as a school subject, one perceives why he called his proposal "neohumanism": "La historia es educativa de la inteligencia, porque es un ejercicio de la memoria, de la imaginación y del juicio" (37) ("History teaches intelligence, because it is the exercise of memory, imagination, and judgment"); "La Historia, en la enseñanza sobre todo, tiene una gran influencia como disciplina moral: tiene la influencia del ejemplo" (39) ("History, in education, has great influence as a moral discipline: It has the influence of providing example"). This objective is achieved through the study of the biographies of national heroes. Let us add in passing that this indoctrinating use of the *vita* (here constructed for the hero) and some of the techniques for the expression and control of the self exemplified by Lenz's "cuaderno de composición" are among the modern legacies and continuities of the technologies of the self originated in antiquity and in early and medieval Christian education (see Foucault).

What at the lower level of education was for Rojas still a somewhat general if nationalized morality becomes at the upper level more and more precise and localized. Alluding indirectly to Marxism, "el innoble veneno" ("ignoble poison"), Rojas formulates a critique that for him can be extended to any of the supranational forms of thought well exemplified by socialism, anarchism, and Catholicism: "esa fórmula contraria a la patria implica substituir el grupo humano concreto por una humanidad en abstracto que no se sabría como servir" (Rojas 1971, 44 and 18) ("this formula, which was contrary to the nation, implied a concrete human group with an abstract humanity that no one would know how to serve"). For Rojas, then, history is fundamentally the teaching of modern patriotism based on a political and territorial concept of the nation, which according to him is itself the only actual and viable way of living within modernity. This strong moral bond is based on the knowledge (acquired in school) of common traditions, the forms of discourse and the collective interests of the nation as administered by the state. This political patriotism is not to be confused with a more base and coarse form he calls "patriotismo instintivo" ("instinctive patriotism"). The main difference between them is the productive nature of political patriotism. Thus the main goal of the homogenizing extension of territorial and civic solidarity and of collective memory is not simply the protection it affords the nation, but the way in which it literally produces new citizen-subjects, that is, "hombre[s] en determinadas condiciones de tiempo y lugar" (Rojas 1971, 147) ("men in the specific conditions of time and place"). According to Rojas, as we have said, this is particularly needed in Argentina:

> Bástenos recordar que una cantidad exhorbitante de brazos italianos trabaja nuestros campos y que una cantidad extraordinaria de capitales británicos mueve nuestras empresas. . . . [In the midst of this cosmopolitanism, he continues,] El momento aconseja con urgencia imprimir a nuestra educación un carácter nacionalista por medio de la Historia y las humanidades. (Rojas 1971, 83–84)

> Suffice it to remember that an extraordinary number of Italian arms work our fields and that an extraordinary amount of British capital moves our industries. . . . The present moment urges us to stamp a national character on our education by means of the teaching of history and the humanities.

The place of history notwithstanding, the teaching of Spanish language and literature was a crucial component of these humanities. Here Rojas criticizes first the classical paradigm of traditional humanities. This is succinctly expressed in his book *Eurindia* (1924):

> Los retores clásicos reverenciaban una norma gramatical, sin patria ni cronología, a la cual ajustaban su juicio. La crítica encerrábase para ellos en un sistema de modelos escritos, dogmas y cánones que nadie podía violar. (Rojas 1980, 1: 50)

> Classical commonplaces abounded in our grammatical norms, without there being a nation, without historical chronology on which to anchor judgment. Criticism was locked into a system of models, texts, dogmas, and canons that no one could violate.

It is characteristic of Rojas, who had called the immigrants "hordas cosmopolitas" ("cosmopolitan hordes"), to attack first what he considered to be the supranational, ahistorical, and atemporal nature of classical studies in Argentina. Then comes the charge against scholasticism, which is implicitly contrasted with the enriching possibilities for nationalized forms of literary expression. We have now come full circle from Caro's Catholic ideal. Whereas Caro valued poetry for its natural relationship to the metaphysical essence of a universal truth, Rojas called for a nationalized aesthetics and aesthetic education. Truth had thus in Argentina finally merged with the nation-state and its intellectuals.

Spirituality was then nationalized. Speaking of the teacher of national language and literature, Rojas recommended:

> El profesor deberá hacer comprender a sus discípulos que en el idioma patrio están los elementos espirituales más duraderos de la tradición nacional y que la conservación del castellano será necesaria a la unidad de nuestra fisonomía histórica. (Rojas 1971, 163)

> The teacher ought to make his students understand that in the national language there reside the most lasting spiritual elements of the national tradition and that the continuance of the Spanish language will be necessary for the unity of our historical identity.

Instead of the mechanistic learning of routinized rules, it was necessary "hacer ver al alumno que cuanto él habla es manifestación de su personalidad y temperamento" (Rojas 1971, 163) ("to make the student understand that when he speaks he expresses his personality and temperament"); but in contrast with the psychological postulates of the previous educational Positivism, this pedagogy was a search for orational expression that was the very identity of the national subject. In 1909 Ricardo Rojas perceived with great clarity that a profound understanding of nationalism had to start by analyzing pedagogical proposals, apprehending at the level of the (desired) transformations in the practice of teaching the forms through which the subject became a subject of a historically constructed notion of self, citizenship, and political participation.

I have successively considered the pedagogical constitution of a nationalized space for the expression and control of the self in the work of Rudolf Lenz (Chile); the Catholic proposal of Miguel Antonio Caro for a supranational, translocal form of literary republic and citizenship based on the model of poetry and the Classics (Colombia); and, finally, the work of Ricardo Rojas, with his neohumanist reclaiming and refashioning of the moral and political potential of history and literature for nation building, both as discourses and as the subjects of pedagogical practices. In so doing I have had to deal with the multiple overlapping of traditionalists, Positivists, and nationalists in conflict over the control of the educational space within that set of institutions we call the state. The result of these conflicts in each Latin American country has been the formation of a reading and writing public who made possible the production of a national literature that in turn became one of the important components of the transcultural processes led by the state in its search for the creation of a national hegemony.

Works Cited

Amunátegui Solar, Domingo. "La Doctrina ideal sobre el Instituto Pedagógico en 1892." *Homenaje a Domingo Amunátegui Solar, Anales de la Universidad de Chile.* Santiago: Universidad de Chile. 213–20.

Brunner, José Joaquín. 1985. *Los Orígenes de la sociología profesional en Chile.* Santiago: FLACSO.

Burchell, Graham et al., eds. 1991. *The Foucault Effect: Studies in Governmentality.* London: Harvester Wheatsheaf.

Caro, Miguel Antonio. 1888. "La Religión y la Poesía." *Artículos y Discursos* by Miguel Antonio Caro. Bogotá: Librería Americana. 307–32.

——. 1928a. "Americanismo en el lenguaje." *Obras Completas de Don Manuel Antonio Caro.* Vol. 5: *Estudios filológicos y gramaticales.* Ed. Victor E. Caro and Antonio Gómez Restrepo. Bogotá: Imprenta Nacional. 120–36.

——. 1928b. "Del Uso en sus relaciones con el lenguaje." *Obras Completas de Don Manuel Antonio Caro.* Vol. 5: *Estudios filológicos y gramaticales.* Ed. Victor E. Caro and Antonio Gómez Restrepo. Bogotá: Imprenta Nacional. 234–75.

——. 1952. "Fundación de la academia colombiana." *Ideario Hispanico.* By Miguel Antonio Caro. Ed. Antonio Curcio Altamar. Bogotá: Instituto Colombiano de Cultura Hispánica. 81–96.

———. 1962a. "Discurso al instalar la juventud católica de Bogotá." *Obras*. Vol. 1: *Filosofía, religión, pedagogía*. Bogotá: Instituto Caro y Cuervo. 727–33.

———. 1962b. "Lo que va de ayer a hoy en materia de educación." *Obras*. Vol. 1: *Filosofía, religión, pedagogía*. Bogotá: Instituto Caro y Cuervo. 1450–59.

———. 1962c. "Oración de estudios pronunciada en el acto de la solemne distribución de premios del Colegio del Espíritu Santo el día 15 de noviembre de 1880." *Obras*. Vol. 1: *Filosofía, religión, pedagogía*. Bogotá: Instituto Caro y Cuervo.1374–85.

———. 1962d. "Raza latina." *Obras*. Vol. 1: *Filosofía, religión, pedagogía*. Bogotá: Instituto Caro y Cuervo. 734–37.

Deas, Malcolm. 1993. "Miguel Antonio Caro y amigos: gramática y poder en Colombia." *Del Poder y la gramática: y otros ensayos sobre historia, política y literatura colombianas* by Malcolm Deas. Bogota: Tercer Mundo Editores. 25–60.

Farrell, Robert V. 1974. "The Catholic Church and Colombian Education: 1886–1930. In Search of a Tradition." Diss. Columbia University.

Foucault, Michel. 1980. *History of Sexuality*. Trans. Robert Hurley. 3 vols. New York: Vintage.

Gagliano, Rafael S. 1990. "Nacionalismo, inmigración y pluralismo cultural. Polémicas educativas en torno al Centenario." *Sociedad civil y Estado en los orígenes del sistema educativo argentino*. Vol 2: *Historia de la Educación Argentina*. Ed. Adriana Puiggrós et. al. Buenos Aires: Editorial Galerna. 281–307.

Gonzalez G., Fernán. 1979. *Educación y estado en la historia de Colombia*. Bogota: Centro de Investigación y Educación Popular.

Gracia, Jorge. 1984. "Philosophical Analysis in Latin America." *History of Philosophy Quarterly* 1:111–22.

Jaramillo Uribe, Jaime, J. G. Cobo Borda, and Santiago Mutis Durán, eds. 1979. *Manual de Historia de Colombia*. 3 vols. Bogota: Subdirección de Comunicaciones Culturales, División de Publicaciones.

Jocelyn Holt, Alfredo. 1992. *La Independencia de Chile*. Madrid: MAPFRE.

Laclau, Ernesto. 1990. *New Reflections on the Revolution of Our Time*. London: Verso.

Lenz, Rudolf. 1924. *La Composición escolar en lengua patria*. Santiago: Imprenta Cervantes.

———. 1940. "Dialectología Hispanoamericana." *El Español en Chile*. By Rudolf Lenz, Andrés Bello, and Rodolfo Oroz. Trans. Amada Alonso and Raimundo Lida. Buenos Aires: Instituto de Filología. 7–48.

———. 1894. "Ensayos filológicos americanos." *Anales de la Universidad de Chile* 87: 113–32, 353–67.

———. 1899. *Proyecto de Programa de castellano*. Santiago: Imprenta Cervantes.

Loy, Jane Meyer. 1971. "Primary Education during the Colombian Federation: The School Reform of 1870." *Hispanic American Historical Review* 51 (May): 275–94.

Manganiello, Ethel M. 1980. *Historia de la Educación Argentina*. Buenos Aires: Librería del Colegio.

Martín Barbero, Jesús. 1987. *De los medios a las mediaciones: comunicación, cultura y hegemonía*. Mexico City: Gustavo Gili.

Molina, Gerardo. 1971. *Las Ideas liberales en Colombia 1849–1914*. Bogota: Ediciones Tercer Mundo.

Nueva Historia de Colombia. 1989. 11 vols. Ed. Jaime Jaramillo Uribe, Alvaro Tirado Mejía, Jorge Orlando Melo, and Jesús Antonio Bejarano. Bogota: Planeta.

Nuñez, Rafael. 1980. "La sociología." *Pensamiento positivista latinoamericano*. Vol. 2. Ed. Leopoldo Zea. Caracas: Biblioteca Ayacucho. 235–42.

Park, James William. 1985. *Rafael Núñez and the Politics of Colombian Regionalism, 1863–1886*. Baton Rouge: Louisiana State University Press.

Pike, Frederick B., ed. 1964. *The Conflict between Church and State in Latin America*. New York: Knopf.

Poviña, Alfredo. 1959. *Nueva Historia de la Sociología Latinoamericana*. Cordoba: Imprenta de la Universidad.

Prieto, René. 1996. "The Literature of *Indigenismo*." *The Cambridge History of Latin American Literature*. Vol. 2: *The Twentieth Century*. Ed. Roberto González-Echevarría and Enrique Pupo-Walker. Cambridge: Cambridge University Press. 138–63.

Rama, Ángel. 1995. *La ciudad letrada*. Montevideo: ARCA.

Rivas, José Manuel. 1977. *El Latín en Colombia*. Bogota: Instituto Colombiano de Cultura.

Roig, Arturo Andrés. 1989. "Eticidad, conflictividad y categorías sociales en Juan Montalvo." *Coloquio Internacional sobre Juan Montalvo*. Quito: Fundación Friedrich Naumann. 189–215.

Rojas, Ricardo. 1980. *Eurindia: ensayo de estética sobre las culturas americanas*. Ed. Graciela Perosio and Nannina Rivarda. Buenos Aires: CEAL.

———. 1971. *La restauración nacionalista. Crítica de la educación argentina y bases para una reforma en el estudio de las humanidades modernas*. Buenos Aires: A. Peña Lillo Editor.

Romero, Jose Luis. 1970. *El Pensamiento político de la derecha latinoamericana*. Buenos Aires: Paidós.

Solar Correa, Eduardo. 1934. *La Muerte del Humanismo en Chile*. Santiago: Nascimento.

Subercaseaux, Bernardo. 1981. *Lastarria, ideología y literatura*. Santiago: Aconcagua.

Tedesco, Juan Carlos. 1986. *Educación y sociedad en la Argentina 1880–1945*. Buenos Aires: Ediciones Solar.

Terán, Oscar. 1983. *América latina: positivismo y nación*. Mexico City: Katún.

Therborn, Goran. 1976. *Science, Class and Society on the Formation of Historical Materialism*. London: NLB.

Uribe, Antonio José, ed. 1919. *El primer congreso pedagógico nacional de Colombia*. Bogota: Imprenta Nacional.

Walde Uribe, Erna von der. 1997. "Limpia, fija y da esplendor: el letrado y la letra en Colombia a fines del siglo XIX." *Revista Iberoamericana* 63.178–79 (Jan.–June): 71–83.

Zea, Leopoldo. 1965. *El pensamiento Latinoamericano*. Mexico City: Editorial Pormaca.

———. 1980. *Pensamiento Positivista latinoamericano*. 2 vols. Caracas: Biblioteca Ayacucho.

Zuluaga de Echeverry, Olga Lucía. 1979. *Colombia: dos modelos de su práctica pedagógica durante el siglo XIX*. Medellín: Universidad de Antioquia.

———. 1987. *Pedagogía e Historia*. Bogota: Ediciones Foro Nacional por Colombia.

CHAPTER 26

MESTIZAJE AND THE INVERSION OF SOCIAL DARWINISM IN SPANISH AMERICAN FICTION

Julie Taylor and George Yúdice

Introduction

This essay examines the legacy of Social Darwinism in the discourses of *mestizaje* and transculturation that became prominent in Latin America from the 1920s to the 1940s. A close reading of these discourses reveals that the degenerative diagnoses of nineteenth-century Social Darwinism are never fully exorcized from the celebratory constructions of hybrid national identities that arose in this era of emerging populism. Until recently, transculturation was characterized by (mostly literary) critics as an apt recognition of the contributions made by indigenous, African, and European peoples as they mixed, physically and/or culturally, in the national formations of Latin America. The term, coined by Fernando Ortiz (1881–1969) in 1940 but already evident in reflections on race and national identity in the late nineteenth century, was received positively by critics concerned with the democratization of culture. It signaled for them the importance of the popular "stock" in which the ingredients of the national *ajiaco* ("stew") were blended (F. Ortiz 1939, 6). More recently, however, the emphasis on synthesis inherent in this model has been criticized for its subordination of the constituents that went into the melting pot. Indeed, a less nationally based conception of democracy has put the emphasis on the ingredients themselves rather than on their absorption for the sake of union. In accordance with this contemporary critique of transculturation, we see the legacy of Social Darwinism as a critical factor in the suppression of individual constituents in the process of narrating a hybrid nation.

In the late nineteenth century, many Latin American intellectuals and statesmen worried about their nations' hybrid populations, which, according to the reigning ideological discourse of Social Darwinism, would retard the nations' progress into modernity. One solution to this predicament was to imagine a scenario in which the hitherto condemned *mestizos* could contribute to a nation's progress. The proposed viability of the *mestizo* as a national subject became, in fact, a dominant theme in literary and political discourse, as intellectuals across the continent envisioned nations in which modernity and *mestizaje* converged in the trajectory toward progress. These were would-be societies in which previously unintegratable *mestizos* attained a stability and order that made them suitable candidates for modernity. In the process, however, we detect in these discourses a hierarchizing imaginary that relegates the original "backward" elements, as well as many "unstable" hybrids, to extinction. They are left behind on the road to progress; their destiny, in the narrative economy of transculturation, is to disappear for the sake of a balanced national character: Neither too African, nor too Indian, nor too European.

Modernity and *Mestizaje*

Mestizaje, or miscegenation, was seen in the nineteenth century as an obstacle to modernization. By the 1930s many Latin American countries had reversed the valence of *mestizaje,* as new historical projects required the acknowledgment of the contributions of subaltern classes, most of mixed-race heritage. This reevaluation turned Social Darwinism on its head, although as we argue throughout this essay, it didn't eliminate it. Social Darwinism is of a piece with the evolutionary thinking at the heart of notions of modernization. It has some very specific features: It maintains that biological laws govern organic nature, including human nature; that the increase in population tends to produce a struggle among organisms; that the physical and mental features that aid in this struggle can be generalized to the entire population; that the accumulated effects of selection and inheritance through time result in the emergence of new species and the elimination of others; and that the deterministic force of these laws acts not only on physical properties but also on social and psychological characteristics of human beings, such as reason, religion, and morals (Hawkins 31). This last premise is fundamental to Herbert Spencer's theory of social evolution, which posits a movement from a primitive state characterized by animality, immorality, irrationality, vice, and mendacity to higher stages of differentiation, specialization, and individuation (Spencer). For Spencer, children, the lower classes, tribal peoples, and women constitute, together with prehistoric man, the "dangerous classes" that hinder social progress. Inheritance, which is operative in the fittest, is what distinguishes those who progress from those who vegetate and regress (Hawkins 98–99).

In the nineteenth century, Social Darwinism was extremely influential in the discourse of the social sciences. In both Europe and Latin America, its pervasive influence could be felt in the work of intellectuals in a variety of fields. Discourse on race, in particular, was affected by this theoretical orientation, as theories of Social Darwinism combined with positivist ideals of progress and modernity in assigning different values to different races. Social Darwinism legitimized the imperial and class projects of European bourgeois elites and their Latin American epigones. Following the English historian Henry Thomas Buckle (1821–1862), the Swiss-U.S. naturalist Louis Agassiz (1807–1873), and French social observers such as Arthur de Gobineau (1816–1882), Gustave Le Bon (1841–1931), and Louis Couty (Skidmore 27–33), Latin American thinkers such as the Brazilian Raymundo Nina Rodrigues (1862–1906), the Bolivian Alcides Arguedas (1879–1946), and Argentines Carlos Octavio Bunge (1875–1918) and José Ingenieros (1877–1925) predicted that "inferior" races would likely disappear due to their inability to adapt to modernity. Particularly discredited were people of mixed race, who were considered degenerate and inappropriate for modern life. Arguedas, presumably defending the *mestizos,* saw them as less adaptable than the Spanish and the Indians:

El *cholo* de Bolivia, Perú y Colombia; el *roto* de Chile, el *gaucho* de la Argentina y del Uruguay, etc., son una clase de gentes híbridas, sometidas ya a un lento proceso de selección, pero que todavía no han alcanzado a eliminar de sí las taras de su estirpe. . . . Por todas las transformaciones del mejor sistema de instrucción: en cien años no haréis de él un obrero inglés que trabaja, consume, vive digna y confortablemente. (438–39)

The *cholo* from Bolivia, Peru, and Colombia; the Chilean *roto*; the Argentine and Uruguayan *gaucho*, etc. are a class of hybrid people, subject to a slow process of selection that has not yet succeeded in eliminating the defects of their stock. . . . In one hundred years, no matter how much education, you will not transform them into proper English laborers who work, consume, and live with dignity and comfort.

The pathological implications of miscegenation for many nineteenth-century Latin American intellectuals can perhaps best be seen in the early writings of the Cuban Fernando Ortiz. Despite the fact that Ortiz would later become a champion of *transculturación*, and in fact would coin the term, his early criminological studies depict *mestizaje* as degenerative. In one of his first books, *Hampa afro-cubana: Los negros brujos (Apuntes para un estudio de etnología criminal)* [1906; Afro-Cuban Underworld: The Black Witches (Notes for a Study of Criminal Ethnology], he expresses concern that cultural transactions between blacks and whites would lead to the moral regression of all. Cultural hybridization does not elevate blacks; instead, he argues, it makes whites regress, especially those who belong to deficient psychic strata. Transculturation is, therefore, pathological, as it is a precarious moral bridge between the races. So long as the communion of ideas, superstitions, and prejudices held by both races flourishes, racial and cultural co-penetration will result in social degeneration. Whites, despite their relatively developed psychological advance, succumb to the vertigo produced by the superstitions and thus fall to their depths from the heights of their civilization; they regress to a primitive state, they turn black (F. Ortiz 1973, 174).

It has become conventional wisdom that in many Latin American countries the pejorative characterizations of racial mixture typical of nineteenth-century Social Darwinism and scientific racism gave way to affirmative portrayals of the *mestizo* in the constructions of the ideal national subject of the 1920s, 1930s, and 1940s. This is evident in the writings (1925) of the Mexican José Vasconcelos (1881–1959), who coined the term the "cosmic race"; the Brazilian Gilberto Freyre (1900–1987), who in *Casa Grande e Senzala* [1933; *The Masters and the Slaves*] inverted the belief in the inferiority of blacks and invented the term "racial democracy"; and Fernando Ortiz, in whose later work the theory of "transculturation" gave recognition to the contribution of blacks in the formation of Cuban culture (1940, 92–97; 1995, 97–103).

In addition to these individual thinkers, whole movements developed in Latin America celebrating various aspects of transculturation. *Indigenismo* in Mexico, *modernismo* in Brazil, *negrismo* in Cuba, and even *gauchismo* in Argentina were expressions of the popular base that presumably embodied the nation. These optimistic portrayals of *mestizaje* are, of course, not divorced from the political and economic context of the years in which they arose. The turbulence of the period–conflicts between oligarchies and mercantile bourgeoisie, the increasing activism of labor unions, a deepened interest in national politics, all in the context of the expansion of export economies and U.S. intervention–generated the

need for a symbolics that could transcend the rifts and accommodate increasingly vocal subordinate sectors. This emergent nationalist symbolics did not become a serious contender for hegemony (in the Gramscian sense of providing a language through which a series of social, political, and economic conflicts could be discussed and debated) until the 1920s and 1930s. The economic and political programs of the late nineteenth and early twentieth centuries, which included Positivist modernization, emulation of the United States, and encouragement of European migrant laborers to compensate for the "inferior" masses of black, indigenous, and mixed-race people thought to be inappropriate for industry and citizenship, were dismissed, as intellectuals and politicians sought nationalist solutions in a post–World War I political-economic context.

Progress now required the inclusion of formerly despised segments of the population as part of the work force. In countries such as Brazil and Argentina, nativist movements decried the immigration policies of the late nineteenth and early twentieth centuries. Politicians and intellectuals in various countries proposed *mestizaje* as a way of recreating national identity, responding, at least at the symbolic level, to the demands of new elites, the working classes, and the newly displaced peasantry. In some countries, the symbolics of *mestizaje* helped downplay class conflict and legitimize the continued hegemony of elites in this period of crisis or transition marked by the Depression and the turn to a new economic project. *Mestizaje* might be understood in those cases (e.g., Brazil and Mexico) as the ideological discourse that covered over the split in the emerging populist governments (e.g., those of Getulio Vargas and Lázaro Cardenas) between those elites who promoted nationalist import-substitution industrialization and those responding to pressures to meet the demands of the increasing work force. *Mestizaje* was thus the mask of a contradictory, nationalist common sense that would only crack when the definitive failure of import-substitution industrialization, quite visible by the 1950s, made it evident that different economic and social projects were necessary.

In other countries, such as Venezuela, *mestizaje* was not an official or quasi-official discourse. Unlike the regimes of Vargas (1930–1945) or Cárdenas (1934–1940), the long dictatorship of Juan Vicente Gómez (1908–1935) was not characterized by a nationalist state that could contain the contradiction between economic elites and popular demands. The dictatorship, in effect, was marked by a failure to turn a nationalist economic project based in the oil boom that became the mainstay of the economy into a political compromise with the "most dynamic sectors of the Venezuelan middle classes" (Halperin Donghi 269). Despite the unification of the country by a network of highways built during Gómez's regime and the construction of schools, health services, working-class housing projects, and so on, populist ideology was not articulated successfully with Gómez's rule, as it was in Brazil or Mexico in the 1930s, but rather against it. Rómulo Gallegos (1884–1969), whose novels we examine below, was an important political force in the search for alternatives. After Gómez's overthrow, Gallegos became the second candidate from the Democratic Action party to accede to the presidency. His presidency was, however, short-lived; a new dictator, Pérez Jiménez, overthrew him. Nevertheless, Gallegos represented a potentially new national consciousness rooted in the educability and creativity of the new *mestizo* national identity. He "enthusiastically endorsed *mestizaje*, which he considered to be a part of the core process of civilization" (Howard 102).

Yet whether they were promoted by the nationalist-populist states of Brazil and Mexico or used symbolically as part of the opposition against repressive, dependent states like those of Cuba and Venezuela, the positive portrayals of *mestizaje* do not completely escape Social Darwinist–inspired prejudices. In the work of Vasconcelos, Gilberto Freyre, and Fernando Ortiz, for example, traces of white superiority or non-white inferiority remain in the eulogies of a hybrid culture. Vasconcelos, for example, hypothesizes that the white component of the "cosmic race" will prevail over the negative aspects of the other races: "Quizás entre todos los caracteres de la quinta raza predominen los caracteres del blanco, pero tal supremacía debe ser fruto de elección libre del gusto y no resultado de la violencia o de la presión económica" (65) ("Perhaps the traits of the white race will predominate among the characteristics of the fifth [cosmic] race, but such a supremacy must be the result of the free choice of personal taste, and not the fruit of violence or economic pressure") (25–26). We see in this passage the reason that Vasconcelos appeals to an "aesthetic selection" rather than a "natural selection" as the engine of evolution toward cosmic perfection. Vasconcelos's concept of hybridization requires a principle of selection to limit it to those who have or can acquire "superior faculties." In Freyre's case, despite his positive account of black influence on Brazilian culture, he also feels that the new national culture could be purged, through a process of "whitening," of its "cacogenic, mongrel, repulsive aspect" (1974, 111). Similarly, in Fernando Ortiz's economic allegory of national identity, *The Cuban Counterpoint*, the white has to marry the black in order to mitigate the pathology or mixture. For transculturation to take place, racial balance should not be upset–an imminent danger given the encouragement of migration of black workers as a result of foreign domination (see Chapter 2 on transculturation, *The Cuban Counterpoint*). Evolutionism, buttressed by education, is what will enable the backward, racially mixed characters of Gallegos's novels to overcome the determinism of natural and social circumstances. His politics of conciliation and harmony are consistent with the notion of a *mestizo* society in which the different racial ingredients might blend; this political project depends, however, on the normativity of the educators and civilizers, as in *Doña Bárbara*.

Mestizaje and Literature

The increasing prominence of *mestizaje* from the 1920s to the 1940s is not limited to social and political discourse in Latin America. The influence and lure of models of transculturation is also strongly felt in the field of literature; these decades witness a proliferation of novelistic representations of *mestizaje* by authors across South America. In this era of national reconsolidation and the rise of populist regimes, fiction became a forum in which to explore the relationship between issues of racial and cultural mixture and the national past and future. As Latin American countries struggled to define and implement nationalist projects, biological and cultural mixture played a privileged role as a site in which to address and mediate issues of national difference. Doris Sommer has described the importance of *mestizaje* in the foundational fictions of nineteenth-century Latin America: "Miscegenation was the way of redemption in Latin America, a way of annihilating difference and constructing a deeply horizontal, fraternal dream of national identity" (39). The era of populist nationalist projects provided an even greater impetus for

national reconciliation, as is evident in the recourse to *mestizaje* in Latin American novels that have been variously classified as *novelas de la tierra* (novels of the land), *indigenista* novels, *criollista* novels, and Afro-Hispanic literature.

Not surprisingly, the representation of *mestizaje* offered by the authors of these novels varies from novel to novel, both with regard to the image of the *mestizo/a* subject and to the potential of transculturation as a national solution. Taken together, the novels afford us various types of relocation, sundry mixed-race protagonists, and denouements that oscillate between national consolidation and national destruction. In Gallegos's (1884–1969) *Doña Bárbara* (1929), for example, the part-indigenous Marisela is the raw material that Santos Luzardo can tame and educate into the young wife capable of restoring his failing family lineage and the legitimacy of his claims to property. Through Marisela, a union is achieved between the civilized rationality of the Caracas-educated, progress-minded law student and the violent and barbaric but important spirit of the *llanura*, a union that bodes well for the modernization of Venezuela. In fellow Venezuelan Arturo Uslar Pietri's (1906–2001) *Las lanzas coloradas* [1931; *The Red Lances*, 1963], however, the mulatto *mayordomo* (overseer) is a far cry from Gallegos's impressionable *mestiza*, "recia y dúctil a la vez, . . . una personalidad del alma de la raza, abierta como el paisaje a toda acción mejoradora" (1977, 106) ("alternately rude and docile . . . a personification of the soul of the Plainsman, open as the prairie and improved by every experience") (1948, 185). Presentación Campos is, instead, a violent and indomitable man who demonstrates disdain toward both the masses of slaves he oversees and the white plantation owners: "Don Fernando y Doña Inés podían ser los dueños de la hacienda, pero quien mandaba era él. No sabía obedecer. Tenía carne del amo" (Uslar Pietri 1979, 8) ("Don Fernando and Doña Inés might be the owners of the plantation, but he was the one who gave the orders. He did not know how to obey. Commanding was in his blood") (1963, 8). Rather than respecting and legitimizing Don Fernando's claims to property, Presentación Campos rapes his sister, burns his estate, and forcibly leads his slaves off to the bloody Wars of Independence. Adding insult to injury, he fights on the side of the Royalists.

Falling midway between Marisela and Presentación Campos is Pedro Miguel, the mulatto protagonist of Gallegos's later novel *Pobre negro* [1937; Poor Black Man]. The son of a courageous insurgent slave and the white mistress of the *Casa Grande* (Great House), Pedro Miguel initially harbors a dark resentment, seeking revenge against the white landowners. Over the course of the novel, however, he falls in love with his white cousin, Luisana, and realizes that liberating Venezuela from the landowning class requires compromise rather than hate. Leaving behind his obsessive hatred for the landowners, he becomes a leader in the civil wars on the side of the liberals. Mediating between the enlightened republican ideals of Luisana's family and the demand for freedom and equality of his slave father, Pedro Miguel plays an important part in the struggles to democratize Venezuelan society in the early to mid-nineteenth century.

Another example of interracial political solidarity forged through the intercession of a mulatto can be found in Ecuadorian Adalberto Ortiz's (1914–2003) *Juyungo* [1942; *Juyungo: A Classic Afro-Hispanic Novel*, 1982]. In this novel, the protagonist's nickname identifies him with Ecuador's black community, for "Juyungo" is presented as a pejorative term for

Afro-Ecuadorians. The main character's life, however, challenges the stable racial and cultural identity this name suggests. As a child, Juyungo is taken in by an indigenous tribe that is supposedly the enemy of the black population, and as an adult, he takes a white woman as his wife and fathers a mulatto child. Like Pedro Miguel, Juyungo initially distrusts and resents all white people, becoming involved with his future wife only to humiliate a white rival. Through his relationship with his wife and his friendship with a light mulatto student, however, Juyungo comes to realize that class rather than racial affiliations should determine his loyalties. As his mulatto syndicalist friend Nelson Díaz explains, "Ten siempre presente estas palabras, amigo mío: más que la raza, la clase" (A. Ortiz 88) ("my friend, always remember these words: class before race"). Although Gallegos's and Ortiz's novels end somewhat less conclusively than *Doña Bárbara* and *Las lanzas coloradas,* they each manage to propose a model of interracial political alliance.

In a rather late representation of *mestizaje* that places as much emphasis on cultural as biological (or political) mixture, Ramón Díaz Sánchez's (1903–1968) *Cumboto* (1950) envisions a harmonious synthesis of the races. This novel's hope for the future comes in the form of a mulatto son who fulfills his white father's and mulatta mother's dreams by composing an American *mestizo* music, one that would "[a]malgamar el alma de esta tierra con el espíritu clásico" (Díaz Sánchez 1984, 181) ("combine the classical spirit with the essence of this soil"; 1969, 260). The regenerative potential of this unnamed mulatto is clear, as the first-person narrator informs us: "Este joven trae un secreto . . . un secreto de vida" (Díaz Sánchez 1984, 185) ("This young man has a secret . . . a secret of life") (1969, 266). In Peruvian Enrique López Albújar's (1872–1966) *Matalaché* (1928), another potentially promising union, between the young mulatto José Manuel, raised and educated by a previous master supposed to be his father, and María de la Luz, the daughter of his current owner, is cut short. Like Díaz Sánchez's mulatto, José Manuel expresses his hybridity through music, winning the title of best guitarist in the land because of his innovative music, which incorporates both Cuban and traditional Venezuelan rhythms. Despite María's father's liberalist leanings, the romance ends in tragedy. When Don Juan Francisco discovers that his daughter is pregnant with his mulatto slave's child, he sentences José Manuel to death in a vat of boiling rubber (one of the plantation's principal products) and bars the gates to the property, leaving the fate of María and her *mestizo* child unknown.

The national context of these depictions of *mestizaje* is unmistakable. A glance at the résumés of some of the authors is enough to determine their interest in a national project. Díaz Sánchez would become the director of culture and fine arts of the Ministry of Education. Uslar Pietri filled various positions within the López Contreras and Medina Angarita governments, from director of the Instituto Nacional de Inmigración y Colonización (National Institute of Immigration and Colonization) in 1938 to Secretaría de la Presidencia de la República (Secretariat of the President of the Republic) in 1941 and Minsterio de Relaciones Interiores (Minister of the Interior) in 1945. Rómulo Gallegos became President of Venezuela on a democratic, anti-dictatorial platform in 1947, only to be overthrown the following year by a military junta that paved the way for a new dictatorship by General Pérez Jiménez in 1952. Subsequently, Gallegos became president again, this time in the first legal representative democracy in Venezuela (1959–1964), issuing in a new era of populist politics.

Rómulo Gallegos's politics and his writing complement each other. In fact, reference to his politics can shed light on his literary work. The change from dictatorship to democracy under the Trienium (1945–1948) is usually explained by reference to economic conditions particular to the opportunities opened up by and the displacements and needs generated by Venezuela's petroleum economy within the larger economy of World War II. But these changes can also be understood through the lens of Gallegos's ideology, which was pitted against that of the positivist apologists for the dictator Juan Vicente Gómez. Laureano Vallenilla Lanz, the most important intellectual apologist of Gómez's regime, believed that only a strong *caudillo* could channel the forces inherent in the natural environment and in the various races and racial combinations that comprised the nation (Howard 88–89). Progress would only be gained by the strong and, it was hoped, enlightened arm of the dictator.

Although there was an economic boom resulting from the privileged position of the oil industry in the 1930s and 1940s, Gómez did not turn out to be enlightened. He repressed and alienated liberal and socialist tendencies. Gallegos formed part of the opposition and proposed a democratic developmentalism, based in part on the recognition and promotion of *mestizaje*, which was seen as the constructive capacity needed for progress. Gallegos therefore appealed to folklore precisely when the new petroleum economy was choking off the active production of folklore. Folklore functions in Gallegos's work as a kind of transitional object and is embodied in the *mestizo*. Folklore and *mestizaje* were ideological constructs in Gallegos's work; they functioned to counterbalance the changes wrought by the petroleum economy, particularly exploitation in the new petroleum-producing cities.

Education, particularly education by the State, was a major part of Gallegos's "civilizing" ideology. He advocated expansion of an "enlightened elite," a nationalist version of DuBois's "talented tenth." Precisely because Gómez did not use the state to construct a new civility, Gallegos considered him regressive, characteristic of a bad mix of modern and archaic pathologies. A new articulation was necessary, one that was nationalist, anti-Eurocentric, anti-imperialist, liberal, statist, and populist.

The articulation of these themes is evident in the works of the novelists considered in this section. It manifested itself in the almost obsessive return to national wars. *Matalaché*, for example, is situated on the eve of Peruvian independence when Republican ideas are beginning to make their way to the interior. The conflicts between the Royalist and Republican factions in Venezuela form a crucial backdrop to the family history in *Cumboto* that creates the crisis in legitimacy the mulatto son will mend. These same factions are at work, although at a different historical moment, in *Pobre negro*, in which blood relations cut across races and political affiliations. *Las lanzas coloradas* is certainly the most dramatic of the Venezuelan novels, chronicling the creole organization leading up to revolution and ending with a prolonged battle scene between the generals Boves and Bolívar. *Juyungo*, too, ends with a battle scene, in which the hopelessly underequipped Ecuadorian troops attempt to defend Guayaquil against the encroaching Peruvians. The recourse to an era of national independence, consolidation, or defense performs a double function, on the one hand returning to a national origin or legend in order to garner patriotic sentiment and on the other hand using past wars as a way to address contemporary political and national issues, particularly under regimes such as that of Venezuela's Juan Vicente Gómez.

The resurrection of South American wars brings with it a resurrection of historical rivalries. The novels are not only about mediations between *criollos* and black or indigenous characters, but also about confrontations between Royalists and Republicans, *godos* and *criollos*. In *Matalaché*, the institution of slavery functions explicitly as a metaphor for colonial oppression, as in José Manuel's attempt to explain *criollo* politics to a fellow slave: "[M]e he referido a esos que son a la vez amos y esclavos como nosotros. . . . Porque aquí, ño Parcemón, no hay más hombres libres que los godos" (96) ("I have referred to those who are both masters and slaves as us. . . . Because here the only free men are the godos"). The problematic implications of this comparison are, of course, the appropriation of a racial identity or cause for a largely *criollo* agenda. While Spanish imperial power was no longer the threat it had been, a project for garnering broad-based national support against the "godos" can be translated fairly easily into the twentieth century by substituting the U.S. neo-colonial threat for the *godos* and twentieth-century Latin American anti-imperialist sentiment for nineteenth-century revolutionary spirit.

These anti-imperialist sentiments are also evident more explicitly in several of the novels. Unfavorable representations of foreigners, for example, abound–Mr. Danger, for instance: the unscrupulous Yankee business partner of Doña Bárbara, from whom the local people expected so much: "[S]e le abrieron todas las puertas en espera de los ríos de dólares que iban a correr por la llanura" (Gallegos 1977, 85) ("all other doors had opened to him in expectation of the flood of money about to over-run the Plain"; 1948, 140). Instead, Mr. Danger hunts alligators, usurps Luzardo Santos's cousin's property, and lusts after Marisela. *Las lanzas coloradas* presents a different type of satirized foreigner: the nostalgic Englishman David who has traveled the world fighting for freedom and who reads Inés's death like a romantic novel. When faced with actual battle, however, David, unaccustomed to the climate, comes down with a fever and spends the battle on a cot in the church. In *Matalaché*, the economics of nationalism is an issue, as two plantation owners debate whether to buy national or Chilean goods. And in *Pobre negro*, Pedro Miguel's shaping of the nation from within is contrasted to the "foreign models" that have hitherto led the nation astray (165).

Another highly charged relationship that runs through these texts is that between the urban or metropolitan, often intellectual, figure and the rural population. Almost unanimously, the character responsible for initiating modernizing influences and conceiving of the national potential of *mestizaje* is himself a hybrid figure to a certain extent, mediating between the metropolitan and the regional. Santos Luzardo, José Manuel's first master, the Cecilios of *Pobre negro*, and *Cumboto*'s Don Federico are all characters who manage to resolve this complicated relationship productively for the national future. The failures of Don Juan Francisco, who orders José Manuel's death, and of Don Fernando of *Las lanzas coloradas* seem to be related at least in part to their inability to successfully ally these two worlds. Don Juan Francisco wants to believe in liberal ideas, but cannot accept them when his daughter's honor is at stake. And for all of Don Fernando's good intentions, he cannot commit himself to war until his property and family are destroyed and he has nothing left to lose. In the alliance proposed between the mulatto or *mestizo* and the *criollo*, then, one could also read a desired alliance between the urban and the rural *criollo*, the capital and the interior, an alliance that would benefit national modernization. This modernizing impulse is perhaps most clearly portrayed in *Doña Bárbara*, in which Santos's goal is to bring the Venezuelan *Llano* (prairie) into modernity.

Despite the often optimistic portrayals of *mestizaje*, the traces of Social Darwinism present in the theoretical apparatus of the discourse of transculturation can also be found in the novels themselves. The concept of whitening, for example, and the Social Darwinist progress it implies are clearly present in many of these novels. In *Matalaché*, María de la Luz's initial daydreams about José Manuel empty him of color: "[L]a decoloración de la broncínea faz, la cual, después de perder aquel tinte caracerístico del híbrido cruce, terminaba adquiriendo el blanco codiciado de la raza dominadora" (50) ("[T]he decoloration of his bronzed face, which after losing the characteristic bronze-like tone of a person of mixed race, ended up acquiring the much desired whiteness of the dominant race"). His whitening results in a division between José Manuel and the other slaves of the plantation, a division that awakens both envy and animosity in the latter (López Albújar 71). Significantly, it is a Congo slave, the one with the most recent and strongest ties to Africa, who denounces José Manuel to Don Juan Francisco. In *Cumboto*, too, we can observe a division that occurs because of whitening. The first-person narrator Natividad's story provides his account of a life in limbo between white and black worlds. While Natividad's actual racial composition is ambiguous (he refers to himself as a black as opposed to a mulatto, but his parents are unknown and at one point he speculates on the possibility that Doña Inés is his mother), culturally he is *mestizo*. Raised on German fairy tales in the plantation owners' big white house, he has been cut off from the black community. When he is sent back to the blacks' quarters to live, Natividad's difference from the other blacks causes resentment among them and leads him at times to adopt an almost anthropological tone when speaking of them (e.g., Díaz Sánchez 1984, 20; 1969, 106–7). Natividad narrates his struggle between reason and superstition, describing his soul as the small white figure of his desire to improve himself struggling in a swamp of darkness (Díaz Sánchez 1984,102; 1969, 189).

Perhaps the most striking carry-over from Social Darwinism in these novels is the persistence of a discourse of degeneration. Despite the fact that *mestizaje* takes on redemptive, regenerative connotations in several of these texts, there are abundant, almost obsessive, examples of degeneration. And the degeneration represented does not only stem from hopelessly backward racialized masses or decadent lines of inbred Europeans. Rather, the potential for degeneration still seems to be linked to racial mixture in spite of its regenerative possibilities. In *Doña Bárbara*, for example, an entire history of degenerative interracial sexual encounters leads up to the regenerative union between Luzardo Santos and Marisela. Doña Bárbara was conceived in a violent racial encounter: "Fruto engendrado por la violencia del blanco aventurero en la sombría sensualidad de la India" (Gallegos 1977, 21) ("Fruit of the sowings of white adventurers in the dark passion of the Indian") (1948, 30). Her own monstrous sexuality is explained as a result of the gang rape that initiated her into interracial love. And the relationship between Santos's cousin and Doña Bárbara, through which Marisela is conceived, is itself degenerative. As a result of his contact with Doña Bárbara, Santos's cousin, previously a brilliant law student, becomes a disillusioned drunk, an "ex hombre" ("degenerate man"), "repugnante ruina" ("repugnant image of ruin"), and an "espíritu envilecido" ("debased spirit") (Gallegos 1977, 68–69; 1948, 113–15).

Doña Bárbara is not the only novel in which racial mixture appears to retain its monstrous and degenerative possibilities despite its rehabilitation as a potentially unifying national metaphor. In *Cumboto*, at least five interracial affairs occur, only one of them yielding the unifying results of the novel's end. Doña Inés, for example, goes insane as a result of her tragic love affair with a mulatto whom her father kills. And Don Federico's and Natividad's experiences with sexual and cultural *mestizaje*, despite bearing fruit in the form of the mulatto hero and the text, respectively, are contaminated by images of degeneration and doom. Don Federico, frustrated by his inability to produce a *mestizo* music, begins to drink and to deteriorate: "Su rostro mostraba también las huellas de una devastación progresiva" (Díaz Sánchez 1984, 181) ("His face began to show the signs of his progressive deterioration") (1969, 261). Natividad, equally obsessed with his dream of union between rationality and superstition, between his *amo* (master) and himself, turns into the shadow that follows Don Federico on his nightly walks. Critic Ian Smart points out the nihilistic menace implicit in this idea (51) despite Natividad's attempt to rationalize his "enfermiza devoción por el amo" (Díaz Sánchez 1984, 184) ("unhealthy devotion to my master") (1969, 264).

Although the friendship established between Juyungo and Nelson Díaz in *Juyungo* points to a potentially productive *mestizo* relationship, the novel's interracial amorous affairs are not similarly blessed. Juyungo's happy mixed-race family does not last long; his mulatto infant is killed by the landowner's thugs and his white wife goes insane upon the child's death. And Juyungo's melancholic mulatto friend, Antonio, so despises his black heritage that he pressures his wife to abort the child who would inherit his miserable status: "Ni quiero que mi hijo sufra lo que yo he sufrido. . . . Mi generación empieza conmigo y terminará conmigo" (A. Ortiz 263) ("Nor do I want my son to suffer what I have suffered. . . . My generation begins and ends with me"). *Pobre negro* is also spattered with examples of degeneration. Both Luisana's uncle and her brother, each named Cecilio, are disqualified from their potential roles as political leaders. Cecilio the younger, groomed to lead the fractious nation on the road to modernity and democracy, falls ill with leprosy; and Cecilio the elder, an enlightened anarchist, is too much of a bohemian to lead the nation. For her part, Ana Julia, Pedro Miguel's mother, suffers from a pathological relationship to interracial contact that oscillates between hysterical repulsion and the obsessive attraction that leads to Pedro Miguel's conception. Although these examples occur among members of the white landowning classes, it is significant that Ana Julia's condition resulted from an early confrontation with *mestizaje*, in which she witnessed a chained and bloody black slave being dragged through the streets to jail for the crime of raping a white woman.

The fact that *mestizaje* can still pose the threat of degeneration in novels that celebrate its regenerative power demonstrates that racial mixture is not the only issue at stake. These novels by no means advocate an uncontrolled *mestizaje*, but rather support the national potential for *mestizaje* under specific circumstances. Not any mulatto or *mestizo* child will do, but only one who, through some combination of circumstance or birth, is in a position to form an alliance advantageous to a nationalist project. Part of the criteria for the "successful" *mestizos* in these novels is certainly genealogical. Marisela, as Doña Bárbara's heiress, restores to Luzardo Santos through legitimate means the land that was usurped by his neighbor. But through her part-indigenous heritage she also goes a long way toward legitimating Santos's presence on that land, land that was originally usurped from her people. Similarly, the arrival of the mulatto son in *Cumboto* reaffirms Don Federico's jeopardized legitimacy as a landholder. His mulatto status allows him to represent the original Africans the novel claims as the first inhabitants of the region. But he is also the grandson of Ana, the slave woman left with the inheritance of the plantation's original owners when they went off to war. The crisis in legitimacy that comes when Don Federico realizes his family came to the land through unscrupulous means is annulled by his union to the descendants of the old slave woman. Rosemary Geisdorfer Feal points out that of all the mulattos in *Cumboto*, the successful one is born of a white father and a dark mother, not the reverse. Thus this unnamed mulatto hero also secures the patriarchal order against potentially subversive alliances between white women and black men (Geisdorfer Feal 27–28).

In *Pobre negro*, genealogy is once again an important part of Pedro Miguel's conciliatory potential. While Pedro Miguel's and Luisana's return home is only suggested at the end of the novel, their union signifies Pedro Miguel's eventual possession of the land his father worked and his mother's family owned. His status as the son of a renegade slave and of the daughter of the landowners and his marriage to Luisana allows him to reconcile his parents' diverse claims to the land. In this novel, then, incest does not lead to a tragic end, but rather to a reconciliation between la Blanca (Ana Julia) and Negro Malo. Finally, the bond that forms between *Matalaché*'s José Manuel and his first master is also genealogically based; José Manuel is not only his master's slave, but also his son. While this relationship is cut short by the master/father's death, it promises to yield a political alliance supporting Peruvian independence.

In addition to genealogy, a certain degree of education or training often seems necessary in order to prepare the *mestizo* for his or her role as national redeemer. José Manuel's unique position is a result not only of birth, but also of specialized training. He is separated from the other slaves, working in his master/father's office instead of in the fields. It is here that he learns about *criollo* politics and the rumors of revolution, and here that he forms his opinions about his role with regard to blacks and *criollos*. *Juyungo*'s Nelson Díaz has a (truncated) university education, presumably the source of his socialist ideas. And although we do not know the childhood of *Cumboto*'s unnamed mulatto, we know from his musical abilities that he has been instructed in both classical and African music. Gallegos's novels in particular emphasize the education or training that helps form the ideal *mestizo* subject. *Pobre negro* depicts above all the education of Pedro Miguel, begun by the enlightened yet disqualified *mantuano* landowners, the two Cecilios. This role is later taken over by Luisana herself, who acts as a surrogate for the two Cecilios's liberal ideas, working this time from within, through the agency of love:

[E]n Pedro Miguel había todo un mundo por crear. La materia prima era de calidad excelente, incluso su misma resistencia a ser moldeada desde afuera, conforme a un modelo extraño, que había hecho imposible la obra de debastamiento emprendida por

Cecilio, quien al fin hubo de desistir de su empeño en meter ideas suyas dentro de aquel espíritu; pero la que fuese comprendida desde adentro, para que de esa manera espontánea se desenvolviesen todas las íntimas formas posibles, encontraría sustancia maleable. (Gallegos 1965, 165)

There was an entire world to be made in Pedro Miguel. The basic material was of excellent quality including his very resistance to external pressure to make him over in accordance with another's model. It was this resistance which had made all of Cecilio's efforts impossible to realize to the point that in the end he had to give up his idea of instilling his own thoughts into that individual. However the task could be accomplished internally so that [Pedro Miguel's] most intimate feelings could be developed spontaneously into malleable material.

Doña Bárbara contains another explicit example of this tutorial relationship. Luzardo Santos begins his interaction with Marisela as her teacher, instructing her in everything from manners and diction to hygiene. Throughout the novel, Marisela's education is compared to the taming of a horse, and at its conclusion, Santos regards her as a work (*obra*) of his: "su verdadera obra . . . lo mejor de sí mismo, puesto en otro corazón" (Gallegos 1977, 229) ("his real accomplishment . . . part of him, the best part, sown in another heart") (1948, 413, 414).

The narcissistic and appropriative connotations of this remark cannot be overlooked. Through Santos's instruction, Marisela is incorporated into his social and political world. The final depiction of the two of them reads as follows: "habían concluído de comer; él hablaba y ella escuchaba, mirándolo embelesada, los codos sobre la mesa, las mejillas entre las manos" (Gallegos 1977, 240) ("They had finished dinner; he was speaking and she was listening to him, gazing at him in delight, her elbows on the table and her cheeks in her hands") (1948, 435). Marisela's unconditional alliance with Santos has been secured, her subversively rough edges have been smoothed, and her incorporation into Santos's familial and national plans is complete. Similar alliances are achieved in the other situations. José Manuel decides he must ally himself with the *criollos* instead of the slaves–the *criollos* who are themselves fighting for liberty from the *godos*. He explains: "Cuando ellos [los republicanos] se levanten yo les acompañaré y entonces José Manuel sabrá ver por ustedes [los esclavos]" (López Albújar 80) ("When they [the Republicans] take up arms I will join them and then José Manuel will know how to look after you [the slaves]"). In this statement, José Manuel positions himself as an ideal political ally. He takes up the Republican cause, putting it before his own, and offers the masses of less fortunate slaves a way of identifying with that cause also. Even the aesthetic *mestizaje* of *Cumboto*'s mulatto has both social and political implications. Through his music, this mulatto links the White Mansion of the landowners to the slave quarters: "Negros y mulatos, atónitos, comienzan a salir de los galpones, de las chozas, de entre los matorrales, y miran hacia la Casa Blanca" (Díaz Sánchez 1984, 186) ("Astonished Negroes and mulattoes are beginning to pour out of the sheds, the huts, the bushes; they stand and stare in the direction of the White House") (1969, 268). The inequality inherent in the novel's closing scene, in which the plantation's frenzied and entranced black population gaze upon and dance around the "godlike" mulatto heir, promises to reestablish the feudal relationship threatened by the delegitimized generation of Don Federico's father.

The mechanisms of Darwinist development are still at work in these representations of *mestizaje*, but instead of

nature, it is the coordinating idea of the nation that enables the selection of the fittest to bring about a popular revolution. *Natural* selection gives way to *national* selection. In *Pobre negro*, set during the civil wars of the mid-nineteenth century, white upper-class liberals could not be given the leading role in keeping with the agency of selection. They had the "impulso renovador" ("impulse to renew") but lacked the inclusionary spirit that would integrate all sectors into the new nation (Gallegos 1965, 134). The novel offers a variety of permutations, only one of which can evolve to a further stage of progress. In this novel, written in the 1930s, the selection of a mulatto to embody the possibilities of national consolidation is a compelling, albeit wily, symbolic compromise. The liberals of the 1920s and 1930s sought to construct a populism that would be effective in their opposition to the dictator Juan Vicente Gómez. This populism is carefully worked out in Gallegos's novel. It is a mulatto who is most likely to command the allegiance of this largely mixed-race country, but with the guiding ideology of the liberals. Far from leading to a radical outcome, such as an autonomous nation for non-whites, this popular project would leave the *mantuanos* in a position of economic power while ceding symbolic, and to some degree political, power. In the process, the activism on behalf of the blacks, represented by Pedro Miguel, and Luisana's proto-feminism are rechanneled in the service of the nation created in the image of the mulatto, animated in this desired new start by the creative breath of liberalism.

Music, *Mestizaje*, and Melancholia

In Díaz Sánchez's *Cumboto*, music is the medium through which a model of nationally productive *mestizaje* might be created. This premise, which is evidence of a change in emphasis between the nineteenth and twentieth centuries from a specifically biological to a more cultural understanding of mixture, has a long tradition in Latin America, to which Fernando Ortiz gave the name *transculturation*. This tradition may be best observed in the writings of Cubans, particularly Ortiz (*Los bailes y el teatro de los negros en el folklore de Cuba* [1951; Black Dance and Theater in Cuban Folklore]) and Alejo Carpentier (*La música en Cuba* [1946; Music in Cuba]), as well as in the novelistic and ethnographic work of the Peruvian José María Arguedas. Indeed, music and language become two privileged grounds of transculturation. Materially, they most embody the processes of hybridization evident in the degenerations decried by Social Darwinists as well as the positive *mestizajes* celebrated by those who sought to lay bridges between the different constituencies of the nation. In his famous statement on transculturation, Ortiz states: "La verdadera historia de Cuba es la historia de sus intrincadísimas transculturaciones" (F. Ortiz 1940, 93) ("The real history of Cuba is the history of its intermeshed transculturation") (1995, 98) from the Indians to the Spaniards, Africans, Asians, and others. Citing the Brazilian Mário de Andrade (1893–1945), Ortiz elaborates on the "constancy and variety" of transculturated music (1981, 90). Transculturation can be seen at work, technically, in the rhapsodic form of Andrade's "novel" *Macunaíma* (1928), which gathers into a collage the disparate parts of the nation, much as Brazilian folkloric music accumulates features of other music (Mello y Souza xx).

Music and dance are also fundamental to national culture in José María Arguedas's (1911–1969) writing, which Ángel Rama (1926–1983) characterizes as exemplary of literary transculturation. For Rama, the narrative process in books such as these functions as an intermediary, bridging the disruptions set off by modernization (Rama 94–103). Through much of his anthropological and literary career, Arguedas held up Quechua music and dance as the proof that the indigenous populations of Peru had not degenerated from the "admirable" culture of the pre-Hispanic past but had actually evolved a superior, hybrid culture. His research led him to believe that music and dance, transculturated from the bottom up, so to speak, made the post-Hispanic present richer and wider-ranging than the ancient arts, because it has assimilated and transformed excellently the instruments of European expression, which are more perfect than the pre-Hispanic ones (J. M. Arguedas 1976, 216). Precisely because it is transculturated, Arguedas believed, this culture is more resilient in modern times. The Indians of the coast assimilated rapidly, learned Spanish, and donned Western clothing. They did this in order not to disappear. Indo-Spanish miscegenation became widespread in the highlands and, because of racial prejudice, the *mestizos* made sure to differentiate themselves from the Indians, in order to attain their ideals and goals (J. M. Arguedas 1987b, 91). Nevertheless, the anti-Indian prejudice, according to Arguedas, did not go very deep, and in their spiritual life, the *mestizos* manifested many Indian forms of expression, particularly in music (J. M. Arguedas 1987b, 92). Arguedas characterizes popular music as the reservoir where traces of what is lost in other spheres of life persist. Indeed, the reservoir swells to include what comes from without: "El quechua vive en su alma [de Kilko] con toda la savia antigua y con toda la amplitud del kechwa que ha incluido en su vocabulario centenares de palabras mixtas" (J. M. Arguedas 1987a, 66) ("Quechua lives in his soul [Kilko's] with all the ancient sap and all the expanse of the Kechwa language, which has incorporated in its vocabulary hundreds of mixed words"). Although *mestizo* romance is not central to Arguedas's novels as it is to the novels of the 1920s through the 1940s discussed above, transculturated language and music serve a similar function, not so much in the service of *criollo* elites. In Arguedas's work, language and music have the potential to preserve traces of nature, which is considered to be the source of unalienated or authentic existence. In "El carnaval de Tambobamba" ["The Carnival of Tambobamba"], Arguedas offers a romantic vision of Andean song, which he characterizes as surpassing in natural power the rumble of the Apurímac River, which penetrates the heart, mind, memory, and love of those who hear its plaint. The songs, which echo the force of the river, are probably of pure Indian origin. Yet they are sung by "gente española modelada a lo indio por el río" ("Spaniards modeled after Indians by the river"). These *mestizos* are, paradoxically, the "gente más autóctona del Perú" ("most autochthonous people of Peru") (J. M. Arguedas 1987c, 152). In Arguedas's understanding, the force of the river, which is conveyed by these songs, creates a

> deseo de luchar y de perderse, como si la noche lóbrega dominada por la voz profunda del río se hubiera apoderado de nuestra conciencia, y se canta sin descanso, cada vez con más ansia y con más angustia. Es un desenfreno de tristeza y de coraje. Toda la esencia del vivir humano agitada con ardiente violencia en todo nuestro mundo interior sensible. Los que no saben el quechua escuchan el canto con mucha gravedad y adivinan todo lo trágico y cruel que es su contenido. (J. M. Arguedas 1987c, 154)

creates a desire to struggle and to lose oneself, as if the dark night, dominated by the deep voice of the river, would have taken hold of our conscience as the river sings continuously with increasing anxiety and anguish. It is a rampage of sadness and courage. All of the essence of human life is agitated with burning violence in our interior sensible world. Those who do not know quechua listen to the song with seriousness and divine the sense of tragedy and cruelty in its message.

If music or language seems capable of providing a positive transculturation that would heal the rifts of a multi-ethnic nation, in Arguedas's last novel the potential of this transculturation breaks down. In *El zorro de arriba y el zorro de abajo* [1969; *The Fox from Up Above and the Fox from Down Below*], the displacement of highland Indians to the coastal factory town Chimbote is characterized by a breakdown in language, a hodgepodge of languages that finds no synthesis. The umbilical cord that music and dance provided between the community and nature is sundered. The novel juxtaposes the narrative of a heterogeneous cast of characters who exemplify the disparity of the hellish capitalist enterprise with entries from a diary in which the author wonders whether he will be able to bring the novel to a positive conclusion, that is, to what Silverio Muñoz has called "salvation by culture." This would be a transmission of a knowledge rooted in nature, as in "El carnaval de Tambobamba" or in novels like *Yawar Fiesta* (1941). *El zorro* presupposes this cultural transmission of knowledge rooted in nature:

> Un árbol de . . . mi pueblo . . . [c]onoce la materia de los astros . . . y ese conocimiento se transmite directamente en el sonido que emite su tronco, pero muy cerca de él; lo transmite a manera de música, de sabiduría, de consuelo, de inmortalidad.
> (J. M. Arguedas 1975, 206)
>
> One of those trees . . . in my hometown . . . is familiar with the stuff the heavenly bodies are made of . . . and that knowledge is transmitted directly in the sound this trunk makes, but only quite close to him; he transmits it like a kind of music of wisdom, of consolation, of immortality. (J. M. Arguedas 2000, 185)

In the novelistic part of *El zorro*, however, characters such as "Muda" (Mute) and "Tarta" (Stutterer) embody breakdown: She is a prostitute, he a homosexual and a coward, and their very names attest to the dissolution of effective communication. In the autobiographical section of the work, the novel ends with the author's (fictional and real-life) suicide.

The redemptive promise of transculturation characteristic of Arguedas's earlier fiction and of the earlier sections of *El zorro* is ultimately not realized. Indeed, Alberto Moreiras has signaled Arguedas's work as the end ("fin") of transculturation, characterizing the breakdown that occurs in this novel as a radical critique of the possibility of transculturation (Moreiras 218). Undermining the utopic potential of *mestizaje* that supposedly characterizes Arguedas's earlier works (and a strong theoretical tradition among Latin Americanists), Arguedas's last book enacts the failure–or, as Moreiras (219) argues, the refusal–of the ideology of cultural conciliation, thus serving as an indictment of the power relations this ideology helps to mask.

Moreiras's opposition of *El zorro* to celebratory portrayals of transculturation offers potential insights not only into the work of Arguedas, but also into the novels on *mestizaje* discussed earlier. In particular, Moreiras's characterization of Arguedas's final text as melancholic suggests a reading of those novels based on the theories that have developed around the concept of mourning. Moreiras's analysis of Arguedas's text, from its refusal to accept healing or consolation to its characterization as narcissistic (Moreiras 220–21), identifies it with the characteristics of melancholia explained in Freud's "Mourning and Melancholia," to which Moreiras refers directly when he describes "the shadow of the object that falls upon the ego" (Freud 249; Moreiras 220). The melancholia attributed to Arguedas is contrasted in Moreiras's article with the celebratory portrayals of transculturation in Latin America, while in Freud's text melancholia is contrasted with what he terms normal mourning. A complication that arises when attempting to use *mourning* and *melancholia* as terms of analysis is the considerably vague definition of the difference between the terms. This vagueness or ambiguity has been noted by critics such as David Krell, Juliana Schiesari, and Judith Butler; it goes back to a lack of clarity in Freud's original text (Krell 285; Schiesari 37; Butler 62). Despite similarities in exciting causes, symptoms, and processes, a few differences seem fundamental to Freud's understanding of the two terms. The most obvious of these differences is a normative one, in which melancholia is characterized as pathological compared with its normal or healthy counterpart, mourning. Another difference is the emphasis on progress in "normal" mourning, a slow process of de-cathexis in which memories of the lost object are dredged up at the expense of considerable psychic energy but one that eventually results in a complete withdrawal of libido from the lost object that can then be transferred to a new object. As Freud writes, "when the work of mourning is completed the ego becomes free and uninhibited again" (245). Melancholia, on the other hand, is characterized by a regression to the more primitive state of narcissism, in which the withdrawn libido remains within the ego itself, converting the ego into an object of the superego's judgment, which can result in a heightened sense of self-criticism and even in suicidal tendencies (Freud 246–50). The emphasis on progress in the distinction between mourning and melancholia is, then, double: Not only does healthy mourning represent progress along the normative developmental path (one does not regress to primary narcissism), but in its own process it repeats this pattern of progress that encourages one to get over the losses of the past and move on toward the future, to new relationships. It is, above all, an encouragement and an acceptance of substitution.

The fact that Moreiras identifies Arguedas's final novel as melancholic suggests a comparison of the earlier literature on *mestizaje* with Freud's normal mourning, a concept that does help explain certain tendencies of this literature. For example, in its normative emphasis on progress and productivity, the discourse of normal mourning approaches that of transculturation (and that of Social Darwinism). Over and over again, the exemplary mulattos or *mestizos* in these novels are those who can contribute to the progress of the nation. They are encouraged to leave behind old relationships, ways of life, and communities to devote themselves to a progressive national project. These novels encourage de-cathexis from an originary community and transition in a time of modern development. The novels of Gallegos or Díaz Sánchez, for example, reenact the War of Independence and the ensuing civil wars between Conservatives and Liberals, thus eliding the capitalist context that drives the integration of popular sectors as workers into their liberal alternative to the dictatorship of Gómez or Pérez Jiménez. In effect, they seek to create a new normativity that subordinates workers and excludes the unproductive and hence not integratable. This observation induces us to reflect on the relationship between the creation

of new normativities and the function of normal mourning. To the degree that blacks and Indians are able to melt into *mestizos* who embody a national project, they are recognized, but as the traces of what disappears in the transitional object.

In Moreiras's reading, Arguedas questions the ethical implications and the possibility of this substitution that cancels out "radical heterogeneity" (218). In doing so, Arguedas's melancholic failure, or refusal of the consolation proposed by healthy mourning, exposes the normative and progressive model implied in "mourning" in Freud's essay, traces of which can be found in the pro-transculturation novels examined above. In them, the excluded elements–Doña Bárbara and Santos Luzardo's cousin (*Doña Bárbara*), Presentación Campos (*Las lanzas coloradas*), Ana Julia and the two Cecilios (*Pobre negro*), Juyungo's friend and wife (*Juyungo*)–are often characterized as melancholic, hysterical, excessive, and so on, implying their contrast to a psychoanalytically normative model. Another perspective, however, would perhaps suggest that Arguedas's suicide and Moreiras's characterization of his text as melancholic are symptomatic of, rather than a break with, the project of transculturation. Both Judith Butler and Bonnie Honig, in quite different projects, have suggested that some of society's most normative identifications are, in fact, melancholic in structure and not examples of "healthy" mourning. In *Gender Trouble*, Butler describes the melancholic nature of certain normative heterosexual gender identifications that can arise from a repression of an original homosexual desire. For her part, Bonnie Honig argues in "Ruth, the Model Émigré: Mourning and the Symbolic Politics of Immigration" for the melancholic character of nationalism, which relies on the repression of the immigrant and his or her relationship with the homeland. Like the normative discourses of gender and nationalism analyzed by Butler and Honig, the discourse of transculturation relies on a repression of certain elements: The backward racialized masses, the decadent European lines, the various unstable or uncontrollable hybrids. The degenerate lines we identified in the novels of the 1920s to 1940s are reminders of precisely what is being left behind, selected against, and repressed in the project to make a diverse society more manageable.

Despite the ambiguous nature of the definitions of melancholia and "healthy" mourning, the theoretical discourse on these concepts helps point out the issue of loss at stake in the project of transculturation, a project that is perhaps less purely celebratory and more authoritative than it was once considered to be. We see, then, that *mestizaje* is caught in a double bind that only the force of a normalizing social order can prevent from catapulting society into the recognition of its violent foundation. The recognition that this originary and continuing violence can be given a "healthy" or cathartic practice is an endeavor that continues to compel Latin American and other societies to repeat the narratives of evolution. To the degree that this is the case, the demon of Social Darwinism has not been exorcized.

Works Cited

Arguedas, Alcides. 1959 [1919]. *Pueblo enfermo. Obras completas.* Mexico City: Aguilar.

Arguedas, José María. 1975 [1969]. *El zorro de arriba y el zorro de abajo.* 5th ed. Buenos Aires: Losada.

——. 1976 [1962]. "El monstruoso contrasentido." *El Comercio.* Sunday Supplement. Lima: 24 June. Rep. in J. M. Arguedas. *Señores e indios. Acerca de la cultura quechua.* Ed. Angel Rama. Montevideo: Arca. 215–19.

——. 1987a. "La canción popular mestiza, su valor documental y poético" 1940. *Indios, mestizos y señores.* 2nd ed. Lima: Editorial Horizonte. 65–72.

——. 1987b [1941]. "La canción popular mestiza, su valor documental y poético." *Indios, mestizos y señores.* 2nd ed. Lima: Editorial Horizonte. 89–94.

——. 1987c. "El carnaval de Tambobamba." *Indios, mestizos y señores.* 2nd ed. Lima: Editorial Horizonte. 151–55.

——. 2000. *The Fox from Up Above and the Fox from Down Below.* Ed. Julio Ortega. Trans. Frances Horning Barraclough. Pittsburgh PA: University of Pittsburgh Press.

Butler, Judith. 1990. *Gender Trouble: Feminism and the Subversion of Identity.* New York: Routledge.

Carpentier, Alejo. 1946. *La música en Cuba.* Mexico City: Fondo de Cultura Económica.

Díaz Sánchez, Ramón. 1984. *Cumboto.* Caracas: Panapo.

——. 1969 [1950]. *Cumboto.* Trans. John Upton. Austin: University of Texas Press.

Freud, Sigmund. 1953–74. "Mourning and Melancholia." *The Standard Edition of the Complete Psychological Works.* Trans. J. Stanley. 24 vols. London: Hogarth. 14: 243–58.

Freyre, Gilberto. 1946 [1933]. *The Masters and the Slaves.* Trans. Samuel Putnam. New York: Knopf.

——. 1974. "Toward a Mestizo Type." *The Gilberto Freyre Reader.* Trans. Barbara Shelby. New York: Knopf. Orig. in *The Racial Factor in Contemporary Politics.* Sussex: Research Unit for the Study of Multi-Racial Societies, University of Sussex, 1966.

Gallegos, Rómulo. 1948 [1931]. *Doña Barbara.* Trans. Robert Malloy. New York: Peter Smith.

——. 1965 [1937]. *Pobre negro.* 6th ed. Buenos Aires: Espasa-Calpe/ Austral.

——. 1977 [1929]. *Doña Bárbara.* Venezuela: Biblioteca Ayacucho.

Geisdorfer Feal, Rosemary. 1983. "Patriarchism and Racism: The Case of *Cumboto.*" *Afro-Hispanic Review* 2.1: 25–28.

Halperin Donghi, Tulio. 1993. *The Contemporary History of Latin America.* Ed. and Trans. John Charles Chasteen. Durham, NC: Duke University Press.

Hawkins, Mike. 1997. *Social Darwinism in European Thought and American Thought 1860–1945.* Cambridge: Cambridge University Press.

Honig, Bonnie. 1988. "Ruth, the Model Émigré: Mourning and the Symbolic Politics of Immigration." *Cosmopolitics: Thinking and Feeling Beyond the Nation.* Ed. Pheng Cheah and Bruce Robbins. Minneapolis: University of Minnesota Press. 192–215.

Howard, Harrison Sabin. 1976. *Rómulo Gallegos y la revolución burguesa en Venezuela.* Caracas: Monte Avila.

Krell, David. 1990. "Of Ashes: The Promise of Memory in the Recent Thought of Jacques Derrida." *Of Memory, Reminiscence and Writing: On the Verge.* Bloomington: Indiana University Press. 277–314.

López Albújar, Enrique. 1977 [1928]. *Matalaché.* Havana: Casa de las Américas.

Mello y Souza, Gilda, ed. 1979. "El tupí y el laúd (Ensayo de interpretación de *Macunaíma* de Mário de Andrade)." *Mário de Andrade. Obra imagável: novela, cuento, ensayo, epistolario.* Trans. Santiago Kovadloff and Márgara Russotto. Caracas: Biblioteca Ayacucho. 1 M.

Moreiras, Alberto. 1997. "José María Arguedas y el fin de la transculturación." *Ángel Rama y los estudios latinoamericanos.* Ed. Mabel Moraña. Pittsburgh PA: Instituto Internacional de Literatura Iberoamericana. 213–31.

Muñoz, Silverio. 1987. *José María Arguedas y el mito de la salvación por la cultura.* Lima: Editorial Horizonte.

Nina Rodrigues, Raymundo. 1957 [1894]. *As raças humanas y a responsibilidade penal no Brasil.* Salvador: Livraria Progresso.

Ortiz, Adalberto. 1970 [1942]. *Juyungo: Historia de un negro, una isla, y otros negros.* 3rd ed. Guayaquil, Ecuador: Editores Libreria Cervantes.

Ortiz, Fernando. 1939. "La cubanidad y los negros." *Estudios Afrocubanos* 3: 3–15.

——. 1940. *Contrapunteo cubano del tabaco y el azúcar.* Havana: Jesús Montero.

——. 1973 [1906]. *Hampa afro-cubana: Los negros brujos (Apuntes para un estudio de etnología criminal).* Miami: Ediciones Universal.

——. 1981 [1951]. *Los bailes y el teatro de los negros en el folklore de Cuba.* Havana: Letras Cubanas.

——. 1995. *Cuban Counterpoint: Tobacco and Sugar.* Trans. Harriet de Onís. Durham, NC: Duke University Press.

Rama, Ángel. 1982. *Transculturación narrativa en América Latina.* Mexico City: Siglo XXI.

Schiesari, Juliana. 1992. *The Gendering of Melancholia: Feminism, Psychoanalysis, and the Symbolics of Loss in Renaissance Literature.* Ithaca, NY: Cornell University Press.

Skidmore, Thomas E. 1993. *Black into White: Race and Nationality in Brazilian Thought.* Durham, NC: Duke University Press.

Smart, Ian I. 1988. "The Trickster *Pícaro* in Three Contemporary Afro-Hispanic Novels." *Afro-Hispanic Review* 7.1–3: 49–52.

Sommer, Doris. 1991. *Foundational Fictions: The National Romances of Latin America.* Berkeley: University of California Press.

Spencer, Herbert. 1969 [1884]. *The Man versus the State, with Four Essays on Politics and Society.* Ed. D. Macrae. Harmondsworth: Penguin.

Uslar Pietri, Arturo. 1963. *The Red Lances.* Trans. Harriet de Onís. New York: Alfred A. Knopf.

——. 1979 [1931]. *Las lanzas coloradas y cuentos selectos.* Caracas: Biblioteca Ayacucho.

Vasconcelos, José. 1979 [1925]. *La raza cósmica/The Cosmic Race.* Trans. Didier T. Jaén. Los Angeles: Department of Chicano Studies, California State University.

CHAPTER 27

MEXICO-U.S. BORDER TRANSCULTURATION AND STATE DISCOURSES
NINETEENTH AND TWENTIETH CENTURIES

Marcus Embry

The last two centuries have resulted in various redrawings of the frontier between the United States and Mexico and, implicitly, between the United States and Latin America. In the colonial era, the border between the English colonies and Spanish territory in Florida was a site of subtle Spanish colonial politics. Escaped slaves were welcomed into freedom in Spanish territory much to the fear of southern English colonists, especially since such pressures resulted in events like the Stono Rebellion of 1739, a slave uprising in South Carolina (Wood). Likewise, the regions beyond the boundaries of the young United States provided a young domestic U.S. literature with a region beyond the Indian/British/French/American polarities of James Fenimore Cooper. Instead, the Latino frontier provided a region heavily marked by Catholicism and an implicit assumption of degeneracy among its inhabitants. It thus also provided a space in which to explore questions of miscegenation that were anathema to U.S. Transcendentalists as well as space for representing the Puritan struggles of the young nation with either the ocean or Indians as Nature and wilderness (Franchot 3–34; Bercovitch). However, even though the Latino frontier is central to the work of minor novelists such as William Bird and Helen Hunt Jackson, until the twentieth century the frontier between the United States and Mexico was elided in the majority of U.S. fiction.

On the other side of that frontier, the emerging dominance of the United States as a cultural and political colossus is evident in the work of Domingo Sarmiento (1811–1888) and other early Latin American writers. However, the ideas of the frontier itself–first, the boundaries of Mexico's northern territories along the Rocky Mountains; second, the Sabine River on the border of Louisiana; and third, the Rio Bravo (Rio Grande)–were at first generally far from the literary imaginations of those in Mexico City and the Central Plateau. Although, again, there is some literature available by writers such as María Amparo Ruiz de Burton (1832–1895), who was a survivor of the U.S. invasion of California.

Certainly the twentieth century has seen enormous growth in the prominence of the frontier as a literary subject, culminating in the various transculturations of Chicano discourse in both the United States and Mexico. Beyond Chicanismo, the frontier, the borderlands, has emerged as a theme in mainstream cultural production in the United States, as in Cormac McCarthy's (b. 1933) fiction and John Sayles's (b. 1950) movie *Lone Star* (1996). As well, the frontier has produced alternative literary voices in Mexico, categorized often as a subgenre such as the Tijuanense writers. But to link the contemporary literary presence of the borderlands with the history of the frontier, we must map a different trajectory than literary influence or "discovery." Rather, the frontier has been present all along in state discourses on both sides of the frontier, but these discourses have found elided and distorted expression in literature. Thus, approaching the literary history of the frontier requires a historical perspective across or through which literature can then be reread, revealing both the frontier's subtle presence in the nineteenth century and also the redeployments of this presence in the twentieth century.

Geographically, the greatest changes in the frontier occurred in the nineteenth century as a result of the Mexican-American and Spanish-American wars. Yet during the twentieth century the meaning attached to the frontier has continued to change after the reallocation of land and governmental authority. Specifically, the frontier has come to dominate various discourses of the borderlands both as a model of anti-essentialist constructions of postmodern identity and also as a geopolitical region where militarization and paranoia grow proportionally with the dissolution of the national economic borders in the age of expanding globalization. This essay will examine the discourses of the frontier in the nineteenth and twentieth centuries by focusing on three specific discourses: Slavery, outlaws, and labor. As these discourses developed on both the U.S. and the Latin American side of the frontier, they alternately opposed and complemented each other, and ultimately they comprised a dialogue of transculturation, a dialogue in which national, industrial, and academic concerns were articulated on both sides of the border in remarkably reciprocal ways. In effect, the border, the frontier, became a site of transculturation, a geopolitical nexus where state discourses crossed and seemingly borrowed from each other to form a web, a net of cultural crossings.

Slavery

State discourses regarding slavery dominated U.S. relationships with Latin America during the antebellum period of the nineteenth century. Antebellum U.S. literature features not only U.S. Transcendentalist (Ralph Waldo Emerson, Henry David Thoreau), Renaissance (Nathaniel Hawthorne, Herman Melville), and Sentimental (Susan Warner, Harriet Beecher Stowe) writers, but also African American writers such as Charles Brockden Brown and Frederick Douglass. And in this latter category, the border of Latin America is most strongly seen in Martin Delany's (1812–1885) *Blake, or the Huts of America*, a text advocating revolution and whose protagonist, Blake, is a free Cuban black who foments revolution after attempting to rescue his wife who has been sold into slavery in the United States. However, the border of Latin America is also present in the work of white writers. Regarding Herman Melville's (1819–1891) short story *Benito Cereno*, Eric J. Sundquist argues that "it has been easy for readers since then [the Civil War] to miss the full implications of Melville's invocation of Caribbean revolution or to misconstrue the historical dimensions of his masquerade of rebellion" (138). Sundquist's point is that the Haitian revolution was terrifyingly present for antebellum U.S. writers and readers as a result of slave-holding and its attendant neuroses, but that the cessation of slavery relieved this pressure and thus changed the subsequent readings of Latinidad in antebellum texts. Nevertheless, even in contemporary attempts to read Latinidad into antebellum U.S. literature, Texas and Mexico are absent, while the Caribbean and South America are left to carry the burden of Latin American representation through issues of slavery and the slave trade.

On the border of the United States, however, a remarkably similar discourse developed in Mexico and the northern neighbor. Beginning with Thomas Jefferson's attempts to quiet the slavery debates through a policy of Conditional Termination, the United States entered into fifty years of legislation that first attempted to free slave children via *post-nati* laws; it then sought legislative balance in acts such as the Missouri Compromise and Kansas-Nebraska Act (Freehling). Eric Lott sums up these years of legislation as "party politics swallowed up by sectional feeling" that resulted in the Compromise of 1850 wherein "Congress attempted through legislation to forestall an ultimate crisis of sectional division" (211). The famous sectional division of the antebellum United States, however, did not include the issues of Texas, Mexico, or Mexicans and slavery.

During the rise of colonization as a national discourse in the United States, beginning in 1816 and resulting in the founding of Liberia in 1818, the Caribbean and Mexico were widely viewed as available territory in which to settle freed slaves. And though abolition replaced colonization as a dominant state discourse by 1831, various Abolitionists such as Benjamin Lundy traveled to "Texas and parts of Mexico, negotiating land grants and agreements for Negro settlements" (Filler 26). After Texas independence, threats of British remuneration for emancipation of slaves became a major national issue in admitting Texas to the United States as a state:

President John Tyler, a partisan of annexation, . . . feared anti-slavery British influence in Texas would present a threat to southern slave holders. Early in 1844 formal annexation negotiations began between the United States and Texas. Tyler, at the same time, initiated a propaganda campaign to convince abolitionists that annexation coincided with their interests. (Schwartz 28-29)

In fact, the Mexican-American War was a source of racial discourse considerably different than the issue of slavery. "The war's large opposition, which consisted of an unstable coalition of abolitionists, conservative Whigs, and a significant number of southerners [was] reluctant to assimilate the racially suspect populations of Mexico" (Franchot 42). Moreover, in addition to the Underground Railroad, there was another route to freedom for U.S. slaves–through Texas and into Mexico. In fact, "by 1851, an estimated 3,000 fugitive slaves had crossed the Rio Bravo, and another 1,000 escaped between 1851 and 1854" (Barr 30).

In fact, the issue of slavery and the power to pursue runaway slaves prevented the United States from signing a Treaty of Friendship with Mexico until the 1850s. In Mexico, the issue of slavery was subject to as many legislative hurdles as it was in the United States, except that the contortions invariably resulted from the colonization of Texas. Miguel Hidalgo demanded immediate manumission of all slaves in 1810, and in 1813, José María Morelos proclaimed slavery forbidden forever. However, these pronouncements were in conflict with the colonization policies regarding Texas, particularly since they affected the original Austin party, who brought slaves with them when they emigrated. Agustín de Iturbide's 20 August 1821 colonization policy allowed settlers to bring slaves but ordered that children be freed at age fourteen. A new Constitutional Congress of 1823–24 decreed that "commerce and traffic in slaves proceeding from any country and under any flag whatsoever, is forever prohibited in the territory of the United Mexican States." But the Texas colonists raised questions about the issue of commerce; specifically, what if slaves were "personal property" and not meant for commerce and traffic (Campbell 16)? Moreover, settlers in Austin's original colony were required by Iturbide's law to free children at age fourteen, but later settlers were not so obligated. In 1826 the Constituent Congress for the new state of Coahuila and Texas modified laws to read "no one shall be born a slave in the state, and after six months the introduction of slaves under any pretext shall not be permitted" (Campbell 21). This resulted in Austin's efforts during 1828 to attract non-slave-holding settlers from Ohio and Pennsylvania. Finally, the colonists proposed in 1828 that blacks were to be brought into Texas and held as indentured servants who were working to pay their former owners for freedom. To further complicate matters, on 15 September 1829, President Vicente Guerrero declared immediate emancipation everywhere in the republic. But another decree on December 2 exempted Texas from the September 15 decree.

Without further belaboring the point, the legislation in Mexico was just as convoluted as the legislative contortions occurring in the United States at the same time. Randolph Campbell sums up the period: "Mexican leaders showed disapproval of slavery but did nothing effective to abolish it" (Campbell 17). President Anastacio Bustamantes April 1830 prohibition of further immigration from the United States and the April 1832 new colonization law of the government of Coahuila and Texas decreeing that no service contracts could exceed ten years eventually led to the war for Texas independence. But the various laws and strategies of resistance that had occurred led to a blurring of the distinction between slaves and indentured servants and freedmen, resulting in a very indeterminant status for black people in Texas. And it was this indeterminant status, and the presence of, for example, Seminole colonies in northern (contemporary) Mexico, that assisted in the route to freedom for U.S. slaves.

Combining the literary elision of Texas and Mexico in the United States and the indeterminacy of blackness in Texas, we can locate historical aspects of the frontier in literature. In Mexico, there were some very strange border texts that alluded to the issue of slavery and the odd status of citizens neither Mexican nor Estadunidense, (citizen of the United States) for example, Victoriano Salado Alvarez's (1867–1931) *De cómo escapó México de ser Yankee* [1968; On How Mexico Escaped Becoming Yankee]. From the U.S. side of the border, a similar, though later, text is José Policarpo Rodríguez's (1829–1914) *The Old Guide* (1898). In both these texts, national identity is construed as both a question of residence–on which side of the national border one lives–and as a question of race and culture. Rodríguez's Yankee or Gringo identity is formed not only by his assistance to the cavalry but also by his conversion to Protestantism. The mobility of identity is not only attributable to the black free(d)men and Seminoles who assisted the Mexicans in "controlling" Indian populations, but it is also evident on the U.S. side of the border and in a form of passing that Lundy witnessed when he visited various former slaves, such as Felipe Elua and William Goyens, who lived successfully in mixed-race communities (Earle 64, 116-17; Barr 4, 10):

> Some mulattos sought with considerable success to pass the color line in frontier Texas. A slave pointed out two well-dressed men among the whites at a dance in Bastrop as persons of African descent. Others felt no need to disguise their racial heritage.... Intermarriage among whites, blacks, and Indians in Mexico proved fairly common, since Spanish immigrants remained rather limited, and virtually eliminated Negroes as a separate ethnic group by the late eighteenth century. (Barr 5)

After Texas joined the United States, Texas newspapers gradually attributed to Mexicans darker and darker skin color, effectively constructing a racial difference that was interpretable through a discourse of blackness and slavery in the US (Montejano).

Thus, the issue of slavery in the nineteenth century contributed to both an elision and a partitioning of the frontier. Texas and Mexico were too close to the United States and too disruptive of a black-white racial dichotomy to write into anti-slavery texts such as *Uncle Tom's Cabin*. And in Mexico, the frontier was seen as both tremendously distant and legislatively different (a set of problems different from concerns of the nation as a whole). In Mexico's colonization policies regarding Texas and in the employment of Seminoles and freedmen to patrol and guard the frontier, as well as in the U.S. interpretation of racial and cultural identities of the frontier and its people, a discourse from opposite sides of the frontier envisioned it as a distinct area populated by a *mestizo* population that served as a buffer zone between national and cultural interests.

Outlaws

In addition to slavery, frontier discourses also circulated around issues of outlaws. Not only did Mexico have to contend with postbellum Confederate soldiers who sought to continue their struggle from Mexican soil, but both the United States and Mexico had to contend with revolutionary fervor in the lower valley of the Rio Bravo. Américo Paredes gives a sense of a region that considered itself as different from central Mexico:

> Santa Anna overthrew the Federalist constitution of 1824, which had given Tamaulipas, formerly Nuevo Santander, a great deal of autonomy. The year before, Santa Anna had ordered the disarming of local militias, a decree that caused serious resentment on the frontier. Texas revolted, and though the official government of Tamaulipas declared in favor of Santa Anna, the Rio Grande people favored Texas rather than Mexico. . . . Like the Texans, the Rio Grande people revolted. As early as January 1836 Centralist troops had to return from Texas to put down a Federalist uprising at Mier (132–33).

Thus began what Paredes labels the *corrido* century, a time when the people celebrated border heroes through *corridos*. Importantly, the heroes were not all considered *innocent* of the various alleged crimes that brought them into conflict with the law. Instead, the *corridos* celebrate acts of resistance both against the Anglos and Anglo laws and institutions in Texas and against the laws and institutions of central Mexico.

In fact, there were many uprisings against the Mexican government that began along the lower Rio Bravo. In 1838, Antonio Canales, a Monterrey lawyer, led an uprising in an attempt to form a Republic of the Rio Bravo, and Santa Anna's troops battled local rancheros until 1840 (Paredes 133). In 1851, José M. Carvajal led a revolt that sought to declare Tamaulipas the Sierra Madre Republic. He "announced a plan of constitutional reforms [and] the reduction of import duties, and demanded the withdrawal of the Federal army from the north" (Schwartz 132–33). They received support from residents on both sides of the Rio Bravo, and the revolution lasted until 1853.

On the northern side of the Rio Bravo, *corridos* tell the stories of various 'heroes' who also rebelled, in these cases against both U.S. law and central Mexican authority. Juan Cortina briefly occupied Brownsville, Texas, in 1859 and won a few engagements with U.S. troops before he fled across the border. But Cortina was not safe across that border. When Porfirio Diaz came to power in 1877, he was

> committed to co-operation with the United States, from whose southern borders would come any successful uprising against his power. He was, therefore, eager to help pacify the Border. He withdrew Cortina to Mexico City and kept him a prisoner for the rest of Cortina's life. (Paredes 135)

The Diaz regime changed the nature of the Rio Bravo as a border and altered the sanctuary offered by Mexican soil. Paredes explains that Diaz began his career from Brownsville and so was very conscious of the border and the instability it could create for his government. In 1877, two Tejanos who were charged with murder were broken out of jail and disappeared across the border. The Rangers demanded the extradition of both the prisoners and those who assisted their escape. Paredes writes that

> Tamaulipas Governor Servando Canales, a staunch Diaz supporter but a Border man, refused to obey Diaz's order to comply with the demand for extradition. Three of the men were somehow turned over to the Rangers, and Border sentiment against Diaz grew bitter. Diaz sent regular troops against Canales, but these joined Canales's forces when they reached the Border. For a while, Diaz's months-old dictatorship was in danger. (Paredes 136)

And finally, in 1890 a newspaper editor named Catarino Garza, from the area around Eagle Pass, Corpus Christi, and Palito Blanco, marshalled a group of men and set out across the border to overthrow the Díaz regime. Defeated by Mexican army troops, they returned to Texas to resupply and were met at the border by Texas Rangers and U.S. troops, sent there by the U.S. government at the request of the Mexican government (De León 93). Governments on both sides of the Río Bravo were in close contact and were establishing a growing relationship of economic ties that necessitated peace and control of the border.

At the same time, José Martí (1853–1895) was gradually building a public awareness of revolutionary struggle that laid the groundwork for arguments regarding U.S. imperialism and the annexation of Puerto Rico and the Philippines. With his articulation of Nuestra America and his prominence in New York City from 1881 to 1895, Martí helped found a discourse of the Americas that is still in circulation today (Kutzinski, Pérez Firmat, Rostagno, José David Saldívar 1991). And yet for Martí, the frontier between the United States and Latin America was economic, military, and ideological but was not located on the geopolitical boundary between the United States and Mexico. Certainly, the Mexican-American War was central in his conception of U.S./Latin American relations, but only in that it was emblematic of the ideologies of a nation determined to call itself "America":

> [W]hen one lives and must continue living face-to-face with a country which, because of its erroneous and customary reading matter, its easy theft of a good part of Mexico, its prejudice against halfbreeds, and the Caesar-like and rapacious character it has been developing in conquest and luxury—then it is a continuous and urgently necessary duty to stand erect every time there is reason or occasion (Martí 357-58).

Likewise, Samuel Clemens (Mark Twain) found in Mexico, principally in the Mexican-American War, a terrifying historical precedent for the imperial violence the United States unleashed during and after the Spanish-American War.

Outlawry along the frontier reached a zenith of public awareness during the Mexican Revolution because of Pancho Villa's dubious raid on the town of Columbus, New Mexico. Although the Mexican Revolution was cause for an increased presence of U.S. troops along the border and various strategies to both hinder and help the federal and revolutionary forces, including Pershing's futile mission to capture and punish Pancho Villa, the frontier was of little fictional merit or presence, and writers such as Stephen Crane chose the Spanish-American War instead as a conflict through which to explore their maturation and the dominant literary themes of realism and naturalism. Frank Norris and Helen Hunt Jackson both addressed the U.S./Mexican frontier, but they did so by addressing the underpopulated state of California, a location not famous for its outlaws and border heroes. In Mexico, too, writers of the early twentieth century dwelled on the Revolution and its aftermath, but the frontier is merely a northern boundary in their work. Only in more recent fiction, such as Carlos Fuentes's (b. 1928) Gringo viejo [1985; The Old Gringo], has a hero marched across the northern national border and entered the Revolution.

Nor did the discourses of outlaws cease with the resolution of the Mexican Revolution. Rather, the discourses that developed around Pancho Villa were reanimated for zoot-suiters in California in the 1940s and for the Cuban Revolution (1957–1959).

Discourses of outlaws currently focus on illegal immigration into the United States, while Mexico struggles with new urban youth identities such as Cholos and punks–illegal immigration of another sort. In A la brava, ése, [To the fight, that one]. Mexican sociologist José Manuel Valenzuela Arce focuses on the appropriation of punk and Cholo identities by young Mexicans not only in border cities, but also in the largest central Mexican cities. Valenzuela Arce documents specific communities and people within Mexican cities who find expression in symbolic representations that are not indigenous to Mexico. (See Ch. 32, Vol. 2, this History.) Punk identity is a Euro-U.S. phenomenon, and Cholo identity is specific to the United States (estadunidense), coming from the barrios of East Los Angeles and the history of the Pachucos and zoot-suiters. And yet the Cholo identity is full of Catholic iconography and images, including the Virgen de Guadalupe surrounded by little angels wearing Pendleton shirts buttoned at the neck, long baggy trousers, and bandannas; exactly the same images evident in movies about Cholo barrios in East Los Angeles. Valenzuela Arce argues that the Catholicism of Mexicanidad managed to jump across the border with those Mexican Americans in the 1940s who became the Pachucos and zoot-suiters. And amazingly, this identity, replete with its Catholic imagery, has now managed to jump back across the national border and become an identity claimed by inner-city Mexican youths, most of whom have only seen U.S. Cholos in movies and magazines. For the Cholos, Catholicism is appropriated and changed as a cultural signifier, a sign on the same level as lowrider cars and the clothing of the zoot-suiters. In interviews with Mexican youths, Valenzuela Arce illustrates that the Cholo Catholic symbols represent religion, specifically Catholicism, and yet their manner of appropriation is the same as the other symbols of Cholismo. While in the U.S. paintings of the Virgin and angels symbolize cultural and ethnic difference from a Protestant Anglo hegemony, in Mexico these symbols mark class and cultural difference, but not one based on an opposition between Catholicism and Protestantism. Instead, the Cholito angels signify an identity of difference that crosses over the U.S./Mexican geopolitical border.

And in this last comparison, the issue of outlawry is imbricated on the issue of culture and perhaps interpretable through García Canclini's theories of cultural reconversion. At the least, the image of the Pachuco as formulated by Octavio Paz in 1950 has been replaced by a trans-bordered commodification of the Cholo image. Even more, outlawry has provided literature with an avenue into the borderlands. In the U.S. mainstream, from Orson Welles's 1958 classic Touch of Evil to John Sayles's 1996 Lone Star, the frontier has harbored outlaws and heroes. The presence of the border in Hollywood and in spaghetti westerns is self-evident, but through the work of writers as diverse as Malcom Lowry, Benito Traven, Katherine Ann Porter, D.H. Lawrence, and Willa Cather, Mexico and the frontier provided an arena in which to continue the Modernist project of épater le bourgeois. More recently, writers such as Cormac McCarthy and Montserrat Fontes have also addressed the border through outlaws and heroes who transgress and traverse the borderlines. And in fact, transgressions by outlaws have even centered the frontier in the U.S. academy itself through the development of Chicano and Chicana Studies in the 1960s and 1970s and through the development of Chicano literature in those and subsequent years. Furthermore, the development of Chicana criticism and literature by writers such as Gloria Anzaldúa

(b. 1942) and Cherríe Moraga (b. 1952) has continued this discourse of outlaws–in their case outlaws in terms of racial, linguistic, gendered, and sexual identities.

Labor

Before the nineteenth and twentieth centuries, labor practices in the borderlands were established first by colonial practices, especially, as Ramón Gutiérrez and Cynthia Radding demonstrate, through the influence and control of the Franciscan and Jesuit missionaries. Differences between English and Spanish colonial practices with regard to Native Americans, coupled with the environmental exigencies of the borderlands themselves, resulted both in various forms of slavery and indentured servitude across the region and in conflations of racial, ethnic, and "national" status for the various residents of the regions. But the linking of labor with issues of culture and identity also resulted in patterns of movement, migration, and dislocation that resulted, for example, in the mass deportation of Yaquis both to Yucatan and across the national border to Arizona during the Mexican-Yaqui Wars of the late nineteenth century. As well, the U.S. war with the Apaches resulted in numerous crossings of the national borders by both the Apaches and the U.S. cavalry as they attempted to capture the Apaches in the Sierra Madre of Mexico (Roberts).

The issue of labor arose in national discourse during the Cardenas administration. Héctor Aguilar Camín argues that "the definitive clash between the government and the oil companies . . . [originated] in a confrontation between the companies and their workers" (151). This conflict led to a consolidation of oil-field workers' unions and ultimately to the expropriation of the oil fields in 1938. Then, in response to a growing labor shortage in the United States during the Second World War, Presidents Avila Camacho and Franklin D. Roosevelt in 1942 allowed Mexican workers to enter the U.S. and serve as agricultural workers (Meyer 633). The Bracero Program lasted until 1964 "and brought five million Mexican workers" to the United States (Heyck 6). However, the U.S. recession in 1953 "and fears of overwhelming immigration led to Operation Wetback in 1954, during which one million Mexicans were returned to Mexico, including some US citizens caught in the indiscriminate roundup" (Heyck 7). After the end of the Bracero Program, illegal immigration increased and the populations of Mexican border cities swelled dramatically. In response to the burgeoning population and the issue of illegal immigration, in 1966 the Mexican government created manufacturing districts along the border; this

> Border Industrialization Program (BPI) led to the proliferation of *maquiladoras*, foreign-owned assembly plants that require labor-intensive work. In 1970, there were two hundred *maquilas* with 19,000 workers; by 1986, there were nine hundred *maquilas* employing 255,000 people (Heyck 319).

At the same time, while *maquiladoras* have entered the consciousness of the United States during the planning and implementation of the North American Free Trade Agreement (NAFTA), filmmakers such as Gregory Nava (*El Norte* 1983) have focused attention on the labor awaiting illegal immigrants in the United States: some piecework in factories, but mostly menial labor and service and domestic work. In fact, Nava focuses on the dilemma facing Central American illegal immigrants who attempt to appear Mexican to the U.S. Border Patrol in order to avoid being deported back to political turmoil and grave danger in their Central American homelands. The imbalance in the growing commercial relations is

well illustrated in Tom Sullivan's summary of frontier ideologies: "In Anglo America frontiers often precede expansion; in Latin America frontiers often limit growth" (1). Or, in other words, NAFTA revealed the frontier to be a source of market growth for the United States and of little help for Mexico in terms of illegal immigration and growing populations in the northern cities.

Discourses that arose concerning slavery and outlaws have found rearticulation in discourses about labor, once again demonstrating the transculturation, the dialogues, of State discourse between the Americas across the frontiers. From a cultural-nationalist perspective, the discourses in question share a sense of contamination, a sense of cultural anxiety and paranoia, related to increasing globalization and the porosity of national borders, of which the infamous California legislation Proposition 187 is only one example. As Carl Gutiérrez-Jones formulates the problem, the United States is creating an illegible discourse around the border, by opening the border economically with NAFTA, while at the same time militarizing the border; in effect, the United States creates a discourse in which the border is said to be open and welcoming of Mexico and Mexican industry, but it is also even more closed to Mexican peoples.

Patterns of migration and border-crossing for labor are amply represented in literature, from José Antonio Villarreal's (b. 1924) *Pocho* (1959) to Graciela Limon's (b. 1938) *The Memories of Ana Calderón* (1994), from Tomás Rivera's (1935–1984) *Y no se lo tragó la tierra* [1971: The Migrant Earth] to Helena María Viramontes's (b. 1954) *Under the Feet of Jesus* (1995). But more importantly, this brief review of literary succession invokes not only labor issues in the factories and the fields, but also the vibrancy of literature in the borderlands, the rewritings that constantly occur and that illustrate the movement of state discourses into both the fiction and the cultural-identity politics of the borderlands. While we can trace theories of the frontier from Hegel's notion of a frontier as an empty space preventing a culture from folding back on itself, to Turner's thesis of the frontier as the "meeting point between savagery and civilization" (133), to Anderson's formulation of the frontier as the border of an imagined community, we can also conceive of the frontier as a geopolitical space where discourse slips between public and private spheres, where national and thematic historiographies find application in literature highly conscious of the inscription of official discourse upon the individual bodies of those who dwell in the frontier.

Precisely in these inscriptions can we find the presence of labor and the shadows of *braceros*, outlaws, and slaves. The contradictory and collusive state discourses of labor cast the frontier as pretechnological, as a place of *maquiladoras* in contrast to the laboratories in Los Alamos, New Mexico, and they cast frontier Latinos as neither Mexican nor American from the perspective of the home countries, and as Pochos and Wetbacks from the perspective of the foreign countries (Gómez-Peña; Lozano Rendón). This in-between status, neither one nor the other, and attendant myopic responses from both nations resulted in early attempts to formulate Chicano issues around a concept of "internal colonialism," that is, reading Chicano issues as Third-World issues within the national boundaries of the United States. With the introduction of gender politics into the region, the designation of labor has been redefined to include not just industry and the workplace, but also the daily responsibility and burden of maintaining the home (Herrera-Sobek).

Conclusion

On the one hand, the state discourses of the frontier in the nineteenth and twentieth centuries presents us with a multi-faceted network of historiographies that we can find echoed and shadowed in the literature of the region. On the other hand, in the literature of the region we can find new historiographies of the frontier, as Ramón Saldívar and Hectór Calderón have demonstrated. And in the relationship of historiography and literature we can see the transculturation that so powerfully permeates issues of the frontier and that is currently appearing as a borderlands hermeneutic in surprising and distant issues and places (Jay). But although the Saldívars, Calderón, and others seek to articulate the frontier in terms of a dialectic between the United States and Mexico or the United States and Latin/o America, transculturation on the frontier has given rise to literary and critical discourses that rearticulate the lines of historiography outlined above. In other words, in Gloria Anzaldúa's often-quoted phrase, "the U.S.-Mexican border *es una herida abierta* ("is an open wound") where the Third World grates against the first and bleeds" (3). Anzaldúa's use of blood imagery allows her to interpolate her experience into the various historiographies of the frontier, those concerning slavery, outlawry, and labor. In effect, the blood of the border invokes the strangeness of the region and its peoples, their indeterminate status and elided histories, and the issues of gender and sexuality that can also form the basis of a historiography of the frontier. The frontier and contemporary Chicana and Latina theory and literature recenter Ortiz's notion of transculturation onto the strange bodies that dwell in the borderlands, and a historiography of state discourses illustrates how the bodies came to be made so strange.

Works Cited

Aguilar Camín, Héctor and Lorenzo Meyer. 1993. *In the Shadow of the Mexican Revolution: Contemporary Mexican History, 1910–1989.* Tr. by Luis Alberto Fierro. Austin: University of Texas Press.

Anderson, Benedict. 1983. *Imagined Communities: Reflections on the Origin and Spread of Nationalism.* London: Verso.

Anzaldúa, Gloria. 1987. *Borderlands/La Frontera: The New Mestiza.* San Francisco: Aunt Lute Books.

Barr, Alwyn. 1996. *Black Texans: A History of African Americans in Texas, 1528–1995.* Norman, OK.: University of Oklahoma Press.

Bercovitch, Sacvan. 1975. *The Puritan Origins of the American Self.* New Haven, CT: Yale University Press.

Calderón, Héctor, and José David Saldívar, ed. 1991. *Criticism in the Borderlands: Studies in Chicano Literature, Culture and Ideology.* Durham, NC: Duke University Press.

Campbell, Randolph B. 1989. *An Empire for Slavery: The Peculiar Institution in Texas, 1821–1865.* Baton Rouge: Louisiana State University Press.

Delany, Martin Robison. 1970. *Blake; or, The Huts of America.* Boston: Beacon Press.

De León, Arnoldo. 1983. *They Called Them Greasers: Anglo Attitudes Toward Mexicans in Texas, 1821–1900.* Austin: University of Texas Press.

Earle, Thomas, ed. 1969. *Life, Travels and Opinions of Benjamin Lundy.* New York: Arno Press.

Filler, Louis. 1960. *The Crusade Against Slavery, 1830–1860.* New York: Harper.

Franchot, Jenny. 1994. *Roads to Rome: The Antebellum Protestant Encounter with Catholicism.* Berkeley: University of California Press.

Freehling, William W. 1990. *The Road to Disunion.* Vol. 1: *Secessionists at Bay, 1776–1854.* New York: Oxford University Press.

García Canclini, Néstor. 1989. *Culturas Híbridas: Estrategias para entrar y salir de la modernidad.* Mexico City: Consejo Nacional para la Cultura y las Artes.

Gómez-Peña, Guillermo. 1991. "Border Brujo: A Performance Poem." *TDR: The Drama Review* 35.3: 48–66.

Gutiérrez, Ramón. 1991. *When Jesus Came, the Corn Mothers Went Away: Marriage, Sexuality, and Power in New Mexico, 1500–1846.* Stanford, CA: Stanford University Press.

Gutiérrez-Jones, Carl. 1995. *Rethinking the Borderlands: Between Chicano Culture and Legal Discourse.* Berkeley: University of California Press.

Hegel, Georg Wilhelm Friedrich. 1956. *The Philosophy of History.* Translation by John Sibree. New York: Dover.

Herrera-Sobek, María and Helena María Viramontes, ed. 1988. *Chicana Creativity and Criticism: Charting New Frontiers in American Literature.* Houston, TX: Arte Publico Press.

Heyck, Denis Lynn Daly. 1994. *Barrios and Borderlands: Cultures of Latinos and Latinas in the United States.* New York: Routledge.

Jay, Paul. 1997. *Contingency Blues: The Search for Foundations in American Criticism.* Madison: The University of Wisconsin Press.

Kutzinski, Vera M. 1987. *Against the American Grain: Myth and History in William Carlos Williams, Jay Wright, and Nicolás Guillén.* Baltimore, MD: Johns Hopkins University Press.

Limón, Graciela. 1994. *The Memories of Ana Calderón: A Novel.* Houston, TX: Arte Público Press.

Lone Star. 1996. Dir. John Sayles. Perf. Chris Cooper, Kris Kristofferson, Elizabeth Peña. Columbia TriStar.

Lott, Eric. 1993. *Love and Theft: Blackface Minstrelsy and the American Working Class.* Oxford: Oxford University Press.

Lozano Rendón, José Carlos. 1992. "Identidad nacional en la Frontera Norte." *Historia y Cultura.* Vol 6. Tijuana: El Colegio de la Frontera Norte. 51–76.

Martí, José. 1977. *Our America: Writings on Latin America and the Struggle for Cuban Independence.* Edited by Philip S. Foner. Translated by Juan de Onis and Roslyn Held Foner. New York: Monthly Review Press.

Meyer, Michael C. and, William L. Sherman. 1995. *The Course of Mexican History.* New York: Oxford University Press.

Montejano, Davíd. 1987. *Anglos and Mexicans in the Making of Texas, 1836–1986.* Austin: University of Texas Press.

Moraga, Cherríe. 1993. *The Last Generation: Prose and Poetry.* Boston: South End Press.

Norte, El. 1983. Dir. Gregory Nava. Perf. Zaide Silvia Gutiérrez, David Villalpando. Independent Productions.

Ortiz, Fernando. 1995. *Cuban Counterpoint: Tobacco and Sugar.* Trans. Harriet de Onís. Durham, NC : Duke University Press.

Paredes, Américo. 1958. *With His Pistol in His Hand: A Border Ballad and Its Hero.* Austin: University of Texas Press.

Paz, Octavio. 1950. *El laberinto de la soledad.* Mexico City: Fondo de Cultura Económica.

Pérez Firmat, Gustavo, ed. 1990. *Do the Americas Have a Common Literature?* Durham, NC: Duke University Press.

Radding, Cynthia. 1997. *Wandering Peoples: Colonialism, Ethnic Spaces, and Ecological Frontiers in Northwestern Mexico, 1700–1850.* Durham, NC: Duke University Press.

Rivera, Tomás. 1996. *Y no se lo tragó la tierra.* Houston, TX: Piñata Books.

Roberts, David. 1994. *Once They Moved Like the Wind: Cochise, Geronimo and the Apache Wars.* New York: Simon and Schuster.

Rostagno, Irene. 1997. *Searching for Recognition: The Promotion of Latin American Literature in the United States.* Westport, CT: Greenwood Press.

Rodriguez, José Policarpo. 1898. *The Old Guide: Surveyor, Scout, Hunter, Indian Fighter, Ranchman, Preacher*. Nashville, TN.: Publishing House of the Methodist Episcopal Church, South.

Ruiz de Burton, María Amparo. 1992. *The Squatter and the Don*. Edited by Rosaura Sánchez and Beatrice Pita. Houston, TX: Arte Público Press.

Salado Alvarez, Victoriano. 1968. *De cómo escapó México de ser Yankee*. Edited by Ana Elena Rabasa de Ruiz Villalpando. Mexico City: Editorial Jus.

Saldívar, José David. 1991. *The Dialectics of Our America: Geneology, Cultural Critique, and Literary History*. Durham, NC: Duke University Press.

Saldívar, Ramón. 1990. *Chicano Narrative: The Dialectics of Difference*. Madison: University of Wisconsin Press.

Schwartz, Rosalie. 1975. *Across the Rio to Freedom: U.S. Negroes in Mexico*. El Paso: Texas Western Press, University of Texas at El Paso.

Sullivan, Tom R. 1990. *Cowboys and Caudillos: Frontier Ideology of the Americas*. Bowling Green, OH: Bowling Green State University Popular Press.

Sundquist, Eric J. 1993. *To Wake the Nations: Race in the Making of American Literature*. Cambridge, MA: Belknap Press of Harvard University Press.

Touch of Evil. 1958. Dir. Orson Welles. Perf. Orson Welles, Charlton Heston, Janet Leigh. Universal Studios.

Turner, Frederick Jackson. 1969. "The Significance of the Frontier in American History." *The Structure of Political Geography*. Edited by Roger E. Kasperson and Julian V. Minghi. Chicago: Aldine. 132–39.

Valenzuela Arce, José Manuel. 1988. *A la brava, ése*. Tijuana: El Colegio de la Frontera Norte.

Villarreal, José Antonio. 1959. *Pocho*. Garden City, NY: Doubleday.

Viramontes, Helena María. 1995. *Under the Feet of Jesus*. New York: Dutton.

Wood, Peter H. 1974. *Black Majority: Negroes in Colonial South Carolina from 1670 through the Stono Rebellion*. New York: W.W. Norton and Company.

CHAPTER 28

A PARADIGM FOR MODERNITY
THE CONCEPT OF CRISIS IN *MODERNISMO*

Jorge Luis Camacho

Two tendencies have prevailed among the critics of *modernismo*. The first persists in seeing *modernismo* as a school that emerged in 1888 with the publication of *Azul* [Blue] and culminated in 1916 with the death of Ruben Darío (1867–1916). This first attempt at categorization puts the emphasis on formal, stylistic aspects and sees *modernismo* as a school, interpreting it as a more or less successful copy of foreign groups of poets, especially of the French Parnassians, Symbolists, and Decadents. This aestheticist view of Hispanic *modernismo*, without being rejected in its totality, has been questioned by those who see in the movement a more general tendency whose origins are rooted in the crisis period that occurred at the end of the nineteenth century. While the first version subjected Spanish American literature to French models, the second integrated Spanish American *modernismo* into a broader process characterized by the economic, political, and social breakdown familiar to us under the label of modernity. Those who see a more general tendency in *modernismo* point to the heterogeneous and not just the aesthetic character of its poetics. Nevertheless, critical work on poetic language and the search for the maximum originality will always remain the common denominators of definitions.

Here, the hermeneutic project centers on the discussion around the debates that surround the concepts of modernity, postmodernity, and *mestizaje*. This text covers the literary historiography of *modernismo* in our problematic present (the start of the twenty-first century and thus the postmodern). It is understood that we cannot simply recreate the context of any one of the *modernista* writers by considering only those texts which provide meaning that is limited or conditioned by our own historical experience (according to Hans Robert Jauss [148]). The search for meaning from our present position *can* allow us to make an archaeological excavation of the idea of modernity and *modernismo* and the critical formulations that surround both phenomena. To speak of *modernista* writers is to refer to a linguistic and cultural community that shares certain values. In this sense, it would be interesting to focus attention on definitions of identity constructed by the *Modernistas* in their writings. For example, in his poem "A Colón" ["For Columbus"] from the volume *El canto errante* [1907; The Errant Song], Darío speaks of America as a passionate Indian maid, virgin and beautiful. There are, however, other poems in this book of a pronounced indigenist tenor, such as the poem dedicated to Momotombo, the volcano of his native land, or the poem to the legendary King Tutecotzimi. Similarly José Santos Chocano (1875–1934), who earned the soubriquet "The Poet of America" for his epic poems, frequently refers to the saga of the Spanish conquistadors and the struggle of the Amerindians, declaring himself to be the heir of both cultures. In all cases, the *modernistas* speak of their mestizo heritage (Spanish and indigenous), which has been an element in the identity question within Americanist discourse from Simón Bolívar (1783–1830) to the present day. However, it should also be taken into account that the concept of *mestizaje*

in José Martí's (1853–1895) writings refers not only to skin color but also to culture.

The idea of a literary crisis resulting from the breakdowns taking place at the end of the nineteenth century was first mentioned by Enrique José Varona (1849–1933) in an article on D'Annunzio dated 1899. In this brief but lucid essay, the Cuban philosopher stated his surprise at the rapidity with which schools of art (Romantic, Parnassian, Symbolist, Decadent) followed and replaced one another. This, according to him, revealed the "intensidad de la vida moderna, que hace variar tanto el gusto" (666) ("intensity of modern life that forces aesthetic tastes to change so rapidly"). The fundamental sign that Varona observes is that of the crisis of individualism in a period in which all tends toward socialization. The artist therefore took refuge from the tumult of this crisis in the work of art, in aesthetic form. Despite Varona's having used this taxonomy to refer to the aesthetic currents of the nineteenth century and the fact that the same topic appears in *modernista* literary criticism, it was Federico de Onís who is attributed with having reconsidered the name *modernismo* from a critical perspective and whose work has been the point of departure for the majority of reformulations that aim to define this subject. Onís pointed out in his much-quoted prologue to the *Antología de la poesía española e hispanoamericana* [Anthology of Spanish and Spanish American Poetry] that "el modernismo es la forma hispana de la crisis universal de las letras y del espíritu, que inicia hacia 1885 la disolución del siglo XIX" (xv) ("*Modernismo* is the Hispanic form of the universal crisis of literature and the spirit that around 1885 initiated the dissolution of the nineteenth century"). Thus the basic organizing metaphor for the epochal study of *Modernismo* is that of crisis and rupture. Ricardo Gullón, Iván Schulman, Manuel Pedro González, and Cintio Vitier have all supported Onís's thesis, seeing *modernismo* as a contradictory and multifaceted movement that begins from this historical crisis.

Gutiérrez Girardot delves more deeply into this same concept of crisis in his discussion of the process of secularization in modern societies at the end of the nineteenth century. The gradual enthronement of the Enlightenment ideal of the eighteenth century marks the beginning of modernity. With modernity humanity becomes the subject of attention and reveals its profound separation from the world and nature. There was a progressive generalizing of mathematical method: Logic, physics, and mathematics became the new gods of thought. Faith in the power of reason that accompanies the process of rationality would establish Bacon's *novum organum* as the ruling principle. Following the German sociologist Max Weber, Gutiérrez Girardot affirms that *krausismo* and Positivism are the two forms that the secularizing of the world took (79). While Positivism had launched a crusade against religious dogma, installing the rationalist method and the desire for exactitude as principal guidelines, *krausismo* tried to redefine and recodify the forms in which modern subjects related to God and to their fellow beings.

Julián Sanz del Río (1814–1869) was responsible for introducing Krausist doctrine into Spain and, with fellow thinkers including Francisco Giner de los Ríos (1839–1915), Nicolás Salmerón (1838–1908), and Gumersindo de Azcárate (1840–1917), created La Institución Libre de Enseñanza (Free Institution of Advanced Study) in Madrid. *Krausismo*, a derivative of Hegelian idealism, was totally transformed into one of the many forms of positivist liberalism. Secular in terms of religious issues, it gave the impression in Spain of having a profoundly ethical character. From the sixteenth century on, Spain had largely distanced itself from the general European spirit, through both its persecution of Protestant heretics and its evident suspicion of science. At the end of the nineteenth century, *krausismo* represented a break with anti-modern Spain in which an enthusiasm for disseminating secular ideas (and a democratic and scientific spirit) was thus generated among the various intellectual groups. The Krausists as much as the Positivists aspired to bring progress to their respective countries with the aim of reinforcing the national conscience and allowing them to create the material bases that would make them the equal of other European nations.

The implications of that process of secularization, as Gutiérrez Girardot stated, was the abandonment of faith in a transcendental being, the rejection of the concept of nature as an imitation of the divine, and a process of secularization of the world that transferred the energy of faith to that of patriotic symbols, the nation, moral perfection, and scientific progress (82). Juan Ramón Jiménez (1881–1958) referred to the same process of secularization in his lectures on *modernismo* given at the University of Puerto Rico, obsessively repeating that the beginnings of the movement must be sought in the theological disputes with the Church and the intention of the former to incorporate scientific discoveries into theology. He states:

> protestantes, católicos, judíos, inician un movimiento de protesta algo semejante a lo que Lutero en otra época hizo cuando la Reforma, contra Roma. Es decir, los teólogos modernistas dicen: "Nosotros queremos unir los dogmas, los dogmas de la Biblia, con los descubrimientos científicos contemporáneos; queremos unir la teología con la ciencia moderna." (250)

> Protestants, Catholics, Jews, all started up a protest movement somewhat similar to that of Luther in a previous epoch when he initiated the Reformation against Rome. In other words, the *Modernista* theologians stated: "We wish to unite all the dogma, the dogma of the Bible, with contemporary scientific discoveries; we wish to unite theology with modern science."

According to him, the genesis of *modernismo* should be sought in the tensions between faith and reason in Catholics who accepted both the rationality of science and the papal encyclical of Pius X condemning it in 1907.

Together with this process of secularization, a neo-spiritualism made an appearance in the literary circles of the end of the nineteenth century that attempted to throw light on the mystery of life and the supernatural. According to Díaz-Plaja, through the renaissance of idealism *modernistas* escaped the dominance of sociology and Positivism that surrounded their inception (136). The vacuum left by the erosion of metaphysical and religious thought provoked by modern scientific concepts was filled by Orphism, Theosophical ideas, Pythagoras, Buddha, Christ, and a feeling of universal harmony and cosmic commitment (Gullón 107–54).

In 1882, the same year that *Ismaelillo* was published, José Martí published one of the seminal documents of Spanish American *modernismo*, the essay-prologue to "Poema del Niagara" ["Poem to Niagara"] by the Venezuelan Juan Antonio Pérez Bonalde (1846–1892). On this occasion Martí offers an analysis of the modern spirit, the problem of faith, and the way that this problem has been translated into literature. He wrote: "nadie tiene hoy su fe segura. Los mismos que lo creen, se engañan. Los mismos que escriben fe se muerden, acosados por hermosas fieras interiores, los puños con que escriben" (7: 287) ("no one today has a sure faith. Those who believe so are fooling themselves. Those that write on faith, harassed by exquisite inner demons, gnaw the very fists with which they write"). To express the anxiety of the modern poet over the loss of faith, Martí brings into play the visionary poetry of Dante. Modern poets are obliged to fall back on themselves and live within their own inferno, gnawing their fists and constantly being pursued by beautiful but savage inner demons. In another fundamental text, "Contemporary Spanish Poets," originally published in English with the eloquent subtitle "The Influence of a Progressive Epoch," Martí analyzes the form and the causes of the discourse of doubt; what he called "la poesía de la duda" (5: 25) ("the poetry of doubt") had influenced Spanish contemporary poets. His analysis led him to suggest that "la poesía española hoy en día no es literatura española" (15: 28) ("Spanish poetry today is not Spanish literature"). Speaking of Núñez de Arce (1834–1903), Martí commented that

> Su poema sobre Lutero, "La visión de fray Martín," es sin duda la obra en que ha puesto mayor cuidado, fuerza y originalidad. Haciendo del fraile la personificación del estado del espíritu humano, ha tratado de pintar el alma rebelde que, cual un niño que lucha en el umbral de la vida, golpea rudamente una bóveda poblada de sombras queridas, y una vez sobre ruinas, llora por esas sombras que huyen ante el derrumbe que él mismo ha ocasionado. (15: 30)

> His poem on Luther, "La visión de fray Martín," is without doubt his most carefully written, strongest and most original work. In making Luther the personification of the state of the human spirit, he has tried to depict the rebellious soul that, like a child who fights on the threshold of life, strikes at the dome of beloved shadows, and once he is amidst ruins, weeps for these shadows that fled at the collapse that he himself has occasioned.

The essay revolves around the state of the human spirit that Martí particularly associated, as in the case of Nuñez de Arce, with the rebellious soul of the Protestant revolt led by Luther and the subsequent erosion of traditional concepts that this provoked in Spain. In 1880 Martí found various reasons to reject and criticize the influence of traditional poetry in contemporary Spain. His argument was all-embracing and accented the differences in social and political character that differentiated Spain from the rest of Europe: The weakness of the feudal regime whose monarchy, according to the Cuban, was an enlightened despotism, the Counter-Reformation, and the tradition of an absolutist rule. As Martí declared:

> No fue en la tierra de las Isabeles donde el Viejo Mundo fue sacudido, volcado, y vencido. En España, ni se predicó la reforma, ni se vio sobre el cadalso una familia de reyes, ni hubo matanzas colectivas de sacerdotes, ni se cambió bruscamente el curso de la vida, ni fueron puestos los hombres a un mismo nivel bajo una hecatombe de señores y una hecatombe de siervos. (15: 27)

> It was not in the territory of the Isabellas where the Old World was shaken up, turned upside down, and defeated. In Spain, the Reformation was never preached, nor was a family of kings seen

on the scaffold; there were no collective murders of priests nor was the course of life changed brusquely; nor were men placed on equal standing beneath a slaughter of lords and a slaughter of servants.

The radical differences that fundamentally separate the history and culture of Spain from those of the rest of Europe would be taken up, according to Medardo Vitier, by Menéndez Pidal and other Spanish philologists (72). Following Martí's original exposition, Octavio Paz (1975) would also return to it in his writings on the Spanish anti-modern spirit and *modernismo*.

Fina García Marruz returns to this same discourse of essential difference in her study of Paz, with an emphasis on the implicit division between a religious Spain of certainty and the discovery of the New World by a Europe dedicated to the quest implicit in research and the critical modern spirit. In a lecture that tries to bring out the premonitory and messianic character of the Conquest, García Marruz suggests that

> La "búsqueda" es lo propio de la modernidad crítica europea; el "encuentro" raíz de nuestra apertura al mundo, fue lo que permitió no al "hombre del Renacimiento" sino a España, que no lo tuvo, encontrar algo realmente nuevo, es decir, la América, al amparo de la teocracia todavía medieval. No fue la Europa la que destronó al Dios de la Edad Media para entronizar al Hombre, sino la España de los Reyes Católicos, la del Descubrimiento. (24)

> The "quest" is a feature of European critical modernity; and "encounter" is the basis of Latin America's entry into the world. This was what allowed not "Renaissance man" but a Spain that never experienced the Renaissance to now find something really new, in other words, America at the mercy of a theocracy that was still medieval. This was not the Europe that had dethroned the God of the Middle Ages to enthrone Man, but the Spain of the Catholic Kings, the Spain of the Discovery.

In his analysis of Núñez de Arce, Martí says of the Spanish poet that he "ha deseado en realidad pintar el estado presente del siglo en Europa, con sus penas y remordimientos. . . . El aliento de una duda real se respira en todo él" (15: 30) ("desired in reality to paint the present state of the century in Europe with its sorrows and regrets. . . . The breath of authentic doubt can be sensed in him"). However, some facts can be clarified from Martí's interpretation of Núñez de Arce. First of all, his reading is nostalgic; it tries to maintain the vision of a tradition in the face of what could be understood as a metaphysical rupture. That rupture demonstrates to Martí–and it seems to be his major fear–a discontinuity in history in terms of identity of the Spanish spirit and, as a result, that of Latin America. His concern is directed toward maintaining an alternative ethic that marks the difference between the Hispanic world and the rest of the West (North America, Europe). At the same time, he attempts to overcome the influential model provided by earlier literature, notably Baudelaire, Augusto Barbier, and Núñez de Arce himself. I have elsewhere analyzed in *Ismaelillo* the form in which Martí dramatizes this discourse of otherness in the panorama of secularized modernity (see Camacho). Martí here criticizes the dogmas of the Church, praises the faith of the primitive Christians, shows himself to be deeply anticlerical, reads Luther, and is convinced that there is a life beyond the earthly one. At the same time he places the heart of his faith in the *patria* (fatherland), poetry, liberty, and the necessity of virtue. For the Cuban poet, religious matters are poetic. Faced with a desacralized modernity, Martí imbued modern symbols with sanctity. In

the discourse of Martí's desire, the Statue of Liberty in New York would acquire a hallowed atmosphere. Man should revere that liberty and adore it. José Enrique Rodó (1871–1917) would react in a not dissimilar way; in his famous book, the statue of Ariel would also acquire a sacred character. In both, the religious discourse shifts from its original field to the secularized one of culture and ethics. Its statues are the new altars, the true gods before whom all should be sacrificed.

In that article on Núñez de Arce, Martí makes a connection between the generation of French Romanticism and Spanish poetry, grouping together Musset, Augusto Barbier, and Baudelaire as "almas nacidas para creer, que lloran la perdida de la fe" (15: 26) ("souls born to believe, that weep over the loss of faith"). In his commentary on this passage Alejo Carpentier (1904–1980) confirms that there was "en efecto, como una añoranza de fe perdida–de Paraíso perdido–en el Musset que dice: 'ya no creo, oh Cristo, en tu palabra santa'" (533) ("in fact, a longing for lost faith–for Paradise lost–in Musset when he says: 'I no longer believe, Oh Christ, in Your holy word'"). For this reason the tensions between reason and faith run throughout *modernismo* as seen in the poems "Desolación" ["Desolation"] by Julión del Casal (1863–1893) or Darío's "Lo fatal" ["Fatality"]. In the first poem, the soul describes a gloomy chapel, empty and abandoned. The objects dedicated to the celebration of faith are in disuse. The censer no longer smokes, nor does the long waxen candle shine brightly. Faith and God have been forgotten and everyone manifests only indifference. Casal writes: "Y ha tiempo no resuena en el santurario/ni la plegaria de la joven pura,/ni la blasfemia horrible del ateo" (89) ("And time has passed since there resounded in the sanctuary,/Either the prayers of the pure young women,/Or the horrible blasphemy of the atheist"). Years later Federico Bermudez (1884–1921) returned to this theme in a poem also entitled "Desolación." There the poetic voice awakens the same doubt, the loss of the notion of harmony, now that "derramó su veneno sobre el labio/la copa aterradora de la duda" (102) ("the terrifying chalice of doubt/has poured its poison onto the lips"). In "Letanías de Amor" ["Litanies of Love"], which appears to be a curious resemantization of the decadent *femme fatale*, simultaneously cold and desired, Bermudez sees that "es fiel y es eterna mi amada . . . ¡La Duda!" (129) ("faithful and eternal is my beloved . . . Doubt!"). In Darío's poem, on the other hand, not only did the presence of a God who gave purpose to existence vanish, but all the Platonic imaginary that the poet had previously displayed in "Coloquio de los Centauros" ["Colloquium of the Centaurs"] disappears as well. The rocks have lost their animistic character, their pneuma; in this text the prose becomes profane. Paradoxically, in his ode "A Roosevelt" ["For Roosevelt"], Darío does not hesitate to confirm his Christian-Catholic heritage in the face of the primitive-modern Anglo-Saxon. While the North American has the Protestant Bible, the Nicaraguan knows that the "América ingenua que tiene sangre indígena/aún reza a Jesucristo y aún habla español" (1994, 331) ("innocent America that has indigenous blood/prays yet to Jesus Christ and still speaks Spanish"), and armed with such a hope invokes a God that will not permit Spanish America to fall into the iron claws of the powerful hawk (1994, 331). In this poem Darío confronts the symbols of Spanish American identity with those of the powerful neighbor to the north that had already revealed its expansionist character in the Mexican-American War and by intervening in the Cuban War of Independence. In this sense, the praising of Hispanism, the indigenous world, and the Catholic religion would help create resistance, a true counter-culture to North American modernity. But the fact that not all those in favor of Cuban independence opposed the North American intervention cannot be forgotten. Such was the case of Federico Uhrbach (1873–1932), who in "La visión de las cimas" ["Vision of the Summit"], a poem dedicated to Varona, stated while speaking of the Unites States that the "voz de Sam/pone en nuestras almas, vidente y redentor,/una luz de enseñanza y un perfume de amor" (269) ("voice of Uncle Sam/places in our soul, prophet and redeemer, /a light of teaching and a fragrance of love").

According to Onís the genesis of *modernismo* was in the aesthetic currents that preceded it: Realism and Naturalism. As the Spanish professor has commented, "el límite entre la literatura anterior, o sea, la literatura realista y naturalista . . . [y modernismo] es fácil de determinar porque el modernismo nació como una negación de la literatura precedente" (xiii) ("the boundary between the previous literature, in other words, Realist and Naturalist literature . . . [and *modernismo*] is easy to determine because *modernismo* was born as a negation of the preceding literature"). For Onís, Realism and Naturalism were the previous literature, the line that divided one form of thinking and writing from another. Realist and Naturalist literature were the dominant aesthetic of world prose. This dual taxonomy was later reinforced by Octavio Paz (1914–1998). In his Charles Eliot Norton Lectures (1971–1972) delivered at Harvard University, the poet included the terms Naturalism and Realism as used by Onís under the heading of Positivism, while simultaneously accentuating the negativity of the latter. Paz understood that the same process of rationalization that extended from the sixteenth century to the end of the eighteenth century continued into Positivism and kindred literary currents in the nineteenth century. He wrote of *modernismo*: "por haber sido una respuesta de la imaginación y la sensibilidad al positivismo y a su visión helada de la realidad, por haber sido un estado de espíritu, pudo ser un auténtico movimiento poético. El único digno de este nombre entre los que se manifestaron en lengua castellana durante el siglo XIX" (Paz 1993, 127) ("having been the answer of imagination and sensitivity to Positivism and its frozen view of reality, having been a state of mind it became an authentic poetic movement–the only one, in fact, among all those in our language during the nineteenth century, worthy of the name" [translation mine; equivalent English can be found in Paz 1974, 89]).

Onís and Paz agreed on three fundamental points in the debate over the periodization of *modernismo*. First, *modernismo* arose as a reaction, a response to a previous means of writing and thinking (Naturalism, Realism, Positivism). Second, these antecedent forms of literatures offer only a limited vision (frozen according to Paz) for they are less imaginative and sensitive. Imagination and sensitivity, according to Onís and Paz, can only access the imaginative reserves of what was Romanticism. From this point, both coincide in calling *modernismo* another form of Romanticism, the reaction *par excellence* to the Enlightenment period. The response of Spanish American *modernistas* would be seen as a return to non-Spanish Romantic strategies. The third point of agreement is that both reject the possibility of the survival of elements belonging to previous aesthetics in the new movement. A vacuum exists between the previous literature and that which followed it, a dramatic break, which is precisely what characterizes the difference

between them. If modernity is distinguished by evading irrational, imaginative, and religious elements, *modernista* poets will be anti-modern. This is precisely the position taken by Paz in *Los hijos del limo* [1974; *Children of the Mire*]. In this well-known text, the Mexican poet argues that the modern tradition is presented as an aesthetic of rupture, "una tradición hecha de interrupciones y en la que cada ruptura es un comienzo" (1993, 15) ("a tradition composed of interruptions in which each break is a new beginning"). The period of crisis that Varona considered as a continuation of artistic schools and Onís described as the genesis of *modernismo*, in Paz's work is transformed into a tradition that extends, as he suggests, from the English and German Romantics to the avant-garde movements of Latin America. However, his ideas on *Modernismo* revolve fundamentally around the notion of the absence of the Enlightenment in Latin America, and instead stress the presence of an anti-modern tradition that began in the sixteenth century. From this, Paz also derived the idea of the absence of a true Romanticism. According to the Mexican poet, both Spanish and Spanish American Romanticism were late imitations of the French original. *Modernismo* around 1880 would find a variant of European Enlightenment in the Positivist doctrine that swept through Latin America and would react against it as a previous Romantic generation had done before in rejecting the rationalism of the Enlightenment. The new Romanticism would bring new rhythms as well as an occult tradition to literature that would contrast with the modern scientific spirit. Paz described various characteristics of this new Romanticism, including a rejection of technology and science, a taste for ornamentalism, a vision of the other (the child, the woman), a subversive eroticism, a certain critical passion, and an anti-imperialist spirit: "La única experiencia de la modernidad que un hispanoamericano podía tener en aquellos días era la del imperialismo" (1993, 130) ("The only experience of the modern age that a Spanish American could have in those days was of imperialism"; 1974, 91). The poet understood that the reevaluation of the indigenous and the Spanish past marked two manifestations of this anti-imperialism. Paz considered the emphasis given to pre-Hispanic poetry to be more an aesthetic appreciation; he sees Netzahualcóatl to be a rejection of U.S. modernity and, in particular, the idea of progress (U.S.-style). Anti-imperialism could be seen in both the fear and the anger provoked by the influence and domination of the United States over the continent (1993, 131). Though Paz was thinking of Rubén Darío and his ode to Roosevelt, there were also two essays on the theme of anti-imperialist *modernismo* that should be mentioned, Martí's "Nuestra América" ["Our America"] and *Ariel* (1900) by the Uruguayan poet Rodó.

As a result of the Spanish-American War, the crisis in international politics in Latin America became more acute. In the face of a voracious capitalist modernity, a discourse of the racial superiority of the Anglo-Saxon, and a political policy of "Manifest Destiny," some *modernistas* waved the banner of indigenist culture, tradition, and difference as identifying signs of Spanish American cultural identity. Even so, the idea of identity that they constructed was based on very different ideas. On the one hand, it could be of a political nature, as in Martí's case; or it could be based on old myths already well known in Europe that arrived in Latin America with the Conquest–such as the utopic America of the "Atlántida," whose name "nos llega resonando en Platón" (Darío 1994, 332) ("arrives resounding of Plato")–in other words, myths and names that had been used in Europe from the time of the first explorers along with later fantastic constructions of the Europeans to try to explain the reality of the new continent. In any case, the revaluation of these myths from a Latin American perspective was equivalent to the search for a separate identity and the construction of a foundational imaginary.

On the other hand, when we compare *modernista* writings with the European texts of the same period, their discourses on race, for example, frequently appear to be permeated with ideas of European provenance, notably the Positivism of Comte, Taine, Spencer, and other *fin-de-siècle* philosophers who argued the power of inheritance and environment in determining the prospects of nations and peoples. The debate over the hereditary aspects of race (against what is acquired from culture) is one of the most recurrent and least explored topics of *modernismo*. A case that perfectly demonstrates these tensions is that of the Venezuelan Pedro Emilio Coll (1872–1947), who in his essay *Decadentismo y americanismo* [1891; Decadentism and Americanism], stated that "hasta en los que suponemos que rinden un culto exclusivo a las hegemonías extranjeras, obra la energía que brota de las entrañas de las razas y del medio" (89) ("even among those we suppose pay exclusive homage to foreign hegemonies, there is an energy that bursts forth from the very depths of race and environment"). When we read statements such as these, it is impossible not to recall the critics pointing an accusatory finger at a Eurocentric Darío (Coll 245). It is precisely in the "palabras liminares" ("liminal words") of *Prosas profanas* [1896 and 1901; Profane Prose] where, at the same time as he accepts the possibility of his mestizo origin, Darío affirms that "si hay poesía en nuestra América" ("if there is poetry in our America")– and this possessive is fundamental in the context of Martí's essay–"ella está en las cosas viejas: Palenke y Utatlán, en el indio legendario y el inca sensual y fino, y en el gran Moctezuma de la silla de oro" (1994, 246) ("it lies in ancient things: Palenke and Utatlám, in the legendary Indian and the sensual and refined Inca, and in the great Moctezuma of the golden throne"). For Pedro Emilio Coll, the European literatures to which the *modernistas* pay homage did not just represent an abundance of aesthetic and literary resources or an agenda of ideas, but were also in practice a school of artistic development that helped refine the senses and train perception and taste, a project that Latin American writers had not yet had time to achieve. For this reason he states that while the contact with European literatures "nos aleja un tanto de la raza, es lo necesario para apreciar mejor sus relieves, matices, y rasgos característicos" (89) ("distanced us somewhat from the race, it is necessary for the better appreciation of the characteristic reliefs, textures, and features of culture"). In other words, what the indigenous writing could not supply was complemented by European literature. It was necessary to see Latin America through the eyes of others from Europe to discover the thousand hues of landscape, given that "los sentidos, como todas las fuerzas de la vida, están en perpetua evolución, y a las literaturas extranjeras les debemos en gran parte el aceleramiento de aquellas" (89) ("the senses, like all forces of life, are in a state of perpetual evolution, and to a large extent we owe their acceleration to foreign literature"). There was no need to search very deep to find the ideas of Darwin, Spencer, and others on the evolution of the senses in the writings of the *modernistas*. It was deemed necessary to acculturate the Indian and the mestizo by whatever means available and as soon as possible.

In the twentieth century (taking into account the implications of domination and subalternity contained in the concept of acculturation), Fernando Ortíz (1881–1969) suggested replacing this idea of assimilation with transculturation. This latter process does not aim at the cancellation of the previous culture but rather at a dialectical transfer whereby the cultural values of one social group are transferred to another, thereby forming "infinite *mestizajes*." The most well-known culinary metaphor employed when discussing transculturation is that of the Cuban *ajiaco* (a form of stew). However, Ortíz's concept has very little to do with the idea of race or *mestizaje* as understood by the *modernistas* at the end of the nineteenth century. These writers were the product of a period and set of circumstances that were not those of Cuba in the 1930s and 1940s, then characterized by the xenophobic discourses of the Second World War and the frustrations of a new republic with all its political and racial complexities. The motives of the groups, if examined closely, were basically very different.

It is exactly in the midst of these circumstances that Ortíz makes common cause with Martí; he pointed out Martí's anti-racist and democratic thinking as an example to be imitated in the 1940s. In Ortíz's opinion Martí demonstrated the folly of speaking of racial hostility since, according to Martí, races did not exist, while a symbolic common cultural imagination did. In fact, Martí spoke on several occasions of a mestizo America and a mestizo literature that superseded the discussion of racial characteristics in order to move into the realm of the symbolic and cultural. In his writings, as in those of Darío, modern and ancient sources of expression were fused with the imaginative history of the continent: myths, symbols, legends. In his essays, speeches and political writings, such as the well-known "Madre América" ["Mother America"] and "Nuestra América," there abound symbols of the original Latin American and Caribbean culture: the great Semi, the elder as a natural man of letters, and the Andean condor, among others. In a fragment quoted by Ortíz, Martí states that he "se siente correr por las venas la sangre enardecida de Tamaco y Paracomani, y se ve como propia la que vertieron por las breñas del cerro del Calvario" (8: 336) ("feels that the fiery blood of Tamaco and Paracomani flows in his veins and that he sees as his own blood that which poured onto the rough ground on Calvary"). Here Martí is referring to the ethnic and cultural composition of the continent and identifying with the indigenous past, not only for what he has in common as cultural heir but also for the desire to be and form part of the same linguistic and cultural community. It is worth recalling that Martí was the son of a Valencian father and mother from the Canary Islands, born in Cuba a long time after the aboriginal culture was exterminated. Fernando Ortíz commented that "sobre la sangre heredada vuelan los espíritus de la historia y de los pueblos, que en cualquier ambiente social hacen de la humanidad un hervor de carnes y mentes, con los sabores de mestizajes infinitos" (1996, 38) ("over inherited blood hover the spirits of history and of the people that in any social milieu make humanity a seething mass of flesh and mind with the flavors of infinite *mestizajes*"). Ortíz published this essay a year after writing *El contrapunteo cubano del tabaco y el azúcar* [1940; *Cuban Counterpoint: Tobacco and Sugar*], in which his seminal concept of transculturation in Caribbean culture appeared for the first time.

It is clear from Ortíz's essay that Martí proposed to challenge, from the perspective of his own roots, the racist theories that affirmed white superiority over the black, and presented himself as the heir of both indigenous and Spanish culture on an equal basis. For him access to education and the standards of morality were the true factors that created differences among peoples. But above all, to be understood Martí's comments on race have to be read in the sociopolitical context in which they were written, that of the War of Cuban Independence. The independentist leaders proposed that the Cuban War of Independence simply expressed the right that Cubans had to end the colonial rule of Spain; it was not an issue of whites or blacks, but rather of Cubans. The partisans of the crown, on the other hand, insisted that it was fundamentally a question of racial struggle between white Europeans and armies commanded by blacks (Quesada and Davenport Northrop 529). The effort to wipe out the fears of the former slaveholders and to found the nation on a basis of equality for all and for the good of all could not be separated from the independentist need to minimize the differences between social groups to seek consensus over and above racial differences.

Returning to the idea of desacralization of the world, we might say that despite the signifiance of Gutiérrez Girardot's use of this concept from a sociological perspective, it was Paz who had already noted that the use of inference and the emphasis on the human body were diametrically opposed to "materialismo positivista y cientista tanto como al espiritualismo cristiano" (1993, 135) ("positivistic and scientific materialism just as much as to Christian spirituality"; 1974, 95). In the oscillation of Ruben Darío from cathedrals to pagan ruins, Paz sees the survival of the remnants of Christianity. As he says:

> la otra creencia de los modernistas no es el cristianismo, sino sus restos: la idea del pecado, la conciencia de la muerte, el saberse caído y desterrado en este mundo y en el otro, el verse como un ser contingente en un mundo contingente. No un sistema de creencias, sino un puñado de fragmentos y obsesiones. (1993, 135)

> the other belief of the modernists is not Christianity but rather its remains . . . the idea of sin, the awareness of death, the knowledge that man is fallen and exiled in this world and in the next, the vision of oneself as an accidental being in a world of contingency. Not a system of beliefs but a handful of fragments and obsessions. (1974, 95)

For Paz, the eruption of the body into poetry destabilized traditional religious codes. The body is politics, and its expression within the poem crosses, subverts, and corrupts those boundaries imposed by the Church and by Positivist doctrine on literature. No one would better exemplify that opposition of the eroticized body in the face of Christian aestheticism than Fabio Fiallo (1865–1942) from Santo Domingo: The Bacchanals of Pan confront the Holy Christian mass. In the countenance of Christ, Fiallo found "tal expresión de goce mundanal,/que a veces pienso si el genial artista díole a su Cristo el alma de don Juan" (64) ("such an expression of worldly pleasure,/that at times I wonder if the talented artist gave his Christ the soul of Don Juan"). The echoes of a sexual demonism are equally heard in "Yo seré tu sequito" ("I will be your entourage"), in which the Dominican poet is asking why kindness, piety, and meekness still live in his soul, if "Eros, más fuerte que Jesús, me impuso/mi renuncia a la gracia celestial?" (62) ("Eros, stronger than Jesus, impelled/my renunciation of celestial grace?"). The demonism of these poets gradually united with theosophical beliefs, dreams, the supernatural, and subversion of religious codes. An example of this appears in the sonatas of Valle Inclán (Litvak 109–18), the poems of Fiallo and Darío, and the work of *fin-de-siècle* painters.

Michel Foucault (1926–1984) has also observed that the experience of sexuality is linked to the process of secularization of the world. In his essay on the eroticism of Georges Bataille, "Préface à la transgression" ["Preface to Transgression"], published in 1963, Foucault links the erotic experience, so fundamental to our culture since de Sade, to the death of God—a death that, according to the French philosopher, opens up the self to an experience both *internal* and *sovereign* (125). But this space for liberty did not exist in a vacuum, but rather was constantly being restricted by restraining elements such as self-censure, social criticism, and the opposition of religious, political, and academic orthodoxies. It was an autonomous space through which literature tried to cross over the threshold of prohibition imposed by a divided ethics. For this reason the liberation of the body in literature and the break with inflexible codes of sexuality are two of the most provocative and important features of *modernismo*. With this the *modernista* poets created an imaginary space where masculine and feminine come together and where poetry acquired the character of a heretical prayer. It was a zone of tension where such transgressions were simultaneously praised and rejected.

Apart from the process of desacralization and transgression of sexual codes that took place at the end of the nineteenth century, the other factor that created *modernismo* was the response to the development of science and technology. The critical formulations of Paz, Gullón, and Litvak remind us that the scientific spirit is opposed to mysticism, neo-spiritualism, and occult beliefs. Paz refers to the scientific technological impact on society in his essay "La modernidad y sus desenlaces" ["Modernity and Its Developments"], where he opportunely notes the change of the "imagen del mundo" ("image of the world") confronted by the *Modernista* poets at the end of the nineteenth century: "la tierra y el cielo que la filosofía había despoblado de dioses se cubre paulatinamente con las formidables construcciones de la técnica" (1975, 13) ("the heaven and earth that the philosopher had depopulated of their gods was slowly being covered by the formidable constructions of technology"). Paz makes it clear that *modernista* poets had no interest in technology and industry, stating that "[a los modernistas] no les fascina la máquina, esencia del mundo moderno, sino las creaciones del *art nouveau*. La modernidad no es la industria, sino el lujo" (1975, 20) ("[the *modernistas*] were not fascinated by the machine, the essence of the modern world, but rather by the creations of *art nouveau*. Modernity is not industry, but luxury"). He went on later to say: "La modernidad que seduce a los poetas jóvenes al finalizar el siglo es muy distinta de la que seducía a sus padres; no se llama progreso ni sus manifestaciones son el ferrocarril y el telégrafo: se llama lujo y sus signos son los objetos inútiles y hermosos" (1993, 129) ("The modernity which seduced the young poets at the close of the century is very different from that which seduced their fathers; it is not called progress nor are its outward manifestations the railroad and the telegraph; it is called luxury and its signs are useless and beautiful objects"; 1974, 91). Following the same line of thought, Ángel Rama (1926–1983) discarded the notion of the *modernistas* having any interest in science, adding that "en todo caso, los poetas del siglo XIX no cantaron a las conquistas científicas como lo hicieron los poetas del XVIII. . . . [L]a ciencia y la técnica se ofrecieron como antitéticas de la poesía hasta la aparición, entrado el XX, de Marinetti" (23) ("in any case, the poets of the nineteenth century did not praise scientific achievements in verse as did those of the eighteenth century. . . . [S]cience and technology were antithetical to poetry until the appearance of Marinetti's Futurism in the twentieth century"). The opinions of these critics, occasionally somewhat exaggerated, are in tune with the antinomies that structured the process of modernity in Spanish America: faith/reason, spirit/materialism, tradition/development, and the constructions of metaphysics/the scientific spirit.

However, one has to ask if our contemporary opinion on the role of science and technology in *modernista* writing is not marked by the strong skepticism of our own culture, especially that of the 1960s and 1970s, provoked by an antiscience backlash in response to the dangers of scientific experiment, nuclear tests, the Cold War, and the consequences of development in Latin America. This distrust of science manifests itself very clearly in the poetry and essays of Octavio Paz during the 1970s, when he returned to Mexico from India, and in C. P. Snow's facile proposition of the chasm separating the two cultures (a notion Rama utilized to support his own proposals [23]). If, at the turn of the nineteenth century, *modernistas* rejected scientific discourse and that of Positivism in its most aggressive forms, there was also a somewhat muted attempt to reconcile science and religion.

It is an unwarranted exaggeration to stress any visceral antagonism between poetry and technology, typical of the formulations of English Romanticism, or to state that the poets of the nineteenth century did not recognize scientific achievement. Not only did José María Heredia (1803–1839) and other Latin American Romantics celebrate scientific discoveries, but Martí and other *modernistas* applauded science and technological advances in the light of the enhancement of life these brought. It is primarily for this reason that the *Modernista* reaction to scientific modernity was both critical and celebratory. Such is the case of Amado Nervo (1870–1919), the principal poet of Mexican *modernismo,* who in 1910 wrote "Pájaro milagroso" ["Miraculous Bird"], an ode to the airplane so arranged as to not mention the word at all. The poem is eloquent in its admiration for the celestial bird. According to Nervo, the new invention would give man the wings that he had lost in his fight against the gods; the poem ends in a prayer for the new technology not to be used for military ends, as the Wright Brothers had also wished, but to contribute to peace and the realization of man's oldest dreams of travel.

> un gran signo de paz entre los pueblos!
> ¡No mancilléis al pájaro celeste con misiones
> de guerra!
>
> *(205)*
>
> A great sign of peace among the people!
> Do not sully the celestial bird with missions
> of war!

In the editions of Nervo's poetry in which this poem appears it is noted that the ode was written "después de un concurso de aviación" (1910, IX: 205) ("after an air show"). However, Isaac Goldberg is confident that it was penned "a raíz de haber hecho el poeta una ascensión en aeroplano" (100) ("as a result of the poet having gone up in an airplane"). Despite the use of airplanes in the First World War, the poet did not lose the hope he had expressed that the airplane would improve life, not destroy it. As Goldberg states, Nervo,

> después de la guerra, tenía visiones de un cielo nocturno, iluminado por señales sostenidas por anchas alas, con leyendas *de París a Nueva York–de Londres a Méjico–de Madrid a Buenos Aires.* "El aeroplano"–decía en el mismo artículo–"nos restituirá el regazo de la noche, la majestad de los astros olvidados". (Goldberg 100)

> after the war, had visions of a night sky illuminated by signs borne aloft by broad wings carrying the captions *Paris to New York–London to Mexico–Madrid to Buenos Aires.* "The airplane," he said in the same article, "will restore to us the depth of night, the majesty of the forgotten stars."

The poet who a year before had declared "je ne suis pas même un futuriste" (194) ("I am not even a futurist") ended up dedicating verses to technology, and wishing to retire to an imaginary monastery where no dogmas existed but only books and a telescope to look at the sky (207). Thus the hymn to technology in Nervo remained associated with the spiritualizing of religion. The symbols that he used to describe it came from that immense reservoir of mysticism which he knew well. In this way the discourse of the miraculous was displaced from the religious context to that of the world of technology and science. Nervo used this awe of technology to approach Futurism, the aesthetic of Marinetti, as published in the first of his famous "Manifestos" the previous year (20 February 1909). Similarly, in "Amor de ciudad grande" ["Love of the Big City"], another major *Modernista* poem executed in the midst of the rush of New York City life, José Martí made reference to lightening rods, the communication media, and the airplane in verses written in an exuberant Baroque style:

> En alta aguja
> Cual nave despeñada en sirte horrenda
> Húndese el rayo.
>
> *(Martí 1985, 89)*
>
> On lofty spire
> As a ship hurled onto horrendous sandbank
> The lightning6 flash is buried deep.

In both Martí and Nervo's work the technological emblems of modernity are not called by their real names, perhaps because they were too recent and for this reason devoid of poetic resonance. It is evident that there is a certain tension between the subject and the poetic objects registered in the written work, simultaneously offering a field of conflict and conciliation. Within the adjustments provoked by modernity, the city and technology would be places of encounter and separation as well as allowing a shifting discourse of displacement. In fact, in *modernista* poetry these poets understood that they could transgress the limits of common language and use the allusion to material objects as poetic imagery. This linguistic tension between things not named yet present in the poetic image could be characterized as a kind of poetic aphasia, the incapacity to name something, in particular the new and marvelous, while yet enunciating its presence. The impossibility of addressing the object by name produces in its place an explosion of signifiers with the sole aim of fulfilling this addressing task. The airplane in Nervo's poetry is successively a miraculous bird, a dove, an eagle, Pegasus, a heavenly bird, Icarus, and a sign of peace. Similarly, the lightning rod in Martí's eponymous poem brings together plural images of the needle, the marine abyss (sandbank) and the ship hurled like a flash of lightning. While Nervo had hope and asked that technology be used for the common good, with his metaphors Martí appears to criticize the violence that had transformed his former sense of the world; he appears to censure the speed of life and the sexual frenzy of the North American city with its suppression of a human scale of living.

But it is perhaps in his descriptions of electric light and the machines that generate it, that one can most strongly appreciate Martí's admiration for scientific discoveries. In the poem "Odio al Mar" ["Hatred of the Sea"], Martí describes a man reading on the bridge of a ship by light generated from electricity. Once again the same poetic process takes place that we have noted above, as a verbal periphrasis simultaneously conceals and replaces the emblem of modernity:

> Y a la luz de los astros, encerradas
> En globos de cristales, sobre el puente
> Vuelve un hombre impasible la hoja de un libro.
>
> *(Martí 1985, 104)*
>
> And by the light of the stars, enclosed
> In crystal globes, on the bridge
> A man impassively turns the page of a book.

In the beginning Martí proposes a contrast between nature and artificiality, between the light of the stars and the crystal globes. Even so, the material object has replaced the star and transformed it into the other source of light. With these words, Martí follows the same process of the denaturalization of the world witnessed by modern man. To create a bridge between stars and technology, the poet encloses starlight within the artificial electric light, finding a new balance for the impassive reader. The verses arise from an astonishment in the face of the new invention, and the possibility, at that time a very recent one, of carrying electric batteries "a bordo de los buques, que se surten de ella y se alumbran a su hermosa luz durante la travesía" (23: 309) ("on board ships, so that they can store electric power and generate beautiful light during the voyage").

The discovery of the transformative capacities of modern man at times seems to have enchanted the Cuban. Modern man empowered with new technology becomes a Promethean demigod, who hurls the changes of progress over the globe. In one of those bizarre passages that Darío adored in Martí's prose, the Cuban pointed out:

> el hombre echa por los mares sus serpientes de cabeza parlante, que de un lado se prenden a las breñas agrestes de Inglaterra, y de otro a la riente costa americana; y encierra la luz de los astros en un juguete de cristal; y lanza por sobre las aguas y por sobre las cordilleras sus humeantes y negros tritones. (7: 228)
>
> man casts his serpents with the talking head over the seas; on one side they illuminate the rugged cliffs of England and on the other the smiling coasts of America; and can enclose the light of the stars in a crystal toy, and throw black smoking tritons on the waters and across the mountains.

In these lines, filled with a pagan vitalism, Martí concentrated all the imagination of a new world captured in three words descriptive of movement: *echa* (throw), *encierra* (enclose), and *lanza* (hurl). The writing thus through classical allusion describes the emblems of modernity in an attempt to close the gap between it and his poetic vision, thereby invigorating poetry with technology. This is the power that gives birth to an age in which the telegraph, electric lamps, steamboats, and steam locomotives were an increasingly needed—and desired—part of everyday life. Although these technological innovations were represented as mythological monsters, it was humanity itself that was responsible for their creation and control. The metamorphosis of the modern emblems not only shows the violence of the machine but also its insertion into the natural world. If in Martí there is always a steely criticism of the social and economic maladjustments that accompanied the project of modernity, there is also a mythology based on the machine and a decided faith in modern humanity. Science that can advance equality and strengthen the hopes and fears of humanity by promoting parity in terms of living conditions can never in itself be antithetical to poetry. It is for these reasons that Martí insisted on a scientific-technical education for "our America," criticizing the excesses of literary and lettered education from which all of Latin America suffered (23: 302). His desire to instruct new generations led him to introduce vignettes on modern exhibitions in his children's magazine. Writing for *La Edad de Oro* about the Paris World Exhibition, Martí once again offered a defense of the machine, imbuing science with a touch of the supernatural and grandiose:

> ¡Pues da ganas de llorar, el ver las máquinas desde el balcón! Rugen, susurran, es como el mar: el sol entra a torrentes. De noche, un hombre toca un botón, los dos alambres de la luz se juntan, y por sobre las máquinas, que parecen arrodilladas en la tiniebla, derrama la claridad, colgado de una bóveda, el cielo eléctrico. Lejos, donde tiene Edison sus invenciones, se encienden de un chispazo veinte mil luces, como una corona. (18: 426)
>
> It makes one want to cry to see the machines from the balcony! They roar, and murmur like the sea: the sun floods in. At night a man touches a button, the two electric wires join together, and the light pours down from the electrified sky suspended from the vault above the machines that seem to be kneeling in the darkness. In the distance, where Edison houses his inventions, twenty thousand lights, like a crown, flicker into life.

At the end Martí describes the relationship between man and machine as that of a god who creates light and brings light into the darkness. On pressing the electric switch the electric light transmutes itself and lights the hall, illuminating "las máquinas, que parecen arrodilladas en la tiniebla" (18: 426) ("the machines that seem to be kneeling in the darkness"). Rapture and faith are the same images that the poet used years before to describe the position of the speaker and the ships in front of the "Estatua de la Libertad" (Statue of Liberty) in New York. It is therefore clear that Martí's attitude toward modernity was anti-modern when dealing with its alienating, dehumanizing, and racist dimensions, but in favor of it when modernity offered effective advances in terms of living conditions and the satisfaction of human needs.

A third aspect is the poet's encounter with the city and the growing artificiality of the modern world. González Echevarría has said that with "Amor de ciudad grande" ["Love of a Big City"], Martí initiated the poetry of the city within *Modernismo*. Taking up the ideas of the German sociologist Georg Simmel concerning the intensification of nervous tension, Gutiérrez Girardot analyzes this aspect in *modernismo*, counterpointing the public space of great cities to the construction of spiritual inner worlds, Antonio Machado's (1875–1939) galleries of the soul, and Miguel de Unamuno's (1864–1936) anxiety over eternity (126). Like Martí, José Enrique Rodó finds a basis for fear in the incipient expansion and utilitarian space of the cities, since the cities that guard the glory of heroes and the promises of its tribunes could end up being Sidon, Tyre, or Carthage (96). In keeping with this vision of alienation, the poem "Amor de la ciudad grande" acts as a broken mirror in which the crisis of modernity, fragmented both ethically and morally, is reflected back, especially in terms of sexuality, the status of woman, and the sexual commerce of the North American metropoli. The spirit of the poet, exiled from the city, seems to live within it like a wounded deer or docile greyhound on a game preserve. Among the characteristics of the modern city that Martí condemns are the vertiginous speed at which everything happens and its fleeting, transitory nature, a Baudelairian topic *par excellence* symbolized by the lightning bolt, the ship hurled into the sea's abyss, and the rumor that moves like light. He also criticizes the fact that the female has become transformed into a luxury object, a painting, or a carved goblet in his Ibsen-like critique of the bourgeois demand for accumulation of possessions—and with it a new love ethic and, above all, the commercialization of the body. However, despite all this, it must not be forgotten that Martí also writes an apologia for the modern city in another poem, "Estrofa nueva" ["New Strophe"], published in the same volume, in which he praises individual liberty and the creative toil of the worker in lines that clearly show the influence of Whitman. In this way one could speak of a two-faced city in which one face reveals the signs of *eros dominandi* and the debasing power of money, and the other that of work, love for others, and charity.

Darío's approach to modernity is not naive. His tropology of modernity is nourished by materials created by industry and science: x-rays, the photographic camera, elephantine locomotives, and mythological airplanes such as those appearing in "Canto a la Argentina" ["Song to Argentina"]. This is how the image of poets as heavenly lightning rods and breakwaters of eternities can be understood; these are neologisms that Darío uses to describe the function of the seer in the cosmopolitan city in another seminal poem of *modernismo*, "¡Torres de Dios!" ["Towers of God"] (1994, 333). Moreover, the desire for specialization, the detailed observation, and the search for an objective and impersonal style are characteristics shared as much by *fin-de-siècle* poets as by scientific researchers. The poet also incorporates luxury objects with those of modernity as the continuous process of industrial expansion increasingly filled the Spanish American market and its storehouses with the necessities for a new bourgeois, the king of a consumer society. *Modernista* poetics were transformed by him into a kind of machine that produced the same incredible rhythms as skillfully made artifacts. Darío seemed to transform all that he touched into artificial, manufactured articles. The same process of the metamorphosis of natural reality into the artificial, factory-made reality is featured in "Sinfonía en gris mayor" ["Symphony in Gray Major"]: "El mar como un vasto cristal azogado,/El sol como vidrio redondo y opaco,/Las ondas que mueven su vientre de plomo" (1994, 333) ("The sea like a vast looking-glass coated with quicksilver,/The sun like a round, opaque glass,/The waves that move its leaden entrails"). The equivalences made between sea and "looking-glass coated with quicksilver," the sun and a "round, opaque glass," are only a periphrastic way of calling the sea a mirror and the sun a lamp. The comparison between the sun and the electric lamp was not new; it appeared frequently in the newspapers and discussions of Edison's marvelous invention. Martí also mentions a lamp that bore this name and adorned the great Parisian salons. In *La isla de oro* Darío did not hesitate to return to such comparisons when he described the tiny salon where he read, in which an electric lamp had created daylight (see Torres Bodet 351). Darío, Casal, and occasionally Martí eliminated an idealized landscape to substitute for it an artificial one. In the first poet's work, the sumptuous interior of the small salons, the anterooms, the ideal museums, the Chinese albums, and the spirit of the poet are all counterpoised to nature. In Martí, a double process takes place: an artificial nature that is progressively naturalized within the poem and an inverse movement in which what is natural becomes artificial, as occurs in the case of the representations of the female in "Amor a la ciudad grande." Flesh acquires the glistening of gold, hair the hardness of metal or the delicacy of fabric; it is either a Damascus blade or a curtain that falls from the sky. The woman herself is a carved goblet. In this way Martí tries to offer a critique of what he believes is a woman's natural inclination for beautiful and decorative objects. At the same time he expresses her value as an object in the magnate's house: the woman as object, monstrous in her aggressive appearance, and converted into a part of the sumptuous furniture of bourgeois life.

But this process of artificialization of the natural order is not only aimed at criticism or celebration, according to the individual case, but also contains an aesthetic proposal. In *modernista* prose and poetry, the fragmentation of the object into its essential components (crystals, surface of quicksilver, round lamp shade, circular piece of glass) and the complex of accompanying associated images offer the poet the possibility of experimenting with language, rhythm, and chromatic hues, thus eliminating any fall into facile imitation. Like musical solos, the parts shine on their own, increasing their expressive capacity. Landscape is a painting, a musical score, an orchestration of visions and spectacular objects. Thus modernist writing functions like a play of tensions, a metalanguage that allows the transmutation of some codes into others. This reconversion already appears in the work of Gertrudis Gómez de Avellaneda, in whose sonnet entitled "A las estrellas" ["To the Stars"] we read, "purísimas estrellas/De la noche feliz lámparas bellas,/Bordáis con oro su luctuoso manto" ("purest stars/By happy night beautiful lamps/ You weave with gold a mournful mantle"); in another poem, the sea is also called a blue mirror (*Poetisas* 39). Some similarities between Avellaneda's poem and Darío's "Sinfonía en gris mayor" are discernible: Both reveal the tensions between the natural and the artificial in a world that was rapidly losing its animistic character to gain artificial and aesthetic properties. It was with Avellaneda that the value of nature began to be lost. The new pattern of beauty was no longer nature but art, beautiful manufactured objects, and the advances of science. The process of denaturalization and experimentation that had been generated within the Latin American Romanticism years earlier, now joined by the search for a new rhythm and an increasingly original language—these are the characteristics of *modernismo*.

Translation by Jessica Johnson

Works Cited

Bermúdez, Federico. 1986. *Todas las poesías de Federico Bermúdez: homenaje en su centenario*. San Pedro de Macorís, República Dominicana: Universidad Central del Este.

Camacho, Jorge Luis. 1998. "Interpretando la historia: la metáfora del desierto/destierro en *Ismaelillo*, de José Martí." *Revista Canadiense de Estudios Hispánicos* 23.1: 119–31.

Carpentier, Alejo. 1974. "Martí y Francia (Primer intento de aproximación a un ensayo posible)." *En torno a José Martí. Coloquio Internacional [Bordeaux, 1972]*. Bordeaux: Editions Bière. 511–39.

Casal, Julián del. 1993. *Poesías completas y pequeños poemas en prosa (en orden cronológico)*. Ed. Esperanza Figueroa. Miami: Ediciones Universal.

Coll, Pedro Emilio. 1980. "Decadentismo y americanismo." *El modernismo visto por los modernistas*. Ed. Ricardo Gullón. Barcelona: Guadarrama. 82–90.

Darío, Rubén. 1965. *El canto errante*. Madrid: Espasa-Calpe.

———. 1994. *Poesía*. Havana: Editorial Arte y Literatura.

Díaz-Plaja, Guillermo. 1966. *Modernismo frente a noventa y ocho: una introducción a la literatura española del siglo XX*. Madrid: Espasa-Calpe.

Fiallo, Fabio. 1935. *El balcón de Psiquis*. Havana: Cultural.

Foucault, Michel. 1996. "Prefacio a la Trasgresión." *De lenguaje y literatura*. Intro. Angel Gabilondo. Barcelona: Editorial Paidós. 123–42.

García Marruz, Fina. 1991. "Modernidad, modernismo y orbe nuevo." *Anuario del centro de estudios martianos* 14: 16–35.

Goldberg, Issac. 1922. *La literatura hispanoamericana; estudios críticos*. Trans. R. Cansinos-Assens. Madrid: Editorial América.

González Echevarría, Roberto. 1987. "Martí y su 'Amor de ciudad grande': notas hacia una poética de *Versos Libres*." *Nuevos asedios al modernismo*. Ed. Iván A. Schulman et al. Madrid: Taurus Ediciones. 160–73.

Gutiérrez Girardot, Rafael. 1983. *Modernismo*. Barcelona: Montesinos.

Gullón, Ricardo. 1990. *Direcciones del Modernismo*. Madrid: Alianza Editorial.

Heredia, José María. 1990. *Niágara y otros textos: poesía y prosa selectas*. Ed. Angel Augier. Caracas: Biblioteca Ayacucho.

Jauss, Hans Robert. 1982. *Toward an Aesthetic of Reception*. Trans. Timothy Bahti. Minneapolis: University of Minnesota Press.

Jiménez, Juan Ramón. 1962. "Clases de Juan Ramón Jiménez sobre el modernismo." *El Modernismo. Notas de un curso (1953)*. Ed. Ricardo Gullón and Eugenio Fernández Méndez. Mexico City: Aguilar. 197–266.

Litvak, Lily. 1979. *Erotismo fin de siglo*. Barcelona: Editorial A. Bosch.

Martí, José. 1985. *Poesía completa*. Ed. Cintio Vitier, Fina García Marruz, and Emilio de Armas. 2 vols. Havana: Editorial Letras Cubanas.

———. 1963–1973. *Obras completas*. 28 vols. Havana: Editorial Nacional de Cuba.

Nervo, Amado. 1982. *Poesías completas*. Barcelona: Teorema.

Onís, Federico de. 1961. *Antología de la poesía española e hispanoamericana (1882–1932)*. New York: Las Américas.

Ortiz, Fernando. 1996. *Martí humanista*. Ed. Issac Barreal and Norma Súarez Súarez. Havana: Fundación Fernando Ortiz.

———. 1978. *Contrapunteo cubano del tabaco y el azúcar*. Caracas: Biblioteca Ayacucho.

Paz, Octavio. 1974. *Children of the Mire: Modern Poetry from Romanticism to the Avant-Garde*. Trans. Rachel Phillips. Cambridge, MA: Harvard University Press.

———. 1975. "La modernidad y sus desenlaces." *El signo y el garabato*. Mexico City: Juaquín Mortiz. 11–30.

———. 1993. *Los hijos del limo: del romanticismo a la vanguardia*. Barcelona: Editorial Seix Barral.

Quesada, Gonzalo de, and Henry Davenport Northrop. 1896. *The War in Cuba, Being a Full Account of her Great Struggle for Freedom*. [N.p.]: Liberty Publishing Co.

Rama, Ángel. 1973. "Sueños, espíritus, ideología y arte. Prólogo." *El mundo de los sueños*. By Rubén Darío. Ed. Angel Rama. Rio Piedras, PR: Editorial Universitaria. 5–54.

Rocasolano, Alberto, ed. 1985. *Poetisas cubanas*. Havana: Editorial Letras Cubanas.

Rodó, José Enrique. 1912. *Ariel*. Valencia: Prometeo.

Sanz del Río, Julián. 1945. "Ideal de la Humanidad." *Antología del pensamiento de lengua española en la edad contemporánea*. Ed. José Gaos. Mexico City: Editorial Séneca. 362–68.

Schulman, Iván A., and Manuel Pedro González. 1969. *Martí, Darío y el Modernismo*. Madrid: Editorial Gredos.

Torres Bodet, Jaime, ed. 1967. *Rubén Darío: Antología*. Mexico City: Universidad Nacional Autónoma de México, Fondo de Cultura Económica.

Uhrbach, Carlos Pío, and Federico Uhrbach. 1907. *Oro*. Havana: Imprenta Avisador Comercial.

Varona, Enrique José. 1945. "D'Annunzio y la crisis actual." *Antología del pensamiento de lengua española en la edad contemporánea*. Ed. José Gaos. Mexico City: Editorial Séneca. 666–68.

Vitier, Cintio. 1969. "En la mina martiana." *Martí, Darío y el Modernismo*. Madrid: Gredos. 9–21.

Vitier, Medardo. 1954. *Martí, estudio integral*. Havana: Publicaciones de la Comisión Nacional Organizadora de los Actos y Ediciones del Centenario y del Monumento de Martí.

CHAPTER 29

TEXTUAL TRANSCULTURAL MEDIATIONS AND THE FORMATION OF REGIONAL IDENTITY

Ileana Rodríguez

From an hacienda house fronting the San Juan river, the frontier between the republics of Costa Rica and Nicaragua, the local inhabitants watch travelers passing through: "aventureros, contrabandistas, especuladores, mineros, madereros, compradores de hule, empleados de compañías bananeras, tratantes de ganado, evangelistas, andarines . . . pescadores de tiburones, atrapadores de fieras vivas, exportadores de micos carablancas y de papagayos, botánicos y zoólogos" (Coronel Urtecho 153) ("adventurers, smugglers, speculators, miners, lumberjacks, rubber buyers, banana company employees, cattle dealers, evangelists, hikers . . . shark fishermen, trappers of live wild animals, exporters of white-faced monkeys and parrots, botanists and zoologists"). These are the leftovers from the Californian Gold Rush, "los últimos *fortyniners*" (143) ("the last forty-niners"), similar to the men who travelled in the ships under the command of Commodore Vanderbilt. The local writer immediately establishes a contrast between these travelers and others, like the individual that

> tenía el ojo fresco para el paisaje tropical y las pequeñas
> peculiaridades de nuestra vida . . . míster Squier, primer
> Encargado de Negocios de los Estados Unidos en Nicaragua,
> quien pasó por el río hace más de cien años, haciendo el viaje
> desde Greytown hasta Granada en un bongo . . . feliz en los
> tortuosos meandros y lagunas de la desembocadura del río que le
> recordaban los *bayous* del Mississipi. (145)

> had a fresh eye for the tropical landscape and the small peculiarities
> of our existence . . . Mr. Squier, chargé d'affaires for United States
> in Nicaragua, who made the river journey almost a century ago,
> crossing from Greytown to Granada on a bongo [large dugout
> canoe] . . . rejoicing in the tortuous meanders and lakes of the
> river delta that reminded him of the Mississippi bayous.

Mark Twain also fits into this category, traveling in 1886 from San Francisco to New York with a notebook to which he gave the title: "From San Francisco to New York by way of San Juan and Grey Town Isthmus" (Coronel 150).

From this viewpoint, anchored as much in a regional-geographical approach as in literary regionalism, the retrospective gaze of the local writer is skeptical since, in the "depopulated" and "remote" creeks of this river,

> la soledad es cada vez mayor y más bella . . . . Tal vez . . . se
> pueble un día, como pensaba Squier, naveguen barcos y
> gasolinas; pasten caballos y ganados de raza en sus llanos y en los
> gramales de las lomas; se miren en sus orillas hermosas casas
> tropicales y en muchas de ellas libros americanos y retratos de
> poetas. Tal vez la soledad y la belleza primitiva queden sólo en los
> libros. Tal vez la selva vuelva a cubrirlo todo. Todo depende. (164)

> solitude grows increasingly greater and more attractive . . . .
> Perhaps . . . one day it will be populated, as Squier thought,
> navigated by vessels and motor boats; horses and breeds of cattle
> will pasture on the level ground and on the Bermuda grass of the

hillsides; beautiful tropical houses will be seen on the banks, many with American books and portraits of poets. Perhaps the solitude and the primitive beauty will survive only in books. Perhaps the jungle will return to cover everything. It all depends.

The dream of modernity crosses the river, not to return since no one stays; no one is interested in speaking to the natives. The travelers pass by, "envueltos en su propia esquivés, sintiéndose aventureros solitarios en la jungla, donde no hay teóricamente hombres civilizados, y pensando en nada más que en la historia que contarán al regresar a casa" (Coronel Urtecho 156) ("wrapped in their own aloofness, feeling themselves to be solitary adventurers in the jungle, where theoretically no civilized men exist and thinking of nothing else, than on the story that they will tell on their return").

What is the story that they will relate and who are the transmitters? José Coronel Urtecho (1906–1994) makes a distinction between different types of narrative within the discourse of modernity; in a series of narrative subjects he distinguishes the uninformed idlers or travelers from the educated. The latter are characterized by having a "ojo fresco para el paisaje tropical y las pequeñas peculiaridades de nuestra vida" (145) ("fresh eye for the tropical forest and the small peculiarities of our existence") and a capacity for expressing their vision. Ephraim George Squier is one of these, Mark Twain (Samuel Clemens) another, and a third, Milton A. Douglas, was a student of zoology at Harvard. These three, together with numerous other travelers mentioned as a group, reconstructed regional identities in the nineteenth century, engaging with the most relevant colonial historiography, categorized into events of greatest significance, as well as responding to contemporary historiography. Works of geography, zoology, botany, and books by well-informed travelers (Mark Twain, as well as visitors such as John Lloyd Stephens, Alfred Maudslay, Désiré Charnay, Carl Bovallius and Pablo Levy, who would establish the archaeological context) are linked in the nineteenth century to the work of commodores, admirals, and businessmen (e.g., Orlando Roberts, Bedford Pim, Thomas Young), working together in the reshaping of the region according to the parameters of positivist science.

These occasional visitors came to narrate a story that described the regions they visited as future sites of economic exploitation. The traveler's report thus becomes an economic inventory of all the visible, measurable and collectable material elements of the region in terms of topography, geography, and above all the market value of natural resources as well as an early evaluation of the classic Mayan cities, first written into the discourse of positivistic science as ruins and later discussed by cultural anthropology under the heading of cities, ceremonial centers, and museums. The new sciences–physical geography (assuming pre-eminence on the basis of being the dominant discourse that expressed identity), botany, zoology, and archaeology—came to represent the method of collecting information that would later be transformed into knowledge, science, power, and prestige. This methodology would establish lines of legitimacy and illegitimacy for the knowledge generated by both local and foreign intellectuals.

I have chosen this textual moment as a point of departure for discussing the creation of regional identities as products of transculturation. Textual transculturation is here understood as an overlapping of texts, as a dialogue that is realized within a bibliographic body of texts, characterized by a "configuración diversa y múltiplemente conflictiva" (Cornejo Polar 13) ("diverse and multiply conflictive configuration"). These transcultural axes provide information on a bibliography that is "especialmente escurridiza por su condición multi y transcultural" (14) ("particularly elusive with regard to its multi- and transcultural condition"). Its processes of production "intersectan conflictivamente dos o más universos socio-culturales" (17) ("intersect in conflict with two or more socio-cultural universes"), while heterogeneity infiltrates the internal configuration of each because they are "portadoras de tiempos y ritmos sociales que se hunden verticalmente en su propia constitución, resonando en y con voces que pueden estar separadas entre sí por siglos de distancia" (18) ("carriers of social times and rhythms that are vertically buried in their own constitution, resonating in and with voices that can be individually separated by centuries of distance").

The Method and the Bibliographies

Ephraim George Squier (1821–1888) was the individual responsible for establishing the parameters of positivistic geographic science in Central America. The contrast between its practices and the colonial tradition lies in a methodology. Positivist science established exactitude as standard practice: Precise measurements, clear descriptions, exact numbers. For example, a league could not be a subjective measurement that depended on the topography of terrain that in San Salvador and the plains rarely exceeded two English miles, while in the mountains it was considered less than a mile and a half. For Squier, crucial details presenting "a clear idea of the landscape of the country and the architecture of her people" (xi) could not be reliant on past knowledge characterized by inadequate representations, a "complete lack of order, gross negligence and dishonest destruction . . . to confound and defeat all investigation" (xi). As Ángel Rama comments, "sólo un cientificismo consagrado a la aplicación del sistema racionalista extremado, podía desarrollar formas mentales que se adecuaran y propiciaran la construcción de una sociedad moderna" (137) ("only a kind of scientism dedicated to the application of an extremely rationalist system could develop mental forms that are suited to and promote the construction of a modern society").

This method was what established the demarcation between colonial and modern. Colonial texts, beginning with the narrative of Pedro de Alvarado on the Conquest of Utatlán (García Grandados), Colonial texts agree with the observations made by Squier. The latter comments that

> not only were important places erroneously located, but also topographic features . . . were placed where nothing existed while others that did exist were left entirely to one side. The majority of the maps of America were made in Europe and filled with names unknown in the country itself. Such errors are perpetuated and frequently it ends up being difficult to surmise their origin. (xi)

Later he partially retracts this general criticism with regard to place-names when stating that "the original place names, even so, have been preserved here [in Central America] with the greatest tenacity and provide a guide to defining the extension of the territory occupied by the various aboriginal nations" (319). The entire geographic network was therefore created by the people whom Squier admires. For this reason, even though the moment of transculturation (when the geographic narratives of the Conquest are inserted into his text) is important, the geography itself is represented here as being without precedent, a science without history, characterized by the total absence of bibliographical and archival knowledge. And even when Squier recognized in his bibliography the work of British captains, French naturalists, and North American businessmen, he still stated that what was known about Central America had been produced by foreigners whose observations—lacking scientific foundation—followed the conventions of such genres as travel writing and adventure literature. Thus they lacked accurate calculation and were merely superficial points of view "in which their authors err by not specifying the exact origin of what they record, let alone make their meaning explicit" (xvi).

For Squier the new positivist science began with Heinrich Karl Wilhelm Berghaus, the Prussian geographer who made the first precise map of the region in 1840. This tradition is contrasted, on the one hand, with that established by colonial historiography (specifically monks' chronicles that are considered to be erroneous, slavish, and inexact repetitions) and, on the other, with that of local historiography as represented by Domingo Juarros, the Guatemalan historian commissioned by the English to write about his native land and whom Squier disqualified on account of his work being merely "a transcription of conventual municipal chronicles of Guatemala. Rarely does [Juarros] make any reference to the physical characteristics of the country, and even in such rare cases it is in an exaggerated and fascinated way that always denotes the absence of positive knowledge" (xv).

According to these criteria, the archival knowledge produced by the collaborative work of monks and indigenous people acquires a different status. The naturalist Arthur Morelet, for example, disqualified Francisco Ximénez, grammarian of the Mayan-Quiché languages and promoter of the *Popol Vuh*, saying "never have [I] seen him quoted—perhaps because he has never had the good fortune to have a reader" (389). This is a perfect example of a *tabula rasa* created by the positivist sciences whose corollary is the idea of the ahistoricity of America. The new methods try to begin at point zero, reducing previous knowledge and information to either preliminary and exploratory collecting or to erroneous information and for this reason to be subsumed under the category of fiction. In this way the information that monks were given by indigenous people in testimonial formats (originally reliable data on geography, jurisdictions, and genealogies), once absorbed and set down, went from being knowledge to being considered a kind of fiction. Regarding these acts of transculturation Ángel Rama stated that

> [p]or un deslizamiento derivado de la creciente especialización y tecnificación del discurso historiográfico, que se caracteriza . . . por una incesante cancelación de los discursos anteriores reemplazados por los nuevos mejor fundados, la literatura ha venido recibiendo una considerable masa de materiales que ha abandonado su originario cauce disciplinario, trasladándose a otro encuadre que le proporciona significación y valor perviviente. (89)

because of a shift derived from the growing specialization and technicalization of historiographic discourse that is characterized . . . by an incessant cancellation of the previous discourses which are replaced by new better based ones, literature has come to receive a considerable mass of material that has abandoned its original disciplinary source and transferred to another framework that gives it meaning and enduring value.

Thus, one of the functions of the discourse of modernization is the revision of colonial history and the demarcation it sets up between military discourse (which is incorporated as exploratory fact, subsumed within the heroic) and the testimonial, collected by the monks (which is given the status of fiction, exaggeration, and the marvelous). In differentiating between the functions of the military and the religious, the modern revision transforms military narrative into popular tales and anecdotes. This historical revisionism introduces a kind of intellectual dysphasia whereby words have no meaning or have an opposite meaning to what had been formerly accepted, for example, war becomes exploration. Narratives by conquistadors such as Pedro de Alvarado, Pedrarias Dávila, Francisco Hernández de Córdoba, Hernán Cortés, and Bernal Díaz de Castillo are all read in this way. A denunciation of the brutality of conquest is transformed into pacification (as in the revisionist interpretation that is given to the work of Bartolomé de Las Casas, Antonio de Remesal, Pedro Cortés y Larraz, Antonio Vázquez and Ximénez). The narrative of exploration is also transformed; it becomes a racist ethnology that supports the positivist demands for knowledge (the reports of commodores, captains, and European businessmen are read thus). Seen together, these narrative transformations come to formulate new population policies that press for the exclusion of the indigenous people from consideration in development, progress, and the politics of the citizenry (as managed by local and foreign intellectuals such as José Milla and Domingo Juarros, along with Arthur Morelet, Ephraim George Squier, and John Lloyd Stephens).

Another important function of the discourse of modernity is to disqualify local intellectual and scientific discourses in favor of often flawed European studies. In the production of maps, for example, this is evident in the prominence given in cartographic bibliographies to maps by Berghaus and Alexander von Humboldt and to the dismissal of those of Juarros. In all cases the selection of information produces and expresses a tradition that legitimizes the European and delegitimizes the local production, with the result that what is accepted as knowledge presents a reinvention of America as a massive supermarket of raw materials for the market economy. The region is reduced into a terrain for exploitation and ready for investment, above all in the form of the installation of communication services, agricultural products, and the transportation systems necessary to market them.

In this discussion, transculturation is distinguished by the selection of materials that are to be recycled and make their presence felt in the form of notes, citations, bibliographies, and the reproduction of anecdotes. The rewritten fragment is a discourse different in nature from that of the discourse of the written text and, as Cornejo Polar explains when commenting on the oral tradition: "cada versión oculta una arqueología propia y distinta, como si acumulara internamente estratos formales y de significación que corresponden a sus confusos itinerarios de actualizaciones espacio-temporales, consistentemente cargadas de contenidos étnicos y sociales" (59) ("each version conceals its own unique archaeology, as if

it internally accumulates formal strata and meanings that correspond to its confused itineraries of spatio-temporal actualizations, consistently charged with ethnic and social content"). My thesis is that the process of trans-textualization or discursive mediation constitutes transculturation as a cultural inversion constituting archives of knowledge. This is the same process that demarcates modes of thought, interpretation and meaning, as knowledge or pseudo-knowledge, and that establishes the gaps that lie between information and knowledge, between the marvelous and psuedo-knowledge. The early twentieth century returned to this pseudo-knowledge. It accepted as true what was merely non-reflexive description and rejected all aspects of an incipient modernity. In other words, discourse was purged of all utopian developmental elements.

The task now is to consider the criteria of selection. How did the new scientists differentiate precision from non-precision in the information that was passed on? What are the distinguishing criteria that help to differentiate one thing from another? A careful reading of the rewritten fragments suggests that the selection criteria for transculturation are what will be deposited as cultural wealth; this involves the coincidence of opinion, function, and projects. Even though the awareness of the difference between cartographers in Europe (Berghaus) and European cartographers in America (Humboldt) was specified, the aim was to reevaluate the production of knowledge in Europe and America, and in America to trace the direct line between the European culture transmitted by the conquistadors and that imparted by the monks, between what was channeled by local and by foreign intellectual cadres, in particular regarding all that refers to the relationship between physical and ethnic topography.

Mestizaje as Dubious Evidence of Transculturation

Who is who in ethnic terms is another of the measurements of transculturation and a fundamental aspect of the results of any investigation that has to express both physical and human geographies. The ethnic is now an interrelationship between indigenous, white, and its mixtures. The mestizo subject is established as dubious evidence of transculturation, a heraclitean subject that Cornejo describes as "ferozmente contradictorio . . . excepcionalmente cambiante y fluido" (20) ("ferociously contradictory . . . exceptionally changeable and fluid"). *Mestizaje*'s existence throws into disarray the idea of racial purity that, for indigenous populations, is transferred to the past and situated in a discussion of historically distant versus living Indians, organized around a concept of the classic period (i.e., the classic Mayan period was between 500 and 800 CE) and rooted in archaeology (see Stephens, Brinton, and Thompson). In this construction of indigenous ethnicity as a monument is to be found the residue of discussions on the ideology of taste (approximations to theories of sensibility understood as aesthetics) that would emerge to promote and enlarge the disciplines of archaeology, ethno-history, and anthropology. These disciplines would return to engage classic foundational indigenous texts (the *Popol Vuh*, *El Rabinal Achi*, *El memorial de Sololá* [*The Annals of the Cakchiquels*] from Sololá, with archaeological sites and ritual dances), just as Spanish scholarship and subsequently the *criollo* lettered tradition had done. In the nineteenth and twentieth centuries travelers and cultural critics had also engaged in this conceptual identity-making until they were absorbed by the contemporary post-modern narrative of the national and international development agencies, above all with regard to agriculture and tourism. Aesthetics and geography are thus situated on the same semantic plane as literary naturalism to the extent that they constitute great data banks. If the residue of tradition is minimal, as García Canclini (16) states, it circulates within folklore (popular literature, fiestas, craftwork)–not to write history but to dance it, as Cornejo (89) describes the process. If it is great, then it becomes part of the national heritage in the form of monuments and museums. In transcultural terms these cartographic bibliographies represent physical space as an open frontier and the ethnic as an impossible limit to cross. My argument is that *mestizaje* is debated as a dubious example of acculturation in terms of the cartographic corpus. For this reason the methodologies of positivist science are concerned with carefully establishing the percentages that measure the mixtures of possible ethnic grades of trans-, neo-, or acculturation.

As in the colonial past, the minute observation of local indigenous people is used above all to re-build a framework for their physical and cultural localization and the reconversion of "the ethnic" into the native in socio-regional terms. Thus ethnic identities are discussed in various ways: In terms of the land, agriculture, and agricultural products, the relationship between subsistence and export economies, and methods of government and authority that compare patriarchal and constitutional systems (see Young, Squier, and Pim). Ethnic mixing is openly discussed as a source of political tension, as the site of struggle between the white Liberal *criollos* (like Francisco Morazán) and ethnically indeterminate Conservatives (the figure of Rafael Carrera) (see Stephens). Thus while the white population represents civilization and progress, contemporary Indians are merely the ship of state's ballast, and mestizos an arguable bridge between them. Social systems, in contrast to those based on ethnicity, remain circumscribed by urban space and described as mere imitative governments ruled by political constitutions of a Republican cut that have established what Silviano Santiago calls the contemporary version of the unity concept: "one God, one king, one language" (5) or, put in other words, one nation, one government, and one language.

If from this perspective we return now to the notion of transculturation as the presence of fragments from other texts and as cultural inversion as a means of transforming one narrative into another, we see, for example, that Hernán Cortés's expedition to Honduras (known as Las Hibueras, Las Higueras, the Audiencia de los Confines), one of the narratives of exploration and conquest that is trans-textualized, does not contribute much to the exploration of space as physical geography. Instead it serves as a means of inserting epic elements within the representation of an heroic landscape that allows for the entry, through the back door, of ideas of progress linked to Europe. The meaning of the epic insertion results from (and thus is intimately linked to) the difficulties encountered at the crossroads of unmapped geographies and uncertain ethnographies: "This expedition, due to its distance as well as the difficulties encountered and overcome in its pursuit, remains and will always remain without precedent and without comparison in the history of martial adventure" (Squier 66). The exemplary nature of the moment and its causal connection oversee the conversion of a narrative of war into one of geography and act to reconstitute indigenous communities within the new paradigm of Positivism. Thus it was that social practices, culturally part of local cultures, "se

transmutan en monstruosos salvajismos al ser trasladados a otros parámetros culturales" (Rama 157) ("are transmuted into monstrous savagery on being transferred to other [Positivist] cultural parameters").

The idea of the marvelous–as registered by colonial prose with reference to the natural world of America–is now portrayed as unprecedented, lacking both history and archives. This move simultaneously localizes and wipes out indigenous presence and establishes an identity that is produced though not necessarily perceived. For example, uninhabited lands are constituted by Positivism as non-productive land (see Seed, Bunzel, Tax). Hence the choice of names and adjectives that re-establish the framework of the route of the conquistadors through what is described as "unknown jungle" and "frontiers" through "deep swamps, broad and almost impassable rivers, lofty and uninhabited mountains . . . [crossed with] almost superhuman courage and fortitude" (Squier 66). Positivist science performs the (con)fusion of the martial and the scientific, conquistador and explorer, soldier and geographer, neo- and post-colonialism. The subtext is the enduring nature of the savage Indians on the point of being modernized and transformed again into the underdeveloped natives, an ontological state contrary to the projected plans for "civilizing" them.

Nineteen undifferentiated ethnic identities are divided, first, into the indigenous and non-indigenous (the suspect mestizos), *ladinos* and *criollos*, and second, into a civilization of ancient Indians (the classical Maya), non-Indian Indians (i.e., Spanish-speaking), contemporary Indians, guides (acculturated Indians), human beasts of burden, bodies limited to the land (plantation Indians), and anthropological specimens. The first distinction was refined and reworked by Positivism; the second, the revision of ancient documents, was undertaken by the disciplines of Mayan anthropology and archaeology whose recognized "father" is John Lloyd Stephens. The prose of the conquistadors had already established the coordinates for distinguishing between upper- and lower-status Indians, between Quichés, Kachiquels, and Nahuas of the central Mexican plateau and the "nomadic fishing tribes that inhabit the low lands of the Caribbean, now called the Mosquito Coast" (Squier 224). In separate chapters Squier speaks of other "aboriginal elements," "native tribes," Xicaques, Payas, Guatusos, Miskitos, Sambos, Caribs, Lempas, Itzas, etc.

With reference to these groups, we can see the outlines of a questionnaire intended to establish with precision the inhabited areas and occupations of their inhabitants. It tried to identify if they lived within the territories marked out for progress (or not) and if they are mixed, assimilated, acculturated, or "retain their original ways of life" (Squier 223). The replies provide information on the general composition of ethnic societies and specify whether the white population had been assimilated (a kind of *mestizaje* and transculturation) or if they have assimilated the indigenous population (yet another variety of *mestizaje* and transculturation). The indigenous aspect is one of the components of *mestizaje*, a biological percentage registered in the column of debits in the table of racial investments in culture. Here confusion abounds, since the eye that classifies registers that "in some districts of the state it is difficult to say if the White population has assimilated the Indians into their way of life or the Indians have assimilated the white population" (Squier 223).

This confusion occurred on the Bálsamo Coast in El Salvador where disquiet existed over a desire to resolve whether the indigenous inhabitants were modern or primitive, without reference to whether they were Indians or mestizos. The difficulty of classification lay in the convergence of transcultural elements since, while their houses had straw roofs, their churches were covered with tiles; and supposedly they read and wrote Spanish, yet they understood little of the mechanical arts and practiced them even less. To Squier's eyes, the confusion abounds, because they professed the Catholic religion and cultivated music but their needs were few and they walked about naked from the waist up. They married, but their ceremonies were peculiar to the Europeans, and they practiced incest. They had a dual notion of government, respecting civil authority along with that of their *Ahuales*. They obeyed the state but did not consult it for internal civil or criminal conflicts. They only cultivated maize. Their sole wealth was balsam, but there was little or no commerce. Their physical features were unattractive and lacking in symmetry; dark in color, they were taciturn and said to be less intelligent than the non-Indians. It is not known whether the narrator here was selecting the phenotype that most promoted *mestizaje* or pointing out the aporias of classification. Ethnographers identify the issue of *mestizaje* as something that is underlying what is transcultural, the hybrid that preserves the indigenous element within *mestizaje*.

Banana Republics

Seen from the transcultural viewpoint and understood as a lettered exchange between the local and outside (the universal, global, European, North American), Central American spaces are described as depositaries of wealth–initially in the form of the population (and in the best of cases, of the workforce), and in terms of land and, later, food products. The area was also regarded either as a storehouse of tropical species and specimens (such as indigo, sugar cane, coffee, and bananas) that could promote the development of Positivism, or as that geographical space that could link north and south, east and west. The metaphors that result from this exchange are fixed as regional identities (e.g., brown brother republics, banana republics). The legitimization of such images can be read in their local reconfiguration in the social imagination of twentieth-century writers–in the "Rápido Tránsito" ["Rapid Transit"] (canals, inter-oceanic railways) of Coronel Urtecho; in the geological metaphors of "Balcanes y Volcanes" ["Balkans and Volcanos"] by Sergio Ramírez (b. 1942) or Carlos Cilas' "Volcanes y Terremotos," ["Volcanoes and Earthquakes"]–all of which underline the construction of means of transport, the wildlife of the isthmus, and the nature of the subsoil. These are the geographies that are handed down as transcultural bequests from explorers and scientists to essayists, historians, and literati.

The formation of socio-cultural identities, the processes of acculturation (Ortiz), transculturation (Rama), hybridization (García Canclini) and *mestizaje* (Cornejo Polar) are all inscribed within a geographical tropicalism. Here the predominant explanations refer to the influence of the climate on cultures and to a kind of orientalism, still not well studied, that extrapolates and compares populations in analogous situations (including that of Arabs and Africans). Such a tradition is already inscribed in the work of the anonymous *Isagoge* as well as in the prolific writings of Las Casas summarized by Stephens and Charnay when comparing Mayan monuments with those of Egypt and Mesopotamia.

The first great attempt at geographic and ethnic transculturation was the conversion of *milpas* into haciendas that produced the reconfiguration of Maya-Quiché identity as "Indians"–what

Cornejo Polar calls the construction of the macro-ethnic image that "descubre el verdadero carácter de la conquista" (50) ("discovers the true character of the Conquest") and identifies Spanish hegemony. The second attempt registered the move from the hacienda to plantations, units marked by the intense cultivation of products, while the third was the local recuperation of ownership or co-participation in the processes of production and the constitution of nations and nationalities to defend local interests. Severo Martínez Peláez calls this *patria criolla* or fatherland. In other words, *criollo* production, in collaboration with other agencies, aimed at development. Societies were areas destined for research in terms of capital development, while the majority of local intellectuals acted as collaborators in the great enterprise of modernity. The society of Amigos del País (Friends of the Country) can be studied in this way for it included a group of rich Liberal *criollos* who collaborated with such institutions as the Royal Geographic Society in London (Juarros) or the Natural History Museum in Paris (Morelet). At the end of the twentieth century another kind of discourse denoted the reconfiguration of the cultural landscape in terms of a critique of colonialism and an affirmation of revolution. The dominant metaphor at this time was that of the mountain as something more than an immense green steppe, that is, as seen in guerrilla testimonies such as those of Omar Cabezas (b. 1950) and Mario Payeras (1940–1995), by indigenous people like Rigoberta Menchú (b. 1959), and sympathetic mestizos such as José de Jesús Martínez (b. 1929).

Among the most outstanding works by guerrillas in Central America is the testimony of Omar Cabezas in *La montaña es algo más que una inmensa estepa verde* [1984: *Fire from the Mountain: The Making of a Sandinista*, 1985]; and the extensive memorial by the same author in *Canción de amor para los hombres* [1988; Song of Love for Humanity], which concludes in the most humble cemetery of León, Nicaragua, where the author's father and three brothers are buried, all victims of the dictatorship: "Nunca nadie habló ni preguntó nada. A lo mejor sabían, o sospechaban, que la respuesta estaba en el viento que soplaba esa noche" (1988, 573) ("No one ever spoke or asked anything. Perhaps they knew or suspected that the response would be in the wind that blew that night"). The testimony of Mario Payeras differs in the sense that *Los días de la selva* [1980; Days of the Rainforest] has a didactic aspect regarding military and political strategy, apart from being an autobiographical story of guerrilla warfare in the jungles and mountains of Quiché in northern Guatemala (1972–76):

> Entre ellos llegó Xan Lam, uno de los primeros cuatro líderes ixiles conocidos por la guerrilla, en los años de la selva . . . . Las experiencias con los ladinos, siempre signadas por menosprecio y engaño, pesaban enormemente en quienes conocían la organización y tardaban en asimilar el hecho de que ésta no podía ser únicamente el instrumento político de los indígenas, sino sobre todo de los guatemaltecos pobres. (110)

> Among them arrived Xan Lam, one of the first four Ixil leaders known by the guerillas in the years in the jungle . . . . The experiences with the *ladinos*, always marked by disdain and trickery, weighed strongly among those knowing the organization and they took time to assimilate the fact that this might not only be the political instrument of the indigenous but above all poor Guatemalans.

The Panamanian José de Jesús Martínez has a considerable number of works to his name. He has published volumes of poetry such as *Hacer la paz* [1964; Make Peace] and dramatic works including *Caifas* [1961; *Caiphas*] *Enemigos* [1962; Enemies], *El mendigo y el avaro* [1964; The Beggar and the

Greedy], *La venganza* [1965; Vengeance], and *La retreta* [1964; The Retreat], as well as the biography of the military general and political leader of Panama, Omar Torríjos in *Mi general Torríjos* [My General Torríjos] that won the Casa de las Américas prize in 1987. A few lines from Torríjos' biography recall some of the zealousness of this period in Central America:

> Había que matarlo. El enemigo considera la calidad moral como una ofensa personal, como un insulto a su ruindad. Y encima de bueno era poderoso, porque contaba con esa fuente de fuerza y convicción que da el pueblo. Y encima de eso, además, tenía razón. Razón, historia, paciencia, talento. Había que matarlo, definitivamente. Y lo mataron. (317)

> He had to be killed. The enemy considered moral quality as a personal offense, as an insult to their own baseness. And beyond being good he was powerful since he relied on this source of strength and conviction that came from the people. And more than this, he was in the right. Reason, history, patience, and talent. He had to be killed, quite definitely. And they killed him.

During the Colonial period, to be successful meant to take possession of the land and install oneself, reduce the native population, construct cities and reorganize jurisdictions, while in the early post-Independent period, it meant drawing with precision physical and economic maps that would support commercial investments and organizing the collection of specimens of flora and fauna for naturalist compendiums as well as inventories of social and cultural phenomena in order to swell the historiographic corpus that produced the required information for the investor. Already, by the eighteenth century, Antonio Fuentes y Guzmán had established the bases of a native tradition in which the description of the land signified its possession; this was one of the means by which land was inscribed within the register of properties and thus certified in its physical and symbolic ownership. In the same way the production of narratives for development incorporated the exploratory moment of war literature, creating a cultural legacy that took possession of indigenous history as its own tradition, as in the case of Cortés and Alvarado in the works of Squier and Morelet. Ethnic narrative remade that of the chroniclers, principally Las Casas and Ximenéz, in order to devalue what is indigenous. Positivist narrative only gave credit to Stephens and to Frederick Catherwood (by including his landscapes and drawings).

For geographers, naturalists, and travelers, Central America is a complex of parts, of balkanized republics, a corridor between the eastern and western continental coasts of the United States, a territory marked by the power of its metonymic representation, one that established the relation between time and space and kept to the rhythm of modernity to prove that time is money when it comes to reducing distances. Central America is an accountable, numerical space. It consists of distances, curves, heights, speeds, longitudes, population counts, and tallies of mixtures, all that Certeau calls "its very own" as "triumph of place (geography) over time (history)" (36), and corresponds to what he calls operations that are both "discursive (in and via language) and the Other without discourse" (64); also, there is no clear referent in the sentence for "the other." Central America is thus a great reserve of what is still not modernity but whose data can already be incorporated into the storehouse of Positivism through the use of descriptions that will later become a theory of exploitation.

Translation by Jessica Johnson

Works Cited

Anonymous. 1934. *Isagoge Histórica Apologética de las Indias Occidentales.* Edited by J. Fernando Juárez Muñoz. Guatemala City: Biblioteca Goathemala de la Sociedad de Geografía e Historia, Tipografía Nacional.

Berghaus, Heinrich Karl Wilhelm. 1852. *Allgemeiner anthropographischer Atlas. Eine Samnlung von vier Karten, welche die Grundlinien der, auf das menschen-leben bezuglichen Erscheinungen nach geographischer Verbreitung und Vertheilung abbilden und versinnlichen.* Gotha: Justus Perthes.

Bovallius, Carl. 1886. *Nicaraguan Antiquities.* Stockholm: Kongl. Boktryckeriet, P.A. Norstedt & Söner.

——. 1977. *Viaje por Centroamérica (1881-1883).* Trans. Camilo Vijil Tardón. Managua: Fondo de Promoción Cultural, Banco de América.

Brinton, Daniel G. 1882. *Library of Aboriginal American Literature.* Philadelphia: Brinton's Library.

Bunzel, Ruth. 1952. *Chichicastenango: A Guatemalan Village.* Seattle: University of Washington Press.

Cabezas, Omar. 1983. *La montaña es algo más que una inmensa estepa verde.* Havana: Casa de las Américas.

——. 1988. *Canción de amor para los hombres.* Managua: Editorial Nueva Nicaragua.

Casas, Fray Bartolomé de las. 1951. *Historia de las Indias.* Ed. Agustín Millares. Mexico City: Fondo de Cultura Económica.

——. 1967. *Apologética historia sumaria.* Edited by Edmundo O'Gorman. Mexico City: Universidad Nacional Autónoma de México.

Certeau, Michel de. 1988. *The Practice of Everyday Life.* Trans. Steven Rendall. Berkeley: University of California Press.

Charnay, Désiré. 1887. *The Ancient Cities of the New World: Being Travels and Explorations in Mexico and Central America: From 1857–1882.* Trans. J. Gonino and Helen S. Conant. London: Chapman and Hall.

Cornejo Polar, Antonio. 1994. *Escribir en el aire: ensayo sobre la heterogeneidad socio-cultural en las literaturas andinas.* Lima: Editorial Horizonte.

Coronel Urtecho, José. 1972. "Rápido Tránsito." *Prosa de José Coronel Urtecho.* Edited by Carlos Martínez Rivas. San José, Costa Rica: Editorial Universitaria Centroamericana. 141–295.

Cortés y Larraz, Pedro. 1958. *Descripción geográfico-moral de la diócesis de Goathemala.* Guatemala: Biblioteca Goathemala de la Sociedad de Geografía e Historia, Tipografía Nacional.

Fuentes y Guzmán, Antonio. 1883. *Historia de Guatemala o Recordación Florida. Escrita en el siglo XVII por el capitán D. Francisco Antonio de Fuentes y Guzmán, natural, vecino y regidor perpetuo de la ciudad de Guatemala.* Edited by D. Justo Zaragoza. Madrid: Luis Navarro Ed.

García Canclini, Néstor. 1992. *Culturas híbridas: estrategias para entrar y salir de la modernidad.* Buenos Aires: Editorial Sudamericana.

——. 1995. *Hybrid Cultures: Strategies for Entering and Leaving Modernity.* Trans. Christopher L. Chiappari and Silvia L. López. Minneapolis: University of Minnesota Press.

García Granados, Jorge, editor. 1934. *Libro viejo de la fundación de Guatemala y papeles relativos a D. Pedro de Alvarado.* Guatemala City: Biblioteca Goathemala de la Sociedad de Geografía e Historia, Tipografía Nacional.

Humboldt, Alexander von. 1818–1829. *Personal Narrative of Travels to the Equinoctial Regions of the New Continent during the Years 1799–1804.* Trans. Helen Maria Williams. 7 vols. London: Longman, Hurst, Ress, Orme and Brown.

Juarros, Domingo. 1825. *A Statistical and Commercial History of the Kingdom of Guatemala, in Spanish America.* Trans. John Baily. London: G. Cowie and Company.

Levy, Pablo. 1873. *Notas geográficas y económicas sobre la República de Nicaragua.* Paris: E. Denné Schmitz.

Martínez Peláez, Severo. 1981. *La Patria del Criollo: ensayo de interpretación de la realidad colonial guatemalteca.* Guatemala City: Editorial Universitaria Centroamericana.

———. 1991. *Motines de Indios.* Guatemala City: Ediciones en Marcha.

Maudslay, Alfred. 1889–1902. *Archaelogy Biologia Centrali-Americana, or, Contributions to the Knowledge of the Fauna and Flora of Mexico and Central America.* Vol. 58–63. London: R. H. Porter and Dulau.

Menchú, Rigoberta and Elizabeth Burgos Debray. 1983. *Me llamo Rigoberta Menchú.* Havana: Casa de las Américas.

Milla, José. 1976. *Historia de la América Central.* Guatemala City: Biblioteca Centroamericana de las Ciencias Sociales.

Morelet, Arthur. 1871. *Travels in Central America: Including Accounts of some Regions Unexplored since the Conquest.* New York: Leypoldt, Holt & Williams.

Ortiz, Fernando. 1940. *Contrapunteo cubano del tabaco y el azúcar.* Havana: J. Montero.

Payeras, Mario. 1982. *Los días de la selva: relatos sobre la implantación de las guerrillas populares en el norte del Quiché, 1972–1976.* Mexico City: Nuestro Tiempo.

Pim, Bedford. 1863. *The Gate of the Pacific.* London: L. Reeve & Company.

Popol Vuh: The Definitive Edition of the Mayan Book of the Dawn of Life and the Glories of Gods and Kings. 1985. Trans. Dennis Tedlock. New York: Simon & Schuster.

Rama, Ángel. 1982. *Transculturación narrativa en América Latina.* Mexico City: Siglo XXI.

Ramírez, Sergio. l983. *Balcanes y volcanes.* San José, Costa Rica: Editorial Universitaria Centroamericana.

Remesal, Fray Antonio de. 1932. *Historia general de las Indias occidentales, y particular de la gobernación de Chiapas y Guatemala.* Guatemala: Biblioteca Goathemala, Tipografía Nacional.

Roberts, Orlando W. 1827. *Narrative of Voyages and Excursions on the East Coast and in the Interior of Central America.* Edinburgh: Constable.

Santiago, Silviano. 1973. *Latin American Literature: The Space in Between.* Special Studies. No. 48. Trans. Stephen Moscov. Buffalo: Council on International Studies, State University of New York.

Seed, Patricia. 1995. *Ceremonies of Possession in Europe's Conquest of the New World: 1492–1640.* Cambridge: Cambridge University Press.

Squier, Ephraim George. 1858. *The States of Central America: Their Geography, Topography, Climate, Population, Resources, Productions, Commerce, Political Organizations, Aborigines, etc., etc., Comprising Chapters on Honduras, San Salvador, Nicaragua, Costa Rica, Guatemala, Belize, the Bay Islands, The Mosquito Shore, and the Honduras Inter-Oceanic Railway.* New York: Harper & Brothers.

Stephens, John Lloyd. 1971. *Incidentes de viaje en Centroamerica, Chiapas y Yucatán.* Trans. Benjamin Mazariego Santizo. San José, Costa Rica: Editorial Universitaria Centroamericana.

———. 1993. *Incidents of Travel in Central America, Chiapas, and Yucatan.* Edited by Karl Ackerman. Washington D.C.: Smithsonian Institution Press.

Tax, Sol. 1952. *Heritage of Conquest: The Ethnology of Middle America.* Glencoe, IL: The Free Press.

Thompson J. Eric S. 1970. *Maya History and Religion.* Norman, OK: University of Oklahoma Press.

Ximénez, Francisco. 1857. *Las historias del origen de los indios de esta provincia de Guatemala, traducidas de la lengua Quiché al castellano para más comodidad de los ministros del S. evangelio.* Viena: Gerold e Hijo.

Young, Thomas. 1847. *Narrative of a Residence on the Mosquito Shore, with an Account of Truxillo, and the Adjacent Islands of Bonacca and Roatan; and a Vocabulary of the Mosquitian Language.* London: Smith, Elder, and Company.

CHAPTER 30

ANATOMY OF THE LATIN AMERICAN "BOOM" NOVEL

Brett Levinson

The Latin American Boom, as I will examine it in this essay, is the name of a conglomerate of well-known Latin American writers who penned key novels in the 1950s and early 1960s, burst onto the world stage in the late 1960s and 1970s, and through their extremely visible works (translated into many languages), became synonymous with Latin American culture as a whole–often for Latin America itself. The three general characteristics of these novels are: (1) intense formalist experimentation; (2) the portrayal of state, local, or regional concerns and events as reflections of larger (though not necessarily more important) Latin American and global matters; and (3) the world-wide reception just mentioned, one that is not an after-effect of the works, but part and parcel of their emergence.

This general definition does not tackle an important, if not familiar question: Which texts and authors fall into this category of the Boom? A catalog of Boom writers would most likely include Gabriel García Márquez (b. 1927), Alejo Carpentier (1904–1980), Guillermo Cabrera Infante (b. 1929), José Lezama Lima (1910–1976), Mario Vargas Llosa (b. 1936), Carlos Fuentes (b. 1928), Juan Rulfo (1918–1986), José Donoso (1925–1996), Julio Cortázar (1914–1984), Ernesto Sábato (b. 1911), and Augusto Roa Bastos (b. 1917). As to who else might be placed on the list, I shall leave that to others. My purpose is to lay out the framework by means whereby one might arrive at a response.

Critical understanding of the Boom has taken four connected but distinct paths. Perhaps none has completely satisfied Latin American scholarship, yet all have contributed to the general understanding of the Boom phenomenon. The first, commonly known as "*vida y obra*" [life and works], maps both the authors and the texts. Charted are, on the one hand, those aspects–personal, intellectual, artistic–of the writer's life that shape his work, and on the other hand, the author's appropriation of, break with, and place within previous Latin American and Western novelistic tendencies. A second school examines the Boom as a vanguard movement, usually through its formal innovations. Here vanguardism (even if at times renamed postmodernism) and modernity are linked: The Boom is seen as an expression of Latin America's development, compensating for, supplementing, or completing an otherwise failed modernization process. A third critical endeavor, a response to the second, associates this vanguardist vision with elitism; it champions a critique of the Boom. I shall lay out the precise nature of this position in a moment. Finally, criticism has deployed the Boom as a means to derive theories for the Latin American cultural identity and for Latin American thought. Such elaborations range from endeavors that seek to locate in the Boom a deconstructive project to ones that, focusing on the Boom as the expression of cultural, demographic, ethnic, and class intersections, seek to develop theses on Latin America as "transculturated" or hybrid *topos*.

As the Boom grew more and more visible both in Latin America and throughout the West in the 1960s and 1970s, the vanguard perspective came to dominate. Hyper-innovative and hyper-modern, seemingly defying the laws of language, breaking with previous European and North American narrative molds, the Boom novel, often associated with the Cuban Revolution, signaled the arrival of those from below, the liberation of a Latin American self or self-expression. Through its technique or technological brilliance, the Boom even came to embody Latin America's potential for industrial progress, however symbolically. Latin Americans, the Boom seemed to announce to the world, should no longer be viewed as followers or latecomers who borrow from the West–who use already antiquated Western products and models (narrative techniques)–but as innovators.

This reading of the Boom was not always explicit in literary and cultural criticism. Yet even the formalist discourses that, more interested in aesthetic than in social matters, only attempted to describe the narratological, semantic, or lexical novelties of the Boom texts did so–still following the developmental model–by situating the new Latin American literature one step beyond, or at least on par with, the aesthetic advancements of Western high modernism (and in more recent years, those of postmodernism). Indeed, it is telling that this progression was frequently articulated through notions of parody or pastiche: Latin America, now matured, had ceased to imitate, and was mocking the West, remolding it, "one upping" it.

This reading slowly found itself under assault, yielding the third school mentioned above (the critique of the Boom as elitist), which by 1990 assumed a powerful if not dominant status. The Boom, the critics contended, is artistically innovative but politically conservative. For as the aesthetic moves ahead, actual Latin American existence remains mired in atrocities: The annihilation of indigenous peoples, the abuse of labor, the torture of those on the left, the widening of the gap between the rich and the poor, the suppression of women, the advent of the neoliberal state, the terror of dictatorship. These calamities occur not *despite* the progress represented by the Boom but precisely *because of* that discourse of progress–the discourse in which the well-being of the advantaged peoples swells in the name of progress, yet does so at the expense of the disadvantaged. The Boom narrative, difficult in form, seemingly removed from everyday life and contemporary political concerns in content, almost exclusively male in profile, and meta-literary (wrapped within itself) by nature, was dubbed elitist, an example of hegemonic culture. Far from symbolizing the Latin American revolution from below, the Boom–whose authors, while often leaning toward the left, consistently indexed the problems of the Latin American and European leftist movements–was reproached for reproducing the divisions upon which the above-mentioned political outrages

345

were founded: Between the Western metropolis and the margins, aestheticism and material reality, the State and the underprivileged classes, the Great Book and popular forms of representation. The Boom, in short, was cast as a project in which metropolitan, European-influenced production or fiction, and by extension, the metropolitan, European-influenced *person*, embodies the whole of Latin America's population and actuality, hence the progress of the entire region, erasing in the process—or even worse, aestheticizing, rendering tolerable and even amusing—concrete political horrors.

These two seemingly opposing visions of the Boom are in fact grounded in similar principles. Both conflate aesthetic shifts with sociological movements, alterations in artistic form with the social progression from the nineteenth through the twentieth century. The nineteenth-century novel, in fact, is typically characterized by a linear story, relatively transparent presentation, a single narrator, social realism or critique, and the marked distinction between the real and the imaginary or fantastic. The Boom narrative advances by creating texts that are rarely linear, that deploy multiple narrators, that are irreducible to social realism (and therefore go beyond local or temporary concerns), and that blend the fantastic and the real (through magical realism or the marvelous real). In addition, Boom works often include the break-up (production of neologisms) or intensification (the neo-Baroque) of the signifier; far from clear, their presentation labors to disrupt common sense, to estrange. The disparate Latin Americanist critical models, agreeing that these modifications are synonymous with societal transformations, disagree only as to whether such changes are radical or conservative emblems of a break with antiquated nineteenth-century European models or signs of a "sell-out" to a Western aestheticism that abandons the political. In dispute are not the products at hand, but their respective values.

All of these various critical narratives are rooted in Latin Americanism's general tendency to confuse literature or the literary with the Great Book. The Great Book, particularly the novel—always reminiscent of the Great Book, the Bible—is the modern cultural artifact that has been posited as the representation of all culture and all cultural production. The Book is the artifact-supposed-to-be-All. Monumental, the Great Book transcends the works that belong to a particular time and place, the passing trends, the productions that pass through history but do not endure, so as to reflect and preserve eternally the entirety, the very being, of culture and history. Therefore, criticism that suggests that Boom or post-Boom authors (Vargas Llosa, Cabrera Infante, Rulfo, Manuel Puig (1932–1990) often subvert the Great Book by incorporating the low into the high, popular forms of speech or mass culture into the classic novel, the transient into the monumental, fail to understand that such incorporations are precisely why particular texts (such as *Don Quixote*) stand as Great Books, as classics.

As a classic, the Latin American Boom novel is not Latin America's Being (truth, freedom); it is the always enduring testimony to such a Being, the promise of Being. This is why the Boom writers emerged as national and international heroes in the 1970s. Like all heroes, these authors supposedly overcame their (Latin American or Third World) circumstances with their imagination and creativeness, performing acts that went beyond their limits, beyond the times—indeed, beyond time itself. The authors did not free Latin America; they revealed that Latin America could be free, and testified to that freedom.

Materializing here is still another matter: That of identity. The Boom text, as just noted, is the embodiment not of Latin American cultural production, but of enduring production: Being. This Being, as Being, cannot emerge as a mere spin-off of Western discourse, for it would then stand as an unnecessary and dispensable copy—no more a Being, no more actual, no more true, no more necessary than a mirror image. But neither can this literary production be viewed as so particular, so tied to a certain time and place, so provincial or disconnected from universal culture that one could allege that it belongs to its time and place, that it has its interest but possesses no essential or permanent value. This explains, at least in part, the symbolic importance, however problematic, of the aesthetic and formal innovations for which the Boom is recognized. The Boom work puts forth a blueprint for an artistic practice that is not a copy of Western forms (even as it dialogues with those forms), but one that the West (and other Third World sites) copies—a copying act that acknowledges a Latin American originality, that is, a Latin American essence. And in a postcolonial site such as Latin America, this originality, this freedom of expression, enjoys special significance. It points not to any prior time or place, but to one that pre-existed or that resists colonization. Aesthetic originality, in Latin American cultural thought, bears witness both to a once-extant de-colonized Latin American self-determination and to the promise of its return.

The Boom, however, is a global phenomenon. It does not simply reflect Latin America's Being/Necessity/Identity but situates that Being alongside and in relation to the Being of the West. With the advent of the Boom, world history emerges as a bookstore holding the many great works, each of which attests to an episode within the history of Western Being. With the arrival of the new books from abroad and below—in short the Boom—the works on the shelves part to allow the Latin American reflection of that Being to squeeze in.

In short, the promise of the Boom is a Latin America that takes its place in Great Western culture while at the same time asserting its true Being, its autonomy and self-determination—its break from the West. From any site on the globe, the Boom beams back to Latin America its own (Latin America's) liberation. Latin America no longer contemplates itself in a Western mirror but sends its own mirror (the Book), its representative, to the West, where it sees itself as itself. The Latin American Being that the Boom brings into view, a being free from the false limitations imposed by the colonizer, is also the Being that leaves Latin America behind, that goes global. Latin America emerges as particular, unique, local, and autonomous only and precisely because it situates itself in the universal. It is this understanding of the Boom that led to the original celebration of the novels but that also fueled the counter-discourse: The very idea that the Boom could pass off fictional works as the entire Being or Truth of Latin America, the notion that the metropolitan elite's freedom of expression within a global context that has so denigrated the Third World could stand for the liberty of a local called Latin America—these were the very ruses that induced the wrath of certain cultural critics.

It must be re-emphasized, however, that the above visions of the Boom are contingent on the reduction of Boom literature to the Great Book and its counterpart: The Third World Author as postcolonial hero. But in fact, and as we will now see, the Boom (at times despite itself) stages not the Book but its disappearance—not the discourse of Latin America's Being but that of the death of such a Being.

In order to explore this thesis, let us reconsider the text that best stands for the aestheticism and hyper-modernization that cultural critics have challenged and literary critics have espoused: Julio Cortázar's *Rayuela* [1963; *Hopscotch*]. The very example of aesthetic innovation, seemingly the most overt manifestation in Latin America of the attempt to present radical narratological experimentation as radical political praxis, as well as an expression of freedom, *Rayuela* is today dated. It has not ceased to be a classic, but it stands as a dying classic: As a unique fashioning of the discourse of the novel that, like all fashionings and fashion, had its day but was also the guarantee of its own passing. But like all fashion as well, *Rayuela* was and is the promise of its own return. Indeed, fashion, as even common sense reveals, is both a sign of the times (times that have their day and will expire) and the sign of the overcoming of time, because a mode is both what passes and what endlessly comes back: Death and resurrection. In fact, *Rayuela*, revolving around its protagonist's transience and return (home), is largely about the transience (or passing) and return of itself. A fashionable novel whose main subject is its own novel fashion, *Rayuela*'s concern is actually fashion as such: The death and non-death, the non-death of death, that (re)marks all fashion.

In other words, *Rayuela* is both a classic—a monument—and a copy of the classic, dispensable and aleatory like every copy or fashionable entity. The fact that *Rayuela* is a novel within a novel (it pivots or jumps around the story of a missing text written by a figure named Morelli) is not therefore unexpected, for Cortázar's work is both the double of the novel and a double novel (at least double, as Cortázar points out in the "manual of instructions" that precedes the first chapter). It is novel, new, trendy, and therefore not entirely a Latin American classic (as is, say, Gabriel García Márquez's *Cien años de soledad* [1967; *One Hundred Years of Solitude*, 1970], which seems never to grow old). Yet at the same time, it is a classic precisely because it is (a) novel, new and trendy. *Rayuela* is not dated after the fact, after its "day," because it dates itself—it is that dating in action. It is a dated classic but also the dating of the classic, the dating of the monument. *Rayuela* in fact shows that every monument is dated, indeed must be dated in order to become a monument, in order—like a tombstone—to memorialize. The condition of eternal endurance, ironically, is the stamp of finitude, a temporal register: The sign of death.

In brief, *Rayuela*, literally safeguarding (as its foundation) a dead novel inside its tomb/tome, is a classic novel that both memorializes and performs the passing of the novel, a passing that the Classic supposedly transcends. Or better still: *Rayuela* is a timepiece representing the death and resurrection of a Latin American project of death and resurrection. It does not only complete or compete with European modernism and, through these struggles, place Latin America into world history by overcoming both a certain history—a colonial/postcolonial one—and historicity itself (time, death) in the name of Latin America's sovereignty, essence, or Being. It also spells the demise of this venture.

The Boom, to put this analysis of *Rayuela* into more general terms, represents both the further opening and the closure of the Latin American project of Being and identity. This termination, like all terminal points or borders, stands also as the discovery of a new understanding of Latin America—Latin America not as a collection of independent, sovereign States but as part of a globalized network. Of course, the Latin American nation-state (like all nation-states) has always been caught within global or transnational *topoi*. But up until the period marked by the Boom, Latin America's Being (its autonomy, sovereignty, and truth) was imagined in terms of a break from the global or universal. This imaginary dictated both cultural production and political activism and thus formed a key component of material reality (governments, institutions of civil society, youth movements, knowledge production, and so forth).

Mestizaje, transculturation, hybridity, indigenism: All of these represent names geared to orienting efforts to forge Latin American nations that, in their plurality, would be irreducible to, and would in effect, alter the Latin American state governments. Liberty received from the West was succeeded by a yearning for emancipation from the homogeneous state, the West's representative.

The Boom pushes this logic to its limit: It continues but disrupts it. The locus advocated by the Boom, in fact, is not quite that of the nation-State or even the nation-continent; it is that of the nation-(inter)continental. This nation-(inter)continental project does not set up the Boom as the Latin American collective *qua* the nation, threatening (from below) Western aesthetics or global capital, although this reading of the Boom is not uncommon and is worthy of further exploration. The Boom, that is, does not represent a simple remodeling of transculturation enterprise but points to a novel undertaking for Latin American cultural politics: That of *transliteration*. In other words, the ultimate difference between the Boom and the production of transculturation is one that may not seem like a difference at all: In the Boom, literature rather than culture emerges as Latin America's key force of intervention.

By literature I am not alluding to books; I am referring to *poisis*, to a making. Latin Americ's existence, the Boom shows, no longer hinges on the building of cultural productions that, like the Book, reflect the given: The popular classes and productions, the pre-European worlds, the imported European forms, and Latin America's natural hybridity. For the Boom, there is no autonomous or true Latin America that culture can reflect, because Latin America's site of freedom must first be *made*, and that making, that *poisis* is the task of this process that I am calling "transliteration."

Transliteration marks the relationality of the West. The West did not pre-exist and then encounter the site that is now called Latin America. It came into being through that relation and similar relations with Africa and the "East," and it could not exist without it. The West's sovereignty, because bound to Latin America, is relative not absolute; its freedom swings upon, is enchained and indebted to, the Other. This disclosure is crucial because the condition of possibility of any Latin American production or political operation that is not a mere epiphenomenal reflection of the West depends on the fact that the West cannot stand as the transcendental essence or ground of Being itself. Only if the West's foundation can be shown to be relative or relational, hence mortal and contingent, does the condition for a Latin American intervention even exist.

Transliteration, secondly, turns to the problem of difference in a new fashion. Precisely because the *poisis* that results from the transliteration cannot be squeezed into existing signs (Western or Latin American), to any *habitus* or common sense, it puts difference in relief. The phrasing between domains, irreducible to those fields, highlights the bind between them: Their contact, contamination, and difference; and that phrasing—I am thinking of terms such as *lo real maravilloso* ("the marvelous real"), which tries to articulate the "interrelationship" of the fantastic, realism, and the avant-garde superrational–is the work of transliteration.

Can we therefore say that a phrase such as *real maravilloso*, breaking from all previous idioms, marking the limit of those discourses (realism, fantastic, avant-garde), serves as a proper name for a part of Latin America, testimony to an autonomy, proof that Latin America is free? But the task of transliteration is not to free Latin America. It is to disclose, to offer a sign of the possibility of freedom–to bring the difference out, an outing that is conceivable only insofar as the Same (the West and all of its discourses or signifiers) is marked as the not-All. *Poisis* does not liberate Latin America; it makes public this potential for freedom. The Boom's *poisis*, that is, is one of the conditions of a Latin American *praxis*–without the exposure of the possibility of liberty, no activism in that direction will surface–and is therefore part and parcel of that *praxis*.

The third function of transliteration, however, is to cancel this same promise of emancipation. In fact, there is no pure *poisis*, no language, form, or neologism that is not drawn from the established senses of the West or of Latin America. Ultimately, one must mark the relation of names or beings that have no name with a name from the tradition. Neither *real* nor *maravilloso* are new words or concepts; nor is the idea of combining the marvelous and the real new (on the contrary, the combination is as old as the West itself). Every new device deployed by the Boom is a repetition–therefore a standardization, formalization, and normalization–of the Western *habitus* into which it intervenes.

All of this is a way of saying that in the Boom, Latin America discovers that its excess or heterogeneity is not another identity but its encounter-with-the-other. The excess is exposure-to-death *qua* the brush-with-the-other, which the Boom tries to stylize into a cultural heterogeneity. The Boom, overblown and excessive according to many of its critics, does not go too far because of an aestheticist drive but because too far is precisely where it wants to go.

Perhaps the best illustration of the difference between transculturation and transliteration is the famous insomnia scene in *Cien años de soledad*. Rebeca, it is to be recalled, arrives in Macondo with a letter indicating that she is a relative of the Buendía family. In the wake of the death of Rebeca's parents (whose unburied bones she carries), the epistle is a request that the Buendías take the young girl into their custody. Upon her arrival, Rebeca is without name. Aureliano reads to her all the names of the saints in the hope of learning her true appellation, ultimately settling on Rebeca when the little girl recognizes herself in none of them. Later it is learned that Rebeca, seemingly unable to speak or hear, actually speaks both Spanish and an indigenous language, easily communicating with the servant Visitación.

We might therefore assume, given that her name is not among those of the saints, that Rebeca was not born a Christian but is indigenous. Yet we certainly cannot know this for sure, especially because descriptions of anyone's skin color or references to race are almost entirely absent from García Marquez's novel.

In any case, Rebeca's arrival brings along with it the insomnia plague–a plague that the servant Visitación recognizes, for the same illness had previously led to the downfall of her indigenous family, the former nobility of a now-vanished cosmos. Gradually, the inhabitants of Macondo lose a good part of their memories. The question is: Why does García Márquez include Rebeca in this narrative?

In the discourse of transculturation, Rebeca's ethnic background would be clarified. Either a critique of the forgetting and loss of the indigenous worlds (hence of Latin America's heterogeneity) or the re-insertion of the Other (Rebeca) into the Christian universe of Macondo (hence the discussion of a hybrid culture) would move the narrative or part of it. Emphasized would be the idea that the truth of Latin America is the pluralism that is either denied by the *criollo* State/the West (eventually represented by Macondo itself) or retrieved by the mixed nation/people.

But García Márquez chooses to emphasize something else entirely. Latin America is struck by a forgetting not of specific identities but of a "thing" that *cannot be identified or traced*, in this case, Rebeca's origins. Even if we were to name Rebeca as indigenous, this term would only mark the erasure of her previous existence because, obviously, the society from which Rebeca–and/or Visitación–comes did not know itself as indigenous. Indeed, to dub Rebeca indigenous is akin to calling her Rebeca: The designation inserts Rebeca into Macondo, but it also buries the prior name. The name Rebeca (like indigenous) thus serves as a placeholder not of a loss–Rebeca, and what she represents, is not lost or missing: the little girl is alive in Macondo–but of a presence that cannot be represented or erased.

Such a reading is proven by two points. One is that Ursula, matriarch of the Buendía family, will eventually recollect the image of Rebeca's parents in a dream but will not recognize these people. The relationship or kinship between Macondo and the other world survives in the memory bank. But the meeting or intersection of the two families is unfamiliar, unrecognizable, unrepresentable. Macondo, through Ursula, retains the idea that a relation to another cosmos exists, but it has no language to realize that relation, no means to bring the memory into full presence. Not unlike Rebeca herself–this almost immortal Buendía sister who is not a Buendía sister at all–the relation stays eternally but cannot be forgotten, remembered, or accounted for.

Secondly, one should not overlook the fact that the insomnia plague never leads, for the populace of Macondo, to full amnesia. Such an event could happen, as the inhabitants of Macondo themselves remark, only if language itself were forgotten. The irony of this proposition should not be missed. For the most part, the deletion of indigenous languages has already taken place in Latin America, meaning that, the obliteration of these cultures' modes of representation (hence of the possibility of *naming* the intersection or relation of indigenous and Christian forms except with Christian names), is indeed nearly absolute. Again, the relations persist, but they have no name.

For García Márquez, Latin America's heterogeneity is not indexed by the natural combination or relation of cultures, identities, or groups, because the kinship itself will always be conceptualized by the Judeo-Christian worlds/tongues, which hence will appropriate and/or entomb alive such affinities. (It is not for nothing that, eventually, Rebeca will inter herself alive) Indeed, since there is no proper image by means of which this presence without re-presence could be turned into a memory, into something of the past, the possibility of initiating a process of mourning or forgetting is forfeited. This is why illness, or melancholia, sets over Macondo when Rebeca arrives. It is also why Rebeca cannot, at first, bury her ancestors. The bones she carries recall the intersection of worlds that serves as a skeleton or frame for Latin American cultural production but is not itself part of that production. The incapacity to represent, hence turn into a memory, that foundational intersection literally plagues Macondo.

García Márquez's Latin America comprises a single identity (this is why ethnic and linguistic differences are not emphasized in *Cien años de soledad*) that cannot account for itself or for its community, because it cannot properly designate the relations by means of which that identity came into being. The outside forces, which eventually inundate Macondo, are not the cause of the fall of this world but the symptom that is foundational to that world. The Boom strives to index, to keep in relief, an originary encounter (the insomnia plague is one such mark). Its concern is the One-plus, the more than identity, the kinship or heterogeneity of the West to which Latin America must bear witness, keep extant. Too Western to be Third World and too Third World to be Western, the *plus* falls to Latin America.

As just suggested, it is easy to view Macondo as an ideal, virgin utopian city that is gradually overrun by Western capitalism and colonial injustices. But the insomnia scene indicates the error of such a reading. The Macondo family is constructed on top of the violation of cultural relations it *has not even forgotten*. The Macondo family damages its own kind and kin in order to materialize (this damage is left out of the Book, out of the archive Melquíades has compiled: It is the archive's condition and limit) and is never done addressing that damage. Capitalism does not pervert Macondo but stands as a perversion that allows for the further erasure of a more anterior perversion, one trapped at the border, at the slash, of the Western/Latin American archive.

The relationality of Being, which the Boom's transliteration works to put in place, includes not only the affinities of cultures but other affinities as well. Magical realism and *lo real maravilloso*, both key aesthetic modes within the Boom, illustrate this point. I am referring to texts such as *Cien años de soledad*, Alejo Carpentier's *El reino de este mundo* [1949; *The Kingdom of this World*, 1967], Juan Rulfo's *Pedro Páramo* [1955; English translation, 1994], Rosario Castellanos's (1925–1974) *Balún-Canán* [1957; *The Nine Guardians*, 1960], and Mario Vargas Llosa's *El hablador* [1987; *The Storyteller*, 1989]. Magical realism (and *lo real maravilloso*) materializes when Latin American history reveals itself as incapable of accounting for its own origin, an incapacity that traditionally–though not here–represents a demand for myth: Mythos as a means to explain the beginnings that escape history's narrative. We know that the Latin American narrative movement prior to magical realism, the so-called *novela de la tierra* ("novel of the earth")–works such as Mariano Azuela's (1873–1952) *Los de abajo* [1915; *The Underdogs*; 1963] and Rómulo Gallegos's (1884–1969) *Doña Bárbara* [1929; English translation, 1942], operate largely by means of demythologization. It strips away the utopian ideals that sit at the base of nineteenth-century Latin American politics, culture, and aesthetics–the myths of revolution, of innocent nature, of progress, of civilization, of the state, and even of the popular classes–leaving the characters face to face with the harshest realities: brutal history or cruel nature.

This demythologization project is continued in the magical realist texts. Yet magical realism undertakes another task as well: De-historicization. By de-historicization I am not alluding to the avoidance of history but rather to the removal of history as ground. Once the myths are demythologized, we are not left with the severity of Latin American history as

truth but with a third topos: The stubborn trace of the past, irreducible to a representation or to the narrative that history is. These are not historical entities but their wandering ghosts, unable to take root, to take their place, to rest within history.

Magical realism reveals, in other words, that Latin America's past is at once too tenaciously present, too strong, to yield to myth, to permit myth to serve as its ground or origin, and also too ineffectual, too destroyed, to do without myth. It is, therefore, a poetics that strives to phrase the limit of the two modes, the bond, boundary, or third term between myth and history (the institutions of myth and history), an articulation that is itself not reducible to either. Thus, the prototypical magical realist figure may well be the axolotl of Cortázar's short story "Axolotl," historical animal and Aztec mythical creature, hence the incarnation of the figure that marks the intersection of these sites.

The Boom, one might therefore say, is the last Book of the State and the first production of the market. The movement represents the last book of the nation-state because it stands for the monumentality, irreducible to fashion, publicity, global circulation, and all that passes–as the book that rises above time and space, thereby standing as the representative of the sovereign, independent Latin American nation. But it is also the first production of the market because it reveals that freedom and sovereignty are no longer conceivable without the publication (the appearance on the bestseller list) which produces the recognition that, because neither the book nor state can dictate it, marks the finitude of both the state and of the Book.

If it did not emerge as the last Book of the Nation-State, as the Book that bears witness to a Latin American sovereignty from below, the Boom never would have taken place–not, in any case, as the Boom. Conversely, without a strong global reception, this narrative of the state is powerless. The Boom, in other words, does not expose the Latin American Being to the outside, where it is ravaged by time, fashion, Western reception, academic receptions, and so on. Rather, it discloses the fact that, just as (by a logical necessity) there can be no local that is not recognized by the universal, no literariness without publication or publicity, no nation-state without global circulation, so there can be no essence or Being that does not open itself to contamination, temporality, circulation, and death. The Boom does not only expose Latin America. It also ex-poses the West as not a position but an ex-position, as a collection of beings outside themselves, with Others.

Let us, on this note, return one last time to *Rayuela*. It should be becoming clear that this novel is not merely about its formal trends or trendiness. It is not an effort to outdo the aesthetics of modernism. It is, on the contrary, about the exhaustion of trendiness, represented for Cortázar by the avant-garde and the French new novel. The aesthetic question posed by *Rayuela*, particularly in the sections that meditate on the fragments of the Morelli text, might be worded as follows: What of literature after technical innovation, after the disruptions of linearity and signification themselves emerge as trendy–not as the resistance to the market but as the essence of the modern classic's marketability?

We do well to recall the basic principle that lies at the base of modern art, beginning at least with the avant-garde: After all the stories are told, only formal innovations will separate *poisis* from the common sense of the establishment (*qua* the state). *Rayuela* reveals that even this formal innovation, in the wake of the project of modernism, has been subsumed into such an establishment. Formal experimentation is just one more tale or narrative that has run its course.

In his own way, José Lezama Lima conducts this same inquiry, first in Chapter 12 of *Paradiso* (1966), which parodies the new-fangled new novel, and then in *Oppiano Licario* (1977), where the sequel to the novel, the post-novel, Licario's *Súmula, nunca infusa, de excepciones morfológicas* [Compendium, Never Infused, of Morphological Exceptions], appears only in the form of a blank box. Cortázar and Lezama, in other words, do not answer the question they pose—Does literariness survive within the Great Book after its last vestige, technicity, falls to publicity?—but can only mark (via erased texts that, while offered up as the post-novel, are presented only as traces), the conclusion of the modern novel's effort to distinguish the literariness of the great work from its publication, circulation, or marketability: Work from Book, self from fashion, Being from death.

The whole world-debate around the canon, it should be noted, pivots on these ideas. Once the components of the classic novel—the imagination, social critique, technical innovation producing estrangement, and implosion/explosion at the level of the signifier which presumably transcend the limits of the social and the common—themselves emerge as culturally and historically determined, as part and parcel of the contingencies of fashion and ideology, then the classic opens itself to its collapse, inviting the anti-canonical attacks that feed off that demise. As soon as the literariness of the work can be exploited for publicity, publication, and propaganda (ideology)—and this has certainly occurred within the Latin American Boom, as the novels' formal and thematic devices, such as magical realism, are publicized, ritualized, and banalized—then the classic surfaces not as a ground for aesthetic value, but as one value among others, one text among others, one view amongst others, and so forth.

Let us, with these last ideas in mind, reconsider one of the foundational moments of the Boom: The thirty-two wars fought by Colonel Aureliano Buendía in *Cien años de soledad*. Originally battling on behalf of the liberal revolutionary cause during a nineteenth-century Latin American civil war, Buendía soon forgets why he is fighting at all. For Buendía, liberalism, conservatism, and radicalism emerge as equally despotic, in no small part because of his own actions. García Márquez, with this narrative, clearly means to suggest that Latin-American politics is an endless series of battles between factions that ultimately reproduce each other. Individuals fight in the name of conservatism or liberalism, of the left or right, of this or that. But sooner or later, all names reveal themselves as capable of serving as a ground for the same terrors. This thesis is reiterated in many other Boom texts, most notably in ones that deal with revolution: Carlos Fuentes's *La muerte de Artemio Cruz* [1962; *The Death of Artemio Cruz,* 1989], Alejo Carpentier's *El siglo de las luces* [1962; *Explosion in a Cathedral,* 1991], Juan Rulfo's *Pedro Páramo* (1955), Agusto Roa Bastos's *Yo, el supremo* [1974; *I, the Supreme;* 1986] and almost all of the narratives of Mario Vargas Llosa. Narratologically and thematically, these works, like *Cien años*, comprised a series of circles (revolutions) that revert to their origin, implying in part that Latin American political revolutions have always been about the return to the regimes against which the outbreaks were initiated. Latin-American history is the endless repetition of itself.

García Márquez, Carpentier, Rulfo, Vargas Llosa, and Fuentes, however, are not merely discussing the failure of

Latin-American revolutions. They are outlining the demise of revolution itself. If they reveal the hypocrisy of conservatism, liberalism, and radicalism, it is to mark the end of all these political ideologies—not because such ideologies can no longer be advocated, but because the distinctions between the belief systems are no longer a given, and the terms have therefore ceased to signify, to mean, to distinguish. Lost is an in-the-name-of to take up politics, which is precisely the problem Aureliano Buendía eventually confronts: Not that political ideologies have melted together, but that no banner exists under which to fight. Freedom, democracy, the family, identity, the nation, the good, the true, revolution, the left, the right, Marxism, anti-imperialism, development, Westernization, autonomy, resistance—all of these words, and many more, have yielded their exalted positions, have depleted themselves. What Colonel Buendía exhausts in his thirty-two wars is not all the ideologies or all the causes, but all the names. It is no longer a matter of hypocrisy, in which high names are uttered but actions do not match these words. It is not that politicians or generals say one thing but their actions are empty. The case is just the opposite: the names are empty, and although the actions try to inform those names with a meaning (to fill them up), they cannot do so.

The Boom novel that pursues this matter with the greatest ferocity is perhaps Ernesto Sábato's *Sobre héroes y tumbas* [1961; *On Heroes and Tombs,* 1981]. Sábato is the Latin American writer who most espoused the principles of existentialism. As an existentialist, he held that all transcendental grounds—not just God, but everything held as sacred—have been stripped from the modern scene. Modern man is reduced to his historical, temporal existence. However, according to Sábato, mankind finds this thesis intolerable. Released from the Master (God), mankind trembles before the very freedom it always thought it desired. Modernity, according to Sábato, is therefore an endless effort to reinstall a new sanctified sphere, name, or Master, one that will always eventually be abjected, because it will necessarily fail to resurrect the transcendental ground it was supposed to deliver. (Sábato's main characters thereby tend to posit the mother, who could be embodied by any woman, as this figure of transcendence. This is why Sábato's male characters are almost invariably misogynists: women always disappoint, betray, and therefore are scapegoated as the cause of the modern existence because they fail to offer the transcendence they are imagined to possess.)

Sobre héroes y tumbas translates these theses into a meditation on Peronism, on an Argentinean populism that Sábato viewed as the model of all contemporary institutionalism. In populism, according to Sábato, a signifier ("Perón") is hoisted to the heights of the sacred and then a mass following ensues. For Sábato nothing is more religious than the secular State or secular organizations. The Argentine obsession with Perón, on the part of the left and on the part of the right, both points up the desire for a name that will fill in the lost space and yields the terror that ensues when a fallen name, an empty and meaningless signifier such as "Perón," is forced into this lofty position.

Crucial to this thesis is a point made in the most famous section of *Sobre héroes y tumbas*, that entitled "El informe de los ciegos" ("Report on the Blind"). Not only does modernity, as well as Latin-American politics, lack a direction/name that would orient a proper project; it does not even possess a name for the despot or problem that blocks that liberation.

Unaware of the origin of the terror he faces, modern man does not know what to look for or what to critique, much less what to espouse. There are many problems, but none is *the* problem, the thing that if ousted would free man or Latin America. In *Sobre héroes y tumbas*, then, "Perón" is a fill-in both for the sacred name that would ground a project of liberation and for the terrible force on which one could ground a critique. "Perón" is deified and vilified, the terror and the scapegoat; this allows Argentines to overlook the fact that "Perón" (and, of course, "Evita"), like all modern names, is banal. There is no God and no Despot, only existence, only freedom: fear of this fact grounds modern political atrocities.

Vargas Llosa's *Conversación en la Catedral* [1969; *Conversation in the Cathedral*, 1975], from its famous opening sentence, pursues this same inquiry: Not only "What is the solution?" but "What is the problem in Latin America?" Criticism of the 1980s and 1990s tended to present Vargas Llosa as a right-wing writer, especially given late texts such as *Historia de Mayta* [1984; *The Real Life of Alejandro Mayta*, 1986], *El hablador* (1987), and *Lituma en los Andes* [1993; *Death in the Andes*, 1996]—all of which put forth a decidedly anti-Marxist message. The view is certainly worthy of exploration; here, I would like to offer a point that might lend itself to that inquiry. In his novels (both of the early period and of the late period), Vargas Llosa exposes the evils not just of the left but of all political ideologies, of the State and of the market, of religiosity and of the end of religiosity. Even as a leftist (which he was in his younger years), Vargas Llosa opposed the ideology of the left, for he clearly saw true politics as the disruption not simply of the right, but of ideology as the discourse of the right.

None of the ideological topoi just named, then, are for Vargas Llosa the problem, and none is the solution. If Vargas Llosa's novels are conservative, it is less because they espouse the wrong ideology than because they are paralytic; they advocate no position, for they can find none that is not ideological. Vargas Llosa spins dazzling narratives that endlessly undermine every political belief. But in his texts no narrative names the cause of Latin-American atrocities, and none can point to an exit. For Vargas Llosa, the terror of Latin America is not absent; it exists at the limit of the name. His writing circulates around that limit, always falling short of or bypassing what it desires to designate.

García Márquez articulates a similar dilemma in *El otoño del patriarca* [1975; *The Autumn of the Patriarch*, 1976]. The novel is the first-person recount of the life and death of a dictator, a pure totalitarian. And yet the I is not a single I but endlessly shifts. At times it is the dictator, at times his lovers, at times his victims, at times his aides, at times common citizens, and so on. García Márquez's point is that there is no place to see the dictator as such, which is to say, to grasp the reason for or ground of despotism. There exists endless subjective perspectives on the despot. Yet none can capture the total picture, the dictator's claim on totality. Again, every evaluation of the political atrocity, every effort to name the cause of terror, to name the terror itself, misses the mark and, indeed, turns heads away from that cause by presenting effects as causes, banalities as reasons, personal experiences and opinions as universal truths.

This is why, for García Márquez, dictatorship does not die with the dictator but, through that death (the autumn of the patriarch), emerges as all the more forceful and totalizing. Terrible is not only the dictator's reign but also the fact that the dictator cannot be buried, placed into the past, removed. He

is total because he lives on forever. In the absence of a signifier big enough to mark or memorialize the dictator, adequate for his memorial, the dictator is never mourned, his death never marked. The monument, the great novel *El otoño del patriarca* itself, fails to serve as a tombstone. The dictator thereby lives on, the death of one dictator does not remove the figure of the dictator, who endlessly returns. This paradigm reappears throughout Boom narratives: The Boom is the effort to mark Latin American atrocities, to memorialize, and thus to mourn them, to place them into history; and yet since that terror lies at the limit of the word and work, the project is an endless one.

It should be apparent, once more, that the technical novelties of the Boom cannot simply be associated with aestheticism and developmentalism—neither with their espousal nor their critique. The disruption of linearity, the break-up and condensation of the signifier, the neo-baroque deployment of aberrant rhythms—these and various other Boom devices, which are not reducible to signification, represent efforts to mark the limit of the signifier: the fact that there is no name for either the Latin American good-to-come or for the cause-of-the-bad. In other words, technical innovation struggles to do the work (the work of mourning, of putting the past into the past, and thus the labor of opening to the future) that the signifier, because of the missing "in the name of," can no longer execute.

Yet just as there is no "in the name of" to take up politics (including politics itself) in the late twentieth century, so there is no clear technique, barely any literariness, by means of which writers might mark the finitude of publication and circulation. When the history of the twentieth-century novel is written (if it is written), people will perhaps see that the great hyper-technical modernist novel, embodied by the works of Joyce, Proust, Celine, Woolf, Faulkner, and others, accomplishes a project, that of exposing the limit of signification, which the Latin American novel brings to a close, by indexing the marketability, hence the death, of even that mark. The modern novel preserves literature in, but over against, the Great Book and aestheticism; the Boom exposes the end of that preservation. Literature has not ended, for it is that prior condition which is ending: By means of and after the Boom, literature borders on literature, and the Boom is the literature of that border, that hinge.

All of this brings us back to the Latin American existential situation, always present but unveiled by the Boom in a unique fashion. There is no great name, no grand narrative for the relation of names, just as there is no great cultural project for the encounter of cultures. Transliteration reveals that both the problem and the solution of Latin America lies in the relation of the various common senses and discourses whose advent Latin America's birth puts in play. Similar to the West as it is exposed by the Boom's ex-position, Latin America is not a combination of common senses. It is instead an endless encounter at the limit of sense (which is not nonsense) that it (Latin America) never fails to face and, because it is missing a proper name, never fails to bypass.

Works Cited

Carpentier, Alejo. 1962. *El siglo de las luces.* Mexico City: Compañía General de Ediciones.

Cortázar, Julio. 1963. *Rayuela.* Mexico City: Fondo de Cultura Económica.

Fuentes, Carlos. 1962. *La muerte de Artemio Cruz.* Mexico City: Fondo de Cultura Económica.

García Márquez, Gabriel. 1967. *Cien años de soledad.* Buenos Aires: Editorial Sudamericana.

——. 1975. *El otoño del patriarca.* Esplugas de Llobregat: Plaza y Janés.

Lezama Lima, José. 1966. *Paradiso.* Havana: Unión Nacional de Escritores y Artistas de Cuba.

Roa Bastos, Augusto. 1974. *Yo, el supremo.* Buenos Aires: Siglo XXI.

Rulfo, Juan. 1955. *Pedro Páramo.* Mexico City: Fondo de Cultura Económica.

Sábato, Ernesto. 1961. *Sobre héroes y tumbas.* Buenos Aires: Compañía General Fabril Editora.

Vargas Llosa, Mario. 1969. *Conversación en la catedral.* Barcelona: Seix Barral.

——. 1984. *Historia de Mayta.* Barcelona: Seix Barral.

——. 1987. *El hablador.* Barcelona: Seix Barral.

——. 1993. *Lituma en los Andes.* Barcelona: Planeta.

CHAPTER 31

THE MODERN IMAGINARY AND TRANSCULTURATION

Eneida Maria de Souza

The issue of cultural dependency was engendered by Latin American critical discourse and began to emerge in its more definitive outlines in the 1950s, when intellectuals gave it more systematic treatment. The close articulation of the concepts of modernization and transculturation, which we shall explore in this essay, led to differing views on dependency theory. These oscillated between a focus on the disjunction of imported ideas and their local acclimatization versus an acceptance of local backwardness as the necessary price for the acquisition of borrowed cultural goods. The Uruguayan critic Ángel Rama (1926–1983) developed the concept of literary transculturation in the 1970s from the Cuban Fernando Ortiz's (1881–1969) study of Cuban culture. Inspired by Latin American neo-regionalist narratives by writers such as Alejo Carpentier (1904–1980), José Maria Arguedas (1911–1969), João Guimarães Rosa (1908–1967), and Gabriel García Márquez (b. 1927), Angel Rama pointed out the need to study cultural transference or transitivity. His work examined and explored the relationship in ideological dyads such as universality and national identity, modernization and the politics of social homogeneity, as well as the constitution of countercultural discourse in neocolonial, marginalized, and dependent societies. Although Rama's notion of transculturation was initially applied to literature, once literary production is understood as cultural praxis and cultural discourse, as Mabel Moraña observes, the concept leads to developments and formulations that take it beyond any narrative text. Transculturation comes into play when literature is seen as a response at the level of symbolic criticism, or as an ideological project in face of modernizing acceleration (Moraña 139). The concept could, however, be extended to the more ample sphere of literary/cultural relations in general, irrespective of its application to the narrow confines of issues pertaining to politics and the modern order.

The trajectory of the concept of the modern throughout twentieth- and twenty-first-century Brazil, from the Modernism of 1922 to this day, includes a series of definitions and redefinitions. These coalesced in the complex interweaving of vanguard ideas freshly imported from Europe and the United States, and the construction of local nationalisms that, in their turn, were intricately linked to certain pretensions of participation in the "concert of nations" as an equal with Western European nations and the United States. The subsequent transition of a discourse based on state-ordained nationalism to present-day globalization brings back delicate issues pertaining to nationalism, since, to a certain extent, it postulates a return to production at a local level without the mediation of values sanctioned by the state. The current replacement of the hegemony of the state with the hegemony of the market brings about an epistemological shift of once-dominant paradigms between the early 1920s and the late 1970s.

We shall try to reconstruct an imaginary of transculturation by using as our parameters the metaphor of geography–Latin America, the originator of an epistemology conditioned by its peripheral, historically defined geography–to which we shall add other contributing metaphors. We shall use the temporal metaphor to articulate the selective memory and oblivion of Colonialism, the historically delayed adoption of metropolitan modernity in the nations of the periphery, and the ideology of development and dependency. This last issue unfolds in diverse planes of discourse (pertaining to economics, development, and dependency) and is thereby understood as a system of exchange between cultures, a system of gains and losses brought about by colonization and interpreted in terms of wealth, profit, debt, and loans. The additional metaphor of the national organism translates into a system of natural processes and elements transported to the realm of culture–terms such as roots, ramifications, fruit, rhizomes, transplants, and grafts. Commerce is another metaphor to explore the development-dependency dyad as a cultural operation in which traffic, contraband, plagiarism, and stealing of ideas become strategies of resistance to the literature of colonizing nations. In the realm of native ritual, through the metaphor of cannibalism, we can find the incorporation of indigenous practices for strengthening national strategies that compete with colonizing forces, the metropolis as the Other, exemplified in Oswald de Andrade's (1890–1954) *Antropofagia* [1972: Anthropophagy] and Glauber Rocha's (1939–1991) *Estética da Fome* [1979: Esthetics of Hunger].

To achieve a greater understanding of the origins of these various operative concepts and their subsequent adoption, one should take into account the Latin American cultural position regarding modernity as it was instated in hegemonic centers. Latin America is situated geographically on the periphery of the North American-Western European center, while on the temporal axis, the continent is historically behind the times. The inherent contradictions of Latin American culture, now exhibiting a slow and gradual process of social modernization (limited as it is by continuing economic underdevelopment), instigate a contemporary rethinking of the production of local knowledge, as well as its relations to knowledge on a global scale. The social, cultural, and economic changes we now identify as globalization and postmodernism provoked a change in the concept of the modern in the sphere of culture. The theories related to dependency underwent a transformation when the concept of temporal linearity in universal history was replaced by the notion of the "simultaneidad espacial de las historias locales" (Mignolo 94) ("spatial simultaneity of local histories"). One should note that this formulation is a theoretical construct that was developed in cultural criticism. Cultural criticism relies on the interpretation of concepts in a contextual socio-historical field. Analysis, in this discipline, means a *ressemantização* [semantic refiguration] of the concept under study, both of its traditional usage and of its diverse revisions in the culture of the nation. The intention here is to analyze critical discourse within the historical parameters that will reveal a multi-dimensional understanding at the start of the twenty-first century. A two-way street, this procedure observes the transit between the value conferred on concepts at the time of their emergence and the possible transformations and ramifications, as realized in their later trajectories.

The Ills of Dependency and Anthropophagic Elation

To understand the relationship between Brazilian and foreign culture in the 1950s one must begin by considering underdevelopment as a commonplace of world capitalism. It is Antonio Candido's premise (1972, 40–62) that the period during which Brazil openly identified itself with being a new nation coincided with a passive acceptance of the nation's backwardness. This would change with the advent of World War II and, impelled by the nation's modernizing drive, that passive acceptance was replaced by a new "consciência do subdesenvolvimento" (consciousness of underdevelopment) which was militant. For the Brazilian nation to take on development under the guidelines of international capitalism meant to jump over the hurdles of long-standing indifference and become, from one moment to the next, an active member of the capitalist world.

Silviano Santiago (b. 1936), in analyzing Brazilian identity politics throughout the twentieth century in his essay *A atração do mundo* [1996: The World's Attraction], correlates Antonio Candido's theoretical position to the one held by his early twentieth-century compatriot, Joaquim Nabuco (1849–1910). The turn-of-century thinker Nabuco, Eurocentric by nature, was divided between advocating for a solid European tradition for Brazil and accepting Brazilian reality, devoid of that heritage and therefore deemed inferior. It was an inferiority that destined Brazilian culture, in the face of any contact, to be subsumed by the other culture (considered as superior). Nabuco concluded that "desde que temos a menor cultura, começa o predomínio destas [das camadas estratitificadas] sobre aquele [o sedimento novo]" (Santiago 1996, 34) ("since we have the lesser culture, this means a predominance of these [the stratified layers of European culture] over Brazilian culture [new sediment]"). Santiago goes further in his analysis of this synthesis of Brazilian culture: In spite of Nabuco's awareness of Brazilian reality, he was given to universalist Eurocentric ideas. Half a century later, Candido defined Brazilian literary production as a secondary branch of Portuguese literature, which in itself amounted to no more than a bramble bush of inferior quality in the garden of the Muses: "Comparada às grandes, a nossa literatura é pobre e fraca. Mas é ela, não outra, que nos exprime" (qtd. in Santiago 1996, 37) ("In comparison to the great literatures, ours is poor and weak. It is nevertheless the only one that can express who we are").

The use of organic metaphors–tree, branch/offshoot/sprigs, and bush–to explain Brazilian cultural dependency is in keeping with the reasoning of the European Enlightenment, especially as it was disseminated in Latin America. This metaphor develops the ideology of a causal and chronological order of cultural influences on (backward) Latin America. The metaphor of the organism-nation furthermore establishes (in keeping with Naturalist criteria) a connection between Brazilian and European literature that mimics the nature of the placenta, and therefore suggests a relationship devoid of choice. The use of the notion of organic growth as the metaphor chosen to illustrate the constitution of Brazilian culture, through its inherent implications of verticality and hierarchy, reinforces the image of the root, of a beginning, a source. This is the semantic network that enables us to conceive the systemic relations capable of integrating the various stages of the great genealogical tree of national culture. Renato Cordeiro Gomes, in his article "Para lá das fronteiras: literatura e subdesenvolvimento, de Antonio Candido" ["Crossing Boundaries, Antonio Candido's Literature and Underdevelopment"] puts it clearly:

> O atraso cultural leva ao tópico da dependência. Aqui, retoma Candido a metáfora da *árvore* explicitada no "Prefácio" da *Formação da literatura Brasileira* e mostra serem as literaturas latino-americanas "galhos das metropolitanas." São literaturas dependentes. Não se trata de camuflar as influências em nome de uma autonomia só justificada historicamente na fase do nacionalismo romântico, fase da consciência amena do atraso do "país novo." Se a literatura é fenômeno de civilização, a influência é inevitável, sociologicamente vinculada à nossa dependência desde a colonização e o transplante das culturas. O vínculo com as literaturas européias é placentário, não é opção. . . . É a maneira de nossa inserção no universal, visto como o ocidental europeu. (Gomes 123)

Cultural backwardness leads us to the topic of dependency. At this point Candido returns to the metaphor of the tree which had been used in the "Preface" to *Formação da literatura Brasileira* [1969; Development of Brazilian Literature] and demonstrates that Latin American literatures are offshoots of the literature of the metropolis. They are dependent literatures. This is not an attempt to camouflage external influences through a purported autonomy, as was done during the period of Romantic nationalism, a period of acceptance of the sense of backwardness of the new nation. If literature is to be considered a phenomenon of civilization, then influences are inevitable; they are sociologically linked to the nation's dependency and its transplanted cultures from the time of colonization. Our connection to European literatures mimics the reality of the placenta, it is not a question of choice. . . . This is the form of our insertion into the universal context, understood as Western Europe.

Antonio Candido (b. 1918) has shown uncommon sensitivity to the duality that characterizes the mentality of intellectuals in nations of the periphery. From his work in *Formação da literatura Brasileira* (1959) to his most recent publications, one finds a persistent discussion of the dialectical identity of Brazilian culture, a culture condemned to oscillate between the local and the universal, the self and the other, civilization and primitivism, the modern and the archaic. Paulo Eduardo Arantes, in his important essay "Sentimento da dialética" [1992; Sense of Dialectic], analyzes both Antonio Candido's and Roberto Schwarz's (b. 1938) positions with respect to resolving this oscillation of literary movements and major authors in Brazil's national historiography. The discussion returns partly to the concept of Latin American transculturation and its effects, sometimes manifest in the positive dialectics of Oswald de Andrade and the *Pau-Brazil* poetics, but also in the *tropicalismo* of the 1960s, and sometimes in the negative dialectics of Machado de Assis (1839–1908) and the lesson learned from the disjunction between the march of modernizing capitalism and Brazilian reality (Arantes 9–22). Candido's and Schwarz's theoretical positions can be summed up as a radically new evaluation of the vanguards in the process of national de-colonization, or in Candido's view a freedom from a sense of inferiority. Schwarz, for example, considers Oswald de Andrade's *Pau-Brazil* poetry a literary form based on the myth of progressive conservatism. Rachel Esteves Lima in *A crítica literária na universidade brasileira* [1997; Literary Criticism in Brazilian Universities] analyzes these issues in the work of Schwarz and Candido:

Mas, se Candido, em sua trajetória adaptativa aos padrões estéticos europeus, valoriza as experiências das vanguardas que surgiram a partir do movimento modernista, o mesmo não ocorre com Schwarz, que não admite um questionamento da visão teleológica sobre a qual constrói sua análise. O problema com o modernismo, de acordo com a visão de Schwarz, é que a superação das contradições se daria apenas ao nível da linguagem, enquanto no contexto social o otimismo de um Oswald não teria como persistir. . . . Para Schwarz, o *desrecalque localista* não passa de uma forma de legitimação da cópia de modelos europeus de uma maneira acrítica, em que a "interpretação triunfalista de nosso atraso" acaba se fundando numa ilusão. (Lima 194–95)

Candido, in a trajectory that adapts European esthetic standards, comes to value the vanguard experiences that began to make their appearance with the Modernist movement. Schwarz, however, does not follow suit, and will not admit putting in question the teleological vision on which his analysis is based. According to Schwarz, the problem with Modernism is that the contradictions true of the period could only be overcome in the realm of language, while in the social context an optimism such as Oswald's would hardly be able to persist . . . . Candido's expression of *desrecalque localista* was no more, in Schwarz's eyes, than a critical form of legitimizing copies of European models, in which the "triumphant interpretation of our backwardness" is ultimately founded in illusion.

Paulo Emílio Salles Gomes formulated the *mal-estar* (ill feeling) of Brazilian society in the face of the process of modernization as a reaction to the simultaneous mutual identification with, and dissolution of, the self and the Other. This argument was made during the discussions on dependency theory in vogue in the 1960s and 1970s. The paradoxical intertwining of these dialectical categories, he argued, causes a permanent sentiment of inadequacy on the part of the person condemned to straddle two cultural realities—a by-product of Brazil's peripheral destiny: "Não somos europeus nem americanos do norte, mas destituídos de cultura original, nada nos é estrangeiro, pois tudo o é. A penosa construção de nós mesmos se desenvolve na dialética rarefeita entre o não ser e o ser outro" (Gomes 1980, 77) ("Neither European nor North American, we are bereft of an original culture, nothing is foreign to us, for everything, in fact, is. The difficult construction of ourselves unfolds in the rarefied dialectics of not being and being the Other").

The inadequacies and ills of Brazilian culture caused by the confrontation between receiving and updating theory from the European and North American mainstream, certainly form one of the crucial points of the problematics of transculturation, as adapted to Latin America. Roberto Schwarz develops the notion of "As idéias fora do lugar" [1987b; Ideas Out of Place] through his reading of Machado de Assis, based on Marxist sociological ideology, and through a questioning of the contradictions brought about by the modernization of the nations of the periphery. Expressions such as *descompasso* (disjunction), *mal-estar* (ill feeling), and *torcicolo cultural* (a cultural crick in the neck) voice Schwarz's preoccupation with pointing out the discrepancy and discontinuity between imported ideas and their reception in a social context that differs from the European reality. While European modernity was based on the autonomy of individuals, universal law, and an established work ethic, Brazil differed in the most fundamental of social values: Its culture was based on the exchange of favors, a position as anti-modern as the institution of slavery; while preaching a sense of personal dependency, exceptions to

the rule and rewards for personal favors were in fact the norm. Free men were still tied to a social structure that would not break with colonial principles of privilege and *clientelismo* (favoritism)—the obstacles to creating the modern state (Schwarz 1981, 13–35).

Silviano Santiago's 1971 essay "O entre-lugar do discurso latino americano" [The In-between Space of Latin American Discourse] subverts longstanding antinomies and hierarchies inherent in the discourse that results from Western colonization. Santiago proposes a reflection on cultural dependency based on a critical approach derived from French philosophy and the work of Jorge Luis Borges (1899–1986). Santiago considers Borges to be a master deconstructor of the origins and models of world literature. Concepts such as source and influence, original and copy, localism and universalism are taken out of the prevailing analysis of Positivism and are now inscribed under the sign of contradiction and paradox, with the result that rigid oppositions break down. The concept of "entre-lugar" (liminality or in-between space), far from being a "fora do lugar" (misplaced) philosophical abstraction (alluding to Schwarz's famous essay), constitutes a positioning that represents Brazilian culture as one reality among many, thereby bringing a new theoretical consideration into Brazilian literary culture.

This essay became an important tool in the national polemics on dependency theory. The concept of *entre-lugar* is closely related to Modernist theories such as Oswald de Andrade's *antropofagia* and Mário de Andrade's (1893–1945) *tração à memória* (memory betrayed), which were responsible for initiating a transcultural dialogue that transmuted the nation's backwardness and underdevelopment into a joyful positive response. It constituted a "sábia e poética" (wise and poetic) assimilation of some of the insights of modernity. This is the sense in which transcultural practice is seen as a joyful dialogue that does not bear the past burden of disjunction or ill feelings, notwithstanding the certainty that the dialectic is open and will not be resolved in a "dialética positiva" (positive dialectics) and is devoid of *ufanismo* (high nationalist sentiment), a point highlighted in Schwarz' interpretation of *Pau-Brazil* poetry and *tropicalismo*:

> Já com Oswald o tema, comumente associado a atraso e desgraça nacionais, adquire uma surpreendente feição otimista, até eufórica: o Brasil pré-burguês, quase virgem de puritanismo e cálculo econômico, assimila de forma sábia e poética as vantagens do progresso, *prefigurando a humanidade pós-burguesa*, desrecalcada e fraterna; além do que oferece uma plataforma positiva de onde objetar à sociedade contemporânea. Um ufanismo crítico, se é possível dizer assim. (Schwarz 1987a, 13)

> Oswald de Andrade subverts topics commonly associated with Brazil such as backwardness and national calamities, awarding them a surprisingly optimistic outlook, joyful even: pre-bourgeois Brazil, practically unspoiled by puritanism and economic calculations, assimilated poetically and wisely the advantages of progress, *prefiguring a post-bourgeois humanity*, a humanity unrepressed and brotherly. Further still, it offers a positive platform from which to place contemporary society under analysis. *Ufanismo* of a critical sort, were it not a contradiction in terms.

Confirming his divergence from Schwarz's Marxist perspective, Santiago's essay "Apesar de dependente, universal" [1982; "Universality Despite Dependency"] relies on French philosophy to refute the concept of origin and subvert criteria such as time and space, in order to constitute a new cultural discourse of the periphery. In search of greater clarity for the unique boundaries of different cultures, Santiago breaks away from the sociological perspective and looks toward anthropology for a new response to the issue of cultural dependency. This strategy, far from restricting the universe of historical, social, and literary exchange, increases the power of the so-called colonized literary output. Santiago's antidotes to a version of the polemics of Dependency theory follow the Modernist lineage: *antropofagia* (anthropophagy), *traição à memória* (memory betrayed), and *concretismo* (concretism) in Brazilian poetry.

Roberto Schwarz's 1987 article "Nacional por subtração" ["National by Way of Subtraction"] takes yet a different position with respect to the redefinitions of nationality and cultural dependency, in opposition to both Santiago and Haroldo de Campos (1929–2003). Schwarz chooses to confront Santiago's above-mentioned article, on the one hand, and Campos's 1983 "Da razão antropofágica: diálogo e diferença na cultura brasileira" ["On Anthropophagic Reason: Dialogue and Difference in Brazilian Culture"]. These essays do show points of convergence, however. They agree on the usefulness of returning to *antropofagia* as an operative concept to deconstruct foreign cultures, to place Brazilian literature on equal standing, and in competition with foreign literature; and both essays place their confidence in the positivity and joy of transculturation. Both essays deconstruct philosophical notions such as original, copy, and simulacrum, inverting the causal process of historical interpretation. Eneida Leal Cunha provides us with a synthesis of Schwarz's and Santiago's positions in her article "Leituras da dependência cultural" ["Interpretations of Cultural Dependency"], offering a clear exposition on their respective lineages and analytical preferences:

O confronto entre os ensaios "Apesar de dependente, universal" e "Nacional por subtração," além de pôr em cena sistemas interpretativos divergentes ou convergentes do pensamento ocidental, expõe o esboço de duas linhagens de intelectuais brasileiros e de dois modos de ler e avaliar as formações de identidade e a experiência da dependência cultural. Ponto nuclear de uma dessas famílias de avaliadores da literatura e da cultura no Brasil, a qual pertence Roberto Schwarz, pode ser identificado na ascendência ilustrada da "Formação" de Antonio Candido e no interesse comum quase excludente pela produção literária datada a partir de 1850, ou, dito mais largamente, pela produção moderna e pós-colonial. As leituras de Silviano Santiago vêm-se empreendendo da história cultural, desde a década de 70. Em contrapartida, operam inversões, reversões e deslocamentos de ênfases, pondo o foco, reincidentemente, em produções coloniais como a carta de Pero Vaz de Caminha, articulando-as à produção modernista e contemporânea. (Cunha 134)

On comparing the two essays "Universality Despite Dependency" and "National by Way of Subtraction," apart from placing before us divergent, or convergent, interpretive systems of Western thought, the confrontation makes explicit two lineages of Brazilian intellectuals and two modes of reading and evaluating the development of identity and the experience of cultural dependency. Considering that each of these authors is the scion of two different traditions of interpreters of literature and culture in Brazil, Roberto Schwarz could be identified as a member of the illustrious descent of Antonio Candido's "Formação" as well as sharing in Candido's interest, almost exclusively, in the literary production of the modern period from 1850 to the present, or, put more amply, modern and post-colonial production. Silviano Santiago's readings, on the other hand, arise from cultural history, which he has developed since the 1970s. Both authors, however, make use of inversions, reversals and changing emphasis,

focusing repeatedly on colonial literary products such as Pero Vaz Caminha's famous Letter informing Portugal on the discovery of Brazil in 1500, and linking them to Modernist and contemporary writings.

Luiz Costa Lima (b. 1937), one of the principal exponents of Brazilian literary theory, sees the problem of cultural difference as a question to be examined from the perspective of the control of the imaginary in Western thought. The task of the critic, in his view, is that of theorizing the transposition of Western thought to colonial space, and the creation of tools for entering into dialogue with foreign cultures. His article, "Da existência precária: o sistema intelectual no Brasil" [1981; "On a Precarious Existence: The Intellectual System in Brazil"], is a searing criticism of the Brazilian discursive tradition, which according to him, has been characterized by a form of auditory culture that is inimical to the clear exposition and development of arguments in philosophical systems. In denouncing the strain of orality and improvisation present in this discursive form–which would include the work of, for example, Gilberto Freyre (1900–1987)–Costa Lima argues that the genre is rich in profuse talk and seductive artifice, these being the signs of a culture that is transmitted orally, that does not make demonstrative structures explicit, and that stages, instead, *palavra teatralizada* (verbal theatricality).

According to Costa Lima, Brazilian intellectual life, shaped by the habit of the stage and the judicial tribunal, lacks the spirit of debate and deeper reflection, because it believes in the seductive power of discourse and is content with idle discussions. Improvisation, then, serving like a double-edged sword, works both to maintain the colonial status of Brazilian culture and to foster an emphasis on pragmatism and experimentalism in opposition to theoretical reasoning (E. M. de Souza 1992, 12). Extending the argument to issues such as cultural dependency, Costa Lima believes that disorganization and a lack of method in a people's thinking process is a conditioning factor in the Brazilians' subordination to other cultures:

E do ponto de vista do sistema intelectual, o pior do autoritarismo é que ele acostuma a *intelligentsia* ao pensamento impositivo, que não precisa demonstrar, pois lhe basta apontar, mostrar com o dedo, "a verdade." No caso das nações econômica e culturalmente periféricas, como a nossa, esta conseqüência ainda se torna mais intensa, porque o seu horror à teorização própria as deixa duradouramente sujeitas à teorização alheia.
(E. M. Souza 1992, 15)

From the point of view of the intellectual system, the worst characteristic of authoritarianism is that it gets the *intelligentsia* accustomed to thought based on imposition, thought that is not in the habit of demonstration. It is a system in which it is enough to merely point out, to put a finger on, the "truth." With respect to nations situated culturally and economically on the periphery, such as ours, the consequences are even more intense, because the aversion these nations have to their own theorizing leaves them continuously subjected to the theorizing of others.

Able to lucidly express the dangers of considering Latin American critical discourse solely through the "Macondo" (in a reference to *Cien Años de Soledad*) lens of magic and intuition, Costa Lima also brings to the fore its inherently naïve presuppositions, while at the same time denouncing the totalitarian vision that has been responsible for its continuation. Cultural dialogue between Brazil and the Other must be based on an inter-subjective exchange between all interlocutors, so that the cultural exchange in due course will not unduly privilege either one of the sides involved. Costa Lima deconstructs the notion of anteriority or posteriority in the production of knowledge, since there is a common historical context even if with distinct characteristics. The identity the critic searches for will result from the encounter with, and tension between, intercultural voices.

If Modernism gave rise to the economic metaphor transplanted to literary discourse (poetry as an export product)–an illustration of which is Oswald de Andrade's *Pau-Brasil* poetry (1925)–the idea of poetry as an export product was at first a reaction to the isolation of colonial domination, but then it became a desire to free Brazilian verse by concentrating on national values. Oswald de Andrade's *antropofagia* (anthropophagy) meant a critical devouring, a critical incorporation, aimed at breaking up regional boundaries by making Brazilian poetry and culture international and establishing an egalitarian dialogue with European culture. It is not surprising that among other popular celebrations the *carnaval* (carnival), became a favorite motif to represent joy, the *dança da raça* (expression of the [black] race) and social inversions–all through a popular celebration versed in humor. The Modernist response to transculturation was still guided by the devouring of what was good in foreign culture (the culture of the Other represented by Europe); Europe, however, was being cooked in the pot. The binary relationship established between Brazil and other cultures was basically restricted to Europe, the matrix from which all Brazilian ideas originated. As a consequence, international exchanges were limited, and the nation's close dependency on Europe meant a constant Westernizing of Brazilian culture.

One can, however, explore the dialectic interior/exterior (local vs. foreign) by taking a closer look at the notion of exterior. "Exterior" here means "from overseas," and is traditionally linked to a notion that represents power, origin, and superiority over cultures like that of Brazil (which are local and autochthonous). Once the concept of exterior is extricated from what strictly belongs to the category of foreign imports, one can then examine it and, in fact, reverse it on a national basis, because it was in fact made to include everything, that is, everything that was different for Brazilian elite white culture, such as aspects of indigenous and African cultures. In this sense Oswald de Andrade's *Antropofagia* entangles the traditional antipodes exterior/from overseas and interior/local, in a search for an identity that is not circumscribed by the culture of the native but is driven by the need to create a culture of difference, free from the imitation of imported models. Roberto Corrêa dos Santos, commenting on Silviano Santiago's "Oswald de Andrade: ou o elogio da tolerancia racial" [1991; "Oswald de Andrade: Or in Praise of Racial Tolerance"] emphasizes Santiago's reading of Andrade as the Modernist intellectual calling for a remaking of Brazil. Dos Santos follows Santiago's example in articulating paired oppositions so that they are in a dialectical relation to each other and thus are complementary in his new interpretation of Brazil in the Modernist project:

> Ao contrário do romântico, o projeto modernista esquadrinhado no convite à Antropofagia de Oswald requer, conforme ainda leitura de Silviano, uma segunda colonização, esta agora decidida pela vontade livre dos agentes sociais. Para tanto, será necessário, ao invés de se exteriorizar o interior, trabalhar no sentido inverso: interiorizar o exterior. O exterior, pensando-se exclusivamente em termos de formação cultural, diz respeito ao estrangeiro, às forças do Ocidente, ao progresso, à produção européia, à

atualização, à modernidade das novas conquistas. A nacionalidade brasileira poderia, com tal operação antropofágica, aí sim, tornar-se forte e autêntica. Mais avançada ainda é a reflexão modernista quando considera sendo o exterior não só a cultura européia, mas também as culturas negra e indígena. Todas elas devem ser introjetadas para gerarem a nossa independência, a nossa identidade, o nosso interior forte. (Santos 100)

In a reversal of Brazilian Romanticism, the Modernist enterprise framed by Oswald's *antropofagia*, as interpreted by Silviano Santiago's reading, demands a second foundation of Brazil, this time determined by the free will of social agents. To that end, instead of externalizing the *interior* [local], it is necessary conversely, to interiorize the exterior. The *exterior*, represents what is foreign, the forces of the European, the notion of progress, current, in sum at the cutting edge of modernity. Brazilian culture could, through the appropriation of the exterior, in the sense of *antropofagia*, become strong and authentic. The Modernist proposal goes even further when it considers not just the *exterior*, the foreign, as culture, but also includes the indigenous and African cultures. All of them [the long-excluded Brazilian other as well as the European] must be introjected so as to generate Brazilian independence, identity, and a strong *interior*.

The Brazilian Modernist concept of nation is built, therefore, through an incorporation of the indigenous–of the primitive and different elements of the nation's native culture–that is capable of creating a "strong interior." Modernism therefore re-interprets the concept of what is national by eliminating European, white, or ethnocentric domination. "Sou um tupi tangendo um alaúde" (Andrade 1987, 83) ("I am a Tupí strumming a lute")–Mário de Andrade's emblematic line–expresses certain ambiguities brought about by this "anthropophagic" transculturation, and echoes Oswald de Andrade's dramatic phrase quoted in the "Manifesto Antropófago": "Tupí or not Tupí, that is the question" (Andrade 1972, 6: 13). *Macunaíma, o herói sem nenhum caráter* still stands as a masterpiece of Modernism. It deconstructs the problem of the alienation of indigenous identity by questioning and enlarging its subject: the hero reaches transnational dimensions, which allows him to enter into the larger Latin American scene.

The Argentine novelist and critic Ricardo Piglia (b. 1941), in a 1991 analysis, linked Borges's family biography and his writing, in the process created the concept of "mirada estrábica" ("strabismic gaze," a visual defect in which one eye cannot focus with the other). The idea of the Argentinean writer looking askance at the world, his oblique perspective–one eye turned to his country and the other to Europe–expresses the ambivalent nature of great part of Latin American literature: "hay que tener un ojo puesto en la inteligencia europea y otro puesto en las entrañas de la patria" (Piglia 61) ("one must have one eye trained on European intelligence and the other on the heart of one's nation"). One cannot, however, think that Latin American literary culture is defined by either Oswald de Andrade's *Antropofagia* or Borges's doubled vision. Hegemonic centers undergo gradual transformation, and the well-established and ever-changing flux of cultural transferences force us into a constant rereading of the different targets contained within the concept of *mirada estrábica*.

The strategy of building on the disjunction between the drive toward modernization and the relentless force of transculturation is one of the developments with which sociocultural conflicts are to be faced, instead of merely endeavoring to ignore or oppose them. This view has been inherited by Brazilian writers who follow the Modernist agenda as defined by Oswald and Mário de Andrade. From the 1930s onwards the

Modernist movement's concept of nation was associated with the state-ordained program, and thus suffered the fate of having become the rationalizing, organizing force of state policy, while still trying to foster the native local cultural memory and coping with the invasion of a global culture arriving with modernization. Mário de Andrade, together with other members of the Modernist movement, was to live the dilemma caused by the need to create a national identity, born of "interiorização do exterior" (interiorization of the exterior) and the rationalist position manifest in the thirties and forties in the state-controlled culture. The contradictory relationship established between Modernist intellectuals and the modernizing project of the Vargas dictatorship (1937–1945) led to the development of a Modernist system of thought that adhered to a critical and deconstructive appropriation of European vanguard discourse, while also committing itself to the state's desire to preserve national cultural principles. The Modernist intellectuals were caught between keeping the writers' independence, on the one hand, and answering the call to participate in the state's politics of cultural nationalism, on the other. For writers, these responsibilities implied a belief in the freedom of expression and the creation of works that emphasize the playful and unfettered aspects of Brazilianness; whereas, for intellectuals, there was an obligation to transcend individualism and join the project of advancing a systematic treatment of the national heritage, which included popular art, ethnographic material, and the rethinking of museums.

During the thirties, while the nation was still under the influence of the Modernist project (which had started in 1922) and its aesthetic renovation (of which the regionalist novel is an example), Brazil was at the same time structuring itself around a modernizing model that was authoritarian and elitist in character. Mário de Andrade's work illustrates the level of complexity with which the Modernist project faced the dilemmas inherent in transculturation. In both his creative work and his enterprising attitude as a public figure, he revealed the contradictions of opposing positions regarding cultural memory. Leaving behind his avowed goals of abandoning foreign models and discovering an autochthonous cultural tradition in Brazil, he instead, in a complete reversal, came to privilege a negativism toward native culture that focused on the avant-garde—to the detriment of the Brazilian legacy.

Macunaíma, however, remains Mário de Andrade's main work and it is a prime example of Brazilian cultural deconstruction; it is based on a revision of national folklore and displaces both the official canon and its dogma through parody. A Modernist vampire, sinking its teeth into institutionalized knowledge, *Macunaíma* represents the revolutionary force of a learning process in action, mixing erudite culture and a national popular imaginary made of legends, folk tales, and indigenous myths. When personal memory fails, the gap of oblivion serves, in a manner similar to the Greek rhapsodists and the *cantadores* of the Brazilian Northeast, to stimulate invention and improvisation. The act of creation is defined by going beyond tradition's inherited models, in a cunning game of memory and improvisational anarchy in the cultural archive (E. M. de Souza 1988, 24–28).

Andrade's vision of a pragmatic nationalism involved a search for the constituting elements of Brazilian identity in local culture, refusing passively to accept models imported from the European avant-garde. For that same reason, Modernism's nationalism turned out to be transitory and changed during the course of Andrade's intellectual development.

Pragmatic nationalism is exemplified in the transformation the main character *Macunaíma* goes through when he is described as having the "brilho inútil das estrelas" (useless light of the stars) because of having slighted the civilization of lights represented by the character Vei, the Sun. The hero's failure results from his inability to carry out any task. He is punished for allowing himself to be overcome by tropical sloth and existential abandon. This *macunaímic* attitude expresses both a concern with ethics and a solution to an intellectual impasse. Applying himself to the task of restoring the country's national heritage, Mário de Andrade developed a different strategy regarding European cultural influence; he advocated imaginative improvisation, which went hand in hand with an appreciation of personal brilliance and intelligence. This creative strategy—which he called "traição à memória" (betrayal of memory)—offered a way for the artist to forgo the models of a past that imitated European culture and, instead, be spurred on by the intuitive spirit of *Macunaíma* (see G. M. Souza 1979). Mário de Andrade builds a concept of Brazilian nationality in tune with the politics of his time; instead of being rejected, the nation's past now emerges as the authentic cultural legacy that is to be preserved and institutionalized through governmental agencies created for that very purpose. The sense of cultural competition with Europe gave new impetus to advancing policies for the protection of national heritage. That this was in fact a principle of the Enlightenment was not recognized as the betrayal that it was of the *Estado Novo's* (the Vargas regime's) modernizing process (E. M. Souza 1993a, 136–37).

Carlos Sandroni has written on the period in which Mário de Andrade headed the Department of Culture of the State of São Paulo. Entitled *Mário contra Macunaíma* [Mário against Macunaíma], this study emphasizes the writer's inclination to value the gradual and slow political perfecting of cultural nationalism versus the rapid and breathless pace of avant-garde writing. Because of his belief in the precariousness of literature and life itself, he did not disdain the know-how brought by the new European and North American scientific innovations. A new, technical consciousness was introduced into Brazil at this time with the establishment of universities in Brazil; this encouraged a new way of thinking of the nation's cultural scene. Intuition now gave way to a rational cognitive system, in the same way that the Hegelian synthesis of polarities differed from analysis (Sandroni 46).

It is nevertheless clear that Mário de Andrade, faced with the imperative to intervene in the country's process of modernization, went against his own revolutionary and democratic convictions and had to turn his back on his own past. His modern discourse coincided with the State's authoritarian discourse that, while opposing improvisation in praise of scientific organization, still paradoxically relied on the brilliance and intuition of its most representative artists. It was a conflict that was to accompany Mario de Andrade for all his life, and which lends an added dimension to his fascinating and difficult dialogue between the universalizing ideas that came with European culture and the need to transcend them with a solution that was both literary and particularized to Brazilian reality. Helena Bomeny, author of "Guardiães da razão" ["Guardians of Reason"] analyzes how Modernists from the State of Minas Gerais reacted to the policies of constituting a nationality in the political sense, and comments on Mário de Andrade's position:

"Passada a revolta, continua a tradição. . . ." Ela continuava agora, nos anos 30, pela novidade de envolver a cultura em um projeto de Estado. O que resultaria do empreendimento? Uma modernidade que informou a política do Estado Novo, como sabemos, deixaria muito pouco espaço às categorias do pensamento romântico e as iniciativas culturais diversificadas, especialmente pela tensa relação que se estabeleceu entre propostas e institucionalização; entre diversidade e uniformização. Nossos intelectuais literatos, nossos modernistas, inscreveram-se distintamente na experiência política do vanguardismo estadonovista. As sucessivas e públicas frustrações de Mário de Andrade e o silêncio de Drummond são mais do que apenas reações de personalidades diferentes. (Bomeny 114)

"At revolt's end, tradition remains. . . . " And still it persisted, in the Thirties, with the novelty of making culture an affair of State. What was to result from this enterprise? A modernity that informed the policies of the *Estado Novo*, as we know, would leave little margin for the categories of Romantic notions of national identity, especially in the tense relations that have developed between theory and institutionalization; between diversity and uniformity. Our intellectual literati, our Modernists, enrolled themselves differently in the political experiment of the *estadonovista* vanguard. Mário de Andrade's successive public frustrations, and Drummond's silence, amount to more than the mere reactions of different types of personalities.

The conflictual relationship Mário de Andrade had with the cultural gap between Europe and the nations of the periphery (like Brazil) can still be translated into an optimistic response to, but nevertheless also a denouncement of the contradictory aspect of the Brazilian spirit. Conscious of the responsibility of promoting the construction of a modern nationality through his essays and fictional work, independently of his participation in government projects, Andrade took responsibility for the paradox of the situation, and by doing so became emblematic of the process of transculturation. The paradox inscribes itself in a Naturalist explanation of Brazilian social behavior, a behavior that hesitates in choosing between Macunaíma's destiny—encoded in the warm regions of the world, with their predisposition toward sloth—and the one of inhabitants of temperate regions, predisposed to work, sobriety, and morality. The basic elements of this equation are intuition versus reason, but the concept of nationality in *Macunaíma* cannot be understood solely from the point of view of what we have been calling the *interior*. The conflict between Mário de Andrade's nationalist proposals during the last years of his life, steeped in Enlightenment rationality, and the transgressive and combative impulse of the 1920s, reflects the struggles within Modernism as an international cultural reality.

Mário de Andrade engaged the contradictions he lived, between work and leisure, intuition and reason or, on a political and cultural level, between national and universal, periphery and metropolis, through solutions that were equally contradictory—at times involving pragmatic nationalism (see Gilda de Mello e Souza), at times the rationalism of the Enlightenment. In taking a position against *Macunaíma*, for instance, Mário de Andrade reflected the other aspect of the rationalist process of modernization and the *avant-la-lettre* effects of globalization and transculturation. In favor of Macunaíma, however, the author dreams of a utopian place, far from the obligations of timetables and city life, a way to break with the illusion of progress and the desires that are motivated by social modernization. In 1933, on answering a questionnaire sent by a U.S. publisher, Andrade expresses the desire to distance

himself from civilization and live in the Amazon forest, repeating the fictional destiny of his character Macunaíma:

> Detesto os climas moderados, e por isso vivo pessimamente em São Paulo. Também não aprecio a civilização, nem muito menos, acredito nela. Tanto o meu físico como as minhas disposições do espírito exigem as terras do Equador. Meu maior desejo é ir viver longe da civilização, na beira de algum rio pequeno da Amazônia, ou nalguma praia do mar do Norte brasileiro, entre gente inculta, do povo. Meu maior sinal de espiritualidade é odiar o trabalho, tal como ele é concebido, semanal e de tantas horas diárias, nas civilizações chamadas "cristãs." O exercício da preguiça, que eu cantei no Macunaíma, é uma das minhas maiores preocupações. (1983, 41)

> I hate moderate climates and for that reason live very badly in São Paulo. I also do not enjoy civilization, much less believe in it. My physical as well as my spiritual disposition pines for the lands of the Equator. My strongest desire is to live away from civilization, at the margins of some small river in Amazonia, or at some small beach on Brazil's Northern coastline, among uncultured people, our people. My greatest sign of spirituality is that of hating work, as it is conceived of weekly and apportioned in daily hours, in the so-called "Christian" civilizations. The exercise of indolence, as I had praised in *Macunaíma*, is one of my greatest desires.

A resistance to a culture of work and Christian ideology imposed by the colonizer at the time of the "discovery" of the New World and an opting for the exercise of indolence, for indigenous nature, far from becoming a solution for the ills of civilization, reinforces the ambiguous nature of the proposal forwarded by Mário de Andrade himself and his fellow Modernists (compared with, for example, Oswald de Andrade and the utopian "matriarcado de Pindorama" [*Pindorama* matriarchy]). *Macunaíma* is unquestionably the most important work of Brazilian Modernism, among other reasons, for its reflections on the impasse between the culture of leisure and a culture of work, as well as on the anthropophagic devouring of indigenous and European culture. If this conflict could be resolved in literature, we might, according to Silviano Santiago, define the process of transculturation of the Modernist movement of 1920 as pragmatic nationalism:

> Oscilando entre o que é pioneiro e o que é etnocêntrico, aflora o nacionalismo pragmático de Mário de Andrade, que não é uma "resposta definitiva," mas uma "solução provisória," como alerta Gilda de Mello e Souza em "Vanguarda e nacionalismo na década de vinte." Pelo sim e pelo não, é no nacionalismo pragmático que fica a lição de atualidade de Mário. Uma estratégia desconstrutora do processo infernal de ocidentalização do Brasil.
> (Santiago 1988, 22)

> Oscillating between the pioneering and the ethnocentric, we find Mário de Andrade's pragmatic nationalism, which is not a "definitive answer" but a "provisional solution," as Gilda de Melo e Souza warns us in her article "Vanguard and Nationalism in the 1920." Provisional or not, we are left however, with pragmatic nationalism as Mário de Andrade's enduring legacy. A deconstructing strategy of the infernal process of Westernization in Brazil.

Avant-Garde and Underdevelopment

Modernist poetry and prose reinterpreted colonial literature through the European avant-garde using concepts from Cubism, Expressionism, and Futurism. This interpretation made special use of the technical resources of modernity as well as addressing the ever-present confrontation between man and machine. The contradictions between these avant-garde movements that arose in the nations of the periphery and the reality of underdevelopment in which these very nations found themselves were always internally conflictual and were taken up once more in the 1950s by *Concretismo*, the Concretist poetry movement in São Paulo. Haroldo de Campos points to the discussion around *Concretismo* about the avant-garde and underdevelopment in his article entitled "A poesia concreta e a realidade nacional" ["Concretist Poetry and the Nation's Reality"]: "Pode um país subdesenvolvido produzir uma literatura de exportação? Em que medida uma vanguarda universal pode ser também regional ou nacional? Pode-se imaginar uma vanguarda engajada?"(1979, 28) ("Can an underdeveloped nation produce a literature for export? To what extent can a universal vanguard also be regional or national? Can one imagine a vanguard movement that is politically committed?"). Placing himself in Oswald's tradition, Haroldo de Campos defends *antropofagia* as a means of artistic minimalism and incorporation, in which the concept of the national expands to an international dimension, not allowing any space for cultural inferiority complexes. Campos's artistic minimalism was of course quite selective of what it took from *antropofagia*, which is thereby transformed into cultural wealth, art for export–it offered a positive solution for a provincial nation like Brazil in the 1920s. The end of the denial of underdevelopment, combined with the realization of Brazil's unique culture, proved to be one of the most fecund results of dependency theory in the 1960s, a theory which had been sketched out in Oswald de Andrade's *antropofagia*, as we have seen.

Mário da Silva Brito in his "História do modernismo brasileiro" [1978; "History of Brazilian Modernism"] assesses the importance of the movement, seen as a first attempt at awaking Brazilian literature from the sleep of alienation in its own formal "Paradise Lost" and placing it back into history (see Campos 1979, 28):

> O desejo de atualizar as letras nacionais–apesar de para tanto ser preciso importar idéias nascidas em centros culturais mais avançados–não implicava uma renegação do sentimento brasileiro. Afinal o que aspirava era tão somente a aplicação de novos processos artísticos às inspirações autóctones, e, concomitantemente, a colocação do país, então sob notável influxo de progresso, nas coordenadas estéticas já abertas pela nova era. (Brito 32)

> The desire to update national letters–although it would still depend on importing ideas from more advanced cultural centers–did not imply a denial of Brazilian sentiment. It simply aspired to apply new artistic processes to autochtonous inspiration, and, concomitantly, to place the nation, then already undergoing a notable increase in progress, into the esthetic coordinates open to the new era.

What can be called the utopic period in Brazilian arts and politics culminates in the construction of Brasília, a city that conjoined a utopic ideal of progress to the modern functionalism necessary for the development of such a massive project, which was headed by the then President Jucelino Kubitschek de Oliveira. The internationalization of national values was then justified by a capitalist economic development that was responsible for opening cultural frontiers and securing loans from developed nations. Concrete poetry, geometric abstraction in the visual arts, *bossa nova* and *cinema novo*, all represented a minimalist artistic style and the attempt to use an artistic language that could both be understood internationally and yet carry the mark of Brazilian nationality. This national mark, closely articulated with the State's political program, was the result of a social campaign characterized by its optimism and intent on integrating and planning a true national order.

In the words of the art critic Mário Pedrosa, the construction of Brasília represented a synthesis of the arts, because it represented the carrying out of a utopian project in the form of a work of art. Contrary to the reigning pessimism of *individualistic* art, it postulated *collective* work in the service of a social and political cause. The concept of the national responds to the concept of the modern in so far as the State's political project promoted the advancement of art and technology–as a strategy for control. Without ignoring the paradoxical relationship among aesthetics, technology, and politics, it is necessary to reflect on the coexistence, instated by the modernizing discourse of the time, of industrialization and the artistic avant-garde. Abstract art was a refusal, from the outset, to use the past as a model; it expressed the need to build nationality through international and cosmopolitan values. Brasília's modern construction, involving a heterogeneous union of disparate elements, led to a predictable contradiction between its revolutionary *form*, which elevated it to the same plane as constructions of the First World, and the social reality of the nation's backwardness and poverty. The euphoria that characterizes the eternal desire for change became an epidemic fever of the new, caused by the joint efforts of art and politics to redefine the meaning of national identity (E. M.de Souza 1993b, 152). Silviano Santiago, in "Poder e alegria–a literatura brasileira pós-64–reflexões" [1989; "Power and Joy–Brazilian Literature post-1964–Reflections"] provides us with an analytical summary of what he sees as the capitalizing of a knowledge born in Brazil of the period pre-1964 (the year of the military coup), comparing it to the period that followed immediately after:

> Perdendo o otimismo social edificante e construtivo, a literatura pós-64 não pode também ser aproximada, por movimentos de semelhança, da sua precedente imediata a produção dos chamados anos democráticos, que vão de 1945 a 1964. Seja na construção de Brasília a partir do nada, sonho de todo arquiteto e metáfora ideal para o artista de vanguarda, seja no transplante maciço de uma indústria automobilística estrangeira para o país, seja nas palavras de um teórico da poesia concreta que pedia aos pares para construírem "poemas à altura dos objetos racionalmente planejados e produzidos"–em tudo perpassava um otimismo construtor do tipo internacionalista que dizia que o bem e o bom estavam na *capitalização*. Na capitalização dos recursos econômicos estrangeiros e nacionais, aí também estava a "capitalização" de um saber brasileiro que trabalharia em favor de um Estado nacional forte e pujante, atrevido e esperançoso, que se lançaria a uma inédita explosão internacional. (1989, 18–19)

> Literature post 1964 loses its previous edifying and constructive social optimism, and cannot be understood by virtue of any similarities to its immediate precedents–the literary production of the so-called democratic years stretching from 1945 to 1964. Be it in the erection of the capital city Brasília from virtually nothing, every architect's dream and ideal metaphor for the avant-garde artist, be it in the wholesale transplanting of a foreign automobile industry to the country, be it in the words of a theorist of *concreta* [Concretist] poetry asking his colleagues to build "poems that measure up to rationally planned and produced objects," it was a period in which everything was threaded together by a constructive, internationalizing optimism that believed that all that was fair and good rested on *capitalization*. The capitalization of foreign and national economic resources coincided with the "capitalization" of a Brazilian knowledge that was to work in favor of a strong and powerful, audacious and hopeful national State, which would project itself into an international explosion of expression never before seen.

Published in 1965, the renowned film director Glauber Rocha's *Uma estética da fome* [An Aesthetics of Hunger] constituted one of the most important manifestos of the cultural situation of Latin American nations during that decade. Not restricting itself to the point of view of cinema, but crossing over into politics, the manifesto made its central point the impossibility of considering the *cinema novo* movement in Brazilian film apart from the political, cultural, and economic dependency the nation was subjected to (as, for that matter, was all of Latin America). The particular conditions of the period in which the manifesto was written–the military dictatorship and the ever-present spectre of the United States's imperialism–motivated Glauber Rocha to use an artistic medium for a critical denunciation of the absence of social liberties and, at the same time, for an exposition of the miseries of the Latin American continent. There is some common ground between the issues brought up in the aesthetics of hunger and *concretismo*'s proposals, such as the question of whether it is possible to produce art in an underdeveloped nation in face of the modernizing technological advances of First World nations. This issue is framed in the reality of underdevelopment in which luxury and penury share the same space, in which the new and the archaic are always in juxtaposition, and the pre-modern and post-modern are conjoined. *Concretismo* and Glauber Rocha's proposals diverge, however, when the former accepts a critical (and anthropophagic) incorporation of international aesthetics and the appropriation of foreign techniques as a necessary condition of artistic universality, since "o patrimônio mental é cada vez mais posto em termos universais, como se verifica cotidianamente nos domínios da ciência" (Campos 1979, 30) ("the mental heritage is ever more expressed in universal terms, as is verified daily in the dominions of science").

This concept was strongly rejected by Glauber Rocha, who in his *cinema novo* believed the greatest efficacy in making film for export resided in defending that aesthetics of hunger. Glauber's motto was "*uma camera na mão e uma idéia na cabeça*" ("an idea in [our] head and a camera in [our] hands"). Instead of *anthropophagic* incorporation, this is more *autophagic*, a self-devouring process of culture. He postulated the creation of a cultural imaginary of poverty to counter the trend of cinema of conspicuous consumption, of "filmes que se opõem à fome, como se, na estufa e nos apartamentos de luxo, os cineastas pudessem esconder a miséria moral de uma burguesia indefinida e frágil, ou se os próprios materiais técnicos e cenográficos pudessem esconder a fome que está enraizada na própria incivilização" (Rocha 16) ("films that do not show hunger, as if Brazil lived in the greenhouses and luxury apartments, as if it were possible for moviemakers to hide the moral poverty of an undefined and fragile bourgeoisie, or as if the very technical and cinematographic materials would be able to obfuscate the hunger that is rooted in our own denial civilization"). This was an esthetics that imposed itself through revolutionary violence at the service equally of truth and of the important causes that mark the political and artistic panorama of the time:

> A fome latina, por isto, não é somente um sintoma alarmante: é o nervo de sua própria sociedade. Aí reside a trágica originalidade do Cinema Novo diante do cinema mundial: nossa originalidade é nossa fome e nossa maior miséria é que esta fome, sendo sentida, não é compreendida. . . . Sabemos nós–que fizemos estes filmes feios e tristes, estes filmes gritados e desesperados onde nem sempre a razão falou mais alto–que a fome não será curada pelos planejamentos de gabinete e que os remendos do tecnicolor não escondem, mais agravam seus tumores. Assim, somente uma cultura da fome, minando suas próprias estruturas, pode superar-se qualitativamente: e a mais nobre manifestação cultural da fome é a violência. (Rocha 16–17)

Latin American hunger, therefore, is not just an alarming symptom: it's the very nerve of its society. That is where the tragic originality of *cinema novo* resides in world cinema: Our originality is our hunger, and the immense misery that is this hunger, that is felt but not understood. . . . We know–we who produce these sad and ugly films, these screaming, desperate films, in which we do not always mirror the triumph of reason–that hunger will not be resolved in cabinet meetings and that Technicolor will not disguise but only aggravate its tumors. It is therefore only a culture of hunger that, by undermining its own structure can overcome hunger, but we must remember that the most noble cultural manifestation of hunger is violence.

If a solution was advocated in the 1930s in the state's modernizing projects instituted with the aid of Modernism's foremost intellectuals, the reverse side of the coin reflects not only the disjunction between literary ideals and state nationalization, but also that nations on the periphery of economic and political power have opened up to cultural universalization, which is translated into an undifferentiated and homogenizing modernization. A consciousness of the conceptual complexity that dominates this form of reasoning allows Brazilians, to confront the continuous development of postmodern positioning which is responsible for today's discussion of transculturation.

Translation by Lis Horta Moriconi

Works Cited

Andrade, Mário de. 1983. *Entrevistas e depoimentos.* Edited by Telê Porto Ancona Lopez. São Paulo: T. A. Queiroz.

——. 1987. "O trovador." *Paulicéia desvairada. Poesias completas.* Edited by Diléa Zanotto Manfio. Belo Horizonte: Itatiaia; São Paulo: Editora da Universidade de São Paulo. 83.

——. 1988. *Macunaíma: o herói sem nenhum caráter.* Edited by Telê Porto Ancona Lopez. Paris: Association archives de la littérature Latino-Américaine, des Caraïbes et Africaine du XXe siècle; Brasília: CNPq.

Andrade, Oswald de. 1966. *Poesias reunidas.* São Paulo: Difusão Européia do Livro.

——. 1972. "Manifesto antropófago." *Obras completas.* Vol 6: *Do Pau-Brasil à antropofagia e às utopias.* Rio de Janeiro: Civilização Brasileira. 11–19.

Arantes, Paulo Eduardo. 1992. *Sentimento da dialética na experiência intelectual brasileira: dialética e dualidade segundo Antonio Candido e Roberto Schwarz.* Rio de Janeiro: Paz e Terra.

Bomeny, Helena Maria Bousquet. 1994. *Guardiães da razão: modernistas mineiros.* Rio de Janeiro: Editora da Universidade Federal do Rio de Janeiro, Edições Tempo Brasileiro.

Brito, Mário da Silva. 1978. *História do Modernismo Brasileiro: antecedentes da Semana de Arte Moderna.* Rio de Janeiro: Civilização Brasileira.

Campos, Haroldo de. 1979. "A poesia concreta e a realidade nacional." *Arte em Revista* 1.1 (São Paulo): 27–31.

——. 1983. "Da razão antropofágica: diálogo e diferença na cultura Brasileira." *Boletim Bibliográfico da Biblioteca Mário de Andrade.* 44.1–4 (São Paulo): 107–27.

Candido, Antonio. 1969. *Formação da literatura brasileira: momentos decisivos.* 2 vols. São Paulo: Livraria Martins.

——. 1972. "Literatura e subdesenvolvimento." *América Latina em sua literatura.* Edited by César Fernández Moreno. São Paulo: Perspectiva. 343–62.

Cunha, Eneida Leal. 1997. "Leituras da dependência cultural." *Navegar é preciso, viver: escritos para Silviano Santiago.* Edited by Eneida Maria de Souza and Wander Melo Miranda. Belo Horizonte: Editora da Universidade Federal de Minas Gerais; Salvador: Editora da Universidade Federal da Bahia; Niterói: Editora da Universidade Federal Fluminense. 126–39.

Gomes, Paulo Emílio Salles. 1980. *Cinema, trajetória do subdesenvolvimento.* Rio de Janeiro: Paz e Terra.

Gomes, Renato Cordeiro. 1987–1988 "Para além das fronteiras: literatura e subdesenvolvimento, de Antonio Candido." *Ensaios de semiótica* 18–20 (Belo Horizonte): 117–25.

Lima, Luiz Costa. 1981. "Da existência precária: o sistema intelectual brasileiro." *Dispersademanda: ensaios sobre literatura e teoria.* By Luiz Costa Lima. Rio de Janeiro: Livraria Francisco Alves Editora. 30–56.

Lima, Rachel Esteves. 1997. "A crítica literária na universidade brasileira." Diss. Universidade Federal de Minas Gerais.

Mignolo, Walter. 1997. "Espacios geográficos y localizaciones epistemológicas o la ratio entre la localización geográfica y la subalternización de conocimientos." *Anais [do] 5o. Congresso Abralic: cânones & contextos.* Rio de Janeiro: Associação Brasileira de Literatura Comparada. 1: 91–105.

Moraña, Mabel. "Ideología de la transculturación." *Angel Rama y los estudios latinoamericanos.* Pittsburgh, PA: Instituto Internacional de Literatura Iberoamericana, Universidad de Pittsburgh. 137–45.

Piglia, Ricardo. 1991. "Memória y tradición." *2o Congresso Abralic: literatura e memória cultural: anais, Belo Horizonte 1991.* Belo Horizonte: Associação Brasileira de Literatura Comparada. 1: 61–64.

Prado, Paulo. 1966. ""Poesia Pau-Brasil." *Poesias reunidas.* By Oswald de Andrade. São Paulo: Difusão Européia do Livro. 59–63.

Rama, Ángel. 1982. *Transculturación narrativa en América Latina.* Mexico City: Siglo XXI.

Rocha, Glauber. 1979. "Uma estética da fome." *Arte em Revista* 1.1 (São Paulo): 15–17.

Sandroni, Carlos. 1988. *Mário contra Macunaíma: cultura e política em Mário de Andrade.* São Paulo: Edições Vértice; Rio de Janeiro: Instituto Universitário de Pesquisas do Rio de Janeiro.

Santiago, Silviano. 1978. "O entre-lugar do discurso Latino-Americano." *Uma literatura nos trópicos: ensaios sobre dependência cultural.* By Silviano Santiago. São Paulo: Editora Perspectiva. 11–28.

———. 1982. "Apesar de dependente, universal." *Vale quanto pesa (ensaios sobre questões político-culturais).* By Silviano Santiago. Rio de Janeiro: Paz e Terra. 13–24.

———. 1988. "Si eu soubesse." *A pedra mágica do discurso: jogo e linguagem em Macunaíma.* Edited by Eneida Maria de Souza. Belo Horizonte: Editora Universidade Federal de Minas Gerais. 15–22.

———. 1989. "Poder e alegria. A literatura brasileira pós-64–reflexões." *Nas malhas da letra: ensaios.* By Silviano Santiago. São Paulo: Companhia das Letras. 11–23.

———. 1991. "Oswald de Andrade: ou o elogio da tolerância racial." *2o Congresso Abralic: literatura e memória cultural: anais, Belo Horizonte 1991.* Belo Horizonte: Associação Brasileira de Literatura Comparada. 67–77.

———. 1996. "Atração do mundo (políticas de identidade e de globalização na moderna cultura brasileira)." *Gragoatá* 1 (Niterói): 31–53.

Santos, Roberto Corrêa dos. 1995. "O político e o psicológico, estágios de cultura." *Oswald Plural.* Edited by Gilberto Mendonça Teles et al. Rio de Janeiro: Editora da Universidade do Estado do Rio de Janeiro. 99–106.

Schwarz, Roberto. 1981. *Ao vencedor as Batatas: forma literária e processo social nos inícios do romance brasileiro.* São Paulo: Duas Cidades.

———. 1987a. "A carroça, o bonde e o poeta modernista." *Que horas são?* São Paulo: Companhia das Letras. 11–28.

———. 1987b. "Nacional por subtração." *Que horas são?* São Paulo: Companhia das Letras. 29–48.

Souza, Eneida Maria de., ed. 1988. *A pedra mágica do discurso: jogo e linguagem em Macunaíma.* Belo Horizonte: Editora Universidade Federal de Minas Gerais.

———. 1992. *Luiz Costa Lima: A crítica em palimpsesto.* Belo Horizonte: Faculdade de Letras da Universidade Federal de Minas Gerais.

———. 1993a. "Preguiça e Saber." *Cartas a Mário.* Edited by Eneida Maria de Souza. Belo Horizonte: Faculdade de Letras da Universidade Federal de Minas Gerais. 136–47.

———. 1993b. "Paisagens Pós-Utópicas." *Utopias: sentidos, Minas, margens.* Edited by Andrés Aparecida. Belo Horizonte: Editora Universidade Federal de Minas Gerais. 147–54.

Souza, Gilda de Mello e. 1979. *O tupi e o alaúde: uma interpretação de Macunaíma.* São Paulo: Livraria Duas Cidades.

PART THREE

LIMINALITY AND CENTRALITY OF LITERARY CULTURES IN THE TWENTIETH CENTURY

SECTION I

AMERINDIAN LITERARY CULTURES

Elizabeth Monasterios

toconitlacozq
in veve tlamanjtiliztli?

(Coloquios y doctrina cristiana)

¿destruiremos
la antigua regla de la vida?

(qtd. in León-Portilla 1986, 152–53)

Are we [now] to destroy
the ancient norm of our life?

(qtd. in Dussel 1995, 114)

In contrast to the nineteenth century, which concluded by celebrating Liberal Positivism, whose cultural logic was aimed at the extermination of indigenous cultures and the usurpation of common lands, the twentieth century ended in a conflict-ridden revitalization of indigenous history. "No more history without us" was the message in cultural terms of the most recent mass declarations emerging from Chiapas in Mexico and the Mapuche people in Chile. In both cases the protagonists demanded a place within the nations that had excluded them and stated the relevance of conserving their cultural heritage, that complex of knowledge accumulated throughout their history. These new events not only created a problem for the imminent emergence of globalization (characterized by the cultural standardization of a civilizing project proposed from the viewpoint of the interests of the free market) but also confronted a still unresolved problem in Latin American literature: The recognition and incorporation of the considerable wealth of the Amerindian cultural imaginary that had remained foreign to the canonical and lettered narrative. For a long time in Latin America it was thought that it was sufficient to broaden the parameters of literature to take into account the folkloric features or native vocabulary that produced a vivid effect in canonical texts. But the epistemological insufficiency of such strategies, and the theoretical lacunae that generated the difficult dialogue with cultures that bring colonial memories in their wake, suggested that the problem of incorporation posed by indigenous "literature" above all lay in the challenge of confronting cultural diversity from different theoretical frameworks, or at least ones more broadly based than those institutionalized by academic criticism in recent years (*mestizaje,*

hybridity, transculturation, heterogeneity, etc.). To produce this kind of reflection is to confront something that academic theory still has not been able to either take on or resolve: The destabilizing presence of different *cultural grammars* that are unknown to the literary canon but without which any attempt to understand Latin American literature remains inconclusive and in a state of self-denial.

The inclusion in this literary history of a section dedicated to the indigenous cultures and literatures springs from a desire to actualize this change experienced in Latin American studies, which permits theoretical formulations that were simply inconceivable a few years ago. For this to occur, the combined efforts of numerous researchers have been necessary—prior to the current project—in order to outline the viability of an indigenous literary corpus and to point out the relevance of including it in the history of Latin American literature outside the theoretical frameworks imposed by classic Indigenism. I am referring as much to those who initiated such a reflection (José Alcina Franch, José María Arguedas [1911–1969], Angel María Garibay, Dick Ibarra Grasso, Jesús Lara, Miguel León-Portilla, María Rostworowski, and Amos Segala, to name a few notable instances) as to those who continued the work by stating the problems and theorizing on postulates (Xavier Albó, Gordon Brotherston, Sara Castro-Klaren, Verónica Cereceda, Amaryll Chanady, Beatriz Garza Cuarón, Serge Gruzinski, Jorge Klor de Alva, Martin Lienhard, Carlos Montemayor, Alberto Moreiras, Luis Millones, Jürgen Riester, and William Rowe among others). Thanks to those mentioned, today it is no longer necessary to justify the consideration of an indigenous text or its inclusion in literary history. Our task has been to emphasize that from such a text (and the interpretations derived from it) a deeper understanding of the Latin American cultural process is possible and, at the same time, to reject the ethnocentrism that has characterized modernity throughout the twentieth century. The first hint of the destabilization of ethnocentrism arises from the new meaning acquired by indigenous cultural history once it is investigated from the viewpoint of its own discourse, in other words, within the cultural grammar that both organizes and explains it. This grammar can be accessed through the great historical-cosmogonic narratives (which Brotherston calls the books of the Fourth World and that include the

Watunna [*Celebration*] of the Soto Carib, the *Ayvu Rapyta* [*Origin of the Human Language*] of the Tupi-Guarani, the *Tatkan ikala* [*Way of the Ancestors*] of the Kuna, the *Runa yndio* or *Manuscrito de Huarochirí* of the Quechuas (see *Dioses y hombres de Huarochirí*), the *Popol Vuh* [*Book of Counsel*] of the Quiché Maya, the *amoxtli* [painted books] written in Nahuatl, the *Ritual de los Bacabes* [*Ritual of the Bacabs*] and *El libro de los libros de Chilam Balam* [*Books of Chilam Balam*] of the Maya, *La palabra de Esnwerta* of the Chamoco people, etc.), but it can also be accessed by pursuing the cultural strategies with which indigenous peoples have responded to the different forms of aggression they have been subjected to by Western modernity. It is specifically in these strategies of survival that indigenous subjects incorporate knowledge that refers back to their narratives and calls attention to the extraordinary continuity and transformation of epistemologies that to this day has been little understood outside of these communities.

Both procedures have been tackled in this section of the book. The contribution of Miguel León-Portilla, which sums up a lifetime of extremely demanding research initiated in 1964 with the publication of *Las literaturas precolombinas de México* [*Pre-Columbian Literatures of Mexico*, 1969], provides ways of access to the indigenous cultural logic through an interdisciplinary study of the great Nahuatl, Maya, Mixtec, Zapotec, Tarascan, and Otomi narratives. Implicit is the idea developed by nineteenth-century Eurocentric pseudo-science purporting that the unlettered condition of indigenous antiquity reduced Amerindians to the status of primitive societies; this cultural blindness had not lost all validity and authority even by the mid-twentieth century. Writing, as will later be emphasized by the contribution of Denise Arnold and Juan de Dios Yapita, exists in all parts of Latin America, ranging from the landscape, textiles, and ceramics to systems equivalent to alphabetic writing such as the Andean *quipus,* the Mesoamerican *amoxtli,* or the dry paintings of the north of the continent. León-Portilla's contribution invites us to rethink the dichotomy of *orality* and *writing* that to date has oriented the study of indigenous cultures and a good part of Latin American cultural studies, a practice that in truth is deceptive, given that it conceals knowledge of pre-Hispanic writing practices. As Brotherston observes in *Book of the Fourth World*, this involves the risk of denying these cultures the capacity for self-reflection and symbolic representation. Bearing these factors in mind and through dialogue with Gruzinski and Klor de Alva, León-Portilla achieves his own self-criticism in *El destino de la palabra* (1996, 21–24 [*Destiny of the Word*]), where he admits the possibility that his work as translator of the *antigua palabra* ("ancient word") might have been produced in a climate of cultural contamination that adulterated the indigenous vision of the world. The road now lies open for investigating that vision without the superimposition of cultural logics alien to it.

The contributions discussed so far are very useful for broadening the limits of cultural theory, given that, without limiting themselves to theorizing the colonial or subaltern condition of the indigenous subject, they approach it instead as a subject of knowledge. Indigenous literatures are made relevant not only because they involve colonial memories of exploitation and cultural marginalization but also because they are capable of producing knowledge. To respond to that knowledge, thereby admitting it as an interlocutor in the cultural dialogue within the academic community, is the challenge posed by the contribution of León-Portilla. Dialogue with the Amerindian culture, if it is to succeed, must

also listen to the great historic-cosmogonic narratives from ancient sources as well as in their contemporary versions. Despite the manipulations of evangelization, the reduction to Western alphabetic writing, and the arbitrariness of interpretation imposed by anthropology and ethnography during the 1960s, the ancient narratives survive and challenge the monopoly of sixteenth-century narratives (Spanish chronicles of the Conquest) as well as cultural historiography to give an account of indigenous cultural histories. Through these narratives we learn that the traditional Amerindian world, which the occidental began to know at the end of the fifteenth century by means of the work of missionaries and their native informants, created a coherent and compact cultural worldview that had knowledge of itself. The epicenters of this new world were four zones that from ancient times had functioned as important cultural and migratory nuclei: The islands and coasts of the Caribbean, Mesoamerica, Amazonia, and the Andes. Each of these zones had developed systems of agrarian technology, communications networks, techniques of representation, and writing systems that ensured the survival and cultural continuity of the region. The different expansions and migrations that took place from these nuclei have drawn attention to the existence of autonomous cultures outside of the hegemonic powers, such as those of the Chaco, Chiquita, and Mapuche, which to date have been little studied and even excluded from the Amerindian canon.

In these great historical-cosmogonic narratives we also find the first indigenous reflections on colonial enslavement. The final pages of the *Popol Vuh*, for example, register the social collapse suffered as a result of the arrival of the Spaniards and how this disarticulated the internal logic of the indigenous world, demanding from its inhabitants a cultural readjustment whose principal aim was to eradicate the spiritual foundation that explained and conceptualized the Amerindian world. More incisive, the *Watunna* of the Sotocarib perceived Columbus as the cause behind the "homicidal madness" known as *kanaima* that destroyed the people of the Caribbean. In the same vein, the *Tatkan ikala* of the Kuna tells how the Spanish conquistadors tortured indiscriminately in their lust for gold (Wassén 22–25). In Mexico, many Nahuatl *cuicatl* (poems) included in the manuscript of the *Cantares mexicanos* lament the loss of the Mexica nation and adopt a historically based awareness of the radical alienation of all their children. In a very similar manner, *El libro de los libros de Chilam Balam* [*Books of Chilam Balam*] express profound grief: "entristezcámonos porque vinieron, porque llegaron los grandes amontonadores de piedras . . . que estallan fuego al extremo de sus brazos" (qtd. in Dussel 1994, 144) ("Let us mourn because they came, because these great gatherers of rocks arrived . . . who explode fire from their arms' extremities" [qtd. in Dussel 1995, 114]). In all cases, recurrent themes appear with variants symptomatic of the history of each region in the register of ethnography but also in those of writers and local scholars who, without concerning themselves about publication, process the historical reality that has fallen to their lot (see Millones).

The cognitive value of these narratives lies in the effectiveness with which they continue to develop elements of self-criticism, which would appear to indicate that our consideration of them would require something more than the current postcolonial perspective. Although postcolonial criticism grants these stories legitimate places of enunciation (Mignolo 509–24), it has the limitation of privileging them as discourses of difference and, as such, converting them into an object of study, thus leaving in second place the confrontation with the Western concept of representation and production of knowledge. We still need to develop an approach to learn the dialogue of these narratives and to make contact with the cultural grammar that organizes them. This is precisely what the European concept of cultural superiority rejected as a possibility, despite the effort of the conquered to make the rationality of their own thought intelligible to the conquerors.

The manuscript of *Coloquios y doctrina cristiana*, produced three years after the fall of Tenochtitlan, reflects like no other historical document the argumentative skill with which the last survivors of the Aztec *calmecac* demonstrated their rationality in the face of the discourse of nascent European modernity. Its authors are the last of the *tlamatinime* who, interrogated by the twelve Franciscan friars, presented their *palabra* ("word"). The culminating moment of this argument arrives when the Aztec elders rejected the evangelizing project with a vigorous argument on the issue of truth:

Anqujmjtjtalhuja
ca amo tictiximachilia
in tloque navaque
in ilhuicava in tlalticpaque.
anqujmjtalhuja
ca amo nelli teteu in toteuvan.
Ca yancuic tlatolli
in anqujmjtalhuia,
auh ic titotlapolotia,
ic titotetzauja.
Ca in totechiuhcava
yn oieco, yn onemjco tlalticpac,
amo iuh qujtotiuj,
ca iehoantin techmacatiuj
yn jntlamanjtiliz,
iehoantin qujneltocatiuj,
quintlaiecultitiuj,
qujn maviztilitiuj in teteu:
iehoantin techmachtitiaque
in ixquich intlaiecoltiloca
Auch cujx ie teoantin,
toconitlacozq
in veve tlamanjtiliztli?
in chichimeca tlamanjtiliztlj?
in tolteca tlamanjtiliztli?
in colhuaca tlamanjtiliztli?
in tepaneca tlamanjtiliztli?
Huj, tetecujoane,
ma itla anqujchiualtihtin
in amocuitlapiltzin, yn amatlapaltzin,
quenoc quilcavaz,
quenoc qujpoloz.

Vosotros dijísteis
que nosotros no conocíamos
al Dueño del cerca y del junto,
a aquél de quien son el cielo, la tierra
Habéis dicho
que no son verdaderos dioses los nuestros.
Nueva palavra es esta,
la que habláis,
y por ella estamos perturbados,
por ella estamos espantados.
Porque nuestros progenitores,
los que vinieron a ser, a vivir en la tierra
no hablaban así.
En verdad ellos nos dieron

sus normas de vida,
tenían por verdaderos,
servían,
reverenciaban a los dioses.
Ellos nos enseñaron
todas sus formas de culto
Y ahora, nosotros,
¿destruiremos
la antigua regla de la vida?
¿la regla de vida de los chichimecas?
¿la regla de vida de los toltecas?
¿la regla de vida de los colhuacas?
¿la regla de vida de los tecpanecas?
Señores nuestros,
no hagáis algo
a vuestro pueblo
a vuestra cola, vuestra ala,
que lo haga perecer . . .

(qtd. in León-Portilla 1986, 148–53)

You have said
that we do not know
the lord-of-intimate-which-surrounds-us,
the one from who the-heavens-and-the-earth come.
You have said
that our gods are not true gods.
We respond that
we are perturbed
and hurt by what you say
because our progenitors
never spoke this way.
Our progenitors passed on
the *norm of life*,
they held as *true*,
and the doctrine that we should
worship and honor the gods.
They taught us
All their forms of worship.
Are we now
to destroy
the ancient *norm of our life*?
For the Chichimecs,
the Toltecs,
the Acolhuas,
and the Tecpanecas?
listen liege lords,
do not inflict
on your people, something
that brings disgrace,
that will cause us to perish.

(qtd. in Dussel 1995, 113–14)

As Enrique Dussel suggests, this document has rarely been studied for what it really is, an extraordinary demonstration of poetic rhetoric ("Flower and Song") and a way to gain an awareness of how the Aztec elders comprehended the fact that the Conquest had produced the first cultural rupture of the colonial condition. In contrast to the Franciscans, who with simple-minded optimism predicted the success of evangelization, the last *tlamatinime* foresaw the immeasurable destruction of the project, understanding that "destruir la antigua regla de la vida" ("to destroy the ancient rule of life") would not be without long-lasting spiritual wounds and that no culture changes its imaginary horizon without the intervention of violence. The Aztec learned class, who were familiar with "the Lord-of-nearness-that-surrounds-us," would not "tomar por verdad" ("accept as truth") the words of the conquistadors. The Spanish response to this sophisticated argument was a campaign of intensified destruction of the cultural memory of the people to convert each *tlamatine* into an idolator (and his truth into idolatry) and therefore to be condemned as irrational enemies.

Three centuries later, with the advent of the first republics and the intellectuals of the Enlightenment, Indian subjects became the agents of barbarism who had to be exterminated or civilized. In the first years of the twentieth century, Positivist racist ideology and political Liberalism considered the indigenous population as a biological problem that was an obstacle to the progress of modern societies. The solutions that were then provided for the "Indian problem" emerged from rationalizing discourses bolstered by the pseudo-science of the late nineteenth century that "scientifically" proved the racial inferiority of the Indians. In the first decades of the twentieth century, *mestizaje* became the solution of choice for diluting the barbarism of the Indian with the civilization of the white population. The racism of the previous century was just as destructive as this "benign" solution, since the only "rational" thought that was recognized as valid was the Eurocentric epistemology of positivist pseudo-science. The first works of literary Indigenism were written precisely within these theoretical frameworks, attaining their most negative expression with Alcides Arguedas's (1879–1946) *Pueblo enfermo* [1909; Sick Nation] and *Raza de Bronze* [1919; Bronze Race].

In the second half of the twentieth century literary *indigenismo* had moved a considerable distance from its nineteenth-century models, but only occasionally (for example, in the case of José María Arguedas (1911–1969)) was it able to express a cultural logic different from that of the dominant class. *Indigenismo* created a complex literary corpus parallel to the Latin American "boom" of the 1960s but was excluded from literary histories because it was considered ethnography, as opposed to literature–in the limited idea of this that still prevailed. José María Arguedas himself, while writing the novel that would take him outside the theoretical framework of *indigenismo* (*El Zorro de arriba y el zorro de abajo* [*The Fox from Up Above and the Fox from Down Below*, 2000], published posthumously in 1971), presented the complex process of readjustment that affected the Andean cultures in their confrontation with capitalist modernization. But while this awareness was accompanied by an increasing sense of an immeasurable and nonterritorial reality, which began to constitute symbolic territories of representation, José María Arguedas experienced, as the *tlamatinime* had centuries before, the rending impossibility of harmonious cooperation between antagonistic cultural camps. The transcultural model, which during these same years had been outlined by Ángel Rama (1926–1983) and, at least theoretically, promised to open up possibilities for participation to the Amerindian cultures that had been marginalized by the machinery of modernization, also remained outside Arguedas's horizon–which demanded more radical theories. Other Latin Americanists, however, adopted transculturation and from the academic world launched theoretical proposals that, based on Rama's interpretations, saw in Arguedas's novel the first symptoms of a changing, protean, and uncontrollable reality that would later be recognized as postmodern and transnational. In this context, the indigenous subject was now no longer defined in terms of traditional identities but in terms of degrees of belonging to multiple cultural identities or as an authentic subject belonging to no specific national entity. The most important

issue was to demonstrate that between an indigenous subject and Western modernity there are multiple encounters and evasions with subsequent cultural fractures and continuities that are far more important than obvious physical movement from closed to open communities. Concepts such as transculturation (see Ortiz; Rama), heterogeneity (see Cornejo Polar), and hybridity (see García Canclini) have been successively proposed to hypothesize this condition of extreme plurality and multiculturalism.

The cultural debate in Latin America outlines the necessity of taking on the study of indigenous cultures and literatures that exist and have existed on the fringes of a discursive logic that is foreign to them; it is incumbent on Latin Americanists to employ the conceptualization and forms of understanding of the indigenous people themselves and of their history, daily life, and worldview. The contribution of Denise Y. Arnold and Juan de Dios Yapita is set up specifically from this perspective. Focused on the Andean region, with particular emphasis on the Aymara context (which is less known than the Quechua), this research consolidates the opening of new directions for the study of indigenous cultures and literatures. Putting to one side both the idea of an unlettered Andean America and also the structuralist postulate that orality manifests a primitive culture, which must become a culture of written texts if it is to achieve its own mission as a civilization, Arnold and Yapita assert that in these cultures "writing" has always been everywhere (from the configuration of a handful of coca leaves to an engraving in stone, the design of a textile, a glyph, and the alphabetic script itself, which, in this order of things, occupies a relative position that is by no means exclusive), and its function has always been that of producing knowledge. From these premises they investigate the nature of Andean literature, its broad tradition of nonoccidental "writing," its methods of transmission and cultural resistance, its conflict-ridden contacts with modernity, and its difficult process of incorporation into the national institutional sphere. The analysis that they offer indicates that, despite considerable achievements, the study of Andean literatures continues to be guided by the idea of a cultural rescue operation of subaltern expression without proposing that the Andean indigenous world constitutes a mass ethnicity that has for centuries been acting on its own account and establishing its historical interlocutors. It would therefore be with some violence to the reality of the indigenous peoples that we continue to narrate for them or try to incorporate their cultural languages into our incompatible Western cultural and theoretical models. One can only hope that this new century begins by finally producing occasions for open dialogue between distinct subjects and their distinct approaches to knowledge, so that cultural difference will not be a problem to be eliminated but a challenge to be addressed, and that the knowledge produced by the indigenous people will finally take its place as part of the rich heterogeneity that is Latin America. The impact of these theories on the conceptualization of indigenous cultures was to have a markedly deterritorializing effect. Not only did they not generate significant changes in the perception of the indigenous peoples (whose cultural logic continued to be an enigma to the majority of the population) but they also constructed the theoretical category of the *marginal hybrid* as a product of transculturation; inclusion or exclusion from this category is based on the degree of liminality these groups have in the different worlds in which they live. In its most dramatic configuration, the image is determined as a subject trapped in the dialectic of capitalist reterritorialization that reproduces the subaltern other to the extent that this other is incorporated into a socio-cultural order whose only discursive memory is global production and the international marketplace (Kraniauskas 150; Mariaca 44).

Translation by Jessica Johnson

Works Cited

Arguedas, Alcides. 1909. *Pueblo enfermo.* Barcelona: Viuda de Luis Tasso.

——. 1945 [1919]. *Raza de bronce.* Buenos Aires: Editorial Losada.

Arguedas, José María. 1990 [1971]. *El zorro de arriba y el zorro de abajo.* Ed. Eve-Marie Fell. Madrid: Archivos.

Ayvu Rapyta. 1959. Ed. León Cadogan. São Paulo: Faculdade de Filosofia, Ciencias e Letras, Universidade de São Paulo.

The Books of Chilam Balam of Chumayel. 1913. Ed. G. B. Gordon. Philadelphia: U of Pennsylvania P. Facsimile.

Brotherston, Gordon. 1992. *Book of the Fourth World: Reading the Native Americas Through their Literature.* Cambridge: Cambridge UP.

Cantares mexicanos. 1994. Facsimilie edition of the anonymous manuscript conserved at the Biblioteca Nacional de México. Ed. Miguel León-Portilla. Mexico City: Universidad Nacional Autónoma de México.

Cornejo Polar, Antonio. 1978. "El indigenismo y las literaturas heterogéneas: su doble estatuto socio-cultural." *Revista de crítica literaria Latinoamericana* 7–8:7–21.

Dioses y hombres de Huarochirí. Narración quechua recogida por Francisco de Avila. 1966 [1598?]. Ed. José María Arguedas and Pierre Duviols. Lima: Museo Nacional de Historia e Instituto de Estudios Peruanos.

Dussel, Enrique. 1994. *1492. El encubrimiento del otro: hacia el origen del mito de la modernidad.* La Paz: Plural Editores y Facultad de Humanidades y Ciencias de la Educación, Universidad Mayor de San Andrés.

——. 1995. *The Invention of the Americas: Eclipse of "the Other" and the Myth of Modernity.* Trans. Michael D. Barber. New York: Continuum.

García Canclini, Néstor. 1990. *Culturas híbridas: estrategias para entrar y salir de la modernidad.* Mexico City: Grijalbo.

Klor de Alva, Jorge. 1988. "Sahagún and the Birth of Modern Ethnography: Representing, Confessing, and Inscribing the Native Other." *The Work of Bernardino de Sahagún: Pioneer Ethnographer of Sixteenth-Century Aztec Mexico.* Ed. Jorge Klor de Alva, H.B. Nicholson and Eloise Quiñones Keber. Albany: State U of New York. 31–52.

Kraniauskas, John. 1992. "Hybridism and Reterritorialization." *Travesía* 1/2: 143–51.

León-Portilla, Miguel. 1964. *Las literaturas precolombinas de México.* Mexico City: Pormaca.

——, ed. 1986. *Coloquios y doctrina cristiana: los diálogos de 1524.* Mexico City: Universidad Nacional Autónoma de México.

——. 1996. *El destino de la palabra. De la oralidad y los códices mesoamericanos a la escritura alfabética.* Mexico City: Fondo de Cultura Económica.

El Libro de los libros de Chilam Balam. 1965. Ed. Alfredo Barrera Vásquez. Trans. Alfredo Vásquez and Silvia Rendón. Mexico City: Fondo de Cultura Económica.

Mariaca, Guillermo. 1999. *Los refugios de la utopía. Apuntes teóricos para una política inter-cultural.* La Paz: Embajada Real de los Países Bajos y Ministerio de Desarrollo Sostenible y Planificación.

Mignolo, Walter. 1995. "Occidentalización, imperialismo, globalización: herencias coloniales y teorías postcoloniales." *Memorias. Jornadas Andinas de Literatura Latinoamericana.* La Paz: Plural editores y Facultad de Humanidades y Ciencias de la Educación, Universidad Mayor de San Andrés. 509–24.

Millones, Luis. 1998. "Perspectiva andina de las culturas literarias de América Latina: la tradición oral." The Formation of Literary Cultures in Spain, Portugal, and Latin America. Third International Colloquium of the Nortel Ibero-American Professorship, University of Toronto, 19 May.

Ortiz, Fernando. 1963. *Contrapunteo cubano del tabaco y el azúcar.* Havana: Consejo Nacional de Cultura.

Popol Vuh. 1989. Ed. Carmelo Saenz de Santa María. Madrid: Historia 16.

Rama, Ángel. 1982. *Transculturación narrativa en América Latina.* Mexico City: Siglo XXI.

Ritual de los bacabes. 1987. Ed. Ramón Arzápalo Marín. Mexico City: Universidad Nacional Autónoma de México.

Wassén, S. Henry, G. Haya, and Rubén Pérez Kantule, ed. *Original Documents from the Kuna Indians of San Blas.* Goteborg: Ethnografiska Museum.

Watunna: Mitología makiritare. 1970. Ed. Marc de Civrieux. Caracas: Monte Avila.

CHAPTER 32

LITERATURES OF MESOAMERICA

Miguel León Portilla

Over the past few decades, the literary production of ancient Mexico has attracted the attention of scholars and intellectuals in all fields of knowledge. The existence of codices and other literary texts, together with the intensive work undertaken in archaeological zones, has clarified chronological sequences and cultural models that were unknown until recently. On the basis of this research, a number of specialists have begun to evaluate the various artistic forms underlying pre-Hispanic works. Specialized criticism has recently focused on researching the world of symbols and ideas underlying the cultural legacy of ancient Mexico.

Linguists, philologists and historians, guided by a new critical awareness, have made significant contributions to the analysis and study of manuscripts, annals, and chronicles, which contain numerous hymns, poems, songs, accounts by village elders, legends, and examples of pre-Hispanic prose. Although this work has only just begun, its potential scope can already be gaged. Some years ago (1964), I published an initial approach to this theme entitled *Las literaturas precolombinas de México* [*Pre-Columbian Literatures of Mexico*]. I returned to this work on several occasions, with the aim of updating the information in it and disseminating the new discoveries of texts and other ancient works. In 1969, I expanded the original version for its translation into English. In 1978, at the invitation of the Ayacucho Library, I published a more extensive version of the Náhua context in *Literatura del México antiguo* [*Literature of Ancient Mexico*]. In *Literaturas de Mesoamérica* [*Literatures of Mesoamerica*], published in 1984, I included testimonies that had not been studied until then. The second English edition of *Las literaturas precolombinas de México* was eventually published in 1986. This chapter is a summary of these publications, my aim here being to acquaint contemporary readers with the central nucleus of what could be described as a corpus of Mesoamerican literary production. This corpus is part of the Aztec or Mexica cultural legacy and that of its closest neighbors and predecessors, who spoke the same Náhuatl language (the lingua franca of ancient Mexico), and also that of certain groups of the great Mayan family. I shall also refer, to a lesser extent, to the literary productions of the Mixtecs and Zapotecs of Oaxaca, the Tarascans of Michoacan, and the forgotten Otomís of Central Mexico.

A brief look at the evolution of these cultures over the centuries, focusing on the aspects that led to their literary expression, will serve to begin to explain their meaning, their origins, and the way they were preserved. Starting from a paradigmatic historical event (the arrival of the Spanish conquerors in 1519), this analysis will delve into the past to discover the oldest faces of pre-Columbian civilization in Mexico. Those unfamiliar with the wealth of materials available to explore and assess pre-Hispanic literary creations will undoubtedly wonder how these peoples were able to conceive, preserve, and transmit their cultural legacy. What strategies did they use to protect them from destruction during the Conquest, and enable them to survive, at least partially, until the present? What and where are the principal native literary works? Did the Indian scholars describe and conceptualize the various forms of their own literary expression?

Studying the sources–codices and ancient texts–provides the answer to these questions together with an appreciation of the literary works themselves. In this essay, I shall explore a broad selection of texts, including religious myths and rituals, lyric poetry, the first expressions of theater art, and various forms of prose, together with the most dramatic Indian literary testimony: The native chronicles of the Conquest with their permanent record of what I have called *Visión de los vencidos* [1963; *The Broken Spears,* 1992]. I should also point out that I am more interested in this text in acquainting contemporary readers with the marvelous symbolic world of these literatures than in providing an in-depth study.

Early Sixteenth-Century Aztecs

When the Spanish conquerors reached Central Mexico in November 1519, they were astonished by the splendor of the Aztec metropolis, México-Tenochtitlán. Both Hernán Cortés (1485–1547), in his letters to Charles V, and Bernal Díaz del Castillo (1492–1584), in his *Historia verdadera de la conquista de la Nueva España* [1632; *The Discovery and Conquest of Mexico, 1517–1521,* 1956], like other Spanish chroniclers of the Conquest, speak admiringly of the beauty of Tenochtitlán–its wide causeways linking the island to land; its palaces and temples; its markets, gardens, and orchards; its canals; and, above all, its extraordinary central enclosure, with the seventy-eight ceremonial buildings of the Templo Mayor. Today, one can see the remains of its successive constructions, thanks to the archaeological excavations undertaken since 1978. However, the conquerors not only were dazzled by the plan of the city, its architecture and innumerable monuments and paintings; they soon noticed the complexity of the Aztec people's social, economic, religious, political and cultural organization.

The first conquerors were witnesses to the greatness of Moctezuma and perceived the shrewdness of the traders, the strength of the warriors, and the wisdom of the priests and leaders, who, in addition to presiding over religious affairs, played an important role as political advisors. Veritable fonts of knowledge, the priests were responsible for the education of the youth, and for preserving esoteric knowledge, the calendrical tradition, and the art of writing in painted books and manuscripts. Bernal Díaz del Castillo described the houses, schools, and temples where they kept "muchos libros de su papel, cogidos a dobleces, como a manera de paños de Castilla" (1955, 1: 143) ("many paper books doubled together in folds like Spanish cloth"; 1933, 140).

A few years later, the first Franciscan missionaries were even more impressed by the discovery of the existence of historical records, myths, and traditions, which the Aztecs preserved in books made from the bark of fig trees, or deerskin that had been treated and covered with white pigment. There is no need to repeat what happened to the majority of these books as a result of the friars' religious zeal, but it is worth noting that, although many missionaries devoted themselves to burning the manuscripts, others, such as Bernardino de Sahagún (1500?–1590) or Andrés de Olmos (ca. 1491–1571?), managed to save some ancient texts in order to study the native past. In these books, the Aztec scholars preserved their knowledge and the memory of their past and, through them, educated young people.

In México-Tenochtitlán and throughout the country, there were many types of schools, the best known of which were the *telpochcalli* (schools for young men) and the *calmécac* (centers of higher education). In both cases, but particularly in the *calmécac,* painted books were studied and memorized. These contained myths, chronicles, accounts of historical events and divine interventions, and even certain religious doctrines expressed in ideograms. Sahagún described the teaching methods used by the Aztec scholars as follows: "enseñaban todos los versos de canto, para cantar, que se llamaban divinos cantos, los cuales versos estaban escritos en sus libros por caracteres. . . . (También) enseñaban la astrología indiana, y las interpretaciones de los sueños y la cuenta de los años" (Sahagún 1956, 1: 307) ("they taught the songs, which they called the gods' songs. They were inscribed in the books in characters. . . . And as well they were all taught the reckoning of the days, the book of dreams, and the book of years"; 1933, Part 4: 65). Through this double procedure of transmission and systematic memorization, the Aztec priests and scholars disseminated and preserved their literary and religious legacy as it had been recorded in the codices through pictograms and ideograms.

Before proceeding to describe this type of writing in detail, it is worth asking whether the Aztecs were the creators of this educational system and the writing used in their codices. The question is crucial, particularly if one recalls that the Aztecs, the best known face of ancient Mexico, had been the lords and masters of the pre-Hispanic peoples for only a relatively short time. In fact, they had only reached the Valley of Mexico in the mid-thirteenth century CE. In 1325, they established their capital on the island in the center of the lake, yet they became independent only in 1428, after defeating the previous rulers, the Tepanecs of Azcapotzalco. Incredibly, in less than a century, they consolidated their dominance over the central and southern regions of what is now Mexico. The period of Aztec splendor that preceded the Spanish Conquest was historically brief.

The answer to our question above is provided by archaeology and by Indian historical sources. The Aztecs, like the Texcocans, the Tlaxcaltecans, and many other Náhuatl-speaking groups, were heirs to a much older culture. Many of their religious ideas, their social and political organization and their other institutions, particularly their plastic arts, the basis of their writing system, their calendrical calculations, and their teaching methods had been directly or indirectly obtained through contacts with more advanced cultures. In the case of the Aztecs, these contacts arose as a result of their settlement, during the twelfth and early thirteenth centuries, in territories belonging to the Tepanecs of Azcapotzalco and the more advanced Culhuacanos, who in turn had inherited much of early Toltec culture.

The Toltecs and Post-Classic Culture

According to the Indian chronicles and archaeological findings, the Toltec metropolis of Tula, located approximately one hundred kilometers north of Mexico City, experienced its flowering between the end of the ninth century and the eleventh century CE. The Toltecs, like the Mixtecs of Oaxaca and the Maya of northern Yucatán, had mastered the art of writing, as evinced, among other things, by their stone glyphs and

inscriptions from various periods showing the influence of the three cultures. Archaeology places the start of the post-Classic period of these cultures at the beginning of the tenth century CE.

In their texts, the Aztecs declared that the Toltecs were followers of the great scholar and priest Quetzalcóatl, who taught them many of their most important arts and religious doctrines. Legend has it that as a result of internal conflicts and external pressures, Tula was abandoned in about the twelfth century CE and that groups of Toltec migrants took their knowledge and arts with them to their various destinations. Some reached Yucatán; others remained in the vicinity and mingled with the peoples that already inhabited the central tableland, such as the Culhuacanos, who had settled along the south-east of the lake in the Valley of Mexico. The Culhuacanos became the main transmitters of Toltec culture to the groups that arrived from the north, such as the Aztecs.

The Mixtecs of Oaxaca, the source of the largest number of pre-Colombian codices that have been preserved, exerted a great influence over the peoples of central Mexico. The Mixtec art of writing and painting books was very similar to that used subsequently by the Aztecs and their neighbors, including the Texcocans. According to Indian sources, many Mixtec scholars settled among the Texcocans, who learned several skills from them, including writing (Fernando de Alva Ixtlilxóchitl, *Obras históricas* [1975–1977; *Historical Works*] 1:117). These scholars were called *tlailotlaque*, "those who had returned," probably in reference to the Toltecs who had joined the Mixtecs after Tula was abandoned. Central Mexico also contains signs of possible Mayan influence, such as the bas-reliefs on the pyramid at Xochicalco, near the city of Cuernavaca, where certain carved glyphs are reminiscent of calendrical calculations of Mayan origin. Despite this, evidence of Mayan presence is still inconclusive. What is certain is that the peoples who lived in the central zone of Mexico during the Aztec era received the Toltec and Mixtec cultural legacy.

Thus if, as a result of available testimonies of the Toltecs, Mixtecs, and Maya from the ninth to the eleventh century CE., we know that the writing in the codices, the stone inscriptions, and indeed the centers of education date back to the Post-Classic period, then we can formulate another question: Were these the peoples who invented the calendar, the writing, and the other systems of preserving knowledge? Or had the art of writing and the systems of oral education been handed down to them from even more ancient cultures? The answer lies in what archaeologists call the Classic period of splendor in Mesoamerica. The term *Mesoamerica* designates the area of high culture that, at the time of the Spanish Conquest, extended from the central zone of what is currently known as Mexico to the Central American regions in which the Maya and other groups lived in pre-Hispanic times (see **Map 1**).

The Classic Period—First Century to Tenth Century CE

In the central region of Mexico, not far from the Toltec metropolis of Tula, another culture, that of the Teotihuacanos, had flourished earlier, overlapping to a considerable extent with the Classic splendor of the Maya. It is in the City of the Gods, Teotihuacan, that archaeologists have found undeniable evidence of writing. One can therefore say that the systematic transmission of an ancient cultural tradition, together with the creation of various forms of writing, had already existed since the Classic period of pre-Columbian cultures among the Teotihuacanos, and above all in the Zapotec and

Map 1.

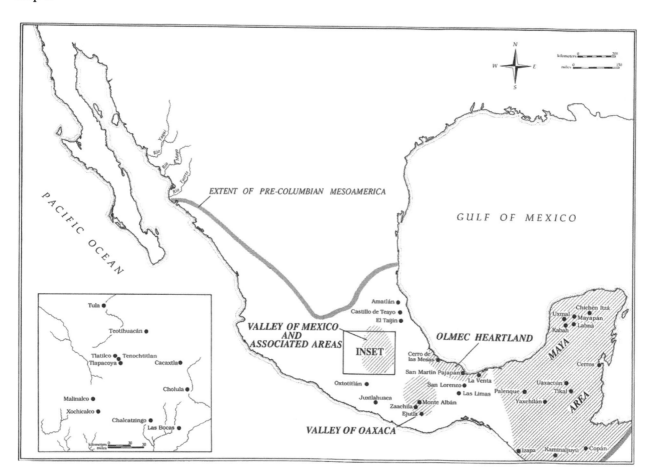

Map of Mesoamerica by Leonardo Manrique Castañeda. (Courtesy of Manrique Castañeda)

Mayan cultural centers. In Oaxaca, for example, near the area where the Mixtecs later achieved their splendor, lies Monte Albán, the most important remains of another extremely ancient culture. The Zapotecs, their descendants, continue using the language of their forebears to this day (see Chapter 11 in Volume I for an example). Mayan groups that had settled a long way from Yucatán, in the forests of Central America, had built important ceremonial centers in Copán, Tikal, Uaxactún, Yaxchilán, Palenque, and other places. All these archaeological sites have yielded temples and palaces built by pre-Columbian architects that, in addition to suggesting urban life, provide ample proof of writing, a calendrical system, and a definite historical awareness.

One can therefore conclude that the Classic period left countless inscriptions on stelae, temples, palaces, and even ceramic objects. Although most of the Mayan hieroglyphic texts have yet to be deciphered, those concerned with the system for counting the years and the representation of certain deities and famous governors, show a lengthy cultural sequence beginning with the Classic period and ending with the inscriptions in the three existing Mayan codices. In the case of the Teotihuacanos and Zapotecs, a number of inscriptions and dates have been found. As Alfonso Caso has shown, the Teotihuacanos were familiar with the ritual and astrological calendar that the Aztecs called *Tonalpohualli* and that the Maya referred to as *Tzolkin* and the Zapotecs as *Piye* (Alfonso

Caso 1936, 131–43 and César Lizardi Ramos 220–23). The builders of Teotihuacán, the City of the Gods, used the same glyphs that would subsequently be employed in the Aztec codices to depict flower and song, an expression meaning poetry; water and fire, meaning war, and other glyphs that expressed the idea of movement, certain attributes of the gods, and other concepts. The Zapotecs of the Classic period utilized an older form of writing, as shown by inscriptions dating from before the Common Era, found in the great center of Monte Albán. Late forms of Zapotec and calendrical writing would appear to derive from this ancient form.

Archaeology has established a lengthy sequence in the transmission of writing and the calendar, from the Classic period of Mesoamerica, showing a common concern shared by various cultures with preserving the memory of the past. From the study of architecture, sculpture, painting, ceramics, and the ancient worldview (as found in the inscriptions, codices, and texts existing among these peoples), one can assume that, despite local differences, they shared the same cultural origin, which is probably the oldest source of literary creation in late pre-Colombian Mexico. The problem of origins is always extremely complex, and in this case, archaeology has yet to find the final answer. However, there is evidence that sheds light on the possible mother culture from which so many peoples obtained, among other things, the precious knowledge of writing and ways of measuring time.

Figure 1.

Stelae 12 and 13 at Monte Albán, Oaxaca, c. 500–400 BCE. (Archive of the author)

The Olmecs

On the coasts of the Gulf of Mexico, on the borders of the present states of Veracruz and Tabasco, a region known to the Aztecs as rubber country (i.e., "the place of rubber trees"), the Olmec culture flourished. This people date from approximately 1,400 years before the Common Era, and archaeologists have found traces of their presence, or at least their influence, in many other regions, some far removed from the rubber country or the actual land of the Olmecs. Among these remains are some of the oldest inscriptions found to date in ancient Mexico. It is worth mentioning Stela C found in Tres Zapotes, Veracruz; the inscriptions found in the famous jade figure in Tuxtla, Veracruz; and the glyphs, older still, found in the ceremonial center of Monte Albán, Oaxaca, in the stela belonging to the group known as "The Danzantes" or dancers (see **Figure 1**). These Olmec-type inscriptions, regarded as the oldest in pre-Columbian Mexico, bear out the invention of an ancient system of writing or art of recording the past. Alfonso Caso provides a precise summary of what is known about the origins of writing and the calendar in ancient Mexico as a result of archaeological findings:

> De acuerdo a la prueba 14 de carbón, se ha determinado que existía una escritura y un sistema calendárico en Mesoamérica por lo menos a partir del año 600 antes de la época cristiana. Pero como el calendario de esa época muestra una perfección extraordinaria y está relacionado a muchos otros aspectos de la cultura mesoamericana (cerámica, escultura en piedra, jade, pirámides, palacios, etc.), se puede afirmar que fue el resultado de un largo proceso de desarrollo que comenzó muchos siglos antes de la era cristiana. (1962, 167–68).

> Carbon 14 testing has shown that writing and a calendrical system existed in Mesoamerica from at least 600 BCE. However, since the calendar of that time was extraordinarily accurate and was linked to many other aspects of Mesoamerican culture (ceramics, stone

sculpture, jade, pyramids, palaces, etc.), then it can be said to have been the result of a lengthy process of development that began many centuries before the Common Era.

The Aztecs appear to have been aware of the antiquity of the invention of writing and the calendar. In a text describing the origin of their culture, they note: "En un cierto tiempo que ya nadie puede contar, del que ya nadie ahora puede acordarse . . ." ("At a time that no one can reckon, that no one can remember . . ."), many years before the construction of Teotihuacan, on the Gulf coasts, there lived a people whose scholars and priests possessed many books of paintings and knowledge of how to measure time. This tribe appeared on the northern coast, not far from the mouth of the river Pánuco, and among them were

> aquellos que
> trajeron consigo
> la tinta negra y roja,
> los manuscritos y los libros de pinturas,
> la sabiduría.
> Trajeron todo con ellos,
> los anales,
> los libros de cantos, y sus flautas.

> those who
> brought with them
> the black and red ink,
> the manuscripts and the books of paintings,
> knowledge.
> They brought everything with them,
> the annals,
> the books of songs, and their flutes.

(Códice Matritense de la Real Academia, VIII, fol. 192r.)

It is impossible to tell whether these "knowers of things" were the Olmecs, to whom archaeology attributes the most ancient writing. However, archaeological research supports the Aztec belief that prior to the time of Teotihuacan, there were people on the Gulf Coast who possessed the art of writing and calendrics. It is universally accepted that the methods of preserving knowledge and the memory of the past among the native groups of Mexico have been developed within a cultural sequence and that its roots date back over 2,000 years (see **Figure 2**).

This brief review of Mexico's past shows that the various Aztec nations or Náhuatl speakers, as well as the Maya, the peoples of Oaxaca, and other groups I have not mentioned, were the cultural heirs of people who had already created a historic awareness and highly developed institutions. They were completely isolated from the ancient European and Asian civilizations, and they had their own culture hundreds of years before their contact with the Western world that would destroy them. When the Spanish conquerors came into contact with the Aztecs and Maya, these peoples still preserved much of their ancient cultural heritage. In order to understand how they managed to preserve the memory of their past and to continue producing art and literature, even after the Conquest, it is necessary to analyze their writing methods and their oral tradition, as they were taught in the pre-Columbian centers of education. (See Vol. 1, Ch. 46, this *History*.)

The Writing of Codices and the Memorization of Texts

Several of the Indian chroniclers and friar historians who arrived as a result of the Conquest mention the way in which oral teaching and the memorization of texts in pre-Hispanic schools served as an irreplaceable complement to

Figure 2.

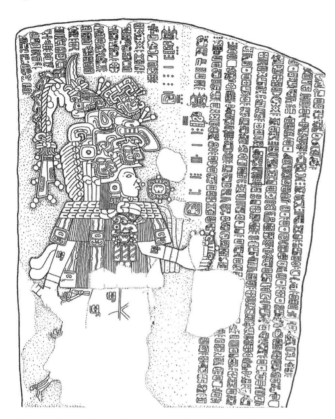

Olmec stela, La Mojura. Dates inscribed are 21 May 143 CE and 13 July 156 CE. (Archive of the author)

the transmission and preservation of the histories and doctrines contained in the Indian codices. Fray Diego de Durán (1537–1587), for example, noted that the Náhua teachers had "grandes y hermosos libros de pinturas y caracteres de todas estas artes por donde las enseñaban . . . " (1867, 2: 229) ("beautiful, large books of paintings and characters on all these arts by which they were taught . . . "). Realizing the impossibility of everyone having access to the books and codices, and aware of the inherent limitations of their writing system, teachers and scholars insisted on systematic memorization as a means of preserving tradition and knowledge. Teachers made their students memorize songs, poems, and speeches that contained an explanatory commentary on what the codices represented. Those who had memorized the texts, conceived as commentaries on the codices, and learned the doctrine, could appropriate the words of the Náhua poet:

Yo canto las pinturas del libro,
lo voy desplegando,
soy cual florido papagayo,
hago hablar a los códices,
en el interior de la casa de las pinturas.

I sing the paintings of the book,
I unfold it,
I am like a flowery parrot,
I make the codices speak,
within the house of the paintings.

(Cantares en Idiomas Mexicanos, Biblioteca Nacional de México, fol. 14 V).

Codices or paintings always formed the basis of teaching. In them, as another Indian text points out: "están escritos los cantos, por eso se despliegan junto a los atabales . . . " ("The songs are written, which is why they are unfolded next to the kettledrums"). And, as we shall see below, the Indian teachers used writing to record information about any event or doctrine. They could indicate the precise date, year, and day of any event, and they were able to symbolize abstract concepts about their religious doctrines, ceremonies, and legal regulations (see **Figure 3**). In short, they were able to produce charts of their doctrines and historical events. To show how these Náhuatl-speaking peoples did this immediately before the time of the Conquest, let us take a closer look at their writing. The Aztecs, the Texcocans, and the Tlaxcaltecans all used three main forms of writing: pictograms, ideograms, and another, partially phonetic system.

Pictographic writing, which is purely representative, is the most elementary form of pre-Columbian writing. In virtually all the Aztec codices which mention the pilgrimage of the seven Náhua tribes from the North, the *teomamas* (priests), who carry their protective gods on their backs, are painted schematically. The *calli* (houses), *tlachtli* (ballgames), *tlatoque* (lords) seated on their *icpalli* (thrones), and various tributes, such as blankets, feathers, cacao, sacks of maize, and other products are also drawn schematically.

As in other ancient cultures, the Náhua scribes progressed from the pictographic stage to that of ideographic glyphs, which are symbolic representations of ideas. Indian ideograms can be divided into three main groups; numerical, calendrical, and those representing abstract ideas such as movement *(ollin)*, life *(yoliliztli)*, and divinity *(teotl)*. The use of color is also symbolic. In the human figure, for example, yellow nearly always denotes the female sex; violet suggests the nobility of the *tlatoani* or principal lord; Blue represents the south, while black and red indicate writing and knowledge. Knowledge and interpretation of these ideographic glyphs require a depth of study that exceeds the aim of this text. Suffice it to say that among the Nahuatl-speaking peoples, as among the Maya, the Mixtecs, and the Zapotecs, writing on the basis of ideograms, particularly as regards numbers and calendrics, had enormous currency as a form of representation that was extremely precise, as well as expressive, even from a purely aesthetic point of view. Since there is no room for a detailed explanation here, I would refer readers to the work by Charles E. Dibble cited in the bibliography and to one of my own texts, *Los antiguos mexicanos a través de sus crónicas y cantares* (1961, 48–75) [*The Aztec Image of Self and Society: An Introduction to Nahua Culture,* 1992].

In addition to pictographic and ideographic glyphs, the ancient Mexicans' writing contained representations of sounds, in other words, the beginnings of phonetic writing. Nahuatl phonetic writing, known from the few extant codices, was primarily used to represent the names of persons and places. Native scribes developed a system of symbolic glyphs representing endings that indicated places, such as the well-known *-tlan* (place of), and *-pan* (on top of). The Nahuas eventually symbolized certain sounds of letters such as "a," "e," and "o", represented by means of the stylization of the pictographic glyphs *a-tl* (water); *e-tl* (bean) and *o-tli* (way). Using these forms of writing, the ancient Mexicans produced codices that, as Fray Diego de Durán points out, preserved "sus memorables hechos, sus guerras y victorias . . . todo lo tenían escrito . . . con cuentas de años, meses y días en que

Figure 3.

Page from a tonalámatl or book of divination. (Archive of the author)

habían acontecido" (1867, 2: 257) ("all their memorable deeds, their wars and victories . . . they had written it all down . . . with glyphs for the years, months and days on which they had taken place") (see **Figure 4**). Comparing the cultural development of these civilizations with that of other civilizations, the North American anthropologist Alfred Kroeber wrote,

> . . . if one thinks of the invention of the first idea of part-phonetic writing, it is conceivable that all the ancient systems of the Old World derive from a single such intervention; although even in that event the Maya-Aztec system would remain as a wholly separate growth. (268)

Yet even though the pre-Hispanic Nahua world, utilizing its Toltec and Teotihuacan heritage, arrived at this form of writing, one should not forget that the peoples of the Mayan family also had their own system, which was even more highly developed than that of the central region of Mexico. A great many inscriptions on stone stelae, lintels, stairways, the inside walls of certain temples and palaces, and even ceramic objects (see **Figure 5**) have been preserved from both the Classic and the later Mayan period. The three Mayan codices discovered to date, the Dresden, Paris, and the so-called Tró Cortesianus codices, held in Madrid, date from a later period, although still prior to the Conquest. As for understanding Mayan writing, in recent decades significant contributions have been made, begun by the Russian scholar Yuri Knorosov and continued by other North American, German, and Mexican researchers. As a result of these findings, it is now possible to talk of a logo-syllabic form of writing among the Maya–in other words, a form of writing that included syllabic glyphs as well as glyphs that represented an idea or a word. This writing system also had

Figure 4.

Figure 5.

The Leiden Plaque, which depicts the King of Tikal, Moon-Zero-Bird. The text on the reverse side gives 17 September 320 CE as the date of his accession to the throne. (Archives of the author)

Page from Diego Durán's Historia de las Indias de Nueva España, written between 1560 and 1565, depicts the calendric system. (Archive of the author)

Figure 6.

glyph affixes that served as markers for morphological and syntactic relationships. Several inscriptions have recently been deciphered (see **Figure 6**). The Maya–who discovered the concept of zero in a mathematical system, and a calendrical system that is a ten-thousandth of a day closer to the astronomical year than the current Gregorian calendar–were certainly past masters in the art of writing and calculating time (see **Figure 7**).

Despite researchers' efforts, however, there are still many Mayan glyphs whose meaning has yet to be deciphered. The deciphering of further inscriptions will probably open the way to knowledge of additional texts of literary value. The same can be said of inscriptions by other peoples such as the Mixtecs and the Olmecs. One should also recall that, the Maya, like the other peoples in the central region of Mexico, also had centers of education in which, through systematic memorization, ancient knowledge was transmitted and preserved through painted books. Fray Diego de Landa states that "Usaba también esta gente de ciertos caracteres o letras con las cuales escribían en sus libros sus cosas antiguas y sus ciencias, y con estas figuras y algunas señales de las mismas, entendían sus cosas y las daban a entender y enseñaban" (1938, 207) ("These people also used certain glyphs or letters in which

Maya carvings on stone tablets, Palenque, depicting the Mayan King Chan-Bahlum's accession to the throne, 10 January 690 CE. Temple of the Foliated Cross. (Archive of the author)

Figure 7.

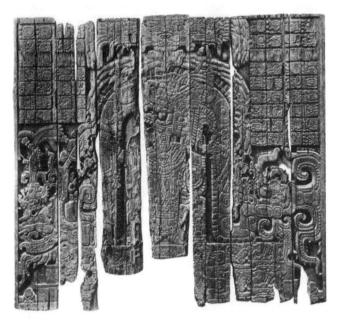

Carved wooden lintel from Temple IV, Tikal, Guatemala. Length is 6 feet 9 inches; it is dated 747 CE. (Archive of the author)

they wrote down their ancient history and sciences in their books; and by means of these letters and figures and by certain marks contained in them, they could read about their affairs and taught others to read about them too"; 1975, 124).

As a result of these teaching methods, also prevalent among the Náhua, valuable literary texts belonging to what is now known as the Mayan family of languages were preserved and survived until the present. Because, as we shall see, certain Indian scholars who had survived the Conquest, remembering the pre-Hispanic teachings and perhaps using some of the codices which they had managed to preserve, wrote texts in their own language, in the alphabet brought from Europe, and in the mid nineteenth century, these texts began to be discovered and translated. These are the texts that friars such as Andrés de Olmos and Bernardino de Sahagún managed to salvage from the violence of the Conquest. Comparing the literary legacy of ancient Greece and Rome with the Indian texts that he was beginning to know, Bernardino de Sahagún observed that "Esto mismo se usaba en esta nación indiana, y más principalmente entre los mexicanos, entre los cuales los sabios retóricos, y virtuosos, y esforzados, eran tenidos en mucho" (1956, 2: 53) ("The same was practiced in this Indian nation, and especially among the Mexicans, among whom the wise, superior, and effective rhetoricians were held in high regard"; 1982, 1: 65).

The Sources

The first attempt to preserve literary texts from the Indian world in the central region of Mexico dates from the period between 1528 and 1533. During this time, a number of Náhua scholars who had already learnt the Roman alphabet, perhaps as a result of the teachings of the first twelve friars who arrived in New Spain, wrote explanations and commentaries on various codices or historical annals in their own language, using Roman script. These texts, written on Indian paper, are preserved in the Bibliothèque Nationale, Paris, under the title of

Anales de Tlatelolco [Annals of Tlatelolco] or *Unos Anales Históricos de la Nación Mexicana* [Some Historical Annals of the Mexican Nation]. The manuscripts record the genealogies of the governors of Tlatelolco, Mexico-Tenochtitlan, and Azcapotzalco, as well as the oldest Indian view of the Spanish Conquest, as experienced by some of its survivors. The Spanish translation of the Indian chronicle of the Conquest contained in this document has been published in *Visión de los vencidos* (1959).

Fr. Andrés de Olmos, who arrived in New Spain in 1528, also compiled a considerable number of *huehuetlahtolli*, talks or speeches in Nahuatl delivered by the elders prior to the Conquest. These speeches were delivered on important occasions, such as the death of a king, the election of a ruler, the birth of a child, or a marriage, or they documented parents' advice to their sons and daughters, and teachers' homilies to their students. Recorded orally from the surviving elders who had memorized them during the pre-Hispanic period, these texts are extraordinarily valuable for the study of Nahuatl thought. Some of these are held in the Library of Congress in Washington and others in the National Libraries of Mexico, Paris, and Madrid. The first complete Spanish version of these texts was published on the occasion of the commemoration of the Meeting between Two Worlds in 1992.

Even more important than Olmos's work of compilation, however, was the large-scale research undertaken by Fray Bernardino de Sahagún. A few years after his arrival in Mexico in 1529, Sahagún, deeply interested in exploring the Indian psyche, drew up a questionnaire on all the points about which he sought to obtain information. Among the issues that most intrigued him were the hymns to the gods, the secular chants, the ancient speeches, proverbs and sayings, religious doctrines, myths and legends, the calendar, the customs of the lords, and texts describing the various professions of priests, scholars, artists, and merchants as well as the discourse of ordinary people. As he himself noted, he was interested in finding out about "las cosas divinas, o por mejor decir idolátricas, y humanas y naturales de esta Nueva España" (1956, 1: 28) ("the divine, or rather idolatrous, human, and natural things of this New Spain"; 1982, 1: 46). With the help of his Indian students from the Colegio Imperial de Santa Cruz in Tlatelolco, Sahagún began collecting hundreds of texts from various places in the central region of Mexico; he described the way he gathered this material: "Todas las cosas que conferimos me las dieron (los ancianos indígenas) por pinturas, que aquella era la escritura que ellos antiguamente usaban" (Sahagún 1956, 1: 106) ("They [the Indian elders] gave me all the matters we discussed in pictures, for that was the writing they employed in ancient times"; 1982, 1: 54). As his elderly informants recited their ancient doctrines and texts to him, the young students from Tlatelolco recorded the information in their own language, using Roman script. As far as possible, they also copied many of the figures and glyphs, which were jealously protected by the elders. With a critical sense unusual for the time, Sahagún repeated his research several times, putting the material he had compiled through a triple sieve, as he called it, to ensure its authenticity.

The result of this lengthy, well-planned research, to which Sahagún devoted most of the sixty years he spent in New Spain, was an enormous collection of nearly a thousand folios, two-sided, with pictures and texts in Nahuatl. This material, which suffered numerous vicissitudes, served as the basis for Sahagún's *Historia general de las cosas de la Nueva*

España [1560; *General History of the Things of New Spain,* 1950–1982], which is not a translation of the Nahuatl texts but rather an annotated summary of them. The Nahuatl documentation, confiscated from Sahagún by order of Philip II, ended up in Spain. The original manuscripts, known as the Codices Matritenses, are kept in the Real Palacio and in the Biblioteca de la Academia de la Historia. In my introduction to *Ritos, sacerdotes y atavíos de los dioses* (9–37) [Rituals, Priests and Attire of the Gods], I refer to this material in detail. The most complete manuscript of Sahagún's history in Nahuatl and Spanish is preserved today as the Codex Florentino, so called because it is held in the Laurenziana Medicean Library in Florence. In 1979, the Archivo General de la Nación (General Archive of the Nation) in Mexico published a facsimile edition of this precious manuscript.

Sahagún's work had still further consequences. Several of his Indian disciples, interested in their ancient culture, continued the work of transcribing and preserving the texts on their own: Antonio Valeriano, of Azcapotzalco; Martín Jacobita and Andrés Leonardo, of Tlatelolco; and Alonso Begerano and Pedro de San Buenaventura, of Cuautitlán, transcribed several collections of poems and a whole series of historical annals into an Indian language, using Roman script. These documents include the *Anales de Cuautitlán* and the *Leyenda de los soles* [Legend of the Suns], included in the Codex Chimalpopoca. These manuscripts contain cosmogonic myths, a version of the legend of Quetzalcóatl, and historical annals from the main towns in the central region of Mexico. These same students, together with others (such as Juan Pomar), were responsible for the compilation and transcription of three important poetic texts: *La Colección de cantares mexicanos* [Collection of Mexican Poems], held in the Biblioteca Nacional de México, the so-called *Manuscrito de los romances de los señores de la Nueva España* [Manuscript of the Ballads of the Lords of New Spain], kept in the Latin American collection at the University of Texas, and another collection of poems held at the Bibliothèque Nationale, Paris. The paleography and the Spanish version of these manuscripts were the work of Ángel María Garibay Kintana (*Poesía Náhuatl,* I–II). Several hundred poems, mainly of pre-Hispanic origin, can be studied in these documents. Some of them are compositions by such famous poets as Nezahualcóyotl of Texcoco and Tecayehuatzín of Huexotzinco.

Another important work is the *Libro de los coloquios* [Book of Colloquia], with its transcription of the dialogues that took place in the atrium of the Convento de San Francisco in Mexico City in 1524 between the first friars who came to Mexico and some of the principal Indian scholars and priests who defended their way of thinking and their beliefs. The text was discovered in the Vatican's Secret Archives by Father Pascual Saura in 1924, and I have edited, translated, and annotated it.

All these texts are important, but the collections of poems in Nahuatl are of particular interest, since they show contemporary readers a world of artistic sensitivity radically different from that of the West. The pre-Hispanic *Tlamatinime* and *cuicapicque* (scholars and composers of poems) classified these forms of expression either under the rich variety of *cuícatl* (songs and poems) or *tlahtolli* (stories or discourses). These two categories, which are perhaps partly related to those of poetry and prose, gave rise to a vast number of variations, which I shall mention briefly.

The *cuícatl*, as the songwriter Ayocuan Cuetzpaltitzin notes, come from the inside of the sky and are both inspiration and sentiment. They contain memories and a dialogue with the heart. Their rhythm, their meter, and sometimes their intonation, accompanied by music, are their outer qualities. In ancient cultures, it was common for sacred compositions, preserved by oral tradition, to include features in their meter or rhythm that facilitated their memorization. The Náhuas produced a wide range of compositions with these features, implicitly evoked by the word *cuícatl.* Foremost among these were the numerous *teocuícatl* (divine poems or poems to the gods). These constituted essential material for the teaching provided at the *calmécac.* A closer examination of the texts that have survived until the present shows that the ancient hymns in honor of the gods, together with the twenty compiled by Sahagún in Tepepulco, in what is now the state of Hidalgo, were genuine *teocuícatl* (León Portilla 1984, 99–102). A literary analysis of these compositions reveals some of their features: In addition to rhythm and meter, they also contain parallelism and the repetition, with variations, of the same thought. The characteristic expression of the *teocuícatl* is necessarily solemn, often esoteric. They do not contain any superfluous words, and are the recollection of important events, or invocations of the gods. Although the theme of divine realities is present in the majority of these compositions, the genre known as *cuícatl,* did not constitute sacred hymns or *teocuícatl* in the strict sense. Thus, *teponazcuícatl* was a term generally used to denote songs that required musical accompaniment. Indeed, many of them contained the germ of the first forms of dramatic representation. *Cuauhcuícatl* (songs of eagles), *ocelocuícatl* (songs of ocelots), and *yaocuícatl* (war songs) were the various terms used to designate the compositions praising heroic deeds.

Also common, albeit different from this type of poetry, were the *xochicuícatl* (songs of flowers), the *xopancuícatl* (songs of spring), and the *icnocuícatl* (songs of sadness), all with a lyrical tone. Some of these songs celebrated the goodness of the earth, friendship between humans, and the beauty of flowers and songs, while others contained sad, intimate reflections on the instability of life, or on death and the great beyond. Indeed, the existence of these poems, which pose questions similar to those asked, at other times and in other latitudes, by the first philosophers, shows that among the pre-Hispanic *tlamatinime,* there were also people who cultivated similar forms of thought in their reflections on the enigmas of human destiny, divinity, and the value that should be placed on the ephemerality of what exists. And since the Nahuatl manuscripts sometimes give the names of those who formulated these thoughts, it has been possible to link some of the poems with their authors, thereby debunking the supposedly universal anonymity of pre-Hispanic literature.

Another literary category, with a different generic concept, was the one described by the Nahuas as *tlahtolli* (word, discourse, story, history, exhortation). The term includes everything that was offered as the result of investigation and knowledge, rather than being based on poetic inspiration or recollection. The principal forms of *tlahtolli* cultivated by the Náhuas contained sharp differences among themselves and included the *huehuetlahtolli* (discourse of the elders); the *teotlahtolli* (divine words often included in the *huehuetlahtolli*); the *ye uecauh tlahtolli* (stories about ancient matters), a native version of what we call history; the *tlamachilliz-tlahtol-zazanilli* (oral accounts of what is known, in other words, legends and narrations often linked to traditions with a mythological content); the *in tonalli itlatlahtollo* (discourse of the astrologers, who predicted destiny); and finally, the *nahuallahtolli* (magic spells).

A number of discourses of the elders are still in existence. Their transcriptions, primarily by Olmos and Sahagún, enable one to assess this peculiar form of Nahuatl expression. In the opinion of Sahagún, they contain the finest testimony of the rhetoric, moral philosophy, and theology of the Mexican people; their significant characteristics include giving a sense of the beauty of the Nahuatl language and delineating many subtle and delicate aspects regarding moral values. This peculiarity of the *huehuetlahtolli*, which shows, as Sahagún notes, the beauty of the language, possesses several remarkable features. First of all, it is one of the most highly refined of all forms of *tlahtolli*. The entire range of formulas of courtesy, of which there were so many in this culture, are contained in the *huehuetlahtolli*. They also include an extraordinary variety of metaphors: Human beings are nearly always described as possessors of a countenance and a heart; the words *icpalli* and *petlatl* (chair and matting) are used to refer to power and command; the supreme deity is always referred to as *Yohualli, Ehécatl*, or the night and the wind, while a small girl is referred to as *chalchiuhcózcatl, quetzalli* (a necklace of precious stones and quetzal plumage). And the *huehuetlahtolli*, like many *cuícatl*, often include parallelism, in other words, the repetition of the same thought with slight variations, in order to make the words easier to recall. The study of the *huehuetlahtolli* is undoubtedly one of the best means of approaching pre-Hispanic intellectual culture.

Other forms of discourse have also been discovered which, because of their content, should be classified more specifically as *teotlahtolli*, dissertations on divinity. This is the case with several of these forms of discourse addressed to Tloque Nahuaque, the supreme god, master of proximity and closeness, in the form of a prayer, or those which specify his various powers and attributes. The *teotlahtolli*, with rhythm and meter, also included the texts that recalled the creations of the different ages or suns, and the well-known text on the origin of the fifth sun in Teotihuacan or those describing the accomplishments of Quetzalcóatl the god, or the priest among the Toltecs.

Náhua testimonies with historical content are also fairly common. On the one hand, there were certain books, such as the *xiuhámatl* (papers of the years), in which the most important events were recorded and painted in the form of annals, with the corresponding date. Some of these manuscripts, either those of pre-Hispanic origin or copies dating from the early part of the Conquest, are still extant. In every case, the oral account served as an essential complement to what was recorded in the codices, and it must be understood that the memorization of these accounts was given great importance in the centers of Education.

In contrast with these plain annals, the *ye uecauh tlahtolli* were often enriched with narrations and legends, as well as genuine *tlamachilliz-tlahtol-zazanilli* (accounts of what was known) which provided a more detailed account of the lives and performance of governors and of what had happened in the entire community at different times. Examples of this are the famous legends on Quetzalcóatl, included in Sahagún's Codex Matritense and in the *Anales de Cuauhtitlán*, or the description in the latter of the life of the wise man of Texcoco, Nezahualcóyotl. Other forms of *tlahtolli* included the *in tonalli itlatlahtollo* or astrologers' speeches. This material constitutes

the entire contents of the Fourth Book of the Codex Matritense de la Real Academia, which contains the Nahuatl testimonies which Sahagún obtained from his informants. They also contain remnants of another form of esoteric expression, known as *nahuallahtolli*, the *tlahtolli* of the *nahualli*, the secret or magical language of shamans. Material for studying this is available in the *Tratado de las supersticiones y costumbres gentílicas que hoy viven entre los indios naturales de esta Nueva España: escrito en 1629* [1892; Treatise on the Heathen Superstitions and Customs that Today Live Among the Indians Native to This New Spain, 1629] by Hernando Ruiz de Alarcón (fl. 1592). This text also contains the original version of some of the spells recorded and compiled by the author among the Nahua shamans who were still active in the early seventeenth century.

In addition to those mentioned earlier, there are other documents worth mentioning, such as the Toltec-Chichimec history, preserved in the Bibliothèque Nationale, Paris; the Codex Aubin, written partly using the ancient system of writing and partly with Nahuatl annotations, using Roman script. Since it is not possible to include other partly literary manuscripts here, I would refer readers to Ángel María Garibay Kintana's catalogue of these texts in his scholarly *Historia de la literatura Náhuatl* [History of Nahuatl Literature]. All that remains to be said is that, after the end of the sixteenth century and the beginning of the seventeenth century, several Indians and *mestizos*, such as Don Fernando Alvarado Tezozómoc (1530–1600), Chimalpain, and Ixtlilxóchitl, already familiar with the European way of writing history, produced their own works, based on documents of pre-Hispanic origin. (I have dealt with these works in detail in *Literaturas indígenas de México* [1992; Indigenous Literature of Mexico].)

These are, very briefly, the principal sources of Nahuatl Indian literature that are still in existence. As can be seen, they are far more varied and richer than might at first appear. I shall now turn to the principal Indian texts in other pre-Columbian cultures, particularly the various groups in the Mayan and Mixtec families. Among the Yucatán Maya and the Quichés and Cakchiqueles of Guatemala, there were also scholars who had descended from priestly or noble families who, after the Conquest, embarked on the task of transcribing both the traditions learned in their pre-Hispanic centers and the contents of some of their ancient codices, primarily those of an historical or calendrical nature. This determination to preserve their knowledge partially offset the loss of Mayan pre-Hispanic codices, of which, as I mentioned earlier, only three remain. As a result of this work, several chronicles, some books on Indian medicine, and an entire series of texts known by the general title of the books of *Chilam Balam*, were preserved in Indian languages, although in Roman script.

The oldest Mayan manuscript is probably the one known as *Crónica de Chicxulub* or *Chac-Xulub-Chen*, the name of the town in which it was written by the Indian noble Ah Nakuk Pech in the mid-sixteenth century. Despite being a relatively short text, of a mere twenty-six pages, it is extremely important because it contains, among other things, a Mayan testimony of the Conquest of Yucatán. According to this testimony, on two occasions

se aposentaron los españoles en la tierra de Ichcaansihó. . . . En la tercera vez que vinieron fue cuando para siempre se asentaron y, a saber, fué en 1542 años; año en que para siempre se aposentaron aquí, en la tierra de Ichcaansihó, siendo el 13 Kan el porta-año, según la cuenta. . . . 1543 años fue el año en que los españoles fueron al norte hacia la tierra de los cheeles a buscar

hombres mayas para siervos . . . [,] en 1544 . . . en Cauacán, después, cuando encerraron en la prisión al letrado Caamal, de Sisal, y pidieron la cuenta de todos los pueblos.
("Crónica de Chicxulub," in *Crónicas de la Conquista* 204-206)

The Spaniards settled in the land of Ichcaansihó. . . . The third time they came was when they settled there permanently, and this was in 1542, the year when they settled there permanently in the land of Ichcaansihó, when 13 Kan was the year bearer-sign, according to our reckoning. . . . In 1543 the Spaniards went to the north, to the land of the Cheeles to look for Mayan men as slaves . . .[,] in 1544 . . . in Caucán they imprisoned the learned man, Caamal, of Sisal, and asked for an account of all the towns.

Mayan writings on Indian medicine, generally of a later origin, include *El Libro de la Medicina* [Book of Medicine], the *Cuaderno de Teabo* [Notebook of Teabo], *Noticias de varias plantas* [Information on Various Plants], the *Libro de los Médicos* [Book of Doctors], and the *Ritual de los Bacaab* [Ritual of the Bacaab], all by unknown authors and only minimally studied to date.

However, the books of the *Chilam Balam* are the most important part of the Mayan literary legacy. The *chilames* (or rather, the *chilamoob*) were high-ranking priests in pre-Hispanic times. They served as teachers as well as prophets. Balam, as Alfredo Barrera Vásquez notes, "es el nombre del más famoso de los chilames que existieron poco antes de la venida de los europeos al continente. *Balam* es un nombre de familia y signififca jaguar o brujo en un sentido figurado" (*El Libro de los libros de Chilam Balam* 14) ("is the most famous name of the *chilames* who lived just before the arrival of the Europeans on the continent. Balam is a family name meaning jaguar or sorcerer in a figurative sense"). According to the Indians who still preserve copies of them, the books of *Chilam Balam*, attributed to various descendants of the ancient priests, contain the testimony of tradition and ancient knowledge, occasionally blended with Christian and biblical ideas interpolated into the ancient text. Eighteen books of *Chilam Balam* have been discovered to date, only four of which have been even partially studied and transcribed. They contain several chronicles and prophecies of the days, and of the years and longer periods. They also contain mythical and historical passages and a number of hymns and poems. The best-known of all these is the *Libro de Chilam Balam de Chumayel*, of which there is only one late copy dating from the end of the eighteenth century. According to an analysis of this manuscript by Antonio Mediz Bolio, it contains sixteen different books. Its titles give some idea of the richness of this most important Indian text: "Libro de los linajes," "de la Conquista," "Katún o veintena de años," "de las pruebas," "de los antiguos dioses," "de los espíritus," "el trece Ahau Katún," "principio de los itzaes," "libro del mes," "el Katún de la flor," "libro de los enigmas," "rueda de los Katunes," "serie de los Katunes," "crónica de los Dzulez," "vaticinio de los trece Katunes," and "libro de las profecías" ["The Book of Lineages," "The Conquest," "Katun or Twenty Years," "Tests," "The Ancient Gods," "The Spirits," "Thirteen Ahua Katún," "The Beginning of the Itzaes," "The Book of the Months," "The Katún of Flowers," "The Book of Enigmas," "The Wheel of Katunes," "The Series of Katunes," "The Chronicles of the Dzules," "The Prophecy of the Thirteen Katunes," and "The Book of Prophecies"]. The *Chilam Balam de Chuyamel* alone, studied in depth by several researchers, provides evidence of the richness of Mayan literature and shows the importance of analyzing it in depth.

Another of the most important books of *Chilam Balam* is *Tizimín*, a twenty-six-page manuscript, with mythological, prophetic, historical and astrological sections. An English version of the *Tizimín* text exists, prepared by Munro Edmonson. There have also been Spanish translations of the *Chilam Balam de Maní*, part of the *Libro de Ixil*, and the *Crónica de Oxkutzcab*, all documents which form part of the Codex Pérez, so-called in honor of the Mayan scholar, Juan Pío Pérez, who compiled and translated them. The contents of all these texts are fairly similar. They include chronicles, prophesies of the various *Katunes* (scores of years), and certain poems and songs. Despite the evident interpolation of ideas and phrases of a biblical and Christian nature, these documents contain authentically Indian texts, the result of the historical tradition of the ancient Maya.

In addition to the aforementioned books of *Chilam Balam*, several others have been discovered (León Portilla 1984, 38), the best known being the Codex Calkiní, also called *Chilam Balam de Calkiní*, published by Alfredo Barrera Vásquez in a facsimile edition. It is an ancient manuscript about the Maya who populated Calkiní, in the state of Campeche, and describes their resistance to the Spanish conquerors. Barrera Vásquez published *El libro de los cantares de Dzitbalché* [Book of the Poem of Dzitbalché], which contains fifteen *h'kay*, hymns and lyrical and religious songs, of the ancient Maya. These include "La ponzoña del año," "Vamos al nacimiento de la flor," "Canto de la flor," "El canto doliente," "Canto del jaguar," and "Canción de la danza del arquero flechador" ["The Poison of the Year," "Let Us Go to the Birth of the Flower," "Song of the Flower," "The Sorrowful Song," "The Song of the Jaguar," and "The Song of the Dance of the Archer"]. Some of these songs have a significant dramatic content.

In addition to these texts from Yucatán, Indian documents written in other languages of the Mayan family have also been preserved. One text of considerable interest was written in Chontal, and transcribed in the early seventeenth century. It describes the arrival of Hernán Cortés in the Acalán region, on the Gulf coast, with Cuauhtémoc as prisoner. What is interesting about this text is that it mentions Cuauhtémoc's intention of gaining the support of the Chontales against the Spanish conquerors.

There is also an important literary tradition among the Quichés and Cakchiqueles currently living in Guatemala, who form a cultural unit with the rest of the groups in the Mayan family. The most important manuscripts written in Quiché are the famous *Popol Vuh* or "Book of Counsel," the *Título de los señores de Totonicapán* [Entitlement of the Lords of Totonicapán], and the *Rabinal Achí*, a play with essentially pre-Hispanic characteristics. The *Popol Vuh* is probably the best-known American Indian text in the world. Although written after the Conquest, with interpolations of a Christian nature, it contains histories and traditions of a pre-Hispanic origin. It was not discovered until the beginning of the eighteenth century, when Fray Francisco Ximénez (1666– ca. 1722), a priest from Chichicastenango in Guatemala, found this book in Quiché in an old cupboard in the vestry. Fascinated by these ancient Indian texts, Father Ximénez immediately transcribed the text and prepared a Spanish translation, which he called *Las historias del origen de los indios de esta provincia de Guatemala* [1857; Histories of the Origins of the Indians of this Province of Guatemala]. The original manuscript subsequently disappeared, leaving only Ximenez's transcription.

As regards the likely author or authors of the *Popol Vuh*, or rather, the compiler of these texts during the second half of the sixteenth century, a number of hypotheses have been put forward. Although some scholars believe they should be attributed to the Indian Diego Reynoso, according to the authorized opinion of Adrián Recinos, "mientras no se descubran nuevas pruebas que hagan luz en la materia, el famoso manuscrito tiene que seguirse considerando como un documento anónimo, escrito por uno o más descendientes de la raza quiché, conforme a la tradición de sus antepasados" (36) ("until further evidence is discovered that will shed light on the issue, the famous manuscript will have to continue being regarded as an anonymous document, written by one or more descendants of the Quiché race, according to the tradition of their forebears"). Foremost among the many studies and editions of the *Popol Vuh* is the French translation, albeit not entirely faithful, prepared by the famous Abbot Carlos Esteban Brasseur de Bourbourg. Scholars who have studied this book include Karl Schertzer, Max Müller, H. Bancroft, Daniel G. Brinton, Francisco Pi y Margall, Georges Raynaud, Miguel Angel Asturias, Antonio Villacorta, Leonhard Schultze-Jena, Adrián Recinos, Munro Edmonson, and Dennis Tedlock. The book has been translated into Spanish, French, German, English, and Japanese.

The contents of the *Popol Vuh* are divided into an introduction and four large sections. In the introduction, the Indian compiler declares his aim of describing the beginning and origin of everything that was done in the city of Quiché; he wishes to reveal what was hidden, and what was done at the beginning of life and at the beginning of history. He mentions that there was an original ancient book, which was hidden from researchers and thinkers after the arrival of the Spaniards. For this reason, so that the memory of that book would not be lost, the Indian compiler embarked on the task of writing, "dentro ya de la ley de Dios, en el cristianismo" ("within the law of God, in Christianity"), this new *Popol Vuh*. The first part deals with the cosmic origins of the various types of human beings created by the gods, as well as their subsequent destruction. It also includes the legendary history of two demigods, Hunahpú and Ixbalanqué, sent to earth to destroy Zipacná's pride. The second part of the book offers other mythical narrations, the most important being a description of the adventures of the *ahup*, when they went to play ball, in the land of the lords of Xiblabá, the land of the dead. Another extremely interesting legend concerns the maiden Ixquic, who became pregnant from the saliva spat out from the skull of one of the lords conquered in the ballgame. The third and fourth sections contain the histories of the first four Quiché leaders, their travels and attempts to take possession of fire, their rites and traditions—in short, the consolidation of Quiché dominion. The manuscript ends with an appendix entitled "Papel del origen de los señores quichés" ("Role of the Origin of the Quiché Lords").

The *Título de los señores de Totonicapán* was also written in Quiché, apparently in about 1554. Its author, although influenced by Christian ideas (as well as those that assumed that the Indians were the descendants of the ten lost tribes of Israel), transcribed ancient chronicles and genealogies that were clearly Indian. Among other things, it mentions the pilgrimage of the three nations or separate groups of the Quiché people who reached Guatemala, where they separated into various communities. The organization of the latter, their struggles, the genealogy of several of the lords, and the distribution of the lands, constitute the main themes of the manuscript. Far shorter than the *Popol Vuh*, this manuscript is nonetheless of interest since it confirms, at least partially, the data provided by the sacred book of the Quichés. Unfortunately, the Quiché text of the *Título de los Señores de Totonicapán* has disappeared, meaning that its contents can be appreciated only as a result of the Spanish translation made in approximately 1834 by the parish priest of Sacapulas, Dionisio José Chonay, who was apparently well-versed in Quiché.

The last of the three most important Quiché manuscripts is the *Rabinal Achí*, compiled by the Abbot Brasseur de Bourbourg in the village of Rabinal in about 1856, from the oral version by the old Indian, Bartolo Ziz, who both knew it by tradition and also possessed a written copy in Quiché. The *Rabinal Achí*—in other words, "The Lord of Rabinal,"—is perhaps the only Indian play in which forms of representation of pre-Hispanic origin survive. When translating it into European languages, the various researchers who have studied this text have divided it into various acts and scenes, following its original structure as far as possible. Without wishing to impose an inappropriate criterion on this form of Indian theater, it is possible to divide it into two main parts or acts, the first of which can be subdivided into three scenes.

The theme of the play is reduced to the capture, lengthy dialogues and interrogations, and the eventual death of a warrior, the lord of the Quichés. The work begins with repeated parleys between the lord of the Quichés and Rabinal Achí. As the dialogue—which sometimes seems interminable and abounds in Indian forms of courtesy, parallel expressions, metaphors, and rich pre-Columbian symbolism—proceeds, we obtain information about the actions and heroic deeds of the prisoner as well as the reasons why he has fought. Meanwhile, a group of dancers whirls continuously around the two speakers. Rabinal Achí eventually throws a rope around the lord of the Quichés, tying him to a tree where he is forced to listen to the heroic deeds of the people of Rabinal. The music and the dances recommence. Rabinal Achí reminds the prisoner of the damage he has caused his people. The lord of the Quichés tries to obtain his freedom, and after a few attempts at attacking his captor, is led before Lord Hobtoh, the father of Rabinal Achí, to whom he announces that he is prepared to accept his death, while requesting the honors due to him because of his rank as a lord. He recalls his heroic deeds once again. Not wishing to humiliate himself, he opts for sacrifice. He obtains permission, according to the ritual, to dance with the maiden, "Madre de los verdes pajarillos" ("the Mother of the Green Birds"), as well as with the eagle and tiger knights. He also obtains permission to bid farewell to his valleys and mountains.

The last part concerns the return of the lord of the Quichés, who, before dying, regrets his inability to turn into a squirrel or a bird, for they die on the branches of a tree, contemplating the mountains and the valleys where they were born. The eagle and tiger knights surround the lord of the Quichés, while the dance continues, and one assumes that the sacrifice is carried out. Despite any reserves one might have about the text, the *Rabinal Achí* should be regarded as one of the most genuine examples of Indian theater prior to the Conquest. The drama of this work and its intense poetic content are evident from the dialog, in which the Lord of the Quichés requests permission to bid farewell to his valleys and mountains. Here is the final speech:

> ¡Ah, oh cielo! ¡Ah, oh tierra! Ya que es necesario que muera, que fallezca aquí bajo el cielo, sobre la tierra, ¡cómo no puedo cambiarme por esa ardilla, ese pájaro, que mueren sobre la rama del árbol, sobre el retoño del árbol donde consiguieron con qué

alimentarse, con qué comer bajo el cielo, sobre la tierra!
¡Oh águilas! ¡Oh jaguares! Vengan, pues a cumplir su misión, a
cumplir su deber; que sus dientes, que sus garras me maten en un
movimiento, porque soy un varón llegado de mis montañas, de
mis valles. ¡El cielo, la tierra, estén con todos! ¡Oh águilas! ¡Oh
jaguares! (*Rabinal Achí* 91)

Oh sky! Oh land! Since I must perish, and die beneath the sky, on
the ground, why am I unable to turn into a squirrel or a bird who
die on the branches of a tree, in the new growth of a tree where
they forage for food, and eat under the sky, on the earth!
Oh eagles! Oh jaguars! Come and fulfill your mission, come and
do your duty, let your teeth and claws kill me in one fell swoop,
because I am lord of my mountains and valleys. Be with us, sky
and earth. Oh eagles! Oh jaguars!

The Cakchiqueles, another group from the Mayan family, also preserved texts that are at least partly of pre-Hispanic origin. The *Memorial de Sololá*, also known as the *Anales de los Cakchiqueles* or the *Memorial de Tecpan Atitlan*, is the most important manuscript. Like the books of *Chilam Balam*, it was written by various Indians who were the custodians of their ancient traditions. The text mentions "de quienes engendraron a los hombres en la época antigua, antes que estos montes y valles se poblaran" ("those who engendered men in ancient times, before these mountains and valleys were populated"). It also tells of the great travels of the tribes and their journey through the great city of Tula, until their arrival in what is now Guatemala. The history of the pilgrimages and accounts of the founding of the cities and of the struggles with the Quichés often embellished their ancient epic poems. The manuscript also describes the Cakchiqueles' contacts with the Spaniards who arrived in Guatemala under Alvarado. As in the Nahua texts, this text notes that "las caras de los españoles no eran conocidas y los señores los tomaron por dioses" (*Anales de los Xahil*) ("the faces of the Spaniards were unknown, and so the lords took them to be gods"). The *Memorial de Sololá* or the *Anales de los Cakchiqueles,* also known as the *Anales de los Xahil* (since their authors were people from this Cakchiquel group), provides data on the preaching of Christianity by the friars, the rebellion of the Cakchiqueles, Alvarado's acts of violence, the founding and destruction of the city of Guatemala, and the death of doña Beatriz de la Cueva, Alvarado's wife.

Other documents of literary interest in the Cakchiquel language include the *Historia de los Xpantzay de Tecpan, Guatemala,* and a text which Adrián Recinos called *Guerras comunes de quichés y cakchiqueles,* which describes the wars between these two pre-Hispanic nations.

In addition to all these codices and documents in the Nahuatl and Mayan languages, there are also certain literary texts, albeit fewer in number, belonging to other Indian peoples who inhabited and indeed continue to inhabit what is now the Mexican Republic, namely the Otomís, Tarascans, Mixtecs, and Zapotecs.

The Otomís, speakers of a language that is totally different from Nahuatl, have lived in the central region of Mexico for several millennia and have been distinguished by their artistic skills. They were not, it is true, the creators of a high culture, and fared rather poorly, as far as luck was concerned: Exposed to direct contact with the great creators of culture (Toltecs, Teotihuacanos, and other subsequent rulers, such as the Texcocans, the Tlaxcaltecans, and the Aztecs), they sometimes mixed with them but were usually dominated by the various states which succeeded each other throughout

pre-Hispanic history. This gave the Otomís the privilege, if one can call it that, of observing the rise and fall of many states or "empires" and of cultivating a permanent smile, with no rancor. Despite being dominated and subjected to numerous influences, they maintained their own cultural appearance and identity. Indeed, to this day, they constitute one of the most numerous Indian groups in several states in the center of Mexico.

The texts of Otomí origin are preserved in three main documents. The first is the aforementioned *Manuscrito de Cantares mexicanos*, kept in the Biblioteca Nacional de México, where an annotation in Folio 6 shows that some of the songs included in it are merely Nahuatl versions of various Otomí lyrical compositions. The note literally refers to them as "cantares antiguos de los naturales otomíes que solían cantar en los convites y casamientos, vueltos en lengua mexicana, siempre tomando el jugo y el alma del canto, imágenes metafóricas que ellos decían" (*Cantares mexicanos*, fol 6 r.) ("ancient songs of the Otomí natives that used to be sung at banquets and weddings, translated into the Mexican language, yet preserving the essence and soul of the song, and the metaphorical images which they contained"). These Otomí songs, veritable literary jewels, are known only in their Nahuatl version. In order to give some idea of their quality, I shall quote a composition described in the Indian text as a "Song of Otomí Sadness":

Cuando yo sufro,
me hago fuerte a mí mismo.
Si estamos tristes,
si andamos llorando en la tierra,
en verdad en un breve instante esto terminará.

When I suffer, I make myself brave.
If we are sad,
if we weep on earth,
we should remember that this will end in an instant.

(*Cantares mexicanos, fol. 5 r.*).

The other two manuscripts in which texts of Otomí origin are preserved are in fact two pictorial codices that were at least partially copied from pre-Hispanic sources. One of these was the *Codex Huamantla*, painted on an enormous canvas, six fragments of which are held at the Museo Nacional de México and three of which are kept in the Humboldt Collection, Berlin. The other is the *Codex de Hueychiapan*, with a calendar and various pages of annals with explanations written in Otomí. Although neither of these two codices has been properly analyzed (nor have the Otomí annotations been fully translated), the *Codex de Hueychiapan* in particular contains historical passages of considerable literary value. Pedro Carrasco Pizana has analyzed the content of this codex, particularly its calendrical annotations.

The Tarascans, who, in pre-Hispanic times, inhabited much of what is now the state of Michoacán and some of the areas bordering the present states of Guanajuato, Querétaro, Guerrero, Colima, Jalisco, and Mexico, were a powerful nation never subdued by the Aztecs. Also known as the Purépechas, they speak a language which has not been able to be linked to any other Indian language in Mexico to date. Their culture, however, has many similarities with that of the inhabitants of the central region. The little that is known about Tarascan literature comes from the so-called *Relación de Michoacán* [The Chronicles of Michoacan], which dates from the sixteenth century. This document was drafted by a missionary, probably the Franciscan Jerónimo de Alcalá, on the basis of oral accounts transmitted by the Indian elders. The missionary who compiled these texts at the request of the first viceroy of New Spain, don Antonio de Mendoza, was fully aware of the significance of his work. In the prologue to the *Relación*, he writes, "yo sirvo de interprete de estos viejos y hago cuenta que ellos lo cuentan" ("I serve as an interpreter for these old men, and I try to write as though they were the narrators"). In the view of Federico Gómez de Orozco, this chronicle was probably written in 1538 or 1539 in Tzintzuntzan, on the shores of Lake Patzcuaro. The same anonymous compiler outlines his aim in the prologue: The first part deals with the principal gods and celebrations, the second with the way the Tarascans settled and conquered their domains, and the third with their form of government prior to the arrival of the Spaniards and the death of Lord Caltzontzin.

The first part has unfortunately been lost; the other two comprise a total of 264 pages. They include several color paintings, in which the Indian technique has been fairly well preserved. Paul Kirchhoff, who has prepared a preliminary study of the *Relación de Michoacán*, points out, after a detailed analysis, that "nuestro texto es, indudablemente, no sólo en su contenido, sino también en su lenguaje, obra de los indígenas que lo dictaron al fraile. Y aún más: se puede afirmar que se trata de un texto cuyas dos terceras partes, según hemos calculado, tienen carácter de palabras fijadas por la tradición . . ." (xx) ("our text is undoubtedly, not only as regards its content, but also as regards its language, an Indian work dictated to the friar. Moreover, according to our calculations, two thirds of this text consists of words established by tradition . . .").

The Mixtecs from the state of Oaxaca are another Indian group of whom significant testimonies exist. The codices that have survived undoubtedly constitute some of the most important collections of books of pre-Columbian paintings with a primarily historical and genealogical content. Walter Lehmann and particularly Alfonso Caso and Mary Elizabeth Smith have made significant contributions to the study of these codices. Alfonso Caso has published a detailed analysis of the genealogies contained in the *Codex Bodley* and the *Codex Selden* (held in the Bodleian Library at Oxford University) and many other works related to this group of pre-Columbian texts. These books, which, at first sight, would appear to be excessively schematic, are of immense documentary value, since they contain a series of historical records in which the pre-Hispanic Mixtecs preserved their oral tradition, legends, and accounts in the Mixtec language, some of which appear to contain ancient traditions handed down from generation to generation. Some of the most recent examples of this literature include the Mixtec texts compiled by Anne Dyck.

Another significant cultural legacy is that of the ancient Zapotecs, whose stone inscriptions were mentioned earlier. Neighbors of the Mixtecs and inhabitants of the present state of Oaxaca, the Zapotecs possessed extremely ancient forms of writing, prior even to the period of Classic splendor. Unfortunately, very little remains of their tradition and knowledge. In the Archivo General de Indias in Seville, José Alcina Franch has discovered various manuscripts dating from the seventeenth century, containing transcriptions of ancient ceremonies related to the astrological and ritualistic calendar. Dating from a later period is a beautiful Zapotec legend compiled by Paul Radin in the village of Zaachila that tells the story of the marriage of the daughter of the Mexica king Ahuítzotl to the great Zapotec lord Cosijoeza.

This description of the texts preserved in Nahuatl and in the Mayan language of Yucatán, in Quiché, Cakchiquel, Otomí, Tarascan, Mixtec, and Zapotec, reveals the principal themes in Indian literatures. They include myths and legends, sacred hymns, various forms of epic, lyrical and religious poetry, early forms of theater, chronicles and history, didactic prose, doctrines concerning the gods, and even the beginnings of what might be called pre-Hispanic philosophy. There are also texts written on the Conquest, in which it is possible to study the vision of the conquered, the testimony left by those who contemplated and were aware of the destruction of their ancient culture and way of life. The languages in which the majority of these texts were written were not only a suitable medium but one that was both rich and elegant. Thanks to the juxtaposition of roots and numerous suffixes and prefixes, these languages are capable of expressing any idea, however apparently abstract or complex. The Indian scholars, artists of the word, were aware of the literary possibilities of the languages they spoke. In the Aztec schools, for example, particular emphasis was placed on the art of rhetoric and on the cultivation of *techillahtolli*, a noble and precise form of expression.

The names of some of the finest poets and historians in ancient Mexico are known. Since I have written about them at length elsewhere, in this essay I shall merely transcribe a brief text that describes the ideal *tlaquetzqui* or narrator, "aquel que, al hablar, hace ponerse de pie las cosas" ("he who, when he speaks, makes things stand up"). By contrasting descriptions of good and bad narrators, this text reveals the Indian ideals regarding the art of rhetoric:

El narrador:
donairoso, dice las cosas con gracia,
artista del labio y la boca.
El buen narrador:
de palabras gustosas, de palabras alegres,
flores tiene en sus labios.
En su discurso las consejas abundan,
de palabra correcta, brotan flores de su boca.
Su discurso: gustoso y alegre como las flores;
de él es el lenguaje noble y la expresión cuidadosa.
El mal narrador
lenguaje descompuesto,
atropella las palabras;
labio comido, mal hablado.
Narra cosas sin tino,
dice palabras vanas,
no tiene vergüenza.

The witty narrator
has an elegant turn of phrase,
and is an artist of speech.
The good narrator:
uses pleasant words, happy words,
and has flowers on his lips.
In his speech, elegantly expressed legends abound,
flowers spring from his mouth.
His discourse is as pleasant and happy as flowers;
his language noble, his expression careful.
The bad narrator
uses disorganized language,
his words come out in a rush;
he bites his lips and uses bad language.
He makes pointless remarks,
and says useless words,
and has no shame.

(Códice Matritense de la Real Academia, fol. 122)

The good narrator was a veritable artist of speech. It was said that he made a great effort to achieve noble language and careful expression. Emphasis was placed on the fact that flowers, in other words, metaphors and symbols, sprang from his lips. All these metaphors, so characteristic of Indian languages, gave to their literary expressions an unmistakable stamp. As a result of these and other resources characteristic of these languages– such as parallelism or expressions that repeat the same idea in different ways, the juxtaposition of words, the "clasp" phrases that open and close a particular text–the ancient poets, orators, historians, and scholars were able to create extraordinary texts in which the abstract and the concrete appear to combine to give new life to myths, legends, stories, and doctrines.

Literary creations were held in such high esteem by these peoples that they conceived an aesthetic view of life formulated through poetry or "flowers and song," as it was called. It is therefore not unusual to find texts in which the poets themselves spoke of their anguish in trying to find a means of expressing their intuitions and thoughts. Lord Ayocuan, the poet from Tecamachalco, in what is now the state of Puebla, says that the origin of his songs lay in the heavens but that he, despite his yearning, is unable to say what he wants:

> Del interior del cielo vienen
> las bellas flores, los bellos cantos.
> Los afea nuestro anhelo,
> nuestra inventiva los hecha a perder.
>
> From the inside of the heavens come
> the beautiful flowers, the lovely songs.
> Our desire makes them ugly,
> our inventiveness destroys them.

(Cantares mexicanos, fol. 9.v.)

Inspiration and intuition, longing or inventiveness; flowers and songs, in other words, metaphors and symbols, are the soul of Indian literature. The culture from which the largest number of literary texts have been preserved is undoubtedly the Nahuatl. It is no exaggeration to say that there are several thousand folios in Nahuatl kept in libraries and museums in Mexico, the United States, and Europe. Manuscripts by the various Mayan groups have also been preserved, some of which have already been translated into European languages, while others continue to wait for scholars to reveal their contents. Although little remains of other cultures such as the Mixtec and Zapotec, Otomí, and Tarascan, it is at least possible to surmise what their forms and methods of literary expression were.

In short, it is no exaggeration to say that many of these texts, particularly those of a religious nature, were extremely ancient and, in the strict sense of the word, millennary. They often contain the key to understanding the meaning of the great institutions–that is, the art of Indian culture. An example of these aspirations in the field of art is provided by the following text which describes the ideal artist, given the title of *toltécatl* (Toltec), since it was thought that all that was virtuous derived from the times of the great priest, the cultural hero Quetzalcóatl:

> Tolteca: artista, discípulo, abundante, múltiple, inquieto.
> El verdadero artista: capaz, se adiestra, es hábil:
> dialoga con su corazón, encuentra las cosas con su mente.
> El verdadero artista todo lo saca de su corazón;
> obra con deleite, hace las cosas con calma, con tiento,
> obra como un tolteca, compone cosas, obra hábilmente, crea;
> arregla las cosas, las hace atildadas, hace que se ajunten.

(Códice Matritense de la Real Academia de la Historia, fol. 175 v.)

> Toltec: artist, disciple, abundant, multiple, restless.
> The true artist: is capable, practices and is skillful;
> he dialogues with his heart, and finds things in his mind.
> The true artist finds everything in his heart;
> he works with pleasure, he does things calmly and
> with a steady hand,
> he works like a Toltec, he composes things, he works
> skillfully and creates;
> he arranges things, he tidies them up, and corrects them.

The ideals of the artist, the Toltec, continue to live on in the souls of many contemporary Amerindian artists. Five centuries after the Conquest, there are still potters, weavers, feather artists, singers, and dancers–individuals capable of dialoguing with the heart who, working calmly and with a steady hand, despite their poverty and neglect, are in fact the possessors of ancient pre-Columbian inspiration. In the field of literature, contemporary Indian works abound. In them, one not only finds the echo of ancient times but expressions with a new meaning. These compositions, both in poetry and narrative, reflect the voices of the men and women who are the descendants of peoples who were conquered, and who now live in a world of contrasts and violent cultural shock. In recent years a number of us have made a renewed effort to bring contemporary indigenous literatures in Mexico to the attention of all interested persons. (See, for example my text "No acabrán mis cantos . . ." [1992; "My Songs Will Never End"] and also the twenty-two volumes of *Lenguas de Mexico* first published in 1994 and reissued in 2002 and my recently published *In the Language of Kings: An Anthology of Mesoamerican Literature–Pre-Columbian to the Present*. These literatures, both ancient and contemporary, reflect the message of those who have managed to give meaning to their lives and to the eternal enigmas of death, divinity, and the universe, so often symbolized in their own individual colors in their books of paintings. Instead of trying to reduce these expressions to somewhat arbitrary rules or principles, I would like to invite those who are interested in them to discover for themselves the literary and human value of the Indian "flowers and songs" which, as the Nahua scholars said, will exist forever. In the words of the wise Nezahualcóyotl:

> No acabarán mis flores,
> no acabarán mis cantos.
> Yo cantor los elevo:
> se reparten y se esparcen. . . .
>
> My flowers will not end,
> my songs will not end,
> I, the bard, lift them up:
> they are dispersed and spread around. . . .

(Cantares mexicanos, fol. 16 v)

Translation by Suzanne Stephens

Works Cited

Alva Ixtlilxóchitl, Fernando de. 1975–1977. *Obras históricas: incluyen el texto completo de las llamadas Relaciones e Historia de la nación chichimeca en una nueva versión establecida con el cotejo de los manuscritos más antiguos que se conocen.* 2 vols. Ed. Edmundo O'Gorman. Mexico City: Universidad Nacional Autónoma de México, Instituto de Investigaciones Históricas.

Anales de los Xahil. 1946. Ed. and trans. Georges Raynaud, Miguel Angel Asturias and J. M. González de Mendoza. Mexico City: Universidad Nacional Autónoma de México.

Cantares en idioma mexicanos, reproducción facsimiliaria del manuscrito original existente en la Biblioteca Nacional, que se imprime por acuerdo del Sr. Gral. Don Manuel González Cosio, secretario de fomento en el taller de fototipia del mismo ministerio bajo la dirección del Dr. Antonio Peñafiel. 1904. Ed. Antonio Peñafiel. fol. 14 v. Mexico City: Oficina Tipográfica de la Secretaría de Fomento.

Carrasco Pizana, Pedro. 1950. *Los otomíes, cultura e historia prehispánicas de los pueblos mesoamericanos de habla otomiana.* Mexico City: Universidad Nacional Autónoma de México, Instituto de Historia en colaboración con el Instituto de Antropología e Historia.

Caso, Alfonso. 1930. "Un códice en Otomí." *Proceedings of the XXIII International Congress of Americanists*, New York, 17–22 September 1928. 130–35.

———. 1936. "¿Tenían los teotihuacanos conocimiento del *Tonalpohualli*?" *El México antiguo* 4. 3–4: 131–44.

———, ed. 1960. *Interpretación del Códice Bodley 2858.* Trans. Alfonso Caso. Mexico City: Sociedad Mexicana de Antropología.

———. 1962. "Relaciones entre el Viejo y el Nuevo Mundo. Una observación metodológica." *Cuadernos Americanos* 21.125.6: 160-75.

———, and Mary Elizabeth Smith. 1966. *Interpretación del Códice Colombino.* Mexico City: Sociedad Mexicana de Antropología.

———, and Federico Gómez de Orozco. 1979. *El Códice de Huamantla. Trabajos inéditos del Dr. Alfonso Caso y el Prof. Federico Gómez de Orozco.* Cuadernos de la Biblioteca Nacional de Antropología e Historia. Serie Codices, no. 7. Mexico City: Instituto Nacional de Antropología e Historia.

Códice Aubin. 1980 [1576]. Ed. Bernardino de Jesús Quiroz. Mexico City: Editorial Innovación.

Códice Chimalpopoca. 1975. Ed. and trans. Primo Feliciano Velázquez. Mexico City: Universidad Nacional Autónoma de México.

Códice Florentino. 1905. Ed. facs. Francisco del Paso y Troncoso. Vol. 5. Madrid: Fototipia de Hauser y Menet.

———. 1950–1955. *Florentine Codex. General History of Things of New Spain.* 13 vols. By Bernardino de Sahagún. Trans. Arthur J.O. Anderson and Charles E. Dibble. Santa Fe: School of American Research.

El Códice Huichapan. 1976. Ed. Manuel Alvarado Guinchard. Mexico City: Instituto Nacional de Antropología e Historia.

Códice Matritense de [Bernardino de] Sahagún. 1964. Madrid: Porrúa Turanzas. Colección Chimalistac 19 and 20.

Códice Matritense de la Real Academia de la Historia. 1907. Ed. facs. Francisco del Paso y Troncoso. Vol. 8. Madrid: Fototipia de Hauser y Menet.

Códice Pérez: traducción libre del maya al castellano. 1949. Ed. and trans. Emilio Solis Alcalá. Mérida: Ediciones de la Liga de Acción Social.

Códice Selden 3135 (A.2) *Interpretación.* 1964. Ed. Alfonso Caso. Mexico City: Sociedad Mexicana de Antropología.

Colloquios y doctrina christiana con que los doce frayles de San Francisco enbiados por el papa Adriano sesto y por el emperador Carlos quinto: convertieron a los indios de la Nueva España. En lengua Mexicana y Española. 1986. Ed. Miguel León Portilla. Mexico City: Universidad Nacional Autónoma de México y Fundación de Investigadores Sociales.

Crónica de Chicxulub. *Crónicas de la conquista de México.* 1939. Ed. Agustín Yáñez. Mexico City: Ediciones de la Universidad Nacional Autónoma de México. 191–215.

Díaz del Castillo, Bernal. 1933. *The Discovery and Conquest of Mexico, 1517–1521.* Ed. Genaro García. Trans. A. P. Maudslay. London: Routledge.

———. 1955. *Historia verdadera de la conquista de la Nueva España.* Mexico City: Editorial Porrúa.

Dibble, Charles E. 1940. "El antiguo sistema de escritura en México." *Revista Mexicana de Estudios Antropológicos* 4: 105–28.

Durán, Fray Diego de. 1867. *Historia de las Indias de Nueva España y Islas de Tierra Firme.* 2 vols. and Atlas. Ed. José F. Ramírez. Mexico City: Imprenta de J. M. Andrade y F. Escalante.

Dyck, Anne. 1959. *Mixteco Texts.* Ed. Elson Benjamin. Norman, Okla.: Summer Institute of Linguistics of the University of Oklahoma.

Garibay Kintana, Angel María, ed. 1943. "Huehuetlahtolli, Documento A." *Tlalocan* 1.1: 31-53, 1.2: 81-107. Rptd. 1971. New York: Johnsons Reprint Corporation.

———. 1953-1954. *Historia de la literatura náhuatl.* 2 vols. Mexico City: Editorial Porrúa.

———, ed. 1964. *Poesía Náhuatl.* Trans. Ángel María Garibay Kintana. 3 vols. Mexico City: Universidad Nacional Autónoma de México.

Gómez de Orozco, Federico. 1940. *Crónicas de Michoacán.* Mexico City: Universidad Nacional Autónoma de México.

Historia tolteca-chichimeca. 1942. Vol. 1. *Corpus Codicum Americanorum Medii Aevi.* Ed. Ernst Mengin. Copenhagen: Sumptibus Einar Munksgaard.

Kirchhoff, Paul. 1956. "La relación de Michoacán como fuente para la historia de la sociedad y cultura tarascas." *Relación de las ceremonias y ritos y población y gobierno de los indios de la provincia de Michoacán, 1541.* Ed. José Tudela. Madrid: Editorial Aguilar. xix–xxxiii.

Kroeber, Alfred Louis. 1923. *Anthropology.* New York: Harcourt, Brace and Company.

Landa, Diego de. 1938. *Relación de las cosas de Yucatán.* Ed. Héctor Pérez Martínez. Mexico City: Editorial Pedro Robredo.

———. 1975. *The Maya: Diego de Landa's Account of the Affairs of Yucatán.* Ed. and trans. A. R. Pagden. Chicago: J. Philip O'Hara.

León-Portilla, Miguel. 1956. *La filosofía náhuatl, estudiada en sus fuentes.* Mexico City: Instituto Indigenista Interamericano.

———. 1958. *Ritos, sacerdotes y atavíos de los dioses.* Bilingual ed. Náhuatl-Spanish. Mexico City: Universidad Nacional Autónoma de México, Instituto de Investigaciones Históricas.

———. 1961. *Los antiguos mexicanos a través de sus crónicas y cantares.* Mexico City: Fondo de Cultura Económica.

———. 1963. *Visión de los vencidos: relaciones indígenas de la conquista.* Mexico City: Universidad Nacional Autónoma de México, Imprenta Universitaria.

———. 1963. *Aztec Thought and Culture Study; a Study of the Ancient Nahuatl Mind.* Trans. Jack Emory Davis. Norman: University of Oklahoma Press.

———. 1964. *Las literaturas precolombinas de México.* Mexico City: Editorial Pormaca.

———, ed. 1978. *Literatura del México antiguo: los textos en lengua náhuatl.* Caracas: Biblioteca Ayacucho.

———. 1984. *Literaturas de Mesoamérica.* Mexico City: Secretaría de Educación Pública.

———. 1986. *Pre-Columbian Literatures of Mexico.* Trans Grace Lobanov and the author. Norman, Okla: University of Oklahoma Press.

———. 1992. *The Broken Spears: The Aztec Account of the Conquest of Mexico.* Ed. and intr. by Miguel León-Portilla. Boston: Beacon Press.

———. 1992. "No acabarán mis cantos: El destino de la palabra indígena." *Literaturas indígenas de México.* By Miguel León Portilla. Madrid: Editorial MAPFRE. 293–336.

León-Portilla, Miguel, and Earl Shorris, with Sylvia S. Shorris, Ascensión H. de León-Portilla, and Jorge Klor de Alva. 2001. *In the Language of Kings: An Anthology of Mesoamerican Literature–Pre-Columbian to the Present.* New York: W. W. Norton.

El Libro de Chilam Balam de Chumayel. 1930. Ed. and trans. Antonio Mediz Bolio. San José de Costa Rica: Imprenta y Librería Lehmann (Santier & Co.)

El Libro de Chilam Balam de Chumayel. 1987. 1st ed. Trans. Antonio Mediz Bolio. Mérida, Mexico City: Consejo Editorial de Yucatán.

El Libro de los cantares de Dzitbalché. 1965. Ed. Alfredo Barrera Vásquez. Mexico City: Instituto Nacional de Antropología e Historia.

El Libro de los libros de Chilam Balam. 1948. Ed. and trans. Alfredo Barrera Vásquez. Mexico City: Fondo de Cultura Económica.

Lizardi Ramos, César. 1955. "¿Conocían el Xíhuitl los Teotihuacanos?" *El México antiguo* 8: 219-23.

Memorial de Solola. Anales de los cakchiqueles. Título de los señores de Totonicapán. 1950. Ed. and trans. Adrián Recinos. Mexico City: Fondo de Cultura Económica.

Olmos, Andrés de. 1972. *Arte para aprender la lengua mexicana*. Ed. Rémi Siméon. Guadalajara: E. Aviña Levy Editor.

Popol Vuh: Las antiguas historias del Quiché. 1953. Ed. and trans. Adrián Recinos. Mexico City: Fondo de Cultura Económica.

Rabinal Achí. Teatro indígena prehispánico. 1955. Ed. Francisco Monterde. Mexico City: Ediciones de la Universidad Nacional Autónoma de México.

Radin, Paul. 1935. *An historial legend of the Zapotecs*. Berkeley: University of California Press.

Relación de Michoacán, La. 1980. (atribuida a fray Jerónimo de Alcalá). Ed. Francisco Miranda. Morelia: Fimax Publicitas.

Ruiz de Alarcón, Hernando. 1900. "Tratado de las supersticiones de los naturales de esta Nueva España." *Anales del Museo Nacional de México* 6. Mexico City. 123–223.

Sahagún, Fray Bernardino de. 1956. *Historia General de las Cosas de la Nueva España*. Ed. A. M. Garibay K.. 4 vols. Mexico City: Editorial Porrúa.

——. 1950–1982. *General History of the Things of New Spain; Florentine Codex*. Part 1: *Introductions and Indices*. Ed. and trans. J. O. Anderson and Charles E. Dibble. 13 vols. Santa Fe: N. M., School of American Research.

The Ancient Future of the Itza: The Book of Chilam Balam of Tizimín. 1982. Ed. and trans. Munro S. Edmonson. Austin: University of Texas Press.

Ximénez, Fray Francisco, trans. 1857. *Las historias del origen de los indios de esta provincia de Guatemala*. Ed. K. Scherzer Viena: En casa de Carlos Gerold é Hijo.

CHAPTER 33

THE NATURE OF INDIGENOUS LITERATURES IN THE ANDES

Denise Y. Arnold and Juan de Dios Yapita

In this essay, we focus on Andean literatures, but from a less usual stance: That of foregrounding Aymara language and literatures, which we know from first-hand experience. However, there are several other reasons why we have adopted this perspective. As compared to Quechua literature, with its many studies (José María Arguedas 1957; Lara 1947, 1957, 1969; Leinhard 1992, Cornejo Polar 1980, 1994; and so on), Aymara literature is less well known. It is all but ignored in some recent literary studies of the Americas (for example, in Lienhard's *La voz y su huella* [The Voice and Its Traces]), although there are ample sources for its study. Rivet and Créqui-Montfort in their four-volume *Bibliographie* (1951–1956), Van den Berg 1984, 1988, 1994, Albó, Briggs, Jemio, Arnold, and many others have written on Aymara sources.

The actual reasons for this lacuna, then, are more complex. They have to do with the particular history of the Southern Andes, above all with the origins and expansion of Inca culture and the way that Spanish colonial rule was then implemented. And they have to do with the higher status of Quechua as the "language of the Incas" and the subsequent expansion of literary Quechua in the hands of a Cuscocentric *criollo* and *mestizo* elite. Written Aymara, in comparison, is sparse (at least in the colonial and republican periods), and the Aymara-speaking world, in general, has been more isolated culturally until recent decades.

But we must remember that at the heart of Cusco Quechua is an Aymara underlay. The origin myth of the Incas is grounded in the journey of Mama Uqllu and Manku Qapaq from Aymara speaking Colla territory, at the southern end of Lake Titicaca. Many scholars have pointed out the Aymara substratum below the Cusco dialect of Quechua; there are suggestions that, at one stage, Aymara may have been the court language of the Inca elite. So it is likely that Quechua literatures, at least around Cusco, might also have emerged from this common source.

In addition, at the time of the Spanish invasion, Aymara-speaking Charkas, with its two large provinces of La Plata (now Sucre) and La Paz in present-day Bolivia, was on the linguistic and cultural fringe of the new Spanish Andean empire, whose main administrative centers were in Cusco and Lima (see **Map 1**). Charkas was at some cultural distance from the efforts of the new colonial state to implement a program of literacy, based on the alphabetic script, first in Quechua and later in Spanish. And it was relatively immune to the new Cuscocentric *mestizo* practice of writing Quechua in a resistance literature harking back to Inca rule. In fact, Aymara-Charkas (including Chayanta) and Quechua-Cusco have often been viewed as rival cultural centers in the development of Andean literary and cultural history. Quechua literature, as a window onto the exotic Inca world, has become more known and more mainstream. But in their own distinct form of resistance to Spanish and alphabetic domination, Aymara literary forms, far from the public gaze, have been able to continue more forcefully, right up until modern times.

Map 1.

Map of Andean cultural centers in present-day Colombia, Ecuador, Peru, Bolivia, and Chile. (Courtesy of the authors)

Part One: The Nature of Andean Literatures

The vitality of Andean literatures, whether Aymara, Quechua, or others (Uru-Morato, Chipaya, Jaqaru, and Mapuche, to name just a few), like the very invisibility of these literatures to the Western world, challenges those canons of "literature" or "text" based exclusively on the written word. Andean literature emerges from woven origins; the explicitness of its woven ontology was taken in the Andes to extraordinary limits and was uniquely expressed.

With Jacques Derrida, we can easily dismiss the structuralist idea that orality is prior to text, since in the Andes "writing" is everywhere: From the patterned scattering of coca leaves, to rock images engraved by lightning, to weaving designs, glyphs, and alphabetic script. Curiously enough, the *mestizo* chronicler Santacruz Pachacuti Yamqui, whose own hybrid text moves between visual, non-verbal, ritual, and written codes, implies that the Incas were aware of "writing" before the time of the Spanish invasion, a view widely held even today. He mentions certain pre-Hispanic *capítulos* and a mysterious *libro grande* that was brought to the Cusco palace by a messenger (Harrison 58). Modern Andeans, too, are just as likely to call "writing" the Inca knotted threads called *khipus*, along with other Andean textual practices.

This broader non-Western definition of "writing" is echoed in Andean terminology. *Qillqa,* in the sense of an engraved or painted image, was transposed to writing from the early colonial period. Today, modern weavers readily adapt their terminology of weaving techniques to the writing skills of modern young women, so that the Aymara word *p'itaña* can be used just as well for "picking out threads" with a bone weaving pick as for "picking out writing" with a pencil (Arnold 1997, 114).

This wider definition of Andean literature compels us to revert to the etymology of text as a woven device. Such woven devices must have underlain the spread of similar literary forms throughout the whole region, where distinctly Andean textual practices–whether patterned designs, braiding, knotted cords, painted images, choreography, speech, libation, music, or drama–are all generated from a predetermined, additive sequencing grounded in cloth. Recent archaeological work has shown how this cultural expansion into new regions might have taken place. Key routes into new Tiwanaku (or Inca) territories are characterized by the presence of distinctive state-level designs on ceramics, drinking cups, and textiles, which differentiated them from the more local patterns; as coded literary forms, these must have transformed textual practices at these new centers of power, just as writing was to do much later under the Spanish.

Continuities with older traditions are evident, too, in Andean literatures. John Rowe (1980, 313–17) conjectured that the iconographic coding of the early Chavín culture might have been directly related to narrative structures. The important essay by Mary Frame on "The Visual Images of Fabric Structures in Ancient Peruvian Art," concerning the structures of early Andean sprang textiles, implies the possible storytelling functions of cloth, through the spatial and temporal markers of character (perhaps even of voice) in the cloth designs at certain junctures, for example, the use of the serpent-head image as a ubiquitous structural element where threads cross. Contemporary ethnographic work by Silverman Proust in Q'eros, Peru, on the acknowledged expression of narrative images (above all, the decapitated Inca's head) in certain weaving designs reinforces this view.

Knotted cords had already been used as tallies in other parts of the Americas, including the Andes (in the case of the Mapuches), reaching more complex woven forms in Tiwanaku and other early Andean cultures. Nevertheless, under the Incas, the *khipu* cords were highly systematized, becoming templates for state rule and administration; some have argued that they made the notion of empire possible.

Within this wider context, it is not surprising that the detailed analyses of Aymara discourse, stylistics, and literary devices have encountered this world of woven devices, with its historical continuities (and ruptures). For example, the three and four linked threads of the early sprang textiles, described by Frame, seem to have become transposed in time to the three- and four-voice motifs in contemporary Aymara tales, such as this *Tale of the Snake* from rural Oruro in Bolivia,

told by Doña Lucía Quispe (Arnold and Yapita 1992, 33–34). Here, the embedded voices of Andean reported speech (N, the narrator; A, the ancestors; G, the girls; and S, the snake) are layered in time, to let us know the ultimate source of the tale:

```
      (N)   Kataris jaqïriw
      (A)        siw.
      (N)   Q'alituriw uka
      (A)        sika.
   5  (G)              «Kawkinkarakta q'alitu»
                  siriw
      (N)   Imillanakar jikjatir
      (A)        sika.
      (N)   Imillanaka parlay.
  10  (G)              «Kawkinkarakta»
      (S)                   «Nä aka manqhankta»
      (G)        siriw–
      (S)                   «nä jutani»
      (G)              «Iyaw».
  15  (S)                   «Mä ch'ankha muruq'u churasitay»
                        siriw,
      (A)        sika.
      (N)   Yast ukat
            ch'ankha muruq'u imilla
  20        irkatasitäwi
      (A)        si.
      (S)                   «Uka ch'ankhat katjitäta»
      (G)              «Iyaw»
                  sasaw,
  25  (N)   Yast,
            uka ch'ankhat arkantatäwi
            imillanaka
      (A)        si.
      (N)   Ukat,
  30        mä qala p'iyan
            katarikiw qhurqhuski.
            Kunas utjit
      (G)              si.
      (N)   Mä akan jikjatakirakitäw,
  35  (A)        si.
      (N)   Ukat,
            mä ukan jikjatakirakitäwi,
            si.
            Janiw kunas utjitï katarikiskiw.
  40  (N)   Ukat,
            chachasti,
      (S)                   «Ukatpi»
                        sakitäwi
      (A)        siw ....
  45  (N)   Uk isapirït nä


      (N)   The snake used to be a person,
      (A)        they say.
      (N)   That one used to be naked,
      (A)        they say
   5  (G)              –Where are you, little naked-one?–
                  they used to say.
      (N)   He used to meet girls,
      (A)        they say.
      (N)   The young girls spoke.
  10  (G)              –Where are you then?–
      (S)                   –I'm here inside–
      (G)              he used to say
      (S)                   –I shall come–
      (G)              –OK then–
  15  (S)                   –Give me a ball of thread–
                        he used to say,
```

```
    (A)            they say.
    (N)    That's it, and then
           the young girl had given him
20         a ball of thread,
    (A)            they say,
    (S)                    –From that thread you shall find me–
    (G)            –Alright–
           saying.
25  (N)    Then,
           they'd followed that thread
           the young girls
    (A)            they say.
    (N)    And,
30         a hole of the rocks
           a snake was snoring.
           There was nothing (else) there
    (G)                    they say,
    (N)    Once more they met him
35  (A)            they say.
    (N)    Then,
           once more they met him,
           they say,
           There was nothing there, only a snake.
40         And then,
           the man,
    (S)                    –I am really that thing–
           he'd said,
    (A)            they say...
45  (N)    I used to listen to that.
```

"Tale of the Snake" by Doña Lucía Quispe Choque. Recorded in Oruro, Bolivia, in August 1990.

Added to this, Aymara stylistics often appeals to "tripartition" (three-threadedness) as an expressive and emphatic feature.

Other modern studies, such as those of Huanca (1989, 139ff.), have indicated the "interlaced" (*k'anata*) nature of Aymara sentences, which can become transformed at critical junctures into "hidden threads" (*taypi ch'ank"a*) deep inside the text, as ideas that will come to fruition later on (see Yapita 1992, 52).

For these reasons, López G. U. (39–42) argues that the basis of Andean discourse is a dialogue between at least two people; as in musical performance, one person guides (*ira*) and the other follows (*arka*), filling in any lapse in oral memory. According to Dedenbach (1999), similar features organize the suffix discourse-markers that pick out the thread of a narrator's point of view, the evidentiality, throughout a tale. Likewise, there are woven links between themes constituting what Huanca calls "illustrative topics of opening and closure" (Huanca 1989, 136-37), or woven connectors between different tales to make up a whole rhapsodic cycle (Arnold and Yapita 1992, 9).

In Andean textual practices, these woven features function as communication devices at multiple levels. Thus, "braiding" (*k'anata*) not only marks the moments in contemporary wedding songs when sling and hair-braids are named; it also functions to bind together couples in an interlinked clasping of hands and, in the larger scale, the braiding and weaving together of whole families, with their animals and food products, living at the different ecological levels (Arnold and Yapita 1998a, 553):

Sisters: Ipalitay ipalita
Brothers: Tiyulitay tiyulita
Sisters: Liriyu k'ana k'ant'añani
Brothers: Chhichhillqhäta qhatt'añani
Sisters: Ipalitay ipalita
Brothers: Tiyulitay tiyulita
Sisters: Liriyu k'ana k'ant'añani

Brothers: Chhichhillqhäta qhatt'añani
Sisters: Ch'akhurüta aküruka
            Jum wiñay saya
            Awki tayka surwin tiwula
            Liriyu k'ana k'ant'añani
            Apsu qhata qhatt'añani,
            Larit tiwulay . . .

Sisters: Sister, sister
Brothers: Brother, brother
Sisters: Let's braid a multi-colored plait
Brothers: Let's tighten a fly-brown sling
Sisters: Sister, sister
Brothers: Brother, brother
Sisters: Let's braid a multi-colored plait
Brothers: Let's tighten a fly-brown sling
Sisters: This very day they become loom-stakes
            You both, standing there forever
            Father, mother, nephew, uncle-fox,
            Let's braid a lily plait,
            Let's tighten a decorated sling,
            Uncle-fox . . .

In areas of the Southern Andes where weaving is still practiced, the popular *wayñus*, as pan-Andean song-and-dance displays during courtship, draw their inspiration and compositional modes from the woven garments of the participants and the braiding dance-patterns of their movements (Arnold 1992b, 40ff; see **Figure 1**). Their woven structure becomes evident at all levels, from the patterns of versification, to the musical patterns of reflection and repeats, to the lyrical content and the patterns of formal exchange between partners:

Figure 1.

Wayñu dance with braided hands (Qaqachaka, Oruro, Bolivia). (Archive of the authors)

Tuka tuka charanguituy
  Asusina sawsisitay
Uka llijlla pagasqayki
  Asusina sawsisitay

Play charango, play
  Little lily, little willow
I shall pay you with that mantle
  Little lily, little willow

The ontology of all these woven devices derives from fleece, at once the means of communication *par excellence* and the basis of production. So McLuhan's famous dictum, "the medium is the message," applies here in the Andes to fleece and textile instead of to paper and Western script. If the Andean textile closest to "writing," in a Western sense, was the Inca system of knotted threads called *khipu*, this was essentially a pastoral discourse, a tally of flocks, as Brotherston affirms in his *Book of the Fourth World* (1992, 194). In this way, economic origins in camelid herds were inseparable from the very origins of the Inca state. Moreover, the *khipus*, according to Andean theorists such as Murra (245), not only had a mnemonic function as numerical tallies but also worked through a logical predetermined system of ordering; Pärssinen, in *Tawantinsuyu* (Chapter 1), suggests they might even have had a phonetic reading.

Khipus still provided the source documentation for many written accounts of communal provisions, well into the colonial period. Thus the *mestizo* chronicler Felipe Guamán Poma de Ayala (1524?–1613) announces at the beginning of his 2,000-page letter to the king of Spain (*Nueva Corónica y Buen Gobierno* 8), written in around 1613, that his account was based on the reading of *khipus* and other woven devices. He also underlines the fact that, for him, the *khipu* was able to express so much more than mere writing.

Even today, modern Andean storytellers "read" their tales with directional suffix markers, as if reading from a *khipu* or its Aymara counterpart called *chinu* (Arnold and Yapita, 1992, 23–27). The directionality, colors, textures, type, and sequencing of knots seem to have marked not only the quantity, gender, and class of objects annotated, but also the underlying spatial logic of Andean hierarchy. Libation sequences to the animals still draw on the logic of *khipu* organization in parts of the Southern Andes, the final knots in a sequence serving to "bind" the herds into their pens so as not to lose them, just as the Inca "binders" (*uatacamayoc*) brought straying objects to justice and prison (Arnold, Yapita, et al. 2000, Chapter 11).

The medium of fleece gives rise to Andean grammatical categories and discourse markers. Mannheim (67–69) describes as the actual grammar of Andean language the pervasive use of woven devices in modern Quechua folksongs and their patterning throughout these songs in a woven language of rotation, reflection, parallelism, slide, and duality (or *yanantin*). Even beyond the semantic, musical, and grammatical parallelism of the immediate couplet, contemporary Andean singers develop, in the formal organization of discourse, entire episodes in their songs to the animals based on the production of fleece by paying particular attention to the qualities of grazing grounds and waters necessary to develop the coats of their flocks (Arnold and Yapita 1998b, 275–76), just as an Aztec poet might have drawn on the ontological roots of his scriptural material in references to the fibers of his screenfold paper page (Brotherston 1992, 46). Color, too, is an important element in their songs. The following example compares the fleece color of the animals going in file with white or red ribbons unfurling:

1	Mamalita, *Mamala paw paw*
2	Jumapiña, *Mamala paw paw*
3	Saratmakay saratma, *Mamala paw paw*
4	Janq'u sinta jaquta, *Mamala paw paw*
5	Saratmakay saratma, *Mamala paw paw*
6	Wila sinta jaquta, *Mamala paw paw*
7	Umay katükam sariri, *Mamala paw paw*
8	Parway katükam sariri, *Mamala paw paw*
9	Uma katükam sariri, *Mamala paw paw*
10	Parway katükam sariri, *Mamala paw paw*
11	Janiw ququy shamati, *Mamala paw paw*
12	Janiw wiskhuy shamati, *Mamala paw paw*
13	Janipiniw pisi pis iñtantati, *Mamala paw paw*
14	Altupiniw saranta, *Mamala paw paw*
15	Kancha puqha saranta, *Mamala paw paw*
16	Jira puqha saranta, *Mamala paw paw*
17	Jawkha wawan jaqïta, *Mamala paw paw*
18	Jawkha allchhin jaqïta, *Mamala paw paw*
19	Jumapiniw Awkñata, *Mamala paw paw*
20	Jumapiñay Taykñata, *Mamala paw paw*
21	Kuna sataki, *Mamala paw paw*
22	«Chita Qallu» sataki, *Mamala paw paw*
23	Kuna sataki, *Mamala paw paw*
24	Jumapiñay «Chitäta» *Mamala paw paw*
25	Pantish t'ikha, *Mamala paw paw*
26	Rusas t'ikha, *Mamala paw paw. . .*

1	Mamalita, *Mamala baa baa*
2	You are our real wealth, *Mamala baa baa*
3	How lovely you go! *Mamala baa baa*
4	A white ribbon unfurled, *Mamala baa baa*
5	How lovely you go! *Mamala baa baa*
6	A red ribbon unfurled, *Mamala baa baa*
7	Who wanders 'til you gulp water, *Mamala baa baa*
8	And wanders 'til you pluck bunch-grass, *Mamala baa baa*
9	And wanders 'til you gulp water, *Mamala baa baa*
10	And wanders 'til you pluck bunch-grass, *Mamala baa baa*
11	I shan't beg food from you, *Mamala baa baa*
12	I shan't beg sandals from you, *Mamala baa baa*
13	Oh, that you'll never seem less in numbers, *Mamala baa baa*
14	That you'll walk in the heights always, *Mamala baa baa*
15	That you'll walk in a full fold, *Mamala baa baa*
16	That you'll walk the full dung-circle, *Mamala baa baa*
17	You're someone with flocks of children, *Mamala baa baa*
18	Someone with flocks of grandchildren, *Mamala baa baa*
19	You really are my Father, *Mamala baa baa*
20	You really are my Mother, *Mamala baa baa*
21	What are you called? *Mamala baa baa*
22	You are called Little Pet, *Mamala baa baa*
23	What are you called? *Mamala baa baa*
24	You are always Little Pet, *Mamala baa baa*
25	Crimson flower, *Mamala baa baa*
26	Rose-red flower, *Mamala baa baa. . .*

Sung in Qaqachaka, Bolivia, on 14 April 1989 by Doña Asunta Arias

The recent discovery in some Jesuit documents from the seventeenth century of an early Colonial drawing of a *khipu*, reputedly by the Quechua-speaking *mestizo* priest Blas Valera, reveals how the grammatical and stylistic elements of Andean languages (a syllabic model of organization based on suffix position and rhythm) were used in the knotted cords to transmit not only numerical tallies but also literary forms, for example, in the famous "Rain Goddess" hymn, which he translated from Quechua into a parallel Latin text. The hymn was already known from El Inca Garcilaso's rendering of it into Spanish:

Súmac ñusta
Torralláiquin

Puiñuyquita
Paquir cayan
5   Hina mantara
Cunuñunun
Illapántac
Camri ñusta
Unuiquita
10 Para munqui
Mai ñimpiri
Chichi manqui
Riti munqui
Pacharúrac
15 Pachacámac
Viracocha
Cai hinápac
Churasunqui
19 Camasunqui

Pulchra Nimpha
Frater tuus
Urnam tuam
Nunc infringit
5   Cuius ictus
Tonat fulget
Fulminatque
Sed tu nympha
Tuam limpham
10 Fundens pluis
Interdunque
Grandinem, seu
Nivem mittis
Mundi Factor
15 Pacha cámac
Viracocha
Ad hoc munus
Te sufficit
19 Ac praefecit

Fair maiden,
Thy brother
Thine urn
Is now breaking.
5   And for this cause
It thunders and lightens
And thunderbolts fall,
But thou, royal maiden
Their clean waters
10 Shalt give us in rain;
And sometimes too
Shalt give hail
And shall give snow.
The world's Creator,
15 Pachacámac,
Viracocha,
For this office
Has appointed thee,
19 And has created thee.

(Brotherston 1992, 78)

In his *Comentarios Reales* [1609, 1617; *Royal Commentaries*] (Book 2, Chapter 27), Garcilaso (1539–1616) tells how he obtained a copy of this hymn, composed originally by an Inca poet and astrologer, based on the knots and accounts of certain annals that were in threads of diverse colors. He mentions a comment by Blas Valera that the verses, composed with four syllables each, had a spondaic quality, as if they were used to remember a particular sequence of libations.

This example of a literary *khipu*, with its own particular rhythms, reminds us of the varied uses of *khipus* as mnemonic devices. The same recently rediscovered document also describes how *khipus* were used historically to express different kinds of knowledge: from the general *khipus* used by everyone for numbering and daily communication to another for keeping all religious and caste secrets, known only to the Kings, the Virgins of the Sun, the Priests, and the Philosophers—and presumably Father Blas Valera. Further research by Hyland and others seems to confirm this tradition of literary *khipus* in the court of Ataw Wallpa (Laurencich 57).

Gendered Differences in Andean Textual Media and Practices

This variety suggests there was not only a class but also a gendered difference in the reading and interpreting of *khipus*, whether as archives, as numerical systems, or as literary media. As the original woven textual basis for the more bureaucratic tradition of memorized recitation in record-keeping, *khipus* were most likely read by the hands and voices of men, as were the recited genealogies and exploits of great warlords.

This is still the case in modern times for written records. Rappaport describes how in Cumbal, Colombia, a textual community of specialized memorizers of oral history recite, with reference to colonial title documents, the place names along boundary markers, mentioning any important peacekeeping treaties with their land gains (or losses). She indicates how the recitations of these particular memorizers are regarded as more canonical, whereas those further removed from the original textual sources are believed to manage a more mythical discourse (77–80).

A similar tradition of territoriality and male enunciation in the specialized shamanic commentaries on the meaning of cloth can be heard in Silverman Proust's study of Q'eros, Peru, *El tejido andino. Un libro de sabiduría* [Indian Textile. Book of Wisdom]. These commentaries emphasize the function of cloth in situating local places in relation to Cusco, at the cosmological center of the sun's pathways; it related local territorial markers to their celestial counterparts, in many instances as a part of a broader mythic strategy to record the eternal return of the Inkarríy, the decapitated Inca-King. A similar emphasis is evident in the ancestral memories of the sacred trophy heads called *wak'a* and the narrated exploits of *ayllu* ancestors who first brought them within *ayllu* territory, all re-enacted in modern ritual in the area around Jesús de Machaqa in Bolivia, as described by Astvaldsson (214–17).

Women's cloth, and women's own discourse about it, appears to be distinct, and any numerical system embedded within it seems to be under the exigencies of design and a broader system of meanings in which the weft threads and heddle-mouth play a key role. According to our studies in Qaqachaka, Bolivia, there is in addition a different body-centeredness, having to do with knowledge that comes from the heart rather than head (Arnold and Yapita 1996, 321–24). This Andean corporality, too, is expressed in cloth; from the textile itself emerge new woven-beings that communicate the voice of the ancestors.

These characteristics would suggest that any relationship with the notion of *Logos* must be quite distinct in Andean textiles from that of Western writing. Rather, the very interrelatedness of woven ideas makes cloth the ideal vehicle for what Boone (15–17) has denominated a meaning-centered graphic system, a semasio-graphics, quite distinct from phonetically based and logocentric writing. In this way, weaving as bound-up meaning provides a clear bridge between oral tradition and modern literacy while at the same time defying the Ong-Goody position that primitive cultures are incapable of expressing or thinking so-called abstract thought.

Traditional Andean Modes of Literary Organization

Such different literary modes of expression must have demanded quite different kinds of institutional support from those of alphabetic writing. We know that Inca ideology emphasized work, particularly agricultural and pastoral production, as a ritual act through which each person contributed to the maintenance of equilibrium in the cosmos and to the reproduction of society. An ideology of hierarchical obligation also pervaded Inka relations with their subordinate groups. The godlike status of Inca and Coya was presented through a language of caring for their subjects, providing them with ample food and drink in return for tribute in agricultural and pastoral labor and, in some cases, warfare. This formal and hierarchical reciprocity as gift exchange was a dominant mechanism through which Andean state power was exercised.

As a field of cultural production and action (in Pierre Bourdieu's terms), this apparently reciprocal set of exchanges would have exercised control through the threat–and enactment–of both real and symbolic violence. Traditional Andean modes of literary organization were subject to such means of control; they might even be regarded as a part of the performative paraphernalia surrounding the return of gifts given for the original exchange. There is much evidence to support such a view, particularly the immense power of sacrifice and ritual bloodshed to move the participants to adopt certain stylistic forms of speech and song (often characterized by forms of parallelism), when dialogic exchanges around the sacrificial offering link specific kin groups to their deceased ancestors and gods (Arnold and Yapita, 1998b, Chapter 3).

These institutional mechanisms of Andean state power were developed the most with Inca expansion, when they became organized into nested levels of hierarchy; from the center of the Inca empire in Cusco, state power enveloped pan-Andean ties as well as local ones at the levels of chiefdom, local village, and hamlet. Inca power was ubiquitous: under Inca rule, transmitted coded artifacts in stone and thread were disseminated through extensive communication systems of roads and way stations (*tambos*) into all corners of the empire. Inca institutional mechanisms controlled not only space but also time, regulating annual and larger cycles according to common state goals. They also controlled literary genres and their expression, uniting the Andes into one extensive cultural center stretching from Ecuador to Argentina, with distant echoes deep into the Amazon basin and the Mapuche territories of what is now southern Chile.

Quechua, Aymara, and other language groups were drawn into the same orbit of power relations. In *La identidad aymara* [Aymara Identity, 171ff.], Bouysse-Cassagne describes a historical Aymara mode of institutional control of local literary performance at the level of chiefdom. Here, the word of the ancestors was recited by Aymara chiefs in front of their vassals, as they drank beer, sang and danced, and narrated their war victories, mostly genealogies of chiefs, and chiefdom boundaries. Garcilaso describes similar practices among Quechua-speaking groups under Inca hegemony. The same practice still occurs in modern times, when elected *ayllu* authorities–above all the *alcaldes mayores*–recite the *ayllu* boundaries, naming all of their boundary stones, or when the church *mayordomos* recite the

journeys of the saint-gods and their resting places along fixed routes before they came to stay in the *ayllu* church, all in sequence (Arnold, 1993, 67–71). In what Abercrombie has called an Andean ethnopoetics of space, the formal pattern of recitations is always a pathway of memory (*amtañ thakhi*) leading back to the central Inca gods, who must first be lubricated by plentiful food and drink (Abercrombie 1993, 146).

These kinds of literary preoccupations explain why Inca ceremonial centers, such as Huánaco Pampa, are characterized by the ubiquitous presence of drink (Morris and Thompson, 90-91), why the threads of *khipus* in Inca iconography dip into drinking cups, and why modern *kipu* threads are thought to be hollow (like leaves of grass)–as they must channel in this way the flow of libations that are focused on its "pathway" (Arnold, Yapita et al. 2000, Chapter 11). (See **Figures 2** and **3**.)

Even so, the precise content of oral narratives and libation sequences depends on which side of the boundary, hill, or valley you are on and on what your territorial intentions might be (see **Figure 4**). At a local level, then, these oral literatures may have a multi-voiced quality and may echo local land claims; you may even make land wars with tales (Howard-Malverde 1994). But the larger state ideological and institutional focus remains the same: Of pathways leading toward a ritual center.

Gendered differences in memory, discourse, and performance are patterned by the same criteria. In present day rural *ayllus* of the Southern Andes, the men, who travel more, name in the libation sequences places they have actually visited on the routes to the valleys or the mines and map them verbally from memory; women name these places from a distance, mapping them in cloth. Men follow the men's pathway to the Sun Father, and women follow the women's pathway to the Moon Mother (Arnold 1991, 61–62; 1993, 72–73). For men, the following of these pathways provides a rhythm and template for remembering their territorial conquests; for women, these pathways provide a more corporal map of continuity:

Ukham mamalña umirïna sas,
jupas umaskäkipini,
jupas ukham wawachakirakini,
ukat ukhamas wawapas umaskakirakini
Nanaka akhamäptwa, ukaw nanakan thakhika.

My mother drank so, saying,
and she will continue to drink so,
and she will give birth to her children so,
afterward, her children will continue to drink in this way.
We are so. This is our pathway.

The annual journeys to the valleys with the llama trains, the regional networks of communication in roads and pathways, the *tambo* way stations are all recorded in contemporary oral tradition, in memory of these older historical ties. Men, and male llamas, traditionally traveled more than women to barter and obtain food products, herbs, and weaving looms in the distant valleys. Thus, men's rhetorical practices value land claims (or land gained in war) in exchange for their work as beasts of burden fetching wealth from a distance and moving it about. The women left behind emphasize their own role, and that of their animals, in the generation and reproduction of *ayllu* wealth from within. So they recall in song the trekking llamas and mules as beasts of burden, and ridicule the lazy men left behind. The following version by Doña Lucía Quispe from Qaqachaka is in Aymara:

Figure 2.

Woven khipu with carved headpiece. (Courtesy of the Museum für Volkerkunde, Berlin)

Figure 3.

Detail of the khipu shown in Figure 2, with khipu reader and drinking cup.

Way away Tatala

Kawkiy uka tirantay
      Iñt'at jan iñt'at marka
            Way away Tatala
Muntirupini sut'unttaka
            Way away Tatala
Chuchi thamathama
      muntirupini thamantanta
            Way way Tatala . . .

Figure 4.

Drawing by Guamán Poma de Ayala depicting the Inca making libations to the Sun Father in El primer nueva corónica y buen gobierno (1615). (Courtesy of the authors)

Wayfaring Father

Where will you trek to?
      To towns, known and unknown
            Wayfaring Father
You'll plunge by habit into the dense forest always
            Wayfaring Father
Easy-going bay-one
      You'll plod into the dense forest always
            Wayfaring Father

(In Arnold and Yapita 1998b, 95)

The same idea is expressed in Quechua in this version of the llama leavetaking (*llama kacharpariy*) collected by Hiroyasu Tomoeda in the region of Apurímac, Perú, in 1985:

Kaylluchallayta churakapuway
Sillwichallayta churakapuway
Viajero kachkani, pasajero kachkani
Wasichallanchi pasallasaqña
Ama pañallay waqapuwankichu
Hermanullayiki kallachkaniraq
Qari qariraq kapullawan
Chicurumillay jovenchallaqa
Riqsisqalla kachkani
Llaqtan llaqtan puriamunaypaq

Put on my chest adornment
Put on my saddlecloth
I am a traveler, I am a passer-by
I am already leaving our house
Don't cry for me, my little sister
I am still your brother
Very brave
Is the young man from Chicurumi
For going from town to town
For strutting from street to street

Similarly, the valley food products and their highland counterparts are recorded in the cycles of songs to the food products, especially the all-important maize for beer production (Arnold, Jiménez, and Yapita 1991, 117):

1   P'aqulay, p'aqulay, jumapinïway, Mamalä
     Juma janq'u lak'utanitaway
     Khitiraki jawsani
     Taqituqut jawsani
5   Janq'u lak'utmaxay munatay, Mamala
     Uka laykuxay jutixa
     Jumapinixay taqi apaniri, phaxsima
     Jumaraki tilantir jawsiri
     P'aqula . . .

1   Red-one, red-one, it is you truly, Mamala,
     You are the white-haired one,
     Who will call, then?
     Who will call from all sides?
5   Your white hairs are loved, Mamala,
     For this reason they come,
     You ever the bringer of all, of moon-money,
     You, too, who calls the leading male llama,
     Red-one . . .

The moral imperative to serve the Inca and other Andean states is a binding obligation, recorded in oral tradition as a part of an "Andean pact" in exchange for land. Its institutional framework is regarded as a source of increase. Thus, women sing to augment the fertility of their herds, and men to increase the production from their fields.

Similarly, the *wayñu* courtship songs and dances play off the in-marrying of Inca warriors to local weavers, whereas those of the actual marriage ceremony, and then of house-building some years afterwards, enact and recall these nested obligations, from the newly married couple, to their next of kin, on to their *ayllu*, and on to the larger regional ties of the state, the empire, and their gods. We hear these obligations in the typical formulaic couplets of both oral traditions, Aymara:

Janiway inatakiti, janiway qhasitakiti
Awksa Tayksa sirwiñataki . . .

It isn't in vain, it isn't for nothing
To serve the Sun Father and Moon Mother.

(Arnold and Yapita 1998a, 532)

and Quechua (Tomoeda 298):

Apamuchkani karguchalla ruwananchipaq
Obligacionllata rurachkanchik
Santo Santata servichkanchik

I am bringing it to pass the cargo
So that we discharge our obligations
To serve the saints

Even the songs and narratives of the *ayllu* saint-gods in the local fiesta cycles help reproduce this larger institutional network, in which local saints (as colonial substitutes for mummy

bundles) still serve as microcosms of the Inca gods of Sun Father and Moon Mother.

Aymara and Quechua Literatures

In its allusions to its woven roots, Aymara literature, like that of Quechua, records in many instances the greatness of the Inca, a curious fact since the Incas were present in the predominantly Aymara-speaking Colla nation of the Southern Andes for a period perhaps as brief as fifty years. However, this elevation of Inca status was undoubtedly a part of formal Inca state policy, which sought to erase the memory of other groups, forbade the recounting of other tribal histories in favor of their own, and exercised a fierce control over public discussion. Inca policy throughout the empire also enforced the spread of Quechua and prohibited the use of former languages, thus exerting an incursion of Quechua, particularly for administrative purposes, into former Aymara-speaking areas.

At the same time, this Pan-Andean state formation acknowledged and encouraged other local differences. During this time, the Collas became the southernmost quarter of Tawantinsuyo; a local fair on the former border between the two empires still celebrates the alliance between Colla and Inca as a part of local custom, and libations made there echo the coming together of the two chiefs and the distinctiveness of each domain. In the following example, recorded by Santacruz Pachacuti Yamqui in about 1613, the Aymara Lord of Colla addresses the Inca in Quechua, in an attitude of obeisance:

Cam cuzco capaca
ñuca colla capaca,
hupyasu, micussu, rimassu,
ama pi rima, &c.
ñuca collquetiya
cam colquetiya
cam Viracocha
pachayachi muchha
ñuca inti muchha &c.

You, Lord of Cusco,
I, Lord of Colla
Let's drink, let's eat, let's talk
Don' talk to me etc.
I have silver,
you have gold,
You, Viracocha,
You kiss the whole world,
I kiss the Sun etc.

In reciprocal fashion, an Aymara version recorded by Guamán Poma seems to have been the Colla equivalent among themselves:

hauisca mallco
capaca colla
hahuisca hila
collasana capacasana
yncapachat
tiapachat
mallcosana
capaca collasana
hilauiri mallcouiri
quirquiscatan mallco
aca marcasan pachasan
tiusa hunpachitan
nra. sra. taycasan hunpachiucin...

Welcome, Lord
Wealthy Colla

Welcome brother,
Our Collas, our wealth,
From the time of the Incas
From the twilight of time
Our Lords
Our wealthy Collas
Elders, Lords,
We sing, Lord,
In this our pueblo, our territory
We worship God,
Let us worship Our Lady, Our Mother . . .

Perhaps these Incaic memories remind Aymara speakers of their own herding history, of when animal fleece provided the very roots of their own literature. Brotherston makes this connection in his *Book of the Fourth World*. Citing Matienzo (1567), he tells us how historically, the Colla nation claimed that the Inca made off with Colla animals in order to build up herds of their own (195, 388 n. 5). Of the four *suyos*, theirs was the one that retained the most rights of local herd ownership under Inca rule, and after the European conquest and the collapse of Cusco, the Colla even recovered some of the llama wealth that had been taken by the Inca.

There was deference to the Colla llamas during Inca royal initiation and other ceremonies. And under the Incas, Aymara literary forms praising these herd animals, received state patronage. In his *Nueva Corónica*, Guamán Poma describes the festivals typical of the Inca and of the four *suyos* of the empire; he shows how the pastoral songs of Colla-suyo were held in particular esteem at the royal court of Cusco, to the extent of being sung at these festivals in Aymara, the Colla language (Guamán Poma 315). The term used by Guaman Poma, *Aymarana*, is still used in parts of the Southern Andes for this particular song genre, sung by women during the annual marking ceremony and the giving of female inheritance in animals, when they record the Inca origins of this tradition (Arnold 1995, 92).

Brotherston also remarks how the organization of llama herds became a founding model for the Inca state: The Inca was viewed as divine herder and his empire as an enormous corral, with its pasture inside the walls. Referring to the regional collection of tales from Waruchiri (whose opening line gives it its Quechua title, *Runa Yndio),* Brotherston suggests that even the sky became pasture, allocated to Yaqana, the Celestial Llama at its center (Brotherston 1992, 198). The Inca hymns sung at the Zithuwa festival in the month of *Quya Raymi* in September (as analyzed by John Rowe and others) make this explicit connection between "flock" and "folk" (to use Brotherston's expression), implying that human organization simply echoes this llama mode. This view of the Inca state is still remembered in contemporary libations in the southern Andes, when male and female herders are explicitly compared to male and female animals and they both record the Inca state as one common corral (Arnold and Yapita 1998b, 31).

The pastoral herder-songs heard at the Inca court, like those sung today, have themes characteristic of this pastoral mode, a literary pastoralism that survives today in Aymara and Quechua poetry, narrative, song, and drama, such as these verses collected by José María Arguedas in 1938 (42–43):

Yank'achu kuyallark'ani
yank'achu wayllullark'ani
itantat kichkachallay!
kay runapa churichallanta

kay runapa wawachallanta
¡Tantat kichkachallay!
¡muradu sisaschallay!

Why should I love that stranger
Why did my heart choose him
Without knowing the name of his parents
nor the road by which he came
nor the day when he arrived!
Ay thorn of the mountains!
Ay purple flower!

Brotherston names Western scholars who have classified these conventions, for example, Kelm, who calls the oral tradition of pastoral legends concerning herder-lovers *Hirten-märchen*. But other terms for these same literary genres function within a more Andean taxonomic tradition. Just as a pastoral love story recounted by Martín de Murúa (1590) reveals the pastures beyond the edge of town as a place of transformation and fantasy, so too do the modern Aymara folktales called *sallqa*, meaning wild and yet timid, like a fox. Such tales, as in the following excerpt of "The All-Night Wayñu Dance" by Doña Lucía Quispe, capture the atmosphere of this transitional world, in the rustlings of a cold twilight between the dark age of the Chullpa-ancestors and that of the birth of the Sun, when the animals were still human-like and could speak. The voices are those of the narrator (N), the ancestors (A), the girls (G), and the foxes (F):

(N) Ukat
    mayninaka wintanat llupakipasji
30 (A)   si,
(N) kuna thanthallanakanti,
    kawkinakanti qhanantaniramäki
(A)   sik.
(N) Män thuqkim mayni chha,
35   ukat,
(F)   «Kullaka»
(G)   «Kuntara wich'inkamt kun takxätsma»
(F)   «Janiw»
(G)   «Kunat kunakij shi»
40 (F)   «Ukakiskipï, kullaka,
    alala wayña,
    parlaqt'asikiñani, kullaka
    apur apuray parlaqt'asiñani, kullaka,
    alala wayña, alala wayña»
45   sas,
(N) thuquntkiriw
(A) sika.

(N) Then,
    others coverered the windows
30 (A)   they say,
(N) with some old clothes
    just where the light usually came in
(A)   they say.
(N) In another moment the other-one would dance,
35 and
(F)   "Sister,"
(G)   "Whatever's this? Have I trodden on our tail?"
(F)   "No!"
(G)   "What is it then? Whatever can it be?"
40 (F)   "It's really just that, sister,
    Brrr, how cold!
    Let's talk a little, sister,
    Hurry, hurry, let's talk a little, sister,
    Brrr, how cold, brrr, how cold!"
45   saying

(N)   they used to dance,
(A)   they say.

(In Arnold, Jiménez. and Yapita 1992, 226–67)

In Chapters 4 and 7 of our *Río de vellón, río de canto*, we show how the classification of modern *aymart'aña*, as songs to the animals, have their own Aymara subgenres, and how these, too, are based on different herding activities, the ages and sex of the animals, and their distinct characteristics within the herd, whether they are sung to "Leading Girl" (or "Leading Man") or "Girl at the Rear." Modern collections and recordings of *aymart'aña* reveal the longevity of this oral tradition throughout the Southern Andes. We also show (in Chapter 5 of the same book), the longevity of the philosophical tradition behind the songs, rooted as it is in an Incaic past. In their exegeses on the songs, the singers note this continuity of ideas, particularly those centered on the Black Llamas (dark clouds in the Milky Way) that remind us of the seventeenth century *Runa Yndio*.

Runa Yndio, The Tales of Waruchiri

The Quechua narratives of *Runa Yndio* were originally compiled in about 1608 by Father Francisco de Avila (ca. 1573–1647) (or by local scribes under his charge) in an area north of Lima as evidence of native religious practices to be wiped out in his pioneer program of extirpation of idolatries. In spite of their purpose, their very existence allows us to hear the native voices of this period at the mercy of these state imperatives:

> cay yacana ñiscanchik llamap camaquin çielo ñiqta chaupicta purimon ñocanchic runacunapas riconchicmi ari yanalla hamocta chaymanta chay yacana ñis Canchicsi mayo hucocta purimon ancha atunmi ari yanayaspa çielo ñicta yscay ñauiyoc concanpas ancha hatun captin hamun caytam runacuna yacana ñincu

> They say the Yacana, which is the animator of the llamas, moves through the middle of the sky. We native peoples can see it standing out as a black spot. The Yacana moves inside the Milky Way. It's big, really big. It becomes blacker as it approaches through the sky, with two eyes and a very large neck. This, we know, is what native people call the Yakana. (Salomon 132)

These tales are particularly interesting for their view from the periphery. When compared with sumptuary royal power as seen in metropolitan Cusco, they seem to express a more shamanic, locally based religion centered on regional deities (*wak'a*), above all the great Paria Caca and his children, the subjects of the plot. This local history seems to have been that of the Yauyo ethnic group, precursors of the Aymara (or Jaqi); there are still islands of speakers of related languages in the zone. Yauyo political space was centered initially on Waruchiri, and the tales seem to trace the feats of a Yauyo expansion down from the highlands into the warmer coastal valleys of Quechua speakers, through battle, marriage alliances, and rights to land and waters. In his *Introductory Essay*, Salomon goes so far as to treat the manuscript, with its traces of Aymara-like lexicon and phonology, particularly in the ritual terminology, as "substantially an artifact of Yauyo culture" (7), suggesting that, "at a minimum," the text has been modified from a more Jaqi-influenced speech toward a Church-influenced "general" Quechua (31).

If this is so, then a substratum of Jaqi literary forms must have given rise to such continuities as that described above. Jaqi influence might also explain the nature of the hero Huatya

Curi, a poor "Baked Potato Gleaner" (Aymaras are the potato growers *par excellence*), unlike his rich future father-in-law:

> 39.   chay pacha cay huatyacuri ñisca huacchalla micuspapas huatya cuspalla causaptinsi sutiachircan huatyacurim ñispa . . .

> They say that fellow called Huatya Curi subsisted at the time just by baking potatoes in earth pits, eating the way a poor man does, and people named him the "Baked Potato Gleaner." (Salomon 55)

It might also explain the nature of the local variant of Viracocha as a miserably poor and friendless man:

> 9.   Cay cuniraya viracochas ancha ñaupa huc runa ancha huaccha tucospalla purirca yacollanpas cosmanpas lliqui lliquesapa runacunapas huaquin mana ricsicnincunaca huaccha husaçapa ñispa cayarcab cay runas canan tucoy llactakunakta camarcan chacractapas rimaspallas pata patactapas allin pircascacta tucochircan rarcactas canan llocsimu nanamanta huc pupuna sutioc cañavelarpa sisayninchucas pallas yachacuchirca chaymantari yma aycactapas ruraspas purir can huaquinin llacta huaca cunactapas yachascanhuan allcuchaspa . . .

> A long, long time ago, Cuni Raya Vira Cocha used to go around posing as a miserably poor and friendless man, with his cloak and tunic all ripped and tattered. Some people who didn't recognize him for who he was yelled, "You poor lousy wretch!" Yet it was this man who fashioned all the villages. Just by speaking he made the fields, and finished the terraces with walls of fine masonry. As for the irrigation canals, he chaneled them out from their sources just by tossing down the flower of a reed called *pupuna*. After that he went around performing all kinds of wonders, putting some of the local huacas to shame with his cleverness. (Salomon 46)

Such oppositions between wealthy Quechua-speaking valley dwellers and poor Aymara-speaking herders from the highlands are still a characteristic feature of Andean oral traditions.

"Traditional" Andean Genres

By juxtaposing historical and modern Andean literary genres, we challenge former categorizations, which followed predetermined Spanish (and other European) literary forms—poetry, histories, narratives, fables, myths, and so on—and tended to reserve Andean terms for pre-Conquest conventions. Such evolutionist models, in their uncritical acceptance of rupture with the Conquest, failed to perceive the many continuities in Andean literary traditions that did exist.

However, the study of the Andean classification of literary genres also confirms a degree of local variation, and in many cases the use of hybrid forms, borrowed from Spanish through centuries of contact (*kuñtu, parla*, etc.). One local system of classification of Aymara literatures we know (from *ayllu* Qaqachaka in Oruro, Bolivia) identifies the following genres: oral history (*layra parla*) includes the mythic tales of the battle between the Incas and the Chullpas and the legendary tales of the *ayllu* ancestors and saint-gods. Common tales (*kuñtu*) include bets (*apustaña*) between different animals, birds, and sometimes flowers; the most wellknown are the ubiquitous tales of the Condor and the Fox, who bet together on the ice who will survive better the freezing winter. These also include tales of the idiot (*sunsu parla*) and those of the wild beasts, said to have taken place in the dark time before the sun arose. (Of these, the tales of the condor are called *kuntur parla*.) Then there are the darker tales of the inner world (regarded as belonging to the Devil and the mines), called sometimes by the name of the hummingbird (*jurüru*); they include stories about the greasesuckers (*kharisiri* or *khari khari*), the condemned ones (*condenado*), and Snake-Woman (*Chukir Qamir Wirnita*). Such formal groupings are still used by modern storytellers, such as the young Elvira Espejo (168–72), to organize their tales.

As in other Amerindian societies, these common tales about wild animals and wild spirits are not only storytelling devices but also philosophical propositions. As plays on variable appearances and spiritual essences, on beasts that turn into humans and humans that change back into beasts, they communicate an omnipresent process in the highly transformational world proposed by Andean ontologies, where to be "clothed" (or not) is one of the privileged expressions of this constant metamorphosis. Here, the differentiation between "culture" and "nature" is not between human and animal, as in the Western canon, but rather suggests a common origin in humanity, where animals subsequently lose their human attributes.

As a whole, it is worth emphasizing that modern pan-Andean genres do not differ much from those mentioned by Guamán Poma in the early seventeenth century. Included in the generic category of song (whether *kirki* or *wayñu*) there are still the feast songs (wedding songs, house-roofing songs, etc.), songs to the gods (both local saints and more global sky- and earth-gods), war songs, songs of production (planting and harvesting, weaving and spinning), and songs to the animals. The modern war songs (*wayli*) and songs of production echo a former group called *jaylli*, the harvest celebrations as songs of victory.

The pan-Andean category of popular music and song, called *wayñu* in both Quechua and Aymara, still flourishes too. *Wayñus*, with their Inca origins, are said to have been an Inca courtly dance, introduced into different regions as a way of bringing dominated areas under Inca control (Lira 327). In the southern Andes, they are still said to be inspired by Inca ancestral (but devilish) spirits, in a dual division of musical and song performance, according to the seasons. *Wayñus*, related to the dead, are played during the rainy season, whereas in the dry season another, lighter and happier kind of song is played; each song type is played on different instruments and has a different musical form (Harris 60; Stobart 1996a, 415ff.). *Wayñu* performance also demands a gendered and age difference in approach and attitude; men and young women play the popular *wayñus*, whereas older women give more importance to the songs to the animals as "another more primordial kind of *wayñu*" (Arnold and Yapita 1998b, 55-6).

Nevertheless, the detailed study of these Andean literatures has challenged the usefulness of the term *genre* as such. Research on the processes of oral composition and memorization has shown that the additive nature of the constituent units of orality (the formulas, strophic episodes, etc.), just like the elements of weaving designs, often cross traditional genre boundaries, blurring genre definitions and boundaries (in ways that Bakhtin had predicted from his studies of written forms). Thus, the repetitive formulas found in one genre, such as the songs to the animals or food products, might be found in the wedding songs or feast songs. And a spoken land claim may become embedded in song, transformed into rhyming couplets (Arnold and Yapita 1998b, 378–81).

Regional Andean Genres

Modern regional variations in Andean literary genres, their modes of performance, and relative emphasis, just as in the days of the Tales of Waruchiri, are often related to immediate ethnic differences in the region.

In the case of Aymara, certain genres seem to follow the boundaries of former chiefdoms and federations. This is particularly notable in relation to the ritual terms and drinking names used in libation sequences and in the song cycles to the animals and food products, of which common subtypes can be found in a region stretching from the north of Chile to southern Oruro, along the borders of the former Killakas Asanaqi federation.

The presence of other genres, or local attitudes to these genres, may have resulted from the importation of particular groups (*mitimae, mit'ayos,* or *yanakunas*) into these areas in Inca times, changing their allegiances from local to more pan-Andean and Inca, and introducing more Quechua literary forms (see, for example, Hartmann 1998). For instance, there are distinct regional differences in the taking of sides in the common *Tales of the Battle Between the Incas and the Chullpas*, which might reflect the presence of pro-Inca *mit'ayos* in certain regions.

A regional emphasis of one genre over another may also reflect localized economies. Distinct genres are narrated in the mining areas around Oruro, Northern Potosí, and Colquechaka, regions characterized in the past by a mobile and mixed population. Examples are the geo-anatomical *Tales of Chuqir Qamir Birnita*, concerning Snake-Woman, a gold-toothed female anti-hero, and her devilish offspring, her wealth, and her dubious ties to the underworld, prevalent in the region of Los Yungas, the city of La Paz, and the mining centers of Oruro. This genre has recently become the subject of a film script.

In other cases, local linguistic differences are used to heighten regional differences. In *Historia y drama ritual en los Andes bolivianos* [History and Ritual Drama in the Bolivian Andes], Beyersdorff has found that the *Dramas of the Death of Ataw Wallpa* are often performed in Cusco Quechua, even in the Aymara-speaking areas of Oruro, as if to emphasize the invasive element of an Inca presence there in the past. In other examples, the Quechua and Aymara languages are used interchangeably in the same tale or song to differentiate episodes that take place in the high, cold, Aymara-speaking *puna* as opposed to the lower and warmer Quechua-speaking valleys. The Fox protagonist, characteristically, speaks in Quechua in his bet with the Aymara-speaking Condor (Yapita 1992, 53–54):

Ukat maynisti,
«Mallku, jum thayjtamti.
Alalay, karaju, alalay chirishawan»
sjiw sika, qhichwat sij sha.

Then the other one [spoke],
"Lord Condor, are you getting cold?
How cold, damn you. Brrr, I'm getting so cold!"
he said, they say; in Quechua they say that he said it.

Modern literary studies (Jemio's *Literatura oral aymara*, or Schramm's *Symbolische Logik in der mündlichen Tradition del Aymaras*) are now making it possible to compare variants of the same tale found in different regions. In this way, recent studies of the *Greasesucker Tales* (Gose; Ansión; Briggs 1994; Spedding) have shown them to be concentrated in certain regions, possibly as the result of heightened economic differences in these places combined with memories of warring factions there in the more distant past.

Local studies have also uncovered the historical specificity of what seem to be timeless tales, in Andean examples of the invention of tradition. In some cases, supposedly historical tales disguise their recent formation, in order to justify access to newly gained lands. In others, new sanctuaries or miracle sites arise as tales woven around a new, miraculous god form part of an economic package intended to bring pilgrims and wealth to an up-and-coming area (Sallnow 1987).

A more diachronic approach reveals local variants of key historical tales (*stemma* in a linguistic sense). Thus, Briggs (1989) was able to analyze an Aymara tale, the *Dog That Speaks Latin*, in the region of Zepita in Peru, and compare it to the story of Huatya Curi (Watiya Ucuri) from the seventeenth-century *Runa Yndio* (Tales of Waruchiri). The Aymara of Zepita still has phonemes from the Jaqi languages, as Waruchiri is thought to have had.

Institutional Modes of Transmission

Traditional Andean institutional modes of power must also have controlled the learning of literary forms. We know that, at the state level, the required level of reading and interpretation of state *khipus* formed a component part of four years of formal learning in an institutional setting. Even today, the specialized readers of colonial texts (the "title-bearers") must learn their art through a period of apprenticeship.

At regional and local levels, there are still formal pathways of learning verbal arts and other skills, harking back to older forms, such as the *kalli* described by Guamán Poma in the seventeenth century. In parts of Oruro and Northern Potosí, young people learn weaving, music, and song according to one pathway (called *jaynu*), while older people after marriage follow another pathway (called *thakhi*) of making libations and passing feasts for the gods (Arnold and Yapita 1996, 327). Feast sponsorship is yet another institutional device for older community members to learn certain genres; they pair with their counterparts of the former year and learn verbatim the appropriate libations, songs, and speeches.

Learning in childhood continues to follows this formal pattern referred to as "pathway." In rural areas, grandparents teach small children traditional narratives and verbal wisdom at bedtime. Isbell and Roncalla (1977) have described how older Quechua-speaking children in rural Ayacucho, Peru, learn riddles as didactic devices for sexual and intellectual exploration, according to another herding analogy, of *vida michiy*, "putting your life out to pasture." Later on, in a gendered division of learning, older girls in rural Oruro, Bolivia, (now on their "girl's pathway") learn songs while they acquire animals and visit feasts; boys (now on their "boy's pathway") learn to play musical instruments while they participate in fiestas. In adolescence, young women weave beautiful mantles that incorporate the aesthetics of the color red, and they sing the latest *wayñus* to the young men's musical accompaniment, both of them performing these courting devices to get the desired partner (Arnold 1992b, 38ff.; Stobart 1996a, 422).

Throughout this period of youth, both sexes appeal to traditional sources of inspiration for their verbal and musical arts. In many regions of the highlands, young men acquire their musical inspiration from the local sirens: special places where water pounds on rocks, enchanted sites often associated with the Inca spirits. The Peruvian writer José María Arguedas (1911–1969) opens his short story *La agonía de Rasu Ñiti* [1962; *The Agony of Rasu-Ñiti*] with an allusion to this special power:

> El corazón está listo. El mundo avisa. Estoy oyendo la cascada de Saño. ¡Estoy listo!–dijo el dansak. Rasu Ñiti." (7)

> "The heart is ready. The world informs me. I am hearing the falls of Saño. I am ready!" said the dansak. "Rasu-Ñiti."

Young women, too, derive their inspiration in song from these places, but they also acknowledge an ancestral knowledge that comes from the dark lakes of the heavens.

Part Two: Cultural Contact

Institutional Changes and the Introduction of Writing, Phase I

With the Spanish invasion, many–but not all–of the traditional institutional patterns of Andean literary organization were severed from their central Andean centers of power and brought under Spanish administrative control. In this way, they were brought under the scrutiny of outsiders–travelers, priests, bureaucrats, and military men–who wrote a new kind of Andean-based literature for a Spanish audience about an exotic other-world at odds with their own. Cusco became the Rome of a dying empire, in what Mariátegui (1894–1930) has considered new but not organically national literatures.

Andean textual practices and literatures became the subject of fascination for Europeans. But from an Andean perspective it was the introduction into the Andes of European alphabetic writing that was revolutionary. This mutual reflection on other textual practices gave rise not only to the new heterogeneity of Andean literary forms but also to a confrontation between them. The nature of this confrontation between different textual practices was such that Cornejo Polar (1994, 88–89) warns of the dangers of viewing it "from only one side"; instead, the real object of literary study should be the crossing of contradictions through contact, their mutual alimentation and interpretation. So if on the one hand, many of these strangers grappled with the new Andean texts (weavings, tapestries, *tocapu, khipu,* pictography, painted boards, etc.), comparing them with writing, on the other hand, Andeans themselves were to compare writing to their own textual practices and to adapt writing in the image of their own forms of expression.

Typically, José de Acosta (1540–1600) in his *Historia natural y moral de las Indias* [*The Natural and Moral History of the Indians,* 1880], written in 1590, insists that the Indians of Peru, before the arrival of the Spanish, had no kind of writing, neither with letters nor with signs. However, he still admires the way in which the knotted *khipus* "complemented" the books of the Old World, how the practical use of *khipus* was like that of books, and how knotting threads was comparable to alphabetic writing, in that the diverse knots and colors signified different things (6: viii). He even compares the handling of the *khipu* knots to a European rosary. He saw a handful of these threads, with which an Indian woman brought a general "written" confession of her whole life, and confessed from them, just as one would do from writing on paper. Acosta's observation reminds us that many remaining *khipus,* as mnemonic devices, had been subject to an intense catechization by the church, in the hope that their previous (and more suspect) uses had been extirpated in the immense conflagration that occurred under Acosta's instructions immediately after the Third Council of Lima in 1583. As Mignolo (235–36) points out, Europeans had already forgotten the roots of their own textual practices. There was also the contemporary colonizing ploy of seeing in writing the only acceptable expression of the word of God. So Acosta's own definition of writing precluded him from applying the term to such Andean texts. Instead, the new colonial encounter initiated centuries of struggles over textual forms. The introduction of alphabetic writing–and European numeracy–prompted an official drive toward an Andean literacy in the European sense and prompted the production of a colonial Andean literature for the initial purposes of Spanish-Andean contact and then for greater penetration and domination. This process began in earnest with the Toledan state reforms of the 1570s, hand in hand with ecclesiastical reforms initiated in the Third Council of Lima (1582–84).

From then onwards, Aymara-speaking Charkas was governed ecclesiastically from the Archbishopric of La Plata (founded in 1552) and administratively from Lima. Even so, in the southern Andes, the new state and ecclesiastical boundaries still followed those of former Aymara and Inca provinces, chiefdoms, and federations (Lupaqa, Charkas, Larecajas, Karankas, Qhara Qhara, Killakas-Asanaqi, and Pakaji). These conglomerations of multilingual ethnic groups did not think of themselves as "Quechuas" or "Aymaras" but rather as distinct social groups, with their own social, cultural–and literary–histories and practices, which continued in adapted forms. Under the Toledan reforms, their own chiefs, or *caciques*, were left to govern them and extract taxes in a new form of indirect rule. The main change, however, was the massive reinstatement of Indian populations in new reduction towns around a central plaza–where the *pax toledana* could be most forcibly appreciated–facilitating the local administration of tax collection and indoctrination. Under the new administration, Andean languages became fiscal and political categories for tax calculations and linguistic categories for conversion.

Early documents written in Aymara or Quechua are therefore ecclesiastical works with the intention of conversion and indoctrination. The Council of Trent (1563) and various papal bulls charged the Spanish Crown with the conversion of the natives and stipulated that the holy sacraments should be explained to the Indians in their native tongue. So in the late sixteenth century, Aymara and Quechua were designated as "religious languages," the church being directly responsible for expanding these languages to new groups of speakers and extending their functions to include written materials, religious rituals, and sermons. The preparation of the first doctrinal materials in Andean languages, already put in motion during the First Council of Lima, was under the direction of Father José de Acosta, who worked with a team of translators; the Aymara translators probably included the *mestizo* priests Blas Valera (1551–1597), Bartolomé de Santiago, and Francisco Carrasco, with Father Alonso de Barzana as collaborator (Cerrón Palomino 86). Catechisms were written in the two principal languages of Peru, and a *Doctrina cristiana y catecismos para la instrucción de los indios* [1584; Christian Doctrine and Catechism for the Instruction of Indians], a *Tercero Catecismo* [Third Catechism], and a *Confesión* [1585; Confession] were written in trilingual versions (Spanish-Quechua-Aymara). Another work, the *Symbolo Catholico Indiano* [1598; Indian Catholic Symbol] by Luis Jerónimo de Oré (1554–1630), was written in Spanish, Aymara, Quechua, and Pukina. The annotation of these texts reveals the degree of normalization of the Andean languages that had already taken place in these first translations, a policy initiated as an ecclesiastical brake on any possible deviations and errors from doctrinal teaching on the part of local priests and local teachers of church doctrine (*doctrineros*).

Access to Andean languages continued to be a prerequisite for priests working in the region, as well as a form of ecclesiastical control over their teaching. In 1547, the Emperor Carlos V requested the pope to consider bestowing special recognition on those who learned to teach and preach in Indian tongues (Levillier 2: 66–7). In 1599, the archbishop of

Cusco, Don Antonio de la Raya, requested that Jesuits interrogate the priests of *indígenas* under their charge in Quechua, Aymara, and Pukina (Torero, 226). Then, in 1603, a chair of university studies in Quechua, Aymara, and Pukina was planned in the University of Cusco. As a whole, though, the first Aymara texts were written some fifty years after the equivalent Quechua works (such as the vocabulary of Fray Domingo de Santo Tomás). While the church preferred the use of indigenous languages for purposes of conversion, the Spanish Crown had always been more interested in the spread of Spanish as the language of empire. The two interests coincided only when later generations of priests were less enthusiastic about learning native languages, so that finally, in 1634, the Crown ordered the teaching of Spanish, and of Christian doctrine, to all Indian children.

The Rise of a New Andean "Literacy"

In spite of the immediate goals that these new doctrinal materials served, they reveal something of the literary richness of this period. The Italian Jesuit Father Ludovico Bertonio (1555–1628), who worked around Juli (now Peru) on the edge of the lake, dedicated a whole chapter to what he called the ornate particles of Aymara, in which he emphasizes repeatedly the elegance and potential stylistics of this language. With his principal collaborator, Martín Santa Cruz (who was a well known teacher in the province), he wrote seven works between 1603 and1612, from grammars and vocabularies to catechisms. In the same period, the Jesuit Torres Rubio (d. 1637?) wrote an *Arte de la lengua aymara* ([1616, *Art of the Aymara Language*], republished in a modern version in 1967 by Mario Franco Inojosa). Rivet and Crequí Montfort's *Bibliographie* also mention a primer in Quechua-Spanish of 6,000 copies, for doctrinal purposes.

In general, though, the early colonial period is dominated by Spanish intents to indoctrinate native speakers of Andean languages with their own scripts, the Bible and books of catechism, rather than appreciating any linguistic and cultural value of Andean texts in their own right, seeing them only as sources of practices to be changed. One of the few secular exceptions is an anonymous phrase book dealing with different topics, such as writing a letter and buying and selling animals, written in a bilingual Andean Spanish-Aymara edition in which each language shows the influence of the other. This was recently re-edited by Lucy Briggs (1995). These translations, mainly from Spanish to Aymara or Quechua rather than vice versa, tell us more about Spanish concerns than Andean ones. However, even the most intimate confessions extracted by priests in their intent to extirpate idolatries are now yielding other voices below the colonized surface, in the Andean underlayers of religious ideas and experiences retranslated (see, for example, Barnes 1992). Another result of these heterogenous texts of Spanish intents to translate Andean ideas was the new level in Andean literacy that developed. This, too, can be appreciated from two distinct points of view.

Andean languages were transformed in order to accommodate the new linguistic and scriptural dominance. The increased pressure of daily contact, translation, and bilingualism provoked an initial stage of lexical borrowing. Then, by the mid-seventeenth century, written (and spoken) Andean languages passed into what Melià and later Cerrón Palomino, with reference to Guaraní and Quechua respectively, have called a "conquered and reduced" version, in which semantic changes reflect its new status under colonial rule. As Albó points out (1992, 14), another characteristic change was that some terms became Christianized (so that Pachamama became *Santa Tira*), whereas others became demonized (into *supay* or *saxra*). Later still, Andean languages were to incorporate more Spanish modes of sentence subordination, as they passed from the paratactic structures of orality toward the more periodic structures of written texts.

Mestizo Writing, Social Memory, and the New Baroque

At the immediate interface between Andean languages, cultures, and textual practices and the various intents to translate them into Spanish emerged a new form of writing, whether in the adapted and colonized Andean languages or in Andean Spanish. Some argue that these new hybrid forms of syncretism and cultural assimilation simply imitated the new colonial norms. Others, such as Dillon and Abercrombie, see them as the creation of a new postcolonial *mestizaje*, in which the notion of conquest has been incorporated. And still others see in them experiment and cultural resistance, plays between orality, drawn images, and icons and European script, characterized by intents to preserve aspects of social memory and the language of the ancestors; Harrison's essay in *Signs, Songs and Memory in the Andes* takes this view.

But instead of drawing such hard and fast boundaries between different textual practices and their ideological content, it is helpful to peruse the actual situations of textual contact. At one extreme, Spanish influence in spoken and musical genres occurred at many levels. Informal contact on encomiendas and haciendas, in mining, urban, and pilgrimage centers, would have been accompanied by gossip and chatter; barter and exchange there would have included the interchange of remedies and tales. In this way, European genres arrived, spread, and adapted to their new setting. As Halushka (42–43) notes, European stories, such as *El águila y la zorra* [*The Eagle and She-Fox*] from the Golden Age, became Andeanized as *El condor y el zorro* [*The Condor and the Fox*]. At another level, more formal church and state pomp and ceremony demanded the introduction of new musical instruments (or the retuning of old ones) and the learning of new genres to honor the new gods (Stobart 1996b, 476–77).

The new Toledan reduction towns became the focus of a reorganized religious life, built around the annual feast cycles of the Catholic saints rather than the former Inca gods. New *caciques*, often *mestizos*, became patrons of the new forms. But even so, former practices of social memory continued in new guises, such as the extended libation pathways (*thakhi*) of Aymara feasting (which still echoes its older common root with the Quechua usage of the term). These drinking pathways, with their spondaic rhythms, are also important structuring devices for the song verses they often initiate (Arnold and Yapita 1998b, 125).

Most early written experiments with the new script, in Andean Spanish, occurred around Cusco, in a predominantly Quechua domain. Of the early chroniclers, Juan Santa Cruz Pachacuti Yamqui (from *ayllu* Waywa in the Kanchis area, halfway between Cusco and Lake Titicaca) probably had Aymara ancestors, although his chronicle is clearly written in the cultural ambit of Cusco Quechua. Guamán Poma (from Sondondo in what is now the Lucana province in the department of Ayacucho, and with lands in the area around Huamanga) is the only chronicler known to have collected Aymara texts with pre-colonial roots. Besides Quechua and Andean Spanish, he is now thought to have spoken an Ayacucho variant of Aymara; certainly Ferrell's glosses of his texts into this variant have been much more successful than those of contemporary Aymara speakers who have attempted to translate them into a modern (and urban) Collavino variant (Ferrell 415).

After the mid-seventeenth century, when Quechua became the general language of Perú and the drive by the Spanish Crown to implement the teaching of Spanish gathered pace, little more was written in Aymara in alphabetic script. In this sense, a dramatic difference emerged between Aymara and Quechua literary forms. As the Aymara-speaking world shrank in scope, drawing in upon itself, the domain of Quechua expanded. New Quechua literary forms emerged, in the hands of a Cuscocentric *criollo* and *mestizo* elite that drew on Andean tradition but began to appropriate and subsume it (Salomon 25).

The Incorporation of Other Scripts

From an Andean point of view, the immediate shock of decipherment of alphabetic script (with its inscrutable animal-like forms on white corn-husks, as perceived by the soothsayer Waylla Wisa) and of Spanish textual practices (the peering at and talking to the "white cloths" they had in front of them, as the Inca Titu Cusi and Guamán Poma would have it) was to give way gradually to an Andean way of reading and writing. In this way, European writing was incorporated into Andean textual practices, but according to Andean criteria of interpretation. This happened, in part, because of the precise colonial techniques of teaching Christian doctrine. In order to teach the new fixed scripts of the Christian Mass and prayer to parishioners unversed in this medium, in the more rural regions of the Andes where European writing was less influential, there were various historic experiments with Quechua and Aymara presented in glyphic scripts for conversion purposes. Found on rock, hide, and parchment, such glyphic-catechisms are popular devices for non-literate parishioners even today (Miranda 1988; see **Figure 5**). Hartmann (1991) has suggested that as didactic devices, these glyphic scripts have certain similarities with the Testerian Franciscan texts from early colonial Mexico, and that the sophisticated word-plays, in many instances, echo a phonetic reading, similar to that which Pärssinen has intimated for the historical Incaic *khipus*. As in the case of the Testerian examples, it is highly probable that such glyphic systems had pre-Columbian roots. So if Andeans were actually incorporating written catechisms into their own forms of writing, then Ibarra Grasso is justified in calling these glyphs *Escritura Indígena Andina* (Indigenous Andean Writing).

This high degree of mobility between different textual practices at the colonial interface between different media is often many-layered. Beyersdorff (1992), among others, has implied that what were once thought to have been an oral tradition of Inca prayers (in the case of the texts collected by Molina or parts of the Santacruz Pachacuti chronicle) were really a part of a much more complex sequence of textual formulations, in which written Spanish doctrinal texts were first translated into Quechua, then adapted to the oral tradition of local ritual needs, and then compiled in writing as examples of this same oral tradition.

A part of this debate, raised by Duviols and Itier in their edition of Pachacuti's *Relación*, hinges on the status of Viracocha, the Andean god of weaving and waters (whether or not he was an Andean high god, on a par with the Christian deity,

Figure 5.

A page of an Aymara glyphic catechism from Miranda (1988). (Courtesy of the authors)

or only an Andean culture hero), and onto what degree the verses dedicated to him draw directly on Biblical imagery (see also Itier, 1992):

> A ticsi uiracochan
> caylla uiracochan
> tocapo acnapo uiracochan
> camac
> churac
> cari cachon huarmi cachon nispa . . .
>
> O Viracocha, origin of this world
> Viracocha, reaching to its furthest limits
> Viracocha, adorned in fine and elegant garments
> who fills with life in due measure
> who assigns each thing its place
> saying "let there be man, let there be woman" . . .

(Translated by Lindsey Crickmay)

Even so, as Brotherston (1973, 203) and Szeminski (1997) have shown, the hymn is composed of the paired or contrasted formulas characteristic of an oral tradition: "origin/fundament" (*ticsi*) and "furthest limits" (*caylla*), "fine cloth" (*tocapu*) and "elegant cloth" (*acnopu*), "creator" (*camac*) and "establisher" (*churac*), "man" (*cari*) and "woman" (*huarmi*), and so on.

The range of textual practices and textual practitioners required in the colonial period to teach (and learn) the new fixed scripts must also have adapted to local needs, giving rise to a new era of mixed genres and mixed performers. A new generation of bilingual *mestizos* worked in official and non-official capacities as translators of Andean tradition, whether as local teachers and interpreters of church doctrine (*doctrineros*) for rural Andean parishioners or as go-betweens in legal settings (*tinterillos*), translating written Hispanic law into oral forms for their rural Andean clients. Spanish-speaking Indians, too, acted as scribes (*escribanos*) and rememberers (*memeronas*) in official settings of the new town councils, although they sometimes kept their former name of *khipu*-keeper (*quipucamayoc*). Bilingual Indians were preferred as leaders and interpreters and were employed officially from 1552 onwards by the New World Audiencias.

The modern descendants of these former go-betweens are the non-literate experts in the teaching of Christian doctrine, who are still versed in the techniques of orality (of sound and gesture and of modeling in clay) in order to communicate the fixed scriptures they cannot read. Their use of oral word-plays as didactic devices must have created some of the characteristic features of Andean Christianity, for example, the association of Pachamama and her Christianized version, the Virgin Mary, with a toad (probably because of the processes of learning catechisms, in which the Hail Mary, *Jamp'atit Mariya* in Aymara, reminds parishioners of the Aymara word for "toad," *jamp'atu*). Even now, Andean schoolteachers use such oral techniques of recitation and memorized repetition to ensure legitimate textual transmission.

Other descendants are the textual community of Andean title-bearers, versed in the oral readings of written colonial documents, and the shamanic community of modern healers, whose oral prayers play on and echo the discourses of colonial law and ecclesiastical doctrine (described by Rappaport, Platt, and others). Their modern literary descendants are writers such as the Peruvian José María Arguedas and the Argentine Héctor Tizón (b. 1929), both of whom were very familiar with the terms of this legal discourse.

Still other descendants are the modern *escribientes* (public writer) of Peru, Ecuador, and Bolivia. From Noriega's point of view (1995, 128–40), these "recopiladores, arreglistas, traductores, imitadores y, escritores" ("compilers, editors, translators, imitators, and writers"), urban intellectuals with their roots in Andean rural cultures, have transformed mythical and marginal subjects (whether the Quechua poet Juan Wallparrimachi [1793–1814] or the illiterate strapper Gregorio Condori Mamani [b. 1908]) into Western-style authors, orality into writing and then back again, and collective modes of creation into individual ones. In doing so, they have helped define in a new way the notions of text and author, orality and writing (Noriega 1996, 316).

An Andean Literature of Resistance

These Andean interpretations of other scripts constantly rework older Andean textual forms in new and unexpected guises, even though they are written predominantly in Spanish. In this way, European letters become subjected to Andean criteria of oratory and poetics and to memorized recitation. To recite alphabetic script (even when it is not comprehended in a Western sense) orally thus becomes a fertilizing act that draws on the ancestral powers located in head and heart, in seed element and generating filament. At the same time, this Andean reinterpretation of European writing becomes a curiously disguised act of resistance.

We have already seen how different Andean literati faced this challenge. Guamán Poma, in his *Nueva Corónica y Buen Gobierno* [c.1613; *New Coronicle [sic] and Good Government*], developed a literary form of Andean writing and illustration (based on the organization of a *khipu*), to persuade the King of Spain of his subjects' errors in the treatment of Andean peoples, and to encourage him to reconsider "good government" on more Andean lines. Pachacuti, in his *Relación de antigüedades deste reyno del Pirú* [c. 1613; *Report on the Ancient Ways of This Kingdom of Peru*], developed a more ecclesiastical form of writing to justify the standing of Andeans as Catholics. And the "Huarochiri [Waruchiri] Manuscript" (c. 1608), on the periphery of both the Inca and Spanish Empires, expressed local history and religion according to an Andean "counter-Bible," complete with origin myths, an Andean Flood, and a sacrifice episode reminiscent of the story of Abraham and Isaac (Salomon 2).

Even earlier, the Inca Titu Cusi Yupanqui (16th century), in his *Relación de la Conquista del Perú* [1570: *Report on the Conquest of Perú*], had used writing as a final act of resistance after years of failed rebellion (including the period of *Taqui Onqoy*, when even the sacred *wak'as* were begged to return). His own text, written in collaboration with an Augustinian catechist and a private secretary of the Inca, uses European writing and canons to disguise yet another agenda, in that he uses the language, logical framework, and stylistic norms of a Spanish politico-legal *apologia* to express Inca political ideology and Inca norms of succession and legitimacy (Salomon 12).

Similarly, Betanzos (1510–1576), in his *Suma y Narración de los Incas* [1551: *Narrative of the Incas*], with his close ties to the Inca court, insists that he cannot write his account as other chroniclers do, because he must keep the manner and order of speaking of the indigenous people. For Leinhard (1992a, 147), this conscious prerequisite suggests that his account drew directly on his memories of the epic character of Inca narratives, triumphal songs, rites of victory, and dances of war, of the royal line, or *panaka*, of Pachacuti, into which he had married. Both he and Titu Cusi might also have drawn on Inca theater in its function of praising Inca royalty in the context of war victory or funereal pageant.

These Andean literatures of resistance had a common goal of speaking through two qualitatively different systems of thought and textual practice at one and the same time (Salomon 32). Many drew their power from the vital confrontation between cultures, religions, and textual practices at Cajamarca in November 1532. They dwelt on the new power relations expressed in the first meeting between the monarch Inca Ataw Wallpa and Captain Francisco Pizarro, and on the religious conflict at the heart of the different modes of communication in the famous dialogue between Father Valverde and the Inca Ataw Wallpa before the latter's execution–what Cornejo Polar (1994, 26) has called point-zero of the colonial encounter.

From the incomprehensible encounter at Cajamarca emerged two decades later (in 1555) the first known dramatizations of the Death of Ataw Wallpa (*Atawallpap wañuynin*), according to a 1705 account collected by Bartolomé Arsanz de Orsúa y Vela (1676–1736). The drama, still performed today in villages in central Peru and in the department of Oruro, Bolivia, focuses on the mutual incomprehension between two differently textualized worlds (that of the Holy Word in writing and that of Inca divination and orality). The modern "strapper," Gregorio Condori Mamani, may or may not have seen the play, but its memory echoes in this excerpt from his life history, as recorded by the Peruvian anthropologists Ricardo Valderrama and Carmen Escalante:

Bueno, totalmente ambicionaspas españakunaqa Inkanchista wañuchisqaku. Inkakunaqa manan papelta reqsirankuchu, qelqata, taytacha papelta qoyta munaqtinpis paykuna rechazasqayu; porque paykunaqa mana noticiasta papelpichu apachinakuranku, sino wik'uña q'aytukunallapi; mana allin notiçikunapaq yana q'aytukunapi, allin notiçiakunapaqta karan yuraq q'aytukuna. Kay q'aytukunan karan libro hina, pero españakuna mana kananta munasqaykuchu hinaspa Inkaman huk papelta qosqaku:
–Kay papelmi riman, –nispa:
–Maytaq rimsqan? Sonseras; engañayta munawankichis.
Panpamantaq papelta wikch'upusqa. Inkaqa manan papelkunamanta entenderanchu. Imaynatatq papel rimanman karan, manataq leeyta yacharanchu chayri? Khaynatan Inkanchis wañuchichikusqa. Chaymanta pachan Inkarrey chinkapun.

Well, these greedy Spaniards were hungry for power. So they killed our Inca. The Incas didn't know anything about paper or writing, and when the good Lord wanted to give them paper, they refused it. That's because they didn't get their news by paper but by small, thick threads made of *vicuña* wool: They used black wool cord for bad news and for the good news, white cords. These cords were like books, but the Spaniards didn't want them around; so they gave the Ina a piece of paper.
"This paper talks," they said.
"Where is it talking? That's silly; you're trying to trick me."
And he flung the paper to the ground. The Inca didn't know anything about writing. And how could the paper talk if he didn't know how to read? And so they had our Inca killed. Inkaríy disappeared and has been gone ever since.
(Condori Mamani 57)

Although colonial Hispanic intent had originally developed such theatrical spectacles to flaunt before Andeans the death of their king, and, with him, their world, nevertheless, in practice, the performance of these spectacles was to have an opposite effect. Rather more like the religious pageants of the Crucifixion than the ecclesiastical authorities might be prepared to admit, these dramas, as forms of resistance, recorded an alternative theology based on the regenerative force of the Inca's sprouting seed-head and the continuity of his voice through new generations.

There was evidently a flowering of these theatrical intents to incorporate an Inca presence during the whole period of rebellion in the eighteenth century, with an even greater intensification toward the end of the century following the 1781 capture and death of Túpac Amaru II (José Gabriel Condorcanqui). Paralleling these were the official intents to extinguish any kind of Inca memory in these Andean fiestas. For example, the royal dramas were banned in 1781, and the Spanish *visitador*, José Antonio de Areche, prohibited Andeans from even dressing as Incas, for fear of rebellion. The problem was, as Intipampa explains (116), that although many indigenous feasts had always counted in one way or another on an Inca presence at a symbolic level, since the Conquest this Andean royal presence had been extended into a Spanish public domain, in the nocturnal masquerades and theater that accompanied any marriage or rite of succession of the kings of Spain.

Many (see, for example, works by Lara, Millones, Ossio, López-Baralt, and others), have interpreted these dramas as a part of the Andean messianism based on the much broader Inkarriy cycle (of tales, elegies, *wankas, cantorales* etc.), focused on the rebirth of an Inca presence. Flores Galindo, in *Buscando un Inca* [*Searching for the Inca*], recognizes in these dramas aspects of an Andean "utopian thought," while contemporary critics read in the plays a historical Andean debate on the status of writing. They are probably all of these.

In her book *Historia y drama ritual en los Andes bolivianos* [*History and Ritual Drama in the Bolivian Andes*], Beyersdorff, armed with more details of the local histories of their performance, often in disputed territories, suggests that they might in fact interpret the historical demands of the Spanish *Requerimiento* (a piece of legislation empowering their nation to subjugate another, read out before battle) according to the formulaic patterns of a much older genre, having to do with inter-ethnic land claims when the fertility of the earth (and hence the future food-seeds) was at stake. For her, then, their ritualized gestures and locutions would stand among the reformulated ancient protocols between groups who have contended for millennia for land and natural resources, perhaps on a par with the Tupi *carbet* as speeches of the defiant or with the ceremonial dialogues uttered when rival lowland groups meet (see Brotherston 1992, 48).

In an alternative but related view, Cornejo Polar (1994) thinks these dramas might also draw on pre-Hispanic funerary customs, the speeches and choreographic patterns (whether *tinku* or *wanka*) between rival groups that were performed over the bones of the dead (1994, 57 n. 86). As such, their performance was a way of dancing history rather than writing it, at once more dynamic, unfixed in meaning, and open to other interpretations.

Another neo-Inca colonial theatrical work, performed in Quechua, was the drama of *Apu Ollantay*. Although the most well-known version was written in the eighteenth century by a priest, Antonio Valdez, the drama obviously draws on prior Andean sources and names resonant of Andean history (on the different versions, see Meneses). Brotherston (1992, 204) suggests that, as a genre, *Apu Ollantay* was probably one of the Inca kingship or royal dramas, those performed in the Inca court to celebrate their rule over the provinces. The plot focuses on the love between an Inca princess and a warrior from Antisuyu, rejected by her father since he is of a lower social status. However, the play clearly locates and defines its characters according to Inca power relations, and in its emphasis it is overtly Cuscocentric.

Like Guamán Poma's *Corónica*, the play is influenced by Inca *khipu* literacy and numeracy. For Brotherston, Inca hierarchy and rules of law especially are expressed visually and aurally in two particular scenes in which knotted *khipus* are displayed (1992, 208–9). The accompanying speeches by the *khipu* readers make of them a corporal template of the destiny of the rebel Ollantay. In the first, the main *khipu*-cord is compared to Ollantay's bound head and the pendant knots to his men as fruit stones, the mere remains after the flesh has been eaten. In the second, the black *khipu* threads are compared to his burnt body and the knots to the Inca's hands that hold him:

cayca llauta
nam kahuahua cay umanpi huatascana
cay rurucanari runam tucuy payman tinkiscana.

As to the main cord,
so the skeins that are bound to his head;
as kernel-knots the men all united with him.

Scene 5

cay kipupim can killimsa
nam Ollantay rupascana
cay kipupakmi kimsa piscucuna huatascana
nam Antisuyu hapiscu
nam Inca makeykipina:
chaymi huatacuncuyptou
kinsa piscu tucuypinas.

As the *khipu* is carbon-black,
so Ollantay is burnt;
as the *khipu* is bound with three quintuple knots,
so the Antisuyu is taken
so it is in the Inca's hand;
here the quintuple knots,
three fives altogether.

Scene 14
Translation in Brotherston (1992, 208–9)

Quechua theater and opera have also been inspired by a well-known love story, *Manchay Puytu*, originally a poem accompanied by music and composed by an unknown priest with Indian origins in the middle of the eighteenth century. In this case, the poem, an Andean version of the Orpheus myth, tells the tragic story of the forbidden love between the priest-author and his young Indian servant, who dies while he is away in Lima. In another image of Andean regeneration, he digs up her body and makes a flute of her femur, with which he dreams and plays melodies in her memory:

Uj k'ata kusiyniy kajta
Mayqen jallp'a mullp'uykapun

What kind of earth has grasped
her who was my only joy?

(Lara 1985, 133)

Like that of the *Tragedia del fin de Atawallpa* [*Death of Ataw Wallpa*], the performance of these dramas might have had the official intention of revealing fundamental flaws within the Inca empire, but in practice they served more to perpetuate social memories in a new guise. There were other Quechua colonial dramas (*El hijo pródigo* [*The Prodigal Son*], *El rapto de Proserpina* [*The Rape of Proserpina*], *El sueño de Endimión* [*The Dream of Endimión*], *Yawri Titu Inca, Utqha Paucar,* and *Usca Paucar, El pobre más rico* [*The Richest Poor Man*]), but *Apu Ollantay* and *Tragedia del fin de Atawallpa* had more powerful Andean resonances. As an Andean appropriation of European theater, they reworked past memories into a millennial vision. Like the *autos-da-fé* and grand colonial theatrical fiesta-spectacles, they used European genres as convenient overlays, unsuspect occasions in which Andeans continued to celebrate an Inca presence. But they were also contemporary rites of entrance and exit into written form as a temporary convenience, a passing medium that allowed–and allows–Andeans to appeal again to the Inca's voice as the ultimate source of power (see **Figure 6**).

Part Three: Literatures of the Andean Nations

Criollo identity was to use writing in much more prosaic ways. On the eve of Independence of the Andean Republics, during the eighteenth century, there was less occasion for recording Inca power and glory and more for emerging *criollo* concerns. The prior struggle between France and Spain, the rise of mercantilism–these were more pertinent worries.

Echoes of the fascination with the Inca *khipu* as an alternative form of literature now came from Europe. For instance,

Figure 6.

The "iukas" from a Diablada dance at Carnival, Oruro, Bolivia. (Courtesy of the Ricardo López Collection)

the popular *Lettres d'une péruvienne* of Mme de Grafigny (1695–1758) (which went through four editions between 1747 and 1764) is a series of letters from Europe between a captured Inca princess and her Peruvian lover, based on contemporary ideas about *khipus* and their possible alphabetic rendering. These European-derived *khipus* were examined earlier this century in a study by Lock and have recently become the subject of another re-scrutiny as a part of the debate surrounding the Blas Valera documents.

Only a few exceptional poets of independence, such as Juan Wallparrimachi Mayta, provided an alternative voice to what Lara (1947) calls a deaf peninsular traditionalism, and even then, Wallparrimachi's work was not known until it was rediscovered by intellectuals from Sucre (Bolivia) in the 1870s. Predictably, Wallparrimachi's rediscovered life was as much mythical as real, his supposed descent bridging the Spanish Crown and Cusco *indigenismo*; in reality he was born in *ayllu* Macha in Charkas. Reared by a *criollo* warrior of independence, Manuel Asencio Padilla, and his wife, Doña Juana Azurduy, the young Wallparrimachi learned to read and write in both Spanish and Quechua. He also became a worthy warrior (and slinger of some note) for independence and died young in battle in 1814, leaving behind poems (reminiscent of *Ollantay* or *Machay Puytu*) to his early love, Vicenta Quiroz, already married to a wealthy miner and sent in shame to a nunnery in Arequipa:

Chajra musmurej
Sumaj t'ikantan
Siminqa phanchin;
Misk'inraykuri
Muyupayaspa
Q'enti musparin.

Her lips open
beautiful, like the flowers
that make fragrant the fields;
And, eager for their sweet nectar,
They are craved and surrounded
By the warrior hummingbird.

(Lara 1985, 146)

However, when the new Andean Republics finally came into being, the expression of *criollo* identity was founded more on the printing press and what Benedict Anderson (in *Imagined Communities*) has called the beginnings of print capitalism, making use of written Indian languages only to the degree that this helped their project of national identity and integration. The *criollo* leaders of the new Andean states had already drawn on the support of the indigenous populations for their cause in the intermediate period of struggle between colonial rule and independence, when they published forced translations into Aymara and Quechua of some political documents, such as pamphlets on tribute and the Declaration of Independence. Now the performance of Aymara and Quechua versions of national works, such as national and regional hymns of identity, became commonplace in schools and colleges, an obligation in this nationalizing project.

After the Wars of Independence, these early political tracts were accompanied by a new wave of religious literature, this time Protestant translations of Biblical texts. The most well-known translator into Aymara was Vicente Pazos Kanki (1779–1851?), an educated diplomat and traveler who also knew Spanish, Latin, and English; he even translated an early proclamation of independence into Aymara. A Catholic reaction followed, mainly from Bolivian priests. However, the first books of Protestant hymns written in Aymara occured from 1870 onwards, by authors and translators such as Carlos Felipe Beltrán (1816–1898) from Oruro, in his numerous pamphlets to civilize the Indian, and Doctor Nuñez Butrón from Juliaca, editor of the periodical *Runa Soncco*.

The Consolidation of a New Textual Community

Where the jural and ceremonial systems of Inca and other Andean states had once formed a vital domain of institutional control over textual practices, now the administrative apparatus of Spanish law, and the written archives of legal discourse and the notarial arts, were to form a new substratum for Andean oral history and literature.

Under the new republics, Spanish and Indian languages (Aymara or Quechua) remained for a time the medium of litigation in local *ayllu* government. However, written Spanish soon became the accepted genre for public legal discourse by Indians, even in cases concerning rural areas. The necessity of formulating arguments that could withstand appeal to the highest levels of the colonial and republican administration meant that rural speakers of Indian languages (or their representatives) had to adopt Spanish legal conventions and concepts. For these reasons, even the 1780s rebellion, focused on the Indian leader Tomás Katari (ca. 1740–1781), was determinedly legalistic in its demands for justice.

In Andean communities, this was done through the formation of a special group: the title-bearers, or *apoderados*, empowered to keep and recite on occasion the colonial title documents of community land claims. These men were versed in the content of written documents, although they recited then orally to their *ayllu* audience. In Bolivia, their skills became even more important toward the end of the nineteenth century, in local attempts to counter the usurpation of *ayllu* lands in another wave of hacienda development under President Melgarejo, when they too were called upon to form regional, national, and trans-Andean alliances in order to defend their territory. Many of these *apoderados* were the same protagonists who led the struggle to found rural schools toward the end of the nineteenth century and beginning of the twentieth. They viewed this need for education as a part of the wider struggle to defend and recuperate Andean territories in a double-edged battle that was to assimilate Andean communities into the Spanish world in unsuspected ways even while it followed a much more Andean agenda.

During the same period, the jural discourse of many of these title-bearers, based on written Spanish law, became the textual basis for many rural Andean oral histories. Now, young urban intellectuals had found a powerful source of Andean indigenous literature, reworked once again in a modern fervor of textual reformulations, in the collection and recording of the oral life histories of certain leading figures of this movement at the turn of this century and in the memories of survivors of some of the most important Indian rebellions of this period. Members of the Taller de Historia Oral Andina (THOA, Workshop on Andean Oral History) in La Paz documented the life of the title-bearer "Santos Marka T'ula," (1984), the *escribano* Leandro Condori Chura (1992), and other indigenous leaders (see, for example, Huanca 1991). With a similar enthusiasm, Antonio Males of Ecuador, in *Villamanta ayllucunapac punta causi*, studied the oral history of the Imbayas of Quinchuqui-Otavalo.

Another result of this articulation between native speakers of Andean languages and the Spanish legal system has been the interest in *testimonio* (testimony) as a genre of oral narration and history. In his book *Testimonios, cartas y manifiestos indígenas* [*Indigenous Testimonies, Letters, and Manifestos*], Leinhard has shown the long history of this genre. Now, with a new lease on life, it became particularly popular in indianist organizations such as THOA in Bolivia. Although this is essentially a Spanish jural medium, its popularity might nevertheless have to do with its particular style, which pays attention to the Andean linguistic postulate that distinguishes between "seen" and "unseen" knowledge. Popular works such as that of Ana María Condorí–*Nayan uñatawi: Mi Despertar* [*My Awakening*]–draw on this medium.

Andean speakers were able to adapt the new jural medium of written Spanish to their own ends in other ways. Platt (1992) describes how the legal discourse of jurisprudence became the basis not only for land claims against the state but also for shamanic interventions into these matters, which could in certain instances erupt into real moments of rebellion.

Part Four: The Incorporation of Andean Indigenous Writing into Literary Modernism

Mestizaje, Identity, and the "Cultural Rescue" of Indigenismo

In the twentieth century, a new kind of writing about the Andes emerged, and a new breed of writer–and reader–began to scrutinize Andean rural life, drawing into its sphere of interest not only Andean textual practices but also Andean characters, literary forms, images of landscape, and the ever-present question of land. Whereas in the first centuries after the Conquest the question of land, from an indigenous point of view, was still tied to the rights of the Inca and, less directly, to the confrontation between different textual practices, now the same question became abstracted from its source, polarized between different class interests.

On the one hand, there was a gradual alliance between a wider anti-oligarchic movement (at once anti-*gamonalista* and anti-clerical) and a socialist plan grounded in the economic basis of the peasantry (the so-called *problema de tierras* ["problem of the lands"]), influenced by Mariátegui, director of the periodical *Amauta* and author of the pioneering *Siete ensayos de interpretación de la realidad peruana* [1928: *Seven Interpretive Essays on Peruvian Reality*]. On the other hand, a new expression of rural Andean life and its oral traditions, in written form, began to form part of the agenda of literary modernism, in new genres suitable for an urban bourgeoisie and a rising literate class of urban intellectuals with provincial roots. This process was related to wider economic and social changes that had to do with urbanism, but also with the change from a dominant *criollo* national ideology towards a more *mestizo* one. The country was now seen from the city (to use Kristal's expression), and an Andean form of *indigenismo* was to emerge from the relative safety and comfort of an armchair and access to books.

So at one extreme, the 1920s and 1930s witnessed the rise of various popular movements in the Andes. In Peru, the Cusco group Resurgimiento was founded in 1927, APRA (Alianza Popular Revolucionaria Americana) in 1928, and the Communist Party in 1930. These popular movements were to develop in parallel with the rise of other indigenous movements and return to Andean languages, at least in part, as their means of expression. In Bolivia, the indigenous schools movement, especially that focused around the *ayllu*-school of Warisata (founded in 1931 by the *mestizo progresista* [leftist] Elizardo Pérez), promoted economic and social changes to give more rights to rural people, facilitated by a last generation of rural *mestizo* teachers who spoke Aymara inside the classroom and in the community. This same movement also grew out of a wider political alliance with *apoderado* leaders, with the aim of wresting writing from *criollo* and *mestizo* hands and using it in defence of *ayllu* lands. Later, in the 1930s and 1940s, in the wake of these various indigenous movements, there was a wave of periodicals and magazines reproducing texts in Aymara and Quechua: *Pututo* started in Puno in 1922, and in Cusco the magazine *Waman Puma* started in 1941. This was still a *mestizo* literature, produced by urban intellectuals of the upper class or by literate *mestizos* who had come to the cities from the provinces. Nevertheless, from these origins began the so-called *indigenista* movements, which were to develop their own literary forms. In this way, the sociocultural heterogeneity that formed the basis of *indigenismo*, already prefigured in the early chronicles of the New World, came into its own.

Although literary *indigenismo* had begun much earlier, it was to flourish in the 1930s. In *La novela indigenista* [*The Indigenist Novel*], Antonio Cornejo Polar (1936–1997) notes how the novel, the most bourgeois of literary forms, suited to an urban elite, was transformed in *indigenista* hands so that the Hispanic novel was drawn into the sphere of this new *mestizo* literature with Andean roots. Cornejo Polar perceives in the novel's system of production an interplay between Andean and bourgeois needs and requirements, a two-way process of composition and form whereby urban literary producers were compelled to appropriate the cultural forms of the rural referents around which their works revolved. In this manner, the first tentative encounters with Andean textual practices of the colonial period were to give way to a full-scale incorporation of Andean songs and tales as the basis of these literary forms. The later *mestizo* novel was characterized by these Andean literary forms, for example, the additive series of independent episodes rather than sequential plot of representation (their so-called internal disorder).

The Orkopata poetry group in Puno had already experimented with these Andean literary forms. Now, in *El pez de oro* [1927: The Golden Fish], Gamaliel Churata (1894–1969) from Arequipa, with his close ties to the Puno region, was to incorporate other familiar Andean details (the *retablo* [series of images] and an inherent dualism) to subvert conventional written forms and help create this recognizably new *mestizo* genre.

Perhaps César Vallejo (1892–1938) went furthest in his search to express heterogeneous Andean textual practices in writing and so to bridge the gap between them. He was intensely conscious that the thread or knot of a *khipu*, just as much as the written line, expressed vital notions of personhood, that a gesture could be writing in the air, such as in these lines from *Trilce* (1923):

Hilo retemplado, hilo, hilo binómico
¿por dónde romperás, nudo de guerra?

Revived thread, thread, binomial thread
Where will you snap, knot of war?

(202)

In other instances, he sensed the futility of so many words, or of writing too saturated with an imposed catechism, as in "El dolor de las cinco vocales" [1919: "The Pain of the Five Vowels"]:

Ves
lo
que
es
pues
yo
ya
no.
La
cruz
da
luz
sin
fin. (156)
See
what
it
is?
I
can't
any
more
The
cross
gives
light
without
end

For him, behind all this futility was the memory of a once-woven empire, for example, in his poem "La Araña" ["The Spider"] in *Los heraldos negros* [1918: *The Black Heralds*]:

Es una araña enorme que ya no anda;
una araña incolora, cuyo cuerpo,
una cabeza y un abdomen, sangra.

(37)

It is a huge spider that no longer moves;
a colorless spider, whose body,
a head and a stomach, bleeds.

In "Comunión" ["Communion"] in *Los heraldos negros*, he compares hair to "roots," a singularly Andean image of regeneration that reminds us of the agricultural process by which the Inca's head and body can be united once more:

Tu cabello es la ignota raicilla
del árbol de mi vid.

(23)

Your hair is the undiscovered root
of my grapevine tree.

These powerful images of Andean regeneration, at their most lyrical, abound in descriptive passages about Andean terrain, for example, in José María Arguedas' *Ríos profundos* [1958: *Deep Rivers*, 1978]. The Quechua-speaking Arguedas, an anthropologist and writer, was to develop these hybrid/syncretic forms of *misti* identity to their fullest. The mythic dimension of Andean culture he had known from his youth is present, whether he is writing in Andean Spanish or in Quechua, in *Todas las sangres* [1964: All the Bloods], in his reworking of the tale of Inkarríy in *La agonía de Rasu Niti* [1962: The Agony of Rasu Ñiti], and in the poem *Tupac Amaru* (1962):

Uyariy Hatun Tayta, karu qeswakunamanta, kita weraqochakuna, pampa, chiri, qoñeq allpaykuna qechuwasqankunamanta, ayqespa, mastarinakuniku lliu tawantin suyupi.

(16–17)

Listen, Great Father: we've fled from the distant valleys, from the cold or scorching pampas that the false *viracochas* took away from us, and we've spread ourselves throughout the four quarters of the world.

(17)

Arguedas's writing and anthropological studies influenced a whole generation of Peruvian intellectuals, from writers to those in the plastic arts. As a part of the general mood of consciousness raising, the writers (for example, Salazar Bondy [1924–1965]) published translated volumes of Quechua poetry (1978), while the artists (for example, Fernando de Szyszlo [b. 1925]) began to study the Andean roots of their culture, treating Andean cultural objects and handicrafts on a par with European ones. In *La construcción de un artista peruano contemporáneo* [*The Making of a Contemporary Peruvian Artist*], Rebaza Soraluz suggests that their aesthetic focus, their drive to translate Andean materials and their language, directed at the cultural rescue of Andean treasures, was yet another facet of cultural appropriation; it was certainly a legitimizing discourse for the new social compromise that intellectuals found themselves in from the 1950s to the 1970s (see also Salazar Bondy 25, 28). But the result, according to Rebaza Soraluz, was simply the creation of a new Andean classicism.

This movement went far beyond the borders of Peru, in the development of an Andean *misti* or *criollo* vernacular. In Bolivia, Jesús Lara (1900–1970), a Quechua-speaking provincial lawyer, began to study and collect *Poesía Quechua* [1947; Quechua Poetry] and *La literatura de los Quechuas* [1969; Literature of the Quechuas], including a written version of the *Tragedia del fin de Atawallpa* (1957). The Bolivian Alcides Arguedas (1879-1946) wrote *Pueblo Enfermo* [1908; Sick People] and *Raza de bronce* [1919; Bronze Race], citing Aymara passages, folkloric themes, and lexicon. Like his Peruvian namesake, he used Andean Spanish (with its ample lexical and grammatical influences from Andean languages) in a conscious attempt to create a regional literary vernacular. In a similar vein, the Quechua-speaking Bolivian writer Carlos Medinacelli (1899–1949), from San Javier de Chirca in Chuquisaca, wrote *Ch'askañawi* (1948), full of "nuestro castellano popular" ["our popular Spanish language"] directed at a regional and national audience.

The Development of Popular Texts

The cultural rescue of Andean texts, in their original form, now became an end in itself. A new period of cultural production, which was to include several new grammars of Andean languages, witnessed the publishing of a wealth of folkloric collections, such as the Aymara collections of Rigoberto Paredes (1870–1950) and of the self-styled *aymaristas*, Luis Soria Lens

and Antonio González Bravo. La Paz, as an Aymara-speaking city, became the center of this cultural drive, and Aymara texts filled the pages of the new periodicals (*Inti Karka, Kjana Aru,* and *Pututu*) and of Paceño Presses.

Other Aymara-speaking *mestizos* began to publish collections for more popular consumption. The folklorist Antonio Paredes Candia (in the tradition of his father Rigoberto), began to publish collections of popular tales together with vocabularies of Aymara terms in popular Spanish. Even so, these collections were characterized by what Briggs (1981) has called "Patron-Aymara," with its notorious lack of politeness markers. Many of the Aymara terms used are incorrectly translated and are, in fact, insulting to Aymara speakers, so these works should be treated more as sourcebooks of *mestizo* and *criollo* usages. Paredes Candia also had no qualms about editing Aymara texts into Spanish literary forms, as if to imply that the original Aymara is not worthy of literary study in and of itself (Albó 1984, 21).

Revolution, World Markets, and Foreign (Academic) Intervention

Gradually, too, another, more distant perspective on Andean life had been in the making. Individual travelers accounts and random scholarly interest in the Andes had continued throughout the nineteenth and early twentieth century. However, in the revolutionary period of the 1920s and 1930s, and then with the rubber demands of the 1940s, the Andean region gradually came within the sphere of influence of North American imperial claims and interests, as a distant extension of their Caribbean backyard.

As a direct result, there was an increasing anthropological and linguistic interest in the Andes on the part of North American scholars. Many eminent scholars of this period (Tschopik, Sebeok, and Carter, to name a few) had direct institutional ties to the U.S. State Department, and in some cases to the Evangelical churches, while the Peace Corps Development Program, which required teaching materials in Andean languages, was a part of this same drive. The Aymara- and Quechua-speaking regions of the southern Andes became the focus of this new wave of interest.

One goal of these scholars was to provide study materials for the increasing interest of North American Centers of Latin American Studies in the Andean region. A part of this material production was to include the collection of Andes texts and a cultural collaboration on their translation. In the case of Aymara, Harry Tschopik Jr. (1948), with the help of a *mestizo* bilingual, collected Aymara tales from the Chucuito region and the life story of a local Aymara woman, Manuela Ari (later re-edited by Briggs and Dedenbach). Weston La Barre (1950) collected Aymara tales in the Pacasa dialect from nearby Tiwanaku, and Thomas Sebeok (1951) collected an Aymara version of *Little Red Riding Hood* from the city of La Paz. Some decades later, William Carter collected several Aymara songs and prayers in *Irpa Chico*, the name of a village near La Paz, home of his collaborator, Mauricio Mamani.

Another facet of this same interest was the beginning of the "Protestant offensive," when evangelical sects from the North penetrated the Andean region. From the late 1930s onward, Canadian Baptist missionaries began to translate the Bible into Aymara (as well as Quechua), providing a new source of written materials in quantity in rural areas. They adapted spoken Aymara language with the new postulates of evangelism to create what Briggs (1981) has called "missionary Aymara," and the different sects created a wealth of modern Aymara written scripts, leading not only to a regional battle over alphabets but also a debate about the best kind of spoken Aymara. Now it was argued that the Aymara of the Baptist hinterland around Huatajata, on the shores of Lake Titicaca, which was mixed with Hispanic missionizing concepts, was far superior to the more rural varieties. At a later stage, between 1967 and 1973, the Summer Institute of Linguistics, with school projects in Ayacucho, La Paz, and Cochabamba, produced primers in Aymara and Quechua (Albó 1979, 320 n.11).

This political and religious interest in Andean languages, above all on the part of the United States, generated a popular reaction against the work of foreign anthropologists in the region. It was claimed that Andean linguistic studies had allowed Aymara to become a "coding language" in the Vietnam War, and Hispanics living in the United States were quick to pass on the information that Quechua was being spoken by spacemen in *Star Wars*.

Part Five: National Revolutions and Their Aftermath

The Rise of Aymara and Quechua Identity and Nationalism

The terms "Aymara" and "Quechua," as they are used today, are modern political categories. Echoing a similar process that occurred under Toledan colonial rule, the modern idea of a monolithic Aymara or Quechua language and culture emerged in the revolutionary period of language and cultural revitalization initiated in the 1940s.

In Bolivia, this particular notion of Andean identity was recognized officially in 1952, under the patronage of the National Revolutionary Party (MNR), in return for the vital role played by peasants and peasant unions during the revolutionary period. After 1952, new modernist economic and educational policies generated a massive wave of migration to the cities, where country people struggled to find a new identity as they encountered the *criollo* and *mestizo* city dwellers already grouped into ranked social classes. They began to think of themselves as "Aymara" (or "Quechua"), rather than by their former local village names, and they were in turn called "Aymara" (or worse, "Indio") by the city elite, lending momentum to this process of regional identity that would later develop into an incipient Aymara nationalism.

This ethnic fervor was accompanied by a new relationship between city and countryside. Waves of migrants now settled in city *barrios* (neighborhoods) created a new world of *barrio* identity. Just as Andeans had used their displacement and re-territorialization into the reduction towns of the colonial period to rework Andean feast cycles into the Catholic calendar, so the new Aymara *barrios* developed their own feast cycles, to dance their identity rather than write it (Abercrombie 1991). Although this process had already begun with the rise of the *cofradías* (brotherhoods) of the urban enclaves of the colonial period (based on colonial theater and *autos da fé*), it now passed into the hands of a new Aymara middle class of resident migrants with economic power, for example the "Senõres de Gran Poder," examined by Albó and Preiswerk, who patronized a new language of expression based on the military brass band and the *danza folklórica* (folkloric dance). Albó and Preiswerk describe how older Aymara speakers expressed their ethnic identity in the *Morenada* dance of Gran Poder, evoking the prestigious image of colonial slave drivers (and their women), the lackeys of Aymara lords, in contrast with the more pitiful state of the black Yungas slaves being led to the mines of Potosí (see **Figure 7**). The younger generation expressed it in the vigorous dance of the Caporales, who controlled the black slaves.

Just as the regional feasts of Gran Poder in La Paz and of Carnival in Oruro were extending their range and degree of internal class and ethnic differentiation, so an added impetus to this process of regional and national identity came from a new alliance between urban *mestizos* and urban Indians with rural backgrounds, with the common aim of promoting tourism as a vital facet of modernization and of greater economic power for the regions. The anthropologist Julia Elena Fortún learned the necessary skills when she visited the first Festival Folklórico in Argentina in 1965, accompanied by a group of folkloric Bolivian musicians and dancers. As director of anthropology in the newly formed Ministry of Education and Culture, she applied this knowledge in the first regional folkloric festival in Bolivia (that of Compi, held in June 1965), when busloads of city dwellers descended onto a small town on the shores of Lake Titicaca to celebrate local folklore and handicrafts. The National Folklore Festival of Cochabamba was held later the same year in the presence of the president. From then onward, regional folklore was to have presidential patronage. Later still, university students from rural backgrounds introduced the same institutional framework of ethnic identity onto their university campuses, and then onto the city streets, as a part of this same search for a multicultural identity–the "Indian within" a modern state formation, to use Abercrombie's memorable expression.

These emerging tendencies were seized upon, and reinforced by, the new political parties that emerged in the same period, with their Katarista and Indianist overtones. Unlike parallel movements in Peru (such as Shining Path), a part of the Katarista propaganda machine (called after the hero Tupaj Katari, killed in 1781) was the production of Aymara literature, in written form as *folletos* (pamphlets) and in spoken form on the radio, to reach an ever wider audience. It was these parties that appealed to the notion of Aymara language and culture, for the first time, as unifying forces.

The sentiments of urban Aymara (and Quechua) identity were thus echoed in the mass media of radio channels, directed in Andean languages at this new audience. Abercrombie has gone so far as to suggest that the idea of an Aymara culture only extends as far as the wavelengths of the Catholic Radio "San Gabriel," the *Voz del pueblo Aymara* (Voice of the Aymara People). This is true to the extent that in the countryside further afield, *campesinos* still think of themselves as Charkas or Laymi, Jukumani or Killakas.

Andean cultures of the rural areas have adapted their orality to the new technologies, their stories (now written down by Aymara writers such as Pedro Quispe, the *Amuyiri*) becoming transformed into a new modernized orality: As radio novels on the air. Aymara-speaking radio buffs or TV crews broadcast Aymara news over the air, echoed by dozens of smaller radio stations throughout the highlands. Local radio, traditionally a powerful instrument of resistance in the Andes, provides an alternative medium to the commercial media and to writing, steeped as these other media are in a different order of things.

These new forms of production in the mass media also gave rise to a new variant of Aymara language, what Briggs calls "radio Aymara," as a direct result of Aymara broadcasters writing their original scripts in Spanish and then translating them live into Aymara over the air. This pidgin Aymara,

Figure 7.

Morenada dance from the celebration of the feast of the Candelaria (Candlemas, Feb. 2nd) in Puno, Peru. (Archive of the authors)

with its Spanish grammatical and lexical structures, had high status as an "oralect" of Paceño Aymara, giving it the impulse to spread into other, more ordinary, kinds of speech throughout the regions reached by the same radio wavelengths.

New Identities, Old Nostalgias

This conscious reformulation of local Andean identity within a regional and national framework was to return to the countryside (from whence it had come) when local folkgroups integrated these regional and national trends into their own festive repertory.

Solomon describes how modern Quechua folksongs from Panacachi in Northern Potosí layer these territorial identifying marks. Local hamlets make themselves known by naming their local toponyms as they enter the plaza dance floor of their pueblo; regional *ayllu* groups name their own ethnic affiliations; and in even wider regional settings, Indian identity is broadcast on radio and contrasted with *mestizo* and *criollo* identities:

Hermanitos campesinos ay siwar Sarita
Ñak'aripi rikhukunchis ay siwar Sarita
Ch'ikipampiña qhuchalita suwakapusqayki
Kay gobierno MIRi galloqa ay siwar Sarita
Llakiy phutiy decretamun ay siway Sarita
Ch'ikipampiña qhuchalita suwakapusqayki
Tukuy yachay wasinchista ay siwar Sarita

Privatisayta munashan ay siwar Sarita
Ch'ikipampiña qhuchalita suwakapusqayki . . .

Brother campesinos, ay siway Sarita
We've got problems, ay siway Sarita
I'll capture you, Cochalita from the green pampa
This government of MIR-gallo, ay siway Sarita
Sadly decrees, ay siway Sarita
I'll capture you, Cochalita from the green pampa
Wants to privatize, ay siwar Sarita
All our schools, ay siway Sarita
I'll capture you, Cochalita from the green pampa . . .

(Solomon 72)

Turino, in *Moving Away from Silence* (1993), describes another institutional facet of this same nation-building process: national service in the armed forces, which was to have a profound effect on the performance and content of ethnic genres. National service forced the integration of Aymara and Quechua men, both *campesinos* and migrants, into national life through their military service in army barracks, when their skills as musicians adapted to the new instrumental medium of brass bands. The national status of these instruments was later to silence the quieter Andean instruments of the rural areas, drowning them out in the fervor of nationhood (with perhaps echoes of a more distant past of an Inca military presence in the region).

With the economic crisis of the 1980s, local *barrio* fiestas flourished to an even greater degree; in parts of La Paz they now take place most weekends between June and September. They have come to provide not only an alternative means of artistic expression to the dominant *criollo* national norms but also an alternative means of economic survival. Women and children who sell drinks and sweets receive a modest income, while men can circulate their modest economic wealth within a limited system of generalized exchange.

But there is another side of this same coin. This is the literature of nostalgia that emerged in both rural and urban worlds, social memories of a former world order to which modern and mobile Andeans are now but "orphans." These began to echo in the narratives of urban migrants (such as Gregorio Condori Mamani and his wife, Asunta Quispe Huamán), of rural women who have achieved not only liberation but also a political voice, and in what Noriega calls the "poetics of deterritorialization" in the songs of travelers and migrants (Noriega 1996, 317-21). The following example in Aymara is by Juan de Dios Yapita:

Kunakipunirakipacha
    sarañ sarañchakituwa
Kunakipunirakipacha
    jachañ jachañchakituwa

Whatever can it really be
    that makes me want to wander?
Whatever can it really be
    that makes me want to weep?

Monumental anthologies, such as the collection of the Montoya brothers, *La sangre de los cerros* [*Blood of the Mountains*], testify to the sheer scale of this literature.

Aymara "Speakers" Learn to Write

In contrast to Quechua literature, which had been written in Western script by bilingual *mestizos* since the early colonial period, the publishing of alphabetic texts in Aymara by

Aymara speakers themselves only gathered pace in the twentieth century, particularly from the 1970s onward. Albó describes the eventual flourishing of this writing as an "exuberant awakening," inspired as it was by various factors (1992, 17).

On the one hand, this awakening, as we have seen, had to do with the rise of the Katarista movement within Aymara national politics and with the conscious use of popular means of mass communication in the Aymara language as a way of extending party influence. On the other hand, there was the priestly and paternal lead of men such as Father Soria Lens and Father Federico Aguiló (Aguiló published a book of tales collected in Potosí). There was also the ecclesiastical patronage of institutions such as CIPCA (Centro de Investigación y Promoción Campesina (Research and Promotion Center of Rural Life) under Xavier Albó, and the Fundación San Gabriel (formerly under Padre Canut). Some of these sponsored their own radio stations at a national level with broadcasts in Aymara and Quechua, such as Radio San Gabriel and Radio Fides in La Paz and Radio Siglo XX in the mining zone of Llallagua.

According to Albó (1992, 17), the 1970s marked this irruption of Aymara into public life and into the national mass media. On radio, there were competitions to present the best work in Aymara oral literatures, in radio novels, and even in psychodramas. Then in the 1980s, a new generation of Aymara intellectuals (patronized by THOA) produced radio novels on the life of the rebel Tupaq Katari, on the *apoderados* Santos Marka T'ula and Leandro Nina Quispe, on the lives of migrant women, an Aymara version of Antonio Díaz Villamil (1897-1948) novel *La niña de sus ojos* [1948; *The Girl of His Dreams*], and many more.

Where there was an emphasis in writing, there was often priestly or international patronage. In Peru, the publishing house of another ecclesiastical organization, Bartolomé de Las Casas in Cusco, encouraged young Quechua-speaking intellectuals to publish life stories and communal accounts of rural life, their task made easier by developments in the technology of tape recording. In 1977, Valderrama and Escalante published their Quechua/Spanish bilingual edition of the life story of the Cusco strapper Gregorio Mamani (and later of his wife, Asunta), which became such a success that it was translated into several other languages, including an English version by Paul Gelles and Gabriela Martínez Escobar. This first experiment in a new genre was followed by Gow and Condori's edition of regional tales, *Kay Pacha* (1982), several other works by Valderrama and Escalante themselves (such as *Ñuqanchik runakuna* [1992: We the People]), and Itier's edition of *Karu Ñankunapi*, forty tales by storytellers from the region of Quispicanchi, Cusco (1999).

Other sources of Andean literature were the pastoral and evangelical centers, which increased their production of written texts in the field of popular education. As a part of the more general "Protestant offensive" of these years, evangelist sects were to penetrate even further into the rural and urban areas of the Andes. Their teaching of the scriptures in written texts provided a new source of education for adults and children alike, enabling new generations of migrants to enter the workforce at a more skilled level. In Bolivia, ceplay (Centro Pastoral y Liturgia Aymara [Aymara Pastoral and Liturgical Center]) in La Paz published three cycles of annual celebrations in Aymara under the direction of Vicente Quispe; in Peru, the Instituto de Estudios Aymaras (IDEA) in Chucuito (Puno) published a double series of more than fifty works in the 1970s under the direction of the rural schoolteacher Victor Ochoa.

But there were other institutional sources of patronage and interest in Andean languages, based less on writing, such as the world of cinematography. The Ukamaw group under Jorge Sanginés initiated a series of film scripts translated into Aymara in the tradition of a socialist critique of existing society. Their first full-length film, *Ukamaw* (1965), used Quechua-speaking actors trained by an Aymara speaker (Juan de Dios Yapita) to pronounce the Aymara script. Then, in the 1980s, Silvia Rivera made the short film *Khunuskiwa* with THOA, on the life of the Bolivian musician Patiño. Later films by the Ukamaw group (such as *El Coraje del Pueblo* [The Courage of the People]) have continued this trend up until the present, with *La Nación Clandestina* [Clandestine Nation] and *Recibir el canto de los pájaros* [To Receive Bird's Song], as has *Ajayu* (by Francisco Ormachea, 1996). In each case, these films are directed at a predominantly Spanish-speaking audience but have episodes in Aymara with Spanish subtitles; the film *Sayariy*, in a similar vein, has parts in Quechua. Other exceptions to the norm of writing were the collaborative ventures into recorded tapes for children, such as that of UNICEF, and Discos Heriba's sponsoring of the singer Luzmila Carpio to sing *Vida para los niños andinos* [Life for Andean Children].

So while a new kind of social realism provided the framework for the production of literatures in Andean languages, the struggle between different textual practices to express this literature continued, with different protagonists adopting different practices. In the ongoing struggle to recuperate their lands, *apoderado* leaders worked closely with peasant communities and educators to end the *mestizo* and *criollo* domination of reading and writing. On another front, *criollos* and later *mestizo* intellectuals had their own interests in incorporating the indigenous as an exotic other into a nation bent on literacy as its primary mode of expression. Meanwhile, a more popular group of urban Aymara and Quechua speakers began to write, or simply switched directly to newer forms of communication, in their search for alternative means of expression.

Institutional Means of Patronage in the Introduction of Writing, Phase II

Popular Education and the Capacitación of the Masses

Finally, in the 1970s, these scattered projects of social realism and popular education were brought together under the aegis of a more international agenda of modernization. In this phase, the *capacitación de las masas* ("training of the masses") was found to be necessary as part of a new economic drive to extinguish Third World poverty and integrate the Andean countries into more extensive world markets. This drive included more formal state interventions in the question of writing Andean languages, just as there had been at the beginning of the colonial period.

With the international financing of aid projects, there began a new process of literacy training of the masses, not only in Spanish but also in the Andean languages, mainly under the democratizing rubric of bilingual education. A fleet of experts (but non-speakers of Andean languages) came to direct the application of these programs in the Andean countries and, as a part of this drive, to supervise the production of materials in these languages.

International finance now began to pour in large quantities into the Andean countries in the name of cultural and linguistic rescue and revival. At the upper end of this new market, the large multinational organizations UNICEF and UNESCO financed many new collections of Andean literatures throughout the Andean countries. In another example, the Peruvian-German bilingual education project in Puno, Peru, financed by the German development institution GTZ, began to "rescue" popular literature and folksongs in Aymara and Quechua.

Finally as a part of this same drive, there was official recognition of an alphabetic script–the so-called *alfabeto único*–for Aymara and Quechua, first at a national level and then at an international pan-Andean one (in 1983).

National Patronage

At a national level, the first official intents to collect and publish texts in native languages came from the educational organs set up for the application of bilingual education. Typical of this drive, Julia Elena Fortún, as director of anthropology in a subsidiary of the Ministry of Education and Culture in Bolivia, began to collect recordings of Andean music and oral literature. Later on, the Instituto Nacional de Estudios Lingüísticos (INEL), after an initial period of collaboration with the University of Florida at Gainesville in which the basic skills of modern linguistics were taught to a select group of Aymara speakers, went on in the 1980s to collect and publish stories in Aymara (such as *Wiñay Arunaka*) and Quechua. The educational team at SENALEP (Servicio Nacional de Alfabetización y Educación Popular [National Service for Literacy and Popular Education]) also began to prepare school texts in Aymara and Quechua (as well as Guaraní and Spanish). Parallel developments occurred in Peru and Ecuador. For example, the Ministry of Education in Peru supported the collection of tales upon which Alejandro Ortiz later based his *Adaneva a Inkarri*.

The Rise of the Non-Governmental Organizations

Within this new institutional framework of financial support, a number of educational establishments run by native speakers for native speakers were able to expand their activities. With their official recognition as non-governmental organizations (NGOs), they were able to seek out their own sources of finance (patronized by bodies as diverse as the Inter-American Foundation, the sympathetic governments and NGOs of countries such as Holland and Canada, and later, with the quincentennial celebrations, of Spain itself). Thus, organizations such as ILCA (Instituto de Lengua y Cultura Aymara [Institute of Aymara Language and Culture]) and later Jayma both in La Paz, were able to collect, transcribe, and publish Aymara oral literature, even newspapers (in Aymara, in the case of ILCA's *Yatiñasawa*, and in a bilingual Spanish/Aymara edition, in the case of *Jayma*).

These new institutional settings provided an increased level of sponsorship for collected works of Andean literature, whether poetry or prose. In an Aymara domain, another source of sponsorship came from the Municipality of La Paz, when it was occupied by the populist party CONDEPA under Mayor Julio Mantilla. Volumes of poetry in Aymara were published by the Bolivians Rufino P'axsi, Clemente Mamani, and Abraham Triguero Coronel, and by the Peruvian José Luis Ayala. In a new phase of *indigenista* writing, Ayala also published a *chroninovela* (a hybrid of a *crónica* and a novella) called *Wancho Lima* (1989), about the La Paz uprising in 1923. This institutional mode of production of Andean literatures has continued apace in Ecuador, Bolivia, and Chile; it was much more controlled in Peru in the years of the civil war, with the general fear of indigenous organizations and their activities.

The Andean Academies

A number of informal Andean academies already flourished from the *indigenista* period of the 1940s, mainly as loose associations of *mestizo* intellectuals, *aymaristas*, or *quechuistas*. In the 1900s, as the study of Andean languages became increasingly respectable and lucrative, Andean "literacy" was to spread into higher levels of education in the Andean countries in order to train a new generation of students in native languages.

In La Paz in 1979, Juan de Dios Yapita, with José Mendoza, initiated the special subject area in Native Languages in the Linguistics Department of the UMSA (Universidad Mayor de San Andrés). Then in 1981, in a critical moment in the Facultad de Literatura–what Albo called "todo un símbolo" ("a unique symbol")–Nancy Paredes defended her licentiate thesis, a structural analysis of Aymara folktales, against a committee of staff opposed to the very idea of oral traditions as literature. After a heated debate, the thesis was approved, thereby opening the doors for many other students to follow. The Department of Native Languages in the UMSA has since approved several theses in Andean linguistics and modes of expression in oral texts (such as that of Alavi M. on the use of metaphor in Aymara). The Department of Literature, too, has produced a number of studies based on the collection and analysis of Andean oral texts, such as the structuralist analysis of *Toad Tales* by Jemio (1986) and the semiotic study of the *Tale of Juan el Oso* by Weitüchter (1984). A part of an ongoing Investigation Project, an archive of Andean oral literature has been set up, recording oral literature and transcribing it onto paper. The same department organized the first international meetings on Andean Literatures: the *Jornadas de Literatura Andina* (JALLA).

Similar tendencies occurred in southern Peru, and later in northern Chile and the north of Argentina. The Universidad del Altiplano in Puno started a master's-level course in Bilingual Education and Linguistics in the late 1970s to train technicians for the implementation of the associated programs in bilingual education. Financed by GTZ, they produced a number of publications of Andean folktales and folksongs, including local variants of the *Tales from Waruchiri* (collected and edited by López and Sayritupac Asqui), and wrote a regional vocabulary of the Aymara around Puno. More recently, the Centro "Bartolomé de Las Casas" in Cusco set up a progam in Andean studies that includes the study of Andean languages and literatures. Similar ventures in northern Chile (in Arica and later in Iquique) were geared more to the relation between local values and national education, in the context of development.

Part Six: New Approaches, New Theories

These new institutional approaches to the collection of Andean literatures had certain characteristics that warrant comment. In the initial enthusiasm for collection, oral traditions were too often collected in a piecemeal fashion, disembedded from their original social and cultural context. Even the recent approach of organizations such as THOA–inviting storytellers to national gatherings replete with modern recording techniques of video and tape recording, while giving priority to orality as a medium of communication–nevertheless do not take into account the original social functions of oral literatures. The modes of compiling collections, through lack of linguistic training, were often improvised and poorly informed, even by native speakers themselves, so that collectors transcribed their own recollections of a tale (in so-called *recopilaciones*), rather than original versions, which they often sought to "improve" by editing out what they thought were superfluous appendages.

At a more theoretical level, the approaches were too often imported (from Paris or New York) and tended to focus on the analysis of content rather than on the performative or linguistic aspects of Andean literatures. Structuralist studies from Europe (under the influence of Lévi-Strauss) and the United States were incorporated uncritically into Andean studies (as in the theses by Paredes and Jemio mentioned above), as were semiotic ones (Blanco and Bueno, Ballón Aguirre). The Finnish school of tale collection and classification also influenced Halushka, Jemio, and Ballón Aguirre. The studies of these decades, then, rarely examined texts within their own terms. A typical volume of Aymara tales from Radio San Gabriel in La Paz has commentaries *post facto* about what they might mean but does not consult the storytellers themselves.

Under educational patronage, especially that of international institutions such as UNICEF and UNESCO, oral traditions (whether from Ecuador, Peru, Chile, or Bolivia) were collected and transcribed into written script (as they had already been in the West) with the sole aim of making them literacy materials for Andean children, thus delimiting the broadly didactic Andean genres of tales and songs into "just stories for children," as if they were no more than that. A bureaucratic translation of texts (even in the current teaching materials of the Educational Reforms in the Andean countries) also fails to identify Andean grammatical markers, or the Andean grammar of orality, so that what might actually be Andean poetry is expressed in unstructured prose.

At a more linguistic level, as translation teams of bilingual technicians came to be active and directed from above by non-speakers, a situation very much like that of the missionizing fervor of the early colonial period occurred (a connection made by Brice Heath and LaPrade). Andean languages and written scripts were "normalized" in a random and non-directed way, untried in practice, and certain dialectal variants became dominant. Directives from above even re-named Andean literary genres for normative purposes, so that all songs (or tales) from now on were to be called *jarawi* (or *jawari*), a term taken from early colonial dictionaries for just one genre among many. Similarly, all books were to be called *panka*, "leaves of maize," presumably in memory of Waylla Wisa's dismay at writing as depicted in the drama of the *Death of Ataw Wallpa*. The fact that most translation teams were composed of urban men produced a gendered bias in the approach to Andean literatures, as well as a dominance of city dialects, for example, Paceño (dialect of La Paz); these dialects were applied throughout the regions, as grapholects (in Ong's terms). This has meant that many teaching materials were limited in scope and incomprehensible in regional application. Critiques of the general limitations of approach in this period, and its undermining of Andean literatures as a whole, can be found in Yapita (1994) and Arnold, Yapita et al. (2000).

Center and Periphery

The gradual realization by regional groups that the new educational materials, although directed at them, had severe limitations of communication, because of their grapholectic use of urban dialects as script, led to an increasing reaction against a centralized approach to Andean literary production. As a result, from the mid-1980s onwards, there were two dominant tendencies.

From the top down, there were new attempts to normalize Andean scripts and textual practices even further, backed up by the publication of guides for doing so. In the case of written Aymara, the so-called Aymara of the Educational Reform is now so far from spoken Aymara that a new mode of Aymara speech has developed, almost incomprehensible to fellow speakers because of its lack of syntax. Meanwhile, from the bottom up, regional groups struggled to write and publish their own forms of Aymara and Quechua and have them recognized at a national level. As in other countries (such as Uruguay) that were suffering this forced intrusion into their textual practices, the struggle was now rephrased as one between a language that unites and a language that separates.

The gradual recognition on the part of Aymara speakers of the internal differentiation of Andean language and culture drew at first on existing academic studies of regional variation. The original collection of oral traditions (out of context) by foreign linguists now served as an important vehicle for linguistic studies into the social and regional variations of Aymara, and studies such as those of Porterie-Gutiérrez were used to this end. A key text in the movement was the doctoral thesis by Lucy Briggs on social and regional variation in Aymara, published in Spanish in 1993. Aymara speakers themselves. especially the NGOs composed of young urban intellectuals from provincial backgrounds searching for their roots, collected texts from their own areas. Aymara linguists (for example, Yapita 1992) began to carry out studies into regional dialects. One result of this movement was the publication of a book of tales in the Oruro dialect of Aymara by the young storyteller Elvira Espejo, *Jichha nä parlt'ä: Ahora les voy a narrar* [Now I Am Going to Tell You a Story], in what has come to be known as the New Realism; the fact that it gained international recognition first in Cuba (as a finalist in the Casa de las Américas competition in indigenous literatures) ensured its publication in Bolivia, with a vice-presidential book presentation to the public.

Another aspect of these changes was the realization that many institutional frameworks, by their nature, patronize an approach to Andean literatures that sees in this task the cultural rescue of a subordinate group, giving a unifying voice of identity to subalternity, or ethnicity, en masse, but that in so doing, they necessarily ignore the individual voices that make up these groups. The Aymara "tribe" or Aymara "Indians" of earlier decades might have been replaced by Andean "women," or "such-and-such-an-Andean-group," but studies or biographies of individual Aymara speakers with exceptional narrative skills that might affect the performance of whole genres, even push them into new directions at one historic moment in time, were to come much later.

Some New Directions

As a result of the increasing pressure from speakers of Andean languages to have their languages, cultures, and textual practices recognized at an official level, new kinds of guides to educational practice had to include not only the recognition of orality as a didactic device but also descriptions of methodological approaches for collecting and analyzing oral literatures. A flutter of workshops and conferences in the Andean region on these themes followed, in NGOs and universities.

At national levels, the continuing international finance from the NGOs ensured the longer-term production of Andean texts. New publishing ventures were to rescrutinize colonial texts; in Peru, the series "Monumentos Lingüísticos" the center from Bartolomé de Las Casas in Cusco re-edited key colonial documents, while in Bolivia Radio San Gabriel's new edition of Ludovico's Bertonio's seventeenth-century vocabulary retranscribed it into the modern Aymara alphabet. At an international level, the series of pan-Latin American Conferences on Andean literatures, JALLA (Jornadas Andinas de Literatura Latinoamericana), held first in La Paz in 1993, allowed scholarly debate (and the publication of their *Memorias*) to range from the concerns of orality and literacy to regional needs and frustrations to the theoretical and methodological approaches necessary to develop a heterogenous and non-centered approach. Further regional debates on local issues included the needs of local Aymara speakers, and, as a part of a regional collaboration, there emerged an exchange of ideas between local regional Aymara-speaking centers in Puno, La Paz, Arica, and Jujuy, with the northern part of Argentina now firmly entering a pan-Andean sphere of influence of Aymara identity and nationalism. At an international level, many new studies and anthologies of Andean oral literature appeared, taking into account these new directions in scholarship and debate (*Literatura Aymara* [Aymara Literature] by Albó and Layme; *Hacia un orden andino de las cosas* [1996; Toward an Andean Order of Things] by Arnold, Jiménez, and Yapita; *Tradiciones orales andinas* [Andean Oral Traditions, 1994] by Beyersdorff and Dedenbach-Salazar, *Tradición oral y mitología andinas* [Andean Oral Tradition and Mythologies] by Itier, to name but a few).

An important part of these new directions has been the formal collaboration between international scholars and native speakers of Andean languages, in dialogue over a common task, in a dialogical anthropology that had already begun some years before in Aymara and Quechua circles (Briggs and Llanque Chana, Briggs and Yapita, Gow and Condori, Valderrama and Escalante, etc.). These collaborative efforts were followed by written studies by Aymara speakers themselves, often those trained in linguistics and anthropology, of their own literatures in context, taking into account the analysis of certain features of Aymara discourse and stylistics, with their woven ontologies. Cipriana Apaza's collection of potato origin myths, *Ch'uqin uñstatapa*, is typical. These writings, using alphabetic scripts developed through general consensus by Aymara speakers, are quickly absorbed by a student body and other interested parties of speakers.

One dominant trend that cannot be ignored is the increased presence of the performers of Andean verbal arts and literatures within written texts. From being the passive victims of colonial indoctrination, or the exotic backdrop of the accounts of travelers and anthropologists, or even the appropriated backdrop of Indianist and *indigenista* texts, Andean performers have now become (whether as historians, writers, poets, musicians, or singers) not only authors in their own right but also commentators on, and critics of, their own literary genres. Their exegeses of their verbal arts have become a vital part of a new Andean order of things.

Another trend is the appropriation of new technologies as a vehicle for the expression of the interests of incipient Aymara and Quechua Nations. The newspaper *Presencia* (in La Paz, Bolivia) now has regular features written in Aymara and Quechua, soon to be expanded into Sunday supplements. Aymara and Quechua linguists are generating dictionaries, lexicon, and translation services on the Web, Andean computer experts are generating there the virtual reality of Aymara origins in Tiwanaku (see for example Aymara Qullana at *http://www.virtualsolarsystem.com/members/chahuita/*), while Aymara and Quechua activists are debating pan-Andean issues in Web pages such as *Aymar lista*. In Chile, Aymara lessons have already been inscribed into interactive IT teaching tools. And in Bolivia, traditional Aymara tales such as *Jukumari*, the Bear-Man, have been animated, and the Bear-Man converted into a culture hero charged with environmental protection (Arnold, Yapita, et al. 2001). At the same time, a blossoming of new textile projects in communities and schools of the region is challenging the current stranglehold of Western forms of literacy. In this way, an Andean vanguard is already abandoning the transitory phase of expressing their words in Western alphabetic script, and turning to state-of-the-art multimedia presentations as a way to explore new virtual modes of oral tradition and the verbal arts, perhaps with the potential to inscribe into its mold more Andean ways of doing things in the future.

Works Cited

Abercrombie, Thomas A. 1991. "To Be Indian, to Be Bolivian: Ethnic and National Discourses of Identity." *Nation-States and Indians in Latin America*. Ed. Greg Urban and Joel Sherzer. Austin: University of Texas Press. 95–130.

——. 1992. "La fiesta del carnaval postcolonial en Oruro: Clase, etnicidad y nacionalismo en la danza folklórica." *Revista andina* (Cusco) 10.2: 279–325.

——. 1993. "Caminos de la memoria en un cosmos colonizado. Poética de la bebida y la conciencia histórica en K'ulta." *Borrachera y memoria: la experiencia de lo sagrado en los Andes*. Ed. Thierry Saignes. La Paz, Bolivia: Hisbol; Lima, Perú, Instituto Francés de Estudios Andinos. 139–70.

——. 1998. *Pathways of Memory and Power: Ethnography and History Among an Andean People*. Madison: University of Wisconsin Press.

Acosta, José de. 1940 [1590]. *Historia natural y moral de las Indias, en que se tratan de las cosas notables del cielo, y elementos, metales, plantas y animales dellas: y los ritos, y ceremonias, leyes y gobierno, y guerras de los Indios, compuesto por el padre Joseph de Acosta*. Mexico City: Fondo de Cultura Económica.

Aguiló, Federico. 1980. *Los cuentos: ¿tradiciones o vivencias?* La Paz: Editorial Los Amigos del Libro.

Albó, Xavier. 1979. "The Future of the Oppressed Languages in the Andes." *Peasants, Primitives, and Proletariats: The Struggle for Identity in South America*. Ed. David L. Browman and Ronald A. Schwarz. The Hague: Mouton. 267–88.

——. 1984. "Entrevista a Javier Albó. Diálogo." *Hipótesis, revista boliviana de literatura*. (La Paz) 20–21, 4.4, 5.5: 17–30.

——. 1992. "Introducción." *Literatura Aymara. Antología*. Ed. Xavier Albó and Félix Layme. La Paz: CIPCA/Hisbol/JAYMA. 11–32.

——, and Félix Layme, ed. 1992. *Literatura Aymara. Antología*. 1, *Prosa*. La Paz: CIPCA/Hisbol/JAYMA.

——, and Matías Preiswerk. 1986. *Los señores del gran poder*. La Paz: Centro de Teología Popular.

Anderson, Benedict. 1983. *Imagined Communities: Reflections on the Origin and Spread of Nationalism*. London: Verso.

Ansión, Juan, ed. 1989. *Pishtacos: de verdugos a sacaojos*. Lima: Tarea.

Apaza, Cipriana. 1996. "La aparición de la papa. Ch'uqin uñstatapa." *Madre Melliza y sus crías Ispall Mama wawampi: Antología de la papa*. Ed. Denise Y. Arnold and Juan de Dios Yapita. La Paz: Hisbol and ILCA.

Arguedas, Alcides. 1979. *Pueblo enfermo*. La Paz: Ediciones Puerta del Sol.

——. 1986. *Raza de bronce*. La Paz: Ediciones Puerta del Sol.

Arguedas, José María. 1938. *Cantokechwa*. Lima: Editorial Club del Libro Peruano.

Arguedas, José María, ed. 1957. *The Singing Mountaineers: Songs and Tales of the Quechua People*. Trans. Ruth Walgreen Stephen. Austin: University of Texas Press.

——. 1958. *Los ríos profundos*. Buenos Aires: Editorial Losada.

——. 1962. *La agonía de Rasu Ñiti*. Lima: Icaro.

——. 1962. *Tupac Amaru Kamaq Taytanchisman: haylli-taki; A nuestro padre creador Tupac Amaru; himno-canción*. Lima: Ediciones Salquantay.

——. 1964. *Todas las sangres*. Buenos Aires: Editorial Losada.

Arnold, Denise Y. 1991. "The House of Earth-Bricks and Inka-Stones: Gender, Memory and Cosmos in Qaqachaka." *Journal of Latin American Lore* 17: 3–69.

——. 1992a. "Introducción." *Hacia un orden andino de las cosas: tres pistas de los andes meridionales*. Ed. Denise Y. Arnold. La Paz: Hisbol and ILCA. 13–30.

——. 1992b. "At the Heart of the Woven Dance Floor. The Wayñu in Qaqachaka." *Iberoamericana* (Frankfurt) 16.3–4, 47–48: 21–66.

——. 1993. "Adam and Eve and the Red-Trousered Ant: History in the Southern Andes." *Travesía, Journal of Latin American Cultural Studies* 2.1: 49–83.

——. 1995. "Las canciones a los animales por las mujeres de Qaqachaka, Bolivia: una taxonomía preliminar." *Memorias: Jornadas andinas de literatura latino americana*. La Paz: Plural Editores Facultad de Humanidades y Ciencias de la Educación, Universidad Mayor de San Andrés. 87–102.

——. 1997. "Making Men in Her Own Image: Gender, Text and Textile in Qaqachaka." *Creating Context in Andean Cultures*. Ed. Rosaleen Howard-Malverde. New York: Oxford University Press. 99–131.

——. 1992. *Hacia un orden andino de las cosas: tres pistas de los Andes meridionales*. La Paz: Hisbol e ILCA.

——. 1996. "Los caminos de género en Qaqachaka: saberes femeninos y discursos textuales alternativos en los Andes." *Ser mujer indígena, chola o birlocha en la Bolivia postcolonial de los años 90*. Ed. Silvia Rivera Cusicanqui. La Paz: Subsecretaría de Asuntos de Género and CID. 303–92.

——, and Juan de Dios Yapita. 1998a. "*K'ank'isiña*: trenzarse entre la letra y la música de las canciones de la boda en Qaqachaka, Bolivia." *Parentesco y género en los Andes*. Vol 2: *Gente de carne y hueso: las tramas de parentesco en los Andes*. Ed. Denise Y. Arnold. La Paz: CIASE and ILCA. 525–80.

——, and Juan de Dios Yapita. 1998b. *Río de vellón, río de canto: cantar a los animales, una poética andina de la creación*. La Paz: Hisbol, Universidad Mayor de San Andrés and ILCA.

——, and Juan de Dios Yapita. 1992. "'Foxtalk'": Addressing The Wild Beasts in the Southern Andes." *Latin American Indian Literatures Journal* 8.1: 9–37.

——, Juan de Dios Yapita, et al. 2000. *El rincón de las cabezas: luchas textuales, educación y tierras en los Andes*. La Paz: Universidad Mayor de San Andrés and ILCA.

——, and Juan de Dios Yapita, et al. 2001. *Jukumari*. Interactive CD-ROM. La Paz: ILCA and Crearte Producciones.

——, Domingo Jiménez A., and Juan de Dios Yapita. 1991. "'Scattering the Seeds': Shared Thoughts on Some Songs to the Food Crops from an Andean Ayllu." *Amerindia* (A.E.A. Université Nancy II–Faculté des lettres, Paris) 16: 105–78.

Arzans de Orsúa y Vela, Bartolomé. 1965 [1705]. *Historia de la villa imperial de Potosí*. Ed. Lewis Hanke and Gunnar Mendoza L. Providence, RI: Brown University Press.

Astvaldsson, Astvaldi. 1998. "The Powers of Hard Rock: Meaning, Transformation and Continuity in Cultural Symbols in the Andes." *Journal of Latin American Cultural Studies* 7.2: 203–23.

Ayala, José Luis. 1980. *Jake Aru*. Lima: El Pez de Oro.

——. 1989. *Wancho Lima (croninovela)*. Lima: Kollao Editorial Periodística S.R.

Ballón Aguirre, Enrique. 1995. "Identidad y alteridad en un motivo etnoliterario amerindio e indoeuropeo: La doncella fecundada." *Revista andina* 13.1 (July): 43–81.

Barnes, Monica. 1992. "Catechisms and Confessionarios: Distorting Mirrors of Andean Society." *Andean Cosmologies Through Time: Persistence and Emergence*. Ed. Robert Dover, Katharine E. Seibold and John H. McDowell. Bloomington, Indianapolis: Indiana University Press.

Berg, Hans van den. 1984, 1988, 1994. *Material bibliográfico para el estudio de los aymaras, callawayas, chipayas, urus*. 3 vols. Cochabamba: Universidad Católica Boliviana.

Bertonio, Ludovico. 1879 [1603]. *Arte y grammatica muy copiosa de la lengua aymara*. Roma: Luigi Zannetti. Facsimile edition. Leipzig: Julio Platzmann.

——. 1984 [1612]. *Vocabulario de la lengua aymara*. Juli, Chucuyto: Francisco del Canto. Facsimile edition. Ed. Xavier Albó and Félix Layme. La Paz and Cochabamba: CIDES, IFEA, CIDES, MUSEF.

Betanzos, Juan de. 1987 [1551]. *Suma y narración de los Incas*. Ed. M. del Carmen Martín Rubio. Madrid: Ediciones Atlas.

Beyersdorff, Margot. 1992. "Ritual Gesture to Poetic Text in the Christianization of the Andes." *Journal of Latin American Lore* 19: 125–61.

——. 1998. *Historia y drama ritual en los Andes bolivianos: (Siglos XVI–XX)*. La Paz: Plural Editores; Universidad Mayor de San Andrés.

——, and Sabine Dedenbach-Salazar Sáenz, ed. 1994. *Tradiciones orales andinas: discurso y literatura*. Bonn: Holos.

Blanco, Desiderio, and Raúl Bueno. 1980. "De la carencia a la abundancia en un relato andino." *Metodología del análisis semiótico*. Lima: Universidad de Lima. 161ff.

Boone, Elizabeth Hill. 1994. "Introduction: Writing and Recording Knowledge." *Writing Without Words: Alternative Literacies in Mesoamerica and the Andes*. Ed. Elizabeth Hill Boone and Walter D. Mignolo. Durham, NC: Duke University Press. 3–26.

Bouysse-Cassagne, Térèse. 1987. *La identidad aymara: aproximación histórica (Siglo XV, Siglo XVI)*. La Paz: Hisbol.

Briggs, Lucy Therina. 1981. "Missionary, *Patrón*, and Radio Aymara." *The Aymara Language in Its Social and Cultural Context: A Collection of Essays on Aspects of Aymara Language and Culture*. Ed. Martha J. Hardman. Gainesville: University Press of Florida. 175–84.

——. 1985. "A Critical Survey of the Literature on the Aymara Language." *South American Indian Languages: Retrospect and Prospect*. Ed. Harriet E. Manelis Klein and Louisa R. Stark. Austin: University of Texas Press. 546–94.

——. 1989. "Wat'iya y el perro que habla latín: de un mito andino antiguo a uno contemporáneo." Conference paper presented at MUSEF (Museo de Etnografía y Folklore), Reunión Anual de Etnología, La Paz, 22–25 August.

——. 1993. *El idioma aymara: variantes regionales y sociales*. La Paz: Ediciones ILCA.

——. 1994. "El k'ari k'ari en dos textos de lengua aymara: análisis morfosintáctico y del discurso." *Andean Oral Traditions: Discourse and Literature*. Ed. Margot Beyersdorff and Sabine Dedenbach-Salazar Sáenz. Bonn: Holos. 161–97.

——. 1995. *Vocabulario para saber hablar, y pronunciar la Castellana compuesta á la Ydioma Aymará. A Colonial Bilingual Text in Spanish and Aymara*. St. Andrews: Institute of Amerindian Studies, University of St. Andrews.

——. In press. "Wat'iya Uquri y el perro que habla latín: de un mito andino antiguo a uno contemporáneo." *Cognitive Patterns of Andean Continuity*. Ed. N. Ross Crumrine et al.

——, and Sabine Dedenbach-Salazar Sáenz, ed. 1995. *Manuela Ari: An Aymara Woman's Testimony of Her Life*. Bonn: Holos.

——, and Juan de Dios Yapita. 1980. "The Origin of the Charago: an Aymara Tale (as told by Bertha Villanueva)." *Latin American Indian Literatures* (Pittsburgh) 4.2: 96–102.

——, and Domingo Llanque Chana. 1986. "El humor en el cuento aymara." *Identidades andinas y lógicas del campesinado*. Ed. Lucy T. Briggs et al. Lima: Mosca Azul Editores. 13–24.

Brotherston, Gordon. 1973. "Inca Hymns and the Epic-Makers." *Indiana* 1: 199–212.

——. 1992. *Book of the Fourth World. Reading the Native Americas Through Their Literature*. Cambridge: Cambridge University Press.

Carpio, Luzmila. 1995. *Vida para los niños andinos*. La Paz: UNICEF, Bolivia and Discos Heriba.

Carter, William, and Mauricio Mamani. 1982. *Irpa Chico: individuo y comunidad en la cultura aymara*. La Paz: Editorial Juventud.

Cerrón-Palomino, Rodolfo. 1987. "Unidad y diferenciación lingüística en el mundo andino." *Lexis* (Lima) 11.1: 71–104.

Condori Chura, Leandro, and Esteban Ticona A. 1992. *El escribano de los caciques apoderados. Kasikinakan Purirarunakan Qillqiripa*. La Paz: Hisbol and THOA.

Condori Mamani, Gregorio, and Asunta Quispe Huamán. 1996. *Andean Lives: Gregorio Condori Mamani and Asunta Quispe Huamán*. Ed. Ricardo Valderrama Fernández and Carmen Escalante Gutiérrez. Trans. Paul H. Gelles and Gabriela Martínez Escobar. Austin: University of Texas Press.

Cornejo Polar, Antonio. 1980. *Literatura y sociedad en el Perú: la novela indigenista*. Lima: Editora Lasontay.

——. 1994. *Escribir en el aire: ensayo sobre la heterogeneidad socio-cultural en las literaturas andinas*. Lima: Editorial Horizonte.

Dedenbach-Salazar Sáenz, Sabine. 1999 "*Jichhaxa sikuyay pikt'itasma, kayñarak pikt'itasma. . . . Un aporte al análisis textual aymara.*" *Tradición oral andina y amazónica. Métodos de análisis e interpretación de textos*. Ed. Juan Carlos Godenzzi. Lima: Centro de Estudios Regionales Andinos "Bartolomé de Las Casas." 187–228.

Dillon, Mary, and Thomas A. Abercrombie. 1988. "The Destroying Christ: An Aymara Myth of Conquest." *Rethinking History and Myth: Indigenous South American Perspectives on the Past*. Ed. Jonathan D. Hill. Urbana: University of Illinois Press. 50–77.

Doctrina Christiana y catecismo para instrvuccion de indios . . . traduzido de las dos lenguas generales, de este Reyno, Quichua y Aymara. 1984. Ciudad de los Reyes (Lima): Antonio Ricardo, 1584–5. Facsimile edition. Lima: Departamento de Relaciones Públicas de Petro Perú, S.A.

Espejo Ayka, Elvira. 1994. *Jichha nä parlt'ä Ahora les voy a narrar*. Ed. Denise Y. Arnold and Juan de Dios Yapita. La Paz: UNICEF; Havana: Casa de las Américas.

Ferrell R., Marco A. 1996. "Textos aimaras en Guamán Poma." *Revista andina* 14.2: 413–55.

Flores Galindo, Alberto. 1986. *Buscando un Inca: identidad y utopía en los Andes*. Havana: Casa de las Américas.

Frame, Mary. 1986. "The Visual Images of Fabric Structures in Ancient Peruvian Art." *The Junius B. Bird Conference on Andean Textiles, April 7 and 8, 1984*. Ed. Ann Pollard Rowe. Washington DC: The Textile Museum. 47–80.

Gose, Peter. 1986. "Sacrifice and the Commodity Form in the Andes." *Man* 21.2: 296–310.

Gow, Rosalind, and Bernabé Condori. 1982. *Kay Pacha*. Cusco: Centro de Estudios Rurales Andinos "Bartolomé de las Casas."

Guamán Poma de Ayala, Felipe de. 1989 [1613]. *Nueva corónica y buen gobierno*. Codex péruvien illustré. Facsimile Edition. Paris: Institut D'Ethnologie.

Halushka, Delina Aníbarro de. 1976. *La tradición oral en Bolivia*. La Paz: Instituto Boliviano de Cultura.

Harris, Olivia. 1982. "The Dead and the Devils Among the Bolivian Laymi." *Death and the Regeneration of Life*. Ed. Maurice Bloch and Jonathan Parry. Cambridge: Cambridge University Press. 45–73.

Harrison, Regina. 1989. *Signs, Songs and Memory in the Andes: Translating Quechua Language and Culture*. Austin: University of Texas Press.

Hartmann, Roswith. 1991. "Christian Religious Pictographs from the Andes: Two Examples." *Latin American Indian Literatures Journal* 7.2: 172–91.

——. 1998. "El papel de los mitimaes en el proceso de la quechuización–El caso del Ecuador y la problemática de las fuentes." *Actas del XI Congreso Internacional de AHILA* (Liverpool, 17–22 September 1996). Vol 1. Ed. John R. Fisher. Liverpool: Institute of Latin American Studies, The University of Liverpool. 330–50.

Heath, Shirley Brice, and Richard LaPrade. 1982. "Castilian Colonization and Indigenous Languages: The Cases of Quechua and Aymara." *Language Spread: Studies in Diffusion and Social Change*. Ed. Robert L. Cooper. Bloomington: Indiana University Press; Washington DC: Center for Applied Linguistics. 118–47.

Howard-Malverde, Rosaleen. 1994. "'La gente más bien hace guerra con los cuentos': estrategias narrativas en una comunidad quechua del Perú central." *Tradiciones orales andinas: discurso y literatura*. Ed. Margot Beyersdorff and Sabine Dedenbach-Salazar Sáenz. Bonn: Holos. 117–35.

Huanca, Tomás. 1989. *El yatiri en la comunidad aymara*. La Paz: Ediciones CADA.

——. 1991. *Jilirinakasan arsüwip–Testimonios de nuestros mayores*. Ed. Tomás Huanca. La Paz: Taller de Historia Oral Andina.

Hyland, Sabine. 2002. "Woven Words: the Royal Quipus of Blas Valera." *Narrative Threads: Accounting and Recounting in Andean Khipu*. Ed. Jeffrey Quilter and Gary Urton. Austin: University of Texas Press.

Ibarra Grasso, Dick Edgar. 1953. *La escritura indígena andina*. La Paz: Biblioteca paceña, Alcaldía municipal.

Instituto Nacional de Estudios Lingüísticos (INEL). 1980. *Wiñay Arunaka. Cuentos andinos*. Ed. Juan Carvajal Carvajal. La Paz: INEL.

Intipampa, Carlos. 1991. *Opresión y aculturación: la evangelización de los aymara*. La Paz: Hisbol.

Isbell, Billie Jean, and F. A. Roncalla Fernández. 1977. "The Ontogenesis of Metaphor: Riddle Games Among Quechua Speakers Seen as Cognitive Discovery Procedures." *Journal of Latin American Lore* 3.1: 19–49.

Itier, César. 1992. "Algunos conceptos quechuas prehispánicos: la raíz yacha-, sus derivados y Pacha Yachachic, atribuido del héroe cultural Viracocha." *Religions andines et langues indigènes: Equator, Pérou, Bolivie, avant et après la conquête espagnole. Actes du Colloque III d'études andines*. Ed. Pierre Duviols. Aix-en-Provence: Université de Provence. 95–113.

——, ed. 1997. *Tradición oral y mitología andinas*. Paris: Bull. Instituto Francés de Estudios Andinos.

——, ed. 1999. *Karu ñankunapi. 40 cuentos en quechua y castellano de la comunidad de Usi (Quispicanchi)*. Cusco: Centro de Estudios Regionales Andinos "Bartolomé de Las Casas"; Lima: Instituto Francés de Estudios Andinos.

Jemio, Lucy. 1986. "Literatura oral aymara. Estudio del cuento jamp'atuta/María-Sapo." Diss. Universidad Mayor de San Andrés.

——. 1993. *Literatura Oral Aymara*. La Paz: Universidad Mayor de San Andrés.

Kelm, Antje, ed. 1968. *Vom Kondor und vom Fuchs*. Berlin: Mann.

Kristal, Efraín. 1987. *The Andes Viewed from the City: Literary and Political Discourse on the Indian in Peru, 1848–1930.* New York: Peter Lang.

La Barre, Weston. 1950. "Aymara Folktales." *International Journal of American Linguistics* 16.1: 490–45.

Lara, Jesús. 1947. *La Poesía Quechua.* Mexico City: Fondo de Cultura Económica.

———. 1957. *Tragedia del fin de Atahualpa.* Cochabamba: Imprenta Universitaria.

———. 1969. *La Literatura de los Quechuas: ensayo y antología.* La Paz: Editorial Juventud.

———. 1985. *La literatura de los Quechuas: ensayo y antología.* 4th ed. La Paz: Librería y Editorial Juventud.

Laurencich, Laura. 2001. *Il linguaggio magico-religioso dei numeri, dei fili e della musica presso glo Inca. Una nota.* Bologna: Società Editrice Esculapio.

Levillier, Roberto, ed. 1919. *Organización de la iglesia y órdenes religiosas en el Virreinato del Perú en el Siglo XVI: documentos del Archivo de Indias.* 2 vols. Madrid: Sucesores de Rivadeneyra.

Lienhard, Martin. 1992a. *La voz y su huella: escritura y conflicto étnico-cultural en América Latina, 1492–1988.* Lima: Editorial Horizonte.

———. 1992b. *Testimonios, cartas y manifiestos indígenas, desde la conquista hasta comienzos del siglo XX.* Caracas: Biblioteca Ayacucho.

Lira, Jorge A. 1982. *Diccionario kkechuwa-español.* 2nd ed. Bogota, D. E. Colombia: Secretaría Ejecutiva del Convenio Andrés Bello.

López, Luis Enrique, and Domingo Sayritupac Asqui. 1985. *Wiñay pacha. Aymara arut Qullasuyun kwiñtunakapa.* Bilingual ed. Chucuito, Puno, Peru: Instituto de Estudios Aymara.

López G. U. Ricardo. 1998. "Rito y memoria en la transmisión de conocimientos y socialización de los niños(as) aymaras en Carangas (Bolivia), en el contexto de la Reforma Educativa." Final Report to PIEB-Multimedia, November.

Males, Antonio. 1985. *Historia oral de los imbayas de Quinchuqui-Otavalo: 1900–1960. Villamanta ayllucunapac punta causai.* Quito: Abya-Yala.

Mannheim, Bruce. 1986. "Popular Song and Popular Grammar, Poetry and Metalanguage." *Word* 37.1–2 (April–August): 45–75.

Mariátegui, José Carlos. 1969. *Siete ensayos de interpretación de la realidad peruana.* 17th ed. Lima: Amauta.

Meliá, Bartomeu. 1986. *El guaraní–conquistado y reducido: ensayos de etnohistoria.* Asuncion: Universidad Católica.

Menéses, Teodoro. 1983. *Teatro quechua colonial: antología.* Lima: Edubanco.

Mignolo, Walter. 1994. "Signs and Their Transmission: The Question of the Book in the New World." *Writing Without Words: Alternative Literacies in Mesoamerica and the Andes.* Ed. Elizabeth Hill Boone and Walter D. Mignolo. Durham and London: Duke University Press. 220–70.

Miranda, Juan. 1988. *Catecismo. Diuswan munanakuypi kawsanapaj.* Sucre: Talleres Gráficos "Tupac Katari."

Montoya, Rodrigo, Edwin Montoya, and Luis Montoya. 1987. *La sangre de los cerros: Urqukunapa yawarnin (antología de la poesía quechua que se canta en el Perú).* Lima: Centro Peruano de Estudios Sociales, Mosca Azul Editores, Universidad Nacional Mayor de San Marcos.

Morris, Craig, and Donald E. Thompson. 1985. *Huánaco Pampa: An Inca City and Its Hinterland.* London: Thames and Hudson.

Murra, John V. 1975. "Las etnocategorías de un khipu estatal." *Formaciones económicas y políticas del mundo andino.* By John Murra. Lima: Instituto de Estudios Peruanos. 243–54.

Murúa, Martín de. 1946 [1590]. *Historia del origen y genealogía real de los reyes incas del Peru.* Ed. Constantino Bayle. Madrid: Consejo Superior de Investigaciones Científicas.

Noriega, Julio E. 1995. "La 'oralización' de la escritura en el mundo andino quechua." *Latin American Indian Literatures Journal* 11.2: 128–47.

———. 1996. "La poética quechua del migrante andino." *Asedios a la heterogeneidad cultural. Libro de homenaje a Antonio Cornejo Polar.* Ed. José Antonio Mazzotti and U. Juan Zevallos Aguilar. Philadelphia: Asociación Internacional de Peruanistas. 311–38.

Ortiz Rescaniere, Alejandro. 1973. *De Adaneva a Inkarrí: una visión indígena del Perú.* Lima: Retablo de papel.

Paredes J., Nancy. 1981. "La literatura oral a través del cuento aymara. Análisis del cuento: *Mä Condorampi mä tawakopmi.*" Diss. Universidad Mayor de San Andrés.

Pärssinen, Martti. 1992. *Tawantinsuyu: The Inca State and its Political Organization.* Helsinki, Finland: The Finnish Historical Society.

P'axsi Limachi, Rufino. 1973. *Aymar yarawiku: poesía aymara.* La Paz: Instituto Nacional de Medicina Natural del Qullasuyu-Bolivia.

Platt, Tristan. 1992. "Voces de Abya-Yala. Escritura, chamanismo e identidad." *Revista Unitas* (La Paz) 7(September): 61–73.

Rappaport, Joanne. 1994. "Textos legales e interpretación histórica: una etnografía andina de la lectura." *Iberoamericana* 16. 3–4, 47–48: 67–81.

Rebaza Soraluz, Luís. 1996. "Arguedas y Salazar Bondy. La poesía quechua, el "espíritu" andino y la construcción de un personaje artista." *Cuadernos hispanoamericanos* 551 (May): 19-39.

———. 2000. *La construcción de un artista peruano contemporáneo: poética e identidad nacional en la obra de José María Arguedas, Emilio Adolfo Westphalen, Javier Sologuren, Jorge Eduardo Eielson, Sebastián Salazar Bondy, Fernando de Szyszlo y Blanca Varela.* Lima: Pontificia Universidad Católica del Perú, Fondo Editorial.

Rivet, Paul, and Georges de Créqui-Monfort. 1951–1956. *Bibliographie des langues aymará et kiçua.* 4 vols. Paris: Institut d'Ethnologie.

Rowe, John. 1953. "Eleven Inca Prayers from the Zithuwa Ritual." *Kroeber Anthropological Society Papers* 8–9: 82–99.

———. 1980. "Form and Meaning in Chavin Art." *Pre-Columbian Art History: Selected Readings.* Ed. Alana Cordy-Collins and Jean Stern. Tunbridge Wells, Kent: Costello Educational. 307–31.

Salazar Bondy, Sebastián. 1978. *Poesía quechua.* Montevideo: Editorial Arca.

Sallnow, Michael. 1987. *Pilgrims of the Andes: Regional Cults in Cusco.* Washington D.C: Smithsonian Institution Press.

Salomon, Frank, ed. 1991 [ca. 1608]. *The Huarochirí Manuscript: A Testament of Ancient and Colonial Andean Religion.* Trans. Frank Salomon and George L. Urioste. Transcription George L. Urioste. Austin: University of Texas Press.

Santa Cruz Pachacuti Yamqui Salcamaygua, Joan de. 1993 [c. 1613]. *Relación de antigüedades deste reyno del Pirú.* Ed. Pierre Duviols y César Itier. Lima: Institut Français D'Études Andines; Cusco: Centro de Estudios Regionales Andinos "Bartolomé de Las Casas."

Schramm, Raimund. 1988. *Symbolische Logik in der mündlichen Tradition del Aymaras. Von schwierigen Übergängen und richtigen Abständen.* Berlin: D. Reimer.

Sebeok, Thomas. 1951. "Aymara 'Little Red Riding Hood' with Morphological Analysis." *Archivum Linguisticum: A Review of Comparative Philology and General Linguistics* 3.1: 53–69.

Silverman Proust, Gail. 1994. *El tejido andino. Un libro de sabiduría.* Translation by Javier Flores Espinoza and Mariana Pease Mould. Lima: Banco Central de Reserva del Perú, Fondo Editorial.

Solomon, Tom. 1993. "Creando etnicidad por medio de la música en el Norte de Potosí." *Reunión Anual de Etnología (Naciones y pueblos originarios, ecología y medio ambiente).* La Paz: Museo Nacional de Etnografía y Folklore. 2: 47–76.

Spedding, Alison. n.d. "El kharisiri: un enfoque epidemiológico." Unpublished manuscript.

Stobart, Henry. 1996a. "Los wayñus que salen de las huertas: música y papas en una comunidad campesina del Norte de Potosí." *Madre Melliza y sus crías. Ispall mama wawampi: antología de la papa,* Ed. Denise Y. Arnold and Juan de Dios Yapita. La Paz: Hibol/Ediciones ILCA. 413–30.

——. 1996b. "The Llama's flute: Musical Misunderstandings in the Andes." *Early Music,* Oxford 24.3 (August): 470–82.

Szeminski, Jan. 1997. *Wira Quchan y sus obras: teología andina y lenguaje, 1550–1662.* Lima: Instituto de Estudios Peruanos.

Tales from Waruchiri. *Runa yndio ñiscap machoncuna ñaupa pacha . . .* MS. 3169. Madrid: Biblioteca Nacional, ca. 1608. [See also Salomon Frank 1991 (ed.).]

THOA, Taller de Historia Oral Andina. 1984. *El Indio Santos Marka T'ula, Cacique Principal de los ayllus de Qallapa y Apoderado General de las Comunidades Originarias de la República.* La Paz: Universidad Mayor de San Andrés.

Titu Cusi Yupanqui, Inca Diego de Castro. 1916. *Relación de la conquista del Perú y hechos del Inca Manco II.* Ed. Horacio H. Urteaga and Carlos A. Romero. Lima: Imprenta y Librería Sanmarti.

Tomoeda, Hirayasu. 1985. "The Llama Is My Chacra: Metaphor of Andean Pastoralists." *Andean Ecology and Civilization.* Ed. Shozo Masuda, Izumi Shimada, and Craig Morris. Tokyo: University of Tokyo Press. 277–99.

Torero, Alfredo. 1972. "Lingüística e historia de la sociedad andina." *Actas del XXXIX Congreso Internacional de Americanistas* Vol. 5 (Lima). 231–64.

Triguero Coronel, Abraham. 1981. *Wiñaya Aymara. Markasana Arupa. Cantares de ayer y de esperanza. Poesía de la gente aymara. El alma de una cultura andina.* La Paz: Proyecto Satawi–MLAL.

Tschopik, Harry Jr. 1948. "Aymara Texts: Lupaca Dialect." *International Journal of American Linguistics* 14: 108–14.

Turino, Thomas. 1993. *Moving Away from Silence: Music of the Peruvian Altiplano and the Experience of Urban Migration.* Chicago: University of Chicago Press.

Valderrama Fernández, Ricardo, and Carmen Escalante Gutiérrez, ed. 1977. *Gregorio Condori Mamani: autobiografía.* Bilingual text Quechua and Spanish. Cusco: Centro de Estudios Rurales Andinos "Bartolomé de Las Casas."

——. 1992. *Ñuqanchik runakuna. Nosotros los humanos: testimonio de los quechuas del siglo XX.* Cusco: Centro de Estudios Rurales Andinos "Bartolomé de Las Casas."

Vallejo, César. 1988. *Obra poética.* Ed. Américo Ferrari. Nanterre: Colección Archivos

Vega, El Inca Garcilaso de la. 1991 [1609]. *Comentarios reales de los Incas.* Lima: Fondo de Cultura Económica.

Weitüchter, Blanca. 1984. "El guerrero aymara." *Hipótesis* (La Paz) 4–5: 41–62.

Yapita, Juan de Dios. 1992. "*Kunturinti liq'uchinti*: análisis lingüístico de un *sallqa* de Oruro." *Latin American Indian Literatures Journal* (LAILJ), Pennsylvania State University 8.1 (Spring): 38-68.

——. 1994. "Hacia una educación bilingüe en Bolivia: un repaso actual." *Revista UNITAS* (La Paz) 13–14 (June): 49–60.

HISPANIC CULTURES IN THE UNITED STATES: DIVERSITY, HYBRIDISM, AND CONSTANT TRANSFORMATION

INTRODUCTION

Juan Villegas

Despite the fact that cultural production by descendants of Hispanic peoples within U.S. territories occurred prior to the existence of the United States as a nation, the official history of North American culture has not considered this factor as integral to the traditions or culture that are generally defined as "American." The study and history of such production has been relegated to a handful of researchers who have tended merely to document its existence. Indeed the general approach has been to view the subject as running parallel, but marginal and unrelated to official culture, if not excluded from it.

As is true for all cultural production, that linked to Hispanic culture in the United States corresponds to transformations of the social sectors producing these cultures and the changes in their relationships with producers and receivers from other cultures. Thus, in general terms, the tremendously varied provenance of the productive sectors of Hispanic cultures in the United States is highly evident, as are the historical transformations of the groups themselves, their different relationships with the dominant cultures (their potential receivers), and the diversity of political positions of these groups at different historical moments. Shortly after the arrival of the Spaniards in the sixteenth century, the Hispanic settlements of what is today the United States were established and, from the beginning, have been characterized by a great variance in ethnicity, in economic conditions, in their public interests, and their relationships with the original cultures of Spain or pre-Hispanic Mesoamerica.

In more specific terms, the issue has been the predominance of some groups during particular historical periods in the defining of Hispanic culture north of the Rio Bravo. Prior to the twentieth century, for example, as in the Spanish Florida and Mexican areas of the Southwest and California, there was a strong contemporary Spanish and Mexican culture. Even within this general characterization, no uniformity existed, owing to the social and ethnic diversity of the areas appropriated from the former Spanish empire. Today there is considerable cultural production aimed at both middle-class and popular sectors, a range which in turn implies a diversity of artistic tendencies. There are clear differences between Hispanic immigration to Florida and New York and the descendants of those from what was Northern Mexico (before 1849) in Texas, California, New Mexico, and Arizona. These distinctions are the result as much of geographic origin as they are to the dominant cultural features of each grouping. Frequently even immigrant groups from the same country have had different social and cultural backgrounds, depending on the main reason for their exodus. For example, during the early twentieth century Mexican immigration to the United States consisted of groups from all social classes as a consequence of the Revolution of 1910. This was then followed by campesino immigrants who settled in agricultural zones. More recently, immigration has been due to economic reasons and the immigrants tend to work in urban environments. This is also true for the Salvadorians, Guatemalans, Hondurans, and Dominicans in recent years. Puerto Rico as a U.S. Commonwealth is another case altogether, but there is no doubt that Puerto Ricans are a powerful Hispanic presence in the country.

In general terms one can speak of both mass immigration and that of minority groups, each one of which has affected cultural production in a different way. Examples of the former include the Mexicans in Southern California and the Southwest, Cubans in Florida, and Puerto Ricans in New York. During the last fifty years the most notable immigration waves have been of Puerto Ricans after the Second World War, Cubans after 1960, and Mexicans, Guatemalans, and Salvadorans in the 1970s and 1980s. This immigration reinforced or increased the populations of those nationals already present in the United States and has meant a rapidly growing and now significant Hispanic presence within that nation's social and cultural panorama. The number of Spanish-speaking radio and television channels increased tenfold in the last quarter of the twentieth century, while advertising in Spanish also increased in tandem with the buying power of these communities. This increase in population of Hispanic origin, with variations in different zones of the United States, has in addition contributed to a stronger presence of Hispanics in business and the universities.

Minority immigrations are always the result of specific social, economic, and political situations, but they also are responsible for the arrival of Hispanic intellectual and artistic groups in the United States. In turn these have moved into U.S. cultural institutions, thereby having greater opportunities to influence the cultural preferences of intellectuals or even the producers of culture in the United States. The Spaniards who arrived after the Spanish Civil War (1936–39) were few in number but highly influential; from positions of cultural power, they would have an influence on the forms and selection of cultural objects within the academy. This shift indirectly contributed to either privileging or marginalizing cultural production of Hispanic origin. The influence of the

Spanish exiles, for example, meant that there was a greater focus on the peninsular cultural canon, with a strong emphasis on the Golden Age and the cultural icons (such as García Lorca, Antonio Machado) of the Republic. However, this did not generate a greater interest in the Latin American or Chicano culture in the North American universities. The next group of Hispanic intellectuals to make a mark were young academics from Latin America, who were imported in the 1960s to take part in promoting Spanish-language studies in the United States. This was the result of a perceived need for expanding international studies as a response to Cold War rivalry with the Soviet Union. The dictatorships in Latin America, and especially the Southern Cone countries (Argentina, Chile, and Uruguay), in the 1970s and 1980s were responsible for still another migration of Latin American intellectuals, many of whom moved into positions of influence on a cultural level. Most of these South American immigrants had a tradition of strong social commitment, and rapidly identified with the movements of social liberation among Chicanos and Latinos in the United States.

This series of immigrations did not necessarily blend easily with those of previous groups or with second and third generations of Hispanics in the United States. On the contrary, there were frequently enormous differences in terms of interest or culture, whether at the personal or collective levels. Despite these conflicts, the multiplicity of experience and diversity of cultures has been responsible for a culture of enormous vitality and plurality of forms, of diverse meanings as well as public. The plurality of cultures means that messages can be shaped for a specific audience in search of the means of expression and communication that correspond to the historical changes and new conditions of production and reception.

Not all immigrant groups are immediately able to create cultural products that have the potential of being aesthetically valued by those wielding cultural power. In some instances, the basic concern of these groups is survival, and there is a tendency to reproduce the cultural objects of their own countries. With time, and according to cultural rhythms that fluctuate according to social and historical periods and circumstances, cultural objects are produced that are more representative of the new social and cultural conditions in the Unites States. In the majority of cases, Hispanic cultures have not affected or, at best, have only indirectly affected the hegemonic cultures within the United States. In some instances, intellectuals and artists tend to identify with existing groups that are both familiar and highly visible. In the 1960s and 1970s, at the time when the Chicano culture was moving toward its highest visibility, Central American writers (or those with Central American origin) tended to identify themselves as "Chicanos," because of the need for identification as much as because of a perceived similarity between the emancipatory struggle of the marginalized in their countries of origin and those of the United States.

Even though there has always been a strong tendency to identify with the particular country of origin (i.e., Cuba, Mexico, the Dominican Republic), up until fairly recently researchers referred to immigrants or descendants of immigrants of Hispanic origin by the collective term "Hispanics." This word acquired negative political connotations during the 1970s, suggesting social and racial discrimination. The tendency was to distinguish almost exclusively between Chicanos and Puerto Ricans. Despite their long history within the country, the Cuban or Cuban-American presence was ignored until the South Florida community acquired a political voice. On the other hand, the continuity of Mexican-American identification, dating back to the eighteenth century, has more recently led to other descendants of Latin American peoples seeking a more broadly-based identity. The designations that have received the widest acceptance among these are those of "U.S. Latino" and "U.S. Latina." These are meant to be quite different from the term "Chicano," with specific different historical and cultural circumstances at the core. "Chicano" maintains its initial connotations of a subversive discourse: socio-political protest, and strong associations with Mexico. The terms "U.S. Latino" and "U.S. Latina" appear to include the descendants of all other Hispanic nationalities, and suggest increased possibilities of entering the mainstream and a broadening of the political base, including the demands of lesbian, gay, and women's groups. Even more recently, there are those who prefer to use the expression "Latino" in the political sphere as well.

In this continual process of change, substitution, and appropriation, the artist often reuses elements of contemporary legitimized or alternative cultures to create cultural objects that integrate the materials and codes of various cultures. These artistic objects are culturally hybrid. Frequently some of the problems or simply conventions characteristic of the country of origin are repeated. Nineteenth century Cuban theater of the Florida region (in Tampa, for example) showed a continuity with the theatrical tradition of the island, since it used similar themes and procedures. However, as time passed, this tradition adapted to the changes experienced by its public, to the new historical conditions and the new personalities of the new social environment. Nevertheless, legitimation always emerges from the insertion of such intertextualities with the cultural space legitimized by hegemonic discourses. Another instance can be seen in Chicano literature from the 1960s, which identified with Mexico as the dominant cultural influence. Chicano poetry of the period mainly used the cultural codes of Mexico, without rejecting the influence of U.S. or European poetry, and also found its inspiration in pre-Hispanic rites and myth. This search for roots and a relationship with the world of myth was not only a Chicano move; on the contrary, it was a common means into the legitimized discourses of the time. Myth, for instance, represented one of the most valued critical and investigative trends (Jung, Lévi-Strauss, Campbell). However, as far as the novel is concerned, at one point it was the novel of the Latin American "boom" that constituted the basic model; even there, however, it is still possible to observe the integration of elements of U.S. or European literary tradition in Chicano fiction.

The cultures of pre-Hispanic origin have been and continue to be marginalized in the United States. This rich and all but invisible literary culture has not been studied in the kind of systematic manner that would include investigating the interrelationship between these cultures and the dominant culture of the United States; the participation of representatives of marginal cultures within those of the hegemony; the consumption and appropriation by the dominant groups of the work of marginal cultures; the acceptance of icons from the latter; or the use of elements of dominant cultural practices by marginal producers in order to access recognition by representatives of the dominant cultures.

A key aspect of Hispanic literatures is their public. The selection of the language determines, in principle, the potential readers and the chances for recognition and acceptance. For the major part of their history, productions in Spanish have been directed to audiences of Hispanic origin, despite differences in cultural practices and history as well as social and economic grouping. A practice like the *corrido* (traditional Mexican ballad) has remained in the popular domain; folkloric dance, on the other hand, has aspired to more diverse audiences. In contrast, the writing of novels, poetry, or drama has perforce sought a literate public.

The last thirty years have witnessed some significant changes. Along with greater awareness of cultural marginalization, there has been a conscious effort to reach out to the dominant culture. This transformation is most clearly seen in the use of English as a literary language, but also in the appropriation and retooling of the artistic codes of the dominant culture, even though this implicit acceptance of other codes in many instances means the inclusion of the stereotype of the other that the dominant culture has assigned to the Latino. This is to be seen in a number of works categorized as Magical Realist, but also in the identification of the Chicano or Latino with the *barrio* (neighborhood) or in the isolated use of words in Spanish as indices of the presence of the Latino. In many cases, this usage is signaled by irony and parody.

Recently, the immense increase in the Hispanic population in numerous states, in the political power linked to a greater number of electoral registrations of Latinos, in the purchasing power of these groups, and in the spread of the communications media on a global and international level (television in particular) has produced an increase in the Hispanic or Latin presence in television and radio, with the consequent massive exposure of cultural practices associated with or directed towards Hispanics and Latinos. The numerous radio programs in Spanish in Los Angeles or Miami, for instance, present Latino, Latin American, or Spanish artists and feature other activities linked to Hispanic culture. In some cases, the economic impact of this focus is revealed in the visibility of artists from the Hispanic cultures in the mass media of the dominant culture. In California supermarkets or record superstores, a large section is given over to Latin music. The impact of such a presence, for example, is even noticeable in newspapers that incorporate a growing number of news items that concern Latin America or Spain. The *Los Angeles Times* is a case in point, having dedicated segments of its cultural section to artists of Hispanic origin. On 28 February 1999, one of these (the "Sunday Calendar") carried a full-color front-page image of the Mexican singer Juan Gabriel with the comment: "Juan Gabriel, the undisputed king of Latin pop[,] says he'll never make records in English. He doesn't need to." In addition, throughout the country, theaters exist that stage texts exclusively written in Spanish.

From the viewpoint of its legitimizing role at the cultural level, the university acts as a source of power. Up until a few years ago, Hispanic cultures in the United States were not subjects for course study in Spanish, English, or Comparative Literature departments. The Chicano movement and organizations linked with this movement, plus the enormous transformation made possible by policies linked to Affirmative Action and the recognition of the cultural and ethnic minorities in the country, have all been responsible for a partial acceptance of the existence of the cultures of these minorities. As a result, academic areas were established, such as Chicano Studies or Ethnic Studies, which usually included Chicano or multicultural modules, or courses in Chicano literature were taught in Departments of Spanish or Hispanic Studies. Very recently, in some English Departments, courses on Chicano literature are offered, often along with courses on African-American literatures; but such ventures still constitute a minority at the national level, at least. Yet, during recent years, many of the Chicano writers of both sexes of the contemporary generation have graduated from U.S. universities or have been contracted as regular or guest lecturers. This transformation, predominantly at a political level, has had positive consequences for the study of Hispanic cultures in the United States, changing their power relationship with official institutions. Thus at the moment there is considerable support for the inclusion of Chicano writing or, to a lesser degree, that of the *nuyorqueñas* (Puerto Rican writing in New York) in these institutions. Even if other writing from more recent immigrants or those with less access to the institutions that wield cultural power continue to be largely excluded (for example, Guatemalans, Salvadorans, Hondurans), at least they are incorporated as part what is culturally accepted by these institutions. The term "U.S. Latinos" has ended up being the term of preference; taking the place of "Hispanics," it has had an inclusive, not exclusive connotation, even though it is increasingly used to refer primarily to the cultural production of Hispanic artists in English.

The academic programs of universities have now incorporated the study of texts by male and female writers of Latino origins. These programs include those in Spanish departments as well as in Latin American Studies, English, Comparative Literature, or Ethnic Studies, and Chicano/Latino or Latina Studies. This phenomenon is undoubtedly contributing to the diffusion and legitimation of Spanish/Hispanic or Latino writing. Another notable change is the fact of the Latina woman's visibility. This presence is seen as much in the business sphere as in the cultural, whether in art, literature, or the academy.

The essays included here provide evidence of the diversity of the literary corpus of Hispanic cultural groups in the United States, a diversity that emerges both from the cultures associated with writers of both sexes and from their historical conditions. The diversity of their public is equally notable. From an ideological viewpoint, these are all discourses that legitimize the culture of the producers and utilize the cultural codes that correspond to that culture–but accommodated or brought up to date with the trends dominant at the moment. This is legitimization with respect to the dominant culture. Historical transformations, however, are responsible for the displacement of a public, a shift that in turn conditions the language of the texts. The move from the use of Spanish to English generally suggests a change in the reading public and, in consequence, a different function for literary discourse. All the contributions here give significant coverage to Latino women's cultural production (which has been considerably more valued during recent years). Finally, each essay treats the considerable productivity, the processes of hybridization, and the constant appropriation of those dominant in the United States and their relationship, whether of proximity or distance, with the other cultures with Hispanic roots.

Translation by Jessica Johnson

CHAPTER 34

REINVENTING AMERICA
THE CHICANO LITERARY TRADITION

María Herrera-Sobek

Within the territorial boundaries of the United States, we find a multiplicity of cultures that, to a large extent, have been excluded from this country's cultural imaginary. These marginal groups have not been considered "authentically American" from the perspective of the hegemonic Anglo-Saxon culture. Some of these minority cultures, such as the Chicano, include within their repertoire traditional as well as modern and even postmodern elements. These marginal cultures coexist within a paradigm of heterogeneity. The heterogeneous ancestral memory of Chicanos/as implies a crossing over and intermingling of both indigenous and *criollo* colonial elements. In addition, Chicano/a culture is privy to aspects of modernity transmitted by both the United States and Mexico in a continuous modernization process.

In this crucible of cultural "isms"–that is, modernity and postmodernity–that characterizes contemporary U.S.A. society are inscribed the symbolic, literary, iconographic, and specular models gleaned from minority cultures. There is a complex articulation extant between tradition and postmodernity, particularly (although not exclusively) as this articulation relates to Chicano cultural manifestations. Even though seldom acknowledged, the Mexican American population in the United States has been a significant force in the development of their country at both the material and cultural levels. This study explores the Hispanic/Mexican/Chicano literary heritage and its role in the reinvention of U.S. literature.

Chicanos/as insist on their right to a radical vision of their reality in which tradition, ethnicity, modernity, and postmodernity coexist. They view and value their own culture as a hybrid culture, a *mestizo* culture in the widest sense of the word: *mestizaje*, both rural and urban, characterized by language mixing, and so forth. In fact, they give special privilege to *mestizo* culture above all other cultural manifestations, judging it as paradigmatic of all cultures because there is no such thing as a "pure" culture: Cultures and peoples have been mixing with each other since time immemorial. Furthermore, they conceive of *mestizaje* as indicative of what the future holds for all humanity: Chicano culture is a hybrid culture that is constructed in the postmodern era by means of heterogeneous models of time and space.

The Chicanos'/as' world view, inscribed in their creative writings, celebrates a historical past in order to reaffirm themselves in a transnational and cultural present. In this present, the reconstitution and recomposition of U.S. urban cultures are being influenced by migratory movements of people that constantly define and redefine concepts of nation, race, and identity.

The transformation and reinvention of contemporary U.S. culture by Chicanos/as and other heretofore marginalized groups began to burst forth in the early 1960s. This creative explosion, however, did not happen by chance; it is rooted in centuries-old literary tradition dating back to the Colonial period and situated geographically in what is today the U.S. Southwest. The early Hispanic colonizers left their descendants a literary tradition rich in writings related to the expansion of New Spain's colonial culture. The *conquistadores*, awed by their new and fabulous experiences in what they perceived to be a "new world," wrote exhaustively to European audiences about their adventures, trials, and conquests. Housed in the library archives of the United States, Mexico, and Spain are epics, *relaciones* (relations), diaries, journals, memorials, manuals, entries, narratives, poems, plays, letters, accounts, and so forth related to the explorations of the Southwest. Possibly one of the most interesting and well known is Alvar Núñez Cabeza de Vaca's (1490–1558) relation, *La relacion que dio Aluar Nuñez Cabeca de Vaca de lo acaescido en las Indias en la armada donde yua por gouernador Panphilo de narbaez desde el año de veynte y siete hasta el año treynta y seis que boluio a Seuilla con tres de su compañia* [1542; *Cabeza de Vaca's Adventures in the Unknown Interior of America,* 1961]. More popularly known as *La relación* [The Report] or *Naufragios* [Shipwrecks], Cabeza de Vaca's story recounts the numerous adventures and misadventures experienced during his 10-year journey across the U.S. South and Southwest after he was shipwrecked in 1527 off the coast of Florida. The author lived among the Indians and learned to understand and respect them. He learned their languages and the intricacies of their traditions and became a highly sought-after shaman among them. He was one of the first Europeans to be assimilated into southwestern cultures and, because of his intimate knowledge of various Native American nations, was able to serve as an intermediary between Native Americans and Spaniards.

Cabeza de Vaca was not the only early Spanish colonizer to narrate his adventures. Gaspar Pérez de Villagrá (1555–1620), the soldier-poet from Spain, authored the first U.S. epic, *La historia de la Nuevo México, 1610* [1610; *History of New Mexico,* 1992]. In this epic poem, he details the conquest and settlement of New Mexico by Captain Juan de Oñate (1549?–1624) and his soldiers and settlers.

Along with the *conquistadores*, the Catholic clergy was heavily involved in the colonizing project and also left us a splendid legacy of historical and literary writings. Fray Marcos de Niza (1495–1558) provided a riveting account of his explorations in the Southwest in his now famous diary, *Descubrimiento de las siete ciudades por el P. Fr. Francisco de Niza* [1539; *The Journey of Fray Marcos de Niza,* 1987]. Father Alonso Gregorio de Escobedo (fl. 1587) expounded on his experiences in Florida in his journal, and Fray Gerónimo de Zarate Salmerón (fl. 1610) described in his *Relaciones* [1856; *Relaciones, an Account of Things Seen and Learned,* 1966] his journey into New Mexico. Twenty years later, in 1630, Fray Alonso de Benavides (fl. 1630) wrote his *Memorial* [1630; Memorial], describing the Pueblo Indians, their lands, and their customs. Arizona and California are represented in the writings of Father Eusebio Francisco Kino (1644–1711), who left us a rich legacy of journals, recently translated and published by Friends of the Bancroft Library as *Three Memoirs of Mexican California* (1988).

And one of the most famous missionaries, Fray Junípero Serra (1713–1784), left several volumes of writings regarding his role in the founding of twenty-one missions in California. Fray Isidro Félix Espinosa's (1679–1755) *Crónica apostólica y seráfica de todos los colegios de propaganda fide de esta Nueva España* [1746; Apostolic and Seraphic Chronicle of All the Loyal Religious Schools of This New Spain] provides a stimulating history of the colonization process in Texas.

Aside from the chronicles written by the missionaries and the explorers, there is also a rich oral tradition inherited from the Colonial period and still with us today. The Southwest is fortunate to have a solid tradition of folk theater, which includes such plays as the *pastorelas* (shepherds' plays) *Los moros y cristianos* [The Moors and the Christians], *Los Comanches* [The Comanches], and *Las cuatro apariciones de la Virgen de Guadalupe* [The Four Apparitions of the Virgin of Guadalupe]. All of these works date from the Colonial period. Other genres dating from the Colonial period are *romances* (Spanish ballads), folk tales, proverbs, religious songs such as *alabados*, and other types of folk song.

The Colonial period was a period of feverish *mestizaje*, both at the biological level and at the literary level. The chroniclers came in contact with the Native American cultures and received an infusion of new ideas, images, and world views. For the Spanish *cronistas de Indias* (chroniclers of the Indies), the "new" world presented daunting challenges in the linguistic sphere. The Europeans encountered myriad plants, animals, and geographic terrains for which they had no words, since these objects and landscapes were not part of the flora, fauna, and geography of the old world. The Spanish language began a transformation into American Spanish. This *mestizaje* of Native American languages with Spanish was to set the pattern for later linguistic hybrids, such as that of Spanish and English. The *mestizaje* also appeared in the performing arts, where both the characters in the dramas and the actors playing them were a mixture of Spaniards, Indians, and *mestizos*. Hybridity and syncretism became evident in other cultural manifestations, such as religion, dress, food, and politics.

Although the names of women do not figure prominently in the literary canon of colonial writings, we do know that women were involved in the colonization project and in the production and transmission of oral literature. Subsequent oral histories, such as those published by the Friends of the Bancroft Library (*Three Memoirs of Mexican California*) demonstrate the splendid repertoire of orally transmitted traditions possessed by colonial women in California. *Décimas*, recipes, *coplas*, folk narratives, legends, folk poetry, and so forth were part of the rich oral traditions of Hispanic-Mexican southwestern women.

New hybrid forms emerged in the beginning of the nineteenth century with the founding of Anglo settlements in Texas soon after the Wars of Mexican Independence (1810–1821). The newly formed Mexican republic wished to populate its northern frontier lands and approved land grants to Anglo settlers such as Stephen Austin in Texas. Incursions by Anglo-Americans in California also began to transform the Hispanic/Mexican cultural landscape. A new form of *mestizaje*—English and Spanish—loomed on the southwestern horizon.

The historical jolt that transformed Hispanos/Mexicanos into U.S. citizens occurred in 1848 with the signing of the treaty of Guadalupe Hidalgo after the Mexican-American War and the subsequent loss of one-third of Mexico's national territory. The former Hispanos/Mexicanos from the Colonial period had to reinvent themselves as U.S. citizens. They did so, but they proudly insisted on retaining their language and their culture. In his seminal study on the Gregorio Cortez (1875–1916) *corridos*, *"With a Pistol in His Hand": A Border Ballad and Its Hero* (1958), Américo Paredes points out how the *corrido* tradition crystallized in southern Texas and northern Mexico and became part of the U.S. ballad tradition after the 1848 debacle. The *corrido* proved to be a useful tool in the dissemination of the political, social, and cultural events transpiring in the country. The second half of the nineteenth century saw a boom in *corrido* production. The ballads produced include such classics as the "Corrido de Kiansas" ["Corrido of Kiansas"] and its many variants (see Paredes 1976). These ballads detailed the cattle drives taking place in the Midwest, in which Mexican *vaqueros*, or cowboys, were an important labor force. The Joaquín Murrieta (d. 1853) legend appeared in California and ballads were penned in his honor (see Herrera-Sobek 1993). Other Chicano resistance fighters, such as Gregorio Cortez and Jacinto Treviño, were commemorated through the lyrics of the *corrido*. Songs depicting the railroad workers' travails came to the fore in the late nineteenth century.

It is also in the nineteenth century that we find an outstanding California woman author, Amparo Ruiz de Burton (1832–1895), who left us two important novels—*Who Would Have Thought It?* (1872) and *The Squatter and the Don* (1885)—as well as a substantial collection of letters and a play.

The first half of the twentieth century was a tumultuous period of settlement, disruption, and expansion. The *corrido* tradition continued unabated, recording important historical, political, and social events. Immigration was a common topic; numerous *corridos* appeared that narrated the immigrant experience. One such was the "Corrido de los Norteños" ["Corrido of the Northerners"] (see Herrera-Sobek 1993). A second favorite topic in *corrido* production was the acculturation and assimilation of the Mexican into Anglo-American culture and society. Such songs as "Los Norteños" ["The Northerners"] poked fun at the "agringado," or assimilated Mexican (see Herrera-Sobek 1993). However, by the 1930s the playful bantering and poking fun at the "agringado" gave way to *corridos* depicting the sad fate of Mexicans and Mexican Americans who were being deported during the period of the Great Depression.

The period between the 1920s and the early 1950s witnessed the involvement of women writers from New Mexico in literary endeavors and the social construction of the Hispano (whence the term "Hispanic" is derived). The old Hispano/Mexicano families, some tracing their ancestry to the original colonizers and settlers of the U.S. Southwest, became cognizant of the cultural transformations being effected by Anglo culture. Amparo Ruiz de Burton, a descendent of the landed aristocracy in California, wrote novels in the 1880s depicting the decline of the California class and the loss of land and culture to the aggressive new Anglo colonizers. In New Mexico, the loss of land and culture was slower than in California but was nevertheless inexorable. Under the stimulus of the Federal Writers' Project in New Mexico, the 1930s experienced what Tey Diana Rebolledo calls a "flowering of a literature of resistance" (16). Writers such as Cleofas Jaramillo (1878–1956) (*Romance of a Little Village Girl*, 1955), Fabiola Cabeza de Baca (1894–1991) (*We Fed Them Cactus*, 1954), Ninà Otero-Warren (1881–1965) (*Old Spain in Our Southwest*, 1936), and Jovita González Mireles (1904–1983) (*Caballero*, written

1930–1940, published 1996) left their imprint in Chicano literary history. These works reflect the concern for the passing of an era and for the necessity of Mexican Americans' reinventing themselves if they were to survive in a new society hostile to their language, their culture, and the Hispano way of life.

In spite of the continuous resistance to the acculturation and assimilation processes in the first half of the twentieth century, the reinvention of the Mexican American did not come into full force until the 1960s. For the contemporary period, it is the decade of the 1960s that marks the renaissance of Chicano/a letters. In fact, the term "Chicano" itself gained currency during this effervescent time. Previously, terms such as "Mexican American," "Spanish American," "Latin American," and "Mexican" had been variously used to designate Mexican Americans. The Chicano student movement in the 1960s adopted the vocable "Chicano," in spite of its previously pejorative meaning, to replace the more commonly used "Mexican American." The latter was disdained because it carried connotations of assimilationist tendencies. The 1960s Chicano cultural revolution took place along two pathways: First, the drive by César Chávez to unionize the farm workers and achieve social justice in the agricultural fields, and second, the political discourse of both literary and visual artists. The two directions coincided in challenging the benevolent but self-serving image of the United States, invented and established by the Anglo-Saxon majority as the dominant exclusivist concept of the nation.

Although the 1959 novel *Pocho* by José Antonio Villarreal (b. 1924) marks the modern epoch of Chicano literature, and despite the fact that writers such as John Francisco Rechy (b. 1934) had been making tentative inroads into the literary scene, it was not until 1965 that the Chicano *qua* Chicano literary movement exploded. The Teatro Campesino, with its founding director, Luis Valdez, can be pinpointed as the initial driving force behind the Chicano/a literary renaissance. Valdez, a young playwright in the 1960s, had been inspired by the works of Bertolt Brecht and other avant-garde playwrights of the period. César Chávez (1927–1993) and the farm workers' unionizing efforts galvanized Valdez to form the Teatro Campesino and to join Chávez in his efforts to *concientizar* (raise the consciousness of) the workers regarding their plight in the rich agricultural fields of the United States and see what could be done about it. The Teatro Campesino's *actos* (skits) were performed on flatbed trucks and in the agricultural fields, at union organizing rallies, at sites of demonstrations, and at schools and universities throughout the nation. These *actos* were simple performances depicting some aspect of the farm workers' hard life. "Las dos caras del patroncito" ["The Two Faces of the Little Boss"], "Los Vendidos" ["The Ones Who Sold Out"], "Bernabé," "Vietnam Campesino" ["Vietnamese Peasant"], "Soldado Razo" ["Buck Private"], "La gran carpa de los rasquachis" ["The Great Tent of the Rasquachis"], and "El fin del mundo" ["The End of the World"] were among the first Teatro Campesino performances. Soon thereafter, other *teatro* groups, such as Teatro de la Esperanza, came together to present their works throughout the United States. (See Ch. 35, this volume.)

Male authors dominated literary production in the 1960s and early 1970s. In prose, the names of Tomás Rivera (1935–1984), Rolando Hinojosa (b. 1929), Rudolfo Anaya (b. 1937), and Ron Arias (b. 1941) come to mind as the founding "fathers" of the contemporary Chicano novel. Tomás Rivera belongs to the first generation of Chicano writers who were acutely aware of the oppressive social conditions under which Chicanos lived in U.S. society, and who chose to write about it. A committed educator, Rivera advanced as an administrator until he became the chancellor of a major university, the University of California, Riverside (1979–1984). He achieved fame, however, through his writings. His book . . . *Y no se lo tragó la tierra/. . . And the Earth Did Not Part* won the first Quinto Sol Literary Prize in 1970 and was published in 1971. The book is a collection of short stories but has the unifying thread of the voice of a child narrator, who recounts the events that transpire in the course of a year. Rivera tries to depict the hard life migrant farm workers have despite living in the most affluent society in the world. The novel shows the influences of Anglo-American authors such as Walt Whitman and John Steinbeck. Even more evident in Rivera's writing is the influence of the Mexican writer Juan Rulfo (1918–1986), author of *Pedro Páramo* (1955) and of the collection of short stories *El llano en llamas* [1954; *The Burning Plain*, 1967]. We see this influence both in the laconic style of writing and in the subject matter: The farm worker protagonist caught in the web of tragic events as a result, for the most part, of the impoverished, discriminatory, and oppressive conditions he or she is forced to live under.

Hybridity in the twentieth century for the Chicano population consisted of incorporating cultural influences from Anglo-Saxon cultural production as well as those from Mexico, Latin America, and Spain. The Native Mexican influence became more pronounced after the 1960s, when Chicanos began to be inspired by their Aztec and Maya heritage.

Just as Tomás Rivera represents the Texas migrant experience in his narrative, Rudolfo Alfonso Anaya narrates the New Mexican way of life and its disappearance under the Anglo onslaught in *Bless Me, Ultima*. Anaya's first novel received the second annual Quinto Sol Literary Prize in 1971 and was a resounding success after its publication in 1972. The New Mexican novelist has written several novels since then, including *Heart of Aztlán* (1976) and *Tortuga* [1979; Turtle]. More recently he published *Albuquerque* (1992) and *Zia Summer* (1995).

Like Rivera and Anaya, Rolando Hinojosa-Smith was also a recipient of a literary prize—the prestigious Premio Casa de las Américas for 1976, a Cuban international award, which he received for his work *Klail City y sus alrededores* [1976; Klail City and Its Surroundings] (later renamed *Generaciones y semblanzas* [1977; Generations and Portraits]). In a similar vein, Hinojosa-Smith portrays the life of the pueblo in a mythical southeastern Texas county. Hinojosa-Smith has been a prolific writer and has published more than ten novels, including *Partners in Crime* (1985), *The Useless Servants* (1993), and a detective novel, *Ask a Policeman* (1998).

While Hinojosa-Smith, Rivera, and Anaya present the rural landscape of the Chicano experience in the early years of the Movement, Ron Arias and Alejandro Morales (b. 1944) focus on the urban southern California experience, in particular the *barrio* experience of the Mexican American communities that surround Los Angeles. Arias's magic realist work *The Road to Tamazunchale* (1975) deviates from the rural-realistic form of narrative to create an imaginary realm. Nevertheless, Arias keeps both feet on the ground by asserting within the magic-realist structure of his work a note of social protest similar to García Márquez's (b. 1927) *Cien años de soledad* [1967; *One Hundred Years of Solitude*].

Morales's work portrays the Californian urban experience in its most degrading form in *Caras viejas y vino nuevo* [1975; Old Faces and New Wine]. He has written five novels in the last two decades: *La verdad sin voz* [1979; Truth Without a Voice], *Reto en el paraíso* [1983; Challenge in Paradise], *The Brick People* (1988), and *The Rag Doll Plagues* (1992).

In poetry, two of the most outstanding poets of the first generation of Chicano writers were Alberto Baltazar Alurista (b. 1947) and Gary Soto (b. 1952). Alurista's poetry is characterized by heterogeneous language; his poems liberally mix Spanish, English, and *caló* (barrio slang) throughout. Soto is more of a traditional poet, using polished language, imagery, and style. Other early poets include Juan Felipe Herrera (b. 1948), Sergio Elizondo (b. 1930), and Rodolfo "Corky" Gonzales (b. 1928).

Although Chicanos dominated the first stage of the Chicano literary renaissance, it should not be assumed that Chicanas were not heavily involved in the political struggles, literary endeavors, and cultural transformations of the period. As Chicana scholar Tey Diana Rebolledo has pointed out, women were writing and were politically active. Chicana writers and activists were marginalized in the early stages of the Chicano movement; they were (and are), in the words of Martha Cotera, a "double minority" (Mirandé and Enríquez 12–13). Teresa McKenna pointedly addressed this issue in her 1997 book, *Migrant Song: Politics and Processes in Contemporay Chicano Literature:*

> In the few analyses published about the Chicano Student Movement, only rarely does the contribution of women emerge as part of the historical record, although women have been and continue to be at the core of political activity. During the years I was involved in student organizations (1967–1980), including MASC (Mexican American Student Committee), UMAS (United Mexican American Students), and MECHA (Movimiento Estudiantil Chicano de Aztlán), women comprised at least half, and often more, of the membership; these women stood in picket lines, were arrested, mailed newsletters, recruited students, raised bail money, and supported strikes. Women were active participants in central UMAS and attended EICC (Educational Issues Coordinating Committee) meetings, as well as Black Student Union and LUCHA activities. These are the political actions that defined the nature of student activism at the time. (109–10)

McKenna proceeds to name several women political activists, such as Ana Nieto Gómez, Adelaida del Castillo, Elsa Iris García Escribano, and Betita Martínez, and asserts that "[t]heir activism continually challenged the definition and scope of Chicano politics" (110).

During the early years of the movement, one Chicana writer did distinguish herself: Estela Portillo Trambley (b. 1936). Originally from El Paso, Portillo Trambley has written in three of the major genres: drama, the novel, and the short story. Her works include *Rain of Scorpions and Other Stories* (1975); *The Day of the Swallows* (1971); a collection of plays, *Sor Juana and Other Plays* (1983); and a novel, *Trini* (1986).

Male writers, however, constituted most of the first generation of contemporary Chicano authors, and they began to disseminate the concepts of multiculturalism and plurality of cultures. The United States's concept of the "melting pot" began to be challenged by the Chicano movement, whose members refused to melt down in the Anglo-Saxon pot. The cultural cartography establishing white society as the dominant culture began to acquire additional hues of black, brown, yellow, and red under the political stimulus of various civil rights movements. The invention of America as an Anglo-Saxon country colonized by the pilgrims began to be deconstructed through the Chicanos'/as' scrutinizing optic. Mexican Americans began to assert their legitimacy as early pioneers who explored and populated what is today perceived as U.S. territory, decades before the Anglo-Saxon population arrived in America. Their legitimacy as pioneers and settlers was based on two historical facts: the Chicanos' Hispanic identity and their indigenous roots. The concept of the land of Aztlán–that is, the Aztecs' homeland in the Southwest before they migrated south to Tenochtitlan or Mexico City–was unfurled within the Chicanos'/as' political banner.

It is in the second generation of Chicano scholars reinventing the U.S. that Chicanas have taken a leadership role. According to McKenna,

> As women's voices begin to be heard, the political and social struggle must alter to accommodate their view. Women's literature gives renewed force to Chicano/a . . . literature and begins to direct a vital dialogue within Chicano politics as well . . . . Chicana literature marks a qualitative change in the root metaphor that provided the context for the development of the literature. Women writers are challenging the male-dominated form of the corrido by asserting the female logos as the center of communal resistance, survival, continuity, and, most importantly, political strength. Their voice transforms the dimensions of sociopolitical consciousness and, by extension, the processes of literary activity itself. (22)

In the 1980s, Chicana scholars and writers began to reinvent the U.S. from various perspectives. Chicana scholars and writers challenged the moral and ethical systems established by the Anglo and Chicano patriarchal institutions. Authors such as Cherríe Moraga (b. 1952), Gloria Anzaldúa (b. 1942), Sandra Cisneros (b. 1954), Ana Castillo (b. 1954), Lorna Dee Cervantes (b. 1954), Helena María Viramontes (b. 1954), Alma Villanueva (b. 1944), Lucha Corpi (b. 1945), Pat Mora (b. 1942), and Denise Chávez (b. 1948) constructed through their literary discourse a new feminist moral and ethical system. This new system can be apprehended in the moral and ethical perspectives posited in the Chicana authors' creative writings, and it is conceptualized within the framework of the relationship of Chicanas to society. I have identified four categories within this relationship: (1) Chicanas and the family, (2) Chicanas and the community, (3) Chicanas and the nation, and (4) Chicanas and the world. Within the category of family relationships, Chicanas began to question the stereotypical roles of the abnegated woman, the suffering mother or *mater dolorosa*, the faithful, silent, obedient wife. The concept of machismo is challenged in Helena María Viramontes' short stories included in the collection *The Moths and Other Stories* (1985); it is also challenged by Ana Castillo in such poetry as *Women Are Not Roses* (1984) and *My Father Was a Toltec* (1995) and in her novel *The Mixquiahuala Letters* (1986). Angie Chabram-Dernersesian exposes the machismo within the very roots of the Chicano movement itself in her article "'I Throw Punches for My Race, but I Don't Want to Be a Man': Writing Us–Chica-nos (Girl, Us)/Chicanas–into the Movement Script"(1992).

Taking a different tack, Chicana lesbians Cherríe Moraga and Gloria Anzaldúa began to question the concept of loyalty to La Raza, or ethnic community, in their writings *This Bridge Called My Back* (1983, edited by both), *Loving in the War Years: Lo que nunca pasó por sus labios* (1983, by Moraga), and *La Frontera: The Borderlands* (1987, by Anzaldúa).

The concept of nationality is challenged in Ana Castillo's *The Mixquiahuala Letters*, Pat Mora's "Legal Alien," and Alma Villanueva's "Mexican Memos." On a larger scale, Chicanas began to question genocidal wars and the destruction of the environment. The harm done to ecological systems and use of insecticides are strongly criticized by Cherríe Moraga in her play *Heroes and Saints* (1994). Alma Villanueva underscores her concern for the protection of the earth throughout her collection of poetry, *Bloodroot* (1977).

Chicanas have been deeply involved in redefining and reconstructing concepts of race, nationality, ethnicity, and gender. They have been at the forefront of reinventing the U.S. McKenna perceptively points out that

> Chicana voices are directing their critical eye to another dimension of the experience: time. Their social commentary is beginning to redefine the historical moment as one no longer tied to place or event, such as the Mexican American War, nor to precursors like the Aztecs, but rather to the historical moment as it is connected to gender relations. (22)

Indeed, Chicana creativity and criticism have been highly instrumental in placing Chicano studies on the national and international maps.

The 1990s proved to be a landmark decade for Chicano/a literature. During this period Chicana authors solidified their reputation as outstanding writers and were recognized by mainstream publishing firms. The New York publishing establishment acknowledged the importance of Chicano and other U.S. Latino literature and aggressively pursued young talented writers of Latino descent. Ana Castillo published *So Far from God* (1993) with Norton and *Sapogonia* with Anchor-Doubleday; Denise Chávez published *Face of an Angel* (1994) with Farrar; Helena María Viramontes published *Under the Feet of Jesus* (1995) with Dutton; and Sandra Cisneros published *Woman Hollering Creek* (1991) and a poetry collection, *Loose Women* (1994), with Random House. Pat Mora's poetry collection *Agua Santa/Holy Water* (1995) and novel *House of Houses* (1997) were both published by Beacon Press in Boston.

Chicanos also did quite well in the 1990s. Most spectacular was the positive critical response given to Luis Rodríguez's (b. 1954) novel *Always Running: Mi Vida Loca–Gang Days in L.A.* (1993).

There are two salient trends evident in Chicano/a writing: continued interest in autobiography and experimentation with new forms, such as the detective novel. Chicano autobiography traces its roots to the Colonial period, when both the colonizers and the missionary *padres* wrote in their journals of their experiences journeying to the United States, and sometimes sent memorials to the king of Spain detailing their experiences. More recent Chicano/a autobiography shares structural and thematic commonalities with nineteenth- and twentieth-century *corridos* that depicted the Mexican immigrant recounting his or her experience traveling from Mexico, crossing the border, and working in the United States. The Chicano novel has tended to initiate its narratives with the journey a family undertakes to the border; its crossing of the border; and its eventual settlement in the United States, usually in the Southwest.

The paradigmatic novel about Mexican immigration, Daniel Venegas's (b. 1928) *Las aventuras de Don Chipote: o cuando los pericos mamen* [The Adventures of Don Chipote, or When Parrots Breast-Feed], first appeared in 1926. The novel was written in autobiographical form, in Spanish; it depicted the travails of a Mexican immigrant coming to work in the United States with great expectations and dreams, and finding only hardships and ill treatment. Novels from the 1970s, 1980s, and 1990s with Mexican immigration as the point of departure are written mostly in English, and include Ernesto Galarza's (1905–1984) *Barrio Boy* (1971), Richard Vasquez's (b. 1928) *Chicano* (1970), Victor Edmund Villaseñor's (b. 1940) *Macho* (1991) and *Rain of Gold* (1991), Estela Portillo Trambley's *Trini* (1986), and Miguel Méndez's (b. 1930) *Peregrinos de Aztlán* [1991; Pilgrims in Aztlán].

Contemporary Chicano/a narratives continue to follow the paradigmatic immigrant trajectory. However, many of the current immigrant novels are written by racially mixed Chicano/a-Anglo writers. The basic structure of the current immigration novel consists of the recounting of the journey from Mexico undertaken by the immigrant, his or her integration in U.S.A. society, and the subsequent generations descended from the original immigrant. Within this group we can include *The Dark Side of the Dream* (1995) by Alejandro Grattan-Domínguez (b. 1934), a Chicano-Irish writer. As its title indicates, this novel presents a very negative view of the immigration experience. The "American dream" turns out to be more of a nightmare for Mexican nationals.

In the second group of novels with Mexican immigrant themes we can include those novels in which the immigrant is a secondary character playing an important role in the plot. Of particular interest are those novels produced by Chicana writers. Helena María Viramontes's novel *Under the Feet of Jesus* features the character of Perfecto Flores, a Mexican immigrant who joins Estrella's family in the migrant fields of California. Estrella, a young adolescent girl, is the main protagonist in the novel. Norma Cantú (b. 1947) also introduced the immigrant theme through various characters, not just through a single immigrant. The Texas-Mexico border in Laredo and Nuevo Laredo, and the crossing of the characters to Mexico and the United States are integral parts of Cantú's 1995 autobiographical vignettes. An innovative novel by Tina Juárez (b. 1942), *Call No Man Master* (1995), is structured as a historical novel with the action taking place in the nineteenth century during the Mexican Wars of Independence (1810–1821) and up until the 1830s. The novel is set in Guanajuto, Mexico, and features a brave *soldadera* protagonist, Carmen Rangel, who has joined the rebel soldiers of the priest Miguel Hidalgo y Costilla. When she is captured by the Spanish army, she escapes to San Antonio, Texas, where she takes up residence.

A second major trend in Chicano narrative production in the 1990s was the detective novel. María Teresa Márquez points out this boom and notes that

> Raza writers have shaped and reshaped the detective/mystery genre for specific cultural, political and social purposes to comment on issues of class, gender, race, and sexual orientation or preference. These writers are producing new literary models that may be viewed as forms of social criticism and cultural representation. Moreover, these writers are modifying the genre by transforming the detective protagonist from white and middle- or upper-class, as in the classical tradition introduced by Edgar Allen Poe and honed by Sir Arthur Conan Doyle, to Raza working-class personas. (Lomelí, Márquez, and Herrera-Sobek 298)

Chicano/a authors who have written detective novels include Rudolfo Anaya (*Zia Summer* and *Rio Grande Fall* [1996]), Lucha Corpi (*Eulogy for a Brown Angel* [1992] and *Cactus Blood* [1995]), Max Martínez (b. 1943) (*White Leg* [1996] and *Layover* [1997]), and Rolando Hinojosa-Smith (*Partners in Crime*). The most prolific Chicano writer in this genre is Manuel Ramos (b. 1948), who has published four detective novels to date: *The Ballad of Rocky Ruiz* (1993), *The Ballad of Gato Guerrero* (1994), *The Last Client of Luis Móntez* (1996), and *Blues for the Buffalo* (1997). María Teresa Márquez underscores how Manuel Ramos expresses the idealism of the Chicano movement and its struggle against greed and corruption and at the same time how he gives prominent exposure to the Chicano cultural ties of family and Mexican-American culture that give the community its identity (see Lomelí, Márquez, and Herrera-Sobek 298–302).

The Chicano detective novel continues to present the Chicano experience in the United States. The authors, through new discursive strategies, underscore the continued marginality and the social, economic, and political oppression of this ethnic group in Anglo-American society. With legislation such as Propositions 187, 209 (denying services to undocumented immigrants), and 227 (anti–affirmative action, anti-bilingual) recently approved by voters in California, one can be sure that writers will continue to expound on these issues.

Chicanos/as continue to reinvent themselves through their discursive strategies, and they are leaving a significant imprint on U.S. letters. More recently, they are making their mark in European literary circles, specifically in Spain. The Chicano/Latino population in the United States is one of the fastest-growing groups in terms of overall numbers. It has been pointed out that the U.S. Latino population will surpass African Americans as the largest minority by the year 2006. Without a doubt, Chicano/a literary production will continue to transform and reinvent U.S. society.

Works Cited

Alurista. 1971. *Floricanto en Aztlán.* Los Angeles: University of California, Chicano Studies Cultural Center.

——. 1972. *Nationchild Plumaroja.* San Diego, CA: Toltecas en Aztlán Productions.

——. 1980. *Spik in Glyph.* Houston, TX.: Arte Público Press.

——. 1994. *Et tú . . . raza?* Tempe, AZ.: Bilingual Review Press/ Editorial Bilingue.

——. 1995. *Z Eros.* Tempe, AZ.: Bilingual Review Press/Editorial Bilingue.

Anaya, Rudolfo Alfonso. 1972. *Bless Me, Ultima.* Berkeley, CA: Quinto Sol Publications.

——. 1976. *Heart of Aztlán.* Berkeley, CA.: Editorial Justa.

——. 1979. *Tortuga.* Berkeley, CA.: Editorial Justa.

——. 1992. *Albuquerque.* Albuquerque: University of New Mexico Press.

——. 1995. *Zia Summer.* New York: Warner.

——. 1996. *Rio Grande Fall.* New York: Warner.

Anderson, Benedict. 1991. *Imagined Communities.* New York: Verso.

Anzaldúa, Gloria. 1987. *Borderlands/La Frontera: The New Mestiza.* San Francisco: Spinsters/Aunt Lute.

Arias, Ron. 1975. *The Road to Tamazunchale.* Reno: West Coast Poetry Review.

Benavides, Fray Alonso. 1954. *Benavides' Memorial of 1630.* Trans. Peter P. Forrestal. Washington, DC: Academy of American Franciscan History.

Cabeza de Baca, Fabiola. 1954. *We Fed Them Cactus.* Albuquerque: University of New Mexico Press.

Cantú, Norma. 1995. *Canícula: Snapshots of a Girlhood en la Frontera.* Albuquerque: University of New Mexico Press.

Castillo, Ana. 1984. *Women Are Not Roses.* Houston, TX: Arte Público Press.

——. 1986. *The Mixquiahuala Letters.* Binghamton, NY: Bilingual Review Press/Editorial Bilingue.

——. 1993. *So Far from God.* New York: W. W. Norton.

——. 1994. *Sapogonia.* New York: Doubleday/Anchor Books.

——. 1995. *My Father Was a Toltec and Selected Poems.* New York: W. W. Norton.

Chabram-Dernersesian, Angie. 1992. "'I Throw Punches for My Race, but I Don't Want to Be a Man': Writing Us–Chica-nos (Girl, Us)/Chicanas–into the Movement Script." *Cultural Studies.* Ed. Lawrence Grossberg. London: Routledge. 81–95.

Chávez, Denise. 1994. *Face of an Angel.* New York: Farrar.

Cisneros, Sandra. 1983. *House on Mango Street.* Houston, TX.: Arte Público Press.

——. 1991. *Woman Hollering Creek and Other Stories.* New York: Random House.

——. 1994. *Loose Woman.* New York: Random House.

Corpi, Lucha. 1992. *Eulogy for a Brown Angel.* Houston, TX: Arte Público Press.

——. 1995. *Cactus Blood.* Houston, TX: Arte Público Press.

Escobedo, Fray Alonso Gregorio de. 1963. "La Florida." *Pirates, Indians and Spaniards: Father Escobedo's "La Florida."* Ed. James W. Covington. Trans. A. F. Falcones. St. Petersburg, FL: Great Outdoors.

Espinosa, Aurelio M., ed. 1907. *Los Comanches: A Spanish Heroic Play of the Year Seventeen Hundred and Eighty.* Albuquerque: University of New Mexico Bulletin. 1.l: 27–46.

Espinosa, Fray Isidro Félix. 1746. *Crónica apostólica y seráfica de todos los colegios de propaganda fide de esta Nueva España. Primera Parte.* Mexico City: Viuda de Don Joseph Bernardo de Hogal.

Galarza, Ernesto. 1971. *Barrio Boy.* South Bend, IN: University of Notre Dame Press.

——. 1964. *History of Texas 1673–1776.* Trans. Carlos E. Castañeda. Washington, DC: Academy of American Franciscan History.

González Mireles, Jovita. 1996. *Caballero: A Historical Novel.* Ed. José E. Limón and María Cotera. College Station: Texas A&M University Press.

Grattan-Domínguez, Alejandro. 1995. *The Dark Side of the Dream.* Houston, TX: Arte Público Press.

Herrera-Sobek, María. 1993. *Northward Bound: The Mexican Immigrant Experience in Ballad and Song.* Bloomington: Indiana University Press.

Hinojosa-Smith, Rolando. 1976. *Klail City y sus alrededores.* Havana: Casa de las Américas.

——. 1977. *Generaciones y semblanzas.* Berkeley, CA: Justa Publications.

——. 1981. *Mi querido Rafa.* Houston, TX: Arte Público Press.

——. 1985. *Partners in Crime.* Houston, TX: Arte Público Press.

——. 1993. *The Useless Servants.* Houston, TX: Arte Público Press.

——. 1998. *Ask a Policeman.* Houston, TX: Arte Público Press.

Jaramillo, Cleofas. 1955. *Romance of a Little Village Girl.* San Antonio, TX: Naylor.

Juárez, Tina. 1995. *Call No Man Master.* Houston, TX: Arte Público Press.

Kino, Fray Eusebio Francisco. 1948. *Kino's Historical Memoir of Pimería Alta: A Contemporary Account of the Beginnings of California, Sonora, and Arizona.* Ed. and trans. Herbert Eugene Bolton. Berkeley: University of California Press.

Lea, Aurora Lucero-White, ed. 1953. "Las cuatro apariciones de la Virgen de Guadalupe." *Literary Folklore of the Hispanic Southwest.* San Antonio, TX: Naylor. 86–106.

——. 1953. "Los moros y cristianos." *Literary Folklore of the Hispanic Southwest.* San Antonio, TX: Naylor. 107–12.

Lomelí, Francisco A., Teresa Márquez, and María Herrera-Sobek. 2000. "Trends and Themes in Chicana/o Writings in Postmodern Times." *Chicano Renaissance: Contemporary Cultural Trends.* Ed. David R. Maciel, Isidro D. Ortiz, and María Herrera-Sobek. Tucson: University of Arizona Press. 285–312.

Martínez, Max. 1996. *White Leg.* Houston, TX: Arte Público Press.

——. 1997. *Layover.* Houston, TX: Arte Público Press.

McKenna, Teresa. 1997. *Migrant Song: Politics and Processes in Contemporary Chicano Literature.* Philadelphia: Temple University Press.

Méndez, Miguel. 1974. *Peregrinos de Aztlán.* Tucson, AZ: Editorial Peregrinos.

Mirandé, Alfredo, and Evangelina Enríquez. 1979. *La Chicana: The Mexian-American Woman.* Chicago: University of Chicago Press.

Mora, Pat. 1995. *Agua Santa/Holy Water.* Boston: Beacon Press.

——. 1997. *House of Houses.* Boston: Beacon Press.

——. 1993. "Legal Alien." *Infinite Divisions: An Anthology of Chicana Literature.* Ed. Tey Diana Rebolledo and Eliana S. Rivero. Tucson: University of Arizona Press. 95.

Moraga, Cherríe. 1983. *Loving in the War Years: Lo que nunca pasó por sus labios.* Boston: South End Press.

——. 1994. *Heroes and Saints and Other Plays.* Albuquerque, NM: West End Press.

Moraga, Cherríe, and Gloria Anzaldúa. 1983. *This Bridge Called My Back: Writings by Radical Women of Color.* New York: Kitchen Table, Women of Color Press.

Morales, Alejandro. 1975. *Caras viejas y vino nuevo.* Mexico City: Editorial Joaquín Mortiz.

——. 1979. *La verdad sin voz.* Mexico City: Editorial Joaquín Mortiz.

——. 1983. *Reto en el paraíso.* Ypsilanti, MI: Bilingual Review Press/ Editorial Bilingue.

——. 1988. *The Brick People.* Houston, TX: Arte Público Press

——. 1992. *The Rag-Doll Plagues.* Houston, TX: Arte Público Press

Niza, Fray Marcos de. 1864–1884. "Descubrimiento de las siete ciudades por el P. Fr. Francisco de Niza." *Colección de documentos inéditos relativos al descubrimiento, conquista y colonización de las provincias españolas en América y Oceanía.* Vol. 3. Ed. Joaquín F. Pacheco, Francisco de Cárdenas, and Luis Torres de Mendoza. 42 vols. Madrid: Manuel B. de Quirós. 325–51.

Núñez Cabeza de Vaca, Alvar. 1542. *La relacion que dio Aluar Nuñez Cabeca de Vaca de lo acaescido en las Indias en la armada donde yua por gouernador Panphilo de narbaez desde el año de veynte y siete hasta el año de treynta y seis que boluio a Seuilla con tres de su compañia.* Zamora: n.p.

Otero-Warren, Nina. 1936. *Old Spain in Our Southwest.* New York: Harcourt Brace Jovanovich.

Paredes, Américo. 1976. *A Texas-Mexican "Cancionero": Folksongs of the Lower Border.* Champaign: University of Illinois Press

——. 1958. *"With a Pistol in His Hand": A Border Ballad and Its Hero.* Austin: University of Texas Press.

Pérez Villagrá, Gaspar. 1992. *La historia de la Nuevo México, 1610.* Ed. and trans. Miguel Encinias, Alfredo Rodríguez, and Joseph P. Sánchez. Albuquerque: University of New Mexico Press.

Portillo Trambley, Estela. 1971. "The Day of the Swallows." *El Grito* (Spring): 4–47.

——. 1975. *Rain of Scorpions and Other Writings.* Berkeley, CA: Tonatiuh International.

——. 1983. *Sor Juana and Other Plays.* Ypsilanti, MI: Bilingual Review Press/Editorial Bilingue.

——. 1986. *Trini.* Binghamton, NY: Bilingual Review Press/Editorial Bilingue.

Ramos, Manuel. 1993. *The Ballad of Rocky Ruiz.* New York: St. Martin's Press.

——. 1994. *The Ballad of Gato Guerrero.* New York: St. Martin's Press.

——. 1996. *The Last Client of Luis Móntez.* New York: St. Martin's Press.

——. 1997. *Blues for the Buffalo.* New York: St. Martin's Press.

Rebolledo, Tey Diana, and Eliana S. Rivero. 1993. *Infinite Divisions: An Anthology of Chicana Literature.* Tucson: University of Arizona Press.

Rechy, John Francisco. 1963. *City of Night.* New York: Grove Press.

——. 1967. *Numbers.* New York: Grove Press.

——. 1977. *The Sexual Outlaw: A Documentary.* New York: Grove Press.

——. 1979. *Rushes.* New York: Grove Press.

Rivera, Tomás. 1971. *. . . Y no se lo tragó la tierra/. . . And the Earth Did Not Part.* Berkeley, CA: Quinto Sol Publications.

Rodríguez, Luis. 1994. *Always Running: Mi Vida Loca–Gang Days in L.A.* New York: Simon & Schuster.

Ruiz de Burton, Amparo. 1992 [1885]. *The Squatter and the Don.* Houston, TX: Arte Público Press.

——. 1995 [1872]. *Who Would Have Though It?* Houston, TX: Arte Público Press.

Serra, Junípero. 1955. *Writings of Junípero Serra.* 4 vols. Ed. Antonine Tibesar. Washington, DC: Academy of American Franciscan History.

Soto, Gary. 1977. *The Elements of San Joaquín.* Pittsburgh, PA: University of Pittsburgh Press.

——. 1978. *The Tale of Sunlight.* Pittsburgh, PA: University of Pittsburgh Press.

Three Memoirs of Mexican California. 1988. Carlos N. Hija, Eulalia Pérez, Agustín Escobar. Trans. Vivian C. Fisher et al. Berkeley: Friends of the Bancroft Library, University of California Press

Valdez, Luis. 1971. *Actos.* San Juan Bautista, CA: Cucaracha.

Vasquez, Richard. 1970. *Chicano.* New York: Doubleday.

Venegas, Daniel. 1998. *Las aventuras de Don Chipote: o cuando los pericos mamen.* Houston, TX: Arte Público Press.

Villanueva, Alma. 1977. *Bloodroot.* Austin, TX: Place of Herons Press.

——. 1977. "Mexican Memos." *Bloodroot.* Austin, TX: Place of Herons Press. 67–68.

——. 1988. *The Ultraviolet Sky.* Tempe, AZ: Bilingual Review/Editorial Bilingue.

Villarreal, José Antonio. 1959. *Pocho.* New York: Doubleday.

Villaseñor, Edmundo. 1973. *Macho.* New York: Bantam Books.

——. 1991. *Rain of Gold.* Houston, TX: Arte Público Press.

Viramontes, Helena María. 1985. *The Moths and Other Stories.* Houston, TX: Arte Público Press.

——. 1995. *Under the Feet of Jesus.* New York: Dutton.

Zarate Salmerón, Fray Gerónimo de. 1966. *Relaciones.* Trans. Alicia Ronstadt Milich. Albuquerque: Horn and Wallace.

CHAPTER 35

CHICANO/LATINO
THEATER TODAY

Claudia Villegas-Silva

The terms *Chicano* and *Chicano theater* are generally associated with political and cultural movements of empowerment in the Hispanic, predominantly Mexican, communities of the United States of America that started in the 1960s; Luis Valdez (b. 1940) is one of the most accomplished of its founding fathers. Although these terms are still used, they have been deconstructed by subsequent dramatic codes, spectators, and cultural spaces in which they are put into practice. Some still use this terminology or identify with it, but most playwrights and members of the theatrical profession prefer the term *U.S. Latino/a theater*. What both forms have in common is that their producers' culture is rooted in or associated with Hispanic cultures, and both present themes and issues related to the descendants of Hispanic peoples living in the United States. They have, moreover, been transformed as the audience, the aesthetics of drama, and sociopolitical conditions have changed. The discourse of the two modes has shifted from addressing a very specific cause and audience to reaching a plurality of causes and audiences. In general terms, this is still protest theater, and particularly addresses political and feminist issues, as well as those of sexual and cultural otherness (depending on the historical context of the audience of the moment). In the beginning, Chicano theater was performed in a marquee or in the open air. Subsequently, its spaces grew to include the street, the community and commercial theater, secondary schools, museums, universities, cultural venues, and even television. As the audience has changed, so have the dramatic codes. As the aesthetic codes have changed, the critic and historian have found they have had to replace the traditional critical terms for others that enable them to explain the new discourses. For this reason, we should now speak of theatricality and performance, because the traditional components of theatrical communication have been exchanged for other media. Verbal language is often displaced by the visual; Italian-style or tent-show performances by informal staging; and an empty stage, multimedia staging, and body language take the place of conventional stage scenery. Thus, the Chicano and U.S. Latino theater of today takes many different forms.

Chicano Theater

In the early years, specialists insisted that Chicano drama follow the norms of Hispanic theater as it had been performed in the Colonial period, particularly in the southwestern part of the United States. They even tried to root it, whenever they could, in a much earlier tradition: "Cuando hablo de 'grupo chicano original' no quiero decir con esto que antes de 1965 los chicanos no tuvieran una tradición teatral. Por el contrario, podemos considerar los dramas rituales precolombinos como parte de nuestra herencia espiritual y teatral" (Huerta 1988, 326) ("When I speak of the 'original Chicano group,' I am not saying that before 1965 the Chicanos did not have a theatrical tradition. On the contrary, we might argue that the pre-Colombian rituals form part of our spiritual and theatrical

heritage"). In this sense of tradition, the defining components were the use of the Spanish language and delivery to an audience, mainly from Spanish-speaking cultures. For example, Nicolás Kanellos states that professional Spanish-speaking theater started over 150 years ago in the United States and has taken very different forms. He explains that theaters were established in several cities–Los Angeles, San Francisco, San Antonio, Tampa, New York–which traveling companies would visit regularly to perform their works in Spanish. This is, as he suggests, a long and diverse theatrical tradition, with an obvious relationship with the modes and tendencies of Mexican theater.

Nevertheless, the term *Chicano theater* tends to be restricted to that theater which arose in the 1960s, because its authors defined themselves as Chicanos, their theater had a specific function, and they appropriated theatrical and cultural modes, which constructed, as a rule, an image of Chicano identity. These images, in conjunction with those developed by other intellectuals, served as a frame of reference for the works that were self-identified as Chicano. The founding of Chicano theater is generally associated with the creation of El Teatro Campesino ("Farmworkers' Theater") by Luis Valdez in 1965. There are various schools of thought regarding the origin of Chicano theater, but most scholars accept what Juan Bruce Novoa calls the "origin myth," which is that Luis Valdez founded it in 1965 as a means of collaborating with César Chavez, founder of the National Farm Workers Association (NFWA), and supporting the strike of rural workers. The idea was to entertain the workers, raise their social consciousness, and maintain the strike spirit. Valdez himself outlines several characteristics and, in an enthusiastic synopsis, states that Chicano theater is "as beautiful, *rasquachi* (decrepit), human, cosmic, broad, deep, tragic, comic, as the life of La Raza itself" (Valdez 6).

At that time, the work of Teatro Campesino was generally created collectively, borrowing devices from popular theater and reworking some of Brecht's techniques and those of Latin American protest theater, such as music, masque, satire, parody, and political criticism. It laid greater emphasis on performance and the oral tradition than on the dramatic text. Its focus on improvisation enabled the spectators to detach themselves from and also ridicule the authorities, and in so doing reveal to themselves that they were in fact in collusion with the landowners. As Valdez says, the work of Teatro Campesino lies "somewhere between Brecht and Cantinflas" (Huerta 1982, 18). One example of this kind of theatrical form is the *actos*, which are satirical and parodic interludes, generally in English with phrases intercalated in Spanish. Among the best known and most performed works are *Las dos caras del patroncito* [*The Two Faces of the Boss*], *Los Vendidos* [*The Sellouts*], and *Soldado razo* [*Private*], first performed in 1965, 1967, and 1971, respectively. *Los Vendidos* depicts several Chicano stereotypes, in terms of their physical appearance and their integration to the dominant sectors. The title of the play

Figure 1.

Performance by the Teatro Campesino, c. 1965. (Courtesy Juan Villegas.)

Soldado razo is a play on words in Mexican Spanish, since *soldado raso* means "buck private" and *soldado razo* means "Mexican-American soldier" (*la raza* [the race] is the self-designation of Mexican-Americans). Both words are pronounced the same in Mexican Spanish. These *actos* stereotypes frequently reappear in Chicano and Latino theater.

As the Teatro Campesino evolved, its themes and audience changed. After ties were severed with the UFWOC in 1967, performances were put on in universities and community centers, and new themes were developed of relevance to these communities, such as the consumption of drugs, police violence, education, ethnic stereotyping, and the Vietnam War. The theater's focus, in other words, was to express the community's concerns. Like other Chicano arts, it incorporated, around 1970, images and figures from the Aztec and Mayan cultures. (Valdez calls this his ritual period.) Some of the best-known works include *Los corridos* [The Ballads] and *I Don't Have to Show You No Stinking Badges! Los corridos*, a 1987 television production for PBS, foregrounds the stories of the traditional Mexican *corridos*, especially those from the time of the Mexican Revolution, sung by Linda Ronstadt. Set in 1985, *I Don't Have to Show You No Stinking Badges!* by Luis Valdez was first produced in 1986; it presents the conflicts of a middle-class family who live in Hollywood. The parents, Buddy and Connie Villa, are successful actors, even if they always play the roles of employees, gardeners, workers, and so on, because of their ethnic physical appearance. Their daughter is a physician and their son Sonny is at Harvard. The conflict surfaces when Sonny comes home with his girlfriend and announces that he wants to leave university and become an actor. The subsequent questioning of identity focuses on Sonny's realization that his only possibility of success is as a fringe Hollywood actor; he can never be a star. Critic Jorge Huerta says of this work, "From melodrama-within-a-play to video-within-a-play, the playwright takes us on a theatrical exploration that offers no easy solutions. The earliest *actos* offered clearly defined action: 'Join the Union,' 'Boycott grapes,' etc. But what to do about distorted history or negative portrayals of Chicanos in the media?" (1992, 12).

Valdez is an iconic figure of Chicano culture. He has been invited to any number of the universities and institutions of the hegemonic culture, and his artistic works have thrived in different cultural sectors. He went to Hollywood determined to become a movie and television producer, and he achieved his goal. In each of his works one can find links with his original themes and motifs, especially the construction of historical figures from the so-called Hispanic tradition in the United States, revealing how the descendants of Mexicans have contributed to the history and culture of the United States. His movie *Zoot Suit* (1979) is a musical comedy, in which he attempts to represent urban Chicano experience using melodrama and Brechtian techniques. He also produced and directed the movie *La Bamba* (1987). Although these movies were extraordinarily successful–in that they rendered visible the particular problems of the urban Chicano–they also reinforced the psychological and visual stereotyping of the alleged people of the *barrio* by identifying them, as did Octavio Paz (1914–1998), with the *pachuco*, a popular Mexican stock character of the 1940s. Valdez produced a television version of the *Pastorela* [Shepherd's Play], in which he updated this popular Mexican genre by setting it in California and adding a touch of magic realism to some of the many religious and folkloric motifs. It is not surprising, therefore, that *Soldierboy* (1982), by Judith Pérez (b. 1945) and Severo Pérez (b. 1941), was also staged by Valdez and the Teatro Campesino. The play begins in 1945 and describes, in a style between dream and reality, the return of Frank from World War II and the adjustments the family must make.

The beginning of Chicano theater is also associated with the Teatro de la Esperanza, which began in 1969 as a student group–Teatro Mecha–at the University of California, Santa Barbara. Its *Guadalupe*, a collective work, was directed by Jorge Huerta, the founder of the group. It utilizes Brecht and concepts of Latin American protest theater, especially those of theorists like Augusto Boal and Enrique Buenaventura, for the purpose of highlighting the injustices committed against the Latino community in a small Californian town. The director thought it resembled documentary theater, because "educaba y entretenía" ("it educated and entertained") and provided "constantes indicaciones al público de que lo que estaban viendo había ocurrido realmente" ("constant demonstrations to the public that what they were seeing had really happened") (Huerta 1988, 329). This group, which moved to San Francisco, and the Teatro Campesino are, in Huerta's opinion, the most important and longest-standing in Chicano theater. After 1970 many other Chicano theater groups sprang up all over the country, and in ideological terms, they generally served as the vehicles for the formation of a Chicano consciousness and identity. They were part of the Chicano movement for self-empowerment but also demonstrated the particular concerns of the Latino community at large. Several institutions have played a key role in the history of Chicano theater and its diffusion. TENAZ, or the Teatro Nacional de Aztlán, serves as a central coordinating organization of a number of theater groups; it finds venues in different parts of the country for Chicano performances.

Even though people associate Chicano theater with Luis Valdez, the cultural movement also has a number of other playwrights. For example, Carlos Morton (b. 1947), a professor at the University of California, Riverside, has had success with several plays inspired by Mexican myths. *Johnny Tenorio* (staged in 1983) adapts the theme of Don Juan by making the protagonist a Chicano. Morton's transformation of Don Juan includes elements from popular and indigenous Mexican cultures. As Lee A. Daniel notes, the character Berta "can also be interpreted as the Aztec goddess Coatli-cue–'la diosa de las inmundicias' and eater of the sins of man" (10–11). Although Morton's treatment of Don Juan in the Chicano and Latino cultures ends in condemnation, the protagonist's construction within the *corrido* tradition of the antihero paradoxically recognizes and, indeed, encourages his social defiance and his undermining of convention, thereby making him a rebel. The dominant language of this work is English, but there are also many expressions in Spanish and much play with both the English and Spanish traditions of the ballad. Morton's other plays (and dates when they were staged) are *Rancho Hollywood* (1979), *The Savior* (1986), *Pancho Diablo* (1987), *The Foundling* (1988), and *The Miser of Mexico* (1989). One of his most frequently performed works is the docudrama *The Many Deaths of Danny Rosales* (1974). This prolific playwright also has a number of one-act plays that have been performed throughout the United States, Mexico, and Europe. His plays generally deal with Chicano identity, discrimination, otherness, and power relations.

A constant frame of reference for Chicanos is the militant past of the 1960s. *The Last Angry Brown Hat* (1997) by Alfredo Ramos represents this nostalgia for the heroic past of the political struggles in California and the Southwest, but at the same time touches on the conflictive theme of gender relations. It was performed at the Phoenix College meeting of the M.E.Ch.A. (Movimiento Estudiantil Chicano de Aztlán) and at the State M.E.Ch.A. Leadership Conference in March 1997. The work explores brotherhood and the struggle of the Brown Berets. Four friends meet in their *barrio* after the death of one of their childhood friends. The play captures the spirit of the past in terms of both its masculine heterosexuality and the traditional and rigid social structure. It is interesting that there are no women characters in this play; they are only alluded to as ex-girlfriends or wives. The irony lies in how, despite (or because of) the exclusion of women, the play sums up the history of the marginalization of women during the turning points of the Chicano movement (see Broyles-González). The action revolves around one man's declaration of his homosexuality, which his friends readily accept.

Homosexuality has always aroused a great deal of controversy in Chicano culture. Luis Alfaro (b. 1961) is one of the authors who has focused on his own homosexuality in his plays, short stories, and poetry. He is a member of Teatro Viva, which aims at promoting education about AIDS. He describes himself as follows:

I call myself a Gay Chicano. I create work that asks questions about identity and social power and addresses the intersection of nationality and sexuality. More than all of that, I am trying to tell the story of my people, of what it means to live in a city like Los Angeles, to give voice to the stories that have not been heard. (316)

In 1997 he wrote *Chicanismo* for PBS, which was nominated for an Emmy award. In her discussion of Alfaro's work, Michelle Habell-Pallan writes:

Alfaro's performance pieces help to invent a new Chicano(a) subject whose identity is not necessarily based on the ideology of static Chicano cultural nationalism which posits an essential Chicano subject (always heterosexual), but instead is based on nuance understanding of how cultural identity and identification is in constant flux. This new Chicano(a) subject is rooted in Chicano culture but, unlike cultural nationalism, is also committed to the politics of anti-homophobia and anti-sexism. (34)

Among the new playwrights who call themselves Latinos, we should mention Guillermo Reyes (b. 1962) in Chile, who is very much aware of the difficulties of producing Latino texts: "The investment of time and resources on any new play is already a miracle in the U.S. theater, but the blatantly discriminatory attitude of Latino theaters make it even more difficult, if not impossible, for a gay Latino play to be produced" (1997, 39). His *Men on the Verge of a Hispanic Breakdown* (1996) was a great success in Off-Broadway theater, as well as in Los Angeles, San Francisco, and San José. It is structured around nine monologues that "depict different forms of gay Hispanic identity" (Foster 103). *Deporting the Divas*, directed by Jorge Huerta, was staged in Los Angeles in 1997. This comedy develops several traditional themes of Chicano and Latino theater, such as oppression, deportation, violence, discrimination, and identity, but it also explores sexuality, homosexuality, and transvestism. According to the author, it is a social satire "on border identity issues, including that of sexual identity" (Reyes 1997, 38). His most recent work is *Queen of the Tango* (1999).

There are many excellent directors, actors, and actresses working in Chicano and Latino theater. José Luis Valenzuela, currently a professor at the University of California, is one of the most active and best-known Latino directors. *La Victima* [The Victim], a work of documentary collective theater and the first he directed, was performed in 1986 by the Teatro de la Esperanza, but was first staged in 1978. It tells the story of the threat of deportation, the separation of families, and the economic difficulties experienced by a Mexican-American family. In 1995 he directed *August 29*, a collectively authored work presented under the pseudonym Violeta Calles, in the Theater Center's Latino Lab in Plaza de la Raza, Los Angeles. The play describes the events surrounding the death of Rubén Salazar, a Chicano journalist who was killed during a demonstration and thus became a martyr to the cause. It focuses on the memories of a professor of Chicano studies who reflects upon her own commitment and on what the Chicano movement has become. Working on several levels, the play presents Salazar's life in the context of the history of the movement and captures the social consciousness of the period very well. Various multimedia techniques are used to demonstrate the violence of the social confrontations. One of the most striking strategies involves scenes filmed or recorded on video in Los Angeles at the time. This work questions the loss of commitment and social activism, as well as the need to understand the past. In 1996 Valenzuela directed *Luminarias* [Luminaries] by Evelina Fernández, also a kind of documentary collective theater, which was produced by the Latino Theater Company in Los Angeles.

The Rise of Chicana Women's Dramaturgy

Women have been active participants in the birth and development of Chicano and U.S. Latino theater. While some critics and playwrights have discussed their importance, the dominant trend during the early years of the Teatro Campesino was to exclude them–other than to offer them the traditional female roles, as Yolanda Broyles González has pointed out. With time, women began to form independent theater groups; women playwrights and performance artists soon gained recognition. In 1996 Jorge Huerta noted that the work of Chicana playwrights was

> being produced all over the country today. Certainly, there were many women participating in the collective creation of earlier acts and plays, but they were not singling themselves out as writers until the 80s. Furthermore, it appears that the Chicanas have been getting their plays produced by a variety of companies, more than their male counterparts. (1996, 94)

Estela Portillo Trambley (b. 1936) was probably the first Chicana writer to publish a play. Her *The Day of the Swallows* (1971) is a classic of Chicano theater. Set in a small town, the play focuses on the lesbian relationship between the protagonist and a young woman who was once a prostitute.

Cherríe Moraga (b. 1952) is undoubtedly one of the most distinguished Chicana playwrights in the United States today. Her plays are constantly performed; she has been interviewed on television, and there have even been documentary programs about her. Her works have attracted the attention of Chicano/a critics and, especially, of academics interested in gender studies. While most Chicana dramatists explore domestic themes, family relationships, the social conditions of Hispanic women, or the relationships between men and women, Cherríe Moraga is one of the first to pose the question of women's sexuality. It has been said that Moraga writes from a threefold marginal position: As a woman, a Chicana, and a lesbian. She launched her career with *Giving Up the Ghost* (1986), which was followed by *Heroes and Saints* (1989), *Shadow of a Man* (1990), and *Watsonville* (1996). *Shadow of a Man* is about a Mexican family living in Los Angeles. Its principal focus is on the women of the family, their direct or indirect relation with the Church, machismo, and the figures of the priest and other men, whether as husband or father. However, it also explores homoeroticism, first through the feelings of two male characters, Manuel and Conrado, and second, through the figure of Lupita. The conflict of the sexual orientation of these characters arises from the social conditioning in the Chicano community.

Josefina López (b. 1969) is another important playwright. Her most frequently performed work, as much by Chicano and Latino groups as by Anglo-Saxon groups, is *Real Women Have Curves* (1988). Her first play, *Simply María, or The American Dream*, was performed by the Teatro Campesino in 1989. In *Real Women Have Curves* the action centers on a group of women who work as seamstresses in a sweatshop. Tension is created within the context of financial hardship, the fear of immigration officials, and personal problems. Conflict emerges from the contrast between the Chicana woman and

the lanky woman from the dominant U.S. culture. Margo Milleret suggests that the text constitutes a feminist reflection on Mexican cultural reality: "López's plays counteract simplistic either/or solutions to assimilate or to resist dominant culture by advocating a hybrid cultural identity. Because the search for this hybrid cultural identity is conducted by girls growing up, it also becomes a search for feminine identity" (109–10).

Edith Villarreal (b. 1944) is another playwright who has made her presence felt. Her *My Visits with MGM* was performed in 1989 at the Hispanic Playwrights Project South Coast Repertory Theater. It deals with the personal relationships among Marta, the grandmother, her sister Florinda, and her granddaughter Marta, the protagonist of the play. It calls into question the different lifestyles and spirituality of each woman, and centers on the young Latina, who leaves the family home. Milcha Sánchez-Scott's (b. 1955) plays *Latina* (1989) and *Roosters* (1987) (which was adapted for the screen) have also met with considerable success. She specifically calls herself a Latina: "I'd always been grouped as a Chicana writer, and part of me is. But a larger part is not. My roots are in South America" (246). Although she was not born in the United States of America, she grew up in San Diego and Los Angeles, where her personal and work experience put her in touch with the world of women workers. She deals with the basic aspects of life for Chicanas in her play *Latina*, which in Huerta's view accurately presents the attempts at economic survival of Chicanas employed as domestic workers and their sense of identity: "Told simply and humorously, this play, based on the playwright's own experiences, explores the prevailing theme through pathos and comedy, farce and satire, to achieve its goals" (Huerta 1989, 10). Other well-known plays include Amparo García's *Claws and Wings to Fly* (1992) and Evelina Fernández's *How Else Am I Supposed to Know I'm Still Alive?* (performed by the Teatro Campesino in 1992).

Chicana/Latina writers have expanded on the traditional concept of theater by creating a form known as *teatro-poesía* (theater-poetry), which is as much theater as poetry, and which began at the end of the 1970s in the work of such artists as Dorinda Moreno and Rose Cano. In 1974, Dorinda Moreno (b. 1935), with the group "Las Cucarachas," put on *Chicana*, a spectacle that combined dance, poetry, music, and prose. We should also include such well-known writers as Sandra Cisneros (b. 1954) and Denise Chávez (b. 1948) in this mode, because many of their poems are performed as monologues. The theater-poetry format is not the province of women alone; male dramatists have also participated in the development of this genre (which has been studied in depth by Yvonne Yarbro-Bejarano, especially with regard to performances in San Francisco).

From Traditional Theater to Comedy Troupes and Performance Art

This review of Chicano and U.S. Latino theater would be incomplete if we did not examine the ways in which it has prospered by means of nontraditional forms. In academic circles, some might challenge the inclusion of these modes in a historical review of theater, but drama studies have, for some time now, been examining diverse forms of theatricality. The consideration of such alternative modes as social and street theater, religious fiestas, and social spectacles has broadened the field considerably. One might say that this diversification of Chicano/Latino theater is in keeping with its primary goal of reaching the popular sectors, including those from what is perceived as the dominant U.S. culture.

Comedy Troupes

Chicano or Latino comedy troupes have become very popular and represent the broadening and diversifying of Chicano theater audiences: performances in comedy clubs, night clubs, and universities have even led to television programs. These comic performances make the spectators laugh by using irony, parody, or satire to make fun of commonplace social incidents. Parody and/or irony often functions as a means of ridiculing the ways in which the dominant culture perceives or has perceived the Chicano or Latino; this resembles the technique used in Valdez's *actos*, as mentioned earlier. Notable among these groups are Culture Clash (Berkeley), Latins Anonymous (Los Angeles), Chicano Secret Service, and Chusma.

Culture Clash has perhaps the longest history and is best known. Founded in May 1984 in San Francisco by Richard Montoya, Ricardo Salinas, and Herbert Sigüenza, it depicts itself as surveying contemporary Latino/Chicano culture in the U.S. from its own outrageous and unique perspective, and as blending the best traditions of Charlie Chaplin, Lenny Bruce, the Marx Brothers, and Cantinflas while transforming vaudeville into a political weapon. *The Mission, A Bowl of Beings, S.O.S., Carpa Clash,* and *Radio Mambo: Culture Clash Invades Miami* are several of its most successful performances. *Bordertown,* one of its most recent creations, was performed under Buen Teatro in the Festival de la Frontera 98 in Tijuana.

One of the most successful groups is Latins Anonymous. It was founded in Los Angeles in 1987 by Luisa Leschin, Armando Molina (b. 1957), Rick Najera (b. 1960), and Diana Rodriguez, who created a new dimension of sketch comedy in Chicano/Latino theater. Edward James Olmos has described them as a combination of "'Saturday Night Live' sketch comedy with the fundamentals of *teatro*, which was based on the Mexican vaudeville *tanda* that was honed on the back road farmlands of Central California, Arizona and Texas. They created an amalgam which was truly their own by mixing *ganas* (guts) and purpose of *teatro* with the slickness of American sketch comedy" (Olmos 1996, 4–5). Their best-known sketches are *The LA LA Awards,* a satire on Latino presence in Hollywood, and *Latins Anonymous,* a parodic and ironic spectacle structured around the Twelve Steps of the Alcoholics Anonymous program. It presents a series of characters who are at different stages of recognizing their Chicano, Latino, or Mexican-American selfhood. It aims at humorously demonstrating how, in the dominant society, Latinos are forced to hide their true identity and integrate themselves into so-called U.S. culture. The satirical representation of stereotypes conveys the message that Latinos should recognize their Latino identity and be proud of it. The basic situation bears a striking resemblance to that of the character Miss Jimenez in Valdez's *Los Vendidos.* The radio noisily announces: "It's 3:00 A.M. and you're staring bleary-eyed into a bowl of matzo ball soup. Your girlfriend Buffy hands you a corned beef on rye. You're trying to forget that your name is Hernández. You've got a problem. Try Latins Anonymous. Only a phone call away" (*Latins Anonymous* 58–59).

Performance Art

Performance art is a highly effective mode of expression among Chicano and Latino artists. Numerous critics have discussed the history and meaning of the terms *performance* and *performance art* (see Schechner; Birringer 1998, Taylor; Villegas), but I shall restrict the meaning here to the way they have been used in the field of Chicano studies. Performance in this context is a spectacle in which the actor generally communicates his or her own present experience and, thus, dramatizes it. The main means of communication are body language and monologue, often in combination with multimedia procedures. Inevitably, this is seen as an alternative to traditional theater. In 1991 María Teresa Marrero argued that the most courageous and inventive work in Latino theater in Southern California was taking place within this lesser-known field of performance art, a form that deconstructed the stereotypical images of the Chicano/Latino as well as those of the Anglo-American "other," rather than creating developed characters that are what mainstream paying audiences want to see and hear (147). Alicia Arrizón defines this theatrical form succinctly: "performance art significaría el proceso mismo de la teatralización personal, donde el 'yo' subjetivo se apodera del espacio mediante el acto de representación" (22) ("performance art signifies the very process of personal dramatization, during which the subjective 'I' appropriates the space through the act of performing"). Although she generally restricts her commentary to performance art by women, Arizón regards this as an art of protest and a response to marginalization: "El caso es que el sujeto femenino se representa como sujeto de su propia historia, consciente de su biografía personal en relación casi siempre a sistemas dominantes" (22) ("The female subject is portrayed as the subject of her own story, aware of her personal biography as nearly always being in relation to dominant systems"). In practice, irrespective of Arizón's restrictions, this is an art performed by both men and women throughout Latino culture and, in fact, is a significant part of the creative expression of completely unrelated marginalized groups throughout the world.

Guillermo Gómez-Peña (b. 1955) has gained national and international renown as a performance artist. Born and educated in Mexico, he considers himself a Chicano as well as a Mexican. As he explains in "A Binational Performance Pilgrimage," "I am Mexican part of the year and a Chicano the other part. I cross the border by foot, by car, and by airplane, as often as ten times a month" (23). This artist has concentrated on themes related to the Mexico–U.S. border culture, as well as to cultural borders, whether they be geographical or ethnic. His performances and installations are, without question, always spectacular and always dramatic; the scenic spaces he explores are both internal and external. "Border Brujo" (1988) offers a multicultural criticism of the hegemony of the United States of America, which Gómez-Peña articulates as he goes through a rite of passage across the Mexico–United States border. His installation created with the Cuban-American Coco Fusco (b. 1960) under the title of "Two Undiscovered Amerindians" has perhaps received the greatest critical attention. It considers cultural stereotypes through the device of museums and zoos dedicated to the exhibition of other cultures, and turns the idea of social reductionism around and has us look at U.S. Anglo-Saxon and other dominant cultures as exotic.

Coco Fusco's contributions to the scenic presentation and the development of a theoretical framework are crucial. Indeed, her essay "The Other History of Intercultural Performance" is one of her most illuminating works on the subject.

"The New World Order (B) Order" is another of this artist's unsettling performances. Johannes Birringer describes its presentation in Chicago (1992–1993): "Using the vibrant irreverent, sarcastic humor of *rasquachismo*, Gómez-Peña wore grotesque wrestling masks, wigs, uniforms, and kitsch paraphernalia while haranguing his audience . . . , playing with conventional stereotypes, and inventing bizarrely intertwined cultural bastardizations in several mediums" (1996, 61). Gómez-Peña is a cultural critic; he is also a reflective artist whose work is intellectually part of contemporary cultural theories, especially post-colonialism. Speaking of his work as a performance artist, Gómez-Peña explains:

> There are a lot of elements [in the performance] that come from MTV, Rock-n-Roll culture, media, Western performance art . . . , there are many sources of inspiration besides Chicano studies. Although the imagery is Mexican, pop-culture and Chicano pop-culture, it is also true that a lot of images are extremely transgressive and they defy Chicano iconography.
> (qtd. in Huízar 1998, 209)

It is this dual role as artist and critic that gives Gómez-Peña his particular perspective in his creative work. As a creator, he is very aware of the meaning and message of his productions. The greatest contribution Gómez-Peña has made to Chicano art has been his intellectual impact on the United States, Mexico, the rest of Latin America, and Europe. This has enabled him to foreground such significant themes as cultural identity and cultural liminality as a way of life.

One of the most innovative performance groups is named About Productions and was founded in Los Angeles by Theresa Chávez, Rose Portillo, and Alan Pulner. About Productions is distinguished by its extensive use of multimedia techniques. Like most Chicano/Latino work, "Memory Rites" (June 1998) addresses the themes of the self, identity, and family relationships. It transmits the message that the present is constantly changing and that the past–the moment it ceases to be (the) present–is forgotten. Video presentation serves the function of projecting memories, enabling the characters to capture (and grasp at) remembrances of times past together with the public.

The use of the term *Chicano and U.S. Latino theater* does not imply that there is only one kind of theater for these distinct groups. On the contrary, this is a theatrical practice that continually changes the codes used, the spectators it addresses, and the spaces in which its performances are staged. The majority of its productions share the common purpose of rejecting or questioning the dominant structures of Anglo-American society, of incorporating aspects of Hispanic cultures into U.S. culture, and of adapting to new modes of theatrical communication. The language most often used is not Spanish, although most performances contain Spanish expressions and words; the language of this theater is English. Chicano and U.S. Latino theater includes traditional theater, performance art in its various modes, comedy troupes, and visual and multimedia artists. Its themes range from the condemnation of social injustice to the denunciation of social and sexual discrimination. In sum, the multiple dramatic modes used form part of an avant-garde in experimental theater. This theater poses the social problems of a large and heterogeneous community within an overwhelming powerful Anglo-American culture that dominates the world at the beginning of the twenty-first century. In the United States, Latinos are a minority, albeit a large one, and for many and distinct reasons they cannot or do not choose to identify with the political and cultural hegemony.

Translation by Charlotte Broad

Works Cited

Alfaro, Luis. 1998. "Downtown." *O Solo Homo: The New Queer Performance* Ed. Holly Hughes and David Román. New York: Grove Press. 313–48.

Arrizón, Alicia. 1996. "Chicanas en la escena: teatralidad y performance." *Ollantay* 4.1: 21–32.

Birringer, Johannes. 1996. "Border Media: Performing Postcolonial History." *Gestos* 11.21: 49–66.

———. 1998. *Media and Performance: Along the Border.* Baltimore: Johns Hopkins University Press.

Broyles-González, Yolanda. 1994. *El teatro campesino: Theater in the Chicano Movement.* Austin: University of Texas Press.

Bruce-Novoa, Juan. 1992. "Chicano Theater: Editing the Origin Myth." *Gestos* 7.14: 105–16.

Daniel, Lee A. 1992. "Introduction." *Johnny Tenorio and Other Plays.* By Carlos Morton. Houston, TX: Arte Público Press. 7–23.

Foster, David William. 1999. "Guillermo Reyes Deporting the Divas." *Gestos* 14.27 (April): 103–8.

Fusco, Coco. 1994. "The Other History of Intercultural Performance." *Drama Review* 38.1 (Spring): 143–67.

Gómez-Peña, Guillermo. 1991. "A Binational Performance Pilgrimage." *Drama Review* 3.3: 22–45.

Habell-Pallan, Michelle. 1996. "Family and Sexuality in Recent Chicano Performance: Luis Alfaro's Memory Plays." *Ollantay* 4.1: 32–42.

Huerta, Jorge, ed. 1982. *Chicano Theater: Themes and Forms.* Ypsilanti, MI: Bilingual Press.

———. 1988. "El teatro chicano contemporáneo: redefinir la revolución." *Escenario de dos mundos: inventario teatral de Iberoamérica.* Ed. Moisés Pérez Coterillo. Vol. 2. Madrid: Centro de Documentación Teatral. 324–32.

———, ed. 1989. *Necessary Theater: Six Plays about the Chicano Experience.* Houston, TX: Arte Público Press.

———. 1992. "Introduction." *Zoot Suit and Other Plays.* By Luis Valdez. Houston, TX: Arte Público Press. 7–20.

———. 1996. "Professionalizing *Teatro*: An Overview of Chicano Dramaturgy Since *Zoot Suit.*" *Ollantay* 4.1: 91–103.

Huízar, Angélica J. 1998. "Performance, Identities and Transgressions: An Interview with Guillermo Gómez-Peña." *Gestos* 13.25: 205–15.

Kanellos, Nicolás, ed. 1990. *A History of Hispanic Theater in the United States: Origins to 1940.* Austin: University of Texas Press.

Latins Anonymous: Two Plays. 1996. By Luisa Leschin et al. Houston, TX: Arte Público Press.

López, Josefina. 1988. *Real Women Have Curves.* Seattle, WA: Rain City Projects.

Marrero, María Teresa. 1991. "Chicano-Latino Self-Representation in Theater and Performance Art." *Gestos* 6.11: 147–63.

Milleret, Margo. 1998. "Girls Growing . . . Up, Cultural Norms Breaking Down in Two Plays by Josefina López." *Gestos* 26 (November): 109–25.

Moraga, Cherríe. 1992. *Shadow of a Man. Shattering the Myth: Plays by Hispanic Women.* Ed. Linda Feyder. Houston, TX: Arte Público Press. 9–49.

Morton, Carlos. 1992a. *Johnny Tenorio. Johnny Tenorio and Other Plays.* Houston, TX: Arte Público Press. 25–52.

———. 1992b. *The Miser of Mexico. Johnny Tenorio and Other Plays.* Houston, Tex.: Arte Público Press. 105–51.

———. 1992c. *Pancho Diablo. Johnny Tenorio and Other Plays.* Houston, TX: Arte Público Press. 153–92.

——— 1992d. *The Savior. Johnny Tenorio and Other Plays.* Houston, TX. Arte Público Press. 53–103.

Morton, Charles. 1983. *The Many Deaths of Danny Rosales and Other Plays.* Houston, TX: Arte Público Press.

Olmos, Edward James. 1996. "Introduction." *Latins Anonymous: Two Plays.* By Luisa Leschin et al. Houston, TX: Arte Público Press. 4–6.

Reyes, Guillermo. 1997. "What I've Discovered." *Ollantay* 5.2: 38–40.

———. 1999. *Deporting the Divas. Gestos* 14.27 (April): 110–58.

Sánchez-Scott, Milcha. 1987. "Roosters." *On New Ground: Contemporary Hispanic-American Plays.* Ed. M. Elizabeth Osborn. New York: Theatre Communications Group. 243–80.

Schechner, Richard. 1998. *Performance Theory.* New York: Routledge.

Schechner, Richard, and Willa Appel, eds. 1990. *By Means of Performance: Intercultural Studies of Theater and Ritual.* Cambridge: Cambridge University Press.

Taylor, Diana. 1994. "Opening Remarks." *Negotiating Performance: Gender, Sexuality and Theatricality in Latin/o America.* Ed. Diana Taylor and Juan Villegas. Durham, NC: Duke University Press. 1–16.

Trambley, Estela Portillo. 1971. *The Day of the Swallows.* Berkeley, CA: Quinto Sol Publications.

Valdez, Luis. 1990. "Notes on Chicano Theater." *Luis Valdez–Early Works: Actos, Bernabé and Pensamiento Serpentino.* Houston, TX: Arte Público Press. 6–10.

Villarreal, Edith. 1992. "My Visits with MGM (My Grandmother Martha)." *Shattering the Myth: Plays by Hispanic Women.* Ed. Linda Feyder. Houston, TX: Arte Público Press. 143–208.

Villegas, Juan. 1994. "Closing Remarks." *Negotiating Performance: Gender, Sexuality and Theatricality in Latino/a America.* Ed. Diana Taylor and Juan Villegas. Durham, NC: Duke University Press. 306–20.

Yarbro-Bejanaro, Yvonne. 1990. "The Female Subject in Chicano Theatre: Sexuality, Race, and Class." *Performing Feminisms: Feminist Critical Theory and Theatre.* Ed. Sue Ellen Case. Baltimore: Johns Hopkins University Press. 131–50.

CHAPTER 36

PUERTO RICAN LITERATURE
IN THE UNITED STATES

Carmen Dolores Hernández

Long before the island of Puerto Rico was ceded by Spain to the United States as a consequence of the Spanish-American War of 1898, Puerto Ricans had been migrating to the New England states and to New York, mostly in connection with the rum, molasses, and tobacco trades. And although New Orleans had been, up until the Civil War, a center for Caribbean political activity, New York afterward became a haven for emigrés and revolutionaries who plotted from there the Spanish island's independence from Spain. In the 1890s, the New York–based Puerto Rico Section of the Cuban Revolutionary Party became a focus of such activity. In the course of the century Cubans and Puerto Ricans established in New York several other associations, mostly for political purposes, although some were of a cultural, social, or literary nature. From the 1880s on there was also considerable journalistic activity; the numerous newspapers and magazines published there gave the community an even greater cohesion (Bernardo Vega 55–67, 75–89).

After the Spanish-American War, and particularly after U.S. citizenship was granted to Puerto Ricans by the Jones Act in 1917, migration to the mainland increased. In 1940 there were about 70,000 Puerto Ricans living in the United States, the majority of them in New York. From 1940 to 1950, the numbers went up to more than 300,000, and they reached nearly a million and a half by 1970. According to the 2000 Census, there are now 3.4 million Puerto Ricans in the United States, slightly less than the Island's inhabitants, who number 3.8 million (Rivera-Batiz and Santiago 11).

At the beginning of the century the migrants were generally artisans, mostly cigar makers who flocked to the many factories that flourished in New York City at that time. Although mostly illiterate, cigar makers acquired a substantial degree of literary and political knowledge because of the practice of being read to in the factories while they rolled tobacco. During the decades that spanned the middle of the century, the migrants were above all peasants displaced from the land and from their livelihoods by the new policies of the Popular Democratic Party in Puerto Rico, which sought to turn a rather primitive economy based on one all-important crop, sugar, into a modern, industrialized economy. And although that ruling party implemented strategies–such as the founding of a Migration Division within its Department of Labor–to promote a seasonal migration of farm laborers to the northeastern states, hoping to alleviate Puerto Rico's problems of chronic unemployment and overpopulation, most immigrants continued to favor New York City. No substantial body of literature emerged from the Puerto Rican community in the United States before the 1960s, when both the more recent arrivals (those who came after World War II) and the communities that had been established before that time had attained some degree of schooling. There were exceptions. An important one is Arturo Alfonso Schomburg (1874–1938), a black Puerto Rican cigar maker who arrived in New York in 1891 and who, from the turn of the century on,

published a steady stream of articles and essays on Caribbean and North American black culture. In 1911, together with other African American scholars, he founded the Negro Society for Historical Research to further the study of black history and to collect books, photographs, letters, and works of art dealing with African American culture. His own collection of black literature and art, donated in 1926 to the New York Public Library, became the basis for the Schomburg Center for Research in Black Culture, now located in Harlem.

Jesus Colón (1901–1974), another black tobacco worker, who had arrived in 1918 from the Puerto Rican mountain town of Cayey, wrote down–in English–a series of sketches describing his experiences in the city as a black man from Puerto Rico. His *A Puerto Rican in New York and Other Sketches* (published in 1961) and fellow cigar maker Bernardo Vega's (1885–1965) *Memoirs* are two books that document the experiences of the Puerto Rican community in New York at the beginning of the twentieth century. Colón's is probably the first full-fledged book by a Puerto Rican in the United States to have been written and published in English. Vega, on the other hand, who lived in New York from 1916 until his death, wrote in Spanish. His memoirs were published posthumously in Puerto Rico in 1977 by César Andreu Iglesias (1915–1976) as *Memorias de Bernardo Vega*.

Some writers from Puerto Rico, mostly poets such as Clara Lair (1895–1973), Felipe Arana (1902–1962), José Dávila Semprit (1902–1958), Graciany Miranda Archilla (1911–1991), and José I. de Diego Padró (1896–1974), the last also an important novelist–wrote part of their work while living sporadically in New York during the 1920s and 1930s. This also was the case with noted poet Julia de Burgos (1914–1953), who lived in the United States at different times during the 1940s and 1950s. Their literature, however, written mostly in Spanish (de Burgos wrote at least two poems in English), belongs to the mainstream Puerto Rican literary canon. One exception is Clemente Soto Vélez (1905–1993), who wrote vanguardist poetry in Puerto Rico during the 1920s, was imprisoned in the United States for taking part in Nationalist meetings and activities in 1935, and, after his release from prison in 1942, stayed in New York and became an integral part of the Puerto Rican community there. He continued to write his most important poetry in Spanish but has been recognized as a key literary figure whose influence upon English-speaking Puerto Rican writers in the United States was great.

On the other hand, during the 1940s and 1950s, some Puerto Rican novelists developed an increased literary social consciousness that was making them take note of marginalized groups on the Island. It was perhaps natural that they should turn their attention to their even more marginalized countrymen in New York. Many of these novelists traveled back and forth between Puerto Rico and the United States. A spate of novels and stories were written in Spanish dealing with Puerto Ricans in the United States: Pedro Juan Soto's (1928–1999) *Spiks* (1956), Guillermo Cotto-Thorner's (b. 1916) *Trópico en Manhattan*

434

[1951; Tropics in Manhattan], Emilio Díaz Valcárcel's (b. 1929) *Harlem todos los días* [1978; *Hot Soles in Harlem*, 1993], and many of José Luis González's (1926–1996) short stories.

It was not, however, until 1967 that the literature written in English by Puerto Ricans in the United States achieved momentum and began to be recognized as distinct both from mainstream Island literature and from U.S. literature. In that year, Knopf published a "shocking" book. It was a novelized memoir narrated in the first person, depicting the life of a young black Puerto Rican delinquent who, having grown up in the streets of Harlem, ends up in jail after attempting an armed robbery. Reviewed in major newspapers and periodicals, it was hailed as a major work. Piri Thomas's (b. 1928) *Down These Mean Streets* (1967) tells a tale of fall and redemption. It has points of contact with one aspect of the literature being written by African Americans at that time, especially Claude Brown's *Manchild in the Promised Land* (1965), *The Autobiography of Malcolm X: With the Assistance of Alex Haley* (1965), and Eldridge Cleaver's *Soul on Ice* (1968). Like those narratives, it documents an impoverished urban community and highlights within it the predicament of a young boy besieged by contradictory imperatives that affect his image of himself and of his place in society. To the dichotomy between life in the streets of *El Barrio* (Spanish Harlem), where he finds violence by prejudiced gangs and a home ambience that instills values that seem to be obsolete, a further complexity is added. Because he is black-skinned as well as of Puerto Rican origin, Piri Thomas is doubly stigmatized by U.S. society, and his place within the Hispanic community is affected by this perspective, which is not shared by all its members (not even by members of his own family, because he is the blackest of five children). Piri is made to choose between belonging to the Puerto Rican community and belonging to the black community in a climax that introduces race as a psychological factor and not only a social one in the literature written by Puerto Ricans on and off the Island.

As in *The Autobiography of Malcolm X* and *Soul on Ice*, the protagonist's rage is turned into a life of commitment to a cause after a stint in prison. Piri Thomas's book—which was autobiographical—tells about his time served in Sing Sing and Comstock prisons. There he turns both to religion and to a writing career. His story, full of anger and grace, is written in a strangely poetic and compelling manner, using both "black" English and abundant Spanish. Its strange poignancy surprised and attracted readers:

> I'd stand on a corner and close my eyes and look at everything through my nose. I'd sniff deep and see the *cuchifritos* and hot dogs, stale sweat and dried urine. I'd smell the worn-out mothers with six or seven kids, and the nonpatient fathers beating the hell out of them. My nose would go a high-pitch tingling from the gritty wailing and bouncing red light of a squad car passing the scene like a bat out of Harlem, going to cool some trouble, or maybe cause some. (Thomas 106)

Down These Mean Streets—unequaled by Thomas's later works—established the parameters for a genre of novels set in the New York ghettos (especially Spanish Harlem) where most Puerto Ricans lived, spawning a tradition, one of whose latest offshoots is Abraham Rodríguez, Jr.'s (b. 1961) *Spidertown* (1993). These novels document, narrate, and dramatize the life conditions of a marginalized sector of society that has had serious problems adjusting to a white, Anglo-Saxon, and English-speaking majority. This sector has not only remained in relative poverty, but has also had to deal on a daily basis (having remained in great numbers in the inner cities) with crime, violence, and temptation in the streets. Its young people tend to suffer from a confusion between two conflicting codes of behavior: A Puerto Rican ethos that puts loyalty to the family before everything else and that also encompasses a male code of *machismo,* and a fierce individualism and energetic enterprise fostered in the United States (often subverted in the ghetto into criminal enterprise).

Within this genre of adventure and violence in the ghetto, certain variations have appeared, such as in Edwin Torres's (b. 1931) novels, especially *Carlito's Way* (1975). Torres, who is a justice of the Supreme Court of the State of New York and who has also written *Q & A* (1977) and *After Hours* (1979), combines the Puerto Rican–cum–gangster formula novel with another kind of street delinquency from a far different time and place: Seventeenth-century Spain. It was there and then that the picaresque novel developed, a curious type of narrative told directly, in an autobiographical guise, by a main character who is typically a small-time delinquent and whose aimless life (within a society of dramatic contrasts between rich and poor, projecting grandiose international state schemes that contrast with the decaying conditions of its cities) takes him from "master" to "master," and often from licentious freedom to prison.

Besides the suggestive parallels that could be made between two hegemonic nations–Spain and the United States–whose politics each shaped an era but whose economic policies each gave rise to a floating population of unemployed drifters, there are certain similarities in the respective situations of marginalized sectors of each society. Torres has used *El Lazarillo de Tormes* (published shortly before 1554; author unknown) as a model of sorts for *Carlito's Way*. As in *El Lazarillo,* there is in this novel a sort of philosophical resignation to a life eschewing accepted conventions. The first-person narrative underscores a likeness that is also emphasized in the way the protagonist moves from one "patron" to another (in Carlito's case, the patrons take the form of gangs with bosses of different ethnicities).

Savagely realistic, even naturalistic, in its portrayal of atmosphere, the picaresque novel seems to be a mirror in which the urban Puerto Rican novel in the twentieth century can recognize its outlines. Much as Torres grafts a very different literary tradition from the U.S. mainstream onto his gangster novels, the young writer Abraham Rodríguez created in *Spidertown* (1993), his first novel, a Dickensian atmosphere especially close to that of *Oliver Twist* with its vivid portrayal of Fagin's school for crime. When he describes the world of present-day Puerto Rican junkies and pushers in the South Bronx, Rodríguez refers to a highly structured community in which the young are instructed by a master and live according to his rules. This master is a small-time drug lord (nicknamed Spider because of his building-climbing abilities) who, not so coincidentally, loves to read *Oliver Twist* and is anxious for the story of his life to be written down.

The society described in Torres's novel is a mirror image of the legitimate one in its hierarchies, differentiated tasks, progress, and rewards. It is just as exacting, competitive, and stressful as that other one, prompting Miguel, the main character, to wish for a less pressured life. He describes his "boss" in the following terms:

Spider says he can grab a ten-year-old kid and turn him into a successful businessman faster than IBM or ITT. He sounds like a proud camp counselor, talking about giving kids the chance they need, providing the incentive that gets them involved and functioning for themselves. . . . He gets young kiddies to scour the streets looking for discarded crack vials that he pays them a dime apiece for. He knows the dream of every little kid is to have his own car, so he promises them one. (Rodríguez 66–67)

Not all "early" Puerto Rican novels deal with crime and violence. A narrative such as Edward Rivera's (b. 1931) *Family Installments* (1982) has the bittersweet tone of a childhood memoir combined with a Puerto Rican's tale of trouble and adaptation to a different environment. It describes the ambience of a Puerto Rican family newly come to the United States and the conflicts between the children and their parents as both sides adapt–with different rhythms–to a new reality.

Other prose writers such as Ed Vega (b. 1938) have picked up from where these bildungsromans leave off. Vega's long novel, *The Comeback* (1985), and his book of short stories, *Mendoza's Dreams* (1987), use humor and irony to play up the contrasts and misunderstandings of life in an environment that persists in seeming alien even though years have elapsed since the first shock of discovery. The barrier between the host society and the Puerto Ricans seems to be the lack of acceptance that the latter are met with. One of the possible responses to this situation is given in Vega's writings. Prejudice, in Vega's works, does not prove the inferiority of the marginalized minority but rather the ignorance of the unaccepting Anglo majority. The difference is emphasized in the stories of *Mendoza's Dreams,* in some of which New York turns into a surreal city as it tries to deal with people who have a different cultural frame of reference from that which provides the organizing principle in society. The space between stereotype and expectation becomes the characters' field of action. They are thus able to subvert and turn to their advantage the blind spot society has toward their distinctness. Mercury Gómez, for example, in the story that bears his name, creates a flourishing messenger business by using to his advantage the physical stereotyping of his ethnic group. Vega's work examines prejudices and conventions on both sides of the cultural divide and plays each side against the other, implying a constant contrast.

In a book of short stories published some years later, *Casualty Report* (1991), Vega focuses almost exclusively on the Puerto Ricans themselves and explores the deep wound left by the "original sin" of having been uprooted from their natural social environment. Even if the wound seems healed and the past forgotten, it can burst forth in an agony of violence or unexplained grief with any unexpected provocation, bringing a sudden consciousness of irreplaceable loss.

Focusing solely on the Puerto Rican as part of U.S. society, without much reference to the Island itself, Jack Agueros (b. 1934)–who was born in New York of Puerto Rican parents and is a playwright and poet as well as a short story writer and translator of Julia de Burgos's poetry into English–explores, in the short stories included in *Dominoes* (1993), the ways in which Island migrants and their descendants try to position themselves in society. His characters deal with their particular background as just one more condition to be taken into account while they search for their individual places under the sun. Their experiences can be seen as a variant of a wider U.S. experience. These characters are not so much typical as common, in the sense of being men and women who seem

well adjusted within an already established sector of society that may not be central but is nevertheless accepted. Subtle signs remain, however, of an underlying difference waiting to erupt at a provocation or a temptation (as in the title "Horologist"). Normality for Puerto Ricans in the United States may not be as normal as for other, more established groups. They sometimes shun, as Max Vázquez, the main character, does in the wonderful story "Horologist," any symbolic representation that may single them out as spokespersons for their particular group, taking them out of their settled routines of work.

At about the time that Piri Thomas was publishing *Down These Mean Streets,* some New York Puerto Rican poets were expressing in a different literary idiom the gap between the mythic American Dream and the harsh realities encountered by their families upon migrating. Drawing upon a centuries-old oral tradition of poetry common to the rural parts of Puerto Rico, where troubadours can improvise verses at a moment's notice, singing them to the strains of a *cuatro* (a guitar-like instrument), the poetic movement that was later to be called "Nuyorican" began as a performance. The "father" of Nuyorican poetry seems to have been Jorge Brandon, a poet who could be seen in the streets of the Lower East Side pushing a shopping cart full of discarded odds and ends and making up poems–some very patriotic–as he walked through the streets.

Another "foreign" tradition was thus made part of the New York City scene, which took to it with the fervor accorded to similar manifestations coming from the black Southern traditions of song and oral literature. The impromptu audiences that gathered on street corners and in parks responded enthusiastically, and the resonance of this poetry quickly expanded beyond specific neighborhoods as the poets–among them Miguel Algarín (b. 1941), Pedro Pietri (b. 1943), Miguel Piñero (1946–1988), Lucky Cienfuegos (d. 1987), Sandra María Esteves (b. 1948), Bimbo Rivas (1939–1992), Jesus Papoleto Meléndez (b. 1950), Louis Reyes Rivera (b. 1945), and Tato Laviera (b. 1950)–wrote down and published their work.

These poets were in the right place at the right time. New York during the late 1960s and the 1970s was not only a hotbed of protest against the Vietnam War and of activism for civil, racial, feminist, and homosexual rights, but it had also just been through a literary commotion. A group of writers had taken the city–and eventually took the country–by storm. They exhibited a contempt for conventions, including those in the sexual sphere; a profound dissent in relation to established society, which they dubbed materialistic and conformist; and a denunciation of the dominance of the military-industrial complex that seemed to have driven the country into the Vietnam War. They also exhibited considerable enthusiasm for altered states of mind provoked by drugs. Known as the Beat Generation (the name plays on the connotations of the word *beat*: Down and out, beat up), Allen Ginsberg, Jack Kerouac, William Burroughs, Gregory Corso, and John Clellon Holmes, among others, were committed to a "New Vision" in art, especially literature. In their poetry and their narratives, they drew on their experiences of bohemian city life, writing about jazz musicians and Times Square junkies while projecting, in various genres, a mood of cultural disaffection with the prevailing central currents of thought and the moral values of the United States. Many experiences that had until then been alien to U.S. literature became part of this movement: Homosexual sex, drugs, and the low street life of a sector of society.

In introducing these themes in literature, the Beats had set the stage on which the young Puerto Rican–New York poets would appear. The fact that these new poets lived in New York was, then, central to their poetry. The name *Nuyorican*, which they adopted as a definition of a state of mind and a purpose, referred both to that city and to the Puerto Rican origins that gave them their particular perspective. It was coined by Miguel Algarín as a reaction to the rejection he perceived in Puerto Rico toward English-speaking Puerto Ricans from New York: "I came to Puerto Rico once with Miguel Piñero [a poet and playwright] and when we came out of the plane. . . I heard the word 'newyorican.' . . . They were looking down on us, as if we were nothing. We were Puerto Ricans talking in English, and that to them was contemptuous" (Carmen Dolores Hernández 39–40). When he was looking for a title for *Nuyorican Poetry: An Anthology of Puerto Rican Words and Feelings*, which he edited with Miguel Piñero in 1975, they agreed on the word *Nuyorican* to describe the poetry written in English by Puerto Ricans. "What I did was to take the insult that the islander threw at me and take away its sting" (Carmen Dolores Hernández 39–40).

But although the Puerto Ricans could relate directly to the Beats' literary scene, it was they who–unlike Burroughs (who was a Harvard graduate), Ginsberg, or Kerouac (who attended Columbia)–were "the real thing." Literally as well as figuratively "beat up" by their place as the children of poor, uneducated migrants who knew no English, their protests took a literary turn but referred to a very concrete situation. They also found U.S. established values wanting, not because of surfeit but because of privation. It was a time of solidarity against the perceived "enemy." Of the group, Pedro Pietri was sent to the Vietnam War and Miguel Piñero landed in prison, an experience that later served him well for his award-winning prison drama, *Short Eyes* (1974).

Nuyorican poetry used the everyday speech of Puerto Ricans in New York, popularly known as "Spanglish" but more aptly described as "code switching." It is a back-and-forth shift between English and Spanish, using the words and phrases of one and the other within a framework that is predominantly English. It also entails the juxtaposition of two distinct cultural sets of references implicit in the respective languages, both of them highly developed and of European origins. These poets used this language to poetic advantage, "playing" one language against the other and incorporating multiple allusions from one or the other tradition. Their themes were also commonplace among Puerto Ricans: the frustrations of daily life, the sting of prejudice, the incomprehension of bureaucrats, the nonadaptation to life in the city. Like the Beats, they wrote highly erotic poetry, either heterosexual or homosexual, and dealt with the culture of drugs in their poems.

And so, just as Spanish Harlem–*El Barrio*–had become identified with the group of Puerto Rican novelists already mentioned, the Lower East Side (dubbed *Loisaida* by Puerto Ricans, loosely following the Spanish pronunciation of the name) became the place where Nuyorican Poetry was born. In 1972 the poets had begun to meet in Miguel Algarín's apartment on the Lower East Side to read their work. Algarín, one of the more prolific of the Nuyorican poets, with four published volumes of poetry–the most recent of which is *Love Is Hard Work: Memorias de Loisaida* (1997)–soon realized that they needed a more public place. He then opened the Nuyorican Poets Café in a small locale on East 6th Street. It quickly became a gathering place for the poets and their ever-larger audiences. The popularity of the place was helped, of course, by the fact that writers such as Allen Ginsberg and William Burroughs were often to be seen at the café, as was the black playwright Amiri Baraka.

Plays began to be performed there on a regular basis along with the poetry readings. In 1980 the café moved to 3rd Street but closed three years later, to reopen in 1989. Since then it has become a cultural haven not only for Latino poets but for those from all ethnicities and persuasions. The well-attended weekly poetic competitions (called "poetry slams") are broadcast on the last Saturday of every month to Tokyo, Chicago, and San Francisco. Miguel Algarín has widened both his aesthetics and his audiences, becoming ever more universal in his themes. (His book *Time's Now,* published in a trilingual version–English, Spanish, and Japanese–in 1992, contains highly spiritual poetry.) The plays and poetry featured at the Nuyorican Poets Café have been collected in two anthologies, *Aloud: Voices from the Nuyorican Poets Café,* edited by Miguel Algarín and Bob Holman (Henry Holt 1994), and *Action: The Nuyorican Poets Café Theater Festival,* edited by Algarín and Lois Griffith (Simon & Schuster 1997).

Other poets and prose writers not fully identified with the "Nuyoricans" share some aspects of their aesthetics in terms of language and rhythm. Most of the Puerto Ricans who have migrated to the United States speak Spanish at home–it is the language of feelings and affection–while English has been learned at school and in the streets. Many of them claim, however, not to have sufficient command of literary Spanish to write in it. On the other hand, some thought that to write in English would signal a surrender of their cultural personality, so Spanglish provided a solution as the language of the Puerto Rican community, both in the Lower East Side and in El Barrio. They also strove to express through it a resistance to a norm or standard imposed by the two "uncontaminated" groups: the Spanish-speaking Island writers, seen as an elite who defended that language as a symbol of the nation (the immigrants were mostly excluded from the concept of nation, having physically left their homeland, thus breaking away from the Puerto Rican "family"), and the English-speaking writers of mainstream United States literature. Neither of those languages by itself could transmit the experience of the Puerto Rican migrant in New York. Code switching thus became a response to a sociocultural situation (Aparicio 147–60). In the introduction to *Nuyorican Poetry*, Miguel Algarín writes: "The poet is responsible for inventing the newness. The newness needs words, words never heard before or used before. The poet has to invent a new language, a new tradition of communication" (9).

One aspect that distinguishes Puerto Rican literature in the United States from that of the Island is its self-conscious role in documenting a unique experience. In a poem from Tato Laviera's *La Carreta Made a U-Turn* (1992) (he has also published *Enclave* [1981], *AmeRícan*, and *Mainstream Ethics* [1989], besides having written several plays), the author writes: "I am nothing but a historian" (13). His poetry is an affirmation of Puerto Ricans in the United States as neither wholly U.S. nor wholly Puerto Rican–nor even Nuyorican, since Puerto Ricans began to migrate to other cities and states, especially during the 1980s–but "AmeRícan," as reads the title of another of his books.

The documentary role is assumed with an intuition that is born out of a cultural substratum (as a result of a long-standing yet understated resistance to colonialism on the Island itself) by

Puerto Ricans who, like the narrator of the stories in the *Arabian Nights*, write "to forestall death" (Foucault 102). Their writing is an affirmation of individual and collective survival that may be assured, or at least aided, by recording the life of this largely forgotten community, marginalized within a host country that has refused to take into account the community's particular experience within the country's accepted repertory of images. This community has also been forgotten–or, for all practical purposes, ignored–in its society of origin. In a way, this situation has actually driven these poets into writing. In effect, their U.S. experience, although bitter because of the spectacle of the American Dream gone awry, may paradoxically have contributed to their becoming the important writers they now are, relevant both to the multicultural experience in the United States and to the culture of the Island itself.

The fact that their new environment was changing fast was another important stimulus for Puerto Rican writers in the United States. As Edwin Torres remarks: "[M]y writing is an offshoot of . . . the fact that I lived a very tumultuous, extraordinary era . . . . [T]he things that were happening in the Barrio in the thirties, the Depression, and then in the forties with the war and then in the late forties and early fifties, the advent of drugs . . . as my father used to say, 'No one knows we're here, no one is writing this.' So I ended up writing them, by default, since no one else did" (Carmen Dolores Hernández 188). Silence, in the case of these Puerto Ricans, could be equivalent to nonexistence, oblivion, and forgetfulness, because there would be no other record of the impact of their lives and feelings and of their process of collectively forging a new identity.

Besides assuming a documentary role, Puerto Rican literature in the United States can also be an advocacy. Such is the poetry of Martín Espada (b. 1957), committed as a lawyer not only to the Puerto Rican community in Massachusetts but also to Latinos in general. His poetry, published in books such as *Rebellion Is the Circle of a Lover's Hands* (1990), *City of Coughing and Dead Radiators* (1993), and *Behold the Angels of Bread* (1997), is strongly anecdotal, forging individual poetic "cases" to illustrate a state of injustice that must be remedied. His verse acquires at times the solemnity of legal discourse and the resonance of biblical writing.

These diverse literary manifestations give a widespread voice to a people at the fringes not only of U.S. but also of Island society. Historically, writers in Puerto Rico had belonged, with exceptions, to a bourgeoisie that had access to the means of intellectual and artistic production (universities, libraries, learned societies, some amount of leisure, publishing houses). Most of the Puerto Ricans who began writing in the United States during the 1960s and 1970s came from a working-class background and had little or no academic tradition in their families. The overwhelming majority–if not all–of them belonged to their family's first generation to attend university. Some were self-taught.

Many of their experiences were unique. When poet Victor Hernández Cruz (b. 1949) writes about a journey in time as well as in place, he is aptly describing what it must have been like to go from a little backwater town in the center of the island of Puerto Rico in the 1940s and 1950s to the center of New York, a city at the height of its power and influence. "We took a trip into the future," reads a verse of a poem in his book *Red Beans* (1991). He has also published *Snaps* (1969), *Mainland* (1973), *By Lingual Wholes* (1982), *Rhythm, Content and Flavor* (1989), and, most recently, *Panoramas* (1997).

The shock of such a change could be devastating, especially if we consider that it was compounded by language difficulties and by enormous differences in climate, landscape, and social mores. The documentation that some of this writing provides about the encounter between two such different stages of development is invaluable, because the experience may never be repeated again in quite the same terms. No matter how many Puerto Ricans migrate now to the mainland and no matter from where they come, the Island's industrial development during the last fifty years and its wealth of communications has turned it into a country aware of what is happening in the rest of the world, and particularly in the United States.

One aspect of the New York Puerto Ricans' creative literature of the 1960s and 1970s that was not amply documented was the women's perspective. Women's lives were subject to another kind of oppression than that experienced in the violence-ridden lives of young males in the streets of the ghetto. They were doubly invisible, both because they came from a segment of society marginalized by poverty and ignorance and because their roles were circumscribed to the home by male dominance within their community. Although they were often heads of families and worked outside the home, their need to support and care for their children kept many of them from taking part in artistic and social projects. Their range of both experience and action has been different, therefore, from that of men. Rather than being the direct subjects, or objects, of street violence (although many have certainly been the victims of the domestic variety), they have often suffered its after-effects.

Sandra María Esteves (b. 1948) in her poetry, and Nicholasa Mohr (b. 1935) in her novels and short stories, were among the first Puerto Rican women to become successful writers. Esteves was the most visible, if not the only, woman among the early Nuyorican poets. Her poetry has been published in books such as *Yerba Buena* (1981), *Tropical Rains: A Bilingual Downpour* (1984), and *Bluestown Mockingbird Mambo* (1990).

Using the Nuyorican poets' emphasis on colloquialism and their continuous references to a specific context, Esteves and other Puerto Rican women poets have explored the conflicting identities of the Latino woman and her growing self-awareness within both the marginalized Puerto Rican community and North American society as a whole. Poems like Esteves's *María Christina* express that conflict, referring to the place of woman as a repository of cultural values that she passes on. The implied subservience to a culture imbued with the feeling of male dominance was resented, however, by another Puerto Rican woman poet, Luz María Umpierre (b. 1945), who answered that stance in a poem titled "My Name Is Not María Cristina" in her book *The Margarita Poems* (1987). Other Esteves poems, such as "From the Commonwealth" (1980), express a greater distance from some of the time-honored traditions of Latino culture.

There is now, however, a large group of Puerto Rican women poets who live in the United States–the aforementioned Luz María Umpierre and Giannina Braschi (b. 1954), Magdalena Gómez (b. 1954), Rosario Morales (b. 1930), Aurora Levins Morales (b. 1954), and Marithelma Costa (b. 1955), among others–who are creating a strong body of poetry in different styles, with different themes and emphases, a poetry that mirrors the complex issues involving race, gender, nationality, and migration. Many write in Spanish or use the two languages with some degree of prominence.

Women who write prose are also striving to overcome their invisibility. They seem to prefer autobiographical novels (or bildungsromans), which have the effect of placing the feminine subject at the center of the action, thus overcoming her marginality but also reducing the scope of women's experience to a single individual's insight.

Nicholasa Mohr was the first to document migrant Puerto Rican women's lives in a semi autobiographical mode in *Nilda* (1973), a novel about a girl who grows up in the Barrio in a hard-working lower-middle-class family. The gently developing story line follows Nilda's growing consciousness of the family's economic hardships and the disruption of traditional ties. A different street culture is seen encroaching on the atmosphere of the home. Nilda becomes conscious of that difference while she is kept somewhat shielded from the turbulence of the first line of confrontation taking place outside the apartment, the school, and the summer camp. In some of her other books, *El Bronx Remembered* (1975), *In Nueva York* (1977), *Felita* (1979), and *Rituals of Survival: A Woman's Portfolio* (1985), Mohr has continued to explore women's lives in relation to their cultural and social context. In 1994 she published a full-fledged memoir, *In My Own Words: Growing Up Inside the Sanctuary of My Imagination.*

Recent novelized memoirs or semi-autobiographical novels by Puerto Rican women in the United States have established a continuity of sorts with Mohr's *Nilda. The Line of the Sun* (1989) by Judith Ortiz-Cofer (b. 1952), who lives in Georgia, develops two parallel stories. On the one hand, there is a somewhat mythical Puerto Rico constructed out of family tales and folklore, with a family black sheep at its center. On the other hand, there is a young girl growing up divided between a Latino household and a typical U.S. education in Paterson, New Jersey. The book reclaims the unusual past of the first part for a girl in the United States who is in the process of getting used to a different way of life from that of her forebears.

Ortiz-Cofer, who has also written poems and essays, has achieved a powerful metaphor for the discrepancies of Puerto Rican migrants within U.S. society in the essay "Silent Dancing." In it, a home movie of people dancing is being shown without sound. The familiar experience of dancing becomes incongruous when done without music, seeming to allude to the way Puerto Ricans go through the motions of their own culture without an adequate context while living in the United States: "It is both comical and sad to watch silent dancing. Since there is no justification for the absurd movements that music provides for some of us, people appear frantic, their faces embarrassingly intense" (Ortiz-Cofer 95).

Another narrative, avowedly autobiographical, also has a young feminine protagonist, this time in a rags-to-riches story. Negi, in Esmeralda Santiago's (b. 1948) *When I Was Puerto Rican* (1993), starts out her life in a rural community on the Island. The deteriorating relationship between her parents determines her mother's move, with her numerous brood, to the United States. There they all have to come to grips with the wider social issue of discrimination before ultimately attaining one of the biggest rewards the United States has to offer: A college education at prestigious Harvard University.

The usual course of the American Dream narrative is reversed, however, because academic success and financial independence U.S.-style, even though they seem to pave the road to fame and fortune, or at least to full integration within U.S. society, also exact a price. Negi's goal is only to be achieved, it seems, at the expense of a profound uprooting and an implied break from her origins, as indicated by the past tense used in the title and the nostalgic tone of the prologue.

(A similar implied critique of U.S. values can be found in Alba Ambert's (b. 1946) 1995 first novel, *A Perfect Silence*. This writer, who is also a poet and has published short stories, has her protagonist attain a Harvard education that cannot save her from a crushing breakdown brought on by inner and outer alienation.) In *Almost a Woman* (1998), the second part of Esmeralda Santiago's memoirs, she continues the exploration begun in *When I Was Puerto Rican*, concentrating on the teenage years. The usual adolescent trauma of breaking away is compounded by a deeper break with a collective past associated with another culture, one that is aptly called a "mother" culture.

Racial considerations are also an important aspect of Puerto Rican writing in the United States. Present in Piri Thomas's and Tato Laviera's works (they are both black men), race and its implications are also central in Louis Reyes Rivera's poetry, of which he has published three volumes: *Who Pays the Cost* (1977), *This One for You* (1983), and *Scattered Scripture* (1996), all of which have come out of his own small publishing house, Shamal Books. In this poetry, Reyes Rivera emphasizes the common historical, cultural, and aesthetic roots of Antillean and U.S. people with African ascendancy as the source of similar experiences that give rise to specific rhythmic patterns and other literary resources that do not depend on language itself: "We came to use the language as difference, but language is not a difference because all five languages that are spoken in this hemisphere were imposed on all of us. So we cannot really use Spanish as a defense because it is not genuinely our language" (Carmen Dolores Hernández 125). Reyes Rivera is aware of the nuances of racism, from the Caribbean variety (which appears to be subtler and less aggressive but is nevertheless present and limiting in the social and professional fields) to the North American variety. If it is all part of one same situation of injustice and oppression, then "black" poetry comes from the same tradition, be it written in English or in Spanish. It was the Harlem renaissance and the resurgence of a black political affirmation that first seemed to point this way. Writers Claude McKay—whose book of poetry, *Harlem Shadows,* was one of the first literary successes of that movement—and Wilfred Adolphus Domingo were born in Jamaica. Also born there was Marcus Garvey, who during the early 1920s galvanized African American political sentiment in the United States, thus setting the stage for an increased racial cultural consciousness that occurred simultaneously with a burst of literary production. Langston Hughes, on the other hand, went to Cuba in 1931 and became acquainted with Afro-Caribbean poetry. He translated many of Nicolás Guillén's writings into English.

The poetry of both Louis Reyes Rivera and Tato Laviera is indebted not only to Afro-Caribbean poetry and to the Négritude movement but also to African American poets like Ishmael Reed and Imamu Amiri Baraka (LeRoi Jones). The latter used his writing as a political instrument and founded the Black Repertory Theater of Harlem, with which Sandra María Esteves was closely associated, thus bringing together the Nuyorican and "black" aspects of Puerto Rican poetry in the United States, both of which were entirely open to including different ethnic responses to the challenge posed by the New York style of U.S. experience.

Where have these writers found their models? What stimulated them to resort to the written word as a form of expression and communication? Their work shows a pervasive influence of the oral tradition, which may have been received by direct means such as by the telling of family stories and traditional lore or through the influence of the radio, which many refer to as crucial in their artistic development. (The presence of Spanish-speaking radio in the United States dates back to the 1920s.)

Popular Puerto Rican music, which was recorded to a significant extent in New York during the 1930s and 1940s, is also an influence. The Puerto Rican music scene in the United States, especially in New York, provides, in fact, sharp contrasts with the literary scene. In the 1920s–and even before, when Puerto Rican musicians were recruited to form part of the African American military bands that went to Europe with the troops during World War I–there began a fertile, creative intermingling of different musical traditions, especially noticeable in the relationship established between African American and Puerto Rican musicians: "Within the context of World War I began a process of migration and a cultural exchange between two groups, African-Americans and Puerto Ricans, that would last for many years" (Glasser 32). In 1934 Augusto Coen organized a band with Puerto Rican musicians, Augusto Coen y sus Boricuas, which developed a distinct style, using the American big band sound and adapting it to the type of popular music played in the Spanish Caribbean: *boleros, guarachas, sones, plenas,* and *danzas* (Glasser 82). The quintessential Puerto Rican composer of popular songs, Rafael Hernández (1891–1964), spent a good part of his life in New York, where he formed the Trío Borinquen in 1926 and the Cuarteto Victoria in 1932. Pedro Flores (1897–1979), another well-known composer of *boleros,* also lived and worked there for a time, as did Manuel "Canario" Jiménez (1895–1975), identified with the *plena.* "During the thirties," according to music scholar Jorge Javariz, "there was a virtual invasion of Puerto Rican musicians in New York . . . to understand the magnitude of that exile, suffice it to say that the major part of popular Puerto Rican music . . . was written in New York, which makes Puerto Rico . . . the only Latin American country whose music was composed in another country with a different language and culture" (Javariz 52). "Puerto Rican music," affirms Glasser, "came into its own in the context of the migration experience. While musical eclecticism and social boundaries existed in Puerto Rico, they were different in New York . . . . Music that Puerto Rican migrants could identify as their own gave them an enduring heritage and . . . immortalized a way of life that back home was fast disappearing" (Glasser 92).

This situation is relevant to the topic of Puerto Rican literature in the United States in two ways. First, it seems somewhat ironic that such highly patriotic songs as "Lamento borincano" (Hernández), "Sin bandera" (Flores), and "En mi viejo San Juan" (Estrada) were composed and first recorded in New York (it was Canario y su Grupo who first recorded "Lamento borincano" there in 1930). Although these songs have been accepted and cherished on the Island as quintessential national productions, the same thing has not happened with Puerto Rican literature written in the United States. Second, the fact that there has been such a wealth of Puerto Rican–and Caribbean–popular musical activity going on in New York since the 1920s points to the strong oral tradition that nourished Puerto Rican writers there. Indeed, many of them speak of such music (and also that of the country's *improvisadores,* or troubadors, who made up verses as they sang) as a much stronger influence in their writing than a strictly literary tradition.

For most Puerto Rican writers in the United States, the Island has been a problem both in itself and in relation to the society in which they find themselves. Some have a love-hate relationship with Puerto Rico and look back in anger and disappointment; others look back with some degree of sadness and longing. Still others mythologize the Island as a lost paradise from which they were forcibly ejected.

Yet although second-generation Puerto Ricans in the United States (or even first-generation ones) are already different from those who live on the Island, they are not, in many instances, being assimilated into the famous "melting pot." What makes migrants from a second or even a third generation retain a distinctive Puerto Rican identification? Why the resistance to melting away?

Some writers, such as Ed Vega (b. 1938), allude to race as the reason Puerto Ricans will not assimilate fully into the U.S. mainstream. (They would have to identify themselves as black or white. Since many of them are not, in fact, white and since to be identified as black would entail a considerable amount of prejudice, they prefer to remain Puerto Rican.) Since Puerto Ricans are already U.S. citizens, there is no need to make any further effort to blend in, according to Esmeralda Santiago. A more generalized view is that the frequency and ease with which Puerto Ricans go to and from the Island to the mainland constantly renews their contact with their "roots" and keeps alive the hope of returning. During the 1970s, there was a reversal of the migratory trend from the Island to the United States, as some studies have shown (Hernández Cruz).

Writers must help the nascent community to re-imagine itself through new perspectives. Having reclaimed a distinctive past through their own texts and by referring to common traditions, they must define, in imaginary terms, their present and project the future. Their position is two-edged; it often applies to the island of origin the critical stance to which those who have championed a cause through thick and thin are entitled. They can possibly see more clearly than those who are immersed in Puerto Rican society the changes that have occurred and the transformations that are taking place. Moreover, the close contact with other cultures has given them a breadth of outlook difficult to attain within insular confines. Perhaps a new kind of *mestizaje* could promote a broader comprehension of a hybrid kind of society, where contact and conflict result in a dynamic, energetic culture. U.S. Puerto Ricans are constantly crossing over the linguistic and cultural frontier between the Island and the mainland. Their experience may be immensely valuable since, in the words of Homi Bhabha,

> a range of contemporary critical theories suggest that it is from those who have suffered the sentence of history–subjugation, domination, diaspora, displacement–that we learn our most enduring lessons for living and thinking. There is even a growing conviction that the affective experience of social marginality–as it emerges in non-canonical cultural forms–transforms our critical strategies. It forces us to confront the concept of culture outside *objets d'art* or beyond the canonization of the "idea" of aesthetics, to engage with culture as an uneven, incomplete production of meaning and value, often composed of incommensurable demands and practices, produced in the act of social survival. (Bhabha 172)

How does Puerto Rico relate to these writers? It has, for the most part, ignored them. Save for a few scholars who have studied and anthologized the writings of U.S. Puerto Ricans (mostly their poetry), a void has surrounded their texts, the immense majority of which are not even translated into Spanish and have not been distributed in Puerto Rico. The main reason for this is that they write in English. Spanish is not only the language commonly used in Puerto Rico, but it has also become a symbol of the Island's national identity, in conflict with what is traditionally considered, especially by an important intellectual and artistic elite, to be an encroaching cultural imperialism on the part of the United States:

In the early twentieth century, as the United States overhauled Puerto Rican institutions by fiat, Puerto Ricans' sense of difference was reinforced, and so were their opposition to U.S. domination and their attachment to symbols felt to be under attack. Language is paramount here. . . . Throughout the century, language has both engendered opposition and provided an excuse for it (Morris 153). Within this context, which directly affected the elite from which most writers emerged in Puerto Rico, literature has traditionally been assigned the mission to preserve linguistic integrity and purity. There is thus little room for English-speaking and -writing Puerto Ricans in traditional cultural circles, no matter how passionately those writers might also resist assimilation into the U.S. reality. Their language represents a problem that not many people know how to face. The easiest way out is simply to ignore their existence, developing a blind spot toward their literary production. Although this attitude is changing, especially among younger intellectuals, many of whom have been educated in the United States, the consensus is still against an English-language Puerto Rican literature. There is, however, a slowly growing perception that while the preservation of a community's language is very important for a colonized people, there is also danger in "the fixity and fetishim of identities within the calcification of colonial cultures" (Bhabha 9).

The cultural contribution of Puerto Ricans in the United States must be acknowledged on both the Island and the mainland as part of the continuous transactions that culture must engage in if it is to endure as a living, dynamic force that inflames and inspires a society. Besides enriching U.S. literature with the traditions born of the contradictions of a Spanish-speaking Caribbean island relocated to the largest city in the United States, the literature written by Puerto Ricans in the United States can still contribute something to the Island's cultural diversity. To be closed to new experiences is a neoconservative stance "associated with a past that is no longer recoverable except by denying or somehow downgrading the lived experience of those who, in Aimé Césaire's great phrase, want a place at the rendezvous of victory" (Said 12). This goes for both sides of the cultural frontier that the Puerto Ricans are straddling.

Works Cited

Agueros, Jack. 1993. *Dominoes & Other Stories from the Puerto Rican.* Willimantic, CT: Curbstone Press.

Algarín, Miguel. 1975. "Introduction: Nuyorican Language." *Nuyorican Poetry: An Anthology of Puerto Rican Words and Feelings.* Ed. Miguel Algarín and Miguel Piñero. New York: Morrow. 9–20.

Aparicio, Frances R. 1988. "La vida es un Spanglish disparatero: Bilingualism in Nuyorican Poetry." *European Perspectives on Hispanic Literature of the United States.* Ed. Geneviève Fabre. Houston, TX: Arte Público Press. 147–60.

Bhabha, Homi K. 1994. *The Location of Culture.* New York: Routledge.

Colón, Jesús. 1961. *A Puerto Rican in New York, and Other Sketches.* New York: Mainstream Publishers.

Esteves, Sandra María. 1980. "From the Commonwealth." *Yerba buena: dibujos y poemas.* New York: Greenfield Review Press. 49.

Foucault, Michel. 1984. "What Is an Author?" *The Foucault Reader.* Ed. Paul Rabinow. New York: Pantheon Books. 101–20.

Glasser, Ruth. 1995. *My Music Is My Flag: Puerto Rican Musicians and Their New York Communities 1917–1940.* Berkeley: University of California Press.

Hernández, Carmen Dolores. 1997. *Puerto Rican Voices in English: Interviews with Writers.* Westport, CT: Praeger.

Hernández Cruz, Juan. 1994. *Migratory Trends in Puerto Rico.* San Germán, PR: Universidad Interamericana de Puerto Rico.

Javariz, Jorge. 1998. "Músicos puertorriqueños en Nueva York: 1898–1960." *La marcha de los jíbaros, 1898–1997: cien años de música puertorriqueña por el mundo.* Río Piedras, PR: Plaza Mayor. 47–82.

Laviera, Tato. 1991. *La Carreta Made a U-Turn.* Houston, TX: Arte Público Press.

Mohr, Nicholasa. 1973. *Nilda: A Novel.* New York: Harper & Row.

Morris, Nancy. 1995. *Puerto Rico: Culture, Politics, and Identity.* Westport, CT: Praeger.

Ortiz-Cofer, Judith. 1990. *Silent Dancing: A Partial Remembrance of a Puerto Rican Childhood.* Houston, TX: Arte Público Press.

Rivera-Batiz, Francisco L., and Carlos Santiago. 1994. *Puerto Ricans in the United States: A Changing Reality.* Washington, DC: National Puerto Rican Coalition.

Rodríguez, Abraham. 1993. *Spidertown: A Novel.* New York: Hyperion.

Said, Edward. 1994. *Representations of the Intellectual: The 1993 Reith Lectures.* New York: Pantheon Books.

Santiago, Esmeralda. 1993. *When I Was Puerto Rican.* Reading, MA: Addison-Wesley.

———. 1998. *Almost a Woman.* Reading, MA: Perseus Books.

Thomas, Piri. 1967. *Down These Mean Streets.* New York: Knopf.

Torres, Edwin. 1975. *Carlito's Way.* New York: Saturday Review Press.

Vega, Bernardo. 1988. *Memorias de Bernardo Vega: contribución a la historia de la comunidad puertorriqueña en Nueva York.* Ed. César Andreu Iglesias. 4th ed. Río Piedras, PR: Ediciones Huracán.

Vega, Ed. 1985. *The Comeback.* Houston, TX: Arte Público Press.

———. 1987. *Mendoza's Dreams.* Houston, TX: Arte Público Press.

———. 1991. *Casualty Report.* Houston, TX: Arte Público Press.

CHAPTER 37

CONSTRUCTION OF NEW CULTURAL IDENTITIES

PUERTO RICAN THEATER IN NEW YORK

Grace Dávila-López

The theater produced by Puerto Ricans in New York is rooted in two cultural traditions: Spanish-language Puerto Rican theater and English-language Anglo-American theater. The terms coined to name it (Nuyorican, U.S. Puerto Rican, AmeRican, American–Puerto Rican, *neoyorican, neorriqueño, nuyorriqueño*) reflect its intrinsically hybrid history. They also show the complexity of classifying and analyzing a theater that, although derived from specific national roots (Puerto Rico), has been transformed by its relationship with a new geosocial environment (the poor sectors of New York City) and the U.S. social, political, and cultural structures that have determined it.

Since the 1980s, a pro-multicultural movement in the United States and especially in New York City has fostered the development and dissemination of Hispanic work, although this does not necessarily mean that sufficient effort has been made to understand its complexity. It is not uncommon for Chicano, Cuban-American, or Nuyorican plays, as well as translations of Latin American theater produced in the United States to be regarded as if they were all the same, often simply as ethnic theater. This homogenizing reductionism overlooks the national origins of these theaters and their function in the communities that produced them. The case of the Puerto Rican theater produced in New York is highly unusual, in that the members of this community arrived in the United States carrying their naturalization papers. The scant critical attention paid to the development of Puerto Rican theater in New York reveals the political and cultural processes and the strategies of exclusion of a cultural expression condemned to liminality.

It is difficult to discuss this new theater in terms of either the aesthetic or ideological ideals of the United States or Puerto Rico. For Puerto Rican critics, English-language plays serve as a metaphor for the colonial domination of the island. The use of English jeopardizes the nationalistic interests that have used Spanish as a means of resisting U.S. dominance. At the same time, U.S. critics see Puerto Rican theater as yet another variant of Hispanic theater. References to the island, the peculiarities of Latin life, the process of social and cultural survival, presented with a smattering of Spanish words, are features that afford the thematic possibility of validating the co-existence of the Puerto Rican as other. To these critics, this theater's legitimization celebrates U.S. cultural diversity and the possibility of integrating new groups socially, but without having to consider that there are real political problems involving a separate Puerto Rico. Response to this theater is thus torn between two opposing forces that correspond to specific political and cultural motivations: Homogenizing U.S. criticism and Puerto Rican criticism, which seeks reinforcement of its own policy of resistance. Yet the reality of this unique theater is that it has evolved in a myriad of ways into expressions adjusted to the changing needs of its community, continuously struggling against simplistic typecasting and seeking a more profound self-definition.

A Bifurcated Theater Moving in Multiple Directions

Mass Puerto Rican migration to New York is a phenomenon associated with the 1950s and the well-known political strategy Operation Bootstrap. It is, however, a phenomenon that began much earlier. Nicolás Kanellos, in *A History of Hispanic Theater in the United States: Origins to 1940,* explains that New York had been the seat of expatriate Spanish families since the 1820s. This elite, consisting of the well-to-do, politicians, and artists, formed a community that produced cultural activities from the outset. It is hardly surprising, then, that the wave of Caribbean political expatriates that arrived during the second half of the nineteenth century should have met with social and cultural acceptance in this community. The Puerto Rican *criollos* were the last Caribbeans to join these elites, at a time when there was already a cultural apparatus and theatrical spaces that served as a forum for the political ideas of the time. When Puerto Rico became a U.S. territory in 1898, and particularly after Puerto Ricans obtained U.S. citizenship in 1917, Puerto Rican migration to the United States increased, concentrating in New York, where cultural links already existed. From the beginning of the twentieth century, this city had attracted the attention of Puerto Rican intellectuals and artists pursuing their studies as temporarily resident there.

Puerto Ricans also have a long history, dating back to the end of the nineteenth century, of migration to other parts of the United States, to as far away as Hawaii. The waves of immigration increased after the Second World War and reached epic proportions from the 1950s onward, thanks to Operation Bootstrap. Its aim was to create an escape valve that would solve the acute problem of unemployment on the island as a result of the transformation of an agricultural into a primarily manufacturing economy. For the Puerto Rican nationalists, the economic project constituted a form of cultural aggression. Writers who visited New York used the theme of migrating to the metropolis as a metaphor for this loss of identity, although their messages were aimed at educated Puerto Ricans rather than poor, uneducated workers.

René Marqués's (1919–1979) *La Carreta* (1951) marked the formal start of the history of Puerto Rican theater in New York. It is interesting to note that this text constitutes a landmark in the history of Puerto Rican theater, but it is also the beginning of Nuyorican theater, because this quintessentially Puerto Rican play actually opened in New York City. Its premiere in Spanish (1953), as well as its performance in English over a decade later (1966) as *The Oxcart,* was extremely well received. Through three acts called "Vignettes," the play tells the story of a peasant family forced to leave the countryside for the slums of San Juan and, subsequently, New York City in search of a better life. Life in San Juan exposes them to a degree of poverty that leads to the ruin of both the younger son, who is sent to reform school, and Juanita, the daughter, who attempts suicide after having an abortion. The journey to

New York appears as an opportunity to improve their lives, but these hopes are dashed when Luis, the older son, dies in a factory accident, a victim of the very notion of progress that brought them to New York. The despair of life in the city surpasses that of the countryside, and the poverty of their situation in New York, together with the cold, the isolation, the racism, and the loss of human values, lead to the moral destruction of the family. The final words of the play, uttered by the matriarch Doña Gabriela, serve as a criticism of the cultural loss represented by migration and suggest returning to the island: "Hay que volver a lo que dajamoh pa que no nos persiga máh la mardisión de la tierra" (1975, 171) ("We must go back to what we left behind so that the curse won't pursue us anymore"; 1969, 153).

This image of a poor family destroyed by succumbing to the illusion of progress became the national metaphor for cultural loss and for the dilemma of the individual having to choose between financial security and personal and national dignity. *La Carreta* created the thematic basis for Nuyorican theater, although it was not itself Nuyorican. Its message was that life in New York City brought about the moral and spiritual degradation of this transplanted family, and even destroyed its identity. The underlying idea was that Puerto Ricans in New York actually had the choice of remaining or returning. This response served patriotic, pro-Independence interests, without dealing with the real economic reasons for the migration or the possibility of creating an alternative identity.

The reason *La Carreta* is considered part of the history of Nuyorican theater is the polyvalency of its message. It is important to understand that the fact that certain Puerto Rican texts have become part of the history of Nuyorican theater does not mean that they will be interpreted in the same way in the Puerto Rican and New York contexts. The return to the island suggested in *La Carreta* is a more appropriate solution for the nationalist interests that had lost ground to U.S. interests than for actual farm workers who never owned their native soil. For Puerto Ricans on the island, the text warns of the danger of migration. For Puerto Ricans in New York who will not return to the island, it serves to boost positive feelings of Puerto Rican identity and the newfound personal power these feelings give. The cultural imagination of the new community is developed through a symbolic return to their roots rather than through their actual return to the island.

The 1970s saw the emergence of a Puerto Rican theater in English. Inspired by the U.S. black civil rights struggles of the 1960s, the flamboyant demonstrations of the Young Lords, and the empowering openness to various social problems, the new playwrights focused on the specific issues faced by the poor sectors with which they identified. Texts from this period depict the harsh life of the streets, poverty, racism, domestic violence and, above all, the generation gap between first-, second- and third-generation Puerto Ricans. Although the islander Jaime Carrero (b. 1931) and the Nuyorican Miguel Piñero (1946–1988) have both explored these issues, it is interesting to see how the ideological messages of their texts in fact diverge.

Despite the fact that Jaime Carrero writes in Spanish, he identifies strongly with the Nuyorican community and is also regarded as a leading figure in the development of Puerto Rican theater. His texts describe the negative aspects of the life of Puerto Ricans in New York, who are regarded as second-class citizens. He criticizes the forced economic migration and other effects of an unresolved economic and political situation on the island. *Flag Inside* (1973), for example, takes place in Puerto Rico and concerns a family's dilemma around burying a son who has died in Vietnam, the victim of a war in which he did not believe. The family is forced to decide whether or not the coffin should bear the U.S. flag or else religious ornaments, respectively representing external and internal values. *Pipo Subway no sabe reir* [1973; Pipo Subway Does Not Know How to Laugh] depicts the frustrated life of a child of the slums, showing how the violence of the streets of New York, poverty, frustration, and apathy lead him to kill for the sake of a bicycle. The violence and the obscene language that characterize these plays have become a tradition in Nuyorican literature in English, but in Puerto Rico they both serve as warnings against life in New York and, ultimately, adversely affect the social image of Nuyoricans.

In *Short Eyes* (1974), Miguel Piñero cultivated this dramaturgy of violence, expressing what he experienced himself during his stay in a New York prison. His stark portrait of the relationship between criminals in a New York prison earned critical recognition for its uncompromising style. Joseph Papp, the godfather of Latin theater in New York, supported the launching of his career because, as he notes in the introduction to the published text, he quickly detected the dramatic honesty of Piñero's crude, corrosive style, which was sometimes difficult for the U.S. middle class to tolerate. The play soon earned widespread recognition, after it received the Obie Prize and the New York Drama Critics' Circle Award for the best U.S. work during the 1973–1974 season. Ironically, the openness that this drama achieved in U.S. critical space distanced it from Puerto Rican theater because of its failure to incorporate island spaces, motifs, or references. Its characters speak English street slang and have established means of survival that are inherent to their surroundings. The text has never been translated into Spanish or performed on the island, and so constitutes the beginning of a cultural, aesthetic, and ideological divide. Whereas Pipo Subway or the dead soldier of *Flag Inside* are the victims of their surroundings, Piñero's characters have managed to survive their environment, which they now control, and have become the contemptible heroes of an upside-down world in which survival must be achieved at all costs. This text marks the transition from Puerto Rican theater in New York to Nuyorican theater.

Theater of New Attitudes

The high profile achieved by Nuyorican theater cannot be attributed to a mere handful of dramatists. The 1960s saw the emergence of artistic and cultural groups and activities that promoted the incipient performing arts. Joseph Papp not only boosted the careers of authors such as Piñero, but he also incorporated Spanish translations into his New York Shakespeare Festival. This openness was crucial to the success of the Latino Festival in New York, held every year since the mid-1970s. The Puerto Rican Traveling Theater (PRTT) was created in 1967. Its founder, actress, and director, Miriam Colón (b. 1936), originally formed a traveling theater group that took performances to Hispanic neighborhoods in New York. Once the group acquired permanent premises, she stepped up her efforts to make theater of Puerto Rican, Latin American, and classical Spanish origin known to a growing and highly diversified audience. Her work expanded to include acting and drama workshops, providing the Hispanic community with theater models, and promoting dramatists, including Jaime Carrero, Edward Gallardo (b. 1949), and, more recently, Federico Fraguada (b. 1952).

In 1967, Pedro Santaliz (b. 1938) founded the New Poor Theater of America. Influenced by the dramaturgy of Jerzy Grotowski (b. 1933) and his concepts of transformative, minimalist theater, he took performances on popular themes to poor communities in New York and Puerto Rico. *Olla* (1986), for example, is about characters who are so overwhelmed by their personal problems that they have become alienated from themselves. Interaction draws them into a vibrant, enjoyable ritual ceremony that transforms them into a community. Santaliz continues to organize creative workshops for members of poor communities. Miguel Algarín (b. 1941), who has been credited with coining the term *Nuyorican,* inaugurated the Nuyorican Poets' Café in 1974. Except for a few interruptions, this has provided space for poetic and dramatic readings, for literary gatherings, and for listening to and improvising music. It spawned *Olú Clemente* (1979), a collective musical text by Algarín and the poet Tato Laviera (b. 1950) on the life of the baseball player Roberto Clemente. More recently, this center has hosted its own theater festival. The Puerto Rican Bilingual Workshop, created by Carlos Pinza in 1973, began by performing island theater in Spanish, but subsequently incorporated Hispanic theater in English. Grupo Pregones, created in 1979, has performed Puerto Rican plays in Spanish and produced group theater. Its participation in U.S. and international tours and festivals, with its versatile performance of *Quíntuples* [1985; Quintuplets] by Luis Rafael Sánchez (b. 1936), has given it considerable exposure. There are also mixed U.S.-Hispanic theater groups that have benefited the new Nuyorican playwrights and actors; this is why it is now possible to speak of cross-influences and hybrid models. The Spanish Repertory Theater has been active since 1969, with the performance of classical Spanish and Latin American theater, as well as *zarzuelas.* Since 1977, INTAR (International Arts Relations) has promoted the development of Hispanic playwrights. Its organizers and members have come from various countries, but participants such as the Cuban María Irene Fornés (b. 1931) have exercised a particularly strong influence over the new generations. Teatro Cuatro (1974), organized by the Argentinian Oscar Ciccone and the Salvadoran Cecilia Vega, served as a link between Latin American and U.S. Hispanic theater, incorporating several Nuyorican actors and themes into its repertoire. Although the group dissolved, Ciccone continued to organize the Latino Festival.

Over the years, with the interaction between drama groups and workshops, the history of Nuyorican theater has become inextricably linked with other groups with which it shares dramatic styles and themes. What still characterizes the cultural development of Nuyorican theater is its focus on themes that reveal an awareness of the changing identity of New York's Puerto Ricans. During the 1970s and 1980s, Edward Gallardo explored the theme of uprooting, particularly focusing on intergenerational conflicts and the feeling of guilt they produce, in works like *Simpson Street* (1979) and *Women without Men* (1985). *Simpson Street* concerns the return home of Michael, a mentally disturbed youth who has attempted suicide. Now he must once again face this world of fixed social values and family expectations he does not share, and cope with his own sense of guilt. His decision to leave, because of his rejection of the stifling conditions at home, will not surprise an Anglo-American public, for whom leaving home is a sign of independence. However, the character's decision to go off to California constitutes a significant break with the expectations articulated in *La Carreta,* where the response is to return home,

to the island. Michael's decision to go anywhere but Puerto Rico and his optimism about the possibility of starting a new life reflect a change of attitude characteristic of Nuyorican theater. The break with the family values that constrain him heralds the emergence of a new identity, one that is not created by geographical space but by a sense of personal worth.

The bilingual musical comedy, *Charge It to My Account/Cárguelo a mi cuenta,* staged in 1991 by Carlos Gorbea (b. 1940), is a good example of how the theme of returning to the island has been dealt with at the popular level. This amusing performance by the Puerto Rican Traveling Theater depicts the complicated life of a widow who discovers the power of credit cards. When she falls dangerously into debt, her relatives suggest she flee the country to avoid her creditors. The widow, who had hitherto appeared as a weak character, in a moment of great determination offers an unexpected musical response: "To go back never. I have lived and I have learned. Now I know better." Escaping to Puerto Rico is depicted as an act of personal cowardice; she decides to deal with her financial problems in order to be able to remain in her home, New York. This type of comedy has been extremely well received in New York's popular theaters, where the audience identifies with characters who have to carve out their own future, overcome obstacles, and adjust to their new situation.

The anthology *Recent Puerto Rican Theater: Five Plays from New York* (1991) contains texts by Federico Fraguada, Juan Shamsul Alam (b. 1946), Richard Irrizary (1956–1994), Ivette Ramírez (b. 1969), and Cándido Tirado (b. 1950). John Antush, the editor, summarizes the new attitude of these playwrights as a desire to become integrated into U.S. culture without betraying their Puerto Rican roots; this marks a radical change from the time when, according to Antush, the identity crisis was the greatest cultural export produced on the island.

Bodega (1986), by Federico Fraguada, provides an example of this new attitude toward New York as a permanent home. The play describes the tensions in a grocer's family; after he has achieved a degree of financial stability in a neighborhood that has become violent, Elena, his wife, begs him to return to the island for the children's sake. The grocer is reluctant to leave what he regards as his home. Moreover, he is bound by his duty toward the members of his community who rely on his credit and support when times are hard. When the grocer is killed by a drug addict toward the end of the play, Elena thinks things over and decides to stay in New York: "I'm not letting anybody run me out of my home" (79). This attitude clearly differs sharply from that of Doña Gabriela and her daughter in *La Carreta.*

Racism is another theme that has been explored by Nuyorican playwrights. In *Vejigantes* (1958), Francisco Arriví (b. 1915) had denounced the Puerto Rican obsession with whitening—in other words, the desire to improve one's stock by marrying someone with paler skin. This obsession entailed hiding relatives whose complexion betrayed the family's racial history. In *Women without Men* (1985), Edward Gallardo explores the theme of the dark family secret that still threatens a pro-white society, and denounces the hypocritical racism that attempts to make amends for the social transgressions of the past. Richard V. Irizarry's *Ariano* (1984) is the first work that openly deals with the theme of racial self-hatred. Ariano is a light-skinned mulatto who marries Dolores (also a mulatto); the couple have a child, who is much darker-skinned than either of them. This lack of racial "improvement" unhinges Ariano, who is ashamed of his black heritage. Dolores, however, makes an effort to understand this form of racism: "All my life the same thing. And from my own people! *Que sí* who's from Spain, who's not from Spain" (224). She concludes that Ariano's lack of affection for his son is due to his self-loathing, a complex that must be dealt with before coping with external prejudice. Dolores, in the affirmative ending, explains to her son: "You're not black. And you're not white! You're not red or yellow or any one color! You are all of these! That is the beauty of what a Puerto Rican is, and don't you let anybody ever tell you any different! You tell them, . . . yo soy el nuevo puertorriqueño! I'm the new breed! And . . . I respect myself! And . . . whoever doesn't like it, que se vaya pa la mierda! Straight to hell!" (226). The Spanish version of this play was well received on the island. Its energetic, direct treatment of racism, rarely explored in Puerto Rican theater, emerged as a model for the construction of national and racial identity that has made a positive contribution to the treatment of the theme in both places. Despite this, it is worth noting that Irizarry's characters never question racism in New York; yet their self-construction as new Puerto Ricans (Nuyoricans) sets them apart and serves as a source of affirmative power.

The Case of Female Playwrights

The relations between female Puerto Rican theater and that of Nuyoricans has not been well documented. Very few women have achieved national recognition in the history of the theater of the island. The best-known and most frequently studied has been Myrna Casas (b. 1934), who has written plays since the 1960s. Some of her plays have been performed in New York, such as "El gran circo EUKraniano" [*The Great USkranian Circus*] (Latino Festival, 1989) with its anti-colonial message, which has recently been translated into English. Lydia Milagros González (b. 1942), wrote and directed street theater in Spanish in the 1960s and 1970s and was deeply involved with the Nuyorican community. Her texts, with their social criticism and nationalist Puerto Rican message, compiled in *Libretos para el Tajo del Alacrán* [1980; Librettos for the Tajo del Alacrán], were performed in poor neighborhoods in Puerto Rico and New York. Although her street theater sought to explore street characters and reaffirm their positive qualities, her ultimate aim was to aid the Puerto Rican social struggle and, above all, to depict the U.S. establishment as the enemy of the interests of Puerto Rican workers.

The plays produced by Migdalia Cruz (b. 1958) and Ivette Ramírez, two of the handful of female Nuyorican playwrights to have published texts, are quite different from the social-pro-nationalistic tone of Casas, González, or any playwright from the island. These contain references to Puerto Rican roots without becoming plays about any crisis of identity. Instead, they focus on the female experience in a changing world and the search for solutions to personal or familial conflicts. Ivette Ramírez's *Family Scenes* (1989) deals with the theme of the generation gap between women. The play concerns two sisters living with their mother, a divorcée who nonetheless holds traditional values. The elder sister, Paula, wants to invite their estranged father to her wedding. At this uncomfortable reunion, the father threatens to reveal that Paula is an illegitimate daughter to whom he gave his surname so that the mother would marry him. The play's predictably tragic ending is given a sudden twist when Paula reveals that his false paternity is not a secret and that she has also had to struggle with a pregnancy as a single woman.

Paula, however, dealt with it differently than her mother: "I wasn't going to make your mistake. I wasn't going to have a kid without being married. So, I had an abortion" (254). Faced with the shame of being an unmarried mother, her mother had accepted a marriage of convenience; faced with the same situation, the daughter opted for an abortion. Whereas in *La Carreta*, Juanita's "sin" was synonymous with moral degradation, for the new generations, abortion is an option. Although this medical procedure is not depicted as a happy solution to an unwanted pregnancy, it exemplifies a change in attitude toward personal and social problems. Lynette Serrano also deals with the issue of abortion. Her text *Broken Bough* was performed by the Hispanic Playwright Project in California in 1988. In this play the protagonist, Angela, feels guilty about an abortion she had when she was very young and feels pursued by an evil spirit; she resorts to a witch-doctor, but finds relief in her husband's love.

In *The Have-Little* (1996) and *Miriam's Flowers* (1992), Migdalia Cruz explores the world of poverty in the South Bronx based on her personal experience. Her works are characterized by the intimate, direct style with which she develops the tragic situations in which her young characters are trapped. In her first work, *The Have-Little*, Lilliana Rivera, a fourteen-year-old girl, has to balance an incestuous relationship with her alcoholic father, the generational conflict with her dying mother, and her boyfriend's death from a drug overdose with her wish to have a child. This depressing scenario is relieved only by the warmth of Lilliana, who keeps a diary in an attempt to put some order in the tumultuous world of her feelings. Although the situation is desperate, and her wish to have a child is immature and irresponsible, the humanity and tenderness with which the character responds to her circumstances reveal an unusual beauty that can only be appreciated in contrast to Lilliana's harsh reality.

Miriam's Flowers portrays the disintegration of a poor family from New York when the younger son is run over by a train. The father blames himself and becomes violently overprotective of Miriam, who is just entering adolescence. The mother closes herself off in a world of long, hypnotic baths that evoke her childhood on the island. Miriam responds with strange sexual rites, the horror and pain of which bring her closer to the memory of her brother. She carves beautiful flowers into her skin that make her cry, and she says: ". . . and I like that, 'cause when I get those tears on my hands and on my arms, they sting, and then I know I'm alive, 'cause it hurts so bad" (71). In Cruz's texts, poverty reduces the characters' world to increasingly alienated and restricted spheres. The ultimate refuge or consolation of the young female characters is their body, an instrument of survival that entails pain and living. The images of dismembering and physical and emotional pain unexpectedly acquire a depth of feeling, a tender, upside-down logic that challenges and moves the imagination. These few plays produced by women explore female situations often arising from the familial circumstances of the playwrights themselves. These include social problems related to poverty, sexuality, and the generation gap—as related to the obvious fact of being Puerto Ricans. Puerto Rican identity, however, does not seem to be the main issue. As in the examples in the other sections, these plays face life on the basis of new attitudes.

Concluding Remarks

Some Puerto Rican playwrights, such as José Rivera (b.1955) or Marga Gómez, have expressed their discomfort with their classification as Nuyoricans, Hispanics, or Latinos. They feel that these terms create barriers and restrict expectations, and that their production in English, their relocation outside New York, and their acceptance in non-minority spheres have helped them to overcome this narrow classification. In other words, they do not want to carry the weight of being Hispanic. José Rivera's *The House of Ramón Iglesia* (1983) won the FDG/CBS New Play Award and was part of the televised series *American Playhouse* in 1986. Its main character, Javier Iglesias, has just obtained a university degree and wants to become part of U.S. society. At the same time, however, he has to cope with the fact that his whole family has decided to return to the island. Although he decides to stay, a part of him realizes that he has still not been fully integrated into a society that tells him, "Dance for us, Javier. Salsa for us . . . Javier" (242). Although the text partly takes up a theme explored by Gallardo in *Simpson Street,* becoming integrated into Anglo society is depicted as a challenge to be overcome. *Marisol* (1992) offers an allegory of the emptiness and desolation faced by the protagonist when she moves from the Bronx to Manhattan. Although Rivera resents ethnic stereotyping, he continues to be concerned with issues of social integration.

Marga Gómez, born in Harlem of a Puerto Rican mother and a Cuban father, has pursued an acting career in San Francisco. She has achieved considerable recognition as a comedienne in groups such as the San Francisco Mime Troupe, Lillith Feminist Theater, and Culture Clash, and has performed stand-up comedy and given readings at the Mark Taper Forum in Los Angeles. Her solo "Memory Tricks" (UC San Diego Multicultural Festival, 1990) is a biographical commentary on memory at a time when her mother was suffering from Alzheimer's disease. "Marga Gómez Is Pretty, Witty and Gay" (San Francisco, 1991) is also a performance piece that traces the author's process of accepting her lesbian identity. Its style and content have attracted the attention of feminist critics.

Reinaldo Povod (1959–1994), also "Cubarican," is the author of *Cuba and His Teddy Bear* (New York 1986), while John Leguizamo, a Colombian–Puerto Rican actor and author of the vignettes in *Mambo Mouth* (1993), describes the complex task of compiling an anthology of Puerto Rican plays in the United States. Alberto Sandoval (b. 1954) was born in Puerto Rico and brought up in Wisconsin and Minnesota. Having then lived in Massachusetts for many years, he does not fit into the geosocial Nuyorican mold. *Side Effects,* first performed in South Hadley in 1993, uses dance, theater, and poetry to explore the mysterious world of AIDS. Although the Angel of Memory transports the Dancer character back to his childhood in Puerto Rico, the text focuses on a present in which the border between life and death is explored. The theme of AIDS has also been dealt with by Edwin Sánchez (b. 1955) in *The Road* (1991) and by Yolanda Rodríguez in *Rising Sun, Falling Star* (1991), from the point of view of its impact on family relations. Although these authors share a new attitude toward life in the United States, the term *Nuyorican* has been rejected by some of them; their plays and theater performances are based on their bicultural experience and are designed to appeal to a diverse audience, making an impression on the theatrical, aesthetic, and thematic transformations of their time.

Two decades ago, Puerto Rican migration to the mainland consisted mostly of people from the educated and professional classes, with no specific geographical destination of preference; it is now possible to see shifts in the cultural manifestations of this changing community. Another factor that it is certainly not too early to consider is the political future of the island and the impact this will have on its cultural expression. The 1998 referendum was expected by many to hasten the granting of statehood to Puerto Rico, but for now it continues to be a territory of the United States. Roberto Ramos-Perea's (b. 1959) text *Malasangre/Bad Blood* (1987) deals with the flight to the United States of the educated Puerto Rican class, and the Nuyorican Pedro Pietri (b. 1943) has published a bilingual edition of his play *The Masses Are Asses/Las masas son crasas* (produced at the PRTT workshops, 1986). These developments clearly complicate the writing of a history of Nuyorican theater.

At the beginning of the twenty-first century, however, despite its short history, Nuyorican theater can already be perceived as a particular phenomenon. It emerged from the concrete concerns of Puerto Rican theater, but with new generations its themes, perspectives, and attitudes shifted toward the particular themes of this constantly developing community. Many playwrights have decided to take up elements that reaffirm the islanders' identity while discarding those values they regard as retrograde. Their theater is being pulled in opposite directions by polarizing forces that maintain strict underlying political and cultural agendas: on the one hand, nationalistic island theater culture that recognizes the production of the diaspora as its own yet regards it as dangerous because of its increasing use of English and its increasingly integrative outlook, and on the other, U.S. theater culture, with its conciliatory construction of an integrative, multicultural environment. This struggle has spawned new expressions, known variously as Nuyorican, New York Puerto Rican, or U.S. Puerto Rican. This theater, like its themes, constitutes a process of cultural survival.

Translation by Suzanne D. Stephens

Works Cited

Algarín, Miguel, and Tato Laviera. 1989. "Olú Clemente." *Nuevos Pasos: Chicano and Puerto Rican Drama.* Ed. Nicolás Kanellos and Jorge A. Huerta. Houston, TX: Arte Público Press. 151–71.

Antush, John V., ed. 1991. *Recent Puerto Rican Theater: Five Plays from New York.* Houston, TX: Arte Público Press.

Arriví, Francisco. 1959. *Vejigantes.* 2nd ed. San Juan, PR: Editorial Tinglado Puertorriqueño.

Casas, Myrna. 1997. *The Great USkranian Circus. Women Writing Women: An Anthology of Spanish-American Theater of the 1980s.* Ed. Teresa Cajiao and Margarita Vargas. New York: State University of New York Press. 125–86.

Carrero, Jaime. 1973. *Flag Inside; Capitan F4C; Pipo Subway no sabe reir; El caballo de Ward.* Río Piedras, PR: Ediciones Puerto.

——. 1988. "Escribir sobre el filo de la navaja." *Escenarios de dos mundos: inventario teatral de Iberoamérica.* Vol. 4: Portugal, Puerto Rico, República Dominicana, Uruguay, Venezuela, bibliografía, quién es quién, agenda. Madrid: Centro de Documentación Teatral. 306–30.

Cruz, Migdalia. 1992. "Miriam's Flowers." *Shattering the Myth: Plays by Hispanic Women.* Selected by Denise Chávez. Ed. Linda Feyder. Houston, TX: Arte Público Press. 51–84.

——. 1996. *The Have-Little. Contemporary Plays by Women of Color: An Anthology.* Ed. Kathy A. Perkins and Roberta Uno. London: Routledge. 108–26.

Fraguada, Federico. 1991. *Bodega*. *Recent Puerto Rican Theater: Five Plays in New York*. Ed. John Antush. Houston, TX: Arte Público Press. 25–79.

Gallardo, Edward. 1990. *Women without Men*. *Simpson Street and Other Plays*. Ed. John V. Antush. Houston, TX: Arte Público Press. 148–225.

———. 1990. *Simpson Street and Other Plays*. Ed. John V. Antush. Houston, TX: Arte Público Press.

González, Lydia Milagros. 1980. *El Tajo del Alacrán*. San Juan, PR: Instituto de Cultura Puertorriqueña.

Gorbea, Carlos. 1991. "Charge It to My Account." Unpublished.

Irizarry, Richard V. 1991. "Ariano." *Recent Puerto Rican Theater: Five Plays in New York*. Ed. John Antush. Houston, TX: Arte Público Press. 167–226.

Kanellos, Nicolás. 1990. *A History of Hispanic Theatre in the United States: Origins to 1940*. Austin: University of Texas Press.

Leguizamo, John. 1993. *Mambo Mouth: A Savage Comedy*. New York: Bantam Books.

Marqués, René. 1975. *La carreta*. 12th ed. Río Piedras, PR: Editorial Cultural.

———. 1969. *The Oxcart*. Trans. Charles Pilditch. New York: Scribner.

Papp, Joseph. 1986. "Preface." *Outrageous: One Act Plays*. By Miguel Piñero. Houston, TX: Arte Público Press. 5.

Perkins, Kathy A., and Roberta Uno, eds. 1996. *Contemporary Plays by Women of Color: An Anthology*. New York: Routledge.

Pietri, Pedro. 1997. *The Masses Are Asses/Las masas son crasas*. Trans. Alfredo Matilla Rivas. San Juan, PR: Instituto de Cultura Puertorriqueña.

Piñero, Miguel. 1975. *Short Eyes: A Play*. New York: Noonday Press.

Povod, Reinaldo. 1986. *Cuba and His Teddy Bear*. New York: Theatre Communications Group.

Ramírez, Ivette M. 1991. "Family Scenes." *Recent Puerto Rican Theater: Five Plays in New York*. Ed. John Antush. Houston, TX: Arte Público Press. 227–55.

Rivera, José. 1987. *The House of Ramón Iglesia*. *On New Ground: Contemporary Hispanic-American Plays*. Ed. M. Elizabeth Osborn. New York: Theatre Communications Group. 191–242.

———. 1994. *Marisol*. New York: Dramatists Play Service.

Sánchez, Edwin. 1994. *The Road*. *Ollantay* 2.2 (Special Issue: *Latino Theater on AIDS*): 83–111.

Sánchez, Luis Rafael. 1985. *Quíntuples*. Hanover, NH: Ediciones del Norte; San Juan, PR: Editorial Cultural.

Sandoval, Alberto. 1997. "Puerto Rican Identity Up in the Air: Air Migration, Its Cultural Representations, and Me. *Cruzando el charco*." *Puerto Rican Jam: Rethinking Colonialism and Nationalism*. Ed. Frances Negrón-Muntaner and Ramón Grosfoguel. Minneapolis: University of Minnesota Press. 189–208.

Santaliz Avila, Pedro. 1992. "Olla." *Teatro*. San Juan, PR: Instituto de Cultura Puertorriqueña. 11–60.

Serrano, Lynette. 1988. *Broken Bough*. Costa Mesa, CA: Hispanic Playwright Project Publications.

CHAPTER 38

COLONIAL FIGURES IN MOTION
TRANSLOCALITY, TROPICALISM, AND TRANSLATION IN CONTEMPORARY PUERTO RICAN LITERATURE IN THE UNITED STATES

Arnaldo Cruz Malavé

Because they make doors out of pure space
and you have to swing them open
so they know
you are around the wind,
you are in the wind with your own dance.
You never know who stabs your shadow full of holes.
You gotta have your tips on fire
Victor Hernández Cruz (1973, 3–4)

[Y]a es hora de que al son de la plena baile[n]
It's about time they danced to the beat of the *plena*
Manuel Ramos Otero (1979a, 81)
(See **Figure 1**.)
En el '98, para mis sobrinos Kiko, Gina,
Steph y La Cuchicusa, y para mi ahijado Matt

Figure 1.

Gina Benitez and Iván Rives of the Pepatián Dance company in Merián Soto's "Así se baila un son." (Photograph by Jack Vartoogian. Courtesy of Jack Vartoogian)

In 1974, shortly before the publication of their "anthology of Puerto Rican words and feelings," *Nuyorican Poetry,* and at the height of what would later be baptized the "Nuyorican" poetic movement, Miguel Piñero (1946–1988) and Miguel

Algarín (b. 1941) visited Puerto Rico. To their astonishment and outrage, Piñero, then famous as the author of the award-winning prison drama *Short Eyes,* and Algarín, later cofounder of the performance space the Nuyorican Poets Cafe, would not be accorded the immigrant son's triumphant homecoming welcome; instead, they would be greeted with a word previously not heard by them that defined them, fixing them at a (safe) distance–in their place: New York Rican . . . Newyorican . . . Nuyorican. U.S. Puerto Rican literature, so often charged with regressive tropicalism or essentializing nostalgia by Island critics, may be said to be born, or reborn, from this confrontation with a refractory origin, with an origin that rejects and "abjects." After the confrontation, Piñero would defiantly assert in a poem, "puerto rico 1974/this is not the place where i was born" (1985, 13) and would reclaim instead the "concrete tomb" of the Lower East Side, or Loisaida, and its spectral womb as his "home" (7). Algarín, for his part, would declare himself a member of a "tribe of nomads/that roam the world without/ a place to call home" (Algarín and Piñero 55) and later project himself from the impotent or *mongo* condition of rootlessness onto a future "liberated" space of subjective and national identification that is often prefigured in his writings in proper homosocial embraces:

I loved you
viejo negro
I would have slept
in your arms to weep
. . . .
old man with the golden chain
and the medallion with an indian
on your chest
I love you
I see in you
what has been
what is coming
and will be

(Algarín and Piñero 56–57)

448

Piñero's and Algarín's attempted return to their Puerto Rican roots "in search of spiritual identity" (Piñero 1985, 14) ends in what may be retrospectively read as a productive instance of disidentification. Confronted with the collapse of their past, Piñero and Algarín, like Benjamin's historical angel, find other means to propel themselves forward, to ground their expression: Piñero in the fierce embrace of a spectral and "queer" locality in all of its rawness, materiality, and abjection; Algarín in its utopian projection.

Years later, toward the end of the decade, another collapse would begin to register in Puerto Rican cultural practices in the United States: That of the future. The history of the various struggles that Puerto Ricans engaged during the 1960s and 1970s in an attempt to transform, translate, or transfigure heterogeneous popular cultural and social practices into the telos of community control (in the United States) or national sovereignty (in Puerto Rico) is rich and complex (see, for example, Laó, and Torres and Velázquez, eds.). Yet by the end of the 1970s the assault of a globalizing U.S. economy that reduced state support of social institutions and privatized public space–thereby divesting communities, already impoverished by the flight of industrial manufacturing, of crucially needed communal institutions and resources–would, if not completely dissolve the dream of community control and national sovereignty, at least devalue it politically and defer it. In U.S. Puerto Rican literature, as I have argued elsewhere (Cruz-Malavé, "Teaching Puerto Rican Authors" [1988] and "What a Tangled Web!" [1996]), devaluation and deferral signal a transition from the decolonizing and demystifying aesthetics of early Nuyorican writing, best exemplified perhaps by Pedro Pietri's (b. 1943) 1973 call to Puerto Ricans to "withdraw" from the addiction to the "empty dreams" promoted by "this dept. store/called America" in *Puerto Rican Obituary* to an aesthetics of translations, tropicalisms, and translocality, of cultural, racial, generic, and sexual entanglements. The transcendent foundational space that grounded the dream of an autonomous self-referential community and nation has been, one might say, imploded.

Contemporary Puerto Rican cultural practices in the United States may be seen then to inhabit the space between these two implosions: That of origins and that of a certain future. Between them, Puerto Rican cultural practices deploy figures of movement, tropical swaggers, perambulating struts, and rhetorical acrobatic stunts or *maromas* (as Edward Rivera suggestively calls his characters' survival strategies in his coming-of-age novel *Family Installments*) in order to emerge from a space of double deterritorialization and banishment–of silence. In a manner not unlike that of the stowaway or contraband land crabs in Luis Rafael Sánchez's (b. 1936) brilliantly uproarious essay "La guagua aérea" (1985, "The Air Bus"), whose "con caminares de hampón tofete y buscabullas, jaquetón . . . por el pasillo alfombrado de la guagua aérea" (24) ["tough, cocky, bullying gangsterlike . . . swagger down the carpeted aisle of the air bus" (my translation)] breaks through the imposed silence of the modern colonial Puerto Rico–New York air route; or that of the Puerto Rican drag queens in "Paris Is Burning," whose protracted, warlike struts down the runway break through the social invisibility of their lives to shimmer briefly in the gaze of the balls and of the film's image; or the performances of *plena* (traditional Puerto Rican dance music) promoted by the vernacularly styled *casitas* (improvised sites) in previously vacant lots in the midst of the devastated urbanscapes of Loisaida or the South Bronx

(see Flores, "Salvación Casita"; and Aponte-Parés), Puerto Rican cultural practices step out, as it were, emerge from their condition of banishment, deploying and displaying translational, translocal moving figures.

Movement, translation, translocality, tropicalism: These have become the mark of contemporary Puerto Rican literature in the United States (see Flores and Yúdice, Sandoval Sánchez, Santos-Febres, Julio Ramos, Marzán, Acosta-Belén and Santiago, López-Adorno 1991, Aparicio, Ríos Avila, and La Fountain-Stokes). Examples of this translocal tendency are numerous: From Jorge Brandon's troubadour recitations of politically engaged poetry, in traditional meter in subversive form, to Pedro Pietri's complication of street oratory through playful aporia and other rhetorical collisions in *Traffic Violations* (1983) and Tato Laviera's (b. 1950) resignifying of contradiction through a syncopated aesthetics of reaccentuation in *Enclave* (1981) and *AmeRícan* (1985); from the universalizing avant-garde aesthetics of nationalist poet and activist Clemente Soto Vélez's (1905–1998) *Caballo de palo* [1959; The Wooden Horse] and *La tierra prometida* [1979; The Promised Land] to Víctor Fragoso's (b. 1944) minoritized revolutionary subject in *Being Islands/Ser islas* (1976) and Giannina Braschi's (b. 1954) conquering crossgendered *auteur* in *El imperio de los sueños* [1988; *Empire of Dreams*, 1994] and her radically dialogical author in *Yo-Yo Boing!* (1998); from Julia de Burgos's (1914–1953) liminal speaking subject in *El mar y tú* [1954; The Sea and You] to Manuel Ramos Otero's strategically assumed abjection in multiple geographic, generic, and sexual contact zones in *Página en blanco y staccato* [1987; Blank Page and Staccato] and Rane Arroyo's productively dislocated poetic persona in *Pale Ramón* (1998); from José Luis González's (1926–1996) and Pedro Juan Soto's (1928–1999) localized representations of subaltern voices in *El hombre en la calle* [1948; The Man in the Street] and *Spiks* (1956), respectively, to Martín Espada's (b. 1957) migratory documentation of alternative histories through a filmlike montage of subaltern testimonials in *Rebellion Is the Circle of a Lover's Hands* (1990) and *City of Coughing and Dead Radiators* (1993); from Pedro Juan Soto's and Piri Thomas's (b. 1928) failed search for an autonomous space of national or racial belonging in *Ardiente suelo, fría estación* [1961; *Hot Land, Cold Season*, 1973] and *Down These Mean Streets* (1967), respectively, to Abraham Rodríguez, Jr.'s (b. 1961) exploration of the possibilities of complicity and implication in *The Boy Without a Flag* (1992) and *Spidertown* (1993); from William Carlos Williams's (1883–1963) ironic and distant translations of his Puerto Rican linguistic heritage in *Yes, Mrs. Williams* (1959) to Victor Hernández Cruz's (b. 1949) passionate tropicalizations of English in *By Lingual Wholes* (1982) and *Red Beans* (1991) and Pedro López-Adorno's (b. 1954) neo-Baroque appropriations of the literary codes of medieval and Golden-Age Spanish in *Concierto para desobedientes* [1996; A Concert for the Unruly]; from Bernardo Vega's (1885–1965) grounding of his authorial voice in shared collective experience in *Memorias* (posthumously published in 1977; trans. *Memoirs of Bernardo Vega*, 1984) to Nicholasa Mohr's (b. 1935) unveiling of the artist's "secret garden" or true self in *Nilda* (1973) to Edward Rivera's (b. 1941) formation of his authorial self through a folk, *jaiba* poetics of parodic citation and carnivalization in *Family Installments* (1983) and Esmeralda Santiago's (b. 1948) construction of a "hybrid" identity through performative mimicry in *When I Was Puerto Rican* (1993); from René Marqués's (1919–1979) phobic exhaustion of the possibilities of migration in *La carreta* [1952; The Oxcart,

1966] to Luis Rafael Sánchez's uncovering, in colonial travel, of multiple routes for national, communal, and self-expression in "La guagua aérea" [1985; "The Air Bus"]; from Miguel Piñero's embrace of his local Loisaida in his anticanonically canonical "A Lower East Side Poem" (*La Bodega Sold Dreams*, 1980) to the scattering of his provident ashes by the multiethnic performance artists of the new Nuyorican Poets Cafe in Algarín and Holman's anthology *Aloud* (1994) (see also anthologies by Barradas and Rodríguez, López-Adorno, and Turner). Ever since its abject beginnings in the appropriated term "Nuyorican" in the early 1970s, U.S. Puerto Rican literature has been deepening its translational, translocal character, willfully bifurcating itself between the imposed colonial routes of global capital and the uncanny, uppity routes of deterritorialized homecomings.

Certainly translation, transculturation, and translocality are not recent phenomena in U.S. Puerto Rican cultural practices. However, one may say that contemporary translational strategies in U.S. Puerto Rican culture have a different *sentido*, the Hispanicism designating both a difference in "meaning" and in "direction." Translation no longer means what it did when Algarín, in his introduction to the first anthology of *Nuyorican Poetry*, fretted about the possibilities of turning "outlaw" street cultural practices (e.g., Spanish-English code-switching or Spanglish, characterized by their ability to "hustle" or "juggle" dominant social structures) into an "alternative street government" (10). As befits an anthologist, Algarín would end up affirming the "legalization" or institutionalization of street cultural practices ("legalize your 'risks'"; 13): He would advocate for the Puerto Rican community's control of its "geographical identity" (14) ("To stay free is not theoretical. It is to take over your immediate environment"; 12) even as he warned against a too-hasty standardization of "Nuyorican language" that would "stunt its childhood and damage its creative intuition" (19).

Today U.S. Puerto Rican translational strategies have less to do with the attempt–hasty or otherwise–to metaphorically subsume subaltern cultural practices under a communal or national government. They do not seek to subvert the power structure of a given social space, taking it over and totally transfiguring it on the basis of a "geographical identity" between its cultural practices and its ideological state apparatuses. Instead, contemporary U.S. Puerto Rican translational strategies attempt to mobilize power relations in contextually specific social spaces, creating new moving figures and routes, transforming without transfiguring or transcending. If in the late 1960s Eduardo Seda Bonilla, the Puerto Rican anthropologist, denounced the apparently disorganized, multidirectional, and evasive character of Puerto Rican social practices as a sign of the Island's pathological colonial heritage, or what he termed its *condición* "jueyera," (171–79) ["crab syndrome"], contemporary Puerto Rican cultural practices in the United States instead seem to revel in it, as Luis Rafael Sánchez's "Air Bus" uproariously attests. Contemporary U.S. Puerto Rican translational strategies, one may suggest then, are like the Puerto Rican popular practice known as *jaibería* (from the *jaiba* or mountain crab's sidestepping forward movement), nonconfrontation and evasion in negotiating asymmetrical power relations recently promoted by Ramón Grosfoguel, Frances Negrón-Muntaner, and Chloé S. Georas as a potentially transforming strategy for a "postnationalist" Puerto Rico (26–33): These strategies do not oppose dominant structures frontally; rather, they deploy themselves laterally, in a move-

ment that, despite its fitful, disjunctive character, is more than an avoidance of dominant restrictive maneuvers. It is also a style, an art. (See **Figure 2**.)

Sidestepping contrapuntally to dominant discourses, rather than taking over a territorially-based center of power, seems a more fruitfully transformative strategy in today's globalized world, as Grosfoguel, Negrón-Muntaner, and Georas, among others, contend. Yet precisely because power in a globalized world is no longer territorially based, one can also suggest that U.S. Puerto Rican cultural practices are neither primarily concerned with sidestepping nor with opposing the demands of territorial nationalist or territorial colonialist discourses. Instead their energies seem to be principally directed toward what Néstor García Canclini has called, after Bourdieu, the "reconversion" of traditional knowledge and practices in a struggle over the *sentido* of a global postmodern culture (45) whose power resides between sites, as a master translator.

In its struggle with a traditional patriarchal and Hispanophile nationalism, contemporary Puerto Rican cultural criticism has frequently posited and celebrated an idealized form of unobstructed travel or nomadism, setting this ideal against the exclusionary demands of territorial nationalist or territorial colonialist discourses. Yet as it privileges and deploys this idealized form of nomadism, contemporary Puerto Rican cultural criticism has run the risk of turning the diasporic experience into a mere figure for, or instrument of, its struggle with a nationalism that is, by its own accounts, ineffectual and defunct; it fails thereby to engage with that experience. For the experience that Puerto Rican cultural practices in the United States seek to redress and *rican*-figure is not of the territorial kind; it is rather a paradoxically "modern colonial" condition (see Pierre-Charles) that anticipates and parallels the very postmodern condition of contemporary transnational travel, in which labor fluctuates between (ex-)colony and metropole_along asymmetrically racialized axes (Grosfoguel 282–83). As in Manuel Ramos Otero's (1948–1990) paradigmatic story of the aftereffects of the American invasion of Puerto Rico in 1898, "Vivir del cuento" [1987d; "The Scheherazade Complex," 1987c], the "modern colonial" experience that Puerto Rican cultural practices in the United States seek to reconfigure is not a liberatory flight from territorial constraints but a certain mobility within abjection and markedness; aboard a ship, on his way to a Hawaiian sugar plantation to work as an indentured servant, Monserrate, the protagonist of Ramos Otero's story, understands that his new identity as a "Porto Rican" is now defined by the mass relocation of workers along racialized routes that the new geopolitical remapping of the world, affected by the "Spanish-American" War of 1898, has brought about:

> y me enteré que el mismo año de 1898 cuando los Estados Unidos invadieron a Puerto Rico también se quedaron finalmente en Hawaii. Ya me olía que salíamos de Guatemala para meternos en Guatepeor. Yo nunca había ido a la escuela pero hasta un analfabeto entendía cuando aquellos hombres trazaban sus destinos sobre un mapa maltratado y húmedo, diciendo que miráramos la línea casi recta que se puede trazar desde Puerto Rico hasta Hawaii y que la misma pasaba un poquito más al norte del mentado canal de Panamá, y quién no había oído hablar del canal en esos tiempos, todo iba a ser canal de mar a mar . . . . Aprendí a leer lo suficiente como para leer las palabras "Porto Rican"debajo de la silhueta dibujada de un criminal enmascarado, armado con cuchilla y pistola, que había aparecido en un

periódico hawaiiano, y saber que "Porto Rican" pronosticaba lo malo . . . . Yo siempre he dicho que nací al revés. Tuve que salir de Puerto Rico para aprender a leer y escribir en español y en Hawaii no había más de mil y pico de puertorriqueños incluyendo el cargamento del cual yo era parte. Nadie sospechaba que estábamos destinados a ser una amenaza para los otros trabajadores y los otros eran muchos: japoneses, portugueses, chinos . . . con toda la mala leche, la Sugar Planters Association de Hawaii había trazado nuestra imagen de pillos de barrio, desorganizados y vagos aunque siempre armados y alertas a la pelea, la apuesta y la bebida, con una historia temerosa de rebelión. (52–53)

I found out that in the same year the United States invaded Puerto Rico, 1898, they also took over Hawaii, and I could already tell we were jumping out of the frying pan and into the fire. I'd never gone to school, but even an illiterate could understand, when those men traced their destiny on a battered and soggy map, asking us to look at the almost straight line that can be traced from Puerto Rico to Hawaii, passing just North of the so-called Panama Canal, that it was all going to be a canal from sea to sea . . . . I learned to read well enough to understand the words "Porto Rican" under the cartoon figure of a masked criminal, armed with a knife and a gun, that appeared in a Hawaiian newspaper, and to realize that "Porto Rican" spelled evil . . . . I've always said that I was born upside down. I had to leave Puerto Rico to learn to read and write in Spanish, and in Hawaii there were no more than a thousand Puerto Ricans, including the cargo I was a part of. No one suspected we were meant to be a threat to the other workers, and there were many of them: Japanese, Portuguese, Chinese . . . . [W]ith premeditation the Hawaii Sugar Planters Association had sketched our image as petty thieves, lazy and disorganized but always armed and ready for a fight, gambling or liquor, with a fearful history of rebellion. (my translation)

Set against the architectural metaphor with which José Luis González, the Puerto Rican writer and cultural critic, reimagined Puerto Rican culture as a sedimented "four-storied" edifice in his 1980s classic, *El país de cuatro pisos* [The Four-Storied Country, in Ramos Otero 1987d, 55], Ramos Otero's Scheherazade-inspired tale reconceives Puerto Rican writing, and by extension Puerto Rican culture, as rhetorical strategies that delay, protract, and rhizomically extend the imposed abject routes of colonial migration. Instead of a liberatory flight from territorial constraints, U.S. Puerto Rican cultural practices may be seen then, following upon Ramos Otero's paradigmatic tale, as describing rhetorical figures in motion, figures that attempt to redirect, retard, and expand colonialism's imposed routes of translocation and translation, that answer hegemonic routes with counterhegemonic moves.

How to intervene then in global capital's master translations/translocations? How to redirect their *sentido*? How to redefine what counts for them as transfer points, both as source and as target? How to extend and historically and culturally deepen their routes of relocation? How to retard their transparently swift travel to include other temporalities and localities as the strategies identified by Doris Sommer do in subaltern texts? How to render the target "foreign," as Benjamin recommends (80–81), so that the source being translocated is translated but not translated away? How to participate, that is, in global capital's modern colonial (or postcolonial) routes without being "equalized," discarded, or effaced?

These are the questions that contemporary U.S. Puerto Rican literature and cultural practices insistently address. In the 1960s and 1970s Puerto Rican nationalist discourses in the United States attempted to transform what Gloria Anzaldúa has so poignantly described for Chicanos as a borderland

Figure 2.

New York-Rican dancer and choreographer Arthur Aviles in his solo dance "Pichón." (Photograph by Lois Greenfield. Courtesy of Lois Greenfield)

condition of double expulsion from Latin American and U.S. territorial discourses into an enabling geographical identity. Today that interstitial space is increasingly being preempted as dominant discourses, theory included, migrate from their territorial centers. The Caribbeanization of the world (Clifford 173) may not then be an entirely celebratory phenomenon; it has, not so unexpectedly, a cannibalistic ring to it. To ward off such appropriating moves while participating in the flow of global culture, Puerto Rican literature in the United States deploys uncanny translational figures of motion. In the following pages, I will briefly turn to some of these.

The Adversarial Conjunction's Pause

Any meditation on subaltern strategies deployed by contemporary Puerto Rican literature in the United States may well have to start with the inverted dictum of one of Ramos Otero's stories: "Vencida pero jamás acorralada" (1971) [Defeated but never cornered] ("Loca la de la locura" [1990; "Queen of Madness," 1992]). Transposing the participles "defeated" and "cornered" in this perverse reprise of a homosexual tale of awakening, Ramos Otero frustrates the narrative's teleological movement from confinement to liberation—a movement implicit in the more conventional saying, "Acorralada pero jamás vencida" [Cornered but never defeated] in order to suggest instead the possibility of movement within defeat. He proposes therefore a movement that does not need to lead inexorably to liberation in order to be productively resistant. Separated yet linked by the adversarial conjunction *pero*, the two participles of Ramos Otero's inverted phrase describe not a fusion but an encounter, a counterpoint in which defeat, rather than being metaphorically transfigured or transcended, serves to fuel mobility.

Defeat–not the defeated but defeat itself in its most abject forms–is variously figured in most of Ramos Otero's stories (see, for example, "Loca la de la locura," "Vida ejemplar del esclavo y el señor" [1992; *The Exemplary Life of the Slave and the Master,* 1991], "Inventario mitológico del cuento" [1979b; Mythological Inventory of the Short Story] "Vivir del cuento," (1987d), "Página en blanco y staccato" (1987b), and "Descuento" [1987a; The Untelling]) as the spectral, outcast condition of migrant, homosexual, black, and female bodies. It rises out of social banishment, like the undead rising from disturbed ashes, to give testimonial, to seek vengeful redress. But narration's ambivalent, weblike, Borgesian stratagems lie in wait to provide the testimonial subject with both a voice for self-expression and an "epitaph." As the "leprous" character of "Vivir del cuento" ironically states:

> Y entonces, de repente, llega una carta desde la colonia de Puerto Rico hasta la colonia de leprosos de Molokai devolviéndome de pronto la humanidad y ahora sí valgo como personaje de cuento, como trabajador inmigrante, como puertorriqueño, como leproso, y ya están revolcando la basura incoherente de mi historia para que esa tumba que todavía no reclama su inquilino reclame el epitafio que Uds. han escrito. (68)

> And then, suddenly, a letter from the colony of Puerto Rico arrives in the leper colony of Molokai giving me back my humanity, for now I count as a character in a story, as an immigrant worker, as a Puerto Rican, as a leper, for now they are plowing through the incoherent rubbish of my history so that that plot that hasn't yet claimed its tenant may lay claim to the epitaph that you have written for me. (my translation)

Most of Ramos Otero's stories are post-liberatory meditations in which the necessity of self-expression is fiercely asserted while the cost of social visibility is made murderously palpable. They are also intricately woven narratives, like the subaltern testimonials discussed by Sommer, constructed around pauses, digressions, etymological speculations, and genealogical reconstructions based on the most minoritarian of objects, the most peripheral of traditions–a passing reference in one of Palés Matos's poems (Marie Cafolé), a Chinese name found by chance in New York's Spanish Yellow Pages (Sam Fat), "the stones from an African river passed down from [mother to daughter]" (Ramos Otero 1987b, 77), a coconut cup. As Monserrate, the Puerto Rican migrant to Hawaii, passionately claims in "Vivir del cuento": "la taza de coco que Flor María me había hecho. . . . Todavía la conservo y mejor no desayuno si no puedo beberme el café negro en ella. Esa taza es toda mi tradición" (62) ["the coconut cup [my mother] Flor María made for me. . . . I still keep it and I'd rather not have breakfast if I can't drink my morning coffee in it. That cup's all my tradition"]. These works linger on the adversarial conjunction's pause between defeat's invisibility or "blank page" and social visibility's murder or "staccato." Like Scheherazade's life-saving art, they turn the pause into a rhizomic relay point that protracts both the narrative and the subaltern subject's passage into normalized sociality, both momentarily cheating sociality of its prey and postponing death.

Ramos Otero's early writing sought to break out of static discourses of subjectivity by privileging dispersion, mutation, travel, and even dissolution (see "Concierto de metal para un recuerdo" [Brass Concert for a Memory], "Piel mutada" [A Change of Skin], "Alrededor del mundo con la señorita Mambresi" [Around the World with Miss Mambresi] and "Hollywood Memorabilia" in *Concierto de metal para un recuerdo y otras orgías de soledad* [1971; Brass Concert for a Memory and

Other Orgies of Solitude]; Cruz-Malavé, "Para virar el macho" [Flipping the Macho]; Gelpí; Sotomayor). His later writing, already located within movement, in migration, assumes the routes of social visibility assigned to colonial migrants and other outcasts in order to retard, redirect, and expand them (*El cuento de la mujer del mar* [1979c; The Tale of the Woman of the Sea], *Página en blanco y staccato*, and the posthumous *Cuentos de buena tinta* [1992; Written in Fine Ink/ Reliable Trees]). Thus, in what is one of the most intensely brilliant passages in all of Puerto Rican literature, Ramos Otero's transvestite character, Loca la de la locura (or Queen of Madness), steps out of "Oso Blanco" State Prison in Puerto Rico. And as if she were walking in a New York drag queen ball, she pauses and turns the imposed route of social normalization and visibility, with its concommitant repudiation (or "eviction") of difference, into proliferating moving figures that trace other histories, other genealogies:

> Después del almuerzo me dijeron, Loca la de la Locura, la calle es toda tuya. Me duele que se queden pellejos de esta vida pegados al seto de la celda. Es otra orden desahucio. El hogar donde por tantos años he vivido, de pronto desaparece. Aquí he pagado con creces el robo del divino tesoro de mi juventud y ya es tarde para ablandar los garbanzos. Se abren los primeros portones. Ahí va Loca la de la Locura, con el alma pura. Pero más dura que una tiburona sin dientes, con las encías en llagas de tanto masticar la rueda apolillada de su destino turbio. Se abren los segundos portones. Y los inquilinos de Oso Blanco se encaraman como garrapatas para ver pasar a la Loca la de la Locura por última vez, la que cantaba boleros en la jaula del despecho. Se abren los terceros portones. No se peguen que no es bolero, es Loca la de la Locura a paso de tango resentido con los callos adoloridos de tanto esperar. Se abren los cuartos portones. . . . Carcamal y talcualita va caminando solita Loca la de la Locura, el recuerdo atrincherando las cajas de dientes carcomidas, angustiada entre pellejos y cutículas, sin navajitas de doble filo para suavizar los bosques intolerables de los sobacos ni los jamones invadidos por venas varicosas, muy ansiosa pero con gesto ecuánime, organizando pensamientos marchitos debajo de su calva mohosa, soñando que fue (que todavía es) más fresca que una lechuga, inalterada y fiel como una musa emborujada en magníficos chifones y volantes gitanos, acalorada y rebuscada sin fruncir el ceño más pálida que una magnolia encarcelada. Se abren los séptimos portones y la luz de la tarde deja ciega a Loca la de la Locura, clavada en el precipicio de la soledad, como diría mi madre, que en paz descanse. A carta cabal!
> (Ramos Otero 1990, 238)

After breakfast they told me, Queen of Madness, the street's all yours. It hurts to leave behind pieces of skin from this life of mine stuck to the walls of the cell. Another eviction notice. The where I've lived in for so many years suddenly disappears. . . . The first gate opens up. There she goes, Queen of Madness, pure in soul. But tougher than a toothless old shark, gums scabbed from chewing so long on the termite-bitten wheels of her troubled destiny. The second gate opens up. The tenants of Oso Blanco jump up like tics to see Queen of Madness go by for the last time, she who sang them boleros in her cage of spite. The third gate opens up. Don't get too close, this is no bolero; it's Queen of Madness dancing to a resentful tango, her corns aching from waiting so long. The fourth gate opens up. . . . Ailing and nonchalant, Queen of Madness is walking out all alone, her memories entrenched in her worm-eaten dentures, anxious amidst loose skin and cuticles, with no double-edged razor to soften the unbearable forests of her underarms or her ham-hock legs invaded by varicose veins, worried yet composed, filing wilted thoughts under her rusty, bald head, dreaming that she was (still is) fresher than a head of lettuce, unaltered and faithful as a muse wrapped in magnificent chiffons and Gypsy flounces, hot and exotic, without a hint of a frown on her brow, paler than a jailed magnolia. The seventh gate opens up, and the afternoon light blinds Queen of Madness, now pinned to the precipice of her solitude, as my mother would say, may she rest in peace. All the way! (my translation)]

Syncopated Reaccentuation

Ramos Otero redirects the routes of colonial travel and normalization through an aesthetics of pausing and digression; Tato Laviera does so through a practice of syncopated reaccentuation. Ramos Otero pauses, differs and defers, strikes a fearsome pose; Laviera skips a beat, altering, as do African-derived rhythms, from traditional Puerto Rican *plenas* to contemporary salsa and hip-hop, through syncopation, the very system of accentuation that regulates value in hegemonic discourses. Like Bakhtin, Laviera understands hegemonic value to reside not merely, or even primarily, in the signs of a discourse but in its regulated movement or rhythm, which determines what is marked and unmarked, what counts as weak and what as strong. His practice of reaccentuating the beat therefore can be a powerful strategy for the formation of alternative identities (see Zavala on Bakhtinian reaccentuation). Without altering the signs of a given discourse, but by skipping its accented beat and displacing it toward unmarked linguistic elements, Laviera can turn hegemonic statements—as the titles of his books of poems, *AmeRícan* and *Enclave*, suggest—into productive sites for other subjective and communal affirmations. "American" can also be, through Laviera's syncopated reaccentuation, productive of an otherwise invisible U.S. Puerto Rican agency: AmeRícan, or the syntactically full sentence "am a Rican," as Laviera himself has proposed (Hernández 80). And "Enclave," which suggests the colonial state of enclosure of a subaltern community within a larger national order (Flores 1981, 6), can also become, through reaccentuation, an imperative to reread that state syncopatedly: *En clave* (both "in code" and "in the key"), which is how the off-beat rhythmic pattern that organizes Afro-Cuban and U.S. Puerto Rican music is known.

Syncopation or its grammatical equivalent, syncope, which consists of skipping a phoneme, is, after all, Laviera's recommended tactic for assimilation:

assimilated? qué assimilated,
brother, yo soy asimilao,
así mi la o sí es verdad
tengo un lado asimilao.
you see, they went deep . . . . Ass
oh . . . . they went deeper . . . SEE
oh, oh, . . . they went deeper . . . ME
but the sound LAO was too black
for LATED, LAO could not be
trans*lated*, assimilated,
no, asimilao, melao,
it became a black
spanish word but
we do have asimilados
perfumados and by the
last count even they
were becoming asimilao

(1985, 54)

It is the syncope at the heart of assimilation's translational process—the untranslatable missing *d* in "asimilao," for example—that allows, rather than impedes, the subaltern subject's assimilation. This willfully omitted, untranslatable element

provides the subaltern subject with the necessarily differential leverage to engage in and with the translocational process of assimilation without risking disappearance or erasure, without forfeiting agency. In his poem, Laviera identifies *asimilao* as a black Puerto Rican linguistic form ("déles gracias a los prietos/que cambiaron asimilado al popular asimilao" [54]). Whether he is dialectologically correct or not (the omission of the *d* in Spanish past participles is certainly standard in Castilian speech), his argument is pitched here not so much at the level of linguistic form as at the level of cultural practice. The signal contribution of Puerto Rican black culture to Puerto Rican culture in the United States, Laviera's poem seems to demonstrate, is not merely the maintenance of specific cultural idioms but its insistence on a practice of engaging with assimilation by retaining untranslatable difference, by tactically deploying unassimilable traditional, premodern, or minoritarian elements in order to negotiate and redirect assimilation's translational process.

Clearly Laviera's literary project is heir to Jorge Brandon's and Pedro Pietri's politically engaged "street" poetry. The aim of this poetry is to arrest its listeners with its metrically intricate verse (Brandon) and grotesque language games (Pietri) in order to awaken them from their alienated colonized mentality by invoking a utopian communal vision to which the poet's prophetic voice has privileged access. In Pietri's early classic, *Puerto Rican Obituary*, this process of awakening is metaphorically figured as an act of resurrection and redemption:

Here lies Juan
Here lies Miguel
Here lies Milagros
. . .
Never knowing
the geography of their complexion
. . .
If only they
had turned off the television
and tuned into their imaginations
. . .
[they] will right now be doing their own thing
where beautiful people sing
and dance and work together
. . .
Aquí Se habla Español all the time
Aquí you salute your flag first
. . .
Aquí to be called negrito
means to be called LOVE.

(134–38)

And in Laviera's most ambitious poem, "Jesús Papote," in *Enclave*, and in his touching "migración" in *Mainstream Ethics'Ética corriente*, redemption continues to define the "street" poet's task. As in much Puerto Rican literature (in José Luis González's "Una caja de plomo que no se podía abrir," René Marqués's *La carreta*, Pedro Juan Soto's *Ardiente suelo, fría estación*, Edward Rivera's *Family Installments*, and Magali García Ramis's (b. 1946) *Felices días, tío Sergio* [*Happy Days, Uncle Sergio*, 1995], for instance) and popular song (in "En mi Viejo San Juan" [In My Old San Juan] for example, which is on the subject of "migración") redemption is consistently represented here as the attempt to restore the migrant's dead or mutilated body to the wholeness of national belonging by returning it to its "home," utopian or otherwise (see Sandoval Sánchez).

454 ARNALDO CRUZ MALAVÉ

Yet there is a striking difference in Laviera's reprise of the migrant poet's redemptive task. For one, Laviera's poetic voice, unlike Pietri's early prophetic I, does not assume a privileged, transcendent stance with regard to an ostensibly "colonized" audience; on the contrary, Laviera's poetic personae in "Jesús Papote" and "migración" are deep inside abjection: One is the unborn fetus of a drug-addicted dying mother, the other the wandering specter or *calavera* [skull] of a street artist. Thus, the sometimes over-the-top quality of these and other poems by Laviera derives from his willingness to risk sentimentality and kitsch in order to accurately convey what is admittedly an impossible mission: To speak with a prophetic, transcendent, collective voice from a state of social invisibility and banishment. In the end, however, Laviera's fidelity is much rewarded: In tarrying with poetry's redemptive task, he finds new forms of redemption that are not mortgaged to a transcendent vision but are fueled instead by the syncopated movement of relationships in dialogue, by dance. Redemption in Laviera is no longer merely the business of a prophetic voice. It is the likely effect of a dialogical counterpoint, an Afro-Caribbean *soneo*, an African-American call and response in which the poet's unborn voice does not offer the ultimate solution but a question, a demand:

with your permission Mami
i ask for one gift one magi gift
inside these heavy odds
. . . I tell you
with pride that I am proud to
have been your son, to have come
from you, with the tenderness
of my grandmother's prayers,
with the silent love of all my
people, with the final resolution
of our nationhood, i am asking
for my blessings BENDICION
BEN . . . DI . . . CI . . . ON.

(Laviera 1981, 20–21)

And this demand does not have to be symmetrically answered but may be responded to in motion, syncopatedly, by skipping a beat:

she woke up she saw she startled she warmed she
protected she cried she broke the umbilical cord
she got up to follow the bells the bells the bells.

(21)

Refusing Signification

Ramos Otero's and Laviera's subaltern strategies set out to resignify abjection through an aesthetics of pausing and through syncopated reaccentuation. To a large extent the resignification of abjection in U.S. Puerto Rican literature has been, with the notable exception of Julia de Burgos's insistence on seeing herself reflected and refracted in the mirror of death (*El mar y tú*), a male affair (consider, for instance, the meditation on male subjection, impotence, and martyrdom that runs through the classic works of Thomas and Piñero to that of contemporary novelist Abraham Rodríguez, Jr.; see Cruz-Malavé, "Toward an Art of Transvestism" and "What a Tangled Web!"). Among women writers (for example, Mohr, Santiago, Carmen Valle [b. 1948], Luz María Umpierre [b. 1945], or Judith Ortiz Cofer [b. 1952]) and in the portrayal of female characters, in both women's and men's fiction, an

attitude closer to that identified by Flores and Yúdice in the poetry of Sandra María Esteves (b. 1948) seems to prevail (202): the fending off of abjection takes the form of a double negative–the refusal to be refused or to refuse, aptly represented by Esteves as an assertion of being, as in the title of one of her most suggestive poems, "Not Neither" (1984, 26).

Perhaps Edward Rivera's carnivalesque bildungsroman, *Family Installments*–certainly the most accomplished novel by a U.S. Puerto Rican–and Esmeralda Santiago's enlightening memoir, *When I Was Puerto Rican*, best illustrate subaltern strategies whose mobility derives not from resignifying but from refusing to identify with abjection. Central to both novels is a mutilated, martyred, or economically dispossessed father figure. Yet while the novels register the father's attempt to assume and metaphorically transcend his abject position through an idealized discourse of peasant values or *jibarismo*, it is the mother's voice–pragmatic, skeptical, metonymic–that drives the protagonists' journeys into American society, their resources for negotiating assimilation, and the novels' rhetorical styles.

In this sense the novels' opening scenes are both literally and literarily instructive. Contrasting the father's and mother's accounts of the family patriarch's death that open and close his novel, Rivera introduces the mother's preferred rhetorical tactic of grotesque degradation in resisting the father's attempt to universalize paternal abjection through representational synecdoche. This is the tactic that will later become the son's, and the novel's, primary rhetorical tool in carnivalizing the process of assimilation (see, for example, the chapter titled "First Communion"):

Xavier F. Alegría starved himself dead when my father, Gerán, his third child and second son, was barely five. That was Papi's version, and my mother's. Papi said it had been a common occurrence all over Puerto Rico–all over the world, as a matter of fact. Mami, who claimed she knew little about the world, said sardonically that there had been nothing unusual in Abuelo Xavier's crash-diet death. She said that 1919, the year it happened, had been a good year for meeting the All Merciful, but not an exceptional one. "I could tell you stories, Santos," she told me, "that would make the little hairs on your *fundillo* stand straight out." (Rivera 13)

Similarly, in Santiago's memoir the mother's refusal to elevate metaphorically her abject *jíbaro* home–as do the *criollista* poem "Claroscuro" by Luis Lloréns Torres (1878–1944) that introduces the book, Jack Delano's sepia-colored photograph on its cover (see **Figure 3**), and the *jíbaro* songs and poems associated with the father–constitutes the protagonist's first coming-of-age lesson. She will later put this lesson to unexpectedly effective use in dealing with the process of assimilation into American society. Parodying perhaps the metaphorically hyperbolic beginning of Gabriel García Márquez's (b. 1927) *Cien años de soledad* [1967; *One Hundred Years of Solitude,* 1970], as Hugo Rodríguez Vecchini has suggested (147), the mother's first painful lesson will be to warn the protagonist not to let herself be lured by the search for metaphorically abstracted deep meanings but to beware and be aware of surfaces:

We came to Macún when I was four, to a rectangle of rippled metal sheets on stilts hovering in the middle of a circle of red dirt. Our home was a giant version of the lard cans used to haul water from the public fountain. Its windows and doors were also metal, and, as we stepped in, I touched the wall and burned my fingers. "That'll teach you," Mami scolded. "Never touch a wall on the sunny side." (Santiago 7)

Figure 3.

Passengers from Puerto Rico disembarking in New York, 1941.
(Photograph by Jack Delano. Courtesy of El centro de estudios puertorriqueños)

And indeed wariness of the search for deep meanings in abjection would seem to be the mother's advice as she asks the protagonist to close the eyes of a dead child in a floating shack over the fetid waters of modernization's ultimate dumping ground, El Mangle (El Fanguito), in what is certainly the most brilliant episode in Santiago's memoir (142–49). Evoking José Luis González's classic tale "En el fondo del caño hay un negrito" [At the Bottom of the Lagoon There Is a Little Black Boy], Santiago rewrites here González's black Narcissus myth by forcing her protagonist to stare death in the face, to touch it, while refusing to identify with it.

To touch, to stare, to perform while deferring identification's metaphorical telos is the mother's singularly creative legacy to the novels' protagonists. Orpheus plays the lyre; Aeneas wields the phallic golden bough; the mother, unarmed, recommends moving along meaning's variegated surfaces in order to pass through death. The lesson is heeded both by male and female characters as they traverse the social invisibility of migration. At the end of the novels, as Rivera's protagonist prepares to leave for his U.S. destination, he pauses and lingers over misquoted fragments of his canonical literary education, keeping the ultimate signified of his identification at bay. And Santiago's younger literary persona emerges from social invisibility by engaging in the most archetypically American of activities as pure performance, as mimicry:

"Do you know what a pantomime is?" the woman asked. I nodded. "You and Bonnie are sisters decorating a Christmas tree."
. . . My family had never had a Christmas tree, but I remembered how once I had helped Papi wind colored lights around the eggplant bush that divided our land from Doña Ana's. We started at the bottom and wound the wire with tiny red bulbs around and around until we ran out; then Papi plugged another cord to it and we kept going until the branches hung heavy with light and the bush looked like it was on fire.

Before long I had forgotten where I was, and that the tree didn't exist and Bonnie was not my sister. She pretended to hand me a very delicate ball, and just before I took it, she made like it fell to the ground and shattered. I was petrified that Mami would come in and yell at us for breaking her favorite decoration. Just as I began to pick up the tiny fragments of nonexistent crystal, a voice broke in. "Thank you." (265–66)

These are after all Christmas stories, stories of birth and rebirth; and what Diana Fuss, following Fanon, has called mimicry without identification–or better yet mimicry that *exceeds* identification's logic (28)–may also clear the way for other temporalities and genealogies in which the father's territorial legacy may now return as performance or mime or, as in the end of *Family Installments*, "Bourne Aerial" or aerial born (299).

1998 marked the centennial of the Spanish-American War, which resulted in the U.S. colonial occupation of Puerto Rico, Cuba, Guam, and the Philippines and in the transformation of Puerto Rico into a territory of the United States. But, as Ramos Otero has so brilliantly reminded us in "Vivir del cuento," 1898 also signaled the beginning of a violent process of globalized modernity that established certain migratory routes, dispersing and channeling populations along specifically racialized axes. One hundred years later Puerto Ricans continue to travel along these colonial routes, and their migratory colonial condition has not only not been settled, it has been exacerbated, giving Puerto Ricans' migratory patterns the dubious (in the present global economy) distinction of anticipating contemporary transnational migrations.

It is from the context of this deterritorialized colonialism, and not from one of territorial colonialism, that Puerto Rican cultural practices in the United States speak to us today. U.S. Puerto Rican cultural practices have not only not accepted passively the obligatory routes of colonial travel nor reveled in the deterritorialized nomadism of unobstructed movement nor retreated to the homey comforts of a paralyzing nostalgia but they have also answered travel with travel, hegemonic routes with counterhegemonic moves. Seeking to redirect, retard, and expand colonialism's imposed translations and translocations, they have armed themselves–or, in that suggestive Puerto Rican Spanish verbal expression in which resistance is a form of acting out, the body the ultimate weapon, *se han armao*. Turning and pausing, or skipping a beat, or moving willfully along meaning's variegated surface, Puerto Rican cultural practices in the United States have preserved not only specific idioms but Puerto Ricans' agency and joy–a legacy to pass on and to enrich.

Works Cited

Acosta-Belén, Edna, and Carlos E. Santiago. 1998. "Merging Borders: The Remapping of America." *The Latino Studies Reader: Culture, Economy and Society*. Ed. Antonia Darden and Rodolfo D. Torres. Malden, MA: Blackwell Publishers. 3–26.

Algarín, Miguel, and Miguel Piñero, ed. 1975. *Nuyorican Poetry: An Anthology of Puerto Rican Words and Feelings*. New York: William Morrow.

Algarín, Miguel, and Bob Holman, ed. 1994. *Aloud: Voices from the Nuyorican Poets Cafe*. New York: Henry Holt.

Anzaldúa, Gloria. 1987. *Borderlands: The New Mestiza. La frontera.* San Francisco: Spinsters/Aunt Lute.

Aparicio, Frances, R. 1997. "On Subversive Signifiers: Tropicalizing Language in the United States." *Tropicalizations: Transcultural Representations of Latinidad.* Ed. Frances R. Aparicio and Susana Chávez-Silverman. Hanover, NH: Dartmouth College, University Press of New England. 194–212.

Aponte-Parés, Luis. 1998. "What's Yellow and White and Has Land All Around It? Appropriating Place in Puerto Rican *Barrios.*" *The Latino Studies Reader: Culture, Economy and Society.* Ed. Antonia Darden and Rodolfo D. Torres. Malden, MA: Blackwell Publishers. 271–80.

Arroyo, Rane. 1998. *Pale Ramón.* Cambridge, MA: Zoland Books.

Bakhtin, Mikhail M. 1981. *The Dialogic Imagination: Four Essays.* Ed. Michael Holquist. Trans. Caryl Emerson and Michael Holquist. Austin: University of Texas Press.

——. 1986. [V. N. Voloshinov]. *Marxism and the Philosophy of Language.* Trans. Ladislav Matejka and I. R. Titunik. Cambridge: Harvard University Press.

Barradas, Efraín, and Rafael Rodríguez, ed. 1980. *Herejes y mitificadores: muestra de poesía puertorriqueña en los Estados Unidos.* Río Piedras, Puerto Rico: Ediciones Huracán.

Benjamin, Walter. 1969. "The Task of the Translator." *Illuminations.* Ed. Hannah Arendt. Trans. Harry Zohn. New York: Schocken Books. 69–82

Brandon, Jorge. 1994. *Aloud: Voices from the Nuyorican Poets Cafe.* Ed. Miguel Algarín and Bob Holman. New York: Henry Holt.

Braschi, Giannina. 1988. *El imperio de los sueños.* Barcelona: Anthropos.

——. 1994. *Empire of Dreams.* Trans. Tess O'Dwyer. New Haven: Yale University Press.

——. 1998. *Yo-Yo Boing!* Pittsburgh, PA: Latin American Literary Review Press.

Burgos, Julia de. 1954. *El mar y tú: otros poemas.* San Juan, Puerto Rico: Puerto Rico Printing and Publishing Co.

Clifford, James. 1988. *The Predicament of Culture: Twentieth-Century Ethnography, Literature and Art.* Cambridge, MA: Harvard University Press.

Cruz, Víctor Hernández. 1973. "You Gotta Have Your Tips on Fire." *Mainland.* New York: Random House. 3–4.

——. 1982. *By Lingual Wholes.* San Francisco: Momo's Press.

——. 1991. *Red Beans: Poems.* Minneapolis: Coffee House Press.

Cruz-Malavé, Arnaldo. 1988. "Teaching Puerto Rican Authors: Modernization and Identity in Nuyorican Literature." *ADE Bulletin* [Association of Departments of English of the MLA] 91 (Winter): 45–51.

——. 1993. "Para virar el macho: La autobiografía como subversión en la cuentística de Manuel Ramos Otero." *Revista Iberoamericana* 59.162–63 (Jan.–June): 239–63.

——. 1995. "Toward an Art of Transvestism: Colonialism and Homosexuality in Puerto Rican Literature." *Entiendes? Queer Readings, Hispanic Writings.* Ed. Emilie L. Bergmann and Paul Julian Smith. Durham: Duke University Press. 137–67.

——. 1996. "What a Tangled Web!: Masculinity, Abjection, and the Foundations of Puerto Rican Literature in the United States." *Differences* 8.1: 132–51.

Espada, Martín. 1990. *Rebellion Is the Circle of a Lover's Hands* [*Rebelión es el giro de manos del amante.*] Trans. Camilo Pérez Bustillo and Martín Espada. Willimantic, CT: Curbstone Press.

——. 1993. *City of Coughing and Dead Radiators.* New York: W.W. Norton.

Esteves, Sandra María. 1984. *Tropical Rains: A Bilingual Downpour, Poems.* Bronx, NY: African Caribbean Poetry Theater.

Flores, Juan. 1997. "'Salvación Casita': un *performance* puertorriqueño y de arquitectura vernácula en el sur del Bronx." *La venganza de Cortijo y otros ensayos.* Río Piedras, PR: Ediciones Huracán. 105–30.

——. 1981. "Prefacio." *Enclave.* By Tato Laviera. Houston, TX: Arte Público P. 5–7.

Flores, Juan, and George Yúdice. 1993. "Living Borders/Buscando América: Languages of Latino Self-Formation." *Divided Borders: Essays on Puerto Rican Identity.* Ed. Juan Flores. Houston: Arte Público Press. 199–224.

Fragoso, Víctor. 1976. *Being Islands/Ser islas.* Trans. Paul Orbuch. New York: Editorial El Libro Viejo.

Fuss, Diana. 1994. "Interior Colonies: Frantz Fanon and the Politics of Identification." *Diacritics* 24.2–3 (Summer–Fall): 20–42.

García Canclini, Néstor. 1997. "El debate sobre la hibridación." *Revista de Crítica Cultural* 15 (November): 42–47.

García Ramis, Magali. 1986. *Felices días, tío Sergio.* Río Piedras, PR: Editorial Antillana.

——. 1995. *Happy Days, Uncle Sergio.* Trans. Carmen C. Esteves. Fredonia. NY: White Pine Press.

Gelpí, Juan. 1993. *Literatura y paternalismo en Puerto Rico.* San Juan, PR: Editorial de la Universidad de Puerto Rico.

González, José Luis. 1948. *El hombre en la calle.* San Juan, PR: Editorial Bohique.

——. 1980. *El país de cuatro pisos y otros ensayos.* Río Piedras, PR: Ediciones Huracán.

——. 1990. "En el fondo del caño hay un negrito." *Antología personal.* Río Piedras, PR: Editorial de la Universidad de Puerto Rico. 27–32.

——. 1990. "Una caja de plomo que no se podía abrir." *Antología personal.* Río Piedras, PR: Editorial de la Universidad de Puerto Rico. 33–43.

Grosfoguel, Ramón. 1998. "Caribbean Colonial Immigrants in the Metropoles: A Research Agenda." *The Latino Studies Reader: Culture, Economy and Society.* Ed. Antonia Darden and Rodolfo D. Torres. Malden, MA: Blackwell Publishers. 281–93.

Grosfoguel, Ramón, Frances Negrón-Muntaner, and Chloé S. Georas. 1997. "Beyond Nationalist and Colonialist Discourses: The *Jaiba* Politics of the Puerto Rican Ethno-Nation." *Puerto Rican Jam: Rethinking Colonialism and Nationalism.* Ed. Frances Negrón-Muntaner and Ramón Grosfoguel. Minneapolis: University of Minnesota Press. 1–36.

Hernández, Carmen Dolores. 1997. *Puerto Rican Voices in English: Interviews with Writers.* Westport, CT: Praeger.

Laó, Agustín. 1994–1995. "Resources of Hope: Imagining the Young Lords and the Politics of Memory" *Centro; Journal of el Centro de Estudios Puertorriqueños* 7.1: 34–49.

La Fountain-Stokes, Lawrence. 1998. "Culture, Representation, and the Puerto Rican Queer Diaspora." Diss. Columbia University. Ann Arbor: UMI. 99–16, 938.

Laviera, Tato. 1981. *Enclave.* Houston, TX: Arte Público Press.

——. 1985. *AmeRícan.* Houston, TX: Arte Público Press.

——. 1988. *Mainstream Ethics. Ética corriente.* Houston, TX: Arte Público Press.

López-Adorno, Pedro. 1991. "Papiros de Babel: pesquisas sobre la polifonía poética puertorriqueña en Nueva York." *Papiros de Babel: Antología de la poesía puertorriqueña en Nueva York.* Río Piedras, PR: Editorial de la Universidad de Puerto Rico. 1–16.

——. 1996. *Concierto para desobedientes.* Río Piedras, PR: Editorial Plaza Mayor.

Marqués, René. 1968 [1952]. *La carreta: drama en tres actos.* Río Piedras, PR: Editorial Cultural.

———. 1969 [1966]. *The Oxcart.* Trans. Charles Pilditch. New York: Scribner.

Marzán, Julio. 1994. *The Spanish American Roots of William Carlos Williams.* Austin: University of Texas Press.

Mohr, Nicholasa. 1973. *Nilda; A Novel.* New York: Harper & Row.

Ortiz Cofer, Judith. 1990. *Silent Dancing: A Partial Remembrance of a Puerto Rican Childhood.* Houston, TX: Arte Público Press.

Pierre-Charles, Gérard. 1981. *El Caribe contemporáneo.* Mexico City: Siglo XXI.

Pietri, Pedro. 1973. *Puerto Rican Obituary.* New York: Monthly Review Press.

———. 1983. *Traffic Violations.* Maplewood, NJ: Waterfront Press.

Piñero, Miguel. 1975. *Short Eyes: A Play.* New York: Hill and Wang.

———. 1985 [1980]. *La Bodega Sold Dreams.* Houston, TX: Arte Público Press.

Ramos, Julio. 1996. "Migratorias." *Paradojas de la letra.* Caracas: Ediciones eXcultura. 177–86.

Ramos Otero, Manuel. 1971. *Concierto de metal para un recuerdo y otras orgías de soledad.* San Juan, PR: Editorial Cultural.

———. 1979a. "It's About Time They Danced to the Beat of the *Plena.*" *El cuento de la mujer del mar.* Río Piedras, PR: Ediciones Huracán. 81.

———. 1979b. "Inventario mitológico del cuento." *El cuento de la mujer del mar.* Río Piedras, PR: Ediciones Huracán. 71–86.

———. 1979c. *El cuento de la mujer del mar.* Río Piedras: Huracán.

———. 1987a. "Descuento." *Página en blanco y staccato.* Madrid: Playor. 89–111.

———. 1987b. "Página en blanco y staccato." *Página en blanco y staccato.* Madrid: Playor. 69–88.

———. 1987c. "The Scheherazade Complex." *The Portable Lower East Side.* Trans. Joe Chadwick. New York: The Portable Lower East Side. 6.1: 131–62.

———. 1987d. "Vivir del cuento." *Página en blanco y staccato.* Madrid: Playor. 49–68.

———. 1990. "Loca la de la locura." *Cuentos de buena tinta.* San Juan, Puerto Rico: Instituto de Cultura Puertorriqueña. 233–40.

———. 1991. "The Exemplary Life of the Slave and the Master." *High Risk.* Ed. Amy Scholder and Ira Silverberg. Trans. Gregory Kolovakos. New York: Plume. 195–99.

———. 1992. "Queen of Madness." *The Portable Lower East Side.* Trans. Amy Prince. New York: The Portable Lower East Side. 7.1: 113–23.

———. 1992. "Vida ejemplar del esclavo y el señor." *Cuentos de buena tinta.* San Juan, PR: Instituto de Cultura Puertorriqueña. 175–77.

Ríos Avila, Rubén. 1998. "Migrant Hybridity" *Postdata* 13 (May): 45–47.

Rivera, Edward. 1983. *Family Installments: Memories of Growing Up Hispanic.* New York: Penguin Books.

Rodríguez, Jr., Abraham. 1992. *The Boy Without a Flag: Tales of the South Bronx.* Minneapolis, MN: Milkweed Editions.

———. 1993. *Spidertown: A Novel.* New York: Hyperion.

Rodríguez Vecchini, Hugo. 1995. "Cuando Esmeralda 'era' puertorriqueña." *Nómada* 1 (April): 145–60.

Sánchez, Luis Rafael. 1985. "La guagua aérea." *Imágenes e identidades: el puertorriqueño en la literatura.* Ed. Asela Rodríguez de Laguna. Río Piedras, PR: Ediciones Huracán. 23–30.

Sandoval Sánchez, Alberto. 1997. "Puerto Rican Identity Up in the Air: Air Migration, Cultural Representations, and Me 'Cruzando el Charco.'" *Puerto Rican Jam: Rethinking Colonialism and Nationalism.* Ed. Frances Negrón-Muntaner and Ramón Grosfoguel. Minneapolis: University of Minnesota Press. 189–208.

———. 1992. "The Air Bus." Trans. Diana L. Vélez. *Catalogue of Antonio Martorell's Exhibit, "La Casa de Todos Nosotros" September 1992–January 1993.* New York City: El Museo del Barrio. 24–39.

Santiago, Esmeralda. 1994 [1993]. *When I Was Puerto Rican.* New York: Vintage Books.

Santos-Febres, Mayra. 1991. "The Translocal Papers: Gender and Nation in Contemporary Puerto Rican Literature." Diss. Cornell University. Ann Arbor: UMI. AAT 9333263.

Seda Bonilla, Eduardo. 1970. *Réquiem por una cultura: ensayos sobre la socialización del puertorriqueño en su cultura y en ámbito del poder neocolonial.* Río Piedras, PR: Editorial Edil.

Sommer, Doris. 1996. *Proceed With Caution: A Rhetoric of Particularism.* Working Papers on Latin America, No. 96–2. Cambridge, MA: The David Rockefeller Center for Latin American Studies, Harvard University Press.

Soto, Pedro Juan. 1956. *Spiks.* Río Piedras, PR: Editorial Cultural.

———. 1961. *Ardiente suelo, fría estación.* Río Piedras, PR: Editorial Cultural.

———. 1973. *Hot Land, Cold Season.* Trans. Helen R. Lane. New York: Dell.

Soto Vélez, Clemente. 1976 [1959]. *Caballo de palo.* San Juan, PR: Instituto de Cultura Puertorriqueña.

———. 1989 [1979]. *La tierra prometida. Obra poética.* San Juan, PR: Instituto de Cultura Puertorriqueña.

Sotomayor, Aurea María. 1995. "Genealogías o el suave desplazamiento de los orígenes en la narrativa de Manuel Ramos Otero." *Nómada* 1 (April): 92–106.

Thomas, Piri. 1967. *Down These Mean Streets.* New York: Knopf.

Torres, Andrés, and José E. Velázquez, ed. 1998. *The Puerto Rican Movement: Voices from the Diaspora.* Philadelphia: Temple University Press.

Turner, Faythe E., ed. 1991. *Puerto Rican Writers at Home in the USA: An Anthology.* Seattle, WA: Open Hand.

Umpierre, Luz María. 1987. *The Margarita Poems.* Bloomington, IN: Third Woman Press.

Valle, Carmen. 1983. *Glenn Miller y varias vidas después.* Mexico City: Premiá.

Vega, Bernardo. 1977. *Memorias de Bernardo Vega: contribución a la historia de la comunidad puertorriqueña en Nueva York.* Ed. César Andreu Iglesias. Río Piedras, PR: Ediciones Huracán.

———. 1984. *Memoirs of Bernardo Vega: A Contribution to the History of the Puerto Rican Community in New York.* Trans. Juan Flores. New York: Monthly Review Press.

Williams, William Carlos. 1959. *Yes, Mrs. Williams: A Personal Record of My Mother.* New York: McDowell, Obolensky.

Zavala, Iris M. 1996. *Escuchar a Bajtín.* Madrid: Montesinos.

CHAPTER 39

CUBAN THEATER IN THE UNITED STATES

José A. Escarpanter

Three Periods

Cuban theater, which first appeared in the United States in the nineteenth century, has always been linked to important events in the history of the island. There were two main phases: During the Guerra de los Diez Años (The Ten Year War) of 1868–1878 and later the movement that culminated in the War of Independence (1895–1898). Theater in the twentieth century, linked to the Revolution of 1959, began in the 1960s and continues to the present day. This period, the longest and most productive of the three, clearly presents rather different characteristics from the first two. It is important to note that Cuban theater during the nineteenth century was concentrated in cities of the United States that were located near the island. Cities such as Tampa, then the capital of the rebels, and Cayo Hueso were both inhabited by a significant population of Cubans. The situation is rather different today. Cuban theater has flourished particularly in Miami, currently the capital of Cubans in exile, but also has a place in the New York area and Los Angeles. When Joanne Pottlitzer interviewed 101 Hispanic theater groups in the United States in 1984–1985, she discovered twenty-one of Cuban extraction, of which seventeen were based in Miami.

This twentieth-century phase can only be compared, in terms of recent history, with the experience of those Spaniards exiled as a result of the Spanish Civil War. The majority of the latter settled in Spanish-speaking countries in which they could continue their theatrical work supported by companies and a public that shared the same language and many of the same cultural traditions. On the other hand, those individuals dedicated to the theater who left Cuba for the United States have established themselves in a nonnative medium in both cultural and linguistic terms. Yet the theater they produce is included for linguistic, ethnic, and cultural reasons within the ambit of Hispanic theater in the United States, as this is developing in the southwest of the country: That of the Chicano and Mexican-Americans, along with that of the "*neoyorricans*" (New York-based Puerto Ricans). Fundamental differences nevertheless exist between Cuban theater and the latter, which tend to represent a theater of protest against their situation as minorities within the United States. Cuban theater is largely the consequence of a political situation, however.

Meanwhile Cuban theater is also related to that of other Spanish American nations (e.g., Argentina, Chile, Uruguay), whose writers in recent decades have been forced to abandon their countries as a result of military dictatorships. These artists have responded intellectually in terms of the principles of Leftist affiliation, which in the 1970s gave them international visibility, especially in Western Europe. In contrast, in most instances those Cuban artists who rejected the Cuban Revolution from the start were dubbed political reactionaries, denied an audience for their work, and have endured scorn and ostracism for decades. Fortunately this situation has recently changed. In most cases the survival of this theater is the result of the enthusiasm and idealism of a handful of individuals of

very different origins. Some were educated in Cuba prior to the Revolution; others have been given a solid academic grounding in U.S. universities, whereas another group, those belonging to the youngest generation, have graduated from the excellent schools established by the Revolution in Cuba. Most of the participants in Cuban theater are not professionals in the sense that they do not regard their work as a means of earning a living. Indeed the theater on U.S. soil has regressed to the conditions of the "heroic" period of the Havana movement of the 1940s and 1950s when participants worked in the theater for love of it, and plays were performed in tiny halls (Muguercia 46–47). The situation is similar today for the overstretched resources of Cuban theaters in Miami, New York, and Los Angeles, since these groups receive little funding from official organizations and considerably less from the private sector. Indeed many depend entirely on the box office for survival, a situation that makes them compete with commercial theater. This total dependence on box office revenue, very prevalent in Miami, abandons the development of a theater with true artistic merit. The paying public thus holds the key to success. Apart from a small group who shares the concept of theater as an aesthetic manifestation, most of the public attending the shows has had its taste shaped by the ideas of entertainment and escapism that predominate in the United States. This public, moreover, is only looking for light entertainment and is not open to considering formal innovations or polemical themes that are too dramatic or require intellectual effort.

Another thing lacking here is serious theater criticism. Except for notable exceptions, comments tend more toward a simplistic summary, either praising or censuring, rather than an intelligent analysis of the production itself. This absence goes hand-in-hand with another disadvantage, the lack of critical writing on Cuban theater. Four journals do exist, however, in this particular cultural wilderness whose titles deserve mention: The theater bulletin *Dramaturgos*, the consequence of the enthusiasm of Matías Montes Huidobro and Yara González Montes; *Ollantay: Theater Magazine* under the editorship of Pedro Monge-Rafuls; Belkis Cuza-Malé's *Linden Lane Magazine;* and *Círculo*, edited by Elio Alba-Buffill. For two years (1987–1988) *Dramaturgos* tackled the work of Hispanic authors in the United States with intelligence and sensitivity, placing particular emphasis on those of Cuban origin. From 1993 *Ollantay: Theater Magazine* published intelligent articles on the development of theater and playwriting by Hispanics in the United States. *Linden Lane Magazine*, founded in 1981, showed an interest in Cuban dramatists, publishing brief texts by them as well as articles of academic quality, and included retrospective reviews of the best dramatists. *Círculo*, first published in 1971, has similar aims, with university faculty predominating among its contributors. The brief but excellent information provided by *AHA!*, the voice of the Association of Hispanic Arts of New York, also deserves mention, since from 1975 this organ has periodically reported on the activities of

458

Hispanic artists in that city. The survival of dramatic texts is a serious problem because publishing houses interested in publishing plays in Spanish barely exist. Those few that have undertaken such a task include *Arte Público Press, Bilingual Press, Ediciones Universal,* the now defunct *Senda Nueva de Ediciones, Persona,* and the *Presbyter's Peartree.* Notable publishers of this kind of material in Spain are *Betania and Verbum.*

Marked differences in staging style are evident within this larger theatrical movement, depending on the different cities in which the drama is produced. It is noticeable that Cuban American dramas produced by New York theater companies have frequently led to combining resources with those of other Hispanic theater groups. In New York the majority of the groups have had recourse to private donations as well as federal, state, and community aid awarded as part of State support of the arts. This is a subsidized theater that allows for the pursuit of aesthetic concerns, permits a certain margin of experimentation, and makes possible the existence of a few stage professionals. In Los Angeles and Miami, on the other hand, such activity, with very few exceptions, has been entirely the work of private initiatives. This situation forces the theater to orientate itself completely within the parameters of commercial light entertainment, dependent on the box office, as previously noted. This factor, which cannot be ignored, means that in general terms Cuban theater in Los Angeles and Miami, despite the enthusiasm and quality of its personnel, does not achieve the artistic level observable in New York theater.

The contribution of various cultural institutions in the latter city have been outstanding. These, apart from staging plays from the Hispanic repertory (with an emphasis on Cuban work by playwrights both from the island and in exile), also mount exhibitions of Latino artists as well as offering conferences and workshops for the development of new dramatists. Among those institutions worthy of mention are INTAR (International Arts Relations), founded in 1966 under the artistic directorship of Max Ferrá; Duo Theater created in 1969 by Manuel Martín Jr. and Magaly Alabau; LATE (Latin American Theater Ensemble-El Portón) established in 1970 by Mario Peña, Margarita Toirac, and Víctor Acosta; the Centro Cultural Cubano, active between 1972 and 1979, and Ollantay, Center for the Arts, which has published work on Hispanic writers in the United States and, in 1993, as mentioned earlier, first published *Ollantay: Theater Magazine.* Among those groups specifically dedicated to the theater, the most outstanding are Repertorio Español, under the administration of Gilberto Zaldívar and artistic direction of René Buch, founded in 1968. Another notable group was the Spanish Dumé Theater that functioned from 1969 to 1979 under the directorship of Dumé, one of the most outstanding Hispanic theatrical talents of his generation. The company Prometeo (along with a magazine of the same name), headed by Francisco Morín (a key figure in Havana theater before the Revolution), was revived by him and operated between 1976 and 1981. In 1977 Thalia Spanish Theater appeared under Silvia Brito in the Queens area of New York. Among the most successful companies specializing in children's theater have been the Bubbles Players, who were also based in Queens until 1986, and the Don Quixote Experimental Theater, founded in 1974 and directed by Osvaldo Pradere.

The only organization with an official subsidy in Los Angeles is The Bilingual Foundation of the Arts, created in 1973 by Carmen Zapata, Margarita Galbán, and Estela Scarlata.

Among the private groups in this city three merit special mention: The Patronato del Teatro, Havanafama, and the Avellaneda Actor's Theater. The first was founded in 1964 by Efrén Besanilla and Marie Curi, the second in 1989 under the directorship of Juan Roca, and the last in 1998 by Jorge Folgueira and Ivonne López Arenal. Four institutions in Miami produce outstanding work, notably, Prometeo, Teatro Avante, the Hispanic Theater Guild, and La Má Teodora. Founded in 1972 by Teresa María Rojas, Prometeo adopted its name as a sign of homage to the work of the previously mentioned Francisco Morín in Havana. Prometeo is based at Miami-Dade Community College and constitutes the most important center of stage education for the Hispanic population of the city. Apart from classes, the company stages various works every year. Teatro Avante was set up by Mario Ernesto Sánchez in 1981. Thanks to the contribution of private donors and official organizations, the Festival Internacional de Teatro Hispano (The International Festival of Hispanic Theater), inaugurated in 1985, has continued to this day. La Má Teodora, a company founded in 1996 by Alberto Sarraín, has focused on staging texts by dramatists still based in Cuba. The efforts by Dumé in recent years to present work by Cuban playwrights in exile should also be pointed out. The Chicos company, created by Marta Llovio in 1977, has performed outstanding work in children's theater. Bellas Artes has proved the most noteworthy of the theaters in the area. As mentioned earlier, most of the other theaters are commercially oriented, as is the case with Las Máscaras and the various auditoria of the Teatro Martí, both of which have been running since 1968.

Playwrights and Their Work

Cuban theater in the United States constitutes a heterogeneous body of work, both in terms of theatrical styles and ideological positions. However, beyond these important differences there is a common element, the premise of possessing a specific cultural identity, notably that of being identified in the majority of cases as Cuban, or at least Hispanic or Cuban-American (as remarked upon by Carlos Espinosa Domínguez [65]). Moreover, as Montes Huidobro states (1987), these texts present continuity in terms of style and thematic content with Cuban theatrical tradition. Alienation, the presence of the absurd, ridicule, the play-within-a-play, and the historical eroticization that Montes Huidobro points out as defining features of theater tradition on the island (1973, 19–65) are present in the work of these authors. Such continuity, nevertheless, does not imply stagnation. The writing of these plays has evolved along with that of contemporary theater. Despite the difficulties mentioned previously, the number of authors (forty-five appear in the anthology by González-Cruz and Colecchia) and the diversity of styles demonstrated are both astonishing.

These writers belong to various generations. The most well known was José Cid Pérez (1906–1994) who, influenced by the European avant-garde, lived out his exile in Indiana, where he wrote a single work, *La última conquista* [1968; The Last Conquest], in which he reinterpreted the myth of Don Juan. Leopoldo Hernández (1921–1994) initially resided in Los Angeles and later in Miami. His intensive creativity manifests in his application of new stage techniques and his profound ethical commitment, characterized by a pessimistic view of contemporary political reality (as in *No negocie, señor presidente* [1977; Do Not Negotiate, Mr. President]) and a particular emphasis on the Cuban situation (*Infierno y duda* [1977; Hell and Doubt]). But Hernández also focused on the experience of the Cuban family in exile, as in *940 S.W. Segunda Calle* [1979; 940 S.W. 2nd Street]. Hernández was also the first Cuban playwright to treat the theme of the encounter between those who left Cuba and those who remained, in *Siempre tuvimos miedo* [1981; *We Were Always Afraid,* 1992]. His work is amongst the most articulate of those produced by Cubans in the United States.

The next generation of playwrights witnessed the triumph of the Revolution at the start of their literary careers and were obliged to take sides; for this reason they were dubbed the "divided generation" (see Escarpanter). Many remained on the island, while others departed at different times into exile. Matías Montes Huidobro (b. 1931) lived long years in Hawaii until he retired and subsequently moved to Miami. *Gas en los Poros* [Gas in the Pores], *La sal de los muertos* [Salt of the Dead], and *La Madre y la guillotina* [*The Guillotine*], all written in 1961, variously reflect the impact the Revolution had on his work. The personal trauma of exile left its mark on the rest of his plays, albeit in metaphorical form in *Ojos para no ver* [1979; Eyes to Not See], and more directly in *Exilio* [1988; Exile], in which he traces the lives of some friends from the period of Batista's dictatorship to life in exile in New York. The playwright has also made forays into the area of stereotypes imposed on Hispanics living in the United States in *Su cara mitad* [1989; *Your Better Half,* 1991], Afro-Cuban issues in *La navaja de Olofé* [1982; *Olofé's Razor,* 1992], and the games inherent in postmodern parody in *Funeral en Teruel* [1990; Funeral in Teruel].

Julio Matas (b. 1931), based for years in Pittsburgh but now established in Miami, has written a number of one-act plays. Among the most notable are *Juego de damas* [1973; Ladies at Play, 1973] and *El cambio* [1977; Penelope Inside, Out] in which he includes elements of the theater of the absurd. In *Diálogo de Poeta y Máximo* [1992; *Dialogue of the Poet and the Supreme Leader,* 1992], his only work on an explicitly political theme, he alludes to the struggle between intellectuals and the Cuban regime. The most outstanding of his full-length works is *El extravío* [1990; *Deviations,* 2000], which takes place in a Caribbean setting.

The work of José Triana (b. 1931), though a resident in Paris, is tightly linked to Cuban theater. Various of his plays have been staged in the United States, including *Revolico en el campo de marte* [1971; Revolt in the Parade Ground], a brilliant homage to the dramatic works of the Golden Age and one of the best examples of postmodern parody in Cuban theater. *Palabras comunes* [Common Words], first performed by the Royal Shakespeare Company in 1986, has proved to be the most profound analysis in Cuban theater so far of the genesis of an independent Cuba. *La fiesta o Comedia para un delirio* [1992; The Fiesta or Play for a Delirium] was his first venture into the area of the life of a Cuban family in the United States.

Mario Martín (b. 1934) and Pedro Román (b. 1938) are two genuine men of the theater. It is only fair to note a dividing line in their work, since both have produced a considerable number of commercial plays for the Miami theater. However, occasionally other plays appear that demonstrate the greater creative capacity of both dramatists. *Hamburguesas y sirenazos* [1962; Hamburgers and Sirens] by Román is perhaps the first full-length play written and staged during the period of the postrevolution 1960s. A comedy about a family in exile, this work laid the foundations for a genre

that flourishes to this day. Martín is best known for two works connected with documentary forms of theater: *Resurrección en Abril* [1981; Resurrection in April] was based on the voyage of El Mariel from Havana to Miami in 1980 and *Réquiem por una jinetera* [1992; Requiem for a Prostitute], a pathos-laden monologue delivered by a prostitute in contemporary Cuba.

Costumbrista (costumes and manners) comedy is a field well tilled by Raúl de Cárdenas (b. 1938), resident in Los Angeles, who recalls (with a Cuban sense of humor) details of the past in plays such as *Las Carbonell de la calle Obispo* [1986; The Carbonnell Women from Obispo Street]. While this playwright describes life in exile in Miami in *Las pepillas de El Vedado* [1988; The Girls from El Vedado] with equal insight, he has also attempted to deal with larger issues. In *Recuerdos de familia* [1988; Recollections of a Family], the life of a family from 1944 until the Revolution is evoked with penetrating critical perception. In *Las sombras no se olvidan* [1989; Shadows Are Not Forgotten], he portrays the Cuban political penitentiary in the form of a documentary drama. Finally *Un hombre al amanecer* [1988–1989; A Man at Dawn], which was awarded the Letras de Oro prize for 1988–89, pieces together in a felicitous monologue the final hours of José Martí in the Cuban countryside.

José Corrales (b. 1937), a resident of New York, bases his work on the theater of the absurd, on drama as celebration, and on the tradition of Cuban vernacular theater. He collaborated with Manuel Pereiras (b. 1950) to write *Las hetairas habaneras* [1977; Prostitutes of Havana], which resulted in the most violent dramatic satire ever written against the current Cuban government. In *Un vals de Chopin* [1985; A Chopin Waltz], Corrales initiated a peculiar dramatic technique rich in ambiguity and fantasy that he developed in later works, such as *Orlando* (1987), *Miguel y Mario* and *De cuerpo presente* [Present and Accounted For] (both 1989), and *Nocturno de cañas bravas* [1994; Nocturne of the Wilderness]. In this latter play Corrales recreates the Cuban world on the eve of the Revolution without sentimentality in one of the most innovative plays to be seen on the contemporary Cuban stage.

All of the previous writers have written in Spanish, but three other members of this generation–emigrants rather than exiles, since they arrived in the United States prior to the Revolution–have elected at times to write in English. All three live in New York. Despite using English, María Irene Fornés (b. 1931) reveals a very tropical Baroque style in her work: In the themes (*machismo* [male chauvinism], violence, and the abuse of power) developed in *The Conduct of Life* (1985), which won the Obie Prize; in her innovative staging techniques, as seen in *Fefu and her Friends* (1977); and in her use of the grotesque, her presentation of life as an absurdity, and her fondness for parody. The Hispanic world frequently appears as the setting for her plays (*Tango Palace* [1962], *Sarita* [1984]). Fornés's dramatic oeuvre, which takes a strong feminist direction, often uses aspects of the musical theater, but her work is very far from the Broadway style of musical comedy (e.g., *Promenade* [1965], which won the Obie Prize, and *Molly's Dream* [1968]).

Manuel Martín, Jr. (1934–2000) bases his playwriting on his fascination with history and contemporary myths. His career as a playwright began with *Francesco: The Life and Times of the Cenci* (1973) and *Rasputin* (1976), texts that demonstrate an effective use of multimedia. However, a return to Cuba in the late 1970s inspired his writing on the life of ordinary Cubans after the Revolution, as can be seen in *Swallows* (1980) and *Sanguivin in Unión City* (1983), which was translated into Spanish by Randy Barceló. The former presents testimonies by Cubans living on the island and in exile with the aim of creating an understanding between the two groups. *Sanguivin in Unión City* analyzes family conflicts with both sensitivity and courage. *Rita and Bessie* (1988) offers a warm and dramatic homage to two popular black singers, the Cuban Rita Montaner and Bessie Smith from the United States.

Renaldo Ferradas (b. 1932) has tackled a variety of subjects. *In Search of an Empire, Hernan Cortes in Cuba* (1990) probes the Spanish conquest of Cuba. In *La visionaria* [1984; The Visionary] he constructs a kind of autosacramental (seventeenth-century mystery play) that operates within a contemporary world of dreams, whereas in *The Cuban Lady* (1986), *La puta del millón* [1987; A Million Dollar Whore], and *Birds Without Wings* (1987) he reflects on the social problems faced by Hispanics living in the United States.

The next generation was made up of those who left Cuba, almost all in childhood or adolescence. Once again some preferred to write in English. These writers, like those mentioned previously, are those who, in my opinion, constitute a real Cuban-American theater. It is not useful or accurate to include all the Cuban playwrights working in the United States in this category, as urged by Professor Rodolfo Cortina (7). Most of the playwrights using English live in the environs of New York City. Dolores Prida (b. 1943) focuses on Hispanic life in general in the city (*Bótanica* [1990; Botany]) and places her emphasis on the situation of women in such an environment. This is the motivation behind *Beautiful Señoritas* (1977), an ingenious musical play that satirizes Latin "machismo" and certain stereotyped concepts held by Latinos of the United States. *Coser y Cantar* [1981; Sewing and Singing], a superb experiment in bilingual theater, materializes the divided personality of a Hispanic woman in New York into two characters. Luis Santeiro (b. 1947) handles the possibilities of *costumbrista* comedy with great skill and humor. His plays underline the generational and cultural confrontations among resident Hispanics in the United States (*Our Lady of the Tortilla*, 1987; *The Lady from Havana*, 1990).

Manuel Pereiras (b.1949) is one of the most prolific playwrights of his generation. His work centers either around marginalized individuals from Cuba's provincial past whom he recalls without nostalgia (*The Chronicle of Soledad as Told by Manacabuya's Town-people and Suffered by Her Daughters*, 1986; *Michaela's Daughter*, 1987) or on the contemporary New York scene (*Washington Heights*, 1987). He deals with homosexuality with total sincerity in other of his works, notably *Bebo and the Band, Ira Evans*, and *The Dones of Central Park*, all from 1986. The majority of his plays are very daring in their exploitation of controversial themes. In both *The Marriage of Hippolyta* (1986), in which the myth of Phaedra is developed in the relationship between mother and daughter, and *Santiago* (1990), based on a love triangle, he illustrates the violence and lack of ethical values that dominate contemporary society.

Eduardo Machado (b.1953) in his tetrology entitled *The Floating Island Plays* (*The Modern Ladies of Guanabacoa; Fabiola; In the Eye of the Hurricane; Broken Eggs*, 1991) describes two Cuban families from 1928 to their exile, covering a period of fifty years. This diachronic journey, as in Cárdenas' *Recuerdos de familia* [Recollections of a Family], allows him to offer an interpretation of Cuban history and at the same time to develop a very negative analysis of the families.

Pedro Monge-Rafuls (b. 1943) writes in English and Spanish. His works, like those of Dolores Prida, are outstanding for their interest in the conflicts affecting not only the Cubans (*Trash*, 1989; *Recordando a mamá* [1990; Remembering Mom]) but also other Hispanic immigrants (*Solidarios* [1989; In Solidarity]). He also takes up themes of homosexuality and AIDS, as in *Noche de ronda* [1990, Night on the Town], which in 1991 won the New York City Prize. His visit to Cuba inspired *Nadie se va del todo* [1991; No One Leaves Completely], conceived as a theatrical melange that seamlessly blends time and space to achieve a cinematographic fluidity that is only rarely achieved on the contemporary stage.

René R. Alomá, another member of this generation (1947–1986), educated in Canada and resident there until his death, is the playwright who first took up the theme of re-encounter in *A Little Something to Ease the Pain*, in which the rivalry between two brothers is demonstrated within a family with unerring shrewdness. First presented in English in 1980, the play was translated into Spanish by Alberto Sarraín as *Alguna cosita que alivie el sufrir* (1986).

Though a resident of New York, Iván Acosta (b. 1943) has always written his texts in Spanish, achieving tremendous success with aspects of *costumbrista* theater elaborated through a grotesque style comedy, which can be seen in *El súper* [1979; The Super]. Guided by a frequently politically slanted irony and a strong sense of Caribbean humor, Acosta has also produced other plays of interest. *Un cubiche en la luna* [1989; A Cuban Guy on the Moon] is reminiscent of the comic theater of the past, whereas *Recojan las serpentinas que se acabó el carnaval* [1986; Pick up the Streamers, the Carnival Is Over] is set in an indeterminate country in Latin America and deals with the corruption wrought by power.

Two other playwrights belong to this generation, both of whom lived in Miami until their deaths, and alternated in their use of English and Spanish. Miguel González-Pando (1941–1998) pursued both realistic theater and farce. The life of Hispanic immigrants in the United States is the subject of plays such as *La familia Pilón* [1982; The Pilón Family] and *A las mil maravillas* [1990; translated by the author as *Once Upon a Dream*, 1991]; he has also written plays in English, which are somewhere between traditional farce and the theater of the absurd and offer cutting criticisms of certain xenophobic attitudes prevalent in U.S. society today. *The Great American Justice Game* (1987) attacks the English-only campaign, and a broader canvas is adopted in *The Torch* (1987) in which he satirizes the victimization of humanity because of the demands of a dehumanized society.

Rafael Blanco (d. 1998) wrote plays about contemporary life for Cubans in the United States, such as *La caída* [1991; The Fall] and *Mama's Last Waltz* (1995); *Lola* (1996)–all well within the range of traditional comedy. However, his most interesting contribution lies in the various works aimed at a younger public concerning contemporary problems, such as violence in schools (*BX Blues*, 1996), domestic violence (*Breaking the Circle*, 1994), and the danger posed by AIDS for future generations (*Burning Dreams*, 1996).

Julie de Grandy, still living in Miami (b. 1956), deals with very contemporary themes, without allusion to the Cuban political problem, and often develops them within the coordinates of traditional theater (*Conexión sin Hilo* [1991; Wireless Connection]). In other plays she experiments with more daring subjects and appropriates the suspense techniques of a murder mystery (*Doble fondo* [1989; False Bottom], *Trampa mortal* [1995; Mortal Trap]).

Two further playwrights of this generation, who (unlike the rest) left Cuba around 1980 as adults, are Héctor Santiago (b. 1944) and José Abreu Felippe. Based in New York, Santiago is the most prolific of all Cuban playwrights in the United States. His range of themes is enormously varied and always treated with imagination, humor, and intense feeling. Satirical comedy is handled with finesse in *El loco juego de las locas* [1995; The Crazy Game of the Queers]. His historical play *Vida y pasión de La Peregrina* [Life and Passion of La Peregrina] was awarded the Letras de Oro prize for 1995–96. He writes politically slanted farce (*Madame Camille: Escuela de la danza* [1994; Madame Camille: School of Dance]) and treats specifically Cuban issues as in *Balada de un verano en Habana* [1992; Ballad of a Summer in Havana]. His handling of homosexuality at times can verge on the grotesque, as in *Las noches de la chambelona* [1992; Nights of La Chambelona], or, at other times, quietly follow the canon of dramatic comedy as in *Camino de ángeles* [1992; Path of the Angels]. Finally, he has also written children's theater (*El día que se robaron los colores* [1995; The Day They Stole the Colors]).

José Abreu Felippe (b. 1947) made his debut as a playwright with *Amar así* [1988; To Love This Way], which is conceived on two levels, one eminently documentary (the moment of the Mariel's departure, described with tremendous vigor) and the other subjective. In this work his solid literary grounding is evident: His love of the stylistic avant-garde flourishes, and his admiration for the theater of the absurd in most recent plays clearly confirm this.

A new crop of playwrights has appeared in recent years, all of whom have provided evidence of mature talent. These include Nilo Cruz (b. 1960) in New York (*A Park in Our House*, 1996) and in Miami, Larry Villanueva (b. 1966) with his *Allá afuera hay fresco* [1997; Outside It Is Cool], and Jorge Trigoura (b. 1969) with *Si las balsas hablaran... o Juicio final a teatro lleno* [1998; If Boats Could Speak or Final Judgment in a Full Theater].

Fundamental Characteristics of Cuban Drama in the United States

Certain traits in terms of both semantics and technique stand out within the vast panorama described previously. The themes and settings tend to focus on three periods delimited by the revolutionary phenomenon: One is prior to 1959; the second is the Revolution and its aftermath; a third runs parallel to the latter but is located in exile. Some texts that use a diachronic structure include all three periods (*Recuerdos de familia*; *Exilio*). Very few plays depart from these historical frames and move to other contexts. One of these, however, is undoubtedly Héctor Santiagos's *Las noches de la Chambelona*, (1992). Others reflect on the human condition itself, either in the abstract or linked to contemporary life, as in the case with *The Conduct of Life* (1985) by María Irene Fornés.

The numerous texts that recall the Cuba that existed prior to the Revolution present a variety of focal points, among which the most important are

1. The approach from a nostalgic perspective that underlines the beautiful and picturesque aspects of the setting being evoked along with a *costumbrista* tendency that, of course, does not exclude criticism, comedy, or farce (e.g., *Las Carbonell de la calle Obispo*).

2. The selection of a few important figures from this past, such as José Martí (*Un hombre al amanecer*), with the aim of introducing them to younger generations or, as in the case of Gertrudis Gómez de Avellaneda (1814–1873) in *Vida y pasión de La Peregrina*, to interpret them in the light of the contemporary context. Such a procedure falls within the metaphorical technique that is very much used in historical plays of all periods, which calls on the complicity of the reader/spectator to get the immediate references.

3. The use of imaginary characters who are related to historical events that have a decisive effect on the plot (*Recuerdos de familia*, *Exilio*). This is the most common procedure.

It must be emphasized that the majority of the plays that tackle the topic of Cuba prior to the Revolution adopt a severely critical attitude toward this past. They present political, social, and family problems, such as dependence on the United States, political corruption, labor injustice, and social inequalities and prejudices, almost always set within a family context–both in the capital and in the provinces. The playwrights who cultivate this theme are perhaps proposing to research past incidents to arrive at an understanding of the events of recent decades. Those plays featuring Cuba after the Revolution share a fundamental element. Two strategies are at work in these works: The metaphorical technique mentioned above (*La madre y la guillotina*; *Las hetairas habaneras*) and a direct approach (*Las sombras no se olvidan*; *Amar así*; *Réquiem por una jinetera*). The methods employed in their execution are very diverse, ranging from the fast-moving one-act farces prompted by contemporary conditions that belong to commercial theater to plays with highly complex structures (*Ojos para no ver*). Every phase of the revolutionary process is illustrated within this work.

Another frequently mined thematic vein is life in exile, once again circumscribed within the context of the home. Here attention is given to two basic aspects, the analysis of family relationships that frequently gives rise to complex and bitter reflections (*Sanguivin in Unión City*) and the presentation of conflicts that emerge from adapting to the U.S. way of life, with its numerous comic, ridiculous, and dramatic incidents (*El súper*). These plays usually deploy the conventions of realism, but some experiment with new techniques. Other themes of interest to this group dedicated to life in exile include the previously mentioned topic of the re-encounter that once again has the family sphere as its focus (*Alguna cosita que alivie el sufrir*; *Siempre tuvimos miedo*; *Nadie se va del todo*) and the study of Cubans living together with other Hispanics and non-Hispanics in the United States (*Solidarios*). Numerous plays exist in all these categories and, for the first time in the history of the theater of the two Cubas, cover the issue of homosexuality with frankness–almost always from the homosexual point of view (*Bebo and the Band*; *Noche de ronda*). One could say that this theme is strongly linked to that of the family, which, as can be observed, is predominant in these works.

The dramatic treatment of the family can be subdivided into the three ways pointed out by Montes Huidobro when referring to theater in Cuba (1973, 25–36): the rebellion against paternal authority, the struggle between Cain and Abel, and the importance of the matriarchy. It must be stated that of the three, the first and the last are never tackled with the same intensity as they are in plays written and produced in Cuba. The father does not seem to be an all-powerful figure anymore; in the United States he is almost always a character who has trouble adapting and seeks the help of others to survive in an alien society. These circumstances frequently invest him with a comic or grotesque dimension, accentuated by the fact that in ideological terms, he struggles within the bounds of a radical conservatism. This version of the father has gained in honesty and positive emotions in comparison with his depiction in Cuba, and for this reason the confrontation between him and his children lacks high drama. The mother now fulfills neither an authoritarian nor the more impassioned role that links her with the matriarchy but rather is a sensible woman who frequently seeks the advice of her husband. But this change of attitude affects her dramatic situation in the text: She is no longer the more prominent character, as she is in Cuban plays. Instead it is the grandmothers who stand out amongst these new-style mothers and perform essential functions within the plot. They symbolize and defend tradition, which in turn leads to an intensification of nostalgia for a lost world (*Sanguivin in Unión City*), and they bring together, along with the sentimental flavor of this nostalgia, the important element of humor (*Mamá cumple ochenta años* [1984; *Mother is Eighty Years Old*]). The sheer abundance of grandmothers in these plays contrasts with the minimal presence of the grandfathers (*La caída*).

Of all these themes, the struggle between Cain and Abel is maintained with an energy that equals or even surpasses that of the island plays, a living reflection of the schism created by the Revolution. But even though animosity between siblings is presented in all its possible combinations (*La caída; Siempre tuvimos miedo; Sanguivin in Unión City*), in some plays (*Alguna cosita que alivie el sufrir; Balada de un verano en La Habana*) this antagonism is finally overcome, as the protagonist of *Balada de un verano en La Habana* attests: "Al final el amor nos hará olvidar y tendremos que perdonar cuando miremos hacia atrás no habrá victimas ni verdugos. Sencillamente, gente que estuvo atrapada en un mal sueño" (Leal 214) ["In the end love will make us forget and we will have to forgive. When we look back there will be neither victims nor executioners. Just people who were trapped in a bad dream"].

The frequency of the homosexual motif is a logical result of the social freedom allowed in the 1960s when this theater came to the fore. There are two tendencies here: The first deals with the familiar secular repudiation, sustained by the Judeo-Christian tradition (*Así en Miami como en el cielo* [1988; In Heaven as in Miami] by Raúl de Cárdenas; *Sanguivin in Unión City*), whereas the second refers to the open lifestyle of the gay communities, especially in New York (*Bebo and the Band*), even though occasionally traces of repression and secular hypocrisy make an appearance here too (*Canciones de la Vellonera* [*Songs of the Vellonera*] by Randy Barceló; *Las noches de la chambelona* [*Nights of the Chambelona*]). AIDS plays a prominent role in both treatments of this theme (*Camino de ángeles; Noche de ronda*).

Within this homoerotic universe there occurs a substitution of symbols. The black and mulatto are transformed into the epitome of sexuality (*Orlando; Nocturno de cañas bravas; Trash*), replacing the mulatto female of the vernacular theater and the Cuban *zarzuela* (Spanish style musical comedy). This is related to a detail that merits mention, notably the only sporadic presence of blacks and thus the limited inclusion of the vigorous reservoir of Afrocuban culture in the plays' plot lines. Various playwrights, however, have taken on the subject during the last decade, and their work forms the basis of an anthology by Armando González-Pérez. Those plays worthy of mention that have tackled religious themes related to race are *Ireme o las débiles potencias* [1976; Ireme or the Weak Powers] by Leopoldo Hernández and *Las hetairas habaneras* [The Prostitutes of Havana], *La navaja de Olofé* [The Knife of Olofé], and *Otra historia* [1995; Another Story] by Pedro Monge-Rafuls. *La eterna noche de Juan Francisco Manzano* [1995; The Eternal Night of Juan Francisco Manzano] by Héctor Santiago places its emphasis on the social aspect of black marginalization. It must be remembered that Cuban culture is mixed, basically mulatto, and to depreciate the strong black elements of which it is composed is to weaken it.

Translation by Jessica Johnson

Works Cited

Abreu Felipe, José. 1998. *Teatro*. Madrid: Editorial Verbum.

Cortina, Rodolfo J. 1991. *Cuban American Theater*. Houston: Arte Público Press.

Escarpanter, José A. 1988. "El teatro cubano fuera de la isla." *Escenarios de dos mundos: Inventario teatral de Iberoamérica*. Ed. Moisés Pérez Coterillo. Vol 2: *Chile, Cuba, Ecuador, El Salvador, España, Estados Unidos de América*. Madrid: Centro de Documentación Teatral. 333–41.

Espinosa Domínguez, Carlos. 1992. "Una dramaturgia escindida." *Teatro cubano contemporáneo: antología*. Ed. Carlos Espinosa Domínguez. Madrid: Centro de Documentación Teatral-Sociedad Estatal Quinto Centenario-Fondo de Cultura Económica. 13–77.

González-Cruz, Luis F., and Francesca Colecchia, ed. 1992. *Cuban Theater in the United States: A Critical Anthology*. Tempe, AZ: Bilingual Press.

González-Pérez, Armando, ed. 1999. *Presencia negra: Teatro cubano de la diáspora*. Madrid: Editorial Betania.

Leal, Rine, ed. 1995. *Teatro: 5 autores cubanos*. Jackson Heights, NY: Ollantay Press.

Montes Huidobro, Matías. 1973. *Persona, vida y máscara en el teatro cubano*. Miami: Ediciones Universal.

———. 1987. "Editorial." *Dramaturgos* 1.2: 3–6.

Muguercia, Magaly. 1988. *El teatro cubano en vísperas de la Revolución*. Havana: Letras Cubanas.

Pottlitzer, Joanne. 1988. *Hispanic Theater in the United States and Puerto Rico: A Report to the Ford Foundation*. New York: Ford Foundation.

CHAPTER 40

CUBAN AMERICAN PROSE

1975–2000

María Cristina García

There are over one million people of Cuban descent living in the United States today, the majority of them in south Florida. Most immigrated after 1959 and regard themselves as political exiles, people who were pushed out of their country by the radical policies of Fidel Castro's revolution. Unlike most immigrants, they did not come to the United States to begin life anew as *estadounidenses* [citizens of the United States] but rather to wait for the time when they could resume their lives back in their homeland. Over the years, as they waited for the improbable political change, they created institutions and networks and practiced the customs and traditions that had given their lives order and meaning in Cuba. To outsiders, it seemed that the Cubans had transplanted to Miami–and to Union City, Chicago, and other areas where they settled–a piece of their beloved country. Some observers in the United States interpreted the emigrés' obsession with the homeland, as manifested in issues of politics and language, as a disconcerting sign of their refusal to assimilate. However, the assimilation process was alive and well in the Cuban community. The "little Cubas" the emigrés created were as much invented as transplanted, providing enough familiarity to offer stability and comfort but also creatively responding to the unique needs of life in the United States. Over time the Cubans established ties to the United States that gave them refuge in spite of their original intentions. And eventually the voices of the first generation were rivaled by the voices of the second, for whom the United States was as important as–or even more important than–Cuba.

Nowhere is this process of dislocation and adaptation articulated as well as in the literature of this community. In many ways, Cuban exile and Cuban American novels and short stories serve as historical documents. Using Cuba, the revolution, and migration to the United States as backdrop for their fictional plots, these authors challenge our interpretations of history. At the same time, they give us insight into the psychological world of exile and biculturalism.

Comparatively few novels and short stories were published during the first decade of exile. Emigrés wrote almost exclusively in Spanish, which limited their audience in the United States. Unless you were an internationally acclaimed author, such as Guillermo Cabrera Infante (b. 1929), editors at mainstream U.S. publishing houses were not interested in looking at your work, much less in translating it for domestic marketing. Most writers sent their manuscripts to publishing houses in Mexico or Spain, where they had better luck; more often than not they ended up financing the publication of their work themselves. In the wake of the revolution, when most of Europe and Latin America regarded Cuba to be the model socialist state, few wanted to read the views of the so-called reactionaries. Fame did not always guarantee that you would be published. Some of Cuba's best writers, including Enrique Labrador Ruiz (1899–1991), Lino Novás Calvo (1905–1983), and Lydia Cabrera (1900–1991), had to finance the publication of their works during their first years in exile

(Arenas 43). By the early 1970s, a small number of publishing houses, most notably Editorial Universal, were founded by Cuban exiles in Miami, New York, and San Juan for the specific purpose of publishing the work of emigré authors.

In general, the works produced during the 1960s and early 1970s were of mixed quality. The more established authors, poets, and playwrights continued to experiment with their craft and produced some of their best work in exile in the United States, Europe, and Latin America. Many of them chose to settle far from the center of Cuban exile, Miami–some, because they had appointments in academic institutions in other cities; others, because they wished to live in vital cultural centers such as London, New York, or Paris; still others, because they wished to avoid the *politqueo*, or the political bickering, of their compatriots. These authors wrote about what they knew best: Cuba and Latin America. As in much of their earlier works, they explored what literary critics have termed *lo real maravilloso* (Carpentier's "marvelous real") of the Latin American experience: The geography, folklore, and exchange of cultures in Cuba, the Caribbean, and South America. Their plots and characters evolved within a Cuban or Latin American setting. They continued to view themselves as Cuban writers, but ones who, like other expatriates, were forced to live outside their homeland.

A number of "anti-revolutionary" novels emerged during the 1960s written by lesser-known authors, some writing for the first time. The first of such novels was Andrés Rivero Collado's (b. 1936) *Enterrado Vivo* [1961; Buried Alive], published in Mexico in 1960. It was followed by a host of other novels by such writers as Angel Castro Martínez (b. 1930), Emilio Fernández Camus (b. 1897), Ramiro Gómez-Kemp (b. 1914), René G. Landa (b. 1922), Raúl A. Fowler (b. 1905), Miguel F. Márquez y de la Cerra, and Luis Ricardo Alonso (b. 1929) (Lindstrom 225; Kanellos). The majority of these novels are valuable more as documentary texts than as literature. They are stories about the revolution and the displacement it caused. These authors vehemently opposed–or came to oppose–Fidel Castro's regime and gave graphic accounts of the abuses of the revolution: The imprisonment and executions of government opponents, the general climate of suspicion and harassment, and the suppression of civil liberties. Some of the accounts are semiautobiographical, and there is no doubt that for many authors, writing these novels served as a means of exorcizing personal demons. However, the writing is uneven and the dogmatic tone unsettling, forcing the non-Cuban reader to question the validity of the information. Hence, non-Cubans generally dismissed these works as propaganda. These novels had only a limited circulation and lifespan. Forty years after the revolution, however, they helped to explain the mindset of one segment of the exile community and to shed light on the reasons for their disaffection.

By the late 1970s, many emigré authors began focusing their creative energies on the United States rather than on Cuba, reflecting the general trend in the community itself.

This was especially true of those who came of age in the United States–the "1.5 generation," as some sociologists called them–for whom Cuba was a beautiful and stirring memory but who had spent most of their formative years in U.S. society. Their social and political development was different from both their elders and from the Cubans on the island, as was the Cuban culture they claimed.

The cultural revolution of the 1960s and early 1970s encouraged this creative shift. The civil rights movement and the counterculture focused new attention on the experiences of groups on the margins of society, and there was a new interest in "minority" art and literature. Suddenly, young Cuban American writers, like other Latinos, had opportunities to develop and showcase their creative work: Grants provided them free time to write; journals recruited their work; and academic appointments offered institutional support. This further encouraged their thematic and linguistic separation from the first Cuban exile generation of writers. Some of their colleagues and critics in the United States unfairly labeled them "fascists" for the political views they were assumed to have. However, since their work focused on the more neutral themes of identity and accommodation, they avoided the censure and ostracism that many exile authors encountered in their careers.

The distinction between Cuban exile and Cuban American literature was sometimes a subtle one. Some authors alternated between the two, refusing to be pigeonholed. The principal concern of Cuban American literature was the issue of identity. What did it mean to be Cuban? Could one retain one's national identity despite the overwhelming pressures to conform, to "Americanize?" Conversely, what did it mean to be an American? How did race, gender, and sexuality shape identity and experience? How did one maintain a balance between multiple worlds? By the 1980s, most of the 1.5 generation–and all of the second generation–were writing in English. With humor, they turned a critical eye to Cuba and the country they now claimed as their own. They gave voice to the experiences of a generation that felt varying degrees of pride, guilt, ambivalence, annoyance, and alienation at being both Cuban and U.S. citizens. Writing as immigrants or minorities in the United States, they were labeled "ethnic" writers rather than Cuban or Latin American writers. However, in seeking to define what *cubanidad* (Cubanness) meant for them, they were linked to generations of Cuban authors dating back to the nineteenth century, who were equally concerned with defining a personal or national identity.

Some writers used the mediums of memoir and biography to explore identity. Pablo Medina's (b. 1948) *Exiled Memories* (1990) and Gustavo Pérez Firmat's (b. 1949) *Next Year in Cuba* (1995) reflect on their authors' childhoods and coming of age in Cuba and the United States. María del Carmen Boza's *Scattering the Ashes* (1998) and Josefina González's *A pesar de todo* [1997; In Spite of All] use biography to discuss what the experience of exile has meant to women and families. In juvenile literature, Alma Flor Ada's *Under the Royal Palms: A Childhood in Cuba* (1998) and *Where the Flame Trees Bloom* (1994) exposed young readers, and especially the newest generation of Cuban Americans, to the people, traditions, and customs that shaped the author's life.

Fiction, however, was the medium most Cuban American writers chose to explore the themes of dislocation, adaptation, and identity. Some of these fictional works can be categorized as historical novels, and they serve as important complements to the numerous academic studies of the revolution and of migration. Virgil Suárez's (b. 1962) *The Cutter* (1998), for example, looks at the first decade of Cuba's revolutionary society. The reader is presented with information about the day-to-day functioning of 1960s Cuban society that will not ordinarily be found in an academic text. The novel describes the pain of families separated by emigration. It gives a sense of how the Cuban bureaucracy worked–or didn't work, as the case may be–and of the petty and annoying obstacles that the Interior Ministry placed in the way of those who wished to emigrate. It describes the *actos de repudio* [acts of rejection] that applicants for emigration were forced to endure, as well as the harassment by the Committees for the Defense of the Revolution (CDR), the neighborhood watch committees. It describes the frustration of losing one's business to the state and the frustration one felt at seeing the confiscation of property and belongings. Finally, it describes the frustration that compelled Cubans to risk everything and *tirarse al mar* (take to the seas) on any craft that floated. The protagonist's story is the story of many people both on and off the island. It seems like oral history.

Achy Obejas' (b. 1956) story "We Came All the Way from Cuba so You Could Dress Like This?" (1994 from a collection with the same title) provides a wonderful account of migration through a child's eyes. It is a story that elicits many painful memories from just about every Cuban emigré who reads it. Obejas' narrator gives us the details of those first days–and years–in exile, details that are not part of academic texts. She tells of fleeing Cuba on a boat and of being picked up by a freighter, of filling out forms at the Cuban Refugee Center, and of being given old clothing and toys to tide them over until her father found a job. She tells us of eating her first meal, a Royal Castle hamburger; of staying at an old hotel for transients; and of being unable to find a permanent place to live because no one wanted to rent to Cubans. She tells of having to take welfare and of her mother having to work as a maid in a luxury hotel; she tells of her father's suicide attempt when he realized that they would not be returning to Cuba any time soon. She tells of having to give money to exile counterrevolutionary groups to show one's patriotism, only to learn that the group members were buying expensive luxuries for themselves. She tells of being placed in a special education class because her lack of English proficiency prevented her from doing well on the IQ test. More poignantly, she tells of her inability to be the person that her parents wanted her to be. When her parents were asked at the Refugee Center why they fled Cuba, they pointed to her and said that they came for her so that she could have a future. And she grew up with that burden all her life because the truth is that her parents came to the United States as much for themselves as for their child, and they projected all their frustrated hopes and dreams onto her.

Of the Cuban American writers who write in Spanish, Roberto G. Fernández (b. 1949) has attracted the most attention. His novels *La vida es un special* [1983; Life is a Special], *La montaña rusa* [1984; Roller Coaster], and *Raining Backwards* (1988) are each a series of satirical vignettes about life in exile. Fernández pokes fun at the older generation of Cuban emigrés who cannot–or refuse to–adapt to life in the United States. Like so many travelers from the United States who constantly complain when traveling overseas, these emigrés constantly complain about life in the United States. For them, Cuba is the most beautiful country, with the finest people; the United States can never compare. In indulging their nostalgia, the characters' memory is selective. Like so many emigrés, they ignore the social and economic problems that brought on the revolution. They claim that there was no racism or poverty in their homeland, no abuses or terrorism. Their lives were comfortable so they ignore the fact that not all shared in Cuba's prosperity. They exaggerate how good they had it back home. In the normal day-to-day exchange between compatriots, emigrés–particularly those who were upwardly mobile in Cuba–oftentimes exaggerate how much property and wealth they owned in Cuba and subsequently lost to the revolution. Psychologically, it is a means of distinguishing their experience from that of the rest of their compatriots. A popular joke in south Florida states that if Cubans had had as much land prior to the revolution as they said they had, Cuba would have been the size of the Soviet Union. Fernández and other authors satirize this propensity to distort reality. In *Raining Backwards* one character insists that her mother's cocoa plantation "would have put the Ponderosa to shame" (36). A character in Omar Torres's (b. 1945) *Fallen Angels Sing* (1991) insists that Cuba never had as many flies as the United States and that no one ever died from cancer there: "That's an American illness," she says (32, 60).

If older emigrés indulge in excessive nostalgia, it is because they feel alienated and marginalized. Their lives have been turned upside down. They have had to uproot themselves from their jobs, their homeland, their friends and neighbors, and, in some cases, their families. They have had to adapt to a new language, a new social and economic status, and a new lifestyle. Despite their attempts to recreate in south Florida the society they left behind, life in exile can never be what it was, at least for the older generation. For those who settled outside south Florida, far away from familiar institutions or supportive countrymen, the feelings of uprootedness can be even more acute. In Torres's *Fallen Angels Sing,* one character insists on being buried in Cuba when she dies. When asked what difference it makes where she is buried, she says, "It makes a lot of difference. I don't belong here. We don't belong here" (65). In Elías Miguel Muñoz's (b. 1954) *Crazy Love* (1988), Julián and Johnny believe that their mother should never have left Cuba. She is terrified of society in the United States; it is too large and threatening. "Take a plant or a fruit tree that only grows in the tropics and plant it in a cold land," says Julián. "It will die, or go crazy, turn poisonous" (111–12). In Virgil F. Suárez's (b. 1962) *Latin Jazz* (1989), the elderly grandfather, Esteban, spends his time reminiscing, unable to adapt to life in Los Angeles. Suárez writes that Esteban "has never forgotten the past, for in the past he lost, as he says, his identity, dignity, his respect for humanity" (12).

Alienation and the clash between cultures are central themes in Cuban American literature as in most ethnic literatures. Despite the U.S. cultural presence on the island before the revolution, the average Cuban had little social contact with people from the United States. In exile, the emigrés find people in the United States puzzling, their customs alien. U.S. idiomatic expressions in English make no sense; the U.S. lifestyle is too fast-paced; U.S. morals are found lacking. "We should never have left," says one character in Roberto G. Fernández's (b. 1949) *Raining Backwards* (1988). "This country changes people. I think it's the water. It makes them crazy!" (85).

The second generation does not share their parents' obsession with the past because it isn't *their* past. It doesn't have a hold on them. While the older emigrés consider Miami to be home because it has the second-largest Cuban population in

the world and because it is the closest they can get to Cuba, figuratively speaking, the younger generation is more cognizant of its limitations. The exile community nurtures and supports its own, but it also has the potential to suffocate. Behavior and political beliefs are dictated by the powerful institutions of the exile community, and those who go against the tide are marginalized. They are dismayed by what they perceive to be the provinciality and narrowmindedness of the community. The older generation sees the world in black and white: One is either a communist or an anti-communist; and if one does not "oppose" Fidel, then one is a communist. Such simplistic reasoning contributes to the climate of censorship in south Florida that inhibits serious and sophisticated political discourse.

It is not surprising, then, that exile politics come under heavy fire in Cuban American literature. Authors poke fun at the political factions and the war games. The work of Roberto G. Fernández once again provides some of the most humorous examples. In *La montaña rusa,* he ridicules both the obsession with communism and the myriad political groups that have emerged in exile. An advertisement for the C.A.A.F.D.P.C.P.M.P.B. ("Cuban-American Alliance for Freedom and Democracy and for the Prevention of Communism and the Preservation of Moral Principles and Biculturalism") states, "We are an Affirmative Action/Equal Opportunity Organization, no communists nor similar degenerates need apply" (80). In *Raining Backwards,* he pokes fun at the "weekend warriors" who train to overthrow Castro, as well as at the inconsistencies in U.S. foreign policy. One character bombs the Cuban presidential palace in Havana with grenades dropped from a large homemade kite, which he maneuvers from his apartment in Little Havana (thanks to a fast-moving cold front). He is subsequently arraigned before a federal magistrate for violating the Kennedy-Krushchev accords–a case that remains pending for the next fifteen years. While he awaits his fate at the hands of the judicial system, Congress awards him a Purple Heart (87–88).

Other authors poke fun at what they perceive to be the emigrés' lack of political sophistication, despite their obsession with politics. The narrator of Omar Torres's *Fallen Angels Sing* ridicules emigrés who claim that they *always knew* Fidel Castro was a communist: "There weren't ten people in Cuba at the time who could tell a communist from a fascist; the only Marx they heard of was Groucho, and even him they didn't understand" (74). In *Raining Backwards,* a character compares bugs to communists: "This year with all this rain they are like the communists: Everywhere. You think you have killed every single one, and bang, they pop in where you least expect them, just like the communists" (86).

Omar Torres is also intrigued by those of his generation who become embroiled in exile politics. As the narrator in *Fallen Angels Sing* states, it is understandable for older emigrés to yearn to return to Cuba (and work toward that end), but unusual for younger emigrés to be as obsessed. The younger generation left as children and had less time to establish strong connections. The narrator concludes that these younger emigrés are trying to invent a past for themselves. They are pulled to a "myth of a country": "It was nothing tangible or tactile; it was a nostalgic longing for something they never had, but wished they had had; it was a life they had been robbed of, even if that life was worse than the one they were living in the United States" (83–84). Like that of the older emigrés, their political ideology was sometimes vague and undefined. Their principal goal in life was to see Fidel's overthow. They had no specific program to propose as an alternative other than a vague insistence on democracy: "They were right-wing in their political thinking because the left had taken over their places; they abhorred communism because it had stripped them of all they had known as a normal way of life. Given the right circumstances they could, perhaps, be more liberal than any man, more progressive than any man, but not as exiles, not as pariahs" (85).

A number of authors have explored the question of whether one can ever really return home. This is a question of particular importance to the Cuban American generation. Most of them left Cuba as children or teenagers before they had a clear understanding of who they were. The decision to leave Cuba was made for them by their parents, and their identity was defined later by others, by the exile community and by the larger U.S. society. For many, particularly those who were teenagers, the separation from Cuba was as traumatic as it was for their parents and grandparents. Miguel, the principal character in *Fallen Angels Sing*, articulates the feelings of many of Torres's generation:

> Mine was a generation drifting among fading memories, uncertainties and a sense of not belonging. It was a generation wishing time would either stop in pre-Castro Cuba–1958–or, to the contrary, speed ahead full blast; wishing the Revolution had never taken place or, better still, that it would end tomorrow; wishing we were back in our homeland, in our hometowns, with our loved ones. We were exiles within an exile, having been caught in the middle: hearing the unchanging voices of our parents chanting songs of yesteryear; watching boys and girls our age living the lies of old; willing to give anything to have had a choice. (14)

As adults, the Cuban Americans had to define for themselves who they were and where they fit. The search for "home" led many Cuban Americans back to Cuba. In 1978, the Cuban government reversed its policy and permitted exiles to briefly return to the homeland for "family reunification trips." In 1979 alone, over 100,000 emigrés returned to Cuba to visit family. For those who chose to return, these trips gave them the opportunity to answer these questions, both in their personal lives and in their creative work.

In Flora González Mandri's "El Regreso" [1990, The Return], the first person narrator returns to Cuba after an eighteen-year absence. The trip offers her the opportunity to determine for herself the accomplishments and failures of the revolution and to reestablish ties to the extended family she left behind. The narrator is struck by how familiar and yet how alien Cuban society seems. The old landmarks are still there, but after a tour through the historic cemetery in Santiago to see the tombs of Martí and Estrada Palma, she realizes that the interpretation of those landmarks and of Cuban history have changed. Her compatriots raised under the communist system have a very different way of looking at the world. The Cubans' day-to-day routines in the revolutionary State are also starkly different from hers, and yet the Cuban sense of humor and *joie de vivre* remain intact, offering a sense of continuity. The narrator is impressed with many of the accomplishments of the revolution, especially with regard to education and health care, but she is dismayed by the shortages in basic consumer goods and by the ever-watchful police presence, as well as by the revolution's inability to eradicate certain social attitudes, especially with regard to women. She had hoped to define her relationship to Cuba during her trip; but instead of answers, she leaves with even more questions. She is certain only about one thing: that there is a great misunderstanding between Cubans on opposite sides of the Florida Straits. Each group has failed to understand the sacrifices that the other has had to make. Despite the ideological differences, there was much that bound Cubans together.

Margarita Engle's two novels, *Singing to Cuba* (1993) and *Skywriting* (1995), at times seem more like travel diaries than fiction. In both novels, a female narrator returns to Cuba to visit family and is confronted by the harsh realities of life in Castro's revolutionary State. In *Singing to Cuba,* for example, we see the more sordid side of Cuba. The narrator tells us what she sees and does in Cuba and juxtaposes her stories with the story of her great-uncle Gabriel, a peasant farmer in Oriente province, who was erroneously accused of assisting counterrevolutionaries and sent to prison. Together, these stories take the reader from the early years of the Castro government all the way into the early 1990s. Here is a family that has been deeply affected by the revolution. Engle's narrator becomes more and more critical of Cuban society as she becomes aware of how wounded her Cuban relatives are. Her family lives in a constant state of fear: Of not having enough to eat, of being accused by their neighbors, of disappearance and death. Her cousin, Miguelito, a composer, is afraid to sing his songs, afraid that they will be misunderstood and that they, along with him, will disappear. The narrator's vision of Cuba is a nightmare. She tells us of the writers and poets who disappear and are later found tortured and maimed in the bowels of some ancient prison. She tells us of the paranoia that inhibits Cubans from even confessing their sins to a priest for fear that he may be a government informant. She tells us of the inhumane economic structure that depends on tourism, providing visitors with all the amenities that Cuban citizens do without.

Engle's second novel, *Skywriting,* takes us to 1994. The idea for the book was developed one summer in Cuba while Engle and her relatives waited for news of two cousins who had fled the island on a homemade raft. This time she tells us about life under Option Zero: a Cuba without Soviet subsidies. We learn about the drastic shortages, about the underground tunnels built in preparation for a rumored U.S. invasion; we begin to understand the deep disillusionment felt by even the most committed revolutionaries in this society. We learn of the misconceptions that people in Cuba have about life in the United States–and about the U.S. population in general. We learn of the emotional suffering and ostracism that families in Cuba experience when a loved one chooses to emigrate or is imprisoned for *conducta impropia* [improper conduct].

For those who have never lived in Cuba, Engle's novels sound like right-wing propaganda; for those who have been unfortunate enough to experience the scenes she describes, the novels are biographical. The stories her narrators tell are the stories Cubans in the United States have lived or heard from friends and family returning from the island. They portray a side of the revolution that is passed over in analyses of State policies.

Cristina García (b. 1958) also addresses the theme of returning to Cuba in her fictional work *Dreaming in Cuban*. The novel revolves around three generations of women of the Pino family. Celia, a staunch revolutionary, her daughter Felicia, and her three children live in Cuba; Celia's other daughter, Lourdes, an equally staunch counterrevolutionary, lives in Brooklyn with her husband and daughter, Pilar, where they run the Yankee Doodle bakery, a gathering place for Cuban political extremists. Relations between the two families are strained because they cannot understand each other's political worldviews. Letters are the only communication between the families in Brooklyn and Havana, and even these are cursory. Lourdes sends her mother photographs of the bakery: "Each glistening éclair is a grenade aimed at Celia's political beliefs, each strawberry shortcake proof–in butter, cream, and eggs– of Lourdes's success in the U.S., and a reminder of the ongoing shortages in Cuba" (117).

Pilar does not share her mother's hatred of communist Cuba. She longs to return to Cuba to see it through her own eyes. When the opportunity to travel to Cuba finally arises in 1980, Lourdes and Pilar return to visit their family. For Lourdes, the trip is an opportunity to make a political statement. She spends her time in Cuba criticizing the revolution and mocking her compatriots. She dreams of assassinating Fidel Castro. For Pilar, on the other hand, the trip is a journey of self-exploration, an opportunity to fill in missing pieces. Like so many Cuban Americans, however, Pilár comes to realize that her ties are to New York–not *instead* of Cuba, but more than to Cuba. She must find a way of maintaining her connection to both worlds. Similarly, the heroine of Teresa Bevin's *Havana Split* (1998) finds that her trip to Havana, after twenty years of exile, becomes a journey of rediscovery, an opportunity to remember and to reconcile her past with her present.

The issue of language–in what language one writes, dreams, and communicates–is naturally a theme and concern for Cuban American writers seeking to define their cultural and artistic identity. From the moment they arrived in the United States, they have been pressured to learn one language and retain another. The challenge was to be truly bilingual in order to maintain connections to both cultures, both societies. Spanish provided a link to the past, but English represented the future and an opportunity for a reinvention of self. As "minority" writers in the United States, language determines their audience and degree of exposure. While many of them began their careers writing in Spanish, most made the transition into English, both because it expanded their audience in the United States and because it reflected their growing ties to North American society.

Bilingualism represents adaptation. Roberto G. Fernández pokes fun at those Cubans whose English skills are so lacking that they don't even know when they are being insulted. In one vignette in *Raining Backwards*, a Cuban couple mistake a harassing phone caller for a salesman. The caller declares open season on Cubans. "We are going to be hunting you down. We are going to purify this land of trash. You fucking Cubans." The Cuban responds: "Chi no jiar. Ron, number. Senquiu" (153). Conversely, Fernández satirizes the forces in south Florida–and ultimately the United States–that would eradicate the use of Spanish and impose monolingualism. In many ways, they are a mirror image of the emigrés they are trying to control. In *Raining Backwards,* the speaking of English in Miami is enforced by the local "Tongue Brigade." According to a Supreme Court decision, speaking in any other tongue, and especially in Spanish, is a form of disglosia, a degenerative disease of speech centered in the brain. The White House promises to secure one hundred million dollars from Congress to establish education programs to help curb the spread of the disease. The goal of this fictional English-only movement is to eradicate any sign of the Cuban presence. Other measures are passed: In the neighboring city of "Gables by the Sea," an ordinance is passed prohibiting the playing of dominoes and the wearing of colored underwear.

The "Miss Calle Ocho" beauty pageant is forced to require English fluency of its aspirants. Unfortunately, Fernández's satire is all too real. Although the nativists in south Florida have not yet lobbied for the banning of domino playing (or of the wearing of colored underwear), they *have* tried to ban the use of Spanish in public settings, as seen in the prohibiting of Spanish among employees in some businesses and institutions and in the successful move to repeal Dade County's bilingual-bicultural ordinance in 1980.

If defining their ties to Cuba is important for this generation of writers, so is defining their relationship to the United States. For those who came of age during the 1960s, the Civil Rights Movement and counterculture radicalized their perception of society as much as–or even more than–the Cuban Revolution. Like other Latino and minority authors, they became concerned with issues such as race, class, gender, and sexuality and with how these defined their identity and experience. They became equally concerned with the problems of poverty, violence, war, racism, and sexism.

Roberto G. Fernández, in *La montaña rusa*, satirizes the way the Cuban exile media has tried to dictate women's proper roles and behavior. During the 1960s and early 1970s, Cuban exile women were bombarded with contradictory messages in the popular media. On the one hand, they were expected to contribute to their family's economic well-being; on the other, they were warned that too much success would sacrifice their femininity and their marriages or their marriage prospects. Magazine articles and radio shows advised them on the proper way to dress, to keep their households, to raise their children, and to keep their husbands "interested." They received similar advice in the mainstream U.S. media, which was equally concerned with controlling women. In one of Fernández's vignettes, a popular radio show advises women on the art of conversation. The host advises her female audience not to express opinions, much less in an aggressive fashion:

> A woman should have a topic rehearsed in which she feels confident. For example: "The Beach certainly was lovely yesterday." A woman should speak little since most of the time we talk and talk without knowing what to say. A woman should listen more and talk less in order not to commit the mistakes that lead one to lose one's male audience. (143)

The radio-show host also advises women not to become involved in the "masculine" forum of politics: "Only in an unavoidable situation might you murmur 'Yes, communism smells like poop'" (143).

In *Crazy Love*, Elias Miguel Muñoz explores the conflict that results when women adapt to new roles in a new society. While many Cuban women have found life in the United States to be liberating, allowing them to develop themselves in ways they think they might never have in Cuba, they also must often deal with resentment from their spouses, parents, and even children. In the novel, Julián's mother undergoes a radical transformation in exile. Life in the United States has forced her to become more assertive and independent, and she is determined that her daughter, Geneia, be so as well. The mother's upbringing in Cuba did not prepare her for the realities of life in the United States, and she does not want her daughter to be weighed down by outmoded cultural expectations. This new attitude in the mother inevitably leads to conflict between the mother and the grandmother, who has very definite opinions about a woman's role and a daughter's responsibilities:

"What's gotten into her?" asks Abuela. "She used to be such a docile creature, never raised her voice, never talked back to me, always listened and took my advice." It's all because of this damned country, she says. This evil world has turned her darling daughter into a monster. Because Mami won't call her ten times a day, and she won't consult with her when a major decision has to be made, and she won't allow her to put ideas about femininity and little-girl-duties into [Geneia's] head. Because she fights her, and hangs up on her when Abuela starts telling her what to do. (11)

While women's roles have adapted to the realities of life in exile, men's roles have not adapted accordingly, at least not among the older generation. Male roles are still strongly prescribed. Men are expected to be the principal breadwinners, or at least the ones who hold the most desirable jobs and the highest incomes. Attitudes toward sexuality remain as rigid as they did in Cuba. A man who cheats on his spouse is forgiven more quickly than a woman who is unfaithful; homosexuality is taboo. Of the Cuban American authors, Elías Miguel Muñoz best articulates the demands made of men and the intolerance of homosexuality within Cuban exile culture. In *Crazy Love,* Julián, a bisexual artist, tells how upon his first demonstration of artistic behavior, his parents took him to a doctor for hormone shots. Afterwards, his father, who was obsessed with penis size, checked his son's penis to make sure that it was developing properly. Julián envies his sister: "You're a lucky girl who knows only psychological torture: long silences, violent screaming and prohibitions" (16). In *The Greatest Performance* (1991), two childhood friends, Rosa and Marito—one a lesbian, the other a gay man—are reunited in California after years of separation. Exile took them each to separate cities, and they had to come to terms with their identities, both cultural and sexual, on their own. Rosa becomes the caregiver of Marito, who is dying from AIDS. "After searching Heaven and Earth for a true love, for a generous homeland, for a family who wouldn't abuse us or condemn us, for a body who wouldn't betray our truest secrets, we found each other: A refuge, a song, a story to share" (149).

In trying to define their relationship to both Cuba and the United States, most Cuban American authors have come to terms with their hybridness; others have concluded that they don't fit anywhere. However, the upheaval and dislocation that could have easily silenced them was transmuted through the creative art of writing. In the process, they not only articulated the concerns of their generation but also vitalized the literature of the country in which they live. The works of the authors I have treated in this text are just a sample of the rich body of work produced by this generation. Like historians and sociologists, they have chronicled the lives of Cubans both on and off the island—discovering, remembering, reinterpreting.

Works Cited

Ada, Alma Flor. 1991. *Where the Flame Trees Bloom.* New York: Atheneum Books for Young Readers.

———. 1998. *Under the Royal Palms: A Childhood in Cuba.* New York: Atheneum Books for Young Readers.

Arenas, Reinaldo. 1986. *Necesidad de libertad.* Mexico City: Kosmos-Editorial.

Bevin, Teresa. 1998. *Havana Split.* Houston, TX: Arte Público Press.

Boza, Maria del Carmen. 1998. *Scattering the Ashes.* Tempe, AZ: Bilingual Press.

Engle, Margarita. 1993. *Singing to Cuba.* Houston, TX: Arte Público Press.

———. 1995. *Skywriting: A Novel of Cuba.* New York: Bantam Books.

Fernández, Roberto G. 1981. *La vida es un special.* Miami: Ediciones Universal.

———. 1985. *La montaña rusa.* Houston, TX: Arte Público Press.

———. 1988. *Raining Backwards.* Houston, TX: Arte Público Press.

García, Cristina. 1992. *Dreaming in Cuban.* New York: Alfred A. Knopf.

González, Josefina. 1997. *A pesar de todo: nostalgias y reflexiones de la mujer cubana en el exilio.* Miami: Ediciones Universal.

González Mandri, Flora. 1990. "El Regreso." *Paradise Lost or Gained? The Literature of Hispanic Exile.* Ed. Fernando Alegría and Jorge Ruffinelli. Houston: Arte Público Press. 38–60.

Kanellos, Nicolás, ed. 1989. *Biographical Dictionary of Hispanic Literature in the United States: The Literature of Puerto Ricans, Cuban Americans, and Other Hispanic Writers.* New York: Greenwood Press.

Lindstrom, Naomi E. 1982. "Cuban American and Continental Puerto Rican Literature." *Sourcebook of Hispanic Culture in the United States.* Ed. David William Foster. Chicago: American Library Association. 221–45.

Medina, Pablo. 1990. *Exiled Memories: A Cuban Childhood.* Austin: University of Texas Press.

Muñoz, Elías Miguel. 1989. *Crazy Love.* Houston, TX: Arte Público Press.

———. 1991. *The Greatest Performance.* Houston, TX: Arte Público Press.

Obejas, Achy. 1994. *We Came All the Way from Cuba So You Could Dress Like This?* Pittsburgh, PA: Cleis Press.

Pérez Firmat, Gustavo. 1995. *Next Year in Cuba: A Cubano's Coming-of-Age in America.* New York: Anchor Books.

Suárez, Virgil. 1989. *Latin Jazz.* New York: Simon and Schuster.

———. 1991. *The Cutter: A Novel.* New York: Available Press.

Torres, Omar. 1991. *Fallen Angels Sing.* Houston, TX: Arte Público Press.

PART FOUR

LITERARY CULTURE IN
THE TWENTIETH CENTURY
INTRODUCTION

Renato Cordeiro Gomes, Djelal Kadir, and
Marília Rothier Cardoso

The twentieth century poses particular challenges to comparative historiography. The accelerated volatilities of the century's cultural formations bend historical perspective on relativity's warped axis of time and on the equally relative axis of space, where relation of center to periphery shifts, and different centers implode into diachronic prisms. It becomes especially challenging to track the continuities and transformations at contact points of local and universal matrices. No less difficult is the task of measuring different rates of change and tracking their attendant discourses: Their emergence and development, their derivations and linkages, their advancements and retrogressions, their endurance and transformations.

The strategies of a comparative history could be defined by the particular ways one privileges dislocation as a narrative principle. This is a principle that will consistently guide our historiographic procedures as we examine the case of twentieth-century cultural formations in Latin America in this part of our history. Here, the modern period will be considered in its various stages and through a variety of lenses: The legacy of a nineteenth-century liberal ideology; the genesis of modernity and the project of nation building; the emergence of diverse modernisms as national discourse and as regional avant-garde movements; the consolidation of certain aesthetic experiments; the critique of certain conservative impulses within modernity; and the recasting of tradition itself into a tradition of the new that eventually founders on its own cult of novelty as postmodern self-parody.

Modernity's first stage renders dislocation into rupture in contestatory pursuit of what might be new. Endowed with an acute historical awareness and anxiety about time, this investment in the future denies the past identified with tradition and facilitates the emergence of peripheral cultural practices and products that, in turn, pollinate the artistic production of hegemonic centers. In later stages, this negativity loses its radical impulse and is partially neutralized by the incorporation of traditional elements and their aesthetic *topoi*. These elements are recuperated, in turn, by the resurgence of diverse artistic procedures that broaden the criteria of taste and judgment. Once the modernist impetus is consumed, once the attitudes of transgression become formulaic and ritualized, the postmodern displaces "the tradition of rupture," as Octavio Paz termed the modernist impulse. Critical passion, then, gives way to certain resonant values. By the same token, the sharp and growing presence of technological developments in artistic production and the rapid succession of dislocations

end by relativizing the differences between times and spaces. History then becomes de-centered and acutely problematic. This predicament of the historical becomes even more exacerbated as cultural imaginaries and their virtuality displace belief in, or reliance on, stable concepts of focus, locus, and movement.

Such radical translocations oblige us to read twentieth-century cultural formations in Latin America interstitially. That reading takes place between the fault lines of reality, where literary life, the intellectual career of artists and writers, and interregional and international exchanges come together; in the aesthetic and ethnic plane, where one witnesses the discoursive relations of appropriation, transculturation, reduction, transfiguration, and deflection; and in the ideological plane, where cultural practices and products are subsumed and must be read as historical symptoms of particular social and political contexts.

Thus, in order to trace the outlines of literary culture in twentieth-century Latin America, as with cultures elsewhere, the emphasis moves from "belles lettres" to a broader cultural textuality comprised of such cultural artifacts as travel books, diaries, chronicles, correspondence, autobiography, and narrative experiments that revolutionize traditional genres. Within this reading process, travel itself becomes a determinative and transformative element in the field of literary culture. Ideas and cultural practices are disseminated by virtue of elective travel by tourists, cultural diplomats, and curious adventurers, or by dint of obligatory displacement of intellectuals and artists into exile or "insile," as well as by massive migrations, both internally and across borders and oceans.

The routes of translocation are diverse and they crisscross. Their impact, however, as the record and the narratives it has elicited from historians show, is unmistakable: The effects of European ideas on Latin American travelers; indelible Latin American effects on Europeans and North-Americans who ventured into Latin America as diplomats, teachers, or as exiles and repercussions of intra-American sojourns between Brazil and Hispanic America. Just as significant are the journeys of writers, intellectuals, and artists into the interior or into the backlands of their own countries. The forays by Brazilian modernist writers in search of their own country and its regional traditions as part of their modernist project are exemplary in this regard.

Geographical displacements have their concomitant parallels in discoursive dislocations. These conceptual deterritorializations serve as indices to modernity, to the various forms of modernism, and its localized permutations. Thus, the historical (time, avant-garde, revolution) and the geographical (space, simulacrum, globalization) converge. The space of that convergence emerges as the contested site of transformations in the poetic diction of the avant-garde, articulated most often by the numerous literary manifestos and programmatic proclamations of what will become a "tradition of the new."

From the 1960s onward, such manifestos give way to a proliferation of theoretical discourses that interrogate instituted canons just as forcefully as their focus shifts to categories of class, ethnicity, and gender. Such concepts as the new, repetition, originality, and rupture become recuperated in discoursive practices that prefix avant-garde movements with "post-" and "neo-" prostheses. In the process, figures of literary appropriation and revisionism become strategies of textual construction and deconstruction that continue to interrogate institutional traditions and the effects of canonization. The private sphere of artistic creation and the public sphere of aesthetic and cultural legitimation continue their dialectical counterpoint, with the confrontation and contradictions between social establishment and private appropriation continuing unabated. These contestations, articulated often through screens of ideology (Marxism, liberalism, neo-conservatism, authoritarianism, capitalism) emerge as the dramatic enactments of individual and collective identity formations. Acted out in the public arena, these acts are as vehemently rehearsed in the textual discourses, particularly in the genres of essay and fiction writing, during the second half of the twentieth century. It is yet another symptom of the twentieth century's irony, an irony that is tragic as often as it is parodic, that in the twenty-first century we can only locate this complex historiographic diagnosis in the context of dislocation–geographical–spatial, historical–temporal, discoursive and ideological.

CHAPTER 41

HISTORIC DISPLACEMENTS IN TWENTIETH-CENTURY BRAZILIAN LITERARY CULTURE

Renato Cordeiro Gomes, Ana Lúcia Almeida Gazolla, Ana Maria de Alencar, Antonio Arnoni Prado, Edson Rosa da Silva, Eneida Leal Cunha, Everardo Rocha, João Cezar de Castro Rocha, Marília Rothier Cardoso, Nádia Battella Gotlib

Travel and Transformations in the Cultural Field

Born of the tension of contact between heterogeneous cultures, Brazilian literature (in the manner of its sibling Latin-American literatures) demands a theoretical perspective that will provide us with an adequate model for criticism and historical interpretation. Silviano Santiago points out the errors in conventional modes of interpretation in his essay "O entre-lugar do discurso latino-americano" ["The In-Between Place of Latin-American Discourse"]. Conventional approaches confer excessive value on sources and influences, and inevitably relegate the literatures of colonial regions to a secondary plane. Santiago proposes to privilege difference–as it is formulated by post-structuralism–as an effective alternative for the canon's predilection for emulation, continuity, and similarity. Latin American literature's place in the literary landscape should be appreciated for having produced ruptures with Eurocentric models on which it has been inevitably based. An unprejudiced look at these ruptures promptly uncovers the positive interference of extraneous elements (foreign, exotic, wild) in the deployment of the West's artistic and intellectual legacy. Interpreted from this perspective, Latin-American cultures have historically prefigured a model of deconstructing of ethnocentrism that was later to be legitimized by post-Modernist theory.

To better establish the measure of difference that characterizes Latin-American literary products, according to Santiago's proposal, it is necessary to redirect our interpretive tools, to eschew the intellectual products of stability and focus instead on the disruption of travel, measuring its aesthetic and cultural consequences. Journeys–whether through geographic or virtual space–are effectively responsible for the confrontation between groups with different cultural lineages. In order to follow the historical course of Latin-American literatures, we must arm ourselves with interpretive tools sensitive to the impact of travel (in its various forms: Migration, exile, diaspora, conquest, tourism, research) on the components of literary text–choice of topics, stylistic procedures, and aesthetic-philosophical criteria.

The demand for a Brazilian cultural identity–framed by universal standards–arises in a tradition of travel writing that makes its first appearance in the sixteenth century, when a plethora of narrative practices produced representations of the non-European world for European consumption. Many of the writings prior to the nineteenth century reveal a recurrence of the tropes and strategies of colonial discourse, and formulations based on premises intended to legitimize the construction of a non-European identity. The principles of similarity, analogy, and self-reference are the conditioning factors that allow for the representation of the other. Conceptual modes established traditionally by European thought defined a shared understanding of objective reality and determined the selection of what could be included for description. These conceptual modes were responsible, therefore, for the topics and motifs that circulated within texts, the structure of these very texts, and the authors' own strategic positioning with respect to the object. Travel narratives evince a form of apprehension that comprises a totalizing vision and a perspective that expects confirmation. They project a model for representing the other of such far-reaching epistemological and political influence that their repercussions are felt in twentieth-century texts.

The vast majority of travel writings up until the beginning of the twentieth century that bridged the zone of contact between Brazil and Europe or the United States had as its subject a construction of Brazil from the point of view of a foreign traveler. Once the incipient phase was over, most of the Colonial period was witness to the experience of travelers in transit from Europe and the United States to Brazil. The eighteenth century saw a great expansion in the geographic mobility of European travelers, motivated by commercial interests that introduced large numbers of visitors to travel to Latin America. (The few records found of Brazilian travelers in Europe, such as those of students enrolled at the University of Coimbra in Portugal, do not present us with narratives in the form of travel writings.) The transference of the Portuguese crown to Rio de Janeiro inaugurated a new cycle of journeys. Stiff protectionist policies were dropped and the tight restrictions that had virtually closed off the nation to non-Iberians were lifted. This new cycle gained intensity throughout the nineteenth century. The English, Portugal's allies during the Napoleonic Wars, had gained privileged access to Brazil, but it was by no means exclusive. In fact, while the largest group was comprised of Englishmen, visitors of various nationalities, male and female, traveled across the nation. Scientists, artists, diplomats, traders, military men, and engineers composed the Capitalist vanguard that was to revise the logic of the European civilizing mission. Toward the end of the century communities of expatriates had already been formed in the larger Brazilian cities, creating uniquely differentiated contact areas. From the gaze of the settler to the eye of the tourist–men on commercial trips or prolonging their stay in temporary or definitive residence, from the narrative of the first colonizers, to a Brazil observed by high-class ladies nicknamed "social explorers"–the interplay of these cultural exchanges contributed to the imprinting of the images of Brazil that informed a national identity marked by the notion of other. Such images were based on an imperial *locus*, whether expressed in the criticism of specific aspects of Brazilian or Iberian culture or in the more favorable visions that presupposed that Brazil was moving toward an ideal of progress (at first represented by Western Europe, and later by Anglo-Saxon North America). A sense of national or racial superiority dominated a reductive process that stereotyped, homogenized, and belittled a projected Brazilian cultural identity. The compromised character of these representations was due to underlying interconnections, of varying intensity, with the expansionist projects of Europe and the United States, and emerging international relations. The travel narratives written by Brazilians in transit through Europe or the United States during the twentieth century are largely (and tellingly) a response to these representations, which were crystallized in tradition and strengthened by the new balance of power in international relations. This was the context in which the first definitions of national identity were established.

Travel Experiences:
EuroCentrism and Its Deconstruction

We suggest a strategic return to the nineteenth century as a platform from which to better launch the project of revising the current theories of identity in post-structuralist and multicultural thought at the dawn of the twenty-first century. Nineteenth-century travel was cumbersome; precarious transportation and poor communications led to a relative isolation of politically and geographically delimited regions. It was a period in which partial isolation invited the mythicizing of borders and the characteristics of the nation, coexisting with aggravated clashes between imperialist forces and emancipatory reactions. This historical conjuncture gave increasing importance to the question of identity and yoked the notion of an individual subject to the concept of nation, in accordance with the period's prevailing Romantic-Liberal model. With respect to Brazil, the nineteenth century was characterized by a double effort–to bring about a consciousness of nationality and to create a literature with particular characteristics, a medium for writers to reaffirm their identities. These pursuits were largely based on travel experiences, specifically the experiences of members of the intellectual and social elite. A trip to Europe became, in this manner, decisive in the education of the leaders of Brazilian society, and in contrast, the narratives of foreign travelers in Brazil functioned as a mirror in which Brazilian culture reflected itself–creating a self-portrait, whether by copying, comparison, or confrontation.

The beginning of the twentieth century, the heyday of Modernist vanguards, which had at best a contradictory relationship with neo-colonialism, was also the period in which the Romantic-Liberal definition of national identity was first seriously questioned. A parodic rereading of narratives left by foreign travelers, in conjunction with the travels undertaken by Brazilian writers and artists–themselves into and out of Latin America–challenged the notion of national hegemony and legitimized a model for a culture of miscegenation. It is important to note, however, that although Modernists were members of an individualist and elitist class of travelers, they were rigorous critics of the great orchestrated migrations–movements of conquest and colonization that imported Africans in shackles, that encouraged the migration of Europeans and Asians for labor–movements which, in the long run, constituted Brazilian society.

Aware of the potential for reflection and criticism inherent in the genre of travel narratives, the leaders of the Modernist revolution practiced a mixed form of fiction, autobiography, and travelogues in their literary careers, experimenting with a discourse that was to question and redefine national and individual identity. It was a generation that found support in the macro-narratives of modernity, as readers of Freudian psychoanalysis and the trend for self-criticism in anthropology, on the one hand, while demonstrating great affinity with left-wing sympathizers or even militants (anarchists, socialists, and communists), on the other hand. It was a group that–in the 1920s and 1930s–became a vanguard at the helm of the deconstruction of Eurocentrism and of its precursors. They carried out this exercise in deconstruction through a caricature of types, such as the ever-present traveler in awe of Europe, as well as by venturing into an aesthetic appraisal of travel in Brazil (i.e., travel itineraries that had otherwise been appropriated by science or tourism). Consequently, this created an art of difference.

The legacy of second-generation Modernists in Brazil was, most important, their literary exercises centering on the internal migrations caused by drought in the Northeast. The 1930s and 1940s were decades in which the regional version of colonialism and the beleaguered survival of small landowners and agricultural workers were depicted in renderings at times critical, at times mythicizing. Toward the mid-twentieth century, as grand theories began to be seriously challenged, the link between literature and nationality became increasingly tenuous. The nation began to lose its privileged position as the main framework for identity, being replaced by regional practices, multiplicity, difference, and the fragmentation of cultural space. Guimarães Rosa's (1908–1967) work published in the 1950s and 1960s is the best Brazilian example of these changes; in it he develops a complex writing technique that is self-reflective and combines grand Western theories with non-Western anti-theory. In more recent decades, and in the face of new political and historical circumstances–borders and distances being erased by mass media, colonialism transformed into financial and cultural globalization–Brazilian literary production has minimized the meaning of travel and turned to the exploration, in subject matter and techniques, of virtual reality. This shift in values corresponds to a deconstruction of ethnocentrism and, further still, signals the deconstruction of the aesthetic parameters based on the unity of the rational subject. For a greater understanding of the artistic and cultural consequences of travel literature in the twentieth century, one should look to their nineteenth-century matrices. An analysis of travel journals and narratives reveals the watershed that was the Eurocentric stance; texts fell either in accord with or in opposition to it.

Foreign travelers to nineteenth-century Brazil who can best illustrate the form of intellectual exchange that was eventually established, passed through the territory between 1810 and 1830. They witnessed the nation's political independence and, in the manner of their precursors, provided the foundations for a portrait of the nation. The Frenchman Ferdinand Denis is an outstanding example in view of his contributions toward developing—in collaboration with local literati—a history of Brazilian literature. In his theoretical foundations, however, although committed to voicing the culture of the Americas, he could not free himself from the canon. As the testimony of a traveler, Denis's discourse is emblematic of the Eurocentric vision of tropical poetry. This Eurocentric discourse, as represented in the sixteenth century by Montaigne—less a traveler himself than a reader of travel literature, who "teve a brilhante idéia de retirar do Outro . . . o seu potencial contestário" (Santiago 1989, 190) ("had the brilliant idea of subtracting from the other . . . its potential for challenge")—finds no real opposition in the ranks of Brazilian travelers, even in the nineteenth century. We can find, however, in the Englishwoman Maria Graham, an observer who is less ideologically compromised. Although her *Diário de uma viagem ao Brasil* [Diary of a Journey to Brazil] cannot be considered a work of deconstruction, it has turned out to be a promising resource for current research in counter-ethnocentric discourse.

Among the Brazilian writers who explored travel as an educational experience or a literary topic, three names exemplify, in turn, the three faces of the literary construct: The Eurocentric matrix, a deconstructive stance, and finally, an intermediary position. Three writers published their main works at the turn of the twentieth century and created a discourse that became paradigmatic for future Modernists who opted to either establish continuity through difference, or break with it completely. Joaquim Nabuco (1849–1910), with his acknowledged educational background of French and British standards, provides us with the Eurocentric matrix; Euclides da Cunha (1866–1909) and his pioneering *Os Sertões* [1902; *Rebellion in the Backlands*], shouldering the philosophical baggage of determinism and positivism, constitutes our middle-of-the-road alternative; and finally, Machado de Assis (1839–1908), an armchair enthusiast of travel narratives as well as of Montaigne's *Essays*, provides us with a model of deconstructive writings.

Foreigners in Brazil: Matrices of Text and Image

Any nineteenth-century or even current history of Brazilian literature and culture must mention the polymath Ferdinand Denis (1798–1890), who—taking up residence in Brazil from 1816 to 1820—was among the first and main sources of incentive for the emancipation of Brazilian fine arts and letters. He translated historical documents of Brazil's Colonial period into French, and published travel notes and interpretations of Brazilian society that could be of interest to his compatriots then involved with commercial and industrial enterprises linked to imperialist expansion. A European Romantic, his enthusiasm for the peculiarities of the American continent experienced during the early period of political independence won him the admiration and respect of the Brazilian elite. *Cenas da natureza sob os trópicos e sua influência sobre a poesia* [1824; Scenes of Tropical Nature and Its Influence on Poetry] and *Resumo da história*

do Brasil [1826; A Summary of Brazilian History] are two of his important contributions as a Luso-Brazilian specialist. Denis was influenced by Humboldt and Mme de Staël, and combined his curiosity about tropical nature and native peoples with a desire for autonomy and progress that he witnessed during his contact with Brazilian society. He created a literary model out of these ingredients that served both for the appreciation of seventeenth-century works as well as for creating contexts for appreciating new poets. Denis functioned, therefore, as a civilizing agent: Much like a traveler coming back from abroad, he returned the lyrical, wild raw material, duly interpreted by Western standards, back to its regional origins.

Denis' proposition, however, must be analyzed from two perspectives, namely (1) that of the consequences in terms of control (domestication) implied in the very recognition of ethnic and cultural difference and (2) that of the incentive thus instilled in the other that it should search for its own identity. These are terms that strike us today as being contradictory, but which in fact characterize Romanticism and its themes: Exoticism, national consciousness, and a search for origins. In the explicitly universalist *Formação da literatura brasileira* [Development of Brazilian Literature], Antonio Candido (b. 1918) exercises caution when observing a taste for exoticism "que eivou a nossa visão de nós mesmos até hoje, levando-nos a nos encarar como faziam os estrangeiros, propiciando, nas letras, a exploração do pitoresco no sentido europeu, como se estivéssemos condenados a exportar produtos tropicais também no terreno da cultura espiritual" (1969, 2: 324) ("that suffuses our self-understanding even to this day, leading us to see ourselves as foreigners saw us, favoring in our literature the exploitation of the picturesque in the European sense, as if it were our fate to export tropical goods even in the terrain of spiritual culture"). As historian and critic, Candido pays a great deal of attention to the role Ferdinand Denis played; his own work, however, focuses on reconstructing the initial phases of Brazilian literature, articulating the balance struck between the integrating gesture typical of neo-Classicism and the differentiating impulses of Romanticism.

In the first few decades of the nineteenth century (between the arrival of the Portuguese royal family and the nation's post-Independence organization), neo-Classicism and Romanticism converged, or were superimposed, thanks to the activities of foreign visitors. The observations and proposals Denis drew from his private travels became a significant factor in the development of Brazilian Romanticism (Candido 1969, 1: 283). The French Mission of 1816, consisting of a troupe of artists traveling under official contract, instituted the School of Fine Arts in Rio de Janeiro under the aegis of neo-Classicism. In the case of the fine and applied arts, the progressive European intervention of individual travelers was not left to chance; it was planned by the Count de Barca in name of D. João VI and carried through with the leadership of Joachim Le Breton (1760–1819). A museologist, a critic, and a man well versed in the fine arts, Le Breton organized a group in 1816 that counted among its members Nicolau Taunay, a painter famous for his landscapes; Jean Baptiste Debret, a painter of historical themes; Grandjean de Montigny, an architect; Auguste Taunay, a sculptor; Charles Pradier, an engraver; François Ovide, a professor of mechanics; and three master craftsmen. His teachings presupposed a fusion of the fine and applied arts, and this group would be completed, in the next few months, with the arrival of the Ferrez brothers—one a sculptor and the other an engraver.

This notable artistic immigration eventually led to, once various difficulties were surmounted, the foundation of the Academia e Real Escola das Artes (the Academy and Royal School of Arts) in 1820; its influence, even if questionable in certain respects, was lasting and decisive for the Brazilian cultural scene. Its artist professors were in the majority affiliated with neo-Classicism, a style whose formal characteristics and themes conflicted with the surviving colonial canon that was predominantly religious, aristocratic, and Baroque. Eurocentric neo-Classicism, for its part, with its bourgeois and lay foundations, conceived of the artist as a free man, who belonged to the elite that could at times also be revolutionary.

As the Mission established itself, it brought with it an atmosphere of confrontation; its most successful branch was architecture, possibly because this combined art and functionality. A disciple of the French masters of neo-Classicism of the Napoleonic age, Auguste Henri Victor Grandjean de Montigny (1776–1850) spent long years in Brazil and oversaw the most stable and consistent of the group's endeavors. His sober lines marked, among other works, the Academia de Belas Arte's own first residence in Rio de Janeiro, located in the Praça do Comércio, at the Rossio Pequeno fountain, and are also present in his proposals for urbanizing downtown Rio (such as opening up a great avenue). Having an enduring influence in the work of his disciples, he became the source of neo-Classical cultural and technical models (Barata 1: 391). The respect that Grandjean's work has always inspired is a demonstration of the quick assimilation of neo-Classical values by the Brazilian elite. This style rapidly became popular throughout the nation, visible in numerous buildings designed by Portuguese architects, and in some cases by French visitors–Pezerat, Palliére, and Vauthier, famous for defining the Recife's new cityscape from 1840 onward.

The French masters in art had a predominantly neo-Classical education with an emphasis on the so-called historical paintings (including portraiture). Pre-Romantic tendencies were relegated to secondary status in the Brazilian school's initial period. Regionalist lyricism–or the lyricism of the local ambience–that influenced the fine arts in their interpretation of nature was to be found only in the work of Nicolau Taunay (1755–1830), the sole landscape painter of the group, whose sojourn in Brazil was relatively short. On returning to France in 1821, Nicolau Taunay left his sons, Teodoro and Felix Emilio (1795–1881), in Brazil. The latter took his place in the Academia and eventually became the drawing and French teacher of the future emperor, Pedro II. Since there was no landscapist in Brazil during the next few years, aesthetic interest gravitated more toward the human form. In the company of French compatriots, the Taunay family settled in Tijuca on the then outskirts of Rio, a healthy suburb of exuberant vegetation. Between 1820 and 1830 this French enclave was home to writers, painters, and *dilettantes* (the Count de Gestas, *chargé d'affairs* for foreign business and relative by marriage to Chateaubriand), creating a type of pre-Romantic intellectual environment. The enthusiastic following of Rousseau and Chateaubriand was therefore allied to Ferdinand Denis's lessons, and the enthusiasm of the naturalists, especially the German naturalists, with the tropical landscape. This attitude of foreigners in Brazil was contagious, and Brazilians too became enthusiastic–though still insecure regarding the differentiated traits of their environment. One should note in passing that *Inocência* [1872; Innocence], one of Brazil's most popular Romantic novels, which combined lyricism

and naturalist observations in a simple plot, was written by Alfredo d'Escragnolle Taunay (1843–1899), a grandson of Nicolau, who was raised in Tijuca. But the person to attain greatest fame was Jean Baptiste Debret (1768–1848) and not accidentally, he attained his reputation as an historical painter. A relative of Jacques-Louis David, he was influenced by Napoleonic neo-Classicism and produced solemn official paintings with strong chromatic qualities. His more personal work as an observer of the quotidian, known as the *Aquarelas Brasileiras* [Brazilian Watercolours], is however, characterized by lightness and spontaneity. Debret's work has some affinity with the pre-Romantic (and Romantic) tendency for exoticism–revealing, instead of correcting, nature's imperfections. He becomes a mediator between the Realist revolutionary ideals of 1789 and the great eighteenth-century movement of French Enlightenment. The volume *Viagem pitoresca e histórica ao Brasil* [A Pictorial and Historical Voyage to Brazil], published between 1834 and 1839, was an integral part of the great effort to popularize and increase the general accessibility of culture in the nineteenth century (Barata 1: 388). In the line of Ferdinand Denis, Debret's art compels a conscious and public affirmation of Brazilian nationality by intervening in the transition from the Luso-Colonial era to the modern, cosmopolitan period. The contradictory role performed by both French travelers is emblematic of the ambiguities of Brazilian culture, both proud and ashamed of the differences that prevent it from conforming to the universalized canon.

One can evaluate the outcome of the *Academia imperial de belas artes'* training by analyzing the work of the first generation of Brazilian artists that it trained: Augusto Müller, Simplício Rodrigues de Sá, and especially Manuel de Araújo Porto Alegre (1806–1879)–Debret's favorite student, who followed him to France in 1831. Like his master, Porto Alegre painted portraits and historical scenes, but he also painted landscapes clearly influenced by a Romanticism that found its expression in canvases, albums, and scenography. In the company of writers such as Domingos Gonçalves de Magalhães (1811–1882) and Francisco de Sales Torres Homem (1812–1876), Porto Alegre launched the journal *Nichteroy, Revista Brasiliense* (1836) in Paris. The journal was a symbol of an ambiguous adherence to Romanticism and a Eurocentric initiative to construct Brazilian culture.

Porto Alegre's influence in the artistic world ensured that the officially academic style, as exemplified by Debret and his colleagues, was transmitted to future artists. Among the most noteworthy painters of the nineteenth century are Vitor Meirelles (1832–1903) and Pedro Américo (1843–1905), who left a mark on the eclecticism of turn of the century Brazil. It was left to the Modernism of the 1920s to break with this sterile legacy. Tracing a history of the Modernist movement of 1922, Aracy Amaral (b. 1930) summarizes Oswald de Andrade's (1890–1954) position as one of radical opposition to servile academic obedience: "em conferência em Paris, [Oswald] denunciou, pela primeira vez, . . . a funesta influência da escola baseada em modelos franceses de ensino das artes, deformando a criatividade nacional em função de um padrão internacionalista superado" (Amaral 26) ("in a lecture in Paris, [Oswald de Andrade] denounced, for the first time, . . . the stifling influence of the school based on French models of artistic instruction that deformed national creativity in name of an internationalizing standard which was already outdated").

The unprejudiced sensibilities of Oswald himself, of Mário de Andrade (1893–1945), Tarsila do Amaral (1886–1973), Gilberto

Freyre (1900–1987), and Rodrigo Melo Franco de Andrade (1898–1969) rescued the freedom, audacity, and memorializing essence of Debret's work. Although the importing of foreign instructors to establish educational and cultural practices had obvious limitations, the Modernist intellectual elite was not entirely opposed to it. This initiative eventually contributed indirectly to the foundation of a pioneering research group in 1934 by establishing the Universidade de São Paulo. Imbued with progressive ideals, this institution's objective was to systematize Brazilian cultural production, and included in its first measures was the hiring of French and Italian cultural missions (Mota 33). Some of the members of these cultural missions (e.g., Fernand Braudel, Claude Lévi-Strauss, P. Monbeig, Roger Bastide, Ungaretti–young professors in the 1930s) became leaders of critical thought in the 1960s. These men, twentieth-century travelers all, deconstructed Eurocentric and logocentric methodologies, and radicalized the effects of the tropical shock on their culture of Enlightenment. In a repetition-through-difference of the trajectory of Denis or Debret, the generation that visited during the 1930s made of South American eccentricities the instruments for imploding the universal canon.

Mário Barata has reevaluated the role played by the 1816 Artistic Mission in the transformation of the Brazilian cultural scene during the first half of the nineteenth century, and has pointed out the need to clarify the interrelations between the collective work carried out by masters on commissions and the individual and self-determined activities of itinerant foreign travelers who made note of and transmitted their observations. He referred to the statements of various artists and scientists who cited the influence of Alexander von Humboldt in motivating their travels across the American continent. The painters who joined scientific expeditions were essential for the development of landscape painting, which had been considered of little value in the past but was to become the visual basis for Romanticism. This was the context in which Tomas Ender was invited to join the von Spix and von Martius group for a time, and in which Langsdorff relied on the similarly temporary collaboration of João Maurício Rugendas (1802–1858) and Hercule Florence (1804–1879). This practice resulted in numerous richly illustrated travelogues.

Today, tracing back the circumstances under which Eurocentric reasoning was first undermined in the 1800s, one can see that the American exotic, both as an object of science and as a subject for artistic experience, began a process of subverting unequivocal concepts and multiplying aesthetic standards. On the one hand, the increase in European scientific expeditions to other continents was both cause and consequence of the imperialist expansion during the nineteenth century. On the other hand, the products of this wide-ranging scientific and artistic survey needed legitimization, and it became imperative that they attain a degree of independence from economic interests. In fact, those involved became increasingly critical of imperialism, as well as self-critical of their very own epistemological preconceptions. Anthropology, a discipline that came into being in the nineteenth century, had to acknowledge its internal contradictions; although it developed in the heart of ethnocentrism (which acted as a justification for the colonial enterprise itself), it became the discipline's obligation to deconstruct ethnocentrism, so as to fulfill its proposal of knowing the other–the wild man. Commenting on *Tristes tropiques* [1955; *A World on the Wane*, 1961], the book in which Lévi-Strauss (b. 1908) relates his work in

Brazil during the 1930s, Silviano Santiago (b. 1936) ventured that "O antropólogo seria a *consciência infeliz* do viajante e do colonizador europeus" (1989, 200) ("[t]he anthropologist then embodied the bad conscience of the traveler and European colonizer"). This perspective of dysphoria, from which Lévi-Strauss and his contemporaries brought about the de-centering of anthropological discourse, in a reversal of eighteenth-century euphoria, was at the same time the culminating point of a critical discourse that had been initiated when von Martius, Wied-Neuwied, or Burton came into contact with the indigenous peoples.

There is an extensive list of European naturalists who chose Brazil as a topic of their writings after having visited it during the nineteenth century. From Humboldt to P. V. Lund, and including the likes of Baron Langsdorff, Saint Hilaire, von Martius, and von Spix, the list included geographers, geologists, mineralogists, archaeologists, botanists, and zoologists. There were even a few notable female naturalists, such as the Princess of Bavaria and Elizabeth Agassiz. We may also note that in the history of scientific research in Brazil, travelers often departed from their fields of specialty to make important anthropological observations. Maximilian von Wied-Neuwied had a background that enabled him to make sound and reliable contributions to anthropology; for that reason he saw the Brazilian native through the prism of ethnographic criteria that were only beginning to be adopted in substitution of less rigorous models (Schaden and Pereira 427).

Various Brazilians, mostly self-educated, traveled the interior of the nation on research trips. The poet Antônio Gonçalves Dias (1823–1864) dedicated himself to the study of indigenous languages and gathered material for ethnographic collections; the botanist João Barbosa Rodrigues (1842–1909) studied many tribes from the Amazon region; the writer Escragnolle Taunay collected ethnographic data from indigenous peoples in the Mato Grosso region; and General Couto de Magalhães (1837–1898) worked persistently to investigate linguistics and ethnography as registered in *Viagem ao Araguaia* [1863; Journey to the Araguaya] and *O Selvagem* [1876; The Wild Man]–the latter an obligatory work of reference until the middle of the twentieth century. Some of the most interesting travel narratives, however, were not written by scientists, but by highly educated laymen who both were talented in critical observation and had great narrative skills. Maria Callcott Graham (1785–1842) is exemplary of this group of travelers. Married to a sea captain, this Englishwoman's South American sojourn, between 1821 and 1825, was only interrupted by a single trip to England. The circumstances were such that she witnessed important political events: the Confederação do Equador (the Pernambuco Insurrection) and Brazilian Independence. She became a widow and was briefly a candidate for the position of governess to Princess Maria da Glória, but competitiveness and intrigue in the court quickly put an end to that. Graham, however, was able to benefit from this experience and write an impartial description of D. Pedro I. She corresponded regularly with the Empress Leopoldina before and after her short stay at the court. During the years in which she lived in Brazil, she wrote and painted; she was an herbalist and made contributions as a naturalist. (Her name is listed as a collector in Marius's publication *Flora brasiliensis.*)

Author of travel books and literature for children, a translator, and an artist, this English lady employed her eclectic gifts in *Journal of a Voyage to Brazil* (1824), in which anthropologists, as well as social and cultural historians, can find rich material for an understanding of the Brazilian nineteenth century. From Gilberto Freyre in the 1940s to Flora Süssekind in the 1990s, the most rigorous and less conventional scholars have availed themselves of the products of Maria Graham's narrative verve. Devoid of literary or scientific pretensions, her writings display a humorous and even-handed approach–mixing an attachment to the rigid European social hierarchy and perspicacious observations of tropical social mores, preconceived notions about the institution of slavery and a humanitarian interest in the plight of black men and women, a sophisticated aesthetic sense and certain more frivolous preoccupations, a personal investment in being well received by the court and a deep curiosity about the young nation's politics. For these reasons, her writings are included in the collections of eminent naturalists and historians who traveled to Brazil. In this context, her journal serves as a necessary critical counterpoint to the excesses of erudition, the Romantic exoticism, and the ethnocentric prejudices of so many other accounts.

Comparative historiography in its present-day deconstructive perspective has a different approach to its subject matter, a large interdisciplinary discourse that juxtaposes traditional literary genres and those with more use value (letters, diaries, research logs). It combines biographical facts and intellectual products, and compresses time and space, creating descriptive depictions through delicate sketches and exquisite literary language. From such a theoretical methodological position, the selection of the topic of travel can function as a strategy for approaching the relationships between cultures in the form of a (paradoxically) continuous act of displacement. Correspondingly, historical-critical work must be developed incrementally, as sketches drawn from the canon and from popular cultural practices, so as to finally deconstruct what would have been the fixed markers of center and periphery.

The Three Matrices of Brazilian Travel Literature

A trip to Europe became the obligatory rite of initiation in the lives of Brazilian writers during the nineteenth century. Candidates for political or intellectual life were educated or had their studies complemented in France, England, or Portugal. Immersed in a European setting, they reinforced their ties to literature, deepening their knowledge of the standards of the canon as well as those of vanguard movements. They were stimulated in this way to reflect on differences between canonical Western civilization and the practices that had been transposed into their cultural life in the tropics. This process resulted in the construction of a consciousness of being Brazilian, formulated at times as a progressive project for national letters, at times as a lyrical representation of their experience of cultural displacement.

Domingos José Gonçalves de Magalhães's (1811–1882) articles and those of his companions written for the *Nichteroy* journal (1836) began the intellectual debate on this topic. Gonçalves Dias'emblematic poem "Canção do Exílio" [1843; "Song of Exile"] opened the discussion to a wider audience. Successive generations in the 1800s left Romantic, Realist, or Parnassian accounts of their impressions during their student travels. One can get a sense of their acquisitions, doubts, and problems by reading *Minha Formação* [My Education] by Joaquim Nabuco (1849–1910). His work, written between 1893 and 1899, was one of the first Brazilian ventures into autobiography and was published, tellingly, in 1900. It is a work in which a mature writer reflects on the various stages of his political and literary education, granting special importance to his

first trip to Europe (Nabuco 1963, 43) between August 1873 and September 1874.

In the opening pages of *Um estadista do império* [A Statesman of the Empire], an historical and biographic study written during the same period, Joaquim Nabuco observed that nothing broadens a person's spirit more quickly than travel: A change of customs, societies, and nations heightens awareness of one's own culture. In this sense he believed that even though he was brought up with French and English texts, it was the experience of direct contact with Europe that brought about a personal metamorphosis that was akin to the transmutation of the chrysalis into the butterfly (36). Nabuco referred to his travel journals to reconstruct his itinerary, which included the classical landscapes of France, Italy, Switzerland, and England. He came to the conclusion, retrospectively, that on contemplating landscapes and famous works of art, and in making the acquaintance of the political and literary personalities of the time, he could in fact evaluate the decisive impact that the European heritage had had in his intellectual education as a South American. Before embarking for the Old World, during his studies in the academy, far from Catholic and aristocratic ideals, he had allowed himself to be fascinated by the Republican regime and by the democracy of the United States of America. During those student days he even went so far as to suggest, as his self-critical recollections note, that the emperor would benefit more from a trip to the young republic of the United States of America than one to old Europe (27). This expression of youthful passion soon died away, and was replaced by the more traditional values of monarchy and European culture. Indeed, the 1873 trip did strengthen these values in the young graduate, who discovered that his interests were predominantly cosmopolitan. Nabuco's autobiography contains descriptions of scenes in which his role was not so much that of a participant in local politics, but that of a spectator for whom politics is a play, staged in the theater of the nation (33). From his perspective, what was human corresponded to what was European. The New World was isolated from the aesthetic or historical imagination (41).

Reflecting on his most meaningful recollections (the French National Assembly, Swiss landscapes, Italian Renaissance Art, the English Parliament), Nabuco referred to having the sensation of irreparable alienation from Brazil. This is a clear formulation of the dilemma that afflicted the intellectual careers of Brazilians, from colonial times to the dawn of the twentieth century: On one side of the ocean, one feels the absence of all that matters in the world; on the other, the absence of the homeland (40). If the majority of Nabuco's contemporaries produced work that conformed to this doubled exile, the subsequent generation–actively engaged with the Modernist program–tried to find a resolution to the dilemma. Oswald de Andrade presented a parody based on the fictional character João Miramar and his European education. Mário de Andrade much more radically, however, made fun of what he called Nabuco's tragedy (a Brazilian who would prefer to be European) and created in his character Macunaíma–a fantastic traveler in South America. Silviano Santiago, with his usual perspicaciousness, contrasts the positions of Nabuco and Mário de Andrade in a 1995 article. Not content to frame the topic from the point of view of a distant commentator of Brazilian history, as a rigorous critic of the past, Santiago detects the insidious persistence of Nabuco's malady in the present-day fascination with globalization. In order to prevent the degeneration caused by that illness, he prescribes the urgent adoption of Mário de Andrade's program for systematically acquiring Brazilianness, certain that there is not one civilization but many, as Mário declared in a letter to his friend the poet Carlos Drummond de Andrade (1902–1987).

From the 1920s onward the action of Modernist writers as travelers and authors of travel literature marks a change in the notion of a twentieth-century writer's education. Much of this shift was prefigured in the aesthetic and biographical experiments of one of Nabuco's contemporaries, Euclides da Cunha (1866–1909). A mere two years after the publication of Nabuco's memoirs, da Cunha shook the Europeanized environment of turn-of-the-century Brazil with his publication of *Os Sertões*. Trained as a military engineer, the young Euclides, well versed in French literature, developed an attachment to scientific and republican ideals and, like the majority of his peers, was passionately progressive and impatient with conservative practices and traditional values. This led him to develop an interest in the insurrection that took place in the barren region known as "Sertões" (in the interior of Bahia State), under the leadership of the mystic Antônio Conselheiro. In his journalistic articles written between 14 March and 17 July 1897, he offered an analysis of the *sertanejo* region's geography and climate, and tried to give an explanation for the *jagunços'* fanatic combat with the Republican army. Agreeing with the prevailing view of the São Paulo and Rio de Janeiro press, Euclides considered the revolt to be monarchic, comparable to the 1789 peasant reactionaries who opposed the libertarian projects of the French Revolution.

These articles had such an impact that da Cunha was eventually invited to cover the military campaigns for the newspaper *O Estado de São Paulo*. He joined the fourth military expedition, which was sent out after the previous three had been defeated. These were the (unexpected) circumstances of what would be the decisive voyage of his intellectual and artistic education. He endured the hardships of isolation in Canudos (where the battles were fought) and witnessed the confrontation to its bitter end, accomplishing the journalistic task that he was commissioned to do. The correspondence he sent during that period already revealed a language of sweeping dimensions and an epic style, capable of interweaving scientific information with civic enthusiasm in a daring and meticulously written text. The articles show that his presence at the scene of war dealt a serious blow to the certainties he had held as a journalist. His main preoccupations were still reflected in his progressive republican ideals, in as much as he spared no effort in arguing for the eradication of a rebellion that he insisted was a retrograde insurrection. But he was equally committed to deciphering the enigmatic identity of the *sertanejo* (people born in the *Sertões* region), whose resistance to modern weaponry and the prolonged siege seemed to defy belief. In the end he was made to understand that Conselheiro and his followers were not, indeed, monarchists. He was brought to a heightened understanding of the *jagunços* by analyzing their behavior under the violent and inefficient onslaught of the army; they were quiet and dignified as prisoners, and possessed admirable courage and efficiency when under attack.

The lesson he took from his voyage to the interior anticipated his future work, once his research had been duly assimilated and reflected on. In the years following the campaign, while overseeing the construction of a bridge over the river

Pardo as an engineer, Euclides da Cunha took on the task of writing *Os Sertões*, a study in interpretation and an experiment with style, motivated by the shocking experience of being a witness to life and death in the *caatinga* (scrub savannah). Developing beyond his journalistic experience, Euclides refined his knowledge of geography, anthropology, and sociology. He transformed his work as a writer into an art of monumentalization, an art that was in keeping with his tendency to find dimensions of greatness and glory in historical characters and landscapes—as Gilberto Freyre once accurately pointed out. The product of these peculiar literary tactics, *Os Sertões* was a passionate denunciation of the disregard with which Brazil treated the disenfranchised of its population.

The publication of *Os Sertões*, a daring work in terms of style and theme, had a great impact on the tepid literary scene at the turn of the nineteenth century. Its author's own polemical notoriety associated him inevitably with the *Canudos* war itself. From our present-day standpoint, it is important to contrast this to Mário de Andrade's work. While the *sertanejo* recreated in da Cunha's rhetoric is the radical opposite of the subject of Modernist parody, one can identify in both authors the decisive stages that led to that rupture with Eurocentrism that marked Brazilian culture in the nineteenth century, and of which there are still lingering remnants today. If science served da Cunha well in helping him rethink the differences between life on the Atlantic coast and in the Brazilian interior, it also contained clear racist presuppositions. It was, however, his integrity as a writer that intervened and led him to question these presuppositions.

It is useful to note that the other journeys he made during his career also found him in the interior of Latin America. Between December 1904 and January 1906 he traveled the Amazon as head of the Reconnaissance Commission of the *Alto Purus* region. It was a trip that became emblematic for the history of Brazilian culture: The Amazonian itinerary would be retraveled in the 1920s by Mário de Andrade. Both writers observed the region with interest and confronted what they saw with more or less conventional images they had drawn from their readings. In his search for consistency and intellectual rigor, da Cunha composed a series of essays on the geography and society of the settlements along the river. The same epic tone is present in his later writings collected in *Contrastes e confrontos* [1907; Contrasts and Confrontations] and *À margem da história* [1913; The Margins of History], but he uses a more sober style to denounce the exploitation of rubber harvesters and other workers. While Nabuco traveled throughout Europe, feeling at once nostalgic for his fatherland and reintegrated into the culture of civilization, da Cunha discovered in the geography of the *Sertão* the nation that he would willingly serve as a writer. These are opposing but not mutually exclusive strategies. They constitute the two basic matrices that contributed to the formation of Brazilian writers—men and women who felt divided between the universal canon and the mixed and bewildering diversity at the margins. They correspond also to recurrent motifs in Brazilian literature—the heroic adventure, intellectual activity romantically offered in the service of a just cause, the discovery of national origins or, conversely, of a national destiny. Notwithstanding, one must—in the name of accuracy—contrast these two types of travel against a third, the one in which the journey through space is minimal or, in fact, nonexistent: that of armchair travelers who rely on the written word for their virtual itinerary. Rather than serving as a motif or point of reference for geographical wanderings, knowledge in books becomes the substitute for travel. The sedentary reader takes on a special dimension in Brazil's literature and cultural life when one considers that one of its principal exponents was none other than Joaquim Maria Machado de Assis (1839–1908). His perspective would constitute the counterpoint to the other two travel matrices. Machado's work has been widely recognized for its unique and significant contribution to the novel as a genre, and one must interpret his denial (literally and figuratively) of travel as a meaningful indication of a conscience that had awakened to a critical stance regarding the nation and the world.

In letters to fellow writers who had been appointed to diplomatic missions in Europe, Machado lamented not having seen the monumental beauties of Rome and Paris. On the other hand, he showed himself to be entirely at ease with the art and philosophy of the metropolis, thanks to the wealth of his experience as a reader. Dom Casmurro, one of his most famous fictional characters, never failed to be irritated at the enthusiasm foreign travelers expressed about the tropical landscape. Machado's article for the newspaper *Gazeta de Notícias* (on 20 August 1893) is brimming with disappointment at the much-applauded stage diva Sarah Bernhardt's praise of Brazil's natural beauties: "*ce pays féerique*" ("this magical country"). To confront the great actress's banalities, he felt obliged to take his readers on a guided tour of *carioca* culture, from the architecture of churches and forts to the rhythm of *capoeira*. Even more well known is the article he wrote, commissioned by the United States publication *Novo Mundo* [New World] (24 March 1873), in which he discarded palm trees and *tapuias* as emblematic of Brazil; the sense of nationality, he contended, was a much more subtle and complex issue. Taking these various aspects into account, what emerges is a clear depiction of the aesthetic and political position of a Latin American writer. He is neither ignorant of nor does he minimize Europe's classical and modern intellectual products, but he feels free to reinvent them through humor and parody. He does not reject the uncultivated traditions of his people, but neither does he feel compelled to idealize them in name of creating his own literary identity.

Flora Süssekind, in searching for the emergence and initial transformations of the fictional narrator in Brazilian prose, points to cartography and foreign travel narratives as constituting the models and the interlocutors of the first novelistic exercises. She examines how different forms in verbal and visual representations of travel (to and throughout Brazil) will eventually coalesce to create a narrator whose role is that of fitting landscapes into the schematics of a plot or producing actions that will reveal the tropical scenario. This narrator's first rudimentary and awkward engenderings later develop into caricature or various comic versions, in its transitional form, and to eventually more sophisticated renderings in the historical and fictional works of Varnhagen and Alencar. Such has been the trajectory of the Brazilian traveling narrator: Adventurous plots, mysteries, and marvelous landscapes eventually confer glory, whether in serious drama or parody, on the protagonist. This inheritance from the model of travel writing was ruptured by Machado de Assis. Its narrators (as Flora Süssekind has shown) were subversive; they broke with presiding standards for the chroniclers of social mores and landscape artists and instead came into existence by journeying according to the cartography of their own selves. This expedient, practiced in texts such as *Memórias Póstumas de Brás Cubas* [1881; *The Posthumous Memoirs of Brás Cubas,* 1997] and

Quincas Borba (1891), compressed the space-time of travel to anachronistic fantasy or vertiginous delirium. In other terms, the Realist illusion was undone so as to free narrator and protagonist to travel the virtual plane of language. As a consequence the Machadian matrix, in contrast to the other two literary matrices, corresponds to a more extreme version of modern deconstructive aesthetics, and has today been validated in the age of the post-Modernist texts' use of quotation and pastiche.

Foreign Intellectuals in Brazil

Journeys to the tropics can be considered an instrument of cultural dialogue, but they can merely be ascribed simple motivations. They were not, in fact, merely accidental in nature, nor were they the by-products of business ventures; they also could not be entirely summed up in the tourist's gaze, so desirous of exoticism. At the turn of the nineteenth century and in the early years of the twentieth century, the transit of foreign intellectuals in Brazil was an integral part of a concerted strategy led by the Baron de Rio Branco (1845–1912). The Baron, then Head of the Ministry for Foreign Relations (Ministério das Relações Exteriores) of the recently inaugurated republic, developed a policy to give culture a new public dimension. Rio Branco's internal policy was responsible for transforming the *Itamarati* (as the Ministry for Foreign Relations was nicknamed) into a gravitational center for many of the most representative names of the intellectual life of the republic. His corresponding plan for foreign policy was to help Brazil cross the threshold into the *belle époque*–a plan that coincided with the modernization of the capital city, Rio de Janeiro, already under way and epitomized by the slogan "Rio civilizes itself." It included inviting illustrious members of the international intellectual elite in the hopes that they would return the favor by offering favorable impressions of the nation in their own circles of influence. Brito Broca claims that it was a period in which Brazilians hosted some of the greatest names of European culture: Guglielmo Ferrero, Anatole France, and George Clemenceau were some of the illustrious men whose visit to Brazil owes much to Rio Branco's initiative (Broca 1956, 157).

The historian Guglielmo Ferrero visited Rio de Janeiro in September 1907. The visit was arranged by Machado de Assis in his capacity as president of the Academia Brasileira de Letras and authorized by Rio Branco. A public meeting, which included lectures entitled "Cultura latina no momento atual" ["Present-day Latin Culture"] and "Corrupção e progresso no mundo antigo e moderno" ["Corruption and Progress in the Ancient and Modern World"], was held at the Palácio Monroe and was attended by intellectuals and members of the officialdom, as well as the president of the republic himself, Afonso Pena. On concluding this successful visit to Rio de Janeiro, the Italian historian left for São Paulo, curious to see the Italian community's contribution to the great civilization that was being forged in that state (Broca 1956, 160); there he was received with public acclaim.

Anatole France's visit soon followed, adding to the cultural effervescence. The French author stopped twice in Brazil, en route to and returning from Buenos Aires, in 1909. Thematically in tune with Ferrero's lectures, Anatole France's talks centered on a discussion of Latin culture as well. On his first sojourn he was received in a solemn session of the Academia Brasileira de Letras and greeted with a salutation in French proffered by Rui Barbosa. During his second stay, Anatole

France gave two lectures; went to São Paulo, where he visited schools, academies, and other cultural institutions; and made a trip to the interior to fulfill his desire to see a coffee plantation. He displayed a curiosity for the exotic that was truly French and European in fashion, as was aptly noted by Brito Broca (1956, 166).

Clemenceau's 1910 visit ratified what quickly became an established itinerary for European intellectuals in search of Latin American exoticism, as well as some hard cash in return for their lectures. From the Brazililan perspective it was expected that these lectures would bring intellectual as well as cultural excitement to life on their side of the Atlantic. While the three lectures given by Clemenceau dwelt on the topic of democracy, Paul Adams's 1911 talks in Brazil focused on the question of race in Latin America. He granted great significance to the term *Latinidade* (Latinity), exalting the kinship among Latin peoples resulting from common origins, shared qualities, and a single genius. Spiritual bonds were easily transformed into material relations and came into play in a treaty between France and Brazil (Broca 1956, 168). This trip, during which Adams made excursions to São Paulo, Santa Catarina, Minas Gerais, and the Amazon region, resulted in the book *Visages du Brésil* [1914; Faces of Brazil], published in Paris. Commissioned to make Brazil better known in Europe, he did not limit himself to a narrative of his impressions as a traveler, but also wrote on Brazilian history and the country's social and political development.

The Nicaraguan poet Rubén Darío (1867–1916) came to Brazil in 1912. This was his second visit; he had first come to Brazil in 1906 as the Nicaraguan delegate to the Pan-American Conference. His second visit was under the auspices of *Mundial* magazine, which he directed and published in Paris. In his salutation to the poet, given at the Academia Brasileira de Letras, the critic José Veríssimo called attention to the mutual ignorance that characterized the relations between Brazil and other Latin American nations, in spite of a similar cultural background and shared interests.

The decade of 1910 was, therefore, a decade of decidedly French influence for Brazil. If Brazilians lived and wrote by the dictates of French fashion, it naturally followed that a trip to the City of Lights became almost compulsory for Brazilian intellectuals. The Rio–Paris route, as we have seen, became one of the matrices of the cultural travel to hegemonic centers. The inverse trajectory, nevertheless, continued throughout the twentieth century—a period in which the dominant European vision began to show signs of necessary revision, when the gaze turned toward the tropics began to shed its predictable exoticizing bias and to result in artistic production. The intercultural encounters provided by artists traveling to Brazil opened a range of possibilities for the productive interaction among peers—until then almost unknown to one another.

One of these artists was Darius Milhaud (1892–1974), the French composer, who arrived in Rio de Janeiro in February 1917 as a member of the diplomatic corps during Paul Claudel's tenure as ambassador (1917–1919), a particularly troubled period in world politics. As Silviano Santiago points out in his article "A tristeza de um é a alegria do outro" ["One's Sorrow Is Another's Contentment"], the fact that diplomats of such stature were sent to Brazil certainly was not without its implications. The objective behind these appointments was the liquidation of the "Brazil Railway" that annually swallowed up thousands of gold francs of French and Belgian savings. During the negotiations carried out with the Brazilian elite and members of Parliament, in which confiscated German ships were exchanged for the commitment to buy two million bags of coffee, the origins of the Modernist movement of São Paulo and the trip of another important French intellectual, the poet Blaise Cendars, took place.

Claudel did not have very positive feelings about Brazil: The excessive summer heat obliged him to take up residence in the hills on the outskirts of Rio; the sound of the Portuguese language he likened to an amalgam of buzzing noises and whistles. Claudel wove an image of Brazil as a sad paradise. (Note the similarity to Paulo Prado's ethno-pessimistic conception in *Retrato do Brasil* [1928; Portrait of Brazil], which considers Brazilians to be a product of three melancholy races.) Claudel took refuge in the hills of Petrópolis and Teresópolis, where, surrounded by colleagues and illustrious European visitors, he led a life far removed from the lives of Brazilians. He filled his letters with statements about the allure of the landscape and the charm of its people, but his diplomatic position, which fused commercial interests with Franco-Brazilian friendship, could hardly be overlooked.

Darius Milhaud arrived in Brazil amid carnival celebrations, and quickly joined in the enthusiam and euphoria of the festivities. In contrast to Claudel, he identified himself with Brazilian music and was fascinated with its rhythms–those of the *maxixes, sambas,* and *chorinhos*–which he reproduced on the piano. Darius praised the work of Ernesto Nazaré (1863–1934) as an expression of the Brazilian soul, and on returning to Paris felt a growing nostalgia for Brazil. This French composer, in his prodigious output, wrote music inspired by South American themes and rhythms. "Boeuf sur le toit" (opus 58), for example, which was wildly successful in Paris, marks the transition from Romanticism to a new musical form in which one can perceive a certain *joie de vivre*. His "Notes sans musique" ["Notes without Music"] depicts the French diplomatic colony in Rio de Janeiro, as well as wartime Brazil. And of course, Milhaud's 1921 composition "Saudades do Brasil" ["Nostalgia for Brazil"] marks the high point of his musical involvement with Brazil.

Yet Brazil left hardly any traces in the work of the other French artists who passed through–practically null in Claudel's case. The exception was Milhaud. Their presence did not leave any mark on the work of Brazilian artists either. Their tropical sojourn did not contribute at all to the climate of Modernist rebellion that was slowly taking over groups in São Paulo and in the Northeast. In this sense one could argue that ideas travel ahead of their creators. Futurism, for example, came to Brazil well ahead of its prime exponent Marinetti, who arrived in Brazil in 1926.

Marinetti's South American Tour

Never one to miss a chance at self-promotion, Filippo Marinetti (1876–1944) proclaimed that his thirty-five lectures given throughout South America in 1926 had generated a groundswell of support for Futurism. The only problem with his enthusiastic declaration was that his tour was considered a complete fiasco by the critics; most of them were in agreement with Mário de Andrade's negative view, as expressed in his *Diario Nacional* column dated 11 February 1930 (Andrade 1976, 191–92). These were two contradictory versions: On one side, Marinetti's narcissistic-triumphant narrative; on the other, Mário de Andrade's version, full of nationalist disenchantment with the Italian poet. Modernist circles were already in strong support of Mário's writings, and Marinetti's association with Fascism made them uncomfortable. Annateresa Fabris's most recent work on Futurism, however, has brought new insight to the encounter, suggesting that instead of analyzing Futurism's influence on Brazilian Modernism, it is in fact more important to examine Brazilian modernity's own futuristic moment (see Poggioli 69), which had little to do with Marinetti's 1926 lectures. In other words, Fabris suggests that one should try to examine the more general social and cultural atmosphere that is specific to the emergence of the modern city, instead of comparing the doctrine of Italian Futurism or even its artistic products with those of Brazilian Modernism's: "É nossa hipótese que o futurismo é assumido pelos modernistas como arma de combate, desde 1921, em virtude da carga negativa de que era portador" (Fabris 1990, 71) ("Our hypothesis is that futurism is taken up by Modernists as a weapon of combat, in 1921, because of the negative connotations it carried").

This hypothesis leads her to suggest the existence of a *Futurismo Paulista* (Futurism originating in São Paulo), in other words, to posit the existence of a movement of joint Modernist forces that appropriated for themselves futuristic principles as an instrument for confrontation. Fabris has reconstructed the tumultuous reception of Marinetti in São Paulo, granting that it is impossible to reduce Marinetti's passage through São Paulo to a purely negative perspective (1994, 259). It was a trip with primarily commercial ambitions; in the course of two months Marinetti went to Rio de Janeiro, São Paulo, and Santos, and also lectured in Buenos Aires and Montevideo. The contract signed by Nicolino Viggiani, an important impresario and organizer of shows in Rio de Janeiro and São Paulo, stipulated that the lectures were to be held in the best theaters of these cities, and implying at least a week's stay at each city in order to ensure that the lectures would be successful and that time allowed for interviews and so on. The impresario, who had had little contact with literary circles, chose to announce the lectures as an attraction comparable to that of a visiting concert pianist or and opera singer. Despite his financial success, Marinetti was coldly received by critics in São Paulo. In Rio he elicited a much warmer response, being received quite favorably by intellectuals such as Manuel Bandeira (1886–1968), Graça Aranha (1868–1931), and Ronald de Carvalho (1893–1935), as well as by the civic authorities. The press coverage he received also provides us with examples of parodies created by the reporters. This would suggest that Marinetti's ideas attained a penetration into public awareness (through parodies) that could only been dreamed of by the other vanguard groups. The *Estado de São Paulo* newspaper printed a caricature of Marinetti on 23 May 1926. His head is depicted transformed into a makeshift stage and across it, in bold lettering, is the name of a consumer product, *guaraná espumante* (a soft drink made of *guaraná*), with a list of the product's various attributes in verse to one side.

Marinetti's tour, in sum, brought about many important innovations that possibly can only be fully evaluated from our present-day standpoint. On the one hand, the commercial nature of his trip represented a clear threat to the South American lecture circuit that functioned predominantly through cordiality, personal relations, and the dynamics of the exchange of favors. On the other hand, the fact that the Futurist aesthetic sense had been assimilated, both in journalistic parody and in advertisement strategies, suggests that the exchange between the vanguard and mass culture was already beginning through Marinetti's unorthodox practices. The mentor of Futurism was a man who desired nothing less than to transform his ideas into the future of all vanguard movements.

Cendrars: The Man, His Travels

While the use of the term *Futurism* and references to Marinetti's ideas caused some embarrassment to Brazilian Modernists, the innovating seeds of Blaise Cendrars's (1887–1961) literature found rich soil among the youth intent on renovating Brazilian aesthetics in the 1920s. Cendrars's presence and his discursive practices became emblematic in the history of Brazilian Modernism. His propensity for travel and constant movement became a trademark of his personality and of his poetry, contributing much to enrich the dialogue he held with Brazilians. Cendrars's literary presence in Brazil predates his physical presence. His translated writings *Páscoa em Nova Iorque* [1912; Easter in New York], *Prosa do Transiberiano* [1913; Prose for the Transiberian (railway)], and *Kodak* (1923) had already been carefully read by the Brazilian vanguard long before his memorable trip to Brazil at the invitation of the diplomat and patron of Paulista Modernism, Paulo Prado (1869–1943). Cendrars, who together with Valéry Larbaud (1881–1957) had been responsible for introducing Walt Whitman (1819–1892) to the French, now had an important role in promulgating Brazilian literature in France, because he foresaw the importance of the Modernist literary movement that was about to make its appearance. The way was opened to the meeting of important Brazilian Modernists in Paris in 1923–Sérgio Milliet (1898–1966), Emiliano Di Cavalcanti (1897–1976), Victor Brécheret (1894–1955), João de Souza Lima (1898–1982), Hector Villa Lobos (1887–1959), Anita Malfatti (1889–1964), Tarsila do Amaral (1886–1973) and, most evidently, Oswald de Andrade (1890–1954). They became acquainted with Cocteau, Supervielle, Paul Morand, and Giraudoux; but their empathy was immediate with Blaise Cendrars, who, having already published the *Antologia negra* [Black Anthology], showed great interest in Brazilian culture. At Cendrars's studio in Place de Clichy, Tarsila would host dinners for guests as illustrious as Fernand Léger, Brancusi, Robert Delaunay, Vollard, Rolf de Maré, and Darius Milhaud.

On 12 January 1924, embarking at Le Havre, Cendrars began his journey to a Brazil that he envisioned as a terrestrial paradise–a view based on his familiarity with sixteenth-century texts about the country. He devoted himself utterly to an experience that would amplify his perception and contribute to his stature as a person and as a writer. At ease in the circles of the high bourgeoisie of São Paulo, Cendrars was equally comfortable in the company of young bohemian writers. He traveled throughout Brazil in the company of São Paulo Modernists, the famous Modernist caravan; they considered this trip a second discovery of Brazil. Brazilian vanguard artists and the European poet departed in search of a Baroque tradition that had adapted to local conditions and that they saw, with liberated perception, as something new. His Modernist hosts introduced him to Carnival in Rio, the religious event of racial pride, followed by a tour of the goldsmith's art in Minas Gerais. During that trip they met young Modernists from the Minas Gerais region such as Carlos Drummond de Andrade (1902–1987), Emílio Moura (1902–1971), João Alphonsus (1901–1944), Pedro Nava (1903–1984), and Abgar Renault (1908–1995). Cendrars was greatly impressed with the Baroque churches and Aleijadinho's sculptures, but the state of deterioration of these colonial treasures upset him deeply. Cendrars was instrumental in establishing the Sociedade de Amigos dos Monumentos Históricos do Brasil (Society for the Preservation of Brazilian Historical Monuments), which would be in charge of protecting and registering artifacts as the cultural heritage in the name of the State. This project had as its objective the development of cultural tourism, aiming at providing an incentive for museums and for the commercial exploitation of popular celebrations, particularly Carnival. Quite different from the paternalistic attitude and centralized bureaucracy so characteristic of Latin America, his proposal was based on the Anglo-American capitalist formula. Cendrars's Brazilian experience was registered in such works as Notas de viagem [Travel Notes] and Mulheres sul-americanas [South American Women], as well as in dispersed articles that he published collectively as Ao Coração do mundo [At the Heart of the World].

The Flux of Immigration:
Anarchism's Ideological Production

Although travelers who go to the tropics return to their nation of origin having experienced a potentially rich exchange between different cultures, rarely does such travel engender anything enduring; but the situation is very different in the case of actual immigration to Brazil. Transplanted permanently, with differing intensities and unique rhythms, immigrants left their mark on Brazilian culture or participated in a process of transculturation in their adopted homeland, which influenced both cultures that came into contact. The worldwide migratory flux toward areas such as the United States, Australia, and Latin America was certainly not motivated by intellectual reasons. These migrations were the outcome of the European crisis that aggravated political, economic, and social problems in the nineteenth century. In the hopes for a better life, the immigrant populations gravitated to regions in need of laborers. The end of slavery was what brought Brazil into this scenario (Holanda 274).

The first wave of immigrants to come to Brazil during the nineteenth century initially came from Germany, Switzerland, and Spain and were later followed by immigrants from northern Italy, who provided much-needed manual labor for coffee plantations. Southern Italians were to arrive in significant numbers later, during the Republic, and settled mainly in cities, especially São Paulo (Holanda 278). Brazilian life was actually subject to a wide range of influences–on its language and culture–and this was not restricted to the Italian influence. From 1911 to 1920 more than 800,000 immigrants entered the nation and joined a work force of close to three million foreigners already living in Brazil. Although large numbers of these wage workers were destined to work in agriculture, they found that the coffee plantations underwent periodic crises from the beginning of the twentieth century onward and that living conditions were precarious; this led them ultimately to gravitate toward the cities. This was a period of significant urban growth that coincided with the appearance of thousands of small industries throughout the nation, most especially concentrated in the Rio–São Paulo region. Terrible work conditions, however, spurred workers to strikes; there was much popular unrest. There was a contingent of politically active foreigners engaged in labor union militancy, especially in São Paulo. From 1912 onward workers began to organize in order to face the crisis, and protest movements sprang up around the country. The Confederação Operária Brasileira (Brazilian Confederation of Workers) was founded in 1908. Side by side

with socialist movements and the *trabalhismo reformista* (labor reform movement), it was the *anarco-sindicalistas* (anarchist-unionist) group that led the workers' movement up until the 1920s. The 1922 foundation of the Partido Comunista do Brasil (Communist Party of Brazil) would precipitate the decline of Anarchism in the nation. Such is the context of Anarchism's most intense cultural activity in Brazil from 1890 to 1935.

To obtain a full appreciation of the role that Anarchism played in Brazil and of its cultural manifestations–especially with respect to literature and theater–it is necessary to add these Anarchist ideological concepts to the others that were part of the lively influence of European culture. These ideas traveled to Brazil in the literary baggage of militants, intellectuals, and journalists, originating above all in Italy and Spain and to a lesser extent Portugal and France. São Paulo, the greatest point of convergence for immigrant labor, witnessed a great number of newspapers, magazines, and cultural centers that were associated with the Anarchist movement–a movement that grew with the advance of industrialization and the expansion of the coffee industry. It also showed significant growth in Paraná, Rio Grande do Sul, Rio de Janeiro, and in the northeastern states, especially Pernambuco, with its great libertarian tradition.

There is a vast collection of ideological texts from this movement still awaiting analysis, such as literary forms of propaganda and indoctrination, literary and musical *soirées*, the *agitprop* theatrical stage productions in streets and factories, and the reviews of and commentaries on books–all part of the drive for literacy, a basic tenet of Francisco Ferri's project for modern schooling and education. This also helps to explain the fact that Anarchist writers in Brazil traditionally were nonprofessional. From their perspective, their work was the outcome of collective experience rather than the result of an aesthetic process. The text's conceptual content was secondary to a militant's decision to write; an author's motivations outweighed the formal aspects of his or her writings. These were writers who typically attributed great relevance to the role of culture, to morality, and to a humanitarian commitment in intellectual activity. It follows, therefore, that the dignity of one's own message had great significance for anarchist writers; attention was paid to issues of judgment, statements of fact, and social denunciations. Of importance too was the fervor (to the point of exhibitionism) with which they exalted the nobility of the proletarian cause in a nation where representations of the oppressed were generally either deformed by erudite literature or transformed into the extravagant characters of the criminal pages of yellow journalism. The Anarchist press showed a frequent preference for thinkers such as Pierre Joseph Proudhon, Peter Kropotkine, and Mikhail Bakunin; authors such as Emile Zola, Pio Baroja, and Maxim Gorki; and poets such as Percy Bysshe Shelley and Victor Hugo. This press also published extensive works on revolutionary topics in the form of chronicles and short stories, verse, and dramatizations, whose vivid illustrations constituted an important contribution to the development of figurative art in the Brazilian press.

On first approaching the literary material created by the Anarchist strategy of direct action, one finds in prose the short story and the *relato-flagrante* (flagrant story) on the one hand, and on the other, *crônica* (chronicle, a Brazilian form close to the short story) and poetry; to these we must add brief occasional essays, parodies, and plays that owed their inspiration to the great authors of universal literary canon.

Between resistance and liberty, these may be characterized as genres of ideological intervention, organized around the three main goals of what became known as *arte em situação* (situational art): to reproduce reality so as to make it accessible to all, to expose concretely the causes of its contradictions, and to show people the elementary conditions for a fruitful coexistence with a changing social order.

More abstract, and using an allegorical structure, the *conto* (short story) can be differentiated from the *relato-flagrante* according to Lily Litvak; the latter is a brief narrative grounded in an ideological base, situating the reader in a scenario that allows the recognition of social injustice. Neno Vasco, Félix Lázaro, Felipe Gil, José Oiticica, and Mota Assunção (following the models of narratives by Pi y Arsuaga, Baroja, and Paul Lafargue) are some of the most important militant writers of fiction in the magazines and newspapers of the time: *Kultur* (Rio de Janeiro, 1904), *Liberdade* (Rio de Janeiro, 1919), *O internacional* (São Paulo, 1924), and *A Plebe* (new phase, São Paulo, 1935). Militant authors like these produced texts such as the *conto "Fogo!"* ["Fire!"], published in *A Barricada* (Rio de Janeiro, 1916), or irreverent fictional protests such as the narrative *"Maluquices"* ["Crazy Things"], signed by a "group of alienated people" from the newspaper *Guerra Sociale* [Social War] (São Paulo, 1916); there was also a vast collection of writings signed by people representing different categories of urban workers. These narratives describing the hardship of factory work bore such signatures as "anonymous hat maker," "industrial p.," "photographer," "glass maker," or simply "a worker." This militant writing resulted in a wealth of material for the pages of newspapers such as *Aurora Social* (Recife, 1901), *O Baluarte* (Rio de Janeiro, 1906), *Novo Rumo* (Rio de Janeiro, 1906), *A Luta Proletária* (São Paulo, 1908), *O Despertar* (Curitiba, 1904), and *A Plebe* (São Paulo, 1917). Anarchists also wrote daily combative editorials and columns such as those, for example, in the section "Quadros Sociais" ["Social Portraits," or "Social Cadres"], signed by Santos Cruz, and "Letras e tretas" ["Words and Epithets"], authored by someone with the unlikely name of Moxila, both appearing regularly in the newspaper *O Cosmopolita* (1915–1918), and "Entre Operários" ["Among Workers"], signed by Anco Márcio, in the newspaper *Aurora Social* of Pernambuco around 1901–1902.

The *relato-flagrante* was written ostensibly as a piece of fiction, but its style leaned openly toward that of the pamphlet form; portraying the exploitation of labor, they were signed by militants close to the top echelons of the movement. This was the case of Florentino de Carvalho, a school teacher from São Paulo who authored "O banquete dos chacais" ["Banquet of Jackals"] (*Guerra Sociale*, 1917); J. Romero, the writer of "As Operárias" ["The Female Workers"] (*Novo Rumo*, 1906); and Manoel Tato, author of "O pior enemigo" ["The Worst Enemy"] (*O Congresso*, 1905). To these we can add translations such as that of Paul Lefargue's "A oficina é pior do que a prisão" ["The Workshop Is Worse than Prison"], published in the newspaper *O Baluarte* in July 1917.

A different aspect of the *relato-flagrante* developed in the *crônica* form of the Anarchist movement, with its accounts of conflicts and confrontations with the established order. We can include in this category the episodes narrated by militant intellectuals or leaders of the movement, almost always alternating between figurative language and the vivid strokes of an empirical exposition, as illustrated in "A nossa explusão" ["Our Expulsion"] by Florentino de Carvalho, published in *A Plebe*; and the narratives written by activist Astrojildo Pereira and "Reinvidicações da Canalha" ["The Demands of the Scoundrels"] by Everardo Dias (1883–1966), both published in *A Plebe*, as well as the texts "Um conto extraordinário" ["An Extraordinary Story"] by the militant Luigi Damiani and "A Lição do abutre" ["The Vulture's Lesson"] by Sílvio de Almeida (1867–1924), published respectively in the newspapers *O Despertar* and *Guerra Sociale* (1917).

The *relato-flagrante* shares a niche with the competing literary forms of *crônica*, and poetry, each one endowed with unique dimensions that had no point of convergence at the time, though they would later in contemporary literature. The *crônica* published in the libertarian newspapers had the same form of a subjective tone and lyrical language as the relato; it also maintained an open ideological slant in its fragmented recounting of current affairs. Maria Lacerda de Moura (1887–1945), Domingos Ribeiro Filho, José Oiticica (1882–1957), and Fábio Luz (1864–1938)–whose work was published in periodicals such as *Emancipação* (1905), *O Baluarte* (1907), *A vida* (1914), and *A Plebe* (1934)–are some of the principal representatives of this genre, which, in two brief columns, acquaints the daily reader with the notion of the incorruptibility of human values, the superior order of the cosmos, and the redemptive function of love and solidarity–understood as the supreme aims of the destiny of every free human being, and seen here as an irradiating center of force, beauty, love, and wisdom.

Poetry, curiously enough, makes its appearance in an entirely different tone, in the ambit of the humorous chronicle or chronicle of farce, which was generally written by anonymous readers or militants struggling against the limitations imposed by the dominant order, as was the case of the majority of the combative writings of the day-to-day direct action. The following merit note: "Na cretinolândia" ["In Scoundrels-land"], written by a certain Lancetta (*Guerra Sociale*, 1917); "Placas Fotográficas" ["Photographic Plates"] (*Novo Rumo*, 1906), signed by "an anonymous photographer"; "Os dois burros" ["The Two Asses"], by the deported Italian militant Luciano Campagnoli (*Luta Proletária*, 1908); "Um sonho" ["A Dream"] (*O Baluarte*, 1907), written by an anonymous hat maker; and "O adulador" ["The Flatterer"], signed by "industrial p." in the newspaper *Aurora Social* (Recife, 1901). Anarchist poetry, however, emerging from the irreverent semi-anonymity described above, was still shackled to the conservative forms of the ode and the sonnet, when not functioning under the constraints of rigid epic meter in celebration of the freedom of the masses; whether in newspapers or in rare published works, this poetic work brought little new to the form, from its Romantic version to its latest manifestations in Symbolism. At first Anarchist poetry was advanced by the work of a few intellectuals who adhered to the movement, such as Benjamim Mota ("Rebeldias" [1899; "Rebel Acts"]), Pereira da Silva (*Vae soli!*, 1903), and José Oiticica, with his two series of sonnets "Sonetos" (1911 and 1919), who, in the company of Otávio Brandão (1896–1979), Ricardo Gonçalves, Martins Fontes (1884–1937) (*O Vulcão*, 1926), and Afonso Schmidt (1890–1964), among others, articulated the first images of both resistance and union of the dispossessed against the oppressors in the workplace and in institutional life.

Later, from the 1920s onward, when the idea of freedom inspired Anarchist hymns and songs that circulated freely about the cultural centers and workers' associations, this poetry of resistance and direct action grew stronger and came to be written by workers and militants who lived the dream of equality in the streets, in the factories, and in their own homes. Among them—as they are remembered today in Edgard Leuenroth's (1881–1968) anthology—are those of Maura de Sena Pereira (on the redemption of the black); Bezerra da Cunha, Carlos Benevenga, and Carlos Bacelar (exalting the dignity of factory workers); Raimundo Reis (defending the female worker); Albino Bastos, Angelo Jorge, and Adalberto Viana (on proletarian education); as well as those of Pedro Catallo, Paulo Torres, Domingos Brás, and Lírio de Resende, who wrote on the great themes of Anarchism, from the First of May and the Chicago heroes, from proletarian organization to the symbolic rethinking of the factory as the place of martyrdom and the degradation of people in need.

Nevertheless, to an even greater extent than poetry, theater became the great genre of the mobilization of libertarian ideals in Brazil. Celebrated in festivals, where poems and lectures were also publicly read, theatrical shows gained increased importance as cultural centers multiplied; the origin of this rapid growth can perhaps be found in the traditional love for the theater of Italian immigrants. From 1906 onward, drama groups began to make their appearance in Rio de Janeiro, where Mota Assunção staged the five-act play *O Infanticídio* [The Infanticide], a play that marked a turning point in the trajectory of Anarchist cultural action in Brazil. The Grupo Filodramático Libertário de São Paulo (Libertarian Filo-Dramatic Group of São Paulo) made its appearance the year after, followed by the group of Curitiba and other important associations in a short time span, such as the Grupo Dramático Máximo Gorki (Maxim Gorki Drama Group) (1913), the Grupo de Teatro Social Primeiro de Maio (First of May Social Theater Group), the Grupo Dramático de Teatro Livre da Associação de Operários Sapateiros (Free Theater Drama Group of the Shoemakers' Workers Association) (1914), the Grupo de Teatro Germinal dos Operários Alfaiates (Germinal Theater Group of Tailor Workers), the Núcleo Filodramático Libertá (Filo-Dramatic *Libertá* Nucleus) (1920), and the Clube Dramático Libertário de Sete Lagoas (Libertarian Drama Club of Sete Lagoas) (1921), which brought the writer Alvelino Fóscolo's (1864–1944) theatrical works to prominence. This combination of poetry, song, lectures, and drama created famous venues, such as the Salão Celso Garcia in São Paulo, whose festivals became a conduit for some of the plays that best illustrated proletarian ideals; two examples are the drama *O pecado de simonia* [The Sin of Simony] by Neno Vasco and the play in verse *Avatar* by Marcelo Gama (1878–1915).

The libertarian theater's origins were closely linked to the Italian theater and the theater of the Universidade Popular de Ensino Livre (loosely translated as the Popular University for Free Education). Compiled by Luigi Molinari in 1908, works were sent that were authored by men such as R. Rousselle (*Il maestro* [The Teacher]), Antona Traversi (*L'assolto* [Absolved]), Jean Grave (*Responsabilità* [Responsibility]), and Carlo Malato (*Una commédia sociale* [A Social Comedy]). Of course, Pietro Gorki's works (especially *Primo Maggio* [First of May] and *L'ideale* [The Ideal]) were frequently staged in Brazil. An entire generation of playwrights and militant producers flourished in this libertarian theater, putting on the stage Anarchist moral dramas that confronted the opposing factions of bosses and servants, the State and free men, war and the voluntary organization of those who produced wealth, and the power of popes and prelates and the faith of the common people. They depicted large networks of people opposed to war as the scourge of humankind; factories for devouring people like the

mouth of an insatiable monster; the metaphor of the destitute yet pure; hungry female workers seduced by their bosses; soldiers caught up in an onslaught, like bloodthirsty animals; harvest bounty and endless abundance at Fourier's tables and in the communes of free workers. These are some of the basic images found in the theater of Fábio Luz (1864–1938) (*Terror noturno* [Nocturnal Terror]), José Oiticica (1882–1957) (*Pedra que rola* [Rolling Stone], *Quem os salva* [Who Will Save Them]), Neno Vasco (*Greve de inquilinos* [Renter's Strike]), Pedro Catallo (*A Casa dos milagres* [House of Miracles], *Como rola uma vida* [How a Life Happens]), Marino Spagnolo (*Bandeira proletária* [Proletarian Flag], *Os immigrantes* [The Immigrants]), Avelino Fóscolo (1864–1944) (*O semeador* [The Planter of Seeds]), A. Andrade Silva (*Sua Santidade* [His Holiness]), Felipe Gil (*Último quadro* [The Last Portrait]), Batista Dinis (*Veteranos da liberdade* [Veterans of Freedom]), and Afonso Schmidt (1890–1964) (*Ao relento* [In Open Air]).

Conceived in a Manichean universe of ideologically redundant and schematic characters, this form of theater shares the confines of action of the protagonists of the so-called *romance social* (socially conscious novel), generally set within a libertarian utopia projected onto the countryside (*Regeneração* [1903; Regeneration] by Geonísio Curvelo de Mendonça (b. 1877) or *Redenção* [1911; Redemption] by Viega Miranda) or in the abstract space of ideological projection (*O ideólogo* [1903; The Ideologue] by Fábio Luz; *No hospício* [1905; At the Asylum] by José Francisco da Rocha Pombo [1857–1933]). Others offered a more immediate recreation of the effects of social struggle: *Mártir da fé* [1899; Martyr of Faith] by Pausílipo da Fonseca; *Os emancipados* [1906; The Emancipated] by Fábio Luz; and *O cravo vermelho* [1907; Red Carnation] by Domingos Ribeiro Filho.

Still in the throes of nineteenth-century Realism, these novels are narrow in focus, and only broaden much later through the satirical writings of Lima Barreto (1881–1922) (*Numa e a ninfa* [1915; Numa and the Nymph], *Os Bruzundungas* [1923]), through the humorous view and parodic resources of *Galabáro* (1917) by Juó Bananere (1892–1933) and A. Paes, or through the more pessimistic treatment of *O Gororoba* [1931; Grub] by Lauro Palhano, which, next to *Parque Industrial* [1933; Industrial Complex] by Patrícia Galvão (1910–1962) and *Navios Iluminados* [1937; Luminous Ships] by Ranulfo Prata (1896–1942), offered a less conventional vision of the excessively rhetorical narratives of these first fiction writers.

Reaching a much larger audience than the novel, however, the *novella* or *folhetim* (serial) was the genre that played a decisive role in the ideological prose of the beginning of the century; its outreach was comparable to that of the chronicle and even the short story itself. Interspersed with translations of *folhetins* authored by European writers such as Zola, Anselmo Lorenzo, and Azorín, the *novelas* soon impressed themselves upon their readers; some representative works are *A vitória da fome* [1911; The Victory of Hunger] by Pausílipo da Fonseca, *Miserere* (1919) by Domingos Ribeiro Filho, *No circo* [At the Circus] and *A vida* [1913 and 1921; Life] by Avelino Fóscolo, and *Nunca!* [1924; Never!] by Fábio Luz.

Jewish Immigrants and Brazilian Intellectual Life

A great number of Jewish men and women took refuge in Brazilian lands: In the fine arts, Axl Leskoschek (1889–1976), born in Austria–painter, illustrator, and creator of etchings and drawings–was active in Rio de Janeiro between 1940 and 1948, where he acted as an artist and professor of the Fundação Getúlio Vargas (Getúlio Vargas Foundation), having illustrated books by Carlos Lacerda and Graciliano Ramos; Fayga Ostrower, born in Poland in 1920, a painter and engraver, was honored with a prize in the *IV Bienal de arte de São Paulo* (São Paulo Biannual Fourth Art Competition). For their contributions to the Brazilian world of letters, we must mention Otto Maria Carpeaux and Paulo Rónai. Carpeaux (1900–1978) was born in Vienna and earned a doctorate in philosophy and literature; he was forced into exile with the Nazi occupation of Austria, emigrating to Belgium and eventually to Brazil in 1939. Carpeaux played an important role in the literature and culture of Brazil: He was director of the library at the Faculdade Nacional de Filosofia (National Faculty of Philosophy) (1942–1944) and the library of the Fundação Getúlio Vargas (1944–1949); he was a writer for and editor of the newspaper *Correio da Manhã* and published, among other works, *História da literatura ocidental* [1953; History of Western Literature] and *Pequena bibliografia crítica da literatura brasileira* [A Short Critical Bibliography of Brazilian Literature]. He also headed up a section of the *Grande Enciclopédia Delta-Larrouse* [Great Delta-Larrouse Encyclopedia] and was one of the editors of the *Enciclopédia Mirador Internacional* [1977; Mirador International Encyclopedia], an enterprise linked with the *Encyclopedia Britannica.* He also became famous as a political polemist, and his collected *crônicas* were edited under the titles *Brasil no espelho do mundo* [1964; Brazil in the World's Mirror] and *A Batalha da América Latina* [1965; The Battle of Latin America]. The writer, translator, critic, and professor Paulo Rónai (1907–1990) also merits attention for his contributions to intellectual life in Brazil. Arriving in Brazil from Hungary, Rónai fled the horrors of war to become one of the most important men of letters of the Brazilian postwar period. Completing his higher studies in Paris and Perugia, he became interested in Brazilian literature before his first visit to the nation, as can be seen by his anthology of Brazilian poetry *Mensagem do Brasil* [1939; Message from Brazil], which earned him an invitation to visit Brazil by the *Itamarati*, the Ministry for Foreign Relations. Rónai's arrival in 1941 was followed shortly by his naturalization in 1945. Books he wrote include *Balzac e a Comédia Humana* [1947; Balzac and the Human Comedy], *Escola de Tradutores* [1952; School of Translators], *Como Aprendi o Português e outras aventuras* [1956; How I Learned Portuguese and Other Adventures], and *Encontros com o Brasil* [1958; Encounters with Brazil], as well as the complete translation of the *Human Comedy* by Balzac, published by *Editora Globo* in Porto Alegre. Like Carpeaux, Rónai placed his erudition at the service of Brazilian culture.

Zbigniev Mariev Ziembinski (1908–1978), born in the region of Krakow, participated in various theater groups and, having directed a number of plays in Rio de Janeiro, became an important point of reference in the history of the national theater. Possibly one of the most famous Jewish refugees, the writer Stefan Zweig (born in Vienna in 1881), came twice to Brazil as a visitor before taking up residence in Petrópolis (in the mountains near Rio de Janeiro) on his third trip in 1941, in the company of his second wife, Lotte; he remained there until his suicide on February 22 of the following year. From his first trip (in August 1936) Zweig expressed surprise at how unlike his preconceptions Brazil was: He had expected a republic with chaotic politics and shaky finances. Instead, he was taken with the beauty of Guanabara Bay, and the warm hospitality of the authorities and of the thousands of Brazilians who came to listen to him. His impressions of Ouro Preto, Salvador, Recife, and Belém are described in *Brasil,*

terra do futuro [Brazil, A Land of the Future], written in the United States. Although Zweig's opinion changed, his view of Brazil as a marvelous nation and his enthusiasm for its pacifism and what he saw as the absolute nonexistence of racism did not break with the conventional stereotypes of Latin American nations held by Europeans. In fact, Zweig never believed he could be happy in this nation of the future. His letters reveal the suffering and anguish of a person condemned to live in exile, far from friends and family because of Nazi persecution. If Brazil offered him a haven and even surprised him, it did not offer him a new life, as can be seen by his decision to take his own life. Zweig's farewell letter is a clear testimony that he could not bear to distance himself from his European roots; unable to live in his fatherland and share the universe of his native tongue, he felt his life was bereft of meaning. This nation of the future–Zweig's conception of Brazil in his moments of enthusiasm–could not be a substitute for his Vienna; although providing him with safety, it became an empty refuge. He was incapable of effectively envisaging himself as part of Brazil.

The French Cultural Mission in Brazil and the Foundation of the Universidade de São Paulo

Other Europeans in Brazil were better able to resist the temptations of tropical exoticism and to offer more accuracy in their views of Brazilian reality. Such was the case of Claude Lévi-Strauss (b. 1908) and Roger Bastide (1898–1974), who were part of the French mission that assisted the São Paulo government in creating the foundations for its state university (USP) in 1934. Teaching at the university from 1934 to 1939 and 1938 to 1953, respectively, Lévi-Strauss and Bastide both found Brazil to be a prodigious terrain on which to develop their reflections and research in their particular fields of interest. Roger Bastide, who published various articles and studies, including the well-known *O Candomblé da Bahia, rito nagô* [Candomble in Bahia, the Nagô Rite], *O sonho, o transe e a loucura* [Dreams, Trance, and Madness], and *As religiões africanas no Brasil* [*The African Religions of Brazil*], was interested mainly in ethnology of religion, acculturation, and social psychiatry. Lévi-Srauss–who shared a background in philosophy with Bastide–discussed totemism and primitive systems of classification in his USP courses. His now classic *Tristes Trópicos,* published in 1955, combined an analysis of indigenous groups and São Paulo society of the time, in a language that was accessible to a nonspecialist reading public. His future work, its articulation of categories of perception with logical processes, as well as his comparative analysis of myths, could not have been what they are without what provoked the first impulse of his professional life as an anthropologist–his sojourn in Brazil. In his narrative of his arrival in Rio de Janeiro, where he notes the disconcerting effect the abundance and density of the tropical landscape has on Europeans, Lévi-Strauss provides us with a glimpse into the differences that will motivate his research and his imagination. According to him, Europeans are ignorant of unspoiled nature, and their landscapes are dominated by human intervention. As he himself would say, journeys are not merely travel through space, but the simultaneous dislocation in space, time, and hierarchy. When Ferdinand Braudel was invited to work at USP in 1935, he declared that the sights that met his eyes in the two years he spent in Brazil sufficed to give him a new understanding of life and, to a certain extent, brought about an intellectual transformation. It was more important for him to visit Brazil than it was for Brazilians to go to Paris. Braudel believed his Brazilian students forced him to think in a different manner. The lack of organized archives, in contrast with his previous experience in Mediterranean countries, allowed his concept of a three-tiered view of historical time and *long durée* to be engendered in Brazil, where, according to Marc Ferro, the seeds of the *Annales* school were planted.

Jean Mangüé also worked at the Universidade de São Paulo. A colleague of Jean-Paul Sartre and Raymond Aron at the École Normale Supérieure, he was invited by Georges Dumas, then in charge of recruiting professors for the French mission in Brazil. The courses he taught had a great impact: He taught the great thinkers (Kant, Hegel, Marx, Freud, Alain, and others), and his teachings emphasized reflection. It was Mangüé's belief that the aim of the College of Philosophy, Science, and Literature was not to produce philosophers but to create an atmosphere conducive to critical thought. His courses included references to current events, cultural affairs, and episodes of daily life. His students created the magazine *Clima*, attesting to his enthusiasm, academic excellence, and critical acuity.

The *Tristes Tropiques* under the Deconstructing Gaze of Anthropologists

"I hate traveling and explorers." This radical statement is the first sentence of the most important travel narrative written by an anthropologist on Brazil. Moved by great curiosity, the reader must ask why *Tristes tropiques* by Claude Lévi-Strauss starts with such an outright repudiation of journeys and exploration, and why the author hesitates even to write the book. The lines that follow provide some indication:

> yet here I am, all set to tell the story of my expeditions. But at least I've taken a long while to make up my mind to it: fifteen years have passed since I left Brazil for the last time and often, during those years, I've planned to write this book, but I've always been held back by a sort of shame and disgust. (1961, 17)

This author's shame, in principle, has a rather simple explanation and is directly associated to the great anthropologist's unpretentiousness. It took Lévi-Strauss fifteen years–from the trip in the early 1930s to the publication of his book in the mid-1950s–to decide on the importance of recounting his experiences. He asks himself whether, amid valid ethnographic observations, there is not too much "dross":

> It may be that we shall have spent six months of travel, privation, and sickening physical weariness merely in order to record–in a few days, it may be, or even a few hours–an unpublished myth, a new marriage-rule, or a complete list of names of clans. But that does not justify my taking up my pen in order to rake over memory's trash-cans. "At 5:30 a.m. we dropped anchor off Recife while the seagulls skirled around us and a flotilla of small boats put out from the shore with exotic fruits for sale." (1961, 17)

The illustrious anthropologist's shame might be explained by what he feared were trivial circumstances and insignificant happenings. These doubts, however, are rooted in greater complexities that must be examined in order to offer an explanation of the journeys anthropologists undertake, of the meanings they take on in the discipline's literature, and in the Brazilian case, of the importance of texts–such as *Tristes tropiques*–that tried to break with the Eurocentrism pervasive in so many such narratives. Further still, these doubts speak to us of a sophisticated intellectual movement that could be one of the hallmarks of present-day anthropology. Let us proceed to examine this in stages.

First we must ask: Which aspect of travel narratives troubles the author to the point of having him doubt the importance of his own narrative? Rather than naming explorers or speculating on their identities, he points out:

> Doubtless there are exceptions, every age has its authentic travelers, and among those who today enjoy the public's favors I could point to one or two who deserve the name. My aim, however, is neither to expose the one nor to authenticate the other, but rather to understand a moral and social phenomenon which is peculiar to France and is, even there, of recent origin. (1961, 18)

In fact, the motive for repugnance is in neither the journey nor the explorer, for they are inevitable and, more especially, intrinsic to ethnology. What brings about this reservation is not the journey as an act or principle, but as a style of traveling and of recounting it. The style that troubles Lévi-Strauss has two characteristics that, combined, result in a perverse perception of the other. One of them is present in the travel narrative or explorer's lecture and brings about a magical transformation of the other: transmuted into the exotic, comical, picturesque, in preferably color photographs or film, domesticated as in a child's almanac, endowed with a circus-like quality, and, finally, timidly genuflecting at the feet of civilization. This style moves Lévi-Strauss to deep repulsion:

> Amazonia, Africa, and Tibet have invaded all our bookstalls. Travel-books, expeditionary records, and photograph-albums abound; and as they are written or compiled with an eye mainly for effect the reader has no means of estimating their value. His critical sense once lulled to sleep, he asks only to be given "more of the same" and ends by devouring it in unlimited quantity. Exploration has become a profession; not, as one might suppose, that it's a matter of unearthing new facts in the course of several years' laborious study–not at all! Mere mileage is the thing; and anyone who has been far enough, and collected the right number of pictures (still or moving, but for preference in color), will be able to lecture to packed houses for several days running. Platitudes take shape as revelations once the audience is assured that the speaker has sanctified them by traveling to the other side of the globe. (1961, 17–18)

This transformation of the other into the picturesque in travel narratives is the first characteristic of the ethnocentric style to be repudiated by Lévi-Strauss; but it may not be the most complex aspect of such narratives. Lévi-Strauss was especially concerned with the violence contained within the concept of ethnocentrism. It is important to note, in the discussion of this topic, that at approximately the same period in which Lévi-Strauss was considering (and hesitating over) writing *Tristes tropiques*, he was involved in another project: the famous text *Race et histoire* [*Race and History*]. Published in 1952, commissioned by UNESCO, and written between October 1954 and March 1955, *Race et histoire* is probably the text on ethnocentrism that has had the greatest influence in anthropology. His text benefited from the discussions held two years previously, which allowed him to position himself clearly regarding some concerns expressed in *Tristes tropiques*. The proximity of these two texts in time may allow us to capture a significant intellectual movement present in the perspective Lévi-Strauss adopted in his understanding of travel narratives of the other, ultimately leading to a rupture with an ethnocentric world-view on reality, culture, and social data.

Brazil–and along with it travel, observation, narrative, and the report–takes on a particular relevance in this process. The nation's internal diversity served as a stage on which to verify his cultural thesis, a privileged place for ethnographic study and anthropological practice to start from. Brazil was well suited as an anthropologicial site when the discipline took up topics such as racial miscegenation, interethnic friction, rapid expansion, urbanization, cultural confluence, or tribal societies. *Tristes tropiques* is, therefore, a dense study–as well as a travel narrative–marked above all by the preoccupation to evade the quagmire of ethnocentrism. Lévi-Strauss offers us a profound insight into his objectives in the writing of his text. His view of Brazil must be free of prejudice; he does not intend to write another version of the picturesque and is not interested in producing reified certainties. Therefore, *Tristes tropiques* does not offer the reader the familiar tourist guide intent on providing a sequence of scenes conforming to the anthropologist's or traveler's expectations. Lévi-Strauss's structuralist theory was largely in the process of being created, and his experimental gaze on Brazilian culture–as well as the Caduveo, Bororo, Nambikwara, and Tupi Kawahib cultures–was consequently opening up a dialogue with ideas that were in gestation, as he mined new intellectual veins. All this hinged on the realization of the greater journey, the one to engage the other as self, well distanced from ethnocentrism.

Evidently Lévi-Strauss was not alone in his attraction to a relativizing stance, capable of harboring the experience of the other as a condition of anthropological knowledge. His travels were in part–a substantial part to be sure–a deconstructive process applied to the Eurocentric imaginary usually imposed on the Brazilian people and culture, which could generally be interpreted against a background of late nineteenth-century racist evolutionism. This was also the sort of ethnocentrism denounced in Skidmore's exasperation at the comments made by Louis Agassiz, after his famous trip to Brazil at the end of the nineteenth century:

> Let any one who doubts the evil of this mixture of races, and is inclined, from a mistaken philanthropy, to break down all barriers between them, come to Brazil. He cannot deny the deterioration consequent upon an amalgamation of races, more widespread here than in any other country in the world, and which is rapidly effacing the best qualities of the white man, the Negro, and the Indian, leaving a mongrel nondescript type, deficient in physical and mental energy. (qtd. in Skidmore 31–32)

This may be the key to understanding the phrase "I hate traveling and explorers." Comments such as those of Agassiz and others by Gobineau and Buckle with direct reference to Brazil have to be taken into account. Lévi-Strauss correctly sees them as responsible for creating the Eurocentric image. *Tristes tropiques* became a cornerstone in the process of deconstruction, in which Lévi-Strauss was capable of both voicing pride in being a French professor and unleashing powerful criticism of a European imaginary that exported little French girls as erotic representations of dubious taste. *Tristes tropiques* shows us a careful anthropologist at work in his articulate rendering of Brazilian cities, their historical dimension and cultural traits, capturing the complex and subtle contrasts, such as those between countryside and urban centers. We see passages in which Lévi-Strauss's intellectual creativity is at work, as he planted the seeds of ideas that would eventually result in important anthropological developments.

Above all, the reader can witness the emphatic use of relativization on the very ethnocentric discourse that engendered, at a certain period in time, the generic notion of a nation doomed because of interracial mixing. One of the main causes of Eurocentrism's undoing is *Tristes tropiques*. Lévi-Strauss, however, as mentioned previously, was not alone in this task, and foreign visitors to Brazil–social scientists in general, and anthropologists in particular–performed a role of great importance in this deconstructive process, in the gradual elevation of the debate on Brazil to higher levels of complexity, and finally to a progressive breaking away from ethnocentric limitations that had kept Europeans in the dark for centuries and Latin Americans in the self-denial characteristic of marginal peoples. One of the first contributions of note is that of Curt Nimuendaju, who changed the prevalent anthropological approach of attempting a totalizing reading of race; his studies on individual groups of the *Jê* people made the traditional anthropological concern for totality obsolete. His work was important because, among other things, it prefigured the monograph as a professional tool, as a mode of study that entailed an ethnographic proximity that led to a relativizing vision of culture and social practice.

Another important point of reference, still during the first decades of the century, is the project that established the *Lycée Français* in Brazil, firmly backed by both countries. This embryonic movement led to a notable outcome in the 1930s with the foundation of USP, the Universidade de São Paulo. The founding of USP is thus ineluctably linked to the Lévi-Strauss's journey, which only came to life with the publication of the book in the 1950s. The same period, of course, is also marked by Roger Bastide's work on Afro-Brazilian religions, among other topics, and his major contribution to the deconstruction of evolutionism.

The contributions of North American sociology should also be noted here. First, one should consider Donald Pierson's lengthy stay, a total of eighteen years in Brazil. Pierson was influenced by Robert Park, his advisor at the University of Chicago, and believed that Brazil was a privileged space for the analysis of intercultural contact. Pierson's work was also instrumental in the process of deconstructing Brazilian Eurocentrism. One should also mention Charles Wagley (1913–1991), Melville Herkovits (1895–1963), Anthony Leeds (b. 1925), Marvin Harris (1927–2001), and so many others who, in one form or another, were associated with the great flux of North Americans linked to Columbia University's Programa de Pesquisas Sociais Estado da Bahia (Social Studies Program in Bahia State). Much more recently, and of great significance for the deconstruction of ethnocentrism and its impact as a basis for considering Brazil, is the Harvard–Brasil Central project. Under the leadership of David Maybury-Lewis, this project was decisive in setting up the postgraduate program in Social Anthropology of the Museu Nacional, which to this day is a center of excellence, responsible for the education of several generations of Brazilian anthropologists. It is important to note that many of these authors' comments on Brazil were made as by-products of their research and analysis of tribal societies within Brazil. In this sense they result from conventional travel narratives and are not social scientific studies. The typical case involves observations made with respect to Brazilian culture as incidental to the research process on other cultures, namely tribal cultures. We have, therefore, a travel narrative within a travel narrative as a by-product. The ensemble of these cultural annotations, created by such a diverse group of authors, served to draw up the blueprints of a new intellectual approach. These authors relativized the image of Brazil, deconstructing the well-established ethnocentric perspective of the exotic tropics.

Other Frenchmen in Transit through the Tropics

The French writer Georges Bernanos (1888–1948) also searched Latin America for a terrestrial paradise. He left France to escape the deleterious political climate that dominated the nation at the eve of the Munich Accords. His disappointment with Paraguay led him to take up residence in Brazil in 1938. Bernanos elected to live in smaller cities such as Juiz de Fora and Pirapora, working in cattle rearing and agriculture, and enjoying the intimacy of a life close to nature. Written in the manner of a diary of his travels throughout Brazil, *Les enfants humiliés* [1949; *Tradition of Freedom*] vividly evokes the virgin wilderness that extended far into Mato Grosso, and the landscape at the margins of the São Francisco River. In August 1940 Bernanos moved to Cruz das Almas, a small town close to Barbacena, Minas Gerais. The depth of his relationship to Brazil is evident in the book *Le chemin de la Croix-des-Âmes* [1944; The Road of the Croix-des-Âmes], which includes his *Journal* (1940) as well as a great number of articles and letters. Bernanos took part in the popular celebrations of D-Day on 6 July 1944 and decided to return to France the following year. We know that Bernanos had close relationships with Brazilian intellectuals such as Alceu de Amoroso Lima (1893–1983), Jorge de Lima (1899–1953), and Augusto Frederico Schmidt (1906–1965).

Albert Camus (1913–1960) traveled in South America from June to August 1949 as part of a cultural mission. The vast expanses of unspoiled nature also impressed him, and his notes expressed the rather utopian notion that a new culture, more primitive and natural, might overcome the excesses of progress. His interaction with Brazilian intellectuals revealed some evidence of his interest in Brazilian culture, especially in Oswald de Andrade's (1890–1954) theories on *antropofagia* (anthropophagy) and matriarchy. He visited *terreiros de Macumba* (Afro-Brazilian religious ceremonies) in Rio de Janeiro. In Recife he attended shows of folklore, such as the *bumba-meu-boi*. In São Paulo he visited the *Rádio Cultura* in search of documents on theater, since part of the purpose of his trip was to acquire some knowledge of Brazilian theater.

On his visit to Brazil between 24 and 29 August 1959, as head of the Ministry for Culture of France, invited by the government of President Juscelino Kubitschek de Oliveira, André Malraux (1901–1976) also expressed the idea that Brazil was the nation of hope. Apart from its cultural objectives, his visit also had a political aim: To defend the colonialist politics of the Fifth Republic. Malraux's official status, however, was unable to shield him from the reaction of various sectors of society, spurred on by events that had taken place in the Algerian War during that week. Malreaux was warmly received by president Kubitschek during their August 25 meeting, and his speech on Brasília was rapidly published and translated to many languages. In the speech–the only one given in Brazil to be widely known–the Minister for Culture of France sees the new capital of Brazil as the city of the future, the first of the capitals of the new civilization. The Brasília speech endeavors to provide an incentive for Latin America's struggles in defense of its own culture, a struggle that Malreaux himself had always championed in his efforts to value other cultures and their works of art. Malreaux imagines a future of both epic and mythical dimensions for Brasília. We may well ask, however, how much of this idea of a mythical young nation was not, in fact, the construct of a European viewpoint marked by its own ancient culture.

Michel Foucault (1926–1984) was one of the most frequent travelers to Brazil in the 1960s and 1970s. An internationally renowned philosopher and man of action, Michel Foucault visited Brazil during the difficult period of the military dictatorship. For a thinker whose work was so deeply concerned with power, Foucault was faced in 1975 with a nation of repression, prison, and political violence. This was precisely the same period in which the journalist Valdimir Herzog was killed in São Paulo (25 October 1975). Foucault even expressed his solidarity by being present at the famous *Praça da Sé* mass, one of the moments of resistance to the military dictatorship. The escalating violence nevertheless forced Foucault to discontinue his lectures as a form of protest. His public declaration to the university stated that he refused to teach in a nation where there was no freedom.

From even this brief exposition, one can develop a synthesis to interpret and evaluate the effects of the confrontation of diverse cultures and experiences in Brazilian culture. Once foreigners established themselves in the South American continent, they were involved in a process of sociological and cultural interaction that had unmistakable consequences for both sides. Referring to the French mission in Brazil, Leyla Perrone-Moisés asserts that French intellectuals, rather than bringing to Brazil what it lacked, instructed it in what it possessed and how it could make use of it. Grouped together by daring and polemical ideas, foreign artists and intellectuals contributed through their work and their presence to a new cultural horizon in Brazil. The fact that a particularly large group took part in founding the Universidade de São Paulo allows us a privileged venue to analyze this exchange, which was no less meaningful than the role played by these individual travelers in Brazil. It was, as we have seen, a role of extreme importance, not only for the experience they brought to bear, but also, in many cases, for the experience they came to acquire in Brazil. Their names, inscribed in permanent memory, will not be ignored in future studies of Brazil's literary culture.

The Brazil–United States Cultural Exchange

The principal works to attempt a definition of the complex and ambivalent relations between Brazil and the Anglo-Saxon world (particularly the United States) in the twentieth century reach back to a tradition initiated in the sixteenth century, and have as their main points of reference the same criteria used to legitimize imperialist expansion over the last four centuries. Brazilian authors were no more likely than Anglo-Saxon travelers writing on Brazil to be neutral or disinterested in their treatments of reality. Comparisons of the two nations' different historical trajectories entailed a consciousness of shortcomings regarding Brazil and projected a mix of admiration and misgivings toward the rather unfriendly northern "brother" (see Bellei 1988 and 1992). The definition of a national identity for Brazil arises, in the writings of various travelers, mediated by the prototype of a nation that is economically more powerful–whether it is expressed as an aim to be reached or as a denunciation of limitations. Contrasted to the United States, Brazil could only be known as the nation of the future, an expression coined, as we have seen, by travelers on visits to Brazil. An ambivalent comparison is set up between two stages of the development of the two nations: The image of the United States as the home of democracy, wealth, and social equality favors the assimilation of many of the North American values, but it sparks a strong reaction in many Brazilian intellectuals to the subsequent *Americanization* of

Brazilian culture (Santiago 1976, 25–26). In the postwar period, when the attempt to create a pan-American vision of the continent became the explicit front for an underlying project of universalizing the "American Way of Life," the Good Neighbor policy launched a new cycle of travel.

The Good Neighbor policy, at the end of the 1930s and the first half of the 1940s, marked a temporary diminishment of the politics of interventionism that had intensified because of the commercial interests of the United States in Latin America. The high cost of fiscal and military interventions was no longer justifiable during the period of deflation that followed the great depression, and the growing threat of the Axis powers led the United States to a new diplomatic and commercial orientation, this time bilateral in character, in which American nations were deemed allies and preferential partners. Latin American nations were in a precarious economic situation caused by the decline of commerce, the devaluation of currency, and the increased impoverishment of the masses; and they saw Roosevelt's example, materialized in the New Deal and his social welfare program, as a reason for accepting a new political strategy–strengthened by the need for North American support to enable any form of industrial development. Interest in the Good Neighbor policy, therefore, was bilateral, even if this was an unequal partnership, based on a growing dependency on the part of Latin America on the United States.

This is the context in which the new cycle of travels took place. These were primarily cultural missions that came and went between Brazil and the United States in the first years of the 1940s. Goodwill ambassadors, writers, artists, and intellectuals circulated between the two nations, in charge of negotiating complementary national policies, establishing affinities and commonalities, enhancing a potentially mutual empathy, and projecting visions of reciprocal solidarity and the pan-American dream. Brazil sent to the United States a wide range of representatives from Carmen Miranda to exhibitions such as "Brazil Builds: Architecture New and Old, 1665–1942." It also sent journalists, editors, students on scholarships funded by the United States government, and professors and writers who taught Brazilian literature in U.S. universities–as was the case, for example, with Erico Veríssimo. The United States, in its turn, emphasized journalism, radio, and the film industry, considering these to be the privileged vehicles for anti-Nazi propaganda. Among the numerous visitors who produced visual images of Brazil *para americano ver* ("for U.S. eyes") were the photographer Genevieve Naylor, Orson Welles (1942, 1943; *It's All True*), and Walt Disney (1942; *The Three Caballeros*, featuring Zé Carioca, a cartoon character created by Brazilian J. Carlos, who shared the spotlight with Donald Duck and Pancho Pistolas). The Good Neighbor policy, nevertheless, signified a gaze turned to the other. Naylor's photography was an interesting counterpoint to this tendency. Although linked to the Office of Inter-American Affairs of the U.S. Department of State, which funded his 1940–1943 stay in Brazil, Naylor had worked in social projects such as the Harlem Document Project and had photographed the plight of the homeless and farm workers in the United States after the Depression. Naylor's relationship to the Department of State was controversial, and the vision of Brazil, depicted as contradictory, anguished, and problematic, hardly conformed to the expectations of the image of Brazil that, it was hoped, could be tailored for the United States public. Naylor resisted the pressure to present a homogeneous vision of Brazil, and

refused the simple paternalistic and exotic stereotyping of it as a nation of tropical forests, gigantic coffee plantations, samba, and perpetual Carnival. The photographs depict a social world that is multiple and diverse, making a synthesis impossible: Rural and urban worlds, cosmopolitanism and traditional religiosity, wealth and destitution, backwardness and development. This was a society in transformation, which would lead to the disappearance of cultural communities, dominated by an urban, cosmopolitan, and exclusionary culture. Naylor's record of the multiracial character of the Brazilian population and the extraordinary photographic perception of the nation's contradictions clashed with the expectations held by both the Vargas dictatorship and the Office of Inter-American Affairs: The nation depicted was not one of aseptic, de-historicized landscapes or of racial harmony and complete progress and development. It was the nation of counterpoints, of a modernizing process that sharpened inequalities, where the *Estado Novo* (New State) regime's cult of personality (Getúlio Vargas's omnipresent portrait as Head of State or Father) was an indication of, and fused with, the State's tutelage. Naylor also photographed those disinherited by the Father/State: the inhabitants of *favelas* (shantytowns) and the workers in the large cities, the indigenous peoples and rural workers, showing the hardships of the countryside and the deep religiosity of the masses; there were images of families grouped together on Sundays, Baroque art, and the campaign against leprosy, images of processions and popular music as meeting points and celebration. Naylor's work echoes the social realist depiction of the anonymous plight of the poor, and at the same time shows an affinity to the social expressionists of the 1940s, such as Lazar Segall (1891–1957), Tarsila do Amaral (1886–1973), Ermiliano Di Cavalcanti (1897–1976), and Candido Portinari (1903–1962); in sum, Naylor created a powerful portrait of Brazil's unequal modernity.

Elizabeth Bishop's (1911–1979) approach to Brazil had different origins. Arriving at first with a tourist's gaze–and armed with a literary project that took shape in her many travel notebooks–her contact with Brazil was mediated by the various travel writings she had read prior to her arrival and during her stay, hoping to achieve a better understanding of the nation (Brown 302). For Bishop it was a growing attachment to relationships in Brazil (initially with Lota de Macedo Soares) that eventually led her to choose to remain in a country in which she would not have previously chosen to live. Bishop's changing cultural experiences of Brazil ultimately became an inquiry into her own identity. The taste for the new and exotic, as well as the strangeness elicited by her first contacts, eventually changed into a sense of not being an outsider and her complex articulation of notions of home, origins, exile, and the other began. This understanding acted as a catalyst for her own memories through identifications and analogies that were expressed in the introduction Bishop writes to her translation of *Minha vida de menina* [*The Diary of Helena Morley*] by Helena Morley, but which also betrayed her resistance to–and fear of–losing her own U.S. cultural background. This fear was eventually justified, since on her return to the United States in 1966, all seemed alien; her sporadic visits home failed to keep her in step with the changes that were overtaking the United States. Her presence in Brazil led her to acquire a taste for the grandiose in the manner of nineteenth-century travelers; but on the other hand, she shared Lévi-Strauss's disenchantment with the cultural dissolution he wrote about in *Tristes tropiques*. In part, her revulsion might be explained in the feverish urge for cultural mimicry that had overtaken the Brazilian elite in the 1950s and 1960s. If one disregards the naïve notion of cultural freedom in the face of the onslaught of the "American Way of Life" as a symptom of a growing U.S. hegemony in the Western world, and in South America in particular, it is interesting to note Bishop's preoccupation with the death of local cultures and her almost ethnographic attempt to fight for their preservation, in collecting Brazilian craftwork, the products of popular culture, be it in transforming them into the topics of her poetry (such as in *The Riverman*) and essays (articles on Carnival music) or in conceiving of books she would not in fact write, such as her planned anthology of translations of samba lyrics. Elizabeth Bishop nevertheless accepted Time-Life's proposition to write the volume entitled *Brazil* as part the Life World Library series, which was eventually co-authored and censored by the Time-Life editors. Bishop was eventually to repudiate the book, pointing out changes made to her style and even her conclusions, noting the use of photographs taken from the film *Black Orpheus*, the new and tendentious titles substituted for her own, as well as additions that pontificated about U.S. values. Time-Life's invitation had taken Elizabeth Bishop on a comprehensive tour of the country, which included the Amazon region, and this was an opportunity she valued in spite of the book. It is what prompted her to decide to write a second book, in the manner of nineteenth-century travelers (a project present in her notes and letters for many years, but which never came to fruition).

Elizabeth Bishop's unadulterated vision of Brazil can be found in her poetry. Most of the poems that express her interpretation of Brazil were edited together in *Questions of Travel*. Framing herself as a tourist in search of answers in "Arrival in Santos," she asks for a different world and a better life. In a vision that is overwhelmingly spatial, the poet registers her first impressions of the new world—a world deemed imprecise, weak, and frivolous; she finds herself surprised that this nation should have a flag! In the poem "Questions of Travel," which lends its title to the book, Bishop then questions the locus of her gaze and the imperialist perspective that constituted it. An observer of differences, both human and natural, Bishop perceives herself as being external to the experience she portrays, and recognizes the bias in her own gaze. The poet recognizes the loss entailed in not experiencing the new and the other, and registers in her poetry the ambiguous relationship between the self and other.

For better or worse, Bishop continues to observe the *commédie humaine* of Brazil's impoverished population with her characteristic poet's eye, moving back and forth from closeness to distance. Bishop creates an intentionally visual depiction in the poem "Manuelzinho or Squatter's Children" while keeping herself on the outside. Her vision of the Conquest, the arrival of the Portuguese, is the topic of the poem "Brazil, January 1st, 1502," and here she transforms the historical past into visual imagery. Finally, one must mention the poem in which Bishop explicitly distances herself aesthetically—as well as socially and politically—from the reality she has experienced. In "The Burglar of Babylon" the poet takes on the point of view of one of the wealthy men who entertain themselves by following a police chase through binoculars. This is indeed a strange stage for strange players and stranger audiences, among them the poet herself.

The last form of literary connection between the poet and Brazil is through Bishop's translation of Brazilian authors. In the *Diary of Helena Morley*, in poems by Manuel Bandeira (1886–1968), Carlos Drummond de Andrade (1902–1987), and João Cabral de Melo Neto (1920–1999), among others, and in Clarice Lispector's (1925–1977) short stories, Elizabeth Bishop's translations created a literary dialogue with Brazilian culture; at times as an insider, at other times as an outsider, the poet moves between distance and proximity, and mediates through the voices of third persons her own vision of Brazil—other stages, different others, but strangers whose vision of life became part of her own, since no one can remain alien to what one sees.

Translation by Lis Horta Moriconi

The Twentieth Century: Brazilian Intellectuals and the Discovery of Brazil

Roteiros. Roteiros. Roteiros. Roteiros. Roteiros. Roteiros. Roteiros.

Routes. Routes. Routes. Routes. Routes. Routes. Routes.

(Oswald de Andrade 1972, 15)

One of the most significant factors in the establishment and consolidation of the Modernist movement in Brazil throughout the 1920s was the amount of traveling undertaken by the authors linked to it. Traveling was a generating and creative force, especially after the change took place in the usual route followed by artists and scholars—those who yearned for European civilization. The traditional itinerary of Rio de Janeiro–Lisbon–Paris–Rio de Janeiro was displaced in favor of new routes to Europe (which included the more direct São Paulo–Paris–São Paulo) as well as trips to other regions of Brazil and the rest of South America. Whatever their destination, however, writers endeavored to discover Brazil.

For the leaders of the Modernist movement, traveling both abroad and around Brazil gave them a privileged opportunity to widen their philosophical and aesthetic perspective, and thus to break with their elitist or provincial assumptions. They incorporated a sense of adventure into their everyday work, aiming to bring it up-to-date and give a Brazilian identity to the cultural production of the country. When, in the late 1920s and early 1930s, a younger generation began to take part on various fronts of the avant-garde, a wave of change (and liberation) hit the areas of political ideology, of the economic organization and social roles of both men and women. Besides influencing the travel itinerary of two generations of Modernist artists, this ideology also emerged, but with a new dimension, during the 1960s and 1970s when people had to go into exile as a result of the repressive military regime that began in 1964. After the restoration of the democratic process in 1979, their return to Brazil gave rise to a series of works in which those who had been exiled now criticized their own radical commitments and dramatized in a heterodox way their rediscovery of Brazil.

Brazilian Writers of the Belle Époque and the Appeal of Paris

The nineteenth-century elitist practice of traveling to Europe was multiplied and trivialized by the Brazilian writers of the first two decades of the twentieth century. Reading the newspapers of the period, it is possible to see how their impressions of Paris sound like a caricature of that cosmopolitan spirit that Joaquim Nabuco (1849–1910) called the attraction of the world. However, in his autobiography, that diplomat questioned the possible lack of cultural values in America and endeavored to justify, from an ethical and aesthetic point of view, his universalist formation according to European models; whereas the members of the generation that succeeded him had an acritical position and were seduced by the Paris of Art Nouveau and the café-concert scene. This generation suffered, in fact, from a serious attack of "Nabuco's malaise," a lingering depression caused by an absence of Paris.

Writing about Olavo Bilac's (1865–1918) annual trips to Paris, Nestor Vítor's (1868–1932) long stay there, and the fascination that José Joaquim de Campos Medeiros e Albuquerque (1867–1934) felt for the boulevards, Brito Broca–the meticulous National Library scholar who compiled the history of Brazilian literary life of the turn of the nineteenth century–concluded that "o chique era mesmo ignorar o Brasil e delirar por Paris, numa atitude afetada e nem sempre inteligente" (Broca 1956, 92) ("what was chic was to ignore Brazil and rave for Paris, with an artificial yearning which was not even clever"). At the time of his research in the 1950s, Brito Broca had established as his critical framework the Modernist project of cultural nationalization, which radically opposed the *belles lettres* aestheticism of the intellectuals dazzled by Europe. Even though he shared the nationalism of figures like Mário de Andrade (1893–1945), Broca was neither intolerant nor radical. With his characteristic sense of humor, he could emphasize the ridiculous nature of the more ineffective writers, but was also able to appraise, for example, the significant contacts established by Henrique Coelho Neto (1864–1934) with foreign journalists and editors. He argued that in spite of his critical limitations and numerous mistakes, Coelho Neto opened the way for the dissemination of Brazilian literature "ao . . . interessar os europeus e os confrades hispano-americanos" (Broca 1991, 311) ("by . . . making Europeans and Latin Americans interested") in Brazilian literature. He also showed that in spite of his enthusiasm for the Old World, he could recognize the talent of João do Rio (1881–1921), who was deeply concerned with the lack of interest and knowledge Brazilians demonstrated *vis-à-vis* the native elements of their own country–a point that was to be one of the main concerns of the Modernists.

Therefore, thanks to Brito Broca's research, it is possible today to have a more balanced appraisal of the Eurocentric attitude of the writers who preceded the 1922 Modern Art Week. On the one hand, we can value their aesthetization of everyday life and their occasional writings, which are in some way similar to postmodern artistic practices; on the other, when considering them individually and not as an undifferentiated block, we can deconstruct their French-like affectation and develop a self-critical Brazilian position with regard to today's globalizing forces.

Because intellectuals began to travel more to Europe at the turn of the nineteenth century, there was a proportional increase at that time in the importation of ideas, fashions, and styles, which changed the Brazilian public space. All aspects of the social order followed European models, from urban reforms to the expansion of the leisure and information networks, passing through aesthetic and epistemological contexts. It was during a trip to Paris, at the end of the nineteenth century, that Pereira Pasos discovered the urban model of Baron Hausmann, which inspired him to modernize Rio de Janeiro. (See Vol. 2, Ch. 49, this *History.*) Other Brazilian cities also acquired a French style as a result of the trips of their mayors. For example, Medeiros e Albuquerque, a member of that privileged class that was educated in Europe and could constantly travel because of his political posts, now became a major disseminating agent of Parisian values and practices. He also introduced the interview format to Brazilian newspapers. In 1904, when he had just returned from Europe, he introduced the young journalist Paulo Barreto (1881–1921), who was also known by the pseudonym of João do Rio, to the journalistic genre of investigative reporting, which was very popular with the Parisian newspapers of the day. Medeiros suggested to his disciple that he make a survey of the Brazilian intellectual landscape by interviewing the main writers of the period, and even gave him the questions to be asked. João do Rio carried out the task and compiled the answers of forty writers. The interviews were published one by one in the *Gazeta de Notícias* and two years later were edited by Garnier in a single volume called *O momento literário* [The Literary Moment] (Magalhães Junior 42, 43).

João do Rio inaugurated the "special feature" in Brazilian journalism in 1904. He went into all kinds of *terreiros* (places where Afro-Brazilian cults were practiced) in Rio de Janeiro and, combining research with a certain sensationalism, he revealed the secrets of all the cults practiced at the time (such as sorcery and Satanism), but he also added details about Positivism, Judaism, the Protestant Evangelical movement, and the sect inspired by Swedenborg. Published in the *Gazeta de Notícias*, this series of features later formed the book *As religiões no Rio* [1904; Rio de Janeiro's Religions]. His journalistic work made him well known among the general public and confirmed him as a curious observer of the city. His pseudonym ended up replacing his own name, thus consecrating him as the privileged witness of the Brazilian capital during its process of modernization. Beginning in 1901, when he moved from the evening to the morning newspaper, he became a "notívago, descrevendo, muitas vezes, o modo pelo qual perambulava pelas ruas e becos cariocas" (Gomes 114) ("a wandering observer, often describing the way in which he roamed around the streets of Rio"). Whereas the illustrious precursors of the serial story–José de Alencar (1829–1877), Joaquim José da França Júnior (1838–1890), Olavo Bilac, and especially Machado de Assis (1839–1908)–were writers who worked in their studies, João do Rio worked outside in the streets and transformed Brazilian journalism. But his most significant contribution was the fact that he put into practice and professionalized a kind of urban commentary that was the result of two modern perspectives–that of the *flâneur* and that of the detective. He thus transformed European journalistic practices into a means of exploring his own city. He was able to perceive the exotic dimension of the domestic scenery and wandered around the city with a detective-like attention to detail and the critical perspective of *flânerie*. He became an expert in this kind of geographical dislocation and developed a style that made the commonplace exotic, which constituted his trademark in the series of features called *A alma encantadora das ruas* [1908; The Charming Soul of the Streets]. For the modern reader these articles dealing with the streets of Rio–written precisely at the time when the city was being transformed, following the Parisian inspiration of Pereira Passos–acquired the emblematic significance of the double consciousness that characterized intellectuals at the turn of the nineteenth century.

Published in the elegant magazine *Kosmos*, next to articles in which Bilac praised the civilizing reforms, João do Rio's features about the *bas-fond* added a daring and mordant tone to the cosmopolitan setting. In their demythicizing attitude to progressive improvement, such features come close to Lima Barreto's articles published in small newspapers of socialist inspiration, in which he reacted with indignation to the degrading shanty towns. Somewhere between the French-like sedentary writer (Machado de Assis) and the bohemian rebel (Lima Barreto), João do Rio represents the lively and observant *flâneur*, the eminent stylist. In this intermediate position he precedes the 1920s avant-garde, which came to consider urban Brazil through the Cubist-Futurist texts of Oswald de Andrade (1890–1954), as well as the humorous travel writings of Mário de Andrade. However, João do Rio's scope surpassed the modern experience and "com a argúcia do fisionomista [que] representa a ficção sombria da cidade" ("with the subtlety of the physiognomist [who] conveys the somber fiction of the city"), he also invested the reader with the role of *flâneur*, thus offering what would come to be seen as a postmodern perspective (Gomes 69, 70).

João do Rio's mentor, Medeiro e Albuquerque, introduced another Parisian fashion to Brazil's intellectual circles–the literary talk. Inviting some writers with French tendencies, such as Olavo Bilac and Coelho Neto, Medeiros organized the first talks in 1905 at the National Institute of Music. His purpose was to supplement the income of writers and to help them establish a direct contact with the heterogeneous audiences of Rio (Magalhães Junior 132, 133). The format was very successful, and it became so popular that João do Rio satirized it in his writings, exhibiting once more the contradictions of the Brazilian elite. He compiled some of his own talks in the book *Psichologia urbana* [1911; Urban Psychology] and employed the preface to caricature the genre, trivializing Western culture.

The title of Medeiros e Albuquerque's posthumously published memoirs is *Quando eu era vivo*... [1942; When I Was Alive...]; this is an interesting document that shows the restless and innovative personality of the man who was a journalist, federal congressman, and one of the founders of the Brazilian Academy. In it he describes his life as a student in Lisbon between 1880 and 1884, as well as his endless trips and long stays in foreign countries during the first decades of the twentieth century. He does not hide his enthusiasm for European modernity, or the means he employed to keep his public positions in Brazil while comfortably living in Paris. Olavo Bilac is a significant character in these memoirs, praised for having perfect tone and diction. One episode tells of their encounter in Paris, where Medeiros spoke about his lack of interest for nature and dismissed the Romantic concept of poetry; Bilac, it seems, also confessed his profound dislike for nature–an attitude opposed to the conventional models of the time, which he had, therefore, kept to himself. Medeiros ends the passage revealing that his friend loved huge cosmopolitan cities and spent long periods visiting them.

In his book *Mocidade no Rio e primeira viagem à Europa* [1956; Youth in Rio and First Trip to Europe], Gilberto Amado (1887–1969) told of an education based on the French model. In 1912 he was sent by the newspaper *O País* to Holland to study the processes of colonization employed in this country's Asian possessions. First, however, he traveled throughout a number of other European countries. In Paris, his first stop, he was seduced by the sites, monuments, shows, and people, which he recreated later in his books. Aware of the ways in which France and especially Paris had been represented in others' writing, he acknowledged in his memoirs that he used the same themes, references, and clichés, justifying the process as an affectionate exercise in recording his own remembrances. In this sense, his writing is an intellectual portrayal of several generations of Brazilians who, in spite of having been educated in the wilderness of the *sertão*, came to breath the spiritual air of France. Amado's style reveals the aestheticism of the turn of the century, when he summarizes his impressions with eloquence. The sentence "Uma rua de Paris é um rio que vem da Grécia" (Amado 207) ("A street in Paris is a river from Greece") reflects the main aim of Brazilian travelers of the time in Europe: to have an encounter with the classical past through the beauty of Paris. It was only during the 1920s, when the avant-garde movements turned to non-Western traditions, that Latin-American writers became aware of their artificial Hellenism and of their inferiority complex. Writers like Amado, however, were indifferent to the avant-garde's rupture with this Parisian seduction, explicitly emphasizing his "alheamento ao chamado modernismo, ronaldismo, mário-de-andradism, verde-amarelismo" (301) ("detachment from the so-called Modernism, Ronaldism, Mario-de-Andradism, Green-Yellowism"). It should be pointed out that this assertion appears only some pages after the counterpoint established between the art of the Louvre and revolutionary art that came after World War I. Regarding the latter, Amado describes his visits to the workshops of modern painters, accompanied by Tarsila and Oswald de Andrade, and how he saw "Léger, de pincel na mão, concretizar suas primeiras formas geométricas" (Amado 1956, 238) ("Léger make his first geometric shapes, brush in hand"). However, none of this changes his conventional cosmopolitan attitude; he continued to be tied to academic art and did not show any kind of interest in the European rediscovery of African and Amerindian cultures.

José Pereira Graça Aranha (1868–1931) offers an interesting contrast to Amado with his disregard of avant-garde manifestations. Collaborator of Joaquim Nabuco and member of the Brazilian Academy of Letters, Aranha endeavored to attain a leading position in the 1922 Modernist movement, and was always torn between a cosmopolitan attraction and an attachment for Brazilian forms. Older than Gilberto Amado and, like him, a graduate of the law school at Recife, Graça Aranha first traveled to Europe in 1899 as part of the diplomatic mission which, headed by Nabuco, was to defend Brazil's concerns in the border dispute with English Guyana. In spite of the fact that he was fascinated by Europe's cultural soundness and progress, he firmly rejected the inferiority complex of his countrymen. He disagreed with the philosophical assumptions of *Minha formação*, which considered that the human spirit was univocally European. Immune to "Nabuco's malaise," he vindicated the Brazilian in the intellectual values of the twentieth century, as is demonstrated in his 1913 conversations with young Brazilians (among them his own son, Temístocles, and Alceu Amoroso Lima [1893–1983]) in Paris, warning against an excessive devotion to the French and urging them to contribute to the development of Brazilian letters (Azevedo 139).

Graça Aranha's relative independence from Eurocentric canons left a significant mark on his literary oeuvre, which includes accounts of his travel as a Brazilian diplomat in Europe and his remembrances as a young man traveling in Brazil. His unfinished memoirs, *O meu próprio romance* [1937; My Own Novel], conveys the enthusiasm he felt when he arrived in Recife as a teenager coming from São Luís do Maranhão. He also describes how he endeavored to become integrated in the intellectual life of Rio de Janeiro in 1891. As a result of ties to his law professors and the leading figures of Brazilian culture and his ability to adapt and learn, in 1890 he was able to present himself for the position of municipal judge in Porto do Cachoeiro, a region in Espíritu Santo where there was significant German colonization. Very concerned about the encounter between European civilization and Brazilian primitive exuberance (Azevedo 32), he recorded his observations, which served as the basis for his novel *Canãa* (1901). His biographer Maria Helena Castro Azevedo has studied both the production stages of *Canãa* and the author's growing lack of interest for the European cities visited by the diplomatic mission. The ideological confrontation underlying the novel is based on an anarchistic humanism that could "ultrapassar o círculo estreito da discussão sobre raças, naquele momento adscrito à definição da superioridade e inferioridade raciais" (Azevedo 28) ("surpass the narrow limitation of racial debate which at the time was circumscribed in the definition of racial superiority and inferiority"). According to Azevedo, Aranha dismissed the biological basis of racial theories and looked for sociological and historical reasons that would explain progress as the result of successful ethnic mixtures. Thus, *Canãa* not only represented Aranha's response to the racist attitudes of his contemporaries, but also developed the idea of a progressive utopia where diverse ethnocultural groups could live together in freedom with mutual benefit.

If Graça Aranha's career shows a turn to Brazil and a detachment from Eurocentrism, and the travel writings of Bilac, Coelho Neto, Medeiros e Albuquerque, and Gilberto Amado show only an exacerbation of Nabuco's Eurocentrism, then the wanderings of João do Rio in the cosmopolitan geography of the *belle époque* take on an ambiguous meaning– neither Brazilianist nor Eurocentric. Behind the dandy's mask with which he traveled around Europe to get to know his models, there was a refined Eurocentric frivolity that was, however, always linked to his professional concerns. Posing as a *flâneur* wandering the dark corners of cities such as Lisbon or Rio de Janeiro, Rome or Buenos Aires, he typifies the kind of attitude that deconstructs any thoughtful centering of cultural power. His critical-aesthetic point of view engages all races, all irrationalisms, both sexes, all perversions. The dream of all journalists at the turn of the nineteenth century was to combine work and tourism in Europe. João do Rio fulfilled his dream for the first time in 1908. Unlike most people, he visited Europe via Portugal, a route he continued to follow during his next three trips, before and after the First World War. In 1908 he was sent by the *Gazeta de Notícias* to Lisbon to report on the Portuguese political crisis that had arisen as a result of an attempted assassination of the king and was fueled by Republican ideas (Magalhães Junior 94, 95). Apart from covering these events, João do Rio discovered a number of cultural activities typical of Lisbon, Brazil's former metropolis, which offered him material for a series of books (which were to be published by Garnier in Paris). He not only became part of Portuguese literary life–publishing some of his own work at Lello & Irmão, giving conferences and staging his plays in Lisbon–but also became a spokesman of sorts for Portuguese immigrants established in Brazil. The Portuguese colony in Brazil, made up of successful merchants, turned João do Rio into an idol, because he helped to minimize the prejudice that Portuguese people had endured ever since Independence. In his 1908, 1911, 1913, and 1919 trips, João do Rio also traveled to London and Paris, where he learned new printing techniques. Attracted both by aristocratic, conservative values and by modern, progressive ideas, he built his own literary career upon his journalistic work and was always up-to-date with the novelties introduced by the mass media of his time. Since he frequented the Côte d'Azur and Venice, and visited Russia, Greece, Turkey, and Egypt, he was able to present Brazilian readers with a series of travel chronicles, some of which were collected in book form. In what turned out to be his last trip at the end of the war, he covered the 1919 Paris Peace Conference for *O País*. He sent almost eighty feature articles, written in his rapid, daring, and artistically elaborate style. As the most influential Brazilian journalist of his day, he contributed greatly to the internationalization of Brazilian journalism (Magalhães Junior 319).

When Joaquim Nabuco reflected upon the attraction of the world that would have such a decisive role in the intellectual activities of Latin America, he attributed this need for universality as a carryover from the fascination exerted by European literary celebrities on Latin America during the eighteenth and nineteenth centuries. Be that as it may, the need to be part of the cultural life of the world has continued in Latin American journalism to this day. In August 1899 Nabuco took his disciple and secretary, Graça Aranha, on a pilgrimage to visit the houses of Rousseau, Voltaire, and Mme. de Stäel. Many Brazilian writers who went to Europe at the start of the twentieth century followed this tendency, making it almost obligatory to visit the houses and graves of their cultural idols and to record their experiences in their chronicles and memoirs. For example, Gilberto Amado describes his trip to Rouen, paying homage to Flaubert, and his frequent visits to the Panthéon in Paris, where Zola and Victor Hugo are buried. Both Amado and João do Rio went to Germany with the intention of going to the places where Nietzsche wrote *Thus Spake Zarathustra*.

Brito Broca's history of Brazilian literary life follows the literary fashions at the turn of the nineteenth century and singles out the names of Wilde, Nietzsche, Tolstoy, Ibsen, and Eça de Queiroz as the most enthusiastically imitated and cultivated figures (1956, 109). After all, João do Rio translated Wilde; Graça de Aranha adopted a form of socialism following Tolstoy, and based his dramatic play *Malasarte* on Ibsen's theater. All of them, in one way or another, paid tribute to the philosophic daring of Nietzsche. When considering the Nietzschean cult of the period, scholars of the 1990s have been intrigued by the contradictory progressive and reactionary ideas attributed to the philosopher. Before it was appropriated by Nazism, Nietzsche's thought had been domesticated by neo-colonialism: In 1910 writers read him as a confirmation of European superiority. Today, this interpretative tendency sounds like an ironical mistake by the writers of the period. Later twentieth-century thinkers like Jacques Derrida and Michel Foucault have reread Nietzsche and developed the deconstructive perspective by which they were able to decenter the legitimizing foundations of Western hegemony: patriarchy, Aryanism and, in general, the logocentric thinking with which the twentieth century began. In this sense Foucault's visits to Brazil during the 1960s and 1970s, when his lectures showed an evident neo-Nietzschean inspiration and questioned logocentrism and ethnocentrism, constitute a counterpoint to the pilgrimages of Brazilians to Engadine, St. Moritz, and Davos in 1900. Posing as intellectual innovators, Gilberto Amado, João do Rio, José Bento Monteiro Lobato (1882–1948), and Graça Aranha accumulated considerable politically reactionary baggage. Their successors had to undertake many trips, both geographical and virtual, in order to get rid of it.

Aboard the Transatlantic Liner: Oswald, Tarsila and Pagu

The multiple trips undertaken by the artists linked to the Modernist movement constituted an undeniable source of new critical perspectives and creative energy. First, there was the displacement of the cultural center from Rio de Janeiro to São Paulo–and to the Europe of elegant sites and avant-garde *ateliers*. Writers were able to make these regular trips because they mostly belonged to the coffee-estate oligarchy and they were always ready to board the luxury liners traversing the Atlantic. In the 1920s two of them met on artistic and personal terms, traveling together both before and after they were married: Oswald de Andrade and Tarsila do Amaral, the Modernist couple Mário de Andrade affectionately called "Tarsiwald." For them, traveling to Paris had a shared significance: More than the simple leisure trips of the old elite, their trips symbolized an artistic and intellectual position, because it was through them that Brazilian artists learned about modern art and the latest artistic tendencies–for instance, Futurism and Cubism–which were centered in Paris, though the artists were from many nations (e.g., Klee, Kandinsky, Picasso). There they saw Japanese engravings and heard African music; they attended the Russian ballet of Diaghilev with Stravinsky's music; they enjoyed Picasso's Cubist paintings inspired by African masks. Artists from several continents came together in the burgeoning creativity of Paris, which Tarsila do Amaral described in a number of articles published in São Paulo starting in the 1930s.

The contact with the European avant-garde gave rise to another kind of creative experience: Artists began to rediscover Brazil within the very heart of Paris artistic circles. Brazilian Modernist artists were open to genuinely national expression, and it was through their work that native cultural values, which up to then had been ignored by an official culture inspired by universal academic models and canons (Candido 1976, 121), were exposed. The making of a national identity, which had been started by Brazilian intellectuals and artists in the nineteenth century, now took place in the opposite direction; instead of looking to imitate Europe in Brazil, artists undertook the rediscovery of Brazil, by visiting *in loco* the regions and places that had been excluded from the usual artistic routes of Brazilian intellectuals. These journeys were made by the intellectuals of São Paulo in 1924 and had two obligatory stops that today have been definitely incorporated into the national artistic calendar: Carnival in Rio de Janeiro and Holy Week in the historic cities of Minas Gerais. Such trips around Brazil became the basis of Modernist works that, in spite of being in an autobiographic register, already belonged to a fictional (or, in the case of painting, to an eminently plastic) Brazilianist context.

Oswald de Andrade started to travel in 1912; at the age of twenty-two, he went first to Europe and from that moment onward, the displacement of space by means of traveling became the subject matter of his writings in letters, poems, memoirs, and novels–all of which share one determining feature: a mixture of reality and fiction (i.e., a mixture of descriptions of his own real trips and fictional portrayals of the imaginary trips made by his characters). During his first trips, he also fell in love. On his first journey to Europe he met the young ballerina Landa Kosbach (or Carmen Lídia). However,

when he returned to Brazil, he was accompanied by a French girl, Kamiá (Henriette Denise Boufflers), who gave him a son, Nonê. Without worrying about big intellectual and artistic projects, during the seven months spent in Europe he enjoyed his freedom and lived the bohemian life, economically supported by his parents. His aim was to acquire a traveling knowledge of the world, as the mother of his character João Miramar puts it. Thus, he was able, as he wrote in the preface to *Serafim Ponte Grande*, to spend time in London without even catching a glimpse of Karl Marx (Andrade 1971, 132).

When in 1922 he traveled to Europe for the second time, he was already a man with ten years of experience as a writer of journalism and a literary piece–*O perfeito cozinheiro das almas deste mundo* [The Perfect Cook of the Souls of this World]–jointly composed with the friends who frequented the bachelor flat in Líbero Badaró Street. Andrade took an active part in the Week of Modern Art, which took place at the Municipal Theater in 1922, when he published his novel *Os condenados* [The Condemned] and began his relationship with Tarsila, who had just arrived from Paris and with whom he formed the so-called group of five: Oswald, Tarsila, Anita Malfatti, Menotti Del Picchia, and Mário de Andrade.

If the first trip was a liberation from the rigid sexual and moral principles held by his traditional São Paulo family, the second trip was guided by financial concerns, for he intended to get in touch with European entrepreneurs who could administrate his inheritance, which included the coffee business and real estate. He also took part in intellectual activities, such as the lecture given at the Sorbonne "O esforço intelectual do Brasil contemporâneo" ["The Intellectual Endeavor of Contemporary Brazil"]. He and Tarsila also added Portugal and Spain to their European repertoire.

Tarsila do Amaral had started to travel when she was very young. She was the daughter and granddaughter of wealthy landowners of the Capivari region, and she spent her childhood within a French-inspired world in Brazil, which included French perfumes, wines, literature, and music, as if living in an imaginary Paris within the province of the state of São Paulo. When she was sixteen she was sent to Barcelona to study, and two years later finally visited France, which did not impress her at all. On her return to Brazil, she got married and later separated. She then departed for Europe with her daughter and studied art in Paris. Therefore, when she went to Paris for the second time, toward the end of 1922, her friends had already introduced her to modern art, which she studied in depth thanks to her new Paris companions and her affair with Oswald de Andrade. Oswald and Tarsila started to live together in Paris in 1923 and traveled extensively, including to the Far East in 1926. This was an extremely busy period, which included organizing Brazilian parties at her workshop, close to the Place Clichy, where people ate the Brazilian national dish *feijoada*, drank *caipirinha* and *pinga*, and smoked straw cigarettes. This was the meeting place of famous artists, such as writers Jean Cocteau and Jules Supervielle, painter Marie Laurencin, musician Eric Satie, and Tarsila's teachers, the Cubist painters Albert Gleizes and Fernand Léger. One of the most assiduous visitors was Blaise Cendrars, who later traveled to Brazil and formed part of the group of Brazilian Modernist artists.

However, the Brazilian Modernist movement was only consolidated in 1924, when the famous São Paulo caravan went to the Carnival in Rio de Janeiro and Holy Week in Minas Gerais–a journey that became the catalyst of the Modernist tendencies so carefully acquired in Paris. Apart from Tarsila and Oswald, the group consisted of Mário de Andrade, Olívia Guedes Penteado, René Thiollier, Gofredo da Silva Telles, as well as Blaise Cendrars, recently arrived from France, and Nonê, Oswald's son. The travel notes of these traveler-artists became part of their future work–such as the book *Pau-Brasil* [1925; Brazil Wood], which included poems by Oswald de Andrade, drawings by Tarsila, and a preface by Paulo Prado (1869–1943), and was published in Paris in 1925. Another example was Blaise Cendrars's book, *Feuilles de route* [*Poems of Road and Sea*], which had as subtitle the name of the ship that took him to Brazil, *Le Formose*. This book was also illustrated by Tarsila and featured the drawing *A Negra* [A Black Woman] on the cover. Oswald de Andrade's *Pau-Brasil* may well be the most significant book of the period, a Brazilian version of the collective literary and pictorial creation of Blaise Cendrars's *Prose du transsibérien et de la petite Jeanne de France* [1912; The Prose of the Trans-Siberian and the Little Jeanne of France], which was illustrated by Sonia Delaunay (1885–1979). In 1926 Antônio de Alcântara Machado (1901–1935) also published the journalistic record of his excursion across Europe, *Pathé Baby*, in which Paim's illustrations were incorporated into the careful construction of the book.

The "Pau-Brasil" art, announced in the 1928 manifesto, gave Brazilians a new awareness of their country through a general review of its history, with new insight into the quotidian reality of Brazil. In this and other writings of the period, traveling was not just another subject for the futuristic cult of machines and mass media. Rather, traveling was an aesthetic process that used artistic devices such as collage, so evident in the poems of Oswald de Andrade (like the montage in Eisenstein's films, which were so admired by the Brazilian Modernists), or in the juxtaposed prose images used in his *Memórias sentimentais de João Miramar* [Sentimental Memoirs of João Miramar]; this was a form of writing that attempted to abolish the use of conjunctions in order to achieve a sort of telegram style in which words are juxtaposed as occurs in the visual language of the plastic arts, where an elimination of perspective favors the juxtaposition of elements in the composition of the drawing or painting.

The artistic insight gained by the Brazilian Modernists on their travels reached a much deeper level when they saw that everybody was in passage, facing passing landscapes, observing them as if from a train window. And landscapes, as "aerial palm trees" (an image taken from the poem "Morro azul" in the book *Pau-Brasil*), became collaged metaphors of juxtaposed cultures–France-Brazil, Cubism-*caipira*–which fused into a transfiguring synthesis, and became more violently yoked together in the last stage of the Modernist movement, after the 1928 Anthropophagy Manifesto, which offered new interpretations of Brazilian culture, now understood as a symbolic appropriation of other cultures. Thus, the symbolic act of eating another takes its conceptual force from the ritual practice of Brazilian anthropophagous Indians, the *abaporu*. (Tarsila do Amaral gave this title to one of her most famous paintings.)

The revolutionary alternatives of the 1930s, either that of Oswald de Andrade (now accompanied by the passionate Pagu [Patrícia Galvão]) or that of Tarsila do Amaral (including the politically active psychiatrist Osório César), involved taking different routes. Tarsila traveled to Communist Russia and to proletarian sectors of French cities in order to paint walls in several architectural projects. Oswald continued to write in left-wing journals and became involved in various scandals,

albeit without any of the energetic radiance or the financial fortune of the Jay Gatsby–like escapades played out by the wealthy elite of the 1920s.

In both cases, it is possible to recognize stages in these literary travel routes. The trip to rediscover Brazil made by Tarsila do Amaral is present in the subject matter of paintings such as *E.F.C.B. (Estrada de Ferro Central do Brasil)* [Brazil's Central Rail Station] and *A Gare* [The Station]; witty and joyful, these offer pleasure in their geometrical arrangements and openness of design, but also unfold the deepest areas of Brazilian mythical roots, revealing through winding forms states of unconsciousness and semiconsciousness, the harsh and tropical reality of cacti and scalding sun, or the never-ending sequence of winding lines in the landscapes called *Sono* [Sleep] and *Sol poente* [Sunset]. But there is a third stage, during the 1930s, when she places on a train platform a group of people as if posing for a portrait, traveling second class, and shows the viewer their poverty and distress.

In the taut atmosphere of the 1930s, during the "segunda dentição" ("second teething") of the *Revista de Antropofagia*–the most radical manifestation of Modernism–the figure of Patrícia Galvão (1910–1962) (better known in literary circles as Pagu) stands out as a result of her publication of small verbal-visual texts. Shortly after, at the side of Oswald de Andrade, Pagu took part in a rebellion of the Left, where she revealed herself to be a rebel in life and in art, thanks to her never-ending drive to break taboos, in the name both of the proletariat and of women. During most of her life she was either in flight, in prison, or in exile. In order to understand and evaluate Patrícia Galvão, it is fundamental to read *Pagu: vida-obra* [1982; Pagu: Her Life and Work], an anthology, biography, and critical study edited by Augusto de Campos.

In December 1930 Pagu traveled to Buenos Aires, where she lectured and met writers such as Jorge Luis Borges (1899–1986), Eduardo Mallea (1903–1982), Victoria Ocampo (1890–1979), and especially the revolutionary leader Luis Carlos Prestes (1890–1990). This encounter had an impact on her artistic commitment to the working class, and on her return to Brazil she became a member of the Communist Party. As part of her precocious and passionate political-intellectual militancy, Pagu made a special kind of trip in 1932: She went to live in a poor part of Rio de Janeiro, working for a proletarian agency. This experience became a novel, *Parque industrial* [Industrial Park], published in 1933 under the pseudonym of Mara Lobo.

Starting in 1931, she carried on intense journalistic activity, either in the main bourgeois newspapers or in small left-wing ones (where she wrote, for instance, a section called "A mulher do povo" ["The Woman of the People"]). In 1933, she traveled around the world as a correspondent for newspapers from Rio de Janeiro and São Paulo. On her own she traveled to the United States, Japan, China, Russia, Poland, Nazi Germany, and France, always showing her bravery as an emancipated woman and her skill as a competent journalist; she played a variety of roles, such as interviewing Hollywood film stars and directors, covering the crowning of the last Chinese emperor, procuring *soja* bean seeds to be introduced in Brazil, and meeting Sigmund Freud; her tour around Asia was organized by Raul Bopp (1898–1984), who was then the Brazilian consul in Osaka, Japan. On her arrival in Moscow, after a long journey in the Trans-Siberian Express, her Marxist enthusiasm suffered a shock when she faced the poverty in the streets, which made manifest the contradictions of the

Communist regime. Even so, she did not abandon her militancy and, during her stay in Paris, she worked as a translator, studied, and took part in protest demonstrations as a member of the French Communist Party. She was detained several times by the authorities, often risking her life as a Communist. On the other hand, she was also very active in her other form of militancy—as an avant-garde artist. When she returned to Brazil at the end of 1935, she resumed journalism and her left-wing contacts, which led to her being imprisoned several times during the New State. Decades later, in 1961, having left the Communist Party, she widened her cosmopolitan learning by traveling at the service of the theater in order to get to know European dramaturgy and scenography.

With her second novel, *A famosa revista* [The Famous Magazine], written in 1945 in collaboration with Geraldo Ferraz (1905–1979), Pagu endeavored to get away from the established patterns of Brazilian narrative forms in order to deal with a more universal subject matter and thus also renew the aesthetics of the novel. Having built up her political-aesthetic thought through her extensive trips abroad and having participated in international artistic and political movements, Patrícia Galvão was not worried about the opposition to her activities in support of peripheral traditions. Her role in Brazil was to disseminate the most daring products of the avant-garde of the West. Even though such works were unknown in Brazil, they were already forming part of the European canon during the 1950s and 1960s, when she spent most of her time translating and working as cultural journalist. If it is true that the results of this kind of work had an important impact on the libertarian turmoil of the 1960s, it is also true that appreciation of her literary achievements continues to be limited to a very small circle of admirers and specialists.

Like Tarsila's and Pagu's, Oswald de Andrade's life went through stages. He worked on his *Pau-Brasil*, constructed through trips to the provinces to see an unknown five-centuries-old Brazil and trips across a modern Brazil in touch with the Modernist tendencies of Europe. This work of consuming Brazil was a kind of fictional autobiography similar to Oswald's *Serafim Ponte Grande*. The latter work was written well into the 1930s and exploited an even more conclusive formal radicalism, deconstructing, by means of parody, a variety of canonical discourses and narrative genres. The protagonist Serafim's pursuit of mindless travel, ranging from Europe to the Far East, reached an unexcelled climax when he returns to Brazil and plunges into rapture aboard the ship El Durasno, where he remains, moving endlessly, permanently traveling in circles.

Mário de Andrade: The Apprentice Tourist and Ethnographical Traveling

As an activity that contributed to the intellectual and artistic renewal of the country, traveling represented for Brazilian Modernism a wish both to break with the academic canon and to rescue noncanonical traditions. In this case the conventional route to the European capitals took turns with excursions to the inner regions of the country, because the aim of the leaders of the avant-garde movement was to bring Brazilian culture into the twentieth century by means of a process of Brazilianization. Mário de Andrade played a central role by taking to the extremes his reaction against the Eurocentric perspective, which prevailed in interpretations of Brazil. Not happy with the fact that his predecessors and contemporaries literally behaved like European exiles, Andrade diagnosed that they suffered from "Nabuco's malaise," a state

of mind that he fought in his writing by setting an example and choosing South America as the focus of his observation and research.

Andrade's best-known text, *Macunaíma*, reveals the real Brazilian hero in its parody of the Brazilian artist who suffers from "Nabuco's malaise." That is the reason why, when he is unable to put into practice his traveling plans, Macunaíma says, "não vou na Europa não. Sou americano. . . . A civilização européia de-certo esculhamba a inteireza do nosso caráter" (Andrade 1988, 114–15) ("I won't go to Europe, after all. I'm an American. . . . Without a doubt, European civilization would play havoc with our unspoiled nature" 1984, 108). This is an ambiguous statement within the humorous context of the narration; however, the hero, albeit torn between foreign attractions and nostalgia for his native Uiraricoera, ends up by concentrating his fantastic displacements in the geography of America, where he manages to recover its wealth, represented by the *muiraquitã* amulet.

Even within the obvious limitations of this brief passage, it is possible to grasp the significance of the author's travels, his way of facing the contradictions that marked his intellectual career, in which his adventures in reading were added to his adventures of travel. Thus, his cosmopolitan nature as a tenacious reader exists side by side with his concern for regional values, observed in his careful field work on Brazilian popular culture. The conservative tendency of the collector of myths and rituals is counterbalanced by the curiosity of the writer published in avant-garde journals. The inevitable Eurocentrism that prevailed in his education is questioned in the light of his reevaluation of Brazilian culture that resulted from his ethnographic research. Andrade traveled across pages and kilometers in order to become a writer, and the stages and strategies underlying that process can be found both in the plot and in the composition of *Macunaíma*. It is also significant that the story was the result of a single writing stint during December 1926, after an intense period of reading books on anthropology and aesthetics; there were subsequently a number of revisions carried out in 1927 and 1928, before and after a long trip to the Amazon region. The records of these trips, found in diaries, letters, and other writings, form part of the Mário de Andrade archive, established at the Institute of Brazilian Studies of the University of São Paulo, and are being published in several volumes—such as *O turista aprendiz* [1983; The Apprentice Tourist]—organized by Telê Porto Ancona Lopez (1972; 1996).

Within his own program for building a Brazilian literary language, de-regionalized and mixed, Andrade experimented with many semantic regional differences in *Macunaíma*. However, unlike his hero, he was not magically displaced. Scholar, poet, and lecturer, he was constantly immersed in the everyday life of São Paulo; yet each trip became more and more decisive for his work. He also found another way to compensate for the periods he spent in São Paulo: He wrote letters, thousands of letters, which for years crisscrossed the country, and established a number of continuing dialogues with writers and artists he had met during those trips. Mário de Andrade took his first study trip in 1919 to fulfill a long-standing desire to know Brazil. The 26-year-old poet was already a skilled writer with a mature and independent critical mind. After having met other young intellectuals from São Paulo who defended certain avant-garde forms of expression (such as the painting of Anita Malfatti and the sculpture of Victor Brecheret), he decided that the true Brazil was neither in

Europe nor in the cosmopolitan capital. Instead, he went to Minas Gerais, where the decline of eighteenth-century gold production had left several cities in ruins; those he visited on his own, with an inquiring mind, and rescued two unexplored treasures–Baroque churches and the poetry of Alphonsus de Guimaraens (1870–1921). He later wrote his commentary on Alphonsus's poetry as "um jardim esquecido no meio do Brasil" (Andrade 1974, 72) ("the forgotten achievement in the middle of Brazil"), thus acknowledging the significant, if ignored, value of his contribution to literary Symbolism amidst the apathy of the end of the nineteenth century. When, in 1921, he systematized his critical view of this forgotten patrimony inherited by his generation, he considered the Symbolist writers as masters of the past.

Trying to keep up-to-date with developments in Europe, especially in German and French culture, Andrade prepared himself to become a new kind of *bandeirante*, an explorer who opened the ground for the aesthetic values that had been abandoned by progress. The rediscovery of Brazilian Baroque art by Andrade–the inventive quality of its local appropriation of Iberian Baroque–was slowly assimilated in Brazilian intellectual circles. In 1919 he wrote an article entitled "Arte religiosa no Brasil em Minas Gerais" ["Brazil's Religious Art in Minas Gerais"], but it was not until 1928, when he published his long dissertation "O Aleijadinho," on the Baroque sculpture, that he had a lasting impact. By then he had returned to Minas Gerais with his colleagues in what became known as the trip of discovery of Brazil. (The documents related to the author's trips to Minas Gerais and his letters to local intellectuals have been studied in *Mário de Andrade: carta aos mineiros* [Letter to the People of Minas Gerais], edited by Eneida Maria de Souza and Paulo Schmidt.) In 1924, two years after the Week of Modern Art–when the larger Brazilian public was able to see the avant-garde project of young and energetic artists–he organized a train excursion to São João del-Rei, Ouro Preto, Belo Horizonte, Congonhas do Campo, and other surrounding cities. Mário de Andrade, together with Oswald de Andrade, Tarsila do Amaral, and other people from São Paulo, wanted to introduce Brazilian culture to their French-Swiss friend Blaise Cendrars. Surely realizing the contradiction they were facing, the Modernist group was in search of art and of the past, as Mário wrote in the eighth of his "Crônicas de Malazarte" ["Malazarte's Chronicles"], where he recorded a lyrical account of the trip. Attributing their new insight in part to their break with conventional aesthetic patterns, the 1922 Modernists were able to see with liberated vision and to appreciate the mixture of primitive and learned elements so typical of Baroque architecture and sculpture. This enriching experience of aesthetic renewal had begun some months before with the participation of the group in the Rio de Janeiro Carnival. The fact that they took an active part in the parades, dancing to the Afro-Brazilian rhythms on the old paths that passed by ruins from the Colonial period of slavery, gave rise to a series of sketches in poetry, drawings, and aesthetic reflections that transformed not only their own works but the very concept of Brazilian art for years to come.

After the 1924 trip, Mário de Andrade's double role as cultural researcher and leader, which he had acquired in his mature years, grew considerably. The poetic experiments of "Paulicéia desvairada" ["Hallucinated Paulicéia"] and "Losango cáqui" ["Khaki Lozenge"] (see *Poesias completas*), where urban colloquialisms and the musicality of free verse

are combined, were refined and made more complex by the incorporation of forms, genres, and rhythms belonging to popular traditions. Symbolized in the "Noturno de Belo Horizonte" ["Belo Horizonte's Nocturn"], this poetic form was extended in the poems of "Clã do jaboti" ["Jaboti's Clan"] and from there to *Macunaíma*. In the following years he wrote extensively to young writers encouraging them to join in the creation of a Brazilian literature. He encouraged the Minas Gerais group *A revista* (where poet Carlos Drummond de Andrade [1902–1987] stood out) to become the consolidating force of Modernism. In the long term his concern for the knowledge and preservation of artistic and historical sites resulted in the draft law for an institution to preserve the national heritage.

Andrade's 1927 trip to the Amazon region with a small group, although perhaps less significant for Brazil's literary history, was rich in its aesthetic implications. Well prepared for this enterprise, Andrade wrote a fictional-reflective-documentary diary from which he selected certain episodes to be transformed into journalistic chronicles. In 1943 he prepared a series of articles and comments to be published under the title of *O turista aprendiz*, the first part of which was to going to be presented as "Viagem pelo Amazonas até o Peru, pelo Madeira até a Bolívia e por Marajó até dizer chega" ["Journey along the Amazon River up to Peru, along the Madeira up to Bolivia and along the Marajó up until Saying It Is Enough"]. Although the narrative is presented from the point of view of an inexperienced traveler (or apprentice, according to the title), its diary form is constructed with the skilled confidence of a great master. The information gained and the sensations felt during the trip are given a fictional treatment within a wide range of registers, from realistic satire to fantastic humor, and employing the techniques of caricature, stylization, and allegory. There is an evident intertextual relationship between the text resulting from the Amazonian tourist journey and *Macunaíma*, the rhapsody based on Amazonian myths. In both cases anthropological research (field work in *O turista*, archival research in *Macunaíma*) is filtered through the aesthetic experimentation of the avant-garde. The geographic journey is made to appear in the textual journey through the appropriation of the discourse of travel books, which include classical texts going back to the chronicles of the colonization of Brazil.

When Mário de Andrade left his office in São Paulo, curious to know other Brazils through his intellectual form of tourism, he was systematically moving through each of the stages he had planned for his two projects–the outline of the character of Brazil's culture, and the remaking of a Brazilian language to be used in modern literature. In this regard one of his most productive moments was on his trip to the northeastern region between December 1928 and February 1929, his last research trip. Choosing his itinerary in order to be able to attend as many traditional celebrations as possible, he traveled on his own, but was guided at each stage by writers linked to Modernism or by folklore specialists with whom he had corresponded (such as José Américo de Faria de Almeida [1887–1980], Ademar Vidal [b. 1900], Antonio Bento [1875–1959], and Luís da Câmara Cascudo [1898–1986]). As contributor to São Paulo's *Diário Nacional*, he regularly wrote chronicles or sketches in which he evaluated certain examples of colonial architecture, described local mores, and recorded music, dance, and folkloric rituals, collecting information on the techniques used by instrumentalists and singers, and thereby establishing a possible genealogy of rhythms and themes to compare them with popular manifestations of other regions or states. The compilation of these chronicles or sketches, completed in 1943, was to form the second volume of *O turista aprendiz* with the subtitle of "Viagem etnográfica" ["Ethnographic Trip"].

The material researched during the 1920s had much wider implications than his other work, because it helped to change the direction of Brazil's literary culture. Andrade's trips outside of Brazil throughout South America must also be considered as foundational for his experiences with Spanish-speaking America and helped to establish the complex reflections on art, society, and culture, which marked his work as a whole and had wide implications. This can be seen in his discussions with his closest friends, who later carried on his work and became the editors of the research. Indeed, his correspondence with young writers was his legacy to the following generations.

Political Exiles and Their Reappraisal of Brazil

Journalist Fernando Gabeira's (b. 1941) book *O que é isso, companheiro?* [What's This, Comrade?] was published in Brazil in 1979, at a time when the military regime governing the country since 1964 still continued to exert its domination, but when a slow and gradual thaw—which had started in 1974—was increasing significantly, as the State's political control relented. Taking advantage of the recently declared amnesty, this narrative—written in exile by one of the participants of the urban guerrilla war—brought into the intellectual and political circles the voice of those who had been tortured by the dictatorship, and encouraged the publication of similar testimonial statements. This launched an open debate about the first fifteen years of the regime. A popular slogan, which was endlessly repeated at the time, demanded a wide, general, and unlimited amnesty for the people who were either imprisoned, banished, exiled, condemned, or clandestinely living within the country. The peculiar form of amnesty allowed—achieved by means of negotiations between the military government, on the one hand, and civil society and the more democratic political sector, on the other—exonerated from trial and punishment both those who opposed the regime and those who, on its behalf, exerted the systematic violence of repression that turned the State, in the eyes of society, into a powerful and indestructible force. As a result of this wide and unrestricted agreement, which encompassed past and present responsibilities, many personal and political stories that had been condemned to silence were able to emerge. Thus, the immediate and poignant impact of Fernando Gabeira's book was mainly due to its consequences: the compulsion to break the imposed silence, at least within intellectually aware circles, that had been unbearable, finally to respond to the government versions of the acts of resistance against the regime between 1968 and 1972, and to denounce the critical inertia or complicity of the so-called armed struggle of the less radical Left.

The fact that *O que é isso, companheiro?* and other, similar works received such a welcome was a result not only of their sense of immediacy, but also of the familiarity of Brazilian readers with hybrid narrations: Ever since the Modernist movement of the 1930s, they had accepted the forms of historical-documentary exercises and recollections, ambiguously offered as autobiographies, journalistic essays, or fictional narrations. The innovative nature of such memoirs rested on the literary portrayal of life histories, which were published not because of their authors' fame but because they were a part of

the community's life. This opened up a demand for publications and gave rise to a cultural and socioeconomic polyphony, where the experiences of the minorities and marginalized—either because of class, gender, race, or sexual orientation did not need scholarly mediation and were sought for themselves. Fernando Gabeira's story stands between personal testimony and the collective memory of political exiles; it emblematically recollects the experience of forced dislocation, which was common to many Brazilians at the time. Sentimental, political, and cultural movement between journalism and political militancy, between a wide social movement and the secrecy of the armed struggle, between the urban guerrilla and torture, between prison, banishment and exile, are all narrated from the perspective of a sharp analysis of the outlook of the country between 1964 and 1970, when the character-author remained in prison, and up to the late 1970s, when he finished writing the book and returned to Brazil under the general amnesty.

As can be perceived in the text, the intention to write a book telling how things happened, an expression that was immediately checked and corrected to say (or, better to tell what went on and is remembered), had its origin in exile when, "uma tarde de setembro de 1973, em Santiago de Chile . . . a apenas alguns minutos do toque de recolher" (Gabeira 9) ("one afternoon of September 1973, in Santiago de Chile . . . just a few minutes after curfew"), the author looked for asylum at the Argentinean Embassy. The text oscillates between the narrator—who controls the narrated matter—and the author, who identifies himself as one among many possible voices, creating a fluctuation that both opens up and filters the narration. Thus, as the title indicates, the book can be read as a detached and critical analytical recovery—often ironic, at times bitter and pained—of an individual life story as well as of the recent history of Brazil, without losing sight of external, contemporary episodes that had an impact on the political movements of the Left. The narrative starts during the bewildering events of 1964—when a military coup disrupted the democratic order by overturning president João Goulart, claiming the existence of Leftist movements of resistance that were never confirmed—and it covers the hardening brutality of the dictatorial regime as well as the obstinacy of the forms of resistance that emerged between 1966 and 1969, up to the early 1970s, when the political groups were replaced by more paramilitary activities of resistance.

Thus, underlying the narrative is the debate, among the diverse groups and militants of the Left, on the role of revolutionary leadership and the road that would finally free Brazil from the military and capitalist yoke. Simultaneously, other international events—such as the 1967 OLAS (Organization of Latin American States) conference at Havana, the May 1968 demonstrations in France, the USSR's invasion of Czechoslovakia, the publication of Régis Debray's *Revolution and Counter-Revolution*, and the guerrilla activity in Latin America—are also introduced into Gabeira's story and serve to underline both the programmatic efficacy of Marxist-Leninism and the legitimacy of the most powerful of modern hybrid narrations.

If it is true that the book sharply criticizes the bureaucracy of the traditional partisan organs, as well as the revolutionary inefficacy of the wide alliances with a variety of social sectors defended by the Communist Party and the fragility of progressive parties, such as the then Labor Party—with which the author was quite familiar before the coup—it is also true that the author exercises broad and detailed self-criticism that focuses on his personal belonging to a political organization with paramilitary inclinations. The book also indicates the extent of the armed attacks on the military dictatorship–most of the time amounting to assaults on banks and military headquarters, looking for arms and funds, or else kidnapings with which to obtain money in order to rescue comrades in prison. Gabeira not only critically condemned the divorce between the radical militancy and its popular bases–the proletariat during urban actions or the peasants in their attempts at rural guerrilla warfare–but also lamented and condemned the solitude and impoverishment of revolutionary experience; the absence of a theoretically sound reflection upon the country's complexity by means of which it would have been possible to break with the linear and totalizing social models of the Right; the lack of awareness of other social movements that emerged all over the world; the absence of information about the sophisticated repressive apparatus of the dictatorship they were fighting against; and the contempt shown toward the efficacy of the mass communication of the dictatorial State's propaganda–instead of learning from it how to effectively oppose the military scourge that beset the Brazilian people.

In this text the critical memory of a militant group mainly formed by people who had taken part in student movements is alternately expressed by a first-person-singular narrator–an always reflective *I*–and a first-person-plural one–a more active *we*. But the work also includes many references to *them*, that is, "Aquela geração de jovens políticos [que] tinha uns dez anos menos que eu. . . . Eram capazes de localizar todas as intenções escondidas num discurso político, apontar as causas econômicas" (52) ("That generation of young politicians who were ten years younger than me. . . . They could single out all the hidden intentions underlying a political discourse, and point out the economic causes behind the scene"). He thus offers a vantage point that is more sensitive and better informed than the circumstance of exile and the historicity of the narration would allow. The prevailing sense of an appraisal of experience conveys the immediacy of the very instant of living, of the action narrated, and through the narrator reinforces the plot of a testimony that tells an exemplary story–exemplary since it is rich both in bearing witness to experience and in giving a clear description of the facts, and can thus enter into the multiple regenerative process of orality; it can be continued in other stories, it can be complemented by other tales, or supplemented by another version: "Sou apenas um guia que vai apontar para que lado foi a caravana. Os atalhos que tomou vão aparecendo nos outros casos que forem contados" (25) ("I am only a guide who will show the road taken by the caravan. The shortcut taken will be evident in the other cases told").

As was to be expected, many other works followed in the wake of Gabeira's. Both Alex Polari's (b. 1950) *Em busca do tesouro* [In Search of the Treasure] and Herbert Daniel's (1946–1992) *Passagem para o próximo sonho* [Passage to the Next Dream] were published in 1982 and must be taken into account not only because of the political activity of their authors between 1967 and 1971 in Rio de Janeiro, but also because they are narrations that offer the point of view of the younger militants–the students. They share with Gabeira's book a self-critical attitude toward armed-struggle resistance; however, unlike Gabeira, these writers emphasize their personal history and present the typical dilemmas of their generation regarding relationships, sexuality, politics, and intellectuality.

Alex Polari was a high school student under 18 when he was taken prisoner in 1971. His story opens with the loud sentence heard at the moment of cross-examination and reiterated during the endless sessions of torture–"Fala, guerrilheiro filho da puta" (11) ("Talk, guerrilla son-of-a-bitch"). It is as if, by the very act of writing, the words themselves took the torturer's words and used them against him. Torture, which destroyed the body and condemned individuals to extreme solitude, also encouraged lucidity. As an act of survival and in order to keep silent to protect the rest of the comrades who were still free, he forced himself to disassociate from his body and his memory, to make a separation between himself as protagonist and his reader as the spectator of a kind of mindless, gratuitous cruelty. In Gabeira, a similar torture experience–with the inevitable morbid interaction between torturer and tortured–resulted in a dry tale and the precise appraisal of the moment's fragility, in contrast with the sophisticated repressive apparatus of the dictatorship's military torturers based on behavioralist theories of mental weaknesses. In Polari the violence suffered was transformed into a link that structured his recollection by means of a process of associations with a body in pain but without images and emotions, a flux of consciousness, which allowed him to build the lived experience in a generational context that could be shared. With its narcissistic emphasis and characterization filtered by an awareness of his own body, the narrative of the young hero establishes a radical counterpoint to Gabeira's text and approaches the genre of the novel, as the ambiguous subtitle suggests: "Uma ficção política vivida" ["A Lived Political Fiction"]. If in *O que é isso, companheiro?* there is a kind of wisdom that needs to be conveyed, in *Em busca do tesouro* it is possible to read an experienced perplexity that has to be shared.

Herbert Daniel's *Passagem para o próximo sonho* can be situated between that very perplexity over what has been lived and the wisdom of experience. The book is introduced as a possible self-critical novel about exile–about being banished for clandestine militancy, exiled in Europe, and degraded because of one's homosexuality. A university student during the late 1960s and early 1970s, Daniel took part with Polari in the Vanguarda Popular Revolucionária, VPR (Popular Revolutionary Vanguard), which at the time was considered as the most Leftist organization in Brazilian politics. Daniel created a paradoxical text that is presented as a novel, often marred by excessive or gratuitous literary devices attempting to achieve depth through technique, but which also contains both very precise information about political militancy and the most implacable condemnation of this chapter in Brazilian history. Although a large part of the novel explores the interdiction of homosexuality, incompatible with the everyday life of the armed struggle and with the phallocentric and conservative ideas of the Left, this is in fact the book that has the least personal register and form, as if repressing sexuality were the main element of quotidian activity reiterated in hiding and in exile.

Historical evaluations differ about how the dictatorial and military regime was confronted by armed actions and the subsequent radicalization of such activities–either through remembrances, in testimonial narrations by some of the participants, or else through a retrospective analysis by others. They share, however, the imperative to build a discourse to deal with failure, either as a prognosis in the case of armed intervention or as a diagnosis in the writings. The forecast of failure emerged from the open discrepancy between the armed struggle and the revolutionary Marxist-Leninist program, which was manifest in axioms such as the pre-eminence of relations of production, the class struggle, the universalization of the proletariat consciousness, the party's regimented leadership of the masses, or the establishment of objective conditions for the Revolution. It thus emerged from the difference between a revolutionary program, requiring certain philosophically and historically preestablished conditions, and an armed struggle, which, on the contrary, was characterized by an isolation from the people and by the radicalization of the idea of a revolutionary vanguard. These policies had to be replaced (as the revolutionary movement diminished and lost its resonance) by the continued questioning and the eventual destabilization of the military dictatorship.

These authors do not disagree on the prognosis of that in which they took part, at least at the level of rational justification and evaluation. Their recollections bring to light the compulsion to understand themselves as actors in a political and historical event that reached its high point either in death, for some, or for others, in being tortured and imprisoned (such as Fernando Gabeira and Alex Polari), or in just surviving the violence of the military police (as was the case for many others, such as Herbert Daniel); or else in a ten-year exile or in clandestine living. To live with failure and to assimilate it did not force these writers (though it might be the response of their readers) to give up all teleology, all totalizing, all expectation of linear and regenerating social progress moving in a universally preestablished direction–to give up, in short, the project of a future whose logocentric logic was in crisis.

Herbert Daniel wrote, "A decisão quixotesca de afrontar-se militarmente à ditadura vale pouco pelas suas formas, nada pelos seus resultados, mas é inestimável pela ruptura que estabelece: a partir daí não é mais possível fazer política como 'antigamente'" (33) ("The quixotesque decision to face militarily the dictatorship is worth little as an act in itself and nothing in its results, but is invaluable because of the rupture it creates in the sense of inevitable movement forward: It is no longer possible to engage in politics as before"). Alex Polari, on the other hand, offered significant clues about the assimilation of this failed experience into the cultural outlook of the period when he underlined among its many elements the passionate, the fragmentary, the unforeseen, and the improvised in order to conclude, "O Tropicalismo e suas diversas ramificações já eram sem dúvida a expressão cultural perfeita para aquilo que incipientemente representávamos na política" (Polari 121) ("Tropicalism and its branches were certainly the perfect cultural manifestation of what we had begun to represent in politics"). In historiography, the narrations of the failed experience of armed struggle are like the coming to consciousness of the history of the defeated, a counterpointed history that needs to be read symptomatically, beyond the "lições politicas e das vicissitudes históricas" (Polari 256) ("political lessons and the historical vicissitudes"), or to be read from an aesthetic point of view like the possible counter-epics of contemporary times. Today, it is possible to recognize that the urban guerrilla–with its ambiguous throbbing of life and death–set up a logic of resistance and operated with a logic from show business, staging short but vehement confrontation scenes in the streets, which forced the dictatorship to expose itself in all its violence and arbitrariness and to unmask the mores it prohibited by means of its censorship.

Translation by Nair María Anaya Ferreira

Works Cited

Agassiz, Louis. 1868. *A Journey in Brazil.* Boston: Ticknor and Fields.

Amado, Gilberto. 1956. *Mocidade no Rio e primeira viagem à Europa.* Rio de Janeiro: José Olympio.

Amaral, Aracy. 1970. *Artes plásticas na semana de 22.* São Paulo: Perspectiva.

Andrade, Mário de. 1972. "Cronicas de Malazarte." *Brazil: 1 tempo modernista–1917/1929.* Ed. Marta Rossetti Batista, Têle Porto Ancona Lopez, Yone Soares de Lima. São Paulo: Instituto de Estudos Brasileiros. 109–15.

———. 1974. "Artigo de Mário de Andrade sobre Alphonsus de Guimaraens (1919)." *Itinerários: cartas a Alphonsus de Guimaraens Filho.* By Mário de Andrade and Manuel Bandeira. São Paulo: Livraria Duas Cidades. 67–72.

———. 1975. "O Alejandinho." *Aspectos das artes plásticas no Brasil.* São Paulo: Martins. 13–46.

———. 1976. *Táxi e Crônicas no Diário Nacional.* Ed. Telê Porto Ancona Lopes. São Paulo: Duas Cidades.

———. 1983. *O turista aprendiz.* Ed. Telê Porto Ancona Lopez. São Paulo: Livraria Duas Cidades.

———. 1984. *Macunaíma.* Trans. E.A. Goodland. New York: Random House.

———. 1987. *Poesías completas.* Ed. Diléa Zanotto Manfio. Belo Horizonte: Itatiaia; São Paulo: Editora da Universidade de São Paulo.

———. 1988. *Macunaíma: o herói sem nenhum caráter.* Ed. Telê Porto Ancona Lopez. Paris: Association Archives de la Littérature Latino-américaine, des Caribes et Africaine du XXe siècle; Brasilia: CNPq.

———. 1993. *A arte religiosa no Brasil: crônicas publicadas na Revista do Brasil em 1920.* Ed. Claudéte Kronbauer. São Paulo: Experimento/Giordano.

Andrade, Oswald de. 1971. *Obras completas.* Vol. 2: *Memórias sentimentais de João Miramar/Serafim Ponte Grande.* Rio de Janeiro: Civilização Brasileira.

———. 1972. "Manifesto antropófago." *Obras completas.* Vol. 6: *Do Pau-Brasil à antropofagia e às utopias: manifestos, teses de concursos e ensaios.* Rio de Janeiro: Civilização Brasileira. 11–19.

Azevedo, Maria Helena Castro. 1997. "Um jóquei no seu cavalo: uma biografia do escritor Graça Aranha." Diss. Pontifícia Universidade Católica do Rio de Janeiro.

Barata, Mário. "A arte no século XIX: do neoclassicismo e romanticismo até o ecletismo." *História geral da arte no Brasil.* Vol. 1. Ed. Walter Zanini. São Paulo: Instituto Moreira Salles. 379–81.

Bastide, Roger. 1979. *Brasil, terra de contrastes.* Rio de Janeiro: Difusão Européia do Livro.

Bellei, Sérgio L. P. 1988. "American Culture in Brazil: The Search for Strategies of Reading." *American Studies International* 26.2 (October): 3–9.

———. 1992. "Brazilian Visitors to the U.S.: 20th-Century Perspectives." *North Dakota Quarterly* 60.1 (Winter): 81–101.

Bishop, Elizabeth. 1965. *Questions of Travel: Poems.* New York: Farrar, Straus and Giroux.

Broca, Brito. 1956. *A vida literária no Brasil–1900.* Rio de Janeiro: Ministério da Educação e Cultura.

———. 1991. *Naturalistas, parnasianos e decadistas.* Ed. Alexandre Eulalio. Campinas: Editora da Universidade Estadual de Campinas.

Brown, Ashley. 1983. "An Interview with Elizabeth Bishop." *Elizabeth Bishop and Her Art.* Ed. Lloyd Schwartz and Sybil P. Estess. Ann Arbor: University of Michigan Press. 289–302.

Callcott, Maria Graham. 1969. *Journal of a Voyage to Brazil and Residence There During Part of the Years 1821, 1822, 1823.* New York: Praeger.

Candido, Antonio. 1969. *Formação da literatura brasileira: momentos decisivos.* 2 vols. São Paulo: Martins.

———. 1976. *Literatura e sociedade: estudos de teoria e história literaria*. São Paulo: Companhia Editora Nacional.

Cendrars, Blaise. 1924. *Feuilles de route–I: Le Formose*. Illust. by Tarsila. Paris: Au Sans Pareil.

———. 1969. "Prose du Transsibérien et de la petite Jeanne de France." *Oeuvres complètes*. Vol. 1. Paris: Denoël. 16–32.

Da Cunha, Euclides. 1913. *À margem da história*. Porto: Chardon.

———. 1939. *Canudos. Diário de uma expedição*. Intro. Gilberto Freire. Rio de Janeiro: José Olympio.

———. 1963. *Os sertões*. Rio de Janeiro: Francisco Alves.

Daniel, Herbert. 1982. *Passagem para o próximo sonho: um possível romance autocrítico*. Rio de Janeiro: Codecri.

Fabris, Annateresa. 1990. "A questão futurista no Brasil." *Modernidade: Vanguardas artísticas na América Latina*. Ed. Ana Maria de Moraes Belluzzo. São Paulo: Memorial da América Latina: UNESP. 67–80.

———. 1994. *O futurismo paulista: hipóteses para o estudo da chegada da vanguarda ao Brasil*. São Paulo: Perspectiva.

Gabeira, Fernando. 1979. *O que é isso, companheiro?: depoimento*. Rio de Janeiro: Editora Codecri.

Galvão, Patrícia (pseud. Mara Lobo). 1982. *Pagu, Patrícia Galvão: vida-obra*. Ed. Augusto de Campos. São Paulo:Brasiliense.

———. N.d. *Parque industrial*. Fascim. ed. São Paulo: Alternativa.

Galvão, Patrícia, and Geraldo Ferraz. 1959. *Dois romances: A famosa revista/Doramundo*. Rio de Janeiro: José Olympio.

Gomes, Renato Cordeiro. 1996. *João do Rio: vielas do vício, ruas da graça*. Rio de Janeiro: Relume Dumará.

Holanda, Sérgio Buarque de, ed. 1967. História geral da civilização brasileira. Vol. 2: *O Brasil monárquico*. São Paulo: Difusão Européia do Livro.

Lévi-Strauss, Claude. 1952. *Race and History*. Paris: UNESCO.

———. 1955a. *Tristes tropiques*. Paris: Plon.

———. 1955b. *Tristes tropiques*. Trans. Jorge Constante Pereira. Lisboa: Livraria Martins Fontes.

———. 1961. *A World on the Wane*. Trans. John Russel. New York: Criterion Books.

Litvak, Lily. 1982. *El cuento anarquista (1880–1911): antología*. Madrid: Taurus.

Lopez, Têle Porto Ancona. 1972. *Mário de Andrade: ramais e caminho*. São Paulo: Duas Cidades.

———. 1996. *Mariodeandradiando*. São Paulo: Hucitec.

Machado, Antônio de Alcântara. 1982. *Pathé Baby*. Fascim. ed. São Paulo: Imprensa Oficial; Arquivo do Estado.

Machado de Assis, Joaquim María. 1995. *Quincas Borba*. São Paulo: Editora Ática.

———. 1998. *Memórias póstumas de Brás Cubas*. Rio de Janeiro: Ed. Record.

Magalhães Junior, R. 1978. *A vida vertiginosa de João do Rio*. Rio de Janeiro: Civilização Brasileira.

Maybury-Lewis, David. 1988. *The Savage and the Innocent*. Boston: Beacon Press.

Molinari, Luigi. 1908. *Il teatro popolare*. Milano: Tip. della Università Popolare.

Mota, Carlos Guilherme. 1977. *Ideologia da cultura brasileira (1933–1974): pontos de partida para uma revisão historica*. São Paulo: Ática.

Nabuco, Joaquim. 1963. *Minha formação*. Intro. Gilberto Freire. Brasília: Editôra Universidade de Brasília.

———. 1969. *Um estadista do Império*. Rio de Janeiro: Aguilar.

Oiticica, José. 1970. *Ação direta (meio século de pregação libertária)*. Ed. Roberto das Neves. Rio de Janeiro: Germinal.

Poggioli, Renato. 1968. *The Theory of the Avant-garde*. Cambridge, MA: Belknap Press of Harvard University Press.

Polari, Alex. 1982. *Em busca do tesouro*. Rio de Janeiro: Codecri.

Prado, Antonio Arnoni, ed. 1986. *Libertários no Brasil: memória, lutas, cultura*. São Paulo: Brasiliense.

Rio, João do. [Paulo Barreto]. 1911. *Psicologia urbana*. Rio de Janeiro; Paris: Garnier.

———. 1976. *As religões no Rio*. Rio de Janeiro: Editora Nova Aguilar.

———. 1994. *O momento literario*. Ed. Rosa Gens. Rio de Janeiro: Edições do Departamento Nacional do Livro.

———. 1997. *A alma encantadora das ruas: crônicas*. Ed. Raúl Antelo. São Paulo: Companhia das Letras, Fundação Biblioteca Nacional.

Santiago, Silviano. 1976. "Brazil/Estados Unidos: Relações Culturais de Dependência." *Vozes* 9: 25–26.

———. 1978. "O entre-lugar do discurso latino-americano." *Uma literatura nos trópicos*. São Paulo: Perspectiva. 11–28.

———. 1989. "Por que e para que viaja o europeu?" *Nas malhas da letra*. São Paulo: Companhia das Letras. 189–205.

———. 1995. "Atração do mundo." *Jornal do Brasil. Idéias* (Rio de Janeiro, December 2).

———. 1997. "A tristeza de um é a alegria do outro." *Jornal do Brasil. Idéias*. (Rio de Janeiro, May 17).

Schaden, Egon, and João Batista Borges Pereira. 1967. "Exploração antropológica." *História geral da civilização brasileira*. Vol. 2: *O Brasil monárquico*; Vol. 3: *Reações e transações*. Ed. Sérgio Buarque de Holanda. São Paulo: Difusão Européia do Livro. 425–43.

Skidmore, Thomas. 1974. *Black into White: Race and Nationality in Brazilian Thought*. New York: Oxford University Press.

Souza, Eneida Maria de, and Paulo Schmidt, eds. 1997. *Mário de Andrade: carta aos mineiros*.Belo Horizonte: Editora Universidade Federal de Minas Gerais.

Süssekind, Flora. 1990. *O Brasil não é longe daqui: o narrador, a viagem*. São Paulo: Companhia das Letras.

CHAPTER 42

SIGNS OF IDENTITY
LATIN AMERICAN IMMIGRATION
AND EXILE

Clara E. Lida and Francisco Zapata

In just over a century Latin America has changed from being a continent known to receive millions of immigrants, largely from Central and Eastern Europe and the Mediterranean coasts, to becoming one that–from the 1960s–has exported populations *en masse,* especially to the United States but also to other countries within the continent and to Europe. Though it would be impossible to estimate the exact number of individuals who have sought work opportunities outside Latin America, the total certainly amounts to many millions. Continental and intercontinental immigration, exile, and displacement have left a permanent impression on the collective and individual experience of Latin Americans. These population movements–the majority compelled by political, social, or economic realities, and in some cases by chance personal circumstances–have rupture and discontinuity as their common denominator, and have brought about a redefinition of self-awareness on an individual and group basis.

Such ruptures, whether voluntary or not, include mandatory encounters (and nonencounters) with places of arrival as much as with those of origin. The separation from a circumscribed and habitual world, as well as the discovery of and encounter with other places and people, while provoking nostalgia for a lost world, also demand adaptation to a new environment, with the subsequent need to explain the other and the obligatory need to revise one's idea of oneself. Rupture and encounter inevitably create an urge to define and fix personal identity, even though such a process is never static, but rather is a continuous experience searching for signs of that personal identity on both an individual and collective basis. Seen from this perspective, these dynamics are inherent in all demographic movements. Hence, it is crucial to understand both the historical and social processes that frame these experiences, as well as the images that emerge from the ruptures, displacements, and encounters taking place among those who move to new environments and those who welcome them on arrival. Immigrants are not just displaced people; they also acquire a consciousness of change that is in turn communicated to those who receive them, frequently creating a shared sense of relocation.

This essay proposes to analyze the discontinuity provoked by exodus as well as the integration that results on arrival, understanding that transit from one point to another does not have a strictly measurable time-frame, since it is not a question of a simple crossing but rather of a complex journey along the invisible and difficult paths of experience, emotions, and intellect. On a parallel trajectory, it will endeavor to reconstruct the cultural world of the subjects of these transitions, so as to attempt an approximation of a definition of the individual and collective imagination that emerges from these processes. Its aim is to specify the complex and plural signs of identity that emerge in the Latin American world and that are rooted in the immigration, exile, and displacement of populations. In speaking of *immigration* here we

will be referring to the movements of considerable numbers of people, generally international in origin, but in every case involving a nationality different from that of the new country. Such migrations are generally characterized by a free and voluntary displacement, usually for economic motives, even though more or less direct political causes can lie in the background, including: Flight from ethnic persecution (pogroms and massacres); racial, religious, or, as in the case of Puerto Rico, colonial reasons; heavy taxation; exclusive agrarian policies; the marginalization of citizens under authoritarian, oligarchic regimes or those run by caciques or on the basis of patronage; or the evasion of military service, among many other motives. In every case it is relevant to note that the participants in these migrations are usually individuals with scarce or irregular economic resources and incomes, coming from minimally privileged or marginal social strata; the majority are of rural or agro-urban origin or, to a lesser extent, are small artisans, qualified in various urban or semi-urban posts, or are in employment within the lower echelons of the service sector. Even so, in the case of immigrations provoked by persecutions prompted by ideological or religious motives, participants may belong to *any* social class.

The term *exiles,* on the other hand, will be used here to refer to a population that was forced to abandon their mother country to seek refuge in other lands for political reasons or as a direct result of war. In other words, this is an involuntary exodus of groups of individuals who normally would not contemplate emigration, if it were not for the need to flee from violence or political repression and its consequences within their country of origin. While in general these groups represent the socially and culturally advantaged, consisting of highly educated intellectuals, artists, professionals, technicians, and workers, exile also affects ethnic groups, such as the Maya groups of Guatemala who were forced to take refuge in vast numbers in southern Mexico in the 1980s (see Aguayo). In contrast to immigrants, exiles present a social, occupational, and cultural profile that indicates no future intention to abandon their country; nor would they have done so *motu proprio* had they not experienced violent circumstances that forced them into exile. In the case of the European refugees of the 1930s and 1940s and that of the Guatemalans of the 1980s, the xenophobic and racist political regimes that forced them into exile (and the genocidal initiatives of the Guatemalan armed forces, committed to engineer the disappearance of the indigenous majorities of that country) should also be taken into account (see LeBot).

Displacements, the third term of central importance to this essay, is here understood as a process of internal migration implying a massive transfer of populations of predominantly rural origin to regions boasting more modern economies (e.g., mining and industry) and the principal urban centers. In the case of Latin America these internal migrations also imply a considerable ethnic displacement of Indians or *mestizos* from different groups and, as a result, of diverse cultures and languages. One particular case mentioned above that combines the characteristics of immigration with that of displacement is that of the Puerto Ricans who–from the 1950s, as a result of the colonial and subaltern character of their country–moved from their own dominated territory to the urban zones of the dominating metropolis. Taking these three definitions as a framework of historical and cultural reference, this essay proposes to try to make sense of the processes of rupture and interaction that, throughout the twentieth century, took place within the vast geographic space of the continent, but without trying to undertake an exhaustive analysis of one or other country in particular; rather, an attempt shall be made to define principal lines of inquiry. Moreover, in reconstructing this process we propose to contextualize the particular and collective experience of immigrants, exiles, and displaced persons and explore the historical bases that could explain the complexities of these separations, movements, encounters, and nonencounters. Finally, this essay endeavors to act only as a background source of information for those concerned to examine how these experiences of rupture, movement, and encounter are created within the various literary texts that have been produced on the continent.

Intercontinental Immigrations

The migrations to and from Latin America have an internal periodicity that permits the establishment of a general typology of these population movements, even given continental diversity. The point of departure will be the mass transatlantic migrations of the last two decades of the nineteenth century, and the end point will be the population movements within Latin America during the last decades of the twentieth century. This periodization does not ignore the fact that America, from its initial appearance in Western consciousness over five centuries ago, has essentially been a continent on the receiving end of foreign populations, mostly European, but also African and Asian. Even so, the population flow from the arrival of the Spaniards in 1492 until the first half century of Independence can be characterized as a continuous, low-intensity migratory process with numerically limited crossings in which Latin America took on more of the role of passive receptor than dynamic protagonist, deciding on its own demographic transformation through the pursuit of active policies.

The Transatlantic Crossings

It was not until after the new American republics had gained political stability and begun development, sustained by the existence of the nation-state in the second half of the 1800s, that the perception of their own demographic and material characteristics impelled them toward an aggressive population policy linked to the need for territorial consolidation and the supplying of labor for the mines and factories that had begun to spring up. This population policy sought, on the one hand, to "whiten" the aboriginal population through *mestizaje* and, on the other, to provide a cheap work force. In this sense various countries of the Pacific and the West Indies organized the forced transfer of Asians, especially Chinese, to work in the exploitation of *guano* on the Peruvian coast, on extending the railway in the Andes and the Ecuadorian, Bolivian, and Mexican highlands, and in harvesting on Cuban sugar cane plantations. It is worth emphasizing the difference that existed between the policies applied to the European colonies (see Pérez Rosales) in Argentina, Brazil, and Chile and those imposed on the Asians, who were thus subjected to intolerable working conditions.

Mexican intellectuals (see Andrés Molina Enríquez [1978] and Agustín Basave [1992]) or intellectual politicians, such as Domingo Faustino Sarmiento (1811–1888), tried to emulate the United States, which–during the mid-nineteenth century–had developed an active immigration policy to populate and exploit its vast, recently acquired (1846–1848) but scarcely populated territories (which until then had been inhabited by Indians and, in the Southwest and California, by a small number of Mexicans). The immigrants were brought to supply the incipient industries with cheap manual labor. The U.S. model became a paradigm for the Latin American countries that, populated or not, tended to want to open up and attract the surplus populations in Europe and displace or eliminate the aboriginal population that hampered this enterprise, which occurred in southern Argentina and Chile.

The River Plate countries and Brazil were extreme cases in this mass importation of European populations, mostly from Italy, Spain, and Portugal. They all possessed vast, barely populated tracts of land that the local agrarian oligarchies wanted to incorporate into the expanding arable and animal husbandry market. In this context the policy of "gobernar es poblar" [to govern is to populate], conceived by the Argentine Liberals and formulated by Juan Bautista Alberdi (1810–1884), became the driving force to attract immigrant populations. Thus, between 1880 and 1930 more than three million foreigners from overseas arrived with the intention of settling in Argentina, Uruguay, and Brazil, in both the richest farming regions (the humid pampas lands and Brazilian coffee plantations) as well as the main capital cities and urban (i.e., commercial, manufacturing, and administrative) centers that needed workers (see Sánchez-Albornoz; Walter). Almost the opposite took place in those countries with an abundant native population, where the rural environment could already count on extensive human settlements and a surplus of cheap farm labor. Moreover, there was a very limited need for the importation of manual labor into their underdeveloped urban centers. Possible examples are Mexico, Peru, or Colombia–countries that received an insignificant flow of immigrants in numerical terms and were never the beneficiaries of mass overseas migration.

Between these two extremes can be situated countries such as Chile, which instigated an extensive foreign immigration (mainly of German extraction) to colonize the lands in the south of the country, or Cuba, which was a Spanish colony from 1511 until the 1890s. Both received a considerable number of Spanish immigrants whose principal object was to ethnically "whiten" a sizable Indian population in Chile and a predominantly African population in Cuba. (For Chile, see Solberg; for Cuba, see Naranjo Orovio and García González, and Casanovas Codina). During this period broad swathes, in generational terms, of Spanish, Italian, Portuguese, Jews (largely from Central and Eastern Europe as well as from the Southern and Eastern Mediterranean), Croats, Poles, and Austro-Hungarians, along with, to a lesser extent, Germans, British, Armenians, Syrians, Lebanese, Japanese, and Chinese, all moved from their respective countries of origin to different territories in the Americas. They all brought with them vastly different social, cultural, linguistic, ideological, and ethnic experiences, and incorporated themselves in different ways into the already varied Latin American environment. Only by taking into account the immensity of these diverse worlds coming together can one understand the plural and complex impact on the cultures of the continent of those men and women who emigrated from the last two decades of the nineteenth century until the Great Depression of the 1930s. The enormously varied parade of human types that appear in Latin American literature is consequently overwhelming. These include fictional characters, such as *La gringa* [1904; *The Foreign Girl*] transplanted from Mediterranean Europe to the *porteño* theater of Florencio Sánchez (1875–1910); those of *Los inmigrantes* [1922; The Immigrants] in the short novel of the same title by Rómulo Gallegos (1884–1969); *Los gauchos judios* [1910; The Jewish Gauchos] of Alberto Gerchunoff (1883–1950), who arrived in the farming colonies of the Argentine Mesopotamia established by Baron Maurice von Hirsch; the Jews, Chinese, and Turks who appeared in ethnophobic and racist literature, largely in pamphlets or journalism; the figure of the peninsular *gachupín* [peninsular Spaniard] in the Mexican novel; and many more. Their daily presence in real life, from Patagonia to the Río Bravo, were authentic proof of the varied experiences of encounter and nonencounter between those who arrived and those who received them.

In this way the phenomenon of *extranjeridad,* or foreignness, was solidified, with the obligatory questions on the part of those on the receiving end: Who are they? What do they want? Where do these foreigners come from? (see Derrida and Dufourmantelle). We might add the interrogatory counterpart as phrased by the new arrivals: What are they like? What might they want? How will these strangers welcome us? This dialogue of crossed questioning, frequently lacking a response until after the passage of long years, undoubtedly lies at the root of all migratory exchange and permeates it throughout the course of mutual contact. Theatrical representations (especially variety shows) and popular music (from the tango to the bolero), as well as literature, reflected this theme of *extranjeridad* ["foreignness"]. A new culture was being created, based on the interactions between foreigners and natives, and it flourished above all in the marginal neighborhoods, the *arrabal amargo* ["bitter urban slum"] of the great cities, creating an urban subculture on the margins of traditional elite cultures. These interactions, initially difficult if not hostile, were reflected, for example, in the stereotyped characterization or caricatured personalities depicted in variety comic theater that were easily identified with individuals and groups in real life: The *gringo* or *tano* and the Italians; the *gachupin* or *gallego* and the Spaniards; the *turco* and the Lebanese; and the *ruso* [Russian] and the Jews. The tango and the bolero for their part not only reflected the means of expressing relations between men and women, but also alluded to the nostalgia of origin and the coming together of those who arrived and those already there. Songs like *Madame Ivonne* and *Peregrina* are classic examples of such encounters and nonencounters, from both the social and the emotional point of view. It is clear that the rapid incorporation of the immigrant as subject into diverse forms of cultural expression revealed the significant impact that they exercised. But it is no less certain that the stereotyped and grotesque representations of these recent arrivals in the new cultural imagination also encouraged caricature, if not xenophobic demonization; they incarnated the subaltern role of the new populations, as well as their fragmented representation that frequently set up situations of confrontation between one group of recent arrivals and another. To sum up, in this complex process, we can observe both inclusion and ethnic conflict. But regardless of the particular case, it might be fitting to ask whether the much referred to "melting pot" of peoples and races existed–and when and where.

From the First World War to the Great Depression

The direction taken by overseas immigration after the First World War was very different from that of previous decades. The great foreign immigrations were reduced as a result of the political and social experiences by both the sending and receiving countries during the second and third decade of the century. On one side, as a result of the 1914 War, many American countries benefited from the increased demand for foodstuffs, raw materials, minerals, and manufactured products by the war-torn countries. Meat, corn, copper, tin, nitrates, and so on generated a considerable expansion in the export markets (see Albert). On the other hand, countries such as Mexico, with its Revolution of 1910, and to a lesser extent Peru, Chile, and Argentina, with their unrest in response to the opposition to the domination of the local oligarchies, can be identified as nations that included immigrants in their social and political life. Thus, the final years of the Great War marked the immigrants' progressive settling-down of permanent roots in the Latin American countries and many of them, including their descendants, now identified themselves as nationals of Chile and Mexico, Argentina and Peru, or of one country or another in this vast Latin American continent.

The result was the recognition of a new citizenry, and with this the practice of a new political and electoral participation that–depending on the individual national case–would influence to a greater or lesser degree a new correlation of power and political parties. This explains in part the success of the movements and parties that erupted onto the Latin American political scene, such as Argentina's Partido Radical, with Hipólito Irigoyen (1852–1933) backed by the *petit bourgeois*, made up of new citizens and their children; the expansion of the Argentine workers' movement through their anarchist branch; and the Federación Obrera Regional Argentina (FORA) and the Partido Socialista Obrero Argentino (PSOA), both supported by the country's expanded working class. In Uruguay the triumph of José Batlle y Ordoñez's (1856–1929) partisans over the most conservative *criollo* sectors grouped under the Partido Blanco and the most traditional wing of the Partido Colorado was undoubtedly due to the growth of its forces thanks to new immigrant members (see Vanger 1963 and 1980 for Batlle y Ordoñez's political biography). When Arturo Alessandri (1868–1950) became President of Chile in 1920, he credited the *chusma dorada* ["golden rabble"] with being the origin of his triumph (as will be seen later in the discussion of internal displacement), but he was also partly supported by new immigrant voters and their descendants. Similar phenomena can be observed in the political transformations in Brazil during these years or the significant labor union activities in Cuba after partial Independence (U.S. occupation lasted until 1902, and again from 1906–1909 and in 1912) in which workers of African origin came together and collaborated with others of peninsular origin (see Casanovas Condina).

The European Exiles

It is well known that the Great Depression that began in 1929–and continued into the decade that followed, affecting every continent–was a watershed in the history of international migrations. Not only was there a reduction in economic opportunities abroad, but also the contraction of the national economies had varied and multiple effects both in countries that traditionally exported populations as well as in receiving nations. This process of economic recession was combined with powerful political disruptions throughout Europe. For the purposes of this study we will target two moments when these worldwide upheavals (during the decade 1935–1945) provoked migrations to Latin America, first from Spain and then from Central and Eastern Europe. Both involved vast contingents of people who were forced to escape from their countries of origin as a result of political repression and violence. The first case was the great exodus of Spanish Republicans provoked by the Spanish Civil War (1936–1939) and the triumph of the Fascist nationalist forces under Francisco Franco. The second major exodus was rooted in the rise of the repressive and racist totalitarianism of German Nazism and Italian Fascism.

(i) Spanish Exile in Latin America

Mexico was the only Latin-American country that supported the Second Spanish Republic in the spring of 1936–at the very start of the military uprising–providing both material support as well as diplomatic solidarity in the League of Nations and other international forums (for Lázaro Cárdenas' government's support of the Spanish Republic, see Lida 1995 and Matesanz's unpublished doctoral thesis, 1995); this support never wavered. In May 1937 some 460 children were evacuated and subsequently given asylum in a school in the city of Morelia; from this came the name by which these first refugees were known in Mexico: los niños de Morelia [the children of Morelia] (see Solorzano; Pla Brugat). From 1937 on, asylum in Mexico was organized for Spanish intellectuals, displaced by the Civil War, who could not continue living in Spain; Mexico received the most illustrious of the writers, artists, scientists, and humanists of Spain who fled into exile (Lida 1988, 44–45). With the great migratory flood that began in the spring of 1939, Mexico welcomed refugees on a massive scale from every profession and occupation. (For the occupations of those who arrived in the first ships, see the suggestive essay by Matesanz 1982, 163–175; and Llorens 1976, 127–28). From 1940 on, at the behest of President Lázaro Cárdenas' government (1934–1940), Mexican citizenship was extended to all those refugees who wished it; it has been calculated that from that date approximately 80 percent took up the offer. Thus, it can be said that from the start of the Civil War to the beginning of the Second World War, in addition to refugees of other nationalities, Mexico received possibly more than 20,000 refugee Spanish Republicans of adult age who arrived either alone or in family groups.

Even though Mexico was an exceptional case in being the only Latin-American country whose government protected émigrés in such a comprehensive fashion, there were others that also helped, although under peculiar conditions and with certain hesitations. For example, from 1939–1940 until the end of the Second World War, the Dominican Republic was the country that–in proportion to its native population–welcomed the greatest number of Spanish Republican exiles. This was because the Dictator Rafael Leónidas Trujillo (1891–1961) decided to receive some 4,000 refugees as a means of pacifying the League of Nations, which had condemned his government after the brutal murder of Haitians by Dominican troops in 1937. Santo Domingo provided only a brief asylum, however, in the nightmare of Trujillo's barbarous dictatorship. By 1945 only a handful of exiles remained in the Republic; the majority left for Mexico, others for Venezuela, and the remainder departed rapidly for other American countries, including Puerto Rico and the United States (see the studies written by temporary refugees in the country: Llorens 1975 and Malagón).

In the rest of Latin America the reception of Spanish refugees was even more limited since–behind many governments giving the impression of democracy–there was actually more sympathy for the Axis powers than for liberal and progressive ideologies. For this reason help was rarely official but rather the result of private initiative and mostly confined to mere handfuls of highly qualified individuals. Such was the case in Argentina where–after the start of the Spanish Civil War– there was a poorly dissembled official sympathy for Francisco Franco's (1892–1975) nationalist forces and a speedy diplomatic recognition of the Franco Regime in 1939. In this context it was difficult for émigrés to arrive other than in trickles– most from the professional, academic, artistic, and scientific elites, as well as some journalists and actors. Firm support came from the old Spanish immigrant organizations, such as the Institución Cultural Española, founded in 1914, and the Asociación Patriótica Española, which helped fellow countrymen, both personally and economically (Méndez 77–95).

Despite the official coolness, those who arrived in Argentina at this time found a country that seemed to correspond to their dreams: Cultural and economic vitality appeared firmly rooted; socially, the large cities seemed to have consolidated an urban democracy; and the cultural environment was apparently propitious for the development of those scientific and artistic activities familiar to the new arrivals. For these individuals Argentina's material and cultural expansion promised to make the country a pleasant home in which to grow roots, despite official authoritarianism and political obstinacy. Few could have anticipated the destruction that the years and decades to come would bring. In fact, Argentina was passing from political instability to military barbarism, from depression to economic chaos, and from cultural and academic crisis to the vastest continual and impoverishing "brain drains" that any Latin-American country has undergone to date. In this context it was to be expected that the new refugees would also suffer the consequences of the social and political instability experienced by their Argentine friends and colleagues. With very few exceptions, the Spanish Republican emigration to Argentina was gradually reduced by further emigration to other locations offering better working conditions and political stability–in United States and postwar Europe. By the 1970s very few Spanish exiles remained in Argentina.

Chile, on the other hand, presented a unique contrast to Argentina, thanks to the decision of President Pedro Aguirre Cerda (1879–1941) and the Spanish solidarity efforts by the Chilean poet and life-time Spanish consul Gabriela Mistral (1889–1957), who sought help from many countries and knocked on many doors to alleviate the plight of the refugees. Moreover, Pablo Neruda (1904–1973), despite the opposition of many Chilean Right-wing politicians and officials, as Consul General in Paris, succeeded in organizing the exodus of some 2,000 refugees from Spain who traveled on the steamship Winnipeg to Valparaíso, arriving on 2 January 1940 (for Mistral and Neruda, see Teitelboim 1984 and 1991, respectively). This contingent was characterized by a low proportion of liberal professions (though they did exist) and an abundance of working-class men and women. Neruda recalls in his Confieso que he vivido: memorias [1974; Memoirs, 1977] that "eran pescadores, campesinos, obreros, intelectuales, una muestra de la fuerza, del heroísmo y del trabajo" (1974, 200–01) ("they were fishermen, peasants, laborers, intellectuals, a cross section of strength, heroism, and hard work"; 1977, 147). Llorens rightly states that the emigration to Chile was "la más proletaria de toda América" (1975, 160) ("the most working-class emigration of all America"). At the start of the Spanish Republican diaspora, Venezuela and Colombia also received many émigré professionals, but proportionally fewer than Argentina and many fewer than Mexico. While instability in Colombia meant that the number of Spanish refugees in that country gradually diminished, Venezuelan development and economic expansion facilitated resettlement for many professionals and academics in that country.

The presence of the exiled Spaniards of the Spanish Republic in greater or lesser concentrations throughout all Spanish America was conspicuous; indeed there was no single country, however small, that did not provide some home for the émigrés in these difficult times (and this included Portuguese-speaking Brazil). It is also notable, as has been mentioned above, that the majority of these refugees belonged to highly qualified sectors of the population–intellectuals and artists, as well as technicians and skilled workers. Had there not been the tragedy of the Spanish Civil War, this part of the population would never have emigrated on such a massive scale; they were not from the social sector that emigrates for material advancement. Their integration into their new homes was a long process, since Franco's dictatorship was a protracted one (thirty-six years, 1939–1975); but they left an indelible mark in many of their new havens. Intellectuals and artists familiarized themselves with American themes, including the pre-Hispanic origins, and then chose to portray Latin America. Meanwhile technicians and workers contributed daily to the development of industries, agriculture, and mining. To sum up, these émigrés who had arrived in a Latin America of which they were totally ignorant had–after the passage of years–made the continent the dominant subject of their attention and labors, and had established homes in their American host country.

(ii) The Refugees from European Totalitarianism

There are no data available on the number of refugees who arrived in different Latin-American countries escaping from European Nazism and Fascism or, to a lesser extent, Soviet Stalinism (among these latter, the most famous was Leon Trotsky who sought refuge in Mexico, where he was assassinated); nor does there exist specific information on their distribution throughout the continent. What is known is that between 1933 and 1945 almost half a million individuals emigrated from Central European countries, such as Germany, Austria, and Czechoslovakia; of these 94 percent were Jewish refugees. Those from other areas of Europe who were being eradicated and exterminated in their places of origin came as well. Though the statistics vary enormously, more than 100,000 of these were distributed throughout Latin America, not without great difficulty and suffering, particularly in Argentina, Brazil, Chile, Uruguay, and Cuba (see Elkin; Strauss and Röder; Elkin and Merkx; Rojer 1989). What we do know is that these European exiles were intellectuals, politicians (both social democrats and socialists), and militant unionists, as well as technicians, merchants, artisans, and so on. The majority, but not all, were the survivors of ethnic groups that had been persecuted and displaced, particularly Jews, but including Gypsies and other ethnic minorities who had been identified by totalitarian governments as being responsible for the tensions and political and economic crises current in their respective countries. Thus, they were made into scapegoats and used to exacerbate the anti-democratic

and anti-unionist ideological cohesiveness of these governments. This was combined with a strong entrenched xenophobia and racism that served to kindle an ethnic nationalism and mythical national self-definition in terms of racial and historical uniqueness and superiority.

The process of integration for the exiles of European origin into Latin America was not only difficult but also of relatively short duration. From the end of the Second World War and in the wake of the various political upheavals within Latin America, many of these refugees returned to their countries of origin or re-emigrated to other countries (for example, the transfer of some families to Santiago de Chile from Buenos Aires) when re-entry on a social and political level was possible, as occurred with the majority of the refugees from France and Italy. Others re-emigrated to other continental regions that offered more stability and material security, especially the United States, where possible, as in the case of those Jews who had taken refuge in Bolivia (see Behar; Spitzer). Representative of such movements on an intermediate scale might be Cuba, which Ruth Behar (b. 1956) sums up so well through the experience of her family, who had sought asylum on the island–though their ideal destination had been the United States. But the latter had rigorously limited the immigration of Jews and other refugees by passing a restrictive law on immigration in 1924. For this reason when strong Jewish pressure was exerted during the 1930s, the U.S. government in turn urged the Latin-American countries to absorb the thousands of desperate Jewish immigrants who were being systematically prohibited entry into the more northern nation. Many Jewish émigrés initially viewed Cuba as a stopover to the United States, but by the beginning of the 1940s the great majority had remade their lives, and Cuba had become their America. The Jews who stayed in Cuba became Robinson Crusoes–shipwrecked sailors on an island that many years later, after the Revolution of 1959, forced them into a second exile; they would always recall with nostalgia their paradise lost.

Through the experience of her own family, Behar takes us back to the conflicts and contradictions that produced the "deterritorialization" of the exiled and the difficult search for a new "territoriality." In other words she sets out the problem of the redefinition of a new identity in a world radically distinct from the one left behind, in this case with all the resultant ethnic, religious, and linguistic tensions. From this experience new terms arise to represent the amalgam of European Jews within Cuban *criollo* culture or *Jubanos*. (Although the flight of German Nazis to South America after the war is not well documented and the numbers were low, it must nonetheless be mentioned as a factor in the future development of authoritarian regimes in the Southern cone countries.)

Displacements within the Continent

In the same way that international immigration affected social, political, and economic development within the receptor countries, the massive internal displacements occurring within different Latin-American countries during the twentieth century had a decisive impact not only in demographic terms but also with regard to the social and cultural transformations in the relevant countries and particularly the urban environments that received these populations. We have already seen how, in the case of Chile, the political change represented by the election of Arturo Alessandri to the Presidency in 1920 was made possible by, among other constituents, the so-called *chusma dorada*. (See Vial who interprets the rupture in Chile's political regime as occurring from the 1920 presidential election.) This was composed of migrants who had left the farms of the Central Valley and the Mapuche communities of Araucania to work in the coal mines of Lota and Coronel and the saltpeter deposits and copper mines of the Atacama Desert. Others moved to Santiago and started to work there, eventually incorporating themselves into the social movements that emerged under the shadow of the deplorable living conditions in the *conventillos*, the poorest tenement housing of Chilean cities (well described in novels by Guzmán and Lillo).

Something similar, but with very different connotations, occurred in Bolivia with the shifts of indigenous populations (Aymaras and Quechuas) of rural or artisan background to the zinc mines or Pacific saltpeter deposits, especially in Tarapacá and Antofagasta (González 1991). As in other areas of the continent, from the end of the nineteenth century onward, the development of the railways was undoubtedly a contributing factor: The tracks tightly linked different regions of Bolivia, Chile, and Peru to mining areas, like the Patiño Mines, and made the extraction of zinc into the cause for attracting numerous internal migrants. Without a doubt, this constituted the bases for the mobilization of workers that culminated in the Revolution of 1952, with its subsequent agrarian reform and the nationalization of the mines–all of which temporarily interrupted these tremendous internal displacements of the population. However, the return of oligarchic-military governments in the mid 1960s meant a reversal of many of the social gains and the restimulation of internal migration. Now migration also flowed toward the agricultural industries in Santa Cruz and coca cultivation in Chapare, as well as to the service industries and small, microcommercial activities in the principal urban centers of the country (see Rodríguez Ostria and Solares Serrano; Rodríguez Ostria).

It could be said that Juan Domingo Perón's (1895–1974) assumption of power in Argentina in 1945 expressed the political will of the majority of those who had experienced the great demographic shifts from the provinces to Buenos Aires from 1930 onward. A massive mobilization of workers without a solid union tradition, the so-called *descamisados* ["shirtless ones"] occurred, and migrants within the Argentine Republic poured into the capital to provide Perón with massive support on 17 October 1945. The displacement of these *mestizo* and indigenous populations within the country–people described disparagingly in racist terms by the Argentine oligarchy and bourgeoisie as *cabecitas negras* ["little black heads"]–together with the growing influence of the Peronist workers' movement that organized the *descamisados* and collaborated in the repression of independent unions, transformed traditional power relationships and generated a split between privileged traditional society and modern mass society (see Germani 1973; also Murmis and Portaniero). Something similar occurred in Brazil with the Northeast migration to São Paolo and Río de Janeiro in the 1930s and 1940s that made up the social base of the mobilization that led to the constitution of the *Estado Novo* headed by Getulio Vargas (1883–1954) between 1930 and 1945 (well described by Jorge Amado; for historical background, see Skidmore).

Internal migration in Peru took on a new aspect, especially during General Juan Velasco Alvarado's government (1968–1975). In this period the impact of internal migrations (that date back to the 1950s) on the processes of transformation within Peruvian society can be seen clearly. In fact, the massive shift of Andean population that took place between 1960 and 1980 changed the face of Peru. From an urban population in 1961 equivalent to 23 percent of the total, it increased to 65 percent by 1980. Given that Peru had a total population of 20 million in 1984, this would mean that around 13 million were city dwellers, of which more than 5 million lived in Lima. (For an outline of the impact of this migration in the context of the socio-demographic development of Peru, see Matos Mar.) The presence of Andean peoples in Lima and other coastal cities modified the urban cultural patterns and threw into relief aspects that until then had been relegated to the Cordillera Central and its dust-ridden and arid provincial climate. Not only were the peasants dazzled by the possibilities that the cities offered for a better future, but it was through them that the Quechua way of life and worldview arrived in the cities. In short, the new Lima dweller of the 1960s or 1970s was a *mestizo* Quechua speaker who contributed to the creation of a new urban space. The social, economic, and political results had an intense impact and contributed to the formation of a new country. To a certain extent and in its own way, Lima was for these migrants what Buenos Aires had been for the Peronist *cabecitas negras*.

Perhaps it was the writer and anthropologist José María Arguedas (1911–1969) who best plumbed the depths of these issues, particularly in *El zorro de arriba y el zorro de abajo* [1971; *The Fox from Up Above and the Fox from Down Below*, 2000], whose plot is set in the *pueblos jóvenes* [young towns] of the port of Chimbote to the north of Lima. But Arguedas does not limit himself to just depicting these problems, but goes further to become a key interpreter of the effects of agrarian Quechua migrations and the penetration of the indigenous people into the Peruvian urban environment. (For a reconstruction of this trajectory conducted in the depth that the topic deserves, see Escobar.)

The great number of these population movements reflects the frequent and extreme levels of social and political exclusion among broad sectors of Latin-American societies, and reveals the explosive nature of the great social problem that underlies any construction of society here. The willingness of people to break with their rural origins was not only because of a desire to better their immediate material situation (for that did not always improve, but in fact often worsened), but it reflected a longing and striving for a different future. In a certain sense the image of rupture, transfer, and the quest for a new social universe signified the creation of an imaginary whose formulations were well realized in literary descriptions. Mariano Azuela (1873–1952), Ciro Alegría (1909–1967), Jorge Amado (1912–2001), José María Arguedas (1911–1969), Rómulo Gallegos (1884–1969), Federico Gamboa (1864–1939), Nicomedes Guzmán (1914–1964), Baldomero Lillo (1867–1923), Volodia Teitelboim (b. 1916), Jorge Icaza (1906–1978), and Luis Orrego Luco (1866–1948) are only some of the authors who provided deep insight into life in the mines, haciendas, factories, suburban *barrios*, tenements, or neighborhoods; it was here that those who had moved from the rural periphery to the marginalization of urban life lived jammed together, worked, and then rebelled. Gradually they would become the central actors of dramatic social processes or active protagonists in the development of political parties of the nascent Socialist and Communist Left in various countries of the continent.

The Continental Exiles: From the Search for American Identity to the Internationalization of the Exodus

In its transition from traditional oligarchic to modern mass society, social upheavals apart, Latin America endured political convulsions from the time of the Mexican Revolution, and more particularly from the 1930s, that produced shock waves throughout the entire continent. As a result different streams of political exiles would emerge, migrating from one country or other within Latin America itself, as well as, in more recent decades, emigrating abroad. Once more the contingents that made up these diasporas were predominantly composed of highly qualified professionals whose destiny would not have included emigration–had favorable political conditions existed in their country of origin.

While exile had been a feature of independent Latin America from its beginnings, the last fifty years of the twentieth century was a period in which the weight of enforced displacement was practically uninterrupted until the last decade. The rupture provoked by these states of exile, beyond the personal and collective dramas involved, generated new perceptions of nationality versus continentality, as well as Latin-American versus patriotic consciousness. Moreover, it contributed to a re-evaluation from outside the country as well as an attempt to construct a continental awareness. In other words, from rupture and distance, an identity and a plural vision was generated to define a personal identity that left behind the purely endogenous perspective. Thus, what at the start appeared as a break could in the end result in an expansion of experience; it could also mean the loss of the discontinuity of exile and the acquisition of a broader Latin-American identity within a new continental community without borders.

In this way the serious consideration of exile can be seen as a prerequisite for the lucid recuperation of the events that caused the exodus and as a way to understand the collective and universal experience from the basis of the individual. This occurred through the conscious search for those symbols of Latin American identity that could serve to unite and not to divide. This cultural emigration, forced by repressive circumstances, has in the end contributed to the development of a consciousness of Latin-American diversity and noncentrality–in opposition to the pretensions of hegemonic political and cultural nationalisms.

Conceptualization of the contributions that Argentines, Bolivians, Brazilians, Chileans, Cubans, Guatemalans, Mexicans, Salvadorans, and others have made to this continental awareness has been undertaken by sociologists, anthropologists, politicians, writers, and artists from Gabriela Mistral to Rigoberta Menchú (b. 1959), from Pablo Neruda to Victor Raúl Haya de la Torre (1895–1979), from Gino Germani (1911–1979) to Ruy Mauro Marini (1932–1997), and from René Zavaleta (1932–1997) to José Leandro Urbina (b. 1949), to mention only a handful of men and women marked and transformed by the contradictions of territoriality and exile, by the internal divisions at the national level and the recuperation of a language and a cultural imaginary without frontiers.

But such ruptures also point out the emotional necessity of preserving the forms of speech, the cultural daily round, and the values that are shared. An attempt thus is made to fix identities on different planes, permitting the maintenance of stability within rupture, transfer, and socialization in the new environment. This tension between the recognition of a Latin American continental dimension and the maintenance of a local identity lies at the heart of the exiled condition and has been recognized on a creative level with tremendous sensitivity by Salman Rushdie, the *depatriated* exile who was pursued for believing in freedom of speech in the face of religious fundamentalism. Despite the experiences of new lands, exiled writers, immigrants, and the displaced are fundamentally obsessed by the desire to look behind, at the risk of turning into pillars of salt. In the end they cannot create real cities or peoples but rather invisible fictions; they are condemned to dwell in and reflect on what Rushdie calls *imaginary homelands.* (Obviously this is an expression derived from the *imagined communities* addressed by Anderson.) In these intellectual constructions, there is also the risk of transforming exile into a metaphor of the spiritual condition without an explicit relationship to material and social conditions or into an ontological reflection on the borderland of the historical coordinates from which it arises and to which it belongs; in an excess of belonging, this can end up converting the exile into someone who does not belong anywhere but rather everywhere (see Ahmad).

In the case of Latin America the rupture induced by these exiles, immigrations, or displacements, beyond that of the dramas that produced them, also generated new themes and perspectives whose contribution to the development of a continental awareness was fundamental. Thus, in the start of the twenty-first century, the connotations, the symbols of identity, and the literary and linguistic expressions now associated with what it means to be Latin American were the direct result of these experiences of personal reconstruction and the incorporation of the foreign in an undreamed of synthesis that has created new signs of Latin American identity.

The Most Recent Migrations and Displacements

In the last decades of the twentieth century the conditions of poverty, de-ruralization, economic and political instability, and demographic explosion, as well as the general deterioration of living conditions had a direct effect on vast sectors of the population of Latin America, stimulating them to emigrate to neighboring countries with more developed economies (primarily to the United States). These shifts were much more massive than those to Latin America from the end of the nineteenth century to the first postwar period in the twentieth century. For example, the number of Mexicans who currently live in the United States, according to the most up-to-date statistics of the Commission for Binational Studies (Binational Study 1997), is 7.5 million. This total represents nothing less than 8 percent of Mexico's population in 1990 (and for the cultural impact of this development, see Part III of this volume). If we add the Argentine, Brazilian, Chilean, Colombian, Cuban, Dominican, Honduran, Peruvian, Salvadoran, and other Latin American migrants to the United States, this statistic would increase considerably (without counting the millions of Puerto Ricans working there, far from their island). In more reduced proportions, something similar could be said of the Bolivians, Paraguayans, and Peruvians now working in Argentina, the Paraguayans in Brazil, the Bolivians and Peruvians in Chile, the Guatemalans in Mexico, the Dominicans in Puerto Rico, and so on.

This migration also differs from the ones that took place before the first postwar period in terms of the communication between those who were displaced and their country of origin. The transformative effect of transport, mail, telephone, and the internet include not only reducing real distances but also doing so in emotional and cultural terms, allowing stronger and more continuous links to be maintained with the world left behind. Some researchers have begun to use the term *transnational* to describe the displacement of those who cross national frontiers but continue to be connected by strong ties and frequent visits to their communities of origin (see Michael Peter Smith; Duany). In some way this label also underlines the fact that the social spaces of the displaced do not correspond to national borders. Instead, those who come to and go from a socio-geographical space are migrants who—while lacking strongly internalized national frontiers and having both a certain cultural duality and ambivalent relationships, in terms of citizenship with both countries—maintain a broad network of relationships and friendships that extend beyond national frontiers (see Schiller, Basch, and Blanc; Basch, Schiller, and Blanc). Transnational characteristics have only recently begun to be conceptualized and conceived as hybrid socio-cultural systems that cross territorial frontiers and national cultures to create a new transnational regionalization and communities whose imaginary functions on the fringes of the official discourse of a nation-state. (Appadurai 1991, 1990; García Canclini; Flores).

Another aspect of the redefinition of national space is that in a country receiving much immigration, despite the idea that all people are equal, the situation inevitably ends in an internalized confrontation (and even racism). This can be seen in the antagonism between the Peruvian and Bolivian, the Bolivian and the Paraguayan, the Cuban and the Puerto Rican, the Puerto Rican and the Dominican, and so on—until the arrival of the next "other." Throughout this complex process, however, there are constant contrasts and parallels between cultural imaginaries and real transnational migrations. These developments create new social and material universes that refer us to those *imagined communities*, so suggestively explored by Benedict Anderson.

Conclusion

It is clear that whoever wishes to study the cultural history of Latin America on any level cannot do so without taking into account the immigration, political exile, displacement, and internal migrations that have emerged at different times and in different geographical areas over more than a century. These social ruptures take on great significance, not only in terms of their number but also, above all, because of the deep impression they have left on the construction and elaboration of the mixed and complex identities of the cultural communities within the continent. To be able to reconstruct this contemporary Latin American identity beyond that of the specific social groups involved, it is essential to take into account that plurality of experiences accumulated through transplantation and separation, whether voluntary or enforced. In this sense, an essential part of Latin American consciousness is made up of such experiences as fear of persecution, threats, prison, torture, solitary confinement in jail, and clandestine hideouts; it also includes violent and radical breaks with the past (in the case of political exiles), the uncertainty derived from lack of work, the precariousness of finding housing, marginality (in the case of internal migrants), ignorance of the language and local customs, which often result in frequent cultural clashes (in the case of those transferring both within and outside the continent).

The intensity of and tension produced by the processes described here—processes that include encounters and mutual recognition—not only make up the social texture of Latin America but are also an intrinsic part of its culture and identity. National consciousness, inseparable from references to "the other" and to "origin," is the product of a reality that integrates diversity. For this reason it is possible to affirm that anthropological and sociological, but above all literary, reflection at the start of the twenty-first century passes necessarily through the invention of complex interweavings and ruptures resulting from these different currents and energies. In other words the immigrations, exiles, and displacements not only provide demographic or statistical data, but also constitute substantive aspects of what during the twentieth century became the signs of Latin American identity.

Translation by Jessica Johnson

Works Cited

Aguayo, Sergio. 1989. *Los refugiados guatemaltecos en Campeche y Quintana Roo*. Mexico City: El Colegio de México.

Ahmad, Aijez. 1992. *In Theory: Classes, Nations, Literatures*. London: Verso.

Albert, Bill. 1988. *South America and the First World War: The Impact of the War on Brazil, Argentina, Perú and Chile*. Cambridge: Cambridge University Press.

Amado, Jorge. 1963. *Os subterrâneos da liberdade*. 3 vols. São Paulo: Martins.

Anderson, Benedict. 1991. *Imagined Communities: Reflections on the Origin and Spread of Nationalism*. London: Verso.

Appadurai, Arjun. 1990. "Disjuncture and Difference in the Global Cultural Economy." *Public Culture* 2.2:1–24.

———. 1991. "Global Ethnoscapes: Notes and Queries for a Transnational Anthropology." *Recapturing Anthropology: Working in the Present*. Ed. Richard G. Fox. Santa Fe, NM: School of American Research Press. 191–210.

Arguedas, José María. 1971. *El zorro de arriba y el zorro de abajo*. Buenos Aires: Losada.

———. 2000. *The Fox from Up Above and the Fox from Down Below*. Ed. Julio Ortega. Trans. Frances Horning Barraclough. Pittsburgh, PA: University of Pittsburgh Press.

Basave, Agustín. 1992. *México mestizo*. Mexico City: Fondo de Cultura Económica.

Basch, Linda, Nina Glick Schiller, and Cristina Szanton Blanc. 1994. *Nations Unbound: Transnational Projects, Postcolonial Predicaments, and Deterritorialized Nation-States*. New York: Gordon and Breach.

Behar, Ruth. 1996 "América jubana." *Casa de las Américas* 202 (Oct.–Dec.): 128–38. [English translation in *Poetics Today* 16.1 (1995): 151–70.]

Casanovas Codina, Joan. 1998. *Bread or Bullets!: Urban Labor and Spanish Colonialism in Cuba, 1850–1898*. Pittsburgh, PA: The University of Pittsburgh Press.

Derrida, Jacques, and Anne Dufourmantelle. 1997. *De l'Hospitalité*. París: Calmann-Levy.

Duany, Jorge. 1996. "Imagining the Puerto Rican Nation: Recent Works on Cultural Identity." *Latin American Research Review* 31.3:248–67.

Elkin, Judith Laikin. 1980. *Jews of the Latin American Republics*. Chapel Hill: The University of North Carolina Press.

Elkin, Judith Laikin, and Gilbert W. Merkx, eds. 1987. *The Jewish Presence in Latin America*. Boston: Allen & Unwin.

Escobar, Alberto. 1984. *Arguedas o la utopía de la lengua*. Lima: Instituto de Estudios Peruanos.

Flores, Juan. 1993. *Divided Borders: Essays on Puerto Rican Identity*. Houston, TX: Arte Público.

García Canclini, Néstor. 1990. *Culturas híbridas: estrategias para entrar y salir de la modernidad*. Mexico City: Grijalbo.

Germani, Gino. 1962. *Política y sociedad en una época de transición: de la sociedad tradicional a la sociedad de masas*. Buenos Aires. Paidos.

——. 1973. "El surgimiento del peronismo: el rol de los obreros y de los migrantes internos." *Desarrollo Económico* 13.51 (Oct.–Dec.): 435–88.

González, Sergio. 1991. *Hombres y mujeres de la Pampa: Tarapacá en el ciclo del salitre*. Iquique: Ediciones Especiales Camanchaca.

Guzmán, Nicomedes. 1943. *La sangre y la esperanza*. Santiago de Chile: Editorial Nascimiento.

LeBot, Yvon. 1992. *La guerre en terre maya: Communauté, violence et modernité au Guatemala*. Paris: Karthala Éditeur.

Lida, Clara E. 1988. *La Casa de España en México*. Mexico City: El Colegio de México.

——. 1995. "Lázaro Cárdenas y la Guerra Civil española." *Claves de la razón práctica*. Madrid (Nov): 66–72.

Lillo, Baldomero. 1904. *Sub-terra*. Santiago de Chile: Editorial Nascimiento.

Llorens, Vicente. 1975. *Memorias de una emigración. Santo Domingo: 1939–1945*. Barcelona: Ariel.

——. 1976. *La emigración republicana de 1939*. Vol. 1. *El exilio español de 1939*. Ed. José Luis Abellán. Madrid: Taurus.

Malagón, Javier. 1991. "El exilio en Santo Domingo (1939–1946)." *El exilio de las Españas de 1939 en las Américas*. Ed. José María Naharro-Calderón. Barcelona: Anthropos. 154–77.

Matesanz, José Antonio. 1982. "La dinámica del exilio." *El exilio español en México: 1939–1982*. Mexico City: Fondo de Cultura Económica. 163–75.

——. 1995. "México ante la Guerra Civil española, 1936–1939." Diss. El Colegio de México, Centro de Estudios Históricos.

Matos Mar, José. 1984. *Desborde popular y crisis del Estado*. Lima: Instituto de Estudios Peruanos.

Méndez, Jesús. 1985. "Impact of Spanish Republican Exiles on Intellectual Life in Argentina." *SECOLAS Annals. Journal of the Southeastern Council on Latin American Studies* (March): 77–95.

Molina Enríquez, Andrés. 1978. *Los grandes problemas nacionales*. Mexico City: Editorial Era.

Murmis, Miguel, and Juan Carlos Portantiero. 1971. *Estudios sobre el peronismo*. Buenos Aires: Siglo XXI.

Naranjo Orovio, Consuelo, and Armando García González. 1996. *Racismo e inmigración en Cuba en el siglo XIX*. Aranjuez: Doce Calles.

Neruda, Pablo. 1974. *Confieso que he vivido: memorias*. Buenos Aires: Editorial Losada.

——. 1977. *Memoirs*. Trans. Hardie St. Martin. New York: Farrar, Straus and Giroux.

Pérez Rosales, Vicente. 1993 [1853]. *Recuerdos del pasado, 1814–1860*. Madrid: Ediciones de Cultura Hispánica.

Pla Brugat, Dolores. 1985. *Los niños de Morelia: un estudio sobre los primeros refugiados españoles en México*. Mexico City: Instituto Nacional de Antropología e Historia.

A Report of the Binational Study on Migration between Mexico and the United States. 1997. Commission on Immigration Reform, United States Secretaría de Relaciones Exteriores, Mexico.

Rodríguez Ostria, Gustavo. 1991. *El socavón y el sindicato: ensayos históricos sobre los trabajadores mineros, siglos XIX–XX*. La Paz: ildis (Instituto Latinoamericano de Investigaciones Sociales).

——, and Humberto Solares Serrano. 1990. *Sociedad oligárquica, chicha y cultura popular*. Cochabamba: Serrano.

Rojer, Olga Elaine. 1989. *Exile in Argentina, 1933–1945: A Historical and Literary Introduction*. Nueva York: Peter Lang.

Rushdie, Salman. 1991. "Imaginary Homelands." *Imaginary Homelands: Essays and Criticism 1981–1991*. New York: Viking. 7–21

Sánchez-Albornoz, Nicolás. 1994 [1973]. *La población de América Latina: desde los tiempos precolombinos al año 2025*. Madrid: Alianza.

Schiller, Nina Glick, Linda Basch, and Cristina Szanton Blanc, eds. 1992. *Towards a Transnational Perspective on Migration: Race, Class, Ethnicity, and Nationalism Reconsidered*. New York: New York Academy of Sciences.

Skidmore, Thomas. 1967. *Politics in Brazil: 1930–1964*. New York: Oxford University Press.

Smith, Michael Peter. 1994. "Can You Imagine? Transnational Migration and the Globalization of Grassroots Politics." *Social Text* 39: 15–34.

Solberg, Carl. 1970. *Immigration and Nationalism in Argentina and Chile 1890–1914*. Austin: University of Texas Press.

Solórzano, Viuda de Cárdenas, Amalia (1982): "Aquellos niños. Entrevista con Amalia Solórzano Viuda de Cárdenas." *El exilio español en México: 1939–1982*. Mexico City: Fondo de Cultura Económica. 891–95.

Spitzer, Leo. 1998. *Hotel Bolivia: The Culture of Memory in a Refugee from Nazism*. New York: Hill and Wang.

Strauss, Herbert A., and Werner Röder, eds. 1983. *International Biographical Dictionary of Central European Emigrés, 1933–1945*. Vol. 2. Munich and New York: K. G. Saur.

Teitelboim, Volodia. 1984. *Neruda*. Santiago: BAT.

——. 1991. *Gabriela Mistral Pública y Secreta: truenos y silencios en la vida del primer Nobel latinoamericano*. Santiago: BAT.

Vanger, Milton I. 1963. *José Batlle y Ordoñez of Uruguay, the Creator of his Times, 1902–1907*. Cambridge, MA: Harvard University Press.

——. 1980. *The Model Country: José Batlle y Ordoñez of Uruguay, 1907–1915*. Hanover, N.H.: Brandeis University Press–University Press of New England.

Vial, Gonzalo. 1980. *Historia de Chile (1891–1973)*. Vol. 1. Santiago: Editorial Santillana del Pacífico.

Walter, Richard J. 1993. *Politics and Urban Growth in Buenos Aires (1910–1942)*. Austin: The University of Texas Press.

Zapata, Francisco. 1990. *Ideología y política en América Latina*. Mexico City: El Colegio de México.

CHAPTER 43

EXILE IN THE NARRATIVE OF THE SPANISH AMERICAN DIASPORA IN THE TWENTIETH CENTURY

Ivan Almeida and Cristina Parodi

Introduction

This essay looks into some of the most important approaches for the historical study of literature of exile in the twentieth century. This project does not involve an encyclopedic panorama nor does it merely exhibit a simple gallery of portraits or impose rigid criteria of classification. Above all, our plan is to suggest a semiotic and epistemological exploration of the problem of literature of exile, and we trust that to the extent that it furthers the elucidation of its object, we will reevaluate some of our own presuppositions. Literature of exile is considered in this study as literature produced by Latin American writers who are physically displaced from what is pragmatically defined as their "country of origin." This criterion excludes consideration of the so-called "inner exile," despite the great pertinence of such a category in certain countries; in contrast, it does include the diaspora provoked by other than political reasons. The selection of authors and texts we examine does not depend on criteria of either social status or a perceived requirement of geographical parity, but rather of a certain aesthetic representative function in the history of literary culture. (Given our linguistic competence, this study is limited to narrative literature written in Spanish.)

Literature and its historical representation are not determined by empirical causality. For this reason, inquiry into the causes of exile literature could be considered as arbitrary or sterile. Another difficulty arises with the choice of an acceptable definition of exile that is workable in the context of literary studies. On the one hand, if we take the narrow definition of "exiled for political reasons," we unduly restrict the phenomenon, thereby obscuring all attempts to discuss it within a larger context. Taking this definition would be tantamount to entrusting dictators with the task of establishing literary guidelines and typologies, for in this case political action would preempt all other considerations. Moreover, it would make literature a phenomenon to study *per causas,* and it would also exclude representative writers of the literature of exile, such as Cortázar, who was said to have left Argentina because of the difficulties he had hearing the quartets of Alban Berg in peace. In other words, human motivation cannot be studied according to the laws of empirical causality. A more fruitful approach might be to consider exile in terms only of departure—for sufficient reasons, whatever they may be. On the other hand, if one assumes a too broad definition of exile, the category would be "metaphorized" to the point of triviality through an excess of generality. Covering this topic would then demand covering the entire history of literature. Writers from all regions have been on the move more often than not. It is nevertheless not to be doubted that the figure of the "exile" is an essential ingredient of all approximations to understanding Latin American literature and that such a figure is to a certain extent linked to the phenomenon of diaspora.

The word "figure" here has a meaning derived from the Kantian notion of "schema" or the point of union between experience and concept. In this case, it is an attempt to organize what could relate a text to an experience in the quest for what Wittgenstein called "a family resemblance." The schema of exile conceived as a "family resemblance" will determine common features that, once conceptualized, could be applied to human beings, texts, literary themes, linguistic options, and aesthetics. In order to give a historical account of this cultural context, we have turned to the interaction of two classes of cognitive schema: The prototype and the paradigm. The concept of prototype acts to select the area of relevance, whereas that of paradigm is applied to the conceptualization of the area so determined.

The Determination of the Prototype

The modern theory of prototypes, particularly that proposed by Eleanor Rosch, allows the cognitive sciences to take up ideas without the need to resort to abstract definitions. One tries to select an indisputable "case" of the phenomenon under study and, as an extreme antithesis, an "anti-case" to then establish a series of concentric circles that proceed from the totally pertinent to the nonpertinent through gradations and approximations. This epistemological approach permits a pragmatic approximation to the phenomenon being studied. One begins by trying to bring together all that could act as a symptom of the selected prototype within the pragmatic model and then proceed in a more globalizing way, deriving or refining these characteristics through comparison with other cases. For instance, Julio Cortázar (1914–1984) could be put forward as a central prototype of the literature of exile, not only because he is among those writers to have spent the longest periods outside his place of origin and his prime linguistic area, but also because he made exile one of his themes; he developed his own theories on the subject and to a certain extent he even gave it aesthetic expression.

As an extreme antithesis (the "anti-case") an author such as José María Arguedas (1911–1969) could be selected because he does not seem to correspond, either in his themes or his personal situation, to a lifestyle or an aesthetic of exile. Between these two extremes can be placed cases that are more or less attenuated. Borges (1899–1986), for example, is an atypical case deserving our consideration. Far from being a political exile, he nevertheless spent, according to Edna Aizenberg, what were the most "important" years in terms of his entire system of thought and aesthetics, his adolescence, in Geneva. Carlos Fuentes (b. 1928) is another atypical but less pertinent case whose presence abroad—as a diplomat's son—does not necessarily carry with it the ingredients of exile.

To establish an idea of the exiled writer without reference to politics is a difficult task because of the risk of vagueness. Taking the most generalized viewpoint, if narration implies the creation of new worlds, all fiction therefore becomes an act of exile and implies an experience of being uprooted: "Deracination, exile, and alienation in varying forms are the conditions of existence for the modern writer the world over" (Gurr 14). There are, moreover, experiences of exile that do not depend on physical displacement outside one's country. While it is true that the particular political situation of Latin America during the twentieth century confronts its writers with examples of repression, torture, proscription, and exile, the phenomenon of artistic diaspora and its consequent production of a literature of exile obey many varied etiologies. Martin Tucker, for example, proposes a good dozen categories of exile: Accidental exile; as a result of crime; cultural exile; for diplomatic, medical, or professional reasons; because of expatriation; for historical or religious reasons; for legal reasons or requirements; social exile; political exile; problematic exile; sexual exile; etc. (789–810). A more simple division is provided by Mary McCarthy, who differentiates between "voluntary expatriates" and "forced exiles." Taking up this distinction, Andrew Gurr suggests a literary version of both types, according to which the voluntary expatriates would be fundamentally poets and the forced exiles novelists (19). But such a correspondence is not only simplistic it is also impossible to apply to Latin American writers.

On the other hand, it must be pointed out that because of its historical and linguistic heterogeneity, all Latin American literature, even that produced by writers who have not moved from their native soil, provides accounts of the conditions of exile: "America," writes Héctor A. Murena, "está integrada por desterrados y es destierro y todo desterrado sabe profundamente que para poder vivir debe acabar con el pasado, debe borrar los recuerdos de este mundo al que le está vedado el retorno, porque de lo contrario queda suspendido de ellos y no acierta a vivir" (24) ["is made up of exiles and is itself exile, and as every exile knows on a deeper level, to be able to survive one must put an end to the past, must wipe out the memories of that world to which it is forbidden to return, because otherwise the exiled individual remains trapped by his or her memories and cannot find a way to remake his or her life"]. A quite different view is that of Borges, who claims that every Latin American is a European in exile, or that of Cortázar, for whom "ser argentino es estar lejos" (1968, 198) ["to be Argentine is to be far from Argentina"]:

> Un viajero del continente americano–escribe Jorge Andrade–que como yo se había sentado en silencio en las gradas de Epidauro, se preguntaba perplejo por qué la tragedia de Sófocles que se representaba ante sus ojos lo emocionaba mucho más que los testimonios más evolucionados de las culturas indoamericanas. La respuesta es sencilla: por éstas sentía el aprecio intelectual del visitante extranjero respetuoso; por el teatro de Epidauro y por Sófocles experimentaba el apasionamiento del viajero que tras muchos años vuelve a casa siguiendo la huella de sus antepasados. (116)

> A traveler from the American continent–wrote Jorge Andrade– who, like me, has sat in silence on the tiers at Epidauros, asked himself, perplexed, why the tragedy of Sophocles performed in front of his eyes moved him far more that the more evolved testimonies of Indo-American cultures. The answer is simple: for the latter he felt the intellectual appreciation of the respectful foreign visitor; for the theater at Epidauros and for Sophocles he experienced the passionate enthusiasm of the traveler who after many years returns home following the footsteps of his ancestors.

Faced with such a panorama, the prototype presented here requires that we pass over the motives for exile, be they personal or political. In other words, we shall only discuss here the case of writers who, for whatever motive, have spent a long period outside their own country (not only their region). In the work of such writers, there is a constant play to maintain equilibrium between what in Cortázar's *Rayuela* [1963; *Hopscotch*, 1966] are called *el lado de acá* ("this side") and *el lado de allá* ("that side"), although it is no easy matter to specify which of the two corresponds to the concept of country.

This phenomenon of seeking to find a balance is a permanent aspect of exile literature, independent of the specific theme developed. And even within temporary stability acquired in exile, a new point of instability emerges: Writers who have managed to establish themselves in the heart of a new community gradually lose contact with their original points of reference and with it the particular characteristics that defined their identity. The need to reposition themselves creates new tensions that are at times artificial. It is these tensions that generate the so-called "literature of exile." Sometimes the *allá* (over there, the place of origin) is recovered as a new element of individuation that replaces exile and the artists acquire "exotic" features (of the type exemplified by "An American in Paris") that were irrelevant to them up to that point; in other words he or she becomes a type. On other occasions, the place of origin carries on only as a reference point and their artistic work begins to acquire new "imported" values from the new community. Even so, in the majority of cases, despite this enthusiasm for new points of reference, exile is adopted as a style, a theme, and literary form. The relationship between the *el lado de allá* (the other side, place of origin) and *el lado de acá* (this side, place of exile) involves less of a reference to a native land then a literary dynamic. María Zambrano (1904–1991) describes her own exiled condition thus:

> De destierro en destierro, en cada uno de ellos el exilado va muriendo, desposeyéndose, desenraizándose. Y así se encamina, se reitera su salida del lugar inicial, de su patria y de cada posible patria, dejándose a veces la capa al huir de la seducción de una patria que se le ofrece, corriendo delante de su sombra tentadora; entonces inevitablemente es acusado de eso, de irse, de irse sin tener ni tan siquiera adónde. Pues de lo que huye el prometido al exilio, marcado ya por él desde antes, es de un dónde, de un lugar que sea el suyo. (37–38)

> From exile to exile, in each, one is dying, dispossessing oneself, uprooting oneself. And thus one sets out, repeating the departure from the first place, from one's own country and from every other possible country, at times leaving behind personal property to flee from the seduction of a country offering such enticements, fleeing before its tempting shadow; the exile is then inevitably accused of this, of just leaving, of leaving without having anywhere else to go. What the exile seeks, which is always already there, is a place that might become one's own.

George Steiner calls this condition of the exiled writer "unhousedness" (viii); little by little, artistic work becomes the only place of "residence on the earth" for writers; it becomes their house, or rather ship, since like sailors, they find there the place equidistant from all nostalgias. From there, the exile creates a literature that, independently of the more or less conservative thematics of *patria* (whether real or virtual), acquires a certain decentralized form that is the almost universal characteristic of works of the diaspora. The time and space of the action, the time and space of the phrase, the time and space of the work itself are all dislocated and thus spread the contagion of exile to the very experience of reading.

Julio Cortázar as a Prototype

Initially an "aesthetic" exile, Cortázar began to take on the role of political exile when some of his works were prohibited in Argentina. Before considering his particular way of representing exile, it might be useful to review briefly his own statements on political exile in relation to his literary work. In his extensive theorizing of exile, Cortázar ceaselessly took his positive valuation of the exiled condition to the level of paradox: "Haré del disvalor del exilio un valor de combate" (1994a, 168) [I will take the negativity of exile and make it into the valor of combat]. Exile is a "siniestra beca" [perverse scholarship] awarded by dictators that must be taken advantage of to refine one's writing:

> El hecho está ahí: nos han expulsado de nuestras patrias. ¿Por qué colocarnos en su tesitura y considerar esa expulsión como una desgracia que sólo negativamente puede determinar nuestras reacciones? ¿Por qué insistir cotidianamente en artículos y en tribunas sobre nuestra condición de exiliados, subrayándola casi siempre en lo que tiene de más penoso, que es precisamente lo que buscan aquellos que nos cierran las puertas del país? Exiliados, sí. Punto. Ahora hay otras cosas que escribir y que hacer, como escritores exiliados, desde luego, pero con el acento en escritores. Porque nuestra verdadera eficacia está en sacar el máximo partido del exilio, aprovechar a fondo esas siniestras becas, abrir y enriquecer el horizonte mental para que cuando converja otra vez sobre lo nuestro lo haga con mayor lucidez y alcance. (169)

> The fact is there: they have expelled us from our countries. Why should we assume their mind set and consider expulsion as a disgrace that can only negatively determine our reactions? Why insist daily in articles and from public platforms on our condition as exiles, almost always emphasizing what is most unpleasant, which is precisely what they sought when they closed the doors of our country against us? Exiled, yes. Full stop. Now there are other things to write about and do, as exiled writers, of course, but with the accent on writers. Because our true efficacy lies in squeezing the maximum benefit from exile, taking the utmost advantage of these perverse scholarships to open and enrich the mental horizon so that when it once again converges with our own it does so with greater lucidity and scope.

The writer should respond to the bitterness of exile with an authentic literature that broadens the ontological framework, prepares the future, and mocks the reach of weapons because "la grande y hermosa paradoja está en que cuanto más literaria es la literatura, si puedo decirlo así, más histórica y más operante se vuelve" (1994e, 238) ["the great and beautiful paradox is that the more literature is literary, if I can put it this way, the more historical and the more operative it becomes"]. Cortázar counterpointed the liberating force of creative literature with the sterility of endless testimony of one's plight that can transform the writer into a scribe of bitterness:

> Hasta hoy no me ha sido dado leer muchos poemas, cuentos o novelas de exiliados latinoamericanos en los que la condición que los determina, esa condición específica que es el exilio, sea objeto de una crítica interna que la anule como disvalor y la proyecte a un campo positivo. Se parte casi siempre de lo negativo (desde la deploración hasta el grito de rebeldía que puede surgir de ella), y apoyándose en ese mal trampolín que es un disvalor se intenta el salto hacia adelante: la recuperación de lo perdido, la derrota del enemigo y el retorno a una patria libre de déspotas y de verdugos. Personalmente, y sabiendo que estoy en el peligroso filo de una paradoja, no creo que esta actitud con respecto al exilio dé los resultados que podría alcanzar desde otra óptica, en apariencia irracional pero que responde, si se la mira de cerca, a una *toma de realidad* perfectamente válida. Quienes exilian a los intelectuales

consideran que su acto es positivo, puesto que tiene por objeto eliminar al adversario. ¿Y si los exiliados optaran también por considerar como positivo ese exilio? No estoy haciendo una broma de mal gusto, porque sé que me muevo en un territorio de heridas abiertas y de irrestañables llantos. Pero sí apelo a una distanciación expresa, apoyada en esas fuerzas interiores que tantas veces han salvado al hombre del aniquilamiento total, y que se manifiestan entre otras formas a través del sentido del humor, ese humor que a lo largo de la historia de la humanidad ha servido para vehicular ideas y praxis que sin él parecerían locura o delirio. (1994a, 167)

> To date I have not read many poems, short stories or novels by Latin American exiles in which the condition that determines them, the specific condition of exile, might be the object of an internal critique that annuls this condition as valueless and projects it as a positive field of operations. They almost always begin from a negative viewpoint (moving from deploring exile to the shout of rebellion that can burst forth from it) and putting themselves onto this bad trampoline, which is without value, they try to make a leap forward: to recover what was lost, to defeat their enemy, and to return to a country free of despots and torturers. Personally, and knowing that I am on the dangerous edge of a paradox, I do not believe that this attitude with respect to exile provides the results that could be achieved from taking another viewpoint, apparently irrational but which responds, if one observes it closely, to a positive perspective on reality that is perfectly valid. Those responsible for exiling intellectuals consider that their act is positive, given that their object is to eliminate the adversary. And what if the exiles also opt to consider that exile as positive? I am not making a joke in bad taste, because I know that I operate in a territory of open wounds and unquenchable tears. But I am calling for a definite distancing, backed up by these internal strengths that so often have saved humanity from total annihilation and that manifest, among other ways, through a sense of humor, that humor that throughout humanity's long history has served to communicate ideas and praxis that without it would seem madness or delirium.

It is clear, then, that Cortázar's position is that of confronting exile in literature. Ironically, doing so transgresses the implicitly political meaning of the title of his story "The Pursuer" to give it the meaning of a musician who pursues other rhythms.

The hero of his short story "El perseguidor" ["The Pursuer"] is Johnny Carter, saxophonist, ontological jazz musician who places *tempo* over *time*: "Esto lo estoy tocando mañana" (227) [This I am playing tomorrow]. Salvation is through *swing*, through oscillation. While tyrants establish frontiers, the poet pursues a reality made of porous space, of reversible, condensable, expandable time. Johnny discovers that in the minute-and-a-half that separates two stations of the subway he can think of something that takes more than fifteen minutes to tell and takes several days to live: *tempo*:

> . . . si vos tenés un tiempo de cuatro por cuatro, el músico de jazz adelanta o atrasa instintivamente esos tiempos, que según el metrónomo deberían ser iguales (excelente definición de lo liso y lo estriado). Y entonces, una melodía trivial, cantada tal como fue compuesta, con sus tiempos bien marcados, es atrapada de inmediato por el músico de jazz con una modificación del ritmo, con la introducción de ese swing que crea una tensión . . . . Y mutatis mutandis, eso es lo que siempre he tratado de hacer en mis cuentos. (Prego 169–70)

> . . . if you have a four four tempo, the jazz musician moves these tempos forward and back instinctively that according to the metronome should be equal (excellent definition of the smooth and rough). And then, a trivial melody, a song just as it was composed, with its tempos clearly marked, is immediately

trapped by the jazz musician in a modification of rhythm with the introduction of this swing which creates a tension . . . . And *mutatis mutandis,* this is what I have always tried to do in my stories.

The jazz of which Cortázar speaks is a happily irreverent literary theory, as well as an ontology, comprising short cuts and prolongations. Where others put ladders and lifts, Cortázar places a plank between two buildings and by this plank his characters circulate between two worlds (*Rayuela*). Another extreme, the highway that others use to go between two cities, is transformed by Cortázar into a waiting room: "Los pasajes y las galerías han sido mi patria secreta desde siempre" (1994c, 590) ["Passages and galleries have always been my secret homeland"].

One of these galleries is used, literally, to change the sky. "El otro cielo" is perhaps the story in which Cortázar most eloquently creates his aesthetic of oscillation. The imposing building of the Bourse, the French Commercial Stock Exchange, is located in the center of Paris. A few steps from this monument to realism is a series of covered arcades where love and fantasy can flow freely, the most celebrated and evocative being the Galérie Vivienne. For the Argentine in Paris, this configuration evokes that of the Buenos Aires of his youth; thus thanks to a secret urban complicity, there is, near the Bolsa de Comercio, another covered arcade, the Pasaje Güemes. Why, then, not parody reality and make these two galleries connect? The individual who will make the crossing can be an employee of either stock exchange. A young man enters the Pasaje Güemes in Buenos Aires; he is postponing marriage with his girlfriend Irma by reliving erotic fantasies he experienced in the Pasaje in 1928 when he was about to leave his childhood behind. It is now the closing year of the Second World War, prior to the Perón regime. The man who leaves from the Galérie Vivienne is an Argentine in Paris who has preserved as remembrances of his country only a silver maté gourd and an almanac; he seeks to live out his sexual fantasies with the prostitute Josiane. But it is now around 1870, and the Prussian invasion threatens Paris. The two periods and the two firmaments are connected by a "stucco sky," that of the low roofs of the arcades. The title of the story, "El otro cielo" is an approximate translation of "Lautréamont," the pseudonym of Isidore Ducasse, *l'autre mont* (the other ascent), whose *Chants de Maldoror* act as an inspiration and provide the epigraphs to the story. On the other hand, redundant details allow us to identify Ducasse himself in the personality of the "South American" of the Galérie Vivienne; he is the inverted double of Cortázar, a European born in South America (who liked to call himself *el montevideano* [the man from Montevideo]), just as Cortázar was a South American born in Europe. The tale is presented in part as a logical but fantastic mechanism to resolve the issue of exile. The man of Lautréamont's Galérie Vivienne will be crossed with the image of the mysterious "South American." There will be periods of delay and absence on both sides of the gallery; history will intervene in both periods. Cortázar says he has discovered, thanks to reading Villers de l'Isle Adam, that a few steps from the hotel where Ducasse died there is a street that preserves five pavement stones larger than the rest; on these the guillotine once stood. There is to be a capital execution: The man to be sentenced will be of confused identity and in the description of his death is recapitulated that of many other deaths the text only mentions. In "El otro cielo," however, nothing happens, or almost nothing. The only thing that happens is one death, which is in turn many, and a constant interplay of nonidentification, transfer, syncopation, and *jazz.*

Cortázar conceived the literature of exile as a step toward cosmopolitanism; extraterritoriality is seen as an ontological uprooting. The poet who is capable of continuing to dream nevertheless experiences exile, a rupture with his past. For Cortázar, this extreme ontologization of the uprooting that in exile is not a gesture of political rejection. On the contrary: "nada me parece más revolucionario—escribe—que enriquecer por todos los medios posibles la noción de realidad en el ánimo del lector de novelas o de cuentos" (1994b, 123) ["nothing seems to me more revolutionary than to enrich through all possible means the notion of reality in the soul of the reader of novels or stories"]. In his celebrated polemic with Oscar Collazos on the political commitment of the writer, Cortázar clearly defines his point of view, stating that "la novela revolucionaria no es solamente la que tiene un 'contenido' revolucionario sino la que procura revolucionar la novela misma, la forma novela y para ello utiliza las armas de la hipótesis de trabajo, la conjetura, la trama pluridimensional, la fractura del lenguaje" (1987, 134) ["the revolutionary novel is not only that which has a revolutionary 'content' but also that which succeeds in revolutionizing the novel itself, the novel form, and for this uses the weapons of hypothesis, conjecture, multi-dimensional plot and fragmented language"]. This revision of what is a revolutionary novel is also a way of fighting against the exiles. The epigraphs to the two parts of *Rayuela* reveal to what extent one is dealing with a variation on the theme of exile: "Rien ne vous tue un homme comme d'être obligé de représenter un pays" (Vaché 1970, 44) ["Nothing kills a man so much as having to be a representative of a country" (1993, 35)]; "Il faut voyager loin en aimant sa maison" (Apollinaire 875) ["One must travel a long way in order to love one's home"]. Cortazar's aesthetic (exemplified by jazz improvisation), Apollinaire's verse: "Il faut voyager loin" and "en aimant sa maison" is the free movement between time and space. "*Rayuela* ha sabido destruir un espacio para construir un espacio, decapitar el tiempo para que el tiempo salga con otra cabeza. Es una novela muy americana que no depende de un espacio tiempo americano" (Lezama Lima 193) ["*Rayuela* knew how to destroy a space to construct a space, decapitate time so that time emerges with another head. It is a very American novel that does not depend on an American space time"].

Un tal Lucas will serve to illustrate the salvation through *jazz* that Cortázar preaches and practices, a salvation through humor: "El exilio y la tristeza van siempre de la mano, pero con la otra mano busquemos el humor: él nos ayudará a neutralizar la nostalgia y la desesperación. Las dictaduras latinoamericanas no tienen escritores sino escribas: no nos convirtamos nosotros en escribas de la amargura, del resentimiento o de la melancolía . . ." (1994a, 169) ["Exile and sadness always hold hands, but with the other hand we can search for humor; it will help us to neutralize nostalgia and desperation. Latin American dictatorships do not have writers but rather scribes; do not let us be converted into scribes of bitterness, resentment or melancholy . . ."]. The features of the aesthetic of exile offered by the study of Cortázar's work can be refined through the consideration of other authors in the attempt at classification that follows.

Paradigms

Paradigms provide operational instruments that allow a certain serialization, at least provisional, of the phenomenon under study. Given that the present essay is exclusively dedicated to narrative literature, the construction of paradigms perhaps ought to obey an *ad hoc* narrative schematization. In his celebrated essay "Der Erzähler" ("The Storyteller"), Walter Benjamin suggests *travelers* and *old people* as prototypes of the narrator. One group narrates what does not happen *here* and the other what is not happening *now*. This means that narration always has its origin (whether real or fictitious) in a displacement; the narrator is always displaced in time and space. In a certain way a bit of exile is inherent in the possibility itself of narrative. This first axis of displacement (spatial *versus* temporal) can be conjugated with another in which the pertinent aspect is the axiology given to the poles of the displacement: overvaluation of what has been left behind *versus* overvaluation of what has been acquired.

The ordering of the space-time axis and the one based on axiology reveals the first two pairs of categories of the representation of exile. The overvaluation of what is lost produces both nostalgic literature, which integrates and restores what happened *there*, and *ethnologist literature*, which integrates and restores what had happened *before*. Both tendencies give a priority to politics; essentially conservative, they crystallize in the theme of "national identity." Conversely the overvaluation of what is acquired produces a *literature of adoption* that integrates and restores the situation of the new arrival *here* (in general, Europe), and a *literature of innovation* that directs a critical gaze toward tradition is open to new forms of thinking and writing. These two last tendencies give a priority to the aesthetic; essentially progressive, they lead to the theme of "extraterritoriality." We can reduce these alternatives to two paradigms: *nostalgia* and *extraterritoriality*. Both present themselves in the themes as well as in the forms of writing. It would be worthwhile, in the case of the Latin American narrative of the twentieth century, to add to these two paradigms another two, more specific to the phenomenon under study: the paradigm of *nomadism*, which involves an almost autobiographical thematization of exile, and the paradigm of *double displacement*, which is more an issue of literary reception.

The examination of some exemplary cases will show to what extent these paradigms serve to help us understand the exceptions. For example, the most localist of novels will not necessarily imply an aesthetic of nostalgia. The response to Kipling's aggressive question "What should they know of England, who only England know?" (221) could be Joyce's answer, almost anticipating Borges: "For myself, I always write about Dublin, because if I can get to the heart of Dublin I can get to the heart of all the cities of the world. In the particular is contained the universal" (in Gurr 21). The same reaction provoked Mario Vargas Llosa's (b. 1936) question as to whether *Los cuadernos de Don Rigoberto* [1997; *The Notebooks of Don Rigoberto*, 1998] could be considered as a Latin American novel because it was set in Peru:

> Escogí Lima porque es el terreno que más conozco. Yo creo que hablar de novela latinoamericana, mexicana o peruana es una reducción que de alguna manera niega la esencia de la literatura, que es la universalidad. Una novela escrita por un peruano o por un latinoamericano sí, de alguna manera, refleja ese matiz que representa a Cuba, a América Latina. Pero si una novela es sólo eso, creo que es una novela frustrada, fracasada. Una buena novela debe ser legible por lectores de cualquier cultura, de cualquier constelación, sin justificaciones geográficas. Si hubiera justificaciones geográficas, para mí, esa novela no sería una obra de arte. (Peralta 20)

I chose Lima because it is the territory I know best. I believe that to speak of the Latin American, Mexican or Peruvian novel is a reduction that in some way denies the essence of literature, which is universality. A novel written by a Peruvian or a Latin American in some way does reflect this nuance that represents Cuba or Latin America. But if a novel is just that, I consider it to be a frustrated, failed novel. A good novel should be readable by readers of any culture, any constellation, without geographical justifications. If there are geographical justifications, for me that novel is not a work of art.

The Paradigm of Nostalgia

The nostalgic representation of exile, exalting the values of "national identity," has perhaps its most illustrious example in the Psalms of the Jewish diaspora:

> By the rivers of Babylon, we sat down and wept as we remembered Zion. On the willow trees there we hung up our lyres, for there those who had carried us captive asked us to sing them a song, our captors called on us to be joyful: 'Sing us one of the songs of Zion.' How could we sing the Lord's song in a foreign land? If I forget you, Jerusalem, may my right hand wither away; let my tongue cling to the roof of my mouth if I do not remember you, if I do not set Jerusalem above my chief joy. (Bible, Psalm 137:1–6)

And the following words by the Cuban Reinaldo Arenas (1943–1990) belong to the same vein of melancholy:

> El universo perdido, aquel país que era nuestro paraíso, aunque en la realidad fuese un infierno, lo volvemos a recuperar una vez que estamos lejos de él. Lo mitificamos, lo reconstruimos, y lo recreamos a través de la palabra. Esa visión totalizadora de una realidad sólo la tenemos cuando la podemos observar desde lejos. . . . Un exiliado es, en el mejor de los casos, una sombra. Cuando yo me paseo por el malecón de Cádiz o visito el Museo del Prado, hay dos personas: una sombra que está paseando o visitando esos lugares, y otra persona que fui yo, que se quedó en Cuba y que me está llamando, reclamando. Un exiliado nunca podrá recuperar su total autenticidad. Imposible. Estamos hechos de un conjunto de connotaciones y referencias a una época y a un país, el nuestro, con las cuales nos vamos a seguir relacionando a través de la memoria. Un exiliado es una persona que vive en las sombras; su verdadera luz está en la patria que dejó. (Espinosa 61)

We will recover that lost universe, that country that was our paradise, even though in reality it was an inferno, once we are far from it. We mythify it, rebuild it, and recreate it in words. We only have that total vision of a reality when we can observe it from a distance . . . . An exile is at best only a shadow. When I walk along the harbor at Cadiz or visit the Prado Museum there are two people, a shadow that is sightseeing or visiting these places, and another person that I once was who remained in Cuba and is calling, reclaiming me. An exile never will be able to recover his authenticity completely. Impossible. We are composed of a complex of connotations and references to a period and a country, ours, to which we will continue to relate through memory. An exile is a person who lives in the shadows; his true light remains in the country he left behind.

In Latin America, the paradigm of nostalgia has produced a few novels and many testimonial essays. Generally, the former group combines the theme of nostalgia with a challenge to existing narrative forms. Guillermo Cabrera Infante (b. 1929) is an exemplary and complex case. Apart from two books published in Cuba (short stories: *Así en la paz como en la guerra* [1960; In Peace as in War] and film criticism: *Un oficio del siglo XX* [1963; A Twentieth Century Profession]), the rest of his work has been written and published in exile. Despite this, he tenaciously recreates colloquial speech and certain Havana haunts of the mid-twentieth century (in *Tres tristes tigres* [1967;

Three Trapped Tigers, 1971], *La Habana para un infante difunto* [1979; *Infante's Inferno*, 1984]):

> La marca que ha dejado esta circunstancia [no escribir ni publicar ni ser leído en Cuba] en mi literatura es enorme. *Tres tristes tigres* es el libro que es porque lo empecé en La Habana en 1961, lo continué en Bélgica y lo terminé en Madrid. Está marcado por las lecturas que tenía entonces: Dante, textos esotéricos a los que me aficioné en Bruselas. No es un libro lleno de color local; las palabras cubanas, las situaciones, los modismos y los personajes de mi país están escogidos voluntariamente. Pensaba que la función del libro en términos de lenguaje era reproducir el habla de La Habana, concretamente el lenguaje de la noche habanera. Y ése fue un proceso, como todos los procesos literarios, hecho esencialmente a partir de la memoria. (Alfieri 93)

> The effect that this circumstance [that of not writing, publishing or being read in Cuba] has had on my writing is enormous. *Tres tristes tigres* is the book that it is because I started it in Havana in 1961, continued it in Belgium, and finished it in Madrid. It is influenced by the books I had then: Dante, esoteric texts that I became enthusiastic about in Brussels. It is not a book full of local color; the Cuban words, situations, idioms and people of my country are chosen voluntarily. I thought that the function of the book in terms of language was to reproduce the speech of Havana, in fact the language of Havana at night. And that was a process, as with all literary processes, essentially created from memory.

Formally, Cabrera Infante participated in Cortázar's aesthetic of *jazz*, creating a shifting literary homeland by freeing up words and playing with them well outside their referential territory. It is important here to emphasize a particular trait that Cabrera Infante shares with the great Spanish American narrators that is, in its own way, another form of banishment. Like so many others, Cabrera Infante's writing owes much to non-Spanish influences, and his cultural exile actually began in Cuba with his reading of Faulkner, Hemingway, and Steinbeck. He brought an end to his voyage of expatriation with *Holy Smoke* (1985), a book written directly in English, that the author does not consider translatable into Spanish.

The case of Miguel Ángel Asturias (1899–1974) is paradoxical. Central to his work is a magical combination of themes *del lado de allá* (here, pre-Columbian America) blended with a narrative form that is markedly *del lado de acá* (in this case, literary Europe): "Durante los años que pasé en París vi el ejemplo de muchos escritores cosmopolitas que escribían en París sobre Versalles. Desde entonces sentí que era mi vocación y mi deber escribir sobre América, que algún día interesaría al mundo" (Harss 127) ["In the years I spent in Paris I saw examples of many cosmopolitan writers who wrote in Paris on Versailles. From then on I felt that it was my vocation and my duty to write about Latin America, which would one day interest the world"]. Thus after long ethnological studies in London and Paris, in 1926 he completed a new translation of the *Popul-vuh* based on the French version by G. Raynaud. From this moment on, his most important works would use the pre-Columbian world and Maya cosmogony (*Leyendas de Guatemala* [1923–1928; Legends of Guatemala], *Hombres de Maíz* [1949; *Men of Maize*, 1975]) as a theme. His intention was not only to revive this world but also to restore its voice. With this, the condition of exile became a fruitful one once more. In the ancient indigenous texts, words not only possess ritual value but are the very substance of religious practices: They are the food of the gods who can only nourish themselves thereby. The result is a poetics that indistinguishably blends dream and reality, like the nascent European Surrealist movement. Paradoxically, therefore, the nostalgic recreation of an indigenous language that he had never learned led him to an aesthetic of formal rupture, breaking up syntax to achieve new rhythms, based on pre-logical associations that concealed secrets and occult or forgotten realities. To recreate the pre-Colombian American voice Asturias would have recourse to the practice of automatic writing employed by the Surrealists: "Lo que obtengo con la escritura automática es el apareamiento o la yuxtaposición de palabras que, como dicen los indios, nunca se han encontrado antes. Porque así es como el indio define su poesía. Dice que la poesía es donde las palabras se encuentran por primera vez" (Harss 105) ["What I obtain with automatic writing is the pairing or juxtaposition of words which, as the Indians say, have never before been connected. Because it is thus that the Indian defines his poetry. He says that poetry exists where words find each other for the first time"].

The Paradigm of Extraterritoriality

The artist has the advantage of converting the almost always painful conditions of exile into a motive for energizing the intellect, a trampoline to leap further, in order to exile the spirit from all kinds of localisms and dependencies. This liberating representation of exile brings with it a glorification of the values of extraterritoriality. The history of universal literature offers two outstanding examples, from Ovid (*parve nec invideo sine me liber ibis in urbem* [Ovid, *Tristia* I, 1] ["Little book, you are off to town without me"]) and, above all, Dante, for whom one consequence of political exile was the assumption of the whole world as his homeland:

> To me, however, the whole world is a homeland, like the sea to fish–though I drank from the Arno before cutting my teeth, and love Florence so much that, because I loved her, I suffer exile unjustly–and I will weight the balance of my judgement more with reason than with sentiment. And although for my own enjoyment (or rather for the satisfaction of my own desire), there is no more agreeable place on earth than Florence, yet when I turn the pages of the volumes of poets and other writers, by whom the world is described as a whole and in its constituent parts, and when I reflect inwardly on the various locations of places in the world, and their relations to the two poles and the circle at the equator, I am convinced, and firmly maintain, that there are many regions and cities more noble and more delightful than Tuscany and Florence, where I was born and of which I am a citizen, and many nations and peoples who speak a more elegant and practical language than do the Italians. (Book I, VII, 3)

Cortázar takes a stance of ironic resignation–"ese libro prohibido o quemado no era del todo bueno: escribamos ahora otro mejor" (1994a, 172) ["the book that was prohibited and burned was not all that good; now we will write a better one"]–a step further: "el exilio enriquece a quien mantiene los ojos abiertos y la guardia en alto. Volveremos a nuestras tierras siendo menos insulares, menos nacionalistas, menos egoístas; pero esa vuelta tenemos que ganarla desde ahora y la mejor manera es proyectarnos en obra, en contacto, y transmitir infatigablemente ese enriquecimiento interior que nos está dando la diáspora" (1985, 136) ["exile enriches whoever keep their eyes open and guard up. We will return to our countries less insular, less nationalistic, less egotistical; but we have to earn that return from now on and the best way to do that is to project ourselves in our work, keep in touch and tirelessly transmit this inner wealth that we have been given as a result of exile"].

For George Steiner extraterritoriality, like "loss of center," is an eminent characteristic of Jorge Luis Borges (1899–1986) in whom he sees "[one of] the three representative figures in the literature of exile–which is perhaps the main impulse of current literature" (viii). Even though Borges's exile was during his youth and bore no relationship to politics, his stay in Switzerland and Spain during his adolescence seems to have determined all his aesthetic opinions. Borges could be localist but only when adopting an attitude of decentralization in the face of the provincialism of certain movements within Spanish thought. His voice could express both the sober pride of the malicious *porteño* (inhabitant of Buenos Aires) and the confessions of a Nazi official, or the thoughts of an oriental Buddhist monk, an Aztec priest, Shakespeare, an Irish criminal, a professor of English in China, Averroes, and so on. His extraterritoriality is not cultural but ontological. His is a different mindset from that of Cortázar. Time, space, and identity, which are responsible for the rigid ontology of mimetic representation, are dislocated but in turn engender, with Borges, an "illustrious uncertainty" that serves as the only act of faith. His geographical paradigms are rarely those of displacement; they are rather those of the labyrinth, the mirror, the spiral, the map within the map, the universe concentrated into one point. He persists in expressing a tone of nostalgia but always accompanied by renunciation as if the only paradises were the lost ones. This is perhaps the great novelty of Borges' writing from the point of view of the literature of exile: the overcoming of nostalgia through renunciation. Choosing Moses' destiny, he feels that the "promised land" only remains thus if it can be contemplated from a distance–without possessing it. This option, which implies the giving up of love, homeland, and paradise, is translated into a constant celebration of what disappears rather than what one possesses: "Borges sees himself as the celebrator of things in their farewell" (Bloom 475).

Another complex and paradoxical case is that of Alejo Carpentier (1904–1980). His exile began, like that of Borges, in the cradle, but later it became permanent in political exile. Constantly torn between two continents (origin and residence), he spent his exile in France to research the anthropological and aesthetic roots, above all musical, of his native Caribbean. The impetus, shared with Asturias, to recreate an aesthetic landscape that reunited these two worlds offered him opposing aesthetic choices. Unlike Asturias, he had no faith in either a simple return to indigenism or a move to the richness of European Surrealism. His original project germinated during a journey to Haiti during which he discovered old monuments dating from the French occupation: America was not the cultural opposite of Europe, but was rather a place for all kinds of encounters and a still unextinguished source of new mythologies. His notion of the *real maravilloso americano* [marvellous American real] marked the interface that permitted him to maintain both his European roots and his American identity. Geographical journeys were translated for him into voyages in time, making the Venice of Vivaldi and Louis Armstrong's trumpet contemporaries. "Personalmente" [Personally], he points out,

> he tratado de especular a mi manera con el tiempo, con el tiempo circular, regreso al punto de partida, es decir, un relato que se cierra sobre sí mismo, en *Los pasos perdidos* y en el *Camino de Santiago*, el tiempo recurrente, o sea el tiempo invertido, en retroceso, en el *Viaje a la semilla*, el tiempo de ayer en hoy, es decir, un ayer significado presente en un hoy significativo, en *El siglo de las luces*,

en *El recurso del método*, en el *Concierto barroco*, un tiempo que gira en torno al hombre sin alterar su esencia, en mi relato 'Semejante a la noche' en que se asiste a la partida de un hombre para la guerra. Lo que se mueve en torno a él es la época; él es perfectamente inmutable, en una acción que comienza en la guerra de Troya y termina en la guerra de Troya, pasando por las Cruzadas, la conquista de América, el desembarco de los norteamericanos en Francia durante la segunda guerra mundial, etcétera. (156)

I have tried to speculate in my own way with time, with circular time I return to the beginning, that is, with a story that closes in on itself in *Los pasos perdidos* [1953; *The Lost Steps*, 1956] and "Camino de Santiago" [1958; The Road to Santiago]; recurrent time, or rather inverted time, going backwards in "Viaje a la semilla" [1944; Trip to Origin]; a time of yesterday today, in other words yesterday signified present in a significant today in *El siglo de las luces* [1962; *Explosion in the Cathedral*, 1963], *El recurso del método* [1974; *Reasons of State*, 1976], and *Concierto barocco* [1974; *Baroque Concert*, 1988]; a time that circulated around man without altering his essence, in my story "Semejante a la noche" [1958; The Same as Night] in which a man's departure for war is witnessed. What moves around him is the epoch; he is perfectly immutable, in an action that begins in the Trojan War and ends in the Trojan War via the Crusades, the Conquest of America, the disembarkation of the North Americans in France during the Second World War, etc.

His aesthetic of extraterritoriality consists of seeing one thing always with the eyes of another: the history of a dictator according to Cartesian methodology; harassment in Cuba through the musical sonata form; space in America as a geography of time.

The Paradigm of Nomadism

Like a river whose waters do not change as it passes through different landscapes or the snail that travels with its own house, there are times when exiled artists decide to emigrate to literature, taking their own image with them by thematicizing exile as themselves exiles and making literature the autobiographical fictionalization of their own uprooting. Such a practice tends to preserve individual identity over cultural identity and adapts to new identities. It is a means of protecting oneself simultaneously from both nostalgia and formal rupture, even though often using nontraditional forms of narration. Alfredo Bryce Echenique (b. 1939) is the most celebrated example of the Latin American novelist who, in order to resolve the difficulties of permanent exile (that in his case were already begun by his Scots-Basque origins), decided to enter fiction by bringing his own life into the equation. Bryce is the Woody Allen of literature who shares with the filmmaker not only the same kind of hypochondriacal and self-deprecating humor but also the art of incarnating himself in the biography of his personages. From his constant disorientation, existential more than geographical (in his family, in the environment of Lima, in Europe), he extracts a literature that is decidedly nomadic and that acquires its literary distinctiveness through the creation of calamity. His characters mourn a paradise that they have chosen to lose and Bryce gleans the essence of his aesthetic from that loss. The existential calamity of his alter ego Martin Romaña, in his celebrated self-referential diptych (*La vida exagerada de Martín Romaña* [1981; The Exaggerated Life of Martín Romaña] and *El hombre que hablaba de Octavia de Cádiz* [1985; The Man Who Spoke of Octavia from Cádiz]) amounts to a rupture of narrative and textual structure of the work along the lines of the work of Sterne, Diderot, and Bustos Domecq. Bryce Echenique in a journey with a nostalgia full of a contagious delight. José Donoso (1925–1996), Manuel Puig (1932–1990), Luisa Valenzuela

(b. 1938), and Cristina Peri Rossi (b. 1941) are other examples of writers who, in different ways and using different modes of representation, incarnate this aesthetic of literary nomadism.

The Paradigm of Dual Displacement

This last type of representation of exile is related to literary reception. The (real) exile of the author, contrary to Ovid's, is less relevant than that of his work. Certain themes and narrative forms considered as ordinary in Latin America play the role of a displaced element within a North American or European context and return to their place of origin, creating the effect of a second-level displacement. This is a complex phenomenon. The globalization of exile for intellectuals during the mid-twentieth century has made for new resonances for the imagination. Literary reception acts as the base of shared expectations, a knowledge that is instrumental in defining the idiosyncrasy of cultural communities that could be confirmed, pacified, displaced, or frustrated by a new text. The simple migration from one area of reception to another causes a book to engender different imaginary worlds. Outside its Caribbean home, the Macondo of García Márquez (b. 1927), for example, acquires the dimensions of a mythical *topos* comparable with Troy, Ithaca, or Babel in the Western cultural imaginary. On returning to the Caribbean, it arrives charged with these new connotations and demanding a new parallelism with regard to these expectations. This phenomenon of imaginary *mestizaje* is complicated when the work itself is already the fruit of displacement on various levels. Mario Vargas Llosa provides a superb example of this proposition. *La ciudad y los perros* [1963; *The Time of the Hero,* 1979] is located in Lima, written by a Faulknerian pen, and concludes in Barcelona.

If multiple migration counts as an aesthetic category in the work of great writers, such as those mentioned above, the complicated mechanisms of reception and transplantation can also be exploited as an easy recipe to trivialize by cheap exoticism what originated as real exile. Think of Auden's ironic verses: "A poet's hope: to be,/like some valley cheese,/ local, but prized elsewhere" (639). Jorge Edwards (b. 1931) recognizes that some of his fellow countrymen have known how to cultivate and exploit the image that Europe always seeks in the Latin American, the primitive man, fruit of a virgin, exuberant, whether from the extreme south of the continent or from the tropical jungle, which has added the very contemporary ecological elements to the myth of the Noble Savage. Not only the themes but also the forms of writing are transformed into a sales strategy while cheap pastiches of García Márquez multiply. The case becomes more serious when what is trivialized is the suffering of the political exile. Hernán Valdés analyzes the complexity of this phenomenon with great lucidity. He distinguishes between the perception of the Latin American writer in general and that of the Latin American writer in exile. The first corresponds to a strictly literary curiosity in global terms, whereas the second functions in accordance with specialized canons in which the aesthetic is subordinated to the humanitarian. This situation creates a new system of expectations that conditions reception. Humanitarianism and denunciation become exotic and negotiable products. The writer who has decided not to sell his soul and for whom the heart-wrenching experience of exile has acted as a healthy leap to extraterritoriality, engenders a lack of confidence or perplexity in others. Valdés writes, "cuando nos situamos en el plano de víctimas o denunciantes de situaciones políticas específicas despertamos la adhesión o compasión de unos, pero . . . cuando volvemos a situarnos en el simple plano de escritores, sin apelativos patéticos, despertamos ya sea el desconcierto, ya el recelo de los unos y los otros" (18) ["when we put ourselves in the place of victims or denouncers of specific political situations, we inspire followers or the compassion of others, but . . . when we return to put ourselves in the simple role of writers without pathetic appeals, we provoke either bewilderment, or jealousy from others"]. He concludes:

Pedir que la solidaridad política se extienda a la solidaridad literaria, a una literatura no funcionalmente vinculada a fines políticos concretos, denotaría no sólo ingenuidad, sino además arrogancia; sin embargo, pedir a quienes tienen un interés general por la literatura que se atrevieran de tiempo en tiempo a desafiar e incluso a romper los estereotipos que surgen en su imaginación cuando se trata de nosotros, los escritores latinoamericanos en el exilio, especie particular dentro de los escritores latinoamericanos y más particular aún e incluso algo dudosa en comparación a los escritores exiliados de los países del este—pedir a nuestros anfitriones ese acto de emancipación de sus ideas preconcebidas sería, creo yo, enteramente apropiado en esta ocasión. (18)

To ask that political solidarity should extend to literary solidarity, to a literature that does not functionally connect to concrete political ends, would denote not only foolishness, but arrogance; nevertheless, to ask those who have a general interest in literature to dare from time to time to challenge and even break stereotypes that arise in their imagination when they are dealing with us, the Latin American writers in exile, a particular species among Latin American writers and more particular even and moreover dubious in comparison with the exiled writers of eastern countries—to request from our hosts this act of freeing themselves from their preconceived ideas would be, I think, entirely appropriate on this occasion.

This essay has endeavored to show that such an augury is not utopian and that the experience of exile has been assumed by the great Latin American writers as a source of aesthetic fecundity, as providing the distance necessary for all artistic creation.

Translation by Jessica Johnson

Works Cited

Aizenberg, Edna. 1984. *The Aleph Weaver: Biblical, Kabbalistic, and Judaic Elements in Borges.* Potomac, MD: Scripta Humanistica.

Alfieri, Carlos. 1997. "Guillermo Cabrera Infante: el regocijo de la palabra. Entrevista." *Cuadernos Hispanoamericanos* 560 (February): 91–100.

Alighieri, Dante. 1996. *Dante, De vulgari eloquentia.* Ed. and trans. Steven Botterill. Cambridge: Cambridge University Press.

Andrade, Jorge. 1998. "Carta desde Argentina: la nostalgia." *Cuadernos Hispanoamericanos* 574 (April): 115–17.

Apollinaire, Guillaume. 1965. "À Howard." *Les mamelles de Tirésias. Oeuvres poétiques.* Préface par André Billy. Ed. Marcel Adema and Michel Décaudin. Paris: Gallimard, Ed. de la Pléiade. 875.

Auden, W. H. 1976. "Shorts II." *Collected Poems.* Ed. Edward Mendelson. London: Faber and Faber. 639.

Benjamin, Walter. 1968. "The Storyteller, Reflections on the Works of Nikolai Leskov." *Illuminations.* Trans. Harry Zohn. New York: Harcourt, Brace & World. 83–109.

Bible. 1989. *The Revised English Bible with the Apocrypha.* Oxford: Oxford University Press.

Bloom, Harold. 1995. *The Western Canon: The Books and School of the Ages.* London: Papermac.

Carpentier, Alejo. 1981. *La novela latinoamericana en vísperas de un nuevo siglo y otros ensayos.* Mexico City: Siglo Veintiuno.

Cortázar, Julio. 1963. *Rayuela*. Buenos Aires: Sudamericana.

——. 1966. *Hopscotch*. Trans. Gregory Rabassa. New York: Pantheon Books.

——. 1968. *La vuelta al día en ochenta mundos*. 2nd ed. Mexico City: Siglo Veintiuno.

——. 1985. "El escritor y su quehacer en América Latina." *Textos políticos*. Barcelona: Plaza & Janés. 121–37.

——. 1987. "Literatura en la revolución y revolución en la literatura: algunos malentendidos a liquidar." *Julio Cortázar: al término del polvo y el sudor*. Montevideo: Biblioteca de Marcha. 105–37.

——. 1994a. "América Latina: exilio y literatura." *Obra Crítica*. Vol 3. Ed. Saúl Sosnowsky. Barcelona: Alfaguara. 161–223.

——. 1994b. "El intelectual y la política en Hispanoamérica." *Obra Crítica*. Vol. 3. Ed. Saúl Sosnowsky. Barcelona: Alfaguara. 113–30.

——. 1994c. "El otro cielo." *Todos los fuegos el fuego. Cuentos completos*. Vol. 1. Madrid: Alfaguara. 590–606.

——. 1994d. "El perseguidor." *Las armas secretas. Cuentos completos*. Vol. 1. Madrid: Alfaguara. 225–66.

——. 1994e. "Realidad y literatura en América Latina." *Obra Crítica*. Vol. 3. Ed. Saúl Sosnowsky. Barcelona: Alfaguara. 225–38.

Espinosa Domínguez, Carlos. n.d. "La vida es riesgo o abstinencia. Entrevista con Reinaldo Arenas." *Quimera* 101: 54–61.

Gurr, Andrew. 1981. *Writers in Exile: The Identity of Home in Modern Literature*. Sussex: Harverster Press.

Harss, Luis. 1971. *Los nuestros*. Buenos Aires: Sudamericana.

Kipling, Rudyard. 1994. *The Works of Rudyard Kipling*. Ware: Wordsworth.

Lezama Lima, José. 1985. "Cortázar y el comienzo de la otra novela." *Julio Cortázar*. Ed. Pedro Lastra. Madrid: Taurus. 191–206.

McCarthy, Mary. 1971. "Exiles, Expatriates and Internal Emigrés." *The Listener* 86: 705–8.

Murena, Héctor A. 1954. *El pecado original de América*. Buenos Aires: Sur.

Ovid. 1986. *The Tristia of Ovid*. Trans. David R. Slavitt. Cleveland, OH: Bellflower Press.

Peralta, Braulio. 1998. "El erotismo y las formas. Entrevista con Mario Vargas Llosa." *Cuadernos Hispanoamericanos* 574 (April): 15–20.

Prego, Omar. 1985. *La fascinación de las palabras. Una conversación con Julio Cortázar*. Barcelona: Muchnik.

Rosch, Eleanor. 1977. "Classification of Real-World Objects: Origins and Representations in Cognition." *Thinking: Readings in Cognitive Science*. Ed. P. N. Johnson-Laird and P. C. Wason. Cambridge: Cambridge University Press. 212–22.

Steiner, George. 1972. *Extra-territorial: Papers on Literature and the Language Revolution*. London: Faber and Faber.

Tucker, Martin, ed. 1991. *Literary Exile in the Twentieth Century: An Analysis and Biographical Dictionary*. New York: Greenwood Press.

Vaché, Jacques. 1970. *Lettres de guerre: précédées de quatre essais d'Andrée Breton*. Paris: Losfeld.

——. 1993. *War Letters: With Four Introductory Essays by André Breton*. Trans. and ed. Paul Lenti. London: Atlas.

Valdés, Hernán. 1982. "Escritores en el exilio y el exilio de la escritura." *Quimera* 25 (November): 27–28.

Vargas Llosa, Mario. 1997. *Los Cuadernos de don Rigoberto*. Madrid: Alfaguara.

——. 1998. *The Notebooks of Don Rigoberto*. Trans. Edith Grossman. New York: Farrar, Straus and Giroux.

Wittgenstein, Ludwig. 1958. *Philosophische Untersuchungen/Philosophical Investigations*. Oxford: Basil Blackwell.

Zambrano, María. 1990. *Los Bienaventurados*. Madrid: Siruela.

CHAPTER 44

POLITICAL EXCLUSION/
LITERARY INCLUSION
ARGENTINE AND URUGUAYAN WRITERS

Saúl Sosnowski

The pivotal dates of 27 June 1973 in Uruguay and 24 March 1976 in Argentina mark these nations' descent into unforeseen levels of violence and repression. The dates memorialize the coups; they also designate breaking points in a process of institutional deterioration that had already led many to seek exile in neighboring countries and elsewhere in Latin America and Europe. State terrorism was to combat the remnants of already defeated guerrilla forces and to cancel out any possible resistance to the new economic order that was being drafted on the heels of armed repression and a growing culture of fear.

The internal wars waged in Argentina and Uruguay in the 1970s and 1980s were couched in terms of defending national interests and values. As urban confrontations increased and abductions and massacres became commonplace, the Juntas' pernicious rhetorical twists were to place responsibility for the emptiness created by disappeared bodies upon the very dead, upon families and educators, upon deviant ideologies and alien forces. Official arguments transferred the burden of criminal acts from the perpetrators to the victims. Invoking the spiritual force granted the defenders of the Nation, the Armed Forces took over governmental functions—a rather familiar procedure in Argentina but not in Uruguay. As on many other occasions, the military intervened in the name of democracy and for the sake of restoring order to the country.

Claiming that anarchy generated by armed insurrection had to be halted by drastic means, the military appealed to a common metaphor of health and disease to interpret and justify policies against guerrilla movements and, more extensively, against those who challenged or disregarded their parameters for political life. These parameters included the fact that opposition parties, and many people from other responsible civilian sectors, had called on the military to intervene and safeguard some semblance of constitutional order so as to enable a return, in due course, to democratic normalcy. Large segments of the population sided with the junta headed by Gen. Videla when Isabel Martínez de Perón was removed from power, including many who would pay dearly for their initial endorsement and others who, in exile, would soon forget their political lapse and later bathe in redemocratization.

Upon seizing power in the 1970s, as on previous occasions, the military proclaimed, in quasi-Messianic tones, the legitimacy of their actions in defense of the nation and democracy, of Christian values, and of the corps' own historical responsibility. To restore the health of the Nation and to mold the citizenry were among the Armed Forces' charges. Accordingly, radical surgery to extirpate the cancerous cells of ideologies foreign to the Nation's character were not only justified, but mandated by their reading of the Constitution. The military, along with its civilian and ecclesiastical allies, and supported by international interests, seized for itself the aura of healers.

Exclusion is based on intolerance and on the contempt that authoritarianism breeds for any obstacle to its power. Methods used to impose a single version of reality have varied according to historical moments and in response to national marketing needs and international acceptance.

Gross violations of human rights led to denunciation of the Juntas and their practices. World opinion was at stake; although it did not necessarily affect investments or alter national policies, its impact was increasingly felt by de facto regimes in the region. For instance, the Argentine victory at the 1978 World Soccer Cup, hosted by the dictatorship, also served the Junta and its allies to cynically cheapen international demands for human rights with the slogan "Los argentinos somos derechos y humanos" [We Argentines are Right and Human].

Against a background that aimed at the appropriation of resources, economies, and peoples—a goal shared across regional borders by the ruling authoritarian mindset—literary-cultural exclusions are to be viewed as a component in the struggle to achieve "purity of mind" and compliance to a higher authority. Efficient publicity campaigns addressed world opinion and also persuaded the citizenry of the normalcy both of their political condition and of the financial benefits to be reaped from newly imposed economic policies. Legislation and education were already firmly in hand; only the future needed to be submitted to rigid control. And it was on the battleground for this future that cultural production would be engaged.

The rhetoric of the Juntas left no room for those who doubted and certainly none for those who questioned. Their arguments were posed in terms of confrontation between titanic forces. It followed that in a war between the forces of light and darkness, good and evil as signifiers of the struggle for the appropriation of the national destiny, all means were justified. From exile, and particularly within the territory occupied by the military, demands were made on behalf of the imprisoned and disappeared—a task that the Madres and Abuelas of the Plaza de Mayo, joined now by the Hijos, have continued to eloquently carry out. Marches, protests, and legal appeals addressed the immediacy of life in the present. Both at home—in a region made uniform by repression—and in exile, there was also a conviction, which found its way into numerous literary works, that to answer back to a doctrine of death was to design a response to a country that would surely emerge from this cycle of violence transfigured and fractured—ethically and humanly poorer.

The absence of writers and of their books under repressive conditions is to be seen as symptomatic of more radical conflicts. In the republic of letters, however, these conflicts are at the very core of issues that include censorship, marginality, and exclusion. Intellectuals have focused on the substantial number of murdered, imprisoned, and exiled writers, artists, scientists, journalists, and other intellectuals. Rodolfo Walsh

521

(1927–1977), Haroldo Conti (1925–1976?), and Francisco Urondo (1930–1975) are frequently mentioned both as a sign of the dictatorship's brutality and as paradigms of the void created by their absence. As dramatic as each case has been, this community constituted a fraction of the victims of repression. Still, it is in their voices, and the absence thereof, that nations have been able to gauge their changing times–a more than sufficient reason for a heightened awareness of their destiny.

Exclusion implies restrictions in the literary-cultural system. It also implies being barred from participation in the public sphere. It means to be silenced and, if taken to an extreme, to be obliterated from a Nation's memory. Exclusion embodies self-censorship, survival in a culture of fear, or life in exile. It includes internal exile through marginalization and also through the penalizing silence of censorship, the excruciating experience of prison, and the uncertainty of illegal detention. It generates a sense of alienation and of being foreign in one's own home. Under authoritarian rule, the Nation is divided; it turns into an ideological construct to be inhabited solely by those who agree with a newly imposed version of history and national destiny. Dissenters meet silence, life on the fringes, exile, jail, death. Within the country or outside its borders, exile and *insilio*–a term coined by Uruguayans for internal exile–are marked by a sense of pervasive distance from all others. To these "border differentiations", Mauricio Rosencof (b. 1933) added the literature that was produced in prison.

In most cases, exile expressed a decision to live, as well as a response to an increasingly repressive, uncertain, and vicious climate. In the historical context of the 1970s and early 1980s–particularly in light of subsequent debates within the intellectual community–it is convenient to differentiate between writers who opted to move overseas, even long before these times, and political exiles, between literature written out of the country and that produced under conditions of exile. The difference does not necessarily reside in thematics but rather in the process of production, in the context, and in the limited access readers in the home country had to those texts. As Julio Cortázar has indicated, exile affects authors and also the public whose ability to access literature from exile is subject to the rule of the censor. It is noteworthy that, whether written by an "exile" or by a "transterrado"–leaving aside readership in the country of residence, across Latin America, and, through translations, in other markets–the resulting works are integral components of national literatures whose immediate frame of reference is both the Nation and its public. Literature produced in exile may be marked, as it were, by the author's place of residence, by the inclusion of motifs that exceed national allusions, by a freedom to state that which those who stayed cannot utter. But as long as it is produced in the same language, and as long as it is articulated in circuits that include the national reading public, it does not cease to be, for the case under study, Argentine or Uruguayan literature. The emphasis, though, is placed on "literature," and not solely on the exilic condition. Juan Carlos Onetti argues that exile does not create good writing nor does it diminish a good writer's talent; it changes the existential situations of the writing (see Onetti 1985).

In terms of national affiliation, it should suffice to recall that although they are physically far from the dramatic conditions that led many into exile in the 1970s, the works of Julio Cortázar (1914–1984) and Juan José Saer (b. 1937), written in France, are read as Argentine literature, as much as the works of Juan Carlos Onetti (1909–1994) and Cristina Peri Rossi (b. 1941), who left their country because of the dictatorship and wrote in their Spanish exile, never ceased to be part of Uruguayan letters. In this sense, the repressive regimes that ruled their nations failed to create a permanent schism in the intellectual field. Nevertheless, particularly in the Argentine case, heated discussions, threats, a chilling gap resulting from ideological and partisan positions, and a growing intolerance for dissenting opinions are part of the legacy of authoritarianism (see Sosnowski, 1988).

Life in exile is a radically transforming experience, whether under sustained hardships or while enjoying readily achieved comforts. An explicit or veiled sense of longing for the lost home is a universal motif, as is the incorporation (or rejection) of the new site into the exile's cultural system. Nuances of the same language, features that define a culture that is being assimilated, nostalgia, and inclusion of newly acquired locales add up to a process and redefinition of both a personal and a national history (Pedro Orgambide [1929–2003], David Viñas [b. 1929], Humberto Costantini [1924–1987], Eduardo Galeano [b. 1940], Carlos Martínez Moreno [1917–1986], among many others). For Manuel Puig (1932–1990), exile in Mexico and Brazil allowed him to further open up his concerns over the exercise of patriarchal power, as signified in sexuality and in military-political domination.

As many of the writers have indicated in essays and interviews, as well as through their literary texts, no one–not even those who attempted to shut their new reality out–returns home unchanged. Multiple factors condition attitudes toward exile, integration, re-entry, or the decision not to return. At times, texts evidence melancholy and despair, and also acceptance of the challenge to remain creative amidst (initially) unknown people and while hearing voices that differ from childhood echoes. Free from immediate danger, exiled writers have also been able to speak directly of conditions that those who remained behind had to translate into elliptical forms. Soriano and Martini compared with Piglia is an example frequently given for Argentina; a case could also be made across locations and generations between Mario Benedetti (b. 1920) in exile and José Pedro Díaz (b. 1921), Amanda Berenguer (b. 1921), and Teresa Porzecanski (b. 1945) in Uruguay.

While living under repression, with a sense of isolation and often with a knowingly self-inflicted blindness to the immediate surroundings, writing itself could be an act of defiance, an affirmation of life. During the subsequent stages of redemocratization, writing became a challenge, an ethical imperative to share in the reconstruction of the Nation amidst increasingly partisan confrontations. These were times of reckoning with conduct at home and overseas, of appraisal of individual and collective conduct, of the limits of the word and of risks taken or shunned (testimonial examples and analyses in Iparraguirre, Sosnowski, Balderston, et al., A.I.D.A. (Asociación Internacional para la Defensa de los Artistas víctimas de la represión en el mundo [International Association for the Defense of Artists and Victims of Repression in the World]), Brocato, Kohut and Pagni, and Spiller).

Often at significant personal risk, the terms and limits of censorship were tested by mentioning restricted names and by discussing issues that were at the edge of the allowable. What the military in the region used to consider adjustments or relaxations of strict rules of censorship were, in fact, reactions to increased vulnerability and to their more tenuous hold of power. This could be documented through María Elena Walsh's (b. 1930) call to awareness of the "país-jardín-de-infantes" [Nation-Children's Garden] and at another level through changes in leading journals, such as *Punto de vista* (1978), directed by Beatriz Sarlo (b. 1942) in Argentina, and Carlos Quijano's (1900–1984) legendary *Marcha*, which was launched in Uruguay in 1939 and promptly became a reference point for the Hispanic world. *Marcha* was forced to close in 1974; it reopened in exile in Mexico as *Cuadernos de Marcha* under Quijano's leadership (see Rocca).

A highly visible case in point was Argentina's "Teatro abierto," which called on twenty-one leading playwrights–among them Griselda Gambaro (b. 1928), Osvaldo Dragún (1929–1999), Carlos Somigliana (b. 1932), Roberto Cossa (b. 1934), Aída Bortnik (b. 1942), and Eduardo Pavlovsky (b. 1929)–to produce brief plays to be staged at the rate of three per day in a weekly series that was to be repeated over an eight-week period. It was a major test of wills and limits, as well as of courage, and an affirmation that culture was not to be submitted to the Juntas' definition of prevailing theatrical norms. It opened on July 28, 1981, and produced three seasons under dictatorship and two during the Alfonsín government before deciding that its goals had been met. A week after Teatro Abierto opened at the Teatro Picadero, it was burned down. A spectacular show of solidarity from leading intellectual quarters and the human rights community allowed it to continue at the Tabarís, a centrally located theater with an audience capacity that doubled that of Picadero's. In 1982, and as a result of its success, it inspired parallel movements in poetry, film, and dance. A similar testing of limits also took place in Uruguayan poetry (see Mántaras Loedel) and song. A singular example can be seen in Leo Masliah's (b. 1954) oblique and outrageously daring look at established conventions.

During the dictatorships' collapse (Argentina) and transition to democracy (Uruguay), the urge to evaluate the immediate past and bring to justice those responsible for State terrorism led to a daily exercise of revelations and to an obsession to preserve memory. The Argentine government-sponsored *Nunca más* [1984; Never Again] and the Servicio Paz y Justicia's *Uruguay Nunca más* [1989; Uruguay Never Again] were part of a national need to learn and to teach, to cleanse the Nation from collective responsibility by bringing the criminals to justice or, at the very least, to public knowledge of their acts. In Argentina, members of the Juntas were tried, convicted, and subsequently pardoned; others involved in crimes against humanity were shielded from prosecution by presidential edicts. In Uruguay, a plebiscite and negotiated pacts settled claims to prosecution and justice. In both cases, as elsewhere in the Southern Cone, the argument for limited or no prosecution of the military was that a fragile democracy needed protection from additional pressures. It should be noted that civilian accomplices of State-sponsored terrorism, including the chief architects of an imposed economic model that lay at the core of the coups, were not brought to justice. Internalized fear, concrete threats, and tangible attempts to restrict or overthrow the restored democracies, as much as a balancing act between ethics and survival, politics, and justice, entered into play.

In spite of limited and largely partial legal outcomes, a trial did take place in Argentina, and a plebiscite in Uruguay expressed the state of the nation. These were necessary steps in the reconstruction of political institutions and of the social fabric, particularly where, as in Argentina, the disappeared numbered from 9,000 to 30,000; in Uruguay–a state with a small population that had become a country of emigration–

approximately 150 people were killed by the dictatorship and one in every 54 citizens experienced prison. Beyond these formal documents, there was to be a stream of testimonies, political accounts, and analyses, fiction, poetry, and drama to account for the missing, the tortured, and exiled–to address the fall into the countries' violent abyss. Although revelations and legal proceedings in Argentina sustain the public's interest, days and nights have been overtaken by routine, by economic and other immediate concerns. For many, a different literary registry now obviates or sidesteps what, for them, has become an annoying emblem of contemporary history.

Each in their own way, Argentines and Uruguayans have been falling back to their pre-1970s delusionary self-perceptions. For Argentina, it means to hold on to a privileged rank within the Latin American landscape and, increasingly, within the Western alliance. For Uruguay, it has meant to revert to the notion of a "model state"–the "Switzerland of America"–to its singularity among all neighbors (Achugar and Caetano). Memory has not served well the promoters of national preeminence and uniqueness (Bergero and Reati; Reati 1992).

As concerns shift with new priorities, exile and the transition to democracy now hold greater interest for academics than for those concerned with current political and cultural transformations. Democracy itself is being played out and negotiated–as much as before and across the globe–in the corridors of power. Everything can be, and is being, said. Long gone, it seems, are the days in which censorship was exercised on issues of morality, sex, family, religion, and national security (see Avellaneda)–namely, when a prescription was being drafted to define the individual's social and political place in the national fabric.

Historical references date back to some of the region's earliest literary production and have served to document an era's ideological tensions, character, and cultural taste. For authors who remained in Argentina, history became a seemingly mandatory escape route for speaking of daily life under repression. In recent years, an abundance of historical novels have become trendy. Some authors worked on history and the artifice and limits of language to retrieve the present; some rebuilt national myths out of debris; some pretended to build links to another dimension. Cognizant of the historical version that was implemented to serve the ruling interests, Viñas engaged in narrative and critical exercises to demythify Argentina's official legacy. While in exile, moreover, he produced a number of projects that encompassed other regions of Latin America. Orgambide reworked Argentina's immigrant roots by retrieving his own legacy and by incorporating his Mexican haven into a literature that until then had a single, Argentine register. This widening of literary, artistic, and intellectual horizons has been common to most exiles, who opted not to remain impervious to their new milieu, whether in Latin American countries or in cultures that were uniquely dissimilar to their own heritage (Juan Gelman [b. 1930], Noé Jitrik [b. 1928], Marta Traba [1930–1983], Néstor García Canclini [b. 1939], Angel Rama [1926–1983], Jorge Ruffinelli [b. 1943], Hugo Achugar [b. 1944], among many others). In Spain, for instance, Daniel Moyano (1930–1992) wrote of the reverse migration caused by the dictatorship. Antonio Di Benedetto (1922–1986) and Héctor Tizón (b. 1929) also left unequivocal statements of exile's impact on them and their work. In France, Osvaldo Soriano (1943–1997) was able to be sardonically and bitterly more explicit about a fractious Peronism and the painful deceit meted out to embodiments of

Argentine popular culture, while Juan Carlos Martini (b. 1944) crafted in Barcelona a masterful narrative of corruption. From Mexico, Mempo Giardinelli (b. 1947) pursued political and erotic literary veins that would have been silenced were he not exiled. As a member of the same literary group, Vicente Battista (b. 1940) was able to enunciate freely from exile what Liliana Heker (b. 1943) and Abelardo Castillo (b. 1935) had to negotiate locally.

The military's own emphasis on its foundational stages, and not solely the inability to speak openly of the present, may explain why a number of writers who remained in Argentina during the repression turned to the nineteenth century to reflect precisely on the forces and ideologies that shaped a history that ended in yet another dictatorial round. The notion of another round in itself provides an opening to understanding why a literary radicalization did not take place in any genre as a result of the gravest wave of violence to envelop the country. While violence did reach new depths in the perverse execution of victims and in the manipulation of survivors and the country at large, the political process itself was not perceived to be outside the periodic cycle of electoral politics and military interventions. It is noteworthy that Uruguay and Chile, countries with longstanding democratic processes and traditions of stability, did not initially witness a pronounced literary shift beyond reflective documents and testimonial narratives.

Years of fear and of ethical corruption (cynically disguised as moral superiority), of deceit, suspicion, and betrayal, had a severe impact on the population and on language itself (Corradi, Dassin and Garretón; Perelli and Rial). Language itself had to be cleansed and the common use of words restored to their proper meaning. In this context, we may ponder whether it was a task left to some survivors of the dictatorship, and to the generation that grew up under repression, to rework power relations, historical statutes, new social contracts, and a view of themselves in the concert of first-world nations. Moreover, caught up in the triumphant economic order that resulted from dictatorial rule, participants in a globalized version of Western civilization and willing practitioners of the postmodern, a number of writers were to have scarce attention for anything but the immediacy of tomorrow. Furthermore, we should also ask whether the emphasis on the postmodern that defines a number of intellectual exercises is not just a way to stay tuned to the First World, to be contemporaries of all Western metropolitan concerns, but also a response to a "traditional Argentina"/"traditional Uruguay" anchored in the oligarchy, held fast by the military, and tied to failed myths.

Works Cited

Achugar, Hugo. 1992. *La balsa de la Medusa. Ensayos sobre identidad, cultura y fin de siglo en Uruguay*. Montevideo: Trilce.

Achugar, Hugo, and Gerardo Caetano, ed. 1992. *Identidad uruguaya: ¿mito, crisis o afirmación?* Montevideo: Trilce.

A.I.D.A. [Asociación Internacional para la Defensa de los Artistas víctimas de la represión en el mundo]. 1981. *Argentina—cómo matar la cultura. Testimonios: 1976–1981*. Madrid: Revolución.

Avellaneda, Andrés. 1986. *Censura, autoritarismo y cultura: Argentina 1960–1983*. 2 vols. Buenos Aires: CEDAL.

Balderston, Daniel et al. 1987. *Ficción y política: La narrativa argentina durante el proceso militar*. Buenos Aires: Alianza.

Battista, Vicente. 1975. *Como tanta gente que anda por ahí*. Barcelona: Planeta.

——. 1984. *El libro de todos los engaños*. Buenos Aires: Bruguera.

Benedetti, Mario. 1982. *Primavera con una esquina rota*. Mexico City: Nueva Imagen.

——. 1984. *Geografías*. Mexico City: Editorial Nueva Imagen.

——. 1985. *El desexilio y otras conjeturas*. Buenos Aires: Nueva Imagen.

Bergero, Adriana J., and Fernando Reati, ed. 1997. *Memoria colectiva y políticas de olvido. Argentina y Uruguay, 1970–1990*. Rosario: Beatriz Viterbo.

Brocato, Carlos A. 1986. *El exilio es nuestro*. Buenos Aires: Sudamericana-Planeta.

Conti, Haroldo. 1975. *Mascaró, el cazador americano*. Havana: Casa de las Américas.

Corradi, Juan, Joan Dassin, and Manuel Antonio Garretón, ed. 1992. *Fear at the Edge: State Terrorism and Resistance in Latin America*. Berkeley: University of California Press.

Cortázar, Julio. 1973. *Libro de Manuel*. Buenos Aires: Sudamericana.

——. 1984. *Argentina: años de alambradas culturales*. Barcelona: Muchnik Editores.

——. 1994. "América Latina: exilio y literatura." *Obra crítica/3*. Ed. Saúl Sosnowski. Madrid: Alfaguara. 161–80.

Costantini, Humberto. 1979. *De dioses, hombrecitos y policías*. Mexico City: Editorial Nueva Imagen.

——. 1984. *La larga noche de Francisco Sanctis*. Buenos Aires: Bruguera.

Di Benedetto, Antonio. 1981. *Caballo en el salitral*. Barcelona: Bruguera.

——. 1983. *Cuentos del exilio*. Buenos Aires: Bruguera.

——. 1985. *Sombras nada más*. Buenos Aires: Alianza.

Galeano, Eduardo. 1978. *Días y noches de amor y de guerra*. Havana: Casa de las Américas.

——. 1982–1986. *Memoria del fuego, I, II, III*. Madrid: Siglo Veintiuno de España Editores.

Gambaro, Griselda. 1976. *Ganarse la muerte*. Buenos Aires: Ediciones de la Flor.

——. 1995 [1973]. *Información para extranjeros. Teatro 2*. Buenos Aires: Ediciones de la Flor.

Gelman, Juan. 1975. *Obra poética*. Buenos Aires: Corregidor.

——. 1985. *La junta luz. Oratorio a las Madres de Plaza de Mayo*. Buenos Aires: Libros de Tierra Firme.

——. 1994. *De palabra*. Madrid: Visor.

——. 1994. *dibaxu*. Buenos Aires: Seix Barral.

——. 1997. *Unthinkable Tenderness. Selected Poems*. Ed. and trans. Joan Lindgren. Berkeley: University of California Press.

Gelman, Juan, and Osvaldo Bayer. 1984. *Exilio*. Buenos Aires: Legasa.

Gianelli María, Fernando Beramendi, Ana Luisa Valdés, ed. 1984. *Fuera de fronteras*. Stockholm: Nordan/Comunidad.

Giardinelli, Mempo. 1980. *La revolución en bicicleta*. Barcelona: Pomaire.

——. 1986. *Qué solos se quedan los muertos*. Barcelona: Plaza & Janés.

——. 1991. *Santo oficio de la memoria*. Bogota: Grupo Editorial Norma.

Iparraguirre, Sylvia, ed. 1993. *La cultura argentina. De la dictadura a la democracia*. Monographic issue of *Cuadernos hispanoamericanos* 517–19.

Jitrik, Noé. 1975. *Producción literaria y producción social*. Buenos Aires: Sudamericana.

——. 1984. *Las armas y las razones: Ensayos sobre el peronismo, el exilio y la literatura*. Buenos Aires: Sudamericana.

Kohut, Karl, and Andrea Pagni, ed. 1989. *Literatura argentina de hoy: de la dictadura a la democracia*. Frankfurt: Vervuert.

Martínez Moreno, Carlos. 1981. *El color que el infierno me escondiera.* Mexico City: Nueva Imagen.

———. 1994. *Ensayos.* 2 vols. Montevideo: Cámara de Senadores.

Martini, Juan Carlos. 1981. *La vida entera.* Barcelona: Bruguera.

———. 1988. *Composición de lugar.* Buenos Aires: Legasa.

———. 1989. *La construcción del héroe.* Buenos Aires: Legasa.

Mántaras Loedel, Graciela. 1989. *Contra el silencio. Poesía uruguaya 1973–1988.* Montevideo: Tupac Amaru.

Masliah, Leo. 1987. *Historia transversal de Floreal Menéndez.* Buenos Aires: Ediciones de la Flor.

Moyano, Daniel. 1974. *El trino del diablo.* Buenos Aires: Sudamericana.

———. 1981. *El vuelo del tigre.* Buenos Aires: Legasa.

———. 1983. *Libro de navíos y borrascas.* Buenos Aires: Legasa.

Onetti, Juan Carlos. 1970. *Obras completas.* Mexico City: Aguilar.

———. 1985. *Dejemos hablar al viento.* Barcelona: Bruguera.

———. 1993. *Cuando ya no importe.* Madrid: Alfaguara.

Orgambide, Pedro. 1977. *Aventuras de Edmund Ziller en tierras del Nuevo Mundo.* Mexico City: Grijalbo.

———. 1983. *El arrabal del mundo.* Buenos Aires: Bruguera.

———. 1984. *Hacer la América.* Buenos Aires: Bruguera.

Perelli, Carina, and Juan Rial. 1986. *De mitos y memorias políticas. La represión, el miedo y después.* Montevideo: Ediciones de la Banda Oriental.

Peri Rossi, Cristina. 1976. *Diáspora.* Barcelona: Lumen.

———. 1984. *La nave de los locos.* Barcelona: Seix Barral.

———. 1985. *La tarde del dinosaurio.* Barcelona: Plaza y Janés.

———. 1988. *La rebelión de los niños.* Barcelona: Seix Barral.

Piglia, Ricardo. 1980. *Respiración artificial.* Buenos Aires: Pomaire.

Puig, Manuel. 1973. *The Buenos Aires Affair.* Buenos Aires: Sudamericana.

———. 1976. *El beso de la mujer araña.* Barcelona: Seix Barral.

———. 1979. *Pubis angelical.* Barcelona: Seix Barral.

———. 1980. *Maldición eterna a quien lea estas páginas.* Barcelona: Seix Barral.

Rama, Angel. 1982. *La novela latinoamericana. Panoramas 1920–1980.* Bogota: Colcultura.

———. 1984. *Más allá del boom: literatura y mercado.* Buenos Aires: Folios.

———. 1978. "La riesgosa navegación del escritor exiliado." *Nueva sociedad* 35 (March–April): 5–15.

Reati, Fernando. 1992. *Nombrar lo innombrable. Violencia política y novela argentina 1975–1985.* Buenos Aires: Legasa.

Rocca, Pablo. 1993. "35 años en *Marcha*: escritura y ambiente literario en *Marcha* y en el Uruguay, 1939–1974." *Nuevo texto crítico* 6.11: 3–151.

Rosencof, Mauricio. 1998–1990. *Teatro escogido.* 2 vols. Montevideo: TAE.

———, and E. Fernández Huidobro. 1989. *Memorias del calabozo.* 3 vols. Montevideo: TAE.

Saer, Juan José. 1980. *Nadie nada nunca.* Mexico City: Siglo XXI.

———. 1983. *El entenado.* Mexico City and Buenos Aires: Folios.

Soriano, Osvaldo. 1982a. *Cuarteles de invierno.* Buenos Aires: Bruguera.

———. 1982b. *No habrá más penas ni olvido.* Buenos Aires: Bruguera.

Sosnowski, Saúl. 1988. *Represión y reconstrucción de una cultura: El caso argentino.* Buenos Aires: Editorial Universitaria de Buenos Aires.

———, ed. 1987. *Represión, exilio y democracia: la cultura uruguaya.* College Park: University of Maryland; Montevideo: Ediciones de la Banda Oriental.

Spiller, Roland, ed. 1991. *La novela argentina de los años 80.* Frankfurt: Vervuert.

Tizón, Héctor. 1984. *La casa y el viento.* Buenos Aires: Legasa.

Traba, Marta. 1979. *Homérica Latina.* Bogotá: Carlos Valencia.

———. 1981. *Conversación al sur.* Mexico City: Siglo XXI.

Valenzuela, Luisa. 1975. *Aquí pasan cosas raras.* Buenos Aires: Ediciones de la Flor.

———. 1983. *Cola de lagartija.* Buenos Aires: Bruguera.

Viñas, David. 1958. *Los dueños de la tierra.* Buenos Aires: Losada.

———. 1968. *Los hombres de a caballo.* Mexico City: Siglo XXI.

———. 1979. *Cuerpo a cuerpo.* Mexico City: Siglo XXI.

———. 1982. *Indios, ejército y frontera.* Mexico City: Siglo XXI.

Walsh, María Elena. 1995. *Desventuras en el país-jardín-de-infantes. Crónicas 1947–1995.* Buenos Aires: Seix Barral.

Walsh, Rodolfo. 1981. *Obra literaria completa.* Mexico City: Siglo XXI.

———. 1995. *El violento oficio de escribir. Obra periodística (1953–1977).* Ed. Daniel Link. Buenos Aires: Planeta.

CHAPTER 45

WRITERS UNDER (AND AFTER) THE CHILEAN MILITARY DICTATORSHIP

Javier Campos

Political Exclusion and the New Writer

Tejas Verdes: Diario de un campo de concentración en Chile [1974; *Diary of a Chilean Concentration Camp,* 1975] by Hernán Valdés (b. 1934) is one of the earliest testimonial diaries written outside the country within a few months of the military coup d'état in Chile (1973) that gives an account of the impact political exclusion had on Chilean literature. The effect of this exclusion has been one of the main themes that runs through much of Chilean art and literature. For some fifteen years it cast its huge shadow over every genre, from the most traditional (poetry, narrative, theater, cinema, and painting) to other alternative nonprint modes of expression born of these circumstances (videos, tapestries, urban street art, poetry on cassettes, and so on). The total exclusion of the political voice became obsessive and dominated texts written as much within as outside the country, no matter the genre. The authors who remained in Chile had to abide strictly by State censorship (and self-censure) if they wished to be published; this often led them to create a language that implied "the unsayable." Of course, the situation was quite different for those who went into exile. Five years after the coup, Jaime Concha (b. 1938) and Antonio Skármeta (b. 1940) summarized what had been happening to Chilean literature written in this new environment and provided a prognosis, which in hindsight from the turn of the new century, is quite accurate:

> En el desierto cultural que la Junta Militar intenta imponer a sangre y fuego, ya no existen más las diferencias entre lo político y lo literario (esas diferencias que, en los buenos tiempos democráticos, eran materia de infinitas controversias escolásticas). El simple hecho de escribir es, ahora, literario y político a la vez. (Concha 98)

> In the cultural desert in which the military junta attempts to impose at any cost, there are no longer any differences between the political and the literary (those differences which, in the good democratic days, gave rise to endless academic controversies). The act of writing is now both literary and political.

Antonio Skármeta wrote at the same time:

> Mirada en conjunto, la narrativa chilena de estos últimos cinco años se ocupa predominantemente del movimiento político y sus personajes centrales son de la burguesía o de la pequeña burguesía. El proletariado, protagonista y víctima de la historia, aparece marginalmente falseado en la visión de los escritores no revolucionarios, o excesivamente idealizado en aquellos más comprometidos, donde abundan poetizaciones voluntaristas. Los artistas de izquierda asumen masivamente temas vinculados a la historia urgente de su patria y abandonan asuntos sutiles y temporales. (94)

> Seen as a whole, the narrative of the last five years is predominantly concerned with the political movement, and its central characters are from the bourgeoisie or from the petite bourgeoisie. The proletariat, as protagonist and victim of history, appears marginal and distorted from the perspective of

non-revolutionary writers or excessively idealized in the more committed works, charged with willful lyricism. The artists of the Left all embrace themes related to the immediate history of their country and abandon subtle and temporal matters.

Even if Hernán Valdés's testimony is a good example of the fate Concha and Skármeta describe during the dictatorship, within the first few pages of *Tejas Verdes* his author/narrator clearly establishes the interrelations of the physically and emotionally helpless person with the absolute and repressive power of the State. Political exclusion, understood as the violent overthrow of a government constitutionally elected by popular vote, dramatically affects the whole of society. *Tejas Verdes* does not explain everything, however, nor does the rest of Chilean literature written during those fifteen years of military dictatorship. Hernán Valdés's testimony is, however, the precursor of the new writing that emerges from the conflict written by a petit bourgeois who has experienced political exclusion in his own country and in his own body; that is to say, he has suffered torture and the loss of his freedom as a citizen within his homeland. In the case of *Tejas Verdes,* the author/narrator is sent to a concentration camp for several days. He begins to awaken conflictively, for the first time, to his new role as a writer in a society in which the freedom, including artistic freedom, he had previously taken for granted, is, as he perceives it, besieged, broken, and plunged into the subterranean depths of the demonic desire of Chilean fascism (see Dorfman 1986, 198–225).

This nascent writer's narrative gaze oscillates between his new emotional and physical responses and those of the torturer, who, brutalized on his journey to the depths of horror, in his turn brutalizes both the tortured detainee and the population whose most basic human rights have been removed indefinitely. The writer fluctuates between the initial anger of feeling imprisoned and the despair of having to leave his homeland. The testimonial genre *Tejas Verdes* introduces into Chilean literature at the time of the coup d'état, constitutes, for almost two decades, one of the main and primary modes of representing Chilean political reality, and as a result both men and women writers took on the responsibility of the committed writer. There is broad consensus on this among critics, one of whom characterizes the Chilean narrative written within and outside the country during the dictatorship in the following way:

> Esta (1) *cuestiona la retórica del discurso oficial* y se propone como otro discurso alternativo además de enfrentarse a la debilidad del discurso populista anterior (*El paso de los gansos* (1975); *Coral de guerra* (1979) y *Una especie de memoria* (1983) de Fernando Alegría (1918)); (2) *desconstruye la familia patriarcal burguesa y el exilio territorial interno* ("Casa de campo" (1978) y "El jardín de al lado" (1981) de José Donoso (1924–1996)); (3) *refiere al fracaso histórico del discurso populista* ("La visita del presidente" (1983) de Juan Villegas (b. 1934));

y *(4) desconstruye los valores de la burguesía tradicional y la inhumanidad del golpe* ("La casa de los espíritus" (1982) de Isabel Allende (b. 1942)). (Jara 131–32)

(1) Besides confronting the ineffectiveness of the earlier populist discourse, it *questions the rhetoric of official discourse* and proposes itself as an alternative discourse (*El paso de los gansos* [1975; *The Chilean Spring*, 1980], *Coral de guerra* [1979; Chorus of War], and *Una especie de memoria* [1983; A Kind of Memoir] by Fernando Alegría [b. 1918]; (2) *it deconstructs the bourgeois patriarchal family and internal exile* (*Casa de campo* [1978; *A House in the Country*, 1983] and *El jardín de al lado* [1981; *The Garden Next Door*, 1992] by José Donoso [1924–1998]); (3) *it exposes the political failure of populist discourse* (*La visita del presidente* [1983; The President's Visit] by Juan Villegas [b. 1934]); and (4) *it deconstructs the purported family values of the bourgeoisie and the inhumanity of the military* (*La casa de los espíritus* [1982; *The House of the Spirits*, 1985] by Isabel Allende [b. 1942]).

These characteristics may be applied equally to other genres and to the alternative and unprecedented richness of new forms of expression of the prolific artistic production of this period.

In his studies of Chilean narrative during this period, José Promis has written the best expositions of the narrative of political exclusion–even though he omits the four important novels of Diamela Eltit (b. 1949) (*Lumpérica* (1983; *E. Luminata*, 1997), *Por la patria* [1986; For the Fatherland], *El cuarto mundo* [1988; *The Fourth World*, 1995], *El padre mío* [1989; My Father]). In his words,

Obligada a sobrevivir bajo dichas condiciones, la novela chilena publicada en el interior del país ha exhibido dos fundamentales orientaciones discursivas de acuerdo a la actitud con que el narrador se ha enfrentado a las exigencias del discurso oficial: el discurso *acomodado* y el discurso *contestatario*.
Como su nombre lo indica, la novela acomodada es aquella que ofrece un "artificio" narrativo y una visión de mundo congruentes con los presupuestos ideológicos del discurso elaborado por la dictadura. . . .
El discurso "contestatario" es aquel que se desarrolla como reacción a los contenidos ideológicos encerrados en el discurso oficial. . . .
Por razones obvias, se podría decir que hasta mediados de los años ochenta la mayoría de las novelas escritas en el exterior desarrollaban este tipo de discurso con una libertad mucho más amplia que la exhibida por las novelas contestatarias escritas en Chile durante la primera década de la dictadura militar. Estas últimas debieron enfrentarse desde muy temprano después de 1973 a la vigencia de la censura y de la autocensura que se generó como consecuencia natural de la primera. De aquí entonces que mientras existió oficialmente en Chile la censura de libros los novelistas disidentes del interior se vieron obligados a desarrollar diversos "registros" narrativos para textualizar su inconformismo hacia la norma social imperante y hacia el discurso oficial que la transmitía. (Promis 21–23)

Forced to survive under adverse conditions, the Chilean novel published in that country developed two fundamental discursive patterns depending on the attitude taken by the narrator with respect to the imperative demands of official discourse: *accommodating* and *contestatory* discourses.
As the word indicates, the accommodating novel is one that develops a narrative "artifice" and a worldview commensurate with the ideological presuppositions of the official discourse elaborated by the dictatorship. . . .
"Contestatory" discourse is that which develops as a reaction to the ideology contained in official discourse. . . .
For obvious reasons, until the mid 1980s, novels written outside Chile developed with a far richer freedom of expression than was the case with the contestatory novels written in Chile during the first decade of the dictatorship (1973–1983). These novels had to confront censorship and self-censorship (which is a natural result of the former) very soon after the take-over in 1973. Consequently as long as official censorship existed in Chile for the dissident novelists in the country, the writers had to develop various narrative registers in order to textualize their opposition to the dictatorship's imperative social norm and the official discourse that transmitted it.

Political Exclusions and Inclusions

Literary critics must exclude certain texts from critical studies in order to maintain their focus, although they often later discover that the omitted texts are crucial works. Nevertheless, in the context of political exclusion (which includes the whole country), our focus is on how literary and cultural workers wittingly or unwittingly provide a theoretical justification for this exclusion. Personally affected by the ideology of political exclusion, these develop theories for the purpose of determining what is and what is not literature that meaningfully contests the official discourse of the dictatorship. In other words, they turn on themselves; in a futile effort to outdo each other, they inadvertently further the aims of the dictatorship.

In January 1987, fifteen years after the coup d'état, Spanish intellectuals organized a grand celebration of the art and culture produced in Chile under the title of *Chile Vive: Memoria Activa* [Chile Lives: Active Memory]; this was "quizás la mayor y más ambiciosa empresa de difusión cultural chilena" (6) ("perhaps the greatest and most ambitious promotion of Chilean culture ever undertaken in Spain"). There were painting, sculpture, photography, and architecture exhibitions, poetry recitals, music, performances put on by three theater companies, videos, colloquia, and debates; also participating was a group from the *Vicaría de la Solidaridad* [Vicariate of Solidarity], the most liberal wing of the Chilean Catholic Church, which had defended political prisoners and sought information on those missing. However, there were no representatives of the *Canto nuevo* [New Song]–Chilean rock music–or any exhibits of the literature, cinema, art, or music produced in exile. In fact, literature was hardly represented at all. What had certainly been rendered invisible was the work of women writers and of those who had developed different styles from those of the successful Boom, the like of which had not been seen before (see Bianchi; Zurita; Campos 1987; Berchenko; Campos 1990; Hurtado; Epple; Moors; Fernández). Literature had continued along the lines described by Concha and Skármeta ten years earlier, lines that were still completely relevant at the time of the *Chile Vive: Memoria Activa* exhibition in Spain, as René Jara and others confirmed at the time and throughout the next decade (see also Alonso *et al.* and Triviños 1992a, 1992b). That is to say, the writers created an esthetics of rupture that fitted in perfectly with the testimonial mode used to express political exclusion under the dictatorship.

Among the young invited writers, who were considered the most representative of the literature produced in the country, there was only one poet, Raúl Zurita (b. 1951), who had, at the end of the seventies, proposed a new language with nine other poets for the purposes of responding to, deconstructing, and denouncing political exclusion. Nicanor Parra (b. 1914) and Enrique Lihn (1929–1988) were among the poets invited from the *Generación del 38* and from the *Generación del 50*. Not one fiction writer from the post-coup group was represented, and perhaps the most inexplicable absence was that of Diamela Eltit, who had already published her two most important works: *Lumpérica* (1983) and *Por la Patria* (1986).

However good one's intentions may be, the mere act of creating a cultural work under a dictatorship does not instantly and automatically make it a lasting work of art. This is where the theme of political exclusion as the subject-matter for literary production under dictatorial regimes becomes a more thorny issue. Wherever there is censorship and repression, sometimes necessarily exaggerated differences of opinion emerge concerning which artistic products should be included and which excluded in the contestation of political exclusion. Which are the most representative artistic works? How can one separate the wheat from the chaff? When will criticism and an appropriate cultural policy under a democratic state be able to cope with the cultural tragedy of exclusion and still recognize relative artistic merit?

Among the publications produced after the *Chile Vive* exhibition in Spain, an article by Enrique Lihn written in Madrid at the time stands out; he reflects on Chilean literary production during the dictatorship:

> Me concierne, en particular, la poesía y la literatura que hemos hecho los chilenos en el exilio interior. Más, es claro, que la obra de los escritores de la diáspora, quienes, por obvias razones, han sido poco leídos dentro de Chile y que han hecho también en general, literatura explícitamente comprometida, de servicio, ocasionalmente panfletaria. Y también documentos de gran valor literario (*Tejas Verdes* de Valdés) o muy buena poesía política o no. (Lihn 1987)

> What particularly concerns me is the poetry and literature that we have written in internal exile. [It clearly concerns me] more than the work of the diaspora writers, who for obvious reasons have hardly been read in Chile and have generally written overtly committed literature, which occasionally serves the purposes of pamphleteering. Although among these [works of the diaspora writers] there were also documents of great literary value (*Tejas Verdes* by Valdés) and very good poetry, be it political or not.

According to this sweeping generalization, it appears that after fourteen years of dictatorship the only literature of exile was, as a rule, committed literature (that is, resembling socialist realism), of which *Tejas Verdes,* published thirteen years earlier, is the one work worth mentioning. Lihn ignores a large number of writers, perhaps because they were, in his eyes, pamphleteers or they did not display what he considered representative artistic value—such as Fernando Alegría, Antonio Skármeta (b. 1940), Isabel Allende, Ariel Dorfman (b. 1942), and José Donoso, who had all published more than one novel and other collections of short stories during those fifteen years. Lihn's reference to the poetry written in exile is unexpectedly misleading. It is surprising that a poet such as Lihn, who had often travelled abroad during these years, who was a discerning reader and a critic conversant with theoretical stances, should be so ill-informed about the Chilean poetry that was being written outside the country (in the United States of America, France, Spain, and Canada, to mention only a few of the important places). In relation to the poetry, "be it political or not," written in exile, which Lihn mentions in passing, without giving any further explanation when he speaks of the poets Gonzalo Millán (b. 1947) and Waldo Rojas (b. 1944), he makes another generalization, finally giving the impression that the literature produced in exile was very different (and Lihn is also ambiguous in this respect) to that written in internal exile.

What is curious is that Lihn's opinion and analysis coincides with Raúl Zurita's theoretical stance concerning *literariness* developed in his essay *Literatura, lenguaje y sociedad (1973–1983)* [Literature, Language and Society] published in 1983, where he discusses ten years of literary production in Chile. Both of these writers brought their influence to bear on the exclusion of some works (and the inclusion of others) that were considered to represent cultural production under the dictatorship from 1973 to 1987. What is most peculiar about this disinterment and archaeological interpretation of *Chile Vive* of 1987 is Lihn's appraisal of the literature of internal exile, which highlights its merits and differentiates it artistically from that of external exile:

> Escritores y poetas hemos aguzado el espíritu de negación en Chile. Fascinados negativamente por la realidad de hecho, hemos establecido con ella distintas relaciones mediatas, muy alejadas casi todas de los referentes habituales o propios del realismo; pero relaciones *profundas*, que nos inscriben a muchos en el espacio de la dictadura y nos hacen legibles si se atiene a esa inscripción. Se ha insistido en la literaturidad de la obra literaria y se ha puesto en juego la relación del arte con la magia, la profecía, el delirio carnavalesco o esperpéntico.

> As writers and poets we have sharpened the spirit of denial in Chile. Negatively fascinated by reality, we have established different mediated relations with it, almost all of which are far removed from the familiar referents of realism. These relations are profound, they inscribe many of us in the space of the dictatorship and make us intelligible if attention is drawn to this inscription in denial. The literariness of the literary work has been insisted upon and the relationship of art to magic, prophecy, carnivalesque, and grotesque delirium has been brought into play.

Looking at this from the distance of the start of a new century, one might find surprising that this important poet's judgment, analysis, and interpretation (which had great influence on young Chilean poets living under the dictatorship) practically formed a manifesto for poetry and fiction alike. Lihn insisted upon the term *literariness,* which he describes in the above passage so as to privilege the one circle of writers who took this route.

In another part of the same article, (which was not dashed off with journalistic haste but was well thought out because it appeared in Madrid's *Diario 16*), he put the finishing touches on his esthetic manifesto by directly expressing his empathy with Raúl Zurita, who became—in the words of another Chilean critic, Ignacio Valente (pseud. José Miguel Ibañez Langlois [b. 1936], a writer for the newspaper *El Mercurio*)—the spokesman of dissident poetry under the military dictatorship, precisely because his writing worked out this literariness most successfully:

> Raúl Zurita es uno de los diez poetas jóvenes de vanguardia que, según dos de sus exegetas—Zurita mismo y otro de ellos—son los protagonistas de la poesía del período. De este grupo se distinguen como personalidades literarias definidas el sofisticado Juan Luis Martínez—poeta secreto, Diego Maquieira, autor del sorprendente libro *La Tirana*, y el autor primeramente nombrado. Esto es lo que puedo decir desde adentro sobre *Chile Vive*. (Lihn 1987)

> Raúl Zurita is one of ten young poets of the avant-garde who, according to its exponents—Zurita himself and others—are the leaders of the poetry of the period. The outstanding figures in this group are the sophisticated Juan Luis Martínez (1942–1993), a secret poet, Diego Maquieira (b. 1953), the author of the surprising book *La Tirana*, as well as the aforementioned writer. This is what I can say from within about *Chile Vive*.

Despite the subtle irony in these remarks, there is no doubt in his mind that out of all those writing poetry in internal exile during the fifteen years of dictatorial rule, only three men are worth even naming: Zurita, the most important figure, Juan Luis Martínez (1942–1993), and Diego Maquieira. According to Lihn's pronouncement, they were the only voices that had expressed aesthetically the rupture caused by the military dictatorship; they alone represented the vanguard of that poetic manifesto. It would be pointless, for obvious reasons, to insist upon the issue, but Lihn does not mention one woman poet or fiction writer. What is true is that this discriminatory selection made by an important Chilean poet was, at the time, so arbitrary that it had the most negative repercussions on later critical assessments that set out to determine who were the most representative writers of the dictatorial regime. At this time, at the start of the twenty-first century, with some distance from the dictatorship and in the midst of this critical re(-)vision of Latin American literary history, it would be most sensible to recognize that these were very different literary times, times that saw an astounding proliferation of poetry (Campos 1987, 11–14; Carrasco 31–46; Campos 1994, 891–912). Such an expansion did not occur in fiction during this period; however, the two novels written by Diamela Eltit are excellent examples of Lihn's aesthetic characteristics.

Popular theater (see Diego Muñoz) and professional theater of this period can be characterized as follows:

> Una representación que aludía críticamente a la realidad a través de un decir sin decir, lo implícito, lo metafórico, eran elementos centrales en el teatro, favorecido por la ansiedad del público de encontrar claves de reconocimiento y alusión a las interpretaciones silenciadas de la realidad; . . . en su mayoría fueron obras realistas y sus protagonistas personajes del pueblo. El tema central es los efectos sociales de la cesantía que provoca Pinochet, y los despidos por razones políticas. Se indaga en la angustia existencial que genera esta situación por los quiebres en la identidad y sociabilidad; por los cambios de roles y aprendizajes de la mujer al entrar al campo informal en suplencia del marido; por las penurias del hambre y la escasez; por los abusos e insensibilidad social de las autoridades; por el ambiente de miedo que se vive cotidianamente . . . . [A]lgunas de estas obras eran ejemplificadoras, en el sentido de mostrar un camino de salida a los problemas: apelaban a la unidad de los trabajadores, a la organización social, a la lucha por los derechos, etc. Otras, en cambio, mostraban una situación de desesperanza sin salida cuyo desenlace posible era la muerte o la locura. En las primeras el humor era constante. En las segundas, el melodrama y el absurdo. (1990, 153–54)

What was central to theater were performances that alluded critically to reality by using such strategies as the saying without saying, the implicit, and the metaphorical, which most aptly met the audience's desire to discover the codes for deciphering the references that were muted interpretations of reality [;] . . . they were mostly realistic works and the dramatis personae were working-class people. The central themes were the social effects of lower-class unemployment caused by the Pinochet government and of the dismissals for political reasons. What was explored was the existential anxiety caused by the loss of identity and social freedom; by women's changing roles as they were forced to enter the work place to supplement their husbands' incomes; by the wretchedness caused by hunger and scarcity of basic goods; by the military authorities' constant abuse of power; and their social insensitivity by the pervasive sense of fear . . . . [S]ome of these works were exemplary in the sense that they indicated a solution to the problems: they proposed unity among workers, a renewal of social organization, and a struggle for human rights, and so on.

Others indicate a situation of hopeless despair ending in death or madness. Humor is the constant of the former, while melodrama and the absurd rule the latter.

This saying without saying or covert "literariness," which Zurita and Lihn had both looked for in poetry, had its antecedents in the theater.

In relation to fiction, the prose style of choice was not, as the critic René Jara has pointed out, difficult to find. Most works followed, I would suggest, one of the routes that María de la Luz Hurtado proposes drama had taken; that is, during the early years of the dictatorship (1973–1980), narrative fiction generally demonstrated precisely that hopeless despair probably ending in death or madness and tended to use melodrama or the absurd as its generic model. Rodrigo Cánovas has undertaken the task of exploring these earlier studies and is, moreover, among the first to include the "avant-garde transgression" of some women's fiction, which critics had sorely neglected as an important part of the response to the unprecedented tragedy of Chile. This transgression, typical of the fiction published during the 1980s, is essential to an understanding of Chilean women´s narrative, but it was never mentioned by earlier critics and had to wait, especially in the case of Diamela Eltit, until women critics began to study it. The narrative discourse of *Lumpérica, Por la patria,* and *The Fourth World* revisit the experience of childbirth using a combination of genres that subsequently are broken down. Family relations are combined with a de-maternalized and de-paternalized biography of a collective I, completely rejecting the traditional model of family identity.

Political Exclusion and Artistic Censorship

Dissident artistic production began shortly after the dictator seized power. In hindsight, it might seem inexplicable that this appeared in its different modes (poetry, theater, tapestry, *arpilleras* [a kerchief with motifs embroidered on it], the visual arts, popular music, and rock and roll) under the very noses of the military authorities who were imposing measures of harsh repression and authoritarian abuse throughout Chilean society. In Carlos Catalán's opinion, this alternative culture emerged from a pressing necessity of survival experienced by a culture with a genuine national identity. The regime completely erased Chilean culture from all the media it controlled and had at its disposal (that is, all the mass media, publishing houses, academic spaces, museums, bookstores, and libraries). Although Catalán's argument is valid, it also implies that wherever there is an authoritarian regime, there has to be an alternative artistic culture—an assertion that is not warranted. There may well be a spirit of national identity (individual and collective) to challenge the regime in power, but it does not necessarily have to express its contestation artistically. The Chilean situation is unique—and very different from that in Argentina and in Uruguay—among the authoritarian regimes of the Southern Cone in the 1970s, precisely because of the proliferation of artistic expression that was not as pronounced among its neighbors (see Catalán and Rivera; Mella et al.; Zurita; Rojo 1985; Campos 1987; Diego Muñoz; Subercaseaux 1987).

The development of this alternative artistic production within the authoritarian space of the Pinochet dictatorship cannot be understood without bearing in mind that the Chilean socio-political and historical situation had, before the coup d'état, exerted a powerful influence on most popular and certain middle-class sectors (see Borón). The artists and intellectuals who remained in the country after 1973 and the younger intelligentsia who evolved in the new circumstances imposed by the government had similarly been influenced by this situation. In sum, most Chileans still remembered the political freedom and social consciousness learned from social militancy during the Allende years; they had experienced life before the dictatorship, and it is clear today that if they had buried their heads in the sand, it would never have been possible to unseat the military regime in 1988 and 1989 (by plebiscite and elections, respectively) or to return to what is really "la democracia pactada" [negotiated democracy] (see Letelier). More significant than any of the other factors Catalán mentions is this earlier empowered political culture, which had such an impact on artistic production. In the case of Chile, this had begun at the end of the nineteenth century and reached its height during the three years of Salvador Allende's rule. The socio-political, but not necessarily militant, consciousness of many artists and intellectuals who remained in Chile after 1973 (including the younger writers, who had, in one way or another, to pick up the information from their elders) was a significant factor in the alternative cultural production that began underground in the early years of the dictatorship and was much more visible at the beginning of the 1980s. What is most important is that this work (circulating underground under conditions of official censorship until 1983) emerged and was developed within a space absolutely controlled by the dictatorship. I certainly do not wish to belittle the extreme conditions of repression in other countries under which artistic expression can exist, but in the case of Chile there is a complex relationship between the pre-dictatorship artistic, political, and generational experience and the later political experience of a repressive social structure. It is this relationship and not simply the fact of living under a state of repression that gave rise to the unprecedented explosion of contestatory alternative art under the Chilean dictatorship.

All the above raises one question in particular: How could this prolific and diverse alternative culture evolve in such an authoritarian regime, which was licensed to prevent any subversive activity under the so-called Doctrine of National Security introduced by the military regime? (See O'Donnell.) The answer is the authoritarian mind of the Chilean military; this alternative culture was irrelevant because it had no power to challenge the political, ideological, and economic project or make any radical changes to it. For example, a poem, novel, painting, play, song, or *arpillera* was not, from the point of view of the junta, going to destroy a regime that considered itself legally constituted by the time it initiated its comprehensive transformation of the institutions and the *Estado de Compromiso* [The Committed State] (that is to say, the notorious seven modernizations that affected the State, economy, administration, health, education, labor relations, and agribusiness from 1979 onward). In fact, the Constitution drawn up by the military junta in 1980 confirms the absolute power of the regime and its almost total indifference to artistic dissidence. Moreover, the regime permitted this alternative production to continue because it did not want "international observers" to condemn it for repression of artists (see Promis). Despite the relative freedom artists enjoyed and the reluctance of the junta to persecute them, art was still produced quietly and on the fringes during the first phase of the dictatorship (1973–1976); the openness, originality, and diversity of the work written during the second phase (1976–1982) eventually gave way to the incredibly free production of the third phase

(from 1983 onward), in part perhaps because official censorship was suspended in 1983. The alternative culture or artistic expression the regime "permitted" consisted of all the forms mentioned earlier: poetry, theater, novels, short stories, tapestries, visual arts, and cultural research–(principally at Centro de Indagación y Expresión Cultural y Artística [Center for Research and Cultural and Artistic Expression]) (see Catalán and Munizaga).

In the case of Chile, there was thus no general or constant repression or persecution of artists *for what they created.* Some did, however, receive anonymous letters, or telephone calls issuing death threats (especially the men and women returning from exile, such as the poet Omar Lara [b. 1941]), and a number of plays and *arpillera* exhibitions were sabotaged. The performers of the Chilean "Nueva Canción" [New Song] deserve particular mention, however, because their lyrics were expressly political and had been immensely popular during Allende's time in power. The singer Victor Jara (1932–1973) was assassinated in the National Stadium a few days after the military coup; other well-known singers, such as Ángel Parra (b. 1943), Isabel Parra (b. 1937), and Patricio Manns (b. 1937), for example, and popular groups, such as "Quilapayun" and "Inti-Illimani," had to flee into exile because they would otherwise have met the same fate. The situation was very different under the dictatorships in Argentina and Uruguay, where there was no alternative culture of any consequence coexisting with the dominant culture of the regime.

Literature of Democratization or Neoliberalism: Inclusion in and Exclusion from the Market

In 1991 under the first government of Patricio Alwyn, voted in under the free elections after sixteen years of dictatorship, Alberto Fuguet (b. 1964), a 27-year-old writer, published an important novel, *Mala Onda [Bad Vibes,* 1997]. I say important because the novel introduces a new theme: that of the difficult and beautiful youth of the affluent upper and upper middle classes during the decline of the Chilean dictatorship, when the Neo-Liberal model and the new order of global economy were in full swing. The innovative and youthful style of this novel has nothing in common with that of earlier Chilean narratives (whether testimonial or exile literature, let alone Latin American magic realism). What we might call the *McOndo* world of the difficult yet marvelous virtual youth in times of globalization, described so well in the prologue to the book, acts to set an atmosphere for all its stories (see Fuguet and Gómez 1996, Campos 1999 and 2000a). It is worth quoting an extract from the prologue to *McOndo* (1996) in order to gain an insight into this new Chilean narrative within the diversity of today:

> [Esta] es una nueva generación literaria que es post-todo: post-modernismo, post-yuppie, post-comunismo, post-babyboom, post-capa de ozono. Aquí no hay realismo mágico, hay realismo virtual.
> Los cuentos de *McOndo* se centran en realidades individuales y privadas. Suponemos que ésta es una de las herencias de la fiebre privatizadora mundial.
> . . . estos escritores se preocuparan menos de su contingencia pública . . . .
> [Los cuentos] no son frescos sociales ni sagas colectivas.
> Si hace unos años la disyuntiva del escritor joven estaba entre tomar el lápiz o la carabina, ahora parece que lo más angustiante para escribir es elegir entre Windows 95 o Macintosh.
> En *McOndo* hay MacDonalds, computadores Mac y condominios, . . . hoteles cinco estrellas construidos con dinero lavado y *malls*

gigantescos.... [D]igamos que *McOndo* es MTV latina [porque] Latinoamérica [es MTV latina], es Televisa, es Miami, son las repúblicas bananeras y Borges y el Comandante Marcos y la CNN en español y el Nafta y Mercosur y la deuda externa...
(Fuguet and Gómez 10, 13, 15, 16)

(This) is a new literary generation that is post-everything: post-modernism, post-yuppie, post-communism, post-baby boom, post-ozone layer. There is no magic realism, but there is virtual realism.
The stories of *McOndo* focus on individual and private realities. We assume that this is one of the legacies of world privatization fever.... [T]hese writers are less concerned with their public contingency.... [The stories] are not social frescoes or collective sagas.
If the young writer's dilemma of the past was whether to take up a pencil or a gun, it now appears that the most distressing choice for the writer is between Windows 95 and Macintosh.
In *McOndo* there are MacDonalds, Mac computers and condominiums ... five-star hotels built with laundered money, gigantic malls.... [L]et's say that *McOndo* is Latino MTV (because) Latin America (is Latino MTV), it is Televisa, Miami, the banana republics, Borges, *Comandante* Marcos [sic], CNN in Spanish, Nafta, Mercosur, the foreign debt....]

In this so-called manifesto, this new prose narrative (developed exclusively by men) excludes, denies, suppresses, and eliminates any reference to all that has no direct bearing on it. In the current context of globalized inequality in Latin America and the rest of the world (see Hopenhayn; Bhalla et al.; Rodríguez Araujo; García Canclini 1999a and b; Martín Barbero; Ortiz), these writers feel closer to their generation—on a global scale—than to the national society to which they belong (see Subercaseaux 1997). What seems to concern them particularly are stories about the global culture of modern cities (in Chile or any other Latin American country) at the turn of the millennium.

Chilean literature written and published during the move toward democracy has grown more and more diverse, multicultural, and conflictive. Many of the new publishing houses, which are often well organized and have good national and international distribution (depending on the strength of their economic resources) exclude some writers and include others (see Pohl). The critics who adopted the National Reconciliation Policy and who emerged with the return to democracy assert that artistic circles in general have not been sufficiently outspoken in exposing and condemning the atrocities committed by the military regime's security agencies (see Lillo). It has also been pointed out that the modernizaton imposed by the military regime has excluded thousands who have remained on the margins in towns and cities (women, indigenous peoples, young and elderly people) (see Sosnowski *et al.*). The current neo-Liberal context privileges changes in the market; the current government has, to date, failed to devise a cultural policy that has the power to contribute to the design of a real and open politics of remembrance. In this light, those who have still not come to terms with the multicultural conditions caused by globalization are apparently encouraging the exclusion of that other diversity of the "subaltern" (see Beverly and Sanders).

Conclusion

The theme of political exclusion in Chilean literature, written both at home and in exile, at the time of the dictatorship created narrative, poetic, and dramatic voices that became obsessively concerned with deconstructing fascism or with returning to the past as the *via crucis* to understand what had led to this collective (and individual) breakdown of Chilean society. Critics have insisted on these characteristics for almost twenty years (see Concha, Skármeta, Dorfman 1996, Epple, Bianchi, Jara, Campos 2000a, and Rojo 1989, among others) when describing the literature written both at home and in exile. At the beginning of the seventies, some began to point out that several writers were promoting a new aesthetic, which they called literariness. This stance, which opposed the facile and worn-out socialist realism, was considered the best aesthetic representation of the deconstruction experienced while living under dictatorial oppression. It proposed, moreover, an original artistic response to political exclusion within Chile and, without belittling other voices, allowed for appreciation of the valuable contributions of such poets as Juan Luis Martínez, Raúl Zurita, Gonzalo Muñoz (b. 1956), etc., as well as the novelist Damiela Eltit. However, this is not the only convincing deconstruction of that context; many newer critical studies, from 1987 onward, have provided a greater sense of the real diversity of literary practices used to represent political exclusion in the different genres and alternative modes of expression, giving us a fuller picture of the vast and heterogeneous artistic production in Chile under the military dictatorship.

There is now a further diversification of artistic practices in the new context of democracy and the neo-Liberal economic model of today, for this has brought globalization with it. Some writers have been newly excluded because they are not prepared to meet the demands of the publishing market or because there is still no cultural policy designed to include the multiplicity of marginalized voices (see Campos 1999; 2000a; 2000b). Chile will have to live with this galloping globalization in the next millennium; but if less than half of the population can enjoy or indirectly take part in it, artistic production will continue to be negatively affected.

Translation by Charlotte Broad

Works Cited

Alegría, Fernando. 1975. *El paso de los gansos*. Long Island City: Ediciones Pulche.

———. 1979. *Coral de guerra*. Mexico City: Editorial Nueva Imagen.

———. 1983. *Una especie de memoria*. Mexico City: Editorial Nueva Imagen.

Allende, Isabel. 1982. *La casa de los espíritus*. Barcelona: Plaza & Janes.

Alonso, María Nieves, Juan Carlos Mestre, Mario Rodríguez, and Gilberto Triviños. 1989. *Las plumas del colibrí: quince años de poesía en Concepción, 1973–1988*. Santiago de Chile: Instituto de Promoción y Desarrollo.

Beverly, John, and James Sanders. 1997. "Negotiating with the Discipline: A Conversation on Latin American Subaltern Studies." *Journal of Latin American Studies* 6.2: 233–57.

Berchenko, Pablo. 1987. "Elementos para un índice bio-bibliográfico de las últimas promociones de poesía chilena." *Ventanal* (U de Perpignan) 12:141–70.

Bhalla, Bharat, et al. 1994. "The Paradox of Economic Globalism: The Myth and Reality of the 'Global Village'–The Changing Role of Multinational Corporations." *Business & The Contemporary World* 4. 131–42.

Bianchi, Soledad, ed. 1983. *Entre la lluvia y el arcoiris: algunos jóvenes poetas chilenos*. Rotterdam: Instituto para el Nuevo Chile.

Borón, Atilio. 1975. "Notas sobre las raíces histórico-estructurales de la movilización política en Chile." *Foro Internacional* 16.1: 64–121.

Campos, Javier. 1987. "Prólogo." *La joven poesía chilena en el periodo 1961–1973*. Minneapolis: Institute for the Study of Ideologies and Literature. 11–14.

———. 1990. "Arte alternativo y dictadura." *Cuadernos Hispanoamericanos* 482–83: 55–56.

———. 1994. "Lírica chilena de fin de siglo y (post) modernidad neoliberal en América Latina." *Revista Iberoamericana* 168–69: 891–912.

———. 1999. "Literature and Globalization: Chilean Narrative in the Time of Marvelous Neoliberalism." *Meditations* 22:150–63.

———. 2000a. "Literatura y globalización: la nueva narrativa chilena en los tiempos del *neoliberalismo maravilloso*." *Literatura Chilena Hoy: La difícil transición*. Ed. Karl Kohut and José Morales Saravia. Frankfurt and Madrid: Vervuert/Iberoamericana. 221–34.

———. 2000b. "Poesía y narrativa chilena/latinoamericana del tercer milenio o ¿cómo escribi(re)mos la globalización?" XXXII Congreso del Instituto Internacional de Literatura Iberoamericana. Universidad de Salamanca (July).

Cánovas, Rodrigo. 1991. "Una reflexión sobre la novelística chilena de los años 80." *Revista chilena de literatura* 38: 101–07.

Carrasco, Iván. 1989. "Poesía chilena de la última década (1977–1978)." *Revista chilena de literatura* 33: 31–46.

Catalán, Carlos. 1982. *Espacios de producción cultural alternativas en regímenes autoritarios*. Santiago de Chile: Centro de Indagación y Expresión Cultura y Artística.

Catalán, Carlos, and Giselle Munizaga. 1986. *Políticas culturales estatales bajo el autoritarismo en Chile*. Santiago de Chile: Centro de Indagación y Expresión Cultural y Artística.

Catalán, Carlos, and A. Rivera. 1979. *Canto popular. Periodo 1973–1978*. Santiago de Chile: Documento de Trabajo Centro de Indagación y Expresión Cultural y Artística.

Chile vive: memoria activa. 1997. Ed. Paulina Gutiérrez. Santiago de Chile and Madrid: Centro de Indagación y Expresión Cultural y Artística e Instituto de cooperación iberoamericana. n.p.

Concha, Jaime. 1979. "Testimonios de la lucha antifacista." *Casa de las Américas* 112: 95–105.

Donoso, José. 1978. *Casa de campo*. Barcelona: Seix Barral.

———. 1981. *El jardín de al lado*. Barcelona: Seix Barral.

Dorfman, Ariel. 1986. "Código político y código literario: el género testimonio en Chile hoy." *Testimonio y literatura*. Ed. René Jara and Hernán Vidal. Minneapolis: Institute for the Study of Ideologies and Literature. 170–234.

———. 1996. "Perspectivas y limitaciones de la novela chilena actual." *Anales de la Universidad de Chile* 140: 110–67.

Eltit, Diamela. 1983. *Lumpérica*. Santiago de Chile: Ediciones del Ornitorrinco.

———. 1986. *Por la patria*. Santiago de Chile: Ediciones del Ornitorrinco.

———. 1988. *El cuarto mundo*. Santiago de Chile: Editorial Planeta.

———. 1989. *El padre mío*. Santiago de Chile: Francisco Zegers Editor.

Epple, Juan A. 1994. "Acercamiento a la literatura testimonial de Chile." *Revista Iberoamericana* 168–69: 1154–59.

Fernández, Teodocio. 1996. "Medio siglo de narrativa chilena contemporánea." *República de las letras* 48: 153–66.

Fuguet, Alberto, and Sergio Gómez, ed. 1996. "Presentación del país MacOndo." *McOndo*. Barcelona: Grijalbo. 9–18.

———. 1999a. *La globalización imaginada*. Buenos Aires: Editorial Paidos.

———. 1999b. "La épica de la globalización y el melodrama de interculturalidad." *Nuevas perspectivas desde/sobre América Latina. El desafío de los estudios culturales*. Ed. Mabel Moraña. Santiago de Chile: Editorial Cuarto Propio e Instituto Internacional de Literatura Iberoamericana. 31–41.

Hopenhayn, Martín. 1994. *Ni apocalípticos ni integrados: aventuras de la modernidad en América Latina*. Santiago de Chile: Fondo de Cultura Económica.

Hurtado, María de la Luz. 1990. "Presencia del teatro chileno durante el gobierno militar." *Cuadernos Hispanoamericanos* 482–83: 149–60.

Jara, René. 1987. "Los límites de la representación, la novela chilena del golpe." *Para una fundación imaginaria de Chile: la obra literaria de Fernando Alegría*. Stanford: Stanford University Press. 131–38.

Letelier, Fabiola. 1996. "Impunidad y sus efectos en los procesos democráticos." Discurso de Apertura: Seminario Internacional < http://www.derechos.org/koaga/iii/3/apertura.html >

Lihn, Enrique. 1987. "*Chile vive*, visto por un chileno." *Diario 16* (Madrid, 1-02-87).

Lillo, Gastón. 1995. "El cine y el contexto político-cultural en el Chile de la posdictadura." *Revista canadiense de estudios hispánicos* 20.1: 31–42.

Maquieira, Diego. 1983. *La tirana*. Santiago de Chile: Ediciones Tempus Tacendi.

Martín Barbero, Jesús. 1999. "Globalización y multiculturalidad: notas para una agenda de investigación." *Nuevas perspectivas desde/sobre América Latina. El desafío de los estudios culturales*. Ed. Mabel Moraña. Santiago de Chile: Editorial Cuarto Propio e Instituto Internacional de Literatura Iberoamericana. 17–29.

Mella, Luis, et al. 1980. *Seminario de la canción popular chilena 1973–1979*. Santiago de Chile: Documento de Trabajo Centro de Indagación y Expresión Cultural y Artística.

Millán, Gonzalo. 1984. "Promociones poéticas emergentes; el Espíritu del Valle." *Posdata* 4: 2–9.

Moors, Ximena A. 1994. "Para una arqueología del testimonio: el rol de la Iglesia Católica en una producción textual (1973–1991)." *Revista Iberoamericana* 60.168–69: 1161–76.

Muñoz, Diego. 1987. "Problema en torno al teatro poblacional." *Poética de la población marginal. Teatro poblacional chileno (1978–1985): antología crítica*. Minneapolis, MN: Prisma Institute. 12–75.

Muñoz, Gonzalo. 1981. *Exit*. Santiago de Chile: Ediciones Archivos.

O'Donnell, Guillermo. 1982. "El estado autoritario en el Cono Sur de América Latina." *Revista de la Universidad de México* 12.

Ortiz, Renato. 1999. "Diversidad cultural y cosmopolitismo." *Nuevas perspectivas desde/sobre América Latina: el desafío de los estudios culturales*. Ed. Mabel Moraña. Santiago de Chile: Editorial Cuarto Propio e Instituto Internacional de Literatura Iberoamericana. 43–54.

Pohl, Burkhard. 2000. "El discurso transnacional en la difusión de la narrativa latinoamericana." *Cuadernos Hispanoamericanos* 604: 43–51.

Promis, José. 1990. "Balance de la novela en Chile: 1973–1990." *Hispamérica* 55: 15–26.

Rodríguez Araujo, Octavio. 1996. "Estados-nación y mundialización económica/II." *La Jornada* Mexico City (23-03-96).

Rojo, Grinor. 1985. *Muerte y resurrección del teatro chileno*. Madrid: Ediciones Michay.

———. 1989. "Veinte años de poesía chilena: algunas reflexiones en torno a la antología de Steven White." *Crítica del exilio. Ensayos sobre literatura latinoamericana actual*. By Grinor Rojo. Chile: Pehuén. 55–75.

Skármeta, Antonio. 1979. "Narrativa chilena después del golpe." *Casa de las Américas* 112: 83–94.

Sosnowski, Saúl, Bernardo Subercaseaux, and Antonio Garretón. 1993. *Cultura, autoritarismo y redemocratización en Chile*. Santiago de Chile: Fondo de Cultura Económica.

Subercaseaux, Bernardo. 1987. *Sobre cultura popular: itinerario de concepciones operantes*. Santiago de Chile: Centro de Indagación y Expresión Cultural y Artística.

———. 1997. "Canto a Chile. América Latina: nuevos escenarios culturales, nuevas mirada." *Cuadernos Hispanoamericanos* 560: 107–12.

Triviños, Gilberto. 1992a. "Cierta oscura poesía de provincias." *Cuatro poetas chilenos.* Ed. María Nieves Alonso, Mario Rodríguez, and Gilberto Triviños. Concepción: LAR. 13–45.

———. 1992b. "Poesía en Concepción: 1973–1988." *Cuatro poetas chilenos.* Ed. María Nieves Alonso, Mario Rodríguez, and Gilberto Triviños. Concepción: LAR. 49–90.

Valdés, Hernán. 1974. *Tejas Verdes: diario de un campo de concentración en Chile.* Esplugues de Llobregat, Barcelona: Editorial Ariel.

———. 1975. *Tejas verdes. Diary of a Chilean Concentration Camp.* Trans. Jo Labanyi. London: Gallancz.

Villegas, Juan. 1983. *La visita del presidente, o, Adoraciones fálicas en el valle del pueblo.* Mexico City: Editorial Centauro.

Zurita, Raul. 1983. *Literatura, lenguaje y sociedad (1973–1983).* Santiago de Chile: Centro de Indagación y Expresión Cultural y Artística.

SECTION II
MODERNITY, MODERNISMS, AND THEIR AVATARS

CHAPTER 46

NATIONS OF MODERNITY

Javier Lasarte Valcárcel

Postmodernity and the Nation

At the end of the twentieth century, it has become common-place among Latin American intellectuals to criticize the ideas of nation, national culture, and national identity. These intellectuals are torn by perplexity and disillusionment, decentered in their quest to redefine their *place* in the national scene; it is like "avanzar a tientas, sin mapa o con un sólo mapa *nocturno*" (Martín-Barbero 1991, 229) ("exploring in a tentative almost groping fashion without a guiding map or with only an obscure, nighttime map"; 1993, 212); they are normally residents of the academy and propose that we read an(other) history (or histories) and question our immediate past, dissolving everything that only a decade earlier underpinned their convictions, beliefs, basic ideas, and sites of discourse.

Historical change and the crises in cultural and political models have made nationalism—and its extended version, Latin Americanism, which draws fervent throngs of Left-wing intellectuals—a "relic from the past" (Schwarz 1995, 268). In a post-catastrophic society, "lo que se encuentra a la orden del día no es el *abandono* de las ilusiones nacionales, sino su crítica específica, que acompaña su desintegración, *la cual es uno de los contenidos reales de nuestro tiempo*" (Schwarz 1994, 32) ("what is on the agenda is not the *renunciation* of national illusions but criticism of the same, which goes hand in glove with its disintegration; *this is one of the real topics of our times*").

The rationalist criticism of Latin American intellectuals—the cornerstone of the invention of national and continental cultural authenticity and specificity—is on the agenda at the turn of the new century—at times in ironic (if not sarcastic) versions, as in the case of Castro-Gómez, who talks about the "síndrome de las venas abiertas" ("syndrome of open veins"), or in the case of José Joaquín Bruner, who coined the idea of *Macondoamérica* (Castro-Gómez 57). Nevertheless, this criticism has, on other occasions, given rise to powerful reconsiderations of such crucial notions as culture, identity, nationality, and popularism for the purpose of presenting them not so much as abstractions or substantial essences but as practices permeated by the avatars of modernizing processes throughout the century. Such texts as *Culturas híbridas. estrategias para entrar y salir de la modernidad* [1990; *Hybrid Cultures: Strategies for Entering and Leaving Modernity,* 1995] by Néstor García Canclini or *De los medios a las mediaciones. comunicación, cultura y hegemonía* [1991; *Communication, Culture and Hegemony: From the Media to Mediations,* 1993] by Martín-Barbero are indisputable

examples of this tendency, even if they were, in one way or another, anticipated by the discussions of Ángel Rama (1926–1983) and Antonio Cornejo Polar (1936–1997). The idea of a fixed reading that orders the whole of Latin American culture has been undermined: "El todo se encuentra hecho trizas" (Ortiz 87) ("the whole has been torn to shreds"). This reading of the present emphasizes disintegration, deterritorialization, and decentralization—exactly the opposite of the desires imagined by the national projects. According to Renato Ortiz, "[d]e ahí proviene la sensación de crisis que atraviesa el debate contemporáneo. Las fronteras de la nación no pueden contener más los movimientos identitarios que existen en su seno" (89) ("(t)his gives rise to the sense of crisis that runs through our current debate. National borders can no longer contain the shifting identities within them").

It seems that three main factors are responsible for this change. The first consists of the processes of transnationalization of mass society; if borders do not implode, they will explode, thus underlining their complexity and their unstable and illusory nature. The second factor concerns the exhaustion as much of political models—from progressive nationalism to orthodox Left-wing ideologies—as of reading strategies (Martín-Barbero 203), which have proposed significant redefinitions of intellectual discourses in the current social dynamics. The third consists of the pressures of those "de los sujetos sociales largo tiempo silenciados, marginados y olvidados por ejercer la memoria colectiva y construir un espacio público y privado democrático y multicultural" (Achugar 1994a, 100) ("social subjects, who have been, for some time, silenced, marginalized and forgotten because they have exercised collective memory and constructed a democratic and multi-cultural public and private space").

The idea of nation has also lost its aura or magic. For this reason, there is no way that a discourse on nationality or on any of its other variants can evade the postmodern debate; the immediate result is the criticism of the term and its inevitable historicization.

In recent years, Benedict Anderson's model of the "imagined community" (1991) of a nation has gained recognition in academic circles. Nevertheless, over fifty years earlier, in 1928, José Carlos Mariátegui (1894–1930) had envisaged in his *Siete ensayos de interpretación de la realidad peruana* [1976; *Seven Interpretive Essays on Peruvian Reality,* 1971] that future discourses would ground their theoretical discussions on the understanding that the concept of the nation was a historical form of social and cultural organization (and domination) of communities in a country, but it was also a discursive artifact, which belongs to the imaginary (Larsen 869).

Several decades later, Jorge Luis Borges (1899–1986) reinforces this line of argument in his prologue to Pedro Henríquez Ureña's *Obra Crítica* [1960; Critical Works] by saying that nations are nothing more than an idea.

At the other end of the twentieth century and armed with another theoretical arsenal, Hugo Achugar notes that national discourse is a narration since it "presupone un relato. Y como todo relato propone un comienzo, un origen, una fundación. Como todo relato postula héroes y villanos; como toda narración histórica presupone, además, el olvido y el silenciamiento" ("presupposes a story. And, like every story, it proposes a beginning, an origin, and a foundation. Like every story, it suggests heroes and villains; like every historical narrative, it also presupposes oblivion and silencing"), an oblivion that "se identifica con el horizonte ideológico y teórico desde donde se organiza el relato" ("identifies with the ideological and theoretical perspective from which the story is organized") (Achugar 1994a, 100–101). Achugar thus makes the point that as much in the historical construction of this political project as in the play of discursive representations, the configuration of a nation is based on a conflictive process of inclusions and exclusions, whether they are linguistic, social, ethnic, sexual or cultural.

Martín-Barbero takes a similar approach when he reads the nation-state as the place that "se justifica e institucionaliza la desvaloración y desintegración de lo popular" (Martín-Barbero 1991, 96) ("justified and institutionalized the devaluation and disintegration of everything popular"; 1993, 86), thereby creating through the homogeneous national culture a "movimiento por el que la Nación al *dar cuerpo* al pueblo acaba *sustituyéndolo*. Del plural de los pueblos a la unidad del pueblo convertido en Nación . . ." (Martín-Barbero 1991, 98) ("process by which the nation, in constituting the people as a corporate existence, replaced the people. Moving from the 'plurality of peoples' to the 'unity of the people' now transformed into nation . . ."; 1993, 87). And if the nation offers a conflictive scenario, the symbolic constructions that play an active role in its constitution and its criticism will also reflect this state of affairs. For this reason, national memory should not, in the future, be treated as some kind of sacred reserve or record but as "un terreno de disputas, en el que se baten las diversas concepciones que habitan la sociedad" ("a terrain of dispute, which stages the struggle among the different concept of society"); intellectuals will be seen in these interpretations as their first "mediadores simbólicos" ("symbolic mediators"), who are in charge of legitimizing their approach (Ortiz 80–81).

Critical Antecedents from the Turn of the Nineteenth Century to the 1920s: Nation and Modernization

Ángel Rama, like José Luis Romero and Rafael Gutiérrez Girardot (see both 1983 and 1987) before him, points out that in the final decades of the nineteenth century, a sector emerged within the space of the learned city as a consequence of the democratization that had partially eroded its isolation, if not its foundations, a sector that would shape critical and dissident thought (Rama 1985a, 80). If, throughout the nineteenth century, most intellectuals had agreed that Latin American nations should be incorporated into modernity–with the

nation-state as its basic instrument–the process of modernization, the signs of which were rendered visible before the turn of the century, would undermine that agreement and the project supporting it. Intellectuals such as Romero, Gutiérrez Girardot, Rama, Franco, Osorio, and Sarlo, among others, offered a diversity of not always compatible perspectives that would reconstruct the social process of modernization and of constituting a modern culture in Latin America. These aspects are central to the debate, but I must leave the reader, for reasons of space, to consult these specialists who have competently explored this complex area of research.

The new subjects of written works, which frequently disguise the reconversions of the writing tradition (as I shall try to demonstrate), have suggested that there is a crisis in the discourses of Liberalism. When discussing the 1920s, Mabel Moraña alludes to the relation between this crisis and the important and contradictory changes in representation, a relation that has exerted its influence over half the century:

> . . . la reelaboración de los conceptos de *nación, pueblo* y *tradición,* y sus distintas formas de articulación dentro del discurso ideológico del período, así como la búsqueda de raíces y modos de expresión de la "americanidad" deben ser vistos
> . . . como momentos de un diálogo complejo y muchas veces contradictorio sostenido entre las diferentes tendencias ideológicas de la época, ante la crisis del liberalismo. (Moraña 7)
> . . . the re-thinking of the notions of *nation, people* and *tradition,* and their different forms of articulation within the ideological discourse of the period, as well as the quest for roots and modes of expression of 'Americanness' should be regarded . . . as instances of a complex and usually contradictory dialogue between the different ideological tendencies of the period in light of the crisis of liberalism.

A few years later, Hugo Achugar points out how the development of Americanist or nationalist discourses were, in the interwar period, responding to a new historical epoch, in which the key elements were the presence of a social and cultural reality unique to the New World and the emergence of new social sectors, which would stimulate discussion and discourse, from multiple perspectives, "en torno a nuestra América" ("concerning our America") (1994b, 641). From that point on, polemic confrontation and diversity characterized the new modes of written expression, on the significance of the nation. In different circumstances and places from those with which the intellectuals of the nineteenth century were socially concerned–that is, in the sphere of modern cultures–other ideas of the nation and its actors were constructed. These imaginary projects of identity had one common denominator: A radical critique of political modernization. And as they developed, these projects offered a multiplicity of responses, from a defense of *culturalismo* to proposals of new national political utopias, from the reformulation to the demolition of the old nation. Finally, springing from disillusionment or survival in the new sordid world of the city, there were others who could not contemplate the possibility of a national identity that meant anything more than the exercise of political power.

Studies focusing on the nation started at the end of the nineteenth century. The grotesque image the Cuban José Martí (1853–1895) sketches in his overview of the nineteenth century in "Nuestra América" [1891; Our America]–"Éramos una visión, con el pecho de atleta, las manos de petimetre y la frente de niño . . ." (Martí 30) ("We were a sight, with our athletic chests, delicate hands and childlike brows")–unmasks the post-Independence Liberal project of the nation by stressing the insufficiency and impropriety of its own fiction of the nation. There is no theoretical questioning of the idea of nation in his criticism, but it certainly offers quite a direct attack on the educated élite of his century—typified perhaps by Sarmiento—who had constructed an artificial nation, by no means grounded on any real community, and had made no attempt whatsoever to create the links of solidarity so essential for institutional legitimacy. For this reason, Martí demands, undoubtedly addressing young educated men, that they return to "los factores reales del país" (28) ("the real factors of the country")–the history of the Incas and banana wine, for example–and underscores the dangers of a nation erected upon the exclusion of the popular classes, when he observes that the solution "hubiera estado en hermanar . . . la vincha y la toga; en desestancar al indio; en ir haciendo lado al negro suficiente; en ajustar la libertad al cuerpo de los que se alzaron y vencieron por ella" (Martí 30) ("is to bond . . . the kerchief and the gown; to release the Indian; to make room for the competent black; to tailor freedom to the bodies of those who rose up and won it"). Following these instructions, the "hombre natural" ("natural man") would vanquish the "letrado artificial" ("artificial learned man") (Martí 28) and the national project would be naturalized. Although Martí's critical humanism still tended toward the hierarchy implied in the Liberal and Christian values of his tradition–brotherhood and charity–he did lay the foundations for the criticism of this tradition and its institutions.

However, Martí was not the only critical mind pondering the idea of nation. Three years earlier in 1888, the Peruvian Manuel González Prada (1844–1918) had highlighted the inconsistent and illusory nature of the Liberal nation in a talk given in the Politeama Theater. Once again, the idea of the exclusion of the popular sector provided the basis for his criticism: "No forman el verdadero Perú las agrupaciones de criollos y extranjeros que habitan la faja de tierra situada entre el Pacífico y los Andes; la nación está formada por las muchedumbres de indios diseminadas en la banda oriental de la cordillera" (45–46) ("The real nation of Peru does not consist of communities of *criollos* and foreigners who inhabit the stretch of land between the Pacific and the Andes; the nation is composed of the large number of Indians scattered throughout the eastern side of the mountain range"). His fellow countryman José Carlos Mariátegui would later make a similar statement: "El sentimiento y el interés de las cuatro quintas partes de la población no juegan casi ningún rol en la formación de la nacionalidad y de sus instituciones" (1976, 88) ("The feelings and interests of four-fifths of the population play almost no role in the formation of the national identity and institutions"; 1971, 78). It appears that none of these three men realized that exclusion was central to the Liberal project of the nation and was not merely a perversion or an erroneous part of the model in Latin America. What is true is that by criticizing it, they had placed their finger on the central point of the great republican utopia of nineteenth-century Liberalism: The modern nation.

There are thus indisputable antecedents to Martí's discussion. If this criticism of the traditional discourses on the nation had, at the start in 1900, to make a connection with the extremes on one and the other side, by the 1920s it was the convergences of the discourses that most clearly demonstrated the complex plot of the national drama, further complicated by an increasingly transnational culture and by internal pressures that new social subjects exerted on their

imaginary frontiers–their value-systems, institutions, and hierarchies. These years were characterized by a "*cultura de mezcla*, donde coexisten elementos defensivos y residuales junto a los programas renovadores; rasgos culturales de la formación criolla al mismo tiempo que un proceso descomunal de importación de bienes, discursos y prácticas simbólicas" ("*melting-pot culture*, in which defensive and residual elements coexisted with renovating programs; there were cultural traits of *criollo* formation at the same time as the massive importation of goods, discourses and symbolic practices"); it was "período de incertidumbres pero también de seguridades muy fuertes, de relecturas del pasado y de utopías, donde la representación del futuro y la de la historia chocan en los textos y las polémicas" ("a period of uncertainty but also of great security, of rereadings of the past and of utopias, in which the representations of the future and that of history clashed in the texts and debates") (Sarlo 1988, 28–29).

My aim now is to describe the ways in which literary discourses overtly or covertly render visible the idea of nation during the early decades of the twentieth century. A comparative study shows how this imaginary national space is dramatized as a discursive terrain of dispute, which stages the struggle for cultural legitimacy; in some cases, as we shall see, these discourses even announce the postmodern bankruptcy of meaning of the idea of nationality and of other factors and related images, such as identity and national culture, cultures and excluded social subjects, modernity, modernization, and so on. For obvious reasons of space, I shall study only a few texts that focus on the River Plate region and that were published between the end of the nineteenth century and the 1930s; these form part of what is conventionally known as *modernismo* and the avant-garde, and are particularly appropriate for the purpose of my argument. The nation is the "*lugar metodológico* desde el cual releer la historia" (Martín-Barbero 1991, 74) ("*methodological* perspective which provides a new reading of the meaning of history"; 1993, 63) or at least a fragment of the history of this phase of Latin American modernity.

The Nation of the Spirits

Anarchy and barbarism, menace and aversion are some of the genetic keys to the scholarly writers' representation of the new illegitimate children of modernization. Martín-Barbero suggests that this image is reconceived, with several variables, in the work of Gustave Le Bon (1841–1931) and Ortega y Gasset (1883–1955), but he might just as well have included J. K. Huysmans (1848–1909) or Henrik Ibsen (1828–1906). It is curious that he does not mention authors who promoted this view in Latin America, such as the Uruguayan José Enrique Rodó (1871–1917) in *Ariel* (1900)–a work launching (ironically?) the new century– or the Argentinian Leopoldo Lugones (1874–1938) in *El payador* [Gaucho Folk-Singer] of 1916, among others.

When contextualizing the work of Rodó, Carlos Real de Azúa (1916–1977) mentions that at the time of *Ariel*, "el momento incipiente, pero que ya parecía amenazador, de la revolución de las expectativas y las demandas de bienestar y de una difusa, reptante masificación y materialización de los comportamientos sociales" ("the nascent moment of an already threatening revolution in the expectations and demands for well-being as well as a diffuse yet widespread massification (of values) and materialistic orientation of social life"). He recalls the response of those sectors that felt their authority and the emblems of civilizing modernity to be at risk: A "melancólica postura de protesta y retaguardia" ("rearguard melancholic stance of protest") (Real de Azúa xv). One wonders whether Rodó's response is not similar but it can be interpreted as an attempt on the part of the intelligentsia to restore its social legitimacy in relation to the anonymous masses and "el odio de la mediocridad envalentonada por la nivelación y la tiranía irresponsable del número" (1985, 28) ("hatred for the mediocrity enshrined by the levelling process, and for the irresponsible tyranny of numbers"; 1988, 64) before the empire of his highness Nobody (1985, 26; 1988, 61). These masses provide the historical backdrop for the negative symbol of a democratic and utilitarian Caliban.

Although Rodó has been associated with the Ariel-Caliban opposition that would significantly alter the civilization-barbarism formula popularized by Sarmiento, it is Rubén Darío's (1867–1916) text entitled "Edgar Allan Poe" from *Los raros* [1896; The Rare], which came out four years before *Ariel* and contains the same opposition between Shakespeare's characters, that serves as the model for Rodó's reading of the pairing. Whereas Caliban is modernization, crystallized in the cosmopolis of New York, "la sanguínea, la ciclopea, la monstruosa, la tormentosa, la irresistible capital del cheque" (1993, 10) ("the blood-red, colossal, monstrous, stormy, irresistible capital of the cheque"), "el imperio de la materia" (1993, 12) ("the empire of matter"), and Ariel is Poe, the artist, "Ariel hecho hombre" (1993, 15) ("Ariel made man"). Some scholars have been tempted to place Rodó's Caliban within the frontiers of the United States of America–as Darío did in his biographical sketch of Poe–ignoring, so it seems, that Rodó had surmised that migration, cosmopolitanism, and the emergence of democracy in Latin America were signs that the reign of chaos was imminent and that the enemy was being reared at home.

As he later wrote: "Necesario es temer . . . que ciudades cuyo nombre fue un símbolo glorioso en América . . . puedan terminar en Sidón, en Tiro, en Cartago" (1993, 50) ("We might well fear . . . that cities whose names were once a glorious symbol in America . . . may end as Sidon, Tyre, Carthage"). In Rodó's work, Caliban is, first and foremost, a political figure of democracy. He also stands for the perversion of the process of modernization, which development has rendered increasingly effective and visible and which traditional Liberalism sought and advocated as the key to its utopian project: The civilized and modern nation. (It is significant that one of the few specific allusions in *Ariel* to the nineteenth-century tradition of Latin American thought critically evokes Alberdi's maxim, "*gobernar es poblar*" (Rodó 1985, 25) ("to govern is to populate"; 1988, 60).

In his attempt to cope with the real nation, that of the Calibanesque present, Rodó poses the need for an "autoridad moral que la depure y la encauce" (Rodó 1985, 24) ("moral authority to refine and channel it"; 1988, 59). Endorsed by honorable impartiality and full of religious conceits (Real de Azúa xi), the words of the sermon of the master Próspero provide his devoted followers with a rough sketch of the new Ariel utopia, the nation of the spirit, inspired by the longing to restore a vertical nation based on consecrated hierarchies and an intellectual aristocracy; access is restricted to those who survive the curious Darwinian and Nietzschean method of selection (Rodó 1985, 26, 31). This is the superior nation of culture, the educational antidote to Caliban (Rama 1985a, 118; 1996, 78) that the new intellectuals would preach. Perhaps this is the great novelty of *Ariel* within a Latin American intellectual context: The conversion of the term civilization into that of culture in light of the revitalized siege of barbarism, now

interpreted as a perversion of the civilizing project. Rodó's thesis of the superiority of culture and the arts above all other social spheres–particularly politics–is the systematic crystallization of an idea shared by many of the most important modernist writers. For example, Martí's early texts also articulate this oppositional scheme–culture/Latin America versus materialism/United States–and the privileged role to be played by the arts and culture: "Los pueblos inmorales tienen todavía una salvación: el arte" ("Immoral peoples still have one means of salvation: art"), "La América del Norte desconoce ese placer de artista que es una especie de aristocracia celestial" (213) ("North America ignores the artist´s pleasure, which is a kind of celestial aristocracy"). As we have seen, Rubén Darío does, to a great extent, second these statements, as does the Venezuelan Manuel Díaz Rodríguez (1871–1927), who exemplifies in his novel *Ídolos rotos* [1901; Broken Idols] the tensions of the Modernist period between the sphere of professional politics and the superior sphere of the arts and culture within the nation at the turn of the century. These and other convergences among the Modernists have been explored in the well-known studies of Ángel Rama (1985b), Rafael Gutiérrez Girardot (1983, 1987), and Julio Ramos.

In his search for models of an alternative nation, Rodó turns elsewhere and reconceives the imagined space of the nation; he changes their boundaries and organizing principles. From history, he salvages what he perceives to be authentic origins, the only authorities from a remote past with the power to counter the drive of the Calibanesque cosmopolis of the present: Greece and Christianity. The other sources he uses in constructing the nation of culture obviously come from literature, specifically Shakespeare (1564–1616) and from the voices of the historian Ernest Renan (1823–1892) and critic Hippolyte Taine (1828–1893), and guarantee that the foundations of the nation will include a history of culture. It is in a private and pure space where Próspero, inspired by the monument of Ariel, delivers his speech; it is also the slums of the spirit of the large city, where one finds "la lámpara que acompaña la soledad de la vigilia inquietada por el pensamiento" (Rodó 1985, 49) ("the lamps it lights by night in the vessel that accompanies the solitary wakefulness incited by thought"; 1988, 92).

The inner realm redefines the name of America when crowned by the statue of Ariel. America (i.e., Spanish America) is the natural territory at the service of the spirit, the nation of culture; Rodó (paradoxically) repeats the contradictory gesture made by the so-called intellectual emancipators–Sarmiento, Echeverría, Alberdi–that of constructing the politics of the nation on desert land, devoid of culture, and history. This desert has now been transformed into the wastelands of a large city, into the democratized culture of modernization. As González Echevarría (16) points out, Rodó founds the utopic nation of Latin American culture by turning his back on, excluding, and eliminating the commotion and threat posed by real culture, which the masses are constructing beyond his control. By eradicating history and politics from the desired nation, Rodó opens the modern chapter of "the patriarchal appropriation of culture" (Montaldo 1989, 26), moving towards the idea of substituting the nation for a culture run by the new patriarchs, the teachers.

Illustrious Men and Shadows: The Virile Nation

Another series of scholarly lectures, another teacher, and another statue attempt to compensate for one of the blind spots in Rodó's vision; now the aim is to create the illusion of constructing a (purified and authentic) national culture, that is, of proclaiming, in the light of modernization, not only the existence of a timeless and transcendent *criollismo* but also the need to found it. The project is so ambitious that Leopoldo Lugones is considered the "*escritor nacional por antonomasia*" (Gramuglio 5) ("*national writer* par excellence"). The pioneering gesture made by Lugones in *El payador* springs from the teachings of the gaucho Martín Fierro in *La vuelta de Martín Fierro* [1879; The Return of Martín Fierro]. But José Hernández's (1834–1886) program for converting the gaucho into a citizen is endowed with other characteristics in Lugones's text. Taking culture as his starting point, he defines the keys of nationality, which include the illustrious men and their "soul." The fatherland can only become a fixed concept when the master poet (as well as the historian and philologist) has put the finishing touches on it, thereby ensuring "culto de los antepasados, la conservación territorial, la raza y la posesión del idioma" ("reverence for the ancestors, territorial protection, race and possession of the language"); the result is the creation of a national "espacio ficticio de la identidad" ("fictitious space of identity") (Monteleone 165–66). This endeavor is stimulated by an in-depth study of the context at the beginning of the century. Lugones's response is, in public terms, inherited from *Ariel* (Montaldo 1993, 67), but it also presupposes radicalizing Rodó's defensive language on account of the social effects of modernization.

In the demarcation between "virile gaucho" and "the dismal rabble of the city," heroic legend and degrading reality, superior individuals and the barbaric masses, Lugones outlines his task as an act of sanitization, of racial and national purification. His rejection of the democratizing processes of the present leads Lugones to undergo a journey to his roots. Like Rodó, he treats not only Hellenism as the cradle of civilization but also the whole Western tradition of epic poetry from Homer to Milton as the source material for the national epic poem, a cultural space that endows the nation with meaning and a soul of its own. Lugones's response entails bringing the past up-to-date and making of it a live tradition, a political model to counter the politics of the present: "¡La política! He aquí el azote nacional" (Lugones 155) ("Politics! Behold the national scourge"). The ghosts to be resurrected are the heroic figure of the gaucho Martín Fierro and, obviously, Hernández's poem.

Graciela Montaldo has rightly observed that this move to found a tradition goes beyond an expression of nostalgia:

Se vuelve a la tradición, pero a la tradición entendida como un conjunto de discursos, prácticas y valores, que fijando sentidos sobre el pasado, se activan en el presente y se colocan respecto de los contemporáneos con pretensiones hegemónicas, para suturar parte de la armonía perdida o para ponerla en escena. (1993, 25)

One goes back to tradition, but to a tradition understood as a set of discourses, practices and values, which by fixing the meanings of the past, are activated in the present and are located by contemporary writers with hegemonic aspirations in order to recapture part of the harmony lost and to act it out.

Ángel Rama, in turn, saw the proposal of a pact (in texts such as *El payador*) by means of which

. . . la clase superior aceptaría la ruda poesía popular y su cosmovisión, la haría suya, la protegería, a cambio de que la clase inferior . . . reconociera que debía ser conducida por los cultos. Del pacto quedaba exceptuada exactamente la mitad de la población del país. (Rama 1977, xxi)

. . . the superior class would accept crude popular poetry and its worldview, they would make it theirs, protect it, if the inferior class . . . would recognize that they should be led by the educated. Exactly half the population of the country was excluded from this pact.

Perhaps Rama's calculations are not quite right, because the nation Lugones proposes in his exclusive cultural pact is even more restrictive. As in Rodó's *Ariel*, the illusion of a group, in this case defined as a national group, incorporates the void of the excluded others. The scenario that endorses—and dramatizes—the pact, granting identity to national culture, is represented in the text itself. Lugones acts as "el agente de una íntima comunicación entre la poesía del pueblo y la mente culta de la clase superior" ("the agent of intimate communication between the poetry of the people and the cultivated mind of the superior class"). He goes on to say, without a trace of irony, that "que es así como se forma el espíritu de la patria" (Lugones 201) ("this is the way the spirit of the fatherland is formed"). To Lugones the beauty of the performance of the people's poetry is in its harmony, and its unity is possible because the two issues at stake—the epic form and the audience—cannot come into conflict: The epic is the heroic gesture of culture, and the audience becomes Lugones' hall of mirrors.

The illusion of the representativity of the national community is constructed in the text because of the figurative identification with Martín Fierro; this creates an apparent pact between the educated and the popular, which in reality is not an alliance with the historical gaucho but rather with his literary portrayal in Hernández's poem. It is the transformation of *Martín Fierro* into an epic poem—and thus a national and popular poem—that makes possible the representational illusion, because Hernández's poem does not depict the popular classes of his time—the breed of the masses, that is, the mulattos and mestizos, the foreign plebs because they have been transfigured by the learned poet: "La materia es tosca; . . . el mérito capital del arte consiste en que la ennoblece espiritualizándola" (Lugones 145) "(The subject-matter is crude; . . . [but] the main value of art is its power to ennoble and spiritualize it"). The intervention of the so-called erudite artist (and of the values running through his work) is indispensable, even if he is to adopt the pose of being in touch with popular poetry: "Así se cumple con la civilización y con la patria. Movilizando ideas, no escribiendo sistemáticamente en gaucho" (197) ("Civilization and the fatherland are served by mobilizing ideas rather than by writing systematically in gaucho"). Not only popular poetry but also speech, the oral world, are salvaged insofar as they serve as a pretext for nationalizing the work of the artist, that is, the scholar. This pretext takes the form of constructing the one thing the nation lacks to be complete, what Borges would later call the Argentine language: "Formar el idioma, es cultivar aquel robusto tronco de la selva para civilizarlo, vale decir, para convertirlo en planta frutal" (Lugones 197) "(To create a language is to cultivate that robust trunk in the forest so as to civilize it and, it is worth adding, to turn it into a fruit tree"). In this way, Lugones transforms popular expression into "pieza de museo" (Montaldo 1993, 69) ("a museum piece"), conversing not with the popular but with the monuments, which are said to represent or evoke it. It is in this sense that *El payador* also becomes itself a creator of monuments. To the known and renowned statues of illustrious military and political figures such as San Martín, Lugones adds another statue so as to complete this nation of monuments: That of Martín Fierro/José Hernández (Lugones 187–88), the literary hero, and his minstrel, the cultural forefathers. Once again, this is a construction of a national culture based on the historical tradition of the country, not on the present; the "triste chusma de la ciudad" ("dismal rabble of the city"), the politicians, and the popular classes are not his concern.

This illusory operation actually proposes extensions to and corrections of the tradition of scholarly discourse. It also enables Lugones, despite what he writes in his Prologue, to present himself as a champion of the mestizo gaucho, who is associated, at least since Sarmiento's work, with barbarism. However, Lugones advocates as the desirable formula for the society of his times, not *mestizaje* but rather pseudo-*mestizaje*, which is constructed through the filter of cultural discourse as a union between a remote, diffuse, and rectified popular legacy and that of the illustrious élite who inherits the patriarchy. Lugones' defense of the mestizo gaucho is grounded in the same narcissistic and phantasmal bases as that theatrical pact. Just as the national epic poem does not represent either popular poetry or popular expression, so the mestizo gaucho does not play the part of the transcultural masses of these times in Argentina. For this reason, barbarism is limited to the indigenous peoples in this reading of history (Lugones 39), and the gaucho, a "sub-raza de transición" (Lugones 42) ("sub-race in transition"), is now perceived as a legendary hero, an astute, virile, independent, and free frontiersman; wrapped in Martín Fierro's mantle, he has become a monument.

Similar to Rodó's approach, Lugones's lectures set a mechanism in motion that completes (once it has taken root in the nation—*his* nation) the defensive and restoring gesture. In relation to the former, the epic poem, its language, and commentary act as an emotional force to counter threats of modernization and to articulate a new legendary and purified nation. In relation to the latter, the writer attempts, from the superior space of culture, not only to recuperate the social standing of the learned men of the generation of 1837 (Rodríguez Pérsico 27) but also to honor them.

If Lugones' *El payador* was publicly recognized in 1926 through the idealization of Ricardo Güiraldes's (1886–1927) *Don Segundo Sombra* and represented the updating of traditionalism within an avant-garde militancy (Masiello 191), it also completed the reconciliation of the Argentinian intelligentsia to the negative roots of their national literature. This consisted of domesticating the terrible shadow of Facundo and making it beneficent by assigning to Don Segundo Sombra the function of the symbolic father of nationality. In this sense, *Don Segundo Sombra* could be understood as the novel of the construction of the father, as well as being a novel of formation of a "guacho" who is transformed into a gaucho when he discovers his identity as the *estanciero* Fabio Cáceres, who, from the perspective of urban modernity, constructs the memory of his tradition in the form of an homage to his learning process. The phrase that opens and closes the novel and that is uttered when the narrator and Don Segundo Sombra meet and bid each other farewell—he is "más una idea que un hombre" (Güiraldes 1983, 297) ("more an idea than a man"; 1995, 203)—as well as the final diffusion of the character into the imaginary and mythical world, the confirmation of "la presencia ilimitada de un alma" (Güiraldes 1983, 297) ("the limitless presence of a soul"; 1995, 203), both support a possible allegorical reading of this text: The adopted father would here stand for the timeless spirit of the nation.

In the light of its immediate predecessor—Lugones' work—*Don Segundo Sombra* offers the additional attraction of

revitalizing the Martín Fierro of *La Vuelta* and places him in an everyday reality recalled by the narrator; this suggests a shift from the illusion of cultural verisimilitude to experienced truth, interiorized as a psychic state. The knowledge and moral values—such as the will, enterprise, courage, liberty, respect, and astuteness—of Don Segundo Sombra, the adopted father, are assimilated willingly by the narrator in the course of the novel. The narrative permits the reader to interiorize these values, and so the novel achieves its didactic purpose of revealing a double destiny. In order for Don Segundo to be adopted as the father, he must display endless wisdom, as well as pacify and domesticate the gaucho, so that the gaucho may teach himself this new mode of conduct. Respect for one's master and a change in attitude—from a violent reaction to a more astute response—are the lessons taught as means of surviving in this environment, lessons taught both directly and by example—as well as by the morals derived from parables, which are introduced, nesting like a Russian doll, into the tales Don Segundo relates (intentionally, of course), such as that of Dolores and Constancia and of Miseria (Masiello 187–88).

In this (hi)story of nations, *Don Segundo Sombra* takes the form of an open-air virile representation of the cloistered courtly projects of Rodó and Lugones. And this is not only because it is set in the countryside. The figures of Próspero's apostles and the senatorial monumental statues are complemented in Güiraldes' novel by the pastoral mode and the provision of a *vade mecum*, which serves the new citizen as a spiritual guide in the wilderness of cement. This is one reason among others for the popularity of the novel upon its publication; its author was almost immediately awarded the National Prize for Literature.

As a historicized space, the modern city is almost completely absent from this world; it is reduced to being the site from which the narrator, now transformed into an "effete gaucho," an "educated man" (Sarlo 1988, 296), constructs his memories. Everything he encounters, such as dangers, invading newcomers, and immigrants, only appear briefly to suggest a grotesque image of this strange and incomprehensible modernity (Sarlo 1988, 214–15, 286). These ephemeral absences and presences are part of the general strategy of this text, to minimize the signs of strangeness, almost to the point of erasing them, in order to construct a narrative with a rural setting representing a *criollo* Arcadia (Sarlo 1988, 34–35).

The countryside represents the absence of conflict; it is the context within which manhood can be forged. "Be tough, boy!" is the main slogan of the novel—and of the fictionalized song of the (truly) virile nation, as opposed to the other allegedly artificial and effeminate space. Indeed, the main conflicts in the novel involve the avatars and obstacles that nature places in the path of those attempting to control it: There are benign open roads, backwaters, and starry nights and imponderable, unexpected evils, such as the grotesque and voracious *cangrejal* or black crab marsh (perhaps a metaphor of modernization). The inhabitants are made in the image and likeness of nature. On the one hand, there are the generous masters and supportive friends and workmates; on the other, there are the resentful, effeminate cowards who, like a kind of human marsh-dwellers, generate absurd violence and are doomed to failure, and ridicule. The structure of the novel organizes the scenes in the learning process from the outset around taming horses (significantly also the point of closure). In order to acquire the recognizable and stable identity of a gaucho, the "gaucho" should be able to fall and rise again triumphant. In the end, the gaucho adopts that other new identity of the *estanciero* Fabio Cáceres and is thus prepared for his encounter with the intelligentsia and the urban world; although he feels uncomfortable with the name imposed by his real father and with his anti-natural world, he now belongs to a lively and superior culture that will permit him to overcome whatever accidents of history. No longer becoming, he has now become an Argentinian (Rodríguez Pérsico 39).

By closing the cycle started by Rodó and Lugones, Güiraldes opens the door to populism. The nation of the new patriarch, who lords over the territory and not just over the land, is that of the man who (now that he is equipped with deeply ingrained roots of tradition that he has left for posterity in his memoirs) can move freely through the spaces of modernity and overcome its grotesque scenes. These vital, imaginary displacements of identity mean that the new patriarch represents a peaceful union of both the old with the new and the erudite with the popular—unions, to paraphrase Güiraldes, that is more an idea than a reality. This union also prepares the way for a certain kind of *mestizaje,* which is not social or ethnic but cultural, by interfusing different times, spaces, and (aesthetic) cultures: Tradition and modernity, countryside and city, *criollismo* and cosmopolitanism.

Rafael Gutiérrez Girardot has shown how figures identified as philosophers of history emerged in the heat of the modernizing process, which implied, on the one hand, intense transformations in social life and, on the other, an equally intense reordering of the types and functions of literary subjects and their writing (1987, 503). In his opinion, such intellectuals as Rodó, Martí, and Lugones are the first of these. Writers of this kind took the initiative of both giving meaning and social space to intellectual functions and also of defining the major problems, engaging and understanding them, and thus identifying the symptoms and even suggesting possible solutions. They had many a task on their hands. Appropriating the spiritual sphere (theirs since the recent strengthening of culture) and equipped with their weapons—their words and ideas—they tackled their task as a mission devoted to the activities of writing combative lectures and criticism in order to provide the community—or *their* community—with new utopias. Likewise, they constructed readings of Latin American and national history, invented traditions and futures, and set up strategies for confronting and surviving modernity and social change.

It is in this context that I have argued the case of the authors of the spiritual renewal of the nation. Rodó's Ariel phobia of modernity, the masses and materialism, Lugones's epic and nationalistic phobia (of universality, democracy, and of new subjects, and social spaces), and Güiraldes's more political phobia of differences all attempt to fix identity, whether national or continental, mythical or utopian, but always guarding against the new times ahead, unfailingly interpreted as a danger (anarchy, new barbarism, linguistic chaos, and challenges to mediocrity) or as a disease (decadence, deformity, effeminacy, and madness). The task of the cultural supermen is to return to the origins—Greece, Christianity, Martín Fierro—and to resurrect them. Interpretation and other similar activities—to help cure the national or continental disease by recovering origins and essences and understanding them—also exist in other Latin American countries, as in the identities articulated by Alcides Arguedas (1879–1946), Francisco García Calderón (1883–1953),

and the Venezuelan Right-wing *Cesarismo Democrático*, ideologues such as Laureano Vallenilla Lanz (1870–1936) or César Zumeta (1860–1955). As the creators of pacts, alliances, and partnerships with various groups that contained specific figures and images that apparently embraced the people but unavoidably belonged to the past or were represented as socially vacuous or impotent entelechies, they entrusted their effectiveness to the power of the I, the place of enunciation of discourse, that is, the new patriarchs and narcissistic scholars of nationhood and culture (see Fell).

Nevertheless, from a perspective closer to us in time, specifically from the turn of the twentieth century to the 1920s, other formulas for continental and national identity were being devised that on occasion coincided with earlier ones. In historical terms, these were probably more socially and politically successful, at least until the 1960s. If it is possible to detect forms that border on the ideas of *mestizaje* and populism in the manifestos of Lugones and Güiraldes, these forms were, as I have tried to demonstrate, particularly weak and undefined, and in the last instance, they were authoritarian and conspicuously exclusive, on account of their almost obsessive consistency. Another line of patriarchs who succeeded these intellectuals not only sought to obliterate the signs of modern social conflicts, but on the contrary, they put them at the center of their discourses. Although they agreed with their culturist or Caesarian contemporaries' reading of the present as a danger or disease and believed in the need for regeneration, they were different in that they championed a *mestizaje* of a social and populist kind. In light of the difficulties of the period—social tensions and imperialistic advances—they proposed the need for a new order whose utopian objectives were to construct an original version of modernity, one that would take their own cultural tradition as a starting point and be grounded in the harmony of all social factors. They were undoubtedly stimulated by such ideas as those expressed by Martí in "Nuestra America," and by the influence his discourse exerted on the thought of intellectuals at the beginning of the twentieth century, those who produced such theses as that of the cosmic race (José Vasconcelos [1881–1959]) and of Indo-America (Victor Raúl Haya de la Torre [1895–1979]). These formed part of the quest for our expression, which Pedro Henríquez Ureña (1884–1946), Mariano Picón Salas (1901–1965), José Carlos Mariátegui, and José Lezama Lima (1910–1976) all embarked upon from their different perspectives.

A comparison of two passages from one of the typical novels of this time, *Doña Bárbara* (1929) by Rómulo Gallegos (1884–1969), illustrates the novelties and limitations of populist Latin American *mestizaje* apropos the construction of the modern nation. Chapter II of Part 2 "Los amansadores" [The Trainers]—parallel in more ways than one to an episode in Part 1, "La doma" [The Horse-Breaking]—describes the well-known scene of Santos Luzardo's attempt to tame Marisela's vocabulary. Luzardo is depicted here as a rigid and inflexible conquistador, willing to correct and control rustic spoken Spanish until it is transformed into standard language: "te perseguiré diciéndote: no se dice jallé, sino hallé o encontré; no se dice aguaite, sino mire, vea" (Gallegos 1977, 151–52) ("I'll come after you with: Don't say 'seen' but 'saw' or 'met'; don't say 'looka' but 'look' or 'see'"; 1948, 182). On the basis of this passage alone, Gallegos's novel belongs to the nineteenth century. In contrast to the conventional readings of this novel as a mere narrative translation of Sarmiento's thesis, however, others argue that Gallegos has extended or rectified the conflict between civilization and barbarism and may even have interfused these opposed terms (Castro-Urioste 129–32). In other words, even though the novel opens with a radical opposition between the characters of Santos Luzardo and Doña Bárbara, Gallegos's purpose may be detected in the transformations of the characters throughout the novel, or even more aptly, in what the mestiza Marisela symbolizes. In fact, the scene does not end there. It closes in Chapter XII of Part 3: "A pesar de la gravedad del asunto, Santos no pudo menos que sonreír: al dios de *Pajarote*, como al amigo del cuento de ño Pernalete, no le producían escrúpulos los puntos sobre las haches" (Gallegos 1977, 318) ("In spite of the gravity of the matter, Santos could not help smiling. Pajarote's God, like Ño Pernalete's friend, had no scruples about dotting e's"; 1948, 422). Significantly, Santos's smile is his last real intervention in the novel. The change from one scene to the other makes us aware of the transition from harassment to leniency, from the figure of the authoritarian patriarch to the father figure. Using this gesture as a starting-point, we can reconstruct the process of and the solution to the fictional allegory.

The coexistence of speech and writing, and the acceptance and awareness of the former by the latter, amount to civilization's recognition of barbarism, the illustrious élite's recognition of the popular sectors. Of course, the hierarchy never disappears and the dominant discourse will never be other than a "discurso de conquista" ("discourse of conquest") that "busca construir la imagen de una nación homogénea" ("seeks to construct the image of an homogenous nation") (Castro-Urioste 128), but the parameters of legitimacy have been transformed. If the nation is to be a legitimate nation, an operation resembling that of Martí should be performed: "hermanar, con la caridad del corazón y con el atrevimiento de los fundadores, la vincha y la toga"; "desestancar al indio; . . . ir haciendo lado al negro suficiente; . . . ajustar la libertad al cuerpo de los que se alzaron y vencieron por ella" (Martí 30) ("bond, with the charity of the heart and with the defiance of the founders, the hair-band and the lawyer's gown"; "release the Indian; . . . make room for the competent black; . . . tailor freedom to the bodies of those who rose up and won it"). In other words, there should be social *mestizaje*.

Some might, perhaps rightly, argue that this is suggested in Güiraldes's novel. The political pact is of a significantly different kind, however. Gallegos's implicit pact foregrounds the social conflicts of his time and the imperialistic threat, not the silence; like that of Martí, it necessarily presents some level of self-criticism by the intellectuals; and finally, it aspires, charitably, to complement the social actors of the novelistic present who are the future of the nation, rather than those of an irretrievable past, which can only be reconstructed through the act of memory.

Staging of Conflicts of the Nation

The avant-garde is, in many cases, a movement that "fragmenta la identidad nacional, [que] hace estallar ese concepto globalizador" (Rodríguez Pérsico 38) ("fragments national identity, [which] shatters the concept of globalization"). Even if the authors who participated in the avant-garde movement–both artistic and political–plotted this rupture they were not alone nor was the avant-garde the only element that undermined the idea of a nation unified against the upheavals and turmoil caused by modernity. Earlier and contemporary writers such as Mariano Azuela (1873–1952), José Rafael Pocaterra (1890–

1955), and Teresa de la Parra (1889–1936), who would, in the end, oppose the vanguard movement or remain on its margins, began this radical or subtle task of subversion and did so by contributing to Mariátegui's idea (which was gaining greater plausibility) of perceiving the nation as "una abstracción, una alegoría, un mito, que no corresponde a una realidad constante y precisa" (Mariátegui 1976, 192) ("an abstraction, an allegory, a myth that does not correspond to a reality"; 1971, 188). For example, David Viñas points out the role of Macedonio Fernández (1874–1952), a writer on the periphery of the vanguard movement, although he was, paradoxically, one of its best exponents in Argentinian literature; he was reduced to that of playing "en contrafigura de la espectacularidad lugoniana por su rechazo de los gestos categóricos, del tradicionalismo chovinista, e incluso, por su cuestionamiento de todo espesor positivista" (Viñas 1989, 14) ("the counterpart in the Lugonesque spectacular because of his rejection of categorical assertions and chauvinist traditionalism, and his positivistic questioning"). In *Papeles de Reciénvenido* [1929; Papers of the Newly Arrived] Macedonio Fernández will name the nation at the outset so that he can omit it in the rest of his work.

When Borges, a visible actor in the vanguard of Argentinian literature, states in "his" *Evaristo Carriego* (1930), "La dolencia es general: no queda plaza que no esté padeciendo su guarango de bronce" (Borges 1995, 23) ("The malady is widespread: There is no square that does not have to put up with its bronze lout" (1984, 43)), he is also contributing to this discursive demolition of the sense of monumental nationality, which Lugones, for example, attempts to establish. In her comparison of the discourses of Borges and Ricardo Rojas (1882–1957), Graciela Montaldo argues that "frente a la monumentalidad de la obra de Ricardo Rojas, las prosas [de Borges] son fragmentarias y no acumulativas, arbitrarias en sus ordenamientos de la historia y la cultura e implican una nueva forma de leer la tradición cultural" (1989, 220) ("the monumentality of Ricardo Rojas' work creates a contrast with [Borges's] prose pieces, which are fragmentary and not cumulative, are arbitrary in their ordering of history and culture, and suggest a new form of reading cultural tradition"). Sarlo's discussion of Borges's universalist aesthetics reveals how Borges, from *Carriego* onwards, decides to "colocarse, con astucia, en los márgenes, en los repliegues, en las zonas oscuras, de las historias centrales. La única universalidad posible para un rioplatense" (1988, 49) ("place himself, astutely, on the fringes, in the folds and dark regions of central histories. The only universality possible for someone from the River Plate"). The quotation from De Quincey at the beginning of *Evaristo Carriego* is a significant indicator of this attitude: ". . . a mode of truth, not of truth coherent and central, but angular and splintered" (n.p.).

This does not mean that Borges's detachment from the fabricators of monuments and shadows–Lugones and Güiraldes–is a radical stance. They have points in common, such as the same social phobias and the retaliation reserved for the children of the country, as he puts it (Borges 1995, 39). His contempt, particularly for the gringo (immigrants of Italian origin) and, in general terms, for the poverty-stricken, the underdogs, and those on the margins cannot be ignored. The space of Maldonado and the riffraff there summarize his contempt. The "milonga" (a type of song), for example, is presented as truly representative: Despite its poor musicality and monotony (Borges 1995, 86), it [the milonga] had a resonance of eternity (Borges 1995, 88), as opposed to the tango, which is not "el natural sonido de los barrios; lo fué de los burdeles nomás" (Borges 1995, 86) ("the natural expression of the outlying neighborhoods, since it originated in brothels"; 1984, 88); "redactado en el sedicente idioma popular, es un acertijo" (Borges 1995, 85) ("written in the would-be popular idiom, it is a riddle"; 1984, 88). Borges thus compares two forms of popular urban culture: One is presented as typical and genuine, whereas the other is false and foreign (terms he uses to designate, inclusively and exclusively, the respective social actors). He also rejects the perverse effects of modernization, as do the other writers of his age. The post-centenary city, which Borges describes two decades later, is definitely the object of his irony: "Palermo . . . era una cosa decentita, infeliz como cualquier otra comunidad gringo criolla" (Borges 1995, 79) ("Palermo . . . was a place of genteel poverty, like any other mixed community of immigrants and native Argentines"; 1984, 82).

Borges adds the premodern and urban *criollo,* a component missing from the fabric of his tradition. But what really distinguishes Borges from Lugones and Güiraldes is the nature of his response. In this case, nostalgia releases his writing practice from the prison house of political consciousness. This act of writing, which devises the same exclusions as its predecessors, is presented as an operation (at once major and minor) that guarantees survival in a world that does not deserve political gestures. Writing is to the reality of the modern city what the "retaliation" of the *criollo* is to the gringo: "Esa benevolencia con fondo completo de sorna" (Borges 1995, 10) ("This tolerance, rooted as it is in concealed irony"; 1948, 54). From there, from that place on the page, Borges constructs another nation. And if "*calle Honduras*" ("Honduras Street") seems more real when seen in print (Borges 1995, 50; 1984, 62), we can detect that in *Evaristo Carriego* Borges sets out to superimpose on the insubstantial nation a paradoxical identity, arbitrarily "más real" ("more real"), because it is fictitious and unreal. Ironic inversion is his device.

Nation and national identity are thus deconstructed: The former by its synecdoche Palermo and the latter by the absurd character and minor writer, Evaristo Carriego. Carriego, the symbol chosen for this (anti-)identity, not only has tuberculosis, that fatal and degenerating illness, but is also a double bastard: His *criollo* father, who comes from Entre Ríos, is almost Uruguayan, whereas his mother has some Italian blood (Borges 1995, 38–39). A combination of the Romantic *criollismo* of the east and the resentful *criollismo* of the suburbs (Borges 1995, 38), Carriego is a *mestizo*; his *criollismo* as a choice is shown to be a pretense learned from an impostor. Likewise, Palermo demonstrates its spurious and paradoxical origins: It was founded by an Italian and its name is also the final destination of the immigrants. The air of the nation wafts through an abattoir; evoking Echeverría, this is the first narrative space that prefigures the denaturalization of modernity. Palermo and Evaristo Carriego thus suggest at once refoundation and parody: The fatherland is a dismal place and its symbol, a writer with very bad taste.

This paradoxical enterprise also enters, in terms of structure and purpose, into a dialog with *Facundo: Civilizacion y barbarie* [1845; *Life in the Argentine Republic in the Days of the Tyrants; or Civilization and Barbarism,* 1868], the seminal book on nationality. In fact, Borges's book cancels Sarmiento's political and writing project. On the one hand, Palermo/Buenos Aires of 1912 is the realization of his political project. On the other hand, *Evaristo Carriego*, like *Facundo*, constructs an identity based on a lack of self; it abounds in digressions, which reach such a point in Borges' book that digression is the main device. The organization of the sequence of events is also similar: Environment, man, works, progeny. Both are, moreover, biographies. The difference is that the testimony of Borges's character is a matter of pure speculation. This biography insists on its arbitrariness and on the gratuitousness of its writing. Human life is "Una vida de Evaristo Carriego" ("A Life of Evaristo Carriego")–the title of Chapter II–and whatever is remembered is ungraspable and unstable: "recuerdos de recuerdos de otros recuerdos" (Borges 1995, 35) ("memories of memories of other memories"; 1984, 51). Carriego is a passing whim: "idiosincrásico sabor que llamo Carriego" (Borges 1995, 35) ("the particular flavor that I call Carriego"; 1984, 51).

Nevertheless, the real Carriego as much as the real Palermo functions as a pretext in this critical parody for the construction of an invisible nation; in his perverse manner, Borges also constructs his fragmentary authority, a new authority over history.

The unreality on the fringes is Borges's subject matter. Carriego is portrayed as a fatuous and pathetic impostor. His life, as Borges describes it, is almost a caricature: His goal involves an unscrupulous and inept quest for fame; he learns his style from a professional *criollo* friendship with the *caudillo* Paredes (Borges 1995, 47); his commitment to his neighborhood is born of rancor; his works' themes include the fragility of the immediate and the "pobrerío amargo" (Borges 1995, 40) ["bitter lot of the poor" (1984, 55)]; his library is culturally invalid (Borges 1995, 42–43); and his literary success springs from the critics' blindness and his readers' bad taste: "Los pobres gustan de esa pobre retórica" (Borges 1995, 61) ("Poor people relish this sorry rhetoric"; 1984, 69). In this way, Borges corrects, adjusts, retells and systematically draws a line of demarcation between the parvenu and the true masters of knowledge and taste. Following Sarmiento, he destroys Carriego's barbaric rhetoric, as well as that of those who identify with it, such as his addressees, readers, critics, and literary disciples–that is, the international and populist Left-wing embodied by Boedo, the underlying enemy of the book. By these means, Borges reestablishes literary order.

Paradoxically, it is the shift in critical line of demarcation that transforms his social phobia into myth; on the margins of writing, even falsehood is mythologized. For example, Carriego is converted, on the one hand, into the legendary victim of tuberculosis: "dedicado a la muerte y sin otra posible inmortalidad que la de sus palabras escritas" (Borges 1995, 49) ("pledged to death and that no other immortality was open to him than that of his writing"; 1984, 61), as if anticipating the futile enterprises of Funes or Pierre Menard; and on the other hand, he becomes Carriego the writer, the founder, the "inventor" of a style, that of his neighborhood. This line of demarcation also transforms the image of this urban neighborhood and provides it with its own myths and memory: The *milonga* versus the tango, the outlaw, the coterie of troublemakers and guitarists, the evil *criollo* versus the treacherous Calabrian; in other words, the marginalized *criollo*. The same thing happens with narrative space: As opposed to Palermo with its *art nouveau*, the abject Maldonado is poetized in the spaces of the *Tierra del Fuego* and the store *La Primera Luz* ("The First Light"), the location of "Escombros del principio, esquinas de agresión o de soledad, hombres furtivos" (Borges 1995, 30) ("A shambles from the outset, street corners either menacing or deserted, furtive men"; 1984, 48). Just as "Carriego" is the threshold on which the real Carriego–the drunkard of *Los Inmortales*, who "pertenecerá a la ecclesia visibilis de nuestras letras" (Borges 1995, 44) ("will . . . take its place in the *ecclesia visibilis* of Argentine letters"; 1984, 35)–meets the essential Carriego (or unreal, as Borges puts it), so Palermo–slums, suburbs, frontier–is, from the time of Rosas, "naipe de dos palos, moneda de dos caras" (Borges 1995, 18) ("stacked deck, a two-headed coin"; 1984, 40), a Janus space on the fringes between countryside and city, tradition and modernity, *criollismo* and cosmopolitanism. This is only possible so long as it does not leave the page, with its conscious and intentional deception. For history and nation as objects of irony and parody are ambiguously illusory.

Recalling the past, the narrator of *Las memorias de Mamá Blanca* [1929; *Mamá Blanca's Memoirs,* 1959] by Teresa de la Parra constructs her disavowal of the virile nation by drawing a parallel between the father figure and the father of the nation, both of which remain estranged and distant. Although on the surface this novel is a pleasant, inoffensive and funny text, its irony and parody can also be interpreted as a critique of the idea of nation. Like the other texts discussed here, it rejects the politics of modernization as represented at the end of the novel upon the narrator's arrival in Caracas, the deadly and dehumanized "Vale of Tears" and the subsequent modernizing transformation, the fall from the paradisaical rural space of Piedra Azul. Like Borges, de la Parra criticizes the monumentalistic severity of official history. The memoirs are employed to create an alternative nation rather than to establish an order. These are forgetful memoirs, and, with many an aside to the reader, they forget or conceal dates and historical incidents (Lasarte 16–17); they play with distinguished historical personages and transform, as they transgress, the meanings of the words of power, such as "government," "command," "republic," and so on, when applied intentionally to the insignificant avatars of domestic life in the Arcadia of childhood. Teresa de la Parra also has other things in common with Borges, such as her praise of lying and writing, not to mention the ambiguities and hierarchies in her text. Unlike him, however, she is totally opposed to the idea of a virile nation. Her criticism of the new era includes one almost unprecedented component: The idea that the rejected and distant nation–including that of the republic of letters–is a nation constructed by the power of men or by men in power (see Garrels). This liberal, rational, progressive, and modernized nation is, however, a space that excludes women.

Texts by other Latin American writers support this deconstruction of the idea of nation from very different perspectives. Uslar Pietri (1906–2001) does it, in *Las lanzas coloradas* [1931; *The Red Lances,* 1963] and some stories of the thirties, by presenting national history as the result of irrational collective impulses and by accentuating the images of madness and the grotesque in his reading of the Independence movement. Using sarcastic and cynical irony, Juan Carlos Onetti (1909–1994) defines the nation and its history as a vacuum in *El pozo* [1939; The Well]: "Detrás de nosotros no hay nada. Un gaucho, dos gauchos, treinta y tres gauchos" (91) ("Behind us there is nothing. One gaucho, two gauchos, thirty-three gauchos"). The national epic is also reread in *La invención de Morel* [1940; *The Invention of Morel,* 1964] by Adolfo Bioy Casares (1914–1999), an author in exile.

In the Margin: Forgetting the Nation

Los de abajo [1916; *The Underdogs*] by Mariano Azuela presents a visual image of the assault on the city of letters, the core, at first, of the Mexican revolutionary movement. This novel is like a double-edged sword. On the one hand, it celebrates grotesqueness and bestiality as a mode for representing the people and, to a certain degree, the nation. In this sense, the novel follows the line of those narratives that identify American territory as a barbaric space that confirms the apocalyptic and nihilistic tone that runs through the novel. On the other hand, it presents an attack on the lettered men–embodied, particularly, by the upstart Luis Cervantes–and on the injustices of social power, the first and last effect of which is the ambushed nation of the underdogs.

Whereas grotesque description is one of the dominant modes of representing the people in discourses of every kind–from *teatro criollo* to cinema and soap operas–in the twentieth century, criticism of social power has inspired another line of reflection, and this has led, with the passage of time, to Marxist and/or socialist Americanist discourses–to the social realism of the thirties, and to the so-called transcultural narrative of such authors as José Carlos Mariátegui, César Vallejo (1892–1938), and José María Arguedas (1911–1969), to mention only a few distinguished Peruvian writers. From the first decade of the last century, criticism of the power of the nation, often from an ironic, parodic, or humorous perspective, is a common thread drawing together a series of Latin American authors and texts, besides that of Azuela, which have, in one way or another, been disregarded; among these are Roberto Payró's (1867–1928) seminal novel, *Las divertidas aventuras del nieto de Juan Moreira* [1910; The Entertaining Adventures of Juan Moreira´s Grandson], *Después de Ayacucho* [1920; After Ayacucho] by Enrique Bernardo Núñez (1895–1964), and the narrative oeuvre of José Rafael Pocaterra. The pioneers in this critical line of thought are probably to be found in "La ida" [The Going] of *Martín Fierro* in fiction and Manuel González Prada's essays, if not the disconcerting texts of Simón Rodríguez (1771–1854).

The novel *El juguete rabioso* [1926; The Rabid Toy] by Roberto Arlt (1900–1942) begins with the assault on the city of letters in fiction began in 1926, when the Club de los Caballeros de la Media Noche (Club of the Knights of Midnight) burgled a school library. In the operation, Leopoldo Lugones's head rolled in the dust–*Las montañas del oro* [1897; Mountains of Gold] was sold out and thus became a collector's item, but it was destined to be sold by petty thieves–and Baudelaire's head was crowned; this new transgressive style erased, moreover, the divisions between art and science, between serious and popular literature (Arlt 1995b, 116–17).

Arlt accomplishes most convincingly the "cross-punch to the jaw" that he sought as the main effect of his writing. In the chapter that gives the title to the novel, a young homosexual, who is apparently from a wealthy background, confesses the intimate secrets of the dark side of his life to Silvio Astier: His arrangements with the owners of cheap hotels, his desire to find the man of his dreams and to get pregnant. His agonies and fantasies are as grotesque, pathetic, and moving as those of any other wretched character in the novel, including Silvio Astier. Not content with this, the young man confesses the origin of his so-called perversion. When he was fourteen, a teacher–talented and demonic–seduced him and he fell in love; the teacher was called Próspero (Arlt 1995b, 187), an insidious coincidence or intentional resonance? Of all the names Arlt could have chosen, he selects precisely that of the master of *Ariel*. This blow (below the belt) to the temple of culture could not have been more categorical or more blasphemous. In the first chapter the novelistic voice draws attention to

Silvio's intellectual superiority and emphasizes that the Club de los Caballeros de Media Noche, like Rodó's disciples, was founded by the desire to form an association of young intellectuals (Arlt 1995b, 93, 101). What is even more capricious is that the date of the publication of *Ariel* coincides with that of Arlt's birth. A sort of rebellious son, apparently!

Like his protagonist, Arlt appropriates literature for the purpose of dramatizing the conflict between writing and populist writing, between the official and the damned, between metaphor and cliché. He attacks, devours, and reorders literature in order to expose the implicit opposing powers: The exclusiveness of Arielism and the transgressor of what Benjamin calls apache poetry. When describing the literary project of *El juguete rabioso*, Ricardo Piglia (b. 1941) says that "el robo es la metáfora misma de la lectura arltiana" (Piglia 24) ("burglary is the metaphor par excellence of an Arltian reading") and Gerardo Mario Goloboff (b. 1939) speaks of an "asalto a la literatura" (38) ("assault on literature"). Criticism during the last few decades has tended to associate it with the powerful expressions of urban culture in Buenos Aires during the 1920s and 1930s; Noé Jitrik compares Arlt with Carlos Gardel (108), whereas Viñas associates him with the Discépolo brothers (1971, 72–73). Arlt responds to the construction of the sanctuary of national literature with its "secularization" (Gnutzmann 44). His prologue to *Los lanzallamas* [1931; The Flame Throwers] and such *aguafuertes* ("ironic sketches") as "El conventillo de nuestra literatura" [1928; The Tenement of Our Literature], "¿Cómo quieren que les escriba?" [1929; How Would You Like Me to Write?] or "El idioma de los argentinos" [1930; The Language of the Argentines] are some of the most explicit examples of the polemic nature of Arltian writing. The power of the literary nation was his favorite target–Lugones, in particular. Alan Pauls describes Arltian language as "una amalgama de piezas discordantes ... en la que se metamorfosean jergas, idiomas prestados o robados, lenguas extranjeras, discursos filosóficos y científicos, literaturas altas y bajas, todo un flujo de elementos heterogéneos y conflictivos que nunca terminan de solidificarse y que permanecen, siempre, abiertos a nuevas irrupciones" (316) ("an amalgam of discordant pieces ... which metamorphose jargon, borrowed and stolen idioms, foreign languages, scientific and philosophical discourses, high-brow and low-brow literatures, a whole flux of heterogeneous and conflictive elements which never solidify and which remain forever open to new additions"). Rita Gnutzmann points out this "superposición y yuxtaposición de diferentes estilos" (65) ("superposition and juxtaposition of different styles") in *El juguete rabioso*, but Ana María Amar Sánchez sees another innovation here: By combining promiscuously, and almost obscenely, high and low, elite culture and mass culture, Arlt pioneers the Latin American tradition of the pastiche. In its movement, its fusions of the imagination and flight, this novel seduces first one and then the other side only to betray them both, so as to propose itself finally "como un relato *diferente*" (Amar Sánchez 49–50) ("as a *different* story"). Other critics have also pointed out this ambiguous (ideological) displacement, which suggests an unstable fusion of the erudite and the popular in Arlt's literary quest for a differing space (see Viñas 1971; Pastor; Sarlo 1988, among others). And it is more than likely that these interpretations are indeed moving in the right direction. What is certainly true is that Arlt's work establishes a margin, which is, by its very characteristics, the opposite of the margin offered by Borges's fringe culture. Among other things, this is because the Arltian margin represents what would constitute, in the latter part of the century, the nucleus of the postmodern critique of the ideas of the nation and of national culture. In this sense, Martín-Barbero describes the distinguishing features of mass culture as "la hibridación y la reelaboración, la destrucción ... del mito de la pureza cultural" ("the process of cultural hybridization and the re-elaboration ... that destroys the myth of cultural purity").

Arlt's irreverent, melancholic, amoral, naïve, and preexistentialist stance also casts doubt on the purity of the culture that national literature attempts to construct as only local, unified, allied with tradition, and purged of modern social reality, which was growing ever more urban and heteroclitic.

A comparison of Güiraldes's *Don Segundo Sombra* and Arlt's *El juguete rabioso* reveals several coincidences: The date of publication, the protagonist's autobiographical narrative (Gnutzmann 31), and, finally, the fact that Arlt finished his novel, started seven years earlier, when he was Güiraldes's secretary. It is worth noting that both are also *Bildungsromans*. What is more interesting, however, is that Arlt's novel is not only written in the shadow of the *Sombra*, but is its flip side, an antithetical staging. As a "city novel," it creates a contrast between the "desgarramientos, discrepancias, enfrentamientos materiales ... se oponen a la unilateral placidez campesina" (Jitrik 124) [ruptures, discrepancies, and material confrontations (of urban life) opposed to the unilateral placidity of rural life]. In relation to Borges, Arlt embodies the bastard progeny of Carriego, his bad taste, his irregular, incorrect and adulterated language, which is impregnated with the ungovernable hybridity of modernized space. Arlt and his characters are the products of emigration, representing the dangers of the democratic rabble, of the treacherous suspension of tradition. Arlt's favorite focus is on the grotesque decadence of the city itself, its gloomy rooms and interiors, the foils for urban magnificence.

Arlt's criticism of the works of those authors who founded the tradition of adopting a defensive intellectual strategy against the threat of modernization presupposes as much the presence of a new writing subject as the representation of other social subjects, the other side of the national coin: "Baldía y fea como una rodilla desnuda es mi alma" (Arlt 1995b, 153) ("My soul is an ugly wasteland like a naked knee"), Silvio Astier says in a soliloquy that takes place after one of his failures. This work represents (an)other social site of expression: In this case, the abandonment of the children of modernization. It responds to the character's request: "Busco un poema que no encuentro, el poema de un cuerpo a quien la desesperación pobló súbitamente en su carne, de mil bocas grandiosas, de dos mil labios gritadores" (Arlt 1995b, 153) ("I am looking for a poem I do not find, a poem of a body suddenly filled with desperation in its flesh, a desperation of a thousand grandiose mouths, of two thousands lips that shout"). As long as this poem does not appear–it perhaps could be *La rueda del hambriento* [1937; The Wheel of the Hungry] by Vallejo–the Arltian narration assumes the responsibility of imagining this expression and desire.

Silvio Astier, dreaming rogue (a *criollo* male Bovary), wretched worker, failed inventor, and despicable traitor, finds it impossible to fulfill his bourgeois dreams of both transgression and social climbing, of scrounging a blue space in the skies of modernization–money, maidens, recognition, and power. So he becomes a writer of himself; by converting himself into the subject matter of his own writing, he eventually discovers a means of survival he has never found outside or inside the law, a way of transcending the effects of madness and confinement in the filthy life of society. This autobiographical memoir reaches a negative point of closure in Astier's learning process. It ends with an image of the fall of the character, in the form of betrayal and delirium, as he realizes that modern urban life is ruled by the law of ferocity (Arlt 1995b, 237). Writing represents one possible way of overcoming failure; it provides him with a job that removes him from the inferno of business and that precariously protects him from the injustices of power. The novel criticizes the character's ingenuous dreams of social climbing and recognizes the social mechanisms involved and develops an ambiguous strategy, which at once permits insertion into social normality and, thanks to the distance of literary language, allows the symbolic recuperation of transgressive dreams–the conspiratorial utopia (Rivera 792)–on which the original identity was grounded. These operations had been tested by the literary model of Baudelaire, as personage and as writer (Rivera 793). If one cannot be a transgressor or an inventor, perhaps one can invent the esthetics of transgression, misery, and urban cruelties.

The way in which Arlt most succinctly foreshadows the postmodern debate is his foregrounding of the relations of power. This then had been silenced or subordinated to others from the time of Lugones to that of Borges. Goloboff, among others, has spoken of the double-edged sword of Arlt's writing practice: In relation to the goods and norms of the double nation, he minimizes, on the one hand, the power of language and the literary world and, on the other, the power of social legality (Goloboff 38).

A passage in Sarlo's *Una modernidad periférica: Buenos Aires 1920 y 1930* [1988, A Periphera; Modernity: Buenos Aires 1920 and 1930] identifies the key to the setting of *El juguete rabioso*: "La 'vida puerca' es la otra cara ... de la ciudad moderna: el paisaje del Buenos Aires inmigratorio" (61) ['Filthy life' is the other side ... of the modern city: The immigratory landscape of Buenos Aires]. In search of a social and literary space, the author and his novel constitute entities and identities that *re-present* as much by voice and writing as by action the threat and danger to the nation, posed by Lugones's "breed of the masses," the incomprehensible voices in Güiraldes's novel and the decadence of Palermo/Buenos Aires in Borges's work. Besides being a transcultural and deterritorialized outsider, the immigrant stands for the ostensible rupture within urban life of ignorance represented by the rules, in part because of the desire to gain access to the "good life" the city has to offer (Martín-Barbero 1991, 172). The writing has identified this menace as the urban masses, the new barbarism that Próspero/Rodó would have deplored.

Arlt hardly ever mentions the nation in his work, except for a reference to Neuquén and Comodoro; it appears that the nation is reduced to the city, a city without history or tradition. This may be because his questioning of the relations of power makes the city itself inaccessible or indifferent. What is at stake is not belonging to a nation or its defense or construction, but a survival strategy against the destruction caused by power–in the face of the desire to reap its benefits as well. In *El juguete rabioso* Arlt reads the city as a machine that accepts only two extremes: The topdogs and the wretched and delirious underdogs. Houses, clothes, women, and the words of those who wield power unlawfully, or exploit the fringes of society, are perceived as both sources of desire and agents of contempt; and the urban spaces and its infamous beings are portrayed as grotesque and tragicomic. The law of money and the struggle to survive rule urban life; the modern jungle is depicted as an unchanging and almost fatal power. The alternative proposed is as cynical as that to be found in any of his *aguafuertes.*

Even if references to the nation in *El juguete rabioso* are merely made in passing, this does not mean that they are insignificant, insofar as they allude to the different orders of power, that is, to the military, economic, political, educational, and cultural orders. Besides the burglary of the school library (the educational order), there are three other indirect references. The military order is mentioned toward the end when the protagonist is rejected from the army because he is *not* "bruto para el trabajo" (Arlt 1995b, 178) ("a brute for work"). Another example occurs when in the Club de los Caballeros de la Media Noche, Lucio suggests that they should rob the national bank (an economic reference) (Arlt 1995b, 111). Lucio, who engenders the idea of the treachery of dreams throughout the novel, speaks about organizing clubs throughout the Republic (a political reference). Silvio defines the proposal as nonsense (Arlt 1995b, 103). The movement of rejecting, assaulting, and despising the nation introduces into literature the vacuum at its foundation (or counter-foundation). The Club de los Caballeros de la Media Noche represents yet another level of transgression. To the assault on the literary nation it adds the image of a naïve group of intellectuals, who skilfully undermine, almost a century later, the efforts of the generation of 1937, the builders of the political nation. By highlighting the failure of the Club, the time of the narrative memory erases the possibility of establishing a negative epic, but in turn it suggests it is the origin and adopts it as the subject matter in and from the margin.

Translation by Charlotte Broad

Works Cited

Achugar, Hugo. 1994a. *La biblioteca en ruinas: reflexiones culturales desde la periferia.* Montevideo: Trilce.

——. 1994b. "La hora americanista o el discurso americanista de entreguerras." *Palavra, literatura e cultura.* Ed. Ana Pizarro. São Paulo: Memorial/Campinas: Editora da Universidade Estadual de Campinas. 635–62.

Amar Sánchez, Ana María. 1997. "Canon y tradición: Literatura vs. cultura de masas." *Revista de Crítica Literaria Latinoamericana* 23.45: 43–53.

Anderson, Benedict. 1991. *Imagined Communities: Reflections on the Origin and Spread of Nationalism.* London: Verso.

Arlt, Roberto. 1978. *Los siete locos. Los lanzallamas.* Caracas: Biblioteca Ayacucho.

——. 1995a. *Aguafuertes porteñas.* Buenos Aires: Corregidor.

——. 1995b. *El juguete rabioso.* Madrid: Cátedra.

Azuela, Mariano. 1992. *The Underdogs.* Trans. Frederick H. Fornoff. Pittsburgh, PA: University of Pittsburgh Press.

——. 1996. *Los de abajo.* Mexico City: Fondo de Cultura Económica.

Borges, Jorge Luis. 1960. "Prólogo." *Obra crítica.* By Pedro Henríquez Ureña. Mexico City: Fondo de Cultura Económica. vii–x.

——. 1984. *Evaristo Carriego: A Book about Old Time Buenos Aires.* Trans. Norman Thomas di Giovanni. New York: Dutton.

——. 1995. *Evaristo Carriego.* Buenos Aires: Emecé.

Castro-Gómez, Santiago. 1996. *Crítica de la razón latinoamericana.* Barcelona: Puvill Libros.

Castro-Urioste, José. 1994. "La imagen de nación en *Doña Bárbara.*" *Revista de Crítica Literaria Latinoamericana* 20.39: 127–39.

Darío, Rubén. 1993. *Retratos y figuras.* Caracas: Biblioteca Ayacucho.

——. "Edgar Allan Poe." *Los raros.* Mexico City: Dirección de Difusión Cultural. 21–34.

Fell, Eve-Marie. 1994. "Primeras reformulaciones: del pensamiento racista al despertar de la conciencia revolucionaria." *Palavra, literatura e cultura.* Ed. Ana Pizarro. São Paulo: Memorial/Campinas: Editora da Universidade Estadual de Campinas. 577–95.

Franco, Jean. 1985. *La cultura moderna en América Latina.* Mexico City: Grijalbo.

Gallegos, Rómulo. 1948. *Doña Bárbara.* Trans. Robert Malloy. New York: Peter Smith.

——. 1977. *Doña Bárbara.* Caracas: Monte Avila Editores.

García Canclini, Néstor. 1990. *Culturas híbridas: estrategias para entrar y salir de la modernidad.* Mexico City: Grijalbo.

Garrels, Elizabeth. 1986. *Las grietas de la ternura: nueva lectura de Teresa de la Parra.* Caracas: Monte Avila Editores.

Gnutzmann, Rita. 1995. "Introducción." *El juguete rabioso.* By Roberto Arlt. Madrid: Cátedra. 9–83.

Goloboff, Gerardo Mario. 1975. "La primera novela de Roberto Arlt: el asalto a la literatura." *Revista de Crítica Literaria Latinoamericana* 1.2: 35–49.

González Echevarría, Roberto. 1985. *The Voice of the Masters: Writing and Authority in Modern Latin American Literature.* Austin: University of Texas Press.

González Prada, Manuel. 1985. *Páginas libres. Horas de lucha.* Caracas: Biblioteca Ayacucho.

Gramuglio, María Teresa. 1993. "Literatura y nacionalismo: Leopoldo Lugones y la construcción de imágenes del escritor." *Hispamérica* 23.64–65: 5–22.

Güiraldes, Ricardo. 1983. *Don Segundo Sombra. Prosas y poemas.* Caracas: Bibliotec Ayacucho.

——. 1995. *Don Segundo Sombra: The Great Novel of the Argentine Pampa.* Trans. Patricia Owen Steiner. Pittsburgh: University of Pittsburgh Press.

Gutiérrez Girardot, Rafael. 1983. *Modernismo.* Barcelona: Montesinos.

——. 1987. "La literatura hispanoamericana de fin de siglo." *Historia de la literatura hispanoamericana. Del neoclasicismo al modernismo.* Ed. Luis Iñigo Madrigal. Madrid: Cátedra. 2: 495–506.

Jitrik, Noé. 1987. *La vibración del presente: trabajos críticos y ensayos sobre textos y escritores latinoamericanos.* Mexico City: Fondo de Cultura Económica.

Larsen, Neil. 1996. "Indigenismo y lo postcolonial: Mariátegui frente a la actual coyuntura teórica." *Revista de Crítica Literaria Latinoamericana* 62.176–77: 863–73.

Lasarte Valcárcel, Javier. 1992. *Sobre literatura venezolana.* Caracas: Edics. La Casa de Bello.

Lugones, Leopoldo. 1979. *El payador y antología de poesía y prosa.* Caracas: Biblioteca Ayacucho.

Mariátegui, José Carlos. 1971 (1928). *Seven Interpretive Essays on Peruvian Reality.* Trans. Marjory Urquidi. Austin: University of Texas Press.

——. 1976. *Siete ensayos de interpretación de la realidad peruana.* Barcelona: Editorial Crítica.

Martí, José. 1977. *Nuestra América.* Caracas: Biblioteca Ayacucho.

Martín-Barbero, Jesús. 1991. *De los medios a las mediaciones: comunicación, cultura y hegemonía.* Mexico City: Gustavo Gili.

——. 1993. *Communication, Culture and Hegemony: From the Media to Mediations.* Trans. Elizabeth Fox and Robert A. White. London; Newbury Park: SAGE Publications.

Masiello, Francine. 1986. *Lenguaje e ideología: las escuelas argentinas de vanguardia.* Buenos Aires: Hachette.

Montaldo, Graciela. 1989. "Introducción: El origen de la historia." *Yrigoyen entre Borges y Arlt (1916–1930). Historia social de la literatura argentina.* Ed. Graciela Montaldo. Buenos Aires: Contrapunto. 7: 23–30.

——. 1993. *De pronto, el campo. Literatura argentina y tradición rural.* Buenos Aires: Beatriz Viterbo Editora.

Monteleone, Jorge. 1989. "Lugones: Canto natal del héroe." *Yrigoyen entre Borges y Arlt (1916–1930). Historia social de la literatura argentina.* Ed. Graciela Montaldo. Buenos Aires: Contrapunto. 7: 161–81.

Moraña, Mabel. 1984. *Literatura y cultura nacional en Hispanoamérica (1910–1940).* Minneapolis, MN: Instituto para el Estudio de Ideologías y Literatura.

Onetti, Juan Carlos. 1965. *El pozo.* Montevideo: Arca.

Ortiz, Renato. 1996. *Otro territorio. Ensayos sobre el mundo contemporáneo.* Buenos Aires: Universidad Nacional de Quilmes.

Osorio, Nelson. 1988. *Manifiestos, proclamas y polémicas de la vanguardia literaria hispanoamericana.* Caracas: Biblioteca Ayacucho.

Parra, Teresa de la. 1982. *Obra. (Narrativa, ensayos, cartas).* Caracas: Biblioteca Ayacucho.

Pastor, Beatriz. 1980. *Roberto Arlt y la rebelión alienada.* Gaithersburg, MD: Hispamérica.

Pauls, Alan. 1989. "Arlt: La máquina literaria." *Yrigoyen entre Borges y Arlt (1916–1930). Historia social de la literatura argentina.* Ed. Graciela Montaldo. Buenos Aires: Contrapunto. 7: 307–22.

Piglia, Ricardo. 1973. "Roberto Arlt: una crítica de la economía literaria." *Los libros* 29: 22–27.

Rama, Ángel. 1977. "El sistema literario de la poesía gauchesca." *Poesía gauchesca.* Ed. Jorge B. Rivera. Caracas: Biblioteca Ayacucho. ix–liii.

——. 1985a. *La ciudad letrada.* Montevideo: Fundación Ángel Rama.

——. 1985b. *Las máscaras democráticas del modernismo.* Montevideo: Fundación Ángel Rama.

——. 1996. *The Lettered City.* Ed. and trans. John Charles Chasteen. Durham, NC: Duke University Press.

Ramos, Julio. 1989. *Desencuentros de la modernidad en América Latina. Literatura y política en el siglo XIX.* Mexico City: Fondo de Cultura Económica.

Real de Azúa, Carlos. 1985. "Prólogo a *Ariel.*" *Ariel. Motivos de Proteo.* Caracas: BibliotecaAyacucho. ix–xxxv.

Rivera, Jorge. 1994. "Textos sobre Roberto Arlt y la ciudad rabiosa." *Palavra, literatura e cultura.* Ed. Ana Pizarro. Sao Paulo: Memorial/Campinas: Editora da Universidade Estadual de Campinas. 787–803.

Rodó, José Enrique. 1985. *Ariel. Motivos de Proteo.* Caracas: Biblioteca Ayacucho.

——. 1988. *Ariel.* Trans. Margaret Sayers Peden. Austin: University of Texas Press.

Rodríguez Pérsico, Adriana. 1993. "Las fronteras de la identidad." *Hispamérica* 32. 64–65: 23–48.

Romero, José Luis. 1976. *Latinoamérica: las ciudades y las ideas.* Buenos Aires: Siglo XXI.

Sarlo, Beatriz. 1988. *Una modernidad periférica: Buenos Aires 1920 y 1930.* Buenos Aires: Nueva Visión.

——. 1994. *Escenas de la vida postmoderna.* Buenos Aires: Ariel.

Sarmiento, Domingo Faustino. 1961. *Facundo: civilización y barbarie.* Buenos Aires: Editorial Universitaria de Buenos Aires.

——. 1868. *Life in the Argentine Republic in the Days of Tyrants; or Civilization and Barbarism.* Trans. Mrs. Horace Mann. New York: Philosophical Society.

Schwarz, Roberto. 1994. "La referencia nacional." *Las culturas de fin de siglo en América Latina.* Ed. Josefina Ludmer. Buenos Aires: Beatriz Viterbo Editora. 27–33.

——. 1995. "National by Imitation." *The Postmodernism Debate in Latin America.* Ed. John Beverley, José Oviedo and Michael Aronna. Trans. Michael Aronna. Durham and London: Duke University Press. 264–81.

Viñas, David. 1971. *Literatura argentina y realidad política: de Sarmiento a Cortázar.* Buenos Aires: Siglo Veinte.

——. 1989. "Presentación: Algunos protagonistas, nudos y crispaciones." *Yrigoyen entre Borges y Arlt (1916–1930). Historia social de la literatura argentina.* Ed. Graciela Montaldo. Buenos Aires: Contrapunto. 7: 7–21.

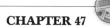

CHAPTER 47

AESTHETICS OF RUPTURE

Eneida Maria de Souza

E começar tudo de novo é sinal dos novos tempos, a modernidade em pessoa. Se antes nos deprimia tudo o que havia de postiço numa civilização mimética, a teoria do oásis vinha reabilitar os sucessivos enxertos que nos permitiam estar *à la page.* (Forçando um pouco a nota, seria o caso de lembrar que, naqueles anos de 50, o espírito do tempo corria a favor das importações que ajudassem a queimar etapas, como se dizia, da indústria automobilística à arte abstrata).

(Arantes 22)

And to start over from scratch is a sign of the times, of modernity itself. If the artificial character of a mimetic civilization had immersed us in gloom, Oasis theory rehabilitated the successive grafts that would allow us to be *a la page* [abreast of things]. (Dwelling further on this point, one should note that in the 1950s there was widespread approval for using foreign models as a mechanism to aid us in taking a leap forward, *queimar etapas*–skipping [evolutionary] stages as we termed it–in all fields, from the automotive industry to abstract art.)

Any historical interpretation must be based on two premises: a description of events within their own context, and their reconstruction from a contemporary perspective. To write literary history means to reflect on the official character of legitimizing discourses entailed in historical and artistic practices, and to take into consideration the exclusion of nonartistic manifestations, as a result of the hegemonic significance granted to documents of official history. Such an interpretation is, furthermore, subject to the constantly recurring crisis of present cultural authority. The operative concepts deployed therefore suffer transformations according to the dictates of the moment and of circumstance, and their spectrum of connotations shifts accordingly. In this chapter I intend to proceed toward a critical relation of past and present, by the doubly threaded weft of tradition and rupture.

The aesthetics of rupture, in my analytic perspective, comprises the artistic and literary manifestations that begin with Brazilian Modernism in the 1920s, unfold throughout the 1940s and 1950s with the *concretismo* (Concretism) and *neo-concretismo* (neo-Concretism) movements and traverse the 1960s and 1970s with *tropicalismo* (Tropicalism). Dear to Octavio Paz (1914–1998), the term *tradição da ruptura* ("tradition of ruptures") signifies both the emergence of a tradition under the signs of rupture, and a dilution of the stasis usually conferred upon the procedure. Broaching a new perspective for criticism allows us to engage in dialectic interpretation, an approach that releases events from being confined to historical periods. Modernism, the vanguard, and postmodernism are historically determined periods in Brazilian literature, but it is their relationships that will be the main focus of our dialectic interpretation. This approach will consider temporal boundaries when analyzing the different aesthetics of rupture, but, by so doing, will tend to dissolve such boundaries.

The pace of epistemological ruptures coincides with the appearance of ruptures in the language of the arts. There are new paradigms in the discourse of the social sciences that have direct bearing on literary criticism, politics, and philosophy. Both the social revolutions and the literary theory of the twentieth century cultivated novelty as a sign of scientific progress and a break with past ideological principles. The dictatorship of the new was a trend shared by Brazilian vanguard theorists, who tried (in the manner of their European counterparts), to create a cultural mirror that would keep up with the modernizing transformations of the technical and the industrial revolutions.

The discourse on metropolitan modernity sprang to life in Brazil with the Modernist movement of 1922, which brought together poets, artists, musicians, and writers. To the minds of

many critics, the as yet precarious plan for modernization perceived in the trajectory of this discourse, revealed the mismatch of foreign ideas transplanted into national soil. Roberto Schwarz's (b. 1938) polemic notion of *As ideias fora do lugar* [1977; *Misplaced Ideas,* 1992] (introduced in his book *Ao vencedor, as Batatas,* whose title, taken from a notion created by Machado de Assis (1839–1908), loosely means "winner takes all") is representative of the way the contradictions of modernity and modernization were played out in Latin America, as illustrated in the relationship between the culture of metropolitan centers and the periphery. Schwarz demonstrates that while liberalism allowed for the emergence of a class of independent professionals in Europe at the end of the nineteenth century, the corresponding phenomenon did not occur in Brazil. The Brazilian "free man," although occupying a much more agreeable position than during slavery, was in fact dependent on the *cultura do favor* ("culture based on exchange of favors"), a sign par excellence of individual subjection to the powerful and the antimodern (Schwarz 1981, 13–25).

One must add to Schwarz's thesis a reflection on Brazilian Modernism, which, although influenced by the aesthetics of the foreign vanguard, is of marked nationalist sentiment. Renato Ortiz, in analyzing the modern movement, reaches the conclusion: "só seremos modernos se somos nacionais" (34) ("we will be modern if we are national"). This is why the Modernist artistic program, while facing its own contradictions, imposes itself, in Ortiz's words, as "uma idéia fora do lugar que se expressa como um projeto" (34) ("an out-of-place [mismatched] idea that expresses itself as a project"). Modernism, subject to its own discrepancies and internal contradictions, and open to European vanguards, was able to conjugate varying degrees of contemporaneity in art, these being a result of the temporal mismatch that characterized the avid reception and adoption of foreign intellectual ideas into the nation.

In the current reality of postmodernity, new questions arise to take the place of modernist concerns; these new questions include contemporary culture as the expression of the hegemonic power of a single, central nation from which all ideas are produced and exported. In Néstor García Canclini's understanding, it is not a question of verifying whether Latin America implemented an incomplete or late version of the modernization model that had been carried out in Europe. Nor is it a question of searching for an alternative, independent paradigm through traditions already transformed by the expansion of world capitalism (221). It is necessary to demystify both the notion of center and that of a modern model that can be implemented. The ideology that has arisen around this concept does not allow us to see the center as a construction, in which the exclusions and cracks inherent to all implementations of the modernizing process are forgotten and suppressed.

The question of the aesthetics of rupture in Brazil must be interpreted through the return to the Modernist movement of the 1920s in connection with the literary criticism of the 1960s and 1970s, a period that coincides with the arrival of structuralist and poststructuralist theories: semiotics, Bakhtin, Derrida's philosophical deconstruction, and the epistemological break created by the works of Gaston Bachelard, Louis Althusser, Gilles Deleuze, Claude Lévi-Strauss, and Michel Foucault. A great deal of Brazilian literary criticism centering on the notion of rupture as an important criterion found rich material in Mikhail Bakhtin's work. The Russian theorist, who explored concepts such as carnivalization and dialogism in literary discourse, provided Brazilian critics with powerful new instruments for an interpretation of Brazil's own reality and its particular artistic methods, such as Oswald de Andrade's (1890–1954) *antropofagia*, with its parody, humour, pastiche, decentering of values, and aesthetic transformation of the quotidian.

This critical lineage includes Haroldo de Campos (1929–2003) and Augusto de Campos (b. 1931), translators, poets, and critics who have been responsible for rehabilitating authors excluded by official history, such as Joaquim de Sousândrade (1833–1902), Gregório de Matos (1633?–1696), Pedro Killkerry (1885–1917), and the Modernist Oswald de Andrade, whose work was revived in the 1960s. The creation of a *paideuma*, a composite of Gustave Mallarmé, James Joyce, Ezra Pound, Vladimir Mayakovski, and Paul Valéry, among others, exemplifies the principle of rupture. Haroldo and Augusto de Campos must be included, by virtue of their singular poetry, in the aesthetical tradition that eventually led to *concretismo*. This neovanguard movement was created in the 1950s, when the new capital city, Brasília, *a cidade concreta* ("the city of concrete" the city itself is a Concretist poem) was built. Theorists established in Rio de Janeiro, such as Luiz Costa Lima (b. 1937), Affonso Romano de Sant'Anna (b. 1937), and Silviano Santiago (b. 1936), a group that disseminated structuralist and poststructuralist thought in universities, have been analyzing contemporary Brazilian literature through the lens of the aesthetics of rupture, an interpretation that has its starting point in the Modernist movement of the 1920s.

Differing from the Rio de Janeiro group, the intellectuals of the University of São Paulo have valued not only the aesthetic rupture with past values, but with tradition itself, the counterpart in the process of constructing modernity. We present on one side the example of Haroldo de Campos, whose rereading of Brazilian historiography validated a tradition in rupture by rehabilitating writers who were excluded from the national canon. As a critical counterpart, we submit the work of Antonio Candido, whose 1970 essay "Literatura e subdesenvolvimento" ["Literature and Underdevelopment"] posited that a national identity would develop only if it hinged on a mechanism of internal causality, through which one could, starting with modernism, "produzir obras de primeira ordem, influenciados não por modelos extrangeiros imediatos, mas por exemplos nacionais anteriores" (1979, 354) ("produce works of the first order, influenced by previous national examples not by foreign models," 1995, 131).

In a work decisive in its rereading of modernist texts in light of postmodernism, Silviano Santiago points out the return of the discourse on tradition in Modernism during the 1980s, identifying himself as a member of the Modernist school of criticism centered on the concept of rupture. This position became necessary, he explains, due to the need to draw together the material that had been excluded from the literary canon for not fitting into a priori aesthetic principles. For example, poetry of a religious nature by authors such as Murilo Mendes (1901–1975) and Jorge de Lima (1893–1953), and essays on messianismo (messianic movements) by Oswald de Andrade were excluded; these texts, among many others, are as yet unstudied and yet comprise a wide-ranging and complex part of the Brazilian Modernist movement. The 1980s signaled an effort to better situate the postmodern aesthetics of parody–respecting its own more radical and transgressive nature–due to conceptual shifts arising from Brazil's own social and political transformations moving from the military dictatorship to democracy. It was a decade of democratic restructuring for the nation, and entailed recycling intellectual positions within a culture that demanded a new language and a different mode of insertion of its social practices, even if this was merely necessitated by the circumstantial demise of its old enemy, *censura*, the government-enforced censorship of free speech. Silviano Santiago expresses himself thus:

> Estamos mais acostumados a encarar o Modernismo dentro da estética da ruptura, para usar a expressão de Octavio Paz, ou dentro da estética do *make-it-new*, de Pound, ou ainda a tradição do novo, de Rosenberg, e assim no infinito. A nossa formação esteve sempre configurada por uma estética da ruptura, da quebra, a uma destruição consciente dos valores do passado. "La destruction fut ma Béatrice," escreveu Mallarmé, declarando o nome da musa moderna. Dessa forma é que um dos discursos mais privilegiados do Modernismo, sobretudo nos últimos 20 anos, tem sido o da paródia.... Esse tipo de estética–da ruptura, do desvio, da ironia e do sorriso, da transgressão dos valores do passado–é que tem o direito de cidadania, por assim dizer, na revalorização dadaísta por que passou o Modernismo desde 1972. (Santiago 1987, 113)

> We are better accustomed to framing Modernism within the aesthetics of rupture, to use Octavio Paz's expression, or in Pound's "make-it-new" aesthetics, or even in the tradition of the new as conceived by Rosenberg, and so forth ad infinitum. We always have been characterized by the aesthetics of rupture, of dissolution, of a conscious destruction of past values. "La destruction fut ma Béatrice" ("Destruction has been my Beatrice"), wrote Mallarmé, giving the muse of modernity a name. This is how parody has become one of the privileged forms of Modernism, especially during the last 20 years.... This form of aesthetics–of rupture, of deviance, of irony, and of the smile [tongue in cheek], of transgressing the values of the past–is what should be given citizen's rights, so to speak, in the Dadaist reevaluation that Modernism underwent after 1972.

It becomes increasingly difficult within this revisionist perspective of the aesthetics of rupture (not limited to what the aesthetics meant at that time, but also including the critical response that shapes it and forms its poetics currently), to establish, precisely and faithfully, the original conception of the vanguard principles in Brazil. The historical process of reinterpretation of these concepts is filled with obstacles that impede us from considering them in their uniqueness, because research on the topic is based on documents and texts that already have been contaminated by the interpretation of others. The impossibility of conceiving a total, overarching history of Modernism is, in part, due to contemporary epistemological conditions, which are no longer directed toward synthesis and generalization, and to the recognition that any analytical frame is at best fragmentary and acts selectively on the construction of the theoretical subject. Modernism, like other cultural events of importance in Brazilian historiography, still merits the attention of its critics, since the official content of its history continues to exclude to this day what was left out by the literary historians of the time.

In the 1950s, *antropofagia* ("anthropophagy," cannibalism), the concept Oswald de Andrade (1890–1954) created in his 1928 "Manifesto Antropofágico" ["Anthropophagic Manifesto"] and used to title the movement's magazine *Revista de Antropofagia*, again became a philosophical and existential *Weltanschauung* in *A crise da filosofia messiânica* [1950; *The Crisis of Messianic Philosophy*]. As a concept, it has remained active to this day, through its appropriation by the *Tropicalismo* movement of the 1960s, and in the rereading of dependency theory found in recent comparative studies in Brazil. Haroldo de Campos, in "Da razão antropofágica: diàlogo e diferença na cultura brasileira" [1983; "On Anthropophagic Reason: Dialogue and Difference in Brazilian Culture"] argues that *antropofagia* should be considered one of the most insightful strategies for conceiving the national in dialogic and dialectic relation to the universal (109). De Campos uses the anthropophagic metaphor of cultural devouring as a justification for his own practices as a translator: His translations are inventive and free from a commitment to be faithful to the original. Haroldo, like Augusto de Campos, assumes the role of coauthor of the original text in his translations. Translators became coauthors in this anthropophagic stance, because of the degree to which, in the process of translating, they devoured the culture of the Other. The intention to merge with the Other's artistic product through translation brings us to the issue of whether Latin American literature is the result of transculturation.

Antropofagia as an operative concept was well incorporated into the translation practices of members of the Concretist poetic movement without, however, ever moving radically to the center stage as a main coordinating principle of the criticism of the 1950s. *Antropofagia*'s current return as an astute weapon for addressing the issue of international cultural borrowings, means breaking out of a closed nationalist position and adopting the strategy of openly embracing multiple national cultural manifestations. As Caetano Veloso (b. 1942) put it in *Verdade Tropical* [1997; *Tropical Truth*, 2002] *antropofagia* meant, at the time, breaking with the roots of Brazilian culture, with the cult of the authentic and the primitive, by accepting without prejudice the most recent musical products of the United States and Europe. This new sense that *antropofagia* acquired in the 1960s, differing from its conception in the 1920s, was stressed further by Veloso. Since the songwriter was opposed to a decontextualized interpretation of artistic methods, he favored taking into account the distinctive characteristics of their context of reemergence.

> A idéia de canibalismo cultural servia-nos, aos tropicalistas, como uma luva. Estávamos "comendo" os Beatles e Jimi Hendrix. Nossas argumentações contra a atitude defensiva dos nacionalistas encontravam aqui uma afirmação sucinta e exaustiva. Claro que passamos a aplicárla com larqueza e intensidade, mas não sem cuidado, e eu procurei, a cada passo, repensar os termos em que a adotamos. Procurei também e procuro agora relê la nos textos originais, tendo en mente as obras que ela foi concebida para defender, no contexto em que tal poesia e tal poética surgiram.

> Nunca perdemos de vista, nem eu nem Gil, as diferenças entre a experiência modernista dos anos 20 e nossos embates televisivos e fonomecânicos dos anos 60. (Veloso 1997, 248)

The notion of cultural cannibalism fit us *tropicalistas* like a glove. We were "eating up" the Beatles and Jimi Hendrix. We found that our arguments against the defensive posture of the nationalists were stated succinctly and convincingly. We, of course, applied Tropicalism generously and intensively, but not carelessly, and I tried, at every step I took, to rethink the terms in which we adopted it. I also tried and still try to reread it in its original sources, taking into consideration the work that *antropofagia* was conceived to defend, the context in which that poetry and poetics emerged. We never lost sight, neither Gilberto Gil nor I, of the differences between the Modernist experience in the 1920s and our televised and audiobroadcast contestations in the 1960s. (2002, 271)

Much in the same manner that Oswald de Andrade's *antropofagia* was criticized by Roberto Schwarz, so was *tropicalismo* to be the object of his disaffection. Reiterating the argument he used to explain the mismatch of the procedure of imitation, Schwarz stated that mismatch was in effect universal because "imitation" as a procedure was always carried out by a single social class. Without entering into an actual discussion of *antropofagia*, Schwarz's essay "Cultura e política: 1964–1969" ["Culture and Politics: 1964–1969"], originally published in the French review *Les temps modernes*, states that the movement was responsible for creating an aberrant image of Brazil, affirming the absurd as its essence. As Evelina Hoisel puts it, "se Schwarz detecta lucidamente essas ambiguidades e tensões inscritas nas produções tropicalistas, a postura ideológica assumida não lhe permite compreender claramente o sentido preciso da Tropicália e sua estratégia de ruptura e desconstrução de determinados valores sócio-culturais" (44) ("If Schwarz lucidly detects these ambiguities and the tensions inherent in the output of *Tropicalismo*, the ideological posture [Schwarz] takes up will not allow him to develop a clear understanding of the precise sense of the *Tropicália* and its strategy of rupture and deconstruction of certain social and cultural values").

Oswald de Andrade's gesture of rupture as expressed in the "Manifesto Antropofágico," in its attack on the rhetoric of the "learned classes," on the presence of the *sacred* enemy (the Church), on the Portuguese colonizer, and on all preconceived self-professed truths, clearly specified its aims, which were distinct from the *tropicalismo* of the 1960s and 1970s. Armed with its dadaist inheritance, the Manifesto had the same tonic of social violence, while advocating a devouring of the past as a strategy to break away from colonialist ideology and the purported culture. Jorge Schwartz (b. 1944) in *Vanguardas latino-americanas* (1994) affirms that the Manifesto's strategic use of aphorisms enables it to trace a national profile of incomparable synthesis, demonstrated in the way it covers Brazil's ethnic diversity, its colors, its culinary practices, its sexuality and religion. Here, Schwartz discusses the Manifesto's revolutionary and utopian character:

> A assim denominada descida antropofágica" é antes de mais nada um ato de consciência. O dilema nacional/cosmopolita é resolvido pelo contato com as revolucionárias técnicas da vanguarda européia, e pela percepção da necessidade de reafirmar os valores nacionais numa linguagem moderna. Assim, Oswald transforma o bom selvagem rousseauniano num mau selvagem, devorador do europeu, capaz de assimilar o outro para inverter a tradicional relação colonizador/colonizado. (Schwartz 140)

The so-called *descida antropofágica* (descent into anthropophagy) is above all an act of conscience. The national-versus-cosmopolitan dilemma finds a resolution through the revolutionary techniques of the European vanguard, and the perception of the need to reaffirm national values in a modern national language. Thus, Oswald transforms Rousseau's noble savage into a cannibal who will devour Europeans, and thereby assimilate the Other so as to invert the traditional relation colonizer/colonized.

In the terms employed in the anthropophagic equation colonizer/colonized–terms like the indigenous devouring of the European, and the revolutionary techniques of the European vanguard–the modernist's enemy appears ambiguously in the form of the European man. It is the European who provides the prerequisites for the revolutionary leap, and it is he who will be devoured, because of these very same forces. The European Other, irrespective of national specificities, is historically taken up by Oswald de Andrade as a functional denominator so that Brazilian culture may impose itself over foreign culture. Seventy years after the Manifesto was published we find that the discourse of rupture has remained in Brazilian national thought, as is the case with the concretismo movement and with Caetano Veloso's tropicalismo as well as with various other sympathizers in diverse arts, although the notion of anthropophagy merits being revisited and examined by new theories. The conceptual developments should therefore receive differentiated treatment according to the historical, aesthetic, and political conditions that are brought up. In the specific case of comparative literature the Oswaldian concept of antropofagia became, from the historical point of view, a part of the debate on cultural dependency.

Ismail Xavier (b. 1947) interprets *tropicalismo* in his *Alegorias do subdesenvolvimento* [1993; *Allegories of Underdevelopment*, 1997] in the context of the changes that occurred in the 1960s, and explains the power that the movement had in terms of the intertextuality it established in its rereading of Brazilian national culture. Xavier points out that the new guise that *antropofagia* assumes in the *tropicalismo* movement is its successful entry into contact with the electronic media (Xavier 20). Caetano Veloso, who was both well adapted to and critical of mass culture, combined the daring experimentalism of the artistic vanguard with the sentimental nostalgia of tradition, in reinterpreting the repertoire of Brazilian popular music. The "Carmen Miranda, Chacrinha" movement (Chacrinha was a famous television host) explored icons of mass culture and inserted popular traditions into the media to such a degree that it was very successful as an aesthetic technique of creating a collage of cultural facts, conferring on the method a character that was increasingly national and cosmopolitan. Veloso's musical compositions simultaneously interacted with kitsch elements from the media, a device that dissolved textual barriers and also creatively transgressed the boundaries of erudite music with music that belonged to popular tradition and was meant for mass consumption (Souza 1994–1995, 23).

One cannot therefore, accurately access the importance of *antropofagia* as an articulating concept in the various manifestations of the artistic and literary vanguards without first analyzing its relationship to the issue of cultural dependency, and its implicit positioning on the insertion of Brazilian culture in an international context. The subversion of ethnocentric values and the belief in the inevitable character of dependency lead to what Silviano Santiago termed "Apesar de dependente, universal" ("universality despite dependency"):

[N]ão se faz de conta que a dependência não existe, pelo contrário frisa-se a sua inevitabilidade; não se escamoteia a dívida para com as culturas dominantes, pelo contrário enfatiza-se a sua força coerciva; não se contenta com a visão gloriosa do autóctone e do negro, mas se busca a inserção diferencial deles na totalização universal. (Santiago 1982, 22)

[W]e did not try to ignore the issue of dependency; quite the contrary, its inevitability is underscored; there is no attempt made to evade our debt to the dominant cultures and their coercive force, there is no compromising of reality by accepting a glorified vision of the autochthonous or of the black, there is instead an effort to find a differential inclusion of them in the universal summation.

Taking an opposing strategy to Roberto Schwarz's recognition of the unremitting *mal-estar* (ills) of dependency, Santiago elects *antropofagia*, allied to Mário de Andrade's (1893–1945) *traição a memória* ("betrayal of memory/heritage") and the *concretismo* movement, as the antidote prescribed by Modernism to cure the bad conscience of the colonized through creative incorporation of foreign products (Santiago 1982, 21). Once texts produced in Brazil opted to engage in the deconstruction and decolonization enterprise by combining the three antidotes, two important points came to the fore: 1) Universality is attained by responding to the values of the hegemonic centers (colonizers) in a nonethnocentric manner; and 2) the subversion of the colonizer's text implies a rupture in the tradition of imitation and the creation of a literature richer than the texts of the dominant literature. In defense of the *displaced* construction of the text in the dominated culture (e.g., Brazil) by an inversion of the traditional criteria with regard to the European original and the Brazilian copy, historical canons and tradition are openly questioned. Historical hierarchy is relativized, and the internal causality of tradition is challenged.

The three antidotes of Santiago responsible for opening up national culture to foreign culture come from a historical and anthropological perspective, a position that takes us to Octavio Paz's formulation *tradição da ruptura* and one that coincides with Haroldo de Campos and opposes the ideas of Roberto Schwarz and the São Paulo school.

One of Brazilian modernism's most representative novels, because of its originality and subversive content, is Mário de Andrade's *Macunaíma: o herói sem nenhum caráter* [Macunaíma: A Hero Without Character] published in 1928, the same year as the "Manifesto Antropofágico." Mário de Andrade's personal differences with Oswald de Andrade prevented him from admitting that his novel was shaped in true antropophagic spirit, but literary critics eventually established *Macunaíma* as one of the movement's finest aesthetic products. It is a rhapsody composed of amalgamated texts from national folklore, ranging from fairytales to indigenous myths, and it includes a vast repertoire of popular, foreign, and native literature. In this work, national origins are forgotten and boundaries confused, leading to a process of reversals in the novel's content, especially with respect to its language. Mário de Andrade's betrayal of memory was an artifice that he employed in positioning himself with respect to foreign models and national aesthetic paradigms, a device that certainly corresponds to the procedure of anthropophagic devouring as it was carried out within the aesthetics of rupture in Brazil during the 1920s. Forsaking all sources is a device common in the recitative practices of the ancient Greek rhapsodists and the *cantadores* [minstrels from Northeastern Brazil]; it is propitious to invention and improvisation. To create is to forget models, to dodge verses that have been memorized, it is to play with the cultural archive so as to generate a state of anarchy within its parasitical structure (Souza 1993, 83).

In order to recreate oral culture in the literary text, Mário de Andrade's open challenge to textual fidelity propelled him toward a creative disrespect for the texts of others that resulted in a work consisting heavily of parody and deconstruction of icons; these were to become principles that he shared with other Modernist authors such as Oswald de Andrade. The subversive quality of this aesthetic enterprise was largely characterized by a radical revolution of the artistic procedures and language inspired by the European avant-garde and the wealth of Brazil's popular cultural tradition. This was recognized as the need to reaffirm national values in a modern language, which became the overarching challenge that the Modernists would attempt. They wanted to create the new with eyes set on the future, and use Brazilian history as material for a critical rereading of the nation's present and past cultural expression.

The relationship of the Modernist movement with the European avant-garde shifted according to the demands of the moment and the diverse predilections and disaffections of their respective exponents. In the first period of the Modernist movement, there was an effusive relationship with Futurism, Cubism, Expressionism, and Dadaism: the ideas of the European avant-garde traveled in the baggage of Brazilians circulating in Europe, and satisfied the national penchant for all such novelties. Mário de Andrade always denied any affiliation to Futurism, notwithstanding the fact that its influence can be perceived clearly in his work; the author appropriated for himself, at different times, Cubist and Expressionist aesthetics. It was Mário de Andrade's firm intent to rethink Brazil's culture through modern artistic expression, and to that end he combined Brazil's eighteenth-century Baroque poetics with Europe's newest avant-garde.

Mário de Andrade's poetics succeed in combining the Baroque poetics of Minas Gerais with German expressionism in an attempt to affirm the national through the universal, thereby condensing and displacing Brazilian and European aesthetic values. In de Andrade's examination of the Baroque as a significant expression of Brazilian culture and his comparison of it to the revolutionary power of expressionism, he found a similar structure in which the deconstructive eye of the subject deforms its object. Both artistic movements caught the writer's imagination because they revealed the emergence of the new man. Expressionism becomes a tool for better explaining the national, "sem que essa postura traduza uma forma de prisão ao modelo europeu. Pelo contrário, essa postura acena para o procedimento astucioso do esquecimento como saída para se criar o desenho simultâneo de dois momentos historicamente distintos" (Souza 1993, 84) ("mindful that this posture does not become imprisoned in the European model. On the contrary, this posture points to the astute procedure of forgetfulness as a solution for creating the simultaneous outline of two historically distinct moments").

The caravan of intellectuals from São Paulo that visited Minas Gerais, home of the Brazilian Baroque-in the company of the illustrious Frenchman, Blaise Cendrars (1887–1961), contributed decisively to the Modernist revision of the new and its relation to the past. The speed brought about by progress, a belief in the future, and the forgetting of the past, were all strategically suspended during the slow passage of the train toward the interior of Minas Gerais. The Brazilian Baroque tradition, itself imported from Europe and recreated throughout Latin America, became a call for broadening the concept of the national from the Eurocentric to include the primitive and the exotic. Oswald de Andrade's 1924 *Manifesto Pau-Brasil*, a reference to the tree after which the nation was named, proposed a cultural revision of the nation by granting enhanced value to its primitive elements, and thus anticipating the fusion of simplicity and novelty with the tradition of invention using the devices of surprise and shock. In 1925, Oswald published *Poesia Pau-Brasil* [*Brazil Wood Poetry*], a result of his experiments with cubism and his own travels to Minas Gerais.

Silviano Santiago, in an article mentioned previously, reinforces the opinion Brito Broca expressed, according to which Modernism could be interpreted from its tortured position between the futuristic aesthetics that preached a break with the past and the contact with the old as new, as represented by the Baroque tradition of Minas Gerais: "A contradição entre Futurismo, no sentido europeu da palavra, e Modernismo, no sentido brasileiro, já existe em 24, no momento mesmo em que os novos estão tentando impor uma estética da originalidade entre nós" (Santiago 1987, 127) ("The contradiction between Futurism, in the European sense of the term, and Modernism, in its Brazilian version, is already present in 1924, in the very moment at which os novos [proponents of the new] endeavour to impose an aesthetics of originality upon us"). To understand the failings and limitations of cultural and literary criticism throughout the years is to contribute to the construction of a history of cultural formations within a margin of dubious generalizations and synthesis.

In 1944, invited by the mayor of Belo Horizonte (and future President of Brazil) Jucelino Kubitschek, a new caravan of intellectuals from São Paulo returned to the state of Minas Gerais. Their objective was to visit the state capital's new modern architectural creation, *Pampulha*, designed by Oscar Niemeyer and Lucio Costa. An exhibition entitled *Exposição de Arte Moderna* [Modern Art Exhibition], comprising art from the exponents of the Modernist movement from the 1920s and its subsequent followers, reinforced the desire to bring the artistic vanguard to an urban landscape and into the realm of political ideals. In an attempt to break with conservatism, tradition in its most stereotypical sense, there was a resurgence of the modern as a concept tailored under the sign of rupture with dominant ideas of the past and industrial development, following the literary and artistic revolution of the 1920s. The architecture of Belo Horizonte in the 1940s, belatedly conceived as modern, functioned to counteract what was felt to be the cultural emptiness of the moment: it became a reconstruction of the idea of the new and a rehabilitation of the concept of progress.

The man to receive an invitation to the festivities that would bring together members of the artistic vanguard at both moments was not Mário de Andrade, however, but Oswald. Representing a position that was more anarchist, both in literature and politics, the author of *Memórias sentimentais de João Miramar* [1964; *Sentimental Memoirs of John Seaborn*, 1971] became during the visit the ambassador of modernism, legitimizing the continuity between past and present, in the conference. "O caminho percorrido" ("Paths Traveled")

Em 22, São Paulo começava. Hoje, Belo Horizonte conclui. Porque enquanto Minas procura unificar o Brasil, São Paulo se dispersou em setenta panelas e foi preciso virmos a Belo Horizonte para darmos o espetáculo duma família solidária e respeitável. (Oswald de Andrade 1972, 93)

In 1922, São Paulo began what today, Belo Horizonte concludes. Because while Minas endeavoured to unify Brazil, São Paulo dispersed itself in seventy factions and it was necessary for us to travel to Belo Horizonte so we could show the world the wonder that we are, a family of respectability and solidarity.

In reality, the pretense of continuity served Kubitschek's political agenda, disposed as he was to associate himself with modernity. Any deletions or temporal mismatches were erased in the name of the continuation of the real Brazil, a procedure that was contingent on satisfying the parties concerned with the historical redefinition of nationalism and populism.

The passion for modern ideas in Brazil, intermittently renewed by the concept of rupture, serves to explain Jucelino Kubitschek's modernizing political program, which was established in the 1950s with the construction of Brasília, the nation's new capital. This same period coincided with the beginning of *concretismo*, led by Haroldo and Augusto de Campos and Décio Pignatari. *Concretista* poetry assumed a radical break with past poetic traditions, while electing Oswald de Andrade as one of its precursors, and preaching the death of verse and the inclusion of visuality into the poetic composition. It opened the intersemiotic horizon of literature and also reinforced the internationalist and cosmopolitan aspects of art no longer circumscribed by regionalist and centralizing limitations. The abstract dimension of the new aesthetics repudiated the figurativism of high modernism as a form of composition suitable for nationalist landscapes and drew sustenance from the political and artistic model of Brasília's *plano-piloto* [the capital's airplane-shaped urban plan], a concrete-poem installed in the central plateau of the country.

The notion of a capital planted in the arid backlands is a repetition, in Mário Pedrosa's (1900–1981) interpretation, of our ancestors' gesture in transplanting their own European culture to Brazil. The *mata virgem* (virgin forest) itself and its stylized version became invitations to the avant-garde's tabula rasa, and imitation became tantamount to privilege (Arantes 22). Modern from birth, with the power to perfect the absorption of all our cultural loans, it would be reasonable to expect that the conservative spirit, responsible for seeing historical evolution as spontaneous and organic, would be forever banned from what pertains to Brazil. Moreover the concept of modern was redefined as a counterpart to political projects and inevitable attempts to redefine national identity.

Let us return to the Otília de Arantes quotation that opened this chapter, taken from the introduction to Mário Pedrosa's collected essays. It mirrors the author's conceptual stance on the occasion of Brasília's inauguration, and it includes a reflection on the role of cultural imports. To conceive of the city as an oasis planted in the middle of the central plateau region reinforced the notion of the manifestation of the new and the ambitious rush toward progress. In this sense, the modern issue reappears in light of the relationship between national and foreign, utopia and progress, rupture and tradition.

To accept Brazil's condition as a nation of the periphery, and its position described as Universality despite dependency, becomes a check on the prejudice enclosed in the notion of mismatched ideas, and it reactivates the debate on the impossibility of bringing the cycle of modernity to a close. The unexpected and belated irruption of early twentieth-century artistic manifestations of the Modernists imposes a constant revision of the social and cultural factors at play in this resurgence. This analytical stance is vital to preventing a conservative and reductionist interpretation of this process of retrospective consideration. As the avant-garde of the 1960s and 1970s disappear on the horizon, their artistic and technical inventions have now been absorbed by mass culture, which, impelled by the thrust of the culture industry, has succeeded in transforming the quotidian of the twentieth century.

Translation by Lis Horta Moriconi

Works Cited

Andrade, Mário de. 1988. *Macunaíma: o herói sem nenhum caráter*. Ed. Telê Porto Ancona Lopez. Paris: Archives; Brasília: CNPq.

Andrade, Oswald de. 1928. "Manifesto Antropófago." *Revista de Antropofagia* 1.1 (São Paulo): 3 and 7.

——. 1925. *Pau-Brasil*. Paris: Au Sans Pareit.

——. 1972 [1950]. A crise da filosofia messiânica. In *Obras Completas de Oswald de Andrade*, vol. 6. *Do Pau-Brasil á Antropofagia e às Utopias. Manifestos, teses de Concursos e ensaios*. Rio de Janeiro: Civilização Brasileira.

——. 1972. "O caminho percorrido." *Ponta de Lança. Obras completas*. Rio de Janeiro: Civilização Brasileira. 93–102.

Arantes, Otília, ed. 1995. "Introdução." *Textos escolhidos*. Vol 3: *Acadêmicos e modernos*. São Paulo: Editora da Universidade de São Paulo. 15–37.

Campos, Haroldo de. 1983. "Da razão antropofágica: diálogo e diferença na cultura brasileira." *Boletim Bibliográfico: Biblioteca Mário de Andrade*. 44.1/4 (São Paulo): 107–27.

Candido, Antonio. 1979. "Literatura e subdesenvolvimento." *América Latina em sua literatura*. Ed. César Fernández Moreno. São Paulo: Perspectiva. 343–62.

——. 1995. "Literature and Underdevelopment." *On Literature and Society*. Ed. and trans. Howard S. Becker. Princeton: Princeton UP. 119–41.

García Canclini, Néstor. 1990. "La modernidad después de la postmodernidad." *Modernidade: Vanguardas Artísticas na América Latina*. Ed. Ana Maria de Moraes Belluzzo. São Paulo: Memorial/Unesp. 101–37.

Hoisel, Evelina. 1994. "Tropicalismo: algumas reflexões teóricas." *Brasil/Brazil. Revista de Literatura Brasileira*. (Brown/Porto Alegre): 39–63.

Ortiz, Renato. 1988. *A moderna tradição brasileira*. São Paulo: Brasiliense.

Paz, Octavio. 1974. *Los hijos del limo: del romanticismo a la vanguardia*. Barcelona: Seix Barral.

Pedrosa, Mário. 1995. *Textos escolhidos*. Vol 3: *Acadêmicos e modernos*. Ed. Otília Arantes. São Paulo: Editora da Universidade de São Paulo.

Santiago, Silviano. 1982. "Apesar de dependente, universal." *Vale quanto pesa: ensaios sobre questões político-culturais*. Rio de Janeiro: Paz e Terra. 13–24.

——. 1987. "Pernanência do discurso da tradição no Modernismo." *Cultura brasileira: tradição/contradição*. Gerd Bornheim et al. Rio de Janeirio: Jorge Zahar/Funarte. 111–45.

Schwartz, Jorge. 1994. *Vanguardas latino-americanas: polêmicas, manifestos e textos críticos*. São Paulo: Editora da Universidade de São Paulo/Fapesp.

Schwarz, Roberto. 1970. "Remarques sur Culture et Politique au Brésil: 1964–1969." *Les Temps Modernes* (January). 37–73. Published in English: 1992. "Culture and Politics in Brazil, 1964–1969." *Misplaced Ideas. Essays on Brazilian Culture*. Ed. and Trans. John Gledson. London Verso. 126–59.

——. 1981. *Ao vencedor, as batatas: forma literaria e processo social nos inicios do romance brasileiro*. São Paulo: Duas Cidades.

——. 1987. "Nacional por subtração." *Cultura brasileira: tradição/contradição*. Ed. Gerd Bornheim et al. Rio de Janeiro: Jorge Zahar/Funarte. 91–110.

———. 1992. "Culture and Politics in Brazil, 1964–1969." *Misplaced Ideas: Essays on Brazilian Culture.* Ed. and Trans. John Gledson. London: Verso. 126–59.

Souza, Eneida Maria de. 1993. "Preguiça e saber." *Revista de Letras* 33 (São Paulo): 81–89.

———. 1994–1995. "Jeitos do Brasil." *Ensaios de Semiótica* 28/30 (Belo Horizonte): 14–26.

Veloso, Caetano. 1997. *Verdade tropical.* São Paulo: Companhia das Letras.

———. 2002. *Tropical Truth: A Story of Music and Revolution in Brazil.* New York: Alfred A. Knopf.

Xavier, Ismail. 1993. *Alegorias do subdesenvolvimento: cinema novo, tropicalismo, cinema marginal.* São Paulo: Brasiliense.

CHAPTER 48

THE POSTMODERN IN BRAZILIAN LITERARY THEORY AND CRITICISM

Italo Moriconi

Readings

In Brazilian intellectual debate, interest in the postmodern, postmodernity, and postmodernism can be dated back to the early to mid 1980s. This interest was motivated not only by an internal need to redefine the dominant categories of cultural historiography but by the need to bring local scholarship up to date with theoretical dislocations then occurring in the larger context of Western humanistic knowledge: The abandonment of structural and Marxist formalisms in favor of deconstruction and linguistic pragmatism. Within the realm of ideology and political science in Latin America and in particular Brazil, the 1980s proved to be a period when intellectuals turned their attention to socio-political themes, such as citizenship, representative democracy, access to the justice system, and the ideological constitution of the public sphere. Though Left-wing critics frequently deemed that an interest in postmodernism represented a capitulation to the neo-Liberal agenda, the course of the debate demonstrated that neo-Conservative and traditionally Liberal sectors of society were the most ardent in their rejection of the validity of the questions brought to light by the postmodern. This trajectory is clear in the work of José Guilherme Merquior (b. 1941), who welcomed literary postmodernism during the 1970s but later became one of the most vociferous voices in the resistance to this and related concepts.

Thus in Brazil the resistance to postmodernity came to be dominated by a Right-wing interpretation claiming that the postmodern represented a new or hyper-radical debate identified with the irrational and politically irresponsible currents in post-structuralism. The bitter tone of the Habermasian critiques of postmodernity was acclimatized in Brazil though the voices of Liberalism (such as that of Sérgio Paulo Rouanet) and (at first) also by the remaining Marxists, such as Leandro Konder. Ironically, it was the painting of postmodernity as radical nihilism that attracted Marxists to the debate, for they found that this discursive space admitted and even presupposed critical evaluations of end-of-century capitalism. Fredric Jameson was important to the development of this debate; in Brazil his formulations were adopted by Marxists, post-Marxists, and neo-Marxists.

One should note that Brazilian academic thought (and anthropology, in particular) also entertained reactionary readings of postmodernity–reactionary in the sense that they were related to religious reactionary movements. Neo-Conservative forces sought to reactivate ties between artists and intellectuals and the great traditional religious institutions–Catholic, Protestant, and Jewish–in the aftermath of counterculture movements that valued hallucinatory experiences, ecological mysticism, and the so-called new or alternative communitarian faiths. In both of these cases, what is presented under the rubric of the postmodern, in fact, represents a rejection of modernity, a position

mourning the fragmentation and commercialization of ethics under the pressures of modernity. Thus this religious reaction to the postmodern recalls the ideology first proposed in the 1930s by militantly Catholic literary intellectuals such as Tristão de Athayde (1893–1983), Murilo Mendes (1901–1975), and Augusto Frederico Schmidt (1906–1965). Recently Brazilian sociologists have actually interpreted the expansion of evangelical sects through the intense use of mass media as a postmodern phenomenon.

In the 1980s, a debate on postmodernism took place simultaneously in the Brazilian academy and in the media, and soon acquired the contours of a movement characterized by the reception of ideas from abroad. Although this debate proved to be ephemeral as a media event, as might have been expected, it nonetheless left traces that survived well into the following decade. The term *postmodern* came to define certain stylistic traits in the discourses and practices of both artistic production and aesthetic criticism. Among the constitutive elements that formed the postmodern imaginary in Brazil, one may cite Wim Wenders' cinema, hypertextual fiction, mass media's universal mediation of culture and subjectivity, the universalization of popular culture, consumption as a libidinal phantasmagoria, the idea of an infinite proliferation of signs, an emphasis on paradoxical rhetoric and paratactic syntax, and the fragmentation of fixed identity and meaning.

Mário Pedrosa and *Arte em Revista*

The publication of the seventh volume of the cultural and aesthetic journal *Arte em Revista* in 1983 marked the start of the reception of the postmodern in the Brazilian academy. The greatest challenge was somehow to avoid the characterization of this inaugural event as the passive importation of a foreign idea. This concern was all the more acute given that the journal was published under the auspices of the University of São Paulo (USP), whose philosophy, as first elaborated by humanist intellectuals following the university's foundation in 1934, entailed the questioning of what was then thought of as the traditional model of passively importing ideas from abroad. Direct heir to the intellectual inheritance of São Paulo's Modernist movement, university intellectuals proposed that Brazilian writers engage foreign ideas critically. USP laid the intellectual foundations for a national pedagogical project based on the elaboration and fostering of local intellectual and aesthetic traditions. Thus local traditions were to be read not within the realm of the folkloric, but rather as original and diversifying interpretations of universal precepts. This approach was centered on the quest for a Brazilian difference, which would at once systematically construct Brazilian identity and deconstruct the universal. USP pioneered, within the academic elite, the organization of the whole nation around this notion of a Brazilian difference.

In Mário Pedrosa's (1900–1981) criticism the journal *Arte em Revista* found the source which made possible the thinking of postmodernity not merely as a foreign idea but as a significant category internal to a genuinely national artistic tradition. *Arte em Revista* privileged Pedrosa's mode of criticism by favoring the contemporary Brazilian art history espoused by USP professor of aesthetics Otília Beatriz Fiori Arantes. While *Arte em Revista* took up Mário Pedrosa as a focal point for Brazilian art criticism, alongside him it also published influential translations from the key works in the philosophical and aesthetic polemic of postmodernity which was then being voraciously consumed by academics the world over: The work of Habermas, Peter Bürger, Jean-François Lyotard, and Paolo Portoghesi. This postmodern canon was formed in response to the need to rethink aesthetics as a function of questions raised by postmodern architecture and the need to conceive of the historiographic status of contemporary art within the context of the exhaustion of the avant-gardes.

In the work initiated by *Arte em Revista*, Pedrosa was rediscovered as the author of an original formulation of the theory of the exhaustion of the avant-garde during the 1960s–when the confusion of the historical moment (that many read paradoxically as the apex or the return of the avant-garde) became evident. Pedrosa, in sharp contrast, recognized the end of what he termed the historical cycle of modern art; he even coined the term "postmodern art" to describe the present and future of aesthetics in articles published from the mid-1960s to the end of his life. Nonetheless, as Otília Arantes notes both in essays published in *Arte em Revista* and in the monograph she later dedicated to Pedrosa in 1991, this sketch of postmodernity hovered between celebration and rejection, creating a tension that would characterize many discourses of postmodernity, beginning with the work of Lyotard himself.

The cleavage between modernity and postmodernity is evident in the evolution of Mário Pedrosa's thought (see 1975; 1981). In the thirties he championed social art without relinquishing formal and structural concerns, and in the forties he valued abstraction and the autonomy of art as axes of modernity. During the fifties he voiced an enthusiasm for modern architecture as an artistic utopia capable of totally revolutionizing human life and sensibility, a project articulated in an exemplary manner in the construction of the country's new capital, Brasília. During this time Pedrosa's criticism embraced modernity as a transformative and totalizing project, a claim that would later be criticized, relativized, and deconstructed with the advent of postmodernity and, in particular, of postmodern architecture. For Pedrosa, Otília Arantes notes, modern art's utopian project was surpassed by reality: The reality of consumer society and of the culture of electronic communication and information. The artist's revolutionary task no longer entailed forging the new through formal innovation, but rather engaging the processes that make up reality, what in today's vocabulary we might term virtual reality. This reality produces a sensorial acceleration, an inability to differentiate between the work of art and consumer goods within the realm of objects, and a new type of enlightenment governed by the media. Thus, the univocal and utopian space of modern art is dissolved, invaded by the hyper-real and multifaceted reality of the media's virtual space. In envisioning positive roles for the artists in this new context–both in the realm of knowledge and aesthetics–Pedrosa adopts what Otília Arantes terms the optimism of the media. This constitutes the celebratory moment in Pedrosa's diagnosis

of postmodernity. According to Arantes, Pedrosa himself would come to be disquieted by this vision of postmodernity, for it reduced the artist to a mere operator within the system's logic of meaning and its technology.

Pedrosa's critical thought developed in a direction that reaffirmed the autonomy of art and the dissident role of the artist within society. He sought a path of resistance–a path not utopian but, to use the vocabulary of the 1970s, alternative or marginal. But after the initial optimism and celebration, his diagnosis of postmodernity achieved a certain synthesis: It moved from the utopian Modernism of the avant-garde in the fifties to a proposal for a guerilla theater of cultural resistance. To this end art, or rather the combination of cultural practices that come to take up the creative function in society, had to be directed by a radical critique of postmodern society. Thus is Pedrosa's acceptance and rejection of postmodernity configured: It is the fruit of both an Adornian negation of the modern and a postmodern neo-Nietzschean affirmation of life's values against the alienating phantasmagoria of consumer goods. Pedrosa elaborates his universal theory of art with reference to the history of contemporary Brazilian art after the utopian surge of the 1950s. He sees in neo-Concretism–particularly in the work of Lygia Clark and Hélio Oiticica–the moment in which the postmodern breaks with the modern (see Oiticica; Favaretto; Milliet). Central to this passage from the one to the other is the abandonment of an aesthetic of the formal contemplation of the object in favor of an aesthetic of participation. With Lygia Clark's animals and Hélio Oiticica's installations and *parangolés* (wearables), the postmodern space of aesthetic experience is no longer that of the relation between subject and object, but rather that of intersubjectivity. In contrast to the repetition and functionality of postmodern culture, there are guarantees here of artistic autonomy in the installations and unannounced performances that reflect on the peripheries (or margins) of society, the city, and the body.

Neo-Concretism forces a crisis in what Martin Jay has called the ocularcentrism of art; the counter-culture substitutes the artistic for art. Art's fixed place is now occupied by what Pedrosa calls constant movement between doing and creating; it is in this sense that he writes of experiments in aesthetic experience. These movements are experimental exercises in freedom, and they constitute an alternative to the totally utopian fable that has lost its significance to virtual reality. Overwhelmed by the power of the real, the dream of utopia is replaced by a Benjaminian *Jetztzeit* (now time) evident in intense moments of liberation of the cathartic, the playful, and critical. Pedrosa writes from within a revolutionary and heroic moment, an anti-pedagogical moment of beginnings. What prevails is the aim to destroy the aesthetic of good form. It appears that the only way to escape the fetish of consumerism is to seek to interfere with it through the creative violence of scream or shock-gesture–as brute affirmations of an ethics of difference. Yet, in truth, this counter-cultural and liberationist postmodernism was itself soon absorbed by cultural and academic institutions: The consumerist and academic fetishization of postmodernism began in the 1980s.

In this light Pedrosa's postmodernism still appears ambiguous and beholden to the values of an enlightened modernity, if not to those of modern art strictly speaking. Whether art heeds the injunctions of technology, or reacts and offers itself to the political or erotic body, for Pedrosa art is supported by meta-narratives of emancipation. Today the question is no longer that of alternating between a celebration and a rejection of the postmodern. Rather it is a question of redefining art, removing it from the ground of epistemology, and conceiving it as an eminently ritualistic and political practice. It is a question of permanently staging the conflicts of difference: Between barbarism and civilization, exception and rule, transgression and the academic establishment, criticism and catharsis.

From Neo-Concretism to the Poetry of Marginality: From the Literary-Aesthetic to the Political-Cultural

One may extend Pedrosa's suggestion to identify a lineage of movements comprehensible within the postmodern as it was rearticulated within the Brazilian context. Alongside the dominant discourses of modernity there was an alternative space sketched out by neo-Concretism, a counter-culture of marginal poetry. This postmodern space was increasingly differentiated from the dominant discourses of modernity. Neo-Concretism had emerged as a crack that widened without rupturing the limits of institutional art. Hélio Oiticica's (1937–1980) experimental, conceptual, and environmental works were situated in a zone of promiscuity and attrition somewhere between art and non-art. Marginal poetry can only be contextualized as a tribal response of an alternative culture, as the emergence of pop in the structures of lettered knowledge. In Brazilian culture, the dominant discourses of modernity legitimized projects that sought to include the nation in the world system. In Latin America a fundamentally economic discourse of modernity (of development, of import substitution for the domestic, of globalization) propelled cultural discourses of cosmopolitan enlightenment. To become modern was to become civilized, Westernized. Within Brazilian culture postmodern space represented distance and dislocation from two dominant discourses of modernity: The Modernist discourse of the 1920s and 1930s and the discourse of the Concretist avant-garde. While in the 1920s and 1930s, Modernism provided the hegemonic discourse for both officially-sanctioned State culture and canonical academic culture, Concretism was a discourse of the opposition which fought for space within the hegemony of Modernist discourse. In sharp contrast to the traditionalism and nationalism of classic Modernism, Concretism sounded a cosmopolitan note which brought it into the utopian form of Modernism of the 1950s. In sum, Modernist discourse can be understood as the meta-narrative of Brazil's modernization from the 1920s to the 1940s, the period of the establishment of the modern corporate State, while Concretist discourse—though possessing a much more limited reach geographically and historically—was supported by the meta-narratives engineering technological modernization set in motion by Kubitschek.

There is also a literal geographical dimension to the postmodern cultural space configured in Brazil by neo-Concretism and the marginal poetry: Here the point of reference is the reaction in Rio against the Modernism centered around São Paulo. Neo-Concretism was a response to the extreme rationalism of São Paulo's industrial utopian fable, denouncing the utopia of industrialization and pressing into service a humanist discourse that only the structuralism of the 1960s would render obsolete (see Brito). While São Paulo's Concretism movement of the 1950s made aesthetics an objective field for formal research, it operated within the realm of the optimism about the media that Otília Arantes criticized in Pedrosa's first phase. Rio de Janeiro's neo-Concretism, in contrast, privileged the concerns of the phenomenological aesthetics of the 1950s which were attentive to problems of consciousness and perception. In the development of their work, Lygia Clark (1920–1988) and Hélio Oiticica were increasingly interested in the interaction between the body and art, between the body and the remnants of the environment excluded from the triumphalist projects of São Paulo's dehumanizing industrialism and Kubitschek's modernity. In sharp distinction to the glamorous pop art of Andy Warhol emerged this Third-World imaginary composed of discarded materials, the detritus of the peripheries. In Clark and Oiticica's work, the body was pressed into service in support of the sign. Neo-Concretism represented a movement still inscribed in what Clement Greenberg defined as the historical and self-reflexive character of modern art. Clark and Oiticica, however, went beyond this movement: Post-neo-Concretism moved outside the history of modern art into that of postmodernism.

This cultural group of Rio—as represented by the work of Clark and Oiticica—directly confronted canonical modernity and the cultural hegemony of São Paulo. Further, Rio's artistic innovators salvaged the intuitive and emotional elements that had been excluded from aesthetic and theoretical debates in Brazil by the rationalism of Modernist meta-narratives. This re-evaluation had occurred in Rio even earlier in the 1930s, albeit in a reactionary vein quite distinct from the revolutionary force of this configuration in the 1960s and 1970s. In the 1930s a Catholic reaction to Modernism had been to reclaim sentimental and ethical values as eternal and hence more truly universal than the rationalist and nationalist ideals purported to be universal by São Paulo's Modernism from 1922 through the 1930s.

The generation of poets that emerged in Rio de Janeiro in the 1970s—one that came to be known as the marginal generation—was distinguished by its direct emphasis on the body and its unmitigated subjectivity. At the level of anecdotal evidence it is important to remember that Hélio Oiticica was the first patron of Chacal, a Rio poet and performer who remained an iconic symbol of marginal poetry. Oiticica's installation *Tropicalismo* lent its name to a movement that interposed itself between neo-Concretism and the marginal poetry. *Tropicalismo* came to encompass important manifestations in the realm of theater (through the troupe Grupo Oficina) and cinema (with the film *Macunaíma*), though its historical importance rests with the work of the lyricists and poets, Torquato Neto (1944–1972), and above all the composers and lyricists, Caetano Veloso (b. 1942) and Gilberto Gil (b. 1942).

The counter-culture and *Tropicalismo* were in opposition to the *status quo* of the police State that dominated the country's politics from the Fifth Institutional Act of 1968 to the last imprisonment of Leftist militants in 1977. The counter-culture and *Tropicalismo* were nonetheless distinct from the traditional cultural movements of the Left, until then marked by a doctrinaire populism, schematic nationalism, and an unreflective anti-U.S. position, taken by both Stalinists and Maoists. As a stylistic trait and an aesthetic of performance, *Tropicalismo* privileged hybridity, mixing national cultural forms with those of global culture; it even encompassed some forms of revolutionary behavior. As Pop took the place of the popular, *Tropicalismo* sought to differentiate its intervention in Brazil's cultural industry from a mere adherence to Anglo-American forms and values, hence its emphasis on an awareness of the peripheral character of Pop music in Brazil. Though it did contribute to the internationalization of Brazilian culture,

Tropicalismo also criticized cultural hegemony and parodied both the Brazilian and the foreign. It showed no nostalgia for any allegedly more authentic or essential national identity. In the counter-culture of the time, *Tropicalismo* inscribed the body as an aesthetic and historical sign. The spectacle of the body was inserted into the logic of the market, and *O rock* (a mixture of music, dance, performance, and the sung poem) became the universal basis for aesthetic expression. Culture could no longer be comprehended outside the sphere of the media and each aesthetic act possessed an immediate impact on behavior. The marginal poetry represents the literary side of this process.

From the vantage point of cultural history it is perhaps more important to note that *Tropicalismo* allowed for a productive dialogue between the emerging, non-erudite culture of the media and the specialized knowledge of academic culture. This entailed a veritable subversion of the relations between these two poles of the production of contemporary culture. Writing literary criticism that could not help but be cultural criticism, the principal contemporary interpreters of this process were Heloísa Buarque de Hollanda (b. 1939), Carlos Alberto Messeder Pereira (b. 1951), and Silviano Santiago (b. 1936). The first two are the major scholars and advocates of Marginal Poetry, removing it from alternative circles and bringing it into the universities and to the publishing houses. Both sought to ground their reading of Marginal Poetry in Octavio Paz's (1914–1998) theoretical writings on the exhaustion of the avant-garde. In 1976 Heloísa Buarque de Hollanda edited what can be considered the first anthology of postmodern Brazilian poetry, *26 poetas hoje* [26 Poets Today].

Silviano Santiago provided a retrospective look at this turning point in Brazilian literary and cultural studies (which coincided with the passage from the 1970s to the 1980s) in a paper presented at a meeting of the Latin American Studies Association in Guadalajara, Mexico, in April 1997. He emphasized how the production of art was to be understood within the more general context of Brazilian society at that time. Amnesty had been granted indiscriminately both to the torturers or accomplices of the police State and to those who had been persecuted, the victims of the military regime now in the throes of self-extinction. This situation would culminate in a massive (yet ultimately frustrated) campaign for direct presidential elections in the early 1980s. Democratization ensued because of a pact between the democratic opposition and the inheritors of the military regime, allowing Congress to elect Tancredo Neves president in 1985. Santiago incorporated into this retrospective look ideas that had formed part of his postmodern criticism. From this vantage point, Santiago contrasted those participants in cultural life who were nostalgically confined to questions of the past (namely how to create a united front against the military regime) with the members of a new generation of artists and academics who constituted a truly democratizing movement, in the sense of questioning old hierarchies between the erudite and the popular, between knowledge and experience. Brazilian culture went through a struggle between the old and the new, in which the old was represented by authoritarian forms of dedication to public causes, while the new turned toward manifestations linked to the politics of everyday life encompassing a plurality of social subjects. For Santiago this was the moment—which he insisted on locating precisely between 1979 and 1981 as evident in the representative texts he discusses—in which Brazilian art ceased to be literary and sociological and became predominantly cultural and anthropological. Art could no longer be interpreted as the exclusive manifestation of the belles lettres, but rather as a multicultural phenomenon that served to create new and plural social identities.

A displacement in what one might call cultural archeology took place, constituted by Caetano Veloso's pop music, the academic recovery of samba and even sentimental songs, the black power movement, the raising of women's voices, the first eruptions of gay power, the Marginal Poetry, and the privileging of the interview and the testimonio as texts of self-representation and self-mapping. This archeological dislocation not only revealed humanistic knowledge as a cultural phenomenon (in the anthropological sense) but also politicized the practice and exercise of this knowledge. In contrast to canonical modernity and the avant-garde movements that spoke with one voice, postmodernity identified practices that questioned centers and hierarchies, and furthered democratization. Postmodernity proposed the politics and aesthetics of everyday life in contrast to the historical consciousness regulated by the development of the national State.

The Question of Modernism:
Silviano Santiago and the New Literary History

If one can measure the impact of postmodernity in the realm of the theory of aesthetics as a displacement of the rationalist modernity of Concretism, in the field of literary criticism the contrast must be made with the hegemony of canonical Modernism. In this sense one may speak of a confrontation between the two principal groups within Brazil's second generation of academic critics. The first group comprises the critics and professors of the University of São Paulo, disciples of Antonio Cândido, and the beneficiaries of the strong sociological formation that structures the organization of knowledge at that university. Among the principal exponents of this school one may cite Roberto Schwarz (b. 1938), Davi Arrigucci Jr. (b. 1943), Walnice Nogueira Galvão (b. 1937), and João Luiz Lafetá (b. 1946). Peripheral to this group, but possessing critical orientations that do not differ significantly from the first group, one may cite also João Alexandre Barbosa and Alfredo Bosi (b. 1936).

The second group is formed of university critics based in Rio's academic institutions, yet who came from the most varied parts of the country and had often pursued postgraduate studies abroad. Given their eclectic intellectual formation, these critics did not owe any significant intellectual debt to Rio and its past (a past which included names such as Alceu Amoroso Lima [1893–1983], Tristão de Athayde, and Afrânio Coutinho, [1911–2000]). In this group of intellectuals based in Rio, one can mention Luiz Costa Lima (b. 1937), Silviano Santiago, Affonso Romano de Sant'Anna (b. 1937), Eduardo Portela (b. 1932), Heloísa Buarque de Hollanda, and Gilberto Mendonça Teles (b. 1931). In this second group we should also include critics even more distant from the nucleus of the University of São Paulo, such as José Guilherme Merquior (b. 1941) and Sérgio Paulo Rouanet (b. 1934), diplomats by trade and only occasionally professors at the University of Brasília (though their writings make evident their academic training and discipline). It is worth noting that—from the first writings of these critics at the beginning of the 1960s—academic criticism came to encompass all critical reflection on literature in Brazil. The news media no longer printed literary criticism, only book reviews, and these were often penned by young faculty or staff writers.

For the circle of critics in São Paulo, the fundamental task entailed reaffirming Modernism as central to the canon and as part of a broader project of constructing a complete canon of Brazilian literature according to the values defined by Antonio Cândido in his *Formação da literatura brasileira* (1959). Cândido understood the canon as the Brazilians' will to build a literature. In contrast, the critics based in Rio appeared less organically linked to this task, though all of them devoted minor or even major studies to the most important authors of Brazilian Modernism. It seems significant that critics *not* based in São Paulo took at least a passing interest in the postmodern question, even if for some this took only the form of articles or courses taught at the university—and even if some came to reject it. Two scholars based in Rio were most consistently engaged in the construction of a literary postmodernism: Silviano Santiago, through the influence of his extensive criticism, fiction, and poetry, and Heloísa Buarque de Hollanda, through her editorial activity and leadership of various research institutions affiliated with Rio's Federal University such as CIEC–Centro Interdisciplinar de Estudos Contemporâneos [Interdisciplinary Centre for Contemporary Studies] and PACC–Programa Avançado de Cultura Contemporânea [Advanced Program for Contemporary Culture]. The research groups associated with these institutions have been developing aspects of a postmodern agenda for some time now. In addition, Francisco Foot Hardman and other researchers at the University of Campinas (São Paulo) have revised the theory of historiography with results that approximate the perspectives of postmodernity.

Silviano Santiago's first collection of essays, *Uma literatura nos trópicos* [A Literature in the Tropics], published in 1978, grouped together two series of articles that point in genuinely postmodern directions. Santiago postulated his fundamental insights into literary theory and methodology in a final essay, "Análise e Interpretação" [Analysis and Interpretation], in which he supports his argument with reference to thinkers such as Foucault and Derrida. In fact, within the field of letters Silviano Santiago was practically the only professor in the 1970s to read systematically all the poststructuralist theorists who constitute today the main points of reference for postmodern thinking; his interventions in the debates surrounding postmodernity contrast with the activity of his colleagues at the Catholic University in Rio (PUC). During this period Luiz Costa Lima drew, in his work, first from the structuralism of Lévi-Strauss and later from the Konstanz school's reader reception theory, while Affonso Romano pressed into service a psychoanalytic repertoire of critical tools. Anthropology rather than sociology governed literary theory's engagement with the social sciences in Rio's academic scene—here again note the marked contrast with São Paulo. While sociology had proved instrumental to debates over the ideologies that configured the modern Brazilian state, the new emphasis on anthropology represented a movement toward the democratization of the image of Brazilian society in a plural and multi-racial sense. This move of literary study in the direction of cultural studies, by some exponents of this new generation of researchers in the 1980s, reflects not only the broader political context but also the intellectual outlook of Rio's foremost schools of literature.

The first group of essays of *Uma literatura nos trópicos* encompass the texts that justify the book's subtitle, "essays on cultural dependency." This subtitle indicates a revisionary position with regard to the perspective formulated in the critical and historiographical work of Antonio Cândido. With rare exceptions, Cândido's former students at the University of São Paulo have inherited or left unquestioned the governing principles of his work–though it should be noted that his work was not without brilliance. In contrast, various aspects of Silviano Santiago's research originated in a stance that at once approached Cândido's work from a distance and deconstructed it. This démarche can be seen in the opening essay of *Uma literatura nos trópicos*, "O entre-lugar do discurso latino-americano" [The In-Between Space of Latin-American Discourse], originally published in 1971, and which contains the outline of a whole theory of comparative literature. Taking up the theme of cultural dependency posited by the thinkers at the University of São Paulo, Santiago works an inversion in the discursive hierarchy by envisioning a world literature rooted not in European hegemony (as in the canon privileged by USP) but rather in the dislocating perspective of the Latin-American periphery. The opening essay establishes the basis for a methodology of deconstructive reading that is then applied in the four subsequent chapters to both Brazilian authors and to the relation between Portugal's Eça de Queiroz and Flaubert. One of the fundamental principles postulated by these essays is the idea that the act of reading itself is constitutive of literary value contesting the canonical a priori assumptions about texts that create the exclusive political status of the lettered elite.

A practical mode of cultural criticism informs Santiago's second series of essays in *Uma literatura nos trópicos*. Here he becomes a cultural critic not only in a political or theoretical sense (as in section 1), but also in a more practical sense, drawing connections between literature, cinema, and popular music. This section encompasses articles on Marginal Poetry, Caetano Veloso as superstar, and on the language of fiction linked to the counter-culture. One of the main threads of his always provocative and wide-ranging essays in his two subsequent volumes (*Vale quanto pesa* [1982; Worth Its Weight] and *Nas malhas da letra* [1989; The Network of Letters]) is a rigorous yet personal re-reading of Modernism from the perspective of renewal rather than canonicity. These essays make evident Santiago's tense dialogue with the type of historiographical criticism practiced by his colleagues at the University of São Paulo. While *Vale quanto pesa* boasts dedications to his colleagues at USP and even an essay that systematically engages the ideas then advocated by Walnice Nogueira Galvão (b. 1937), a greater sense of distance informs Santiago's dialogue with USP toward the end of the 1980s. The game of references and dedications in *Nas malhas da letra* suggests that this distancing from São Paulo corresponds to a period of broadening and intensification of relations between criticism in Brazil and abroad.

In effect, the postmodern preoccupations voiced by Silviano Santiago came to dominate academic criticism at the end of the 1980s. Brazil's range of academic institutions then reflected the emergence of new centers of literary reflection outside the Rio–São Paulo axis (Rio Grande do Sul, Minas Gerais, Santa Catarina) and the start of a generational transition marked by retirement in the nineties of the second generation of literary critics and professors. Taking into account the average age of the professors when they retired (sixty), this wave of retirements was relatively premature, though it was dictated by the peculiarities of Brazilian legislation. Many retired professors continue to be linked to academia as associated researchers or are under contract, a process that delays indefinitely the conclusion of the transition from one generation to the next. One might call this indecision regarding the completion of the substitution of one generation by the next a very Brazilian ambiguity. Despite these developments, the nucleus of scholars at the University of São Paulo seems to have remained in the same place. As attested by their most recent works of criticism, they continue to canonize Modernism, revisiting the most unanimously consecrated poets and novelists of twentieth-century Brazilian literature.

Santiago's re-readings of Modernism in the mid 1970s and, with renewed intensity, in the 1980s are marked by an effort to recontextualize works and authors. Thus he was foremost in his generation in his criticism of the neglect of history and biography by Brazilian academic criticism, then dominated (following world trends) by the dogma of a purely textual approach. Santiago's effort to reintroduce historical and biographical contexts to literary study did not, of course, represent a return to old-fashioned models. The type of history that interested Santiago was the history of the material circulation of culture. To this end, some of the essays collected in *Vale quanto pesa* and *Nas malhas da letra* point to the relations between the Modernist literary canon and the structural characteristics of the largely illiterate society it sought to express. To this same end, Santiago pressed biography into service to promote a critical perception of the insertion of Modernist writers into the Brazilian intellectual system, radically criticizing the authoritarianism of this system. Santiago sought to reinterpret the importance of autobiography and the memoir in modern fiction–concerns developed by Antonio Cândido and Alfredo Bosi, but which Santiago worked out in a different direction, moving toward the reconstitution of the subject rather than society. He also sought to incorporate into a critical and historical analysis of Modernism an account of the professionalization of Brazilian intellectuals under the Leviathan-like State erected by Getúlio Vargas and reinforced by the military regime. The critical force of Santiago's essays has greatly contributed to Brazilian intellectual history.

Still within the realm of Silviano Santiago's critical re-readings, we may cite his most clearly postmodern readings of Modernism in the essays "Fechado para balanço" [Closed for Inventory] and "A permanência do discurso da tradição no modernismo" [The Permanence of the Discourse of Tradition in Modernism], both included in *Nas malhas da letra*. In this regard one should also consider an essay never collected in any anthology, "Caleidoscópio de questões" [Kaleidoscope of Questions]. In these, his reflections are postmodern to the extent that he formulates questions that examine Modernism as a tradition, and thus brings out the interest in tradition latent in Brazilian Modernism, for it neither breaks with tradition nor can it be completely comprehended within the key of the avant-garde. To paraphrase Mário de Andrade (1893–1945), Brazilian Modernism was not Futurism. Santiago's criticism corrected once and for all a mistake that had been repeated by many in academia, due less to the influence of the University of São Paulo than to that of Haroldo de Campos's (1929–2003) decontextualized reading of Oswald de Andrade (1890–1954) in the 1960s.

Written in 1982, "Fechado para balanço" meaningfully gestured toward closure for the history of Modernism, bringing to light and opening the way for other aspects that had remained forgotten in Brazilian literary culture, because of the perceived necessity of continuing the unfinished project of Modernism. To perceive Modernism as a closed entity allows it to be relativized within history and also permits other perspectives to emerge. Santiago's essay proved prophetic in relation to what would happen within the field of literary history in Brazil in the coming years. In suggesting an

understanding of Modernism as a closed chapter, he treats it like an object of historical and necessarily distanced and deconstructed knowledge (through contextualization). The essay also proves prophetic in turning to authors usually deemed to be pre-modern and establishing links between the virtuality of Lima Barreto's (1881–1922) aesthetic and Euclides da Cunha's (1866–1909) ideological position on the intellectual necessities of the time in which these texts were produced. Lima Barreto's language is defended as a model for a type of fiction less exclusively directed at the elite, hitherto the privileged audience of Modernist fiction. Euclides da Cunha's intellectual development in *Os sertões* [1902; *Rebellion in the Backlands*] through his painful exposition of the tragedy of Canudos is cited as an example of an open attitude toward the multiplication of social voices in Brazil. The new Brazilian literary history developed in the 1980s and 1990s possesses as a central trait a decentering with regards to the Modernism of São Paulo and the Concretist avant-garde.

With respect to Brazil's literary and cultural past, this new literary history uncovers other moderns that add to or deconstruct the canonical moderns projected by those two critical movements. Thus the politicization of knowledge–central to the concept of postmodernity (with its plurality of social subjects)–politicizes the very comprehension of the past, rendering a more complex understanding of the links between Brazilian culture and modernity. Brazilian cultural and literary Modernism can no longer be reduced to the ceremonies of consecration of São Paulo's Modernist movement, nor to a triumphalist celebration of the Concretist avant-garde. The greatest victim of this dislocation within literary history has been the category of the pre-modern. What canonical interpretations of Modernism had interpreted as "pre" and as a mere preparation for Modernism is now perceived in its own specificity. This task is carried out by a new generation of academics, the third since the emergence of the modern university in Brazil. In this context one may single out, among Santiago's former students, Flora Süssekind and in particular her work *Cinematógrafo de Letras* [*Cinematograph of Words*]. In this work the very concept of modernity in the Brazilian context is expanded. A new vision of the country's cultural life in the first decades of the twentieth century emerges with the recovery of writers hitherto forgotten or considered to be of minor importance, such as João do Rio. Süssekind's critical approach is centered on the consideration of material aspects of cultural circulation. Nonetheless, we must also mention others among the great number of researchers dedicated to re-reading the impact of modernity on different phases of Brazilian culture that predate the Week of Modern Art in São Paulo (considered by canonical readings to be the genesis of Modernism in Brazil): Raúl Antelo, Francisco Foot Hardman, Nicolau Sevcenko, Roberto Ventura, Beatriz Resende, Renato Cordeiro Gomes, and Vera Lins. Their work represents a new historiography, disseminated in monographs and journal articles, a growing bibliography that relocates the values and vocabulary of literary history, particularly with reference to the manuals and other products of the literary history produced under the sphere of influence of the University of São Paulo in the 1960s and 1970s.

Translation by Paulo Lemos Horta

Works Cited

Arantes, Otília Beatriz Fiori. 1991. *Mário Pedrosa: itinerário crítico*. São Paulo: Scritta.

Brito, Ronaldo. 1985. *Neoconcretismo: vértice e ruptura no projeto construtivo brasileiro*. Rio de Janeiro: Funarte.

Cândido, Antonio. 1959. *Formação da literatura brasileira: momentos decisivos*. 2 vols. São Paulo: Martins.

Clark, Lygia, and Hélio Oiticica. *Cartas, 1964–1974*. Ed. Luciano Figueiredo. Rio de Janeiro: Ed. Universidade Federal do Rio de Janeiro.

Favaretto, Celso. 1992. *A invenção de Hélio Oiticica*. São Paulo: Editora da Universidade de São Paulo.

Milliet, Maria Alice. 1992. *Lygia Clark: obra-trajeto*. São Paulo: Editora da Universidade de São Paulo.

Oiticica, Hélio. 1986. *Aspiro ao grande labirinto*. Rio de Janeiro: Rocco.

Pedrosa, Mário. 1975. *Mundo, homem, arte em crise*. Ed. Aracy A. Amaral. São Paulo: Perspectiva.

——. 1981. *Dos murais de Portinari aos espaços de Brasília*. Ed. Aracy A. Amaral. São Paulo: Perspectiva.

Santiago, Silviano. 1978. *Uma literatura nos trópicos: ensaios sobre dependencia cultural*. São Paulo: Perspectiva.

——. 1982. *Vale quanto pesa (ensaios sobre questões político-culturais)*. Rio de Janeiro: Paz e Terra.

——. 1983. "Caleidoscópio de questões." *Sete ensaios sobre o modernismo* Sérgio Tolipan et al. Rio de Janeiro: Funarte. 25–28.

——. 1989. *Nas malhas da letra: ensaios*. São Paulo: Companhia das Letras.

——. 1998. "Democratização no Brasil–1979–1981. Cultura versus arte." *Declínio da arte, ascensão da cultura*. Ed. Raúl Antelo. Florianópolis: Letras Contemporâneas; Abralic. 11–23.

——. 1997. "Crítica cultural, crítica literaria: desafíos de fin de siglo." XX International Congress of the Latin American Studies Association, Guadalajara, Mexico. (19 April).

Süssekind, Flora. 1987. *Cinematógrafo de letras: literatura, técnica e modernizacão no Brasil*. São Paulo: Companhia das Letras.

CHAPTER 49

LITERATURE AND REVOLUTION IN LATIN AMERICA

Hermann Herlinghaus

> I believe that experiences are only engaged in collectively. But when collective bodies are
> organized, in such a way, that those experiences are immediately suppressed. It is a case of
> preventing or rendering null that process of suppression.
> —*Heiner Müller, recalling Bertolt Brecht 32*

Taking up the word *revolution* when announcements of its crisis have become commonplace is one way into the historical perspective. If the term is assumed to be a mobile set of narratives and symbols, its "strategic" (oppositional) referentiality is diluted as (relational) asymmetries are made visible. The asymmetries of any discourse reveal the "interactiveness" of its codes, through which what Foucault called its *episteme* emerges. This essay starts from the thesis that the narratives of revolution develop their own particular *episteme* in Latin America, which is why they do not fit into fixed models. Establishing links in this way between the literary and the ideological is a common phenomenon in the periphery. If revolution was invented as a modern concept in Europe, in Latin America it simply filled an ideological vacuum. As one can see from José Martí (1853–1895) in Cuba to Sub-Commander Marcos in Mexico, there were different visions of how it can be filled historically. Symbolically speaking, these differences imply an imbalance: Modernity in Latin America arose as a discourse of a modernity already in crisis (see Herlinghaus 2000, 43–52), with different "hermeneutical dramas" accompanying the various political and social projects implemented since Independence. This latent historical crisis prefigured the ideological imaginary of the twentieth century and explains why certain foreign ideologies were avidly welcomed. Revolutions may be "hijas del concepto de tiempo lineal y progresivo" ("daughters of the concept of linear and progressive time"), models for "el cambio violento y definitivo de un sistema por otro" ("the violent and definitive replacement of one system by another") (Paz 1990, 26). Yet this still does not help to analyze either its peculiar trajectory of symbolic circularity or its anachronistic presence in the most varied discourses and cultural practices in the continent. Any dualism that establishes the alienness of the idea of revolution in the Latin American sphere is as unproductive as the stereotype that vindicates the natural right of these lands to revolution.

When we focus on the dynamics of writing, its discourses, and institutions, the Latin American problem regarding modernity appears to be expressed in aporias. It is often through literature that cultural authorizations and political legitimacies are

negotiated; there is therefore a constant fluctuation between aesthetic-philosophical ideals and the materiality of collective dreams, between the traditional popular and the new mass culture, between identity and otherness. Narratives, exacerbated not by the themes but by the problems of modernity, are inserted into the imaginaries of revolution and pass through them (Kadir 1992, x); both are temporarily metamorphosed. One ideal side is hardly ever identical to the material side, yet they are not distant poles either, and this incongruence is a specifically Latin American sign, one of the greatest ideological constituents of its modernity.

In view of the developments and ruptures that characterized the twentieth century, four historical nuclei have been chosen here: The Mexican Revolution, Peronism in Argentina, the Cuban Revolution, and the conflicts in Chile and the Southern Cone which, as a result of the impact of neo-Liberal modernization in recent decades, led to one of the most radical dislocations in the experience of narrating identities. From a point of view that favors the multiplication of different perspectives to take in gender, ethnic group, class, education, or locality, such a choice may seem limited. However, the politicization of the social subject during the twentieth century has been more explicit and comprehensive in Latin America than in the United States, for example, and has been expressed in more collective imaginaries. The nuclei that will be discussed below do not fit into one common register; they merely help us imagine a map of the "mistimings" of revolution on the continent. Through them, however, the ideological, shot through by these contestatory agencies of gender, ethnic group, and various class mediations, emerges as a phenomenon that resists generalization: The politico-cultural pacts that go to make up the hegemonic will be seen to be plural and changeable.

The hermeneutically open perspective selected to carry out this study will operate through the transversal interpretation of literary discourses from the canon and its margins, and will be oriented toward the relations between the literary and the cultural matrices that (pre)figure (Valdés 27) what are here called revolutionary imaginaries. It is hardly surprising that, among the culturally significant mediators of any Latin American revolution, the phenomena of the popular and the mass culture should have such resonance, their symbolic presence so attractive. In order to contextualize these phenomena historically, we start from the premise, formulated by Jesús Martín-Barbero (1994), that dualistic thinking must be overcome. The cultural discontinuities that, from the 1920s and 1930s on, helped displace the agencies of cultural modernity in Latin America profoundly altered the relationship between the cultural, the popular, and the masses. Mass communication failed to eliminate popular traditions. With the advent of radio, cinema, and subsequently television, the urban–and national–imaginaries were (re)constituted outside both the lettered city and the spheres of tradition. Reconceiving the problem of identity through the mediation of the mass and the popular entailed a radical shift. To paraphrase Hayden White, the melodramatic imaginary of those who "melodramatically" suffered the avatars of modernization acquired the status of a meta-historical emplotment.

The various twentieth-century Latin American revolutions exercised a significant influence on the imaginary through a strong appeal to popular and mass codes. Here, the literary is regarded, as far as the circulation of social energy is concerned (see Greenblatt), as a subconscious or an archive of ideological processes, discursively constituted as a (re)creative form of narrative, that dramatize a cultural "other." Its role is somewhat precarious, as attested to by the material links between literature and revolution. The literary is less concerned with the actual rhythm of structural results of revolutions than with the assumptions that precede them and the authority from which they emanate. Strangely enough, this brings literature closer to a non-instrumental concept of "public opinion" which, as Walter Lippmann wrote at the beginning of the revolutionary era (59), fictionalizes experiences in order to deal with the complexity of the social.

Traumas, Plots, and Narrators of the Mexican Revolution

Both the specifically Mexican imaginary and the larger spheres of cultural memory in Latin America are shot through with reverberations of the Mexican Revolution. When it broke out in 1910, creating a landscape of war until 1917, there did not seem to be a literary or intellectual tradition capable of describing its events. Classical, *Costumbrista*, Naturalist, or Symbolist conventions could not deal with the eruption of the popular masses as a reality or conceptual category. Out of the ruins of all that was known, new cultural authorities emerged; the Revolution broke with the established Positivist notion of the perfectibility of the spirit, and literature gradually appeared as a modern institution with a lettered public, networks of publishing houses, and specialized critics. But what was to become one of the distinctive, albeit virtually ignored, features of Latin American literature during the twentieth century began to unfold here–as an imbalance between the socially precarious nature of the incipient "lettered city" (Rama 1984) and the eruption of the masses. This historical experience would thrust the marginalized classes and the forgotten regions into the center of the new collective imaginaries. Out of this imbalance was born what critics would call the novel of the Mexican Revolution, a phenomenon involving the narrativization of socially significant experiences that appeared during the decade and reached its peak when the armed conflict had ceased, that is, from the mid-1920s to the late 1930s.

Among the chroniclers of these early experiences, Mariano Azuela (1873–1952) is a revealing, if atypical, writer. His *Los de abajo* [*The Underdogs,* 1992], whose title recalls those of Emile Zola, reflects the inclination of its author toward the style of the French naturalistic novel. It was written as a "narrative of experience" that was first published in serial form (in 1915) and subsequently as a book (in 1916); eventually it came to be declared a paradigm because it contributed to the institutionalization of a theme that became a national symbol. Yet prior to the construction of the myth of nationality, the book was ignored for almost a decade. Its text, which is only 150 pages long, describes a cycle of actions and experiences of the revolutionary guerrilla war in the decisive years of 1914 and 1915. The struggles against General Huerta, the Porfirian restorer, ended in a sovereign convention between the Northern Division, led by Pancho Villa and the forces of the "Liberator of the South," Emiliano Zapata, which held Venustiano Carranza in check (at the 1914 Aguascalientes Convention). In 1916, Carranza's military triumph put an abrupt end to the anti-feudal and democratically communitarian tendencies of the Revolution. It paved the way for a centralizing, reformist modernization of Mexico that created a new bourgeoisie:

> Y esa nueva clase opone a las pretensiones aristocráticas de la oligarquía porfiriana su entusiasmo por encumbrarse. Generales que se convierten en financieros, sargentos que se desdoblan en hacendados o banqueros ... lo que hoy vemos como oportunismo ... puede ser también un beneficio de la oportunidad, la movilidad que permite ... llegar a viejo y no en la miseria. (Monsiváis 1977, 25)

> And this new class used its desire for advancement to oppose the aristocratic aspirations of the Porfirian oligarchy. Generals who became financiers, sergeants recast as landowners or bankers ... what is now viewed as opportunism ... might simply have been a question of taking advantage of opportunity, or the mobility that allowed them ... to grow old in comfort rather than poverty.

Eighty years later, in 1994, the revolutionary convention at Aguascalientes would be symbolically reinstituted at San Cristóbal de las Casas (Chiapas), when the National Zapatista Liberation Army, the first postmodern guerrilla army on the continent, organized a meeting with representatives of civil society.

Mariano Azuela, born in Lagos de Moreno, Jalisco, a physician by profession, managed to participate in literary history as a writer from the margins. At the age of forty-one, he witnessed the triumph of Villa's troops in his native town, and in July 1914 contacted General Julián Medina, who made him head of the troops' medical services. As a result, he found himself in the center of the conflicts on the side of the revolutionary forces. He took part both in the capture of Guadalajara by Medina in late 1914 and in the withdrawal in the face of the offensive by Carranza's supporters who occupied it in January 1915 (Dessau 211), during which time he witnessed the triumphs, defeats, and constant displacements of Villa's men. He assessed the morality of Medina's officers as follows:

> Muy pronto la primitiva y favorable impresión que tenía de sus hombres se fue desvaneciendo en un cuadro de sombrío desencanto y pesar. El espíritu de amor y sacrificio que alentara con tanto fervor como poca esperanza en el triunfo a los primeros revolucionarios, había desaparecido. ... Nadie pensaba ya sino en la mejor tajada del pastel a la vista. (Azuela 1958, 3:1080–81)

> Soon the early, favorable impression I had formed of his men was replaced by somber disenchantment and grief. The spirit of love and sacrifice that, with as much fervor as there was little hope of

triumph, had animated the early revolutionaries, had disappeared. . . . No one thought of anything but a larger slice of cake that was in view.

The much longed-for "spirit of love and sacrifice" was linked to the Liberal legacy of the previous century that filtered into the Revolution through its petitbourgeois sectors, and *Los de abajo* reflects the abandonment of this ideal.

The story is as follows: A revolutionary guerrilla band gathers around the peasant Demetrio Macías and enjoys the support of the rural population; it sets off to fight against the troops of the dictator Huerta and heroically joins the battle of Zacatecas, where Huerta is defeated. In the second part, the group then enters a period of disorientation and crude means of self-satisfaction. In the third part, the band repeats the same excesses against the civil population as had the federal troops it once fought. At the end, Demetrio's band falls victim to a rival group at the exact spot where their triumph had begun two years earlier. This macro-narrative implies a fatalistic attitude. But a more positive aspect can be found in the narrative perspective that incorporates a group of voices, with no single protagonist. Through the resources of the orality of a collective protagonist—the group of guerrilleros—the text incorporates a popular and plural "other," becoming polyphonic. Azuela's skill lies less in his literary technique as such than in his ability to capture a sense of collective experience in motion. For Azuela, inserting himself into the revolutionary dynamics, suspended between the destabilizing chaos of an old order and the move toward a new order emerging from this very chaos, involved using new narrative resources to dramatize the action, and narrate situations in such a way as to create continuous suspense.

The Mexican Revolution's influence on literature was a result, first, of the forces of chaos that unleashed a popular-mass phenomenon (where *popular* was no longer merely synonymous with backwardness and isolation): These anachronistic forces suddenly found themselves fighting for progress. Unlike subsequent twentieth-century revolutions and even the October Revolution in Russia, here there did not seem to be any ideological preconception capable of organizing what was happening. The continuing quest for an inner *telos*, a profound sense of the meaning of the Revolution, that began with Azuela and was prolonged by his literary successors during the 1920s and 1930s, is part of the history of Mexican literary culture. The roots of this search can be seen in the first attempt at modernization under Porfirio Díaz, and Azuela was not entirely free of this legacy. He developed his ethical standards from the cultural system in which he had been educated:

el porfiriato, con . . . sus mezclas de positivismo y catolicidad y su amor siamés a la dictadura y el progreso. Al pasado se le encomienda el juicio moral sobre el presente. Esta "paradoja," una de nuestras constantes históricas, se explica también por el carácter inconcluso de las transformaciones sociales y políticas. (Monsiváis 1977, 27)

the Porfiriato, with . . . its blend of Positivism and Catholicism and its twin love of dictatorship and progress. The past was entrusted with the moral judgment of the present. This "paradox," one of our historical constants, can also be explained by the unfinished nature of social and political transformations.

Another feature of Mexican intellectual history was the sense of the proximity of the notions of socialism and common justice: "La Revolución es el socialismo, que pretende la cooperación de todos para todos, el salario proporcional, la casa higiénica, la escuela común, etc. La Revolución tiene como meta la felicidad de vivir" (García qtd. in Dessau 6) ("The Revolution was socialism that sought everyone's cooperation for everything, proportionate salaries, decent housing, common schools, etc. The goal of the Revolution was the happiness of living").

The reverberations of Azuela's novel heard in subsequent novels of the Revolution are due, to a significant extent, to the hybrid nature of *Los de abajo* and to its incorporation of the popular. On the one hand, its classic dramatic cycle—the rise, decline, and death of the guerrilla fighters—suggests a sense of fatality. On the other, much of the action is related through spoken communication, which transmits the intensity of the colloquial speech of the illiterate protagonists (the peasants who become rebel soldiers); this is a speech of action governed by the immediate relations between the collective hero and the social and historical environment. Actions appear to be governed more by mimicry than by cause and effect. Demetrio is able to become the leader of the group through venting feelings that everyone feels:

–!Me quemaron mi casa! . . .
–Dios nos da licencia, dijo Demetrio, mañana o esta misma noche les hemos de mirar la cara otra vez a los federales. . . . Los hombres semidesnudos saltaron dando grandes alaridos de alegría. Y luego redoblaron las injurias, las maldiciones y las amenazas.
–. . . Julián Medina, en Hostotipaquillo, con media decena de pelados . . . les hizo frente a todos los cuicos y federales del pueblo. . . .
–¿Qué tendrán algo los de Medina que a nosotros nos falte? (1958, 1: 324)

"They burned my house! . . ."
"God willing," said Demetrio, "tomorrow or even tonight we'll get our chance to look the *federales* in the face again. . . .
The half-naked men leapt up whooping with joy. Then they renewed the chorus of insults, curses, and threats.
. . . "Julián Medina, in Hostotipaquillo, with only a half dozen poor devils, armed with knives sharpened on the *metate*, stood up to all the police and *federales* in the village, and chased them out. . . ."
"What have Medina's men got that we don't?" (1992, 9)

The descriptive interludes read like pastiches, combining panoramic images that would proliferate during the 1920s in film melodramas:

El torbellino del polvo, prolongado a buen trecho a lo largo de la carretera, rompíase bruscamente en masas difusas y violentas, y se destacaban pechos hinchados, crines revueltas, narices trémulas, ojos ovoides. . . . Los hombres, de rostro de bronce y dientes de marfil, ojos flameantes, blandían los rifles o los cruzaban sobre las cabezas de las monturas. (1958, 1: 389–90)

The whirlwind of dust, covering a long stretch of the road, would suddenly break into diffuse, violent masses, and then you could see the panting chests, wind-tossed manes, trembling nostrils, and wild, almond-shaped eyes, hooves extending and contracting to the rhythm of the gallop, and men with bronze faces, ivory teeth, and flashing eyes, rifles brandished aloft or slung across the saddles. (1992, 85)

In the narrative world of *Los de abajo* the masses' primitive sense of right and wrong masked a basic notion of getting what is one's due. Azuela attempted to give a philosophical gloss to these sentiments in paragraphs of narrative summary. Literary critics have concentrated on these passages in their search for a thematic summing up to the novel. However, there is a deeper hermeneutic problem that has all but been ignored, and this is the extent to which the novel creates a creative tension between the narrative development and the unpredictable, explosive social action of the reality of the revolution. It is thus that we ask, where does the extensive literary influence of this novel in Mexican literature come from? Is it from the novel's fatalism or from its description of the dynamics of the anarchistic chaos of the revolution? And how can we explain its place in literary history as the forerunner of Mexican modernity? The answer seems to lie somewhere in the range of ideas that the modern Mexican nation could only be built out of the ruins of the old order.

From the 1920s onward, several texts that focused on the Revolutionary War were published. One of these was a short novel, whose phenomenological openness to life and narrative effectiveness appear to be have been drawn from direct experience. *Cartucho: Relatos de la lucha en el norte México* [1931; *Cartucho;* and *My Mother's Hands,* 1988] by Nellie Campobello (1900–1986) is the testimony of a six- or seven-year-old girl, drawn from memory at the later age of twenty. An unusual psychological situation provides access to the unmentionable aspects of the story's events. In a childhood that lacked social normality, the implausible acquires the status of reality and blends with the fantastic and natural elements that fill the girl's mind. The book consists of thirty-three scenes (each between one and three pages long) in which violent death appears as a constant. In 1915 and 1916, the author's family lived in Parral and in nearby villages in Chihuahua, controlled by Villa's troops. Here the federal army subsequently began to execute people. In the introduction, Campobello writes that, as a young girl, "acostaba a mis fusilados, los valientes del norte, en un cuaderno: Mis fusilados, dormidos en la libreta verde. Mis hombres muertos. Mis juguetes de la infancia" (iv) ("I used to put the men who had been shot, the brave men of the north, to sleep in a notebook. All my shot men, fast asleep in my green notebook. My dead men. My childhood toys"). One of the many death scenes, which speaks of Villa's troops, evokes one woman, Nacha Ceniceros, among all the men who died:

Junto a Chihuahua, en X estación, un gran campamento villista. Todo está quieto y Nacha llora. Estaba enamorada de un muchacho coronel de apellido Gallardo, de Durango. Ella era coronela y usaba pistola y tenía trenzas. Había estado llorando al recibir consejos de una soldadera vieja. Se puso en su tienda a limpiar su pistola, estaba muy entretenida cuando se le salió un tiro. En otra tienda estaba sentado Gallardo junto a una mesa; platicaba con una mujer; el balazo que se le salió a Nacha en su tienda, lo recibió Gallardo en la cabeza y cayó muerto.
—Han matado a Gallardito, mi General.
Villa dijo despavorido:
—Fusílenlo.
—Fue una mujer, General.
—Fusílenla.
—Fue una mujer, General.
—Fusílenla.
—Nacha Ceniceros.
—Fusílenla.
Lloró al amado, se puso los brazos sobre la cara, se le quedaron las trenzas negras colgando y recibió la descarga.
Hacía una bella figura, imborrable para todos los que vieron el fusilamiento.
Hoy existe un hormiguero en donde dicen que está enterrada. (1931, 55–56)

A large Villista encampment at station *X* near Chihuahua. All was quiet and Nacha was crying. She was in love with a young colonel from Durango by the name of Gallardo. Nacha was a *coronela* who

carried a pistol and wore braids. She had been crying after an old woman gave her advice. She went to her tent where she was busily cleaning her pistol when, all of a sudden, it went off. In the next tent was Gallardo, sitting at a table and talking to a woman. The bullet that escaped from Nacha's gun struck Gallardo in the head and he fell dead.
"Gallardito has been killed, General."
Shocked, Villa replied, "Execute the man who did it."
"It was a woman, General."
"Execute her."
"Nacha Ceniceros."
"Execute her."
She wept for a lover, put her arms over her head, with her black braids hanging down, and met the firing squad's volley.
She made a handsome figure, unforgettable for everyone who saw the execution. Today there is an anthill where they say she was buried. (1988, 21)

The narrative style that in artistic terms works with avant-garde brevity, also sketches a kind of subjectivity that gains importance in literature until it becomes a source of authority in works such as the testimonial novel *Hasta no verte Jesús mío* [1969; *Here's to You, Jesusa!,* 2001] by Elena Poniatowska (b. 1933), which articulates a popular feminine subjectivity that vibrates like a hitherto repressed other.

During the 1930s and 1940s, melodramatic cinema drew its themes of paternalism and *machismo* from the epic conflicts of the Revolution. In the film *Enamorada* [1946; In Love] by Emilio Fernández (1904–1986)–a director with an enormous talent for portraying folk environments–an unassuming, upstanding revolutionary general manages to win the love of an aristocrat (played by María Félix), who becomes the self-sacrificing champion of the poor. Through a series of ups and downs that (eventually) alter the aristocrat's mentality, the latter says to the general:

"Vaya con sus soldaderas. "
El general replica:
"Si somos diferentes, no es por culpa mía ni por méritos de usted. Como tampoco son mujerzuelas aquellas soldaderas que usted desprecia porque no las conoce. Pero yo sí las conozco. Son humildes y abnegadas, y saben trabajar y sufrir y morir sin esperar nada–nada más que el cariño del hombre que quieren."
(Cita de la película)

"Why don't you just run along with your female camp followers?"
The general replies:
"If we're different, it's not through any fault of my own or thanks to you. Just as those women you scorn because you don't know them. But I do know them. They are not loose women They are humble and self-sacrificing, and are able to work and suffer and die without expecting anything in return–other than the affection of the man they love." (Quoted from the film)

The scene quoted earlier from *Cartucho* shows how, on the one hand, Nacha Ceniceros surrenders to the sacrifice of dying. On the other, despite minimizing the fact, the text still does not hide the fact that this woman plays an active role. Presumably, Nacha Ceniceros does not share the hopes of the female camp followers portrayed by the screen general José Juan. The theme of female camp followers established a theme that for many years was part of the national rhetoric: the story of the active entry of poor, peasant women into the whirlwind of modernization.

The year 1928 saw the publication of *El águila y la serpiente* [*The Eagle and the Serpent,* 1930] by Martín Luis Guzmán (1887–1977), a novel which, by maintaining the author's testimonial relationship with events, was able to achieve considerable complexity. One passage highlights the cultural effect caused by the experience of the cinema in milieux that had been abruptly democratized by the new prominence of the masses. During the Aguascalientes Convention, an audience of soldiers and officers attended the first performance of documentary sequences showing the leaders of the struggles:

> Apareció Carranza, corpulento, solemne, hierático, en el acto de entrar en triunfo en Saltillo. Otra voz dijo:
> ¡Viva el Primer Jefe!
> Pero en vez del grito entusiasta y multitudinario, respondió el desorden. . . .
> Y a renglón seguido, como si el operador lo hiciera adrede, caracoleó bañada en luz, sobre su caballo magnífico, la magnífica figura de Pancho Villa. . . . El clamor unánime ahogó las voces y sólo como coletilla de la salva de aplausos logró imponerse este grito:
> —!Viva la División del Norte! . . .
> Así todos los otros. Durante cerca de una hora . . . se prolongó el desfile de los adalides revolucionarios y sus huestes, nimbados por la luminosidad del cinematógrafo y por la gloria de sus hazañas.
> . . . Don Venustiano, por supuesto, era el personaje que más a menudo aparecía en la pantalla. Sus apariciones . . . habían venido haciéndose . . . más y más ingratas para el público convencionista . . . al proyectarse la escena en que se veía a Carranza entrando a caballo en la ciudad de México, una especie de batahola de infierno . . . culminó en dos disparos.
> Ambos proyectiles atravesaron el telón, exactamente en el lugar donde se dibujaba el pecho el Primer Jefe. (1941, 339)

> Carranza emerged on the screen, corpulent, solemn, hieratical, at the moment of his triumphant entrance into Saltillo.
> Another voice cried:
> "Long live the First Chief."
> But instead of the enthusiastic, unanimous chorus, disorder followed. . . .
> Then immediately afterward, as though the operator had planned it so, astride his superb, prancing horse and bathed in light, came the magnificent figure of Pancho Villa. . . . The unanimous applause drowned out the voices and only like a postscript to the salvo did this cry manage to make itself heard:
> "Long live the Division of the North!" . . .
> For one hour . . . the parade of the standardbearers of the Revolution and their hosts went on, haloed by the light of the screen and the glory of their deeds.
> . . . Don Venustiano, naturally, was the figure who most frequently returned to the screen. His . . . appearances . . . were becoming more and more displeasing to the Convention audience . . . in the scene where Carranza was making his entry on horseback into Mexico City. At this point it became a kind of hellish din that culminated in two shots.
> Both of them perforated the curtain at the height of the First Chief's breast. (1965a, 290–91)

This intense participatory reaction cannot simply be explained by the captivation of an illiterate public by the magic of the screen. The Revolution created dramatic scenarios that involved the popular masses at the same time as it offered them an image of themselves. Fighting in isolation at the beginning, units like those in *Los de abajo* eventually formed one immense movement that became a hurricane (Azuela 1: 362), placing peasants, shepherds, shopkeepers, railway men, or schoolteachers in thitherto unexpected situations, as they joined the Revolution. The masses savored their performing skills: "su hambre por acceder a una visibilidad que les confiere un espacio social de cualquier índole, el que . . . integrarán y agrandarán con los métodos a su disposición" ("their longing to gain access to some form of visibility that would grant them some kind of social space, that they would . . . integrate and expand with the methods at their disposal"). At the intersections between social action and their experience as mediated by the incipient cultural industry, poor people recognized and celebrated themselves for the first time with a national voice and face (Monsiváis 1978, 100–101). This new experience was perceived to be a political resource by the new leaders, a resource that would be used to help create a post-Revolutionary, exceptionally monolithic State. The popular world of peasants and, to a certain extent, of the proletariat, achieved symbolic importance for the country as a whole, which is why it could be made part of the national culture in so effective a way.

During the 1930s and 1940s a paradoxical feature of Mexican literary culture emerged from the political reality of the country: the perceived need to legitimize the Mexican Revolution. This led to a sort of canonization of *Los de abajo* as the prototype of a new genre, the novel of the Mexican Revolution. There was a concerted effort to establish the aesthetic features of the genre in order to distinguish it from narratives that dealt with social unrest and rebellion. The emergence of new cultural matrices of revolutionary culture readied its apex with the celebration of forty years of this culture of the revolution in 1950 (which is not to be confused with revolutionary culture such as that which followed the victory of Fidel Castro and his comrades in 1959). The intellectual search for cultural legitimacy was taken up by critics and historians alike. There was a fascination with the social upheaval of the revolution (especially with the now heroic figures of Pancho Villa and Emiliano Zapata); this was a revolution, an archaic response to a patently contemporary problem of social injustice, but it was much more. This was a revolution with permanence; it had been institutionalized (PRI, the political party of the institutionalized revolution) and now became the foundation of Mexican culture and society. This led to a proliferation of assessments not only of witnesses to the action, but even of the writings of armchair revolutionaries–the petty clerks who had been elevated to assessors of the generals. Azuela again serves us well to capture the moment: "¡Qué hermosa es la Revolución, aun en su misma barbarie!" (1958, 1: 368) ("How beautiful the revolution is, even in its savagery"; 1992, 58). At the same time Azuela's contemporaries suffered from an acute case of a need to have a moral purpose, as Azuela himself demonstrated:"¡Pueblo sin ideales, pueblo de tiranos! . . . ¡Lástima de sangre!" (1958, 1: 368) ("A people without ideals, a land of tyrants! . . . All that blood shed in vain!"; 1992, 58).

Once the novel of the Revolution became an approved genre, the (auto)biographical (albeit non-introspective) novel became dominant. This proves that the literature of the Revolution was produced as a result of cultural authorization, rather than a particular artistic configuration. It was fiction which, as a discourse based on specific dynamics of modernization, was distinguished from and actually opposed to Modernist discourse, for it put collective experience at the center of novels as different as *El águila y la serpiente* and *Memorias de Pancho Villa* [1938–1940; *Memoirs of Pancho Villa*, 1965] by Martín Luis Guzmán, *Desbandada* [1934; The Rush], *Mi caballo, mi perro y mi rifle* [1936; My Horse, My Dog, and My Rifle], and *La vida inútil de Pito Pérez* [1936; *The Futile Life of Pito Pérez*, 1966] by José Rubén Romero (1890–1952), or the "bombastic" memoirs (Molloy 461) of José Vasconcelos (1881–1959) *Ulises Criollo* [1935; *A Mexican Ulysses, an Autobiography*, 1963] and *La tormenta* [1936; The Storm]. Interpreted according to Ferdinand Braudel's theories, these approaches could be said to reveal a notion of history based on events, favoring narratives of a biographical inclination that tend to construct visions of organic time. It is hardly surprising that the majority of these canonized texts naturally incorporate elements of the serial form.

El águila y la serpiente resembles a war report: "Villa…, el Águila azteca, que ha clavado su pico de acero sobre la cabeza de la víbora Victoriano Huerta" (Azuela 1958, 1: 365) ("Villa…, the Aztec Eagle who has buried his iron beak in the head of the serpent, Victoriano Huerta"; 1992, 54). It offers a chronology of events dating from 1913 to 1915, in which outstanding or typical representatives of the Revolution receive the most attention. This concern with the personification of the icons of the Revolution leads the author to a second monumental work– *Memorias de Pancho Villa*. The hero figure is one of the most effective and ambivalent creations of popular culture, paving the way for modernity, not so much through the figure of the traditional boss who tended to merge with that of the irresponsible politician, but through the unusual mythical aura given off by the figures of Emiliano Zapata and Francisco Villa ever since the social radicalization of this Revolution. During the nationalistic, revolutionary era of Lázaro Cárdenas (1934–1940), a mass idolatry based on the film industry brought the myth of these heroes to the fore. By contrast, Guzmán devoted himself to the task of verifying Villa's role. In 1913 and 1914, the author had visited the military fields of the Revolution and had met Villa personally and been on fairly close terms with him. He has also "[habiendo] tenido entonces el cuidado de poner por escrito, y con cuanta fidelidad textual me era dable, lo que decía él en mi presencia" (Guzmán 1967, 3) ("committed myself to the greatest possible exactness in writing down all that he said in my presence"; 1965b, x). When, fifteen years later, Guzmán had access to Villa's archives, he chose to adopt the device of a first-person narrator to bring the general's actions and experiences to life. Guzman's aim was to re-authenticate his hero, in other words, to replace the lofty language used by Villa's learned chronicler (Bauche Alcalde) with Villa's original lively, rustic form of speech. He sought to recapture its tone, the way "como Villa hubiera podido contar las cosas en su lenguaje, castellano de las sierras de Durango y Chihuahua, castellano excelente, popular, nada vulgar, arcaizante, … cargado de … frases pleonásticas ricamente expresivas, de paralelismos recurrentes y de otras peculiaridades" (Guzmán 1967, 4) ("in which Villa was able to tell things in his own language, the Castilian of the sierras of Durango and Chihuahua. It is excellent Castilian, popular but neither vernacular nor archaic… it was full of … highly expressive redundancies, recurring parallelisms, and other peculiarities"; 1965b, xi). Adopting a first-person narrator for Villa is a tribute to a sort of "poetics of orality" (in Zumthor's terms) that nonetheless, remains within the limits of the literary. Due to this narrative logic, when Guzmán himself emerges as a character in the text, he too is dealt with from Villa's supposed point of view. And indeed, Guzmán makes his character appear at a key moment, giving the popular general his opinion on Carranza's maneuvers, in a chapter entitled "En espera del triunfo definitivo de la Revolución, Pancho Villa se prepara al probable rompimiento con Carranza" ["Expecting the Final Triumph of the Revolution, Villa Prepares for the Probable Break with Carranza"]. This attempt to provide a true version of history shows that the author regards himself as an ethical agent in a frankly enlightened sense of the historical past, although, in his ideological passion for his subject matter, he becomes unintentionally comic. Writer and hero join forces in the discoursive undertaking:

> Sucedió así, cayendo la tarde de aquel 18 de julio de 1914, que mandé llamar al … licenciado Martín Luis Guzmán y le dije:
> —Muchachito, ¿no le falta ánimo para trabajar conmigo en favor de la causa del pueblo?
> Me contestó él:
> —Señor general, yo estoy a sus órdenes como buen hombre revolucionario.
> …
> —Dígame muchachito: ¿qué anticipa usted de mis desavenencias con el Primer Jefe y del futuro de nuestra causa para cuando lleguemos al triunfo?
> …
> Me habló él estas palabras:
> -Señor general, soy de opinión que ya no tienen cura las discordias de usted con nuestro Primer Jefe. … Usted cumplirá los convenios que se hagan: él hallará siempre forma de decir que los convenios no eran suyos. No afirmo yo, señor, que Venustiano Carranza sea hombre poco patriota, … pero considera que sólo él conoce el alcance de nuestra Revolución, y que sólo tienen derecho a reflexionar lo que nuestra Revolución sea, y a expresar cómo deba ella desarrollarse en su triunfo, los hombres que él escoge como buenos porque lo lisonjean y acarician, y no todos los hombres que andamos en esta pelea por nuestro propio ánimo. (1967, 540–41)

> It happened like this. At dusk on July 18, 1914, I sent for Martín Luis Guzmán and I said:
> "Young man, are you up to fighting with me on behalf of the people?"
> And he answered:
> "General, I am at your service, like a good revolutionary." …
> "Tell me, lad, what do you expect from my disagreements with the Great Leader and of the future of our case when we triumph?"
> …
> To which he replied, "General, I am of the opinion that there can be no solution to the disagreements between yourself and our General Leader. … You will fulfill the agreements signed; he will always find a way of saying that he had nothing to do with the agreements. I am not saying, sir, that Venustiano Carranza is unpatriotic … yet I feel that only he knows the scope of our Revolution and that only he has the right to reflect on what our Revolution will be and to decide how it should develop after its triumph. He has chosen his men because they flatter and praise him and not all of us are in this fight of our own volition.
> (my translation)

By "correcting" Villa's image using the gestures of an historical reporter, Guzmán saves him from the suspicion of political maneuvers that Guzmán, "'rectificando' la imagen de Villa con gestos de reportero histórico, la deja a salvo de dudas frente a las maniobras políticas que dañaban tanto la causa de nuestra Revolución" (1967, 907) ("were damaging the cause [of our Revolution] so much"; 1965b, 478).

This blend of strategies that were at once aesthetic (devising a discourse capable of authenticating popular language), political (lending eloquence to the forces of justice of the Revolution or weighing up the betrayal of their true nature), and didactic (highlighting the heroic deeds committed at the heart of an uncultured, primitive people) characterized this heterogeneous set of writings that date from Azuela's first fictional writing to texts produced in the late 1930s and which would be given the status of novels of the Revolution. These helped to lend a legitimate cultural status to a new theme and establish a new moral order for a modern Mexico. Their conversion into representative novels assimilate a heretofore relatively unknown body of texts into the sanctioned genre of the novel. The significance of appropriating the mass theatricality of revolution as a new subject, one which addressed the crucial matters of society as a whole, should not be lost on us today." One is struck by the radicalizing aspect of that new canon, since it managed to displace the followers of the "Ateneo de la Juventud" (critics of nineteenth-century Positivism, defenders of Humanism and Classicism) whose cultural notion spoke of the antithesis:

> El tema de la Revolución no creará nunca para nosotros la literatura revolucionaria. . . . Lo que logró la Revolución Mexicana con la nueva generación de escritores . . . fue convencerlos de la existencia de una sensibilidad personal, mientras más personal, más genuinamente mexicana, en donde había que ahondar sin retrasarse con la cultura del mundo. (Ortiz de Montellano qtd. in Dessau 80)

> The theme of the Revolution will never create revolutionary literature for us. . . . What the Mexican Revolution achieved through the new generation of writers . . . was to convince them of the existence of a personal sensibility, the more personal, the more genuinely Mexican, which they would have to explore without being set back by comparison to the culture of the world.

Antonio Caso's (1883–1946) concern in 1925 could well be seen as an intuition of the consolidation of the new canon; he saw the development as contemporary democracy, as the debasement of higher human achievement in order to give the people the benefits of a national culture–and with it greater possibilities of expression–but also leading to less than profound reflection. The didactic personification of heroes and foundational positions espoused by the novels of the Revolution proved how the national was rapidly transformed into a desire for collectivity (the desire for the imagined community) which, at the same time, responded to the policies of partiality and exclusion that national capitalism would practice from the time of Calles's presidency onward. And it was this desire for a true community, different from that which was created as a result of the Revolution, that the authors subsequently continued to express. As one of the characters in Carlos Fuentes's (b. 1928) novel *La region más transparente* [1958; *Where the Air Is Clear*, 1960] says:

> al recoger todos los hilos de la experiencia histórica de México, nos propuso metas muy claras: reforma agraria, organización del trabajo, educación popular. La Revolución Mexicana fue el primer gran movimiento popular de nuestro siglo que supo distinguir este problema básico: cómo asegurar la plena protección y desarrollo de lo comunitario sin herir la dignidad de la persona. ¿Por qué nos quedamos con las soluciones a medias? No puedo pensar que el único resultado concreto de la Revolución Mexicana haya sido la formación de una nueva casta privilegiada, la hegemonía económica de los Estados Unidos y la paralización de toda vida política interna. (1958, 273)

> on recovering the threads of our historic experience, the Revolution gave us very clear objectives: land reform, unionization, public education. The Mexican Revolution was the first great popular movement of this century to face the basic problem: how to insure the community protection and growth without sacrificing personal dignity. Why were we satisfied with half solutions? I can't believe that the only concrete result of the Revolution had to be the rise of a new privileged class, economic domination by the United States, and the paralyzing of all internal political life. (1960, 221)

The desire for collectivity produced various trajectories. The melodramatic cinema of the 1930s to the 1950s placed the greatest importance on a "community in suffering and luck"

since, prior to the advent of television, it was there that the notions of history and the "newspaper serial" were linked in an effective semblance of identity. The cultural balance of the cinema of this period proves decisive because, if "la mayoría de los mexicanos hemos sido entrenados en el empeño de captar . . . la dimensión anecdótica de la historia . . ., se ha llegado, en una conmovedora confusión populista, a identificar historia con melodrama, historia con despliegue interpretativo" (Monsiváis 1970, 40) ("the majority of Mexicans have been trained in the task of capturing . . . the anecdotal dimension of history . . ., then, as part of a moving, populist confusion, we have come to identify history with melodrama, and history with interpretative deployment").

Mexican literature continues to be permeated by the themes and symbols of the Revolution in a myriad of ways. The Revolution has become a critical part of what, through the populist nationalism of the State, the press, the radio, and the prosperous cinematographic industry, became first an organic metaphor of a changing country and, second, a more ambivalent commonplace. The greatest modernization of the sectors of education, cultural administration, and the promotion of the arts and sciences dates back to the final stages of the repoliticization of the popular masses during the reforms and nationalizations of President Cárdenas (1934–1940) and is linked to the consolidation of the new bourgeoisie and the rise of a party that called itself by the ridiculous name of the "Institutional Revolutionary Party." After the Revolution developed into a strong State, "la síntesis de la Nación se inicia en las exclusiones y los primeros segregados son los indígenas, la peonada mestiza, los parias urbanos y las mujeres" (Monsiváis 1985, 39) ("the synthesis of the Nation began to practice exclusion and the first to be segregated were the Indians, the mestizo farm workers, the urban pariahs and women"). The fact that centralized political discourse repressed the historical subconscious of the nation produced traumatic situations. This marked the start–in the links between what was inferred and what was actually repressed in the revolutionary tradition–of a consolidation of critical energies that has extended to the immediate present which resound today.

Did the Revolution serve to reveal what modern Mexico not only failed to accept but did not even acknowledge? The alternative politics of gender and sexuality put forward in the discourse of authors such as Elena Poniatowska, Rosario Castellanos (1925–1974), Ángeles Mastretta (b. 1949), Carmen Boullosa (b. 1954), Laura Esquivel (b. 1950), and others are characterized by a marked re-historicizing of the Revolution, sometimes in search of popular-female elements. These authors do not reject popular narrations as the cradle of *machismo* a priori; they decenter them from within. The novel-testimony *Hasta no verte Jesús mío* could be called hetero-biographical in the sense that its ethical position consists of the impossibility of including and representing another personality. The text, based on a wide range of interviews, develops, from a first-person perspective, the hybrid imaginary of Jesusa Palancares, a woman from Oaxaca, marginalized from history and society, who served as a camp follower and soldier during the Revolution, and in subsequent decades was forced to join that anonymous multitude in modern Mexico that only barely manages to survive. A later text, "Vida y muerte de Jesusa" [1900–1987; "Life and Death of Jesusa"], summarizes, on the death of a person who actually existed, Josefina Bórquez (1987), the richly ambiguous relationship that developed between the writer and her informant, a poor, illiterate woman, who, contrary to the traditional image of Mexican women, had maintained a high degree of nonconformism and independence, from the time of her participation in the armed struggle until the end of her life.

> La Jesusa no tuvo límites, tanto que se enfrentó a su propio marido, el capitán Pedro Aguilar. . . . Sin las soldaderas no se sostiene la Revolución, pues ¿quién mantenía a los soldados? Sin ellas, todos hubieran desertado. . . . ¡Qué ambiente sabían crear las soldaderas! Además de cacerolas, gallinas, puerquitos, ollas, sarapes, sartenes, municiones, teteras, rifles, metates, cachorritos que andaban criando, llevaban guitarra y en la noche se ponían a cantar. Caminaban horas sin cansarse, más aguantadoras que los mismos tamemes. . . . Maternales, acogían al hombre, lo hacían reir, lo entretenían además de lo mero principal. . . . Muchas de ellas morían de tuberculosis, peritonitis y chorrillo. . . . Se lanzaban atrabancadas a desafiar a la muerte. Sin embargo nunca perdieron su mala fama. (Poniatowska 1994, 47–48, 64)

> There was nothing that could hold her back, so much so that she stood up to her own husband, Captain Pedro Aguilar. . . . The Revolution would have collapsed without the female camp-followers, who would have maintained the soldiers? Without them (the women), they would all have deserted . . . . What a wonderful atmosphere the female camp followers created! In addition to their pots and pans, chickens, pigs, shawls, frying pans, munitions, kettles, rifles, flat stones for grinding, and children they were raising, they brought their guitars and used to sing at night. They walked for hours without getting tired, and had more stamina than the bearers themselves. . . . Maternally, welcoming their men, making them laugh and keeping them entertained in addition to their main function. . . . Many of them died of tuberculosis, peritonitis and diarrhea. . . . They used to hurl themselves recklessly into the fray to challenge death. Nevertheless, they never managed to shake off their bad reputation.

Hasta no verte Jesús mío raises the question of whether the Revolution was in fact a purely male undertaking. In *Juchitán de las mujeres* [1988; Juchitán of the Women], the belief in a sort of female popular power produced a particular style that involved the eroticization of the social (Franco 1992, 72). This literary problematization treated the historical aspects of the Revolution in an ambivalent manner, as well as questioning the interpretive capacity of the intellectual: "Al terminar me quedé con una sensación de pérdida; no hice visible lo esencial, no supe dar la naturaleza profunda de la Jesusa. . . . No puede adentrarme en su intimidad, no supe hacer ver aquellos momentos en que nos quedábamos las dos en silencio" (1994, 50) ("At the end, I was left with a feeling of loss; I had failed to make essential aspects visible or reflect the profound nature of Jesusa. . . . I was unable to penetrate her intimacy, and I failed to depict the moments when the two of us sat there in silence"). Herein lies the difference between the apparent lack of a testimonial figure in Poniatowska, on the one hand, and the elevation of a new narrative mode into a sort of alternative model of representation provided by Miguel Barnet (b. 1940) in Cuba.

A clear look at the incongruities of the Mexican Revolution—which had broken out even before the October Revolution in Russia—can be found in *El laberinto de la soledad* [1950; *The Labyrinth of Solitude*, 1962] by Octavio Paz (1914–1998), who points out the lack of ideological predecessors and the shortage of links with a universal ideology (124). However, and bearing in mind the years from 1910 to 1915, it is possible to detect inherent anarchistic features in the subject of the action. The engine was the people who could not be reduced to a concept of class, yet, at the same time, challenged the

class view to be extended to the unstructured heterogeneity of the people. (The revolutionary armies consisted primarily of peasants, whose reasons for taking up arms varied from region to region.) Latent in nineteenth-century anarchistic thought was something that European Marxism rapidly rejected–a tendency when dealing with political issues to assume chaos as a possible matrix of conflict in view of the non-calculability of events, a problem that no theory of revolution has been able to resolve. These inherent anarchistic features, however, had lent the novels of the Revolution their unusual phenomenological force of lived experience and a political subconscious that was barely concealed by the position of fatalism.

It is striking that Octavio Paz should have given particular importance to the southern Revolution led by Emiliano Zapata. In an attempt to found an alternative *telos* of Mexican history in "nuestra raíz, . . . la porción más antigua, estable y duradera de nuestra nación: el pasado indígena"(1959, 120) ("our roots, . . . the most ancient, stable and lasting part of our national being: the indigenous past"; 1985, 144), he holds that Zapatismo provided a corrective force to twentieth-century Mexican history, the alternative force to the Liberal project that began with the Reform. The "Plan de Ayala" (1911), the Zapatistas' political document, demanded that the indigenous people of the states of Morelos and Guerrero should be given back their common lands and the respective property deeds of which they had been stripped. In Zapata's isolation from the current ideas of his time, Paz detects a requirement for gaining access to the historical other:

> Pues la verdad de la Revolución era muy simple y consistía en la insurgencia de la realidad mexicana, oprimida por los esquemas del liberalismo tanto como por los abusos de conservadores y neo-conservadores. El zapatismo . . . en un sentido profundo niega la obra de la Reforma, pues constituye un regreso a ese mundo del que, de un solo tajo quisieron desprenderse los liberales. (1959, 120)

> The truth of the Revolution was actually very simple: It was the freeing of Mexican reality from the constricting schemes of liberalism and the abuses of the conservatives and neo-conservatives. The zapatista movement . . . [was a] denial of the work of the Reform, in that it was a return to the very world from which the liberals had wanted to cut themselves loose. (1985, 144)

Zapata's project was so clear and simple that the inability of Mexican intellectuals to formulate the conflicting popular aspirations into a coherent system (1959, 121) made Liberalism politically irrelevant. According to Paz, the historical normality established by the ruling classes, allied with the imperialism of the north, led a modern nation–that had begun to live inauthentically with a mere "mask of the Revolution" (1959, 122)–into alienation from itself.

The works of two writer-thinkers, who have always targeted monolithic ideologies, has contributed one of the characteristic tensions of Mexican modernity: two concepts of intellectual resistance that reveal a comparison between the poet and essayist Octavio Paz and the chronicler Carlos Monsiváis (b. 1938). It is no accident that Jürgen Habermas called Paz "un compañero de ruta de la modernidad" (134) ("a traveling companion of modernity"), since his conceptualization of the critical resources of an aesthetic modernity seemed to revive a tradition that was no longer dominant: "Tradición de lo moderno: heterogeneidad, pluralidad de pasados, extrañeza radical" (Paz 1981, 18) ("A tradition of the modern: Heterogeneity, plurality of pasts, radical unusualness"). By exploring the decentered history of Mexico, citing its omissions and drawbacks, and denouncing its political authoritarianism, Paz placed himself at one extreme of the authority that demanded allegiance to universal literature. This ensured him an enormous symbolic power made public through the journal *Vuelta*. Conversely, Monsiváis is a writer whose radicalness, aimed at decentering the culturally exclusive, beggars comparison. In his essays, political and learned discourses are metamorphosed. His fascination with the popular culture of cities, their subcultural jargon, codes, and images has immunized him against any aseptic intellectual form of criticism. His discourse has become a national institution in Mexico within the margins of legitimacy: "Con sagacidad e ingenio, con ironía y con lucidez, Monsiváis escucha cantar a Juan Gabriel, apoya causas populares, se alía a marginados y minorías, escribe todo el tiempo y se burla de todo" (Sefchovich 203) ("With wisdom and ingenuity, irony and lucidity, Monsiváis listens to the romantic songs of Juan Gabriel, supports popular causes, is the ally of minorities and the marginalized, writes all the time and mocks everyone"). One of his chronicles, "Alto contraste/A manera de foto fija" [1977; "High Contrast/In the Manner of Still Photography"] draws a moral portrait of the Mexican Revolution that extends to the present and resembles a parodic parade of the protagonists, situations, and memories (both literary and cinematographic) of the country's political mythology. Spurred on by the crisis that shook Mexico after the massacre of students in Tlatelolco (in 1968), the text invokes and dramatizes what it also dismantles. One of the sequences ridicules the personification of the Party which, as a result of the Revolution, became a State:

¡Detente oh momento! Eres tan irreparable. El país afirma su estabilidad con la creación en 1929 del Partido Nacional Revolucionario que se rebautizará Partido Revolucionario Mexicano y que devendrá Partido Revolucionario Institucional. En el tránsito de las siglas (PNR/PRM/PRI) se efectúa el sometimiento. Fuera y dentro, el Partido de la Revolución, tótem burocrático-político, suministra, alquila y proclama mitos: se masifica el método viable de acercarse a las fuentes dispensadoras de bienes, prestigios y recompensas. EL PRI se vuelve un partido (un modo de vida) que—sobre todo en provincia—ha de suministrar patrones de conducta, gesticulaciones, dicciones. Lecciones morales y visuales: se habla como el PRI, se mueven los brazos como el PRI, se logra la indignación instantánea a la manera del PRI, se obtiene el lugar de privilegio mediante el impulso atlético de los priístas. Termina el monopolio de la preceptiva religiosa: el PRI obtiene discípulos igualmente fieles y más ambiciosos. (Monsiváis 1977, 32–33)

Stop, oh moment! You are so irreparable! The country affirms its stability through the creation in 1929 of the National Revolutionary Party, which was renamed the Mexican Revolutionary Party and subsequently became the Party of the Institutional Revolution. The shift in acronyms (PNR/PRM/PRI) reflected the gradual subjection of the people. Inside and outside, the Party of the Revolution, that bureaucratic-political totem, supplied, and proclaimed myths: the viable means of approaching the sources of goods, prestige and rewards was effected on a vast scale. The PRI became a party (a modus vivendi) which, particularly in the provinces, provided patterns of behavior, and even of diction. It also offered moral and visual lessons: people talked like the PRI, they moved their arms like the PRI, they whipped themselves up into a state of instant indignation like the PRI, and they obtained a privileged position through the athletic impulse of PRI members. The church's monopoly on religious followers was over: the PRI was able to obtain equally faithful and more ambitious disciples.

This prose blends critique with an enactment of what was criticized. This narrative montage would have been unthinkable without the great changes that took place in the public sphere from the 1960s onward—the polyphony produced by the multiple political rituals. This kind of writing has its own "popular-cultured" agency; despite its constant irony, it takes ordinary events seriously, and investigates the voices, sociolects, myths, and even eroticism of the collective imagination. Monsiváis takes risks with cultural populism without being trapped by it (Kraniauskas 1997a, 11).

The writings and political activities of Monsiváis, who, following the creation of the National Zapatista Liberation Army, was invited to be one of its first mediators with the government, show how radical the change in the notion of literature has been. Both in Mexico and within a broader Latin American context, he is associated with the literary intellectual's shift from his traditional role, a shift that accompanied the changes that took place in the sociocultural sphere from the 1960s to the 1990s, such as the move from the purely intellectual registers of the Revolution to others that reflect a reformulation of the problem of democracy. Paz expressed the disillusionment of the intellectual in the form of an elegy. Monsiváis experiences it with effective modesty: He rejects the role of representing or educating the oppressed or being the bearer of universal values, following instead the alternative heterodox movements that emerge within civil society—such as:

La luna es una pastilla mal cortada,
arrojada encima de la mesa que la madrugada
pone sobre las montañas del sureste mexicano
(abajo el río semeja una serpentina plateada,
olvidada y rota después de una fiesta).
. . .
Esta es la mesa para los arrojados de la modernidad.
Una larga y oscura sombra,
herida de luz por alfileres de cabeza erizada.
Una sombra, mesa de sombras, cuyo acceso es selectivo a la inversa:
todos los que pueden evitarla lo hacen.
Acuden a ella aquellos quienes sólo tienen
la memoria por alimento y la dignidad por cuchara y tenedor.
Una gran y solitaria mesa.
La atribulada mesa de los de abajo.

(Marcos 1998a)

The moon is an unevenly broken tablet
thrown onto a table that the early morning
has placed on the mountains of the Mexican south-east
(below, the river resembles a silver streamer,
lying forgotten and torn after a party).
. . .
This is the table for the rejects of modernity.
A long, dark shadow,
pierced by the light from bristly-headed pins.
A shadow, a table of shadows, to which access is inversely selective:
all those who can avoid it, do so.
It attracts only those who have nothing but memory for food, and dignity for knives and forks.
A vast, solitary table.
The grieving table of the underdogs.

On 10 April 1997, a text was published on the Internet and in various Mexican magazines entitled "Carta de Marcos a Emiliano Zapata" ["Letter from Marcos to Emiliano Zapata"] signed by "Insurgent Sub-commander Marcos," spokesman for the National Zapatista Liberation Army. In it, the historical Zapata emerges as both the addressee and referent:

> Ya usted se acuerda de lo que le escribió a un presidente de los gringos que se llamaba Woodrow Wilson, porque es bueno que los gobiernos extranjeros sepan y entiendan de la lucha de los mexicanos. Y entonces usted le escribió aquello de . . . "Y es que los hacendados, de despojo en despojo . . . han ido absorbiendo todas las propiedades que legítimamente pertenecen y desde tiempo inmemorial han pertenecido a los pueblos indígenas, y de cuyo cultivo estos últimos sacaban el sustento para sí y para sus familias." Y eso fue en 1914. Ahora, en 1997, la historia no ha cambiado.

> You will recall what you wrote to the president of the United States by the name of Woodrow Wilson, because it is good that foreign governments know about and understand the Mexicans' struggle. You wrote to him that . . . "The landowners have plundered and plundered . . . thereby acquiring all the properties that legitimately belong and have belonged, since time immemorial, to the indigenous people and from the cultivation of which they obtained food for themselves and their families." You wrote this in 1914. It is now 1997 and nothing has changed.

This is not a form of commemorative rhetoric that uses and alienates its historical subject, but rather a discourse in which the subjectivity of one of the most brutally marginalized groups, the indigenous peoples, moves to agency. The rhetorical presence of the dead in the living (so that the latter can live), a principle practiced within the neo-Zapatista group, harken back to the narrative culture of the Maya. Focusing here on Marcos's discourse is intended less as a gesture of reference to an anthropological position than as the signaling an awareness of culture as text. The challenge lies in reformulating the links between politics and literature, understanding the former as political culture and the second in terms of narrative and the aesthetic at the same time. At the beginning of the twenty-first century in Latin America, the project of "revolution" (now in lower case) reemerges where one would least have expected–within concepts of democracy, in other words, linked to the concept of a fair, participatory "civil society," linked to the EZLN (Ejercito Zapatista de Liberación Nacional [Zapatista Army of National Liberation]), which was founded in 1983 and burst onto the political scene in 1 January 1994 with fighting in the state of Chiapas, declaring that democratic change is the only alternative to war.

The events in Chiapas, which have caused a reaction in "civil society" in favor of the insurgents, had a perplexing and a mythologizing aspect. No one appeared to understand anything well enough to be able to analyze the phenomenon, as borne out by the initial comments of the best-known writers. Octavio Paz declared that "parecen relativamente claros: retazos de las ideas del maoísmo, de la Teología de la Liberación, de Sendero Luminoso y de los movimientos revolucionarios centroamericanos" (1994) ("its ideological origins [of the EZLN] . . . appear to be relatively clear: they include snippets of Maoist ideas, Liberation Theology, Shining Path, and the Central American revolutionary movements"). Carlos Fuentes, who perceived the political sensitivity of the Zapatistas and the innovativeness of their language, regarded their unexpected emergence on all the political scenarios as the first post-Communist movement of the era which was shortly changed to the first postmodern guerrilla war.

Marcos's discourse can be linked to a specific communicative situation: He speaks from a clandestine place in the Lacandona forest in the Mexican South-East controlled by the Zapatistas (Guadalupe Tepeyac, Chiapas). But the aim of the EZLN has not been to seize power but to cause irritation and force a response from a national political system that has blocked political reforms, kept the opposition in check, and ruthlessly neo-liberalized the country (see Méndez). The Zapatista movement's stand on the social inequalities of its region (by demanding that land be returned to the indigenous people) spurred a move to promote a new national and democratic project to be constructed, not by guerrilla fighters, but by the entire country with all the creativity and legitimacy of every social actor. This distinguished it from the guerrilla model that spread in the 1960s at both the representational level (the focus being the cell and the disciplined voice of all oppressed peoples) and the level of political conception (the violent suspension of democratic mechanisms). Neo-Zapatismo converted military issues into a political gesture. Their inadequate weapons were primarily symbols aimed at contributing to the symbolic reorganization of politics.

It became the first Latin American guerrilla group to develop a multimedia discourse as a political message that circulated on the Internet. This discourse was easy to understand thanks to its creation of specific images (beginning with the covered faces and balaclavas of the Zapatistas) and narrative figures (Old Antonio). It used a wide range of linguistic devices, such as those of the language of children, colloquial terms, and an elliptical style, constantly resorting to literary allusions (from Cervantes and Shakespeare to José Saramago and Umberto Eco) and quoted particular intellectuals such as Paul Ricoeur's *Métaphore vive*. This discourse offered an alternative to the instrumental rationality of political discourse. When Sub-commander Marcos addresses civil society and the international community through his communiqués, letters, and hybrid stories, accessible from all over the world, he is not understood as a representative voice but as the oral storyteller of the indigenous people, a concept of narration that modernity had managed to exclude from history, but recalling a phrase by Walter Benjamin: "the narrator is a person in whom the fair man finds himself"(410). In reflecting on a concept of narration subsequently explored in depth by Paul Ricoeur, Michel de Certeau, and Hayden White, Benjamin noticed the strangeness of the assumption about the isolation of the modern novelist and reader. In the case of Marcos, Zapatista discourse speaks through his voice, and the cultural (and political) task assumed here is the translation of indigenous thought into Western rationalism and vice versa. Marcos constructs a flow of stories, facilitated as much by technology as by the world-views of Mayan origin that he adapts. One of structuring principles (and ethical sources) he uses is an imaginary dialogue with Old Antonio, a figure from collective memory.

Zapatista discourse employs a historical perspective that might seem essentialist in its invocation of a repressed past. The point, however, is to open up the concept of history through a narration that encourages the participation of various subjectivities: "Marcos es feminista en los partidos políticos, comunista en la postguerra fría, chavo banda en Neza, machista en el movimiento feminista, ama de casa un sábado por la noche en cualquier colonia de cualquier ciudad de cualquier México" (Reguillo 7) ("Marcos is a feminist in the political parties, a communist in the post–Cold War period, a gang member in Neza, a male chauvinist in the feminist movement, and a housewife any Saturday evening in any neighborhood in any city at any social level in Mexico").

Marcos the storyteller tells stories to be listened to and understood, and narrates so that others may narrate through him:

Cuentan que los primeros dioses, los que nacieron el mundo, tenían muy mala memoria. . . . Así que . . . los más primeros dioses . . . hicieron una copia de todo lo que habían hecho y de todo lo que sabían. Esa copia la escondieron bajo el suelo. . . . El mundo primero está bajo la tierra.
Le pregunté al Viejo Antonio si es que el mundo subterráneo era una copia idéntica a la del mundo que conocemos.
'Fue', me respondió el Viejo Antonio, 'ya no'. Y es que—explicó—el mundo de afuera se fue desordenando y desacomodando al paso del tiempo. 'Cuando los más primeros dioses se fueron, nadie de los gobiernos se acordó de mirar abajo para ir arreglando lo que se iba desacomodando. Así que cada nueva generación de jefes pensó que el mundo que le tocaba así era de por sí y que no era posible otro mundo. . . .'
Dijo el Viejo Antonio que por eso es costumbre de los hombres y mujeres verdaderos el enterrar el ombligo del recién nacido. Lo hacen para que el nuevo ser humano eche un vistazo a la historia verdadera del mundo y sepa luchar para acomodarlo de nuevo . . . como debe ser. (Marcos 1998b)

They say that the first gods, those who created the world, had a very bad memory. . . . So . . . the earliest gods . . . made a copy of all that they had done and of everything they knew. They hid this copy under the ground. . . . This first world lies under the ground.
I asked Old Antonio if the underground world was an identical copy to the world we know.
"It was," replied Old Antonio, "But not any more." And the thing is—he explained—that, over time, the outside world got into a mess. "When the first gods left, none of the first governments agreed to look underneath to see what was going wrong. So every new generation of leaders thought that the world they had to look after was just like that and that no other world was possible. . . ."
Old Antonio says that this is why true men and women bury the newborn baby's umbilical cord. They do it so that the new human being will have a look at the true history of the world and will be able to fight to restore it . . . to how it should be.

The task of translation that the Zapatista discourse has set itself is, inspired by the other, to avoid transmitting the dominant rules of Western rationality. It continuously produces mediations in order to reach a world of legitimate discourse. In Benjaminian terms, Marcos rejects the authorship of the writer who is a tool of the autonomization of the individual and rejects the solitude of the modern writer. Paradoxically, assuming a narrative practice as a *modus vivendi* enables neo-Zapatismo to survive as a guerrilla group under conditions of worldwide electronic communication. Throughout the world, peoples, groups, and communities have emerged who have assumed Marcos's project as their own, becoming in turn interlocutors and communicators of this narrative imaginary.

Numerous interpretations of the Zapatista project are possible. Here, the concepts of literature and revolution, and literature and history confront hybridized new contexts. On the one hand, the Zapatista discourse did lead to the start of a national negotiation of a different future for Mexico. On the other, the critical review of Mexican national identity following the massacre in Tlatelolco in 1968, led by intellectuals such as Elena Poniatowska, Carlos Monsiváis, Roger Bartra (b. 1942), and many others, has had a different fate. A few years ago, Roger Bartra was still able to write,

La concepción dualista de México es una verdadera obsesión que comparten escritores, políticos y antropólogos. Hay dos Méxicos: uno es rural y bárbaro, indígena y atrasado; el otro es moderno y urbano, industrial y mestizo . . . aunque no es posible reducir las expresiones estéticas a esta única polaridad, es evidente que el modelo dual está siempre presente en la narrativa mexicana posrevolucionaria. (1996, 159)

The dualistic conception of Mexico is a veritable obsession shared by many writers, politicians and anthropologists. There are two Mexicos: one is rural and barbarous, indigenous and backward; the other is modern and urban, industrial and *mestizo.*. . . In modern Mexican literature the duality is expressed in very complex and subtle forms; although it is impossible to reduce aesthetic expression to this unique polarity, it is clear that the dual model is always present in post-revolutionary Mexican narrative. (1992, 137–38)

The Zapatista narrator Marcos has exploded this dualism. His place of enunciation is so remote, so open and yet so near on a basis of everyday life that it has fully preserved its true mythical impact.

Peronism and Literary (Non)Encounters in Argentina

Si los treinta son años claves para América Latina, tanto o más que por los procesos de industrialización y modernización de las estructuras económicas lo son en lo político, por la irrupción de las masas en la ciudad. . . . El mantenimiento del poder era imposible sin asumir de alguna manera las reivindicaciones de las masas urbanas. El populismo será entonces la *forma* de un Estado que dice fundar su legitimidad en la asunción de las aspiraciones populares y que, más que una estratagema *desde* el poder, resulta ser una organización *del* poder que da forma al compromiso entre masas y Estado. La ambigüedad de ese compromiso viene tanto del vacío de poder que debe llenar el Estado—con el autoritarismo paternalista que ello produce—como del reformismo político que representan las masas. (Martín-Barbero 1987, 170–71)

If the 1930s were important years in Latin America for the economic processes of industrialization and modernization, politically they were even more important for the "irruption" of the masses in the cities. . . . The maintenance of power was impossible without assuming in some way the vindication of the demands of the urban masses. Populism became the form of a state which sought to strengthen its legitimacy by taking upon itself the popular aspirations. This was not a strategy from a position of power, but rather an organization of power which expressed concretely the contract between the masses and the state. The ambiguousness of this contract resulted both from the vacuum of power which the state was supposed to fill—with the paternalistic authoritarianism which this produces—and from the political reformism which the masses demanded. (1993, 156–57)

Peronism in Argentina (1943–1955) is regarded as the populist phenomenon par excellence in Latin America, the one that has elicited heated debates about problems that seem to resist classification by political theory or any other academic discourse. Like other major political movements, it had sympathizers, but it does not seem to have generated its own organic intellectuals, perhaps because of its lack of a coherent ideology. As a result of its taste for grand gestures, it was also rejected by writers and artists. The social sciences have tended to place it in the same category as the Fascist regimes of Europe, a view supported by Juan José Sebreli (68–69). It was not until the 1980s that populism was reassessed within the framework of a debate that, under the sign of postmodernism, permitted the new historicization of modernity. In Ernesto Laclau, the inspirer of a form of self-criticism of the Left which he called (post-)Marxist, the reconsideration of populism was one of the bases for theorizing the political processes of the 1960s and 1970s involving the rapid disintegration and multiple politicizations of the established political and social issues (1978, 33–39). He separated the problem of political identity from structurally homogenizing goals that are also totalizing when it comes to representation. By making the concepts of hegemony and social movement more flexible (1990, 179–80 and 230–31), he developed a theoretical approach to the unstable, opaque aspects of the ideological referent in the midst of what the theorists of peripheral (post)modernity would call political culture (Herlinghaus and Walter 29–30). It was by abandoning the usual dualistic schemes that the historicization of Latin American processes between 1930 and 1960 managed to articulate the more complex tensions among national(istic) discourses, the State, mass media, and cultural democratization. Laclau's reflections on the massive, urban, and intercultural displacements helped strip the notion of "popular" culture of its former aura of purity (García Canclini 150).

Operating at the service of a land-owning bourgeoisie, the regime that preceded Juan Domingo Perón's (1895–1974) was closed, cynical, and highly unpopular. Unlike Mexico, Argentina had not undergone a democratic-bourgeois revolution. It was, however, the Latin American country with the largest number of immigrants and a site of major urban transformations. It was the first country to have to cope with cultural modernity, with its thitherto unprecedented consumption of cinema, radio, paperbacks, and popular magazines (Sarlo 1988, 18–27), the beginnings of an advertising aesthetics, and even techno-myths (see Arlt), in the manner of major European and North American cities. These changes created new desires, while recycling old habits (Sarlo 1992, 15–16). By 1939, the annual number of feature films produced had reached fifty (Fox 56), thanks to a cinematographic industry which, together with Mexico's, was the most developed in the continent. By the 1930s, though, it was the turn of radio, a fact that would prove crucial to understanding the phenomenon of Peronism: It would eventually take over this medium. Despite these culturally democratizing dynamics and a nationalistic climate reinforced by the Second World War, until the 1950s Argentina lacked the institutions and political subjects capable of organizing any real national project. The founding myth of a civilized Argentina (see Sarmiento) that emerged in that symbiosis between a writer and a national legitimizer during the nineteenth century would be dismantled by the writers of the "Boom" during the 1960s (Sommer 1–4).

It was in the middle of the 1940s that Perón made enormous inroads, showing urban workers, farm workers, and part of the middle class the road to justice: "Para colmo, el nuevo Líder les hablaba del espíritu y de sus valores, no les predicaba la lucha entre el capital y el trabajo sino la cooperación, y aun les decía que era necesario poner en la práctica los viejos principios olvidados del cristianismo" (Perón 1997, 92) ("To crown it all, the new Leader spoke to them of the spirit and of its values, preaching not of the struggle between capital and labor, but rather of co-operation, and even told them that it was necessary to put the old, forgotten principles of Christianity into practice"; 1978, 77). These words, uttered by Eva Perón (1919–1952) in 1951, stressed the Leader's skill in implementing a nationalistic social project that encompassed a variety of political aims. And many Argentineans experienced the phenomenon as a revolution, the "Peronista Revolution."

The autobiographical novel *Se dice hombre* [1952; Identified As Male] by Jorge Perrone offers an insight into the events of 17 October 1945, the day when Colonel Perón, then Vice-President, Minister of War, and Secretary of State for Labor and Social Welfare–after being detained by military rivals along with whom he had come to power in 1944, and who had later allied themselves with oligarchic interests–received the mass popular support that secured his release, and later enabled him to be elected President in 1946:

> La revolución. Suena un poco espectacular y se te ocurre que no tiene nada que ver con los porteros o los arrepentidos, que no tiene nada que ver con las palabras.
> La cosa te alcanzó sorpresivamente. . . .
> -¡Queremos a Perón! ¡Queremos a Perón!
> No supiste por qué, mas estabas seguro que ese grito era tuyo.
> . . .
> Al llegar la noche la multitud desbordaba hacia la Avenida, por la Diagonal, a lo largo de las calles adyacentes. Y una grita fue tomando cuerpo. Empezó con un rumor apretado y ronco y el vocerío invadió todo el aire de la ciudad.
> ¡Queré-mos-a-Pe-rón! ¡Queré-mos-a-Pe-rón! ¡Queré-mos-a-Pe-rón!
> . . .
> A veces la multitud ofrece un curioso aspecto. Asume la condición de un animal fabuloso con el hocico hacia el suelo, un hocico que percibe los olores más sutiles, más imposibles de alcanzar. Vos solo, vos en tu condición de hombre solo, nunca serías capaz de alcanzar, de ubicar, los olores en tal forma. La multitud siempre es un instinto. Está en posesión de la pureza. Aunque incendie tranvías o balee a otros hombres. Tal vez los ataque porque inconscientemente sepa que son hombres solos.
> (Perrone, qtd. in Borello 64–66)

> The revolution. It sounds a bit spectacular and it occurs to you that it has nothing to do with the porters or those who have repented, that it has nothing to do with words.
> The thing creeps up on you unexpectedly. . . .
> "We want Perón! We want Perón!"
> You didn't know why, but you were sure that that shout was yours.
> . . .
> At nightfall, the crowd surged toward the Avenida, along the Diagonal, along the adjacent streets. And an uproar gradually began to be heard. It began as a dull roar and the shouting gradually filled the city air.
> "We want Pe-rón! We want Pe-rón! We want Pe-rón!"
> . . .
> Sometimes the crowd looked strange. It resembled a fabulous animal with its snout on the ground, a snout that perceived the most subtle smells, the ones that were almost impossible to detect. You alone, as just one man, would never be able to pick out or locate the smells in such a way. The crowd is always based on instinct. It possesses purity. Even though it sets streetcars on fire or shoots other men. Perhaps it attacks them because it unconsciously knows that they are men on their own.

According to Rodolfo Borello, the writers who witnessed this era mainly discussed the appearance of this radically politicized crowd (64–68). It was not a question of a natural sociopolitical phenomenon, but rather a problem of reconfiguring one's sense of everyday life. In his novel *El uno y la multitud* [1955; One and the Crowd], we can see this in how Manuel Gálvez (1882–1962) returns to that same day in October, describing the experience of a member of the upper class:

> Claraval soportó con angustia el tremendo entusiasmo de la multitud. A sus vecinos se les multiplicaban los cuerpos, los brazos, las contracciones, los olores. Lo distraían las antorchas erguidas en la

plaza. Él sentíase contento, por el espectáculo grandioso a que estaba asistiendo, y desgraciado por las molestias que experimentaba. Sentíase enfermo de multitud. (Gálvez, qtd. in Borello 102)

The tremendous enthusiasm of the multitude made Claraval anxious. The bodies, arms, contractions and smells of his neighbors multiplied. He was distracted by the lighted torches in the square. He felt happy, because of the marvelous spectacle he was witnessing, and unhappy because of the discomfort this caused him. He felt sick because of the crowd.

In 1947, a story signed "H. Bustos Domecq," the pseudonym of Jorge Luis Borges (1899–1986) and Adolfo Bioy Casares (1914–1999)–a typed copy of which was circulated among a small group of readers (Vázquez 200)–described this same phenomenon as grotesque. In "La fiesta del monstruo" ["The Monster's Party"] a vulgar character with a visceral mind (a *greaser* or a worker), given to speaking a distorted version of Buenos Aires slang, tells an imaginary interlocutor, Nelly, how he and other demonstrators walked to the Plaza de Mayo to enjoy the "celebrations of the monster," an allusion to the country's new leader. Along the way, the group bumps into a Jewish student and kills him in an act of brutal racism ("Todos bramábamos como el pabellón de los osos y nos rechinaban los dientes" [Borges 1981, 463–64] ["We all bellowed like the bears in the pavilion and our teeth chattered"]). This is a caricatured version of José Ortega y Gasset's (1883–1955) claim that the masses, in their modern rebellion, annihilate everything that is different from themselves (12).

One of Julio Cortázar's (1914–1984) first stories, "Omnibus" (1956), explored a similar theme though in a different way, but the story by Borges and Bioy Casares satirizes the crowd's agitation:

Presto, gordeta, quedó relegado al olvido ese episodio callejero. Banderas de Boitano que tremolan, toques de clarín que vigoran, doquier la masa popular, formidável. En la Plaza de Mayo nos arengó la gran descarga eléctrica que se firma doctor Marcelo N. Frogman. Nos puso en forma para lo que vino después: la palabra del Monstruo. Estas orejas la escucharon, gordeta, mismo como todo el país, porque el discurso se trasmite en cadena. (465)

That street episode was soon forgotten, love. What with Boitano flags fluttering, bugle calls livening up the atmosphere, and the masses standing all around, it was wonderful. In Plaza de Mayo, we were harangued by the great electric shock that Dr. Marcelo N. Frogman ordered. It prepared us for what followed: the Monster's words. I heard him with these very ears, just like the rest of the country, because his speeches were broadcast by a network of radio stations.

This frontal attack, which exposes its object through a comic tone that degrades and despises, operates from a distance. It is hardly surprising that satire is constructed on the basis of a stereotypical view of Peronism cultivated by both authors, since Borges had supported the intellectual position of anti-Peronism. The psychological-social prejudice that marks "La fiesta del–monstruo"–as is clear from its title–tends to preserve the core of liberalist aestheticism intact. A few years later, in the fragment "El simulacro" ["The Mountebank"] (in *El hacedor* [1960; *Dreamtigers*]), Borges classifies Peronism as the perfect code for an unreal era (1977, 789).

The literary witnesses of the time became negotiators with visions of different worlds, not so much of different events but of the myths events provoke. The paradoxical fact is that in the case of Borges, Bioy Casares, and Cortázar, the actual process of the rise of Peronism was made into part of the fantastic, and therefore made unreal. The story "Casa Tomada" [1956; "Occupied House"] by Cortázar tells the story of a brother and sister whose life centered on a spacious house that preserved the memories of several generations of the family. An obscure force, "los ruidos se oían más fuerte pero siempre sordos" (in Cócaro 162) ("the sounds [which] became louder, but were always muffled"), invades this family space until it strips them of everything, leaving them defenseless and impoverished on the street. The possibly incestuous relationship between Irene and her brother (the narrator) helps create in the atmosphere of the house (a surrogate mother) the charm of a world unconcerned by events that nonetheless take place; in this sordidness, however, lies the eroticization of politics by Eva Perón.

Why was Peronism treated as though it was a myth? What was seen as surprising and incalculable, in these early literary expressions, particularly by these three writers? The first of possible reasons was its lack of a clear and therefore censurable discourse, a discourse that would correspond to usual register of Argentinean politics. A second might be the scandalous symbiosis in which the movie idol–like couple of Perón and Evita managed to ritualize the desires of a collectivity, gathered together as never before in Argentina. As Eva Perón wrote: "Y fue el mismo Perón quien me dijo: Los pueblos muy castigados por la injusticia tienen más confianza en las personas que en las instituciones" (1997, 131) ("And it was Perón himself who told me: 'Peoples much smitten by injustice have more confidence in persons than in institutions'"; 1978, 112). It is worth recalling that "La fiesta del monstruo" ends with the blunt phrase "el discurso [del monstruo] se trasmite en cadena" ("the [monster's] discourse is broadcast by a network of radio stations"). In other words, the "monster" becomes a monster with the support of a new medium–radio. Out of the mass media's enchantment with political discourse a new power was born. Its effectiveness was the result of the "virtualization" of ritualistic celebrations, the hybridization of politics with theater through radio broadcasts. This "secondary orality" (see Ong), created through a pact between Peronism and a pillar of the cultural industry, heralded a new era different from the dramatization of the "primary orality" of the Mexican Revolution.

Argentina was a pioneer in the development of radio, having installed a commercial network of radio stations in 1936; there were a million and a half radio sets and, by the 1920s, there were weekly journals devoted to the new medium (Martín-Barbero 1987, 183). Ernesto Sábato (b. 1911) noted that during this period, the rhetoric of radio novels was a false and degraded one and that, together with their forerunner, the newspaper serial, these narratives poisoned the public. From his more romantic notion of the people–also present in *Sobre héroes y tumbas* [1961; *On Heroes and Tombs*, 1981]–he regretted the fact that "enorme foso . . . se ha abierto entre el pueblo y la belleza" (1976, 63) ("a yawning gap . . . has opened up between the people and beauty"). Recalling Perrone's phrase quoted earlier–that the multitude "possesses purity" but in reverse–this shows the two poles of the Romantic interpretation of the popular among writers: their positive identification with the masses, on the one hand, and on the other, the relegation of them to "las primitivas comunidades . . . cuando el pueblo estaba aún entrañablemente unido a los hechos esenciales de la existencia: al nacimiento y la muerte, a la salida y puesta del sol, a las cosechas y al comienzo de la adolescencia, al sexo y el sueño" (62) ("primitive communities . . . when the people were still closely linked to the essential facts of existence:

birth and death, sunrise and sunset, harvests and the start of adolescence, sex and dreams"). In the incompatibility between major writers and the phenomenon of Peronism, there was less political struggle than cultural resistance: Certain developments seemed to traumatically contradict the symbolic capital of learned culture. To prevent this from happening, it was essential to opt for an "uncontaminated popular art" (Sábato 1976, 65). Primitive beauty was attributed to the people as a way of overlooking their "cultural modernization," a gesture that reflected a profound irritation (the main source of anguish in Cortázar's story) with the authority achieved by popular narratives, even in the field of politics. Manuel Puig (1932–1990) was one of the few writers to explicitly deal with the phenomenon of the modernization of the popular by the mass media.

The literary, cinematic, and musical reemergence of the figure of Eva Perón from the 1980s onward does not indicate the recycling of a symbol of the mass imaginary that lacked a political referent, in Baudrillard's terms. Perhaps, instead, this process proves that such a referent has in fact proved extremely effective. Although Peronism appealed to the popular masses as an active political interlocutor, its achievement was largely cultural in that it opened up a new dimension for the masses to articulate their feelings about the nation. The predecessors of Juan Domingo Perón were not so much the politicians as the fictional newspaper serial heroes of Eduardo Gutiérrez (1851–1889), who oscillated between the *criollo* circus performers and actors of radio melodramas, or the legendary bandits demanding social justice who peopled the gaucho stories of González Pulido (Martín-Barbero 1987, 184–85). The crucial role of "Evita" in the success of Peronism lay in the fact that it was she who managed to become the voice and image of politics. She spoke regularly to the workers via Radio Nacional from a microphone at the Ministry of Labor and Social Welfare, which was her domain, at the same time as she received the petitions of thousands and thousands of people who filed past her desk. Through the diminutive form "Evita," the leader's wife became the finest "political troubadour" that Latin America has ever had. In her words: "Recuerdo que, siendo una chiquilla, siempre deseaba declamar. Era como si quisiese decir siempre algo a los demás, algo grande, que yo sentía en lo más hondo de mi corazón" (Perón 1997, 24) ("I recollect that, as a child, I always wanted to recite. It was as though I always wished to tell others something–something great which I felt, deep of my heart"; 1978, 11). Before meeting Perón, Eva Duarte had worked as an actress for a series of cinema and radio companies. In the radio series *Heroínas de la historia* [Heroines of History], she had played Sarah Bernhardt, Isadora Duncan, Catherine the Great, Josephine Bonaparte, Mary Stuart, and Madame Chiang Kai-shek. When she emerged in the political arena, her appearance was as disconcerting as it was effective. She had the sense to engage in political discourse using her most effective weapon–her melodramatic speech. Her notions of justice, participation, and love were not drawn from some ideologically differentiated realm, but rather from popular narrative memory. Few critics have realized that, behind the demagogic propaganda that praised the "humanistic Christianity" and "revolutionary justice" of her husband, lay a remarkable narrative talent.

Months before she died of a virulent form of cancer in July 1952, she dictated fragments of her memoirs in which she said, "Yo sé que mi obra es . . . una gota de amor en medio del mar. Mejor dicho: es una gota de amor cayendo sobre un inmenso océano de barro, que es este mundo lleno de odios y de luchas" (Perón 1997, 182) ("I know that my work is like a drop of water in the ocean. Or rather: it is a drop of love falling on that immense muddy ocean which is the world of hatred and strife"; 1978, 161–62). The former actress succeeded in establishing a strange, mixed discourse at the center of which love figured as an eminently political issue. The link here is to the petit-bourgeois tradition of melodrama; with Pixérécourt, from the French Revolution onward, melodrama became the "other" of enlightened modernity, representing on stage the desire for happiness of the plebeian subject, and, even more so, of the female plebeian subject. This is what was collectively dramatized, but on the margins of political and artistic institutions; as a "chameleonic story," it was at the heart of the newspaper serial, cinema, and radio (Herlinghaus 1994, 111). The petit-bourgeois melodrama was not just a secularized form of classical tragedy; it became a place to articulate anger about the injustices of society. And at its core was not only–as so often suspected–the threat and reinstitution of virtue, but the conflict around an amorous relationship presented specifically as a problem of justice.

The autobiography of Evita contains simple, redundant metaphors and begins with the author placing herself within the ranks of the "shirtless ones": "yo no era ni soy nada más que una humilde mujer . . . un gorrión en una inmensa bandada de gorriones. . . . Y él [Perón quién la elevó a su misión] era y es el cóndor gigante que vuela alto y seguro entre las cumbres" (Perón 1997, 13) ("I was not, nor am I, anything more than a humble woman . . . a sparrow in an immense flock of sparrows. . . . But Perón was, and is, a gigantic condor that flies high and sure among the summits and near to God"; 1978, v]. Although there was a real happy ending here (the marriage between the leader and the actress), Evita was always quick to add that this was nothing more than the image of another, more important happy ending–the happiness of the poor. Until this happened, she would always be a sparrow, a weak woman who rejected behaving like a privileged wife, Eva. The task of the condor was to personify the myth of the good hero so that Evita, the sparrow, would not play her role as the president's wife but instead continued to keep the melodrama going, playing her virtual role and carrying out her symbolic function. The imaginary pact, always renarrated and dramatized in this manner, between the sparrow (a childish-female position) and the condor is the ideological story that fed both collective desire and belief. It was the perfect eroticization of politics through a triadic emplotment.

> Cuando un pibe me nombra 'Evita' me siento madre de todos los pibes y de todos los débiles y humildes de mi tierra.
> Cuando un obrero me llama 'Evita' me siento con gusto 'compañera' de todos los hombres que trabajan en mi país y aun en el mundo entero.
> Cuando una mujer de mi patria me dice 'Evita' yo me imagino ser hermana de ella y de todas las mujeres de la humanidad.
> (Perón 1997, 75)

> When a street-urchin calls me "Evita," I feel as though I were the mother of all the urchins, and of all the weak and the humble of my land.
> When a workingman calls me "Evita," I feel glad to be the companion of all the workingmen of my country and even of the whole world.
> When a woman of my country calls me "Evita," I imagine myself her sister, and that of all the women of humanity. (1978, 62)

The melodrama that she wielded as a weapon gave a populist ideological image to Peronista "justice," whose aim was, according to Eva, "hacer desaparecer la lucha de clases y sustituirla por la cooperación entre capital y trabajo" (1997, 98) ("to end the class war and substitute cooperation between capital and labor"; 1978, 83), to create a single class of men who would be both non-proletarian and non-bourgeois, although "para mí la justicia está un poco más allá de la mitad del camino" (1997, 99) ("[a]lmost always justice for me is a little farther than the middle of the road"; 1978, 84).

The Peronist project failed both economically and politically. It did, however, create one of the most enduring myths of national sentiment that stood in contrast to the Enlightenment's fiction of the nineteenth century, which promised to turn barbarism into civilization. The Peronista myth was based on a radical and confused blend of dreams that sought to represent the soul of the poor, of workers and women. One of the most dismaying paradoxes of the figure of Eva Perón has been, and continues to be, her multiple transgressive role. On the one hand, she set up a female platform from which she loudly denounced the "feminist" mimicry that, in her view, represented a growing imitation of male culture. In her handling of power, however, she used excessively "male" behavior. This ambiguity that became the axis of the literary and cinematic discourse about her which, a few decades later, rediscovered Evita. Recalling a 1944 radio play starring Eva Duarte, Juan José Sebreli noted an earlier self-reflexive moment: "La novela se llamaba *500 años en blanco*, y se transmitía por Radio Belgrano a las 18:30 horas. El tema era de ciencia ficción, se trataba de un viaje al planeta Marte realizado por un grupo de astronautas, entre ellos una intrépida mujer interpretada por Eva Duarte" (241) ("The radio novel was called *500 años en blanco* [A Blank 500 Years] and was broadcast by Radio Belgrano at 18:30. The theme was science fiction and it was about a journey to Mars undertaken by a group of astronauts, including a brave woman played by Eva Duarte").

Peronism had no intellectualized ideology, but it used cultural mediations to regulate and create new political hegemonies. Latin American processes of modernization, as Peronism showed, both generated and inverted models of modernity, in a manner that was difficult to classify. The sense of nation, as a feeling and mass desire for nationality, exceeded the legitimation encoded by Liberalism. The enormous importance of the new mass media in the 1930s, 1940s, and 1950s cannot be reduced to their roles as an ideological instrument, though that role was political in its mediation of new subjectivities. Because of their opaqueness and ambivalence, these subjectivities escaped being subjected to the Romantic goals with which Liberal intellectuals continued to construct their notion of the people. The media were part of the other negotiation with modernity—a carnivalization of oligarcho-bourgeois society. In terms of literary history, the period involved unusual challenges: It encouraged the shift from purely literary hierarchies to cultural ones that reflected a greater social heterogeneity.

A novelist who became one of the translators of the literary into the social in the era of Peronism during the Boom years was Manuel Puig (1932–1990). Puig's initial rejection by the critics, a response that would be transformed into enthusiasm through the canonization of postmodern writing, enacted the institutional drama of an epistemological change. A typical early assessment was that Puig was a critic of the alienation that the Argentinean middle classes experienced from their contact with cinema and radio drama (Rodríguez Monegal; but see also Pope 1996, 266). But wasn't Puig himself a devoted fan of the great divas of Hollywood and of popular songs? This is where a concept of literature and the function of the intellectual based on a "high art" hierarchy reveals its drawbacks: The popular and the mass can only be judged negatively in terms of high art (as in the example of Sábato): "Cuando Puig empieza a escribir sobre 'temas argentinos,' comprende que es necesario operar un desplazamiento en la voz. Frente a la superstición . . . de 'ser la voz de los que no tienen voz,' Puig nota lo que cualquier vecina haría notar: que la gente tiene voz y se reconoce a través de ella" (Lorenzano 64) ("When Puig begins to write about 'Argentine themes,' he understands that it is necessary to effect a displacement of the voice. Faced with the image . . . of 'being the voice of those who have no voice,' Puig notes what anyone might note: that the people have a voice and know themselves through it").

Puig transposed this voice to literature. He showed that popular psychology rising above all forms of bad taste was not the only option for serious writing (Piglia 115). He painted–"mouths"–*Boquitas pintadas* [1969; *Heartbreak Tango*]–offering rhetorical instead of poetic imaginaries, opting for the polyphonous "second-hand" story, a combination of prefabricated fragments from everyday speech and bits of everyday mythology, and therefore gave us "do-it-yourself" stories. Puig initiated a self-reflection on cinematic "bad taste" in Latin American literature. *La traición de Rita Hayworth* [1968; *Betrayed by Rita Hayworth*] describes how the myth of this prima donna is experienced by the lower middle class of Río de la Plata during the Peronist era. The "betrayal" of the title consists in the fact that the longed-for loves, those that manage to cross or fill abysses, fail in everyday life. This constant renarration of what happens even to favorite heroes also echoes the form of the plot of poor people's lives. Their bad taste is a way of experiencing the precarious conditions of modernity without sacrificing fantasy. Puig situates himself as the interlocutor of Peronist discourse from the culture of those very people to whom it appealed, the marginalized.

The name and image of Evita Perón provided postmodern culture with an unmistakable icon from the periphery. Three of the many factors that contributed to her rediscovery during the 1980s are the post-dictatorial climate in Latin America that linked the need for a democratic political culture and the repressive impact of globalization, the conversion of the gender issue into a political one, and an excess of populist symbols at the level of the semiotics of audiovisual culture. The political referent disappears into musical and theatrical illusion as in the case of Alan Parker's film *Evita*, starring Madonna and Antonio Banderas, though an alternative image and politics appealed in Juan Carlos Desanzo's *Eva Perón*. Interestingly, both were produced in 1996. Various literary approaches also reinforced the new political tone of the "metafictional paradox" (Hutcheon), reciprocally deconstructing both the (macro)politics of Peronism and the Liberal aestheticism. This goal, attempted in a novel such as *El beso de la mujer araña* [1976; *Kiss of the Spider Woman*, 1979] by Manuel Puig, was subsequently taken on by Miguel Bonasso (b. 1940) in *Recuerdo de la muerte* [1984; Remembrance of Death] and above all in his *La novela de Perón* [1985; *The Perón Novel*, 1988], as in *Santa Evita* (1995) by Tomás Eloy Martínez (b. 1934).

Borges had already given some idea of how thought-provoking the theme could be beyond its immediate sphere. The fragment "El Simulacro" which figures in *El hacedor* the real reason for the scandalousness felt by liberal literati–a politically transgressive fetishism:

El enlutado no era Perón y la muñeca rubia no era la mujer Eva Duarte, pero tampoco Perón era Perón ni Eva era Eva sino desconocidos o anónimos (cuyo nombre secreto y cuyo rostro verdadero ignoramos) que figuraron, para el crédulo amor de los arrabales, una crasa mitología. (Borges 1977, 789)

The man in mourning was not Perón, and the blonde-haired mannequin was not the woman Eva Duarte, but then Perón was not Perón, either, nor was Eva, Eva—they were unknown or anonymous persons (whose secret name and true face we shall never know) who acted out, for the credulous love of the working class, a crass and ignoble mythology. (Borges 1998, 301–2)

During the post-history of Evita, various political forces fought over her body–which endured a spectacular series of kidnappings and displacements, and which even toured Europe: "Eva was alternatively the Actress, Cinderella, First Lady, Comrade, Martyr, Saint and embalmed monument, mobilizing and demobilizing within an elastic political horizon of expectations . . . embodying forces that have completely transformed the Argentine political field. . . . She must be contained" (Kraniauskas 1997b, 3). But she could not be contained. In the light of the military coup of 1966 that provoked the resistance of a rejuventated Left-wing Peronism, in *El fiord* [1969; Fiord]–the name of a pornographic puppet play– Osvaldo Lamborghini (1940–1985) used the satirical tone and allegorical mode of "La fiesta del monstruo" by Borges and Bioy Casares to invert the story and create a sort of "snuff-story," a kind of cruel theater that enacts yet another Argentine revolution, a porno-Revolution that, through sacrifice, reinstalls Peronist law.

The text that most obviously marks a watershed in the metahistorical recovery of Evita is the short story: "Esa mujer" [1965; "That Woman"] by Rodolfo Walsh (1927–1977), published in *Los oficios terrestres* [The Terrestrial Trades]. It is a hybrid narrative halfway between a detective story and fictional testimony, and takes place during the events that followed the death of Eva Perón. Her body had been transported from the presidential residence to the headquarters of the CGT (Confederación General del Trabajo) to be housed in a monument that was never built. After the military coup against Perón in 1955, the secret service of the new regime seized the body to prevent the resistance forces from using it as a symbol of their struggle. Referring to this history, Walsh poses the question, "Where is that woman?" in a conversation between "the Colonel" and the narrator. The military character is supposedly Colonel Carlos Eugenio Moori-Koenig, head of the information services of the coup government, who was given the task of taking possession of the body. The narrator expresses an overwhelming if strange desire:

Algún día (pienso en momentos de ira) iré a buscarla. Ella no significa nada para mí, y sin embargo iré tras el misterio de su muerte, detrás de sus restos que se pudren lentamente en algún remoto cementerio. Si la encuentro, frescas altas olas de cólera, miedo y frustrado amor se alzarán, poderosas vengativas olas, y por un momento ya no me sentiré como una arrastrada, amarga, olvidada sombra. (11–12)

One day (I think during moments of anger), I shall go and find her. She means nothing to me, and yet, I shall go after the mystery of her death, and her remains that are slowly rotting in a remote cemetery. If I find her, new, high waves of anger, fear and frustrated love will rise up, powerfully vengeful waves, and for a moment, I shall no longer feel like a bitter, forgotten shadow that has been dragged along.

The Colonel, in turn, claims his right to "that woman" whom he intends to protect from an invisible mob of offenders:

"Pero esa mujer estaba desnuda. . . . Tuve que taparle el monte de Venus, le puse una mortaja y el cinturón franciscano" (17) ("But that woman was naked. . . . I had to cover her mount of Venus, I covered her with a shroud and a Franciscan belt"). "That woman" is narrativized, to use Hayden White's term, as something that brings together political and sexual desire, something rather like a fetish. The narrator says, "Pero no es ninguna forma concebible de amor lo que nos ha reunido . . . es apenas una fantasía . . . perversa" (11) ("But we have not been joined by any conceivable form of love . . . but rather, by a perverse fantasy"), a fantasy that had also affected Borges when he relegated her to unreality. The Colonel in Walsh's story, attuned to authoritarian Liberalism, wishes to avoid a new wave of barbarity, worse than that which rejected Sarmiento. That is why he cuts off the inquiring voice of the narrator: "¡Está parada!–grita el coronel–. ¡La enterré parada, como Facundo, porque era un macho!" (21) ("She's standing up!" shouted the colonel. "I buried her standing up, like Facundo, because she was a male!"). The authority of "Facundo" signals the reemergence of the symbolic guarantor of masculinity, since the worst thing of all would be a "Female Facundo" (Kraniauskas 1993–1994, 112). Walsh reveals the sexual dimension of an ideological imaginary that recuperates Evita as a phallic woman and, through this, "un espacio político que ha sido rigurosamente codificado como masculino" (Kraniauskas 1993–1994, 113) ("a political space that has been rigorously encoded as male"). The Colonel's retention of the body (and its symbolic domestication, which the narrator discovers) is a cultural rather than an aesthetic act. What is at stake is nothing less than a utopian vision, creating a "happy ending" for a society that still appears to be waiting for one. A related Eva-image appears in Tomás Eloy Martínez's *Santa Evita*, a hybrid gothic novel whose main character is a body that is multiplied in the desires of the people who do not wish to say good-bye to her. This novelist, who had accompanied Rodolfo Walsh to Bonn in 1970 in search of the body of "that woman" (113), is said to have made the best use of irony to reveal the literary unconscious of Peronism. For our purposes, however, the issue can also be posited the other way around: What clues does Peronism provide for defining the political unconscious of literature?

The Cuban Revolution: The Reality of the Myth, the Critical Experience, and Debate

With the overthrow of Fulgencio Batista's regime in 1959, Cuba achieved national independence for the second time. A period of social change began that, given the combined impact of economic isolation and the threat of war with the United States, rapidly led to a political radicalization. This has produced the only socialist state in Latin America to have had a prolonged development, one whose extraordinary capacity for survival and self-defense was still intact at the start of the twenty-first century. In 1977 Cintio Vitier, in the literary tradition of *Orígenes* (the journal founded by José Lezama Lima in 1944), wrote about the ideological peculiarity of a socialist Cuba:

The collapse of socialism in Eastern Europe and the former Soviet Union has not provoked in Cuba, despite the enormous economic trauma we now suffer, the ideological void hoped for by the United States. . . . The reason is simple: no matter how important our alliance with Soviet socialism was, it was never more than just that– an alliance. Where the Soviets hoped to find an ideological void, the community of Céspedes, Maceo and Martí was waiting for them. It was more than an ideology; it was a true vocation for justice and freedom. The popular interpretation of Marxist-Leninist socialism was put to the service of the same vocation that had been declared by our founders. (215–17)

Seen from inside Cuba, in the early years, the Revolution's validity, for the vast majority of people, had already acquired the status of a fact, and was inseparable from a sense of romantic heroism. During a visit to Cuba in 1960, Sartre declared that he was surprised by the apparent lack of ideology in comparison with countries in eastern Europe. He remarked,

> Sin embargo, no son las ideologías lo que falta en este siglo; aquí mismo tienen representantes que os ofrecen por todos lados sus servicios. Vuestros dirigentes no las ignoran: simplemente no las emplean. Sus adversarios les formulan los reproches más contradictorios: para unos, esa ausencia de ideas no es más que un engaño; . . . algún día, los cubanos se quitarán la máscara y el comunismo se instalará en el Caribe, a pocos kilómetros de Miami. Otros enemigos . . . los acusan de no pensar nada en absoluto: 'Están improvisando', . . . 'y luego de haber hecho algo elaboran una teoría'. (Sartre 4)

> What is missing in this century, however, is not ideologies; in this very place, they have representatives who offer you their services everywhere. It is not that your leaders are unaware of them: they simply do not use them. Their adversaries devised the most contradictory reproaches: for some, this lack of ideas is merely a deception; . . . one day, the Cubans will unmask them and Communism will set up shop in the Caribbean, a few miles away from Miami. Other enemies . . . accuse them of thinking about nothing at all: "They are improvising," . . . "after they have done something, they devise a theory for it."

The situation at the beginning of the Socialist Revolution in Cuba was one that political thinking in the West found difficult to comprehend. It was a new situation offering a real alternative for social development, in other words, of a radically different political model. And it would survive, despite the havoc and deformations that geographical fatalism, economic realism, and political centralism continued to inflict. At the start of this Revolution, a powerful legend helped both to prefigure its ideology and to nourish a mythic sense of the state that was then being established: the journey by land and sea undertaken by the young lawyer Fidel Castro, the bearded hero, following the assault on the Moncada barracks to fight Batista's army (and subsequently the invaders of Playa Girón). Another mythical figure of the Revolution–along with Castro and the literary apostle of Independence and anti-Imperialism, José Martí–was Ernesto Che Guevara (1928–1967). Following the failure of his goal of a continent-wide guerrilla war in 1967, his image became that of a "Christ of the Revolutionaries" (Castro 1968, 96–105).

The historically spectacular birth of a new Cuban society became a paradigm for writers and intellectuals in Latin America; it crystallized the desire for the representation of a dream of another modernity. This other vision of modernity lacked the shape of complex modernization, but was legitimized as the right of the majority to social and national justice. It was a time of crisis and change that fed into a sense of the political exoticism of difference. Latin America took on the role of the rebellious subject of the Third World. This was the time of the greatest cultural politicization the century experienced. Later on, as the intellectual desire to differ from orthodox models ran up against an implacable state centralism in Cuba, one of the most heated debates about socialism, democracy, and aesthetic creation would take place. Before

reflecting on this debate, however, we must consider three literary options offered by the new Revolution. The first can be seen in a novel by Alejo Carpentier (1904–1980) that contains a metaphor of emancipation–a drama of individual tragedy and historical optimism; the second is clear in a text by Miguel Barnet (b. 1940) that includes an ethnographic romance transformed into the odyssey of the moral ascent of an ex-slave; in the third, Jesús Díaz (b. 1941) describes the disintegration of a revolutionary dream because of the everyday traumatization of the individual–a story that relocates the conflict of subjectivity in those minor quotidian tragedies that in effect take away the heroic gloss of the revolutionary epic and make it merely one more authoritarian state in Latin America.

In 1979 the novelist Alejo Carpentier, one of the founding theorists of the new Latin American novel, developed an impressive macro-narrative. In an essay called "La novela latinoamericana en vísperas de un nuevo siglo" ["The Latin American Novel at the Dawn of a New Century"] he declared:

> nuestro novelista, deberá admitir ciertas evidencias molestas–y digo 'molestas' porque lo obligarán a aceptar tres elementos inseparables de la vida actual que la novela europea, ávida de asepsia, de distanciamiento, de fría objetividad en el enfoque de las contingencias humanas . . . se ha empeñado en desterrar de la narrativa, levantando, ante el novelista moderno, una muralla de interdictos. . . . [E]sos tres elementos son: 1. el melodrama; 2. el maniqueísmo; 3. el compromiso político. (1981, 25)

> our novelist will have to admit certain annoying pieces of evidence–and I say "annoying" because they will force him to accept three elements that are inseparable of present-day life which the European novel, keen not to be contaminated by reality with distancing and cold objectivity in its approach to human contingencies . . . has striven to eliminate from narrative, erecting a wall of prohibitions in front of the modern novelist. . . . These three elements are: 1. melodrama; 2. manichaenism; 3. political commitment.

His inclination toward manichaenism is based on a philosophical assumption, "El mundo es el teatro de una perpetua lucha entre el Bien y el Mal, la Luz y las Tinieblas, Ormuzd y Archiman" (27) ("The world is the theater of a perpetual struggle between Good and Evil, Light and Darkness, Ormuzd and Archiman"), and leads to a committed "pedagogy"–"la Historia toda no es sino la crónica de una inacabable lucha . . . entre opresores y oprimidos" (28) ("all of history is nothing but the chronicle of an endless struggle . . . between oppressors and the oppressed"). Carpentier adds that in a continent housing many different opinions, such as Europe, "la elección entre causas justas y causas injustas se hace sumamente difícil, . . . pero, en América Latina, la elección se vuelve sumamente fácil, puesto que se reduce a elegir entre dos posibilidades: 1. la de estancamiento . . .; 2. la de un progreso real en el plano nacional y colectivo" (28) ("the choice between just and unjust causes becomes extremely difficult, . . . but in Latin America, the choice becomes extremely easy, since it is reduced to choosing between two possibilities: 1. stagnation . . ., or 2. real progress at the national and collective level").

The arguments offered by Carpentier reaffirm a vision that has, in fact, fostered numerous ideological visions throughout the twentieth century. They aim to establish identity by demanding a macro-collective antidote to dependency and neocolonialism. In his opinion, this ideological principle is recognized in many literary texts as an intrinsic form of manichaenism, a sign that they must fight developed countries for the rights to progress: "Era todavía posible para un escritor latinoamericano, ser apolítico en tiempos de Rubén Darío. Pero, a partir de la Revolución mexicana . . . a partir del general despertar universitario de los años 20, ser apolítico es imposible para un escritor nuestro" (31) ("It was still possible for a Latin American writer to be apolitical in the times of Rubén Darío. But, after the Mexican Revolution . . . following the general awakening of university students in the 1920s, being apolitical was impossible for our writers"). Carpentier also wrote "[Es casi] 'inconcebible' que un tal compromiso político conllevara opciones derechistas" (29) ("[It is] virtually 'inconceivable' that such political commitment should have implied a Right-wing option"). The allusion to the Mexican Revolution moves from a specific reference to assume a more general historical meaning (31).

Carpentier's words set up an equation between cultural identity and a collective national identity, but a paradox soon became evident. By the middle of the century, modernity as a utopian discourse (or compensatory modernity as an aesthetic discourse) was increasingly undermined by the process of modernization that was accompanied by the anachronistic rise of the masses. As a result, the writer's politicization became not merely a problem of affiliation or non-affiliation with a particular political movement, but was necessarily inserted into the larger scale of cultural hierarchies and legitimacies. Underlying Carpentier's position is the supposition that there can be a homogeneous commitment that attempts to eliminate any conflict between the political revolutionary and the cultural elite. Here, he poses raising the question of whether "el compromiso político pone en peligro la calidad de la obra literaria o artística" (29) ("political commitment threatens the quality of the literary or artistic work"). To prove that this is not the case, he links—with diachronic abandon— Dante's *Inferno,* Eisenstein's *Battleship Potemkin,* and Picasso's *Guernica* as great works of political passion. From one paragraph to the next, he has changed his notion of politics.

The Latin American valuation of political commitment among writers and artists, based on then current post-Independence and pedagogical thought, is part of the context of Carpentier's penultimate novel *La consagración de la primavera* [1978; The Consecration of Spring]. Following the outbreak of the Cuban Revolution, which made him return to Cuba from Venezuela, his ideological position had been characterized by two contradictory assumptions. In 1962 he declared that his novels were not about any successful popular revolution, since he lacked the proper personal experiences to write about that. Shortly afterward, however, he balanced that view: "La Revolución cubana no me ha cambiado; yo la esperaba desde los días de mi juventud sin saber de qué manera iba a llegar" (1985, 160) ("The Cuban Revolution has not changed me; I had been waiting for it from the time when I was very young, without knowing what form it would take"). This novel was generally rejected by critics, in part because of its necessarily heterogeneous nature. But it is this artificial blend of autobiography, historical novel, melodrama, and a declaration of principles that reveals the unconscious drama of revolutionary universalism. Melodrama provides the structure of the main story. Two characters who share Carpentier's autobiographical wealth are the Russian Vera and the Cuban Enrique. Vera, a Russian ballerina from an upper-class family, flees the events of the October Revolution, leads an existence in Paris that brings her into contact with the Spanish Civil War and the advent of Fascism in Europe, and eventually arrives in the Caribbean where she witnesses the victory of the bearded ones in Cuba. Enrique, an architect and the son of a family from the Cuban upper middle class, is committed to the student protests against the dictator Machado and thus is exiled to Paris. He enlists in the Lincoln Brigade to defend the Spanish Republic, leaves Europe on the eve of the Second World War, and returns, with his lover Vera whom he met in Spain, to Cuba, where he helps conspire against Batista. In 1962, he participates against the invaders of the Bay of Pigs. Roberto González Echevarría attributes the failure of the novel to the fact that the writer fell into melodrama (282). Yet here melodrama is a consciously deployed form whose aesthetic potential lies, from the outset, in its obstinate lack of realism. When political events become conflicts within gigantic theatrical scenarios, a notion of history is evoked, drawn from previous works by this author, works that oscillate thematically between illustrative ethics and individual tragedy. Implying the metaphor of the great theater of the world suggests a *Weltanschauung* that sees the fatalism in human cycles. In order to place the Cuban Revolution in the period, forming part of a trio with the October Revolution and the defense of the Spanish Republic, the destiny of the protagonists is portrayed in melodramatic terms. Melodrama—a cathartic exploration of the unreal or the unlikely, of what is desired or dreamt of—is a sign of the political dedication of the novel. After experiencing the great historical events of the century, Vera and Enrique also bring an enormous amount of artistic knowledge with them to Cuba. And it is there, in the Caribbean, that this heritage acquires a new legitimacy: Europe was losing its hold on the universals of culture (Carpentier 1978, 81). This is also where Vera fulfills her life's ambition of staging Stravinsky's *Rite of Spring.* She produces an Afro-Cuban version of the ballet, a version in which "habría poco que añadir. Entenderían muy pronto la rítmica de Stravinsky, y se vería una danza realmente sometida a pulsiones elementales, primordiales, bien distintas de las birrias coreográficas que hemos visto hasta ahora" (262) ("there would be little to add. The [black dancers] would soon pick up Stravinsky's rhythm and one would produce dance that was really subjected to elementary, primordial drives, quite different from the choreographic rubbish we have seen so far"). The multicultural springs is what offers the right to reinterpretation here, but the Revolution also holds an ontological fascination (120). This ontological desire assumes a reflexive being-in-the-world under conditions of the market and cultural autonomy. It is the fundamental solitude of the modern novelist (as Benjamin noted) that makes one aspire to tellurian (186), outward-directed drives (136) linked to a "tengo la impresión de integrarme *en algo,* de hallarme a mi mismo *en algo* que, envolviéndome, arrastrándome, tonificándome, me trasciende" (120) ("far more copious and universal collectivity. I have the feeling of becoming incorporated into something, of finding myself *in something* which, by enveloping me, dragging me along and invigorating me, transcends me"). The novel reads like a veritable compendium of the politicizing of the spheres of art, like a didactic discourse that pushes the bourgeois intellectual over the threshold of Caribbean Socialism. From Vera's perspective the myth of origin is potent: "Miro y vuelvo a mirar a esos hombres de la Sierra y me parecen como gente de otra raza—raza distinta. . . . Acaso una raza nueva, capaz de hacer algo nuevo" (494) ("I look and I look again at those men from the mountains and they seem to me like people from another race. . . . It may perhaps be a new race, capable of doing something new"). At the same time, the Cuban Revolution was destined to confirm a totalizing view of history; revolution in peripheral countries authorizes a late, political universalism.

From Cuba, Miguel Barnet conceived a project that contributed decisively to the development and legitimization of the new Latin American form of testimony, a democratic mode of autobiography that emerges from an encounter with the informant. At its center lies a real-life character, who has been socially and historically marginalized, who lacks the resources, authority, and skill to make her- or himself heard. A hybrid text is created from a narrative encounter between a writer or an ethnographer (who brings the modern medium of writing) and a speaker whose oral memory reveals an other repressed by modernity. The concept appears to be genuinely Latin American because the anti-individualistic focus of this type of autobiography and the radicalization of an ethnographic position on oral history combined to create a new, literary utopian form.

In 1970 Barnet published his programmatic essay "La novela testimonio: socio-literatura" ["The Testimony Novel: Socio-Literature"]. Basing authority on authentic persons, and rejecting artistic formalism, he called for an integrated art that did not separate reality from fantasy, politics from religion or individual from collective memory (1970, 125–27). He attributed the supposed crisis in the Western novel (with the exception of North American literature) to the belief that for many years in Western Europe, there was no significant social movement or political explosion, and so literature had to reflect this innocuous state of things (128–29). The concept of the testimony novel reestablishes a fresh link between the literary (understood as popular stories) and those social facts that marked a watershed in the culture of a country (134).

Barnet's work, which, together with the well-known work of Elena Poniatowska and Elizabeth Burgos (b. 1940)/Rigoberta Menchú (b. 1959), indicated a shift to an alternative canon (Walter 204–5), was *Biografía de un Cimarrón* [*The Autobiography of a Runaway Slave*, 1968], published in 1966 by the Instituto de Etnología y Folklore (Institute of Ethnography and Folklore) of Havana. The author describes the background of his central character, the old former slave, Esteban Montejo:

> Así, el Cimarrón, luego de una infancia esclava entre cochiqueras y látigo, entra en una etapa de libertinaje al hacerse cimarrón; más tarde obrero asalariado y finalmente mambí. Es decir: esclavitud, cimarronería, patronaje, Guerra de Independencia. Cada uno de estos períodos ha dejado una huella profunda en la psicología del cubano, ha contribuido a formarlo, le ha atribuido una historia. Y no son hechos marginales, aislados, sino conmociones sociales, hechos colectivos, épicos, que sólo pueden ser reconstruidos en base a la memoria histórica. Y para eso nada mejor que un protagonista representativo, un actor legítimo. (134)

> Thus the runaway slave, after a childhood as a slave among pigsties and lashings, entered a phase of licentiousness when he became a runaway slave; then a salaried worker and eventually a rebel. In other words: slavery, running away, becoming a boss, and the War of Independence. Each of these periods has left a deep mark on the psychology of the Cuban, has helped train him and given him a history. And these are not marginalized, isolated facts, but social upheavals, collective, epic events that can only be reconstructed on the basis of historical memory. And what could be better for this than a representative protagonist, a legitimate actor?

The history of the "informant" Esteban Montejo, 104 years old when Barnet interviewed him between 1964 and 1965, was admittedly unusual, atypical, and ideal, since his biography was linked to historically decisive events of over half a century. The discovery of this person inaugurated an ethical project, in which the narrator of the history had to be the person who legitimately participated in it. Thus, *Cimarrón* provides a detailed account of an historical world with lots of interruptions and chronological leaps, yet with a continuity guaranteed by morally admirable aspects of a very human rebellion against the inhumanity of slavery.

The narrative development of the novel avoids being schematic about the revolution and succeeds in elucidating rebellious awareness as a way of life for black people in Cuba. The protagonist's belief in social liberation and national independence is based on very "simple truths." When the autobiographical voice of the runaway slave refers to the end of the War of Independence and in particular, to the so-called guerrilla death groups that had fought on behalf of colonial power, he clarifies his notion of justice:

> Antes de la guerra yo conocí a muchos guapos; guapos de pueblo que vivían del truco. Eran hombres ambulantes y los sábados y domingos se fajaban y alardeaban y buscaban odios y se emborrachaban. . . . Casi todos esos hombres, negros y blancos, fueron guerrilleros. No tenían otra salida. Sabían que la guerra no era cosa de juego y buscaban la comodidad. León era uno de ellos, fue práctico de las guerrillas y había sido amigo íntimo, uña y carne, de Valentín el Verdugo, el que mató a medio mundo en el garrote. Esos eran los guerrilleros. . . .
> Cuando me pongo a pensar en estos hombres sin madre, mientras uno estuvo peleando con hambre, metido en el fango, y en toda la podredumbre de la guerra, me dan ganas de guindarlos. Lo más triste es que en Cuba nunca se castigaron guerrilleros. El propio Máximo Gómez los quiso igualar. Dicen que eso era por conveniencia. Pero yo digo la verdad, a mí no me convence esa palabra de conveniencia. Yo le hubiera dado paredón a esos hombres. . . .
> Y no acabo de entender, nunca lo entendí, por qué Máximo Gómez dijo en la Quinta de los Molinos, al acabarse la guerra, que en Cuba no había vencidos ni vencedores. Esa fue la frase. Yo la oí, porque estuve presente en ese discurso.
> (Barnet 1966, 199–200)

Before the war I knew lots of roughs, village roughs who lived by trickery of one sort or another. They were drifters, bums, and on Saturdays and Sundays they made trouble and boasted and got into fights and got drunk. Almost all those men, blacks as well as whites, became guerrillas. It was the only way out for them. They knew war wasn't a game, and they wanted safety. León was one of them, he acted as guide to the guerrillas and he was once the intimate, hand-in-glove friend of Valentín, the executioner, who must have bumped off a hell of a lot of people with the garrote. That's what the guerrillas were like. . . .
When I think of those bastards, at a time when people like me were fighting against hunger, struggling through mud and all the foul stink of war, I feel like hanging the lot of them. But the sad thing is they never punished the guerrillas in Cuba. Máximo Gómez even tried to make them equal with the rest of us. He said this was only for convenience, but I'm telling you, that word "convenience" doesn't impress me. I would have given them the same treatment the murderers in the last government got. . . . And I never have and never will understand why Máximo Gómez said, in his speech at Quinta de los Molinos at the end of the war, that in Cuba there were neither victors nor vanquished. That was what he said. I heard him say it, because I was there at the time.
(1966b, 209–10)

This "participatory" narration of the historical emancipation of Cuba acquires its thickness through revealing the political elements in the disorder of everyday social normality. But Barnet's gesture goes beyond this, seeking to convert the narrative of lived experience into foundational literature, to go from the exclusive Latin American *I* to the inclusive Latin American *we* (1983, 19). Anyone who has read *Biografía de un cimarrón* will be astonished to find the following phrase in his programmatic essay "La novela testimonio": "las consecuencias del fenómeno son más importantes que el fenómeno mismo; su presente es más importante que ser pasado" (1970, 138) ("the consequences of the phenomenon are more important then the phenomenon itself: its present is more important than the past"). This is followed by: "Debemos superar la sociología, el didactismo, con personajes que encarnen su época.... [N]uestros personajes como tales deben permanecer, sobreviviendo a su tiempo. Deben servir como hitos para un futuro distinto y nuevo" (1970, 41) ("We must go beyond sociology and didacticism, with people who embody their era.... [O]ur characters as such must remain, surviving their time. They must serve as landmarks for a distinct, new future"). This establishes an obligatory secondary referent reflecting a greater need, to build a bridge between the marginal in history, between the Socialist Cuban nation in a more just international situation. The novel *Cimarrón* speaks for itself, with the voice of the unusual experience of a subaltern subject who becomes a macrohistorical protagonist.

The life of Esteban Montejo was not, as subsequently proved, as honestly accounted as the testimonial narrativization of Miguel Barnet suggested. Studying archives in Havana in the early 1990s, Michael Zeuske was able to suggest a different view of the character. He confirms his spectacular participation in the Wars of Independence, while questioning the writer's omission of nearly sixty years of a long life. Zeuske notes that a rebellious attitude was not the only thing to condition the former slave's life. He also established pacts with doubtful village chieftains and sought to obtain small financial advantages that led him to make the occasional opportunistic decision (57). This fact does not make Barnet's experiment any less noteworthy, for it shows, on the contrary, the affinities and resistance of popular culture to ideology. The testimony novel is a shared narration whose logic is intercultural; it seems to resist the hegemonic assimilating of difference into a telos of revolution. Certain questions remain unanswered: Do the practices of self-representation of the socially and culturally other actually manage to drive the various testimonial projects? Or do they simply generate a new model of intellectual appropriation that, through the ethnographically committed gesture, proves to be an even more refined version of colonial discourse? Finally, can a construct of identity shared by the writer and the social informant really exist, when they have diverse ideological cultures? And how does one analyze these literary epistemologies that demand that the literary be rethinking against literature itself? (See Beverley 99.) These questions demand a radical relocation of the coordinates that locate Latin American imaginaries within literary history—as was implied, of course, by the narrative project of Subcommander Marcos in Chiapas.

In their writings mentioned above, Carpentier and Barnet projected a revolutionary awareness (in the present) onto prerevolutionary contexts (in the past). In contrast, Jesús Díaz (b. 1941) explored the Cuban Revolution within its own context; *Las iniciales de la tierra* [1986; The Initials of the Land] is a novel that takes place within the very experiences of the Revolution. One of the inaugural principles proclaimed by Fidel Castro in "Palabras a los intelectuales" ["Words to Intellectuals"] in 1961 states: "Dentro de la Revolución, todo; contra la Revolución ningún derecho" (11) ("Within the Revolution, everything; against the Revolution there are no rights"). This was conceived, at the beginning of the Revolution, as the basis for a cultural policy that would permit a broad consensus among different positions. In *Las iniciales de la tierra*, Díaz took up that initial premise, searching behind the famous commonplace for the conflicts that, within the Revolution, were experienced personally and artistically. The novel may be intended as an antidote to another one which, published in the extremely difficult year of 1971, had become an example of socialist realism: *La última mujer y el próximo combate* [1971; The Last Woman and the Next Battle] by Manuel Cofiño (1936–1987). In Cofiño's book, the individual eventually finds the meaning of life in the (fulfilling) act of participation in agrarian reform, in the armed defense against the invaders of Playa Girón, and in the collective shift from superstition to revolutionary rationalism. Conversely, for the protagonist of *Las iniciales*, participatory commitment gives rise to an individual attempt at subjective appropriation.

Here, Carlos Pérez, the son of a landowner, is 18 years old in 1959. It is a time when he watches the heroes who fight for justice and love and who peopled his childhood imaginary move from the cinema screen to real life. The conflicts of the early years emerge, particularly those of a violently politicized university, while the pressure of the American-led blockade and the threat of invasion lead to the rapid formation of a Socialist state in Cuba. Díaz describes how the political changes from 1959 to 1970 exercise a powerful influence on personal experience. Fragments from a series of memories show Carlos in the Revolutionary Militia, at military school, as a student of architecture, and as a worker at a center for international studies. He dreams of joining a Latin American guerrilla group and, as a self-sacrificing reaction to the death of Che, decides to work in the sugar harvest for three consecutive years, until the highly publicized dramatic sugar harvest of 1970. He occupies positions of political responsibility in all spheres, and eventually finds himself at a hearing of the Communist Party Assembly that will decide whether he deserves to be called an exemplary worker and incorporated into a military cadre. At the end of the novel, the result of this collective hearing is left open. Carlos's story is chaotic in that he seems to leap from one revolutionary challenge to the next, but it is coherent as search for constant ethical and social standards in the midst of a confusion caused by the changes in society. The ambiguity of the main character lies in the fact that he likes the advantages that life offers him, while at the same time feeling irritated by the opportunism made possible by State bureaucracy. When Carlos has to consult a physician, he realizes that

padecía de un mal infantil que entre los adultos solía tener consecuencias desastrosas. Y lo peor era que lo había atacado en su variante china, desgraciadamente la más virulenta y la que mayor índice de morbilidad estaba causando entre nosotros. Sufría ... el Síndrome del Izquierdismo, una enfermedad psíquico-política común, pero muy perniciosa; por suerte, en su caso no venía acompañada de ciertas manifestaciones parásitas como el oportunismo, aunque sí de una fortísima incidencia egolátrica que, por otra parte, no era lo peor. Todo jóven soñaba con ser un héroe, luego la vida hacía su trabajo. (Díaz 267)

he was suffering from a childhood illness that usually had disastrous consequences among adults. And the worst of it all was that he had caught the Chinese strain, which was unfortunately the most virulent and the one that had caused the highest rate of mortality among us. He was suffering from ... the Leftist Syndrome, a common psycho-political disease that was highly pernicious. Fortunately, in his case, the disease was not accompanied by certain parasitic manifestations such as opportunism, although it did have an extremely high incidence of egotism which, on the other hand, was not the worst. Every young man dreamed of becoming a hero, then life took its toll.

Jesús Díaz not only presented a dramatized narration but also cultivated his documentary obsession. He noticed how the ideological became part of the scenes of life itself, and so combined in his work the most contradictory aspects of Cuba's experiment in social modernity: direct support of the heroism that emanated from the figures of Fidel and Che Guevara (making possible the effectiveness of the foundational myth), a personal identification with the precariousness produced by military defense and the economic struggle against the U.S. embargo (establishing the compensatory myth of resistance), and an unusual, effervescent, popular-democratic sense of subjectivity in the midst of the forced centralization of the Socialist state. What from an external rationalizing perspective might constitute either an aberration or an anti-democratic sign was transformed, within the internal imaginary of the novel, into something inevitable, in other words, the revolutionary disease.

The narration ends at the point where a political apparatus that functioned in institutions, workplaces, and neighborhoods, and that was in a phase of social naturalization, prepared to rediscipline people. The mechanism of "tell-me-your-life" to a legitimate group of male and female comrades involved detecting the thread of a politically correct life, through marginalization, those who admitted ideological weakness, self-sufficiency, or sectarianism. Carlos seeks the approval of the collectivity gathered there and talks frankly of the ambiguities of his life. If Carlos emerges purified from this ritual—and this remains unclear—his life as an individual will be restricted, although in keeping with the collectivity of believers; he will experience tragedy as a social need.

The disciplining apparatus turns out to promote a sexist ideology and a rhetoric of the double standard: Carlos is also judged for having made love to a secretary while occupying an important post. At the level of stereotype, here is a sacred law of the tribe of which every Cuban is aware (403): machismo, in its purest form. A comrade reproaches Carlos for having violated this law by going back to his ex-wife Gisela after she too has engaged in extramarital relations: "Cómo concebir un revolucionario cornudo y contento? Ser revolucionario era ser hombre a todo, macho, varón, masculino, pingú hasta la muerte" (326) ("How could a revolutionary possibly be cuckolded and happy? Being a revolutionary meant being a man above all, macho, male, masculine, promiscuous until his deathbed"). When Gisela confessed she had been with another man,

> Carlos sabía que estaba obligado a divorciarse. Imaginó a Gisela engañándolo tantas veces como él la había engañado a ella, o peor aún, haciéndolo y diciéndoselo, y pensó por un instante que se había acostado con un negro o con un extranjero y sintió un fortísimo dolor en el pecho. No, no le salía de los mismísimos verocos aguantar eso porque, gracias a Dios, había nacido macho, blanco y cubano, y por lo mismo tampoco iba a serle fiel a ninguna mujer. A cada buena hembra que se le pusiera a tiro, china, negra o blanca le daría jan, pero la suya, su esposa, tendría que andar al hilo, derechita derechita. El no era el hombre nuevo ni un carajo para aceptar ese igualitarismo que cualquiera podría confundir con mariconería. (327–28)

Carlos knew he was obliged to get a divorce. He imagined Gisela cheating on him as often as he had cheated on her, or worse still, doing it and then telling him about it, and he thought for a moment that she had slept with a black man or a foreigner and felt a sharp pain in his chest. No, he wouldn't put up with that because, thank God, he had been born male, white, and Cuban, and as a result, he wasn't going to be faithful to any woman. He'd lay any good-looking female, whether Chinese, black, or white, but his wife would have to toe the line. He wasn't a new man or a namby-pamby who would put up with that sort of equality that could well be mistaken for effeminacy.

Yet thanks to Gisela, Carlos manages to reduce his macho obsession and begins to wonder about whether both sexes should have the same rights, if one wishes to assume major revolutionary changes as changes in one's life. And it is precisely at this public-personal intersection that the novelist places the most sensitive ideological critique, a critique directed at the Revolution. What Carlos has learned—so painfully—so as not to sacrifice his personal happiness—runs the risk of appearing to be male weakness. It may cost him the approval of the assembly, which seems to be dominated by macho discourse of the male comrades. Here, ideology speaks frankly. The male position in the private and public domains is an important factor in Cuban society, its most distinctive popular element. And the popular is, throughout the country, a source of the particular strength of revolutionary change. On the one hand, in the words of Miguel Barnet, the Revolution needs the living source of popular memory that reflects resistance to suppression and intolerance, and authorizes subjects neglected by history. At the same time, the fact of "having been born male, white, and Cuban" speaks of a common revolutionary spirit. Upholding, at all costs, an order that coercively institutionalizes one definition of social justice for the majority of the population and yet taking part in the fight against intolerance, exclusion, and racism—this creates a vicious circle that both female and male writers, like other Cuban artists, continue to endure to this day. (The film *Fresa y chocolate* [1993; Strawberry and Chocolate] by Tomás Gutiérrez Alea and Juan Carlos Tabio has only recently been able to raise the issue of homosexuality publicly in Cuba.) *Las iniciales de la tierra* is a postmodern novel, in both the artistic and the political sense. The problems it explores reveal a microanalysis of Socialist power, worthy of the precision of Michel Foucault (1926–1984). Its fragmented style captures and transmits a traumatic experience that could well mark the threshold of the pathology of the system. If Díaz leaves the ending open, failing to disclose the comrades' judgment of Carlos, then this is a calculated move: Decisions matter little when performance guarantees the ideological mechanism—the modeling of a collective subconscious.

A decade after its beginning, the Cuban Revolution had become the center of a heated intellectual debate. A second, pro-Socialist experience had emerged in the Southern Cone—a project implemented by the Unidad Popular de Chile [1970–1973; Popular Unity of Chile]. At the same time, as a result of the Soviet invasion of Prague, socialist states in Europe were experiencing what one might call a certain loss of legitimacy. In November 1970, shortly after the Socialist Salvador Allende had assumed the presidency in Chile, the writer Jorge Edwards (b. 1931) was sent to Cuba. His diplomatic mission was to renew official relations between the two countries. With the exception of Mexico, which had not followed the decision of the Organization of American States in

1964, Chile was the first Latin American country to break the Cuban embargo. Edwards provided a detailed account of the events that took place from his arrival until he left Havana four months later. The memories of his diplomatic odyssey, which proved to be a diplomatic failure, were published as *Persona non grata* (1974). In the introduction, Edwards writes:

> Era uno de los momentos más difíciles de la Revolución, un momento en que las ilusiones de los primeros años se estrellaban contra realidades económicas implacables. En esa situación, mientras observaba los comienzos de la experiencia chilena desde el interior de la crisis cubana, me tocó vivir en carne propia, en la doble condición de escritor y diplomático que tenía entonces, el conflicto dramático entre la razón de Estado y las razones o sinrazones del pensamiento independiente y de la creación artística. (1973, 9–10)

> It was a very difficult time for the Revolution, as the illusions of the early years came up against harsh economic realities. It fell to me then, in my dual capacity as writer and diplomat, to watch the early days of Chile's new experience from inside a crisis-torn Cuba, and to experience personally the harrowing conflict between the interests of the state and the sometimes irrational demands of independent thought and creation. (1977, 1)

This book has been virtually ignored by historians of the Revolution. Edwards's subjective assessment, affected by the complicated political relations between Cuba and Chile, involved articulating the incongruities between these revolutionary projects and showing the degree to which certain assumptions had changed as a result of the shift from utopian ideals to implacable social and geopolitical realities. The wave of euphoria that had lasted throughout the 1960s had practically disappeared by the time he arrived. The symbolic fascination of a relatively monolithic conception of revolutionary commitment had become an anachronism thanks to the enormous practical obstacles that threatened Cuba.

A selection of poems by Pablo Neruda (1904–1973) marked the *literary* inauguration of the "long decade of the 1960s" as a decade of "Revolution" (whose historical limits stretched from 1959 to 1973). The poems were composed between January and April of 1960 in the weeks after the triumph of the rebel army over the dictator Batista. In *Canción de gesta* [*Epic Song*], he wrote, "fui el primer poeta que dedicó un libro entero a enaltecer la Revolución Cubana" (1993, 445) ("I was the first poet to dedicate a whole book to the Cuban Revolution"). By the time he wrote the prologue to the 1968 edition, however, he was already fairly bitter (see 1993, 441–46). Yet his disillusionment with the Cuban authorities did not dampen his enthusiasm for the Cuban Revolution, which he continued to defend until his death five years later.

In these poems, which provided the euphoric prelude to the politicization of the decade, it seemed one could "touch Utopia with one's hands." Neruda, in honor of the Sierra Maestra, asks:

> "Un minuto cantando para Sierra Maestra"
> por una vez toda la voz de América,
> sólo un minuto de profundo canto
> . . .
> Bajaron invencibles los barbudos
> a establecer la paz sobre la tierra
> . . .
> por eso pido este minuto unánime
> para cantar esta Canción de Gesta
> y yo comienzo con estas palabras
> para que se repitan en América

> 'Abrid los ojos, pueblos ofendidos,
> en todas partes hay Sierra Maestra'

> *(1962, 86–87)*

> "One minute to sing for the Sierra Maestra"
> for once the whole voice of America,
> I ask for only one minute of deep song
> . . .
> And invincible bearded men came down
> to establish peace over the land
> . . .
> which is why I ask for this unanimous minute
> to sing with all of you this *Epic Song*,
> and I will begin with these words
> that they may resound over and over throughout America:
> "Open your eyes, offended peoples,
> there is a Sierra Maestra in every land."

> *(1998, 83–84)*

Metaphors of nature and a sense of reverence for those who fought for the poor and the helpless, indicate the arrival of an era of fulfillment. In "La Gesta" ["The Epic"] he writes of:

> . . . el ejército puro de los pobres
> creció y creció como la luna llena

> *(1962, 18)*

> . . . the poor army of the poor
> grew and grew like the full moon

> *(1998, 20)*

In "Cuba aparece" ["Cuba Appears"],

> surge la mano de Fidel y en ella
> Cuba, la rosa limpia del Caribe.
> Y así demuestra con su luz la Historia.

> *(1962, 15)*

> Fidel's hand reaches forth and in it
> Cuba, pure rose of the Caribbean.
> Thus history with her light teaches us.

> *(1998, 18)*

This discourse, by "speaking on behalf of," becomes a sermon. It is a lament and hope about a cosmogonic view of eternalized injustice "in our pure land." In "Tierra central" ["Central Land"], he describes

> Pobre América en sangre sumergida
> a medio cuerpo en tantos cenagales,
> clavada en una cruz y con espinas,
> maniatada y mordida por los canes,
> despedazada por los invasores
> herida por torturas y desmanes,
> arrasada por vientos fabulosos,
> ventas sacrílegas, robos colosales.
> Oh delgada cadena de dolores,
> oh reunión del llanto de dos mares.

> *(1962, 22)*

> Poor America up to her waist
> in blood in so many slums,
> crucified on the cross, with thorns,
> handcuffed, gnawed at by dogs,
> ripped to shreds by invaders,
> wounded by torture and outrage,
> lashed by false winds,

sacriligious deals, massive plundering.
Oh narrow chain of sorrows,
Oh meeting place for the rush of tears of two oceans.

(1998, 23)

Faithful to this style, the poet speaks with the voice of a singer authorized by those subjects whose suffering is recorded in history as a mission of the future. This marks the point of convergence of expressions of a universal desire for modernity and religious metaphors shot through with the idea of continental and social liberation. In a monumental gesture of self-representation, Neruda expresses his own faith:

> Yo represento tribus que cayeron
> . . .
> pero yo continúo sus acciones
> y por toda la tierra americana
> sacudo los dolores de mis pueblos,
> . . .
> porque, de qué me serviría el canto,
> el don de la belleza y la palabra
> si no sirvieran para que mi pueblo
> conmigo combatiera y caminara?
> . . .
> mi poesía tiene ojos de aurora,
> puños de piedras y corazón con alas
> . . .
> a establecer la claridad del mundo
> y dar la luz a los que la esperaban
> y a acercar la victoria a los que luchan
> y a dar tierra a los que la trabajan.

(1962, 33–35)

> I represent the tribes that fell
> . . .
> but I continue their actions
> and throughout America
> I stir up my people's sorrow,
> . . .
> I mean, what purpose does my song serve,
> this gift of beauty and words
> if it doesn't serve my people
> to fight and walk with me?
> . . .
> my poetry has the eyes of dawn,
> fists of stone and a winged heart.
> . . .
> to establish clarity in the world
> to give light to those who hope for it
> to bring victory to those who struggle for it
> to give the earth to those who work it.

(1998, 33–35)

Ten years later, the paradigms of literary representation, literary authorization, and the belief that the Cuban Revolution was capable of crystallizing the standards of all those who longed for a fairer Latin America, had undergone a crisis. Among writers, disillusioned, even offended voices began to be raised (e.g., that of Mario Vargas Llosa), yet many other writers opted for a virtually unconditional solidarity with Socialist Cuba (such as Julio Cortázar and Gabriel García Márquez); there were other intellectuals whose skepticism regarding real Socialism had never ceased (e.g., Octavio Paz). The immediate incentive for a vigorous debate was the "Caso Padilla" referred to by Edwards, who had visited Havana in

January of 1968 and participated in the jury for the short story competition sponsored by the Casa de las Américas, which awarded the young Cuban writer José Norberto Fuentes (b. 1943) a prize for his "Condenados de Condado" ["Condemned of the Region"]. Another prize was awarded to Heberto Padilla (1932–2000) for "Fuera del juego" ["Outside the Game"]. In late 1968, Fuentes, Padilla, and Antón Arrufat came into conflict with the Union of Cuban Writers and Artists (UNEAC) and the army journal *Verde olivo*. They were accused of cultivating nihilist writings and engaging in anti-Communist behavior. As a result, as Edwards observed with some surprise, Padilla chose to continue to make his public appearances as a gesture of insubordination to the State (1973, 312–13). On 20 March 1971, Padilla was detained for thirty-seven days for "conspirar contra los poderes del estado" (Padilla 12) ("conspiring against the powers of the State"). He was subsequently forced to submit to an embarrassing public self-criticism. Edwards, in turn, whose mission as the first commercial attaché lasted from 7 December 1970 to 22 March 1971, had unwittingly become a "persona non grata." Official Cuba thought that the Allende government, whose triumph did not represent the political position of the radical Chilean groups that had thitherto cooperated with Cuba, had chosen a "bourgeois intellectual" for the diplomatic post (Edwards 1973, 409). Padilla had been addressed in the same terms. Edwards, who, on his arrival in Havana, was not sufficiently aware either of Cuba's internal problems (which culminated in the failure of the Sugar Harvest Program of 1970) or of certain coercive measures at the level of public behavior that State Socialism had introduced as normative rules, experienced his contact with the first Socialist revolution in Latin America as traumatic. His book reflects an asynchrony that is as real as it is irreducible. It describes the difference between the restrictive internal realities that the Socialist State established and the external expectations of all those who were prepared to see this Revolution as the model for an alternative to a dependent form of capitalism. At an everyday level, at the intersection of historical meaning, collective values, and practical identifications, Socialist reality was becoming inconceivable for many who had not learned to live through it and naturalize it from the inside. Edwards remarked that what proved least useful at this time was the widest dissemination of social principles–without a doubt in the early days of the Unidad Popular government, Jorge Edwards along with most intellectuals of all political persuasions considered the Cuban Revolution to be the political paradigm for the future of Chile. Although by 1970 the Castro government was in the midst of a crisis, the Chilean Left somehow managed to keep this situation from the Chilean public. Some would say that the Chilean propagandists were so successful that they were able to deceive themselves (Edwards 1973 and 1977).

One of the conditional and cautious sympathizers with Cuba was Julio Cortázar, who, shortly after Padilla's critique, in a discussion with Mario Vargas Llosa (b. 1936) and Oscar Collazos (b. 1942)–in *Literatura en la revolución y revolución en la literatura* [1970; Literature in the Revolution and Revolution in Literature]–maintained that the debate about revolution should not be based on totalizing criteria. Cortázar implicitly expressed his differences from another text that Vargas Llosa had published in 1966 entitled *Una insurrección permanente* [A Permanent Insurrection] (see Vargas Llosa 85–88). Cortázar wrote:

el papel del escritor *como crítico* varía fundamentalmente según que se esté situado en una sociedad burguesa, de la que el buen escritor es casi invariablemente opositor, o en una sociedad revolucionaria dentro de la cual el escritor ha de situarse constructivamente, criticando para edificar y no para echar abajo. Esta diferencia esencial, que muchos escritores de izquierda europeos no se deciden a comprender del todo . . ., no debe ser confundida con el problema de la creación en sí, por completo diferente de esa función crítica aunque ambas cosas puedan darse simultáneamente. (1970, 53–54)

the role of writer *as critic* varies fundamentally according to whether he lives in a bourgeois society, which good writers invariably oppose, or in a revolutionary society within which the writer has to operate constructively, criticizing in order to construct rather than to destroy. This essential difference, which many European Leftist writers have not yet fully understood . . . must not be confused with the problem of creation in itself, which is completely different from this critical function, although both things could occur simultaneously.

According to Cortázar, creation itself does not fit into a sociocultural and political context and warrants its own criteria of ferment, a multiform imaginary, and a certain nonconformism: "Pocos dudarán de mi convicción de que Fidel Castro o Che Guevara han dado las pautas de nuestro auténtico destino latinoamericano; pero de ninguna manera estoy dispuesto a admitir que los *Poemas humanos* o *Cien años de soledad* sean respuestas inferiores, en el plano cultural, a esas respuestas políticas" (1970, 44) ("Few will doubt my conviction that Fidel Castro or Che Guevara have provided the guidelines for our true Latin American destiny; but I am by no means prepared to admit that *Poemas humanos* [Human Poems] or *Cien años de soledad* [One Hundred Years of Solitude] are inferior responses, at the cultural level, to these political responses").

For Mario Vargas Llosa, the masquerade of the self-criticism of Padilla, his wife, and three other writers during the public ceremony of UNEAC provided immediate grounds for drawing up a letter of protest, together with several European writers, to Fidel Castro. The letter stated that the ceremony recalled the most sordid moments of the era of Stalinism, and ended with the following request: "Quisiéramos que la revolución cubana volviera a ser lo que en un momento nos hizo considerarla un modelo dentro del socialismo" (166–67) ("We would like the Cuban Revolution to return to what it once was, which made us regard it as a model within Socialism"). This direct criticism gained some force from the fact that sixty European and Latin American writers (including Jean-Paul Sartre) had signed the letter.

Edwards describes his consternation over the fact that, during the years of crisis, the revolutionary regime was unable to negotiate a consensus between the State and critical writers. His decision to publish *Persona non grata* was taken at the end of 1973 in Spain, after Pinochet's military coup had stripped him of his position as Neruda's secretary in the Chilean embassy in Paris (see Neruda, *Confieso* 464) and forced him into exile there. Neruda, meanwhile, was in Chile, where he was unable to survive the bloody annihilation of Allende's government.

The Short-Lived Chilean Socialist Regime and Military Authoritarianism: The Crisis of the Literary Institution and the Irruption of New Political Paradigms of Culture

The political sign of the neo-Liberal modernization undergone by Brazil, Chile, and other countries in the Southern

Cone–the shift from a revolutionary climate to a dramatic struggle for (re)democratization–indicated the collapse of previous models of collective identity. Various mechanisms then came into play in the change of cultural imaginaries. On the one hand, these countries experienced the imposition of military regimes–as a result of which, conflicts seemed to be exacerbated to new extremes. At the same time, they experienced the disintegration of the very possibility of commitment. The paradigms of a political imaginary on the continent, of either a nationalistic nature or involving a Socialist revolution, not only lost their practical validity but found their symbolic potential destroyed as well. These factors had a shattering impact on the very premises of a literary culture.

In Chile, following the presidential triumph of Salvador Allende (1908–1973) in September 1970, an anti-Imperialist policy had been declared, along with plans for the development of Socialism based on the rule of law. The Basic Program of the Unidad Popular Government proclaimed the acceptance of democratic conventions and of freedom of opinion, the press, and organization for all citizens according to the 1925 Constitution (40). This led to an almost immediate division within society, a kind of ideological hysteria. In the midst of their frenzied anguish, the middle classes expressed their fear that the middle-of-the-road policies produced by Eduardo Frei Montalvo's (1964–1970) reforms in previous years was threatened. A factual (if impressionistic) paragraph from the novel *La casa de los espíritus* [1982; *The House of the Spirits,* 1985] by Isabel Allende (b. 1942) gives one some idea of the situation:

Mientras el pueblo celebraba la victoria dejándose crecer los pelos y las barbas, tratándose unos a otros de compañeros, rescatando el folklore olvidado y las artesanías populares y ejerciendo su nuevo poder en eternas e inútiles reuniones de trabajadores donde todos hablaban al mismo tiempo y nunca llegaban a ningún acuerdo, la derecha realizaba una serie de acciones estratégicas destinadas a hacer trizas la economía y desprestigiar al gobierno. . . . El pueblo se encontró por primera vez con suficiente dinero para cubrir sus necesidades básicas y comprar algunas cosas que siempre deseó, pero no podía hacerlo, porque los almacenes estaban casi vacíos. Había comenzado el desabastecimiento, que llegó a ser una pesadilla colectiva. (1982, 307–8)

While the people were celebrating their victory, letting their hair and beards grow, addressing each other as *compañero,* rescuing forgotten folklore and native crafts, and exercising their new power in lengthy meetings of workers where everyone spoke at once and never agreed on anything, the right was carrying out a series of strategic actions designed to tear the economy to shreds and discredit the government. . . . For the first time in their lives, people had enough money to cover their basic needs and to buy a few things they had always wanted, but now they were unable to do so because the stores were nearly empty. (1985, 294–95)

Another, more recent recollection, by the sociologist Tomás Moulián, summarizes the contradictions of that change in society:

El carácter profundamente retórico de la Unidad Popular se revela . . . cuando se analizan los componentes de su aleación de poder: un poder jurídico débil . . . que no permitía procesar ninguna reforma por la vía institucional; un poder-saber fuerte como construcción teórica y capacidad comunicativa segmentada, que había alimentado desde la revolución bolchevique las ilusiones de millones de trabajadores, pero que le otorgaba el protagonismo histórico a una clase particular en contra de las otras clases, que no hablaba a nombre de universales comunes; un poder-terror inexistente, aún en las formas más débiles de la mera capacidad coercitiva. . . .

En el período de la Unidad Popular, en vez de terror, hubo tolerancia y libertinaje. Un gobierno constantemente superado por los grupos ultraderechistas o ultraizquierdistas que se tomaban la calle. Sin embargo, se produjo temor, porque el discurso sobre la organización del futuro Estado socialista (dictadura del proletariado) y sobre la necesidad (teórica) de la violencia atemorizaban, producían miedo. . . . El peso semántico de las palabras amenazantes . . . impedía[n] ver . . . lo que había tras las palabras. (23–24)

The profoundly rhetorical nature of the Unidad Popular is revealed . . . when one analyzes the nature of their political power: a weak juridical power, . . . that did not allow any reform to be processed by institutional means; a great power of knowledge as a theoretical construction and a segmented communicative capacity that, since the Bolshevik Revolution, had fed the illusions of millions of workers, yet granted a particular class historical supremacy over the other classes, which did not speak in the name of common universals; a non-existent ability to terrorize, even in the weakest forms of coercive ability. . . . The administration of the Unidad Popular was characterized by tolerance and licentiousness rather than terror, together with a government that was constantly outwitted by the far-right or far-left groups that took the streets. However, an atmosphere of fear was created, because the discourse concerning the organization of the future Socialist State (the dictatorship of the proletariat) and the (theoretical) need for violence, scared people and produced fear. . . . The semantic weight of threatening words . . . prevented people from seeing what lay behind words.

In Chile, the myth of the Revolution lost none of its luster. Its effect was both inspiring and disorienting in a society where the means for ensuring the cohesiveness of bourgeois society–law, education, the press, the various political groups, and cultural institutions–proved incapable, in their interaction, of promoting a revolutionary project. Following the nationalization of copper production, they did not even appear to continue guaranteeing the balance between the forces in conflict. The upheavals, the great expectations, the social fears, during the brief administration of the Unidad Popular, failed to be significantly reflected in literary texts; they only became important in literary terms when, after General Pinochet's military take over, writers were driven into a marginal culture world by hiding or the alien territories of exile. It was thus the central concern of Chilean writers after 1973, whether in exile or in hiding in their own country, to try to rescue the significance of Chilean Socialism and its promise to construct a new society that was based on fairness to all and privilege to none.

In Norbert Lechner's words, "En ningún país el fracaso de la visión heroica, casi prometeica, del desarrollo está tan a la vista como en Chile" (113) ("In no other country was the failure of a heroic, almost Promethean vision of development as visible as in Chile"); during the twentieth century, few societies experienced such a brutal destruction of an institutional literary system by a military dictatorship. The Unidad Popular had respected the bourgeois legislation and had legally exceeded it by permitting the explosion of an imaginary world of possibilities (Brunner 84). Its concept of opening up the spheres of an elite culture to the everyday use of poorer people achieved the greatest results at the level of the production, distribution, and consumption of books. Thus, the "task" of literature focused on a democratization of the public sphere according to fully clear and open criteria, on condition that high culture be made available for use by the poorer sectors

of society. During the period from 1970 to 1973, Chile was the country with the highest per capita consumption of books in the region (with the exception of Cuba) and was the second largest importer of foreign books (after Argentina). The publishing house "Zig Zag" was acquired by the State and turned, under the name of Quimantú, into a grassroots institution for this new cultural policy. A series of popular books was inaugurated, in which major works of Latin American and world literature were published in illustrated paperbacks. Costing the same as or even slightly less than a pack of cigarettes, these paperbacks were distributed by means of a broad system of kiosks, making them available to trade unions, Leftist mass organizations, and public demonstrations. Although the population's purchasing power had increased, there was a dearth of consumer goods, and so books found their way into the homes of workers, peasants, and the lower middle classes. While during the 1960s, the print runs of well-known titles of *belles lettres* had fluctuated between 2,000 and 4,000, they subsequently increased ten- to twenty-fold. A few months after the publishing house Quimantú opened (in February 1972) a million books had been sold. It was not unusual for 80,000 copies of a single title to be sold in a week. Between August 1971 and August 1972, in just two of its popular series, "Minilibros" and "Quimantú para todos," Quimantú published 5,700,000 copies, including works by Federico García Lorca, Jack London, Thomas Mann, Boccaccio, Nicholai Gogol, O. Henry, Mikhail Sholokov, Jules Verne, and Edgar Allan Poe (Skármeta 1977, 85–86). Quimantú also published the novels and short stories of writers who were committed to change, such as Hernán Valdés (b. 1934), Antonio Skármeta (b. 1940), Ariel Dorfman (b. 1942), Carlos Droguett (1912–1996), Poli Délano (b. 1936), and Fernando Alegría (b. 1918).

The political project of the Unidad Popular was linked to the strategy of making a system for the democratic production and distribution of books work within the framework of cultural life. At the heart of this "educational archaeology" (to use Michel de Certeau's idea) was a monolithic discourse, a kind of macro-metaphor. All Chilean men and women supposedly dreamed the same dream. And the profound, legitimate voice that spoke the essence of this dream was poetry: "Las batallas políticas han sido inseparables de la poesía. La liberación del hombre pasa a veces por la sangre, pero siempre por el canto. El canto humano se enriquece cada día en nuestra gran época de martirio y de liberación" (Neruda 1978, 421) ("Political struggle is an integral part of poetry. Man's liberation often flows in blood, but always in song. And human song is every day enriched in our great era of martyrdom and liberation"; 1983, 377–78). On receiving the Nobel Prize in 1971, Neruda declared:

Hace hoy cien años exactos, un pobre y espléndido poeta, el más atroz de los desesperados, escribió esta profesía: *A l'aurore, armés d'une ardente patience, nous entrerons aux splendides Villes.* (Al amanecer, armados de una ardiente paciencia , entraremos a las espléndidas ciudades.) . . . debo decir a los hombres de buena voluntad, a los trabajadores, a los poetas, que el entero porvenir fue expresado en esa frase de Rimbaud: sólo con una ardiente paciencia conquistaremos la espléndida ciudad que dará luz, justicia y dignidad a todos los hombres. Así la poesía no habrá cantado en vano. (1978, 434–35)

Exactly a hundred years ago, a poor but splendid poet, the most tortured of the damned, prophesied: "A l'aurore, armés d'une ardente patience, nous entrerons aux splendides Villes."

... I say to all men of good will, to workers, to poets, that the future of man is expressed in Rimbaud's phrase: only with fiery patience will we conquer the splendid city that will shed light, justice, and dignity on all men.

Thus, poetry shall not have sung in vain. (1983, 388–89)

Poetry literally "sang" when Neruda, during the months of the 1970 presidential campaign and later as the "poet of the Unidad Popular" traveled throughout Chile to recite his poetry, nearly always beginning with *Veinte poemas de amor y una canción desesperada* [1924; *Twenty Love Poems and a Song of Despair*]. This practice, which belonged to a poetic era from the past (Skármeta 1989, 103), aimed to restore literature to its oral status as part of a political mission. Neruda was famous and inspired people's hope for change, creating wide familiarity with the folkloric tradition of Chile. It is hardly surprising that his motifs of justice and dignity should have been directly assimilated by the new government as the beacon of a politically committed culture. But it overlooked the fact that modern secularization and differentiation had created in Chile different assumptions from those adopted by the Cuban Revolution at its inception. The paradox was that the democratizing project of Salvador Allende was based on Enlightenment pedagogical goals, with a faith in the revolutionary potential of literature, whereas in the public sphere, it was the various different mass media that interacted, and cultural consumption rapidly diversified.

With the implementation of the military state on 11 September 1973, Chile became the model for the neo-Liberal capitalist revolution, the model for the entry of a marginalized country onto the scene of globalization. The political opposition, driven into exile or hiding by the military regime, denounced the chaos caused by repression, destruction, and denial. But for many years, the Left underestimated the power of the projection onto reality of these new protagonists, who created the conditions for a technocratic modernization based on authoritarianism. Like the model implemented in Brazil under General Castello Branco in 1964, that of Augusto Pinochet declared its moral right to effect major utopian transformations ("Declaración" 20–24). Reading and the mass distribution of books were classified as subversive, luxury activities, according to its doctrine of national security. Books must be destroyed because of their potential to create attitudes, emotions, and ideas taken from foreign, hostile, or neutral groups acting against the national mission (Mattelart 419). The crisis of literature began during the coup with the search of the Quimantú publishing house and the burning of books, the repressing of authors and editors, total censorship, and the forced emigration of many of the lettered intellectuals; the crisis was prolonged through the atrophy of the country's literary institutions and the reorganization of the publishing industry (Mansilla 205): "Writers experienced a complex social collapse. It was an earthquake, a biological break, the collapse of the everyday atmosphere and further pressure on the respiratory organs that were forced to adapt to survive the fear, terror, insecurity and grief" (Skármeta 1977, 78). Because of the political exile of so many artists and intellectuals, this whole region (if one also includes Argentina, Uruguay, and Brazil) lost much of that sphere of human work in which the ideas and emotions of national identity had been defined.

In the case of Chile, the first five years of the dictatorship were characterized by political repression and the reorganization of social structures. The following years saw the spectacular domination of the audiovisual realm. In Brazil, this development had functioned as follows:

Tiro certeiro o da estratégia autoritária no primeiros anos de governo militar. . . . Certeiro e silencioso: deixava-se a intelectualidade bradar denúncias e protestos, mas os seus possíveis espectadores tinham sido roubados para televisão. . . . Enquanto isso, uma população convertida em platéia consome o espetáculo em que se transforman o país e sua história. A utopia do 'Brasil Grande' dos governos militares pos-64 é construída via televisão, via linguagem do espetáculo. Sem os *media* e sem público, a produção artística e ensaística de esquerda se via assim transformada numa espécie de Cassandra. Podia falar sim, mas ninguém a ouvia. A não ser outras idênticas Cassandras. (Süssekind 259)

The authoritarian strategy of the military government was absolutely on target. . . . Perfect, silent shot but a bull's eye: intellectuals were allowed to voice their denunciations and protests loudly, while television took care of its anchormen and viewers. . . . A population that had been turned spectators watched the show into which the country and its history had been transformed. The utopia of the "Great Brazil" of the post-'64 governments was constructed by television through the language of TV shows. With no media or audience, the artistic and literary production of the Left was transformed into a sort of Cassandra.

The brutality of the participants in the coup and the compulsory change in the notion of the public confirmed that in Socialist Chile, there had indeed been an important link between the literary and the popular. The Unidad Popular was unable to use this phenomenon to bring about political consensus, but its adversaries feared that its idea of a new social order might become a reality: the links between popular expectations and cultural legitimization (in other words, both pedagogical and learned) might prove too explosive. On the basis of this, the "Neruda" phenomenon can be understood as a broadly cohesive, rhetorical-poetic agency. Fascination with Neruda would reemerge during the 1980s in the imaginaries of writers as different as José Donoso (1924–1996), Isabel Allende, Antonio Skármeta, Volodia Teitelboim (b. 1916), Jorge Edwards (b. 1931), and various others. The new government of Chile combated "literature" as popular rhetoric, as an element of underlying, incalculable orality in the midst of a collective effervescence (and the presence of the trade union and students in the public sphere). The aim of the regime was to close this politically open "performance." In 1985, the poet Raúl Zurita (b. 1951) summarized the extraordinary symbolic force of the name "Pablo Neruda":

[La obra de Neruda] encarna todo el trayecto del movimiento popular chileno hasta su quiebre en septiembre de 1973, constituyéndose en el portavoz no sólo de un modo particular de escribir poesía, sino de todo un sistema de entendimiento que terminó por tener acceso al gobierno con Salvador Allende el año 70. . . . [E]l 'tono nerudiano' sobrepasó el ámbito de la escritura literaria para ser parte integrante de la retórica con que dichos movimientos acceden . . . al poder. . . . [L]a obra nerudiana se nutre de una realidad de clase y es apropiada partidísticamente, pero, a su vez, al nominar esa realidad, comienza a ejercer su influjo autónomo sobre ella y deviene de esa manera una causa más del desarrollo concreto que tuvo una historia. (304)

[Neruda's work] embodies the course of the Chilean popular movement until its collapse in September 1973, becoming the mouthpiece not only of a particular way of writing poetry but of an entire system of understanding that eventually gained access to the government through Salvador Allende in 1970. . . . [T]he Nerudian tone went beyond the sphere of literary writing, becoming an integral part of the rhetoric with which these movements gain access . . . to power. . . . Neruda's work is based on a class reality and is appropriate, as far as the party is concerned, yet at the same time, by naming this reality, it begins to exercise its autonomous influence over it, thereby becoming yet another cause of the specific development that had a history.

This describes an experience that contrasts with the claim of Cortázar in the debate with Vargas Llosa over Cuba. That one should not confuse a writer's immediate commitment to a revolutionary undertaking within the world of creativity. In Chile, within a climate of change, such confusions were widespread, a sign of the transforming power of a popular force in the conflicts of peripheral modernity. The military regime, which in turn provided access to the icons of the global market, set about neutralizing the agency of "Neruda"–the popular heroic capable of merging with the needs of a social movement.

> Al otorgarle al movimiento popular una retórica accesible, lo hizo más visible y, en cierto modo, se constituyó en factor dinamizador de ese movimiento. . . .
> [E]s en el mismo momento en que la retórica nerudiana y toda su secuela de consignas, afirmaciones y programas, entraba, por así decirlo, a La Moneda, . . . cuando el coloquialismo poético alcanza su mayor presencia y se carnaliza en prácticamente todos los ámbitos de la intelectualidad chilena. (Zurita 304–5)

> By granting the popular movement an accessible rhetoric, it made it more visible, and to a certain extent, it became a factor that galvanized the movement. . . .
> (I)t took place at the same time that Nerudian rhetoric and all its attendant watchwords, affirmations and programs entered La Moneda [Government House], so to speak, . . . when poetic colloquialism achieved its greatest presence and was embodied in virtually all spheres of Chilean intellectuality.

The mechanisms of ideological control introduced by the military government began with coercion and moved increasingly toward a specific control of all public means of communication. The use of censorship shows this process of the culturalization of a dominant ideology. During the initial stage of the dictatorship, censorship, unconditionally imposed, was part of a direct attack on literature. By 1977, censorship had already become a bureaucratized procedure operated by the Justice Department. By 1983, it was formally suspended, still during the dictatorship. The government was convinced that literature had been turned back into an hermetic, elite sphere. It had great faith in its ability to neutralize culture through focusing on consumption and television. With the growing participation of artists and intellectuals in audiovisual and media culture, a process of re-democratization also began to reemerge, but by the mid-1980s, it was still a long way from affecting political macrostructures.

Modern paradigms began to falter during the military regime; literary creation began to shape the outlines of a postmodern writing. In general, literature began to investigate the diffuse realities of the micro-politics of power, since the macro-projections not only produced fear and rejection, but also suddenly no longer said anything, lacking the capacity for language. However, it was not only a question of the deconstruction of identity-based referents and narratives; the matrices that shaped ideology had changed. What symbolic frameworks, what mediators would enable writers to connect with the new realities? Among those who managed to find a way are José Donoso, Isabel Allende, Antonio Skármeta, and Diamela Eltit (b. 1949).

José Donoso's *La desesperanza* [1986; Hopelessness] is a conceptually hybrid novel that does not really fit into the Donosian aesthetic universe in which critics have tended to place it. It emerged, after the writer had returned from exile in 1981, as a "narration of encounter" with an unknown Chile, a novel with mimetic features, a blend of memories, ideological references and a plot that dramatized psychological aspects–with obvious allusions to detective novels. The protagonist is from the 1960s protest generation, a combination of a political singer and a rock musician who was once the idol of Leftist demonstrations and who, after 13 years of exile, returned to an unfamiliar, phantasmagorical Chile. The date of his return, as "Mañungo" finds out at Santiago airport, coincides with the wake for Matilde Urrutia, the widow of Pablo Neruda (5 January 1985). Abroad, "Mañungo" had been the "profitable cliché" of the Chilean Revolution, a "cantante guerrillero . . . poseído por la potencia de su guitarra-sexo-metralleta" (14) ("guerrilla singer . . . possessed by the power of this guitar-sex-machine-gun"); in the eyes of those in the "new Chile," he does not represent them and is only a ridiculous mask. In the house of "La Chascona" in Santiago, the wake draws old friends of the Neruda family as well as a few somewhat questionable characters. Matilde Urrutia seemed to be the personification of dignity during the years of the dictatorship, a character from an earlier era whose world, at her death, ended forever; the wake becomes a performance where all nostalgias are mutually deconstructed. The person who questions the singer's image as inauthentic is a member of the Communist Party, "Lisboa":

> la aparición del ídolo, un ídolo de pacotilla . . . de yeso o cartón-piedra . . ., había alterado un instante . . . el recogimiento establecido en el patio, . . . y todos y todas . . . acudían a saludar y a tocar al astro como si se tratara de un icono milagroso. . . .
> Mañungo Vera se fue a Europa a triunfar con la palabra 'Revolución', aunque sin participar en ella como los exiliados de veras . . ., se fue transformando en el cliché del revolucionario más revolucionario de todos . . ., utilizó al Partido para hacerse carrera si bastaba recordar que fue gracias a una invitación del Partido que salió de Chile a un festival en San Francisco . . . un año antes del 11 de septiembre. Cantó con Joan Baez en esa ocasión. . . . Mañungo se constituyó en el 'super-palomo' de exportación, maniquí de muestra de las posibilidades de esa imagen que entonces parecían infinitas. (61–63)

> the appearance of the idol, a shoddy idol . . . of plaster or plasterboard . . . had momentarily disturbed . . . the group of people gathered in the patio, . . . and each and everyone of them . . . walked up to greet the star and touch him as though he were a miraculous icon. . . .
> Mañungo Vera went to Europe to triumph with the word "Revolution," without having participated in it like those who were really exiled . . ., was gradually transformed into the cliché of the most revolutionary of all revolutionaries . . ., using the Party to get ahead, particularly if one recalls that it was thanks to an invitation from the Party that he left Chile to attend a festival in San Francisco . . . a year before September 11. On that occasion, he sang with Joan Baez. . . . Mañungo became the "super dove export," a mannequin of all the possibilities of this image that seemed unlimited at the time.

The government official who expresses this view is obsessed with discipline and rejects any popular cultural discourse. He tries to use the funeral of Neruda's widow to help the Party recover its leading role: "Ese funeral . . . debía ser la primera manifestación política de la izquierda de un Chile en estado de sitio, un reto frontal al régimen, el planteamiento por fin de una resistencia activa . . . que el Partido debía encabezar" (66) ("The funeral . . . should be the first political expression by the Chilean left during a state of siege, a direct challenge to the regime, to finally put forward a proposal for active resistance . . . that the Party should lead").

The novel becomes an allegory of the political stereotypes that thrived in the Chilean Left. Neruda is dismantled as a monumental figure, yet no one stops claiming him as "theirs." At the time of this novel, a series of commemorative fictions had begun to emerge, such as *Neruda* (1984) by Volodia Teitelboim and *Adios, Poeta . . .* [1990; *Farewell Poet*] by Jorge Edwards. Neruda was re-assessed as an individual with foibles and the creator of commonplaces such as those described in *La Desesperanza*: "esta América nuestra a que nos había condenado la maravillosa poesía nerudiana era más nerudiana que verdadera" (Donoso 25) ("this America of ours to which Neruda's poetry had condemned us was more Nerudian than true").

The novel *Ardiente paciencia* [1985; *Burning Patience*] by Antonio Skármeta, written in the form of a film script (and in 1994 made into the film *Il postino* by Michael Radford), tells the imaginary story of a close friendship between the poet and his postman in Isla Negra. The starting point here is the everyday presence of *Veinte poemas de amor . . .* in the imagination of many young people. During the Socialist government, Mario the postman takes advantage of his closeness to the illustrious character to ask for some new poems for his beloved. The postman wishes to pass himself off as the writer of these poems, which leads to an amusing debate between the fake poet and Neruda: Whom do the poems belong to, once they have become public? And is literature capable of becoming a tool for helping to resolve practical conflicts in life? A friendship develops between these two characters from two different worlds, which helps the great poet to understand the culture of those who transform this marginal precariousness into a discovery of resourcefulness. The novel suggests "cómo lo político desborda la política, o al menos ensancha de tal modo su esfera que la vuelve irreconocible para los 'especialistas'" (Martín-Barbero 1994, 103) ("how the political goes beyond politics, or at least, broadens its scope to such an extent that it becomes irreconcilable for 'specialists'"). This change in the notion of the political, its decentering and dissemination through everyday spheres of action is one of the themes constantly taken up by writers in Chile and the Southern Cone during the decade of the 1980s.

In 1980, the Christian Democrat lawyer Máximo Pacheco Gómez (b. 1924) published the book *Lonquén* in Santiago; it was banned a few days after it appeared, but was re-published in 1986. It describes the discovery, in a mine fifty kilometers outside the capital, of fifteen bodies of people who had been assassinated and had previously been declared missing. The case was brought to the notice of the national and international press by the Chilean Church under Archbishop Silva Henríquez. Pacheco's principle of strict truth in his text was an ethical Christian response. The book includes literal transcriptions of the sessions of the trial; documents containing the Church's revelations to the Supreme Court of Chile; testimonies of civil and military figures; petitions from relatives of the victims; the verdict of the Supreme Court declaring the accused military men innocent; and finally, a newspaper column reporting the destruction of the mine as an incriminating piece of evidence. Bravery and a moral imperative had produced a text distinguished by its total objectivity. Yet it used such highly specialized legal language and ways of thinking that special knowledge was actually required to understand it. Pacheco's factual book, however, served as the basis for a political melodrama, *De amor y de sombra* [1984; *Of Love and Shadows*] by Isabel Allende. Its epigraph summarizes her credo: "Esto es la historia de una mujer y de un hombre que se amaron en plenitud salvándose así de una existencia común" (1984, 7) ("This is the story of a woman and a man who love one another so deeply that they saved themselves from a banal existence"; 1987, i). The "Lonquén" case reemerges as the center of the conflict in the life of a young intellectual couple, and was serialized on radio and television. According to *El Mercurio*, the novel version, written in Caracas, became one of the most successful best-sellers in Chile in 1985. In aesthetic terms, it is a hybrid text. Melodrama does not rule out the principle of resistance, although it does strip it of its usual rationale. In ideological terms, the book offers imaginary participation in the most dramatic conflicts of the present.

The warm reception of international critics for another Chilean writer helped ensure a new avant-garde voice. In the words of Diamela Eltit herself, "El hecho de intentar mantener un discurso cultural, centrado en los dilemas que presenta la escritura, me ha dado la paradójica mala fama de ser percibida como 'muy intelectual'. Y ese 'muy intelectual' no es de ninguna manera halagador, sino el modo de descartar un canal de comunicación" (1993, 24) ("The fact of attempting to maintain a cultural discourse, based on the dilemmas of writing, has paradoxically led to my being perceived as 'highly intellectual.' And being thought of as 'highly intellectual' is by no means a compliment but rather a way of rejecting a channel of communication"). Before becoming a novelist, Eltit worked with a group of writers and visual artists who were the first to organize, in the middle of the dictatorship, a public debate on social concepts of life and practical workshops to analyze the new intersections of art, media, and everyday life. Her first novel, *Lumpérica* (1983), contains a photograph showing her in a performance, cutting her arms. The anti-establishment aesthetics of this novel-scenario (an excessively fragmented text) demand an insider's sense of the traumatizing conflicts of Chile. Eltit conceived of the novel as a triple gesture; a gesture of separation that assumes the fragmented history of a fractured country; a gesture of performance in a public place at night where the protagonist performs (both in symbols and in language) with other people from the "lumpen proletariat"; a gesture of the increased marginalization of a female character. The incoherence of the text is expressed at the level of language (hybridization of languages and jargon), synecdoche (the protagonist who interacts with the lumpen proletariat), media (the theatricality of narrating); scenes are presented from different perspectives, and symbols proliferate (the creation of a ritual place within a sphere occupied by power). The novel creates a virtual spectacle, open to its own decentering: "Es revelador que *Lumpérica* (título que nombra una virtualidad: la saga por formularse sobre el lumpen, es decir, una contra-retórica) presente a su sujeto como un pre-sujeto, como una hipótesis en la intemperie, en la distancia promediada de la plaza pública ceremonial" (Ortega 56) ("It is revealing that *Lumpérica* [a title that names a virtual situation; the saga to be written about the lumpen proletariat, in other words, a counter-rhetoric] depicts its subject as a pre-subject, as a hypothesis in bad weather, in the average distance from the ceremonial public square").

Eltit wrote of the experience of the trauma of the forced marginalization that she faced as a woman and a literary figure. Her notion of protest opened up the text to the performance of a (counter-)act that was a ritual and intermediate discourse which consequently took literature to the edge of its own limits. Her strategy was to politicize writing as the subversion of any significant identity. It entailed a decentering of the media without utilizing the codes of mass culture. Did this imply an end to the possibility of ideologizing? Or was it merely an attempt to survive, an exorcism of the dominant culture, by a female Latin American writer? Perhaps this history of literary culture will finally put to rest the question of whether literature and ideology are ever far apart in Latin America. What we can say is that the cultural heterogeneity of Latin America is explosive in both literature and politics, as the twentieth century has so amply demonstrated.

Translation by Suzanne D. Stephens

Works Cited

Allende, Isabel. 1982. *La casa de los espíritus.* Barcelona: Plaza y Janés.

———. 1985. *The House of Spirits.* Trans. Magda Bogin. New York: A. A. Knopf.

———. 1984. *De amor y de sombra.* Barcelona: Plaza y Janés.

———. 1987. *Of Love and Shadows.* Trans. Margaret Sayers Peden. New York: Knopf.

Arlt, Roberto. 1995. *El juguete rabioso.* Madrid: Cátedra.

Azuela, Mariano. 1958. *Obras completas.* 3 vols. Mexico City: Fondo de Cultura Económica.

———. 1992. *The Underdogs: The Classic Novel of the Mexican Revolution.* Trans. Frederick H. Fornoff. Pittsburgh, PA: University of Pittsburgh Press.

Barnet, Miguel, ed. 1966. *Biografía de un cimarrón.* Havana: Instituto de Etnología y Folklore.

———. 1966b. *The Autobiography of a Runaway Slave.* Trans. Jocasta Innes. London: The Bodley Head.

———. 1970. "La novela testimonio, socio-literatura." *La canción de Rachel* [and] *La novela testimonio, socio-literatura.* Barcelona: Editorial Estela. 125–50.

———. 1983. *La fuente viva.* Havana: Editorial Letras Cubanas.

Bartra, Roger. 1992. *The Cage of Melancholy: Identity and Metamorphosis in the Mexican Character.* Trans. Christopher J. Hall. New Brunswick, NJ: Rutgers University Press.

———. 1996. *La jaula de la melancolía. Identidad y metamorfosis del mexicano.* Mexico City: Grijalbo.

Baudrillard, Jean. 1994. *Simulacra and Simulation.* Trans. Sheila Faria Glaser. Ann Arbor: University of Michigan Press.

Benjamin, Walter. 1974. *Illuminationen.* Frankfurt: M. Suhrkamp.

Beverley, John. 1993. *Against Literature.* Minneapolis and London: University of Minnesota Press.

Borello, Rodoldo A. 1991. *El peronismo (1943–1955) en la narrativa argentina.* Ottawa: Dovehouse Editions.

Borges, Jorge Luis. 1977. *Obras completas 1923–1972.* Madrid: Ultramar.

———. 1981. *Obras completas en colaboración.* Vol. 1: *Con Adolfo Bioy Casares.* Madrid: Alianza.

———. 1998. "The Mountebank." *Collected Fictions.* Trans. Andrew Hurley. New York: Viking.

Brunner, José Joaquín. 1988. *Un espejo trizado: ensayos sobre cultura y políticas culturales.* Santiago: FLACSO.

Campobello, Nellie. 1931. *Cartucho: relatos de la lucha en el norte de México.* Mexico City: Ediciones Integrales.

———. 1988. *Cartucho; and, My Mother's Hands.* Trans. Doris Meyer and Irene Mathews. Austin: University of Texas Press.

Carpentier, Alejo. 1981. *La novela latinoamericana en vísperas de un nuevo siglo y otros ensayos.* Mexico City: Siglo XXI.

———. 1985. *Entrevistas.* Ed. Virgilio López Lemus. Havana: Letras Cubanas.

———. 1978. *La consagración de la primavera: novela.* Madrid: Siglo XXI.

Castro, Fidel. 1968. *Oraison funèbre pour "Che" Guevara.* Paris: Eric Losfeld.

———. 1961. *Palabras a los intelectuales.* Havana: Ediciones del Consejo Nacional de Cultura.

Cócaro, Nicolás, ed. 1970. *Cuentos fantásticos argentinos.* Buenos Aires: Emecé Editores.

Cofiño, Manuel. 1971. *La última mujer y el próximo combate.* Havana: Casa de las Américas.

Cortázar, Julio. 1970. "Literatura en la revolución y revolución en la literatura: algunos malentendidos a liquidar." *Literatura en la revolución y revolución en la literatura (polémica).* Ed. Oscar Collazos, Julio Cortázar, and Mario Vargas Llosa. Mexico City: Siglo XXI. 38–77.

"Declaración de principios del Gobierno de Chile." 1977. *Constitucionales: antecedentes y textos actualizados al 20 de marzo de 1977.* Ed. Eduardo Soto Kloss and Gustavo Fiamma Olivares. Santiago: Editorial Jurídica de Chile. 19–31.

Dessau, Adalbert. 1972. *La novela de la Revolución Mexicana.* Trans. Juan José Utrilla. Mexico City: Fondo de Cultura Económica.

Díaz, Jesús. 1987. *Las iniciales de la tierra.* Madrid: Alfaguara.

Donoso, José. 1986. *La desesperanza.* Barcelona: Seix Barral.

Edwards, Jorge. 1973. *Persona non grata.* Barcelona: Barral Editores.

———. 1977. *Persona non grata: An Envoy in Castro's Cuba.* Trans. Colin Harding. London: Bodley Head.

———. 1990. *Adiós, Poeta . . .* Barcelona: Tusquets.

Eltit, Diamela. 1983. *Lumpérica.* Santiago: Ediciones del Ornitorrinco.

———. 1993. "Errante, errática." *Una poética de literatura menor: la narrativa de Diamela Eltit.* Ed. Juan Carlos Lértora. Santiago: Para Textos/Editorial Cuarto Propio. 11–25.

Fernández, Emilio, dir. 1946. *Enamorada.* Perf. María Félix and Pedro Armendáriz.

Fox, Elizabeth, ed. 1989. *Medios de comunicación y política en América Latina: la lucha por la democracia.* Mexico City: Gustavo Gili.

Franco, Jean. 1967. *The Modern Culture of Latin America: Society and the Artist.* London: Pall Mall Press.

———. 1992. "Going Public: Reinhabiting the Private." *On Edge: The Crisis of Contemporary Latin American Culture.* Ed. George Yúdice, Juan Flores, Jean Franco. Minneapolis: University of Minnesota Press. 65–84.

Fuentes, Carlos. 1958. *La región más transparente.* Mexico City: Fondo de Cultura Económica.

———. 1960. *Where the Air Is Clear: A Novel.* Trans. Sam Hileman. New York: Ivan Obolensky.

———. 1994. "El estallido zapatista." *La Jornada del Campo* (February 22).

Gálvez, Manuel. 1956. *El uno y la multitud.* Buenos Aires: Theoria.

García Canclini, Néstor. 1982. *Las culturas populares en el capitalismo.* Havana: Casa de las Américas.

González Echevarría, Roberto. 1990. *Alejo Carpentier: The Pilgrim at Home.* Austin: University of Texas Press.

Greenblatt, Stephen. 1988. *Shakespearean Negotiations: The Circulation of Social Energy in Renaissance England.* Oxford: Clarendon Press.

Gutiérrez Alea, Tomás, and Juan Carlos Tabío, dir. 1993. *Fresa y chocolate.* Cast. Jorge Perugorría, Vladimir Cruz, and Mirta Ibarra.

Guzmán, Martín Luis. 1941. *El águila y la serpiente.* Mexico City: Editorial Anahuac.

———. 1965a. *The Eagle and the Serpent.* Trans. Harriet de Onis. Garden City, NY: Doubleday.

———. 1965b. *Memoirs of Pancho Villa.* Trans. Virginia H. Taylor. Austin: University of Texas Press.

———. 1967. *Memorias de Pancho Villa.* Mexico City: Cía. General de Editores.

Habermas, Jürgen. 1989. "Modernidad, un proyecto incompleto." *El debate modernidad-posmodernidad*. Ed. Nicolás Casullo. Buenos Aires: Puntosur. 131–44.

Herlinghaus, Hermann. 1994. *Intermedialität als Erzählerfahrung. Isabel Allende, José Donoso und Antonio Skármeta im Dialog mit Film, Fernsehen, Theater.* (Intermedialidad como experiencia narrativa). Frankfurt am Main.: Peter Lang.

———. 2000. *Modernidad heterogénea. Descentramientos hermenéuticos desde la comunicación en América Latina.* Caracas: Ediciones CIPOST.

Herlinghaus, Hermann, and Monika Walter. 1994. "¿'Modernidad periférica' versus 'proyecto de la modernidad'? Experiencias epistemológicas para una reformulación de lo 'pos'moderno desde América Latina." *Posmodernidad en la periferia. Enfoques latinoamericanos de la nueva teoría cultural.* Berlin: Langer Verlag. 11–47.

Hutcheon, Linda. 1984. *Narcissistic Narrative: The Metafictional Paradox.* New York and London: Methuen.

Kadir, Djelal. 1992. *Columbus and the Ends of the Earth: Europe's Prophetic Rhetoric as Conquering Ideology.* Berkeley and Los Angeles: University of California Press.

Kraniauskas, John. 1993–1994. "Rodolfo Walsh and Eva Perón: 'Esa mujer'." *Nuevo Texto Crítico* 6.12–13 (July–June): 105–19.

———. 1997a. "Introduction: Critical Closeness: The Chronicle-Essays of Carlos Monsiváis." *Mexican Postcards.* By Carlos Monsiváis. Ed. and trans. John Kraniauskas. London and New York: Verso. ix–xxii.

———. 1997b. "El fiord: The State and Literary Form." *Latin American Studies Association. Latin America Towards the Fin de Siècle.* Guadalajara, April 17–19.

Laclau, Ernesto. 1978. *Política e ideología en la teoría marxista: capitalismo, fascismo, populismo.* Mexico City: Siglo XXI.

———. 1990. *New Reflections on the Revolution of Our Time.* Trans. Jon Barnes et al. London and New York: Verso.

Lechner, Norbert. 1990. *Los patios interiores de la democracia: subjetividad y política.* Santiago: Fondo de Cultura Económica.

Lippmann, Walter. 1997. *Public Opinion.* New York: Simon & Schuster.

Lorenzano, Sandra, ed. 1997. *La literatura es una película: revisiones sobre Manuel Puig.* Mexico City: Universidad Nacional Autónoma de México.

Mansilla, Luis Alberto. 1979. "Reminiscencias." *Araucaria de Chile* 8: 203–11.

Marcos, Subcomandante Insurgente. 1994. *Primera y segunda "Declaración de La Selva Lacandona.": Comunicados: del 1 de enero al 23 de marzo.* Mexico City: El ejército. (June 10). < http://www.nodo50.org/pchiapas/documentos/selva.htm >.1

———. 1997. *Carta de Marcos a Emiliano Zapata.* (April 10). < http://www.fzln.org.mx/archivo/ezln/1997/marcos-19970410.htm >.

———. 1998a. "Tres mesas para la cena de fin de siglo." *La Jornada* (February 26).

———. 1998b. "Un periscopio invertido (o la memoria, una llave enterrada)." *La Jornada* (February 24).

Martín-Barbero, Jesús. 1987. *De los medios a las mediaciones: comunicación, cultura y hegemonía.* Mexico City: Gustavo Gili.

———. 1993. *Communication, Culture and Hegemony: From the Media to Mediations.* Trans. Elizabeth Fox and Robert A. White. London: SAGE Publications.

———. 1994. "Identidad, comunicación y modernidad en América Latina." *Posmodernidad en la periferia: enfoques latinoamericanos de la nueva teoría cultural.* Ed. Hermann Herlinghaus and Monika Walter. Berlin: Langer Verlag. 83–110.

Mattelart, Armand, and Seth Siegelaub, eds. 1979. *Communication and Class Struggle: An Anthology in 2 Volumes.* Vol. 1: *Capitalism, Imperialism.* New York: International General; Bagnolet, France: International Mass Media Research Center.

Méndez Asensio, Luis, and Antonio Cano Gimeno. 1994. *La guerra contra el tiempo: viaje a la selva alzada.* Mexico City: Ediciones Temas de Hoy para Espasa Calpe Mexicana.

Molloy, Sylvia. 1996. "The Autobiographical Narrative." *The Cambridge History of Latin American Literature.* Vol 2: *The Twentieth Century.* Ed. Roberto González Echevarría and Enrique Pupo-Walker. Cambridge: Cambridge University Press. 458–64.

Monsiváis, Carlos. 1970. *Días de guardar.* Mexico City: Ediciones Era.

———. 1977. *Amor perdido.* Mexico City: Ediciones Era.

———. 1978. "Notas sobre cultura popular en México." *Latin American Perspectives* 16.5.1: 98–118.

———. 1985. "De algunos problemas del término 'Cultura Nacional' en México." *Revista Occidental* 2.1: 37–48.

Moulián, Tomás. 1997. *Chile actual: Anatomía de un mito.* Santiago: ARCIS Universidad, LOM Ediciones.

Müller, Heiner. 1989. *Material. Texte und Kommentäre.* Leipzig: Verlag Phillip Reclam.

Neruda, Pablo. 1962. *Canción de gesta.* Montevideo: Editorial El Siglo Ilustrado.

———. 1978. *Para nacer he nacido.* Ed. Matilde Neruda and Miguel Otero Silva. Barcelona: Seix Barral.

———. 1983. *Passions and Impressions.* Ed. Matilde Neruda and Miguel Otero Silva. Trans. Margaret Sayers Peden. New York: Farrar, Straus, and Giroux.

———. 1993. *Confieso que he vivido: memorias.* Barcelona: RBA Editores.

———. 1998. *Epic Song.* Trans. Richard Schaaf. Falls Church, VA: Azul Editores.

Ong, Walter J. 1988. *Orality and Literacy: The Technologizing of the World.* London and New York: Routledge.

Ortega, Julio. 1993. "Diamela Eltit y el imaginario de una virtualidad." *Una poética de literatura menor: la narrativa de Diamela Eltit.* Ed. Juan Carlos Lértora. Santiago: Para Textos/Editorial Cuarto Propio. 53–82.

Ortega y Gasset, José. 1958. *Der Aufstand der Massen (La rebelión de las masas).* Hamburg: Rowohlt.

Pacheco, Máximo. 1986. *Lonquén.* Santiago: Aconcagua.

Padilla, Heberto. 1981 *En mi jardín pastan los héroes.* Barcelona: Argos-Vergara.

Parker, Allan, dir. 1996. *Evita.* Cast: Madonna, Antonio Banderas.

Paz, Octavio. 1959. *El laberinto de la soledad.* Mexico City: Fondo de Cultura Económica.

———. 1981. *Los hijos del limo: del romanticismo a la vanguardia.* Barcelona: Seix Barral.

———. 1961. *The Labyrinth of Solitude.* New York: Grove.

———. 1990. *El ogro filantrópico, historia y política, 1971–1978.* Barcelona: Seix Barral.

———. 1994. "Comentario." *La Jornada* (January 5).

Perón, Eva. 1978. *Evita: Eva Duarte Perón Tells Her Own Story.* London: Proteus.

———. 1997. *La razón de mi vida y otros escritos.* Barcelona: Planeta.

Perrone, Jorge. 1953. *Se dice hombre: novela.* La Plata: Ministerio de Educación.

Piglia, Ricardo. 1993. *La Argentina en pedazos.* Buenos Aires: Ediciones de La Urraca.

Poniatowska, Elena. 1984. *Hasta no verte Jesús mío.* Mexico City: Alianza Tres.

———. 1994. *Luz y luna, las lunitas.* Mexico City: Ediciones Era.

Pope, Randolph D. 1996. "The Spanish American Novel from 1950 to 1990." *The Cambridge History of Latin American Literature.* Vol. 2: *The Twentieth Century.* Ed. Roberto González Echevarría and Enrique Pupo-Walker. Cambridge: Cambridge University Press. 226–78.

"Programa básico del Gobierno de la Unidad Popular." 1970. *Índice* 280–81 (Madrid). 37–42.

Rama, Ángel. 1984. *La ciudad letrada.* Hanover, NH: Ediciones del Norte.

Reguillo, Rossana. 1995. "Chiapas: El otro rostro de la 'modernidad' mexicana." *Nómada.* San Juan, PR. 1: 3–10.

Rodríguez Monegal, Emir. 1978. "Tradición y renovación." *América Latina en su literatura.* Ed. César Fernández Moreno. Mexico City: Siglo XXI. 139–66.

Romero, José Rubén. 1957. *Obras completas.* Mexico City: Ediciones Oasis.

Sábato, Ernesto. 1969. *Sobre héroes y tumbas.* Buenos Aires: Sudamericana.

——. 1976. *La cultura en la encrucijada nacional.* Buenos Aires: Sudamericana.

Sarlo, Beatriz. 1988. *Una modernidad periférica: Buenos Aires, 1920 y 1930.* Buenos Aires: Nueva Visión.

——. 1992. *La imaginación técnica: sueños modernos de la cultura argentina.* Buenos Aires: Nueva Visión.

Sartre visita a Cuba: ideología y revolución. Una entrevista con los escritores cubanos. Huracán sobre el azúcar. 1960. Havana: Ediciones R.

Sebreli, Juan José. 1992. *Los deseos imaginarios del peronismo.* Buenos Aires: Sudamericana.

Sefchovich, Sara. 1987. *México, país de ideas, país de novelas: una sociología de la literatura mexicana.* Mexico City: Grijalbo.

Skármeta, Antonio. 1977. "Kunst und Kultur in Chile während der Regierung Allende." (Arte y cultura en Chile durante el gobierno de Allende). *Kunst und Kultur des demokratischen Chile.* Ed. Martin Jürgens and Thomas Metscher. Fischerhunde: Atelier im Bauernhaus. 76–92.

——. 1985. *Ardiente paciencia.* Buenos Aires: Sudamericana.

——. 1989. *Heimkehr auf Widerruf. Chile im Umbruch? Politische Reflexionen.* (Retorno condicional). München: Piper.

Sommer, Doris. 1991. *Foundational Fictions: The National Romances of Latin America.* Berkeley: University of California Press.

Süssekind, Flora. 1985. "Polêmicas, retratos & diários. Reflexões parciais sobre a literatura e a vida cultural no Brasil Pós-64." *Fascismo y experiencia literaria: reflexiones para una recanonización.* Ed. Hernán Vidal. Minneapolis: University of Minnesota Press. 255–95.

Teitelboim, Volodia. 1984. *Neruda.* Madrid: Ediciones Michay.

Valdés, Mario J. 1995. *La interpretación abierta: introducción a la hermenéutica literaria contemporánea.* Amsterdam and Atlanta, GA: Rodopi.

Vargas Llosa, Mario. 1983. *Contra viento y marea (1962–1982).* Barcelona: Seix Barral.

Vázquez, María Esther. 1996. *Borges: esplendor y derrota.* Barcelona: Tusquets.

Vitier, Cintio. 1997. "Martí and the Challenge of the 1990s." *The South Atlantic Quarterly. Bridging Enigma: Cubans on Cuba.* Ed. Ambrosio Fornet. (Special Issue). Durham, NC: Duke University Press. 96.1: 213–20.

Walsh, Rodolfo. 1965. *Los oficios terrestres.* Buenos Aires: Jorge Álvarez.

Walter, Monika. 1992. "El cimarrón en una cimarronada." *La voz del otro: testimonio, subalternidad y verdad narrativa.* Ed. John Beverley and Hugo Achugar. Lima, Peru; Pittsburgh, PA: Latinoamericana Editores. 201–5.

White, Hayden. 1987. *The Content of the Form: Narrative Discourse and Historical Representation.* Baltimore and London: Johns Hopkins University Press.

Zeuske, Michael. 1997. "The *Cimarrón* in the Archives: A Re-Reading of Miguel Barnet's Biography of Esteban Montejo." *New West Indian Guide/Nieuwe West-Indische Gids* 71.3–4: 265–79.

Zumthor, Paul. 1990. *Oral Poetry: An Introduction.* Minneapolis: University of Minnesota Press.

Zurita, Raúl. 1985. "Chile: Literatura, lenguaje y sociedad (1973–1983)." *Fascismo y experiencia literaria: reflexiones para una recanonización.* Ed. Hernán Vidal. Minneapolis: University of Minnesota Press. 299–331.

CHAPTER 50

IMAGINING NARRATIVE TERRITORIES

Lucille Kerr

When in the early 1960s Octavio Paz rhetorically posed the question "Spanish American literature or literatures?" (7), he was interrogating not only the relationships among literary works produced in Spanish American countries but also the stories that might properly be told about Spanish American literary production, and about developments during the twentieth century. Paz argued that "the multiplicity of situations, races, and landscapes does not deny the unity of our language and culture. Unity is not uniformity. Our literary groups, styles, and tendencies do not coincide with our political, ethnic, or geographic divisions; on the contrary, there are families, lineages, spiritual or aesthetic traditions, universals" (7). Notwithstanding Paz's answer and his eloquent argument in favor of the idea of a collective literature in Spanish America, Spanish American literature, and perhaps Spanish American narrative in particular, persistently returns to this kind of question. But this query compels a return not so much to a choice between the different responses implicit in Paz's question, but rather to a recognition of the complexity and diversity that have characterized Spanish American literary production. Consequently, Paz's rhetorical interrogation recognizes that Spanish American literature resists the homogenizing narratives and normalizing categories to which critics unavoidably turn to talk about literary tradition.

That the territory of Spanish American narrative is a difficult region to assay is perhaps all too clear from the diverse stories that have aimed to map its terrain. Many, if not most, of those stories have been formulated since the 1960s, when "the Boom" of the Spanish American novel occasioned new interest in Spanish American literature, and especially in Spanish American fiction. Some of the benchmark stories written around that period survey a wide area. They focus on the Spanish American novel, on short narrative forms, or on both, from their origins through mid-century and beyond (e.g., Alegría 1974 and 1986; Gertel; Goic; Leal; Sánchez) or target twentieth-century currents (e.g., Brushwood; Fuentes 1969; Rama 1986; Rodríguez Monegal 1972c; Zum Felde). Other versions of the Spanish American story told since the 1960s aim to expand, if not sometimes to revise, the standard narratives. Some propose comprehensive views of modern narrative traditions in Spanish America (e.g., Lindstrom 1994; Peden; Shaw 1981; Vidal); others concentrate on specific periods and currents or on proposed new ways to read individual texts if not also the critical stories told about them (e.g., Brotherston; Foster; González Echevarría 1985; Kadir 1986; Mac Adam; Ortega). Still others aim to tell stories about the theoretical and critical enterprises undertaken by Spanish American narrative itself (e.g., Borinsky; Echavarren; González; Kadir 1993; Kerr), or propose overarching theories about the whole of Spanish American narrative (González Echevarría 1998). That there are so many different stories, and also different ways of telling stories about Spanish American narrative literature, may well reflect not only the complexity of the tradition but also the resistance that tradition offers to conventional ways of talking about literary production and reception.

The difficulties presented by Spanish American narrative are perhaps more readily figured by the competition among the different taxonomic systems and descriptive terms to which literary critics have turned in their attempts to organize this unruly and heterogeneous textual aggregate. We recall that there is a variety of organizational models available for laying out any such history (e.g., genre, theme, author, period, movement, or school). Equally varied are the underlying concepts of division and identification that would authorize different ways to talk about literary production in general and the Spanish American tradition in particular (e.g., chronological order, geographical particularity, political history, cultural development, or critical ideology). Understandably, then, the response to a question such as the one posed by Paz might naturally aim to construct an all-inclusive narrative whose logical structure could persuasively account for and embrace the heterogeneity of Spanish American literature. Such is of course the task assumed in the telling of the story of any literary tradition; such order can only be imagined from without, from the field of critical reception, rather than from within, from the territory of creative production. If our critical narratives would have us imagine that the story of Spanish American narrative, for example, lies already constructed, if not encoded, within the space of literature itself, the Spanish American tradition would have us recall that the literary landscape, and especially the unsettling territory of modern Spanish American imaginative literature, cannot be easily contained within any one organizing story or taxonomic order.

The stories told about Spanish American fiction draw on the competing—sometimes complementary, sometimes contradictory—models of coherence that have traditionally been deployed to talk about the production and reception of narrative literature. The competition among different stories is also a competiton for authority over the territory's complex landscape, around which critics have plotted a variety of paths (e.g., generic, cultural, historical, thematic, or rhetorical). Such stories derive their authority both from the realm of the literary, where specific authors, texts, and currents appear already to have distinguished themselves in competition with one another either in the academy or in the marketplace, and from the domain of criticism, where different theoretical, ideological, and discursive models have at one time or another dominated the field. For example, Spanish American literary critics have talked about "old" versus "new" narrative forms, "Boom" versus "post-Boom" poetics (see, e.g., González Echevarría 1997, 243–53; Marcos; Rodríguez Monegal 1968–1969; Shaw 1998; Swanson; Vargas Llosa 1987; Williams). They have plotted the movement of different "isms," some deriving from European models (e.g., realism, naturalism, vanguardism) and some endemic to Spanish American literary culture (e.g., *criollismo, indigenismo, modernismo, realismo mágico, regionalismo*) (see, e.g., Chiampi; González Pérez; Rodríguez-Luis; Unruh). They have organized texts around thematic and discursive rubrics (e.g., *la novela de la tierra* [novel of the land], the novel of the

Mexican Revolution, *la novela del dictador* [dictator novel], detective novels, fantastic fiction, the "new" historical novel, testimonial narrative), identified works in terms of rhetorical properties (e.g., irony, parody), and grouped texts around authorship and gender (see, e.g., Alonso; Franco 1989; Jitrik; Lindstrom 1989; Magnarelli; Menton; Pons; Rama 1976; Simpson; Sklodowska 1991 and 1992; Sommers; Souza; Tittler). The proliferation of organizational models and critical vocabularies, themselves varied if not also unwieldy, may well occasion as much confusion as comprehension for a wide range of readers.

It could be argued that such proliferation of terms, concepts, and categories deployed to tell those stories is itself an important, if not necessary, component of the history of twentieth-century Spanish American narrative fiction. Indeed, from the turn of the century onward–through the ruptures represented by Spanish American *modernismo* (1880s–1910s), vanguard literature (1920s–1930s), and the new narrative (1950s–1960s and beyond)–Spanish American literature, and Spanish American prose narrative in particular, has been situated in an oddly consonant and conflictive relation with both the European and U.S. traditions and models. Spanish American authors have drawn on those traditions and models while also interrogating their underlying principles and practices. While recent literary theory has provided valuable methods for making sense of literary texts and traditions, the unruly nature of Spanish American narrative literature has also revealed the limitations of the modern critical concepts brought to bear on them. One might argue that it is precisely such disquieting aspects of Spanish American narrative–its difference from other traditions, its resistance to being described adequately by modern literary theory, and by Anglo-American or European vocabularies–that identify and define it, and in some sense also tell its story. The uneasy, somewhat asynchronic relationship between Spanish American narrative and the discourses available for talking about it has also shaped how the tradition has (or has not) been analyzed and explained. Spanish American imaginative literature seems always to be ahead of literary theory and criticism. Arguably, critics and theorists have neither yet imagined nor invented the concepts and terms that would be capable of entirely encompassing Spanish American narrative fiction (Kerr 21).

That critical discourse frequently has turned to metaphorical language, as well as to allegorical figures, to tell such stories is evident; and that concepts from the natural sciences (e.g., biology, botany, geology, geography) have often been privileged in the writing of literary history is also clear. It has not been uncommon for theories of literature and literary criticism to propose associations between the idea of literary development and biological evolution, or between the movements of literary genres and the cycles of nature, and to draw on the discourses, if not the methods, of science and related disciplines for their proposals (e.g., Frye; Wellek and Warren). If, in general, metaphors of nature seem to lend themselves well to the discourse of literary history, in the case of Spanish America they might seem a particularly apt way of speaking about its literary tradition. It may well be that such figures naturally fit the Spanish American terrain, given the images cultivated for Spanish America from the time of discovery until the present, not only in European and Anglo-American descriptions of fantasies about this part of the New World but also in the vocabulary of literary critics who have talked about its narrative tradition (e.g., González Echevarría 1988, 1–4, 42; Rama 1986, 26ff).

When appropriated by Spanish American writers, these figures of discourse have sometimes taken provocative turns to suggest diverse images for the tradition. For example, if Paz's essay implicitly recognizes the difficulties of telling the Spanish American story, it also deploys just this sort of natural metaphor as an organizing figure for that story at least through mid-twentieth century. This poetic figure, moreover, opens onto a field of related figures also well suited to the Spanish American story and to the continuation of the story Paz himself tells. In the response to his own question, Paz expands, a botanical figure, a critical commonplace, which had been used to characterize Spanish American literature as a branch from the Spanish trunk. Stating that the tradition that began as a branch "has grown so much that it is now as big as the trunk . . . [a]ctually it is another tree" (7), Paz appropriates this figure of subordination and turns it into an independent figure. This figure, capable of spreading beyond its own borders, might seem a natural one for representing the Spanish American tradition; indeed, Spanish American literature has continued to grow beyond that figure in the years since Paz's essay was written. The increased and ever-increasing dimensions of Spanish American literature have extended the field of that figure from the idea of an enormous and enormously productive tree rooted in a particular terrain to that of an abundant and abundantly varied territory whose perimeters it is difficult to set and whose forms it is difficult to seize. One might see this territory as unsettling, disorderly, precisely because it would resist as much as it would seem to require an organizing survey of its varied terrain. To settle such a complex territory, to differentiate or group together Spanish American narrative's constituent currents in one form or another–into a generic, chronological, thematic, or ideological body or combination thereof–is not, however, permanently to control or contain this tradition.

Spanish American narrative literature (especially its development during the twentieth century) is a territory whose internal borders have been remapped and whose ground has been recultivated principally from within, by literary production, but also from without, by literary criticism. It seems an unsettling territory precisely because it persists in producing unfamiliar forms and in shifting its terrain in unexpected ways; it persists in cultivating currents that counter as well as respond to each other, tendencies that combine apparently contradictory principles. Although the current cultural and linguistic borders of the Spanish American literary tradition may well endure if the tradition continues to be understood as comprising only texts that are written in Spanish and are produced by authors whose cultural formation is Spanish American, the generic, thematic, discursive, and structural boundaries of its narrative traditions are likely to shift in unanticipated ways (see Díaz). One might propose that Spanish American narrative (in and of itself as well as in relation to the critical systems brought to bear on it) alternately destablizes and institutes the discursive frames that would encircle it. The unstable divisions and distances according to which one might try to organize Spanish American narrative literature are instructive inasmuch as they draw the kinds of boundaries that Spanish American narrative ignores (in the etymological sense of "not knowing" or "not recognizing"), or refuses to respect. While Spanish American writers have persistently questioned the prevailing discursive, structural, and thematic borders of imaginative literature, critics have continually tried to draw new ones. Critical discourse has had to adapt to the complex changes within those borders, changes that regularly redefine the landscape of Spanish American prose narrative. But while Spanish American imaginative literature refuses a totalizing narrative, a master map, it may at the same time call for the telling of stories about that refusal.

Like other literary traditions, that of Spanish American narrative constitutes itself as a set of stories here told about Spanish America–stories that Spanish America tells about itself. Those stories speak about Spanish American history, society, and culture and about the literary culture that frames the production and reception of imaginative literature in Spanish America. Spanish American narrative in the twentieth century, like prose generally, has the capacity to tell all of those stories, or any story at all. The narrative tradition in Spanish America tells us how Spanish Americans have told stories about themselves and about their culture, and how they have formulated new ways of telling such stories. The variety of literary currents that inform twentieth-century Spanish American narrative at once responds to different narrative needs and creates possibilities for different ways to narrate. That variety, moreover, recalls that different types of stories about Spanish American culture and society have been privileged at different times; different narrative models have been valued for their capacity to tell certain kinds of stories. It also recalls that different kinds of authors, different narrative figures, have competed for authority and legitimacy within Spanish American literary culture as well as within Spanish American society. The voices through which Spanish American stories are told are the voices of specific authors and groups of writers, individual and collective subjects with different interests and claims, projects and positions, which during some periods have gained legitimacy, indeed hegemony, within the culture and which during others have been denied it. If prose writing in general produces a space in which a differentiated society's heterogeneity can be embraced or held together, and if narrative literature is the form of prose through which a culture can effectively stage its own differences as well as negotiate the distances between component currents and causes, the stories told by Spanish American narrative also tell the story of the differences and distances about which Spanish American culture has authorized (or not) its writers to speak (Kittay and Godzich 182ff, 205ff).

Like the development of prose more generally, Spanish American narrative does not have a linear history. Rather, its routes are sometimes simultaneous and sometimes overlapping; its currents are sometimes coherent and sometimes contradictory. Throughout the twentieth century many such overlapping and divergent paths have been visible, the competition for authority among them appreciable. For example, in the first two decades of the century the aestheticizing principles and practices of *modernista* prose overlapped, and competed, with the poetics of realist and naturalist narrative that dominated Spanish American imaginative literature from the early 1900s until around 1930 and retained considerable authority well beyond that era. In the 1920s and 1930s, and beyond, the space of literary culture was shared, sometimes uneasily, by writers in the multi-generic avant-garde movements (seminal were the activities of the *ultraísmo* and *estridentismo* groups in the 1920s, the former in Buenos Aires and the latter in Mexico City) and by authors dedicated to literary realism. If as a whole the vanguard group declared a breach with that regionalist past, with the poetics of literary realism, and thereby identified itself with avant-garde currents in Europe, the movement also incorporated another tendency that was

concerned with Spanish American realities rather than with European artistic projects and that unhinged regionalist themes from the realist poetics that characterized the writing of *criollista* authors (see, e.g., Brushwood 31–144; Lindstrom 1994, 34–139; Rama 1986, 99–163). Around mid-century, as early as the 1930s and 1940s and still more noticeably in the 1960s, writers challenged the conventions of literary language and narrative structure that prevailed during the first half of the century, and also renounced literary realism and regionalism. However, despite the conscious refusal of realist poetics and the concerted embrace of more self-conscious or self-critical narrative models by many of these writers, neither regional themes nor rural settings nor local problems were abandoned, nor was the analysis or criticism of the political and social order that had also been central within realist and naturalist works. Likewise, writers who focused explicitly on historical events and social issues, not unlike the century's early novelists, did not ignore–indeed, their work incorporated as well–the interrogation of language and form that was foregrounded especially in benchmark texts of the 1960s.

These parallel and overlapping, conflicting and converging, projects and practices distribute themselves throughout the complex territory of Spanish American narrative in the twentieth century. Stories about the tradition's competing currents therefore also find themselves in disagreement, or competition concerning how best to represent the Spanish American tradition. Stories about regionalist novels parallel and encounter stories about texts from avant-garde, cosmopolitan, fantastic, or magical realist currents. That is, stories about novels "of the land," such as José Eustacio Rivera's *La vorágine* [1924; *The Vortex*, 1935] and Rómulo Gallegos's *Doña Bárbara* (1929; 1931); or about novels of the Mexican Revolution, such as Mariano Azuela's *Los de abajo* [1916; *The Underdogs*, 1929], Martín Luis Guzmán's *El águila y la serpiente* [1928; *The Eagle and the Serpent*, 1930], and Agustín Yáñez's *Al filo del agua* [1947; *The Edge of the Storm*, 1930]; or about Indianist and *indigenista* novels, such as Alcides Arguedas's *Raza de bronce* [1919; Bronze Race], Jorge Icaza's *Huasipungo* (1934; 1964), Ciro Alegría's *El mundo es ancho y ajeno* [1941; *Broad and Alien Is the World*, 1941] , Rosario Castellanos's *Balún Canán* [1957; *The Nine Guardians*, 1960], and José María Arguedas's *Los ríos profundos* [1958; *Deep Rivers*, 1978]–those stories run parallel with, and sometimes traverse, the stories told about other, often contrary, narrative currents. These practices encounter very different narrative enterprises in texts such as Teresa de la Parra's *Ifigenia* (1924; *Iphigenia*, 1993), Macedonio Fernández's *Papeles de recién venido* [1930; Papers of One Recently Arrived], Adolfo Bioy Casares's *La invención de Morel* [1940; *The Invention of Morel*, 1964], Jorge Luis Borges's *Ficciones* [1944/1956; *Ficciones*, 1962] or *El Aleph* (1949/1952), María Luisa Bombal's *La última niebla* [1935; *House of Mist*, 1995], Leopoldo Marechal's *Adán Buenosayres* (1948), or Ernesto Sábato's *El túnel* [1948; *The Outsider*, 1950].

Similarly, the rupture with realist narrative principles and practices effected by texts of the 1960s were anticipated by certain works from the 1930s to 1950s, which are often identified as precursors or even originators of that rupture, and which chronologically coincided with works that represent the narrative models rejected by Boom authors. Novels such as Juan Carlos Onetti's *El pozo* [1939; *The Pit*, 1991], Miguel Angel Asturias's *El Señor Presidente* [1920s/1946; *Mr. President*, 1963], and Alejo Carpentier's *Los pasos perdidos* [1954; *The Lost Steps*, 1967], for example, have often been incorporated into the stories told about the later period of the Boom and about the new narrative more generally. They have sometimes been identified as the first works to formulate a poetics of narrative that anticipates or initiates the radical writing of texts such as Carlos Fuentes's *Cambio de piel* [1967; *Change of Skin*, 1968], Julio Cortázar's *62: modelo para armar* [1968; *62: A Model Kit*, 1972], Mario Vargas Llosa's *Conversación en la Catedral* [1969; *Conversation in the Cathedral*, 1975], and many others. In the 1970s and 1980s the return to the referent, or to history, undertaken by testimonial texts and historical novels—that is, the apparent move away from, though not total rejection of, the reflexive narrative models cultivated by Boom texts—was contiguous with the self-critical linguistic and literary excursions of texts that continued the projects of the most celebrated authors of the 1960s and 1970s. Thus works such as Roque Dalton's *Miguel Mármol* (1972; 1987), Hernán Valdés's *Tejas Verdes: Diario de un campo de concentración en Chile* [1974; *Diary of a Chilean Concentration Camp*, 1975], Jorge Ibargüengoitia's *Los pasos de López* [1982; *López's Footsteps*], and Antonio Benítez Rojo's *El mar de las lentejas* [1985; *Sea of Lentils*, 1990], which arguably represent post-Boom currents, appeared at the same time as texts such as Reinaldo Arenas's *El mundo alucinante* [1969; *Hallucinations: Being an Account of the Life and Adventures of Friar Servando Teresa de Mier*, 1976], Manuel Puig's *Boquitas pintadas* [1969; *Heartbreak Tango*, 1973], Severo Sarduy's *Cobra* [1972; *Cobra*, 1975], Luis Rafael Sánchez's *La guaracha del Macho Camacho* [1976; *Macho Camacho's Beat*, 1980], Luisa Valenzuela's *Cola de lagartija* [1983; *The Lizard's Tail*, 1983], and other works whose filiation is with the family headed by writers such as Cortázar, Fuentes, and García Márquez. However, when one looks at individual texts, one often sees that they straddle, or spill beyond, the borders that would otherwise differentiate, if not oppose, one literary project or current, one ideological position or proposal, to the other (e.g., *El mundo alucinante* or *Cola de lagartija*). The complex literary affiliations between many of these disparate texts are numerous. The virtual dialogue among such texts, as well as the multiple lines of descent that would define them, potentially confounds the categorical oppositions they might otherwise seem to represent.

The ups and downs of competing narrative models and groups of writers tell a story that seems to repeat itself as it moves from one critical juncture to another. One might read the Spanish American story as a story of negotiations not only between competing literary currents but also between different ideologies, between competing ideas about literature, and as a story about prose narrative in particular. In that contest the view of literature as entertainment, as existing for its own sake (i.e., "art for art's sake") or for pleasure, contends with the view of literature as instructive, as functioning to depict and teach readers about social reality. The idea of narrative as necessarily referential, as obligated to refer to and to represent the real world, or to take positions about social issues and historical events, struggles against the idea of narrative literature as self-sufficient and constitutive of its own reality, as obliged to recognize its own artifice and to engage the generic and discursive principles governing its production and reception. Such discussions about literature, about its nature and function—which, beginning with the Horatian distinction between poetry as *dulce* and as *utile*, have informed many Anglo-European literary and critical debates over the centuries—remain palpable within Spanish America, where writing and politics have been intertwined since the time of the Colonial

period. The tension or conflict between currents and critical enterprises that seem to privilege either the referential or the artistic function of literature, or that subscribe to the idea of prose narrative either as necessarily representing extra-textual reality or as inevitably reflecting upon the art of literature itself, is therefore also an ideological tension or conflict. One way of reading the story of Spanish American narrative might be as the story of the dialectical movement between those views—or, better, as the story of those pivotal moments when such tensions have been forcefully articulated, when such conflicts have marked the passages between different currents, between different ways of reading the nature and function of imaginative literature in Spanish America.

It has been suggested that since the end of the nineteenth century there have been perhaps three such critical moments in the history of modern Spanish American literature, moments when such encounters between coetaneous currents, competing literary models, and ideological positions have been all too visible. Such instances—when, having turned a critical eye to their own tradition, writers consciously aim to do something new, to diverge from the past—mark the eruption of modernity into Spanish American literary culture. The periods of *modernismo*, *vanguardismo*, and the Boom of the Spanish American novel are those moments. They mark turning points for Spanish American literature; they stand out as moments when writers turned in new literary and linguistic, as well as cultural, directions. Arguably, these periods of rupture reflect and repeat, restage and reproduce one another (see Rama 1986, 100–136; Rodríguez Monegal 1972b, 139–45). *Modernista*, *vanguardista*, and Boom authors—all, in a sense, avant-garde writers—openly proclaim their turn toward the new and their break with the old. Connected to and informed first by an international dialogue with European cultures (in the case of *modernista* and vanguard writers) and later also with Anglo-American traditions (in the case of Boom or new narrative writers), these currents have taken Spanish American literature, and Spanish American prose narrative, well beyond local borders.

If only because of the international recognition it brought to the Spanish American literary tradition, the Boom, the most recent of those critical developments, has had perhaps the most far-reaching consequences. Also the most conspicuous of the Spanish American tradition's complex, and also controversial, developments, this phenomenon of the 1960s represents the extraordinary production and dissemination of Spanish American literature, and primarily Spanish American narrative, after mid-century. Indeed, the Boom of Spanish American narrative changed the map of Spanish American literature and literary culture between the early 1960s and the 1970s. The figures at the center of that change, and considered almost its official figures, were Julio Cortázar (Argentina, 1914–1984), José Donoso (Chile, 1924–1996), Carlos Fuentes (Mexico, 1928–), Gabriel García Márquez (Colombia, 1927–), and Mario Vargas Llosa (Peru, 1936–). Undeniably, the Boom was a pivotal—some would say *the* pivotal—moment in twentieth-century Spanish American narrative. However, what is important about this moment is perhaps not so much that many Spanish American critics saw it, correctly or not, as inaugurating a revolutionary writing that successfully moved away from the era's dominant models of narrative fiction (i.e., realism, regionalism, *criollismo*) (Rodríguez Monegal 1970). Perhaps more important is that, because of the widespread attention brought to Spanish American literature by the Boom novels during this period, there was also a burgeoning, parallel boom of writing about Spanish American fiction, and about Spanish American literature more generally both inside and outside the academy.

The term *the Boom*, a *sui generis* phrase coined to name a spectacular publishing and marketing phenomenon as well as significant developments in Spanish American literary culture, recalls again the terminological variety and logical difficulties that inform attempts to author a coherent and consistent story about Spanish American narrative. (The term was coined by Luis Harss, an Argentine critic who used it in 1966 to refer to the success of the Latin American novel, which had been transformed during the immediately preceding decades; within a few years the term had passed into the general vocabulary, along with the terms *new novel* and *new narrative*, with which it was often conflated; see Harss 1966, 68 and 1980, 197; Rodríguez Monegal 1980, 186–87 and 1972a, 24–29.) This phrase, which is neither chronological, historical, cultural, generic, thematic, nor structural, cannot be assimilated into any established theoretical order nor into the critical vocabulary customarily deployed in the writing of literary history. It is a disruptive term, and has also engendered its own family of words, which have since grafted themselves onto the family tree of categories and concepts deployed to describe surrounding currents in Spanish American narrative (the term's offshoots are *pre-Boom* and *post-Boom*).

Debates have been waged around the term's value and validity. Both critics and writers have focused on its origins in the language of the marketplace and, specifically, in talk about the burgeoning economy of the 1960s. They have also disagreed about whether the economic metaphor correctly characterizes the production, reception, promotion, and publishing of the Spanish American new novel (see Rodríguez Monegal 1972a, 11–36; Viñas). If, for some, the Boom referred not to a flourishing of literary texts but rather to the successful promotion and marketing of some authors' works, for others it represented a period of extraordinary, indeed unprecedented, literary production, represented by the internationally celebrated Spanish American "new novel." And for some it was neither solely a commerical nor solely a literary phenomenon, but both a "publicity venture" and a "literary event" (Rodríguez Monegal 1984, 34).

Undeniably, the phenomenon of the Boom itself, along with the emergence of Spanish American new narrative into an international as well as a continental arena, is bound up with economic, social, and political factors as well as with developments in Spanish American literary culture. Indeed, the decades preceding the phenomenon brought changes in the reading public and in the publishing industry that made possible the extraordinary production and reception of Spanish American literature beginning in the 1960s. In the period following the Second World War, when the economies of Latin American nations began to share in the prosperity that European countries and the United States were then enjoying, there were a number of conditions created that readily supported and actually advanced the production and reception of Spanish American literature. During the 1960s especially, following the rise of large urban populations and the expansion of the educated middle-class, publishers in Spain and in Latin America found a large reading public ready to consume new titles and to demand new texts. On the political front, the 1959 Cuban Revolution brought Latin America as a whole into the international spotlight; it was a strategic Cold War

territory, in which the United States and the Soviet Union could compete for ideological influence or even military power. The potentially critical role of Latin America as a strategic geopolitical territory focused considerable attention on Spanish American topics and opened up new spaces for its writers and intellectuals to speak and be heard beyond their own borders. In the early 1960s, the events surrounding the Cuban Revolution brought Spanish American writers together in unified support of its anti-imperialist project; however, only a decade later events thrust these authors into divisive disagreement over the ideological demands placed on intellectuals by Cuba's revolutionary government (i.e., the Padilla Affair: the 1971 imprisonment of the poet Heberto Padilla for his criticism of the Revolution begun in 1968). Political differences or no, for many this was the period during which Spanish American writers began to see their work within a common continental tradition rather than as separate national projects (see Halperin Donghi 292–337; see also Donoso 17–37, 45–46; Rodríguez Monegal 1972a, 13–36; Viñas 21–25, 38–39).

The internationalization of Latin American literature and its writers produced significant changes in Spanish American literary culture and in the way that the Spanish American author came to be seen. During the 1960s and after, these authors were acclaimed in foreign as well as in home regions, and disparate forces both inside and outside Spanish American culture began to determine the value of its literature. The discovery and valuation of Latin American fiction by readers abroad, mainly in the United States and in Europe, spurred demand for their work, and the number of translations of Spanish American writers' texts into other languages rapidly increased. These translations (especially of the Boom authors' novels) were promoted by the publishing industries in foreign markets (especially in the United States and in Europe) and by literary agents, translators, academics, and the Spanish American writers themselves. Spanish American literary culture was thereby shaped by a variety of forces not only from within its continental borders but also from outside. It was fashioned at once by the mechanisms of the international marketplace, which bestowed more or less recognition on different writers and texts; by academic institutions, where authors and texts were chosen (or not) for incorporation into the literary canon and curriculum; by the networks of publishers, agents, and critics, whose approval (or lack thereof) could effectively determine individual authors' cultural value; and by foreign writers within whose literary circles Spanish American authors and texts often found valued readers, interlocutors, and friends (see Mudrovcic 1997, 55–80; Rama 1986, 235–54, 271–90; Viñas esp. 18–29; Vidal 9–27, 65ff)

The Boom virtually catapulted Spanish American literary figures (and through them the Latin American literary tradition as a whole) onto the world stage and "into the mainstream" of literary culture (see Harss and Dohmann). Initially, these renowned figures were those authors directly associated with the Boom, and also the venerable master-figure of Jorge Luis Borges (Argentina, 1899–1986), whose *Labyrinths* (1961), published just after Borges shared the International Publisher's (or Formentor) Prize with Samuel Beckett, was among the first of the translated titles to gain recognition for the Latin American literary tradition. The list of translated authors rapidly grew to include many lesser-known, but no less talented, figures in addition to Borges and the original Boom group. Arguably, outside Latin America attention was drawn to

Spanish American literature, and to the new narrative as a whole, because of its difference from the U.S. and European traditions. Consequently, writers such as Borges, Cortázar, Donoso, Fuentes, García Márquez, and Vargas Llosa stood as fascinating, even exotic, figures. Inside Latin America questions were raised precisely about such differences. Some critics argued that the new novel was but a borrowing of techniques from Anglo-American and European literatures; others discussed the complex tradition of narrative literature out of which the new narrative had emerged and how this most recent development in that tradition marked significant differences within Spanish American narrative itself (see, e.g., Blanco Amor 13–25; Rama, 1986, 99–202, 235–39, 255–60, 264–65; Rodríguez Monegal 1972a, 37–85; Viñas 30–39).

Discussions about these and related issues concerning the writers and literature of the Boom as well as about Spanish American literary culture more generally were given wide display in many serial publications dedicated to the Spanish American literature and culture of the period. Through such discussions the Boom also became a competition among journals, a contest of competing ideologies that was staged for diverse audiences inside and outside Latin America. *Casa de las Américas* and *Mundo Nuevo* were the most important of those publications, not only because of the space they devoted to the Boom and to new narrative generally but also because of their struggles for cultural authority, and hegemony, in the late 1960s. *Casa de las Américas* was founded in Havana in 1960 as a literary journal, and was directed by Antón Arrufat during its first five years of publication. Under the editorial guidance of Roberto Fernández Retamar from 1965 to 1971, it became an ideologically focused publication that promoted Cuba's revolutionary culture. Many of the articles it published were written about new narrative authors, whose own essays in the journal often touched on different aspects of Latin American literary culture. *Mundo Nuevo* was founded in Paris in July 1966 by Emir Rodríguez Monegal, who directed the journal for two years (nos. 1–25). Under Rodríguez Monegal's editorship, the journal identified itself with the Boom and explicitly eschewed identification with any ideological position or political agenda. In a sense, the journal expropriated the Boom from the Cuban publication by laying claim to the new narrative, which it positioned beyond politics, and to many of its authors, whom the journal promoted as international rather than solely Latin American literary figures. These publications' opposing ideological positions promoted different readings of the Spanish American novel, different images of the Spanish American author, and different programs for Spanish American literary culture in general. *Casa de las Américas*, committed to the principles of the Revolution, placed Spanish American literary culture within its own ideological framework and provoked significant discussion about the writer's role in relation to the Revolution in particular and to political activity in general; in its pages the Spanish American author was seen as necessarily committed to social and political action. *Mundo Nuevo*, bent on creating a literary, as opposed to a political, forum for the discussion of Spanish American culture, focused on purely literary topics in critical essays about new-narrative writers and texts and in interviews with authors; in its pages the Spanish American author was seen as dedicated solely to the art of literature (see Collazos, Cortázar, and Vargas Llosa; Mudrovcic 1997; Weiss).

The competing stories about Spanish American narrative and the competing images of the Spanish American author or intellectual, and particularly the novelist, that were promoted by these journals are arguably emblematic of competing, but also complementary, currents not only within Spanish American literary culture but also within Spanish American criticism during the twentieth century. Arguably, throughout the development of the latter there have been movements dedicated principally to the transformation of artistic models or aesthetic principles and movements interested mainly in depicting, taking a critical position about, social reality. As already noted, the story of Spanish American narrative recalls, however, that the neat opposition between literary art and social reality–which has often produced critical alliances among, on the one side, notions such as art for art's sake, art as entertainment, and reflexive or self-conscious writing and, on the other, concepts such as committed literature, art as instruction, realist or referential writing–is a precarious one. The same is true for characterizations of any literary period as promoting only the principles of one or the other of those positions or practices (e.g., vanguardism, regionalism). Indeed, the confluence as well as competition between those principles within currents primarily identified with one or the other project, and the convergence within a single current of texts governed apparently more by the principles of the one than by those of the other, suggests the complexity not only of the story of Spanish American narrative literature but also of the stories about specific developments such as the Boom or the new narrative.

The debates and discussions about the Boom as a term and as a phenomenon are therefore important because they are in their essence concerned with literary history and with the differences out of which any such history is constituted. Furthermore, these discussions draw attention to the difference, the unassimilability, of the Spanish American tradition in relation to Anglo-American and European stories about literary development. Through this term, through discussions about it, questions are posed concerning whether Latin America's difference can be accommodated by European and Anglo-American terms–whether the differences within Spanish American narrative can be subsumed at all by literary history. One might, on the one hand, object to *the Boom* as a term either because it seems to designate a commercial rather than a literary phenomenon or because it suggests, all evidence to the contrary, that there was little if any notable narrative tradition in Spanish America prior to the 1960s. On the other hand, one might argue that the term is one of the ways that the difference of Spanish American literature from other Western traditions has been marked, and maintained, within critical discussion. Regardless of either position, *the Boom* is an overdetermined term, around which there can be heard the voices of writers and critics with decidedly disparate critical views and ideological projects, and for whom what is at stake in the term, and in the representations or misrepresentations it makes about Spanish American narrative literature, is nothing less than the proper (in the sense not only of "correct" but also of "belonging to" or "being the property of") conception of the Spanish American tradition overall.

If the term *the Boom*–or *new novel* or *new narrative*–has any value, such value might reside more in what it does than in what it says. That is, as differential terms, these phrases mark breaks or divisions within the territory of Spanish American narrative as well as in the field of Spanish American literary history and criticism. If *the Boom* marks a difference, almost a division, within Spanish American narrative, it records the visible (even metaphorically audible) passage from what has been characterized, correctly or incorrectly, as new and old narrative practices in Spanish America. As a critical tag the term perhaps finds its most appropriate place in a position subordinate to that of *the new narrative*, the term that more properly designates the body of writing of which the Boom is but an early, albeit the most visible, phase. Together, the two expressions can be understood to name two facets of the same phenomenon: the coming of age, the maturity of Spanish American narrative overall (Brushwood 211; Rama 1986, 32, 73, 75; Rodríguez Monegal 1972a, 58). The locution has nonetheless persisted within, and moreover has shaped, critical discussions that aim to describe what precedes and what follows the apparent explosion of Spanish American narrative in the 1960s–that is, "pre-Boom" and "post-Boom" writing or poetics (see, e.g., González Echevarría 1987, 243–53; Shaw 1981 and 1998; Swanson). Despite its reference to nonliterary matters, the phrase "the Boom of the Spanish American novel" has also stood for a specific narrative practice, a new poetics of narrative, whose importance and impact are as much ideological and political as they are literary and cultural. In its synecdochal function, moreover, the term *Boom*, or rather the reducing of the new narrative to the production of but a decade or so of literary activity, has virtually effaced the complexity of Spanish American narrative since mid-century, along with the complicated currents that shape Spanish American narrative literature during the twentieth century's first three decades.

If *the new narrative* is read as synonymous with *the Boom*, its narrative poetics is identified with the literary and linguistic experiments characteristic of the novels produced by the most celebrated authors of the period, that is, texts such as those by Cortázar, Donoso, Fuentes, García Márquez, and Vargas Llosa. And it would also incorporate writing by other authors whose innovative work, produced during the Boom years or in the years immediately preceding or following them, was clearly affiliated with that of the Boom authors. Such work would include texts such as *Pedro Páramo* (1955; 1959) by Juan Rulfo (Mexico, 1918–1986); *La traición de Rita Hayworth* [1968; *Betrayed by Rita Hayworth*, 1971] by Manuel Puig (Argentina, 1932–1990); *Tres tristes tigres* [1965; *Three Trapped Tigers*, 1971] by Guillermo Cabrera Infante (Cuba, 1929–); *De donde son los cantantes* [1967; *From Cuba with a Song*, 1994] by Severo Sarduy (Cuba, 1937–1990); and *Paradiso* (1966; 1974) by José Lezama Lima (Cuba, 1912–1976).

However, it was principally the novels of this group of five Boom authors that came to represent all of Latin American narrative for a reading public that extended far beyond Latin America. Consequently, for the general readership as well as for students of Spanish American literature, not only was Latin American literature subsumed into the Latin American novel, but the Latin American authors were conflated into one literary figure, a figure that was cast in the image of a select group of writers who dominated the Spanish American literary landscape during the 1960s and into the 1970s, and beyond. Inside and outside Latin America these writers were praised–indeed canonized–by critics and scholars. They were promoted by literary journals, editors, and agents, and for a time they were viewed as revolutionary, even heroic, figures. However, these authors, and the phenomenon with which they were so identified and which they inevitably helped to shape and sustain, were also characterized as an elite and exclusionary group, a literary "mafia" or "club," who did not actually represent all the literary and cultural realities of Latin America during this period (see, e.g., Blanco Amor; Donoso 56–57; Rama 1986, 264; Rodríguez Monegal 1980, 188–89; Viñas). (Additionally, within Spanish American literary circles, Donoso's slot was seen as a "rotating seat," filled alternately by him and by other writers such as Carpentier and Lezama Lima [Rama1986, 264].) Nonetheless, from the work of these most celebrated, even "consecrated" authors or "superstars" (Franco 1981; Viñas 28), a new narrative canon emerged, its cornerstones being Fuentes's *La muerte de Artemio Cruz* [1962; *The Death of Artemio Cruz*, 1969], Vargas Llosa's *La ciudad y los perros* [1962; *The Time of the Hero*, 1967], Cortázar's *Rayuela* [1963; *Hopscotch*, 1966], García Márquez's *Cien años de soledad* [1967; *One Hundred Years of Solitude*, 1970], and Donoso's *El obsceno pájaro de la noche* [1970; *Obscene Bird of the Night*, 1973].

Despite the lengthy careers of each of these writers, who, since the Boom period, have produced an extraordinarily wide range of texts connected to diverse narrative currents, and despite the many differences within the work of each as well as between the work of one and that of the others, the so-called Boom authors have become identified with a determinate set of titles that have themselves come to represent, or delimit the enterprises subsumed by, the new narrative. Notwithstanding the trajectory of their work after the Boom years, these writers had a common literary project, which included an interrogation of Realist narrative conventions generally and a rejection of the assumptions governing Latin American realism and regionalism specifically. We recall that these are the narrative models and concepts that had dominated the continent's literary landscape from the 1910s to 1930, and even beyond, and were represented by well-known texts such as *La vorágine* (1924; 1935) by José Eustasio Rivera (Colombia, 1888–1928), *Don Segundo Sombra* (1926; 1935) by Ricardo Güiraldes (Argentina, 1886–1927), and *Doña Bárbara* (1929; 1931) by Rómulo Gallegos (Venezuela, 1884–1969). These are the texts whose literary poetics dominated during the first decades of the century; these are the texts that represented the "old" canon, which was situated in a terrain far from the "new." Let us recall what the old terrain looked like to Boom authors and critics.

The stories about Spanish American narrative that see twentieth-century authors and texts separated by a chasm divide the territory against itself, into dichotomous, Manichaean oppositions between what are described as old and as new formal, thematic, and linguistic vocabularies. We recall that, in general terms, the so-called old group of texts comprises realist and regionalist narratives of the *novela de la tierra*, the early novels of the Mexican Revolution, and the *novela indigenista*. The thematic rubrics under which such titles have been organized tell their own kind of story inasmuch as they draw attention to the referential, sometimes reportorial or even prosecutorial, projects undertaken by their authors. These *criollista* narratives represented specific and separate "home" territories whose cultures and histories and geographies were depicted by authors who spoke for their own particular regions, when not for national traditions. Such texts told stories about geographical areas, historical events, political systems, economic conditions, and cultural traditions. When authors such as Azuela, Gallegos, Güiraldes, and Rivera have been read as speaking for such territories, they have virtually been seen as defenders of the innocent and the powerless and as prosecutors of the guilty and the powerful. As these texts directly engage social and political issues of their own times, they pursue a kind of writing characteristic of Spanish American literature. For they can also be read as indictments of the abuses of power, and as interrogations of the discourses of legitimation, not unlike the kind of interrogation undertaken by the chronicles of conquest and later expanded in the nation-building narratives of the nineteenth century (see, e.g., González Echevarría 1998, 43ff; Sommer).

Having been read as vehicles for taking positions about real-world situations, regionalist texts would seem to commit themselves to the representation of real-world truths rather than to the development of specifically literary programs. That such texts focused on rural rather than urban landscapes, that their fictional characters were more symbolic than they were psychologically complex, that the novels' language may be seen more as a transparent medium through which ideas could be communicated and fictional worlds could be produced than as an opaque material to which attention had to be drawn as well–that such are the features held in common by many of the regional novels and that those are the features later writers aimed to reject has been suggested repeatedly by critics and writers alike. The devaluation of many texts produced in this earlier period was the result of the temporal division itself; that is, the division into "old" and "new" narrative models suggested a qualitative rather than a merely chronological distinction between the two groups. However, the flourishing of Spanish American narrative in the later period which promoted such distinctions, also produced new readings of the earlier period. Some of those readings restored value to the very same texts that Boom writers and some earlier critics had disparaged. Indeed, it has been proposed that some of the canonical "old" texts bear within their narrative structures and strategies a kind of self-consciousness that later became the hallmark of the "new" novel, from which these earlier texts would otherwise seem so distant (see Alonso).

In very general terms, when the new narrative became recognized as such, the Boom authors appeared to privilege a reflexive form of narrative, that is, a writing for which the literary text (its language, its formal structure, its narrative strategies) is an object (in some instances the principal object) of its own inquiry and in which an inquiry into Latin American reality appears to be a secondary, though still important, project. The canonical Boom novels presented themselves as totalizing narratives whose fictional worlds were self-sufficient as linguistic and literary constructs. While also referring to the real-world contexts of Mexico, or Chile, or Colombia, for example, to many readers these texts appeared to examine their own status as literature rather than extra-literary reality; they appeared to subordinate any correspondence with extra-literary reality, with real-world social situations or historical events, to an inquiry concerning literary principles and practices. The authors of the Boom novels aimed, as they often said they did, to reject conventional forms of narrative in which a text's structure and language are at the service of a natural or historical or social reality external to the literary text; they reclaimed value for the literary as such, rescuing the Spanish American novel from a position subordinate to that of extra-textual reality (e.g., Donoso 21ff; Vargas Llosa 1969). Even when they told stories about the social, historical, or cultural realities of Spanish America, the Boom novelists were heard by some, correctly or not, to speak as individuals and

as elite figures, rather than as members of a larger society. Nonetheless, that these authors' concerns were indeed literary, and that their projects constituted a challenge to the narrative poetics to which they were expected to conform but which they resisted, or altogether refused to accept, did not mean that they did not also direct attention to those realities. One could go further and say that the Boom writers' projects resisted the facile distinction between narrative literature that engages cultural and social issues or depicts political and historical realities and narrative literature that challenges prevailing aesthetic principles and practices or undermines conventional models of narrative form and language.

One could also underscore the changes wrought in all of these celebrated authors' literary production beyond the immediate period of the Boom; one could remark on the difference between the canonical Boom novels' literary poetics and the principles governing their authors' later works, which both descended and diverged from the narrative models of their most celebrated texts. For example, one might consider Cortázar's, Donoso's, Vargas Llosa's, García Márquez's, and Fuentes's explorations of forms of the historical or political novel in *El libro de Manuel* [1974; *A Manual for Manuel*, 1978], *Casa de campo* [1978; *A House in the Country*, 1984], *La guerra del fin del mundo* [1981; *War of the End of the World*, 1984], *El General en su laberinto* [1989; *The General in His Labyrinth*, 1990], and *La campaña* [1990; *The Campaign*, 1991], respectively; Vargas Llosa's, Donoso's, and García Márquez's ventures into memoir writing in *El pez en el agua* [1993; *A Fish in the Water*, 1994], *Conjeturas sobre la memoria de mi tribu* [1996; *Conjectures on My Tribe's Memory*], and *Vivir para contarla* [2002; *Living to Tell the Tale*, 2003], respectively; Donoso's and Vargas Llosa's forays into the territory of the erotic novel in *La misteriosa desaparición de la marquesita de Loria* [1980; *The Mysterious Disappearance of the Little Marquise of Loria*] and *Elogio de la madrastra* [1988; *In Praise of the Stepmother*, 1990], respectively; García Márquez's reportorial and testimonial projects in *Relato de un náufrago: que estuvo diez días a la deriva en una balsa sin comer ni beber, que fue proclamado héroe de la patria, besado por las reinas de la belleza y hecho rico por la publicidad, y luego aborrecido por el gobierno y olvidado para siempre* [1970; *The Story of the Shipwrecked Sailor: Who Drifted on a Life Raft for Ten Days without Food or Water, Was Proclaimed a National Hero, Kissed by Beauty Queens, Made Rich through Publicity, and then Spurned by the Government and Forgotten for All Time*, 1986], *La aventura de Miguel Littín clandestino en Chile* [1986; *Clandestine in Chile: The Adventure of Miguel Littín*, 1987], and *Noticia de un secuestro* [1996; *News of a Kidnaping*, 1997]; Donoso's engagement with feminist issues in *El jardín de al lado* [1981; *The Garden Next Door*, 1992] and with social protest in *El mocho* (1997); Fuentes's engagement with topics and forms of popular culture in *La cabeza de la hidra* [1978; *The Hydra Head*, 1978], and Vargas Llosa's *La tía Julia y el escribidor* [1977; *Aunt Julia and the Scriptwriter*, 1982] and *¿Quién mató a Palomino Molero?* [1986; *Who Killed Palomino Molero?*, 1987]. Arguably, given the remarkable transformations of these writers' literary production, one might instead read their careers as telling the story of the many transformations that characterize Spanish American narrative as a whole from the 1960s forward rather than as merely representative of one moment in that complex history–that of the Boom.

If one were to look at the novels that now represent the Boom, the cornerstone texts mentioned above, one would also see that they are perhaps rather more complex than the conventional descriptions of Boom novels would suggest.

One would perhaps discern the gaps between some of the stories told about these texts and the texts themselves; between the fixed, if not monolithic, images literary critics have assigned to these authors and the varied faces projected by their overall production. Not only might one see so-called post-Boom novels as continuing and further transforming the narrative models of the Boom; many Boom novels might also be seen as anticipating, or already instituting, the acute (and artistically innovative) interrogations of Spanish American society, culture, and history that post-Boom currents have emphasized, indeed privileged. For example, Cortázar's *Rayuela*, set between Paris and Buenos Aires about a would-be writer, is designed to challenge traditional narrative conventions through its "Table of Instructions," which pretends to invite the reader to choose the order in which the novel's chapters will be read, and through a complex and self-conscious narrative structure. But it is also an inquiry into the cultural values that characterize Argentine, if not Latin American, society around mid-century. Fuentes's *La muerte de Artemio Cruz*, set in Mexico City concerning the eponymous figure of a wealthy industrialist, presents its protagonist's story, and that of the betrayal of the Mexican Revolution (1910–1917) by the dominant classes, through a series of achronological narrative fragments and through three narrative voices, and thereby pushes into the foreground its own formal structure and strategies. But it is also, perhaps essentially, the story of Mexico from the Mexican Revolution to the late 1950s, if not from the time of the conquest until the Cuban Revolution of 1959. Vargas Llosa's *La ciudad y los perros*, set in Lima of the 1950s and concerning a group of teenage cadets in a military academy, tells its story through the fragmentary performances of several narrators, whose voices cut across multiple temporal frames and whose tale in the end resembles a murder mystery that remains unsolved. But it is also a powerful depiction of the structures of power that have governed the social and political order in Peru.

Thus, if one were to read the new narrative as identical to the Boom novel, one would see that the radical interrogation of literary principles and practices that dominates the Boom authors' texts also allows and not almost always encourages an interrogation of Spanish American culture, society, and history. However, to privilege the complex phenomenon called the Boom through such a restrictive identification would be to sever that era from the family of texts and authors of which it is an integral part; it would be to disinherit, as it were, parallel and overlapping narrative currents that, while diverging from Boom projects, either are descended from or anticipate them. Although the Boom lasted but a brief period, the new narrative has endured as a tradition of literary transformations that have enlarged as they have interrogated the limits of imaginative literature in Spanish America. Thus, if one were to read the new narrative as encompassing not only the Boom but also other—antecedent, simultaneous, and subsequent—narrative currents, which, since mid-twentieth century, effect a series of breaks with earlier traditions, one would see its territory broadened and greatly diversified, but not disconnected from previous currents.

Although the diversification and proliferation of narrative forms in the 1970s and 1980s signal perhaps a democratization of the tradition, it also recalls the variety of directions in which Spanish American narrative moved simultaneously in the twentieth century, if not from the beginnings of Spanish American literature. The diverse forms of narrative that have gained ascendancy from the 1970s onward (some of which are briefly mentioned above as among those to which the Boom authors also turned their talents) include historical novels and testimonial narratives, "popular" genres, and writing by women. While these texts also continue the transformation of literary language and structure that was one of the most visible hallmarks of the Boom authors' early projects, they also interrogate more pointedly and privilege matters specific to the Spanish American social, cultural, and political context. That is, they interrogate directly the systems of value that inform Spanish American culture; they focus explicitly on specific historical figures and events; they take direct aim at the structures of class, race, and gender that inform Spanish American society; and they focus on ideological positions and political projects that have shaped the course of Spanish American history and society in the past and in the present. All this, arguably, appears as the primary concern of these recent currents.

With the development of trends such as these, a variety of narrative forms have gained wide readership and recognition for their authors. The narrative models of these so-called post-Boom texts recognize that the aims and assumptions of the "totalizing" Boom projects are in a sense impossible if not absurd. That is, despite Boom novels' notions to the contrary, global truths cannot be told; the total reality of and truth about an entire culture or national history or literary genre cannot be revealed or represented. These recent currents interrogate the discourse of truth itself and attack those discourses that propose to tell any such truth. These post-Boom narrative models inventively interrogate the discourses of history and of the natural and social sciences; they also put into question the discourses of literary criticism and the Boom novel itself (see, e.g., Lindstrom 1994, 197–221; Jitrik; González Echevarría 1988, 166–86; Williams).

Arguably this further transformation of narrative poetics during the post-Boom years is a turn away from international or continental frames and toward national and regional concerns. It is a return home, in a sense, to local realities of culture, history, and society. Moreover, it is a return that perhaps (as suggested above and below) repeats similar returns home that characterized previous moments in Spanish American literary and cultural history (i.e., *modernismo* and vanguard movements) (see Rama 1986, 132; Rodríguez Monegal 1972b, 139–45). If the return home in the 1970s and 1980s and beyond is, for some, essentially a return to the referent, it is not a return to conventional models of realism and representation. Indeed, the artistic framework within which this return has been undertaken is the one also fashioned by the Boom authors' interrogation of traditional generic forms and discoursive models, by their transformation of literary principles, and by their challenge to received notions about social and cultural values.

Like the Boom phenomenon, these narrative currents emerge within a complex set of conditions that frame and also help to shape literary production. If one considers the economic circumstances and political events that precede and surround this return, the resurgence of interest in local issues and immediate problems seems unavoidable and the changes in narrative models as well as the shifts in anecdotal material seem inevitable. Indeed, after decades of growth, the 1970s and 1980s brought a number of economic, political, and cultural crises that moved Spanish Americans' attention away from international spaces and toward national settings, away from global contexts and toward individual countries' social problems, political history, and cultural values. When the prosperity and optimism of the 1960s ended with the economic downturns of the 1970s and 1980s (with oil crises, rising inflation, decreasing economic resources) and with the rise of repressive governments (the military dictatorships in Chile, Uruguay, and Argentina); when the common political and cultural ground that was forged among Latin American writers during the early phase of the Cuban Revolution was broken up by political if not also personal disagreements (the Padilla Affair in 1971); when numerous writers are forced into, or chose, political or personal exile from their own countries; when feminist principles and practices began to challenge the patriarchal social order, its organization and values–the circumstances that made possible and sustained the literary, cultural, and critical activity during the previous decade or two, and especially during the height of the Boom, all but disappeared, and the apparent cohesion of new narrative texts and the surrounding culture seemed to crumble.

That the image of a cohesive group of writers and texts may itself have been but one of the fictions produced by the Boom era's promotion is arguable; but that that image obscured other realities of the Spanish American tradition's varied literary enterprises is perhaps not. Undoubtedly, the territory of Spanish American narrative became a much more varied territory in the 1970s and 1980s, but its variety, the differences within that territory, were in fact already present and producing significant trends even in the 1960s, when the new novel was so widely disseminated and Boom authors became international figures. Or, rather, the variety of literary currents and real-world concerns that had also been informing Spanish American narrative literature during the 1960s, when the attention of the reading public and literary critics was primarily directed at a small group of writers, became more visible in the 1970s and 1980s. During these decades it becomes more possible to see the enduring complexity of the new narrative currents of which the Boom was but an episode, albeit the most noticeable one. Indeed, if the Boom put Spanish American narrative, and by extension Spanish American literature, on the map, as it were, that phenomenon also made it difficult to see other currents of narrative literature that were developing simultaneously but virtually behind the scenes. With the retrospective, and sometimes necessarily recuperative, glance through which literary history is written, the variety of texts and authors that have shaped the diverse currents in Spanish American narrative literature since mid-century have since become visible not only to Spanish American readers but also to the international reading public.

The story about the narrative literature produced in the 1970s and 1980s, and beyond, follows different paths and authors who, to some degree, have little in common. During this period, Spanish American narrative comprised texts by a diverse group of writers: texts by both women and men, by educated middle-class authors and unschooled writers, by individuals who produced a considerable body of work and others who have authored but a few (in some cases even as few as one or two) titles. The stories these texts tell may well be local, as well as personal, stories, but many draw on and give new and unexpected turns to established and well-known narrative models and currents. The models taken up might be identified mainly with two currents, that of the political novel, which incorporates the "new" historical novel, testimonial narratives, and journalistic novels, and that of popular literature,

which includes detective fiction, and romance novels, as well as other narrative forms (Mudrovcic 1993).

The return to national, more local, issues is also a return to canonical "high" and "low" forms of narrative. The development of the detective novel model (which derives from the hard-boiled model of detective fiction that originated in the United States with the work of writers such as Raymond Chandler) since the 1960s is both an appropriation of a popular foreign model and a reformulation of the forms of criminal fiction that prevailed in Spanish America during earlier periods. This reformulation is not only literary but also ideological, for the detective texts take a decisive turn away from the classical detective form (i.e., the British enigma model that focuses on abstract intellectual analysis), which had been cultivated by Borges and other writers beginning in the 1940s. Whereas the classical genre served to reassure readers that order could always be restored because crimes could always be solved and the truth could always be found, whereas in its beginnings crime fiction upheld the social order, declared its faith in public institutions (e.g., the legal and criminal justice systems), and reinforced the prevailing ideology–the new detective novel, like its hard-boiled models, revealed the harsh realities of those institutions and systems. Taking shape as a "trivial" or popular genre, the Spanish American detective novel nonetheless constructs a powerful, and often graphic, portrait of the dark side–the institutionalized corruption, greed, violence–of the region's social and political order from the late 1960s onward. This kind of ideological interrogation or fierce critique is undertaken in texts such as *Morirás lejos* [1967; *You Will Die in a Distant Land,* 1991] by José Emilio Pacheco (Mexico, 1939–), *El agua en los pulmones* [1973; Water in the Lungs] by Juan Carlos Martini (Argentina, 1944–), *Los asesinos las prefieren rubias* [1974; Assassins Prefer Blonds] by Osvaldo Soriano (Argentina, 1943–1997), *Días de combate* [1976; Days of Combat] by Paco Ignacio Taibo II (Mexico, 1949–), if not also *Novela negra (con argentinos)* [1990; *Black Novel with Argentines,* 1992] by Luisa Valenzuela (Argentina, 1938–) (see Simpson).

Most conspicuously new, perhaps, is the "new" historical novel, whose name differentiates the late twentieth-century narrative production from the original forms of the genre that arose in the nineteenth century. The interrogation of the discourse of history, the reexamination of the lives and feats of historical figures, the reconsideration of official or state versions of historical events, that are undertaken by these texts, constitute a general critique of the discourses of truth that have been presumed to underlie official history (see, e.g., Jitrik; Menton; Pons). Such is the endeavor of texts that take as their subject historical figures; for example, the Paraguayan dictator Dr. José Gaspar Rodríguez de Francia (1766–1840) is the subject of *Yo el Supremo* [1974; *I the Supreme,* 1986] by Augusto Roa Bastos (Paraguay, 1917–); Christopher Columbus (1451–1506) is the protagonist of *El arpa y la sombra* [1979; *The Harp and the Shadow,* 1990] by Alejo Carpentier (1904–1980); the Emperor Maximilian (1832–1867) is the subject of *Noticias del Imperio* [1987; Notices from the Empire] by Fernando del Paso (Mexico, 1935–); Juan Perón (1895–1974) is the figure at the center of *La novela de Perón* [1985; *The Perón Novel,* 1988] by Tomás Eloy Martínez (Argentina, 1934–). Such is the undertaking of texts that audaciously rewrite historical events or refashion historical periods. For example, *Crónicas del descubrimiento* [1980; Chronicles of the Discovery] by Alejandro Paternain (Uruguay, 1933–), tells of the discovery of Europe by an expedition of Indians from the New World; *Lope de Aguirre:*

Príncipe de Libertad [1979; Lope de Aguirre: Prince of Liberty] by Miguel Otero Silva (Venezuela, 1908–1985), retells the story of the eponymous figure's rebellion against Philip II; *1492: Vida y tiempos de Juan Cabezón de Castilla* [1985; 1492: Life and Times of Juan Cabezón de Castilla] by Homero Aridjis (Mexico, 1940–) tells the story of a *converso* at the time of the Inquisition.

If in the popular or formulaic models, of which the detective novel is an example, there appears to be a separation between political and literary goals (politics being but a set of instrumentalized facts at the service of a literary project), in the "new" historical novel, and perhaps even more so in testimonial narrative, there seems to be a fusion of the political and the literary (novelistic discourse being a means by which the text takes a critical, or even prosecutorial, position in relation to historical figures or official versions of history) (Mudrovcic 1993, 449, 457–59). In fact, among the openly political forms of narrative, it is testimonial literature that has had the widest dissemination outside Latin America and perhaps even the greatest immediate impact in Spanish American countries. Indeed, the Nobel Prize for Peace received in 1992 by Rigoberta Menchú (Guatemala, 1959–), co-author with Elisabeth Burgos-Debray (b. 1940) of *Me llamo Rigoberta Menchú y así me nació la conciencia* [1983; I, Rigoberta Menchú: An Indian Woman in Guatemala, 1984], brought recognition to its author and attention to the plight of the indigenous culture and people about which Menchú speaks in that text. The work also created an interest, indeed a demand, for testimonial texts by other Spanish Americans, and became a privileged text for analysis within the industry of academic criticism that in a short time has grown up around testimonial writing (see, e.g., Beverley and Achugar; Gugelberger).

Situating itself at the borders between the novel, autobiography, journalism, and historical narrative, testimonial literature is a disruptive form of writing within the Spanish American tradition, not only because of the stories it tells, but also because of the challenge it poses to generic categories, such as the category of literature itself. Given that this kind of writing constitutes, unwittingly or not, an interrogation of the boundaries of narrative fiction, if not all of literature, testimonial writing arguably has an affiliation with Boom and other new narrative texts in which such interrogation is conspicuous and in relation to which testimonial narrative situates itself at an opposite ideological and discursive pole. Although frequently produced in collaboration with a professional writer or partially shaped by the hand of an editorial figure, testimonial texts are presented as first-person accounts of events witnessed or lived by testimonial subjects themselves. These narratives give voice to stories that would otherwise find no space in which to be told and to subjects who would otherwise have no opportunity to tell their stories. In general, testimonial subjects speak from the margins of history and society, from the edges of dominant culture. They tell personal and collective stories about social and political struggle, about historical events they have witnessed or in which they have participated. They speak to accuse and to defend, to indict and to vindicate, to testify to events and to the truth of testimony itself; they speak to bear witness for others as well as for themselves. Testimonial writers tell stories about imprisonment and exile, about political resistance and revolutionary activity, about natural disasters and massacres of innocent civilians in texts such as *La noche de Tlatelolco* [Mexico, 1971; Massacre in Mexico, 1975] by Elena Poniatowska (Mexico, 1933–), *"Si me permiten hablar…": testimonio*

de Domitila, una mujer de las minas de Bolivia [1978; Let me Speak! Testimony of Domitila, a Woman of the Bolivian Mines, 1978] by Domitila Barrios de Chungara (Bolivia, 1937–), *"Somos millones…": La vida de Doris María, combatiente nicaragüense* [1977; Inside the Nicaraguan Revolution of Doris Tijerino as Told to Margaret Randall, 1978] by Margaret Randall (United States, 1936–) and Doris Tijerino (Nicaragua, 1943–), *Preso sin nombre, celda sin número* [1981; Prisoner without a Name, Cell without a Number, 1981] by Jacobo Timerman (Argentina, 1923–1999), and *The Little School* (1986) by Alicia Partnoy (Argentina, 1955–). (See Vol. 2, Ch. 23 and 24, this *History*.)

Although testimonial texts such as these seemed to take Spanish American narrative literature in new directions in the 1970s and 1980s, they are part of a lengthy tradition of narratives that produce firsthand documentary representations of historical events and accounts of personal travails. Arguably, Spanish American literature is founded in such texts, in the chronicles of discovery and conquest and stories of shipwrecks and servitude during the Colonial period. Moreover, well-known texts such as *Operación masacre* [1957; Operation Massacre] by Rodolfo Walsh (Argentina, 1927–1977), *Biografía de un cimarrón* [1966; The Autobiography of a Runaway Slave, 1966] by Miguel Barnet (Cuba, 1940–), and *Hasta no verte Jesús mío* [1969; Here's to You, Jesusa!, 2001] by Elena Poniatowska, which are anchored in the discourses and practices of reportorial writing ethnography, are also the immediate antecedents for the concentrated production of testimonial writing during the 1970s and 1980s. Thus testimonial literature may be read not only as a turn in a direction radically different from, but nonetheless also affiliated with, Boom novels of the same period, but also as a return to an important tradition already firmly established within Spanish American letters. While testimonial texts position themselves as having a direct and unproblematic relation to the referent, and therefore seem to declare their difference and distance from fictional narrative in general, they have nonetheless become situated within the tradition of Spanish American narrative literature and have been incorporated into, and privileged within, the academic canon. However, as they are so situated, these texts compel an interrogation about the nature of the literary and about the parameters of Spanish American literary culture, and also about Spanish American literary criticism. Testimonial narratives unsettle Spanish American literary history by introducing into the Spanish American narrative tradition a form of writing that seems to undermine the privileged position held by fictional narrative; such texts also challenge, and perhaps dismantle, conventional critical concepts, such as that of the author. Yet, in the interrogation of that particular concept, testimonial literature installs powerful new figures of authorship and authority within the Spanish American tradition.

Among those figures are those of women who attempt to bear witness to, by writing about, their own experience, which would otherwise remain unheard and unrecognized. These female voices of testimony arise from around the margins of literature and history to speak as individual voices that are also the voices of a collectivity. Indeed, women's stories predominate among testimonial narratives; testimonial writing seems to have been taken up naturally, as it were, by women, whose personal and private stories, even when virtually identical to that of the collectivity they would represent, have gained legitimacy through this form of writing. Moreover, when these female figures, as well as those of other writers formerly excluded from the story of Spanish American writing, appeared as especially strong figures during the 1970s and 1980s, they dethroned, as it were, the conventional figure of the Spanish American author and, in some sense, disrupted traditional stories about Spanish American narrative literature (see Kerr 16–64, 165–70). (See Vol. 1, Ch. 35, this *History*.)

Thus, if one reads Spanish American new narrative as a tradition that encompasses all the disruptions and new directions taken by Spanish American narrative literature since the middle of the century rather than as only the production identified with the Boom novel written around the 1960s, one will indeed see that tradition as an inherently complex and broad territory. While at one time the figures of the principal Boom authors seemed to permit and promote the construction of a single image of "the Spanish American author" (the image of an upper-class, white male well schooled in, and identified with, European and Anglo-American literature as well as conversant with Spanish American traditions), the figures to be found in this broader new narrative territory defy consolidation into a single image. This more recent new-narrative figure is, on the contrary, a figure of heterogeneity, and it speaks from disparate positions throughout Spanish American narrative literature, and in myriad texts spanning several decades (Kerr 164–69). That figure derives from many different authors in addition to those mentioned above. Those authors are as diverse as José Agustín (Mexico, 1944–), Isabel Allende (Chile, 1942–), Gustavo Alvarez Gardeazábal (Colombia, 1945–), Albalucía Angel (Colombia, 1939–), Arturo Arias (Guatemala, 1950–), Carmen Boullosa (Mexico, 1954–), Alfredo Bryce Echenique (Peru, 1939–), Julieta Campos (Cuba/Mexico, 1932–), Carlos Cerda (Chile, 1942–), Hiber Conteris (Uruguay, 1933–), Emilio Díaz Valcárcel (Puerto Rico, 1929–), Salvador Elizondo (Mexico, 1932–), Diamela Eltit (Chile, 1949–), Rosario Ferré (Puerto Rico, 1938–), Eduardo Galeano (Uruguay, 1940–), Isaac Goldemberg (Peru, 1945–), Augusto Monterroso (Guatemala/Mexico, 1921–2003), Cristina Peri Rossi (Uruguay, 1941–), María Luisa Puga (Mexico, 1944–), Gustavo Sáinz (Mexico, 1940–), Juan José Saer (Argentina, 1937–), Antonio Skármeta (Chile, 1940–), Manuel Vargas (Bolivia, 1952–), Ana Lydia Vega (Puerto Rico, 1946–), and many more.

This alphabetical list of authors' names, which might initially strike one as something of a Borgesian enumeration, is purposely deployed to give a sense of the chronological and cultural scope of the heterogeneous literary activity that has in fact constituted the Spanish American narrative tradition. It is also deployed to figure an expandable terrain whose space remains open to the addition of names of other Spanish American writers. (That is, in accordance with their alphabetic place, an unlimited number of names can be inserted into the spaces between the names that appear in this enumeration.) This list also raises the question of how best to group authors and texts so as to identify in other than chronological or national terms the currents that have shaped Spanish American narrative during the twentieth century, especially since the 1950s or 1960s. This question has, of course, been addressed in many Spanish American literary histories, and it is a question that seems to elicit incomplete responses, as inevitably it must. The answers provided are not unexpected: Some critics have attempted to organize writers into "generations," or "groups," or "schools" or "movements"; or to differentiate between "older" and "younger" writers or among "precursors" and "initiators" and "masters" or between "fathers" and "sons"; others have put into question

such schematic representations altogether, even disputing that "the new narrative" has anything but a metaphoric value (see, e.g., Rodríguez Monegal 1972a; Viñas 29–33; Swanson 1–20). These are conventional concepts, of course, which have derived from, and also fostered, the evolutionary and genealogical narratives that characterize the discourse of literary history. These narratives seem naturally to map the territory of Spanish American imaginative literature as a path from older to newer terrain, from the land of the fathers to those of the sons, and so on.

With regard to stories about the new narrative, for example, one well-known genealogical scheme proposes four generations of new novelists. The first, that of "the founders" of the 1940s, would comprise Miguel Angel Asturias, Jorge Luis Borges, Alejo Carpentier, Leopoldo Marechal, and Agustín Yáñez; the second, which overlaps with that of the "masters" of the previous group and whose authors published some of their most important works in the 1950s–1960s, would include José María Arguedas, Julio Cortázar, José Lezama Lima, Juan Carlos Onetti, and Juan Rulfo; the third, which was virtually simultaneous with that of the second "promotion" and whose authors published their most successful titles in the 1960s, would contain some famous and some lesser-known authors, such as Guillermo Cabrera Infante, José Donoso, Carlos Fuentes, Gabriel García Márquez, Salvador Garmendia, Mario Vargas Llosa, and David Viñas; the fourth, that of the youngest and at one time "newest of the new" group whose work began to appear in the late 1960s, would include writers such as José Agustín, Reinaldo Arenas, Fernando del Paso, José Emilio Pacheco, Manuel Puig, Gustavo Sáinz, Néstor Sánchez, Severo Sarduy, and Rodolfo Walsh (Rodríguez Monegal 1969, 155–62 and 1972b).

This genealogical sketch is instructive not only because it produces a succession of affiliated literary figures, a family tree that gives shape to the story of modern Spanish American prose fiction. It is also instructive because the lineage it sketches is a strictly filial one (in the etymological sense of the word). That is, the family tree laid out here is literally that of a family of "fathers" and "sons"; there are no "mothers" or "daughters" to be found within its genealogy. Such stories about Spanish American literary generations, until the 1970s and the 1980s, told stories about virtually autogamous families of writers, about an apparently autogenic literary clan that has dominated Spanish American literary culture and seemed to populate the whole territory of Spanish American modern narrative literature. That the wide territory of new narrative, and that of twentieth-century Spanish American fiction more generally, was once mapped as a patriarchal territory became evident mainly in the last decades of the twentieth century. And just as we can read the story of Spanish American narrative as having been reshaped during the 1960s and early 1970s by the phenomenon of the Boom and by the rereading of Spanish American literary history occasioned by the emergence of the new novel, for example, we can see that story as having been revised again because of the discovery of contemporary Spanish American women writers, at least since the 1980s.

The emergence of women writers in Spanish America in recent decades, and the subsequent recuperation of antecedent figures, and a Spanish American tradition of writing by women, has disrupted the conventional generational stories previously told about Spanish American narrative literature. (See Vol. 1, Ch. 31, 32, 34, this *History*.) The belated insertion of women's names and texts into those stories has produced new and different versions of the tradition, stories that have grafted new branches onto the Spanish American family tree. Arguably, these changes have been effected as much by the writing of feminist literary critics and the institutionalization of women's studies more generally in the academy as by the production of the women authors themselves. Likewise, the development of Latin American feminist criticism has been reinforced by the increased publication of texts by women writers as well as by the theoretical and political projects in which feminists, regardless of their professional identity, have become involved. It may therefore seem necessary to talk about women's writing in specifically feminist terms and to theorize about how to do that, precisely because women's writing in Spanish America frequently constitutes itself not only as a literary practice but, in some cases more explicitly than others, also as a political activity. To talk about the writing of figures such as Rosario Castellanos, Cristina Peri Rossi, Luisa Valenzuela, and Ana Lydia Vega, among others, is to talk about individual as well as shared literary itineraries and about political acts as well as artistic projects. Like the "new" historical novel, for which the political and the literary are inseparable, like testimonial literature, in which to bear witness is to take political action, the voices of feminist writers and critics have affirmed that the act of writing itself, as well as what gets written about, is a way of taking power and of being political (see, e.g., Castillo; Lindstrom 1989; Kaminsky; Castro-Klarén, Molloy, and Sarlo).

It may also seem necessary to tell the story of women writers as a story unto itself, to formulate a descriptive, or explanatory, category that would be constituted solely by gender. Although the work of many women writers might be incorporated into discussions about literary movements and tendencies more generally, one of the effects of feminist critical studies has been to authorize the telling of the story of writing by Spanish American women as a story separate from the canonical stories about Spanish American narrative and about its literature more generally. Nonetheless, to talk about women writers and women's writing is also to talk about a diverse body of work that cannot be subsumed by any single critical theory or ideological position. The exclusion of women from most of the traditional stories about Spanish American literature has constituted those writers as a separate group. Their belated, if not outspoken, entry into those stories has made them more visible, and audible, than they might otherwise have appeared, and they therefore stand as important figures of difference. However, to segregate or separate women writers from the tradition overall, to deny that theirs is also a heterogeneous body of writing and a diverse group of voices that converge, and converse, with the writing and voices of male writers, together with whom they have come to shape Spanish American literary culture at the end of the twentieth century, may well erase the important and original differences among them.

Some of these female figures seek to straddle different regions within the broad territory of Spanish American narrative literature, identifying themselves both as women writers who tell stories that only women can tell and as writers whose stories converse with currents otherwise dominated by male authors. For example, some of the writers who have published important works and who have received recognition since the 1960s, have written texts that pertain to the established tradition of fantastic fiction (e.g., Luisa Valenzuela), some have been central figures in the production of testimonial writing (e.g., Elena Poniatowska), some have become

identified with the current of magical realism (e.g., Isabel Allende), some have explored new paths between historical figures and fictional texts (e.g., Carmen Boullosa), and so on. But the differences within the writing of each of these authors, like those of their male counterparts, also put into question the identification of each with but one literary current, thematic concern, or generic model. In their writing one also sees the wide array of literary experiments and real-world problematics that shaped Spanish American narrative overall during the final decades of the twentieth century.

To talk about women's writing not as an isolated region but as part of the broad territory of Spanish American narrative is to insert into that tradition's story somewhat unruly figures and texts that have compelled a rewriting of much of what has been told by earlier stories. Indeed, if the difference imprinted by women's narratives, the unassimilability of their writing, once marked a region for exclusion and for subordination, since the 1970s and 1980s the territory of Spanish American narrative literature has been remapped. The difference figured, and expressly cultivated, by women writers has become a constitutive part of the territory rather than an area beyond its canonical borders. The stories that can now be told about that territory, and about Spanish American literary culture more generally, are stories about a different kind of family and different kinds of affiliations.

The prominence of contemporary women authors such as Isabel Allende or Elena Poniatowska or Luisa Valenzuela and the concomitant recuperation, and also the repositioning, of earlier women writers have had a transformative effect. That group would include figures such as María Luisa Bombal (Chile, 1910–1980), Marta Brunet (Chile, 1897–1967), Silvina Bullrich (Argentina, 1915–1990), Lydia Cabrera (Cuba, 1899–1991), Rosario Castellanos (Mexico, 1925–1974), Sara Gallardo (Argentina, 1931–1988), Elena Garro (Mexico, 1917–1998), Beatriz Guido (Argentina, 1925–1988), Silvina Ocampo (Argentina, 1903–1993), Yolanda Oreamuno (Costa Rica, 1916–1956), Elvira Orphée (Argentina, 1930–), Lucila Palacios [Mercedes Carvajal] (Trinidad/Venezuela, 1902–1994), Teresa de la Parra (Venezuela, 1889–1936), Armonía Somers [Armonía Etchepare de Henestrosa] (Uruguay, 1914–1994), and Marta Traba (Argentina, 1930–1983). The diverse figures and voices of these writers inevitably tell different stories about Spanish American culture and society and about its literary figures. The recuperation of what might arguably be called a tradition of women's narrative literature in Spanish America has changed the landscape of writers and topics and texts that would make up the whole territory of Spanish American narrative (see, e.g., Lindstrom1989; Castro-Klarén, Molloy, and Sarlo). Not only has the entrance of women writers into the territory of Spanish American narrative literature opened the terrain to authors from earlier periods and to a reexamination of how the Spanish American tradition has been constructed, but these writers have also turned the Spanish American territory into a terrain where gender both makes all the difference (i.e., women writers may be valued because they write as women and about women's experience) and doesn't matter at all (i.e., women writers may be valued because their writing is an interrogation of the established order, whether literary, social, cultural, or political).

The reformulation of the story about Spanish American prose narrative that has been provoked by contemporary women writers has also involved the refashioning of the image of the Spanish American writer. In representing–that is, both in depicting and in speaking for–their own culture, Spanish American authors, like authors more generally, have played important roles in Spanish American society at least since the nineteenth century. Indeed, in Spanish America it has not been uncommon for political figures to be writers, or writers to be political figures (e.g., Bello, Bosch, Gallegos, Martí, Sarmiento); it is not uncommon for authors to address audiences outside their own countries about political, economic, and social issues, as well as about literature and culture (e.g., Dorfman, Fuentes, García Márquez, Paz). That the figure of the Spanish American author was necessarily a male figure was perhaps taken for granted until recent decades. The female figures that now talk about and speak for Spanish American culture and society are figures invested with new authority, and their appearance (as well as that of other groups of writers) has changed the figure of the Spanish American author itself. The different faces that figure now bears have changed the appearance of Spanish American literary culture as well as its literature.

Oddly, the shift in that appearance is also something of a return, for it carries with it a reaffirmation of a role the Spanish American author had assumed early in the twentieth century. It has been understood that during the early decades of the twentieth century, when the poetics of literary realism predominated and regionalist narratives were privileged, the (male) author was at the same time journalist, legislator, revolutionary, and intellectual, who documented physical reality, defended the exploited masses, and denounced social injustice (Fuentes 1969, 12). During the last decades of the century, when political narratives (and perhaps especially testimonial and feminist literature) were much in evidence, the (male and female) author appeared as a figure who again speaks for others as much as for him- or herself, again seeking to expose national, regional, and local problems. However, while the political or social role of the Spanish American author has been newly foregrounded, indeed privileged, while a certain figure of the author has been recovered from the story of Spanish American culture, that role and that figure have been recuperated with a difference. Whereas the regionalist writer or the *indigenista* author, for example, spoke from on high and from a position virtually untouched by the realities he aimed to expose and denounce, the testimonial subject, as in the case of some women writers, spoke from a marginal position and sometimes even directly from within a site of conflict, and suffering. The voicing of the stories of subjects who would now speak for themselves, even as representatives of a collectivity, has therefore also been the voicing of resistance to the established order, which is sometimes social, sometimes political, sometimes cultural.

The widening and democratization of Spanish American literary culture, as well as the broadening of the territory of Spanish American narrative, has introduced into national, continental, and even international spaces figures and stories that are oddly both new and traditional, original and familiar. Indeed, although some of the most powerful narratives at the end of the twentieth century are narratives of resistance, they are also narratives of recuperation. Each of the significant literary developments or currents of the last half of the twentieth century has also compelled a rereading of and return to earlier traditions and trends, sometimes to recover lost or marginalized stories or figures, sometimes to reread, or reconstruct, the relationship between the newest project and the traditions that have preceded it. One could argue that it is this retrospective gaze, this rereading of earlier writers, texts, and stories, that has repeatedly been undertaken by Spanish American authors, as well as by the literary critics who have attempted to tell their stories. It is that glance backward that links all of these narrative currents and regions with one another; it is that review of the past that connects them with the overall project that has been called the new narrative, as well as with the entire tradition of Spanish American narrative from its origins to the present.

Spanish American narrative literature from the 1950s and 1960s onward is grounded in a return to earlier texts, authors, and currents, even if only to negate or reject them, as well as in a move into new and unexplored regions. This return, which may be read as a repetition of other returns (as noted above) also marks, or emerges from a conscious, indeed self-conscious, separation from "the old" that accompanies the invention of "the new." Since the Boom and the idea of the new narrative became current within literary culture and academic discourse, critics have attempted to describe and discern, theorize and thematize, precisely what makes "the new" new, what constitutes the break that legitimizes, if at all, the distinction and opposition between earlier and later aesthetic principles and narrative practices, between past and recent conceptions of imaginative literature's relation to social reality, and between former and current ideas about the role of the Spanish American author. Whether twentieth-century Spanish American narrative is read according to an evolutionary model or not, whether it is understood as merely unfolding in time or as maturing into an adult state or as evolving from lower to higher forms, the question has repeatedly been asked about how–when, with which writer or writers, in which text or texts–the territorial divides can be demarcated, how the differences between these different regions can be mapped, and whether they in fact represent qualitative rather than merely chronological divisions. For example, where neat oppositions have been proposed between older or more traditional or primitive novels and newer or creative narratives (Vargas Llosa 1969), or where attempts have been made to map the Spanish American tradition directly onto European and Anglo-American currents and categories (i.e., the Boom and the post-Boom, modernism and postmodernism), writers as well as critics have struggled not only to define the differences, but also to describe the space between seemingly contrary positions and to map the region between different terrains. Such projects involve not only assigning places to authors and texts on either side of a virtual divide, but also describing the in-between territory, the space straddled by writers and texts who would appear either to break with one current or to initiate another or both (e.g., Asturias, Borges, Carpentier, Onetti, Rulfo).

Where discussion focuses on the Boom and other new-narrative authors, and attempts are made to organize systematically the authors and texts that constitute new-narrative production (understood here in the broader sense), writers and critics have been induced to turn simultaneously to chronological, generational, and generic models (e.g., "la generación del medio siglo" ["the generation of mid-century"], "la novela testimonial" ["the testimonial novel"]), or to use reflexively relativistic, sometimes also redundant, rubrics ("new new novel," "los novísimos" ["the newest"]; "El *boom* I," "El *boom* II"; "el *boom* junior"; the post-Boom) to tell the Latin American story (see, e.g., Rama 1986, 26–32; Rodríguez Monegal 1968–1969; Shaw 1981). What such schema recall, however, is that the Boom in particular has to some extent been the impetus for the rereading and the rewriting of the history of Spanish American narrative in recent years, although the same could be said about the continued production that has shaped the new narrative overall since the 1950s and 1960s. Those projects are an attempt to explain the new narrative in terms of a tradition from which its authors are viewed as having distanced and differentiated themselves, but to which their own stories, as well as that of the whole tradition, clearly belong. Whether they write about the Boom or Spanish American narrative more generally in order to explain their own literary careers or to describe the texts and writers that have constituted the tradition in which they are also included, when some of these authors glance back at the Spanish American imaginative writing they perform a characteristically retrospective, recuperative, reading that has itself also shaped the Spanish American literary story (e.g., Donoso; Fuentes 1969; Vargas Llosa 1969). (See also Vol. 2, Ch. 32, this *History*.)

The new narratives, and especially Boom novels, do appear to design a break from the past; new novelists do seem to anchor themselves in a present that differentiates and dissociates itself from their literary culture's past. But these writers also construct their own literary family romances in their own rereadings of the Spanish American narrative tradition. Through those readings, the Boom writers both respond to and refuse, reject, and reclaim the Spanish American narrative tradition (or, perhaps, stereotypes thereof). It is a tradition they may seem to disown but to which they inevitably return. The personal and critical stories told by these "native informants" arguably stand as authoritative representations of the period and of the literary culture that supported their projects (e.g., Donoso; Fuentes 1969 and 1993, 9–31; Vargas Llosa 1969 and 1987, 202). The stories told–also invented–by Donoso, Fuentes, and Vargas Llosa, especially, have themselves been incorporated into the official critical stories about Spanish American narrative literature in the twentieth century.

As controversial as it is, then, the Boom has in a way functioned as a point of departure for the construction of the story of Spanish American fiction perhaps more than it has served as a point of arrival. To try to understand this phenomenon is to reread, and thus return to and also recuperate, texts and trends that earlier might not have seemed so significant. Oddly, the Boom retroactively revalues the narrative tradition its authors would refuse but to which they are obliged to return; the phenomenon that would present itself as appearing from nowhere occasions the kind of reading, and rereading, that would ground it as a logical, though extraordinary, step in the story of modern Spanish American narrative. It is this activity of rereading and returning to earlier traditions and texts that informs not only critical views of Spanish American prose narrative, but also some of the tradition's recent literary enterprises (e.g., the new historical narrative). Thus this idiosyncratic phenomenon, and its odd name, demands (depends on) odd forms of reading as well as writing simultaneously in several directions. This apparently anomalous development has compelled both writers and literary critics to try to construct a comprehensible, comprehensive frame around the production and reception of the new narrative. It has compelled attempts to make sense of the whole of the Spanish American narrative tradition, especially since the nineteenth century (see, e.g., Sommer). The route around Spanish American narrative literature might therefore seem a naturally reversible route that moves back as logically as it moves forward, taking its authors to foreign territories while also returning them to the home terrain in which Spanish American narrative is, to recall Paz's metaphor, inevitably rooted and to which Spanish American writers continue to return as they tell stories about individual national cultures or about continental concerns and currents.

Indeed, the story of the past constructed by readers and writers of the Boom is largely a story projected backward from the present of the new developments; it is itself an effort by writers and critics to find, and construct, the complex origins of a later episode that has yet to be completely accounted for or assimilated into the total story of Spanish American narrative literature. The retrospective glance implied by the phrase "new narrative" and the critical return to previous narrative forms and authors occasioned by this new writing finds, of course, neither a linear route to the origins of the new texts or a straight path back to contemporary literary production. The routes backward and forward, on the contrary, might be figured as overlapping and superimposed (also forking) paths through a territory of multiple narrative trends and currents. The simultaneity of narrative directions and literary currents complicates further the return, by literary historians as well as by literary authors, to the forms of narrative that appeared in the early decades of the twentieth century and from which "the new" ostensibly made its dramatic break.

The break marked by the newest forms of narrative is arguably as much (if not more) a breach in reading, that is, a break with the readings that had constructed the dominant stories about Spanish American narrative and with ways of reading literature generally. The rereadings undertaken by writers and critics alike have produced new currents in Spanish American narrative as well as in the stories told about the tradition. One finds no better example, perhaps, than in the rereading, or rewriting, of stories about Spanish American narrative that has been occasioned by the emergence of women writers in the late twentieth century. However, while the extraordinary emergence of women authors and imaginative literature by women plots new paths through the territory of recent Spanish American narrative, it also plots a returning route that converges with the routes taken by other major currents in Spanish American narrative since mid-century. Moreover, if this example stands out, it is perhaps because this transformation has been effected simultaneously in the space of critical discourse and in the sphere of literary production. It recalls for us that the Spanish American enterprise is at once literary and critical, theoretical and practical; it has been constituted by different, overlapping and, mutually dependent concerns.

At every stage of Spanish American narrative, and also in the discrete critical enterprises that have burgeoned around the tradition, one finds a potentially confounding overlay and intersection of diverse currents. Since mid-century, the complexity of the tradition's trajectory has become more visible not only because of the Boom itself, but also because the Boom (as a phenomenon) and the new narrative (as both a cause and an effect of that phenomenon) have occasioned a virtual boom in the industry of literary criticism both inside and outside Latin America, and especially in the academy. In a sense, the task of explaining these developments–the task that has generally fallen on literary critics–is also an imaginative task, for it entails, in a sense, imagining Spanish American narrative, which is itself essentially a territory of the imagination.

Works Cited

Alegría, Fernando. 1974 [1959]. *Historia de la novela hispanoamericana.* 4th ed. Mexico City: Ediciones de Andrea.

———. 1986. *Nueva historia de la novela hispanoamericana.* Hanover, NH: Ediciones del Norte.

Alonso, Carlos J. 1990. *The Spanish American Regional Novel: Modernity and Autochthony.* New York: Cambridge University Press.

Beverley, John, and Hugo Achugar, eds. 1992. *La voz del otro: testimonio, subalternidad y verdad narrativa.* Lima, Peru/Pittsburgh, PA: Latinoamericana Editores.

Blanco Amor, José. 1976. *El final del "boom" literario y otros ensayos.* Buenos Aires: Ediciones, Cervantes.

Borges, Jorge Luis. 1981 [1951]. "Kafka and His Precursors." *Borges: A Reader.* Ed. Emir Rodríguez Monegal and Alistair Reid. New York: Dutton. 242–43.

Borinsky, Alicia. 1993. *Theoretical Fables: The Pedagogical Dream in Contemporary Latin American Fiction.* Philadelphia: University of Pennsylvania Press.

Brotherston, Gordon. 1977. *The Emergence of the Latin American Novel.* Cambridge, England: Cambridge University Press.

Brushwood, John S. 1975. *The Spanish American Novel: A Twentieth-Century Survey.* Austin: University of Texas Press.

Castillo, Debra. 1992. *Talking Back: Toward a Latin American Feminist Literary Criticism.* Ithaca, NY: Cornell University Press.

Castro-Klarén, Sara, Sylvia Molloy, and Beatriz Sarlo, eds. 1991. *Women's Writing in Latin America: An Anthology.* Boulder, CO: Westview Press.

Chiampi, Irlemar. 1983. *El realismo maravilloso: forma e ideología en la novela hispanoamericana.* Trans. Agustín Martínez and Margara Russotto. Caracas: Monte Avila.

Collazos, Oscar, Julio Cortázar, and Mario Vargas Llosa. 1970. *Literatura en la revolución y revolución en la literatura.* Mexico City: Siglo XXI.

Díaz, Roberto Ignacio. *Unhomely Words: Foreign Tongues and Spanish American Literature.*

Donoso, José. 1983. *Historia personal del "boom."* 2nd ed. Barcelona: Seix Barral.

Echavarren Welker, Roberto. 1992. *Margen de ficción: poéticas de la narrativa hispanoamericana.* Mexico City: Joaquín Mortiz.

Foster, David William. 1979. *Studies in the Contemporary Spanish-American Short Story.* Columbia, MO: University of Missouri Press.

Franco, Jean. 1981. "Narrador, autor, superestrella: la narrativa latinoamericana en la época de cultura de masas." *Revista Iberoamericana* 47.114–115: 129–48.

———. 1989. *Plotting Women: Gender and Representation in Mexico.* New York: Columbia University Press.

Frye, Northrop. 1957. *Anatomy of Criticism.* Princeton, NJ: Princeton University Press.

Fuentes, Carlos. 1969. *La nueva novela hispanoamericana.* Mexico City: Joaquín Mortiz.

———. 1993. *Geografía de la novela.* Mexico City: Fondo de Cultura Económica.

Gertel, Zunilda. 1970. *La novela hispanoamericana contemporánea.* Buenos Aires: Columba.

Goic, Cedomil. 1972. *Historia de la novela hispanoamericana.* Valparaíso: Ediciones Universitarias.

González, Eduardo. 1992. *The Monstered Self: Narratives of Death and Performance in Latin American Fiction.* Durham, NC: Duke University Press.

González Echevarría, Roberto. 1985. *The Voice of the Masters: Writing and Authority in Modern Latin American Literature.* Austin: University of Texas Press.

———. 1987. *La ruta de Severo Sarduy.* Hanover, NH: Ediciones del Norte.

———. 1998 [1990]. *Myth and Archive: Toward a Theory of Latin American Narrative.* Durham, NC: Duke University Press.

González Pérez, Aníbal. 1987. *La novela modernista hispanoamericana.* Madrid: Gredos.

Gugelberger, Georg M., ed. 1996. *The Real Thing: Testimonial Discourse and Latin America.* Durham, NC: Duke University Press.

Halperin Donghi, Tulio. 1993. *The Contemporary History of Latin America.* Trans. John Charles Chasteen. Durham, NC: Duke University Press.

Harss, Luis. 1966. "Literatura: Latinoamérica despierta." *Primera Plana* 9 (August): 68–70.

———. 1980. "Balance y visión de conjunto." *Requiem for the "Boom"–Premature?: A Symposium.* Ed. Rose S. Minc and Marilyn R. Frankenthaler. Montclair, NJ: Montclair State College. 197–202.

Harss, Luis, and Barbara Dohmann. 1967. *Into the Mainstream: Conversations with Latin-American Writers.* New York: Harper & Row.

Jitrik, Noé. 1995. *Historia e imaginación literaria: Las posibilidades de un género.* Buenos Aires: Biblos.

Kadir, Djelal. 1986. *Questing Fictions: Latin America's Family Romance.* Minneapolis: University of Minnesota Press.

———. 1993. *The Other Writing: Postcolonial Essays in Latin America's Writing Culture.* West Lafayette, IN: Purdue University Press.

Kaminsky, Amy. 1993. *Reading the Body Politic: Feminist Criticism and Latin American Women Writers.* Minneapolis: University of Minnesota Press.

Kerr, Lucille. 1992. *Reclaiming the Author: Figures and Fictions from Spanish America.* Durham, NC: Duke University Press.

Kittay, Jeffrey, and Wlad Godzich. 1987. *The Emergence of Prose: An Essay in Prosaics.* Minneapolis: University of Minnesota Press.

Leal, Luis. 1966. *Historia del cuento hispanoamericano.* Mexico City: Andrea.

Lindstrom, Naomi. 1989. *Women's Voice in Latin American Literature.* Washington, DC: Three Continents Press.

———. 1994. *Twentieth-Century Spanish American Fiction.* Austin: University of Texas Press.

MacAdam, Alfred J. 1977. *Modern Latin American Narratives: The Dreams of Reason.* Chicago: University of Chicago Press.

Magnarelli, Sharon. 1985. *The Lost Rib: Female Characters in the Spanish-American Novel.* Lewisburg, PA: Buckness University Press; London: Associated University Presses.

Marcos, Juan Manuel. 1986. *De García Márquez al postboom.* Madrid: Origenes.

Menton, Seymour. 1993. *Latin America's New Historical Novel.* Austin: University of Texas Press.

Mudrovcic, María Eugenia. 1993. "En busca de dos décadas perdidas: la novela latinoamericana de los años 70 y 80." *Revista Iberoamericana* 164–165: 445–68.

———. 1997. *Mundo Nuevo: Cultura y Guerra Fría en la década del 60.* Buenos Aires: Beatriz Viterbo.

Ortega, Julio. 1984. *Poetics of Change: The New Spanish-American Narrative.* Trans. Galen D. Greaser and Julio Ortega. Austin: University of Texas Press.

Paz, Octavio. 1968–1969 [1961]. "A Literature of Foundations." Trans. Lysander Kemp. *Tri-Quarterly* 13–14: 7–12.

Peden, Margaret Sayers. 1983. *The Latin American Short Story: A Critical History.* Boston, MA: Twayne.

Pons, María Cristina. 1996. *Memorias del olvido: la novela histórica de fines del siglo XX.* Mexico City: Siglo XXI.

Rama, Ángel. 1976. *Los dictadores latinoamericanos.* Mexico City: Fondo de Cultura Económica.

———. 1986. *La novela en América Latina. Panoramas 1920–1980.* Montevideo: Fundación Rama; Xalapa, México: Universidad Veracruzana.

Rodríguez-Luis, Julio. 1980. *Hermenéutica y praxis del indigenismo: la novela indigenista, de Clorinda Matto a José María Arguedas.* Mexico City: Fondo de Cultura Económica.

Rodríguez Monegal, Emir. 1968–1968. "The New Latin American Novelists." *Tri-Quarterly* 13–14: 13–32.

———. 1970. "A Revolutionary Writing." *Mundus Artium* 3.3: 6–11.

———. 1972a. *El boom de la novela latinoamericana.* Caracas: Tiempo Nuevo.

———. 1972b. "Tradición y renovación." *América Latina en su literatura.* Ed. César Fernández Moreno. Mexico City: Siglo XXI. 139–66.

———. 1980. "El Boom de la novela latinoamericana: diez años después." *Requiem for the "Boom"–Premature?: A Symposium.* Montclair, NJ: Montclair State College. 186–96.

———. 1984. "The Boom: A Retrospective." *Review* 30–36.

Sánchez, Luis Alberto. 1968. *Proceso y contenido de la novela hispano-americana.* 2nd ed. Madrid: Gredos.

Shaw, Donald L. 1981. *Nueva narrativa hispanoamericana.* Madrid: Cátedra.

———. 1998. *The Post-boom in Spanish American Fiction.* Saratoga Springs, NY: SUNY Press.

Simpson, Amelia S. 1990. *Detective Fiction from Latin America.* Rutherford, NJ: Fairleigh University Press; London: Associated University Presses.

Sklodowska, Elzbieta. 1991. *La parodia en la nueva novela hispanoamericana.* Amsterdam/Philadelphia: John Benjamins.

———. 1992. *Testimonio hispanoamericano: Historia, teoría, poética.* New York: Peter Lang.

Sommer, Doris. 1991. *Foundational Fictions: The National Romances of Latin America.* Berkeley: University of California Press.

Sommers, Joseph. 1968. *After the Storm: Landmarks of the Modern Mexican Novel.* Albuquerque: University of New Mexico Press.

Souza, Raymond D. 1988. *La historia en la novela hispanoamericana moderna.* Bogotá: Tercer Mundo Editores.

Swanson, Philip. 1995. *The New Novel in Latin America: Politics and Popular Culture after the Boom.* Manchester, England: Manchester University Press.

Tittler, Jonathan. 1984. *Narrative Irony in the Contemporary Spanish-American Novel.* Ithaca, NY: Cornell University Press.

Unruh, Vicky. 1994. *Latin American Vanguards: The Art of Contentious Encounters.* Berkeley: University of California Press.

Vargas Llosa, Mario. 1969. "Novela primitiva y novela de creación." *Revista de la Universidad de México* 23.10: 29–36.

———. 1987. "The Boom Twenty Years Later: An Interview with Mario Vargas Llosa." With Raymond Leslie Williams. *Latin American Literary Review* 29: 201–6.

Vidal, Hernán. 1976. *Literatura hispanoamericana e ideología liberal: surgimiento y crisis (una problemática sobre la dependencia en torno a la narrativa del boom).* Buenos Aires: Hispamérica.

Viñas, David. 1981. "Pareceres y digresiones en torno a la nueva narrativa latinoamericana." *Más allá del boom: literatura y mercado.* Ed. David Viñas et al. Mexico City: Marcha. 13–50.

Weiss, Judith A. 1977. Casa de las Américas*: An Intellectual Review in the Cuban Revolution.* Chapel Hill, NC: Hispanófila.

Wellek, René, and Austin Warren. 1963 [1949]. *Theory of Literature.* 3rd ed. New York: Harcourt Brace Jovanovich.

Williams, Raymond L. 1995. *The Postmodern Novel in Latin America: Politics, Culture, and the Crisis of Truth.* New York: St. Martin's Press.

Zum Felde, Alberto. 1964. *La narrativa en Hispanoamérica.* Madrid: Aguilar.

CHAPTER 51

UTOPIC THEORIES IN BRAZIL

Vera Follain de Figueiredo

With regard to the nature of Brazilian culture, it is not possible to leave aside the centuries of self-inflicted anguish of Brazilians thinking of their country as being peripheral and the degree to which such a condition determines a vacillating, irregular, and paradoxical way of experiencing modernity. This experience differs, quite radically, from the way in which the hegemonic, capitalist countries underwent this experience. In *A Revolução Burguesa no Brasil* [1975; The Bourgeois Revolution in Brazil] Florestan Fernandes (1920–1995) has noted that in dependent societies that have undergone a colonial process, capitalism was neither born nor grew out of the internal differentiation of the preexistent economic order (the colonial economic system), which was introduced long before the establishment of a competitive social order. This notion of the anteriority of the colonial economic system has been considered and developed by a number of scholars who underline, among other related issues, the fundamental importance of the discordance among certain ideals that have been part of the cultural horizon of the elite, such as, for example, the Liberal utopia and the existing socio-economical conditions. Renato Ortiz has emphasized how modernity acquired the character of a national aim-to-be-achieved in the Brazilian imaginary, drawing attention to the frequent ideological inversion between the superstructure (the national economic indicators) and the infrastructure (the substandard living conditions of the majority), an inversion caused by the very modernizing desire that constituted the national project of building the country.

We are concerned here with interrogating such a discordance, not as a result of the ideological issues (Schwarz)—which have been widely discussed—but rather insofar as it allows us to link it to a specific way of experiencing historical temporality. That is, if the modernizing imaginary is characterized by the dream of conquering the future, the cult of anticipation is even stronger in those countries experiencing slow modernization. The anticipatory attitude that often led Brazilians to try to exceed their own set pace is related to the fact that Brazilians always want to keep up with what they take to be the rhythm of Western civilization—a position that is concomitant with the feeling that Brazil is living in the past (of the hegemonic world). Therefore, instead of emphasizing the resolution of the contradictions of the present, the emphasis has fallen on the creation of anticipatory devices built in order to quickly implant the future idealized by the elite.

The Brazilian urgency to be modern was born together with the political independence of the country, when Romantic ideals prevailed. In this sense, the positions assumed by Joaquim Nabuco (1849–1910) and José de Alencar (1829–1877) are representative because they point toward the paradigms that shaped for a long time this modernization project. Both of these writers looked toward developed countries and took from them the models that were to guide the construction of the Brazilian nation. Nabuco looked toward England and France, and following a universalist perspective, decided that Brazil should be completely Westernized following their examples. Alencar, on the other hand, privileged the kind of

symbiosis that would take into account the particularities of Brazil. Both were eager to transform the current order, without serious modifications. From that time on, it is possible to say that, with certain variations and operating under other theoretical proposals, Brazil's modernizing projects tended, on the whole, not to modify the basic assumptions of these paradigms.

At the turn of the nineteenth century, certain notions, such as progress, rupture, or revolution, increasingly prevailed in the intellectual discourse and also in the projects for social intervention in Brazilian society. Thus, the first years of the twentieth century were characterized by specific formulations marked by the predominance of racial and geo-climatic determinisms based on a vague scientific ideology that permitted the identification of "modernizing" with "civilizing," with all the connotations of moral superiority implicit in the latter term. The aim was to defeat backwardness and to introduce the capitalist ethos following the model of the hegemonic countries. Euclides da Cunha's (1866–1909) *Os Sertões* [1902; *Rebellion in the Backlands*, 1944] placed before readers the dilemma experienced by the writer, when he attempted to interpret the heterogeneous nature of Brazilian society from the standpoint of evolutionist criteria, which could not, it seemed, account for the issues arising out of the local context. A great part of the power of this work lies precisely in the tension on which it is structured: One pole is the context that generated the problem from which the book arose–the uneven and excluding process of modernization–whereas the other, resulting from this, is the role and the formation of the intellectual in countries where the development of modernity occurs intermittently, thus marginalizing large sectors of society.

Therefore, the social drama of *Os Sertões* is not linked to the emancipating and rational stage of the modernizing project, but to the stage that becomes confused with a sacrificial myth, justifying violence. As a result, it is related to the question of the place of production of theoretical thought in the modern world. Linked to European expansion, the construction of the idea of modernity involved the constitution of a privileged, hegemonic, geo-cultural place where knowledge is produced; that is, the place of theoretical production came to be identified with the so-called First World. Those countries with only a peripheral modernity would be destined to create culture, but the metropolitan centers would produce the intellectual discourse that would interpret that colonial cultural production, asserting themselves thus as the only place where valid epistemological categories would be defined. According to Walter Mignolo, no significant theoretical thought is expected to emerge from an economic and technologically underdeveloped country, for it is limited to a derivative way of thinking. In this respect, Euclides da Cunha lived the impasse of attempting to adjust the Eurocentric theories current at the time to a Brazilian reality these theories could not explain. In *Os Sertões*, the use of literary figuration and the use of a hybrid discourse fill the empty spaces left by the inadequacy of the positivist theoretical apparatus to deal, in a more direct way, with the issues created by the rebellion. Literary images and metaphors give flexibility to the rigidity of abstract positivist concepts and gave rise to a border discourse between fiction and theory, where the author places himself in the middle with the intention of constructing a philosophical position of his own, yet at the same time, without daring to articulate a different theoretical apparatus, a theoretical approach that could allow for the emancipation of the categories of knowledge, that is, one that would respond to reality and result in better understanding of Brazilian contradictions. In other words, as Walnice Nogueira Galvão states:

> Euclides denota oscilar entre concepções diversas daquilo que está ocorrendo. É preciso lembrar que nunca se livrou de todo dessas oscilações, que aparecem mais tarde n' *Os sertões* e cujo exemplo mais notável é aquela extraordinaria antítese que coloca o Conselheiro 'indo para a História como poderia ter ido para o hospício.' É assim que o esforço firme de enxergar com seus própios olhos e entender com sua própria razão alterna-se com recaídas nas idéias feitas. (Galvão 72)

> Euclides fluctuated between a variety of interpretations of what was happening. It is necessary to remember that he never got rid of those fluctuations–they emerge later in *Os Sertões* and their most remarkable example is that extraordinary antithesis which places the "Counsellor" 'walking towards History as he could have walked towards an asylum.' This is how the steady endeavor to see with his own eyes and to understand with his own reason alternates with relapses into the received Eurocentric ideas.

Thus, *Os Sertões* stage two different dramas: That of the *sertanejo*, the individual living in the *sertão*, who is excluded from the process of modernization, and that of the intellectual of a peripheral country who lives the clash between his European theoretical formation and the reality that defies it. But in fact, they can be considered two sides of a single drama: That of being outside the centers where decisions are taken, either in socio-economical or in intellectual terms.

In *A América Latina: males de origem* [1903; Latin America: Evils of Origin], Manoel Bomfim (1868–1932) experienced similar difficulties to those lived by Euclides da Cunha because he tried to revise the models of scientific thought of the time in order to denounce the exploitation suffered by the continent. With a more daring counterdiscourse, he kept the biological metaphors favored by the current theories but developed the concept of an Iberian parasite culture living off its host–the American colonies. This is how he characterized the kind of plundering that was colonial reality, a relationship that was responsible for the formation of conservative and reactionary ruling elites. The price Bomfim had to pay for the defiance of expressing a nationalistic critical thought that went against the ideas favored by his Brazilian elite (including his condemnation of ideas of the superiority and inferiority of the races) was, apart from Sílvio Romero's negative criticism of the book, the fact that his intellectual production was ignored for a very long time. According to Dante Moreira Leite (1992), in a later book–*O Brasil Nação* [1931; Brazil Nation]–Bomfim denounced Gobineau's racism precisely at the time when Oliveira Viana (1883–1951), whose work was extremely successful, referred to the French count as a mighty genius and discussed the whitening of Brazil.

Already in the 1920s and 1930s, motivated by the economic, political, and cultural transformations that took place in Brazil and Europe, the modernizing project acquired a more nationalistic outlook, both to the right and to the left. During this period, intellectual production stood out because of its endeavor to understand and explain Brazil,

either in a conservative way, looking back toward the past in order to appraise the Portuguese-Brazilian roots and to privilege certain aspects related to continuity, or else looking back toward the past but in order to find arguments that could oppose the conservative tendencies of the present. Oswald de Andrade's (1890–1954) *Antropofagia* [Anthropophagy], which emerged in the 1920s and was taken up again in the late 1940s, constituted a new tendency in Brazilian thought, one that aimed at overcoming both Romantic idealism and determinist pessimism founded on ethnocentrism. The proposal to "ver com olhos livres" ["see with free eyes"] expressed in the 1924 *Manifesto Pau-Brasil* acquired a strong critical sense: The eyes must be freed from Eurocentric epistemological categories for the better understanding of Brazilian society. Oswald de Andrade's cultural political attitude turned against the colonialist mentality of passively accepting the values of Western civilization–which separated from their original European historicity were now imposed as universal. According to Florestan Fernandes (1987), in Latin America, the anticolonialism found in the privileged groups of society was only evident in one aspect, that of conquering the legal and political conditions for acquiring power. In all other aspects, the local elite promoted a freeze on decolonization. Thus, Oswald de Andrade aimed at fostering a thaw of such an attitude by offering a new interpretation of history: He opposed the acceptance of the sacrificial myth that emerged with modernity, the sense that the European mission was to bring civilization to primitive and barbarous peoples even if it was necessary to employ violence in order to submit them. He proclaimed his anticolonialist position: "Contra todas as catequeses. E contra a mãe dos Gracos" (1972, 6:13) (Against all forms of catechism. And against the mother of the Gracos), he stated in the *Manifesto antropófago*. The turmoil in Europe at the turn of the century weakened the totalizing, incorporating and universalizing codes created by the big metropolitan centers, and opened a space for new representations that acted as counterpoints to the dominant rhetoric:

> Neste momento a Europa viveu uma crise psicológica em face da tecnização, mercantilizaçao, alienação e violencia generalizada, expressas em termos de contradições marxistas, decadência splengleriana e invasões freudianas do subconsciente. A tomada de consciência latino-americana exigia precisamente esta dissolução dos motivos evolucionistas e reformistas. A Europa agora oferecia patologias e não apenas modelos. O desencanto no centro motivava a reabilitação na periferia. (Morse 183)

> At that time, Europe underwent a psychological crisis as a result of a general process of technologization, mercantilization, alienation, and violence, all of which were expressed in terms of Marxist contradictions, Splenglerian decadence, and Freudian invasion of the subconscious. The Latin American process of awareness demanded precisely the dissolution of these evolutionist and reformist motives. Europe now offered pathologies, not just models. The center's disenchantment fostered the rehabilitation of the periphery.

Oswald took advantage of this opportunity in order to propose the revision and the deconstruction of Western representations of the non-European world, thus asserting the latter's right to narrate and construct its own images of modernity. In this sense, he announced the critical position that underlies magic realism, which emerged two decades later in Spanish America. Andrade's ideas are close to those expressed by the Cuban José Lezama Lima (1910–1976) in the 1957 conferences compiled in the book *La expresión americana* [1969; The (Spanish) American Expression]. In order to develop Spanish American history, Lezama Lima dissolved dichotomies and hierarchies that violate and distort Latin American culture. He replaced temporal order by free analogies, repetition by creative recurrences, and national thinking by imagination and memory.

The "anthropophagic" idea is inscribed within this context, and by this means it is possible to reread the paradigm of modern reason without necessarily being antimodern. Oswald avoided the methodology of binary oppositions, which tended to repeat, one way or another, the formulation coined by Domingo Faustino Sarmiento (1811–1888)–civilization or barbarism. Instead of proposing disjunctive polarizations, he propounded a dialectical hybridity; instead of "or" he said "and": "o misto de dorme nenê que o bicho vem pegá e de equações", "a floresta e a escola" ("the mixture of lullabies and equations; the forest and the school"). Cultural hybridization or miscegenation thus becomes a crucial category of analysis: The *Manifesto Antropófago* is, on the one hand, a Brazilian futurist song–the rupture of the internal code. Even if more concentrated in São Paulo, the demands for economic and political transformations and the increasing process of industrialization gave rise to the hope that Brazilians would be able to catch up with contemporaneity. On the other hand, it is also a primitivist song, as well as a break with Europe to promote a self-appraisal of what does not fit the European rational model. While adopting the paradox of primitivism-modernism, Oswald de Andrade also adopts a culturally decentered perspective: Recognizing the importance of modern technology is useful in neutralizing the comfortable temptation to interpret backwardness as the manifestation of some original creative force, not polluted by European vices. The valuation of the hybrid or *mestiço* aspects of Brazilian culture–not just restricted to the indigenous inheritance, but extended to the whole range of differences that result from mixing races and values–is useful to control the Brazilian nature of "do grito imperioso de brancura en mim" (203) ("the imperative shout of whiteness within me"), as can be seen in the poem "Improviso do mal da América" [The Improvised Evil of Latin America] written by Mário de Andrade.

The "anthropophagic" proposal does not just juxtapose São Paulo's enthusiasm for progress with a reappraisal of Indian origins. It also expresses the wish to decolonize a culture, rejecting European-Latin American polarizations. The praise for "Latin American irrationality" as a primitive alternative for the maladies of civilization comes from Europe, as does the unconditional cult of progress that excludes those countries whose modernization process is not completely achieved. "Anthropophagic" thinking criticizes the evolutionary and linear view of history of the West, which is alien to Latin America's multitemporality, its concurrent cultures that are centuries apart:

> Em Nietzsche e Kierkegaard, inicia-se no século XIX um dramático protesto humano contra o mundo lógico de Hegel e a sua terrível afirmação de que tudo que é racional é real. Hegel, que completa a metafísica clássica de Kant, promete e sagra a imagem dum mundo hierarquizado e autoritário que terminará nas delícias do Estado Prussiano e dialeticamente en Nüremberg. Com ambos tudo acabaria azul e legal, em catecismo e presepe. (O. de Andrade 1991, 102)

During the nineteenth century, Nietzsche and Kierkegaard began a dramatic outcry against the logical world of Hegel and his terrible assertion that all that is rational is real. Closing Kant's classical metaphysics, Hegel promises and venerates the image of a hierarchical and authoritarian world which will end in the pleasures of the Prussian state and dialectically in Nüremberg. Everything would be blue and nice, everything would end in catechism and cradle.

Marked by a cultural revolution that opened up new perspectives for Brazil (the national State asserted itself, industry was in the process of development, and a unique urban style was established), the 1930s announced the emergence of new ideas that would give a new dimension to the modernizing project, starting from the expectations that the hitherto excluded masses would be introduced to the idea of national participation. The increasing influence of Marxist thinking over Brazilian writers framed certain issues related not only to the artist's social commitment, but also to the political function of art itself. Oswald de Andrade became a member of the Communist Party (and remained active for almost fifteen years) and revealed his change of direction in his famous self-criticism, written in 1933, in the preface to *Serafim Ponte Grande* [*Seraphim Grosse Pointe*], when he declared he had been a clown of the bourgeoisie and asserted his desire to become, at least, a warrior in the Proletarian Revolution. Mário de Andrade (1893–1945) read texts about Marxism, and was receptive to socialism as an idea, although he did not fully accept Marx's philosophy. Nevertheless, he recognized in it a great deal of truth and often employed in his own works certain Marxist concepts as tools for analysis. At the end of his life, in *O banquete* [1977; The Banquet], through a dialogue between his characters, he developed the ethical and aesthetic issues that had confronted him, torn between the conviction that the artist should preserve his autonomy and the feeling that art had to be committed to the construction of a better world, an issue also explored (with a different approach, nearing social romance) in Oswald de Andrade's *Chão* (1945), the second volume of *Marco Zero*. Leandro Konder has shown the variety of paths taken by many Brazilians throughout their lives in response to Marxism:

> uns aderiram entusiasticamente a seus princípios (embora interpretando-os em termos diversos); outros lhe reconheceram aspectos estimulantes e trataram de assimilá-los, em diferentes graus e sob formas distintas; outros, ainda, prestaram-lhe a homenagem de discutir com ele, recusando-o de maneira global, mas freqüentando-o como interlocutor incômodo porém útil, ao qual se volta sempre para o exercício da discórdia. (11)

> some enthusiastically adhered to its principles (although interpreting it in a variety of ways); others recognized in it some stimulating aspects and tried to assimilate them in different degrees and under different forms; others paid the tribute of arguing with it, globally rejecting it, but frequenting it as a troublesome, though useful, notion that could always be addressed for the sake of debate.

In the atmosphere of the 1930s and 1940s, the issue of the interplay between aesthetics and politics assumed ever-increasing importance and emphasized, in those artists involved in the climate of revolutionary utopia, a sense of mission and a conviction that sacrifice was needed for the success of collective causes. These feelings led Mário de Andrade to question himself in his 1942 conference "Movimento Modernista" and to demand of himself a more serious endeavor in the social struggles of his time:

E si agora percorro a minha obra já numerosa e que representa uma vida trabalhada, não me vejo uma só vez pegar a máscara do tempo e esbofetea-la como ela merece. Quando muito lhe fiz de longe umas caretas. Mas isto, a mim, não me satisfaz.
(Mário de Andrade [1964?], 253)

And if I now look at my already extensive work, which represents an entire life of writing, I do not see myself even once getting hold of the mask of time and slapping it as it deserved. At most, I made, from afar, some faces at it. But this, to me, is not enough.

The idea that art was committed to a change of direction to be taken by Brazilian history–which at that moment was measured by writers of the Left (they did so in a narrow political sense and held to the attitude that the conscious sacrifice of the transitory creative aspects of art was necessary so that the work could be useful)–had aesthetic consequences which in certain ways can be seen as retrogressive in relation to earlier literary and artistic achievements. One of these retrogressive measures that emerged was the link established between committed art and Realist art; this was not to be the Realism of another reality, Brazilian reality, but rather that imported Realism that basically corresponded to the cognitive structures of the nineteenth-century European bourgeoisie, that is, a Eurocentric Realism, full of systematic logic, which was not capable of capturing the contradictions of Brazilian life. Brazilian intellectuals of the day were also engaged in defending collective social causes and therefore tended to attribute to themselves the role of cultural consciousness, that is, the role of a superior person who holds the truth and must enlighten those who look up to him. This explains the didactic register (in the style of Socialist Realism) that from time to time affects Brazilian fiction: The omniscient narrator speaks as the voice of the committed writer. The narration is not problematized and, as Antônio Cândido (b. 1918) has observed, the singular humanity of the protagonists is sacrificed to the didactic imperative.

Marxist thought also contributed to the process of recovery of a capitalist perspective by which it was assumed that social or cultural backwardness, instead of being a feature of Brazilian culture, was the result of Brazil's economic backwardness. It was thought that it was necessary to attain a capitalist modernity, carrying out the bourgeois democratic revolution based on the model of the hegemonic countries– something that forced a temporary alliance with a financial and industrial bourgeoisie–in order to create the necessary conditions for the following stage, socialism. This modernizing attitude created a chasm between the past and the future one wanted to build, thus becoming an excluding, Westernized position that did not contemplate the multifaceted aspects of a hybrid culture like Brazil's. All the endeavors of the "anthropophagic" proposal–in the sense of working in the area of culture through accumulation and breaking down hierarchies–were left aside. In this sense, the novel *Jubiabá* (1935), considered by Jorge Amado (1912–2001) as the start of his mature work, can be taken as an example of the artistic impasse generated in fiction by such a political commitment. A novel dealing with the formation of a man of conscience, the Brazilian hero of low origins, *Jubiabá* describes the evolutionary course of Balduíno, from being a rogue to becoming the leader of the workers (see Duarte). Roguery is seen as a stage of prerevolutionary revolt. Balduíno does not accept entering the working world because, intuitively, he rejects the condition of slave, which characterized Brazilian workers. At this stage, his behavior mirrors the stereotype of Brazilian man, according to the project of a national-popular culture:

Balduíno the black man is strong, brave, sensual, musical, and a good athlete, he follows an Afro-Christian religion, and he is not attached to material values. However, when he becomes aware of the notion of class and learns about the principles of capitalist exploitation he breaks with his racial and social stereotypes and begins to look at them with contempt, as the fruits of ignorance:

Meu povo, vocês não sabe nada. . . . Eu tou pensando na minha cabeça que vocês não sabe nada. . . . Vocês precisam ver a greve, ir para a greve. Negro faz greve, não é mais escravo. Que adianta negro rezar, negro vir cantar para Oxóssi? Os ricos manda fechar a festa de Oxóssi. . . . Negro não pode fazer nada, nem dançar para santo. Pois vocês não sabem de nada. (Amado 299)

My people, you don't know anything. . . . I am thinking in my head that you don´t know anything. . . . You need to strike, to go on strike. The black man can strike, he is no slave no more. What's the use of the black man praying, of singing to Oxóssi? The rich here ordered an end to the celebration of Oxóssi. . . . What can the black man do? Blacks can't do anything, not even dance for the saints. You don't know anything.

In order to become a revolutionary militant, the protagonist has to leave behind the characteristics that shaped his cultural identity. The profound transformation of his worldview, which aims at didactically showing the steps that the Brazilian people must take in order to change the face of the country, is artificial and produces an imbalance in the novel, thus affecting its internal coherence.

Although also interested in Marxist thought, Graciliano Ramos (1892–1953) followed a different path. For the author of *Vidas Sêcas* [1938; *Barren Lives;* 1965], writing committed to collective ideals is the place where tensions are staged and where the ways to be followed are demonstrated. Thus his novels, in contrast to Amado's, do not have an absolute narrative voice that submits the characters to preestablished norms, imprisoning them inside an ideological logic for didactic purposes, according to a doctrinaire view. On the contrary, his novels incorporate a worldview that belongs to society undergoing uneven modernization, thus showing contempt for any communist utopia; the author's pessimism did not allow him to work, at least in the field of fictional narrative and chronicle, with a teleological view of history. Historical reality and fiction are entertained in the world of the characters, which lies beyond the center where decisions are taken, at the margins of significant events. Within the modest environment of these characters, national history is felt as something that takes place somewhere else; it is just the news in the newspaper that does not affect the everyday life of people; but socioeconomic facts become intermingled with the fictional world, and past and present, too, become confused, as can be seen, for instance, in *Infância* [1993; Childhood]:

Fatos antigos se renovavam, confundiam-se com outros recentes, e as notícias dos jornais determinavam perturbações nos espíritos. Debatiam-se Canudos, a Revolta da Armada, a Abolição e a Guerra do Paraguai como acontecimentos simultâneos. A república, no fim do segundo quadriênio, ainda não parecia definitivamente proclamada. Realmente não houvera mudança na vila. Os mesmos jogos da gamão e solo trasmitiam-se de geração a geração; as mesmas pilhérias provocavam as mesmas risadas. (Ramos 47)

Old events were renewed, and became confused with other more recent ones, and the news in the newspapers determined the disturbances of the spirits. Certain events like the Canudos Rebellion, the Army Revolt, the abolition of slavery and the

Paraguay War were discussed as if they were simultaneous. At the end of the second four-year term, the Republic still did not seem definitely proclaimed. The village had not changed at all. The same games of backgammon and cards were transmitted from one generation to the next; the same jokes produced the same laughter.

And, further on, the narrator adds:

> A política nacional era um romance que os meninos barbados folheavam, largavam, retomavam, deturpavam. Versáteis, não permaneciam nas alturas, caíam nos sucessos vulgares, que eram também contos de fadas. . . . Abaixo dessa classe andavam criaturas que não liam journais, ignoravam D. Pedro II e o Barão de Ladário. (Ramos 49)

> National politics was a novel which bearded boys discussed, abandoned, took up again, and spoiled. Being versatile, they did not stay with it, falling back to vulgar events, which were also fairy tales. . . . Below this class were the people who did not read newspapers, and did not know King Pedro II or Baron de Ladário.

The cultured writing of the author is in touch with the oral narratives of the predominantly unlettered context that surrounds him. Without adopting a populist attitude, Graciliano Ramos endeavored to rescue the wisdom of the oral universe that social change tended to extinguish, as can be seen in the presentation of *Alexandre e outros heróis* [1962; Alexander and Other Heroes]. The narrative lets us see, by means of the severe criticism of the bourgeois capitalist world and the relativization of its values, that modernization and progress are not values in themselves, and that they come at a price. The future is woven from the threads of the past; hence the significance of memory in his work. By means of memory, he rearticulates and re-invents what was lived, looking for the meaning that cannot be obtained from a mere succession of facts resulting from collected data; memory can emerge from the free rearrangement of selected features that depend on the point of view of the narrator.

The commitment that artists of the Left felt toward the socio-political process in the 1930s has a parallel (keeping in mind the differences between two historic moments) in the atmosphere of commitment of the 1960s. During the latter period, fertilized by the ideas of the 1950s, especially those produced by the intellectual group of the Instituto Superior de Estudos Brasileiros (ISEB) (Brazilian Institute of Advanced Studies), the artistic avant-garde of the Left set itself the task of fighting cultural alienation as a form of struggle against U.S. imperialism, which is clearly expressed in the program of the Centros Populares de Cultura (CPC) (Popular Centers for Culture), which was organized by the National Union of Students.

In the 1960s atmosphere, arts for mass audiences, such as cinema and theater, assumed a predominant role in the cultural landscape. People believed in their capacity to change socio-economic reality by the power of the word, by creating a new consciousness among the people and certain sectors of the bourgeoisie. They believed in the power of art to place the revolutionary word centerstage: An art whose modernity was fuelled by the very obstacles it faced, which grew out of the very lack of resources, as was defined in Glauber Rocha's (1939–1981) "Uma estética da fome" [1965; An Aesthetics of Hunger]. Within the teleological perspective of history that accompanied the revolutionary utopia, the link between the cunning of the intellectual and the astuteness of the historian announced the possibility of building a new reality where progress would be at the service of social justice. Either seen from a revolutionary or a reformist perspective, what can be observed is that the varied ideological currents of the Left that marked Brazilian thought during the twentieth century mostly tended to work with the idea of discordance, of anachronism in the social structure of the country, and tended to attribute to intellectuals and certain sectors of the national bourgeoisie the role of an avant-garde capable of creating strategies to speed up Brazil's development, anticipating more advanced stages, but unfortunately blind to the historical limits of their efforts. Thus, the inversion of the superstructure and infrastructure, pointed out by Renato Ortiz, continued to be a constant feature throughout the century. Besides favoring an uncritical view of Western modernity, the will to be modern has led Brazilians to put aside their own rhythm and has ended up generating an uncomfortable sense of fragility for social projects, as if Brazilians' build great stages for a political denouement that never comes and that is always overcome by the legacy of the denial of the imported European utopias. In order to convey this pessimistic feeling, there is no better example than the situation lived by Gil, a character in the novel *Bar Don Juan* (1971), written by Antonio Callado (1917–1997), who during the 1960s set out to write the great novel of the Brazilian Revolution: He registered everything, arranged all, created round characters, and placed them in their positions, ready to act, and waited for the leading thread of the story. Since it never came, he abandoned fiction, declaring that he did not want to write a book about people who imagined themselves chosen to produce history but who lived in a pre-historical country. At the beginning of the twenty-first century, when the significant changes that have taken place in the Western world seem to turn the modern dream into something obsolete, leaving behind historical, libertarian notions in order to assume directly a more pragmatic approach, we have created as compensation a new aim—that of managing to be completely postmodern, whatever that means for Brazilian society, thus overcoming our *eterno anacronismo* ("eternal anachronism").

Translation by Nair María Anaya Ferreira

Works Cited

Amado, Jorge. 1984. *Jubiabá*. Rio de Janeiro: Ed. Record.

Andrade, Mário de. [1964?]. *Aspectos da literatura brasileira*. São Paulo: Livraria Martins Editora.

—— 1966. "Improviso do mal da América." *Obras completas*. Vol 2: *Poesías completas*. São Paulo: Martins. 203.

——. 1977. *O banquete*. São Paulo: Livraria Duas Cidades.

Andrade, Oswald de. 1972. "Manifesto antropófago." *Obras completas*. Vol 6: *Do pau-Brasil à antropofagia e ás utopias*. Rio de Janeiro: Civilização Brasileira. 11–19.

——. 1974 [1945]. *Chão*. Rio de Janeiro: Civilização Brasileira

——. 1991. *Estética e política*. São Paulo: Editora Globo.

Bomfim, Manoel José do. 1903. *A America Latina: Males de origem*. Rio de Janeiro: H. Garnier.

——. 1931. *O Brasil nação: Realidade da soberania brasileira*. Rio de Janeiro: Livraria F. Alves.

Cândido, Antônio. 1967. *Literatura e sociedade: estudos de teoria e história literária*. São Paulo: Companhia Editora Nacional.

Duarte, Eduardo de Assis. 1996. *Jorge Amado: romance em tempo de utopia*. Rio de Janeiro: Editora Record.

Fernandes, Florestan. 1976. *A revolução burguesa no Brasil: ensaio de interpretação sociológica*. Rio de Janeiro: Zahar Editores.

———. 1987. "O problema da descolonização." *América Latina: 500 anos da conquista*. Ed. Paulo San Martin, Carlos Eduardo Dias Camargo and Augusto Lanzoni. São Paulo: Ícone Editora. 29–39.

Galvão, Walnice Nogueira. 1976. *Saco de Gatos: ensaios críticos*. São Paulo: Livraria Duas Cidades.

Konder, Leandro. 1991. *Intelectuais brasileiros e marxismo*. Belo Horizonte: Ed. Oficina de Livros.

Leite, Dante Moreira. 1992. *O caráter nacional brasileiro: história de uma ideologia*. São Paulo: Editôra Ática.

Lezama Lima, José. 1969. *La expresión americana*. Madrid: Alianza Editorial.

Mignolo, Walter. 1996. "La razón postcolonial: herencias coloniales y teorías postcoloniales." *Revista Gragoatá* [Editora da Universidade Federal Fluminense] 1: 7–29.

Morse, Richard M. 1990. *A volta de McLuhanaíma: cinco estudos solenes e uma brincadeira séria*. Trans. Paulo Henriques Britto. São Paulo: Companhia das Letras.

Ortiz, Renato. 1988. *A moderna tradição brasileira: cultura brasileira e indústria cultural*. São Paulo: Editora Brasiliense.

Ramos, Graciliano. 1993. *Infância*. Rio de Janeiro: Editora Record.

Schwarz, Roberto. 1977. *Ao vencedor as batatas: forma literária e processo social nos inícios do romance brasileiro*. São Paulo: Livraria Duas Cidades.

CHAPTER 52

CONSERVATISM AND MODERNIZATION IN BRAZIL

Victor Hugo Adler Pereira

The Crisis of Patriarchal Thought

Some original points in the ideology of the Getulio Vargas's "New State" (1937–1945) must not overshadow the fact that it marks a continuity with a particular line of traditional Brazilian authoritarian thought. If the ideology of the New State was linked to and supported by a fascist mentality, both in Brazil and abroad, it developed and even extended some of the basic elements of that discourse. The New State discourse was simultaneously constituted by the pronouncements, icons, and propaganda offered in a variety of media; without question these administrative measures constituted the active part of the state's attempt to control the production of the imaginary. The authoritarian modernization of the New State introduced projects to organize educational and cultural activities that will be explored in this text in relation to the ideology associated with such measures. The New State's project was framed both in a populist critique of traditional intellectuals and in an attack on their separation of culture from everyday life.

Some significant studies of New State ideology in Brazil emerged in the late 1970s during the gradual return to democracy, which eventually cast off the controls of the military regime. The large number of these studies suggests that this research was the turning point for Brazil's political life as well as its culture; it is summarized in the question "Quando é que a coesão das esquerdas, alcançada na resistência à repressão e à tortura, cede lugar a diferenças internas significativas?" (Santiago 1998, 11) ("When does the cohesion of the left, attained during the resistance to repression and torture, give way to significant internal differences?"). The close study of the New State shows a break in that cohesion of the left and marked differences in the various interpretations of national origins and the nature of authoritarianism in Brazil.

Some outstanding works of the 1970s contributed to the critical revision of the relationships between authoritarian ideas and the role of intellectuals in a position of political power, which is still a part of Brazil's present debate. Jardim de Moraes's *A brasilidade modernista: Sua dimensão filosófica* [1978; Modernist Brazilianness: Its Philosophical Dimension] identifies matrices of thought common to two radically different groups in the political establishment: On the one hand, the leftist *Pau-Brasil/Antropofagia* movement and on the other, the rightist *verde-amarelista/Anta* (green-yellow Anta group). Although both proposed the dissemination of similar aesthetic principles, they represented very different political positions and projects to transform the country: The former group embodied the intense intellectual activity of Oswald de Andrade (1890–1954), and the latter the fascist militancy of Plínio Salgado (1895–1975). There was a deeper common denominator that Jardim de Moraes identified in the works of Graça Aranha (1868–1931), especially in *A estética da vida* [1921; Life Aesthetics]. Some features from which modernist ideology developed (Moraes 11) have been characterized by an emphasis on the problematization of what is "national" and by the idea of social integration and its emphasis on intuition in

place of reason. The introduction of these ideas by Graça Aranha occurred as part of his critique of positivism, an attack based on a monist and vitalist perspective inherited from the Recife School, where Tobias Barreto (1839–1889) had taught Aranha's generation. Graça Aranha argued that

> a ciência é via de acesso a uma compreensão parcelada da realidade; ela decompõe e analisa, mas não permite ao espírito humano a compreensão do universo em sua realidade essencial. (Moraes 21)

> science gives society a divided comprehension of reality; on the one hand, it decomposes and on the other it analyzes, but it does not allow the human spirit to understand the universe in its essential reality.

Human suffering results from abandoning a sense of wholeness, a sense of the universe that results from an awakened consciousness; this sense of the whole is what frees humanity from the terror of the unknown. The solution is the recovery of an integration with the cosmos, which, in Graça Aranha's mind, could be attained only "pelo sentimento, por vias emocionais como a religião, a filosofia, a arte e o amor" (Moraes 24) ("by feeling, by using the emotional channels such as religion, philosophy, art, and love"). It is important to underline the central role played by intuition in such ideas, because it is a way of carrying out intellectual activities and communicating such issues as nationalism. Jardim de Moraes distinguishes among these implications in the use of the term "intuition":

> A intuição sentimental da realidade, e não a reflexão a respeito dos fragmentos de que a compõe, que seria o caminho da ciência, é o que permite a Graça Aranha apreender a nacionalidade brasileira. Esta nacionalidade, captada de forma intuitiva, como o será também nas vertentes oswaldiana e verde-amarelista do modernismo ou no *Retrato do Brasil* de Paulo Prado, se define através dos traços psicológicos coletivos que constituem a alma brasileira. (31)

> The intuitive feeling about reality, and not the reflection on the fragments that shape it (which would be the ways of science), is what Graça Aranha advocates with regard to Brazilian nationalism. Such sense of nation, intuitively apprehended or the same way, as was proposed by Oswald de Andrade and the verde-amarela (green-yellow) current or in Paulo Prado's (1869–1943) *Retrato do Brasil* [1920; Portrait of Brazil], is defined as a collective psychological configuration that constitutes the Brazilian soul.

Moraes argues that there is a continuity of modernist ideas into the late twentieth century that can be seen by looking beyond the ruptures to a real ideological development. This continuity opens the way for postmodernism, according to Silviano Santiago (1987, 114), as he stated in his lecture "Discurso da tradição no modernismo" ["Traditional Discourse in Modernism"]. He points out that the continuing and intimate contradiction between the spirit of nationalist deconstruction and the search for cultural roots has been present since 1924, during the first modernist generation, and was openly expressed by Oswald de Andrade, Mário de Andrade

(1893–1945), Tarsila do Amaral (1886–1973), and Blaise Cendrars (1887–1961) on their visit to Ouro Preto:

> A contradição entre . . . Modernismo, no sentido brasileiro, já existe em 24, no momento mesmo em que os novos estão tentando impor uma estética da originalidade entre nós. A emergência do discurso histórico no Modernismo visa a uma valorização do nacional em política e do primitivismo em arte. (Santiago 1987, 127)

> The contradiction within . . . modernism, in the Brazilian sense, was already present (in 1924), precisely at the time when the newcomers were trying to impose the aesthetics of originality among us. The emergence of historical discourse of modernism looks for a reappraisal of the national in politics and of primitivism in art.

Considering the rethinking of the national, by means of the search for what was genuine in the past, it is not surprising that the modernists from the Ministry of Education and Health, headed by Mário de Andrade during the 1930s created the Serviço do Patrimônio Artístico Nacional (SPHAN) (National Art Heritage Service), as Silviano Santiago reminds us (1987, 125).

Jardim de Moraes emphasizes the continuance of Graça Aranha's ideas in the work of both Oswald de Andrade and Plínio Salgado, and after examining the debates that separated the followers of the anthropophagic movement and the *verde-amarelistas*, he concludes that such political differences cancelled each other out, at the level of ideas, because they were based on "solo comum" (Moraes 164) ("a common ground"). In his conclusion, Moraes points to the new direction taken by these ideas when they responded to Graça Aranha's appeal to an intuitionist philosophy aimed at social action: "Em 1932 Plínio Salgado lança a Ação Integralista, e Oswald de Andrade já aderira ao Partido Comunista" (Moraes 169) ("In 1932, the Fascist leader Plínio Salgado launched his Integral Action program, and Oswald de Andrade had already joined the Communist Party"). Silviano Santiago (b. 1936) considered the lines of difference, in relation to tradition, in the discourse of Oswald de Andrade, starting from his philosophical texts, in which he discussed his utopian proposals of returning to a matriarchy. He concludes,

> . . . para Oswald o Brasil é por excelência o país da utopia, desde que—como pensavam os modernistas—se atualizasse pela industrialização. Voltando ao Matriarcado de Pindorama, à origem do Brasil e da utopia moderna na Europa, chegamos ao futuro. Dessa maneira, Oswald tenta conciliar a visão linear progressiva em direção ao futuro com o retorno ao Matriarcado. Seria o que se pode chamar de eterno retorno em diferença. Não seria o eterno retorno do mesmo, já que Oswald não quer, como Policarpo Quaresma, que o Brasil volte a ser um país indígena. (Santiago 1987, 128–29)

> . . . for Oswald, Brazil is the country of utopia par excellence, from the moment—as the modernists thought—it was modernized through the process of industrialization. By turning back to the matriarchy of Pindorama, which is Brazil's origin and that of Europe's modern utopia, Brazilians would arrive at the future. In that way, Oswald tries to reconcile the progressive, linear move towards the future, with a return to matriarchy. This would constitute what could be called the eternal return with a difference. It would not be an eternal return in itself, because Oswald does not want, like Policarpo Quaresma, Brazil to become a country of Indians again.

Santiago underlines the non-conformity of such discourse, its opposition to traditionalism, and establishes a parallel between the utopia of Oswald and the research carried out by Pierre Clastres on Brazilian indigenous societies, in which the French anthropologist confirmed that the construction of social structures had taken place in Brazil without being imposed by European power. He emphasizes that this was a non-conformist perspective that incorporated irrationality, an idea that became a central point in the reappraisal of conservative thought in Brazil during the 1970s. For example, Marilena Chauí (b. 1941), in her 1978 philosophical study, explored the discourse of the Ação Integralista Brasileira (Brazilian Integralist Action) led by Plínio Salgado. Unlike Moraes, Chauí analysed the kinship of the integralist proposal within the context of the historical and social modernist transformations that preceded the establishment of the New State. Discussing the efficacy of the process by means of which imported ideas were adapted to specific functions in Brazil, Chauí states,

> . . . a admissão de que pensamos por importação de idéias pressupõe, implicitamente, que há uma ideologia "correta", isto é, aquela que tem a função de espelhar invertida, . . . por isso mesmo, frágil e ridícula, ainda que sirva para sustentar processos históricos como a Abolição, a República, a Constituinte de 1934 ou a democratização de 1945. (28)

> To admit that we think on the basis of imported ideas assumes, implicitly, that there is a "correct" ideology, that is, an ideology that has the effect of an inverted mirror, . . . for that reason, such an ideology is fragile as well as ridiculous, even if it serves to support historical processes such as the Abolition of Slavery, the Republic, the 1934 Constitution, or the 1945 democratization.

According to Chauí, therefore, the role played by ideas closely tied to political practices is what legitimates those ideas as ideology, and not the other way around. We could add that to the degree to which capitalism is international, there is a circulation of ideas that accompanies the movement of goods, technology, and those practices transplanted in response to the needs of capital. The discourse to maintain the New Order is accompanied by counter-discourses, a by-product that cannot be controlled. The concern for establishing the links of discourses with specific political practices that are inherent in them alerts us to the serious discordance between the political role played by AIB (Brazilian Integralist Action) and the fragility of the theoretical formulations of the movement:

> É sempre tarefa ingrata acercar-se dos textos em que se expressa o pensamento autoritário no Brasil. Mesmo para um leitor que raramente se surpreenda, momentos há em que não poderá evitar uma interrogação: como um pensamento cuya debilidade teórica é gritante pode ser contraponteado pela eficácia prática? Ou, ao contrário, como uma dominação eficaz pode suscitar expressões teóricas tão inconsistentes?(Chauí 31)

> It is always an ungrateful task to approach the texts in which Brazil's fascist thought is expressed. Even for a reader who is rarely surprised, there will be moments in which he or she will not be able to avoid posing the following questions: How is it that such obviously theoretically weak thought can be counter-pointed by practical efficacy? Or, on the contrary, how can an effective political control give rise to such inconsistent theoretical expressions?

Chauí herself offers the key to interpret such an apparent contradiction when, some pages later, she analyses the intellectual production related to the Brazilian Integralist Action:

[Os textos integralistas] são, como diria Espinosa, textos onde as conclusões se sucedem com total ausência de premissas. Tal ausência engendra a debilidade teórica e sua contrapartida, isto é, a eficácia prática, pois, ausentes as premissas, o discurso torna-se normativo e programático-pragmático, o dever-se ocupando, assim, o lugar do ser, e as técnicas de ação, o lugar do agir. Não e surpreendente que, entre nós, formular um projeto de governo sempre apareça como a única via para fazer política e história. (Chauí 34)

(Integralist texts) are, as Spinoza would say, texts where the conclusions take place in a total absence of premises. Such absence engenders a theoretical weakness and its consequences, that is, it has immediate practical efficacy, because, unencumbered with long range plans and premises, the discourse becomes normative and programmatic with a pragmatic aim; immediate demands thus take the place of policy, and techniques for action take the place of action. It is not surprising that for Brazilians the decision to formulate a government project always appears as the only way to develop politics and history.

Marilena Chauí's approach to studying the integralist discourse involves a consideration of the specific modes of reception inherent to fascist ideology. The first point that I would want to stress in describing Chauí's conclusions is that integralist discourse operates with images instead of concepts (Chauí 40). Chauí describes some of the consequences of operating with images; among them, there is the creation of an illusion of knowledge (46) as a result of the ordering effect that such discourse produces in its elimination of the sense of fragmentation of immediate experience. Thus, concludes Chauí, images conveyed by this discourse have a persuasive and even constricting power; she adds,

Abolindo a distância entre o mundo e o discurso, as imagens soldam o real e a palavra fazendo com que o primeiro se organize de acordo com os parâmetros da segunda que se torna, então, organizadora da realidade e da ação. Quando se trata especificamente desta última, o papel das imagens é claro: pretendem criar no destinatário não só o sentimento da necessidade de agir, e de agir de maneira determinada, mas ainda convencê-lo de que aqueles que proferem o discurso podem ser os condutores da ação. (Chauí 47)

Abolishing the distance between the world and discourse, the images fuse the real and the word, organizing the real according to the criteria of the word, which becomes, then, the prime organizer of reality and action. Where action is concerned, the role of images is clear: They pretend to create in the addressee not just the feeling of the need to act, and to act in a determinate way, but they even try to convince him of the fact that those who utter the discourse can be the agents of social action.

The need to manipulate the public efficiently by persuasion and even aggression in order to convince or to instill loyalty was explicitly assumed by Plínio Salgado, who believed that this strategy was necessary because of the state of brutalization of the masses. He explained:

Não podemos de maneira nenhuma cortejar a massa popular. Ela é o monstro inconsciente e estúpido. Pelo contrário, devemos irritar o monstro para que ele nos agrida. Precisamos provocar agressões violentas, sem o que não poderemos exercer ação decisiva. (quoted in Chauí 48)

There is no way in which we can woo the masses. The masses are an unconscious and stupid monster. On the contrary, we must provoke it so that it attacks us. We must provoke violent aggressions, otherwise we will not be able to exert decisive action.

This statement articulates the nature of his political proposal of using direct action to overcome the backwardness of the masses; it would be an integralist struggle for social redemption, thus diminishing the earlier policy of defending the masses, seen as having been victimized by the abuses of capitalism imposed by neoliberal ideology. If the defense of the masses were emphasized, as it was and still is by leftist groups, it would lead the movement to take a definitive position in the class struggle, something that was ruled out in the discourse of rightist authoritarianism. In integralist discourse, for example, the word "class" was always substituted by the word "profession." This strategy was linked to the appeal to a national reconstruction by means of the participation of the different professions, something that was considered a radical initiative. In political practice, this proposal corresponded to Italian fascist corporativism, which had been absorbed by the New State and taken as a structuring principle of the relations between the state and the workers. Once the labor union movement that had represented workers' interests was eliminated, the New State organized and controlled its own network of professional union organizations.

If Marilena Chauí concentrates on the procedures that are characteristic of the integralist discourse, she does not overlook identifying its addressee. Discursive devices were created in order to mobilize a certain segment of the middle-class population, trying to foster their adhesion to specific government projects. According to her, class struggle was defused through a moralizing crusade based on the trinity of God, country, and family, which was the way of sensitizing specifically the urban middle classes to the redemptive feature of the New State. The middle classes had to take a position with regard to the turmoil of the 1924 Revolution and *tenentismo*; they did not want to keep the oligarchic privileges of the Old Republic, but they feared assuming a position on the left. Integralism offered the middle-class ideologues a way to respond to the impasse arising from such contradictions. Their discursive strategies, as was pointed out before, were not exclusive to Brazil; in fact, there are striking similarities among the discourses of fascist Spain, Italy, and Brazil.

Plínio Salgado (1895–1975) was fully aware of the manipulative nature of his policies. In October 1930 he wrote to Augusto Schmidt (1906–1965),

A bandeira que imagino que a Nação deve contemplar—será o Nacionalismo. Porque com ela captaremos os sentimentos. O sentimentalismo é a única força positiva da economia social brasileira. Com ele fizemos a Independência. Com ele fizeram-se todas as revoluções. Esta energia é incontestável no caráter nacional. Recrutemo-la. Ela, como sempre, caminhará às cegas. Nós a dirigiremos. Antes que outros a venham dirigir. (quoted Chauí 72–73)

The flag that the Nation must salute is Nationalism. With it we will capture the feelings. Sentimentalism is the only positive force of Brazilian social economy. With it we attained Independence. With it we launched the revolutions. This energy is indisputable in the national character. Let us recruit it. As usual, it will walk blind-folded. We will lead it. Before others come to lead.

Chauí's interpretation of the appeal to irrational elements in fascist discourse is linked to a distinction established by Moraes between the production of two kinds of intellectuals: The intellectual in whom the analytical perspective prevailed (represented by the work of Sílvio Romero (1851–1914) and Mário de Andrade), and those in whom a synthetic view predominated (exemplified by Oswald de Andrade and Plínio Salgado) (Moraes 124). Moraes distinguishes a discourse of a totalitarian nature in the work of the latter group of synthetic intellectuals, and links it to the way in which they developed the notion of intuitive knowledge and proposed the configuration of Brazil as a synthetic whole. He states that in the 1927 work *O curupira e o carão* [The Curupira and the Ugly Face], in which essays by Plínio Salgado, Menotti del Picchia (1892–1988), and Cassiano Ricardo (1895–1974) were compiled, the latter declared his contempt for scholarship and proposed instead an intuitive approach to the nation (147). The irrational nationalism of Brazilian fascist thought is explained lucidly by Marilena Chauí when she characterizes the construction of two opposed series of texts on Brazil: The artificial, that is, rational, legalistic, and foreign texts, on the one hand; and texts formed around the ideas associated with the natural, the real, and the national, on the other. She describes an operation of myth-substitution, which purports to give authenticity to the fascist discourse, overruling the obvious original links to European thought by means of the invention of a purportedly autochthonous mythology:

> Confundindo as imagens nativas com o movimento da história, acreditam que a substituição dos mitos de origem européia por outros, caboclos, é uma operação teórica suficiente para liberar o pensamento nacional das "influências" alienígenas. (Chauí 36)

> They believed that confusing native's images with historical ones, and replacing European myths by indigenous ones, was enough to free national thought from foreign "influences."

Another study on Brazilian thought, published around the same time—Carlos Guilherme Mota's (b. 1941) *Ideologia da cultura brasileira (1933–1974)* [Ideology of Brazilian Culture]—explores the relationship between intellectuals and power, examining the formation of the category "Brazilian culture," which, by virtue of official discourse and of its recurrence in a number of fields, was naturalized; that is, it became Brazilian ideological thought. Mota's analysis provides the historical dimension and shows the commitment to the interests and ideology of the conservative elites. Official government ideas, even in some texts of the 1930s that express an urge to political renewal, nevertheless stress the formation of a deep commitment that would be characteristic of the New State. This is the case, for instance, of the ideas of Fernando de Azevedo (1894–1974), who took a stand against capitalism and defended public education. Yet he also supported the 1937 Constitution and the educational project established by the New State by means of which the less favored classes were obliged to receive technical training, rather than post-secondary education—which meant they were destined to the subaltern positions of the industrial sectors. Azevedo's project for higher education reveals his elitist perspective and the mixing of traditionalism with a will to modernize Brazil. He proposed the centralization of university courses in the Faculty of Philosophy, because in that way Plato's academy in Greece and the university of the middle ages would be linked with modern research (Mota 79), thus enhancing the tempering of the cultural legacy by means of modern technological research from Europe and the United States. The commission that created the University of São Paulo in 1932, led by Fernando Azevedo and Júlio Mesquita Filho (1892–1969), invoked the aristocratic principle inherent in all higher culture on behalf of the nation, thus revealing an underlying rejection of the levelling effect of the masses (Mota 79). Such is the outlook of this influential New State thinker, clearly revealing that the fears of the uneducated urban and rural masses (which had been a part of patriarchal ideology dating back to the earliest colonial fears of a slave revolt) were very much alive in the worries about the possibility that the democratization of culture could take away absolute control from the elite.

It was not surprising, then, that in the 1930s there emerged a series of studies in conjunction with the New State that aimed at establishing an overview of Brazil that incorporated the presence of the lower classes, but were strongly marked by a patriarchal outlook. Mota demonstrates a parallel between Gilberto Freyre's (1900–1987) *Casa grande & senzala* [1933; *The Masters and the Slaves*, 1946] and Giuseppe Tomasi di Lampedusa's (1896–1957) *Il gattopardo* [1958; The Leopard], as works that offer a testimony to the crisis of the oligarchy, laying bare the implicit difficulties with traditional social relations and institutions. A taste for the popular gave a peculiar expression to this aristocratic view of the world; thus it is that Paulo Prado's *Retrato do Brasil* [1920; Portrait of Brazil], Sérgio Buarque de Holanda's (1902–1982) *Raízes do Brasil* [1936; Roots of Brazil], with their populist imagery, reveal the divided sentiments experienced by society at the turn of the 1930s (Mota 63).

The publication of Gilberto Freyre's *Casa grande & senzala* in 1933 and of Sérgio Buarque de Hollanda's (1902–1982) *Raízes do Brasil* in 1936 are thus interpreted as symptoms of an aristocratic nostalgia. In spite of the fact that in the context of the intellectual life of the time they seemed innovative, both works reveal that they are firmly committed to conservative thought. In the case of Gilberto Freyre, for instance, his work with the U.S. anthropologist Franz Boas allowed him to substitute for the traditional categories (in aristocratic ideology) of lineage and blood a new emphasis on the relations of race, culture, and environment. As Mota (61) points out, Freyre gave much greater psychological weight to "race" than did Boas. Sérgio Buarque de Hollanda's focus was also on the rural aristocracy and the psychological factors in the interpretation of situations of social life. Mota identifies the critical issues that arise because of his disciplinary formation:

> Segundo Emília Viotti da Costa, seria um trabalho de Psicologia Social, ou simplesmente uma obra ideológica sobre o caráter do brasileiro, cuyo foco estaria localizado na descrição intuitiva do brasileiro de classe alta, segundo Dante Moreira Leite. (31)

> According to Emília Viotti da Costa, it [*Raízes do Brasil*] belongs to Social Psychology, or it is simply an ideological work about the character of Brazilian people, concentrating on the intuitive description of upper-class Brazilians, according to Dante Moreira Leite.

The method of analyzing Brazilian reality adopted by these scholars—whose perspective was determined by a patriarchal bias—was committed to the study of origins developed into an ideological discourse, which they considered to be as generalizing explanations applicable to different regions of the country and all social classes, and covering very long historical periods. As Chauí has stated, they aimed to gain support in the established academic institutions of knowledge, which, quite clearly, was necessary to legitimate their interpretation of the Brazilian people as a whole, an interpretation whose function was both to guarantee and when necessary to impose the modes of control of the intellectual elite. And, according to Mota, "Sob a capa de um tratamento científico, às vezes buscando instrumental na Antropologia e na Sociologia, deixam escorrer sua ideologia—como é o caso do luso-tropicalismo de Gilberto Freyre" (30) ("Under the guise of scientific study, applying methodologies borrowed openly from Anthropology and Sociology, these apologists for the State allow their ideology to become the dominant factor in their writing, as is the case with Gilberto Freyre's tropicalism").

One of the aspects that link the discourse of these 1930s scholars to the conservative thought of Brazil's colonial past is the fact that their arguments are founded on intuitionist, irrational factors in order to explain what is considered to be Brazilian reality. Like Moraes, Mota points to huge intuitive syntheses as the main feature of these thinkers, that is, what to Moraes would also constitute the intellectual basis for the authoritarian practices made possible by such discourses.

Another revisionist study of the 1930s intellectuals was Sérgio Miceli's (b. 1945) *Intelectuais e classe dirigente no Brasil (1920–1945)* [Intellectuals and the Ruling Class in Brazil], which was also published in the late 1970s. Miceli's study agrees with the others in its main thesis about the relationships between intellectuals and power. His concern for recovering Brazilian cultural history seems to be closely linked to his concern to analyze the degrees of commitment to which the intellectual would submit himself in the 1970s if he had to face the end of the military regime and thus enter a period in which the positioning of diverse initiatives of cultural production would once again become as intense as it was in the 1930s. His approach is to analyze the mechanisms that explain the course taken by cultural production during the 1930s: Apart from the generally repressive nature of the New State bureaucracy, he includes its propaganda and, most importantly, its promotion of cultural activities. This perspective allows him to identify the signs of rationalization of such activities, a rationalization that would reveal the appeal of modernization. What becomes clear is that modernization was promoted in an authoritarian way, but it was given legitimacy by establishing ties with the old oligarchic elites. The paradox was that this was a populist promotion of cultural activities that sought an alliance with the ruling elite in order to maintain control.

In the political bargain put forward by Vargas, the state centralized control over all strategic cultural activities and prepared the way for large scale industrialization. Already in 1930, for example, the government established the Ministry of Labor, implementing a paternalistic policy of control in this area and enacting advanced legislation in social terms, but at the price of controlling social production by means of the so-called *pelego* unions. In 1931, the government began to invest in agriculture, creating the Conselho Nacional do Café (National Coffee Council) and the Comissão de Defesa da Produção do Álcool (Commission for the Protection of Alcohol Production). In 1933, the Instituto do Açúcar e do Álcool (IAA) (Sugar and Alcohol Institute) was founded. All of these were symptomatic of the country's drive to administrative centralization. One should not lose sight of the rationalization of modernization at all costs that these administrative measures of control implied, when criticizing the ineffectiveness of such state policy from today's neoliberal point of view.

According to Miceli, there was neither artistic complicity with state power in the organization of cultural activities nor a timidity in revealing the state's commitment to culture, such as that expressed by the bureaucracy in support of poet Carlos Drummond de Andrade (1902–1987) (and received with indignation by the poet). Miceli's research concentrates on the field of symbolic production (Pierre Bourdieu's concept). Because of the fragility of cultural activities in Brazil, artists and writers were extremely receptive to the intervention of the state and to the control over an unmediated market. In

Antônio Cândido's (b. 1918) *Formação da literatura brasileira* [1971; Formation of Brazilian Literature], the idea of structuring a literary system demonstrates a similar concern for establishing a series of internally determined relationships with the state, with the result of gaining larger Brazilian autonomy in literary production.

The Ideological Matrices of the New State

The fascist ideas in the regime's public articulation resulted in the fact that ideological issues were very important for the New State. I have already pointed out how Plínio Salgado's fascist proselytizing was disguised as cultural transformation. Similarly, the proposal for the creation of a National State, which can be considered as the core of the New State's political thought, also implied the elaboration of a unitary culture that would bring together different social and regional contrasts. The push toward erasing an ideological, and even cultural, plurality resulted in authoritarian and centralizing procedures that were explained (as in the case of European Nazism and fascism) as a strong response to the failure of liberal democracies. In that sense, it is curious to note the contradictions arising out of the performance of the Vargas government regarding its links with Nazi Germany. The political closeness and the mutual affection shown between the two countries did not stop the repression against the use of the German language in Brazil's southern region in an attempt to eliminate groups of German-speaking immigrants who might otherwise not fully integrate into the national unity.

Regarding the *content* of cultural manifestations, two parallel mechanisms of control and production were established: On the one hand, there was a team with refined training formed by liberal professionals and public figures who remained faithful to the regime and who were in charge of elaborating the criteria of the official discourse; on the other hand, there were means of controlling the dissemination of information and official statements that would describe and interpret situations considered strategic by the authorities. Thus, there was a mechanism of production and dissemination of information that, based on a theoretical foundation, contributed to producing the ideological matrix, adapting it to the various means of communication that were directed to the distinct social levels. The consequence of this policy was the establishment of a hierarchy for the creation of information sponsored by the state, according to respective responsibility for elaborating the ideological discourse.

Mônica Pimenta Velloso has concluded that "o discurso veiculado pelo conjunto dos meios de comunicação tem a sua matriz na imprensa escrita" (73) ("the discourse conveyed by diverse means of communication has its matrix in the print media"). She adds that of the journals created by the regime for propaganda purposes (*Estudos e conferências, Dos Jornais, Brasil novo, Planalto, Ciência política*, and *Cultura política*), it is *Cultura política* that can be singled out as the prime producer of the New State discourse. Placed at the top of the hierarchy, its function was therefore to define and clarify the course of Brazilian socio-political transformations, giving the coordinates of the discourse that was to be disseminated. Significant figures were linked to it, such as Francisco Campos (1891–1968), Azevedo Amaral (1881–?), and Almir de Andrade (1911–1991), whom Velloso identifies as New State intellectuals because they were the creators of the regime's ideology. Nelson Werneck Sodré (1911–1999), Gilberto Freyre, and Graciliano Ramos (1892–1953) collaborated with *Cultura política* (see Editorial 1942a), representing different political currents and thus showing the intellectual autonomy of this publication and the fact that it was directed to a reading public for whom the dissemination of texts with clear ideological differences (albeit always controlled) would be enlightening.

The journal *Ciência política* played a lesser role, since it had fewer of the important intellectuals who could be characterized as disseminators. The aim of this journal was to acquaint a wider audience with the foundations of the New State, operating as a bulletin of the Instituto Nacional de Ciência Política (INCP) (National Institute of Political Science), which was a national cultural entity that aimed to gather the intellectual elite around the ideas of the New State. In a speech given in November 1940, Getúlio Vargas defined the members of the Institute as his most direct and efficient collaborators and thanked them for their participation in disseminating the teachings of the new regime's doctrine (quoted in Velloso 81). However, the praise given by the President must not be taken as an indication of any strategic role played by *Ciência política*, linked as it was to the Institute, and given the larger circulation of *Cultura Política*. It did offer more accessible language and functioned well to popularize ideas; this led it to be assigned to the Departamento de Imprensa e Propaganda (Printing and Propaganda Department).

Preserving Order and the "New Man"

There were some recurring subjects and concerns among the intellectuals who spoke on behalf of the regime—writers such as Azevedo Amaral, Rosario Fusco (1910–1974), and Cassiano Ricardo (1895–1974). These issues gravitated around the proposal of the creation of the *homen novo* (new man), who would be the result of the new political order based on the "raízes da brasilidade" ("roots of Brazilianness"). One of the central topics of such discourse was the proposal of preserving order, which was fundamental to the theoretical thinking of the regime and played a significant role as the foundation of a series of measures that were not restrictive because they merely involved censorship and limited an individual's performance, and because they also gave rise to the emergence of particular government propaganda identified with the proposal. The preservation of order was justified as the necessary condition for productive activities. Rosário Fusco, one of the renowned speakers of the regime, stated in 1941 that "[a] ordem social, a paz, o trabalho, a tolerância política favorecem o desenvolvimento de todas as capacidades criadoras da coletividade" (quoted in Gomes 1996, 135) ("[s]ocial order, peace, work, and political tolerance favor the development of all the creative skills of the collective").

The issues related to labor organization and the figure of the worker were articulated in the proposal to preserve order in New State discourse. As Ângela de Castro Gomes has observed, the New State saw the emergence of the idea that citizenship and labor were indistinguishable; that is, the citizens were the workers, and the legal guarantees created by the regime were there to protect them. Those who were excluded or rejected by the labor market did not have rights and did not deserve protection—they were suspected of not wanting to contribute to the construction of a better society. Gradually, this idea was complemented by the view that unions were the vehicle of citizenship, especially after 1942 during the second stage of the New State (Gomes 1988, 201).

This period is characterized by certain changes in the way of approaching labor issues, which accompanied the redefinition

of politics that occurred as Brazil moved closer to the United States in the Second World War and therefore needed to diminish the tone and the intensity of pro-German sentiment and—if possible—to keep those fascist-leaning individuals who were part of the government from making any public display of pro-German ideas. The fact that Waldemar Falcão was replaced by Marcondes Filho in the Ministry of Labor exemplified these changes, which were more a relative rearrangement of forces than any real change in the regime (Gomes 1988, 201). A new style in the way of conducting labor issues was introduced by Marcondes Filho, one more atuned to the government's endeavor to appear democratic and to the international order led by the United States. Apart from this, it became necessary gradually to establish a regime of wider popular participation, which Ângela Gomes would describe as "o esforço de abrir mão de um regime autoritário, sem abrir mão das posições de poder então detidas por seus mentores" (1988, 201) ("an effort of opening up the authoritarian regime without letting go of the positions of power held by its members").

The strategic significance of the concept of "worker" is evident in the fact that it was applied, on the one hand, to intellectuals, resulting in a loss of the aura the group once enjoyed with its autonomy in the face of political power. And on the other hand, the industrial "worker" became part of the elaboration of the forms of social representation of workers in general. Starting from theoretical ideas whose social features needed to be promoted, the state developed public images according to planned programs; some images proposed in order to correct popular tendencies, were considered negative to the state. Such corrective measures were applied to the image of the rogue conveyed in Rio de Janeiro's samba. The continued praise of the cunning of this character, who manages to live off of trickery and dodges work, was considered pernicious to society; this rogue contradicted the image of the "new man," which was being disseminated by the government. Music competitions promoted on National Radio only-accepted the promotion of sambas that praised work and a decent life. These remarks expressed in an article about radio published in the journal *Cultura política* in August, 1941, reveals the official perspective and practices:

> O samba que traz em sua etimologia a marca do sensualismo, é feio, indecente, desarmônico e arrítmico. Mas paciência: Não repudiemos esse nosso irmão pelos defeitos que contém. Sejamos benévolos, lancemos mão da inteligência e da civilização. Tentemos, devagarinho, torná-lo mais educado e social. Pouco nos importa de quem seja ele filho. . . . O samba é nosso; como nós nasceu no Brasil. É a nossa música mais popular . . .[;] representa a alma do povo na sua simplicidade pura e encantadora. Não toleramos os moleques peraltas, dados a traquinagens de toda a espécie. Entretanto, não os eliminamos da sociedade: pedimos escolas para eles. A marchinha, o samba, o maxixe, a embolada, o frevo, precisam, unicamente, de escola. (Salgado 86)

The samba, which has as its origin the mark of sensuality, is ugly, indecent, discordant, and unrhythmical. However, let us be patient: Let us not repudiate this expression of our brother because of its defects. Let us be benevolent and take advantage of intelligence and civilization. Let us try, very slowly, to make samba more educated and social. It does not matter who samba's parents are. . . . The samba is ours; like us it was born in Brazil. It is our most popular music. . . [;] it represents the soul of the people in its pure and charming simplicity. We cannot, however, put up with rogues who commit all kinds of deceit. But we will not banish them from society; we have to educate them in our schools. The Brazilian dances–*marchinha, samba, maxixe, embolada, frevo*–need only to be educated.

The proposal to disseminate state-approved models of citizenship resulted in the decision to choose the Duke of Caxias as the example of patriotic behavior to be exalted by the official channels. The Comédia Brasileira, the state-sponsored theater company funded by the Serviço Nacional do Teatro (SNT), therefore staged the play *Caxias*, which became one of the company's biggest financial failures. The state's policy of preserving social order was put into action through a number of governmental measures that all reflected the state's ideology. Ângela de Castro Gomes (b. 1948) observes that what was at stake was finding the link between "politics" and "nationality," as is clear in Rosário Fusco's comment:

> Hoje, podemos afirmar que existe uma política brasileira que é uma autêntica expressão do nosso espírito nacional. Nesse espírito social ajustaram-se as necessidades do nosso presente às conquistas do nosso passado, para formarem esta permissão tríplice da política, que nos concede agir, pensar e criar o Brasil. (quoted in Gomes 1996, 140)
> We can affirm today that there exists a truly Brazilian political expression, which is the true expression of our national spirit. This social spirit comprises both the needs of our present and the conquests of our past, which were organized in order to create this triple political permission, which allows us to act, think, and create Brazil.

The need to legitimate the New State's political practices by means of an appeal to the national spirit is clear. The use of the term "permission" is significant–giving the state the power to grant the most basic conditions, such as being able to act, think, and create Brazil. Thus, a hierarchy was established as the starting point of the country's political organization. At the theoretical level of this discourse, there were attempts to base the exercise of authority on cultural legitimacy, something that would curb the state's power. For Rosário Fusco,

> o "progresso" da coletividade advém da tutela política sobre a ordem sociocultural em todos os tempos, o que se pode efetivar pela pura força da autoridade ou por um "acordo tácito" em que a ordem social não exorbita de suas limitações e a ordem política não se afasta das "fontes de formação do povo." (Gomes 1996, 136)
> The "progress" of the community comes from the state's political tutelage of the socio-cultural order, which is, at all times, based on something that can be carried out by the use of force or by "tacit agreement" as long as the social order does not go beyond its limitations and political order does not detach itself from "its source in the people."

According to Gomes (1996, 140), the notion of the spirit of nationality, which shapes Rosário Fusco's thought, is just a construct, simultaneously thought up and created by him and other intellectuals. This interpretation means two significant things: In the first place, it means that intellectuals were engaged in the creating of nationalism; in the second place, it presupposes that these intellectuals took it upon themselves to select what must be preserved as characteristic of the Brazilian cultural formation and what can be rejected. Without a doubt the national spirit is a synthetic construction alluding to a past that never existed; such a construction is a practice endemic to conservative ideology. In this discourse, the "past" has two meanings: It refers either to the specific interpretations of social mores, race, and language or to the memory of critical events of the country's history (Gomes

1996, 143). Regarding the former, Gomes notes that, among the intellectuals who wrote in the journal *Cultura política*, the notion of race did not simply reproduce the biological argument of the turn of the nineteenth century (which still prevailed in the sociocultural beliefs of that period), but their ideas also served a construction of race that fit not only the specific features of the country but also the populist nature of the regime. This specifically Brazilian version of fascist nationalism can be read alongside a passage from Adolf Hitler's *Mein Kampf* [1925; "My Struggle," 1943]:

> . . . the highest purpose of a folk state is its concern for the preservation of those original racial elements which bestow culture and create the beauty and dignity of a higher mankind. (394)

This fragment is part of the chapter entitled "The State," which offers a proposal for the foundation of a new Germany based on enhancing ethnic purity. Both countries, therefore, shared the view that the state should select and support those elements that are more important for national development. During the Brazilian New State, both in its legislation and in the actual measures enacted, discriminatory notions based on ethnic origins or on the mere condition of being a foreigner, were a general part of domestic policy.

In addition to overt or covert persecution motivated by anti-Semitism, the regime established strictly controlled limits on the movement and activities of foreigners in the country by means of its labor laws. The xenophobic mentality that accompanied this legislation can be deduced from its consequences in all aspects of life. In the theater, for instance, it meant a labor incentive for Brazilian actors, who had previously had to face the competition and prestige of foreign companies whose activities were now restricted. Witness this police report announcing in the newspaper *Diário Carioca*–on 1 September, 1937, months before the promulgation of the New State–some measures that would restrict all foreign companies:

> . . . considerando que decorre no não cumprimento das leis prejuízos injustos aos artistas brasileiros, aos quais a legialação do trabalho vai amparar; considerando que enquanto artistas de outras nacionalidades são para aqui trazidos de maneira ilegal e aqui exploram sua profissão com lucros apreciáveis, os artistas nacionais são relegados para plano secundário pelos empresários quase todos estrangeiros, contrariando, assim, a lei de nacionalização do trabalho . . .
>
> 1. O Serviço de Censura Teatral e de Diversões Públicas não aprovará programas que lhe forem apresentados quando os artistas estrangeiros que nestes tomarem parte não estiverem quites com o parágrafo 6 do artigo 14 do decreto 24,258 de 16.05.1934.
>
> [Seguem-se outras exigências concernentes a legislação trabalhista, encerrando-se com o seguinte aviso:]
>
> 5. Constatada qualquer irregularidade, o Serviço da Censura Teatral e de Diversões Publicas suspenderá imediatamente a exibição, de acordo com o regulamento e encaminhará a este gabinete uma representação circunstanciada para serem tomadas as providências requeridas. Cumpra-se. (Instruções 11)
>
> . . . and considering that these violations of the law constitute unfair competition for Brazilian artists, whom the labor legislation aims at protecting; considering that artists of other nationalities are brought to the country in an illegal way and exploit Brazilians to considerable profit, national artists are left aside on a secondary plane by the managers who are also mostly foreigners, thus in violation of the law of labor nationalization . . .

1. The Service of Theatre Censorship and Public Entertainment will not approve programs presented to it when the foreign artists who take part in them are not fully in accordance with paragraph 6, of article 14 of the decree 24,258 of 16/05/1934.

[Other requirements concerning the labour legislation follow here, and this closes with the following notice:]

5. If there is any irregularity, the Service of Theater Censorship and Public Entertainment will immediately suspend the exhibition, according to the regulations, and will submit to this office a detailed report in order to carry out the required dispositions. Let it be enforced.

It is important to note here that the emphasis is on the need to protect national artists against the foreign companies who visited the country. One can deduce from this administrative procedure that censorship was in fact enforced through labor legislation. There also emerges a link between cultural production–understood in the sense of theatrical performances–and other kinds of national cultural production. In this case, it was necessary to defend the market for the Brazilian professional actor; the issue with regard to the foreign theater companies reveals the attention given only to the allocation of labor and profit, without giving any further considerations to the particular characteristics of the theater companies or their role in the socio-cultural context of the country's capital. These juxtaposed planes (of labor and culture) were not considered to be separate in the administrative decisions of the fascist bureaucracy. This policy had been developed by the regime's ideologues as something that appealed to xenophobic nationalism and at the same time guaranteed the ideological control of the authoritarian regime. New State cultural policies transformed matters related to culture into police issues–the result of the fascist ideological make-up of the public administration, which was more extreme than the regime in general.

Filters and Obstacles in the Production and Circulation of Culture

The New State authorities resorted to more direct means when simple persuasion did not reduce those cultural manifestations that they considered harmful to the interests of the state. Apart from strictly controlling the press and censoring all public entertainment–actions that eliminated all political criticism and imposed a rigid code of morality–the government rigorously intervened in order to preserve its ideological policies and to impose them on the population. Some of these extreme actions were given support by the controlled press. For example, the Rio de Janeiro newspaper *Diário Carioca*, on 1 April 1941, announced the detention of more than thirty "*pais de santo*" ("priests") in a *Blitzkrieg* against Afro-Brazilian cults. The operation had been planned for over two months by Rio de Janeiro's Chief of Police, Filinto Muller, whose links with Nazi-fascism were publicly known. According to the *Diário Carioca*, he had decided to eliminate Afro-Brazilian religious rituals when he was told that some people had been interned in psychiatric hospitals after performing their practices. The newspaper justified the repression and accused the priests of taking advantage of the good faith of the population for economic gain. The government's Director of General Enquiries, Dr. Cesar Garcez, declared to the same newspaper that legal Afro-Brazilian religious groups had nothing to fear because their activities were registered.

This episode reveals but one of the numerous ways in which the New State dealt with any form of popular culture it did not

consider to be part of its cultural plan: The aim was to control such cultural manifestations by imposing registration and regulations. This also happened to the official Carnival parade of the samba schools, which were forced to perform themes related to Brazil's history; their exuberant nature was controlled in order to incorporate them into the project of building a national culture. In the suppression of the *terreiros* (premises where Afro-Brazilian religious rituals were performed), two kinds of cults of African origin were identified: Those that were linked to Christianity, such as the *umbanda*, as distinct from the *candomblé*, which kept its ties with African traditions. All of this became evident in the government records of the detained priests, who gave declarations about their religious activities, as well as in the newspaper's description of the ritual objects that were confiscated–typical of the *candomblé*.

The implementation of the government's cultural policy was carried out through unilateral decisions; the government did not feel the need to consult the concerned groups, their representatives, or those sections of the population that could be affected by official measures. In an apparent contradiction to the Eurocentricity of this policy, the propaganda put out by ideologues of the New State presented popular and regional culture as the necessary starting point of erudite art; popular foundations would be transformed into works of art commensurate with Western artistic canons. This proposal implied a change in the role of the intellectual, who now acquired the political role of building national culture by distinguishing what should be promoted from what should be suppressed in the popular traditions. The intellectual thus became the link between popular and learned culture. Villa-Lobos was considered the best example: His artistic work rescued and disseminated popular elements, in an educational crusade, by means of encouraging choral singing. Therefore, his work was seen as one of the best examples of the civic education of the masses. As in other areas of cultural production, the decision that a specific kind of music was to become the national model was part of the New State's authoritarian cultural policy. Let us examine, in this light, the public declaration that demanded the termination of the government's financial help to presentations of foreign operas, signed by the most prominent figures of erudite music, beginning with Villa-Lobos himself. The document claimed that the people linked to foreign opera even spoke among themselves in foreign languages. It is possible to see here the exploitation of a xenophobic nationalism associated with the defense of New State concerns; public resources were to be used for only those musicians who supported the project of the development of a characteristically Brazilian erudite music.

Complementing these control mechanisms, the official policy was to give public thanks to the support given by different sectors of society. One example of this was the case of the theater company managed by Walter Pinto, who helped the regime in a variety of ways: First, by creating, from the early 1940s to almost the end of the New State, increasingly luxurious and magnificent stage productions that reflected a self-satisfied patriotism and by using an actor who specialized in imitating Getúlio Vargas, which, through the pleasant parodies of the president, fixed his friendly character in the minds of the population.

The Role of the Departamento de Imprensa e Propaganda (DIP) (Press and Propaganda Department)

During the New State, the government's dual role in controlling and promoting cultural production led to its intervention into the development of a national cultural industry. It improved the ways of controlling mass media and entertainment, and at the same time, promoted productions that fit official proposals. Such was the case of the Rádio Nacional (National Radio), which represented the concern of the ruling class elite with the creation of an official vehicle that would direct the modernizing tendencies of the mass media. Acquired by the federal government in 1940, national radio broadcasting was placed under the direction of playwright Gilberto de Andrade, who was a promoter of the National Security Tribunal. This official radio station managed to get and keep the largest audiences with programs that included popular soap operas and public talent shows, in which popular stars were created. The station was expanded into a national network and was closely linked to its sponsoring industries, thus creating the first examples of Brazil's new mass culture. Radio broadcasting was one of the most significant elements in the creation of the New State's official culture. In a process similar to what happened to telecommunications during the 1970s, during the 1930s the Vargas regime officially ordered that radio broadcasts had to cover the whole of the country and communicate the political proposals of the government.

The regulation of broadcasting services by the New State became law with decree number 1.915 of 27 December 1939, which mandated that the DIP would henceforth be in charge of regulating broadcasting operations in the entire national territory. The following regulatory tasks of the Broadcasting Division of the DIP should be highlighted:

> fazer a censura prévia de programas radiofônicos e de letras para serem musicadas e levar através do rádio, às aglomerações que se acham situadas em zonas afastadas dos centros irradiadores de cultura no país, elementos capazes de aumentar o contingente de conhecimentos práticos necessários a uma evolução social rápida. (Salgado 91)

> to censure radio programs and the lyrics of songs to be broadcast to the people located in the far-away corners of the country's irradiating centers of culture, as well as to encourage elements which can increase the practical knowledge necessary for rapid social evolution.

Therefore, the government played the roles of both censor and producer, even of musical presentations. Without a doubt, government policy in this area had a didactic nature. At the time, one issue that was often debated was that of the role and limits of educational programs in relation to popular taste and the expectations of the audience, as can be seen in Álvaro F. Salgado's essay "Radiodifusão, fator social" ("Radio Broadcasting, Social Factor), which appeared in the journal *Cultura política* in August 1941. By controlling the broadcasting services, this government department brought to the surface previously existing conflicts regarding the jurisdiction of the Ministry of Education and Health in relation to educational broadcasting. Such conflicts had already emerged in 1938, when Minister Capanema tried to explain to President Getúlio Vargas the distinction between the "difusão escolar" ("school broadcasting"), which should be the responsibility of the Ministry of Education and Health, and broadcasting in general as means of advertising and propaganda (Schwartzman 88)—a distinction Roquette Pinto advocated in 1942 for the National Institute of Educational Cinema, which he directed (Schwartzman 89). Because the press and propaganda department had exclusive jurisdiction on all ideological questions, especially regarding the preservation of the regime's image and the integrity of its projects, the functions

of this department were virtually unlimited. A semi-official text, published in the journal *Cultura Política*, explained the role of the DIP starting with the law number 1915, 27.12.39:

> centralizar, coordenar, orientar e superintender a propaganda nacional, interna ou externa; fazer a censura do teatro, do cinema, de funções recreativas e esportivas de qualquer natureza, da radiodifusão, da literatura social e política e da imprensa, quando a esta forem cominadas as penalidades previstas por lei; estimular a produção de filmes nacionais e classificar os de caráter educativo e os nacionais para a concessão de prêmio e favores, sugerindo ao governo a isenção ou a redução de impostos e taxas federais, além de outras vantagens especiais para seu transporte. (Editorial 1942b, 173)

> to centralize, coordinate, guide, and oversee national propaganda, either internal or external; to censure theater, cinema, entertainment, sports, and activities of any kind, as well as radio broadcasting, social and political literature, and the press, whenever it was warranted imposing the penalties foreseen by the law; to promote the production of national films and to classify both those of an educational nature and national entertainment films by bestowing prizes and grants, and suggesting that the government increase or reduce federal taxes, as required apart from granting other special advantages for its dissemination.

The role of the DIP in relation to the theater went in two directions: to control the content of productions, by means of censorship, and to oversee the enforcement of the labor legislation. In fact, the direct interference the DIP demonstrated regarding radio broadcasting and newspapers could be found only, occasionally, in the theater, as happened shortly after the Brazilian government decided to take part in World War II. In November 1942, the Council for National Security, the DIP, and the management of the National Theater Service carried out the necessary procedures so that this agency could be in charge of presenting certain patriotic messages–supporting the participation of Brazil in the war–and of arranging theatrical performances for soldiers. The National Theater Service's communication of 27 November 1942 specified the proposals put forward by Abadie Faria Rosa for the implementation of a politics of civic conscience during the war. All pertinent documents are in the Administrative Archive of the National Art Foundation (CEDOC/FUNARTE) in Rio de Janeiro. It can thus be seen that conservative, patriarchal thinking and its more extreme authoritarian expression has been an important part of Brazil's literary culture in the twentieth century.

Translation by Nair María Anaya-Ferreira

Works Cited

Cândido, Antônio. 1971. *Formação da literatura brasileira (momentos decisivos)*. 2 vols. São Paulo: Livraria Editora Martins.

Chauí, Marilena de Souza. 1978. "Apontamentos para uma crítica da Ação Integralista Brasileira." *Ideologia e mobilização popular*. By Marilena de Souza Chauí and Maria Sylvia de Carvalho Franco. Rio de Janeiro: Centro de Estudos de Cultura Contemporânea/Paz e Terra. 17–149.

Editorial 1942a. "As atividades culturais do DIP (Departamento de Imprensa e Propaganda)." *Cultura política* 2.20 (Rio de Janeiro): 207–16.

Editorial 1942b. "A imprensa e a propaganda no qüinqüênio 1937–1942." *Cultura política* 2.21 (Rio de Janeiro): 169–87.

Freyre, Gilberto. 1933. *Casa Grande e Senzala*. Rio de Janeiro: Schmidt.

——. 1946. *The Masters and the Slaves*. Trans. Samuel Putnam. New York: Random House.

Gomes, Angela Maria de Castro. 1988. *A invenção do trabalhismo.* São Paulo: Vértice; Rio de Janeiro: Instituto Universitário de Pesquisas do Rio de Janeiro.

———. 1996. *História e historiadores: A política cultural do Estado Novo.* Rio de Janeiro: Fundação Getúlio Vargas Editora.

Hitler, Adolf. 1943. *Mein Kampf.* Trans. Ralph Manheim. Boston: Houghton Mifflin.

"Instruções ao Serviço de Censura Teatral e Diversões Públicas." 1937. *Diário Carioca.* (1 September, Rio de Janeiro): 11.

Miceli, Sergio. 1979. *Intelectuais e classe dirigente no Brasil (1920–1945).* São Paulo: Difel.

Moraes, Eduardo Jardim de. 1978. *A brasilidade modernista: Sua dimensão filosófica.* Rio de Janeiro: Edições Graal.

Mota, Carlos Guilherme. 1977. *Ideologia da cultura brasileira.* São Paulo: Editora Ática.

Salgado, Álvaro F. 1941. "Radiodifusão, fator social." *Cultura politica* 1.6 (Rio de Janeiro): 79–93.

Santiago, Silviano. 1987. "Permanência do discurso da tradição no modernismo." *Cultura brasileira: tradição/contradição.* Ed. Gerd Bornheim et al. Rio de Janeiro: Jorge Zahar Editor/Fundação Nacional de Arte. 111–45.

———. 1998. "Democratização no Brasil-1979–1981 (cultura versus arte)." *Declínio da arte, ascensão da cultura.* Ed. Raul Antelo et al. Florianópolis: Associação Brasileira de Literatura Comparada/Letras Contemporâneas. 11–23.

Schwartzman. Simon, et al. 1984. *Tempos de Capanema.* Rio de Janeiro: Paz e Terra; São Paulo: Editora da Universidade de São Paulo.

Velloso, Mônica Pimenta. 1982. "Cultura e poder político: Uma configuração do campo intelectual." *Estado Novo: Ideologia e poder.* Ed. Lúcia Lippi Oliveira et al. Rio de Janeiro: Zahar Editor. 71–108.

CHAPTER 53

POST-UTOPIAN IMAGINARIES

Flávio Carnelro

The poet, critic, and translator Haroldo de Campos (1929–2003) defined well, and in a single word, the general sentiment of recent times marked by lack of faith in the aesthetic and ideological project proposed by Modernism. We inhabit, according to him, a *post-utopian* period. The term seems more appropriate than *postmodernism* in the sense that it avoids certain ambiguities–the supposition, for example, that we are dealing with a period which aims to bring Modernism to its conclusion with the prefix "post" suggesting a complete break rather than Jean-François Lyotard's suggested redefinition of cultural trajectories. Haroldo de Campos's term *post-utopianism* also points to the main difference between that imaginary imprinted on the general aesthetic arena, not exclusively the literary, of the first half of the twentieth century, and the one through which (from the end of the 1960s) we have been living. Campos takes up the "hope principle," an expression coined by Ernst Bloch in his definition of modernity, and in the case of Brazil, applies it to the avant-garde imaginary that dominated culture between 1920 and 1960, interspersed with intervals of conventional literature (such as the work of the generation of the 1940s). It is this principle, this programmatic hope, as Campos defines it, that sustains the Modernist imaginary. Both the generation of the 1920s and the generation of the 1930s, the latter best known for the novels of the Northeastern region of Brazil, were guided by a definite and decidedly bold project: The struggle to bring Brazil into modernity. There was, in each case, something to fight against: For the 1920s Modernists it was the rejection of aristocratic taste and *bourgeois* mediocrity; for the generation that followed, it was political backwardness, social inequality, and oppression. Although there were many differences between the generations, they shared what one could identify as a *missionary* zeal.

Oswald de Andrade (1890–1954), and especially Mário de Andrade (1893–1945), in their subsequent summing up of the Modernist movement were critical of what they perceived as its superficial character, its "festiveness," its lack of commitment to more serious basic issues. The Modernist movement had not squarely faced the social, political, and economic problems that afflicted the nation; in retrospect, they believed these issues had to be considered first and foremost. Even if one duly recognizes the invaluable contributions made by the Modernist movement, in the sense that it prepared the way for the social and political changes that followed, a sober evaluation must point out that it was also largely unaware of the nation's true social conditions during that period; had it had such an awareness, it would have demanded a different form of engagement (see Mário de Andrade 252). This criticism, however, should not diminish the fact Modernism was an investment, a struggle, a project, and indeed a mission of renewal (Andrade 253). On concluding his evaluation of the movement, Mário de Andrade had already taken up the spirit of a new epoch; his 1942 lecture "O movimento modernista" [The Modernist Movement] was marked by a rigid distinction of ideologies: The Right and the Left. There was no room for the luxury of subtleties for the intellectual who was committed to the future of the nation. It was a time of struggle, just as

in 1922, but the battles were now on an altogether different terrain (Andrade 253).

Whether combating the bourgeoisie or the military's politics, the Modernists had been involved in a struggle. There was an enemy and the enemy had a face. Much in the same way that, in the 1950s and 1960s, the adversary of the *concretista* movement had a face: The social and economic backwardness as it was represented in the poetry of the generation of 1945. The musicians of the *Bossa Nova* were also well aware of what was in store for them when they decided to upset the tradition of the elaborate, theatrical voices and dramatic verses of the radio singers; similarly, the directors of *Cinema Novo* were fully aware of the challenge ahead, as they confronted U.S. film as the enemy, but also targeted the excesses of the Brazilian government. All these movements were filled with the desire to impose novelty, to break up existing structures, and to inaugurate a new imaginary.

We are today post-utopian, to use Haroldo de Campos's expression. The newspaper *Folha de São Paulo* published a short story, a *crônica*, by the film director Arnaldo Jabor (b. 1940) in 1993 (later reprinted in the anthology *Os canibais estão na sala de jantar* [1994; The Cannibals Are in the Dining Room]), that provides us with a vivid sense of the more recent time. Jabor gives us a detailed interpretation of a photo: It depicts the shirtless Glauber Rocha (1939–1981) armed with a lightweight camera, while directing the film *Barravento* on location at the beaches of Salvador in 1961. He is standing in the sun, his body against the wind, with the sea in the background; his face radiates an intense smile. It is only a photo, but as Jabor sees it, in it are the signs of the *Cinema Novo*'s future for the twenty years to follow:

> um mulato-índio do sertão, o sol, o vento, o sal, a câmera como arma, o braço armado do utopia (*ut topos*–outro lugar), o riso debochado, a pele nua contra o figurino, o grão da foto estourada, a câmera movente, a idéia na cabeça, a atitude de guerra, o cinema de autor, a miséria e o ouro, o choro e a dança, o precário assumido, o horror ao posado, a estética da fome, e, não sabíamos ainda, a morte nos esperando fora de quadro. (52)

> A mulatto-Indian in the *sertão* [backlands region], the sun, the wind, salt, the camera a weapon, the battling arm of utopia (*ut topos*–another place), irreverent laughter, naked skin in place of costumes, a photo of overexposed grain, flighty camera shots, *uma idéia na cabeça* [reference to the motto of the *cinema novo*, 'an idea in our heads a camera in our hands'], a warrior's stance, *auteur* cinema, destitution yet gold, dance and despair, a precarious situation, that repudiates posing, that posits an aesthetics of hunger, and, we did not yet know it, death, it was expecting us, standing just outside the picture.

Jabor places the Glauber Rocha's photograph in context. He sees the photograph as the sign of an imaginary marked by euphoria:

> No momento em que esta foto foi feita, havia uma euforia no país. Brasília tinha sido inaugurada, a Bossa Nova soava no mundo e Fidel Castro podia ser visto do outro lado do mar que se encapela atrás de Glauber. Este é um cartão-postal político, um correio metafísico que Glauber nos manda do passado para hoje. E por

627

esta câmera entraram outras imagens, do mar para o sertão. Por estas lentes entraram os miseráveis de *Vidas Secas*, os loucos de *Os fuzis*, e os negros de *Ganga Zumba*. Uma longa fila de mais de 300 filmes foi feita durante 20 anos, seguindo este braço de Glauber. E em todos estes filmes ficou esta lição salina, ventosa, de areia branca e mar batido. (51)

This photograph was taken at a time in which there was euphoria in the nation. Brasília had just been inaugurated, *Bossa Nova* was being heard throughout the world and Fidel Castro could be seen at the other end of the rough sea that stretches out behind Glauber. It is a political postcard, a metaphysical letter Glauber posted to us from the past into the present. And through his camera other images also emerge, from the sea to the *sertão* [backlands]. Through this lens the destitute of *Vidas Secas* come before us [Graciliano Ramos's novel, *Dry Lives*], the insane of *Os fuzis* [*The Rifles*] and the black men and women of *Ganga Zumba*. A long line of more than 300 films made during 20 years, by Glauber and his camera. And in all these films there remained these images of sea salt, of the wind, of white sands, and of lapping seas.

Jabor makes a telling choice in selecting this picture for comment, he writes at the beginning of the 1990s when Brazilian cinema was going through a difficult period. The nation was living the nightmare of President Fernando Collor's (b. 1949) tenure in office (1990–1992). Both *Embrafilme* and *Concine* were eliminated and with them disappeared any market protection for national films, a move that served well the interests of the great foreign distributing companies and led to a significant decline in Brazilian film production.

This was the context of Jabor's commentary on an image taken at the beginning of the 1960s; it seems like an attempt at understanding the roots of destruction, at divining the cracks that brought down the house, or perhaps, at just finding a way out. During a time in which it was impossible to move ahead, this was a return to another time, rich in possibilities. One should note, in passing, that the article's original title (changed for re-publication) was: "O primeiro take da euforia" ["The First Shot of Euphoria"]. Jabor's article demonstrates one of the marks of the post-utopian period: A return, through criticism, to utopia. This return is no longer prompted by a definite aesthetic and ideological project; quite the contrary, it is the absence of an overarching project that motivates it. Nelson Brissac Peixoto and Maria Celeste Olalquiaga, in a short essay "O futuro do passado" [1987; "The Future of the Past"], carry out a comparative analysis of films produced in the 1950s and the 1980s—specifically those in the science-fiction genre. They investigate how these two distinct periods project their respective concepts of the future, analyzing their iconography and their ideological traits and tracing, in sum, the aspirations that each period projected onscreen when attempting to create a narrative that unfolds in the future. Their analysis of this futuristic imaginary reveals a close relationship to present cultural conditions. In other words, the authors consider that one of the most authentic forms of mapping the present is to be found in the projections that we create for the decades to come.

This theory can be explored in comparing films such as *The Day the Earth Stood Still* (Robert Wise, 1951), or *The War of the Worlds*, (Byron Haskin, 1953), with more recent productions such as *Back to the Future* (Robert Zemeckis, 1985), and *Alien* (Ridley Scott, 1979), *Aliens* (James Cameron, 1986), or even the highly successful *Blade Runner* (Ridley Scott, 1982). In the films of the 1980s one sees a prevalence of references

to earlier periods, to precisely those periods in which the dreams of modernity were being engendered: Consider the two historical periods into which the protagonists of *Back to the Future* travel, the 1950s and a nineteenth-century Wild West. Both periods provide us with an expansionist ethic in which an advanced civilization conquers space, and both offer portraits of an imaginary dominated by faith in technology and progress. Peixoto and Olalquiaga's first paragraph quickly presents us with the issue and a draft of a possible answer:

A ficção científica é, ainda que pareça paradoxal, um viés privilegiado para retratar a pós-modernidade. Como uma época marcada pelo fim das grandes empresas e utopias pode pensar o futuro? Em primeiro lugar, como catástrofe, um mundo em ruínas, saturado de lixo, onde a mais sofisticada tecnologia convive com a decadência urbana absoluta. Mas também o futuro pode aparecer, na medida em que não há nada à frente, como passado. Futuro, reciclado pelo olhar nostálgico do contemporâneo, não como possibilidade efetiva de porvir, mas como *imagerie* e simulação. (75)

Science fiction is, although it might seem a paradox, a privileged space for portraying postmodernism. How can a time marked by the death of the great enterprises and utopias think of its future? Firstly, as a catastrophe, a world in ruins, intoxicated with waste, where the most sophisticated technology co-exists with complete urban decadence. But it could also be a future that can appear–in so far as there is nothing ahead of us–as the past. The future, recycled for the nostalgic contemporary eye, can take the guise of not so much the effective possibilities of the time to come, but of imagery and simulacra. . . .

Haroldo de Campos has stressed that it is precisely this programmatic hope that allows us to glimpse in the future the postponed realization of the present, allowing the passage from the modern to the post-utopian: The hope principle, turned toward the future, is succeeded by the reality principle, turned to the present (269).

Whether the issue of Modernism and postmodernism should (or should not) be framed in such a manner–if a post-utopian world is caught up in the eternal recycling of utopian periods, in a play of simulacrum, or if, in truth, the issues of this paradigm shift do not constitute a crisis, but simply a different order, one which does not call for global solutions– is a topic for discussions of much greater depth. In this brief study, the most relevant point is to show that there is a difference, that we live today in a way that is quite different from what was foreseen both by the Modernism of 1922 and the euphoria of the 1950s (which had assimilated the difficult ideological message of the 1930s). It is a difference that may best be described by the term displacement, or more precisely by the idea of a shift, a paradigm shift in the established ideologies–Left and Right– to a stance that is pluralistic, multifaceted, and possibly the legacy of countercultural movements. This means a shift from great projects and meganarratives to specific projects, created with less pretentious aims, in which the role of the *missionary,* the spokesperson of the new, is now taken up by the ordinary citizen, preoccupied less with radical ruptures than with just a possible coming to grips with one's own present.

This is a time populated by characters portraying solitary men of diminished ambitions, roaming city streets intent on no more than getting themselves through another day, displaying not the slightest interest in formulating definite questions or answers to anything. These are characters such as the anonymous narrator of João Gilberto Noll's (b. 1946) novel *O quieto animal da esquina* [1991; The Quiet Animal at the Corner]. Noll's narrator is at the start an unemployed nineteen-year-old who lives with his mother in a shanty, constantly under threat of being raided by the police, and who is in the habit of walking the streets of Porto Alegre in such a state of alienation that at times he forgets where he is going (7). The events that are to change his life—making a young woman pregnant, being sent to jail, being freed by a German couple who then adopts him—all of these events have not yet taken place. But when they do occur, he takes no notice of them; he only perceives them once they are over, and even then in a hazy, uncomprehending manner. He does not have the desire or strength to allow himself to be seduced into thinking. At times, especially from the second half of the novel onward, the narrator does make an effort to understand what is going on, to lucidly apprehend what takes place around him. But his attempts are doomed to failure and are foreign to his nature. Faced with his lover Amalia's hatred, when she calls him a cold-blooded killer, he contents himself with the comment: "percebi no fundo dos seus olhos um sinal de alarme, e conclui que eu não teria a disposição de decifrá-lo" (33) ("I noticed that in the depths of her eyes there was a note of alarm and concluded that I was not in the mood to decipher it").

The little energy he has is taken up by two activities: Writing poems and attempting to distance himself from his miserable past. He offers no commentary on or criticism of his poems, as if he did not, in effect, think about either them or the act of writing. Nor does he have any strategy worthy of note that will help pay for his bed, his food, and his comforts. Noll's narrator belongs to a family of disenchanted men and women, like the protagonist of *Estorvo* [1991; Turbulence] written by Chico Buarque de Hollanda (b. 1944). These are characters who experience the anonymity of large cities, absolute solitude, and the senselessness of all things. They wander into public libraries; across bustling streets; into cinemas, bars, and cabarets, impervious to understanding how they function or what purpose they might serve. They are characters waiting, without much conviction, for something to happen. Noll's narrator, in this, as in his other novels, does not find any question that warrants the effort of thinking of an answer. City, countryside, death, people, political manifestations, and love—all are just words in a text that have no meaning. Only poetry can offer a modicum of pleasure or relief, but only if it is not analyzed.

The shift that occurs from an imaginary that is ideologically committed, especially one charged with an optimistic view of the future, to another, where there are no long-term projects, but only the minute-to-minute unfolding of the everyday, can be perceived in such things as the characterization of the investigator in detective novels. The prototype of the modern detective is certainly Poe's well-known Dupin. Thomas Narcejac (1908–1998), in *Une machine à lire: le roman policier* [1975; A Reading Machine: The Detective Novel] defines the genre, as indicated by the title of his book, as a reading machine, as writing so skillfully wrought that the text becomes a trap, a machine, that imprisons readers from start to finish and does not allow readers a single moment away from the plot. It follows that Dupin is truly a thinking machine, a machine that uncovers crimes that defied and defeated the intelligence of the citizens of Paris and even of its police department. Dupin's discoveries do not rely on intuition or on the mere physical involvement with the crime (such as repeated visits to the location, witness interrogations, etc.), but they come about through a dispassionate and meticulous analysis of the data on hand, data that may have come from the crime scene or even from newspaper clippings. Dupin's method is scientific: To observe, to deduce, and to confirm. It was not by chance that Umberto Eco and Thomas Sebeok (1991), among others, noted the affinity between Dupin's and Sherlock Holmes's methods and the method anticipated by Charles Sanders Peirce, the philosopher of the early days of semiotics—when semiotics purported to be a science of signs.

Poe's detective is a personification of the scientific spirit of his time, of the love of detailed and rational observation of facts, of the irresistible allure of discovery. Dupin—followed by Sherlock Holmes—is the portrait of a period infatuated with science, technological progress, and discovery, a time with a great project for the future. Brazilian literature did not find its model for a detective in Poe; it went instead to Dashiel Hammet. Sam Spade is the detective who serves as a model, and it is U.S. literature from the turn of the century, Hammet and Chandler's *noir* narratives (among others), that supplanted Poe in Brazil's contributions to the genre. Dupin and Spade are very different fictional men. Dupin with his asceticism, makes Sam Spade, in contrast, a much more human character, less of a machine and more akin to the common man, one who smokes and drinks and frequents prostitutes; he is a detective moved by intuition rather than by scientific method. Spade is the image of the U.S. crisis at the end of the 1920s when the American Dream seemed to have become a nightmare and a detective such as Dupin would have been incongruous. This is a post-utopian period, inspiring the creation of a detective more subject to doubt, uncertainty, and especially skepticism, and one who sees no reason for believing in a better future.

José Roberto Campos (1983) highlights the differences between the two schools of fiction as representations of two distinct imaginaries. On the one hand, there is the detective novel centered on an enigma, in the fashion of Poe, and on the other, the U.S. *roman-noir* that is much closer to the spirit of contemporary skepticism. Raymond Chandler (1888–1959) and Dashiel Hammett (1894–1961) put an end to the conservative and well-behaved detective novel of their predecessors. They took crime away from an ascetic, logical environment and took it into the streets. They inscribed its human characteristics and dirtied the hands and consciences of the detectives and policemen, who had been veritable models of positivism. There are no winners in the *roman-noir* crime hunt. The detective, isolated and in conflict with the police, neither concludes his work with the satisfaction of having carried out his duty, nor does he provide, as catharsis, the sensation of relief that comes from handing over diabolic villains into competent hands in this less than perfect world. Chandler's Philip Marlowe or Hammet's Continental OP and Sam Spade know their world well enough to be suspicious of the effectiveness of their services. Cynicism is this detective's trademark. Cynical and wary, these detectives embody the spirit of a time of disenchantment and lack of faith—quite the opposite of their book-bound colleagues Dupin, Holmes, and Poirot. This class of skeptics will become the core of the late-emerging detective novel in Brazil. With the exception of a couple of experiments in serialized publications in the 1930s, the detective novel and short story were only truly established in Brazil during the 1980s, as a genre founded in Rubem Fonseca's writings.

Vera Follain Figueiredo (1988) comments on the failure of the earlier detective novel to take hold in Brazil, in contrast to the *roman-noir,* which gained great popularity at this time.

> O descrédito nas instituições, a consciência do relativismo das leis, entrava a criação de obras nos moldes do romance clássico, em que 'a burguesia triunfante olhava a vitória da sua *ratio* sobre as forças da obscuridade'. . . . Nesse sentido, o chamado *roman-noir* , cujo iniciador, segundo Raymond Chandler, seria situando o crime num mundo sem valores autênticos, numa sociedade corrompida, pode ser facilmente adotado por nós. (21)

> A lack of faith in institutions and an awareness of the relativism of the law are the elements that entered into the creative process of works fashioned after the demise of classic detective model in which the triumphant bourgeoisie had witnessed the victory of nationalism over the forces of darkness. . . . In this sense, the *roman-noir,* according to one of its creators, Raymond Chandler, was a genre that placed crime in a world devoid of authentic values, within a corrupt society, which could be easily adopted by Brazilians.

Rubem Fonseca's (b. 1925) work, as Figueiredo points out, does not attempt to imitate but rather to enter into a dialogue with the U.S. detective novel of the 1930s, travelling the more sophisticated and complex paths that, in a certain sense, would lead to the work of Alain Robbe-Grillet (b. 1922) and Jorge Luis Borges (1899–1986). This affiliation is of interest because it gives us a measure of the degree of skepticism with which the authors of *roman-noir* and the authors of Brazilian detective novels considered any scientific project. It is a skepticism perceived in Rubem Fonseca's detectives. Mandrake, in *A Grande Arte* [1983; High Art] in blatant contradiction to the classic methodology, prefers to *imagine* the situation in his search for clues that will lead him to potential solutions of the crimes under investigation. Similarly, Canabrava, the character from Fonseca's *Bufo & Spallanzani* (1985), becomes Gustavo Flávio, a writer of fiction, in order to solve a case of insurance company fraud. *Agosto* [1990; August] deals with the events of August 1954—beginning with the killing of a businessman in Rio de Janeiro and culminating in President Getúlio Vargas's suicide—real events that serve as the background for the novel. The detective Mattos suffers from a prosaic ailment that would never afflict a detective such as Dupin: an ulcerated stomach. Mattos is a common man, emotionally involved with the events taking place around him, and caught in a political web that defies his understanding. Although he is well intentioned, he leads a life of stress in a world of uncertainty and error. He does not find the criminal, as would be the commonplace denouement of the classic detective novel, but on the contrary, the criminal, a black man named Chicão, finds and kills Mattos, putting an end to a life of trouble and empty of ambition. (For the detective novel in Spanish America, see Vol. 1, Ch. 59, this *History.*)

With a literature aimed at a wider public, as is the case with the detective novel, another factor attests to what we have been referring to as a paradigm shift. Different approaches to the media were developed on the one hand, by the Modernists of 1922 and the avant-garde of the 1950s, and on the other by contemporary literature. Both Modernists and current writers have entered into dialogue with the media, but there are interesting differences. Modernists were fascinated by the aesthetic potential of the new artistic languages, especially cinema at the beginning of the century and advertising in the 1950s. Yet they tempered their enthusiasm with criticism of the manufactured mass appeal that resulted from these media. The *concretismo* movement made it especially clear that its interest in advertising was purely aesthetic, and that interest was kept on a tight leash given the group's firm ideological opposition to capitalism. Décio Pignatari's (1958) poem illustrates the Modernist position very well:

beba coca cola	drink coca cola
babe cola	slobber cola [glue]
beba coca	drink coke [cocaine]
babe cola caco	slobber cola [glue] *caco* [shards, junk]
caco	*caco* [decayed tooth]
cola	cola [glue]
cloaca	cloaca [cess pool]

(n.p.)

Certain similarities to such a position could already be observed in Oswald de Andrade's work in the 1920s. The language of film was already a significant presence in his work, making its appearance through techniques of editing and montage, but it was never his intention to write for a public as wide-ranging as the one reached by cinema. It seems, to the contrary, that both Modernists and the *concretistas* included in their intellectual baggage a disdain for the masses. Their fascination was with a language that was fast and fragmented and with the discovery of images as aesthetic resources to be exploited and administered to the written word in the construction of poetry; these novelties were not, therefore, tied to any desire to reach a greater public.

Today's literature functions differently: Now there exists a new language of the masses—television—that has a greater range than cinema and promotes a mixture of styles hitherto unimaginable, both in its genres—news, soap operas, variety shows, audience participation, talk shows, and sports—as well as in its advertisements. The greatest difference between the Modernist experience and that of the twenty-first century, however, is in a new, growing rapport between literature and mass media. Having shed its previous animosity, literature today no longer sees an aesthetic discourse created for the masses as being of an intrinsically lower value. Criticism based on ideological positions has become a thing of the past, vanishing almost completely or disappearing into degrees of subtlety. A new literature is born with its antenna aimed to the market—in other words, a literature that not only makes use of the linguistic resources of the media, but is also interested in having a share of the same public.

Rubem Fonseca's first writings provide us with a good illustration of this new stance, especially *Lúcia McCartney* (1969). The short story that lends its title to the book is created almost entirely in the language of the media, through the appropriation of certain *clichés* derived from the language of radio and the use of shorthand typical of television scripts; the very concision and speed of the text echo journalistic language. But yet another factor links *Lúcia McCartney* to the media: It is a remarkably sellable product, as proved by its many re-editions, and its transposition to stage and television. Even if it is possible to detect in this work, as well as in other examples of current literature, some criticism of the role of the media in generating a state of alienation, there is no concern comparable to that of the Modernists who avoided any resemblance in their work to literature for the masses; the Modernists were committed to maintaining a sharp distinction between high and low literatures. *Bufo & Spallanzani, A grande arte,* and *Agosto* are novels that refuse any such distinctions, in the sense that they appeal both to readers who simply want a well-crafted detective story, as well as to those who would look for greater sophistication, perhaps a text with allusions to the literary world.

Another interesting example is Sérgio Sant'Anna's (b. 1941) collection of short stories entitled *A senhorita Simpson* [1989; Miss Simpson]. The short story or novella that gives its title to the volume is preceded by a clarification: "Esta é uma história do gênero... como aquelas publicadas na *Seleções do Reader's Digest*. O meu tipo inesquecível é a senhorita Simpson" (109) ("This is a story of the genre... much in the line of the stories published in *Selections from Readers' Digest*"). This statement would naturally lead us to expect that a parody were to follow, a parody of the cloying genre of sentimental narratives dispersed throughout magazines such as *Readers' Digest*. What we are faced with, however, is a text in which the same ingredients of that genre are present—and with no parody whatsoever—and yet there is a sophistication in the narrative technique that has little to do with narratives of the *Readers' Digest* genre. *A senhorita Simpson* is one of the author's bestselling books. In other words, Sérgio Sant'Anna makes use of a peculiar language and a narrative form drawn from the mass media—elevating it to a greater level of sophistication while sharing the same objective for which the language of the media strives: reaching a wider audience and carving out a place for the author in the publishing market. Authors such as Rubem Fonseca and Sérgio Sant'Anna in prose and Arnaldo Antunes in poetry reinforce this new dialogic stance between literature and the media, one in which the preoccupation with establishing boundaries and taking a definitive ideological position disappears and is replaced with finding a place in the market.

To conclude by returning to the notion of post-utopianism, if there is no such thing as a dominant trend in literature today—no "hope principle" such as that guided the projects of Modernism—and if the belief in the great redemptive projects is no longer part of our imaginary, there is, however, a glimpse of a new path in the very terrain of doubt, uncertainty, smallness, and incompleteness. Nicolau Sevcenko's essay *O enigma pós-moderno* [1987; The Post-Modern Enigma], maps out the diverse interpretations afforded by its title's elusive concept and stresses the importance of unresolved enigmas—thus, putting itself quite at variance with the Modernist desire for determinant structures. Sevcenko champions the existence of a beautiful, generous, and multifaceted hope to come to terms with the death of Modernist hope. This is hope encompassed in:

> O anseio de uma justiça que possa ser sensível ao pequeno, ao incompleto, ao múltiplo, à condição de irredutível diferença que marca a materialidade de cada elemento da natureza, de cada ser humano, de cada comunidade, de cada circunstância, ao contrário do que nos ensinam a metafísica e o positivismo oficiais. A sensibilidade para a expressão inevitável do acaso, do contraditório, do aleatório. O espaço para o humor, o prazer, a contemplação, sem outra finalidade senão a satisfação que o homem neles experimenta. O aprendizado humilde, que já tarda, da convivência difícil mas fundamental com o imponderável, o incompreensível, o inefável--depois de séculos de fé brutal de que tudo pode ser conhecido, conquistado, controlado. (54)

Aspirations toward a system of justice that is sensitive to the small, the incomplete, and the multifarious, one that respects the irreducible difference that characterizes the material reality of each element of nature, of each human being, of each community, and of each circumstance, contrary to what we are taught by the official metaphysics of positivism. A sensitivity to the inevitable expression of the fortuitous, of the contradictory, and of random occurrences.

A space for humor, for pleasure, and for contemplation, with no other purpose than the satisfaction of the person who experiences it. The humble apprenticeship, already late, of the difficult but fundamental coexistence with the imponderable, the incomprehensible, and the ineffable–after centuries of brutal faith that everything can be known, understood, and controlled.)

The gradual abandonment of rigid ideological delimitations has now shifted to a concern for the diverse possibilities of power. There is, therefore, a preference (to the detriment of the positivist model) for the *roman noir*, reinvented to represent the temper of the times in the great Brazilian cities. This is a love affair, more than mere flirtation, between literature and the media; the literary text is now part of a competitive market. These are some of the traits of Brazilian literature that emerge at the end of the 1960s, to which we could add still others not addressed explicitly in this essay, but which come under the sign of the *post-utopian*: A taste for the historical novel, reconstructed from a new point of view; humor; the deconstruction and reinvention of the concept of nationality; and a dialogue between the essay form and fictional writing. This effervescence, as Jair Ferreira dos Santos has often said, becomes a space where some see a picnic in the garden of delights and others, the last tango on the verge of chaos, but in between the delights and chaos, the future makes itself known.

Translation by Lis Horta Moriconi

Works Cited

Andrade, Mário de. 1978. "O movimento modernista." *Aspectos da literatura brasileira*. 6th ed. São Paulo: Martins. 231–55.

Campos, Haroldo de. 1997. "Poesia e modernidade: da morte do verso à constelação. O poema pós-utópico." *O arco-íris branco: Ensaios de literatura e cultura*. Rio de Janeiro: Imago. 243–69.

Campos, José Roberto. 1983. "O fim dos anjos positivistas." *Folhetim*. São Paulo: Folha de São Paulo (11 December). 360.

Eco, Umberto and Thomas Sebeok. 1991. *O signo de três: Dupin, Holmes, Peirce*. São Paulo: Perspectiva.

Figueiredo, Vera Lúcia Follain. 1988. "O assassino é o leitor." *Revista Matraga*. Rio de Janeiro: Universidade do Estado do Rio de Janeiro. 4–5.

Fonseca, Rubem. 1969. *Lúcia McCartney*. Rio de Janeiro: Codecri.

——. 1983. *A grande arte: Romance*. Rio de Janeiro: Francisco Alves.

——. 1985. *Bufo & Spallanzani*. Rio de Janeiro: Francisco Alves.

——. 1990. *Agosto*. São Paulo: Companhia das Letras.

Hollanda, Chico Buarque de. 1991. *Estorvo*. São Paulo: Companhia das Letras.

Jabor, Arnaldo. 1994. "O primeiro take do Cinema Novo." *Os canibais estão na sala de jantar*. São Paulo: Siciliano. 49–52.

Lyotard, Jean-François. 1986. *Le postmoderne expliqué aux enfants: Correspondance, 1982–1985*. Paris: Galilée.

Narcejac, Thomas. 1975. *Une machine à lire: Le roman policier*. Paris: Éditions Denoël-Gonthier.

Noll, João Gilberto. 1991. *O quieto animal da esquina*. Rio de Janeiro: Rocco.

Peixoto, Nelson Brissac and Maria Celeste Olalquiaga. 1987. "O futuro do passado." *Pós-modernidade*. Ed. Roberto Cardoso de Oliveira et al. Campinas: Editora da Universidade Estadual de Campinas. 73–88.

Pignatari, Décio. 1986. "Beba Coca Cola." *Poesia, pois é, poesia, 1950–1975; Poetc, 1976–1986.* Ed. Décio Pignatari. São Paulo: Ed. Brasiliense. [n.p.]

Sant'Anna, Sérgio. 1989. *A senhorita Simpson: Histórias.* São Paulo: Companhia das Letras.

Santos, Jair Ferreira dos. 1986. *O que é pós-moderno.* São Paulo: Brasiliense.

Sevcenko, Nicolau. 1987. "O enigma pós-moderno." *Pós-modernidade.* Ed. Roberto Cardoso de Oliveira et al. Campinas: Editora da Universidade Estadual de Campinas. 43–55.

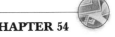

CHAPTER 54

SCENES OF THE TWENTY-FIRST CENTURY
THE ROUTES OF THE NEW

Julio Ortega

How can we assure that literary history does not transform our reading of the present into another version of the past? Above all, how can we interpret the signs of the future, the forces for change, or the shape of the new from the facts of history? Broadly speaking, can the anxiety-ridden and non-normative nature of culture at the end of the twentieth and start of the twenty-first centuries also deconstruct the established sanctions of the historical archive with the traditional fluidity of events that are taken for granted? Ideology has operated for the most part in modern Latin American literature as an archive (a discursive matrix), with configuring functions of representation that frequently determine the nature of its narrative. In what follows I propose to revise the Latin Americanist theoretical paradigm in order, on the one hand, to begin a debate on the model or interpretation sanctioned by the archive (the genealogical model that explains everything through origins) and, on the other, to suggest a reading of new literature (based on an aphoristic model that does not exhaust textual signification but articulates the signs of change) through counter-canonical projected scenarios.

What stance can we take to discuss the future? As far as Latin America is concerned the only solution, it has to be said, is to assume the viewpoint of uncertainty. The historian Paul Kennedy could be said to have discovered the future by studying the English nineteenth century: He believed he found a disturbing symmetry between the predictions of Malthus and the demographic explosion foreseen for 2025. The population of the United States will grow by 25 percent, while that of Mexico and Guatemala will increase by 88 percent. The 5-million population growth of countries of southern Europe will correspond to 108 million in the countries in North Africa. Only the unlikely possibility of another industrial revolution in the peripheral countries will disprove Malthus's argument. For this reason the first documentation of the future will come from these countries on the periphery. The migration of the undocumented workers is already responsible for a resurgence of violence. Denounced by Juan Goytisolo (b. 1941) on the Spanish–African frontier and by Carlos Fuentes (b. 1928) on the United States–Mexico border, such violence can do no more than multiply both inside and outside these chaotic boundaries or, as they say in Mexico, *la borda*. Paul Virilio reminds us that the technology of vigilance once used in Vietnam is now employed on the Mexico–United States border and that the wall between San Diego and Tijuana has been constructed with steel plates used in the Gulf War.

All things considered, migration is more than victimization. The migration of peoples has its own maps and strategies, resistances and alliances and is capable of converting limits into thresholds and what lies outside into yet another encirclement. Migrations now reshape the map of citizenries, the practices of ethnic territorialization, and oblige both sides to search for an understanding; it is the first cultural strategy of the new century. We are witnessing the powerful social forces of the disfranchised sectors of civil society articulate a vast crisis situation within the public sector, which forces us to negotiate and reorient ourselves within the fabric of the dialogue. One can for this reason state that some contemporary evidence allows one to envisage future directions, decipher current events to codify the future. Here is the Hispanic paradox: Uncertainty makes us slightly more certain.

Contemporary disciplinary models of reading and processing social life and cultural forms have revealed themselves to be insufficient. To declare oneself today a social scientist is to assume the anxieties endemic to objectivity, since disciplines and methodologies now do not define cultural objects. Here lies the central question of interpreting the concurrent signs of the present: Both the social sciences and the humanities have been losing control of their fields of study. The cultural object is no longer a fixed, measurable entity to be catalogued; it has been transformed into a kind of information process, a hasty form of hybridism. This process-oriented social condition demonstrates the precariousness of standard interpretations as well as the changing power of the claim to objectivity. The disciplinary pretensions by which the object is fully legible are now for us naive and perhaps authoritarian. In this post-theoretical epoch of post-modern relativism and decentering, the useful question to ask is how to read the texture and resonance of the new cultural object taking into account its workmanship and its mutations, as well as its projections into unforeseen and unforeseeable situations.

Almost everywhere academic rational inquiry has been made intellectually less pertinent. A good part of academia today risks suffering from becoming irrelevant in the future.

Much research seems to be based on the principle of filling empty spaces without suspecting that they might be empty for a reason. The market dictates the values of the supposedly recovered voice of the marginalized: One moment it is women's writing; then it is the subaltern of the colonial period followed by the national foundational structures of the nineteenth century. No minor indication of this irrelevancy is the fact that the computer is taking over from field work; I fear greatly that the next generation of Latin Americanists in Europe and the United States will no longer need to visit Latin America.

If the national model of interpretation of Latin American literary cultures has shown itself to be grossly inadequate, this is because the future is no longer that of the nation; globalization is relentless in power and scope. At the same time, globalization, in whatever form, has not ceased to inspire strong regional counter-responses. The result is that the future links Latin American nations even more, but difference distinguishes them. This double movement gives the lie to both theories of the homogenization of the market and of regressive isolationism. Thus, if the standard models of interpretation are suffering a crisis of legitimacy and belonging, this is because the uncertainty over the future, with which this present is being planned, demands the effort of imagining hybrid forms of analysis, and multiple assessments; it demands that we pay attention to the horizon of virtuality and the images through which cultures project their self-recognition, their cultural identity. One cannot know a people, warned Lévi-Strauss, without understanding their horizon of expectations, and this has never been more appropriate than for Latin America in the twenty-first century.

The suspicious reading that superimposes the burden of the past onto textual and cultural objects of the present has been no less impoverishing in Latin America than elsewhere; but in Latin America it has also clouded the future relevance of these cultural products. I am referring here to the persistent cultural theory that narrates the Latin American experience, time and time again, as failure. Notorious in Mexico (not only in the traumatic thesis expressed by Octavio Paz (1914–1998) on the bastard origin of Mexicans and the determinism of violence, but also in the idea of the loss of the colonial world as being anti-national) and in Peru (where the ideology of this malaise, naturalized as representation and interpreted as negativity, solidifies in the novels of Mario Vargas Llosa (b. 1936)), this cultural hypothesis has been widely spread. It is repeated in Argentina (with a defeatist vision of history as corruption) and in Venezuela (with a racist ideology of the delay of the modern as a result of the incompatible races that share the same space and the still incomplete mixing of races). I feel that the irrationalism of these theses and their self-derogatory complacency are clear; suffice it to say, they are signs of the difficulty of formulating the constitutive antagonism of disputed nations and nationalities in the sphere of power as much as in the field of discourse and interpretative authorities.

This complacency–seen in terms of images, verdicts, and sanctions of failure–therefore enacts the functional crisis of a way of interpreting culture that cannot achieve dialogue or be inclusive. It is not accidental that such an ideology of exclusions reflects the national formation of excluding societies. It is nationality defined through non-similarity with the other who is then marginalized and deprived of citizenship. This powerful model–working through discursive representation– processes, registers, and evaluates the different versions of origin, subjects of history, the vicissitudes of change, and scenes of daily life in traumatic terms. Supposedly tragic, this ideological representation of trauma and lack is nevertheless an impoverishment of the present and of the cultural work undertaken to make it viable. A number of writers have fallen back on this self-abasing indulgence: Believing themselves to be critical, they have actually done no more than propagate a kind of neo-*costumbrismo* (made up of types, topics, and too much local color), where violence, frustration, and misery conclude in a melodramatic but picturesque scenario. Today this reading is backwards-looking, and through contrast, demonstrates the value of other artists who affirm pleasure, exuberance, and desire, aspects that are not determined by an externally derived code and that are projected inexhaustibly. I am reminded of the work of José Lezama Lima (1910–1976) and Enrique Molina (1910–1997), Severo Sarduy (1937–1993) and Luis Rafael Sánchez (b. 1936), Alvaro Mútis (b. 1923) and José Balza (b. 1939).

Of course, there also exist great works inspired by a radical nihilism of representation. Such is the case of *Pedro Páramo* (1955) by Juan Rulfo (1918–1986), probably the one Latin American novel that, in the middle of that century, made the drama of a Latin American ideology of representation most obvious and, at the same time, most universal. In fact, if we understand ideology as the articulation of configured forces of representation played out within discourse, we can see that this novel ideology (as social historical experience) represents the world from the viewpoint of popular religiosity. Rural Catholicism is here assumed as a coherent cultural formation; the fictive world is configured from this discourse. The paradise transformed into desert is thus a radical dismantling of another cultural construction; in this sense Rulfo is telling us that ideology is false consciousness, but also the only world possible for the alienated subject. In other words, ideology takes the form of daily life.

Rulfo thus sets the archive alight in the most radical gesture of Latin American literature in the mid-twentieth century. It is true that the great deconstructer of the Western archive is Jorge Luis Borges (1899–1986), who reduced the museological authority of history to that of an equivalent and exchangeable text. Rulfo, on the other hand, as a result of an extreme act of historical plunder, emptied historical representation itself of meaning, converting its discourse into a phantasm. For this reason his burning of the archive does not propose an alternative condition but rather a strategy of refutation. The novel is the instrument of modernity most suitable for eliminating the archive. The technique of the story leaves us without a familiar discourse, without familiar terms of reference, but it grants us the proved efficacy of a narrative form capable of reconfiguring meaning.

For this same reason José María Arguedas's (1911–1969) work is considered to have such a close relationship with that of Rulfo. In *Los ríos profundos* (1958; *Deep Rivers*) Arguedas directly confronts the national ideological program and responds to each authority responsible for configuring the discourses of society: The church, the educational system, the military state, ethnic culture, the public arena, and popular revolution. What Louis Althusser would call these ideological state apparatuses are unfolded by Arguedas through his power to represent cultural antagonism and debate; in formal terms they are incarnated in an authoritarian monologue. The adolescent educated in this ideological repertory comes from another national realm, the ethnic world, where the model is not authority but dialogue and where subjects and societies speak and sing of a more joyful identity. Communication here is the non-socialized space in which those in dialogue can humanize discord and thus perpetuate culture. Thus the novel is transformed into an instrument for the representation of a cultural force that is an alternative to state social standardization. In fact, the novel changes allegiances, passing from Modernity to the place of the subaltern, and assumes the mythic perspective of revolt as the response that goes beyond the project of the subject of modern reason.

When speaking of new directions, a primary hypothesis might be that neither catastrophic futurology (a calculation of probabilities) nor redemptionist millennarianism (an act of faith) seems sufficient. In *The Illusion of the End*, Jean Baudrillard (b. 1929) states that perhaps the poor countries of the south are going too far in their enthusiasm to produce catastrophes, another kind of raw material that the north processes for its own sense of moral well-being. But in Baudrillard's view, Latin America cannot maintain a monopoly on catastrophe indefinitely. What is certain is that Baudrillard's hyperbole is answered by a strategy of resistance in the south: Each catastrophe generates an immediate and collective rebuilding of the social fabric. The Mexican earthquake of 1985 is a good example. Civil society was reconstructed and the political map of the country was also rebuilt; the community was re-established through the humanization of death. Historically, Hispanic cultures have been expert at this: They have a reserve of this civic medicine of repairs and sutures that helps to rearticulate dispossession as a new beginning, as habitable space. This is the first way to negotiate with violence and the symbolic loss it brings.

A new connective way of reading is required that could articulate the space between borders, perhaps be nomadic, and thus try to recognize scenarios created by change, by texts with anti-canonic power. This would be a mode of interpretation situated in the radically new, the inter-mediating, and the cross-connecting. This reading can be only a process-oriented one (including various migrations of meaning), border-based (observing diversity and nomadism) and pluri-generic (acknowledging the hybridism of cultural forms). We would thus be facing a heterogeneous new subject that speaks from between borders, from disciplinary disenchantment, and against defeatist complacency–two of the expressions of which today are discursive saturation and the exacerbation of firmly held opinion. For this reason, seeing the present as a reading of the future and then seeing current writing as an empirical affirmation of what will come both require a critique of the fundamental ideology of the marketplace, especially its crude Latin American authoritarian version that postulates a Darwinian approach to technological competence. In discursive terms, this supposed market-driven freedom is in fact appropriated by products that give some form of elementary satisfaction, symbolic products that in passing create a complacent and simple public, whose cult of the best-seller seems to prove Adorno's thesis of a reified ideology as a product of the marketplace.

Faced with the amount of space (and attention) that the best-seller products take up, new writers are creating their own networks of communication, often with limited opportunities at the national level but gradually winning new audiences on the Internet. In the disputed mercantilist space of Latin America today, cultural objects become illegible, and literature must seek alternative positions, converting itself into more compact forms of expression. The short story, public recitals, regional seminars, the newspaper (one-page) mini-story, and the serialized novel are the new ways to communicate a counter-ideological imaginary. I also suspect that the genre of the newspaper story (which has ended up by trivializing the use of the first person) and that of the biographical testimonial (which has concluded by postulating that popular subjectivity is legible by simplifying and reshaping it, in a maneuver equivalent to that of the extirpator of idolatries) will also, for this reason, cease to have future relevance.

The new imaginary of doubt resists cartography, since its fluidity is the result of independence. This exercise in uncertainty is difficult to remember in cultures such as these, created by disciplinary authorities and fundamentalist convictions. The Hispanic intellectual is forged, not by the methodology of doubt but in incarnated opinion, not in the interweavings of dialogue but in polemical disqualification. Certainly modernity gave the writer the notion of playing the hero in the context of discourse; Ezra Pound believed he could delay the Second World War if he were given an appointment at the White House. And there are those who promote the market as destiny and compulsive modernization as a cultural filter. Yet, given the possibility of having any future, every truth-claim is contaminated with doubt. An exploration of uncertainty can start by making connections to the subject of identity in the postmodern debate. If group identity is based on shared narratives, as Paul Ricoeur (b. 1913) argues, the Latin American archive has enunciated a national ideology of a *mestizo* identity. However, it has also discriminated against ethnic diversity and has naturalized racism. New operative, functional identities should decenter this history and be defined by the position that they occupy within a dialogue. This is not the identity of the same; it is not a mere identification of what is homogeneous; rather, this is the identity of difference, which is the re-identification of heterogeneity. This is where the processes of mutual self-recognition are forged.

Identity is not a matter of one's *being* (which pacifies things) but rather of one's *being there*, being located in time and space (and so changing names and things in a here and a now). Eduardo Subirats has written on these operations of constructing subjectivity through the exchange of signs in the unequal history of power. In his *El continente vacío* (The Empty Continent), both Spain and Latin America are treated as having common wounds with a shared remedy. The notion of identity in psychology is a form of personalization and in psychoanalysis, more of a non-identification through lack; both are contested by an idea of identity based on ideology, which is, above all, a loss of subjectivity through alienation but presuppose places from which one or another reading of identity can be declared and archived. In other words, there must be codes to read identity as articulated in the subject, in personal desire, or in language itself, which distinguishes it as Mexican, Argentine, etc., or is responsible for its loss. Carlos Fuentes in *Cristóbal Nonato* and Julián Ríos (b. 1941) in *Larva* have suggested the transformation of the narrative "I" into an idiomatic mask, according to which the identity of the speaker is revealed in his or her recovery of the speech of the other, to the extent that the subject is not only pluri-lingual but also speaks in tongues. Thus the subject is not a rational entity, but a permanent substitute of the heroic "I" by whoever is speaking. It is not coincidental that Spanish literature, from Juan Goytisolo and José Angel Valente (b. 1929) onwards, now engages in a dialogue with Latin American letters on this level of essential non-identifications or process-based identifications. Another

Spanish literary actuality can be seen to exist if we start from the dismantling of discursive logic in the subversive maps drawn up by José Miguel Ullán (b. 1944). We can immediately recover the parodic comedy of J. Leyva (b. 1938), who denounces everyday discourse as absurd, and continue, from José Antonio Millán (b. 1954) with his stories of urban identity of auspicious elite to Julio Llamazares (b. 1955), with his lyricism, to perceive a distinctive regional world. It is also possible to take up again the Colombian thread of Gallician exile, which Pedro Sorela (b. 1951) reconstructs as a question aimed at the future that can now no longer resolve the past. Or we can linger with Nuria Amat (b. 1950) and her narrative that links up with Juan Rulfo, wherein she encounters the limits of language in attempting to recreate the family pantheon, to speak and cure herself of origin. It is not happpenstance that in recent years a new genre of fiction from exiles has appeared, telling the tale of those who return and documenting departures–in other words, constructing an identity of an "I" in transit, without lineage and without a personal language.

When Jacques Derrida (b. 1930) states that the declaration "I am" means "I am mortal" (*Speech and Phenomena*), he does not just confirm Borges's intuition in "El inmortal" ["The Immortal"]. In truth he returns to the archive of the "I," proving that the subject that makes the assertion does so provisionally: That subject coincides with the word "I" in time, in the duration that it takes for the voice to state and articulate the word "I." The declaration "I am immortal," which is redundant, like the blink of an eye ("I") in the moment of its utterance is the truth uncovered. For this reason the presence of the other is only possible among various voices, among others; to invent the other is to imagine oneself invented. One might say that the "I" is the place of a superficial agreement, a glance at what lies between: The interview, the inter-mediate, that is, mediated and open to this recognition, to this mutuality. We could also read the statement "I am" not as a palindrome (repetition) but as an anagram (rewriting): I am = today I am. To be is to be here–in the Mexico of Fuentes, in the Lima of Alfredo Bryce Echenique (b. 1939), in the San Juan of Edgardo Rodriguez Juliá (b. 1946), in the Caracas of José Balza, in the Buenos Aires of César Aira (b. 1949); all these cities appear massively inhabited at the end of the last century, by this sum of frontiers and thresholds. The city itself has been transformed into a not entirely legible, representative, or inexpressable scenario. The novel that de-represents thus competes with today's speed of communication to reveal the measure of its artificial and transient nature.

How then can we interpret the borderlines between discourses dialogically? In the first place, we can revise our models of analytical interpretation. Currently two of these, the genealogical and the process-based models, seem to alternate. The genealogical model is that which seeks to reconstruct the origins of a discourse or a text. It is based on the concept that a text echoes its sources and is the end result of different discoursive levels of semantic fields that are articulated like a causal history. Certainly, despite the influence of structuralism and Michel Foucault's (1926–1984) "archaeology of discourse," texts have been explained through sources. This genetic recomposition of another discourse beneath any given text sets up a suspect mode of interpretation that converts the reader into a semantic policeman, someone who confirms a typology of meaning through the signs of identity. In my opinion this is a melancholic kind of machinery, since its symmetry demands the filling in of space, the providing of all the answers. And when this occurs, questions no longer exist, only authority–in

other words, the museum and the archive, the past. The other dominant method is process-orientated and proposes to read toward discovery, to search for signs of the new. It is interested in the work of the signs, the distinctive operations of writing, the spaces of textuality, and the constructing of an interpretation made on the threshold of another interpretation. While the genetic model of interpretation tends to be canonic and sanctioning, this second one is anti-canonic and relative. Roland Barthes and Lyotard had already proposed to read texts as a process of signification, not as its validation–looking forward and outwards, beyond common sense and the market. Following the new in its general outlines, in its connections, disconnections, and tentative spaces, goes beyond the tradition of novelty and overvaluation of change that is characteristic of the avant-garde. This outline takes advantage of highly contextualized and relative poetics of interpretation with their liminality and hybrid configuration.

In Peru recent writers such as Fernando Ampuero (b. 1949), Guillermo Niño de Guzmán (b. 1955), Alonso Cueto (b. 1954), Mario Bellatin (b. 1960), Iván Thays (b. 1968), Alejandro Sánchez Aizcorbe (b. 1954), and Rocío Silva-Santisteban (b. 1963) among others, renounce global interpretations to propose different scenarios of uncertainty and defensiveness, of a transient sense of life and a complicity in a rootless nomadic existence, full of obsessive emotion and skepticism of all explanations. What is innovative in these writers is a deliberate will to restart the story in a present time, without a history to purge or a vision to prove. They are the first generation of Peruvian writers, acting independently, who practice the emotional empathy of the period and reveal a taste for the immediate and for the fertility of the hybrid. In his anthology of short stories entitled *Bicho raro* (1966; Rare Creature), Fernando Ampuero communicates a saga of uncertainty as the space of identity that is put to the test. In his short novel *Salón de belleza* (1994; Beauty Salon), Mario Bellatin offers a moving tale of the plague of this *fin de siècle*, AIDS, in order to give a name to the marginal humanity with a common cause. This documentation of anguish nevertheless underlines the subjectivity of the new, notably the demands of desire, the renewed gamble involved in starting again and stripping the word down to its most vulnerable–on the subject of feelings. This value placed on emotion communicates the best dimension of the characters of these books, their subjectivity hemmed in by mapped spaces. They are characters who seek each other through non-encounters, who explore opportunities for consolation and pleasure, agreement and vehemence, and who inscribe themselves as inhabitants of a discourse in action. Thus these books of fiction, with their shared ethos of doubt, document the actual construction of the liminal subject at the end of the twentieth century. They operate on the fringes of a society without a civil discourse and during a debased time that needs to be recreated as elemental material from the immediacy of shared emotions. Everything in this reinvented Peruvian writing indicates that the new is an extreme act of non-identification. In contrast to the writers of previous generations, who, in order to process the violence of the real, were obliged to deploy cultural memory and explore the genealogy of malaise and the ideologies of consolation, these new writers eliminate memory and cling fast to the present, seeking to construct a symbolic corpus that does not derive from any disciplinary archives but from border crossings, from open and baffling spaces, and from the anxious speech of subjectivity. They are more alone, but also freer.

A considerable number of Latin American intellectuals have resigned themselves to a determinist interpretation of the continent usually based in the sanctioning weight of tradition, race, colonialism, psychologism, and, frankly, dependency and frustration. It is their habit to see Latin America as more traditional than modern, as more archaic than innovatory. D.H. Lawrence believed he saw the tip of an obsidian knife in each Mexican he met; Toynbee saw the Conquest as having occurred only yesterday in Peru. Yet I would argue that a large part of Latin American history has been animated by a certain will toward the future. The recurrence of this utopian vision cannot be ignored, lying as it does so near to the modern version of a Latin America derived from future expectation and the reasoning behind those reforms. In 1943 Jorge Basadre (1903–1980) complained about the absence of utopianism among Peruvian thinkers and essayists, and demanded a reorientation towards the future, the dream, not of a lost paradise, but of one still to be discovered. Nevertheless, this history can be read as a revelatory future broken down periodically into its independent, republican, new world, revolutionary, and pluralist phases. Although often limited by factionalist politics, this is a cultural memory that is worth keeping. This emancipatory modern paradigm has played a major role in each one of the great and easily interpreted historical events of Latin America, including the Liberal Republic, populist trades unionism, cultural heterogeneity, and popular modernity. Latin Americans are the products of that prolonged reform: The promise of the modern project, and at the same time, again and again, its contradiction. As Agnes Heller puts it, postmodernity is more obvious in the countries on the periphery where the modern program is repeatedly not delivered. For the same reason, to whatever extent the inquiry into origins has characterized Latin American self-reflection, there still exists that emancipatory concept that true history has yet to be made and democratic nationality is still to be established.

This projection into the future was translated into a political culture of virtualities, foundations, and new beginnings. As a paradoxical memory of the future, it solidified in the great novels of the 1960s and 1970s, linking cultural history to the avant-garde, as well as to the discourse of civil society and its projects of negotiation and its networks of connections. But the future's archive is also insufficient because one is not dealing now with cartography but with the unprotected nature of interpretation, whose future is created by nomadic interpreters such as the Venezuelan Simón Rodríguez (1771–1854), the teacher of Bolívar. These interpreters seek to formulate their readings outside the archive and the museum. These practices cross over borders, suggesting a map of migrations (both literary and figurative), the crossing of borders and boundaries (moving in every direction like the decentering force of the desire to transgress the standardization of dominant authorities).

Seen from this vantage point, the future to be interpreted appears as a conflictive temporality whose factual documentation (demographic, economic, educational, urban, or labor-based) declares, as we know all too well, an abyss between actual reforms and readjustments and the excluded masses—an inverse relationship between population and resources, between technology and a trained populace. If the Mexico–U.S. border will in time have produced another human geography (the impossibility of a map), it will also have produced another language. Everything indicates that the future of the United States is going through a Hispanic redefinition (at the start of the twenty-first century, 20 percent of the country is Spanish-speaking). The future of Latin America is certainly undergoing a major renegotiation with the United States. Many voices are now expressing the urgent issues represented by these creative intersections. The Mexican-American performance artist Guillermo Gómez-Peña (b. 1955), for example, who re-writes English into Spanish, represents well these hybrid times. If the future, in understandable (or statistical) terms, is unthinkable because it is surrounded by catastrophic signs, it is, in turn, imaginable in cultural terms, in the cross-disciplinary practices and dialogues in which the twenty-first century has already created an anticipated language. In the most recent literature, a sense of the new century has become clear in at least the following scenarios.

1. The scenario of postmodern disenchantment, in which we read of the often celebratory fragmentation of the grand novel (e.g., the first novel of Yván Thays and short stories by the two Venezuelans, Juan Calzadilla Arreaza (b. 1931) and Armando Luigi Castañeda).

2. The scenario of migratory flows, where the cultural nomadism implicit in the exploration of a border is evident (as well illustrated in the poetry of the Peruvians Magdalena Chocano (b. 1957) and Montserrat Alvarez (b. 1969) and the stories of the Venezuelan Miguel Gomes (b. 1964) and the Mexican Naief Yehya (b. 1963)).

3. The scenario of the de-socialization of the "I" reveals the subject as seeking to reject the social destiny imposed by modern statistics (e.g., the short stories of Guillermo Niño de Gúzman (b. 1955) and those of Venezuelan Ricardo Azuaje (b. 1959), inspired by generational differences, and those of the Mexican Pablo Soler Frost (b. 1965), which find their inspiration in an ironic gloss).

4. The scenario of uncertainty that reveals the disconnectedness of subjectivity but also the loss of the repertoires of predicted consolations (as in the fluid and free-floating stories of Fernando Ampuero (b. 1949) and the Mexican writer Ana García Bergua (b. 1954), where the subject is discovered in the shifting vicissitudes of everyday life).

5. The scenario of emotions, wherein communicative space re-establishes a fugitive but more concrete order (e.g., the shiver of the immediate truth expressed in the poetry of the Peruvian Giovanna Polarollo (b. 1952), the engravings of the Venezuelan Antonio López Ortega (b. 1957), and the empathetic humor of the Argentine Rodrigo Fresán (b. 1963).

6. The scenario of negotiations concerning the subject, in which young men reconstruct their identity, their family nucleus, their place in relation to the language of authority (as evident in the pilgrimage to divest themselves of learning that moves the small heroes of Alonso Cueto (b. 1954), the somnambulant adolescents of the Chilean writer Tito Matamala (b. 1963), and the uninhibited characters of the Argentine Cristina Civale (b. 1960)).

With these writers, the oldest form of *criollismo*, as a topical and stereotypical explanation of social malaise, comes to an end. And it shows, in passing, that *criollismo* (the painting of local color into which much Peruvian cinema has lapsed, perhaps as a result of the influence of the populism of Cuban cinema) is perhaps nothing more than a dead-end cultural interpretation of a stereotypical conflictive society: It perpetuates the picaresque, compulsive violence, and self-negation, for want of sharp criticism and poetic vision. But it still is not atypical that some Chilean and Mexican writers fall back on this easy *costumbrismo*, given that Latin America has become more difficult to grasp imaginatively and the old formulas do make its literary interpretation somewhat easier. The Cuban film *Guantanamera*, in my opinion, is an example of such a limited vision for this very reason; it reduces reality to stereotypical humor.

The creative coming together of these new scenarios can be verified in the work of Fernando Ampuero and Alonso Cueto, two of the Peruvian short story writers mentioned above. In "Criaturas musicales" ["Musical Creatures"], Ampuero constructs the communicative environment of a family (father, mother, and daughter) as one of anxiety: An effective language of uncertainty through which the subjects experience wounding, even though they have at their disposal all the instruments of communication technology. They appear as if they are psychologically incapable of dialogue. In the short story "Julio y su papá," ["Julio and his Father"], Alonso Cueto chronicles a non-traumatic negotiation of identity: The boy without a father, harassed by the violence of others, seeks a substitute father. In both stories television plays the role of the public arena (as Paul Virilio dubs it). In "Criaturas musicales," the father finds a program on television in which Maria Callas is singing; that moment of communicative fullness reveals, in contrast, the loss of even the possibility of everyday dialogue. In "Julio y su papá" the child uses sports' programs to attract his new father and give him a place (in terms of language). In the feminine world sharply delineated by Ampuero, the desire for liberation from social constraints comes from the voice of the other, the liberated speaker. In the masculine world of social comedy chronicled by Cueto, the desire for communication becomes a simulacrum in which society is revealed as comprising cruel and empty statements and pronouncements.

This problem of the crisis and anxiety of communication (and non-communication) confers on new writing its lineage in process, its sense of a new kinship. A free rewriting of the canon responds to a crisis in the systems of national representation and moves towards the "internationalism" of a world increasingly diverse and pluri-national, one that requires community networks capable of resisting the new hegemonies. On the other hand, the new Latin American writers can also be seen to illustrate the end of a traumatic period of Latin American culture: The concept of the subject that emerges from these authors' work is no longer explained by the culturalist thesis of substandard origins as compared with Western Europe and the United States, a thesis that was elaborated in the middle of the last century to describe a social history of lack and self-destruction. The gratuitously destructive hypotheses that Latin America is the product of a historical rape, that it is socially ancillary to that violence, that the republican failure, the progressive defeats, dependence of every kind, and the globalization of the marketplace have defined its destiny— all these have been transformed at the end of the twentieth century into mere myths, simplifications of historical complexities that ignore the imaginative quality of the arts, the creative capacity of popular cultural resistance to exploitation, and the negotiating strategies of civil society. Above all, these negativities are oblivious to a daily life capable of renewing itself in the context of interpersonal communication. Against all reason, this everyday existence continues to humanize the violence that proceeds from lack and to reappropriate dominant languages.

The fatalist determinism of Octavio Paz (1914–1998) in *El laberinto de la soledad* [1959; *The Labyrinth of Solitude*, 1962], for example, colored the portentous vision of Mexican history, over-interpreted for too long as pure violence and bastardy. The betrayed mother and mocking father summed up not a creative family romance but rather a clinical melodrama. Curiously, today the "children of the Malinche," reduced to "the children of the raped woman," the orphans of national

discourse, reappear–after Venezuelan soap operas and Mexican *ranchera* music–in the films of Pedro Almodóvar (b. 1949) as the social subjects of "Euro-trash" comedy, a recycled subgenre in which the urban "harlot's children" are the agents of metropolitan romance (as occurs in *Carne trémula* [1997; *Live Flesh*], when a Peruvian waltz is sung Flamenco style by a Catalan group). For the rest, the rhetorical authority of Mario Vargas Llosa or Emilio Azcárraga (founder and owner of Televisa, who once described Mexico as a country of "screwed people" compensated with televisual rubbish) is not only self-depreciatory but also lacking in any sense of the present or the future. The violence and frustration have not disappeared; on the contrary, they have increased everywhere as a result of endemic poverty, the reinforcing of *machismo*, and a buoyant racism. And civic amorality still prevails (through egoism, amnesia, even to the point of cultural autism) because, for the youngest generation, all global explanations have proved to be insufficient–whether starting from the paradigm of a Latin America on the road to modernization (an illusion that perished with the flagrant corruption of the government of Carlos Salinas and his promise of a Mexico ranked in the "First World") or from authoritarian versions (such as the orthodoxies of state communism as well as those expressed by the barbarous capitalism of a global market). The concept of an enlightened intellectual, capable of imposing an abusive system with equal pitilessness, whether initially in terms of Marxist destiny or subsequently a neoliberal future, has been put to rest: first, because the writer-as-Olympian-judge has ended up becoming a mere soap-box orator offering his ineffective opinion and second, because the mass-media genres that propagate the authority of the expert (the impressionistic chronicle that is presented as public-affairs commentary, the absolute truth-claim based on partial information, opinion based on political beliefs disguised as moral superiority) have so trivialized individual authority that today expert commentary is nothing more than a commercial message. If the writers and artists who are now constructing the future have something in common, it is their non-adherence to the powerful will of one or another dominant discourse.

Under the persuasion of the future, all supposed truth becomes relative. This is not as a result of mere skepticism but rather because of the need to return to words, to names, to begin again in a fragmentary fashion with humor and tolerance–not without indignation, but with hope. For this reason, it is a revelation that objectivity is pared down in the hands of writers who no longer need to give us a grand construction in the style of Flaubert or a historicist version; nor need they specify a realist or a magical-realist environment. Objectivity seems to depend on new subjectivities that see daily existence as being exceptional, the trivial as ritual, and socialization as reversible. Finally, the experience of the close of the twentieth century was not seen as a forgone catastrophe or apocalypse, but rather as a test and a challenge. This time, the beginning of the century is not one of nostalgia and decadence, but the trance of a hypersensibility that, without illusions but with a calling for clarity, explores the emotive quality, the capacity for dialogue, the mundane intelligence of a subject that goes beyond the archive, beyond the norms, toward the openings within the process where innovation allows a mutual language.

One conclusion to be drawn from all this is that younger writers are driven by another mode of representation. For them, the world is less remote, more immediate, and manifests reality as a daily experience. But this is also the result of another temporality: The page is an emotive register; language is more enunciated than textual; the speaker is closer to the reader; the poetic act is less a performance and more a dialogue. Even though this interpretation is limited to the most recent works, I am not ignoring the fact that the new does not lie in novelty, since the force for change, the desire to transgress, a critical will, and a passion for rupture all install the new wherever one is capable of finding it. The great Venezuelan painter Miguel von Dangel found it in a triptych by Uccello.

On the horizon of national interpretation, the work of Andrés Bello (1781–1865), Rómulo Gallegos (1884–1969), and Teresa de la Parra (1889–1936) can be retrieved. The sense of futurity that exists, for example, among the great Peruvian writers (the Inca Garcilaso de la Vega (1539–1616), José Carlos Mariátegui (1894–1930), Vallejo, and José María Arguedas), is of an actuality that exceeds the present time, despite the fact that some interpreters may wish to convert these paradigms of change into sealed archives, imaginary museums, and even to mere archaisms. Garcilaso understood that his readers formed part of the future cultural *mestizaje* of Peru; Mariátegui spoke from the viewpoint of the pressing and fertile historical approach to Peru; César Vallejo (1892–1938) took various liberties with the future, calling us brothers in terms of future action and pretending that only death would die; Arguedas finally incarnated the flow itself of the unequal Peruvian social order and his work tells us that Peru's people of both the literate and oral traditions are knowable by reading aloud, as an imminence of the shared voice. Each one of these writers, in some decisive moment of his work, set fire to the archive of standardization that sanctions and to the over-codification that saturates.

For this reason, it is worth lingering on the artistic and poetic work of the Venezuelan Juan Sánchez Peláez (b. 1922) and that of the Peruvian Jorge Eduardo Eielson (b. 1924). As if he were faced with a Paracas weaving, Eielson unpicks the thread of the radical space of desire, renewing it and signaling its color; but in this case to interpret the desert is to convert it into a time that is strung together as habitable. In contrast, Sánchez Peláez tries to make a clearing in the forest of discourse. In both poets' work, vital reaffirmations, flexible form, and lyrical clarity forge the nomadic language that is an outline of the road ahead for Spanish American poetry.

The most pertinent question in cultural theory at the end of the twentieth century concerned the asystemic nature of texts and critical works. How, then, do we interpret cultural objects that exceed the present and are projected into the future? How do we make legible that which still is not configured? The dominant genealogical model dating back to the archive was a melancholic operation, since it was believed that in each element of the text there was a previous one explaining it. This philological causality nevertheless ended up saturating the texts and converting criticism into a museological activity. The process-based alternative method of interpretation, the one that seeks to point out the processes of change and does not conceive of the work as concluded and closed, but rather as in an ever-changing flow, does not cease to be problematic, given that to read is almost a divinatory activity of speculative participation elaborated with tools that are developed even as one reads. Cultural objects have lost their standardized rules, their prearranged disciplinary typology, or their family of retraceable images; this is equivalent to saying that they lie outside the logic of identity or similarity and beyond methodological causality. The act of interpretation is thus an attempt to discover a new route, lying open between the flux of exploration and the text's formal features, which demands new articulation and contextualization. These scenarios of independence and these diverse places of recognition require the exercise of a measured reading—not as transparent illusion or with the anxiety provoked by influences but rather as the construction of an intermediary object of interpretation that emerges between the reader and the text.

Writers do not necessarily invent their precursors from the causality of literary lineage, as Borges believed. Instead, writers invent future readers. In this case, in the shared temporality of poetry, poets choose the great practitioners of a model interpretation where their own writing begins to decipher itself, to make itself legible. For this reason the new Cuban poets interpret themselves through the poetry of José Lezama Lima—not from the viewpoint of a style of writing but in a demand for interpretation. These poets are not only fine writers but are also poets of empathy, to such an extent, in fact, that they have demonstrated the courage of an artistic option as valid as any other vital project, as certain as any notion of the future in today's world. They belong to those few poetic generations that have been capable of influencing their elders, demonstrating to them that in independent art there is an internal validation and a creative gamble against all limitations. But this does not only apply to Lezama. Also belonging to this category are Cintio Vitier (b. 1921) and Fina García Marruz (b. 1923), César López (b. 1933), Manuel Díaz Martínez (b. 1936) and Reina María Rodríguez (b. 1952). More than precursors, they are post-cursors because they set the course for a city of anticipated speech. Cuban poetry, both inside and outside Cuba, is one of the great flames that Latin American literature has been capable of kindling, fanned by every contrary wind.

The case of the youngest Peruvian poets is not very different. Jorge Eduardo Eielson, Blanca Varela (b. 1926), and Pablo Guevara (b. 1930) are not so much examples of a current tradition but more the practitioners of a liberty to come. A parallel experience of complicity and empathy can be found in the work of Juan Sánchez Peláez (b. 1922), Rafael Cadenas (b. 1930), Ramón Palomares (b. 1935), and Hanni Ossot (b. 1946), who are intermittently visited by the younger Venezuelan poets. These young poets are re-interpreted in the work of these great artists of the poetic word that neither stays on the page nor is exhausted by it, and what the poetic word says keeps changing as if the formal context of the poem were not a sufficient correlate and these articulations did not generate a necessary knowledge. Like a page still without history but already from a present of latent future, this coming literature is actualizing literary historicity as the memory of the future. It is thus writing a history of the present by means of the summation of the new.

Translation by Jessica Johnson

Works Cited

Ampuero, Fernando. 1966. *Bicho raro*. Lima: Jaime Campodónico.

Arguedas, José María. 1958. *Los ríos profundos*. Buenos Aires: Losada.

Balza, José. 1995. *Después Caracas: Ejercicio narrativo*. Caracas: Monte Avila.

Basadre, Jorge. 1943. *Pequeñeces*. Lima: np.

Baudrillard, Jean. 1994. *The Illusion of the End*. Trans. Chris Turner. Stanford: Stanford University Press.

Bellatin, Mario. 1994. *Salón de belleza*. Lima: Jaime Campodónico.

Bryce Echenique, Alfredo. 1971. *Un mundo para Julius*. Barcelona: Barral Editores.

Cueto, Alonso. 1996. *Cinco para las nueve y otros cuentos*. Lima: Alfaguara.

Derrida, Jacques. 1973. *Speech and Phenomena, and Other Essays on Husserl's Theory of Signs*. Evanston: Northwestern University Press.

Eielson, Jorge Eduardo. 1989. *Poesía escrita*. Mexico City: Vuelta.

Fuentes, Carlos. 1987. *Cristóbal nonato*. Mexico City: Fondo de Cultura Económica.

Gómez-Peña, Guillermo. 1996. *The New World Border: Prophecies, Poems, and Loqueras for the End of the Century*. San Francisco: City Lights.

Heller, Agnes. 1996. *The Postmodern Political Condition*. Cambridge: Polity Press.

Kennedy, Paul. 1993. *Preparing for the Twenty-First Century*. New York: Vintage Books.

Leyva, J. 1990. *Picasso, ¿estás allí?*. Madrid: Libertarias.

Llamazares, Julio. 1985. *Luna de lobos*. Barcelona: Seix-Barral.

Millán, José Antonio. 1990. *La memoria: Y otras extremidades*. Madrid: Sirmio.

Paz, Octavio. 1950. *El laberinto de la soledad*. Mexico City: Fondo de Cultura Económica.

Ricoeur, Paul. 1992. *Oneself as Another*. Chicago: The University of Chicago Press.

Rios, Julián. 1983. *Larva*. Barcelona: Ediciones del Mall.

Rulfo, Juan. 1956. *Pedro Páramo*. Mexico City: Fondo de Cultura Económica.

Sánchez Peláez, Juan. 1993. *Poesía*. Caracas: Monte Avila.

Sorela, Pedro. 1997. *Viajes de niebla*. Madrid: Alfaguara.

Subirats, Eduardo. 1994. *El continente vacío: La conquista del Nuevo Mundo y la conciencia moderna*. Mexico City: Siglo Veintiuno Editores.

Ullán, José Miguel. 1979. *Soldadesca*. Valencia: Pre-textos.

Vargas Llosa, Mario. 1974. *Conversación en la Catedral*. Barcelona: Seix-Barral.

Virilio, Paul. 1986. *Speed and Politics: An Essay on Dromology*. New York: Columbia University Press.

———. 1991. *The Lost Dimension*. New York: Semiotext(e), Columbia University.

LIST OF CONTRIBUTORS

Hugo Achugar
Universidad de la República,
Montevideo

Willem F. H. Adelaar
Leiden University

Fernando Ainsa
UNESCO

E. Marianne C. Akerberg
Universidad Nacional Autónoma de
México

Ana Maria de Alencar
Universidade Federal do Rio de
Janeiro

Leila Mezan Algranti
Universidade Estadual de Campinas

Ivan Almeida
Aarhus University

Ivia Alves
Universidade Federal da Bahia

Lizir Arcanjo Alves
Universidade Católica do Salvador

Ana María Amar Sánchez
University of California, Irvine

Gail Ament
University of Washington

Raúl Antelo*
Universidade Federal de Santa
Catarina, Brazil

Olga Araujo-Mendieta
Wilfred Laurier University

Denise Y. Arnold
Instituto de Lengua y Cultura
Aymara, La Paz

Idelber Avelar
Tulane University

Luigi Avonto
Universidad de la República,
Montevideo

Jeferson Bacelar
Universidade Federal da Bahia

Daniel Balderston
University of Iowa

Jon Beasley-Murray
University of Aberdeeen

José Joaquín Blanco
Instituto de Estudios Históricos,
UNAM

Mario Blaser
McMaster University

Lisa Block de Behar*
Universidad de la República,
Montevideo

Violette Brustlein-Waniez
CREDAL-CNRS, France

Heloisa Buarque de Hollanda*
Universidade Federal do Rio de
Janeiro

Ana Maria de Bulhões-Carvalho
Universidade do Rio de Janeiro

Julianne Burton-Carvajal
University of California, Santa Cruz

Luiz Roberto Velloso Cairo
Universidade Estadual Paulista
(UNESP)

Jorge Luis Camacho
Arkansas Tech University

Maria Lucia de Barros Camargo
Universidade Federal de Santa
Catarina, Brazil

Javier Campos
Fairfield University

Augusto de Campos
São Paulo, Brazil

Maria Consuelo Cunha Campos*
Universidade do Estado do Rio de
Janeiro

Luisa Campuzano
Casa de las Américas, Universidad de
La Habana

Marcelino Canino Salgado
Universidad de Puerto Rico

Dionisio Cañas
Baruch College, City University of
New York

Marília Rothier Cardoso*
Pontifícia Universidade Católica do
Rio de Janeiro

Flávio Martins Carneiro
Universidade do Estado do Rio de
Janeiro/Pontifícia Universidade
Católica do Rio de Janeiro

Tania Franco Carvalhal*
Universidade Federal do Rio Grande
do Sul

Debra Castillo
Cornell University

Sara Castro-Klaren
Johns Hopkins University

Daniel Chamberlain
Queen's University, Canada

Magdalena Chocano Mena
Barcelona

Jorge Coli
Universidade Estadual de Campinas

Félix Coluccio
Comisión Internacional Permanente
de Folklore, Buenos Aires

Marta Isabel Coluccio
Comisión Internacional Permanente
de Folklore, Buenos Aires

Rildo Cosson
Universidade Federal de Pelotas

Eduardo Faria Coutinho*
Universidade Federal do Rio de
Janeiro

Arnaldo Cruz-Malavé
Fordham University

Célio da Cunha
Universidade de Brasília

Eneida Leal Cunha
Universidade Federal da Bahia

Maria Zilda Ferreira Cury
Universidade Federal de Minas Gerais

Leslie H. Damasceno
Duke University

---

* indicates a contributor who is also a coordinator

Grace Yvette Dávila-López
Pomona College

Rita De Grandis
University of British Columbia

Jean-Paul Deler
Unité Mixte de Recherche, UMR,
CNRS/ORSTOM, Bordeaux

Silvia Delfino
Universidad de Buenos Aires

Angela Maria Dias de Brito Rocha
Universidade Federal do Rio de
Janeiro

Tânia Dias
Pontifícia Universidade Católica do
Rio de Janeiro

Marco Dorfsman
University of New Hampshire

Marcus Embry
University of Northern Colorado

José A. Escarpanter
Auburn University

João Roberto Faria
Universidade de São Paulo

Rosemary G. Feal
State University of New York, Buffalo

Luzila Gonçalves Ferreira
Universidade Federal de Pernambuco

Jerusa Pires Ferreira
Pontifícia Universidade Católica de
São Paulo

Vera Follain de Figueiredo
Universidade do Estado do Rio de
Janeiro

Ettore Finazzi-Agrò
Università de Roma "La Sapienza"

Sibylle Fischer
Duke University

María Cristina García
Cornell University

Beatriz Garza Cuarón*
El Colegio de México, Centro de
Estudios de Literatura y Lingüística

Ana Lúcia Almeida Gazolla
Universidade Federal de Minas Gerais

Claudia Gilman
Universidad de Buenos Aires

José Antonio Giménez Micó
Concordia University, Montreal

Guillermo Giucci
Universidade do Estado do Rio de
Janeiro

Renato Cordeiro Gomes*
Pontifícia Universidade Católica do
Rio de Janeiro

Roberto González Echevarría
Yale University

Pablo González Casanova
Universidad Nacional Autónoma de
México

Aníbal González-Pérez
Pennsylvania State University

Beatriz González Stephan
Rice University

Nádia Batella Gotlib
Universidade Federal da Bahia

Eva Grosser Lerner
Instituto Nacional de Antropología e
Historia, México

Júlio Castañon Guimarães
Fundação Casa de Rui Barbosa

João Adolfo Hansen
Universidade de São Paulo

Regina Harrison
University of Maryland at College
Park

Milton Hatoum
Universidade de Amazonas

Lucia Helena
Universidade Federal Fluminense

Hermann Herlinghaus
Geisteswissenschaftliche Zentren
Berlin

Carmen Dolores Hernández
San Juan, Puerto Rico

María Herrera-Sobek
University of California, Santa
Barbara

Lori Hopkins
University of New Hampshire

Linda Hutcheon
University of Toronto

Noé Jitrik
Universidad de Buenos Aires

Djelal Kadir*
Pennsylvania State University

Lucille Kerr
Northwestern University

Gwen Kirkpatrick
University of California, Berkeley

K. Alfons Knauth
Ruhr Universität de Bochum

Jon Landaburu
Centro Colombiano de Estudios de
Lenguas Indígenas/CNRS, France

Javier Lasarte
Universidad Simón Bolívar

Cesar Leal
Universidade Federal de
Pernambuco

Horacio Legrás
Duke University

Ilka Boaventura Leite
Universidade Federal de Santa
Catarina

Miguel León-Portilla
Universidad Nacional Autónoma de
México

Brett Levinson
State University of New York at
Binghamton

Emmanuel Lèzy
ATER, Université de Paris X

Clara Lida
El Colegio de México, Centro de
Estudios Históricos

Yêdda Dias Lima
Universidade de São Paulo

Rachel Esteves Lima
Universidade Federal de Minas Gerais

Yone Soares de Lima
Instituto de Estudos Brasileiros/
Universidade de São Paulo

Daniel Link
Universidad de Buenos Aires

Denilson Lopes
Universidade de Brasília

Fábio Lucas
President, Associação de Escritores do
Brasil

William Luis
Vanderbilt University

Leticia Malard
Universidade Federal de Minas Gerais

Leonardo Manrique Castañeda
Instituto Nacional de Antropología e
Historia, Mexico

Stephen A. Marlett
University of North Dakota

Reinaldo Marques
Universidade Federal de
Minas Gerais

Alexis Márquez Rodríguez
Monte Avila Editores, Caracas

Jesús Martín-Barbero
Universidad de Guadalajara

Elena Martínez
Baruch College, City University of
New York

Luz María Martínez Montiel
Instituto Nacional de Antropología e
Historia/Museo Nacional de las
Intervenciones, Mexico

Leda Maria Martins
Universidade Federal de
Minas Gerais

Claudia Neiva de Matos
Universidade Federal Fluminense

Marie-Claude Mattéi Muller
Centre National de Recherche
Scientifique, Paris

José Antonio Mazzotti
Harvard University

Stephanie Merrim
Brown University

Eugenia Meyer*
Universidad Nacional Autónoma de
México

Marlyse Meyer*
UNICAMP/Universidade de São
Paulo

Walter D. Mignolo
Duke University

Luis Millones*
Universidad Nacional Mayor de San
Marcos

Kenneth R. Mills
Princeton University

José Mindlin
Universidade de São Paulo

Wander Melo Miranda*
Universidade Federal de
Minas Gerais

Eduardo Lucio Molina y Vedia
Mexico

Elizabeth Monasterios*
State University of New York at Stony
Brook

Carlos Monsiváis*
Mexico

Graciela Montaldo
Universidad Simón Bolívar

Alberto Moreiras*
Duke University

Mabel Moraña
University of Pittsburgh

José Moreno de Alba
Universidad Nacional Autónoma de
México

Italo Moriconi
Universidade do Estado do Rio de
Janeiro

Josefina Muriel
Universidad Nacional Autónoma de
México

Alain Jean Musset
École des Hautes Études en Sciences
Sociales

Kathleen A. Myers
Indiana University

Gizelda Melo do Nascimento
CIEC/Universidade Federal do Rio
de Janeiro

Margarida de Souza Neves
Pontifícia Universidade Católica do
Rio de Janeiro

Kathleen Newman
University of Iowa

Gabriela Nouzeilles
Duke University

Benedito Nunes
Universidade de Belem

Marcela Orellana
Universidad de Santiago de Chile

Silvia Oroz
Universidade de Brasília

Julio Ortega
Brown University

José Emilio Pacheco
Colegio Nacional, México

Aparecida Paiva
Universidade Federal de Minas Gerais

Sylvia Paixão
Universidade Federal do Rio de
Janeiro

Cristina Parodi
Aarhus University

Maria de Lourdes Parreiras-Horta
Museu Imperial, Petrópolis Brasil

Gilberto Pinheiro Passos
Universidade de São Paulo

Alcir Pécora
Universidade Estadual de Campinas

Marta Peixoto
New York University

Victoria Peralta*
New School for Social Research, New
York City

Victor Hugo Adler Pereira
Universidade do Estado do Rio de
Janeiro

Leyla Perrone-Moisés
Universidade de São Paulo

Marina Pianca
University of California, Riverside

Zuzana M. Pick*
Carleton University, Ottawa

Luz Aurora Pimentel
Universidad Nacional Autónoma de
México

Juan Poblete
University of California, Santa Cruz

Elena Poniatowska
Mexico

Randolph Pope*
Washington University

Antônio Arnoni Prado
Universidade de Campinas

Jussara Menezes Quadros
Universidade do Vale do Rio dos
Sinos

Beatriz Resende*
Universidade Federal do Rio de
Janeiro

Laura Barbas Rhoden
Wofford College

**Everardo Pereira Guimarães
Rocha**
PUC-Rio e Universidade do Estado
do Rio de Janeiro

João Cezar de Castro Rocha
Universidade do Estado do Rio de Janeiro

Ileana Rodríguez
Ohio State University

Luz Rodríguez-Carranza
Rijks Universiteit, Leiden

Adriana Rodríguez Pérsico
Universidad de Buenos Aires

Denis Rolland
Université de Paris III, Sorbonne

Eduardo Romano
Universidad de Buenos Aires

Adriana Romeiro
Universidade Federal de Minas Gerais

Eduardo Rosenzvaig
Universidad Nacional de Tucumán

Susana Rotker †
Rutgers University

Maria Helena Rouanet
Universidade do Estado do Rio de Janeiro

Nicolás Sánchez Albornoz
Emeritus New York University; Madrid

Idelette Muzart Fonseca dos Santos
Université de Paris X

Rita T. Schmidt
Universidade Federal do Rio Grande do Sul

Laszlo Scholz
Oberlin College/University Eötvös Loránd, Budapest

Cíntia Schwantes
Universidade Federal de Pelotas

Nicolau Sevcenko
Universidade de São Paulo

Edson Rosa da Silva
Universidade Federal do Rio de Janeiro

Elzbieta Sklodowska
Washington University

Doris Sommer*
Harvard University

Saul Sosnowski
University of Maryland at College Park

Eneida Maria de Souza*
Universidade Federal de Minas Gerais

Heloísa Maria Murgel Starling
Universidade Federal de Minas Gerais

Cynthia Steele*
University of Washington

Nicomedes Suárez Araúz
Smith College

Flora Sussekind*
Fundação Casa de Rui Barbosa

Julie Taylor
New York University

Hervé Théry*
École Normale Supérieure

Heloisa Toller Gomes
Universidade do Estado do Rio de Janeiro

Consuelo Triviño Anzola
Instituto Cervantes, Madrid

Noemí Ulla
Universidad de Buenos Aires

Tamara Underiner
Arizona State University

Nicasio Urbina
Tulane University

María Elena de Valdés
University of Toronto

M. J. Valdés*
University of Toronto

José Manuel Valenzuela
Colegio de la Frontera Norte, Tijuana

Wendy van Es
Rijks Universiteit, Leiden

Monica Pimenta Velloso
Fundação Getúlio Vargas, Brasil

Sébastian Velut
École Normale Supérieure

Roberto Ventura
Universidade de São Paulo

Ana Cláudia Coutinho Viegas
Pontifícia Universidade Católica do Rio de Janeiro

Nelson H. Vieira
Brown University

Else Ribeiro Pires Vieira
Universidade Federal de Minas Gerais

Juan Villegas*
University of California, Irvine

Claudia Villegas-Silva
University of Kansas

Richard Walter
Washington University, St. Louis

Ivete Lara Walty
Pontifícia Universidade Católica de Minas Gerais

Marcelo Rocha Wanderley
Universidade Federal do Rio de Janeiro, Programa de Estudos Americanos (PEA)

Maria Helena Werneck
Universidade de Rio de Janeiro

Gareth Williams
Wesleyan University

Susane Worcman
Universidade Federal do Rio de Janeiro

Juan de Dios Yapita
Instituto de Lengua y Cultura Aymara

George Yúdice
New York University

Francisco Zapata
El Colegio de México, Centro de Estudios Sociológicos

Iris Zavala*
University of Utrecht

Leopoldo Zea
Universidad Nacional Autónoma de México

For reasons of contractual obligations thirty-three texts have not been included in this edition. They will appear in the Spanish-language edition by Fondo de Cultura Económica (Mexico).

LIST OF PERSONS INCLUDED IN
LITERARY CULTURES OF LATIN AMERICA
WITH BIRTH AND DEATH DATES
COMPILED BY MARÍA ELENA DE VALDÉS

A

Abadía, Guillermo, b. 1912
Abalos, Jorge Washington, 1915–1978
Abeijón, Asencio, 1901–1991
Abente, Victoriano, 1846–1935
Abreu, Caio Fernando, 1948–1996
Abreu, Casimiro José Marques de, 1839–1860
Abreu, João Capistrano de, 1853–1927
Abreu, José Antonio, b. 1939
Abreu, Luciana de, 1847–1880
Abreu Felippe, José, b. 1947
Abreu Gómez, Ermilo, 1894–1971
Accioly, Marcus, b. 1943
Acevedo, Jesús T., 1822–1918
Acevedo Bernal, Ricardo, 1867–1930
Acevedo Díaz, Eduardo, 1851–1921
Achugar, Hugo, b. 1944
Acosta, Agustín, 1886–1979
Acosta, Cecilio, 1818–1881
Acosta, Iván, b. 1943
Acosta, José de, SJ, 1540–1600
Acosta, María Teresa, 1906–1990
Acosta de Samper, Soledad, 1833–1913
Acosta Saignes, Miguel, 1908–1989
Acuña, Cristóbal de, 1597–1675?
Acuña, Manuel, 1849–1873
Acuña de Figueroa, Francisco Esteban, 1791–1862
Adán, Martín [Rafael de la Fuente Benavides, pseud.], 1908–1985
Adão, José, b. 1924
Adet, Carlos Emílio, 1818–1867
Adet, Walter, 1931–1992
Adolph, José, b. 1933
Adorno, Juan Nepomuceno, d. 1814
Adorno, Theodor Wiesengrund., 1903–1969
Agassiz, Louis, 1807–1873
Agia, Miguel, fl.1563–1604
Agorio, Adolfo, 1888–1965
Agrestes, Perfiles, b. 1941
Agudo, María Adela, 1912–1952
Agueros, Jack, b. 1938
Aguiar, Cláudio, b. 1944
Aguiar y Seijas, Francisco, d. 1698
Aguilar, Rosario, b. 1938
Aguilar Mora, Jorge, b. 1946
Aguilera Malta, Demetrio, 1909–1981
Aguinis, Marcos, b. 1935
Aguirre, Isidora, b. 1919
Aguirre, Juan Bautista, 1725–1786
Aguirre, Nathaniel, 1843–1888
Aguirre Cerda, Pedro, 1879–1941
Aguirre y Fierro, Guillermo, 1887–1949

Agustín, José, b. 1944
Agustini, Delmira, 1886–1914
Aira, César, b. 1949
Aires, Matias, 1705–1763
Aita, Zina, 1900–1968
Ajzenberg, Bernardo, b. 1959
Ak'abal, Humberto b. 1952
Alabau, Magaly, b. 1945
Alagoano, Altino [Maria das Neves Bastista Pimentel, pseud.], 1913–1995
Alarcón, Francisco X., b. 1954
Alarcón, Rolando, 1929–1973
Alberdi, Juan Bautista, 1810–1884
Alberti, Rafael, 1902–1999
Albuquerque, Maria Cristina Cavalcanti de, b. 1943
Aldrete, Bernardo José, d. 1645
Alegre, Francisco Xavier, 1729–1788
Alegría, Ciro, 1909–1967
Alegría, Claribel, b. 1924
Alegría, Fernando, b. 1918
Aleijadinho, Antônio Francisco Lisboa, 1730–1814
Alemán, Mateo, 1547–1615
Alemás, Mayra, b. 1957
Alencar, José Martiniano de, 1829–1877
Alessandri, Arturo, 1868–1950
Alfaro, Luis, b. 1961
Alfaro Siqueiros, David, 1896–1974
Alfau, Felipe, 1902–1999
Alfieri, Vittorio, 1749–1803
Alfonseca, Miguel, 1942–1994
Alfonso X, (king of Spain), 1221–1284
Algarín, Miguel, b. 1941
Allende, Isabel, b. 1942
Allende, Salvador, 1908–1973
Almafuerte [pseud. of Pedro Bonifacio Palacios], 1854–1917
Almaraz, Sergio, 1928–1968
Almeida, Abílio Pereira de, 1906–1977
Almeida, Jose Americo de, 1887–1980
Almeida, Julia Lopes de, 1862–1934
Almeida, Manuel Antônio de, 1831–1861
Almeida, Silvio de, 1867–1924
Almodóvar, Pedro, b. 1949
Alomá, René R., 1947–1986
Alonso, Dámaso, 1898–1952
Alonso, Manuel Antonio, 1822–1889
Alonso y Pacheco, Manuel Antonio, 1822–1889
Alphonsus, João, 1901–1944
Altamirano, Ignacio Manuel, 1834–1893
Altolaguirre, Manuel, 1905–1959
Alurista, Alberto Baltazar, b. 1947

Alva Ixtlilxóchitl, Fernando de, 1568–1650
Alvarado, Lisandro, 1858–1929
Alvarado Tezozómoc, Fernando, 1530?–1600?
Alvarenga, Manuel Inácio da Silva, 1749–1814
Alvarenga, Oneyda, 1911–1984
Alvarenga Peixoto, Ignacio José de, 1748–1798
Álvarez, José Sixto [Fray Mocho], 1858–1903
Álvarez, Julia, b. 1950
Álvarez, Monserrat, b. 1969
Álvarez, Soledad, b. 1950
Álvarez Bravo, Manuel, 1902–2002
Álvarez de Toledo, Fernando, 1550?–1633
Álvarez Gardeazábal, Gustavo, b. 1945
Álvarez Henao, Enrique, 1871–1914
Álvarez Sosa, Arturo, b. 1935
Alves, Antônio de Castro, 1847–1871
Alvim, Francisco, b. 1938
Amado, Gilberto, 1887–1969
Amado, Jorge, 1912–2001
Amália, Narcisa, 1852–1924
Amaral, Aracy Abreu, b. 1930
Amaral, Tarsila do, 1886–1973
Amaral, Antonio José Azevedo, d. 1881
Amaru, Tupac II [pseud. of José Gabriel Condorcanqui, Tupac Amaru], d. 1781
Amat, Nuria, b. 1950
Amaya-Amador, Ramón, 1916–1966
Ambert, Alma, b. 1946
Ambrogi, Arturo, 1874–1936
Ambrosetti, Juan Bautista, 1865–1917
Américo, Pedro, 1843–1905
Amor, Guadalupe, 1920–2000
Amorim, Clóvis, 1911–1970
Amorim, Enrique, 1900–1960
Amparán, Francisco, b. 1957
Ampuero, Fernando, b. 1949
Amunátegui, Miguel Luis, 1828–1888
Anaya, José Vicente, b. 1947
Anaya, Rudolf A., b. 1937
Anchieta, José de, 1534–1597
Ancona, Eligio, 1836–1893
Anderson Imbert, Enrique, 1910–2000
Andrade, Almir de, 1911–1991
Andrade, Carlos Drummond de, 1902–1987
Andrade, Joaquim de Sousa, 1833–1902
Andrade, Jorge, 1922–1984
Andrade, Mariano, 1734–1811
Andrade, Mário de, 1893–1945

Andrade, Oswald de, 1890–1954

Andrade, Rodrigo Melo Franco de, 1898–1969

Andrade, Ruda de, b. 1930

Andrade e Silva, José Bonifacio de, 1763–1838

Andreoni, João Antonio, 1650–1716

Andrés, Avelino, 1899–1974

Andreu Iglesias, César, 1915–1976

Ángel, Albalucía, b. 1939

Angelino, Diego, b. 1944

Angelo, Ivan, b. 1936

Anghiera, Pietro Martire d', 1457–1526

Angulo Guridi, Alejandro, 1818–1906

Angulo Guridi, Javier, 1816–1884

Anicet-Bourgeois, Augusto, 1806–1871

Anjos, Ciro dos, 1906–1994

Anteo, Mario, b. 1955

Antequera y Castro, José de, 1690–1731

Antillano, Laura, b. 1950

Antipoff, Helena, 1892–1973

Antonil, André João [Andreoni, pseud.], 1650–1716

Antonio, Nicolás, 1617–1684

Anzaldúa, Gloria, b. 1942

Anzoátegui, Ignacio Braulio., 1905–1978

Aparicio, Carlos Hugo, b. 1935

Appleyard, José-Luis, b. 1927

Arana, Felipe N., 1902–1962

Arango, Doroteo [Francisco "Pancho" Villa, pseud.], 1878–1923

Aranha, Bento de Figueiredo Tenreiro, 1841–1918

Aranha, José Pereira da Graça, 1868–1931

Aráoz Anzoátegui, Raúl, b. 1923

Araripe Junior, Tristão de Alencar, 1848–1911

Araújo, Francisco Manuel Alvares de, 1829–1879

Araújo, Max, b. 1950

Araújo, Orlando, 1927–1987

Araújo, Sizenando Barreto Nabuco de, 1842–1892

Araújo Porto Alegre, Manuel de, 1806–1879

Arcaya, Pedro Manuel, 1874–1958

Archanjo, Neide, b. 1940

Arciniegas, Germán, 1900–1999

Arciniegas, Ismael Enrique, 1865–1938

Ardiles Gray, Julio, b. 1922

Areda, Francisco de Sales, b. 1916

Arellano, Jorge Eduardo, b. 1946

Arenales, Ricardo [Miguel Ángel Osorio, pseud.], 1883–1942

Arenas, Braulio, 1913–1988

Arenas, Reinaldo, 1943–1990

Aréstegui, Narciso, 1824–1869

Arévalo, Juan José, 1904–1990

Arévalo Martínez, Rafael, 1884–1975

Argerich, Juan Antonio, 1862–1924

Argote, Jerônimo Contador de, 1676–1749

Arguedas, Alcides, 1879–1946

Arguedas, José María, 1911–1969

Argüello, Santiago, 1872–1940

Argueta, Manlio, b. 1935

Arias, Abelardo, 1908–1989

Arias, Arturo, b. 1950

Arias, Ron, b. 1941

Arias de Saavedra, Hernando, 1561–1634

Aridjis, Homero, b. 1940

Arlt, Roberto, 1900–1942

Armand, Octavio, b. 1946

Arona, Juan de, 1839–1895

Arraíz, Antonio, 1903–1962

Arráiz, Rafael Clemente, 1916–1996

Arreaza Calatrava, José Tadeo,–1970

Arreola, Juan José, 1918–2001

Arrigucci Junior, Davi, b. 1943

Arriví, Francisco, b. 1915

Arrufat, Antón, b. 1935

Arvelo Larriva, Alfredo, 1883–1934

Arvelo Larriva, Enriqueta, 1896–1962

Arzáns de Orsúa y Vela, Bartolomé, 1676–1736

Asbaje y Ramírez, Juana Inés de [Sor Juana Inés del la Cruz], 1651–1695

Ascasubi, Hilario, 1807–1875

Ascher, Nelson, b. 1958

Asís, Jorge, b. 1946

Aspiazu, Agustin, 1817–1897

Assis Brasil, Luiz Antônio de, b. 1945

Astrada, Carlos, 1894–1970

Asturias, Miguel Ángel, 1899–1974

Athayde, João Martins de, 1880–1959

Athayde, Manuel da Costa, 1762–1830

Athayde, Roberto, b. 1949

Athayde, Tristão de [pseud. of Alceu Amoroso Lima], 1893–1983

Aub, Max, 1903–1972

Avelino, Andrés, 1899–1974

Ávila, Francisco de, ca. 1573–1647

Ávila, Francisco Javier, b. 1961

Ávila, Fr. Juan de, 1499–1569

Avilés, Estevan, fl. 1633

Ayala, Eligio, 1879–1930

Ayala, Eusebio, 1875–1942

Ayala, Walmir, b. 1933

Ayala de Michelagnoli, Margot, b. 1935

Ayala Gauna, Velmiro, 1905–1967

Ayala Michelena, Leopoldo, 1897–1962

Ayerra y Santa María, Don Francisco de, 1630–1708

Ayres, Lula Cardoso, 1910–1987,

Azamor y Ramírez, Bishop Manuel de, 1733–1796

Azar, Aquiles, b. 1932

Azcárate, Gumersindo de, 1840–1917

Azevedo, Aluízio, 1857–1913

Azevedo, Artur, 1855–1908

Azevedo, Fernando de, 1894–1974

Azevedo, Manuel Antônio Álvares de, 1831–1852

Azevedo, Manuel Duarte Moreira de, 1832–1903

Azparren, Leonardo, b. 1941

Azuaga, Moncho, b. 1953

Azuaje, Ricardo, b. 1959

Azuela, Mariano, 1873–1952

B

Baca, Jimmy Santiago, b. 1952

Bacellar, Luiz, b. 1928

Bachiller y Morales, Antonio, 1812–1889

Bacon, Sir Francis, 1561–1626

Baena, Antonio Ladislau Monteiro, 1782–1850

Báez, Cecilio, 1862–1941

Baeza Flores, Alberto, 1914–1998

Balaguer, Joaquín, 1906–2002

Balboa Troya y Quesada, Silvestre de, 1563–1648

Balbuena, Bernardo de, 1568–1627

Ballagas, Emilio, 1908–1954

Balmes, José, b. 1927

Balza, Jose, b. 1939

Balzac, Honoré de, 1799–1850

Bananere, Juo, 1892–1933

Banchs, Enrique, 1888–1968

Bandeira, Manuel, 1886–1968

Baquíjano y Carrillo de Córdoba, José de, 1751–1817

Barahona de Soto, Luis, 1548?–1595

Baralt, Rafael María, 1810–1860

Barata, Ruy Guilherme Paranatinga, 1920–1990

Barba Jacob, Porfirio [Miguel Angel Osorio Benitez, pseud.], 1883–1942

Barbosa, Januário da Cunha, 1780–1846

Barbosa, João Alexandre, b. 1937

Barbosa, Domingos Caldas, 1738–1800

Barbosa de Oliveira, Rui Caetano, 1849–1923

Barceló, Randy, b. 1951

Barceló, Simón, 1873–1938

Barco de Centenera, Martín, 1535–1601

Barcos, Julio R., 1883–1960

Bardi, Lina Bo, 1914–1992

Bareiro, Francisco Luis., 1877–1930

Bareiro Saguier, Rubén, b. 1930

Barletta, Leónidas, 1902–1975

Barnet, Miguel, b. 1940

Barnola, Pedro Pablo, 1908–1986

Barra, Francisco León de la, 1863–1939

Barragán, Luis, 1902–1988

Barrán, José Pedro, b. 1934

Barreda, Gabino, 1818–1881

Barrera Linares, Luis, b. 1951

Barrero, Hilario, 1948

Barreto, Belarmino, 1840–1882

Barreto, Chiquita, b. 1947

Barreto, João Paulo [João do Rio, pseud.], 1881–1921

Barreto, Joõ de Cunha Lobo, 1853–1876

Barreto, Paulo Emílio Coelho

Barreto, Tobias, 1839–1889

Barrientos, Raúl, b. 1942

Barrionuevo, Jerónimo de, 1587–1671?

Barrios, Alba Lía, b. 1943

Barrios, Gracia, b. 1927

Barrios Cruz, Luis, 1898–1968

Barrios de Chungara, Domitila, b. 1937

Barros, João de, 1496–1570

Barros, Leandro Gomes de, 1865–1918

Barroso, Gustavo, 1888–1959

Bartolomé, Efraín, b. 1950

Bartra, Roger, b. 1942

Basadre, Jorge, 1903–1980

Bastidas, Antonio, 1615–1681

Bastide, Roger, 1898–1974

Batista, Francisco das Chagas, 1882–1930

Batista, León Félix, 1964

Batlle y Ordóñez, José, 1856–1929

Batres Jáuregui, Antonio, 1847–1929
Batres Mantúfar, Carlos Rivera José, 1809–1844
Battista, Vicente, b. 1940
Baudelaire, Charles Pierce, 1821–1867
Baudrillard, Jean, b. 1929
Bautista, Fr. Juan, 1555–ca. 1613
Bauzá, Francisco, 1849–1899
Bayley, Edgar, 1919–1990
Beça, Aníbal, b. 1946
Becher, Emilio, 1882–1921
Beck Bernard, Lina, 1824–1888
Behar, Ruth, b. 1956
Belda, Joaquín, 1883–1935
Beleño, Joaquín, b. 1922
Belgrano, Manuel, 1770–1820
Bellatin, Mario, b. 1960
Bellessi, Diana, b. 1944
Belli, Carlos Germán, b. 1927
Belli, Giaconda, b. 1948
Bello, Andrés, 1781–1865
Belo, Oliveira, 1851–1914
Beltrán, Carlos Felipe, 1816–1898
Benavides, Alonso de, fl. 1630
Benavides, Wáshington, b. 1930
Bender, Ivo, b. 1938
Benedetti, Mario, b. 1920
Benítez, Fernando, 1912–2000
Benítez, Justo Pastor, 1895–1967
Benítez, María Bibiana, 1783–1873
Benítez Rojo, Antonio, b. 1931
Bentham, Jeremy, 1748–1832
Berenguer, Armanda, b. 1921
Bergamin, Jose, 1895–1983
Berisso, Luis, 1866–1944
Berman, Sabina, b. 1953
Bermejo, Ildefonso Antonio, 1820–1892
Bermúdez, Manuel, b. 1930
Bermúdez de la Torre y Solier, Jose, b. 1665 ?
Bermúdez y Ortega, Federico, 1884–1921
Bernáldez, Andrés, d. 1513
Bernanos, Georges, 1888–1948
Bernardet, Jean-Claude, b. 1936
Bernardez, Francisco Luis, 1900–1978
Beroes, Juan, 1914–1975
Beroes, Pedro, b. 1912
Berro, Bernardo Prudencio, 1803–1868
Berrón, Linda, b. 1951
Bertonio, Ludovico, 1555–1628
Betances, Ramón Emeterio, 1827–1898
Betancourt, José Victoriano, 1813–1875
Betanzos, Juan Díez de, 1510–1576
Betanzos Palacios, Odón, b. 1926
Bethléem, Louis, 1869–1940
Bezerra, Jaci, b. 1944
Bianco, José, 1908–1986
Bibliowicz, Azriel, b. 1949
Bielsa, Rafael, b. 1953
Bilac, Olavo, 1865–1918
Bilbao, Francisco, 1823–1865
Billini Mejía, Lourdes, b. 1950
Bioy Casares, Adolfo, 1914–1999
Bishop, Elizabeth, 1911–1979
Bittencourt, Aurelio Verissimo de, 1849–1919
Bittencourt, Carlos, 1890–1941
Bitti, Bernardo, 1548–1610

Blanco, Andrés Eloy, 1897–1955
Blanco, Eduardo, 1838–1912
Blanco Fombona, Rufino, 1874–1944
Blanco, Rafael, d. 1998
Blanco, Tomás, 1896–1975
Blanco y Crespo, José María [Joseph Blanco White, pseud.], 1775–1841
Blanes, Juan Manuel, 1830–1901
Blanqui, Louis Auguste, 1805–1881
Blasco Ibáñez, Vicente, 1867–1928
Blest Gana, Alberto, 1830–1920
Blonda, Máximo Avilés, 1931–1988
Boal, Augusto, b. 1931
Bocage, Manuel Maria do, 1765–1805
Bocaiúva, Quintino de Sousa, 1836–1912
Bocanegra, Matías de, 1612–1668
Boccanera, Sílio, b. 1863
Boggio, Emilio, 1857–1920
Bolaños, Fr. Luis, 1539?–1629
Bolet Peraza, Nicanor, 1838–1906
Bolio de Peón, Dolores, b. 1880
Bolívar, Simón, 1783–1830
Bombal, María Luisa, 1910–1980
Bomfim, Manoel José do, 1868–1932
Bonaparte, Napolean, 1769–1821
Bonasso, Miguel, b. 1940
Bonfil Batalla, Guillermo, 1935–1991
Bonfioli, Igino, 1886–1965
Bonnet de Condillac, Etienne, 1715–1780
Bonnet de Mendoça, Neida, b. 1933
Booz, Mateo [pseud. of Miguel Angel Correa], 1881–1943
Bopp, Raul, 1898–1984
Bor, Modesta, 1926–1998
Bordao, Rafael, b. 1951
Bordoli, Domingo Luis, b. 1919
Borello, Rodolfo A., 1930–1996
Borge, Tomás, b. 1930
Borges, Jacobo, b. 1931
Borges, Jorge Luis, 1899–1986
Borges, Ricardo, 1886–1975
Borrero, Juana, 1877–1896
Borsella, Donald, 1926–1986
Bosch, Juan, 1909–2001
Bosi, Alfredo, b. 1936
Botero, Juan Carlos, b. 1960
Botnik, Aida, b. 1942
Boullosa, Carmen, b. 1954
Bouterwek, Friedrich, 1765–1828
Bracho, Coral, b. 1951
Braga, Teófilo, 1843–1924
Brailovsky, Antonio Elo, b. 1946
Bramón, Francisco, 17th c.
Brandán Caraffa, Alfredo, 1897–1987
Brandão, Ambrósio Fernandes, b. ca. 1555 [fl. 1585–1613]
Brandão, Ignácio de Loyola, b. 1936
Brandão, Otavio, 1896–1979
Brannon Vega, Carmen [Claudia Lars, pseud.], 1899–1974
Braschi, Giannina, b. 1954
Brasseur de Bourbourg, Charles Etienne, 1814–1874
Brathwaite, Edward Kamau, b. 1930
Braudel, Fernand, 1902–1985
Bravo, José Antonio, b. 1937
Bray, Arturo, 1898–1974
Brecheret, Victor, 1894–1955
Brecht, Berthold, 1898–1956

Brennand, Débora, b. 1928
Brennand, Francisco, b. 1927
Briceño Iragorri, Mario, 1897–1958
Brindis de Salas, Virginia, 1908–1958
Brito, Francisco de Paula, 1809–1861
Brito, Pedro Francisco Xavier de, d. 1751
Briviesca, Francisca, 1550?–1610?
Broca, José Brito, 1903–1961
Bru, Roser, b. 1923
Brunet, Marta, 1897–1967
Bryce Echenique, Alfredo, b. 1939
Buarque de Hollanda, Chico, b. 1944
Buarque de Hollanda, Sérgio, 1902–1982
Buchin, Mirko, b. 1932
Buckle, Henry Thomas, 1821–1862
Buenaventura, Enrique, b. 1925
Bueno, Cosme, 1711–1798
Buffon, Georges Louis Leclerc, comte de, 1707–1788
Buitrago, Fanny, b. 1943
Bullrich, Silvina, 1915–1990
Bulnes, Francisco, 1847–1924
Bunge, Carlos Octavio, 1875–1918
Bunge de Gálvez, Delfina, 1890–1953
Buñuel, Luis, 1900–1982
Burciaga, José Antonio, b. 1940
Burgain, Luís Antônio, 1812–1877
Burgos, Fausto, 1888–1953.
Burgos, Julia de, 1914–1953
Burgos-Debray, Elisabeth, b. 1940
Burnett, W.R., 1899–1982
Burton, Sir Richard Francis, 1821–1890
Bustamante, Carlos María de, 1774–1848
Bustamante, Ricardo Jose, 1821–1886

C

Caballero, Fernán [Cecilia Bohl de Faber, pseud.], 1796–1877
Caballero, José Agustin, 1762–1835
Caballero, Manuel, b. 1931
Caballero Calderón, Eduardo, 1910–1990
Cabello de Carbonera, Mercedes, 1845–1909
Cabeza de Baca Gilbert, Fabiola, 1894–1991
Cabezas, Omar, b. 1950
Cabral, Alfredo do Valle, 1851–1894
Cabral, Astrid, b. 1936
Cabral, Manuel del, 1907–1999
Cabral de Melo Neto, João, 1920–1999
Cabrales, Luis Alberto, 1902–1974
Cabrera, Lydia, 1899–1991
Cabrera Infante, Guillermo, b. 1929
Cabrioto, Alfonso, 1884–1955
Cabrujas, José Ignacio, 1937–1995
Cadenas, Rafael, b. 1930
Cadícamo, Enrique, b. 1906
Cadogan, León, 1899–1973
Caetano, João, 1808–1863
Caicedo Rojas, José, 1816–1898
Calado, Manoel, 1584–1654
Calancha, Antonio de la, 1584–1654
Calcaño, Julio, 1840–1918
Caldas, Francisco José de, 1768–1816
Calder, Alexander, 1898–1976
Calderón, Fernando, 1809–1845

Calderón de la Barca, Pedro, 1600–1681
Calderón de la Barca, Marquesa [Fanny Erskine Inglis], 1804–1882
Callado, Antônio, 1917–1997
Callcott, Lady Maria, 1785–1842
Calleja, Diego, 1638–1725?
Calvetti, Jorge, b. 1916
Calvo, César, b. 1940
Calzadilla Arreaza, Juan, b. 1931
Camacho Ramírez, Arturo, 1910–1982
Câmara Filho, João, b. 1944
Camargo, Oswaldo, b. 1936
Camba, Julio, 1882–1962
Cambacérès, Eugenio, 1843–1890
Cambours Ocampo, Arturo, 1908–1996
Caminha, Adolfo, 1867–1897
Caminha, Pero Vaz de, 1450?–1500
Camino Galicia, León Felipe, 1884–1968
Camões, Luis de, 1524?–1580
Campbell, Federico, b. 1941
Campo, Estanislao del, 1834–1880
Campobello, Nellie, 1900–1986
Campos, Augusto de, b. 1931
Campos, Francisco, 1891–1968
Campos, Haroldo de, 1929–2003
Campos, Humberto de, 1886–1934
Campos, Julieta, b. 1932
Campos, Milton, 1900–1972
Campos, Paulo Mendes, 1922–1991
Campos, Rubén M., 1876–1930
Campos Cervera, Hérib, 1908–1953
Camus, Albert, 1913–1960
Canabrava, Luiz, b. 1926
Cañas, Dionisio, b. 1949
Cançado, Maura Lopes, b. 1930
Candela, Félix, 1910–1997
Candelaria, Cordelia, b. 1943
Candelier, Bruno Rosario, b. 1941
Cândido, Antonio, b. 1918
Cané, Miguel, 1851–1905
Caneca, Fr. Joaquim do Amor Divino, 1779–1825
Cantú, Norma, b. 1947
Capdevila, Arturo, 1889–1967
Capetillo, Luisa, 1879–1922
Capote, Truman, 1924–1984
Caraguti, Dirma de, b. 1922
Cardenal, Ernesto, b. 1925
Cárdenas, Nancy, 1934–1994
Cárdenas, Ramiro, b. 1925
Cárdenas, Raúl de, b. 1938
Cardim, Fernão, d. 1625
Cardona, Lazaro, fl. 1550
Cardoso, Fernando Enrique, b. 1931
Cardoso, Lúcio, 1913–1968
Cardoza y Aragón, Luis, 1904–1992
Cardozo, Efraím, 1906–1973
Cardozo, Joaquim, 1897–1978
Carneiro, Edison de Sousa, 1912–1972
Caro, Gabriel Jaime, b. 1949
Caro, José Eusebio, 1817–1853
Caro, Miguel Antonio, 1843–1909
Caro, Rodrigo, 1573–1647?
Carpeaux, Otto Maria, 1900–1978
Carpentier, Alejo, 1904–1980
Carpio, Manuel, 1791–1860
Carranza, Eduardo, 1913–1985

Carrascal, José María, b. 1930
Carreño, Inocente, b. 1919
Carreño, Manuel Antonio, d. 1874.
Carreño, Teresa, 1856–1917
Carrera, Arturo, b. 1948
Carrera Damas, Germán, b. 1930
Carreras, Roberto de las, 1875–1963
Carrero, Jaime, b. 1931
Carrero, Raimundo, b. 1947
Carriego, Evaristo, 1883–1912
Carrió de la Vandera, Alonso, b. ca.1706
Carrión, Benjamín, 1898–1979
Cartagena Portalatín, Aída, 1918–1994
Carvajal, Fray Gaspar de, 1504–1584
Carvajal, José M., b. 1961
Carvalho, Bernardo, b. 1960
Carvalho, Flávio de, 1899–1973
Carvalho, Ronald de, 1893–1935
Carvalho, Trajano Galvão de, 1830–1864
Carvalho Oliva, Homero, b. 1957
Casaccia Bibolini, Gabriel, 1907–1980
Casal, Julián del, 1863–1893
Casal, Manuel Aires de, 1754?–1801?
Casals, Pablo, 1876–1976
Casas, Fray Bartolomé de las, 1474–1566
Casas, Myra, b. 1934
Casassanta, Mário, 1898–1963
Casasús, Joaquín Demetrio, 1858–1916
Cascudo, Luis da Câmara, 1898–1986
Caso, Antonio, 1883–1946
Casola, Augusto, b. 1944
Casona, Alejandro, 1903–1965
Castellano, Gonzalo, b. 1926
Castellanos, Evencio, 1915–1984
Castellanos, Juan de, 1522–1607
Castellanos, Pablo, 1917–1981
Castellanos, Rosario, 1925–1974
Castello, José Aderaldo, b. 1921
Castelnuovo, Elias, 1893–1982
Castelo Branco, Camilo, 1825–1890
Castilla, Manuel J., 1918–1980
Castilla, Ramón, 1797–1867
Castillo, Abelardo, b. 1935
Castillo, Ana, b. 1945
Castillo, Cátulo [González], 1906–1975
Castillo, Florencio del, 1760–1834
Castillo, Francisca Concepción [Madre Castillo, pseud.], 1671–1742
Castillo, Roberto, b. 1951
Castillo de González, Aurelia, 1842–1920
Castillo Solórzano, Alonso de, 1584–1648?
Castiñeira de Dios, José María, b. 1920
Castro, Augusto de, d. 1896
Castro, Carlo Antonio, b. 1930
Castro, Dolores, b. 1923
Castro, Fidel, b. 1927
Castro, Francisco de, d. 1740
Castro, Luis, 1909–1933
Castro, Luis de, 1863–1920
Castro Alves, Antonio de, 1847–1871
Castro Leiva, Luis, 1943–1999
Castro Martínez, Ángel, b. 1940
Castro Pozo, Hildebrando, 1890–1945
Casuso, Teté, b. 1912
Catarina de San Juan, 1608?–1688

Catherine of Siena, 1347–1380
Cavalcante, Alberto, 1897–1982
Cavalcante, Rodolfo Coelho, 1919–1986
Cavalcanti, Valdemar, 1912–1982
Cavo, Andrés, 1739–1803
Cea, José Roberto, b. 1939
Cela, Camilo José, 1916–2002
Celso, Afonso Celso de Assis Figueiredo, conde de Afonso, 1860–1938
Cendrars, Blaise [Frederic Sausir-Hall, pseud.], 1887–1961
Centeno, Israel, b. 1958
Centeya, Julián, 1910–1974
Centurión, Juan Crisóstomo, 1840–1902
Cerda, Carlos, b. 1942
Cernuda, Luis, 1902–1963
Cerro, Emeterio, b. 1952
Cerruto, Oscar, 1912–1981
Certeau, Michel de, 1926–1986
Cervantes, Lorna Dee, b. 1954
Cervantes, Miguel de, 1547–1616
Cervantes de Salazar, Francisco, 1514?–1575
Césaire, Aimé, b. 1913
César, Ana Cristina, 1952–1983
César, Guilhermino, 1908–1993
Céspedes, Augusto, 1904–1996
Céspedes del Castillo, Guillermo, b. 1620
Cetina, Gutierre de, 1514?–1557
Cevallos, Pedro Fermin, 1812–1893
Cevallos, Petrorio Rafael, b. 1953
Chabran, Angie, b. 1952
Chagas, Carlos, 1878–1934
Chalbaud, Román, b. 1932
Chamie, Mario, b. 1933
Chandler, Raymond, 1888–1959
Charlot, Jean, 1896–1979
Charry Lara, Fernando, b. 1920
Chauí, Marilena, b. 1941
Chaves, Federico, 1881–1978
Chaves, Julio César, 1907–1989
Chávez, César, 1927–1993
Chávez, Denise, b. 1948
Chejfec, Sergio, b. 1956
Chiacchio, Carlos, 1884–1947
Chirinos, Orlando, b. 1944
Chirveches, Armando, 1883–1926
Chocano, José Santos, 1875–1934
Chocano Mena, Magdalena, b. 1957
Chocrón, Isaac, b. 1932
Chungara, Domitila Barrios de, b. 1937
Churata, Gamaliel [Miguel Ángel Huaman, pseud.], 1894–1969
Cícero, Antônio, b. 1945
Cid Pérez, José, 1906–1994
Cienfuegos, Lucky, d. 1987
Cieza de León, Pedro de, 1518–1554
Cinta-Larga, Pichuvy, d. 1988
Ciria, Alberto, b. 1943
Cisneros, Antonio, b. 1942
Cisneros, Sandra, b. 1954
Civale, Cristina, b. 1960
Clark, Ligia, 1920–1988
Clairville, M., 1811–1879
Claudel, Paul, 1868–1955
Clavijero, Francisco Javier, 1731–1787
Clemanceau, Georges, 1841–1929
Cliff, Michelle, b. 1951

Clifford, James, b. 1945

Coaraci, José Alves, Visconti de, 1837–1892

Cobo, Bernabé, 1580–1657

Cocco de Filippis, Daisy, b. 1949

Codina, Iverna, b. 1934

Coelho, Ruy, 1920–1990

Coelho, Teixeira, b. 1944

Coelho Neto, Marcos, 1740–1806

Coelho Netto, Henrique, 1864–1934

Cofiño Lopez, Manuel, 1936–1987

Cohen, Marcelo, b. 1951

Coiscou-Weber, Rodolfo Juan, b. 1924

Colasanti, Marina, b. 1937

Coll, Pedro Emilio, 1872–1947

Collazos, Oscar, b. 1942

Collor, Fernando, b. 1949

Coll y Toste, Cayetano, 1850–1930

Colmán, Narciso Ramón, 1878–1954

Colón, Cristobal, 1451–1506

Colón, Fernando, 1488–1539

Colón, Jesús, 1901–1974

Colón, Miriam, b. 1936

Columbus, Christopher, ca. 1451–1506

Comte, Auguste, 1798–1857

Conceição, Sônia Fátima, b. 1951

Conceiçao da Silva, Jônatas, b. 1952

Concha, Jaime, b. 1938

Concolorcorvo [pseud. of Alonso Carrió de la Vandera], fl. 18th Cent.

Condé, Maryse, b. 1937

Conde, Rosina, b. 1954

Condesa de Merlin, Santa Cruz y Montalvo, Ma de las Mercedes, 1789–1852

Condorcanqui, José Gabriel [Tupac Amaru II, pseud.], d. 1781

Condori Chura, Leandro, b. 1905

Condori Mamani, Gregorio, b. 1908

Conget, José María, b. 1948

Connolly, Cyril, 1903–1974

Conrad, Joseph, 1857–1924

Constant, Benjamin, 1767–1830

Constantini, Humberto, 1924–1987

Conteris, Hiber, b. 1933

Conti, Jorge, b. 1935

Conti, Haroldo, 1925–1976?

Contín Aybar, Pedro René, 1907–1981

Contreras, Hilma, b. 1913

Contursi, Pascual, 1888–1932

Corallini, Juan Carlos, b. 1925

Cordeiro, João, b. 1914

Cordero, Luis, 1833–1912

Cordovez Moure, José María, 1835–1918

Cornejo Polar, Antonio, 1936–1997

Coronado, Jesús, 1850–1919

Coronel Urtecho, José, 1906–1994

Corpi, Lucha, b. 1945

Corrales, José, b. 1937

Corrêa, José Celso Martinez, b. 1937

Corrêa, Julio, 1890–1953

Correa, Miguel Angel [Mateo Booz, pseud.], 1881–1943

Corro, Gaspar Pio del, d. 1923

Cortázar, Julio, 1914–1984

Cortés, Alfonso, 1893–1969

Cortés, Hernán, 1485–1547

Cortez, Gregorio, 1875–1915

Cortijo Verdejo, Rafael, 1928–1982

Cortina, Juan Nepomuceno, 1824–1894

Cosío Villegas, Daniel, 1898–1976

Cossa, Roberto, b. 1934

Costa, Antonio Joachim Rodrigues da, b. 1833

Costa, Cláudio Manoel da, 1729–1789

Costa, Francisco Augusto Pereira da, 1851–1923

Costa, João Cruz, 1904–1978

Costa, Julio Dias de, 1878–1935

Costa, Jurandir Freire, b. 1944

Costa, Lúcio, 1902–1998

Costa, Luiz Edmundo, 1878–1961

Costa, Marithelma, 1955

Costa, Sosígenes, 1901–1968

Costantini, Humberto, 1924–1987

Costa Pereira Furtado de Mendonça, Hippolyto José da, 1774–1823

Cota, Raúl Antonio, b. 1949

Cotto-Thorner, Guillermo, b. 1916

Coutinho, Afrânio, 1911–2000

Coutinho, Azeredo, (bishop of Olinda), 1742–1821

Coutinho, Edilberto, b. 1938

Coutinho, Sônia, b. 1939

Couto, Rui Ribeiro, 1898–1963

Crapanzano, Vincent, b. 1939

Cravioto, Alfonso, 1884–1955

Crespo, Luis Alberto, b. 1941

Croix, Charles François de, 1699–1786

Crosthwaite, Luis, b. 1962

Cruls, Gastão, 1888–1959

Cruz, Ernesto, b. 1898

Cruz, Francisco de la, 1530–1578

Cruz, Manuel de la, 1861–1896

Cruz, Migdalia, b. 1958

Cruz, Nilo, b. 1960

Cruz, Oswaldo, 1872–1917

Cruz, Sor Juana Inés de la, 1651–1695

Cruz, Victor de la, b. 1948

Cruz Diez, Carlos, b. 1923

Cruz e Sousa, João, 1861–1899

Cruz Varela, Juan, 1794–1839

Cuadra, Jose de la, 1903–1941

Cuadra, Manolo, 1907–1957

Cuadra, Pablo Antonio, 1912–2002

Cuauhtlehuanitzin, Domingo Francisco de San Antón Muñón Chimalpahin [Chimalpahin, pseud.], 1579–1660

Cuéllar, José Tomás de, 1830–1894

Cuervo, Rufino, 1801–1853

Cuervo, Rufino José, 1844–1911

Cuesta, Jorge, 1903–1942

Cueto, Alonso, b. 1954

Cueva, Juan de la, 1543–1612

Cunha, Adalmir, b. 1930

Cunha, Alberto Coelho da, 1853–1939

Cunha, Delfina Benigna da, 1791–1857

Cunha, Euclides da, 1866–1909

Cunha, Helena Parente, b. 1929

Cunha, Luiz da, 1662–1740

Cuoto, Ribeiro, 1898–1963

Curiel, Nicolás, b. 1928

Cuzzani, Agustín, 1924–1978

Cytrynowicz, Roney, b. 1964

D

Dalton, Roque, 1935–1975

Damata, Gasparino, b. 1918

Daniel, Herbert, 1946–1992

D'Anna, Eduardo, b. 1948

Darío, Rubén, 1867–1916

Darwin, Charles, 1809–1882

Dávalos, Jaime, 1921–1981

Dávalos, Juan Carlos, 1887–1959

Dávalos, René, 1945–1968

Dávalos y Figueroa, Diego, 1550?–1608?

Dávila, Amparo, b. 1928

Dávila Padilla, Agustín, Obispo de Santo Domingo, 1562–1604

Dávila Semprit, José, 1902–1958

Debret, Jean Baptiste, 1768–1848

Délano, Poli, b. 1936

Delany, Martin Robison, 1812–1885

Delaunay, Sonia, 1885–1979

Delfino, Luis, 1834–1910

Delgado, Rafael, 1853–1914

Delgado, Wáshington, b. 1927

Delgado Aburto, Leonel, b. 1965

Delgado Senior, Igor, b. 1942

Delille (Jacques), abbé, 1738–1813

Del Paso, Fernando, b. 1935

Del Valle, Aristóbulo, 1845–1896

Denis, Jean-Ferdinand, 1798–1890

Denser, Márcia, b. 1949

Derrida, Jacques, b. 1930

Descartes, René, 1596–1650

De Sola, Otto, 1912–1975

Dessalines, Jean Jacques, 1758–1806

D'Halmar, Augusto, 1880–1950

Dias, Antônio Gonçalves, 1823–1864

Dias, Cícero, 1907–2003

Dias, Everardo, 1883–1966

Díaz, Eugenio, 1804–1865

Díaz, Jesús, b. 1941

Díaz, José Pedro, b. 1921

Díaz, Junot, b. 1968

Díaz, Leopoldo, 1862–1947

Díaz, Nidia [Ma. Marta Valladares Mendoza, pseud.], b. 1952

Díaz, Porfirio [dictator of Mexico, 1876–1880, 1884–1911], 1830–1915

Díaz Bagú, Alberto, b. 1919

Díaz Casanueva, Humberto, 1907–1992

Díaz de Guzmán, Ruy, 1558?–1629

Díaz del Castillo, Bernal, 1492–1584

Díaz Grullón, Virgilio, 1924–2001

Díaz Martínez, Manuel, b. 1936

Díaz Mirón, Salvador, 1853–1928

Díaz Niese, Rafael, 1897–1950

Díaz-Pérez, Rodrigo, 1924

Díaz Polanco, Héctor, b. 1936

Díaz Rodríguez, Jesús, b. 1941

Díaz Rodríguez, Manuel, 1871–1927

Díaz Sánchez, Ramón, 1903–1968

Díaz Solís, Gustavo, b. 1920

Díaz Valcárcel, Emilio, b. 1929

Di Bella, José Manuel, b. 1952

Di Benedetto, Antonio, 1922–1986

Di Cavalcanti, Emiliano, 1897–1976

Dickens, Charles, 1812–1870

Diderot, Denis, 1713–1784

Diego, Eliseo, 1920–1994

Diego-Padró, José Isaac de, 1896–1974

Díez de Betanzos, Juan, 1510–1576

Díez de Games, Gutierre, ca. 1379–ca. 1450
Díez de Medina, Fernando, 1908–1990
Dines, Alberto, b. 1932
Discépolo, Armando, 1887–1971
Discepolo, Enrique Santos, 1901–1951
Domecq, Brianda, b. 1942
Domingo de Santo Tomás, Fray, 1499–1570
Domínguez, Franklin, b. 1931
Domínguez, Manuel, 1869–1935
Domínguez Camargo, Hernando, 1606–1659
Domínguez Charro, Francisco, 1910–1943
Domínici, Pedro César, 1873–1954
Donato, Ada, b. 1933
Donoso, José, 1925–1996
Dorantes de Carranza, Baltasar, fl. 1550–1604
Dorfman, Ariel, b. 1942
Dornal, Jules, [archbishop of Belge], 1846–1924
Dorra, Raúl, b. 1937
Dourado, Autran, b. 1926
Draghi Lucero, Juan, 1897–1970
Dragún, Osvaldo, 1929–1999
Droguett, Carlos, 1912–1996
Drummond, Roberto, 1937–2002
Drummond de Andrade, Carlos, 1902–1987
Duarte, Paulo, 1899–1984
Du Bois, W. E. B. [William Edward Burghardt], 1868–1963
Dueñas, Guadalupe, b. 1920
Dumas, Alexandre [Pére], 1802–1870
Dumas, Alexandre [fils], 1824–1895
Duncan, Quince, b. 1940
Durán, Fray Diego, 1537–1587
Durán Bóger, Luciano, b. 1904
Durão, José de Santa Rita, ca. 1720–1784
Dürrenmatt, Friedrich, 1921–1990

E

Echagüe, Juan Pablo, 1877–1950
Echavarren Welker, Roberto, b. 1944
Echavarría de Del Monte, Encarnación, 1812–1890
Echeverría, Esteban, 1805–1851
Eco, Umberto, b. 1932
Edwards, Jorge, b. 1931
Eguiara y Eguren, Juan José de, 1696–1763
Eguren, José María, 1874–1942
Eichelbaum, Samuel, 1894–1967
Eielson, Jorge Eduardo, b. 1924
Eiró, Paulo, 1838–1871
Eliot, T. S., 1888–1965
Elizondo, Ricardo, b. 1950
Elizondo, Salvador, b. 1932
Elizondo, Sergio, b. 1930
Eltit, Diamela, b. 1949
Encina, Juan del, 1468–1529?
Ennery, Adolphe d', 1811–1899
Erauso, Catalina de [Monja Alférez, pseud.] 1582?–1650
Ercilla y Zuñiga, Alonso de, 1533–1594

Escobar y Mendoza, Antonio de, 1589–1669
Escobedo, Alonso Gregorio de, fl. 1587
Escofet, Cristina, b. 1945
Escoiquiz, Juan de, 1762–1820.
Eslava, Fernán González de, 1534–1601
Espada, Martín, b. 1957
Espina, Concha, 1869–1955
Espinal, Valentín, 1803–1866
Espino, Fernando, ca. 1597–1676
Espínola, Lourdes, b. 1954
Espinosa, Alfredo, b. 1954
Espinosa, Isidro Felix de, 1679–1755
Espinosa, José María, 1796–1883
Espinosa Medrano, Juan de [El Lunarejo, pseud.], 1620?–1688
Espronceda, José de, 1808–1842
Esquivel, Laura, b. 1950
Esteves, Sandra María, b. 1948
Estévez, Abilio, b. 1954
Estévez, Antonio, 1916–1988
Estrada, Genaro, 1887–1937
Estrada, Luís Gonzaga Duque, 1863–1911
Estrada y Zenea, Ildefonso, 1826–1912
Estrela de Villeroy, Frederico Ernesto, 1837–1897
Estupiñán Bass, Nelson, 1912–2002
Eugeren, José María, 1874–1942
Eulálio, Alexandre, 1932–1988
Eulate Sanjurjo, Carmela, 1871–1961
Evia, Jacinto de, b. 1629
Ezeiza, Gabino, 1858–1916

F

Fabini, Eduardo, 1882–1950
Faillace, Tânia, b. 1939
Falla, Manuel de, 1876–1946
Fallas, Carlos Luis, 1909–1966
Fanon, Frantz, 1925–1961
Faraco, Sergio, b. 1940
Faras, João, 15th/16th cent.
Faria, Antonio Bento de, 1875–1959
Faria, Francisco de, b. 1653
Faria, Otavio de, 1908–1980
Farias, Elson, b. 1936
Fariña Nuñez, Eloy, 1885–1929
Feierstein, Ricardo, b. 1942
Feijoo, Benito Jerónimo, 1676–1764
Feinmann, José Pablo, b. 1943
Feira, Lucas da, 1807?–1849
Felinto, Marilene, b. 1957
Felipe, Carlos, 1911–1975
Felipe, Luis, 1884–1968
Felipe II [king of Spain], 1527–1598
Fellman Velarde, José, 1922–1982
Fernandes, Carlos Dias, 1874–1942
Fernandes, Florestan, 1920–1995
Fernandes, João Damasceno Vieira, 1850–1910
Fernandes, Millôr, b. 1924
Fernández, Emiliano Rivarola, 1894–1949
Fernández, Emilio, 1904–1986
Fernández, Macedonio, 1874–1952
Fernández, Roberto G., b. 1949
Fernández Camus, Emilio, b.1897
Fernández de Lizardi, José Joaquín, 1776–1827

Fernández de Oviedo, Gonzalo, 1478–1557
Fernández de Santa Cruz, Manuel, 1637–1699
Fernández Mejía, Abel, b. 1931
Fernández Moreno, Baldomero, 1886–1950
Fernández Moreno, César, 1919–1985
Fernández Retamar, Roberto, b. 1930
Ferradas, Renaldo, b. 1932
Ferraz, Geraldo, 1905–1979
Ferré, Rosario, b. 1938
Ferreira, Alexandre Rodrigues, 1756–1815
Ferreira, Athos Damasceno, 1902–1975
Ferreira, Aurélio Buarque de Holanda, 1910–1989
Ferreira, Luis Gomes, 18th cent.
Ferreira, Alexandre Rodrigues, 1756–1815
Ferreiro, Alfredo Mario, 1899–1959
Ferrer, Rafael, 1570–1611
Ferrer, Renée, b. 1944
Feuillet, Octave, 1821–1890
Fiallo, Fabio, 1865–1942
Fião, Jose Antonio do Vale Caldre e, 1821–1876
Fielding, Henry, 1707–1754
Fierro, Enrique, b. 1942
Figari, Pedro, 1861–1938
Figueiredo, Jackson de, 1891–1928
Figueirôa, Amália dos Passos, 1845–1878
Figueras, Francisco, 1853–?1909
Figueroa, Baltasar de, ca. 1560–1659
Figueroa, Pablo, b. 1977
Figueroa, Pedro Pablo, 1857–1909
Filgueira Sobrinho, Francisco Antonio, 1842–1878
Filho, Godofredo, 1904–1992
Finot, Enrique, 1891–1952
Florence, Hercules, 1804–1879
Flores, Celedonio, 1896–1947
Flores, José Felipe, 1751–1814
Flores, Pedro, 1894–1979
Flores de Oliva, Isabel [saint Rosa de Lima, pseud.], 1586–1617
Flores Suárez, Alfredo, b. 1897
Floresta, Nísia, 1809–1885
Flórez, Julio, 1867–1923
Florit, Eugenio, 1903–1999
Fombona-Pachano, Jacinto, 1901–1951
Fombona Palacio, Manuel, 1857–1903
Fondane, Benjamín, 1898–1944
Fondizi, Arturo, 1908–1995
Fonollosa, José María, 1922–1991
Fonseca, José da, 1788–1866
Fonseca, José Ruben, b. 1925
Fonseca, Reynaldo, b. 1925
Fonseca, Rubem, b. 1925
Fontanarrosa, Roberto, b. 1944
Fontella, Orides, b. 1940
Fontenelle, M. de [Bernard Le Bovier, pseud.], 1657–1757
Fontes, José Martins, 1884–1937
Fornés, María Irene, b. 1931
Forster, E. M., 1879–1970
Fóscolo, Avelino, 1864–1944
Foucault, Michel, 1926–1984
Fraga, Myriam, b. 1937

Fragoso, Maria, 1866–1947
Fragoso, Víctor, b. 1944
Fraguada, Federico, b. 1952
Franca, Leonel, 1893–1948
França Júnior, Joaquim José da, 1838–1890
Francia, José Gaspar Rodríguez de, 1766–1840
Francisca, Concepción del Castillo, 1671–1742
Francisco, Ramón, b. 1929
Franco, Francisco [dictator of Spain, 1939–1975], 1892–1975
Franco, Luis Leopoldo, 1898–1988
Francovich, Guillermo, 1901–1990
Frank, Waldo David, 1889–1967
Fray Mocho [pseud. of José Sixto Alvarez], 1858–1903
Frazer, Sir James George, 1854–1941
Freire, Luis José Junqueira, 1832–1855
Freire, Paulo, 1921–1997
Freire de Jaimes, Carolina, 1844–1916
Fresan, Rodrigo, b. 1963
Frexieiro, Fabio, 1931–1984
Freyre, Gilberto, 1900–1987
Frías, Heriberto, 1870–1925
Frota, Lélia Coelho, b. 1937
Frugoni, Emilio, 1880–1969
Fuentes, Carlos, b. 1928
Fuentes Mares, José, 1919–1986
Fuentes y Guzmán, Francisco de, ca. 1643–1699 or 1700
Fuguet, Alberto, 1964
Furtado, Celso, b. 1920
Fusco, Coco, b. 1960
Fusco, Rosário, 1910–1977
Futoransky, Luisa, b. 1939

G

Gabeira, Fernando, b. 1941
Gaitán, Jorge Eliécer, 1898?–1948
Gaitán Durán, Jorge, 1924–1962
Galán, Raúl, 1913–1963
Galarza, Ernesto, 1905–1984
Galeano, Benita, 1905–1995
Galeano, Eduardo H., b. 1940
Galeno, Juvenal, 1836–1931
Galiano, Alina, b. 1950
Galindo, Francisco E., 1850–1896
Galindo, Néstor, 1830–1865
Galindo de Vera, León, 1819–1889
Gallardo, Edward, b. 1949
Gallardo, Sara, 1931–1988
Gallegos, Rómulo, 1884–1969
Galliano, Alina, b. 1950
Galton, Francis, 1822–1911
Galván, Manuel de Jésus, 1834–1911
Galvão, Benjamim Franklin [Barão de Ramiz, pseud.], 1846–1938
Galvão, Patrícia [Mara Lobo Pagu, pseud.], 1910–1962
Galvão, Walnice Nogueira, b. 1937
Gálvez, José, 1885–1957
Gálvez, Manuel, 1882–1962
Gálvez Ronceros, Antonio, b. 1931
Gama, José Basílio da, 1740–1795
Gama, Luíz, 1830–1882
Gama, Marcelo, 1878–1915

Gama Malcher, José Candido de, 1853–1921
Gamarra, Gregorio, fl. 1600–1630
Gambaro, Griselda, b. 1928
Gamboa, Federico, 1864–1939
Gamez, José Dolores, 1851–1918
Gândavo, Pero de Magalhães, d. 1576
Gandolfo, Elvio E., b. 1947
Gandolfo, Francisco, b. 1921
Gante, Pedro de, 1486–1572
Gaos, José, 1900–1969
Garay, Blas, 1873–1899
Garay, Epifanio, 1849–1903
García, Cristina, b. 1958
García, Germán Leopoldo, b. 1944
García, Gregorio, d. 1627
García, Iván, b. 1938
García, Santiago, b. 1929
García, Uriel, 1884–1965
García Bacca, Juan David, 1901–1992
García Bergua, Ana, b. 1954
García Calderón, Francisco, 1883–1953
García Calderón, Ventura, 1886–1959
García Canclini, Néstor, b. 1939
García de Coronado, Domitila, 1847–1937
García del Rio, Juan, 1794–1856
García Hevia, Luis, 1816–1887
García Lorca, Federico, 1898–1939
García Maffla, Jaime, b. 1944
García Márquez, Gabriel, b. 1927
García Marruz, Fina, b. 1923
García Monge, Joaquín, 1881–1958
García Montero, Luis, b. 1958
García Ramis, Magali, b. 1946
Garcia-Roza, Luiz Alfredo, b. 1936
García Velloso, Enrique, 1880–1938
Gardea, Jesús, b. 1939
Gardel, Carlos, 1890–1935
Garet, Enrique Ricardo, 1904–1979
Garfia, Pedro, 1901–1967
Garibay, Ricardo, b. 1923
Garibay Kintana, Angel Maria, 1892–1967
Garmendia, Julio, 1898–1977
Garmendia, Salvador, 1928–2001
Garrido de la Peña, Carlota, 1870–1912
Garro, Elena, 1917–1998
Garvey, Marcus, 1887–1940
Garzón, Eugenio, 1849–1940
Gatón Arce, Freddy, 1920–1994
Gavidia, Francisco, 1864–1955
Gaviria, Víctor Manuel, b. 1955
Gaya, Ramón, b. 1910
Gayoso, Milia, b. 1962
Gelly, Juan Andrés, 1815–1904
Gelman, Juan, b. 1930
Gent, Pedro de, 1500?–1572?
Genta Dorado, b. 1957
Gerbasi, Vicente, 1913–1992
Gerchunoff, Alberto, 1883–1950
Germani, Gino, 1911–1979
Getrudis de San Ildefonso, 1652–1709
Ghiraldo, Alberto, 1874–1946
Ghivelder Zevi, b. 1934
Giaconi, Claudio, b. 1927
Giannotti, José Arthur, b. 1930
Giardinelli, Mempo, b. 1947
Gibson, Percy, 1908–1969

Gil, Gilberto, b. 1942
Gil, Lourdes, b. 1951
Gil-Albert, Juan, 1904–1993
Gil Fourtoul, José, 1861–1943
Gil Gilbert, Enrique, 1912–1973
Gili, Carlos E., b. 1938
Giménez, Carlos, 1945–1993
Giménez, Herminio, 1905–1991
Giner de los Ríos, Francisco, 1839–1915
Ginés de Sepúlveda, Juan, 1490–1573
Girondo, Oliverio, 1891–1967
Girri, Alberto, 1919–1991
Glantz, Margo, b. 1930
Gobineau, Arthur de, 1816–1882
Godino, Rodolfo, b. 1936
Godoi, Juan Silvano, 1850–1926
Godoy, Emma, 1921–1989
Goes, Clara, b. 1956
Gola, Hugo, b. 1927
Goldemberg Isaac, b. 1945
Goloboff, Gerardo Mario, b. 1939
Gomes, Angela María de Castro, b. 1948
Gomes, Carlos, 1836–1896
Gomes, Dias, 1922–1999
Gomes, Eugenio,1897–1972.
Gomes, Miguel, b. 1964
Gomes, Paulo Emílio Salles, 1916–1977
Gomes de Barros, Leandro, 1865–1918
Gomes de Lima, Mário Hélio, b. 1964
Gómez, Juan Carlos, 1820–1884
Gómez, Magdalena, b. 1954
Gómez, Máximo, 1836–1905
Gómez Carrillo, Agustín, 1842–1915
Gómez Carrillo, Enrique, 1873–1927
Gómez-Correa, Enrique, 1915–1995
Gómez de Avellaneda, Gertrudis, 1814–1873
Gómez de Guevara, Luis, 1611–1675
Gómez Kemp, Ramiro, b. 1914
Gómez Montero, Sergio, b. 1945
Gómez Morín, Manuel, 1897–1972
Gómez-Peña, Guillermo, b. 1955
Gómez Restrepo, Antonio, 1869–1947
Gómez Restrepo, Francisco, 1884–1924
Gómez Rosa, Alexis, b. 1950
Gómez y Hermosilla, José Mamerto, 1771–1837
Gondra, Manuel [president of Paraguay, 1910–1911, 1920–1921], 1871–1927
Góngora y Argote, Luis de, 1561–1627
Gonsalves de Mello, José Antonio, b. 1916
Gonzaga, Armando, 1889–1954
Gonzaga, Tomás Antonio, 1744–1807?
Gonzáles Castillo, Cátulo, 1906–1975
González, Joaquín Víctor, 1863–1923
González, José Luis, 1926–1997
González, Jovita, 1904–1983
González, Juan Vicente, 1810–1866
González, Lidia Milagros, b. 1942
González, Luis J., 1912–1990
González, Natalicio, 1897–1966
González, Otto Ral, b. 1921
González, Pedro Gaspar, b. 1945
González, Ray, b. 1952
González, Rodolfo "Corky", b. 1928
González Bocanegra, Francisco, 1824–1861
González Castillo, José, 1885–1937

González de Bobadilla, d. 1587
González de Eslava, Fernán, 1534–1601
González Holguin, Diego, b. 1552
Gonzalez Lanuza, Enrique, 1900–1984
González León, Adriano, b. 1931
González Martínez, Enrique, 1871–1952
González Mireles, Jovita, 1904–1983
González Pacheco, Rodolfo, 1882–1949
Gonzalez-Pando, Miguel, 1941–1998
Gonzalez Peña, Carlos, 1885–1955
González Prada, Manuel, 1844–1918
González Rojo, Enrique, 1899–1939
González Santín, José Ma., 1819–1899
Gonzalez Stephen, Beatriz, b. 1952
Gonzalez Suárez, Federico, 1844–1917
González Tuñón, Enrique, 1901–1943
González Tuñón, Raúl, 1905–1974
González Viaña, Eduardo, b. 1941
Gorbea, Carlos, b. 1940
Gordon, Arturo, 1883–1944
Gori, Gastón [Pedro Marangoni, pseud.],
    b. 1915
Gorodischer, Angélica, b. 1929
Gorostiza, Celestino, 1704–1767
Gorostiza, José, 1901–1973
Gorostiza, Manuel Eduardo, 1789–1851
Gorriti, Juana Manuela, 1816–1892
Gottberg, Carlos, b. 1929
Goyena, Pedro 1843–1892
Gracián, Baltasar, 1601–1658
Grafigny, Madame de [Françoise
    d'Issembourg d'Happoncourt],
    1695–1758
Gramcko, Ida, 1924–1994
Grandy, Julie de, b. 1956
Grases, Pedro, b. 1909
Grattan Domínguez, Alejandro, b.
    1934
Greiff, León de, 1895–1976
Gresset, Jean-Baptiste-Louis, 1709–1777
Griaule, Marcel, 1898–1956
Grieco, Agripino, 1888–1968
Grillo, Max, 1868–1949
Grondon, Gonzalo "Payo", b. 1945
Grossman, Judith, b. 1931
Grotowski, Jerzy, b. 1933
Groussac, Paul, 1848–1929
Guamán Poma de Ayala, Felipe,
    1524? –1613
Guanes, Alejandro, 1872–1925
Guaramato, Oscar, 1916–1987
Guardia, Gloria, b. 1940
Guarnieri, Gianfrancesco, b. 1934
Guasp Cervera, Ignacio, 1810? –1874
Guayasamín, Osvaldo, 1919–1999
Gudiño Kramer, Luis, 1898–1973
Guedes, Lino, 1906–1991
Güell y Mercader, José, 1839–1905
Guerra, Guy, b. 1932
Guerra Trigueros, Alberto, 1898–1950
Guerrero, Julio, 1862–1937
Guevara, Antonio de, d. 1545
Guevara, Ernesto "Che", 1928–1967
Guevara, Laureano, 1889–1968
Guevara, Osvaldo, b. 1933
Guevara, Pablo, b. 1930
Guevara y Basoazábal, Andrés de,
    1748–1801
Guido, Beatriz, 1925–1988

Guido y Spano, Carlos, 1827–1918
Guillén, Jorge, 1893–1984
Guillén, Nicolás, 1902–1989
Guimaraens, Alphonsus de, 1870–1921
Guimarães, Bernardo, 1825–1884
Guimarães, Emanuel, 1871–1907
Guimarães, Francisco Pinheiro,
    1832–1877
Guimarães, Geni, b. 1947
Guimarães, Hilda Leite, 1860–1916
Guimarães, Ruth, b. 1920
Guimarães Júnior, Luís, 1845–1898.
Guimarães Rosa, João, 1908–1967
Guinsburg, Jacó, b. 1921
Güiraldes, Ricardo, 1886–1927
Guirao, Ramón, 1908–1949
Gullar, Ferreira, b. 1930
Gurjão, Henrique Eulálio, 1834–1885
Gusmán, Luis, b. 1944
Gutiérrez, Carlos María, b. 1926
Gutiérrez, Eduardo, 1851–1889
Gutiérrez, Franklin, b. 1951
Gutiérrez, Joaquín, 1918–2000
Gutiérrez, Juan Maria, 1809–1878
Gutiérrez, Manuel Socorro, 1758–1818
Gutiérrez, Miguel, b. 1940
Gutiérrez Girardot, Rafael, b. 1928
Gutiérrez González, Gregorio,
    1826–1872
Gutiérrez Nájera, Manuel, 1859–1895
Gutiérrez Vega, Hugo, b. 1934
Guzmán, Martín Luis, 1887–1977
Guzmán, Nicomedes, 1914–1964
Guzmán Blanco, Antonio, 1828–1899

H

Haenke, Tadeás, 1761–1817
Halperín Donghi, Tulio, b. 1926
Hammett, Dashiell, 1894–1961
Harare Duque, Francisco, 1929–1991
Harris, Marvin, 1927–2001
Harss, Luis, b. 1936
Hatoum, Milton, b. 1952
Haya de la Torre, Víctor Raúl,
    1895–1979
Hebreo, León, b. ca. 1460
Hecker Filho, Paulo, b. 1926
Hegel, Georg Wilhelm Friedrich,
    1770–1831
Heker, Liliana, b. 1943
Helme, Elizabeth, d. 1814?
Henestrosa, Andrés, b. 1906
Henríquez, Camilo, 1769–1825
Henríquez de Guzmán, Alonso,
    1499–1547
Henríquez Ureña, Max, 1885–1970
Henríquez Ureña, Pedro, 1884–1946
Heraud, Javier, 1942–1963
Herbert, Daniel, 1946–1992
Herder, Johann Gottfried, 1744–1803
Heredia, José Francisco de, 1776–1829
Heredia, José María de, 1842–1905
Heredia y Heredia, José María,
    1803–1839
Herkovits, Melville Jean, 1895–1963
Hernández, Camilo, 1769–1825
Hernández, Felisberto, 1902–1964
Hernández, José, 1834–1886
Hernández, Josefina, b, 1928

Hernández, José Manuel, 1853?–1921
Hernández, Juan José, b. 1932
Hernandez, Leopoldo M., 1921–1994
Hernández, Natalio, b. 1947
Hernández, Oscar, b. 1974
Hernandez, Rafael, 1891–1965
Hernández Bustamante, Juan Fabri-
    ciano, 1844–1890
Hernandez Cruz, Victor, b. 1949
Hernández Franco, Tomás, 1904–1952
Herrera, Catalina Luisa, 1717–1795
Herrera, Fernando de, 1534–1597
Herrera, Juan Felipe, b. 1948
Herrera, Pablo, 1820–1896
Herrera Luque, Francisco J., 1927–1991
Herrera-Sobek, María, b. 1942
Herrera Toro, Antonio, 1857–1914
Herrera y Obes, Manuel, 1806–1890
Herrera y Reissig, Julio, 1875–1910
Herrera y Tordesillas, Antonio de,
    1559–1625
Heureaux, Ulises, 1870–1938
Hidalgo, Alberto, 1897–1967
Hidalgo, Bartolomé, 1788–1822
Hidalgo, Diego, b. 1888
Hidalgo, María Luisa, 1918–2000
Hidalgo y Costilla, Miguel, 1753–1811
Hierro, Jose, b. 1922
Highsmith, Patricia, 1921–1995
Hijuelos, Oscar, b. 1951
Hilst, Hilda, b. 1930
Hinojosa-Smith, Rolando, b. 1929
Hinostroza, Rodolfo, b. 1941
Hojeda, Diego de, 1570?–1615
Holanda, Heloísa Buarque de, b. 1939
Hollanda, Martha de, 1903–1950
Hollanda, Sérgio Buarque de,
    1902–1982
Homem, Francisco de Sales Torres, Vis-
    conde de Inhomerim, 1812–1876
Homem Lopo, fl. 1517–1565
Honório, José Carlos, b. 1946
Hortigoza, d. 1796
Hostos, Eugenio María de, 1839–1903
Houaiss, Antonio, 1916–1999
Houston, Matilda Charlotte Fraser,
    1815?–1892
Hoyos, Angela de, b. 1945
Huerta, Efraín, 1914–1982
Hugo, Victor, 1802–1885
Huidobro, Vicente, 1893–1948
Humareda, Victor, 1920–1986
Humboldt, Alexander von, 1769–1859
Humboldt, Baron de Wilhelm von,
    1767–1835
Hume, David, 1711–1776
Huneeus y Gana, Jorge, 1866–1926.
Hurtado de Mendoza, García, Marques
    de Cañete, 1535–1609
Huysmans, Joris-Karl, 1848–1907

I

Ibáñez, Sael, b. 1948
Ibáñez Langlois, José [Ignacio Valente,
    pseud.], b. 1936
Ibarbourou, Juana de, 1892–1979
Iberico, Mariano, 1892–1974
Ibsen, Henrik, 1828–1906
Icaza, Jorge, 1906–1978

Iglehart, Fanny Chambers Gooch, 1842–1913
Iglesias, Francisco, 1923–1999
Iglesias Prieto, Norma, b. 1959
Ignacio de Loyola, Saint, 1491–1556
Igreja, Francisco, b. 1949
Illescas, Carlos, 1918–1998
Incháustegui Cabral, Héctor, 1912–1979
Inclán, Luis G., 1816–1875
Inés de la Cruz, 1588–1663
Infante, Angel Gustavo, b. 1959
Ingenieros, José, 1877–1925
Inglis, Frances Erskine, Marquesa Calderón de la Barca, 1804–1882
Insausti, Rafael Angel, 1916–1978
Insfrán [see Ynsfrán]
Insúa, Alberto, 1883–1963
Ipuche, Pedro Leandro, 1889–1976
Irigoyen, Hipólito [president of Argentina, 1916–1922, 1928–1930], 1852–1933
Irisarri, Antonio José, 1786–1868
Irrizary, Richard V., 1956–1994
Isaacs, Jorge, 1837–1895
Isaías, Jorge, b. 1946
Isla, José Fracisco de, 1703–1781
Islas, Maya, b. 1947
Iturbide, Agustín de, 1783–1824
Iturralde, Iraida, b. 1954
Ixtlilxóchitl, Fernando de Alva, 1578–1650
Izaguirre, Enrique, b. 1929
Izidora, Francisca, 1855–1918

J

Jabor, Arnaldo, b. 1940
Jaimes, Carolina Freyre, 1827–1881
Jaimes Freyre, Ricardo, 1868–1933
Jansenius, Cornelius, 1585–1638
Jara, Victor, 1932–1973
Jaramillo, Cleofas, 1878–1956
Jaramillo Levi, Enrique, b. 1944
Jardiel Poncela, Enrique, 1901–1952
Jardim, Rachel, b. 1928
Jarry, Alfred,1873–1907
Jerez, Francisco de, 1497–1564?
Jerónima de la Trinidad, 15??–1616
Jerusalem, Ignacio de, 1707–1769
Jesús, Carolina Maria de, 1914–1977
Jijón y Caamaño, Jacinto, 1890–1950
Jiménez, José Alfredo, 1926–1974
Jiménez, Juan Ramón, 1881–1958
Jiménez, Manuel, 1895–1975
Jiménez, Mayra, b. 1938
Jitrik, Noé, b. 1928
Joachim, Sébastien, b. 1933
João do Rio [psedu. of João Paulo Barreto], 1881–1921
John, Climacus, Saint, 6th c.
Jolis, José, 1728–1790
Juana Inés de la Cruz, 1648–1695
Juan de la Cruz, Saint, 1542–1591
Juan de los Angeles, Fr. 1536–1609
Juárez, Benito, 1806–1872
Juárez, María Elena, b. 1917
Juárez, Tina, b. 1942
Juárroz, Roberto, 1925–1995
Junqueiro, Abilio Manuel Guerra de, 1850–1923

K

Kahlo, Frida, 1907–1954
Kamenszain, Tamara, b. 1947
Karlik, Sara, b. 1935
Katari, Tupak, 1750–1781
Katari Maria, Tomás, ca 1740–1781
Kaufman, Moisés, b. 1954
Kiefer, Charles, b. 1958
Kilkerry, Pedro, 1885–1917
Kino, Eusebio Francisco, 1944–1711
Koch-Grünberg, Theodor, 1872–1924
Kock, Paulo de, 1783–1871
Koellreutter, Hans Joachim, b. 1915
Kordon, Bernardo, b. 1915
Korn, Alejandro, 1860–1936
Koseritz, Carlos von, 1834–1890
Kozer, José, b. 1940
Krauze, Esther, b. 1954
Kundera, Milan, b. 1929

L

Labrador Ruiz, Enrique, 1902–1991
La Condamine, Charles Marie de, 1701–1774
Lacunza, José María, 1731–1801
Ladeira, Julieta de Godoy, b. 1935
Lafetá, João Luiz, b. 1946
Laforgue, Jules, 1860–1887
Lagunas, Alberto, b. 1940
Lair, Clara, 1895–1973.
Lalou, Ferdinand, d. 1850,
Lam, Wifredo, 1902–1982
Lamarche, Angel Rafael, 1900–1962
Lamas, Andrés, 1817–1891
Lamborghini, Osvaldo, 1940–1985
Land, Eduardo, b. 1941
Landa, Diego de, 1524–1579
Landa, René G., b. 1922
Landivar, Rafael, 1731–1793
Lange, Norah, 1906–1973
Lara, Agustín, 1900–1970
Lara, Jesús, 1898–1980
Lara, Omar, b. 1941
Larbaud, Valéry, 1881–1957
Larra, Mariano José de, 1809–1837
Larrañaga, Dámaso Antonio, 1771–1848
Larrea, Carlos Manuel, 1887–1983
Larreta, Enrique, 1875–1961
Larreynaga, Miguel, 1771–1847
Lars, Claudia [Carmen Brannon, pseud.], 1899–1974
Lasarte, Javier, b. 1955
Lasso de la Vega, Gabriel, 1559–1615
Lastarria, Jose Victorino, 1818–1888
Latcham, Ricardo, 1903–1965
Latorre, Mariano, 1886–1955
Laus, Harry, b. 1922
Lautréamont, Isidore Ducasse, comte de, 1846–1870
Lavandera, Beatriz R., b. 1942
Laverde Amaya, Isidoro, 1852–1903
Laviera, Tato, b. 1950
Lazzaroni, Alicia, b. 1954
Leal, Fernando, 1896–1964
Leal,Weydsin Barrios, b. 1921
Le Bon, Gustave, 1841–1931
Le Breton, Joachim, 1760–1819
Lebrón, Maybell, b. 1923
Lebrón Saviñón, Mariano, b. 1922

Lecuna, Juan Vicente, 1891–1954
Ledesma, Luis Manuel, b. 1949
Leeds, Anthony, b. 1925
Leguia, Augusto B., 1863–1932
Leguizamón, Martín, 1858–1935
Leite, Maurício Gomes, b. 1936
Leiva, Raúl, b. 1934
Lejter, Herman b. 1935
Lelpi, Rafael Oscar, b. 1939
Leme, Pedro Taques de Almeida Paes, 1714–1777
Leminski, Paulo, 1944–1989
Lemos, Antônio José de, 1843–1936
Lemos, Miguel, 1854–1917
Leñero, Vicente, b. 1933
Lenz, Rudolf, 1863–1938
León, Carlos Augusto, 1914–1997
León, Fr. Luis de, 1527–1591
Leonard, Irving Albert, 1896–1996
León de Hazera, Lidia, b. 1927
León Díaz, José Luis de, 1940–1984
León Felipe [pseud. of Camino Galicia], 1884–1968
León Pinelo, Antonio de, 1590?–1660
León Portilla, Miguel, b. 1926
Lequerica Perea, b. 1931
Lerdo de Tejada, Sebastián, 1823–1889
Lerner, Elisa, b. 1932
Lerner, Gabriel, b. 1953
Lerner, Jaime, b. 1959
Léry, Jean de, 1534–1611
Leskoschek, Axl, 1889–1976
Lessa, Origenes, 1903–1986
Leuenroth, Edgard, 1881–1968
Levi Calderón, Sara, b. 1942
Levi Carneiro, 1882–1971
Levin, Eliezer, b. 1930
Levins Morales, Aurora, b. 1954
Levi-Strauss, Claude, b. 1908
Levrero, Mario, b. 1940
Lewis, Oscar, 1914–1970
Leyva, José, b. 1938
Lezama Lima, José, 1910–1976
Lieber, Francis, 1800–1872
Liendo y Goicoechea, José Antônio, 1735–1814
Lihn, Enrique, 1929–1988
Lillo, Baldomero, 1867–1923
Lima, Alceu Amoroso [Tristão de Athayde, pseud.], 1893–1983
Lima, Barreto Afonso Henrique de, 1881–1922
Lima, João de Souza, 1898–1982
Lima, Jorge de, 1893–1953
Lima, Justiniano José, 1812–1862
Lima, Luiz Costa, b. 1937
Lima, Manoel de Oliveira, 1867–1928
Lima, Silviano Pirauá, 1848–1913
Lima Sobrinho, Alexandre José Barbosa, 1897–2000
Limeira Marinho Santos, José Carlos, b. 1951
Limón, Graciela, b. 1938
Linning, Samuel, 1888–1912
Lins, Álvaro, 1912–1970
Lins, Joanna Tiburtina de Silva, 1840–1905
Lins, Osman, 1924–1978
Lins, Paulo, b. 1958

Lins do Rego, José, 1901–1957
Linyera, Dante A. [Francisco Bautista Rimoli, pseud.], 1902–1938
Lira Luciano, d. 1840?
Lisboa, Antônio Francisco da Costa [Aleijadinho, pseud.], 1730–1814
Lisboa, Henriqueta, 1904–1985
Liscano, Juan, 1915–2001
Lispector, Clarice, 1925–1977
Lispector, Elisa, 1911–1989
Littin, Miguel, b. 1942
Lizardo, Pedro Francisco, b. 1920
Llamazares, Julio, b. 1955
Llano Zapata, José Eusebio de, 1721–1780
Llerena, Cristóbal de, O.P., 1545–1616
Llinás, Julio, b. 1929
Llona, Numa Pompilio, 1832–1907
Lloréns Torres, Luis, 1878–1944
Loayza, Luis, b. 1934
Lobato, José Bento Monteiro, 1882–1948
Lobo, Luíza, b. 1948
Lobo, Tatiana, b. 1939
Locke, John, 1632–1704
Lockward Artiles, Antonio, b. 1943
Lombardo de Miramón, Concepción, 1835–1921
Lopes, Ascanio, 1906–1929
Lopes, Valentim José da Silveira, b. 1830
Lopes Neto, João Simoes, 1865–1916
López, Carlos Antonio, 1792–1862
López, César, b. 1933
López, Gregorio, 1542–1596
López, Josefina, b. 1969
López, Lucio V., 1848–1894
López, Nacho, 1923–1986
López, Nila, b. 1954
López, Rafael, 1875–1943,
López, Vicente Fidel, 1815–1903
López-Adorno, Pedro, b. 1954
López Albújar, Enrique, 1872–1966
López Decoud, Arsenio, 1867–1945
López de Enciso, Bartolomé, fl. 1586
López de Gómara, Francisco, 1511–1564
López de los Ríos, José, fl. 1684
López de Mesa, Luis, 1884–1967
López de Ubeda, Juan, fl. 1579–1582
López Méndez, Luis, 1863–1891
López Ortega, b. 1957
López Portillo y Rojas, José, 1850–1923
López Velarde, Ramón, 1888–1921
López y Fuentes, Gregorio, 1897–1966
Loureiro, João de Jesus Paes, b. 1939
Louzeiro, José, b. 1932
Loveira, Carlos, 1882–1928
Loynaz, Dulce María, 1902–1997
Loyola, Martín de, d. 1606
Lozano, Pedro, 1697–1752
Lozano, Wilfrid, b. 1950
Luaces, Joaquín Lorenzo, 1826–1867
Lucas, Fabio, b. 1931
Luco Cruchaga, Germán, 1894–1936
Luft, Lya, b. 1938
Lugones, Leopoldo, 1874–1938
Luis, de Granada, 1504–1588
Luna, Francisco, b. 1956
Luna, Pedro, 1894–1956
Lussich, Antonio Dionisio, 1848–1928

Luz, Fabio, 1864–1938
Lynch, Benito Eduardo, 1880–1951
Lynch, Marta, 1925–1985

M

Macedo, Francisco R., b. 1921
Macedo, Joaquim Manoel de, 1820–1882
Macedo Júnior, José Joaquim Cândido de, 1842–1860
Maceo, Antonio, 1845–1896
Macera, Pablo, b. 1929
Machado, Alcântara, 1875–1941
Machado, Alexandre Ribeiro Marcondes [Juó Bananére, pseud.], 1892–1933
Machado, Ana María, b. 1942
Machado, Aníbal, 1894–1964
Machado, Antonio, 1875–1939
Machado, Antônio de Alcântara, 1901–1935
Machado, Dyonelio, 1895–1985
Machado, Eduardo, b. 1953
Machado, Gilka, 1893–1980
Machado, Lourival Gomes, 1917–1967
Machado, Luz, 1916–1999
Machado, Simão Ferreira, fl. 18th century
Machado, Wilfredo, b. 1956
Machado de Assis, Joaquim Maria, 1839–1908
Macías, Elva, b. 1944
Maciel, Pedro Nolasco, 1861–1909
Madariaga, Francisco José, 1927–2000
Madero, Francisco I., 1873–1913
Madiedo, Manuel María, 1818–1888
Madrid, Antonieta, b. 1939
Madureira, Paulo Sena, b. 1947
Maecenas, Caius Cilnius, d. 8 B.C
Magalhães, Antônio Valentim da Costa, 1859–1903
Magalhães, Domingos José Gonçalves de, 1811–1882
Magalhães, Fernão de, d. 1521
Magalhães, José Vieira Couto de, 1837–1898
Magalhães Júnior, Raimundo, 1907–1982
Magariños, Santiago, b. 1902
Magdaleno, Mauricio, 1906–1986
Maggi, Carlos, b. 1922
Malamud, Samuel, 1908–2000
Maldonado, Pedro Vicente, d. 1748
Malfatti, Anita, 1889–1964
Malinowski, Bronislaw, 1884–1942
Mallea, Eduardo, 1903–1982
Mallet, Pardal, 1846–1894
Malraux, André, 1901–1976
Mañach, Jorge, 1898–1961
Maneiro, Juan Luis, 1744–1802
Manns, Patricio, b. 1937
Manrique, Jaime, b. 1949
Mansilla, Lucio, 1792–1871
Mansilla, Lucio Victorio, 1831–1913
Manso, Eduardo Vieira, b. 1931
Manso, Juana Paula, 1819–1875
Manzano, Juan Francisco, 1797–1854
Manzi, Homero, 1905–1951
Maples Arce, Manuel, 1898–1981

Maquieira, Diego, b. 1953
Márceles Daconte, Eduardo, b. 1942
Marcos, Juan Manuel, b. 1950
Marcos, Plínio, b. 1935
Marcus, George E., b. 1943
Marechal, Leopoldo, 1900–1970
María Anna Águeda de San Ignacio, 1695–1756
María Antonia Lucía del Espíritu Santo, 1646–1709
María de Estrada, b. 1620?
María de Jesús de Agreda, 1602–1665
María de Jesús de Puebla, 1579–1637
María de San José [née Juana Palacios Barruecos], 1656–1719
Mariana de Jesús, Saint, 1618–1645
Mariana de la Encarnación, 1571–1657
Mariani, Roberto, 1892–1946
Mariátegui, José Carlos, 1894–1930
Marichal, Leopoldo, 1900–1970
Marinello, Juan, 1898–1977
Marinetti, Filippo Tommaso, 1876–1944
Marini, Ruy Mauro, 1932–1997
Mármol, José, 1817–1871
Marmontel, Jean François, 1723–1799
Marques, Afonso, 1847–1872
Márques, René, 1919–1979
Marques, Xavier, 1861–1942
Marques Rebelo [pseud. of Eddy Dias da Cruz], 1907–1973
Márquez, Carlos, b. 1964
Márquez, Pedro José, 1741–1820
Márquez Rodríguez, Alexis, b. 1931
Marrero Aristy, Ramón, 1913–1959
Marroquín, José Manuel, 1827–1908
Marset, Juan Carlos, b. 1963
Martí, José, 1853–1895
Martín, Carlos, b. 1914
Martín, Manuel, Jr., 1934–2000
Martín, Mario, b. 1934
Martínez, Gregorio, b. 1942
Martínez, José Luis, b. 1918
Martínez, José de Jesús, b. 1929
Martínez, Juan Francisco, fl. 1807
Martínez, Juan Luis, 1942–1993
Martínez, Max, b. 1943
Martínez, Tomás Eloy, b. 1934
Martínez Campañón, Baltasar Jaime, 1735–1797
Martínez Correa, José Celso, b. 1937
Martínez de Castro, Inés, b. 1954
Martínez de Irala, Domingo, 1486–1557
Matínez de Nisser, María, 1812–1872
Martínez Estrada, Ezequiel, 1895–1964
Martínez Gamba, Carlos, b. 1939
Martínez Moreno, Carlos, 1917–1986
Martínez Rivas, Carlos, 1924–1998
Martín Gaite, Carmen, 1925–2000
Martini, Juan Carlos, b. 1944
Martins, Carlos Estevam, b. 1936
Martins, Luciano, b. 1934
Martins, Luís, 1907–1981
Martins, Wilson, b. 1921
Martins de Athayde, João, 1879–1959
Marx, Burle, 1909–1994
Masferrer, Alberto, 1868–1932
Maslíah, Leo, b. 1954
Massacese, Magda, b. 1945
Massiani, Francisco, b. 1944

Mastretta, Angeles, b. 1949
Mata Gil, Milagros, b. 1951
Matamala, Tito, b. 1963
Matamoro, Blas, b. 1942
Matos, Julio, b. 1931
Mateo, Eduardo, 1940–1990
Mateos, Juan M., 1831–1913
Matienzo, Juan de, 1520–1579
Matos, Eusebio da Soledade, 1626–1692
Matos, Gregório de, 1633?–1696
Matos, Nemir, b. 1949
Matta, Roberto, 1911–2002
Matto de Turner, Clorinda, 1852–1909
Mattos, Aníbal, 1889–1969
Mattos, Tomás de, b. 1947
Mattoso, Glauco, b. 1951
Matus, Macario, b. 1943
Matus, Manuel, b. 1949
Maudsley, Ann, 1854–1939
Mauro, Umberto, 1897–1983
Mautner, Jorge Henrique, b. 1941
Maximilian [emperor of Mexico, 1864–1867], 1832–1867
Maya, Alcides, 1878–1943
Maya, Rafael, 1897–1980
Mayorga Rivas, Ramón, 1862–1925
Mayz Vallenilla, Ernesto, b. 1925
McCarthy, Cormac, b. 1933
McHatton-Ripley, Eliza, 1832–1912
Medeiros e Albuquerque, José Joaquim de Campos de Costa, 1867–1934
Medina, José Ramón, b. 1921
Medina, José Toribio, 1852–1930
Medina, Pablo, b. 1948
Medinacelli, Carlos, 1899–1949
Médiz Bolio, Antonio, 1884–1957
Medoro, Angelino, 1547–1631
Medrano, Marianela, b. 1964
Meireles, Cecilia, 1901–1965
Meirelles, Vitor, 1832–1903
Mejia Lequerica, José, 1775–1813
Mejía de Fernángil, Diego, 1565–c. 1620
Meléndez, Jesús Papoleto, b. 1950
Melgar, Mariano, 1790–1815
Meliá, Bartomeu, b. 1932
Mello, Evaldo Cabral de, b. 1936
Mello, Pórcia Constança de, 1824–1894
Mello, Thiago de, b. 1926
Mello Franco, Afonso Arinos de, 1905–1990
Mello Franco, Francisco de, 1757–1823
Mello Moraes, Alexandre José de, 1816–1882
Melo, Alberto Cunha, b. 1942
Melo, Antonio Francisco Dutra e, 1823–1846
Melo, Rita Barém de, 1840–1868
Melo Neto, João Cabral de, 1920–1999
Melville, Herman, 1819–1891
Mena, Juan de, 1411–1456.
Menchú, Rigoberta, b. 1959
Mendes, Agrário de Sousa, 1885–1954
Mendes, Manuel Odorico, 1799–1864
Mendes, Murilo, 1901–1975
Mendes Campos, Paulo, 1922–1991
Méndez, Evar, 1888–1955
Méndez, Miguel, b. 1930
Méndez Capote, Renée, 1901–1989
Méndez de Cuenca, Laura, 1853–1928

Méndez Nieto, Juan, 1530–?
Méndez Plancarte, Alfonso, 1909–1955
Mendieta, Jerônimo de, 1525–1604
Mendive, Rafael María, 1821–1886
Mendonça, Geonísio Curvelo de, b. 1877
Mendonça, Lucio de, 1854–1909
Mendonça de Spinzi, Lucy, b. 1932
Mendoza, Jaime, 1874–1939
Menéndez Pidal, Ramón, 1869–1968
Menéndez y Pelayo, Marcelino, 1856–1912
Meneses, Guillermo, 1911–1978
Menezes, Agrário de, 1834–1863
Menotti del Picchia, Paulo, 1892–1988
Mera, Juan León, 1832–1894
Mercado, Tununa, b. 1939
Merchá, Rafael Maria, 1844–1905
Merchan, Rafael María, 1844–1905
Merlin, María de las Mercedes Santa Cruz y Montalvo, comtesse de, 1789–1852
Merquior, José Guilherme, b. 1941
Mesonero Romanos, Ramón, 1803–1882
Mesquita, José Joaquim Emerico Lobo de, 1746–1805
Mesquita Filho, Júlio, 1892–1969
Mexía, Pedro, 1496?–1552?
Meyer, Augusto, 1902–1970
Miccolis, Leila, b. 1947
Micelli, Sérgio, b. 1945
Michaux, Henri, 1899–1984
Michelena, Arturo, 1863–1898
Michelena, Margarita, 1917–1998
Mier, Servando Teresa de, 1763–1827
Mieses Burgos, Franklin, 1907–1976
Miguel, Maria Esther de, 1930–2003
Mijares, Augusto, 1897–1979
Milán, Eduardo, b. 1952
Milhaud, Darius, 1892–1974
Miliani, Domingo, b. 1930
Mill, John Stuart, 1806–1873
Millá, José, 1822–1882
Millán, Gonzalo, b. 1947
Millán, José Antonio, b. 1954
Miller, Henry, 1891–1980
Milliet, Sérgio, 1898–1966
Milton, John, 1608–1674
Mir, Pedro, 1913–2000
Miramontes y Zuázola, Juan de, 1550–1614
Miranda, Francisco de, 1750–1816
Miranda, Graciany Archilla, 1911–1991
Miranda, Luiz de, b. 1945
Miranda, Murilo, 1912–1971
Miró, Ricardo, 1883–1940
Mistral, Gabriela [Lucila Godoy, pseud.], 1889–1957
Mitre, Bartolomé, 1821–1906
Modesto, Tomás, b. 1951
Mohr, Nicholasa, b. 1935
Moleiro, Moisés, 1905–1979
Moleiro, Rodolfo, 1898–1970
Moliere [né Jean-Baptiste Poquelin], 1622–1673
Molina, Armando, b. 1957
Molina, Cristóbal de, 1494?–1578

Molina, Enrique, 1910–1997
Molina, Juan Ignacio, 1740–1829
Molina, Juan Ramón, 1875–1908
Molina, Pedro, 1777–1854
Molina, Tirso de, 1571?–1648
Molina Enríquez, Andrés, 1866–1940
Molinari, Ricardo E., 1898–1996
Molinas Rolón, Guillermo, 1892–1945
Moliner, Luis, b. 1949
Molloy, Sylvia, b. 1938
Monasterios, Rubén, b. 1943
Monesterolo, Oscar, b. 1953
Monge Medrano, Carlos, 1884–1970
Monge-Rafuls, Pedro R., b. 1943
Monsiváis, Carlos, b. 1938
Montaigne, Michel de, 1533–1592
Montale, Eugenio, 1896–1981
Montalvo, Juan, 1832–1889
Montaña, Antonio, b. 1932
Monte, Domingo del, 1804–1853
Monte, Félix María del, 1819–1899
Monteagudo, Bernardo, 1785–1825
Monte Carmelo, Luís de, d. 1785
Monteiro, Ângelo, b. 1942
Monteiro, Fernando, b. 1949
Monteiro, Maciel, 1804–1868
Monteiro, Vicente do Rego, 1899–1970
Monteiro Lobato, José Bento, 1882–1948
Montejo, Esteban, 1860–1973
Montejo, Eugenio, b. 1938
Montejo, Víctor, b. 1951
Montemayor, Carlos, b.1947
Montemayor, Jorge de, 1520–1561
Montépin, Xavier de, 1826?–1902
Monterroso, Augusto, 1921–2003
Montes Huidobro, Matías, b. 1931
Montesinos, Antonio de, 1470–1520
Montesinos, Fernando, 17th cent.
Montesinos, Jaime, b. 1938
Montesquieu, Charles de Secondat, Baron de 1689–1755
Montes Vanucci, Wolfgango, b. 1951
Montigny, Auguste Henri Victor Grand-jean de, 1776–1850
Montoya, José, b. 1932
Moog, Vianna, Clodomir, 1906–1988
Moore, Rachel Wilson, fl. end 19th cent.
Mora, José María Luis, 1794–1850
Mora, Luis María, 1869–1936
Mora, Pat, b. 1942,
Morae, Rubens Borba de, 1899–1987
Moraes Filho, Evaristo de, b. 1914
Moraga, Cherríe, b. 1952
Morais, Frederico, b. 1936
Morales, Alejandro, b. 1944
Morales, Antonio, b. 1955
Morales, Francisco, b. 1940
Morales, Rosario, b. 1930
Morales Bermúdez, Jesús, b. 1956
Morales Carrión, Arturo, 1913–1989
Morán de Buitrón, Jacinto, 1688–1749
Mora Serrano, Manuel, b. 1940
Moreira, Álvaro, 1888–1964
Morejón, Nancy, b. 1944
Morell de Santa Cruz, 1684–1768
Morelos y Pavón, José María, 1765–1815
Moreno, Fulgencio R., [Fulgencio Ricardo], 1872–1933

Moreno, Mariano, 1778–1811
Moreno de Gabaglio, Luisa, b. 1949
Moreno Durán, Rafael Humberto,
    b. 1946
Moreno Fraginals, Manuel, 1920–2001
Moreno Jiménez, Domingo, 1894–1986
Moreno Villa, José, 1887–1955
Moreyra, Alvaro, 1888–1964
Moriconi, Italo, b. 1953
Morla Vicñuna, Carlos, 1846–1901
Moro, César [Alfredo Quíspez Asín,
    pseud.], 1903–1956
Morón, Guillermo, b. 1926
Morrison, Mateo, b. 1947
Morton, Carlos, b. 1947
Mosca, Stefania, b. 1957
Moscona, Myriam, b. 1955
Moscovich, Cíntia, b. 1958
Mota, Carlos Guilherme, b. 1941
Mota, Valdo, b. 1959
Motolinia, Toribio, 1490?–1565?
Moura, Caetano Lopes de, 1780–1860
Moura, Emilio Guimarães, 1902–1971
Moura, Ignácio Baptista de, 1857–1929
Moura, Reynaldo, 1900–1965
Moutinho, Rita, b. 1951
Moyano, Daniel., 1930–1992
Moya Pons, Frank, b. 1944
Mugaburu, Josephe de, d. 1686
Mujía, Maria Josefa, 1812–1888
Mujica Láinez, Manuel, 1910–1984
Muñiz, Angelina, b. 1936
Muñoz, Elias Miguel, b. 1954
Muñoz, Gonzalo, b. 1956
Muñoz, Rafael F., 1899–1972
Muñoz Camargo, Diego, ca. 1529–1599
Muricy, José Cândido de Andrade,
    1895–l984
Murria, Roseana, b. 1950
Murrieta, Joaquín, 1809?–1832?
Mutis, Alvaro, b. 1923
Mutis, José Celestino, 1732–1808

N

Nabuco, Joaquim, 1849–1910
Nájera, Rick, b. 1960
Najera Yanguas, Diego de, 1580–1635
Najlis, Michèle, b. 1946
Nalé-Roxlo, Conrado, 1898–1971
Naranjo, Carmen, b. 1928
Narcejac, Thomas, 1908–1998
Nariño, Antonio, 1760–1823
Nascimento e Silva, Josino, 1811–1866
Nava, Pedro, 1903–1984
Navarrete, Carlos, b. 1945
Navarrete, Manuel de, 1768–1809
Navarro, José Gabriel, 1881–1965
Nazareth, Ernesto, 1863–1934
Nazoa, Aquiles, 1920–1976
Nebrija, Antonio de, 1444–1522
Neruda, Pablo, 1904–1973
Nervo, Amado, 1870–1919
Neto, Torquato, 1944–1972
Neves, Guilherme Santos, b. 1906
Neves, Inácio Parreiras, 1730–1793
Neves, Jaime Santos, b. 1908
Nezahualcóyotl Acolmiztli, 1402–1472
Nicholas of Cusa, Cardinal, 1401–1464
Nicotra, Alejandro, b. 1931

Niemeyer, Oscar, b. 1907
Nieremberg, Eusebio, 1595–1658
Nietzche, Friedrich Wilhelm, 1844–1900
Nimuendaju, Curt, 1883–1945
Nina Rodrigues, Raymundo, 1862–1906
Niño de Guzmán, Guillermo, b. 1955
Niser, María Martínez de, 1812–1872
Nissan, Rosa, b. 1939
Niza, Marco da, 1495–1558
Nóbrega, Manoel da, 1517–1570
Nogueira, Hamilton, 1897–1981
Nogueira, Lucila, b. 1950
Noguera, Carlos, b. 1943
Nolasco Cordero, Francisco, b. 1932
Nolasco Crespo, Pedro, 1734–1807?
Noll, João Gilberto, b. 1946
Novais, Faustino Xavier de, 1820–1869
Novás Calvo, Lino, 1905–1983
Novo, Salvador, 1904–1974
Nucete Sardi, José, 1897
Nunes, Benedito, b. 1929
Nunes, Feliciano Joaquim de Sousa,
    1734–1808
Nunes, Paulo, b. 1944
Núñez, Enrique Bernardo, 1895–1964
Núñez, Juan Carlos, 1895–1964
Núñez, Rafael, 1825–1894
Núñez Cabeza de Vaca, Alvar,
    1490–1558
Núñez de Arce, Gaspar, 1834–1903.
Núñez de Pineda y Bascuñán, Francisco,
    1607?–1676
Nuño Montes, Juan Antonio, 1927–1995

O

Obejas, Achy, b. 1956
Obeso, Candelario 1849–1884
Obligado, Rafael 1851–1920
Ocampo, Florián de, 1499?–1555?
Ocampo, Silvina, 1903–1993
Ocampo, Victoria, 1890–1979
Ocaña, Diego de, 1565–1608
Ochoa, Enriqueta, b. 1928
Odália, Nilo, b. 1929
Odio, Eunice, 1922–1974
Oesterheld, Héctor, 1919–1977
O'Gorman, Edmundo, 1906–1995
Oiticica, Hélio, 1937–1980
Oiticica, José, 1882–1957
Olavide, Pablo de, 1725–1803
O'Leary, Juan Emiliano, 1879–1969
Olimpio, Domingos, 1850–1906
Oliva, Aldo, 1927–2000
Olivari, Nicolás, 1900–1966
Oliveira, Eduardo de, b. 1926
Oliveira, Manuel Botelho de, 1636–1711
Oliver, María Rosa, 1898–1971
Ollé, Carmen, b. 1947
Olmedo, José Joaquín de, 1780–1847
Olmos, Andrés del, 1491–1571?
Oña, Pedro de, 1570?–1643?
Oñate, Juan de, 1549?–1624
O'Neill, Eugene, 1888–1953
Onetti, Juan Carlos, 1909–1994
Onís, Federico de, 1885–1966
Operto, Walter, b. 1937
Oquendo de Amat, Carlos, 1899–1936
Oquendo de Amat, Carlos, 1899–1973
Ore, Luis Jeronimo de, 1554–1630

Oreamuno, Yolanda, 1916–1956
Orfila, Arnaldo, 1897–1997
Orgambide, Pedro, 1929–2003
Orozco, José Clemente, 1883–1949
Orozco, Olga, 1920–1999
Orozco y Berra, Manuel, 1816–1881
Orphée, Elvira, b. 1930
Orrego Luco, Augusto, 1848–1933
Orrego Luco, Luis, 1866–1948
Ortega, Eulalio María, 1820–1875
Ortega, Francisco, 1793–1849
Ortega, Julio, b. 1924
Ortega y Gasset, José, 1883–1955
Ortigão, Ramalho, 1836–1915
Ortiz, Adalberto, 1914–2003
Ortiz, Fernando, 1881–1969
Ortiz, José Joaquín, 1814–1892
Ortiz, Juan L., 1896–1978
Ortiz-Cofer, Judith, b. 1952
Ortiz de Montellanos, Bernardo,
    1899–1948
Ortiz Saralegui, Juvenal, 1907–1959
Osorio, Amilkar, 1940–1985
Osorio, Miguel Ángel [Ricardo
    Arenales, Porfirio Barba Jacob,
    pseuds.], 1883–1942
Osorio Lizarazo, José Antonio,
    1900–1964
Ossott, Hanni, b. 1946
Ostrower, Fayga, 1920
Otero Muñoz, Gustavo, 1894–1957
Otero Reiche, Raúl, 1906–1976
Otero Silva, Miguel, 1908–1985
Otero Warren, Nina, 1881–1965
Othón, Manuel José, 1858–1906
Ovalle, Alonso de, 1601–1651
Ovalles, Caupolicán, b. 1936
Oviedo, José Miguel, b. 1934
Oviedo y Baños, José de, 1671–1738
Oviedo y Herrera, Luis Antonio, Conde
    de la Granja, 1636–1717
Owen, Gilberto, 1905–1952

P

Pacheco, João, 1910–1966
Pacheco, José Emilio, b. 1939
Pacheco Gómez, Máximo, b. 1924
Padeletti, Hugo, b. 1928
Padilla, Herberto, 1932–2000
Pagaza, Joaquín Arcadio, 1839–1918
Pagés Larraya, Antonio, b. 1918
Palacio, Ernesto, 1900–1979
Palacios, Alfredo Lorenzo, 1878–1965
Palacios, Antonia, 1915–2001
Palacios, Lucia, 1902–1994
Palacios, Lucila [Mercedes Carvajal de
    Arocha, pseud.], 1902–1994
Palacios Fajardo, Manuel, 1784–1819
Palafox y Mendoza, Juan de, 1600–1659.
Palatnik, Roza, 1904–1979
Palés Matos, Luis, 1898–1959
Palhano, Lauro, fl. 1930s-1940s
Pallais, Azarías H., 1884–1954
Pallotini, Renata, b. 1921
Palma, José Joaquín, 1844–1911
Palma, Ricardo, 1833–1919
Palomares, Ramón, b. 1935
Pane, Ignacio Alberto, 1880–1919
Pané, Fray Ramón, d. 1571

Pantin, Yolanda, b. 1955
Pardo, Luis, b. 1927
Pardo, Miguel Eduardo, 1868–1905
Pardo y Aliaga, Felipe, 1806–1868
Paredes, Américo, 1916–1999
Paredes, Rigoberto, 1870–1950
Pareja y Diez Canseco, Alfredo,
　1908–1993
Parra, Ángel, b. 1943
Parra, Isabel, b. 1937
Parra, Marco Antonio de la, b. 1952
Parra, Nicanor, b. 1914
Parra, Teresa de la, 1889–1936
Parra, Violeta, 1917–1967
Parra del Riego, Juan, 1894–1925
Parrado, Gloria, 1927–1987
Partnoy, Alicia, b. 1955
Pasos, Joaquín, 1914–1947
Pasos Kanki, José Vicente, 1779–1852?
Passos, Francisco Pereira, 1836–1913]
Pastori, Luis, b. 1920
Paternain, Alejandro, b. 1933
Patrocínio, José do, 1853–1905
Patroni, Felippe, 1789?–1866
Patterson, Aline, b. 1938
Pauw, Cornelius de, 1739–1799
Pavlovsky, Eduardo, b. 1933
Payeras, Mario, 1940–1995
Payno, Manuel, 1810–1894
Payró, Roberto J., 1867–1928
Paz, Octavio, 1914–1998
Paz, Senel, b. 1950 [Cuba]
Paz Castillo, Fernando, 1893–1981
Pazos Kanki, Vicente, 1779–1851?
Paz Paredes, Margarita, b. 1922
Paz y Mateos, Alberto, 1915–1967
Pecar, Samuel, b. 1922
Pederneires, Paranhos, 1860–1890
Pedreira, Antonio S., 1889–1939
Pedroni, José, 1899–1968.
Pedrosa, Mário, 1900–1981
Pedroso, Regino, 1896–1983
Pedrozo, Mabel, b. 1965
Peixoto, Luiz, 1889–1973
Pellegrini, Aldo, 1903–1973
Pellegrino, Hélio, 1924–1988
Pellicer, Carlos, 1899–1977
Pena, Domingos Soares Ferreira,
　1818–1888
Peña, Mario, b. 1973
Pena, Martins, 1815–1848
Peña Batlle, Manuel Arturo, 1902–1952
Peña Montenegro, Alonso de la,
　d.1688
Peña Villa, Ricardo León, b. 1962
Pena y Pena, Manuel de la, 1789–1850
Peña y Reinoso, Manuel de Jesús,
　1834–1913
Penna, Cornélio, 1896–1958
Pensón, Nicolás, 1855–1958
Penteado, Darcy, 1926–1990
Peralta, Alejandro, 1899–1973
Peralta Barnuevo, Pedro de, 1664–1743
Peraza, Luis, b. 1908
Perdomo, Omar, b. 1944
Perdomo y Heredia, Josefa Antonia,
　1834–1896
Pereda, Prudencio de, b. 1912
Pereda Valdés, Ildefonso, 1899–1996

Pereira, Carlos Alberto Messeder,
　b. 1951
Pereira, Edwiges de Sá, 1885–1954
Pereira, Gustavo, b. 1940
Pereira, Lúcia Miguel, 1901–1959
Pereira, Nuno Marques, 1652–1731
Pereira da Costa, Augusto, 1851–1923
Pereira da Silva, João Manuel,
　1817–1898
Pereiras, Manuel, b. 1949
Perellón, Carlos, b. 1957
Peres, Fernando da Rocha, b. 1936
Pereyra, Nicandro, b. 1914
Pérez, José Joaquín, 1845–1900
Pérez, Judith, b. 1945
Perez, Odalis G., b. 1952
Perez, Renard, b. 1928
Pérez, Severo, b, 1941
Pérez Bonalde, Juan Antonio,
　1846–1892
Pérez Castellanos, Manuel, 1743–1815
Pérez Coterillo, Moisés, b. 1988
Pérez Chaves, Emilio, b. 1950
Perez de Alesio, Mateo, 1547–1616
Pérez de Holguin, Melchor, 1660?–1732
Pérez de Villagrá, Gaspar, 1555–1620
Pérez Díaz, Amalia, b. 1923
Pérez Escrich, Enrique, 1829–1897
Pérez Firmat, Gustavo, b. 1949
Pérez Galdós, Benito, 1843–1920
Pérez Perdomo, Francisco, b. 1930
Pérez Petit, Victor, 1871–1947
Pérez Ramírez, Juan, b. 1544?
Pérez Rosales, Vicente, 1807–1886
Pérez Triana, Santiago, 1858–1916
Pérez Vila, Manuel, 1912–1991
Peri Rossi, Cristina, b. 1941
Perlongher, Néstor, 1949–1992
Perón, Eva [Duarte; Evita], 1919–1952
Perón, Juan Domingo [president of
　Argentina, 1946–1955 and
　1973–1974], 1895–1974
Pesado, José Joaquín, 1801–1861
Pesante, Edgardo A., b. 1932
Pessoa, Fernando, 1888–1935
Petion, Alexandre, 1770–1818
Petterson, Aline, b. 1938
Peza, Juan de Dios, 1852–1910
Pezoa Véliz, Carlos, 1879–1908
Philip II [king of Spain, 1592-1598],
　1527-1598
Piar, Manuel Carlos, 1782?–1817
Picabia, Francis, 1879–1953
Picasso, Pablo, 1881–1973
Pichardo, Esteban, 1799–1879
Pichardo Moya, Felipe, 1892–1957
Picón-Febres, Gonzalo, 1869–1918
Picón Salas, Mariano, 1901–1965
Pietri, Pedro, b. 1943
Pigafetta, Antonio, ca. 1480/91–ca.
　1534
Piglia, Ricardo, b. 1941
Pignatari, Décio, b. 1927
Pimentel, Francisco, 1889–1942
Piñera, Virgilio, 1912–1979
Piñero, Miguel, 1946–1988
Piñero, Sergio, d. 1931
Pinheiro, Joaquim Caetano Fernandes,
　1825–1876

Pinheiro, Luis Gonçalves, d. 1727
Piñón, Nélida, b. 1937
Pino Suárez, Josè Marìa, 1869–1913
Pinto, Antísthenes, d. 1929
Pinto, Heraclito Sobral, 1893–1991
Pinto, Walter, 1910–1994
Piva, Roberto, b. 1937
Pizarnik, Alejandra, 1936–1972
Pizarro Suárez, Nicolas, 1830–1895
Plá, Josefina, 1903–1999
Pla, Josep, 1897–1981
Plá, Roger, 1912–1982
Plácido, Valdés [Diego Gabriel de la
　Concepción, pseud.], 1809–1844
Planchart, Enrique, 1894–1953
Planella, Gabriel, b. 1958
Plaza, Exequiel, 1892–1944
Plaza, Juan Bautista, 1898–1961
Plinio, Marcos, b. 1935
Pocaterra, José Rafael, 1890–1955
Poe, Edgar Allan, 1809–1849
Pol, Osvaldo, b. 1935
Polari, Alex, b. 1950
Polarollo, Giovanna, b. 1952
Poleo, Héctor, 1918–1989
Policastro, Cristina, b. 1955
Polo, José Toribio, 1841–1918
Polo de Ondegardo, d. 1575
Pomar, Juan Bautista, fl. 1582
Pombal, Sebastião José de Carvalho e
　Melo, Marquês de, 1699–1782
Pombo, José Francisco de Rocha,
　1857–1933
Pombo, Rafael, 1833–1912
Pompéia, Raul, 1863–1895
Ponce, Aníbal, 1898–1938
Ponce, Manuel M., 1882–1948
Ponce, Mary Helen, b. 1938
Poniatowska, Elena, b. 1933
Pontes, Joel, 1926–1977
Poppe, René, b. 1943
Porras Barrenechea, Raúl, 1897–1960
Portal, Magda, 1903–1989
Portella, Eduardo, b. 1932
Portillo Trambley, Estela, b. 1936
Portinari, Candido, 1903–1962
Pôrto Alegre, Apolinário, 1884–1904
Porto Alegre, Aquiles, 1848–1926
Porto Alegre, Manuel de Araújo,
　1806–1879
Porzecanski, Teresa, b. 1945
Posada, José Guadalupe, 1852–1913
Possevino, Antonio, 1533–1611
Post, Franz, 1612–1680
Pound, Ezra, 1885–1972
Povod, Reinaldo, 1959–1994
Pozas, Ricardo, 1912–1994
Prada Oropeza, Renato, b. 1937
Prado, Adélia, b. 1932
Prado, Décio de Almeida, 1917–2000
Prado, Eduardo Paulo da Silva,
　1860–1901
Prado, Paulo, 1869–1943
Prado Júnior, Caio, 1907–1990
Prados, Emilio, 1899–1962
Prata, Ranulfo, 1896–1942
Pratt, Hugo, 1927–1995
Prego, Irma, b. 1933
Prescott, William Hickling, 1796–1859

Prestes, Luís Carlos, 1890–1990
Prestol Castillo, Freddy, 1913–1981
Price-Mars, Jean, 1876–1969
Prida, Dolores, b. 1943
Prieto, Adolfo, b. 1928
Prieto, Guillermo, 1818–1897
Prieto, Justo, 1897–1982
Puente, Diego de la, 1586–1663
Puga, María Luisa, b. 1944
Puig, Manuel, 1932–1990
Pulido, José, b. 1945

Q

Queiroga, Antonio Augusto, 1811–1855
Queiroz, José Maria Eça de, 1845–1900
Queiroz, Dinah Silveira de, 1910–1978
Queiroz, Maria Amélia de, 1860?–1923
Queiroz, Rachel de, 1910–2003
Quental, Antero de, 1842–1891
Queremel, Angel Miguel, 1900–1939
Quesada, Ernesto, 1858–1934
Quessep, Giovanni, b. 1939
Quevedo, Francisco de, 1580–1645
Quijano, Carlos, 1900–1984
Quintana, Mário, 1906–1994
Quintana Roo, Andres, 1787–1851
Quinteros, Lorenzo, b. 1945
Quiroga, Horacio, 1878–1937
Quiroga, José Salomé, 1810–1878
Quiroga, Juan Facundo, 1790–1835
Quiroga, Pedro de, fl. 1560
Quispe Tito, Diego, 1611–1681
Quiteño, Serafín, 1906–1987

R

Rabasa, Emilio O., 1856–1930
Rabelo, Laurindo, 1826–1864
Raiol, Domingos Antonio, 1830–1912
Rama, Ángel, 1926–1983
Ramírez, Ignacio, 1818–1879
Ramírez, Ivette, b. 1969
Ramírez, Sergio, b. 1942
Ramírez Heredia , Rafael, b. 1942
Ramos, Artur, 1903–1949
Ramos, Graciliano, 1892–1953
Ramos, José Antonio, 1885–1941
Ramos, José Luis, 1785–1849
Ramos, Luis Arturo, b. 1947
Ramos, Manuel, b. 1948
Ramos, Samuel, 1897–1959
Ramos Mejía, José María, 1849–1914
Ramos Otero, Manuel, 1948–1990
Ramos-Perea, Roberto, b. 1959
Ramos Sucre, José Antonio,
    1890–1930
Ramponi, Jorge Enrique, 1907–1977
Randall, Margaret, b. 1936
Rangel, Alberto, 1871–1945
Rawet, Samuel, 1929–1985
Rawlings, Norberto James, b. 1945
Raynal, Guillaume-Thomas, 1713–1796
Real de Azúa, Carlos, 1916–1977
Rechy, John Francisco, b. 1934
Recinos, Adrián, 1866–1962
Rega Molina, Horacio, 1899–1957
Regen, Jacobo, b. 1935
Rego, José Lins do, 1901–1957
Reis, Maria Firmina dos, 1825–1917
Reis, Vicente Torres da Silva, 1870–1947

Rejano, Juan, 1903–1976
Renan, Ernesto, 1823–1892
Renau, Josep, 1907–1982
Renault, Abgar, 1908–1995
Rendón, Ricardo, 1894–1930
Requena, Andrés Francisco, 1908–1952
Resende, Enrique de, 1899–1973
Resende, Garcia de, ca. 1470–1536
Resende, José Camelo de Melo, d. 1964
Restivo, Paulo, 1658–1741
Reverón, Armando, 1889–1954
Reyes, Alfonso, 1889–1959
Reyes, Carlos José, b. 1941
Reyes, Guillermo, b. 1962
Reyes, Osvaldo, b. 1919
Reyes Rivera, Louis, b. 1945
Reyles, Carlos, 1868–1938
Reynoso, Oswaldo, b. 1932
Rezende, Otto Lara, 1922–1992
Ribeiro, Darcy, 1922–1997
Ribeiro, Eduardo [governor of Amazo-
    nas, 1892–1896], 1862–1900
Ribeiro, Francisco Bernardino,
    1814–1837
Ribeiro, João, 1860–1934
Ribeiro, João Ubaldo, b. 1941
Ribeiro, Júlio, 1845–1890
Ribeiro, Santiago Nunes, d. 1847
Ribeyro, Julio Ramón, 1929–1994
Ricardo, Cassiano, 1895–1974
Riccio, Gustavo, 1900–1942
Rich, Adrienne, b. 1929
Richardson, Samuel, 1689–1761
Ricoeur, Paul, b. 1913
Riestra, Gloria, b. 1929
Riestra, Jorge, b. 1926
Rimoldi, Francisco Bautista [Dante A.
    Linyera, pseud.], 1902–1938
Rio, João do, 1881–1921
Rio Branco, José Maria da Silva Para-
    nhos Júnior, Barão do, 1845–1912
Ríos, Julián, b. 1941
Rios Reyna, José Antonio, 1905–1971
Ripa, Cesare, 1560?–1623?
Ripley, Eliza McHatton, 1832–1912
Riquer, Martín de, b. 1914
Risco Bermúdez, René del, 1937–1972
Riserio, Antonio, b. 1953
Ritter, Jorge, 1907–1977
Riu Farré, Federico, 1925–1985
Riva Agüero, José de la, 1885–1944
Rivadavia, Bernardino, 1780–1845
Riva Palacio, Vicente, 1832–1896
Rivarola Matto, Juan Bautista,
    1933–1991
Rivas, Bimbo, 1939–1992
Rivas Mercado, María Antonieta,
    1900–1931
Rivera, Andrés, b. 1928
Rivera, Diego, 1886–1957
Rivera, Edward, b. 1941
Rivera, Francisco, b. 1933
Rivera, José, b. 1955
Rivera, José Eustasio, 1888–1928
Rivera, Tomás, 1935–1984
Rivera Martínez, Edgardo, b. 1934
Rivero, Juan, b. 1940
Roa Bastos, Augusto, b. 1917
Robbe-Grillet, Alain, b. 1922

Robertson, William, 1721–1793
Roca, Julio Argentino [president of
    Argentina, 1880–1886, 1898–1904],
    1843–1914
Rocha, Glauber Andrade, 1939–1981
Rocha, Justiniano José da, 1812–1862
Rocha, Octavio, 1910–1985
Rocha, Ruth, b. 1931
Rocha Pita, Sebastiao da, 1660–1738
Roche, Regina Maria Dalton,
    1764?–1845
Rodó, José Enrique, 1871–1917
Rodrigues, Amélia, 1861–1926
Rodrigues, João Barbosa, 1842–1909
Rodrigues, Lupicinio, 1914–1974
Rodrigues, Nelson, 1912–1980
Rodrigues Ferreira, Alexandre,
    1756–1815
Rodríguez, Abraham, Jr., b. 1961
Rodríguez, Guillermo, b. 1931
Rodríguez, José Policarpo, 1829–1914
Rodríguez, Luis J., b. 1954
Rodríguez, Lupicínio, 1914–1974
Rodríguez, Manuel Alfredo, b. 1929
Rodríguez, Manuel del Socorro,
    1758–1818
Rodríguez, Reina María, b. 1952
Rodríguez, Simón, 1771–1854
Rodríguez Acosta, Ofelia, 1902–1975
Rodríguez Castelo, Hernán, b. 1933
Rodríguez de Francia, José Gaspar,
    1766–1840
Rodríguez de Montalvo, Garci, fl. 1500
Rodríguez de Morales, Catalina,
    1835–1894
Rodríguez Demorizi, Emilio, 1904–1986
Rodríguez de Tió, Lola, 1843–1924
Rodríguez Freyle, Juan, 1566–1642
Rodríguez Galván, Ignacio, 1816–1842
Rodríguez Juliá, Edgardo, b. 1946
Rodríguez Monegal, Emir, 1921–1985
Rodríguez Objio, Manuel, 1838–1871
Rodríguez Ortiz, Oscar, b. 1944
Rodríguez Torres, Alvaro, b. 1950
Rodríquez, Alberto, b. 1925
Roffé, Mercedes, b. 1954
Roffé, Reina, b. 1951
Roffiel, Rosamaría, b. 1945
Rojas, Cristóbal, 1857–1890
Rojas, Fernando de, 1470–1541
Rojas, Gonzalo, b. 1917
Rojas, Jorge, 1911–1995
Rojas, Manuel, 1896–1973
Rojas, María Teresa, b. 1902
Rojas, Ricardo, 1882–1957
Rojas, Waldo, b. 1944
Rojas González, Francisco, 1904–1951
Rojas Guardia, Armando, b. 1949
Rojas Guardia, Pablo, 1909–1978
Rojas Paz, Pablo, 1896–1956
Rojo, Grínor, b. 1941
Rokha, Pablo de, 1894–1968
Roldán, Belisario, 1873–1922
Román, Jerónimo, 1536–1597
Román, José, 1906–1983
Román, Pedro, b. 1938
Román, Sabrina, b. 1956
Romano-Sued, Susana Nelly,
    b. 1947

Romero, Denzil, 1938–1999
Romero, Elvio, b. 1926
Romero, José Luis 1909–1977
Romero, José Rubén, 1890–1952
Romero, Luis Alberto, b. 1944
Romero, Manuel, 1897–1954
Romero, Silvio, 1851–1914
Romero Brest, Jorge, 1905–1989
Romero de Terreros, Manuel, 1880–1968
Romerogarcía, Manuel Vicente, 1865–1917
Rónai, Paulo, 1907–1992
Roos, Jaime, b. 1953
Roquette, José Ignacio, 1801–1870
Rosa de Lima [née Isabel Flores de Oliva], 1582–1617
Rosales, Alberto, b. 1931
Rosas, Ernani, 1886–1955
Rosas, Juan Manuel José Domingo Ortiz de, 1793–1877
Rosas de Oquendo, Mateo, b. ca. 1563
Roscio, Juan Germán, 1763–1821
Rose, Juan Gonzalo, 1928–83
Rosenblat, Ángel, 1902–1984
Rosencof, Mauricio, b. 1933
Rosende de la Sierra, Petrona, 1787–1845
Rosenfeld, Anatol, 1912–1973.
Rosenzweig, Carmen, b. 1925
Rossi, Vicente, 1871–1945
Rouanet, Sergio Paulo, b. 1934
Rouède, Emilio, 1848–1908
Rousseau, Jean-Jacques, 1712–1778
Rovinski, Samuel, b. 1932
Roxlo, Carlos, 1860–1926
Rozenmacher, Germán, 1936–1971
Ruas, Tabajara, b. 1942
Rubião, Murilo, 1916–1991
Rueda, Manuel, 1921–1999
Rueda, Salvador, 1857–1933
Ruffinelli, Jorge, b. 1943
Rugana, Leonel, 1949–1970
Rugendas, João Mauricio, 1802–1858.
Ruiz Belvis, Segundo, 1829–1867
Ruiz de Alarcón, Hernando, fl. 1592
Ruiz de Alarcón, Juan, 1581–1639
Ruiz de Burton, María Amparo, 1832–1895
Ruiz de Montoya, Antonio, 1585–1652
Ruiz Martínez, José, 1873–1967
Rulfo, Juan, 1918–1986

S
Saavedra, Bautista, 1870–1939
Saavedra Fajardo, Diego de, 1584–1648
Saavedra y Guzmán, Antonio de, fl. 1599
Sábato, Ernesto, b. 1911
Sábato, Magaldi, b. 1927
Sabines, Jaime, 1926–1999
Sabino, Fernando, b. 1923
Saco, José Antonio 1797–1879
Sada, Daniel, b. 1953
Sáenz, Jaime, 1921–1986
Sáenz, Manuela, 1793–1859
Saer, Juan José, b. 1937

Saguier, Raquel, b. 1940
Sahagún, Fr. Bernardino de, 1500?–1590
Saint-Pierre, Bernardin de, 1737–1814
Sáinz, Gustavo, b. 1940
Salado Alvarez, Victoriano, 1867–1931
Salas, Tito, 1887–1974
Salas y Montes de Oca, Esteban, 1725–1803
Salazar, Eugenio de, 1530–1602
Salazar, Luis, b. 1924
Salazar, Ramón A., 1852–1914
Salazar Arrue, Salvador, 1889–1975
Salazar Bondy, Augusto, 1924–1965
Salazar de Espinosa, Juan de, 1508–1556
Salazar Martínez, Francisco, b. 1925
Salazar Tetzagüic, Manuel, b. 1948
Saldanha, Nelson Nogueira, b. 1933
Sales, Antônio, 1868–1940
Salgado, Plínio, 1895–1975
Salinas, Fr. Buenaventura de, d. 1653
Salinas, Pedro, 1892–1951
Salles, Vicente, b. 1931
Sallust, 86–34 B.C.
Salmerón, Nicolás, 1838–1908
Salterain, Joaquín de, 1856–1926
Salvador, Vicente do, Father, 1564–1639?
Sambrano Urdaneta, Oscar, b. 1929
Sam Colop, Luis Enrique, b. 1953
Sampaio, Francisco Moreira, 1851–1901
Sampaio, José da Silveira, 1914–1964
Samper, Darío, 1909–1984
Samper, José María, 1828–1888
Samper, Miguel 1825–1899
Samper, Soledad Acosta de, 1833–1913
Sanabria Fernández, Hernando, 1909–1986
Sánchez, Edwin, b. 1955
Sanchez, Efrain, b. 1955
Sanchez, Enriquillo, b. 1947
Sánchez, Florencio, 1875–1910
Sánchez, Luis Alberto, 1900–1994
Sánchez, Luis Rafael, b. 1936
Sánchez, Néstor, b. 1935
Sánchez, Rosaura, b. 1941
Sánchez Aizcorbe, Alejandro, b. 1954
Sánchez Bustamante, Daniel, 1871–1933
Sánchez Juliao, David, b. 1945
Sánchez Lamouth, Juan, 1929–1968
Sánchez Peláez, Juan, b. 1922
Sánchez Quell, Hipólito, 1907–1986
Sánchez Requejo, Miguel, d. ca. 1615
Sánchez Valverde, Antonio, 1734–1790
Sandoval, Alberto, b. 1929
Sanín Cano, Baldomero, 1861–1957
San Martín, José de, 1778–1850
Sanoja Hernández, Jesús, b. 1930
Santa, Eduardo, b. 1927
Santa Anna Nery, Frederico José de, 1849–1902
Santacilia, Pedro, 1826–1910
Santa Cruz, Marcelo Quiroga, 1931–1980
Santa Cruz Pachacuti Yamqui, Juan de, b. end of 15th c.
Santa Cruz y Espejo, Francisco Xavier Eugenio de, 1747–1795

Santa Cruz y Montalvo, María de las Mercedes, Condesa de Merlin, 1789–1852
Santaliz, Pedro, b. 1938
Santana, Rodolfo, b. 1944
Sant'Anna, Affonso Romano de, b. 1937
Sant'Anna, Sérgio, b. 1942
Santareno, Bernardo, 1924–1980
Santayana, George, 1863–1952
Santiago, Esmeralda, b. 1948
Santiago, Héctor, b. 1944
Santiago, José Alberto, b. 1934
Santiago, Silviano, b. 1936
Santiago Villarejo, José, b. b. 1907
Santoro, Roberto Jorge, 1939–1976
Santos, Nelson Pereira dos, b. 1928
Santos, Roberto Corrêa dos, b. 1949
Santos, Theotônio, b. 1937
Santos Chocano, José, 1875–1934
Santos Discepolo, Enrique, 1901–1951
Santos-Dumont, Alberto, 1873–1932
Santos Vargas, José, 1796–1853
Sanz del Río, Julián, 1814–1869
Sarduy, Severo, 1937–1993
Sarlo, Beatriz, b. 1942
Sarmiento, Domingo Faustino, 1811–1888
Sarmiento de Gamboa, Pedro de, 1532?–1608?
Sasturain, Juan, b. 1945
Satz, Mario, b. 1944
Savary, Olga, b. 1933
Sayles, John, b. 1950
Scalabrini Ortiz, Raúl, 1898–1959
Schmaltz, Yêda, b. 1941
Schmidel, Ulrich, 1510?–1579?
Schmidt, Afonso, 1890–1964
Schmidt, Augusto Frederico, 1906–1965
Schomburg, Arturo Alfonso, 1874–1938
Schon, Elizabeth, b. 1921
Schottus, Andreas, 1552–1629
Schutel, Duarte Paranhos, 1837–1901
Schwartz, Jorge, b. 1944
Schwarz, Roberto, b. 1938
Scliar, Moacyr, b. 1937
Scliar-Cabral, Leonor, b. 1929
Scorza, Manuel, 1928–1983
Seabra, Bruno, 1837–1876
Sefchovich, Sara, b. 1938
Segall, Lasar, 1891–1957
Segovia, Ramón, b. 1927
Segura, Manuel Ascensio, 1805–1871
Seligson, Esther, b. 1941
Selva, Salomón de la, 1893–1959
Semprún, Jesús, 1882–1931
Sención, Viriato, b. 1941
Senghor, Léopold Sédar, 1906–2001
Senna, Homero, b. 1919
Sepúlveda, Luis, b. 1949
Sepúlveda Leyton, Carlos, 1895–1941
Serna, Jacinto de la, d. 1691?
Serra, Fr. Junípero, 1713–1784
Serra, Joaquín, 1838–1888
Serrano, Andrés, b. 1950
Serrano, Jônatas, 1885–1944
Serrano, Pablo, 1908–1985
Sesto, Julio, 1879–1960
Sganzerla, Rogério, b. 1946
Shakespeare, William, 1564–1616

Shamsul Alam, Juan, b. 1946
Shimose, Pedro, b. 1940
Shúa, Ana María, b. 1951
Sicardi, Francisco, 1856–1927
Sierra Méndez, Justo, 1848–1912
Sigüenza y Góngora, Carlos de, 1645–1700
Silén, Iván, b. 1944
Silva, Agostinho, 1906–1996
Silva, Aguinaldo, b. 1944
Silva, Antônio Joaquim Pereira da, b. 1878
Silva, Antonio José, o Judeu, 1705–1739
Silva, Astrogildo Pereira Duarte de, 1890–1965
Silva, Caetano Cosme da, b. 1927
Silva, Deonisio da, b. 1948
Silva, Francisco Pereira da, 1817–1898
Silva, João José da, 1922–1997
Silva, João Pereira da, 1817–1898
Silva, João Pinto da, b. 1889
Silva, Joaquim José da [O sapaterio Silva], 1775–1825
Silva, José Asunción, 1865–1896
Silva, Ricardo, 1836–1887
Silva Alvarenga, Manuel Inacio da, 1749–1814
Silva Estrada, Alfredo, b. 1933
Silva Herzog, Jesús, 1891–1985
Silva Santisteban, Rocío, b. 1963
Silva Valdés, Fernán, 1887–1975
Silva Xavier, Joaquim José da, [Tiradentes] d. 1789
Silveira, Alvaro Ferdinando de Sousa da, 1883–1967
Silveira, Tasso da, 1895–1968
Simón, Fr. Pedro, 1574–1637
Sinán, Rogelio, 1904–1994
Sinzig, Pedro [Petrus], 1875–1952
Siqueiros, David Alfaro, 1896–1974
Sismondi, J.C.L. Sismonde de, 1773–1842
Skármeta, Antonio, b. 1940
Soares de Sousa, Gabriel, ca. 1540–ca. 1591
Soca, Susana., 1907–1959
Sodre, Lauro, 1858–1944
Sodré, Nelson Werneck, 1911–1999
Sojo, Vicente Emilio, 1887–1974
Solar, Alberto del, 1860–1921
Soler Frost, Pablo, b. 1965
Sologuren, Javier, b. 1921
Somers, Armonía, 1914–1994
Sorela, Pedro, b. 1951
Soriano, Osvaldo, 1943–1997
Sosa, Roberto, b. 1930
Soto, Gary, b. 1952
Soto, Hernando de, ca. 1500–1542
Soto, Jesús Rafael, b. 1923
Soto, Luis Emilio, 1900–1970
Soto, Pedro Juan., 1928–1999
Soto Borda, Clímaco, 1870–1919
Soto Vélez, Clemente, 1905–1993
Sousa, Augusto Fausto de, 1835–1890
Sousa, Herculano Inglês de, 1853–1918
Sousa, Pero Lopes de, ca.1500–1539
Sousa, Otávio Tarquinio de, 1889–1959
Souza, Gilda de Mello e, b. 1919
Souza, Márcio, b. 1946

Souza, Rita Joana de, 1696–1718?
Souza e Silva, Joaquim Norberto, 1820–1891
Spencer, Herbert, 1820–1903
Spota, Luis, 1925–1985
Squier, Ephraim George, 1821–1888
Starosta, Isaac, b. 1933
Steimberg, Alicia, b. 1933
Stirling Maxwell, Sir William, 1818–1878
Storni, Alfonsina, 1892–1938
Suárez, Clementina, 1902–1991
Suárez, Marco Fidel, 1855–1927
Suárez, Ursula, 1666–1749
Suárez, Virgil, b. 1962
Suárez Araúz, Nicomedes, b. 1946
Suárez de Peralta, Juan, 1536–1589?
Suárez y Romero, Anselmo, 1818–1878
Suassuna, Ariano, b. 1927
Subercaseux, Elizabeth, b. 1945
Sucre, Antonio José de, 1795–1830
Sucre, José Francisco, b. 1931
Sucre Figaralla, Guillermo, b. 1933
Sue, Eugène, 1804–1857
Sujo, Juana, 1913–1961
Suro, Rubén, 1916–1999
Swain, Regina, b. 1967
Sylvester, Santiago E., b. 1942
Szichman, Mario, b. 1945
Szpumberg, Alberto, b. 1940
Szyszlo, Fernando de, b. 1925

T

Tablada, José Juan, 1871–1945
Taboada Terán, Néstor, b. 1929
Tafolla, Carmen, b. 1951
Taibo II, Paco Ignacio, b. 1949
Taine, Hippolyte Adolphe, 1828–1893
Talamates, Melchor de, 1765–1808
Talavera, Natalicio, 1839–1867
Tallenay, Jenny, 1860–1928
Tallet, José Zacarías, 1893–1985
Talma, François Joseph, 1763–1826
Tamayo, Franz, 1879–1956
Tamayo, Rufino, 1899–1991
Tanco Bosmeniel, Felix M., 1797–1871
Tapajós, Renato, b. 1943
Tapia y Rivera, Alejandro, 1826–1882
Taunay, Alfredo d'Escragnolle Taunay, Visconde de, 1843–1899
Taunay, Felix Emilio, 1795–1881
Taunay, Nicolau, 1755–1830
Tavares, Constantino do Amaral, 1828–1890
Tavares, José Nilo, 1935–1997
Taveira Júnior, Bernardo, 1836–1892
Tavira, Luis de, b. 1948
Teitelboim, Volodia, b. 1916
Teixeira, Anésio, 1900–1971
Teixeira, Bento, ca. 1560–1618
Teixeira, Mucio Scevola Lopes, 1858–1926
Teixeira, Pedro, b. ca.1570–1610
Teixeira de Melo, José Alexandre, 1833–1907
Teixeira e Sousa, Antonio Gonçalves, 1812–1861
Tejada Sorzano, José Luis, 1882–1938
Tejeda, Luis de, 1604–1680
Tejera, Emiliano, 1841–1923

Tejera, María Josefina, b. 1930
Teles, Gilberto Mendonça, b. 1931
Telles, Lygia Fagundes, b. 1923
Tello, Julio César, 1880–1947
Tenório de Albuquerque, Terêza, b. 1949
Teresa de Ávila, Saint, 1515–1582
Teresa de Mier, Fray Servando, 1763–1827
Terrazas, Francisco de, ca. 1524–1600
Tesauro, Count Emanuele, 1592–1675
Thays, Iván, b. 1968
Thénon, Susana, 1937–1990
Thomas, Piri, b. 1928
Tiempo, César [Israel Zeitlin, pseud.], 1906–1980
Tijerino, Doris, b. 1943
Timerman, Jacobo, 1923–1999
Tirado, Cándido, b. 1950
Tirso de Molina, 1571?–1648
Tizón, Héctor, b. 1929
Tojeiro, Gastão, 1880–1965
Tomasi di Lampedusa, Giuseppe, 1896–1957
Tomlinson, Henry Major, 1873–1958
Toro, Fermín, 1807–1865
Torquemada, Juan de, ca.1557?–1664
Torres, Ana Teresa, b. 1945
Torres, Camilo, 1766–1816
Torres, Camilo, 1929–1966
Torres, Carlos Arturo, 1867–1911
Torres, Edwin, b. 1931
Torres, Juan, b. 1955
Torres, Omar, b. 1945
Torres Bodet, Jaime, 1902–1974
Torres Caicedo, Jose Maria, 1830–1889
Torres-García, Joaquín, 1874–1949
Torres Méndez, Ramón, 1809–1885
Torres-Rioseco, Arturo, 1897–1971
Torres Rubio, Diego de, d. 1637
Torri, Julio, 1889–1970
Tostes, Theodemiro, 1903–1986
Tovar, Juan de, ca. 1546–ca. 1626
Tovar, Manuel José, 1831–1869
Tovar y Tovar, Martín, 1828–1902
Traba, Marta, 1930–1983
Tracy, Antoine Louis Claude Destutt, comte de, 1754–1836
Trancoso, Gonçalo Fernández, 1515–1596?
Traven, B., 1882–1969
Travieso, Martín J., b. 1820
Trejo, Nemesco, 1802–1916?
Trejo, Pedro de, 16th c.
Treviño Carranza, Celia, b. 1912
Trevisan, Armindo, b. 1933
Trevisan, João Silverio, b. 1944
Triana, José, b. 1931
Triggoura, Jorge, b. 1969
Trinidade, Solano, 1908–1973
Tristán, Flora, 1803–1844
Troche, Julio César, b. 1927
Trueba, Antonio, 1819–1889
Trujillo, Gabriel, b. 1958
Trujillo, Rafael Leonidas [dictator of Dominican Republic, 1930–1961], 1891–1961
Truque, Carlos Arturo, 1928–1970
Tsuchiya, Tilsa, 1936–1984
Tufic, Jorge, b. 1930

Viscardo Guzmán, Juan Pablo, 1748–1798
Vitale, Ida, b. 1926
Vitier, Cintio, b. 1921
Vitor, Nestor, 1868–1932
Víttori, José Luis, b. 1928
Vives, Juan Luis, 1492–1540
Voltaire, François Marie Arouet de, 1694–1778
Voscos Lescano, Jorge, 1924–1989

W

Wagley, Charles, 1913–1991
Wainberg, Paulo, b. 1944
Walcott, Derek, b. 1930
Waldseemüller, Martin, 1470–1521
Wallparrimachi Mayta, Juan, 1793–1814
Walsh, María Elena, b. 1930
Walsh, Rodolfo, 1927–1977
Weffort, Francisco, b. 1937
Westphalen, Emilio Adolfo, 1911–2001
White, Joseph Blanco, 1775–1841.
Whitman, Walt, 1819–1892
Wilde, Eduardo, 1844–1913
Wilde, José Antonio, 1813–1885
Williams, William Carlos, 1883–1963
Wilson, Carlos Guillermo, b. 1941
Woolf, Virginia, 1882–1941

X

Xavier, Ismail, b. 1947
Ximénez, Francisco, 1666–ca.1722.

Xirau, Joaquín, 1895–1946
Xirau, Ramón, b. 1924
Xirgú, Margarita, 1888–1969

Y

Yáñez, Agustín, 1904–1980
Yáñez, Francisco Javier, 1777–1842
Yapuguay, Nicolás, b. 1680
Yehya, Naief, b. 1963
Ynsfrán, Pablo Max, 1894–1972
Yrigoyen, Hipólito, 1852–1933
Yun, Sui, b. 1955
Yunque, Alvaro [pseud. of Arístides Gandolfi Herrero], 1889–1982
Yupangui, Diego de Castro, Titu Cusi, 16th c.
Yupanqui, Atahualpa, 1908–1992
Yupanqui, Francisco Tito, 1540?–1608?
Yupanqui, Tupac, 1460?–1532
Yupanqui, Tupac, Inca, 1471–1493

Z

Zalamea, Jorge, 1905–1969
Zalamea Borda, Eduardo, 1905–1963
Zaldumbide, Gonzalo, 1885–1965
Zaluar, Augusto Emílio, 1825–1882
Zambrana, Antonio, 1846–1922
Zambrano, María, 1904–1991
Zamudio, Adela, 1854–1928
Zapata, Luis, 1526–1595
Zapata, Luis, b. 1951

Zapata Olivella, Manuel, b. 1920
Zarate, Armando, b. 1933
Zárate Salmerón, Gerónimo de, fl. 1610
Zarratea, Tadeo, b. 1947
Zavaleta, Carlos Eduardo, b. 1929
Zavaleta, René, 1932–1997
Zaya, Octavio, b. 1949
Zayas, María de, 1590–1650
Zayas, Marius de, 1880–1961
Zea, Leopoldo, b. 1912
Zeballos, Estanislao Severo, 1854–1923
Zeitel, Amália, 1933–1992
Zenea, Juan Clemente, 1832–1871
Zeno Gandia, Manuel, 1855–1930
Zentella, Arcadio, 1844–1920
Zepeda, Eraclio, b. 1937
Zérega Fombona, Alberto, b. 1968
Ziembinski, Zbigniew Mariev, 1908–1978
Zitarrosa, Alfredo, 1936–1989
Zola, Emile, 1840–1902
Zorrilla, Rafael Augusto, 1892–1937
Zorrilla de San Martin, Juan 1855–1931
Zubizarreta, Carlos, 1904–1972
Zumarraga, Fray Juan de, 1468–1548
Zumeta, César, 1860–1955
Zum Felde, Alberto, 1889–1976
Zurita, Raúl, b. 1951
Zweig, Stefan, 1881–1942

Afro-Brazilians (*continued*)
   Frente Negra Brasileira, **I:**256
   growing influence of, **I:**257–58
   oral tradition of, **I:**248–49
   outside concern for, **I:**249–50
   portrayal of in abolitionist literature, **I:**251
   stereotypes of, **I:**251
   in theater, **I:**256–57
   umbanda, **I:**464
Afro-Brazilian studies, **II:**41
Afro-Cuban movement, **III:**270
Afro-Hispanic literature, **I:**241
   in Caribbean, **I:**468–70
Afro-Hispanics
   defined, **I:**241, 244
   in Latin American literary history, **I:**240–44
Afro-Hispanic studies, **I:**240
Afro-Hispanism, **I:**240
Afro-Latin American cultures. *See also* African culture; Afro-
    American culture; Afro-Brazilian culture
   in Brazil. *See* Afro-Brazilian culture
   construction of folklore of, **I:**551
   festivities and, **I:**551
   French influence on, **I:**465
   "folkloricization" and, **I:**552
   hybridism and, **I:**553
   hybridization with other Latin American cultures, **I:**548
   importance of drums to, **I:**476, 479–80
   importance of rhythm to, **I:**480
   incorporated into Cuban cultures, **I:**548
   legitimization of, **I:**551–52
   localization of, **I:**548
   "La Mama Negra" and, **I:**551
   marginalization of, **I:**548–49
   material expressions of, **I:**477
   in Peru, **I:**552
   poetic genres of, **II:**44
   popular narrators, **II:**44
   Protestant influences on music of, **I:**480
   religious rites, **II:**43
   representations of, **I:**551
   revindication of values of, **I:**465
   in Spanish Caribbean, **I:**466
   sugarcane and, **I:**480
   survival of, **II:**44
   transitory nature of, **I:**478
Afro-Latin American theater, **I:**548–53
   during colonial period, **I:**550
   Congo rituals in, **I:**550
   dances in, **I:**549–50
   festivities and, **I:**551
   government control of, **I:**550
   El juego de los congos, **I:**550
   masked dances in, **I:**550
   masquerades and, **I:**550
   negritos, **I:**551
   spirit dolls and, **I:**550
   in 20th century, **I:**551
Age of Enlightenment
   criollos in, **III:**205
   in Latin America, **I:**372
   in Mexico, **III:**201–11
   role of Jesuits in, **III:**205
   in Spain, **III:**204–5
Age of Spectacle, **II:**65
Agosto (Fonseca), **I:**603, 604–5; **III:**630
Agreda, María de Jesús de, **I:**284
Agudeza y arte de ingenio (Gracián), **II:**260
Águeda de San Ignacio, María Anna, **I:**285

Agüero, Riva
   and efforts to eradicate indigenous cultures, **III:**90
   on indigenous people, **III:**90
   on literary gallicization, **III:**92, 97
Agueros, Jack, **III:**436
Aguilar, Jerónimo de, **I:**440
El águila y la serpiente (Guzmán), **I:**641; **III:**568
Aguirre, Juan Bautista, **II:**467
Aguirre Beltrán, Gonzalo, **III:**202
Agustini, Delmira, **II:**184–85
   letters of, **I:**323
AHA!, **III:**458–59
AI-5 Generation, **I:**206
AI-5 law, **I:**542; **II:**123
Ainsi parla l'oncle (Price Mars), **I:**463
Aira, César, **II:**667
Aires, Jacinta Rodrigues. *See* São José, Jacinta de
Aita, Zina, **II:**605
Akab', Q'anil, **I:**220
Ak'abal, Humberto, **I:**221
Akawaio language, **I:**86
Alabau, Magaly, **I:**343–44
El Alacrán, **II:**467
Alagoano, Altino [Maria das Neves Bastista Pimentel, pseud.],
   I:615
Albó, Xavier, **III:**408
Alboroto y motín de México (Sigüenza y Góngora), **III:**187
Álbum de Familia (Rodrigues), **I:**568
Albuquerque, Doña Brites de, **I:**338
Alcazar Lyrique, **I:**559
Alcedo, Antonio de, **II:**467
Alcor, **II:**624
Alderado, Cego (The Blind Man), **II:**43
Aleandro, Norma, **I:**321–22
Alegría, Ciro, **I:**227; **III:**228, 234
Alegría, Fernando, **I:**353
Alegría, Ricardo E., **II:**393, 421–22
Alegro Desbum (Vianna Filho), **I:**570
Aleijadinho, Antônio Francisco Lisboa, **II:**599
"O Aleijadinho" (Andrade), **III:**498
Alemán, Mateo, **I:**121–22
Alencar, Godofredo de. *See* Barreto, Paulo Emílio Coelho
Alencar, José Martiniano de
   abolitionist plays of, **I:**251
   and abolition of slavery, **I:**158
   and anti-colonialist attitude, **III:**110
   awareness of the invented character of the nation, **III:**104
   and the Black man, **I:**248
   and Brazilian nationalism, **I:**252
   and creating a national imaginary, **III:**104
   and creation of Brazil's national imaginary, **III:**102–10
   and the European literary tradition, **III:**103
   foundational myths created by, **III:**107–10
   and *O Guaraní,* **I:**158–59; **II:**26–27; **III:**107–**9**
   and the historical novel, **II:**253
   and the importance he placed on a national literature for
    Brazil, **III:**104
   and *indianista* themes, **III:**105
   and *Iracema,* **I:**105
   and "O Jesuíta," **III:**104–5
   and *Luciola,* **I:**328; **II:**279
   memoirs of, **II:**152
   and *Minas de Prata,* **II:**274
   plays of, **III:**127
   and proto-history of Brazil, **III:**101–2
   response to accusations, **III:**103
   role of legend in the work of, **III:**107
   and romantic movement, **I:**105, 573
   and treatment of Amerindian, **I:**159

Dance of the *Cabrita*, **I:**522
Elenco Teatro Libre del Paraguay, **I:**522
European attitudes towards, **I:**515
Fragua Theater, **I:**523
El Güegüense, **I:**520
of Incas, **I:**517
Jesuits' influence on, **I:**517–18
Laboratorio de Teatro Campesino e Indígena de Tabasco, **I:**521
in Mayan Carnival celebrations, **I:**526
of Mayans, **I:**525–30
"Moors and Christians" mock battles, **I:**523
national and international visibility of, **I:**522, 523
in 19th Century, **I:**520–21
performance of *Bodas de Sangre*, **I:**521
pre-Conquest, **III:**379–80
present day, **I:**522–24
purpose of, **I:**515–16
Rabinal Achí, **I:**525
Teatro de la Fragua, **I:**521
in 20th Century, **I:**521–22
Amigos de la patria, **I:**155
Amnesis, **II:**528
Amora (Roffiel), **I:**346–47
"Amor de ciudad grande" (Martí), **II:**185; **III:**335–336
De amor y de sombra (Allende), **III:**590
Ampuero, Fernando, **III:**636–38
Anais Pernambucanos (Costa), **II:**50
Anales de los Cakchiqueles, **III:**380
Anales de Tlatelolco, **I:**112; **III:**375
Anarchism
in Brazil, **III:**483–85
in Brazilian theater, **III:**485
poetry of, **III:**484–85
the *relato-flagrante* in, **III:**484
Anaya, Rudolf Alfonso, **II:**325; **III:**422
Anchieta, José de, **I:**104, 127; **III:**141–42
Tupi writings of, **III:**143
Las Andariegas (Angel), **I:**346
Andean academies, **III:**409
Andean centralism, **II:**407
Andean cities, **II:**414–16
cultural elitism in, **II:**406
growth of, **I:**34–36
population of (1990s), **I:**36
poverty in, **I:**36
United States' influence in, **II:**405–6
values of colonial society in, **II:**417
Andean Community, **I:**36
Andean countries. *See also* Andean cities
Amerindian population in, **I:**29
Andean Community in, **I:**36
appreciation of Quechua in, **I:**226–27
difficulty in unifying, **I:**33–34
of the intertropical zone, **I:**28
linguistic diversity in, **I:**96–102
modern concerns of, **I:**36
placement of cities in, **I:**30
printing press in, **I:**33
Andean cultural centers, **III:**385
Andean culture
Andean utopia in, **I:**476–77
centers of, **II:**406
Christian influence on, **II:**410
collaboration and resistance in, **I:**475
during colonial period, **I:**474–75
contempt of Spanish and *criollo* elites for works of "common people," **I:**479
creation of national identities in, **II:**408
criollo aristocracy, **II:**408

dancing in, **III:**387–88
distinguishing features of, **II:**405
dual nature of, **II:**405
effect of Spanish colonialism on, **II:**405
elitism in, **II:**405
inclusion of indigenous heritage in, **II:**408
Independence struggles of, **II:**405
outside influences on, **II:**405
painting in, **II:**408
popular festivals in, **I:**476
progress of, **II:**405
of rural areas, **III:**406
social actors in, **II:**406
syncretism and, **I:**475
Andean holocaust, **II:**426
Andean indigenous writing, **III:**403–6
Andean languages
Aymara. *See* Aymara language
Catholic Church's use of, **III:**397–98
collection of writings in, **III:**409
emphasis on literacy in, **III:**409
extinction of, **I:**97
new community of, **III:**403
non-governmental organizations (NGOs) for, **III:**409
"normalization" of, **III:**410
Quechua. *See* Quechua
U.S. interest in, **III:**405–6
in world of cinematography, **III:**408
Andean literature, **III:**401–3
Aymara. *See* Aymara literature
and cultural contact, **III:**396–403
development of popular texts in, **III:**405
educational development in, **III:**410–11
educational materials, **III:**410
first book printed in southern Americas, **I:**224
gendered differences in textual media of, **III:**389–90
importance of "braiding" in, **III:**387
importance of color in, **III:**388
indigenous literary texts, **I:**224–29
influence of indigenous people on, **I:**224
institutional modes of transmission, **III:**396
international meetings on, **III:**409
introduction of European alphabetic writing to, **III:**396
from journeys of Incan men, **III:**390–92
nature of, **III:**385–96
new approaches to collection of, **III:**409–11
new directions for study of, **III:**366–67
non-governmental organizations (NGOs) in support of, **III:**409, 410–11
performance of, **III:**411
Quechua and, **I:**224–29
quipus as, **III:**386–89
"Rain Goddess" hymn, **III:**388–89
regional genres of, **III:**395–96
resistance to European writing, **III:**399–401
Runa Yndio, **III:**394
Tale of the Snake, **III:**386–87
traditional genres of, **III:**394–95
traditional modes of organization of, **III:**390–92
20th-century, **III:**407–8
woven devices in, **III:**387–88
Andean music, **II:**441
Andean novel, **I:**35
Andean pact, **III:**392
Andean primacy, **II:**527–28
Andean region. *See also* The Andes
abuse of natural resources in, **II:**411
alliance between urban *mestizos* and urban Indians in, **III:**406

Buenos Aires (*continued*)
  contemporary problems of, **II:**642
  as democratic center, **II:**642
  as described by José Vasconcelos, **II:**231
  federalization of, **II:**658
  first subway in Latin America, **II:**640
  founding of, **II:**639
  French influence on, **I:**53
  future of, **II:**642
  housing problems in, **II:**641
  immigration in, **II:**660, 661, 662
  impact of automobile on, **II:**641
  influence of Baron Hausmann on, **II:**658
  and the Institutio Torquato Di Tella, **II:**665
  and José S. Alvarez, **II:**660
  and Julio Argentino Roca, **II:**658–59
  leisure activities in, **II:**639, 641
  literacy in, **II:**664
  literary discourse of Jorge Asís, **II:**667
  Marcos Sastre bookshop, **II:**658
  middle class in, **II:**660
  modernization of, **II:**660, 662
  North American influence on, **II:**641
  as Paris of Southern Hemisphere, **I:**53
  persecution of psychoanalysis, **II:**667
  as political center, **II:**662, 663–64
  political involvement with Paraguay, **II:**620
  population of (1887), **II:**661
  population of (20th century), **II:**641
  port expansion in, **II:**659–60
  presses in, **II:**664
  remodeling of, **II:**657
  role of exiles living in, **II:**661
  and Rubén Darío, **II:**661–62
  second foundation of, **I:**49
  suburban growth of, **II:**641
  tango culture in, **II:**661
  territorial importance of, **I:**50–51
  violence in (1960s and 1970s), **II:**642
  writers moving to, **II:**667
  writings on modernization of, **II:**658–59
Buenos Aires, desde setenta años atrás (Wilde), **II:**659
Bufo & Spallanzani (Fonseca), **III:**630
Bunge, Carlos Octavio, **I:**422
Burciaga, José Antonio, **II:**327
Burgain, Luís Antônio, **I:**556
Burgos-Debray, Elisabeth, **III:**604
Burgos, Julia de, **II:**688
burletas, **I:**563
bush blacks, **I:**465
Bustamante, Anastacio, **II:**314
búzios, **II:**60

C

El caballero encantado y la moza esquiva, **II:**133
Caballeros de Espuelas Doradas, **II:**9
"*Los caballos de Abdera*" (Lugones), **I:**397
Cabeza de Vaca, Alvar Núñez, **III:**420
Cabezas, Omar, **III:**342
Cabichuí, **II:**621
caboclização, **I:**46
Cabral, Alfredo do Valle, **II:**26
Cabral, Pedro Álvaro, **II:**65
  discovery of Brazil, **I:**37
Cabrera Infante, Guillermo, **II:**302–3
  exile literature of, **III:**516–17
  satire from, **II:**241–45
Cabrujas, José Ignacio, **I:**544
Cachuela Esperanza, **II:**526

Cadenas, Jesús, **I:**456–57
Caderno de Sábado, **II:**631, 633
Cadernos Brasileiros, **II:**113
Cadernos Negros, **I:**259
Cadícamo, Enrique, **I:**493
Cadogan, León, **I:**101, 486–87
Caetano, João, **I:**555–56
Caetés (Ramos), **II:**102
cafés
  as cultural centers, **II:**454
  flow of ideas within, **II:**41–42
The Cage of Melancholy (Bartra), **II:**233
caicara, **II:**505
Cakchiqueles, writings of, **III:**380
Calandria, costumbres campestres (Leguizamón), **III:**226
Calcagno, Francisco, **III:**236
Caldas, José, **II:**466
Calder, Alexander, **II:**422
Calderón, Antonio, **II:**19
Calderón, Bernarda, **I:**324
Calderón, Ventura García, **II:**435
Calderón de la Barca, Marquesa [Fanny Erskine Inglis], **I:**323
Calderón de la Barca, Pedro, **I:**148
calenda, **II:**646
Calendario manual y guía universal de forasteros en Venezuela para el año de 1810 (Bello), **II:**415
Calibán: apuntes sobre la cultura en nuestra América (Fernández Retamar), **II:**240
Caliban, in José Enrique Rodó's work, **III:**538
El calidosopio de Hermes (Rojas Guardia), **I:**352–53
California
  siege of Los Angeles, **II:**315
  U.S. invasion of, **II:**315
Callado, Antônio, **I:**126; **II:**79; **III:**615
calmécac, **III:**369
Calmon, Pedro, **II:**50
Calvo, César, **II:**500, 502, 503
En Câmara Lenta, **II:**79
Camarena, Sergio Ordóñez, **II:**339
Camargo, Oswaldo, **I:**258
Cambridge History of Latin American Literature, **II:**199
Camelo de Melo Rezende, José, **I:**615–16
Camêo, Hélza, **II:**236
Camila o la patriota de Sudamérica (Henríquez), **I:**536
Caminha, Adolfo, **I:**357–58
Caminha, Pero Vaz de, **I:**128; **II:**216; **III:**21–22, 146
O caminho da porta (Assis), **I:**558–59
caminos reales, **I:**25
Camp
  critical positions on, **I:**607
  defined, **I:**607
Campbell, Federico, **II:**329
Campobello, Nellie, **I:**319; **III:**566
Campos, Augusto de, **II:**1, 4, 189, 193
  broadening definition of translation, **II:**143
  and the Concretist movement, **II:**140
  metalanguage of, **II:**141
  similarities to Ezra Pound, **II:**143
  and theories on translation, **II:**141
  translation of "The Apparition," **II:**141
  translation of "The Sick Rose," **II:**142
  translation paideuma, **II:**143
Campos, Haroldo de, **II:**4; **III:**356, 360, 549–50, 627
  on *antropofagia*, **III:**550
  and the Concretist movement, **II:**140
  connection between translation and original text, **II:**144
  in contrast to Ezra Pound, **II:**143
  metalanguage of, **II:**141
  and parody as "parallel song," **II:**143–144

similarity to Ezra Pound, **II:**143
and theories on translation, **II:**141, 144
translation of Hebrew Bible, **II:**142
translation paideuma, **II:**143
Campos, Humberto de, **II:**103
Campos, Paulo Mendes, **II:**595
Campos, Pedro Albizu, **II:**399
Campos, Rubén M., in José Guadalupe Posada's workshop, **I:**579
Campoy, Rafael, **III:**205
Camus, Albert, **III:**489
Camus, Marcel, **I:**653–54
Canãa (Graça Aranha), **III:**494
Canales, Antonio, **III:**323
Cañaris, **I:**136
Canción de gesta (Neruda), **III:**584
Canción de Rachel (Barnet), **II:**202–3, 224
Cândido, Antonio, **II:**105, 115, 120, 125, 225, 243, 554, 570; **III:**549
    as Angel Rama, **II:**115
    on essay genre, **I:**412–16, 419, 423
    on exoticism, **III:**475
    focus on *Letras* courses, **I:**415
    on link between foreign and local influences, **I:**127
    on national identity, **III:**549
    on significance of literature, **I:**412
    on Silvio Romero, **I:**410
Candomblé, **II:**560, 563
Cané, Miguel, **II:**447
canonization
    comparative approach of, **II:**158
    of testimonio, **II:**199–200
canons
    English-American, **II:**157
    inclusion of works in, **II:**157
    Western, **II:**157
El cantar del payador (Seibel), **I:**490–95
Cantares de Dzibalché, **I:**445–49
Cantares Mexicanos, **I:**188, 440–42
Cantinflas, **I:**594–95
Cantinflismo, **I:**642–43
"Canto a la Argentina" (Darío), **I:**386, 391, 395; **II:**662
Canto de amor (Lira), **I:**228
"Canto de pájaros" (Ak'abal), **I:**221
Canto encomiástico de Diogo Pereira Ribeiro de Vasconcellos (Menezes), **II:**23
El canto errante (Darío), **I:**391, 395; **III:**328
Canto General (Neruda), **II:**175, 179, 185, 197, 202
Canto Kechwa (Arguedas), **I:**228
Cantolla y Rico, Joaquín de la, **I:**578
canto popu, **II:**654
Canudos
    in *Os Sertões,* **II:**99
    vs. Republican army, **II:**98, 100
    and the *Tomochic* uprising, **II:**286
capacitación de las masas, **III:**408
"La capilla aldeana" (Huidobro), **II:**193
capital cities, as port cities, **I:**3–4
"Capitanias Hereditárias," **III:**20
Capitan Paul (Dumas), **II:**269
Capote, Truman, **II:**210
Capuchins, **III:**259
Caracas
    Banco Consolidado, **II:**422–23
    beginning of revolution, **II:**415–16
    as center for political refugees, **II:**415
    central importance of, **II:**416
    El Cojo Ilustrado, **II:**418–19
    Creole novel, **II:**420

description of, **II:**414, 418
founding of, **II:**413
geographic/climatic conditions of, **II:**413
important writers from, **II:**416
Independence Generation, **II:**415
intellectual movement, **II:**415
journalism in, **II:**417, 418
link between literary and political movements in, **II:**419
Maundy Thursday, **II:**415
musical movements in, **II:**422–23
people of, **II:**414
politically influential books in, **II:**415
population of (1723), **II:**413
printing press in, **II:**418, 423
publishing industry of, **II:**423
radio network of, **II:**423
recent population growth in, **II:**424
Seminario de Santa Rosa de Lima, **II:**414
Sociedad Patriótica, **II:**415
television networks in, **II:**423
Teresa Carreño Cultural Complex, **II:**422
theaters in, **II:**422–23
El Venezolano, **II:**417
Caras viejas y vino nuevo (Morales), **III:**423
Caras y Caretas, **II:**660
Cardenal, Ernesto, **II:**360–61, 689
Cárdenas, Gilberto, **II:**329
Cárdenas, Lázaro, **II:**346
Cárdenas, Nancy, **I:**344–45
Cárdenas, Raúl de, **III:**460
Cardoso, Lúcio, **II:**225
Cardoza y Aragón, Luis, **III:**201
Cardozo, Joaquim, **II:**544–45
    Trivium 1952–1970, **II:**547
The Carib, **II:**392.
    languages, **I:**94
    in Venezuela, **I:**86
Caribbean
    African languages in, **I:**465
    African orality in, **I:**460–70
    Baroque influences in, **III:**174–76
    as battling arena of hegemonies, **III:**177
    black Brazilian festivities on mainland of, **I:**466
    criollo in, **II:**229
    criollo languages in, **I:**465
    cultural area of, **I:**460
    European influence in, **I:**460, 462
    French possessions in, **I:**463
    influences in, **III:**177–79
    musical discourse of, **III:**178
    negrismo in, **III:**269
    Negritude movement in, **I:**463, 468
    racial diversity of, **I:**460
    runaway slave culture in, **I:**465
    slave labor in, **I:**460
    slave population in, **I:**460
    U.S. interventions in, **I:**162
    various languages spoken in, **III:**177
Caribbean Antilles
    architecture of, **II:**367
    carnivals in, **II:**367
    changed conditions upon reign of Carlos III, **II:**395
    common culture of, **II:**366–68
    communication between, **II:**368
    Creole culture in, **II:**367
    Cuba. *See* Cuba
    cuisine of, **II:**366–67
    Maundy Thursday (19 April 1810), **II:**415–16
    mourning customs of, **II:**367

Caso, Antonio, **I:**195; **III:**569
  on preserving freedom, **II:**347
el castellano, as school subject in Chile, **III:**301–2
Castellanos, Rosario, **I:**203, 212, 308, 323, 545
Castello, José Aderaldo, **I:**126–27
Castelo Hill, demolition of, **II:**571–72
Um castelo no pampa (Assis Brasil), **II:**636
Castillo, Ana, **II:**325–27
Castillo, Francisca Concepción [Madre Castillo], **I:**296
Castillo de González, Aurelia, **I:**320
Castro, Fábio, **II:**511, 514
Castro, Fidel, **II:**346, 373, 703
Castro, Vicente Félix de, **II:**272
Castro-Klarén, Sara, **I:**240
Casualty Report (Vega), **III:**436
Catalina de Erauso. *See* Erauso, Catalina de
Catalogue of Rare Works, **II:**24
Catarina de San Juan, **I:**292, 296–98, 301–2
  biographies of, **I:**293
  life events of, **I:**293
Catay (Valencia), **II:**136
Catechistic theater, **I:**474
Catecismo breve para rudos y ocupados, **II:**618
Catedral de Santa María la Menor, **II:**381
Cathedral of Santo Domingo, **II:**390
Cathedral of Zacatecas, **III:**176
Catholic Church
  acculturation of Amerindians, **I:**181–82
  in Andean region, **III:**397–98
  basic education in, **I:**279
  biographies in, **I:**282
  in Brazil. *See* Brazilian Catholic Church
  catechized uses of *quipu* in, **III:**399
  and censorship in Brazil, **I:**401, 404–6, 409, 415–23
  in Central America, **II:**355
  changing role of women as threat to, **I:**408
  Christianization of Mayans, **I:**525
  chronicles in, **I:**281–82
  and control of the printed word, **I:**405–6
  control of women by, **I:**184
  Counter-Reformation in, **I:**289–90
  criticism of, **II:**285
  early response to indigenous languages, **I:**273
  and education in Brazil, **II:**69
  and efforts to eliminate indigenous religions, **I:**475–76
  and evangelized indigenous people, **III:**157–70
  expansion of Aymara and Quechua languages, **III:**397
  and extirpations of idolatry in the New World, **III:**157–70
  and the family, **I:**403, 408
  and founding of convents in colonial America, **III:**62
  and indigenous theater, **I:**520–21
  internal conflicts in 17th-century Brazil, **III:**61
  loss of power in Latin America, **I:**535
  during Luso-Brazilian colonial period, **II:**61–62
  and Mexican culture, **I:**576
  Mexican popular music and, **I:**584
  outlook toward reading, **I:**401–7
  political moves of, in Brazil, **I:**401–3
  preservation of indigenous oral and written discourses, **I:**180
  and protection of cultural possessions, **II:**449
  religious changes in (17th century), **III:**169–70
  and separation of Church and State in Brazil, **I:**401–2
  and social discourse, **I:**401–9
  in Spanish America, **II:**34
  and spread of European ideas during Colonial period, **III:**163–64
  teaching reading to Amerindians, **I:**180–81
  theatrical discourses of, **I:**533
  and use of Catechistic theater, **I:**474
  and use of Quechua language in colonial period, **I:**477, 521
  and views on modern society, **I:**404
  women of importance in, **I:**291–301
  women writers and, **I:**408
Catholic Confederation of Rio de Janeiro, **I:**402
Catholicism
  Africans' adoption of, **I:**464
  discretio, 262
  effect on cultural development, **II:**309
  as represented by *Cholos,* **III:**328
Catholicism (17th Century)
  architecture of the churches, **II:**262
  benevolentia, **II:**264
  consensio, **II:**264
  Counter-Reformation, **II:**262
  Eucharist, **II:**261–62
  hermeneutics, **II:**258
  hierarchies and, **II:**265–66
  historical events and, **II:**258
  Iberian Catholic sermon, **II:**258. *See also* sermons
  Incarnation of Christ, **II:**265
  intentionality, **II:**258
  love, **II:**264
  sacramental mystery, **II:**258–59
  sacred oratory, **II:**258, 271, 273
  unifying purpose of the sacrament, **II:**263–64
  union of men, **II:**264
Catholic universities, **II:**37
caudillista tradition, in Argentina, **II:**246–47
"La cautiva" (Echeverria), **II:**180; **III:**247
El cautiverio feliz (Núñez de Pineda y Bascuñán), **III:**188
Ceará, and spread of Naturalist ideas, **III:**121
Cecilio del Valle, José
  library of, **III:**219
  life of, **III:**219
Cédula de Gracia, **II:**396
Celso, Afonso [Celso de Assis figueiredo, condede, Afonso], *Ufanista* thought and, **III:**26, 29
Cenas da vida Amazonica (Sousa), **II:**513
Cendrars, Blaise [Frederic Sausir-Hall, pseud.], **II:**585–86
  in Brazil, **II:**607
  as focal point for Modernist Brazilian culture, **II:**587–88
  reception in Brazil, **III:**482–83
El censor, **I:**155
censorship
  abolition in Brazil, **II:**26
  banned books in Brazil, **II:**81, 84
  in Brazil, **II:**2, 580
  in Chile (1973–1991), **III:**530
  by Chilean Socialist regime, **III:**586
  and copyright law, **II:**84
  effect on Brazilian society, **II:**80
  effect on Brazil Literary System, **II:**80–82
  of immoral themes, **II:**81
  imprisonment of writers, **II:**79
  "Index of Prohibited Books," **II:**15
  influence on literary styles, **II:**79
  of literature vs. other arts. **II:**79
  and the press (18th and 19th centuries), **I:**373
  resistance against, **II:**3
  self-censorship, **II:**2
  state sponsorship as, **II:**83
  and underground translations, **I:**373
  under military dictatorships, **II:**79
Centennial Farroupilha Revolution Exhibition, **II:**630
Center for Amazonian Literature and Culture, **II:**501
Center for Popular Culture, **II:**579
Center of Cinematographic Studies, **II:**611

essayism
  in Brazilian intellectual life, **I:**413–14, 416
  influence on Latin American identity, **I:**419
essays
  colonial attitude within Latin America in, **II:**231
  European dominance of, **II:**227
  European versus Latin American, **II:**238
  national psychology in, **II:**231–33
essays on identity, **III:**285–86
Um estadista do império (Nabuco), **III:**478
estancias, defined, **I:**5
"Estatutos do Recolhimento de Santa Teresa" (Jacinta de São
    José), **I:**305
Uma estética da fome (Rocha), **III:**361
Esteves, Sandra María, **III:**438
Estigarribia, J. F., **II:**623–24
Estrada Medinilla, María de, **I:**282
estradas boiadeiras, **I:**38
estridentismo, **II:**192
El eterno femenino (Castellanos), **I:**545
Eucharist, **II:**259, 261
  unity of the Trinity, **II:**263
Euclides Da Cunha, **II:**286
EUDEBA (*Editorial universitaria de Buenos Aires*), **II:**665–66
Eugénie Grandet (Balzac), **II:**26
Europe
  American rebuke of, **II:**183
  classifying the New World, **II:**67
  consolidating link between colonies and, **II:**17
  decline of Positivism in, **II:**291
  ensuring colonial control, **II:**307
  homogenization of Latin America, **II:**308–9
  imposing freedom on America, **II:**45
  and inferiorization of the New World, **III:**215
  restrictions imposed on Brazil by, **II:**58
  strategies for conquest of new territories, **II:**65
  transculturation of Latin America, **III:**174–79
  transfer of institutions to America, **II:**4
  transfer of libraries to America, **II:**45
European art, export to Latin America, **II:**431
European avant-garde, in Latin American poetry, **II:**191
European boutique Paris, **II:**510, 511
European culture
  and expectation of islands in the Sea of Darkness, **III:**140–
    41
  impact of discovery of New World on, **III:**139
  loss of centrality and, **III:**140
European education, of Amerindians, **II:**238–39
European essay
  historical value of, **II:**238
  universality of, **II:**238
European literary culture, transmission to conquered nobility,
    III:202
European literature
  influence on Brazilian novel, **II:**267
  translation of, **II:**267–68
European museums
  function of, **II:**65
  post Middle Ages model for, **II:**65
European naturalists, who chose Brazil as topic of their writ-
    ings, **III:**477
European pirates, and composition of defensive forces against,
    III:8, 11, 12
evaluative impressionism, **II:**101
Evaristo, Conceição, **I:**255, 256, 259, 261
Evaristo Carriego (Borges), **III:**542–43
Evia, Jacinto de, **II:**464
Evohé (Peri Rossi), **I:**342
d'Evreux, Ivo, **III:**259

Una excursión a los indios ranqueles (Mansilla), **I:**485
exegesis, **II:**258
  interpretation of Christ's life, **II:**259
  memorial of expiatory death, **II:**259
The Exhibition of Modern Art of 44, **II:**608
exile
  defined, **III:**503
  from Latin America, **III:**503
  and the Maya groups of Guatemala, **III:**503
exile literature
  in Argentina, **III:**522
  from Brazil, **III:**499–501
  defined, **III:**512–13
  of Julio Cortázar, **III:**514–15
  paradigm of dual displacement in, **III:**519
  paradigm of extraterritoriality in, **III:**517–18
  paradigm of nomadism in, **III:**518–19
  paradigm of nostalgia in, **III:**516–17
  paradigms of, **III:**515–19
  in Uruguay, **III:**522
"Da existência precária: o sistema intelectual no Brasil" (Costa
    Lima), **III:**356–57
exoticism, **II:**160–62
La expression americana (Lezama Lima), **III:**613
extinct languages, **I:**96–97
La Extraña Muerte de Fray Pedro (Darío), **I:**396–97
extranjeridad, **III:**505
EZLN (Ejercito Zapatista de Liberación Nacional), **III:**572

F

Fábulas quechuas (Vienrich), **I:**226
Face to Face with the Mexicans (Iglehart), **I:**320
Facundo o civilización y barbarie (Sarmiento), **II:**239; **III:**257,
    292–93, 543
  orientalism in, **III:**242
fairs, literary and musical competitions at, **II:**43–44
A Falecida (Rodrigues), **I:**568
Fallen Angels Sing (Torres), **III:**466, 467
Family Installments (Rivera), **III:**436, 452
Family Scenes (Ramírez), **III:**445
famine, in relation to "free" countries, **II:**209
A famosa revista (Galvão), **III:**497
Fanon, Frantz, **III:**201–2, 210
Los Fantasistas, **I:**552
the fantastic play, role of sets and costumes in, **I:**559–60
Faraco, Sergio, **II:**634
Farfán, José María Benigno, **I:**228
Farroupilha Revolution, **II:**634
  and liberal ideology, **II:**627–28
fazendas, defined, **I:**5
Feast of Corpus Christi, **I:**532
Federal University of Bahia, **II:**536, 561–62
Federal University of Pernambuco, **II:**544, 549
Feijó, Diogo Antonio, **II:**574–75
Felinto, Marilene, **I:**255, 259–60
Felipe, Carlos, **I:**552
Felipe V de Borbón, coronation of, **I:**549
Felipillo, **I:**135
Félix, María, **I:**590, 594
female poets, **I:**282, 296
  themes in works of, **I:**283
female writers
  best selling, **II:**268–69
  literary historians' treatment of, **I:**202–4
feminism, in Latin American theater, **I:**545
Feria del Libro (Book Fair), **II:**390
Fernandes, Florestan, **I:**414; **III:**611
Fernández, Emiliano R. (Rivarola), **II:**623
Fernández, Emilio, **III:**566

Hollanda, Sérgio Buarque de, **I**:6; **II**:536, 566, 592; **III**:620
and European culture in Brazil, **I**:411–12
Holy Smoke (Cabrera Infante), **III**:517
"Hombre de las esquina rosada" (Borges), **II**:662
Hombres de maíz (Asturias), **II**:358
homosexual literature. *See* gay literature; lesbian literature
homosexuality, in Cuban theater, **III**:461, 462, 463
homotextuality
in Brazil, **I**:356–65
defined, **I**:356
Honduras, **II**:354–55
book production in, **II**:360–61
cultural centers of, **II**:360–61
geographical books on, **II**:355
journalism in, **II**:356
literary centers of, **II**:359
Modernista revolution in, **II**:357
newspapers in, **II**:356
theater in, **I**:521
A hora da estrela (Lispector), **I**:277
Horcasitas, **I**:74
horses
importance to colonists, **I**:11
increasing number in Latin America, **I**:10
Hostos, Eugenio María de, **III**:238
The House of Ramón Iglesia (Rivera), **III**:446
House of the Americas, **II**:379
Houston, Matilda Charlotte Fraser, **I**:322
Huarochirí manuscript, **I**:100
editions and translations of, **I**:225
Huascar, **I**:145
Huasipungo (Icaza), **I**:227, 424–25 **III**:227–28
Huave language, **I**:78
huayno, **I**:101
huehuetlatolli, **I**:440–41, 443, 450; **III**:375, 376, 377
Huehuetlatolli. Plásticas morales de los indios para doctrina de sus hijos, en mexicano (Bautista), **I**:443–44
Huerta, Jorge, **III**:428
Huerta, Victoriano, writers who supported, **II**:343
Hugo, Victor, **II**:26, 27, 410
Huidobro, Vicente, **II**:190–91, 674
Huilliches, location of, **I**:138
Humboldt, Alexander von, **II**:170–71, 450, 466–67
in Caracas, **II**:414
redefinition of America as New World, **III**:240
Huneeus y Gana, Jorge, and efforts to eradicate indigenous cultures, **III**:90–91
hybridity, defined, **III**:137
hysteria, as a literary topic, **III**:123–24

I

Ibarbourou, Juana de, **II**:652
Ibirapuera Park, **II**:594
"Ibum de Pagu," **II**:29
Icaza, Jorge, **I**:227; **II**:469, 470
Indigenist novel of, **III**:227–28
icnocuícatl, **I**:443
"iconogrammical" aesthetic, **II**:4
Iconología (Ripa), **II**:38
Idea del valor de la isla Española y utilidades que de ella puede sacar su monarquia (Sánchez Valverde), **II**:387
El ideal de un calavera (Blest Gana), **I**:186
La identidad aymara (Bouysse-Cassagne), **III**:390
ideographic glyphs, **III**:372
Ideologia da cultura brasileira (Mota), **III**:620
El idioma guaraní: Gramática y antología de prosa y verso (Guasch), **I**:101
I Don't Have to Show You No Stinking Badges! (Valdez), **III**:428
igarapes, **II**:517–19

Igarassu, **II**:539
Iglehart, Fanny Chambers Gooch, **I**:320
the Igneri, **II**:392
illegal publications, in Brazil, **II**:149
The Illusion of the End (Baudrillard), **III**:635
illustrated novels
in Brazil, **II**:150
European versus Brazilian, **II**:150
from France, **II**:150–51
Imagen de la Virgen María Madre de Dios de Guadalupe, milagrosamente aparecida en la Ciudad de Mexico . . . (Requejo), **III**:220
Imagens do Brasil (von Koseritz), **II**:568
imitative novel, **II**:156
immigration
to Brazil, **III**:483
causes of, **III**:503
the Great Depression and, **III**:505–6
of Jews to Brazil, **III**:485–86
to Latin America, **III**:503
modern technology and, **III**:509–10
social spaces and, **III**:510
transnational trends and, **III**:510
to United States, **III**:503
Imperial Eyes: Travel Writing and Transculturation (Pratt), **I**:371; **II**:166
Imprensa Régia, **II**:23
different names of, **II**:26
first publication of, **II**:26
literature found in, **II**:26
publishing program of, **II**:26
Impresiones y recuerdos (Gamboa), **II**:340
El Inca Garcilaso de la Vega. *See* Garcilaso de la Vega, El Inca
Incan culture
aránway, **I**:473
collaboration and resistance in, **I**:475
dances, song, poems, and plays in, **I**:472–73
and expansion of Quechua language, **I**:473
and introduction of Spanish language, **I**:473
and limited documentation of pre-Hispanic literature, **I**:473
oral versus written systems and, **I**:473–74
popular festivals in, **I**:476
syncretism and, **I**:475
wanka, **I**:473
Incan empire
map of, **I**:31
map of (1532), **I**:97
size of, **I**:29
Incan literature
common tales of, **III**:394
of the inner world, **III**:394
for journeys, **III**:390–92
oral history in, **III**:394
Incan settlements, **II**:462
Incan values, opposed to European values, **II**:236
Incas. *See also* Amerindians
account of origin of, **I**:143
archives and libraries of, **I**:472
Aymara literature and, **III**:392
ceremonial practices of, **III**:390
chronicles of, **I**:144–46
colonial theatrical work of, **III**:401
Coya, **II**:33–34
development of state power, **III**:390
historical accounts of, **I**:136–37
importance of llamas to, **III**:393
journeys of, **III**:390
languages of, **I**:29; **II**:33; **III**:385. *See also* Quechua
mamacuna, **II**:34

Júnior, França, **I:**560
Júnior, Raimundo Magalhães, **I:**564
Junta Defensora de los Derechos de Fernando VII, **II:**415
Juntas, **III:**521
    in Argentina, **III:**523
Jurupari, **I:**235
Juventud, **II:**623
Juyungo (Ortiz), **III:**312–13
    interracial affairs in, **III:**315
    melancholia in, **III:**318

K

Karuncharay (Wallparrimachi), **I:**477
katarismo movement, **II:**493–94
the Keynesian state
    Borges's interpretation of, **III:**135
    globalization and, **III:**135
Khipukamayuq, role of, **I:**472
khipus. See quipus
Kirchhoff, Paul, study of *Relación de Michoacán,*
    III:381
Kitsch
    critical positions on, **I:**607
    defined, **I:**607
Knopf, lack of Latin American titles, **II:**131
Koch-Grünberg, Theodor, **II:**522
Kodak (Cendrars), **II:**588–89
Koseritz, Carl von, (also Carlos) **II:**568, 631
Kosmos, **II:**568
Kotz'ib': Nuestra literatura maya (González), **I:**222
krausismo, **III:**329
Krieger, Murray, **II:**199–200
Kubayanda, Josaphat, on *negrismo,* **III:**269, 272–74
Kubitschek, Juscelino
    creation of Brasilia, **II:**609
    as mayor of Belo Horizonte, **II:**609
    modernizing political program of, **III:**553
    as president of Brazil, **II:**611
the Kurripako language, **I:**87

L

El Laberinto de la Soledad (The Labyrinth of Solitude) (Paz),
    I:198; **II:**229, 232–33; **III:**570, 638
Laboratório de Teatro Campesino e Indígena, **I:**528–29
Laboratorio de Teatro Campesino e Indígena de Tabasco, **I:**521
Laçador statue, **II:**634
Laclau, Ernesto, **III:**573–74
Laços de Família (Lispector), **I:**330–32
Lacunza, José María, **II:**165, 337
Ladder to Paradise (Climacus), **I:**283
Lafetá, João Luiz, **II:**92
Landi, Giuseppe, **II:**506
landowners, establishment of power, **I:**4–5
landscape
    defined, **II:**174
    see also landscape representation
landscape poetry. *See* landscape representation
landscape representation
    of America versus Europe, **II:**183
    in Europe, **II:**174
    examples of, **II:**178
    and framing of history, **II:**174
    and the indigenous past, **II:**179–81
    and Latin American poetry, **II:**174
    in Mexico, **II:**177
    recording history through, **II:**177
Las langostas (Sánchez Chan), **I:**530
Las lanzas coloradas, melancholia in, **III:**318
Lapa (Martins), **III:**120

Lapa
    fear of contamination and, **III:**121
    prostitution and, **III:**121
Lara, Agustín, **I:**585–86; **II:**190
Lara, Jesús, **I:**226, 227–28
    and *Relato del Inca,* **I:**473–74
Lares Insurrection, **II:**397
Larra, Mariano Jose de, **II:**418
Larriva, Alfredo Arvelo, **II:**421
The Last Generation (Moraga), **II:**326
Laterza, Moacyr Filho, **I:**509–10
Lathrap, Donald, **II:**525
latifundios, **II:**384
the *latifundio* property system, **I:**10–11, 12
    role of the peon in, **I:**11
Latin
    in Chilean schools, **III:**303
    in Latin American schools, **III:**301
Latina (Sánchez-Scott), **III:**430
Latin America
    abolition of slavery in, **III:**217
    Afro-Hispanic writers in, **I:**240–44
    agricultural model for, **I:**4–5
    anti-French discourses in, **I:**195
    anti-Hispanic sentiment in, **II:**411
    Asian peoples in, **I:**7
    and the attempt to construct a continental awareness,
        III:509
    Baroque culture in, **III:**174–79, 191–99
    Baroque style as a national style in, **III:**184
    bilingual education in, **I:**100
    black population in, **I:**6–7
    book smuggling, **II:**431
    canonization of French literature, **II:**136
    carnival in, **I:**625–29
    centers of control in, **II:**309
    centers of foreign trade, **I:**16
    change from oral to written culture, **II:**130
    changes in political order at end of 18th century, **III:**240
    and the Cold War, **I:**541
    colonial animal breeding in, **I:**10–11
    colonial encounters in, **III:**20–29
    colonial semiosis, **I:**181–82
    communism, **I:**426
    conflict over rule of, **I:**389
    consequences of expulsion of Jesuits for, **III:**204–5
    contract workers in, **I:**7
    and the Cordilleras, **I:**7–10
    correlation between language and social status in, **III:**82
    cost to general population of modernization in, **III:**85
    creolization in, **I:**7
    criollos and Spaniards in Colonial period, **III:**33
    cultural centers of, **I:**159–60, 163, 169–70; **II:**307–11. *See also*
        cultural centers
    as a cultural construction, **I:**3
    cultural dependency and, **III:**353–61
    cultural development of, **II:**2
    cultural journalism, **II:**3
    decline of autochthonous languages in, **I:**61
    dependency theory in, **I:**426
    developing high culture in, **II:**240
    development of mining cities in, **I:**21–22
    development of nation-states in, **III:**88–89
    development of painting and religious transculturation in,
        II:430
    development of roads in, **I:**11, 14
    difficulties of constructing a self-image in, **I:**194–97
    diversity of climates in, **I:**9
    diversity of language in, **II:**446

Montevideo, **I:**49–50
  beef livestock, role of, **II:**645
  blanco party, **II:**649–50
  British influence in, **II:**640
  colorado party, **II:**649–50
  contemporary, **II:**655–56
  contemporary problems of, **II:**642
  cultural activity during crises, **II:**651–52
  culture. *See* Montevidean culture
  as democratic center, **II:**642
  early educational institutions in, **II:**645
  economic crisis of 1982, **II:**655
  effect of Great War in, **II:**647
  end of dictatorship in, **II:**655
  etymology of, **II:**644
  exiled Argentinean intellectuals in, **II:**647
  foreign cultural institutions, **II:**655
  founding of, **II:**639, 644–45
  as frontier region, **II:**645
  future of, **II:**642–43
  gambling in, **II:**649
  growth of, after War of the Triple Alliance, **II:**648
  growth of religion in, **II:**655
  housing problems in, **II:**641
  immigration in, **II:**640
  immigration to, **II:**641, 642, 648, 649, 653, 654
  impact of automobile on, **II:**641
  after independence from Spain, **II:**639
  industrialization of, **II:**640
  layout of, **II:**639
  leather, **II:**645
  leisure activities in, **II:**641
  literature. *See* Montevidean literature
  local literature, development of, **II:**645–46. *See also* Montevidean literature
  Mercosur, **II:**656
  middle class in, **II:**640
  modernization of, **II:**640
  municipal records and colonial life of, **II:**645
  19th-century cultural institutions in, **II:**639–40
  19th-century demographic growth, **II:**640
  North American influence on, **II:**641, 642
  as political center, **II:**640, 641–42
  political culture of the 1990s, **II:**655
  population increase, **II:**650
  population of (20th century), **II:**641
  President José Batlle y Ordoñez, **II:**650–51
  President Julio María Sanguinetti, **II:**655
  restoration of, **II:**655–56
  return of exiles to, **II:**655–56
  role of exiles living in, **II:**639
  shopping malls in, **II:**655
  slums in, **II:**655, 656
  socialism in, **II:**640
  Statutory Limitations Law, **II:**656
  suburban growth of, **II:**640
  and the Treaty of Tordesillas, **II:**644
  and Uruguay's independence from Spain, **II:**648
  violence in (1960s and 1970s), **II:**639
  war in, **II:**654
  World Cup of soccer in, **II:**651
Montevideo Group, **II:**635
Montévideo ou la nouvelle Troie (Dumas), **II:**647–48
Montoya, Edwin, **I:**229
Montoya, Luis, **I:**229
Montoya, Matilde, **I:**518
Montoya, Rodrigo, **I:**229
Montufar, Juan Pío, **II:**466
"Monumentos Lingüísticos," **III:**410–411

Moog, Vianna Clodomir, **II:**232
Moore, Rachel Wilson Barker, **I:**322
Moraes, Eduardo Jardim de, **III:**617
Moraga, Cherríe, **II:**326–27; **III:**423
Morales, Alejandro, **III:**423
Morales, Antonio, **II:**455
Moreira, Álvaro, and proposal for new Brazilian dramaturgy, **I:**562
Moreiras, Alberto, analysis of José María Arguedas's texts, **III:**317–18
Morelos y Pavón, José María, **I:**452; **III:**227
Morenada dance, **III:**406
A Moreninha (Macedo), **I:**251; **II:**147, 148–49, 150, 152–53, 154, 253, 267
Moreno, Gabriel García, **II:**467
  schools founded by, **II:**468
Moreno, Mario. *See* Cantinflas
Morín, Gómez, **II:**344
  and the Mexican Revolution, **II:**343
A morte de D.J. em Paris (Drummond), **I:**610
Morte e Vida Severina (Melo Neto), **I:**573
Morton, Carlos, **III:**429
El Mosaico circle, **II:**454
Mota, Carlos Guilherme, **III:**620
the Motilón language. *See* the Barí language
Motivos de son (Guillén), **III:**269
Mott, Maria Lúcia de Barros, **I:**259
Motta Coquiro ou a Pena de Morte (Patrocínio), **I:**252
Moura, Ignácio Baptista de, **II:**509
"O movimento modernista" (Andrade), **III:**627
Moving Away from Silence (Turino), **III:**407
Moxos, **II:**525
  and the House of Suárez, **II:**527
  Pedro Ignacio Muiba, **II:**528
Moya Pons, Frank, **II:**381, 389–90
La muerte de Artemio Cruz (Fuentes), **III:**602
"La muerte del cisne" (Reyles), **I:**400
La muerte no entrará en palacio (Marqués), **I:**542
Muerte sin fin (Gorostiza), **II:**189
Mugaburu, Josephe de, diary of, **III:**35
"A Muhuraida" (Wilkens), **II:**501
Muiba, Pedro Ignacio, **II:**528
Muiscas (or Chibchas), **II:**445–46
  artistic tradition of, **II:**448
La mujer, **I:**324
La mujer desnuda (Somers), **I:**312–13
Las mujeres no hablan así (Matos), **I:**343
Mujica, Barbara, **I:**241
mulattoes
  as standard for feminine beauty, **I:**250
  stereotypes of, **I:**249
A mulher no espelho (Cunha), **II:**564
A Mulher Sem Pecado (Rodrigues), **I:**567
Mullen, Edward, **I:**241
multiculturalism, in Bolivia, **II:**495
Las multitudes argentinas (Ramos Majía), **I:**398–99; **III:**293
El mundo es ancho y ajeno (Alegría), **I:**227; **III:**228
Mundo Nuevo, **III:**599
Muñoz, Elias Miguel, **III:**468–69
Murillo, Pedro Domingo, revolt of, **II:**483
Musa Joven, **II:**674
Museo de Historia Nacional, **II:**436
Museo de la novella de la eternal, (Fernández), **II:** 241–245
museological discourse
  Latin American conflict in, **II:**68
  after World War II, **II:**67–68
Museum of Modern Art in São Paulo, **II:**593–94
museums
  archaeological, **II:**46

oral literature (*continued*)
  in Mexico, **I:**436–57
  moral tales in, **I:**454
  mythopoeics, **I:**496–97
  versus oralized literature, **I:**437–38
  a paradox in, **I:**438
  poetry genres in, **I:**455
  prayers in, **I:**454
  pre-Hispanic period of, **I:**471–73
  preservation of, **I:**471
  problems with transcribing, **I:**438
  pseudo, **I:**449–50
  puns in, **I:**455
  recovering, **I:**433–35
  simulacra and, **I:**471
  singing of, **I:**499–500
  and status of minority languages in Mexico, **I:**436
  Teufel literatur, **I:**497–98
  versus verbal discourse, **I:**436
  versus written literature, **I:**438
oral poetics, **I:**496
  understanding, **I:**502
  the unmaking in, **I:**500–02
oral poetry, prophecy in, **I:**498–99
oral tradition. *See* orality
De Orbe Novo (Charles V), **II:**11
Orçamento Participativo (OP), **II:**635
Ordaz, Gustavo Díaz, **II:**349
Ordaz, Luis, **I:**515
A Ordem, **I:**402–3
ordem e progresso, **II:**37
O'Reilly, Alejandro, **II:**395
Orellana, Francisco de, **II:**14
Orestes (Alfieri), **II:**536
Orfeu na roça (Vasques), **I:**559
Orfeu negro (Camus), **I:**653–54
Orígenes, **II:**89, 192
origins, defined in terms of Bogotá, **II:**445
Orinoco river, **I:**57
Orkopata poetry group, **III:**404
Orozco, José Clemente, **I:**582
Orphée aux enfers, **I:**559
Orquesta Típica, **I:**586
Ortiz, Adalberto, **III:**312–13
Ortiz, Fernando, **II:** 256, 293; **III:**234, 284, 287, 297, 312
  and Afro-Cuban cultures, **I:**549–50
  anthropological research of, **III:**270
  ideas for transculturation, **III:**332
  on miscegenation, **III:**311
  on modernization, **III:**234–35
  opinions on José Martí, **III:**332–33
  and transculturation, **III:**129, 180
  on transculturation, **III:**234–35
Ortiz-Cofer, Judith, **III:**439
Ortiz Rescaniere, Alejandro, **I:**494–95
  on the Inkarrí, **I:**494
Osorio, Antonio de, **II:**383
Osorio, Miguel Ángel [Ricardo Arenales; Porfirio Barba Jacob, pseud.]. *See* Barba Jacob, Porfirio
Otomanguean languages, **I:**77–78
Otomís, **III:**380
El otoño del patriarca (García Márquez), **III:**351
Otra Tempestad, **I:**553
"El otro cielo" (Cortázar), **III:**515
Our Lady the Virgin of Guadalupe, **III:**42, 220
  importance to indigenous and *mestizo* people, **I:**576
  role in Mexican national identity, **I:**576
  widespread acceptance of, **III:**205–6
Ouro Preto, **II:**597, 612. *See also* Vila Rica

architecture of, **II:**599–600
  importance of, **II:**598
  photograph of, **II:**598
Our Time, **II:**377
outlawry, on Mexico-U.S. border, **III:**323–25
Ovalle, Alfredo, **I:**186
Over (Marrero Aristy), **II:**384
Oviedo, José Miguel, **II:**407
Oviedo y Baños, José, **II:**413–14
Oviedo y Herrera, Luis Antonio de, **III:**10

P
"Pablo Neruda," symbolic importance of, **III:**588–89
Pachacamac, **II:**426
Pacheco Gómez, Máximo, **III:**590
pachuco, **II:**321–22
Pachuquismo, **II:**322
El pacto de Cristina (Nalé-Roxlo), **I:**539–40
Padaria Espiritual, and Brazilian cultural traditions, **III:**121
Padilla, Herberto, **III:**585
El padre Horán (Aréstegui), **II:**285, 410, 435
Paeces, **I:**92
Pagu
  in Buenos Aires, **III:**496
  individuality of, **III:**496
  world travels of, **III:**496–97
Pagu: vida-obra, **III:**496
painting
  European education in, **II:**430
  importance to Lima, **II:**430
  religious iconography in, **II:**430
  during the Republican period, **II:**435–36
El país de los cuatro pisos (González), **II:**400
A paixão segundo (Lispector), **I:**276–77
Palace of Fine Arts, **II:**347
Palace of Justice, **II:**300
Palacin, Luis, **III:**59, 61
Palácio da Cultura, **II:**577
Palacios Berruecos, Juana. *See* María de San José
palafittes, **II:**521
Palenque, **II:**298
Palés Matos, Luis, **II:**193; **III:**269, 270, 272–74
  anticolonial counterdiscourse of, **III:**274
  and *negrismo,* **III:**272–74
Palma, Ricardo, **II:**432, 444; **III:**255–56
  costumbrista sketch by, **III:**255
  and transculturation of the past, **III:**255
palo de Brazil, **I:**104
Pampas
  livestock growth in, **I:**49
  resourcefulness of men in, **I:**51
Pampulha, **II:**609–11
Pan-Africanism, **I:**465
Panama, **II:**354
  building of canal, **II:**356–57
  carnival in, **I:**627–28
  literary journals in, **II:**356
  national cultural figure of, **II:**357
Panama Canal, **II:**356–57
  significance of, **II:**236
Panama City
  establishment of, **II:**354
  population of, **II:**361
  universities of, **II:**361
the Pan-American Highway, **I:**11
the Panares language, **I:**86
Pancho Villa, **III:**324, 564
Pané, Fray Ramón, **II:**289–90

Puerto Rico (*continued*)
  indigenous people of, **II:**392
  Instituto de Cultura de Puerto Rico, **II:**399–400
  issues of language in, **III:**441
  José M. Lázaro Library, **II:**400
  Lares Insurrection, **II:**397
  leaders of revolutionary movement, **II:**397–98
  location of, **II:**392
  National Library of Puerto Rico, **II:**400
  negrismo in, **III:**270
  obligatory agenda of, **II:**113
  "Operation Serenity" festival, **II:**400
  political future of, **III:**446
  population of (1839), **II:**396
  printing press in, **II:**395–96
  religious schools in, **II:**394
  slavery in, **II:**393–94
  social divisions of, **II:**396
  theater in, **I:**542
  and United States, **III:**434
  U.S. Bills that influenced, **II:**399
  U.S. invasion of, **II:**398
  U.S. occupation of, **II:**401–2
  and U.S. Puerto Rican writers, **III:**440–41
  Venezuelans exile to, **II:**401
  the Warrant of 1815, **II:**396
  writers from, **II:**396–97
Puig, Manuel, **I:**351–52, 645–46
  literary efforts of, **III:**577
the Puinave language, **I:**87
Puquina language, **I:**96–97

Q

Quadragesimo Anno (Pope Pius XI), **I:**417
Quadro de historia natural, civil y geográfica del Reyno del Perú, **I:**225–26
Quando eu era vivo . . . (Medeiros e Albuquerque), **III:**493
Quarto de despejo (de Jesus), **I:**207
Quarup (Callado), **I:**126, 132
Quechua, **I:**94, 96, 97
  in armed forces, **III:**407
  Catholic Church's use of, **III:**397
  in Christian church, **I:**142
  in Cuzco, **I:**148
  designation as religious language, **III:**397
  early material written in, **I:**225, 226
  early 20th-century periodicals and magazines written in, **III:**404
  expansion of, **I:**97
  first full-length film in, **III:**408
  huayno, **I:**101
  literature involving language and culture of, **I:**226–29
  love story in *Manchay Puytu,* **III:**401
  map of expansion of (1700–1800), **I:**102
  modern speakers of, **I:**29
  in northern South American nations, **I:**90
  number of speakers of, **I:**97
  as an official second language, **I:**100
  presented in glyphic scripts, **III:**398
  published texts in, **I:**101; **III:**405
  relation to Aymara, **III:**385
  Spaniards' use of, **I:**473
  Spanish syntax limiting translations of, **I:**228
  spread of, **I:**141–42
  structure of, **I:**98
  Wallparrimachi's poetry in, **II:**484
Quechua fable, conservation of, **II:**42
Quechua literature, **II:**409
  during colonial period, **I:**474–75

José María Benigno Farfán and, **I:**228
  for a journey, **III:**391–92
  Ollantay, **I:**519
  regional genres of, **III:**395–96
  Runa Yndio, **III:**394
Quechua music, José María Arguedas's observations of, **III:**317
Quechua theater, **I:**101
O que é isso, companheiro? (Gabeira), **III:**499
Queiroga, Salomé, **I:**250
Queiroz, María Amélia de, **I:**339
Queiroz, Raquel de, **I:**205, 335, 339
Quental, Antero de, **II:**542
Quesada, Gonzalo Jiménez de, **II:**445
Questions of Travel (Bishop), **III:**491
Quetzalcóatl, **III:**369, 382
El que vendrá (Rodó), **I:**391
the Quiché, **III:**154–56
  the *Popul Vuh* and, **III:**154–56
"Quiché Achí guerrero" (Sam Colop), **I:**220
Quiché language, important manuscripts in, **III:**378–80
Quijano, Carlos, **I:**420
quilombos, **I:**246
Quimantú, **III:**587
  censorship of, **III:**588
Quincas Borba (Assis), **II:**274; **III:**124
Quintana, Mário, **II:**637
O Quinze (Queiroz), **I:**339
quipucamayos, **I:**136
quipus, **II:**407
  Andean, **I:**472
  as Andean literature, **III:**386–89
  in *Apu Ollantay,* **III:**401
  Church's destruction of, **II:**426
  gender issues in reading of, **III:**389
  ideographic, **I:**472
  pictures of, **III:**391
  "Rain Goddess" hymn in, **III:**388–89
  Tale of the Snake, **III:**386–87
  as viewed by José de Acosta, **III:**396
Quiroga, Don Vasco de, **I:**20
Quiroga, Horacio, **II:**15
Quispe, Doña Lucía, **III:**393
Quito, **II:**462–72
  architectural additions to, **II:**467–68
  convents in, **II:**464–65
  as educational center of Spanish colonies, **II:**463
  first movie in, **II:**469
  first newspaper of, **II:**466
  Franciscan Riot of 1747–1748, **II:**465
  historical descriptions of construction in, **II:**462, 470
  independence from Spain, **II:**467
  Indian protests in, **II:**471
  indigenous rights movement in, **II:**471
  and influence of cultural modernity, **II:**407–8
  landscape of, **II:**462
  libraries in, **II:**466–67
  modern change of, **II:**468–69
  Pedro V. Maldonado's study of, **II:**467
  religious architecture in, **II:**462–63
  religious influences in, **II:**463
  religious texts in, **II:**464
  Santa Catalina revolt in, **II:**464
Quito Rebellion, **II:**465
Quito Society
  as center for the exchange of ideas, **II:**466
  closing of, **II:**466

Rocha, Oswaldo Porto, **III:**118
Roche, Regina Maria Dalton, **II:**268–69
Rodó, José Enrique, **I:**161, 391, 395–96; **II:**240, 650; **III:**222
  historical/cultural setting for *Ariel,* **III:**537–38
  on the nation as a concept, **III:**537–38
Rodrigues, Nelson, **I:**562, 565, 566, 567–68; **II:**577
  concern with secrets of human privacy in works of, **I:**568
  influence of the works of, **I:**568
  and process of psychic unveiling in works of, **I:**567
  public opinion as plot factor in works of, **I:**568
Rodrigues Alves Municipal Forest, **II:**510
Rodríguez, Abraham, **III:**435–36
Rodríguez, José Policarpo, **III:**323
Rodríguez, Lorenzo, **III:**176
Rodríguez, Manuel del Socorro, **II:**446
Rodríguez, Manuel Díaz, **II:**418
Rodríguez Cabrillo, Juan, **II:**14
Rodríguez de Morales, Catalina, **I:**320
Rodríguez Freyle, Juan, **III:**47–49, 188
Rodríguez Galván, Ignacio, **I:**536–37; **II:**180
Rodríguez Lozano, Manuel, **I:**323
Rodríguez Pérsico, Adriana, **I:**368
Rodríquez Monegal, Emir, **II:**90, 108, 109
Roffé, Mercedes, **I:**343
Roffé, Reina, **I:**345
Roffiel, Rosamaría, **I:**346–47
Rojas, Ricardo, **I:**209
  and the development of Argentine culture, **I:**393–94
  national revolution of, **III:**307
  neohumanism of, **III:**307–8
  pedagogical plan for Argentina, **III:**306–7
Rojas Guardia, Armando, **I:**352–53
Román, Pedro, **III:**460
"Romance a Cortés" (Ramirez), **III:**6
"Romance de Jiménez de Quesada," **II:**445
Romance do Pavão Misterioso (Camelo de Melo Rezende), **I:**615–16
romanceiro, **I:**498
"Romance negro" (Fonseca), **I:**602–3
Los romances basados en La Araucana, **III:**6–7
roman-feuilleton, **II:**269–70, 279
Romans à lire et romans à proscrire (Bethléem), **I:**405
Romantic Indigenism, **I:**232
Romanticism
  in Brazil, **III:**100
  in Latin American theater, **I:**536–37
Romantic literature, interaction with nature, **II:**159–60
Romero, Silvio, **I:**253, 410; **II:**548; **III:**121–122
  conflicting attitudes in works by, **I:**394
Romero de Terreros, Manuel, **I:**576–77
Rómulo Gallegos, prize of Caracas, **II:**109
  of 1972, **II:**110
Rónai, Paulo, **III:**486
A Rosa, **I:**339
Rosa, João Guimarães, **I:**165; **II:**294, 610
Rosa de Lima
  canonization of, **I:**291–92
  mystical musings of, **I:**292
  public life of, **I:**291
  religious calling of, **I:**291
  writings of, **I:**292
Rosa de Santa María, **III:**10
Rosário, Antônio do, **II:**63
Rosas, Juan Manuel José Domingo Ortiz de, **II:**282
  European influences on Argentina due to barbarous reign of, **III:**248
  implementation of *caudillista* tradition in Argentina, **III:**246–47
Rosas de Oquendo, Mateo, **III:**50, 51–52

Rosenblat, Angel, **II:**407
Rosende de la Sierra, Petrona, **II:**647
Rosicrán, **II:**622. *See also* Colmán, Narciso Ramón
Rothschilds' loan, **II:**591
Rousseau, Jean-Jacques, anti-literature literature, **I:**184–85
Royal Authority, endurance of, **II:**59
Royal Botanical Expedition Academy of Drawing, **II:**450
Royal Charter of 1688, **II:**50
Royal Havanan Trading Company, **II:**371
Royal Library of Portugal, relocation of, **II:**24
Rozitchner, León, **I:**266
rubber boom in Bolivia, **II:**527
rubber economy
  in Belém, **II:**50–512
  center of, **II:**519
  and English rubber plantations, **II:**507
  of Manaus, **II:**517
The Rubén Darío Theater, **II:**361
Las ruinas circulares, **I:**553
Ruiz de Alarcón, Juan
  plays of, **III:**186
  status of, **III:**186
Ruiz de Burton, María Amparo, **III:**421
Rulfo, Juan, **II:**320
runaway slave movement, **I:**465
runaway slaves, **I:**246
Runa Yndio, **III:**394
rupture
  aesthetics of, **III:**548–53
  historical process of reinterpretation of, **III:**549–50
  Oswald de Andrade's "Manifesto Antropofágico" as discourse of, **III:**550–51
  Silviano Santiago's views on, **III:**551
Rushdie, Salman, **III:**509
Russian literature, link between poets and artists, **II:**28–29
Rusticatio Mexicana (Landívar), **II:**354

S

Saavedra Fajardo, Diego de, **II:**259, 264–65
Saavedra y Guzmán, Antonio de, **III:**13
Sab (Avellaneda), **I:**123; **II:**185
Sábato, Ernesto, **I:**198
  as existentialist, **III:**350–51
  on rhetoric of radio novels, **III:**575–76
Sabina, María, **II:**215
Sabogal, José, **II:**437
Sacred Congregation of the Roman Inquisition, **I:**401
SADAIC (*Sociedad Argentina de Autores y Compositores de Música*), **II:**665
Sáenz, Jaime
  analysis of works of, **II:**490–91
  artistic vision of, **II:**490–91
Sáenz, Manuela, **I:**322
Sagarana (Rosa), **II:**610
Saggio de Storia Americana (Gilij), **I:**88
Sagrario Chapel, **III:**176
Sahagún, Fr. Bernardino de, **III:**15, 220
  Christmas sermon of, **I:**463–64
  pseudo-oral literature, **I:**463–64
  research on Mesoamerican texts, **III:**375–76, 375
Sainetes, **II:**433
Saint Domingue. *See* Haiti
Saint-Domingue. *See* Santo Domingo
Saint Hilaire, Auguste de, in Porto Alegre, **II:**627
Saint Pierre, **I:**26
Saint-Pierre, Bernardin de, **II:**160
Saint Thomas Aquinas, **II:**61
"Saker-Ti" group, **II:**357
Salado Alvarez, Victoriano, **III:**323